W9-AJM-718

A DICTIONARY OF ASIAN CHRISTIANITY

A Dictionary of ASIAN CHRISTIANITY

Edited by

SCOTT W. SUNQUIST

Associate Editors

David Wu Chu Sing *and*
John Chew Hiang Chea

William B. Eerdmans Publishing Company
Grand Rapids, Michigan / Cambridge, U.K.

Wm. B. Eerdmans Publishing Co.
255 Jefferson Ave. S.E., Grand Rapids, Michigan 49503 /
P.O. Box 163, Cambridge CB3 9PU U.K.

Printed in the United States of America

07 06 05 04 03 02 01 7 6 5 4 3 2 1

Library of Congress Cataloging-in-Publication Data

A dictionary of Asian Christianity / edited by Scott W. Sunquist; associate editors,
David Wu Chu Sing and John Chew Hiang Chea.
p. cm.
Included bibliographical references.
ISBN 0-8028-3776-X (alk. paper)
1. Christianity — Asia — Dictionaries. I. Sunquist, Scott, 1953-

BR1065.D52 2001
275′.003 — dc21

2001033224

www.eerdmans.com

This volume is dedicated to two communities of faith.

First, this volume is dedicated to the hundreds of Asian church leaders who, seeing the importance of telling the stories of Christian faith in Asia, made the sacrifices necessary to write for this volume. These are the storytellers of Christianity in Asia. Many of the people who have written for this volume are Christians living in a minority context. As a result they sometimes face very difficult economic and political circumstances. Some who have made uniquely valuable contributions are aware that their faith communities are at risk and have therefore requested that their names be omitted. With this dedication go our prayers for these Christian communities across Asia.

Secondly, this volume is dedicated to my local community of faith, my family. My wife, Nancy, and our four children, Caroline, Bethany, Elisha, and Jesse, have patiently believed with me that such a project was possible and that, by God's grace, it would be done. When this project was started, eleven years ago, our children were five, seven, nine, and eleven and living in Singapore. They have patiently waited as dad traveled, worked late, and often seemed preoccupied for these many years.

May this work be blessed to the glory of the triune God.

CONTENTS

LIST OF ENTRIES

ACKNOWLEDGMENTS

The *DAC* represents a ten-year project involving more than five hundred people. It would be impossible to recognize all those who have made this volume possible. Many contributions, however, have been particularly noteworthy. We wish to acknowledge first of all the contribution of the many Asian church leaders who, often with very pressing schedules and limited resources, have understood the importance of this resource and have taken the time to write articles. Surely the degree of their sacrifice and the extenuating circumstances they faced in carrying out this task will be known only by God.

Much of the material on Japan comes from the *Historical Dictionary of Christianity in Japan,* edited by Ebisawa Arimichi, and is used by permission of the publisher, Kyobunkwan Press in Tokyo. We are grateful for their cooperation. Translations were made by a former missionary to Japan, Margaret Warren.

From the beginning, the project needed an administrator to keep track of the thousands of letters (faxes, e-mail) of correspondence and the articles being submitted. Three outstanding and energetic administrators guided this project. Ms. Annie Soh, of the Methodist Church in Singapore, helped to organize this project from the beginning. Mrs. Soon Guat Eng (Anglican Church, Singapore) did an excellent job pursuing articles from various parts of Asia and then helped through the years in transferring the articles and correspondence from Singapore to Pittsburgh. Finally, without the capable work of Mrs. Connie Gundry Tappy this work may have ended up in the bottom file drawers in my office. Connie took the thousands of pages of correspondence and articles and pulled them all together so we could bring this work to completion. A good administrator is hard to find, and we have had three.

Special appreciation also goes to the excellent faculty and staff of Trinity Theological College in Singapore. Ms. K. K. Chia kept track of our finances for more than five years. Books and articles were quickly found by the kind and careful librarian Ms. Lau Jen Sin. Dr. David Wu Chu Sing, working on the editorial team, kept the project going in the early years, providing the needed linguistic facility in English, dialects of Chinese, and Bahasa Indonesia. His organizational abilities and translations have been invaluable. Bishop John Chew Hiang Chea of the Anglican Church in Singapore facilitated the delicate task of working with teams from the Roman Catholic and Protestant Churches in China and the groups from Taiwan. This work would have been far weaker without his patient and wise labor. Ms. Bonnie Tan of the Methodist Church in Singapore produced the early drafts of the maps by hand. Theology students at Trinity Theological College did early research to help guide the project even before the first regional meetings were held.

As with all major works that involve a lot of communications and travel, this work would never have been completed without the financial support of people and organizations committed to the Asian church. In the early years, the support of the Evangelisches Missionswerk in Deutschland and Missionswissenschaftliches Institut Missio supported the regional consultations and communications. The Rivendell Stewards' Trust (USA), with the encouragement of Dr. Walter Hansen, also provided ongoing support in the early years. In addition, support was provided by the following: Covenant Presbyterian Church (Singapore), The Institute for the Study of Religion and Society (Singapore), South East Asia Graduate School of Theology, Presbyterian Church (USA), United Methodist Church (Board of Global Ministries), Paoli Presbyterian Church (USA), and the faculty development fund of Pittsburgh Theological Seminary. In the final years the project was supported by the World Mission Initiative of Pittsburgh Theological Seminary. The editors wish to thank them all.

A final note of appreciation goes to the Luce Foundation of New York. It has provided invaluable funding to complete the project and to make copies available to Asian seminary libraries and to our Asian authors. I am particularly glad that the final support comes from the foundation related to a missionary in China, Henry Winters Luce (1868-1941), who, like me, was a father of four, came from Pennsylvania, studied at Princeton Theological Seminary, and worked in Asia.

Thanks and blessings are offered to all who made this project a reality. The credit for the wonder, joy, and discovery that this book engenders belongs to the faithful Asian authors and supporters of the project. The final shortcomings I shoulder myself.

Scott W. Sunquist

PREFACE

A Dictionary of Asian Christianity (DAC) is both a reference work and a study in Christian theological and historical method. In fact, the *DAC*, through the global Christian fellowship it has engendered, has even become part of the Christian history it describes. The project did not start out as such, but through ten years of traveling, corresponding, translating, editing, and searching, Christians have been brought together, in Asia and around the world, to discover afresh how the Gospel has been proclaimed and expressed in Asia for these past two millennia. Such Christians, who seldom have the luxury of meeting together — Koreans and Chinese, Pentecostals and Roman Catholics, Karen Baptists and Singaporean Methodists — have spent time struggling to understand what it means to talk about a truly ecumenical Christian history of Asia.

The *DAC* was born out of two senses of frustration. First, professors of church history in Myanmar (Burma), Thailand, Malaysia, and Singapore expressed frustration that they had so few basic resources for teaching Asian church history, a requirement in most Asian curricula. Although in the last decades of the twentieth century regional church histories were being written by groups such as those associated with the Church History Association of India and the Roman Catholic church in Jakarta and Bangkok, there was no place to go to look up names, dates, or themes to get an overview of some topic mentioned in a lecture. *The Historical Dictionary of Christianity in Japan* (in Japanese) was a valuable exception to this general lack. If a professor mentioned something about the Mennonites in Indonesia or the Franciscans in the Philippines, a student had very few resources available to find further information. It was of course embarrassing that students would at times express more interest in British, Scottish, or American church history than they would in their own, simply because of the many reference works available on the Western churches. The Asian story was available, but it was difficult for our students to find. As a result we all inadvertently reinforced the notion that Christianity was a Western imposition on Asia even though we knew this was really not the case.

The second frustration was the ongoing struggle with nationalism and racism that our scholarship had to critique. When we, as Asian Christian historians, gathered together, we discovered that national and political church divisions as well as language differences made it difficult for pastors and scholars to see the Christian faith as truly ecumenical. It was hard to view it as international and interconfessional. For example, Japanese scholars have done excellent work on Christianity in Japan, but because of language differences they know very little about Christianity in China. It is true, of course, that no country is completely isolated from others. Through the ages Christians from one country have often influenced the development of Christianity in neighboring, and indeed even in distant, countries. The divisions that made it difficult to discover this interdependence were a stumbling block to our theological reflection. However, today publications like Samuel H. Moffett's *A History of Christianity in Asia* help to bring Christians together in Asia, with the added benefit of providing a fresh perspective on the misleading assumption that Christianity is a Western religion.

With these twin concerns in mind faculty members from Trinity Theological College (TTC; Singapore) and Seminari Teoloji Malaysia (STM: Kuala Lumpur) held a consultation in 1987. Although they called the meeting to discuss regional cooperation in theological education, one of the main issues was the development of new resources for theological study in Asia. All three of the Asian church historians present noted that a priority must be placed on the production of basic reference works to help students in the study of Asian Christianity. Such works would be used both to provide basic resources to encourage study of Asian Christianity and to express the unity of the church. The consensus of all of the participants was that an Asian-produced dictionary or encyclopedia was an important first step.

In 1990 three members of the faculty of Trinity Theological College (Drs. John Chew, David Wu, and Scott Sunquist) decided to take up the project. They immediately agreed that such a dictionary would approach the story of Christianity in each area from the perspective of the people in that area. This meant that Christian historians and theologians from every country would need to be involved. We did not realize at the time the difficulty of this commitment. But neither did we foresee what a wonderful experience it would be to receive articles from the far corners of Asia. With the encouragement of Dr. Yeow Choo Lak of the Association of Theological Education in South East Asia, we decided to hold regional meetings with local church leaders. They would help to determine what topics would be included in the *DAC* and provide valuable suggestions for qualified authors. This meant that within each country or region we would try to bring together scholars who represented as many traditions and church movements as possible. For many people attending our consultations this was their first exposure to Roman Catholic, Anglican, Methodist, Presbyterian, Lutheran, Baptist, Pentecostal, Orthodox, Salvation Army, and other Christians. And we were discussing something about which we all care deeply: Asian Christianity. These regional meetings were held in Jakarta, Yangon, Seoul, Chiang Mai, Bangkok, Madras, Manila, Tokyo, Hong Kong, Lahore, Nanjing, Taipei, and Singapore. In addition, a special meeting was held in Singapore to identify major Roman Catholic congregations (orders) that should be included and to find authors for these articles.

The regional meetings were as diverse as are the cultures and languages of Asia. Our first meeting in Jakarta brought together an encouraging group of mostly younger scholars from places as diverse as Batakland in Sumatra, East Java, and Minahasa in Sulawesi. As in Myanmar with Karen, Chin, Kachin, and ethnic Myanmar participants, all of the scholars were concerned that their church's story be represented. At our meetings in Chiang Mai and a later meeting in Bangkok we worked to represent the different streams of Christianity in Thailand, and at the same time to include some other countries and tribal groups in neighboring Indochina. Each of these meetings ended with thanksgiving to God for bringing us together and for reminding us of the saints who have gone before us.

Each consultation also sought to include the issues that would help to explain Christianity in Asia. Thus we identified both "survey terms" — movements or institutions that would cover all of Asia — and "local terms" for leaders, institutions, and movements known only in a particular region. Western missionaries were included only if they had a significant impact upon the development of Christianity as understood from the perspective of local church leaders. In addition, we decided that Protestant mission societies would not be included. This was done to prevent the *DAC* from becoming a dictionary of Christian missions. Some of our discussions were memorable as we wrestled over the relative importance of particular people or movements. We felt that in a sense history was being written as decisions were being made.

Often our decisions for one region did not fit the others. As a result we had many mid-course corrections to make. One of the major decisions concerned local Christian institutions. In the early regional meetings (Jakarta, Singapore/Malaysia) we sought to include entries on Christian colleges, universities, seminaries, and major churches in the *DAC*. It quickly became clear, however, that the inclusion of major churches (buildings as well as local church groupings) would not be possible. When it came to colleges and universities, seminaries and Bible colleges, no one at first had any idea how many institutions were involved. It turned out to be several thousand. Thus, after the articles came in, we had to reevaluate: enough material was collected on seminaries and colleges to publish a separate two- to three-hundred-page dictionary of Asian Christian colleges and seminaries. As a result, survey articles were written from the material submitted to describe some of the trends and generalizations in Asian Christian colleges, universities, and seminaries.

One of the major issues concerned the amount of material to allocate for each country. The editors used the following questions to guide their decisions: How long has the church been present in the country? How influential has the church been in the general history? How large is the Christian presence? Thus China, India, Indonesia, and the Philippines have a great deal more space in the *DAC* than Nepal, Thailand, or Japan. While some compromises had to be made in this process, the *DAC* does reflect the relative importance and impact of the Christian faith in the various regions of Asia.

The compilation of the articles represented a special challenge. As they were submitted, decisions had to be made about their use. We found out that in some cases they had to be combined. Thus articles on specific topics were sometimes turned into more comprehensive essays. No one could do an adequate job on such large topics as Jesuits in Asia, colonialism in all of Asia, or Methodist churches in Asia. Thus we commissioned compiled articles on Jesuits in Japan, China, and India and then we had another author weave the articles together into a single survey article. On the other hand, some specific articles had to be omitted. This was particularly the case if a certain article from one country could not be balanced by articles on the same theme from other countries. We did this because we felt that the overall presentation of Christianity in Asia should have as much symmetry as possible. Other topics seemed to be so important that, in the final analysis, we did turn to scholars in Europe and North America to ensure their inclusion. In the end, we included 1,260 separate entries. Another 464 articles were written and incorporated into these 1,260 entries.

INTRODUCTION

In some ways this *Dictionary of Asian Christianity (DAC)* is not really about Asia (at least not all of it); nor is it, strictly speaking, a dictionary. A dictionary defines terms in a fairly concise manner so that the reader can get the information needed and then move on. Nor is it an encyclopedia. An encyclopedia tries to cover an area of knowledge in a thorough and systematic manner. Although this work is not truly encyclopedic, it does move beyond the strict definition of a dictionary. In sociological terms, the *DAC* tries to provide a type of "thick description" of Christianity in Asia. One can, in this volume, study various social and political influences upon Christianity as well as look up facts about particular Christian leaders.

Strictly speaking, the *DAC* does not cover all of Asia. Asia, topographically speaking, stretches from Turkey to Siberia and south to Papua. This volume does not use a strictly topographical or geographical definition for Asia but instead adds cultural and historical tests to determine the extent of Asia. After some exploratory consultations concerning the possibility of including West Asia (Lebanon, Palestine, and Turkey), we decided that most West Asians in the modern period look to the Islamic and Mediterranean world more than to the East. This has not always been the case though, which complicates matters a bit. In the early centuries of the Christian era, Asian Christianity was the area outside, to the east of, the Roman Empire. Indian Christians today have a very close identity to those Christians in Syria and "Persia" (Edessa, Osrohene, Selucia-Ctesiphon, and Baghdad) since this is regarded as the region from which St. Thomas came. In the early centuries Asian Christianity was composed of those churches that were to the east of the Roman Empire. Thus, we decided that the *DAC* should cover this Persian area of western Asia until the Arab conquest of the seventh century, and from that point on it should cover the area from Pakistan to the east. Language (Urdu is spoken in India and Pakistan), culture, and empire decided this as much as geography. Russia is not included, nor are the Pacific Islands. While this may seem to be somewhat arbitrary, it is confirmed by the way in which Asian church history is taught in most seminaries in Asia today.

A Basic Understanding of Christianity

This volume is built around the understanding that Christianity develops in each context in dialogue with the local cultures. There is a central or core concern (the person and work of Jesus Christ as taught in Scripture) that, through this dialogical process, becomes expressed locally. Thus, to understand the local Christian piety, church order, worship, or theology, one must know something about the broader culture. In Pakistan the Islamic context is very important, as is the Buddhist context in Thailand and the particular Communist context of Vietnam or Laos. For most of East Asia, wars have had a tremendous influence on Christian development. Some of these cultural influences, or forces, are collective (the government or religion), and some of them are quite specific and even individual. A king or president or even a great evangelist may have the type of influence on church development that is usually seen only by a collective elite. The *DAC* tries to include many of these forces that have helped to make the various churches what they have become. Two examples may help. First, in reading about Christianity in Sri Lanka*, it quickly becomes clear that various European countries had colonized the island of Ceylon and that this was very important in determining the type of Christianity that was planted. The article on colonialism* will thus help both to identify the unique influences of colonialism in Sri Lanka and to show how this is part of the experience of almost all countries of Asia. Second, in reading about Christianity in twentieth-century Korea* one sees immediately that nearly every article dealing with Korea refers to Japanese influence, the Shinto* shrine controversy, the Pacific War (World War II*), and the later Korean War*. All of these entries can be found in this volume and help to explain their influences upon Korean Christianity.

We mentioned above that Christianity develops in dialogue with the local context. This means that the local context is also affected by the advent of Christianity in that context. Thus our goal was to include some of the prominent features of this dialectical development. This influence on the local context, it must be confessed, has not always been positive. This is because the relationship between Christianity and the basic social institutions has been so complex in the modern period. As a result, the complexity of these relationships is presented here as well. We have thus included articles on opium*, literacy*, colleges and universities*, medical work*, and women's movements*. Christianity has not only brought modern education and medicine to many regions of Asia but has also had an impact on the way peoples of Asia see themselves and the way other religions understand themselves. In the early history of Christianity in Asia, Christian translation projects (Greek to Syriac and then to Arabic) had a significant influence on the development of Islam in western Asia. Hinduism in India and Buddhism in Thailand and Sri Lanka have all been influenced by their contact with Christian communities. Some would say that Buddhism in China and Japan has also been influenced by early contacts with East Syrian (Nestorian*) Christianity. We hope that this volume will therefore help readers understand this two-way dialogue of Christian communities with local cultures.

Using *A Dictionary of Asian Christianity*

This resource is designed to be used in a number of ways. One approach might be to begin with a survey article such as China* or Jesuits* to get an overview of a country or movement. Then as each article notes words or concepts that are also discussed under other topics in the *DAC*, a person could continue her or his research by looking up some of the words that have an asterisk (Matteo Ricci*, colleges*, James Hudson Taylor*, etc.). Another approach might be to focus on suggested references. Someone interested in the ecumenical movement* in Asia or Gospel and culture* might look up these articles and then use the concluding bibliographies for guidance. Some researchers may begin with a more specific topic, region, or person (Islamic Fundamentalism*, Celebes*, or Luo Wen Zao*), and through cross-referencing discover further discussions covering the broader context of their specific subject. What is to be remembered is that the *DAC* is specifically limited to subjects that help to describe Asian Christianity. Thus some subjects (such as mission societies) and some Western missionaries (who are important from the Western perspective) may not be found here.

A Note on Languages and Spellings

Languages are not as easily tamed as one might hope. In our regional meetings, we arrived at no common agreement from Pakistan to Japan as to how to handle historic spellings. In general, we give the spelling of a place or name as it is most commonly used in that area. This means that some of the names might seem unfamiliar at first. When possible, however, we give another, or earlier, or more recent spelling parenthetically. Thus, as an example, we do not have only the Pinyin or only the Wade Giles spelling of Chinese names and places. Where persons or places have two common spellings, we have often listed both in the text for cross-referencing purposes. Since the *DAC* is in English, we tend to use Anglicized spellings unless the Portuguese-, Spanish-, or Asian-language spelling is more commonly understood. Articles were submitted in nine different languages, so the process of standardization was often caught between author, translator, and editor. Even at the end of the project, there were a few brief biographies (written in Chinese) of Western missionaries who worked in China whom we could not identify. The Western names could not be identified from the Anglicized Chinese, and the descriptions were so general in nature that we were not sure about whom we were reading.

A Note on China

When this project was started, Hong Kong was a British Territory, and the editorial committee decided that articles on people or events in the People's Republic of China should preferably be written by Chinese living in China rather than by Taiwanese or residents of Hong Kong. In addition, it took a little extra time to get together two teams of Christian scholars in China (one Protestant and one Roman Catholic). Under the helpful leadership of Bishop John Chew of Singapore, however, this was eventually accomplished. The sensitive nature of much of the material from China meant that the writers should work as a team with their articles signed only as "China Group." Furthermore, it will quickly become clear that the Chinese entries reflect a self-understanding slightly different from that in other countries. Another issue concerned the various articles from China that would be listed under the general heading "Chinese Translations and Writings." We grouped them together under this single heading as a major article in order to reveal something of the literary nature of the development of Christianity in China. Special appreciation should be given to those Chinese scholars who helped to tell the Chinese Christian story in an ecumenical setting at the beginning of a new millennium.

A Final Note, a Future Note

A great deal of material was left out in producing this volume, and at the same time a great deal of material was requested that was never received. This *Dictionary of Asian Christianity* should therefore be seen best as a first edition resource for the study of Asian Christianity as told by Asians. With the rapid growth of Christianity in Asia, the multiplication of institutions, and the proliferation of scholarship about the Asian churches, it is only fitting that research continue. The descriptions of Christianity in Asia in this volume will change dramatically over the course of the next ten or twenty years. Any request for further information about, or suggested contributions to, our ongoing research should be addressed to:

Dr. Scott W. Sunquist
Pittsburgh Theological Seminary
616 North Highland Ave.
Pittsburgh, PA 15260; USA
sunquist@pts.edu

Scott W. Sunquist, *Editor*

David Wu Chu Sing *and*
John Chew Hiang Chea,
Associate Editors

CONTRIBUTORS

D. Stephen Abraham
Associate General Secretary and Secretary, Bible Ministries
Scripture Union and CSSM, India
Madras, India

Thomas Abraham
Adjunct Faculty
Jubilee Memorial Bible College
Kerala, India

T. S. Abraham
General President
The IPC of God
Kerala, India

Bernard Adeney
Program Pascasarjana Agama and Masyaraka
Universitas Kristen Satya Wacana
Salatiga, Indonesia

Stephen Aisthorpe
Deputy Director
International Nepal Fellowship (INF)
Pokhara, Nepal

Solomon D. L. Alagodi
Associate Professor, History of Christianity
Karnataka Theological College
Karnataka, India

K. P. Aleaz
Bishop's College
Calcutta, India

Martin Alphonse
Former Pastor
Wesley Methodist Church
Madras, India

Robert Alter
Retired Presbyterian Church (U.S.A.) Missionary India
Wooster, OH, U.S.A.

Samuel Amirtham
Bishop
Church of South India
Kerala, India

Mariano Apilado
President
Union Theological Seminary
Manila, Philippines

Mar Aprem
Metropolitan, Chaldean Syrian Church of the East
Kerala, India

Jan S. Aritonang
Professor of Church History
Sekolah Tinggi Teologi Jakarta
Jakarta Pusat, Indonesia

Saphir Athyal
Director, Mission and Evangelism
World Vision International
Monrovia, CA, U.S.A.

Aung Khin
Adviser, Myanmar Ecumenical Institute
Myanmar Council of Churches
Yangon, Myanmar

U Aung Than
Bible House
Myanmar

Samuel Azariah
Bishop of Raiwind
Church of Pakistan
Lahore, Pakistan

Pat Babiera
Executive Secretary
AMRSP
Quezon City, Philippines

Stephen Bailey
Country Director
Christian and Missionary Alliance Services Inc.
Nongkhai, Thailand

Peter Barry
Researcher
Holy Spirit Study Centre
Hong Kong, People's Republic of China

John Bathgate
Former Missionary
Presbyterian Church, U.S.A.
India

Leslie Bauzon
Former Professor, Graduate School
University of Tsukuba
Ibaraki-Ken, Japan

Monina Baybay
Provincial Superior
Daughters of St. Paul
Pasay City, Philippines

Ilsa Berner
Lecturer in Church History
Gujranwala Theological Seminary
Pakistan

Stephen B. Bevans, S.V.D.
Professor of Historical and Doctrinal Studies
Catholic Theological Union
Chicago, IL, U.S.A.

William E. Biernatzki, S.J.
Research Director
Centre for the Study of Communication and Culture
St. Louis University
St. Louis, IL, U.S.A.

Amelia A. Boco, O.S.C.
Religious Sister
Monasterio de Santa Clara
Quezon City, Philippines

Jim Bowman
President
Far East Broadcasting Company
La Mirada, CA, U.S.A.

Henry Breidenthal
Lecturer
Bangkok Bible College
Bangkok, Thailand

Sebastian Brock
Reader in Syriac Studies in the University of Oxford and Professional Fellow of Wolfson College
Oriental Institute
Oxford, England

G. Thompson Brown
Professor of Missions and World Christianity, Emeritus
Columbia Theological Seminary
Decatur, GA, U.S.A.

Judith M. Brown
Beit Professor of Commonwealth History
Balliol College, Oxford University
Oxford, England

Frank Budenholzer
Professor of Chemistry
Fu Jen Catholic University
Taiwan, Republic of China

David Bundy
Librarian and Associate Professor of Church History
Christian Theological Seminary
Indianapolis, IN, U.S.A.

Stanley Burgess
Professor of Religious Studies
Southwest Missouri State University
Springfield, MO, U.S.A.

Beverly Butcher
Former Lecturer in Folklore
University of Pennsylvania
Philadelphia, PA, U.S.A.

Esther Byu
Executive Secretary
International Committee for the Fellowship of the Least Coin
Bangkok, Thailand

John Carroll
Director
Institute on Church and Social Issues
Ateneo de Manila University
Manila, Philippines

Chan Hay-Him
General Secretary
Chinese Coordination Centre of World Evangelism
Kowloon, Hong Kong

P. T. Chandapilla
St. Thomas ECI
Poona, India

J. Russell Chandran
Former Principal
United Theological College
Bangalore, India

Chang Te-Hsiang
Professor of New Testament
Tianan Theological College and Seminary
Tainan, Taiwan

Jean Charbonnier
Service Chine Missions Étrangères de Paris
Paris, France

Sunil Kumar Chatterjee
The Carey Library, Serampore College
West Bengal, India

Chaiwat Chawmuangman
President
Thailand Baptist Theological Seminary
Bangkok, Thailand

Chek Yat Phoon
President
Southeast Asia Union College
Republic of Singapore

John Chen Chhong-Fat
Director of Lay Training and Continuing Education
Tainan Theological College and Seminary
Tainan, Taiwan

Chen Nan-jou
Professor of Christian Ethics
Tainan Theological College and Seminary
Tainan, Taiwan

Paul Chen
Anglican Church
Yangon, Myanmar

Cheng Yang-en
Associate Professor of Church History
Taiwan Theological College and Seminary
Taipei, Taiwan

John Chew Hiang Chea
Bishop
Anglican Church in Singapore
Republic of Singapore

Ernest C. T. Chew
Associate Professor, Department of History, Faculty of Arts and Social Sciences
National University of Singapore
Republic of Singapore

Emrys M. K. Chew
Research Student
University of Cambridge, United Kingdom

Chen Chia-Shih
President
Taiwan Theological College and Seminary
Taipei, Taiwan

Luke Chim
Roman Catholic Church
Taipei, Taiwan

Kummool Chinawong
Church of Christ in Thailand
Thailand

Joseph Chinh Vu Kim
Faculty of Theology
Fujen Catholic University
Taipei, Taiwan

Chit Sein, May, M.C.S.
Medical Doctor
Yangon, Myanmar

Choi Hyeong-Mook
The Korea Theological Study Institute
Korea

Chong Tet Loi
Former Pastor
Basel Christian Church of Malaysia
Sabah Malaysia

Choong Chee Pang
Lecturer in New Testament
Trinity Theological College
Republic of Singapore

Charles Christiano
Mennonite Church
Jakarta, Indonesia

Contributors

Chu Sin Jan
Assistant Professor of History
Chinese Culture University
Taipei, Taiwan

Surachai Chumsriphan
Archivist and parish priest
Catholic Mission of Bangkok
Thailand

John Clammer
Professor of Comparative Sociology and African Studies
Ichigaya Campus, Sophia University
Tokyo, Japan

Jean Clavaud
Director
Mission Evangelique Contre La Lepre
France

David Claydon
Federal Secretary
Church Missionary Society, Australia
New South Wales, Australia

Kuchipudi Clement
Director
Sram Ashrams of India
Secundarabad, India

Maria Anicia Co, R.V.M.
Directress
Mother Ignacia Center for Spirituality
Quezon City, Philippines

Teresa Joseph Constantino, O.C.D.
Carmelite Monastery of St. Therese
Quezon City, Philippines

Ralph Covell
Professor of World Missions, Emeritus
Denver Seminary
Denver, CO, U.S.A.

Evelyn Tan Cullarmar
Chairperson, Department of Political Science
Ateneo de Manila University
Manila, Philippines

Joy S. Cullen
Consultant
Baptist Christian Education
Penang, Malaysia

Floyd T. Cunningham
Academic Dean
Asia-Pacific Nazarene Theological Seminary
Rizal, Philippines

Digna Dacanay
Society of the Sacred Heart
Quezon City, Philippines

Saw Daniel
Director of Leadership Promotion; Jayin Baptist Convention
Yangon, Myanmar

Richard M. Daulay
Deputy General Secretary of PGI (Communion of Churches in Indonesia)
Jakarta, Indonesia

Thomas X. Davis
Abbot
Abbey of New Clairvaux
Vina, CA, U.S.A.

Eugenia de Costa
Assistant Secretary of CEID
Sisters of Our Lady of the Missions
Dhaka, Bangladesh

Christiaan G. F. de Jong
Professor of Church History
Sekolah Tinggi Theologia
Jakarta, Indonesia

Victorina de la Paz, M.M.S.
Medical Mission Sisters
Cubae, Quezon City, Philippines

Rolando de la Rosa, O.P.
Priory of St. Thomas Aquinas, University of Santo Tomas
Manila, Philippines

José de Mesa
Religious Education Department, College of Education
De La Salle University
Manila, Philippines

Teodoro M. de Mesa
Officer-in-Charge
Deputy Director for Operations for Mindanao
Task Force Detainees of the Philippines (TFDP)
Manila, Philippines

Frans de Ridder, C.I.C.M.
Church of St. Francis of Assisi
Republic of Singapore

Desmond de Sousa
Secretary, House for Human Development
Redemptorist Community
Goa, India

Archie de Souza
Vicar-General, Professor, Pastor
St. Patrick's Cathedral
Karachi, Pakistan

Teotonio de Souza
Former Researcher
Xavier Centre of Hitorical Research
Goa, India

V. Devasahayam
Professor of Systematic Theology
Gurukul Lutheran Theological College
Madras, India

Alfonso Deza
Editor/Director
ASICC
Manila, Philippines

Antonio Didone
Director
St. Mary's Hopsital
Lotung, Taiwan

Parig Digan
Researcher
Society of St. Columban (SSC)
London, United Kingdom

Anthony Do Nghiem Huu
Historian, researcher
Institute of Social Sciences
Ho Chi Minh City, Vietnam

Say Doh
Myanmar

Conor J. Donnelly
Independent Reseacher
Republic of Singapore

Frederick S. Downs
Professor of History of Christianity, Emeritus
The United Theological College
Bangalore, India

Phuveyi Dozo
Outreach Challenge Ministries
New Delhi, India

Andreas D'Souza
Director
Henry Martin Institute: International Centre for Research, Interfaith Relations and Reconciliation
Hyderabad, India

Christopher Duraisingh
Professor of Applied Theology
Episcopal Divinity School
Cambridge, MA, U.S.A.

Salvador Eduarte
Professor of Church History
Union Theological College
Cavite, Philippines

Eh Wah
Former Principal
Myanmar Institute of Theology
Insein, Myanmar

Fang Chih-Jung
Faculty of Theology
Fujen Catholic University
Taipei-Hsien, Taiwan

Prema Fenn
Union of Evangelical Students in India
Madras, India

Ana Maria Fernandez
Philippines

Pilar Ferrer
President
Teresian Association
Quezon City, Philippines

Michael Fonner
Assistant Professor
Colby-Sawyer College
Hanover, NH, U.S.A.

Joselito Fornier
Professor
Ateneo de Manila University
Philippines

Ann Fox
Thailand Baptist Theological Seminary
Bangkok, Thailand

Jose Mario C. Francisco, S.J.
Director, East Asian Pastoral Institute
Ateneo de Manila University
Quezon City, Philippines

Robert E. Frykenberg
Professor of History, Asian Studies
University of Wisconsin, Madison
Madison, WI, U.S.A.

Robert Fukada
Professor of Practical Theology
Doshisha University
Japan

Awais Gill
Educationist
Senior Secondary School Teacher, Rawalpindi
Pakistan

Manuel Ginete, F.C.M.
Provincial Superior
Congregation of the Mission, Philippine Province
Tandang Sora, Philippines

J. W. Gladstone
Bishop of the South Kerala Diocese
Church of South India
Kerala, India

Goh Keat Peng
Executive Secretary
Christian Federation of Malaysia
Selangor, Malaysia

Michael Goh
The Regional Fraternity
St. Anthony's Friary
Republic of Singapore

Hilario Gomez
General Secretary
United Church of Christ in the Philippines
Philippines

Kathleen Grimley
Instructor in English
Daughters of Charity
Taipei, Taiwan

Harold Gross
Church of Christ in Thailand
Bangkok, Thailand

Christoffer Grundmann
Professor
University of Hamburg
Germany

Amelia de Ntra Guadalupe
Monasterio de Santa Clara
Quezon City, Philippines

Connie Gundy-Tappy
Dictionary of Asian Christianity Project Coordinator
Pittsburgh, PA, U.S.A.

Francis Gustilo
Provincial of the Salesians (S.D.B.)
Commission on Formation
Manila, Philippines

John Hamlin
Emeritus Professor
Payap University, Faculty of Theology
Chiang Mai, Thailand

Saw Hanson Tadaw
Myanmar

George Harper
Associate Professor of Christian History and Thought
Alliance Biblical Seminary
Manila, Philippines

Chris Hartono
Lecturer in Church History
Duta Wacana Christian University, Faculty of Theology
Yogyakarta, Indonesia

Roger E. Hedlund
Director, Mylapore Institute for Indigenous Studies, Chennai; Managing Editor, Dharma Deepika; former Professor of Mission Research, Serampore College
Calcutta, India

Arnold Heredia
Executive Secretary
Idara-e-Amn-O-Insaf
Karachi, Pakistan

Adolf Heuken, S.J.
Writer and publisher
Yayasan Cipta Loka Caraka
Jakarta, Indonesia

Hla Yi
Myanmar

Ho Chee Sin
Former Bishop
The Methodist Church in Singapore
Republic of Singapore

Daniel Ho
Pastor
Damansara Utama Methodist Church
Petaling Jaya, Malaysia

Marvin D. Hoff
Executive Director
Foundation for Theological Education in South East Asia
Holland, MI, U.S.A.

George A. Hood
Retired English Presbyterian Missionary (China, Malaysia) and Mission Board Secretary
Northumberland, England

Fanai Hrangkhuma
Coordinator, Mission Studies
Serampore College
West Bengal, India

Andrew Hsiao
President Emeritus
Lutheran Theological Seminary
Hong Kong, People's Republic of China

Hsu Hsin-te
Program Secretary, Evangelism Committee
The Presbyterian Church in Taiwan
Taipei, Taiwan

Huang Po Ho
Professor of Systematic Theology
Tainan Theological College and Seminary
Tainan, Taiwan

George R. Hunsberger
Professor of Missiology
Western Theological Seminary
Holland, MI, U.S.A.

Robert Hunt
Pastor
English-Speaking United Methodist Church of Vienna
Vienna, Austria

Huon Phan Phat
Former Catholic Chaplain of the Armed Forces of the Republic of Viet Nam
Priest, Congregation of the Holy Redeemer
Long Beach, CA, U.S.A.

Jubil Raplan Hutaurak
Ephorus
Huria Kristen Batak Protestan
Kantor Pusat HKBP
Sumatera Utara, Indonesia

Hwa Yung
Director, Center for the Study of Christianity in Asia
Trinity Theological College
Republic of Singapore

Adai Jacob
Principal
Malankara Syrian Orthodox Theological Seminary
Kerala, India

Plamthodathil Jacob
Professor of Philosophy and Religion,
Union Biblical Seminary
Pune, India

Blesson G. Jacobs
Nepal

Bernard Jagueneau
Philippines

Arthur James
Principal/Executive Secretary
Gujranwala Theological Seminary
Gujranwala, Pakastan

Violet James
Lecturer in Church History
Singapore Bible College
Republic of Singapore

John Jin Jyi-giokk
Christian Institute for Social Transformation
Tainan, Taiwan

Aeries Sumping Jingan
Dean
St. Thomas Cathedral
Sarawak, Malaysia

Merle Jivanandam
Anglican Cathedral
Lahore, Pakistan

T. K. John
Professor
Vidyajyoti College of Theology
Delhi, India

Anne Johnson
Associate Minister, Retired
Bethany Presbyterian Church
Republic of Singapore

M. J. Joseph
Vicar
Mar Thoma Syrian Church
Madras, India

Kang Keun Whan
Professor Emeritus, Church History
Seoul Theological University
Kyunggido, Korea

Contributors

Kang Wi Jo
Wilhelm Loehe Professor of Mission, Emeritus
Wartburg Theological Seminary
Dubuque, IA, U.S.A.

Perry Katoppo
Translation Consultant
Lembaga Alkitab Indonesia
West Java, Indonesia

David Keck
Visiting Assistant Professor of Pastoral Theology
Duke Divinity School
Durham, NC, U.S.A.

Aloysius Kedl
General Archivist
Missionari Oblati Maria Immacolate
Vatican City, Italy

Hugh P. Kemp
Dean of Studies
Manawatu Regional Learning Centre of the Bible College of New Zealand
Palmerston North, New Zealand

Keun Whan Kang
Seoul Theological University
Buchun-shi Kyunggido, Korea

Lillian Kha Nau Daw
Board member
National YWCA
Yangon, Myanmar

Ramesh Khatry
Nepal Bible Ashram
Kathmandu, Nepal

Kim Heung Soo
Mokwon University
Taejon, Korea

Kim In Soo
Professor of Church History
Presbyterian College and Theological Seminary
Seoul, Korea

Kim Kyoung Jae
Professor, Faculty of Theology
Hanshin University
Seoul, Korea

Kim Seung Tae
Institute of Korean Church History
Seoul, Korea

Kim Yong Bok
Chancellor
Advanced Institute for the Study of Life
Seoul, Korea

Kin Huh
President
Korea Baptist Theological University and Seminary
Korea

Vorayuth Kitbamrung
Thailand

John Kleinen
Anthropological-Sociological Center
University of Amsterdam
Amsterdam, Netherlands

Lawrence Ko Jearn Chier
Manager, Christian Emphasis
YMCA
Republic of Singapore

Theodorus Kobong
Pdt. Doctor Theologiae
Sekolah Tinggi Theologi
Jakarta, Indonesia

Symond Kock
Lecturer in Church History
Trinity Theological College
Republic of Singapore

Victor Koh
Director
Campus Crusade for Christ
Republic of Singapore

Onukum Konkaew
Thailand

Jacob Kurian
Vice-Principal
Orthodox Theological Seminary
Kerala, India

Anne Kwantes
Asian Theological Seminary
Philippines

Kwock Sunja
Ph.D Candidate in Theological and Religious Studies
Drew University
Madison, NJ, U.S.A.

Kwok Pui-lan
Professor
Episcopal Divinity School
Cambridge, MA, U.S.A.

Clifford Kyaw Dwe
Myanmar Institute of Theology
Myanmar

Kyaw Nyunt
Director
Myanmar Ecumenical Institute,
Myanmar Council of Churches
Yangon, Myanmar

Kyoung Jae Kim
Hanshin University
Seoul, Korea

Creighton Lacy
Professor Emeritus, Divinity School
Duke University
Durham, NC, U.S.A.

Lai Chun Ming
General Secretary
The Bible Society in the R.O.C. (Taiwan)
Taipei, Taiwan

Lal Nun Tluanga
Interserv, India
Mizoran, India

Lal Pan Liana
Principal
Myanmar Theological College (Methodist)
Mandalay, Myanmar

Lam Wing-Hung
Research Professor, Church History and
Chinese Studies
Tyndale College and Seminary
Ontario, Canada

Victor Larque
Roman Catholic Church
Bangkok, Thailand

Albert Lau
Department of History
National University of Singapore
Republic of Singapore

Earnest Lau
Archivist
Methodist Church of Singapore
Republic of Singapore

Lau Jen Sin
Librarian
Trinity Theological College
Republic of Singapore

Lena S. N. Lau
Former Lecturer in General Linguistics
University of Hong Kong

Maria Goretti Lau
Superior General
Sisters of the Precious Blood
Hong Kong, People's Republic of China

Agnes Lee
Provincial
Sisters of the Infant Jesus
Republic of Singapore

Andrina Lee
Provincial
Franciscan Missionaries of Mary
Taipei, Taiwan

Lee Chee-Kong
Pastor
The Chinese Rhenish Church-Wancai
Hong Kong, People's Republic of China

Lee Chong Kau
Lecturer, Christian Education
Trinity Theological College
Republic of Singapore

Lee Deok-Joo
Vice President
Hyangsan Academy for Korean Christian
Culture Studies
Seoul, Korea

Lee Kam Hing
Department of History
Universiti of Malaya
Kuala Lumpur, Malaysia

Leung Ka-lun
Vice-President (Adacemic Affairs) and
Chief-Editor of *Jian Dao Journal*
Alliance Bible Seminary
Hong Kong, People's Republic of China

James Lewis
Professor of World Religions
Wheaton College
Wheaton, IL, USA

Lim Cheang Ean
Vicar
Christ Church Penang
Penang, Malaysia

Lin Hong-Hsin
Professor
Taiwan Theological College
Taipei, Taiwan

John Liu
Superior General CDD
Catholic Heng Yee High School
Taipei, Taiwan

Linda Lizada
Regional Superior
Cenacle Retreat House
Quezon City, Philippines

Stella-Marie Llerin
Superior General
OND Generalate
Cotabato City, Philippines

Anthony Lobo
Chairman, Office of Education
Federation of Asian Bishops' Conference
Rawalpindi, Pakistan

Joseph Loftus, C. M.
Coordinator, China (PRC) Projects
Catholic Mission
Kan Shan, Taiwan

Loh I-to
Chair, Department of Church Music, President of the Tainan Theological College and Seminary
Tainan, Taiwan

Frank Lomax
Hon. Chaplain
Trinity Theological College
Republic of Singapore

Imti Samuel Longkumer
Lecturer
Indian School of Ecumenical Theology (ISET)
Bangalore, India

Mangal Man Maharjan
Kathmandu, Nepal

Edward Malecdan
Dean
St. Andrew's Theological Seminary
Manila, Philippines

Man Kyu Oh
Samyook College
Seoul, Korea

Mary John Mananzan
Institute of Women's Studies
Scholastica's College
Manila, Philippines

Jeffrey Mann
Vanderbilt University
Nashville, TN, U.S.A.

Mar Cheta Thein
Yangon, Myanmar

Maran Yaw
Pastor
Yangon Kachin Baptist Church
Myanmar

Marip Ja Naw
Executive Secretary
Myanmar Council of Churches
Myanmar

Luke Martin
Retired
Volunteer, Vietnamese Ministries
through the Eastern Menonite Mission
Allentown, PA, U.S.A.

Masao Takenaka
Asian Christian Art Association
Kyoto, Japan

Louis Mascarenhas, O.F.M.
Professor of Mission Theology
National Catholic Institute of Theology
Karachi, Pakistan

Gabriel Massey
General Secretary
Federation of Evangelical Churches in India
Nagpur, India

James Massey
General Secretary
ISPCK
Delhi, India

James K. Mathew
Bishop of the United Methodist Church, retired
Bethesda, MD, U.S.A.

Samuel Mathew
Faith Theological Seminary
Kerala, India

C. V. Matthew
Principal
Jubilee Memorial Bible College in Chennai Madras
Tamil Nadu, India

Johnny Maung Lat
Professor
Myanmar Institute of Christian Theology
Yangon, Myanmar

John McCoy
Media Relations Manager
World Vision International
Monrovia, CA, U.S.A.

Robert McCulloch
Professor of Liturgy and Church History
National Catholic Institute of Theology
Karachi, Pakistan

William McElrath
Baptist Church Head Office
Bandung, Indonesia

Gary McGee
Professor of Church History and Pentecostal Studies
Assemblies of God Theological Seminary
Springfield, MO, U.S.A.

Mark W. McLeod
Professor, Department of History
University of Delaware
Newark, DE, U.S.A.

Chrys McVey, OP
Regent of Studies
The Pastoral Institute
Multan, Pakistan

Jerome Mesina
Augustinain Novitiate and Prayer House
Cebu, Philippines

Edgar Metzler
International Program Director
Mennonite Central Commttee
Akron, PA, U.S.A.

Josef Metzler
Prefect
Archivio Segreto Vatican
Vatican City, Italy

Thomas Michel
Office for Ecumenical and Interreligious Affairs
Bangkok, Thailand

Dominic Moghal
Christian Study Centre
Rawalpindi, Pakistan

Ben A. Moraleda, C.S.S.R.
Program Director
Inter-Congregational Theological Center
Quezon City, Philippine Islands

Domingo M. Moraleda, C.M.F.
Institute for Consecrated Life in Asia (ICLA)
Quezon City, Philippines

Mark Mullins
Professor of Sociology of Religion
Meiji Gakuin University
Tokyo, Japan

A. Mathias Mundadan
Jeevass Kendram; St. Anthony's Monastery
Kerala, India

Lewis Myers
Vice President for World A Strategies
Southern Baptist Convention
Richmond, VA, U.S.A.

Ellen Mary Mylod
Ursulines of the Roman Union of the Order of St.
Ursula
Wen Tzao Ursuline Convent
Kaohsiung, Taiwan

Josefina Nepomuceno
President
Holy Angel University
Angeles City, Philippines

Peter Ng Tze Ming
Acting Director
Centre for the Study of Religion and Chinese Society
Hong Kong, People's Republic of China

Zakaria Ngelow
Sekolah Tinggi Theologia Intim
Ujung Padang, South Sulawesi, Indonesia

Anthony Nghiem Do Huu
Institute of Social Sciences
Ho Chi Minh City, Vietnam

Nguyen Cuong Huu
Academic Dean
Vietnamese Theological College
Westminster, CA, U.S.A.

Bruce Nicholls
Editor
Evangelical Review of Theology
New Zealand

Rene Nicolas
Procureur in Singapore for the
Paris Foreign Missions Society
Republic of Singapore

Frederick W. Norris
Dean E. Walker Professor of Church History
and Professor of World Mission/Evangelism
Emmanuel School of Religion
Johnson City, TN, U.S.A.

Nu Sar
Myanmar

Christopher Ocker
Professor of Church History
San Francisco Theological Seminary
San Francisco, CA, U.S.A.

Graham Ogden
United Bible Society
Canberra City, Australia

Ohtawa Koichi
Associate General Secretary
The International fellowship of Evangelical Students
Tokyo, Japan

Hendrik Ongirwalu
Church Minister, and Adjunct Professor at Sekolah
Tinggi Theologia
Jakarta, Indonesia

George Oommen
Professor, Department of History of Christianity
United Theological College
Bangalore, India

Monette Ouellette
Provincial Superior
Missionary Sisters of the Immaculate Conception
Taipei, Taiwan

Robert Owens Jr.
T. W. Nakarai Professor of Hebrew Bible/
Old Testament
Emmanuel school of Religion
Johnson City, TN, U.S.A.

Peterus Pamudji
President, Professor of Theology
Institut Theologia Aletheia
Jatim, Indonesia

Simon Pandey
General Secretary
National Churches Fellowship of Nepal (NCFN)
Kathmandu, Nepal

Geevarghese Panicker
St. Ephrem Ecumenical Research Institute
Kottayam, Kerala, India

Arnold Parengkuan
Fakultas Theologia UKIT
Manado, Indonesia

Timothy Park Kiho
Associate Professor of Asian Mission and
Director of Korean Studies
Fuller Theological Seminary
Pasadena, CA, U.S.A.

Sutarman Partonadi
Gereja Kristen Jawa, NEHEMIA
Jakarta, Indonesia

Glendora Paul
Mission Volunteer
Pittsburgh Theological Seminary
Pittsburgh, PA, U.S.A.

Julius Danaraj Paul
Bishop, Evangelical Lutheran Church in Malaysia
Kuala Lumpur, Malaysia

William Paw
The National Council of YMCAs of Myanmar
Yangon, Myanmar

Michelle Payette
Secretary General
The Missionary Sisters of the Immaculate Conception
Outremont, Canada

Galende Pedro
Director
San Agustin Museum
Manila, Philippines

Giacomo Pellizzari
Focolare
Tagaytay City, Philippines

M. Basil Pennington
Abbot
Abbey of Our Lady of Holy Spirit
Conyers, GA, U.S.A.

Bernardo Ma Perez, B.M.P, O.S.B.
Rector
San Beda College
Manila, Philippines

Cindy Perry
Director
Himalayan Ministries
Kathmandu, Nepal

Donald Persons
Missionary
Lamp of Thailand (of the Church of Christ in Thailand)
Chiang Mai, Thailand

W. L. A. Don Peter
Educationist, Historian, Oriental Scholar, and former Rector of St. Joseph's College, Colombo, and Aquinas College, Colombo
Ragama, Sri Lanka

Peter Phan
The Warren-Blanding Distinguished Professor of Religion and Culture, Department of Religion and Religious Education
The Catholic University of America
Washington, DC, U.S.A.

A. T. Philip
Pastor
India

Richard V. Pierard
Professor of History
Indiana State University
Terre Haute, IN, U.S.A.

Zinia Pinto
Chairperson, standing committee of Catholic Board of Education, Karachi
St. Joseph's Convent
Karachi, Pakistan

Eileen Poh
Lecturer
Discipleship Training Centre
Republic of Singapore

Edward Poitras
Professor of World Christianity
Perkins School of Theology,
Southern Methodist University
Dallas, TX, U.S.A.

François Ponchaud
General Vicar of Kompong Cham
Catholic Church
Phnom Penh, Cambodia

Pong Singh Konyak
Nagaland Baptist Church Council
Kohima, Nagaland, India

Prasit Pongudom
Office of History
Payap University
Chiang Mai, Thailand

Albert Poulet-Mathis, S.J.
President of Taiwan Conference on Religion and Peace; Executive Secretary of Chinese Regional Bishops' Conference's Commissions for Interreligious Dialogue and Cooperation, and Promoting Christian Unity
Tien Educational Center
Taipei, Taiwan, R.O.C.

Matana Pratipasen
Associate Professor, Faculty of Pharmaceutical Sciences
Chulalongkorn University
Bangkok, Thailand

Frank Quinlivan
Sacred Heart of Jesus Province
Dhaka, Bangladesh

Vinoth Ramachandra
Colombo Theological Seminary
Colombo, Sri Lanka

Apolonio Ranche
St. Andrew's Theological Seminary
Manila, Philippines

John Reid
Avoca Beach, NSW, Australia

Reg Reimer
World Evangelical Fellowship
Chilliwack, B.C., Canada

Ronald D. Renard
Self-employed Consultant
Chiang Mai, Thailand

Evelyn Tan Requiza, E.T.R.
Associate Professor, History and Political Science Departments
Ateneo de Manila University
Quezon City, Philippines

Contributors

S. E. Retnowinarati
Former Librarian
Litbang PGI, Research Department of the Indonesian Council of Churches
Indonesia

Rhee Jong Sung
Director
Institute of Advanced Christian Studies of Korea
Seoul, Korea

Robert F. Rice
Literacy Ministries Consultant and Founder
Literacy Ministries International
Tulsa, OK, U.S.A.

H. L. Richard
Church Worker
India

R. David Rightmire
Professor of Bible and Theology
Asbury College
Wilmore, KY, U.S.A.

Doug Ringer
Director, Baptist Leadership Training
Thailand Baptist Mission
Bangkok, Thailand

Rajendra K. Rongong
Kathmandu, Nepal

John Rooney, M.H.M.
Mission Hill Missionary (Pakistan)
St. Joseph's College
London, UK

A. Rosaria
St. Paul's Convent
Narowal, Pakistan

John Roxborogh
Former lecturer in Asian Church History and Missiology
Studia Teologia Malaysia
Presbyterian School of Ministry, Knox College, Dunedin
New Zealand

Rung Ruengsan-Ajin
Principal
Bangkok Institute of Theology
Bangkok, Thailand

Sang Awr
Myanmar Institute of Theology
Myanmar

Sang Gyoo Lee
Institute of Christian Thought
Kosin University
Pusan, Korea

Luciano Santiago
The Medical City Hospital
Manila, Philippines

Pritam Santram
Bishop of Delhi
Diocese of Delhi, CNI
New Delhi, India

Catherine Sardar
Pastoral Centre
Rawalpindi, Pakistan

Paul Russ Satari

Anna May Say Pa
Principal
The Myanmar Institute of Theology
Myanmar

Frank Schattner
Thailand

Don Schlatter
Thailand

Herbert Schneider
Ateneo de Manila University
Philippines

Olaf Schumann
Professor
Universität Hamburg
Hamburg, Germany

David C. Scott
Adjunct Faculty
Wesley Theological Seminary
Washington, DC, U.S.A.

Israel Selvanayagam
World Church Lecturer
Wesley College (World Church in Britain Partnership Programme of the Methodist Church)
Bristol, United Kingdom

Gam Seng Shae
Translation Consultant
United Bible Societies
Chaing Mai, Thailand

Saw Si Hai
National Director Myanmar Youth for Christ
Yangon, Myanmar

Eric J. Sharpe
Emeritus Professor
University of Sydney
Denistone, Australia

Herman Shastri
Seminari Theoloji Malaysia
Selangor, D.E., Malaysia

Wilbert R. Shenk
Professor of Mission History and Contemporary Culture
Fuller Theological Seminary
Pasadena, CA, U.S.A.

Shin Seung Min
Regional Secretary
World Student Christian Federation, Asia Pacific Region
Hong Kong, People's Republic of China

Godwin Shiri
Director
Christian Institute for the Study of Religion and Society
Bangalore, India

G. R. Singh
Principal
Leonard Theological College
Jabalpur, India

T. Valentino Sitoy
Consultant on History and Theology
United Church of Christ in the Philippines

Sixtus Hiddin Situmorang
Probolinggo, Indonesia

Timothy Skinner
Research Services
Fort Worth, TX, U.S.A.

N. Za Thawng Smith
Associate General Secretary
The Myanmar Council of Churches
Yangon, Myanmar

Bobby Sng Ewe Kong
General Secretary
Fellowship of Evangelical Students, Singapore, Retired
Republic of Singapore

Petrus Soedjarno
Bala Keselamatan (Indonesia)
Bandung, Indonesia

Robert Solomon
Bishop
The Methodist Church in Singapore
Republic of Singapore

G. P. V. Somaratna
Colombo Theological Seminary
189 Dutugamunu Street, Kohewela, Sri Lanka

Soon Guat Eng
Project Director
Dictionary of Asian Christianity, 1992-95

Soon Soo Kee
Rector
Church of the Good Shepherd
Republic of Singapore

Soelarso Sopater
Former Chairman of the Indonesian Council of Churches and Emeritus Professor of Systematic Theology (Adjunct Professor)
Jakarta Theological Seminary
Indonesia

Theodore Srinivasagam
Minister-at-Large
India Missions Association
Bangalore, India

James Stamoolis
Executive Director, Theological Commission
World Evangelical Fellowship
Wheaton, IL, U.S.A.

Brian Stanley
Director, *Currents in World Christianity* Project
University of Cambridge, Westminster College
Cambridge, England

Jean S. Stoner
Partnership Consultant
Presbyterian Church (U.S.A.)
Craftsbury Common, VT, U.S.A.

Stanislaus Su
Superior General
Little Brothers of St. John the Baptist
Taiwan

David Suh
Visiting Professor, Asian Theology
Drew University
Madison, NJ, U.S.A.

Contributors

Suh Jeong Min, S.J.M.
Research Professor
Yonsei University
Korea

Sunand Sumithra
Managing Editor
Theological Book Trust
Bangalore, India

Ebenezer Sunderaj
General Secretary
India Missions Association
Madras, India

Scott W. Sunquist
W. Don McClure Associate Professor of World Mission and Evangelism
Pittsburgh Theological Seminary
Pittsburgh, PA, U.S.A.

Herbert Swanson
Office of History
Church of Christ in Thailand
Payap University Archives
Thailand

Andre Sylvestre
Congregation of the Mission, Province of Toulouse
Taipei, Taiwan

Taizé Community
Taizé, France

Grace Tan
Chairperson, Conference Committee on Church History and Records
Methodist Conference (Lower Myanmar)
Yangon, Myanmar

Agus Tangyong
Majelis Pusat Pendidikan Kristen di Indonesia
Jakarta, Indonesia

Mesakh Tapilatu
Lecturer
Fakultas Teologi, Universitas Kristen Indonesia Maluku
Amboina, Indonesia

Irene Tay Mui Lan
Missionary
Thailand

Pracha Thaivatcharamart
Dean of Students
Thailand Baptist Theological Seminary
Bangkok, Thailand

U Than Htun Myat
General Secretary
The Bible Society of Myanmar

Captain Thangvella
Salvation Army
Myanmar

Peter Thet Lwin
Pastor
St. Francis Parish
Myanmar

Anna Thuc Phan Thi
Congregation of the Lovers of the Cross
Hunei Diocese
Hanoi, Vietnam

Thanaporn Thumsucharitkul
Bangkok Bible College and Seminary
Thailand

Bernard Ticherhoof, T.O.R.
Administrator and Program Director
The Franciscan Spirit and Life Center
Pittsburgh, PA, U.S.A.

Sergio Ticozzi
Spiritual Director
P.I.M.E. International Theological Seminary
Cavite, Philippines

Tin Jyi-Giokk
Christian Institute for Social Transformation
Taiwan

Deetje Tiwa-Rotinsula
Persekutuan Gereja di Indonesia (PGI)
Jakarta, Indonesia

Nipa Todsparint
Vice President
Payap University
Chiang Mai, Thailand

John B. Tran Thu
Congregation of St. John the Baptist
Taichung, Taiwan

Ronnie Tin Tun
Director
Far East Broadcast Radio International, Myanmar
Yangon, Myanmar

Tun Aung Chain
Yangong, Myanmar

Antolin Uy, S.V.D.
Professor of Church History
Divine Word Seminary
Tagaytay City, Philippines

Aart van Beek
Sekolah Tinggi Theologia
Jakarta, Indonesia

Thomas van den End
Missionary in the service of the Reformed Mission League for Literature
On behalf of Churches and Theological Institutions in Indonesia
Apeldoorn, Netherlands

H. A. van Dop
Liturgy and Church Music
Jakarta Theological Seminary
Jakarta, Indonesia

T. I. Varghese
Orthodox Theological Seminary
Kottayam, India

Amelia Vasquez
District Superior
Religious of the Sacred Heart
District Center
Quezon, City, Philippines

Supchai Veerasombat
Thailand Baptist Theological Seminary
Bangkok, Thailand

Lee Wanak
Academic Dean
Asian Theological Seminary
Manila, Philippines

Martin Wang C. C.
Professor of Old Testament
Taiwan Theological College and Seminary
Taipei, Taiwan

Wang Hsien-Chih
Tainan, Taiwan

Margaret Warren
Former Missionary, Japan
Morrison, CO, U.S.A.

I. Ketut Waspada
Protestant Christian Church of Bali (GKPB)
Bali, Indonesia

John Webster
Former Missionary to India
Waterford, CT, U.S.A.

Fred Djara Wellem
Professor of Theology
Fakultas Theologia Universitas Kristen Artha Wacana
Kupang, Indonesia

Philip Wickeri
Flora Lamson Hewlett Professor of Evangelism and Mission
San Francisco Theological Seminary
San Anselmo, CA, U.S.A.

Jean-Paul Wiest
Center for Missions Research and Study at Maryknoll
Maryknoll, NY, U.S.A.

Mark Williams
Senior Lecturer in Japanese Studies
University of Leeds
United Kingdom

Tom Williams
Foreign Mission Board, Southern Baptist Convention
Bangkok, Thailand

John Witek
Associate Professor of East Asian History
Georgetown University
Washington DC, U.S.A.

Christabel Wong
Assistant Librarian
Seminari Teoloji Malaysia
Negeri Sembilan, Malaysia

Danny Wong Tze-Ken
University of Malaya
Department of History
Kuala Lumpur, Malaysia

Timothy Wong Man-Kong
History Department
Hong Kong Baptist University

David Wu
General Board of Global Ministries
United Methodist Church
New York, NY, U.S.A.

Peter Wu Wun-hsiong
Taipei, Taiwan

John Mary Xuan Doan Phu
First Assistant General
Congregation of the Mother Coredemptrix
Ho Chi Minh City, Vietnam

Yap Kim Hao
Former General Secretary
Christian Conference in Asia
Republic of Singapore

Timothy Yates
Canon Emeritus of Derby Cathedral
Derbyshire, UK

Yeoh Seng Guan
Lecturer
Sunway College
Malaysia

Yeow Choo-lak
Executive Director
Association for Theological Education
in South East Asia
Republic of Singapore

Yeow Geok Lian
Former Lecturer in Christian Education
Trinity Theological College
Republic of Singapore

Yoshida Ryo
Associate Professor
Doshisha University
Kyoto, Japan

Thomas Yu
President
China Lutheran Seminary
Hsinchu, Taiwan

Andrina Yuan Lee Bi
Provincial
Franciscan Missionaries of Mary
Taipei, Taiwan, R.O.C.

A. H. Mathias Zahniser
Professor Emeritus
Asbury Theological Seminary
Wilmore, KY, U.S.A.

J. M. Zalei
Director
Evangel Mission, Myanmar
Myanmar

Contributors to "Colleges and Universities" and "Theological Education" Articles

General
Anthony Lobo

China
Tian Wen Zai
Dufresse Chang
Frank E. Budenholzer
Peter Ng

India
F. Hrangkhuma
K. C. Abraham

Japan
Kato Tsneaki
Hubert Cieslik
Yamamoto Joji
Ushimaru Yasuo
Kobayashi Keiko
Takami Tishihiro
Takenaka Masao
Matsukawa Mario
Matsuda Shigeo
Sugii Mutsuro
Ebisawa Arimichi
Yamauchi Ichiro
Izawa Heihachiro
Akiyama Shigeo
Oda Nobundo
Murakami Toraji
Demura Akira
Katakozawa Chiyomatsu
Obata Satoru
Yamazaki Takako
Matsukawa Shigeo
Kuroda Seiko
Suzuki Minako
Yoda Ikuko
Takamichi Motoi
Yanagida Tomotsune
Oguro Kaoru
Honda Shigeru

Korea
Sang Gyoo Lee
Kim Kyoung Jae
Kim In Soo
Jong Sung Rhee
Kang Keun Whan
G. Thompson Brown

Philippines
Francisco Demetrio
Antolin V. Uy
M. Bolasco

Ralph Donato
Ana Maria O. Fernandez
Josefina G. Hepomuceno
T. Valentino Sitoy, Jr.
Lee Wanak
Rodrigo D. Tano
David Keck

Sri Lanka
G. P. V. Somaratna

Indonesia
Agus F. Tangyong
Jan Sihar Aritonang
Adolf Heuken
Thomas van den End

Singapore/Malaysia
Robert Hunt
Violet James
René Nicolas
Ed Carlson
Yeow Choo Lak
Hwa Yung

Myanmar
Daw Hla Yi

Thailand
Henry M. Breidenthal
Pracha Thaiwatcharamas
Vorayuth Kitbamrung
E. John Hamlin
René Nicolas
Rung Ruengsan-ajin
Prasit Pongudom
Herbert R. Swanson
Donald S. Persons
Nipa Todsparint
Kumool Chinawong
Surachai Chumsriphan

Nepal
Ramesh Khatry

Pakistan
Arthur James
John Rooney
Jean S. Stoner

Vietnam
Violet James
Phan Phat Huon

Hong Kong
Sergio Ticozzi

Macau
Sergio Ticozzi

Taiwan
Yang-en Cheng
Martin Wang
Ralph Covell

Aba I, Mar

(b. Hale, Radan; d. 552). Aba served as catholicos of the East Syrian Church from 540 to 552. He grew up as a Mazdaian but converted to Christianity. Having studied Greek at the theological school of Edessa, he went to Palestine, Greece, and Egypt. On his travels, he met and perhaps studied with the renowned scholar and traveler Cosmas Indicopleustes*. After his travels, he settled in as a professor at Nisibis.

While at Nisibis, Aba was elected catholicos; after the closure of the school at Nisibis*, he started a theological school at Seleucia-Ctesiphon. The period of his catholicate was made difficult both by tensions within the church and by the problems between Christians and the Persian government. He worked to heal the schisms in the church. The government sent him into exile in Azerbaijan, and from there he worked to lead the church. About 548, he escaped from detention in Azerbaijan and returned to Seleucia-Ctesiphon. He was imprisoned for about three years, was released in 551, and died within the year.

To Aba are attributed numerous works by later authors. The issues of authenticity relating to these materials are complex and unresolved. Some, such as the commentaries, are known only through quotations used by later writers. Other works survive: administrative canons, synodal letters, hymns, homilies, and liturgical texts. He is credited with a translation of the Old Testament from Greek into Syriac, and the translation of liturgies of Theodore of Mopsuestia* and of Nestorius*, also from Greek into Syriac.

Bibliography

Chabot, J. B., ed. and trans., *Synodicon Orientale, ou recueil des synodes nestoriens* (1902). • Labourt, J., *Le Christianisme dans l'Empire Perse sous la dynastie Sassanide (224-632)* (1904). • Vööbus, Arthur, *The Statutes of the School of Nisibis* (1962); *History of the School of Nisibis* (1965). • Fiey, J.-M., *Jalons pour une histoire de l'Église en Iraq* (1970); *Nisibe: métropole syriaque orientale et ses suffragants des origins à nos jours* (1977).

David Bundy

Abdul Messiah

(b. ?; d. 15 Aug 1915). Patriarch of Antioch (Turkey) who rendered timely help in establishing the catholicate at Malankara.

Abdul Messiah was enthroned in 1895. After 10 years in office, he was denied the political support of the sultan. (The patriarch was dethroned not by the synod but by the political authority.) The struggles of the Malankara church for self-identity and autonomy were brought to Abdul Messiah's notice. He immediately came to Malankara, where he cooperated with the synod and gave direction for the enthronement of the catholicos in 1912. He regularized the matters of the church for its smooth functioning under an autonomous catholicate and then returned in 1913. After two years, he died and was buried at the patriarchal headquarters at Mardin.

Jacob Kurian

Abeel, David

(b. New Brunswick, New Jersey, United States, 12 Jun 1804; d. Albany, New York, 4 Sep 1846). Chaplain for the American Seamen's Friends Society in China, and one of the first missionaries of the American Board of Commissioners for Foreign Missions (ABCFM).

Abeel's family came from Amsterdam, and this Dutch origin influenced him in his later missionary work. He was converted at 17 years of age, and two years later in 1823 he enrolled at the Theological Seminary in New Brunswick, New Jersey. After the completion of his theological studies in 1826, he was licensed to preach and shortly after was called to be pastor in Athens, New York. He continued at this post until 1828, when, because of failing health, he sailed for St. John, one of the Danish West Indian islands. Because of the opposition of government authorities his hopes for ministry here did not materialize.

In 1829, Abeel was invited to serve as a chaplain for seamen in Canton under the American Seamen's Friends Society. He accepted this post with the understanding that after one year he could be appointed as a missionary with the ABCFM. On 14 Oct 1829 he sailed for Canton with Elijah Bridgman, the first missionary appointed by the ABCFM for China*. After their arrival on 25 Feb 1830, Abeel occupied himself in preaching to seamen, in study of the Chinese language, and in encouraging and helping Liang A-fa, the first Chinese Protestant convert.

Concerned to learn more about needs for mission work in eastern and southeastern Asia, Abeel visited Java and Singapore* at the end of 1830. On this trip, wherever possible he distributed Chinese literature* to China-bound ships and ministered to seamen. In Jun 1831 he left Singapore with Jacob Tomlin and went to Bangkok, again to minister to seamen and survey the need for mission work. For the next two years he made repeated trips to Siam, Singapore, and Malacca, often being invited to fill the role of English chaplain.

Because of failing health, Abeel went to England in Oct 1833. For nearly one year he visited in England, France, Germany, and Switzerland. In Holland he encouraged churches to cooperate with the Reformed Dutch Church in America to support missions to eastern Asia. While in England he often spoke on the degradation of women in Asia and encouraged the founding of the Society for Promoting Female Education in the East. In Sep 1834, Abeel went on to America where he was delayed for four years because of recurring ill health. Returning to China in 1838, he spent the next two years in Macau, continuing in his study of Chinese. In 1841, he visited churches of the Reformed Dutch Church in Borneo.

In Feb 1842, Abeel and William Boone*, a missionary surgeon with the Protestant Episcopal Church in America, sailed for Amoy and settled on Gulangsu Island, opposite the city, as the first resident missionaries in that area. Abeel commenced his missionary work among the Chinese and also served for a short time as chaplain to the English troops stationed on the island. During this period he established the Amoy Mission of the Reformed Church and shortly was joined by missionary colleagues Elihu Doty and William Pohlman. While in the Amoy area, he declined an offer to receive the doctor of divinity degree from Rutgers College in New Jersey. Ill health forced him to return to America in 1845, where he died in 1846 in the midst of his activities to promote the cause of missions. He published three works: *A Journal of a Residence in China; A Missionary Convention in Jerusalem;* and *The Claims of China for the Gospel.*

Bibliography

Abeel, David, *Journal of a Residence in China and the Neighboring Countries* (1836); *Memorials of Protestant Missionaries to the Chinese* (1867). • Latourette, Kenneth Scott, *A History of Christian Missions in China* (1929). • Williamson, G. R., *Memoir of the Rev. David Abeel* (1848).

RALPH R. COVELL AND CHINA GROUP

Abella, Guillermo L.

(b. Lumbang, Laguna). Outstanding early Filipino minister.

After his conversion in 1904, Abella left his teaching job to become a Presbyterian* mission clerk and interpreter in 1905 and an evangelist in 1906. He was a pioneer Protestant worker in the Laguna towns of Mabitac, Siniloan, Pangil, Paete, and Lumbang. After studies at Silliman Institute and Union Theological Seminary (Manila; see Education*), Abella was ordained as a minister in 1910. Subsequently he served as pastor of the San Pablo Evangelical Church for more than 20 years. The leading Presbyterian minister in Luzon by 1927, Abella also served as moderator of the Manila Conference of the United Evangelical Church in 1931-37. In 1947-48 he was a member of the Committee on Church Union, which drafted the union plan for the United Church of Christ in the Philippines (see Ecumenical Movement).

Bibliography

"Laguna Station Report," *Philippine Presbyterian Mission Report* (1927). • Rodgers, J. B., *Forty Years in the Philippines* (1941). • Sitoy, T. V., Jr., *Several Springs, One Stream* (1992).

T. VALENTINO SITOY, JR.

Abellera, Elena

(b. 1885; d. 1979). Outstanding early Filipino church leader and pioneer of the Junior Christian Endeavor Society (JCES) movement in the Philippines*.

Wife of Juan Abellera of the United Brethren Church, Abellera organized the JCES in Caba, La Union, in 1907. It served as a model for later, similar societies in the country. By 1914 the JCES had over 200 members, mostly from non-Protestant families. To afford leadership training for the greatest number, its officers were elected every three months.

In 1910, when Filipinas were expected to remain silent, perform household chores, and bear many children, Abellera helped establish the Young Women's Bible Training School in San Fernando. From 1924 to 1929, she served as first president of the United Church of Manila Women's Auxiliary Association.

Bibliography

Roberts, W. N., *The Filipino Church* (1936). • United Church of Manila, *Golden Jubilee Book* (1974). • Sitoy, T. V., Jr., *Several Springs, One Stream* (1992).

T. VALENTINO SITOY, JR.

Abellera, Juan A.

(b. Caba, La Union, 24 Mar 1880; d. Oct 1940). A leading Filipino United Brethren minister.

From Caba, La Union, Abellera began as an outstanding head teacher in the public school and was awarded a gold medal by officials of the 1903 St. Louis World's Fair for sending the best industrial art exhibit. Converted in 1904, Abellera became a United Brethren evangelist in 1906, giving up his position as the highest paid public school teacher in La Union and imminent promotion as the first Filipino provincial supervisor. Abellera translated nearly all of the 200 hymns in the Ilocano hymnal of 1907 shared by three denominations. Ordained the first Filipino United Brethren minister in 1913, Abellera repeatedly served as conference superintendent. An ardent advocate of church union (see Ecumenical Movement), he became the first pastor of the United Church of Manila in 1924-26.

Bibliography

Roberts, W. N., *The Filipino Church* (1936). • Higdon, E. K. and I. W., *From Carabao to Clipper* (1941). • Sitoy, T. V., Jr., *Several Springs, One Stream* (1992).

T. Valentino Sitoy, Jr.

Abgar

A name frequently used by kings of Osrhoene, which had its capital at Edessa. With the conversion of Abgar IX (ca. 177-212), Osrhoene became perhaps the first Christian nation. It was during the reign of Abgar IX that Bardaisan* (the first known Syriac Christian theologian) flourished. The Abgar legend relates to a King Abgar (probably Abgar V) who is supposed to have corresponded with Jesus. This correspondence was supposedly translated from the archives of the city of Edessa and published by Eusebius of Caesarea in his *Ecclesiastical History* (I.13; II.1, 6-7). In the correspondence, which is extant in Syriac, Greek, and Armenian, Abgar asked Jesus to come to Edessa to heal Abgar. Jesus refused but promised that after his ascension he would send a disciple to heal him. According to Eusebius, Thomas (see St. Thomas) sent Thaddaeus (in Syriac, Addai). A Syriac document titled "The Teaching of Addai" provides another perspective on these events. Here it is claimed that Jesus sent a messenger to Edessa with a response. The messenger was said to have painted a portrait of Jesus that served to protect the city. The royal tradition of the Abgar dynasty was brought to an end by the final incorporation of the kingdom into the Roman Empire early in the 3rd c.

Bibliography

Bauer, W., *Orthodoxy and Heresy in Earliest Christianity*, 2nd ed., trans. R. Kraft et al. (1971). • Brock, S., "Eusebius and Syriac Christianity," *Eusebius, Christianity and Judaism*, ed. H. A. Attridge and G. Gata (1992). • Desreumaux, A., et al., *Histoire du roi Abgar et de Jésus* (1993). • Runciman, S., "Some Remarks on the Image of Edessa," *Cambridge Historical Journal* 3 (1929-31). • Segal, J. B., *Edessa: The Blessed City* (1970). • Youtie, H. C., "Gothenburg Papyrus 21 and the Letter to Abgar," *Harvard Theological Review* 23 (1930).

David Bundy

Abiera, Severino B.

(b. 1894; d. Leyte, Philippines, 1951). Filipino pioneer Presbyterian nicknamed "the Scarfaced Evangelist."

A fiery speaker and man of deep faith, Abiera began his evangelistic efforts in 1921 in northern Leyte and Samar and later was ordained as a minister of the United Evangelical Church.

Leyte and Samar being particularly hostile to Protestant preachers at the time, Abiera was twice assaulted by blade-wielding fanatics. The first attack left him permanently scarred on the cheek. The second attack left him with 13 nearly mortal wounds. On each occasion, Abiera astonished everyone by pardoning his assailants. Advised to desist from preaching, Abiera retorted, "I am not afraid even if they take away my life."

In 1951, Abiera was brutally clubbed by an angry mob in Leyte, an attack which eventually led to his death.

Bibliography

Rodgers, J. B., *Forty Years in the Philippines* (1940). • Mancebo, S. T., *Fifty Years in the Making* (1967). • Ramientos, N., "Portrait of (a) Filipino Christian Martyr," *Crusader* IX.3 (Mar 1966). • Sitoy, T. V., Jr., *Several Springs, One Stream* (1992).

T. Valentino Sitoy, Jr.

Abineno, Johannes Ludwig Chrisostomus

(b. Timor, 1917; d. 22 Jan 1995). Abineno studied (in Dutch) at the Higher Theological Seminary in Jakarta. His study was interrupted by the Pacific War and the Japanese occupation. He had his first ecumenical experience as head of the Indonesian delegation to the International Christian Youth Congress in Oslo (1947). In Utrecht, the Netherlands, he married Alberta A. Meijer. He studied in Basel, Leiden, and Bossey (Ecumenical Institute). Abineno graduated from the seminary in Jakarta in 1948. Ordained as a pastor in the Timor* Church, he was chosen as chairperson of its synod in 1950, a position he retained until 1960. For a couple of years, he did postgraduate work in Utrecht, where he wrote a doctoral dissertation on "Liturgical Forms and Patterns in the Evangelical Church of Timor" (1956).

In 1960, Abineno moved to Jakarta, where he became a professor of practical theology at his alma mater; he retained this position until his death. In the same year, he was chosen chairman of the Indonesian Council of Churches and served in that capacity until 1980. Also in 1960, he became a member of the national parliament, which he served until 1975.

In 1962, the Indonesian Bible Society (see Bible Societies) appointed Abineno chairman of the Bahasa Indonesia Translation committee. Under his guidance, the New version of the Bible was finished and appeared in 1973. Abineno was very active in international ecumeni-

Aboriginal Ministry, Taiwan

cal bodies such as the World Council of Churches (WCC) and the World Alliance of Reformed Churches (WARC) (see Ecumenical Movement).

In a period of a little over 30 years, Abineno wrote 67 books on a wide range of theological subjects (practical theology, Bible commentaries, liturgics, church order, history of missions, the presbyter, the deacon, biographies of great theologians such as Zwingli, Calvin, Bonhoeffer, Bultmann, etc.).

Abineno gave much to the churches of his country. He translated and reworked much of Western thought for Indonesian churches. Writing in Bahasa Indonesia, which was a relatively new instrument in which to communicate the old truth, he expected that the regenerative strength of the Good News would bring renewal for people, churches, the state, and society.

Bibliography

Weinata, S. (in memoriam of Abineno), *Berita Oikumene,* Nos. 222-23 (Jan-Feb 1995). • Sopater, Sularso, ed., *Apostole-Pengutusan. Kumpulan karangan dalam rangka memperingati hari ulang tahun ke-7- Prof. Dr. J. L. Ch. Abineno* (1987). • Hoekema, A. G., *Denken in dynamisch evenwicht. De wordingsgeschiedenis van de nationale protestantse Theologie in Indonesie (ca. 1860-1960),* Series Mission No. 8 (1994). (Indonesian edition: *Berpikir dalam deseimbangan yang dinamis. Sejarah lahirnya teologi Protestan nasional di Indonesia [sekitar 1860-1960]* [1997].) (Thinking in a Dynamic Equilibrium: The Genesis of National Protestant Theology in Indonesia.)

Arie de Kuiper

Aboriginal Ministry, Taiwan

The original inhabitants of Taiwan*, until recently referred to as the "mountain tribes," came either from southwest and southeast China* or from the Philippine* Islands and Indonesia. Wherever their origin, they belong to the Malayo-Polynesian linguistic groups. Probably arriving on the island before the time of Christ, they were not mentioned in any Chinese sources until the 2nd c. after Christ. Only during the late Ming (A.D. 1368-1644) or early Qing (A.D. 1644-1911) Dynasties did Chinese settlers arrive in Taiwan in any number.

When the Chinese came, they occupied the best land on the plains and gradually assimilated (Sinicized) the many groups of original inhabitants or drove them into the foothills or high mountains of Taiwan. Eventually, the Sinicized groups were called *Pepohoan,* the Amoy-language term for "savages of the plains." Groups only partially Sinicized or in the process of being Sinicized were called *Sekhoan,* meaning "ripe" or domesticated savages. Those who had been forced to retreat into mountainous areas were referred to as *Chinhoan,* meaning "green," wild, or untamed savages.

These various groups of original inhabitants probably came to Taiwan at widely different times, as evidenced by differences in culture and language. Many of the early groups have disappeared, including one group of very short, dark-skinned people referred to as "negritos." At present, there are 11 subgroups of original inhabitants divided into Atayalic, Paiwanic, and Tsouic major groupings. Even within the major groupings the languages are mutually unintelligible.

The original inhabitants of Taiwan had no contact with the outside world until the Dutch East-India Company arrived in 1624. It gained sovereignty over the island through an agreement with China, gradually pacified many groups of the original inhabitants, and began missionary efforts to establish the "true Christian reformed religion" among them. Those most responsible for the Christianizing were called predikants, chaplains whose main task was to minister to company personnel in the commercial centers.

Despite much turnover of personnel and strong-armed tactics by the predikants, the work of evangelization among those whom they called "Indians" was very successful. Thousands of the original inhabitants made professions of faith, church buildings were erected, portions of Scripture were translated, catechisms were developed, and a beginning was made in establishing training centers for emerging leaders.

Unfortunately, this beginning effort was brought to an end in 1662 as the Chinese rebel Zheng Cheng-Kung (Koxinga), fleeing from the control of the mainland by the new Qing (Ch'ing) Dynasty, came to Taiwan and expelled the Dutch. How much of the Christian faith survived after the Dutch left? Later arrivals reported that some original inhabitants remembered the Dutch language, read Dutch books, and continued to use the romanized alphabet taught them by the Dutch. Some still remembered portions of the catechism. They did not worship idols, but neither did they practice baptism or have any community Christian life.

Two hundred years after the departure of the Dutch, English and Canadian Presbyterian missionaries came to south and north Taiwan respectively (see Presbyterian). Although concerned to minister to the Chinese, they found the greatest response among the Pepohoan, upon whom the Dutch had concentrated their efforts, in south, central, and northeast Taiwan. Converts in the north and south numbered over 4,000 by 1896, and two leaders, one a Pepohoan, were ordained.

In 1895, as a result of the Treaty of Shiminoseki, Japan gained control of Taiwan and imposed a strict rule. The new government constructed a 300-mile guard line around all of the mountain aboriginal territory. Although the Presbyterian churches north and south passed various resolutions to reach the original inhabitants, the strict Japanese control made this impossible. The Amis, one of the original tribes, was not included within this guard line, and missionaries hoped to be able to work among them.

The Taruku (also called Sediq) group of the original inhabitants fiercely resisted the Japanese. When the Japanese attacked their mountain strongholds, rid them of their vice of head-hunting, and moved them to coastal areas to pacify them, the way was prepared for a fresh entrance of the Gospel. Headhunting had been the core of their religious system, and now there was a vacuum. Through the efforts of two Taiwanese pastors, Liu Zhunchen and Li Xiu-zhe, and a Presbyterian missionary, James Dickson*, a 50-year-old tribal woman, Chi Wang, was led to faith in Christ in the late 1920s and was taught in a Bible school the rudiments of the Christian faith. She was well respected by the Japanese, for she had been the peacemaker between her own people and the Japanese.

During World War II, Chi Wang witnessed boldly to her fellow villagers and led many to Christ. In turn, many of these became leaders in raising up Christians throughout the Taruku villages. Despite severe persecution by the Japanese, these leaders continued their witness, gathering together to worship in caves and isolated mountain areas. With the war's end, the believers came by the hundreds from their seacoast and mountain homes to Hualien, a city on the east coast, to be baptized in Presbyterian churches.

Gradually the faith spread from the Taruku tribe to the other 10 groups of original inhabitants, preached not by missionaries but by the people themselves. Referred to as the "miracle of the twentieth century," this movement among the original inhabitants soon resulted in the organization of churches, many fine church buildings, the founding of mountain presbyteries, the translation of the entire Bible into local languages, a full range of church activities, training schools, and even missionary outreach to the Philippines* and Indonesia*.

At present, among the 11 groups there are over 500 Presbyterian churches and nearly 80,000 baptized believers. The Catholic Church began work among the original inhabitants in the mid-1950s and has an equal number of adherents as the Presbyterians (see Roman Catholic Church). A few churches have also been founded by The Evangelical Alliance Mission, the Free Methodists, the Oriental Missionary Society, and the True Jesus Church (see Methodist Church). The original inhabitants number a bit over 300,000, and well over 50 percent claim to be Christians. Facing the challenges of the modern world will be a daunting task for these churches as they move into the second generation of their faith.

Bibliography

Band, Edward, *He Brought Them Out* (1947). • Covell, Ralph, *Pentecost of the Hills in Taiwan* (1998). • Vicedom, George, *Faith That Moves Mountains* (1967). • Whitehorn, John, and Edward Band, *He Led Them On* (1955).

RALPH R. COVELL

Action Union of Chinese Catholics

(*Union de l'Action Catholique Chinoise,* UCCA). National body of believers of the Chinese Catholic Church (see Roman Catholic Church).

The UCCA was first initiated by Friar Chang Yutang of Shanxi (later bishop of the Hong Kong* Diocese), Wang Jinren, Liu Jinwen, and others, who, after consultation by correspondence with Friar Pan Gusheng, editor-in-chief of *Holy Religion Magazine,* Shanghai, published a constitution for the union in the magazine and other Catholic journals in 1912 and urged all Catholics to join (see Literature on Publishing). The UCCA seems to have developed out of the Congregation for the Propagation of the Faith (see Propaganda Fide) as a means to encourage the Chinese to evangelize their friends and relatives. The 12 articles of the constitution included the name of the organization, its objectives, program of action, and rules on the set-up of branch organizations, membership qualifications, and conferences. Local action unions were subsequently established in Tianjin, Lucheng, Shanxi, Shanghai, and elsewhere. Sponsored by the Tianjin Union, the First Joint Conference was held in Tianjin on 18-24 Nov 1914 (attended by approximately 50 representatives), but it failed to form a united national body. Ten years later, only the Shanghai Union remained active. In Aug 1928, Pope Pius XI, in a circular telegram recognizing the Kuomintang government, encouraged the Chinese Catholics to expand the Action Union.

In Jan 1933, with the approval of the Congregation for the Propagation of the Faith, the papacy's first envoy to China*, Gang Hengyi, announced in a circular the "Organic Outline for the Union for Chinese Catholic Action." On 15 Aug 1934, the national headquarters of the Action Union was established, with Lu Behong from the Shanghai Catholic Church as president. The first representative assembly of the UCCA was held in Shanghai on 8-15 Sep 1935, attended by 123 representatives.

The second papal envoy, Cai Ning (Zamin), and more than 10 bishops from Shanghai and other dioceses were at the assembly. A letter from Pope Pius XI was read. Chairman Lin Sen of the Kuomintang government sent a congratulatory telegram. The mayor of Shanghai, Wu Teichang, and the vice chairman of the administrative council were present at the opening and closing ceremony respectively. The assembly discussed issues which included the society, education*, the press, and scholarship. They issued a declaration on the ideals and plans of the Action Union.

The Japanese invasion in 1937 halted the activities of the Union. Some activities were resumed after V-J Day in 1945, but the emigration of several prominent Catholics from China toward the end of the Kuomintang regime in late 1948 and early 1949 led to the voluntary dissolution of the UCCA.

Bibliography

Annals of the Propagation of the Faith, Vols. 74, 77, and 78.

CHINA GROUP

Acts of the Martyrs

Three sets of materials dating to perhaps the 4th c. — two that document martyrs from an earlier period in

Edessa and another that narrates the martyrdom of Persian Christians under the Sassanian kings. The first contains the stories of Sarbel and Barsamja, who were apparently killed during the persecution orchestrated by the Roman emperor Decius. The second tells of the martyrdom of Gurja, Semma, and Habib, who were, according to the text, martyred during the reign of the Roman emperor Diocletian.

Further to the east, Persian Christians were martyred during the reigns of the Sassanian kings who sought to restore the Zoroastrian* traditions. This persecution is attested by imperial Sassanian inscriptions. Although the persecution began earlier, the extant narratives, written in Syriac, cover the period 327-576. The largest group includes those written during the reign of Shapur II* (309-79).

Bibliography

Assemani, S. E., *Acta Sanctorum Martyrum Orientalium et Occidentalium* (1748; repr. 1970). • Cureton, W., *Ancient Syriac Documents* (1864; repr. 1967). • Wiessner, G., *Zur Märtyrerüberlieferung aus der Christenfolgung Schapurs II* (Untersuchungen zur syrischen Literaturgeschichte 1; Abhandlungen der Akademie der Wissenschaften in Göttingen. Philologisch-historische Klasse 67; 1967).

David Bundy

Acts of Thomas

Account of Thomas the apostle of Jesus from perhaps the early 3rd c. (before 226 C.E.) written in Syriac.

Versions of this text survive in Syriac, Greek, Armenian, Arabic, Coptic, and Ethiopic. The best textual witness is the earlier, unrevised Greek version. Allusions to the text are found in a variety of Christian and Manichaean texts (see Mani). Its internal references are to western Asia and to India*. Its closest known literary relationships are to Syriac Christian texts, although it would appear to have influenced later Buddhist (see Buddhism) traditions as well. This text is different from the Gospel of Thomas*, an early Gospel attributed to Thomas that circulated in early Syriac churches, as well as Western churches.

The Greek version contains 171 chapters, concluding with the martyrdom of Thomas. Chapters 1-16 describe the division of mission territories among the disciples. Thomas is assigned to India. Thomas is reluctant to go to India and is sold by Jesus (his twin) to Chaban, an Indian merchant. They pass through the city of Sandrok (Syria), where a royal wedding is in progress. Thomas composes the Hymn of the Bride for the occasion, Jesus (Christ) appears to both bride and groom, both are converted to celibacy, and Thomas leaves the city before the king can respond to the problem.

Chapters 17-29 find Thomas in India being interrogated by King Gundaphor. Assigned to build a palace for the king, Thomas uses the resources to inaugurate a relief program for the poor. Chaban and Thomas are imprisoned. Meanwhile the king's brother Gad, seeking a mansion in heaven, is sent back to earth. Both royal brothers are converted. Thomas anoints the converts, preaches, and celebrates the Eucharist (see Worship).

In chapters 30-38, Thomas resurrects a boy and turns the occasion into an opportunity to preach a series of homilies exhorting the onlookers to adopt an ascetic lifestyle and promising forgiveness of sins to those who would accept this teaching. Chapters 39-41 describe an encounter with and the burial of a talking ass which claims descent from the biblical Balaam's ass. In chapters 42-50, Thomas conducts an exorcism, converts the woman, baptizes her, and celebrates the Eucharist.

Chapters 51-61 describe the resurrection of a prostitute killed by a young Christian when she refused to accept the life of celibacy. He became crippled when he consumed the Eucharist. Both were healed and converted.

The narrative becomes more complex as the text moves to the stories of wealthy women who accept Thomas's message of asceticism against the will of their husbands. The first (chapters 62-81) involves Sipor, who brings Thomas to meet his family to exorcise demons from his wife and daughter. Thomas does so, using a speaking ass as an assistant. The second (chapters 82-138) involves Carish, a royal counselor, and his wife Mydonia. In prison again, Thomas offers a prayer of thanksgiving and creates the remarkable Hymn of the Pearl (chapters 108-13) that is a summary of Thomas's theology and provides a theological reflection on his life.

The remainder of the text (chapters 139-71) involves the narration of successes in gaining converts and the desire of women converts to help Thomas leave the country. They are not successful. King Misdai interrogates Thomas and he is killed. In a farewell speech, Thomas compares his impending death to that of Jesus. After his death, he appears to certain of his followers. The relics of the saint are used to heal and to convert people. The text ends with the transmission of the relics to Edessa by merchants.

While it is often impossible to distinguish fact from fiction, the text is an important witness to the evangelistic traditions of the early Asian churches, both in Syria and in what is now Pakistan*, Afghanistan, northeast India, Iran, and Iraq, the old Kushan and Persian Empires. It provides hymns and contains significant liturgical information. Ablution and anointing are important features of Christian celebration. The oil invokes the Holy Spirit as the feminine aspect of God; the term used is "the merciful mother." As one would expect from a Syriac source, asceticism is an important, even an essential virtue to be adopted by Christian converts. The text also provides access to the early traditions of Asian Christian spirituality. It clearly presents a developmental spirituality and theology (sometimes derogatorily labeled "gnostic" by Latin and Western Christian writers) not unlike that of Origen of Alexandria and Ephrem* of Syria.

Adat and the Christian Faith

Bibliography

Adam, A., *Die Psalmen des Thomas und das Perlenlied als Zeugnisse vorchristliche Gnosis* (Beihefte zur Zeitschrift für die alttestamentliche Wissenschaft 24; 1959). • Bornkamm, G., *Mythos und Legende in den apokryphen Thomas-Akten* (Forschungen zur Religion und Literatur des Alten und Neuen Testaments 49; 1933). • Klijn, A. F. J., "The So-called Hymn of the Pearl," *Vigiliae Christianae* 14 (1960); "Das Thomasevangelium und das altsyrische Christentum," *Vigiliae Christianae* 15 (1961); *The Acts of Thomas* (Supplements to *Novum Testamentum* 5; 1962). • Poirier, P.-H., *L'Hymne de la perle des Actes de Thomas* (*Homo Religiosus* 8; 1981). • Quispel, G., *Makarius: Das Thomasevangelium und Das Lied von der Perle* (Supplements to *Novum Testamentum* 15; 1967). • Segal, J. B., *Edessa the Blessed City* (1970).

David Bundy

Adat and the Christian Faith

Adat, religion, and culture are three aspects of the same concept in Indonesia*. The origin of the word *adat* is Arabic. Before the Arabs came to Indonesia, the ethnic groups used different words for *adat* to express their respective ways of life and culture.

Culture is the pattern for living of a group of people guided by convictions based on religious values or transcendental principles passed from generation to generation. *Adat* is more than the popular customary law, because *adat* includes religion as well as culture. These words can also be used morally. Infringement of *adat* means transgression against the will of the godhead and the ancestors, and punishment must be meted out accordingly.

The transcendence of *adat* can be seen in the concept of *Aluk Todolo* (the religion of the ancestors, *Toraja*). The *aluk* existed already in heaven, created by the godhead to watch over life (including heavenly life). Therefore, the deities and the whole heavenly existence are under the *aluk.* The first performance of the simplest sacrifice was the offering of *piong sanglampa* (a section of bamboo filled with rice) in order to get *Simbolong Manik* (symbol of beauty) out of a granite rock to become the wife of *Usuk Sangbamban* (the floating rib — the second godhead). *Puang Matua* (the third godhead and creator) performed later in the same ritual in order to draw *Arrang di Batu* (another symbol of beauty) out of a granite rock to become his wife. There is nothing which is not regulated by *aluk;* everything has its *aluk.* When the first ancestor came down to earth, the *aluk sola pemali* (regulations and their sanctions, 7,777 in number) were given to him, carried down by his slave, *Pong Pakulando.* This mythical story depicts the origins and destinations of life. Once the performance of the life rituals from birth to death is completed, one then returns to his heavenly origin.

The Batak understanding of *adat* is similar. *Adat* is law and order, derived from *Mulajadinabolon* (the Great Beginner of Genesis, thus the Great Creator, *vide Sinaga*). *Adat* is experienced as an intimate presence of God as the founder and establisher of order, protecting life against disorder or chaos. *Adat* is not religion itself, but its total implementation is needed for the redemption of the past.

According to L. Schreiner, *adat* is of divine origin and, as divine law and order, it comprises the totality of life and determines the harmony of existence (life and death) of a single person, group, or society in relation to God *(vide Sinaga).* Speaking on the *adat* of the Dayak, F. Ukur concludes, "*Adat* is all embracing, including religious rites; a social law which regulates the whole society." The center of *adat* is the ancestors (see Ancestor Worship) who handed down the *adat* by way of tradition and watch over its implementation in life, bringing blessings or curses.

The Christian faith came to Indonesia through missionaries from different agencies, from different cultures, and with different theological backgrounds. They introduced Christianity to different regions and islands, with different cultures, over a 400-year period. The interaction of the Christian faith and *adat* is therefore not uniform. Even in one area with a single missionary board, the way of interaction could be different depending on the missionaries' approach.

The missionaries (mostly Lutheran*) in the southern part of northern Sumatra were not strongly opposed to *adat,* except for ancestor worship. The approach was more or less comprehensive-social. The natives were left their traditional way of life, which could not be separated from the power of *adat.* In other areas, such as Irian, Minahasa, and the Moluccas, the missionaries judged *adat* as darkness and devilish and therefore to be abolished and replaced by the Christian way of life. In some areas, this approach seemed to be successful, but already in the second and especially in the third generation, local Christians began to search for self-identity when all *adat* was purged. Again in other parts, such as in Java, where religious tolerance is regarded as virtue, the symbiosis of the religio-cultural layers is both possible and pragmatic.

Contemporary theological discussions and efforts at contextualizing theology (see Contextualization) in Indonesia show three main trends: syncretism, symbiosis, and rejection (see Syncretistic Movements). Syncretism in this context means combining and blending principles of different origin and content. This is evident in ancestor worship, still uncritically practiced by many Christians. Symbiosis means that cultural values and forms can be continued and transformed into a pattern for living which is not contrary to the Christian faith or to the Gospel. Rejection means a radical repudiation of the elements of a local culture. This is what Niebuhr calls the Christ-against-culture attitude.

The theological discussions concerning contextualization follow the lines of Niebuhr's "gospel transforming culture": transforming *adat* in the sense of living within the *adat*, transforming or rejecting what is incompatible with the Christian faith, and cultivating what is good and does not contradict the Gospel.

Bibliography

Ukur, F., *Tantang-Djawab suku Dayak* (1971). • Kobong, Th., et al., *Aluk, Adat dan Kebudayaan Toraja dalam Perjumpaannya dengan Injul; Evangelium und Tongkonan* (1989). • Schreiner, L., *Telah Kudengar dari Ayahku* (1978). • Sianipar, F. M., *Adat dan Agama dalam Keyakinan dan Perjuangan* (1972). • Nicholls, Bruce J., *Contextualization — A Theology of Gospel and Culture* (1979). • Sinaga, Anicetus B., *The Toba-Batak High God* (1981). • Van den Veen, H., *The Merokfeast of Sa'dan Toraja* (1965). • Scharer, H., *Ngaju Religion* (1963). • Nooy-Palm, H., *The Sa'dan Toraja*, Vol. I (1979). • Pardonti, Sutarman S., *Sadrach's Community and Its Contextual Roots* (1988). • Akkeren, Ph. v., *Sri and Christ* (1970).

Th. Kobong

Addai

Many of the texts relating to the spread of Christianity in West Asia include references to the tradition of Addai. It is a tradition found in the *Ecclesiastical History* of Eusebius (I.13) as well as Syriac histories. According to the legend, Thomas* sent Addai (Thaddaeus) to Edessa to fulfill the promises of Jesus to Abgar* V (probably). These promises were made in the supposed correspondence between Abgar and Jesus preserved by Eusebius. The second half of the text tells of the missionary activities of Addai, how he became a court healer and evangelist. The Liturgy of Addai and Mari is a eucharistic anaphora that is still used in Syria and India as well as Syriac Christian communities in the diaspora. The liturgy was probably developed at Edessa sometime before the 4th c. A text attributed to Addai, *The Doctrina Addai*, is in its present extant form probably from the early 4th c. The Acts of St. Mari the Apostle that supposedly records the efforts of Addai's successor is also probably from the 4th c. These have been viewed as totally mythical by Drijvers (1984) and yet as containing some level of historical accuracy (Chaumont, 1988). There is little contextual material by which to evaluate the claims of the documents or their interpreters. Without doubt, all of the documents are based on earlier oral traditions.

Bibliography

Bauer, W., *Orthodoxy and Heresy in Earliest Christianity*, 2nd ed., trans. R. Kraft et al. (1971). • Bundy, D., "Christianity in Syria," *Anchor Bible Dictionary* 1 (1992). • Chaumont, M. L., *La Christianisation de l'Empire Iranian des origines au grandes persécutions du IVe siècle* (Corpus scriptorum christianorum orientalium 499; Subsidia 80; 1988). • Drijvers, H. J. W., *East of Antioch* (1984). • Macomber, W., "The Oldest Known Text of the Anaphora of the Apostles Addai and Mari," *Orientalia Christiania Periodica* 32 (1966). • Phillips, G., *The Doctrine of Addai* (1876). • Segal, J. B., *Edessa the Blessed City* (1970).

David Bundy

Adeney, David H.

(b. Bedford, England, 3 Nov 1911; d. California, USA, 11 May 1994). Missionary to China* and pioneer student worker.

The second of five sons of a missionary who was also chaplain to the queen of Rumania, Adeney studied history and theology at Queens' College, Cambridge University, where he received his bachelor's and master's degrees. He left for China with the China Inland Mission (CIM) in 1934. In China, he started by living with the people in the villages of Honan Province. During the war with Japan and the Chinese Revolution, he preached and taught in the major universities of China and helped found the Inter-Varsity Christian Fellowship (IVCF) in China. In 1947, China had the largest Christian student movement in the world with 10,000 members. While in China, Adeney met and married Ruth W. Temple, born in the United States. She also worked for CIM. They had four children: Rosemary, John, Michael, and Bernard.

After expulsion from China in 1950, Adeney worked with IVCF in the United States and became its first missions director. In 1956, he was appointed associate general secretary for the International Fellowship of Evangelical Students* (IFES or IVCF International) and moved to Hong Kong. Adeney pioneered IFES student work in Asia, traveling extensively to establish Christian student movements in many Asian countries. In 1969 he moved to Singapore and founded the Discipleship Training Center (DTC), a graduate school in theological studies for Asia.

In 1977 Adeney moved to Berkeley, California, where he served as director of the China program of Overseas Missionary Fellowship (OMF, formerly CIM). He was also adjunct professor of mission at New College, Berkeley. He received the doctor of divinity degree from Wheaton Graduate School in 1983. He was elected president of IFES for two terms. Adeney was the author of several books and many articles. A popular speaker at Chinese conferences and churches in many parts of the world, Adeney made many trips to China during the last 15 years of his life, encouraging Christian leaders in house churches as well as in the official churches of the China Christian Council*. Wherever he went, part of his heart was in China.

Bibliography

Adeney, David, *The Church's Long March*. • Armitage, Carolyn, *Reaching for the Goal: The Life Story of David Adeney* (1993).

Bernard T. Adeney

Adiabene

Located south of the kingdom of Osrhoene*, Adiabene was sometimes an independent buffer state between the

Persian and Roman Empires. Its capital was Irbil (=Arbela). Adiabene had a large Jewish population and, at times, Jewish monarchs. The Jewish monarchs were removed by the emperor Trajan, who took the area in 115-16 C.E. Adiabene was an early center of Christian activity. Tradition ascribes the evangelization of the area to Addai*. It was eventually (2nd Christian c.) incorporated into the Persian Empire. By the time the Parthian Empire was supplanted by the Sassanian Empire (226 C.E.), Christianity was well established. Arbela's first generally recognized bishop, John of Arbela, was martyred in 343 C.E. The second recognized bishop, Abraham, was martyred in 344. The Sassanian persecution of Christians had a major impact on the region. Under the early Arabic administrations, however, the churches flourished. Later Syriac chronicles describe Christian churches and monasteries built in the area.

The major source for Adiabene is the *Chronicle of Arbela.* It claims to recount the lives of the early bishops of Arbela, beginning about 100 C.E. The second bishop, Samson, was martyred by the Parthian king Xosroes (Chosroes) during a period of Parthian occupation. The *Chronicle of Arbela* was published in Syriac by Alphonse Mingana in 1907. Assfalg and Fiey argued against its authenticity and suspected that it was forged by the editor. However, later scholars, including Sachau, Brock (tentatively), Neusner, Kawerau, and Chaumont, have argued that it has some historical worth.

Bibliography

Assfalg, J., "Zur Textüberlieferung der Chronik von Arbela: Beobachtungen zu MS. Or. Fol. 3126," *Oriens Christianus* 50 (1966). • Brock, S., "Alphonse Mingana and the Letter of Philoxenos to Abu 'Afr," *Bulletin of the John Rylands Library* 50 (1967). • Bundy, D., "Christianity in Syria," *Anchor Bible Dictionary* 1 (1992). • Chaumont, M. L., *La Christianisation de l'Empire Iranian des origines au grandes persécutions du IVe siècle* (Corpus scriptorum christianorum orientalium [CSCO] 499; Subsidia 80; 1988). • Fiey, J.-M., "Auteur et date de la Chronique d'Arbèles," *L'Orient Syrien* 12 (1967); *Jalons pour une histoire de l'Église en Iraq* (CSCO 370; Subsidia 36; 1970). • Kawerau, P., *Die Chronik von Arbela* (CSCO 467-68; *Syria* 199-200; 1985). • Mingana, A., "Chronique d'Arbèles," *Sources Syriaques* 1.1: *Msiha Shka* (1907). • Neusner, J., "The Conversion of Adiabene to Christianity," *Numen* 14 (1966). • Peeters, P., "Les passionnaires d'Adiabène," *Analecta Bollandiana* 43 (1925). • Sachau, E., *Die Chronik von Arbela. Ein Beitrag zur Kenntnis des altesten Christentums im Orient* (Abhandlungen der Königlichen Preuss. Akademie der Wissenschaften. Philologisch-historische Klasse 6; 1915). DAVID BUNDY

Adriani, Nicolaus

(b. Oud-Loosdrecht, Holland, 15 Sep 1865; d. Poso, Central Celebes, 1 May 1926). Missionary linguist to Central Celebes, Indonesia*.

Born into a family of ministers, Adriani studied theology at the University of Utrecht (1886-87) and applied for a scholarship from the Netherlands Bible Society to study Oriental languages to become a Bible* translator. He earned his doctorate from the University of Leyden, where he studied from 1887 to 1893. It was already decided in 1887 that he should partner with A. C. Kruyt*, who was preparing to become a missionary to Central Celebes* (Poso district).

In 1893, Adriani married M. L. Gunning, who became an invaluable help assisting him with his linguistic research and the publication of his works. In 1894, they set out for Indonesia, arriving the following year in Poso, where Adriani worked, with intermittent breaks, until his death. From 1902 to 1905 he assisted a missionary in Minahasa, J. A. T. Schwarz, the son of missionary pioneer J. G. Schwarz, with linguistic publications. In 1906-8 and 1914-19 he went to Holland on furlough, the latter furlough being extended because of his poor health. Adriani died while taking leave from Central Celebes to return home.

Adriani's partnership with Kruyt in discovering together the languages and social and religious life of the peoples of Central Celebes was exemplary. They initiated a new missionary approach, which was very influential in the following decades. Adriani himself was of the opinion that the Bible could be translated effectively only if the local language together with all the spiritual concepts behind it was carefully studied and thoroughly understood. The translation of the Bible was for him the final stage of the introduction of a non-Christian people to the Christian faith, because, without proper initiation in the Christian truths and concepts, the Bible would remain strange, even when translated properly. This opinion was reflected in his work. He started to study the language in all its facets, including the religious speech, to determine the grammar and vocabulary. The first stage of translating the Bible consisted of compiling readers with biblical stories (New Testament, 1903; Old Testament, 1907), followed by the translation of the New Testament. In the meantime, the first group of Christians were baptized (1909). Adriani was not able to finish the translation of the New Testament in the language of Central Celebes (called *Bare'e* by him, and *Pamona* by the people themselves) before his death. It was completed in 1933 by A. C. Kruyt and Mrs. Adriani.

During his first furlough, Adriani caused a commotion with a lecture about missionary strategy in the Netherlands Indies. It was his opinion that priority had to be given to the mission among "animistic" peoples in order to prevent them from becoming Muslim (at that time Islam* was advancing in Indonesia). Opposition came from people working among Islamic peoples in Indonesia (e.g., in West Java) who did not understand that he was talking about strategy, not principle.

Bibliography

Latourette, K. S., *A History of the Expansion of Christianity,* V, 6th ed. (1978). • Neill, S., ed., *Concise Dictionary of Christian World Mission* (1971). • Kraemer, H., and A. E. Adriani, *Dr. N. Adriani,* 2nd ed. (1935).

Christian G. F. de Jong

Aerts, John

(b. 1880; d. 1942). Apostolic vicar of Netherlands New Guinea shot dead by the Japanese without any interrogation on the shores of Kei Kecil Island in the Moluccas*.

Four Dutch priests and eight brothers suffered the same fate as Aerts. The reason for the murder of all the missionaries at Langgur, Kei Island, was a slanderous accusation by a man of Arab descent who hated Christianity. In 1951, the bodies were reburied next to a statue of the Sacred Heart of Jesus with great ceremony attended by government and church officials. Adolf Heuken

Aglipay, Gregorio

(b. Batac, Ilocos Norte, Philippines, May 1860; d. Manila, 1 Sep 1940). Filipino revolutionary priest, nationalist, and church leader; first *Obispo Maximo* (supreme bishop) of the *Iglesia Filipina Independiente* (IFI)/Philippine Independent Church (PIC)*.

From a middle-income family of farmers, Aglipay was five days old when he was baptized on 9 May 1860, but from 1902 onward he celebrated his birthday on 8 May. A reputedly strong-willed boy, he grew up in the care of great-aunts, who often castigated him for swimming the swollen rivers and for fracas with his peers. In his adolescent years, his father brought him along on his frequent trips to the neighboring province of Cagayan.

At 16, Aglipay continued his primary education in Manila and did his secondary course as a working student at Letran. He transferred in his third year and became a first-rate student during his final year. Perhaps influenced by progressive university students such as Marcelo H. del Pilar and Jose Rizal, who, according to hearsay, advised him to join the priesthood during a fencing session, Aglipay entered the seminary at Vigan in 1885. Despite repeated reports of misdemeanors, he graduated, was ordained to the priesthood just before Christmas 1889, and celebrated his first sung mass in the following new year. He was transferred four times in six years — evidence, his critics claimed, of an unstable character. But a contrary interpretation is that the transfers were due to the insecurity of his superiors.

Most likely, Aglipay joined the Katipunan* before the outbreak of hostilities in 1896. During the revolution he ministered to combatants on and off the battlefields. In 1897, as parish priest of Victoria, he organized the local Katipunan, using the convent as a meeting place and sanctuary for the group. When the revolutionary government proclaimed Philippine independence on 12 Jun 1898, he was the only priest delegate of the congress which drafted the constitution of the First Philippine Republic. On 20 Oct 1898, President Emilio Aguinaldo* appointed Aglipay military vicar general of the Philippine armed forces. In this position, he immediately sent to the clergy two manifestos urging support for the revolutionary government. Later in the same year, he was appointed ecclesiastical delegate for the dioceses by the Spanish prelate of Nueva Segovia, Jose Hevia y Campomanes. Archbishop Nozaleda excommunicated Aglipay in May 1899 for "usurpation of authority" because of his appointment by a layperson, Emilio Aguinaldo.

On 23 Oct 1899, Aglipay organized a conference of 26 Filipino priests in Paniqui that produced the document *Constituciones Provisionales de la Iglesia Filipina* (Provisional Ordinances of the Philippine Church), placing the highest ecclesiastical authority in the hands of the Filipino clergy during times of trouble and uncertainty. Together with layman Isabelo de los Reyes, Aglipay fought as guerrilla general against the Americans, especially in the Ilocos region, and even after his surrender at the end of Mar 1901 continued to strive for the Filipinization* of the church.

On 8 May 1902, Aglipay celebrated his birthday with several clergymen and wartime subordinates at a place where several major encounters had occurred. They discussed the possibility of a new independent church but decided instead to continue negotiations with the Vatican. The occasion was later referred to as the Kullabeng Assembly. In a surprise move on 3 Aug 1902 at the general council of the *Union Obrera Democratica* (UOD), the head labor leader, Isabelo de los Reyes, Sr. (Don Belong), proclaimed the establishment of IFI and nominated Aglipay, in absentia, its *Obispo Maximo.* Aglipay reluctantly accepted the position which he held until his death in 1940, consistently denying that he was the founder of IFI and explaining that it was "founded by the people of our country . . . a product of their desire for liberty, religiously, politically and socially." As *Obispo Maximo,* he tackled the issues of the unity of faith and revolution and was an early proponent of the indigenization of the local church. He was also a staunch defender of the downtrodden and a severe critic of charlatans.

Aglipay ran for the presidency of the Philippine Commonwealth in 1935 but was resoundingly defeated by Manuel L. Quezon. In his twilight years, he mellowed his criticisms against the Americans and reserved his scathing criticism for local politicians whom he regarded as responsible for the suffering of the people. He was regarded as a patriot and a hero when he died.

Bibliography

Achutegui, Pedro S., and Miguel A. Bernad, *Religious Revolution in the Philippines,* Vols. I and II (1960, 1966). • Iglesia Filipina Independiente, *Our Heritage, Our Response* (1989). • Manaligod, Ambrosio, *Father Gregorio Aglipay: Priest of the Philippine Church of the Patronato*

Real Espanol (1995). • Schumacher, John N., *The Revolutionary Clergy and the Nationalist Movement, 1850-1903* (1981). • Scott, William Henry, *Aglipay Before Aglipayanism* (1987).

APOLONIO RANCHE and TEODORO M. M. DE MESA

Aguinaldo, Emilio

(b. Kawit, Cavite, Philippines, 22 Mar 1869; d. Quezon City, 6 Feb 1964). Filipino patriot and first president of the Philippine Republic.

Aguinaldo was educated by the Dominican* friars at the College of San Juan de Letran, becoming a teacher and later a municipal captain. In 1895, he joined the Katipunan* and became one of its generals in the province of Cavite. At the Tejeros convention, he was elected in absentia the president of the Philippine Republic. There is suspicion that Aguinaldo was responsible for the execution of Bonifacio on 8 May 1897 to eliminate a rival. He went into voluntary exile at Hong Kong, returning in 1898 to collaborate with the Americans against Spain.

Aguinaldo declared the victory of the Filipino people's struggle against Spain by having a decree of independence read in Kawit, Cavite, on 12 Jun 1898. He set up a republic at Malolos, Bulacan, and led a rebellion against the American forces when independence was denied by the Treaty of Paris (1898). He was captured in 1901. In 1935, he ran unsuccessfully for the presidency of the Philippines. He was charged with collaboration after World War II but was never brought to trial. Aguinaldo disappointed the people's aspirations when he failed to redistribute the friar estates to poor peasants.

Bibliography

Agoncillo, Teodoro A., *History of the Filipino People* (1990). • Constantino, Renato, *The Philippines: A Past Revisited* (1975). • Foreman, John, *The Philippine Islands* (1906). • Maring, Ester G. and Joel M., *The Philippines* (1973).

TEODORO MAXIMILIANO M. DE MESA

Ah Fah. *See* Leong Kung Fa

Ah Mya, Francis

(b. Institute Village, Toungoo, Burma, 6 Jul 1904). First Burmese bishop, first archbishop of the Church of the Province of Myanmar (Anglican), and an ecumenical leader.

Ah Mya started his primary education at Bawgalilay Village, continued at St. Luke Anglican Mission School, Toungoo, completed high school at St. John Diocesan High School, Yangon, and attended Judson College, Yangon, for two years. Beginning in 1925, he studied three years at Bishop's College, India. He returned in 1928 and served two years as a catechist at Aihe Village, where he built a parsonage and started a primary school. In 1930, Ah Mya served as a lecturer at Kokaing Bible School and was ordained a deacon. Three years later, he was ordained a priest by the bishop of Yangon and married Naw Katherine Lu Lar Le on 21 Apr 1933.

During the Japanese occupation (ca. 1941-44), Ah Mya ignored the dangers and continued visiting neighboring villages in Hoki, which was temporarily under his pastoral care. The British government conferred on him the Membership of the British Empire (MBE) for his courageous work.

In 1949, Ah Mya was consecrated an assistant bishop. The government conferred on him the title *Thiripyanchi* for his services for the welfare of the country.

In 1956, Bishop V. G. Shearburn sent Ah Mya to the Hpa-An region of Kayin State to begin self-supporting projects there. In 1956-66, he built St. Peter's Bible School, St. Peter's High School at Hpa-An, and the Missionary Middle School at Hlai-Bwe. He also started a press for Kayin literature and began agricultural work in the region. Furthermore, he also accomplished the considerable feat of building brick churches for Hkakpali, Hkwanta, Hkwanbi, and Hkundaw villages.

When foreign missionaries were forced to leave, Ah Mya was elected bishop in 1966. He rewrote the constitution for the Anglican church and in 1967 started a Three-in-One project aimed at producing future leaders for the church. When the Anglican church in Myanmar* had to separate from India, Pakistan, and Sri Lanka, Ah Mya took the lead in establishing the Church of the Province of Myanmar on 24 Feb 1970, which comprises four dioceses. He served as its first archbishop. Striving for church renewal, he started self-supporting projects throughout the province. A keen supporter of church unity, Ah Mya served as chairperson of the Myanmar Council of Churches. Although he retired in 1973 to Institute Village, Toungoo, with his family, he continued to travel throughout the province, advocating church renewal and missionary outreach.

Bibliography

U Aung Hla Tun, "A Personal Interview with Francis Ah Mya," *Golden Jubilee Magazine* (1985).

SAW MAUNG DOE

Ainu People

(Ainujin Dendo).

Catholic. The missionary bishop Alexander Berlioz arrived at Motomachi Church in Hakodate in 1884 and from the beginning had a great interest in ministry to the Ainu people. Upon his arrival he assigned Julian-Jean-Marie Rousseau to Muroran, where he was to work specifically with the Ainu people. Rousseau studied the Ainu language, translated the Roman Catholic catechism into the Ainu language, and set up a mission station in Muroran. He dedicated the station in Jul 1893, but because of poor health was forced to leave Muroran in 1901. The bishop himself often went to Shiraoi, where, living with the Ainu, he made an investigation of their language, customs, and habits. The bishop taught the Ainu how to farm in an attempt to improve their living conditions. He even had them live on the grounds of the Trappist Monastery, but he was not able to establish firmly this lifestyle among people who had always been fishermen and hunters. Using the catechism that Rousseau had earlier translated as a base, Berlioz edited a new translation, *Petit Cathéchisme Aino (Parvus Catechismus Aino).* There were two volumes, a small one with the Ainu language written in Roman letters on the cover, and a large one for the missionary. In 1928, these were published by the Nazareth Printing Company in Hong Kong.

Bibliography

Sato Kenichi, *Muroran Katorikku Kyokai nana-ju-nen no ayumi* (Muroran Catholic Church, a Seventy-year History) (1965). • Ono Tadasuke, *Faurie-Shimpu* (1977).

Ono Tadasuke

Russian Orthodox. Mission work of the Russian Orthodox Church in Chishima began when Russia made plans to expand eastward, and Russians moved out to Sakhalin, Kamchatka, and Chishima. There they made their first contact with the Ainu people. In an investigative study of Etorofu Island, *Henyo bunkaizuko* (Treatise on Frontier Fortification), Kindo Seisai made the following notes: "Teachers of the church sometimes went to the various islands to tend and teach the flock," and "We received that 'god' and amulet (or charm)."

In an exchange agreement related to Chishima and Sakhalin in 1875, all of Chishima came under Japanese jurisdiction. The Ainu people living on Shumushu Island were forcibly moved to Shikotan Island. A number of these people then moved to Sakhalin. The Ainu Orthodox Church believers who stayed behind lost their priest. In 1885, however, Bishop Nikolai sent Komatsu Tozo and Sawabe Teitaro to Shikotan Island to care for the believers there, and in 1897 put them under the jurisdiction of the Nemuro Church. Money was collected for mission work to the Ainu people, and the priest Ignatio Kato was to be sent, but, because of the fog and the limited number of boats making the trip to the islands, he was able to travel only about once per month during the summer. In Aug 1899, Shoin Sergii (Tikhomirov), who accompanied Bishop Nikolai, itinerated to Etorofu and Shikotan Islands, but after that the mission was not actively pursued.

Bibliography

Miyata Yoko, trans., *Doin Sergei Hokkaido junkaiki* (Hokkaido Travels of Doin Sergei) (1972).

Ebisawa Arimichi

Protestant. The persons who most fervently pursued mission work to the Ainu people were Walter Dening, John Batchelor, and others from the British Church Missionary Society. Dening visited the Ainu village of Kotan, on the outskirts of Hakodate, in 1875 — the year after he arrived. His heart went out to the Ainu people, who were being treated cruelly and discriminated against by the Japanese. The following year, he traveled to Hiratori of Hidaka and studied the Ainu language with Penryuku, a knowledgeable elder of the village. Dening discussed with him the possibilities for mission.

Batchelor, who came after Dening, was also taught Ainu by Penryuku. In 1885, he baptized Kannari Taro and asked that the mission work be continued while he went to Hakodate to open Airin School. He worked very hard for the Ainu people, producing about 10 evangelists, including folklorist Kannari Matsu and Mukai Yamao, who became a priest.

The work of such people as Walter Andrews, Lucy Payne, Akutagawa Seigoro, and Nagakubo Hidejiro was also very important. Other workers included George Peck Pierson, a Presbyterian who worked with the Kotan in Asahikawa, and missionaries from the Salvation Army* and the Holiness Church. The work of Miura Masaji, a member of the Sapporo Independent Christian Church and principal of Harutori School (from 1923), in fighting against discriminatory education is especially worthy of mention. During and after World War II*, mission work to the Ainu came to a halt. This was largely due to strict enforcement of the policy instituted by the government in the Meiji Period, which made doing anything with the Ainu almost impossible.

Bibliography

Anglican Church of Japan, *Hokkaido Diocese Kyku kyu-j-nenshi* (Ninety-year History of the Hokkaido District of the Anglican Church of Japan) (1966). • Batchelor, J., *"Ainu Minzoku e no Fukuin"* (Taking the Gospel to the Ainu People), in *Nihon dend megumi no ato* (Mission Work in Japan, After the Grace of God) (1930). • Koike Sozo, *Inaka dendsha Pearson senkyoshi fusai* (Rev. and Mrs. Pearson, Rural Evangelists) (1967). • Matsumoto Narumi et al., *Kotan ni ikiru Ainu Minzoku no rekishi to kyoiku* (History and education of the Ainu people living in Kotan) (1977).

Fukushima Tsuneo

Akaiwa Sakae

(b. Hijikawa Village, Kita-gun, Ehime Prefecture, Japan, Apr 1903; d. 28 Nov 1966). Minister at Uehara Church of the United Church of Christ in Japan (UCCJ).

After leaving Koryo Middle School, Akaiwa entered Kobe Seminary. He transferred to Osaka Seminary but developed a skepticism toward the Christian faith and dropped out before graduating. He then entered Tokyo Shingakusha (seminary). While studying under Takakura Tokutaro, he experienced a conversion. After graduation, he became pastor of the Presbyterian* Church in Japan's preaching point at Sado. At Takakura's request, he returned to Tokyo (1931-33) to edit the magazine *Fukuin to Gendai* (The Gospel and the Present Age). He started the Nakahara preaching point and in 1932 established Uehara Church. He was soon ordained and served at Uehara Church for the remainder of his life.

From 1931 to 1940 Akaiwa published the monthly magazine *Kotoba* (The Word). Drawn to Karl Barth's dialectical theology, he observed such strict church polity that no one was allowed to enter the worship service once it began. He published a number of books, including *Bikosha-Iesu* (Jesus, the One Who Traveled Incognito) in 1937. Following the defeat of World War II*, his keen sense of war responsibility compelled him to social action. In the general election held in Jan 1949, he actively supported Kazahaya Yasoji, leading theorist of the postwar Japan Communist Party (JCP), and announced that he was joining that party, an action that caused waves in and outside the church. He believed Christianity's way of dealing with human existence and Communism's worldview and mode of social action were compatible. But under persuasion by United Church of Christ in Japan leaders, he abandoned his plan to join the JCP, supporting it rather from the outside.

Greatly interested in thought, literature, and art*, Akaiwa led a colorful life as a critic. In 1949, he collaborated with writer Shiina Rinzo, whom he had baptized, in publishing the monthly *Yubi* (Finger). Eventually he became critical of Barth's dogmatics and abandoned Rudolf Bultmann's demythologizing in favor of the historical Jesus. In 1964, he wrote *Kirisuto-kyo dasshutsuki* (Escape from Christianity), defining "faith" as an existential relationship with Jesus before he became the Christ. Meanwhile, in his church he discontinued Sunday school, ritualized offerings, and hymn singing; purging the worship service of all liturgy, he called it simply "Sunday gathering." Shiina saw this development as a forsaking of Christian principles and took leave of Uehara Church.

The hallmarks of Akaiwa's thought were: (1) religion's ascendance over culture; (2) the compatibility of religion and culture; and (3) the development of culture by means of religious negation. Akaiwa may well be called one of the most important contributors to postwar Christian thought.

Bibliography

Akaiwa Sakae, *Shosakushu* (The Collected Works of Akaiwa Sakae), nine volumes, one supplement (1970-72).

Kasahara Yoshimitsu

Akha

A Tibeto-Burman-speaking people akin to the Hani.

Approximately one million Akha live in Yunnan and other provinces of southern China*, Myanmar* (Burma), Thailand*, Laos*, and Vietnam*. Generally, they live in the hills, forests, and remote valleys, distant from urban centers.

The Akha traditional way, known as *Akhazhang*, is a strong unifying factor. Akha see themselves as people of shared descent who follow *Akhazhang* in religion, customs, agriculture, kinship, and other practices which comprise Akha identity.

Akhazhang has lately been pressured by nation formation, modernization, and religious evangelization. Nation formation has ostracized Akha as minorities; modernization has made *Akhazhang* appear outdated; and evangelization has converted many to Christianity and sometimes Buddhism.

Christian missionaries established contact with the Akha in 1869 near the Shan State of Jengtung (in Burma), but it was only in 1909 that American Baptists converted an Akha to Christianity. The first Protestant Akha church opened in 1936. During the early 1900s, other Akha became Catholics. The Pontifical Institute for Foreign Missions (PIME)* began work in Burma in 1868. In Jengtung, where most Catholic Akha in Burma live, the Vicariate of North Burma was established. Thailand's first Catholic Akha was baptized in 1971.

In Thailand, Akha first became Protestants in 1962 following contacts with Christian Tai Ya migrants from China, and then with Jean and Peter Nightingale of the Overseas Missionary Fellowship (OMF) who started working with the Akha in 1955.

Little is known about Akha churches in Burma at present. Thousands of Akha there apparently are Christian, but political life has made staying so difficult. Many churches nonetheless show signs of recent rebuilding. In 1994, Jengtung's Catholic bishop dedicated an Akha church there, and Sunday church services were celebrated without signs of obvious interference.

Reasons Akha become Christian vary. Early converts did so out of genuine belief. Later, many were attracted by monetary and material rewards. As the pressures of highland life in the face of modernization mounted, the costs of traditional practice, often involving pig sacrifices, became prohibitive. Some Akha converted for economic rewards from generous church groups and also for freedom from sponsoring sacrifices.

Akha have joined several Protestant churches, mainly larger bodies in the Church of Christ in Thailand (CCT) and the Evangelical Fellowship in Thailand (EFT)*. These include two districts in the CCT and the Akha Church of Thailand Churches of Christ and independent Akha churches within the EFT.

Although growing steadily, Akha Christians constitute a minority of Thailand's total population. Much growth has come from immigrant Christian Akha leaving harsh political conditions in Burma since the 1960s. The best estimates suggest a Christian population of under 20 percent of Thailand's Akha total, or 7,000-8,000. There are very few Christian Akha in China, Laos, and Vietnam.

Christian Akha have sometimes been explicitly obliged to abandon many customs. Although Catholics since Vatican II have tolerated traditional Akha spirituality, some Protestant missionaries in Thailand have had Akha rework beliefs, rituals, and customs governing marriage and other relationships. Replacing the components of *Akhazhang,* though, is difficult since even partially abandoning *Akhazhang* is disruptive especially in these modern changing times.

As this occurs in Thailand, and also because of strict Thai citizenship and forestry laws, much good in Akha life is lost. As a result, Akha in Thailand are marginalized and suffer more problems of addiction, alienation, and prostitution than do neighboring hill groups.

Paul and Elaine Lewis, American Baptist missionaries who had worked with the Akha in Burma since 1947, came in 1966 to deal with the difficulties in Thailand. They addressed the problems through public health, family planning, and narcotics rehabilitation work while also devising an Akha script and writing a dictionary. They were instrumental in setting up the Development Agricultural and Education Project (DAPA) for the Akha in 1984, which remains the largest indigenous Akha project working to alleviate poverty among the Akha. DAPA has also worked to provide modern education to Akha youth as a viable way to cope with modern Thai life. Recently as Akha have migrated to Thailand from other countries in the region, many have settled in city slums, but a few more fortunate have taken their place among the urban educated elite. The future of the Akha church, its members, and the rest of the community in all countries where it is found remains in doubt.

Bibliography

Kammerer, Cornelis Ann, *Gateway to the Akha World* (1986). • Lewis, Paul, *Akha Village and Political Systems* (1973). • Lewis, Paul and Elaine, *Peoples of the Golden Triangle: Six Tribes of Thailand* (1984). • Nightingale, Jean, *Without a Gate* (1990). • Renard, Ronald D., et al., *Evaluation of DAPA* (1995).

RONALD D. RENARD

Albuquerque, Afonso de

(b. Portugal, 1453; d. Goa, India, 16 Dec 1515). Mariner, military officer, and second governor of Portugal's Asian empire.

The second son of a prominent nobleman and the grandson of an admiral, Albuquerque was raised at the court of the king of Portugal. He began his career of service to the crown while still quite young, spending some years in North Africa fighting the Moors. In 1503 he made his initial voyage to the East, erecting Portugal's first Asian fortress at Cochin, on India's southwestern coast, and establishing a garrison there before returning to Lisbon the following year. In 1506 he sailed again for India*, this time as a captain commanding several vessels belonging to the fleet of Tristão de Cunha. The next year he used his ships to seize and fortify the island of Socotra, at the mouth of the Red Sea. He attempted the same with the island of Hormuz, in the channel between the Persian Gulf and the Gulf of Oman, but was unable to raise fortifications there because of disagreements with several of his officers. King Manuel I appointed him to succeed Francesco de Almeida, first governor of Portugal's Asian holdings, but initially Almeida refused to yield his post, holding Albuquerque prisoner for over a year. Finally gaining his freedom and assuming office in 1509, Albuquerque broke with Almeida's policy of reliance on command of the sea, moving instead to establish Portuguese control of trade by means of a series of strong points around the rim of the Indian Ocean such as he had already built at Cochin and Socotra and attempted at Hormuz. In 1510 he took, lost, then retook Goa, which was to serve as Portugal's bastion. The next year he conquered and garrisoned Malacca*, on the Malay Peninsula. In 1513 he assaulted but failed to capture Aden, at the mouth of the Red Sea. In 1515 he returned to Hormuz, this time winning that island's submission and bringing it under Portuguese control. On arriving again in India, he received word that King Manuel, persuaded by the arguments of Albuquerque's enemies, had deposed him and appointed one of those enemies as his successor. The king later repented of this, but not before the embittered Albuquerque had died and been buried at Goa. Half a century later, his remains were exhumed and returned to Lisbon for a more fitting interment. His strategic vision and policy of toleration for indigenous political and religious practices marked him as "the ablest of the Portuguese viceroys in the East" (S. Neill).

Bibliography

Albuquerque, Afonso de, *Albuquerque, Caesar of the East: Selected Texts by Afonso de Albuquerque and His Son,* ed. and trans. T. F. Earle and John Villiers (1990). • Neill, Stephen, *A History of Christianity in India: The Beginnings to 1707* (1984). • Stephens, H. Morse, *Albuquerque* (1892).

GEORGE W. HARPER

Aleni, Julio

(Ai Ruluo) (b. 1582; d. Yanping area, 1649). Italian and first Jesuit missionary to realize success in Fujian, China.

Aleni arrived in Macau in 1610 and entered inland China* in 1613. Visiting Yangzhou, Shanxi, and Changsu, he propagated Catholicism. He made a special trip to Kaifeng, Henan, to seek classic works on Judaism. In 1624, he met Yie Xianggao, a retired prime minister and a native of Fujian, at the home of Yang Tingjun in Hangzhou. In 1625, invited by Yie, Aleni went from Hangzhou to Fuzhou, bringing with him five Chinese books on Catholicism, including *The True Idea of God,* authored by Matteo Ricci*.

For a period of time, Yie's house became a place for debate on Catholic doctrine between Aleni and some Chinese literati. Twenty-five people were baptized after the first debate, among whom were several *Xiucai* (scholars who have passed the national imperial examination). Within a few years, Aleni had traveled to almost all of the eight major cities of Fujian. While there, he would pay his respects to the local officials of each city. He was acclaimed by some people as the "Confucius from the West," because he was considered by them to be sociable, good-looking, and accomplished in Chinese, while others sent him inscriptions to express their appreciation.

Aleni spent 23 years in Fujian, establishing 22 churches and baptizing more than one million people. He was responsible for turning the two Buddhist temples on Mount Wuyi into Catholic churches.

When Qing troops took Fujian (1647-48), Aleni escaped to Yanping to a remote mountainous area. He died there and was buried at Shizi Shan outside the North Gate of Fuzhou.

Bibliography

Aleni, Julio, *Sanshan lunxueji* (Discussions of Sanshan) (1627); *Wan wu zhenyuan* (The Origin of All Things) (1628); *Zhifang waji* (Geography of Countries) (1623). • Gernet, Jacques, *China and the Christian Impact,* trans. Janet Lloyd (1982/1985). • Ross, Andrew C., *A Vision Betrayed: The Jesuits in Japan and China, 1542-1742* (1994). • Goodrich, L. Carrington, "Aleni, Giulio," in Carrington and C. Fang, eds., *Dictionary of Ming Biography* (1976).

China Group

Allen, Horace Newton

(b. Delaware, Ohio, United States, 23 Apr 1858; d. Delaware, Ohio, 11 Dec 1932). First missionary of the American Presbyterian Church to Korea.

Allen graduated from Ohio Wesleyan College and Miami Medical College, Oxford, Ohio, in 1883. After graduating from medical school, he married Frances Anne Messenger and was appointed as a missionary to China by the Presbyterian* Church in the United States of America (North). He arrived in Shanghai, China*, in 1883, but his wife was sick and had some trouble with the missionaries who worked there. Thus Allen made up his mind to move his mission field. His friends advised him to go to Korea* because there was no medical doctor there. After receiving permission from the board of his church, he moved to Korea in Sep 1884 and became the first missionary to live in Korea. However, he could not work as a missionary, because Korea did not permit mission work. He was therefore appointed as a physician by the American consulate.

In December, there was political revolt, and Young Ik Min, nephew of the queen and the strong man in the government, was seriously wounded by the opposition party. Allen treated him, and he recovered; because of this incident, Allen became acquainted with the king and his family and was appointed the king's physician. He received permission to establish a clinic, *Kwanghewon* (Extended-Grace Clinic). This clinic became a permanent base of the Christian mission in Korea. At the clinic, Allen treated more than 10,000 patients with the aid of other medical missionaries — J. Heron, a Presbyterian missionary, and W. Scranton, a Methodist missionary who arrived in 1885.

Allen could not work smoothly with other missionaries, so when the Korean king asked him to be a foreign secretary of the Korean consulate in Washington, D.C., he accepted the position and resigned from his role as a missionary. He returned to the United States with Jung Yang Park, the first Korean consul to the United States. He worked for two years for the consulate and strove to prevent China's interference in the foreign affairs of Korea.

Allen resigned from the position in 1889 and was reappointed as a medical missionary to Korea. He returned, but in the same year the United States State Department appointed him as secretary at the American consulate general in Korea, so he resigned from his position as a missionary once again.

After two years, Allen was promoted to the position of deputy consul and in 1901 became the consul. In 1905, he had a difference of opinion with the United States State Department regarding the treaty between Japan and Korea, so he was removed from his position and the consulate in Korea was closed.

Allen returned to his hometown in Ohio, where he died. Through his work and experience in Korea for 20 years as a missionary and a diplomat, he gained information and wrote many books and articles about Korea, including *Korean Tales* (1898), *A Chronological Index* (1900), *Korea: Fact and Fancy* (1903), *Korean-American Relations* (1904), and *Things Korean* (1908).

Bibliography

Encyclopedia of Christianity (of Korea) (1994). • Allen, H. N., *Korea: Fact and Fancy* (1903). • *Allen's Diary.* • Dennett, T., *Americans in Eastern Asia* (1922). • Kim In Soo, *A History of Christianity in Korea* (1994).

Kim In Soo

Allen, Young John

(b. Georgia, United States; d. Shanghai, 1907). American Methodist* missionary to China.

Allen was converted during his high school days and subsequently joined the Methodist Episcopal Church (South). After graduating from Emory University (Georgia) in 1858, he was committed to foreign mission work. In Jun 1860, he came to Shanghai. He visited *Tai-ping tian-guo* (Heavenly Kingdom) the following year and tried to preach in the Taiping army. Shortly after, the Civil War in America broke out, and the financial support from his mission board lapsed. Allen had to find his own financial means by teaching in Shanghai's Foreign Language Literature School *(Wai-guo yu-yen wen-zi xue-guan)* and the China Education Committee *(Jiang nan zhi zao ju).*

He also did translation work for 10 years, during which time he translated more than 10 books relating to world history, geography, and natural science. These contributed tremendously to the modernization of China.

In 1868 Allen self-financed the publication of *Jiao-hui xin-bao* (The Church News), originally a weekly publication which later became a monthly. It was later renamed

Wan Kuo Kung Pao (Globe Magazine). Its content informed readers of world news and propagated reformation, and its influence was deeply felt in the government. In 1881, after Allen joined the Methodist Episcopal Church (South) again, he opened *Zong Xi Shu Yuan* (The Anglo-Chinese College), which later developed into Soochow University, in Shanghai. In 1890 he opened Zong Xi Nu Shu, which was well received among the rich and famous who sent their daughters to this girls school. In 1891 Allen became chief editor of *Zhong Xi Jiao Hui Bao* (The Chinese Christian Review), published by the Society for the Diffusion of Christian and General Knowledge among the Chinese *(Guang-xue-hui)*, and also became chief editor of *Jiao Bao*, published by the Methodist Episcopal Church (South). When Allen went back to America in May 1906, he was received by President Theodore Roosevelt. He died the following year in Shanghai.

Bibliography

Allen, Young John, *Zhong Dong Zhan Ji Ben Mo* (War between China and Japan: How it began and ended"); *Wen Xue Xing Guo Ce* (Literature could reform a country); *Wu Da Zhou Nu Su Tong Kao* (Women in all lands"). • Treadgold, Donald W., *The West in Russia and China: China, 1582-1949* (1973). • Chandler, Warren A., *Young J. Allen: The Man Who Seeded China* (1931).

China Group

Alonzo, Ricardo

Filipino Presbyterian evangelist who defected to the Philippine Independent Church* (PIC).

The pioneer Presbyterian* evangelist in Cebu, Alonzo was a well-to-do half-Spanish Filipino converted in 1903. His mother was one of the first two Presbyterian Bible women in Cebu. An eloquent speaker, Alonzo was the chief evangelist in the islands of Cebu and Bohol. Ordained by the Presbytery of Manila in 1907, Alonzo served as pastor of Oslob and Opon.

In 1912 the Congregational and Presbyterian Missions jointly sent him to organize the Alglipayans in Baliangao and Dapitan in northwestern Mindanao, who were turning Protestant en masse. Alonzo was the first pastor of the Baliangao Evangelical Church (1912-14).

Returning to Cebu, Alonzo subsequently came in conflict with the Presbyterian missionaries, leading to his defection to the PIC in 1916.

Bibliography

The Philippine Presbyterian, Vol. 1, No. 1 (Jan 1910). • Sotto, A. C., *Mga Handumanan sa Akong Tinhoan* (1954). • Sitoy, T. V., Jr., *Several Springs, One Stream* (1992).

T. Valentino Sitoy, Jr.

Amantes de la Croix. *See* Lovers of the Cross

Ambedkar, Bhimrao Ramji

(b. Mhow, Central Provinces, India, 14 Apr 1891; d. New Delhi, 6 Dec 1956). Indian statesman and leader of the Dalits ("untouchables").

Ambedkar was born into the untouchable Mahar caste, the son of a *subhedar* in the Indian army. His educational accomplishments were remarkable for a person of his generation and caste background. He received his bachelor of arts from Elphinstone College, Bombay; his master's and doctoral degrees in economics from Columbia University, New York; his master's and doctor of science degrees from the London School of Economics; and his barrister-at-law from Grey's Inn. He became the acknowledged leader of his own and other untouchable castes at the time when Gandhi* and the Indian National Congress were engaged in a mass struggle to win independence for India*.

Ambedkar's career as spokesperson of his people began in 1919 when he testified before a British franchise commission, asking it to give the depressed classes (as the Dalits were then called) separately elected representation in the upcoming constitution. He again argued for separate representation as a depressed-classes delegate at the Round Table Conferences in 1930-31, when the constitution was once more up for revision. This brought him into direct conflict with Gandhi, who not only did not wish to divide Hindus into separate constituencies, but also believed that such separation would perpetuate rather than eliminate untouchability. Ambedkar considered the Dalits to be a very vulnerable minority which needed guaranteed protection and representation under majority rule. The conflict was resolved in a compromise known as the Poona Pact (1932), which gave Dalits a good portion of reserved seats within the general (Hindu) constituency rather than completely separate electorates in the central and provincial legislatures. This agreement was incorporated into both the 1935 constitution and the constitution of independent India (1950).

Politically, Ambedkar went on to form three successive political parties: the Independent Labor Party (1936), the Scheduled Castes Federation (1942), and the Republican Party (1956). He served as a member of the Bombay Presidency Legislative Assembly (1937-42) and then as Labor Member of the Viceroy's Executive Council (1942-46). When India became independent in 1947, Jawaharlal Nehru* invited him to be its first law minister (1947-51). In that capacity, he became the chief drafter of the present constitution of India (1950).

Religiously, Ambedkar became increasingly alienated from Hinduism* during the 1920s and 1930s. In December 1927, he publicly burned the *Manusmriti* in protest against its religious sanction of untouchability. At the Bombay Presidency Depressed Classes Conference on 13 Oct 1935, he announced that he would leave Hinduism. The conference then voted to leave Hinduism for a religion granting them equality. The question which preoccupied Ambedkar, his followers, his critics, and religious leaders for the next two years was which religion they would adopt. In the end, Ambedkar gravitated toward Buddhism* and converted on 14 Oct 1956. About 300,000 followers joined him that day, and over two million more converted within the next five years.

During Ambedkar's lifetime, the histories of Christianity and of the Dalit movement became closely intertwined. Mass conversions to Christianity among Dalits during the last quarter of the 19th c. had helped to make the Dalits' plight a matter of growing public concern. After 1909 when Muslims were first granted separate electorates, it was apparent that mass conversions from one religion to another could affect the communal balance of political power. Hindu reformers and nationalists became alarmed, passed resolutions, and engaged in "uplift work" among Dalits to stem the tide. After 1919, Gandhi was in the forefront of this effort and became increasingly critical of Christian evangelism among Dalits, especially after Ambedkar's announcement in 1935. On this question, Ambedkar sided with the Christians, rebutting Gandhi's arguments and affirming that conversion out of Hinduism was essential to the Dalits' wellbeing.

Ambedkar understood Christianity and its impact upon Dalit converts but did not become a Christian. Perhaps the nationalist in him desired a religion of Indian origin not dominated by foreigners. Certainly the Christian response to his 1935 declaration and its potential consequences for the church was ambivalent. For his part Ambedkar was critical of Christianity for its inability to eradicate both caste within the churches and the "paganism" of its converts, for its failure to agitate for the social emancipation of Dalits, and for its general political ineffectiveness. Today, when at least half of all Indian Christians are Dalits who are increasingly not only affirming their Dalit identity but also seeking unity with Dalits of other faiths in a common struggle for dignity, equality, and justice, they are finding in Ambedkar's example, methods, and social and political philosophy a basis for unity and common action (see Dalit Movements).

Bibliography

Gore, M. S., *The Social Context of an Ideology: Ambedkar's Social and Political Thought* (1993). • Keer, Dhananjay, *Dr. Ambedkar: Life and Mission* (1971). • Moon, Vasant, compiler, *Dr. Babasaheb Ambedkar Writings and Speeches,* Vol. 5 (1989). • Webster, John C. B., *The Dalit Christians: A History* (1994). • Zelliot, Eleanor Mae, "Dr. Ambedkar and the Mahar Movement" (doctoral dissertation, University of Pennsylvania) (1969).

John C. B. Webster

Ambrosi, Louis

(b. Verona, Italy, 1829; d. Hong Kong, 10 Mar 1867). Fourth prefect apostolic of the Hong Kong Catholic Church (1855-67).

Ambrosi was a committed coordinator of mission work in China* and builder of the basic social and educational institutions of the Roman Catholic Church* in Hong Kong.

Diocesan priest of Verona, Ambrosi arrived in Hong Kong in 1854 to help A. Feliciani in the Far East Procuration of the Sacred Congregation for the Propagation of Faith (see Propaganda Fide). He was appointed to succeed Feliciani as procurator and prefect apostolic of Hong Kong with the decree of 20 Jun 1855. He served in this position until his death in 1867.

In 1858, Ambrosi welcomed the arrival of the first members of the Lombardy Seminary of the Foreign Missions (later, the Pontifical Institute for Foreign Missions) as a solution to the staffing of the prefecture, which, up till then, was unstable since it was made up of transitory missionaries destined for mainland China.

In 1860, the prefecture was enlarged to include the entire San On (later, Po On) District in mainland China. In that same year, Ambrosi welcomed the first group of Canossian Sisters, who started educational and social services mainly among girls and women. In 1863, the West Point Reformatory was opened for training young delinquents, while in 1864 the Holy Savior's College started classes for young men.

Bibliography

Hong Kong Catholic Church Directory 1995. • Ryan, T., *The Story of a Hundred Years* (1959); *Catholic Guide to Hong Kong* (1962). • Ticozzi, S., *Historical Documents of the Hong Kong Catholic Church* (in Chinese) (1983).

Sergio Ticozzi

Amirtham, Samuel

(b. Parasala, Kerala, India, 19 Aug 1932). Pioneering theological educator in rural and slum areas of India.

After obtaining a bachelor of divinity degree from the United Theological College*, Bangalore, Amirtham was ordained in 1957. He pursued a master of theology degree in Old Testament in Germany and worked as a lecturer at the United Theological College, Bangalore, from 1963 to 1966. In 1968 he obtained a doctorate in theology from Hamburg University. He did postdoctoral research at Gorat Theological Seminary and Jerusalem University. In 1969, he became the first principal of Tamil Nadu Theological Seminary, Madurai. He experimented with and initiated many reforms in the field of theological education to make it relevant to the local context. In 1978, he left his principalship to take up responsibility with the Rural Theological Institute. In 1980, he became director of the Program for Theological Education (PTE) and held that post until 1989. In 1990 he became bishop of the Church of South India (CSI)*, South Kerala Diocese, and continued to be a leader of the Indian church.

Jacob Kurian

Amity Foundation

(Aide Jijinhui). Development agency established by Chinese Protestant Christians in 1985.

The stated purpose of the Amity Foundation is to promote social development, make Christian presence more widely known to the Chinese people, and serve as a channel for people-to-people sharing and exchanges.

Amity has been seen as a new Christian initiative in Chinese society designed to promote cooperation and understanding between Christians and non-Christians both in and outside of the People's Republic of China*. It has attracted considerable attention among churches and mission agencies all over the world because it represents a new way for them to participate in mission in China and to strengthen the social witness of the China Christian Council*. Amity is not a mission organization in the traditional sense of the word, but rather an expression of social ministry appropriate for the Chinese context.

Amity has been involved in such projects as the sending of foreign-language teachers, the training of rural doctors, integrated development programs, and the promotion of voluntary staff support for orphanages. A polio rehabilitation project in northern Jiangsu Province has received national commendation. In addition, the foundation has sponsored several international conferences on Christianity and social development.

The Amity Printing Company, a joint venture with the United Bible Societies, had produced more than 25 million Bibles for the Chinese church as of Jan 2001.

The headquarters of the foundation are in Nanjing. Amity's president is Bishop K. H. Ting* and its general secretary, Wenzao Han.

Bibliography

The Amity Newsletter (1985-present). PHILIP WICKERI

AMRSP (Association of Major Religious Superiors in the Philippines)

Joint forum (1974) of the two associations of Major Religious Superiors (Men and Women) in the Philippines, both founded in 1955.

The AMRSP forum provides an avenue to share common interests, cooperate in collaborative efforts, and pursue the role of the prophetic witness of being religious in the Philippine church and society. The central emphasis of the AMRSP is justice and peace, hence the birth of Mission Partners, designed to meet the emerging needs of workers, farmers, urban poor, women, human-rights victims, political detainees, and church people. The Mission Partners include rural missionaries, urban missionaries, a task force for urban conscientization, a task force of church personnel, an education forum, a sanctuary desk, a justice and peace commission, and a women's desk. AMRSP has a membership of approximately 150 female and 90 male congregations.

PAT BABIERA

Ancestor Worship

Clarification of Terms. The practice of ancestor worship (AW) has been variably termed "ancestor cult," "ancestor rite," "ancestor veneration," or "ancestral remembrance." The term "ancestor cult" signifies a system of beliefs expressed in rituals and homage to deceased ancestors. The term "ancestor rite" stresses the ceremonial act. "Ancestor veneration" places the focus on the attitude of reverence, though such reverence is usually accompanied by certain rites. As remembrance, AW may mean personal mental recollection or the corporate act of reminiscence through ritual or liturgy.

The word "worship" is problematic. If worship is used in a theological sense to mean the creature's response of wonder and adoration of the Creator, then the act of worship toward ancestors is apparently misplaced. If, however, worship is used in a more religious sense to designate the homage shown by the living to the spirit of the deceased person, "worship" then represents the creature's response to the spiritualized creature. Although the Chinese word *pai*, or worship, can have religious implications, it may also simply mean "reverence," "to pay respects to," "to visit," or "to make obeisance to." It is in this latter sense that we will use the term in our discussion of the phenomenon of ancestor worship.

It should be noted that AW is not to be confused with the cult of the dead, which centers on death, the preservation of the corpse, and the ceremonies related to the burial and postburial; the cult of the dead presupposes the ongoing existence of the departed soul and continuing interdependence between the living and the dead. The dead depend on the living to offer oblation, while the living look to the dead for protection and blessings. Such symbiosis is regarded as providing mutual benefits.

Ancestor Worship in Asia. In Asia, the practice of AW is found in India and is particularly strong in China*, Hong Kong*, Taiwan*, Singapore*, Korea*, Vietnam*, and Japan*.

India. AW in India takes on various forms, differing from area to area among diverse ethnic groups. The Laws of Manu give specific regulations for ancestral offerings. The offering of food for the deceased is a widespread custom. The feast of *sraddha* is observed by all male Hindus. This observance is directed to the deceased parents, grandparents, and great-grandparents. It is intended to assist them in achieving transmigration.

China. The origin of Chinese AW can be traced back to the very dawn of the Chinese civilization. From bone and bronze oracle inscriptions, we find that AW was already a well-established cultus in the Shang Dynasty (1765-1123 B.C.E.).

The ancient Chinese believed in the continued existence of deceased ancestors. At death, the upper soul *(hun)* ascended to heaven, while the lower soul *(p'o)* descended into the earth. According to Julia Ching, such belief "was formulated only in Chou times," but "it was implicit in the religious beliefs of Shang times, and in

Shang practices of divination and sacrifice" (*Chinese Religions,* 1993, p. 35).

From the texts of classic literature such as *Shu-ching* (the Book of Documents) and *Shih-ching* (the Book of Poetry), we see ample evidence of the mutual dependence between the living and the dead. The dead looked to the living for sacrifice and sustenance, and the living anticipated from the dead protection, guidance, and continued blessings upon them and their descendants. Such mutual dependence reduced the sense of isolation and enhanced family solidarity.

Closely tied with the practice of AW in Chinese culture is the virtue of filial piety. The great scholar/teacher Confucius (see Confucianism), or K'ung Fu Tzú (551-479 B.C.E.), incorporated many of the historical records dating from the first millennium before Christ into the Confucian canon. This suggests that filial piety has been an important part of Chinese tradition since 2200 B.C.E. In the Han Dynasty (206 B.C.E.-222 C.E.), government officials sought to revive traditional Chinese values and in the process rediscovered the works of Confucius. As a result, Confucian teachings became the official canonical books and standard texts of the Chinese educational system, and these writings on the significance of filial acts were highlighted as being of monumental significance to the maintenance of traditional Chinese values.

The meaning of the expression "filial piety," called *hsiao* in Chinese, is represented by the character which is composed of the ideogram for "old" with that for "son" placed underneath. This picture symbolizes the obligation of the child to respect and take care of the parents according to what is known as *li,* or the socially acceptable behavior of individuals in all circumstances. The Confucian *Hsiao Ching: Scripture of Filiality* details the way in which children are to respect and show gratitude to their parents. According to *Hsiao Ching,* after the burial of the deceased parents, the children should, in order to show true filial devotion to their parents, "prepare an ancestral temple [to receive the tablet of the departed], and there present offerings to the disembodied spirit [resident in the tablet]. In spring and autumn, they offer sacrifices, thinking of the deceased as the seasons come around."

The most comprehensive code of Chinese ancestor worship is included in the *Li-chi* (the Book of Propriety). In his practice of the ancestral rite, the reverent son was admonished to serve the dead as if he were serving the living. One passage in the *Li-chi* vividly portrayed such piety: "Thus the filial piety taught by the ancient kings required that the eyes of the son should not forget the appearance (of his parents), nor his ears their voices; and that he should retain the memory of their aims, likings, and wishes. . . . So seeming to live and stand out, so unforgotten by him, how could his sacrifices be without the accompaniment of reverence?" (Bk. XXI, Sec. I.4). Children could be put to death if found to be unfilial.

Filial piety has ramifications for an individual beyond the parent/child relationship. Learning to be filial to one's parents prepares a child to be responsible in the other four major relationships that a person has in his or her life as defined by Confucius: ruler and subject, husband and wife, brother and brother, and friend and friend. Filial piety helps to maintain the stability of all these relationships and ideally serves to achieve harmony in society as a whole.

Confucius's disciple Tseng-tzu held the view that, when careful attention is given to perform the funeral rites of the parents and to follow with the regular ceremonies of sacrifice to them, "the virtue of the people will resume its proper excellence" (*Analects,* Bk. I, Ch. IX).

Thus the assumption elaborated upon in the canon is that the ties which exist between parents and children are not severed with death; rather, they continue on afterwards in a different form. In the Li Ki it is stated that a filial child's responsibilities toward his/her parents are shown by nourishing them while they are alive, by performing the rites of mourning when they are dead, and by enacting periodic ancestral rites when the mourning is over (Bk. XXII.3). It is believed that if every individual behaves in accordance with these rules of *li* both before and after death occurs, there will be harmony not only in society, but in the universe.

After Confucianism* was adopted in the Han Dynasty as the state ideology, the ancestral rite was further institutionalized and popularized. Before Buddhism* and Christianity found their way into China, there was a long period of time in which AW was the most practiced quasi-religion in ancient Chinese society. Because of the demand of celibacy for the Buddhist monks and nuns, Buddhism was accused of promoting unfiliality, and Buddhists were persecuted for desertion of their ancestors.

A traditional ancestral veneration ceremony which may be performed in honor of one's ancestors as a form of filial respect may take different forms depending on the specific occasion, location, and economic means of the family involved; however, food and drink, flowers, incense, candles, a tablet, prostrations *(kowtow),* and the burning of paper money are all common elements of the ceremony. The ritual is typically performed at the grave site, in the clan temple (if the family can afford it), and at the family altar located in the home. Some Chinese have traditionally believed that the spirit of the deceased has three souls and that these souls reside in three separate places: in the grave, in the tablet mentioned above, and in the spirit world (although there is variation in this belief). Thus, when a family offers food and drink at the grave site or before the ancestral tablet — which is called by non-Christians *shen wei* (seat of the spirit), or *shen chu* (lodging place of the spirit) — traditional Chinese may believe that the spirit of the deceased is really present and that he or she actually partakes of the food and drink which are offered. At the time of a food offering, words may be spoken in which there is an announcement of some sort: the birth of a child, a marriage arrangement, or the beginning of a journey.

Ancestor Worship

Christianity and Chinese Ancestor Worship. The entry of East Syrian Christianity (Nestorianism*) into China in the 6th century was short-lived. The scarce literature these Persian Christians left behind did not give any indication where they stood on the issue of AW.

When the Jesuits (see Society of Jesus) arrived on the mainland of China in the late 16th c., they — largely led by the founder of the Chinese Catholic Church, the Italian Jesuit Matteo Ricci* (in China 1582-1610) — had to decide how to interpret these traditional ancestral veneration rituals. They needed to discern whether the ceremonies performed in honor of the dead were merely secular rituals of respect or whether there were any non-Catholic beliefs associated with them. In the (no longer extant) Directive of 1603, Ricci described the Jesuit position that the ancestral rites were, in fact, not superstitious in nature, because they had not been conceived as such; however, he recognized that there were a variety of beliefs associated with the rites and qualified this statement in later writings by adding that "perhaps" the rites were not superstitious.

After Ricci's death in 1610, other missionary orders were also given permission by the pope to establish missions in China: Dominicans* began to build missions in China in 1631, and the Franciscans* arrived in 1633. The Augustinians* established themselves on the mainland by 1680, and the Paris Foreign Mission Society* (MEP) joined these other orders in 1683. The arrival of these additional orders not only increased the likelihood of new Catholic converts, but also increased the possibility that there would be disagreement as to how to interpret the ancestral rites. As a result of the extent to which there was disagreement amongst these Catholics in this regard, there came to be what is known as the Chinese Rites Controversy. This controversy within the Catholic Church, which began in the mission field in 17th-c. China, did not remain confined to that time and place by any means, for not only were the archbishop and bishop of Manila involved, but so were 26 popes; the cardinals in the Holy Office of the Sacred Congregation of the Faith; two apostolic delegates; 160 scholars at the Sorbonne; the kings of Spain, Portugal, and France; the Jansenists; the preachers Fenelon and Bousset; the writers Leibnitz and Voltaire; the Jesuit confessor of Louis XIV; as well as two 17th-c. Chinese emperors and 20th-c. government officials from China and Japan over a period of 300 years. That is, the Chinese Rites Controversy formally began in 1633 and did not end until 1939.

The question of whether to interpret the ancestral rites as being civil in nature or as having religious significance for the Chinese was only one of the three major issues of the controversy. The other two matters involved were (a) whether to interpret the ceremonies which were performed in honor of Confucius by the patron of scholars who ritually paid their respects to him — primarily in his *wên miao,* or temple — as being secular or religious in character (these rites closely resembled those ceremonies performed for the ancestors but often added the sacrifice of a pig or bull and/or pantomimes or musical performances, depending on the particular circumstances); and (b) the "Term Question" or the "Term Issue," which was concerned with the difficulties which missionaries had in coming to agreement as to the wisest word choice to indicate the Christian concept of God in the Chinese language.

The church made a series of decrees over the course of the first century of the controversy. The Decree of 1645 — which was made in response to the questions brought to Rome by the Spanish Dominican Juan Baptista Morales — was the first official statement made by the church in regard to the ancestral rites. This decree judged against the Jesuit interpretation of the ceremonies as being secular in nature. Those which followed generally were alternately for, then against, Catholic participation in or attendance at the ancestral rites. Typically, when the Jesuits issued to Rome a series of questions for consideration in regard to the rites, the Sacred Congregation for the Propaganda of the Faith (SCPF) (the organ of the church in charge of the missions) ruled in their favor; whenever a non-Jesuit order issued a series of questions to the holy office describing the situation from their perspective (critical of the rites), the church sanctioned their interpretation.

After the significant church decrees of 1645, 1656, 1669, the 1704 decision, Clement XI's Decree of 1710, his Apostolic Constitution *Ex illa die* of 1715, the 1721 pastoral letter of papal legate Jean Ambrose Charles Mezzabarba*, and the 1735 brief of Clement XII were issued, *Ex quo singulari* of 1742 was the final bull to be issued by the holy office until the 20th c. This bull reiterated the issues contained in the previous documents. Essentially, it confirmed *Ex illa die* of 1715 (based fundamentally on the Decree of 1704), which took a strong stand against the rites, and required missionaries to take an oath promising that they would follow specific guidelines. *Ex quo singulari* also nullified Mezzabarba's "eight permissions" outlined in his 1721 letter, which compromised some of the requirements of *Ex illa die.* The bull attempted to clarify a clause in *Ex illa die* which was ambiguous as to what rites were to be considered civil and political and which ones were not; the bull also indicated that every aspect of this constitution had to be followed under the threat of excommunication and that religious folk would be denied "an active and passive voice" if they broke these vows. An addition made to the oath that was provided in *Ex illa die* of 1715 required the missionaries to follow every aspect of the 1742 bull. The 1742 bull *Ex quo singulari* also disallowed any further official discussion of the Chinese Rites Controversy within the Catholic Church, although ambiguities in that document made this impossible.

The controversy continued in Protestant circles in the last decade of the 19th c. The heated debate between the American Presbyterian W. A. P. Martin* and Hudson Taylor* did not, unfortunately, thaw the icy standstill but caused the machinery of resolution to freeze up even more. Protestant missionary conferences debated the issue into the 20th c.

Japan. The issue became active again due to an incident which occurred in Japan. With the goal of inspiring the spiritual unity and mobilization of the people, state Shinto had been instituted by the Japanese military government in the early 1930s which required that all citizens pay their ritualized respect before a government shrine. In addition, because the Japanese had occupied and seized Manchuria (Manchukuo) and because there the Japanese army had instituted *Wangtao,* a form of Confucianism, in order to unify the spirit of the new regime, all citizens were required to pay homage to Confucian shrines.

As a result of these rulings in Japan, Manchuria, and Korea by the Japanese state, a crisis of conscience was caused for Christians. In Japan, Christians reacted overtly: on 5 May 1932, a few Catholic students from Sophia University refused to pay homage at Yasukuni Shrine. This incident forced the Japanese government to declare in writing to the Catholic Church that the rituals performed before the Shinto shrine in Japan and before the Confucian shrine in Manchuria were not religious in nature but merely of civil significance.

In response to this official governmental statement, on 8 Dec 1939 the SCPF issued a decree which announced that Catholics were now allowed to participate in ancestral veneration (and Confucian) ceremonies, reversing the decree of *Ex quo singulari* of 1742. This 1939 Instruction, known as *Plane compertum est* and approved by Pope Pius XII, declares that the state rites for Confucius and the mortuary and periodic rituals conducted for ancestors are performed to demonstrate honor and respect. It also states that at previous points in history the rites may have had pagan connotations, but with the passing of the centuries these rites are now merely civil expressions. The instruction also permitted the use of an ancestral tablet, but with nothing other than the name of the deceased inscribed upon it. (It is interesting to note that the Emperor K'ang Hsi's Declaration of 1700 stated that the Chinese rites were civil, but Rome gave this government document no credence.)

Vietnam. The Vietnamese cult of the ancestors may be described as the highest expression of pervasive animism* in traditional Vietnamese belief and practice.

Early observers, including missionaries, falsely concluded that the Vietnamese were not a very religious people. To understand ancestor worship, one needs to have some appreciation for the functional role of religion in Vietnamese life.

In 1929, Cadière wrote, "Annamese religion . . . if it can be referred to in the singular . . . gives an impression analogous to what is felt when one enters a large forest of the Annamese Chain . . . a profound vitality in which one feels submerged. Likewise, in all classes of Annamese society, religious feeling is apparent in a powerful way and dominates all of life. It envelopes daily actions, the most important as well as the humblest. . . . Such is the true picture seen not by the traveler who visits a few temples, nor by the scholar who delves into literature . . . but by those who have constantly under their eyes the daily manifestation of the religious life of the Annamese nation." Cadière concluded, "The true religion of the Annamese is the worship of spirits."

Of the special cults which have grown out of the web of this basic animism, the most highly developed and persistent is ancestor worship. It is so universal among Vietnamese that it is accorded a special and primary place in Toan Anh's two-volume *Tin Nguong Viet-Nam* (Religious Beliefs of Vietnam, 1967/68). People are believed to have three *hon* (souls) and nine *via* (vital principles). At death, the soul(s) of the deceased is ritually honored at the ancestral altar and sometimes at the tomb. The souls of those *co hon* (abandoned or orphaned) in death become errant spirits which are considered malevolent. The rituals for honoring ancestors are among the most highly developed Vietnamese cultural institutions.

One common term for the rituals of ancestor worship is *tho cung. Tho* means worship and *cung* means sacrifice. There can be little doubt that "worship" of spirits is involved in ancestor worship, not mere "veneration" of those who have gone before. Traditional ancestral tablets, kept on the ancestral altar in the home, have a small hole believed to be the door by which the ancestral soul comes and goes. And it is the souls of the ancestors which provide the living with a line of communication into the spirit universe where the fortunes of the living are controlled. To orthodox Christian belief, then, this calls for discontinuity and the "radical displacement" discussed by missiologists such as Hendrik Kraemer*.

Both Catholic and Protestant missionaries in Vietnam have often felt it necessary to discontinue even the positive sociological functions of ancestor worship along with the beliefs which are incompatible with Christian doctrine. Doubtless, Christian missions in Vietnam have been greatly affected by their frequent failure to provide meaningful functional substitutes for the positive social dimensions of ancestor worship. The Evangelical Church in Vietnam was often criticized and rejected as *dao bo ong bo ba,* the religion that discards the ancestors.

With a much longer history in Vietnam, the Roman Catholic Church often reflected the great Rites Controversy (see China section above) initiated by Matteo Ricci*, which raged in nearby China for 180 years. The church closed the door on an accommodating attitude toward ancestor worship by a papal bull in 1742.

Struggling with contextualization* in Vietnamese culture will mean dealing with ancestor worship. Years of the secularizing influence of Communism* may have diminished it somewhat, but they have no more erased it than have centuries of previous "isms." The three-century-long Rites Controversy in China has shown that contextualization will be a dynamic and ongoing process. It does seem that in Vietnamese culture, appropriate contextualization of the Gospel will seek to build the connection between the care for parents and elders that is promoted and demonstrated in the Scriptures and the positive functions of traditional ancestor worship, while at the same time requiring the abrogation of its worship dimension.

Indonesia. There are at least 472 forms of primordial religion (see Rachmat Subagio, *Agama Asli Indonesia*) among both the proto- and deutero-Malay ethnic groups in Indonesia. The basic concept of ancestor worship is the continuity between this life and the afterlife. Godheads, deities, spirits, and even nature are conceived of as a totality. The mode of existence may differ, but the basic concept is unmistakably present everywhere. Some examples, mainly from the ethnic groups of the proto-Malays, where neither Islam* nor Christianity was able to bring about substantial change, will illustrate this.

1. *Ngaju* religion (Kalimantan*): the Upperworld (the dwelling place of the supreme deities) is a faithful image of the world, but everything there is richer and more beautiful. The ancestors live in the real village of the dead, which is situated on the edge of the Upperworld, whence they bestow blessings or curses on the living person, family, or clan according to their religious behavior. Ancestor worship is evident in this context.

2. *Aluk Todolo* (Toraja): "This world is but a stay overnight, the eternal abode is in heaven." To die means to go back to one's origins. If the death rituals have been completed, one becomes a deity again, i.e., deification. Those whose death rituals are not yet completed remain in *puya,* the temporary place for the ancestors. From a chant for the deceased, the communion between the living and the dead is evident:

> He has already become a deity above,
> He has become the all-embracing.
> To him sacrifice must be offered,
> He must be worshipped,
> That he may give us blessings,
> All things that bring welfare,
> All profits for the glory and happiness of the family.

The mutuality and the *do ut des* are clear in this chant. The first act at the main ritual is the offering of sacrifice to the ancestors *(to matua)* in general. The ancestors may not be bypassed.

3. *Parmalim* and *Si Raja Batak* (Sumatra): The revival of ancestor worship in Batakland can be seen in the setting up of monuments *(tugu)* for ancestors. The basic concept is primordial, and may even go back to the neolithicum. The Toba area might have been the center of the sarcophago culture. The dynamic behind this culture is ancestor worship. Not every ancestor is the object of ancestor worship, but only those whose *begu* (souls) are transformed into *sumangot* (spirit). The ritual centers on the digging up and gathering of the bones and the skulls of the ancestors after a certain period. They are put in a small box and laid in a new tomb. At this ceremony, food is served and dances are performed to honor the ancestors who in their turn bless the descendants. The special *gondang* (gong) music provides communication with the unseen ancestors. The tomb and the *tugu* become the center of worship on special days when the descendants perform ancestor worship.

For many groups in Indonesia, the impulse toward ancestor worship and devotion to those deceased continues to resurface years and generations after conversion. In some cases (Batakland), devotion to ancestors continues when families become Christian, with Christian prayers and liturgy supplementing and giving new meaning to the family devotion (see Batak Churches).

Ancestor Worship and Missiology Today. As in ancient and modern Jewish culture, so also in most East Asian cultures the family has been the backbone of society. In spite of the surging and unrelenting impact of the social changes experienced over the past three millennia, the family continues to be the most significant source of identity and stability in these cultures. Undoubtedly, the institution and inculcation of filial piety have helped maintain bonds of kinship, a sense of solidarity with all the clan members, living and deceased, and have guarded them against the vicissitudes of life.

The Marxist ideology in the People's Republic of China (PRC) that campaigned against Confucianism and the Four Books, and the process of modernization that fosters individualism and the nuclear family, have considerably weakened these family ties, and thus the observance of AW. In the PRC, the practice is a less and less visible part of society, "but memories of it linger." Despite the far-reaching impacts of modernity, adherence to AW is still strong in Taiwan, Hong Kong, Korea, Singapore, and other communities. According to the survey conducted by Henry Smith in Hong Kong in 1985, "only . . . 14.1% of the sample [households] never sacrifice to ancestors. The cult of the dead, though diluted by forces of change and stripped of much of its structural support, retains a near-ubiquitous presence in family life."

The Roman Catholic Church responded to this reality in the Vatican Council II (1962-65) when, among other issues, the church called for the recognition of the native genius of each and every culture throughout the world as expressed through indigenous traditions in order that the universal church learn from each of its cultural components. The pronouncements made then go beyond the simple allowance of Catholic participation in native traditions, such as is declared in *Plane compertum est* in reference to the ancestral rites in China. "Before the corpse of the deceased or ancestral tablets which record only the name and age of the deceased, Catholics are permitted to bow their heads and perform other gestures of respect." In addition, the Decree on the Missionary Activity of the Church *(Ad Gentes)* advises that native Catholics imbue their national treasures with the Christian message, while the Constitution of the Sacred Liturgy *(Sacrosanctum Concilium)* calls for the creation of new rites within the Catholic Church which clearly express the worldview of a particular people or culture. (Enculturation is the term for these processes: see Contextualization*.)

The decrees of Vatican II mentioned above made it possible for Cardinal Yu Pin to conduct the first ancestral veneration ceremony by a member of the Catholic clergy on 27 Jan 1971. This nationally televised ancestral rite took place in Taipei, Taiwan, before an audience of 1,000 individuals. Many elements of a traditional ceremony were evident: food, drink, candles, incense, flowers, bowing *(jugung)*, and words spoken. The traditional ancestral tablet was omitted, however. Archbishop Lokuang and Bishop Paul Chen Shihkuang, Confucian scholars who created the guidelines for this Catholic performance, integrated words which referred to the Christian concept of God and the Catholic tradition of the communion of saints with words which encouraged reverence and remembrance in the Confucian tradition of filial piety.

The first formal Chinese ancestral-memorial-service liturgical text, known as the "Proposed Catholic Ancestor Memorial Liturgy (for Church and Family Use)," was issued by the Chinese Bishops' Conference in Taipei, Taiwan, on 29 Dec 1974. This liturgical text combines Catholic tradition with ancestor veneration even more thoroughly than did the cardinal's rite. Here, all of the elements of the 1971 public ritual are included; however, this six-part liturgy also includes a statement of objectives, general principles, details of the style of the ancestor tablet (which allow more than the name of the deceased as declared in *Plane compertum est*), and specifics for both the church rite and the home ritual, some of which are here named: both include the traditional offerings and a reading of the Book of Sirach 44:1-15 or "another suitable reading"; the church rite is to be performed during Chinese New Year on the Ching Ming Festival, All Saints' Day, and All Souls' Day; the family ceremony is to be enacted on national holidays and important family occasions; the church rite includes a prayer of the faithful and a homily; the home rite includes prayers for the ancestors and the optional recalling of the deeds of ancestors.

In Cardinal Yu Pin's rite, it is apparent that when the sacrifices were symbolically offered to the ancestors as a sign of veneration and respect in demonstration of filial piety — and that when he, and those gathered, prayed for the ancestors, just as any Catholic would pray for or to the church suffering (those in purgatory) or the church triumphant (those in heaven) within the Catholic tradition of the communion of saints — Confucian tradition and Catholic tradition complemented each other to such an extent that the two became one. In the Bishops' Conference liturgy, this intermingling of indigenous Confucian and Catholic traditions (in accordance with the enculturation goals of Vatican II) was even more complete due to the overt opening statements as to the meaning and significance of the ceremony. The "Objectives" and "General Principles" proclaim that the filial rite serves a Christian purpose: it brings individuals closer to God. In fact, the first objective states that the reason for the ceremony is "to emphasize God's commandment to 'Honor thy Father and thy Mother' as the basic spirit, to encourage filial piety among Catholics, and to increase filial love towards God"; and the first principle named declares that, in order to be truly filial as a Catholic, one must participate in the communion of saints tradition by praying for the deceased: "In honor of the ancestors, to give return for their blessings toward us, we must always pray and offer Mass for their entry into Heaven and to fulfill our duty of filial reverence." Hence, the first two sections of the Bishops' Conference liturgy not only testify that the Catholic performance of the ancestral rite expresses the communion of saints tradition, but also overtly state how the Chinese tradition is a way in which to obey the fifth commandment.

Biblically, the worship of the deceased and the act of necromancy are unequivocally prohibited. Therefore, any effort to develop a biblically acceptable practice of AW must be free of any taint of idolatry. The Confucian understanding of AW, particularly its ethical orientation, is congenial to the Hebraic ethos of honoring the forefathers and of cherishing and transmitting the spiritual heritage handed down from them to succeeding generations (e.g., Gen. 45-47; Exod. 20:12; John 19:26-27; Ps. 37:28, 37-38). However, during the long history of AW, there has been a mixture of animist, Taoist, Buddhist, Hindu, and other superstitious elements with the original practice. These elements must be entirely removed before the creation of a Christian rite of ancestral remembrance can even be considered. Moreover, before such a rite can be designed, there must be formulated a theology of filial piety, a theology of death, and a theology of communion of saints which are biblically sound and contextually relevant. This theological foundation, when properly laid, will furnish a solid underpinning for a Christian practice of ancestral remembrance.

At the same time, clear and specific pastoral instructions concerning what Christians can and what they cannot participate in at a funeral or in the AW of a non-Christian household are badly needed. A Christian alternative to the traditional Chinese rituals which is theologically sound and culturally meaningful to the Christian as well as non-Christian participants is called for to avert the centuries-old accusation that Christians have deserted their ancestors and have no concern for their roots.

Finally, one wonders whether an ambivalent stance with respect to the custom of AW is the chief obstacle to evangelism among the peoples who hold fast to the practice. In the Chinese as well as the Japanese societies, this certainly seems to be the case. However, in Korea the Christian churches took an uncompromising stance and denounced AW as idolatry; yet the churches there still experience phenomenal growth. This does not mean, however, that AW, as a missiological and pastoral issue, is no longer a burning concern, for it will continue to be a point of dialogue for Christians living in cultures that honor or "worship" ancestors.

Bibliography

Addison, James Thayer, *Chinese Ancestor Worship* (1925). • Berentsen, J. M., *Grave and Gospel* (1985). • Ching, Julia, *Chinese Religions* (1993). • Hsu, Francis L. K., *Under the Ancestor's Shadow* (1948). • Huang, Bernard, "Ancestor Cult Today," *Missiology: An International Review*, Vol. V, No. 3 (1977). • Li Chi, *Book of Rites*, Vol. II, trans. James Legge (1967). • Ro, Bong Rin, ed., *Christian Alternatives to Ancestor Practices* (1985). • Smith, Henry N., "Ancestor Practices in Contemporary Hong Kong: Religious Ritual or Social Custom?" *Asia Journal of Theology*, Vol. 3, No. 1 (1989). • Yu, Chi-Ping, "Theology of Filial Piety: An Initial Formulation," *Asia Journal of Theology*, Vol. 3, No. 2 (1989). • Abbott, Walter M., ed., *The Documents of Vatican II* (1966). • Butcher, Beverly J., "Remembrance, Emulation, Imagination: The Chinese and Chinese American Catholic Ancestor Memorial Service" (doctoral dissertation, 1994). • Gutheinz, Luis, "*Christliche Ahnenverehrung* in China?" *Die Katholischen Missionen* (1971). • Legge, James, trans., *The Hsiao Ching* (1899) and *The Li Ki* (1885). • Minamiki, George, *The Chinese Rites Controversy from Its Beginning to Modern Times* (1985); "The Yasukuni Shrine Incident and the Chinese Rites Controversy," *The Catholic Historical Review* (1980). • Noll, Ray R., ed., *100 Roman Documents Concerning the Chinese Rites Controversy (1645-1941)* (1992). • Latourette, Kenneth Scott, *A History of Christian Missions in China* (1929). • Thompson, Laurence G., *Chinese Religion: An Introduction* (1989). • Anh, Toan, *Tin Nguong Viet-Nam* (Religious Beliefs of Vietnam), 2 vols. (1967 and 1968). • Cadière, Leopold, *Religions Annamites et non Annamites* (Annamese and non-Annamese Religions) (1929); *Religious Beliefs and Practices of the Vietnamese*, 3 vols. (1958). • Hickey, Gerald, *Village in Vietnam* (1964). • Reimer, Reginald E., *Vietnamese Religion: Three Articles* (1974). • "The Religious Dimension of the Vietnamese Cult of the Ancestors," *Missiology*, Vol. 3, No. 2 (Apr 1975). • Scharer, H., *Ngaju Religion* (1963). • Van den Veen, H., *The Merofeast of Sa'dan Toraja* (1965); *The Sa'dan Toraja Chant for the Deceased* (1966). • Nooy-Palm, H., *The Sa'dan Toraja*, Vol. I (1979). • Kobong, Th., *Evangelium and Tongkonan* (1989). • Schreiner, L., *Telah Kudengar dari Ayahku* (1978). • Subagio, Rachmat, *Agama Asli Indonesia* (1981). • Sinaga, Anicetus B., *The Toba-Batak High God* (1981).

Reginald E. Reimer, Beverly J. Butcher, Thomas C. P. Yu, Th. Kobong

Anderson, Alan S. Moore

(b. Kensington, London, 1876; d. Muar, Malaya, 1959). English Presbyterian missionary to China, Malaya, and Singapore.

From a family background which included Anglicans*, Presbyterians*, Brethren, and the Society of Friends, Anderson's Christian commitment developed at Cambridge when it was still feeling the effects of D. L. Moody's visit over a decade before. Anderson heard J. R. Mott in 1896 and a year later was certain of his call to ministry, overseas mission, and teaching. He trained in London and at Westminster College, Cambridge, and was ordained in 1902. He began a lifetime of school-building in Chuanchow (Chin-Chew) in Amoy in 1904, naming the school he founded after Westminster College.

Anderson was transferred to Singapore* in 1931. He was shameless in soliciting money for Singapore schools, especially from former Chuanchow pupils around Southeast Asia. At age 65, he went on furlough to South Africa in the summer of 1941. Following the Japanese invasion, he remained in Africa raising money for China* but failed in an attempt to get back there from India*. He returned to Singapore in 1946 and spent his retirement in Katong and then Muar. Anderson never married. He had a strong devotional life, a sense of humor, and gifts of personal evangelism; something of a poet, he accumulated a proverbial collection of puzzles, which he used to strike up conversations with young people. His keen strategic sense of mission included committing his personal funds to obtaining land for church development.

Bibliography

Anderson, Alan S. Moore, *Random Reminiscences* (ca. 1956). • Band, Edward, *Working His Purpose Out: The History of the English Presbyterian Mission, 1847-1947* (1948). • Henderson, John, "The Service in Malaya and Singapore of the Reverend Alan S. Moore Anderson," *The Presbyterian Church in Singapore and Malaysia. 90th Anniversary of the Church and 70th Anniversary of the Synod, Commemoration Volume* (1970).

John Roxborogh

Andrews, Charles Freer

(b. Newcastle-on-Tyne, England, 12 Feb 1871; d. Calcutta, Mar 1940). Missionary, professor of English, and founder of the Indian National Trade Union Congress.

Andrews was one of the most beloved Christian missionaries in 20th-c. India*. He preached the Christian doctrine of love to all not only by word but also by selfless service to suffering societies, irrespective of color or country. He was passionately convinced that there is a love which binds all humankind, transcending nationality, creed, social division, and ideology.

Andrews's father, an East Anglian by birth and descent, was a God-fearing man. His mother set an example of forgiveness and selflessness by praying for, instead of cursing, the man who caused the family acute poverty by misappropriating her inherited capital.

Andrews was a meritorious student and completed his distinguished academic career at Cambridge University. His father desired him to keep up the family tradition by becoming a minister. He was ordained a priest in Jun 1897 and, following the footsteps of his bishop, "C.F." dedicated his service to the poor. He worked for a while among the poor in southeast London. His essay on "The Place of Religion in the Capital and Labor Disputes" won the Barnee Prize at the university.

Andrews arrived in India on 20 Mar 1904 to join St. Stephens College of Delhi as a professor of English. He also joined the missionary work of the Cambridge Brotherhood in Punjab. As he painfully observed the disgruntledness of the Indian society and the unthinkable plight of the poor millions, especially the laborers and peasants, he came to realize that British rule was not doing justice to Indian society and must ultimately lead to moral disaster for both India and Britain herself. The peculiar color prejudices and intolerable ignorance of the British officers shocked him. During the first 10 years of his stay in India, he concentrated on teaching, preaching, and attending to poor, suffering people. He also started writing inspiring tracts for young Indian Christians on the doctrine of Christian love. He called on Christian youth to be peacemakers by spreading Christian love.

In 1912, Andrews went to South Africa, where he developed a lifelong friendship with Gandhi*. He went to Fiji when he heard disturbing reports about the Indians in Fiji. He returned to India to join Gandhi to fight against the recruitment of Indian coolies to work in Fiji. Andrews was involved in India's Nationalist Movement (see Nationalism). His religious and spiritual thinking found a new dimension after his meeting with Rabindranath Tagore*, who infused in him the desire to work among problem-stricken people. Andrews found in Tagore's view moral support for his idea of Christian love.

Before his connection with Tagore's *Shantiniketan,* Andrews was at the forefront of labor movements in eastern countries, especially in India, where he founded the Indian National Trade Union Congress. He fought gallantly to protect the poor laborers and earned the title *Deenabandhu* (friend of the poor).

Andrews spent the closing years of his life in solitude and peace, involving himself in religious and academic writings.

Bibliography

Clark, Ian, *Deenabandhu C. F. Andrews* (1970). • O'Connor, Daniel, *Gospel, Raj and Swaraj: The Missionary Years of C. F. Andrews 1904-14* (1990). • Roy, Malina, *Charles Freer Andrews* (1971). • Tinker, Hugh, *The Ordeal of Love: C. F. Andrews and India* (1978).

Sunil Kumar Chatterjee and John Mathew

Anglican Church

India. The first Anglican initiative in the subcontinent in 1706 consisted of Danish and German Lutheran* missionaries in Tranquebar* supported by the Society for Promoting Christian Knowledge (SPCK) in England. The strong church-state link of the Church of England inhibited independent missionary action by the national church. However, the founding of the voluntary societies — the SPCK in 1699, its sister society, the Society for the Propagation of the Gospel in Foreign Parts (SPG), in 1701, and later, in 1799, the Church Missionary Society (CMS) — forged the instruments by which the church began its missionary task in India*, as well as in other parts of Asia.

Although the "factories" of the East India Company (EIC) were provided with Anglican chaplains, their activities were severely limited by the terms of the company's charter. Nevertheless, under the influence of Charles Simeon's ministry in Cambridge, a number of godly chaplains began to reach out to the Hindus and Muslims among whom they were living. Henry Martyn* (1781-1812) was one of the most outstanding. His great work was the scholarly translation of the New Testament into Arabic, Persian, and Urdu (see Bible Translation).

After a long political campaign by William Wilberforce in England, a new charter of the East India Company included the appointment of a bishop of Calcutta in 1814 and facilitated the opening of direct Anglican missionary work. The CMS sent its first Anglican clergymen to India in 1815. In the meantime, by the early 19th c. 28 Lutheran missionaries had served under the patronage of SPCK and SPG and had established Christian centers in Madras, Trichinopoly, Tanjore, Palamcotta, and Madura. Many of the Lutheran missionaries used the Anglican *Book of Common Prayer* in their church services and translated it into Tamil. In 1825, Martyn's convert, Abdul Masih*, was the first Indian national to be ordained (by the bishop of Calcutta).

Both the CMS and SPG developed extensive missionary work throughout India during the 19th c. and were joined by smaller societies, such as the Cambridge Mission to Delhi (1877), the Oxford Mission to Calcutta (1880), the Dublin University Mission (1892), and the Church of England Zenana Missionary Society (1880). The witness of several Anglican religious communities (e.g., SSJE, the "Cowley Fathers") proved effective, especially in the North Indian setting.

It was especially in South India that the church prospered. By the middle of the century, Tinnevelly had a church of 50,000 members, largely ministered to by Indian nationals. Immense people movements among the "depressed classes" brought large numbers into the church (see Mass Movements). In the Telugu country, north of Madras, around one million people became Christians, of whom about one-fifth joined the Anglican church. Another fruitful field was among the aboriginal, pre-Hindu peoples of India. In the task of witnessing to high-caste Hindus and Muslims, the church colleges proved to be the best instruments, the first of which was Bishop's College, Calcutta (1820). Most of the future leaders of the Indian church were educated in these colleges (see Theological Education).

"Ubi episcopus, ibi ecclesia" proved to be true for Anglicanism in Asia, first because bishops were appointed where there was a proven potential for church planting; second because episcopal leadership provided the direction and impetus which Anglicans accepted and to which they responded; and third because the diocesan focus created a unity of immense importance in the days when the SPG and CMS, with their different emphases, were often working in adjacent areas. For this reason, the pace of growth of the Anglican Church in India and elsewhere in Asia can, in most cases, be measured by the foundation of dioceses. By the end of the 19th c., dioceses had been formed in Madras, Travancore/Cochin, and Tinnevelly in South India, and further north the dioceses of Calcutta, Bombay, Chota Nagpur, and Lucknow had come into being.

In 1930 the Church of India, Burma,* and Ceylon (Sri Lanka*) became an independent province of the Anglican communion and was set free to develop a form of Christianity that would be Asian. Stephen Neill* commented: "The Constitution of the Church of India, Burma and Ceylon (to which, in 1947, Pakistan* had to be added) was perhaps the best of all Anglican constitutions. . . . It offers a method for the selection of bishops which avoids almost all the difficulties experienced in other provinces." The most important decision taken by the Indian church made possible in 1947 the formation of the Church of South India (CSI) through the union of the four South Indian dioceses, comprising nearly half a million Anglicans, along with the Methodist*, Congregational, and Presbyterian* bodies in South India (see Ecumenical Movement). Bishop Azariah* had declared at Lausanne: "Unity may be theoretically desirable in Europe and America. It is vital to the Church in the mission field."

When the Church of North India (CNI) was formed in 1970 with seven participating denominations, the Anglican dioceses joining the Union were (from east to west) Assam, Barrackpore, East Bengal, Calcutta, Chota Nagpur, Bhagalpur, Lucknow, Nagpur, Nasik, Bombay, Delhi, and Amritsar.

Some leading Anglican figures during the 19th and 20th cs. included Bishop Daniel Wilson of Calcutta, Robert Caldwell of Tinnevelly, V. Samuel Azariah of Dornakal (the first Indian bishop), and Stephen Neill, who played a decisive part in bringing the South Indian Church Union to fulfillment. The Indian church initiated the work in Myanmar* (from Calcutta), Sri Lanka (from South India), and Pakistan in the pre-partition diocese of Lahore.

Pakistan. The CMS was responsible for most of the Anglican work in Pakistan. Chaplain Daniel Corrie, one of those influenced by Charles Simeon of Cambridge, established most of the mission stations in the north of the subcontinent. Abdul Masih*, the first ordained Indian clergyman, worked under him as a CMS reader at Agra (1812). From there work was extended to Amritsar in the Punjab (1852), to Multan (1856), and to Peshawar (1858), whence the CMS Afghan Mission was launched. In the meantime, the CMS had already begun Sindhi work in Karachi in 1850. One of the first converts, Abdullah Athim (baptized 1853), became a preacher and translator of the Gospel into Sindhi.

In the second half of the century, the Anglican mission began to extend to the northwest frontier towns on the upper Indus, Dera Ismail Khan (1862), and other towns that faced the mountain passes into Afghanistan. Imad-ud-Din, a Punjabi ordained at Amritsar in 1868, was responsible for many books and tracts in Urdu on the Christian faith as well as New Testament commentaries.

The work in what was to be Pakistan was very slow compared to that in the southern provinces of India; many missionaries died prematurely from disease or violence, but many of the hard-won converts witnessed courageously to their faith, even spreading it into Afghanistan, Kafiristan, and Baluchistan.

The Lahore Divinity School, opened by Thomas Valpy French* (1825-91) in 1870, was to play a leading role in preparing local men for the ministry. In 1877 the diocese of Lahore, comprising Punjab, Kashmir, the Sindh, and neighboring states, was founded, with French as its first bishop.

The CMS established and maintained educational, medical, and pastoral work in the four areas of the Punjab, the northwest frontier, Baluchistan, and Sind, mostly among underprivileged villagers. At Hyderabad, lay training was undertaken with success at the Pakistan Bible Training Institute (founded in 1960) under the leadership of Bishop Chandu Ray of Karachi. Women's work, chiefly through the Church of England Zenana Mission Society (CEZMS; est. 1880), has been a conspicuous feature of Anglican church work since the early days.

The SPG was mainly concerned with educational work in the city of Lahore, but from 1906 medical missionary work was opened in Rawalpindi by the wives (both of whom were doctors) of SPG missionaries C. J. Ferguson Davie* (later bishop of Singapore*) and A. C. G. Cowie. From the beginning of this century, the Society of St. Hilda has cared for the welfare of Anglo-Indians in Lahore.

During this century the Anglican church has grown slowly but steadily under Asian leadership. In 1947 Pakistan was added to the Constitution of the Province of the Church of India, Burma, and Ceylon. In 1970 Anglicans united with Methodists, Lutherans, and the Sialkot Presbyterians to form the Church of Pakistan, consisting of four dioceses: Karachi, Lahore, Multan, and Sialkot, of which Karachi and Lahore were former Anglican dioceses. In 1995 there were eight dioceses in the Church of Pakistan.

Bangladesh. The Anglican Church in Bangladesh (estimated membership of 13,000) was part of the Province of India, Pakistan, Burma, and Ceylon until the union of the Church of Pakistan in 1970. After the independence of Bangladesh in 1971, the Church of Bangladesh, basically an Anglican-Presbyterian union, began operating independently, for all practical purposes.

Myanmar (Burma). The earliest Anglican work in Myanmar* was carried out by British chaplains. In spite of the scruples of the EIC regarding evangelism, the chaplains managed to do missionary work. After the second Anglo-Burmese War (1852-53), C. S. P. Parish, encouraged by the chaplain at Moulmein, established a Burma Mission Fund and requested a trained schoolmaster from England. In 1854 Mr. Cockey, a Eurasian student from Calcutta, was sent to begin educational work. By 1855 Bishop Wilson of Calcutta preached to a congregation of 500 that had to meet in a Buddhist temple. By the time the first SPG missionaries arrived, over 100 students of different races were attending St. Mathew's School.

The first SPG missionaries sent out in 1859 to Moulmein were T. A. Cockey and A. Shears. A young schoolmaster from London, John Ebenezer Marks* (1860), opened several church schools in Rangoon and Mandalay and recruited missionary staff for them. Because of the schools, the church enjoyed royal favor (King Mindon) for several years. In addition to educational work, Marks, Cockey, and Shears translated part of the *Book of Common Prayer* into Burmese. In 1873 mission work was opened among the Karen* in Upper Myanmar. This prospered so that by 1900 there were 12 Karen clergy. The diocese of Yangon (Rangoon) was established in 1877, and work among the Karen, though never as extensive as that of the Baptists*, advanced steadily, in part because of the defection of thousands of Baptists to Anglicanism led by Mrs. Mason.

The diocese of Rangoon was formed in 1877 with a donation of £10,000 from the See of Winchester and a further £10,000 donation from the SPCK, SPG, and Colonial Bishoprics Fund. The Indian government paid for a senior chaplain. Apart from education, there was limited evangelistic outreach because of the language barriers and the entrenchment of Buddhism*. When King Thibaw ascended the throne, the Mandalay mission was broken up in 1878, and the church was converted to a state lottery office. After the British annexed Upper Myanmar in 1885, it was reestablished by James Colbeck, who started the church of St. Augustine in Moulmein (1880), where he was reassigned during the closure of the Mandalay mission.

In 1879 Bishop Titcomb returned to England after a fall while on a tour in the Karen hills. He was succeeded by John Miller Strachan, who consolidated the Karen mission in the Toungoo area. In 1883 a divinity school for the training of catechists was established in Kemmendine, a suburban village two miles from Rangoon, under the charge of Rev. Fairclough. In 1900 St. Barnabas School was opened.

When Arthur M. Knight, Dean of Caius College, Cambridge, was consecrated the third bishop of Yangon in 1892, there were 41 clergy missionaries comprising 10 government chaplains, six chaplains of the Additional Clergy Society, nine SPG missionaries, and 16 native clergy (10 Karen, three Myanmar, and three Tamils). His successor, in 1910, was R. S. Fyffe, the first head of the Winchester Missionary Brotherhood in Mandalay. In Jan 1911 Fyffe reported that, in 1910, 400 candidates were confirmed, six new churches dedicated, and two European schools established, one for boys in Moulmein and the other for girls at Toungoo. Under Fyffe, St. George's Church in Syriam was built with the help of the Burmah Oil Company. In 1916 churches were built in Katha and Kalaw. A blind missionary, William Henry Jackson, founded the Kemmendine Blind School in 1918. In 1929 the children's hospital, Queen Alexandra, was opened in Mandalay. Railway chaplaincies were revived at Insein, Letpadan, Tharrawaddy, Bassein, Yamethin, Pyinmana, and Toungoo. Mission work to the Kachin* at Moynihan was started by Rev. and Mrs. A. T. Houghton of the Bible Churchman's Missionary Society (BCMS) in 1925. In the course of 30 years, G. Whitehead had translated the Bible and *Book of Common Prayer* into Burnese, Chin*, and Car Nicoberese (Car Nicobar is a group of islands south of the Andamans). The *Hymn and Prayer Book* was printed in Burmese, Bwo Karen, and Chin in 1924. A divinity school for men was established at Myittha, and the first school for ordained and lay-teachers was held at Maymo. The Holy Cross Theological College, started in 1929, was dedicated in 1935, with George Appleton as principal. The first degree of bachelor of theology (B.Th.) was conferred on 21 Mar 1939 at the Holy Trinity Cathedral.

Under Bishop Tubbs, consecrated in 1929, the BCMS opened a Deaf and Dumb School in Yangon in 1932 and a station in Arakan. The BCMS also began mission work in Kyaukpyu and Paletwa. The Methodists, Baptists, and Anglicans made an attempt to agree on a translation of the Lord's Prayer in 1930. Tubbs pursued nationalization of the clergy, a policy actively continued by Bishop West and put into effect in Jan 1935.

After World War II*, West created three deaconeries (Delta, Mandalay, and Toungoo) and put them under the charge of Luke Po Kun, J. Aung Hla, and F. Ah Mya respectively. In 1951 both archdeacons, Ah Mya and Aung Hla, were consecrated as assistant bishops. On 28 Aug 1966 Bishop Francis Ah Mya* became the first national to be enthroned at the Holy Trinity Cathedral, and, for the first time, the service was conducted in Burmese.

With national independence and the consequent restrictions on travel abroad imposed by the Myanmar government, it became necessary to form an autonomous province in Myanmar. To enable the transition, the dioceses of Mandalay and Hpa-an were created in 1970 and the missionary diocese of Akyab (now the diocese of Sittwe) was inaugurated on 24 Jun 1972.

Sri Lanka. The Anglican Church is the largest and most influential Protestant denomination in Sri Lanka, with a history of over one-and-a-half centuries. With the British occupation of the island in 1795/96 came Angli-

Anglican Church

can chaplains. In 1799 James Cordiner was appointed chaplain to the Colombo garrison. Under Governor Frederick North, Cordiner took charge of the religious establishment as senior Anglican chaplain from 1804. In 1817 letters of patent placed Sri Lanka under the ecclesiastical jurisdiction of the bishop of Calcutta; J. T. Twisleton was appointed archdeacon. In 1835 the episcopal supervision was transferred to the newly appointed bishop of Madras. The establishment of a separate bishopric in 1945 provided for local episcopal supervision of the diocese of Colombo, which encompassed the entire island.

The Anglican establishment inherited the privileges held by the Dutch Reformed Church during Dutch times. Therefore the registration of births, marriages, and deaths was their monopoly until 1862. The head of the Anglican Church was the chairman of the school commission, which oversaw education in Sri Lanka until the establishment of the department of public instruction in 1880.

There were different Anglican missionary societies working concurrently on the island. In 1817 the CMS sent an initial contingent of four clergymen to the island. They opened stations among the Sinhalese in Kandy, Baddegama, and Kotte and among the Tamils at Jaffna. Progress was slow, but the society and its missionaries persevered, conversions were registered, and among them were those of some Buddhist priests. Congregations gathered, schools were conducted, an indigenous clergy was trained, and a vigorous native church was developed.

From 1876 to 1880 there was a disturbing controversy over some features of episcopal jurisdiction, but eventually this was amicably settled. Between 1929 and 1934 most of the work of the CMS was transferred to the diocese, and its major educational institutions were placed under a board of governors. The CMS gave assistance and supervision to the Kandyan Itinerancy (1853) and Tamil Coolie Mission (1855), begun among Tamil laborers on the coffee plantations and supported in part by non-Anglican planters.

The SPG began work in Sri Lanka in 1840. The first missionary was stationed in Colombo and was transferred to Matara in the south in 1841. Its first missionary was C. Mooyart. The SPG has been a promoter and facilitator of missionary work rather than a proprietor of distinct missions. In some districts it has worked independently but more often it has labored in close conjunction with government chaplains or diocesan clergy rather than to have a staff and mission of its own. In 1851 the SPG opened the famous St. Thomas College for boys in Colombo.

The Church of England Zenana Missionary Society (1889) was also represented, laboring in close conjunction with the CMS. They began educational and evangelical work in Kandy. Hillwood Girls School (1890) in Kandy and the School for the Deaf and Blind at Peradeniya (1911) are among the best known of their schools.

Until the 1880s subsidies from colonial revenues were paid to the Anglican bishop. In 1881, the colonial office decided to withdraw state subsidies from the Anglican Church. It was a limited kind of disestablishment because government ordinance No. 6. of 1885 laid down "that nothing be done at variance with the doctrine and discipline of the Church of England or that will sever this Diocese of Colombo from the said church." It remained so tied until the formation of the Province of India, Burma, and Ceylon of the Anglican Church in 1930. Since then the Anglican Church in Sri Lanka has been referred to as the Church of Ceylon.

The first Sri Lankan bishop of the Church of Ceylon and of the Anglican communion — Lakdasa de Mel* — was consecrated on 8 Nov 1945, the centenary year of the diocese of Colombo. He ruled the newly formed diocese of Kurunegala. The first Sri Lankan to be the bishop of Colombo was Cyril de Soysa (1964).

The Anglican Church in Sri Lanka, known today as the Church of Ceylon, has taken a vigorous role in the ecumenical movement and interfaith dialogue* for a long time. The Margaya Missionary Society (1976), founded by Lakshman Peiris, began as the evangelical wing of the Anglican Church. The dioceses of Colombo and Kurunegala make up the Church of Ceylon.

Singapore and Malaya. After the founding of Singapore* by Stamford Raffles* in 1819, the Anglican Church was chiefly represented by the colonial chaplains working among the British civil servants and merchants. However, in 1856, a sermon by the then residency chaplain, William Humphrey, brought the St. Andrew's Church Mission into being, and work in Chinese, Malay, and Tamil developed under clergy and catechists. The appointment of a bishop of Singapore in 1909 gave fresh impetus to the work.

New churches in the suburbs were built under Archdeacon Graham White, and this policy was continued after World War II*. In the 1970s and 1980s a great expansion of the church occurred as a result of the renewal movement under Bishop Chiu Ban It* and his successors, Moses Tay and John Chew Hiang Chea. In the final decade of the 20th c., Singapore began a new initiative in the outlying parts of the diocese in Indonesia*, Thailand*, and Cambodia*.

Educational work begun in the early days continues today. After World War II, the Anglican Church, together with the Methodists, Presbyterians, and Lutherans, took part in the establishment of Trinity Theological College.

Malaysia. West or Peninsula Malaysia* (Malaya) was part of the diocese of Singapore from the days of the Straits Settlements until the separation of Singapore from Malaysia in 1965, which necessitated the creation of a separate diocese of West Malaysia, with a cathedral church in the capital, Kuala Lumpur. Because of the prohibition of mission work among the Malays (a policy also implemented under colonial rule), the membership

Anglican Church

of the church consists mainly of the Chinese and Indian population of the peninsula. Strong parishes have been developed in the Kuala Lumpur district and in coastal towns such as Penang, Malacca*, and Johor Baru, together with several inland parishes.

CMS missionaries expelled from China* in 1949/50 began work among the Chinese in the New Villages during the Malayan Emergency and established several new parishes. Educational and medical* work has been carried on throughout the history of the diocese. St. Nicholas' School for the Blind has had an extensive ministry since it was established in Penang in 1932. West Malaysia has opened its own theological school, the Seminari Theologi Malaysia, which is also an ecumenical endeavor.

East Malaysia, Sarawak. Responding to the appeal of James Brooke*, the SPG sent out Francis McDougall*, a surgeon and priest, to Kuching in 1848. The mission began first among immigrant Chinese, together with educational and medical work. In 1855 McDougall was consecrated bishop of Labuan* and Sarawak. In spite of early setbacks caused by uprisings, piracy, and disease, the church spread rapidly among the Iban (Sea-Dayak) communities along the rivers of the Second Division. New work in the Bidayuh (Land-Dayak) area began, and the New Testament was translated into both languages. More local ministry was added to the SPG in the early years of the 20th c. The first Bidayuh was ordained in 1920, and the first Iban in 1923. At the onset of World War II, the diocesan membership was about 12,500. After the war, as civil jurisdiction was handed over to the British Colonial Office, the title "Diocese of Borneo" was used for all Anglican work in Sarawak, Labuan, and North Borneo.

The church grew numerically strong among the Iban and Bidayuh communities and the Chinese population in Kuching and in the oilfield towns. In 1963 Malaysia was formed, embracing Peninsula Malaya, Sarawak, and North Borneo (Sabah). Brunei* became a separate state under its Sultan. At this time there were 11 Asian clergy in the diocese and an equal number of SPG missionaries. The Sarawak state government maintained an independent policy of assisting the churches with both church and educational buildings. Anglican membership is over 30,000, of whom 53 percent are Iban, 35 percent Chinese, and 12 percent other Dayak groups.

Sabah. North Borneo was administered by the British Chartered Company until World War II, after which, like Sarawak, it became a colony. In 1888 the SPG sent out William Henry Elton to the then capital, Sandakan. Elton labored there until 1913, opening up schools and churches among the mainly Hakka Chinese in the coastal towns of Sandakan, Kudat, and Jesselton. In Sandakan he built the only stone church in the diocese, the Church of St. Michael and All Angels. In 1902 Fong Hau Kong, stationed at Kudat, was the first Chinese to be ordained a priest in North Borneo. In addition, five Chinese clergy were trained for the ministry in Kudat under E. Parry, and all were ordained by 1928. At Sandakan, Archdeacon Bernard Mercer produced a Hakka liturgy with musical tones that is still in use today (see Music).

In 1957 the first work was done in the interior of Sabah with the help of several Iban missionaries from the Sarawak part of the diocese. This led to the establishment of church centers along the Kinabatangan, Labuk, Sugut, and Segama rivers. Indigenous Christians now form a substantial part of the diocesan community. Extensive training of lay evangelists is carried on at an interior center, Telupid.

In 1954 the CMS Australia sent missionaries to develop the work in the east coast towns of Tawau, Semporna, and Lahad Datu and along the Segama River. In 1962 a separate diocese of Sabah was formed, with its Cathedral in Kota Kinabalu. Membership in Sabah is well over 30,000.

An Anglican province of South East Asia consisting of the dioceses of Singapore, West Malaysia, Sarawak, and Sabah came into being in Feb 1996, with Moses Tay, bishop of Singapore, as its first archbishop.

China. The Chinese Anglican Church was the fruit of no fewer than 12 missionary societies. By 1948 there were 14 dioceses — five had connections with the CMS, two with the SPG, three with the American church, one with the church in Canada, and one with the China Inland Mission; two were from missions of the local Chinese church.

William J. Boone*, a missionary of the American Episcopal Church, has been regarded as the chief founder of the Anglican Church in China. With the opening of China after the Treaty of Nanking (Nanjing), Boone, a qualified lawyer and doctor, arrived in Shanghai (1845) before his ordination. One of his converts, Hwong Kwong-ts'ai, became the first Chinese Anglican to be ordained in China itself (1863). In 1847 Boone was consecrated bishop of Shanghai.

In 1845 the CMS sent two missionaries to South China, and work was begun in Shanghai and Ningbo. One of these missionaries, George Smith, became the first bishop of Hong Kong* in 1849. After 1866 CMS work in Zhejiang (Chekiang) and Fujian (Fukien) grew rapidly. CMS success in church planting was probably due to concentration on evangelism rather than educational work.

An American priest, S. I. J. Schereschewsky*, best known for his Mandarin translations of the Bible and the *Book of Common Prayer,* opened a mission in Beijing in 1863. It eventually fell upon the SPG to continue the work in North China.

The work of the SPG was mainly in the provinces of Hebei and Sandong. In 1862 J. S. Burdon*, a Church Missionary Society (CMS) missionary, went from Hangzhou to Beijing to serve as the first English instructor in the Society for the Diffusion of Christian and General Knowledge among the Chinese and to be a chaplain in the British embassy. With the support of the SPG, Burdon translated works on missions and evangelism.

Anglican Church

Although other CMS missionaries also went to other cities around Beijing, the SPG sent only J. A. Stewart and a few others to work in the Yongqing and Hejian areas of Hebei, but they did not stay long. When Burdon was made bishop of Victoria, Hong Kong, in 1872, the CMS missionaries also went south with him. The SPG then sent C. P. Scott to Beijing and M. Greenwood to Qufu of Shandong in 1878. Together they went to work on the mission fields of Pingyin and Qizhou in Shandong. In 1880 Scott was made bishop of North China and G. E. Moule (CMS) bishop of Mid-China. The North China diocese included Tianjin, Sanhai Pass, Niuzhuang, and some cities outside the Jiaodong Peninsula in Shandong. The Sandong diocese was formed in 1903, with G. D. Illiff as the first bishop.

Anglican Church of Canada. In 1910 Bishop W. C. White came from Fukien and started mission work in Honan, where he set up a diocese. For four decades mission work was done along the railroad track that went through Kaifeng, Zhengzhou, Shangqiu, and other main cities. The most well-known sites were Trinity Church at Kaifeng and the Church of our Saviour in Shangqiu. The mission had its own hospital and a few primary and middle schools. For a short time a Bible school for women was also in operation.

The Church of our Saviour at Shangqiu received new members mainly from the patients who received treatment from St. Paul's Mission Hospital. In 1920 the church built a road leading from the railway station to the hospital in order to keep patients who wished to participate in worship services. White was a man with vision; he proposed that the Chinese church should have its own characteristics. In 1934 he installed an assistant bishop as diocesan bishop — the first Chinese bishop in Anglican church history. Though Honan suffered much under the warlords and experienced the great strike in 1925, these external factors had little impact on the church.

By the turn of the century, Anglican church work had spread inland up the Yangtze into central China and further west to East Szechuan (Sichuan). Practically all the pastoral work was now being done by Chinese clergy, trained for the most part in Ningbo, Chefoo (Yantai), and Wuchang.

By 1912 the dioceses of Shanghai, Hong Kong, Zhejiang, Kiangsu (Jiangsu), North China, Shantung (Shandong), Hankow (Hankou), Sichuan, Fujian, Kwangsi (Jiangxi), Hunan, and Anking (Anqing) had been established, and at the first general synod in Apr 1912 the name *Chung Hua Sheng Kung Hui* (CHSKH; "Holy Catholic Church of China") was adopted as the church's title. The first Chinese Anglican bishop was Shen Tsai-sen, consecrated assistant bishop of Zhejiang in 1918. In 1922 a central theological college was opened at Nanking (Nanjing) to serve all dioceses of CHSKH, and a medical college was founded at the large CMS hospital at Hangchow (Hangzhou). In the same year (1924) Anglicans joined in the formation of Huachung (Central China) College, with Francis Wei Tso-min, an outstanding Anglican scholar, as its first president. Of the 15 Christian universities and colleges in China, only St. John's College Shanghai was purely Anglican, supported by the American church.

At the outbreak of the Sino-Japanese War in 1937, the CHSKH had 12 dioceses, 272 Chinese and 82 Western clergy, and nearly 80,000 baptized and 40,000 communicant members. Over a quarter of this membership was in Fujian. The Sino-Japanese War and the Nationalist-Communist War that followed hard on its heels caused the church great dislocation. The inauguration of the People's Republic in 1949 was followed by the departure of all foreign staff. The Anglican Church in China was soon to become part of the Three-Self Movement*, renouncing all financial support and contacts with the West. Only in recent years have the windows on China been reopened, revealing a church even more numerous than in pre-Communist days and in which the CHSKH is still playing a vital role. Official contacts with Chinese theological colleges have been renewed, and a new era of cooperation, especially between the China Christian Council and the church in South East Asia, has begun.

Hong Kong. Although it is once again part of China, Hong Kong's church history has some distinct lines of development. Missionary work of the Anglican Church in South China commenced at Macau in 1839 and continued in Hong Kong from 1842. In 1849 George Smith was made the first bishop of Victoria, Hong Kong, with oversight of the consular stations and factories in China. The SPG was responsible for the endowment of the bishopric and the provision of a civil chaplain. The first CMS personnel began work there in 1862. Today their missionaries are working chiefly in schools and colleges such as the Anglican St. John's College, attached to the university. Another prominent Anglican ministry has been the leprosy* mission on an island off the coast of Hong Kong. After 1951 Hong Kong became a "detached diocese" of the CHSKH but outside its jurisdiction. The diocese is involved in much educational and welfare work.

Taiwan. Taiwan* (Formosa) was originally part of the Church of Japan (NSKK). With the end of the Japanese occupation in 1945, Japanese clergy and church members returned to Japan*. In 1949 many of those who came from mainland China with the nationalist government were Anglicans and formed the main impetus for the development of the Anglican Church in Taiwan. The Taiwan Church formally came under the jurisdiction of the diocese of Hawaii in 1954 as a missionary district of the American Episcopal Church. St. John's Church, Taipei, the first church building erected by the Taiwan Episcopal Church (1956), became the cathedral in 1965, when James C. L. Wang was installed as the first Chinese bishop. Taiwan is now a diocese in the American Episcopal Church province of the Pacific (province VIII); its membership is under 3,000 and the number of congregations 14. Trinity Hall, founded in 1984 in cooperation with St. Andrew's Theological Seminary, Manila, trains clergy for the diocese of Taiwan.

Korea. In 1890 C. J. Corfe was appointed as the first Anglican bishop in Korea*. Hospitals were opened at Inchon and Seoul by Eli Landis and an orphanage established by an Anglican sisterhood. In the early years the main work of the mission was in hostels for Christian boys and girls studying in Seoul. By 1924 the diocese of Korea had 10 European and eight Asian clergy and about 5,000 baptized Anglicans. The membership grew to 10,000 in 1938, with 24 Korean priests. Religious communities had always been part of the Anglican Church in Korea, and in 1932 the first Korean made her profession in the Sisterhood of the Holy Cross. The first Korean bishop was Paul Lee, consecrated in 1965.

The separation of North and South Korea disrupted all church communications (see Korean War). Four dioceses — Seoul, Pusan, Taejon, and North Korea — form the province of Korea. Clergy are trained at St. Michael's Theological College, located between Seoul and Inchon. Anglicans in Korea are estimated at around 50,000 members, or 0.1 percent of the country's population.

Indo-China: Thailand. Thailand has been part of the diocese of Singapore since its inception. A chaplain was stationed at Bangkok from 1893 on, and some mission work was attempted among the Thai population. However, Christ Church, Bangkok, with its mainly expatriate congregation, has remained the only parish. In the last two decades of the 20th c., mission teams from Singapore parishes have visited Thailand frequently, mostly to work alongside other denominations. However, since the creation of the deanery of Thailand in 1993, new work has begun among the Thai population in Bangkok district with the aim of starting new Anglican congregations.

Laos. Also within the diocese of Singapore, the pre–World War II chaplaincy church of the Holy Spirit in Vientiane has been reopened, but a chaplain/pastor is still needed.

Vietnam. Also made a deanery of Singapore in 1993, Vietnamese Anglicans have been allowed to start an English service for expatriates in Hanoi, but open evangelism among Vietnamese nationals is not permitted.

Cambodia. Since the opening of doors to the Anglican Church in Phnom Penh, a missionary priest from Singapore and another diocesan worker have been stationed there and a small Khmer congregation established and named the Church of Jesus Christ our Peace.

Indonesia. The only Anglican parish in Indonesia is that of All Saints, Jakarta, established over 100 years ago. It serves the expatriate community and a number of Indonesians. For most of its history, All Saints Church has been staffed by CMS missionaries. With the appointment of a dean of Indonesia in 1993, the diocese of Singapore plans to plant churches among the more receptive people groups in Java* and Sumatra.

Japan. The first Anglican missionary to Japan was B. J. Bettelheim, sent by the Loochoo (Ryukyu) Naval Mission in 1846. However, in 1859 the first missionaries who came to the Japanese mainland were John Liggins and Channing Moore Williams, sent out by the Missionary Board of the American Episcopal Church. The ban on Christianity outlawed mission work in the public sphere at that time. Therefore, first in Nagasaki then later in Osaka, missionary work was limited to the translation of the Scriptures and prayers into Japanese and the teaching of the English language. With the lifting of the ban, Williams moved to Tokyo. The CMS sent George Ensor to Nagasaki in 1869. In 1873 the SPG sent William Ball Wright and Alexander Croft Shaw to Tokyo. Thus three different Anglican mission bodies started work in Japan.

At the request of missionaries from both the United States and Great Britain, missionary bishops from each country came to Japan. The church in Japan, however, early on sought to be self-governing, self-supporting, and self-propagating, and at a meeting of the three bodies the structure for the Anglican Church of Japan (NSKK) was approved. It was a long time, however, before the church actually achieved autonomy. In the beginning there were only three Japanese clergymen with the status of deacon. However, with this organizational structuring came the writing of a constitution and canon law. A parliamentary structure was established, but other special characteristics of the Anglican Church, such as the creation of a *Book of Common Prayer,* the Three Orders, and the diocese system, were not approved at the first meeting of the synod, but took lengthy deliberations at a number of later synod meetings to achieve acceptance. The fifth synod, held in 1896, was very important because it finalized preparations for the first organizational structure. Six regional areas, forerunners of the later diocese, were established; the *Book of Common Prayer* and canon law were also revised. The church has changed very little since that time.

In 1912 the Anglican Church of Canada extended its mission work, establishing and assuming responsibility for the central region. From early on, each mission group set up seminaries in the various regions to train Japanese leadership, but, until 1911, they were unable to open a school that combined a strong faculty with adequate facilities. In that year the Anglican Seminary at Tokyu Ikebukuro was opened, and all of the other mission seminaries merged with it.

One of the most epochal occurrences in the NSKK happened in 1923, when dioceses were established in Osaka and Tokyo and Japanese bishops were appointed to them. Soon afterward, the Tohoku and Kobe regional areas were added to the total. Beginning about this time, the number of Japanese who became priests and lay members increased remarkably; whereas there had been only about 200 before, the number soon increased to over 20,000. However, in 1939 the Religious Organizations Law was passed by the government, and the situation for churches deteriorated rapidly. Almost immediately they had to become self-supporting. Foreign

Estimates of Anglican Members in Some Asian Countries

Country	Congregations	Adult Members	Total Members
Bangladesh	42	4,620	13,200
Hong Kong	29	15,900	23,000
India: CNI	3,300	700,000	1,000,000
CSI	9,300	800,000	1,700,000
Japan	277	28,972	57,900
Malaysia	322	87,000	150,000
Myanmar	611	22,995	44,290
Pakistan (Church of Pakistan)	736	184,000	460,000
Philippines	457	48,000	100,000
Sri Lanka	137	20,500	50,000
Singapore	24	10,657	23,700

(Source: Patrick Johnstone, *Operation World* [5th ed., 1993])

missionaries returned to their countries of origin, and churches were forced to deal with the issue of unification.

With the resignation of the foreign bishops came the consecration of Japanese bishops, but only six months later (1942) they were forced to dissolve their organization and pressed to become autonomous local churches. Despite the decision of the house of bishops, one group began to press for admittance to the United Church of Christ in Japan (UCCJ), and, in Nov 1943, about a third of the churches and clergymen joined. The General Synod for Reconstruction of the NSKK was held in Dec 1945, and a great majority of those who had joined the UCCJ returned to the fold.

After World War II the NSKK accepted financial assistance from overseas churches, but it did not change its principle of self-sufficiency. Since 1963, when the entire church passed the principle of "Mutual Responsibility and Interdependence in the Body of Christ," the NSKK has developed a more mature relationship with overseas' churches. With the return of the Okinawa Diocese in 1971, it had a total of 11 dioceses. At this time provinces and the position of primate were instituted, giving the church a more integrated structure. The primate serves as a representative of the NSKK. The 1959 revision of the *Book of Common Prayer* was the first original *Book of Common Prayer* for the NSKK. Receiving stimulation from recent revisions in the Books of Common Prayer from overseas' churches, the church has revised it again.

Philippines. The first Episcopal service in the Philippines* was conducted by a chaplain on 4 Sep 1898 for the American forces. In 1901 the Philippines became a missionary district of the Protestant Episcopal Church of the USA (PECUSA). Charles Henry Brent*, who arrived in 1902, was its first bishop.

Considering himself more a chaplain to the Americans and a representative of the United States than a missionary, Brent bought a choice lot near the government offices in Manila and built the Cathedral of St. Mary and St. John in 1907. He established the Baguio School for Boys (now Brent School) in Baguio City in 1909, a school for Muslim girls in Kawakawa, Zamboanga, and the Brent Hospital in Zamboanga (both in 1912) and St. Luke's Hospital in Manila (now St. Luke's Medical Center in Quezon City) to serve the expatriate community. St. Luke's Hospital began as a dispensary in 1903 and became an eight-bed hospital in 1905. After its renovation in 1907, the hospital included a school of nursing. It was transferred to Cathedral Heights in Quezon City after World War II.

His successor, Governeur Frank Mosher* (1920-40), who had served as bishop in Shanghai, China, prior to his posting in the Philippines, was interested in the development of native clergy. In 1932 he established St. Andrew's Training School (now St. Andrew's Theological Seminary) in Sagada. Under him St. Paul's Mission in Balbalasang, Kalinga Apayao, was established in 1925 and St. Francis of Assisi in Upi, Maguindanao, in 1927.

When Mosher retired because of poor health in 1940, his successor was Norman Binsted. The latter inherited 20 clergy, three of whom were Filipinos, and 9,950 communicants. Of the communicants, 80 percent were Igorots from the Cordillera region (45 percent of whom were in Sagada, Mountain Province), 9 percent were Tirurais and Ilocanos (mostly in Upi, Maguindanao), 2 percent were Chinese, and 9 percent were mainly expatriates in Manila and Zamboanga. After the war, Binsted sold the church property in Manila and moved to Cathedral Heights in Quezon City. St. Andrew's Theological Seminary was moved there in 1947, followed by St. Luke's Hospital and the Cathedral of St. Mary and St. John. Trinity College, established jointly with *Iglesia Filipina Independiente* (IFI) in 1963, completed the three-pronged ministry to be established at Cathedral Heights: hospital, schools, and a cathedral. On 22 Sep 1961, after long negotiations that were led by Binsted, who left the Philippines in 1957 because of ill health, the PECUSA signed the Concordat of Full Communion with IFI at the Detroit general convention. The agreement was implemented in the Philippines between the IFI and the PEC.

In the 1960s church leadership was transferred to the Filipinos, with Eduardo Longid consecrated suffragan bishop in 1963. Benito Cabanban was the first Filipino diocesan bishop in 1967, and Constancio Manguramas became suffragan bishop in 1969.

In the 1970s, because of expansion and the difficulty of pastoral visitation, the diocese was divided into three dioceses — the North, South, and Central. This allowed for better administration and laid the groundwork for autonomy. A house of bishops of the PEC was created, and they elected Cabanban the first presiding bishop when they met on 9 Feb 1972. In 1978 the PEC national convention approved a proposed church constitution. In Mar 1980 the prime bishop formed an ad hoc committee to consult the PECUSA for autonomy. Dean Robert Hibbs resigned, and Henry Kiley became the first Filipino dean of the seminary. On 2 May 1990 the PEC was finally inaugurated as an autonomous province of the Anglican communion, and Richard Abellon was installed as its first prime bishop. The PEC presently has five dioceses led by five bishops, 186 active priests and deacons, and more than 100,000 Filipino Episcopalians. It runs three hospitals, an elementary school, nine high schools, a college, and a seminary.

Epilogue. The Anglican Church in Asia has moved far since the days of British chaplains and colonial bishops. The form it takes varies subtly from country to country, but the distingishing marks of the Lambeth Quadrilateral are still there: the Scriptures, the historic creeds, the Gospel sacraments, and the episcopate. It struggles to understand its own identity and distinctiveness amid a plethora of Christian church forms and a background of other faiths. Perhaps the last word should come from the Asia Regional Conference for Anglican Leaders held in Jun 1995. In the report titled "Vision 2000 and Beyond," the delegates together stated: "God continues to challenge us to partnership with Him to reach the 3,200 million people of Asia. He calls us to sow in tears and He promises that we will reap in joy." Estimates of Anglican members in some Asian countries appear in the table above.

Bibliography

Thompson, H. P., *Into All Lands (History of the Society for the Propagation of the Gospel in Foreign Parts, 1701-1950)* (1951). • Neill, Stephen, *Anglicanism* (1977). • Gray, G. F. S., *The Anglican Communion* (1958). • Clark, Allen D., *History of the Church in Korea* (1971). • Albright, Raymond W., *History of the Protestant Episcopal Church* (1964). • Barrett, David B., *World Christian Encyclopedia* (2000). • Bell, C. K. A., *Christian Unity: The Anglican Position* (1949). • Chatteron, E., *History of the Church of England in India* (1924). • Grimes, C. J., *Towards an Indian Church* (1946). • Anderson, N. K., *Short History of the Cathedral of the Holy Trinity, Rangoon* (1930). • Marks, J. E., *Forty Years in Burma* (1917). • Purser, W. C. B., *Christian Missions in Burma* (1913). • Stock, Eugene, *History of the Church Missionary Society*, 3 vols. (1899) • Sykes, N., *The English Religious Tradition* (1961). • Robinson, C. H., *History of Christian Missions* (1915).

Sri Lanka

Balding, J. W., *The Hundred Years in Ceylon or the Centenary Volume of the Church Missionary Society* (1922). • De Soysa, Harold, ed., *The Church of Ceylon: Her Faith and Mission* (1945). Bewan, F. L., *A History of the Diocese of Colombo* (1946).

Philippines

Gowen, Vincent Herbert, *Philippine Kaleidoscope: An Illustrated Story of the Church's Mission* (1939). • *Journal of the Missionary District of the Philippines* (1907-18; 1921-41; 1972). • *Journal of the Proceedings of the Special Convention and the Primary Synod of the Philippine Episcopal Church* (1990). • *Journals of the General Convention of the Protestant Episcopal Church* (1898, 1901). • *Handbooks on the Missions of the Episcopal Church, Philippine Islands*, Vols. 1-3 (1923). • Norbeck, Douglas, "The Protestant Episcopal Church in the City of Manila, Philippine Islands from 1898-1918" (M.A. thesis, University of Texas, May 1992). • Wentzel, Constance White, *A Half Century in the Philippines* (1952).

Frank Lomax, with contributions from Paul Chen (Myanmar), G. P. V. Somaratna (Sri Lanka), the China Group (China), Tsukada Osamu (Japan), and Edward P. Malecdan (Philippines)

Animism

In the world of religion, the word "animism" serves two separate purposes. It is derived from the Latin *animus*, or more commonly *anima* (spirit or soul), words which belong to a large group of ideas having to do with the concept of "breath" or "wind" as the life-giving principle. The term "animism" (German, *Animismus*) was first coined in the early 18th c. by the German scientist Georg Ernst Stahl (1660-1734) to label the theory that every physical organism is in fact controlled by that which is not physical. But it was not until the late 1860s and early 1870s that "animism" entered the vocabulary of anthropology and religion, in the writings of Edward Burnett Tylor (1832-1917), most notably his epoch-making *Primitive Culture* (1871). The first use of "animism" was as a theory of the nonsupernatural origin of religion, its second as a term to describe a type of religious belief and observance in which the fearful acknowledgement of the powers of a nonphysical order of being is paramount.

According to Tylor, animism consists simply of "the belief in Spiritual Beings" — spiritual, that is, in contrast to corporeal: spirits either without bodies or detachable from the bodies they normally inhabit. In Tylor's view, this belief had arisen out of the human experience of dreams and "altered states of consciousness" (hallucination, trance) in which some part of the human personal-

Animism

ity had temporarily parted company with the body. In sleep, the body could be in one place, the spirit *(anima)* in another, and the dead could return to bless or torment the living. *Anima* is also a life-force, which the healthy young adult possesses in full measure, but which can be stolen, lured away, or overpowered. Without reference to the actual causes, disease is attributed to the clash of supernatural forces. To be healthy is to have the full measure of one's vitality. To fall ill is to have part of that vitality drained away, and in death it departs altogether.

The human being is therefore energized by an *anima;* according to Tylor, other living things are likewise given life in a similar fashion. Tylor insisted that at the dawn of human history no "absolute physical distinction" was drawn between humans and nonhumans: all pass through the same cycles of life and death and are therefore also assumed to have souls; this applies to plants and other natural objects as well. Tylor explained by drawing an analogy with the behavior of children, who readily attribute life to toys and pieces of furniture, as well as to people and pets.

Tylor, followed by most late-nineteenth-century anthropologists, maintained that religion had originated through reflection of this general kind. First there is a simple and generalized belief in "spiritual beings," some of which, being more powerful than others, are eventually elevated to the rank of gods and goddesses. Similar theories have been put forward at intervals ever since the days of the ancient Greeks. They are not altogether false, since we have many examples of powerful, revered, or enlightened men and women who have been admired and feared in their own lifetimes and have been elevated to divine status after death. This, however, is inadequate as a general theory covering the origin of all religion. Between 1870 and about 1914 (Tylor died in 1917), it was generally accepted, nonetheless, as a plausible if not conclusive theory of how religion might have originated — if, that is, one is not disposed to involve God or divine revelation. It was never more than one theory among many: 30 years ago, the anthropologist E. E. Evans-Pritchard listed fetishism, manism, nature-mysticism, totemism, dynamism, and magism together with animism as abandoned theories of the origins of religion, and he added, "Nobody, as far as I am aware, defends any of these positions today" (*Theories of Primitive Religion,* 1965, p. 104).

So much for animism as a nontheistic theory of the origin of religion. There remains the use of the term in a purely descriptive sense, as a general label for a bundle of fundamental ideas and practices relative to sacred things, which not only provide the substance of customary religious belief and practice in parts of the world relatively untouched by urbanization, but are frequently found as a substratum beneath the great traditions themselves, Christianity included. Terminology is an acute problem. Words originally introduced to serve a descriptive purpose become value judgments and are rejected as biased, condescending, and derogatory. "Primitive" and "savage" are the best-known examples. "Animism" tends sometimes to be added to the list. But since it is still used as a blanket term to characterize nonliterate religious systems, and since there is no obvious alternative, except perhaps "shamanism" (which is more functional than belief-centered), it may at least be examined. "Animism" and "animist" are of course very general and also very imprecise words to label some very explicit ideas and attitudes and the actions they prompt.

An *anima* is a "spirit": on the one hand, a life-force within or accompanying a body; on the other, a free agent that may or may not once have had a body, or a sequence of bodies, of its own. Spirits — powerful supernatural presences — attach more to some persons, places, times, and seasons than others. They frequent places of burial and cremation, temples and sanctuaries; they are most active where there is least light; and any of them may be malicious if not treated with due respect (see Ancestor Worship). In years past, the Christian would describe the life of the animist as being a life dominated by fear and devoid of comfort. This may have been overstated, but life on this level had to be lived in a state of constant watchfulness and constant preparedness to take evasive action by (in a manner of speaking) bribing the most influential agents.

Pre-Christian Asia teems, as it always has teemed, with these powers, and where a people's place of residence and means of livelihood have remained unchanged over the centuries, so too will their relationship to their sacred sites and the powers associated with them, even after an acceptance of Christianity. What is sometimes called "archaic" or "popular" religion creates a ladder between heaven and earth, a chain of command, authority, and power passing downward from God, by way of lesser gods and goddesses (for Christians, archangels and angels, saints and martyrs), to the guardian spirits of well and tree, hearth and home, and lower still to the imps who simply make mischief. Within this animistic hierarchy there are male and female beings, static and mobile beings, and helpful and malicious beings. What they have in common is that they are permitted to exist, and though some have been human beings, none is now encased in a parcel of flesh and blood and bones. To take them seriously is to be an animist.

To catalogue "Animism in Asia" would fill an encyclopedia. Animistic beliefs and practices are diverse in form and expression but always serve the same functions. Every power active in the world has, as a rule, its attendant spirit or spirits, varying in potency according to local circumstances. Some may be called "nature-spirits" and are associated with features of the natural environment. Of the others, those most often acknowledged and most generally respected are those having to do with sun, moon, planets, and stars, as well as the ghosts of the dead — especially those who have died by violence or on whose behalf the proper funeral ceremonies have not been carried out. Although belief in reincarnation is common in non-Christian Asia, and practically universal in Hindu* and Buddhist* societies, failure to dispose of a body in the appropriate manner interrupts the process and condemns the spirit to an indefinite wandering and malice against the living.

Where the belief in these spiritual beings dominates, the whole of life is dangerous. Particular danger, however, accompanies transitions from one phase of life to another, each of which — birth, puberty, marriage, death — has to be accompanied by the appropriate rituals to keep malicious spirits at bay. The agricultural community's rituals are of course closely related to the growth cycle of crops, such as rice, with special rituals at the times of plowing, sowing, and harvest. As with sacred rituals generally, it is essential that they be carried out by persons in a state of ritual purity, accurately and reverently. Failure on any count may bring the anger of the spirits — who are, in a sense, morally neutral but demand respect — upon the entire community.

Although it is assumed that Christians in Asia (and elsewhere) no longer believe in an animistic universe, and that they have no further need to defer to the spirits, it is impossible to generalize about how far animistic beliefs and practices survive in Christian contexts. In agricultural communities, the customs — though not necessarily the beliefs behind them — would seem to have a fairly high rate of survival, to judge from Carl Gustav Diehl's studies in South India. The secular urban milieu is much less likely to see their continuation, although even there they continue. Asian animism has, however, survived successive changes of regime and philosophy, including the postwar shift to Marxism. In recent years, it has attracted many new students anxious to trace the course of indigenous religion in Asia. The newer term is "popular religion," as an alternative to imported religion on the one hand, and no religion on the other. It may well be that what former generations believed about animism will resurface in this context, not as a competitor to Christianity, but as a cultural complement, providing an appropriate language in which Christianity can express itself.

Bibliography

Tylor, E. B., *Primitive Culture* I-11 (1871). • Whitehead, H., *The Village Gods of South India* (1916). • Diehl, C. G., *Church and Shrine* (1965). • Evans-Pritchard, E. E., *Theories of Primitive Religion* (1965). • Sharpe, E. J., *Understanding Religion* (1977). • Trompf, G. W., *In Search of Origins* (1990); *Melanesian Religion* (1991). • Van Nieuwenhove, J., and B. Klein Goldewijk, eds., *Popular Religion, Liberation, and Contextual Theology* (1991).

Eric J. Sharpe

Anirun, Yosua

(b. Cigelam, West Java, 9 Nov 1894; d. Jakarta, 15 Oct 1983). Evangelist and minister in the service of the *Nederlandse Zendingsvereniging* (Dutch Missionary Association, NZV) and from 1934 onward of the *Gereja Kristen Pasundan* (GKP).

Born in a Christian village, Anirun was educated at the NZV teacher-training school in Bandung and from 1916 to 1921 worked as a teacher in several mission elementary schools. In 1921, he was appointed an evangelist, but only in 1927 did he enter the two-year evangelists' training course in Bandung. After that, for three years he was trained as a nurse in the mission hospital. It was hoped that he would gain access to the (mainly Muslim) population of West Java more easily if his preaching could be accompanied by the giving of medical care. For several years, he worked as an evangelist in the Bandung mission hospital and in the villages of the Bandung area, besides ministering to the Sundanese Christian congregation in Bandung. In 1940, he was ordained a minister of the *Gereja Kristen Pasundan,* the Pasundan Christian Church, which had been declared independent on 14 Nov 1934, but until 1942 in part was still mission-led.

In 1940, Anirun was appointed treasurer of the GKP and as such was a member of the GKP synodal board. When the Japanese occupied Java (Mar 1942), the Dutch chairman had to resign and subsequently was imprisoned by the Japanese, as were all Dutchmen in Indonesia* in general. Anirun stepped in as chairman of the church. He held this office until 1950. In the following years he continued to occupy a post in the leadership of the GKP.

Anirun had to steer the Sundanese church through the years of the Japanese occupation (1942-45) and the struggle for independence (1945-49). In those years, the church not only went through the hardship the population of Java in general had to endure, but it also suffered from persecution by Muslim groups, especially in 1945-46. Owing to the circumstances, the GKP synod could not convene for a number of years. In 1946-47, the church territory was split in two, because part of it was Dutch-held and part belonged to the fledgling Indonesian Republic. In that time, Anirun struggled to maintain unity by traveling hundreds of kilometers, crossing the demarcation line between the two armies, on a bicycle.

In 1967, Anirun retired, but until his death he served the Bandung congregation as an assistant minister.

Bibliography

Van den End, Thomas, *De Nederlandse Zendingsvereniging in West-Java, 1858-1963* (1991).

Koernia Atje Soejana

Anthing, Frederik Lodewijk

(b. Batavia [Jakarta], 1818; d. 1883). One of several lay Christians on Java who stood at the cradle of Christianity on that island.

Born to a Lutheran* family, Anthing was educated in the Netherlands. He returned to Java and became a member and later vice president of the Supreme Court of the Dutch East Indies in Batavia. From 1852 onwards, he was stimulated by missionaries arriving from Europe to evangelize among the indigenous population of

Batavia and Java. However, his methods differed from those of the pietist missionaries. First, he had a strong conviction that "the nations of the Indies could only be won for Christ by workers from those nations." Consequently, he did not go around evangelizing but trained and sent emissaries who traveled the whole of Java. Realizing the liabilities of the colonial system, he treated his preachers as full equals, and at the end of his life ordained one of them to be his successor (see Colonialism).

Second, Anthing did not agree with the pietist repudiation of indigenous religion and culture. Therefore, he taught his emissaries to use Javanese cultural and religious elements, including white magic, as a means for spreading the Gospel. In this way, he succeeded in establishing a number of small congregations and inspiring a "Javanese Christianity." Most of the teacher-preachers and evangelists employed by the Dutch mission in West Java originated from those congregations.

Third, Anthing did not put his trust in the missionary societies which employed salaried European workers. He evangelized mostly outside of any organizational framework, using all of his personal resources (Anthing remained single until 1881, when he married an apostolic "prophetess"). Initially, he worked together with the societies, motivating them to establish the Depok Seminary, the first mission-run training school for Indonesian evangelists (1878-1926). For several years, he was also a board member of the Batavia Missionary Society and even of the established Protestant Church of the Netherlands Indies. But he found the methods of the Dutch societies still too western and broke off relations in 1872. He had himself called by one of his congregations and after that administered the sacraments. When he had spent his whole fortune on the mission and did not succeed in getting help from Holland, he turned to an apostolic (Irvingian) church in Holland and was ordained apostle for the East Indies (1879). After his death, some of his followers continued to constitute an apostolic church, which in the 20th c. split up into several groups. The majority were gradually absorbed by the Dutch missionary bodies working in Java. However, Anthing's ideas remained as an undercurrent in a number of congregations.

Bibliography

Bliek, A. J., *Mr. F. L. Anthing* (1938). • Van den End, Th., *De Nederlandse Zendingsvereniging in West-Java, 1858-1963* (1991). • Partonadi, Sutarman S., *Sadrach's Community and Its Contextual Roots: A Nineteenth Century Javanese Expression of Christianity* (1990).

Thomas van den End

Aphraates

(Syriac: Aphrahat). One of the first Syriac Christian theologians, who wrote a series of 23 treatises between 325 and 345.

The first 10 treatises of Aphraates, dated 337, deal with theological questions as well as Christian lifestyle, with a focus on asceticism. The fourteenth treatise and the introduction to the collection are in the form of letters, that treatise being a letter to a synod of bishops. The last nine treatises reflect the argument between Christians and Jews in Persia during the early 4th c. The last treatise, number 23, was composed during the winter of 344-45 at the beginning of the persecution of Christians (as well as Manichaeans*, Jews, and Buddhists) by Shapur II*.

The church reflected in the texts differs significantly from the dominant Greek and Latin churches of the early 4th c. The local structures focus around the "Sons of the Covenant" and the "Daughters of the Covenant." These groups are composed of celibate baptized believers. They are to be radical in their asceticism, love of God, and love of neighbor. These protomonastic groups appear to have constituted the bulk, if perhaps not the whole, of the church in the Persian Empire.

It is impossible to ascertain Aphraates' role in the Persian church. He was certainly in discussion with the bishops and an informed theologian, but there is no evidence that he was a bishop. The exegetical methods used to interpret the Scriptures are closely related to the rabbinic traditions of Judaism. His theology is modestly trinitarian, but without the support of the Greek philosophical structures developed in the Western churches.

The treatises, or "Demonstrations" as they are sometimes called, were translated into Armenian and into Ethiopic and circulated under the name of Jacob sometimes specified to be of Nisibis. While the name "Jacob" may have been a baptismal or episcopal name, there is no evidence that the texts were written in Nisibis or by Jacob of Nisibis*. They reflect a Persian perspective and knowledge of Persian life that would be of minimal concern to a bishop in Nisibis, which was, during the life of Jacob of Nisibis, part of the Roman Empire.

Bibliography

Bundy, D., "Christianity in Syria," *Anchor Bible Dictionary* 1 (1992). • Chaumont, M. L., *La Christianisation de l'Empire Iranian des origines au grandes persécutions du IVe siècle* (Corpus scriptorum christianorum orientalium 499; Subsidia 80; 1988). • Murray, Robert, *Symbols of Church and Kingdom: A Study in the Early Syriac Tradition* (1975). • Neusner, Jacob, *Aphrahat and Judaism* (1971); "The Jewish-Christian Argument in Fourth Century Iran: Aphrahat on Circumcision, the Sabbath, and the Dietary Law," *Journal of Ecumenical Studies* 7 (1970).

David Bundy

Apostolic Vicars and the Congregation of Propaganda

The setting up of the Sacred Congregation of Propaganda was an event of major importance in the history of Christianity and especially in the history of Christian mission. Pope Gregory XV called the new congregation into existence on 6 Jan 1622. The papal bull, which was not issued until 22 Jun 1622 (titled *Constitutio*), begins with the words *Inscrutabili Divinae Providentiae Arcano.* The tasks assigned to the new congregation were sweeping: to do everything possible to spread the Catholic faith. Its field of activity was the whole world. The congregation was to bring the two most important events of the 16th c., namely, the expansion of the world through geographical discoveries and the Protestant Reformation, into new relation with the church. In addition, it was to initiate new contacts with the estranged Eastern churches. In later documents, this threefold task is repeatedly spoken of as helping souls that are off the true path of salvation because of schism, heresy, or infidelity.

The word "mission" was used by the congregation in the beginning in its original, proper, and literal sense of "sending out." The congregation sent the apostolic vicars and also the missionaries to fulfill its tasks.

Some inconveniences in the missionary work came from the system of patronage, under which the popes from the late 15th c. on granted many rights and privileges to kings (see Padroado). By the middle of the 17th c., the Portuguese empire was in full decline in the East. Most of the dominions had been lost to the Dutch and the British (see Colonialism). Many of the regions conquered by the Portuguese had by then recovered their independence, and since it was practically impossible for Portugal to exercise an effective patronage in the occupied territories, the Congregation of Propaganda devised the principle of limited patronage; that is, the congregation firmly refused to acknowledge the right of patronage (1) in lands which had never been conquered by the Portuguese, (2) in lands which had recovered their independence and were under their native rulers, and (3) in territories occupied by the Dutch and the British.

A specific application of this principle is the case of China*, where the Congregation of Propaganda never admitted the extension of the diocese of Macau over the Chinese empire as the Portuguese crown had claimed. Pope Innocent XII took a very decisive stand on this issue and supported the congregation's policy with his personal approval.

The other issue which was keenly debated between the Portuguese crown and the Congregation of Propaganda was the institution of apostolic vicars in the Far East. During the long period of Portugal's uncertain political situation and in order to provide for the spiritual needs of the Christians and the evangelization of the pagans, the congregation sent to China and Indochina prelates endowed with the episcopal character and consecrated as titular bishops of a diocese *in partibus infidelium.* These apostolic vicars were, whenever possible, chosen from diocesan priests or from those who were more independent of the patronage and the authority of religious superiors. The congregation also bid all missionaries to follow all the directives given by Rome. So in this way the direction of missionary activity returned to the hands of the supreme pontiff.

The king of Portugal claimed that the appointment of apostolic vicars was an evident violation of the privileges of the patronage. In 1680, the Congregation of Propaganda, with the complete approval of the pope, issued an official statement to the king declaring that the institution of apostolic vicars neither violated the privileges of the Portuguese patronage nor curtailed the jurisdiction of the bishops of those sees subject to the patronage, because the apostolic vicars were not appointed to territories under the actual dominion of the Portuguese. Nevertheless, the congregation also made it clear that the institution of apostolic vicars was, by its very nature, provisional, and that the patronage retained all the privileges granted by the popes.

Toward the end of the 16th c. and the beginning of the 17th c., other problems arose: rivalry among the missionary orders, neglect in preparing a native clergy, and lack of missionary adaptation. The Congregation of Propaganda tried always to unite and coordinate missionary activities by promoting a peaceful collaboration amongst the different orders. Many programs and plans were prepared both to solve the problems and to advance the progress of missionary activities (see Instructions of 1659). Yet the conflicts concerning rites and also the Jansenist theory still existed in the church, and the congregation was never fully able to overcome these theological controversies. SURACHAI CHUMSRIPHAN

Appasamy, Aiyadurai Jesudasen

(b. 3 Sep 1891; d. 2 May 1975). Indian writer, teacher, pastor, and bishop who popularized the spiritual reading of the fourth Gospel.

Appasamy identified himself with the Indian *bhakti* tradition and used its insights for exposition of the biblical text. He challenged the traditional Chalcedonian approach and the Hindu monistic tendency which views the union between the Father and the Son as a metaphysical one. Appasamy served the Indian church in many capacities, notably as a bishop of the Coimbatore Diocese in the Church of South India*.

After graduation, Appasamy left for America in 1915 and spent seven years there. He completed his doctorate in England, where the subject of his Oxford doctoral thesis was "The Mysticism of the Fourth Gospel in Its Relation to Hindu *Bhakti* Literature." During his study abroad, he had contact with Western theologians such as B. H. Streeter and Friedrich von Hügel in the United Kingdom and Rudolf Otto and Friedrich Heiler in Germany. He also met Sadhu Sunder Singh* at Oxford and valued his friendship throughout his life. After returning to India in 1922, he published two books, *Christianity as Bhakti Marga* (1928) and *What Is Moksha?* (1931). These books are an exposition of the fourth Gospel, illuminated by a wealth of illustrations from the Tamil *bhakti* poets. In them he explains what led him in his doctoral studies to concentrate on the relation between the Gospel of John and Hindu *bhakti* literature. He gives a detailed interpretation of the relation between God and the universal *logos* and the incarnate *Logos* in John's Gospel. He also links sin with *karma* and defines salvation as liberation from both through the redemptive suffering and death of Jesus on the cross. Appasamy's creative exegesis keeps *bhakti* spirituality and orthodox theology together in a brilliant synthesis.

On 27 Sep 1950, Appasamy was consecrated bishop of Coimbatore Diocese. The tearing apart of the church by factions and fear drove the new bishop to prayer, which, to him, included the five elements of adoration, confession, petition, intercession, and communion. In 1959, he retired from active service to lead a contemplative Christian life.

More than any other Indian theologian, Appasamy identified himself with the *bhakti* tradition. He was a leading figure in the Indian church for more than 40 years.

Bibliography

Appasamy, A. J., *A Bishop's Story* (1969). • Boyd, Robin, *Indian Christian Theology* (1991). • ISPCK Study Guide, *Readings in Indian Christian Theology* (1991). • Thomas, M. M., and P. T. Thomas, *Towards an Indian Christian Theology* (1992).

Jacob Abraham

Appenzeller, Henry Gerhard

(b. Souderton, Pennsylvania, United States, 8 Feb 1858; d. Korea, 11 Jun 1902). First missionary of the Methodist Episcopal Church, USA, to Korea.

Settling in Seoul in 1885, Appenzeller helped in establishing the first Methodist* churches and schools, while cooperating with other denominations in Bible translation*, publishing, and many Christian projects. He sought to introduce Western culture together with the Gospel, gradually affirming the value of Korean culture and religion, yet always believing that conversion to Christianity was the central missionary goal, both for individuals and for the Korean nation.

Appenzeller had graduated from Franklin and Marshall College in 1882 and from Drew Theological Seminary in 1885. After ordination, he sailed to Korea with his wife Ella (Dodge), landing with Presbyterian* pioneer missionary Horace G. Underwood* at Inchon on Easter Day, 5 Apr 1885. Overt evangelistic activity was forbidden by the Korean king at that time, so Appenzeller pursued educational work, winning royal approval for *Paichai Hakdang,* a school for young men, in 1887. He and others secretly witnessed to the Gospel, however, even baptizing converts. When public worship became possible, he founded Chong Dong First Methodist Church (begun as Bethel Chapel), with Korean leadership and Appenzeller serving as its pastor until his death. He explored mission opportunities in other regions of Korea*, usually in cooperation with Presbyterian missionary colleagues, but concentrated mainly upon a variety of projects in Seoul, including the translation of the Bible into Korean, an ecumenical effort with other Protestant groups.

Appenzeller opened a bookstore in 1894, wrote many religious tracts, edited the *Korean Repository* and *Korea Review* to introduce Korea internationally, and was active in the Korea branch of the Royal Asiatic Society. He helped found and lead organizations to serve the religious and social needs of expatriates in Korea, such as the Seoul Union Church and Seoul Union Club. At the Paichai school he began the Trilingual Press, which published the first Korean-language Christian newspaper, the *Korea Christian Advocate,* and an organ of the Korean independence movement, the *Independent.* Always concerned about political developments, Appenzeller was committed to Korean cultural and political development. Although it sometimes disturbed his missionary colleagues and the home office in America, Appenzeller actively supported the Korean independence movement. This led him into conflict with Korean government authorities, and he even gave sanctuary to persons wanted by the Korean police. Because he sought to train Korean church leaders early on, he fostered the development of theological education* based upon a liberal arts tradition and dreamed of establishing a college and seminary.

While Appenzeller's enduring contributions were made through establishing Methodist institutions and training leaders, his character and views also helped shape Korean Protestantism, with its evangelical spirit, fidelity to the Bible, and concern for social justice and Korean independence. Although he began his career with a firm confidence in the virtues of American culture and the hope of building a westernized Christian Korea, Appenzeller later acknowledged positive values in Korean culture and religion. In his early years, he had commented upon the laziness, dishonesty, and inequality he saw in Korean society, and upon the harmful influence of Confucianism* and other religious traditions, especially ancestor* veneration. Gradually he began to mention the positive contributions of Asian traditions and embarked on a program of study of Asian culture and religions.

Like most missionaries of his day, Appenzeller saw conversion to faith in Jesus Christ as the central purpose of all missionary activity. He affirmed the value of meeting human need on all levels, from the medical to the intellectual, yet saw the preaching of the Gospel of love, power, and hope as the unifying center of mission. He was glad to struggle heroically for the ideal of building a Christian Korea. An activist by nature, Appenzeller left few records of theological reflection except for sermon manuscripts, but we can discover a confident, robust American missionary of the late 19th c., unselfconscious about his American culture, conservative theologically, and comfortable with the missionary triumphalism of his day. He had a deep respect for Korean colleagues and their Christian faith, but he tried to retain the right to decide when they should be given responsibility for ministry and decision making in the churches. He had a passion for personal piety and the ethical life, so he opposed the use of alcohol and tobacco, helping to establish a strict Protestant tradition that has endured in Korea. His cooperative ecumenical spirit was notable at a time when the mission boards in the United States and many missionary colleagues in Korea were highly competitive. Evidence of this ecumenical spirit is illustrated in his leadership in founding *Hankuk Sungko Suhoe* (Korean Religious Book and Trust Society), *Daehan Sungseo Konghoi* (Korean Bible Society), and the Korean Young Men's Christian Association*.

Bibliography

Davies, Daniel M., *The Life and Thought of Henry Gerhard Appenzeller (1858-1902), Missionary to Korea* (1988). • Hunt, Everett N., Jr., *Protestant Pioneers in Korea* (1980). • Griffis, William T., *A Modern Pioneer in Korea: The Life Story of Henry G. Appenzeller* (1912). • Appenzeller's personal papers, Union Theological Seminary Library, New York.

EDWARD W. POITRAS

Aqaq (Acacius) of Seleucia-Ctesiphon

(late 5th c.). Aqaq served as catholicos or patriarch of the Persian church (485-95). He succeeded his relative Babowaï, who was martyred under the Persian king Peroz in 485. A competitor for the position, Barsauma*, bishop of Nisibis, convened a counterelection at Bet Lapat, where both Monophysitism and the Byzantine Empire were condemned. In 485, Aqaq declared the synod of Bet Lapat null and void. He convened the Council of Seleucia-Ctesiphon in 486. This council sanctioned Nestorianism* as the correct theology and condemned divergent views. It confined celibacy to the monks and denied it for priests. Attended by only 12 bishops, not including Barsauma, this council significantly defined the East Syrian church. The *Buch der Synodos* edited by O. Braun (1900) contains translations of the text of the council and six letters between Aqaq and Barsauma.

Bibliography

Chabot, J. B., ed. and trans., *Synodicon Orientale, ou recueil des synodes nestoriens* (1902). • Fiey, J.-M., *Jalons pour une histoire de l'Église en Iraq* (1970). • Gero, S., *Barsauma of Nisibis and Persian Christianity in the Fifth Century* (1981). • Labourt, J., *Le Christianisme dans l'Empire Perse sous la dynastie Sassanide (224-632)* (1904).

DAVID BUNDY

Ardašīr I

(ca. 224-239/42). Conqueror of the Parthian Empire and founder of the Sasanian Empire who took the title "King of Kings."

Ardašīr I appears to have understood his role to be to avenge the defeat of Persia at the hands of Alexander the Great. He moved his armies westward and laid siege to Nisibis in 230 but was unable to capture the city. However, the incursions of Persian forces into Syria brought Roman attention to the area, and Alexander Severus moved to extend Roman hegemony into northern Mesopotamia. This demonstrated the inadequacy of the system of independent Christian, pagan, and Jewish buffer states between the two empires. The war brought hopes for independent city-states in Osrhoene* and Hatra to an end. After the death of Alexander Severus, Ardašīr I again invaded northern Mesopotamia and conquered Carrhae and Nisibis (238-39). Hatra was selected by Ardašīr I as a center for military operations in the area.

There is no evidence of persecution of Christians during the reign of Ardašīr I. Syrian Christianity grew rapidly during the period. The *Chronicle of Arbela** asserts that the power and independence of the Jewish courts and legal system were reduced. Ardašīr I encouraged Zoroastrian clergy to establish religious centers (characterized by the holy fire) throughout the Persian Empire. This was clearly done both to assert Persian social and political control and to encourage conversion to Zoroastrianism*. Mani awaited the death of Ardašīr I to take his religious system into the public arena, perhaps because of fear of persecution.

Bibliography

Tabari, *History* and *Die Chronik von Arbela*, ed. and trans. P. Kawerau (1985). • Labourt, J., *Le Christianisme dans l'Empire Perse sous la dynastie Sassanide (224-632)* (1904). • Frye, Richard N., *The Heritage of Persia* (1963). • *Atti del Convegno internazionale sul Tema: la Persia nel Medioevo; Roma, 31 marzo–5 aprile 1970* (1971). • Chaumont, M. L., *La Christianisation de l'Empire Iranian des origines au grandes persécutions du IV e siècle* (CSCO 499; Subsidia 80; 1988). • Winter, E., *Die sâsânidisch-römischen Friedenverträge des 3. Jahrhundert n. Chr. — ein Beitrag zum Verständnis der aussenpolitischen Beziehung zwischen den beiden Grossmächten* (1988).

DAVID BUNDY

Armenia

The traditions of Christian evangelism in Armenia attribute the first efforts to Addai*, who was supposed to have worked in the early 1st c. Tertullian (*Adversus Judaeos* 7.4) wrote of Christian villages in the area of Armenia, which then comprised not only the present republic, but also much of what is now eastern Turkey. Certainly the early biblical versions and the liturgy demonstrate that the country was first evangelized from Syria. The definitive conversion of the nation took place, according to early Armenian historians, through the efforts of Gregory the Illuminator (ca. 240-332), who converted King Tiridates III in the early 4th c. At that point, Christianity became the official state religion.

The Armenian alphabet was developed by Mashtots and Sahak during the early 5th c., and an ambitious translation project from Syriac was begun. Most of the early Syriac texts were translated into Armenian, followed by significant Greek texts and later Arabic. Thus

Armenian language texts preserve Christian texts that were otherwise lost, including works by Philo, Irenaeus, Ephrem, Severian of Gabala, and Nonnus* of Nisibis, among others. Original literature was also produced. Early Armenian Christian writers include Agathangelos, Korium, Eznik of Kolb, Lazar P'araec'i, Moses of Khorene, and Gregory the Illuminator.

The Armenian church accepted the Councils of Nicaea, Constantinople, and Ephesus, but rejected Chalcedon, being troubled by the language of the "two natures." This theological disagreement was encouraged in order to demonstrate the independence of Armenia from Byzantium, since Byzantine military forces were unable to protect the area from incursions from the south. Throughout the centuries that followed, there would be occasional efforts at reconciliation with the Byzantine imperial church, but without success.

Since the 4th c., the Armenian church has served to unite Armenians against foreign pressures and influences. The catholicate of the Armenian Apostolic Church is located today in Etchmiadzin, Armenia, beside the 5th-c. cathedral.

In 1088, Armenian princes in Cilicia decided their survival in the face of the Crusades required a separate government and patriarchate. Thus with its capital and cathedral at Sis, Cilician Armenia (sometimes on maps as Lesser Armenia) was organized with the approbation of Crusaders and the Byzantines. This kingdom, under Het'um I, was the first to submit to the Mongol* invaders (1250) rather than risk a futile defense. An effort was made to balance the requirements of the Mongols and Crusaders/papacy in order to insure the survival of the kingdom. The kingdom lasted into the late 14th c., when it succumbed to Turkish control. This kingdom produced large numbers of literary works as well as copies of older materials. It was also a center for translating medieval Syriac writings into Armenian. Armenian Christians in both Cilician and Greater Armenia developed important traditions of the arts, including sculpture, architecture, textiles, and metallurgy.

Bibliography

Cox, C., "Biblical Studies and the Armenian Bible, 1955-1980," *Revue Biblique* 89 (1982). • Lyonnet, S., *Les Origines de la version arménienne et le Diatessaron* (1950). • Metzger, B., *The Early Versions of the New Testament* (1977). • Sarkissian, K., *The Council of Chalcedon and the Armenian Church* (1965). • Thomson, R. W., trans., *Agathangelos: History of the Armenians* (1976); *Moses Khorenats'i: History of the Armenians* (1978); *Studies in Armenian Literature and Christianity* (1994).

David Bundy

Aroccia, Giovanni

(Lo Ruowang) (b. 1566; d. 1623). Portuguese Jesuit missionary who entered interior China in the late Ming Dynasty.

Joining the Society of Jesus* at age 17, Aroccia left for India* in 1586, studying philosophy and theology in Goa and Macau, respectively. In 1597, when Lazzaro Cattaneo* temporarily returned to Macau for medical treatment, Aroccia was instructed to look after the residence in Shaozhou and was granted permission to remain in Shaozhou after Cattaneo's return. He then began his preaching career in inland China*.

After Matteo Ricci* had established residences in Nanchang and Nanjing, Aroccia was first called to Nanchang, and then to Nanjing, where he stayed for nine years. In 1603, he baptized Xu Guangqi. He also baptized Qu Taisu*, who had given much help to Ricci. In 1609, Ricci ordered his return to Nanchang. Following an incident in which Chinese officials brought an accusation against missionaries in 1616, Aroccia went into hiding at a convert's home in Jianchang, Jiangxi. He later went to Zhangzhou, Fujian, and Jiading, Jiangsu, to continue preaching. In 1622, he succeeded Longobardo* as the third leader of the Inland China Jesuit missionaries' organization in inland China. He died in Hangzhou.

China Group

Art and Architecture

In the modern period, Christianity came to Asia through the West and only gradually took root. The artistic symbols and expressions of Christianity in which Asians took an interest were mainly those which came from the West. Initially, there was very little indigenization in the field of art and architecture, but not because Asian Christians lacked artistic creativity. In fact, Asian people have very strong artistic traditions and creative ability. Yet in the early period, those who accepted Christianity were more interested in adapting Western forms of Christianity. In this period, the translation* of the Bible and some hymns took a place of primacy. The process of creating indigenous expressions of the Christian faith took place in various Asian countries gradually (see Contextualization).

Daniel Johnson Fleming of the United States was a pioneer in the study of Asian Christian art and architecture. He taught at Union Theological Seminary after serving as a missionary in Asia. He collected some representative Asian Christian art and architectural works in his book *Each with His Own Brush* (1938). The book contains 51 paintings from three Asian countries: China*, Japan*, and India*.

Another pioneer was Arno Lehmann, who worked in India as a missionary and later taught at Martin Luther University, Halle (at that time, East Germany). He published two books, *Die Kunst der jungen Kirchen* (1957) and *Afro-asiatische Christliche Kunst* (1966). Despite the fact that he lived in East Germany, where travel abroad was restricted, he made untiring efforts to gather materials and to write interpretations of them. In his second book, he included 282 works of art from Asia and Africa. Lehmann made this pioneering contribution in hopes of preparing the way for Asians someday to take the responsibility for promoting work in this fascinating field.

After its inaugural assembly in Kuala Lumpur (1959), the East Asia Christian Conference (EACC), now called the Christian Conference of Asia* (CCA), encouraged Asian expressions of the Christian faith through Asian music* and art forms. Influential here was the leadership of D. T. Niles*, general secretary of the EACC in its initial years.

At the working committee of the EACC which met in Brisbane, Australia (Nov 1962), the project of collecting and publishing contemporary Christian art in Asia was initiated, and Takenaka Masao* was asked to undertake it. Takenaka conducted extensive research throughout Asia and abroad and published *Christian Art in Asia* (1975), which became the basic foundation for later developments in this field of study.

Recognizing the significance of the publication of *Christian Art in Asia,* the CCA assembly met in Penang, Malaysia*, in 1977 and endorsed the idea of holding a consultation among Asian Christian artists and theologians. The consultation was held at Dhyana Pura, Bali, Indonesia*, in Aug 1978 with the theme, "The Lord's Prayer in Asia Today." The consultation brought together 43 people, most of whom were Asian artists involved in painting, sculpture, wood carving, flower arrangement, sand painting, and printmaking. At the end of the consultation, they decided to form the Asian Christian Art Association (ACAA) and elected Takenaka as chair and Ron O'Grady as secretary.

IMAGE, a quarterly magazine with the purpose of coordinating and stimulating interest in the field of Christian art and architecture in Asia, has been published by the ACAA since 1979. Its continuous publication to the present has brought attention to various streams of Asian Christian art and has helped form a network among Asian artists and those who are interested in the subject both in and outside Asia.

The second consultation on Christian art in Asia was held at Mt. Makiling, outside Manila, Philippines (Mar 1984) with the theme "The Magnificat in Asia Today." Together with the CCA committee on mission and the Asian Institute for Liturgy and Music (AILM), the ACAA organized a joint consultation on "Art and Mission of the Church in Asia Today" in Chiang Mai, Thailand* (Mar 1991).

The first consultation of women artists was held in Sep 1992 in Hong Kong. It was jointly sponsored by the CCA Women's Concern and the ACAA and provided a forum for Asian women artists to articulate their identity and to build a network of mutual encouragement.

On the international scene, the ACAA has organized exhibitions for several conventions, including the World Council of Churches (WCC) Assembly on World Mission and Evangelism in Melbourne, Australia (May 1980), the assembly of the WCC in Vancouver (1983), and the CCA assembly in Seoul, Korea (1985).

A traveling exhibition of Asian Christian art (1986-87) started in Geneva and extended through Sweden, Denmark, Germany, and the United States. The special catalogue for the exhibition, "That All May Be One," depicted 40 works of art. Many groups, churches, and agencies from various Asian countries were interested in hosting the exhibition and in using its art in their periodicals, on book covers, and in Christian education textbooks.

To celebrate the seventh assembly of the WCC, which was held at Canberra, Australia (Jan 1991), the book *The Bible through Asian Eyes* (1991), co-edited by Takenaka and O'Grady, was published. It became one of the most frequently used resources on Christian art in Asia. Other significant publications in the field of Asian Christian art include: *Your Kingdom Come* (1980); Frank Wesley's *Consider the Flowers: Meditation in Ikebana* (1990), which features 28 pieces of *Ikebana* (flower arrangements) on biblical themes and which was published in three languages (English, Japanese, and Swedish); Naomi Wray's *Exploring Faith with a Brush* (1993); and Carlos V. Francisco's *The Man and Genius of Philippines Art* (1985).

The leadership of the ACAA changed in 1992, when Yuko Matsuoka of Japan became president and Egai Fernandez of the Philippines became vice president. Takenaka became honorary president and O'Grady consultant.

Judo Poerwowidagdo and Ken Hassell have researched Asian church architecture. Their report on churches and chapels was printed in *IMAGE,* No. 7 (Mar 1981). In 1983, the CCA asked Takenaka to carry on studies in the field of Christian architecture in Asia. With the help of architects and photographers, he collected and edited materials for publication in *The Place Where God Dwells: An Introduction to Church Architecture in Asia* (1995). This was, as the subtitle indicates, only an introduction to the field of church architecture in Asia, where rapid growth and development continue today.

Significant works on church architecture at the national level have also been published. The standard work, *Kyokai Kenchiku* (Church Architecture), coauthored by Yasuyuku Takahashi and five others (1985), is one example. Of the six coauthors, two are architects, one is a historian, and three are theologians, representing the Orthodox, Roman Catholic, and Protestant traditions in Japan.

In 1998, Jyoti Sahi, a creative Indian artist, published a provocative book on Indian church architecture titled *Holy Ground: A New Approach to the Mission of the Church in India* (1998). This work is very challenging in that it is not a factual, descriptive survey nor a historical review on the subject, but instead raises critical questions from the perspective of the mission of the church in the Indian context.

Another development in this field is the effort to express the Christian faith through traditional *Noh* drama. Around 1962, an attempt to produce *Noh* drama on biblical themes was made in the Tokyo area under the guidance of Kakichi Kadowaki of Sophia University. In recent years, several biblical *Noh* dramas have been performed at Kansai Seminar House in Kyoto. Yuko Yuasa, who is engaged in the study of Christianity and culture at Doshisha University, has written several scripts of biblical *Noh* drama and put on successful performances of them with Nobushige Kawamura of the Kanse stream of the *Noh* tradition.

At the 20th anniversary consultation of the ACAA (held in Jul 1998 in Bali), along with a dynamic dance on the suffering of Christ by the Bagong Kussudiardja dancing team, "Hannya Miriam," an agnostic story of Moses' sister, was performed on the outdoor stage of Dyana Pura.

Finally, we note that because of Asia's extended geographical area and diverse cultures and traditions, attempts are being made to organize networks and organizations around the theme of Christian art which would include artists from countries such as China, India, Indonesia, Japan, Korea*, Pakistan*, and the Philippines.

Bibliography

Masao Takenaka, *Christian Art in Asia* (1995); *The Place Where God Dwells: An Introduction to Church Architecture in Asia* (1995). • Masao Takenaka and Ron O'Grady, *The Bible Through Asian Eyes* (1991). • Jyoti Sahi, *Holy Ground: A New Approach to the Mission of the Church in India* (1998). • *IMAGE — Christ and Art in Asia* (since 1979). • O'Grady, Ron and Alison, eds., *Twenty Years: A Celebration of the Asian Christian Art Association, 1978-1998* (1998).

MASAO TAKENAKA

Arya Samaj

Pioneer Hindu revivalist movement of the 19th c. popularly known as the church militant in the Hindu fold.

Swami Dayanand Saraswati* (1824-83) founded the *samaj* on 10 Apr 1875 in Bombay as a universal religion open to all, irrespective of caste, color, or nationality. The movement later became a formidable socio-religious force in North India*, with headquarters at Lahore. The Ten Principles of the *samaj*, acceptance of which is essential for membership, are noteworthy: (1) God is the primary cause of all true knowledge; (2) God is absolutely perfect and alone deserves worship; (3) the Vedas are the books of true knowledge; (4) an *Arya* must be ready to accept truth and to reject untruth; (5) all actions must conform to virtue; (6) the objective of the *samaj* is to improve the physical, spiritual, and social condition of humanity; (7) all ought to be treated with love and justice; (8) ignorance must be dispelled; (9) selfishness must be discarded; (10) the common good must prevail over individual interest.

The *samaj* is primarily associated with three programs: (1) *Shuddhi*, the program of purifying non-Hindu converts and former Hindus and taking them into the Hindu fold. Over the years, it has reconverted many Muslims and Christians back to the Hindu religion; (2) *Sanghatan*, "union," a device to organize Hindus for self-defense, which created a militant spirit among members. It endeavors to uplift the depressed castes and bring about Hindu solidarity; (3) educational work (several educational institutions are run to promote Vedic and scientific knowledge).

In 1892 the *samaj* split into conservative and progressive parties. Swami Shraddhananda, Lala Lajpat Rai, and others contributed to the growth of the movement. The cow protection movement *(Gaurakshini sabha)* has aroused Hindu communal consciousness and became a symbol of Hindu resurgence. The *samaj* has mixed religion with politics, and the slogan "India for Indians" has promoted Hindu religious nationalism*. It stands for the defense of the *Arya dharma* — its traditions, Vedas, and orthodoxy. It denounces polytheism, idolatry, animal sacrifice, child marriage, discrimination against women, and untouchability; considers the Vedas alone as true scriptures; and supports the idea of caste by merit instead of by birth. Dayanand's magnum opus, *Satyartha Prakash* (Light of Truth), is very authoritative, second only to the Vedas.

The *samaj* holds the views that the Vedas and Vedic religions alone are true; other religions are false, and *Aryavarta* (India) is the country *par excellence.* It promotes Hindi as the national language and stands for intrareligious reforms, active social service, and an active policy of confrontation against other missionary religions such as Christianity and Islam*. The *samaj* was significantly involved in the Hindu-Muslim communal conflicts and riots in preindependent India. Apologetic and polemic trends are quite evident in the activities of the *samaj.* Since the partition of India in 1947, the headquarters of the *samaj* has been relocated to Delhi.

The *Arya Samajists*, having a holy book (the Vedas), a creed (the Ten Principles), a society of committed members (the *Arya Samaj*), a slogan ("back to the Vedas"), a missionary organization (the *Paropakarini Sabha*), and an agenda *(Shuddhi* and *Sanghatan)*, have contributed significantly to the renewal of Hindu religion, especially its missionary ideology. *The Arya Samaj* considers its mission universal and is quite a strong movement among Hindu expatriates in different parts of the world (see also Hinduism).

Bibliography

Baird, Robert D., ed., *Religion in Modern India* (1981). • De Smet and J. Neuner, eds., *Religious Hinduism* (1968). • Garg, Ganga Ram, ed., *World Perspectives on Swami Dayananda Saraswati* (1984). • Mathew, C. V., *Neo-Hinduism: A Missionary Religion* (1987). • Rai, Lajpat, *The Arya Samaj* (1915). • Sarma, D. S., *Hinduism through the Ages* (1973). • Seunarine, J. F., *Reconversion to Hinduism through Suddhi* (1977). • Zachariah, Aleyamma, *Modern Religious and Secular Movements in India* (1992).

C. V. MATHEW

Asano Junichi

(b. Omuta City, Fukuoka Prefecture, Japan, 12 Dec 1899; d. 10 Jun 1981). Japanese Old Testament scholar, pastor.

Asano graduated from Tokyo Commercial High

School in 1921 and was employed by Mitsui Produce Company. He entered Tokyo Shingakusha (seminary) and studied under Takakura Tokutaro*. In 1926, he went abroad to study at Edinburgh College, studying Old Testament for two years under Adam Cleghorn Welch. Following that, he studied at the University of Berlin for six months. Upon returning to Japan* in 1929, he began teaching at Tokyo Shingakusha. In 1931, he engaged in pioneer evangelism in Aoyama Kitamachi (predecessor to the United Church of Christ in Japan Mitake Church). The same year, he published his first written work, entitled *Yogensha no kenkyo* (A Study of the Prophets). He made many contributions to the development of Old Testament studies, including papers and books such as *Kyuyaku seisho* (The Old Testament), a volume published as part of *Iwanami Dai Shiso Bunko* (Iwanami Great Ideas Library). After World War II, he devoted himself to teaching Old Testament and training pastors at both Aoyama Gakuin University and Japan Biblical Seminary. In 1955, he published *Isuraeru yogensha no shingaku* (Theology of Israel's Prophets), which won him an honorary doctor of literature degree from Kyoto University. In 1962, he published *Yobuki no kenkyu* (A Study of the Book of Job), and between 1965 and 1975, he completed a four-volume commentary on the book of Job, *Yobuki no chukai.*

In addition, Asano was very active in the peace movement, serving as leader of a goodwill envoy to China* in 1957 and as vice-president of the Japan Religionists Peace Council. He also was involved in social welfare programs, founding Izumi Kai, a facility for the employment of disabled persons, in 1956.

Kida Kenichi, Japanese Dictionary

Ashram Movement

Ashram is a settlement of Christians devoted to simplicity of life and fellowship in service.

The word "ashram" in the Hindu religious usage has the meaning of a place or hermitage in which austere life is practiced for spiritual purposes. The modern ashram movement is, however, of recent origin and may be traced back to the Hindu renaissance in the 19th c. Keshub Chunder Sen's* Bharat Ashram, founded in 1872 at Belgharia near Calcutta, could be regarded as the first of this kind. The Santiniketan, founded by Debendranath Tagore* in 1888, was another ashram, although it did not have resident facilities. Both of these ashrams derived inspiration from Christianity as well as Hindu tradition. In 1915, Gandhi* returned from South Africa and founded the Satyagraha Ashram at Sabarmati in Ahmedabad following the methods of Tolstoy Farm and Phoenix Settlement in South Africa. Most of these ashrams emulated the ancient forest hermitages mentioned in ancient epics such as Ramayana.

The idea of Christian ashrams came as an Indian response to the Western expression of Christianity. Some Indian Christian leaders were concerned about their own involvement in the mission in their country. The earliest Protestant experiment with an ashram came in 1917 by N. V. Tilak* at Satara. Tilak referred to Jesus as "guru" and, as the head of the institution, he was the chief servant as well. The first major Protestant ashram, Christukula, was founded by two medical doctors, S. Jesudason and E. Forrester-Paton, in 1921. Only vegetarian food was served, celibacy was the rule, and the membership was confined to males. A long day was kept with fixed hours for work, study, and worship. A full member of the ashram was called a *sevak* (servant). This ashram was popular because of the medical work done by the founders, but it was also successful in evangelism. Among missionaries, E. Stanley Jones* (1884-1973), an American Methodist, was the leader in the Christian ashram movement. His first ashram was started in 1930 at Sal Tat in the Himalayas. His ashrams provide room for religious reflection, Christian worship, and dialogue (see Interreligious Dialogue).

The early founders of the ashrams frequently spoke of them as a "kingdom of God" society. They tried to live by the statement found in the Acts of the Apostles, "Distribution was made according to need." The people gathered together not only to hear about but also to experience the kingdom of God. It was stated that a Christian ashram should combine the spirit of Christ and the *dharma* of vanaprastha for the glory of God.

The earliest ashram among the Roman Catholics* was founded in 1941 in Ranchi by Brahmacari Rewachand Animananda. The Saccidananda Ashram was founded by Abishekananda and Swami Parama Arubi in 1950 at Shantivanam, on the Kaveri near Kulittalai. It was the first major Catholic ashram. The founders of this ashram attempted to integrate the Hindu idea of *sannyasi* into Christianity. They dressed like Hindu monks and worshipped and ate like Hindus. They even meditated like Hindus. Nevertheless, this ashram, which had Benedictine principles, did not attract new recruits.

There were several ashrams in Kerala which emerged after the 1940s without any foreign collaboration. The Christa Panthi Sangh in Sihora (1942) and Chritiya Bandhu Kulam at Satna are Mar Thoma Syrian Church ashrams set up near Jabalpur. They were founded by some theological students. The members were celibate. The mission of the ashram was worship, evangelism, and rural social and economic work. The Sachhidanand Ashram was founded in 1971 in another locale near Jabalpur by a Roman Catholic friar, A. Premananda. It is a rural village ashram which emphasizes farming, praying, studying, and witnessing. It follows the Indian village style of living.

The ashrams have made a disproportionately large contribution to the "Indianization" of the church. A major portion of Indian Christian theology has come from the ashrams. In the field of Indian Christian painting, ashrams have made an equally important contribution. The ashrams have also made use of Indian architecture for Christian buildings. Important Indian liturgical contributions have come from Poona, Shantivanam,

Jyotiniketan, and several other ashrams. The contribution made by N. V. Tilak and the ashrams in Tirupattur to Indian Christian lyrics is invaluable.

However, the ashrams have suffered from one problem. They functioned well during the lifetime of their founding fathers. In the second and third generations, however, the interest has dwindled, and many have not been able to attract new members.

The ashram movement spread from India to neighboring countries. The first ashram in Sri Lanka was opened in Jaffna in 1939 by a minister of the American Mission, S. Selvaratnam. A celibate ashram, its life members took the Franciscan vows of obedience, poverty, and chastity. This was an interdenominational work and was therefore supported by many churches. In the 1950s, another ashram, Joti Nilayam, was founded in the eastern part of the island. In the 1960s the ashram idea was introduced to the Sinhala area by Yohan Devananda, a minister of the Anglican church. This ashram, located at Ibbagamuwa near Kurunegala, was devoted to social work and ecumenism.

The ashrams both in India and elsewhere seemed to lose their vision after the death of their founding fathers. They came into existence through the devotion of one or two Christians of strong character and clear conviction. Celibate ashrams have not attracted many to their community life; hence life membership is low.

Bibliography

P. Chenchiah, V. Chakkarai, and A. N. Sudarisanam, *Ashram: Past and Present* (1941). • Saral K. Chatterji, ed., *Acknowledging the Lordship of Christ: Selected Writings of Richard W. Taylor* (1992). G. P. V. Somaratna

Asia Evangelistic Fellowship

In 1960, evangelist G. D. James, a convert from Hinduism* and immigrant from India, set up the Malaysia Evangelistic Fellowship (MEF) in Malaya. This was to be an indigenous national mission which would equip and send out Asian missionaries to Malaysia* and Singapore*. MEF, which began evangelistic ministry on the Malayan rubber estates with two workers, gradually expanded its scope of ministry and number of workers. G. D. James was a captivating speaker and wrote several evangelistic books. As a result, his ministry spread to other Asian cities and countries, including Thailand, Indonesia, India, and the Philippines; MEF therefore changed its name to Asia Evangelistic Fellowship (AEF) in 1972. National workers were appointed in these various countries.

AEF celebrated its twenty-fifth anniversary by organizing a conference for national evangelists in Singapore on 3-12 May 1985. The theme was "Tell Asia Today." One hundred forty evangelists from 14 countries were present. By then, AEF had 130 workers, missionaries, and evangelists serving in 12 nations (cf. 50 in 1978 and 100 in 1982). Activities included holding city-wide crusades, publishing evangelistic literature, and running training institutes such as the Tamil Bible Institute (principal, Rev. Dorairaja) in Johor, Malaysia, which trained Tamil workers to do village and plantation evangelism in Malaysia. This institute, set up in 1977, was closed down in Apr 1994 due to various circumstances, including demographic changes in Malaysia. The institute was replaced by special evangelism training conducted in local churches and schools of mission and evangelism set up in Singapore (1990), Bombay, Manila, and Yangon (Rangoon, 1992). In 1990, Jonathan James succeeded his father as international director, while G. D. James became honorary president. The AEF headquarters is located in Singapore. The number of full-time and associate workers today is over 100.

Bibliography

Douglas, J. D., ed., *Tell Asia Today* (1985). • James, G. D., *Amazed by Love*, 3rd ed. (1987). • Sng, Bobby E. K., *In His Good Time: The Story of the Church in Singapore, 1919-1992*, 2nd ed. (1993). Robert Solomon

Association of the Like-minded for Moral Cultivation

(*Suyang Dongwu Hoe* [SDH]). Founded in 1929, the SDH was an organization similar to the Young People's Academy (Hungsadan) founded by the eminent Korean nationalist An Ch'ang Ho. As with numerous contemporary reform organizations, the SDH was supported by Protestants, especially those from the northwest. Prominent Protestant members included Song Chang-gun and Yu Hyong-gi. The obvious objective of SDH was the moral cultivation of its members, but its hidden agenda was to realize national independence (see Nationalism).

In May 1937, alerted by a publication which encouraged Christians to take the lead in saving Korea*, the Japanese conducted an investigation and discovered the nationalistic objective of SDH. The following month, people associated with the SDH were arrested. Twenty-two were indicted, but they were declared innocent in a trial held in Oct 1941. Nevertheless, SDH members came under Japanese surveillance. Between appeasement and coercion, the Japanese police succeeded in making many SDH members pro-Japanese. This struck a crucial blow to Korean independence and the church, as many of the members were professionals (lawyers, doctors, ministers, writers, etc.) respected by the Korean populace.

Kim Seung Tae

Assumption Cathedral

The history of the Assumption Cathedral goes back to 1809, when a descendant of a Thai-Portuguese family living in Bangkok, Fr. Pascal, who had been ordained a priest in 1805, raised 1,500 bahts from devoted Catholics and his own extended family for the construction of a church. He entrusted the task to Fr. Florens, who bought a piece of land on the bank of the river opposite the

Santa Cruz Church and north of the Holy Rosary Church in Thonburi for 250 bahts in 1810 and started the groundwork for the construction of a church to be built in honor of the Assumption of the Virgin Mary.

However, the construction was delayed when Florens was appointed an acting bishop in 1810. He succeeded Bishop Garnault when the latter died on 4 Mar 1811 in Chanthaburi.

In 1820, Florens bought a banana field adjacent to the site of the intended church. It is now used by Assumption College; the first modern Catholic school in Bangkok, it was founded by Fr. Colombet in 1885. A second piece of land also purchased in 1820 served as the site of the present Assumption Cathedral, the Cathedral school, the school run by the sisters of St. Paul de Chartres*, the bishop's residence, the Catholic Center, the East-Asiatic Company, and some other Catholic houses.

By late 1820, the donations were insufficient for the church building. Florens raised 1,500 pastros from the cardinals in Rome, and the first Assumption Church, built of brick, was completed in 1822. The bishop's office and residence were also constructed at the same time. The residence of the bishop of Bangkok and the head of the Catholic Church in Thailand has been located in the Assumption compound ever since.

In 1864, the city area of Bangkok expanded to include the Assumption Church and its environs. The number of Catholic families increased, and it was possible to designate a parish of Catholics living near Assumption Church. When a fire in 1864 gutted the compound of the nearby Holy Rosary Church, Assumption was designated a regular parish by Bishop Dupond, and François Joseph Schmitt was appointed its first pastor. The parish registry containing the names of the first baptized persons and the earliest members of Assumption Church was destroyed by a fire in late 1865.

In 1910, Fr. Colombet began the construction of the present building of the Assumption Church. It was completed in 1918. A high altar of French marble was added in 1939 by Fr. Perroudon. The church was consecrated by Bishop Perros on 23 Jun 1940. During World War II, bombs damaged the church. It was restored after the war at a cost in excess of 77,200 baht. Major renovations were made to the cathedral a year before the visit of Pope John Paul II to Thailand (1983-84).

Assumption Cathedral has been, and remains, the center of missionary work in Thailand.

VICTOR LARQUE

Augustinians (O.S.A.)

Background. St. Augustine is one of the founders of the religious life. After his conversion in 386, he set aside all worldly ambitions and, together with his friends, decided to serve God. He returned to Africa where, first as a layman at Thagaste and later as a priest at Hippo, he introduced the monastic life "in keeping with the manner and rule conceived under the holy apostles," living in poverty, chastity, and obedience. Many brothers chose this way of life and have been ordained clerics and consecrated bishops for the service of the church.

Augustinian monasticism was carried to Europe by the African bishops, clergy, and monks who were persecuted or exiled by the Vandals between 430 and 570. As a result, it was known "not only in Africa but also in the lands across the sea," as Possidius writes in his *Life of Augustine.*

Based on the number of monasteries established under St. Augustine's *Rule,* the Apostolic See, in the 13th c., promoted the founding of the Augustinian Order from the union of various groups of hermits. On 9 Apr 1256 the Order of Saint Augustine was confirmed by Pope Alexander IV and providentially destined to serve the church together with the other evangelical orders.

The Augustinian way of life is first and foremost a community in which the brothers live in unanimity bounded by the charity of Christ, serving one another, striving to develop their God-given talents, and working together for the good of the community and the people of God.

Through their religious vows, the Augustinians dedicate themselves to the divine worship, especially in the liturgy, and to apostolic activity according to the needs of the church.

Philippines. The Augustinians came to the Philippines* from Mexico in 1565 in the expedition of Miguel López de Legaspi* and Fray Andrés de Urdaneta. In 1575 they became an independent province of the Order. By the end of the century they already had some 50 houses on six of the islands.

From 1565 to 1898, close to 3,000 Augustinians worked in the Philippines. They founded 328 parishes, 90 of which were turned over to other orders or to the native secular clergy. In 1897 more than 3,500,000 Filipinos were under their care.

In addition to preaching the Christian faith to the Filipinos, the friars made an invaluable contribution to the material and cultural progress of the country. The Augustinians, as did other religious institutions, played the role of pastors, mentors, providers, and protectors of the people. They brought with them the technical know-how of Europe and America, they revolutionized the cultivation of agricultural products already existing in the islands, and they introduced new ones, such as sugar, coffee, cocoa, tobacco, potatoes, and various fruits, from America and from other parts of Asia. They directed the construction of ditches and channels for irrigation, and they worked hand in hand with the people to develop old and new industries vital for the survival of the newly formed Christian communities. The interest and direction of the friars changed the Philippines from a primitive, self-sufficient country into an organized system of towns, for which the religious served as architects, engineers, and farmers. They made it possible to construct drainage systems, bridges, and stone buildings and taught the Filipinos how to make lime, mortar, and bricks. They were the regular directors of primary education until 1863, when the Spanish government published an official plan for a public system of primary instruction. They introduced the printing press in 1593, after which many books were published in the various languages and dialects of the islands. Some of the first books printed in the Augustinian Press are *The Life of Saint Nicholas of Tolentine*, by Fray Felipe Tallada in the Pampango language (1613); and *Arte y Reglas de la lengua Pampanga* (Grammar and Rules of the Pampango Language) (1617) and *Catechism and Christian Doctrine* (1621), by Fray Francisco Coronel, also in the Pampango language. The translation of *The Christian Doctrine of Cardinal A. Agnagan*, by Fray Francisco López, was printed in 1620 at the Monastery of San Pablo (commonly, San Agustin). (See also Literature and Publishing.)

The multiplicity of languages in the Philippines made the missionary work quite difficult in the early years of evangelization. Forced by practical reasons, the Augustinians, and later on the other missionaries, undertook from the very beginning the study of the native languages. Grammars, dictionaries, and catechisms were necessary for the missionary to be able to pass on to the local people the message of the Gospel in a more accurate and effective way. Furthermore, a royal decree of 27 Apr 1594 divided the territory among the various religious orders. The Augustinians worked among the Tagalog-, Pampango-, Ilokano-, Cebuano-, and Hiligaynon-speaking people in whose languages they wrote grammars, dictionaries, catechisms, and religious literature. The Augustinians wrote and printed 12 grammars and four dictionaries in the above-mentioned languages; Bible translation* came much later. Francisco López studied the Iloko language for over 28 years and then came out with *Arte de la lengua Iloca* (Grammar of the Iloko Language), printed in 1627 by the University of Santo Tomas press, Manila. Alonso de Mentrida published in 1628 his *Arte de la lengua hiliguaina de la isla de Panay* (Grammar of the Hiligaynon Language of Panay Island) after 30 years of work and study. They likewise published and translated over 600 books in the above languages and dialects.

Aside from books on philology and religious literature, the Augustinians wrote books on history and the sciences, such as Gaspar de san Agustin's *Conquistas de las Islas Filipinas* (Conquest of the Philippine Islands), published in Madrid in 1698 (with a second edition in Madrid, 1975, and a bilingual Spanish and English edition in Manila, 1998). This book deals with the study of the anthropology, culture, customs, and beliefs of the Filipinos at the coming of the Spaniards; Manuel Buceta and Felipe Bravo's *Diccionario Geografico-Histórico-Estadístico de las Islas Filipinas* (Geographical-Historical-Statistical Dictionary of the Philippine Islands), 2 Vols., Madrid, 1850; Joaquín Martínez de Zúñiga's *Estadismo de las Islas Filipinas*, written at the end of the 18th c. and published in Madrid, 1893, 2 Vols. (published in Manila, 1973, as *Status of the Philippines, 1800*).

In the field of science, the most outstanding work is perhaps *Flora de Filipinas* (Philippine Flora), by Manuel Blanco, published in Manila in 1837. A second edition was printed after his death, in 1845; a third, greatly enlarged, appeared in 4 volumes, 1877-88, in Latin and Spanish, with 470 colored illustrations and the treatise "Medicinal Values of Trees and Plants of This Land" by the Filipino Augustinian Ignacio Mercado. A fourth bilingual edition in Spanish and English came out in Manila in 3 volumes with text and colored lithographs (1993). Blanco's botanical work was acclaimed by French, British, Dutch, Swiss, and Spanish scientists, who named some plants after Blanco. He translated into Tagalog Tissot's treatise on the medicinal plants found in the Islands. In the various towns he administered, he taught the people ways of raising and gathering rice, cotton, coffee, and of dyeing various textile materials.

Still another aspect of missionary activity was to teach the Filipinos to defend themselves against the Muslim pirates, as well as from Europeans invaders. The Philippine archipelago consists of over 7,000 islands, but at no time were more than 5,000 soldiers present. The missionaries, therefore, often assumed the task of military leader to protect the people whom they evangelized. Thus the Augustinian Julian Bermejo, parish priest of the town of Bolhoon (Cebu Island) from 1802 to 1842, built a chain of watchtowers from Cebu to Negros and Bohol islands via a telegraphic system. Through the signals he kept the townspeople informed in cases of impending pirate raids. Watchtowers were likewise built by Augustinians in towns near the sea in various islands of the Philippines.

As part of their social involvement with the people, the Augustinians established orphanages for children who lost their parents during the cholera epidemic of 1882. Orphan girls were housed at Mandaluyong Orphanage (Asilo) under the direction of the Augustinian Sisters, who were invited to come from Barcelona, Spain. They later formed the Congregation of Augustinian Sisters of the Philippines. Today they run the University of Regina Carmeli (Bulacan), six colleges, and 16 schools. Orphan boys were housed first in a building at the San Marcelino district in Manila, later on at Guadalupe Monastery, and in 1890 in Malabon (Bulacan), where a school of arts and trades with a modern printing press was established. This school had a short life since it was destroyed during the uprising of the Filipinos against the Americans in 1899.

At present the Augustinians run the University of San Agustin (Iloilo), *Colegio San Agustin* (Bacolod), *Colegio San Agustin* (Biñan-Laguna), *Colegio San Agustin* (Makati), two schools in the cities of Iloilo and Cebu, a Museum of Filipino-Spanish ecclesiastical colonial art at San Agustin Monastery in Intramuros, Manila, three seminaries, and four parishes. They publish three journals. The San Agustin Church and Museum were declared a World Heritage Site by UNESCO on 11 Dec 1993.

China. The first attempts of the Augustinians to enter China* were made in the 16th c., but their efforts did not materialize due to causes beyond their control. On 12

Jun 1575, Martín de Rada and Jerónimo Marín traveled from Manila to China as ambassadors of the general governor of Manila. They were well received in China and were invited to visit several cities during their stay of almost five months, but they were forbidden to preach the Gospel. Thus they returned to Manila on 28 Oct. Rada wrote *Relación del viage que se hizo a la tierra de la China, de 1575 años* (Report of the Voyage Made to China in 1575; Manila, 1575). This report, much esteemed by scholars, has been published by Rodriguez and Boxer, among others. The latter claims for Fray Rada the glory of being the first to identify Marco Polo's Cathay with China. Most of the work in China during this period was done by the Jesuits*.

In 1681 Alvaro de Benavente and Juan Nicolas de Rivera established a house at Kaokingfu, and two years later in Nanhiung and Foky. In May 1700 Benavente became the first apostolic vicar of the mission. These missions grew gradually, and by the early 18th c. there were some 7,000 converts and 23 mission churches, served by 10 Augustinians, located in three provinces of Kiangsi, Kwantung, and Kwangsi. In addition, the religious took care of the leprosarium (see Leprosy Work) in the province of Canton. But the controversy of the so-called "Chinese Rites" (see Ancestor Worship) and the intervention of the apostolic legate Maillard de Tournon* in 1707 made the work of the Augustinians, as well as of the missionaries of other orders, very difficult. Thus the Augustinians left China and proceeded to Macau*, where Benavente died on 20 Mar 1709. Not until 1734 did the Augustinians return to China. But persecution by Emperor Kia-King forced them to leave China in 1795. The last to leave, after 20 years of work there, was José Seguí, who later became archbishop of Manila. A few Chinese Augustinians were ordained priests, one of whom, Juan Sie Li, was expelled from Canton province and died in Macau* in 1796.

After a few unsuccessful attempts, the Augustinians returned to China in 1879. The first to arrive were Elias Suarez and Agustín Villanueva. They were assigned to the territory of northern Hunan Province, in the districts of Changteh, Lichow, Yochow, and Hofu. The latter district was eventually turned over to the Passionist Fathers. The Augustinians erected parishes and schools in the main cities; these served as mission centers. They also established many "stations" with chapels in the nearby areas under the direction of the central missions. All their efforts fizzled out in 1949 when they were forced by the Communist (see Communism) government to leave China. When the Augustinians started working in the missions in 1879, there were only 45 Christians in a territory of 9,000,000 souls. By 1947 the number of baptized Christians increased to 24,332, with 3,250 catechumens; there were 20 churches in the central missions and 90 in the rural stations, attended by 29 Spanish priests and 25 Chinese priests, both diocesan and Augustinians. In 1925 four Spanish Augustinians sisters arrived in China to take over the schools and orphanages for girls. They administered one major and one minor seminary, 19 schools for boys, 14 schools for girls, three professional schools, three pharmacies, three asylums, one house for the aged, and three clinics.

At present there are only three Augustinian priests and four Augustinian sisters who take care of three parishes, working with the Catholic Patriotic Association.

Japan. Mission work in Japan* began with the arrival of Diego de Guevara and Eustasio Ortiz in Hirado on 12 Aug 1602. They first built a church at Bungo (the present Oita Prefecture). The work of the Augustinians centered around the Nagasaki area, where Hernando Ayala opened the first house in 1612. At the same time a parish of over 10,000 Christians was assigned to the order. In 1614, however, the persecution broke out anew and all the Augustinian missionaries except Ayala were forced to leave the country. Ayala went into hiding and secretly took care of the Christians who had now gone underground. He was captured and beheaded in Omura in 1617 (see Kirishitan Evangelism).

His replacement, Pedro de Zúñiga, was burned to death. He was followed by Bartholome Gutiérrez, who was jailed in Omura, from where he witnessed the tortures and deaths of many of his colleagues and Japanese Christians. He, too, was burned at the stake.

One of the most interesting characters of the so-called "Christian Century" was the Japanese Augustinian priest Thomas Jihioye. Born in Omura in 1602, he studied under the Jesuits* and later became a catechist. As his work became risky, he sailed for Manila in 1622, where he entered the Augustinian Monastery, was ordained a priest, and sailed back to Japan in 1632. He carried out his missionary activities at night while working as a stable helper in the house of the governor. Thomas was finally captured and subjected to the torture of the "pit." He died in Nov 1637. The only Augustinian to outlive Thomas was another Japanese Augustinian, Michael of Bungo, who was also ordained a priest in the Philippines, returned to Japan (1632), and did missionary work near his native place in Bungo. In 1637 he was forced to take refuge in Nagasaki but was captured and placed in the "pit" and killed. With the death of these two Japanese, the Augustinian mission in Japan closed in 1637. In 1874 the Augustinians tried to return to Japan but were prevented by French missionaries staying there. Three Augustinians from the United States, Thomas Purcell, George Kupa, and Edward Robinson, arrived in Nagasaki in Nov 1952 and were given a parish in the Shiroyama district. Soon they built a church, a monastery, and a kindergarten, primary, and junior high school.

In 1961 they arrived in Fukuoka, where they built a kindergarten school and a fairly large monastery, hoping that the house could be used as a seminary. In 1965 they started working in the diocese of Nagoya, and in 1969 they established a workers' mission in the industrial area of the city of Tokyo. At present, besides the schools mentioned above, they run four parishes and a house of formation.

South Korea. On the invitation of the bishop of Inchon, Rev. William McNaughton, two Augustinians

Augustinians (O.S.A.)

from Australia and two from the Anglo-Scottish Province arrived in Korea* in Sep 1985.

After learning the Korean language, they were entrusted with the parish of Song Hyon Dong — the Parish of Christ the King in Inchon. At present there are three Australian and two Filipino Augustinians in charge of three parishes and an Augustinian formation house.

Irian Jaya, Indonesia. The Augustinians started their missionary work in Indonesia* in Jan 1953 with the Dutch Augustinians Peter van Diepen and William Snelting, who arrived in Hollandia (now Jayapura) in the northern part of the island of New Guinea.

Over 30 Augustinians have been working in this mission up to the present. They were entrusted in 1959 with the newly established apostolic prefecture known as Manokwari, a section of the prefecture of Hollandia, with a territory of 63,700 square kilometers, including the Vogelkop and several adjacent islands.

In 1977 there were over 15,000 Catholics out of a population of 200,000 people. Their method of evangelization was to open village schools and teach simultaneously the elementary subjects and Christian doctrine. The Augustinian priests visited the villages regularly, assisted by the lay catechists. Van Diepen, the pioneer of the mission, became the first ecclesiastical superior in 1959, apostolic prefect in 1960, and finally bishop in 1967. Recently the Augustinians turned over several parishes to the diocesan clergy. They run three parishes and a formation center.

India. Since this region was first colonized by Portugal, the Portuguese Augustinian Province founded in 1572 a special "congregation," or vicariate, under the Congregation of the East Indies for mission work. In 1638 it already had 240 members working in its missions, which extended from the west coast of Africa to Macau*. The first 12 missionaries arrived in India* in 1572. Its numerous houses, established in the 17th c. in Iraq, Persia, Georgia, and Pakistan*, were closed before the end of the 18th c.

The Augustinians, nevertheless, continued their regular missionary work in India during the first quarter of the 19th c., even though in Portugal authorities had already begun to limit the number of religious and monasteries in the home country, until 1834, the year Portugal abolished all religious orders. Among the houses established in India, the monastery of Our Lady of Grace is considered one of the outstanding buildings in the city of Goa. Nearby is the College of San Antonio with its main monastery of Our Lady of the People, where the Augustinians taught humanities, philosophy, and theology. Houses were also opened in Calcutta, Meliapor, in Hoogly near the mouth of the Ganges River. A number of houses were founded in Ceylon (Sri Lanka*), Bangladesh*, Burma (Myanmar*), Siam (Thailand*), Malacca*, and Macau.

Like their confreres in the Philippines, the Augustinians working in India wrote works of science and religion. Mention should be made of Manoel da Assunçao, who printed in Lisbon in 1743 a valuable work of popular theology in both the Portuguese and Bengalese languages in the form of a dialogue between a Christian and a Brahman. He also published in Lisbon a dictionary of Portuguese and Bengalese, preceded by the Bengalese grammar. In the 18th c., several Augustinians became bishops in various dioceses in India, the most outstanding of whom was the great missionary Alexis Meneses, appointed archbishop of Goa in 1595 and transferred to the diocese of Braga (Portugal) in 1612.

From 1834 to 1841, the apostolic vicariate of Madras in British India was under the Irish Augustinian bishop Daniel O'Connor, who brought with him a few Augustinians from Ireland. He had the catechism translated into Tamil and founded schools for girls and boys against the wishes of the Hindus. In 1838 he became apostolic vicar of Meliapo, but a few years later he resigned due to poor health and retired to Ireland.

The Augustinians from the Philippines returned to India in 1981 to reestablish the order there. At present there are four Indian Augustinians running two seminaries and two parishes.

Bibliography

Philippines

Blair, Emma H., and James A. Robertson, *The Philippine Islands, 1493-1909,* 55 Vols. (1903-09). • Rodríguez, Isacio, *Historia de la Provincia Agustiniana del Smo Nombre de Jesús de Filipinas* (History of the Augustinian Province of the Most Holy Name of Jesus of the Philippines), 22 Vols. (still in the course of publication) (1965-94). • San Agustin, Gaspar de, *Conquest of the Philippine islands* (Spanish-English ed. Pedro Galende) (1998). • Hernández, Policarpo F., *The Augustinians in the Philippines and Their Contribution to the Printing Press, Philology, Poetry, Religious Literature, History and Sciences* (1998). • Galende, Pedro G., *Angels in Stone: Architecture of Augustinian Churches in the Philippines* (1987).

China

See Rodríguez and San Agustín mentioned in the Philippines • Boxer, Charles R., *South China in the Sixteenth Century: Being Narratives of Galeote Pereira, Gaspar da Cruz, OP, Fr. Martín de Rada OESA (1570-1575)* (1953). • Martinez, Bernardo, *Historia de las Misiones Agustinianas en China* (History of the Augustinian Missions in China) (1918). • Galende, Pedro G., *Apologia pro Filipinos: The Quixotic Life and Chivalric Adventures of Fray Martín de Rada, OSA, in Defense of the Early Filipinos* (1980).

Japan

See Rodríguez and San Agustín mentioned above • Sicardo, Jose, *Cristiandad del Japon* (Christianity of Japan) (1698). • Hartman, A., *The Augustinians in the Seventeeth Century Japan* (1965).

South Korea

Arneil, Stan, *Out Where the Dead Men Lie: The Augustinians in Australia, 1838-1992* (1992).

India
Breve relaçao das cristiandades que os religiosos de nosso padre sancto Agostihno tem a sua conta nas partes de Oriente (A short telling of the Christian Communities which the religious of our Father Saint Augustine have in the regions of the Orient) (1630). • Aparicio, Teófilo, *La Orden de San Agustín en la India (1572-1622)* (The Order of Saint Augustine in India (1572-1622) (1997). • Alonso, Carlos, *Alejo de Meneses, O.S.A. (1559-1617), Arzobispo de Goa (1595-1612)* (Alexis de Meneses, O.S.A [1559-1617], archbishop of Goa [1595-1612]) (1992).

Policarpo Hernández

Aye Myat Kyaw

(b. 10 Oct 1915). Pastor, teacher, educator, translator, and writer in Myanmar.

Kyaw was the son of S'ra Byu and Nant Hnin Yone. His father was a village schoolteacher at first but later joined the ministry to become pastor of a local church. Kyaw had a strict religious upbringing. He attended the Burma Divinity School (Myanmar Institute of Theology) and obtained the bachelor of theology degree in Mar 1939. In that same year, he was assigned to teach at the Pwo Karen Bible Training School in Yangon. He became assistant principal in 1940 and the next year its principal. He was ordained on 28 Jan 1954 and married Maiden Tun on 9 Aug 1969.

Kyaw traveled widely. On 5 Apr 1956, he visited Bangkok, Thailand*, to make a survey of different dialects of Pwo Karen*. In 1959, he was sent as a delegate to Kuala Lumpur, Malaysia*, to attend the East Asia Christian Conference inauguration service. From there, he flew to Thailand to attend the Karen Baptist* Convention. In 1961, he was sent as a delegate to the Third General Assembly of the World Council of Churches at New Delhi, India*.

Kyaw served for six years (1962-67) with the World Council of Churches (WCC). He served two four-year terms as general secretary of the Burma Baptist Convention (1961-69). In 1961, he was privileged to attend the central committee meeting of the WCC in Paris, France. He was also able to attend the Baptist World Alliance executive committee meeting in Norway and visited the WCC headquarters in Geneva.

After his term as general secretary of the Myanmar Baptist Convention (MBC) had expired, Kyaw became general secretary of the Pwo Karen Conference, serving from 1969 to 1995. On 16 Dec 1990, the executive committee of the MBC and the board of trustees of the Myanmar Institute of Theology presented him with the Fellowship of Distinguished Christian Service (FDCS).

As author and translator, Kyaw has written and published a large number of booklets and lecture notes. They were written for use by Pwo Karen schools as well as individuals. Kyaw also helped write the Commentary of the Bible in the Pwo Karen language.

Kyaw gave over 50 years to the Lord. His unfailing service to the church, his interest in theological education, and his devotion to the spread of the Gospel in Myanmar made him exemplary in the eyes of Myanmar Christians.

J. Maung Lat and Anna May Say Pa

Azariah, Vedanayagam Samuel

(b. Vellalavilai, Tinnevelly District, South India, 17 Aug 1874; d. 1 Jan 1945). First bishop of Dornakal and first Indian bishop of the Anglican Church in India.

Azariah's father was Thomas Vedanayagam, a village pastor and a simple, earnest, godly man. However, a far greater influence on Azariah was his mother.

As a student, Azariah was in the first class to take the matriculation examination at Madras University. This enabled him to do two years of college studies in Tinnevelly and then two more years at Madras Christian College. He first worked as a secretary of the Young Men's Christian Association* (YMCA) and eventually served the organization for more than 10 years.

In 1903, Azariah led in the founding of the Indian Missionary Society* of Tinnevelly, one of the first indigenous mission societies in Asia. In 1905, together with K. T. Paul*, Azariah was instrumental in the formation of the National Missionary Society (NMS), or the *Bharat Christya Sevak Samaj*, in Serampore. He traveled widely throughout India* urging young people to commit themselves to the service of Christ, especially in direct missionary work among non-Christians. At one meeting, he was challenged by a student who asked, "Why do you not go yourself?" Thus he decided to go to Dornakal as a missionary. Bishop Henry Whitehead of Madras advised him to be ordained. In 1910, Azariah participated in the World Missionary Conference at Edinburgh, where he had a significant influence challenging Western missionaries in their attitude toward Asian church leaders.

On 29 Dec 1912, the 11 Anglican bishops in India laid their hands on Azariah, and he became the bishop of Dornakal at age 38. Azariah wrote books in Tamil, although he spoke Telugu fluently. He wrote on holy baptism, Christian marriage, and Christian giving.

From his early years, Azariah was concerned with the question of church unity in India. He served as chairman of the National Christian Council of India, Burma, and Ceylon. He served on the committee which was to bring the Anglican*, Presbyterian*, Congregational, and Methodist* churches together into one great united church. Unfortunately, he died at midday on 1 Jan 1945, two years before the Church of South India* came into being in Sep 1947.

Bibliography

Azariah, V. S., *Christian Giving* (1954). • Firth, Cyril Bruce, *An Introduction to Indian Church History* (1961). • Hodge, J. Z., *Bishop Azariah of Dornakal* (1946).

S. Sam Victor

Ba Thaw

(b. Bassein, Myanmar, 1891; d. Myitkyina, 1967). Ba Thaw studied for his bachelor of arts degree in Calcutta, India*. He worked with George J. Geis, a Baptist* missionary to the Lisu* and Kachin*, beginning in 1911. Ba Thaw spoke both Lisu and Kachin fluently after one year of service. He lived with the Lisus*, dressed like a Lisu, and consistently sought to learn more about their language and culture.

At one point, the thought came to Ba Thaw's mind that "a tribe having no literature cannot be improved much in education, social activities, and also in spiritual aspects." So, in 1913, he made a trip across the mountains into China*, visiting Lisu villages. He came finally to Tengyueh, where he spent some time with J. O. Fraser of the China Inland Mission and the few Lisu Christians there. Ba Thaw and Fraser developed a Lisu alphabet using romanized letters. They worked on translating the catechism and the Gospel of Mark (see Bible Translation). Ba Thaw's first Lisu script was completed at the end of 1913 and was printed in 1917 by the American Baptist Mission Press in Rangoon.

Ba Thaw arrived in Myitkyina in 1914 and started a village school at Sadon in 1920. He worked as an evangelist, pastor, and teacher. After retiring in the early 1950s, Ba Thaw lived into his late seventies. He chose to die among the people to whom he had come as a young missionary. Anna May Say Pa

Ba Yin, Stephen, U

(b. Sagaing, northern Myanmar, 12 Oct 1903; d. Sep 1987). Editor of the *Sower,* the bilingual Catholic monthly newspaper in Myanmar*.

Ba Yin was the fifth of the six children of U Pan Bon and Daw Nyein. U Pan Bon passed away when Ba Yin was only three years old, and his mother, a nurse, took her family along with her when she was transferred to Nyaunglebin in Bago Division.

Ba Yin studied at the Roman Catholic mission in Nyaunglebin (conducted by Michael Mignot, a French missionary) through middle school. He completed his high school education at St. Patrick's High School in Mawlamyine, run by the Brothers of the Christian Schools. After his school education, Ba Yin was employed by Mignot as a mission catechist, religious instructor, music master, and all-around handyman. After Mignot's death in 1937, Ba Yin continued serving in the Nyaunglebin Mission under Mignot's successor, Fr. Matthew.

During World War II*, Nyaunglebin Mission was destroyed by bombing. Ba Yin was invited to Pathein by Fr. Perrin in 1947 and employed in the publication of the *Sower,* Myanmar's only Catholic newspaper. In 1949 he went to Yangon (Rangoon), capital city of Myanmar, when the *Sower* office was transferred there. He became editor of the publication, put out in English and Burmese. He continued in this post until 1979. In spite of his heavy duties as editor, he also served on the board of management for the Roman Catholic Church in Myanmar, taught the Myanmar language to seminarians at the Catholic Major Seminary in Yangon, and published several religious books in the Myanmar language.

In 1954 Ba Yin was awarded the Pro Ecclesia et Pontifice Medal for distinguished and faithful service to the church by Pope Pius XII. After his retirement as editor of the *Sower,* he spent his time publishing religious tracts. His health deteriorated in 1986, and in Sep 1987 he died.

Ba Yin is remembered for his years of unremitting service to the cause of disseminating God's Word through the medium of a regular monthly Catholic newspaper. Peter Thet Lwin

Babaylan/Catalonan

In pre-Hispanic Philippines*, the native priest or religious functionary was called *babaylan* by the Visayans and *catalonan* by the Tagalogs. The religion of the early Filipinos did not have a highly developed theology. They venerated the dead and worshipped nature. They had a notion of a supreme being who was the creator and lord of all, but he was relegated to the background by a host of more accessible deities and spirits who could be appealed to by sacrifices. They were deemed his agents and ministers. These deities (the dead ancestors* and environmental spirits) were called *anito* or *diuata*. Idols and images were made of these beings. The *babaylan* or *catalonan*, mostly old women, offered sacrifices to them in ceremonies called *paganito* or *pagdiuata*. They acted as intermediaries, or mediators, between the gods and the people. They performed specific religious duties for which they were paid. This prestigious and highly lucrative office was acquired through friendship, kinship, inheritance, or claims of being selected by the *diuata* and having communion with the gods.

With the coming of the Spaniards and their Catholic faith, acculturation took place. Many Christian terms, rites, and ceremonies found their way into the indigenous religion. The *babaylan* or *catalonan* lost dominance over the people, and her function was taken over by the priest. In 1621 and 1622, Tamblot of Bohol and Bankaw of Leyte led local revolts against the Spaniards. They were former *babaylan* who desired to return to the pre-Hispanic religion. EVELYN-TAN CULLAMAR

Baclaran Fathers. *See* Redemptorists

Baha'i

(Persian, *Bahai*). Religion founded by Mirza Husain Ali (1817-92).

Baha'i is not a sect of Islam* but a spin-off from the Babi movement which revived the early Shia belief that the hidden Imam communicates with the faithful through a medium called Bab (the "door" of communication).

The first Bab, Mirza Ali Muhammad (1820-50), foretold the coming of "he whom God shall manifest." Mirza Husain Ali, an early disciple of the Bab, called himself Bahaullah (glory of God). He was arrested and imprisoned in 1852 for alleged connections with an attempt by Babis to assassinate the Shah, who executed the first Bab in 1850. He was released and deported to Baghdad in 1852, and in Apr 1863 he declared himself to be the manifestation of God foretold by the Bab. Ali believed that his mission was to redeem the world at the end of the age and to communicate God's will. He sent letters to the heads of various states and also to Pope Pius IX inviting their support to his mission. He moved to Constantinople, Adrianople, and finally in 1868 to Acre in Palestine. Later he moved to Banji, near Haifa, and lived there until his death in 1892. The Baha'is consider Palestine as their holy land because of this association of Bahaullah with Israel and also because Haifa was the administrative headquarters of the faith.

After Bahaullah's death, his mission was carried out by Abbas Effendi (1844-1921), who made three missionary journeys to Egypt, Europe, and America, and by Shoghi Effendi Rabbani (1899-1957), who married a Canadian Christian named Mary Maxwell. Since his death, leadership has been provided by a committee, first, by the Council of the Hands of the Cause and since 1962 by the Universal House of Justice.

The opposition and severe persecution that this new faith had to face resulted in its rapid growth. The committed followers took the new faith wherever they could. Baha'i has a following numbering over two million members. The Baha'i religion is the largest religious minority in Iran. The local and national spiritual assemblies and the Universal House of Justice take care of the administration, which is a kind of democratic theocracy.

The Baha'is believe that faith is essential for spiritual life. God is unknowable. However, he manifests himself through messengers such as Abraham, Moses, Zoroaster, Krishna, Buddha, Christ, Muhammad, and Bahaullah. The Baha'is hold the view that religious truth is always relative and not absolute. Therefore, they have a positive approach to all religions as repositories of religious truth, though in embryonic form. The Baha'i faith is a fuller revelation, and of course much fuller revelations will appear, although not before 1,000 years.

In other words, Bahaullah is not the final prophet nor the Baha'i religion the final revelation. But for this age Bahaullah and his teachings will suffice. The Baha'is believe that Bahaullah's writings are inspired, and their religious literature is translated into about 750 languages.

Revelation is progressive and continuing, as is human civilization. In the evolutionary process of time, the unity of humankind is the need of the present age. Anyone who professes belief in Bahaullah is admitted into the faith. There are no initiation rites, no sacraments, and no priests. Religious duties are to pray daily, to fast 19 days a year, abstain from intoxicants, practice monogamy, obtain the consent of parents to validate a couple's marriage, and participate in the Nineteen-Day Fast, a celebration of the spirit of fellowship and oneness. Women are assured full equality of opportunity with men. Though Baha'is have no public worship, they have temples called *Mashriq al-Adhkar* (literally, "place where the uttering of the name of God arises at dawn"), a nine-sided building having a dome of nine sections. This is open to one and all, and is not regarded as a sectarian place.

In the early years of its existence, the Baha'i religion came to India. This occurred during the lifetime of Bahaullah himself. The British colonial policy of religious neutrality and the heightened spirit of the missionary enterprise prevalent among various religions since the second half of the 19th c. were conducive for the work of the Baha'is in India. The faith is more than 100 years old in India and has a vigorous and zealous community of believers. New Delhi has one of Baha'i's most imposing and magnificent temples; it is built in the shape of a lotus flower. Even after 100 years of existence and mission in India, the number of Baha'i members is insignificant in proportion to the imposing demographic reality of India. However, to their credit it must be observed that as a community they are very active in the religious and social realms of life, despite their small numbers. Every member is characterized by what is called the missionary spirit and zeal.

Though an offshoot of Islam, Baha'i's appeal in India seems to be greatly to non-Muslims, especially Hindus, Christians, and the tribals. Services to the community through institutions such as homes for the aged and orphans and schools and hospitals have won the goodwill of the larger society. The all-embracing universalistic approach and acceptance and respect of other religions strike a familiar note to the Indian ethos.

The Baha'i faith respects Jesus Christ as one of the messengers of God and views the mission of Jesus in the progressive economy of God's revelation as one of purifying the souls of individuals. Jesus is viewed as having fulfilled his mission successfully, so Christianity is not a failure. The challenge of the Baha'i is to progress, to move forward, and not to dwell on an already accomplished task. The mission of the modern age is the attainment of the collective sanctity of the entire human race. Bahaullah initiated this mission, and humanity should now join him in realizing this vision. Thus the challenge to Christians is to grow out of their "churchianity" and help the human race in its spiritual evolution. There has not been any major official collaboration or dialogue between the church and the Baha'i faith in India. However, the vigorous Baha'i community finds recruits from among the ranks of the church.

The Baha'is are also active in many of the countries in the Indian subcontinent. Being a universalistic religion, Baha'i is not limited by any language, as in the case of Islam by Arabic. Its translinguistic and cultural stance and its affirmative approach to other religions while calling for further advance in the world of religions will continue to have its appeal in the Asian context.

Bibliography

Cole, Juan R., and Moojan Memon, eds., *From Iran East and West* (1984). • Effendi, Shoghi, trans., *The Dawn Breaks* (1970). • Ferraby, John, *All Things Made New* (1977). • Jones, L. Bevan, *The People of the Mosque* (revised by Dwight Baker) (1988). • Memon, Joojan, ed., *Studies in Babi and Baha'i History* (1982). • "Bahaullah," "Baha'i," in *The Encyclopaedia of Religion, The Encyclopaedia Britannica* (Macropaedia), and *The Encyclopaedia of Islam.*

C. V. Mathew

Baines, Henry Wolfe

(b. England, 7 Feb 1905; d. Wellington, New Zealand, 29 Nov 1972). Anglican bishop of Singapore and Malaysia.

Educated at Repton and Oxford (Balliol), where he played cricket and soccer, and at Cuddleston, Baines was remembered for an ease of relationship, candor, and seriousness in which some saw early the making of a bishop. From 1927 to 1929, he was an ordained Student Christian Movement* (SCM) traveling secretary. He was ordained a deacon in 1930 and a priest in 1931. From 1934 to 1938, he was chaplain at St. John's Cathedral in Hong Kong. He became vicar of St. Nicholas Radford, Coventry, in 1938 and in 1941 rector of Rugby. He married Elizabeth Bartlett in 1944 and in 1949 was consecrated bishop of Singapore*. In 1960, he became bishop of Wellington, New Zealand.

In Singapore for much of the Malayan Emergency, Baines was noted for his strong ecumenical commitments particularly in relation to the Malayan Christian Council, Trinity Theological College, and reunion schemes in Singapore and Malaya. He increased the number of local clergy, and in 1958 Roland Koh was appointed assistant bishop. Baines worked for more positive statements on religious freedom in the new Malaya than was possible to attain but accepted the realities of the situation after 1957. He encouraged greater Christian participation in society and at the same time welcomed evangelicals into a traditionally high-church diocese.

Baines took to New Zealand a depth of interchurch experience and commitment to church union which sometimes ran ahead of others. In the capital city, he provided a strong church voice in civic and national affairs. He visited South Vietnam in 1971 and advocated humanitarian aid and religious contact. He opposed rugby tours to South Africa under apartheid. His breadth of vision gained from Asia was appreciated by other church leaders. He was of imposing stature and gracious manner, had a good voice, and was known as a person of prayer as well as a listener. He had a wide range of friends. When it was discovered that he had cancer, he announced, "my train has come in rather earlier than expected," and with dignity and grace he made peace with his family, his clergy, and with God.

Bibliography

Evening Post, Wellington (30 Nov 1972). • *Singapore West Malaysia Dioceses Association 1971 SWMDA Festival 21 June.* • Baines, H. W., "The Church in Malaya," *East and West Review* 19.3 (1953); "The Church in Singapore and Malaya, 1949-1960," *East and West Review* 26 (1960).

John Roxborogh

Bakht Singh

(b. Punjab, 6 Jun 1902). Indian evangelist and church planter.

"Brother" Bakht Singh is considered the Billy Graham of India* because of his great evangelistic impact on India in the 20th c. He hailed from the Punjab state and was born into a Sikh* family. He brought revival to the established churches and planted many new churches. Presently, across the country and abroad, but mostly in the state of Andhra Pradesh, there are about 1,300 churches which are identified as Bakht Singh's assemblies.

Though he went to a Christian boarding school as a youth, Bakht Singh was opposed to the Gospel and Christians. He even tore apart a Bible that was given to him after his intermediate exam. He went to England in Sep 1926 to study agricultural engineering with the support of his parents. He learned Western customs and had wonderful experiences, and yet he had no joy, nor did he meet anyone who had joy. His first encounter with Christ was aboard ship as he traveled on holiday from England to Canada. He attended a Christian service in the first-class dining salon. "As I knelt down, I felt my body was trembling," he writes in his testimony. "I could feel divine power entering into me and lifting me. . . . I was repeating the name of Jesus and began to say, 'Oh, Lord Jesus, blessed be thy name, blessed be thy name.' The name of Jesus became very sweet to me."

In 1928 Bakht Singh attended his first Christian service in Canada, and then in 1929 he asked a friend for a Bible. He received a New Testament and began reading the Gospels. Deeply convicted of his sins, he was assured of forgiveness through the blood of Jesus Christ by a voice. In two months he had "finished reading the whole Bible once and the New Testament several times." He was baptized on 4 Feb 1932 in Vancouver.

On 19 Oct 1932, Bakht Singh wrote to his father about his conversion. He prayed that the Lord might send someone to explain the letter to his father, since it was long and included many biblical references. An American missionary went to his hometown, met his father, and eventually led him to the Lord. His mother became a believer in Christ soon thereafter.

After completing his engineering studies in 1933, Bakht Singh returned to India and ministered in the northern part, including Karachi (present Pakistan*). He preached in different churches in Madras, and as a result a great revival of prayer and evangelism continued for two years (1938-40). From 1951 on, he labored to establish congregations across Andhra and in other areas of India. He even started some work in the Gulf countries, Britain, Germany, France, Australia, and New Zealand. His sermons were published in book form to give guidance to the churches he started.

These assemblies have some unique features carried over from Bakht Singh's personal practice. Most congregations gather around 10:00 A.M. and begin singing after an opening prayer. By this time only a few individuals, mostly women, have gathered, but as singing is in progress, people continuously come in. As they enter, they kneel down, pray, and then join the rest in singing. One of the leaders then gives an exhortation to worship, which is the first of three sermons. Sermons are interpreted into the local languages from English if it is a city congregation, but in the villages there is no such need. After the exhortation, there is an hour or so for individual worship through song or prayer. The second sermon is an exhortation centered on the Lord's Table or the Lord's Supper. This constitutes the peak hour of the service, after which the third sermon begins. This is the main sermon and the longest and is followed by an offertory, or, as it is often called, "worshipping the Lord by your substance." During the offering, the congregation sings, and then they all kneel down for the benediction. Finally, a small chorus is sung which is related to the final message. After the service, there is often a love feast, a simple meal. Then the congregation go out for open-air preaching and gather again for a smaller Gospel meeting. During the week, there are a Bible study and prayer meeting and a cottage fellowship. On Saturdays there is an all-night prayer for the Sunday worship.

Bakht Singh, who started his Christian life with hunger for the Word, expressed this through all of his life and ministry. When he preached, he quoted numerous Bible passages without any notes. At his first formal sermon, when his notes blew away, he felt God was telling him not to preach from his notes. His accurate memory came to his aid on this occasion. His sermons were very long and were interpreted sometimes into one or two languages. Main sermons ran between two and four hours. Followers of Bakht Singh were so focused on the Word of God that they hung Scripture passages on their walls rather than pictures. This constant emphasis upon Scripture frequently led to allegorical interpretation.

George Verwer, the founder of Operation Mobilization, has said, "I know the secret of this man; he prays every day till after the middle of the night." Even in his travels, Bakht Singh kept up this practice of prayer. When Rajamani, who later became his coworker, had become cold in his spiritual life, he was invited by Bakht Singh's mother to attend Bakht Singh's meetings. He writes, "Bakht Singh was simply clad and unimpressive. . . . That man's prayer went deep into my heart."

Bakht Singh's evangelistic meetings were quite effective and impressive. He would take advantage of every occasion — funerals, marriages, and cottage meetings — to share the Gospel. The Gospel was preached with such simplicity that anyone could understand it and respond. At almost every evangelistic assembly, there was a good response from the people.

Often the whole congregation would go out for open-air preaching. They would march out singing and preach the Gospel at different centers. As they marched and sang, the lay leaders would shout aloud Bible verses. They would stop at strategic centers, kneel on the road, pray, and preach. This scene was very impressive especially during the convocation season when thousands of men, women, youth, and children would joyfully witness for Christ in public. In a context where people are accustomed to political processions and riots, this kind of scene was unusual and captivating. In addition to these efforts, a group of people (sometimes as many as 100) would go on "campaigns" for a number of days preaching the Gospel and encouraging the local believers in towns and nearby villages.

A group of about 40-80 men and women live on Bakht Singh's campus in "Hebron." The young Christian leaders take on-the-job training for ministry. After they are proven in every aspect of Christian life and ministry, they are assigned to different congregations. This is equivalent to seminary training. Formal seminary training is discouraged for fear would-be pastors might become indoctrinated with liberal theology.

Bakht Singh also sponsored holy convocations. The first convocation involved 1,000 people celebrating for nine days. By the 1980s, these gatherings swelled up to 40,000 people meeting for 10 days. No fee was collected, and no appeals were made for funds. Voluntary donations in cash and in kind were sent to Hebron. At the end of this celebration, there were up to 200-300 baptisms in addition to hundreds of conversions.

Bakht Singh's theology and spirituality are focused on Jesus Christ and the need to be separated from sin. Such a concern takes its outward expression in many cultural ways, e.g., in the way men relate to women, in health habits, in dress and in money management. Women do not wear any ornaments. Going to theaters and drinking and smoking are not acceptable; congregants address one another as "brother" or "sister." As far as possible, they encourage segregation of men and women; women are subordinate and express this status by covering their heads with a veil in any public setting. Preachers dress in white, and they do not raise funds for any spiritual purposes. Possession of real estate or church property was avoided until 1958, when property was obtained in the heart of the city of Madras, called Jehovah-Sham. No silly talk of any kind is tolerated, and worshipers sit on mats. The assembly halls and the church premises are kept clean for Sunday worship. Men must not wear women's clothing and vice versa.

Bakht Singh had a deep love for people. Often this love was expressed in the context of hospitality, both providing and receiving it. Whenever people came, they would be invited to dine with him. He would mingle with people after the worship services and pray for their specific needs. Whenever he traveled by road or train, he would have a large contingent with him. At mealtime, he would see that each one was served before grace was offered. In his travels he would assist a blind man who was his coworker. The blind man had a great gift of music, composing songs and playing the harmonium.

Bakht Singh's love was also expressed in his prayer life. He would remember people's names and pray for them by name even if he had met them only once. When he did visitation, he would touch children and joke with them and take care to see that he did not forget their names. He would pray for people and ask for their prayers as well. Often he would pray for them until he received guidance for meeting their needs. His closing prayer, a prayer of intercession, would run for 30-40 minutes at times, and it would be very refreshing.

Bakht Singh's assemblies tended to be heterogenous. He loved the poor and the rich, and so the congregation constituted the rich, the poor, and the middle class without any caste distinctions. Since all sat on mats, this has become a very powerful demonstration of church unity in social diversity.

There is no ordained ministry, for every spiritual elder who has a good testimony is accepted to solemnize baptism and the Lord's Supper. Believers are baptized through immersion. Elders guide the church, and in some cases a full-time elder is called "servant of God." The Lord's Supper is observed every Sunday. Candidates for baptism testify to the congregation before they are baptized. During the baptism, they are interrogated extensively to make sure they have a genuine relationship with the Lord. After baptism, the candidates come to the front and kneel before the platform. The elders lay their hands on each of the baptized and pray for them individually. This ceremony is to symbolize their reception into the body of Christ.

Bakht Singh's assemblies have had a great impact in India for two basic reasons. First, they have sought to be indigenous. Second, they have focused on the basics of the Gospel: prayer, Bible study, holiness of life, Christian fellowship, concern for the poor, and the Great Commission.

Bibliography

Rajamani, R. R., *Monsoon Daybreak: A Stirring of the Spirit of God in South India* (1971). • Bakht Singh, *Joy Unspeakable and Full of Glory; The Skill of His Loving Hands;* and over two dozen other books available from Hebron, Hyderabad.

Kuchipudi Clement

Baldaeus, Philippus

(b. Delft, Holland, Oct 1632; d. 1671). Minister of the Dutch Reformed Church who made an attempt to indigenize the activities of the church in the initial period of the Dutch administration in Ceylon (Sri Lanka).

In 1654, Baldaeus completed his theological studies in Amsterdam, Groningen, and Leyden, applied for a position of predikant (minister) in the Dutch East-India Company, and was accepted in June. He was ordained on 14 Sept 1655, and in 1656 he proceeded to the East. He took up residence in Galle, which the Dutch held at that time, and from there he accompanied Dutch forces as an army chaplain for eight months. In 1658, he was appointed as chief predikant in the province of Jaffna, where he remained till the end of his sojourn in the East. Jaffna was the main theater of his religious activity. The South Indian city of Tuticorin and the ports along the coast of Madura were under the authority of the Dutch governor in Ceylon, and they also came under the pastoral concern of Baldaeus.

Baldaeus worked to wean the people from Catholicism and introduce Protestantism. But the task of keeping the former Catholics from falling back on the Catholic faith was a difficult one. Baldaeus made a study of the Hindu religion, the religion that the Tamil people historically adhered to, and he tried earnestly to learn the Tamil language. The prevailing practice had been to instruct native inhabitants in Dutch and seek to communicate with them through that language. In his effort, Baldaeus was one of the pioneers among Protestants. He prepared a question-and-answer formula containing fundamentals of the faith in an easily digestible form in order to introduce Protestant beliefs. This form was standardized and followed throughout the island in both the Sinhalese and Tamil languages.

Baldaeus translated into Tamil the essentials of the faith: the Lord's Prayer, the Ten Commandments, and the articles of faith. Five years after his departure from Ceylon, they were published in Rotterdam in 1671 as small booklets. He also prepared an elementary grammar of Tamil that listed basic rules such as verbal conjugations, the various cases of the noun, and the use of the singular and plural. Considering the pioneering nature of the work, this volume was commendable.

Baldaeus paid great attention to the establishment of schools and the education of the young. With the assistance of the Dutch government, he provided the 30 schools in Jaffna (formerly Roman Catholic*) with schoolmasters.

Baldaeus came into conflict in 1659 with the Dutch government over matters of church administration. The government turned down his proposal of administering the church by rotation of predikants. It was over the question of the control of schools that the conflicts between Baldaeus and the government came to a head in 1664. He objected to the idea that predikants were to be subordinate to the political authorities.

Baldaeus had to end his services abruptly. He departed for Holland by the end of 1665. However, there is no doubting the value of what he was able to achieve, for succeeding missionaries built upon the approaches and foundations he began.

Bibliography

S. Arasaratnam, "Reverend Baldaeus — His Pastoral Work in Ceylon, 1656-1665," *Ceylon Journal of Historical and Social Studies* 3 (1960). • R. L. Broher, "Philippus Baldaeus," *Journal of the Dutch Burgher Union* 41 (1951).

G. P. V. Somaratna

Baldwin, S(tephen) L(ivingston)

(b. Somerville, New Jersey, United States, 1835; d. Brooklyn, New York, United States, 1902). Missionary of the Methodist* Episcopal Church (North) (MECN) to China*.

Baldwin arrived in Fukien, Foochow, in 1858 and returned to America three years later because of the poor health of his wife, who died on the voyage home. In 1862 Baldwin returned to Foochow and was one of the first missionaries who proposed that Chinese churches should be self-supporting. In 1868 he was put in charge of his denomination's newsletter, *The Missionary Recorder.* He transformed it into an interdenominational newsletter and changed its name to *The Chinese Recorder* *(Jiao Wu Za Zhi).* This periodical became the most important document in understanding foreign missions in China. In 1871, on his third trip to China, he was appointed to be in charge of Foochow mission. After attending the conference organized by the MECN, he pastored churches in New York and New England, United States. In 1889 he was appointed to be in charge of the archives of the MECN. In the following year he was elected honorary secretary at the World Missionary Conference held in New York.

Bibliography

Carlson, Ellsworth C., *The Foochow Missionaries 1847-1880* (1974).

China Group

Bali, Christian Protestant Church in

(Gereja Kristen Protestan di Bali, GKPB). Commonly known as *Gereja Bali* (the Bali Church), GKPB is a relatively young church which marked its beginning with the baptism of 12 people (one woman and 11 men) on 11 Nov 1931 in the Yeh Poh, a small river west of Untal-Untal. This was a surprising event, as the Dutch East Indies government had forbidden any missionary to work in Bali since 1881, when a Balinese, baptized in 1872, inadvertently killed a Dutch missionary, Jacob de Vroom, and the work of the *Utrechtse Zendingsvereniging* (UZV) in Bali (1863-81) was considered a failure.

The Chinese Foreign Mission Union (ChFMU) came to Bali at the beginning of 1931 as an auxiliary body of the Christian and Missionary Alliance Church* (C&MA) and within a year succeeded in baptizing 12 Balinese. Those who had heard Tsang Kam Foek (the ChFMU evangelist) testified that, though Tsang was limited in his command of their language, he preached with power and persuasion so that his listeners were challenged to make a decision.

In 1932, the record showed that 235 Balinese had been baptized. Competition among the mission agencies, beginning in early 1933 with the arrival of Bible teachers from the *Gereja Kristen Jawi Wetan* (GKJW) under the leadership of Hendrik Kraemer*, resulted in division along denominational lines among the Balinese Christians. In 1992, there were more than 20 church organizations registered with the ministry for religious affairs in Bali. Christians comprise 0.8% (0.5% Protestants and 0.3% Catholics) of the population in Bali. The GKPB has 7,000 members.

Initially, members of the Bali Church were by and large evangelical Christians. In 1936, the Dutch *Zending* (mission) initiated a union of Balinese Christians, and the Bali Church inclined toward the Reformed church group, causing some members to seek affiliation with the C&MA. The majority, however, joined the ecumenical movement and formed the GKPB, inaugurated on 11 Aug 1949 with an organization patterned after the Presbyterian synod. GKPB is one of the founding members of *Persekutuan Gereja-gereja di Indonesia** (PGI) and is a member of the World Alliance of Reformed Churches and the World Council of Churches.

Its painful history of schism made GKPB develop an ecumenical* outlook, emphasizing that the church should be separated only because of location, and not because of language, race, or, worse, doctrine. Consistent with its belief, GKPB does not allow its members to establish branches in other regions, even though 75% of the Balinese Christians live outside Bali. Fellowship, theologically and organizationally, is important to GKPB and the ecumenical movement in Bali.

Bibliography

Kraemer, H., *From Missionfield to Independent Church* (1958). • Swellengrebel, J. L., *Kerk en Tempel op Bali* (1948).

KETUT WASPADA

Banerjea, Khrishna Mohan

(b. 24 May 1813; d. 1885). Banerjea was the second son of Jinban Khrishna Banerjea. When he was six years old, his parents sent him to David Hare's vernacular school in Calcutta. In 1824, he was admitted into Hindu College, Calcutta, and graduated in 1829, thereafter serving as assistant teacher in Hare's Pantaldanga School. His education had been financially supported by the Calcutta School Society. For his achievements in the fields of Oriental literature and higher education, he was given an honorary degree of doctor of law in 1876 by Calcutta University.

After hearing the lectures of Alexander Duff*, Banerjea was converted to Christianity and baptized in Apr 1832. From among Duff's Hindu students, he was the first person to embrace the Christian faith. In 1839, he was appointed minister of Christ Church in Calcutta. Within a few years, he baptized 59 youth. His aim was to convert a maximum number in a minimum of time. In 1848, he joined Bishop's College, Calcutta, as its second professor. In 1853, he was appointed examiner in Sanskrit and Bengali at Fort William College. In 1867, he was elected president of the faculty of arts and for several years was university examiner in Oriental languages.

Krishnan Mohan wrote articles such as the "Nature of Female Education," "Kulen Brahman of Bengal," and "Essay on Hindu Caste." These were published in the *Calcutta Review, India Review, Bengal Spectator, Mookeryees Magazine, Bengal Magazine, Way of Vedee,* and various other periodicals. He also wrote a play entitled *Persecuted.*

Banerjea was buried in the grounds of Bishop's College, Calcutta. His last words to his family were "Trust in the Lord."

Bibliography

Philip, T. V., *Khrishna Mohan Banerjea, Christian Apologist* (1982). • Das, Kumar, *The Shadow of the Cross: Christianity and Hinduism in a Colonial Situation* (n.d.).

ONKHOMANG. HAOKIP

Banerjee, Bhavani Charan. *See* Brahmabandhav Upadhyaya

Bangladesh

Bangladesh is located in the northeast of the Indian subcontinent. It became an independent, separate nation in 1971. While the area is ancient in terms of civilization and culture, it had existed as part of both the Moghul and British Empires, both of which left their mark (see Colonialism). It was, as almost all of India*, under British control until independence in 1947. The area of Bengal, home to the Bengali people and language, had been divided by the British into two administrative units: West Bengal (still an important state in India with its capital at Calcutta) and East Bengal (the present Bangladesh). While the people of Bengal are one, they were separated, for both administrative and control reasons, along basically religious lines. East Bengal was predominantly Muslim and West Bengal Hindu.

With independence, Muslim East Bengal was joined with Pakistan* (1,200 miles away) to form one country — Pakistan, East and West. These were people who differed from one another in language, culture, history, and tradition but were united by religion.

The agricultural East, even though it had the greater population, became quickly dominated by the more developed West. The tensions of this situation were magnified when the East won a national election in 1970 but the army refused to allow the new East-dominated government to take power. War broke out in Mar 1971, and Bangladesh declared itself independent. This bloody struggle ended quickly when India joined the war on the side of Bangladesh, and the Pakistan army surrendered on 16 Dec 1971.

Bangladesh became a new country, war-ravaged, agricultural, and poor. Bangladesh is a river delta drained by some of the great rivers of the world. It is still predominantly rural and agricultural, although urbanization and some industrialization are beginning to take place, especially in the capital, Dhaka, which has doubled in size in the last 15 years.

Bangladesh is a small country (55,598 sq. mi., or 143,998 sq. km.) with a population that is estimated as approaching 120 million. There is a staggering population density. It is one of the poorest nations on earth, with an average income of about $220 (US). Life expectancy, according to a World Bank report, is 58 years. The literacy rate is only 32% of the population. There have been fairly continuous political unrest and four separate military coups since independence.

The constitution of Bangladesh guarantees religious freedom, but it also states that Islam is the state religion of the country. Muslims constitute about 86% of the population, Hindus about 12%, Buddhists about .6%, and Christians about .5% (or one half of one percent of the population).

The major Christian denominations are Roman

Catholic*, Baptist*, Church of Bangladesh (Anglican*), Lutheran*, and Presbyterian*. Other denominations include the Assemblies of God and the Seventh-Day Adventist*. The Pentecostals* and the Korean Christians came after 1971.

Christianity, while very ancient on the subcontinent, first arrived in Bangladesh in 1576 through Portuguese missionaries who came along with traders to develop trading posts after Vasco da Gama sailed to the subcontinent around the southern tip of Africa in 1497. It would seem that some of the earliest churches in Bangladesh developed in these Portuguese settlements near what is now Chittagong, its second largest city and port. There were also Christian settlements at Hoshenpur in Mymensingh District and Sripur near Sonargaon, the old capital of Eastern Bengal. The church at Iswaripur, credited with being the first Christian church structure, was dedicated by Jesuit* missionaries on 1 Jan 1600. Only ruins of this church can presently be seen. Father Francis Fernandez was blinded and tortured and died in captivity in Chittagong on 14 Nov 1602. The first Protestant (Baptist) church was built in Dinajpur in 1796.

The oldest existing church is Holy Rosary, in the Tejgaon area of Dhaka, which was built in 1677. While a new church has been built, the old one has been preserved. This was followed by parishes in Nagari (1695), Padrishibpur (1764), and Hashnabad (1777), all of which were under the Portuguese and later the diocese of Mylapore (Madras, India), which was established as a diocese in 1606.

Dhaka was made a vicariate in 1852 and a diocese in itself in 1886. In 1950, Dhaka became an archdiocese. The diocese of Chittagong was created in 1927, as was the diocese of Dinajpur. This was followed by Khulna (formerly Jessore) in 1952, Mymensingh in 1987, and Rajshahi in 1990.

Of the approximately 500,000 Christians in Bangladesh, 200,000 are Catholic. With the coming of British rule, the Baptist and Anglican churches were firmly established. Most of the Bengali Christians of all denominations are converts from Hinduism*.

Today the majority of Christians, perhaps a little over one half, are indigenous tribal peoples, many of whom live on either side of the long Indian border. These people — Mandi, Khasi, Santal, Oraon, Mahali, Mundari, Pahari — have practiced a form of animism*. They have and continue to become Christians in significant numbers.

While very small in number, the Christian community has had a significant impact on Bangladesh, especially through its institutions — colleges, high schools, trade schools, medical* service, development and self-help projects, literacy* programs, and justice and peace efforts. These institutions and programs, while benefiting the Christian community, have served all people irrespective of creed and culture and have made the Christian presence in the country recognizable. Some Christian denominations which have not planted churches in Bangladesh have, nonetheless, contributed much through their development projects; notable here are the Mennonites* and the Christian Reformed World Relief Committee (CRWRC).

While earlier there was a heavy foreign missionary presence to Christianity in Bangladesh, that day is rapidly coming to an end. Christianity is much more indigenous, not only in Bangladesh, but of it. Church leadership across all denominations is now local. The Christian churches of Bangladesh continue, however, to be heavily dependent on foreign monetary assistance to continue their work.

Ecumenical* activities among the various Christian denominations are growing. In some areas, however, where the Christian denominations exist side by side, there is sometimes competition among them, and there is a significant number of marriages across denominational lines, a practice necessitated by the small size of the various communities. In some areas, joint prayer meetings are very popular.

While the churches enjoy freedom of worship, the government tends to be wary of their activities. Sunday is a regular working day in Bangladesh, where, according to Muslim practice, Friday is observed as a holy day.

The urbanization of the country, especially the growth of Dhaka, claimed by many to be the fastest growing city in the world, has also led to the increasing urbanization of the church, which was, like the country, highly rural and village-based. This will be a major adjustment for the Christian community in the years ahead, because the traditional Christian society *(shomaj)* tends to break down rapidly in urban settings.

Christians in Bangladesh are still small in number and poor, as is the country. Christianity is, however, vibrant and increasingly local. It will remain a very small minority of the total population with both the challenges and fears this generates, but Christianity is firmly planted and, by and large, the roots are strong.

Bibliography

D'Costa, Jerome, *Bangladesh Katholic Mondoli* (Catholic Church in Bangladesh), Vol. I (1988). • Clancy, Raymond J., *The Congregation of Holy Cross in East Bengal, 1853-1953,* 2 vols. (1953). • Goedert, Edmund N., *Holy Cross Priests in the Diocese of Dacca, 1853-1981* (1983). • Pinos, Luigi, *Catholic Beginnings in North Bengal* (1994). • Dutta, Denis Dilip, *Banla Churches Itihash* (History of the Church in Bengal) (Literature Department, Chittagong). FRANK QUINLIVAN

Bao Dai

(b. Hue, Vietnam, 1913, d. Paris, France, 31 Jul 1997). Thirteenth and last emperor (1926-45) of the Nguyen Dynasty (1802-1945) of Vietnam.

Originally named Vinh Thuy, Bao Dai, meaning "to preserve the greatness," was the only son of Khai Dinh, the emperor who was put on the throne in 1916. Bao Dai went to France to study and returned to Vietnam* in 1932. Confined to the imperial palace of Hue, Bao Dai acted as a powerless, nominal head of state. He accepted independence from the Japanese after they had removed the French from nominal power on 9 Mar 1945. Tran Tong Kim formed a new government. Several months later, the revolutionary Vietminh forced Bao Dai to abdicate (25 Aug 1945). He became high counselor to the new government of the Democratic Republic of Vietnam, but, in the course of the first Indochina War, Bao Dai opted again for the French. From 1949 to 1955 he held the position of chief of state of the State of Vietnam. He was totally dependent upon the French for financial aid and support. His prime minister, the Catholic Ngo Dinh Diem*, forced him to retire after a national referendum made clear that southern Vietnam opted for a republican form of government. Bao Dai then retired and moved to France. JOHN G. KLEINEN

Baptist Leadership Training, Thailand

(BLT). Program that equips new lay leaders in local areas to teach and care for the new believers in their villages without disrupting their means of support or their services; jointly sponsored by the Foreign Mission Board, Southern Baptist Convention, Thailand Baptist Mission (TBM), and the Thailand Baptist Churches Association (TBCA).

Jerry Hobbs began the work of BLT in 1972 (Bangkhla) with meetings held at the hospital or church and later a vacant missionary residence. The curriculum, taught by both Thais and foreign missionaries, was adjusted to meet the needs of the different leaders. In 1978, courses for seminary credit were offered.

In Nov 1979, BLT was officially recognized as a separate ministry under the newly formed Training Ministries Board. Bob Stewart was appointed as director, with Jerry Perrill, a seminary teacher, as consultant. The following year, the training was moved to Fellowship Baptist Church in eastern Prachinburi Province. There the work grew, and additional subjects were added for emerging leaders. Since that time, BLT work has expanded to include all areas of Thailand. The need for a basic leadership-training manual became evident, and in Feb 1982 missionaries requested BLT to write the course. The manual was not written until 1990, when Doug Ringer and a joint committee of Thais and missionaries wrote, tested, and published the two-part manual. The English version was printed in 1995 for use in other Asian countries.

Training is initiated from the local level, with decisions as to study times and subject matter being determined by the local leaders in consultation with the BLT director. Through the years, TBM has provided the majority of funding, with TBCA doing a smaller part. Local leaders or their group or church provides the transportation expense. Since its beginnings, BLT has proven to be an effective and efficient means of training local leaders of churches who do not meet seminary qualifications and are unable to leave the local setting for further study.

Bibliography

Report of the Thailand Mission (1973, 1979, 1980).

DOUG RINGER

Baptists

The Baptist movement began in England in 1612. Baptists are distinguished by their insistence that the church is made up of autonomous congregations of believers, and their consequent rejection of infant baptism in favor of the baptism of believers. Most Baptist churches in Asia trace their roots to missionary endeavor from Britain or North America.

*India**. The first Baptist churches in Asia were formed in Bengal by missionaries of the Baptist Missionary Society (BMS), led by William Carey* (1761-1834). Carey's first convert, Krishna Pal*, was baptized at Serampore in 1800. However, Carey and his colleagues made slow progress among the Hindu population. The Baptist churches planted in Bengal and other parts of North India tended to be heavily dependent on missionary protection, finance, and leadership. These problems (which Baptists shared with other Christians in the region) are reflected in the continuing relative weakness of the Baptist community today in North India. In parts of North India, some Baptist churches have joined the Church of North India* (CNI, 1970), where they retain their distinctive principles of baptism and worship within an episcopal church. In Orissa, churches of a Baptist tradition within the CNI, many of them comprising tribal people, form the overwhelming majority of the Christian community.

Baptists are most heavily concentrated among the tribal, formerly animistic peoples of Northeast India. The American Baptists commenced work among the Garos of Meghalaya in the 1860s and the Nagas* in the 1870s. The BMS entered Mizoram (see Mizo) in 1903. A series of revivals in the period 1900-14 led to rapid church growth throughout the region. Today the Baptist churches of Northeast India have over 600,000 members. In Nagaland and southern Mizoram, Baptists form the majority of the population.

Baptists are also numerous in parts of South India, where they have shared in the mass movements toward Christianity among the Dalit* (outcast) community. From the late 1860s onwards, the American Baptist mission to the Telegus saw significant growth among the Dalits. Some 30,000 members of the Sudra caste also became Christian between 1925 and 1935. The Samavesam of Telegu Baptist Churches now has a membership of about 430,000. Another large Baptist group in South India is the Convention of Baptist Churches of the Northern Circars, which owes its origin to Canadian missionary work. Today there are about 1.4 million Baptists in

India, which makes the denomination one of the largest Protestant bodies in the country.

*Bangladesh**. In this Muslim nation, Baptists form the largest section (about 30,000) of the tiny minority Christian population. The main groups are the Bangladesh Baptist Sangha (comprising churches planted by the BMS, some of which go back to Carey's day), the Bangladesh Baptist Fellowship (deriving from work by Australian and New Zealand Baptists), and the Garo Baptist Union (located among the tribal Garo people).

Sri Lanka. In Sri Lanka*, the Baptists represent the oldest of the modern Protestant missions. James Chater moved from Myanmar* (Burma) to Sri Lanka in 1812 to found the Baptist Missionary Society's (BMS) Sri Lanka mission. He reported in 1815 that he had yet to find 50 Sinhalese in Colombo to hear a sermon. He was, nevertheless, able to lay the foundation for the mission. He translated the New Testament into Portuguese and collaborated with the Bible Society* to prepare a Sinhala translation (see Bible Translation). He also opened schools for Sinhala, Portuguese, and English elementary education.

Chater's successor, Ebenezer Daniel, who arrived in 1830, initiated a regular program of evangelistic preaching in villages around Colombo. By his death in 1844, the Sri Lanka mission could boast over 500 church members and 1,257 pupils. Charles Carter, who served in Kandy in 1853-81 and 1888-91, is regarded as the best Sinhalese scholar to have arisen among European missionaries. He prepared a fresh translation of the New (1862) and Old Testaments (1876). He produced a Sinhalese grammar (1862), an English-Sinhalese dictionary (1891), and a Sinhalese-English dictionary (posthumously published in 1924).

Despite these eminent personalities, the Baptist mission as a whole stagnated from the mid-19th c. and fell behind the Methodists* and Anglicans*. The paucity of human and financial resources, lack of provision for training pastors, evangelists, and schoolteachers, and the rise of militant Buddhism* are the main causes for this retardation. The revival of Buddhism affected the Baptists most, since they confined their work to the Sinhala-speaking area of the country.

In addition to the activities of the BMS, the Lanka Baptist Mission (1887) and the Ceylon Baptist Union (1895) shared the Baptist mission in Sri Lanka. As a result of the effort made by W. M. P. Jayatunga, a Sinhalese minister, and C. E. Wilson, a missionary of the BMS, the Lanka Baptist Union was formed and the constitution was adopted in 1932.

The Lanka Baptist Union's original goal was to achieve total independence in finances and personnel for the Sri Lanka mission within 10 years. Although the mission found it hard to keep to this ideal when the government imposed restrictions on missionaries in the postindependence era, this became a blessing in disguise.

In 1958, the Sri Lanka Baptist Snagamaya (SLBS) was formed. It became legally independent of the mother mission in England. Nevertheless, as late as 1967 the SLBS remained dependent upon the BMS for financial support. Thereafter, BMS support was phased out, and in 1974 the process of devolution reached its terminus when all property formerly held by the BMS was vested in the SLBS.

The Baptist mission, together with other Christian denominations, suffered when the government took over the assisted schools in 1960. Only Carey College (1915) remained in the hands of the mission as a private school.

Despite the small size of the mission, SLBS has contributed to the national development in many ways. Apart from the contribution of the missionaries to Sinhala language and literature, Sinhalese such as C. H. Ratnaike (secretary of the National Council of Churches), S. J. de S. Weerasinghe (secretary of the Bible Society), and W. G. Wickremasinghe (principal of Carey and Trinity Colleges) have made great contributions to the nation. The Baptists' contribution to ecumenical cooperation is seen in their collaboration with Anglicans and Methodists in the Teachers Training College (1914), the Theological College of Lanka (1963), and several other joint ventures.

Myanmar (Burma). Christianity reached Myanmar as early as the 17th c. The earliest Anglican work began with an army chaplain who came with the British forces in 1825. An American Methodist couple named Carter came from India in 1879, but the British Methodists took over the mission work after the annexation of Upper Myanmar in 1886. The Baptist work began earlier, though unsuccessfully, with the British missionary Felix Carey* but thrived under American missionary Adoniram Judson*, who arrived at Yangon on 13 July 1813.

The Myanmar (Burma) Baptist Convention began as the Myanmar Baptist Missionary Convention in 1865. It was renamed the Myanmar Baptist Convention in 1954. Comprising 14 language and regional groups, it both cooperates with and coordinates the Baptist churches in Myanmar. In 1993, it had 77 associations, 3,513 local churches, 1,076,697 members, and 33 Bible schools.

The Myanmar (Burmese) Baptist Churches Union is a Barmar-speaking church association started as Yangon Baptist Association in Thonze (1860). In 1869, there was a growth in new churches. Between 1884 and 1890, many associations were formed. The Prome-Tharawady (1890) became the Henzada Burmese Baptist Association in 1900. In 1898, Upper Myanmar was represented by the Aunngpinle Baptist Association, which grew from the Tenasserim Mon-Baptist (1882). The Bago (Pegu) Burmese Association expanded with the inclusion of Syriam and Kyauttan. U Lu Din, from the normal school of the Baptist College, initiated a union of the different associations into the Myanmar Baptist Conference. By 1912, the conference had grown countrywide and represented all Barmar-speaking churches. After World War II, the name was changed to Myanmar Baptist Evangelistic Society, then the MBE Committee, and yet again to

Myanmar Baptist Mission Society. In 1964, it acquired its present name. It has six associations, 94 churches, and 25,000 members.

The Kiyin (Karen*) Baptist Convention (KBC) is the largest organization in the Myanmar Baptist Convention with 17 associations, 1,297 churches, and 372,856 members. The *Burmese Annual, 1928* records that the Kiyin Baptist Conference (as it was then known) started its mission work in 1828, beginning with home mission societies that also sent missionaries to other tribes. The Pa-thein (Bassein) Home Mission Society was formed in 1850 and the Yangon Home Mission Society in 1853. Thra Saw Peh of Pa-thein served as a pastor at the first Kachin Baptist Church in Myitkyina. Thra Blah Paw and Thramu Bessie rendered invaluable service to the Shan Buddhists. When Rev. Carson opened a mission station in the Chin* Hills, there were many Kiyin missionaries. Kiyin missionaries also worked with Josiah N. Cushing and Jonathan Wade in northern, southern, and eastern Shan State among the Shans, Lahus, Was, and Akhas. Between 1830 and 1863, KBC also sent missionaries to work among Thai Kiyins. Thra San Dun of the Pa-thein Home Mission worked in Thailand until 1932. Outstanding missionaries to the Kiyins include Mr. and Mrs. Boardman and Rev. and Mrs. Francis Mason, who succeeded them in 1831. Especially remarkable was Mrs. Boardman, who continued the work after her husband's death, going deep into the malaria-stricken jungle of Tavoy to work among the uncivilized Kiyin.

The Mon Baptist Churches Union is one of the smallest associations in the Baptist Convention. During the time of Judson, Mawlamyein (Moulmein), capital of Mon State, and Kyaikkame (Amherst) were mission headquarters for the missionaries, but the church grew very slowly. Rev. and Mrs. James Haswell arrived in 1835 and were the first missionaries to the Mons. One of their daughters, Susan, was the founder of the Mortaon Lane Girls' School, the English Girls' High School, and the Leprosy Home and Hospital. Notable Mon converts were Nai Myat Kyaw and Nai Mahn Boke. Sayama Daw Tin May started a Bible school in 1959. Nai Ba Shin served with the Myanmar Baptist Convention. In 1897, Dr. E. A. Stevens went to Thailand with Nai Taw Thun, Nai Shwe Gyaw, and Nai Di to distribute 500 tracts. Dr. Adamson and Akya Nai Leh started a church with 25 members in the village of Tapawlon, 10 miles south of Ayutthaya. Akya Nai Leh returned to Myanmar in 1910, but his son-in-law, Akya Nai Di, went back and started two Mon churches in Tapawlon and Bangkok with a total of 50 members.

The Arakhan (Rakhine) Baptist Churches Union is related to the Asho Chin Mission. The Asho Chins live mainly along the coast of Rakhine and the western range (the Rakhine Range). The Asho Chins initially resisted the Gospel, but today all the churches in the Rakhine State are Asho Chin churches. Steeped in Buddhism*, the Rakhines are still resistant to the Gospel. James Colmans and Mr. Fink of Serampore were the first missionaries to Rakhine, and Grover Comstock came in 1835; they had little success. Levi and Catherine Hall, teaming with other missionaries, the Barmar preacher Maung Khet, and the Rakhine evangelist Saya Koung Oung, managed to form the first Baptist church in Akyab and a second, smaller church in Kyaukpyu in 1839. Kincaid and Abbot joined them in 1840. Kincaid served the Akyab mission (only 13 members) for two-and-a-half years. By 1841, the Rakhine mission had increased to include several churches and schools.

Kincaid received a request from the chief of the Kamee tribe who lived along the Kaladan River 150 miles north of Akyab to preach and teach the children there. The request was met by his successor, Stilson, who helped the Kamees to develop their own dialect and writing. William J. Knapp prepared a Kamee catechism, and five Kamees were baptized in 1847.

Abbot went to Sandoway, a relatively cleaner and healthier coastal town, to work mainly with the Karen refugees and also the Barmar. Mrs. Abbot won her first Barmar convert in 1843. A small Barmar church with two national preachers was established in 1851.

Mission work in Rakhine State, hampered by poor location and communication, continues to be difficult and challenging. Seventeen missionaries have died for the Gospel. There is only one association, with 23 churches and 8,050 members.

Under the Myanmar Baptist Convention, the Shan Baptist Churches are divided into the south, north, east, and Shweli Valley Shans. The Pa-o are mainly from the south; the north has a mixture of Shan, Kachin*, Wa, and Lahu. In the east are Shans, Chinese, Was, and Lahus. Shans dominate the Shweli Valley, but there are also Kachins, Lahus, and Palaungs.

The Southern Shan Baptists have two associations, 44 churches, and 6,000 members. The Northern Shan Baptists have six associations, 157 churches, and 24,636 members. The Eastern Shan Baptists have three associations, 110 churches, and 15,589 members. Shweli Shan Baptists have one association, 12 churches, and 4,904 members.

The first mission station at Toungoon was started in Mar 1861 by Moses Homan Bixby. In the north, the mission stations were at Bhamo, Hsipaw, and Mongnai, and in the Shweli Valley at Namkhan. Rev. and Mrs. J. A. Freidy went to Bhamo in 1878. Dr. Cushing moved from Bhamo to Hsipaw, where he did extensive travels with Rev. Rose. Hsipaw Sawbwa, who had been helped by Dr. Cushing when he had problems with the British government, invited him to open the mission in Hsipaw, but lack of workers and finance led to its closure. A new station was opened at Namkhan in the Shweli Valley.

Wilbur Cochrane started the Namkhan station in 1892. The year 1914 saw the establishment of a Shan and Kachin church. In fewer than 10 years, a second Shan church was started at Se-lan village and a third in Mu-se. In 1942, there were about 500 Christian Shans in Shweli Valley. Saya Ai Pan opened a Shan Bible training school in Namkhan. It later reopened at Taunggyi in the south. The first Palaungs to be baptized were Soi Kham Binya and his wife in 1952.

The Pwo Kiyin (Karen) Baptist Conference has six associations, 199 churches, and 37,504 members. The Pwo-Kiyin Baptist mission began with Eleanor Macomber at Don-Yin village in 1836. The first convert was Pu Sang Pau, baptized on 12 Jan 1837. The following year, two Baptist churches were formed in Don-Yin village. Macomber was succeeded by Edwin Bullard and Rev. and Mrs. Durlin Brayton. They were assisted by local leaders Sra Kon Luht and Sra Myat Tha. The Pwo-Kiyin Baptist mission was located in three main areas: Pa-thein, Henzada-Danubyu, and Yangon-Maubin. In 1849 H. L. van Meter became the first missionary to work the Pa-thein field. He was assisted by Mahn Shwe Bo, who became the first Pwo-Kiyin ordained minister. The longest-serving missionary among the Pwo-Kiyins was Leonard Cronkhite, from 1884 until his retirement in 1922. By 1947, the Pa-thein field had 8,344 baptized believers and 92 churches with 21 ordained and 52 unordained pastors.

The Henzada-Danubyu field was started in 1854 with the transfer of Durlin L. Brayton from Mergui to Henzada. Within a year, he baptized 75 new converts and the Pwo-Kiyin pastor baptized 50. In 1855, Brayton moved to Yangon, where he served till his death in 1900. He translated and reviewed the Pwo-Kiyin Bible and did extensive evangelism among the Pwo-Kiyins.

The first missionaries in Maubin were Rev. and Mrs. Walter Bushell, who established the normal school. Carrie Putnam arrived in 1887. In 1908, the Pwo-Kiyin Conference was formed in Pa-thein, and Sra Byu was the first honorary secretary. Sra Kwa was elected full-time secretary in 1947.

The Asho Chin Baptist Conference has two associations, 20 churches, and 6,800 members. The Asho Chins are scattered along Rakhine Yoma, Bago Yoma, and the Irrawaddy and Sittang river valleys. Asho Chin Baptist churches initially included churches in the Rakhine State. In 1962, there were four churches, 534 members, and five workers in North Rakhine; seven churches, 557 members, and 11 workers in South Arakan; and 17 churches, 2,178 members, and 39 workers in the Magwe and Bago division.

The Myanmar Baptist Convention sent Mahn Company to work among the Asho Chins. He developed the Asho language. His script was later improved by E. O. Steven. In 1871, Shwe Daung, a Chin, preached in the Mindon area with a Barmar, Maung Htike. They were well received by both groups. In 1886, Arthur E. Carson was officially designated as missionary to the Asho Chins. He served eight years in Thayetmyo and then left for Hakka in the Northern Chin Hills. Rev. and Mrs. Carroll Condict arrived in 1912 and served in Thayetmyo until 1954. World War I and insurrection after independence hindered the mission work. W. F. Thomas of Henzada reopened the Asho mission work in Sandoway. Several missionaries served there for a short term after his departure. But the Asho Chin churches in Rakhine had been isolated for many years from their brothers on the east of the mountain, so they formed the Rakhine Baptist Churches Union. The Asho Chins from the Bago Yoma and along the Irrawaddy River formed the Asho Chin Baptist Conference.

The Kachin Baptist Convention is the second largest group after the Kiyin in the Myanmar Baptist Convention. It has nine associations, 219 churches, and 245,118 members. Mission among the Kachins began with a brief visit by A. Taylor Rose, Francis Mason, and Josiah N. Cushing. Though designated to work among the Shans, Cushing accompanied two Kiyin evangelists to work among the Kachins. On 13 Feb 1878, Mr. and Mrs. Albert J. Lyon arrived at Bhamo for their work among the Kachins. Unfortunately, Lyon fell ill and died within a month. He was succeeded by William Henry Roberts, who arrived on 12 Jan 1879. Prior to Roberts, James A. Friedly supervised the Kiyin evangelists in the hills. Kiyin evangelists to the Kachins were Thra Saw Peh, Thra Ne Hta, Thra Ko Te, Thra Maw Keh, and Thra Shwe Gyaw. In 1892, George Geis and his wife joined Roberts. They set up a new station at Myitkyina, which is still the headquarters of the Kachin Baptist Convention. On 19 Mar 1882, the first seven Kachin converts were baptized. In the span of 25 years, the work expanded: schools, a Kachin catechism and hymnal, leadership training and outreach in the north and south are among the accomplishments. By the second quarter-century, the Kachin Baptist Church became self-supporting and took initiative in assisting missionaries and evangelism among other indigenous groups such as the Lahu, Wa, Palaung, and Naga. Notable missionaries among the Kachins include William Henry Roberts, who worked for 35 years until his retirement in 1914; Ola Henson, who concentrated on literature work and served from 1890 to 1928; and George Geis, who worked until his retirement in 1936. The missionaries who returned after World War II included Herman Tegenfeldt, and the Misses Bonney, Taylor, and Mary Laughlin. They helped to rebuild and reconstruct the Kachin mission field.

The Zomi Baptist Convention was formed in 1953 with Hau Go elected as its first general secretary. It is the third largest group in the Myanmar Baptist Convention with 20 associations, 875 churches, and 182,575 members.

Baptist work among the Chins may be divided into four periods: the first decade until the death of Arthur Carson; from then until 1924; from 1924 to 1941, during which time the churches increased rapidly until World War II stopped missionary work; and from 1942 on.

Carson and his wife, accompanied by Kiyin evangelist San Win from Henzada-Pathein, left Thayetmyo for Hakka in 1899. Shwe Zan served at Khawsak in the Siyin Valley in the Tiddim area. With him was Po Ku, who later moved to Tonzang. Maung Gone worked at Laizo in the Falam district. Other Kiyins were Po Aye at Lumbang,

Maung Lun at Zokhua, Maung Kya at Thlantland, and Kyi Ghine at Hakka. During Carson's time, 100 converts were baptized, a hospital established, and the Hakka language reduced to writing.

In 1908, Herbert J. Cope and his wife succeeded Carson in the Tiddim area. Dr. and Mrs. J. G. Woodin took charge of the Hakka hospital. They started two stations for evangelistic and medical work, the latter of which was not very successful because the Chins are basically healthy and robust and trust in their ancient system of sacrifice and propitiation to ward off sickness. The evangelistic work, however, was successful. By 1915, Chin Christians numbered 600 in eight churches. By 1924, Chin churches had become self-supporting and the Gospel had taken root in many villages. The work was further aided when Dr. and Mrs. Chester U. Strait started a Bible school in Hakka. After learning the language, they began a new translation of the New Testament from both Greek and English. With the help of San Ling, they completed it in 1940. During his 30 years of service, Cope also managed to publish the New Testament and a hymnal in Tiddim Chin in 1934.

The strong foundation laid by missionaries enabled national leaders to continue the work when the missionaries had to leave Myanmar in 1965. The Kachin Baptist Convention celebrated its centenary in 1975 with the baptism of 6,000 people and the launching of the 3/300 mission project (300 volunteers to evangelize Kachin State within three years). The Kiyin Convention celebrated its 150th jubilee and the 125th jubilee of the Kiyin Holy Bible in 1978 in Tavoy. The celebrations included the Kyo Tha Byu 5-year mission project, leadership promotion, and the opening of three mission fields in southern Naga Hill, Bago Yoma, and the Thaton district to work among the Kiyin animists and Buddhists. In the early 1980s, the Chin Baptist Convention also started a special mission project called Chin for Christ in One Century (CCOC). The Shan Baptist Convention celebrated its centenary in Namkhan in 1985.

The Myanmar Baptist Convention belatedly celebrated its 175th jubilee in Dec 1990 (two years late). It brought together 20,000 Baptists from all over Myanmar. The A.D. 2000 Baptist Mission arose from this event. Its objective was to reach everyone in Myanmar with the Gospel of Jesus Christ and at least to double the number of churches and membership by the year 2000.

The Naga Baptist Convention, formed in 1992, was the fruit of the joint efforts from 1979 of the Kiyin Baptist Convention and the Myanmar Baptist Convention. It now has 101 churches, 23,065 members, and 137 ministers.

The Wa Mission is a joint effort of the Baptist Convention Evangelism Department and the Wa Baptist associations of the Eastern Shan State. The first 39 converts were baptized in Feb 1992. The work has now extended to 50 villages.

The Chindwin Baptist Mission was initiated by the Zomi Baptist Convention (ZBC). In Jul 1991, the ZBC teamed with the Myanmar Baptist Convention for greater effectiveness. They were joined in 1992 by the Lisu and Kachin Baptist Conventions and the Myanmar Baptist Churches Union. The focus is the Buddhists in the seven townships of the Sagaing division. Over 100 Buddhists were converted in 1992.

*Thailand**. American Baptist missionaries first entered Thailand in 1833 from Burma. In 1837, they planted what later became the Maitrichit Chinese Baptist Church in Bangkok, the first Protestant church in East Asia. After the opening of China* to Western missions in the 1840s, Thailand tended to be neglected, but the missionary exodus from China after 1949 again focused attention on Thailand. The Southern Baptists arrived in 1949, and the American Baptists returned in 1952. Many of the Chinese Baptist churches in Thailand are affiliated with the ecumenical Church of Christ in Thailand (1934). As in Myanmar, however, the most responsive group have been the Karens; the Thailand Karen Baptist Convention has some 14,000 members. Baptists account for about one-quarter of Thailand's approximately 100,000 Protestants.

The first 13 Southern Baptist missionaries to Thailand were displaced from missionary work in China. Mr. and Mrs. E. D. Galloway arrived in 1949 and found Baptists from China and India. They were encouraged and aided by the Chinese congregation of Maitrichit Baptist Church. While learning the Thai language, these missionaries went to work evangelizing the Chinese population. By the end of the first five years, the foundations of seven churches had been laid.

In 1952, two new couples were appointed specifically for Thailand. The first work outside of Bangkok was begun in the ancient capital city of Ayutthaya in 1952. The Deaver Lawton family moved there in 1953, and Ayutthaya Baptist Church was organized in 1967. Work was opened in Cholburi in 1954 by Ronald Hills, and a church was organized in 1959. Between 1955 and 1960, work was begun in seven new cities outside of Bangkok.

During the 1960s work was opened at Sri Racha (1961), Bangkla (1963), Rayong (1968), and Pattalung (1968). During the decade, eight churches were organized and five new chapels were started.

In addition to church-planting work during this early time, several types of institutional work were begun. The Thailand Baptist Theological Seminary was started by Glenn Morris in Oct 1952 with five students. Today's Baptist Christian Education was started by Mary Gould in 1953 to produce children's Sunday school and vacation Bible school literature. The Baptist Bookstore was begun in 1953 to distribute Christian literature in Chinese, Thai, and English. In 1958, the present-day Christian Conference Center was purchased at Jomtien Beach in Cholburi. Baptist Leadership Training was begun by Bob Spear and Jerry Hobbs, and has been carried to its present-day importance by Bob Stewart. In 1953, the Baptist Student Center was opened to offer English classes to students as an evangelistic outreach ministry.

In 1959, a leprosy clinic was opened. Baptist Mass Communications had its early beginnings in 1960-61. Harold Reeves began a radio ministry that eventually included films and TV. This ministry continues today on a project-by-project basis. Bangkla Baptist Hospital opened in 1964 in a rural area that had no government medical services. Fred Medcalf, Orby Butcher, Harlan Willis, and Rosemary Spessard were the first missionary staff. The hospital rapidly became a center of Christian influence for all of Prachinburi Province.

The 1970s were a period of transition from missionary prominence to a period of growth in national leadership. The Thailand Baptist Convention was organized in 1976 and includes churches in the Thailand Baptist Churches Association (TBCA), Chinese churches from the Church of Christ in Thailand, Karen, and Lahu Baptist Churches. In Jul 1978, there were over 12,000 members of Baptist churches (American Baptists and Southern Baptists) among all ethnic groups in Thailand, with 22 organized churches and 23 pastors. By 1995, there were 40 Baptist churches.

*Philippines**. In 1900, missionaries from the American Baptist Missionary Union were among the first Protestant groups to enter the predominantly Roman Catholic* Philippine Islands following the American annexation of 1898. Their leading pioneer, Eric Lund (1852-1933), was in fact a Swede. The mission founded some major educational institutions and set up the Convention of Philippine Baptist Churches (1935), which remains marginally the largest Baptist body in the Philippines, with approximately 89,000 members in 677 churches. After World War II, partly in response to the missionary withdrawal from China, other Baptist groups entered the Philippines, notably the Foreign Mission Board of the Southern Baptist Convention. The four Southern Baptist conventions of churches now rival the 1935 convention in the size of their membership. Other Baptist groups from the United States, mostly of conservative inclination, have also entered the arena, with the result that the approximately 314,000 Baptists in the Philippines today present a complex and fragmented denominational picture.

*Indonesia**. Baptist work in what is now Indonesia dates from 1813, when the BMS missionary, William Robinson, landed in Java. The outstanding Baptist missionary in the early 19th c. was Gottlob Bruckner, an Englishman who became a Baptist on the mission field. Serving faithfully among the Javanese from 1814 to 1857, Bruckner made the first translation of the New Testament into one of Indonesia's hundreds of tribal languages. (The complete Bible had been available in Malay since 1733.)

Yet no lasting Baptist work developed from the sacrifices made by the early pioneers. The Dutch took over the Indies again and drove out British missionaries. Not until well into the 20th c. (after World War II) did Baptists begin to take root in Indonesian soil, and this time they came from many different countries.

Following is a brief description of the six distinct Baptist associations in Indonesia today:

1. Fellowship of Irian Jaya Baptist Churches *(Persekutuan Gereja-gereja Baptis Irian Jaya, PGBIJ)*. After colonial forces had been driven out by Indonesian freedom fighters in 1945-49, the Dutch held on a while longer in New Guinea, the second largest island in the world. Baptists from Australia worked in the eastern half of the island (Papua New Guinea) and, in 1955, also began to survey the possibility of working among Stone Age tribes in the western half (Irian Jaya, a province of Indonesia).

Evangelization among the Dani (or Lani) of the Baliem Valley began in 1956 and developed into a people movement, as Danis piled up their fetishes for burning. The first converts were baptized in May 1962, but four months later, animists attacked and massacred many believers (see Animism). The church continued to grow, and by 1982 Baptists were baptizing 7,000 Danis in a single year.

Meanwhile the Fellowship of Irian Jaya Baptist Churches had been established in Dec 1966 and later merged with an earlier group, the spiritual heirs of Dutch Baptist missionaries who had labored there from the 1930s to the 1960s.

The Indonesian government, by moving homesteaders from overcrowded Java, has opened new home mission fields for the fellowship. By the mid-1990s, there were 36,000 baptized believers (plus 13,500 potential baptismal candidates) in 170 congregations. Among their ministries were a theological college, two Bible schools, a hospital, and an agriculture/forestry center.

2. Evangelical Baptist Association of Indonesia *(Gereja Perhimpunan Injili Baptis Indonesia, GPIBI)*. About 1925, a persistent Dutch-American named John G. Breman began evangelizing among the Dayaks of western Kalimantan. He led the way toward a national convention (organized in 1956 and first designated "Baptist" in 1965). A self-styled doctor, he laid the groundwork for Conservative Baptist missionaries from the United States who arrived in 1961 and established Bethesda Hospital at Serukam, an outstanding medical institution. Other ministries of Evangelical Baptists include youth hostels, Bible schools, and Theological Education by Extension (TEE).

In 1984, the Evangelical Baptists also began working outside Kalimantan, especially in cooperation with a large nondenominational evangelical seminary in Central Java. By the mid-1990s, they had 5,500 baptized believers in 119 congregations on Java, Sumatra, and Kalimantan, with home mission work on Bali* as well. Evangelical Baptists have not joined the Baptist World Alliance but cooperate with others through the Baptist Fellowship of Indonesia *(Persekutuan Baptis Indonesia, PBI)*.

3. Union of Indonesian Baptist Churches *(Gabungan Gereja Baptis Indonesia, GGBI)*. The closing of China to foreign missionaries in 1949 sent Southern Baptists

(USA) looking for other fields in Asia. On Christmas Day 1951, three old China hands landed in Jakarta, capital of Indonesia. One of their first Indonesian coworkers was Pastor Ais Pormes, who as a youth had flown away from his native Moluccas after helping rescue the crew of a downed American warplane. Getting an education in Australia and America, he then came back to plant what soon became a large Baptist church in the capital city.

During the 1950s and 1960s, Southern Baptist missionaries started many institutions in Java: a seminary, a publishing house, a hospital, and several student centers. Yet Baptist church growth remained relatively slow and weak till the aftermath of the failed Communist* coup in 1965. Then Baptists, like other denominations, capitalized on a phenomenal turning to Christ in Java and on other islands as well.

The Union was established in Aug 1971. It has continued to work with Southern Baptists and also with Baptist missionaries from Japan*, Korea*, and elsewhere. Another hospital and a rural development model have been established on Sumatra, a university in eastern Java, and several more theological schools in various places. Baptist churches have been planted on Java, Sumatra, Bali, Ambon, Ceram, Kalimantan, Sulawesi, Timor, and Moa. By the mid-1990s, the Union's evangelism coordinator estimated 50,000 baptized believers in 625 congregations.

4. Convention of Indonesian Baptist Churches *(Kerapatan Gereja Baptis Indonesia, KGBI)*. In the late 1930s and 1940s, several young people from the old-line Protestant Reformed denomination of Minahasa (northern Sulawesi) studied at a Christian & Missionary Alliance* Bible school in southern Sulawesi. Convicted about the need for personal faith and believers' baptism, they returned home to bring new spiritual life to needy churches. But church leaders did not welcome this new movement. These young evangelicals then formed a new denomination in Oct 1951.

Several young people from the new group studied at the Baptist seminary in Semarang, Java. Gradually they came to realize that they were in fact Baptists and began to use that name in 1979. Characteristically missionary in outlook, they began to reach out to other parts of Sulawesi*, to the Sangir-Talaud Islands, to Halmahera*, to several areas in Java and Sumatra, and especially to western Kalimantan*.

Both Canadian Baptist and Southern Baptist missionaries work with this convention, especially at its seminaries, one in Manado (northern Sulawesi) and another in Pontianak (western Kalimantan). By the mid-1990s the convention claimed 7,000 baptized believers in 214 congregations.

5. Independent Baptists in Indonesia *(Gereja Baptis Independent di Indonesia, GBII)*. Independent Baptist missionaries began to arrive in Indonesia in 1970, sent by World Baptist Fellowship, Baptist Bible Fellowship (USA), Baptist Bible Fellowship (Japan), Macedonia Baptist World Evangelization Crusade, and other groups. Indonesian government policy forced them all to establish a common organization in 1986.

The Independent Baptists' greatest strength is in Jakarta, where a Bible school was started in 1971. However, there are also churches and branch Bible schools in western and central Java and in northern Sumatra. By the mid-1990s, Independent Baptists estimated that they had 5,000 baptized believers in 56 congregations. They have not joined the Baptist World Alliance but cooperate with others through the Baptist Fellowship of Indonesia.

6. Jakarta Synod of the Baptist Christian Church *(Sinode Gereja Kristen Baptis Jakarta, SGKBJ)*. In 1952, a small group left a Mandarin-speaking congregation in Jakarta. Through the influence of a pastor who moved from Hong Kong, these believers became Baptists in 1953. Later they were assisted by an American missionary supported through Baptist Mid-Missions.

Like many other Asian evangelicals, these Indonesians of Chinese descent consider themselves one church with several congregations. By the mid-1990s, they reported 2,000 members in Jakarta and also on Belitung and Sumatra. They assist 28 home missionaries in Java and Irian Jaya, and since 1980 they have published a quarterly magazine. The Jakarta Synod has not joined the Baptist World Alliance, but cooperates with others through the Baptist Fellowship of Indonesia.

*Japan**. The first Baptist church in Japan was formed by four missionaries of the American Baptist Missionary Union in 1873. The American Baptist mission was followed in 1889 by the Southern Baptists, who began work in southwest Japan. Government pressure compelled the two groups of churches to unite in 1940, and in 1941 to join a united Protestant church. After World War II, some churches remained within the united church. Others formed the Japan Baptist Convention in 1947 (related to the Southern Baptists) and the Japan Baptist Union in 1958 (related to the American Baptists). The Convention is now the largest of several Baptist bodies in Japan, with approximately 31,000 members out of a total Baptist population of 48,000.

*Korea**. The Korean Baptist church started with the arrival in Seoul in 1889 of independent missionary Malcolm C. Fenwick* (1863-1935) from Canada. Nondenominational by background, he studied the Korean language during his first 10 months in Seoul and then went through Songchun in Hwanghae Province to Wonsan, where he established residence and began mission work. The mission field of Korea was then divided between the Presbyterians and the Methodists following an earlier comity arrangement. To avoid friction, Fenwick chose to work in Manchuria, Khan Island, and Siberia. In 1893, he organized the Korean Itinerant Mission and attempted to follow the model of the early church in mission as recorded in the book of Acts. In 1901, he took over the mission work of the Baptists throughout the province of Chungchong. In 1906, he organized the Church of Christ in Korea by combining his own itinerant mission with the mission work in Chungchong Province.

The evangelical, indigenous Church of Christ in Korea refused to submit to the oppressive religious measures of the Japanese government in 1944 and thus became disorganized as a denomination. But as soon as Korea was liberated in 1945, the leaders of the former denomination sought affiliation with a Protestant body of similar faith in America. In 1949, the Church of Christ in Korea affiliated with the Southern Baptist Church (America) and became the Korean Baptist Church. It later received mission support from the Southern Baptists of America, enabling vigorous mission activity and church growth. Presently there are about 1,800 Baptist churches in Korea with a membership of over 500,000.

*Hong Kong**. The first two Baptist churches in Hong Kong were formed in 1842 and 1843 by American Baptist missionaries. However, Baptist work in the territory remained on a small scale until the closure of China after 1949, when the first Southern Baptist missionaries arrived to assist the very small Hong Kong Baptist Association (now Convention). This has grown to a current membership of 46,000.

*Taiwan**. The first Baptist church in Taiwan was planted in 1949 from mainland China* by the Southern Baptists. Growth was rapid until the mid-1960s, but then slackened. Current Baptist membership is over 20,000.

*Vietnam**. The first missionaries of the Southern Baptist Foreign Mission Board to South Vietnam were Herman and Dottie Hayes, who arrived with their three children in Nov 1959. They were joined by two other families in Mar and Jul 1960, respectively.

The first Baptist missionaries resided in Saigon (Ho Chi Minh City), and later the city became the headquarters for the Baptist Mission and denomination in Vietnam. In 1961, a language study center for incoming Baptist missionaries was established in Da Lat. In the late 1960s, a more formal language school was established in cooperation with other evangelical groups.

The strategy decided upon was to place missionaries in as many major cities as possible rather than clustering them in Saigon. By 1968, there were personnel residing in Saigon, Thu Duc, Can Tho, Da Lat, Cam Ranh, Nhatrang, Qui Nhon, Danang, and Hue. By the early 1970s, there were 46 Southern Baptist ministries and bookstores.

The Baptist Publications Department, begun in 1962, produced Bible study and doctrinal materials for various age groups as well as pamphlets and tracts, and also operated a chain of book outlets. The Baptist Communications Center was established in 1966. Among other activities, the center produced radio programs with corollary correspondence courses and motion pictures based on biblical concepts.

In 1967, the Vietnam Baptist Theological Seminary was established with a campus at Thu Duc and extension centers around the country. The seminary was the outgrowth of leadership training classes based on a curriculum drawn up in 1964 and conducted wherever missionaries were in residence. The seminary was moved to suburban Saigon in 1968 and had its first three graduates in 1969. It had graduated a total of 32 students by the time of its closure in 1975. In the spring of 1975, its enrollment was 32 resident students and 120 in the Theological Education by Extension program.

In 1969, the Baptist Building in suburban Saigon was dedicated. It housed the Publications Department, a bookstore, meeting rooms, administrative offices, and guest apartments. In 1972, the Christian Social Ministries Department was established primarily to equip local congregations for ministry in their communities. In 1975, land in Saigon was purchased for building facilities to meet the needs of the local ministry and training programs and for the national administrative offices.

In 1971, the United States military at Cam Ranh handed over to the local Baptists an orphanage which they had built and managed. In 1975, Nguyen Xuan Ha, the director, moved the whole orphanage and staff, almost 100 persons, to Dallas, Texas, where adoptive homes were secured for the children.

A Bible study for expatriates begun in 1960 by missionaries in Saigon grew over time into the Trinity Baptist Church, which ministered to thousands of civilian and military expatriates until 1975. When the missionaries and Vietnamese Baptist leaders left South Vietnam in 1975, there were about 50 local Baptist churches, most meeting in homes or temporary facilities. Grace Baptist Church in Saigon, established in 1962, remained open and under the leadership of Pastor Le Quo Chanh.

Overview. Today there are at least three million Baptists in Asia, affiliated with different national Baptist conventions and fellowships. Many of these are members of the Baptist World Alliance (1905). The greatest Baptist concentration is in a belt extending from northeast India across Burma into northern Thailand; in much of this belt, Baptists form the dominant Christian community. It should also be remembered that many Protestants in mainland China follow Baptist principles and practice; this is due partly to government opposition to infant baptism.

Bibliography

Downs, F. S., *Christianity in North East India* (1976). • Fridell, E. A., *Baptists in Thailand and the Philippines* (1956). • Hminga, C. L., *The Life and Witness of the Churches in Mizoram* (1987). • McBeth, H. L., *The Baptist Heritage* (1987). • Maung Shwe Wa, and G. and E. Sowards, eds., *Burma Baptist Chronicle* (1963). • Stanley, Brian, *The History of the Baptist Missionary Society, 1792-1992* (1992). • Wardin, A. W., ed., *Baptists across the World* (1995). • Charter, H. J., *Ceylon Advancing* (1955). • Maung Latt, Johnny, *The Baptists in Burma, 1813-1976* (1977). • Chit Sein, U, *175th Jubilee Celebration of the Myanmar Baptist Convention* (Dec 1990). • Margay Gyi, *The Baptist Mission Today in Myanmar* (1990). • Young, Joshua A., *Report on AD 2000 Mission to 126th Board of*

Management Annual Meeting. • Anderson, Courtney, *To the Golden Shore* (1956). • *Suara Baptist* (The Baptist Voice) (Jan-Dec 1994).

BRIAN STANLEY, with contributions from G. P. V. SOMARATNA, SAW DANIEL, TOM WILLIAMS, WILLIAM N. MCELRATH, KIN HUH, and LEWIS I. MYERS, JR.

Bardaisan

(ca. 154-222). Christian philosopher in the court of Abgar* VIII in Edessa, capital of Osrhoene*; he is known in Latin sources as Bardesanes.

A description by Julius Africanus in about 212 characterizes Bardaisan as an able archer, but it does not discuss his theology. During his lifetime, and soon after by Eusebius, Bardaisan was recognized as a Christian theologian.

Bardaisan, together with his son Harmonius and his disciples, created a significant corpus of original Syriac compositions, including Christian hymns and theological treatises. Because he was declared a heretic by later Christian theologians, most of his works did not survive, except in quotations by his detractors, especially Ephrem of Syria. The primary source for our knowledge of his thought is *The Book of the Laws of the Countries,* which contains a dialogue between Bardaisan and Awida, a student (perhaps a Marcionite); the dialogue was recorded by another student, Phillip. Use of this source in the *Vita Abercii* does not add to our knowledge of Bardaisan. A fragment of a treatise on astronomy was preserved by George, Bishop of the Arabs (*Patrologia Syriaca* 2.612-15). Bardaisan's theology, mistakenly characterized by some as gnostic, encouraged a developmental spirituality (similar to that of Clement of Alexandria) and used Greek and local philosophical and scientific traditions to articulate his faith and understanding of the cosmos. There are interesting parallels with the Pseudo-Clementine and the Thomas traditions.

Bibliography

Text: *Patrologia Syriaca;* English translation from the Dutch in H. J. W. Drijvers, *The Book of the Laws of the Countries: Dialogue on Faith of Bardaisan of Edessa* (1965). • Bundy, D., "The Life of Abercius: Its Significance for Early Syriac Christianity," *Second Century* 7 (1989-90). • Drijvers, H. J. W., *Bardaisan of Edessa* (1966); *East of Antioch* (1984). • Jansma, R., *Natuur, Lot en Vrijheid: Bardesanes, de filosoof der Arameërs en zijn images* (1969). • Teixidor, J., *Bardesane d'Édesse: La première philosophie syriaque* (1992). DAVID BUNDY

Barhebraeus

(1226-86). Known as Grigor bar 'Ebraya in Syriac and Greek, and as Grigor abu-l-Farag ibn al'Ibri in Arabic, Barhebraeus was perhaps the greatest encyclopedist of the Syriac church. He was West Syrian, born at Melitene just as the Mongols (see Mongolia) entered the Middle East. He studied at the Monastery of Bar Sauma at Tagrit and became an active churchman and writer. His most important works were: (1) *The Candelabra of the Sanctuary,* a massive synthesis of Syriac Christian theology; (2) a careful philological and theological biblical commentary which drew upon earlier scholarly traditions, *The Storehouse of Mysteries;* (3) a history of the world, *Chronography;* (4) a history of the church, *Chronicon Ecclesiasticum;* (5) a summary of canon law, *Nomocanon;* and (6) a study of cosmography, *Ascension of the Spirit.* These demonstrate his ease with Syriac, Arabic, and Persian sources. He also wrote treatises on political science, Greek philosophy, grammar, and the natural sciences.

Bibliography

A. Baumstark, *Geschichte der syrischen Literatur* (1922). • Fiey, J.-M., "Esquisse d'une bibliographie de Bar Hebraeus," *Parole de l'Orient* 13 (1986). • Segal, J., "Ibn al'Ibri," *Encyclopedia of Islam* 3 (1971). DAVID BUNDY

Basel Christian Church of Malaysia

Lutheran* church in the state of Sabah (formerly North Borneo) which, together with the Roman Catholic* and Anglican* churches, was instrumental in the modernization of Sabah*.

Originally an offshoot of the Basel Mission in mainland China*, the Basel Christian Church became an appendage in 1902. Fashioned after the Three-Self Movement*, the church attained independence in 1925 and was named the Borneo Basel Self-Established Church. When Malaysia* was formed, the church was renamed as the Basel Christian Church of Malaysia (1964).

Though Reformed in nature, the church opted to join the Lutheran confession in 1975. In 1977 it joined with the Protestant Church in Sabah, the Lutheran Church of Malaysia, and the Evangelical Lutheran Church of Malaysia to form the Federation of Lutheran Churches in Malaysia. It became a full member of the Lutheran World Federation in 1978.

The church began in Nov 1882 when two of its future members landed at Kudat, then capital of the British North Borneo Chartered Company, on a fact-finding mission aimed at resettling Hakka Christian refugees from China. The chartered company, which had secured rights over the whole of North Borneo in 1881, faced a labor shortage in its efforts to open up the territory and requested Rudolph Lechler* to recruit Chinese laborers. Lechler was one of the first two Basel Mission missionaries to China and was helping Hakka refugees escape the reprisal of the Ching Dynasty authorities after the failed Taiping* Revolution. On 4 Apr 1883, 14 Hakka families, 96 persons in all, resettled in the Kudat Peninsula. Other groups followed in 1888, 1913, and 1914, in addition to unaided arrivals, and they spread to other towns. Pious Christians, they gathered for worship every Sunday in different houses and became the founding members of the local congregations in Sabah. They settled into their adopted land and laid the foundation for today's thriving agricultural and economic development in their respective districts. They established Chinese mission schools, and in 1903 the church formally started a school in Kudat. Well-known schools in Sabah are Lok Yuk, Sung Siew, Yuk Yu, and Anglo-Chinese.

After World War II*, the church needed funds for reconstruction. In 1947, chief pastor Lee Wok Sin established ties with the Lutheran World Federation; hence the Federation's modest participation in the education of Sabah until the nationalization of the education system by the Malaysian government in the early 1970s, which greatly reduced the domination of the church in this field.

The church was initially led by laypeople with minimal supervision from the parent mission. Its first pastor, Wong Tien Nyuk, came in 1902. With its first synod in 1925, which also marked its independence, the church assumed a polity akin to a parliamentary democracy with lay leadership. In 1981, Thu En Yu was appointed bishop, marking a new era in the church.

From 1975, the church began to develop a more multiracial outlook when two young laypersons challenged their congregations in Inaman to reach out to the surrounding tribal people. The year 1978 was declared a mission year. The rapid growth in membership led to the establishment of a Bible training center in 1980, which became the Sabah Theological Seminary in 1986 — the only seminary in Malaysia to teach in the local Malay language.

Bibliography

Basel Christian Church of Malaysia Centenary Magazine (1882-1982). • *Basel Christian Church of Malaysia Magazine* (1982-86).

Chong Tet Loi

Baselios, Eldo

Syrian prelate who arrived in India in 1685.

Because of Portuguese opposition to all non-Catholic missionaries arriving in India in the 17th c., Mar Baselios, Mar Ivanios, and two priests arrived first at Surat and then came to Malankara by road. On the thirteenth day after his arrival at Kothamangalam, Baselios died. He was buried at Mar Thomman Cheriapally. Baselios is believed to have been a catholicos (*Maphriana:* a subordinate title created by the patriarch for a bishop to act as rival to the autonomous Persian catholicos). Baselios commanded respect from the people during the few days he stayed in Malankara. Eventually, he was declared a saint, and the church of his final rest is one of the pilgrim centers in Kerala.

Jacob Kurian

Batak Churches

The regional ethnic Batak churches in North Sumatra originated from the mission work of various mission societies from continental Europe and America in the mid-19th c.

The historical development of mission work among the Bataks and the cultural differences of the Batak tribes made it impossible to build a single ethnic Batak (folk) church body. As the number of Batak Christians increased, so did the variety of missionary organizations, with their various doctrinal distinctions, and the variety of Batak churches, with their tribal and cultural differences. The historical development of Dutch colonial rule among the Bataks also supported the process of increasing the plurality of the Batak groups and churches.

The Bataks were divided into six related tribal groups with six distinctive languages. To the south and southwest of Lake Toba and on the island of Samosir lived the most numerous of the Batak people, the Toba-Batak. Their homeland was sometimes called Central Batakland during Dutch colonization and now corresponds to the regency *(kabupaten)* of North Tapanuli. Northwest of the Toba-Batak region lived the far less numerous Pakpak/Dairi-Batak. North of the lake were the Karo-Batak, and to the east of the lake lived the Simalungun-Batak. South of the Toba-Batak, in the districts of Angkola, Mandailing, and Padanglawas, lived another group now most conveniently called the South Tapanuli Bataks, but sometimes they are regarded as two subgroups, the Angkola-Batak and the Mandailing-Batak. The Mandailing- and Angkola-Bataks are largely Muslim. The Bataks to the north are a mixture of Christians, Muslims, and animists (see Animism).

The German Rhenish Mission began its work among the Angkola and Mandailing Bataks in South Tapanuli, and also among the Toba-Batak in North Tapanuli, in the 1860s. The mission work succeeded more among the Toba-Bataks than the Angkola- and Mandailing-Bataks. Due to the ethnic cultural differences, the Rhenish missionaries used both the Angkola- and Toba-Batak languages for church instruction and Christian teaching. The Toba-Batak church body officially came into existence in 1930 with the name *Huria Kristen Batak Protestan* (HKBP; see Batak Protestant Christian Church*). To some extent, the Angkola-Batak Christians tried to build an Angkola-Batak church body in the 1940s, but it became a reality only in the 1970s with the name *Gereja Kristen Protestan Angkola* (GKPA). The main reason for the peaceful separation from the HKBP was the difference in language and custom *(adat*)*. A smaller group of Mandailing-Batak Christians stems from the mission work of the Baptist* Mission, *Doopsgezinde Zendingsvereniging* (DZV), started in 1871, but there was no Mandailing-Batak church. The Toba-Batak church (HKBP) faced difficulties and had schisms in 1927 and 1965 because of internal, personal, and leadership problems.

The Rhenish Mission extended its mission field among the animistic Pakpak/Dairi-Bataks in the 1930s. The Pakpak/Dairi Christians (93 congregations with 27,014 members) belong to the HKBP church and are working toward becoming an independent church. The trend seems clear that in each ethnic subdivision of the Batak Christians an independent church body should eventually be formed.

The Simalungun Protestant Christian Church (*Gereja Kristen Protestan Simalungun*, GKPS) is the fruit of the Rhenish Mission work among the Simalungun-Bataks from 1903 to 1940. Some Toba-Batak pastors and evangelists were sent by the Rhenish Mission to the Simalungun region to accompany the German Rhenish missionaries. August Theis, the first missionary, settled among the Simalungun people at Pematangraya on 6 Sep 1903, the date GKPS considers to be its birthday. By the twenty-fifth jubilee of Christian mission work among the Simalungun people in 1928, the Simalungun Christians had developed a strong ethnic consciousness and awareness and used the Simalungun language in their worship and church life. Through a long process, GKPS became an independent church on 1 Sep 1963. GKPS introduced the traditional Simalungun melodies to enrich its music and liturgy. Certain selected Simalungun musical instruments were also used in some congregations. Currently, GKPS has 178,970 members across North Sumatra and other Indonesian islands.

The Karo-Batak church (*Gereja Batak Karo Protestan*, GBKP) stems from the mission work of the Dutch Mission Society (*Nederlandsch Zendeling Genootschap*, NZG) in 1890. The first initiative came from the large tobacco concerns on the east coast of Sumatra. The Dutch mission was assisted by Menadonese and Minahasan evangelists from the eastern part of Indonesia rather than by Toba-Batak evangelists. The first baptism of the Karo-Batak people was on 20 Aug 1903. The numbers of the Karo-Batak church increased very slowly. In 1950, the Karo-Batak church members numbered only 5,000. But after the 30 September Movement in 1965 (the failed coup of the Communist Party in Indonesia), the number increased rapidly with mass conversions between 1967 and 1969. In 1968, the Karo Batak church had 76,300 members, and in 1971 the number was 94,085. Currently it has over 205,000.

The American Methodist* Church began its missionary work in Sumatra among the Chinese of Medan in 1905, and then among the Simalungun- and Toba-Bataks, who came to the coastal areas in search of a better livelihood, and also among the Pardembanan-Bataks in the region of Asahan and Labuabatu. With increased migration from Tapanuli, the mission work of the Methodist Church grew so rapidly that the work among the Bataks overwhelmed that among the Chinese. Because of different customs, culture, and religious backgrounds, the Batak Christians and the Chinese Christians had separate services on Sundays and, to some extent, a separate church organization until the 1970s. In 1964, the Methodist Church of Indonesia (*Gereja Methodist Indonesia*, GMI) came into being. The Batak Christians made up a considerable part of the Methodist Church, and the smaller number of Chinese Christians provided enormous support for the financial needs of the church.

All Batak churches face the same problems arising from the influence of their customary law, or *adat*, upon the life and destiny of a Batak. The outsider might well ask whether it is not more tribalism than faith in the God revealed in Jesus Christ that accounts for the remarkable social coherence. This is still part of the Batak Christian struggle today.

Bibliography

Aritonang, Jan S., *Mission Schools in Batakland (Indonesia 1861-1940)* (1994). • Hutauruk, J. R., *Kemandirian Gereja. Penelitian historis-sistematis tentang Gerakan Kemandirian Gereja di Sumatera Utara dalam kancah pergolakan kolonialisme dan gerakan kebangsaan di Indonesia, 1899-1942* (1992). • Lempp, W., *Gereja-gereja di Sumatera Utara* (Series: Benih yang Tumbuh, XII) (1976). • Pardede, Jansen, "Die Batakchristen auf Nordsumatra und ihr Verhaltnis zu den Muslimen" (doctoral thesis, Mainz, Germany) (1975). • Pedersen, Paul B., *Batak Blood and Protestant Soul: The Development of National Batak Churches in North Sumatra* (1970).

J. Raplan Hutauruk

Batak Protestant Christian Church

(*Huria Kristen Batak Protestan*, HKBP). The first fruit of the mission work of the German Rhenish Mission (RMG) among the Bataks in Sumatra (1861-1942), HKBP, ecumenically referred to as the "Batak Church," became an autonomous church within the Rhenish mission body in Sumatra in 1930.

Before the work of the Rhenish Mission, there were missionary attempts by English Baptist missionaries Burton and Ward in 1824 and by the mission board of American Congregationalists (Lyman and Munson) in 1834. None succeeded in baptizing the Bataks. In fact, the two American missionaries were killed by the Bataks. Thirty years later, the Rhenish missionaries came and concentrated their mission among the Bataks. Within 14 years (1864-1878), the successful evangelization among the Bataks in the valley of Silindung (about 40 km. from Lake Toba), through pioneer missionaries such as L. I. Nommensen*, was also experienced in other Batak areas. The increasing number of Batak Christians can be seen in the following statistics: 1,250 in 1871; 5,188 in 1881; 21,779 in 1891; 103,528 in 1911. In 1936, the seventy-fifth aniversary of Rhenish mission work among the Bataks, the number of Batak Christians was 368,535.

During World War II, all Germans in the Dutch colony of Indonesia*, including the German missionaries who occupied leading positions in the Batak Church (HKBP), were interned by the Dutch government. Through an extraordinary synod in Jul 1940, a Batak pastor, Kasianus Sirait, was elected as *ephorus* of the HKBP. Thus the HKBP declared itself an independent church body, the equal of its mother mission body, the

Rhenish Mission in Sumatra. The numbers of congregations and members are fast increasing because of the urbanization of the Batak Christians, especially those from around Lake Toba. In 1959, the HKBP had 1,290 congregations, 791,072 adherents, and 202 pastors serving the congregations and other church bodies.

Presently, HKBP has 2,548 congregations spread throughout various parts of Indonesia, as well as Singapore*. The church is served by 601 pastors, 309 teacher-preachers, 146 Bible women, and 54 deaconesses. Since 1982, women have been ordained as pastors. Bible women and deaconesses have the same rights as do the teacher-preachers and may preach and pronounce the benediction. Administration of the two sacraments (baptism and holy communion), however, is limited to ordained pastors. Several congregations form a resort, and the resorts are coordinated under districts. A congregation is led by a teacher-preacher, a resort by a resort-pastor, a district by a *praeses* (superintendent), and the whole HKBP is led by the *ephorus* (presiding bishop), with a general secretary as his partner. There are now 285 resorts and 19 districts. Each resort has its own synod, but the controlling body of the whole HKBP is the general synod, comprising delegates from each resort and led by the *ephorus* and, to some extent, the general secretary, in conjunction with the church central board (*Parhalado Pusat,* comprising pastors and elder members of the synod). The biennial synodical meeting hears reports on the life and work of the church, debates issues, and elects officials.

To organize and administrate its extensive work, the HKBP has several departments (mission, diaconal-social, Sunday school, youth, women, education, pension, health, and business), theological institutes (for pastors, teacher-preachers, Bible women, and deaconesses), and bureaus. Its headquarters is located in the midst of the traditional Batak Land, Pearaja-Tarutung, southeast of Lake Toba. The majority of the 1,600,000 members are rural people living in villages and engaged in small farming, but many live in cities, in Pematangsiantar, Medan, Jakarta, Bandung, Surabaya, and other places outside the Batak homeland. As both Christians and Indonesians, they are making a positive impact on Indonesian national life. The church service is still held in the Toba-Batak language except for some congregations in the big cities where the Indonesian language is used.

Most HKBP congregations are self-supporting. Individual congregations also support the running expenses of the HKBP headquarters. Two offerings are collected at each Sunday service. Since 1970, the second offering has been given to HKBP headquarters to meet general expenses and staff salaries. A special offering is collected on appointed Sundays to support a specific department or institution. Financial aid from ecumenical partners is used to support projects in education, health, mission, and, recently, community development in and outside the church.

The theological seminary, the *Sekolah Tinggi Theologia HKBP* (STT-HKBP), is the center of theological education for pastors with a higher degree. Prior to 1978, the seminary consisted of the theological faculty of the HKBP Nommensen University, which was opened in 1954 and has two campuses, one in Medan for agriculture, economics, technology, and business administration (and more recently music), and the other in Pematangsiantar for education. The total student body of the university is about 10,000.

HKBP celebrated its 125th aniversary on 7 Oct 1986 with various activities and is very much concerned about the social problems connected with the industrialization of Indonesia. HKBP subscribes to the law stipulating that *Pancasila** is the only foundation for regulating societal, national, and state activities, but not religious doctrine. HKBP is also a member of various ecumenical communities. In 1950, it was one of the sponsoring churches of the *Dewan Gereja-gereja di Indonesia* (DGI, Council of Churches in Indonesia), now called *Persekutuan Gereja-gereja di Indonesia* (PGI, Communion of Churches in Indonesia*). HKBP is also a member of the Lutheran World Federation (LWF, 1952), the Christian Conference of Asia (CCA), and the World Council of Churches (WCC, 1962).

Bibliography

Aritonang, Jan S., *Mission Schools in Batakland (Indonesia 1861-1940)* (1994). • Hutauruk, J. R., *Kemandirian Gereja. Penelitian historis-sistematis tentang Gerakan Kemandirian Gereja di Sumatera Utara dalam kanach pergolakan kolonialisme dan gerakan kebangsaan di Indonesia, 1899-1942* (1992). • Lempp, W., *Gereja-gereja di Sumatera Utara* (Series: Benih yang Tumbuh, XII) (1976). • Nyhus, Edward O. V., "An Indonesian Church in the Midst of Social Change: The Batak Protestant Christian Church, 1942-1957" (doctoral dissertation, University of Wisconsin) (1987). • Pedersen, Paul B., *Batak Blood and Protestant Soul: The Development of National Batak Churches in North Sumatra* (1970).

J. RAPLAN HUTAURUK

Batavia. *See* Jakarta

Beateria. *See* Indigenous Religious Congregations; Religious of the Virgin Mary

Beijing Convent

(St. Joseph's Convent). Indigenous convent built to house religious women of advanced age who had no convent in which to stay after the Beijing Diocese was restored in 1979.

Built in 1984 to house 50 women, the Beijing Convent opened a novitiate in 1986 to train young women for the religious life. Thirteen novices entered, the oldest being 30 years of age and the youngest 19, with educational backgrounds ranging from high school to university level. The local church authority requested that Rev. Sister Wang Beren from Wuhan Diocese serve as the mother superior. Newly professed sisters are required to love country and church and consecrate themselves in service to the church and common people. In 1987, there were some 30 septuagenarian sisters. By 1994, young sisters formed the core of the convent.

CHINA GROUP, translated by DUFRESSE CHANG

Beijing Diocese

The oldest Roman Catholic diocese in China*.

The Franciscan* missionaries came to China in the early part of the Yuan Dynasty, and Pope Clement V named John of Monte Corvino* head of the Archdiocese of Khanbaliq (Beijing) in 1307. When the Mongolian Empire (see Mongolia) ceded to the Ming Dynasty, the diocese ceased to exist. When Catholicism reentered China at the end of the Ming Dynasty, there had been no inland dioceses for well over 100 years. The missionary endeavor was subjected to Macau control until 1690, when Pope Alexander VIII named Luo Wen Zao* and Della Chiesa bishops of Beijing and Nanjing respectively. The diocese of Beijing extended to include a great part of China and Korea, resulting in the creation of the apostolic vicariates of Shang-si and Shansi.

Between 1831 and 1839, further districts were separated: Chaoxian, Liaodong, Mongolia, and Shandong. Chili Province, the only region remaining under the jurisdiction of Beijing Diocese, was further divided into the three apostolic vicariates of northern, southwest, and southeast China. Only the northern vicariate bore the name of Beijing. In 1926, the Xuanha apostolic vicariate, under the Scheut* Mission, was created from the northern sector. The Beijing apostolic vicariate became a diocese again in 1946.

The eight successive bishops between 1856 and 1946 were all French Lazarists*. The first Chinese, Cardinal Tin Gengsin, was consecrated bishop of Beijing in 1946. When the cardinal left Beijing in 1948, Vicar General Rev. Li Juinwu took up the administration of the diocese. Yeo Juanyu was elected bishop in 1958, but he died soon afterwards. During the Cultural Revolution, the diocese suffered destruction, and it was only in 1979 that its administration emerged to become the leading diocese of the country. The present bishop is Mgr. Fu Tieshan, and the cathedral is at Nangtang.

CHINA GROUP, translated by DUFRESSE CHANG

Beltran, Francisco Luz

(b. Lucban, Tayabas, ca. 1870). First Filipino Presbyterian minister in Quezon Province.

Beltran was for many years the only Filipino Presbyterian* minister in his native Tayabas (now Quezon) Province. From a middle-class family of hoteliers, Beltran was converted in 1904 and started his labors as a young evangelist in 1905. In 1908 he and another evangelist went on an evangelistic tour of Tayabas, preaching "somewhere almost every night during the years." When Tiaong Evangelical Church was organized in 1909, Beltran, then only recently ordained, became its first minister. He is best remembered as the minister of Lucena Evangelical Church in the provincial capital, which he served for 24 years (from 1914 to 1938).

In 1919 Beltran was elected stated clerk of the Evangelical Church of the Philippine* Islands (Independent Presbyterian). He occupied the post for many years.

Bibliography

Rodgers, J. B., *Forty Years in the Philippines* (1940). • Sitoy, T. V., Jr., *Several Springs, One Stream* (1992).

T. VALENTINO SITOY, JR.

Benedictines

(OSB). Benedictinism has its origins in 6th-c. Italy in the life of Benedict of Nursia (480-547), who as a youth lived as a hermit for three years in Subiaco and later in that same locality founded several small monastic communities. About the year 530 he brought his monks to Monte Cassino and there established the great abbey where he wrote his Rule for Monasteries. During the Middle Ages, this rule was adopted by monasteries in Italy, France, England, Austria, Germany, Switzerland, and Spain. In the course of history, monasteries observing the Rule of Benedict formed congregations based on national or regional groupings or historical bonds. In 1893, the congregations established the Benedictine Confederation, which is popularly called the Order of St. Benedict. The confederation is composed of 21 congregations of monks, 41 of nuns, and 34 of sisters.

It was only in the late 19th and early 20th cs. that Benedictine monks began to implant their way of life in Asia. While the founders of monasteries were Europeans, they developed native recruits so that at present most of the Benedictines in Asia are Asians.

*Philippines**. In Sep 1895, monks from the Abbey of Montserrat in Barcelona, Spain, came to the Philippines to work as missionaries in the province of Surigao on the island of Mindanao in towns that were turned over to them by the Jesuits*. Because of the political situation in the province during the revolution against Spain and during the Philippine-American war, the monks suffered great difficulties. Some of them returned to Spain, some transferred to Manila, and a few remained in Surigao. The remaining missions were turned over to the Missionaries of the Sacred Heart* in 1909.

In 1901, the monks in Manila established San Beda College, a school for boys and young men. At present, the institution, which has 6,000 students, includes a grade school, a high school, a college of liberal arts, accounting, and commerce, and a college of law. In 1904, the Benedictine community was raised to a priory and in 1924 to an abbey, with the title Our Lady of Montserrat.

In 1972, the monks established the Benedictine Abbey School, which in 1995 was renamed St. Benedict College upon the opening of a collegiate department.

In 1981, the abbey founded the Monastery of the Transfiguration in Malaybalay, Bukidnon, in Mindanao. The community is engaged in farming and the production of coffee, as well as in community development projects. It maintains a guest house and retreat facilities. The monastery is known for its boys' choir whose members are the sons of farmers in the vicinity.

The abbey in Manila and the monastery in Malaybalay form the Philippine Pro-Province of the Subiaco Congregation. In 1990 the Pro-Province established the Paul VI Institute of Liturgy, which offers a three-month course on liturgy for clergy, religious, and laypersons. The institute is located in Malaybalay on the monastery premises.

In 1906, the Missionary Benedictine Sisters of Tutzing, based in Germany, came to the Philippines and that same year founded St. Scholastica's College in Manila. St. Scholastica's College, which today has 6,000 students, is one of the leading schools in the Philippines for girls and young women. It is known for its school of music, which has produced many eminent artists. From this one college also began an extensive apostolate that includes 12 schools throughout the country, three of which offer collegiate courses; one hospital; two retreat houses; and nine houses for pastoral ministry. The Philippine Priory has sent Filipino sisters to missions in Angola, Tanzania, Kenya, and Australia.

In 1991 the sisters established their tribal Filipino apostolate for the Aeta, the aboriginal people of the Philippines, who were victims of the eruption of Mt. Pinatubo and its lava flow.

In 1931, the Congregation of the Benedictines of the Eucharistic King was founded by Mother Edeltraud Danner, OSB, in Vigan, Ilocos Sur. Its members included both nuns and sisters. The sisters formed a separate congregation in 1986. The contemplative communities include the abbey in Vigan, monasteries in Salong, Calapan, Oriental Mindoro, and Cogon, Digos, Davao del Sur, and a cella in Nalseb, Tublay, Benguet. The sisters' congregation, which is composed of four priories, oversees 15 mission stations, 13 apostolates (service in various institutions), one retreat house, and the Religion Teachers' Formation Center in Vigan.

In 1945, Mother Mary Agnes of the Sacred Heart founded the Benedictine Sisters Reparatrix of the Sacred Heart, a contemplative congregation which at present has two houses in the towns of Mexico and Lubao in the province of Pampanga.

In 1983, the Congregation of St. Ottilien, a German missionary congregation, established St. Benedict's Monastery in Digos, Davao del Sur, with German and Korean monks; Filipino monks were soon admitted. The community is engaged in pastoral work, maintains a retreat house, and is involved in farming.

*Korea**. In 1909, the Congregation of St. Ottilien founded a monastery in Seoul, which in 1913 became St. Benedict's Abbey. The monks opened a teacher-training and vocational school. In 1927, the abbey was transferred to Tokwon, where a mission had been established in 1920. In Jan 1940, the abbey became as an *abbey nullius*, or territorial abbey, with parishes under its jurisdiction. As in Seoul, the abbey ran a vocational school. The monastery was suppressed by the Communists in May 1946 (see Communism).

In Yenki, Manchuria, the St. Ottilien monks founded a monastery in 1922 which became Holy Cross Abbey in 1934. The monks worked in parishes and founded vocational schools. Yenki became a diocese in 1940. In May 1946, the monastery was also suppressed by the Communists.

The monks from Tokwon and Yenki went to Waegwan, South Korea, and in 1950 established a new monastery which was raised to a priory in 1956 and to an abbey, the Abbey of St. Maur and St. Placid, in 1964. The apostolate of the Waegwan monastery includes parishes, middle schools and high schools, a theological institute for women, retreat houses, and a guest house. Its activities include religious art*, manufacture of church furnishings, a printing press, and work in leper settlements. The abbey also has houses in Seoul, Pusan, Taegu, and Hwajop.

In 1925, the Missionary Benedictine Sisters of Tutzing founded a mission in the northern part of Korea. This was destroyed in 1949. In 1956, the sisters established a priory in Taegu, and in 1976 a priory in Seoul. The Taegu priory has 19 houses, and Seoul has nine. The apostolates of the Taegu priory include two hospitals, pastoral ministry in 22 parishes, two middle and high schools for girls, eight kindergartens, one retreat house, two Bible study centers, and one social welfare center.

Sisters of the Seoul priory are engaged in the pastoral ministry in seven parishes as well as in the campus ministry in one school. Institutes under their care include a retreat house, a school for the deaf and mute, a nursing home, a home for children, two social mission houses, and four kindergartens.

In 1931, the Benedictine Sisters of Mount Olivet, or Olivetans, based in Switzerland, founded a mission in Yenki, which was later suppressed. In 1953 the sisters established a house in Pusan and founded a hospital. The work of the sisters includes catechesis, pastoral ministry, retreats, counseling, social work, and education.

*China**. Fu Jen Catholic University was founded in Nov 1923 in Peking (Beijing) by monks from St. Vincent's Archabbey, Latrobe, Pennsylvania, of the American-Cassinese Congregation. The university was turned over to the Society of the Divine Word* in 1933. The university was later suppressed and reconstituted in Taipei in Sep 1961.

Monks of the Abbey of St. Andrew-Zevenkerken in Bruges, Belgium (of the Belgian Congregation, now Congregation of the Annunciation), founded a mission in Si-Shan in 1929. This was transferred to Chengtu in 1947. The monks subsequently left China and founded a house in Valyermo, California, in 1955.

*Sri Lanka**. The Sylvestrine Congregation founded St. Sylvester's Monastery in Colombo in 1928. The community later transferred to Ampitiya and was raised to a priory in 1983. It founded St. Benedict's Monastery in Adisham, Haputale, in 1962, and St. Anthony's Monastery in Wahacotte in 1973. Dependent houses include St. Anthony's College in Katugastota and the Sacred Heart Church in Colombo. The monks are engaged in pastoral and mission work. The apostolate of the Ampitiya community includes teaching in seminaries and schools.

St. Helen's Convent of the Benedictines, a contemplative community in Wennapuwa, was founded in 1952 by the Benedictine nuns of Olzai in Italy. The nuns make altar breads and raise poultry.

*Vietnam**. In 1940, the Abbey of Pierre-qui-Vire, in Saint-Leger-Vauban, France, of the Subiaco Congregation, founded the Monastery of Thien An in Hue. It became an independent priory in 1959. Thien An has founded the following monasteries: Thien Binh in Saigon (Ho Chi Minh City) in 1960; Thien Hoa in Banmethuot in 1962; and Thien Phuoc in Saigon in 1972. All four monasteries are engaged in agriculture. Thien An has a guest house and an orange orchard. Thien Binh produces rice and fish; its service to the community includes pastoral counseling. Thien Hoa produces rice and coffee. The monastery is involved in pastoral work and accommodates guests. Thien Phuoc produces rice, fish, and vegetables, and manufactures sun hats. The monks' apostolate includes recollections, catechesis, and reception of guests.

In 1954 the Congregation of the Benedictine Sisters of St. Mathilde, based in Paris, founded the Priory of St. Mary in Banmethuot. In 1967 the community transferred to Thu-Duc in Saigon. The nuns make liturgical vestments and are also engaged in farming.

*Japan**. Monks of St. John's Abbey, Collegeville, Minnesota, of the American-Cassinese Congregation, founded St. Anselm's Benedictine Priory in Tokyo in 1947. One of the major parishes in the city, St. Anselm's is also a center for university student meetings and is engaged in ecumenical work. Theological lectures are held in the church, which is outstanding for its modern design. The monks teach in leading Japanese universities.

The Congregation of the Sisters of the Good Samaritan, founded in Australia in 1857, has a provincial house in Nara and dependent houses in Sasebo and Tokyo. The sisters are involved in education and pastoral work.

The Benedictine Sisters of the Federation of St. Benedict, based in the United States, founded St. Benedict's Convent in Sapporo, Hokkaido, in 1950. The sisters' work includes adult education and a kindergarten.

The Sisters of Jesus Crucified, founded in Paris in 1930, established a priory in Shirako-Machi in 1966. Their activities include confectionery, embroidery, and card making.

*Taiwan**. St. Benedict's Convent, St. Joseph, Minnesota, of the Benedictine Sisters of the Federation of St. Benedict, established a community in Peking in 1930. The community transferred to Tanshui, Taiwan, in 1949. The sisters are engaged in retreats and counseling and run a hostel for university students.

Wimmer Priory, in Hsin Chuang, was founded in 1964 by St. Vincent's Archabbey of the American-Cassinese Congregation. The monks teach at Fu Jen University in Taipei.

The Benedictine Priory in Chiayi was founded in 1965 by St. Procopius Abbey, Lisle, Illinois, of the American-Cassinese Congregation. The apostolate of the community includes retreats, ecumenical activities, publications, and the oblates' program.

*India**. The Saccidananda Ashram at Shantivanam was founded in 1950 and in 1980 was affiliated with the Camaldolese Congregation. The Asirvanam Monastery in Bangalore was founded in 1952 by the Belgian Congregation, now the Congregation of the Annunciation. Its activities include retreats and lectures on Scripture, theology, and spirituality. The community is also engaged in farming and cattle-breeding. In 1986, Asirvanam monks founded a house in Changnacherry, which in 1988 was transferred to Kappadu in Kerala. The monks are engaged in biblical and liturgical apostolate and in pastoral work.

In 1962, monks of the Sylvestrine Congregation from Sri Lanka founded St. Joseph's Monastery in Makkiyad, Kerala. The monastery then founded the Monastery of St. Sylvester Abbot in 1973 in Vanashram, Bangalore; the Jeevan Jyoti Ashram in 1982 in Shivpuri; and the Navajeevan domus in 1987 in Vijayawada. The monks at Makkiyad are involved in pastoral ministry and run a college and vocational institutes. The apostolate of the Shivpuri monks includes hospitality and preaching retreats.

St. Cecilia's Abbey at Ryde, Isle of Wight, England, of the Solesmes Congregation, founded the monastery of Shanti Nilayam in Bangalore in 1970. The nuns have a vineyard, poultry, and dairy farm and make altar breads. In 1984, Shanti Nilayam founded the Ishwar Kripa Ashram in Bhanvad.

*Cambodia**. In 1952, four Benedictine monks from Pierre-qui-Vire, France, sent originally to Cochin China to start a monastic community, arrived in Cambodia at the request of Mgr. Chaballier, bishop of the country. "Cambodia is a country of monks; it will only be converted by monks," said the bishop to convince them.

The Benedictines founded the Monastery of the Tranquil Sea *(Santesakoraram)* at Kep beside the sea. In 1970, besides the foreigners, the monastery comprised one monk-priest, Fr. Bernard Chhim Chunsar, and several professed Khmer brothers: André Seng Nimith, André Rath Rumchor, and Michel Suong. In 1970, the war forced the monks to move to Phnom Penh. In 1975, the foreign monks were expelled from the country; the professed Khmer monks were sent out to collective labor, then executed by the Khmer Rouge.

The Benedictine monks attempted to find a formula for the monastic life suitable to Cambodia. One of them, Jean Badre, was sent to a village of Christian peasants to study a mode of monastic life that was more Khmer in nature. The study was cut short as Fr. Badre was executed by the Khmer Rouge on 3 May 1975.

Besides the real spiritual enlightenment radiated by the monastery both in the Christian community and in the Buddhist world, the Church of Cambodia is indebted to the Benedictines for the composition of a number of liturgical chants and for the spiritual formation of a number of young people who were to become leaders in the Christian communities.

Conclusion. Benedictine presence is well established in Asia — in the Philippines, South Korea, Sri Lanka, Vietnam, Japan, Taiwan, and India — extensively in some countries, and to a limited degree, though no less firmly, in others. Six congregations of monks and seven congregations of sisters have houses in the region. There are eight convents of nuns in the Philippines, India, and Sri Lanka. At present, there are over 450 monks, nearly 200 contemplative nuns, and over 1,000 sisters serving the OSB in Asia.

It has been observed that the Benedictine way of life appeals to Asians because of its monastic character and its emphasis on prayer. *Ora et labora* (pray and work) is a principle of Benedictine life. Benedictine work in Asia covers a wide range — agriculture, crafts, education, hospitals, pastoral work, missionary work, ecumenism — so that, as St. Benedict says in his rule, "in all things God may be glorified."

Bibliography

Annuaire des Fondations Monastiques (1988). • *Atlas O.S.B. Benedictinorum per orbem praesentia* (1973). • *Catalogus Monasteriorum O.S.B.*, Edition XVII (1990).

BERNARDO PEREZ, with a contribution on Cambodia by FRANÇOIS PONCHAUD

Bertumen, Julian V.

(b. Balangui, Albany, 25 Jan 1869; d. 29 Mar 1962). Filipino Catholic who became a Presbyterian* evangelist in the Bicol Provinces of the Philippines*.

Prior to conversion to Protestantism, Bertumen had studied three years for the Catholic priesthood and was secretary to the bishop of Nueva Caceres. Turning Protestant at about age 40, Bertumen soon became one of the most revered Presbyterian evangelists in the Bicol Peninsula. Beginning in 1921, he led a systematic evangelistic tour of Sorsogon Province. A tireless worker, Bertumen was responsible for organizing several local churches and the conversion of many of the intelligentsia in the Bicol Provinces, including another ex-seminarian, Policarpo Pelgone*. His influence was so great that his converts were generally fondly called "Bertumen." Later the Presbyterian Mission placed him in charge of all pastoral and evangelistic work in Sorsogon.

Bibliography

Tabios, A. D., J. P. Cruz, and M. G. Pejo, *The Evangelical Church in the Bicol Region: A Brief History* (1974). • Sitoy, T. V., Jr., *Several Springs, One Stream* (1992).

T. VALENTINO SITOY, JR.

Beurel, Jean-Marie

(b. Plouguenast, France, 5 Feb 1813; d. Paris, 3 Oct 1872). French missionary and founder of Catholic Singapore*.

Born in Brittany, France, in the diocese of St. Brieuc, Beurel was already a deacon when he joined the seminary of the Paris Foreign Mission Society* (MEP) on 23 Aug 1838. There he was ordained a priest on 16 Mar 1839 and left the following 28 Apr for the mission of Siam (Thailand*), which was established and entrusted to the MEP in 1669. He arrived in Singapore on 29 Oct 1839. The Portuguese *Padroado** was then claiming jurisdiction over the island. But on 16 Dec 1839, a pontifical decree of Gregory XVI confirming an earlier decree of 22 Sep 1827 gave jurisdiction to the vicar apostolic of Siam over Singapore and the Malay Peninsula.

On 23 Apr 1840, Beurel was given charge of the still new and very small Catholic mission of Singapore. The small chapel, built in 1833, was no longer large enough to accommodate the growing Catholic congregation; at once, Beurel began collecting funds to build a new and bigger church. He obtained a piece of land from the British resident and began building what is now the cathedral. That was a long and difficult task which Beurel carried out with great determination and perseverance, in spite of many setbacks. Money was collected locally and overseas in France, Reunion Island, and even Manila and China*, where Beurel went in 1846. The church, dedicated to the Good Shepherd, was solemnly blessed and opened on 6 Jun 1846. The former small chapel was converted into a boys' school, which Beurel himself directed for some years.

In 1845, Beurel, Bishop J.-B. Boucho, and Fr. P. Bigandet jointly wrote the *Litterae Apostolicae* and *Avis Particuliers aux Missionnaires*, an elaborate directory for the pastoral life and work of the missionaries of the vicariate apostolic of the Malay Peninsula. In Aug-Sep 1847, Beurel and a fellow missionary went to explore the state of Johor, where they found Chinese settlers interested in the Catholic faith. He also went to the Rhio Islands for the same purpose.

As soon as the new church was built, Beurel made plans for the establishment of English schools for boys and girls, for he could foresee the important role education would play in Asia, especially in the British possessions. The project was approved by the bishop in Jul 1849, but the responsibility to finance it was all left to Beurel. He had already written to the Brothers of the Christian Schools (see La Salle Brothers) and the Sisters of the Institute of the Holy Infant Jesus (see Convent of the Holy Infant Jesus), inviting them to manage and staff the schools he was planning to build. Negotiations by correspondence took a long time in those days, even with the help of the MEP directors in Paris. To avoid any more delays, he decided to settle the matter himself. He left Singapore for France on 25 Oct 1850 and returned on 28 Mar 1852 with six brothers and four sisters. The bishop retained the sisters and three brothers in Penang, so Beurel was left with only three brothers to open his school for boys on 1 May 1852, on the site of the old chapel. By year's end, it had 110 pupils; bigger premises were soon needed. The cornerstone of a new building was laid on 19 Mar 1855, on the feast of St. Joseph, and the school placed under his patronage. It is still known today as St. Joseph's Institution*.

Anxious to provide for the education and welfare of girls as well, Beurel applied twice (1849 and 1852) for the grant of a piece of land on which he could build a school. Finally, on 18 Aug 1852, with his own money, he bought a house and land near the new church and built a school, quarters for the sisters, and later an orphanage. The convent opened on 5 Feb 1854.

In 1856, Beurel was appointed pro-vicar of the Malay Peninsula mission. In Sep 1859, he completed the Good Shepherd Presbytery, which is now the archbishop's house. He also held the office of procurator for the neighboring missions and visiting missionaries. When the MEP established a procuracy in Singapore, he bought land and supervised the new building.

All these labors were undertaken at a time when mission and apostolic work were at their very beginning amidst endless difficulties, some coming often from unexpected quarters. At times, Beurel was upset, but he usually let the storm pass by; he always went on with perseverance and success in the way he had determined to follow. Disabled by a stroke and seriously ill, he left Singapore in Dec 1869 for France, and he died at the MEP seminary in Paris on 3 Oct 1872. When the Singapore Catholics heard of his death, they requested that his body be brought back to be laid to rest among them; they even offered to pay for the expenses. This was not agreed to, but they retained a very deep affection for their pastor, who had loved and served them so well. A tireless and skillful apostle endowed with a great spirit of initiative that produced many successful results, Beurel is rightfully considered the founder of Catholic Singapore.

Bibliography

Launay, Adrien, *Histoire générale de la Société des Missions Étrangères,* 3 vols. (1894). • Buckley, Charles Burton, *An Anecdotal History of Old Times in Singapore* (1965).

R. Nicolas

Bhave, Vinoba

(b. Gangode, India, 1895; d. Paunar, India, 1982). Spiritual heir to Mahatma Gandhi* and acknowledged leader of the Sarvodaya Movement.

Drawn to Gandhian ideas as a youth, Bhave accepted Gandhi's invitation to join Sabarmati *ashram** (hermitage) as a *brahmachari* (celibate) in 1916. Gandhi asked him to take charge of its new branch (1921) at Wardha. His experience in meditation and the Gandhian "constructive program" of village industry and new basic education inspired him to meet the challenges of poverty, inequality, and discontent among rural people, especially after Gandhi's assassination (1948). While he was touring the village of Pochanpalli (1951), a group of outcaste laborers sought his help in obtaining land from the government for cultivation. At an evening prayer with the villagers, Bhave asked whether anyone could give a few acres of land for the landless. A farmer offered 100 acres, and this marked the beginning of a great movement, *bhoodan yajna* (land-gift mission), culminating in the gifting of hundreds of thousands of acres for the landless in 1957.

The basis of *sarvodaya* (welfare of all) is all-embracing love, nonviolence, and respect of individual will. All members are equal and committed to sharing the produce of each other's labor. The strong will protect the weak, and the rich shall be the trustees of the poor. Bhave promoted *sarvodaya* through *bhoodan gramdan* (village in gift), *prakhandan* (bloc of villages), and *zilladan* (district). By 1969, he received 10,000 villages, 7,000 blocs, and 17 districts in gift. He wanted the whole of India redistributed with community or semiprivate ownership in the same year (1969 being the Gandhi birth centenary). But Bhave found the selfish and violent nature of men standing in the way of *bhoodan* and *sarvodaya.* He appealed to women to take over the management of villages and dethrone men from the seats of power. He saw women as being better qualified to do this because of their loving nature, nonviolent disposition, and fearless will. If they were *grihadevata* (goddess of the home), creating happiness for the family, they could also become *gramdevata* (village goddess), managing the welfare of all and ushering in the Gandhian ideal of self-sufficient villages. For Bhave, the empowerment of women was the most reliable means for achieving *sarvodaya.*

Bhave provided a spiritual foundation for *sarvodaya* and its form of socialism. Inequality is the consequence of violence and exploitation. The Vedantic (monistic) concept of *Brahman* (God) as the essence of all demands that humans should love one another. He often quoted Christ ("love your neighbor") in support. Socialism should be practiced in human relationships. The real transformation of society will come from change of hearts and the resultant love, persuasion, and education. He experimented with the Indian spiritual practice of *dan* (voluntary giving) for the welfare of the oppressed. The have-nots in turn can offer *sramdan* (gift in labor) for the happiness of all. Bhave's attempt to eradicate injustice and oppression by the application of Indian spiritual principles offers a challenge to Asian Christianity to utilize the rich spiritual heritage of Asian societies.

Bibliography

Bhave, Vinoba, *Bhoodhan Yajna: Land Gift Mission* (1953); *Revolutionary Sarvodaya: Philosophy for Remaking Man* (1964); *Women's Power* (1975). • Ram, Suresh, *Vinoba and His Mission* (1962). • Tilak, Srinivas, *The Myth of Sarvodaya* (1984).

PLAMTHODATHIL S. JACOB

Bhutan

The proud country of Bhutan, "Druk Yul," the Land of the Thunder Dragon, is hidden away in the mountain fastness of the Eastern Himalayas. Surrounded by India* to the south, east, and west, and Tibet (China*) to the north, it has maintained its national sovereignty and the integrity of its Tibeto-Buddhist heritage. Lamaistic Buddhism* is the official state religion and dominates much of modern life.

The land was unified in the 17th c. after Ngawang Namgyel was forced to flee from Tibet. A *Drukpa* of the Kagyupa sect of Tibeto-Buddhism, he brought together the independent principalities and was the principal architect of modern Bhutan. In 1907 a hereditary monarchy was established when Ugyen Wangchuk defeated his enemies and was declared the king of Bhutan. He forged an understanding with the British in India that allowed them to direct Bhutan's foreign affairs but protected Bhutan's national integrity. After India gained her independence, in 1948 she signed a friendship and cooperation treaty with Bhutan. This paved the way for a close relationship between the two countries and became a cornerstone of Bhutan's diplomacy.

Under the leadership of the third king, HM Jigme Dorje Wangchuck, during the 1950s and 1960s Bhutan began to emerge onto the international scene, following centuries of isolation. Entry into the United Nations in 1971 was the hallmark of this new direction. A policy of cautious development and modernization was also embarked upon and carried forward by the current king, Jigme Singye Wangchuk, who was crowned in 1974. Before the 1960s there was no educational system in the country except within the monasteries, no public medical facilities, and no roads or modern communications to connect the isolated hills and valleys of the mountainous kingdom. Various international agencies, including Christian missions, which had served for many years along the Indian border with Bhutan, were cautiously invited to help in the process of development. The door was opened to Nepali laborers for road-building crews and the like and as emigrants to bring the largely uninhabited southern lowlands under cultivation.

Measuring only 47,000 square miles, Bhutan has a diverse ethnic population of nearly 700,000 today. Successive waves of Tibetans made their way into Bhutan between the 7th and 17th cs., populating the high valleys. The Ngalongs *(Drukpas* of Tibeto-Mongol origin) live mostly in western Bhutan. Although not the largest group, they became preeminent from the time of Ngawang Namgyel. The ruling family comes from this group, and their language, Dzongkha, is the official national language. Sharchops, one of the oldest known ethnic groups and the largest in the country, are of Indo-Mongoloid origin and live mostly in eastern Bhutan. Nepalis, the third-largest group, are relative newcomers and known locally as Lhotsampas. They live mostly in the low-lying fertile duars and former jungle area of the south, having settled there since the end of the 19th c. and gradually scattered throughout the country. However, during the past decade official policy has been to reduce drastically the number of Nepalis in Bhutan, as their fast-growing population and increasing political activism, coupled with differences in cultural and religious background (they are mostly Hindu), have been perceived as a threat to the present regime. Today more than 100,000 Lhotsampa (ethnic Nepali) are resident in refugee* camps along the eastern border of Nepal*, waiting for the day they can return to Bhutan. In addition to these three main groups, there are several minority peoples, including the Kyengpa forest people of central Bhutan, Brokpa and Monpa seminomadic shepherds and yak breeders of the highlands, Lepchas mostly in the west bordering Kalimpong, India (former British Bhutan), and others. At least 85 percent of the population lives in rural areas.

Bhutan's first brush with Christianity was during the visit of two Portuguese Jesuit* fathers en route to Tibet during the early 1600s. They were followed by William Carey* and a friend, who ventured to the border in 1797 while investigating the possibility of starting a Bhutan field. William Robinson was chosen to start this field, with a view to translating the Bible* into the Bhutanese language. Between 1808 and 1811 he made five attempts to establish the mission before the effort was finally abandoned following a series of extreme difficulties. A few years later, the first known Bhutanese convert is recorded in Baptist* records, a young man called Kiaba who made his way to Patna and requested baptism. He was employed by the mission but disappeared a year later.

The main early Christian influence in Bhutan came from Kalimpong (formerly British Bhutan, annexed by the British in 1865) to the west, the powerhouse of the Eastern Himalayan Mission (EHM) of the Church of Scotland, and their educational and medical institutions, which were frequented by people from Bhutan. But it was the native Nepali-Lepcha church of Kalimpong that made the first evangelistic expeditions into Bhutan after forming their own mission to Bhutan in 1891. Five successive national missionaries were sent out, of whom the first four died of disease and poisoning, but a base was established at the border town of Todey. To the southwest the Scandinavian Alliance Mission (handed over to the Finnish Alliance Mission in 1929) maintained a small station at Buxa Duars, the gateway to the capital of Bhutan at that time, from 1895. The first local converts in the 1930s formed the beginnings of a mixed ethnic church, including some native Bhutanese, at this border town. But this church became firmly established only from the 1950s with the ordination of three *Drukpa* Christians (two of them sons of the first converts). The earliest Christian witness in southeastern Bhutan was from the 1940s through a Bhutanese teacher (educated, converted, and baptized in Kalimpong) and Nepali and Boro Christians, all encouraged by the Norwegian Santal Mission. Rinchin Lama, the first Bhutanese evangelist in eastern Bhutan, died in 1947 of suspected poisoning, but not before the first church was started in Dewangiri. His work was carried on by Mr. Dhan, an ethnic Nepali married to a Bhutanese Christian, until 1958.

The way was paved for Christian missions to enter Bhutan itself by a Scotsman, Dr. Craig of the EHM, the first to settle inside Bhutan in 1962. Several other missions soon followed, including the Leprosy* Mission, the Salesians* of Don Bosco, the Norwegian Santal Mission, Bible and Medical Mission Fellowship (BMMF; later Interserve*), a Swedish mission, and others; all were invited to do various types of development work and "nation building." But by the mid-1980s the honeymoon period of missions was over. Visas were severely curtailed. Hospitals and other projects were gradually nationalized, and by 2000 mission personnel were out.

A few Christian congregations had grown up alongside the mission work, but the main church growth in the country was through the personal witness and testimony of Nepali, Lepcha, and other Indian Christian professionals, laborers, and settlers. In addition, an Eastern Himalayan Church Council (EHCC) mobile pastor from Kalimpong was allowed to travel in and out to minister to EHCC members in Bhutan during the 1970s. During P. S. Tingbo's tenure in Bhutan, a few hundred baptisms were reportedly performed and four Christian congregations formally organized.

Nepalis have been the most responsive group to the Christian message, and small house fellowships have formed throughout the country wherever a few Christians could gather; the native Tibeto-Buddhist Bhutanese have generally been much less responsive. The strongest church has grown up in the capital of Thimphu, but it is predominantly Nepali and Lepcha in the midst of the Ngalong stronghold.

Christianity is perceived as a threat to the Buddhist establishment, and open evangelism has never been allowed. This has led to various acts of suppression; thus there has been limited church growth, especially among native Bhutanese. Christians employed by mission institutions now face possible loss of their jobs under nationalization; a few Bhutanese have lost their jobs and even their homes due to conversion to Christianity; a few have been imprisoned and experienced harassment by local officials; and the government policy from 1989 of expulsion of "nonnationals" (under which most ethnic Nepalis are lumped) has displaced many Christian Nepalis. Nonetheless, those who have become Christians have a strong vibrant faith, and there is a firm foundation for the future of the church in Bhutan.

Bibliography

BMS Periodical Accounts, Vols. 3 (1806-9) and 4 (1809-11), at the Angus Library, Regent's Park College, Oxford. • Graham, J. A., *On the Threshold of Three Closed Lands* (1897; 2d ed. 1905). • Hamelin, Eila, and Sisko Peltoniemi, *Edellakavijat: Vuosisata Vapaakirkollista Lahetystyota* (The forerunners: One century of the mission of the Free Church) (1990) (in Finnish). • Haugstad, Edel and Magnus, *"Alt Det Jeg Vil, Det Gjor Jeg": Spedalskeaarbeidet Sprenger Grenser I Bhutan* ("I will do all that I will do": The leprosy work expands into Bhutan) (1978) (in Norwegian). • Perry, Cindy L., "Christianity in Bhutan," in *Nepali around the World* (1997). • Pinniger, Rachel, "History of the Church in Bhutan," Confidential TS (late 1980s), Himalayan Collection, CSCNWW, New College, University of Edinburgh. • Tingbo, Panthuk Singh, "Ringing the Gospel Bells at the Foothills of the Himalayas," (Th.M. thesis, Princeton Theological Seminary, Jan 1985). CINDY PERRY

Bhutto, Zulfiqar Ali

(b. Jan 1927; d. 4 Apr 1979). President and prime minister of Pakistan* (1971-77) overthrown in a coup d'etat and subsequently executed after a lengthy trial.

In the landscape of Pakistan's history, Bhutto stands out like a Byzantine mosaic. Educated at the University of California, Berkeley, and Oxford University, England, Bhutto was a Sindhi landlord and lawyer who entered national politics in the 1960s and founded the People's Party of Pakistan. He was a gifted leader with considerable public experience. With the support of the masses, armed with a significant coalition, and counseled by careful advisers, Bhutto was called to administer a nation that had been forced to submit to dismemberment, that seemed to have lost direction and was on the verge of rejecting its own ethos.

Bhutto's goal was to place Pakistan in the forefront of the Muslim nations, and he aspired to be the recognized spokesman for Third World causes. In international relations he was creative and generous, but at home he was deceitful, impulsive, and power-hungry. Bhutto did not apply at home what he practiced abroad. A case in point was the nationalization of several industries in Pakistan and, in particular, the nationalization of schools and colleges throughout Pakistan. As far as churches were concerned, this was a big blow to the standard of education in the country and a hindrance to the missionary charism of education of the poor and the masses, which has been, and continues to be, a service to the country by the minority Christian communities. These minority communities were now pressured by the government to cater to the needs of an elite Muslim majority by maintaining certain elite Christian schools as privately run institutions, while all their schools in rural areas and colleges in city areas were nationalized. This also created a second-class feeling among the minority communities that soured in the years ahead with the processes of Islamization*.

During the Bhutto years, several elements characterized his foreign policy, and certain local innovations left their mark in history. Only months after the debacle in former East Pakistan, Bhutto turned the nation's foreign policy in new and virtually uncharted directions. He labeled his foreign policy "bilateralism," which implied that Pakistan would cease taking sides in the Cold War, would deal equally with the superpowers, would strengthen its ties with China and begin a process of expanding relations with Communist countries in Eastern Europe as well as with North Korea. Standing arrangements with the United States were still to be honored. Above all, the Simla Accords with India and the developments that followed showed that Bhutto had done as well as could be expected. During this period, the Muslim countries became Pakistan's largest market for its exports, as he frequently contacted Muslim heads of state (and governments) and obtained much needed economic and financial assistance from them.

On the home front Bhutto encouraged his people with the slogan *Roti, Kapra, Makan* (bread, clothing, housing) and won over the hearts of Pakistanis. However, not all the elements of this slogan were realized for the masses (the *Awam*), who even heralded him as the *Quaid-E-Awam* (leader of the people).

Bhutto's tragic end will not be forgotten in the history of Pakistan. He was removed from office by a coup d'etat led by the army's chief of staff, General Mohammed Zia Ul-Haq*, on 5 Jul 1977. After a lengthy trial, Bhutto was executed in 1979.

Bibliography

Bhutto, Zulfiqar Ali, *If I Am Assassinated . . .* (1979). • Ziring, Lawrence, "Bhutto's Foreign Policy, 1972-1973," *Contemporary Problems of Pakistan,* ed. Henry Korson (1974). • Zafar, M. D., *A Short History of Pakistan.*

Archie Desouza

Bianchi, Lawrence

(b. Corteno, Italy, 1 Apr 1899; d. Brescia, Italy, 13 Feb 1983). Second bishop of Hong Kong* Catholic Diocese (1951-69).

Bianchi was the "missionary of Hoi Fung" and the bishop who led the Catholic Church throughout the difficult period of the influx of refugees into Hong Kong. He is remembered for having shown an admirable spirit of service, openness, and cooperation with everyone.

Bianchi joined the Pontifical Institute for Foreign Missions* in 1920 and was ordained a priest in 1922. He arrived in Hong Kong in 1923 and was soon assigned to the Hoi Fung District, where he worked until 1952, sharing the many hardships and the few joys of the local people that were the result of the chaotic conditions of those years.

On 10 Oct 1949, Bianchi was consecrated auxiliary bishop of Hong Kong, but soon after he returned to Hoi Fung to remain with his "sheep," to whom he felt he belonged, during the difficult times of the Communist takeover. He himself was arrested with three other priests and kept in custody until Oct 1952, when he returned to Hong Kong. He was warmly welcomed by Catholics there as their bishop, since in the meantime Mgr. H. Valtorta had died.

Bianchi soon had to face the great challenges posed by the influx of refugees from mainland China. Churches, chapels, and spiritual centers mushroomed. In a very unassuming and friendly way, but with a long-range vision, he encouraged and welcomed everyone by providing the services needed both for relief and for education, according to his motto, "We work for today and trust in God for tomorrow." He also made efforts to better coordinate and organize these services. For example, the various welfare agencies were gradually organized under Caritas-Hong Kong*, while the Catechetical Center was set up in 1963.

Taking part in the Second Vatican Council in Rome (1962-65) made Bianchi fully aware of the need for a local and new leadership of the diocese. Therefore, and also in view of his declining health, in 1968 he submitted his resignation, and in Apr 1969 he returned to Italy, hastening the handover of the direction of the church to the local clergy.

Bibliography

Gheddo, P., *Lorenzo Bianchi di Hong Kong* (1988).

Sergio Ticozzi

Bible Society

In 1804, the British and Foreign Bible Society (BFBS) was founded to serve the need for Scripture both in Britain and throughout the world. Its vision was quickly realized with the establishment of a corresponding committee in 1806 in Serampore, Bengal, India*. It was in Serampore that many of the missionary translations of Scripture were printed for the rest of Asia (see Bible Translations). In 1811, the first Bible Society agency in Asia was established in Calcutta. Others quickly followed. In 1812, one was set up in Colombo, Ceylon (Sri Lanka*). In India, the Bombay auxiliary was established in 1813, and the Madras auxiliary in 1819. In the East Indies, the first agency was set up in Batavia (1814), then in the Moluccas* (1815), and in 1818 an auxiliary was formed in Sumatra with Stamford Raffles* as president.

It was not only the BFBS which was active in Bible work. The Netherlands Bible Society (1814) also served the publishing interests of the missionary translators in what today we know as Indonesia*, Malaysia*, and the Philippines*. They worked closely with BFBS throughout the region. They were later joined by the American

Bible Society (1816) mostly in the Philippines, China*, and northeast Asia, and by the National Bible Society of Scotland (1861).

The work of these Bible societies through their agencies in Asia was to support translation activity, then to publish and distribute Scripture. Their work was inseparable from that of the missionary translators, but it was the development of distributors (colporteurs) that ensured that Scriptures were made available to the peoples of Asia. That mission remains the focus of the many national Bible societies which have been established in Asia since 1811.

The links in those early days between Bible societies, missionaries, and the political and trading interests of their national governments cannot be overlooked. However, the BFBS, Dutch, Scottish, and American Bible Societies generally cooperated rather than competed with one another to ensure the provision of Scriptures to all.

In India, the six auxiliaries that were set up served the Scripture needs of most of the subcontinent — today's Pakistan*, India, Bangladesh*, Myanmar*, Nepal*, and Bhutan*. By 1853, they reported distributing over two million copies of Scripture in the first half-century of their ministry. The establishment of a national office eventually coordinated the work of the auxiliaries (now 15). The Bible Society of India is the largest national Bible society in the world. Annual distribution of Bibles and New Testaments in India now exceeds the figure for their first 50 years.

The British and Foreign Bible Society (BFBS) began work for Burma (Myanmar) by publishing the Pali New Testament in Colombo, Ceylon (Sri Lanka). This translation was begun in 1813 and completed in 1835.

Prior to 1889, the BFBS had cooperated with the Myanmar Bible and Tract Society for more than 20 years. The agency for Myanmar was established in 1889. William Sherratt, who had served two years with the Wesleyan Missionary Society in Monywa, took office in Yangon as agent in Jan 1899, and a new Bible House at Sule Pagoda Road, Yangon, was formally inaugurated on 19 Nov 1909, but the work was suspended during World War I. During World War II*, the Burma Agency opened its office in Madras under the charge of H. C. Willans. He returned to Myanmar and reopened the Bible House in Apr 1946. The society has published a number of Bible translations since 1903.

Bible Society work in the East Indies began in 1814. Cooperation between the British and Dutch Bible Societies and missions was very close, and there was a very effective network of colporteurs active in providing Scriptures throughout the islands. Bibles for China and Indochina were printed in Malacca* from 1882. From the establishment of the agency office in Batavia (Jakarta) in 1814, work began throughout Indonesia with the Dutch society eventually taking over responsibilities for distribution from Bandung until 1937. BFBS distribution was to Java and Bali. The National Bible Society was established in 1950 and moved to Jakarta. Work from Singapore* began officially with an auxiliary in 1837, and the first Bible House opened in 1910.

Both the British and the Dutch Bible Societies provided Scriptures to the Philippines even after the islands were ceded to America in 1899, and the American Bible Society began officially to work there. The country was divided between the various agencies to serve the needs of the people better. Vernacular language translations done in Spain were published and distributed from 1899.

China had always been a major focus of Christian activity, and this holds true for the Bible societies as well. Support for the early missionary translators was strong. The work of Robert Morrison*, William Milne*, Karl Gutzlaff*, and others was supported by the Bible societies as well as by their own missions. Distribution in China was made possible through the five treaty ports, but it was not until 1860 with the Treaty of Tientsin opening up more ports to European expansion that wider distribution throughout the country was possible. Chinese converts became increasingly involved in the distribution work. The first auxiliary office was set up in 1868 in Shanghai and printing was done in Hong Kong. This auxiliary became the East China Bible Society with a related office in Hangkow for central China. By 1937, the China Bible Society was established with local leaders in Canton and Hongkow. Not until 1950 was the first indigenous general secretary, a Dr. Lee, appointed in Shanghai.

Although there had been early Christian contact with Japan* from the time of Francis Xavier*, the first official Bible distributor in Japan was a British missionary who arrived in 1878; the American and the Scottish societies had had a presence in the country since 1875. A committee was set up in 1890 to coordinate the work of the three foreign Bible societies, and shortly after they were given permission to circulate Scriptures freely. Many Japanese bought the Scriptures but few seemed to be moved by them, in contrast to Korea*, where work had begun with Scottish missionaries in Manchuria. There the response was much greater. The Japan Bible Society became independent in 1938.

Korean Bible work began with the Scottish missionaries, who also helped develop type for printing, leading to the Gospels being published in 1882 and the New Testament in 1887. Again the British, American, and Scottish Bible Societies worked together until the Americans withdrew to concentrate on work in the Philippines. The Korean Bible Society was established in 1938 while the country was under Japanese occupation. It became autonomous in 1940, though after the Korean War* its activities were confined to the South.

Today, national Bible societies exist in almost every Asian country. They are linked through the United Bible Societies, the global fellowship which began its service and coordination work in 1946. Countries where national Bible societies do not exist for political reasons still are able to have their Scripture needs met through other channels but only with government recognition or sanction.

Bibliography

One-Hundred–Year History of the Japan Bible Society (Nihon seisho kyokai hyaku-nen shi) (1975).

GRAHAM S. OGDEN, with U THAN HTUN MYAT and TANABE MOTOAKI

Bible Translation

Bible translation in Asia has a long history dating back to the mid-2nd c. C.E., when the Gospels were translated into Syriac, and the religious and cultural language centered in Edessa (modern Turkey). The standard, or *Peshitta,* version from the 5th c. was carried by evangelists to Sri Lanka* and China* from the 6th to the 10th c.

Apart from the early Syriac translations, we have only sketchy information of subsequent translation work up to the Reformation. For example, Pope Benedict XII in 1335 refers to a Mongolian Bible, presumably a translation of the New Testament (NT) and Psalms done by a Franciscan* monk at the court of Kublai Khan in 1306. Unfortunately no trace of this text remains. It seems as though Bible translation was essentially a task undertaken in post-Reformation times. The list of the earliest translations which follows makes that clear.

In the major Asian languages, the earliest translation was the Malay translation of 1629. This Gospel of Matthew, published in Dutch and Malay by the Dutch East-India Company, reflects the close relationship between the early European traders and European missionary activity.

Bible Translation and Evangelism. Among the earliest Scripture translations in the Asia region were those undertaken by Roman Catholic missionaries. Their purpose appears to have been largely liturgical, translating passages of the Old Testament (OT), including the Psalms, and the Gospels for use in worship.

One of the earliest Catholic translations was in Japanese, done in Goa, India, by a Japanese exile named Yajiro. Francis Xavier* had met Yajiro in 1548. The following year, Yajiro translated the Gospel of Matthew. Upon arrival in Japan, Xavier discovered that the uneducated Yajiro had produced a translation which was not acceptable in view of its poor level of language and incompleteness. The Jesuits* produced a NT in Kyoto in 1613, but no copies remain. It was not until Protestant missionaries arrived in the 19th c. that other Bible translation work was undertaken there.

Beginning in the 17th c., Protestant missions engaged in Bible translation essentially for evangelistic purposes. They shared the belief that Bible translation was an essential part of the evangelistic task, for without the Scriptures in the hands of the people, the local church could not grow and mature. The Bible in local languages allowed indigenous Christians to interpret the Bible in culturally appropriate ways, strengthened vernacular languages, recognized and affirmed the value of local cultures, and played a significant role in enculturating the faith.

Initially, the translation task throughout Asia was in the hands of foreign missionaries, either individually or as committees. Involvement of indigenous peoples was generally as assistants to the foreigner translators. However, it is certain that the linguistic contribution of the native speakers was much greater than generally recorded in missionary reports. Thus we note that early Bible translations often bear the missionary's name but not that of the nationalist coworker. The early translations were heavily influenced by foreign speakers of the language, resulting in some very unnatural renderings. These early missionary translators were generally committed to putting the Bible text into a form which was bound by the form of the original languages. As a result, the translation was often not natural in the local language. There was in some cases a resistance to using local terms which the missionaries felt had pagan associations, and so they created new terms they believed to be more biblical or religiously neutral. Without denying the significant contributions of these early translators, it is nevertheless important to state that their translations tended to create a church language which was unnatural, through it was accepted by local Christians because of the missionaries' influence and authority.

Among the early missionary translators in Asia certain names stand out. In India, the Danish missionary Bartholomew Ziegenbalg* in 1714 published his Tamil NT using the classical form of the language. By his death, he had completed the OT up to the book of Ruth. Others continued his work, but their work was not of a sufficient standard and needed to be redone. This task later fell to Johann Fabricius* and was completed in 1796, giving India its first Bible in an Indian language.

William Carey*, a British Baptist missionary, arrived in India in 1793 and within five years translated the NT into Bengali. His first attempt was unintelligible, as he had not mastered Bengali idiom. Undeterred, he retranslated the NT. He was joined in 1799 by two others, Joshua Marshman*, a school- teacher, and William Ward*, a printer. Setting up work in Serampore, north of Calcutta, they established the Serampore Press and, during their 30 years together, translated and published six Bibles, 23 NTs, and Bible portions in 10 additional languages. Carey was responsible for Bengali, Sanskrit, and Marathi. Marshman learned Chinese and published the NT, though it was not widely accepted owing to its unnatural expression. Carey also published a Sanskrit dictionary. Nothing is heard of their local assistants.

Among those early arrivals in Serampore was one Henry Martyn. Arriving in 1806 after a Cambridge University education, he studied Urdu and translated the NT. His translation remained current without the need for revision for over a century. Martyn also thoroughly revised the earlier Persian translation. He was engaged in revising the Arabic translation when he died in 1813 at the age of 31 in Persia.

Bible translation into Chinese was undertaken (we presume) by the Jesuits in the early 16th c., but none of their work survives. On the other hand, the discovery of some portions on scrolls is evidence that the Persian (Nestorian*) Christians who came to China during the 7th c. C.E. may have engaged in some Bible translation.

The first Protestant missionary to arrive in China was Robert Morrison* of the London Missionary Society; he reached Canton in 1807. Protected by his appointment as translator for the East India Company, Morrison completed his translation of the NT in 1813 and the Bible in 1819, though it was not published until 1823. He also produced a Chinese dictionary. At the same time, Marshman and Lassar were working on their Chinese translation in Serampore, India. Their Chinese Bible was published in 1822, before that of Morrison and Milne* (who arrived in 1813) in Canton. Early texts were in the literary form known as Wenli, and each page was hand-carved on wood blocks.

Morrison's Bible required revision to make it more idiomatic. It went through several revisions until in 1843 a group of missionaries from different missions was organized to do another revision. Their Gospels appeared in 1850, the NT in 1852, and the OT in 1854. Among the many problems facing this group was the rendering of the words "God" and "spirit." Agreement was not possible, and so the early editions left blank spaces for the different traditions to insert the words they preferred. This translation problem continues, though several versions are now available to meet the needs of different church communities.

The need to translate into Mandarin to make the Scriptures more widely available led to a decision at the end of the 19th c. to form a committee to translate and publish a Bible in Northern or Peking Mandarin. This group produced the Union Version in 1919 in the colloquial style of the time, making it available to all educated Chinese. Translations into the various dialects using romanized orthography or characters was going on at the same time, the first to appear being a Scripture portion in Shanghai dialect in 1847. Other dialect translations appeared throughout the 19th c.

The first Protestant missionary to Myanmar (Burma) was the American Adoniram Judson* in 1813. He set himself to the task of learning Burmese and began his NT translation. Under suspicion of spying when the Anglo-Burmese war broke out in 1824, he was jailed for almost two years, kept alive only by his wife's care. His NT manuscript was hidden in his pillow. His jailers threw it out on one occasion, but the pillow and the manuscript were rescued by a friend who eventually realized its significance. It was preserved and incorporated into the final manuscript. Judson's translation of the Bible was completed in 1834. He also compiled an English-Burmese dictionary.

Melchior Leidekker, a Dutch missionary in Batavia, translated the OT and much of the NT into Malay using the Arabic script. The task was completed by van der Dorm, and the Bible published in 1758. Though regularly revised, it continued to have an impact on the church in Malaya and Indonesia until the early part of the 20th c. It was revised again in 1912 by a group including William Shellabear*.

Bible Translation and Literacy. With its emphasis on education, early mission activity often involved the establishment of schools. There was a close relationship between this activity and the translation of the Bible, because without literacy* the Bible could not be read. In fact, one of the motivating factors in the establishment of mission schools was that people might be taught to read the Bible. In so-called minor language groups, often the only written document available in the local language is some portion of the Scriptures. Literacy for Bible reading has been an important associate of Bible translation.

Earliest Bible Translations in Asia. The list on pages 81-83 gives some of the earliest translations done in the various major languages of Asia. It does not include later revisions or modern translations. Many of the languages listed are spoken in more than one country; country names are generally those extant at the time of the translation.

The translation of Scripture is an ongoing task. As language changes, older translations need to be redone or revised to reflect both those changes and advancing scholarship in biblical and textual studies. Also, in view of the needs of smaller language communities, translations in so-called minor languages are increasingly being given priority.

Most modern Bible translation work is in the hands of native speakers of the various languages. This basic change from missionary to mother-tongue speaker ensures that the resulting translation is a more natural one. Additionally, the focus in translation is on rendering the meaning of the biblical text, rather than its form in the original languages. This means that some biblical idioms and other figurative expressions as well as literary structures are modified to what is more natural in the translator's own tongue.

In 1994, there were 205 translation projects currently being undertaken by the various national Bible Societies* and 151 by other translation agencies within the Asia region. Most of these are in the languages of minority groups, with older translations in dominant languages being revised to address the needs of the younger generation. Altogether there have been 105 Bibles and 168 NTs published in Asia, though many of these have also been revised since their original publication date. Bible societies and other translation agencies regularly update these figures.

It is not possible to provide a complete survey of translations done throughout the Asian region. However, the following brief summaries provide some examples of translation history in Asia.

Japan. The first Bible translation into Japanese was

Country	Language	First Portion	NT	Bible	Translator(s) and Notes
Afghanistan	Dari	1974	1982	—	
	Pashto	—	1818	1895	NT by Serampore missionaries; Bible by Mayer, Hughes, Jukes
Bangladesh	Bengali (see under India)				
China	Cantonese	1862	1877	1894	
	Foochow	1852	1856	1884	
	Hainan	1891	—	—	
	Hakka	1860	1883	1916	
	Hangchow	1879	—	—	
	Hankow	1921	—	—	
	Hinghua	1892	1900	1912	
	Mandarin	1854	1857	1878	Bible was Schereschewsky's OT (1874) + Peking Committee's NT
	Nanking	1854	1857	—	
	Ningpo	1852	1868	1901	
	Shanghai	1847	1870	1908	Medhurst, Farnham
	Shantung	1892	—	—	
	Soochow	1879	1881	1908	
	Swatow	1875	1896	1922	
	Taichow	1880	1881	1914	
	Union Version	—	1907	1919	Representatives of various missions
	Wenchow	1892	1902	—	
	Wenli (easy)	1880	1885	1902	Schereschewsky
	Wenli (high)	1810	1814	1822	1810 — Matthew by Marshman & Lassar; 1810 — Acts by Morrison; 1819 — Bible by Morrison & Milne (pub. 1823); 1822 — Bible by Marshman & Lassar in Serampore
India	Awadhi	1820	—	—	
	Bengali	1800	1801	1809	Trans. by Carey, rev. 1832; 1852 rev. by Wenger
	Dakhini	1747	1758	—	A form of Hindustani spoken by Muslims in Hyderabad, later replaced by Urdu; trans. Schultze
	Gujarati	1809	1820	1823	
	Hindi	1806	1811	1835	
	Jaipuri	1815	—	—	
	Kannada	1812	1823	1831	
	Kashmiri	—	1821	1899	
	Khasi	1816	1831	1891	Serampore missionaries; Bible trans. by Roberts & Welsh Mission
	Kiu	1893	1954	—	
	Kohli	1834	—	—	
	Malayalam	1811	1829	1841	
	Malto	1881	—	—	
	Manipuri	1820	1827	1984	
	Marathi	1807	1811	1821	
	Mizo	1898	1916	1959	
	Mundari	1876	1895	1910	
	Naga	1883	1929	1964	
	Pali	1827	1835	—	
	Panjabi	—	1815	1959	
	Sanskrit	—	1808	1822	Carey et al. in Serampore
	Santali	1868	1887	1914	
	Tamil	1714	1715	1727	Ziegenbalg (Danish Luth.); 1871 revision by Bower known as Union Version; 1949 rev. by Monahan, Bishop Azariah, etc.

Bible Translation

Country	Language	First Portion	NT	Bible	Translator(s) and Notes
	Telegu	1812	1818	1854	
	Tulu	1842	1847		
Indonesia	Balinese	1910	1978	—	
	Batak, Karo	1910	1928	1987	
	Batak, Toba	1859	1878	1894	
	Biak	1870	—	—	
	Bideyu	1887	1963	—	
	Bugis	1863	1888	1900	
	Dayak	—	1846	1858	
	Indonesian	—	—	1959	Swellengrebel + committee; until after World War II, Indonesian and Malay were the same language
	Javanese	—	1829	1854	
	Macassar	1864	1888	1900	
	Nias	1874	1892	1911	
	Sundanese	1854	1877	1891	
Iran	Armenian	1831	1834	1883	
	Azerbaijani	1842	1878	1891	
	Baluchi	1815	—	—	
	Kurdish	1856	1872	—	
	Persian	1546	1815	1838	1546 — Pentateuch for Persian Jews trans. by Jacob ben Joseph Taurus; 1815 — NT by Henry Martyn, often revised; Bible by Thomas Robinson in India
Japan	Ainu	1889	1897	—	Trans. Batchelor
	Japanese	1837	1879	1883	1549 — Matthew trans. by Yajiro, a convert in India, brought to Japan by Xavier; 1613 — NT trans. by Jesuits in Kyoto, no copies remain; Bible trans. by group representing all Protestant missions, including Hepburn and Japanese scholars
Kampuchea	Khmer	1899	1929	1954	
Korea	Korean	1882	1887	1911	NT trans. by Ross; 1911 — Bible by Bible trans. Committee of Korea (missionaries)
Laos	Lao	1906	1926	1932	NT/Bible trans. by Audetat and Willy (Swiss Brethren)
Malaysia	Malay	1629	1668	1733	1629 Gospel is first extant Bible translation into non-European language (diglot Dutch-Malay, publ. by Dutch East-India Co.); 1758 — Bible in Arabic script by Leidekker and van der Dorm, used in Indonesia and Malaya for over 150 years
	Malay (Baba)	1891	1913	—	
Mongolia	Mong., Inner	1872	1952	—	1872 — Matthew trans. by Mongolian lama, rev. by Schereschewsky
	Mong., Khalka	1979	1990	—	
	Mong., literary	1819	1827	—	1827 — NT printed in Russia but not circulated; 1840 — OT trans. by Stallybrass, Swan, and Yuille
Myanmar	Burmese	1815	1832	1835	NT and Bible trans. by Judson
	Karen	1857	—	—	
	Mon	1843	1847	1928	NT trans. by Haswell, OT by Halliday
	Pwo Kayin	1845	1860	1883	
	Shan	1871	1882	1892	Trans. by Cushing
Nepal	Mundari	1876	1895	1910	Bible by Nottrott (German Evangelical Lutheran)
	Nepali	—	1821	1914	NT trans. by Serampore missionaries; Bible by Turnbull, etc.

Bible Translation

Country	Language	First Portion	NT	Bible	Translator(s) and Notes
Pakistan	Marwari	1821	1899	—	
	Panjabi	1815	1959	—	
	Sindhi	1825	1890	1954	
	Siraiki	—	1819	—	
	Urdu	1805	1814	1843	1805 — Gospels in Devanagari script; 1817 — NT trans. by Henry Martyn, rev. 1829, romanized 1836; 1965 — Bible in Arabic script
Philippines	Cebuano	1902	1908	1917	
	Hiligaynon	1900	1903	1912	
	Ilokano	1899	1903	1909	Union Version trans. by committee
	Pampango	1901	1908	1917	
	Pangasinan	1887	1908	1915	Trans. by Lavalle, Basconsillo, and American Methodist missionaries; Bible rev. in 1924-25 as original plates were destroyed in Tokyo earthquake of 1923
	Samarenyo	1908	1928	1937	
	Tagalog	1898	1902	1905	NT trans. by Calderon & Miller
Sri Lanka	Indo-Portuguese	1819	1826	—	Portuguese Creole now extinct
	Pali	1827	1835	—	
	Sinhala	1739	1776	1823	Gospels trans. by Conijin and Wetzelius (Dutch Reformed); 1823 — OT trans. by Tolfrey, etc., including M. Perera; 1938 — Bible rev. by Union Committee
Taiwan	Formosan	1661	—	—	An aboriginal language spoken near Tainan, trans. by Gravius (Dutch Reformed)
	Taiwanese	1852	1873	1884	NT trans. by English Presbyterians; Bible by American Reformed Missionaries; 1933 — Bible trans. by Barclay
Thailand	Thai	1834	1843	1883	1834 — Gospels trans. by Gutzlaff; NT by Jones with Robinson and Caswell
	Thai (Nthn)	1876	1914	—	1876 — Matthew trans. by McGilvary
Vietnam	Vietnamese	1890	1914	1916	1890 — Luke trans. by M. Bonet; Bible by Schlicklin (Roman Catholic)

the Gospel of Matthew done by Yajiro in Goa, under the guidance of Francis Xavier in 1549. It consisted only of brief notes. Roman Catholic missionaries also began in 1549 to translate biblical passages such as the Lord's Prayer and Ten Commandments. By 1552, Juan Fernandez had produced from the Gospels excerpts of Jesus' life and passion, leading to all four Gospels being available in 1563, though the manuscript was subsequently lost in a fire. By 1613, a complete NT was available.

In 1836, K. F. A. Gutzlaff* was among the Protestant missionaries who arrived in Japan. Using Morrison's Chinese text, he worked with assistants to produce a translation of John's Gospel and the letters of John in 1838. A coworker, S. Williams, translated Matthew. The Ryukyu dialect (Okinawa) had a translation of the Gospels and Romans in 1855 thanks to the work of Bettelheim.

Subsequent translation work was undertaken by Channing Williams, James Hepburn, and Samuel Brown, usually from the available Chinese text. The Chinese text played a significant role in determining church vocabulary in Japanese. In 1864, J. Goble began working from the Greek text to produce Matthew's Gospel and published it using woodblock printing.

A General Conference of Protestant Missionaries of Japan was held in 1872. One of their decisions was to appoint a committee, chaired by Samuel Brown, to which various missions appointed translator representatives. Japanese translators were included (Okuno, Matsuyama, and Takahashi Goro, and others). They worked from the *textus receptus* and King James Version, together with a Chinese translation, beginning in 1874. Difficulties in choosing terms for "God" and "baptism" were noted, but in 1879 they completed the NT and published it in Apr 1880. It was known as the Original Meiji Translation.

Nathan Brown, a Baptist who resigned from the original committee over the terminology issue, published his NT in 1879. Renewing their cooperative approach, the committee continued their work and published the Bible in 1887.

The Roman Catholic Church* was also working on Bible translations at the same time. Petitjean published passages from the passion of Jesus (1873), and in 1879-80 Kojima Junji published excerpts from the OT and NT. In 1887, a committee to translate the Gospels was formed and commissioned to submit a draft to a bishops' conference, but due to pressure of other work the members of the committee were unable to complete the task. However, Takahashi Goro produced a translation of the Gospels in 1895 which won praise from the Protestant Meiji translators. An even more comprehensive work was published in 1910 including references and commentary, an explanation of theological terms, and textual notes.

The Orthodox Church* in Japan used the Chinese Protestant Bible through the 1870s, and in 1889 notes were added to the text of the NT. The first original translation for the Orthodox Church was done by Ueda Susumi and published in 1892. It consisted of Matthew's Gospel only, but it gave rise to an Orthodox NT translation being completed in 1896 and revised in 1901.

With the appearance of excellent Catholic, Orthodox, and Baptist translations, the original Protestant Meiji Translation was seen to need revising. A broad-based revision committee was set up in 1909 and, under the leadership of Daniel Greene, began work the following year. In 1911, a test translation of Mark was published, and in 1916 the work was completed, with the official Taisho Revised Version being published in 1917. The use of the Nestle revised Greek text and many linguistic and stylistic factors, as well as the full participation of Japanese Christians, ensured that this version was widely accepted.

Individual translations also have their history from around the beginning of the 20th c., including the first OT translations done from the Hebrew text. These are associated with Sakon Yoshisuke and Yuasa Hangetsu, among others.

Language changes since World War II indicated the need for further revisions and new translations of the Bible. F. Barbaro and A. Del Col of the Salesian order worked on a Bible which was published in 1964 using more colloquial language. At the same time, E. Breitung of the Franciscan order worked with Kawaminami Shigeo and produced an OT with the Deuterocanon for the first time (1954-59). In 1952, the Japan Bible Society began a revision in more colloquial language and completed the work in 1955.

In 1972, work began on an interconfessional translation under Bible Society sponsorship. This milestone work was published in 1987, the first Catholic-Protestant translation in Japan.

Sri Lanka. The Roman Catholics who evangelized Sri Lanka in the 16th c. brought the Bible to the island for use by the priests. Subsequently, portions of the Bible were translated into the vernacular for the instruction of the people.

The Dutch Protestant missionaries were the first to work on a vernacular translation of the Bible into Sinhala (1638-1796). Simon Cat translated Matthew and Acts. It was written on ola leaves and distributed to government schools. This work was revised by William Conijn and J. P. Wetzelius, to which they added Mark and John. These were printed on the printing press newly set up in Colombo in 1732. Following this, Henrick Philips, a Sinhalese minister, translated and published the remaining NT books and the first five books of the OT.

Bible translation was boosted by the establishment of the Bible Society in 1812. A fresh translation was undertaken, and in 1817 a NT was published. It was guided by William Tolfrey and was highly regarded for its scholarship. The OT appeared in three installments (1822-24). Believing that the Bible Society publication was too scholarly, the Church Missionary Society undertook another translation. Their NT was published in 1832 and the OT in 1834. However, this translation (known as the Cotta version) failed to gain popular support because of its incorrect use of honorific terms in the language. A modified version was released in 1855 by the Bible Society. The Baptists disagreed with the use of certain theological terms and so published their own version of the NT in 1862, and the OT in 1905.

In 1938, the Baptist mission worked with the Bible Society to publish a common version, though the result was disappointing in view of the grammatical and syntactical problems it contained. Thus in 1962, a new translation was undertaken, out of which the modern Sinhalese translation grew (NT in 1973 and OT in 1982). This translation was done interconfessionally and is highly regarded even though the Roman Catholic Church had its own translation in 1929. The Apocrypha was first translated in 1986.

Questions of terminology in the 1982 translation caused some Protestant Christians to object to it. They claimed that Buddhist terms were introduced; thus a revision was made in 1992 with evangelical cooperation.

Supply of Tamil Bibles from India have made the question of Tamil translation largely unnecessary. However, in the early days the Dutch did work on a Tamil translation. Philippus Baldaeus* translated Matthew and circulated it among schools. The first printed translation of Matthew was done by A. de Mey in 1741, with the whole NT being published in 1759.

In the north of the country, the Jaffna Auxiliary of the Bible Society undertook a fresh translation supervised by Peter Percival. It produced the Bible in 1850, though it was not very popular among Sri Lankan Tamils, as they preferred the translation from South India.

The Indo-Portuguese language was a dialect spoken by Sri Lankans of Portuguese and Dutch descent. There has been a decline in the number of people speaking this language, but the Bible Society published Matthew's Gospel (1819), the Psalms (1821), the four Gospels (1823), and the complete NT in 1826.

Indonesia. The first portion of Scripture to be translated into an Indonesian language was the Gospel of Matthew, published in 1629. Translated into Malay by a Dutch merchant, A. C. Ruyl, in 1612, it was published as a Malay-Dutch diglot. It was in fact the first portion of the Bible to be published in a non-European language. In 1668, the NT in Indonesian Malay was published. It had been translated by Daniel Brower and was followed in 1733 by the complete Bible translated by Melchior Leidekker. Other Indonesian Malay translations included the complete Bible translated by H. C. Klinkert in 1879 and the NT by W. A. Bode in 1939.

When World War II* ended and Indonesia became an independent nation, Indonesian Malay, *Bahasa Indonesia,* became the national language. Under the auspices of the Netherlands Bible Society and subsequently the Indonesian Bible Society, a new translation was undertaken. The committee began work in 1952 and completed it in 1970. The complete Indonesian Bible was published in 1974 and is widely used.

Meanwhile, translations were being undertaken for the other language groups throughout Indonesia. During the 19th and early 20th cs., the Bible appeared in Javanese, Toba Batak, Macassar, Bugis, Sundanese, Toraja, and Nias, while the NT or portions of the Bible were published in various other languages.

Before independence, the task of Bible translation was largely in the hands of missionaries. A major shift in the approach to translation took place in the 1970s, with the Indonesian Bible Society stressing the need for native speakers to do the translation work. Following this new principle, the Bible has now been published in Indonesian, Karo Batak, Toba Batak, Balinese, Sundanese, and Angkola Batak. The NT has been published in a variety of other regional languages. At the end of 1992, 135 Indonesian languages had at least a portion of the Bible, while translation work in many of the remaining languages continues.

Since 1968, Protestants and Catholics have participated in the revision of the new translation of the 1952 Protestant Bible. An interconfessional (or ecumenical) version of the NT in *Bahasa Indonesia* was published in 1975 by the Bible Society. The entire Bible was published in 1977. A common-language translation of the NT was published in 1977 and the whole Bible in 1988.

Malay. Since the language of modern Malaysia and Indonesia is essentially the same, the list on page 86 identifies translations which were complete, which were significantly different from their predecessors, and which were recognized as Malay rather than other regional languages. This list does not include all the translations of the Bible into languages in the Indonesian archipelago, such as Bugis, Javanese, and Batak.

China. The Bible was partly translated into Chinese during the Tang Dynasty, when Persian Christian missionaries arrived in China during the 7th c. A.D. During the Ming and Ching Dynasties, missionaries from the Roman Catholic and Russian Orthodox Churches also worked on translations of the NT and Psalms. However, it was the Protestant missionaries who first provided a complete Bible in Chinese.

Three types of Bible translation were done: (1) *Wenli* (literary style) included the work of Joshua Marshman and Johannes Lassar, of Robert Morrison and William Milne. Others who produced translations in this form of the language were W. Medhurst*, K. F. A. Gutzlaff, and Elijah Bridgman with Ke Bi-Sheng. (2) *Easy Wenli* (less literary style) was done by Griffith John*, Bao Yue-Han, Bai Han-Li, and S. Schereschewsky*. (3) *Guo-Yu* (national common language) is associated with the names of W. Medhurst, J. Stronach*, J. Edkins*, W. A. P. Martin*, Schereschewsky, and Griffith John.

Marshman and Lassar completed the NT in 1811 and the Bible in 1822 in Serampore, India. The so-called Delegates Version of 1852 was the result of various mission boards and organizations sending delegates to a working committee. They produced the NT. However, during this work a difference of opinion about how to translate the Greek word *theos* (God) arose, resulting in two versions being printed. One version used *Shangti* and the other *Shen.* The terminology issue persists until today.

In 1890, there was a mission conference held in Shanghai and a resolution passed to establish a committee for Bible translation. As a result of this committee's work, the NT Union Version was published in 1906 and the revised NT together with the OT in 1919. This version *(Guo-yu)* still enjoys wide acceptance among the Chinese-speaking churches. Since 1980, the Chinese Christian Three-Self Patriotic Movement* and the China Christian Council (CCC)* have printed this Bible. In Jan 2001, the CCC celebrated the printing of its 25 millionth Bible.

Most of the above translation work was carried out by foreign missionaries, with Chinese help in the discussion and editing. After the Union Version appeared, Zhu Bao-Hui, Wang Xuan-Chen, and Lu Zhen-Zhong also made translations and published their work.

Zhu Bao-Hui's translation was published in Shanghai in 1936. A native of Shandung and a graduate of Nanking Theological Seminary, Zhu taught Greek there from 1927. He began his translation in 1920 and worked until 1929, later revising the draft completely until its publication in 1936. Zhu's translation also included a commentary and exposition at the conclusion of each book.

Wang Xuan-Chen was a graduate of what later became Cheeloo University and was an assistant to C. W. Mateer, who worked on the Union Version translation. Wang began his work of revising the Union Version in 1931 and completed it in 1933. He based his revision on the Vulgate, but it was not a popular translation.

Lu Zhen-Zhong taught at Fukien Theological Seminary and Yenching Graduate School of Religion.

Bible Translations in *Bahasa Malay*

1646	Albert Cornelius Ruyl, Jan van Hasel	The Gospels	(Indonesia)
1651	Justus Heurn	1646 version + Acts of the Apostles	(Indonesia)
1651	Heurn and van Hasel	1651 version + Psalms	(Indonesia)
1668	Daniel Brower	NT (sponsored by Dutch East-India Company)	(Indonesia)
1733	Melchior Leidekker	Full Bible in Malay (romanized script)	(Indonesia)
1758	M. Leidekker	Full Bible in Malay (Arabic script)	(Indonesia)
1832	Claudius Thomsen, Robert Burns, Abdullah bin Abdul Kadir	Gospel and Acts	(Malaysia)
1835	W. H. Medhurst,* D. Lenting	NT in Malay	(Indonesia, Surabaya)
1852	Benjamin Keasberry*	NT in Malay (romanized)	(Malaysia)
1856	B. Keasberry	NT in Malay (Arabic)	(Malaysia)
1863	Cornelius Klinkert	NT (Low Malay)	(Indonesia, Java)
1870	C. Klinkert	NT (High Malay)	(Indonesia)
1879	C. Klinkert	OT (High Malay)	(Indonesia)
1910	W. G. Shellabear*	NT	(Malaysia)
1912	W. G. Shellabear	OT	(Malaysia)
1913	W. G. Shellabear	NT in Baba Malay	(Malaysia)
1938	Werner Bode	NT	(Malaysia/Indonesia Union Version)
1965	Indonesian Bible Society	Full Bible	(NT from 1938 version; OT from Indonesia)
1971	J. L. Abenino R. Soedarmo, O. E. Woewoengan	NT in Modern Indonesian	(Indonesia)
1975	Abenino, Soedarmo, O. E. Woewoengan	Full Bible in Modern Indonesian	(Indonesia)
1976	E. T. Suwito	NT, Today's Malaysian Version	(Malaysia)
1981	Fiona Lindsay, A. Wilding	NT in Pattani Malay	(South Thailand)
1987	E. T. Suwito	Full Bible, Today's Malaysian Version	(Malaysia)
1987	Indonesian Bible Society	Full Bible, Today's Indonesian Version	(Indonesia)

Working from the Greek text, Lu translated the NT, and it was published in 1910. He revised the work and published it in 1951. More recently, the United Bible Societies sponsored a colloquial (common language) translation published in 1975.

Translations into various Chinese dialects have also been undertaken. The full Bible exists in a number of Chinese dialects including Shanghai, Foochow, Ningpo, Canton, Amoy, Hinghwa, Soochow, Hakka, and Taizhou. There are also translations of the NT in some of the minority languages such as Lisu and (Inner) Mongolian.

*Cambodia**. The first known attempt at translating the Bible into Khmer was that by Father Marie-Joseph Guesdon, who published the text of the Gospel readings in the Dominican* liturgy in 1910.

In 1923, A. L. Hammond began to work with Roman Catholic assistance to produce a NT in 1934 and the entire Bible in 1940. After a number of revisions, this was republished in 1954 by the British and Foreign Bible Society.

A new interconfessional translation was planned and work began in 1973, but the project was disrupted in 1975 when the four Cambodian translators died during the revolution and the French priest involved left the country temporarily. A further attempt was made in 1983 at an interconfessional translation using common language, this time sponsored by the French Bible Society. Roman Catholic and Protestant scholars worked together to complete the NT in 1993, and the full Bible (including Deuterocanon) was published in 1998.

Myanmar. Bible translation in Myanmar may be presented under two categories: formal and common-language translations. As with other Asian translations, the earlier translations were completed mostly by Protestant missionaries with local helpers. After the expulsion of missionaries in the 1960s, all translations have been done by local speakers of the languages (see Bible Society).

1. *Formal Translations.* a. *Akha.* More than 100,000 Akha live in adjoining areas of China, Laos, Myanmar (40,000), and Thailand. The New Testament, translated by Paul Lewis and his wife (of the American Baptist Foreign Missionary Society), with the help of Sala Mose and a translations committee, was published in 1968 by the Bible Society of Myanmar (BSM).

b. *Chin: Asho.* The Asho, or Southern Chin, live in the Ayeyawaddy lowlands. The New Testament was translated by Samo Hla U, a Chin, and published in 1954 by the British and Foreign Bible Society (BFBS), Yangon.

c. *Chin: Falam.* The Laizo Chin language, now known as Falam, has been designated the lingua franca of the Falam political subdivision in the central part of the Chin Hills area. J. Herbert Cope, assisted by Saya Dew and Chin pastors, translated the New Testament, published in 1951 by the BFBS.

d. *Chin: Haka.* Haka, the language of the Lai or Baungshe Chin, is the lingua franca of the Haka political subdivision in the southern area of the Chin Hills. The New Testament, translated by Mrs. Arthur E. Carson and Chester Strait (American Baptist missionaries), assisted by Saya Sang Ling (a Chin), was published in 1940.

e. *Chin: Khumi.* Edwin Rowlands, of the North East India General Mission, and E. W. Francis translated the New Testament into the Khumi language with the help of Heng Ngaw, Pra Meaung, and Len Vai. It was published in 1959 by the BFBS.

f. *Chin: Khumi Awa.* Two Lushai evangelists supervised by a missionary of the Bible Churchman's Missionary Society translated the book of John into Khumi Awa; it was published in 1939 by the BFBS.

g. *Chin: Ngawn.* Lung Nun, a Chin preacher, translated the book of Mark into Ngawn; it was published in 1951 by the BFBS.

h. *Chin: Tiddim.* Formerly known as Kamhau, Tiddim is the lingua franca of the Tiddim political subdivision in the northern area of the Chin Hills. The New Testament, translated by J. Herbert Cope of the American Baptist Foreign Mission Society, assisted by Viel Nang, was published in 1932 by the American Baptist Mission Press (ABMP), Yangon.

i. *Chin: Zotung.* Khua Mying, a Chin teacher, supervised by R. G. Johnson, an American Baptist missionary, translated the book of Matthew into Zotung; it was published in 1951 by the BFBS.

j. *Kachin: Jinghpaw.* About 450,000 Kachin live in northern Myanmar and in adjacent Yunnan, China, and Assam, India. Myanmar Kachin is known as Jinghpaw. "Kachin" includes Atsi, Maru, and Lashi. The entire Bible was translated by Ola Hanson of the American Baptist Missionary Union (ABMU) and published in 1927 by the ABMP.

k. *Kayin: Bghai.* About two million Kayin live in eastern, central, and southern Myanmar and the adjacent border areas of Thailand. The largest Kayin groups are the Sgaw, Pwo, Bghai, or Bwe, and Kayah. Francis Mason, of the ABMU, translated the books of Matthew, James, 1-3 John, Genesis, Exodus, and the Psalms, published by the BFBS, Calcutta, in 1857-62.

l. *Kayin: Pwo.* More than half a million Pwo Kayin, a plains people, live in the Ayeyawaddy River Delta and northern Taninthayi, Myanmar. About 20,000 live in adjacent areas in Thailand. The New Testament, translated primarily by D. L. Brayton (of the ABMU) assisted by F. Mason, A. J. Rose, and others, was first published in 1860 in Yangon. A revised second edition was published by the BFBS in 1873. The entire Bible was published in 1883, with a revised edition being published by the ABMU in 1885.

m. *Kayin: Sgaw.* The Sgaw, who call themselves Kanyaw, are the largest Kayin group, numbering more than half a million in Myanmar, where they live both in the lowlands of the Ayeyawaddy Delta and Taninthayi and in the hill areas of the Bago Range. Francis Mason (of the ABMU), assisted by J. Wade, J. H. Vinton, and Saw Kwala, a Kayin, translated the New Testament, first published in 1843. Their translation of the entire Bible followed, being published by the BFBS, Dawai, in 1953.

n. *Lahu.* Approximately 300,000 Lahu live around Kyaingtone, Shan State, Myanmar, and northward into Yunnan, China. The Lahu comprise several groups: Na (Black), Shi (Yellow), and Nyi (Red or southern). The New Testament was published in 1932 by the ABMP, Yangon, having been translated by J. Haxton Telford, assisted by Potun, David Sala, Ai Pun Sala, and Saya Chit Swe. In 1962, the BFBS, Yangon, published a translation of the New Testament done by Paul Lewis and his wife (American Baptist missionaries), assisted by Sya Yi, Saya Yohan, and Saya Ai Pan.

o. *Mon.* Mon is spoken by about 300,000 people in Mon State and in the Ayeyawaddy River Delta. J. M. Haswell, of the ABMU, translated the New Testament, published in 1847. R. Halliday, of the Church of Christ, translated the Old Testament, published by the ABMU, Yangon, in 1928 and reprinted by the BFBS in 1951.

p. *Myanmar.* Myanmar (the official language of Myanmar) is spoken by about 25 million people, the majority of whom are Buddhist. The English Baptist missionary Felix Carey translated the book of Matthew, which was published in 1815. Adoniram Judson (1788-1850) of the ABMU translated the entire Bible, published in 1840. Tun Nyein, a Myanmar Christian, produced a revision of the New Testament, published in 1903. The BFBS further edited Tun Nyein's revision of the New Testament (1909) and added the Old Testament as well (1926). A revision of Judson's translation was completed by McGuire and published by the ABMP in 1933.

q. *Pa Oh.* The Pa Oh, or Taungthu, number about 300,000 and live from southwestern Shan State to northern Mon State. A number of books were translated by

Mrs. W. D. Hackett, an American Baptist missionary: John (1950), Mark (1951), Acts (1955), Ephesians, Philippians, and James (1957), and Luke (1964), published by the BFBS, Yangon. Saya Maung Maung translated the entire New Testament, printed privately in Yangon in 1961.

r. *Shan.* About 500,000 Shan are scattered throughout the northern parts of Myanmar, especially in Shan State. Myanmar Shan, also called Ngio, is spoken with regional dialect differences. J. N. Cushing, of the ABMU, translated the New Testament in 1882 and completed the entire Bible in 1892. He completed a revision of the New Testament published by the ABMP, Yangon, in 1905, later editions of which were published by the BFBS.

2. *Common-Language Translations.* The following translations are either completed, revised, in the process of revision, or in the process of translation into a common language under the supervision of the United Bible Societies (UBS). Common-language translators are native speakers of the languages, and they are aided by review of committees.

a. *Akha.* Noel Kya Heh's Old Testament translation into Akha began in 1983 and was completed in 1994.

b. *Chin.* Aung Thaik began translating the New Testament into Asho in 1980 and finished in 1993. Thang Nagi Om began translating the New Testament into Cho in 1988 and completed it in 1993. S. Hre Kio completed translation work into Falam in 1985, which was printed in 1991. D. Van Bik's translation work into Haka was printed in 1978, and James Sangawi did a New Testament revision between 1988 and 1994. Lung No, Lai Nou, and Lawngthang began translating the New Testament into Matu in 1992 and completed it in 1995. Max Vai Pum began translating the New Testament into Siyin in 1986 and finished in 1993. Kam Khaw Thang translated the Old Testament into Tiddim, publishing it in 1977 with a previous New Testament translation, and completed a revision of the entire Bible in 1991. Khua Mying translated the New Testament into Zotung betwen 1991 and 1993.

c. *Kachin.* La Ja translated the New Testament between 1988 and 1995, with plans to translate the Old Testament as well. S. Haw Ying and Khua Sau translated the New Testament into La Cid from 1992 to 1995. Gyung Hkawng translated the New Testament into Lhaovo from 1992 to 1995. Aye Aye Chit translated the New Testament into Pwo from 1988 to 1993, with plans to translate the Old Testament as well. C. Kyaw Dwe, Marcheta Thein, and Naw Hsi Mu translated the New Testament and Psalms into Sgaw and began translating the Old Testament in 1993.

Enoch Pun began translating the Bible into Lahu in 1991. Sein Pe translated the New Testament and Psalms, printed in 1985, and, with Chit Lwin, translated the Old Testament and produced a revision of the New Testament and Psalms. A revised Bible was done by Aung Than between 1991 and 1994. Htay Htay Yu translated the New Testament into Pa Oh from 1987 to 1996. A New Testament translation into Shan begun in 1972 was completed in 1985, and the Old Testament was translated by Sai Tun Shwe from 1985 to 1995.

Bibliography

Neill, S., *A History of Christian Missions* (1964). • Sanneh, L., *Translating the Message: The Missionary Impact on Culture* (1989). • Nida, E., *The Book of a Thousand Tongues* (1972). • Arimichi, E., *Nihon Seisho Kyokai Hyaku-nen Shi* (One-Hundred-Year History of the Japan Bible Society) (1975); *Nihon no Seisho, Seisho Wayaku no Rekishi* (The Bible in Japan, History of Japanese Bible Translation) (1981). • Fernando, C., *God's Word in Sernedib, 1812-1992.* • Somaratna, G. P. V., "History of the Sinhala Bible," *Journal of the Royal Asiatic Society, Sri Lanka Branch* 34 (1991). • Darlow, T. H., and H. F. Moule, *Historical Catalogue of Printed Editions of the Holy Scripture* (1911).

Graham Ogden, with contributions from Ebisawa Arimichi, G. P. V. Somaratna, P. G. Katoppo, A. Heuken, Robert Hunt, China Group, François Ponchaud, and U Aung Than

Bichurin, Nikita Yakovlevich (Iakinf)

(b. 1777; d. 1853). Russian sinologist and archimandrite of the 9th Orthodox* mission group to Beijing.

Originally named Iakinf, Bichurin graduated from Khazan Theological Seminary. He was first a principal and later an abbot. Heading the 9th Orthodox mission to Beijing in 1808, he remained in China* for 13 years and translated the Orthodox liturgy into Chinese. He dressed in the style of Manchu officials, traveled about the Vassal Administration of the Qing dynasty, and gleaned inside information. He was reprimanded by the Vassal Administration for secretly drawing "The Plan of Beijing City" through range estimation and pacing. He was exiled when he returned to Russia for "dereliction of duty" in Beijing but was later placed in the Asian division of the ministry of foreign affairs to translate Chinese documents. More scholar than monk, Bichurin translated many Chinese classics and historical records and wrote *The Record of Tibet* and *The Reading Notes on Mongolia.* He was an authority on Eastern culture and antiquity.

Bibliography

Skachkov, P. Yeo, *Iakinf Bichurin: Materialy K Biographi* (Materials for biography) (1933). China Group

Binsted, Norman Spencer

(b. Toronto, Canada, 2 Oct 1890; d. Feb 1962). Third missionary bishop (Episcopal) of the Philippines*.

Binsted became a naturalized American citizen when his family moved to Washington, D.C., while he was still a child. Upon ordination to the diaconate in 1915, Binsted was sent to Japan* as a missionary. On 3 Dec 1928, he was consecrated first bishop of the diocese of

Tohuco, northern Tokyo, Japan. Just before the outbreak of World War II*, Binsted was transferred to the Philippines, arriving in Manila on 14 Jan 1941. He was elected missionary bishop of the Philippines by the house of bishops the following year.

Binsted transferred Saint Andrew's Training School from Sagada, Mountain Province, to Cathedral Heights, Quezon City, in 1947. The seminary, now called Saint Andrew's Theological Seminary, opened that year with students from both the Philippine Independent Church* (PIC) and the Philippine Episcopal Church (PEC). It was also through his efforts that the Concordat of Full Communion between the PIC and the PEC (United States of America) was signed in 1961 (see Anglican Church).

Binsted had to resign from the Philippines in 1957 due to ill health. When he left the country, there were 31 Filipino clergy and more than 50 seminarians preparing themselves for the ordained ministry.

Bibliography

Journal of the Annual Convocation of the Missionary District of the Philippine Islands (1948-56).

EDWARD P. MALECDAN

Black, Robert Franklin

American Congregational missionary pioneer in Mindanao, Philippines*.

The first American Board (Congregational) missionary to the Philippines, Black arrived in 1902 and located his work in Davao City, southern Mindanao. He and his wife (nee Gertrude Grainer) labored alone until 1908, when new Congregational missionaries joined them. Black's pioneering tours along the eastern and northern Mindanao coasts from Davao to Dipolog aroused the initial interest in Protestantism among many in these places.

Black organized the Davao Evangelical Church in 1909, and his wife began the first kindergarten in Mindanao. Black's great interest, however, lay with the Bagobos in the district of Santa Cruz near Davao City, where he set up another local church and several elementary schools (see Education). The Blacks labored in Mindanao until 1923.

Bibliography

Rodgers, J. B., *Forty Years in the Philippines* (1940). • Sitoy, T. V., Jr., *The Story of the American Board Mission in Mindanao* (1989). • *Several Springs, One Stream* (1992).

T. VALENTINO SITOY, JR.

Blackmore, Sophia

(b. Goulburn, Australia, 18 Oct 1857; d. Australia, 3 Jul 1945). First woman missionary sent by the Methodist* Women's Foreign Missionary Society to work in Singapore*.

Blackmore was primarily involved with the education and evangelization of Baba Chinese women who were housebound and uneducated. Through their development, her work influenced a very large number of people in Singapore, as well as in Malaya. In her 40 years of service in Singapore (1887-1928), she founded two girls' schools, a girls' hostel, and together with William Shellabear* inaugurated and nurtured the first Baba Malay–speaking Methodist Church.

Blackmore arrived on 18 Jul 1887, and within one month she had started the Tamil Girls' School (15 Aug) at the request of Tamil businessmen. The school eventually became known as the Methodist Girls' School (MGS). Her second school, later known as the Fairfield Girls' School, was started within one year of the first. Although both schools at first found it difficult to recruit women teachers, they successfully expanded to serve all the communities in Singapore and were followed by a number of other Methodist girls' schools in the major towns of Malaya.

The initiative to start a girls' hostel was taken in 1887. Until it was disbanded at the onset of the Japanese occupation on 15 Feb 1942, Nind Home (named in honor of Mary Nind, who had been instrumental in financing Blackmore's appointment) was a thriving and self-funded home with over 100 boarders. Many became Christians, being educated in the MGS, and took their places as professional women, church workers, and leaders of society. Other girls' hostels were similarly planted in a number of Malayan towns with similar success.

Nind Home was also the nucleus from which grew the Baba Church on Middle Road, now known as Kampong Kapor Methodist Church (it moved in 1930). It was the first Methodist church to use Baba Malay, drawing many to its Sunday school (at one time with an attendance of over 800) and worship services. For a time, it was the largest Methodist church in Malaya and Singapore and provided training for lay and pastoral leadership as English education caught on among the community.

Bibliography

Blackmore, Sophia, "Looking Backward," *Malaysia Message* (Jan-Dec 1918); "A Record of 40 Years of Women's Work in Malaya, 1887-1927" (unpublished manuscript, Methodist Archives, Singapore). • Doraisamy, Theodore R., ed., *Sophia Blackmore in Singapore* (1987).

EARNEST LAU

Boon Mark Gittisarn

(b. Rat Buri, Thailand, 1 Sep 1898; d. 20 May 1987). Major figure in the Thai Protestant church before and after World War II*.

Boon Mark received his education at Padongradsr School, Pitsanuloke, and graduated from Bangkok Christian College (BCC) in 1921. He converted to Christianity while at BCC. In 1923, he married Muan Suphaphun. After high school, he was employed as an evangelist by the Presbyterian* mission's Pitsanuloke Station. In 1926, he entered McGilvary Theological Seminary's first advanced class. He graduated in 1930 and continued to work in Pitsanuloke. In 1933, he became evangelist for the Presbyterian Bangkok Station.

The first general assembly of the Church of Christ in Thailand (CCT), held in Apr 1934, elected Boon Mark assistant general secretary. In Aug 1934, he was installed as pastor of Second Church, Bangkok. In his ministry, he emphasized evangelistic involvement. In 1936, he traveled as translator with the Chinese evangelist-revivalist, Paul Lyn, to several cities, and in 1938-39 he served as translator for John Sung's* revivalistic campaigns in Thailand. Boon Mark became Sung's most prominent, outspoken supporter. The CCT elected him general secretary in 1938. Thus, he was a prominent leader in the CCT and acknowledged head of its increasingly influential evangelical wing.

During World War II, Boon Mark traveled extensively, encouraging CCT churches and helping them withstand pressure and oppression. His fundamentalist theology, however, alienated an important part of the church. Postwar tensions with returning missionaries and Thai church leaders led him to resign from the CCT in 1948. He also resigned his pastorate at Second Church. He then founded the Thai Church of Bangkok. Boon Mark remained very active in evangelism and assisted conservative missions in entering Thailand after the war. In the late 1950s, he founded the independent Association of Free Churches with himself as general secretary. By the late 1950s, Boon Mark was increasingly associated with Pentecostalism*. He played a central role in the evangelistic campaign of the American Pentecostal preacher, T. L. Osborn, in Bangkok in 1956. He subsequently associated himself with the United Pentecostal Church (UPC), an American group. Although the UPC in Thailand experienced significant growth at first, it declined rapidly when Boon Mark withdrew from active leadership in the late 1960s. He then remarried and joined the Seventh-Day Adventist Church*.

Boon Mark had a strong impact on the development and fragmentation of Thai Protestantism. He strove to free the CCT of what he considered liberal missionary influences. He thereby promoted increased independence for the Thai church. He played a leading role in promoting revivalism and evangelism among CCT churches. He facilitated fundamentalist missions and also played a leading role in the development of Thai Pentecostalism.

Bibliography

Pongudom, Prasit, *History of the Church of Christ in Thailand* (1984) (in Thai). • Boon Mark Gittisarn, taped interview (Payap University Archives, Chiang Mai, Thailand). • Smith, Alex, *Siamese Gold* (1981). • Jaakko Makela, *Khrischak Issara* (1993). HERBERT R. SWANSON

Boon Tuan Boon Itt

(b. 15 Jul 1865; d. 8 May 1903). Thai Protestant church leader.

The eldest of three children, Boon Itt was born to Boonsooie (father) and Tuan (mother). His mother's father was Quakieng, the first convert to associate himself with the Siam Mission of the Presbyterian* Church USA. His father died in 1874, and his mother became a teacher at the Presbyterian Mission's Wang Lang Girls' School.

Boon Itt studied at the Bangkok Christian Boys' School. In 1876, Dr. Samuel and Mrs. Harriett House*, retiring missionaries, took Boon Itt to the United States, where he completed his education. He graduated from Williams College in 1889 and from Auburn Theological Seminary in 1893. Boon Itt returned to Thailand in 1893 as a regularly appointed Presbyterian missionary.

When Boon Itt returned to Thailand, he had forgotten Thai and had to go through a period of language study and adjustment. He soon began to do church and evangelistic work, and in 1897 married Kim Hoch, a distant relative and graduate of the Mission Girls' School. That same year, the family moved to the Pitsanuloke Station, where Boon Itt played a key role in founding a boys' school while his wife started a girls' school. After a brief time, Boon Itt was the sole missionary responsible for the station.

In 1902, Boon Itt was called back to Bangkok to found a new church, but while still in the process he died on 8 May 1903. Boon Itt was revered by the churches and widely seen as symbolizing the future possibilities for indigenous leadership. His death at an early age was considered a setback for the emergence of the Thai church.

Bibliography

Brain, Bell, "Boon-Itt, A Christian Leader of Asia," *Siam Outlook* (Oct 1928). • Kim Heng Mungkrphun, "A Short Biography of Kru Boon-Itt," *Church News* 1 (Nov 1932) (in Thai). • Anusorn Boon Itt, *Fifty Years of Blessings* (1994) (in Thai). • Eakin, J. A., *Boon Itt in Siam*, Women's Board of Foreign Missions of the Presbyterian Church. • Feltus, George Haws, ed., *Samuel Reynolds House of Siam* (1924). HERBERT R. SWANSON

Boone, William Jones, Sr.

(b. South Carolina, United States, 1 Jul 1811; d. Shanghai, 17 Jul 1864). First American Episcopalian bishop in China*.

Boone was converted while a law student at Charleston, South Carolina, in 1833. Following his studies in law, he graduated from a seminary in Alexandria, S.C., and then studied medicine, graduating with his M.D. in 1836. In 1837, he was ordained a priest by the Protestant Episcopal Church, married Sarah De Saussure, and sailed for Batavia (Jakarta) as a missionary with the Domestic and Foreign Missionary Society of the Episcopal Church.

Boone stayed in Batavia, Indonesia, from 1837 to 1840, learning the Chinese language and witnessing to

Chinese sailors on ships sailing to China. Because of ill health, he went to Macau in 1840 and helped direct the school of the Morrison Education Society. In 1842 he sailed with David Abeel* to Gulang Island, opposite Amoy (Xiamen). While establishing work there, Sarah died from cholera, leaving him with two children.

Boone returned to the United States in 1843 where he was honored with a doctor of divinity degree, and his board consecrated him "Bishop of Amoy and such other parts of China as the Board shall hereafter designate." He returned to China in 1845 with eight other missionaries and his second wife, Phoebe Elliott, and moved his mission to Shanghai because of the better climate and also because Amoy appeared to have sufficient Protestant missionaries.

Churches and schools were opened, and missionary work was developed on the lower basin of the Yangtze River (Yangzi). In September 1851, Boone ordained the first Chinese deacon in Shanghai, Wang Ji (Wong Kong-chai), whom he had brought with him to the United States when he returned for his consecration as bishop. Twelve years later, Wang Ji was ordained a priest.

In 1847, Boone and Walter Medhurst* of the London Missionary Society were appointed Shanghai consultants for the Delegates Version of the New Testament and later the Old Testament. Representatives from the several cities were badly divided over whether to use the term *shen* or *shangdi* for God. Boone was probably the leading proponent for *shen* and wrote long essays arguing his position (see Bible Translation).

Boone and his wife needed to make repeated trips to the United States, Singapore*, and Japan* in seeking to alleviate various health problems. On the way to Europe in early 1864, Mrs. Boone died at Suez, Egypt. Boone returned to Shanghai in June 1864, where he died a month later.

Boone translated Matthew, Mark, John, Romans, and various church materials — catechism, morning prayers, and church prayers — into the Shanghai dialect. Bishop Boone Road in Shanghai, Boone University in Wu Chang, which was first established as a school in 1871, and Boone Divinity School, which opened in 1906, were all named after him.

Bibliography

Boone, Muriel, *The Seed of the Church in China* (1973). • Latourette, Kenneth S., *A History of Christian Missions in China* (1966). • Wylie, Alexander, *Memorials of Protestant Missionaries to the Chinese* (1867).

RALPH R. COVELL, with contributions from THE CHINA GROUP, translated by PATRICIA SIEW

Borneo. *See* Evangelical Church of Borneo

Bos, Pacificus

(b. ?; d. ?). First apostolic prefect (1905) and vicar (1918-33) of Borneo nicknamed *Bapa Misi Kalimantan* (Father of the Borneo Mission).

Bos became head of the Capuchin* missions of Borneo in 1905. Together with five other Capuchin missionaries, he took over the Jesuit* post of Sejiram in western Borneo, which had only about 500 Catholics at the time. He invited the Franciscan* Sisters of the Immaculate Conception to start schools and hospitals (1906), opened new missions on the river Mahakam in the eastern parts of Borneo (1907), intensified the mission among Chinese farmers in western Borneo, and opened a center of schools and educational facilities in Nyarumkop for the Dayak tribes in western Borneo. In 1918, he was appointed apostolic vicar with six parishes, five in western and one in central Borneo. He trekked tirelessly into the dense tropical forests and sailed the long rivers in small boats to found new mission posts and strengthen small and isolated communities. He retired in 1913, handing over the 6,000-strong vicariate of Pontianak to his successor and transferring the greater part of the mission in eastern Borneo to the Missionaries of the Holy Family (MSF). Nine missionaries died during the first 25 years of the mission, but young Borneans were challenged to enter the seminary and novitiates of the Capuchins and Franciscan sisters. ADOLF HEUKEN

Bouvet, Joachim

(b. Le Mans, France, 1656; d. 1730). French Jesuit* missionary serving the Qing dynasty during the reign of Kangxi.

Bouvet was among the first five missionaries ("royal mathematicians") sent by Louis XIV in 1685 to China. Arriving in 1688, he studied Chinese and the Manchu language in Beijing and, together with Jean-François Gerbillon, imparted knowledge of calculus and Western philosophy to Emperor Kangxi. In 1693 Kangxi sent him back to France to thank Louis XIV for the gifts (astronomical instruments) and to recruit more missionaries. Among the gifts that Bouvet brought back to Louis XIV were 49 volumes of exquisitely bound Chinese books. Bouvet reached France in 1697 and returned to China in 1699 with 10 missionaries, including Dominicus Parrenin and other Jesuit missionaries, in addition to more gifts from Louis XIV to Kangxi. In 1708 Kangxi instructed Bouvet, Joan Baptiste Regis, Petrus Jartoux, Xavier Fridelli, and other Jesuits to draw the map of China. They were later joined by de Mailla and several other Jesuits. "The Map of the Empire" took nine years to complete. Bouvet also published *The Historical Account of Emperor Kangxi (Portrait historique de L'Empereur de la Chine).*

Bibliography

Witek, John, *Controversial Ideas in China and in Europe: A Biography of Jean-François Foucquet, S.J., 1665-1741* (1982). • Bouvet, Joachim, *Portrait historique de l'empereur de la Chine* (1697).

CHINA GROUP, translated by DAVID WU

Boym, Michael

(b. 1612; d. Jiao Zhi, China, 1659). Polish Jesuit missionary to China in the late Ming period sent by the imperial palace to deliver a message to the Vatican.

When Boym arrived in Macau in 1650, the household in the imperial palace including the emperor's wife (baptized Anne), the first and second queen mothers (Helen and Mary, respectively), and the infant Prince Chieng had already been baptized (1648). Asked to convey a royal message to Rome, Boym arrived in Venice toward the end of 1652 after a long journey and many difficulties and then had to wait three years to meet the newly chosen Pope Alexander VII. On 28 Dec 1655, the pope sent a reply to the queen mother, calling her "the beloved daughter" and expressing his pleasure with her baptism. Boym returned to China via Lisbon, from where he sailed on 30 Mar 1656, arriving in Siam (Thailand*) in 1658 when the Qing army had occupied the provinces of Quangzhou and Guangxi and the Ming Dynasty was on the brink of collapse. Boym then moved about between the border of Jiao Zhi and Guangxi.

Bibliography

Latourette, Kenneth Scott, *A History of Christian Missions in China* (1929).

China Group, translated by David Wu

Bradley, Dan Beach

(b. western New York, United States, 18 Jul 1804; d. Bangkok, 13 Jun 1873). American missionary doctor, printer, and evangelist; one of the most significant Protestant missionaries to serve in Thailand* and an important agent in Thai Westernization.

Bradley was born during an era of evangelical revivalism which inspired him to become a missionary. After an informal education, he graduated from New York Medical College in 1833. He married Emelie Royce on 5 Jun 1834.

The Bradleys went to Thailand under the American Board of Commissioners for Foreign Missions (ABCFM), arriving in Bangkok in Jul 1835. He pioneered the introduction of Western medical practices by opening a dispensary in Aug 1835. His fame spread rapidly, and he treated hundreds of patients each week, including members of the nobility and monkhood. Bradley's close relationship with certain members of the nobility and royalty, particularly the future King Mongkut*, enhanced his medical reputation. He introduced Western surgery, obstetrics, and hospital practices, and played a leading role in promoting smallpox inoculation and vaccination (see Medical Work).

Bradley also pioneered Western printing and publishing in Siam, having brought a press with him in 1835. He organized the ABCFM's printing office, prepared tracts and books for publication, and learned related skills such as bookbinding. The first Thai government document to be printed came off his press; indeed, he had assisted with the first item ever printed in Thailand. He also produced the first printed materials in the distinct northern Thai script. Bradley further contributed to the modernization of the Thai language by preparing and printing dictionaries and grammars. In the late 1850s, he undertook commercial printing. His press produced important Christian literature, including tracts, Scriptures, hymnals, and theological works. He also edited both English and Thai language newspapers, including the *Bangkok Calendar* and the *Bangkok Recorder.*

Bradley was ordained by the ABCFM mission in 1838. During the 1840s, he and his colleague, Jesse Caswell*, began emphasizing Finney perfectionism, which caused a serious division in the ABCFM. Bradley left Thailand in Aug 1857 for a long furlough, severed his connection with the ABCFM while in the United States, and affiliated himself with the American Missionary Association (AMA). He also married Sarah Blachley in Nov 1848, his wife Emelie having died in 1845. Bradley returned to Thailand in 1850 with two other missionary couples to establish an AMA mission in Bangkok. While continuing his medical and printing work, Bradley gave increased attention to evangelism, but his mission met with little success and had no converts. Bradley also remained a close friend to Prince Mongkut, who became king in 1851. He acted as an adviser and translator as well as physician to the king, whom he had in earlier years tutored in English and scientific subjects. The king supported and facilitated Bradley's work in a number of ways, including gifts of land and funds, even though the two men quarreled often over religion.

Bradley remained a deeply admired figure in Bangkok in later years and continued to have an influence on mission work. His vision for mission stations in Phet Buri and Chiang Mai was fulfilled in the 1860s by his daughter Sophia and her husband Daniel McGilvary*.

Bibliography

Dan Beach Bradley Journals (1830-73) (microfilm from Oberlin College Archives). • Feltus, George Haws, *Abstract of the Journal of Dan Beach Bradley.* • Lord, Donald C., *Mo Bradley and Thailand* (1969). • McFarland, George Bradley, ed., *Historical Sketch of Protestant Missions in Siam, 1828-1928* (1928). • Moffat, Abbot Law, *Mongkut* (1961).

Herbert R. Swanson

Brahmabandhav Upadhyaya

(b. 1861; d. 27 Oct 1907). Indian theologian who sought to express Christianity in a Hindu context.

Brahmabandhav, whose original name was Bhavani Charan Bannerjee, was an eminent Indian Christian theologian of Bengali Brahmin descent. The youngest son of a police inspector, he was influenced by the religious and political climate of Bengal and was very much attracted to Keshab Chandra Sen* and P. C. Mazoomdar and championed the principles of the Brahmo Samaj*. Later he converted to Christianity and was baptized as Theophilus in the Anglican* Church in Feb 1891. In September of that year, he became a Roman Catholic*.

He had moved in the circle of Ramakrishna's* disciples and had inclinations toward the ascetic life. In Dec 1894 he announced that he had adopted the life of a *sannyasin* and taken the name Upadhyay Brahmabandhu (the Sanskrit equivalent of Theophilus). He wanted to express the Christian faith and life in a manner indigenous to India. His proposal to found a monastery for Catholic Hindu *sannyasins,* though supported by the bishop of Nagpur, did not receive the approval of the higher ecclesiastical authorities.

Brahmabandhav was deeply committed to faith in Christ and wanted all of his countrymen to share the same faith. However, he distinguished between the person of Christ and the doctrines of Christ, which he regarded as Western. He held a very high Christology, confessing that Christ was the very incarnation of God, not just an *avatar.* But he did not accept the view that in order to be a disciple of Christ one had to cease to be a Hindu. He preferred to call himself a Hindu Christian or a Hindu Catholic (see Hindu Cultural Christianity).

Trained in the Thomist system of thought, he believed that in India the philosophy of Sankara would be more appropriate than that of Aristotle for the formulation of natural theology. He edited a journal, *Sophia,* to expound his views. He suggested an integration of the social structure of India into the Christian way of life, the establishment of an Indian monastic order, the employment of the Vedanta for the expression of Christian theology, and the recognition of the Vedas as the Indian Old Testament.

In 1902 he went to Europe to discuss his views with both Roman Catholic and Protestant theologians and to explain his views to the Vatican, but he was unsuccessful. After his return to India, he gradually moved away from active contact with the church and became more active in the national movement for political freedom. Upon his death, his body was cremated according to Hindu rites.

During his lifetime, he was not recognized by the church as a Christian theologian. After Vatican II, there was a revival of interest in his teachings, and his prayers and hymns have been rediscovered for use by several Christian groups, particularly in theological seminaries.

Bibliography

Heiler, F., *Christliche Glaube und Indisches Geistesleben* (1926). • Vath, A., *Im Kampfe mit der Zauberwelt des Hinduismus* (1928). • Animananda, B., *The Blade: Life and Work of Brahmabandhav Upadhyaya* (1946). • Boyd, Robin, *An Introduction to Indian Christian Theology,* rev. ed. (1975). • Lipner, Julius, and George Gispert-Sauch, *The Writings of Brahmabandhav Upadhyaya* (1991).

J. Russell Chandran

Brahmo Samaj

The *Brahmo Samaj* was founded by Ram Mohun Roy* in 1828. His objective was to save the people of his country from the evils of Puranic Hinduism* and draw their attention to the original purity of the teaching of Vedanta. In the sphere of religious reform, he repeatedly declared that he had no intention of breaking away from the religion of his ancestors. He only wished to restore it to its original purity. Accordingly, he took his stand on the Upanishads and the Brahma-Sutra as authoritative sources of Hinduism. He founded the *Brahmo Samaj* on what he considered to be the theism of these scriptures. He no doubt condemned idol worship in strong terms, but his argument was that, according to Hindu scriptures, the best means of securing bliss is the pure spiritual contemplation and worship of the Supreme, and that sacrificial rites and idols are intended only for persons of limited capacity.

With regard to social and domestic duties, Ram Mohun insisted on their due performance according to the *Sastras* and *Smritis.* He only wanted to purge Hindu religion and society of certain manifest evils such as polytheism, idol worship, caste, *sati,* polygamy, and the lack of scientific and English education in India*. The system of *Sadhana* he introduced into the *Brahmo Samaj* was modeled on that of the Vedanta. It consisted first in meditating on God with the help of the Gayatri Mantra and some texts from the Upanishads and a few explanatory verses. This meditation was followed by a *Stotra* taken from the *Mahanirvana Tantra.*

The death of Ram Mohun in 1833 brought to a close the first period in the history of the *Brahmo Samaj.* The second period began with the entry of Maharshi Debendranath Tagore into the *samaj* in 1842 as its leader. The Maharshi was no doubt a true religious spirit, but he was primarily responsible for a new rationalism that grew among his followers and widened the gulf between Hinduism and Brahmoism. In the *samaj,* Vedic authority was rejected and a purely subjective authority known as intuition was set up in its place. But in spite of all his rationalism, Debendranath was a conservative Hindu. He did not like the members of the *samaj* being compelled to renounce caste. He did not like the intercaste marriages that were being promoted by Keshub Chunder Sen*, the leader of the younger group in the *samaj,* who had joined the *samaj* in 1857. Above all, he did not like the soft spot Keshub had for Christ.

The two had to part, and in 1866 Keshub founded a separate *samaj* known as the *Brahmo Samaj* of India. Debendranath's group henceforth became known as *Adi Brahmo Samaj.* Keshub's religion was a sort of conglomeration of Brahmo rationalism, Vaisnava emotionalism, Christian supernaturalism, and Vedantic mysticism. In 1878 a group broke away from him and established a third *samaj* known as the *Sadharan Brahmo Samaj* in protest against the doctrine of *adesa,* or "message from God," which he claimed for himself. Keshub renamed his *Brahmo Samaj* of India, "The Church of the New Dispensation" *(Naba Bidhan),* in 1880, designing it to be the consummation of all the religions of the world. Prominent among those who formed the *Sadharan Brahmo Samaj* were Ananda Mohun Bose and Pandit Sivanath Sastri. Later it produced eminent teachers such as Pandit Sitanath Tattvabhushan and Nagendranath Chatterji. Brahmo teaching now moved away more definitely from the intuitional dualistic theism of Debendranath to the rational, nondual mysticism of the Upanishads by admitting the essential unity of the Universal Self and the individual self.

From a historical analysis of Brahmo Samaj, it will be seen that the new theism it established differed from the older Vaisnava, Saiva, and Sakta theism in the following respects: (1) it had no faith in any scripture as an authority; (2) it had no faith in *Avataras;* (3) it denounced polytheism and idol worship as sinful; (4) it denounced caste distinctions; and (5) it made faith in the doctrines of *karma* and rebirth optional. In fact, the new theism of the *Brahmo Samaj* differed from the older theism of India not in what it asserted, but in what it denied. All that the new theism said about the personality of God, the need for divine grace, and the superiority of spiritual worship was found in the old.

One main reason for the decline of *Brahmo Samaj* is the fact that it has no religious canon that it accepts as authority. Its authority is purely subjective reason or intuition, and it uses portions of Hindu and other scriptures as only secondary helps. No wonder, therefore, that in spite of all the invaluable work it has done by way of social reform and in spite of the many distinguished people it has had in its fold, it has remained a mere droplet in the waters of Indian religions.

But, though the *Brahmo Samaj* is almost a spent force now, it has rendered useful service to Hinduism by popularizing social reform, helping to prevent conversions to Christianity through its "halfway house," and rousing the orthodox Hindus to organize themselves and work for a revival of their religion.

Bibliography

Sastri, Sivanath, *History of the Brahmo Samaj,* 2 Vols. (1911-12); *Theistic Church in India* (1966). • Tattvabhushan, Sitanath, *The Philosophy of Brahmoism* (1909). • *Leaders of the Brahmo Samaj* (1926). • Sarkar, Hem Chandra, *The Religion of the Brahmo Samaj* (1911). • Ghosh, N., *The Evolution of Navavidhan* (1930). • *The Father of Modern India* (The commemoration volume of the Ram Mohun Roy Centenary) (1933). • Killingley, Dermot, *Rammohun Roy in Hindu and Christian Tradition: The Teape Lectures, 1990* (1993). • Mozoomdar, Pratap Chander, *The Life and Teachings of Keshub Chunder Sen* (1887); *The Faith and Progress of the Brahmo Samaj,* 2nd ed. (1934). • *The New Dispensation and the Sadharan Brahmo Samaj* (1881). • Farquhar, J. N., *Modern Religious Movements in India* (1924). • Sarma, D. S., *Studies in the Renaissance of Hinduism in the Nineteenth and Twentieth Centuries* (1944).

K. P. ALEAZ

Brent, Charles Henry

(b. Newcastle, Ontario, Canada, 9 Apr 1862; d. Lausanne, Switzerland, 27 Mar 1929). First missionary bishop of the Philippine Episcopal Church (PEC).

Ordained a priest in 1887, Brent moved to New York where he served as a curate and organist at St. John's Church in Buffalo. Brent and Henry Torbert were reviving St. Stephen's Church in the South End, Boston, Massachusetts, when Brent was elected to become the first missionary bishop of the Episcopal Church's Philippine District in 1901.

Brent, who thought of himself more as chaplain to his fellow Americans than a missionary to the Filipinos, openly indicated that he was a representative not only of the Episcopal Church but of America as well. He arrived in the Philippines in 1902 and established the massive and beautiful Cathedral of Saint Mary and Saint John in Manila in 1907 for the American residents of the city. Two years later, he established the Baguio School for Boys, now Brent School, in Baguio City. He also served as the Philippine colonial government's representative to the Opium* Conference in 1903 and was appointed by President Theodore Roosevelt to be a member of the First International Opium Commission (1909) convened in Shanghai. He was elected chairman of the conference. The same year, he was appointed by the Episcopal Board of Missions to be its representative to the World Missionary Conference held in Edinburgh, Scotland. In 1911, he was appointed by President William Howard Taft to head the American delegation to the International Opium Conference in The Hague, which unanimously elected him its president.

For the Filipinos, Brent established schools, hospitals, and churches in places where there were no other churches at work. This was in accord with his view that the church should be an agent of change to improve the standard of life wherever it is established, and that there should be no "building of altar against altar." Brent believed that Roman Catholics were already Christians and there was no need to re-christianize them. "Proselytizing I abhor," he said, "it is a negative and dangerous method of Christian work."

Beginning in 1914, there was a radical reduction of American residents in the Philippines. The replacement of many expatriate civil servants by Filipinos affected the priority of Brent's work. Brent therefore left the Philippines in 1917 to become the bishop of western New York. He first served as chaplain to the American Expeditionary Force in Europe during World War I before starting his duties as bishop of western New York in 1919.

In 1927, Brent was one of the delegates to the first Conference on Faith and Order held in Lausanne, Switzerland. He was elected president of this important ecumenical conference. Two years later, in 1929, Brent represented the Episcopal Church at the enthronement of Cosmo Lang as archbishop of Canterbury. He traveled to Lausanne after this event, where he died while reading the Book of Common Prayer. He was buried on 12 Apr at the Bois de Vaux cemetery in Lausanne.

Bibliography

Clymer, Kenton, *Protestant Missionaries in the Philippines, 1898-1916* (1986). • Halsema, James, *Bishop Brent's Baguio School* (1988). • Kates, Frederick, *Charles Henry Brent: Ambassador of Christ* (1948). • Norbeck, Douglas, "The Protestant Episcopal Church in the City of Manila, Philippine Islands from 1898-1918: An Institutional History" (master's thesis, University of Texas) (1992). • Portuando, Emma J., "The Impact of Bishop Charles Henry Brent upon American Colonial and Foreign Policy, 1901-1917" (doctoral dissertation, University of America) (1969).

EDWARD P. MALECDAN

Brooke, Charles Anthony

(b. England, 3 Jun 1829; d. England, 17 May 1917). Second rajah of Sarawak during whose reign the church played a critical role in developing the country of Borneo.

Brooke served in England's Royal Navy from 1842 until 1852, when he joined his maternal uncle Rajah James Brooke*, whose surname he adopted in 1864. Prior to becoming rajah in Sarawak, Brooke spent most of his time in the interior, often involved in quelling uprisings among local inhabitants but also learning much of the Dayak culture. As a result, he grew more sympathetic to the Dayaks than to his fellow Europeans. Upon the death of James Brooke in Jun 1868, he was proclaimed rajah in August of the same year.

Concerned for the welfare of his people and progress in the country, Brooke promoted Western education through the state as well as Christian missions, beginning initially with the Anglicans. Brooke was determined that education not destroy the traditions of the local inhabitants; he also favored secular education over religious education. This resulted in some tension between Brooke and the Anglican Mission over the purpose of education: was it to achieve secular and humanitarian ends or spiritual and Christian objectives?

Brooke's interest in the development of the country subsequently resulted in the introduction of the Roman Catholic* and the Methodist* missions in Sarawak. The Methodists were encouraged by Brooke to bring in migrants from China*, many of whom were Christians who contributed significantly to the economic development of Borneo. Thus, under Brooke, the church began to play an important role in the spiritual, social, and economic development of the country.

Bibliography

Brooke, Charles, *Ten Years in Sarawak* (1866). • Crisswell, Colin, *Rajah Charles Brooke* (1978). • Payne, Robert, *The White Rajahs of Sarawak* (1960). • Saunders, Graham, *Bishops and Brookes* (1992).

SOON SOO KEE

Brooke, James

(b. India, 29 Apr 1803; d. England, 11 Jun 1868). First rajah of Sarawak who initiated the Anglican* Mission in Sarawak.

Brooke served in the armed forces of the East India Company (EIC) from 1819 to 1825, when he was wounded in the First Burmese War. After his recuperation in England, he returned to the East, inspired by the exploits of Stamford Raffles*. Having an interest in Borneo, he was called by the Sarawak Malays to help them in their fight against their overlords, the Brunei Sultanate, in 1839. Consequently, he ended up being made rajah of Sarawak in 1841.

Although uncertain about his Christian theology, Brooke was certain about the need for a Christian mission amongst the natives in Sarawak. His motive for the mission was not purely spiritual but humanitarian as well. He saw Christianity as a means of introducing Western civilization, with the aim of improving the lives of the natives and consequently building up the country through commerce.

In 1846, the Borneo Church Mission Institute was formed in England to raise funds for the Sarawak mission. Subsequently, the Society for the Propagation of the Gospel in Foreign Parts (SPG) assumed responsibility for the mission in 1853, with the first bishop, Francis Thomas McDougall*, being Brooke's choice.

Personal and policy differences marked the relationship between Brooke and McDougall, but the Anglican Mission, by the end of Brooke's reign in 1868, managed to establish a work among both the Dayaks and Chinese.

Bibliography

St. John, Spencer, *Rajah Brooke* (1899). • Templer, J. C., *The Private Letters of Sir James Brooke,* 3 vols. (1853). • Runciman, Steven, *The White Rajahs* (1960). • Saunders, Graham, *Bishops and Brookes* (1992).

SOON SOO KEE

Brothers of the Immaculate Conception

(*Fratres Immaculatae Conceptionis,* FIC). Founded in 1846 in Maastricht, Netherlands, by L. Rutten for the education of neglected children, the FIC came to Java in 1920 and opened schools, orphanages, and the Roncalli Institute (1968), a training center for all Indonesian religious congregations (brothers and sisters) in Salatiga, Central Java. The FIC congregation presently comprises 120 members working mainly in the educational apostolate (Pangudi Luhur Foundation) on the islands of Java, Sumatra, and Borneo.

Bibliography

Urselmann, August, *Ons Missiewerk op Java 1920-1940; Onder de Japanse knoet. Leven en lijden van de Broeders in Indie tijdens de Japanse bezetting* (1947).

ADOLF HEUKEN

Brown, James David

(b. Landour, Uttar Pradesh, India, 5 Jun 1909; d. 12 Apr 1985). Missionary, chaplain, educator and administrator.

Born to missionary parents, Brown attended the Woodstock School in India until his family moved to New Concord, Ohio, where he attended high school and graduated from Muskingum College in 1931. He earned his bachelor of theology from the Pittsburgh-Xenia Seminary in 1934 and studied further in Edinburgh, Scotland. In 1951 he was awarded an honorary doctorate by Muskingum College, and he conducted further studies at Princeton Seminary while on furlough in 1952.

In 1937, en route to India to serve as a missionary, he visited his sister and her husband, Dr. and Mrs. Horace Griffen, in Egypt. While there, he renewed his friendship with a friend from college, Virginia Liggit, whom he later married in India. Both studied Urdu in Sialkot.

After language studies, Brown's first assignment in 1939 was the chaplaincy at Gordon College, Rawalpindi. He was also professor of English at the college. In 1946 the synod of the United Presbyterian Church of Pakistan invited him to join the seminary in Gujranwala. He joined them in 1949 under the first national principal, the Rev. Prof. Wazir Chand, and served 12 years teaching New Testament theology, Greek, Islamic studies, and homiletics. He was promoted to principal in 1952.

Under his leadership, the seminary became a Union Institution in 1954. He supervised the building construction of the present Union Seminary, and a building was named after him in 1958. He bought a house for the seminary staff. Brown translated Louis Berkhof's *Systematic Theology* for the seminary to use as a textbook. In 12 years of teaching at Gujranwala, he trained about 150 students to become pastors. Some are still actively serving both in and outside Pakistan.

Brown left Gujranwala in 1958 to join the office of the First Representative of Commission of the United Presbyterian Church, USA, in Lahore. A few years later he traveled with his wife to many countries on a consultation mission with missionaries. He then returned to the United States and served for 18 months at the First Presbyterian Church in San Diego, California. He retired to Westminster Gardens in Durate, California, where his wife died in 1973. They had three sons: Dick, Lansing, and Dale. He later married Mrs. Edna Moser in 1976. Brown died from a massive heart attack in 1985.

Bibliography

Nisar, Iqbal, "Biography of J. D. Brown"; Tabbe, R. F., "J. D. Brown Entered God's Rest"; Naman, G. M., "Dr. Jim Brown a Linguist"; and Qaddir Baksh, J. S., "You Will Be with Me," *PASBAN* Newsletter No. 34 — J. D. Brown Number (Gujranwala Theological Seminary, Jun 1985).

Arthur James

Brown, Samuel Robbins

(b. East Windsor, Connecticut, United States, 1810; d. Monson, Massachusetts, United States, 1880). American missionary to China*.

The son of Timothy Hill Brown and Phoebe Hinsdale, Brown graduated from Monson Academy in Massachusetts. He furthered his studies at Yale University. In 1836 he entered Columbia Theological Seminary in Columbia, South Carolina, and finally Union Seminary in New York. He married Elizabeth Bartlett in Oct 1838.

In that same year Brown was sent by the American Board of Commissioners for Foreign Missions (ABCFM) to the Orient, where he joined the Morrison Education Society. His job was to assist in building up Morrison Memorial School in Macau, of which he later became principal. At the end of 1839, when the school opened, five students were enrolled, and in the following year Yung Wing was enrolled. In 1842 this school was moved to Hong Kong* on Morrison Hill.

In 1847, when Brown returned to America, he chose three Chinese boys to go with him to pursue studies in America: Wang Seng, Wang Fun, and Yung Wing. Wang Seng was the first to return to China, due to his poor health; he worked as supervisor of Hong Kong Mission Press. Upon Wang Fun's return to China, he worked in a mission hospital in Canton with distinction until his death. Yung Wing graduated from Yale University in 1854 and worked in the business world as well as in political circles. He was appointed by Li Hong Zhang to set up the Chinese Educational Committee in Shanghai. This institution sent Chinese boys to America for study during the period 1872-81. These boys later contributed tremendously to the development of China. From 1859 Brown was sent by the Protestant Church of America to Japan* for mission work.

Bibliography

Beauchamp, Edward R., "Brown, Samuel Robbins," *Encyclopedia of Japan* (1983). • Drummond, Richard H., *A History of Christianity in Japan* (1977). • Griffis, William Elliot, *A Maker of the New Orient, Samuel Robbins Brown* (1902).

China Group

Brunei "Negara" (State of) Brunei Darussalam

Brunei is a small state (5,765 sq. km.) made up of two sections nestled in the Malaysian state of Sarawak in what was formerly known as North Borneo. The present sultan can trace his lineage back 29 generations (early 15th c.) to the first sultan to embrace Islam*, Sultan Mohammed. Brunei became a fully independent state on 1 Jan 1984, when it stepped out from British protection with the full assurance from Malaysia* that its independence would be honored. The population of Brunei is about 300,000, of which 65 percent are Malay, almost all of whom are Muslim. Other ethnic groups include Chinese (20 percent) and various tribal groups (5 percent), most of whom are Iban (also Kedayan, Kayan, Kenyah, Kiput, Jurut, and Tutung). The final 10 percent is mostly made up of various foreigners living in Brunei and working in the areas of banking, oil industry, and service industries. Economically, Brunei is one of the wealthiest and most stable nations in Asia, with an average yearly income per capita of nearly U.S. $15,000.

The government of Brunei is centered in the sultan. There has been no active legislature in recent decades, and the last general elections were held in 1968. Since 1962, when there was a massive rebellion in Brunei, the government has been run under the status of "emergency rule." With the tight control over the government and economy has also come the advocacy of Islam by the sultan. One of the largest mosques *(masjid)* in East Asia is the Sultan Omar Ali Saifuddin Mosque in the capital city of Bandar Seri Begawan. Not only the building of mosques but also the active promotion of Islam among tribals has been a priority of the government. The promotion of traditional Bruneian values (since 1990) has meant a revival of Islamic ethics and teachings for the country. Since 1990 a number of social issues have been taken up: alcohol is banned from entry into the country, the celebration of Christmas is banned, women are to wear the *tudong* (headdress) when in public, and Christian materials (especially Bibles) are not allowed to be brought into Brunei. In addition, evangelism is not permitted among the Muslims.

Even with these restrictions on religious propagation, the Christian population of Brunei remains stable at about 8 percent of the total population, of which nearly half are Roman Catholic and half Protestant. Most of the Christians in Brunei are Chinese who have migrated from Hong Kong* and other areas of China*. These immigrants are added to the Roman Catholic* and Anglican* communions of various denominations from China (Little Flock* and True Jesus churches) and newer independent local congregations. Church growth continues among the non-Malay in spite of the restrictions imposed by the government.

Bibliography

Hsieh, Peter and Russel Self, "Brunei," in *The Church in Asia*, ed. Donald E. Hoke (1975). • Fahlbusch, Erwin, Jan Milič Lochman et al., "Brunei," in *The Encyclopedia of Christianity*, Vol. 1 (1986/1994).

SCOTT W. SUNQUIST

Bu, U Hla

(b. Padigon, Myanmar, 21 Apr 1897; d. Yangon, 2 Jan 1970). Professor, philosopher, and administrator in Myanmar*.

A simple, sincere, kind, affable, and soft-spoken Baptist layman and son of U Tha Din and Daw Khin Lay, U Hla Bu was a distinguished professor of the University of Yangon and the first national to become principal of Judson College, a constituent of the university, where he had earned his bachelor of arts degree with honors in 1919. U Hla Bu received his M.A. from the University of Calcutta in 1920 and a Ph.D. from the University of London in 1934.

Highly respected, U Hla Bu won many prizes and awards in his lifetime. He represented the Student Christian Association of India, Burma (Myanmar), and Ceylon (Sri Lanka) at the first ecumenical conference of the World's Student Christian Federation in Peking (Beijing) in 1922 (see Ecumenical Movement). A lay ecumenical pioneer in Myanmar, he was elected president of the national Council of Churches, the national Young Men's Christian Association*, the national Student Christian Movement*, and other church-related organizations. After World War II, he served as vice-rector of the university and professor of philosophy. He was honorary counselor to the officers' testing team of the Burma Defense Forces.

When he retired from academic life in 1958, the government of Myanmar honored U Hla Bu with the title *Sithu.* He was approached by the Revolutionary Council that came into power in 1962 to serve as minister of education, but he declined, citing age as his reason. He visited institutions of higher learning in the United States, Europe, India*, and China* with the aim of upgrading the University of Rangoon. He was a visiting professor at Union Theological Seminary in New York in 1959-60. When foreign missionaries had to leave Myanmar, U Hla Bu served as an honorary pastor of the Judson Church on the university campus, and later as its moderator until his death. His motto in life was "Nothing is impossible with God."

Bibliography

U Hla Bu, *The Automatisation of Voluntary Movements* (1934); *Practical Psychology* (1948); *Psychoanalysis: A Critical Appraisal* (1938). • Thet Tun, "My Three Sayas," *The Guardian* (Jul 1970).

KYAW NYUNT

Buchanan, Claudius

(b. Cambuslang, United Kingdom, 12 Mar 1766; d. Broxbourne, 9 Feb 1815). Dutch East-India Company* (EIC) chaplain and missionary publicist.

Buchanan's grandfather had been influenced by the preaching of George Whitefield, and his home was devoutly evangelical, but initially he did not favor service in the church. He attended the University of Glasgow (1782-87) before leaving Scotland for London, where he obtained a position as a clerk. He experienced a personal conversion in 1790 and was nurtured in Christian discipleship by John Newton, the ex-slavetrader who was rector of St. Mary's, Woolnoth. Through Newton, he was introduced to the evangelical circle which included William Wilberforce, Henry Thornton, and Charles Grant. In 1791, Thornton, an evangelical banker and philanthropist, paid for Buchanan to attend Queens' College, Cambridge, favored by the evangelicals on account of its head, Isaac Milner. Buchanan was an assiduous student at Cambridge and became the friend and protégé of Charles Simeon, vicar of Holy Trinity, Cambridge. Wilberforce and Simeon were both fired with the missionary possibilities of India*. Buchanan became one of a number of "Sims," as Simeon's admirers became known, to aspire to missionary service there, and in 1796 he accepted the offer of a VOC chaplaincy made to him through the influence of Grant. He had been ordained a deacon to serve with John Newton in 1795, ordained a priest in 1796, and sailed for India in 1797.

On arrival in India, Buchanan was befriended by another of Simeon's circle, David Brown, who had arrived in India in 1786. Brown's high estimate of Buchanan is on record (Pearson, II, p. 147). The two men cooperated in ministry to the company's employees and to the military garrison. In 1799, the year of Buchanan's marriage to Mary Whish, David Brown was created first provost of Fort William College, designed to produce candidates for the civil service. Its founder, the Marquis of Wellesley, then governor-general, appointed Buchanan as vice-provost. Buchanan's vision for the college included a department for Bible translation*, and in 1801 Wellesley was persuaded to add the Baptist missionary pioneer, William Carey*, admired by Buchanan and Brown, to its staff as professor of Sanskrit and Bengali. By the time of the closure of this department in 1806, the newly founded (1804) British and Foreign Bible Society had become interested in translations into Indian languages.

In order to foster missionary enthusiasm at home, Buchanan set up prizes for essays on missionary subjects. These prizes were awarded at the Universities of Oxford, Cambridge, Edinburgh, Glasgow, Aberdeen, St. Andrew's, and Trinity College in Dublin; and, among the schools, Eton, Winchester, and Charterhouse. By this means, he hoped to interest some of the best minds of the day and devoted the large sum of 1,650 pounds of his own money to the project; it began in 1803, the suggested theme being "The best means of extending the blessing of civilization and true religion among the sixty millions, inhabitants of Hindoostan, subject to British authority."

To strengthen the position of the church in India, Buchanan submitted a plan for an ecclesiastical establishment to the archbishop of Canterbury in 1805 and was invited to become the first bishop in India in 1806, but declined on grounds of poor health. He established good relations with the Syrian churches of South India, which eventually enabled him to donate an ancient Syrian manuscript of the Bible to the library of Cambridge University. His travels in South India and Sri Lanka* (Ceylon) were turned into his popular and widely read *Christian Researches in India,* which ran to 12 editions in two years after its publication in 1811 and did much to publicize the cause of missions.

Buchanan was awarded a D.D. by the University of Glasgow in 1805 and another by Cambridge University in 1809. He had married for a second time in 1809, after his first wife's death in 1805, having himself returned to England in that year. He lived at Moat Hall, Little Ouseburn, in Yorkshire, where he continued to work on his Syriac version of the New Testament. He was influential in supporting Wilberforce in his parliamentary campaign for the admission of missionaries to India under the renewal of the VOC's charter in 1813, the so-called Pious Clause. Buchanan was buried with his second wife, who had died in 1813, at Little Ouseburn.

Bibliography

Dictionary of National Biography, Vol. 7 (1886); Stock, E., *History of the Church Missionary Society,* Vol. 1 (1899). • Neill, S. C., *History of Christianity in India* (1985). • Pearson, H. N., *Memoirs of the Life and Writings of the Reverend Claudius Buchanan D.D.,* 2 vols. (1817). • Gibbs, M. E., *The Anglican Church in India, 1600-1970* (1972). • Davidson, A. K., *Evangelicals and Attitudes to India, 1786-1813: Missionary Publicity and Claudius Buchanan* (1990). • Anderson, G. H., et al., eds., *Mission Legacies: Biographical Studies of Leaders of the Modern Missionary Movement* (1994). Timothy Yates

Buddhism

Buddhism is a so-called missionary religion and is practiced by the followers of Gautama Buddha. It had its origin in ancient times in South Asia. It is based on the teachings of the founder, who lived about 500 years before Jesus Christ. Today, it is widely practiced in Sri Lanka*, Myanmar*, Thailand*, Cambodia*, Laos*, Korea*, and Japan*. It still has an uncertain influence under a state of persecution in China*, Tibet, and Vietnam*. Pockets of Buddhist believers are found in many parts of the world.

Buddhism arose as a nonconformist movement against the prevailing religion in India and gathered momentum as a protest against the dominance of Brahmins, the priestly class of Hindus. It sought reform and egalitarianism in a society where caste hierarchy marginalized and oppressed many through claims of superiority sanctioned by the religious traditions. Arising as an antispeculative and an antisacerdotal radical dissent movement out of Hinduism*, Buddhism rejected the authority of the *Vedas,* the most sacred scriptures of the Hindus.

Siddhartha Gautama, founder of Buddhism, is venerated today as the Buddha, meaning "the enlightened one." He belonged to the Sakya clan and is also remembered as Saky Mun, or the hermit of the Sakya. Many legends are narrated about his birth and life. He was born in 563 B.C.E. at Lumbini and was brought up at Kapilavastu (in Bihar Province in northern India). He was the only son of King Suddhodhana and Queen Mahmya and was brought up in luxury. At the age of 16, he married the beautiful princess Yasodhar, who gave birth to his son Rahula.

As Siddhartha grew up, he saw the cruel realities of

life. As the legend goes, one day he was greatly distressed by seeing an old man with failing eyesight and a toothless mouth living in a state of destitution. Then he saw a sick man suffering with physical agony and groaning with pain. Later he saw a corpse being carried in a funeral procession by mourning relatives. The prince was greatly moved and depressed by these sights and began to reflect about suffering and death. He realized that the despair, pain, and sorrow in the lives of human beings made them miserable. He called this *dukkha* (misery) a fact of human life.

On another occasion he saw a serene and dignified mendicant leading a life of peace in the midst of misery and unrest. This led him to discover the root cause of *dukkha* and to solve the riddle of suffering, sorrow, and human existence. He decided to renounce worldly comforts and attachments. He left his palace, his wife and son, and his royal future in search of peace and liberation from the suffering of the world. He began a rigorously ascetic life. In the final analysis, he found that severe ascetism did not lead him to the solution of his problems. Nevertheless, he continued in meditation. He sat in the traditional posture of meditation under a peepal tree and resolved not to move from there until he found the answer to his search. The Evil One tempted him and frightened him in an effort to get him to abandon his search. But Siddhartha continued to remain in deep meditation. Suddenly, he attained perfect knowledge and enlightenment.

Siddhartha became renowned as the Buddha at a place in India now called Bodh-Gay. Near Vrnasi (Benares) at Srnth in the Deer Park, he delivered his first discourse as the Enlightened One. He advocated a middle way between the two extremes of self-mortification and self-indulgence. After attaining enlightenment, he preached for 45 years his message of salvation from misery and attracted many converts. His followers were bound together in a community called the *sañgha*. One notable feature of the *sañgha* was that its members were free from the rigid caste taboos and observed no caste prejudices. After a hectic preaching and traveling mission, he passed away in 483 B.C.E. at the age of 80 at Kusinra (Kushinagara). His death was called *mahparinirvana*. After his cremation, his disciples began the process of deification. His mortal remains were preserved as relics and were placed in special burial mounds called *stupas* for veneration. In the course of time, the Buddha was elevated to the position of a divine being by his devotees and came to be worshipped as divinity. The Buddha born in historical time was believed also to have had previous incarnations. The Jataka mythology recounts the lives of the *Boddhisattva*, or the "Buddha to be," of the previous age. Buddhists predict that, at a future time, the Promised Buddha, or *Maitreya*, will appear.

Historically, different traditions of doctrinal interpretation developed within Buddhism. A well-defined community of monks *(bhikkhus)* arose at Mahsangha. This was divided into two main schools: (1) *Theravada* comprised 12 branches. Today, the sole surviving branch of this school is known as *Hinayana*, or the "small vehicle," which means carrying only a few to salvation. *Hinayana* actually was a derogatory term invented by its opponents. Today, the followers of this branch are found mostly in southern Asia: Sri Lanka, Myanmar, Laos, Cambodia, and Thailand. Its main scriptures are the Pali Canon. (2) The other school is called *Mahsanghika*, consisting of six branches. It came to be known as *Mahayana*. The followers of the *Mahayana* school are found in Japan, Korea, Mongolia, Nepal, Sikkim, Bhutan, Ladakh, and Vietnam. Its followers are under persecution in China and Tibet. One of its offshoots, Zen Buddhism, is found in Japan. Another branch, Lamaism, is found in Tibet and Ladakh. The scriptural texts of the *Mahayana* school were originally in Sanskrit, but now survive only in Chinese, Tibetan, and other local translations.

After the death of Gautama Buddha, his teachings were preserved and transmitted to succeeding generations in oral form. Over two centuries passed before the oral corpus of his teachings was compiled into five collections. Later, at an important religious council in the 1st C. B.C.E., these collections were committed to writing in Sri Lanka. The Buddha taught in *Magadh*, a people's dialect, but when his sayings were reduced to writing from oral tradition, they were documented in the sophisticated Sanskrit and Pali languages. Out of this corpus of scriptures, only the Pali Canon is extant, and today this is the main scriptural text of the *Theravada* school.

The Pali Canon consists of the *Tripitaka*, or the three divisions, namely *Vinaya Pitaka*, comprising discipline and rules governing the community of *bhikkhus; Sutta Pitaka*, or discourses delivered by the Buddha on various occasions; and *Abhidhamma Pitaka*, or philosophy and ethics. In addition to these texts, there are various commentaries. The *Tripitaka* also incorporates a book of proverbs which describe the Buddhist doctrine in simpler form. It is called the *Dhamapada*. The scriptures of the *Mahayana* school originally written in Sanskrit in North India spread to other countries, and each country adopted and translated them into their local languages, such as Chinese, Japanese, Tibetan, Nepali, Korean, etc. The *Mahayana* scriptures extol the Buddha as an omnipotent god who rules the cosmos.

The fundamental teachings of the Buddha are summarized in the concept of *Chatvri ryasatyni*, or the Four Noble Truths. These Truths were expounded in Gautama's first discourse delivered at Deer Park. They can be summarized as follows: (1) human beings are in a state of misery; therefore, life is full of suffering, or *dukkha;* (2) *dukkha* comes from the desire for "being," which leads humans to the chain of rebirth; this is known as *dukkha-samudaya* and constitutes the wheel of existence; (3) this "being" and ensuing suffering can be overcome with *dukkha-nirodha*, the complete annihilation of desire; (4) the cessation of all desires can be attained by following the Eightfold Path *(ashtñgikka-mrga)* leading to *nirvana (nibawa),* or ultimate salvation. This is *dukkha-nirodha-mrga.*

The Eightfold Path, the middle way between the extremes of self-torture and self-indulgence, consists of the following: (1) right belief *(Samyagdrishti),* which involves understanding things as they really are; (2) right resolve *(Samyaksankalpa),* which involves being calm at all times and not harming any creature; (3) right speech *(Samyakvk),* which involves never telling a lie or slandering anyone and not using harsh language; (4) right behavior *(Samyakkarmñta),* which involves never stealing, killing, or doing anything one may later be ashamed of; (5) right occupation *(Samyagjv),* which involves not choosing an occupation which may cause harm to others; (6) right effort *(Samyagvyaym),* which involves control of the mind and the will, the result of which will be good *karma* and the reduction of desire; (7) right contemplation *(Samyaksmriti),* which involves avoiding evil thoughts and ill-will, lust, cruelty, and untruthfulness; and (8) right concentration *(Samyaksamadhi),* which involves concentrating on a single object so as to induce certain special states of consciousness in deep meditation *(dhyna).*

This Eightfold Path is also referred to as the Way of eight duties to regulate one's conduct. This Path leads to insight and wisdom which remove ignorance. Its results are serenity, knowledge, and enlightenment, which in totality is *nirvana,* or the state of perfect bliss and peace. *Nirvana* is not a gift of divine grace but is a state earned by human beings themselves by their own will, effort, and responsibility. Human beings have to work out their own salvation for themselves. There is emphasis on self-control and self-emancipation. Each person must work out his or her own salvation without the help of a savior. This concept was modified in *Mahayana* Buddhism, which glorified the Buddha as a divine being full of grace and mercy. The meaning of the word *nirvana* is "extinction," as in the putting out of fire (fire of desire and of existence). *Nirvana* is the extinguishing of the flame of desire to exist. This is not annihilation of the self (according to the doctrine of *anatta,* there is no self) but annihilation of the illusion of the self. *Nirvana* is not nothingness. It is an experience of bliss which can be attained in the present life of this world. Everyone is capable of this attainment. There is also a state of bliss after death called *parinirvana,* after which there is no rebirth.

Buddhism teaches the doctrine of *anatta,* namely, that there is no eternal and indestructible entity called the soul. A being is continually changing and is never the same for two consecutive moments. The combination of mental and physical forces creates an illusion that there is a person, but there is no permanent self. This illusion gives rise to the notion of self and thereby produces desire and all other evils.

A human person is a "no-soul," or *anatta.* One question which inevitably arises is, if there is no soul or self or person, who is it that is reborn? Is it the same person that is reborn, or is it another? According to Buddhism, the answer is that one who is reborn is neither the same nor another. The new life is not the same as the previous life, but the new life is not an altogether different one either. Paradoxically, the one reborn is neither the previous one nor a different one. Rebirth will continue as long as there is desire, and it is the law of *karma* which keeps the process going. The law of *karma* may be described as the law of cause and effect. Everything is the result of some prior cause. Good actions produce good results, and bad actions produce evil results. This continued existence, birth after birth, is called *samsara,* or reincarnation.

The goal of liberation, *nirvana* according to *Theravada* or *Hinayana* Buddhism, can be achieved by following the Eightfold Path. Those men and women who attain *nirvana* are called *Arahat.* The path to *nirvana* according to *Mahayana* Buddhism is linked with the concept of the *Boddhisattva,* the Buddha who postpones his *nirvana* out of compassion so that others may be led to it before him. Gradually, a belief grew in the celestial *Boddhisattvas,* who helped others to *nirvana;* these *Avalokitesvara* and *Amitbha* Buddhas dwell in a cosmic paradise called the Pure Land. In China, *Amitbha* Buddha was once prominent. In Japan, *Vairochana* Buddha is supreme.

Underlying the ethical teachings of Buddhism are important philosophical views. One of these views is the concept of the conditional existence of things. According to this view the existence of everything is conditional and dependent on a cause. This is called *Pratitiya-samutpda* in Sanskrit and *Paticcasamuppda* in Pali. This concept is used to solve the problem of the cause and the removal of suffering.

The doctrine of conditionality leads to another important doctrine of Buddhism, i.e., the doctrine of universal impermanence. According to this doctrine, all things are subject to change and decay. Everything has conditional and nonpermanent existence and exists for one moment only. This is also known as the doctrine of momentariness, or *kshanika-vda.*

In spite of Buddha's aversion to theoretical speculation, four philosophical schools came to be developed by his followers: (1) The *Madhyamika* school of *Shny-vda,* or nihilism, maintains that the so-called self or knower, the known or object, and knowledge are mutually interdependent. Thus all perceived things are illusory. There is nothing real, and the universe is *shnya,* or void. Ngrajuna was the founder of this school. (2) The *Yogchra* school of subjective idealism *(vijnnavda)* holds that the things which appear to be outside the mind are merely ideas of the mind like dreams and hallucinations. The followers of this school are called *Yogchras* because they used to practice yoga to realize the reality of mind. Asanga, Vasubandhu, and Dinnga were the most famous *Yogchras. Lankvatrastra* is one of their important works. (3) The *Sautrntika* school of representationism believes in the reality not only of the mind but also of external objects. Their argument is that, without the being of external objects, it is not possible to explain the illusory appearance of external objects. (4) Followers of the *Vaibhsika* school, or the *Bhyapratyaksavadi* school, maintain that, unless external objects are perceived by the knower, their existence cannot be known in any other way. If external objects were never perceived, then they could not even be inferred from their mental forms. This is also called the concept of direct realism, or *Bhyapratyaksavda*.

As Buddhism spread outside India, variations in its doctrines developed. One such variation is Zen Buddhism, which originated in China and then spread to Japan. The word *Zen* in Japanese means "contemplation." Zen doctrine teaches that people can attain enlightenment by contemplation and not by the study of scriptures or from philosophical speculation; rather, it comes as a sudden flash of insight, like lightning, which a person receives during disciplined meditation.

Buddhist piety and spirituality are observed at two levels, that of the clergy and of the laity. The community of the clergy, or *bhikkhus*, responsible for propagating and preserving the teaching *(dharma)*, is closely knit into *sañgha* in the *Theravada* or *Hinayana* tradition of Buddhism. The *bhikkhus* are initiated at an early age and ordained after many years of disciplined living and are called *ther*, or elder. They usually live in monasteries. They are not totally isolated from society at large, but many participate, in addition to spiritual and religious activities, in social and political matters. The *bhikkhus*, the *upsaka* (laymen), and *upsika* (laywomen) recite the three refuges in Pali as an act of piety: I go to the Buddha for refuge *(Buddham Sharanam gachhm)*; I go to the *dharma* for refuge *(Dharmam Sharanam gachhm)*; I go to the *sañgha* for refuge *(Sañgham Sharanam gachhm)*.

The *bhikkhus* and the laypeople have to follow the prescribed rules of the Vinaya. The Buddha images are worshipped at home, at the temple, or at a *stupa* (relic mound or shrine) with flowers, incense, and lighted oil lamps and with meditation. To earn merit, the layperson offers food to the *bhikkhus*, who live on the food thus begged.

Buddhism is again finding its way in India, the land of its origin from where it literally disappeared in the post-Christian centuries. This new movement, aptly called neo-Buddhism, was headed by a convert, Bhimrao Ramji Ambedkar* (1891-1956). He experienced the anguish and humiliation of being born in a low caste, an untouchable community. His writings about the plight of the untouchables express a deep realism and are characterized by bitter denunciation of the classical lawgivers. Some of the neo-Buddhist followers of Ambedkar have adopted a new name, *dalit*, or "the trampled ones," expressive of their identity and existential predicament.

The state of Buddhism in the People's Republic of China has been critical since 1949. In spite of Maoist China's assurance of freedom of religious belief, Buddhists have undergone a ruthless persecution. Many monasteries and shrines have been converted for other uses, and currently Buddhism, along with Confucianism* and Taoism*, is experiencing a phase of repression. Many practice religion in secret, and in recent years there has been new growth in Buddhist practices in China. The same may be true of the fate of Buddhism in Tibet, where a peculiar form of Buddhism mixed with Lamaism is undergoing persecution. The religious head, the Dalai Lama, is in exile in India.

Buddhism in Korea, along with Confucianism, was introduced from China in the early centuries of the Christian Era. Historically it was the court religion. It is influenced by shamanism*, spirit worship, and ancestor worship*. In Japan, Buddhism is influenced by Shinto and Confucian elements and has given rise to aggressive new religious movements. One such major movement with Buddhist roots is Soka Gakkai, founded in 1931 and based on the Lotus Sutra of Nichiren (1222-82). Another, Rissho Kosei-Kai, is based on *Mahayana* Buddhism. These movements have given spiritual help to the Japanese people, who live under the tensions of urban, industrial, and technological progress. The activities of these movements range from medical services to providing educational and recreational facilities and counseling.

Cambodia. Cambodia knew Buddhism in its *Mahayana* form even before the Christian Era. During the following centuries, Brahminism was introduced more or less in symbiosis with Buddhism, the belief in Siva "King of the Gods" *(devaradja)* favoring the royalist ideology and the expansion of the Angkorian empire. It was only in the 13th c. that Prime Tamalinda, son of the great Angkorian king Jayavarman VII, having become a monk in Ceylon, would substitute *Theravada* Buddhism. After a century punctuated by religious revolts, it was under this form that Buddhism was imposed on Cambodia, having integrated harmoniously the preexisting religions. The Buddhist community divided into two orders: the Thomayuk Order, a minority influenced by the Buddhism of Thailand, which officiates in the royal pagodas; and the Mohanikay Order. Two supreme patriarchs, one for each order, are named by the king.

In 1970, the Buddhist monks numbered 60,000, or nearly 1% of the total population. Totally exhausted during the Khmer Rouge period (1975-79), when Buddhist monks were defrocked and pagodas profaned or used as warehouses, Buddhism began gaining ground gradually in the 1980s, and in 1993 the Cambodian constitution again named it the "religion of the state." In 1995, more than 6,000 pagodas were newly opened in the realm of Cambodia.

Relations between Buddhists and Christians have always been stamped with tolerance on the Buddhist side. If the first missionaries were in admiration of the austerity of the monks, their successors have often considered Buddhism as a religion to oppose. Thanks to Vatican Council II, Catholics have reflected on how to understand better and respect Buddhism. In 1992, several sessions were held with a gathering of professors from the

Buddhist Institute. Some common charitable actions took place in 1994.

Myanmar (Burma). Of Myanmar's 42 million people, 89.5% are Buddhists. Tradition says that Buddhism reached Myanmar while Buddha himself was still alive. The inscriptions on three stones, engraved by order of the Mon king Dahmmaceti in 1485 and discovered by Dr. Forchhammer in 1880, tell the story of the Shwedagon Pagoda and claim that the eight sacred hairs of the Buddha enshrined in the pagoda were brought back by two merchant brothers, Taphusa and Ballikha, immediately after meeting with him.

Inscriptions similar to the Kadamba script of the 5th c. have been found on gold plates at Maunggan near Pye (Prome); they indicate that *Theravada* (Pali) Buddhism was thriving in the Prome, Halingyi, and Thaton areas in the 5th or 6th c. Traces of *Mahayana* (Sanskrit) Buddhism were also found in the upper section of the Ayerwaddy (Irrawaddy) River in areas such as Tagadung and Pagan.

Buddhism spread quickly after the conversion of King Anawratha through a young Mon *Theravada* Buddhist monk, Shin Arahan of Tahton, who was well versed in the Pali *Pitaka.* In Upper Myanmar, *Theravada* Buddhism replaced the *Mahayana*-Tantric influence which came from Tibet, Bengal, and Assam in the 7th or 8th c. Myanmar Buddhism focuses on the *Abhidhamma* (philosophy and ethics) and the *Vinaya* (rules governing the community, important aspects of the *sañghas,* which stress discipline and a consolidated monastic life).

Buddhist councils were convened to ensure strict adherence to the original teachings of Buddha as contained in the *Tripitaka.* At the first three councils held in India, the disciples recited from memory. At the fourth council held in Sri Lanka in the year 100, the *Tripitaka* was written in Sinhalese on palm leaves, and later in Pali. The fifth council was held in Myanmar during the reign of King Mindon with the intention of redacting the *Tripitaka.* After a thorough reading and recitation by learned monks, the Pali *Pitaka* was engraved on 729 marble slabs which are in Mandalay today.

Buddhism lost royal support and hence its status as a state religion when the British annexed Myanmar in 1885. But it remained the majority religion and was instrumental in arousing nationalism among the people. When the colonial period ended in 1948, Buddhism once again enjoyed the official support of the state. U Nu, prime minister of Myanmar during the 1950s, was the patron of the World Peace Pagoda and the Great Cave, where the sixth Buddhist council was held (1954) and attended by 2,500 learned monks from five *Theravada* countries. The council revised and edited all the original texts and commentaries in Myanmar Pali script. Myanmar translations were made for the benefit of the Myanmar people.

From 1044 until 1885, the Sañhga Order had been headed by the *Sañgharaja* or the Patron of the *Sasana,* assisted by a 12-member advisory board of the *Sudhamma* Council. The sect-general *(Gaing-Gyoke),* sect-chief *(Gaing-Oke),* and sect-assistant *(Gaing-Dauk)* took charge of the district, township, and ward, respectively; *Vinaya* disputes were settled by such *sañgha* organizations under the supervision of the *Sudhamma* Council. The British disbanded the Sañgha Order until 1949, when the *Vinicchaya* Act was passed and *Vinicchaya* judicial courts were duly established, two at the central, 22 at the district, and 120 at township levels. The act was amended by the revolutionary government on 18 Jan 1965, together with two other acts on the *Pariyatti* Education Examinations. In 1980, a special program for the purification, perpetuation, and propagation of the *Sasana* was convened to encourage unity and cooperation among all sañgha orders in Myanmar.

The first Congregation of the State Central Sañgha Organization (24-29 May 1980) was attended by 1,218 representatives, selected in the ratio of one representative to every 100 sañgha. In 1986, two state *Pariyatti Sasana* Universities were founded in Mandalay and Yangon. At present, there are over 143,000 *bhikkhus* (monks) and over 164,000 Samaneras in the Union of Myanmar.

Sri Lanka. Buddhism has been a dominant force in Sri Lanka since the 3rd c. B.C.E. Although Christianity made a powerful presence in the island in the 6th and 7th cs., its first lasting encounter was in the Portuguese period (1505-1658). The typical Roman Catholic priest did not encourage physical force for conversion of the Buddhists. Yet the behavior of the Portuguese soldiers was harsh and confrontational. The Buddhist religious establishments in the area controlled by the Portuguese were destroyed or gradually fell into disrepair. During this period, many people in the maritime regions of the island embraced the Roman Catholic religion and renounced Buddhism.

The situation was not different under the Dutch (1638-1796), as their religious policy was injurious to the Buddhists. The absence of state patronage brought about the degeneration of Buddhism.

The situation changed in the British period (1796-1948). The liberal policies of the British government allowed freedom of religious practice. This helped both Buddhists and Roman Catholics alike, who had suffered under Dutch rule.

The early missionaries did not know much about Buddhism. Very often, they discounted it by referring to it as the religion of the devil. It was the Methodist* missionaries since the 1840s who made a serious attempt to study Buddhism in a scientific way. D. J. Gogerly, Spence Hardy, and several others learned the Pali language in order to read the Buddhist sacred texts. Their intention was to make a polemical attempt to evangelize the Buddhists. Later, there were others who continued this tradition. Gogerly's publication of *Kristiyani Pragnapti* (Christian Institutes) in Sinhala and English (1848) highlighted the weak areas of Buddhism from a Christian perspective. This publication provoked a polemical response from the side of the Buddhists. The best reply to Gogerly's work came from Bentara Atthadassi (1852), a *Theravada* Buddhist monk.

At first, the Buddhists were paralyzed by the absence of modern propaganda methods such as the printing press, a modern system of schools, and organizational structure. Toward the middle of the 19th c., Buddhists gradually began adopting the methods used by missionaries. They had their first printing press set up in Galle (1862) and the first school in Dodanduwa (1876). Some Buddhist priests, such as Mohottivatte Gunananda, also began to imitate the Christian clergy even in the style of preaching.

Once the Buddhists had the printing press, they used it as an organ to criticize the Christian leadership and the Christian Scriptures. Buddhist newspapers such as *Sarasavi Sandarasa, Riviresa,* and *Lakminipahana* are some examples of Buddhist polemical publications against Christianity. Similarly, the Roman Catholics' *Gnanarthapradipaya,* the Methodists' *Satyalankaraya,* and *Kristiyani Mitraya* were critical of Buddhism and its practices. The Buddhist-Christian controversies came to a head in the 1860s and 1870s as a result of a number of public debates between them. The culmination of this was the *Panadura* controversy (1873), out of which the Buddhist party emerged as a powerful force. With the Kotahena riot in 1883 the controversies between the Buddhists and Christians went a step further. The debates were mainly between Buddhists and Protestants. The riot, on the other hand, took place as a result of hostilities between Roman Catholics and Buddhists.

At the end of the 19th c., Buddhism was fully equipped with organizations similar to those of the missionaries. The arrival of the Theosophists under the leadership of H. S. Olcott was a boost to the Buddhists. They were able to inject much of Western methods into the Buddhist fight against Christianity. In addition to the setting up of Buddhist schools, they opened Sunday schools for Buddhists. The Young Men's Buddhist Association (YMBA, 1886) and the Young Women's Buddhist Association (YWBA) vividly illustrate how the Buddhists successfully took over the Christian institutions. Anagarika Dharmapala, in his attempt to give a code of moral conduct to the Buddhists, adopted a good part of Victorian Protestant ethics. The introduction of monogamy, rituals relating to funerals, and Buddhist festivals reflected similar Christian institutions. Dharmapala's *Maha Bodhi* Society (1891) was dedicated to Buddhist missionary activities.

The emerging nationalist sentiment in the late 19th c. was primarily anti-Christian in its outlook and content (see Nationalism). It entailed a reapportioning of Buddhist values and a reaction against the Christian missionary enterprise. Political overtones of the Buddhist revival were seen in the temperance movement in the first quarter of the twentieth century.

The interwar years constituted a decisive period for the Christian minority, as they had to accept a diminishing role in the affairs of the country. They were beginning to feel the necessity to accept Buddhist dominance of Sri Lankan politics. With the introduction of the universal franchise after 1929, even the educational system dominated by the Christian missions was challenged.

The political situation in the country changed to the benefit of Buddhists after independence in 1948. Buddhists found that Christians enjoyed a disproportionate part of the national pie. At a meeting of the All Ceylon Buddhist Congress in 1954, a committee was set up to inquire into the state of Buddhism in the country and to report on the measures necessary to improve and strengthen the position of Buddhism. This committee, known as the Buddhist Commission, published its report under the title *Betrayal of Buddhism* in 1955. The report emphasized that only by eliminating the power of the Christians over schools, orphanages, and other charitable institutions could Buddhism rise above "the ruins." As a result of slogans in political platforms, Christian nuns were prohibited from serving in hospitals in 1958, and the denominational schools were taken over by the government in 1960.

Only in the early 1960s was the dialogue taken seriously by Christians. Relations between Catholics and Buddhists improved as a result of Vatican Council II. Buddhism was referred to as a path by which humans "can either reach a state of absolute freedom or attain supreme enlightenment by their own efforts or by higher assistance." Michael Rodrigo, Leo Fernando, Antony Fernando, and Tissa Balasuriya are some of the Catholic leaders who entered into dialogue with Buddhists (see Interreligious Dialogue).

Among Protestants, Lynn de Silva (Methodist), Yohan Devananda, and Kenneth Fernando (Anglican) studied Buddhism under Buddhists in order to develop new forms of Buddhist-Christian community living and dialogue. Academic research was undertaken by the Ecumenical Institute for Study and Dialogue (1959) to come up with new initiatives.

Among Buddhists, religious ecumenism was sought by the *Pavidi Handa* (voice of the priests). This body invited even Christian leaders to its deliberations. There is still much to be done in this direction.

Buddhism and Christianity. Early contacts between Buddhists and Christians are not well documented. Definite evidence has been found for close relations along the Silk Route from Syria to China in the 3rd-13th cs., especially at Turfan from 850 to 1250. East Syrian (Nestorian*) monks in China during the Tang Dynasty had extensive contact with Buddhist monks and were eventually severely persecuted by Buddhist rulers. With the arrival of the Jesuits* in East Asia (Matteo Ricci* reached Macau in 1582), more extensive contacts began; a case of significant exchange occurred in the 20th c. between the Buddhist reformer T'ai-hsu and the Christian missionary Karl Reichelt. Today, Tao Fong Shan and the Christian Study Center on Chinese Religion & Culture, which publish *Areopagus* and *Ching Feng* respectively, are important centers.

In Japan, Francis Xavier's* arrival in 1549 initiated a remarkable century of Buddhist-Christian relations. By 1600, Christians numbered over a quarter of a million in Japan when a period of persecutions arose, all but eliminating Christianity by the 1640s. Christian missionaries reentered Japan in 1858, and today Buddhists and Christians enjoy cordial relations. The Nanzan Institute for Religion and Culture in Nagoya and the Center for the Study of Japanese Religions (National Council of Churches), which publishes *Japanese Religions*, encourage dialogue.

In South Asia, relations flourished in the 20th c. Lynn de Silva, a Sri Lankan Christian, founded the journal *Dialogue* in 1963, which originates at the Ecumenical Institute for Study and Dialogue in Colombo and promotes exchange between Christianity and *Theravada* Buddhism. While Thai Buddhism has proved resistant to Christianity, the Protestant missionary Sinclaire Thompson inspired a memorial lecture series which has been given annually since 1963 at McGilvary Faculty of Theology in Chiang Mai. A significant lecture in this series was delivered in 1967 by the Buddhist monk Buddhadasa Bhikkhu, who maintained a lively interest in Buddhist-Christian relations until his death. In Myanmar, the 20th-c. church has experienced isolation; an important figure was Bishop Bigandet in the latter half of the 19th c. whose works on Buddhism remain authoritative.

The International Society for Buddhist-Christian Studies, founded in 1980, publishes *Buddhist-Christian Studies* and provides a channel for global exchange. Buddhist and Christian thinkers who engage in dialogue see in it potential for transformative thinking about central symbols and doctrines.

Buddhist-Christian dialogue has focused on the nature of ultimate reality. The Buddha regarded the question of the reality of God as speculative and an obstacle on the path to enlightenment. Preserving this emphasis is the Sri Lankan Buddhist Gunapala Dharmasiri, who sets forth a critique of the Christian concepts of revelation and God. The Indian Christian Raimundo Pannikar* treats the Buddha's silence on the nature of God as refusal to engage in the disputes of the day and reduction of God to the order of creatures. In Thailand, Buddhadasa Bhikkhu's discussion of God focuses on distinguishing two levels of language and meaning by which he is able to forge a correspondence between *dhamma* (truth) and God. In Japan, such discussions often touch on the distinction between *tariki* (other power) and *kiriki* (self-power); the former is associated with Pure Land Buddhism, the latter with Zen Buddhism. These concepts provide insights for Christian reflection on such topics as faith and works, sanctification, and the atonement.

Concepts related to the issue of ultimate reality are the Buddhist *sunyata* and Christian *kenosis*, both of which concern emptiness and self-emptying. The Japanese Christian Seiichi Yagi employs *sunyata*, which is derived from Indian *pratitya samutpada* (dependent origination), as the basis for the interrelation of these two religious traditions and within all of reality. Masao Abe of the Kyoto School of Buddhist Philosophy (significant figures here include Kitaro Nishida, Tanabe Hajime, and Keiji Nishitani; each has engaged Western philosophy and Christianity) employs *sunyata* to articulate a vision of kenotic theology and Christology, and of the Christian Trinity, as processes of self-emptying love. *Sunyata* has been the basis for identifying *samsara* (the cycles of rebirth) and *nirvana* (the soteriological goal) and, similarly, God and creation, i.e., the creator and the creative process.

Much Buddhist-Christian dialogue revolves around particular topics. The Korean Christian Andrew Sung Park compares *han* (the relational consequences of sin) and sin, and in this process relates shame and guilt. Lynn de Silva employs *anatta* to explore biblical *pneuma;* both are central to understanding human existence. The Japanese Buddhist Takeuchi Yoshinori uses the I-Thou encounter with Amida Buddha in Pure Land Buddhism to comment on Bultmann's understanding of history and the decision of faith. The Sri Lankan Christian Aloysius Pieris examines religious practice, seeking complementarity, rather than contradiction, between Buddhist wisdom and Christian love.

Bibliography

Guha, B. C. *Coronation of Burma's Shingottara Kon* (1946). • Niharranjan Ray, *Theravada Buddhism in Burma* (1946). • Biggs, T. Hesketh, *The Shwedagon Pagoda* (1963). • *The Dhamma of Buddha for Higher Level* (in Myanmar) (1994). • Sao Htun Hmat Win, *Lectures on Basic Principles of Buddhism and Essentials of Burmese Buddhism* (1979). • Thomas, Edward J., *The Life of Buddha as Legend and History* (1956). • Malalgoda, Kitsiri, *Buddhism in Sinhalese Society: A Study of Religious Revival and Change* (1976). • Senanayake, S. G. B., ed., *Buddhist-Christian Dialogue: A Controversy* (1990). • Bhikkhu, Buddhadasa, *Christianity and Buddhism* (1967). • Pannikar, Raimundo, *The Silence of God: The Answer of the Buddha* (1989). • Pieris, Aloysius, *Love Meets Wisdom: A Christian Experience of Buddhism* (1988). • Thelle, Notto R., *Buddhism and Christianity in Japan: From Conflict to Dialogue, 1854-1899* (1987). • Seiichi Yagi and Leonard Swidler, *A Bridge to Buddhist-Christian Dialogue* (1990).

MICHAEL G. FONNER, GODWIN RAJINDER SINGH, FRANÇOIS PONCHAUD, AUNG KHIN, and G. P. V. SOMARATNA

Buencamino, Felipe, Sr.

(b. 1848; d. 1929). Filipino Federalist lawyer who hoped to draw support from the Protestant missionaries in his effort to make the Philippines* a United States state.

A lawyer by profession, Buencamino was the Philippine secretary of foreign affairs in 1898. Captured and imprisoned by the Americans, he was released in Apr 1900 and in 1902 was appointed a member of the civil service board. Supporting the American regime, Buencamino joined the Federalist Party, which sought United States statehood for the Philippines.

Hoping to draw Protestant missionary support, Buencamino and other Tondo Federalists, all friends of the Protestants Paulino Zamora and Luis Yangco, joined the Presbyterian Church. Disappointed that the missionaries, on principle, could not support their cause, the Federalists gradually fell away. Showing genuine interest, Buencamino remained a Presbyterian*, but after 1902 he joined the Philippine Independent Church*. Remaining a close friend, however, he helped greatly in Presbyterian beginnings in Tondo.

Bibliography

Galang, Z. M., *Encyclopaedia of the Philippines* (1936). • DECS, *Bayang Magiliw* (1986). • Agoncillo, T. A., *History of the Filipino People* (1990). • Sitoy, T. V., Jr., *Several Springs, One Stream* (1992). T. Valentino Sitoy, Jr.

Buglio, Louis (Lodovico)

(b. Sicily, 1606; d. Beijing, 1682). First Jesuit* missionary to enter the province of Sichuan, China, and translator of many Christian books into Chinese.

Buglio, from Minco, Sicily, came to China in 1637, learned Chinese in Nanjing, and began to work in Jiangnan in 1639. Not long afterward, he moved to Beijing where an old magistrate, Liu Yu Liang, a native of Jinzhu in Sichuan, introduced him to work in Sichuan Province. In 1640 Buglio left Beijing for Sichuan and began work in Chengdu, baptizing 30 members. In 1642 Gabriel de Magalhaen came to Szechuan from Hangzhou, and they both went to Zhongqing and Baoning to do mission work. During the transition from the Ming to the Qing dynasty, Buglio and Magalhaen were at one time under the authority of the rebel Chinese ruler Zhang Xian Zhong, where they became court astronomers. They were both captured by the Qing army under the Manchu prince Haoge and sent to Beijing in 1648, where the emperor's uncle, Tong Kuo Gang, was much impressed with Christianity and helped in the funding of a second church building in Beijing, the East Church (Dongtang). Buglio stayed in this church and devoted much time to writing, translating 19 works into Chinese, and writing a defense of Christianity. He was the first missionary to translate the theology of Thomas Aquinas into Chinese.

Bibliography

Pfister, Louis, *Notices biographiques et bibliographiques sur les Jesuites de l'ancienne mission de Chine* (1932-34; repr. 1975), pp. 230-43. China Group

Buraku Liberation Movement, Japan (Buraku Kaiho Undo)

Movement in opposition to discrimination and calling for the establishment of human rights for the Buraku people.

The Buraku Liberation Movement was divided roughly into a reconciliation movement and a liberation movement for unifying and rallying the Buraku people themselves. The relationship of Christianity to this movement began as evangelization of the Buraku people. Until the beginning of the 20th c., the Christian teaching that all people are equal was welcomed by the Buraku people, and quite a large number became believers. Being able to identify with the churches had an important meaning. But most of the members of churches that welcomed Buraku believers had not completely conquered their own prejudices against the Buraku. Incidences of persons refusing to share communion vessels (cups) with Buraku people occurred in churches across the country.

From the 1890s, poverty became increasingly prevalent in Buraku areas, prompting medical and educational work along with evangelism, all on a small scale. One such program was the Shoyugikai, run by Kaiho Kumajiro and Yasueda Takeo. Sending specialists into Buraku communities to lead such programs was seen as discrimination against Buraku believers within the church, and in time evangelistic focus shifted to the lower middle class, and the Buraku people were gradually forgotten by the church. The way in which the church world dealt with Buraku discrimination began and ended with a sympathetic attitude, failing to chastise those who discriminated while seeking to smooth over problems and maintain harmony. The work of Takeba Toraichiro and Tomeoka Kosuke was unable to get beyond the level of cooperation to promote harmony with local and other government agencies. Even Kagawa Toyohiko*, who was influential in the founding of the Levellers Society, was clearly prejudiced in his understanding of the Buraku people, something that is evident in the fact that he never dealt with the Buraku people from the standpoint of human rights and liberation.

During the time when the Buraku Liberation Movement was actively developing, the Christian world did nothing to resolve Buraku problems beyond a one-time evangelistic effort. After the war, evangelistic work was started again in new areas, a small part of the church became interested in Buraku issues, and the Buraku Liberation Christian Council, an organization of volunteers, was set up, which resulted in the surfacing of incidents of Buraku discrimination involving churches and believers that had not occurred before. In the 30 years after 1950, more than 50 such incidents occurred.

In May 1975, at the request of the Buraku Liberation League, the United Church of Christ in Japan (UCCJ) began confronting Buraku issues more actively for the UCCJ Buraku Liberation Center. This action also had an effect on other churches and denominations. The remarks on discrimination made by Machida at the Third World Conference on Religion and Peace precipitated actions that brought the discriminatory nature of the Japanese religious world to the forefront. A solidarity meeting of religious groups that engaged in education to promote reconciliation was set up, and Christians undertook more positive participation, as they performed a leadership role. Even so, there was no let-up in the number of discrimination incidents in the Christian world.

When the *Complete Words of Kagawa Toyohiko* became an issue in 1962, the discriminatory nature of Kagawa's faith itself was questioned, which caused serious critiquing of the discriminatory predisposition throughout the Christian world. Discriminatory language is frequently found in Christian literature. There are those who feel that in regional matters like the Buraku issue, it is enough for the church to leave it to the people who feel a special calling to do something about it. Evaluation of this attitude in the church is divided between those who regard it as correct and those who find it negligent and lazy. The discriminatory remarks at the Thirty-eighth General Meeting of the Anglican* Church in Japan (NSKK) were challenged from within, causing Resident Bishop Watanabe Masanao to resign. In his statement of resignation, with a repentant heart he called for a revolutionizing of the discriminatory nature of the church. Along with the challenges from within the Christian world to change, there is also a need for an awakening within the entire church to the Buraku issue.

Bibliography

Kudo Eiichi, *Kirisuto-kyo to buraku mondai* (Christianity and the Buraku Issue) (1983).

KUDO EIICHI, JAPANESE DICTIONARY

Burdon, John S.

(b. Glasgow, Scotland, 1826; d. Royston, 1907). Missionary of the Church Missionary Society for Africa and the East.

Burdon entered the Anglican* Mission College at age 23 and came to Shanghai in 1853. The following year, he was consecrated by the bishop of Victoria, George Smith, as an elder. His mission work was mainly in the cities of Kiangsu and Chekiang. Burdon also visited *Tai-ping tian-guo* (the Heavenly Kingdom; see Taiping Rebellion). In 1862, he was transferred to Peking, where he first set up a chapel in the British embassy and later began a boarding school for Chinese boys. After his furlough, he returned to China* in 1865 and was commissioned to translate the Bible into *guan hua.* In 1874, he was commissioned as bishop of Victoria. Before his commissioning, he went to Fukien and visited almost all of the Anglican churches in the province. In 1876, Burdon went to Japan* and visited the Anglican churches in Tokyo, Nagasaki, Osaka, and other cities. In 1882, he started new missionary districts in the provinces of Kwangsi and Hainan Island. In 1897, he resigned from the episcopate; thereafter he traveled in Europe and did some writing.

Bibliography

Cohen, Paul A., *China and Christianity* (1963).

CHINA GROUP

Burgos, José Apolonio. *See* Gom-Bur-Za

Burma. *See* Myanmar

Butler, William

(b. Ireland, 1818; d. 1899). Methodist mission founder in India and Mexico who also served in India* as a bishop.

A member of the Methodist* Church in Ireland, Butler moved to America in 1850, where he became very much interested in missions. He was commissioned by the Methodist Missionary Society on 8 Apr 1856 and sent to India. Butler and his wife Clementina (1820-1913) chose to remain in the northern territory, embracing the ancient kingdom of Oudah and the province of Rohilkband with Bareilly, Lucknow, and Moradabad as the chief centers of operation. The reasons for this choice were: (1) the field was unoccupied; (2) it was compact and well defined; and (3) there was only one language spoken in these places. With the help of some of the military officers, Butler was able to secure a piece of land for the Methodist mission in 1857. It was unfortunate that by the year Butler settled at Bareilly, the Sepoy Mutiny had broken out and he had to give up everything and escape to Nainital. But the situation became more favorable to missions when India was brought under the British crown in 1858. After the mutiny, the Butlers remained in Nainital, where they opened schools, a church, and a farmhouse. By 1859, Butler had established stations at Lucknow, Bareilly, and Nainital. Several other missionaries came to work in the mission, and, by 1860, the mission had spread to several other locations.

Butler sensed the need for orphanages and schools from the beginning of his ministry. These he started in order to gain ministers for the church. It is noteworthy that, from the beginning of their ministry, the missionaries provided education, which they considered the best means to win converts to the church. Despite his enthusiasm, Butler was not able to penetrate into the upper classes but had significant influence on the lower-class people, who were economically and socially very backward.

One of the major events during Butler's period occurred when the India mission gained the status of annual conference. The Indian Mission Annual Conference was formed on 8 Dec 1864. This helped develop the indigenous leadership. Valsalen notes that Butler was in favor of the ordination of indigenous leadership and gave them equal status. Butler left India in 1865. His dominant, almost dictatorial, personality produced strong leadership for the progress of Methodism in India.

Bibliography

Butler, Clementina, *William Butler: The Founder of Two Missions of the Methodist Episcopal Church* (1924). • Butler, William, *From Boston to Bareilly and Back* (1885); *The Land of the Veda* (1891). • Badley, Brenden, *Visions and Victories in Hindustan: A Story of the Mission Stations of the Methodist Episcopal Church in Southern Asia* (1931). • Valsalen, F. J., "The Missionary Methods of Revds. William Butler, James M. Thoburn and William Taylor of the Methodist Church in India from 1859 to 1893" (M.Th. thesis, Bangalore, United Theological College Archives) (1984).

FRANKLYN J. BALASUNDARAN

Cabanban, Benito

(b. ?; d. 22 Nov 1990). Fifth diocesan and first presiding Filipino bishop of the Philippine Episcopal Church (PEC).

Cabanban was consecrated suffragan bishop on 24 Feb 1959 and diocesan bishop in 1967. When the subsidy from the Episcopal Church (see Anglicans), United States, was substantially reduced, Cabanban embarked on a vigorous campaign to establish an endowment fund in 1970. In 1971 the PEC was divided into three dioceses, with the consequent creation of the house of bishops, because of the expansion of the church, the difficulty of pastoral visitation and administration, and as part of the move toward autonomy. Bishops were elected for the northern and southern dioceses, while Cabanban was retained as bishop of the central diocese. The house of bishops met on 9 Feb 1972 and elected Cabanban as first presiding bishop of the church.

Cabanban retired on 1 May 1978 at age 65. He died of a heart attack shortly after the church gained its constitutional autonomy in May 1990.

Bibliography

Journal of the Annual Convocation of the Philippine Episcopal Church (1967-78). Edward Malecdan

Cabecera-Visita Complex

Parish structure adapted from Latin America by early Spanish missionaries in the Philippines* in response to the reluctance of indigenous peoples from outlying areas to stay permanently in settlement centers.

Initially, the Spanish missionaries tried the Latin-American *reduccion,* the establishment of settlement centers, to facilitate evangelism and conversion, but Filipinos refused to stay permanently in the *cabecera* (centers), which were far from the fields, rivers, and forests, their means of livelihood. The friars then developed the *cabecera-visita* ("visit") system. Small chapels were erected in outlying areas visited periodically by the friars. On major feast days, the people flocked to the *cabecera* to join the fiestas, vending and purchasing wares.

Bibliography

Phelan, John Leddy, *The Hispanization of the Philippines* (1959). • Schumacher, John, *Readings in Philippine Church History* (1979). Apolonio M. Ranche

Cadière, Leopold-Michel

(b. Aix-en-Provence, France, 14 Feb 1869; d. Hue, Vietnam, 1953). Missionary of the *Missions Étrangères de Paris* to Vietnam*; prolific writer and scholar.

Cadière went to Vietnam in 1892 and stayed until his death in 1953. A well-known amateur ethnologist, his extensive and variegated knowledge covered history, archaeology, philology, ethnology, and ethnobotany. He developed a unique sociology of religion of the Vietnamese, based on his research in the villages of his diocese near the imperial capital of Hue in central Vietnam. His extensive knowledge of the Vietnamese language allowed him to study intensively the oral traditions of the Vietnamese peasants he worked with during his long years of service in the country. He was a prolific correspondent of the École Française d'Extrême Orient, which he joined as a permanent member in 1918. Some years earlier, he had founded the prestigious journal *Le Bulletin des Amis du Vieux Hue* (BAVH). He also contributed to the *Revue Indochinoise.*

In 1945, Cadière was taken prisoner first by the Japanese and later by the Vietminh, who subsequently limited his freedom to work and travel for more than six years. In 1953, he refused to be repatriated to France. Shortly after, he died in Vietnam at the age of 84. His tomb in the cemetery of Phu Xuan near Hue has survived calamities and the ravages of war.

Cadière's works amount to more than 250 titles, some containing more than 350 pages. Most renowned is his *Croyances et pratiques religieuses des Annamites dans les environs de Hue,* published in the *Bulletin d'École*

Française d'Extrême Orient (BEFEO) in 1918 and 1919. In an earlier treatise, *Anthropologie populaire annamite* (1915), Cadière undertook a pioneering attempt to engage in symbolic anthropology by comparing different parts of the human body with beliefs and representations, showing the meaning of taste, smell, and sound. In the early 1930s, his interest moved toward the link between social relations and religious practices, focusing upon the family as the locus of religious belief (see "La Famille et la religion en pays annamite," in *BAVH* 17.4 [Oct-Dec 1930]: 353-413).

This and other writings are collected in three voluminous publications, representing the best empirically based research in the French language on Vietnamese religion. By treating several great traditions like Buddhism*, Taoism*, and Confucianism* as a blend of popular beliefs and practices and the ancestor* cult, Cadière developed his own definition of religion, which came close to Durkheim's moral order.

Cadière stressed the internal division of villages by family and lineage interests and devoted a remarkably modern attention to the position of women. He recognized the male-oriented model of social hierarchy but clearly had an open eye for the countervailing power of females who exploit gender roles in their favor ("La Famille . . . annamite"). In spite of his enormous knowledge of the Vietnamese language, however, Cadière never developed a comprehensive treatment of the intricate kinship system, with its many linguistic expressions. Nevertheless, Cadière, who never graduated from a scientific institution, became an experienced ethnographer in his own right.

Unlike many of his contemporaries, Cadière did not regard Vietnamese religious practices as superstition, pointless rituals, or useless but harmless beliefs. He shared some degree of the paternalistic and prejudiced mentality of his contemporaries, but on the whole his scholarly work shows remarkable objectivity. His determination to understand the colonized Other as evidenced by his published speeches and memoirs was remarkable at a time when such attitudes were not accepted by his compatriots.

Bibliography

Condominas, Georges, "Deux grands ethnologues pratiquement inconnus de la profession: Les Pères François Callet et Leopold Cadière," in Britta Rupp-Eisenreich, *Histoire de l'Anthropologie XVI-XIX Siècles* (1984).

JOHN G. KLEINEN

Cadman, William C.

(b. London, England [Rotherhithe], 1883; d. Vietnam, 1948); **Grace Hazenberg Cadman** (b. Fulton, Illinois, United States, 1876; d. Vietnam, 1946). Canadian missionaries of the Christian and Missionary Alliance* (CMA) who pioneered to help establish the Evangelical Church of Vietnam* (ECVN) and made significant contributions in the training of pastors, Scripture translation (see Bible Translation), and literature preparation for the C&MA mission and ECVN throughout Indochina.

William apprenticed to the printer's trade in London. Converted in 1904, he was called to ministry and went to study at the Toronto (Canada) Bible College for one year; subsequently, he graduated from Nyack Missionary Training Institute (New York, United States) in 1910. He was appointed by the C&MA and served four years in South China* before transferring to Annam, French Indochina, in 1914. Grace was raised and educated in South Africa by her missionary parents. After earning a bachelor's degree there, she earned a master of arts degree in Toronto, Canada. In 1913 the C&MA appointed her to Vietnam*, where she met William, whom she married in 1915. The couple had one child, Agnes, born in 1916, but she was stricken with poliomyelitis while the family was on furlough in Canada and later died in Hanoi at six years of age. Through their years of service, the Pennsylvania Conference of the Mennonite Brethren in Christ provided their financial support.

After a brief time in Tourane (Da Nang), the Cadmans moved to Hanoi in 1917, where the mission purchased a residence and erected a church and printing press facility. Initially by bicycle and later by automobile, they traveled out from Hanoi selling Scriptures, distributing Gospel literature, and preaching the Gospel. The Hanoi church's first Vietnamese pastor, Le Van Thai*, became a lifelong colleague, friend, and later fifth president of the ECVN.

The *Imprimerie Evangelique* (Evangelical Press) in Hanoi, under William's supervision, printed *Thanh Kinh Bao* (The Bible Magazine), Scriptures, Gospel tracts, hymnals, Sunday school supplies, and devotional literature in Vietnamese, Cambodian, Lao, and various languages of the highland minorities. By 1927 five million printed pages were turned out annually. In 1915 the Cadmans, Vietnamese scholar Mr. Nho, and others began Scripture translation (see Bible Translation) of the Gospels, Acts, and Romans into the romanized script of Vietnamese (Quoc Ngu*). After a temporary suspension of the work, it was commenced again in 1919 and, with the contributions of John D. Olsen, Tran Van Dong, and noted scholar Phan Khoi, the New Testament was completed in 1922 and printed in Shanghai in 1924. The first complete Bible in Vietnamese was printed in 1926 at the Hanoi Press.

During World War II*, the Cadmans were interned in Mytho by the Japanese in 1943 but remained in Vietnam after the end of the war until Grace's death in 1946. After the French forces returned to retake Indochina, causing great suffering to the civilian population, William bicycled in the south from jail to jail, crossing lines between the French and the Vietnamese guerrillas to rescue Christian and non-Christian Vietnamese alike from firing squads of both sides. He traveled in Dec 1945 to Hanoi from Saigon, where 37 men, women, and children trapped in the ECVN Hanoi church compound were caught in the midst of a battle between French and Vietminh forces. He demanded to see the French commanding officer, whom he persuaded to secure their freedom. His bravery was long remembered by his Vietnamese coworkers.

After Grace's death, William returned to North America and married Anna G. Kegerize in 1948. While there, he raised funds for a new cylinder press from England, but he died shortly after returning to Vietnam before the press could be delivered to Dalat, in central Vietnam, to which the entire printing operation was being moved from Hanoi.

Bibliography

Irwin, E. F., "Grace Hazenberg Cadman: An Appreciation by a Fellow Missionary," *The Alliance Weekly,* 1 Jun 1946. • Le, Phu Hoang, "A Short History of the Evangelical Church of Vietnam (1911-1965)" (Unpublished dissertation, New York University, 1972), 2 Vols. • Snead, A. C. "A Laborer at Rest," *The Alliance Weekly,* 8 Jan 1949.

JAMES F. LEWIS

Calchi, Sigismondo Maria

(b. 1685; d. Myanmar, 6 Mar 1728). Papal legate to China* and Myanmar*.

In 1719, Pope Clement XI sent a delegation led by a 35-year-old prelate, Carlo Ambrogio Mezzabarba*, to Emperor Kangxi of China. The delegation, the cream of the Barnabite Order, chosen for their learning and piety, comprised Onorato Maria Ferrari of Vercelli in Piedmont, Sigismondo Maria Calchi of Milan, Allesendro De Allesandri of Bergamo, Filippo Maria Cesati of Milan, and Salvatore Rasini of Nice.

The papal delegation, bearing precious and useful gifts for the emperor, set out on 5 Feb 1720 on their unpredictable mission and, after a tedious, long, and perilous journey, reached Canton on 22 Aug of the same year. They were granted an audience with the emperor on the last day of 1720. During their stay in the royal city, the papal legate, aware of lurking trouble for missionaries, sent the delegation to look for evangelical possibilities in neighboring countries. He assigned Calchi and Vittoni to the kingdom of Ava and Pegu (present-day Myanmar).

When the two priests landed at Syriam, they found two Portuguese priests, who spoke only their own language, "ministering to the scanty remnants of their fellow countrymen" who had been permitted to remain as captives in Syriam after its seizure by King Anaukpetlun of Ava in 1613. Calchi and Vittoni ran into immediate trouble at Syriam because the Portuguese community regarded them as intruders, and they were denounced to the king as spies of China, with which Myanmar was then at war. The king, Taninganwe, summoned them to his court at Ava, the capital, for judgment. But the officers at the court, descendants of the Syriam captives, acted as their interpreters and defended them before the king. As a consequence, they were received with honor. The Christian captives in Ava were happy to have their new priests.

The king, favorably impressed by Calchi, as reported in a letter dated 11 Mar 1723 from the latter to his superior general, granted Calchi permission to build churches and to preach, and also provided money to build a church. The king showed his desire "to have amity and commerce with all Christian princes, and especially with the pope; to have other missionaries and men well-versed in the arts of painting, weaving clothes, glass-making, astronomy, mechanics and geography to instruct his subjects." He retained Calchi in the royal city and sent Vittoni with some rubies, sapphires, and other precious stones in a red taffeta box to present his compliments to the pope.

Calchi studied the Myanmar language, speaking it at first in elegant style, and later expressing himself in the popular way. He prepared the first Myanmar dictionary in anticipation of the arrival of his fellow priests from Europe, begging his father general to send him good, disciplined, pure, and kind missionaries and to make them study, before coming to Myanmar, "geometry, astronomy, mathematics or some arts; also some carpentry, the art of building fountains and wells, pharmacy, in a word, anything useful, be it cooking, making perfumes, cakes, etc., as everything is new here."

Calchi lived humbly, ate poorly, and worked incessantly, carrying on alone after the departure of Vittoni. Exhausted after eight years in Myanmar, he died at age 43. He was buried in a field belonging to an Armenian Christian outside the walls of Ava. Calchi is rightly called the cornerstone of the Catholic Church in Myanmar.

Bibliography

Thet Lwin, Peter, "The History of the Church in Myanmar (Burma)" (unpublished, Yangon).

PETER THET LWIN

Cambodia

Cambodia, or Kampuchea, or "the country of Khmer" *(srok khmer),* is situated between Vietnam* and Thailand*, sharing some 100 kilometers of common border with Laos*. It has a tropical monsoon climate (rainy season from May to September). The people call themselves Khmer, and they speak the Khmer language, a monotonal language with very rich phonetics. It has its own writing, borrowed from Sanskrit. The Khmer language is not similar to any other Asiatic language, except for the Mon language in Myanmar.

The name "Cambodia" comes from a monk called Cambu who married a divinity named Mera and founded the Tchenla kingdom at the beginning of the 6th c. C.E. In the time when Angkor was its capital (9th-14th cs.), the Cambodian empire extended across almost the entire Indochinese peninsula, from the point of

Camau (Vietnam) up to Louang Prabang (Laos) and Chiang Mai (Thailand), from the China Sea to the isthmus of Kra (Malaysia). During this period, the great temples were built in Angkor and throughout the vast empire. From the 14th c. on, Siam (Thailand) and Vietnam took advantage of the internal dissensions in Cambodia to annex neighboring Cambodian provinces. The glorious past so profoundly shapes the mentality of contemporary Khmer that the loss of these territories has created a lasting resentment toward these two neighbors, especially Vietnam.

Around 1850, the Cambodian king, Ang Duong (Norodom), requested France (at that time looking for a way of access to China*) to "protect" his country from his two invaders. Beginning in 1863 and for 90 years, Cambodia thus became a French protectorate. In the wake of the first Indo-China War waged by the Vietminh (Vietnamese nationalists) against the French presence, and at the conclusion of the "Royal Crusade for Independence" waged by King Sihanouk, the country regained its sovereignty on 9 Nov 1953.

From 1953 to 1970, with peace established, Cambodia experienced a beginning of economic development under the reign of Sihanouk, who followed the political line of "active neutrality" between the Sino-Soviet Communists and the United States then in open confrontation in Vietnam. But the prince was deposed on 8 Mar 1970 by a coup d'état directed by pro-American general Lon Nol. The Vietnamese War then spread to Cambodia: the Vietcong (Vietnamese Communists), who from 1965 had set up bases in Cambodian territory, invaded Cambodia and formed an army of national liberation which they handed over to the Khmer Rouge, revolutionary Cambodians. During five years of civil war (1970-75), over 600,000 people perished.

On 17 Apr 1975, the pro-Chinese Khmer Rouge*, led by Pol Pot, entered Phnom Penh as victors and installed the "Democratic Kampuchea" regime. They emptied all the towns and larger villages and sent their populations to collective labor projects in order to create an irrigation network comparable to that of the Angkor period. Their objective was to introduce an egalitarian, agrarian Communism of the Maoist type. To "purify" the people, they executed all military and public-service personnel and intellectuals. The number of deaths by execution and above all from starvation can be estimated at around 2.5 million (nearly one-third of the population).

After many bloody skirmishes led by the Khmer Rouge along the common frontier, pro-Soviet Vietnam invaded Cambodia on 25 Dec 1978. On 7 Jan 1979, the Vietnamese army installed the populist regime of the People's Republic of Kampuchea and attempted to annex the country. The Khmer Rouge took refuge in the mountains close to Thailand and took the lead in the anti-Vietnamese resistance movement, with the support of the West. A new, 12-year-long civil war began. More than a half million Cambodians sought refuge in Thailand, and many took sanctuary in Western nations.

After 1987, the weakened Soviet Union could no longer give military aid to the Vietnamese occupying forces, a situation which gave rise to negotiations between the two Cambodian camps. The Vietnamese occupation army withdrew completely on 26 Sep 1989, and the country thereafter was called the State of Cambodia. On 23 Oct 1991, 18 countries signed the Paris Accords, which regulated the international aspects of the Cambodian conflict. The United Nations Transitional Authority for Cambodia (UNTAC) contingent — 22,000 strong, including almost 15,000 military personnel — was sent to Cambodia to disarm the factions, control the various government departments, and prepare for free elections. Only the third mission proved successful. "Fair and free" elections took place peacefully on 23-28 May 1993, with more than 80% voting. The Royalist Party (FUNCINPEC) of the resistance came first with 45.5% of the votes; the former Communist Party (Pracheachon), the party in power, was second with 38.2%.

A constituent assembly of 120 elected members drew up and adopted a constitution, by the terms of which Prince Sihanouk was named king on 23 Sep 1993. The king nominated a government which had the special feature of having two representatives from the two principal parties at the head of each ministry. In effect, it is the former Communists of the Pracheachon who continue to rule the country. Prince Ranaridhh and Hun Sen are, respectively, first premier minister and second premier minister. Chéa Sim is president of the national assembly.

The country is now called the Kingdom of Cambodia. Thanks to international aid, the economic infrastructure of the country is in the process of slow reconstruction, but continued internal strife and corruption have undermined economic progress.

The population of Cambodia is estimated at between 9 and 10 million, the last reliable statistics going back to 1962. Ninety percent of the population are Khmer who practice *Theravada* Buddhism* and speak the Khmer language, the national language. The aboriginal proto-Khmer belong to a dozen ethnic groups and number about 80,000; they live in the mountains and practice traditional religion. Some 200,000 Chams, descendants of Champa (a kingdom once situated in central Vietnam and annihilated by the Vietnamese in the 15th c.), practice Sunni Islam and speak the Cham language. They are also called the Khmer Islam. The Chinese community, which was very powerful before 1975, lives in the towns and handles commerce, numbering approximately 400,000. The number of Vietnamese immigrants has risen to around 500,000. They are generally artisans and fishermen and practice ancestor worship*.

History of Christianity. Christianity was first brought to Cambodia in the 16th c. by Portuguese merchants and navigators (beginning in 1553). Gaspar da Cruz, a Portuguese Dominican*, presented himself at the royal court of Longvek in 1555. He came to serve his compatriots. Another Portuguese Dominican, Sylvester d'Azevedo*, who arrived in Cambodia around 1574, became the first missionary among the Khmer.

At the beginning of the 17th c., a group of Japanese Catholics, fleeing from imperial persecution, made their home to the north of Phnom Penh. They were followed some years later in 1660 by a group of Portuguese Eurasians from the Moluccan Islands (Indonesia), who were fleeing from persecution by Dutch Protestants. This group formed the nucleus of the Catholic Church. Around the same time, some 50 Vietnamese Catholics appeared on the scene. Thus the earliest church was made up of a diverse ethnic community whose members brought many of their conflicts into the church. French missionary Louis Chevreal became so frustrated by the Cambodian indifference and European conflicts that he left in 1665. From this time on, the responsibility of the apostolate was entrusted to the Paris Foreign Mission Society* (MEP) created by the vicars apostolic appointed by the pope.

Until the institution of the French protectorate, Siamese and Vietnamese invaders, both laying claim to the country, frequently destroyed communities and churches and carried off Christians into captivity, either to Siam or to Vietnam. Around 1770, Fr. Levavaseur* laid the foundations for the evangelization of the Khmer. In 1770, a catechism in Khmer was published, but no Bible translation* was yet begun. The French protectorate encouraged French missionary work in Cambodia (among Vietnamese and Chinese), but it also discouraged evangelism among the ethnic Khmer.

From 1863 on, French laws authorized population movements within French Indochina, and numerous Vietnamese settled in Cambodia. Many of them were Catholic. This massive presence of Vietnamese Christians in the church has constituted a major obstacle to the evangelization of the Khmer people. While the French could not preach to the Khmer, others could. Therefore in 1922, two Americans, D. Ellison and A. Hammond, from the Christian and Missionary Alliance* settled in Cambodia. Ellison founded a Bible school at Battambang in 1925, and Hammond started Bible translation. The New Testament was printed in 1934 and the whole Bible in 1954. In 1949, the Bible school was transferred to Ta Khmau, near Phnom Penh.

In 1970, the Christian community comprised around 65,000 believers, of whom 60,000 were Vietnamese. Following the deposition of Prince Sihanouk and the invasion of the country by the Vietcong, about 4,500 Vietnamese residents, some 1,000 Catholics amongst them, were assassinated; the rest were expelled, and the church was decimated.

For Cambodian Christians, this ordeal was nevertheless beneficial; they were finally able to be Khmer and Christian without being accused of being tied to the Vietnamese. During the civil war of 1970-75, Cambodian Christians made remarkable efforts to acculturate their liturgy, translate the biblical texts, and dialogue with the Buddhists. The unselfish service they rendered to the victims of war allowed them to build good relations with the authorities, who appreciated their efforts.

Among Protestants, the Overseas Missionary Fellowship sent missionaries to Cambodia in 1973, and an American charismatic preacher started an evangelistic work the same year. In 1975, when the Khmer Rouge took power, all foreigners were obliged to leave. At that time, 14 national Protestant pastors remained in Cambodia. It is estimated that, during the brief reign of the Khmer Rouge, between two and three million Cambodians were killed. In 1979, when the Vietnamese threw out the Khmer Rouge, only three pastors were still alive. Eleven had been killed or died from sickness or malnutrition.

In the Roman Catholic Church, the first Cambodian priest was not ordained until 1957. During the next 16 years, six Khmer entered the priesthood, one a Benedictine monk. In 1968, Paul Tep Im Sotha* was appointed prefect apostolic of the diocese of Battambang. On 14 Apr 1975, Joseph Chhmar Salas* was consecrated bishop coadjutor of the diocese of Phnom Penh.

Beginning in 1975, all of the Cambodian priests and religious leaders, the majority of the nuns, and some parish directors were either assassinated by the Khmer Rouge or died of starvation. All the churches, with the exception of two, were destroyed and administrative buildings erected on their sites by the authorities of the People's Republic of Kampuchea. Christians continued to practice their faith secretly, deprived of any priestly ministry for almost 15 years.

After 1989, several foreign priests managed to visit Cambodia under cover of Caritas* International or other charitable, nongovernmental organizations. On 4 Apr 1990, Christians were once again officially authorized to practice their faith publicly. On 25 Mar 1994, for the first time in 450 years, diplomatic relations were established between the holy see and the kingdom of Cambodia.

Present State of Christianity. At the present time, the Catholic Church comprises about 5,000 Cambodian Christians distributed principally in the regions of Phnom Penh, Battambang, and Kompong Thom. They represent about 0.05% of the country's total population and belong to all social strata. It is estimated there are about 10,000 Vietnamese Catholics, or almost 5% of the Vietnamese community. The vast majority of these Vietnamese Christians live in the towns and provinces adjacent to Vietnam.

Since 1990, about 100 catechumens have been baptized each year. A Cambodian priest was ordained in Jul 1995. A major seminary has been established at Battambang.

Protestant Christian groups have begun to multiply rapidly in Cambodia. Most new missionary work comes from Anglican*, Methodist*, or independent groups in Southeast Asia. A small number of Cambodian Christians have returned from overseas to help rebuild the church.

Bibliography

Ponchaud, François, *The Cathedral of the Rice Paddy* (1990). • Chandler, David, *The History of Cambodia* (1993/94). • Cormack, Don, *Killing Fields, Living Fields* (1996). FRANÇOIS PONCHAUD and JEAN CLAVAUD

Camillians

The Order of St. Camillus, also known as the Order of the Ministers (Servants) of the Sick (MI), was founded in Rome in 1582 by St. Camillus de Lellis (1550-1614), who spent his life in the service of the sick. The church defined his work as "a new school of charity." Pope Leo XIII in 1886 proclaimed St. Camillus, together with St. John of God, "patron of the sick and hospitals." In 1930, Pius XI named him "protector of the hospital personnel."

The Order of Camillians is a clerical institute comprising priests and brothers, equal in rights and obligations, living together in a community, pledged in poverty, chastity, and obedience to minister to the sick. Their headquarters is in Rome. In 1995, the Order of St. Camillus numbered 1,200 males distributed in 14 provinces spread over 29 countries worldwide.

Various female congregations and lay associations have chosen St. Camillus as their teacher and model. In 1841, Maria Domenica Barbantini founded the Servants of the Sick (Camillian Sisters) in Lucca. At the end of the 19th c., Josephine Vannini, in collaboration with Fr. Tezza, founded the Daughters of St. Camillus in Rome. These two congregations are now present in many Asian countries, e.g., India*, Thailand*, Taiwan*, the Philippines*, Indonesia*, and Vietnam*. In 1936, Germana Sommaruga, under the guidance of Fr. Carazzo, established the Secular Institute, Missionaries of the Sick: Christ Our Hope, approved by Rome in 1953 for lay members fully committed to the service of the sick. The Camillian family also includes lay volunteer movements, e.g., Friends of the Sick, Fraternity of the Sick, Auxiliaries of St. Camillus, and At the Service of the Poorest.

Camillians in Asia are of recent origin. Although the Camillian Red Cross first appeared in Asia in 1726 when Frs. Giordani and Signorini were sent to Beijing by the Congregation of Propaganda to work as artisans at the imperial court, it was only in the 20th century that initiatives were taken to extend the order to Asia. The first mission was in China* in 1946, followed by foundations in Thailand, Taiwan, the Philippines, India, and Vietnam. Presently, 12.5% of the entire Camillian order is in Asia, engaged in health care and religious formation. Their ministry comprises health-care institutions (hospitals, dispensaries, leprosaria), social works (centers for the handicapped, houses for the aged, refuge for AIDS victims), educational institutes (nursing schools, youth centers, kindergartens), pastoral centers, hospital chaplaincies, and parishes, with preference for the poor and forsaken sick.

China. The mission in China started in 1946 when the Lombard-Venetian Province sent a group of religious to Zhaotong in northeast Yunnan. With the encouragement of the apostolic administrator J. Kerec, a vast program of activities was undertaken. Hospitals, clinics, leprosaria, missionary centers, etc., were set up in the midst of enormous difficulties. Celestino Rizzi and Claudia Martinelli died in the struggle. Unfortunately, in 1952 all 14 Camillians were expelled from China. They sought new locations in Taiwan and Thailand, proceeding in later years to the Philippines, India, and Vietnam. In 1976, Taiwan and the Philippines were designated as the vice-province of the Far East, while the other foundations continue to depend on the Lombard-Venetian Province (Italy).

Thailand. Headed by G. Dalla Ricca, Camillians first arrived in Thailand in 1952 upon the invitation of the bishop of Ratburi, Msgr. Pasotti, and settled in Ban Pong, a town northwest of Bangkok, where a wealthy Catholic had donated a small hospital which, enlarged many times, underwent a major restructuring in 1994. From Ban Pong, the Camillians also took care of the Christians of Lukke and the lepers of Tawa. Recently they purchased an 86-acre forest in Chombun to house 30 families of former lepers. In 1955, the Camillians began health-care work in Bangkok. In 1982, the modern seven-story, 150-bed Camillian Hospital was built. A school of nursing was later added. In Bangkok, the Camillians also assist the marginalized in the port slums. A house near the National Hospital for Infectious Diseases was bought in 1993 for HIV/AIDS victims. *Suun Banthaojai* (Relief Center) is a leading center in the country in care and prevention. Sri Vicien Village, in Chiang Ray, north Thailand, was built in 1990 for the families of former lepers. In 1994, a center for tribal children was erected in the heart of the village. Sri Vicien Village had 68 families in 1995. Deserving mention is the village of Khokwat, built in 1965, renowned for its organization, therapy program, and lifestyle, where 200 lepers and their families receive free assistance and care. The recruitment of native clergy has always been a principal goal. A seminary was built in 1971 in Sampran. On the seminary compound are an old folks' home and a social center for children at risk. A minor seminary, located in Sriracha, was inaugurated in 1989. The Thai contingent had 40 religious in 1995.

Taiwan. Camillian missionaries first arrived in Taiwan in 1952, after their expulsion from China, and their mission covers two areas: Lotung, Ilan County, on the east coast, and Makung, the capital of the Pescadores Islands. A small dispensary in Lotung has grown, with the collaboration of surgeons like Dr. Janez, to become the present 500-bed St. Mary's Hospital. In Lotung, the Camillians also sponsor a school of nursing, a sanatorium, a center for mentally handicapped children, a Catholic youth center, and the Lanyang Folklore Dance Group. In addition to welfare activities, there is also a commitment to evangelization. The parish of Lotung is surrounded by many Christian communities. Most of the Ayatals (the "Head Cutters"), aborigines living in the mountains, have accepted the Christian faith. Ernesto Valdesolo, the apostle to the Ayatals, spent 40 years among them.

In Makung, the Camillian mission began with an outpatient center and a nursery in 1952. St. Camillus Hospital, built in 1957, was recently restructured to accommodate 120 beds. A new parish church, which also operates a center for the disabled and several kindergartens, was built in 1964 by Antonio Crotti, the apostle of the Pescadores. In 1970, the holy see constituted the Pescadores an apostolic administration.

Philippines. The Camillian community of the Philippines was officially opened in March 1975. The pioneers were Frs. Nidini, Anselmi, and Roman. The health-care institutions include the Home of Charity (Marikina); the polyclinics of Makati, Pasig, and Cogeo; and various clinics, e.g., Boso-Boso in Antipolo and Balugo in Negros Oriental. Two small hospitals are planned for Samar (Calbayog) and Mindanao (Mati). Hospital chaplaincies represent an unlimited opportunity for pastoral care and, in 1995, the Camillians were providing ministry in five large hospitals, where they also offered courses on clinical and pastoral education and inspired the health-care workers. The parish Our Lady of la Paz in the outskirts of Makati is also entrusted to the Camillians. The initiatives of the parish include a program of preventive medicine, a nutrition center, and a dispensary. One group, the Friends of the Sick, regularly visits the elderly and the abandoned of the parish. The St. Camillus College Seminary of Marikina accommodates 120 students for college-level courses in philosophy. At the end of four years, the students go to Baguio, 300 km. north of Manila, for the novitiate. Theology is studied at the Formation Center in Quezon City, Manila. A pastoral year prepares the religious for his final commitments. In 1995, there were 18 Filipino priests and 20 temporary professed scholastics.

India. The mission in India was founded by Antonio Crotti in 1980. The prime concern has been vocation promotion. A minor seminary was opened in 1983 in Mananthavady (Kerala) and a major seminary in Bangalore (1985). A novitiate house is under construction near Bangalore. In 1995, there were seven Indian priests, a growing number of scholastics, and fifty young aspirants. These young religious have the task of giving life to an Indian Camillianism. Many initiatives are in the process of development for the coming years.

Vietnam. A Camillian foundation in Vietnam is just beginning. A church rich in vocations and the challenges of health care encourage the Camillians to make a specific contribution in this land. Already some lay associations venerate St. Camillus and follow his inspiration. A group of young students is aspiring to the Camillian religious life. These are signs of hope for a rapid development of a Camillian presence in Vietnam.

The Camillian presence in Asia, although young, is full of promise. Faithful to the Lord's command to heal the sick and preach the Gospel, the Camillians intend to care for the sick and the poor of this continent in collaboration with the local churches. "The future of the church lies in Asia," said Pope John Paul II in Manila in 1995. This is also an invitation to the Camillians to become more involved with their special charism in the range of missionary activities in Asia.

Bibliography

Vanti, M., *St. Camillus and His Ministers of the Sick* (1990). • Brusco, A., *The Camillian Presence in the Third World: Perspective and Programming* (1991). • Giordan, D., *The First Camillian Mission in China* (1992).

Antonio Didone

Campus Crusade for Christ

When Joon Gon Kim was made the national director for South Korea in 1958, the Campus Crusade for Christ (CCC) ministry was birthed in Asia. By 1970, CCC ministries were established in South Korea, Japan*, the Philippines*, Taiwan*, Malaysia*, Indonesia*, India*, and Pakistan*. New national ministries were being established in Singapore* and Sri Lanka* at the same time.

Bailey and Elizabeth Marks and Kent and Diane Hutcheson came to Singapore in 1970 as CCC missionaries to Asia. Bailey Marks served as the Asia South Pacific director of affairs from 1970 to 1980. In 1972, the first Great Commission Training Center was established in Manila. In the same year, a ministry led by nationals began in Singapore with Victor Koh as the first director.

As the Asia ministries grew, there came a need to divide the Asia South Pacific Area of Affairs for the sake of better development, specialization, and growth of the ministries. So in 1980 the Asia South Pacific Area was divided into the East Asia Area of Affairs and the Central Asia and Pacific Area of Affairs, under the leadership of Joon Gon Kim and Thomas Abraham, respectively. In 1990, Victor Koh succeeded Kim as the East Asia director.

Highlights of CCC Ministry in Asia. The 1970s and 1980s were times when the CCC ministries in Asia took root and shape and began a wide variety of ministries to help fulfill the Great Commission. The 1970s saw the development of campus, high school, lay, church, military, executive, music, and other working adult ministries throughout Asia. Effective training programs, materials, and strategies in evangelism, follow-up, discipleship, and church management were also implemented to help in the growth process.

In the 1970s, Lay Institutes for Evangelism, Leadership Training Institutes (LTI) and Classes, Church Management Conferences for Church Pastors and Leaders, and Institutes of Biblical Studies (IBS) were started as strategies to help train Christians in the areas of evangelism and discipleship. The first major mobilization and training meeting for CCC in Asia occurred in 1974, when EXPLO '74 was held in Seoul, Korea. For one week, over 320,000 Koreans and overseas Christians came together to be trained and challenged to help fulfill the Great Commission. The Here's Life "I Found It!" campaign was launched in Asia, with major citywide campaigns. It was a call for the saturation of the Gospel in all countries in Asia. Ministries in major cities in Asia, such as those in South Korea, Singapore, Malaysia, Taiwan, Japan, Hong Kong*, Macau, Indonesia, the Philippines, Thailand, and India participated in this campaign. It is estimated that by 1976, over 100,000,000 people in the Asia and South Pacific region had been made aware of this campaign.

In the 1980s, the JESUS film was released in the theaters of Asian cities in 22 major Asian languages. This enabled Asians, be they Bengali, Thai, Burmese, or Indonesian, to hear and see JESUS speak in their own language. Film teams were also set up to penetrate villages with the Gospel.

EXPLO '80 in Korea saw three million Christians gather at one time to hear the challenge to be involved in world evangelism. The next global training conference was in 1985, where the worldwide ministry of CCC joined together to have an EXPLO '85 training conference by satellite. This linked the key cities of Asia to the other major cities around the world. Over 600,000 Christians around the world were trained and challenged at one time via satellite transmission.

After EXPLO '85, New Life 2000 World was launched as a global movement to evangelize the world and systematically to follow up, build, train, and send out believers.

The 1990s were years of fine-tuning of local strategies and partnerships with the others in the body of Christ to help fulfill the Great Commission in this generation. In 1990, the Manila '90 project involved about 5,000 staff, disciples, and friends of CCC in the saturation of the city of Manila. The leaders also met during the same time in Manila to develop the Million Population Target Area (MPTA) strategy, which would help in completing the unfinished task of proclaiming the Gospel to every geographical area of the world in a language understood by the various ethno-linguistic people groups.

Partnership became the CCC's key strategy in the 1990s. Therefore, in 1995, all the CCC national ministries in Asia supported and joined in the Global Consultation on World Evangelism (GCOWE) '95. The national directors of the CCC in Asia served as national coordinators of Saturation Evangelism and the Small Group Leadership Development Track (SEL) of the AD 2000 & Beyond movement.

In the 1990s, the ministries in Cambodia and Vietnam were reopened, and ministries began in Mongolia and Laos. In 1996, CCC initiated flood relief and food distribution projects in North Korea, followed by other development projects to help the starving North Koreans.

Bibliography

Marks, Bailey, *Awakening in Asia* (1981). Victor Koh

Caodaism

The only native religion of Vietnam*. Caodaism represents a syncretistic attempt to unite the three Vietnamese religions, i.e., Confucianism*, Taoism*, and Buddhism*, with Western religious elements, in particular Roman Catholic* Christianity, the ultimate goal being to unify all religions. The full name of the new religion is *Dai Dao Tam Ky Pho Do* (the Great Religion of the Third Dispensation of Salvation). The term *Cao Dai* literally means "high tower" or "elevated palace" and by metonymy designates God ("the Most High").

Historical Developments. It is claimed that the founder of Caodaism was God Most High himself, who reveals his holy will through spiritistic seances. Its historical initiator, however, was Ngo Van Chieu. Born on 28 Feb 1878 in Binh Tay, near Cho Lon, Chieu worked as a minor official of the French colonialist government in Saigon from 1899 to 1902 and then moved to the island of Phu Quoc. Tranquillity on the island led him to renew and intensify his earlier interest in spiritism, that is, in communication with the spirits of the dead by means of mediums, especially as this was popularized by the works of Allan Kardec and Camille Flammarion.

In 1919, Chieu allegedly received a message during a seance that God would make himself known with a new name, Cao Dai, that is, God the Most High. On Christmas Eve 1925, during a seance, it was reported that Cao Dai revealed that people should welcome with joy the day of his birth that was being commemorated in the West. Among Chieu's friends was a building contractor, Le Van Trung, reputed to be a materialist and hedonist. During another seance, the spirit of a Chinese poet, Ly Thai Bach (b. 705 B.C.), appeared to him and gave him a religious mission. Another important convert was Pham Cong Tac. Ngo Van Chieu was chosen as the leader of the new religion. In 1926, there were 12 members. Because of his inclination toward solitude, Chieu asked to be relieved of the leadership position, and Le Van Trung was chosen to replace him. To acquire public legal status, on 7 Oct 1926 the new organization presented the French governor Le Fol with a petition for official recognition; it was accompanied by 247 signatures of the faithful. Thus was born a new native spiritist religion.

The new religion spread with surprising rapidity. In less than two years, it acquired 20,000 converts, among whom were important personages. In 1932, it had 128 temples and 200,000 faithful. Its success was due partly to the popularity of spiritism and partly to its irenic spirit, which enabled it to assimilate other religions in Vietnam. In March 1927, a magnificent temple was built in Tay Ninh and was declared the holy see of Caodaism.

When Le Van Trung succeeded Ngo Van Chieu, he organized the new religion along the lines of the Roman Catholic Church, using similar nomenclature, liturgical rites, and vestments. But Trung's ascendancy did not last long; in 1933 he was fiercely attacked for alleged financial irregularities and died the following year. He was succeeded by Pham Cong Tac as "pope," governing both the Cuu Trung Dai (the executive branch) and Hiep Thien Dai (the judicial branch). In 1939, there were several anticolonialist movements in which many Caodaists participated. As a result, on 26 Aug 1940, the French government shut down the holy see of Caodaism in Tay Ninh and on 21 Aug 1941 arrested Pham Cong Tac and exiled him to Madagascar. In 1943, the Japanese invaded Vietnam and, to foment opposition to the French colonialist government, they armed Caodaism under the leadership of Tran Quang Vinh. When Japan was defeated, Caodaism was not militarily strong enough to resist the Vietnamese Communists; Vinh was arrested, and control of the Caodaist army was taken away from him. In 1946, the French repatriated Pham Cong Tac and began arming the Caodaists. In 1953, the Caodaist army was 15,000 strong and the church had 1,500,000 members. Not all Caodaists supported the French, however. One sect at Ben Tre joined the Communists to oppose French rule. Another sect, under the leadership of Trinh Minh The, withdrew into the maquis to fight against both the French and the Communists. In July 1954, after the Geneva Accords divided Vietnam into two parts, the North under the Communist rule, and the South under a democratic, pro-Western government, the Caodaist army was disbanded; Pham Cong Tac went to Cambodia* and died there in 1959.

After its conquest of the South in April 1975, the Communist government set out systematically to persecute Caodaism. It confiscated its properties, secularized its holy see at Tay Ninh, and disbanded its leadership. Many of its adherents left the country and settled in the United States, France, Canada, Australia, England, Germany, Japan, and Congo, where they continue to practice their faith. Currently it is estimated that there are 3,000,000 Caodaists, most of whom are Vietnamese, Chinese, and Cambodians.

Internal Organization. Caodaism believes that there are two authorities. The heavenly authority, that is, the authority of God the Most High and that of the perfect ones, is exercised by the earthly authority, that is, the authority of the creatures, to establish laws for the church (the legislative power). The earthly authority is divided into the popular council, the priestly council, and the supreme council. The popular council consists of representatives elected by all the faithful to present their petitions to the priestly council; the priestly council consists of higher officers of the church whose charge is to deliberate and vote on the petitions of the popular council. The supreme council consists of the highest officers of the church whose duty is to approve the proposals of the popular and priestly councils.

Caodaism is organized in three "towers" or "palaces." The first is invisible and is called *Bat Quai Dai* (Eight-Spirits Tower); it is the world of God the Most High and of the saints, who include the Chinese poet Ly Thai Bach, the French novelist Victor Hugo, the French saint Joan of Arc, the Chinese general Quan De, the Buddhist nun Quan Am, and Sun Yat-Sen*, the founder of the Republic of China. The second tower is semivisible and is called *Hiep Thien Dai* (Communion with Heaven Tower); its officers function in communion with the invisible tower to receive the instructions of God the Most High. Its power is judiciary, and its task is to preserve and implement the teachings of the church. The head of this tower is called *Ho Phap* (guardian). The third tower is the visible organ of the church; its power is executive and its task is to organize the activities of the faithful and to execute the decisions of the church. The head of this tower is called *Giao Tong* (pope).

Caodaism is a highly structured organization and yet is deeply democratic in its operations. Both men and women participate equally in the decision making of the church.

Doctrinal Teachings. Fundamental to Caodaism is the belief in the one God, the Most High *(Cao Dai),* creator of all things. The symbol of Caodist monotheism is the One Eye, which is reminiscent of Freemasonry. Moreover, the one God is professed to be the savior of all things. He carries out his saving work *(Pho Do)* by communicating the Great Doctrine *(Dai Dao)* in three dispensations or stages *(Tam Ky).* Hence the complete name of the new religion is, as mentioned above, *Dai Dao Tam Ky Pho Do.*

In the first stage, the Most High bestowed the universal revelation to all peoples; however, this revelation was not well preserved and transmitted due to the lack of proper mediation. In the second dispensation, the Most High communicated the Great Doctrine in five branches: *Nho Dao* (Confucianism or religion of the human); *Than Dao* (Vietnamese animism* or religion of the spirits); *Thanh Dao* (Christianity or religion of the saints); *Tien Dao* (Taoism or religion of the immortals); and *Phat Dao* (Buddhism or religion of the Buddha). In Caodaism, the third and last dispensation, the Most High purposes to unite all religions and communicates his doctrines and will no longer by means of intermediaries but directly, through spiritistic seances.

Caodaism thus presents itself as the unification of all religions, both Eastern and Western. On the one hand, it adopts many of the elements of the three traditional Vietnamese religions, i.e., Taoism Confucianism and Buddhism. For instance, from Buddhism it adopts the doctrine of karma and reincarnation; from Confucianism it derives much of its individual, family, and social ethics; and from Taoism it borrows many of its rituals. As for its organization, it stipulates that beneath the pope there will be a representative *(chuong phap)* from each of the three religions whose task is to examine the pronouncements of the pope, correct him if necessary, and approve the books of prayers and doctrine for publication.

On the other hand, Caodaism appropriates the Western theosophist practice of spiritism and makes it one of the principal means of obtaining divine revelation. It also adopts many terms of the Roman Catholic sacramental and canonical system, e.g., pope, cardinal, archbishop, bishop, priest.

Ethically, Caodaism urges simplicity of life, mutual charity, and social responsibility. Furthermore, it promotes a strict ethical code. Minimally, all the faithful must abstain from the five prohibitions (no killing of any kind, stealing, sexual improprieties, drinking, and lying) and observe the four commandments (obedience to the superior, humility, financial honesty, and respect for all). It must also be mentioned that Caodaism has played an important role in the war first against French colonialism and then against Communism*, whose atheism it vigorously rejects.

Bibliography

Gobron, Gabriel, *Histoire et Philosophie du Caodaïsme* (1949). • Fall, Bernard, "The Political-Religious Sects of Viet-Nam," *Pacific Affairs* 28 (1955). • Oliver, Victor L., *Caodai Spiritism: A Study of Religion in Vietnamese Society* (1976).

PETER C. PHAN

Caozhou (Chaozhou City) Religious Affair

The Caozhou (He Ze) Religious Affair concerns the killing of two German missionaries in Caozhou, Shandong Province. In 1882 German missionaries of the Society of the Divine Word* (SVD) began their work in Lu Nan. By 1895 their number had reached 34. On 1 Nov 1897 two missionaries, Franciscus Nies and Ricandus Henle, were killed by members of a local society, The Big Knife, in Ju Ye district, under the jurisdiction of Caozhou.

Germany, looking for the opportunity to invade a Chinese seaport, used the affair as a reason to send an armada to the gulf of Jiao Zhou. The Ching dynasty government was forced to sign an agreement on 6 Mar 1898 to demote the viceroy of Shandong Province, execute two of the nine people arrested, compensate Germany with 225,000 ounces of silver, and provide protection for German missionaries. In addition, the treaty of Jiao Ao Territory was signed, allowing Germany the right to use the Gulf of Jiaozhou, to build the Jiao Ji Railroad, and to mine.

Bibliography

Latourette, Kenneth Scott, *A History of Christian Missions in China* (1929). • Stentz, George M., *Life of Father Henle, S.V.D.* (1921); *Twenty-five Years in China 1893-1918* (1924). • Pieper, R., "*Unkraut, Knospen und Bluten auf dem blumigen Reiche der Mitte,*" *Steyl* (1900).

CHINA GROUP

Capitalism. *See* Colonialism; Imperialism; Opium

Capuchins (Indonesia)

In 1905, the Dutch province of the Capuchins took over the whole mission of Borneo from the Jesuits, who lacked manpower for the fast-developing missions in eastern Indonesia (e.g., Flores, the Kei Islands, North Celebes). Six years later, all three parishes of Sumatra were also entrusted to the Capuchin missionaries.

In 1905, Pontianak in western Borneo became the second independent apostolic prefecture (after Batavia, 1808). It was the center of evangelization among Chinese migrants in western Borneo and among the native Dayak tribes around the upper Mahakam River in eastern Borneo. Schools, boarding houses, and a minor seminary were established in Nyarumkop (1916), still the educational center of the present archdiocese of Pontianak (1961). The first bishop, Pacificus Bos* (1918-33), called the Father of the Kalimantan Mission, traveled the whole island on foot. He succeeded in attracting other religious societies to the mission field in Borneo. As a result, since 1938 vicariate after vicariate has been handed over to other groups of missionaries, and the Capuchins by 1982 concentrated on only three districts in the province of West Kalimantan. Here the congregation increased from 5,000 (1905) to 136,315 (1992), led by a Dayak archbishop (since 1977) and a majority of native priests, mostly Indonesian Capuchins.

Even more astonishing was the development of the Sumatra Capuchin mission, from 22 indigenous and four Chinese believers in 1912 to more than a half million believers in 1992, forming the archdiocese of Medan, with four suffragan dioceses. The Capuchins kept only the province of North Sumatra and the Special Region of Aceh. Though Christians in Aceh are practically prohibited from forming congregations and building churches, the two North Sumatra dioceses entrusted to the local Capuchins (Medan and Sibolga) developed into prospering mission fields after the Dutch colonial regime allowed the first Capuchin missionaries to work among Bataks (1933) and the people of the island of Nias (1939).

In the seminaries and novitiates, local friars are educated (since 1950). The theological faculty of Pematangsiantar (1956) has been incorporated into St. Thomas University in Medan (1984). The Indonesian province of the Capuchins presently comprises 326 members working in Borneo, Java, Nias, and Sumatra.

ADOLF HEUKEN

Carey, Felix

(b. Moulton, England, 1785; d. Serampore, India, Aug 1822). Eldest son of William and Dorothy Carey and first Protestant missionary to Burma (Myanmar).

On 10 Nov 1793, William Carey* came to India* along with his family. Felix was much attached to his father; his mother, Dorothy, died in Dec 1807. Felix married a Burmese woman of European extraction, and they had two daughters, Lucy and Dolly, both of whom remained at Serampore. Lucy married Rev. Brunden and Dolly married Mr. Backan.

Under the great efforts of William Carey, Krishna Pal became the first Indian to convert to Protestant Christianity. At the same time, Felix accepted Christ as his Savior. They were both baptized on Sunday, 26 Dec 1800. Felix's ordination took place in 1807.

Felix served on the nine-member Missionary Board Committee formed by John Chamberlin. This committee established guidelines for all missionary-related endeavors. Recognizing Serampore's medical needs, Felix studied at the Calcutta General Hospital. He ministered with the mission for only a short time and soon left for Burma, where he conducted most of his active missionary work.

Felix volunteered to go with Mr. Chater as a missionary to Rangoon, knowing that two previous missions to Burma had failed. The fact was that the Rangoon seaport was at the mercy of a despotic governor. Everything depended on his whims and fancies. Conditions in Burma were very unfavorable toward missionary activities, but Carey was allowed to stay for four years — the only one of four missionary representatives allowed to do so. He was an exception because his wife was Burmese.

In a horrific episode during Carey's tenure, 500 soldiers were buried alive merely because they had been recruited by an officer whom the commander disliked. Later, a large number of rich people from Rangoon bribed the viceroy with large sums of money in exchange for permission to leave. Even Carey was having serious trouble.

Carey began the process of stepping down from missionary employment. He was offered a position in government service at Ava. He decided to accept, but first he wanted to go to Calcutta to consult with his father. A few weeks later, Felix lost his wife in a boating accident. The mission of Serampore that he had directed in Burma was handed over to Adoniram Judson*. Soon after Carey's departure, Judson decided to move out of the mission house to a house inside the city walls.

As a professional doctor, Felix introduced the practice of smallpox vaccination to the area. Realizing the need for good textbooks in the fields of history and science, he also produced a textbook on anatomy and physiology in the Bengali language. An editor noted that he was probably the only person in India qualified to write such a work. The medical practices among the natives became an object of study for the first time. Felix also made a suggestion that a medical department subsidized by the government be attached to Serampore College.

Carey was as linguistically gifted as his father. He was one of the best Bengali scholars of the day. In addition to writing the first Bengali treatise on medicine, he translated *Pilgrim's Progress* and *The Vicar of Wakefield* into Bengali. Carey had planned an encyclopedia, but his death in 1822 ended this ambitious project. He was a master in Sanskrit as well as Bengali. Moreover, he learned the Burmese language and worked on a Burmese dictionary and grammar in addition to translating the Gospels of Matthew and Mark.

Carey resigned from his missionary work to become an ambassador in Calcutta representing the king of Burma. William Carey wrote bitterly that his son had shriveled from a missionary into an ambassador, even though he had the high esteem of the king of Burma, who supported his missionary translation work. Felix arrived in Calcutta in 1814 and began to live in ambassadorial state. In the course of time, he ran into debt and never recovered completely. He became sick both spiritually and mentally, and eventually his father had to draw on his personal savings to pay Felix's creditors. Finally, he was recalled in disgrace to Burma, and he abandoned his position at the court.

In Aug 1822, Felix Carey died of a liver complaint at the age of 37. His death deprived William Carey not only of a beloved son, but also of a much needed translator.

Bibliography

Anderson, Courtney, *To the Golden Shore* (1956). • Chatterjee, Sunil Kunar, *Felix Carey: A Tiger Tamed* (1991). • Daniel, J. T. K., and R. E. Hedlund, eds., *Carey's Obligation and India's Renaissance* (1993). • Pearn, B. R., *Judson of Burma* (1962). • Drewery, Mary, *William Carey: A Biography* (1979).

FRANKLYN J. BALASUNDARAN

Carey, Jabez

(b. Piddington, England, 1793; d. Serampore, India, 1862). The third son of William Carey*, Jabez Carey married Eliza Miltan, and together they had six children, who themselves had large families that today are widely scattered throughout the world. In the mid-19th c. several of Carey's descendants worked in the Indian mission field, in medical work, in surrounding centers, and in the civil administration.

Jabez Carey was 15 years old at the time of his father's remarriage. His stepmother had great affection for him, and she gave him motherly care. In Jan 1814, William Carey had the joy of seeing his son Jabez baptized. Though at first apprenticed to a solicitor in Calcutta, Jabez, much to his father's delight, soon chose to join wholeheartedly in the Serampore mission. After marriage, he went overseas to Ambon in the Moluccas. From there he sent his father many plants and seeds for his Serampore horticultural society. But the political situation soon required that Jabez and family return to India.

In 1817, Jabez began to live at Ajmer, where his work was similar to that of his brother William in Katwa. He established schools, undertook evangelistic work, and developed gardens. After losing his first wife, he married Sarah Hawkins.

Later, Jabez went to Rajputana to carry on mission work. He was then sent to Java, another Dutch possession taken by the English during the Napoleonic wars. Then he moved to Sumalva to join Nathaniel Ward, after which he was again sent to Ajmer to start schools and to train teachers in the Lancastrian system of education.

Having been born just prior to his father's departure for India, Jabez Carey died without ever setting foot in

England again. He has been described as the most overwhelmingly complex personality among William Carey's sons.

Bibliography

Potts, E. Daniel, *British Baptist Missionaries in India, 1793-1837* (1967). • Drewery, Mary, *William Carey: A Biography* (1979). • Carey, Pearce, *Carey Marshall.* • Daniel, J. T. K., and R. E. Hedlund, eds., *Carey's Obligation and India's Renaissance* (1993).

FRANKLYN J. BALASUNDARAN

Carey, William

(b. Panlerspury, England, 17 Aug 1761; d. Serampore, India, 9 Jun 1834). Pioneer English Baptist missionary to India*.

Carey's father, Edmund, was a weaver who later became a parish clerk. Carey grew up during the time when Britain was at the threshold of attaining political supremacy in India. In fact, it was in the year of his birth that the French surrendered Pondicherry to England. This period was an age of awakening and rapid growth of industry and commerce. It was also an age of religious momentum in Britain which focused on organizing missionary societies.

From his earliest years, Carey displayed a passionate interest in his surroundings, particularly in plants and animals, an interest which in his later years led to his becoming a botanist. Since his father was poor, Carey could not continue his studies in school after the age of 12. He started work on a farm and also began learning the art of cobbling shoes, which he continued to practice until he became a Baptist preaching in 1785. At the same time, he was teaching in a primary school and studying other languages such as Dutch, Italian, German, and French. Having been offered the use of a library, he also read about the adventures of Captain James Cook and Columbus, which made him enthusiastic about going abroad to preach Christ in foreign countries.

At a meeting of Baptist* clergy in 1791, Carey put forward a proposal to set up a missionary society with a view to carrying the Gospel to foreign nations. In the following year, Carey published a booklet titled "An Enquiry into the Obligations of Christians to Use Means for the Conversion of the Heathens"; in it he explained the need for preaching Christ in different countries of the world. The same year, on May 30 at the annual meeting of the Northampton Baptist Association, Carey introduced his well-known slogan, "Expect great things from God. Attempt great things for God." His speech impressed many, but no resolution was forthcoming. But on 2 Oct 1792, the Baptist Missionary Society (BMS) was formed with the aim of spreading the Gospel among the "heathen" in foreign countries.

Carey at first wanted to go to Tahiti or West Africa. But his having met John Thomas, who was a physician by profession and had been to India twice, resulted in his going to India, where he arrived on 14 Nov 1793. It was necessary for missionaries to obtain the permission of the East India Company to enter India. Since British ships refused to take passengers without the permission of the East India Company, Carey and his friends managed to get berths on a Danish ship. During their trip, Carey learned Bengali from Thomas, and together they finished the translation of Genesis (see Bible Translation).

Though they did not have permission from the East India Company, Carey and Thomas had no difficulty landing in Calcutta. On the day of his arrival, Carey engaged a Bengali tutor and continued learning the language. Facing financial constraints, Carey took up farming in a village called Debhatta. The acute financial problems afflicted his wife with depression. Carey next secured a job as a manager of an indigo factory at Madnabatty. This was a relief to his family. At Madnabatty, Carey's botanical interests took shape. He started a garden and an agricultural farmhouse where he began his research to improve the agriculture of the country. He started growing English plants in Bengal and sent Bengali seeds to England to be planted there. He studied the Indian agricultural system and later discussed it in his article "Agriculture and Agriculturists in Dinjapore," which was published in the *Asiatic Researcher* in 1811.

At Madnabatty, Carey started learning Sanskrit and Hindustani in addition to Bengali. In 1795, he wrote a grammar as well as a dictionary of the Bengali language. He also continued the translation of the Bible into Bengali. Having become proficient in Bengali and conversant in Hindustani, Carey went around the villages preaching on Sundays and on various other days of the week. In 1796, John Fountain (1767-1800) was sent by the BMS to assist Carey in managing a school and translating the Bible into Bengali. Fountain learned Bengali within a short time and was a special help to Carey. By 1797, the Bengali New Testament was ready for printing. Carey bought an old printing press, which proved to be a great help when the indigo business went through severe losses and the plantation closed.

A team of BMS missionaries consisting of Joshua Marshman*, William Ward*, John Brunsdon, William Grant, and their families arrived on 13 Oct 1799. Having discussed their future activities, they along with Carey were convinced that their purpose would be fulfilled only if they worked at the Danish settlement at Serampore. On 25 Dec 1799, Carey took his printing machine and the manuscripts of the Bible translated into Bengali and left for Serampore.

Serampore was on the bank of the Hooghly River about 20 kilometers north of Calcutta. The villages around began to develop from the middle of the 18th c. when the Danish established a factory there. Serampore became famous as a center of trade, a holiday resort, and a place of refuge for debtors and wastrels. It was said to be populous, healthy, and a beautiful town on the verge of its most prosperous years. Its residents were Hindus, Muslims, Sikhs, Greeks, Portuguese, Danes, Germans, French, and English. The town was predominantly Hindu, and the Brahmin influence was strong.

Before Carey and his associates arrived in Serampore, an attempt had been made to evangelize the area by Moravian missionaries. In 1777, two Moravian missionaries, Karl Friedrich Schmidt and Johannes Grassman, had gone to Bengal and Serampore from Tranquebar. Their only success was a Bengali-German dictionary. They abandoned their mission in 1792, comparing preaching at Serampore to plowing upon a rock.

The Serampore mission was founded on 10 Jan 1800 with six missionary families. All the missionaries looked to Carey as their leader and guide. They started their work from a rented house, but within a short time a big building was purchased in the name of the BMS to accommodate the missionary families and the printing press. All of the missionaries were to adopt an identical lifestyle. Their earnings were to be collected in a common account and disbursed toward the cost of living of all.

The activities of the mission were well coordinated and responsibilities delegated. Principles and guidelines were laid down: (1) Every missionary would contribute funds to the mission for the maintenance of all the families. (2) They would live as a joint family, and the wives of the missionaries would in rotation keep the accounts. (3) Each would assume certain responsibilities: Carey — agriculture, finance, medicine, translation, and overall supervision; Marshman and his wife Hannah — education; Ward, Brunsdon, and Felix — printing; Fountain — library. (4) Each member was to learn the language of the country and engage in preaching in the villages. Thus the mission had the features of a brotherhood, and the missionaries were to sort out their differences every Saturday.

By Mar 1800, the Serampore mission was able to plant a church. Carey was its pastor and Marshman and Fountain its deacons. They had at the same time a regular full-fledged mission work entailing preaching, a boarding school, printing, language learning, and translation. By June the same year, a charity school for the local boys was opened.

One of the most important contributions of Carey's work was Bible translation. By 1796, just a few years after his arrival, he had completed the translation of the New Testament into Bengali, except for a few chapters of Revelation, and the Old Testament up to the book of Numbers. On 17 Mar 1800, the first page of the New Testament was printed. On 7 Feb 1801 a bound copy of the complete New Testament was placed on the communion table. Carey revised it in 1803, and the second edition was published in 1806. By Jun 1832, two years before he died, he had completed the fifth edition of the Old Testament and the eighth edition of the New Testament.

Carey did not limit his literary activity to Bengali. With the help of other scholars of respective languages, he ventured into the translation of the Bible into Sanskrit, Marathi, Oriya, Assamese, Manupuri, Hindi, Nepalese, Gujarathi, Telugu, and several other languages.

Carey took up an assignment with Fort William College, which was founded to train civil administrators in Indian languages, literature, culture, politics, and science and had helped the finances of the mission. This affiliation aided the mission in entering into a positive relationship with the government. Carey taught Bengali, Sanskrit, and Marathi at Fort William. It was during this time that he contributed toward the development of Bengali prose. The first book Carey published apart from the Bible was *Kathopakathan.* It gave a picture of daily life at different levels of Bengali society.

The Serampore mission gave special attention to education (see Colleges and Universities). Charity schools were given priority. In 1794, a charity school was established with 40 boys. In 1800, a Bengali school was established, and the number of schools established by the mission eventually rose to 111 with about 10,000 students. The curriculum of these schools included Oriental languages and philosophy in conjunction with Western science. The Serampore missionaries were sensitive to the lack of female education and started to encourage girls to take up studies as well. By 1830, they had established 23 schools for girls with 582 female students.

In order to provide higher education, the missionaries started Serampore College with the blessings of the Danish governor. Its prospectus for 1818 stated that the aim of the college was to instruct Asiatic Christians and youth in Eastern literature and European science. The syllabus included Sanskrit, Arabic, Western science, and English. The college was considered preeminently a divinity school to raise indigenous leadership for the Indian church. Under Carey's leadership, Serampore College pioneered in many fields under the broad umbrella of Eastern literature and Western science. By 1827, Serampore College had received the right to confer degrees and became the first university on the European model in India.

The garden Carey created at Serampore became a source for cash crops years later in Bengal. Carey initiated two major and significant ventures in the study of natural history in India and its practical application: a catalog of 3,500 species in cultivation by the Royal Botanic Garden, and the setting up of an agri-horticultural society with a farm designed for hybridization and the introduction of better varieties of cereals, vegetables, and fruits.

Under Carey's leadership, the Serampore missionaries pioneered presses that were run with engines. They also established the first paper mill using modern methods. They undertook scientific research as a consequence of which they were able to manufacture a high-quality paper, printing inks, and insecticides.

Carey employed women, especially widows, in the composing section of the Serampore printing press. Carey knew very well that poverty was the greatest problem of the country. To help the poor face the calamities of an adverse period, he started a savings bank in Serampore. He understood that charity and service alone would not solve the problem of poverty. Therefore, he emphasized the improvement of agriculture and industry and insisted that the natives of India be involved in these activities. The accomplishments of the Serampore mission in the area of social welfare included: (1) dispelling ignorance and spreading education; (2) sowing the seeds of the scientific attitude and humanistic frame of mind; (3) preserving health and preventing disease; (4) publishing books and newspapers; (5) developing agriculture and industry using scientific methods; (6) preserving forest resources; (7) eradicating poverty; and (8) resisting social oppression and establishing social justice.

Carey's scientific attitude and humanistic frame of mind motivated him to continue a relentless struggle to remove the evil social practices prevalent in India. Within a few days of his arrival, he had come to witness some of these practices, such as *suttee* and throwing children into the Bay of Bengal, and he vowed to stand against them. Greatly distressed by infanticide, he started a protest movement while he was teaching at Fort William College. Through the joint efforts of Carey and George Woodney, this practice attracted the attention of Lord Wellesley, who in 1802 declared it an act of murder. Carey also prepared a statistical record of widows burned in *suttee*, giving a vivid description of this horrible practice. He sought the help of Hindu pandits to ascertain whether there was a Shastric sanction for this cruel practice, and shaped public opinion by arranging debates on the matter. The Serampore missionaries' movement for the abolition of *suttee* was later carried on by Raja Ram Mohun Roy* and other Bengali intellectuals.

Bibliography

Daniel, J. T. K., and Roger E. Hedlund, *Carey's Obligation and India's Renaissance* (1993). • Dewanji, Malay, *William Carey and Indian Renaissance* (1996). • Drewery, Mary, *William Carey: A Biography* (1978). • Potts, E. Daniel, *British Baptist Missionaries in India, 1793-1837* (1967). • Firth, C. B., *An Introduction to Indian Church History* (1976). • Sunquist, Scott, *The History of the Baptists Missionary Society 1792-1992* (T. & T. Clark, 1992).

Franklyn J. Balasundaran

Caritas. *See* Jesus Caritas

Caritas–Hong Kong

(Hong Kong Catholic Welfare Organization)* Official and central social service organization of the Roman Catholic Church* in Hong Kong*, established for charitable purposes.

The humble beginnings of Caritas go back to 1 Jul 1953, when an emergency cash-assistance scheme was initiated by the director of the Catholic Center, Charles Vath* (1909-74). It was accepted as a member by Caritas International in Mar 1955, and from Dec 1957 it functioned as the Catholic Social Welfare Conference–Diocesan Caritas Organization, which was set up to provide a better coordination of the rather chaotic services to refugees. It was renamed Caritas–Hong Kong in 1961.

Every year, a fund-raising campaign and bazaar were organized in order to involve local resources and foster local responsibility. In 1968, Vath handed over the presidency to Francis Lerda. Since 1971, due to changes in the influx of refugees and improvement in standards of living, Caritas has tried to provide more-specialized services and has gradually become the only official and central welfare organization of the diocese, greatly subsidized by the government. It was incorporated by ordinance in Nov 1981. In 1993, it was given a new constitution.

The main function of Caritas is to improve and coordinate all Catholic social services. Its services focus on bringing help to the neediest in society, victims of disasters, and handicapped and aged people. Caritas provides family services and promotes community development and self-help projects. It aims to foster collaboration and understanding of integral human development and to educate toward "love in the service of hope." Recently, Caritas also started some projects in mainland China.

By Aug 1994, Caritas was operating 14 main centers with various activities: six hospitals with 2,948 beds; 17 clinics and outpatient departments; 17 nursery and child-care centers; 12 homes for the aged; four residential homes for girls; 13 rehabilitation centers; and seven hostels. In addition, it runs nine prevocational, nine vocational, eight special, and 26 adult-education schools. Its total staff is made up of 5,400 full-time employees, plus hundreds of part-time workers and volunteers, thus representing one of the largest employers in Hong Kong.

Bibliography

Caritas–Hong Kong: 40 Years of Partnership in Love and Service, 1953-1993 (1993).

Sergio Ticozzi

Carmelites

Unlike most other Catholic orders, the Carmelites do not have a single founder. The order developed from a group of penitent hermits who were living in the Mt. Carmel region of the Holy Land, hence the name Carmelites. The hermits were following a formula of life set for them between 1206 and 1214 C.E. by Albert, the patriarch of Jerusalem. They observed solitude, silence, continual prayer, and asceticism, and they centered their lives on following Christ. Today, in addition, the Carmelite cloistered nuns observe papal enclosure. In 1229, Pope Gregory IX imposed corporate poverty on the hermits. In 1238, the hermits were forced to emigrate from the Holy Land. They went westward and set up houses in Europe. Pope Innocent IV formalized Albert's formula into the official Carmelite Rule *(regula)*, which is still read today in all Carmelite monasteries every Friday. The hermits became friars — contemplative monks, but on apostolic call. By the end of the 13th c., the Carmelites were studying in established universities in Cambridge, Oxford, and Paris to equip themselves for the ministries of preaching, teaching, and the administration of the sacraments. A continuing major challenge to Carmelites is the delicate tension between pastoral ministry and contemplative solitude.

Two significant figures to the Carmelites are the 9th c. B.C.E. prophet Elijah of the Old Testament, considered their moral founder and inspiration, and the Virgin Mary, for whom they claim the order was founded. Two feasts are held in their honor in the Carmelite liturgical calendar, on 20 and 16 Jul respectively. Carmelites have three attributes: biblical, Elianic (prophetic), and Marian (becoming "fire as God is fire," to quote Cardinal Anastacio Ballesteros).

In 1452, as a result of the efforts of John Soreth, a French Carmelite prior general, women were allowed to join the order. The nuns formed the second order and have made major contributions in defining Carmelite spirituality. In the 16th c., Teresa of Avila (b. 1515; d. 1582; beatified in 1614, canonized in 1622, and declared Doctor of the Universal Church in 1970), aided by a newly ordained friar, John of the Cross (b. 1542; d. 1591; beatified in 1675, canonized and also declared a Doctor of the Universal Church in Mystical Theology), led a reform back to the comtemplative life which resulted in the formation of the Discalced (now called Teresaian) Carmelites. Taking only a few nuns with her, Teresa of Avila, or Teresa of Jesus as she signed her name, left the Monastery of the Incarnation in Spain and established the Convent of St. Joseph to enable a return to a closer observation of the primitive Carmelite Rule. Limiting her nuns to only 13, and at times opposed by her Carmelite superiors, local church authorities, and the townspeople, who feared the financial burden of another convent, she succeeded in forming several communities. By 1600, there were 47 Discalced convents in Spain, 15 of which had been founded by Teresa.

Masters of the interior life and contemplative prayer, Teresa and John provided the classical expression of the mystical dimension in Carmelite spirituality through their writings, which are considered classics in prayer and faith. In the 19th c., the writings of Thérèse of Lisieux (b. 1873; d. 1897; beatified in 1923, canonized in 1925) provided the spiritual inspiration "to do ordinary things extraordinarily well" for the love of Jesus and to have total confidence in the merciful love of the Father. The centenary of her death was celebrated in 1997.

In 1476, Pope Sixtus IV allowed the creation of the Carmelite Third Order (or Secular Order) for the benefit of those who would adopt the Carmelite spiritual ideal but still maintain their secular calling. This is open to both men and women, single and married.

Carmelites first came to Asia in the 17th c. Teresian Carmelites reached India* in 1620. In 1994, there were 670 religious. The first monastery for nuns was founded in 1859, and in 1994 there were 439 nuns in 30 carmels (monasteries). Sri Lanka* presently has three carmels; the first was established in 1935. Carmelites from the monasteries in Kandy and Colombo founded the carmel in Lahore, Pakistan*, in 1983.

In 1861, French Carmelites established the first carmel in Vietnam*, where there are presently three carmels. In 1925, Carmelites from Kampuchea (Cambodia*) founded the first carmel in Thailand*, which now has three carmels. The Bangkok carmel founded the Singapore* monastery in 1938. Malaysia had four carmels in 1995, the first Carmelite nuns having arrived in 1930. In Indonesia*, the first Carmelite monastery for nuns was established in 1939 in Lembang, West Java. At present, there are three carmels. In addition, a Teresian mission started in 1952 has resulted in the formation of three communities with 26 members, six of whom are priests. The Philippines* had its first Carmelite monastery for nuns in 1923. In 1994, there were 22 carmels and 332 nuns. There are now two Carmelite bishops.

In China*, Carmelite sisters are also known as *Sheng Yi Hui* (Sacred Robes Society). Upon the invitation of Vicar Apostolic Languillat, five French Carmelites from the Monastery of Laval arrived in 1869. Two more arrived later. Temporarily put up in an ordinary Chinese house at Wang Jia Tang, Xujiahui, Shanghai, they moved into their first monastery, the Carmel of St. Joseph, in 1874. A few Chinese Catholic girls applied to join the order. In 1900, there were nine foreign and 16 Chinese nuns. At the seventieth anniversary of the Carmel of St. Joseph, there was a total of 21 nuns. Though few in number, the nuns managed to expand to Chongqing, Sichuan (1921), and Jiaxing, Zhejiang (1927), making a total of three Carmelite convents in China before the Communist takeover.

Carmelite nuns first reached Hong Kong* in 1933. The first Carmelite monastery in Stanley was established in 1937 during the time of Henry Valtorta. In 1995, there were 11 Carmelite sisters.

Taiwan* presently has two monasteries for nuns. The first was established in 1954. There are presently two additional religious communities with six priests and seven students.

In Korea*, where the faith was first brought by laypeople from China, French Carmelites established a carmel in 1939. In 1994, there were seven carmels. Four Koreans were sent for training in France, and the first Korean foundation for friars was established in 1974. There were 32 religious in 1994.

The 10 Carmelite communities with a total of 40 religious in Japan* were first established by Carmelites from China, who arrived in 1951.

The essence of Carmelite spirituality is *kenosis* for holiness of life and intimate union with God: to die to oneself, pick up one's cross, and follow Jesus for the glory of God and the salvation of souls through perfect charity in the service of the church. To quote Carmelite Superior General Camilo Maccise, "zeal for external works must be accompanied by a fervent commitment to prayer, the splendor of a pure conscience, patience in adversities, and an ever-active charity watchful for the salvation of souls."

Bibliography

Discalced Carmelites of Boston and Santa Clara, *Carmel: Its History, Spirit and Saints* (1927); Downey, Michael, ed., *The New Dictionary of Catholic Spirituality* (1993). • Catholic University of America, *New Catholic Encyclopedia*, Vol. III (1967). • Primary sources for 1994 statistics: *Servitum Informatium Carmelitanum (SIC) Missionem* No. 11 (Nov 1993); SIC, OCD World Missionary Congress (25 Sep–2 Oct 1994); *The Teresian Carmel and Evangelizing Work in Asia and Australia* (1994).

TERESA JOSEPH CONSTANTINO

Carvaka (Lokayata) Philosophy

The "philosophy of the people," the "philosophy of this-worldliness," or "materialism."

The original works of the *Lokayatikas* being lost beyond any prospect of recovery, we have to reconstruct them mainly on the basis of references found in the writings of their opponents, one of whom was Madhavacarya, whose version of the *Lokayata* in his *Sarva Darsana Samgraha* was not authentic. Today, scholars such as Debiprasad Chattopadhyaya suggest that *Lokayata* originally meant those popular and obscure beliefs and practices that are broadly referred to as Tantrism. Spiritual and otherworldly ideas were subsequently superimposed on Tantrism, but original Tantrism, like its more philosophical version known as the *Sankhya*, was atheistic and materialistic. The original meaning of the word *Carvaka* is not certain. One view is that it is the name of the founder of the school. Another is that it is a descriptive name of a materialist either because he preaches "eat, drink, and be merry" (*Carv* = "eat, chew") or because his words are pleasant and nice (*Carv* = "nice," *vak* = "word"). Materialism is the philosophy which holds that matter is the only reality. Thus mind and consciousness are the products of matter.

According to *Carvakas*, perception *(pratyaksa)* is the only source of valid knowledge *(pramana)*. To establish this, they criticize other sources of knowledge, such as inference and testimony, accepted by other schools. When we infer the existence of fire in a mountain from the perception of smoke in it, we are actually taking a leap in the dark, because our assumption of a universal invariable relation *(vyapti)* between smoke and fire can be established only if we have a knowledge of all cases of smoke and the presence of fire, which is impossible. Some *Carvakas* admit the usefulness of inference in determining the nature of all worldly things where perceptual experience is available, but according to them inference cannot be employed for establishing any dogma regarding the transcendental world, or life after death, or the law of *karma*, which are beyond perceptual experience. For them, testimony relating to unperceived objects is also not reliable.

The *Carvaka* metaphysics follows from its epistemology. We can believe only in the reality of perceptible objects. God, soul, heaven, life before birth or after death, and any unperceived law cannot be believed in because they are all beyond perception. According to *Carvakas*, all living and nonliving organisms are composed of the four perceptible elements, namely air, fire, water, and earth; the fifth element, ether, is rejected as its existence cannot be perceived. They admit that the existence of consciousness is proved by perception. Consciousness is a quality of this body itself. What people mean by a soul is nothing more than this conscious, living body. To the question how consciousness can arise from matter, the *Carvakas* would reply that qualities not present originally in any of the component factors may emerge subsequently when the factors are combined together. The material elements combined in a particular way give rise to the conscious living body. Also, it is the material elements which produce the world; a creator God is unnecessary. The material elements each have their fixed nature. It is by the natures and laws inherent in them that they combine together to form this world.

Carvaka ethics is related to their metaphysics. They reject the view that heaven is the highest goal because belief in heaven is based on scripture. Neither can liberation be the highest goal of human life. There is no soul to liberate from physical existence. If liberation means freedom from pain in this life, it is also an impossible ideal. Pleasure, though mixed with pain, is the highest good. Enjoyment *(kama)* is the ultimate end, and wealth *(artha)* is a means for achieving it. Of course, cultured *Carvakas* could accommodate virtue *(dharma)* also as a human end, and they have contributed to the development of the fine arts in India. The value of *Carvaka* philosophy lies directly in supplying fresh philosophical problems and indirectly in compelling other thinkers to give up dogmatism.

Bibliography

Chattopadhyaya, Debiprasad, *Lokayata: A Study in Ancient Indian Materialism*, 4th ed. (1978); *Indian Philosophy: A Popular Introduction*, 4th ed. (1979). • Sastri, H. P., *Lokayata* (1925); *Absorption of the Vratyas* (1926). • Sastri, D. R., *A Short History of Indian Materialism, Sensationism and Hedonism* (1930). • Kosambi, D. D., *An Introduction to the Study of Indian History* (1956). • Cowell, E. B., and A. E. Gough, trans., *The Sarva Darsana Samgraha* (1914). • Basham, A. L., *History and Doctrines of the Ajivikas* (1951). • Belvalkar, S. K., and R. D. Ranade, *History of Indian Philosophy* (1927). • Dasgupta, Surendranath, *A History of Indian Philosophy* (1922-25). • Chatterjee, Satischandra, and Dhirendramohan Datta, *An Introduction to Indian Philosophy*, 7th ed. (1968).

K. P. ALEAZ

Case, Brayton Clark

(b. Yangon, 18 Aug 1887; d. Indawgyi Lake, Myanmar, 14 Jul 1944). First American Baptist agricultural missionary to Myanmar* and founder of the Pyinmana Agricultural School.

All of the important events of Case's life — his birth, baptism, engagement and marriage, ministry, and, finally, his death — took place in Myanmar. He was very much a Burman except for his color and blood. He found a perfect partner in Lena Tillman, a teacher in the Moulmein English Girls' School, whom he married on 17 Jan 1917; they had an only son, Clark, born on 4 Feb 1918.

During his earlier studies in the United States, Case saw the success of irrigation in the Imperial Valley, and, feeling called to do the same for Myanmar, he took up studies in agriculture. Two years at the University of California, a master's degree in botany from Columbia University, and one year at Union Theological Seminary gave him adequate preparation to be an agricultural missionary. He was ordained in 1912 and sent back to Myanmar as a general missionary in 1913.

On 21 Jul 1918, Case opened his first experimental school in Pyinmana, with half the time spent in field work and the other half in the classroom. The purpose of the school was to uplift the rural life of Myanmar. He organized weekend and vacation trips for his students. They traveled extensively to reach the different ethnic groups and even the lepers.

Case used lantern slides to show his methods and their results. At association meetings, he would preach about effective farming, pigs, hens, and vegetables. Typical topics were: "A Good Pig Is a Friend of Burma," "How to Make Hens Lay Golden Eggs," "Ten Commandments for Rice Growers," and "Vegetables for Victory." He developed plans for the cooperative marketing of pigs and fruits and introduced the rotation of crops. Case used every means available and possible for the communication of the good news for the whole being.

On 28 Dec 1934, Case was awarded the *Kai-Sar-i-Hind* silver medal for his practical agricultural work. Two months after the bombing of the Pyinmana School in 1942, Case, together with General Joseph W. Sitwell and Gordon Seagrave*, made his way to India. Soon after, Sitwell asked him to return to Myanmar as a liaison between the American military force and the people of Myanmar. He was a friend and counselor to the homesick soldiers and also helped rehabilitate the war-ravaged villages of the Hukawng Valley. Case planted many nurseries for the refugees and would search for hidden stores of food and talk the owners into sharing with their less fortunate neighbors.

On 14 Jul 1944, Case was on such a trip and about half an hour out from Chaungwa on Indawgyi Lake when his boat made a very sharp turn and all on board were thrown into the water. He sank and never reappeared. Case died in action and was posthumously awarded the Order of the British Empire in Jul 1945. The American Baptists named one of the buildings at their national assembly grounds in Green Lake, Wisconsin, after him. The farmers of Myanmar still raise "Bo Case Pig" and grow "Bo Case Pe" (beans).

Bibliography

Cramer, Robert E., *Hunger Fighter in Burma* (1946). • Howard, Randolf L., *Lazy Man Rest Not* (1947). • Yu, Mg., *Case of Burma* (1951).

MARCHETA THEIN

Castiglione, Josephus (Giuseppe)

(b. 1683; d. 1766). Famous Italian painter and Jesuit* lay brother.

Castiglione, accompanied by another Jesuit brother (trained in medicine), arrived in China* in 1715 and was instructed by Emperor Kangxi to learn Chinese painting. In 1723, when Emperor Yongzheng ascended the throne, he arranged for Castiglione to reside in Ru Yi Pavilion in the palace compound, although he never granted him an audience. Emperor Qianlong loved Castiglione's paintings so much that he continued to watch him paint at Ru Yi Pavilion even after he ascended the throne. When the Qing government prohibited the spread of Christianity in China, Castiglione, seizing the opportunity, prostrated himself before the emperor, pleaded for leniency toward Christianity, and received a positive response. Castiglione painted in the palace grounds for nearly 50 years. In 1988, the Beijing Museum of Art held an exhibition and published a special volume to commemorate the 300th anniversary of his birth.

Bibliography

Loher, George Robert, *Giuseppe Castiglione* (1940). • Beurdeleym, C. and M., *Giuseppe Castiglione: A Jesuit Painter at the Court of Chinese Emperors* (1971). • Siu, Victoria, "Castiglione and the Yuanming Yuan Collections," *Orientations* 19, No. 11 (Nov 1988). • Mikinosuke Ishida, "A Biographical Study of Giuseppe Castiglione," *Memoirs of the Research Department of the Yoyo Bunko*, No. 19 (1960). • Vath, Alfons, *Johann Adam Schall von Bell S.J. (1592-1666)* (1991).

CHINA GROUP, translated by DAVID WU

Caswell, Jesse

(b. ?; d. 1848). Pioneer missionary in Siam (Thailand*) from 1840 to 1848 under the American Board of Commissioners for Foreign Missions (ABCFM).

An ordained Presbyterian* minister born in Middletown, Vermont, USA, Caswell arrived in Bangkok with his wife Anna on 1 Jan 1840. Emphasizing in-depth contact rather than attracting large crowds, Caswell soon shifted his work from port evangelization to porch-side preaching and book distribution, through which he developed his facility in the Siamese language. Bua and Yoi, both under his care, were the first Siamese applicants for membership in the Congregational Church of Bangkok, which he briefly pastored. Caswell was the first to translate into Siamese a hymnbook, a Bible commentary (six volumes), and a church history (eight volumes).

Caswell taught English and science to many royal monks and officials, including the founder of the Thammayuthika Buddhist reform movement, Prince Mongkut*, and he preached and distributed Christian books at their temple. Prince Mongkut referred to Caswell as teacher or *acharn* (now a title for all Thai Protestant clergy), and later, as King Rama V, broke with many traditions of religious intoleration and radically reformed what is now modern Thailand (see Chulalongkorn).

Caswell's theological shift to Finneyism led to his resignation from the ABCFM in 1847 and the closing of the Siam Mission in 1849 (see Bradley, Dan Beach). He went on salary with the American Missionary Association in Jun 1848 but died of lung inflammation only three months later. In honor of his life, King Mongkut erected a monument over Caswell's grave (1853) and sent large gifts to Anna and his three surviving children.

Bibliography

ABCFM, *Minutes of the Annual Meeting of the American Board of Commissioners for Foreign Missions* (1811-48). • Feltus, George Haus, ed., *Missionary Journals of Rev. Jesse Caswell and of Rev. and Mrs. Asa Hemenway of Siam* (1931). • Pongudom, Prasit, *History of the Thai Church in Thailand* (Church Archives, Payap University, Chiang Mai, 1986). Donald S. Persons

Catalonan. *See* Babaylan/Catalonan

Catholic Action

Term used in Roman Catholic* ecclesiology of the 19th and early 20th cs. to designate the officially mandated participation of the laity in the apostolate of the hierarchy to teach, sanctify, and govern in the church.

Although primarily a part of the Western European understanding of the church, Catholic action greatly influenced Catholicism in Asia, particularly the Philippines*. Its origin can be traced to the writings of Pope Leo XIII (1878-1903), who, at a time of a marked proliferation of Catholic voluntary associations, believed not only that laypeople should "defend their faith and show it forth publicly," but that its effectiveness depended on the control of a single authority. However, it is Pope Pius X (1903-14) who should be considered the true begetter of Catholic action in the sense under consideration. His encyclical *Fermo proposito* (1905) has been regarded as the charter of this lay ecclesiastical activity. But while it urged laypeople to pool their energies to restore Jesus Christ to his rightful place in the family, school, and community, it also stipulated that voluntary associations which directly supplemented the church's spiritual and pastoral ministry were to be subordinated in every detail to the church's authority. It was left to Pope Pius XI (1922-39), who essentially saw the laity as an extension of the priest in a context of shortage of clergy, to articulate the restricted definition of Catholic action.

Catholic action may be seen from two perspectives. On the one hand, it was a legitimate development of the laity's sense of being part of the church in a climate of clericalism. In the 19th c., Western Catholicism was confronted with a world which had become either indifferent or hostile to both religion and the church. Many laypeople and priests realized the necessity and urgency of making contact with this world and influencing it positively. They also recognized that the faith had to be defended and explained in a language intelligible in this new situation. Since society was looked upon as no longer officially Christian, there was a further need to create environments in which spiritual life could develop. These Catholics further knew that upholding priestly authority by power was no longer viable. Reliance henceforth had to be put on a laity who had an apostolic sense of Christian life.

On the other hand, Catholic action could also be regarded as a move by the hierarchy to ensure not only a corporate and coordinated effort by the laity, but also retention of authority in the hands of the clergy. Pope Pius XI vigorously promoted Catholic action when he witnessed the increasing number of lay associations which had similar objectives and means, but which were weakened by rivalry. But for him, Catholic action required a hierarchical mandate since it was a participation in the apostolate of the hierarchy.

While a broad understanding of the concept had been part of the theological development, namely, the application of the notion to any faith-inspired external action of Catholics, a more narrow understanding became popular. This was based on the notion that "the Church of Christ is not a community of equals in which all the faithful have the same rights" (first schema of the Dogmatic Constitution on the Church prepared for Vatican I, 1869-70). Only the hierarchy participate directly in Christ's mission as prophet (teaching), priest (sanctifying), and king (governing); they do so by virtue of their ordination to the priesthood. The unordained laity merely participate, or collaborate according to some interpretations, in the apostolate of the hierarchy through Catholic action.

Catholic action came into existence within an ecclesiology which was largely dualistic and clergy-centered. Internally, this ecclesiology divided the church into an active clergy and a passive laity. It was the prerogative of the clergy to teach, govern, and sanctify by virtue of their priestly ordination; it was the duty of the laity to be taught, sanctified, and governed by virtue of their baptism. It was the clergy that actively proclaimed church teaching, administered the sacraments, and directed Catholic life in an official manner; the laity passively listened to what was taught, received the sacraments, and obeyed the clergy's directives. This attitude was clearly articulated in the writings of Pius X. In *Vehementer nos* (1906), he reiterated the idea that inequality in the church is natural because the church "comprises two categories of person, the pastors and the flocks. The hierarchy alone moves and controls. . . . The duty of the multitude is to suffer itself to be governed and to carry out in a submissive spirit the orders of those in control."

With the coming of Vatican Council II (1962-65), the theological underpinnings of Catholic action were transcended. Participation in the priestly, prophetic, and kingly functions of Christ arises from baptism and not from clerical ordination as stated in the theology of Catholic action. Rather than participate in the apostolate of hierarchy, the laity "carry out their own part in the mission of the whole Christian people with respect to the church and the world" since it is not the hierarchy, but the Lord himself, who gives the laity its mandate to be in mission (*Lumen Gentium*, article 31; *Apostolicam Actuositatem*, article 3).

Bibliography

Geaney, D. J., "Catholic Action," in *New Catholic Encyclopedia* III (1967); "Dogmatic Constitution on the Church" and "Decree on the Apostolate of the Laity," in Walter M. Abbott, ed., *The Documents of Vatican II* (1966). • Aubert, Roger, *The Church in a Secularised Society*, Vol. V, *The Christian Centuries: A New History of the Catholic Church* (1978). • Congar, Yves, *Lay People in the Church* (1965).

José M. de Mesa

Catholic Center, Hong Kong. *See* Hong Kong Catholic Center

Catholic Central Bureau

(Pan-China Catholic Evangelization Committee). Multilateral organization set up by Mgr. Liberi, apostolic delegate to the nationalist government of China*, prior to the founding of the People's Republic of China in 1950.

The overall director of the Catholic Central Bureau, James E. Walsh, had come to China as bishop of the diocese of Jiang Men, Guangdong, in 1918. In 1936, he was elected superior general of the Maryknoll* Catholic Foreign Mission Society of America and returned to its New York headquarters. In 1948, he returned to China to accompany Francis Cardinal Spellman, then archbishop of New York, on his visit. When the cardinal returned to the United States, Bishop Walsh remained in Shanghai. Soon after, he became secretary general to the Catholic Central Bureau founded by Liberi.

Walsh engaged approximately a dozen foreign and Chinese priests from the Shanghai Diocese and elsewhere as his assistants to tackle a variety of responsibilities: publications, unification of Catholic terminology, pictorial media, labor and legal consulting, communication networking, the Chinese Mission Review, the Legion of Mary, and finance. While the Catholic Central Bureau was well on the way to being operative, political turbulence caused the association's activities to be regarded as anti-revolutionary and a hindrance to the liberation of China. The bureau was seized in 1951 by the Military Control Committee of Shanghai.

China Group

Catholic Church. *See* Roman Catholic Church

Catholic Party (Indonesia)

The Catholic Party in Indonesia* grew from the Central Javanese political association *Pakempalan Katolik Djawi*, which was set up by a group of young Javanese students of van Lith* in Yogyakarta (1923), some of whom left the Dutch-dominated *Indische Katholieke Partij* (1917) because of their desire for self-government, which van Lith advocated in his article "De Politiek van Nederland ten opzichte van Nederlandsch-Indie" (1922). For a few years, the indigenous party formed a federation with the Dutch Catholic Party but broke away in 1925 because of the issue of independence. It elected its own representative to the Volksraad (1923) and changed its name to *Persatuan Politik Katolik Indonesia* (1933). Its struggle together with other national parties for the immediate self-government of Indonesia was supported by the apostolic vicar of Batavia, Petrus Johannes Willekens*.

Forbidden during the Japanese occupation (1942-45), the party was reestablished in Surakarta (1945) as the *Partai Katolik Republik Indonesia* (see World War II). Its chairman, I. J. Kasimo, served as minister during the war of independence (1945-49). It was the first party of the republic to hold a national congress (Yogyakarta, 1949) and gained six seats in the first national election (1955) and 10 in the constituent assembly (1956). The party opposed President Sukarno's* policy of taking Communists into the cabinet and supported the *Liga Demokrasi* (1960).

After the Communist coup d'état (1965), the *Partai Katolik* backed the fight of the Catholic Students Organization (PMKRI) against Sukarno's policy of rehabilitating the Communist Party. In 1968, it joined the faction in parliament that wanted to incorporate human rights into the constitution and refused to accept the *Piagam Jakarta* as a constitutional document. In the 1971 election, the *Partai Katolik* was considerably weakened when some of its former cadres joined the government-sponsored Golkar movement. It gained only three seats. In 1973, it had to fuse with *Partai Kristen Indonesia, Partai Nasional Indonesia, Murba,* and *IPKI* into the new *Partai Demokrasi Indonesia* (PDI), which, as a heterogeneous body and under government pressure, is allowed to play only a minor role. Some of its members from the former *Partai Katolik* try to resist policies that harm society, especially any restrictions on religious freedom.

Bibliography

Muskens, M. P. M., *Sejarah Gereja Katolik* IV (1973). • Heuken, A., *Ensiklopedi Gereja* III (1993).

Adolf Heuken

Catholic Social Action. *See* Social Action, Roman Catholic

Catholic Tribal Apostolate in Pakistan

The Catholic Tribal Apostolate carries on the work of the church among the peoples known as the Kholis and Bhils, generally nomadic peoples who move between Pakistan's Sindh Province and the Indian state of Gujarat. They work as farm laborers on the large estates of the Sindh *zamindars* and are kept tied to their employers by systematic debt bondage.

One group, known as the Marawari Bhils or the Thatta Nagar Fakirs, is thought by some scholars (W. G. Young and R. A. Trotter) to be a vestigial Christian remnant of the converts of St. Thomas. Claims are made that they call themselves *Barthamai* (H. D'Souza), that they own secret collections of scripture, and employ rituals that might have a Christian origin. The Catholic missionary F. Vankerkhoven identifies these rituals as death customs and a special prayer formula (*Om Nimo Narain Athiadi* = "in the name of God, the compassionate and merciful, the beginning and the end").

Work among the tribal peoples is conditioned by their exclusive separateness. A missionary who works with one group is not acceptable to the other groups. The groups that have received Christian missionary attention are the Marawari Bhils, the Megwar, the Bagri, the Parkari Kholi, and the Kutchi Kholi. For a short time, the Catholic Church dropped contact with the Marawari Bhils. The Church of Pakistan's reported policy is to restrict itself to the Marawari Bhils and the Megwar. There has been little response from the Marawari Bhils and only limited response from the Megwar.

The first Catholic approaches to the tribal peoples came at Nawabshah in 1935. The Franciscans made contact with a Marawari Bhils village. With the help of the Daughters of the Cross*, they established the Kunwari Maryam hospital to provide maternity and child-care services. Unhappily the town of Nawabshah began to expand and encroach on the tribal settlement. A housing society had to be established to defend the Bhils. Land prices had meanwhile risen to such an extent that the Franciscans* were forced to try to re-establish the village at Nawaz Dhari. These initiatives collapsed in 1948 when the Marawari elected to move to India*.

The Franciscans then turned their attentions to the Kholis near Matli and Mirpurkhas. They continued the Nawabshah policies. They provided medical* aid and endeavored to persuade the tribals to settle in stable villages. To do this, they had to spend a good deal of money on land and on effecting the release of the tribals from debt bondage. Missionary results were, nevertheless, poor. The largesse showered on the tribals was resented by the Goan and Punjabi Catholic communities. The policy had to be drastically curtailed.

In the 1970s, there was a significant rise in the number of conversions among the tribal peoples. The Marawari group that had gone to India returned. They settled near Kotri. The Bagri in Larkhana began to show interest. Large numbers of Kutchi Kholi came into the church. The tribal apostolate was now spread over three dioceses: Karachi, Hyderabad, and Multan. The Franciscans who had pioneered the work were now growing old and the order lacked the personnel to replace them. A national appeal was launched to find priests, catechists, and sisters to carry on the work. As a result, the archdiocese of Karachi took responsibility for the Larkhana-based work among the Bagri. The Mill Hill* Missionaries and the Columban* Missionaries moved into Hyderabad to take charge of the Kholi missions. The Spiritans (Holy Ghost Fathers) came into the diocese of Multan to handle the work among the Marawari.

More recently, missionaries have chosen to change the Franciscan approach. They decided to concentrate on education. A first priority was the opening of boarding establishments to house school-age children. The missionaries did not seek to resettle the tribal people. Instead they formed themselves into itinerant teams that went out to meet the people wherever they were. The teams consisted normally of three individuals: a priest, a religious sister, and a catechist or lay helper. It is hoped that, in time, better education may help the tribes reach an improved standard of living and lead lives of greater stability.

John Rooney

Catholic University Students Organizations (Indonesia)

Catholic university students organizations were established in Indonesia* on a local level in 1947 in Bandung and Yogyakarta. Several student groups formed one national organization in Surabaya in 1951, *Perhimpunan Mahasiswa Katolik Republik Indonesia* (PMKRI). Local branches have since been established in nearly all university cities of the country. The present 26 branches comprise at most 10% of the Catholic students community. After being actively involved in anti-Communist activities in the 1960s and some social issues later on, the PMKRI lost much of its spirit, like many similar organizations, partly because of official regulations.

Adolf Heuken

Catholic Women's Organization. *See* Wanita Katolik

Cattaneo, Lazzaro

(b. Italy, 1560; d. Hangzhou, China, 19 Jan 1640). Italian Jesuit* missionary to China* in the late Ming period and pioneer of the Catholic Church in Shanghai.

First sent to India*, Cattaneo was later transferred to Macau to learn Chinese. In 1594, he was sent to Shaozhou to help Matteo Ricci*. One year later, when Ricci left to go north, Cattaneo was left in charge of the

Jesuit mission in Shaozhou. In 1597, Lung Hua Ming came to assist him. In 1598, leaving Lung behind, Cattaneo moved to Nan Chang to work with Ricci, who had since established a mission there. Failing to gain an audience with and present gifts to Emperor Wan Li, both Cattaneo and Ricci went on to Nanjing.

After the establishment of the Jesuit mission in Nanjing, Ricci sent Cattaneo to Macau to do journalistic work and secure funding for the mission. Cattaneo returned to Nanjing in 1599 with Didace de Pantoja*. In 1600, Ricci, accompanied by Pantoja, went to Beijing for the second time, leaving Cattaneo in charge of the mission work in Nanjing. In 1604, Cattaneo returned to Macau; he returned to Nanjing in 1606. In 1608, acceding to the request of Xu Guang Qi*, Ricci sent Cattaneo to Shanghai to begin mission work there. Cattaneo spent two years in Shanghai and baptized 200 people. This was the beginning of Catholic work in Shanghai.

In 1611, at the invitation of Li Zhi Zao, Cattaneo went to Hangzhou to baptize Yang Ting Jun*. Following this event, Cattaneo spent most of his time in Hangzhou. In 1627, Yang Ting Jun built a church in Hangzhou and a house for priests. Cattaneo spent the latter part of his life in this house. He was buried in the cemetery of Da Fang Jing, having spent 46 years in mission work in China.

Bibliography

Goodrich, L. Carrington, "Lazzaro Cattaneo," in *Dictionary of Ming Biography, 1386-1644* (1976). • Cattaneo, Lazzaro, *Ling-hsing i-chu* (Introduction of the Soul to God); *Hui-tsui yao-chi* (On Contrition and Sorrow for Sin), described in Pasquale M. d'Elia, ed., *Fonti Ricciane,* 3 vols. (1942-49), Vol. I. • Dunne, George, *Generation of Giants: The Story of the Jesuits in China during the Last Decades of the Ming Dynasty* (1962). • Mungello, D. E., *The Forgotten Christians of Hangzhou* (1994). • Vath, Alfons, *Johann Adam Schall von Bell S.J. (1592-1666)* (1991).

CHINA GROUP

Celebes

The Protestant churches in North Celebes, which are now united in the General Synod of the Churches in North and Central Celebes, originated from missionary efforts made in the 19th and 20th cs. From North Celebes, there are the Christian Evangelical Church in Sangihe-Talaud (*Gereja Masehi Injili di Sangihe-Talaud,* GMIST); the Christian Evangelical Church in Minahasa (*Gereja Masehi Injili Minahasa,* GMIM); the Christian Evangelical Church in Bolaang Mongondouw (*Gereja Masehi Injili di Bolaang Mongondouw,* GMIBM); the Indonesian Protestant Church in Gorontalo (*Gereja Protestan Indonesia Gorontalo,* GPIG); and the Assembly of Protestant Congregations in Minahasa (*Kerapatan Gereja Protestan Minahasa,* KGPM). The synod mentioned above also includes four Protestant churches in Central Celebes and three other Pentecostal* Churches in North Celebes. The latter are the Full Evangelical Bethel Church (*Gereja Bethel Injil Sepenuh,* GBIS), the Pentecostal Movement Church (*Gereja Gerakan Pentekosta,* GGP), and the Pentecostal Church Centered in Surabaya (*Gereja Pentekosta Pusat Surabaya,* GPPS).

The GBIS, GGP, and GPPS cannot be called regional churches because their congregations are scattered throughout the Indonesian archipelago. The GMIST and the KGPM, though they have congregations in Jakarta* and several other regions, are still ethnically oriented. Many congregation members of GMIST in Jakarta are Sangirese in origin, and many members of the KGPM in Jakarta come from Minahasa. The congregations of the GMIM, GMIBM, and GPIG can be found only in their respective regions. When a family or individuals from these churches move to another place, they become members of a church in the region where they now live.

The GMIM and the GMIBM were formed through the missionary efforts of the Netherlands Missionary Society (*Nederlandsch Zendeling Genootschap,* NZG). Actually, the Christian communities in Bolaang Mongondouw began in the 17th and 18th cs. when pastors of the Dutch East-India Company* baptized native people in several places. But the congregations which were founded in that period did not receive adequate spiritual care; hence these early Christian communities generally became Muslim.

Ulfers, a Dutch missionary in Minahasa, made an appeal to the NZG to prepare missionaries for this area. In 1904, Dunnebier, the first missionary of the NZG, received approval from the colonial government to enter the area. From 1904 to 1942 there was a process of relocating people from Minahasa to Bolaang Mongondouw, resulting in an increased number of Christians in Bolaang Mongondouw. A similar increase of Christians was seen in 1961 and 1977, when Balinese and Javanese were relocated there. According to a 1990 report, 130 of the 210 villages in Bolaang Mongondouw have their own church buildings, and 70,000 of the 300,000 inhabitants are Christians. The church became independent on 28 Jun 1950, but the congregants are still struggling in the areas of self-support, in establishing schools, and in developing other plans for education.

The congregations of the GPIG were formed by the efforts of NZG missionaries who came from Minahasa between 1861 and 1936. The GMIM took over this effort by sending some Minahasan missionaries from 1936 until 1959. The people of the GPIG live among a Muslim majority with only a few local people originating from Gorontalo. According to a 1990 report, there are 56 congregations in this church with a total of 13,185 members.

The church in Sangihe-Talaud is the product of the missionary work of the Sangihe-Talaud Committee, which was formed in 1885. The committee sent "craftsmen missionaries" from Germany, the first four being Schroder, Steller, Grohe, and Kelling. They worked in several of the islands around the Sangihe-Talaud archipelago. The church became independent on 25 May 1947. The main problems faced by the people of this church relate to the geographical setting of their congregations, which makes church development difficult.

The Assembly of the Minahasa Protestant Congregation (KGPM) has been growing together with the congregations of the GMIM. It can be said that the KGPM is the sister of the GMIM. The GMIM uses the presbyterian* synodical system of organization, whereas the KGPM follows the congregational system of administrating the church. The people who formed the KGPM did not accept the hierarchical system of the Protestant Church in Indonesia during the period of colonial rule. This is the main reason why they always call themselves a national church. This church became a member of the Indonesian Council of Churches on 6 Sep 1979. In 1990, her members numbered about 47,767.

These five regional churches face a variety of challenges. The members of the GPIG and the GMIBM live in the midst of predominantly Muslim societies, whereas the members of the GMIM, KGPM, and GMIST live in predominantly Christian societies, but where the influence of older customs and beliefs derived from ancestors is still strong. Consequently, the Christians who live together with the Muslims in Bolaang Mongondouw and Gorontalo must make their daily Christian practice an example for their community. In Minahasa and Sangihe-Talaud, the problem Christians face is in integrating the old customs and beliefs into Christian practices. Many of the congregants still uphold and practice these customs and beliefs *(Adat*)*.

The General Synod of the Churches in North and Central Celebes, which was formed on 14 May 1989 by these five churches and four other churches in Central Celebes, was formerly the Council of Regional Churches in North and Central Celebes. It aims to solve the problems in this region in an ecumenical* spirit. There are other churches in North Celebes: Pentecostal churches, the Seventh-Day Adventist* Church, the Salvation Army*, and the Baptists*. There are more than 30 Pentecostal churches in North Celebes which are recognized by the government. The largest of them is the Pentecostal Church in Indonesia. Only a few of these churches cooperate with the synod at present.

Bibliography

Müller-Krüger, Th., *Der Protestantismus in Indonesien. Geschichte und Gestalt* (1967). • Barrett, D. B., *World Christian Encyclopedia* (1982). • *33 Tahun PGIW Sulutteng* (1988). • Van den End, Th., *Ragi Carita,* Vol. II (1989). • *Handbook of Reformed Churches Worldwide* (1999).

ARNOLD PARENGKUAN

Cenacle Sisters

Founded by St. Thérèse Couderc and Fr. Stephen Terme in 1826 in La Louvesc, France, as the Congregation of Our Lady of the Retreat in the Cenacle (from the Latin *coenaculum,* referring to the upper room where Jesus ate the last supper with his disciples).

According to the Scriptures, Mary, the holy women, and the disciples returned to the upper room after the ascension of Jesus and "with one accord devoted themselves to prayer" (Acts 1:14) as they awaited the coming of the Holy Spirit at Pentecost. This interval of prayer is seen as a prototype of a retreat, where men and women withdraw from ordinary activities to pray and await a new visitation of the Holy Spirit.

The religious of the Cenacle serve the church mainly through retreats and spiritual direction, using especially the Spiritual Exercises of St. Ignatius; through religious education; and through other forms of spiritual apostolate that aim at awakening and deepening people's faith.

The Cenacle Sisters carry on their ministries in 15 countries. First established in Asia in the Philippines* in 1967, they are found today in Quezon City, Legazpi, and Cebu. The sisters run a retreat house in Quezon City and live in communities from which they minister to other parts of the country.

Although the Cenacle in Asia is found only in the Philippines*, the sisters travel to other Asian countries to run retreats and spiritual programs and to train lay leaders, religious men and women, and clergy in the ministry of spiritual direction and facilitating retreats.

LINDA LIZADA

Center of Church Music

(*Pusat Musik Liturgi,* PML). The Center of Church Music was established by the Jesuits* in 1971 in Yogyakarta (Central Java) as part of the wider Catechetical Center. PML collects and documents religious music all over Indonesia*, fosters inculturation of liturgical hymns and the exchange of local musical traditions in order to promote common Indonesian church hymns and songs, and offers courses for choir leaders, organists, and gamelan players.

ADOLF HEUKEN

Ceylon. *See* Sri Lanka

Chakkarai, Vengal

(b. Madras, India, 1880; d. 1958). Chakkarai was born to a well-to-do Madras family of the Chetty caste. His father, who died when Chakkarai was still very young, was a follower of the Vedanta. His mother, who had much influence on him, was a devotee of the Vaishnava bhakti tradition.

Chakkarai received his early education in a Scottish mission school and his college education at the Madras Christian College, where he was greatly influenced by William Miller, whom he held in the same high regard as did his brother-in-law, P. Chenchiah*. It was through his association with Miller and his own study of the Bible that Chakkarai had a personal experience of Jesus Christ. Jesus' cry of dereliction from the cross challenged him most. Regarding Jesus as a mysterious being, Chakkarai accepted him as his Lord. He made a public confession of his faith and received baptism in 1903.

Chakkarai qualified as a lawyer but worked with the Danish Missionary Society in Madras, helping in the evangelistic work among educated Hindus. In 1906, he joined the national struggle for independence (see Nationalism). In 1917, he joined the Home Rule movement and in 1920 the campaign of Mahatma Gandhi* for noncooperation. Later he took an active part in the labor movement and became one of the best-known Christian public figures. In 1941, he was elected mayor of Madras, and in 1951 he became the chairman of the All India Trade Union Congress.

Along with Chenchiah, Chakkarai was one of the founders of the Madras group known as the *Christo Samaj,* concerned with the Indianization of the church. In 1917, he acquired ownership of a weekly paper, *The Christian Patriot,* which he edited and published until its closure in 1926. He was a prolific writer and published several books, including *Jesus the Avatar* (1927) and *The Cross and Indian Thought* (1932). He also made an important contribution to *Rethinking Christianity in India.*

Chakkarai's understanding of bhakti was greatly influenced by his reflection on the suffering and death of Christ on the cross. For him, Christology was the starting point of theology. He asked whether theology should begin with Jesus or God and formulated what he called "the doctrine of the Christhood of God." The real knowledge of God must begin with the personal experience of Christ, the key to which is the passion and death of Jesus on the cross.

Of all Indian theologians, Chakkarai seems to make the most extensive use of Hindu terminology. He describes Jesus as the *Avatara.* For him, religion cannot begin with *nirguna* or *avyakta Brahman.* The Christian *bhakta* must begin with the *vyakta Isvara,* God made manifest in Christ. "We see God with the face of Jesus. . . . Out of the infinite nebulousness emerges the face of Jesus. God is the unmanifested and Jesus is the manifested. God is the *sat,* or being, and Jesus is the *cit,* or intelligence, wisdom and love which indicates the nature of the being of God" (Chakkarai, p. 32). It is important to note that, while Chakkarai used the concept of *Avatar,* he brought out the "once-for-all-ness" by calling Jesus *the Avatar,* not just one of the repeatedly appearing *avatars,* as in Hinduism*.

Chakkarai's view of the Scriptures has been misunderstood because of the impression that he wanted the Old Testament to be replaced by some of the Hindu scriptures. But he firmly believed in the unity of the whole Bible with both the Old and New Testaments. He wrote, "The Old Testament is even a greater book than even the Church conceived it to be, or even the original apostles like Peter and later on Paul" (Thomas, p. 37).

Chakkarai also took seriously the experience of the Holy Spirit. No one who has not received the Holy Spirit can be considered a *bhakta.* He held that the main function of the Holy Spirit is to reveal the things of Jesus Christ.

Chakkarai was aware of the "Jesus of History" school and took seriously the quest for the historical Jesus. For him, the full humanity of Jesus of Nazareth was important for his divinity. He regarded Jesus as the true man who lived in complete communion with the Father. He regarded the work of the Holy Spirit as the continuation of the incarnation and in a way identified the Holy Spirit with the risen living Christ at work in the world.

Bibliography

Boyd, Robin, *An Introduction to Indian Christian Theology* (1975). • Thomas, P. T., ed., *Vengal Chakkarai,* 6 vols. (1981-92). • Estborn, S., *V. Chakkarai — Hindu Convert* (1965). • Chakkarai, V., *Jesus the Avatar* (1932).

J. Russell Chandran

Chaldean Syrian Church of the East

The Chaldean Syrian Church of the East claims to be the faithful remnant of pre-Portuguese Christianity in India* which, according to tradition, was founded by St. Thomas* in 52 C.E., who built seven churches in South India and is believed to have been martyred in 72 C.E. at Mylapore, near Madras. It is one of the smaller ancient Indian churches tracing its heritage to St. Thomas. The Chaldean Syrian Church is centered in Baghdad under Patriarch Mar Adai. Church divisions that led to the present situation of the Chaldean Church date to the 18th c.

In 1796 the Shakthan Thampuran of Cochin (now part of Kerala) brought 52 families to Trichur with a view to developing Trichur as a center of trade and commerce. The Marth Mariyam Big Church was constructed in 1815 by a Royal *Theetooram* ("Proclamation"), translated as follows: "*Theetooram* issued to Palayail Abraham Kathanar, Archdeacon of our Syro-Chaldeans. Whereas 52 houses have been built in Trichur and the locality has been named Puthenpettah with our sanction and whereas a Church has been constructed at the site sanctioned by us for the performance of their rituals and services, and whereas they have come to us and prayed that you be commanded to proceed to the place and initiate the performance of the rituals and services on 4th Meenom, the day fixed therefore, and have then performed thereafter also, and we do hereby command you to go to the said place and have rituals and services performed in accordance with Syro-Chaldean rite on the 4th Meenom and thereafter. Issued from our Royal Residence at Kanayannur, Kumbhom 990 (Mar 1815), written Pavathil Kunju." The question of the faith of those Christian families had been debated in various litigations in the civil courts. The final settlement of the litigations in the district court of Trichur and the royal court of Cochin was given by C. W. E. Cotton, the British political agent, who was the arbitrator on 18 Apr 1925. The plaintiffs-appellants of the Trichur Church Case later joined the Roman Catholic Church and constructed the "Puthan Pally" near the old church (known as the Lady of Dolors Basilica). In the late 1800s two metropolitans from the Middle East (Mar Thoma Rokoe, 1861-62, and Mar Elia Mellus, 1874-82) and a metropolitan from the neighborhood of Palai (Mar Abdeesho Thondanatt) served the Chaldean Syrian Church. The Chaldean Syrians of Trichur do not claim their origin to be 1815 when the Big Church was constructed, but they claim to be the faithful descendants of the 1st-c. converts of St. Thomas (52 C.E.). Metropolitan Mar Abdeesho died on 16 Nov 1900. From 1900 to 1908, Augustine Cor-Episcopa ruled the church in the absence of a metropolitan. Mar Abimalak Timotheus Metropolitan came to Trichur from Kurdistan in Feb 1908 and ruled the church until his death on 30 Apr 1945. His successor was Mar Thoma Darmo, who arrived at Trichur on 22 Jun 1952. He returned from India to Baghdad on 7 Sep 1968. In the same month Metropolitan Mar Thoma Darmo consecrated in Baghdad a priest of the Indian diocese, George Mooken (studying in the United States), as a bishop on 21 Sep 1968 and as a metropolitan on 29 Sep 1968 with the name of Mar Aprem. The constitution for the Chaldean Syrian Church has been in force since 1953. The metropolitan is the head of the church. Four central trustees (so far, only laymen) are elected from the representatives of all the parishes. All male members above 21 years of age who pay the annual subscription are entitled to vote. The term of office of central trustees, as well as that of the representative council, is three years. Each parish elects two trustees *(kaikkars)* annually for the administration of the respective parishes. Every parish has a priest as the vicar and a deacon as an assistant vicar, appointed by the metropolitan. In most cases, the clergy are transferred every three years.

The Chaldean Syrian Church of the East is under Patriarch Mar Adai in Baghdad. In India it has 20 parishes. Most of the churches are in and around Thrissur. There are churches in Madras, Calicut, Ernakulam, Fort Cochin, and Koraty. There are also touring mission services in Palghat, Coimbatore, Bangalore, Bombay, Alathur, Delhi, Alappy, and Trivandrum. There are 15 deacons, 15 priests, one episcopa, and one metropolitan. There is a 52-acre seminary at Trichur in addition to a Chaldean Syrian College, Mar Timotheus Birth Centenary Technical Training Center, Mar Narsai Press, and M. T. M. Orphanage. The total membership of this church is about 30,000. It is a small fraction of the total strength of the Syrian Christians of Kerala, which is about seven million, including the Catholic, Orthodox*, and Reformed groups.

Bibliography

Mundadan, A. M., *History of Christianity in India,* Vol. I (1989). • Assemani, J. A., *De Catholicis seu Patriarchis Chaldaeorum et Nestorianorum Commentorium Historico-Chronologicum* (1775). • Badgor, George Percy, *The Nestorians and Their Rituals* (1852/1987). • Tisserant, Cardinal Eugene, *Eastern Christianity in India: A History of the Syro-Malabar Church from Earliest Time to the Present Day* (1957). • Auril, Adolphe d', *La chaldée chrétienne* (1892). • Keay, F. E., *History of the Syrian Church in India* (1960).

Mar Aprem

Chao, C. T. *See* Zhao Zi Chen

Chao, Timothy

(Zhao Shi-kuang) (b. Shanghai, China, 1908; d. Toronto, Canada, 17 Sep 1973). The thirty-third generation of Song emperor Zhao Kuang-yin, Zhao's given name was Yuan-Chang. In 1921, at the age of 13, Zhao was brought to Sunday school by his cousin. He was baptized on Christmas Day in 1924.

Zhao dedicated his life to full-time ministry at a revival meeting led by missionary Paget Wilkes. He felt that he was born again by the Holy Spirit, and he thus decided to be a light to the world. He changed his name to Shi-kuang (literally, "world light"). He then entered a Bible college established by the Mission Alliance Society and studied there for three years. In 1928, Zhao was invited by Shanghai Shou Zhen Church of the Mission Alliance Society to become a pastor; he was subsequently ordained in 1932. During these years, he held evangelistic and revival meetings in many places.

In 1934, Zhao married Tang Ling-An, a graduate of Shanghai Chinese Women's Seminary and a great partner in his ministry. They had seven children.

In 1940, Zhao accepted an invitation from missionary Zhai Fu-min to conduct evangelistic meetings in the countries of Southeast Asia. In 1941, while pastoring Shanghai Shou Zhen Church, he received a letter from the church in Jakarta, Indonesia*. Zhao saw a vision and heard the Macedonian call. When he was about to travel to Indonesia, the Pacific War broke out on 8 Dec 1941, preventing his trip (see World War II). In prayer, Zhao then received another mission vision from the Holy Spirit, and together with seven young people founded Ling Liang ("Spiritual Food") Mission Team. In Aug 1943, Ling Liang Church was formed in Shanghai and rented the auditorium of a school for worship services. Between 1942 and 1947, five other Ling Liang churches, a seminary, primary and secondary schools, orphanages, and homes for the elderly were founded in the eastern region of China.

In Jun 1946, at a meeting of all Ling Liang churches, the decision was made to form the Christian World Ling Liang Evangelism Association. In Dec 1948, Le Chuanzhen was sent to Calcutta, India*, for pioneering evangelistic work, and Zhou Zhu-pei was sent to Ling Liang Church in Jakarta, Indonesia, as its pastor. On 1 Jan 1950, Zhao began renting Hong Kong Entertainment Theater as a place to hold worship services. This arrangement lasted for 15 years until the theater was torn down in 1965.

In 1955 and 1956, Zhao received honorary degrees (D.J., D.D., D.Litt.) from three universities in the United States (Taylor University, Boston University, and Baptist Theological Seminary).

In Feb 1956, a Mission Training College was founded in Indonesia, and a university was built in the same year. In Jul 1957, Zhao visited the country for the second time and held evangelistic meetings in many cities. In 1958, the work had to come to a stop due to political changes in Indonesia. In 1980, the Theological College was reopened and took the name of Faith (Iman) Theological Seminary (see Theological Education).

In 1964, Zhao built the International Theological College in Hong Kong* and at the same time traveled worldwide for evangelistic meetings and international conferences.

Throughout his life, Zhao paid special attention to literary evangelism. He wrote 35 exegetical works on biblical books, four biographies, four mission travelogues. He edited two volumes of Ling Liang Gospel Songs and wrote eight books in English.

Bibliography

20th Year Anniversary of The Spiritual Food Christian Church (Jakarta, Indonesia) (1972). • *The 40th Year Anniversary of the World Mission of The Spiritual Food Christian Church* (1990). PETER WONGSO

Charismatic Movements

Three waves of renewal. The 20th-c. Pentecostal* Renewal has impacted every segment of the Christian church in virtually every country with new vitality and fervor. Participants share exuberant worship, an emphasis on religious experience and spiritual gifts, claims of supernatural miracles, signs, and wonders, and a "life in the Spirit" that guides their daily activities. Classical Pentecostals, Charismatics, and Neocharismatics comprise three waves within the renewal — each with unique origins and identity.

The first wave of classical Pentecostalism began on 1 Jan 1901 at Charles F. Parham's Bethel Bible School in Topeka, Kansas, United States, when Parham and his students identified speaking in tongues *(glossolalia)* as the evidence of baptism in the Holy Spirit. Shortly thereafter, William J. Seymour, a black Holiness preacher, traveled to Los Angeles, California, to preach the new Pentecostal message. The ensuing revival at the Azusa Street Mission (1906-9) spawned similar "outpourings of the Holy Spirit" across the United States and around the world.

In 1960 the Charismatic Movement, the second wave of Pentecostalism, emerged shortly after Dennis Bennett, an Episcopal rector in Van Nuys, California, announced to his congregation that he had spoken in tongues. The movement grew rapidly, spreading to other Protestant churches, the Roman Catholic* Church, and finally to the Orthodox* Churches. Charismatics emphasize a "life in the Spirit" and the exercise of extraordinary gifts of the Spirit, including but not limited to *glossolalia,* both in private prayer and in public worship.

The renewal in the Roman Catholic Church can be traced in part to the changes ushered in by Vatican Council II. Officially, the Catholic Charismatic Movement began in 1967, simultaneously at Duquesne University in Pittsburgh, Pennsylvania, and in Bogota, Columbia.

The Neocharismatics, comprising the third wave of Pentecostalism, include vast numbers of independent and indigenous churches and groups (18,810 at last count) that cannot be classified as either Pentecostal or Charismatic. These are Christian bodies with Pentecostal-like experiences that have no traditional Pentecostal or Charismatic denominational connections. They are as diverse as the cultures they represent.

Outnumbering on a worldwide basis the first two waves combined, the Neocharismatics are also by far the largest component in the Asian renewal movement. Neocharismatics account for 79 percent of nearly 135 million Asians in renewal, followed by 16 percent Charismatics and 5 percent classical Pentecostals (Barrett and Johnson, *World Christian Encyclopedia* [2000]).

Unfortunately, because most Neocharismatic groups are new and poor, they have not yet recorded their histories nor maintained needed archives. What follows is a brief overview of Asian Charismatic and Neocharismatic movements, the second and the third waves of the renewal.

Charismatic and Neocharismatic movements in Asia. Asia shares with Latin America and Africa the distinction of having the greatest concentrations of Pentecostalism. This is due mainly to the spread of the renewal in Korea*, India*, the Philippines*, Indonesia*, and mainland China*.

It is generally known that several of the world's megachurches are found in South Korea. In addition to Yoido* Full Gospel Church in Seoul (the world's largest congregation with a membership in 1998 of approximately 720,000, connected loosely to the Assemblies of God), there are 14 Korean megachurches with adult attendance exceeding 12,000. Seven are Charismatic Presbyterian* (both Tong-Hap and Hap-Dong groups), three are Methodist*, two are Assemblies of God, one is Unification Holiness, and one Southern Baptist*.

Such spectacular growth is difficult to explain without recognition of the fervent indigenous Prayer Mountain Movement, which served as an antecedent of and foundation for Korean Pentecostalism. The leadership of Lee Yongdo Lee, a Methodist minister during the 1930s, and Ra Woon Mong, a Methodist elder in the 1940s, set the stage for the explosive growth in the Korean Renewal after World War II*. Korean Pentecostalism clearly reflects local culture, including elements of Buddhism* and Confucianism* (Elder Ra approved Buddha and Confucius as Old Testament prophets). There are over three million Neocharismatics and over two million

Charismatics in the South Korean Renewal, and, possibly, a half million Neocharismatics in North Korea.

The Roman Catholic renewal was begun when Miriam Knutas, a Swedish Pentecostal, traveled to Korea, convinced that she had been divinely called to preach to Catholics there. During 1971 the Catholic Pentecostal Movement was born. It grew under Fr. Gerald Farrell, freshly arrived from experiencing the Catholic renewal in the United States. At present there are more than 700,000 South Korean Catholics in renewal movements.

In India, indigenous churches provided the setting for a strong Neocharismatic movement of over 27 million. The largest is the New Apostolic Church, founded in 1969, with approximately 1.5 million members. The second is the Independent Pentecostal Church of God or IPC (founded in 1924 as a split from classical Pentecostal groups) with approximately one million adherents throughout India (they have missionaries in 10 other countries). Others include the New Life Fellowship, founded in 1968, with almost 500,000 members; the Manna Full Gospel churches and ministries (Portuguese origins) with 275,000; and the Nagaland Christian Revival Churches, a 1952 split from Nagaland Baptists, now with 260,000.

In 1972 Minoo Engineer, a Parsi civil engineer who had been studying at Fordham University and had been converted to Catholicism through his involvement with the Charismatics, brought the Catholic charismatic renewal to India. In that same year two Jesuit* priests, Fr. Fuster and Fr. Bertie Phillips, who had been in the United States for studies and research, returned to India as Charismatics. These leaders formed prayer groups, and the movement spread rapidly throughout the subcontinent. Leading Indian Catholic Charismatic leaders are Fr. Rufus Periera, who has organized national conventions, and Fr. Mathew Naickomparambil, a healing evangelist from Kerala, who has preached to crowds of up to 200,000. In the Protestant Church of South India, the Charismatic Movement has been growing under the leadership of Bishop K. J. Samuel of East Kerala, who has launched a successful program of church planting. Overall, there are more than 5 million Catholic and Protestant Charismatics in India.

In the Philippines, independent Charismatic fellowships have drawn large numbers from all social classes, including businesspeople, educated professionals, corporate executives, government employees, and military officers. Bishop Eddie C. Villanueva, a professor at Polytechnic University, began a small Bible* study in 1978. This became the seedbed of what is the largest non-Catholic Charismatic church in the Philippines, called the Jesus Is Lord Fellowship. At present the church claims 4 million constituents, although regular participants number about 150,000. Other fellowships with significant memberships include Love of Christ, Asian Christian Charismatic Fellowship, Bread of Life, Word for the World, Jesus Reigns Ministries, and Jesus Christ Saves Global Outreach. Overall, 7.5 million are connected with the Neocharismatic Movement in the Philippines.

The Catholic Charismatic Movement came to the Philippines in July 1969, under the leadership of Brother Aquinas and Mother Marie Angela, who began prayer groups and sponsored conferences. The overwhelming success of the new Charismatic "fellowships" — which emphasized distinctively Pentecostal experiences such as baptism in the Spirit, spiritual gifts, and especially speaking in tongues and physical healing — posed a threat to traditional Catholic leadership. Reluctantly, the bishops responded to the steady exodus of Catholic believers to independent Charismatic fellowships and Pentecostal churches by officially providing room within the Catholic Church for such groups as El Shaddai, Couples for Christ, the Community of God's Little Children, and the *Bukas Loob Sa Diyos* (Open to the Spirit of God) Community. At present there are over 11.5 million Catholic participants in the renewal in the Philippines.

Details regarding the present state of the Charismatic and Neocharismatic movements in Indonesia are unavailable generally because of the unstable political and religious situation there. From the beginning, the renewal, whether Pentecostal, Charismatic, or Neocharismatic, has been weakened by numerous schisms and, most recently, by strong opposition from an Islamic majority. Notwithstanding, there are almost one million Charismatics (including Catholic and Presbyterian — the GKI or *Gereja Kristen Indonesia)* and over 7 million Neocharismatics in Indonesia.

Mainland China contains more renewal participants than any single country in the world except for Brazil and the United States. From 1970 to 2000, the Chinese church as a whole grew from about 1.5 million to over 50 million (a rough, conservative estimate). In 1970 only 10 pecent of Chinese Christians were Pentecostal or Charismatic. By 1995 65 percent were in the renewal. At present Neocharismatics make up nearly all of those in the renewal. The explosive growth of the house church movement is largely responsible for this increase. Another cause is the growth of Christian broadcasting, together with Scripture and literature distribution.

In addition to the house church movement, two early indigenous movements, Assembly Hall Churches (Little Flock*) and the True Jesus Church (oneness or non-trinitarian) each number over a million members. Roman Catholic Charismatics also claim over a million, and ethnic minority churches have over a million members.

In Taiwan*, the Prayer Mountain Movement, a nondenominational body, set the stage for spiritual renewal that began in 1982 by sponsoring weekend renewal experiences based on intensive prayer meetings. The True Jesus Church was planted on the island of Taiwan in the 1920s and has produced a large number of missionaries. Neocharismatics make up 74 percent of the 359,000 in the Taiwanese renewal movement.

The Catholic Charismatic Movement began in Japan* in 1972, when Hiroshi Yoshiyama of the Japan Assemblies of God was invited to the Hatsudai Catholic Church in Tokyo for a Holy Spirit Seminar. This was supplemented by visits in 1974 by David DuPlessis. Subsequently, Pastor Paul Yonggi Cho of the Yoido Full Gospel Church in Seoul, South Korea, ministered in Charismatic mass meetings.

Japan has produced several indigenous Neocharismatic groups. Most important are the Original Gospel Movement, the Spirit of Jesus Church, and the Holy Ecclesia of Jesus. At present Neocharismatics comprise 88 percent of the 1.7 million in the renewal in Japan.

Singapore* has been a vibrant center for Charismatic renewal. It began in the early 1970s with an outburst of *glossolalia* among students at the Anglo Chinese School (Methodist) and two other schools. Several of these students were from the Wesley Methodist Church. Their pastor experienced physical healing, and a full-fledged Charismatic outpouring followed. A similar renewal occurred in the Anglican* Church, first under Bishop Chiu Ban It*, baptized in the Spirit in 1973, and then from 1982 under Bishop Moses Tay, assisted by Canon James Wong. In 1975 the Full Gospel Businessmen's Fellowship was reorganized and contributed significantly to the Charismatic Movement. Other influential churches in Singapore are Faith Community Baptist and Calvary Charismatic Center, which has an active missionary program to India and Africa.

The True Jesus Church (from Taiwan) has made a vital contribution to the spread of the renewal in Thailand* since its arrival in 1956. The Hope of Bangkok Churches, under the leadership of Joseph Wonsak, has become important in missions with congregations scattered throughout the world. There also is a significant Charismatic renewal in progress within the Church of Christ of Thailand, a church created by the merger of the Christian Church (Disciples of Christ), Presbyterians, and Methodists. Neocharismatics make up 90 percent of over 800,000 in the Thai renewal.

The renewal movement in Asia is rapidly growing and maturing, pulling away from Western theological direction and control. No comprehensive history of the Charismatic and Neocharismatic renewals in Asia exists at present. Because of the vastness of these movements, such a study is unlikely, and even if it were published, it would be outdated almost immediately because of the rapid growth and ever-changing face of the Asian renewal.

Bibliography

Barrett, D. B., and T. M. Johnson, *World Christian Encyclopedia* (2000). • Bays, D. H., ed., *Christianity in China: From the Eighteenth Century to the Present* (1996). • Burgess, S. M., and E. Van der Maas, eds., *New International Dictionary of Pentecostal and Charismatic Movements* (2000). • Calvary Charismatic Centre, Singapore, *And This Gospel Shall be Preached* (1994). • Francis, Andrew, *Charismatic Renewal in the Philippines* (1980). • Fu Io-Te, *A New Day of the Mountain Church* (1969). • Hackett, R. I. J., "New Directions and Connections for African and Asian Charismatics," *Pneuma*, Vol. 18, No. 1 (Spring 1996). • Hollenweger, W. J., *Pentecostalism: Origins and Developments Worldwide* (1997). • Ikegami, Y., "Okinawan Shamanism and Charismatic Christianity," *The Japan Christian Review*, Vol. 59 (1993). • Lambert, T., *The Resurrection of the Chinese Church* (1991). • Mäkelä, J., *Krischak Issara: The Independent Churches in the Bangkok Metropolitan Area, Thailand: Their Historical Background, Contextual Setting, and Theological Thinking* (thesis, 1992). • Mullins, M. R., *Christianity Made in Japan: A Study of Indigenous Movements* (1998). • Poewe, K., ed., *Charismatic Christianity as a Global Culture* (1994). • Shyong, S., *The Doctrine of the Work of the Holy Spirit: The Study of the Charismatic Movement in Taiwan* (thesis, 1991). • Sng, Bobby E. K., *In His Good Time: The Story of the Church in Singapore, 1819-1992* (1993). • So Kwang-son, "The Theological Understanding of Holy Spirit and Revival Movement of Korean Church," *Hanguk Kyohoi Sungnyung Undoing-ui Hyunsang kwa Kujo* (1982). • Sumual, N. J., *Pantekosta Indonesia: Satu Sejarah* (1980). • Tang, E., and J. P. Wiest, *The Catholic Church in Modern China: Perspectives* (1993). • Trever, H., *Japan's Post-War Protestant Churches* (1993). • Vaughan, J. N., *Absolutely Double! The Story of Miracles and Explosive Church Growth at Sung Rak Baptist Church, Seoul, Korea* (1990). • Wagner, C. P., *The New Apostolic Churches* (1998). • Yoo, B., *Korean Pentecostalism: Its History and Theology* (1988). • Young-gi, Hong, "The Backgrounds and Characteristics of the Charismatic Mega-Churches in Korea," *Asian Journal of Pentecostal Studies*, Vol. 3, No. 1 (2000).

STANLEY M. BURGESS

Cheam Ri Methodist Church

A small village Korean Methodist* church famous because of the Japanese military forces' brutal massacre of its members by setting fire to the church building with the people inside during the 1 Mar 1919 independence movement. Some 20 churchgoers and 30 villagers were killed by the fire and by the bullets of the Japanese soldiers firing at anyone trying to escape the building. The Japanese military sacked the nearby villages and thoroughly searched any Koreans who participated in the independence movement; they arrested some 2,000 people in 64 villages between 2 and 17 Apr 1919. Anyone who resisted arrest was killed on the spot, and after the search the military set fires that destroyed some 275 houses.

Missionaries F. W. Scofield and H. G. Underwood* made investigative visits to the village of Cheam Ri and exposed the Japanese atrocity to the world. A monument was erected at the site of Cheam Ri church to commemorate the victims, and the church building was rebuilt nearby for worship and for pilgrims.

DAVID SUH, with contributions from LEE DUK JOO; original translated by KIM IN SOO

Chelliah, Devasahayam David

(b. Thattanikulam, South India, 14 Mar 1894; d. Singapore, 2 Apr 1979). Educator and Anglican* churchman in Penang and Singapore*.

A leading Christian educator, Chelliah taught for 50 years (1911-61), believing strongly in the "teaching of Scripture as the basis for character building." Ordained in 1940, he became president of the Federation of Christian Churches in Malaya in 1945 and the first Asian archdeacon of Singapore in 1957. His pastoral interests continued to occupy him up to his last days.

Principal of a primary school in Penang at age 17, Chelliah went on to serve as a teacher, vice-principal, and principal in Anglican schools in Penang and Singapore. He also earned his bachelor's degree with honors in mathematics in 1923 and his doctorate in education in 1940, both from London University. He was the first person in the Straits Settlements to be awarded a doctorate by a British university. He was awarded the Order of the British Empire by King George VI in 1950 for his services to education. A man of vision, he was an early advocate of bilingual education in place of monolingualism in a foreign tongue.

The acting dean of St. Andrew's Cathedral in Singapore during the Japanese occupation, it was Chelliah's ministry to a then ecumenical congregation which led to his appointment as president of the Federation of Christian Churches in Malaya. A founding member of the Inter-Religious Organization in 1949 in Singapore, he remained on its council until his death. Concurrently with his teaching and after his retirement, he was actively involved with ministry to lepers, the blind, and the elderly.

Bibliography

The Straits Times (2 Jul 1984). • *The Diocesan Digest* (Singapore) (Jan 1967).

SOON SOO KEE

Chen Chi-Chun

(b. Nuannuan, Taiwan, 14 Nov 1895; d. Taipei, 15 Feb 1990). Prominent Taiwanese church figure.

A broad-minded ecumenical Presbyterian* minister who exercised dynamic spiritual leadership in promoting interdenominational witness by drawing different churches together to cooperate in joint evangelism crusades, retreats, and Bible study work, Chen was highly respected by the ministers of Taiwan's Christian community. He was appointed chairman of almost all joint Christian assemblies in Taipei City and at the national level. In 1975, at the age of 80, he was appointed national chairman of the first Billy Graham Crusade in Taiwan*. As chairman he invited the then Republic of China (ROC) president, Chiang Ching-kuo, to attend.

Chen achieved a number of firsts in the Taiwanese church. He ministered at Shuang-Lien Presbyterian Church (SLPC), Taipei's largest church, for 55 years (1921-76). During this period, the church was rebuilt three times. He was ordained pastor there in 1936, and his funeral service was held there in 1990. His youthful enthusiasm throughout his life is summed up in his nickname, "Pastor Evergreen."

Chen had the foresight and courage to lead his flock at SLPC to build a 12-story combined church and commercial building (1973). He forged a bond between the church and the surrounding business community through the Shuang-Lien Lectures, with topics such as "Faith and Business Management" and "Faith and Interpersonal Relations." He opened up new avenues of evangelism toward the modern business community.

The longest-serving board chair and honorary chairperson of the Bible Society* in the Republic of China to date (1961-90), Chen promoted the translation of the Bible* into the aboriginal* languages, of which the Amis, Taroko, Yami, Atayal, and Paiwan projects have already come to fruition. As the chairman of some dozen national church organizations, he made many contributions to church unity and evangelism among the disabled and ethnic minorities.

Chen died at age 95. At his memorial service, the Rev. Dr. Tsai Jen-Li, United Bible Society Asian Pacific regional secretary, noted: "His sight was not dimmed, nor had his vigor failed" (Deut. 34:7). Like Moses, he remained active until the end of his life, working for Christ.

Bibliography

Lai, David C. M., *An Evergreen Among Men: A Centenary Collection in Memory of the Rev. Chen Chi-Chun* (1994).

LAI CHUN-MING

Chen Meng-nan

(b. 1840; d. 1882). First Chinese Christian to advocate the idea of a self-governing church.

A native of Guangdong Province, Chen was educated in the traditional schooling system of private tutelage. Hence he was well versed in classical Chinese literature, as well as the art of Chinese medicine. He heard the Gospel from a Baptist* missionary, with whom he studied the Sermon on the Mount, and consequently became a Christian. Believing that a Chinese scholar should not be baptized by a Westerner, he hired a boat to take him to the provincial capital of Shao-xing, where he was baptized by the Chinese canon Sin Kwai-Tang. Several years later, he went to Canton, where he had more opportunities to learn the truth.

Chen taught at the charity school run by the church. In 1873, he founded the East Guangdong Chinese Alliance Church and advocated that the Chinese set up their own churches. The following year, he bought property to start a Chinese Alliance church and became its pastor. In his spare time, he edited and translated articles for *Alliance Digest*, e.g., "Brief Commentaries on the Parables of Jesus." His "Showing Forth the Truth" was particularly valued and was reprinted many times after his death for a total of one million copies. His writings were as much respected as his personal integrity. His arduous labors eventually led to his illness, and he had to return to his native home in 1881. He died during one of his evangelistic meetings. The Chinese Alliance Churches won wide support from the Chinese people, eventually reaching a peak of 40-50 local congregations. (See also Three-Self Patriotic Movement.)

CHINA GROUP, translated by LENA LAU

Chen Su Lan

(b. 13 Feb 1885; d. 1972). Anti-opium philanthropist.

The younger son of Chen Hui Mei and Dang Li Ming, Chen was named Nen Ya at birth. His mother, a nurse trained by Methodist* missionaries in Fuzhou, China, was widowed when Chen was still a child. She had to flee with her two sons to the countryside when a foreign gunboat approached the port city of Fuzhou. These experiences shaped Chen's future life.

Schooled in the Chinese classics, Chen sat for the *Xiu Cai* examinations when he was 16, after which he attended the Anglo-Chinese College headed by John Gowdy, a Methodist missionary. Upon graduation in 1905, he studied medicine in Singapore* and was among the first medical graduates there.

Chen was active in the Fuzhou Methodist Church and was a delegate to the Quadrennial Conference in the United States in 1928. He became the first president of the Alumni Association of King Edward VII College of Medicine in 1923 and was later a council member of the college.

Ignoring the threat of deportation, Chen fought against the government's monopolistic sale of opium* and established the Anti-opium Clinic, running it almost single-handedly. About 7,000 addicts were rehabilitated before the clinic was closed at the outbreak of the Sino-Japanese War*.

Fleeing from the Japanese, Chen was shipwrecked on 14 Feb 1942 and captured by the Kempetai. He described his experiences in his book *Remember Pompong and Oxley Rise*. His war experience led him to form the Chen Su Lan Trust. It gave land to the Scripture Union and both property and funds to the Wesley Methodist Church for the founding of the Chen Su Lan Methodist Children's Home.

During the British military administration, Chen was appointed to the advisory council but was discontented with "mere speechmaking" on social issues. He proceeded to found the Chinese Young Men's Christian Association* (YMCA) in his retirement. He received an honorary doctorate from the University of Malaya; the theme of his convocation address was the role of Christianity in the emancipation of women. Chen Su Lan was a person who constantly bridged his faith to the everyday world.

CHEN CHI NAN

Chen Zhonggui

(Marcus Chen) (b. Wuchang, Hubei, 1884; d. 1963). Controversial anti-imperialist, pro-Communist Chinese pastor and one of the founders of the Three-Self Patriotic Movement (TSPM)*.

Chen was the second child of a poor cooper. When he was six years old, his father and uncle opened a lumberyard, and Chen was able to attend a primary school run by charity. His schooling, however, was often interrupted by the need to help out at the lumberyard.

At age 16, Chen entered the Powen Middle School in Wuchang, where he felt inferior and discriminated against because of his poverty*. He graduated at age 21 and worked as an English teacher while doing part-time studies at a small Bible school. In 1907, he became a full-time teacher in Wuchang and in 1909 in Yidu. In 1920, he went to Wheaton College, Illinois, to study for his bachelor of arts degree and returned in 1922 to teach at the Yidu (Chingchow) Theological School. Following the incident of 30 May 1925 in which British troops killed a number of unarmed student demonstrators in Shanghai, he was forced to resign from his teaching post. For the next two years, he served as chaplain in the army of Feng Yu Xiang, the Christian general. When Feng aligned his army with the Kuomintang, Chen resigned from the chaplaincy and visited Europe and America in 1928 upon the invitation of the Swedish Missionary Society. He returned and taught Bible and theology at the Bible school in Changsha, Hunan, until the school was closed during the Japanese War. He then became an independent preacher in Sichuan. He visited Singapore* in 1941, where he stayed for two years because of the Japanese invasion. Later, he returned to Chongqing via Thailand*, Vietnam*, and Guangdong. In Sep 1943, Chen set up the Chongqing Theological Seminary and served as its president until 1953. Together with Wu Yaozong* and others, he initiated the TSPM in 1950.

Chen claimed that his anti-imperialist and nationalistic sentiments traced back to the entry of the eight-nation army into Beijing after the Boxer Rebellion. Following that event, he feared losing his own country. During his middle-school years, he was torn between reform and revolution. He decided in favor of the latter because the revolutionary leader Sun Yat-Sen* was a Christian. Chen was in Yidu, a Manchu garrison city, when the revolution of Oct 1911 broke out, but he managed to escape capture by the Manchu army. His pro-Communist and pro-Russia convictions arose from his reading of Marxist literature and his appreciation of Russian aid to China. His membership in the Sino-Soviet Friendship Association and the People's Alliance shocked many Christians.

In his final years, Chen spoke out against the corruption of the Communist Party of China (CPC) during the "Hundred Flowers" movement (1957). When the 10th plenum of the TSPM (28 Oct–4 Dec 1957) adopted a strong left, socialist agenda, Chen was one of seven church leaders who received intense criticism. Although he was severely criticized until his death, his funeral in

Mar 1963 was conducted by Y. T. Wu*, an indication that he died in good standing with the TSPM.

Bibliography

Documents of the Three-Self Movement (1963). • Wickeri, Philip, *Seeking the Common Ground* (1988).

CHINA GROUP

Chenchiah, Pandipeddi

(b. Nellore, Andhra Pradesh, 8 Dec 1886; d. 1959). Lay writer and theologian in the Indian church.

Chenchiah was one of the most distinguished lay theologians of the Indian church. His father, Adinarayaniah, was a prominent Brahmin lawyer who was appointed munsiff in a Madras court in 1901. In the same year, he and the family became converts to Christianity and were baptized. Chenchiah thus became a Christian as a teenager.

He studied at Madras Christian College and came under the influence of the principal, William Miller, who was a missionary from Scotland. Miller was well known for his theological views, which were both Christ-centered and liberal. Chenchiah was trained to be a lawyer and became quite distinguished in his profession. For a few years, he served as lecturer at the Law College, Madras. He was later appointed a judge of the high court of the princely state of Pudukkottai.

Chenchiah regularly worshipped and occasionally preached at Anderson Memorial Church in Madras. He became very interested in dialogue between Christians and Hindus as well as among Christians themselves. Though he had a deep devotion to Christ, he believed that such devotion did not require him to give up a reverential attitude to his Hindu heritage. He was associated with a group of creative Indian Christian thinkers who came to be known as the "Rethinking Group," a reflection of his publication of the book *Rethinking Christianity in India.* This was an Indian reply to Hendrik Kraemer's *Christian Message in a Non-Christian World,* a book which Kraemer wrote for the 1938 World Missionary Conference at Tambaram.

Though he did not write any major books himself, Chenchiah influenced many people by publishing articles in the periodicals *The Pilgrim* and *The Garden.* He even edited *The Pilgrim* for several years. He was critical of both the institutional character of the church in India* and some of the traditional Christian doctrines. One idea that had tremendous influence on his life was the "integral vedanta" of Aurabindo Ghosh of Pondicherry. Chenchiah also developed a fascination for the use of Yoga for the renewal of human community. His Christology was similar to that of Teilhard de Chardin. Applying the framework of Bergson's philosophy of emergent evolution, Chenchiah interpreted Jesus Christ as the first in the emergence of a new species of human brought into existence by the Holy Spirit. He believed that, through "the Yoga of the Holy Spirit," Christ is now reproduced in humans. He spoke of the "raw fact of Jesus Christ," his expression for the historic Jesus of Nazareth, as the key to the experience of salvation. He also suggested that the scriptures of other faiths be accepted in a similar fashion to Old Testament texts. (See also Interreligious Dialogue; Hinduism.)

Bibliography

Thangasamy, D. A., *The Theology of Chenchiah* (1966). • Burkle, Horst, ed., *Indische Beiträge zur Theologie der Gegenwart* (1966). • Boyd, Robin, *An Introduction to Indian Christian Theology* (1975). • Thomas, P., *100 Indian Witnesses to Jesus Christ* (1974).

J. RUSSELL CHANDRAN

Cheng Jingyi

(Cheng Ching-yi) (b. North China, 22 Sept 1881; d. Shanghai, 1939). Manchu Christian and founder of the China* for Christ movement.

The son of a pastor, Cheng studied the Chinese classics before continuing his education at the Anglo-Chinese Institute of the London Missionary Society (LMS) in Beijing. From 1896 to 1900, he did theological studies in Tianjin and graduated two weeks before the Boxer Uprising. Cheng risked his life as an interpreter and stretcher-bearer for the Allied forces. After the siege ended, he participated in relief work in Beijing.

At age 22, Cheng began to help George Owen of the LMS revise the Chinese translation of the New Testament (see Bible Translation). It was completed in 1906. He received further theological training at the Bible Institute in Glasgow, Scotland, and returned to China after his graduation in 1908. After his ordination in his home church, he pastored a newly independent church, the Mi-shih Hutung Church in the East City of Beijing, which was attended by a number of Chinese academics and professionals.

Cheng was one of the three Chinese delegates at the World Missionary Conference in Edinburgh in 1910. In a seven-minute address, he expressed his hope to see a "united Christian Church without any denominational distinctions" in China. Cheng was appointed secretary of the continuation committee of the National Missionary Conference in China, formed after John R. Mott's visit to China in 1913.

In 1917, Cheng led a campaign against the movement to allow only Confucian teachings for moral instruction in the schools. Realizing the future of the church in China lay in indigenous leadership, he formed the China for Christ movement (1919) and also helped form the indigenous interdenominational Chinese Home Mission Society* to reach the ethnic groups in southwest China. He was general secretary of the National Christian Council from its establishment in 1922 until his resignation in 1933 because of poor health. In 1927, Cheng was elected the first moderator of the Church of Christ in China, a Protestant ecumenical organization comprising

16 denominations. He was on the executive committee of the International Missionary Conference from 1928 until 1938.

Cheng was deeply distressed by the Sino-Japanese war in 1937 because he knew many Japanese Christians and felt the war would do irreparable damage to Christian unity (see World War II).

Cheng worked for an independent, unified Chinese Christian church and desired universal Christian unity. A talented, tireless leader, he received honorary doctorates from Knox College, Toronto, Canada (1916); the College of Wooster, Ohio, USA (1923); and St. John's University, Shanghai (1929). He died in Shanghai after his visit to the mission work in southwest China and Guizhou in 1939.

Bibliography

World Missionary Conference, 1910: Report of Commission VIII. • Boorman, Howard L., ed., *Biographical Dictionary of Republican China,* Vol. 1 (1967). • Boynton, Charles, "Dr. Cheng Ching-yi," *Chinese Recorder* 70 (1939).

China Group

Chew, Benjamin

(b. 1907; d. 10 Oct 1994). Doctor, Bible teacher, and churchman in Singapore*.

Born in Malacca, Chew moved to Singapore at the age of three. His father, Chew Cheng Yong, was a lay pastor and teacher in the Methodist* mission. His mother, Tan Siok Kim, was the mission's first Chinese woman convert in Malacca*. Chew studied at the Anglo-Chinese School where, in 1920, he was converted through the ministry of E. Stanley Jones*. A brilliant student, he studied medicine and graduated in 1929 at the top of his class. He began his medical career in government hospitals, serving in Penang and Singapore. After the Pacific War, he went into private family practice. In 1947, he helped to found the Singapore Anti-Tuberculosis Association. This organization was instrumental in bringing the dreaded disease under control.

Chew had been baptized at Bethesda Gospel Hall (Bras Basah Road) in 1921. He taught Sunday school, played the church organ, and learned to preach. His uncle, Goh Hood Keng*, the first Straits Chinese to be ordained into the pastoral ministry of the Methodist mission, was an effective evangelist, a powerful preacher, and a much-loved pastor whose life inspired all who knew him. Chew proved to be much like his uncle.

In 1931, Bras Basah Road Gospel Hall decided to start an extension work in the Katong area where Chew lived. In 1948, he was appointed an elder of Bethesda Katong Church. The church grew steadily and has since spawned two other churches. Chew was equally respected by leaders outside the Brethren circle. His able handling of the Word made him a much sought after speaker at church meetings and conferences. He played key roles in the formation of various parachurch groups. The Graduates' Christian Fellowship was inaugurated at a meeting held in his home (see International Fellowship of Evangelical Students). He was president of Singapore Youth for Christ from its beginning in 1957. He gave unstinting support to the Overseas Missionary Fellowship (formerly China Inland Mission) when it moved its headquarters to Singapore, and he was chairman of the local home council until 1987. He also gave firm support to the Gideons Camp, Keswick Convention, and Christian Conciliation and Arbitration Ministry.

Chew's gracious and humble disposition made him a natural choice to head the Billy Graham Singapore Crusade (1978), which had the support of 90 percent of the Protestant congregations. When the Evangelical Fellowship of Singapore was formed in 1980, Chew was unanimously elected as its first chairman, a position he held until 1991.

Bibliography

Singapore Youth for Christ, *My Times Are in His Hands* (1991).

Bobby Sng Ewe Kong

Chhmar Salmas, Joseph

(b. Phnom Penh, Cambodia, 1940; d. Taing Kauk, Cambodia, 1977). First Khmer Roman Catholic* bishop in Cambodia*.

Chhmar Salmas was born into a large family, his father being a minor government official. After his primary education, he was sent to pursue his secondary studies in Montpellier, France, because at that time it was too difficult for a Khmer to study at the little seminary of Phnom Penh, where the students were mostly Vietnamese. He followed the program for priests at the great seminary of Paris, Issy-les-Moulineaux, and returned to Cambodia in 1964, where he was ordained in the Cathedral of Phnom Penh by Mgr. Yves Ramousse. (One of Joseph's brothers pursued the same studies in the great seminary in France and was ordained in Cambodia in 1967.)

Chhmar Salmas was first charged with training the catechists and then with teaching the Khmer language in the little seminary of Phnom Penh. Next he was charged with the task of translating Khmer liturgies, furnishing vital support to the church. He took to heart the task of helping Christians reach out to Buddhists.

In 1975, in a sabbatical year in France, Chhmar Salmas was recalled to his country by the bishop of Phnom Penh. He went without hesitation, doubting he would ever be charged with directing the church, but submitting to the fate awaiting him. "I leave for Cambodia in order to die there," he confided at his departure from Paris.

On 7 Apr 1975, a papal bull appointed Chhmar Salmas bishop coadjutor of Mgr. Ramousse, apostolic vicar of Phnom Penh. In view of the desperate situation of the country, his episcopal ordination, initially set for 20 Apr, was advanced suddenly to 14 Apr. Several shells fired by Khmer Rouge surrounded the church where he was ordained.

On 18 Apr 1975, Chhmar Salmas and the other citizens of Phnom Penh were expelled from the city to participate in "work of collective interest." In this desperate situation, he displayed extraordinary courage and faith, strengthening the faithful and celebrating the Eucharist in hiding with his brother priests. Wishing to find his fellow deported Christians, he volunteered to form a band of "mobile troops of the region," work groups which moved according to the needs and orders of the Khmer Rouge*. He found not one loyal Christian and returned exhausted. He died destitute in a pagoda transformed into a hospital. FRANÇOIS PONCHAUD

Chiang, Paul C. C. *See* Zhang Zhijiang

China

First attempts. Ignoring the legend that dated the entrance of Christianity into China at the apostolic age, Christianity was first introduced to the Middle Kingdom by Nestorian* missionary Alopen. He appeared in Chang-an, the capital of the Tang dynasty, in the year 635. The Persian "monk" was well received by the Chinese Emperor Taizong (reigned 627-49). Alopen was permitted to station himself in a temple built by the imperial court, translating the religious materials from Syriac to Chinese with the assistance of secretaries sent by the emperor. The alien religion was later termed "The Luminous Religion."

Nestorianism remained in China for 210 years. Apart from the period of Empress Wu Zetian (reigned 650-705), when they faced a time of most severe testing due to Buddhist predominance, Nestorians were by and large well treated. Missionaries built churches in Chang-an and a few other cities, but it is believed that the church remained primarily a place of foreigners, including merchants, soldiers, and missionaries, who resided in the Middle Kingdom. The number of Han believers was small, with even fewer holding positions in the ecclesiastical hierarchy.

The Nestorian epoch was terminated in the mid-9th c. when Emperor Wuzong decided to expel all foreign religions out of the mainland in 845. The reasons for this measure were both religious and economic. Owing to the Taoist influence at the imperial court, the persecution was applied mainly against Buddhism*. However, all other religions, including Zoroastrianism*, Manichaeanism, and Nestorianism, were affected. Monastic systems were dissolved, monks or priests secularized, and sacred books burned. Nestorianism did not disappear from China overnight. Missionaries nevertheless gradually withdrew from the mainland and survived only among the minority peoples at the northwest border. Some argue that the Christian community was eventually absorbed into the Muslim community.

It was at the time of the Yuan Dynasty (1260-1368), when China was ruled by the Mongols*, that Christianity came to China for the second time. Both Nestorianism and Roman Catholicism (see Roman Catholic Church) were on the scene.

The Mongols had their own religions, mainly Shamanism*, but the rulers adopted a tolerant policy toward all kinds of religions. Missions were facilitated, and religious work was subsidized by the government. The Mongol court employed people of "colored-eyes" from mid-Asia; some of them were Nestorians. Together with the Nestorians of the minority peoples, such as the Uighurs, Naimans, Keraits, and Mongols (the Clan of Onguts), they migrated to the mainland and settled in Beijing (Khanbalik). Nestorian Christianity reentered China with an even better political status compared with the former stage. Some years before 1275, Khanbalik became the seat of a Nestorian metropolitan. Nestorian churches were found both in the capital and in the cities on the main arteries of trade. Although some missionary work was carried on among the native Chinese, apparently very few Han people accepted this alien faith.

In the 13th c., the papal court of Roman Catholicism sought to establish relationships with the Mongol conquerors. The pope sent two Franciscan* emissaries, John of Plano Carpini* and William of Rubruck*, to visit the Mongol capital, Karakorum, in 1245 and 1253 respectively. In 1296 Kublai Khan asked the Polo brothers to bring his letters to the pope on their return journey to Italy, asking for 100 well-educated missionaries. However, it was not until 1289 that Pope Nicholas IV succeeded in sending the first missionary, John of Montecorvino*, a Franciscan, to China. He reached Khanbalik in 1294, and was permitted to stay in China by Khan Timur (1294-1307). John built a church in the capital. By 1305 he could report to the papal court that he had won as many as 6,000 converts. Another church and a school were erected the following year. In 1307 Pope Clement V appointed him archbishop of Khanbalik and primate of Cathay (North China) and the entire Far East. Another bishopric was established in Quanzhou (Zaitun), Fujian, after more missionaries arrived. John died in 1328 after his 34 years of service. It was estimated that believers in China had exceeded 10,000 by then.

Successors of Montecorvino were appointed, but none appeared at the episcopate in Khanbalik. Since then, the popes maintained limited relationships with the Mongol court. The last Mongol emperor, Toghan Timur, sent words to Rome requesting more priests. He was answered by Pope Benedict XII, and an embassy was sent to China in 1338. The Catholic Church in China was given liberty to preach and was supported financially by the royal court. In the city of Quanzhou there were three chapels. The number of adherents reached 30,000, but not many of them were Han people. This was the main reason that the church disappeared when the Mongols, together with the foreign traders and the foreign troops and officials, were driven out of China.

Most of the Nestorian and Roman Catholic adherents were Mongols and "colored-eyes" peoples, members of the ruling classes. At the time when the Mongol court exercised a policy of extreme racial discrimination, it was unimaginable that the oppressed Han people would accept the religion of the oppressors. With the collapse of the Mongols, Christianity in China disappeared completely a second time. In the subsequent centuries, even the peoples in the northwestern border of the empire abandoned their Nestorian faith for Islam* and Lamaistic Buddhism.

The third attempt to spread Christianity in China was made by the Jesuits* during the 16th c., a century of Catholic missionary expansion. Francis Xavier*, one of the earliest followers of Ignatius of Loyola, took the initiative to come to the Fast East 12 years after the new order was founded. After several unsuccessful attempts, the difficult task was accomplished by an Italian, Matteo Ricci* (1552-1610), who arrived at Zhaoqing, a city of South China, in 1583 and established a mission there. In 1601 Ricci reached Peking, the capital of the empire, and was permitted to remain and carry out his missionary work.

Ricci and other Jesuits were well aware that the Chinese people were glued to their culture (particularly Confucianism*). As a result, the missionaries consciously adapted their Christian doctrines to Confucian teachings. They put on robes of the Confucian scholar, acquainted themselves with Chinese learning and customs, and tried their best to persuade themselves and the Chinese people that there were no differences between Christian ethics and Confucian moral principles. Confucian teachings were not to be refuted, but to be supplemented by Christianity. The Jesuits believed that Western science and technology were not just a means to "resurrect Chinese culture" but also an effective tool in assisting missionary work, and particularly in reaching the literary class.

After the death of Ricci in 1610, the mission continued to prosper. His confreres continued to hold a conciliatory attitude toward Chinese culture. In return they won a hearing for their faith. Catholic missions spread from Beijing to Shaozhou, Nanchang, and Nanjing. Many Chinese came to Christ. It has been estimated that, by the year of the downfall of the Ming dynasty (1644), there were about 100,000 Catholics, including members of the royal family and some learned scholar-officials such as Xu Guangqi*, Li Zhizao*, Yang Tingyun*, and Wang Zheng*. The missionary access to the emperor and to the official and educated classes helped increase the impact on the elite strata of the population.

The progress of the Catholic mission was not without its obstacles, however. The first incident occurred in 1606, when a native Jesuit was martyred. The most severe persecution arose in 1616. A chief official of the board of rites charged that mission work was seditious, and this was followed by an imperial decree which ordered the foreigners to be deported. Some missionaries were apprehended and sent to Macau, some even in cages, but most of them hid among the Chinese Christians and continued their work secretly. Another persecution of a similar kind occurred in 1622. All of these tensions were eventually resolved by the Jesuits through their wisdom and patience and did not endanger the propagation of Christianity.

When the Manchu dynasty replaced the Ming in the mid-17th c., religious policies remained unchanged. Catholic missionaries were permitted to preach, and some continued to be employed by the imperial court.

From the beginning, the Portuguese claimed to have the right of patronage in the Fast East, including Japan* and China. They prohibited the Spanish Franciscans and Dominicans* from obtaining a foothold in the Middle Kingdom. Thus missionary work in China was monopolized by the Jesuits. It was not until 1631 that the pope granted freedom to orders other than the Jesuits to go to non-Portuguese territories in China. The late-arriving Franciscans and Dominicans created their provinces in Fujian and other parts of South China, as did the other Catholic orders from France and Italy. However, when missionaries of different orders and nationalities worked together in the same country, their divergent approaches engendered discord and created disputes among themselves. There was no proper mechanism to settle disputes among orders in the mission field. All had to rely on decisions by the papal court thousands of miles away. Misunderstandings and miscalculations were thus inevitable. One notable example was the Rites Controversy (see Ancestor Worship).

Most Jesuits supported the view of Ricci that there was no religious significance in ancestor worship and Confucian rites. Participation in ceremonies in honor of Confucius and of ancestors by Chinese adherents was acceptable. They realized that missionaries had to show respect to Chinese culture in order to succeed in propagating their beliefs. The Dominicans opposed the Jesuits' policy and denounced the Jesuits in front of the pope. In their eyes, this policy was not just a matter of strategy but represented an attempt at East-West syncretism. At that time the papal court was disturbed by the Reformation and other dismemberment movements and was sensitive to all forms of "heretical" tendencies. After several debates, Pope Clement XI finally confirmed the statement issued by the Inquisition in 1704 and forbade Chinese Christians to take part in sacrifices to Confucius or to ancestors. He also sent a special legate, headed by Charles Maillard de Tournon*, to the Far East to ensure the implementation of the decree. Tournon arrived at Peking in 1705. When the decree was heard, Emperor Kangxi was antagonized. He ordered the legate to return to Europe and decreed that only those missionaries who agreed to abide by the practice of Ricci could obtain permission to remain in China. The pope did not concede but commanded obedience of all missionaries. Another legate, led by Charles Mezzabarba*, was sent to China in 1720. When Mezzabarba understood the serious situation the Catholic Church faced, he presented to the emperor a concession in the form of "Eight Permissions" allowing the Chinese Christians to observe those rites of no religious character. However, Pope Benedict XIV annulled the "Eight Permissions" and insisted on the total prohibition of ceremonial participation. Because of the Rites Controversy, the golden age of Catholic missions in China came to an end.

Emperor Kangxi forbade missionaries to preach in China in 1720. In 1727 his successor Yongzheng (1723-36) reiterated the decree, which was severely enforced. Chinese Christians were commanded to renounce their faith. Churches were seized and used for secular purposes. Missionaries, except for those serving in the government, were banished. Native priests were forced to choose between secularization and punishment. Severe persecutions took place sporadically during the following 160 years, but the feeble Christian community remained on Chinese soil. A number of foreign and native clerics carried on their work in the interior. It was reported that there were about 200,000 Christians in all of China in 1800.

Christian missions in the 19th and early 20th centuries. It was when Robert Morrison*, the first Protestant missionary sent by the London Missionary Society, arrived at Macau in 1807 that the fourth attempt to preach the Gospel in China began.

To the newly arrived missionary, the immediate obstacle that had to be overcome was gaining legal status to remain in China. By the imperial decree of 1720, missionaries were forbidden to stay in China. Two years after his arrival Morrison joined the East India Company as a translator, and he worked for the company until his death. By so doing, he associated himself closely with an opium* trading agency. He devoted himself to learning Chinese and completed the translation of the Bible* in 1819. He also compiled the first Anglo-Chinese dictionary and wrote tracts and pamphlets for evangelism with the assistance of Chinese helpers. He had the first Protestant Chinese convert, Cai Agao, baptized in 1814, the year the second Protestant missionary, William Milne*, joined him.

Milne did not stay in China for long before he decided to make his home in Malacca, a European colony with many Chinese inhabitants. One of his goals was to found a Bible college for the training of Chinese evangelists who could be sent back to the mainland. A printing factory was also built for the preparation of evangelistic materials to be delivered in China. One of the factory workers, named Liang Afa*, later became the first Chinese-ordained minister.

More missionaries came to China in the 1820s and 1830s, making their accommodation in Macau and Canton illegal. They faced all kinds of cultural and political problems. Preaching opportunities were scarce, for as foreigners they could hardly find ways to meet ordinary people. They had to hire native assistants, both Christians and non-Christians, to help penetrate the inland to scatter the tracts. Many of these people came to Christ because of the jobs they needed. Called Rice Christians, they caused many problems to the Christian ministries. When Morrison died in 1833, there were only 10 Chinese Christians as the result of 25 years of missionary endeavor.

In order to find means to meet Chinese people, some missionaries set up small schools, mostly in the form of the "one-man-school." Education was an effective means both for evangelism and for the training of native helpers. A dispensary was founded by Peter Parker* in 1836, which signified the introduction of medical* missionary work. The early missionaries were also committed to promoting the knowledge of Chinese culture and society in the West. A periodical called the *Chinese Repository* and books of related subjects were printed. These studies facilitated both the later missionary work and Western invasions to China. Missionaries became the first group of sinologists in the 19th c. The most prominent was James Legge*, who translated the entire Confucian canon into English (completed in 1872).

The history of Western imperialism in China took a sudden leap forward when the Opium War broke out in 1839 and the Treaty of Nanjing was signed in 1842. Since then, Western powers came waging wars against China and forced her to sign unequal treaties that conceded all kinds of privileges and profits to the West. Since missionaries were virtually the only foreigners with knowledge of Chinese, some were employed by their governments in their expeditions to China. They performed duties mostly as translators and magistrates of the occupied regions and helped in the negotiations of treaties. Some even gave up their missionary calls and became consulate employees. John Leighton Stuart*, the last ambassador of the United States to China before 1949, had been working in China as an educational missionary for years before he heeded the call by his government. Not many missionaries exchanged their religious roles for secular ones. The phenomenon nevertheless confused the Chinese, leading them to believe that the Christian missionary enterprise was an integral part of Western imperialism to China.

The accusation of having an intrinsic political agenda within the missionary endeavors was not easy to deny. Most of the time the legal right to preach and to erect churches in the Chinese territories was included in the unequal treaties after wars. These privileges were ensured on the strength of the consular jurisdiction backed by military powers. Catholic missions were, in particular, protected by France, which replaced Portugal and assumed the role of protector in the 1840s. Missionary work was carried out within a treaty framework. Even the Chinese Christians were protected by the treaties so as to prevent them from being discriminated against or ill-treated by Chinese officials and the gentry class. Together with missionaries, they were immune to Chinese laws. In Chinese eyes, these Christians were no longer Chinese. They lived as a segregated group and relied totally on missionaries and the mission enterprise. Catholic communities scattered in the rural areas were, in particular, viewed by Chinese people as foreign colonies. Chinese Catholics were isolated and estranged from their fellow people.

A policy of toleration was decreed by the Chinese government in 1844 and 1846. After the signing of the Peking treaties in 1860, the door of evangelism to the whole of China became wide open. There were no more political obstacles to mission work. However, because of the prevailing anti-foreign and anti-Christian sentiments among the Chinese people, missionaries and native preachers still faced fierce opposition. They were seen as symbols of Western invasions and a threat to the traditional social and cultural order. Even philanthropic efforts administered by the missionaries were regarded suspiciously. Numerous anti-Christian conflicts (Missionary Incidents) broke out in the 19th and early 20th centuries: anti-Christian literature was disseminated, missionaries and native Christians were attacked or even killed, and churches were demolished. Among the 800 incidents or so recorded during the Qing dynasty, the Boxer Rebellion of 1900 was the most tragic of all. During that time over 200 foreign missionaries and over 30,000 Chinese Christians were killed. In response to the tumult, Western consuls intervened and foreign troops were summoned. A new phase of military actions took place. Subsequently, the Chinese government and people were further humiliated, and more political benefits were conceded to the countries to which the missionaries belonged.

From 1860 on, Catholic and Protestant missionaries began flocking to China. Catholic priests of various orders endeavored to rebuild formerly established missions and acquired new territories, most of which were in the interior. Vicariates apostolic set up in different provinces were entrusted to different orders. By 1870 there were 250 European priests. Thirty years later this figure had jumped to 886. The number of Protestant missionaries rose from 81 in 1858 to 1,324 in 1893. It grew to nearly 7,000 in 1920. China became the largest mission field ever in the world. Due to the inconvenience of transportation and communication, as well as concerns for the family members of the missionaries, most of the Protestant work was concentrated in the port cities of the coastal area. Few personnel were assigned to West China. Even after the founding of the China Inland Mission by Hudson Taylor*, this uneven distribution of missionary resources had not changed much.

Missionaries came to China with the objective of saving souls. For them, direct preaching of the Gospel was the first priority. It found its expressions in street evangelism, renting houses for preaching halls, and excursions into the hinterland to spread the Gospel and distribute Bibles and tracts. Nonetheless, owing to differences in language, religion, and culture and the suspicion and vigilance the Chinese held toward Westerners, the effect of this type of "direct evangelism" was not satisfactory. In view of this, missionaries had to look for ways that might change the attitude of the Chinese toward the Gospel. Various approaches were adopted. Education, medical care, and relief and social services were provided side by side with the preaching of the Gospel. This kind of work was called "indirect evangelism." Orphanages and schools were established and administered by numerous Catholic orders. To them, the baptism of infants and children was the easiest way to gain new converts. By 1900 there were over 700,000 Catholics in China. Almost all Protestant societies had organized schools and charitable institutions. Because the Chinese people welcomed these services and the need for such works was vast, ministries of indirect evangelism gradually became a major part of the missionary work. By 1920 it was estimated that Chinese Protestant Christians had reached 360,000, but the mission schools of different levels, including 14 colleges and universities, had enrolled more than 200,000 students. In the same year there were 347 mission hospitals and 473 dispensaries around the country.

In the 19th c., missionaries in general shared the opinion that Chinese culture was heretical and incompatible with the Christian faith and should definitely be rejected. One of the main reasons for this uncompromising approach was their direct involvement with the grass-roots population and exposure to the dark side of society (bribery, a corrupt legal system, foot-binding, blind marriage, and many superstitious practices). Foreigners from a more sophisticated Western society could hardly appreciate these aspects of Chinese culture and concluded that it was the product of heathenism. The true interests of the Chinese people could be served only by means of a fundamental change in their culture and religion. Most of the missionaries believed that Western culture was equivalent to Christian culture and that Westernization should go along with Christianization.

There was no major difference among missionaries in their understandings of the interrelationship between Westernization and Christianization. The only disagreement between the "conservatives" and the "liberals" was a matter of priority: whether missionaries should concentrate their efforts first in preaching the Gospel, on which the wealth and power of the West were rooted; or in helping introduce Western culture so as to smooth the way for Christianization. "Conservatives" such as Hudson Taylor insisted on the priority of direct evangelism and preaching to the masses (from the bottom up). The China Inland Mission also ran schools and charitable institutions. "Liberals" such as Timothy Richard* urged a more strategic effort to reach the educated elite (from the top down) and to participate in social and political reform movements. Taylor's views toward Chinese culture were as negative as Richard's. "To change China" was their common goal.

There were missionaries who had been directly involved in introducing Western learning to the Chinese. Some of them were employed by the Manchu government in those newly formed institutions (arsenals, language schools, and translation bureaus) set up by enlightened officials. These institutions enabled the missionaries to take part in the Self-strengthening Movement in the 1860s. Others propagated Western knowledge through institutions created by the missionaries themselves. The Society for the Diffusion of Christian and General Knowledge among the Chinese, founded in 1887 by a group of missionaries, merchants, and diplomats in Shanghai (renamed the "Christian Literature Society" in the 20th c.), was one of the foreign institutions that endeavored to translate and publish Western books and deliver them to Chinese intellectuals, including the imperial court. The Chinese-language periodical *Chinese Globe Magazine* (later *A Review of the Times)* was influential among the Chinese reformers and revolutionaries who sought ways to reform China. The School and Textbook Series Committee (later the Educational Association of China), founded at The First General Conference of Protestant Missionaries in China in 1877, was also a major supplier of Western knowledge. Missionaries had extensive influences upon the reform and revolutionary movements of the late Qing through their writings as well as through personal contacts with reformers and revolutionaries.

China underwent great changes in the 20th c. After the Boxer Uprisings, the Manchu government carried out an unsuccessful constitutional reform movement that was followed by revolutions in the first decade. In 1911 and 1912 the overthrow of the Qing dynasty was achieved, and the Chinese Republican era began. Sun Zhongshan (Sun Yat-sen*) was elected provisional president of the new government. Christians had long been marginalized by traditional society. Many of them participated in the revolutions actively. In return, many Christians were appointed as officials in the new regime. Although it did not make any significant difference in the deteriorating political situation, it helped to build a good church-state relationship in the early republican era. The years from 1900 to 1920 could be viewed as the golden age of Christianity in China. The number of Chinese Christians rapidly increased from 95,943 in 1900 to 366,527 in 1920.

During the New Culture Movement, which preceded the May Fourth Movement in the 1910s, fundamental changes aiming at the reconstruction of China were the objective of conscientious intellectuals. Many of them perceived Christianity as a tool to the "heart reform" of the nation that was a prerequisite for the genuine reform of culture and society. They believed that the feebleness of the Chinese people could be strengthened by the perfect character of Jesus Christ such that Chinese could shoulder the duties of social and political reform. The Young Men's Christian Association* (YMCA), founded in 1895, was active in promoting this kind of spiritual reform. Their various programs and activities attracted thousands of participants. In 1920 the membership exceeded 60,000. Twenty-four thousand people joined Bible study classes, 2,000 of them converting to Christ in the same year. International leaders such as John R. Mott* and George Sherwood Eddy became prominent speakers throughout the entire nation. The total attendance at Eddy's itinerary speaking trip in 1918 totaled nearly 200,000.

It is not without irony that the same Christianity regarded as "foreign religion" and rejected by most Chinese in the mood of "anti-foreignism" in the 19th c. was seen again as "foreign religion" but was now welcomed in the mood of "antitraditionalism." Christianity in China was (and is still) associated with the West. However, it was when modern atheistic thought was imported to China (mostly in the 1910s) that the Chinese people found it possible to accept Western knowledge and reject Western religion.

The Anti-Christian Movement broke out in 1922 and marked the end of the golden age and the beginning of a new phase of predicament. Initiated by a group of college students who were protesting the convention of the eleventh congress of the World Student Christian Federation held at a Chinese state university, it turned into a national movement against Western imperialism in the form of propagating Christianity. Anti-Christian riots broke out in almost all the major cities. Joined by factory workers and scholars, students organized a "Non-Religious Alliance" with regional branches established in different cities and organized a nationwide campaign with the goal of driving out missionary forces. Christianity was charged with being an anachronism, an obstacle to science, and a deterrent to China's modernization. Mass meetings were held, anti-Christian publications and open telegrams disseminated, parades and demonstrations held, and boycotts against mission schools demanding the withdrawal of their privileges to run educational institutions initiated. In some places missionaries were physically assaulted.

The movement gradually quieted down in 1923, but it was once again renewed in the summer of 1924. A new "Anti-Christian Alliance" was organized in Shanghai, with branches subsequently established in various provinces. After the May 30 Massacre in 1925, the movement came to its climax when patriotic and antiforeign sentiments were at their height. By this time it was no longer a student or youth movement; it was supplanted by political parties (both Nationalist and Communist*) that eventually took over the movement. In 1927, at the instigation of radicals synchronized with the advancement of the Northward Expedition Army, violence erupted in certain localities that caused damage to Christian properties, physical injuries, and the loss of human lives. Thousands of missionaries left China for safety. The number of Protestant missionaries dropped from 8,300 in 1927 to 3,150 in 1928. A number of mission schools and hospitals were closed down or left to the care of Chinese workers. Secondary school students decreased from 11,000 in 1922 to 5,500 in 1927.

During the campaign of 1924-27, missionaries were

accused of being the pioneers and agents of Western invasions. Mission work was but a form of "cultural imperialism." Missionaries used philanthropies as a means to appease Chinese so that the latter were no longer alert to the conspiracies of the Westerners. The spearhead of attack was especially pointed at the educational enterprises operated by missionaries. The Educational Right Movement was launched in 1924 and demanded that all mission schools be brought under government supervision and serve the cause of national revolution. Mission schools should not be permitted to use education for the purposes of evangelism or cultural aggression by foreigners. Supported by most scholars and educators, the Nationalist government passed a set of regulations for private schools in 1928 that required all educational institutions to be registered. The principal and half of the board members of the school had to be Chinese. No compulsory religion class or religious activity could be conducted. There was a total ban of religion both in primary and junior middle education, which resulted in a drastic drop in the number of primary schools operated by Christian churches. In the 1930s only 13 registered Catholic and Protestant colleges remained.

The Anti-Christian Movement in the Republican period was more complicated than in the late Qing period. Participants in the Republican period, mainly young students, were profoundly influenced by Western atheistic thought, including scientism, rationalism, liberalism, anarchism, and Marxism. Christianity was viewed as an outdated ideology, incompatible with modern scientific learning.

The chaotic situation was brought under control when the Northern Expedition was concluded and the government, under the leadership of the Nationalist Party, expelled the Communists from its camp. Social order was restored and religious freedom was reensured. Missionaries were able to return to their stations, but the number was reduced due to severe budget cuts for mission work owing to the Great Depression beginning in 1929. After Jiang Jiashi (Chiang Kai-shek) became a Christian, the church-state relationship warmed up significantly. Christians were invited to play a role in the social and cultural reconstruction programs conducted by the Nationalist government ("New Life Movement") in the 1930s.

The Anti-Christian Movement had the effect of awakening Christians and prodding them to self-examination. They went through a series of measures to adapt Christianity to the Chinese scene. In 1926 an article titled "Characteristics of the Christian Movements," written by the editor of the *China Christian Year Book,* stated that Christians were facing severe challenges from the Chinese people. They demanded answers from two sets of questions. First, "What does the Christian religion mean?" This, in turn, implied the following subquestions: "Was Christianity superstitious and incompatible with modern science? Was it time bound and already antiquated? Was it socially bound and obligated to align itself with capitalistic thought?" Second, "What is the place and function of the church in the life of China?" This also implied other questions: "Was Christianity an opiate of the people that prohibited them from actively participating in social life? What was the role of the church in the process of national reconstruction? Which side would Christians take in the worldwide warfare waged in fighting against Western imperialism?" These questions could serve as the gauge of all the endeavors and activities undertaken by Christians in the 1930s and 1940s with the goal of building an indigenous church.

Indigenization took place in various forms and dimensions, from changing the names of denominations (usually adding the prefix "Chinese" to the original name) to the amalgamation of denominations, from the transference of administrative functions and leadership from missionaries to Chinese Christians to the formation of Chinese independent churches. A "Chinese church consciousness" emerged among Christian communities, with a goal of separating the Chinese church from the missionary enterprise, of removing its foreign character, and of assuming a Chinese image. The advancement of the "Three Self's," namely, self-support, self-propagation, and self-government (see Three-Self Movement), became a consensus among Chinese Christians.

Affirming identification with the national interests of the Chinese people was also seen as imperative. This task was achieved through various social and political actions, including schemes of rural reconstruction, mass education, the hygiene movement, vocational training, anti-prostitution efforts, anti-drug campaigns, and many others. Most of these social reconstruction programs were initiated by the YMCA, Young Women's Christian Association* (YWCA), the National Christian Council (formerly China Continuation Committee), and Christian colleges. Many young intellectuals committed themselves to the national salvation movement and to the integration of Christianity and Chinese society.

Many independent churches emerged. Among them the most notable were the True Jesus Church, the Jesus Family*, and the Little Flock*. All of these gradually became national denominations and extended to Chinese Christians all over the world. Evangelistic campaigns were conducted by the National Christian Council, denominations, independent "evangelistic bands," and individual revivalists/evangelists. The Chinese church was able to present a united front and became a missionary church reaching out to millions.

The church suffered badly along with the entire nation during the Sino-Japanese War (1937-45). In the occupied territories, church facilities were damaged or occupied, people were wounded or killed, and missionaries from the Allied countries (estimated at 1,500 in 1942) were put into concentration camps or repatriated after the outbreak of the Pacific Wars in 1941. Due to political and financial difficulties, most of the philanthropic activities were brought to a halt. Only a few could be transferred to the free zone. In the territories ruled by the Nationalists, missionaries and Chinese Christians engaged in refugee relief work. New evangelistic opportunities were found among the refugee students who left home and went to West China for education. The spiritual needs of the border tribes were then recognized by Christians originally from the East. The most significant incident in the development of the Chinese church was the abolition of extraterritoriality and in the signature of treaties with the Allies in 1943, which implied an end to the privileged position as well as the charges of extraterritoriality given to Christianity in China a century previous.

Civil war (1947-49) broke out two years after the end of the war against Japanese aggression. Economic hardship and the influx of refugees* oppressed the whole country. Reconstruction schemes carried out by Chinese Christians and returned missionaries who resumed their duties after the war (3,500 in 1947) could hardly be accomplished due to the shortage of time and resources. Church service and social services were maintained, but the scope was reduced to its minimum. Future difficulties were anticipated by most Christians with the advancement of the Communists. Many Chinese Protestant leaders (the independent revivalists in particular) fled the country before the turnover of government. Some missionaries decided to remain on the field, but most of them could extend their service only until 1952. Emergency meetings were called by denominations, and plans were arranged and sent down from the hierarchy. In Jul 1949 the Vatican distributed a papal letter to all parishes in China prohibiting Chinese Catholics from accepting Communist doctrines.

The Chinese Church after 1949. The birth of the People's Republic of China in 1949 signified an end to the history of foreign missions in China. The government demanded that Christianity, both Protestant and Catholic, be freed from the domination of colonialism and imperialism and run by the Chinese themselves. The indigenization process accelerated after the outbreak of the Korean War*. The churches had to cut off their links with American and other missions completely. All foreign mission organizations stationed in China had to be pulled out and all missionaries expatriated. Educational and medical institutions founded by foreign missions were taken over by the state. Theological schools were amalgamated and the number reduced from more than 60 in 1949 to only one after 1957. On the Protestant side, several patriotic Christians were appointed by the government to take over the leadership of the church. This was accomplished with the state's assistance by deposing the national and denominational leaders when the denunciation movement began in 1951 and launching a Three-Self Reform Movement afterward. The Three-Self Patriotic Movement Committee* (TSPM) was officially inaugurated in 1954 after the First National Christian Conference was held in Beijing. All churches were required to join the body. Those who opposed to the new leadership were arrested and charged as counterrevolutionaries. On the Catholic side, however, those who tried to break free from the control of the Vatican experienced considerable resistance. It was not until 1956, after a series of political actions to eliminate the counterrevolutionaries in the Catholic Church, that the Chinese Catholic Patriotic Association* was formally established.

The state policy toward religion became more and more radical from the late 1950s on. The Socialist Education Movement was launched in 1957 and was followed by the Great Leap Forward a year later. Church ministers were summoned to attend political study sessions. Many of them were persuaded or forced to leave their pastorates and joined the proletarian class by becoming factory workers. Because the number of pastors and church attendees was reduced, the TSPM called for a Church Union Movement, which resulted in a remarkable reduction in the number of churches. For example, the 200-plus churches in Shanghai were reduced to eight, and in Beijing the number was reduced from 64 to four. Many church buildings were confiscated by or voluntarily offered to the state.

When the Cultural Revolution broke out in 1966, the few remaining churches in the cities were shut down. Religions were regarded as superstitious and incompatible with the new revolutionary society. From 1966 to 1979, institutional Christianity was completely eradicated in China. Bibles were burned, and many pastors and converts were sent to prison. However, a few Christians continued to meet secretly in their homes, especially in the countryside. The house churches gradually grew in size and in number in the late 1970s. Christianity had become deinstitutionalized and declericalized.

Through Deng Xiaoping's open-door policy, churches began to reopen in 1979. The patriotic Christian organizations were revived, and normalization of religious policy was implemented. Seminaries were established, and Bibles and other Christian literature* were printed. Christianity experienced a great revival under Socialism in the 1980s and 1990s and developed notable Chinese characteristics. Christian activities were tolerated by the state with the condition that the church remain under the strict control of the government. Now and then, the state intervenes whenever it sees itself threatened, and then some form of purge takes place.

Bibliography

"Christianity and Chinese Nationalism in the Early Republican Period — A Symposium," *Republican China,* Vol. 17, No. 2 (Apr 1992). • Cohen, Paul A., *China and Christianity: The Missionary Movement and the Growth of Chinese Anti-foreignism, 1860-1890* (1963). • Covell, Ralph R., *Confucius, the Buddha and Christ: A History of the Gospel in Chinese* (1986). • Hunter, A., and K. K. Chan, *Protestantism in Contemporary China* (1993). • Latourette, K. S., *A History of Christian Mission in China*

(1929; reprinted 1975). • MacInnis, Donald E., *Religion in China Today: Policy and Practice* (1989). • Ng Lee-ming, "Christianity in China," in *Christianity in Asia — Northeast Asia*, ed. T. K. Thomas (1979). • Varg, Paul A., *Missionaries, Chinese and Diplomats: The American Protestant Missionary Movement in China, 1890-1952* (1977). • Wickeri, P. L., *Seeking the Common Ground: Protestant Christianity, the Three-Self Movement, and China's United Front* (1988). • Young, John D., *Confucianism and Christianity: The First Encounter* (1983).

LEUNG KA-LUN, with contributions from XU RU LEI, translated by TUNG LUN-HSIEN, and THE CHINA GROUP, translated by DUFRESSE CHANG

China Christian Council

The China Christian Council (CCC) was established at the Third National Christian Conference in Oct 1980. According to its most recent constitution (revised in 1997), the aim of the CCC is "to unite all Chinese Christians who believe in the Heavenly Father and who acknowledge Jesus Christ as Lord, and to run the church well under the guidance of the Holy Spirit, with one heart and unity of purpose, in obedience to the truth of Scripture, the three-self patriotic principle, the Chinese Church Order and the national constitution, laws, regulations and policies."

Together with the national committee of the Three-Self Patriotic Movement* of the Protestant Churches in China (TSPM), the CCC is the national organizational expression of Protestant Christians in China. The TSPM and the CCC are said to function as "two hands of one body," with relationship based on "co-operation and differentiation of function." The former is involved in patriotic education and relationships with the government, while the latter is concerned with the ecclesiastical affairs of Protestant churches in China. The committees of these two national bodies are elected at the National Christian Conference, which meets every five years. *Tian Feng,* the church monthly, is published jointly by the CCC and the TSPM.

The tasks of the CCC are to serve Chinese Christians through publication of the Bible*, hymnals, and Christian literature*; to promote and oversee theological education* and volunteer training; to review the work of Chinese churches and strengthen contact between church bodies at different levels; to advocate "mutual respect" in matters of faith and worship; to strengthen unity and promote mission; and to develop and maintain international Christian relations. The China Christian Council became a full member of the World Council of Churches at its seventh assembly in 1991.

The headquarters of the CCC is in Shanghai, but a Nanjing office has been established to coordinate international ecumenical relationships. K. H. Ting* was president of the CCC from its inception until the Sixth National Christian Conference in 1997, when Han Wenzao was elected to succeed him. Christian councils or church-affairs committees have been set up in most provinces, autonomous regions, and municipalities, and in some cities and towns. The CCC promotes communication, meetings and exchanges between these bodies to enable them to deal with matters of common concern.

Bibliography

Wickeri, Philip L., *Seeking the Common Ground: Protestant Christianity, the Three-Self Movement and China's United Front* (1988). • Hunter, Alan, and Chan Kim-Kwong, *Protestantism in Contemporary China* (1983). • *Chinese Theological Review,* 1985-present.

PHILIP WICKERI, with contributions from CAO SHENG JIE

China Christian Independent Church

(Zhonghua Jidujiao Zili Hui). One of the larger independent denominations among the Chinese Protestant churches.

The China Christian Independent Church flourished mainly in the province of Shandong. In 1885, Zou Liyou, a Presbyterian and graduate of Deng Zhou Huiguan, broke from the Presbyterians and established an independent evangelistic thanksgiving meeting. During the 10 Oct 1911 revolution, elder Liu Shoushan and others initiated the China Christian Independent Church. Shangdong mayor Zhou Liqi showed his support by offering a piece of land of 201 hectares in Jinan and also rescinded the tax on it indefinitely. Elder Zhang, together with others, gradually built churches, hospitals, and schools, and in Qingdao and other locations churches responded to the call for independence. Shandong Chinese Christian Independent Church was officially established in 1915. Liu Shoushan and 12 others were elected to the board of directors. Later in different cities of Shandong Province, independent, self-supporting, self-spreading indigenous churches sprang up one after another. In 1924, the headquarters was established at Jinan, and independent churches that were not under provincial control were called to a district parliament. District parliament meetings were to be held once each year to foster a self-supporting spirit in fundamental churches. According to 1924 statistics, the Independent Church had 12 pastors, 41 elders, and over 2,200 believers. Members' contributions toward the church's net assets amounted to approximately $300,000. CHINA GROUP

China Medical Missionary Association (CMMA)

The CMMA was formed as a professional agency in Shanghai in 1886 by medical* missionaries working in the country, with John Glasgow Kerr, M.D. (1824-1901), as its first chairman. Its aims were to enhance the development of Western-style medical practice and science in China* and to serve as a forum for mutual exhange. Local branches were set up in Shanghai, Manchuria, Wuchang, Canton, Fukien, and Formosa (Taiwan*), and supervisors were appointed for the medical work in the large cities such as Peking, Chefoo, Hangchow, Nanking, Amoy, and Canton. Its committee on publication and translation not only worked on the adequate rendering of technical medical terms into Chinese, but it also provided adequate study materials for Chinese students and published the *China Medical Missionary Journal* (1887-1909), the first professional medical journal in all of Asia. In 1909 this became the *China Medical Journal,* and, finally, when the CMMA merged with the nonmissionary China Medical Association, which published the *National Medical Journal,* the periodical changed its name again to the *Chinese Medical Journal* in 1931, with an edition in Chinese since 1942.

Bibliography

Balme, H., *China and Modern Medicine* (1921). • Cadbury, W. W., and M. H. Jones, *At the Point of a Lancet* (1935). • Wong, Chimin K., and Wu Lien-The, *History of Chinese Medicine — Being a Chronicle of Medical Happenings in China from Ancient Times to the Present Period* (1932). China Group

China Outreach Movement

At the eighth annual meeting of the China Continuing Committee in Sep 1919, the North America Church World Movement aroused an ardent nationwide spirit among church leaders. Looking to China's situation at that time, each church promoted unity for the cause of missions, and the China Outreach Movement came into existence.

In December of the same year, a special meeting was called in Shanghai to bring together representatives from all of China's churches. There were 117 people in attendance at the meeting — approximately 50 percent Chinese and 50 percent Westerners. Lou Bingshen, honorary executive of the China Continuing Committee, talked about the North America Church World Movement's general condition. After much discussion, a unanimous conclusion was drawn, namely, that the China Outreach Movement should initiate a united evangelistic effort and hold a nationwide meeting with the theme "Jesus Is China's Savior." The suggestion was made to invite each Bible society* to help publish the National Phonetic Alphabet Bible so that by 1921 believers would not only be able to read the Bible, but also be able to read evangelistic advertisements in public places, in newspapers, and other media.

After the special meeting, the China Outreach Movement published a booklet at regular intervals. Approximately 100,000 copies of each issue were distributed. After the movement was initiated, many cities began to set up local outreach movements or united revival meetings. The movement's central organization was Zhonghua Xuxing Weiban Hui, under the leadership of the Church of China's chief executive. Financial aspects were taken care of by the North America Church World Movement. The China Outreach Movement imitated the American movement in its effort to perpetuate long-term revivalism and evangelism. However, after the 1930s, the movement gradually disappeared. China Group

Chinda Singhanet

(b. Chiang Mai, Thailand, 15 Jul 1902; d. 15 Aug 1985). Leading figure in the Church of Christ in Thailand (CCT).

Chinda's parents were Duangchuen and Chun Singhanet. He received his early education in Presbyterian missionary schools. He married Bunboon Boonchachaiya, and they had five children. He came under the special care of Dr. Edwin C. Cort, who placed him in the first class of the missionary Chiang Mai Medical School. Chinda was deeply influenced by the John Sung* revivals in Thailand* in 1939. He received further training at the Peking Union Medical College and at Johns Hopkins University, where he was studying when World War II* broke out. Because he was a Christian, Chinda was unable to work in government hospitals upon his return to Thailand, so he founded a private clinic which in 1945 became the first private hospital in Thailand. In 1955, he became director of the McKean Leprosarium and remained in that position until his retirement in 1967 (see Leprosy). He was instrumental in speeding the hospital's recovery from the war.

Chinda was the CCT's first representative to the World Council of Churches (1949). He once served as president of the Chiang Mai city council and was active in community service activities. He was an elder and leader of First Church, Chiang Mai.

Bibliography

Boonruem Singhanet, *Chinda Singhanet* (1985). • Chinda Singhanet, taped interview (1979) in the Payap University Archives, Chiang Mai, Thailand. • Papers of Chinda Singhanet, Payap University Archives, Chiang Mai, Thailand. Prasit Pongudom, translated by Herbert R. Swanson

Chinese Catholic Cultural Association

Organization established ca. 1940 to promote Catholic culture in China*.

During the Sino-Japanese War, Bishop Yu-Bin of Nanjing left his diocese and moved to Chungqieng. In order to help in the task of repelling the invader he founded the Chinese Catholic Cultural Association to promote and improve Chinese culture. The organization was inaugurated on Christmas Eve in 1941 at the Sino-French-Belgian-Swiss Students Union, with well over 1,000 Catholics attending. At the meeting, the constitution was approved and the first board of administrators was elected, among whom were Yu-Bin, Niu Yi-Wei, Kang Si-Cheng, Fang-Ho, Yuan Cheng-Bin, Sou Xue-Lin, Pan Chao-Ying, and eight others. They located their central bureau in Chungqieng, where they held their annual general meetings from 1942 to 1944. After the surrender of the Japanese in 1945, Yu-Bin returned to Nanjing, and, on 29 Dec 1946, the association held a combined fourth and fifth annual general meeting at Hung-Guang Middle School. The association's central bureau was then moved to Nanjing.

Yu-Bin was elected head of the administration board for five consecutive years; among the members of the fifth administration board were Ying Qian-Li, Chen Zhe-Min, Mao Zhin-Xiang, Fan Zheng-Bo, and Liu Hang-Chen. During its first five years the association received four awards of merit from the nationalist government.

China Group

Chinese Catholic Patriotic Association

Organization formed in Beijing in 1957 to direct a united effort by both Chinese Catholic clergy and laypeople to work for the benefit of the country under Communist control.

The association's aims were to unite the clergy and Catholic laypeople under the directives set out by the Chinese Communist Party and the People's Government to uphold patriotism, exalt the socialistic system, and abide by the constitution of the country, observing its laws, regulations, and policies. The association also sought actively to engage in building a twofold cultural structure, assist the government in actualizing the policy of liberty of religion, help clergy and laypeople cultivate a sense of patriotism and socialism, safeguard the legitimate rights of the church, promote social service, engage in self-supporting enterprises, develop a friendly relationship with Catholics worldwide, accelerate the unification of the country, fight despotism, and uphold world peace.

Archbishop Pi Sou-Shi was chairman of the association for two terms. He was succeeded by Bishop Zong Huai-De, who died in 1997.

In January 1998, it was decided to elect separate persons to the presidencies of the Catholic Church Episcopal Conference and the Chinese Catholic Patriotic Association, formerly jointly held by Bishop Zong. Bishop Fu Tieshan of Beijing is now president of the Patriotic Association, and Bishop Liu Yuanran of Nanjing is president of the Episcopal Conference.

Jean-Paul Wiest and China Group,
translated by Dufresse Chang

Chinese Churches in Indonesia

Evangelization among the Chinese in Indonesia was initiated in 1824 by J. Heurnius, who was then working for the *Verenigde Oost-Indische Compagnie* (United East-India Company, VOC; see Dutch United East-India Company). His solo attempt to reach the Chinese bore limited fruit.

Further ventures of evangelization among the Chinese began during the British occupation with the London Missionary Society (LMS) and the American Board of Commissioners for Foreign Missions (ABCFM). By the mid-19th c., there were several Dutch missions, namely, the *Genootschap voor In-en Uitwendige Zending* (GIUZ), working in Jakarta and its vicinity from 1851; the *Doopegezinde Zendingsvereniging* (DZV), in the Muria regency since 1854; the *Nederlandse Zendingsvereniging* (NZV), in West Java since 1884; and the *Zending der Gereformeerde Kerken in Nederland* (ZGKN), in south Central Java since 1892. In addition, evangelistic work was also conducted by various Chinese Christian individuals, e.g., Gan Kwee*.

Early in the 20th c., there were a number of evangelists from the Pentecostal Church (1919), the Tabernacle Church (1928), and others. A well-known missionary from the Tabernacle Church was R. A. Jaffray*, who energetically established the Chinese Foreign Missionary Union (CFMU) in 1929. Makassar (now Ujung Pandang) was later chosen as the central governing base as Jaffray proclaimed the Gospel among the scattered Chinese in Indonesia. For conducting evangelistic work, the CFMU maintained her relationship with the Christian and Missionary Alliance* (C&MA) in New York. Since 1928, the C&MA had also operated in many harbor towns of East Kalimantan*, the west coast of Sulawesi*, East Java, and Bali*.

The first Christian congregation established among the Chinese in Indonesia was the Indramayu parish in 1858. Slowly, several other Chinese congregations were formed in Jakarta (1868), Bogor (1888), and Bandung (1900).

In the next stage of development, some denominational Chinese Christian congregations were instituted. Among the newly founded church bodies were the *Tiong Hoa Kie Tok Kauw Hwee* (THKTKH) in West, Central, and East Java, with a Calvinistic background; the THKTKH in the Muria area (Mennonite); and the *Chung Hua Chi Tuh Chiao Hui* (CHCTCH, Methodist*), the *Sing Ling Kauw Hwee* (SLKH, Pentecostal), and the THKTKHs in Kalimantan, Sulawesi, Bangka, and Biliton (Gospel Tabernacle).

Other Chinese Christian congregations also known as THKTKH or by some similar name later joined with one of the above-mentioned church bodies, e.g., the THKTKH in Ambon merged with the Moluccan Protestant Church, while the Chinese Methodist Church in Sumatra united with the Methodist Church in Indonesia. The established churches continued to be distinctively Chinese. In the 1950s, they were encouraged to adopt more typically Indonesian names. Thus, the THKTKHs in West, Central, and East Java became the *Gereja Kristen Indonesia* (Indonesian Christian Church); the THKTKH in the Muria area became *Gereja Kristen Muria Indonesia* (Muria Christian Church in Indonesia); the CHCTCH became *Gereja Kristus* (Church of Christ); the SLKH became *Gereja Isa Almasih* (Church of Christ the Redeemer); and the THKTKHs from Kalimantan, Sulawesi, Bangka, and

Biliton became the *Gereja Kemah Injuil Indonesia* (Gospel Tabernacle Church in Indonesia).

This institutional development slowly brought about an independent style of worship. The use of the Indonesian language has become common for religious services in the churches in West and Central Java, the exception being some churches where the majority of the members are still Chinese-speaking.

Finally, there still remain some individual congregations as well as small clusters of churches which hold on to their Chinese identity, retaining a separate status on the basis of ethnic, cultural, or linguistic distinctions.

Bibliography

Pouw Boen Giok, *De kerkrechtlijke positie van een ethnisch bepaalde kerk in ander ethnisch bepaald milieu* (1952). • Hartono, Chris, *Gereja di Jawa Barat* (1979). • Van den End, T., *Ragi Carita* 2 (1989). • DGI *(Dewan Gereja-gereja di Indonesia), Buku Pedoman* (1973).

Chris Hartono

Chinese Coordination Center of World Evangelism

(CCCOWE). The CCCOWE was unanimously voted into existence by participants in the Chinese Congress on World Evangelization, 18-25 Aug 1976, Hong Kong*, and was legally established in October of that year. The congress, attended by 1,600 Chinese Christians from various traditions and countries, was a concrete expression of the collective conviction of the 70 Chinese leaders at the International Congress on World Evangelization, 16-25 Jul 1974, Lausanne, who were convinced of the urgency for Chinese churches to be fully involved in world evangelization, and of the necessity for them to unite and cooperate for the kingdom of God. Hence the intention of the CCCOWE is to promote unity and the growth of Chinese churches and to mobilize them for world evangelization.

The CCCOWE defines its role as: (1) servant: not to supervise, but to serve the churches; (2) bridge: to serve as a liaison between (a) the older and the younger generations; (b) the modern and the traditional; (c) the East and the West; and (d) various church traditions; (3) prophet: to stand in the forefront of the age, perceiving the world and the church with prophetic vision, and to share such insight with Chinese churches around the world.

The means to achieving the CCCOWE's objectives are: (1) research and information services, e.g., *World Chinese Church Survey* 1980, 1985, 1994; *Chinese Church Handbook* 1981, 1986, 1991; and an information service related to world evangelization, which the CCCOWE has been offering since 1993; (2) conferences and seminars (e.g., Chinese Congress on World Evangelization '76, '81, '86, '91; Chinese and Western Leadership Cooperation Seminar, Sep 1977; Chinese World Missions Seminar, Mar 1978, Jul 1993; Chinese Church Growth World Seminar, Oct 1978; Chinese Christian Communication Seminar, Oct 1983; Ethnic Chinese Congress on World Evangelism, Jul 1984; Chinese Culture and Gospel Seminar, Jul 1985; Seminar on Chinese Evangelism, Sep 1987; Consultation on Mission Strategy to the Hakka-Speaking Chinese, Feb-Mar 1989; Worldwide Ethnic Chinese Missions Seminar, Oct 1989; and World Chinese Grassroots Ministry Seminar, Jun 1990); (3) expertise service to churches; (4) publications, including (a) three periodicals: *Chinese Church Today,* a Chinese monthly, 16,000 copies per issue circulated in 62 countries; *Chinese Around the World,* an English monthly, 6,000 copies circulated in 48 countries; *Pastoral Sharing,* a bi-monthly for ministers and lay leaders, 5,500 copies circulated in 53 countries; (b) compendia of the various congresses, conferences, and seminars; (c) books related to world evangelization, e.g., *Kingdom Vision and Commission — A Reader of the CCCOWE Movement* (1989); *Who Cares for Them?: A Survey of China's Minorities* (1992).

Since inception, the CCCOWE has depended entirely on donations from individuals and churches. It is governed by a board of directors comprising a member from each of the district committees and a few co-opted senior leaders. A standing committee oversees the center on behalf of the board.

District committees are autonomous bodies, e.g., there is one in Hong Kong, two in Taiwan*, and six among Chinese communities in Canada. There were 29 such committees in 1974. In 1994, the number was 49.

The leaders of the CCCOWE come from various backgrounds: Philip Teng, founding chairperson of the board of directors and a Christian and Missionary Alliance minister; the late Wu Ming-Chieh, founding chairperson of the standing committee, and for many years bishop of the Lutheran* church in Hong Kong; Thomas Wang, founding general secretary and a Methodist* minister; and Chan Hay-Him, general secretary since 1986 and a Baptist minister.

Bibliography

CCCOWE, *CCCOWE Declaration* (1976). • *Kingdom Vision and Commission* (1989). • *Compendium of CCCOWE '76* (1977). • *Marching Toward A.D. 2000: A Survey of World Evangelization* (1991). • Lam, Timothy, *A Historical Study of the CCCOWE Movement (1976-1986)* (1990).

Chan Hay-Him

Chinese Home Missionary Society

During the summer of 1918, a retreat of many Chinese Christian leaders was held in Kiangsi, Lushan. During the retreat, a proposal was brought up by lay leaders requesting that mission work be carried out in Yunnan. As a result, the Chinese Home Missionary Society for Yunnan preparatory committee was formed, and Cheng Jing Yi* was elected its director. Cheng then invited 69 well-known Christians from all over China to sit on this committee, and 18 missionaries were invited as consultants. In the following spring, a team of seven, headed by pastor Ding Li Mei*, was sent to Yunnan, and some missionaries followed in their footsteps at a later date at their own expense.

In 1920, the preparatory committee decided to register the Chinese Home Missionary Society as a formal organization, and Cheng was elected its first chairman. A coordination department was set up in Hong Kong to recruit Chinese pastors and Christian medical doctors to serve in Yunnan, Kweichou, and Manchuria. A periodical, *Fu Yin Zhong*, was published on a monthly basis. After some years, the Chinese Home Missionary Society became a working committee of the National Christian Council. After Cheng's death in 1936, Jiang Chang Chuan and Zhou Zhi Yu* became chairmen. The society ceased its operation in 1958. China Group

Chinese People's Committee Against Opium

(Zhonghua Guomin Juduhui). In the 1920s, the Chinese Christian world established a corporation aiming at the banning of opium*. In early 1924, the Chinese National Christian Council, Chinese National Young Men's Christian Association*, Chinese Medical Society, Chinese Educational Society, and other Christian organizations came together. Taking advantage of the International Association to Restrict Opium organized by the League of Nations, they joined with 30 other groups from different social spheres and formed an organization called People to Oppose Opium, which advocated the banning of opium. It was officially formed on 5 Aug 1924. Roman Catholic scholar Ma Xiang Bo* was invited to be honorary chairman. The renowned Christian Xu Qian* served as chairman, and most of the positions of Chinese and English honorary secretaries and on the board of directors were assumed by Christians. Representatives were also sent to participate in the International Anti-Smoking Conference in Geneva.

After the setting up of the organization, a day was set apart to be the National Judu Day, when speeches and processions were held nationwide. The response was a success, and as many as 248 branches were formed in the first year of the organization. A proposal handed to the International Anti-Smoking Conference bore the signatures of four million members representing more than 3,000 groups. The Committee against Opium later became a member of the China Christian Council* and organized anti-smoking campaigns within the churches regularly. From 1927 on, the organization published an English bulletin, *Anti-Opium Quarterly.* This was terminated in 1931 because of the local situation.

China Group

Chinese Translations and Writings

Christianity in China* has, from its earliest days, depended heavily on Chinese Christian literature* for its propagation and development. The East Syrian monks (see Nestorianism) who first arrived in China in 635 began a program of translating Christian *sutras* in a scriptorium in Xian. Numerous scrolls containing Christian teachings in Chinese have been found in caves along the old Silk Route dating from the 7th to the 13th cs. When the first Roman Catholics* (Jesuits*) came to China, they, too, wrote numerous treatises and translated Western Christian works into Chinese. Many of these early writings were attempts to communicate the Christian message in Chinese cultural patterns (see Contextualization). These writings were so extensive and significant for the Roman Catholic Church that, in 1949, a summary of many of the books written or translated by the Jesuits during the Ming and Qing dynasties was published by a Jesuit priest Xu Zongze under the title *Mingquengjian Yiesouhuishi Yizhoutiyiao.* This collection of about 200 Jesuit writings was published to commemorate the 400th anniversary of the Society of Jesus.

When Protestants began their work in China in the 19th c., they immediately began to work on translating the Bible into Chinese (see Bible Translation). Robert Morrison*, later aided by William Milne*, finished his New Testament translation in 1813 and the complete Bible in 1819 (published in 1823). There would be numerous changes and re-translations in the next 180 years.

Roman Catholic Bible translations began in earnest a little later, in the early 20th c., but other liturgical and sacred writings have been very widely used. *The Six Kinds of Liturgies* (also called *The Collection of Important Scriptural Passages*) is more commonly used among Catholics in China than the Bible. The six liturgies are Morning Prayer, Evening Prayer, The Ritual of Mass, Sunday Worship Scripture, the Rosary, and Adoration of the Way of the Cross. The Sunday Worship Scriptures comprise seven themes, one for each day of the week: In Adoration of the Holy Trinity of the Lord of Heaven, Deliverance of the Souls of the Deceased from Purgatory, Showing Deep Gratitude to the Guardian Angel, Relying on Saint Joseph, Adoration of the Eucharist of Jesus, Adoration of the Sacred Heart of Jesus, and Showing Piety to the Benevolent Virgin Mary. The Rosary is designed for reciting prayers to the Virgin Mary. Adoration of the Way of the Cross is intended for believers seeking spiritual guidance from Jesus to overcome suffering.

A second important spiritual book, which for many Catholics in China is ranked second only to the Bible, is the early translation (1640/1774) of Thomas à Kempis's *The Imitation of Christ (Shizhupian).* The Portuguese Jesuit missionary Emmanuel Diaz* started this four-volume Chinese translation, naming it *Qiengshijinshu.* Diaz completed the first two volumes in 1640, the second two volumes being completed in 1774 by a Michael Jiang (possibly a pseudonym for French missionary Michael Denoit). In 1851 a four-volume common dialect translation was engraved.

Although the Protestant Old Testament had been translated before 1820, the full Roman Catholic Old Tes-

Chinese Translations and Writings

tament (with Apocrypha) was not completed until the 20th c. In fact, during the 20th c. Roman Catholic biblical work was quite extensive. The following are some of the more important Roman Catholic biblical translations of the 20th c.

Shengyongji, a new translation of the Psalms, was done in 1946 by Gabiele Maria Allegra with some Chinese Franciscan* priests in Beijing. In the same year a different translation was produced by a former Protestant, Wu Jingxiong, who converted to the Catholic church. Wu, working only with English, French, German, and Protestant Chinese translations, had his volume published by the Shanghai Commercial Press. Wu submitted his manuscript to Chiang Kai-shek, who at the time was head of the Chinese government in Chongqing, and Chiang read the manuscript through three times. The translation was considered excellent and chantable. The first cardinal of the Chinese Catholic church, Tian Gengxin, added a preface written by Archbishop Yu Bin of Nanjing. Allegra's Psalms were divided into five volumes. Each psalm has an introduction containing information about its author and the period in which it was written, accompanied by a brief summary giving an overall idea of its construction and an analysis with footnotes. The preface contains an explanation of the variety of Psalms, their position and purpose in the OT, and their theological and liturgical value. The end of the book contains a list of 27 works consulted. The book was well received, and 21 copies were sent to the pope, who sent a congratulatory letter.

The Books of Wisdom is a translation of the Roman Catholic portions of the OT done by the Bible Society of Saint Francis Hall, Beijing. The volume was translated from the Greek and was published in 1947 with the approval of Cardinal Tian Gengxin of Beijing, who mentioned in his preface that the translation was for trial use in the hope that, with further revision, it would become the new standard Chinese version. From the 1950s through the 1970s, virtually no biblical work was done in China.

New Bible, a translation of the four Gospels based on the *Jerusalem Bible,* was published by the Shanghai Diocese in May 1986. A record 300,000 copies were printed. Prior to its publication, Chinese Catholics used a translation from the Vulgate that had obscure language in many places and contained a number of inaccuracies.

Zongtudashilu is a translation of the Acts of the Apostles based on the *Jerusalem Bible* and published in 1991 by Guangqi Catholic Press in Shanghai. The 28 chapters of Acts, prefaced by an introduction, are divided into five main sections, namely, the Church in Jerusalem, the Early Church, Paul and Barnabas's Journey, Paul's Second Journey, and the End of Paul's Missionary Journey. Explanatory notes accompany every chapter. In the introduction, the editor remarked that this work would greatly facilitate the proper reading and understanding of the history of the early church.

Baolushuxin, the *Jerusalem Bible*–styled translation of Paul's 14 epistles, was translated by Sheshan Seminary and published in 1992 by Guangqi in Shanghai. The editor in his introduction said that, in comparison with former translations, this one had numerous improvements with regard to paragraphing, titles, and explanatory notes. He added that it would help in deepening the understanding of Paul's theological thought, his fidelity to Christ, and his zeal for the salvation of souls. It is hoped that the publication of this new translation of Paul's epistles will further promote Scripture reading among Chinese Catholics.

Shengjin Xinyue Quanji, a new translation of the New Testament, was done by Shenshan Catholic Seminary and published by Guangqi Press for the Diocese of Shanghai in 1994. This edition, sponsored by the United Bible Societies* and Joseph Homeyer, bishop of Hildesheim, Germany, is not for sale. The foreword to the volume makes its purpose very clear: "The New Testament greatly influences the living faith of believers. In it we find God the Son, Jesus Christ's Holy Word. It is hoped that every believer should have a copy in his hand to read, meditate, discuss and share with others every day, with a view of deepening the faith in, and knowledge of Christ, listening attentively to His teaching to strive to be a Christian worthy of the name, and to reflect in our everyday life our Christian faith, making large strides on the road of sanctity toward perfection to realize God's plan and the mission He has given us." These lines express both the purpose and concern of the translators and the publisher.

Equally important for the study of Christianity in China are the various Chinese Christian writings that have been produced since the first Jesuits began their study of Chinese in the late 16th c. The following publications, given in chronological order, are among the most important Chinese writings, written both by missionaries and Chinese Christian scholars.

The True Meaning of the Lord of Heaven. Originally titled "The True Idea of God," this Chinese work was authored by Matteo Ricci* and printed in Beijing in 1603, its cost subsidized by Feng Yingjing, a reputed intellectual, who also wrote its preface. The book was instrumental in the conversion of Chinese intellectuals such as Xu Guangqi* and others and was translated into Japanese in 1664. It was included in "The First Letters on Divinity," edited by Li Zhizao* in 1629, with more recent editions published by the Catholic Printing Press in Shanghai and Beijing.

In "The True Idea of God," Ricci incorporated Confucian* concepts to propagate Catholicism among the Chinese, especially the literati. Presented as a dialogue between a Chinese and a Western scholar, the book has eight chapters in which the Western scholar drew parallels between Confucian concepts and Catholic doctrines; e.g., Ricci quoted from the Confucian classics to suggest that the Confucian "Shangdi" is the same as the Christian "God" or "Lord of Heaven." Ricci said, "Going over a number of ancient writings, I find 'God' and 'Shangdi' in fact referring to the same Being but with different names." He invited people to peruse his draft manuscript when he was in Nanchang and Nanjing, and it took some time before the book was published.

Qike (Seven Prevailing Powers). This Catholic book on asceticism, published in 1614, was written by Didace de Pantoja*, who accompanied Matteo Ricci to Beijing. According to Catholic moralists, there are seven capital sins, namely, pride, envy, avarice, anger, gluttony, lust, and laziness. *Qike* talks about humility, tolerance, generosity, patience, temperance, chastity, and love of work — in short, all the virtues that prevail over the capital sins. In the preface, Pantoja admitted the difficulty of mastering Chinese, which is "completely different from what we ordinarily use. Through years of hard study, we only know it as children do."

Limadou Zhongguozhaji. This translation of Matteo Ricci's *De Christiana Expeditione apud Sinas* was done by Ho Gaoji, Wang Zuingzhong, and Li Shinggeng. Nicolas Trigault*, an Italian Jesuit missionary, on his return to Europe to give a report of the progress of missionaries in China, translated, from Italian to Latin, Ricci's draft reports on the spread of Catholicism in China at the end of the Ming dynasty, adding the recent events of Ricci's death (1610) and burial. The Latin version of *Christian Expedition to China* was published in 1615. It was soon translated into French, German, Spanish, and other languages. Ironically, the Chinese translation (from an English version), titled *Limadou Zhongguozhaji,* in two separate volumes, was not made until 1982, to mark the 400th anniversary of Ricci's arrival in China. The first edition was published by Zhonghua Press in 1983. The Chinese version includes an introduction in Chinese, translations of the introduction in the English version, and the 1978 French introduction comparing Trigault's Latin translation with Ricci's Italian original.

Book on the Interpretation of Catholic Doctrinal Questions (Dai Yi Bian). This first book on Catholic doctrines by a Chinese Catholic, Yang Tingjun, was written in 1621, 10 years after Yang's conversion from Buddhism*. Yang learned Catholicism from Jesuit missionaries and wrote the book in question-and-answer form to expound Catholic doctrines (God the creator, judgment, the Trinity, heaven and hell, the Lord of Heaven, the incarnation, etc.) and to dispel doubts about Catholicism. He compared Catholicism with Buddhism, refuting the Buddhist discipline of releasing and abstaining from killing living creatures and defending the Catholic rule on eating meat and fasting. He also answered questions on how to look at foreign missionaries. Dai Yi Bian is a valuable resource on the Chinese Catholic literati of the late Ming period.

The Lord Is the Sovereign of the Universe (Zhu Zhi Qun Zheng). This two-volume work in Chinese was written by Tang Ruowang (Johann Adam Schall von Bell*) when he was in Shaanxi, before his posting at the imperial court. It was printed in Jiangzhou in 1629. The book was highly acclaimed by two prominent Catholics, Ma Xiangbo and Ying Qianzhi, who both wrote a preface to the second edition in 1915. A third edition was published in 1919. In his book on the biographies and work of Jesuits in China, Pfister (Fei Lai Zhi) wrote that Schall von Bell translated only the first volume from a Latin work, and the second volume was completed by Martinus Martini* (Wei Kunagguo), who entered China in 1643, more than 20 years later than Schall von Bell.

Chaosheng Xueyiao. This earliest Chinese translation of St. Thomas Aquinas's famous *Summa Theologia* was done by Italian Jesuit missionary Louis Buglio*, who came to China in 1637, and by Portuguese Jesuit Gabriel de Magaihaens, who came in 1640. Buglio translated the first 26 treatises (Part 1). Six on divine nature, three on the Blessed Trinity, and one on the origin of species were printed in 1654. Buglio also wrote an introduction mentioning his regard of theology as the most valuable branch of all sciences, comparing other branches of learning to a flying moth wanting to reach the sun — an impossibility. In 1676 five treatises on angels and one on creation of the "visibles" were printed, followed by six treatises on the human soul, two on the corruptible body, and two on the governing of created things in 1677. Magaihaens translated six treatises (a portion of Part 3, four on the incarnation and two on the resurrection; these were printed in 1677. Magaihaens died in 1677 and Buglio in 1682, leaving the translation incomplete.

A Humble Offering in Time of Prosperity (Shengshichuyiao). This popular Chinese Catholic book on doctrines was written by French Jesuit missionary de Maillac, who was employed by the imperial court in Beijing, and his Chinese Catholic friend, Thomas Yang, during the persecution by the Qing dynasty. The title was deliberately chosen to avert attention from the hostile authorities. The five chapters of the book dealt with origins (knowing God), redemption, the soul (knowing oneself), reward and punishment, and heresy.

Unlike other books by Jesuit missionaries that used the *Wenyianwen* understood only by scholars, this book was written in the local dialect, *Beihuawen,* easily read by the less educated and understood when read to the illiterate. Some church historians believe that the *Shengshichuyiao* was instrumental in helping a large number of ordinary Catholics to persevere in their faith and survive the persecution of Emperor Yongzheng.

Quan Shi Liang Yan. This famous Chinese tract was written by Liang A-Fa* and edited by Robert Morrison*. The first printing was made in Canton in 1832. Since Tai Ping Tian Guo leader Hong Xiu Quan* was inspired by this tract and knew about Christianity, this tract became famous thereafter (see Taiping Rebellion). There were nine short essays. The first, taken from Gen 3, Isa 1, and Matt 5–7, discusses idol worship in China. The second explains John 3:17, Matt 19:23, Isa 8:19, and John 3:1-21. The third is a summary of Psalms, Isaiah, and Genesis and discusses the creator God and redemption in Christ. The fourth explains John 6:27, Rom 2:1, and Gen 6–7.

The fifth deals with Matt 16:26, 2 Cor 5:10, and John 3:16. The sixth discusses Isa 58, Eph 5, and the autobiography of the writer. The seventh talks of Matt 18:6, Heb 12:25, and 1 Cor 1–2 and 13 and explains that those people who walk righteously will receive a blessed afterlife, but those who reject the Gospel will experience a miserable afterlife. The eighth explains 1 Thess 5:22 and 2 Pet 3:10. The ninth uses 1 Tim 1 and 6 and 1 Thess 5 to talk of the final judgment. This tract was later revised and printed as a pamphlet. [Yao Min Quan]

True Religion Propagated with Approval (Zhengjiaofengchuan). This comprehensive collection of documents concerning the propagation of Catholicism in China was first printed at Our Lady of Mercy Church in Shanghai in 1877. Two reprints appeared in 1890 and 1900. The authorship was attributed to a Chinese priest, Peter Huang. It contains two official notices by local authorities at the end of the Ming dynasty (one from Jiangzhou, Shanxi, and the other from Jiannieng, Fujien), 118 documents from the Qing dynasty, including imperial decrees, ministerial reports, treaties, letters between the ministerial office and the French embassy, and the local mandarins' notice. In its preface it mentions that Emperor Wanli of the Ming dynasty granted permission to preach the Catholic religion in the provinces; Emperor Shunzhi of the Qing dynasty ordered the church to be built in Beijing; Emperor Kangxi gave written authorization to missionaries to preach the "true religion" in the provinces and allowed the people to build churches. Emperor Doaguang publicized, both in and out of the country, his permission to teach and learn the religion; Emperor Xianfong granted missionaries the liberty to rent or purchase land to build churches; Emperor Tongzhi granted tax exemption to Catholics in deference to the church ruling against taxes; Emperor Guangxu sympathized and favored the propagation of religion; etc. The author seems to attribute to the emperors a positive attitude toward the propagation of Catholicism in China, hence its title.

Civilization East and West. Authored by Ernst Faber of the Rhenish Missionary Society, this volume includes 73 chapters and was divided into five sections — humanity, righteousness, manners and customs, sciences, arts and commerce, and association — to introduce European Christian civilization to its Chinese readers. Faber associated these five sections with *ren, yi, li, zhi,* and *xin* to make it more attractive to Chinese scholars. For example the section on *ren* includes Christian doctrine and compassion and kindness for the weak. This book was first printed in Hong Kong* in 1884. The Society for the Diffusion of Christian and General Knowledge among the Chinese (SDCGKC) raised funds to reprint many copies of this book, and a set was presented to each of the principal Mandarins throughout Chin, which increased the impact of the book on society at large.

True Church Be Praised (Zhengjiaofengbao). This two-volume collection of historical proofs was written by Chinese priest Peter Huang to show the benevolence of the Chinese emperors toward the missionaries for their technological expertise. It was printed in 1884 at Our Lady of Mercy Church in Shanghai with the approval of Valentinus Garnier, bishop of Shanghai. The book explains the favor shown by the late Ming and early Qing emperors toward missionaries such as Johann Adam Schall von Bell, Ferdinand Verbiest*, and others whom they employed for their expertise in fixing the calendar and casting cannons. The author considered the emperors' respect of the missionaries' talents as a reflection of their high regard for the Catholic Church, hence the title of the book.

History of Christian Civilization. This book was written by Mackenzie and translated by missionary Timothy Richard* into Chinese. It was published by the SDCGKC in eight volumes. The book describes the Reformation in France, Great Britain, Germany, and Italy. It also sets aside one chapter each for missionary movements and the papacy. This book had a great impact on China. After its first printing in 1895, it was reprinted several times. In its first three years 20,000 copies were printed; the 4,000 copies reprinted in 1898 were sold out within two weeks. Missionaries had great expectations for this translation, considering it suitable for Mandarins and scholars and a useful foundation for reform.

War between China and Japan: How It Began and Ended. This book on the Sino-Japanese War (1894) was compiled by missionary Young John Allen* with Chinese scholars Cai Er Kang and others. The first volume, consisting of eight chapters, was printed in Apr 1896 and covered the background history of the war, the development of the war, the situation in northern Korea*, the process of negotiation, the comments made by Chinese and foreigners regarding the war and the negotiations, and the comments made by Allen and Cai and other scholars regarding the reformation of China in military, finance, and education. This book had many direct quotations from historical documents, official and military telegrams, official letters to and from the emperor, and texts of foreign treaties to show its authenticity. It also unveiled certain historical incidents. The book caused a great stir outside the government and was in great demand for almost 20 years. In the spring of 1897 the second volume of the book was released, and the third was released in the spring of 1900 (with alterations and corrections), providing a lengthy list of losses suffered by both China and Japan* during the war.

Women in All Lands. Compiled by American missionary Young John Allen*, this volume focused on a cultural campaign in women's studies. The book was divided into 200 sections, its length exceeding one million words, with more than 1,400 illustrations. This voluminous book was published by the SDCGKC. Young's Chinese assistant, Ren Bao Luo, a young man who had studied in the United States, did most of the translation. This book introduced the customs and systems relating to women, such as marriage, love, family*, offspring, paternal power, being a widow, divorce, adultery, and other topics. The book also touched on politics, law, education, and other customs and proclaimed that it was only through educating and liberating women that China could be saved from its declining status.

The World History. Coedited by Li Si Lun, John Lambert Rees, and China scholar Cai Er Kang, this book was published in three batches (1900, 1904, and 1905), each batch consisting of 10 volumes. Well illustrated, the book has a very useful list of Chinese-English technical terms that runs to 200 pages. The first volume in the first batch was on pre-history and went on to discuss the history of Egypt, Assyria, Persia, the Hebrews, and other ancient civilizations. The second and third batches were on the Middle Ages and the modern history of Great Britain, France, Germany, and Russia.

Brief History of Early Evangelistic Work in Beijing (Yanjing Kai Jiao Lue). Published in 1905 by the Xishiku Catholic Church of Beijing, this work is the Chinese translation of the book in French on the history of Catholicism by Favier* (Fan Guoliang). Favier himself requested someone to translate his book for the benefit of Chinese Catholics. It was published with a preface by Favier that recounted the process of its translation and publication. The book consists of three volumes. Volume 1 covers the period from the West Han, when Jesus was born, until the arrival of Matteo Ricci in the late Ming; Volume 2 covers Ricci until the arrival of the Vincentians* (Qian Si Hui); and Volume 3 covers the Vincentians until the twentieth year of the reign of Emperor Guangshu (1894), when missionaries were under the protection of the French ambassador Gerard.

Shengjiaoshilue. This first two-volume Chinese Catholic church history was first printed in the church at Zhangjiazhuang, Xianxian, Hebei, in 1905. It was written by Joseph Xiao, a Chinese Jesuit priest. The book presents church history in three main periods: early, middle, and late centuries. The "early centuries" covers four centuries from the founding of the church by Christ to the fall of the Western Roman Empire, focusing on the spread of the faith by Jesus' disciples, the persecutions suffered under different Roman emperors, Emperor Constantine's conversion, and the situation of the church. The "middle centuries" begins with the conversion of barbarians until the 15th c., focusing on the successive conversion of the barbarian invaders, the various states in Europe turning Catholic, the Crusades, Catholicism during the Yuan dynasty in China, and the church in Europe throughout the 12th and 13th cs. The "late centuries" starts with Martin Luther's Protestantism until the 19th c., highlighting the development of the New Church, the Council of Trent, the founding of the Society of Jesus, the church under Pope Pius V, the spread of the church in South America and Asia, missionary work in China from the end of the Ming Dynasty until the Boxer Rebellion in 1900, and the invasion of Beijing by the eight Western allies. Written from the viewpoint of the church, a third of the book focuses on the events that affect China. It was revised for the third edition in 1919. Catholic middle schools used it as a text for church history.

The History of Kiangnan Mission (Jiangnan Chuanjiaoshi). This book is the Chinese translation by Ding Zongjie and a few other Chinese priests of the French *Histoire de la Mission du Kaingnan,* by J. de la Serviere, a French Jesuit who came to Shanghai in 1909. The original work was meant to be in three volumes, giving the history of Jesuit missionaries in Shanghai and the two provinces of Jiangsou and Anhui from 1839 to 1900. The first two volumes, covering 1839-78, were printed by Shanghai Tushanwan Press in 1914 with the permission of Prosper Paris, bishop of Shanghai, but he withheld permission to print the third volume since he did not deem it prudent to publish a history in which some of the people involved were still living. The work was not translated into Chinese until 1979, when the Catholic church in Shanghai was allowed to resume its former activities. The historical value of the work was recognized by the Shanghai Translation Press, which published it in Jun 1983.

Yishibao. Yishibao was the Catholic newspaper that first appeared in Oct 1915. It was founded by Belgian Lazarist* Vincent Lebbe*, who had adopted Chinese nationality when he took his residence in Tainjing. During the year of the flood in Hebei the newspaper did its utmost to raise funds for the flood victims. In May 1916 a branch press was established in Beijing. In Jul 1937, when the Japanese took Tianjing, the publication of *Yishibao* was stopped. However, in the winter of the same year, Msgr. Yubin, of the diocese of Nanjing, reorganized *Yishibao* in Kunming. In Mar 1940 Kuming *Yishibao* removed to Chunqieng. In Apr 1945 Xian *Yishibao* appeared. After the victory over Japan, Beijing *Yishibao* returned on 18 Sep 1945; so did that of Tianjing on 1 Dec. On 15 Jun 1946 the paper reached its readers in Shanghai once more. During this period *Yishibao* had on its five-member board of trustees Yubin, Wang Wencheng, bishop of Nanchun Diocese, Sichuan, and three others, with Yubin as chairman. Each district had its own chief director of publication. Shanghai had the largest circulation, with 15,000 for Chunqieng and 30,000 for Tianjin.

The Study of the History of the Propagation of Catholicism in China. Written by Xiao Ruose, a Chinese Jesuit, the book is about the origin and development of the Chinese Catholic Church and was thrice printed between 1923 and 1937. Typeset in the Catholic church in Zhang Jia Zhaung, Xian County, Hebei, it contained eight volumes, arranged chronologically according to the Chinese dynasties: the events in the Han (206 B.C.E.–220 C.E.) and Tang (618-937) dynasties, Yuan dynasty (1271-1368), early Ming to late Wan Li (1573-1620), Wan Li to late Chongzhen (1628-1644), late Ming and early Qing, early Qing to late Kangxi, Yongzheng to late Xianfeng, and late Xianfeng to late Guangshu.

In the first volume, the author remarked that the claim of some archeologists that St. Thomas* had preached the Gospel in China was plausible, and that even if the apostle himself did not reach China personally, his disciples would have done the job. Thus the entry of Christianity into China may be traced to the Han dynasty, an appreciably different view from that of the dominant position that Christianity first reached China during the Tang period.

Outline of the History of Philosophy. This first concise book on Western philosophy, edited and written by Chinese Jesuit Xu Zhongze, was published in 1930 by Holy Religion Magazine Publishing House, Xujiahui, Shanghai. The introduction contained an exposition of the definition, system, and different schools of philosophy, a systematic classification, and the different stages in the history of philosophy. Part 1 of the book contained Greek philosophy before Socrates, philosophy from Socrates to Aristotle, and philosophy afterward. Part 2 discussed scholasticism from the 8th to the 12th cs., the philosophy of the Arabs and Jews, 13th-c. scholasticism, 14th- and 15th-c. philosophy, and the Renaissance. Part 2 enumerated the theories of 32 renowned philosophers, including Bacon, Locke, Hume, Spencer, Kant, Hegel, and Comte, but not Karl Marx, and discussed 18th- and 19th-c. philosophy.

The History of the Propagation of Catholicism in China in the Sixteenth Century. This translation of French Jesuit H. Bernard's original work in French was done by Xiao Junhua (who did not mention the title of the original). Bernard (Pei Huaxing) had taught for several years in Gianjin College of Industry and Commerce (the third Catholic university established in China). Among his works was a book, *Aux portes de la Chine, Les missionaries du 16 siècle,* published in Tianjin in 1933, which was most likely the original of the translation. The book comprises two volumes. Book 1 has eight chapters based mainly on letters sent to Europe by missionaries who went to the Orient (1514-81) when Portugal and Spain were expanding overseas. Bernard discusses how the newly established Society of Jesus, the Franciscans*, Dominicans*, and Augustinians* had successively dispatched their missionaries with little success to China. Book 2 deals mainly with the new method initiated by Valignano* (Fan Lian), who specified that missionaries entering China should learn the Chinese language and script and become "sinicized." Bernard praised Ricci's unflinching willpower to stay on alone and his innovative methods of evangelism through literature and conversational meetings.

The Biography of Jesus. This was the first biography of Jesus written by a Chinese — Zhao Zi Chen — who served on the faculty of Yenching Graduate School of Religion, Yenching Theological Seminary, for many years. The author made full use of the limited text on the life of Jesus, filling in details not in the text, and provided his own interpretation of difficult passages. Zhao portrayed Jesus and the worship of Jesus from the point of view of a Chinese and refused to allow Western theology or doctrines to veil the real Jesus. This book was first printed in 1935. In 1988, in commemoration of the 100th birthday of Zhao, the book was reprinted by the Shanghai Academy of Social Science.

Christianity and Chinese Culture. Written by the principal of Yenching University, Wu Lei Chuan, this book was printed by the Shanghai Youth Association Press in 1936 and was reprinted several times. In the beginning chapter, Wu makes a comparison between Christianity and Chinese culture, pointing out that by looking at the thinking of Jesus, Christianity is a religion that calls for revolution. He saw a distinction between academic thinking and the sociopolitical side of Chinese culture. According to Wu, Christianity should wash away its mistakes in history and return to its original sociorevolutionary spirit, and Chinese culture should work to create a new society. Then Christianity would have its unique role to play. This unique book quoted from many thinkers and was highly regarded by Chinese intellectuals for many years. Wu was a Ju-ren, Jin-Shi, during the Qing dynasty. He was the editor of *Hanlin-yuen,* and after the revolution of 1911 he took a post in the ministry of education.

Hymns of Universal Praise (Pu Tian Song Zan). This hymnbook was compiled by the Protestant Church of China in the 1930s. Six denominations — the Chinese Christian Church, Chong Hua Sheng Kung Hui, Methodist Episcopal Church (North), North China American Board of Commissioners for Foreign Missions), East China Baptist Church, and Methodist Episcopal Church (South) — formed an editorial committee and selected 512 hymns for the hymnbook.

Well-known figures on the committee included Liu Ting Fang, Yang Yin Liu, and Fan Tian Xiang. The aim of the hymnbook was to present the praise and enthusiasm of the Chinese church. A few criteria were set: (1) to try to accommodate all the popular hymns in these six denominations; (2) to include quality hymns: those rich in content, beautiful in word and tune, fine in translation, with attention to the phonetic characteristics of the Chinese language; (3) to include hymns with Chinese tunes (there are 72 hymns using Chinese tunes, either of ancient or folk songs or recent compositions). The hymnbook was published by the Chinese Literature Society for China in Shanghai in 1936. [Cao Sheng Jie]

The Biographies of Jesuits to China. This book is a Chinese translation of French Jesuit missionary Louis Pfister's *Notices biographiques et bibliographiques sur les jesuites de l'ancienne mission de Chine* done by Feng Chengjun, a Chinese historian of modern China. Feng graduated from the department of law, Paris University, France. Believing that the Jesuits had contributed more than just the spread of the Gospel in the late Ming and early Qing dynasties (1522-1773), Feng was eager to translate Pfister's two-volume work, which appeared in 1932 and 1934 respectively. He originally intended to publish each part as the translation was completed; instead, a one-volume translation containing more than 50 biographies was published by the Commercial Press in

1938. He mentioned in the preface that "No unnecessary additions or deletions were made in the translation except some slight abridgment in places where numerous mentions of miracles appeared and due corrections made on some accidental glaring mistakes therein."

Biography of Jesus. This book is a Chinese-edited translation of French Catholic Fr. P. L. Christiani's three-volume *Jesus-Christ, Fils de Dieu, Sauveur.* French Jesuit A. Haouisee, vicar apostolic of Shanghai, considered Christiani's work suited to the needs of Chinese believers and with the author's consent assigned his Chinese secretary, Ding Zhongjie, to translate volumes 1 and 3. Volume 2 was done by Wang Changzhi, a Chinese priest, member of the Society of Jesus, and Ma Siguang of Nanjing Diocese. The translation was completed in 1938 and published by the Tu Shan Wan Publishing House, Shanghai.

Christiani presumed that Chinese believers would be unfamiliar with the history and customs of Palestine and the issues arising from the Bible in Europe and the West. He therefore edited the original for the translation, changing headings and omitting quotes, the introductions to each volume, and the appendices and replacing them with a listing of the important events in the life of Jesus and a catalogue of Scripture readings for the Lord's Day and important religious festivals throughout the year.

Zhongguo Tianzhujiao Chuanjiashigailuing. This 11-chapter book by Xu Zongze, published in 1938 by Shanghai Tushanwan Press, contains articles on the propagation of Catholicism in China. The first 10 chapters are reproductions of 10 long articles on the coming of Catholicism to China written between 1936 and 1937 in the *Catholic Review* when Xu was its chief editor. Chapter 11 is an appendix titled "*Zhongguo Shengjio Zhanggu Shiling*" ("The Compendium of Related Historical Facts with Regard to the Catholic Church in China") and contains 99 shorter articles written from materials obtained from non-Chinese books on the Chinese Catholic Church.

The History of Christianity in China. Written by Wang Zhi Xin, this book was published by the Youth Association Press in Shanghai in 1940. The history of Christianity in China was divided into four periods: the "Nestorians" in the Tang dynasty, Christians under the Mongols, Catholics in the Ming dynasty, and the Protestant church and Catholic Church after Dao Guang. The author pointed out that Christian doctrines could accommodate Chinese culture, and Christianity has done more good than bad in China's history. This was the first book written by a Chinese on the history of the Christian church. Wang had earlier taught in Nanking Theological Seminary, the University of Shanghai, and Nanjing Union Theological Seminary.

Christianity and Literature. Authored by Zhu Wei Zhi, this book was printed by the Shanghai Youth Association Press in 1941 and was reprinted many times. This was the first reference book ever written on the history of Christian literature in China. This book surveys the history of Christianity and its literature and explains the relationship of hymns, prayers, and evangelism to literature, as well as explores how poems, novels, and drama drew from Christian resources. The author had two basic points: (1) ever since the beginning of history, arts have been inseparable from religion; and (2) realism and romanticism were two poles in the history of literature for a long time, but after frequent conflicts they have come to appreciate each other's greatness.

Saint Ignatius Loyola. This Chinese translation by Yang Di, a Chinese non-Jesuit priest of Anhui diocese, was made from French Jesuit P. Victor Barjon's *St. Ignatius of Loyola.* Wu Yingfeng, a Chinese Jesuit and editor in chief of *Sheng Xin Bao* (Sacred Heart Paper), had studied in France and was a schoolmate of Barjon. To commemorate the occasion of the 400th anniversary of the establishment of the Society of Jesus by Saint Ignatius Loyola in 1940, Wu asked Yang, then a student at the Xujiahui monastery, to translate Barjon's book for *Sheng Xin Pao.* The translation first appeared in installments in the paper, and was published in book form in 1941 by Tu Shan Wan Publishing House, Shanghai.

Gaozhong Jiaoli Jiangyi. This represented the first set of Chinese textbooks for teaching religion and was written by Chinese priest Wang Rensheng. It was published in 1943 by Tushangwan Catholic Press, Shanghai. The author, originally from a non-Catholic family, was baptized while attending Xuhui College. Upon graduation he joined the Society of Jesus and was ordained a priest in 1940. At that time all Catholic middle schools both for boys and girls required religion classes and written religious knowledge examinations as part of students' junior and senior final examinations. All those who succeeded were awarded Shanghai Diocese Religious Knowledge Middle Level Certificates. In order to obtain a uniformity of teaching religion in Catholic middle schools, this Jesuit priest used the well-known catechism by A. Boulenger, a French scholar in that field, to help write his set of textbooks. It comprises three books covering dogma, commandments, grace, and sacraments.

A Look at the Vatican (Fa Di Gang Yi Pie). This informational booklet on Chinese Catholicism was published in 1946 in Beijing by Shang Zhi Publishing House. The author, Zhang Tian Song, was editor of the *Nanjing Catholic Daily (Yi Shi Bao).* The book contains 87 themes introducing well-known premises of the Vatican, the pre-Vatican territories and their demise, the Lateran Treaty, the organization of the church, the church's relationship with other countries, Vatican museums and libraries, and so on. It also contains 20 pictures and maps of the Vatican territory of 1860 and two city maps of Vatican City. The preface of the book is a long article by the well-known Catholic church historian Fang Hao on the relationship between China and the Vatican. The appendix contains three short articles on the first Catholic bishop of China, Tian Keng Xin, China's ambassador to

Chinese Translations and Writings

the Vatican, Wu Jing Xiong, and the Vatican ambassador to China.

The Progress of Christianity. Written by Chinese Christian leader Zhao Zi Cheng, the manuscript was completed in 1943, but the book was delayed until 1947, when it was finally published by the Youth Association Press. The book has two sections: dogmatic theology, and Christianity and Chinese culture. The author intended to eradicate the influence of foreigners and build up a theology belonging to China. Zhao thought Christianity and Chinese culture could communicate with one another, the intersection being ethics and the arts. In the final chapter the author touched on the issue of Christianity and the world from the standpoint of Christian ethics. He thought the relationship between countries should be based on justice and peace. This point came out of Zhao's personal experience, for this book was nurtured while he was imprisoned by the Japanese. The book had a great influence among Chinese intellectuals.

Saint Augustine's Confessions. The Chinese translation of the Latin *Confessions,* by Aurelius Augustinus (354-430), was done in 1950 by Chinese Jesuit Wu Yingfeng and published by Tu Shan Wan Publishing House, Shanghai. The translation sold out in less than three months. A second edition, with a foreword by Wu, was printed in 1954 to commemorate the 1600th anniversary of Saint Augustine's birth.

These Fifty Years. This is a memoir of Wang Ming Dao*, a famous Protestant Church Christian pastor in China. It was published in 1950 when he turned 50. During that year Wang began to write his memoir in May, and the manuscript was released portion by portion (seven chapters) when it appeared in his own quarterly periodical, *Spiritual Food.* An article titled "Remember Mother" was added as an appendix when the book was published. In the book Wang traced how he was converted at age 14 and started to hold meetings at home at age 25. The meeting slowly grew into a church, *Ji-du-jiao Hui-tang* (Christian Church). During the Japanese occupation, he refused to join the North China Christians Association (see World War II).

The Approach That the Protestant Church of China Should Endeavor in the Construction of the New China. After the inauguration of the New China, the Protestant Church of China proclaimed a manifesto to enable Chinese to have a clearer understanding of Christianity in China. This manifesto was often called the "Three-Self Manifesto." It proclaimed that, while Christianity was spread in China, it was linked inevitably in certain ways to imperialism. The manifesto declared that the most important task of the Protestant Church in China was to follow the government's policy of anti-imperialism, antifeudalism, and antibureau-capitalism and to support the building up of a new nation that was independent, democratic, peaceful, united, and prosperous. The manifesto also requested all churches and organizations to clear up all the imperialistic influence within themselves and head toward self-support, self-government, and self-propagation. This manifesto, signed by Wu Yao Zong and 40 other Christian leaders, was dated 28 Jul 1950. The manifesto also sent a circular to all Christians in the nation and called for their approval through signing the manifesto. On 23 Sep 1950 the *People's Daily* printed the full article of this manifesto and the first batch of 1,500 signatures. By 1954 the number of signatures on the manifesto exceeded 410,000.

Tianzhujiao Jiaoyi Tantao. This is a contemporary book on Catholic doctrine written in Chinese by Jesuit father Wang Changzhi, originally from Shanghai, who spent years writing and editing Chinese Catholic literature. Early in 1949 he was told to accompany young seminarians from the Chinese department at the Jesuit university to the Philippines*. When he settled in the Philippines, he began writing a three-volume work with the title *Exploring Catholic Doctrine* and had it published. In 1988 a local diocesan priest from Shanghai made a synthesis of the book and had it published by Guangqi Catholic Press, Shanghai. The publisher, in an explanatory note, expresses the purpose of the volume: "It is hoped that the brothers and sisters who have already believed in God, having read this book, will have greater appreciation and be strengthened in their faith. Those who do not believe in God but wish to understand the Catholic church, on reading this book, will not fail to understand the doctrine and belief of the Catholic church."

Catholic Church in China. This is an irregular publication of the Chinese Catholic Patriotic Association* and the Bishop's deputation of the Chinese Catholic Church started in Nov 1980 with about four issues per year. The contents are mainly expositions of the "love-country, love-church" principles, the propagation of independence and self-government for the Chinese Catholic Church, cooperation with the government in the implementation of the policy on religious freedom, the financial and spiritual contributions to the country made by clergy and believers, Catholic doctrines and practice, church history, and news on the activities of the local patriotic associations and religious affairs committees.

Chinese New Hymnal (Zan Mei Shi-Xin Pian). This hymnal was published by the China Christian Council in Shanghai. It was a compilation by the China Christianity Hymnal Committee, which selected a total of 400 hymns. Since the hymnbook is meant for all denominations, the committee adopted the principle of mutual respect and accommodation, with an emphasis on Chinese style. A quarter of the hymns collected were either composed by Chinese or employed a Chinese-style tune. Fifty-six of the hymns were new compositions. The total number of copies printed has exceeded six million. In 1993 *The Compilation of the Chinese New Hymnal* was published by Wang Shen Yin.

Ancient Chinese Christianity and the Jews at Kaifeng. Written by Jiang Wen Han and published in Shanghai by

Zhi-shi Press in 1982, this book consists of three essays: "Nestorian," "The *ye-li-ke-wen* in the Yuen Dynasty," and "The Jews in China." The author used earlier historians, discovered new materials, and used new methods to touch on the three topics. He also made a comparative religion study among the three. The number of reference books that appeared in the bibliography amounted to nearly 200.

Brief History of the Church (Tanzhujiao Jianshi). This is a Chinese translation by Jesuit father Meichengqi of Jean Baptiste Duroselle and M. M. Mageur's *Histoire du Catholicisme*. Published by Guanqi Catholic Press, Shanghai, in 1989, the book has nine chapters, with annotations, beginning with the statement that the Catholic Church is universal and apostolic and continuing with a global account of events from the time of Jesus until Pope John Paul II.

SCOTT W. SUNQUIST and THE CHINA GROUP, with translations by DUFRESSE CHANG

Chins

The Chin group of the Union of Myanmar* live mainly in the Chin State, the northwestern hilly part of the country. The population of the Chins within the Chin State is about 300,000. The Chins are believed to be one of the earliest immigrant groups that came into Myanmar during the first and second centuries A.D. Many Chin groups call themselves "Zo," "Mizo," or "Cho," which supposedly means "the highlanders" or the "hill people." The name "Chin" is believed to connote "a friend" or "fellow people" in Burmese. Their national emblem is the hornbill bird, which symbolizes loyalty and bravery according to Chin legends.

Chins were characterized by Western observers as "feasting people" and "fierce fighters" because the life of a traditional Chin was full of religious rituals, occasional and seasonal feasts, and tribal wars which made them good fighters. Accordingly, their fighting ability was important in the anticolonial movement: although the British officially announced their annexation of Myanmar in 1886, they came to control the Chin Hills only in 1889 after fierce fights and tiresome negotiations.

Remarkable social and religious actions were taken by the Chins at the turn of the 20th c. due to the British colonial administration and the arrival of the American Baptist* missionary couple, Laura and Arthur Carson, on 15 Mar 1899, with the resulting spread of Christianity among the Chins. When the British administration made slavery illegal, many Chins adopted their former slaves as their nearest relatives.

When missionaries strictly prohibited the celebration of the traditional seasonal and occasional feasts, Chin Christians creatively celebrated Christian feasts such as Christmas and Easter in the form of their traditional feasts, that is, socially enjoyable and religiously meaningful.

As a result of the deportation of missionaries and the resurgence of Burmese nationalism* during the 1960s, many Chin Christians resumed celebrating some of their important traditional feasts in Christian forms. For example, when they celebrate the New Year festival, which lasts seven days, a religiously significant day like the "day of the dead" is set aside as the "day of consolation" for recently bereaved families; theological discussion focuses on death and Christian hope.

Chin Christians creatively use their traditional tribal/ethnic spirit as the source of organizing and implementing ambitious and effective racial/ethnic-based mission enterprises. The "Chins for Christ in One Century" (CCOC) mission, launched in 1983, is a good example. This project is probably the most ambitious and effective mission work ever implemented in Myanmar. The same spirit of tribal and racial competition takes another form in Christian leadership promotion, that is, excellence in leadership, good education, and evangelistic outreach. Despite some negative effects (unnecessary splits among Chin Christians), this has been the main cause of the emergence of forceful leaders among the Chins. It is seen as a blessing in disguise or a creative use of cultural dynamics as a means of practical Christian living in the contemporary world.

Bibliography

Carey, Bertram S., and H. H. Tuck, *The Chin Hills: A History of the People, Our Dealing with Their Customs and Manners and Gazettes of Their Country*, Vol. I (1896). • Harvey, G. E., *History of Burma* (1982). • Johnson, Robert G., *History of American Baptist Chin Mission*, Vols. I and II (1988). • Laisum, David, *God's Revelation in Chin Tradition* (B.D. thesis, Myanmar Institute of Theology) (1988). • Lehman, Frederick K., *The Structure of Chin Society* (1963).

DAVID LAISUM

Chit Maung

(b. Okkan, Burma, 1 Apr 1905). Burmese Baptist* theological educator and church leader.

A member of the Kayin (Karen*) tribe, Chit Maung was trained to be a lawyer but entered the ministry instead. He received his theological education at Northern Baptist Theological Seminary in Chicago, Illinois, United States, graduating in 1935. He served as headmaster of a mission high school from 1935 to 1942, when the Japanese occupied Burma. After World War II*, Chit Maung led in the reestablishment of two major theological institutions located at Insein, eight miles north of Rangoon (Yangon): Karen Theological Seminary (Kayin Baptist Theological Institute) and Burma Divinity School (Myanmar/Burma Institute of Theology).

Chit Maung's service to the church was inclusive in scope and not confined to one race or denomination. He was active in the Burma Council of Churches (Myanmar Council of Churches) and, in earlier years, the Young Men's Christian Association* (YMCA). He played an important role in the upgrading of theological* education in Burma and was one of the Asian leaders who brought the Association of Theological Schools in South East Asia (ATSSEA) into existence in 1957. After retiring officially in 1977, Chit Maung continued to be active in the ministry of teaching and preaching. EH WAH

Chiu Ban It, Joshua

(b. Penang, Malaya, 16 Jul 1918). First Asian bishop of Singapore*; introduced charismatic* renewal to the diocese of Singapore.

After completing law studies in London, Chiu trained for the Anglican* ministry and was ordained a priest in England in 1946. From 1947 to 1950, he practiced as a barrister in Penang. He served in Singapore at St. Andrew's Cathedral and St. Hilda's Church from 1950 to 1955 and then as vicar of Selangor from 1955 to 1959.

After three years as home secretary to the Australian Board of Missions, Chiu worked with the World Council of Churches (WCC) in Geneva (1962-65) and then as a fellow of St. Augustine's College, Canterbury, Central College of the Anglican Communion (1965-66).

On 1 Nov 1966, Chiu was consecrated the first Asian bishop of the Anglican diocese of Singapore and Malaya, and, after the division of the diocese in 1970, he continued as bishop of Singapore. During his episcopate, Bishop Chiu was active as chairman of the Anglican Council of the Church of Southeast Asia, member of the Anglican Consultative Council, and a vice-chairman of the East Asia Christian Conference. He was also a member of the Central Committee of the WCC (1968-75).

Chiu was responsible for introducing the charismatic renewal movement into his diocese beginning in 1972. The consequent revival resulted in an unprecedented membership growth as well as in the establishment of many new congregations throughout the island. His influence in this respect extended beyond the Anglican church to other mainline denominations. He retired from the diocese in Oct 1982.

Bibliography

Diocese of Singapore Annual Report. • *Rt. Rev. Joshua Chiu Ban It: Bio-Data* (Church Archives, Trinity Theological College, Singapore). FRANK LOMAX

Choi Byung Hun

(b. Che Chun, Chung Chung Province, 16 Jan 1858; d. 13 May 1927). First Korean minister of Jung Dong Methodist Church, Seoul; theologian of indigenous religions of Korea*.

Choi accepted Christianity as he was reading the Christian tracts given out by a Methodist* missionary, L. H. Jones. He was baptized by H. G. Appenzeller*, an American Methodist missionary pastor of Jung Dong Church. In the same church where he was baptized, Choi organized Epworth League for youth outreach and for the independence movement. He was an active member of the Independence Club. He was founding editor of *Shinhak Wolbo* (The Theological Monthly), the first Korean scholarly journal for theological studies.

In 1902, when H. G. Appenzeller died in a boat accident on his way home after a Bible* translation retreat in the south, Choi succeeded him as the first Korean minister of the Jung Dong Church. Choi was appointed as a professor at Union Methodist Theological Seminary in 1923 to teach world religions. He published more than 60 books both in Chinese and Korean to explain the nature of Christianity and Christian doctrines. His major contribution to Korean theology was his scholarship in comparative religions. He is remembered as the first Korean theologian to indigenize of the Gospel into the Korean religious mind-set. He set the tradition of Korean Methodist scholars' endeavors in "indigenization theology." (See also Contextualization.)

DAVID SUH, with contributions from LEE DUK JOO; original translated by KIM IN SOO

Chok Loi Fatt

(b. ?; d. ?). One of the first local catechists engaged by the Anglican* Church in Singapore*.

Though appointed primarily as a catechist, Chok became involved in the St. Andrew's Mission School in 1864 as the work of the school grew. The school was started in 1862, catering mainly to the Chinese-speaking community. In fact, Chok served as principal of the school for some eight years.

Besides Mandarin and Hokkien, Chok was also fluent in other main Chinese dialects: Cantonese, Hakka, and Hainanese. His singular usefulness was probably the reason most of the other early catechists were dismissed when the mission experienced financial difficulties after 1866. Later, in 1876, Chok also labored in the Jurong area when the Hokkien-speaking work of the mission extended there.

Bibliography

Sng, Bobby E. K., *In His Good Time* (1993).

JOHN CHEW

Chosen (North Korea) Christians Federation

Only association of Protestant clergymen in North Korea.

Founded by Kang Yang Wook* in 1946, the Chosen Christians Federation was organized by the pro-Communist Protestant clergymen to support the forthcoming establishment of the Communist government of Kim Il Sung (1948-94). Those who opposed and refused to join the federation were harassed by the North Korean police, arrested, imprisoned, and finally executed without trial during the Korean War* (1950-53).

The North Korean government's yearbook of 1948 listed the membership of the federation at 85,118. There has been no official number listed in any North Korean publication since. Since 1985, the federation has invited world ecumenical leaders to North Korea to worship together in the newly opened Bong Soo Church. The leaders of the federation, headed by Kang Yong Sup, a son of Kang Yang Wook, attend international meetings to dialogue on the issues of reunification and the role of Christians in Korea and around the world. Since 1974, the federation has been a religious branch of the Democratic Front for the Reunification of the Fatherland.

David Suh with contributions from Kim Heung Soo, translated by Kim In Soo

Christian and Missionary Alliance

The Christian and Missionary Alliance (C&MA) was founded by A. B. Simpson (1843-1919) of New York in 1897 as an amalgamation of the Evangelical Missionary Alliance and the International Christian Alliance, which had been set up in 1887.

The C&MA regards mission as the responsibility of the whole church. It retains characteristics of the Holiness movement of which it was part. It believes in the creation of indigenous churches including the "three-self" formulation (see John Nevius). Caution about the social dimensions of mission has been modified by the reality of human suffering. Local Bible schools are basic to its mission strategy. The C&MA has sought to transfer its missionary passion to other cultures and to future generations through the education of the children of missionaries.

Simpson, as a true postmillennialist, believed that completing the missionary task would "bring back the King." His New York Missionary Training Institute (founded in 1882, later Nyack College and Alliance Theological Seminary) sent missionaries to India* in 1887, China* in 1888, Japan* in 1891, and the Philippines* in 1902. The vision was to go to "unoccupied" areas, including Tibet and Vietnam*. Robert Alexander Jaffray* (1873-1945) was a key leader in South China and Vietnam and then in Indonesian Borneo. From 1906, Pentecostal* gifts were a contentious issue, and some missionaries transferred to new Pentecostal missions. In Japan*, Mabel Francis (1880-1975) worked for 56 years from 1909 and founded 20 C&MA churches.

In China, Shanxi (Shansi) in the north was assigned to Swedish C&MA missionaries. By 1896, there were 60 workers, but many were killed by Boxers, and the area was later transferred to the China Inland Mission (Overseas Missionary Fellowship). In South China, the C&MA became the biggest missionary board in Guangxi Province, with headquarters in Wuzhou, along with the Alliance Bible School (now the Alliance Seminary in Hong Kong) and the South China Alliance Press. The *Bible Magazine* edited by Jaffray circulated among Chinese communities around the world.

After a number of attempts to enter Vietnam, in 1916 Jaffray, at the invitation of the British and Foreign Bible Society, opened a station in Tourane (now Da Nang), and a Bible school was started in 1921. Growth was rapid in the South and slow in the North. Work also began among highland tribes. In 1941, financial support ceased though some missionaries were not interned until 1943. The Bible school and a mission press continued, and the church grew in membership and self-reliance. It also had to cope with the effects of the War of Independence (1946-54) and the Vietnam War*, which ended with the Communist victory in Apr 1975. For over 50 years, the C&MA was the only Protestant church in the region; other Protestant groups came in during the 1960s. The Evangelical Church of Vietnam (ECVN), or *Hoi Thanh Tin Lanh Viet Nam,* was organized as an independent body in 1928 and remains the largest Protestant church body in Vietnam.

From Vietnam, the vision extended to Laos* and Cambodia*. The C&MA began in Battambang in 1923, starting a Bible school in 1925. Bible* translation was begun. By 1965, when missionaries were expelled, the *Église Évangélique Khmère* had about 600 members. Missionaries returned in 1970, and from 1974 the C&MA worked in partnership with the Overseas Missionary Fellowship (OMF). There was very rapid numerical growth before the Khmer Rouge* victory and another missionary evacuation in 1975. In the tragedy of the killing fields, 90% of the Christians, including virtually all the leaders, were killed. After limited activity from the end of the Pol Pot regime in 1979, particularly in refugee camps in Thailand, Christian work has again been possible since 1990.

In east Thailand*, the C&MA began in Ubon in 1929. The response was slow, and by 1941 there were only 75 baptized members in six mission-compound fellowships. A Bible school was moved to Khon Khan in 1936. During World War II*, missionaries were interned and then repatriated, but the work expanded with the addition of couples from China after 1949. The Gospel Church of Thailand was formed in 1951 and a self-support policy introduced in 1953, although the change was difficult for both mission and church. Later the Bangkok Bible College was established as a joint venture with the OMF.

The C&MA began in the south of the Philippines (mostly Muslim areas) with little result, but found significant response among nominal Catholics.

Bibliography

Cormack, Don, *Killing Fields, Living Fields* (1997). • King, Louis L., *Missionary Atlas: A Manual of the Foreign Work of the Christian and Missionary Alliance* (1964). • Reimer, Reginald E., "The Protestant Movement in Vietnam: Church Growth in Peace and War" (M.A. thesis, Fuller Theological Seminary, Pasadena, California, United States) (1972). • Wisley, Tom N., "Towards a Dynamic Indigenous Church," in *Readings in Dynamic Indigeneity,* ed. Charles H. Kraft and Tom N. Wisley (1979).

John Roxborogh, China Group, Reginald Reimer

Christian and Missionary Alliance Church, Indonesia (Gereja Kemah Injil Indonesia, GKII).

The Christian and Missionary Alliance* (C&MA) was founded in 1897. In 1926, the C&MA board in New York decided to start missionary work in what was then the Netherlands East Indies. When it seemed this decision would not be implemented because of lack of funds, Robert A. Jaffray* (1873-1945), who from 1897 to 1927 had worked in South China and had received reports about the thousands of Chinese immigrants in Southeast Asia, together with some Chinese Christians founded the Chinese Foreign Mission Union (CFMU, president Leland Wang, vice president/treasurer R. A. Jaffray).

Beginning in 1928, the CFMU sent several Chinese missionaries to Indonesia*. They worked mainly among Chinese immigrants in urban areas but baptized more than 2,000 in the Mahakam area of East Borneo. In 1930, Jaffray himself settled in Makassar (now Ujung Pandang), which became the center of C&MA work in Indonesia, mainly among ethnic Indonesians. Within a few years, missionary work was begun in a number of regions which had hardly or not at all been touched by the Dutch missionary societies working in the colony, such as East Borneo (1929, George Fisk and David Clench), Lombok (1929, J. Wesley Brill), Bali* (1931, Tsang To Hang and Gustav Woerner), Southern Sumatra (1933, D. Griffin), West Borneo (1935, D. A. Patty and Luther Adipatty), Sumbawa (1937, S. W. Chu), Malaya (1937, Tsang To Hang), North Borneo (1937, Einar Mickelson), West Irian (Paniai region, 1939, W. Post and R. Deibler; Baliem Valley, 1954, E. Mickelson, Elisa and Rut Gobai). Eventually, East Kalimantan and Irian became the most important fields from a statistical point of view. In this mission work, students and graduates from the Bible school which was opened in 1932 in Makassar (*Sekolah Alkitab Makassar,* SAM) played an important part; in some cases (West Borneo, Misool, Buton, South Sumatra), it was these students who opened up new mission fields.

Another important general tool was colportage, the materials for which were provided by the publishing house Kantor Kalam Hidup (1930), the British and Foreign Bible Society (BFBS) and the National Bible Society of Scotland, and the magazine *Kalam Hidup,* with P. H. Pouw as editor (see Bible Societies). Pouw also published a hymnbook, *Nafiri Perak* (The Silver Trumpet). In East Borneo, the work was particularly blessed, so that a second Bible school was founded there (1938). It had the same basic facilities as Jaffray had set up at SAM, so that the students might not become alienated from the environment they came from and were destined for. In 1939, Fisk began using a waterplane to overcome the difficulties of traveling in the jungle.

The mission fields mentioned above were mainly inhabited by adherents of tribal religions, sometimes by Muslims (Lombok, Sumbawa) or Hindus (Bali). In Sumatra and Malaysia*, missionary work was directed to isolated ethnic groups which had not embraced Islam*. Because of lack of funds and personnel, the Dutch and German mission bodies, weighed down by educational and medical* work, had not started work in these fields. However, as a number of SAM who students originated from christianized regions returned home to bring the Gospel as they had come to understand it, C&MA churches came into existence in those regions, too (Toraja, Minahasa, Alor). Preceding this development, the Dutch mission had held the C&MA in low esteem because of the supposedly low level of its theological* education and its American methods. The colonial government was mainly interested in preventing unrest. For that reason, in 1934 the C&MA workers were expelled from Bali.

In 1941, C&MA was working in 139 places. There were 11,694 baptized members served by 20 foreign and 140 Indonesian workers; the SAM had 209 students, and there were 13 lower-level Bible schools with 479 students.

During World War II*, the work survived without funds from abroad and sometimes under heavy Japanese pressure. Four American and 10 Indonesian workers were killed, and two more Americans, including Jaffray, died in Japanese internment. The C&MA churches were forced to join the regional councils of Christian churches *(Kiristokyo Rengokai).*

After the war, the work continued to expand, including to two other christianized regions (the eastern Sunda Islands, Sangir-Talaud) and to Java, where in 1981 an ambitious program was launched to found 500 new congregations within 10 years. In 1947, inhabitants of the Paniai region, Irian Jaya*, were baptized for the first time; in 1964, the Ekagi New Testament was published. In 1954, the first C&MA missionaries (E. Gobai et al.) entered the Baliem Valley by plane. More Bible schools were founded (by 1987 there were 19). The central Bible school in Ujung Pandang was upgraded and became Jaffray Bible College (1958) and *Sekolah Tinggi Theologia Jaffray* (Jaffray Theological Academy) (1966). The mass media continued to be used extensively, including radio. Church workers from 1967 on had their own journal for pastors, the *Sahabat Gembala.*

In 1951, the C&MA congregations were assembled into three regional churches — East Indonesia and East and West Borneo. Five years later, the Indonesian daughter churches were considered to have reached maturity. The foreign workers were put under the supervision of these churches; at the same time, the C&MA stopped the allowances which, until then, were given to a great number of Indonesian church workers. However, the Indonesian church and the C&MA continued to cooperate closely, though separated organizationally. In 1965, the regional churches entered into a fellowship called the *Kemah Injil Gereja Masehi Indonesia,* which, in 1983, was transformed into a united church named *Gereja Kemah Injil Indonesia* (GKII), with its central office in Jakarta. The regional churches which made up the united church included the following: GKII *Bahagian Timur* (KINGMIT, 21,000 members); GKII *Kalimantan Timur* (98,000); GKII *Kalimantan Barat* (62,000); GKII Toraja *(Kerapatan Injil Bangsa Indonesia,* 40,000); GKII *Bahtera Injil Menado* (6,500); GKII Irian Jaya (138,000); and GKII Jawa-Sumatera (3,000). (Membership figures given include those not yet baptized.) The board was all-Indonesian; its first chairman was Matias Abai, from East Borneo. The congregations which had originated from the CFMU mission remained separate and formed several independent churches. The GKII has not joined the Indonesian Council of Churches, but it is a full member of the Indonesian Evangelical Fellowship (PII).

Bibliography

Conley, W. W., *The Kalimantan Kenyah: A Study of Tribal Conversion in Terms of Dynamic Cultural Themes* (1975). • Lewis, Rodger, *Ringkasan Sejarah Gereja Kemah Injil Indonesia, 1928-1987* (1987). • Tozer, A. W., *Let My People Go!* (1948) (Indonesian translation by Robert A. Jaffray: *Lepaskanlah umatKu pergi! Riwayat hidup* [1972]).

THOMAS VAN DEN END

Christian Broadcasting System (CBS), Korea

First civilian broadcasting system in Korea*.

CBS Korea first broadcast on 15 Dec 1954. Otto E. Decamp, an American Presbyterian missionary, had initiated the establishment of a Christian radio station in 1948, but it was curtailed by the Korean War* (1950-53). The radio station was a part of the evangelical mission to reach Christians and non-Christians alike with cultural programs and Christian messages. It was run by an interdenominational body of managers.

The CBS Korea news program was vital to the Korean audience during the military regime of Chun Doo Whan (1980-87). The military government controlled and manipulated all channels of mass media in order to cover up their atrocities and to gain popular support. The Korean people tuned in to CBS for accurate newscasting and some courageous critical comments on the military dictatorship. The government threatened to shut down the system, but instead ordered it to discontinue its newscasting and commercial advertisements on the grounds that it was a religious broadcasting system which should have only evangelical programs.

Due to this pressure, the CBS had to operate without advertising revenue and faced a desperate financial crisis. But churches and individuals came to rescue the operation of the system until the liberalization of the military regime in 1988. It has now moved into a new building in the northwestern part of Seoul and continues functioning as the most responsible mass medium. The CBS Korea has a network in the major South Korean cities and is considered the most reliable and respectable source of news information.

DAVID SUH, with contributions from
SEO JEONG MIN, translated by KIM IN SOO

Christian Conference of Asia

(CCA). The Christian Conference of Asia traces its beginnings to the missionary movement. Mission boards and missionary societies had established churches in several countries in Asia. Later the churches organized national Christian councils to further their fellowship with one another in their own countries. This was a national structure to link the churches together in fellowship, witness, and service.

The national ecumenical experience was extended to the Asian region early in the 20th c. Some of the Asian Christian leaders felt that they ought to form an Asian regional ecumenical* organization. In the past, they had participated in global ecumenical bodies such as the World Council of Churches (WCC) and the International Missionary Council. As so-called younger churches then, and consequently smaller, they were aware of the need to have Asian solidarity in the international arena.

World War II* and the rapid movements of independence in Asia accelerated the need for regional cooperation. After a series of regional discussions and consultations, the leaders of the Asian churches came together in Prapat, Indonesia, in 1957 to establish the East Asia Christian Conference (EACC). The theme of the conference was "The Common Evangelistic Task of the Churches in East Asia." For the sake of the evangelistic task the churches covenanted to share their life together in the region. This was a pioneering effort in the formation of regional ecumenical organizations. Other regions of the world followed the example set by the Asian churches. The formal inauguration of the EACC took place two years later in Kuala Lumpur, Malaysia*. The name was changed to the Christian Conference of Asia in 1973, when the Assembly met in Singapore*.

The basis of membership in the CCA is stated as follows: "Churches joining the CCA must be Churches which confess the Lord Jesus Christ as God and Saviour according to the Scriptures and therefore seek their common calling to the one God, Father, Son and Holy Spirit. National councils or similar bodies joining the CCA must be councils or bodies which approve this basis." The unique feature is that the membership of the CCA is composed not only of churches but of national councils as well. Within some national councils, the Roman Catholic Church* holds membership.

The area covered by the CCA extends from Pakistan* in the west to Japan* in the east and reaches down to Australia and New Zealand. The China Christian Council* enjoys good relations with the CCA but has not applied for membership.

The CCA exists "as an organ of continuing co-operation among the churches and national Christian bodies in Asia within the framework of the wider ecumenical movement." It guards jealously its autonomy and is not a regional branch of the WCC, although it works in close cooperation with the WCC. The CCA also has working relationships with the Roman Catholic Federation of Asian Bishops' Conferences*.

Some of the stated functions of the CCA are "the exploration of opportunities and the promotion of joint action for the fulfillment of the mission of God" and "development of effective Christian response to the changing societies of Asia." The method consists of study and action in mission and evangelism, service and development, urban-rural mission, and international affairs.

Emphasis is placed on the training of ecumenical leaders so that church leaders can capture the ecumenical vision. The sharing of a common life together as Asian churches enables them to support one another in their development and in their involvement in society. Acting in solidarity with one another, they can respond more faithfully to issues within the church and society.

The central office of the CCA is now in Hong Kong. It is run by the general secretariat and the program staff. They cover the areas of communications, development and service, education, international affairs, mission and evangelism, theology, women, and youth. They provide ecumenical perspective in all areas of the life and mission of Asian churches. The CCA is the main agency for the promotion of ecumenism in Asia.

Bibliography

Niles, D. T., *Upon the Earth* (1962). • *EACC Hymnal* (1962). • EACC, *Christian Art in Asia* (1975).

YAP KIM HAO

Christian Education. *See* Colleges and Universities; Theological Education

Christian Evangelical Church in Halmahera (GMIH)

The seed of the Gospel, or Good News, which was sown with great economic and political difficulty by Portuguese missionaries in the 16th c. and by the Dutch in the 19th, produced Christian congregations on the island of Halmahera. The United Utrecht Mission Board (UZV) carried out mission work there most intensively. The UZV was founded in 1859 in Utrecht (the Netherlands) and arrived in Halmahera in 1866 with three missionaries — H. van Dijken*, Klassen, and Van de Bode — after receiving the blessing of the sultan of Ternate. Of these three, van Dijken's name and work became the best known. Like the majority of UZV missionaries, he was not an evangelist with a background in theological education or special ministerial training. His skills were mostly in agriculture, but he was ordained a minister in 1872 in Ternate and lived in the village of Duma until he died in 1899. From there, evangelistic work branched out into all the outlying areas of Halmahera and the surrounding islands. Van Dijken's motto, "From the seen to the unseen," became his chief principle for spreading the Gospel of Jesus Christ in the area.

The congregations in Halmahera and the surrounding islands were granted autonomy of administration and organization on 6 Jun 1949 under the name the Christian Evangelical Church in Halmahera (GMIH). The preamble to the church regulations states that "only by the work of the Holy Spirit have the followers of Jesus Christ who inhabit Halmahera and the surrounding islands gathered together and been set apart to become a fellowship of believers as a materialization of the Body of Christ, called The Christian Evangelical Church in Halmahera and officially constituted on 6 Jun 1949." The central office is in Tobelo, the capital of an administrative district in the North Moluccas. The preposition "in" is used because GMIH is not a church to be identified with a people of a specific ethnic background but one whose members live in Halmahera and the surrounding islands, and until now has worked only in that area.

The sociocultural heritage of Halmahera is very complex, consisting of 21 tribal groups, each with its own characteristics. Twelve ethnic groups live in the coastal regions of West and East Halmahera, i.e., the Galela, Tobelo, Loda, Soe Oeroe, Wayoli, Modole, Tololiku, Isam, Bo Eng, Patani, Maba, and Sawai groups; three live in the interior of West and East Halmahera, i.e., the Togutil, Biri-biri, and Tobaru groups (the first two are still classed as "primitive tribes" or "nomadic societies"); and six others (the Ternate, Tidore, Makean, Kayoa, Bacan, and Sula) inhabit small islands to the west of Halmahera. Each group has its own language and culture. In addition to these varied groups, an immigrant group, the Sangihe Talaud, now lives in the area, especially in West Halmahera and the island of Morotai. All of these groups are included in GMIH's field of service. Because of this great variety of ethnic groups, it has been impossible to choose a local language as the official means of communication in the church, and so the Indonesian national language is used. But there is an exception in that in some of the village congregations the language of the local tribe is used in worship* and official meetings.

The membership of GMIH is over 170,000, distributed among 315 congregations in 17 areas (presbyteries). Serving them are over 100 ministers and about 200 evangelists. A large proportion of the members live in villages. The level of their education is still low. Their income is not assured because they still obtain the fruits of their work in traditional ways, i.e., traditional farming and fishing, so that they are still at the mercy of the elements of nature. In its service to its members, GMIH has used various resources to educate and encourage members to raise their standard of living.

GMIH has a presbyterial-synodal structure. The rule of the congregation is in the hands of local elders (presbyters), who can meet together by arrangement to consider problems, make decisions, and find solutions. The fields of service of GMIH as an institution cover education, farming, and health. Education is organized by the board of education of GMIH, which now includes everything from elementary through tertiary education.

Theological* education was originally established as an academy in 1967 in Ternate, which became the center for education of ministerial candidates. Farming is organized by the Sara Ni Fero Board (SANRO) of GMIH, which is now making an effort to improve farming for members of congregations and for society generally. Health is organized by the Christian board of health of GMIH, which is now developing the Bethesda Hospital in Tobelo.

The teaching of GMIH follows traditional orthodox Calvinism (see Presbyterian and Reformed Churches). Therefore the piety of the individual's life is considered important. Emphasis is put on the sacrifice of Jesus Christ on the cross and the sanctifying work of the Holy Spirit, together with the Reformation principle of *sola Scriptura*. This heritage of orthodox Calvinistic teaching has strong influence in the life of faith of congregations in Halmahera. But this does not mean that the influence of the original beliefs of the people has disappeared completely. Everywhere the spirit of these beliefs is still felt, e.g., in the way congregations understand and celebrate Lent. They are influenced by belief in *dilikene*, i.e., that the spirit of a dead person becomes *gomanga* either by being killed in battle or by experiencing persecution. They have the conviction that Christ is the highest *gomanga*, or Hero, who has undergone the cruel death of the persecuted. The Spirit of Christ, they believe, will protect them from the dangers that threaten their lives. In this and other ways, the Calvinist theology of Halmahera expresses itself in the local context.

In addition to struggling with the context of these traditional beliefs, GMIH also serves in a society where a large proportion of the people are Muslims. Creative interaction between Islam* and Christianity can take place with the deepening of the spirituality of the two great religions. Harmonious relationships can be built up between them in the atmosphere of the village communities of Halmahera society, but these communities can also suddenly explode with ethnic and religious violence.

GMIH is a member of the Communion of Churches in Indonesia* (PGI), the Christian Conference of Asia* (CCA), the World Council of Churches (WCC), and the World Alliance of Reformed Churches (WARC). This membership is seen as GMIH's involvement in ecumenical* movements at the national, regional, and international levels. For GMIH, the unity of the church is expressed in institutions reflecting its essence as one and apostolic. This is clearly expressed in the church's regulations.

In the 1980s GMIH also accepted *Pancasila** as the sole base of society, nation, and state. It is one of the political decisions taken by GMIH together with other member churches of PGI. This political decision is included in one of the chapters of the church regulations. It was done on the basis of theological awareness that Jesus Christ is head of the church, Lord, and Savior of the world.

Some small congregations of other Protestant churches do exist in Halmahera (Pentecostal*, Seventh-day Adventist*, and Tent of God). There is also a congregation of Moluccas* Protestant Church in Ternate and a number of Roman Catholic* congregations. A Roman Catholic missionary performed the first baptism in Indonesian church history in Mamuya, Halmahera, in 1534.

Bibliography

Haire, James, *The Character and Theological Struggle of the Church in Halmahera, Indonesia, 1941-1979* (1981). • Magany, M. T., *Bahtera Injil di Halmahera* (1984). • Fransz, A. L., *Benih yang Tumbuh IX* (1976). • Paterson, Robert M., "Mission and Social Change," *Outlook* (Mar 1978).

JULIANUS MOJAU

Christian Evangelical Church in Minahasa (Gereja Masehi Injili Minahasa, GMIM)

Church in North Celebes, Indonesia*, formed mainly by the missionary efforts of the Netherlands Missionary Society (NZG, *Nederlandsch Zendeling Genootschap*).

In the period of the Dutch East-India Company* (VOC) in Minahasa during the 17th and 18th cs., there were Dutch pastors who baptized a number of the native Minahasan people. The Christian communities born during this period received little care for their spiritual growth and were eventually abandoned. Intensive missionary activity in Minahasa could begin only after NZG responded positively to the appeal for missionaries by the Rev. Hellendoorn, pastor of the Protestant Church in Manado.

Johann Friedrich Riedel and Johann Gotlieb Schwarz were the missionary pioneers to the native people of Minahasa in 1831. They were followed by other missionaries of the NZG who worked in several remote places in the region. The main problem they faced was the religion of the people, which they called *agama alifuru* (a religion of paganism). To communicate with the people, they built schools in almost all of the villages and taught young people sewing and basic crafts. They followed this pattern to attract the people's attention. It can be said that Christianization in Minahasa went hand in hand with the educational effort of the missionaries. Clearly, the Minahasan saw the role of the missionaries as an influential factor in the intellectual development of the people. Through education, the missionaries prepared some of the native people to assist them in educating other Minahasans. The first three Minahasans who became teachers and assistants of the missionaries were Silvanus Item, Adrianus Angkouw, and Eliza Siwij. They were educated in the missionaries' homes, where they lived as *anak piara* (a young native man or woman who lived in the missionary's home as a servant).

Until 1874, the congregations formed by the missionaries' efforts were still in the care of the NZG. Thereafter, the NZG faced financial problems and could not meet the cost of running the schools and the congregations. There was also the general opinion that a mission body which had converted all the inhabitants of a particular region had completed its work and ought to move on elsewhere. These factors led to the integration of the congregations in Minahasa to form the Protestant Church, a recognized state church. The NZG no longer had the right to administrate the local congregations, except in the area of education, where the NZG missionaries continued to serve under the Protestant Church until 1932.

Nationalism* in the early 20th c. influenced the Minahasan congregations to build an independent Protestant church with its own organization and church order managed by native leaders. This desire became a reality on 30 Sep 1934, when the church in Minahasa was declared an independent church within the communion of the Protestant Church in Indonesia (PGI) (see Communion of Churches, Indonesia). Until the beginning of 1942, this church was led solely by Dutch pastors. Although the congregation participated in the missionary efforts of the Dutch, they were not prepared to become a self-supporting church; indeed, the salaries of church workers were still being paid by the Dutch government. When the Japanese navy occupied Minahasa and the Dutch pastors were interned, native pastors were forced to administrate the church. A. Z. R. Wenas* was the first Minahasan pastor to become the moderator of this church (1942). Some of the other Minahasan pastors who played a role in developing the church in the early period of independence were B. Mundung, W. J. Rumambi*, and R. M. Luntungan*. During the Japanese occupation, they motivated the people toward self-support. This spirit of self-support was interrupted when the colonial government returned to rule Minahasa from 1945 to 1950. When the spirit of independence was aroused thereafter, the leaders of the church faced yet another challenge: Communism*. In 1954, seeing its potential to destroy the life of Minahasan society, they issued a formal rejection of Communism.

During 1958-61, the GMIM faced a local civil war, the *Pemberontakan Permesta* (the rebellion of Permesta, i.e., universal struggle), which involved many Minahasans. The church leaders actively sought to resolve the conflict. The executive board of the synod, through its moderator, Rev. Wenas, managed to mediate and establish peace between the rebels and the central government in Jakarta in 1961. The leaders of the church then began the work of healing and rehabilitating the congregations. Four years later, the church leaders encountered the problem of the suppression of the Communist Party in Indonesia, which included many members of the church.

GMIM today participates fully in the ecumenical movement. It is a member of the PGI, the Christian Conference of Asia* (CCA), the World Alliance of Reformed Churches (WARC), and the World Council of Churches (WCC). One form of participation in international affairs in Asia was the sending of two nurses for humanitarian service in Vietnam* in 1968.

Bibliography

Müller-Krüger, Th., *Der Protestantismus in Indoneisen, Geschichte und Gestalt* (1967). • van den End, Th., *Ragi Carita* 2 (1989). • Wenas, A. Z. R., *Pelajan Geredja di Minahasa* (1969). • Barrett, D. B., *World Christian Encyclopedia* (1982).

Arnold Fr. Parengkuan

Christian Federation of Malaysia

(CFM, *Persekutuan Kristian Malaysia*). Federation of the three main sections of the Christian community in Malaysia*: the Catholic Church (as represented by the Catholic Bishops Conference of Malaysia), the Council of Churches, and the National Evangelical Christian Fellowship.

The desire among some Christian leaders for the unity Jesus prayed for in John 17 led to the First National Christian Conference in Malaysia in 1979, the second coming in 1982. Following a resolution passed at the second conference in recognition of the need for a national Christian body, an inaugural meeting was convened on 6 Feb 1985, and the CFM was established. Formally registered on 14 Jan 1986, the CFM organized the third and fourth National Christian Conferences, as well as the fifth held in Sabah in Apr 1995 commemorating the CFM's tenth anniversary.

The aims of the CFM are to bring together all Christians who accept the authority of the Bible and who subscribe to the cardinal doctrines of Christianity as set forth in the Apostles' Creed; to reinforce and extend, wherever possible, through dialogue and consultation, the common areas of agreement among the various Christian groups in the country; to look after the interests of the Christian community as a whole, with particular attention to religious freedom and rights as enshrined in the federal constitution; to represent the Christian community in Malaysia on all matters that affect or are of interest to it; and to consult and work with government and nongovernmental (religious and secular) bodies, at all administrative levels, on matters of common interest and concern. In practical terms, the CFM functions as a kind of embassy for the Christian community. It relates to government, other religious communities, and nongovernmental organizations. It ensures that the Christian community is a full participant in nation building and looks after Christian interests in the context of national integration and goodwill among all Malaysians.

The CFM is a member of the Malaysian Consultative Council of Buddhism*, Christianity, Hinduism*, and Sikhism (MCCBCHS) established in 1985. Membership is open to all legally constituted national bodies of the four religions. The Muslim bodies were invited, but they declined to be part of the organization. The MCCBCHS is a consultative council and neither holds combined religious ceremonies nor denies the distinctiveness of the various religions. It serves as a forum whereby sensitive issues of religion and complaints can be resolved amicably by leaders of the various religious communities. Its aims are to promote understanding, mutual respect, and cooperation, to study and resolve problems affecting interreligious relationships, to make representations regarding religious matters when necessary, to uphold and promote the ideals enunciated in the Rukun Negara (the national philosophy), to organize conferences, seminars, and other channels to achieve harmony and unity among the people of different religions, and to print, publish, and distribute, with approval from the relevant authorities, suitable journals, periodicals, leaflets, or books for the promotion of its objectives. Presently, the MCCBCHS has branches in Penang, Kelantan, Ipoh, Selangor, Negri Sembilan, Melaka (Malacca), Johor, and Sarawak. (See also Ecumenical Movement.)

GOH KEAT PENG

Christian Institute for the Study of Justice and Development

(CISJD). Ecumenical action research center founded in 1979 at the height of the military dictatorship of President Park Jung Hee in South Korea (ruled 1963-79).

The CISJD was founded with the financial support of a consortium of the world ecumenical community in response to the cries of the Korean people for the protection of human rights, democratic development, and reunification of the divided Korea*. The Institute has published various books in *mook* form, that is, nonperiodical publication, on the history of Korean Christian development for national politics. The CISJD has conducted sociological surveys on the character of the Korean church and society. It also organized various dialogues between Christian leaders and political dissident leaders to promote democratic movements under the military dictatorship of the 1980s. The Institute has developed the research resource center, whose database has been widely used by scholars and researchers into the Korean democratic movement.

DAVID SUH, with contributions from KANG KEUN WHAN

Christian Institute for the Study of Religion and Society

(CISRS). Pioneer Christian study center in post-independence India* founded in 1957.

Along with engaging in wide-ranging study, research, and interfaith dialogue, the CISRS unceasingly appealed to churches to participate actively in the process of building a just society in a nation which was in the process of being liberated from colonial rule. The impact of the CISRS's work was soon felt not only within India but also far beyond, including in many Asian countries and in the global ecumenical* movement. The CISRS was considered to be the place where "theological work in India carries its work into the focal points of societal problems" as well as the "study wing of the Indian church" and the "think tank of the Asian churches."

After a long struggle, British rule came to an end and a free India emerged in 1947. On the eve of independence, the national leaders reassured the people of their commitment to building a democratic, secular, and socialistic nation in India. In 1950, the new constitution came into force. The constitution guaranteed justice, liberty, equality, and fraternity to every Indian citizen. A major economic program was launched when the first Five Year Plan came into operation in 1951. The first general elections were held in 1952.

All of these historic events had a tremendous impact on people, including the Christian community. A spirit of patriotism was surging all around. The historical developments which were taking place were deeply challenging. In this context many Christians felt an imperative call to participate in the evolving political life of the country. While many churches, church-related organizations, and individuals saw their role in free India in terms of expansion of traditional social service activities and developmental programs, a number of groups and individuals thought that the urgent and essential task in the changed national scenario was to *study* the national issues and declared national goals, engage in interfaith dialogue, and *develop* a Christian social thought which could help Indian Christians participate meaningfully in nation building. Those groups and individuals who placed more emphasis on study and interfaith dialogue were related to the National Christian Council (NCCI, now National Council of Churches), Young Men's Christian Association* (YMCA), and Student Christian Movement* of India (SCMI), all closely linked with the ecumenical movement. From the early 1950s, they started taking new initiatives and became involved in programs which were directed toward study, research, and interfaith dialogue. Finally, at the initiative of the NCCI and with the merger of the Christian Institute for the Study of Society (CISS), the Committee on Literature on Social Concerns, and the Bombay Conference Follow-up Study on Rapid Social Change in India with the proposed NCCI Center for the Study of Hinduism*, the CISRS was born in 1957.

The purpose of the CISRS was defined as assisting the churches in India in their total task of witness and services by: (1) promoting scholarly study and research in fields of religion and society; (2) establishing contact with non-Christian thought and initiating conversation with those of other religions on vital issues; (3) helping the members of the church to fulfill their responsibilities in church and society; (4) interpreting the social implications of the Gospel in India; (5) producing and distributing relevant literature; and (6) relating these studies to similar programs of study in India and elsewhere. The basic objective of the CISRS can be summarized as Christian concern for people and Christian responsibility in society. If in its early years this was expressed through programs of social research and interfaith dialogue, priority has been given in more recent years to studies and social action related to the most oppressed sections of society — women, Dalits*, and indigenous ethnic groups.

The growing activities of the CISRS may be classified under four broad headings. First, *Studies and Research,* with the results made known in various publications, such as the CISRS quarterly, *Religion and Society,* and several series of books which include the Series on Religion, Social Research Series, Social Concern Series, Indian Christian Thought Series, Pamphlets on Religion, Inter-Religious* Dialogue Series, and Confessing the Faith in India Series. Current studies and research give special attention to the problems of the marginalized and oppressed sections of society.

The second area of activities comprises *Joint Programs.* In cooperation with the William Carey Study and Research Center, Calcutta, the CISRS sponsors a Joint Women's Program, a Joint Caste-Class Program, and a Joint Urban-Rural* Program, dealing with the key issues in these areas. The CISRS also has contact with many churches and nongovernmental organizations and collaborates with them according to need on various issues.

The third heading is *Macro-level Programs,* such as periodic consultations involving leading figures from academic institutions, churches, and the government who come together to discuss such concerns as Plan Perspectives for Women, New Education Policy, New Economic Policy, and Dalit and Tribal Concerns.

Last, *Micro-level Programs* work with grassroots organizations in social education and development.

From the beginning, persons of repute headed the CISRS. Directors have included Paul Devanandan (1957-62), M. M. Thomas (1963-76), and Saral K. Chatterji (1976-). The directorate of the CISRS was shifted from Bangalore to New Delhi in 1983. With regional offices in Calcutta, Bangalore, Bombay, Trivandrum, and Chennai, the work of the CISRS covers a vast area of the country.

During its four decades of existence, the CISRS has been able to stimulate and bring together front- rank leaders of the church, university, government, and people's movements in its activities. Challenged by the socioeconomic and political context and influenced by ecumenical thinking, it has been able to develop a "new climate of opinion" motivating churches, theological circles, and laymen and women toward a dynamic Christian faith and praxis. In recent years, the CISRS's contribution in developing a Dalit theology and its leadership in Christian dalits' struggle for equal rights have been noteworthy. Indeed, the CISRS, which has made such an indelible mark in the church and society through its remarkable contribution, is not a mere organization but a movement.

Bibliography

Hoffman, B. R., *Christian Social Thought in India: 1947-1962* (1967). • Shiri, Godwin, *Christian Social Thought in India: 1962-1977* (1982).

Godwin Shiri

Christian Life Community (CLC)

The three names the CLC has been given during its history reflect the two main periods of its development. It was called Marian Congregations, or Sodalities of Our Lady, until 1967, at which time it took on the name Christian Life Communities. After the World Assembly, Providence '82, its name became Christian Life Community.

The first period of the CLC's life extends from its official beginning in 1563 to 1967, spanning the time when the Society of Jesus* (Jesuits) was suppressed (1773-1814). At first the Sodalities were groups of laypeople inspired by Ignatian spirituality who placed a strong emphasis on devotion to Mary. When the Society of Jesus was suppressed, the Sodalities lost, to a great extent, the element of Ignatian spirituality but retained their devotion to Mary. Later, they gradually recovered the aspect of Ignatian spirituality and a desire to return formally to their origins.

This return officially started in 1922, when Fr. General Ledochowski called to Rome the Jesuits who were working with the Sodalities or Marian Congregations. In the same year, a Central Secretariat was opened in Rome; it promoted National Federations following the old (pre-1773) tradition and also asked the pope for an official document specifying the identity of the Marian Congregations or Sodalities. The document *Bis Saeculari* was promulgated in 1948 by Pope Pius XII.

Though 1563 marks the official beginning of the Sodalities, it seems the real origin of these communities should be traced back to the origin of the Society of Jesus, when groups organized by laypeople who practiced the Spiritual Exercises of Saint Ignatius wanted to come together for the sake of apostolate and Christian life. Awareness of these beginnings sparked the change in name which occurred in 1967. The change from "Communities" to "Community" made in 1982, while minor in appearance, is also very important. Before that time, at the world and national levels, the CLC comprised federations of many small groups or communities (although every Sodality or Marian Congregation was affiliated with the one in Rome, called the *Prima Primaria*). In 1982 they became one world community dispersed in many small groups or communities. The change is being slowly and gradually assimilated and is intended to bring a new vigor into the life and apostolate of the CLC.

The changes described above have not been drastic and clear-cut. After the restoration of the Jesuits, many groups still remained as ordinary pious associations centered on devotion to Mary, with little or no Ignatian spirituality. After 1967, Sodalities continued to exist in many countries, although some gradually affiliated themselves with the World CLC. And after 1982, the mentality and practice of "federation" have continued to persist.

The Christian Life Community has usually developed according to the apostolate of the Jesuits and in territories where the Jesuits have exercised their influence. It is common practice for Jesuits to organize laypeople into groups or communities and for laypeople who have experienced Ignatian spirituality to form such groups or enter into already existing ones. At the same time, the CLC, even after such a long history, has not become legally attached to the Society of Jesus (in contrast to the Franciscans*, the Dominicans*, and others that have the so-called Third Order, namely laypeople legally attached to the religious order). Therefore, though its emphasis on Ignatian spirituality from the very beginning has attracted many laypeople, the CLC clearly maintains lay characteristics.

The Ignatian spirituality of the CLC is expressed in the so-called General Principles, written down for the first time by the World Executive Council and approved by the holy see in 1967. Following the Second Vatican Council and the change from federation to community, the General Principles were revised, and the revisions were approved by the World Assembly, Guadalajara '90 and by the holy see in the year 1990. The same world assembly also approved the General Norms, some basic procedures for the World CLC.

The highest governing body of the CLC is the World Assembly, composed of three delegates from each national community who come together every four years in a different part of the world. One of the delegates is the Assistant, normally a Jesuit priest.

While being a strictly apostolic community, the CLC does not have a definite field of apostolate. It has to discern constantly which are the most important needs of the church and society and the ways to answer those needs. The instrument for this discernment is the so-called consciousness examination, at the personal level, and the revision of life at the group level. This consists basically in trying to find the will of God in daily life. It includes three basic questions: (1) What has happened in my/our life? (2) How is the Lord working on me/us? (3) What is he asking from me/us?

In Asia there have been Marian Congregations or Sodalities in India*, China*, Japan*, and the Philippines* since the arrival of the Jesuits. At present the CLC exists in practically every country in Asia, though in a few it is not yet officially affiliated with the World Community.

In China, Matteo Ricci* founded the first Marian Congregation in Peking in 1609. Fifty years later, there were about 40,000 members nationwide in parishes, schools, and wherever the Jesuits were working. With the arrival of the Jesuits in Taiwan* in the 1950s, the Marian Congregations or Sodalities naturally came with them and became active in practically every parish or apostolic center run by the Jesuits. Included were both adults and young people from middle school on. In 1956, a service center was opened to coordinate all the existing Sodalities. In 1967, faithfully following the worldwide change, the Sodalities became Christian Life Communities. Since that time, the adult Sodalities have declined in number, and few continue to exist, but there has been growth among college students. The Adult Federation comprised mainly young, unmarried adults. Following the World CLC, they became a National Community in 1985. This National Community includes young people of college age and older adults. Some attempts are being made to expand toward middle-school students.

The Christian Life Community is especially lively in Hong Kong, with members serving on the World Executive Council. Their community of over 100 members includes middle-school students and hosted the World Assembly, Hong Kong '94.

Bibliography

Lefrank, Alex, and Maurice Giuliani, *Freedom for Service* (1989). • O'Sullivan, Patrick, Una O'Connor, and Brian Brogan, *An Ignatian Journey for Lay Apostles* (1991). • Dhotel, Jean-Claude, *Who Are You, Ignatius of Loyola?* (1991). • "Centered on Christ," "Walking with Mary," supplements to *Progressio* (May 1988). • Paulussen, Louis, "God Works like That," supplement to *Progressio* (Jun 1979). • "Finding God's will in Community: The Process of Communal Discernment," supplement to *Progressio* (Jul 1993). • Ochagavia, Juan, "The CLC World Community," supplement to *Progressio* (Nov 1982, Apr 1983). • O'Connor, Una, and Brian Brogan, "Reflective Living, God's Plan and the Examen," supplement to *Progressio* (Sep 1989). • "General Principles of the Christian Life Community," supplement to *Progressio* (Jan 1991).

JAIME VALENCIANO

Christian Peace Association (Japan)

(Kirisuto-Sha Heiwa No Kai). Protestant organization founded in Tokyo in Apr 1951 opposing the rearmament of Japan*.

The Christian Peace Association was founded as it issued an "Appeal for Peace" opposing the rearmament of Japan called for by General Douglas MacArthur in Jan 1951. The organization publishes a bulletin titled *Kirisuto-sha heiwa no tomo* (A Christian's Friend of Peace). A list of its presidents includes Asano Jun'ichi*, Omura Isamu, Inoue Yoshio, and Matsuo Kiyoshi. At the time of the United States/Soviet Union confrontation, the bilateral Japan–United States Security Treaty had placed Japan in the Western camp; the Christian Peace Association supported instead a multilateral peace treaty that would include all of Japan's former enemies. The Christian Peace Association emphasized preservation of the peace agreement, repudiation of militarization, establishment of world peace, and the resolution of social contradictions.

This position, which was rooted in a feeling of remorse for the position the church took during World War II*, proclaimed, "It is a Christian's responsibility to make decisions and take action that openly witness to the sovereignty of Christ over all spheres of politics and society." Like-minded people around the country founded regional groups, attaching their regional names to the name of the national group, and in 1954 30 groups came together to form the Japan Christian Peace Association (a remnant still exists). They organized many activities in and outside Japan, including a movement against nuclear weapons and participation in the World Peace Council (Prague), where they expressed solidarity with other Christian and non-Christian peace organizations in a variety of meetings and networking. Their activity had a phenomenal effect on Christian trends in the 1960s and 1970s. But from 1969, factionalism within and outside of the political parties made a united peace movement very difficult. Those energies which were once focused into smaller individualistic efforts that belied the original intent of the Christian Peace Association. Indeed, many of these groups have become frozen in their isolated concerns. Only the movement to promote aid for *hibakusha* (A-bomb victims) retains its nationwide appeal.

IIJIMA MUNETAKA, JAPANESE DICTIONARY

Christian Service Inc.

An international Christian social-service institution.

Kim Chang-whan (Billy Kim) established Christian Service Inc. in Dec 1959. Its headquarters is in Soowon, near Seoul. In 1966, the board of directors was constituted, and in 1969 the Christian Service Center was founded at 86 Maekyo-dong, Soowon, Kyungki Province. This building is equipped with a gymnasium, library, and youth center. Since 1975, Christian middle schools have been constructed for needy children. In 1976, Kyungki Theological Seminary was founded for the education of laymen and ministers. In 1978, Christian Service Inc. began Chung-ang kindergarten. It has also carried out local service action and evangelical ministry. It retains relations with Youth for Christ and the Far East Broadcasting Company*, Korea.

SEO JEONG MIN, translated by KIM IN SOO

Christian Union of India

Nondenominational Christian organization with the objective of mobilizing Christians to be more meaningfully involved in the socio-political concerns of the church in India*.

The Christian Union of India was formed at the All India Conference on Peace with Justice held at Bombay in Jul 1967. The founding members included some important Christian lay leaders, such as M. H. Samuel, Violet Alva (a cabinet minister of the Indian government), A. L. Rallia Ram, and A. K. Thampy. J. Russell Chandran was the union's founding president.

The union is committed to strengthening and promoting the secular democratic character of India and to educating Christians in the rights and duties of citizenship, as well as helping them participate responsibly in the life of the nation. It has both an individual and corporate membership (churches, organizations, and institutions).

The union has as its motto: "To serve India in the name of Christ." In 1990, the union decided to describe itself as a "Christian forum for peace with justice."

Bibliography

Shiri, Godwin, *Christian Social Thought in India: 1962-1977* (1982).

J. RUSSELL CHANDRAN

Christian Village, Pakistan. *See* Pakistan, Christian Villages in

Christians for National Liberation

(CNL). Underground organization for Christians involved in liberation work in and for the Philippines*.

The beginnings of CNL probably lay in the 1960s when some Christians fighting for reforms in church and society became impatient with the moderates and other reformist groups involved in internal conflicts. In 1971, two years after the launching of the National Democratic Revolution, a number of Catholic and Protestant priests, pastors, nuns, seminarians, and young Christians met to discuss the relationship between Marxism and Christianity. Some saw cooperation with and participation in the National Democratic Revolution spearheaded by the Communist Party of the Philippines as an imperative of their faith. On 17 Feb 1972, during the commemoration of the three martyr-priests, Gomes, Burgos, and Zamora (Gom-Bur-Za*), the CNL was formed. It went underground barely one month after its first general assembly in August, when martial law was declared on 12 Sep 1972. It joined with others to form the National Democratic Front in Apr 1973. Quite a number of CNL members joined the New People's Army (NPA) after experiencing the futility of legal means to obtain structural transformation. Many were arrested, tortured, and indefinitely detained; some were extrajudicially executed or reported missing. The lives of CNL members challenged many church people to examine the depth of their Christian commitment and the incarnation of their faith in the Philippines.

Bibliography

CNL, *Second National Congress Documents* (1981); *Basic Framework and Position* (1993). • Fortaleza, Lem, "Giving Flesh and Blood to Christianity," *Liberation* (Jan 1982). • Youngblood, Robert L., *Marcos Against the Church: Economic Development and Political Repression in the Philippines* (1993). • De la Torre, Edicio, ed., *The Philippine Christians and the Politics of Liberation.*

TEODORO MAXIMILIANO M. DE MESA
and APOLONIO M. RANCHE

Christo-Samaj. *See* Indian Independent Church Movements

Chronicle of Arbela

Medieval Syriac history of the church in the East that claims to have been written soon after the events it describes (6th c.).

The editor of this work attributes the chronicle to a certain Msihazka (Msiha Zha). The authenticity of the document is not at all established, and recent scholarly consensus indentifies A. Mingana as the person who produced the work when he published it in 1907. Therefore, all 20th-c. scholarship based even in part on this document must now be rethought. What it purports to describe is the development of the church in the Persian Empire in its earliest years and the relationships between various church leaders, the church, and emperors.

Bibliography

Gero, Stephen, *Barsauma of Nisibis and Persian Christianity in the Fifth Century* (1981). • Mingana, A., ed. and trans., *Sources syriaques* (1908). • Sachau, E., trans., *Die Chronik von Arbela* (1915). • Assfalg, J., "*Zur Textüberlieferung der Chronik von Arbela. Beobachtungen zu Ms. Or. fol. 3126,*" *Oriens Christianus* 50 (1966). • Brock, S. P., *A Classified Bibliography* (n.d.). • Fiey, J.-M., "*Auteur et date de la 'Chronique d'Arbeles,'*" *Or. Syr.* 12 (1967).

Scott Sunquist

Chronicle of Seert

The Chronicle of Seert, an East Syrian (Nestorian) history written in Arabic and concerned primarily with the church in Persia, depends upon two manuscripts, one from the Chaldean patriarchate of Mosul and the other from the Chaldean patriarchate of Seert. The Mosul manuscript is apparently the older and covers selected events from 230 to 422; the Seert manuscript covers 484 to 650.

The Chronicle is anonymous. It dates events according to the Alexandrian calendar. Reference to Išo'barnoun, who died in 828, suggests that composition did not occur before then; an aside which seems to refer to Caliph Thâhir, who died in 1226, makes the mid-13th c. a possible date of composition. Yet like other Eastern chronicles it offers insights much older than its date of writing.

To use the divisions of Scher's edition, the first part, first section, primarily treats Christianity in the Eastern Roman Empire, but also offers tantalizing tidbits about Persia. Mani's parents are named. He wrote four books, claimed to be the Holy Spirit incarnate, and was ordained a Christian priest. Occasional persecutions of Manichaeans* and Christians occurred in Persia, most often by Zoroastrians* who sometimes distinguished between the two communities.

The materials about Paul of Samosata, bishop of Antioch, are uncontaminated by the later Apollinarian forgeries which concentrated on his Christology and disparaged the term *homoousios.* Statements about Arius and Nicaea depend in part on Socrates' church history (Socrates is named), yet have a twist. Arius changed the text of Matthew 28, which spoke of threefold baptism, and preached against the threefold Gloria. Ephrem*, Theodore of Tarsus, Jacob of Nisibis*, Elias of Merv, Simeon bar Sabbae, Mar Sahdost, and others are said to have attended the 325 Council of Nicaea. The information is suspect, but it may represent a list of important Eastern supporters of Nicaea.

The first part, second section, continues the discussion of Greek and Latin figures while highlighting the eleventh through the seventeenth catholicoi, the Nestorian patriarchs. The history of important sees and monasteries as well as the conversion of Nedjran to Christianity suggests the flavor of the church. The rule of Julian the Apostate is described from Greek Christian sources and a novelistic treatment from sixth-century Edessa. Ephrem the Syrian receives the most attention of any theologian primarily through anecdotes and praise of his poetry. Diodore of Tarsus and Theodore* of Mopsuestia are highly praised. Diodore wrote 80 books. Theodore, called the Interpreter, authored commentaries on most of Scripture. Cyril of Alexandria is portrayed as a villain.

The main structure of the second part, first section, continues the history of the catholicoi, the twentieth through the twenty-ninth. Descriptions of rulers from both the Roman and the Persian Empires anchor the piece in political history. Many commentaries on Scripture written by Narsai* are listed, but some students question their existence because they are not mentioned by Barhadbesabba. The career of Mar Aba*, the twenty-seventh catholicos, is richly portrayed. A Zoroastrian convert, he traveled to Alexandria and Constantinople. He founded a school in Seleucia, worked for reform within the church, and baptized several magi.

Part two, section two, completes the chronicle. It covers a shorter period, fewer catholicoi, and far more monastic and theological leaders. The central figure is Mar Sabrišô: monk, catholicos, and saint. While earning the respect of both Roman and Persian rulers, he rallied the church through his life, visions, and miraculous deeds. Monophysite or Jacobite growth created difficulties for the Nestorians, but the worst problems concerned Hnana, director of the school of Nisibis, who differed from Theodore of Mopsuestia on important christological matters. The struggle led to the eventual closing of the school. Babai the Great, who studied medicine at the school of Nisibis, became a monk, then opened another theological school, and wrote many theological books.

The final section also speaks of various aspects of Islam, most importantly a pact between Christians and Muslims in the Najran region along the Persian Gulf that claims to reflect realities under Muslim rule everywhere.

Some asides throughout the chronicle deal with the expansion of Christianity further into Asia. David, bishop of Basra in Persia, resigned his see, went to India*, and won many converts. Catholicos Ahai was sent by the Persian king Yazdagird I* to investigate charges that trade goods — including pearls — which had come by ship from India and China* were stolen by pirates. The story shows how open the trade routes to the Far East were. Ma'na, metropolitan of Persia, translated Greek theological books into Syriac and sent them to churches along the sea routes, including the church of India.

Bibliography

Histoire Nestorienne inédite (Chronique de Séert), ed. Addai Scher, *Patrologia Orientalis* IV.215-312; V.217-344: VII.95-203; XIII.437-639 (1950-73). • Colless, B., "Persian Markets and Missionaries in Medieval Malaya," *Journal of the Malayan Branch of the Royal Asiatic Society* 42 (1969). DAVID BUNDY and FREDERICK W. NORRIS

Chu Kichul

(b. South Kyongsang, Korea, 5 Nov 1897; d. 21 Apr 1944). Korean Presbyterian minister and martyr.

Chu was the fourth and youngest son among the seven children of a church elder, Chu Heyn Sung. After he graduated from Osan High School, founded by Lee Sung-Hun in Jungju, North P'yongan, Chu continued his studies at the Yonhee College (now Yonsei University) until ill health forced him to quit. In January 1921, he attended a revival meeting in his hometown and was inspired by the speaker, the Presbyterian revivalist Kim Ik Doo*, to become a minister. He enrolled at the Presbyterian Seminary in Pyongyang, graduated in 1926, and was ordained.

Chu served the Choryang Church in Pusan for four-and-a-half years (1926-30) and then the Moonchang Church in Masan, Kyungnam Province, for five years. In 1936, he went to Pyongyang to serve the Sanchunghyun Church.

During the next seven years, Chu was arrested, tortured, and imprisoned by the Japanese police for his clear stand against the installation of the Shinto* shrine in Christian homes, which he considered to be idolatry and thus contrary to the teaching of the Bible. The Shinto shrine was imposed upon the Koreans by the Japanese authorities to instill loyalty to the Japanese emperor. Chu was arrested four times and spent altogether almost five years in prison. He did not survive his last imprisonment, which began in August 1940, and was martyred 16 months before the national liberation.

Widowed in 1935, Chu remarried a godly woman of like mind within the year. During his last arrest, Chu's family was evicted from the manse; but they were provided and cared for by loyal church members. One of his sons, Chu Yongjin, who became a lay pastor, disappeared as a result of his opposition to the Communist plan to introduce a "Christian League" (see Chosen [North Korea] Christians Federation).

In 1968, the government of the Republic of Korea declared Chu Kichul an honored patriot and erected a memorial for him at the National Military Cemetery in Seoul.

Bibliography

Kim In Suh, *Chu'kichul Moksa'eui Sunkio-sawha Seol'kiojip* (History of the Martyr Chu Kichul and Collection of His Preachings) (1958). • Kim Chung Nam, *Sunkilja Chu Ki Chul Moksa Saeng Ae* (The Life of the Martyr Chu Kichul) (1970). • Clark, Allen D., *A History of the Church in Korea* (1971). KIM IN SOO

Chuang Ching-Feng

(Chng Chheng-Hong) (b. Tamsui, Taiwan, c. 1849; d. Cho-eng, Taiwan, 24 Apr 1868). Lay preacher and first Taiwanese Christian martyr.

Chuang was the first Taiwanese Christian who was persecuted and brutally killed during the early period of the English Presbyterian* mission in southern Taiwan*. His death signified the identity dilemma of the early converts in being both Christian and Taiwanese, and the hostility and misconceptions of the common Taiwanese towards Catholic and Protestant Christians.

Originally from upper Tamsui, Chuang first heard of the Gospel while conversing with a janitor at Dr. Carnegie's hospital in Amoy, China. Upon his return to Tamsui, he learned about the Presbyterian mission in Ki-au (near present-day Kau-Hsiong), and he immediately embarked on a nine-day journey from Taipei to Tainan. Learning that there would be a Sunday service in Takaw the following day, he went and received Christ at once after hearing the sermon. He was baptized by Leonard William Kip and received his first communion on 10 Mar 1867.

Soon after his conversion, Chuang assisted James Laidlaw Maxwell in the Ki-au Hospital and was appointed an itinerant preacher for San-te-chhu, Pi-tau, and the surrounding areas. He married Kho Un-liang in early 1868 through a matchmaker, Lim Bok-piau, who convinced Kho that Chuang was not a *Jip-kau-e* (one who has fallen into the religion), but a believer in the "highest God." They settled in Ki-au.

A conflict arose when Chuang tried to force his wife (even beating her several times, she claimed) to go to church. After he went to church on Sunday, Apr 23, his wife escaped and hid in a friend's house in Cho-eng. When he tried to compel her to return home the next day, the old woman in the house shouted, "*Jip-kau-e* is seizing people." At that time the rumor was circulating that foreign missionaries were forcing people to join their religion and poisoning them. Chuang was therefore inhumanely beaten and killed by a mob of several hundred people. His body was cut into pieces and his heart was eaten. He was 19 years old and his wife 15.

Bibliography

Lai, Yung-hsiang John, *Topics on Taiwan Church History,* Series II (1990). • Iun, Su-iong, *Short Biographies of Famous Taiwanese Christians,* Vol. I (1966).

CHENG YANG-EN

Chulalongkorn, King

(Rama V) (b. 20 Sep 1853; d. 23 Oct 1911). Fourth son of King Mongkut* and Princess Rampoey (later Queen Thep Sirindra) who played a key role in the modernization of Thailand* after his ascension to the throne.

Chulalongkorn received a mixed traditional and Western-style education and ascended the Thai throne in 1868, with Somdet Chaophraya Si Suriyowong serving as his regent until 1871. He initiated major reforms in Thai government and society, including the gradual freeing of all slaves beginning in 1872. He expanded Thailand's communications and irrigation systems and introduced electricity, a rail system, and a telegraph system. He initiated public health measures, including the founding of a medical school, and he began a Western-style public school system which included Thailand's first university. He also introduced Western administrative methods and structures in a thorough revamping of the Thai government. In the process, he drastically reduced the power of the tributary regional princes, centralized authority in Bangkok, and created a single unified nation-state.

Chulalongkorn supported such Christian missionary activities as he deemed useful to Thai society, including medical* and educational work, and his reforms had a significant impact on foreign missionary work. He helped create the conditions by which Christian efforts contributed to and advanced the government's own efforts in social and political reform. While he supported freedom of religion for Christians, the reforms also reduced the effectiveness of missionary medical and educational institutions as evangelistic agencies through the establishment of competing public institutions. Chulalongkorn died a highly revered monarch.

Bibliography

"Chulalongkorn," *The Thai Encyclopedia,* Royal Institute Edition (1969-70) (in Thai). • Chula Chakrabongse, H. R. H. Prince, *Lord of Life* (1960). • Narong Phuangphit, *Thai History* 3: *History of Thai Rule and Politics* (1980) (in Thai). • Sanun Muang Wongse, *Thai History in the Thonburi-Ratanakosin Era* (1979) (in Thai). • Ware Umphaiwan, *Biographies of the Kings and Queens of the Chakri Dynasty* (1991) (in Thai). • Wyatt, David K., *Thailand: A Short History* (1984). PRASIT PONGUDOM

Chung, Kyung Ok

(b. Jindo, South Chulla Province, 24 May 1903; d. 1 Apr 1945). Methodist* pastor and systematic theologian; Korean neoorthodox theologian who authored the first systematic theology in Korean.

In Seoul, Chung studied at the First High School and the Young Men's Christian Association* English Academy. While he was pursuing theology at Doshisha University, the tragic Kwan-Dong earthquake hit and thousands of Koreans in the area were killed. He returned home and continued to study theology at Union Methodist Theological Seminary. In 1927, he went to the United States to study theology further at Garrett Theological Seminary of Northwestern University and graduated with a master's degree. Upon his return in 1931, he was appointed professor of theology at Union Methodist Theological Seminary and taught there until 1939.

Chung was editor-in-chief of a theological journal, *Shinhak Segye* (The Theological World), to which he contributed some 60 articles. He introduced neoorthodox theology, especially that of Karl Barth, into Korean theological circles. He authored the first Korean text on systematic theology and a book on the historical Jesus. In 1939, he went to Manchuria to serve as president of a theological seminary until he returned to Kwangju to do parish ministry in 1943. Upon his return, Japanese police arrested him on the charge of being a pro-American scholar and detained him in jail for about eight months. DAVID SUH, with contributions from LEE DUK JOO, translated by KIM IN SOO

Church of Christ in Korea, The (Taehan Kitokhyowhe)

First organizational predecessor of the Korean Baptist* Convention.

The Church of Christ in Korea was formed by Malcolm C. Fenwick* and his assistants at Kang Hyung in 1906 with a 46-article constitution. This occurred after Fenwick had merged the Ella Thing Memorial Mission with his Korea Itinerant Mission (1901). The organizational structure of the Church of Christ in Korea was hierarchical, with the entire body under Fenwick, who appointed various officers and dispatched them to several districts. Any denominational notion was avoided, and a concept of the New Testament congregation as being led by the Holy Spirit was emphasized.

There were nine vertically graded officers: superintendent-pastor *(kammok),* circuit-pastor *(ansa),* pastor *(moksa),* supervisory elder *(kamno),* teacher *(kyosa),* evangelist *(chundosa),* captains of 100 *(tongchang),* captains of 50 *(chongchang),* and captains of 10 *(panchang).*

Under the Japanese control of Korea, the Church of Christ in Korea changed its name several times in order to survive, until its dissolution in 1944 by the Japanese government. In 1921 the name became The Church of Christ in East Asia *(Donga Kitokhyowhe).* In 1933 the name was changed again to The Flock of Christ in East Asia *(Donga Kitokdai).* In 1940 its name was East Asia Christianity *(Donga Kitokhyo).* KIN HUH

Church of God in India

The Church of God in India was formed as a result of the work of Robert F. Cook, who came to India in 1913. During his visit to Kerala, he conducted revival meetings and was able to establish several Pentecostal* congregations. Those congregations were known as the Full Gospel Church of God.

With the assistance of other missionaries and national workers, Cook expanded the ministry to various other parts of the country. A large number of people, particularly from the weaker sections of society, accepted the Pentecostal faith. In association with K. E. Abraham, Cook founded the Church of the Full Gospel in Malabar in 1926. He bought a small hill in Mulakuzha for the headquarters of the church and made his residence there. He started a magazine in 1927 and a Bible school in the following year. In 1930, he severed all connections with Abraham and carried on the work independently.

In due course, Cook felt that it was not wise to work independently and decided to join with an organized Pentecostal group. He came into contact with J. H. Ingram, a minister of the Church of God in America, and subsequently joined with the Church of God in 1936.

To expand the work, the Church of God began to send missionaries to different parts of the country. Among them were C. E. French, Dora P. Mayers, William Pospisil, and others. The national leaders also actively participated in the development of the work. During these years, the Church of God established congregations in several cities, built prayer houses, started Bible schools, and undertook various humanitarian activities.

Later, the foreign missionaries began to exit the country, leaving the responsibility to the national leaders. By 1973, there were 150 congregations in Kerala State. To set up a systematic program to evangelize the unreached areas, a project called Church of God Kerala Mission was founded under the leadership of P. A. W. Samuel. This organization did effective evangelistic work in various places, and by the mid-1990s the number of congregations had grown to 400, with over 50 mission stations. The congregations are divided into several districts for administrative purposes.

From the beginning, a large number of Pentecostal believers were drawn from the weaker sections of society, but there was no discrimination based on caste or color. From 1970 onward, the need was felt to organize the members separately to encourage greater involvement in the various activities of the church. As a result, in 1972 the Church of God in India was divided into two sections. The members of the Church of God Kerala State are drawn from the Syrian Christian community; members of the Church of God Kerala Division belong to the weaker sections of society.

The Church of God has several auxiliary ministries such as the Zion Bible School, which has graduated over 500 workers. To equip youth in the ministry of the church, Young People Endeavor was started in 1947. *Suvisesha Nadam* has been the official magazine of the church since 1952.

In the midst of several hardships and financial constraints, the Church of God in India has experienced tremendous development during the short period of its existence and has become one of the major forces in Pentecostal circles. The church continues to grow under the able leadership of national leaders.

Samuel Mathew

Church of North India

(CNI). The Church of North India (CNI) evolved out of the union of six churches on 29 Nov 1970 after nearly 40 years of prayerful negotiations and a quest for visible unity of the church in accordance with Christ's prayer "that they may all be one" (John 17:21).

In the 18th c., foreign missionaries brought to India* all of their denominational divisions. The result was the establishment of a denominationally divided church faced with the enormous task of proclaiming the Gospel of reconciliation and wholeness in a religiously, culturally, linguistically, racially, and socially pluralistic society in India, which was also torn apart by caste divisions legitimized by religion.

The need for mutual cooperation among churches was felt by Protestant missionaries early in the 19th c. The International Missionary Conference of Edinburgh (1910) contributed much to the coming together of churches to cooperate in mission. In 1914, the National Missionary Council (now the National Council of Churches in India) was formed to promote interdenominational consultation and cooperation in mission. In 1919, a conference of church leaders held at Tranquebar in South India brought into clear focus the inherited "unhappy divisions" in the church in India and the need to take concrete steps toward organic union of the churches in India as they "face together the titanic task of the winning of India for Christ." This gave a powerful thrust to the growing movement toward the union of churches in India. The Lambeth Conference of Anglican bishops held in 1920 also sent out an appeal to "all Christian people" which promoted explorations into the possibilities of reunion with Anglicans in several parts of the world.

In the spirit of the Tranquebar Conference, the Congregational churches of the General Aikya and the Presbyterian* Church in India joined together in Dec 1924 to form the United Church of Northern India (UCNI), which subsequently adopted a constitution for itself popularly known as the Blue Book. The First General Assembly of the UCNI (1924) sent out invitations to other churches and mission agencies to explore the possibility of a wider union. The Wesleyan Methodist* Church responded and proposed that invitations be sent to all the churches which were willing to come together for a consultation to discuss the possibility of a union of churches. As a result, the First Round Table Conference on the issue of union was held on 10-11 Apr 1929; the representatives of six churches convened at the Methodist Church's Lall Bagh Girls' School, Lucknow. This meeting paved the way for negotiations for the organic union of churches.

It may be noted that in South India, as early as 1901

and 1903, federal or other kinds of unions between Presbyterian missions, the United Free Church of Scotland Mission, the Arcot Mission of the American Dutch Reformed Church and the Basel* Mission, the Congregational Churches of the London Missionary Society and those of the American Board of Missions in South India and Jaffna (Sri Lanka) had already taken place; in 1908 the South India United Church (SIUC) was formed as a union of Presbyterian and Congregational churches. A strong movement for the union of churches in South India was afoot, which resulted in the formation of the Church of South India on 27 Sept 1947.

In North India, the Second, Third, Fourth, and Fifth Round Table Conferences were held in 1930, 1939, 1941, and 1947 respectively, through which a Basis of Negotiation and an agreement on the mode of unification of the episcopates of the Methodist Church in Southern Asia (MCSA) and the Church of India, Pakistan*, Burma, and Ceylon (CIPBC) were developed; a Negotiating Committee (NC) was also formed. The first meeting of this NC was held at Calcutta on 27-30 Mar 1951 and produced the First Plan of Church Union. This plan was further revised by the NC at meetings held in 1952 and 1953, and the second edition was published in 1954. At the request of the churches in Pakistan, the same plan also provided for an identical union of churches in Pakistan. In 1957, the third edition of the plan was adopted by the NC and was referred to the seven negotiating churches for decision.

In the light of certain suggestions made by the Lambeth Conference of 1958 to facilitate full relations between the proposed united Church of North India/Pakistan and the provinces of the Anglican Communion, the NC met again in 1959 at Jabalpur and incorporated certain verbal and procedural changes in the proposed inauguration service. By 1963, a working committee had been appointed which undertook a revision of the plan in the light of responses from the churches. This was followed by a further review and clarifications by a continuation committee in Feb 1964. In Mar 1965, the NC produced the fourth and final edition of the Plan of Church Union in North India and Pakistan, which became the basis of the union from which the CNI has evolved.

The final plan was drawn up by and referred to the following churches for their decision: Council of the Baptist* Churches in Northern India (CBCNI), Church of the Brethren in India (CBI), Disciples of Christ (DC), CIPBC, Methodist Church (MC, British and Australasian Conferences), UCNI, and MCSA. Although these seven churches had participated in the negotiations, one of them, the MCSA (now known as the Methodist Church in India, MCI), having earlier accepted the plan (1965) with the required two-thirds majority, later in Aug 1970 rejected the plan and opted out of the proposed church union. The remaining six churches (CBCNI, CBI, DC, CIPBC, MC, British and Australasian Conferences, and UCNI), acting through their respective constitutional procedures and appropriate legislative and executive bodies, accepted the fourth edition of the plan (1965) and entered into the union which was inaugurated on Sunday, 29 Nov 1970, at Nagpur, establishing the CNI, and they thereby ceased to exist as separate ecclesial entities. The CNI emerged as their true successor in all respects. This was the first organic union of churches in the history of the church involving as many as six different denominations.

The basis of the churches' union was the plan (fourth edition, 1965) as a whole, which may be summed up as follows: (1) recognition of the fact that God wills the church to be visibly one so that it may be a more effective sign and instrument of God's mission in the world; (2) acceptance of the divinely inspired Scriptures of the Old and New Testaments as the standard of faith and conduct; (3) acceptance of the classical creeds known as the Nicene Creed and the Apostles' Creed as witnessing to and safeguarding the faith of the church; (4) acceptance of the two sacraments of baptism and the Lord's Supper/Holy Communion; (5) mutual recognition and acceptance, by the uniting churches, of each other's ministry; (6) acceptance for the whole CNI of the threefold ministry of bishops, presbyters/priests, and deacons as symbolizing the governing, liturgical, and serving aspects of the church's ministry within the priesthood of all believers; (7) recognition of the united CNI as a church which, while holding to the fundamental faith and order of the one, holy, catholic, apostolic church, would ensure for its members freedom of opinion in all other matters, and also freedom of action in such varieties of practices as are consistent with the faith and life of the church as one organic body.

The inauguration of the union on 29 Nov 1970 was immediately followed by the Representative Act of Unification of the Ministry. In this act, through prayer and a mutual laying on of hands, the united church received from God a unified ministry acceptable to the whole church from the beginning. The episcopate is both historic (i.e., in historic continuity with the early church) and constitutional (i.e., the bishops are appointed, and they exercise their functions in accordance with the constitution of the CNI).

Since Baptist churches are included, the CNI accepts both believers baptism and the baptism of children as two alternative practices for Christian initiation. In the case of parents desiring their children to be baptized when they grow up, there is a provision for the blessing of children in their infancy. Admission to communicant membership for the baptized is through confirmation by a bishop or its equivalent rite.

At the Fourth Synod held in October 1980, the CNI decided to admit women to the ordained ministry. At present there are ordained women in the dioceses of Lucknow, Delhi, Calcutta, Sambalpur, Jabalpur, Cuttack, Patna, and Chandigarh.

The administrative structure of the CNI is composed of (1) congregations and pastorates, which are the basic units of the church under the care of presbyters and administered through pastorate committees, and (2) dioceses, which comprise several pastorates spread over a large area under the care of bishops and administered through diocesan councils. There are 23 dioceses at present in the CNI spread over nearly two-thirds of the country north of Andhra Pradesh. The total membership of the church in 1995 was over one million. The synod is composed of all the diocesan bishops and ordained and lay representatives of the dioceses. It meets once every three years and is presided over by the bishop elected as moderator for a term of three years. Other office bearers are the deputy moderator, general secretary, and treasurer.

For administration and programs of the church and its institutions there are several boards, standing committees, and three commissions on theology, liturgy, and life. At all levels in the organizational structure of the church, both ordained and lay persons participate through various committees. There is also provision for participation of women and young people in the life and mission of the church at various levels and in the various decision-making bodies of the church, but specially through the Women's Fellowship for Christian Service and the Youth Fellowships.

The union has not meant the absorption of one church by another. The united church values, and is enriched by, the diverse spiritual and liturgical heritage of the uniting churches. The unity is in baptism, ministry, sacramental communion, and mission. It is a unity in diversity. Members of the CNI are assured of full freedom of belief and practice insofar as these do not conflict with the faith and order of the whole church and do not disrupt the unity and the fellowship of the church. No form of worship or spirituality is imposed on any congregation. Over the past 25 years, new forms of worship have been evolving in the process of growing together, and preparation of a compact book of common worship is under way.

In 1989, the CNI adopted nine priorities for the last decade of the 20th c.: (1) spiritual renewal; (2) unity within the Church of North India and with other churches; (3) mission and evangelism; (4) development of Christian leadership; (5) socioeconomic and political concerns, particularly the struggle of the oppressed and marginalized sections of society such as women, Dalits*, and indigenous communities (tribals) for their self-development, dignity, and a wholesome life; (6) dialogue with people of other faiths; (7) structural changes leading to decentralization, democratization, and devolution of power; (8) indigenization and contextualization* of the life, work, and worship of the church; and (9) self-reliance in personnel and financial resources.

In 1993, the CNI embarked on Towards a Holistic Understanding of Mission (THUM), a program to mobilize the whole CNI at the grassroots level as a community committed to justice, peace, and the integrity of creation. In its thinking and action, the CNI as a whole is deeply committed to development and justice for the poor, the oppressed, the Dalits, and weaker sections of society, and is slowly striving to become an authentic indigenous church in its theology, spirituality*, ethos, and resources.

Bibliography

Plan of Church Union in North India and Pakistan (1965). • *Forward to Union: The Church of North India: A Handbook* (1968). • Sully, T. D., *A United Ministry for a United Church* (1964). • Marshall, J. W., *A United Church: Faith and Order in the North India/Pakistan Unity Plan* (1968). • *The Constitution of the Church of North India* (1987).

PRITAM B. SANTRAM

Church of South India

(CSI). The Church of South India was inaugurated at St. George's Cathedral in Madras on 27 Sept 1947. It came into being as the result of three different churches in South India* uniting, namely, the Wesleyan Methodist* Church, the Anglican* Church, and the South India United Church (SIUC). The SIUC was itself the result of a federated union which had taken place in 1908 between the Presbyterian* and Congregational churches in South India.

The formation of the CSI can be traced directly to the modern ecumenical* movement and the International Missionary Conference in 1910 at Edinburgh. The recommendation for cooperation in mission among the churches led to joint evangelistic outreach by several churches in South India from 1918. The awareness of the scandal of disunity and the discovery that all the churches had the same Gospel to proclaim and the same testimonies to give induced the leaders of the churches to call a conference on church union at Tranquebar in May 1919. Bishop Azariah* of Dornakal was one of the pioneers of this move. At this conference, a joint committee was formed to plan the union of the churches. It took 28 years of negotiations before the churches decided to unite.

At first, the Anglican churches insisted on the historic episcopate as the basis for union. The SIUC insisted on the spiritual oneness among the churches as the basis. They all finally agreed to adopt as a basis what was known as the Lambeth Quadrilateral, namely, acceptance of the Bible, the two ecumenical creeds (the Apostles' and Nicene), the two universal sacraments of baptism and the Eucharist, and the historic episcopate. The CSI adopted the threefold ordained ministry of bishops, presbyters, and deacons (see Church of North India).

The CSI is the first united church which brought together Episcopal and non-Episcopal churches into a new episcopal church. The ordained ministers of all the united churches were accepted as ministers of the new church. This was based on the affirmation that God had blessed with "undistinguishing regard" the ministries of all the uniting churches, and on the theological insight that ministry belongs to the church and not the church to the ministry. The ministries were considered as having been united when the churches were united. All ordinations in the CSI are by episcopal laying on of hands.

The structure of the CSI consists of local congregations, dioceses, and synod. Each diocese has a bishop, and one of the diocesan bishops is elected as moderator for a two-year term. There are at present 21 dioceses including the Jaffna Diocese in Sri Lanka.

The CSI maintains a close relationship with the churches of the Anglican communion, the World Methodist Council, and the World Reformed Alliance.

Bibliography

Sundkler, Bengt, *Church of South India — The Movement Toward Union: 1900-1947* (1954). • Paul, R. D., *The First Decade — An Account of the Church of South India* (1958). • *Ecumenism in Action — A Historical Survey of the Church of South India* (1972). • Newbigin, J. E. L., *The Reunion of the Church* (1960). • Ward, A. Marcus, *The Pilgrim Church* (1953). • Hollis, A. Michael, *The Significance of South India* (1966). J. Russell Chandran

Church of the Immaculate Conception, China.

See Nantang

Church of the New Dispensation (Naba Bidhan)

In 1878, those who opposed Keshub Chunder Sen* because of the doctrine of *adesa,* or "message from God," which he claimed for himself, seceded in a body and established a third Brahmo Samaj* known as the Sadharan Brahmo Samaj. It was a great blow to Keshub, who fell seriously ill but recovered to live for six more years. While ill in bed, he resolved to revive his Brahmo Samaj of India. He desired to bring all religions in the world under his banner, make himself the prophet of a new universal religion, introduce a rich and complex ritualism which would satisfy the mind of the masses, and send apostles into the world to propagate the new faith. His church would be renamed the Church of the New Dispensation. A proclamation was made in 1880 during a sermon in the *Brahma Mandir* in connection with the anniversary festivities. *Naba Bidhan* would be a consummation of all the religions of the world, something superior to Hinduism*, Christianity, and Islam*.

According to Keshub, the Old Testament sang Jehovah's glory, and the New Testament sang the praises of Jesus, the Son of God. The Church of the New Dispensation of India was to sing the praises of the Holy Spirit. If Judaism taught us the Father, Christianity taught us the Son, and the New Church should teach us the Holy Spirit. The Old Testament was the First Dispensation, the New Testament the Second, and Keshub and his followers were given the Third Dispensation. At one level, he conceived a synthesis of these three dispensations, uniting and amalgamating them.

But Keshub also put forward another type of synthesis when he declared that in the Third Dispensation all the religions of the world were harmonized. Accordingly, on the anniversary day of his Samaj in 1881, he appeared on the platform surrounded by his disciples with a red banner bearing the Christian cross, the Islamic crescent, and the Hindu trident, and on the table were laid the scriptures of all these religions. This was a theatrical rendering of the idea of the harmony of all religions. In order to realize this idea further, Keshub now adopted a number of rites and ceremonies from both Christianity (e.g., baptism, the Lord's Supper, and pilgrimages to the saints) and Hinduism (e.g., *homa, arati*). In adopting the Christian rites, Keshub seemed to come close to making the ritualistic part of his religion look like a ridiculous travesty of Christianity. The new baptismal ceremony was an example. Keshub's adoption of the Hindu rites, on the other hand, made him come very near to justifying idol worship, which was abhorrent to the Brahmo Samaj. Keshub also presented Jesus as the revealer of Sonship and consequently the fulfiller of Hinduism.

When Keshub died, his church broke up into several groups, such as the Lily Cottage Party, the Durbar Party, the Young Men's Party, and the Keshub Academy Party.

Bibliography

Borthwick, Meredith, *Keshub Chunder Sen: A Search for Cultural Synthesis* (1978). • Farquhar, J. N., *Modern Religious Movements in India* (1924). • Ghosh, N., *The Evolution of Navavidhan* (1930). • *Keshub Chunder Sen and His Times* (1917). • Mozoomdar, P. C., *The Life and Teachings of Keshub Chunder Sen* (1887). • Sarma, D. S., *Studies in the Renaissance of Hinduism in the Nineteenth and Twentieth Centuries* (1944). • Sastri, Sivanath, *History of the Brahmo Samaj,* Vol. 2 (1912). • *Slokasangraha: A Compilation of Theistic Texts* (1904). • *The Faith and Progress of the Brahmo Samaj* (1934). • *The Oriental Christ* (1933). • *The Spirit of God* (1918). K. P. Aleaz

Church-State Relationships

St. Thomas Christians: The earliest church-state issues. The ambivalence of church-state relationships as it was experienced by Asian Christians throughout the ages is expressed already in the New Testament. While the apostle Paul in his letter to the Romans favors a civil obedience of Christians toward the state as long as its representatives do not act arbitrarily against the moral and legal principles of God's will (Rom. 13), John in his Revelation describes the state as "the great Babylon, the mother of whores," the archenemy of the righteous, drunken with the blood of the martyrs (Rev. 17), and therefore under the punishment of the Lord.

Both biblical writers envisage a state — the same state, as a matter of fact — which is not a Christian one. This fact comes into play in determining the attitude of the Christians of the early churches toward the state. The state shows by its own morality and acts, not by its religion, whether it can be respected or must be detested by the Christians. This principle is echoed in the Acts of Thomas*, which claims to narrate the apostle's travels to India*. When King Gundaphar (Gondophares) ordered the apostle to build him a magnificent palace, Thomas is said to have distributed the money among the poor. The king angrily ordered the apostle to be imprisoned. Only later did he realize that the apostle, having used the royal wealth in this way, did indeed build a palace for the king, not on earth but in heaven; and, consequently, the king was baptized. Thomas's main area of activities was South India: the Coromandel coast, where he is said to have landed, and the area around Madras, where, either on the command of the local king or due to strong opposition from the Brahmins, he is said to have "earned the crown of martyrdom."

We are concerned here not with the question of the historicity, but the motives in view in the account. A cooperative attitude toward the state has seldom been the norm in Asia. Congregations of the emerging Mar Thoma Christians developed considerably in the 4th c. when the Christians in Persia suffered under a severe persecution instigated by King Shapur II* (309-79), and numbers of them took refuge in South India. They were eager to maintain friendly relations with their non-Christian neighbors, who gave them a high position in the caste system. Their honesty and social concern not only earned them respect and (particularly in the 8th c.) privileges from the local princes, but also added Indian converts to their community. Except for criminal cases, the metropolitans were invested with civil as well as ecclesiastical jurisdiction.

History turned for the worse for the Malabar Christians when the Portuguese established themselves at Goa (1510) and tried to incorporate the Mar Thoma Church into the Roman Catholic* hierarchy. As a result, all East Syrian (Nestorian*) elements in their dogmatics and liturgy were banned by the Synod of Diampar (1599); at the same time the local rulers were encouraged to abstain from any interference in ecclesiastical matters. A series of schisms followed, and the relationships between the different factions and those with political power — first the Portuguese, later the Dutch and British — were determined by the denominational orientation of the rulers.

The first Christian states. Syrian Christianity, to which the Mar Thoma Christians have always been closely related, was the oldest and largest cultural manifestation of the spread of Christianity into western Asia. Osrhoene*, or eastern Syria, with its capital Edessa, is said to have become the first Christian kingdom, with King Abgar* IX (174-214) being considered the first Christian ruler; he declared Christianity to be the religion of his state (around 200).

The other kingdom adopting Christianity before Constantine the Great and the Edict of Milan (313) was that of the Armenians* (Haikh) in eastern Anatolia, where King Trdat (Tiridates) II converted to Christianity and declared it to be the state religion (310). The first catholicos, Gregory the Illuminator (ca. 240-332), organized the church and gave it, after the country had regained its independence from Persia, a national scope, strictly loyal to the ruler, adopting a feudal system of rule. When Armenia was again occupied by the Persians (363) and the influence of the Christian king declined, the church began to represent the identity of the Armenians, religiously and culturally, the latter with the help of Mesrop, a priest (d. 440), who invented the Armenian alphabet and thus enabled his people to record the Bible, liturgies, doctrinal works, and their national literature. Thus the national and the religious (Christian) identities became one, represented in the church, and this helped the Armenian people to survive as a nation until the present.

Christianity in the Persian Empire. Generally speaking, Persia under the Parthians* pursued a tolerant policy in religious matters which provided a secure refuge for Christians who fled the repeated persecutions in the Roman Empire. With the Sassanids ascending to power in 226, a new dynasty emerged which aimed at restoring the old glory of the Persian Empire, based on a revival of the Zoroastrian* religion. A growing enmity with the Roman Empire was the logical consequence. When Christianity became the dominant and favored religion in the Roman Empire, the Persian Christians naturally were distrusted by their rulers, and so they suffered heavy persecutions, particularly under Shapur II (309-79).

After this experience the Persian and the Armenian churches made efforts to strengthen their independence from the Western churches, which increasingly were identified with the Roman state. In 380, the Roman emperor declared Christianity, as defined by the Council of Nicaea (325), the only and official religion in the Roman state. The Council of Constantinople (381) decreed Rome, Constantinople, Alexandria, and Antioch to be the four seats of the patriarchs of the one church, all of them situated in the West. In 410, at the first Asian synod (held in Seleucia), the Persian clerics declared the bishop of Seleucia to be the catholicos of the Persian church, acting as the representative of Persian Christianity at the shah's court. King Yazdegerd I (399-420) responded positively by granting the Persian Christians the status of an officially recognized community. In 424, the Synod* of Markabta declared the catholicos of Seleucia-Ctesiphon to be the sole head of Persian Christianity (in which East Syrian, or Nestorian, theology prevailed, though it was not yet officially adopted). The catholicos now being called patriarch, the administrative separation from the Western church and solidarity with the Persian state were complete.

The Persian church now focused on relations to the east and thus started on its way to becoming the largest church, expanding with its parishes throughout Asia. Dogmatic differences (e.g., between Nestorians and Jacobites*) had to be dealt with as internal affairs of the church, but the shah did not interfere, for he was inter-

Church-State Relationships

ested only in the relationship between the Persian church and his enemy, Byzantium. With the Synod of Gundeshapur in 486, the Persian church turned officially toward Nestorianism, maintaining the Syrian language, thus adding to the estrangement from the Western churches. It stressed its own independent character administratively and dogmatically. The shah was acknowledged to have the right of appointing the patriarch, which made for a history of creative tensions between the *shahinshah* (king of kings) and the church. It was, moreover, strictly forbidden to convert from Zoroastrianism to Christianity. Mar Aba I*, the Great, who guided the Persian church as patriarch from 540 to 552, in spite of repeated tensions with the *shahinshah* and consequent imprisonments, earned deep respect from Shah Chosrau I (531-79) because of his saintliness, personal integrity, prudence, efficiency, and faithfulness to his convictions.

The Christians under Islamic rule. Similar to their situation in the Persian state under the Sassanids, Christians in the Islamic Empire again were considered and treated as a minority group to be protected by the government against external enemies, but with limited civil rights internally, and without the right of self-defense. Their status, however, included the right to practice their religion and establish their own courts for cases which did not involve a Muslim or in which the state had no particular interest. Since the first Islamic conquests extended to Byzantine (Syria, Palestine) and Persian territory alike, the former border between the two ancient kingdoms disappeared, thus bringing together the different Eastern confessions (Monophysite/Jacobite, Nestorian, Greek Orthodox/Melchite) in one empire. The Syrian-speaking Christian communities, which were treated by the Byzantine emperors as heretics (followers of Nestorius or of Eutyches), welcomed the Muslims as liberators, because they were not interested in the details of their quarrels and treated them equally as *ahl al-kitab* (owners of a holy scripture).

Contracts concluded between the victorious Muslims and their new subjects were not uniform. They differed, especially when fixing the *jizya* (tax), according to local conditions. The Abbasid caliphs (750-1258) tended to view the bishops or patriarchs residing in the capital city as legal representatives of their specific denominations at the court, with a certain preference extended to the Nestorian catholicos who, around 1065, was decreed to be superior to the Jacobite and Melchite bishops.

The caliphs continued the right of the Persian shahs to appoint the patriarchs and, to some extent, bishops. A newly elected head of a church had to apply for a diploma. By granting it, the caliphs, and later on local potentates as well, installed him as legal representative of his community with the right of jurisdiction over its members. The caliphs did not much interfere in internal matters of the churches. Organized persecutions seldom took place, except under the mad Fatimid caliph, al-Hakim, which lasted from 1017 to 1020. Local persecutions usually were initiated by personal rivalries between Christian personalities who invited the rulers to interfere.

During the time of the Crusades, Eastern Christians had to make sure their Muslim rulers did not suspect them of being loyal to the "Frank" intruders. This was not so difficult for those churches anathematized in the 5th c. But other Christians, especially in the former Persian territories and among Armenians, hoped to exchange their Muslim rulers for a new Christian rule. These hopes were encouraged when the Tartars (Mongols*) from central Asia started their raids to the south and southwest, some of them having adopted Christianity. Eminent among them was Dokus Kathun, the wife of the Ilkhan Hulagu who conquered Baghdad in 1258; she was compared by some Christians to Helena, the mother of Constantine. While many Muslims were massacred, the lives of the Christians were spared. Some Mongols became bishops or even were appointed as catholicos. Under Kublai Khan, whose mother had been a Christian (although he himself was more inclined toward Buddhism*), the Nestorian church could extend her parishes in China* and Southeast Asia. But the moral decline of Christian dignitaries and their zeal to participate in power finally caused the Mongolian nobility to prefer Islam*, a decision made earlier already by many common people. The devastation under Timur Lenk left the Christians powerless under reestablished Muslim rulers who had not forgotten the hostile attitudes of the Christians during the times of the foreign intruders.

During the period of the Ottoman sultanate the Christians were given again the status of a protected minority. Except for the Thomas church in South India and the remnants of old churches in the Middle East, the Christians originating from the earlier waves of expansion had more or less disappeared. In none of the Asian states could Christianity develop as a state (or even national or tribal) religion, except Armenia, which only briefly enjoyed national independence. Relations with state rulers faced the additional handicap that either Western Christian rulers appeared as enemies or Christians were drawn into their own internal conflicts. These minority communities were persecuted, as in China under the T'ang, or lost favor under the three great Mongol khans, Mangu (ruled over Mongolia), Hulagu (ruled over Persia), and Kublai (ruled over China), three brothers whose mother had been a Nestorian Christian.

Colonial and post-colonial period. (See Colonialism.) When the Portuguese (1510) and then the Spaniards appeared on Asian shores, their colonies and settlements had to comply with the *padroado**. The papal commission required the colonizers to subjugate the territories and their inhabitants to the lordship of Christ under the authority of the pope, to whom their kings were responsible. Thus baptized Christians would be subject to a distant king and pope, not to local kings or chiefs.

The Dutch and British trading companies did not follow this policy. When the Protestant governments took over, especially in the course of the later 18th and

19th cs., Christians under their rule felt a degree of security and responded with a certain, albeit not blind loyalty. Members of state churches which had established new congregations, or of synods such as the Anglican or the (Dutch) Protestant Church, naturally felt more closely linked to their foreign sovereigns than to those of other denominations.

In the Philippines*, at present the only Asian state with a Christian majority, the governmental protection of the Catholics remained until the end of Spanish rule (1898), while under the United States administration a great amount of religious freedom was practiced, excluding the Muslims in the south. The relationship between the Catholic Church and the government improved after independence (1946). But under the dictatorial regime of Ferdinand Marcos the internal situation deteriorated, and so Christian activists (both Protestant and Catholic), and later even part of the hierarchy, took sides with the exploited and oppressed masses.

China, like Korea*, knew a period of relatively close relations between Catholic missionaries and their imperial courts in the 17th c., which, however, was followed by severe persecutions. Since the reopening of the Middle Kingdom to Christian missions was linked to the unequal treaties of 1842, the hatred against foreigners meant a hatred of Christians as well. Their position became more difficult during and after the Taiping* revolution (1849-64), which was considered by the Maoists to be one of the most significant uprisings in prerevolutionary China. Although the leader of the Republican revolution in 1911, Sun Yat-Sen*, was a Christian like many of his followers, the image of Christianity deteriorated again during the corrupt and arbitrary regime of Chiang Kai-shek, whose influential wife was the daughter of a Christian preacher.

After the Maoist takeover in China (1949) and especially after the outbreak of the Korean War* (1950), all Christian organizations had to sever their relations with their foreign partners. Officially, freedom of religion was guaranteed, but practically a freedom from religion was encouraged. In Protestant circles, the Three-Self Patriotic Movement* was inaugurated (1953), comprising members of different Protestant denominations and, depending on the passing waves of strict antireligious and then more tolerant policies, enjoying some official respect as a pure Chinese organization. Those Christian groups which withdrew together with the Kuomintang government from mainland China to Taiwan* remained loyal to the nationalist government, while the Taiwanese Christians, especially the Presbyterians*, favored opposition groups, demanding more external independence and internal freedom and justice. Together with the political opposition, many church people suffered persecution by the Kuomintang government.

In Korea, Catholicism shrunk to a tiny underground community after the severe persecutions in the 18th and 19th cs., which were instigated by the powerful Confucian* administration. The church only started to recover around 1885 when the gate to Protestantism was opened too. Although the Donghak (Tonghak*) understood themselves as an anti-Western, socio-religious movement, Christian elements were essential in shaping its self-understanding. Meeting with some rejection from Western missionaries, a number of Christians continued their opposition against the government from the times of the Yi Dynasty (abolished in 1910) to the end of the Japanese occupation (1945). While after the division of the country (1953) most Christians left North Korea, the Christians in the South of the country were dominant in the social and political movements directed against the authoritarian rule of Rhee Syngman* (1960) and the later military dictators.

When the Dutch government took over the East Indian islands (1818), the Dutch king decreed that the Protestant congregations throughout the archipelago be united in one Protestant Church. This church was governed by a special commission including members of the (colonial) government and financed by the state; its head was the Dutch king. To this church, the congregations (later, churches) in the Moluccas* (Ambon), Minahasa, and Timor* were added, while all other Protestant churches which grew out of the missionary enterprises and, of course, the Roman Catholics developed as churches independent from direct influence or supervision by the state. Although the Dutch government declared an administrative separation between church and state in 1935, it was only after Indonesian* independence (1945) that the Indonesian president (the Muslim Sukarno*) made this Dutch church equal to the other churches. Since the Indonesian constitution declares that all acknowledged religions in Indonesia have equal rights, no interference from the state in the internal affairs of religious communities is allowed. In spite of a traditional allegiance toward those in power, the Christian churches have repeatedly and increasingly voiced their concern about social, economic, and legal measures pursued by the government.

The churches in Malaysia* are in a peculiar position vis-à-vis the state, because none of them is a Malay institution. Thus none of them enjoys those privileges which are reserved by the constitution for the ethnic Malays. Religious freedom is guaranteed, with the exception of the Malay, who have to be Muslims, and no Muslim may be converted to another religion. Until recently, the churches were quite unpolitical, reflecting the mood of their Chinese, Indian, or Bornean members. A growing effort by the government to make Malaysia more Malayan has caused a greater political awareness and more communication between churches and government officials. The churches are concerned that the recent steps by the government may estrange many Malaysians from their traditional cultures, which they consider to be part of what "Malaysia" should mean.

In all Asian countries, except the Philippines, the Christians are tiny minorities which often came into being during the colonial period. Expatriate missionaries, as subjects of the colonizing states, had to be protected; in certain instances, their activities could be restricted or prevented if the internal situation required such steps. Legally or by other means of favor, native Christians could instantly enjoy certain privileges, which, however, have lately decreased as a consequence of ideological and constitutional changes in the West. The widespread image of Christians as loyalists of the colonial powers, however, was destroyed during the independence movements and wars in which many Christians took an active part and died. Therefore, the independent states which emerged after the departure of the colonial armies are considered by most Asian Christians to be their common property along with their non-Christian compatriots. Most of these new nations adopted Western-style constitutions with democratic institutions and a clear guarantee to the freedom of religion. Therefore, the position of the churches toward the state is, generally speaking, that of an independent, loyal, and, if necessary, critical partner.

The minority Christian communities are often significant players in non-Christian nations, depending on the respective constitutional provisions for the freedom of religion, conscience, and expression, and the extent to which the government honors its own constitution. Much depends also on the Christians' attitude, loyalty, and responsibility toward their nations.

The status as minority, often considered the main factor that led to the eclipse of Asian Christianity in the past, has been a problem in countries ruled by absolutist governments. At present, only a few countries are forbidding their nationals to become Christians, such as Nepal* until recently and Saudi Arabia. In revolutionary Iran, Christianity — as the religion of an *ahl al-kitab* — is not forbidden, but adherents of "younger" churches in the country, such as the Anglicans and Baha'is, may be counted as apostates and thus fall under the law of *irtidad*. In Pakistan and Bangladesh*, both referring to themselves as "Islamic states," Christians and other non-Muslims are increasingly situated in a state of — albeit to some extent modernized — dhimmis. But the status of Christians as minorities in the state is not the only criterion for their position in society. A clear Christian identity which lays equal emphasis on faithful confession and practiced ethics, and which is reliable in its solidarity with its people, contributes strongly to the acceptance of Christians in Asia as equal citizens.

Bibliography

Atiya, Aziz S., *A History of Eastern Christianity* (1968). • Browne, Laurence E., *The Eclipse of Christianity in Asia* (1933). • MacInnes, Donald, ed., *Religion in China Today* (1989). • Kawerau, Peter, *Die jakobitische Kirche im Zeitalter der syrischen Renaissance* (1960). • Moffet, Samuel H., *A History of Christianity in Asia*, Vol. I, *Beginnings to 1500* (1992). • Neill, Stephen, *A History of Christianity in India*, 2 vols. (1985). • Vine, Aubrey R., *The Nestorian Churches* (1980). • Young, William G., *Patriarch, Shah and Caliph* (1974). • Forbes, Andrew D. W., ed., *The Muslims of Thailand*, 2 vols. (1988-89). • Esposito, John L., ed., *Islam in Asia: Religion, Politics, & Society* (1987).

Olaf Schumann

Cistercians

The Cistercians (or White Monks) are named after the Abbey of Citeaux, located outside Dijon, in eastern France. This monastery was founded in 1098 by St. Robert of Molesme and 20 of his monks as a renewal of the Benedictine life. The reform quickly caught on, and within a century there were hundreds of Cistercian monasteries established in all parts of Christendom. Historical situations led to the order developing congregations along national and ideological lines. In 1892 under the auspices of Pope Leo XIII, the order was divided into the Cistercian Order of the Strict Observance (commonly called Trappists*), which retains the aim of the founders of the order and seeks to live a contemplative monastic life, and the Order of Cistercians (usually referred to as the Common Observance), which is open to various apostolic activities, especially schools. There are, however, some strictly contemplative communities among the Common Observance.

Cistercian life was sadly in decline when Asia was first being colonized. For their part, the Spanish and Portuguese colonizers wanted only mendicants like the Franciscans* and Jesuits*, who would be active evangelizers, not monks. The rest of the colonial powers had long since cleared their countries of monks.

Beginnings in China. In 1883, the first Cistercians were sent to China* by the abbot of Sept-Fons in France. The Christians of Fan Shan offered them an extensive property 120 kilometers northwest of Peking, 10 kilometers from the Great Wall, in the province of Hopei. Here the French monks founded the Monastery of Our Lady of Consolation — Yang Kai Ping. It was rugged, inhospitable, mountainous land which, along with the harsh weather, made it exceedingly difficult for the monks to provide a living for themselves. By dint of great labor, they developed nut orchards, brought in water by canal, and started herds, producing cheese and milk. The monastery was elevated to an autonomous abbey in 1891, traditional monastic structures were built, and the community grew to become one of the largest in the Cistercian order.

As the community grew, there were constant appeals from other parts of the Orient for foundations. In 1896, Cistercians were sent to Japan* to begin a monastery near Hakodate. Then in 1928, a large group of monks was sent to establish Our Lady of Joy Monastery 300 kilometers south of Peking near Tchengtingfu in Hopei Province. This monastery also flourished and became an autonomous priory, electing the first Chinese superior, Dom Paulinus Lee.

War was to take its toll on these communities — first

the Sino-Japanese War*, with its occupation and the imprisonment of the non-Chinese monks, and then the civil war. The Communists took control of much of the north in 1947. In August, they burned the abbey and led the 77 monks of Yang Kai Ping out on a death march. Thirty-one died a martyr's death, the rest of the priests disappeared into prisons, and in October the surviving brothers were dispersed. They regrouped at Beijing (Peking), and with the help of Dom Paulinus they started a dairy and resumed a regular life. Six years later, the dairy was confiscated and the monks were again sent to prison or dispersed. In 1995, 13 of the monks still lived in dispersion, though an attempt was made to regroup and to hand over the Cistercian heritage to eager young Chinese men and women.

As the Communist forces approached Tchengtingfu, a large number of the monks fled south and established a refuge in Szechuan Province. Here they lived their peaceful monastic life for some time, but in 1949 they again had to flee the approaching Communists. In the end, Dom Paulinus was able to bring only 18 monks out to the freedom of Hong Kong*. The rest were imprisoned or dispersed, and two of them, Vincent Shih and Albert Wei, were martyred. In 1995, six of the monks were still continuing their monastic life in China.

In 1950, Dom Paulinus was able to obtain from the British government a beautiful valley on the island of Lantao. Before his death in 1980, through years of hard labor, the zealous prior was able to fully reestablish the monastery of Our Lady of Joy. Not long after, the novice master of Lantao went with one of the other monks to establish a new foundation in Taiwan* in collaboration with some American Cistercians. Holy Mother of God Monastery is located high in the hills above Taichung. In 1995, Dom Paulinus's successor, Dom Benedict Chao, presided over a community of 20 monks, including four from Hong Kong.

Japan. As mentioned above, Yang Kai Ping sent the first Cistercians to Japan in 1896 to establish the monastery of Our Lady of the Lighthouse on the island of Hokkaido. Additional monks came from the Abbey of Bricquebec in France, which took on the responsibility for the development of this community. Gradually young Japanese entered, and in 1980 eight monks went south to start a new monastery near Beppu, Oita-ken.

India. In 1956, Francis Mahieu, a monk from Scourmont Abbey in Belgium, arrived in Kerala. He was inspired with a call to revive the monastic tradition of the ancient Syrian Church in India*, while assimilating as much as possible the spiritual heritage of India, with its ascetical and contemplative traditions, and a Gandhian vision in regard to the economy of the community. In 1958, the regular monastic life was begun at Kurisumala near Vagamon, Kottayam. Francis adopted the Indian name of Acharya, the saffron cloths of the Hindu *sannyasis*, and many other aspects of the local culture. The monastery has grown and flourished not only as a spiritual center but as an enlivening force in the economy of the area. Since 1968, it has sent out five groups to start similar ashrams*.

Philippines. A young university student in Manila, Pascual Gaba, felt the call to the Cistercian life. He worked his way to the United States on a freighter and finally reached Gethsemani Abbey in Kentucky. After eight years of preparation, Br. José was consecrated a monk, only to die some weeks later. His close friend from college days, Pedro Lazo, responded to the interior call to realize his companion's vision. He entered Gethsemani. However, he was sent to a foundation in South Carolina. Yet he never lost the vision, and finally he was able to recruit five American monks and lead them back to the Philippines* in 1972 to establish the Monastery of Our Lady of the Philippines on the island of Guimaras, south of Iloilo. There they adopted the poverty* of their neighbors, living in nipa huts, building a bamboo church, and making their living from various sorts of farming and fish ponds. Many Filipinos were drawn to the Cistercian life. The monastery became autonomous and elected its first Filipino prior in 1982. It was raised to the dignity of an abbey in 1990.

Korea. Lawrence Musu, a priest of the archdiocese of Seoul, also responded to a call and a vision and went to the Abbey of the Genesee in New York State to receive Cistercian training. After two years there, he returned to his diocese to begin a monastery according to the Cistercian tradition. In 1987, he acquired a beautiful valley near Beob Weon Ri, not far from the demilitarized zone. A monk came from Genesee to help him train the young Koreans attracted to the Cistercian life.

Vietnam. It was a priest of the Paris Foreign Mission Society* (MEP), Benoit Denis, who brought the Cistercian life to Vietnam*. He began a diocesan monastery at Thu-Duc in 1918 following the Cistercian model. The community developed in authentic Cistercian spirit and ways, although it did not respond to all the expectations of the Strict Observance of that time; therefore, it was incorporated into the Common Observance in 1934. In 1936, a group of monks was sent out to start a new monastery at Chau-son. In 1950, another group went forth to Phouc-Ly. In the meantime, the community of Chau-son divided and established a new monastery at Don-Duong.

Finally in 1966, the four monasteries were formed into a new congregation, that of the Holy Family. Another monastery was established in Vietnam by the monks of Lérins (France): the Monastery of My-Ca, near Bangoi. All of these Vietnamese monasteries suffered greatly because of the prolonged warfare in Vietnam and the adaptations necessary to continue monastic life under a Communist regime.

The Cistercian Nuns. The Cistercians of the Strict Observance are the one order in the church in which men and women form one religious body, sharing in the general chapter and together electing their general. This is the fruit of a long evolution that began in the time of the

Cistercian founders. Frequently, a foundation of Cistercian nuns follows the arrival of the monks in an area.

It was only two years after the monks were established in Hokkaido that nuns arrived from the Abbey of Ubexy in France and established themselves in nearby Hakodate. The new monastery was called Our Lady of the Angels: Tenshien. It grew rapidly and became in time the largest monastery in the order. In 1935, it founded Seiboen, Our Lady of Lourdes at Nishinomiya, not far from Kobe and Osaka, and in 1953, Our Lady of the Holy Family at Shindenbaru. This community moved to Imari in 1964. Seiboen in its turn founded Immaculate Conception, Nasu, in 1954, and, far in the south on an island belonging to Okinawa, Our Lady of Miyako.

In the same year that Fr. Lawrence started Beob Weon Ri, nuns arrived from Tenshien to establish a community in southern Korea. In 1995, this community of Sujong had 25 Korean members.

In 1994, the nuns of Soleilmont, the Trappistine convent near Fr. Acharya's native monastery of Scourmont, sent a group to start Our Lady of Joy, Ananda Matha Ashram in Kerala. And in the following year, the community of Vitorchiano in Italy sent a group to establish the Monastery of Our Lady of Matutum on the large southern island of the Philippines, Mindanao. Thus the Cistercian Order in Asia continues to grow both in communities and in the number of monks and nuns within the communities.

The twentieth-century renewal of Cistercian life. The life the new members entered into, even in the 1940s and early 1950s, was very much like what had been in force for many decades. Then the move to return to the simplicity of primitive Citeaux began. Step by step, the duplications and accretions in the liturgical life were removed, reducing the hours in choir from six or seven to three or fewer, allowing more time for *lectio* and contemplation. Only after the Second Vatican Council would the vernacular be allowed and greater freedom be given to the local community to create its own liturgical worship.

In 1969, the first official renewal chapter of the order produced a sweeping Statute on Unity and Pluralism which reduced all the previous rules to little more than suggestions, replacing them with 11 principles that were to lead each community in the creation of its own guidelines and customs.

Contributions. The Cistercians of the Strict Observance have always seen their primary contribution to the church and to the world as lying in their quiet, prayerful lives. At the heart of the church and the particular diocese in which they are established, they devote the largest part of their waking hours to prayer, in choir and in private, and *lectio.* They are also committed to offering an open hospitality, providing a place of quiet and apartness and spiritual guidance for any who come seeking it. In recent years, many of the communities have significantly upgraded their guest facilities and have begun to welcome members of the opposite sex. Retreat programs are simple, offering mainly silence and solitude, with spiritual fathers or mothers available for consultation and instruction in prayer. In the 1970s, there came forth a practical, simple teaching on contemplative prayer that has popularly become known as Centering Prayer.

Bibliography

Jen, Stanislaus, *The History of Our Lady of Consolation: Yang Kai Ping* (1978); *The History of Our Lady of Joy* (1978). • Lekai, Louis J., *The Cistercians. Ideals and Reality* (1977). • Pennington, M. Basil, *The Cistercians* (1992); *Monastic Life: A Short History of Monasticism and Its Spirit* (1989).

M. Basil Pennington

Clapp, Walter C.

First Episcopal Church missionary and educator of Bontoc, Mountain Province, Philippines*.

Clapp was assigned by Bishop Brent in Jun 1903 to Bontoc, where he opened the first Episcopal (see Anglicans) mission station in this part of the Cordillera Central Philippines. He named it All Saints' Mission. Believing that the Christian education of the pagan Bontoc Ogorots ought to be a priority of the church, Clapp started his mission with the education of children, using it as a means to convert them to Christianity, to improve their standard of living, and to produce future leaders for the community (see Education). He said, "One may not hope to do much with the fathers and mothers, but in the children there is hope." This endeavor was in accord with the colonial government's program to educate the people for eventual independence*. Clapp himself believed that America should stay in the Philippines for an indefinite period of time for this purpose.

By 1910 nine out of 10 prizes given by the public school to deserving students went to those from All Saints' Mission School. All Saints' continues to maintain its high academic standards and remains a source of good Christian leadership for both the church and the government. Clapp retired from All Saints' in 1912.

Bibliography

"Report of All Saints' Mission, Bontoc," *Journal of the Annual Convocation of the Missionary District of the Philippine Islands* (1908, 1909, 1910, 1911, 1912). • *Spirit of Mission* (Nov 1904; Aug 1903). • Fry, Howard, *A History of the Mountain Province* (1983). • Clapp to Wood, 22 May 1904, Archives of the Episcopal Church in the United States, Austin, Texas.

Edward P. Malecdan

Claretians

The Congregation of the Claretian Missionaries or Sons of the Immaculate Heart of Mary (CMF), a religious community of priests and coadjutor brothers, was founded by Archbishop Saint Anthony Maria Claret in Vic, Spain, on 16 Jul 1849 and has since been established in over 50 countries. In Asia, there are about 400 Claretians, mostly Asian.

China. In 1929, the Pontifical Institute for Foreign Missions* (PIME) in Milan asked the Claretians to run the Regional Seminary of Kaifeng, Hunan. Nicolas Garcia, the Claretian superior general, accepted the offer and, in 1931, two Spanish Claretians, Joseph Gil Foguet and Anastasio Rojas, arrived in China*; however, the regional seminary was yet to be built. After a few months of uncertainty, Vicente Huarte, a Jesuit bishop, offered the Claretians a mission in his apostolic vicariate of Wuhu. The mission was developed by 19 Spanish Claretians and became the apostolic prefecture of Tunki, Anhui Province, on 21 Feb 1937, with Fr. Foguet as its first apostolic prefect. Besides the development and consolidation of Christian communities, the Claretians became well known for their school of nurses and paramedics, clinics, and dispensaries under the leadership of Jośe Maria Torres, a Claretian coadjutor. Evacuation from China started in 1949 as the situation became difficult, with the last two Claretians leaving in Nov 1952 for the mission of Tunki, Hong Kong. Most Claretians went to the Philippines* or Japan*; a few returned to Spain.

Philippines. Three Claretians (Raymond Catalan, Thomas Mitchell, and Martin Hortelano) arrived in the Philippines from California on 26 Dec 1946 in response to the late bishop Mariano Aspiras Madriaga's letter of appeal on 20 Aug 1945 to the United States Claretian superior, Stephen Emaldia, for English- and Spanish-speaking priests to work as retreat masters, mission directors, and parish priests, and to establish a vocational school. They took possession of the parish of Santa Barbara, Pangasinan, on 9 Jan 1947. More Claretians came later from the United States and China. As a result of a contract between the bishop of Zamboanga, Msgr. del Rosario, and the Claretian superior general, Peter Schweiger, on 21 Sep 1950, the Claretians moved to the missions of Zamboanga and Basilan. In Oct 1963, Basilan became a prelature nullius, with José Maria Querexeta, former missionary in China, as its first bishop. In addition to the formation and consolidation of Christian communities, the Claretians opened schools and a hospital and undertook rehabilitation and development projects, especially for war victims, both Muslim and Christian, in the south Philippines. Claretian Publications in Manila publishes evangelistic and Bible materials in several languages. The Claretians are in the process of establishing the Theological Institute for the Consecrated Life in Asia. Many young Filipinos have joined the community and are now serving in other Asian countries. From the Philippines, the Claretians have expanded to Korea*, Australia, and Indonesia*.

Japan. The bishop of Osaka, Pablo Taguchi Yoshigoro, met the superior general of the Claretians in Rome in May 1950 and requested missionaries for his diocese. On 9 Sep, the first Claretian, Anthony Briskey from the United States, arrived in Japan, followed by Mariano Gonzalez and Romario Jarussi, who were expelled from China. On 9 Dec 1950, they opened the parish of Imaichi, which became the headquarters for the oriental district of the province of Osaka. They founded new parishes and educational institutions. A few years later, they also opened a parish and a school in Nagoya. The Claretians are presently trying to reach the marginalized workers of Kamagasaki, drug addicts, and mentally retarded children. A few Japanese have joined the Claretians, both as priests and as coadjutor brothers, and are actively involved in Claretian missions in Indonesia, Taiwan*, and South Korea.

India. In 1960, Francis Xavier Dirnberger, a German, arrived in India* to establish the Claretian Congregation. Sebastian Vayalil, bishop of Palai, Kerala, offered him several seminarians to be trained in Germany. Some became Claretians and returned after their training to establish the first Claretian House at Kuravilangad, Kerala, in 1970. They have expanded to Karnataka, Tamil Nadu, Andra, West Bengal, Bihar, Orissa, Mehalaya, Manipur, and other places. The mission work in India includes the rehabilitation of prisoners, lepers*, and drug addicts.

South Korea. The first two Claretians in Korea arrived on 8 Sep 1982; they were José Maria Ruiz Marquez and Manuel Tardio from the Philippines. Several others followed, and they established a center in Seoul, a parish in Sogot, Inchon, and a house in Kwanju. In addition to training future priests and missionaries, the Claretians in Korea also work among the poor, sick, and marginalized people.

Indonesia. Since 11 Oct 1983, Claretians have been in Darwin, Australia, working among the refugees* from East Timor*. On 10 May 1990, Orlando Cantillon and Manuel Suñas (Philippines) and James Nadakal (India) arrived in Dili in response to an invitation from the apostolic administrator, Carlos Felipe Ximenez Belo, to the Philippines Claretian superior, Domingo Moraleda, to establish missions in the mountains of Fohorem, province of Covalima, and later Bobonaro in the eastern part of East Timor. Besides consolidating the Christian communities and parishes, the Claretians have also undertaken agricultural and development projects for the benefit of the natives. Many young men from Timor and the Flores Islands have joined the formation centers at Kupang and Fohorem.

Sri Lanka. The German Francis Xavier Dirnberger was also instrumental in establishing the Claretian presence in Sri Lanka*. He recruited several young men from the area of Jaffna during the 1980s and trained them in India and the Philippines. Several returned to Sri Lanka in the early 1990s as ordained priests and started a central house in Colombo, providing pastoral services in several dioceses, and especially Jaffna.

Taiwan. Hoping to return to China, the superior general, Aquilino Bocos, decided to open a Claretian community in Taiwan, and Fathers Pablo Olmedo, Francisco Carin, and Mario Bonfaini arrived in Taipei on 20 Feb 1994.

Bibliography

Lozano, John M., *The Claretians: Their Mission and Spirit in the Church* (1980). DOMINGO MORALEDA

Clark, Edward Winter

(b. New York State, United States, 25 Feb 1830; d. 1911). First American Baptist missionary to the Ao Nagas.

Clark married Mary Mead in New York when he was 28 and was ordained as a pastor the following year at Logansport, Indiana, on 30 Jun 1859. He sailed from Boston for Assam on 20 Oct 1868 and arrived at Sibsagar on 30 Mar 1869, where he was to be in charge of the mission press and relieve William Ward*, who was due for furlough.

Three years later, Clark transferred to the Naga Hills. He reduced the Ao language to writing, using the Roman alphabet. During his stay in Nagaland, he prepared the Ao Naga Hymn Book, an Ao Naga grammar with illustrative phrases and vocabulary, and translated the Gospel and other Bible* portions into Ao Naga. L. A. Perrine dubbed Clark an Apostle to the Headhunters, and the Nagas still acclaim him so. He retired and returned to America in 1911, where he soon died. Clark Theological College was established in 1972 at Mokochung, Nagaland, in his memory.

Bibliography

Philip, P. T., *The Growth of Baptist Churches in Nagaland* (1983). • Puthenpurakal, Joseph, *Baptist Missions in Nagaland* (1984). L. H. SANGA RIVUNG

Clark, Percy and Mary

(b. ?; d. 1957 [Percy]; d. 1963 [Mary]). Baptist missionaries to Siam (Thailand).

In 1891 the Churches of Christ in Great Britain decided to begin overseas missions work. In 1892 Burma was chosen as the site for their first missionary endeavor. The first group of three missionaries included Alfred E. Hudson, Robert Halliday, and William Forrester. Halliday, his second wife, and his daughter Esther were later to play important roles in the early days of the work in Thailand*, then known as Siam. A mission was begun at Yeh, in the province of Tessarim in Burma, a center of the Tailing or Mon people not far from the border of Siam.

In 1903, learning that there was a large group of Mons on the Siamese side of the border who spoke the same language as those in Burma, Alfred Hudson entered Siam to work among them. He was joined later that year by Percy B. Clark from Blackburn, Lancashire, England, who had trained for evangelistic work before his departure for the mission field. Converts were made at Nakhon Choom near the river boundary, and in 1906 the mission headquarters was moved to the Siamese provincial capital of Nakhon Pathom, 60 kilometers west of Bangkok. The station at Yeh was handed over to the American Baptists* in 1909.

Meanwhile, Clark had married Mary Lenore Denley in Singapore* in 1904. She had received some medical training, especially in midwifery, a skill she immediately put into the service of the mission. She was never known to refuse a call, however distant or at whatever hour of the day or night, and was fearless even when called on to enter the villages and homes of suspected bandits.

The Clarks remained at the head of the Nakhon Pathom mission until they were interned all through the years of the Japanese occupation. They developed the work along evangelistic, educational, and medical lines. Percy Clark and Alfred Hudson journeyed along the rivers and canals, spreading the Gospel and establishing small groups of worshippers. Clark was doing this as late as 1930. A Siamese congregation came into existence in Nakhon Pathom, and then another for the Chinese. The Clarks personally supervised all the educational work until 1920. Separate schools were established for boys and girls, and the Chinese congregation opened a school for their children as well. In 1907 a small hospital was begun, and two Christian Chinese doctors supervised its operation for many years. Percy Clark also served on the Nakhon Pathom municipal council for a considerable period of time.

When the Church of Christ in Thailand (CCT) was formed in 1934, the mission of the British Churches of Christ did not feel that it could join the new church. Doctrinal issues and the likely repercussions back home probably constituted the main reasons. However, the Clarks maintained an ecumenical outlook and spirit. In 1930 Percy Clark had been a founding member of the Siam National Christian Council (SNCC). He and Mary had been invited to the conference in Bangkok in 1929 chaired by John R. Mott, which followed the International Missionary Council conference in Jerusalem the year before. The Bangkok conference was called to discuss the implications of the Jerusalem conference for Siam, and the SNCC and the CCT were to be its fruits.

Percy Clark also contributed to *Siam Outlook* (later *Thailand Outlook*), which was published quarterly by the Presbyterian Mission* "in the interests of missionary endeavor in the Kingdom of Siam."

Upon their release from internment in 1945, the Clarks returned to live at Nakhon Pathom and finally retired to Chonburi, east of Bangkok. Percy Clark died in 1957 and Mary in 1963. They were buried at Nakhon Pathom.

Bibliography

McFarland, George Bradley, ed., *Historical Sketch of Protestant Missions in Siam, 1828-1928* (1928). • Wells, Kenneth E., *History of Protestant Work in Thailand, 1828-1958* (1958). • Thompson, David M., *Let Sects and Parties Fall: A Short History of the Association of Churches of Christ in Great Britain and Ireland* (1980).
HAROLD F. GROSS

Clorinda

(b. ?; d. Palayamcottah, India, 1806). Early Brahmin woman convert who built the first Protestant church in India*.

About 250 years ago, a few hundred Marattas came to the Tanjore Kingdom and settled there. Among them, one man was working in the government service. His wife's name was Kokila. She was a Hindu Maratta Brahmin. When her young husband died, her relatives and Hindu pandits attempted to kill her, according to their religious custom called *suttee* or *sati*. But she was miraculously saved from the funeral pyre and brought to the British military camp by some officers.

When Colonel Littleton was transferred to Palayamcottah to command the army there, he was accompanied by Kokola. Christian Friedrich Schwartz* (1724-98) used to come to Palayamcottah to conduct worship and communion services for the military officers. A few years after the incident with Kokila took place, Schwartz visited the neighborhood of Palayamcottah, and Kokila applied to him to be baptized. But he told her that, as long as she continued the illicit connection with Littleton, he could not comply with her request. It appears, however, that the colonel had privately promised to marry her. Meanwhile, Littleton died of a severe illness. As Kokila belonged to the Brahmin caste, was related to the palace, and had lived with the English colonel, others called her *Rani Ammal* (queen).

In those days, there were no churches at Palayamcottah, so Schwartz baptized Kokila at one of the small prayer meetings for military officers. This baptism service took place on 25 Feb 1778, when Kokila was 32 years old. From that day, she came to be known as Royal Clorinda. Clorinda began work around Palayamcottah and, within two years, 42 people had joined her for worship. In the first baptism register of the Palayamcottah Mission (1780), the names of 40 people are mentioned, including the parents of Tanjore Vedanayagom Shastariyar.

Clorinda brought the catechist Sattianadan from Tranquebar to Palayamcottah at her own expense. She gave him a house to stay in and a salary to do the work at Palayamcottah. She built a church at Palayamcottah in 1783, which was dedicated by C. F. Schwartz on 24 Aug 1785. This church exists even today. The local residents call the church *Papathi Ammal Kovil* (the Brahmin Lady's Church).

Clorinda also established a small school at Palayamcottah. This was the first mission school in the district of Tirunelveli. The present-day St. John's College at Palayamcottah originated in the Pial school started by Royal Clorinda. Clorinda also dug a large well from which the general public could draw water. People still use this well and call it *Papathi Ammal Kinaru* (the Brahmin Lady's Well).

Royal Clorinda died eight years after Schwartz's death (13 Feb 1798). She was buried at Palayamcottah near her church.

Bibliography

Kadambavanam, S. Paul, "Origins of the Diocese of Tirunelveli," *Madras* 7 (1967). • Pearson, Hugh, *Memoirs of the Life and Correspondence of the Rev. C. F. Schwartz*, 2nd ed., Vol. II (1835). • Hough, James, *History of Christianity in India from the Commencement of the Christian Era*, Vol. III (1845). Franklyn J. Balasundaran

Cole, Edna S.

(b. Illinois, United States, 1 Jan 1855; d. United States, 23 Nov 1950). American Presbyterian* missionary educator instrumental in the promotion of women's education in Thailand*.

Cole graduated from Western Female Seminary, Ohio, in 1878. She served in the Chiang Mai Station of the Presbyterian Church's Laos Mission, northern Thailand, from 1878 until 1883, where she developed a girls' class into the Chiang Mai Girls' School, the first Western-style school in northern Thailand. In 1885 she took over the Presbyterian Siam Mission's Bangkok Girls' School and made it the leading girls' school in the nation. The school was officially called the Harriet House* School and popularly referred to as the Wang Lang School because of its location.

Cole undertook several major expansions of the school, the most important being in 1888 when the school took over the whole of the mission's Wang Lang property. About that same year the members of royalty began placing their daughters and maids-in-waiting in the school. The school also provided numerous teachers for government schools. Cole emphasized the school's value to the church and trained teachers for mission schools, particularly in northern Thailand. The school also sponsored an annual Conference for Christian Workers and housed Bangkok's Second Church from 1878 onward. Cole initiated the removal of the school to its present location in 1921, where it is now called the Wattana Wittaya Academy. After a long period of illness, she officially retired in 1923.

Bibliography

McFarland, George Bradley, ed., *Historical Sketch of Protestant Missions in Siam in 1828-1928* (1928). • Eakin Family Papers, Payap University Archives, Chiang Mal, Thailand. • Wells, Kenneth E., *History of Protestant Work in Thailand 1828-1958* (1958). Herbert R. Swanson

Colleges and Universities

Education, especially higher education, has been one of the most important and controversial concerns of Christian work in Asia. The earliest missionaries coming from the West realized the importance of translation (see Bible Translation) and literacy*, but in order to prepare indigenous church leaders, higher education was required. Controversy ensued in the 19th c. with an increased em-

Colleges and Universities

phasis, made possible in part by financial support from the colonial governments, on general college education for both Christians and non-Christians. Some reasoned that general education was an obvious path to evangelize the local children; higher education would train strong Christian leaders. Others argued that it was simply part of the Christianizing and civilizing responsibility of the church to provide education. Many mission leaders questioned the huge amounts of money spent for schools to teach young adults physics, biology, and business. They questioned whether this was really the responsibility of Christian missions. In the end, hundreds of schools were started from the middle of the 19th c. until the Pacific War (see World War II). Most of these schools started out as small classes meeting in a missionary's home or on the mission compound, teaching elementary subjects. In time many grew to become colleges, often combining in the 20th c. with other small colleges to form union universities. By 1910 the issue of education, especially higher education, was so important on the ecumenical (see Ecumenical Movement) agenda that the largest volume from the Edinburgh Missionary Conference, 1910, was the report of Commission III, "Education in Relation to the Christianization of National Life." As a result of the proliferation of colleges and universities in Asia, Christian leaders did become trained, and for many countries education became one of the key ingredients in the broader mission of the church. Throughout Asia, the introduction of modern science, mathematics, philosophy, and agricultural studies was the result of Christian schools. Many of these schools planted the seeds of faith along with seeds of doubt through their Western curricula combined with Christian classes and chapel services.

The earliest forerunners of modern colleges in China* began as small schools and orphanages for teaching children. Hangchow University, for example, started out as a boarding school for boys in 1845. By 1897 it had become an accredited college. Between 1879 and 1924 the 13 Protestant Christian Colleges in China were all founded, and during their years of existence as Protestant schools, 26,000 students graduated and another 40,000 attended but did not complete their studies. The 13 Protestent Colleges were Yenching University (Beijing), Shantung Christian University, Ginling College (women's), University of Nanking, Huachung University, West China Union University, Soochow University, St. John's University, University of Shanghai, Hangchow University, Hwa Nan College (women's), Fukien Christian University, and Lingnan University. During the Japanese occupation and the years of student uprisings, many schools had to close or move to the west to stay open. The Christian presence of most of these schools in the broader Chinese society was only a brief chapter in Chinese history (50-60 years), and yet their impact would be difficult to estimate.

Roman Catholic* schools in China developed later and with fewer schools, and yet some of these schools also became important in the training of Chinese leaders. The first Catholic university in China, Aurora University, was founded by a Chinese Christian, Ma Xiang Po*, in 1903. The school was later turned over to the Jesuits*, who expanded the school. Aurora College for Women was established by the Society of the Sacred Heart in 1926, and later joined Aurora University. Other Catholic universities include Catholic University of Beijing (established in 1927 by American Benedictines* with Ma Xiang Po and Ying Qinzhi), Tianjin College of Commerce and Engineering, and Fu Jen Catholic University. After the Communist takeover of colleges in China, Fu Jen was reestablished through the efforts of the Chinese Bishops Conference, Jesuits, the Society of the Divine Word*, and the Sisters of the Holy Spirit* in Taipei, Taiwan*.

Although Jesuits had been training missionaries in India* since the 16th c., it was not until 1819 that the first "College for the instruction of Asiatic, Christian and other youth in Eastern Literature and European Science" was opened by William Carey* in Serampore, India. From the beginning, nearly half of the students were non-Christian (18 out of 37); thus, like many other Christian colleges in Asia, the school would serve the dual purpose of training leaders and evangelizing through education. In 1827 the King of Denmark empowered the college to grant bachelor of arts and bachelor of divinity degrees (see Theological Education). By 1910 the whole Indian territory (including Burma [Myanmar*] and Ceylon) would have 53 Christian colleges. Most of these were related to British churches (16 were Church of England, 10 were related to other English churches, and seven were Scottish churches), and most were Protestant (only seven were Roman Catholic). During the late 19th and early 20th cs., government schools expanded with much greater financial support. As a result, some of the Christian colleges closed, while others struggled for survival and a new sense of purpose. By 1932 there were only 38 colleges in the Indian region, nine being run by American churches. A new problem began to develop in South Asia with more and more local students and staff; the institutions were growing faster than the conversions. It became difficult to find enough local Christian staff to work in the "Christian" colleges. In addition to introducing Western studies, one of the greatest social changes these schools promoted in Muslim and Hindu societies was the education of women. Protestant schools, such as Women's Christian College of Madras, Kinnaird College in Lahore, St. Christopher's Training College in Madras, and Isabella Thoburn* in Lucknow, opened up Indian society to women and women to the larger society. In 1918 the great woman pioneer Ida Scudder* opened the first Women's Medical College (coeducational in 1945). Roman Catholic women's higher education developed, but not until after World War II, and then in rapid succession: Stella Maris College at Madras (1947), Providence College at Udagamandalam and Nirmala College at

Coimbatore (1948), Fatima College at Madurai (1953), Auxilium College at Katpadi (1954), and, finally, Jayaraj Anna Packiam College at Periakulam, Holy Cross College at Tiruchchirappalli, St Mary's College at Tuticorin, and St. Ignatius College at Palayankottai.

The language of education in India was an important issue for the churches. The use of English, it was reasoned, brought all of the fruits of Western learning to India and provided a foundation for those who would do theological studies, but not all mission societies agreed. One result of the extensive and more democratic approach to education in India (including the uniform language of instruction) was the blurring of caste and sex lines to give "outsiders" access to the benefits of society in general. Indian scholars were also prepared for graduate study and thus to take over the leadership of the Christian colleges and universities. An unexpected result of the flourishing of Christian colleges, with their English language medium and Western curricula, was the beginning of Hindu and Muslim schooling to counter the Christian influence (e.g., Hindu College as a response to St. John's College which started in 1880).

Christian education in Sri Lanka* began with the arrival of the first Franciscan* missionaries in 1542 during the Portuguese rule (1505-1658). The Franciscans operated two types of schools: parish schools and colleges. The parish schools were small and provided rudimentary instruction in religion, reading, and writing. Colleges were in fact monasteries where students were given higher education in religion. The Jesuits, who arrived in 1602, had better organized colleges that had three departments: elementary, secondary, and theological. The Augustinians* (1604) and Dominicans* (1605) also established schools in Sri Lanka. Links between education and religion were evident; education was the principal means of introducing Christianity to the local people. The Dutch (1638-1796) took over Portuguese territory in Sri Lanka and found a well-organized parish school system that was confined to oral instruction. The British, who came in 1796, recognized the value of parish schools. When the Colebrooke Commission of 1829 emphasized the necessity for English education, Christian missionaries were made exclusive authorities for education on the island with financial assistance from the government. Besides the parish schools, a teachers' training college was set up in 1914 by the Anglican*, Methodist*, and Baptist* missions.

Eventually, the Christian monopoly on education, the emphasis on English and Westernization, and government funding led to opposition from the Buddhists, Hindus, and Muslims. In 1905, following the Wace Commission's report, the government imposed a "conscience clause" on vernacular mission schools. This permitted non-Christian parents to withdraw their children from Christian schools if necessary. The situation came to a head in 1960, when all assisted schools were taken over by the government, leaving only a handful as private schools.

The roots of Christian schools in Japan* reach as far back as the 16th c. when Francis Xavier* aspired to establish a Roman Catholic university in Japan. A Kirishitan* school for Japanese and Portuguese novitiates was finally started in 1580. However, the school functioned for only 20 years because of persecution and restrictions on Kirishitan activities.

The next phase of school building took place in the 1800s and early 1900s, which saw the mushrooming of many schools, the majority of them Protestant. Two Catholic schools established during this period were Sophia University (1908), opened by German, French, and English Jesuits, and the Sacred Heart Girls' School (1908), founded in Tokyo. Protestant institutions originating in this period include Aoyama Gakuin University (1878), Doshisha (1875), Ferris Girls' School (1870), Kwansei Gakuin University (1887), Rikkyo University (1874), Meiji Gakuin University (1877), Kobe Jo Gakuin Women's University (1875), Hiroshima Jo Gakuin Women's University (1886), Hirosaki Gakuin School (1888), Kinjo Gakuin University (1889), Tsuda Juku University (1900), Tokyo Woman's Christian College (1918), Toyo Eiwa Girls' School, Tohoku Gakuin College, and Kanto Gakuin School. Of special note is Doshisha, which was started by Japanese convert Neesima*, who established the Yamamoto Society to help with the funding of one of the first Christian colleges in Japan in Kyoto.

Over the years, Christian schools encountered many difficulties in Japan. In the 1890s, when many Christian schools were appearing, the rise of nationalism* resulted in a general loss of interest in Christianity. In 1899 the ministry of education issued an order forbidding religion to be taught in private schools. This led Christian schools to switch to professional school status by offering other subjects. Religious teaching in private schools was allowed to resume only when new school regulations were enforced after World War II. During the war, many students and teachers were killed, school buildings were destroyed in bombing raids, missionaries were expelled, foreign financial aid declined, recruiting for English department classes stopped, and teachers were interrogated because of suspected ties with the enemy. Natural disasters, such as the Great Kanto Earthquake of 1923, also caused much damage, but demolished schools were slowly rebuilt.

In many places, Christian schools were the pioneers in higher education. Besides building up Japanese society, Christian schools helped raise the status of Japanese women. Many Japanese women educators, social workers, temperance workers, and women's liberation pioneers were educated in Christian schools. A number of research institutes have also been established, and academies for specialized studies (e.g., Nippon Christian Academy, 1961, and Asian Rural Institute, 1973).

Some of the churches and agencies involved in establishing and operating Christian schools in Korea* include the Presbyterian Church United States South

(Taejon College), Korean Mission of the Presbyterian Church, USA (Yonsei University, 1915), Presbyterian Church in Korea (Hanshin University, 1940, Kosin University, 1946, and Korea Christian Academy, 1966), Northern Presbyterian Mission (Soongsil University, 1897), together with the Methodist Episcopal Church North, Methodist Church in Korea (Mokwon University, 1954), as well as Christian individuals (Pierson University, 1912, later renamed Pyeng-taek University). Several of these schools began as seminaries (Kosin University, Hanshin University, Pierson University, and Mokwon University).

During the Japanese Occupation of Korea, all missionaries were deported. The Japanese took over some Christian schools and shut down others because they rejected Shinto* shrine worship. Many graduates of Christian schools actively participated in the independence movement. After the Japanese left, control of the schools returned to the church. However, due to the Communist regime in North Korea, institutions there were relocated to South Korea or were closed.

Today Christian universities in Korea offer a range of vocational and academic fields which lead to bachelor's, master's, and doctoral degrees. These include theology, liberal arts, medicine, public health, natural science, commerce, and agriculture. Christian schools play an important role in Korean churches and society. Institutions such as the Korea Christian Academy contribute toward the modernization of Korea by training young people for the work of industrial development, political democratization, and social improvement. Some of the strongest movements for social change have come from Christian universities in Korea.

Roman Catholic education in the Philippines* has grown tremendously in the past century. The Catholic Educational Association of the Philippines (CEAP) has a membership that comprises 21 universities, 56 graduate schools, 203 colleges, 1,055 secondary schools, 420 elementary schools, and 31 affiliate educational associations in the 13 regions. Founded in 1941, CEAP supports the teaching function of the Catholic Church and promotes quality education. CEAP also advocates religious education as essential in Catholic character formation and citizenship building.

Ateneo de Manila, originally a public primary school for boys, became a Jesuit school in 1859. The status of the school was raised to college of secondary instruction in 1865, and it was then entitled to confer the bachelor of arts degree. Ateneo de Manila gradually expanded to include a college of law (1936), a graduate school of arts and sciences (1948), and a graduate school of business (1960). It was granted university status in 1959. Three other Jesuit institutions bearing the name Ateneo are Ateneo de Naga, Ateneo de Davao, and Ateneo de Zamboanga. A fourth, Ateneo de Cayagan, renamed Xavier University, operates a museum and has two institutions of international repute: Southeast Asian Rural Leadership Institute and the Research Institute for Mindanao Culture. Other Catholic schools include De La Salle University (1911), established by the Brothers of Christian Schools, and Divine Word University (1929), operated by the Society of the Divine Word*.

The Association of Christian Schools and Colleges (ACSC) is an association for fellowship, cooperation, mutual support, and the maintenance of high academic standards among Protestant schools in the Philippines. Founded in 1946, ACSC also serves as a liaison body with cooperating mission boards, government, and related agencies. By 1993 ACSC had 101 member schools comprising four universities, 23 colleges, and 74 secondary schools. These institutions represent the Philippine Baptist Convention, First Church of God, Independent Baptist Church, Southern Baptist Convention, Philippine Episcopal Church, Philippine Independent* Church, Seventh-Day Adventist* Church, Chinese United Evangelical Church, United Church of Christ in the Philippines, and United Methodist Church.

In Indonesia* the Christian educational system has been significant in the development of the national education system, as well as in church planting and evangelism. The Protestant school system in Indonesia was a joint effort of the church and the Dutch East India Company (*Vereenigde Oost-Indie Compagnie,* VOC) in the early 17th c., reflecting the concept of church and state unity during that period. However, students were solely from the Dutch community. The Dutch colonial government replaced the VOC in 1800, and attention gradually began to be given to educating local people. Protestant missionaries arrived in the early 19th c. and quickly established schools as channels for evangelism. In accordance with the government's principle of religious neutrality, governmental subsidy policies required that religion be kept as an optional subject. This strained relations between the government and Protestant mission bodies.

The foundation of the present Catholic school system was laid in the latter half of the 19th c. by the Ursuline* Sisters, Brothers of St. Aloysius, and Sisters of Mercy. Although anti-Catholic colonial officers often delayed the opening of new schools, many Catholic boarding schools were set up, the first of which was Canisius College (1927). Teachers' training colleges were established in Flores (1862), Celebes (1905), and Central Java (1904).

During the Japanese occupation (1942-45), many schools were confiscated and some destroyed. After the war a considerable number of school buildings were not returned, but the church was able to provide for the increase in students. Many new churches and Christian organizations established schools during the era of independence. Today there are thousands of Christian schools in Indonesia, from kindergarten to high school (both general and vocational), and over 100 Christian universities and colleges. These are required to adhere to the constitution of the national education system, which allows religious schools to be self-managed and to conduct religious instruction. The National Council of

Christian Education (NCCE) was set up by the Indonesian Council of Churches in 1950 to coordinate and promote Christian education on a national level within the framework of the national education system. The NCCE is assisted by the Centers for the Development of Christian Education at Christian University (UKI) and Satyawancana University, the planning board in Jakarta, and the publication department of the NCCE headquarters.

Catholic schools are represented to the NCCE and the ministry of education by the National Council for Catholic Education. More than 400 Catholic foundations in the country run roughly 2,700 primary schools and 1,412 secondary schools. Catholic vocational schools include graphics schools (e.g., SMT Grafika Lenteng Agung, 1970), technical academies (e.g., STMI St. Michael, 1967), carpentry schools (e.g., PIKA, 1968), and secretarial and nursing schools. Several foundations also provide nonformal education to increase employment prospects. There are 10 Catholic universities, among which are Atma Jaya (1960), Parahyangan University (1955), and Sanata Dharma University (1955). Catholic institutions of higher learning also maintain ties with Stichting University in the Netherlands through the Association of Catholic Schools of Higher Learning.

The ministry of Christian schools in Malaysia* and Singapore* was varied in its purposes and method but shared similar results. The majority of Christian schools in West Malaysia and Singapore were built and maintained by the American Methodist Mission, LaSalle Brothers, and Sisters of the Holy Infant Jesus. Anglican missionary bodies (London Missionary Society and the Society for the Promotion of Female Education in the East) introduced the first schools in Malaysia and Singapore at the beginning of the 19th c. Catholic and Methodist education began in earnest in the latter half of the 19th c. In East Malaysia, the Basel Church, Anglican Church, Mill Hill Brothers, and Mission Hill Sisters built the majority of Christian schools, with Methodists and Seventh-Day Adventists each founding a major urban school.

The significance of these schools in Malaysian society overall may be gauged by the fact that, in 1950, they educated nearly half the students in English medium schools in West Malaysia and provided nearly two-thirds of all secondary education in any medium. With the exception of government schools for the Malay Muslim elite, Christian schools were given the primary responsibility for English medium education in the colonies. They were the first girls' school in any medium of instruction and educated two-thirds of the women in West Malaysia up to independence in 1957. In Sarawak the Christian schools educated over half of those attending any school, and all of those who sought a secondary education. In Sabah they were, until independence, the only English medium schools. As a result, the schools played a crucial role in educating the English urban elite throughout Malaysia, particularly the significant class of professional women involved in education, business, and politics. They also helped shape the character of the churches as a largely urban, middle-class body.

Growth of Christian schools in both East and West Malaysia was tied to economic expansion and government grants. Grants were given on condition that the schools prepared children for the annual government examinations and refrained from evangelism during school hours. After World War II*, concerted efforts were made to develop Malaysia. Christian schools grew rapidly in response to greatly increased government grants. By 1960 they were found in almost every urban center. At the same time the percentage of Christian teachers dropped rapidly. After Malaysia became independent in 1957, the mission schools were gradually nationalized. Christian instruction was no longer allowed during school hours, and instruction in Islam* for Muslims was required. They were required to adopt the national system of Malay medium instruction, as English was not a recognized vernacular under the new constitution. East Malaysia schools came under the same policies when Sabah and Sarawak joined the Malaysia Federation in 1963. In 1970 amendments to the Education Act of 1961 brought Christian school management under the control of the ministry of education, although in most cases the property is still owned by the churches. Singapore left the federation in 1965, and after a period when Christian schools were under the control of the education ministry, they were invited to become independent schools operating under their own management. They are now some of Singapore's largest and most prestigious schools.

Prior to British conquest, education in Myanmar* reflected the Buddhist (see Buddhism) religion of the local people. Schools were basically monastic, but in addition to Buddhist philosophy, the curriculum also included the "3Rs," history, Pali, geography, astrology, and medicine. There were also lay schools for children too young to attend the monastic schools. Roman Catholic missionaries first opened vernacular and coeducational mission schools in Myanmar in the mid-18th c. Religious books in the Myanmar language were printed to teach the rudiments of Christianity. The Roman Catholic mission schools, however, were restricted to the Christian community, although there were a few secret Myanmar converts among the students. By the first half of the 19th c., the Roman Catholics were providing education for two groups of people: the European community and the Karens*. The American Baptist Mission (ABM) began educational work in 1824. As soon as Ann Judson, the wife of Adoniram Judson*, had acquired proficiency in the Myanmar language, she administered two schools. ABM schools for boys of various nationalities were later founded in 1826. These schools taught Christianity and the "3Rs" in the Myanmar language. In 1867 the British government set up a department of public instruction to encourage the spread of education. Thus Anglo-vernacular and mission schools were established in principal towns. Although the curriculum led to a university education, it had few facilities for technical and vocational education. As such, employment opportunities for vernacular students were limited, while those trained in English served as minor officials in the British administration. During the Japanese period schools were standardized, with the Myanmar language as the main medium of instruction, and after Myanmar's independence, the state took control of education in the country.

As in Myanmar, higher education in Siam (Thailand*) got an early but weak start by the Roman Catholics. French Catholic missionaries, followed by the Jesuits, set up the first European-style schools in Siam in the mid-1660s. The setting up of schools, both Catholic and Protestant, began in earnest only in the 19th c. A key person in the establishing of Catholic schools was Jean-Louis Vey*, apostolic vicar of Siam. Taking note of the country's move toward progress and modern civilization, Vey encouraged missionaries to set up elementary schools in the respective districts. He also reasoned that literacy was necessary to maintain the Catholic faith of catechumens. By his invitation, teachers from St. Mary's College in London and the Sisters of St. Maur arrived to open and staff schools in Siam. This led to the opening of Assumption College for boys and a Convent School for girls in 1885. Later the St. Gabriel Brothers were appointed to take charge of Assumption College. The American Presbyterian* Mission played a major role in setting up Protestant mission schools in Thailand. These include Bangkok Christian College (1852), Dara Academy (1873), Wattana Wittaya Academy (1874), Prince Royal's College (1888), and the McCormick School of Nursing (1923). During World War II the Japanese seized and nationalized all mission schools, but control was returned to the missionaries after the war. The administration of Presbyterian mission schools and institutions of higher learning were handed over to the Church of Christ in Thailand in 1959. The Thai government made it possible to establish private tertiary level educational institutions in 1970. As such, Payap University was opened by the Church of Christ in 1974 and today comprises the McCormick Faculty of Nursing, the McGilvary Faculty of Theology, the Faculty of Humanities, and the Faculty of Social Sciences.

Receiving royal approval and support from the early days, Christian schools in Thailand have contributed much to the development of Thai society. The schools have played a central role in the education and employment of women in a society that traditionally denied women formal learning. Today Christian institutions in Thailand are some of the leading schools that provide quality education from kindergarten to university level.

Bibliography

Sri Lanka

Sumathipala, K. H. M., *History of Education in Ceylon* (1970). • De Silva, K. M., *University of Ceylon: History of Ceylon*, Vol. 3 (1974). • Don Peter, W. L. A., *Education in Sri Lanka under the Portuguese* (1978).

Japan

Arai Toshitsugu, *Hanashiai ("Discussion")* (1983). • Hiratsuka Masatoku, *Nihon kirisuto-kyo shugi kyoiku bunka shi* (History of Japanese Christian education and culture) (1937). • *Ningen o chushin to shita joshi kyoiku shi* (The people-centered history of women's education) (1965). • Aoyama Nao, *Meiji jogakko no kenkyu* (Study of girls' schools in the Meiji Period) (1970). • Fukaya Masashi, *Ryosai kenbo shugi no kyoiku* (Education to be a good wife and a wise mother) (1966). • *Aoyama Gakuin kyu-ju nen shi* (Ninety-year history of Aoyama Gakuin) (1965). • Iglehart, C. W., *International Christian University — An Adventure in Christian Higher Education in Japan* (1964). • *Rikkyo gakuin setsuritsu enkaku shi* (Historical development of Rikkyo Gakuin) (1954). • *Rikkyo gakuin hyaku-nen shi* (One hundred-year history of Rikkyo Gakuin) (1974). • Washiyama Daizaburo, *Meiji gakuin go-ju-nen shi* (Fifty-year history of Meiji Gakuin) (1927). • *Meiji gakuin hyaku-nen shi* (One hundred-year history of Meiji Gakuin) (1977). • *Akiyama Misao, Kirisuto kyokai shi* (History of the Christian Church [Disciples]) (1973). • Murata Yuka, ed., *Joshi sei gakuin goju-nen shi* (Fifty-year history of Joshi Sei Gakuin) (1956). • *Nihon baptistuto renmei shi* (History of Japan Baptist Convention) (1959). • *Seinan gakuin nana-ju-nen shi* (Seventy-year history of Seinan Gakuin) (1986). • Hana-wa Shozaburo, ed., *Tohoku Gakuin Soritsu Nana-ju-nen-shi* (Seventy-year history of Tohoku Gakuin) (1959). • *Kanto Gakuin go-ju-nen no ayumi* (Fifty years at Kanto Gakuin) (1969). • *Kanto Gakuin shi shiryo shu* (Collection of materials on the history of Kanto Gakuin), Vols. 1-6 (1976-79). • Roggendorf, Joseph, ed., *Jochi daigaku go-ju-nen shi* (Fifty-year history of Sophia University) (1963). • *Jochi daigaku shi shiryoshu* (Collection of materials on the history of Sophia University), Vols. 1-3 (1980-85). • Yoshikawa Toshikazu, *Tsuda Umeko* (1930). • *Tsuda Juku yonju-nen shi* (Forty-year history of Tsuda Jukuege) (1940). • Yamazaki Takako, *Tsuda Umeko* (1962). • Yamazaki Takako, ed., *Tsuda Juku rokuju-nen shi* (Sixty-year history of Tsuda Juku University) (1960). • Yamazaki Takako, ed., *Tsuda Umeko bunshu* (Writings of Tsuda Umeko) (1980). • Friends and Alumni of Tokyo Woman's Christian College, *Nitobe Inazo Sensei Tsuito-roku* (Record of memorial for Professor Nitobe Inazo) (1934). • Aoyama Nao, *Yasui Tetsu Den* (Biography of Ysui Tetsu) (1949). • *Tokyo Joshi Daigaku Go-ju-nen shi* (Fifty-year history of Tokyo Woman's Christian College) (1968). • *Yasui Tetsu to Tokyo Joshi Daigaku* (Yasui Tetsu and Tokyo Woman's Christian College) (1982). • Reischauer, A. K., *Tokyo Woman's Christian College, Tokyo Joshi Daigaku: Its Founding and Early Developments* (1953). • *Toyo eiwa jo gakuin hyaku-nen shi* (One hundred-year history of Toyo Eiwa Girls' School) (1984). • *Ferisu jo gakuin hyaku-ju-nen shoshi* (One hundred ten-year condensed history of Ferris Girls' School)

(1982). • *Seishin joshi gakuin nana-ju-nen no ayomi* (Seventy-year history of Sacred Heart Girls' School) (1978). • *Kobe jo gakuin hyaku-nen shi* (Centennial history of Kobe Jo Gakuin Women's University), 2 Vols. (1976, 1981). • Kondo Buichi, *Kinjo gakuin nana-ju-nen shi* (Seventy-year history of Kinjo Gakuin) (1960). • *Ichimura Yoichi Sensei* (Professor Ichimura Yoichi) (1965). • Mayama Mitsuma et al., *Kinjo gakuin saikin ju-nen shi* (The most recent decade of Kinjo Gakuin) (1980). • Takebayashi Setsuzo, *Nanmi senkyo go-ju-nen shi* (Fifty-year history of Southern Methodist Mission) (1936). • *Hiroshima go gakuin kyu-ju-nen no ayumi* (The ninety-year path of Hiroshima Girls' School) (1976). • *Hirosaki jo gakko rekishi* (History of Hirosaki Girls' School) (1926). • *Hirosaki gakuin hachi-jusshunen kinen shoshi* (Eightieth anniversary book of Hirosaki Gakuin) (1967).

Korea

Kosin University Bulletin for 1993-94 (in Korean) (1993). • Kim, S. S., and S. G. Lee, *The Educational Task of Kosin University* (in Korean) (1994). • Underwood, Lillias H., *Underwood of Korea* (1918). • American Tract Society, "Fifteen Years among the Top-knots" (1904). • Underwood, H. G., *The Call of Korea* (1908). • Rhodes, H. A., ed., *History of the Korea Mission Presbyterian Church USA 1882-1934* (1934). • *Yonsei Daehak'kio Paikyonsa* (History of the 100 years of Yonsei University), Vol. 104 (1985). • *Soongch'un Daehak'kio 80 yon-sa* (The 80 years of Soongch'un University). • Lee Myung Jik, *The Brief History of OMS Holiness Church* (1929). • "Minutes of the General Assembly of the Korea Evangelical Holiness Church." • *The Materials of Theological Educational Institutions in Korea* (1995).

Philippines

Sitoy, T. Valentino, Jr., *Several Springs, One Stream* (1992). • "NCCP Newsletter," Vol. 33, No. 3 (Jun-Aug 1993). • "Ateneo de Manila University Fact Sheet 1994."

Indonesia

Aritonang, Jan Sihar, *A History of Schooling in Batakland, Indonesia* (1993). • Kroeskamp, H., *Early Schoolmasters in a Developing Country* (1974). • *Strateji Pendidikan Kristen di Indonesia* (1989). • Moedjanto, G., *Tiga Dasawarsa Atma Jaya* (1990). • Heuken, Adolf, *Unika Atma Jaya 1960-1990* (1995); *Ensiklopedi Populer Tentang Gereja Katolik di Indonesia* (1989).

Malaysia/Singapore

300 Years of the De La Salle Brothers in Asia, 1652-1980 (1980). • Chelliah, D. D., *A Short History of Educational Policy in the Straits Settlements, 1890-1925* (1960). • Holmes, Brian, ed., *Educational Policy and the Mission Schools* (1967). • Ho Seng Ong, *Methodist Schools in Malaysia* (1963). • Kwan Lee Kun, *Gerakan Missionari Kristian Protestan di Sabah: Satu Tinjauan Mengenai Sumbangan Missionari Protestan di dalam Pendidikan (1880-1962)*. • Ooi Keat Gin, "Mission Education in Sarawak during the Period of Brooke Rule, 1840-1946," *Sarawak Mission Journal*, Vol. 63 (1991).

Myanmar

U Kaung, "A Survey of the History of Education in Burma before the British Conquest and After," *Journal of the Burma Research Society*, Vol. 46, Part 2 (Dec 1963). • "Octennial Report on Education in Burma — 1947/48 to 1954/55," *Supdt* (1956).

Thailand

McFarland, George Bradley, ed., *Historical Sketch of Protestant Missions in Siam, 1828-1928* (1928). • Wells, Kenneth E., *History of Protestant Work in Thailand, 1828-1958* (1958). • Prince Royal's College, *Prince Royal's College 80 Years, 1906-1986* (1986). • Prasit Pongudom, "From Monburi to Bangrak," *Church News*, Vol. 52, No. 397 (Jul 1983) (in Thai). • Satien Thamaraphak, *M. B. Palmer, B.A., B.D. and Bangkok Christian College, 1920-1938* (in Thai). • Persons, Donald S., "Land Management Issues Underlying the International School, Bangkok," unpublished research paper, Chiang Mai: Payap University Archives (1991). • "Records of the American Presbyterian Mission and the Church of Christ in Thailand," Payap University Archives. • *McCormick School of Nursing 60th Anniversary Volume* (1983). • "The History of Payap University," *Payap News*, 3 Dec 1994 (in Thai). • Maen Pangudom and Prasit Pangudom, "Missionary Education in Lan Na Thailand," in *Chiang Mai Teachers' College 60th Anniversary Volume* (1983). • Dara Academy, *One Hundredth Anniversary Volume* (1978) (in Thai). • Swanson, Herbert R., "A New Generation," *Sojourn*, 3 Aug 1988.

SCOTT W. SUNQUIST, compiled by
CHRISTABEL WONG LEE MAY
(see List of Contributors in
the front of this volume)

Colonialism

The West European efforts to colonize Asia were based on two major motivations: first, to gain a direct access to the riches of India*, and, second, to expand the fight against the Muslims to regions outside of southwestern Europe, where the Spanish *Reconquista* finally succeeded in 1492 by capturing Granada — in the very year Christopher Columbus landed on Guanahani Island and opened the New World for Spain.

The direct trading routes to Asia were cut after the Mamluks became rulers of Egypt and the Ottoman Turks started to extend their kingdom in the 14th c. Portugal, after expelling the last Muslims from its territory in 1250, explored the western shores of Africa, and Bartholomeus Diaz successfully circumnavigated the Cape of Good Hope in 1484. In 1498, Vasco da Gama landed in Calicut on the Malabar coast in South India.

In order to avoid conflicts between the Portuguese and Spaniards over the newly discovered territories in the New World, Pope Alexander VI, in a papal bull issued in 1493, divided the world into Spanish and Portuguese spheres of influence; and the Treaty of Tordesillas (1494) laid down a north-south dividing line 100 leagues to the west of the Azores and the Cape Verde Islands. At the same time, the two Iberian sovereigns were entrusted with the *padroado**, or *patronate* (patronage), which gave them the responsibility and authority to administer the church in their new territories.

But also the Protestant countries used religious, or denominational, motivations in their colonial endeavors. In particular the Netherlands, after having achieved independence from Spain, acted against the Catholics in Eastern Indonesia*, then in Malacca*, Colombo (Sri Lanka*), and Taiwan*. Internal European conflicts, too, quite often affected the colonies. It is quite obvious that the predominant motivation behind colonialism was the striving after economic profit, and religion quite often was used as a pretext and propaganda tool. Therefore, the situations of missionaries, local Christians, and churches under colonial rule have been quite diverse.

Portuguese. The Portuguese were the first among the modern European colonialists to set foot in Asia, and they were among the last to leave. In 1961, they were forced out of Goa (where they had been settled since 1510) by the Indian occupation forces, and they left East Timor* in 1975 only after the democratic revolution. They maintained Macau until 1999, when it was returned to China*.

A well-known Portuguese administrator-historian, J. H. da Cunha Rivara, commented on the difference between Spanish and Portuguese colonial rule: "India was not America. Here the European conquerors could not exterminate summarily the natives, because they were not ingenuous and savages, neither replace them with people imported from Europe. Distance from the home country and the undefeatable resistance of huge numbers, among whom there were important groups with a high degree of culture, made the colonialists opt for more subtle forms of violence, though not always mild, in order to attain the same goals" (*Ensaio Histórico da Lingua Concani,* 1858). Portugal, being a small nation, opted for a commercial network or, as historian C. R. Boxer termed it, a "thalassocracy," or "a shoe-string empire," comprising a string of coastal outposts or fortified settlements linked by flotillas of merchant ships and fleets of gunboats. Afonso de Albuquerque* was the architect of this empire that came to be known after his death as *Estado da Índia.* He had captured Hormuz, a key point to control the trade through the Gulf of Aden and the Red Sea; Goa, another central point on the west coast of India, to check the supplies of Arabian and Persian horses to the Indian potentates in the hinterland; and Malacca, yet another strategic point at the Straits through which flowed most of the traditional trade of Southeast Asia and the Far East. The Portuguese tried to block the traditional Muslim enemies of Europe from continuing to benefit from the profitable spice trade of Asia. To achieve this, the Portuguese introduced the passport, or *cartaz,* system of shipping control and resorted to corsair activity on a large scale.

Originally, Cochin in Malabar (South India), and later Goa, were made the headquarters of this far-flung *Estado da Índia,* which extended from East Africa to the islands of the Pacific and Japan. The Dutch, English, and French began making inroads from the early years of the 17th c. This process was made easier by the union of the crowns of Portugal and Spain during 1580-1640. During this period, the administrative autonomy of Portugal and its empire was respected, but insufficient attention was paid to its national interests, and Spanish enemies became Portugal's as well. By 1665, Portugal had lost all but three enclaves of its *Estado,* namely Goa, Daman, and Diu, all in western India. Bombay was presented to the British crown as part of the dowry of the Portuguese princess, Catherine of Brangança, in the hopes of winning British assistance against the Dutch attacks. The Asian native rulers benefited from the rivalry among the European powers until the Industrial Revolution established the British as a superior power able to extend her hegemony over the whole of Asia, which continued until decolonization began in the middle of the 20th c. Other European colonialists in Asia, including the Portuguese, continued only upon British sufferance. None remained long beyond British departure.

The Portuguese colonists, who resented their state mercantilist controls and were usually badly paid for official services, were more involved in the intra-Asiatic trade *(cabotagem)* in partnership with the natives than in trade with the home country *(carreira).* Many Portuguese "went native" in different parts of Asia. Apart from trade, another characteristic feature of Portuguese colonialists was their missionary zeal. They had come ostensibly in search of "spices and Christians," though "Christians" meant Christian allies to fight the Moorish foes from the rear. However, they soon discovered that there were more Muslims in India than they had found in Africa. It was the Tridentine Counter-Reformation and the arrival of the Society of Jesus* in Asia that brought greater zeal to the conversion policy, but the practical and economic interests were not easily sacrificed by the secular authorities. It became a service of God and mammon. Christianity helped as a bonding element in the trade network and administrative controls, just as was the case with the Cholas of India, who had earlier used Hinduism* in Southeast Asia, and with the Muslims, who had used Islam* in the control of trade in the Indian Ocean zone. In the absence of an international law of commerce, trust was based on common faith and community bonds, and that was how the great religions spread effectively in Asia, and not so much through proselytization and violence.

In the pockets where the Portuguese could establish territorial control, as in Goa, the mixture of a "stick and carrot" method was employed to promote Christianization. The traditional class and caste differences and intra-societal conflicts in Asian society were also exploited by the Portuguese in this respect. But the Portuguese undoubtedly took their religious mission and *padroado* seriously, which helped them to ensure their political and commercial interests beyond the areas of their direct military presence. An additional advantage was the Portuguese non-racial policy (even though some amount of white superiority associated with a dominant colonialist complex was never entirely absent), which enabled the Portuguese colonialists to penetrate the native culture more effectively than did other Europeans in Asia. De Albuquerque himself had initiated the policy of mixed marriages with state dowries.

The vestiges of Portuguese language and of their brand of Christianity have remained strong in Asia. Goa is still regarded as the "Rome of the East" because of the number and magnificence of its churches and the strong flavor of Latin culture. A prophetic statement was made by João de Barros, author of *Decades of Asia:* "Time may destroy the monuments the Portuguese may leave in Asia, Africa and in innumerable other islands of the three continents, but it will not succeed in destroying the religion, the habits, and the language we shall leave behind."

Spanish. Spain, driven by its desire to improve its commerce and to maintain the spirit of the *Reconquista* (the movement to destroy Muslim power and influence in the Iberian Peninsula and beyond), sponsored exploratory maritime voyages intended to reach the East by sailing westward from Europe. It had to take this route because, according to the Treaty of Tordesillas, the eastern route, discovered by Vasco da Gama in 1497, was reserved for the Portuguese. The voyage headed by Ferdinand Magellan* brought Spain into contact with the Moluccas* and the Philippines* in 1521 via the Pacific. While the Portuguese could maintain their claim on the Moluccas, Spain succeeded in establishing a colony in the Philippines, its only colony in the Far East, by means of a permanent settlement in 1565.

Understood properly, the aims of the Spanish colonization of the Philippines can be summed up in the phrase "gold, glory and God." Spain, in its expansionist moves, had an eye on economic profit and prestige. It wanted to acquire a share in the spice trade. At this time, *conquistadors* sought riches in the form of precious metals and in the exploitation of native labor. Spaniards of all classes during the 16th c. were driven by an unbounded faith in their nation's power and prestige. It seemed as though Spain and the Spanish race were destined to execute the plans of providence as God's new chosen people. Spain's mission was to forge the spiritual unity of humankind by crushing the Protestants in the Old World, defending Christendom against the onslaughts of the Turks, and spreading the Gospel among the nonbelievers of America and Asia. In its thirst for gold and glory, Spain did not forget the claims of God. Both missionaries and *conquistadors* sincerely desired to share with non-Christians, first of the Philippines and eventually of China* and Japan*, what they considered the benefits of Christianity. Because of this mixture of motives, a certain ambiguity always surrounds any discussion of the Christianization of the Philippines.

One of the striking features of Spanish imperialism was the *Patronato Real,* the inseparable union of church and state. Both remained autonomous, and at the same time inextricably interdependent. The Spanish monarchs were given sweeping powers over the administration of the church's revenues and the deciding voice in the selection of ecclesiastical personnel by the holy see. In addition, the crown took to itself the task of supervising the conversion of the *indios* to Christianity. The colonial church in the islands enjoyed the backing of the state. Although church and state were inseparably linked in carrying out Spanish policy, there was frequent disagreement between the two over the means to reach the common goal. Abuses were committed by both sides, the civil and the ecclesiastical. Theoretically, the friars were the *defensores de los indios;* in practice, they caused much oppression and suffering among the masses because of the multifarious political and economic powers they wielded.

Unwittingly, the Spaniards brought about the unification of the nation, fusing the various regions and the innumerable *barangays* into one people who had begun to share a common national identity. The Muslims *(Moros)* in the south, however, were seen as enemies in line with the *Moros* in the neighborhood of Europe; they considered themselves a distinct nation. The Filipino sense of nationhood was both a product of Spanish rule and, even more, a reaction against it. The people's rebellions were, for the most part, negative responses to economic exploitation and colonial oppression rather than positive movements for the attainment of national goals. The imposition of taxes, with its cruel method of collection, forced labor, usurpation of lands, racial inequality, and many other injustices, drove the Filipinos to fight for their rights. Not exempted from the fury of the native grievances were the religious orders which abused their authority and were, by perception and in reality, one with the Spanish political power.

Eventually, at the end of the 19th c., a revolt of great proportions arose. Its goal was to remove the colonial power itself. Fanned by the ideas of liberty and justice sweeping Europe, and driven by the oppressive rule of a Spanish minority, this movement culminated in the revolution of 1896. A sense of nationhood and solidarity among the inhabitants of the islands had arisen. National independence was proclaimed on 12 Jun 1898 by the Filipino revolutionary forces, and a constitutional republic was established in Jan 1899 (see Nationalism). The tragedy of this drama lies in the fact that the part of the villain was played by the friars, who had been the main instruments in the spread of Hispanic culture and Catholicism, and yet some had risen to the defense of the oppressed people.

Notwithstanding the abuses committed by the Spaniards within the context of the *Patronato Real* and the colonization process, Spain must be credited with having brought the Christian faith to the Philippines. When compared to Spain's bloody conquest of America, its occupation of the islands was much more a missionary rather than a military enterprise. Economically, the occupation of the Philippines turned out to be quite unprofitable.

Although Spanish presence in the Philippines brought some changes for the better in the social, political, and cultural spheres of life, its imposition forced the local peoples to abandon to a great extent their own indigenous traditions and customs for an alien culture. "They declined, degrading themselves in their own eyes; they became ashamed of what was their own; they began to admire and praise whatever was foreign and incomprehensible; their spirit was dismayed and it surrendered" (José Rizal).

Hispanic rule over the Philippines officially came to an end in 1898. That year, in the context of the Spanish-American War, the Spanish fleet under Admiral Montojo was defeated by the American fleet under Commodore George Dewey in the battle of Manila Bay, and the Philippines was sold by Spain for $20 million to the United States under the Treaty of Paris.

American. The victory of the American fleet in Manila Bay and the Treaty of Paris ending the war between the United States and Spain signaled the beginning of American imperialism in Asia. National independence, which was proclaimed on 12 Jun 1898 by the Filipino revolutionary forces and supported by the establishment of a constitutional republic in Jan 1899, was frustrated by the decision of the United States government to take over the Philippines despite the efforts of diplomatic agents sent abroad to work for the recognition of Philippine independence.

The general mood of the United States during that period was influenced by the concept of Manifest Destiny, a providential mission to extend the blessings of American freedom to neighboring peoples who wanted to achieve self-realization. President McKinley* explained to a Methodist* delegation that he had decided through the course of prayer to annex the Philippines. Returning the Philippines to Spain he saw as dishonorable; giving it to France or Germany would be bad business and discreditable; and leaving the Filipinos to themselves would result in anarchy and misrule. The only option left to the US was to educate, civilize, and Christianize the Filipinos as a part of humanity for whom Christ had died; they were considered to be incapable of self-rule. The régime of democratic partnership with the Filipinos, with them as junior partners, was not satisfactory to the Filipino nationalists, but it was a decided improvement over subjection to Spain. Politically, the first stirrings of nationalism were discouraged.

From the beginning, American political leaders who were embarrassed by the stigma and cost of being a colonial power generally agreed that the occupation should last only as long as it took to prepare the people for self-government. In Feb 1899, following an instruction of McKinley to the military commanders, a war of suppression against the Filipino republican forces began. An estimated one million Filipinos died from war injuries and war-related diseases. The war ended in 1901 with the capture of the president of the young republic, Emilio Aguinaldo*.

While control over the Philippines was being pursued militarily, a survey was also conducted. This survey recommended the establishment of a national legislative body, as well as provincial and municipal administrations under overall American control; the early replacement of military rule by a civilian government; the development of natural resources; and, finally, the setting up of a comprehensive system of public education, which became the priority of the US administration.

Some benefits of the American régime were the emphasis on universal education; the promotion of public health and welfare in remote barrios; the impetus given to commerce, industry, and trade; respect for basic individual freedom; improvement of the means of communication and transportation; and the development of political consciousness through the introduction of American political institutions and practices. The negative effects included general economic dependence on the US, the partial loss of cultural heritage, the persistence of a colonial mentality, and a distorted sense of values. Illustrative of the ambivalence was the area of public education. Although the Spaniards had established a system of public schools in 1863, education of the masses began only when 600 American schoolteachers arrived in the Philippines in Aug 1901. While there was an increase in literacy, the introduction of the American educational system appeared to be a subtle means of pacifying the populace and defeating a growing nationalism. Until at least 1935, the educational system was used to create a sense of American cultural superiority while glossing over the abuses of colonial rule. The political tutelage of the Philippines by the US went through the stages of military rule, civil government, and a commonwealth. It lasted a total of 48 years and ended when the Philippines became a republic on 4 Jul 1946.

British. Since the late 1960s, perceptions of the relationship between British colonialism and Christian missions in 19th- and 20th-c. Asia have been shaped by anti-colonial reactions linked to nationalism, decolonization, and the end of the empire. The Christian missionary movement stands accused of operating in consistent partnership with the instruments and exploitative activities of British colonial rule — commerce, conquest, code of law, and "civilizing mission." But in fact, British missionary-colonial relationships were far more complex.

The making of the second British empire (ca. 1780-1830) overlaps with an age of British Protestant missions from the 1790s to the mid-19th c. It was a period in which British knowledge of and interest in the oriental world multiplied exponentially, most notably in India. Indian affairs were often the subject of extended parliamentary and public debate in Britain. The protestations in parliament by Edmund Burke and others that British power in India should be exercised with moral responsibility for the benefit of the native people were mirrored in the plans of evangelicals such as Charles Grant and Claudius Buchanan* for missionary work in India. Meanwhile, published accounts of exploration and discovery (e.g., Captain James Cook's voyages to Australasia and the South Pacific, 1768-79) inspired missionary endeavor; William Carey* later acknowledged that "reading Cook's voyages was the first thing that engaged my mind to think of missions." For their part, the Dutch United East-India Company's* (VOC) officials in India were sympathetic to missionaries who were politically useful — usually as military chaplains or language instructors. In this general sense, British exploration, expansion, and missionary endeavor intertwined, inasmuch as the breadth of the Christian conscience is inevitably related to the scope of secular knowledge of the world and its peoples.

However, the genesis of the British missionary movement is also explained by theological changes that were autonomous of developments in the colonial sphere. The resurgence of Anglican* piety toward the end of the 17th c. raised up societies committed to evangelism at home and overseas (e.g., the Society for Promoting Christian Knowledge, founded in 1699), though, until the 1790s, British missionary concern for the non-European world remained sporadic and geographically limited. It was the evangelical revival of the 18th c. that gave new impetus and direction to British Protestant missions — forming the evangelical party in the Church of England (William Wilberforce and the Clapham Sect in parliamentary circles), transforming the ethos of Calvinistic dissent, and producing the new denominations of Wesleyan and Calvinistic Methodism that saw "the world as their parish."

The missionary awakening is conventionally dated from 1792. During the Victorian Era (1837-1901), the missionary movement developed a new kind of assertiveness. The proclamation of the Gospel came to be increasingly associated with the pursuit of British economic expansion: "commerce and Christianity" (David Livingstone, 1857). Influenced by Enlightenment ideas, evangelicals expressed confidence in the regenerative role of lawful trade within the providential order. Yet most still recognized that commerce by itself was of strictly limited value. In fact, the transfer of Britain's Asian colonies from company rule to direct crown rule after the Indian mutiny (1857) was welcomed by missionaries who hoped that accountability before God rather than commercial profit would be the guiding principle behind colonial policy. Along with British gentlemanly capitalism went the virtues of muscular Christianity. And yet, even in the so-called high imperial period of ca. 1880-1914, the British Christian public were neither uniformly nor consistently preoccupied with either the spiritual or secular implications of the white man's burden (Rudyard Kipling, 1899).

As in the 19th c., the trends in 20th-c. colonial history have been only one influence — and not necessarily the most important — affecting the health of the British missionary enterprise. Thus the downward slide in British missionary numbers in the 20th c. (from 9,014 missionaries in 1899 to 7,490 in 1973) does not accurately reflect shifting patterns of British colonialism, colonial policy, and overseas investment. The decline which affected most denominational societies in the interwar years probably owed more to the effects of the depression and of diminishing theological confidence than it did to any loss of missionary enthusiasm for the British Empire between 1918 and 1939. The progressive shrinkage of the British missionary force since ca. 1960 may also suggest the growing self-sufficiency of the younger Asian churches and, more recently, a significant shift in the evangelical world conscience from evangelistic to liberal-humanitarian concerns.

Throughout the course of British colonialism in the 19th and 20th cs., the Pax Britannica was a precondition of missionary activities. Once they entered colonial societies, missionaries worked to reform or abolish local customs and religious practices, chiefly by preaching the Gospel, by promoting Western education and medicine, and by pressing colonial regimes to act responsibly. Between 1813 (the year licenses were first issued freely for missionary work in the East) and 1857 (the year of the Indian mutiny), missionary-colonial relationships in Asia revolved around issues of humanity and issues of idolatry. In India, there were both missionary-led campaigns against *suttee* (the burning of widows) and missionary agitation against a pilgrim tax that supported Hindu temples. The missionaries pioneered the first comprehensive schemes for education and elementary schooling (e.g., the Church of Scotland mission school, Calcutta). The missionaries' scholarly contributions to literature and classical studies (e.g., dictionaries, translations, etc.) helped to unlock the riches of the indigenous cultural heritage.

Even where the British did not exercise colonial rule in a strictly territorial sense, British commercial imperialism pried open Asian societies in a way that facilitated missions. However controversial in the eyes of the missionaries, Britain's defeat of China* in two opium* wars (1839-42, 1856-60) and the imposition of various unequal treaties first opened the door for free trade and missionary work in the five treaty ports of Canton, Amoy, Foochow, Ningpo, and Shanghai, then gave European travelers virtually unlimited access to the Chinese interior, while guaranteeing security for Christian converts. By 1860, British semi-colonialism enabled missionary organizations already working in China to expand operations, encouraged others to enter China, and made possible James Hudson Taylor's* vision of a mission to inland China (from 1865).

In the long term, the determination of British colonialists to remold Asian societies via Christianity, Western education, and law and order did much to quicken the cultural processes that substituted nationalist for traditional local politics. The attainment of national independence reinforced the view that Christianity should shed its Western aspects, especially the denominational divisions.

Myanmar. Although Myanmar* had been exposed to Westerners before the advent of Christian missionaries, it was never dominated by a Western colonial power until the Anglo-Burmese wars. In the mid-15th c., Myanmar kings had employed Portuguese mercenaries for their expertise in navigation, building, and weapons. With the Portuguese came the first Jesuit* missionaries (ca. 1540). Highly educated, the priests gave priority to Western education, including Latin, grammar, and sciences. In 1599, Portuguese soldiers were allowed to settle in Rakhaing (Arakan) by King Minyazargyi. Among them was Philip de Brito, a Portuguese adventurer, who was later assigned to settle in Syriam, where he established himself as governor. He built a church, destroyed Buddhist pagodas, and forced Buddhists to become Christians.

In the years to come, missionaries from other countries arrived in Myanmar, gradually penetrating into the interior. But in 1618, the Myanmar king of Ava, Maha Damayaza, invaded Syriam, captured Philip de Brito and the Toungoo prince, and executed them as heretics. Four hundred Christian families were forced to resettle in Ava, in Upper Myanmar *naingan,* where they joined "French" Christians from Chiang Mai who had been exiled after Damayaza's victory over Chiang Mai in 1614. King Thalun, his brother and successor, forced some Portuguese to serve at the palace and settled the rest in eight villages in the valley between the Chindwin and Mu Rivers. He and other kings wished to trade with the West and continued to use the missionaries as educators of the people.

The first Protestant missionaries to Myanmar were Adoniram Judson* and his wife. They came to Myanmar in 1813 and settled in Ava. After the first Anglo-Burmese war (1824-26), Tenasserim and Rakhaing were ceded to the VOC, which invited the Judsons to help them select a site for the capital; in 1826 they arrived at Amherst, the chosen capital. Judson agitated in favor of religious freedom for Myanmar nationals, but he had offended the officials by serving as an interpreter to the conqueror.

Lower Myanmar was annexed by the British after the second Anglo-Burmese war (1852-53). While the Upper Myanmar *naingan* still was independent and closed to mission work, King Pagan Min (1846-53) allowed the missionaries to start work again; two of them had stayed in Yangon under his patronage. In 1854, King Mindon allowed work to begin in Pye, and he assured the Baptist missionaries that it would be safe for them to enter "the Golden City," Amarapura. Thus, in spite of the tensions in Anglo-Burmese relations, the Protestant church expanded from the seed sown by Judson, spreading into Mon and Myanmar and developing various churches among the different peoples in Myanmar. British rule ensured missionary presence and protection until well into the 20th c.

At the outset of the Japanese invasion in World War II, all missionaries were imprisoned or left, but they returned after the war.

Indonesia. Western colonialism in Indonesia* can be divided broadly into two periods: monopolistic mercantilism (up to 1800) and political domination (to 1942). In the first period, Western powers (Portuguese and then the Dutch) forced indigenous rulers by military power to accept their monopolistic trade approach. The trade commodities were mostly spices from the Moluccan Islands. After the Dutch trade agent, the VOC, collapsed in 1799, the Dutch government took over Indonesia. This period may again be divided into three sub-periods. First came a period of conservative policy (1800-48, interrupted by the British interregnum [1811-16]) when the colonial government introduced a system of land taxes, which was replaced later by the *Cultuurstelsel* (Forced Culture System, 1830-70). The second period was one of "liberal policy" (1848-1900). The change of 1848 was followed in 1854 by the *Regeerings Regelement.* Non-government enterprises took over the government roles of exploiting the colony, and they scooped up large profits at the expense of the indigenous people. The need for more land to exploit brought about an expansion to new regions outside Java. The local rulers were forced to accept conditions of submission. Formally they were still running the government, but they acted as representatives of the colonial power. This indirect rule was resisted by Indonesians in some unsuccessful armed rebellions, such as the Pattimura rebellion in Saparua (1817), the Padri War in Minangkabau (1819-37), the Java War (1825-30), the Banjar War (1859-66), the Aceh War (1873-1912), and the Pong Tiku resistance in Toraja (1907). There was also popular resistance in the rural areas in the form of messianic or religious movements.

The announcement of the "Ethical Policy" opened the third period. This was an effort to develop indigenous society as a repayment for the economic profits taken out of the country. In this new policy, stress was also laid on the ethical responsibility of the Dutch people to develop the Indonesian people. Aiming at improving the welfare of the colony, the political principle was to change the colonial relationship from ownership to guardianship. The administration was to be decentralized, the people's health improved, emigration, irrigation, and agriculture intensified, and education developed. From this ethical colonial policy emerged the Indonesian nationalist movement demanding independence.

Protestant Christianity in Indonesia, which reduced Catholicism from the 17th c. onward, was responsible to the colonial power, that is, the VOC and, later, the Netherlands' government. In 1835, the king of the Netherlands, William I, proclaimed a unity church, the Protestant Church of the Netherlands' Indies, which was to be fully controlled and regulated as an integral part of the colonial administration. Its Indonesian members included congregations in the eastern part of Indonesia and small congregations in some towns in Java and Sumatra. A century later, before the end of colonial rule, the government church dissolved into some ethnic-regional churches. In the meantime, mission boards from the West with Calvinistic (and some Lutheran*) traditions (especially from the Netherlands and Germany) introduced Christianity among Indonesian ethnic groups in the relatively remote regions; these groups later organized themselves into ethnic churches. At the end of the colonial era, the Protestant Christians amounted to 2.5% of the population (1,546,933 out of 60,728,773).

The relationship between colonialism and Christianity, in particular the missions, cannot be generalized. In some places there was cooperation, e.g., the colonial pacification opened the way for the missions, and the civilizing work of the missions made the tasks of colonial administration easier. There were also obstacles from the government side. But most of the missionaries in Indonesia in the 19th c. were not interested in political matters. Their pietistic views regarded socio-political matters as being outside their mission tasks.

In regard to the colonial policy, some officials supported the idea of Christianization to check the influence of Islam*. This effort to exploit Christianity failed, but it left an image of Christianity as a colonial instrument. In the 1920s, Indonesian Christian youth and students adopted a new attitude of siding with the nationalists against the colonial regime.

Sri Lanka. There are very few countries in Asia with a longer record of Western influence and control than Sri Lanka* (Ceylon). Over 400 years of colonial influence have had a great impact on the government, society, culture, religion, and economy of the island.

The first colonial power to set foot in Sri Lanka was Portugal (1505). In 1518, the Portuguese governor of Goa built a fortress in Colombo. However, the building was dismantled in 1524. Only after the death of Dharmapala, the king of Kotte, in 1592 and the death of Rajasinha, the king of Sitawaka, in 1594 were the Portuguese able to capture the lands in the western coastal area of Sri Lanka. In 1619, they conquered the independent kingdom of Jaffna. Portuguese possessions in Sri Lanka were part of their *Estado da Índia.* The captain general resident in Colombo headed the administration and was subordinate to the viceroy in Goa. The period of Portuguese rule was marked by intense Roman Catholic missionary activity. There was a strong link between the Roman Catholic Church and Portuguese colonial activities in Sri Lanka (see *Padroado*).

The wars of 1638 put some parts of the maritime provinces under Dutch control. In 1656, the capture of Colombo terminated Portuguese rule, giving way to the administration of the VOC, which lasted until 1796. Unlike the Portuguese, the Dutch had very little interest in converting the people to their way of life. Their main interest was the profits from the country's products. They introduced the code of Roman-Dutch law, many elements of which have been retained up to the present time. The Dutch made it necessary for a Sri Lankan to be baptized as a Christian of the Dutch Reformed Church in order to inherit property or to hold a government job. These "government Christians" were Christians in name only.

The British conquered the Dutch possessions in 1796. At first, they were administered by the British East India Company. Because of the unrest of some natives who were mistreated by employees of the company, the British government interfered and made Sri Lanka a crown colony in 1802. In 1815, the independent kingdom of Kandy was also captured by the British, bringing the entire island under their control. In 1832, on the recommendation of the Colebrooke Commission, the British terminated the traditional feudal system and opened the country to a laissez-faire economy, bringing great changes to the social system and judicial administration. Plantation agriculture led to the emergence of a market economy. English was introduced as the language of the administration.

The Legislative Council was set up in 1833 as an advisory body. As a responsible Sri Lankan middle class evolved, it demanded a stronger voice in the government. Riots in 1848 and 1915 were demonstrations against colonialism. The Donoughmore Commission in 1929 recommended a new constitution. Only in 1931 did the Sri Lankans get a fully representative government. However, the constitution did not satisfy the aspirations of the nationalist leaders. The Soulbury Commission in 1945 recommended self-government short of dominion status. The Independence Act of 1947 established a parliamentary representative government, and on 4 Feb 1948, Sri Lanka became independent.

In the post-independence era, the connections many Christian denominations had with the colonial past became a target for criticism by the nationalists and Marxists. Even within the body of the church, the liberation theologians have criticized this connection between colonialism and Christianity. Most denominations have made a serious attempt to indigenize the church in order to separate it from the colonial past.

Japan. Japanese colonialism can be traced to the 16th c. when General Toyotomi Hideyoshi had the ambition to establish his capital city in Beijing, China, and colonize the whole of East Asia. To fulfill this purpose, the Japanese army invaded Korea in 1592 and 1597. Among the generals were some Christians from southern Japan* converted in the first wave of Christian expansion in Japan. But Toyotomi's military ventures met with limited success.

Modern Japanese colonialism was revived after the Meiji restoration of 1868, when the rule of the emperor was restored. It was based in the Japanese Shinto* mythology, which taught that Japan was to be ruled by emperors, the descendants of the creators and living gods.

The imperial military became the agency to colonize the neighboring countries. On numerous occasions, Japan tried to invade and colonize Korea. In Feb 1894, when the Tonghak Rebellion* took place in southwestern Korea, Japan dispatched its military. After the Korean army had crushed the rebellion, all foreign troops were forced to leave Korea. From Korea, however, the Japanese army attacked the British steamer *Kowshing* transporting Chinese troops. This led to the Sino-Japanese War* of 1894, which ended with the victory of the Japanese in the following year and the beginning of Japanese colonial rule over Taiwan* (1895-1945). The Russians challenged Japanese ambitions in East Asia and were supported by the Korean government. This led to the murder of the Korean queen, the dismissal of the government by the Japanese, and the establishment of a new, pro-Japanese cabinet. The victory of the Japanese over the Russians in the war of 1904 strengthened Japanese colonial ambitions and finally led to the annexation of Korea in 1910 as a strategically significant place for defense or expansion of the Japanese empire.

The Japanese government attempted to eliminate the influence of foreign missionaries in the Korean churches. Any church activities of which the government disapproved became an excuse to imprison church leaders or expel missionaries. The annual Day of Prayer, which included a prayer for peace, was accused of being a sign of disloyalty to the Japanese emperor and his government. During the years of the Pacific War (World War II*), the Christian churches were completely controlled by the Japanese colonial government. Churches needed permission from the police to hold meetings or had to safeguard the presence of police representatives. In Oct 1940, all Americans, including missionaries, were evacuated. Church agencies such as the Christian Literature Society and the British and Foreign Bible Society* were closed. On 29 Jul 1945, the government ordered the abolishment of all denominational distinctions, combining denominations into the Japanese *Kyodan*, the united church. Following this forced union, about 3,000 Christian leaders were arrested, and 50 of them suffered martyrdom.

But Japanese colonialism was not limited to Korea. Its ultimate purpose was to colonize most of Asia and the Pacific Rim. The Manchurian Incident on the South Manchurian Railway became the pretext to colonize the entire region of northwestern China, and in 1932 the Japanese established the colonial government of Manchukuo. The year 1937 saw the beginning of the Sino-Japanese War, which was the overture to the confrontation with the United States, the Pacific War, when Japan, or *Dai Nippon*, occupied most of Southeast and East Asia. The Christian churches in the occupied countries had to sever all ties with Western Christianity, and many of them suffered persecution. But relations with the *Kyodan* were sometimes possible. The result was both a setback for Western missionary activity and a rapid strengthening of indigenous Christian leadership and institutions.

Bibliography

Boxer, C. R., *The Portuguese Seaborne Empire, 1415-1825* (1991; 1st ed., 1969). • Subrahmanyam, Sanjay, *The Portuguese Empire in Asia, 1500-1700: A Political and Economic History* (1993). • Thomaz, L. F., *De Ceuta a Timor* (1994). • De Souza, Teotonio R., ed., *Indo-Portuguese History: Old Issues, New Questions* (1985). • Agoncillo, Teodoro, and Milagros Guerrero, *History of the Filipino People*, 4th ed. (1973). • Bernad, Miguel, *The Christianization of the Philippines: Problems and Perspectives* (1972). • Constantino, Renato, *The Philippines: A Past Revisited* (1975). • Phelan, John Leddy, *The Hispanization of the Philippines: Spanish Aims and Filipino Responses, 1565-1700* (1959). • Vreeland, Nena, Geoffrey B. Hurwitz, Peter Just, Philip W. Moeller, and R. S. Shinn, *Area Handbook for the Philippines* (1976). • Anderson, Gerald H., ed., *Studies in Philippine Church History* (1969). • "Mark Twain on American Imperialism," *Atlantic Monthly* (Apr 1992). • Zaide, Gregorio, *History of Asian Nations* (1980). • Ballhatchet, K., and H. Ballhatchet, "Christianity since 1800: Asia," *Oxford Illustrated History of Christianity*, ed. J. McManners (1990). • Neill, S., *Colonialism and Christian Missions* (1966). • Stanley, B., *The Bible and the Flag* (1990). • Monika, "The Roman Catholic Missionary Educational Work in Myanmar from Mid-16th Century to 1885" (M.A. thesis, 1992). • Maung Shwe Wa et al., *Burma Baptist Chronicle* (1963). • Howard, Randolf L., *Baptists in Burma* (1931). • Kartodirdjo, Sartono, *Pengantar Sejarah Indonesia Baru*, Vol. 2, *Sejarah Pergerakan Nasional* (1990). • Ngelow, Zakaria J., "Transformation of Nationalism: A Study on the Encounter of Protestant Christianity and the National Movement in Indonesia, 1900-1950" (Dissertation, South East Asia Graduate School of Theology, 1992). • De Silva, K. M., *The University of Ceylon: History of Ceylon*, Vol. 3 (1974). • De Silva, C. R., *Sri Lanka: A History* (1987). • Kemper, Steven, *The Presence of the Past: Chronicles, Politics and Culture in Sinhalese Nationalism* (1991). • Clark, Allen D., *A History of the Church in Korea* (1971). • Conroy, Hilary, *The Japanese Seizure of Korea: 1868-1910* (1960). • Kang, Wi Jo, *Christ and Caesar in Modern Korea: A History of Christianity and Politics* (1997). • Kim, Eugene C. I., and Han-kyo, *Korea and the Politics of Imperialism, 1876-1910* (1987). • Lee Chong-Sik, *The Politics of Korean Nationalism* (1963).

Olaf Schumann, Teotonio R. de Souza,
Jośe M. de Mesa, Ernest Chew, Emrys Chew,
Daw Tin Aye, Zakaria J. Ngelow,
G. P. V. Somaratna, Wi Jo Kang

Columbans

The Society of St. Columban (SSC), one of the smaller Roman Catholic missionary bodies working mainly in

Asia, takes its name from St. Columbanus (d. 615), Ireland's chief missionary to early medieval Europe.

The Columbans were established in Ireland in 1916 as a missionary society of diocesan priests. First known as the Maynooth Mission to China*, it spread internationally within a couple of years — to the United States (1918), Australia (1919), and New Zealand — and its official name (SSC, later MSSC) came into common use.

John Blowick (1888-1972), a professor of theology at the National Seminary, Maynooth, and Edward Galvin (1882-1956), a Roman Catholic priest, led the society up to 1924, by which time there was a female counterpart, the Columban Sisters. Galvin became bishop in Hanyang, China, and remained there till expelled in 1952 after the Communist Revolution triumphed in 1949.

China. The Columban Fathers began early in the 20th c. with a primary concern for the masses of people in China. Galvin, after three years of ministry in the United States (New York), received permission to serve in China on 25 Feb 1912. He was shocked both by the poverty* and the absence of knowledge of Christ. After an initial work in China, Galvin returned to the United States and then Ireland, receiving approval for the new mission (29 Jun 1918) and beginning to recruit missioners. He arrived in China with his first 16 recruits in 1920. From the beginning, the mission was an Irish and American cooperative work. Galvin began the work in Hanyang, where he later became bishop and labored until his expulsion in 1952.

John Blowick oversaw the work of the society as the first superior general until 1924. In that year he invited lay brothers to membership in the society and, together with Lady Frances Maloney, founded the Missionary Sisters of St. Columban. Sent to China in 1926 to work in the medical* and educational field, the sisters are now in diversified ministries in most of the society's areas of assignment.

Columbans worked in Hanyang, Nancheng, and Huzhou through decades that saw floods, famine, bandits, a war of resistance against Japan*, civil war between Nationalists and Communists, and Communist repression in their last years there. Columban numbers in China were fewer than 100 during most years before 1946, when worldwide membership had reached 600. Total Columban member-years in China counted for a mere 4% of the 52,000 Columban member-years accumulated by 1995.

A change in Columban policy and approach came from outside Asia through new mission experiences. Though a Columban presence began in the Philippines* in 1929, in Korea* in 1933, in Burma* in 1936, and in Japan in 1948, it was in the first SSC Latin American missions that a sort of Columban conversion first took hold. By 1970, Columbans had accepted the preferential option for the poor, which was a religious rallying-cry from Latin America.

Philippines. The largest commitment of the Columbans has been to the Philippines. What was originally intended as a limited charge of the Manila parish of Malate in 1929 eventually extended to 10 provinces including Luzon (1933), Mindanao (1938), and Negros (1950), and by the end of the 1960s had a total complement of over 250 men. In these peak years, Columbans were mainly engaged in parish ministry — staffing 154 parishes — and in the provision of secondary education. This substantial contribution led to the birth of five new dioceses, now under Filipino bishops, and to the maturity of the local church. In Manila, the most notable achievement was Student Catholic Action, which revitalized lay leadership in the church for two generations. Established in 1935 by E. J. McCarthy, a founding member of the society, it came under suspicion during the martial-law regime (1972-81), was temporarily suppressed under tight surveillance by the state, was taken out of Columban hands, and is now defunct.

As the implementation of Vatican II got under way and issues of social justice became more pressing, Columbans engaged in the formation of Basic Christian Communities, land reform, the support of trade unions, and the defense of human rights, especially in the islands of Mindanao and Negros. They were instrumental in the creation of the Mindanao-Sulu Pastoral Conference (1971-82), a novel experiment in co-responsible church policy-making by religious and lay leaders, which was later dissolved by the bishops' act of dissociation on the alleged grounds of Marxist infiltration. In Negros, the growing conflict between the church and the sugar barons came to a head in the Gore-O'Brien murder trial, which resulted in the dropping of charges against the two priests because of lack of evidence.

Since the overthrow of the Marcos government in 1986, church and state have veered a course toward calmer waters without resolving the underlying causes of social unrest. Though Columbans are still actively committed to the poor, the work of the society is less consciously determined by theologies of liberation than by the priorities of a missionary body now in transition. With the decline in membership (120 in the Philippines out of a total membership of approximately 650), attention has turned to providing a viable vehicle of mission for the future. In 1982, the general assembly introduced a policy of inviting candidates from the local churches in which Columbans work to become society members, and the Assembly of 1988 inaugurated a Lay Mission Program. Both of these have been widely implemented in the Philippines and other Columban regions. Education for mission and an associate-priests program have also been developed to foster in local churches an awareness of their missionary responsibility. At the same time, a renewed emphasis has been given to dialogue with Islam* in the prelature of Marawi, Mindanao, and with the tribal peoples, the Subanons of Mindanao and the Aeta of Zambales. Columbans are also active in ecological issues throughout the archipelago.

Korea. At Galvin's suggestion, nine Columbans en route to China were redirected to begin a work in Korea* in 1933. By 1938, they were given full responsibility for two missions: Kwangju and Chunchon. While avoiding the conflict in China, these missionaries encountered Japanese harassment and imprisonment under the Japanese imperial forces. After the Korea partition, six Columbans were martyred by the Communists in the North, and one later died in prison. In 1955, Columban Sisters arrived to help with the overwhelming refugee* problem. During the 1960s and 1970s, Columbans, along with other Christians in South Korea, struggled against the injustices of the military dictatorship. Today, Columban work in Korea focuses on human rights, ministries to the urban poor, workers, farmers, alcoholics, and gamblers. Fifty-eight Columban priests, 30 sisters, and five lay missionaries carry on the Korean work today.

Burma (Myanmar). Columban work in Burma* was initiated in 1936 at the request of Rome and focused on the prefecture of Bhamo in the Mandalay vicariate. Most of the initial work was among ethnic Kachins* and Shans. During the Japanese invasion in 1942, 21 Columbans were arrested, two escaped to China, and two remained serving their people in the jungles. After the war, Columban work concentrated on schools, including a Columban Sisters' School for girls in Myitkyina. Columban work was caught in the middle of the Kachin struggle for independence in the 1960s and the government's nationalization of all schools in 1965. In 1966, all foreign missionaries were expelled, leaving behind 21 Columban priests and no sisters. In 1977, at the age of 38, the Columban Zinghtung (Paul) Grawng became the first Kachin priest. Today Grawng is the bishop, serving 38 Kachin priests and 17 convents of religious sisters from four tribal groups.

Japan. The bishops of Tokyo, Yokohama, Osaka, and Fukuoka requested the help of Columbans in the aftermath of World War II* (1948). Most of the first 22 Columbans who arrived worked in local parishes helping to rebuild both churches and lives. The parish work continues to focus mainly on evangelization through community service and marriage preparation classes. Over 50 Columban priests work in Japan today.

Taiwan. Columban work in Taiwan* did not begin until 1978. Ministry to foreign workers (Thai, Filipinos, Malaysians), day-care centers, and reconciliation between different ethnic groups make up the majority of their labors. Of special note is the Columban work among the Atayals, who live a marginal existence in the mountains of Miaoli County. Eleven Columban priests and four lay missionaries serve in Taiwan.

Pakistan. In 1977, the Columbans accepted the invitation of Bishop Armando Trindade of Lahore to work in that diocese. Earlier requests had been made by the bishops of Faisalabad and Hyderabad to minister in those dioceses.

The first group of six Columbans arrived in Pakistan* in 1979. In spite of episcopal misgivings, the Columbans opted for 18 months of language study before undertaking any pastoral or ministerial work. Since then, Columbans have assumed responsibility for the annual summer language school for newly arrived Catholic missionaries in Pakistan. The number of Columban priests assigned to Pakistan has increased to 14, in addition to one priest associate and five lay missionaries from the Philippines.

The decision to send personnel to Pakistan reflected the Columbans' renewed commitment to Asia. Pakistan was evaluated as a place where the Columban missionary vocation to announce the Gospel to the marginalized poor and oppressed and to engage in dialogue with people of other religious faiths could be positively carried out.

For the first period, Columbans ministered in city and rural parishes in Lahore Diocese, gaining from the experience of the Belgian Capuchins* and the insights of the emerging local clergy. By 1985, they decided to concentrate on two areas, one a neglected slum in the city of Lahore and the other in Sheikhupura, a rural area in the process of rapid industrialization.

In 1983, Columban presence in Pakistan was extended to the diocese of Hyderabad to work amongst the Parkari Koli people. Since late 1981, Timothy Carney, an American Dominican priest stationed at Rahimyarkhan, had continually impressed upon the Columbans the needs and missionary opportunities that existed amongst the scheduled-caste Hindu tribal people of interior Sindh in south-east Pakistan. Retaining the commitment to Lahore Diocese, four Columbans were appointed to Matli and Badin in Hyderabad Diocese to continue and develop the work that had been begun by the Franciscans*. In both dioceses, the number of Columbans assigned has gradually increased.

David Arms, a Columban priest and linguist, was part of the first group appointed to Hyderabad and contributed to the development of the Parkari Koli language, which was at the time an unwritten language without any script. Columbans have also fostered important developments in the area of inculturation: their encouragement has led Parkari people to compose their own religious music* and hymnody. Columbans opened schools and medical programs, all staffed by Parkari men and women whose training and skills they helped develop. The medical programs initiated in 1985 and implemented by trained Parkari Koli who are Christian are the single most important reason for the marked decrease in interreligious hostilities and caste prejudices amongst Muslims, Hindus, and Christians in this part of Hyderabad Diocese.

Charisms. Parallel to Columban developments in Pakistan, the society has sought to focus its energies on specifically missionary apostolates in other parts of Asia. Mission centers have been opened among indigenous peoples in the Sindh and the Punjab. In Taiwan, Columbans have concentrated their efforts on labor problems and an outreach program among the aboriginal mountain people. The remarkable growth of the

Comity Agreement of 1901, Philippines

church in Korea, which accelerated in the aftermath of the Korean War* (1950-53), led to a redeployment of Columban personnel from a mainly rural parish setting to urban ministry in Seoul and Kwangju. Japan, by contrast, has continued to present special difficulties to the growth of the church. While new initiatives in evangelization have become more common, Columbans have generally kept to traditional parish ministry in the dioceses of Tokyo, Yokohama, Osaka, Fukuoka, and Oita.

After years with the Kachin and Shan peoples in northeast Myanmar, the MSSC had to withdraw as a result of General Ne Win's policy of political isolation, which began in 1962. As one chapter of the society's mission was closing, a new page was turned with the decision in 1974 to create a China watch based in Hong Kong. Two years later, a society commission to advise on developments in China was set up, and by 1989 a permanent mission unit was established. At present, this consists of six Columbans, a resource group of three in Hong Kong, and three teaching in mainland China. With the collaboration of others, the unit coordinator, Edward Kelly, launched a program to respond to the need in China for foreign teachers. Known as AITECE (the Association for International, Technological, Economic and Cultural Exchange), the organization has found placements for foreign professionals in Chinese universities. More recently, in response to the request of the bishops of Wuhan and Shanghai, training is now provided for a small number of Chinese church laity in the Philippines.

Bibliography

MSSC, *Columban Mission Today* (1982); *Becoming More Missionary* (1988). • Kinne, W., *The Splintered Staff* (1990). • Barrett, W. E., *The Red-Lacquered Gate* (1967). • Digan, P., *Churches in Contestation: Asian Christian Social Protest* (1984). • McDonagh, S., *To Care for the Earth* (1986). • O'Brien, N., *Seeds of Injustice* (1985); *Revolution of the Heart* (1987).

Parig Digan, Colm McKeating, and Robert McCulloch

Comity Agreement of 1901, Philippines

Agreement entered into by individual members of the Evangelical Union of the Philippine* Islands in order to avoid unseemly rivalry and needless duplication of time, effort, and money.

The Comity Agreement of 1901 entailed the equitable distribution of the country among the various Protestant missions. The apportionment generally followed the main linguistic demarcations: Methodists* — Luzon north of Manila, except the northwest, which was given to the United Brethren and the Disciples; Presbyterians* — Luzon south of Manila, except for certain areas given to the Disciples, and the Visayas, except half of Panay and half of Negros, which were given to the Baptists*; Congregationalists — Mindanao, except a portion in the southwest reserved for the Christian and Missionary Alliance*.

At first, the Disciples missionaries, because of pressure from officers of their home society, did not adhere to the territorial division, resulting in some conflict in the Tagalog areas of southern Luzon. By the early 1920s, however, the Disciples had entered fully into all comity agreements of the Evangelical Union. On the other hand, though given all of northwest Luzon, the United Brethren confined themselves to the provinces of La Union and Abra, with the result that this region subsequently became the most evangelized Protestant mission territory throughout the Philippines. The Episcopalian and Christian and Missionary Alliance missions, though nonmembers of the union, adhered faithfully to the territorial agreement, the former limiting its work to Westerners and Chinese residents, Muslims in Mindanao, and animists in northern Luzon.

Difficulty in maintaining its original terms in the midst of new historical conditions after World War II* caused a breakdown of the agreement in 1953. There were three reasons: (1) the arrival of new evangelical missions, many of which went wherever opportunity opened; (2) the union in 1948 of the United Church of Christ in the Philippines (UCCP), which, by including the breakaway Philippine Methodist Church, made the UCCP an unintentional intruder into United Methodist territory; and (3) the United Methodist settlers' desire to organize their own churches in Mindanao, a traditional territory of the UCCP.

To remedy the situation, the Philippine Federation of Christian Churches created an advisory Board of Christian Strategy, with the task of forging a new comity agreement. Reflecting sentiments similar to those of the Evangelical Union in 1901, this board adopted certain principles: (1) Where a church of a cooperating denomination was already established, the board encouraged that church to continue. (2) If there was a real need for another denomination to begin new work where another already existed, a request was to be made to a subcommittee of the board, which would render the final decision. (3) To facilitate this matter, subcommittees of the board were created for Mindanao, the Visayas, and Luzon, each composed of two representatives from each cooperating denomination. The board made a comprehensive study and plan for introducing evangelistic work into areas not yet reached and also urged cooperating churches to collaborate in evangelizing all communities yet unreached in the Philippines.

Bibliography

Rodgers, J. B., *Forty Years in the Philippines, 1899-1939* (1940). • Laubach, F. C., *People of the Philippines* (1925). • *Minutes of the Biennial Convention of the Philippine Federation of Christian Churches* (19 Jan 1950). • *Minutes, 3rd UCCP General Assembly* (1962). • Sitoy, T. V., Jr., *Comity and Unity* (1989).

T. Valentino Sitoy

Communion of Churches, Indonesia (CCI)

(*Persekutuan Gereja-Gereja di Indonesia,* PGI). National Council of Protestant Churches in Indonesia comprising 64 member churches representing 85% (9,048,147) of the Protestant Christians in Indonesia.

The origin of PGI is related to the history of Indonesian Protestant churches, which developed from two historical backgrounds. First there were the churches which grew along with Western colonial expansion from the 16th c. onward (initially as Roman Catholic* Christianity). These churches consisted mainly of European congregations in several cities and converts from among the Ambonese, Minahasan, and Timorese ethnic groups. These congregations were formed (in 1835) into a government institution (the Netherlands Indies Protestant Church) and finally developed into several ethnic churches. Second, there were the churches which grew through the work of missionary societies from the 19th c. These societies generally worked among ethnic groups. Thus churches were demarcated along ethnic or regional lines. Denominational differences, though not prominent, existed.

Various factors such as the worldwide ecumenical* movement, and in particular the International Missionary Council Conferences, the Indonesian nationalist movement, and the experience of the churches during the Japanese occupation, steered the churches and missionary societies toward the twin aims of independence from missionary supervision and unity among the churches. From 1930, the missionary congregations were formed into institutions, like the government church in 1835, and became ethnic or regional churches. In the meantime, ecumenical efforts were institutionalized. Initially there were several regional councils which subsequently formed the Council of Churches in Indonesia (*Dewan Gereja-gereja di Indonesia,* DGI) on Pentecost Sunday, 25 May 1950. Among the founders were W. J. Rumambi*, Simon Marantika*, Augustine L. Fransz*, and B. Probowinoto. Membership grew from 29 churches (and potential churches) in 1950 to 62 today.

The DGI as a council was a compromise between the desire to be a self-supporting church and the desire to give substance to the unity of the church in Indonesia. Initially, there was strong encouragement to form one Protestant church institution in Indonesia. Subsequently, however, Christians became conscious of the need for unity in diversity, a realization paralleling the national slogan of *bhineka tunggal ika* (differentiated but unified). Unity was understood in terms of a common vision and action. Thus the DGI functioned as a means of cooperation and coordination, and sometimes as a voice for the churches in Indonesia.

The DGI developed various agencies, such as the Institution for Research and Development; the Department of Christian Education; the Department for Participation in National Development; the Department of Unity, Evangelism and Church Development; the Office for Youth Concerns; and the Office for Female Concerns. An important activity of the Institution for Research and Development since 1980 has been the organization of the annual seminar on religions, which helps to develop views on religious pluralism amongst the churches. Another important DGI activity is the organization of the quadrennial National Church and Society Conference (Jakarta 1962, Salatiga 1967, Klender Jakarta 1976, Dhyana Pura Bali 1984, Wisma Kinasih Bogor, 1989).

The DGI has regularly organized general assemblies. These have taken place in Jakarta (1950, 1953, 1956, 1960, 1964), Makassar (1967), Pematang Siantar (1971), Salatiga (1976), Tomohon (1980), Ambon (1984), and Surabaya (1989). These general assemblies discuss common problems facing the churches; for example, the Fifth General Assembly (Jakarta 1964) agreed on the principle of adopting a positive, creative, critical, and realistic attitude toward the dynamics of national life, and the Seventh General Assembly (Pematang Siantar 1971) oriented the churches to the call for national development as organized by the New Order government.

The Tenth General Assembly (Ambon 1984) made the important decision to accept the Five Documents on Indonesian Church Unity, that is, the Principal Tasks of Our Common Call; the Common Understanding of the Faith; the Charter of Mutual Recognition and Intercommunion; the Charter of Independence in Theology, Human Resources and Financial Resources; and the New PGI Constitution. With these documents, the unity of the Indonesian churches was expressed more clearly as a unity in calling, teaching, ministry, and worship. The new constitution changed the DGI from a council into a communion, hence the Indonesian Communion of Churches.

Bibliography

Cooley, F. L., "Bagaimana Terbentuknya D.G.I.?" *Peninjau* II (1975); *Karunia Tambah Karunia. 30 Tahun DGI* (1980). • Ngelow, Zakaria J., "*Jalan Keesaan DGI*" (master of theology thesis, South East Asia Graduate School of Theology) (1982). ZAKARIA J. NGELOW

Communism

The term "communism" is used broadly of that theory of history, society, and economics, espoused by Karl Marx and Friedrich Engels *(The Communist Manifesto,* 1848; Eng. 1888), which has as its goal the "common" sharing and enjoyment of property, amenities, and means of production by all members of a given society. Although "socialism" was the term used earlier by social theorists in the mid 19th-c., both Marx and Engels argued that socialism was still a middle-class movement and an elitist theory that maintained a socially privileged class. Thus socialism may be a step on the way to a truly Communist society from either an agrarian or an imperialist and capitalist society. The proletariat, or working class, must be given the means of production for this egalitarian (classless) society to develop. Communism is a materialist theory that, therefore, has no place for religion, God, or worship. Marx noted that "the existence of religion is the existence of a defect" in society. "We do not change secular questions into theological ones. We change theological questions into secular ones. History has for long enough been resolved into superstition: we now resolve superstition into history." In general, Communist theory sees emancipation from religion and superstition as a necessary evolution of the historical process. "Thus, the struggle against religion is indirectly the struggle against that world whose spiritual aroma is religion. . . . Religion is the sigh of the oppressed creature, the feeling of a heartless world, and the soul of the soulless circumstances. It is the opium* of the people. . . ."

This last phrase had a double meaning for China* at the beginning of the 20th c. The struggle of the masses to be free was very much the struggle of many Asian societies suffering under imperial powers from the West (England, France, Spain, Portugal, the Netherlands, and the United States) and from Asia (Japan*). The opium trade was a powerful symbol of this subjection. By the beginning of the 20th c., the rise of Communist movements coincided with the rise of opposition movements and the rise of national consciousness. The Communist theory of Karl Marx was a totalistic theory in which the historical process moving from capitalist toward Communist societies would be (must be) an international movement. The need for social change in countries such as China, the availability of Marxist theory, and the rise in Western learning came together in the founding of Communist parties in many countries in Asia during the early 1920s. The Communist ideology and strategy was encouraged by the founding in Mar 1919 of the Comintern (Communist International) in Petrograd (St. Petersburg), an international Communist organization to promote and coordinate revolutionary activities worldwide. Decisions of the Comintern were binding upon Communist movements in other countries, creating a unified approach and, for our purposes, a unified view of religions.

In Jul 1921, after a decade of Communist cells forming in various regions of China, the "First Congress" of the Communist Party met in Shanghai. In attendance were 14 Chinese delegates, as well as delegates from Japan and Russia. From the beginning, the various Communist movements in Asia worked closely with the new Soviet Republic of Russia. The spread of Communist principles involved three channels for social change: educating the masses regarding social theory, organizing labor (proletariat) and political parties, and armed struggle. The impact upon Christian history has been quite varied, but in most countries where Communist theory has been victorious, tightly controlled societies, often with unyielding leadership, have been the norm, greatly restricting the Christian communities. In some cases, Christians were caught in a struggle for social change, not because they were Christian but because they were religious (China, Vietnam*); in other cases where Christians were mostly ethnic Chinese, they were persecuted because of their ethnic identity (Malaya, Indonesia*).

In every context of Communist influence or rule, the development of Christianity has been effected. The armed struggle for control of Korea* (see Korean War) meant that the majority of Christians, who had been living in the north, were exiled to the South, imprisoned, and often killed. We must be careful not to identify this as "communist persecution" per se, for the consolidation of power under a dominant leader is not limited to Communist societies. Similar persecution was evident under the Japanese rule in East Asia. The results of this type of Communist victory have generally included: the displacement of Christian populations, a purification of the church, strengthening of Christian resolve and witness, and creation of martyrs.

China. Christianity and Communism have often been intertwined in modern Chinese history. Yet today they coexist with a miraculous vitality.

The Chinese Communist Party (CCP) was first organized with international support in Shanghai in 1921. From the beginning there were two major approaches of the CCP to religion in China: the united front, supported by many Russians, encouraged a type of nationalism to build up China, whereas the "ultra-leftists" felt that religion was a roadblock to progress, and therefore it must be destroyed. Since Christians and many Communists have shared common goals for China (e.g., education, economic progress, and medical care), there have been times of greater or less conflict between religion and Communism in China. Today, Chinese Christians speak of the years from 1949 to 1958 (the Anti-Rightist Movement) as a time in which the united front was practiced. The period from 1958 to 1966 is a time of growing leftism. The time of the "Cultural Revolution" (1966-76/78) is a period of complete suppression of religion. The most recent period (1978 to the present) has been a period of "openness and reform" — a new type of united front. Proof of the newer openness is found in Document 19 (1982), which no longer refers to religion as an opium of the people.

The struggle for Communist control of China was long and slow; it challenged Chinese Christian leaders and missionaries alike. Even during the late 1920s and early 1930s, many Christians saw useful parallels in goals and even in programs of mass education, rural rehabilitation, and moral uplift. The New Life Movement, for example, flourished in the same province of Kiangsi where the Communists established their first "Soviet" republic.

Nevertheless, most missionaries and many Chinese Christians condemned the Communists for their atheism and their occasional attacks on churches and mission institutions. Not until the end of World War II* did it become apparent — and only gradually for most — that the nationalists, despite many Christian leaders, had lost "the mandate of Heaven" and that Communists might more adequately represent the ideals of Luke 1:51-55 or Matt 5:3-12.

A few, however, such as Y. T. Wu* and other Young Men's Christian Association* and Young Women's Christian Association* leaders, recognized the necessity for coming to terms with the new rulers. It was essential for Christians to demonstrate their nationalism* and patriotism by affirming the goal of self-government, self-propagation, and self-support for the church, a goal advocated by much earlier missionaries (see Nevius, John L.). A "Christian Manifesto" denouncing the imperialism of foreign missions was widely circulated. Regrettably — and often regretfully — many Christians were pressured into denouncing fellow church members. Missionaries were allowed to stay at their posts "until their passports or terms expired" — or until the Korean War made their presence a possible danger as well as embarrassment to their friends.

Gradually, churches were closed and pastors assigned to "more productive" labor. Hospitals and schools were taken over as more appropriately government than religious concerns. The Roman Catholic Church* bore the added onus of loyalty to the papacy as well as an "alien doctrine." Yet during the 1950s and 1960s, despite the cruelties and aberrations of the Great Leap Forward and the Great Proletarian Cultural Revolution, China made undeniable material progress in housing, education, health care, agricultural production, and social cooperation — human welfare, which Christians could acknowledge. Some even wondered why Mao's slogan "Serve the People" seemed to be more effective than Christ's admonition to "Love your neighbor."

Nevertheless, while all religious institutions, including mosques and temples as well as churches, were closed during the decade 1966-76, the seeds of the Gospel continued to germinate. A few Christian leaders quietly but firmly defended the professed though limited freedom of religion and patriotism of most believers. In 1977, exactly one year after the death of Mao Tse-tung, churches began to reopen, attracting enormous emotional crowds. What became visible to the public at large is that, during the time of suppression, Christian communities had been purged of their Western structures (denominational loyalty, buildings, etc.) and had grown in numbers often through simple devotional meetings in homes. The growth of Christianity in China in the last decades of the 20th c. has been one of the major Christian movements of the century.

Today, as officially throughout the Communist period, freedom of belief is permitted, but activities are variously restricted to religious programs in approved locations under authorized leadership. Many Christians still prefer to worship in the privacy of their homes. No foreign missionaries are admitted as such.

The 1990s opened up a new period for Christianity and Communism in China during which the party and government downplayed the importance of ideology while maintaining control over religion as a potential source of political and social instability, subject to the influence of "hostile foreign powers." The emphasis is on stressing the "compatibility" between religion and socialism for the benefit of the nation. This new period of "cooperation" in China has also been a period of institutional growth for the Chinese church: seminaries have opened again, and Nanjing publishing house, in cooperation with the Amity Foundation*, has produced tens of millions of Bibles, in addition to hymnals and Scripture portions.

Singapore/Malaya. Communist influence in Singapore* began in the mid-1920s when the Communist Party of China started to send secret agents to the island. Its goal was to build a base of support so that it could spread its influence to other parts of Southeast Asia. In 1930 the Malayan Communist Party (MCP) was set up. Despite attempts to espouse popular grievances by agitating students and workers, the party never made much headway. Generally, people remained indifferent to the revolutionary doctrine, and the party had to contend with its rival non-Communist Kuomintang Party for overseas Chinese support. The invasion of China by Japan in 1937 and the beginning of the Pacific War (see World War II) in 1941 changed the fortune of the MCP. It rallied the people against the Japanese and fought alongside the British. An Allied Forces–supported Malayan People's Anti-Japanese Army (MPAJA), many of whom were communist sympathizers, was hurriedly formed, and it operated in the jungle of Malaya. After the war, the British returned and the MPAJA was disarmed. Over the next few years, the MCP was allowed to function openly. It agitated against further colonial rule and staged mass demonstrations. In Malaya, the Communists retreated to the jungle to recover secret arms caches, attacked outlying police stations, slashed rubber trees, destroyed tin-mining machinery, and killed European planters. In 1948 a state of emergency was declared in Malaya and Singapore.

At its peak, the MCP had some 8,000 armed fighters in the jungles of Malaya. They were supported by thousands of others living in small towns and villages who provided them with food, money, medical supplies, and intelligence. In order to cut off this lifeline, the authorities decided in 1950 to resettle half a million Chinese squatters. These people lived on the fringe of the jungle and were therefore easily given to intimidation by the terrorists. About 600 new villages were built, each securely fenced and guarded at the entrance. Most of the new dwellers had never known community life since they had previously lived freely off their own plots of land. The Malayan authorities welcomed charitable agencies to assist. Basic needs such as health care, education, youth work, recreational facilities, and so on had to be provided. The Christian community responded positively. The Malayan Christian Council (MCC) set up a committee to coordinate services offered by different church groups. From the start, it was apparent that the challenge presented by the new villages was too large for local churches to undertake by themselves. Many were still recovering from the devastation of the Pacific War. Additional help was needed.

During this period momentous events were taking place in China that culminated in the establishment of a new Communist regime. Before long, tightened government regulations forced missionary organizations to withdraw their workers from China and to relocate them elsewhere. The many millions of Chinese in Southeast Asia attracted their attention. For Singapore and Malaya, the 1950s ushered in a new period of church development. Together with these missionaries, most of whom were already conversant in the various dialects, came Chinese pastors, evangelists, Bible teachers, and hundreds of believers, all fleeing the Communist regime. News of mounting Communist insurgencies in different parts of the region only added a sense of urgency to the work of the church.

The new wave of Christian workers who came assisted the MCC in its ministry to the new villages. At its peak, some 220 missionaries representing eight different societies and hundreds of other local workers, labored in just over 300 villages. Together, they initiated new forms of community service and set up scores of churches. Furthermore, others such as China Inland Mission (Overseas Missionary Fellowship) supplied personnel to help the many English-speaking meetings that were springing up in churches that had traditionally been Chinese speaking. China Native Evangelistic Crusade, later renamed Christian Nationals' Evangelism Commission, also helped set up Singapore Bible College. The Lutheran* Church of America and the Foreign Mission Board of the Southern Baptist* Convention in America set up many new churches and bookshops and built a large conference center.

In 1957 Malaya gained its independence from Britain. Over the years the resettlement scheme had succeeded in stemming the Communist uprising. Three years later, the government repealed the Emergency Regulations Ordinance. By then it was apparent that the Communist challenge, both local and overseas, had combined to reshape the church scene in Singapore and Malaya.

Indonesia. Communism was introduced to Indonesia* by H. J. M. Sneevliet, a Dutch leftist activist, during the Indonesian nationalism movement. In 1914, together with some other Dutch leftists, he formed the *Indie Sociaal Democratish Vereeniging* (ISDV, "The Netherlands-Indie Social-Democratist Union") in Semarang, center of the railway workers organization. His party successfully infiltrated the *Sarekat Islam* (SI), a widespread Indonesian political party with members from both the urban and rural population, to propagate their ideology. Indonesian cadres of ISDV, such as Semaun, Alimin, and Darsono, became leaders of the SI branch in Semarang.

In line with the development of international Communism after the COMMINTERN was set up in Moscow in 1919, ISDV made clearer its ideological basics by adopting the name *Partai Kommunist Hindia* ("Netherlands-Indie Communist Party") on 23 May 1920 and in December became *Partai Komunis Indonesia* (PKI, "Indonesian Communist Party"). After COMMINTERN instruction, the PKI developed a network with the nationalist intellectuals and exploited the mass organizations of the colonialized people, including Islamic parties, contrary to COMMINTERN anti–Pan-Islamic movements. But the SI leaders, H. O. S. Tjokroaminoto, H. Agus Salim, A. Muis, and R. M. Soerjopranoto, checked the PKI infiltration and warned the party members to hold only SI membership. Eventually the PKI leaders were excluded from the SI. But the PKI gained from the conflict of the radicals against the moderates within the SI and formed "the Red SI" (infiltrated by the PKI) against "the White SI." The Red SI became the *Sarekat Rakjat* (SR, "The People Union") and was incorporated into the PKI in Dec 1924. The PKI became the largest political party at the time.

The PKI was more radical and stirred rebellion against the colonial government toward the end of 1926 and in early 1927. The premature rebellion, lasting only a few days, was crushed. The PKI was declared a prohibited party, and thousands of innocent people were killed. More than 10,000 people were arrested and imprisoned. Some were exiled to Boven Digul (Irian).

In 1935 the international Communist movement sent Musso to Indonesia to organize the "Illegal-PKI" by recruiting some radical youths such as Aidit, Wikana, Lukman, and Amir Sjarifuddin. Conforming to the Dimitrov Doctrine, the "Illegal-PKI" sought cooperation with available groups (including the imperialist) to fight fascism. But during the Japanese occupation, the Japanese military intelligence uncovered an underground Communist activity led by Sjarifuddin. After Indonesian independence in 1945, the Indonesian Communist Party was reorganized. Mohammad Jusuf reestablished the PKI on 21 Oct 1945 but developed under two experienced leaders who had arrived from abroad — Sardjono from Australia and Alimin from China. Some other communist members registered and eventually dominated three Marxist parties: *Partai Sosialis* ("Socialist Party"), *Patai Buruh* ("Labor Party"), and *Pemuda Sosialis Indonesia, Pesindo* ("Indonesian Socialist Youths"). These parties were incorporated into the PKI in Aug 1948. During the struggle for independence against the Dutch offensive, the PKI under Musso (the PKI leader of the 1920s just arrived from Moscow) rebelled against the Indonesian Republic. The PKI called Indonesia the Soviet Republic of Indonesia on 18 Sep 1948 in Madiun, but this Madiun Rebellion was quickly crushed by the Indonesian army.

PKI leaders such as Aidit, Lukman, Sudisman, and Njoto rebuilt the PKI in the 1950s as a mass political party. In a decade, the PKI developed from about 100,000 to three million members. In the national election of 1955 the PKI emerged as the fourth largest contestant, and in the 1960s it became the dominant political power in rivalry against the army.

The PKI masterminded the coup d'état of 30 Sep 1965 that victimized six generals of the army. The coup was also quickly crushed by the army. Hundreds of thousands of PKI members were arrested and imprisoned as political prisoners or killed. As General Suharto got the power mandate from President Sukarno by the *Surat Perintah Sebelas Maret* (Supersemar, The Letter of Instruction of 11 Mar 1966), the next day he announced that the PKI was a banned party and that Communism was prohibited in Indonesia. Until the 1970s some PKI activists in various places plotted to revive the banned party underground but were foiled by the national security. Some PKI cadres sought their chance abroad. The government warns people of the possibility of latent PKI infiltrations.

Since the 1920s Christian leaders in Indonesia have regarded Communism as dangerous and anti-religious. Christian youth and students have been warned against communist propaganda. At the peak of the PKI in 1950s and 1960s, the threats of Communism were on the agenda of ecumenical meetings. As a result of the intermittent threats from communist political leaders and armed forces, church growth seemed to have been an unexpected by-product. In light of these Communist threats, the government has used and encouraged religious belief as a defense against "atheism." The decades after the 1965 coup attempt have been among the most fruitful periods for Indonesian church growth.

India. In India*, as in other Asian countries, Communism has played a crucial role. The Russian Revolution (1917), the victory of the Communists in China (1949), and the dialectical-materialistic ideology not only influenced Indian politics and society but also theology.

Communism in India emerged under the guidance of the Communist International (CI), when a group led by M. N. Roy* set up the Communist Party of India (CPI) in Tashkent (Central Asia) in Oct 1920. Five years later, several groups united in India to form the CPI, initiating local committees. In 1928 the Workers' and Peasants' Party was built up to work on a legal body, mostly within the Indian National Congress (INC), while the CPI would work clandestinely and was later outlawed.

After the Communists had broken their connection to the "class party of the bourgeoisie" (the INC), they again started to work under reformist leadership because the VII CI-Congress (1935) had worked out a new policy known as the "United Front." As a consequence, the INC and the Congress Socialist Party both opened their doors to the Communists. The Communists succeeded in securing key positions and mostly worked at the grassroots level — for example, with the All Indian Kisan Sabha, a peasant front.

When Germany attacked Russia in 1941, the CPI joined hands with the Allied Forces to fight Nazi Germany. Therefore the CPI did not participate in the "Quit-India Movement," and consequently its reputation declined. After the war, the CPI led an important peasant revolt in South India known as the Telangana Armed Struggle (1946-51).

In 1957, in the state of Kerala, for the first time in the world, a communist government came to power through elections. Two years later the central government took over power from the elected body. The major split in the Indian Communist movement took place in 1964, and the Communist Party of India (Marxist), CPI(M), was formed. Contributing to the break were different approaches to the congress-government and whether elections and the parliamentary system should be used to achieve Communism's larger goals. The CPI later became known as the Moscow-oriented party, while the CPI(M) developed closer links with China.

In West Bengal a United Front Government led by the CPI(M) was formed in 1967. Only there and in Kerala were radical land reforms implemented. In the same year a peasant insurrection broke out and was suppressed by the West Bengal government. It did not spread to other parts of the country but gave birth to a new and third major form of Indian Communism, the "Naxalite movement." Under the leadership of Charu Mazumdar, this movement formed the Communist Party of India (Marxist-Leninist), CPI(ML), in Apr 1969. The party, which was influenced by "Mao Zedong Thought," especially his concept of the "New Democratic Revolution" (modeled for the semi-feudal conditions of China), went underground one year later because of suppression.

After the "Emergency" imposed under Indira Gandhi's government (1975-77), CPI(ML) divisions reemerged. Today one can identify them by the names of their party organs: Liberation, Towards New Democracy, and the like.

While the praxis of different parties did not influence to a large extent the activities of Christians and the church, the ideology has had a strong impact on some Indian theologians, particularly P. D. Devanandan*, M. M. Thomas*, and the Jesuit* S. Kappen.

Laos. Since coming to power in 1975, the communist Lao People's Revolutionary Party (Lao PRP) has been intimately involved in governing the Lao People's Democratic Republic (Lao PDR). It is not uncommon to hear Laos speak of the "Party Government." But governing has not always been easy for the Lao PRP. After taking power, two fateful decisions put a severe strain on the social and economic fabric of the country. First, tens of thousands of former government and military personnel were sent to "seminars" in the remote north for reeducation. The death of the Lao King in a "seminar" camp was particularly demoralizing to the Lao people. The second ill-fated decision was to collectivize nearly all agricultural production. Then, what few processing plants existed were taken over by the state. By the end of 1979, even the Soviet Union was advising the Laos to liberalize their economic policies to reverse the damage to the economy.

But the Party also achieved some significant advances. Education, which traditionally had been available only to Laos of status, was extended into the countryside to all ethnic groups. The literacy rate went from 40 percent in 1975 to 84 percent in 1990. In addition, training of Lao medical personnel replaced the former reliance on direct foreign medical personnel, and a highly successful hydroelectric dam was built on the Nam Ngeum River, providing sorely needed foreign earnings. In 1986 the New Economic Mechanism Policy (NEM) was adopted, introducing a free market and private ownership system. The result has been economic growth generally between seven and 10 percent per year, and foreign investment, which was virtually nonexistent, totaled $2.5 billion at the end of 1994. Since the implementation of the NEM, the Lao PDR has maintained close cooperation with Vietnam* and normalized relations with China (1988) and Thailand*. Consequently, commerce is brisk with all three border countries.

To build confidence in the liberalizing economic policies, the Laos have been working hard at building a legal system. In 1986 the first constitution of the Lao PDR was adopted. Yet lawyers in Laos can only advise their clients, not actively represent them in the People's Courts. Furthermore, the impartiality of the courts is undermined by certain stipulations in the constitution that provide for the National Assembly Standing Committee (a governing body) to be the final interpreter of the law. While the Lao PRP has been mostly faithful in fulfilling its pledge to make Laos independent and more prosperous, it is unfortunate that the habit of fighting enemies in wartime has not yet been completely laid aside. There remains a strong tendency to hunt for "enemies" where they do not exist. The Lao PRP is convinced that Western countries are plotting to overthrow Communism in Asia through "peaceful evolution." The heart of this strategy is believed to be the sowing of discontent in the population through the mass media, business investment, and cultural imperialism. While there are, in fact, a few rightist Lao and Hmong soldiers who continue to pester the country with armed attacks, nothing seems to justify the conviction that there are other "enemies" out there. Ordinary citizens are regularly called to "seminars" for the latest line on who these "enemies" are.

In 1994 one of the "enemies" identified was the Christian church, and consequently churches in several provinces were closed. There has also been an effort to intimidate hundreds of Christians into signing affidavits renouncing their Christian faith. Only a party/government confident in its ability to rule can make the decision to include all ethnic and religious groups in the effort to build a better Lao nation-state.

Summary. Christianity in Asia has been shaped by Communism both indirectly (through its goals, methods, and concerns) and directly (armed revolt, imprisonment, and laws). Both the geography of Christianity in Asia (e.g., Korea) and the theology have been shaped by these movements. Today in countries such as China and Vietnam, Christians are learning to express faithful Christian commitment in the context of a Communist government which gives room for Christian participation. In other Asian countries (Laos and North Korea), this is not yet possible. (For a discussion of capitalism's influence upon Christian development, see Colonialism*, Opium*, and Imperialism*.)

Bibliography

General

Bottomore, Tom, ed., *The Dictionary of Marxist Thought.* • Carew Hunt, R. N., and J. Gould, "Communism," in *A Dictionary of the Social Sciences,* ed. Julius Gould and William L. Kolb (1961). • Bennett, Gordon, "Communism," in *Encyclopedia of Asian History,* ed. by Ainslie T. Embree (1988). • McLellan, David, *Karl Marx* (1975).

China

Brown, G. Thompson, *Christianity in the People's Republic of China* (1983). • Bush, Richard C., Jr., *Religion in Communist China* (1970). • Hunter, Alan, and Chan Kim-Kwong, *Protestantism in Contemporary China* (1993). • Lacy, Creighton, *Coming Home — To China* (1978). • Luo Zhufeng, ed., *Religion under Socialism in China* (1991). • MacInnis, Donald E., *Religious Policy and Practice in Communist China* (1972); *Religion in China Today: Policy and Practice* (1991). • Whitehead, Raymond L., ed., *No Longer Strangers: Selected Writings of K. H. Ting* (1989). • Wickeri, Philip L., *Seeking the Common Ground: Protestant Christianity, the Three-Self Movement and China's United Front* (1988).

Singapore/Malaya

Malayan Christian Council, *The Churches Working Together* (1959). • Miller, Harry, *Jungle War in Malaya* (1972). • Sng, Bobby E. K., *In His Good Time: 1819-1992* (1993). • Wittenbach, H. A., *Working Together in Malaya* (1957). • Yeo, Kim Wah, and Albert Lau, "From Colonialism to Independence, 1945-1965," in *A History of Singapore,* ed. Ernest C. T. Chew and Edwin Lee (1991).

Indonesia

Marwati Djoened Poesponegoro dan Nugroho Notosusanto, eds., *Sejarah Nasional Indonesia,* Vols. 5 and 6 (1990). • Heuken, A., et al., eds., *Ensiklopedi Populer Politik Pembangunan Pancasila* (1984), s.v. "Komunisme." • McTurnan Kahin, George, *Nationalism and Revolution in Indonesia* (1952). • Van der Kroef, Justus M., *The Communist Party of Indonesia: Its History, Program and Tactics* (1965). • McVey, Ruth T., *The Rise of Indonesian Communism* (1965). • Cooley, Frank L., *The Growing Seed: The Christian Church in Indonesia* (1981).

India

Devanandan, P. D., and M. M. Thomas, *Communism and the Social Revolution in India* (1953). • Kappen, S., *Liberation Theology and Marxism* (1986). • Overstreet, Gene D., and Marshall Windmiller, *Communism in India*

(1960). • Thomas, M. M., *The Secular Ideologies of India and the Secular Meaning of Christ* (1976).

Laos

Brown, MacAlister, *Apprentice Revolutionaries: The Communist Movement in Laos, 1930-1985* (1986). • Gunn, Geoffrey C., *Political Struggles in Laos, 1930-1954* (1988). • Radetzki, Marcus, "From Communism to Capitalism in Laos," in *Asian Survey*, Vol. 34, No. 9 (Sep 1994). • Stuart-Fox, Martin, *Laos* (1986).

SCOTT W. SUNQUIST, with contributions from PHILIP WICKERI, CREIGHTON B. LACY (China), BOBBY SNG EWE KONG (Singapore/Malaya), ZAKARIA J. NGELOW (Indonesia), and CARSTEN KRINN (India)

Confession of War Responsibility, Japan

The statement acknowledging the United Church of Christ in Japan's (UCCJ) responsibility during World War II.

The Confession of Responsibility for World War II* was issued in 1967 over the name of the moderator, Suzuki Masahisa. Leading to this statement were a number of earlier actions. At the Third Extraordinary General Assembly in Jun 1946, the members keenly recognized their war responsibility with feelings of confession and repentance; on 8 Dec 1952, the UCCJ issued a Statement on the Issue of Peace, praying for world peace; but these were both very timid statements. Groups like the Christians' Peace* Association conducted peace activities as manifestations of their repentance.

At the pastors' summer study retreat in 1966, the issue of the UCCJ's responsibility during World War II was discussed, and at the Tenth General Assembly in October that year, a proposal drafted by Suzuki Masahisa*, Oshio Seinosuke, and four others was submitted. With the support of six delegates of the same mind, Watanabe Izumi presented the proposal that the UCCJ confess publicly its responsibility during World War II. After much discussion, it was entrusted to the executive committee, and, after further deliberations there, the decision was made to issue it in the name of the moderator. The gist of the statement says that the UCCJ was formed largely because of the Religious Organizations Law of the government, and that the church as the light of the world and the salt of the earth should not have acted in concert with the war effort; yet the church approved of the war, supported it, and neglected the calling to serve as a watchman for the nation. The confession sought the forgiveness of God, of Asian neighbors, and of the Japanese people for mistakes committed in the name of the UCCJ at the time of its formation and during the war years; in the confession the church also asked for God's help and guidance so that it might never repeat its errors.

This confession is the only one of its kind issued by a religious organization in Japan after World War II and has been praised highly by progressive persons everywhere. It has since established one of the directions for the UCCJ and has heightened interest in societal issues of the church. However, from the more conservative parts of the church has come the argument that the issue of war responsibility is not appropriate for the church. A five-member committee, including theologian Kitamori Kazoh, was organized to put the question to a vote.

The confession opened the way for an exchange between Korean Protestants and the UCCJ. Korean representatives came to Japan in 1967, and a covenant of cooperative mission was signed; soon afterward, moderator Suzuki visited Korea. In 1969, the UCCJ merged with the UCC of Okinawa, and the Okinawa District was established. In 1971, Seireien, a home for A-bomb victims, was built in Hatsukaichi-cho, Hiroshima Prefecture. The confession was also a catalyst for a major confrontation within the church between the conservatives and the progressives, which erupted around the issue of the 1970 Expo's Christian Pavilion, and this confusion has not entirely abated.

Bibliography

Dohi Akio, *Nihon purotesutanto kyokai no seiritsu to tenkai* (The Founding and Development of Protestant Churches in Japan) (1975). • Morioka Iwao and Kasahara Yoshimitsu, *Kirisuto-kyo no senso sekinin* (Christian War Responsibility) (1974).

KASAHARA YOSHIMITSU

Confradia de San José. *See* De la Cruz, Apolinario

Confreria Reinha Rosari. *See* Fraternity of the Queen of the Rosary

Confucianism and Christianity

The transcultural study of Confucianism and Christianity may conveniently start from the study of Confucian elements found in Chinese Christian belief. The common denominator primarily lies in the realm of ethical teachings. Christianity is seen as a moral pursuit simply because Chinese culture generally believes that the aim of religion is to make people morally good. In this connection, Chinese Christian faith can be seen as a kind of syncretism, for the Chinese generally take truth as a matter of approximation which anyone can approach with sincerity from his own perspective, i.e., the end is more important than the means. Given such a mentality, Christianity not only provides a transcendental dimension and metaphysical framework for Confucianism, but also validates and strengthens some Confucian values.

Generally speaking, Confucianism is an intellectual tradition based on the classics, which have gone through a long period of endless interpretations. This tradition originates from Confucius (551-479 B.C.E.) himself, and his philosophy provides some humanistic values such as the *dao* (*tao,* way), and *ren* (humanity). Confucius admitted that he was only a transmitter of the *dao,* and his teachings are mostly about being human and social behavior. He was concerned more about things here and now than life hereafter. He was viewed as a sage, the ideal human being. He did not claim to be a religious savior, nor did he intend to lay down his life for the sake of reconciling human beings with heaven. Unlike Jesus, Confucius never declared that he was "the Way, the Truth, and the Life."

Though Confucianism is not a religion, the sense of religiosity is not lacking. *The Mean,* one of the Confucian classics, provides a strong sense of religiosity in terms of self-cultivation, soul-searching, and the practice of sincerity. Confucius had no intention to diminish the importance of heaven. This heaven, though not anthropomorphic, operates in accordance with the law of nature in the universe, which is seen as a harmonious organism. In heaven, a hierarchy is formed based on the harmonious cooperation of all beings concerned. Man can communicate with heaven through his heart (or his mind). Such an interaction dictates the idea of the unity of heaven and man. This idea closely resembles certain types of Christian mysticism.

Human nature is imparted by heaven, and to follow that nature is called the *dao.* In this connection, Confucius did not clearly specify whether human nature was good or evil. He left a vacuum for later debates. Mencius (371-289 B.C.E.) and his followers believed that human nature was originally good. They acknowledged man's possession of an inner faculty of moral discernment that knows what is good and evil. Xun Zi (fl. 298-238 B.C.E.), on the other hand, taught that human nature was originally evil. Nevertheless, he and his followers affirmed the perfectibility of human nature through education. It is Mencius's thought which prevails, and so Confucianism ascribes original goodness to humans. In general, Confucian teaching implies that conscience is inborn and is a gift from heaven. Christianity, however, believes that conscience comes from God, the giver of moral law. It believes in human fallibility or original sin. Self-reliance is impossible, as human beings are totally depraved.

In Confucianism, the ethical end of being human is to be a *junzi* (profound man or gentleman). Such a status can be achieved through practicing *ren* (humanity), an arch-virtue in Confucianism. One can practice it through *zhong* (conscientiousness) and *shu* (reciprocity), as suggested by Liu Baonan (1791-1835) on the basis of Zhu Xi's (1130-1200) teaching. Liu stated that *zhong* was to establish one's own character, and *shu* was to establish the character of others. This *ren* is the characteristic of being human.

However, this *ren* cannot be equated with Christian love, *agapē. Ren* does not have any divine origin. *Agapē* implies universal love without discrimination. *Ren,* on the other hand, is subject to the constraints of Confucian social moralism. The five relationships of Confucianism, ruler-subject, father-son, husband-wife, elder brother–younger brother, and friend-friend, practically limit the scope of the love of mankind. They are mutually and reciprocally obligated, prescribing a basic sense of social hierarchy. They provide a model for social behavior based on familial relations. In Confucianism, then, man's love of others is hierarchically graded and is conditioned by this framework "in accordance with heaven's ordinance." In practice, man extends this love to others in the order of family and friends first, then to those in society, and eventually to the world. A sense of mutual responsibility is to be established in such relationships.

The application of *ren* to actual living is found in the *Great Learning,* which provides the balance and harmony between an individual and society. It consists of a sequence of eight steps ranging from self-cultivation to ruling the country. The application of *ren* is accomplished through investigation of things, extension of knowledge, sincerity of heart, rectification of minds, cultivation of personal lives, regulation of families, bringing order to the state, and manifestation of a clear character to the world. Catholic teaching joins the Confucian theory here in showing this sense of self-reliance. Protestant theology, however, insists upon faith alone and exclusive dependence on God's power. It is also interesting to note here the greater resemblance between Confucian teaching and the traditional Catholic doctrine of a natural moral law based on human nature itself, a law that is written in people's hearts. The doctrine of personal salvation in Protestantism offends Confucianism.

The give-and-take mentality of the Chinese mind is best exemplified by four Chinese Christian intellectuals who held the highest academic degree, *jinshi.* They believed that Christianity could supplement the original Confucianism; sincerity was the way. It was the quality that brought man and heaven together. The first three, Xu Guangqi* (1562-1633), Li Zhizao* (1565-1630), and Yang Tingyun* (1557-1627), were called the three pillars of evangelization in China. As adults they were converted to Christianity by Jesuits*. They did not show any inner tension between their Confucian heritage and their new-found faith. Their acceptance of Christianity never brought them any intellectual difficulty.

Xu, the most prominent, viewed the Christian faith as supplementing Confucianism. He was thinking in terms of universal values, and he attempted to bring the teachings of Confucius under the sanction and guidance of the God of heaven. He also saw that the general reinvigoration of society depended on the individual's actions. Though he believed that the relationship of the self to others was to be based upon Confucian morals and ethics, he affirmed that Christianity was a way to moral reform, and such moral reform occurred at the grassroots level. If everyone believed in the Christian God, all people would become worthies and genteel. The other two shared the same sentiments. Li was convinced that the genuine teachings of Christianity must come from the Confucian classics. Yang, on the other hand, believed

Confucianism and Christianity

that the way to gain true knowledge of heaven was for people to love others as themselves. In doing so, they would first subdue their evil desires and manifest their inner virtues.

The fourth intellectual, Wu Leichuan* (L. C. Wu, 1870-1944), was converted to the Anglican* faith. Wu's rational understanding of Christianity was heavily influenced by *The Mean* and *Mencius.* Following the tone of *The Mean,* he believed that the cultivation of the *dao* was called religion. As such, all teachings and religions would lead to the *dao.* Wu's religiosity, especially the aspect of prayer and meditation, was depicted by *The Mean.* Sincerity was the prime factor in such religious pursuit.

Wu believed that Jesus' self-cultivation and his sacrifice for the sake of his country can serve as a role model for the Chinese. Jesus was far better than Chinese sages because he died for the cause. In Wu's mind, Jesus, an ordinary man, was like a Confucian *junzi* who perfected his personality through his blameless struggle. He was therefore a perfect model for personality development. Wu also identified *ren* with the Holy Spirit, stripping the latter's divine status. In fact, the Christian faith of Wu, like that of Xu, Li, and Yang, was one of sincere intellectual commitment to moral renewal.

The theology of a prominent modern Christian intellectual, Zhao Zi Chen* (C. T. Chao, 1888-1979), sheds some light on Chinese Christianity. Trained at Vanderbilt University in the United States, he was very concerned about a theology of relevance, a theology that related to the Chinese culture and understood the Chinese mind. Zhao apparently was influenced by his contemporary, theologian Paul Tillich, who emphasized the study of religion and culture. Zhao was also exposed to the thoughts of William James, Borden Parker Bowne, and Henri Bergson. Above these, his Confucian heritage directed him to emphasize personality and human growth, which were seemingly compatible with his acquired theological thought.

In the light of Confucian teaching, Zhao saw Christian salvation as an effort of self-renewal in a process of self-cultivation. It was a way of deification, in which one's personality could be perfected. Through self-cultivation, Jesus, an ordinary man, was conscious of his identity as the Christ. Jesus' self-consciousness was not the top-to-bottom process of incarnation, that is, God becoming man, but a bottom-to-top process of striving to attain godliness. Jesus' sincerity and his self-consciousness of his mission serve as a model for humankind.

Wang Ming-tao* (1900-91), though not an intellectual, was an influential preacher and prolific writer. He acknowledged that he was very influenced by the Bible and the Four Books *(Analects, Mencius, Learning,* and *The Mean).* Though claiming unswerving confidence in the Bible, his flow of thought was deeply rooted in Confucian ethics. His preaching and life reflected Wang Yangming's (1472-1529) teaching on the unity of knowledge and action. He was a man of perception and of strong will. He preached the utilization of Christian faith.

Wang Ming-tao's teaching emphasized personal ethics and behavior. He was convinced that human beings cannot help themselves because of their corrupted human nature. Salvation is an act totally dependent on the redeeming grace of Jesus Christ. But Wang's stress on personal ethics made him take sanctification seriously; Christians are primarily responsible for this process through conquering sins and imitating Jesus Christ. This is the ultimate goal of Christians. However, no one can reach that goal in this life. Being born again, on the other hand, is the work of God.

Throughout his life, especially when his life was at stake during the Japanese occupation and his long-term imprisonment under the Communist regime, Wang never gave up his faith for the sake of his safety. He was, as he recalled, a great man *(dazhangfu)* in accordance with Mencius's teaching. A great man would never be dissipated by wealth and honors; neither would he be brought low by poverty or humbleness, nor be subdued by force and might. Wang's strong will against persecutions of course found justification in Jesus' life.

A study of Chinese Christian intellectuals and preachers shows that they all take Christianity seriously. Though they may in one way or another have modified Christian tenets, their sense of sincerity justifies their faith. On the other hand, their Confucian way of reflection on Christian theology shows their concern that Christians, in the pursuit of *ren,* be in relationship to establish their own character and other people's character, as well as to live in harmony with each other and with God. Confucian values, not to mention Confucian logic and language, greatly color their Christian faith. Their Confucian heritage makes them more concerned about personal and social ethics than anything else.

In a transcultural study of Confucianism and Christianity, we must be reminded that both Confucianists and Christians, in varying degrees, are seeking universal truth in which self-transcendence is a key. Such an understanding may be the best starting point for a dialogue between them. In moral pursuit, Confucianism and Christianity do not exclude each other. In the final analysis, Confucianism perhaps needs to say more about human fallibility and the meaning of human suffering in the light of Jesus' crucifixion, while Christianity has need of a more profound inquiry into the question of human responsibility, preferably from the perspective of God's creation.

Bibliography

MacInnes, Donald, *Religion in China Today: Policy and Practice* (1989). • Küng, Hans, and Julia Ching, *Christianity and Chinese Religions* (1989). • Ching, Julia, *Confucianism and Christianity: A Comparative Study* (1977). • Gernet, Jacques, *China and the Christian Impact* (1985).

• Covell, Ralph, *Confucius, the Buddha, and Christ* (1986). • Yang, C. K., *Religion in Chinese Society* (1961).
CHU SIN-JAN

Congregation for the Propagation of the Faith.
See Propaganda Fide Congregation

Conscientious Objection, Japan

(Ryoshin teki Heieki Kyohi). Refusal to serve in the military for reasons of personal conscience or religious beliefs.

There have been many examples of conscientious objection because of Christian beliefs and the militant side of Japanese culture. Historically, conscientious objection was a position taken by many members of three Protestant denominations: the Religious Society of Friends (Quakers), the Mennonites, and the Plymouth Brethren, all known as peace churches. In the 19th c., members of Dukhober, a Protestant group that had settled in Russia, were also conscientious objectors, receiving support from Tolstoy. The first example of such in Japan was Yabe Kiyoshi, a minister who chose to serve as a medic during the Russo-Japanese War. During the Taisho period, Suda Seiki, under the influence of Kashiwagi Gien, sent a letter of withdrawal from the army to the secretary of the army. During the war in China*, Akashi Makoto and Muramoto Issei, both employees of the Watch Tower Society, were arrested because they refused as soldiers to shoot a weapon. During World War II*, Ishiga Susumu of the Non-Church Movement* was a conscientious objector. At the present time, there are many countries that legally recognize conscientious objection. As of 1965, there were 15 countries, including the United States, Great Britain, France, Germany, the Netherlands, Sweden, Canada, and Australia, that accepted such petitions and assigned alternative service.

Bibliography

Japan Fellowship of Reconciliation, *Ryoshin teki heieki kyohi* (Conscientious Objection) (1967). • Abe Tomoji, *Ryoshin teki heieki kyohi no shiso* (The Thinking behind Conscientious Objection) (1969).
KASAHARA YOSHIMITSU, JAPANESE DICTIONARY

Consultative Forum between Religious Groups

(Wadah Musyawarah Antar Umat Beragama). The Consultative Forum between Religious Groups was established in 1981 after long discussions by the Indonesian ministry of religious affairs to promote harmony *(kerukunan)* within, and between, religious groups and with the government. Members of the forum include the National Councils of the Muslims, Protestants, Catholics, Hindus, and Buddhists. The national and regional forums have succeeded in establishing inter-religious communication and better contact with the government agencies.
ADOLF HEUKEN

Contextualization

General Trends. "Ours is the faith of the apostles in the risen Christ." Thus spoke 56 Roman Catholic Asian theologians in a statement issued after a meeting in Pattaya, Thailand*, in Apr 1994. But as Asian Christians — Catholics and orthodox Protestants — have come to realize, to have the faith of the apostolic church is to have a *living* faith, one that emerges from a "living theology" that is done within the Asian context of ancient and rich cultures, venerable religious traditions, teeming populations, oppressive poverty*, struggles with Westernization and modernization, dehumanizing violence, growing nationalism*, and increasing economic importance and power.

Although intentional contextualization has roots that go back to pioneers like Matteo Ricci* and Roberto de Nobili* in the 16th c., the leaders of the Indian cultural renaissance in the 1800s, and some visionary theologians in the early 20th c. (see England and Lee, pp. 36-37), it has only been in the last 50 years that Christian theology and Christian life have begun to understand contextualization as a theological and ecclesial imperative; more specifically, as Asian Catholics began to come to grips with Vatican II's commitment to history, and as Asian Protestants began to take seriously the second and third mandates of the World Council of Church's (WCC) Theological Education Fund (TEF), it became more and more clear that if Christianity did not become Asian it was not a genuine Christianity. One can safely say today that contextualization (or its rough synonyms of "indigenization," "inculturation," and "incarnation") is truly alive and well in Asia. Some efforts may be repetitive, some imitative, some dead ends, as one Asian theologian points out (see Sugirtharajah, p. 42); but there is no doubt that the development of a truly Asian Christianity is a priority of the Asian church.

One indication of the vitality of contextualization in Asia is the proliferation of organizations and institutes all over Asia that devote themselves to producing or promoting a theology and Christian practice which are authentically Asian. Among Protestants, there have developed the Christian Conference of Asia (CCA), the Association for Theological Education in South East Asia (ATESEA), the North East Asia Association of Theological Schools (NEAATS), and the Program for Theology and Cultures in Asia (PTCA). ATESEA has developed the South East Asia Graduate School of Theology (SEAGST) and publishes the important *Asia Journal of Theology* and *ATESEA Occasional Papers.* For over a decade, the PTCA has held annual workshops which have explored doing theology with Asian folk literature, Asian people's movements, Asian cultures, Asian symbols and images, and Asian religious festivals and customs; it has published selected papers from these workshops in the *ATESEA Occasional Papers* and publishes the *PTCA Bulletin*. In 1991, PTCA sponsored a forum of Asian theological librarians in Chiang Mai, Thailand*, which encouraged the development of Asian resources in libraries and forged ties of inter-Asian cooperation (see Batumalai 1991, and England and Lee 1993).

For Roman Catholics*, the Federation of Asian Bishops' Conferences* (FABC) has met regularly since the 1970s and has issued important statements on evangelization, spirituality*, ecclesiology, and the laity. In addition, it has held regular institutes for the missionary apostolate, interreligious affairs, social action, and the lay apostolate (see Rosales and Arevalo 1992). In Manila, Philippines*, the East Asian Pastoral Institute* has been a leader in developing Asian theological reflection; and its publication, the *East Asian Pastoral Review*, is one of Asia's most accessible theological journals. In Japan*, Nanzan University's Institute for Religion and Culture has spearheaded scholarship and interreligious dialogue; in India*, there is Ishvani Kendra in Pune; in Sri Lanka* there is the Tulana Research Center founded by Aloysius Pieris, and in the Philippines there is the Paul VI Institute of Liturgy directed by Anscar Chupungco. These are just a few of a large number of spirituality and dialogue centers, theological research institutes, and pastoral centers that have sprung up all over Asia, making contextualization an ever-growing reality within the Asian church and helping it shape its mission.

On the ecumenical scene, it is important to point out that major contributions to the Ecumenical Association of Third World Theologians (EATWOT) come from Asian theologians, and an important source for Asian feminist* theology is the Asian Women's Resources Center for Culture and Theology which is based in Seoul, Korea*. The semi-annual bulletin *Inter-Religio*, long published in Japan and now published in Hong Kong*, represents a number of East Asian centers of interreligious* dialogue.

Another indication of the vitality of contextualization in Asia is the number of Asian journals that regularly publish serious articles on Asian theological and pastoral topics. Several journals have already been mentioned by name; a longer list can be found in the publication *Theologie im Kontext* from the missiological institute in Aachen, Germany. In addition, one can get a sense of the high level of Asian theological thinking by consulting the quarterly notices on dissertations that appear in the *International Bulletin of Missionary Research*.

Contextualization in Asia has various starting points. Aloysius Pieris (*Vidyajoyoti*, Nov 1993) speaks of involvement with and commitment to the poor of Asia as the one condition of the possibility of a truly inculturated Asian liturgy. Asian members of EATWOT have made that point again and again at their various regional and general assemblies. Other Asian theologians begin their theology by attending carefully to the wealth of Asian culture, traditional folk tales, mythologies, and symbols; still others insist that contextualization in their own Asian situations can be accomplished only as a dialogue with the great Asian religions of Hinduism*, Buddhism*, and Islam*, or with the plethora of traditional religions of Asian tribal minorities. Theology and Christian practice in Asia are also influenced by a growing consciousness of women's oppression, a growing appreciation of subaltern voices such as Indian Dalits* or Japanese Burakumin people, and a growing awareness of the ecological threat and its roots in Western greed (see Buraku Liberation Movement).

What is clear, however, is that *context* — whether social, cultural, or religious — is now regarded, along with Scripture and ecclesial or theological tradition, as an indispensable source for Asian theologizing and Christian life. Asian Christians are increasingly in agreement with what a key statement of the Asian church insisted on some 20 years ago: "Christian theology will fulfill its task in Asia only as the Asian churches, as servants of God's Word and the revelation in Jesus Christ, speak to the Asian situations, from involvement in them" (Batumalai, p. 24).

Southeast Asia. The Republic of the Philippines is the only country in Asia where Christians are in the majority, and so it is not surprising that contextualization has developed quite strongly there. Some of the earliest attempts at contextualization were Douglas J. Elwood and Patricia Magdamo's *Christ in Philippine Context* (1971) and Leonardo Mercado's pioneering works on Filipino philosophy and theology in which he attempted to discover Christian patterns within Filipino culture and language. Theologians such as Cataline Arevalo, Carlos Abesamis, and Edicio de la Torre were inspired by Latin American liberation theology and advocated a Filipino theology that started with a reflection on and analysis of the disenfranchised and marginalized poor. In 1981, Rodrigo D. Tano offered a useful survey of the thought of these and several other Filipino theologians in his *Theology in the Philippine Setting*. More recently, Salvador T. Martinez of the CCA has reflected as a Protestant on the theological possibilities of Filipino popular religiosity, and Catholics José de Mesa and Dionisio Miranda have done important creative work with Filipino culture. Both de Mesa and Miranda have reflected on the rich theological implications of the Tagalog word *loob* (untranslatable, but basically referring to one's inner self). Among his many publications, de Mesa has written seminal reflections on the meaning of Jesus' resurrection, grace, and providence, and, with the Belgian missionary and theologian Lode Wostyn, has produced important books on theological method and Christology. In the last several years, Miranda has published books on Filipino values (*Buting Pinoy*, 1993) and on medical ethics (*Pagkamakabuhay*, 1994). Finally, no survey would be complete without the mention of Filipino feminist theologians, the most notable of whom are Virginia Fabella and Mary John Mananzan, and without the mention as well of Anscar Chupungco and his efforts to contextualize the Catholic liturgy.

Sadayandy Batumalai is a prolific Malaysian theologian who has written an introduction to Asian theology (1991) and has edited a number of books that focus on Malaysian culture as a source for theology. The young Malaysian Jesuit*, Jojo M. Fung, has contributed to the development of Malaysian theological reflection with his "shoes-off" theology. Fung proposes a five-step method of theologizing that begins with the life experiences of Malaysians, moves through a reflection on biblical sources, and ends up with a reflection on possible responses of the Malaysian church.

Contextualization in Indonesia* is rooted in the country's rich culture, in the inevitable dialogue with Islam, and in reflection on what is often a difficult political situation for Christians. One of the great advantages of Indonesian contextual theology is that almost all of it is done in the national language, Bahasa Indonesia; the disadvantage, of course, is that much remains inaccessible to others, Asians and non-Asians alike. Some works by Indonesian theologians have appeared in English, however. Robert Hardawiryana, perhaps the most well-known Indonesian theologian, has recently provided a survey of efforts of Indonesian contextual theologizing (see *Studia Missionalia* 1996, pp. 135-52). A. M. Sutrisnaatmaka has written on the possibilities of celebrating the Eucharist within the Indonesian context. J. B. Banawiratma, together with fellow Jesuit Tom Jacobs, has reported on a 12-step process of theological reflection used in Yogyakarta. Indonesian Marianne Katoppo is considered a leading Asian feminist theologian.

In Thailand*, Koson Srisang takes as his starting point the masses of Thai people and develops a theology with strong political overtones that is rooted in Thai cultural heritage. A creative use of culture, he maintains, can lead people to political action. Employing a method that reflects on Thai folk tales, Maen Pongudom of Payap University in Chiang Mai has tried to interpret passages in the Bible for the Thai people. Traditional Thai drama is also used to theologize and communicate in an appropriate way at Payap in Chiang Mai.

South Asia. Even though the Christian population of the countries of South Asia is quite small, the process of contextualization is perhaps more advanced here than in any other region of Asia, with the possible exception of the Philippines. The relatively small island of Sri Lanka produced Aloysius Pieris, who is perhaps the most widely known Asian theologian today. In a number of books and articles in the last 25 years, Pieris has developed a theology that combines the need to be rooted in the poor and the oppressed with the need to be in dialogue with the wealth of culture and religious faith. "The Asian Church," says Pieris, "must abdicate its alliance with power. It must be humble enough to be baptized in the Jordan of Asian religiosity and bold enough to be baptized on the Cross of Asian poverty" (quoted in Batumalai, p. 208). Other theologians of note are Preman Niles (son of D. T. Niles*), Wesley Ariarajah, and Tissa Balysuria. Catholic theologian A. J. V. Chandrakanthan has recently published an important reflection on contextualization in Sri Lanka.

Contextualization in India, despite its small Christian population, has a venerable tradition which goes back to the time of the early St. Thomas Christians. India can boast of theological giants such as K. M. Banerjee*, Brahamobandhav Upadhyaya, P. Chenchiah*, A. J. Appasamy*, and, of course, M. M. Thomas* and P. D. Devanandan*. Of extreme interest to contemporary Indian theologians is the development of a theology in dialogue with Hinduism; theologians such as Stanley J. Samartha*, Samuel Rayan, and Jacob Kavunkal are heavily involved in this process. Several Indian theologians who make their homes elsewhere — Raimundo Panikkar*, Thomas Thangaraj, and R. S. Sugirtharajah — also do theology in terms of dialogue, and Panikkar's influence in this regard is quite profound. On the other hand, biblical scholar and Jesuit George Suares-Prhabhu believes that more important than this culturally and religiously oriented approach is one that sides with the millions of impoverished and marginalized in India and discovers the God of all peoples in working for human dignity and liberation. This more liberational and political approach is also espoused by Michael Amaladoss in several of his works. Amaladoss has recently published a valuable survey of liberation theologies in several Asian contexts.

Taiwan. In late 1940, the Presbyterian Church in Taiwan* (PCT) began moving toward becoming a contextualized church, that is, a localized church that identifies with and shares the history of the people of Taiwan. In the mid-1950s, the Doubling Movement* (PKU) marked a turning point in the move toward contextualization. By the 1970s, the maturity of the localized church was reflected in the issuance of three public statements.

Although the pioneer missionaries contributed much in terms of education, medical work, and other social services, it was difficult for them to indigenize the Christian faith to the local culture and social context. Their aim was essentially to plant churches working from a base that was associated with Western colonialism*.

Some early missionaries did try to establish a self-supporting church in Taiwan, but the process was long and slow. By 1940, more than 70 years after the first Protestant church was planted, there were only 66 ordained ministers in South Taiwan and 42 in the North.

Indigenization really began in East Asia in 1940, when the missionaries were compelled by the Japanese to leave or were imprisoned. Under the difficult circumstances of World War II*, Taiwanese Christians learned to become self-governing, self-supporting, and self-propagating. The self-reliance and independence of the church was the first step toward contextualization.

Contextualization in Taiwan may be understood in the light of the historical-cultural context of the country, reformation in the church and ecumenism, and the socio-political factor. From a historical-cultural perspective, early attempts at contextualization by the pioneer missionaries began with church architecture (see Art and Architecture) and Bible* translations. Church buildings were patterned after the traditional folk house, no crosses were displayed, and a fence was built around the pulpit, as in the Taiwanese temples. There were even small pagodas on the roof of some churches.

Political factors also played a role in the need to contextualize Christianity in Taiwan. When the government of Taiwan, after being ousted from the United Nations, compelled the PCT to withdraw from the World Council of Churches in 1971, the PCT saw the need to relate the Christian faith to the socio-political context of Taiwan and to erase the perception of Christianity as a Western religion. The PCT responded by issuing three public statements: "Public Statement of Our National Fate" (1971), "Our Appeal" (1975), and "A Declaration on Human Rights" (1977). In essence, the PCT believed that it was essential to "re-experience and re-understand the gospel within our time and culture" and to identify with the "living situation," that is, the hopes and aspirations, the culture, and the history of the people. The PCT saw Taiwan as "a suffering servant" of God for the sake of bringing the gospel of justice, love, and peace to the world and urged the government to recognize the people's desire for Taiwan to be a new and independent nation with the right to self-determination.

The effort to contextualize the Gospel into the socio-political and historical-cultural realities of Taiwan has been criticized in some quarters. The task of understanding its cultural uniqueness is an ongoing process. The challenge remains to construct a theological understanding of church and missions that takes into account Taiwan's unique cultural traditions and practices.

Conclusion. This brief article has provided only a partial glimpse of a number of efforts to produce a living theology — academic as well as pastoral, written and permanent as well as oral, occasional, and ephemeral — all over Asia today. The process of contextualization in Asia continues to give vitality and relevance to Christian communities in each milieu. With greater Asia-to-Asia contact, the work of contextualization will look very different in the coming years — freed up from Western intellectual imperialism. Like African Christians in Africa, like North American and Latin American Christians in the Western Hemisphere, like European Christians in Europe, Asian Christians are succeeding in discovering "the unfathomable riches of Christ" (Eph. 3:8) within their own cultural, religious, and political riches.

Bibliography

Amaladoss, M., *Life in Freedom: Liberation Theologies from Asia* (1997) (contains an extensive bibliography). • Dayanandan, F. T., *Asian Expressions of Christian Commitment: A Reader in Asian Theology* (1992). • Batumalai, S., *An Introduction to Asian Theology* (1991). • England, J. C., and A. C. C. Lee, *Doing Theology with Asian Resources: Ten Years in the Formation of Living Theology in Asia* (1993). • Fabella, V., and S. A. L. Park, eds., *We Dare to Dream: Doing Theology as Asian Women* (1990). • Gnanapiragasam, J., and F. Wilfred, eds., *Being Church in Asia: Theological Advisory Commission Documents (1986-92)* (1994). • Rommerskirchen, J., and W. Henkel, eds., *Bibliographia Missionaria,* 55 vols. to 1991. • Rosales, G., and C. G. Arevalo, *For All the Peoples of Asia: Federation of Asian Bishops' Conferences Documents from 1970 to 1991* (1992). • "Inculturation: Gospel and Culture," *Studia Missionalia,* Vol. 44 (1995); "Local Theologies," Vol. 45 (1996) (articles on Asia contain extensive bibliographies). • Sugirtharajah, R. S., ed., *Frontiers in Asian Christian Theology: Emerging Trends* (1994) (contains an excellent annotated bibliography and a list of Asian Christian journals in English); *Asian Faces of Jesus* (1993); *Voices from the Margin: Interpreting the Bible in the Third World* (1991). • *Theologie im Kontext: Informationen über theologische Beiträge aus Afrika, Asians, Ozeanien und Lateinamerika* (1979-95).

Stephen Bevans and Wu Wun-hsiong

Convent of the Holy Infant Jesus

The Institute of the Sisters of the Infant Jesus, also known as the *Dames de St. Maur,* began in France as a group of laywomen whose aim was to instruct and educate poor and disadvantaged children and young people by enabling them to develop their human and spiritual potential to the fullest so that they could live with dignity, fulfill their vocation in life, and reach their final destiny. Under the able and inspiring leadership of Nicolas Barre (1621-86), these women lived among the poor and began small free schools for the poor in Sotteville, Rouen, in 1662. Soon these were in great demand all over France. Mission expansion outside France brought the sisters to Asia, then to America and Africa. In 1887, the Lay Institute of the Sisters of St. Maur was officially recognized by Rome. From then on, it became a religious institute following a conventual lifestyle.

In the second half of the 19th c., the urgent need of education for girls in Asia was one of the reasons the sisters came to the East. Education was perceived to be the key to human development and the way to build a country where citizens would live in justice, integrity, and racial harmony. This belief prompted the bishops of this region, at different times, to request sisters who could educate and instruct girls.

As early as 1850, upon the appeal of Mgr. Boucho, apostolic vicar of Malaya, Fr. Beurel of the Foreign Missions approached Rev. Mother de Faudoas (1837-77), the then mother general, for sisters to be sent to Malaya. Accordingly, Mother Mathilde Raclot (1814-1911), who started missions in Penang (1852), Singapore* (1854), and Japan* (1872), was sent to Malaya together with three others.

By the close of the century, schools, boarding homes, orphanages, and homes for abandoned babies were established in Penang, Singapore, Malacca*, and Kuala Lumpur. In 1872, these services were made available in

Yokohama, Japan. The mission continued to expand, and by the first half of the 20th c., the Convent of the Holy Infant Jesus (CHIJ) schools were to be found all over Malay and Japan. The year 1885 saw a similar mission in Bangkok, Thailand*. It was closed in 1907 and resumed in 1957 in Cholburi.

Today, the sisters are returning to their original inspiration; and, like the pioneers, their strength lies in their union of heart and spirit in mission. This implies openness to change, freedom, and flexibility, relying totally on divine providence as they collaborate with their lay partners for the human and spiritual formation of children and young people.

The sisters have always been a small band and will probably remain so. At present, there are close to 50 sisters in Singapore, with 11 schools and four education/social centers; 178 sisters in Malaysia, with 69 schools and three educational/social centers; 125 sisters in Japan, with six schools; and 40 sisters in Thailand, with four schools and two education/social centers.

Bibliography

Flourez, Brigitte, *Better than Light* (1994). • *Book of the Institute: Sisters of the Infant Jesus (Nicolas Barre)* (1986). • *Congregation of the Sisters of the Holy Infant Jesus Called Dames de Saint Maur: Mission of the Sisters of the Holy Infant Jesus in Malaya, 1852-1952* (1952). • *The Beginning: Convent Annals 1852-1981* (1987). • Takamine, Mother Cecilia, *Sisters of St. Maur — Japan, 1872-1972* (1972).

AGNES LEE

Cook, J. A. B.

(b. 1854; d. 13 Jul 1926). Missionary to Singapore* (1882-1925) responsible for overseeing the Chinese Presbyterian* churches in Singapore and Peninsular Malaysia*.

Cook decided to become a missionary after reading an account of the death of David Livingstone. In 1881, the English Presbyterian Mission appointed him to take charge of the Chinese Presbyterian Church in Singapore, which had been without missionary oversight after the death of its founder, Benjamin Keasberry*. After studying the Swatow dialect in China* for one year, he arrived in Singapore in 1882. He reformed the existing congregation and then initiated new congregations for Chinese Christians outside the Singapore town area and for those speaking dialects other than Swatow. He established churches among the Chinese in Johore after obtaining land grants from the sultan of Johore through James Meldrum, son-in-law of Keasberry and prominent company manager in Johore. For many years, Cook oversaw a monthly missionary meeting, which carried on the ecumenical work of Sophia Cooke* of the Anglican mission and brought together all of the Protestant church workers in Singapore. These meetings fostered extensive cooperative ministries and were instrumental in helping the Methodists establish their missionary presence. Cook was an influential leader of the anti-opium* and temperance movements in Singapore and was an outspoken critic of the brothel trade in Chinese women. This and his interest in history were reflected both in his books and numerous articles for the Christian press in Singapore.

Bibliography

Cook, J. A. B., *Sunny Singapore* (1907). • Sng, Bobby, *In His Good Time* (1993).

ROBERT HUNT

Cooke, Sophia

(b. Norfolk, England, ca. 27 Feb 1814; d. Singapore, 14 Sep 1895). Anglican English missionary-teacher to Singapore*.

The gross sexual imbalance between males and females in the early days of Singapore resulted in the exploitation and trafficking of women. Cooke, whose ministry spanned 42 years, worked mainly to better the lot of the unfortunate girls.

A governess in the home of a pastor, Cooke heard much about the East through visiting missionaries. Inspired, she joined the Society for Promoting Female Education in the East and arrived in Singapore on 29 Jul 1853 to take charge of the Chinese Girls' School (now St. Margaret's School), a boarding school for unwanted girls. The school flourished under her care and supervision. The girls received a sound education, including religious instruction, and many later married Christian men and continued to serve God in Singapore and beyond with their husbands.

Cooke took a great interest in the General and Military Hospitals, the only two hospitals in Singapore at the time, frequently visiting the sick with her young helpers to spread cheer and the Gospel. She held Bible classes for soldiers, policemen, and sailors, and many destitute sailors were fed and clothed by her. She also started a branch of the Young Women's Christian Association* (YWCA) to draw in European and Eurasian young ladies to join her work.

Despite failing health in her later years, Cooke did not cease to labor. Sophia Road, on which sat St. Margaret's Primary School, was named after her.

Bibliography

Walker, E. A., *Sophia Cooke: Or, Forty-Two Years' Work in Singapore* (1899). • Sng, Bobby E. K., *In His Good Time* (1980, 1993). • Doraisamy, Theodore R., *The March of Methodism* (1982).

YEOW GEOK LIAN

Cordeiro, Joseph

(b. Bombay, 19 Jan 1918). Archbishop of Karachi (1958-94).

When Cordeiro's father, who was a medical officer in Bombay, retired, the family moved to Karachi. Cordeiro was educated at St. Patrick's and the D. J. Science College,

Karachi, and at the Papal Seminary at Kandy, Sri Lanka*. After his ordination on 24 Aug 1946, he read modern classics at Oxford and returned to Pakistan* as rector of the minor seminary at Quetta. He was nominated archbishop of Karachi in Aug 1958 and 15 years later received the red hat from Pope Paul VI in 1973. Cordeiro was viewed publicly as a special representative of the Goan people. When circumstances moved many of these people to emigrate from Pakistan, he felt he still owed them care. He traveled widely to ensure that the churches in America, Europe, and Australasia understood and responded to the needs of Asian Catholics.

A firm believer in quiet diplomacy, Cordeiro served on many international Catholic commissions, such as the International Committee on English in the Liturgy (ICEL) and the Roman Synod Preparatory Commission. He was a consultant whose advice was sought and appreciated even by the popes themselves. At home, he was a hands-on worker who was noted for his pastoral care of the clergy, catechists, and religious, but especially for preparing young engaged couples for marriage. He provided the quiet leadership and inspiration that guided the Catholic community through the social and political challenges of the time. John Rooney

Cosmas Indiclopleustes

(b. Egypt, 6th c.; d. ?). One of the earliest witnesses to travel and geography in West and South Asia: "the Indian sailor."

Cosmas's many travels from Egypt have won him the title "The Indian Navigator." He was a trader who traveled to Persia, Arabia, and India* and was an early witness to the church and to the geography of these areas. His travels to India occurred between 520 and 525 C.E. After his travels, he retired to a monastery and recorded what he had seen and heard, along with various interpretations of biblical texts. Many of his observations about geography would prove to be true, but, against some of the ancients who argued that the earth was round, Cosmas defended the earth as flat. Cosmas wrote about Christian (Nestorian*) communities he had discovered in western India, on the island of Socotra, and on Taprobane (Sri Lanka*). He notes that the priests were ordained in Persia and that the bishop he met in Kallyan (Kalyana) was also sent from Persia.

Bibliography

Cosmas Indicopleustes, "Christian Topography," in *Sources chrétiennes,* Vols. 141, 159, and 197, ed. W. Wolska-Conus (1968, 1970, 1973). • Casey, "The Fourth Kingdom in Cosmas Indicopleustes and the Syrian Tradition," *Rivista di storia e letteratura religiosa* 25 (1989). • Winstedt, E. O., *The Christian Topography of Cosmas Indicopleustes* (1909). • Wolska, Wanda, *La Topographie chrétienne de Cosmas Indicopleustes théologie et science ou VIe siècle* (1962). Scott W. Sunquist

Costantini, Celso (Gang Hengyi)

(b. Italy, 1876; d. 1958). First apostolic delegate of the Vatican to China* and advocate of indigenous church development in China.

Costantini was consecrated in 1899 and made a bishop in 1921. After his arrival in China on 8 Nov 1922, he learned that he had been made an apostolic delegate by Pope Pius XI earlier on 12 Aug. He reached Shanghai on 24 Dec. The Vatican Representative Office was temporarily set up in Hankou and moved to Beijing on 18 Jul 1923. In 1924 there were more than two million Chinese Catholics and over 1,000 Chinese priests, but no Chinese bishop. By 1949 there were almost 30. (Luo Wenzao*, the only Catholic bishop until the 20th c., was consecrated bishop of the Nanjing Diocese in early Qing in 1690.)

In 1926 Costantini led six Chinese bishops to the Vatican to be consecrated by the pope. They were Superintendents Cheng Hede (of Hubei PuQi Superintendent's Diocese) and Sun Deszhen (Hebei Lixian), and Vicars Apostolic Zhao Huiyi (of Chahaer Xuanhua Vicar Apostolic Diocese), Chen Guodi (Shanxi Fenyang), Zhu Kaimin (Jiangsu Haimen), and Hu Ruoshan (Zhejiang Taizhou). In 1927 one of them, bishop Zhao Huai Yi, died. Costantini consecrated another Chinese, bishop Cheng You You, in Xuan Hua Catholic Church the following year. In 1930 Costantini consecrated three more Chinese bishops: Wang Zhi Fu in Chong Ching Catholic Church in Sichuan for the Vicariate Apostolic district of Wan Xian; Wang Wen Zheng in the Nan Chong Catholic Church for the district of Nan Chong; and Liu Jin Wen in the North Church, Beijing, for the district of Fen Yang. By 1933 19 of the 119 ecclesiastical precincts in China were led by Chinese Christians. Costantini's greatest contribution was promoting Chinese leadership in encouraging Chinese expressions of Christian faith.

Bedridden after 1931 because of a serious foot illness, Costantini returned to Italy for rest and treatment at the end of 1932. He resigned from the Vatican diplomatic post in China and was made a cardinal in 1952.

Bibliography

Bruls, Jean, trans. and ed., *Réformé des Missions au XXe siècle* (1960). China Group, translated by David Wu

Covenant of Omar

The Islamic conquests of Christian territory beginning under Umar I* (634-44) necessitated a series of treaties specifying treatment of religious minorities under Islamic rule. The earliest forms of these treaties gave relative freedom to the (majority) Christian population. As the Muslim rulers consolidated their military dominance over formerly Byzantine territories and developed an Islamic administrative system, control over the lives of non-Muslims was considerably tightened. The result was the Covenant of Omar (Umar), which in its traditional form dates to the 9th c. despite being attributed to Umar I.

Versions of the covenant after the 9th c. categorize non-Muslims as *dhimmis* who live under Muslim protection and may follow their traditional religious and communal practices, yet are subject to a variety of prohibitions and social humiliations. Important prohibitions included evangelizing Muslims or marrying Muslim women. *Dhimmis* were also required to pay a special tax in lieu of service to the state, to live in restricted areas, and to wear distinctive clothes, badges, and hair styles to distinguish them from Muslims.

Within the Islamic empire, the provisions of the Covenant of Omar were a major factor in encouraging mass conversion to Islam. The detailed provisions of the covenant had the effect of creating distinct systems of law and government for Muslims and non-Muslims and effectively ghettoizing the non-Muslim population. The Covenant of Omar and its antecedent treaties have been the topic of considerable discussion as Muslims try to form postcolonial Islamic states with substantial Christian minorities. Muslim opinion regarding the authority of these treaties and the covenant for modern Islamic lawmakers varies considerably.

Bibliography

Moffett, Samuel Hugh, *A History of Christianity in Asia*, Vol. I (1992). • Khadduri, Majid, *War and Peace in the Law of Islam* (1955).

ROBERT HUNT

Cuadra, Matias

(b. Siasi, Jolo, Sulu, 24 Feb 1896; d. Polangui, Albay, 20 Sep 1964). First Filipino Muslim convert to become a Protestant minister.

Having grown up a Muslim, Cuadra was baptized a Catholic by a German Jesuit* in Sandakan, Borneo, in 1907. He met the Christian and Missionary Alliance* missionary, David Lund, at Zamboanga in 1913 and turned Protestant in 1914.

Graduating from Union Theological Seminary (Manila), Cuadra was ordained in an interdenominational ceremony in 1920, with 15 American and Filipino ministers from five denominations officiating collegially. Thereafter Cuadra freely preached for some years to Muslims in Siasi and Jolo, converting and baptizing scores of young men.

Subsequently joining the Evangelical Methodist Church in the Philippine Islands (IEMELIF), Cuadra became one of its bishops. In 1948 he led 11 IEMELIF congregations into the United Church of Christ in the Philippines.

Bibliography

The Philippine Presbyterian, Vol. 11 (Feb 1920). • Laubach, F. C., *People of the Philippines* (1925). • Sitoy, T. V., Jr., *Several Springs, One Stream* (1992).

T. VALENTINO SITOY, JR.

Cults

As Christian teachings are carried across cultures in Asia, non-Asian churches are often planted, and new, Christian-influenced movements are started. Some of these Christian-influenced movements have been labeled "cults," "sub-Christian movements," New Religious Movements (NRM), and syncretistic movements. No one label is satisfactory, but the concept of "Christian cult" reminds us that these new religions do revolve around a cultus of religious belief and practice. Each cult reflects local cultural (including religious) life along with newer Christian teaching and/or practices.

Japan. Christian-related new religious movements referred to as cults and regarded as heterodox by most established churches or denominations are also engaged in missionary work in Japan*. Some of these groups originate in the West, others in Asia, but each takes on something of its local context as it missionizes in Asia. The Church of Jesus Christ of Latter-Day Saints (Mormons), the Watch Tower Bible and Tract Society (Jehovah's Witnesses), and the Holy Spirit Association for the Unification of World Christianity (often referred to as the Unification Church*) are three such movements with an active organizational presence in Japan.

The Church of Jesus Christ of Latter-Day Saints' work in Japan began in 1901 with the arrival of four missionaries in Yokohama. Initial activities were limited due to lack of Japanese language training, but with the translation and publication of the Book of Mormon in 1909, the missionaries' determination and efforts began to bear fruit. Through street evangelism and church planting, small groups were established in Tokyo, Sapporo, and Osaka. By 1920, there were 12 missionaries and 124 converts. In 1925, missionary activity in Japan was discontinued due to a deterioration of United States–Japan relations. Evangelistic work among Japanese continued in Hawaii through the war years. Missionary work in Japan resumed in 1948, and steady growth has been recorded in the postwar period. According to 1994 statistics, there are 290 churches with a membership of 106,000. There are also 10 mission centers across the country that serve as a base for 1,600 self-supporting missionaries.

The missionary activity of the Jehovah's Witnesses in Japan began when Akashi Junzo, a convert who had lived in the United States for many years, returned to Japan in 1926. He began propagation activities in Kobe, devoting himself to the translation and distribution of the writings of Joseph Rutherford, the second president of the Watch Tower Society. Membership recruitment was difficult in the nationalistic environment of wartime Japan, and the total membership never exceeded several hundred. The Japan branch was known as Todaisha (the Lighthouse) during this early period. The antiwar declarations and pacifism of Akashi and his followers caught the attention of the special police, and they were subsequently investigated for their subversive ideas. By 1941, the number of Todaisha members arrested reached 122, and 53 of that number were charged with violating the Peace Preservation Law. Akashi was not released from prison until after the war.

In 1946, United States headquarters sent a representative to meet with Akashi and resume missionary activity. After reading the most recent Watch Tower publications, Akashi wrote a letter criticizing the leadership in New York and severed ties with the United States headquarters. In 1949, the United States headquarters sent seven missionaries to start work anew in Japan. Led by Don Haslett, who had been the society's branch coordinator in Hawaii, the movement resumed distribution of literature and engaged in English conversation classes and door-to-door visitation. From 1949 to 1951, their work focused on the major urban centers of Tokyo, Osaka, Kobe, Nagoya, and Yokohama. From 1952 to 1959, work was extended to the cities of Sendai, Hiroshima, Nagasaki, and Fukuoka. In 1973, the Japanese translation of the New World Bible was completed. Although the leadership of the Japanese branch was turned over to Japanese in 1975, there are still 64 foreign missionaries engaged in missionary work. Each month, one million copies of both the *Awake* and *Watchtower* magazines are distributed throughout the country. As of 1994, there were 3,365 congregations divided into 11 districts and an active membership (i.e., those members engaged in proselytizing activities) of 194,608.

The Holy Spirit Association for the Unification of World Christianity, founded in 1954 by Sun Myung Moon in Korea*, expanded into Japan in 1958. The Unification Association of Japan *(Nihon Toitsu Kyokai)* was organized the following year. Under the leadership of Isami Kuboki, a former member of *Rissho Kosei Kai* (a Buddhist-related new religion), the movement grew rapidly in the 1960s and 1970s. The Japanese version of the *Divine Principle* was published in 1967. As in other countries, the movement in Japan was particularly active on university campuses. By the mid-1980s, the movement claimed to have 300,000 members. Outside observers maintain that these statistics are inflated and suggest that fewer than 20,000 are active members. The Unification Association in Japan has been the focus of media attention because of its involvement in right-wing politics, the imprisonment of the founder in the United States for tax fraud, mass weddings, and the claims by many families that their children have been deceived and brainwashed into membership. A number of Christian pastors have been involved in deprogramming activities, assisting both Christian and non-Christian families in retrieving their sons or daughters from the movement. Christian bookstores throughout Japan stock a number of books and pamphlets by evangelical and mainline church leaders addressing the theological and practical problems these three movements represent for Christian mission in Japan.

Vietnam. In traditional Vietnamese belief, especially among peasants, each person is surrounded by the good and evil spirits of all of his deceased ancestors which inhabit animate and inanimate objects. Altars dedicated to ancestors* found in homes, pagodas, and communal houses reflect filial piety, which is highly regarded morally and socially. The ancestral souls live with their children and descendants and share all family vicissitudes. On death anniversaries, relatives gather to present food and incense offerings to the dead in a ceremony presided over by the eldest son; this is followed by a visit to the grave, after which the family returns home for a commemorative meal. The deceased ancestors are invited for every significant family event and invoked for guidance and protection.

In individual families, the god of the hearth and the home genius are also worshipped. At the village level, the communal house is both a worship center and a meeting place for the villagers who worship the village founders, the tutelary genii, heroes and heroines. Besides bimonthly feasts, there are also seasonal ones, such as those at the beginning of planting in the low land, the end of harvest in the high land, the new rice in the ninth month; Thuong Nguyen, Trung Nguyen, Ha Nguyen on the fifteenth day of the first, seventh, and ninth month respectively; the Cold Meal on the third day of the third month; the mid-fall on the fifteenth day of the eighth month, and New Year's Day. The festivities include entertainment such as games, comedies, chess, cockfighting, and buffalo fighting.

In the villages, there are also small temples dedicated to various sacred creatures (a thief, child, tiger, etc.) or pagodas dedicated to the Buddhist pantheon. In some villages, the church seemed to replace the temple or pagoda as cultural center when Christianity was introduced. In other villages, the church became the material center, but the spiritual center remained devotion to ancestors.

At the state level, the cult of heaven was observed by the king and his mandarins. Once each year, the king offered sacrifices of incense, silk, victuals, and wine to heaven, the creator of the universe, at the Nam Giao Altar (a round, elevated place located south of the capital). A buffalo was also burned on the holocaust altar. In the royal temple, where royal ancestors were worshipped, the king had to offer sacrifices to the gods of soil, rice, and the seasons on the Xa Tac Altar, a square at the right of the royal palace. Confucianist intellectuals, saints, and sages were worshipped at the Literary Temple in the capital and at smaller provincial temples.

At the popular level, there are countless cults, a syncretism of Buddhism, Confucianism, Taoism, animism, and Christianity. The legion of spirits worshipped accounts for the presence of diviners, astrologers, chiromancers (palm readers), zoochiromancers, geomancers, and shamans. The last supposedly have the power to exorcise evil spirits believed to be the cause of disease, and amulets for protection may be bought from them.

The first Christian missionary came as early as 1533 under the reign of King Le Trang Ton. Though Christianity has romanized or latinized the national language and introduced modern science to Vietnam*, it has only a limited influence upon traditional animistic beliefs and practices. Animism* still persists to an astonishing degree, evidenced by the permission of the authorities to reconstruct village and town temples dedicated to different deities and patriots.

Bibliography

Boyle, Timothy D., "Jehovah's Witnesses, Mormons, and Moonies: A Critical Look at Christian Heterodoxy in Japan," *Japan Christian Quarterly,* Vol. 57, No. 1 (1991). • Inoue, Nobutaka, et al., eds., *Shinshukyo Jiten* (Dictionary of New Religions) (1990). Scott Sunquist

Da Costa, Arquimino Rodrigues

(b. S. Mateus, Pico, Azores, 8 Jul 1924). Last Portuguese bishop of Macau (1976-88), who gave special care to the formation of local clergy and to the building up of a solid local church.

Da Costa arrived in Macau in 1938 as a seminarian. After philosophical and theological studies, he was ordained a priest in 1949 and remained in the seminary as prefect, teacher, and rector until 1956. He then went to Rome to continue his studies at Gregorian University, where he received a licentiate in canon law in 1959.

Da Costa returned to Macau in 1960 and was appointed prefect and professor at the seminary and rector in the following year. He was appointed administrator of the diocese during the absence of Bishop P. J. Tavares (1920-73), while the latter took part in the sessions of the Second Vatican Council in 1963 and 1965.

When Macau Major Seminary was closed in 1968, da Costa was sent to teach at Aberdeen Seminary, Hong Kong*, as prefect of the philosophy department. After the death of Tavares, da Costa was elected vicar capitular of the diocese in Jun 1973 and in Jan 1976 was appointed bishop.

As bishop, da Costa's priorities were the personal formation of the clergy, social concern for Macau's people, especially for the refugees, and Catholic involvement in the mass media.

In order to speed up the handover of the diocese to the local clergy, da Costa submitted his resignation, which was accepted in 1988. He retired to his native Azores, where he worked as a parish priest.

Sergio Ticozzi

Dalit Movements

The expression "Dalit Movement(s)" itself is an indication that the people known as Dalit are on the move, rejecting the existing societal order in search of a new one. Dalits in the past have been referred to by many contemptuous names by the so-called upper castes: *dasa* (slave), *avarna* (without caste), *panchama* (fifth caste), *achuta* (untouchable), *harijan* (children of God, but without known human father), depressed classes, scheduled castes, and so on. But today the victims have decided to address themselves as Dalit ("oppressed"), which for them is not just a new name meaning poor or low caste, but a pointer to their awakened state of life and an expression of hope for recovery of their past self-identity synonymous with liberation.

In India*, almost every fourth person is an identified Dalit who confesses either Hindu, Muslim, Christian, Buddhist, or Sikh faith. The total number of Dalits presently is around 225 million. Among the Indian Christians, more than 75% are Dalits. The total number of Christians is about 25 million, of which approximately 19 million are Dalits.

Historically, the roots of the Dalit Protest (or Movement) date back to the period of the Rigveda, for the testimonies found in the text of the Rigveda reveal that the Dalits did protest and fight against their oppressors but were defeated and subdued. To worsen the condition of the Dalits, the so-called upper castes, particularly the priestly Brahmin class, in the course of time formulated a number of religious practices and myths in order to support their stand. These included the famous *Purusasukta* hymn of the Rigveda, according to which the Indian fourfold caste system known as *chaturvrnyam* had divine origination (Book X, Hymn XC, verse 12).

During the early period of the Dalit problem, two nonpriestly caste princes, Mahavira (540-468 B.C.) and Gautama Buddha (563-483 B.C.), revolted against the supremacy of the Brahmins and attacked the caste system. After that, during the Muslim rule, the Bhakti ("Devotion") Movements (12th-18th cs.) arose. Through these, a number of Hindu saints made attempts to bring reforms within the Hindu religion. Some Bhakti saints such as Kabir, Nanak, Ramanand, and Ravidas also fought against the tyranny of the caste system. But their efforts were mostly limited to improving the Hindu religion from within. They never attempted to lift the socioeconomic status of the Dalits.

During the British period, starting from the middle of the 19th c., various Christian missionary movements began their work, which attracted thousands of Dalits all over India to the Christian faith because of its egalitarian teachings. In a way, the mass conversion of the Dalits to Christianity really shook the closely guarded Indian religious fabric by giving birth to a number of well-planned and organized movements in other faiths. Among the Hindus, Brahmo Samaj* and Arya Samaj* came into existence. Their purpose was, in part, to improve and change the attitude of the caste Hindus towards Hindu Dalits. In the same way, the Ahmadiya Movement arose among the Muslims and movements such as Singh Sabha among the Sikh. But all these movements, like the Bhakti Movement, could do very little in favor of the Dalits.

However, all of these movements, which included the Christian missions and the various religious reform movements, contributed in creating an awakening among the Dalits, especially through education, which was a major factor for change. Even the conflicts in which the major religions were involved on the question of the conversion of the Dalits, helped them to establish their own separate religious identity, which later on helped them in forming a separate political identity also. The British census policy, particularly from 1881 onward, was another factor which helped the Dalits in establishing their separate identity, because in the census every community was given a separate place. Dalits were also helped by getting employment in the army and other service opportunities outside their own villages. All these factors contributed to the emergence of various Dalit movements, which included Aid-Dravida in Tamil Nadu, Adi-Hindu in Uttar Pradesh, Adi-Dharm in Punjab, Mahar in Maharashtra, Namashudras in Bengal, and Ezhavas in Kerala. Similar movements were started in Karnataka and Andhra Pradesh also. The most recent (1970s) was the Dalit Panther Movement, which was started by young Marathi Dalit writers on the model of the Black Panthers in the United States.

A number of personalities played a special role in the Dalit movements. Of note are Mahatma Phule and B. R. Ambedkar*. Mahatma Phule was an early revolutionary reformer who tried to unite all the Dalits and other members of the various low-caste communities. Ambedkar believed that Dalits should revolt because they lived like slaves; and only by becoming aware of their slavery and inferior status could the Dalits unite and fight for change. He was also a firm believer that only the Dalits themselves can understand their own conditions and needs. He believed in a total rejection of the Hindu social and religious order by the Dalits in order to achieve fuller liberation. According to Ambedkar, education and politics were the main means to achieving equality with others.

By the beginning of the 1980s, the Christian Dalits (doubly oppressed, first by society in general, and then within the church) became aware of their rights. In almost all the churches in India, though the majority of the members are of Dalit background, they do not have any leading role to play, particularly in the decision-making process. Christian Dalits are even deprived of their basic fundamental and human rights on the basis of religion. For example, the government of India gives special economic and political rights to the Dalits belonging to the Hindu, Sikh, and Buddhist faiths, but not to Christians. Certain government laws also are provided for the protection of Dalits belonging to other faiths, but again these do not apply to Christians. To face and fight against these injustices, during the 1980s a number of Christian organizations came into existence, including the Christian Dalit Liberation Movement, Vellore, and the All India Christian People's Forum, Delhi.

One of the most recent efforts of the Dalits is the formation of the interfaith Dalit Solidarity Programme (DSP), which historically owes its existence to the efforts and work of a number of organizations, both church and non-church, but basically it is a result of the awakening of the Dalits themselves. It is also true that a number of international and national partners such as the World Council of Churches and the National Christian Council of India have contributed and are contributing in a major way to the materializing of the program of the DSP.

DSP was born during a national convention held in Nagpur (central India, 28-31 Dec 1992), in which about 150 participants representing Dalits belonging to different faiths (Christian, Buddhist, Hindu, Muslim, and Sikh) took part. These Dalit leaders came together by detaching themselves from their religious and political affiliations to prepare to fight a common fight against suffering and oppression. At the Nagpur convention, a four-point agenda was prepared: first, to strengthen solidarity among all the Dalits; second, to extend its full cooperation to the indigenous communities; third, to liberate the education system, which has been used as an instrument of oppression; and fourth, to internationalize the Dalit issue in order to make the global community aware of it. The DSP program is spreading throughout the country steadily.

Finally, an important point which needs to be remembered is that the Dalit issue has been taken by many as only a social issue which belongs to Hindu society. This was the basis of the non-Dalit reformers (such as Gandhi*) and movements. Therefore, they tried to reform the caste system within the Hindu structure only. On the other hand, the Dalits are concerned about the historical sociocultural oppression in the form of "cumulative domination" to which they have been subjected and which is responsible for their present state. Because of this domination, they are faced with a threefold problem, which includes the state of untouchability (social), powerlessness (political), and poverty* (economic). Therefore, their liberation also has to be threefold, which will give them an equal status as human beings, ensure full citizen's rights, and make them free workers instead of economic slaves. This total liberation is the goal before all the Dalit Movements.

Bibliography

Omvedt, Gail, *Dalits and the Democratic Revolution: Dr. Ambedkar and the Dalit Movement in Colonial India* (1994). • Webster, John C. B., *The Dalit Christians,* rev. ed. (1994). • Shiri, Godwin, *The Plight of Christian Dalits — A South Indian Case Study* (1997). • Massey, James, ed., *Indigenous People: Dalits — Dalit Issues in Today's Theological Debate* (1994). • Robb, Peter, ed., *Dalit Movements and the Meanings of Labour in India* (1993). • Zelliot, Eleanor, *From Untouchables to Dalit: Essays on the Ambedkar Movement* (1992). • Oommen, T. K., *Protest and Change: Studies in Social Movements* (1990).

JAMES MASSEY

Danckaert(s), Sebastiaen

(b. The Hague, 1593; d. Batavia, 2 or 3 Apr 1634). Dutch Reformed minister in Indonesia*.

Danckaerts dedicated his whole life to the Reformed Church in the Dutch East Indies. After a few years of theological education at the University of Leiden (1613-15), he was ordained as a minister by the presbytery of Enkhuizen, one of the presbyteries responsible for the church in the Indies.

At the age of 23, Danckaerts arrived in Indonesia and became a minister in the region of Vanten, West Java, where he started learning Malay. A year later, he was sent to Ambon, where he served the church from 1618 to 1622. Preaching in Malay and Dutch, he drew so many worshippers that a bigger church had to be built in Ambon. His translation of the Heidelberg Catechism into Malay was used by the Reformed Church in the East Indies for many years. He also initiated a training program for indigenous workers in his own house. He wrote a book about the past and the present condition of the church in Ambon. It was printed in Holland (1621) and drew the attention of the Reformed Church in the Netherlands to the church in the East Indies and its need for good order and good ministers. Danckaerts married a Dutch woman in Ambon at the end of his stay there.

In 1622-23, Danckaerts was back in the Netherlands, where he had two books printed, the Malay catechism and a Malay vocabulary. He also drafted a church order for the East Indies based on the church order of the Synod of Dordrecht. The draft was discussed and considered suitable by the provincial synods of North and South Holland.

After Danckaerts returned to Indonesia with a number of new ministers, a meeting was held in Batavia (Jakarta: 1624) between representatives of the church and the government of the Dutch East-Indies Company to discuss a number of church issues, e.g., a church order for the East Indies. With a few changes, Danckaerts's draft was accepted as the order for the church in the East Indies and was then provisionally approved by the governor-general. Its main feature was the replacement of the presbyteries of the Dutch church order with a "church meeting" in Batavia, which in fact gave the church council of Batavia, especially the ministers in it, a determining role in the whole church of the East Indies.

Danckaerts stayed in Batavia as a minister until his death in 1634. Mention is made of some trouble with the authorities of the Dutch East-Indies Company because of illicit trading, and with the church council because of "quarreling." His role as leader of the church was gradually taken over by Justus Heurnius, but he remained highly esteemed. In 1631, the governor-general sent him to Ambon to mediate between two ministers. Together with Adriaan Hulsebos, with whom he had corresponded about the organization of the church, Danckaerts can be considered one of the founders of the Reformed Church in the Netherlands East Indies.

Bibliography

Van Boetzellaer, C. W. Th., "Correspondentie van Ds Adriaan Jacobszoon Hulsebos," *Nederlandsch Archief voor Kerkgeschiedenis,* XXXII (1943). • Müller-Krüger, T., *Der Protestantismus in Indonesien: Geschichte und Gestalt* (1968).

CHRISTIAAN G. F. DE JONGE

Daniel, Kurunthottickal Ninan

(b. Kozhencherry, Kerala, India, 23 Feb 1878; d. Tiruvalla, India, 5 Jul 1965). Indian church historian, liturgist, zealous evangelist, and reformer in the Syrian Church of Malabar.

Daniel was one of the most brilliant teachers and writers of the Protestant churches of Malabar (Kerala). Raised in a spiritual atmosphere of revival movements in the State of Travancore of British India, Daniel developed an interest in church affairs from his boyhood. The metropolitan of the Mar Thoma Church, Titus I Mar Thoma, made Daniel the editor of the official publication of the church, the *Malankara Sabha Tharaka* (Star of the Malankara Church), when he was 29. During his editorship (1907-20), the monthly *Tharaka* grew to its highest fame and subscriptions increased threefold. The magazine became an effective means of communicating relevant contemporary theological and social issues.

Daniel's greatest contribution was in the field of liturgy. He conducted diligent and laborious research into primitive liturgies. His book *A Critical Study of Primitive Liturgies — Especially That of St. James* was the result of scholarly and careful investigation of the liturgical forms of the Indian Syrian Church of Malabar. As a result of his liturgical investigation, he pointed out that those passages in the liturgy of St. James which imply doctrines unacceptable to Christians who glory in the name "evangelical" — such as prayers for the dead, prayers to the Virgin Mary and the saints, and some prayers which attributed a mediatorial function to the priesthood or expressed a magical view of the sacraments — have no liturgical support. Any such doctrines found in the ancient liturgies are later accretions.

As a church historian and liturgist, Daniel became an able exponent of the movement led by Abraham Malpan, often called the Reform of A.D. 1836. Malpan revised the Syriac liturgy, omitting all prayers and passages which did not stand the scrutiny of sound biblical doctrines. He extirpated the heretical tenets prevalent in the church, which was then Jacobite*, and restored the church to its purity.

In later years, when there was a countermove in the Reformed Mar Thoma Church to annul the reforms and bring back Jacobite doctrines and practices, Daniel began a relentless and uncompromising battle against the conservatism. He brought forth book after book to elaborate and to substantiate the beliefs of the Reformed Mar Thoma Church. He did a great service in preserving the evangelical zeal of personal faith in Jesus Christ emphasized in the Reformation.

Daniel stands out as a great champion of evangelical reformation in the 20th-c. Malabar Church over against heretical doctrines and practices. He was an honorary worker in the Mar Thoma Church for 60 years and a bachelor who devoted all his service to the Master.

Bibliography

Daniel, K. N., *A Critical Study of Primitive Liturgies* (1949). • Metropolitan Alexander Mar Thoma, *The Mar Thoma Church* (1986). • Thomas, M. M., *Towards an Evangelical Social Gospel* (1977). THOMAS ABRAHAM

Darmajuwono, Justinus

(b. Godean, Central Java, 1914). First Indonesian raised to the cardinalate (1974).

Darmajuwono entered the *Normaalschool* which had been founded in Muntilan by Franz van Lith*. Baptized in Muntilan, he entered the minor and higher seminaries (1941) and was ordained a secular priest in 1947. After working in a parish and teaching in the minor seminary, he studied missiology at the Gregorian University, Rome, in 1954. He was ordained a bishop in 1964, succeeding Msgr. Soegijapranata, the first Indonesian Catholic bishop (1942-63). After the Second Vatican Council, he became chairman of the Indonesian Bishops' Conference (1965-79). He retired as archbishop of Semarang (1981) to work as a pastor in Banyumanik (Semarang).

Darmajuwono defended the families of former Communists killed or detained after the 1965 coup and pushed for social action among farmers and migrants.

ADOLF HEUKEN

D'Armandville, Le Cocq C. F. C.

(b. Netherlands, 1846; d. Irian Jaya, 1896). Dutch Jesuit* missionary who worked as a pioneer in different areas of the Indonesian archipelago.

Stationed in Maumere and Sika (Flores*), D'Armandville frequently visited the people of the mountains. He was seriously wounded by a gunshot when it was thought that his drilling of artesian wells had stopped the rainfall in the area. When he was transferred to the Moluccas* after nine years, the people of Sika, of whom he had baptized 11,000, forcibly detained him. He worked hard to reform the church of many of the old Portuguese customs which had become mixed with animistic beliefs through the centuries.

In the Moluccas, D'Armandville tried in vain to establish a mission on the remote islands of Seram (1888) and Watubela (1893-95). Thereafter, he set out for the shores of New Guinea (Irian Jaya) and succeeded in converting a few young people in Teluk Berau. Ill health forced him to return to Java, but before doing so he tried to reach New Guinea's south coast with the help of a hired Arab sailor. According to one report, D'Armandville drowned just before boarding the ship while trying to save a native boy from rolling waves. Other reports suggested robbery and murder. Though D'Armandville did not succeed in opening a new mission field among unknown peoples, his death drew attention to the Moluccas (Kei Archipelago) and Irian Jaya, which resulted in mission work a decade later.

Bibliography

"400 Jaaren Missie in Nederlandsch Indie," *Social Leven* Nos. 2-3 (1934). • Steenbrink, Karel, *Catholics in Indonesia, 1808-1942; A Documented History,* Vol. I, *A Modest Recovery, 1808-1903* (forthcoming). ADOLF HEUKEN

Daughters of Charity of St. Vincent de Paul

The Daughters of Charity of St. Vincent de Paul began in France in 1633, when St. Vincent and St. Louise de Marillac brought together three or four country girls to care for and visit the sick and poor in their homes — a novel practice, as all orders of sisters at that time were cloistered. The order spread rapidly, and by 1645, there were about 100 sisters working in the cities and villages of France. In the mid-19th c., a phenomenal growth enabled the community to reach out to foreign countries.

China. The Daughters of Charity from Paris, led by Sr. Durand, arrived in China* in cooperation with the Lazarists*. After losing one sister to typhoid fever on the voyage, the surviving Daughters of Charity first reached Macau in 1848 but did not begin any institutionalized work until 1851, when the vicar apostolic of Zhejiang assigned them to an orphanage in Ningbo. The work actually began in China in 1852. Reinforcements came with the arrival of four more sisters in 1855, and then 14 sisters arrived with the Lazarist bishop of Beijing in 1862. The community gradually spread to Shanghai (1863), Beijing, and Tianjin. The sisters were also active in many smaller towns in Zhejiang, Hebei, and Jiangxi, where they had clinics, orphanages, homes for the aged, and other social services. Ten Daughters of Charity were martyred in Tianjin in 1870.

As the first Catholic sisters in China, the Daughters of Charity attracted many native recruits. By 1950, there were 26 foundations and 287 sisters, mostly Chinese. The most notable Catholic sisters were Sr. de Jaurias, who withstood the Boxer siege of Beitang (Northern Cathedral), along with 500 children and 2,500 adults, from 15 Jun to 19 Aug 1900; and Xavier Berkeley, who worked for 54 years in China, mostly on Zhousan Island, east of Ningbo.

The Daughters of Charity were distinguished by their large white headdress (cornette) and the service they rendered in their hospitals, schools, and orphanages. Vocations were plentiful, but their provincial house in Shanghai and all other institutional buildings were confiscated by the government after the Communist takeover. The foreign sisters either left or were expelled. The Chinese sisters were either dispersed to their own families or hired as lay personnel in the very institutions they had owned.

The surviving sisters, estimated to number about 708, have not been able to regroup and are scattered in various cities and towns. Many may be in government-run homes for the aged.

Philippines. The Daughters of Charity began in the Philippines* with the arrival of a group from Spain in 1862 to work in a military hospital for Spanish soldiers stationed there. The order grew quickly in the Philippines, a predominantly Catholic country. At present, there are about 540 sisters, 90% being Filipinas. They have over 50 foundations, concentrating mainly on health, education, social services for the poor, and pastoral care. Each year, between 10 and 20 candidates enter the community in the Philippines.

Vietnam. Sisters from France reached Ho Chi Minh City (Saigon) in 1928. The Vietnamese mission grew rapidly until the civil war between the North and South in the 1960s and 1970s. When the Communists finally took over the South, the sisters lost their establishments and were sent into the countryside as lay workers in the fields. The sisters have been able to regroup gradually, and, though still under much government control, allowed to accept candidates and resume some of their social, educational, and health services to the poor. At present, there are about 330 sisters in 36 foundations. New recruits are numerous. Among the newer services are the care of street children and job training for poor girls.

Indonesia. The Daughers of Charity from the Netherlands began their work by caring for orphans in Surabaya and Malang in 1931. At present, there are about 75 sisters, most of whom are Indonesian, in 11 establishments, all in Java. Their work includes schools, clinics, orphanages, homes for the aged, rehabilitation centers, pastoral work, and special services for scavengers, factory workers, and rickshaw drivers.

Japan. French sisters arrived in Japan* in 1933 and opened a clinic and a nursery. They stopped in China en route as the infant Japanese mission was considered a foundation of the China province. Growth of the community in Japan depended for some time on foreign missionaries, notably from the United States, but in 1954, Japan became an independent province with a majority of natives. At present, there are over 90 sisters, most of whom are Japanese. The sisters operate a crèche, centers for the handicapped, kindergartens, nurseries, and an orphanage. They serve immigrants and day laborers, do home visiting, and visit patients in homes for the aged and hospitals.

India. The mission in India* was started in 1940 by Spanish sisters who opened a nursery for orphans. Many young women from the southern part of India requested to join the order. The work in India has expanded to include primary and secondary schools, boarding homes for girls and for children of the victims of Hansen's disease, homes for the destitute and for the aged, vocational training centers, centers to treat Hansen's disease, rural hospitals, dispensaries, and homes for the physically and mentally handicapped. At present, there are 33 foundations with about 230 sisters.

Taiwan. The work in Taiwan* was begun in 1959 by four Filipino sisters who ran a kindergarten in Taipei. Sisters from the United States arrived three years later to do clinical and parish work in the south. The two groups were united administratively in 1980 when the Daughters of Charity in Taiwan were set up as a region. There are over 40 sisters comprising an approximately equal number of Filipinas, American, and Chinese in six locations. Their works include a hospital, homes for the aged, and a kindergarten, besides social services and pastoral work in parishes, a prison, and aboriginal villages. They visit the poor and care for the sick in their homes.

Thailand. Four Daughters of Charity (two Americans and two Filipinos) arrived in 1969 to care for the victims of Hansen's disease in response to the request of the Redemptorist fathers. When the American sisters withdrew, the province of the Philippines increased its number of missionary sisters. Meanwhile, native sisters were being accepted into the community. Their work now includes care for the elderly, rehabilitation of disabled children, feeding programs in remote villages, and educational assistance programs for the children of Hansen's patients. There are fewer than 40 sisters in Thailand.

Korea. Two sisters from Japan, who came as volunteers to nurse Hansen's patients, opened the mission in Korea* in 1978. Native recruits soon followed, and by 1995 there were 13 sisters, seven of them Korean. In Jun 1995, the mission in Korea was transferred to the province of the Philippines. In addition to a clinic for Hansen's disease, the sisters in Korea also care for the sick in their homes and do pastoral work, chiefly in catechetics, because of the numerous conversions.

At present, there are approximately 1,350 Daughters of Charity in Asia (not counting those in mainland China). They are most numerous in Vietnam, India, and the Philippines, and relatively scarce in Thailand, Japan, and Taiwan. While there are still some foreign sisters, the growth of the order in Asia largely depends on locals.

The Daughters of Charity are committed to serving the poorest and most marginalized and are increasingly turning over large institutions to lay management in favor of works in more remote areas where the presence of the Catholic Church is minimal.

Bibliography

Baudelet, J. M., ed., *Echoes of the Company* (1994). • M. L. H., *Sister Xavier Berkeley* (1949). • Mazeau, Henry, *The Heroine of Pe-Tang* (1928).

KATHLEEN GRIMLEY, with contributions from THE CHINA GROUP

Daughters of St. Paul

(FSP). Women's religious missionary order dedicated to evangelization using communications media.

Founded by Catholic priest James Alberione in Alba, Italy, on 15 Jun 1915, with co-foundress Teresa Merlo, the Daughters of St. Paul is the female counterpart to the Society of St. Paul (SSP), which was founded in 1914.

The first FSPs in Asia, Srs. Edvige Soldano, Elena Ramondetti, and Cleofe Zanoni, were sent to China* because it had the largest non-Catholic population. They arrived on 11 Feb 1937 but moved temporarily to India* in September because of the Sino-Japanese War. After a futile wait for the archbishop's residence permit, Merlo redirected them to the Philippines* upon the request of SSP-Philippines.

India. Three sisters arrived in Bombay on 18 Aug 1950 upon the request of the SSP superior in India. The book (literature*) missions did not seem to meet the basic needs of the people, but the conditions appeared more favorable after the sisters moved into their new house in Bandra (1958).

Japan. Advised by SSP pioneers in Japan*, Merlo sent four sisters via the United States and Philippines. Arriving on 6 Aug 1948, they started a book mission in Tokyo, disseminating FSP-USA publications among American soldiers, who became the benefactors of the rapidly increasing local members.

Korea. Four sisters, sent by Rome in response to an invitation by a Korean priest, arrived on 13 Dec 1960 and began a small bookstore at their home and book displays at church doors. In 1966, there were two flourishing bookstores at the center in Seoul. Applicants were also increasing rapidly.

Malaysia. Upon the invitation of the apostolic vicar of Kota Kinabalu to FSP-Philippines, four sisters from Manila arrived on 6 Feb 1961. As a result of an invitation from the bishop of Kuala Lumpur, another four sisters arrived on 19 Mar 1965. They left in 1971 when foreign missionaries were expelled, but they returned in 1989.

Pakistan. Invited by Karachi's archbishop, Rome sent four sisters, who arrived on 15 Aug 1965. They helped print a Catholic weekly while studying Urdu and opened houses in Karachi and Lahore.

Philippines. The sisters arrived in Manila on 13 Mar 1938, residing in Lipa and managing the SSP household while studying the local languages. As more sisters arrived, they began a home-to-home book mission with the publications of SSP. When World War II* broke out on 8 Dec 1941, they were evacuated until 1945. The order increased after the war, developed their own publications, and in 1950, upon the directive of Rome, sent out missionaries to other Asian and Australian foundations.

Taiwan. Upon the invitation of China's internuncio, the FSP-Philippines sent four sisters from Manila to Taiwan* on 5 May 1959. They opened a house in Kaoshiung and Taipei and expanded to Macau (1969) and Hong Kong* (1978). Because of diverse needs from the Philippines, they became a delegation under Rome.

Until 1995, Pakistan and Taiwan still remained delegations because of the small number of local members. Macau came under Rome in 1990. The Philippines, Japan, India, and Korea have become provinces or territories with at least four houses, 50 full-fledged members, and the ability to maintain and expand themselves. The Philippine province includes Malaysia*, Papua New Guinea (1989), and Thailand* (1994). Singapore* (1994) is under Rome. The FSP now includes electronic media in its ministry.

Bibliography

Daughters of St. Paul, *Il Nostro Atlante I* (1968). • Zanoni, Cleofe, *Faithwatch* (1988).

MONINA BAYBAY

Daughters of the Cross

In line with the objective to develop indigenous Catholic leaders for Asia, one important early act of Bishop Pierre Marie Lambert de la Motte* (1624-79) of the Paris Foreign Mission Society* (MEP), vicar apostolic of Cochin China, was to establish a community of female religious, whom he called *Amantes de la Croix* (Lovers of the Cross), or "Daughters of the Cross," as they were later more often called. The first convent was established by Lambert in 1671 in the home of a pious Christian Annamese widow named Lucia Ky in Quang-ngai Province. Others were later established in other MEP missions, even in Siam (Thailand*), Burma*, and China*.

The Daughters of the Cross were charged with teaching the catechism to young girls, evangelizing women and attending to their maladies, and baptizing infants (including those of non-Christian parents) in danger of death. In Vietnam, they served as a potent auxiliary force in mission work.

An 18th-c. MEP missionary in Tonkin, Joseph Pavec, noted that many young girls forced by their parents to participate in "superstitious" ceremonies or to marry non-Christian youths (or those they did not love) joined the Daughters of the Cross and "consecrated themselves to God to avoid these dangers." By about 1750, they numbered about 500, of whom some 70 to 85 percent were in Vietnam. One hundred years later, the figure for Tonkin alone had risen to 673.

The Daughters of the Cross contributed more than their full share to the roll of Vietnamese martyrs. In the persecution of 1857-62, about 100 of them perished, while 80 of their convents were destroyed and all 2,000 residents therein dispersed. In the final outburst of persecution in 1885, another 270 were martyred along with some 24,000 other Christians in the vicariate of East Cochin China (Qui-nhon) alone. Vietnamese Catholic statistics in 1898 reported 772 Daughters of the Cross for that year.

Bibliography

Launay, A. C., *Histoire Générale de la Société des Mission-Étrangères,* Vols. I and II (1894); *Memorial de la Société des Mission-Étrangères,* Vol. II (1916). • Piolet, J. B., *Les Missions Catholiques Françaises au XIXe Siècle,* Vol. II (1903). • de Frondeville, H., "Pierre Lambert de la Motte, Évêque de Beryte (1624-1679)," *Revue d'Histoire des Missions,* Vol. I (1924). T. VALENTINO SITOY, JR.

Daughters of the Cross of Liège

The Congregation of the Daughters of the Cross was founded on 8 Sep 1833 in Liège, Belgium, recognized in 1840, and granted approbation by Rome in 1850. The foundress was Jeanne Haze, fifth daughter of Louis Haze, secretary to Prince Bishop of Liège, and Marguerite Tombeur. In religious life, she took the name of Marie Thérèse Haze. She was beatified on 21 Apr 1991. The cofounder of the congregation was Cannon Habets.

The title of the order is significant, because it sums up all that Haze understood of the dual ideal of sacrifice and service, which is at the very heart of Christianity. This is more apparent in the French version, *Filles de la Croix,* for *fille* means servant as well as daughter. In choosing the cross as the emblem, Haze also focused on resurrection, symbolized by the crown on the cross — the Paschal Mystery. The cross with the crown sums up the spirituality of the Daughters of the Cross, who choose humility as the virtue proper to their congregation. By the vows of poverty*, chastity, and obedience, the Daughters of the Cross place themselves at the service of the church as women of prayer in complete loyalty.

When Mother Marie Thérèse took the responsibility of establishing the new congregation, turmoil still rocked Europe in post-revolutionary years. Religion was an altogether unpopular subject with governments of the day, and convents and monasteries made no sense to a society suffering from the devastating ravages of war. Penal laws were passed banning Catholic education and virtually outlawing the religious orders. Belgium was forcibly joined to Holland, whose government at this time was rabidly anti-Catholic. No situation is lasting, and soon the first signs of tolerance were noticed. The people began to flock into the churches.

One of the main needs was education, especially of the poor. Since Mother Marie Thérèse's great desire was to rescue the desperately uneducated and de-Christianized children of the city, education of the poor was her first priority. It was not only the children who needed to be rescued, but the women's prison in Liège was an abyss of despair and corruption as well. Abandoned by society and living in appalling conditions, the women prisoners were in a deplorable state. Mother Marie Thérèse responded to an appeal for help and gave the sisters appointed to this ministry every encouragement. Ignoring the filth, violence, and cursing, they brought order into chaos. When cleanliness and good food transformed the kitchens gradually, serenity superseded turmoil. To avoid the recurrence of crime, Mother Marie Thérèse undertook the work of rehabilitation by providing a refuge and striving to find employment for the recently released. Always ahead of her time, she responded to need, and, trusting in God, she undertook daunting tasks with unquenchable confidence.

Soon the Belgian frontiers were crossed in order to proclaim the love of Jesus to all people by serving him in the weakest and most suffering members of society; the sisters excluded no work of mercy in Germany, undivided India*, England, Italy, Brazil, and California.

The sisters came to India at the invitation of Archbishop Steins, the vicar apostolate of Bombay. The five pioneers on arrival at Bombay were told they were destined for Karachi (Pakistan*). They were asked to help in the girls' section of St. Patrick's School, an English-language school. Many of the pupils were daughters of the soldiers of the Irish regiment stationed at Karachi Cantonment. The sisters wondered whether they were in the right place, since their target population here was not the poor. However, they were soon at peace when they opened a school for the poor and utterly ignorant children from Sindh. Today, the school has 2,000 pupils all seeking education in an English medium.

On the same premises, the Daughters of the Cross of Liège have also run the Marie Thérèse Institute of Arts and Crafts since 1985. The institute prepares women for employment and helps empower the less fortunate and poor women. Education remains the main apostolate of the sisters both in schools run by the congregation and those of the diocese. Instruction is conducted in Urdu or English.

The congregation has moved into interior Sindh (Nawabshah and Badin) and into the Punjab (Mian Channu, Sialkot, and Lahore). In Badin, its focus is on tribals, especially Parkri Kholis. In Pakistan, it has nine communities and 58 sisters in the provinces of Sindh and the Punjab. There are nine novices and one postulant. The main apostolates are educational (formal and nonformal, urban and rural), medical* (diocesan hospitals), pastoral (cathechesis), tribal (preevangelization, evangelization), and developmental (boarding houses, orphanages). The provincial house is in Karachi.

In 1863, the Daughters of the Cross of Liège moved to Bombay and in 1867 to Calcutta. The Bombay Province has 19 communities, four subcommunities, and 220 sisters in three states: Maharastra, Gujrat, and Karnataka. The Calcutta Province has 17 communities, two subcommunities, and 200 sisters in two states: West Bengal and Orissa. They are engaged in identical apostolates with a focus on education and development. They are also engaged in mother-and-child programs. The two provinces have a common novitiate at Bandra Bombay with more than 28 novices. The provincial house for Bombay is in Bandra and for Calcutta in Kidderpore. Almost 500 sisters serve in the three provinces of Pakistan, Bombay, and Calcutta.

Bibliography

Martindale, C. C., *Daughters of the Cross,* ed. Thomas Corbishly. • O'Neil, L. W., *Theodorine Witness to Love.* • See also articles by Mary Emily, F. C., in *Christian Voice* (Feb 1991 to May 1991).

ZINIA PINTO

Day Offering

(Collection of Days). The day offering was a common practice in the early years of the Korean Protestant church when people had more time than material wealth at their disposal. At the end of each Bible study class, participants were requested to offer their time, measured in days, for evangelistic work. The donor would then devote the dedicated number of days to spread the Gospel among unbelievers.

The innovative day offering proved to be an effective strategy for evangelism. During the Great Revival of 1907 (or the Korean Pentecost; see Korean Revival Movement) and the Million Souls* for Christ Movement (1909-10), a total of 100,000 days were offered for evangelism. For example, in a Bible study at Pusan, 35 participants offered a total of 900 days; at another in Sonch'on, 2,200 days were offered; and in Pyongyang, 1,000 people offered a total of 22,000 days for evangelism.

KIM SEUNG TAE

Dayao, Benigno

(b. ?; d. 1914). Second Filipino Presbyterian* evangelist in the Philippines* responsible for much of the early work done in the Tagalog regions in the southern Luzon provinces.

Dayao is first mentioned in Protestant missionary records as one of those present at the first Presbyterian service in Manila held on 7 May 1899. Dayao and his daughter, along with the family of Paulino Zamora*, were baptized by James B. Rodgers on 22 Oct 1899. Late in 1900, Dayao became an evangelist, serving until his death in 1914.

Dayao was one of the earliest assistants of the Presbyterian missionaries. In Nov 1900 he accompanied Rodgers to Malolos, Bulacan. The following years he served as an evangelist for Leonard P. Davidson (1866-1901) in the southern Luzon provinces of Rizal, Bulacan, Pampanga, and Bataan and was responsible for many of the early Presbyterian gains in the Tagalog regions.

Bibliography

Rodgers, J. B., *Forty Years in the Philippines* (1940). • Sitoy, T. V., Jr., *Several Springs, One Stream* (1992).

T. VALENTINO SITOY, JR.

Daybreak Prayer Meeting

Uniquely Korean practice of early morning prayer meetings seven days a week in almost all Korean Protestant churches.

The practice of early morning prayer was first introduced by Kil Sun Joo as part of the 1907 Great Revival. Early morning prayer services had been an indigenous religious practice before the coming of Christianity to Korea*. Mostly women would either climb a nearby hillside or go into the courtyard of the house before dawn and offer clear water to the spirits of the mountain, or other spirits, praying for family blessings, protection of family members, and the success of the family business. This ardent religious practice was transferred to the Korean churches. Today, church pastors are responsible for early morning prayer meeting programs, which may entail a series of Bible studies and/or spiritual guidance of prayers.

DAVID SUH, with contributions from SEO JEONG MIN; original translated by KIM IN SOO

D'Azevedo, P. Sylvester

(b. Portugal, ca. mid-16th c.; d. Cambodia, ca. 1596). Portuguese Dominican* and pioneer of the evangelization of Cambodia*.

The Portuguese merchants established at the royal court of Longvek had suggested to the Cambodian king Ang Chan I (1529-55) that priests be sent to the already authorized religious leaders in Malacca*. It was a veiled way to ask for military aide for Portugal, a new colonial power. Thus in 1555, the Dominican* Gaspar da Cruz arrived at the court of Longvek. He was the first Catholic priest to set foot on Cambodian soil, where he stayed only one year. Around 1573, at the request of King Satha I (1567-74), a successor of Ang Chan I, two other Portuguese Dominicans were sent: Father Lopo Cardosa and Father Joao Madeira. The Brahmins and Buddhist monks opposed the action of the two missionaries, even if the latter did enjoy the royal favor.

P. Sylvester d'Azevedo arrived in Cambodia around 1574. He stayed there some 20 years. As a result of an incident involving slaves entrusted to his superior by the king, he was imprisoned, but still his mission advanced as he converted 500 Japanese, Javanese, and Chinese prisoners while he was in prison.

Liberated, the priest gained the confidence of the king, who made him his counselor and gave him the title of "Father of the King." The religious authorities of

Malacca suspected d'Azevedo of having left the order to become a Cambodian prince and threatened him with excommunication. Nevertheless, his new rank allowed him to build the first Christian church with funds from the royal treasury. His style of life attracted the Buddhist monks, one of whom converted to Christianity and was almost put to death as a result. With two (or four) other Portuguese Dominicans who arrived after him, d'Azevedo composed the first handbook of the Christian religion in the Khmer language. In spite of the intrigues of the petty king of Johore, who succeeded in having him incarcerated once more, he obtained authorization to preach the Christian faith again as well as to publish an edict affording religious freedom to the Khmers. Taken as a prisoner to Ayuthaya (Siam) after the capture of Longvek by Siamese soldiers (1594), he was freed in 1596 and returned to Cambodia, where he died.

D'Azevedo can be considered the first apostle of Cambodia, even if his apostolate was made difficult because it was linked to the Spanish and Portuguese colonial presence.

Bibliography

Groslier, B. P., *Angkor and Cambodia in the 16th Century According to Portuguese and Spanish Sources* (1958).

François Ponchaud

De Abreu, P. Aegidius

(b. 1593; d. 1624). Portuguese missionary destined for Japan but imprisoned by the *Verenigde Oost-Indische Compagnie* (United East-India Company, VOC) in Batavia (Jakarta) when his ship was caught by pirates off Singapore in 1622.

De Abreu was tortured and condemned to heavy labor because he converted other prisoners and left the prison to celebrate mass in three secret chapels in the suburbs of Batavia. His candidature for beatification was raised by the bishop of Malacca. Although witnesses were interrogated and a report sent to Rome (1629), the case dragged on until it was forgotten.

Bibliography

Wessels, C., "P. Aegidius De Abreu SJ, Een geloofsgetuige te Batavia, 1624," *Studien, Tijdschrift voor Godsdienst, Wetenschap en Letteren* (Dec 1933).

Adolf Heuken

De Azevedo e Castro, João Paulino

(b. Lages do Pico, Azores, Portugal, 4 Feb 1852; d. Macau, 17 Feb 1918). Bishop of Macau (1902-18) who guided the church through the fall of the Chinese Empire and World War I.

After his theological formation at the University of Coimbra, de Azevedo e Castro was ordained a priest in 1879 and lectured at the seminary of Angra, becoming its rector in 1888. Consecrated as bishop of Macau in 1902, he arrived in June 1903 with a seminarian, Jóse da Costa Nunes (1880-1976), who later succeeded him as bishop.

Soon after his arrival in Macau, de Azevedo e Castro founded the official diocesan bulletin, *Boletim do Governo Ecclesiastico da Diocese de Macau.* In 1904, he began a pastoral visit of the diocese, first to the Singapore* Mission (laying the foundation stone of St. Joseph's Church on 1 Aug) and then to the Timor* Mission in 1905.

De Azevedo e Castro welcomed the Franciscan Missionary Sisters of Mary* (1903) and the Salesian* Fathers (1906) to work in the diocese. In 1908, he traded Hainan Island with the ecclesiastical authorities of Guangzhou for Zhaoqing and entrusted the northern part of Zhaoqing to the care of the Jesuits* in 1913. In 1917, he published the book *Os Bens das Missoes Portuguesas in China.*

Originally buried in the Church of Our Lady da Penha, de Azevedo e Castro's remains were later transferred to his homeland in the Azores.

Bibliography

Texeira, M., *Macau e sua Diocese,* Vol. II (1940).

Sergio Ticozzi

De Behaine, Pierre Joseph George Pigneau

(b. Aisne, France, 11 Mar 1741; d. Qui Nhon, Cochin China, 9 Oct 1799). Paris Foreign Mission Society* (MEP) missionary to Vietnam and bishop of Adran.

De Behaine was the son of a superintendent of the domain of Origny in the county of La Valliere. He signed his name as Pigneaux-Behaine, after the village territory possessed by his family. The eldest son of a 19-member family, de Behaine entered the MEP seminary in 1765. After his ordination as a priest, he was sent to the East, arriving in Cochin China on 9 Sep 1767. He taught in the seminary at Hon Dat, Ha Tien district, and became its director. He was jailed for two months for allegedly sheltering the Siamese (Thais) who were fighting against Mac Thien T'u, the governor of Ha Tien. He went to Malacca* (in peninsular Malaysia) and Pondicherry (in India), where he reopened the MEP seminary in 1770, the year he was appointed bishop of Adran and assistant to Bishop Piguel. He left the seminary of Virampatnam for Cochin China in 1774 and reached Can Cao, Ha Tien, on 12 Mar 1775.

De Behaine wrote a catechism and an Annamitico-Latin dictionary while in Pondicherry. He started a Christian community in Cochin China that grew to 3,000-4,000. In 1777, he rescued Prince Nguyen Anh from Tay Son's pursuing soldiers. Their friendship further developed when de Behaine moved to the seminary at Tan Trieu. De Behaine helped negotiate the Treaty of Versailles (21 Nov 1787) between Louis XVI of France and Nguyen Anh for French military aid when the latter was a refugee in Siam (Thailand*) in exchange for territorial, commercial, and missionary rights. When the

French defaulted on their promise, de Behaine raised funds and recruited troops himself. When Nguyen Anh subdued Tay Son to become Emperor Gia Long* in 1801, his son Prince Canh became the first Vietnamese prince to be educated by French Catholics at the missionary school in Malacca and was converted to Catholicism.

De Behaine's aim was to convert Nguyen Anh himself to facilitate evangelization. His political involvement, however, created controversy among Vietnamese and foreigners about the pure mission of the Gospel.

Anthony Do Huu Nghiem

De Britto, João

(b. Portugal, 1647; d. Oriyur, Tamilinadu, India, 4 Feb 1693). Jesuit* martyr who served in India*.

The third son of a viceroy sent to Brazil to represent the Portuguese government, de Britto was actually raised in the royal court in Portugal. When he was very young, he became a court page and developed a close friendship with Prince Peter (King Peter II). This friendship would last into adulthood, when the newly crowned king tried to convince de Britto to stay and serve the royal court. Because of these royal connections, we have more material on de Britto than on any other 17th-c. missionary except for Roberto de Nobili*.

De Britto had come to know the lifestyle and work of the Jesuits* and early on hoped, like many Europeans in the 17th-19th cs., to serve in China*. After being accepted by the Jesuits (at age 16) and serving his novitiate, he was redirected in his goal for ministry by the letters of Balthasar da Costa in India. Da Costa made strong appeals for help in the growing and difficult work in the Mathurai mission. In 1673, while da Costa was back in Lisbon reporting on the work in India, de Britto, newly ordained, signed on and made his first trip to India. De Britto barely survived the voyage; da Costa did not.

In India, de Britto completed his theological studies at the Jesuit school in Goa and then in Ambalakat (Ambalakkadu) in Kerala. After his theological training was complete, he traveled with the more experienced Antony Freyre to the region of the Mathurai mission. De Britto adapted quickly to the work of the mission and the culture of the people. He identified with the lowest castes, accepting the role of a *pandaraswamy (pandaraswami),* fully aware of their oppression at the hands of the Brahman rulers. He chose to live in the village of Tattuvancheri, near the Coleroon River. This location offered ". . . a little safety from the troubles of the war, and full freedom to deal with the Paraiyas, the care of whom is so difficult under the eyes of the Brahmans in the big cities." This concern for Brahman oppression and violence was well founded. The location near a river brought de Britto into even closer identification with the poor when the river flooded 17 Dec 1676 and the village was destroyed, the small group of Christians all having survived.

De Britto's missionary work was marked by great risks, undying devotion to the poor, and multitudes of conversions. Some of the details are difficult to verify, but even conservative estimates of his ministry show that his work was very effective. Local rulers were quite aware of his impact. In the midst of political discussions regarding the nationalism of the *padroado**, de Britto was wholeheartedly an advocate of Indian concerns. In 1682 he was appointed superior of the mission, and in 1683 he was nearly martyred. July of 1686 brought the greatest crisis yet in his ministry when de Britto, along with three other Indian Christians and two young catechists, were all arrested. The local Brahmans had no idea that there was a missionary working in the Marava province, and so they planned to put an end to this activity. The prisoners were all beaten, but it seems that the king of Marava, moved by the strength and fortitude of the prisoners, warned them not to preach this doctrine again in his region and then set them free.

From 1687 to 1689, nearly three years, de Britto was back in Portugal representing the mission and pleading for more workers. He proved to be a very effective communicator, and the king again appealed for his services in Lisbon. But de Britto's calling was to the poor of Marava, and so he returned for one last time. This time he moved into a residence on the border of the Marava Province but was still concerned to focus his varied ministry in Marava. Once again many baptisms were registered, mostly among the lower caste, but some Brahman conversions were recorded. One such man was Tadiya Thevar, a relative of Raghunatha Thevar (Kilavan: "the old man"), ruler of Marava. The king tried to have de Britto killed by sorcery and finally had him arrested by a local ruler. On 4 Feb 1693, his head and hands were cut off. Stephen Neill identifies this as one of the few isolated cases of missionaries in India being killed through a (semi-)official process rather than by angry mobs. De Britto was beatified in 1852 (delayed because of the suppression of the Jesuits) and canonized by Pius XII in 1947.

Bibliography

Neill, Stephen, *A History of Christianity in India* (1984-85). • De Britto, F. Pereira, *Historia do nascimento vida e martyrio do Beato J. de Britto da Companhia de Jesus, Martyr da Asia, e Protomartyr da Missiao do Madure* (1772/1852; Eng. trans. Antonia Maria Teixeira, 1932). • Prat, J. M., *Histoire du bienheureux J. de Britto, composée sur des documents authentiques* (1853). • Nevett, A. M., *John de Britto and His Times* (1980). • Sauliere, A., *Red Sand: A Life of St. John de Britto* (1947).

Scott W. Sunquist

De Casal, João

(b. Alentejo, Portugal, ca. 1641; d. Macau, 20 Sept 1735). Bishop of Macau who organized the Macau Church on a solid basis.

Having received a doctorate in theology from the

University of Evora, Portugal, de Casal was appointed bishop of Macau in 1690. He left Portugal soon after the Episcopal consecration in Lisbon and arrived in Macau in 1692 with eight priests. He took advantage of the stable political situation to organize the diocese and established the canonical chapter in 1698. He favored order and cooperation in pastoral work. In 1700 there were 20,500 Catholics in Macau, 18,500 of whom were Chinese.

De Casal became famous in the Rites Controversy because of his zeal in defending his episcopal authority against the accusations of the apostolic delegate Mgr. C. T. Maillard de Tournon* (1668-1710), who was expelled from China* and arrived in Macau in 1705. He curtailed the influence of Mgr. Tournon by expelling the Augustinians* who supported him. But after Tournon's death they were allowed to return in 1721. De Casal welcomed Tournon's successor, Mgr. C. A. Mezzabarba*, both on his way to and from China in 1720-21.

De Casal gave hospitality to many priests and bishops who were sent out of China during the persecutions under the emperors, especially Yongzheng. De Casal was interim governor of Macau from 15 Jan to 24 Aug 1735. Having served as bishop for 45 years, he was buried in the Holy Sacrament Chapel of the cathedral.

Bibliography

Texeira, M., *Macau e sua Diocese,* Vol. II (1940).

SERGIO TICOZZI

De Castro, Francisco

Portuguese captain and lay catechist who converted the chiefs of several Philippine islands.

In 1538 de Castro and two Portuguese secular priests baptized the people of Makassar in Celebes*. In 1539 de Castro was sent by the Portuguese captain-general of Ternate, Dom Anton Galvao, on a reconnaissance and evangelistic mission to Mindanao. They were to lay claim to Mindanao and "other islands north of it" for the crown.

De Castro converted and baptized the chiefs and subjects of Saragani Island, Surigao, Butuan, Pamilara (now Buenvista, Agusan del Norte), and Camiguin Island. De Castro christened each baptized chief "Dom Joao" in honor of King John III of Portugal, except in the case of the Surigao chief, whom he christened "Dom Anton Galvao."

Bibliography

Galvao, A., *Tratado dos descubrimentos* (1944). • "Jacobs, H.," in *Neue Zeitschrift für Missionswissenschaft,* Vol. 31 (1975). • Combes, F., *Historia de . . . Mindanao* (1667), Vol. 1, Bk. 2 (1897). • Sitoy, T. V., Jr., *The Initial Encounter* (1985).

T. VALENTINO SITOY, JR.

De Costa Nunes, José

(b. Concelho de Madalena, Pico, Azores, 15 Mar 1880; d. Rome, 29 Nov 1976). Bishop of Macau; patriarch and cardinal of the East Indies.

De Costa Nunes was one of the most active bishops of Macau (1920-40). He continued the policies and style of his predecessor Mgr. J. P. de Azevedo e Castro (1852-1918), providing the diocese and mainly the Timor Mission with important institutions. He also served as patriarch of the East Indies from 1940 to 1953 and then cardinal beginning in Mar 1962.

De Costa Nunes studied in the seminary of Angra. While still a theology student, he was taken to Macau by Bishop de Azevedo e Castro in 1903. Ordained a priest in the same year, he was put in charge of the orphans of the Santa Casa da Misericordia. He was made administrator of the diocese whenever the bishop was absent, and he became vicar capitular at the death of the latter. He was appointed bishop of Macau in 1920.

De Costa Nunes accepted into the diocese the Sisters of Our Lady of Angels in 1929 and welcomed back the Jesuits*, entrusting them with the direction of St. Joseph's Seminary in 1930. In Macau, de Costa Nunes rebuilt the churches of Our Lady da Penha in 1935 and St. Claire in 1936. He opened the Canossa School (in Praca de Camoes) and restored the cathedral as well as the Bishop's house in 1938.

De Costa Nunes provided the Timor Mission with new personnel and institutions, mainly schools and churches together with a minor seminary, in order to make it autonomous from the diocese of Dili, established in 1940. He also improved the educational services of the Missions of Singapore* and Malacca*. De Costa Nunes retired in Rome, where he spent the last days of his life.

Bibliography

Texeira, M., *Macau e sua Diocese,* Vol. II (1940).

SERGIO TICOZZI

De la Cruz, Apolinario

(b. 1815; d. 1841). Better known as Herman Pule, cofounder of the *Cofradia de San José,* Philippines*; Christian martyr.

From Tayabas (Quezon) Province, de la Cruz was a 19th-c. Filipino religious dissenter, nationalist hero, and pious martyr who served as a lay brother in his early youth at the San Juan de Dios Hospital in Manila. Prevented by racist prejudices from joining a Spanish religious order, he returned home and, with Filipino secular priest Ciriaco de los Santos, organized the Masonic-type *Cofradia de San José,* in 1832 to promote piety, mutual fellowship, and support among its members. The confraternity rapidly spread from Tayabas to Laguna and Batangas.

The jealous Spanish curate of Lucban denounced Herman Pule as a heretic and a rebel. His confraternity being forcibly suppressed by Spanish troops, he was beheaded on 19 Oct 1841.

Bibliography

DECS, *Duyan ng Magiting* (1989). • Agoncillo, T. A., *History of the Filipino People* (1990).

T. Valentino Sitoy, Jr.

De la Motte, Pierre Lambert

(b. La Boissière [Calvados], 28 Jan 1624; d. Ayutthaya, Thailand, 15 Jun 1679). One of the first vicars apostolic, one of the founders of the Paris Foreign Mission Society* (MEP), and first member of the society to leave for the Far East.

De la Motte was a friend of François Pallu*, who begged him to go to Rome to help him obtain their appointment as vicars apostolic. It is reported that he was the one who convinced the secretary of the Congregation of Propaganda of the necessity of this appointment. On 29 Jul 1658, de la Motte was named bishop of Berythe and on 9 Sep 1659 vicar apostolic of Cochin China as well as administrator of the provinces of Chekiang, Fukien, Swangtung, Kwangsi, and the island of Hainan in China*. He was consecrated in Paris by the archbishop of Tours, Victor Le Bouthillier, on 2 Jun 1660 in the Church of the Sisters of the Holy Sacrament.

De la Motte left Paris on 18 Jun 1660 and Marseilles on 27 Nov of the same year, accompanied by two missionaries, de Bourges and Deydier. He arrived in Ayutthaya, capital of Siam, on 22 Aug 1662, two years, two months, and several days after his departure from Paris. The kingdom of Siam was not under his jurisdiction, but he extended Christian fellowship to all the missionaries living there. Elsewhere, the Cochin China mission to which Lambert was to go was exposed to persecution. The bishop thus made Ayutthaya his provisional headquarters.

De la Motte stayed first with a religious order, then established himself in the part of the city inhabited by the Annamites, known as the camp of the Cochin Chinese. Since he was vicar apostolic of Cochin China, he devoted himself first of all to the natives of that country, who were his first contacts. From there, he went on, as Rome had directed him, to examine the situation of the missions. The mission in Siam appeared to him to be in a very poor state. He found the missionaries lacking in zeal, engaging in pursuits forbidden by canon law, and in particular indulging in commerce. He notified the supreme pontiff and the Congregation of Propaganda of this in his letters of 10 Oct 1662, 6 Mar 1663, and 11 Jul 1663. In consequence, he was soon exposed to the animosity of the Portuguese, both civil and religious, who regarded his presence and spiritual powers as contrary to the rights of their king. His life was even threatened. He informed the pope about the situation and in a letter of 3 Oct 1663 offered his resignation.

The arrival of Pallu in 1664 and further reflection changed de la Motte's mind. In concert with the bishop of Heliopolis, he wrote *Monita*, a work which gives missionaries excellent counsels on piety, prudence, conduct, the organization of parishes, education, and indigenous priests. This work was highly esteemed by Rome, where it was printed for the first time in 1669; since then, many new editions have been published. On 13 Jan 1665, the prelate received jurisdiction over Cambodia* and Ciampa.

Having obtained from the king of Siam, Phra-Narai, a property in the camp of the Cochin Chinese, de la Motte had a modest residence built there with a little chapel, which he dedicated to St. Joseph. Another building served as a seminary for young men coming from China, Tonkin, and Cochin China to prepare for the sacred ministry. The first ordination took place in 1668. The two priests ordained were Tonkinese.

The following year the bishop left for Tonkin, which a trip to Europe had prevented Pallu from visiting, although it was entrusted to him. De la Motte ordained seven indigenous priests who had been instructed by Deydier. He founded a women's religious order in Siam, which he called Lovers of the Cross*, whose aims were the education of young women, care of the sick, conversion of women, and baptism of infants.

De la Motte returned to Siam in 1670 and in 1671 paid a visit to Cochin China. He traveled back to Siam in Feb 1672. The situation of the prelate in this mission had from the beginning been a very painful one because of the hostility of the merchants and the Portuguese religious orders, who denied that he was either a bishop or vicar apostolic, refused him obedience, and, to make matters worse, held certain incorrect doctrines of the theologian Quintana Duenas.

On 4 Jun 1669, Pope Clement IX elevated Siam to the status of a vicariate apostolic and entrusted it to the MEP, a decision already taken by a decree of 1665. On 13 Sep 1669, Clement IX, in the Bull *Speculators*, declared that the members of the religious orders owed obedience to the vicar apostolic. On 12 Sep 1671, Clement X, in the letter *Coelestibus*, confirmed the censure pronounced by the bishop against the theses of the theologians Quintana Duenas and Fragoso. On 10 Nov 1673, the same pope condemned, in the letter *Cum ad aures*, the acts of the Commissioners of the Inquisition in Goa. Further letters, on 22 and 23 Dec 1673, reconfirmed the powers of the vicar apostolic.

On 18 Oct 1675, the king of Siam granted a very solemn audience to the three vicars apostolic then at Ayutthaya: Pallu, Lambert, and Laneau (who had just been appointed vicar apostolic and bishop of Metellopolis, but was not yet consecrated). In 1676, de la Motte left again for Cochin China. His stay there was, according to the missionaries, one of the happiest times in the history of Catholicism in that country. Soon after his return to Siam, he fell ill and died in Ayutthaya, where he was buried in the Church of St. Joseph. Unaware of his death, Rome nominated him on 1 Apr 1680 as administrator general of the missions of Siam, Cochin China, and Tonkin.

Bibliography

Memoirs of the Paris Foreign Mission Society (MEP).

Translated by Canon Frank Lomax

De Legaspi, Miguel Lopez

(b. Zumarraga, Guipuzcoa, 1510; d. Manila, 20 Aug 1572). Born a Basque hidalgo, de Legaspi went to Mexico in 1545 and served in the municipal government of Mexico City. On 24 Sep 1559, a royal decree from King Philip II of Spain was sent to the viceroy of Mexico, Don Luis de Velasco, to organize, under the Treaty of Tordesillas, an expedition to the Philippine* Islands and other places where spices could be found. However, de Velasco died before he was able to carry out this undertaking. On 1 Sep 1564, the royal court of Mexico issued instructions to de Legaspi, who was then in his fifties, to head the expedition. His instructions were to explore islands toward the Moluccas*, especially the Philippines; to establish peace and friendship with the natives; to evangelize; to gather information on Portuguese activities in the area; and to find a return route to Mexico. In addition, he would search for and ransom prisoners from former expeditions.

The expedition: veni, vidi, vici. On 21 Nov 1564, de Legaspi sailed from Mexico, a captain-general heading a fleet of four ships, with Fray Andres de Urdaneta as his navigator. On 13 Feb 1565, de Legaspi sighted Samar and anchored near the island of Cebu. A reconnaissance tour of nearby islands, including Mindanao, encountered hostility from the natives. Nonetheless, de Legaspi exercised patience in establishing peace and friendship with the local people, thus making it easier for him to learn about the local customs and seek information regarding the resources of the islands.

On 28 Apr 1565, the leaders of the expedition decided to settle in Cebu, which they had captured by use of arms. De Legaspi initiated a peace pact with its king and chiefs which stipulated that they would recognize King Philip II of Spain as their sovereign and be subject to his laws and protection. They were to observe, fulfill, and obey royal commands through their governor, de Legaspi. This event may be viewed as the beginning of Spanish colonial rule over the Philippines.

With the chiefs' and natives' consent, de Legaspi chose a site to build a settlement, a fort, and a church. De Legaspi took formal possession of the island of Cebu in the name of Spain on 5 May 1565 and called it San Miguel, later, Santisimo Nombre de Jesus. The locals gradually gained trust and confidence in the Spaniards and freely traded with them. As trade flourished, the Spaniards met Muslim traders who came bearing various goods and spices from, and information on, Luzon.

Aside from initiating peace, the Spaniards proceeded to evangelize and convert the local people. Baptism steadily continued in Cebu. However, the village of Mactan, site of Magellan's defeat, remained hostile toward the foreigners. De Legaspi later learned that the hostility from most local people was due to marauding Portuguese who came posing as Spaniards.

With Cebu as his base, de Legaspi traveled to various islands of the archipelago, establishing contact and trade with other inhabitants, and took possession of and founded other towns in the name of Spain.

As these developments unfolded, de Legaspi recommended to the king that the islands be conquered because they were abundant in resources, especially gold and spices. The islands were bountiful and could maintain settlements. Furthermore, conquest would facilitate speedy propagation of the Catholic faith.

In 1570, de Legaspi decided to sail for Manila on the island of Luzon to check the possibility of initiating peace, trade, and the building of a settlement. However, certain groups in Manila were opposed and attacked the Spaniards. De Legaspi and his men retaliated and took possession of a native fort in Manila. De Legaspi then returned to Cebu. In mid-1571, de Legaspi traveled back to Manila with reinforcements, determined to establish a colonial government. After completing peace negotiations and securing the loyalty of the chiefs, de Legaspi formally founded the city of Manila on 3 Jun 1571 and formed a municipal organization. In so doing, de Legaspi laid a firm foundation for Spanish colonial rule over the Philippines for centuries to come.

On 20 Aug 1572, de Legaspi died of apoplexy in the city of Manila. He reportedly died a pauper, but a man of highest distinction.

Bibliography

Agoncillo, Teodoro A., and Milagros C. Guerrero, *History of the Filipino People* (1977). • Blair, Emma, and James Robertson, eds., *The Philippine Islands, 1493-1898,* 55 vols. (1902-9). • De la Costa, Horacio, *Readings in Philippine History* (1992). • Sharp, Andrew, *Adventurous Armada: The Story of Legaspi's Expedition* (1960).

José Mario C. Francisco

De los Reyes, Isabelo. *See* Reyes, Isabelo de Los, Sr.

De Medeiros, Antonio Joachim

(b. Vilar de Nantes, Portugal, 15 Oct 1846; d. Lahane, Timor, 7 Jan 1897). One of the most dynamic Roman Catholic bishops of Macau*, known as the apostle of the Timor Mission (1884-97).

Ordained a priest in 1871, de Medeiros arrived in Macau* in 1872 and taught in the seminary there. In 1875, he was appointed Visitor of the Timor Mission. He became vicar general of the mission in 1877 and invited the Canossian Sisters. He was chosen auxiliary bishop of Goa in 1881. In 1884, he was appointed bishop of Macau, where he returned in 1885.

As bishop, de Medeiras gave priority to the training of local sisters and to the education of youth. The 1886 Concordat between Portugal and the holy see is a faithful copy of proposals he submitted. He launched the weekly *O Voz do Crente* (The Voice of the Believer), published from 1886 to 1895. He succeeded in restoring control of St. Joseph's College to the Jesuits* in 1890, thus ending the secularization of this institution.

In 1895, de Medeiros took part in the Sixth Provincial Council held in Goa. He visited the missions of Singapore*, Malacca*, and Timor* several times, showing great concern and care especially for the latter, his first place of work, where he died at age 50.

Bibliography

Texeira, M., *Macau e sua Diocese*, Vol. II (1940).

SERGIO TICOZZI

De Mel, Lakdasa

(b. Moratuwa, 24 Mar 1902; d. Kurunegala, 23 Oct 1976). First Sri Lankan to be consecrated bishop in the Anglican* Church of Sri Lanka*; later elected metropolitan of India*, Pakistan*, Burma, and Ceylon.

Educated at Royal College, Colombo, and the Keble College, Oxford University, De Mel was ordained in 1927. He served as the incumbent at Baddegama in the southern province of Sri Lanka from 1929 to 1939. During this time he introduced traditional Sinhalese modes of worship* to the church (see Music). He incorporated Sinhalese lyrics into the worship, using local musical instruments for accompaniment. He also practiced the local forms of greeting and encouraged the congregation to do the same. De Mel made it a point to visit the local Buddhist temples and maintain a cordial relationship with the Buddhist monks. He was appointed vicar of St. Paul's Church in the ancient Sinhalese capital of Kandy in January 1940.

De Mel was consecrated assistant bishop of Colombo on 8 Nov 1945 in the midst of centenary celebrations of the diocese of Colombo. During his tenure as assistant bishop, he introduced Sinhalese as the first language of the diocese. He also introduced the Oriental practice of obeisance — prostrating oneself before the altar in the Eucharist of the Anglican Church.

De Mel was selected as the first diocesan bishop of the newly created diocese of Kurunegala in 1950. It was his idea to select Kurunegala as the seat of the new diocese instead of locating it in Kandy, which was the main center of Buddhism*. He continued his indigenization activities by introducing national customs to the church (see Contextualization).

De Mel invited non-Christians to functions at the cathedral in order to demonstrate to them the use of national traditions in the Christian church and to create a cordial atmosphere. His attitude toward Buddhists was friendly, even at the time of the school takeover by the government in 1960. He believed the duty of Christians was to help the nation in the effort of reconciliation.

De Mel was deeply interested in church union. In 1947, he attended the General Council of the United Church of South India*. In the same year he proposed a scheme to the Colombo Diocesan Council for church unity in Sri Lanka. In 1953 he participated in the newly formed North India negotiating committee on church union. In 1962 he went to Jaffna with the East Asia Christian Consultation Council to work out a plan for church union for Sri Lanka.

In May 1962 De Mel was elected metropolitan of India, Pakistan, Burma, and Ceylon. Much of his activity was devoted to work among the Pakistani refugees* in Bengal and matters of ecumenical* concerns in South Asia, in addition to his duties as metropolitan bishop.

De Mel retired in 1970 and returned to Sri Lanka. After his marriage in 1971, he and his wife, Joan, became busy with ecumenical and philanthropic activities. They were instrumental in inaugurating the Sri Lankan chapter of the Samaritans in 1973, which he named Sumitrayo ("good friends"). De Mel died in 1976 at his home in Kurunegala.

Bibliography

De Mel, Joan, *Lakdasa de Mel* (1980).

G. P. V. SOMARATNA

De Nobili, Roberto

(b. Rome, Sep 1577; d. Mylapore (Chennai), 16 Jan 1656). Pioneer Jesuit* missionary to South India who lived as a Hindu among Hindus.

De Nobili was the first missionary to study philosophical Hinduism deeply. He adopted a Hindu lifestyle, including a strict vegetarian diet, and encouraged his converts to remain Hindu in every possible way. A few dozen baptisms demonstrated the potential of his approach before controversy led to a ban on further baptisms. The issues debated are still controversial today despite belated official church approval for de Nobili's methods.

Eighteen months after arriving in India in 1605, de Nobili moved to Madurai, a city of great political, economic, and religious import in South India. A missionary predecessor had resided in Madurai for over a decade, ministering to the Portuguese community and acting as a representative of Portugal in political affairs. He had not seen a single conversion. De Nobili realized that Christ was misrepresented by the European community and the few Indian converts who had migrated to Madurai from the coast. He decided that words would not clear up the misunderstandings; a new ministry model had to be adopted.

Within two months of arrival in Madurai, de Nobili acted on his insights, and controversy flared immediately. Central was the notion that Christianity is a religion for the *parangi*. Historically this term meant "European," but in practice it was also applied to the low-caste Indian converts to Christianity and carried a connotation of "unclean and uncultured." By definition, a *parangi* could not teach a civilized person; thus the resistance to the missionary message and the lack of interest in Christ. Missionary disdain for local attitudes hardly needed demonstration. Two proud civilizations were meeting and competed as to which could most haughtily look down on the other.

De Nobili cut the Gordian knot. He was not a *parangi*, and one need not become a *parangi* to follow Christ. His own identity as an Italian, rather than a Portuguese, and his noble ancestry justified in his own mind his rejection of the *parangi* label. His wearing the dress of a religious teacher (a *sannyasi* or renunciant), eating pure vegetarian food prepared by a Brahmin cook, learning Sanskrit and Hindu lore, and physical separation from regular interaction with *parangis* (including local Christians and his fellow missionaries) convinced the local populace (not without conflict and intermittent persecution) that he was indeed different. Within four years, de Nobili had baptized over 100 new converts, including numerous Brahmins.

Church controversy over de Nobili's methods raged for decades. Already in late 1612, a new provincial leader (Portuguese, unlike his Italian predecessor) ordered de Nobili to cease baptizing until a definitive ecclesiastical ruling was made. Only in 1623 did a final verdict from Rome permit baptisms again under de Nobili's methodology. The Madurai Mission associated with de Nobili's name grew beyond Madurai with more missionary *sannyasis* adopting de Nobili's spirit and method. Soon the mission was deeply involved with the lowest as well as highest castes, and by 1661 there had been 30,000 baptisms, but most from the lower strata of society.

Bibliography

Cronin, Vincent, *A Pearl to India: The Life of Roberto de Nobili* (1959). • Rajamanickam, S., *The First Oriental Scholar* (1972). • Sauliere, A., *His Star in the East* (1995). • Thekkedath, Joseph, *History of Christianity in India*, Vol. II (1988).

H. L. Richard

De Pordenone, Odoric. *See* Odoric of Pordenone

De Salazar, Domingo

(b. ?; d. Madrid, Spain, Dec 1594). First bishop of Manila.

In 1578 King Philip II of Spain appointed de Salazar the first bishop of Manila. De Salazar arrived in Manila in Sep 1581 to establish the diocese of Manila.

In 1582 the bishop convened the first Manila synod, which met intermittently until 1856. The purpose of the synod was to rationalize and justify the Spanish conquest of the Philippines* and to define and establish its colonization. It was described as both a civil and religious assembly which discussed the problems of evangelization and colonization in the Philippines, as it was the king's concern.

The bishop, through his conscience, invoked "supernatural sovereignty" to legitimize the Spanish conquest of the Philippines. Elevated to the spiritual level, it was the moral obligation of the Spanish crown to establish a colonial government in order for them to preach the Catholic faith, de Salazar argued. It was the supreme responsibility of Spain to evangelize and convert the locals to Christianity so that they might gain the grace and salvation of God. It was by this most sacred reason that the Spanish crown could claim title to the islands.

The Manila synod also characterized the laws for governance of Spanish rule. It defined the roles, duties, and obligations of the missionaries, *encomenderos*, and other colonial officials such as the governor, captains, *alcalde mayores*, soldiers, and judges. Any abuses committed by these officials were to be met with retribution.

These laws were basically instituted to curtail abuses of Spanish authorities against the locals, most common of which were the exacting of exorbitant tributes and forced labor. De Salazar reasoned that any cruelty by Spanish officials was an obstacle to conversion. The bishop wanted true converts through peaceful evangelization and not conversion through coercion, which by moral justification nullified the legitimacy of the Spanish conquest of the Philippines.

The *encomenderos* and other Spanish officials sought to oppose the terms to be enforced by the bishop, which created a conflict between them. However, upon review of the matter, King Philip thought it just to implement the bishop's recommendation on the ministration of the *encomiendas* and colonial government.

De Salazar also sought the help of the Spanish crown to establish reforms, spiritual and temporal, in the colony. He requested more missionaries in order to widen the geographical scope of evangelistic work and ministrations in the islands. He also helped build hospitals for the people. He aimed to show the benevolence of Christianity in order to bring about more conversions, thereby further justifying the establishment of a colonial government for spiritual gains.

In 1583 de Salazar wrote to the king of Spain requesting the establishment of a Jesuit college to provide for the growing needs of the colony. He explained that establishing a college in the Philippines where good religious education could train priests in the islands would save the crown great expense. This would lessen if not eliminate the necessity for the Spanish government continually to provide for such needs to the colony.

In 1591 de Salazar traveled back to Spain to report to King Philip personally on the spiritual condition in the Philippines and to request a remedy for the spiritual abuses. He also petitioned for the elevation of the diocese of Manila into an archbishopric with three suffragan dioceses to respond to the expansion and growing needs of the church in the Philippines. But in Dec 1594 he succumbed to an illness and died in Madrid.

In 1595 Pope Clement VIII promoted the diocese of Manila into an archbishopric, with Manila as its see, and created three suffragan dioceses: *Nueva Segovia* (now Lal-lo, Cagayan Valley), Cebu, and *Nueva Caceres.* De Salazar certainly would have been the first archbishop of Manila.

The bishop was often described as upright and just, as dictated by his conscience. He fought for the rights of the people, especially the oppressed locals, and voiced his opposition toward colonial abusers, often arousing conflict with authorities. For this he was described by colonial authorities as obstinate and unbending. More important, the success of the synod of 1582 established and defined the role of the church and the colonial government, which transformed Tagalog social relations in the coming centuries.

Bibliography

Blair, Emma, and James Robertson, eds., *The Philippine Islands, 1493-1898,* 55 Vols. (1902-9). • Fernandez, Pablo, *History of the Church in the Philippines (1521-1898)* (1979). • Rafael, Vicente, *Contracting Colonialism* (1988). • Schumacher, John, *Readings in Philippine Church History* (1979).

Jose Mario C. Francisco

De Silva, J. Simon

(b. Kurana, 27 May 1868; d. Colombo, 16 Feb 1940). Prominent Sinhalese scholar of the Sri Lanka* Methodist* Church.

De Silva entered ministry as a Methodist pastor in 1892. He was the first Sinhalese graduate (Calcutta University) to enter the Methodist ministry. He served in stations at Madampitiya, Badulla, Kurana, Galle, Kalutara, Kandy, and Matara.

In keeping with the Wesleyan tradition, the Methodist ministers took an active part in the drive against the use of alcohol. De Silva was very active in the temperance movement, which had become very popular in Sri Lanka during the first quarter of this century.

He was a prolific writer in Sinhala and English and was able to preach in Portuguese as well. For several years he was the secretary of the Sinhalese Literature* Committee, an ecumenical* body consisting of 21 members of Christian churches in Sri Lanka. He edited two Sinhalese weeklies, *Rivikirana* (first issued in Feb 1907) and *Gnanodaya* (first published in Sep 1923). He was also a hymn writer and general editor of the Christian hymnal used by Methodists, Anglicans*, and Baptists* in their worship* services. He also served as chairman of the revision committee of the Sinhala Bible*. De Silva is credited as chief reviser of the 1938 version of the Sinhala Bible, which is also known as the Union version. It remains the most widely used Sinhala Bible even today.

It would be true to say that de Silva dominated the field of Sinhalese Christian literature in the first quarter of this century. He was for some time actively connected with the Christian Literature Society (CLS) and also with the Bible Society*. He was responsible for numerous tracts, poems, hymns, and lyrics. His Sinhalese works included the *Christian Message, Imitation of Christ, Story of Wesley, Early Methodism, Life Not a Play,* and *Uttamadarasha.* The latter (published by the CLS) contained brief life sketches in Sinhalese of 13 foreign and local celebrities. These books became popular in schools during his time.

De Silva's work in the CLS became the nucleus of ecumenical activity during this time. His contribution to Sinhalese literature had an impact on the Sinhalese reading public at large.

Bibliography

Small, W. J. T., *A History of the Methodist Church in Ceylon* (1970).

G. P. V. Somaratna

De Silva, Lynn

(b. Kurana, 10 Jun 1919; d. Colombo, 22 May 1982). Methodist minister and scholar of Buddhist-Christian dialogue (see Interreligious Dialogue).

Ordained in 1947, de Silva served at the Methodist churches in Kollupitiya-Wellawatta, Kandy, Badulla, Kalahe, Mutwa, Seeduwa, and Matara. He was director of the Study Center for Religion and Society in Colombo and was a member of the World Council of Churches' department for Dialogue with People of Living Faiths and Ideologies. He was founding editor of *Dialogue* (Colombo) and authored many books and articles in English and Sinhala, many of which have been translated into other languages. He is regarded as the first to have written a book on Greek philosophy in Sinhala (1950). Two of his most outstanding contributions to Buddhist-Christian dialogue are *Reincarnation in Buddhist and Christian Thought* (1968) and *The Problem of the Self in Buddhism and Christianity* (1975). Besides these books on dialogue, his scholarship of Buddhism* is evident in his book *Buddhism: Beliefs and Practices in Sri Lanka* (1974).

In 1962 de Silva was selected for the joint project of Protestant and Roman* Catholic translation of the Bible* into contemporary Sinhala, and from 1974 until his death he served as chief translator.

In 1964 he delivered the "Sinclair Thompson Memorial Lectures," a lectureship established to foster mutual understanding and goodwill between Christians and Buddhists, at McGilvary* Institute of Theology, Chiang Mai. In 1970 he was invited to be the William Paton* Lecturer, a lectureship accorded to a "leading academic of standing from overseas," at Selly Oak College, Birmingham, and was also accorded the status of visiting lecturer in Asian religions on the academic staff of the University of Bristol.

De Silva believed that the acknowledgment of spiritual truths in other religions would not weaken one's commitment to the Christian faith; rather, he was convinced that one's own faith could be deepened and broadened by a sympathetic and intelligent understanding of faiths of others. His thesis was that the truths in Buddhism could be absorbed or adapted into Christianity and could fertilize and enrich a Christian's own faith. In his publications and lectures, he tried to facilitate Buddhist-Christian dialogue and help people of these two faiths overcome prejudices and past misunderstandings of each other.

Bibliography

Small, W. J. T., *A History of the Methodist Church in Ceylon* (1970).

G. P. V. Somaratna

De Souza, Polycarpe

(b. 1697; d. 1757). First bishop in Beijing following the banning of Christianity by the Qing emperor Yongzheng.

De Souza joined the Society of Jesus*(Jesuits) in 1712. In 1724 Emperor Yongzheng banned Christianity and deported all missionaries to Macau*, except those in the calendrical bureau and others working in Beijing who were housed in the South Church, East Church, and North Church. In 1726 the Portuguese king, John V, officially sent Allexande Metello to China. Accompanying him were three Portuguese Jesuits, one of whom was de Souza. They were granted audiences with Yongzheng in Beijing on 28 May and 8 Jul 1727. Before leaving Beijing on 16 Jul, Metello recommended the three Jesuits with expertise in calendrical matters to the emperor, who subsequently hired them. De Souza engaged in clandestine religious work and learned of his appointment as bishop of Beijing *(Episcopus Pekinensis)* on 19 Dec 1740. He was consecrated in Macau and returned to Beijing. In 1742 Pope Clement XIV issued the final bull prohibiting the practice of Chinese rites, the *Ex Quo Singulari.* De Souza announced it only in 1744 through a pastoral letter and notices in the three churches in Beijing after strong urging from the Vatican.

Bibliography

Goodrich, L. Carrington, *Dictionary of Ming Biography, 1386-1644* (1976).

China Group, translated by David Wu

De Tournon, Charles Thomas Maillard

(b. Turin, Italy, 1688; d. Macau, 8 Jun 1710). First papal legate to China* during the early Qing period.

Consecrated at St. Peter's, Rome, by Pope Clement XI on 22 Dec 1702, de Tournon left Rome as the patriarch of Antioch and apostolic visitor of the pope on 9 Feb 1703, arriving first in India*, where he issued a decree condemning the Malabar rites. He then sailed to Manila, Philippines*, before reaching Macau* on 2 Apr 1705. He entered the city of Guangzhou in Chinese garments on 5 Apr, and on 9 Sep he took a boat to Beijing, arriving on 14 Dec for an audience granted by Emperor Kangxi (K'ang-hsi) upon the petition of Philippus M. Grimaldi*, François Gerbillon*, and Thomas Pereira*. Kangxi gave him residence in the North Church, and during his eight-month stay in Beijing, he met the emperor twice. When asked about the intention of his visit, he replied that he came to convey greetings and to thank the emperor for the protection given to Christianity. But Kangxi had learned that his real intention was to forbid Chinese Christians to pay homage to Confucius (see Confucianism) and to worship ancestors*. Kangxi maintained that the Chinese could not change the practice of their rites and forsake the teaching of Confucius, which they had observed for 2,000 years. If the Chinese were forbidden to worship their ancestors and pay homage to Confucius, it would be difficult for Westerners to remain in China. He eventually ordered de Tournon to leave. On 28 Aug 1706, de Tournon, in poor health, and his followers left Beijing, arriving in Nanjing on 17 Dec, and made public on 7 Feb 1707 the "Order of Nanjing" *(Mandement de Nankin),* signed on 25 Jan, prohibiting Chinese Christians to worship ancestors and pay homage to Confucius. The order was strongly opposed by the Jesuits (see Society of Jesus) in China. On 18 Mar, de Tournon left Nanjing and arrived in Guangzhou on 24 May. Emperor Kangxi sent two officers on 19 Jun to take de Tournon to Macau within five days. De Tournon died of illness while under arrest in Macau.

Bibliography

Rosso, Antonio Sisto, *Apostolic Legations to China of the Eighteenth Century* (1948). • Rouleau, Francis A., "Maillard de Tournon, Papal Legate at the Court of Peking," *Archivum Historicum Societatis Iesu,* Vol. 31 (1962). • St. Sure, D. F., *100 Roman Documents concerning the Chinese Rites Controversy (1645-1941)* (1992). • Sebes, Joseph S., "China's Jesuit Century," *Wilson Quarterly,* Vol. 2 (1978).

China Group, translated by David Wu

De Ursis, Sabbatino

(b. Italy, 1575; d. Macau 3 May 1620). Italian Jesuit* missionary to China* in the late Ming dynasty.

De Ursis arrived in Beijing in 1606 and learned Chinese from Matteo Ricci*. At the time of de Ursis's arrival in China, Ricci was transmitting Western science to the Chinese intelligentsia. Through Ricci's introduction, de Ursis got to know many Chinese scholars and joined Ricci in introducing Western science to them. In 1611 and 1612, two books on Western science which he introduced were published through the writing of Paul Xu Kuang Qi*: *Jian Ping Yi Shuo* and *Tai Xi Shui Fa.* In 1614 another book, *Piao Du Shuo,* through the pen of Zhou Zi Yu, was published. All of these books, including Xu Guang Qi's *Nong Zheng Quan Shu,* were entered into the encyclopedia of *Si Ku Quan Shu.* De Ursis was opposed by traditionalists in China. In 1616, arising out of the complaint of Chinese magistrate Shen Que, de Ursis was one of four missionaries deported to Macau*. He died there at age 46.

Bibliography

Latourette, Kenneth Scott, *A History of Christian Missions in China* (1929). • Vath, Alfons, *Johann Adam Schall von Bell, S.J. (1592-1666)* (1991). CHINA GROUP

Dean, William

(b. Easton, New York, United States, 1807; d. San Diego, California, United States, 1895). Pioneer church planter in China and Thailand, and theological educator of the American Baptist Foreign Mission Society (ABFMS).

A graduate of Hamilton Literary and Theological Institution (Hamilton Theological Seminary), Dean married Matilda C. Man, who died before he arrived in Siam on 1 Jul 1835. He was appointed to work among the Chinese in Thailand and there founded and pastored the world's first Protestant Chinese church, Maitrichit Chinese Baptist Church, on 1 Jul 1837. He also instituted theological training classes (1838-42). He then married Theodosia Ann Barker in 1838 (who died five years later) and sailed to Hong Kong* in 1842 with preaching students Tang Tui and Koe Bak, helped to organize Hong Kong Swatow Baptist Church and Cheung Chau Baptist Church, and began training many preachers. His third wife, Maria Stofter, whom he met on furlough, had directed school and women's ministries in Siam.

The Deans returned to Siam (1865) and built up the work in Bangkok based on wide experience and respect from both church and society. The Deans' work prospered, peaking in 1882 with 500 baptized Chinese in six churches and seven outstations. In 1881 Maria left for the United States and died there. William then returned to the States in August 1884 after 49 years of ministry. Dean helped globalize Chinese missions, emphasized theological education for the Chinese Baptist churches, ordained Thailand's first indigenous pastors, and sent out scores of Chinese Christian workers. Dynamic and sincere with people, he authored a number of Chinese biblical commentaries.

Bibliography

ABFMS, *Records of the American Baptist Foreign Mission Society.* • Hervey, G. Winfred, *The Story of Baptist Missions in Foreign Lands* (1886). • Kho, Samuel, *150 Years of Thankfulness: A History of the Maitrichit Chinese Baptist Church, 1837-1987* (1987). DONALD S. PERSONS

del Espiritu Santo, Ignacia

(b. Binondo, Manila, 1663; d. Intramuros, 10 Sept 1748). Foundress of the Religious of the Virgin Mary*, the first indigenous religious congregation in the Philippines.

Del Espiritu Santo was born, lived, and died during the Spanish colonial era (1521-1899) in the Philippines. The precise date of her birth is not known. Her baptismal certificate records 4 Mar 1663 as the date of her birth. But since it was the custom at that time to name the child after the saint of the day, it is assumed that del Espiritu Santo was born on 1 Feb, the original feast of St. Ignatius of Antioch. She was the eldest and the sole surviving child of Maria Jeronima, an *yndia* (native), and Jusepe Iucuo, a pure Chinese immigrant from Amoy, China, who was converted to the Catholic faith in 1652 and resided in Binondo, Manila.

When del Espiritu Santo reached the age of 21 in 1684, her parents wanted her to marry. Perhaps heeding a call deep within but not wanting to disappoint her parents, she sought counsel from Fr. Paul Klein, a Jesuit* priest from Bohemia who arrived in Manila in 1682. The priest gave her the spiritual exercises of St. Ignatius. After this period of solitude and prayer, del Espiritu Santo decided to "remain in the service of the Divine Majesty" and resolved to "live by the sweat of her brow." She left her home with only a needle and a pair of scissors, living alone in a house at the back of the Jesuit College of Manila. Her life of prayer and labor attracted *yndias* who also felt called to the religious life but could not be admitted into the existing congregations, which accepted only Spanish women. "Mother Ignacia" accepted these women into her company, and the first community was born. They became known as the *Beatas de la Compañia de Jesus* because they frequently received the sacraments at the Church of St. Ignatius, performed many acts of devotion there, and had the Jesuit fathers for their spiritual directors and confessors.

Mother Ignacia centered her life on the suffering Christ and tried to imitate him by acts of penance. Some of the *beatas* who tried to imitate her got sick. Because of this, she advised moderation in the practice of penance. They supported themselves partly by the labor of their hands and partly by the help offered by pious people. They lived in poverty and sometimes had to beg for rice and salt and scour the streets for firewood.

The growing number of *beatas* called for a more stable lifestyle and a set of rules. A daily schedule was drawn up, and community practices were defined. Following the spirit of St. Ignatius, Mother Ignacia exhorted her *beatas* to live always in the presence of God and develop great purity of heart. She also emphasized charity in the community, which she called the family of Mary. This spirit runs through the 1726 constitutions which were written for the guidance of the *beatas*. By this time, Mother Ignacia had gradually realized that the women of the *beaterio* were called by God not only to a life of prayer and penance but also to a life of service. The *beaterio* admitted young girls as boarders and taught them Christian doctrine as well as works proper to their sex. Mother Ignacia did not make any distinction of color or race but accepted *yndias, mestizas,* and Spaniards as *recogidas.* Women whose husbands were away would stay in the *beaterio* until their husbands' return. The *beatas* were also involved in retreat work and helped the Jesuit fathers by preparing the retreatants to be disposed to the spiritual exercises.

Since the *beaterio* needed royal recognition to continue to exist in the colony, Mother Ignacia submitted the 1726 constitutions to the archdiocesan office for approval. While the *beatas* awaited the response of Spain, Mother Ignacia realized that she could now give up her responsibility as superior. She resigned from the governance of the house and lived as an ordinary member until her death. Murillo Velarde, a Jesuit historian who wrote her biography, saw this as a great sign of her humility. Mother Ignacia had no desire to command or control. Murillo Velarde describes her as a "truly valiant woman who overcame the great difficulties which she met in the foundation from the beginning to the end . . . mortified, patient, devout, spiritual, zealous for the good of souls."

Mother Ignacia died without knowing the response of the Spanish king, but her long life in the *beaterio* must have taught her to trust in the providence of God. Little did she know that the *beaterio* she founded would become a congregation and continue to exist until today, more than 300 years after her death. This congregation, now known as the Religious of the Virgin Mary, is a living testimony to her life as God's handmaid who opened the door of religious life to native women in the Philippines and proved that God is the God of all peoples, of whatever color or race.

Bibliography

Ferraris, Maria Rita, *From Beaterio to Congregation* (1975); *Beaterios for Native Women in Colonial Philippines* (1987). • Murillo Velarde, Pedro, *Historia de la Provincia de la Compañia de Jesus* (1747).

Maria Anicia Co

Delamarre, Louis-Charles

(b. Rouen, France, 11 Jul 1810; d. Han-Keou, China, 3 Oct 1863). First missionary of the Paris Foreign Mission Society* (MEP) to enter China*.

Delamarre entered the seminary of the Paris Foreign Mission Society (MEP) in 1833 and was ordained on 20 Dec 1834. In 1835 he arrived in China from France, entering both Sichuan and Hong Kong* clandestinely. He became the interpreter for the French representative Gros during the second Opium* War. In Oct 1860, when China was forced to sign the unequal Beijing Treaty, Delamarre, taking advantage of his position as translator, personally added to the Chinese translation of Treaty No. 6 the following clause: "and allowing French missionaries the freedom to purchase or rent land for building purposes." When the French soldiers left Beijing, Delamarre, holding a French passport, departed Beijing via Baoding, Henan, and Shaanxi. He arrived in Sichuan in Jan 1862. He was protected through his departure by local Chinese magistrates. Delamarre left behind a handwritten draft of a Chinese-Latin-French dictionary.

Bibliography

Cohen, Paul A., *China and Christianity* (1963).

China Group

Devanandan, Paul David

(b. Madras, 8 Jul 1901; d. Dehra Dun, 10 Aug 1962). Indian theologian and historian of religions, ecumenical* leader, and evangelist.

Devanandan was born into a Tamil pastor's family in which disciplined Bible study was a formative element. He studied at Nizam College, Hyderabad, and Presidency College, Madras. Early on he came into contact with K. T. Paul*, one of the outstanding leaders of the church in India*, who at the floodtide of Indian nationalism* attempted to give it a sense of direction and a Christian content. Impressed with the young Devanandan, Paul took him as his secretary when he went to the United States, providing Devanandan the opportunity of extended firsthand contact with the thought, vision, and work of this pioneer. It also gave the young man an opportunity to widen his horizons and deepen his convictions in circumstances very different from those at home.

After his work with Paul was finished, Devanandan stayed on in the USA to study at Pacific School of Religion, Berkeley, where he completed his B.D. He earned a Ph.D. in comparative religions from Yale University with a dissertation on the concept of *maya* in the Hindu religious tradition. Subsequently, a number of visiting appointments were received, including William Paton Lecturer at Selly Oak, Birmingham; Henry Luce Professor at Union Theological Seminary, New York; and Teape Lecturer at Cambridge University. In 1931, he was appointed professor of philosophy and religions at United Theological College, Bangalore, where today his papers and manuscripts are housed in the college archives. From 1949 to 1956, he worked with the Indian Young Men's Christian Association* (YMCA), most notably as its national literature secretary. In 1954, he was ordained a presbyter in the Church of South India*, and 1956 saw him appointed director of the Center for the Study of Hinduism, which later became the Christian Institute for the Study of Religion and Society* (CISRS), Bangalore. Through his work at the CISRS and his writings in its journal *Religion and Society*, Devanandan, with his associate M. M. Thomas*, sought to guide young Indian Christian leaders in constructive tasks in newly independent India, and to build them into a community of mind and spirit. Here, as well as through his address "Called to Witness" to the third assembly of the World Council of Churches at Delhi (1961), Devanandan gained recognition in the world church.

As a young man, Devanandan had rebelled against a theological liberalism which reduced Christianity to a kind of religious philosophy, and found in Hendrik Kraemer* a basis of renewal of his theology. Later, however, he revolted against Kraemer, searching for a post-

Kraemer approach to the relation between Christianity and other religions. Most of his adulthood was lived in the days of dominance of the Western mission, against which the nationalist in him rebelled. Devanandan had, however, learned two important lessons from Paul: first, that it is possible for a Christian to be a responsible nationalist without surrendering Christian convictions and values; and second, that Christians, while affirming their membership in the worldwide body of Christ, must also take part in nation building with a sense of Christian responsibility and concern. Indeed, he saw more clearly than most in his time that the new day for church and nation was not one of rebellion and revolt, but of reconstruction, whether in theological endeavor, church life, or nation building.

Devanandan's perennial theme was Jesus Christ in the "contemporary world" of religion and society. This and his many contacts with people of faith in other religious traditions, in and through whom he experienced "the surging new life manifest in other religions . . . the creative activity of the Holy Spirit," gave him a clear conviction of the significance and necessity of dialogue with the living religious and secular faiths of people in order to understand the ultimate questions they ask and the meaning of Christ in relation to them. At a time when conversations between Christians and persons of faith in other religious traditions were primarily contentions or, at best, "parallel monologues," Devanandan initiated a series of dialogues with Hindu scholars and thinkers. His intention was to facilitate a deeper understanding of religions based on the actual experience of dialogue. His persistent emphasis on the fact of Jesus Christ reinforced and clarified the common humanity of all women and men. On this basis, he was convinced, all dialogues about humankind, faith, culture, or society become real conversations in Christ and about Christ.

Thus Devanandan prepared the way for a credible theology of religions whose significant themes may be summarized in three basic affirmations. First, the redeeming work of God in Jesus Christ, in a world where persons are involved in nature, society, and history, is all-inclusive in that all things will be summed up in Christ. Second, while believing that God's work is continuing in the world, Christians must never forget that it is not of this world. The Gospel must never be identified with any particular culture, system of thought, or moral ideal. Third, the ongoing work of the living Christ, bringing healing and wholeness to broken humanity today, is a work in which Christians are called to be humble participants. In all of this, Devanandan's fundamental concern was to help the Indian church understand Jesus Christ as the final clue and fulfillment of God's work for the world of Indian religion, culture, and society, and to restate and communicate that truth.

Bibliography

Devanandan, P. D., *The Concept of Maya* (1950); *The Gospel and Renascent Hinduism* (1959); *Christian Concern in Hinduism* (1961); *Christian Issues in Southern Asia* (1963); *I Will Lift Up Mine Eyes unto the Hills: A Collection of Sermons and Bible Studies*, ed. Nalini Devanandan and S. J. Samartha (1963); *Preparation for Dialogue: A Collection of Essays on Hinduism and Christianity in New India*, ed. Nalini Devanandan and M. M. Thomas (1964).

David C. Scott

Development Work, Myanmar. *See* Myanmar — Christian Development Work

Dharma Angkuw, Margaretha

(b. Bogor, West Java, 11 Oct 1925). Pioneer female social activist in Indonesia*.

Dharma Angkuw completed primary and secondary school in Bogor and in 1948 enrolled at the Theological Seminary in that city which is now the *Sekolah Tinggi Theologia, Jakarta.* At that time, she was one of only two women students. She graduated in 1955 and began her work at the synod office of her church, the Protestant Church of Western Indonesia. She was also ordained in that year. Her responsibilities centered on the promotion of diaconal work and women's service. She continued these tasks until 1962, when she began her pioneering efforts in the field of pastoral work in the hospital context, serving as head of the spiritual-care commission at Cikini Hospital, the hospital of the Indonesian Communion of Churches.

For many years, Dharma Angkuw was a member of the executive committee of the Communion of Churches in Indonesia (PGI)*, with responsibility primarily in the area of social health services and especially family planning. She dedicated herself to promoting the government's ambitious, highly successful, and widely copied family-planning program. She also served as one of the treasurers of the PGI.

Dharma Angkuw represented the Indonesian churches twice as a delegate to the general assembly of the World Council of Churches (WCC), in New Delhi in 1961 and in Uppsala in 1968. She was also active in the East Asia Christian Conference (EACC) and in 1958 became one of the founders of the Asian Christian Women's Conference (ACWC), which became a part of the EACC. As a member of the ACWC, she was most active in the area of family planning. She also holds membership in the International Christian Hospital Fellowship.

Dharma Angkuw will remain known for her four pioneering areas of service. First is the area of diaconal service. Her commitment in this area challenged prevailing views that the church was ultimately responsible only for the service of its own members. Thus she helped broaden outreach efforts. Second, her commitment to family-planning education helped popularize the program in Protestant circles. Third, with humor, insistence, and intelligence, she advanced the position of women in the Indonesian church, not in the least through the example of her own service. She believed that women must always give a slightly better performance than men in order to be accepted. At the same time she had a positive response to the obstacles she faced as a woman. She would take whatever opportunity was available to her as a woman at any given time. Fourth, her many years of visibility in pastoral work in the hospital setting opened many eyes in Indonesia to the significance of this service.

Articulate, outspoken, witty, and efficient, Dharma Angkuw has exemplified creative leadership in a crucial era of Indonesian history. She is the widow of John Lie, an admiral in the Indonesian navy who played a prominent role in the struggle for Indonesian independence.

AART M. VAN BEEK

Dharmapala, Anagarika

(b. Colombo, 16 Sept 1864; d. Saranath, India, 1933). The most charismatic Sinhalese Buddhist leader and a national hero in Sri Lanka*.

Dharmapala was known in his childhood as Don David Hewavitarane. He was educated in the leading Catholic and Anglican schools. He worked in a government department until 1886 and later joined the Theosophical Society. He took on the name Anagarika ("homeless") Dharmapala ("servant of the *dhamma*"), giving up the name David because he considered it Christian.

The two main forces that shaped Dharmapala's thinking were Buddhism* and the theosophical movement. He plunged avidly into the activities of the Buddhist Theosophical Society by assuming major responsibilities for their weekly *Sandaresa* (begun in 1880) and the *Buddhist* (begun in 1888). Dharmapala was actively involved in raising funds for the purpose of opening Buddhist schools in order to counter Christian missionary propaganda. He was active in influencing the Sinhalese Buddhists to be proud of their heritage.

In his career as a Buddhist activist, Dharmapala realized the value of setting the Buddhist revival in Sri Lanka in a wider perspective. In May 1891, he founded the Maha Bodhi Society in Calcutta and in January 1892 began publishing the *Maha Bodhi Journal,* which soon became in his hands a powerful vehicle for Buddhist propaganda. From 1892 to 1930, he was occupied with his concern for the rehabilitation of Buddhist pilgrim sites in India.

Dharmapala's missionary work for the cause of Buddhism soon brought him international attention. He attended the Parliament of Religions held in Chicago in Sept 1893. He traveled to America, England, France, Italy, Myanmar*, and Japan* to further the cause of Buddhism. When not involved in propaganda work in other countries, Dharmapala spent a good part of his time in Sri Lanka.

Dharmapala toured all over the island promoting the Sinhalese Buddhist revival. His activities attracted the adverse attention of the British government in India* and Sri Lanka. In the aftermath of the Buddhist-Muslim riots of 1915, he was ordered to remain in Calcutta in 1916. This ban was rescinded in December 1919. He visited Sri Lanka for the last time in 1931, and on his return to India he received ordination as a monk, acquiring the name Devamitta Dhammapala, on 13 Jul 1931. He passed away on 29 Apr 1933 at Saranath.

Dharmapala was not a philosopher but a propagandist. His central concern for nearly half a century (1886-1933) was Buddhism, and he took upon himself the responsibility of rescuing it from its low status and transforming it into an instrument for spiritual revival in Sri Lanka and elsewhere. He imitated the contemporary Protestant Christian institutions to revive Buddhism and to counter Christian missionary activities in Sri Lanka. His criticism of those Sinhalese who embraced Christianity was harsh. Similarly, he was hard on any racial stock which he thought might be harmful to the Sinhalese Buddhists.

Dharmapala's impact on Sri Lanka was much more powerful and sustained than on India and the West despite the fact that he was absent from Sri Lanka most of the time. As a Buddhist propagandist, he strove hard to convince others that Buddhism, in many ways, was far superior to other religions. His influence led to merging the strands of Sinhalese nationalism* and Buddhism into one, thereby alienating Sinhalese Christians from the mainstream.

Bibliography

Sangharakshita, Bhikku, *Anagarika Dharmapala: A Biographical Sketch* (1964). • Guruge, Ananda, *Return to Righteousness* (1965).

G. P. V. SOMARATNA

Dia, Pablo

Pioneer Filipino Presbyterian* evangelist in the Bicol Peninsula.

From Bacon, Sorsogon, Dia had been converted about 1901 and was sent in 1903 to assist P. F. Jansen* of the Presbyterian mission in Cebu. For two years Dia labored as one of the chief evangelists in the city and province of Cebu and for a time also in Leyte.

Recalled to Albay in 1905 to assist Roy Brown, Dia was largely responsible for the conversion of 258 individuals within two years. Ordained about 1908, Dia labored throughout the Bicol Peninsula. The earliest Presbyterian successes in the Camarines, Albay, and Sorsogon provinces (including the conversion of the ex-Catholic seminarian Julian Bertumen*) were due to his untiring efforts.

Bibliography

The Philippine Presbyterian, Vol. 6 (Apr 1915). • Sitoy, T. V., Jr., *Several Springs, One Stream* (1992).

T. VALENTINO SITOY, JR.

Dialogue. *See* Interreligious Dialogue

Diaz, Emmanuel

(b. 1574; d. Hangzhou, China, 1659). Portuguese Jesuit missionary to China* in the late Ming period.

Diaz arrived in Macau in 1605 and entered China in 1611. He was among the people deported to Macau following a complaint filed against the missionaries by a Chinese magistrate in 1616. He reentered China in 1621, residing in Beijing. When Jean de Rocha died, Diaz succeeded him in directing the Jesuit mission in China. In the following years, Diaz visited Nanjing, Songjiang, Shanghai, and Hangzhou. In 1638, Diaz visited Fuzhou, which was in upheaval. When the missionaries were expelled from China, Diaz took temporary refuge in Macau and later returned to Fujian Province. When the Qing government sent troops into Fujian Province, Diaz and Julio Aleni* fled to the mountain region of Yan Ping. In 1648, Diaz did mission work in Yan Ping and devoted himself to writing. He translated into Chinese *Contemptus Mundi,* or *De Imitatione Christi.* This and another book, *Bible Exegesis,* were quite popular among the Catholics. Diaz also wrote *Nestorian Tablet Explained* (see Literature and Publishing).

Bibliography

Treadgold, Donald W., *The West in Russia and China: China, 1582-1949* (1973). • Vath, Alfons, *Johann Adam Schall von Bell S.J. (1592-1666)* (1991). • Goodrich, L. Carrington, *Dictionary of Ming Biography, 1386-1644* (1976).

China Group

Dickson, James Ira

(b. Dalzell, South Dakota, United States, 23 Feb 1900; d. Taipei, 15 Jun 1967). Visionary missionary and church developer sent by the Presbyterian Church of Canada to north Taiwan*.

Dickson was one of the most influential and far-sighted missionaries in Taiwan. His tireless efforts and deep involvement in the society resulted in both the numerical and qualitative growth of the churches. His accomplishments included the founding of the Yu-Shan Theological College (1946) to train aboriginal* ministers; the organization of a local evangelical group (1947) which established more than 320 churches for the aboriginal tribes within 15 years; the starting of the Taipei American School (1949) for the education of foreign residents in Taiwan; the beginning of the Rotary Club (1949) for communication between the churches and the upper class of Taiwanese society; the organizing of the Taiwan Evangelical Fellowship Conference (1951) where all missionaries in Taiwan could share their work and experience; the founding of the Taipei Bible School (1952; it is now known as the Shin-Chu Bible College) to train ministers to cope with the fast growth of churches; and moving the Taiwan Theological College to suburban Taipei and developing it into a school accommodating 250 students (1954). Though suffering from brain cancer, Dickson managed to set up the Burning Bush Missionary Society (1967) to evangelize aborigines both in and outside the island.

After his bachelor of theology studies at Princeton Seminary, Dickson and his wife, Lillian Ruth Le Vesconte, founder of the Mustard Seed Society in Taiwan, were sent to Tamshui in north Taiwan (1927). Though principal of the Theological College (1931-40 and 1948-65; during World War II*, he was sent to British Guinea, 1940-45), Dickson was better known as a practical minister than a theologian. He served on various church committees and often went to the aboriginal people in the mountains on weekends, traveling for hours, even days, on foot. His many friends included President Chiang Kai-shek, the commander of the U.S. Military Assistance Advisory Group in Taiwan, and local gardeners.

Dickson's most satisfying accomplishments were the reestablishment of the Taiwan Theological College and the mission work among the aboriginal people, for which he was awarded honorary doctorates by Macalester College (1953), Knox College of Canada (1960), and Tokyo Union Seminary (1962).

Bibliography

Chai, Jin-Li, ed., *A Collection in Memory of Rev. James Ira Dickson* (1978). • Dickson, James Ira, *Stranger than Fiction* (1948).

Chen Chia-Shi

Didascalia Apostolorum

An important work of pastoral theology and moral admonition in the genre of church orders, the *Didascalia Apostolorum* provides a look at early Christian diversity by describing what was happening and setting out what should be done. It was written in Greek probably during the first half of the 3rd c. somewhere in Syria. Scattered Greek fragments still exist. The fullest text is in a 9th-11th-c. Syriac translation bearing the title "Catholic Teaching of the Twelve Apostles and Holy Disciples of Our Savior." This translation may have appeared as early as the 4th c. Codex Veronensis, which may also date from the 4th c., has about 40 percent of the Syriac text.

The *Didascalia* forms the basis of the later Ethiopic and Arabic *Didascalia* as well as the first six books of the Greek *Apostolic Constitutions,* written in the 4th c. It makes use of much Scripture, free quotations from Psalms, Proverbs, Isaiah, Jeremiah, and Ezekiel as well as Wisdom, Ecclesiasticus, Susanna, and perhaps Tobit. All four Gospels are employed: Matthew dominates but Luke is frequent. Phrases from 1 Timothy and Titus are evident as are similarities to passages from Romans, 1 and 2 Corinthians, Galatians, Ephesians, Philippians, and 1 and 2 Thessalonians, and insights from 1 and 2 Peter, James, 1 John, and probably Revelation. A reference to John 8:3-11 suggests that the author had read Papias or the Gospel of the Hebrews or that he had a text of

John that included the account of the adulteress who was about to be stoned. The author also uses the Sibylline Oracles, the Ignatian Epistles, Hermas, and Barnabas and possibly knows 1 and 2 Clement and Polycarp. Knowledge of the writings of Justin Martyr and particularly Irenaeus suggests that the document could not be much earlier than the beginning of the 3rd c.

The *Didascalia* treats issues raised in the *Didache* about church life and seems to have been written for a group of converts from paganism who were deeply concerned with how Christians should deal with pagan culture and Jewish customs. The writer purports to be Matthew spelling out the results of a conference of the Twelve held in Jerusalem.

Although the *Didascalia* does not offer much specifically doctrinal information, it does appear to be orthodox in ways that the Arian *Apostolic Constitutions* are not. In to the Syriac translation, the readers are six times reminded to worship Father, Son, and Holy Spirit; one of those times the bishop is said to be like the Father, the deacon like the Son, and the deaconess like the Holy Spirit. Where there are parallels, the author of the *Apostolic Constitutions* has worked the confessions into Arian form.

The *Didascalia*'s author does not develop Christology very far. The law of God spelled out in the Old Testament and the teachings of Jesus, which all Christians should follow, are contrasted with the Jewish "second legislation," which is not binding on Christians. Both husbands and wives should avoid finery and bathing with the opposite sex. The husband should cherish his wife and the wife obey her husband.

Every congregation should be led by a bishop, a blameless man of at least 50 years of age. He exercises judgments over the presbyters and the congregation, exhorting them to good life. He has supreme authority to rebuke and to forgive sin. Avoiding too much wine, food, and fancy clothing, his living, like that of the Levitical priesthood, will come from church revenues. In charge of those revenues, he will distribute them justly, particularly to poor widows. He will give judgments in various cases on the second day of the week so that any ill feelings may dissipate by the next Sunday. Presbyters and deacons will always be present at such sessions. Both parties in the dispute must hear all testimony and argument. Serious violations of the law result in being cast out of the church and glory; thus good judgment and mercy are in order.

Presbyters may receive a portion twice that of deacons. Deacons should be the eyes and ears of the bishops. The church building is to be built east to west. Presbyters and the bishop on a throne occupy the eastern end, then laymen, then laywomen. Children stand on one side in a group or with their parents. Special sections allow young women with children to stand and old women to sit. One deacon will stand by the eucharistic oblation, another at the door to see that people go to their proper places. All the deacons will help in serving the Eucharist.

Visiting presbyters from other churches should sit with the presbyters; a visiting bishop should sit with the bishop and be asked to speak. After the service starts, it should not be interrupted to seat a dignitary, but even the bishop should sit on the ground to offer a seat to someone destitute who comes late.

The order of widows includes those over age 50 who will not seek a second marriage. Young widows may be assisted and should be encouraged to marry, but only a second time. The clear commands for women not to teach or baptize, for widows to stay at home and pray, give evidence that in some groups, perhaps Jewish Christians, Montanists, or a different community of the orthodox, women did teach and baptize. Deaconesses are needed to visit houses where a deacon should not go. At the baptism of women, only deaconesses may anoint their whole bodies with oil. If no deaconess is available, only the heads of the women should be anointed.

Orphaned children should be adopted, first by the childless. A girl might be adopted as a wife for a son. Adopted boys are to be taught a craft and paid accordingly. All children should be given skills to avoid indolence.

Christians condemned to death as martyrs should be remembered by the congregation. The resurrection is every Christian's hope. Fasting in preparation for the Pascha is fitting for all Christians, but not on Sunday. Sustenance is gained through bread, salt, and water.

Schismatics condemn themselves to fire. Heresies began with Simon Magus. Like the apostles, so the church should cast out those who persist in such errors, but forgive those who repent. But there is no forgiveness of sins committed after baptism.

Bibliography

Connolly, R. H., *Didascalia Apostolorum: The Syriac Version Translated and Accompanied by the Verona Latin Fragments* (1929). • Vööbus, A., *The Didascalia Apostolorum in Syriac,* I-II, Corpus scriptorum christianorum orientalium (1978), Vols. 401, 407 (text), and 402, 408 (tr.). • Hardin, J. M., *The Ethiopic Didascalia* (1920). • Bartlet, J. V., *Church-Life and Church-Order During the First Four Centuries with Special Reference to the Early Eastern Church-Orders* (1943). • Methuen, C., "Widows, Bishops and the Struggle for Authority in the *Didascalia Apostolorum,*" *Journal of Ecclesiastical History* 46 (1995).

FREDERICK W. NORRIS

Dili

Small village in Indonesia, once the capital of the former Portuguese colony of Timor*.

Evangelization was started on the island of Timor by the Dominican* friar Antonio Taviero, who is said to have baptized about 5,000 people around the year 1556. After the Dutch *Verenigde Oost-Indische Compagnie* (United East-India Company, VOC) occupied the ports of Lewomama on Solor Island (1636) and Kupang

(1653) in western Timor, the few Portuguese and many Catholic Timorese moved to Lifao (now Oikusi) in western Timor, which in 1762 became the center of the Timor mission and the seat of the bishop (or the administrator) of the diocese of Malacca, after that town had been conquered and occupied by the Dutch. Around 1769 Dili was chosen to be the colony's capital by a Portuguese governor who had to leave Lifao because the unruly Black-Portuguese felt they had been cheated by him.

The few and poor Dominican missionaries, mostly Goans from India*, did not work systematically, often meddled in local politics, and hardly spoke the languages of their flock. But some of them were diligent workers and shed their blood for their faith after being tortured by the Dutch or Muslim enemies of the Portuguese.

On eastern Timor, which always remained Portuguese territory, missionary activity was low and inhibited by liberal Portuguese colonial administrators. The Dominicans were evicted in 1834, and afterward only a few priests served the small stagnating Catholic community. From 1834 to 1940, East Timor was administrated by the bishop of Macau, who established the parochial system (1877) and sent a few priests and Canossian sisters (1879) to found schools. Jesuits* have helped in parish and educational work since 1900. Salesians* opened a technical school (1927) in Dili, and a minor seminary was established in Saibada (1936; since 1958, it has been run by Jesuits in Dare). In 1940, Dili became an independent diocese, whose population suffered much during Japanese occupation. Presently, there are 23 parishes with a total congregation of over 540,000 believers.

The incorporation of East Timor into Indonesia (1975) was followed by a long guerrilla war until 1993. This fighting caused heavy suffering, destruction, and antagonistic feelings. Evangelization was intensified with the help of religious men and women of different orders from Indonesia, and new schools of higher learning were established (e.g., for catechists, 1987). Pope John Paul II visited Dili in 1990. Even though C. F. Ximenes Belo and the Church of Dili play an active part in the life of the Indonesian Catholic Church, the diocese of Dili has not been incorporated into the Indonesian Bishops' Conference because political issues have not been settled at an international level. Harsh measures by military units against peaceful young demonstrators in 1991 (Santa Cruz Incident) caused a (temporary) setback in the practice of human rights, and the free elections of 1999 led to extensive violence, migration, and the necessity of international peacekeepers.

Bibliography

Teixeria, M., *The Portuguese Missions in Malacca and Singapore (1511-1958),* Vol. II (1963). • Muskens, M. P. M., ed., *Sejarah Gereja Katolik Indonesia,* Vol. IIIb (1974). • Loedding, W. J., *Die schwarz-weibe Legion* (1974).

ADOLF HEUKEN

Din, U Khin Maung

(b. Thaton, Myanmar, 5 Jul 1931; d. Boston, Massachusetts, United States, 10 Sep 1987). Professor, lay church leader, and composer in Myanmar*.

U Khin Maung Din was a respected academic who was popular among students and youth in general. He may be described as a true successor of his mentor, U Hla Bu, both in the university and in the church. The second of the three children of U Tha U Khin Maung Din and Daw Thein Nyunt, U Khin Maung Din was baptized when he was 11 at the First Baptist Church in Moulmein by Ah Shoo. He matriculated at Morton Lane Judson High School in Moulmein in 1947. He graduated with a bachelor of arts degree in 1953, served as a philosophy tutor in Moulmein College, and in four years secured a master of arts degree in philosophy with first-class honors. He married Daw San San Swe on 7 Aug 1958. They had two sons and an adopted niece.

From 1958 to 1960, U Khin Maung Din was the full-time general secretary of the National Student Christian Movement* of Burma. He attended the general assembly of the World Student Christian Federation at Strasbourg, France. The university invited him back to the philosophy department at its main campus in Yangon, and by 1981 he had become the head of that department. Later in the same year, he was promoted to professor and remained so until his death in 1987.

U Khin Maung Din was active in the Student Christian Movement, the Baptist* church, the Myanmar Council of Churches, and the Myanmar Institute of Christian Theology. He led seminars, presented papers, and deliberated ecumenical issues. He helped the study commission of the Myanmar Council of Churches to formulate a response to the statements of the World Council of Churches on "Baptism, Eucharist and Ministry" and "Education for Ecumenism." He also composed popular hymns and wrote plays on Christian themes, inspiring both young and old. Examples of his work are the song *Hlaung ein de hmar* (The Bloodstained Dove in the Cage) and the play *Metta maingan* (The Country of Love), which focused on the theme of overcoming evil with love. U Khin Maung Din died while on a government study tour in the United States.

Bibliography

The Burman Messenger (Oct/Nov 1987; Jan 1988).

KYAW NYUNT

Din, U Tha

(b. Laung-gyi, Burma, 24 Sep 1871; d. Yangon, 23 Dec 1955). Buddhist convert who became a renowned Christian evangelist, scholar, and theological educator in Myanmar*.

The son of U Tha Maung and Daw Hnin Khaing, U Tha Din converted from Buddhism and was baptized in 1892. He graduated from the Burmese Baptist Seminary two years later and eventually served as its principal for

43 years until his retirement in 1940. He was referred to as Prome Tha U Tha Din to distinguish him from his well-known namesake and contemporary, Mandalay Tha U Tha Din. He traveled widely, even as a student, to proclaim the Gospel, especially to Buddhists, who reacted with hostility. He pioneered the Myanmar Baptist Churches Union, with his namesake as chief evangelist, and also the Myanmar Ministers Association to promote unity and cooperation.

Two of his many books are still used as references today: *Boddhaw-wada thin kaypa kyan* (Comparative Study of Buddhist and Christian Scriptures) and *Kyanoke ee ko-dwe* (Short Evangelistic Sermons). Some of his blunt apologetics against Buddhism* were proscribed by the colonial government to avoid interreligious tensions. On 22 Mar 1954, he was awarded an honorary D.D. degree by St. Andrews University College, London. He and his wife, Daw Khin Lay, raised four distinguished children: U Hla Bu, the eldest, was an educator; the second, Sein Maung, a medical doctor and director of Burma Pharmaceutical Industries; U Khin Maung, a court prosecution officer; and the youngest, daughter Daw Mya Su, married the chief engineer of Burma Railways. U Tha Din's devotion, literary knowledge, and sanctified life made him a unique leader for the churches in Myanmar.

Bibliography

U Tha Din, *My Life* (in Burmese) (1956).

KYAW NYUNT

Ding Guangxun

(Bishop K. H. Ting) (b. Shanghai, 1915). Chinese Anglican* bishop and theologian; former president of Nanjing Union Theological Seminary.

The son of a banker and the grandson of an Anglican priest, Ding received his bachelor's degree from St. John's University, Shanghai, in 1937; his bachelor of divinity degree in 1942; and his master's degree from Union Theological Seminary, New York, in 1948. He was ordained a priest in 1942 and became the bishop of Zhejiang Diocese in 1955.

In Shanghai, Ding served as a student secretary of the Young Men's Christian Association* (YMCA), a curate of the Church of Our Savior, and a pastor to the International Church during the Japanese occupation. In the 1940s, he was student secretary of the Student Christian Movement* of Canada. He also served the World Student Christian Federation in Geneva. He returned to China* in 1951 and became general secretary of the Christian Literature Society in Shanghai. In 1952, he became principal of Nanjing Union Theological Seminary (NUTS). In 1954, he was elected to the Three-Self Patriotic Movement* committee.

A widely traveled man, Bishop Ding was a delegate to the Chinese People's Consultative Conference (1959) and the National People's Congress (1964). During the Cultural Revolution, Bishop Ding was kept under close surveillance by the Red Guards. He and his family were evacuated from their home and resettled in simple quarters. Toward the end of the Cultural Revolution, Bishop Ding and some faculty members of NUTS did some translation work, including the minutes of the United Nations into Chinese. They also compiled a Chinese-English dictionary.

In 1979, Bishop Ding attended the Third World Conference of Religion and Peace in Princeton, New Jersey. In 1981, NUTS was reopened. Bishop Ding was elected chairman of the Chinese Christian Three-Self Patriotic Movement and president of the China Christian Council*. In 1985, he became president of the Amity* Foundation. Bishop Ding was a moving force in the publication of the *Chinese Theological Review,* first issued in 1985. The tenth issue (1995) was a tribute to his eightieth birthday.

Ding's wife, Kuo Siu-may, was also a graduate of St. John's University and earned a master's degree from Columbia University, New York. She was professor of English language at Nanjing University and vice-chairperson of the Jiangsu Women's Federation. She published two books to introduce the Bible to students of English literature. She died in Nanjing in September 1995 at the age of 79.

Bibliography

Wickeri, Janice, ed., *Chinese Theological Review* 10 (1995).

CHINA GROUP

Ding Limei

(Ting Li-Mei) (b. Shandong, 1871; d. 1936). Chinese pioneer in student work.

Ding studied at the Wen Huiguan, the predecessor of Quilu University, in 1883. He finished school in 1894 and taught at the Weihsien Christian Grade School. Together with another preacher, he founded the Wen Nu Zhong (Wenmei Girls' High School) in Shandong. In 1895, he returned to the Wen Huiguan to study theology. In 1898, he took up a pastoral position and began to preach in different parts of Shandong. He suffered for his faith during the Boxer Uprising in 1900-1901.

In 1909, Ding was at the helm of a strong religious revival at Shandong Union College, inspiring more than 100 young men to enter the Christian ministry. He was then invited to institutions in Tianjin, Tungchow, and Beijing, where he inspired over 200 others to enter the ministry. The Student Volunteer Movement, initiated by the Young Men's Christian Association* (YMCA), was formed in Jun 1910 with the motto, "The evangelization of our mother country and the world in this generation." Ding was appointed its first traveling secretary. Ding served the movement for 20 years, traveling all over China, meeting with and encouraging students in Christian schools, colleges, and universities.

Ding spent one year doing evangelistic work in

Yunnan with the China Inland Evangelistic Society and taught at a Bible college in Shandong in 1923. He also founded a Bible college in Tianjin in 1932, serving as its assistant dean until his death.

Bibliography

Latourette, Kenneth Scott, *A History of Christian Missions in China* (1929).

CHINA GROUP

Diokno, José W.

(b. Batangas, 26 Feb 1922; d. Manila, 27 Feb 1987). Filipino patriot, nationalist, defender of human rights, and peace advocate.

Popularly known as Ka Pepe, Diokno exemplified intellectual brilliance and personal integrity in both his government service as a senator and in his personal life. He consistently upheld the rights of the poor and the needy. In 1961, he opted to resign as secretary of justice rather than participate in a travesty of justice in a celebrated case involving high officials. Later, acting on the dictates of his conscience, he resigned from the ruling Nacionalista Party to defend victims of human-rights violations. In his last days, he served as chief peace negotiator for the government of President Corazon Aquino with the National Democratic Front on the issues of food, freedom, jobs, and justice. Ka Pepe and the church shared common views on human rights, justice, and peace.

Bibliography

José W. Diokno Foundation, Inc., *Files on Notes and Newsclippings, 1971-1987.* • Saguisag, Rene A. V., *Six Modern Filipino Heroes* (1993).

TEODORO MAXIMILIANO M. DE MESA

Disabled and Christianity

(Shogaisha to Kirisuto-Kyo). Disabled persons make appearances in both the Old and New Testaments. In the same manner, disabled persons have been evident from the beginning of the history of Christianity in Japan*, even if limited to Protestant history. For example, Samuel Robbins Brown, a missionary who came to Japan in 1859, is known for his work as the first person to educate people with a hearing disability. In 1873, soon after the prohibition of Christianity was lifted, a school for those with sight and speaking disabilities was opened in Tsukiji, Tokyo, by a group of believers, including missionaries. This pattern of mission tied to education was a special characteristic of the relationship between Christianity and the disabled before the war. From a charitable standpoint, they were pitied and seen as persons who needed to be saved.

The democratization of Japan after World War II* brought a change in the way of looking at human character. This was true also for Christians. They no longer viewed the disabled as always being recipients, but also as givers. The disabled are now taking part in the mission of the church. This is the basis for the founding of such organizations as the Japan Christian Mission Society for the Visually Impaired and the Mission Support Group for Physically and Mentally Disabled Christians. The National Council of Churches has a similar perspective on the relation between the disabled and the church. The International Year of the Disabled (1981) served to elevate consciousness of the realities of disability. This raised awareness should lead the church with Christ as its head to see the disabled as indispensable members of the body instead of merely individuals who need to be saved.

SHIMAZAKI MITSUMASA, JAPANESE DICTIONARY

Ditt

In 1873 Nattu, a young Hindu convert of the Jat caste, witnessed to an acquaintance named Ditt, a member of the despised Chuhra caste and a farmer. He was "a dark little man, lame of one leg, quiet and modest in his manner, with sincerity and earnestness well expressed in his face, and at that time about 30 years of age," according to Andrew Gordon, a missionary at that time. Once convinced that God's message was for outcastes, he gave his heart to Christ and asked to be baptized. Although quick baptism was not the policy, he was baptized and returned home, where he was ostracized by relatives. He bore the social pressure and steadily witnessed to relatives. Two months later he again walked the 30 miles to the mission, this time with four converts, including his wife, daughter, and two neighbors. Gradually he made converts of more relatives and friends.

From this beginning he became a valued evangelist. He never asked for support from the mission but undertook many long journeys on foot for the love of his good work. In the end he spent all of his time doing evangelism, and so was given a modest sum by which to support himself. From his humble beginnings, an early "people movement" began in southeast Uttar Pradesh. The rural evangelists like Ditt were selected for their spiritual insight, natural leadership ability, and willingness to serve. Ditt was among those who never mastered the art of reading but acquired some knowledge of the Bible*, basic doctrines, and the ability to transmit these to their people. He was one of the group of rural evangelists who laid the foundation upon which the church in Pakistan grew.

Bibliography

Gordon, Andrew, *Our India Mission* (1886). • *Reports of the Schemes of the Church of Scotland, 1875.*

JEAN S. STONER

Dodd, William Clifton

(b. Marion, Iowa, United States, 15 Oct 1857; d. Yunnan, China, 18 Oct 1919). Missionary evangelist of the Presbyterian Church USA and explorer who played a key role in the expansion of Protestant missions from northern Thailand* into southern China*.

Dodd graduated from Parsons College in 1883 and McCormick Theological Seminary in 1886. He arrived in Chiang Mai to work under the Laos Mission in 1886. He married Isabella Eakin in 1889. Dodd founded the mission's training school for evangelists in 1889, and in 1891 the Dodds established the Lamphun Station near Chiang Mai. In 1897, they helped found the Chiang Rai Station, and in 1904 they pioneered the first Laos Mission station outside of Thailand, that at Kengtung, Burma. The latter closed in 1907, and the Dodds returned to Chiang Rai.

An ardent advocate of mission expansion, Dodd took a number of significant exploratory trips into eastern Burma and southern China. He produced a massive literature of reports and correspondence advocating the expansion of Presbyterian* mission to reach all of the ethnic Tai peoples. Dodds' long journey from Chiang Rai through southern China to Canton in 1910 generated considerable interest in Tai missions and led to the Dodds' founding of the Laos Mission's Chiangrung (Kiulungkiang) Station in Yunnan, China, in 1917. Dodd died there on 18 Oct 1919. He was one of the first ethnologists of the Tai race and accumulated an impressive array of data on the extent, numbers, and culture of the Tai.

Bibliography

Dodd, William Clifton, *The Tai Race* (1923). • McFarland, George Bradley, ed., *Historical Sketch of Protestant Missions in Siam, 1828-1928* (1928). • Swanson, Herbert R., "The Kengtung Question: Presbyterian Mission and Comity in Eastern Burma, 1896-1913," *Journal of Presbyterian History,* Vol. 60, No. 1 (Spring 1982). • *Krischak Muang Nua* (1984). HERBERT R. SWANSON

Dominicans

(Order of Preachers: OP). The name "Dominicans" refers to a large family of friars (6,600), cloistered nuns (4,400), sisters in apostolic congregations (36,000), and laity (70,000 plus), all of whom consider St. Dominic (1172-1221) to be their founder and inspiration.

The early 13th c. was a time of profound cultural transition in Europe from a feudal to a centralized form of government, from rural to urban economic structures, and from monastic schools to urban universities. The Dominican order was founded in 1216 to counter the growth and preaching of the Manichaean Albigensian (Cathari) sects in southern France, but the focus soon expanded beyond the local area. Response to changing needs resulted in a new form of religious life more flexible and more mobile than established monasticism.

The Dominican Order has had, from the beginning, a number of unique characteristics. It is the only religious order whose explicit mission is preaching and whose mandate is universal, thus making it the first truly missionary order. The common life, prayer, and study are all ordered to preaching and take their justification from it; commitment to lifelong study is written into the legislation of the order. The friars make a single vow of obedience to the master of the order, who, as every friar, is himself governed by constitutions which establish a system of democratic government from the local to the international level, providing a balance of power between membership and elected leadership.

Well-known members of the order include St. Thomas Aquinas, Albert the Great, Fra Angelico, Meister Eckhart, Catherine of Siena, Bartolomeo de las Casas, and in recent times M.-J. Chenu, Yves Congar, and E. Schillebeeckx. Today the order of friars is divided into 42 provinces, three vice provinces, and four general vicariates. In the 12 Asian entities, there are 590 friars, 135 nuns, and 3,500 sisters in apostolic congregations.

St. Dominic himself longed to preach to the Cumans in the east, the Moors in his homeland, and the pagans of the north. Eight years after his death, Dominicans were in the Holy Land. By 1300 a congregation of pilgrim friars was founded to work in eastern Europe and Asia. In 1250 a school for Arabic studies was opened at Tunis. Other schools for oriental languages were founded at Barcelona, Valencia, and Murcia. In 1233 the order was established in Constantinople, which became the base for movement to the east. French and Italian Dominicans were in the Near East; French friars were in the majority in 13th-c. Palestine; and Italians were in the forefront in 14th-c. Mesopotamia and Persia. During a 12-year stay in Mesopotamia, Ricoldo of Montecroce preached and debated with Nestorians*, Jews, and Arabs in Mosul and Baghdad, where he met other Dominicans in 1289.

Dominican contact with the Tatars was extended by the plans of Pope Innocent IV. In an attempt to contain the Muslims, the pope inaugurated a plan for an alliance with the Tatars in Asia and their conversion. In 1245 he sent four embassies, two of them Dominican, to the Tatars in southern and central Asia. The Dominican groups contacted Tatar generals in Mesopotamia. Simon of St. Quentin described the experiences in one of the groups. It is incorporated into the *Speculum Maius* of Vincent of Beauvais. Andrew of Longjumeau, the head of one of the groups, even reached the court at Karakorum. The pope's plans came to nothing, and at least one of Innocent's embassies lacked diplomatic finesse when it made demands on the Tatar general as though he were a papal subject. The Dominican emissaries were lucky to escape with their lives. The anger soon died down, and the lengthy stay of the friars among them ended on a happier note. Returning from China, the Franciscan* William Rubruk* met two contingents of Dominicans in 1254 as they were seeking to enter the Tatar dominions. In 1274 two Dominicans made their appearance, possibly as translators, in the company of a Tatar embassy to the Council of Lyons. In the 15th c., the Dominican archbishop in eastern Armenia, John of Sultania, knew Tamerlane, the Khan of the Tatars, and led an embassy to Europe for him.

The Indian subcontinent. The first known Dominican in the subcontinent is Nicholas of Pistoia, who arrived in 1291. With a Franciscan companion, John of Monte Corvino*, he set out for China, touching land at Mylapore in southern India*, where he died a year later. In 1321 Jordan of Severac came to India from Tabriz in Persia with four Franciscan companions. They met martyrdom early, leaving Jordan alone, until he was joined by four other companions in 1323. Others followed and enjoyed great success. In 1323, in his letter to the Franciscan and Dominican communities in Persia appealing for volunteers, Jordan claimed conversions exceeding 10,000. In 1328 Jordan visited Avignon, where Pope John XXII acceded to his request to set up an independent ecclesiastical jurisdiction in India so as to serve in a better manner the Christian communities he had established along the west coast of India and to respond to the needs of the people who seemed ready to receive the Gospel message. Jordan was named bishop of Quilon. Five of his companions were martyred, and in 1330 he himself met a martyr's death.

Portuguese Dominicans arrived in the 16th c., more as chaplains to the Portuguese than as missionaries, but by 1630 there were 70 houses and 320 friars in India, a territory comprising Sri Lanka*, Burma (Myanmar*), Thailand*, Cambodia*, and Indonesia*. The enterprise died out in the 19th c., but the 20th c. saw a revival of Dominican presence in India with the arrival of friars from Ireland in 1959 and the establishment of an independent vice province in 1988 with over 60 friars. Friars staff the major seminary in Nagpur, are involved in pastoral ministry, retreats, spiritual direction, and youth ministry, and publish two English periodicals and a newsletter for the Dominican family.

In 1931 the Italian friars came to work in the diocese of Lahore (now Pakistan*). In 1939 the diocese of Multan was erected, with Benedict Cialeo as its first bishop. In 1956 American friars from New York arrived, and in 1960 the diocese was divided into Multan and Faisalabad. In 1966 the first group of young men from Pakistan entered the order. In 1973 the first friars were ordained, and the independent vice province of Pakistan, erected in 1982, now has 40 friars. Pakistani friars are involved in teaching philosophy and theology in the seminaries in Karachi and Lahore, in formation of laity at the Pastoral Institute in Multan, in writing and publishing an English periodical and a newsletter for Dominicans, and in urban/rural pastoral ministry and are active in interreligious dialogue* and promotion of justice and peace.

East Asia. There were Portuguese friars in Siam (Thailand*) and in East Timor* in 1561, but an organized presence in the region began only with the arrival of the first band of Spanish friars in the Philippines* in 1579. They were Bishop Domingo de Salazar*, appointed first bishop of Manila, and Fray Cristobal de Salvatierra. However, it was on 21 Jul 1587 that the founding fathers of the Religious Province of the Most Holy Rosary of the Philippines arrived in Cavite. Of these, five stayed in Manila, which was later called the Santo Domingo Convent. Four left for Bataan, and the remaining six took the trail to Pangasinan. The missions that the Dominicans established were Baybay, Binondo, and the Parian, located near Manila for the Chinese; almost all the province of Bataan; the province of Pangasinan; some towns in north Tariac; the entire Cagayan Valley, i.e., the present provinces of Cagayan, Isabela, and Nueva Visaya, including the slopes of Central Cordillera and the western side of the Sierra Madre mountain range, and the Babuyan Islands, with interruptions from 1619 on; and the Batan Islands, a permanent mission since 1783. The early Dominicans' lasting contribution, however, can be found in the field of education, with the establishment of the University of Santo Tomas (founded in 1611) and the Colegio de San Juan de Letran (founded in 1620).

The Philippine Dominican Province was established on 8 Dec 1971, 384 years after the arrival of the first Dominican missionaries on the islands. The nationalistic movement (see Nationalism) of the 20th c., oftentimes expressed in mass demonstrations by students, was one of the factors that influenced its emergence. Ultimately inspired by the urging of Vatican Council II to obey the doctrine of missiology and to discern the signs of the times, the province was formally born in Santo Domingo Convent, Quezon City.

Since its establishment, the indigenous province has gained its own personal identity within the Philippine church hierarchy. The main areas of its concern are clearly set forth in Fundamental Statute 4, Statute 28, of the Dominican Province of the Philippines. Its priorities are stated as follows: (1) evangelization principally through education and media apostolate; (2) higher theological reflection applied to the religious, cultural, social, economic, business, labor, political, technological, and scientific situations of the Philippines in Asia; (3) justice and peace; and (4) mission.

From Manila friars went to China. After the arrival of the Franciscans, Spanish Dominican missionaries Angel Cocchi and Juan Baptista de Morales arrived at Fuan in Fujian in 1632 and 1633 respectively. In 1707 Rome designated Fujian as a missionary territory for the Dominicans, who continued to enter China stealthily, even after a ban on foreign religion by Emperor Yongzheng in 1724. Some of them were discovered and suffered severe punishment. After the Opium* Wars, five coastal cities were opened, including Fuzhou and Xiamen.

The Dominicans resumed their missionary effort and in 1883 established two prefectures apostolic, one in Fuzhou and the other in Xiamen. The Dominican Sisters of the Roman Congregation of St. Dominic arrived in Fuzhou in 1889. Between 1913 and 1938 Fuzhou was subdivided into the Funing apostolic prefecture, with three subprefectures: Tingzhou, Jian-ou, and Shawu. Funing was entrusted to the Spanish Dominicans, and the others either to the Germans or Americans, with the exception of Shawu, which came under the Salvatorians (of German origin). In 1946 Pope Pius XII granted the traditional hierarchy to the region. Fujian Xiamen, Funing, and Tingzhou became dioceses with their own bishops, and Fuzhou with a Dominican archbishop.

The names of the first two missionaries who came to Siam (Thailand) were Jéronimo da Cruz and Sebastião da Canto, both Dominicans. They were sent to Siam by their superior, Fernando di Santa Maria, who was also the general vicar at Malacca*. From a letter of di Santa Maria addressed to the General of the Order, Fr. Vincente Justiano and dated 26 Dec 1569, we know that the two missionaries made a two-month journey and arrived at Ayutthaya in 1567. The letter also tells us about the activity of the two missionaries, the subsequent fate of one of them, and the situation of Siam at that time. In the book *Historia Fratrum Praedicatorum*, we find confirmation of the date of the letter. According to the letter, di Santa Maria told the general that the two missionaries were given a befitting residence in one of the best locations in the city. They learned the Siamese language in a very short time and were then able to converse and have social contact with the people. Many local people came to visit them, some women, and also some Buddhist monks.

But the Muslims, the enemies of the Christians and the Portuguese, were jealous and feared that their influence was waning. They could not openly attack the missionaries, who were well respected and well loved, for then they would risk trouble from the Siamese authorities. But finally the Muslims killed Jéronimo by piercing him with a lance, and Sebastião was severely wounded by rioters throwing stones. Sebastião asked the king not to punish the killers because he desired no more bloodshed. The king admired him and showed even greater affection and friendship for the friar.

Sebastião also asked the king for permission to go to Malacca to request and return with more missionaries. Two other priests were given for this task of evangelization, but their names are unknown to us. When the missionaries returned to Ayutthaya, they began to preach the Gospel openly, as before. First they worked among their own countrymen, the Portuguese, and then among the Siamese. In spite of the goodwill and interest shown by the people and despite the many conversations about the religion, which were organized by the missionaries, few people would embrace the Christian faith without the permission of the king.

During the war with Burma (Myanmar*) in 1569, which was to culminate in the fall of Ayutthaya, the Burmese found three missionaries praying in the church and beheaded them on 11 Feb 1569 because they had preached the Gospel in Siam. So the pioneer missionaries were murdered in 1569. Later the same thing happened to Frs. Mota and Fonseca. Finally, Francisco da Annunciçao succeeded in establishing himself from 1601 to 1619, and their mission continued, with some interruptions, until 1783. At present there are no Dominicans working in Thailand.

Dominicans endured bitter persecution in East Asia in the 18th and 19th cs., giving the church large groups of martyrs. Its missionaries were persecuted in Japan* during the 17th c. and in China from 1745 to 1748 and during 1837 and 1838. Members of the province now number almost 350; they are found in the Philippines, Taiwan, Japan, Hong Kong*, and Korea. From the territory of the province, the province of Vietnam* was erected in 1967 and that of the Philippines in 1971. In 1978 Taiwan became a vicariate general. There are also two provincial vicariates belonging to the province of the Holy Rosary and to the German province, with a combined membership of 35. In Japan the 70 friars belong to either the vicariate of Holy Rosary province or that of the Canadian province. These have been joined in recent years by volunteers from the province of Poland.

Indochina. The order has been present in what is now Vietnam since Gaspard de Santa Cruz landed on Ha Tien in 1550. He was followed by two other Portuguese friars who in 1558 went to Annam, where they worked for 10 years before being expelled. The beginning of an organized and continuous activity dates from much later, in 1676, when friars were entrusted with a district in the northeast. In 1693 Raimondo Lezzoli, an Italian friar, was appointed vicar apostolic. In these 300 years 240 Spanish missionaries were sent to Vietnam to expand and consolidate the mission.

The history of the order in Vietnam coincides with the history of persecutions against Christians. The first edict of persecution, promulgated in 1711, meant that friars had to exercise a clandestine ministry. Jacinto Castanedo and Mateo Alonso Liciniana were the first Dominican martyrs, whose number increased in the 19th c. Of the 117 Vietnamese martyrs canonized by John Paul II on 19 Jun 1988, 60 were Dominicans.

With the division of the country in 1954 (see Vietnam War), most of the Vietnamese friars moved south, while the Spanish and French friars either left or were expelled. Despite the war ravaging the country in the 1960s, the independent province of Vietnam was established in 1967. The dream of development was shortlived with the fall of Saigon on 30 Apr 1975. Most of the brothers remained, but some escaped with the "boat people," forming part of the diaspora, especially in the provincial vicariate in Calgary, Canada. With the fall of Communism* in Europe, a certain openness has been introduced into Vietnam, but many restrictions on entry into the order and ordination to the priesthood are still in place. The province now has 129 friars.

The Dominican family. Historically, one of the major strengths of the Dominican Order has been the sense of belonging to one family. In Asia-Pacific, this is witnessed to by the presence of brothers and sisters in almost every country where there is a Dominican presence. Where this is not the case — as in many general chapters of the friars state — there is something missing in the Dominican presence.

There are one or two monasteries of contemplative

nuns in Pakistan, Korea, Taiwan, and the Philippines and four in Japan. In India there are five congregations of sisters, the earliest from 1956 and the most recent in 1994, with a total of about 200 sisters. In Pakistan four congregations of sisters, the earliest from 1934, number over 160. In Vietnam there are five local congregations with numbers exceeding 1,000, in addition to 243 associations of lay Dominicans that number in the tens of thousands. Several young Indonesian men have trained to become friars. The order is represented there by three groups of sisters in Java and East Timor. The largest congregation is entirely Indonesian, with over 100 sisters. In Sri Lanka* two congregations of sisters represent the order. The oldest presence of sisters is found in the Philippines, one of the largest congregations having been founded in 1696 in Manila. There are 16 congregations in all, with over 900 sisters. These Filipina sisters have long been in mission and are to be found in the region in Australia, Guam, Korea, and Taiwan. Pakistani sisters are found in missions in Nigeria, Uganda, and Brazil. There are also sisters from 13 other congregations that are Spanish, Filipina, and Maltese in origin.

The ministry of the sisters is varied: teaching, technical education, health care, care and education of the handicapped, pastoral ministry especially to women, economic empowerment of women, ministry to aboriginals and Dalits*, street children and migrants, involvement in justice issues and interreligious dialogue*, and theological education* and reflection on women (see Women's Movements).

There is regional cooperation among the family in the biennial meetings of the leadership, in frequent meetings of those responsible for forming young Dominican women and men, and in the meetings of promoters of local justice and peace. There is also a center in Manila for men and women teachers. There are signs of growth in the Philippines, India, and Pakistan and in the new foundations formed in Korea. Friars will return to Indonesia, and there are hopes of returning to Thailand, where Dominicans were the first priests. The maturity of the region is seen in the many Filipina and several Pakistani sisters in mission and in the commitment of the friars of Pakistan to reestablishing a presence in Iran.

Bibliography

Williams, R. B., "Dominicans," *The Modern Catholic Encyclopedia* (1994). • Hinnebusch, William A., *The Dominicans, A Short History* (1975). • *Jordan of Severac OP*, ed. by Peter B. Lobo, *Miribilia Descripta* (1993). • *Catalogus Generalis Ordinis Preadicatorum* (1992). • Ashley, Benedict M., *The Dominicans* (1990). • Byrne, Damian, Felicisimo Martinez, and Simon Roche, ed. by Fausto Gomez, *The Dominican Mission Here and Now* (1988).

Chrys McVey, with the China Group (China; translated by Dufresse Chang) and Surachai Chumsriphan (Siam)

Domus Dei. *See* Indigenous Religious Congregations

Dong Bing Seng

(b. 1868; d. 1961). One of the first three Asians to be ordained an Anglican* priest in the diocese of Singapore*.

Because of the lack of dialect-speaking workers, in Jul 1910 Dong was engaged by the St. Andrew's Mission from Foochow, Fukien, China*, to go to Singapore to work among the Foochow-speaking community. He was ordained a deacon in 1916 and a priest in 1918. He took charge of the Foochow service at St. Peter's Church, which stood on the site of the present National Library at Stamford Road. In 1936, he was seconded to Penang to pastor the Hokkien-speaking parish of St. Paul's Church.

Bibliography

Sng, Bobby E. K., *In His Good Time* (1993).

John Chew

Doraisamy, Michael Robert

(b. Madurai, India, 17 Aug 1886; d. Singapore, 26 Sep 1933). Methodist pastor and educator in Singapore* and Malaya from 1912 to 1933.

Emigrating to Singapore in 1912, Doraisamy taught at the Anglo-Chinese School. A confrontation with the person of Christ convinced him to seek ordination. His first appointment, to the Singapore Tamil Church, was characterized by strict personal discipline, including early morning devotions, lyrical singing, and prayer with indigent church members who boarded with him.

Doraisamy was posted to Teluk Anson, Perak, Malaya, from 1924 to 1929 as head of the Anglo-Chinese School (ACS) and pastor of the Tamil congregation. His most innovative and fruitful ministry took place here, as he became convinced that the Methodist* schools were "indispensable for evangelistic work."

Doraisamy's third appointment was to Seremban, Negri Sembilan, Malaya (1929-31), where he served as vice-head of the ACS and pastor of the Tamil church. He enjoyed a happy and fruitful ministry, characterized by his introduction of lyric singing into his preaching and lantern-slide presentations. He drew large and appreciative Tamil audiences wherever he preached and was responsible for the conversion of many, as well as a revival in the life of the local church.

Doraisamy's final appointment saw him return to Singapore's Tamil church and the ACS, where he served until his death in 1933. His eldest son, Theodore, served as bishop of the Methodist Church in Singapore and Malaysia from 1973 to 1976.

Keeping his hands full, Doraisamy threw himself heart and soul into the work, scarcely letting up even in the face of deteriorating health.

Bibliography

Doraisamy, Theodore R., *Michael Robert Doraisamy: Called of Christ* (1989).

EARNEST LAU

Doubling Movement

(*Poe-Ka-Untong*, PKU). An evangelical movement by the Presbyterian* Church in Taiwan* (PCT) in 1954 to double the number of churches and church members in 10 years.

In response to the theme of the 1954 World Council of Churches (WCC) assembly in Evanston, "Jesus, the Hope of the World," a paper titled "Ecumenical Studies: Evangelism in Formosa" was submitted to the south synod of Taiwan by then general secretary Hwang Wutong*. It pointed out that, during the previous 90 years, only .72 percent of the population in Taiwan was converted to Christianity. There were still 161 out of 324 villages that had no church. The statistics prompted the 10-year Doubling Movement in the 13th session of the south synod, with the goal of doubling the number of churches and church members by 1965.

In the first year, 22 churches were founded in the south. Membership increased by 14,718 within two years. After the first two years, the executive office was shifted to the presbytery level, and each presbytery could decide its own mission policy.

The number of churches increased from 454 in 1954 to 864 in 1964, and the membership rose from 86,064 to 177,420. Villages without churches were reduced to 36. It was reported by the PKU secretary that by 1962 nearly 20 million Taiwanese dollars had been given toward the construction of churches, more than twice the amount budgeted in 1954.

The PCT founded two Bible schools, the Taipei Bible School (1952, now Presbyterian Bible College, PBC) and the Bible School Division of Tainan Theological College (1955, merged into PBC in 1964), in response to the increasing need for trained ministers. In 1959, the PCT sixth general assembly embarked on industrial evangelism, student work, and medical evangelism in the coastal areas and among mountain tribes in keeping with the changes brought about by industrialization and urbanization (see Urban Rural Mission).

Although PKU began with the south synod, it spread to the full PCT in 1959 and was eventually supported by most of the Protestant churches throughout the country. The Centenary Celebration of Protestant Christian Witness in Taiwan (1865-1965) was supported by 22 denominations and organizations in Taiwan. It was held on 16 Jun 1965 in Tainan, where the first church was founded in 1865 by the Presbyterian Church of England. PKU was followed by the five-year New Century Evangelical Movement, which emphasized the development of Christian education, student work, lay training, literature, and Christian witness in society rather than simply increasing numbers. Next came the Good Servant Movement (1971-75), the Independence and Cooperation Movement, the Ten Plus One Movement (1978-1985), and the second Ten Plus One Movement (1979-91). In 1991, the Year 2000 Gospel Movement began.

In spite of criticisms, the Doubling Movement marked a turning point in the church history of Taiwan. PKU was a grassroots movement in that the enthusiasm for church growth and propagation came from the local churches and lay leaders. The simplicity of its twin goals of doubling churches and church membership made the movement a success. It also stimulated the PCT, after 90 years of Westernization, to make a survey of the evangelistic needs in the country and respond to the situation. It eventually led to the publication of three statements: "Public Statement on Our National Fate" (1971), "Our Appeal" (1975), and "A Declaration on Human Rights" (1971). PKU was the first post–World War II* interdenominational evangelistic effort. The Taiwan Ecumenical Cooperative Committee (ECC), founded in the late 1960s, is now the National Churches Council in Taiwan (NCCT, 1991).

Bibliography

Lai, John Yung-hsiang, *Topics on Taiwan Church History* (1990). • Tong, Hollington K., *Christianity in Taiwan: A History* (1961). • Hwang, C. H., "P.K.U. and the Centenary Year in Formosa," *Theology in the Church* 5 (1965).

WU WUN-HSIONG

Douglas, Carstairs

(b. Reufreushie, England, 1829; d. Shanghai, Jul 1877). Scottish Presbyterian* missionary who worked with the English Presbyterian Mission in China*.

The son of a Scottish pastor, Douglas studied six years at the University of Glasgow, obtaining his master of arts and doctor of law degrees successively. In 1851, he began studies for the ministry at the Free Church Divinity School in Edinburgh and was recruited by William Burns, who was one of the pioneer English-speaking missionaries to work in China. A celibate, Douglas went to Xiamen, China, after his ordination in 1855. As a Scottish Presbyterian, Douglas worked under the Scottish Auxiliary of the English Presbyterian Mission, initially doing extensive linguistic studies. By 1873, he had produced the first Chinese-English dictionary in the Amoy dialect. In addition, he composed and edited hymns which were widely used in worship in the Amoy region.

On a return trip to the United Kingdom, Douglas stopped off in Taiwan* and, realizing the need for missionaries, convinced J. L. Maxwell to become the first English missionary to Taiwan. For his excellence in missionary work, Douglas was elected co-chair of the Shanghai Missionary Conference in May of 1877. Soon after the conference, in July, Douglas died in Shanghai of cholera. Douglas is remembered as one of the great pioneer missionary linguists in China and as an effective missionary pastor whose single congregation in Bai-chuan grew under his leadership to a regional presbytery of 25 congregations by the time of his death.

Bibliography

Anderson, Gerald, ed., *Biographical Dictionary of Christian Missions* (1998). • Band, Edward, *Working His Purpose Out* (1947). • Douglas, J. M., *Memorials of Revd Carstairs Douglas, MA, LLD* (1877).

CHINA GROUP, translated by SUN XING HONG

Drijarkara, Nikolaus

(b. Central Java, 1913; d. 1967). Founder of *Basis,* a cultural monthly magazine, and also known for his philosophical essays on *Pancasila**, the state philosophy of Indonesia.

Drijarkara studied at the Gregorian University in Rome. He became professor of philosophy at the state universities of Jakarta and Ujung Pandang and the Catholic University of St. Louis (United States). He served for several years as a member of the Peoples' Supreme Consultative Council (MPRS) and the Supreme Advisory Council (DPA) to the president. A philosophical academy (1969) in Jakarta which trains seminarians of different religious orders and dioceses in addition to students of other disciplines, is named after him.

Bibliography

Budi Susanto, A., ed., *Harta dan surga* (1990).

ADOLF HEUKEN

Dryburgh, Margaret

(b. Sunderland, England, 1890; d. Lakat, Sumatra, 21 Apr 1945). English Presbyterian* missionary teacher in Swatow and Singapore*.

Sent to China* by the Women's Missionary Association of the English Presbyterian Church, Dryburgh joined the Swatow mission in 1919. She was involved in teacher training and, after furlough in 1927, was appointed to Singapore to work among Teochow-speaking Chinese. With Alan Anderson, she recognized the need for the Chinese Presbyterian Church in Singapore to be involved in education. In 1937, she became principal of the Kuo Chuan Girls' School. After the Japanese invasion of Malaya, she remained in Singapore until evacuated on 11 Feb 1942. The ship on which she sailed was captured, and she was interned in Banka Island and later moved to Lakat, Sumatra, where she died.

Music was an important part of Dryburgh's life and ministry in schools and churches and as a prisoner. Fellow internees and former pupils remembered her faith, strength of character, astonishing memory for classical music scores, and gifts of leadership and organization. Her music for the women's vocal orchestra she organized with Norah Chambers, including her "Captives' Hymn," was recorded in 1995 from a handwritten score which survived the camps. Her experiences, and those of other Dutch and British women prisoners, are also recalled by the books *Women Beyond the Wire* and *Song of Survival,* as well as by the television series *Tenko* and the feature film *Paradise Road.*

Bibliography

Band, Edward, *Working His Purpose Out: The History of the English Presbyterian Mission, 1847-1947* (1948). • Colijn, Helen, *Song of Survival* (1995). • Warner, Lavinia, and John Sandilands, *Women Beyond the Wire* (1982). • Women's Choir of Haarlem, Holland, "Song of Survival," Mirasound CD 399216 (1995).

JOHN ROXBOROGH

Dudgeon, John

(b. 1837; d. Peking, China, 1901). Scottish medical* missionary to China* from Britain.

After earning his doctoral degree in medicine from Edinburgh University, Dudgeon was sent by the London Missionary Society to China in 1863 at the age of 26. The following year, he succeeded to the medical officer's post at the British embassy and also moved the clinic out of the embassy to accept outpatients. The clinic later became the first public Western hospital in Peking (Beijing) and was named Shuang Qi Gan Hospital (Double Flag-post Hospital). In 1870, Dudgeon was appointed Peking's customs medical officer. In 1871, he became the first pathology and medicine lecturer at Gung Wen Kuan ("School of Combined Learning").

Dudgeon contributed enormously to both Western and Chinese medical studies. He edited *Quan Ti Tong Kao, Xi Yi Ju Yu* (two volumes), and *Yi Xue Ci Hui* (Medical Dictionary; six volumes), and wrote books introducing Chinese medical studies to the West. These writings included *The Art of China's Diagnosis and Therapy; Illness in China: Its Beginnings, Conditions and Spreading, as Compared to Situations in Europe;* and a *Brief History of China and Russia in Politics and Religion.* Dudgeon was also involved in the anti-opium movement in Peking and stood against opium* trading. He was knighted in his old age.

CHINA GROUP

Duff, Alexander

(b. Moulin, Scotland, 1806; d. Scotland, 1878). First Scottish missionary to India* and a pioneer in Christian higher education and mission theology.

Born and brought up in Moulin, Duff studied at St. Andrew's University and was ordained a missionary by his church in 1829. In Calcutta in 1830, he started the first English-medium boys' school with five students under a banyan tree with the help of Hindu reformer Ram Mohun Roy*. He also set up an English-medium girls' school, a residence for Christian students, and a new mission station near Calcutta in 1834. He persuaded Lord William Bentinck that education in India should be in English rather than Sanskrit or Arabic. Duff established a college in Calcutta in 1840, which set a pattern for other Scottish mission colleges such as Madras Christian College, Foreman Christian College in Lahore, Isabella Thoburn College in Lucknow, and Hislop College in Nagpur.

In his first 13 years of ministry in India (1830-43), Duff baptized many converts and dedicated four missionaries, viz., Jagadiswar Bahttacharya, Prassana Kumar Chatterjee, Lalbehari Dey, and Behari Lal Singh. His main efforts were focused on reaching upper-caste Hindus and young secular Hindus who rejected Hinduism*. He produced the *Calcutta Christian Observer* in order to reach thinking Hindus.

Duff had a firm faith in literature, philosophy, and science as well as in modern Christianity. Before he permanently left India on medical leave in 1863, he helped Lord William Bentinck form the government policy of importing Western knowledge to enlighten India. Duff returned to Scotland in 1863, being critically ill. He helped establish the first Protestant chair of mission studies at New College, Edinburgh (1867), and was a continual advocate for responsible mission study and activity.

Bibliography

Carey, S. P., *William Carey* (1923). • Glover, H. Robert, *The Progress of World-wide Missions* (1960). • Mackensie, J., *The Christian Task in India* (1929). • Macnicol, N., *India in the Darkwood* (1930). • Neill, Stephen, and Gerald H. Anderson, eds., *Concise Dictionary of the Christian World-Mission* (1970). • Tucker, Ruth A., *From Jerusalem to Irian Jaya.*

Pratap Digal

Duncan, Moir

(b. 1861; d. Tai-yuen, China, 1906). Missionary to China* of the Baptist* Missionary Society.

Duncan lost his parents at a young age. He went to Scotland Baptist College and later graduated from Glasgow University, where he earned a bachelor of arts degree. He furthered his studies at Mansfield College, Oxford University, and was tutored by James Legge*, a pioneer missionary to China. Showing a natural talent for languages, Duncan learned Wenli from Legge. Duncan came to China in the winter of 1887 and received on-the-job training in Shansi until he could debate in Chinese. During the Yi-he-tuan crisis in 1900, he found shelter in Shanghai. Shortly after, he became a translator for the Eight-Power Allied Forces and went to Shensi, Tai-yuen-fu. After the crisis was over, he worked on relieving famines in Shanxi and Shenxi. In 1902, when Shansi University was founded, he was recommended by Timothy Richard* to be the acting principal. He rejected for admission to the university the nephew of Shansi's governor-general's and was well commended by local Chinese from middle- and high-class society.

Bibliography

Stanley, Brian, *The History of the Baptist Missionary Society* (1994).

China Group

Dunlap, Eugene P.

(b. New Castle, Pennsylvania, United States, 8 Jun 1848; d. Tap Teang, Thailand, 4 Apr 1918). Presbyterian* Church USA missionary evangelist prominent in the expansion of Thai Protestantism into southern Thailand*.

Dunlap graduated from Westminster College, Pennsylvania, in 1871 and from Western Theological Seminary in 1874. He married Emaline Cross in 1875.

The Dunlaps arrived in Thailand in 1875 and served under the Siam Mission. They took up work in Phet Buri in 1878, where they remained until 1888 except for sick leave from 1879 to 1883. Dunlap was in charge of all station work, and his dynamic evangelistic and pastoral style led to rapid growth in the Phet Buri churches. But his success caused controversy among other missionaries, who accused him of buying conversions because of his personal generosity. During these years Dunlap began to develop very close ties with Thai royalty, who often supported his work financially. From 1889 until 1910 the Dunlaps were stationed in Bangkok, from which base he conducted extensive evangelistic touring down Thailand's southern coast. His work led to the founding of a church and then a mission station at Nakhon Si Thammarat. In Nov 1910 the Dunlaps joined another couple in founding another station at Trang, on the western side of the Malay Peninsula. Dunlap died there on 29 Mar 1918.

Dunlap was one of the most successful Presbyterian missionary evangelists to serve in Thailand. He was deeply admired by Christians and others and maintained close contact with Thai nobility and royalty.

Bibliography

McFarland, George Bradley, ed., *Historical Sketch of Protestant Missions in Siam, 1828-1928* (1928). • Eakin Family Papers, Payap University Archives, Chiang Mai, Thailand. • Swanson, Herbert R., *Towards a Clean Church* (1991). • Wells, Kenneth E., *History of Protestant Work in Thailand, 1828-1958* (1958).

Herbert R. Swanson

Dutch Mission, Taiwan

The earliest missionary endeavor in Taiwan* began with the Dutch occupation (1624-61). During their 38 years of rule, the Dutch, under the chartered-company system conducted by the Dutch United East-India Company* *(Verenigde Oost-Indische Compagnie),* sent more than 30 ministers (predicants) and many evangelists (proponents) and schoolteachers to Taiwan. These ministers, all affiliated with the Dutch Reformed Church, formed the

Formosa Consistory and were under the supervision of the Amsterdam Classis.

Basically, these missionaries had to perform three kinds of duties: they were chaplains for Dutch officers and soldiers, interpreters or civil officers serving the Dutch company, and actual missionaries working among the aborigines*. Most of them had to engage in certain civil obligations. Moreover, on matters regarding missionary policy-making and implementation, they often had to comply with the Formosa Council of the company. Inevitably, missionaries with a stronger sense of calling would be in conflict with the company.

The early Dutch missionaries were successful in their missions because they worked hard to study the language, lifestyle, customs, religious rites, and beliefs of the aborigines. On 4 May 1627, Georgius Candidius, the first Dutch minister, arrived in Taiwan and began working among the Siraya aborigines in Sinkan (near present-day Tainan). In 1629, Candidius wrote *An Account of the Inhabitants.* Robertus Junius, the second Dutch minister, baptized 5,900 people and presided at the marriages of 1,000 new couples.

The first period of the Dutch mission (1624-43) was characterized by the work of Candidius and Junius. From the six Siraya tribes surrounding An-Peng (Tainan), they stretched their work northward to Chulo-san (Chia-yi) and southward to Long-kio (Pingtong), covering the major inhabited areas of the southern aborigines. During the second period (1644-61), the Dutch missionaries, probably as a consequence of their strict Reformed tendencies, displayed a less indigenizing attitude toward the aborigines and tried to introduce a more unified Dutch system. Nonetheless, they also extended their missionary enterprise northward to Changhwa and set up missionary posts at Keelung and Tamsui (near Taipei) after the Spanish were forced out of Taiwan in 1642. The Spaniards had occupied northern Taiwan since 1626 and introduced Roman Catholicism* to the northern aborigines.

Dutch missionaries introduced the romanized alphabet system to Taiwan and translated religious materials into aboriginal languages via this system. The list of publications, many presumably lost, includes Candidius's Sinkan dictionary and prayer booklets, Junius's Sinkan dictionary and catechetical booklets, Joannes Happartius's Lord's Prayer and Ten Commandments, Simon van Breen's catechism, Daniel Gravius's *Articles of Faith* and the Gospels of St. Matthew and John, and Jacobus Vertrecht's *Articles* in the Favorlang dialect. It is possible that Gravius's *Articles of Faith* is the Heidelberg Catechism. It is also notable that Dutch missionaries adapted the Ten Commandments to the Taiwanese context, e.g., "One should not go to the field on Sunday (the Sabbath)," "Do not kill, do not abuse children," "Do not commit abortion," etc.

Beginning in 1636, Junius introduced elementary schooling in Sinkan for children between the ages of 10 and 13. Because of its success, the school system was also introduced to the An-Peng area. In order to train native workers for ministry, the missionary council planned to institute a seminary in Moa-tau. This undertaking, however, was aborted by the invasion and capture of Taiwan by Cheng Chheng Kong (Koxinga).

When Koxinga attacked Fort Zeelandia, several Dutch missionaries, including Antonius Hambroek, became martyrs. After the Dutch left Taiwan, Christian activities gradually diminished and were probably abandoned within 50 years. However, the memory of these "red-haired relatives" still lingered in the minds of the Siraya people.

What caused the Dutch mission to disappear from Taiwan? Possible reasons include the ambiguous role of the missionaries and their mingling of religious and civil duties; the neglect of individual instruction and confession of faith, due primarily to the practice of mass conversion among the aborigines; the belated attempt to train local pastors and to translate the Bible* into the native languages; and the intermittent immoral behavior of the missionaries.

Bibliography

Campbell, William, *An Account of Missionary Success in the Island of Formosa* (1889); *Formosa under the Dutch* (1903).

CHENG YANG-EN

Dutch United East-India Company

(*Verenigde Oost-Indische Compagnie,* VOC). Merchant body founded in 1602 after the Dutch, lured by the lucrative spice trade, had discovered their own route to Southeast Asia.

The VOC was granted a monopoly for trading in the Indian Ocean and the Pacific area by the Dutch government, as well as the right of exercising sovereign powers in that area. The VOC was directed by a board in Holland; in the Asian territories, the supreme power was, from 1610, exercised by a governor-general, who from 1618 resided in Batavia (Jakarta). In order to realize the monopoly granted it, the VOC had to drive out its European competitors, the Portuguese and the English. In the area between Ceylon and the Moluccas*, it largely succeeded in doing so.

Originally only a trading company, the VOC became a territorial power by conquering the districts around its trading posts and the areas producing goods vital to its commerce. In this way, parts of the Moluccas, the north coast of Java, the coastal areas of Ceylon, and for some time also Taiwan* came under direct VOC rule. But by concluding treaties with a number of Asian rulers, and if possible forcing them to acknowledge the overlordship of the company, the VOC dominated a much larger area. Because of the ruthless application of the monopoly, VOC power was detrimental to Asian commerce and to the welfare of the population. In the 18th c., the company's power waned, and in 1798, after having lost Ceylon to the English (1795), the VOC went bankrupt. Its possessions were taken over by the Dutch state and became the nucleus of the Dutch colonial empire in Asia (1800-1942).

From the start, the VOC considered religious affairs a matter of its concern, even before the Dutch government made this concern mandatory in the charter of 1623. In the first place, it had to provide religious care for its European personnel on board the ships and in Asia. For that purpose, in the course of two centuries more than 900 ministers and several thousand "consolers of the sick" (poorly trained laypeople who conducted the religious services on the ships and in the forts and trading posts not cared for by a minister) were sent to South and Southeast Asia. In the greater centers, such as Ambon, Batavia, Malaka*, and Colombo, monumental church buildings were erected, church councils were formed, and a regular church life initiated.

This church life was distinctly Protestant in character, the company considering it necessary to actively (and at times violently) suppress Catholicism in its domains. The Netherlands had just freed itself from Catholic Spain in what was partly a religious war. As a consequence, in the mother country Catholicism, if not persecuted, was discriminated against. Moreover, the most important of the company's European enemies in Asia, the Portuguese, were Catholics. So Catholics from Europe were not allowed into the VOC domains, and the Catholic populations in some of the former Portuguese territories, such as Ambon and Ceylon, were made Protestant. In this way, the Christians of the Central Moluccas and several other island groups in present-day Indonesia became thoroughly Protestantized. Most of those in Ceylon, however, reverted to Catholicism after the end of Dutch rule. The effects of the Protestant monopoly in the Indonesian archipelago during the 17th and 18th cs. make themselves felt in religious statistics even today.

In the second place, the VOC charter contained the instruction to look after the expansion of the Christian faith. This instruction was carried out on a limited scale only. The Dutch never suppressed non-Christian faiths by destroying temples or mosques or prohibiting non-Christian religious services, as the Spaniards and Portuguese had done in several places. Missionary activities were undertaken at the initiative of church people and allowed only in areas where they would do no harm to the company's commercial interests, such as the Moluccas and Taiwan* and among the slave population of Batavia. To fulfill the needs of the Asian Christians, the company saw to it that catechisms, volumes of sermons, hymnbooks, and Bible* translations were published in Malay, Portuguese, several Taiwanese languages, Sinhalese, and Tamil. In Colombo, a training center was founded which in the course of a century (1696-1796) produced 23 Sinhalese and Tamil ministers and a large number of catechists and schoolmasters. Similar centers in Jaffna and Batavia did not meet with the same success.

The salaries of the church ministers and all other expenses for church activities were paid by the company. In return, the company required strict obedience from all church servants. As a consequence, the church was not free. It was Reformed (Presbyterian*) in doctrine and liturgy, but not in organization. There were no synods or regional assemblies, the church council of Batavia acting as a central board which on behalf of the churches in Asia maintained the communication with the colonial government and with the churches in Holland. Characteristic of the domination of the church by the state was that all correspondence between the churches in Asia and in Holland had to be under unsealed cover. As a consequence, the church was not in a position to criticize the company's politics or even personal misconduct of its senior officials. When it was considered necessary, church and mission were ruthlessly sacrificed to company interests. Thus in 1607, the VOC concluded a treaty with the Muslim sultanate of Ternate which stipulated that both sides would hand over deserters (which in the context also meant converts) to their lawful ruler. In order to keep the exclusive trade rights granted by the Japanese government, the company's employees on Japanese soil had to refrain from even the smallest religious practice. When the last Japanese Christians arose in defense of their faith, the company sent a ship which bombarded the castle in which they took refuge (1637).

The VOC first introduced Protestant Christianity in Asia, and its personal and financial assistance secured the survival and even a limited expansion of Christianity in some areas (especially the Moluccas), which in the 19th and 20th cs. became bases for the modern missionary movement and recruiting grounds of Asian mission personnel.

Bibliography

Boxer, C. R., *The Dutch Seaborne Empire, 1600-1800* (1965). • Van den End, Thomas, *Ragi Carita* I (1980). • Van Goor, J., *Jan Kompenie as Schoolmaster: Dutch Education in Ceylon, 1690-1795* (1978).

THOMAS VAN DEN END

Dyer, Samuel

(b. Greenwich, England, 20 Jan 1804; d. Macau, 24 Oct 1843). London Missionary Society (LMS) missionary remembered for his printing of Chinese characters and for his daughter Maria, who married Hudson Taylor*.

Dyer's father had been secretary of the Royal Hospital at Greenwich and was later chief clerk of the British Admiralty. Dyer was converted in 1822 and studied mathematics and law at Cambridge. In 1824, he offered to serve with the LMS and trained at Gosport and under Pye Smith at Homerton. Smith's combination of missionary, philological, and scientific interests provided a relevant background. Dyer married Maria Tarn before joining the LMS Ultra-Ganges Mission in 1827.

Based in Penang, Dyer studied Hokkien and tackled the challenge of producing movable metallic types for the thousands of Chinese characters. He began with a systematic analysis of characters and strokes. Initially using wood reliefs to create the clay molds from which type could be cast, he soon moved to steel punches and copper matrices. Dyer's linguistic abilities, meticulous planning, and painstaking attention to detail resulted in Chinese fonts of high quality. They were later passed on to the American Presbyterian Mission Press in China* and played a significant part in its development.

The Dyers moved to Malacca* in 1835 and returned to England in 1839. Dyer was in Singapore* in 1842 and in Hong Kong* in 1843. In addition to articles in the *Calcutta Christian Observer, Chinese Repository,* and *Periodical Miscellany,* his publications included *Vocabulary of the Hokkien Dialect* (1838), *A Selection of Three Thousand Characters Being the Most Important in the Chinese Language for the Purpose of Facilitating the Cutting of Punches and Casting Metal type in Chinese* (1834), and *Aesop's Fables* (in Hokkien, 1843).

Bibliography

Barnett, Suzanne W., "Silent Evangelism: Presbyterians and the Mission Press in China, 1807-1860," *Journal of Presbyterian History* 49.4 (1971). • Bin Ismail, Ibrahim, "Samuel Dyer and His Contributions to Chinese Typography," *Library Quarterly* 54.2 (Apr 1984). • O'Sullivan, Leona, "The London Missionary Society: A Written Record of the Missionaries and Printing Presses in the Straits Settlements, 1815-1847," *Journal of the Malaysian Branch of the Royal Asiatic Society* 57.2 (1984). • Wylie, Alexander, *Memorials of Protestant Missionaries to the Chinese Giving a List of Their Publications and Obituary Notices of the Deceased with Copious Indexes* (1867).

W. John Roxborogh

Dzao, Timothy. *See* Chao, Timothy

E

Eagles Communications

Singapore*-based Christian group formerly known as Eagles Evangelism.

The history of Eagles Communications began in 1968, when Peter Chao was converted. Although only 14 years old, Chao was already recognized as the leader of a gang of rebellious youths. Immediately, he shared his newfound faith with other members of his gang. Within months, most of the gang became Christians, redirecting their youthful energies from acts of vandalism to evangelism. Calling themselves the Eagles Club, they shared their faith with other students. On weekends, they went on door-to-door neighborhood evangelism. A year-end camp in 1970 marked a new turning point. Chao and his colleagues, John Ng, William Tang, Michael Tan, Michael Chan, and a few others, responded to the challenge to serve the Lord full-time. The group conducted Gospel rallies and teaching seminars. Young people by the hundreds, disillusioned with the materialism and academic pressure that plagued society, responded to the Gospel. In 1975, the group held a five-night, nationwide Eagles Crusade, packing the 3,400-seat National Theater, then the largest auditorium in Singapore. Two years later, the group was registered as Eagles Evangelism.

From the beginning, the organization, seeking to address the needs of people in a modern urbanized situation, has used multimedia, music*, and drama. In the 1970s, its target audience was those in their 20s and 30s. But in the 1980s, it began to focus attention on business people and professionals, using dinner concerts with a lecture. Various teaching and training seminars such as Lifestyle Evangelism, Mind and Lifestyle, Saturday Rendezvous, and Leadership Development have sought to equip laypeople for effective service in church and society. Many of these activities received the cosponsorship of churches. The organization also conducted evangelistic rallies, concerts, and teaching seminars in many Asian towns and cities. In 1990, it was renamed Eagles Communications to better reflect its broad-based ministry. Over the years, the small group of teenage pioneers have retained their comradeship and continue to provide leadership to the organization. Their vision and commitment are shared by a large corps of volunteer supporters.

Bibliography

Eagles Evangelism, *With Wings like Eagles* (1988).

Bobby E. K. Sng

Eakin, John A.

(b. Pennsylvania, United States, 28 Feb 1854; d. Bangkok, Thailand, 21 Jan 1929). Presbyterian* Church USA missionary educator and evangelist.

Eakin graduated from Washington and Jefferson College in 1879. He accepted a Thai government position teaching in the Suan Anand School in Bangkok, an experimental school established under royal patronage by Samuel G. McFarland.* He taught from 1880 to 1884 and then entered Western Theological Seminary (now Pittsburgh Theological Seminary), graduating in 1887. Eakin returned to Thailand* in 1888 as a missionary and married Laura Olmstead in Bangkok in 1889. He founded the Christian High School in 1889. In 1892 this school united with the Samray School (founded in 1852) under the name Bangkok Christian High School. The united school soon became one of the leading boys' schools in Thailand. In 1913 its name was changed to Bangkok Christian College.

In 1890 Eakin founded a religious and literary magazine, *Sang Arun*. His wife died in 1897, and Eakin married Altha Lyman in 1899. In 1903 Eakin moved the Christian High School to its present location on the Bangkok side of the river. The Eakins transferred to Phet Buri (Petchaburi) in 1907, where they remained until 1925. They built up the work there, emphasizing evangelism, vaccinations, and the distribution of Christian literature. Eakin also took a leading administrative role in the Presbyterians' Siam mission. He engaged in literature work, particularly revision of the Thai Scriptures, and he retained close ties with Thai nobility. He died after serving as chair of the highly successful Centennial Celebration of Protestant Missions in Siam in 1928.

Bibliography

Eakin, Paul A., *Eakin Family in Thailand* (1955). • Eakin Family Papers (Payap University Archives, Chiang Mai, Thailand).

HERBERT R. SWANSON

Eakin, Paul A.

(b. Bangkok, Thailand, 29 Jan 1890; d. United States, 8 Oct 1966). Presbyterian* Church USA missionary administrator who shaped missionary policy and practice in Thailand* prior to World War II*.

Eakin graduated from Grove City College, Pennsylvania, United States, in 1910 and from Western Theological Seminary in 1912. He returned to Thailand as a missionary in 1913 and began work at Phet Buri in 1914. In addition to evangelistic itineration, he reopened the station's boys' school and engaged in pastoral work. He married Gertrude Shearer in 1917. They transferred to Bangkok in 1924, where he did pastoral and pastoral-training work and established language training for new missionaries.

The American Presbyterian Mission elected Eakin executive secretary in 1929, and he played an important role in the 1933 evaluation survey which set directions for Presbyterian missions in Thailand and in the founding of the Church of Christ in Thailand in 1934. He dealt particularly with the divisive modernist-fundamentalist Presbyterian split in Thailand, including the controversial evangelistic campaigns of John Sung* in 1938 and 1939.

At the outbreak of World War II, Eakin was interned in Bangkok until 1942. The Eakins returned to Thailand in early 1946, and he served as Church World Service director for relief and rehabilitation work in Thailand. A major reorganization of the Presbyterian mission in Thailand relieved him of his position as executive secretary in 1947, and he took up literature* and pastoral work until 1949, when the Eakins left the field. He died in the United States.

Bibliography

Eakin Family in Thailand (Eakin family papers, Payap University Archives, Chiang Mai, Thailand).

HERBERT R. SWANSON

East Asian Pastoral Institute

(EAPI). Training institute in Manila, Philippines*, dedicated to the continuing formation of pastoral agents for the local churches of Asia and the Pacific.

EAPI offers lay, religious, and ordained pastoral leaders an integrated program for growth in ministry and spirituality. It provides them with training courses and a community experience which integrate faith and life and which encourage them to learn from the cultural heritage of the many different countries of Asia and the Pacific.

In 1955, Fr. Johannes Hofinger, who had come to Manila from the Jesuit* mission in China*, pioneered a catechetical, biblical, and liturgical renewal in Asia through publications, courses, and conventions. The aim of his institute was "to render missionaries, laity and religious capable of setting up an intelligent dialogue with the Asian community of the day." Out of this foundation a new institute, the EAPI, was born in Aug 1965, and its headquarters set up on the Ateneo de Manila University campus. In the same year, the institute was included among the interprovincial works of the East Asian Assistancy of the Society of Jesus by Fr. Arrupe, the superior general. Fr. Alfonso Nebreda, S.J., was appointed director of the new institute.

Desiring to implement more fully the directives of Vatican II, and in response to the many requests from bishops and religious superiors, the EAPI structured courses to incorporate the different aspects of the church's pastoral renewal after the council, focusing especially on the church's new awareness of its mission in the world. In order to reach a wider audience in Asia and beyond, the EAPI published three periodicals: *Good Tidings* for pastors and religious teachers; *Amen* to inform the laity and religious about the changes in liturgy after Vatican II; and *Teaching All Nations,* which penetrated more deeply into fundamental questions on liturgy, catechetics, theology of mission, and inculturation. In 1979, these periodicals were replaced by the *East Asian Pastoral Review.*

The participants come from as many as 30 different countries in Asia and the Pacific and live as a multicultural community engaged in theological reflection, united in biblical prayer, group sharing, team learning, and the Eucharist. They are divided into cross-cultural and regional/national groups which provide opportunities and structures for cross-cultural communication and community life. The institute's program of studies is designed for pastoral agents seeking an extended time (from five months to one year) of renewing and updating.

The institute also offers a master's degree in pastoral theology for those seeking a professional qualification in pastoral studies. Its goal is to train participants in research techniques as they probe the complex history, culture, social structure, and religious traditions of the country to which their Christian message is to be made relevant. It therefore requires a substantial project of pastoral research.

More recently, the EAPI has undertaken an extensive evaluation of its policies and programs, clarifying its mission statement, which is as follows:

"The East Asian Pastoral Institute is committed to the continuing formation of pastoral agents for the local churches of Asia and the Pacific region. It hopes to carry out this mission through (i) courses which provide training in theological reflection and in practical pastoral skills; (ii) symposia which promote communication among people with expertise in various fields; (iii) research by both permanent staff members and visiting research fellows; and (iv) the institute's journal, the *East Asian Pastoral Review.*

Bibliography

Nebreda, Alfonso M., "The Beginnings of the EAPI — Reminiscing," *East Asian Pastoral Review* (1987). • O'Gorman, Thomas H., "At the Threshold of the Third Decade: The EAPI Looks Ahead," *East Asian Pastoral Review* (1987). • King, Geoffrey J., "EAPI at Twenty-Five: Evaluation, Mission Statement, Future Plans," *East Asian Pastoral Review* (1991). KATHLEEN COYLE

Ebina Danjo

(b. 18 Sep 1856; d. Tokyo, 22 May 1937). Japanese Christian evangelist, philosopher, educator.

Born into the Chikugo Yanagikawa Feudal Clan, Ebina's birth name was Kisaburo. He studied at Kumamoto School of Western Learning, where he became a Christian. He graduated from the Doshisha in Apr 1879 and served as pastor of Annaka Church (1879-84), Maebashi Church (1885-86), Hongo Mission (1886-87), and Kumamoto Mission (1887-90); president of the Japan Christian Mission Company (1891-93); pastor of Kobe Church (1893-97) and Hongo Mission in Tokyo (1897-1920); chancellor of the Doshisha (1920-28); and honorary pastor of Hongo Church (1930-37).

Ebina taught that the universal religious consciousness of all people has been ultimately realized in Christianity (he explains its continuity with Confucianism and Shintoism) and that human religious consciousness reached its highest development in the person of Christ. For this reason, he had a dispute with Uemura Masahisa, who insisted on the divinity of Christ. In Apr 1902, Ebina was removed from the Evangelistic Alliance, but he had many sympathizers. He supported and promoted the mission of the Japan Congregational Church to Korea* as a preparation for the Korean people to become actively involved in the Greater Japanese Empire. His teaching of the universal religious consciousness of humanity had a remarkable impact on Yoshino Sakuzo, Nakajima Shigeru, and others.

Bibliography

Dohi Akio, *Ebina Danjo no shingaku shiso* (Theological Thought of Ebina Danjo); *Kumamoto bando kenkyu* (Research on the Kumamoto Band) (1965); *Ebina Danjo no seiji shiso* (The Political Thinking of Ebina Danjo) (1982). DOHI AKIO

Ecumenical Movement

Ecumenism in Asia emerged from the missionary movement. Christian mission had aimed to evangelize the world. The material and spiritual resources of the church in Europe and North America, especially in the 19th c., were directed to evangelization. Missionary societies and church mission boards were constituted to carry out the task. They established institutions for social service largely to meet the medical* and educational needs of the people. Eventually congregations were organized and churches were built in different countries in Asia. Because mission was pursued by the churches separately, denominational and national churches were transplanted into the mission fields. Churches themselves were divided, and so mission was not carried out in Christian unity. At times competition took place, and there was often rivalry between churches. Each denomination and national church put forward its own claims and emphasized its own distinctiveness. Therefore, the church divisions of the West were not only exported to Asia, but were even multiplied (e.g., Lutheran* churches came to China* from Germany, Norway, Sweden, and the United States).

Cooperation and comity. During the early 19th c., it became clear that, since resources were limited and the missionary task was vast, churches in mission ought to cooperate in spite of their differences. Mission agencies began to enter into consultation. On the local level, they recognized the duplication of effort and the wastefulness of carrying on work among the same groups of people. Pressure was placed upon their parent bodies to work more cooperatively. Thus the concern for unity was both a pragmatic concern and a theological commitment. This concern led to the calling of the first historic World Missionary Conference in Edinburgh in 1910. As early as 1810, William Carey* had suggested the holding of decennial interdenominational world missionary conferences, recommending that the first be held in South Africa. It took a century before that proposal was finally implemented. Periodically, national and regional missionary conferences were held from 1854. They were the forerunners of Edinburgh, 1910. Mission agencies were well represented in this meeting. In contrast with previous conferences where participation was open to all interested to attend, at Edinburgh official delegates were appointed to represent mission agencies. They were authorized to speak for the mission agencies of their churches. It was a consultative assembly and had no powers to legislate for the missionary societies. One of the eight commissions was given the specific topic of cooperation and the promotion of unity. The attention of the Christian world was brought to the issue of missionary cooperation. It was reported that there was wide agreement on the goal and that it is "the aim of all missionary work to plant in each non-Christian nation one undivided Church of Christ." Kenneth Scott Latourette commented that "Edinburgh 1910 summed up and focused much of the previous century's movement for uniting Christians in giving the Gospel to the world." John R. Mott, chairman of the conference, declared that, in "gathering together from different nations and races and communions" the representatives were made aware of their "oneness in Christ." The significance of this conference lay in the assembling of those who were directly involved in the missionary enterprise. They sensed a common need for cooperation. In the spirit of Christian friendship and in common obedience to mission, they endeavored to discover areas of cooperative action. The call for wider church unity was also heard, and it stimulated movements toward the unity of the church. The direct outcome of this conference was the creation of a Continuation Committee with Mott as chairperson. J. H. Oldham, secretary, regarded the formation of the Continuation Committee as "the decisive event which made possible the growth of the ecumenical movement." The Continuation Committee was charged with the responsibility to "preserve and extend the atmosphere and spirit of the Conference." Mott was directed by the committee to visit the principal mission areas in Asia, which he did from Oct 1912 to May 1913. He visited Sri Lanka*, India*, Myanmar*, Malaysia*, China*, Korea*, and Japan*. In each country Mott visited, local or regional conferences were held which led to larger national meetings, all of them advancing the discussion that began in Edinburgh. National Continuation Committees were set up; they became the National Missionary Councils that later evolved into National Christian Councils and National Councils of Churches. The NCCs in India, China, and Japan were typical examples of such organizational expressions of missionary cooperation.

By 1921 the International Missionary Council (IMC) was constituted, and Asian missionary councils became members of this international body. In 1938 the IMC held its meeting in Tambaram, Madras. This conference further advanced the cause of ecumenism in Asia. One of the statements from the Tambaram conference said that "disunion is both a stumbling block to the faithful and a mockery to those without." Interest was expressed in the visible union of the churches, the goal being observable and organic union, and the urgency for unity was felt strongly by national churches. One important area of cooperation was that of comity arrangements. Comity agreements preceded mission conferences because in pioneering regions in Africa and Asia missions worked out geographic divisions often out of necessity. One of the classic comity arrangements was that made among missions preparing to begin Protestant work in the Philippines*. Edinburgh stated: "these principles of comity are concerned with such matters as overlapping or intrusion, the transfer of agents, the standard of conditions of church membership, and the discipline of the church." It related more to the opening of missionary work in new areas or new projects in existing mission fields. In such cases, there must be adequate consultation in order to avoid overlapping and conflict. The comity principle helped to conserve limited resources and reduce rivalry and competition among different denominational mission agencies working in the same locality or country. However, the various mission agencies generally created different denominational churches in various countries or separate areas in the same country. For instance, the Baptists* are strong in Myanmar; the Presbyterians* dominate in Thailand*, Korea*, and Taiwan*; the Lutherans* and the Reformed churches prevail in different parts of Indonesia*. These different churches came together on the level of consultation for cooperative ventures and following the principle of comity. Comity as a principle deals only with matters about which the churches agree to consult and cooperate with one another. Cooperation does not involve the total life and mission of the church. It is, therefore, inadequate and limited without the sharing of one common life in the one church.

Search for unity. The need for unity was keenly felt by the churches in Asia. The history of division of the churches had little relevance for Asian churches, and so it was felt that new churches were inheriting the contentious issues of the past. The churches were convinced that unity was essential for the mission of the church. Asian churches, as a rule, sensed the urgency of the task of evangelism. Church division was seen as a hindrance to the evangelistic mission. It was difficult for divided churches to communicate the message of reconciliation. V. S. Azariah* brought out this point when he said, "We are unable in our divided state to give an authoritative call to repentance, faith and baptism."

The Tranquebar* Conference in 1919 was credited with providing the impulse for realizing church unity in the formation of the Church of South India. This conference declared: "We face together the titanic task of the winning of India for Christ — one-fifth of the human race. Yet, confronted by such an overwhelming responsibility, we find ourselves rendered weak and relatively impotent by our unhappy divisions — divisions for which we were not responsible, and which have been, as it were, imposed upon us from without, divisions which we did not create, and which we do not wish to perpetuate." Unity of the church and evangelistic mission are interrelated. The task of evangelism provided a motivating factor for the search for unity on the part of some Asian churches. After years of intensive church union discussions, the unity of the church was expressed and celebrated. It happened particularly in the formation of the Church of South India* and later the Church of North India*, the Church of Pakistan*, the Church of Christ in Japan, the Church of Christ in Thailand, and the United Church of Christ in the Philippines. These were spectacularly successful church union efforts, and there was a great deal of excitement over expressing the unity of the church. Some of the united churches were able to bring together churches of episcopal and non-episcopal traditions in one ecclesial family. In the process of church union negotiations, theological, faith, and order issues were discussed. Churches became more aware of their differences but also their unity. The euphoria of church union, however, was soon dissipated. Other church union discussions met with both theological problems and nontheological factors that prevented the consummation of union after years of negotiations. The united churches did not, as was hoped, lead to a great new sense of mission and evangelism. They were larger, but they did not seem to be qualitatively different from the churches that did not unite. New tensions and conflicts emerged in the united churches, and the commitment to organic unity began to wane in the 1970s.

Concern for evangelism. Churches did, however, continue to work together in the common task of evangelism. Since they were minority churches in most Asian countries, church growth was a primary interest. Evangelistic organizations of the West planned mass campaigns and preaching missions. The churches in specific countries provided joint sponsorship for mass evangelistic campaigns such as the Billy Graham Evangelistic Crusades. As countries achieved independence and became engaged in nation building, social problems surfaced. Political and economic developments gave rise to questions related to national goals and the means to achieve them, in part through a united church witness. Human rights became an issue, especially in countries such as Indonesia*, Korea, Singapore*, and the Philippines. Churches wanted to ensure open political participation in the creation of a more democratic society, and they were called upon to defend the fundamental rights of the people — human rights that are often violated in the name of law and order. The drive for economic development raised the issue of workers' rights and the freedom to organize free trade unions. The power and control of multinational corporations were closely monitored. For the sake of profit, wages were kept low, workers' benefits were reduced, and the natural environment was destroyed. Such exploitation was exposed. In the name of development, both people and the environment were being sacrificed. Ecumenism was expressed in churches working together in tackling the problems people face in their specific countries. They had to deal with questions of poverty*, employment, human rights, workers' rights, and political participation. It was in addressing societal problems that some ecumenical groups or communities were formed to express ecumenism at the local level. In some cases, they were experimenting with new forms of church life and seeking to express the common life that cuts across traditional theological and liturgical barriers.

Regional ecumenical organizations. Both denominational churches and National Christian Councils fostered relationships in mission with one another. Previously they had forged strong links with their parent bodies in the West. In working together in their own national situation they related more closely with one another. Regional consciousness among churches was also developing in the post–World War II* era. Churches and councils came together to form the East Asia Christian Conference in Prapat, Indonesia, in 1957. This was one of the main regional organizational expressions of ecumenism in Asia. The name was later changed to reflect its broader representation: the Christian Conference of Asia* (CCA). The CCA exists as "an organ of continuing cooperation." The concerns of the National Christian Councils and the CCA are intertwined. Each has influenced the other. They both began with the evangelistic task in Asia leading to Christian action in Asian society. The CCA is committed to the continued development of ecumenism in Asia. It strives to be comprehensive in its approach and seeks to relate to various aspects of the life and mission of Asian churches. Opportunities were provided for Asian churches to respond together in meeting Asian needs. During the Indochina conflict, they supported Asian Christian Service, a program for emergency relief and rehabilitation in war-torn areas. In times of natural disasters, churches together have offered assistance. Churches have given support for those who are victims in their struggle for human rights and social justice. Support for political detainees and their families and advocacy for their release are other forms of service. Asian theologians have been encouraged to do more creative and original work as they support, theologically, issues of culture and justice. Ecumenism is also being expressed in the creative fields of music*, art*, literature*, liturgy, and church architecture. An ecumenical Asian hymnal was published with many lyrics put to traditional Asian folk tunes. The Asian Institute for Liturgy and Music in Manila guides this creative work. The Asian Christian Art Association has promoted the development of Christian artists and has published books on Asian Christian art. It must be mentioned that ecumenism in Asia is also expressed in other regional organizations which have identified certain tasks of the church such as evangelism, prayer, missions, youth, and work among women*. Included among these are such parachurch organizations as the International Fellowship of Evangelical Students* (IFES), Campus Crusade for Christ*, Youth for Christ, Every Home Crusade, Navigators, Asian Outreach, World Vision*, Operation Mobilization, etc. Of late there has been a proliferation of such Western-based parachurch groups with Asian offices or headquarters. On the one hand, they cut across denominational lines in their work, but on the other, they can create a new rivalry and competition. The more ecumenically minded organizations are InterVarsity Christian Fellowship (IFES), Student Christian Movement* (SCM), and the Asian Church Women's Conference. They, too, advance the cause of Asian ecumenism.

Ecumenical challenge. The primary challenge that ecumenism in Asia faces is in relating Asian churches to Asian cultures and traditions. In the past, the Christian missionary movement often dismissed Asian culture as pagan. They believed that God was exclusively at work in Judeo-Christian history. The missionary movement that came from the West imposed a Western Christian theology and church life. The foreignness of the Christian church was evident in all Asian countries. The ecumenical pioneer D. T. Niles* made the classic comment that "Christianity is a potted plant which needs to be rooted in the cultural soil of Asia." The earthen vessel has to be broken and the plant allowed to grow freely in the new

Asian soil. The process of indigenization and contextualization* attempted to relate the Gospel to Asian culture and history. It was an effort to "give Asian Christianity in Asia an Asian face," or "to see Christ through Asian eyes," or to provide the Gospel with an Asian flavor. Contextualization is the approach of relating the Gospel message (text) to the local situation (context). It is to bring to bear the text upon the peculiar context. The context varies, and therefore the process of contextualization is an ongoing ecumenical endeavor in Asia.

Myanmar. The ecumenical movement began in Myanmar with the arrival of John R. Mott in Yangon (Rangoon) on 13 Jan 1913 during his third mission tour as general secretary of the World Student Christian Federation (WSCF) and as chairman of the Continuation Committee of the Edinburgh 1910 World Missionary Conference. The National Missionary Council of India, Burma, and Ceylon (Sri Lanka*) was founded in 1912. Mott successfully reorganized the missionary leadership to form the Burma Representative Council of Missions (BRCM) in 1914 in Yangon with representatives from eight organizations, namely, the American Baptist Mission, Society for the Propagation of the Gospel (SPG), English Wesleyan Mission, Methodist* Episcopal Mission, Leipzig Lutheran Mission, Young Men's Christian Association* (YMCA), British and Foreign Bible* Society, and Women's Christian Temperance Union. In 1921 the National Missionary Council was changed to the National Christian Council. Likewise, the Burma Representative Council of Mission was also changed to the Christian Council in Burma in 1923. After Burma gained independence from the British in 1948, the Christian Council in Burma was reorganized as the Burma Christian Council. It became, for the first time, an autonomous national council with a stronger leadership and a larger number of nationals participating. Burmese nationals have taken leadership of the council as presidents since 1939 and as general secretaries since 1954. Since the Revolutionary Council took power in 1962 and the consequent expulsion of all foreign missionaries in 1966, the life and mission of the church, as well as the task of the ecumenical movement in Burma, fell entirely upon the shoulders of national Christian leaders. The ecumenical youth movement in Burma has a national background, whereas the SCM has an international background. In the late 1940s some patriotic Christian youth who had strong concerns for nation building formed the All Burma Christian Youth League (ABCYL). ABCYL was transformed into the United Christian Youth of Burma (UCYB) in the mid-1950s, and it was further changed into the Burma Church Youth Fellowship (BCYF) in the mid-1960s. From its inception in 1912, the SCM existed as an autonomous body until the mid-1960s, when it came under the umbrella of the church. It was then renamed the University Christian Fellowship (UCF), a name which it holds currently. The Burma Christian Council was reconstituted as the Burma Council of Churches in 1974, with a membership of 11 denominational churches including the Burma Baptist Convention, the Church of the Province of Burma (Anglican*), the Methodist Church Upper Burma, the Methodist Church Lower Burma, the Presbyterian Church of Burma, the Salvation Army*, the Self-Supporting Karen* Baptist Mission Society, the Lisu* Christian Church, and the Mara Independent Evangelical Church. The following organizations were recognized as cooperating bodies: the National YMCA, the National Young Women's Christian Association* (YWCA), the Bible Society* of Burma, the Christian Literature Society of Burma, and the Burma Medical* Relief Society. The BCYF became the Youth Department of the Council, and the SCM of Burma became the University Christian Work Department of the Council. There were four main program branches: faith and witness, study and education, Christian service and relief, Christian radio audio-visual aids (communication), along with the youth, student, and women's departments. The Buddhistic Study Commission was transformed into Dialogue study groups. Some new projects were introduced, such as adult literacy, Urban Rural Mission*, community development, theological* education by extension, Bible correspondence course, etc. Proposals and discussions about the possibility of a Union Theological Seminary emerged. The Commission for Higher Theological Education was formed, which gave birth to the Association for Theological Education in Burma (ATEB) in 1986. The BCC was restructured in 1988 with the following program units and departments: mission and ecumenism, service and development, education and communication, youth department, student department, and women's department. There were also some special committees, such as the finance personnel and property committee, public relations committee, ecumenical scholarships committee, comprehensive leadership promotion program committee, etc. Member churches of the Myanmar Council of Churches are: the Myanmar Baptist Convention, the Church of the Province of Myanmar*, the Methodist Church Upper Myanmar, the Methodist Church Lower Myanmar, the Presbyterian Church of Myanmar, the Lutheran Bethlehem Church, St. Gabriel's Congregational Church, the Self-Supporting Kayin Baptist Mission Society, the Salvation Army Myanmar Command, the Lisu Christian Church of Myanmar, the Mara Evangelical Church of Myanmar, and the Independent Church of Myanmar.

There are seven ecumenical organizations that cooperate with the MCC: the National Council of YMCAs of Myanmar, the National YWCA of Myanmar, the Bible Society of Myanmar, the Christian Literature Society of Myanmar, the Association for Theological Education in Myanmar, the National Christian Leprosy Mission Board, and the Myanmar Christian Health Workers' Services Association. In 1980 the socialist government successfully convened a historical Assembly of the Buddhist *Sanghas* of all orders, where they launched the process of purification, perpetuation, and propagation (3P) of the

Buddhist *Sasana*. In the following year (1981) the Burma Council of Churches, at the request of the authorities, made parallel efforts to bring together all churches and parachurch groups which were nonmembers of the council for the purpose of mutual fellowship, cooperation, and better understanding. At its Diamond Jubilee celebrations in 1989, the council resolved to form a coordinating committee for evangelistic actions with the aim of promoting understanding, trust, and cooperation. They sought to include representatives from non-MCC member churches and other Christian groups and began with several seminars. The ecumenical movement has been strongly promoted through local and regional councils of churches. There have been over 20 such councils and fellowships of local/regional churches throughout the country. The World Week of Prayer for Christian Unity (held in January) has been regularly observed by these councils for the past several years. The National YMCA was formed in 1950, with over 10 local YMCAs active in Myanmar currently. The National YWCA was organized in 1951 and has about 10 locally active organizations working ecumenically. At the national level, the MCC established cordial relationships with the Roman Catholic Church* through the National Ecumenical Joint Commission between the MCC and the Catholic Bishops' Conference of Myanmar (CBCM). Annual retreat seminars and consultations occurred together. The MCC has participated in the life and activities of both the WCC and the CCA ever since they were founded in 1948 and 1957 respectively. The churches in Myanmar have been blessed with national ecumenical leaders such as U Hla Bu*, U Hla Thwin, Ba Maung Chain, Francis Ah Mya, U Ba Ohn, U Ba Hmyin, Daw Katherine Khin Khin*, Victor San Lone*, U Khin Maung Din*, U Kyaw Than, U Aung Khin, and many others.

Korea. Although churches in Korea were planted along denominational lines, from the beginning there was cooperation among the different mission groups in the peninsula in areas such as Bible translation, hymnal publication, education, and other shared interests. Ecumenical work first started among the different Presbyterian groups. In 1889 the Northern Presbyterians joined with the Australian Presbyterian Mission to form the United Council of the Missions of the American and Victorian Churches. The union was short-lived due to the death of J. H. Davies from smallpox. He was at that time the only male Australian missionary. The Presbyterian Council (more precisely, the Council of Missions holding the Presbyterian Form of Government) was organized in 1893, after the arrival of the Presbyterian Mission of the United States (Southern) in 1892. Its purpose was to have a uniform organization among those who maintained "the Reformed faith and Presbyterian form of Government" in Korea. The Australian and Canadian Presbyterian Missions were also invited to join the Council. In 1892 a set of comity rules was worked out between the Northern Presbyterian and Northern Methodist missions. In general, it was agreed that each would have the monopoly to work in towns with populations of fewer than 5,000. Although disapproved by the visiting bishop, John W. Foster, the agreement provided the practical basis for mission work until a more definite future arrangement could be made. In 1905 the six missions united under the General Council of All Protestant Evangelical Missions in Korea. Its purpose was to establish a united church in Korea. In 1910 Baron Yun Chi Ho, a prominent Korean Methodist layperson, attended the IMC in Edinburgh. As a result, the Presbyterian and the Methodist Church Council of Korea was formed in 1917. A preparatory committee for the formation of the Korean National Council of Churches (KNCC) was formed in 1922. The KNCC was formalized in 1924 with 11 groups in its membership. It joined the IMC in 1926 and sent six delegates to the 1928 IMC in Jerusalem. The KNCC was later disbanded by the Japanese. After liberation, the KNCC was reconstructed and became a member of the WCC in 1948. Under the military regime of the Park Jung Hee, many leaders of the KNCC who opposed Park and who fought for human rights were imprisoned. The KNCC comprises six denominations: the Presbyterian Church of Korea, the Presbyterian Church of the Republic of Korea, the Methodist Church, the Salvation Army, the Anglican Church, and the Korean Evangelical Church. Most of the more conservative denominations refuse to join the KNCC because of its broader theological framework. A member of the WCC and CCA, the KNCC is the official representative organization of the Protestant church in Korea. The KNCC churches do cooperate with nonmember churches in activities such as the Easter Sunday Daybreak* worship and Christian literature and publishing (e.g., the work of the Bible Society and hymnals). The ecumenical movement both unites and divides churches in Korea. On the one hand it is drawing many denominations together, and on the other it is causing splits in churches.

India. India has a long history of ecumenism. The first Protestant mission, the Danish-Royal Tranquebar Mission in the 18th c., was an ecumenical mission involving Christians from Denmark, Germany, Sweden, Italy, and England. In 1808 William Carey suggested to Andrew Fuller, secretary of the Baptist Missionary Society, to call a World Missionary Conference to be held in 1810 at the Cape of Good Hope. His dream came true, but not until 1910 with the Edinburgh World Missionary Conference. Meanwhile, missionaries in India felt keenly the need for fellowship and cooperation. First at the local level, missionary consultations and fellowship came into being in Bombay (1825), Calcutta (1830), and Madras. From 1855 to 1900, five regional missionary conferences were held in various places. From 1872 to 1902, at the national level, decennial missionary conferences were held four times, bringing various mission societies and their missionaries (including a few Indian Christians) together to discuss common missionary interests. In 1914 the National Missionary Council (NMC) was created with the main purpose of acting as a channel for better cooperation between Christians in India. In 1922 the NMC changed its name to the National Christian Council (now the National Council of Churches in India or NCCI), headquartered at Nagpur. The NCCI is supported by 14 regional councils, and its 26 larger churches (Protestant) are its members. The first organic union took place among churches belonging to different missions of the same type of churchmanship. The first was in 1901, when two Presbyterian churches in South India, the American Arcot Mission and two Scottish Presbyterian Missions (the Church of Scotland and the Free Church of Scotland), united. In 1904 this body joined with eight Presbyterian Missions in North India to form a Presbyterian Church of India. Another union was effected in 1905 when the Congregationalists of the London Mission and the American Madura Mission came together. The first interdenominational union was the South India United Church (SIUC), formed in 1908. This was a union of all the Congregationalists and Presbyterians in South India and the Jaffna District of Ceylon (Sri Lanka); in 1919 the Basel Mission of Malabar also joined. The church order was a mixture of Congregationalism and Presbyterianism, governed by eight regional church councils and a general assembly. This agreement provided for local autonomy and differences of practice between one area and another. A parallel union was formed in 1924 in North India by the formation of the United Church of North India (UCNI), a union of Presbyterians and Congregationalists. Eleven missions were represented in it, and its area stretched from Bengal and Assam to Gujarat and Punjab. The constitution was Presbyterian. Each local congregation had its session; there were 25 church councils, representing groups of congregations over particular areas; seven synods, representing the church councils of a linguistic area; and a general assembly. The first serious call for a wider interdenominational union representing episcopal and non-episcopal traditions was sounded under the leadership of V. S. Azariah (Anglican), V. Santiago (SIUC), H. A. Popley (an English missionary), G. Sherwood Eddy (an American Congregationalist), and a few others when they drew up the Tranquebar Manifesto in 1919. The Manifesto was sent to the episcopal synod of the Anglican Church in India and the general assembly of the SIUC, inviting them to consider entering into union on the basis of certain general principles. Consequently, a joint committee was set up and began work in 1920. The Wesleyan Methodist Church joined in from 1925 on. The Scheme of Union was published in 1929. After it went through seven editions, it was finally accepted and, after its twentieth and last session, the Church of South India (CSI) was inaugurated on 27 Sep 1947 in Madras. The CSI maintained the historic episcopate but did not attempt to formulate a new doctrine. It began with a mixed ministry and left the ultimate decision to the united church at some future time. It was provided that all the ministers of each uniting party should be accepted as ministers of the CSI with the right to minister anywhere within it; but a "pledge" was given that no minister would be imposed upon a congregation that could not consciously welcome his ministrations. In addition, it was laid down that, after 30 years, all new ordinations in the CSI would be episcopal. The church should then decide whether it would continue to allow exceptions to the rule of episcopal ordination. Consultation with a view to union began in North India in 1929. Two organizations, the Round Table Conference and the Joint Council, working on different lines and representing partly the same and partly different churches, made preliminary explorations. After sailing a stormy sea, a negotiating committee was constituted in 1951 by the church bodies concerned, namely, the UCNI, the Anglican (the Church of India, Pakistan, Burma, and Ceylon), the Methodist Church of South Asia (MESA), the (British and Australia) Methodist Church, and the Council of Baptist Churches in Northern India. Two others, the Church of the Brethren and the Disciples of Christ, joined in the negotiations from 1957. The plan drawn up in 1933 reached its fourth and final edition in 1965, and on that basis the Church of North India (CNI) was inaugurated at Nagpur on 29 Nov 1970. The MESA, which had announced its acceptance of the plan in Jan 1970, decided in August not to join. From the outset the ministry was unified, adopting the Episcopalian form. All the previous ordinations were accepted as fully valid, but at the inauguration the rite of mutual laying on of hands with prayer was done as a scriptural and traditional symbol of the bestowing of spiritual gifts by God. In the matter of baptism, both infant and believer's baptism have been accepted and practiced. These two organic unions have been followed by numerous union negotiations between them and other denominational churches, but none of them have borne visible union. The impetus seems to be declining recently in favor of conciliar unity. In addition to the above, there arose numerous union institutions in the area of liberal education, theological training, and medical and health care, and a host of cooperative organizations function in India today, serving God and humankind in various ways.

Indonesia. By the 1920s, various attempts had been made to draw congregations and churches together. Initially, these efforts were pioneered by the Chinese. This is quite understandable, as the Chinese in Indonesia had been drawn together by events in mainland China. In 1926 Chinese Christians set up an organization called *Bond Kristen Tionghoa* ("Chinese Christian Association") with the intention of encouraging unity among Chinese Christians in general and, more specifically, among Chinese Christian congregations. In the 1930s some fully self-managed and united non-Chinese churches were also founded. During the Japanese occupation of Indonesia, a number of such ecumenical movements emerged that were intensive in tone, though nearly all of them were initiated by the Japanese. For example, the so-called *Celebes Kiristokyodan Rengokai* was founded in 1942 in Central and South Sulawesi. It was a forced union that later also encompassed North Sulawesi. In 1943 the Unification of the Christian Churches in Ambon was inaugurated. The former proved to be a social agency, but the latter became an actual regional council of churches. Both unions were dissolved when the Japanese were defeated. In the period 1946-47, two councils of churches, functioning as regional councils, were instituted. The first was the Consulting Council of Churches in Indonesia, founded in 1946 in Yogyakarta and covering churches in Java, and the second, the Assembly of Joint Efforts of the Christian Churches, founded in 1947 in Malino and covering a number of churches in Sulawesi* and other parts of East Indonesia. The latter council pioneered the establishment of the future National Council of Churches. Resistance was encountered in the formation of the National Council of Churches. After much struggle (1948-50), the *Dewan Gereja-gereja di Indonesia* (DGI, "Council of Churches in Indonesia") was officially inaugurated on 25 May 1950. Based on the commitment to establish "One Christian Church in Indonesia," the 10th General Assembly of DGI held in 1984 (Ambon) changed its name to the Communion of Churches in Indonesia* (PGI). Other ecumenical bodies in Indonesia include the Indonesian Evangelical Association, founded in 1971, which is both an association and a place for cooperative action among interested persons, bodies, and churches adhering to evangelical principles; the Union of Baptist Churches, founded in 1971, which is actually limited to all extant Baptist Churches in Indonesia; the Indonesian Pentecostal Council, founded in 1979; the Baptist Alliance, founded in 1981; and the Conference of Church's Trustees in Indonesia, founded in 1924 at a meeting of Roman Catholic bishops.

Sri Lanka. The cordiality and friendship between the Church of England and the Methodists is a noted fact in the early years of their missions in Sri Lanka. From the very beginning, the Bible Society was the common meeting ground of the missionaries of various denominations. Baptists and Methodists shared one another's chapels and frequently spoke on the same platforms at public meetings.

The deterioration of these relations was seen in 1841, when E. B. Pusey accused the Methodists of heresy in England. The disagreements between Methodists and Anglicans came to a head with the dispute regarding burial grounds in Moratuwa in 1851. The dispute over Anglican privileges also separated the dissenters and the Anglicans. There was no fellowship between the Protestant denominations and the Roman Catholics during the 19th c.

However, toward the beginning of the 20th c., Christians realized that the divided church was in itself a stumbling block to evangelism. In 1902, the formation of the Christian Alliance with J. A. Spear as first president was important in working toward interdenominational cooperation. The visit of John R. Mott to Colombo in 1912 led to the formation of the All Ceylon Missionary Conference, where Protestants cooperated on common issues. The founding of the Training Colony at Peradeniya in 1914 was the united venture of Methodists, Anglicans, and Baptists. While the situation was improving in the Sinhala areas, similar developments were taking place in the Tamil areas, where the American Congregationalists, Methodists, and Anglicans united for common action. In 1907 the Jaffna Christian Union was founded in order to continue the interdenominational cooperation that was carried out under the auspices of the Jaffna Bible Society. The first United Christian Teachers Training College in Jaffna was inaugurated in 1922.

The SCM, YMCA (1885), and YWCA also brought these denominations together. The National Christian Council formed in 1923 was a practical step toward ecumenical cooperation.

The initial move toward church union was taken in 1934 when church leaders met at Trinity College in Kandy. There was then formed a society in Sri Lanka called Friends of Reunion. The churches invited to this included the Church of Ceylon, the Methodist Church, the Presbyterian churches, the Baptist Church, and the South Indian United Church. The Dutch Reformed Church, which was one of the Presbyterian churches in Sri Lanka, withdrew from the union in 1952. The Jaffna Diocese of the newly formed Church of South India remained in the Sri Lanka Church Union negotiations.

The negotiations for church union in Sri Lanka have been difficult. The churches began educating the masses about the necessity of the union in 1966. There existed a minority of people who were against church union from the very beginning. In 1972 the participating churches voted for the church union scheme of 1971. The intention was to inaugurate the United Church of Sri Lanka on Advent Sunday 1972. It was at this stage that three members of the Church of Ceylon challenged in a court of law the vote taken on Church Union in the diocesan Council of the Diocese of Colombo in Oct 1971. The verdict given on 24 Jun 1974 made it difficult to go ahead with the scheme for church union.

Since then, despite continued negotiations, church union in Sri Lanka has not become a reality. The division has been increased by the emergence of several new denominations and independent churches during the last two decades. The Pentecostal denominations have, thus far, kept aloof from negotiations for unity.

Bibliography

Rouse, R., S. C. Neill, and H. E. Fey, eds., *A History of the Ecumenical Movement,* 2 Vols. (2d ed. 1967, 1970). • Weber, Hans-Ruedi, *Asia and the Ecumenical Movement 1896-1961* (1966). • Yap Kim Hao, *From Prapat to Colombo: History of the Christian Conference of Asia, 1957-1995* (1995). • Clark, Allen D., *A History of the Church in Korea* (1971). • Rhodes, H. A., ed., *History of the Korea Mission Presbyterian Church USA, 1884-1934* (1934). • Rhodes, H. A., and A. Campbell, eds., *History of the Ko-*

rean Mission Presbyterian Church, USA, 1935-1950 (1984). • Chun, Taek Boo, *Hankook Ecumenical Undongsa* (History of the ecumenical movement in Korea). • Arangaden, A. D., *Church Union in South India: Its Progress and Consummation* (1947). • Baago, K., *A History of the National Council of Churches* (1965). • Firth, C. B., *An Introduction to Indian Church History* (1989). • Kellock, James, *Breakthrough for Church Union for North India and Pakistan* (1965). • Paul, R. D., *The First Decade: An Account of CSI* (1958); *Ecumenism in Action: A Historical Survey of the Church of South India* (1972). • Sundkler, B., *Church of South India: The Movement towards Union 1990-1947* (1954); *The Plan of Church Union in North India and Pakistan* (1965). • Hartono, Chris, *Gerakan Ekumenis di Indonesia* (1984). • Van den End, T., *Ragi Carita* 2 (1990). • Wilson, D. Kangasabai, *The Christian Church in Sri Lanka* (1975).

Yap Kim Hao, with Smith N Za Thawng (Myanmar), Kim In Soo (Korea), F. Hrangkhuma (India), Chris Hartono (Indonesia), and G. P. V. Somaratna (Sri Lanka)

Edict of Toleration, Thailand

Although it was hailed by Protestant missionaries in Thailand* as the charter of Christian liberty, later research suggests that the Edict of Toleration, established in northern Thailand in 1878, was of more limited significance. The edict was issued in response to an appeal to the king by Presbyterian* missionaries in northern Thailand for permission to allow Christians to marry without having to pay "spirit fees." Officials of the semi-independent tributary states in the north used these fees to limit Christian conversion and expansion. The king referred the petition back to his viceroy in Chiang Mai, who issued an edict on 8 Oct 1878 addressed to three of the northern states. It affirmed the rights of people to convert to Christianity and observe the sabbath, as well as the right of American citizens to hire as servants anyone they wanted.

The missionaries believed this edict would lead to a period of territorial expansion and growth by reducing official persecution of Christians. Later generations of missionaries and Thai Christians considered it a guarantee of religious freedom. In some instances, the edict did relieve pressure on Christian groups or individuals, but its actual influence was limited geographically and to a relatively short period of time. In a number of instances, local officials openly defied it, and the widespread harassment of Christians continued. The edict may well have had a much more significant impact on the Bangkok government's campaign to extend its power over the northern states, as it afforded the king's viceroy an opportunity to assert central authority.

Bibliography

McGilvary, Daniel, *A Half Century Among the Siamese and Lao* (1912). • McFarland, George Bradley, ed., *Historical Sketch of Protestant Missions in Siam, 1828-1928* (1928). • Swanson, Herbert R., *Krischak Muang Nua* (1984).

Herbert R. Swanson

Edkins, Joseph

(b. Gloucester, England, 1823; d. Shanghai, 1905). English Protestant missionary and sinologist.

A graduate of London University and the Congregational College, Edkins was a missionary with the London Missionary Society (LMS). He arrived in Shanghai in September 1848 via Hong Kong and worked as an evangelist at the LMS hospital. He returned to England in 1858, married and returned with his wife to China*.

In 1860 Edkins and another missionary, Griffith John*, went to Suzhou (Soochow), Jiangsu, to meet with Hong Jen-kan, the Kan Wang (Shield King) of the Taiping Rebellion* and a cousin of Hong Xiuquan. They had met Jen-kan in 1854 when he was studying at the LMS academy in Shanghai. Jen-kan was also, for a time, employed as an evangelist by the LMS. Both missionaries were sympathetic to the Taiping cause because of its Christian overtones and pleaded for neutrality from the foreign powers on its behalf.

Edkins decided to develop mission work in northern China. In 1860 and 1861 he stationed himself in Yantai (Cheefoo) and Tianjin respectively. He made several trips to Beijing in 1862 and baptized three converts as members of the first Protestant church in the capital. In 1863 he and his wife became the first Protestant missionaries to settle in Beijing. He bought a dilapidated Buddhist temple near a grain market and converted it into a chapel from which he preached daily.

He was awarded a doctorate by the University of Edinburgh in 1875 for his knowledge of Chinese culture. He retired from the mission field in 1880 and worked as a translator for the Imperial Customs Service. He was also involved in the translation and revision of the Chinese Bible. He died in Shanghai. His translation of *Treatises on Mechanics* and *History of Greece and Rome* were popular readings among the Chinese intellectuals. A varied writer, his works included *Chinese Buddhism* (1890), *Religious Condition of China* (1859), *China's Place in Philology, Chinese Currency, The Revenue and Taxation of the Chinese Empire* and *Banking and Price in China.*

Bibliography

Barr, Pat, *To China with Love* (1972).

China Group, translated by Patricia Siew

El Padre Capitan

("The Priest-Captain") (b. 1599; d. 1653). Nickname of Spanish father Agustin Rodrigues de San Pedro, first prior of Cagayan (now Cagayan de Oro City), northern Mindanao, Philippines*.

In Spain in 1619, Rodrigues de San Pedro had so devoted himself to mathematics and military science that his superiors ordered him to desist. But his knowledge of these fields proved beneficial in organizing the defenses of northern Mindanao Recollect missions against Islamic raids. He fortified the Cagayan Christian settlement complete with a high stockade, bulwarks, sentry boxes, and redoubts; and he drilled his Christians in the use of arquebuses. About 1627, he led them in beating off 2,000 Maguindanao invaders and also checked the frequent raids of the Maranaws.

Bibliography

De Jesus, L., "Historia General, decada IV," ch. v, no. 3, in E. H. Blair and J. A. Robertson, *The Philippine Islands* XXXV (1903-9). • De la Concepcion, J., *Historia General de Filipinas* V (1788).

T. VALENTINO SITOY, JR.

11th Union of Chinese-Speaking Christian Churches of Singapore

(Xin Jia Po Hua Wen Ji Du Jiao Lian He Hui). The 11th Union of Chinese-Speaking Christian Churches of Singapore* was formed on 10 Oct 1931 from the Singapore Overseas Chinese Christian Evangelistic League *(Xin Jia Po Hua Qiao Ji Du Jiao Nan Yang Bu Dao Tuan),* which had been founded in 1928. When the Union was formed, the League became its department of evangelism.

The 11th Union was first called the Singapore Chinese Christian Inter-Church Union *(Xin Jia Po Hua Qiao Ji Du Jiao Lian He Hui).* Its constitution states, "The Union purposes to work together with the Chinese-speaking Christian Churches of all denominations . . . as well as Chinese-speaking Christian Organizations . . . to advance the relevant works of Christianity and to promote wider deeds of charity."

In 1935, the Union organized the John Sung* Evangelistic and Revival Crusade in Singapore, which resulted in over 1,300 conversions and the formation of the Singapore Christian Evangelistic League *(Xin Jia Po Ji Du Tu Bu Dao Tuan).* It was also instrumental in the establishment of the Chinese Young Men's Christian Association* (YMCA) in 1946 and the Singapore Bible College in 1952. In Jul 1946, it published *The Original Light,* which continued for 15 issues.

The 11th Union was formally registered with the Registrar of Societies on 20 Sep 1971. The inaugural issue of *The Christian Church Union Bulletin (Ji Du Jiao Lian Bao)* was published on Easter 1973. Since then, the Union has published three issues annually on Easter, National Day, and Christmas.

The 11th Union organized annual youth evangelistic rallies from 1975 to 1990 and, since 1982, annual Bible* expositions. Membership in 1994 included 44 churches from various denominations, 15 Christian organizations, and 38 individuals.

Bibliography

Sng, Bobby E. K., *In His Good Time* (1980, 1993).

LEE CHONG KAU

Elias III

(b. 1867; d. Manjinikkara, 13 Feb 1932). Patriarch of Antioch who arrived in Kerala and died there.

Elias III became patriarch on 25 Feb 1917. He was invited by the British viceroy, Lord Irvin, to settle a dispute between two parties in the Syrian Orthodox Church, but his attempts were unsuccessful. Upon his death, he was buried at Manjinikkara, which today is the home of a mission station for the Syrian bishops and prelates.

JACOB KURIAN

Emilia, Simeon S.

(b. 1886; d. 1984). Pioneer Filipino Presbyterian* minister, first and long-serving pastor of the Bais Evangelical Church in the Philippines*.

Emilia was one of the first 15 students of Silliman Institute in Dumaguete, Negros Oriental, in 1901. He started Christian work in 1904, first as a student volunteer and from 1906 on as a full-fledged evangelist. Beginning in 1908, he served as the first pastor of Bais Evangelical Church and held this position for nearly two decades.

Ordained by the Cebu presbytery in 1914, Emilia also became the first moderator of the Dumaguete presbytery in 1918. He held this position several times during the following 35 years, which saw the church unions of 1929 and 1948. Emilia served in this capacity longer than any other minister. He retired in 1951 but continued church work until the late 1960s, marking more than half a century of unbroken Christian service.

Bibliography

73rd Annual Presbyterian Board Report (1990). • Sitoy, T. V., Jr., *Several Springs, One Stream* (1992). • Interview with Simeon S. Emilia, Dumaguete City, 12 Sep 1967.

T. VALENTINO SITOY, JR.

Emperor System, Tennosei

Specialized term to describe the problematic system of control existing in Japan* from the 1920s.

The Tennosei emperor system, in its widest interpretation, refers to the Japanese form of government that makes the emperor the sovereign ruler. As the characteristics and structure are not historically standardized, one can refer to both the emperor system of ancient times and the emperor system of modern times.

Usually, the emperor system at issue is the one which existed from the time of the Meiji Restoration (1868) until the end of World War II*, placing the emperor at the top of everything in Japan — the political system, business, culture, society, and thought. Though the description of the emperor system in the postwar constitution of Japan is fundamentally different from that in the imperial constitution, it is still called "the emperor system" today.

The rule of the emperor system after the Meiji Restoration was extremely authoritarian because of the times and conditions. Though there have been periods in the longer historical span when it possessed power and periods when it did not, the emperor system pervading the whole of Japanese society became stronger with the development of militarism and fascism in modern times. The emperor system placed the emperor at the top of the national power structure (legislative, judicial, administrative, military, and police). In economics, by treating the assets of the imperial family as those of a strong capitalist and great landowner, he became the top capitalist landowner with the economic control system as an ally. In society, he became the head of the Japanese "family" state, with all Japanese taught to consider him as their father and ruler. Nationalizing the Shinto* religion and making the emperor into a god forced other religions into subordinate roles. The emperor system was solidified by making the imperial rescript on education the guiding moral principle and the emperor the primary source of morality, and by absolutizing the people's loyalty to the emperor by placing him at the top of the moral lineage and at the top of the educational structure.

With the new postwar constitution of Japan, even the emperor's position in politics was changed, and a large percentage of imperial family assets became property of the state. A number of remnants of the old emperor system are still in existence, however, especially "the emperor system within the heart of each Japanese person." This means that the people's awareness of the emperor system has not been removed. It is important to note that the criticism of and opposition to the modern emperor system have come mainly from Marxists on the one hand, and some religious leaders on the other, such as Jehovah's Witnesses, Christian Holiness denominations, and new religions like *Tenri Honmichi* (The Real Principle), *Hitonomichi* (The Principle of Men), and *Motokyo* (Imperial Faith).

IISAKA YOSHIAKI, JAPANESE DICTIONARY

Encomienda/Encomendero

Tribute system in the Philippines* during its initial 150 years of colonial rule by Spain.

Originating in Spain itself, the *encomienda* was transplanted by the Spaniards to their colonies in Spanish America. Then via Mexico, they instituted it in the Philippines in order to compensate the Spanish soldiers for rendering meritorious service in the conquest and pacification of the Philippine inhabitants, and to attract Spanish citizens to settle in the colony. Under this system, the *encomiendas* were classified as crown *encomiendas* or private *encomiendas*. The *encomiendas* raised revenue for the colonial government while rewarding those who served king, God, and country in this colonial outpost halfway around the world from Spain.

Spain established the first *encomiendas* in the Philippines on 25 Jan 1571. These *encomiendas* were in Cebu Island. The first governor-general of the Philippines, Miguel Lopez de Legaspi*, created these *encomiendas* on the basis of a royal fiat issued by the Spanish king Philip II on 16 Nov 1568. The recipient of an *encomienda* grant came to be known as an *encomendero*. As an *encomendero*, the grantee enjoyed the privilege of collecting tribute from the pacified and colonized inhabitants of the Philippines. During the initial decades of Spanish colonization, the *encomendero* collected the authorized amount of eight *reales* from every adult residing within the territory covered by his *encomienda* grant. The *encomendero* could keep two *reales* from the eight he collected, with another two apportioned for the missionary personnel in his *encomienda*. The remaining four *reales* went to the government treasury. In subsequent decades, the tribute exacted from the Filipinos increased to 10 *reales* and eventually to 14.

Admittedly, the *encomienda* system and the *encomenderos* caused suffering among the Filipino inhabitants. The tribute could be commuted to its equivalent in kind or to labor, leading to abuses such as the outright confiscation of property and exploitation. As well, the *encomenderos* collected tribute in excess of the prescribed amount and used a heavy hand in making their exactions. Bishops Martin de Rada and Domingo de Salazar*, of the Augustinian* Order and the Dominican* Order respectively, in their own time criticized the system for the hardships it visited upon the Philippine population.

Nevertheless, the *encomienda* system (which started to decline as a source of revenue after 1621 until a royal order issued on 17 Sept 1721 declared that all private *encomiendas* falling vacant throughout the country would no longer be regranted to individuals or to missionary groups, but would instead revert to the crown) performed a vital role as a form of public office at the beginning of Spanish rule. The *encomendero* acted as the personal representative of the Spanish monarch at the local level of his far-flung Philippine colonial domain. In this sense, the *encomendero* represented the first civil authority in the islands. He functioned as the intermediary between the royal government and the colonized Filipinos, and was mandated by crown legislation to provide military protection for the inhabitants of the islands, and to educate them politically and spiritually.

More significant was the role played by the *encomendero* within the sphere of religion and the spread of Roman Catholic Christianity in the Philippines. He performed the functions of a lay apostle. Legally, the *encomendero* carried the obligation to provide prebaptismal instruction to his *encomienda* wards, such as the recitation of the three basic prayers of the Roman Catholic faith (Ave Maria, Pater Noster, and Credo) and the making of the sign of the cross. In certain cases where a priest was not available, the *encomendero* had authority to offer sacraments. As a lay missionary, the *encomendero* was also responsible, as mentioned earlier, for providing from the tribute demanded of each ward two *reales* to pay the salaries of the priests who rendered evangelical labor with him in his *encomienda.* He was to help in the construction of chapels and provide wine for use in religious masses.

Although the *encomendero* did not always execute his quasi-missionary obligations faithfully, he nevertheless did not completely fail in fulfilling his role as a lay missionary. The *encomendero* assisted the friars and priests in teaching the Filipinos the rudiments and tenets of the Roman Catholic, indeed Christian, religion and their duties as newly converted Christians.

There is not sufficient evidence to suggest any connection between the *encomienda* system and the great landed estates, called *haciendas,* which emerged in the Philippines late in the 18th c. and throughout the 19th c. to transform the Philippine economy from an agricultural subsistence economy to an agricultural export economy, and thereby shape the nature of modern Philippine society. The *encomienda* system and the *hacienda* system were two separate institutions having their own respective impact on Filipino societal development and growth.

Bibliography

Bauzon, Leslie, "The Encomienda System as a Spanish Colonial Institution in the Philippines, 1571-1604," *Silliman Journal* XIV, No. 2 (1967). • de la Costa, Horacio V., "Church and State in the Philippines During the Administration of Bishop Salazar, 1581-1594," *Hispanic American Historical Review* XXX (Aug 1950). • Kirkpatrick, Frederick A., "Landless Encomienda," *Hispanic American Historical Review* XXII (Nov 1942). • Phelan, John Leddy, "Pre-Baptismal Instruction and the Administration of Baptism in the Philippines During the Sixteenth Century," *The Americas* XII (July 1955); *The Hispanization of the Philippines: Spanish Aims and Filipino Responses, 1565-1700* (1959). LESLIE E. BAUZON

Ende

Town on the island of Flores (Lesser Sunda Islands) and seat of a Catholic archbishop whose ecclesiastical province comprises the suffragan dioceses of Larantuka and Ruteng in Flores and Denpasar in Bali.

Dominican* missionaries from Goa, who established the Solor Mission, succeeded in founding strong congregations in the eastern part of the Ende Diocese, especially in the Sikka area after 1566. Though these communities were neglected through many decades of the 18th and 19th cs., they kept the faith mainly by means of pious devotions introduced by their Indo-Portuguese missionaries. When Jesuit* missionaries arrived from Larantuka (1863), they were readily accepted, and in a few decades the whole area around Maumere (1873) and the old kingdom of Sikka (1884) became Catholic again. Religious brothers and sisters from the Netherlands established schools, boarding houses, hospitals, and teacher training colleges. Many teachers proved to be very apostolic and brought the faith to western Flores (since 1912) and to many islands of Eastern Indonesia*. The Jesuits handed their flourishing mission over to missionaries of the new Society of the Divine Word* (SVD) (1914-19), and Ende became the seat of the first apostolic prefect of the Lesser Sunda Islands. Petrus Noyen*, a former missionary in China*, proved to be a far-sighted planner of the mission strategy.

In the *Flores-Soemba Regeling* (1913), the colonial government had pledged to support primary mission schools on the whole island of Flores. Many of these schools became the first means of evangelization and social progress. In a period of 40 years (1921-62) the church of Ende grew from 34,084 to 338,964 faithful despite heavy setbacks during the Japanese occupation. By 1992, nearly all of Flores had become Catholic (Ende: 581,364; Larantuka: 224,766; Ruteng: 458,947 faithful). Three minor (since 1926) and two major seminaries in Ledalero (1937) and Ritapiret (1955) educate local clergy for both the diocese of Ende (1961) and other mission areas in and outside Indonesia. The novitiates of several congregations of sisters and brothers are growing in numbers, especially those of indigenous congregations, e.g., the Congregation of the Followers of Jesus (CFJ, since 1935).

During the Japanese occupation, thanks to Captain Sato's understanding and the intervention of the vicar apostolic of Nagasaki, Mgr. Yamaguchi, the German-born bishop, Mgr. Leven, and a few old Dutch priests were allowed to serve the hundreds of thousands of believers. After 1941, they were supported by the first two young Florenese priests. Local congregations of sisters and indigenous sisters of international congregations conduct educational, medical, social, and pastoral work together with a rapidly growing number of secular priests. The diocese of Ende is numerically the largest in Indonesia, with more than half a million faithful in about 73 parishes (97% of the population).

Bibliography

Teixeire, M., *The Portuguese Missions in Malacca and Singapore (1511-1958),* Vol. II (1961-63). • Cornelissen, P. F., *Missie-arbeid oner Japanse Besetting* (1949). • Muskens, M. P. M., ed., *Sejarah Gereja Katolik Indonesia,* Vol. IIIb (1974). • Tennien, M., and T. Sarto, *I Remember Flores* (1957). • Petu, P. P., *Nusa Tenggara, Setengah Abad Karya Misi SVD (1913-1963)* (1966). ADOLF HEUKEN

Endo Shusaku

(b. Tokyo, 27 Mar 1923; d. Tokyo, 29 Sep 1996). Japanese Christian author.

Endo is the best known of a series of authors of Christian persuasion to emerge to literary prominence in Japan* after the Pacific War. Troubled by the sense of unease he experienced when confronted by "the great flow of European Christianity" as one of the first Japanese students to study in France after the cessation of hostilities, and forced to return home prematurely with tuberculosis, he resolved to pursue a literary career in which he sought to "locate God on the streets of Shinjuku and Shibuya, districts which seemed so far removed from Him."

Endo was moved to Manchuria at age three and remained there until he was 10 when, following his parents' divorce, he returned with his mother to Kobe. Inspired by the example of his aunt, he was baptized into the Catholic tradition later that same year and eventually proceeded to Keio University to study the writings of Mauriac and other French Catholic authors. Increasingly "concerned with the conflict and tension created by [his] identity as a Christian, a Japanese and an author," Endo's subsequent *oeuvre* represents a concerted attempt to "retailor the ill-fitting suit of Western Christianity" into something more suited to his needs.

In his early classic, *Silence* (1966), this tension assumes the form of Rodrigues, a Portuguese missionary who enters Japan in defiance of the 17th c. proscription on all proselytization and is there confronted by the image of the country as a "mudswamp," one in which the "roots" of Christianity are destined to "rot and wither." Following his inevitable arrest, Rodrigues is faced with an impossible choice: to trample on the *fumie* (crucifix) in the ultimate act of apostasy or to cling to his faith in the knowledge that such a response will result not only in his own death but also in that of the Japanese peasants whose cries of agony he can hear emanating from the nearby torture pit. The subsequent portrayal of Rodrigues as he accedes to the magistrate's demands was the subject of considerable controversy at the time of publication of the novel, but a close reading of its concluding sections suggests a protagonist ultimately possessed of a faith more personal and more profound than that which had inspired him to risk all in embarking on his mission to Japan in the first place.

In his novels of the 1970s and early 1980s, most notably in the beautifully crafted *The Samurai* (1980), Endo built on this same theme. His next major work, *Scandal* (1986), surprised many of his critics with its apparent shift of focus toward examination of the protagonist, Suguro, himself an elderly Catholic author, troubled by his perceived doppelganger. Especially when read in conjunction with Endo's final work, *Deep River* (1993), however, the view emerges of this as yet one more literary depiction of the individual intent on reconciliation of the various, often seemingly conflicting, aspects of his multifaceted nature. *Deep River,* in particular, is a remarkable work. The portrayal of Otsu, the disaffected young man more at home living in a Hindu ashram and providing practical assistance to those dying beside the Ganges than in the confined circles of the European seminaries in which he had initially sought spiritual solace is a powerful testimony to the potency of the interfaith dialogue which Endo had come increasingly to advocate.

Bibliography

Endo Shusaku, *Silence* (1966); *The Samurai* (1980); *Scandal* (1986); *Deep River* (1993). • Gessel, Van, "Voices in the Wilderness: Japanese Christian Authors," *Monumenta Nipponica,* Vol. 37, No. 4 (Winter 1982). • Williams, Mark, *Endo Shusaku: A Literature of Reconciliation* (1999).

MARK WILLIAMS

Ephrem the Syrian

(ca. 306-73). Ephrem's influence on the entire Christian church can scarcely be overstated. His works were translated into Armenian, Georgian, Latin, Old Slavonic, Greek, Arabic, Chinese, Coptic, and Ethiopic. His influence on the Syriac-language churches was probably the single most determinative factor in their development. He influenced biblical interpretation, theological method, the content of theology, the definition of orthodoxy, liturgy, and hymnody. His criticism of older intellectual and scientific traditions in Syria led to their eventual demise as viable methods of explaining the universe.

Ephrem was born in a Christian home and eventually joined the church, becoming a member of the "sons of the covenant," a quasi-monastic and ascetic community for guiding Christian life. He was never ordained. The title of deacon was given to him by later sources in an effort to make him part of the church hierarchy. Despite his fame and influence, little is known of his life. According to the later hagiographers who supply details otherwise unknown, he left Nisibis for Edessa after Nisibis was surrendered to the Persians by Emperor Jovian upon the death of Emperor Julian in a campaign against the Persians in 363. According to these same sources, he died while organizing and providing relief during a famine in 373.

Ephrem was a prolific writer. He wrote commentaries on the *Diatessaron,* probably on Genesis and Exodus, and perhaps on the Pauline Epistles. The commentaries on the Pauline Epistles are preserved only in Armenian, and their authenticity is debatable. Other exegetical material is attributed to Ephrem in various manuscripts. Most of that material is not authentic. The exegesis in the *Commentary on the Diatessaron* reflects several of Ephrem's concerns: (1) there are two levels of text: the historical narrative and the level of symbolism; (2) there is a balance between Old and New Testament images and symbols as well as a convergence of the two collections; (3) nature is to be considered revelatory of God and of God's intention for the creation.

The prose works attributed to Ephrem include sermons, letters (many of which are inauthentic), and, most important, the *Refutation of Heresies.* The *Refutation of Heresies* is certainly from Ephrem. In this text, he criticizes the approaches to spirituality* and theology found among his religious competitors in Nisibis and Edessa. Those criticized include the Manichaeans, Marcionites, Bardaisanites, and the Arians. He argues that the determinism and tendencies toward dualism lead to an understanding of God and human nature that is counter to the biblical witness. As a determined proponent of both freedom of the will and of a progression toward Christian perfection, Ephrem was quite in the tradition of the Alexandrian theologians Philo, Clement of Alexandria, and Origen.

Most popular were the metrical poems composed by Ephrem to be sung by choirs of women in the churches. More than 450 compositions are extant. These were early organized into cycles or collections of hymns around various themes. The problems of authenticity are significant, as many sought to duplicate his artistry and to have their work passed off under his name. His work is rich in its use of images and symbols, as well as in its evident piety. This corpus was translated into many languages and continues to be used in the Syriac-language churches of the Middle East (and the diaspora), as well as by churches in India.

Bibliography

Editions and Translations: Beck, E., *Ephraem der Syrer . . .* (1955-79). • Brock, S., *The Harp of the Spirit,* 2nd ed. (1983); *St. Ephrem the Syrian: Hymns on Paradise* (1990). • Mitchell, C. W., E. A. Bevan, and F. C. Burkitt, eds. and trans., *Prose Refutations* (1912, 1921). • McCarthy, C., *St. Ephrem's Commentary on Tatian's Diatessaron: A Translation of the Chester Beatty Syriac MS 709* (1993). • Mathews, E. G., Jr., and Joe Amar, trans., *St. Ephrem the Syrian: Prose Works,* Fathers of the Church 91 (1995). • McVey, K., trans., *Ephrem the Syrian: Hymns* (1989).

Studies: Brock, S., *The Luminous Eye: The Spiritual World Vision of St. Ephrem the Syrian,* 2nd ed. (1992); *The Syriac Fathers on Prayer and the Spiritual Life* (1987). • Griffith, S., "Ephraem, the Deacon of Edessa, and the Church of the Empire," *Diakonia: Studies in Honor of Robert T. Meyer,* ed. T. Halton and J. P. Williams (1986). • Hidal, S., *Interpretatio Syriaca* (1974). • Mansour, T. B., *La Pensée symbolique de saint Ephrem le Syrien* (1988). • Murray, Robert, *Symbols of Church and Kingdom: A Study in the Early Syriac Tradition* (1975). • Petersen, W. L., *The Diatessaron and Ephrem Syrus as Sources of Romanos the Melodist* (1986). • Bundy, D., "Christianity in Syria," *Anchor Bible Dictionary* 1 (1992).

DAVID BUNDY

Episcopalians. *See* Anglican Church

Erekhawan

A Mongol word originally meaning "blessed man" or "blessed woman," but later also meaning "presbyter," "clergy," or "priest."

Generally, Erekhawan referred to those Christians who professed the Christianity (actually, Nestorianism*) which spread into China* during the Yuan Dynasty in the 13th to 14th c. At this time, the members of the Order of Friars Minor (Franciscans*) and Nestorian clergymen were also called Erekhawans. Most believers were Alans, Mongolians, and Keraits. There were Erekhawan churches in Gansu Province, Ningxia Province, and some cities such as Beijing, Hangzhou, Xian, Zhenjiang, and Yangzhou. Some missionaries were appointed Chinese officials and received handsome salaries. Their followers enjoyed such privileges as exemption from military service and taxes. According to the statistics in 1330, there were about 30,000 Christians. Erekhawan disappeared from China after the Yuan Dynasty collapsed. Some traces of Erekhawan have been found since the 19th c.

Bibliography

Moule, A. C., *Christians in China Before the Year 1550* (1930). • Moffett, Samuel H., *A History of Christianity in Asia* (1992).

CHINA GROUP

Eschatological Movements, Korea

Korean eschatology has its roots in the literal premillennial interpretation of Rev. 20:1-6 held by the Western missionaries who pioneered Korean mission work. Premillennialists hold the position that Christ's second coming and the first resurrection will herald the thousand-year reign of Christ on earth. It will be followed by a second resurrection and the final judgment. The millennial reign will be preceded by supernatural and catastrophic events.

Influenced by the monthly publication of the Seventh-Day Adventists, *Signs of the Times* (first published in 1910), some Korean Protestant churches began to emphasize eschatology. The Holiness Church (see Korea Evangelical Holiness Church) has always emphasized the second coming of Jesus as one of its four cardinal doctrines. Eschatological preaching was well received by Koreans because of the hardship they endured as a result of the tumultuous national situation, including oppression by the Chinese and Japanese. Eschatological hope provided one of the major impulses toward the great revival movements and the growth of the early Korean church (see Korean Revival Movements). Most of the revival leaders, e.g., Kil Sun Joo*, were firm eschatologists. Kil's favorite subject in Bible classes and revival meetings was "A Study on Jesus' Second Coming." His premillennialism, however, was tainted with D. L. Moody's dispensational beliefs.

In the 1920s, conservative Korean Presbyterian theologians drew a distinction between historic premillennialism and dispensationalism. Dispensationalists see historical periods in terms of dispensations and believe in the secret rapture of the saints and the restoration of the Jews. The two, however, share a common literal understanding of the Bible and a belief in the coming of Christ before the millennium. This has led to much confusion over the understanding of the premillennial period.

In the 1980s, amillennialistic eschatology was gaining influence among many theologians, including some from conservative denominations. Several churches inserted amillennialism into their official confession.

By 1990, three eschatological interpretations could be observed among Korean Protestant churches: historic premillennialism was maintained by the conservative Presbyterian churches and the Seventh-Day Adventists; dispensational millennialism was upheld by the Baptists*, Full Gospel Churches, and the Holiness Church (Sungkyul Church); and amillennialism was the position of the liberal Presbyterian churches and the Methodists*.

While eschatological interests provided the people with hope during difficult times in Korea and contributed toward Christian revival and church growth, they also led to many false messianic movements. The novel eschatological sects may be divided into two types: the false messianic groups and the date setters. Examples of the first are the *Jundogwan* (Hall of Evangelism) of Pake Tae-Sun, who identified himself as the "Olive Tree" of the last days (Rev. 11:4) and the "Righteous One from the East," and the *Tongilkyo* (Unification Church*) of Moon Sun-Myung, who claimed to be the Advent Jesus. An example of the second type is Lee Jang-nim and his followers, who deluded the Korean community with the idea of a secret rapture in 1992.

Bibliography

Chun Gyung-Yun, "Eschatological Beliefs and Korean Churches," *Gidokyo-sasang* (1991). • Kim Gyung-Jae, "The Sense of Crisis and Eschatology to the Korean People," *Gidokyo-sasang* (1991). • "Korean Churches and Heterodoxical Eschatology," *Gidokyo-sasang* (1991). • Kim Sung-Gun, "Sociological Analysis on the Rise of the Eschatological Movement," *Sinhak-sasang* 74 (Theological Thought) (1991). • "Symposium on the Prevalence of Eschatological Beliefs," *Sinhak-sasang* 74 (Theological Thought) (1991). OH MAN-KYU

Espiritu Santo, Ignacia, del. *See* Del Espiritu Santo, Ignacia

Estrella, Monico

(b. 1853; d. 1916). First ordained Filipino Presbyterian* minister; evangelist and pastor.

Estrella graduated from the Jesuits' Ateneo de Manila and was a schoolmaster in 1900 when he became a Protestant. Ordained in 1904 after a rigorous theological examination, Estrella labored in Manila and the provinces of Rizal, Laguna, Cavite, Batangas, and Tayabas, later becoming pastor of the Presbyterians' Tondo Evangelical Church (1908-16). Gifted with the ability to present the Gospel tactfully and pleasantly to casual acquaintances and strangers, Estrella easily gathered groups of eager listeners around him. At his death, he was lauded as "untiring" and persevering despite sneers, insults, stonings, and distress from "weariness, hunger and danger," a worker "always patient, always faithful, always true," and an example of "true consecration" and "devoted service."

Bibliography

Rodgers, J. B., "Monico Estrella, Dean of the Filipino Ministry," *Philippine Presbyterian* VIII (Jan 1917); *Forty Years in the Philippines* (1940). • Sitoy, T. V., Jr., *Several Springs, One Stream* (1992). T. VALENTINO SITOY, JR.

Evangelical Christian Church of Irian Jaya

(*Gereja Kristen Injili Irian Jaya*, GKI-Irja). The GKI-Irja dates back to 1855, when C. W. Ottow (d. 1862) and J. G. Geissler (d. 1870), two German missionaries sent by J. E. Gossner*, started work on the island of Mansinam. In 1863, the Dutch *Utrechtsche Zendings Vereniging* (UZV) came to their assistance. Until 1951, this society (which in 1905 joined a federation named *Samenwerkende Zendingsgenootschappen* (Cooperating Missionary Societies), which from 1917 had its seat at Oegstgeest) was responsible for nearly all Protestant missionary work in Irian; from 1951 to 1956, the responsibility was taken over by the *Nederlandse Hervormde Kerk*.

Indonesian teacher-preachers were brought in from the Moluccas*. The missionaries at once started direct evangelization in religious services and attacked "paganism" head-on, without engaging in serious study of local religion and culture. During the first half century, missionary work was mainly restricted to the west coast of the Geelvink-Baai and made little headway. After 25 years, 20 Irianese had been baptized, but 17 graves of missionaries and members of their families had been dug. An important factor was the permanent state of war, the tribes being involved in a vicious circle of retaliation which could not be broken unilaterally. Nevertheless, the missionaries earned the respect of the population because they stood by the people among whom they lived when attacked; as a result, the Gospel tales were spread to regions not visited by the missionaries.

In about 1900, the coastal regions of Irian were pacified by the Dutch government, and in 1907 a mass movement toward Christianity began. At the same time, missionary work spread to the whole north coast. In 1937, there were 41,237 baptized adult Christians. F. J. F. van Hasselt (1894-1932 in Irian) and F. C. Kamma studied religion and culture; I. S. Kijne (1923-58 in Irian) used his wide range of talents in educating Irianese evangelists and teachers and creating hymnbooks which were used all over Indonesia.

Due to the great number of tribal languages, the language used in the mission was mainly Malay. However, as in most Dutch Reformed mission fields, organizational development was slow. When World War II* broke out, no Irianese had been given authority to administer the sacraments, the leading posts being in the hands of Moluccan evangelists. Of these Moluccans, numbers were killed by the Japanese. After the war, the mission finally started to lead the church toward independence. In 1950, the first Irianese ministers were confirmed, among them F. J. S. Rumainum*, and in 1956, the church became independent. During the first years after independence, the influence of the Dutch missionaries still made itself felt, but in 1963 most of them had to leave because Irian, until then a Dutch colony, was handed over to the Republic of Indonesia*.

Problems faced by the church include the Koreri* movements and other Cargo cults occasionally occurring in its territory, the tensions created during the 1970s and 1980s by an insurrection against the Indonesian government, and the relations with the faith missions working in the interior and with the Roman Catholic Church*, which has its base in Southern Irian. The faith missions tend to cold-shoulder the GKI, while the Catholics attract the most promising youths with their excellent school system. Nevertheless, the GKI-Irja, with its approximately 500,000 members, includes the mass of the population in Northern and Western Irian and is the greatest single church in Irian (about 25% of the total population). In 1957, the GKI-Irja started a mission in the interior of Irian (Galimo Valley).

Bibliography

Kamma, F. C., *Ajaib di Mata Kita,* 3 vols. (1981-94).

THOMAS VAN DEN END

Evangelical Christian Church of Timor

(*Gereja Masehi Injili di Timor,* GMIT). The GMIT, which became an autonomous church on 31 Oct 1947, has 40 dioceses with 1,612 congregations and a total membership of 800,000 people of various ethnicity. It is one of the largest denominations in Indonesia, with 478 pastors (of whom 110 are women) and 1,134 lay preachers. Its ministry covers two provinces, East Nusa Tenggara (with the exception of Sumba Island) and West Nusa Tenggara (excepting Lombok Island).

The history of the GMIT began with the Dutch United East-India Company* (*Verenigde Oost-Indische Compagnie,* VOC). In 1613, the VOC expelled the Portuguese from Kupang (Timor) and stationed troops there. In 1614, the VOC sent its first pastor, M. van Broeck, to cater to the spiritual needs of the soldiers. Taken ill with malaria, Van Broeck did not stay long, and there was no pastoral care until the arrival of Key Serokind 56 years later (1670). He was replaced by A. Corpius in 1687, who died the following year, leaving the congregation in Kupang without a pastor for another 65 years (1688-1753). The church was, however, served by a native medicine man named Paulus Kupang. In 1753, J. R. Wasmuth was placed in Kupang as a result of the expansion of Christian work on Roti Island.

Although Kupang was neglected pastorally, Christianity expanded to distant islands through the initiative of native kings. Christianity came to Roti Island (located west of Timor) in 1729, when one of the kings, King Thieu of Paoura Messa Island, and his family were baptized. Other kings followed suit, resulting in mass baptism throughout the island without proper teaching given beforehand. The conversion to the Christian faith was not the result of repentance but of a desire to obtain the better social status associated with becoming a Christian. The Christian faith of the converts was therefore shallow. The number of Christians on Roti Island grew to 5,870 in 1760.

Christianity came to Sawu Island (west of Roti Island) in 1756. The people here also became Christians en masse. In 1766, there were five congregations with a total membership of 826. During the period of the VOC, the Christians in Timor, Roti, and Sawu were neither properly trained nor taught, were led by schoolteachers, and continued to live under the strong influence of their old tribal religion.

After the VOC was dissolved on 31 Dec 1799, the Dutch government established a national church, the *Indische Kerk,* in 1815 to meet the needs of the congregations in Indonesia*, but there were insufficient personnel for pastoring and evangelism. Pastoral care of the churches and evangelism were then handed over to the *Nederlandsche Zendeling Genootschap* (NZG), which sent the evangelist R. Le Bruijn to Timor in 1819. He revived the long-neglected congregations in Timor, Roti, and Sawu but died in 1829. In 1828 there were only 3,000 members and 12 schools. In 1827, the NZG sent Ter Linden and F. Karbe to Roti, but Karbe died in 1828. When Le Bruijn died, Ter Linden moved to Kupang. D. Douwes joined him in 1830 but died the following year. In 1832, Ter Linden was replaced by G. Heymering, who served until 1866.

In 1850, L. J. van Rhijn, inspector of the NZG, visited Timor and Roti and was disappointed with the work in Timor. Consequently, the NZG abandoned work in Timor in 1854 and returned it to the *Indische Kerk* (1854-1942).

Christianity then expanded rapidly in Timor, spreading into the interior of the island and to Roti, Sawu, and Alor. Congregations were established in Flores and Sumbawa. There were mass baptisms everywhere. The congregations in Timor were organized according to the hierarchical structure of the *Indische Kerk,* with those already working under the *Indische Kerk* given new status as assistant pastors *(Hulp-predikant).* To attract native workers, J. J. Le Grand opened the Teachers' School for Natives (*School tot Opleiding Voor Inlands Leraars,* STOVIL) in Baa-Roti in 1902. It was moved to Kupang in 1926 and closed in 1931. It was reopened in 1936 and closed again in 1942 when the Japanese invaded Timor.

In 1910, the *Indische Kerk* sent Willem Back as chief pastor in Kupang to lead and oversee the entire church ministry in Timor. He served until 1914. His successors were V. L. Visser (1915-16), R. W. F. Kyftenbelt (1916-19), H. A. Loef (1919-21), Hesnik (1921-23), G. C. A. A. van den Wijngaard (1923-27), P. J. Le Bruijn (1927-31), J. Beers (1931-34), G. P. H. Locher (1934-41), I. H. F. S. Enklaar (1942), and E. Durkstra (1946-47).

The rapid expansion of Christianity in Timor was made possible because of the peace established by the

Indo-Dutch government, sufficient Dutch pastors and native workers, the good organizational structure of the *Indische Kerk*, and a contextualized and more comprehensive approach in evangelism, which included the provision of schools, health care, and other services to improve the life of the community. A pastor who contributed much toward contextualization was P. Middelkoop (1922-57). His translations of the Bible*, Bible stories, hymns, and the Book of Worship into Dawan, the Timor language, are still in use today.

The church suffered most during the Japanese occupation (1942-45). Dutch pastors were interned, and native pastors were suspected of spying for the Dutch. Revs. Dekuanan, Riwu, and Mengga were among the first Christian martyrs in Timor killed by the Japanese authorities. The first attempts to build an independent church had begun with the formation of the Church of South Timor, headed by N. Nisnoni, a Kupang king and a layman. The church collected funds to support its ministries during the Japanese occupation, and Christians became aware that they themselves were responsible for the well-being of the church.

Preparation for the establishment of the GMIT began in 1937 under the leadership of Locher and, later, Enklaar, but stopped because of World War II*. When the war ended, E. Durkstra was sent to Timor, and the plan was revived. On 31 Oct 1947, the GMIT was declared an autonomous church under the umbrella of the Protestant Church in Indonesia (*Gereja Protestan Indonesia*, GPI). Durkstra was chosen to be the first chairman of the GMIT synod (1947-50), and he was succeeded by a Timorese, J. L. Ch. Abineno* in 1950. The church was faced with immediate leadership and financial difficulties. The government stopped its subsidy to the GMIT in 1950; although it received aid from some other sources, the funds were quickly exhausted. The GMIT, on its own financially, was able to overcome its problems in 1970 and is now a self-sustaining church without dependence on foreign funds.

To meet the need for workers and church leaders, the GMIT sent pastoral candidates to seminaries outside Timor while starting its own seminary, initially a junior seminary, upgraded to an academy in 1971 (Kupang Theological Academy) and a theological seminary in 1981. In 1985, working ecumenically with the Sumba Christian Church (*Gereja Kristen Sumba*, GKS), the seminary became the theological faculty of the Christian University of Artha Wacana.

Since its founding, the GMIT has been active ecumenically through theological education and affiliation with the Indonesian Council of Churches, the Christian Council of Asia* (CCA), the World Council of Churches (WCC), and the World Alliance of Reformed Churches (WARC).

Bibliography

Dicker, Gordon, *Pengabaran Injil di Pulau Timor* (1960) (published as a stencil, Kupang, 1975). • Brookes, G. F., "Spirit Movements in Timor: A Survey" (master's thesis, Melbourne College of Divinity) (1977). • Noach, M. A., *Langkah Pertama. Suatu tinjauan terhadap periode 25 tahun G.M.I.T., 1947-1972* (published as a stencil, Kupang, 1972). • Peters, George W., *Indonesia Revival: Focus on Timor* (1973).

F. D. Wellem

Evangelical Church of Borneo

(Sidang Injil Borneo, SIB). Fast-growing church in East Malaysia officially organized in 1959 from the various mission congregations of the Borneo Evangelical Mission (BEM) of Australia, and the largest Protestant denomination in Sabah today.

SIB has an illustrious mission heritage with pioneer BEM missionaries such as Hudson and Winsome Southwell, Frank and Inid Davidson, and Carey and Florence Tolley, who obtained permission from Rajah Brooke*, the British colonial governor of Sarawak, and started working in the Limbang area on 29 Nov 1928. By 1942, BEM had established work among the Ibans, Bisayas, Kelabits, Lun Bawang, Muruts, and Dusuns. With the return of the missionaries after World War II*, the church grew rapidly. The missionaries concentrated their attention on building up the congregations, translating the Bible* into various tribal languages including Kayan, Kenyah, and Penan, and developing local leadership. In 1959, Racha Umung, a local leader, became the first president of SIB. The revival movement of the 1960s and 1970s and the charismatic* renewal of the 1980s that swept across the churches in East Malaysia have resulted in significant church renewal and growth for SIB.

SIB practices a congregational system of church government. The local churches support their own ministers and church workers. Training institutions, Sunday school ministry, evangelism, and youth ministry are handled as cooperative projects allowing for a variety of informal styles of worship. A service may last up to two hours. Lively singing of short choruses with hand clapping, prayers said together audibly, and the sharing of thanksgiving or personal testimonies are found in most SIB worship services. Larger churches may use drums or trained Gospel dancers during the worship service.

SIB has a strong tradition of training its members for ministry. Sarawak has six Bible schools and a Bible college. Sabah has one Bible school and at least two evangelist-training centers. SIB is also represented on the board of governors of Sabah Theological Seminary and sends pastors there for advanced training.

SIB strongly emphasizes evangelism. Although the church began among the tribal groups, today there are many Chinese SIB congregations in Sarawak. These churches are reaching out to other Chinese groups in Malaysia*. Kota Kinabalu has an active English congregation as well. The common use of Bahasa Malaysia provides an excellent channel for communicating the Christian message to all groups of people in Malaysia. The church cooperates with the Far East Broadcasting Company* (FEBC) in producing Christian radio messages in Bahasa Malaysia. In addition, SIB is a member of the Sabah Council of Churches. Historically, it has trained leaders for other denominations and shared some of its own trained leaders to help other denominations in their outreach ministries.

A new SIB administration center was established in Kota Kinabalu, Sabah, in 1976; the headquarters moved from Lawas to Miri, Sarawak, in 1988. The church practices adult baptism by immersion. The latest official (estimated) statistics show that there are over 130,000 members worshipping in nearly 700 churches, of which about two-thirds are in Sarawak.

Bibliography

Borneo Evangelical Mission Annual Reports (1988). • Lees, Shirley, *Drunk Before Dawn* (1979). • *Majlis Perasmian Wisma Sidang Injil Borneo Sabah* (1993). • Saging, Robert Lian, "An Ethno-History of the Kelabit Tribe of Sarawak" (1976) (thesis at Kuala Lumpur University) (1976). • Samporoh, Richard Yamin, "The Establishment, Growth, Strengths and Weaknesses of the SIB Church" (thesis at Malaysia Evangelical College, Miri Sarawak, Malaysia) (1992). GAM SEMG SHAE

Evangelical Church of Kalimantan

(*Gereja Kalimantan Evangelis,* GKE). The arrival of the first Protestant missionary in Kalimantan on 26 Jun 1835 is celebrated by the Protestant Church in Kalimantan* as the Day of Mission, the arrival of the Gospel to the island Kalimantan. One of the few non-Dutch mission boards working in Indonesia was the German Rhenish Missionary Society *(Rheinische Missionsgesellschaft),* which had permission from the colonial government to operate in Kalimantan. When the missionary work began to show positive results, and local people, the Dayaks, slowly became interested in the Gospel after more than 20 years of hard labor, a catastrophe occurred. In 1859 there was a revolt against the Dutch. Four missionaries together with three wives and two children were murdered by the Dayaks, who made no distinction between the colonial power and the mission and regarded all whites as Dutch. The colonial government closed the whole area to mission until 1866.

After World War I (1914-18), financial difficulties compelled the Rhenish Mission to give up various mission fields. It continued its work in Kalimantan until 1920, when it was decided that the Kalimantan mission field would be handed over to the Swiss Basel Mission. At that time, there were 3,700 Dayak Christians, 17 missionaries, 72 local teachers and evangelists, 11 stations, and 33 mission posts. The process of transfer took five years before the Basel Mission was able to continue on its own in Kalimantan.

It was not until one century after the arrival of the first missionary in 1835 that the mission field in Kalimantan became independent. During the general synod (2-6 Apr 1935) in Kuala Kapuas, Central Kalimantan, the independent indigenous Evangelical Dayak Church was inaugurated (5 Apr). The following day, five Dayak pastors were ordained, and an executive committee of seven was selected, comprising two missionaries (as president and member), four indigenous laypeople, and one layman as an honorary member. The church had 96 congregations with a membership of 10,012. In theory, the church was fully independent, but in practice she was under the control of the mission board. In 1939, there were 15,000 members served by 16 pastors, 23 evangelists, 158 teachers, 26 assistant nurses, and 40 missionaries (all indigenous workers).

The situation changed radically during World War II*. When Germany invaded Holland, all Germans in Indonesia were imprisoned by the Dutch, including German missionaries working under the Basel Mission in Kalimantan. Later, when the Japanese occupied Kalimantan in 1942, all Dutch people were imprisoned by the Japanese. Seven missionaries were killed by the Japanese army. This meant a total isolation of the church from any relationship with Europe, and she was forced to be on her own. The church had to learn to depend solely on the Lord. Right after World War II, the church was placed in a difficult revolutionary situation in the wave of nationalism*. It had to "be wise as serpents and innocent as doves" (Matt. 10:16).

The church tried to reach all layers of society through its services, including education and various social services. The Evangelical Church of Kalimantan now has a university, including a faculty for religious education, located in Palangka Raya, the capital of Central Kalimantan Province; a theological seminary in Banjarmasin; a training center for religious teachers in Pontianak (West Kalimantan); a technical school in Mandomai; an agricultural center in Tumbang Lahang, which includes both a formal school for agriculture and nonformal training for young farmers, and primary and secondary schools scattered all around Kalimantan.

In the early period, the church also provided medical and public health services. For various reasons, the church no longer runs a hospital but provides medical* service in small clinics in the remote areas. Various commissions at congregational, district, and synod levels serve the needs and interests of the different church groups, e.g., women, young people, men, and children. Lay training is a priority. A center in Kuala Kapuas runs programs throughout the year.

The church has a membership of about 220,000, with 940 congregations in 64 districts and nearly 320 full-time workers.

Bibliography

Ukur, F., *Tuaiannja sungguh banjak. Sedjarah 25 tahun Geredja Kalimantan Evangelis dan 125 tahun Pekabaran Indjil di Kalimantan* (1960); *Tantang-Djawab suku Dajak* (1971). • Witschi, H., *Christus siegt: Geschichte der Dajak Mission auf Borneo* (1942). FRIDOLIN UKUR

Evangelical Church of Vietnam (ECVN). The ECVN, better known as *Tin Lanh* or "Good News" Church, was the work of the Christian and Missionary Alliance* (C&MA). The need for a Protestant witness in the French-controlled peninsula called Indochina (Vietnam*, Laos*, and Cambodia*) was first noted by A. B. Simpson in his missionary magazine in 1887. This challenge was pursued by Robert A. Jaffray* while he was stationed in South China* in 1889. Because of the hostility of both the Vietnamese and the French, the mission was unsuccessful.

In 1911, Jaffray landed in Tourane (Danang), central Vietnam. There he found the representative of the British and Foreign Bible Society (BFBS), who had distributed portions of the Gospel in Chinese and French among the Vietnamese. As the BFBS was relocating its center to Haiphong in the north, its property was sold to the C&MA. The C&MA commenced its work in Tourane and spread to Haiphong and Hanoi in the north and Saigon and Mytho in the south. The mission strategy was to learn the vernacular, translate the Bible* into spoken languages, distribute Bible portions to the villagers, and preach the Gospel.

A Bible school was established in 1921 in Tourane to train the Vietnamese to preach the Gospel in their own languages in areas inaccessible to missionaries. This was the most important contribution of the C&MA ministry. The Bible school was patterned after Simpson's Missionary Training Institute in Nyack, New York. The main objective was to give the national Christians a thorough education in the Bible so that they could evangelize the whole of Indochina and hasten the return of Jesus (a reflection of Simpson's ecclesiology linked to eschatology).

From one member in 1911, the church grew to 4,115 baptized members in 1927. That same year saw the formation of the Evangelical Church of Indochina (renamed the Evangelical Church of Vietnam in 1950). The missionaries taught the Christians to support their own workers, and at an early stage many of the churches became self-supporting. Wherever the church was not self-supporting, it was governed by the mission. At a time when the people had strong anti-foreign feelings because of French colonial rule, the national leaders believed that self-support was the route to independence and self-government.

In 1938, Chinese evangelist John Sung* visited Vietnam, leaving an indelible mark on the people and the church. His preaching was followed by extraordinary revivals adding more than 1,000 members to the church. Sung introduced a method of evangelism called "witnessing bands": new believers were sent out in teams to distribute literature* and invite people to Christian meetings.

The Vietnamese in the Mekong Delta and central Annam were particularly responsive to the Gospel, but work in Tonkin was slow and unproductive. The greatest response, however, was in the South in Mytho and Cantho, where large numbers of people, even entire villages, became Christians. By 1940, there were 123 churches, 86 of which were fully self-supporting.

By the end of World War II*, all the churches were self-supporting. As the work was successful among the Vietnamese, the missionaries sought to reach out to the tribal peoples scattered in the central highlands of Vietnam, Laos, and Siam (Thailand). These one-and-a-half million people spoke over 30 different languages and dialects. In the mid-1950s, the C&MA established two Bible schools for the tribes, one in Dalat and the other in Banmethuot. There was also a short-term program for laypersons in Pleiku. The Dalat school trained workers for the Koho tribe and the minorities living in that vicinity. Banmethuot served the Raday, Jarai, and Muong tribes.

The Koho tribe was the most responsive to Christianity. One third of all the tribal peoples in Dalat Province were Koho. In 1955, the Koho church had 1,500 baptized members and 4,100 followers. By 1965, there were 3,551 baptized members and 12,625 followers.

The Stieng tribe, relatively unreached despite missionary efforts since 1953, experienced a revival where entire villages became Christians.

By 1974, the Tribes Church totaled 45,000 Christians and had a strong presence among all the major groups. This was significant in that while the tribes made up only 16% of the population of South Vietnam, they comprised 33% of the ECVN. Only six tribes with a total of 50,000 people were without a church in their communities.

The wars in Vietnam affected the ECVN physically and financially, but it came of age bringing to birth a core of able C&MA Vietnamese leaders and a strong Vietnamese church. Men such as Le Van Thai* (president of the ECVN during the three wars, 1941-60), Ong Van Huyen* (dean of Nhatrang Bible and Theological Institute and secretary of the ECVN), and Doan Van Mieng (president of the ECVN, 1961-75) were some of the outstanding leaders. Throughout the War of Independence (1945-54) and the Vietnam War* (1959-75), the church adopted a policy of noninterference in politics. It believed that every Christian must be a good citizen and serve his country, but underscored the church's task as spiritual, that is, to preach the Gospel of Jesus Christ. But this was never clarified in the individual's mind. This lack of precision caused the church much suffering and bloodshed. Neither the Vietminh (Communist) nor the French understood on which side the Christians stood.

In 1954, when Vietnam was divided into the Communist North and the American Vietnamese South, both the C&MA and the ECVN identified with the American military presence in the south. The 1,000 Protestant refugees who moved south were absorbed into the Evangelical Church of South Vietnam. Those Protestants who refused to move south remained as the ECVN, with no missionary assistance or church affiliation with the South.

The C&MA cooperated with the American and South Vietnamese governments in creating a peaceful environment in the south for the extension of its spiritual mission. Some of the missionaries believed that, since South and Central Vietnam were more receptive to Christianity, this division might even be providential.

Between 1955 and 1965, the C&MA and the ECVN joined in a two-pronged strategy to reopen churches closed during the war and consolidate the existing churches for evangelism and church planting. The presence of thousands of refugees* and of the Americans in South Vietnam led to a profusion of Protestant missions after 1955. The C&MA, the sole Protestant mission since 1911, and its offspring, the ECVN, were challenged by other Protestant missions and denominations. Many of these missions did not share the same philosophy as the C&MA, nor did they see their role in South Vietnam as solely spiritual. Numerous organizations responded to the refugee situation by extending physical and social relief as their primary obligation. The ECVN was in a dilemma. For more than 45 years, it had believed that the ultimate goal of the church was spiritual and that it must not be distracted by any other option. But new organizations were actively involved in social and educational projects which seemed viable options for the church. As the war escalated (1960-69), the ECVN saw the need to identify with the social and physical needs of the people in order to make the Christian message authentic.

The leprosarium in Banmethuot, a joint project of the C&MA and the ECVN, was later assisted by the Mennonite* Central Committee (MCC). By 1965, the hospital was treating 170 patients, with 41 clinics in surrounding villages, and a total of 5,532 patients. A new hospital was opened in Pleiku, a joint venture between the ECVN and the MCC.

The church also established two primary schools for the tribes in Dalat and a high school in Nhatrang. In 1966, the church cooperated with a multidimensional organization called the Vietnamese Christian Service, with the MCC taking leadership. The church's involvement in social and educational programs was a source of concern for the C&MA, as it believed there was a definite decline in spiritual and evangelistic zeal. The mission did, however, assist the church in radio work, as this was primarily a spiritual ministry. In 1975, when the North liberated the South, the ECVN was broadcasting the Christian message in Southeast Asia 62 times each week.

The Vietnamese Christians suffered heavy losses throughout the protracted war, but the church continued to grow. By 1975, there were 510 churches with 54,000 baptized members, 276 Bible students at Nhatrang, 900 laypeople trained by Theological Education by Extension, and an able president at the helm of the ECVN. In 1975, all the missionaries were repatriated and reassigned new fields. Four Mennonites remained for about one year before they too left the country with hundreds of Vietnamese. All the pastors who remained were ordered by the new government to help rebuild the country. The Bible Institute was shut down. Doan Van Mieng, the church's president, and 500 pastors were given the option of leaving the country, but they chose to remain with their people. One hundred evangelical churches were closed and 90 pastors sent to reeducation camps. Three pastors were executed in 1978. Ninety-nine percent of the tribal churches were closed, and their pastors sent to reeducation camps.

A church leader reported that the church in North Vietnam numbered 13,000 and the church in the South 130,000. The government expressed the desire to have one Protestant church for Vietnam, but the ECVN resisted the government's efforts for unification and paid heavily for it. There is evidence of a revival in several places in Vietnam, resulting in numerous conversions. Thousands of cell groups and Bible study groups are scattered throughout the country, and the numbers are increasing daily.

Bibliography

James, Violet, "American Protestant Missions and the Vietnam War" (doctoral dissertation, University of Aberdeen) (1989).

VIOLET JAMES

Evangelical Fellowship of Thailand

The Evangelical Fellowship of Thailand (EFT) began in 1956 as a fellowship of Christians to help each other in the work of evangelism. At that time, only two groups were recognized by the Thai government as representatives of Christians in Thailand: the Roman Catholics* and the Protestants represented by the Church of Christ in Thailand (CCT). But there were many other newer Christian groups and churches which were not affiliated with the CCT. These groups decided to come together to fellowship and work with each other, recognizing that it would be easier to relate with the government on official matters if they came together as an organized body. So they called themselves the "evangelical fellowship."

Out of this informal fellowship, the EFT emerged when, in 1969, they decided to register with the Thai government as a third representative group of Christians in Thailand*. Under the initiative and leadership of Suk Phongnoy*, the EFT began with a board of four members, one full-time secretary, and one full-time staff person.

In 1976 the Evangelical Fellowship Foundation (EFF) was set up in order to grant scholarships for Bible training and to manage funds and assist in the sale and purchase of properties. In that same year, a special committee consisting of Charan Ratanabutra, Somdii Pusodsi, Wirachai Kower, and Phaitoon Hatamas was established to set the standards and qualifications for confirmation of the title "Reverend." They also set up guidelines for Christian leaders and missionaries working in Thailand.

Over the years, the number of staff in the EFT grew as the work expanded. By 1980, they had a board of directors, an advisory board, and a working board with a full-time director and staff members in charge of membership, finance, government relations, and social services. The number of members has also grown, and at their 25th anniversary in 1993, they recorded a total of 383 members, of which 265 were churches and 118 were Thai and foreign mission groups and organizations. Those who desire to be members of the EFT must subscribe to the principles and practices of the EFT and abide by its objectives: (1) promote the preaching of the Gospel of Jesus Christ; (2) promote fellowship among Christians; (3) promote the spiritual life of Christians; (4) promote social services including health and education; and (5) abstain from involvement in the politics of Thailand.

Today, the EFT functions as a representative body and coordinator for government-related matters, including visas and work permits. Recently, it has also undertaken to help in gathering statistics regarding the church and mission in Thailand. The EFT can step in to help resolve onflicts between members and decide on disciplinary action. The EFT now requires that all missionaries coming to work in Thailand first learn the Thai language and pass the government language exam (primary six equivalent) within two years. A secretary has also been appointed in the EFT to act as a liaison with organizations outside Thailand, such as the World Evangelical Fellowship, the Evangelical Fellowship of Asia, and the Asian Mission Commission. TAY MUI LAN

Evangelical Union, Philippines

(EU). Association of Presbyterian*, Methodist*, Baptist*, United Brethren, Disciples, and Congregational American missionaries and Bible agents in the Philippines for "comity, unity, and cooperation."

The EU was established in 1901 in order to eliminate unseemly rivalry and avoid needless duplication of effort, time, and resources. It drew up the Comity Agreement of 1901*, which divided the country into specific areas of responsibility among the various Protestant missions. The long-range goal of the EU was to have only one Protestant church in the Philippines*. To facilitate the attainment of this objective, it was decided to adopt only one name for all the churches represented in the EU, namely, the Evangelical Church of the Philippine Islands, with the denominational name, if so desired, being appended in parentheses, such as the Evangelical Church of the Philippine Islands (Methodist Episcopal). This goal of only one church has been partially realized in what is now the United Church of Christ in the Philippines.

To satisfy Filipino nationalist demands, Filipino ministers were admitted to the EU in 1921. Under the inspiration of John R. Mott, the EU gave way in 1929 to the National Christian Council of the Philippines, in which Filipinos were the leaders, with American missionaries as advisers.

As the Philippine churches matured, it was thought more appropriate to have a cooperative organization with churches, rather than individuals, as members. The result was an entirely new body in 1938, namely, the Philippine Federation of Evangelical Churches (PFEC), comprising the United Evangelical Church in the Philippines (1929), the Methodist Episcopal Church, the Philippine Baptist Convention, the Churches of Christ (Disciples), and two indigenous groups, the Evangelical Methodist Church of the Philippine Islands (IEMELIF) (1909), and the United Evangelical Church in Christ (UNIDA) (1932). For varying reasons, the Episcopal Church, the Seventh-Day Adventists, and the Christian and Missionary Alliance did not join the federation. Neither could the Philippine Methodist Church (1933), because bad feelings still ran high between its leaders and those of the mother Methodist Episcopal Church.

When the imperial Japanese forces occupied the Philippines during World War II*, they pressured all Protestant churches into a new Federation of Evangelical Churches in the Philippines (1942). In 1943, this federation named itself the Evangelical Church in the Philippines, though several groups left this forced union when the war ended in 1945.

Reconstituted in 1947, the PFEC brought into its fellowship the Philippine Methodist Church. Hoping to draw in the Philippine Independent Church* and the Philippine Episcopal Church (both of which belonged to the Catholic tradition), the PFEC in 1949 renamed itself the Philippine Federation of Christian Churches. The real problem, however, was the continuing goal, dating back to the days of the EU, of eventually having only one Protestant church in the Philippines. In 1963, this goal was made optional, and a new, looser organization with a wider spectrum of membership was created in the National Council of Churches in the Philippines.

Bibliography

Dean, J. M., *The Cross of Christ in Bolo-land* (1902). • "The Evangelical Union," *The Philippine Presbyterian* XII (Apr 1921). • Laubach, F. C., *People of the Philippines* (1925). • Rodgers, J. B., *Forty Years in the Philippines* (1940). • Sitoy, T. V., Jr., *Comity and Unity* (1989); *Several Springs, One Stream* (1992). T. VALENTINO SITOY, JR.

Evangelism. *See* Rural Evangelism (Noson Dendo), Japan

Every Home Crusade, India

(EHC). Interdenominational organization that exists to mobilize the church to participate actively in the systematic presentation of the Gospel of Jesus Christ to every home.

In 1964, Johnee Lee, overseas director of the World Literature Crusade (WLC), which was founded by Jack McLister in 1946, visited India* to explore the possibilities of starting the EHC. He came into contact with Christian leaders from different states. Among them were Donald David from Tamil Nadu, B. A. Prabhakar of

Andhra, J. J. Oliver from Madhya Pradesh, P. N. Kurien from Delhi, and C. George from Kerala. On their initiative, all the necessary preparations were made, and 2 Oct 1964 witnessed the launching of the India EHC in a simple ceremony at the Good News Center Assembly in Secunderabad. In the same year, offices were established in six states and the ministry commenced in Jan 1965.

The first project, Operation Last Home (1965-74), was aimed at placing Gospel tracts in every home. An organized band of pioneer workers visited each house with two Gospel tracts, one specially designed for adults and the other for children. As the work began to develop, new stations were opened in several places, and B. A. Prabhakar was appointed as director for South Asia, with Delhi as his headquarters. Those who showed interest in knowing more about Christ were given a well-prepared correspondence course and other study materials. Occasionally, seekers' conferences were conducted to establish personal contact and to provide them with spiritual assistance.

Project Calvary (1976-84) was the second effort to reach every home with the Gospel message. Along with this, there was a chain of activities among the patients in hospitals, tribals, the blind, and prisoners. The work was mainly carried on with the financial support of the WLC and the generous contributions of friends and well-wishers.

As the work began to expand, Christ Group ministry came into existence, designed mainly for new believers where there were no churches. This was a gathering of new believers for prayer, worship, and fellowship.

In 1992, EHC prepared a mega-plan, Final Thrust 5000, to present the Gospel personally at every doorstep of the 170 million homes in India. It has been designed to confront at last 600 million people individually with the Gospel on a one-on-one basis through the native missionary network. The goal of this project is to plant 300,000 churches across the land. For the fulfillment of this plan, EHC launched a unique project called the ten-year chain prayer. They also began missionary training with an emphasis on personal counseling and soul winning. Training institutes for church planters have been established for eight major Indian languages.

EHC has spearheaded evangelism and reached several peaks of excellence. During the last 30 years, they have covered India twice, presenting the Gospel at almost every doorstep, and are in the process of a third coverage. In these years, their contribution to the Indian church has been substantial, with 5 million responses and 9,000 village churches planted across the land.

SAMUEL MATHEW

Expo '70 Problem

A cluster of problems related to the proposal to erect a Christian Pavilion at the World Exposition in Osaka in 1970; the United Church of Christ in Japan (UCCJ) was especially affected.

In response to an invitation from the World Exposition Committee, the Osaka Christian Council, the National Christian Council in Japan (NCCJ), and the Japan Catholic Bishops' Conference proceeded with preparations to participate. The NCCJ at its Twenty-first General Assembly in March 1968 approved the plan, and in October a vote to support and promote it was passed at the Fifteenth General Assembly of the UCCJ.

When 1969 came, a call was issued to rethink the planned contents of the pavilion, and before long opposition to participating in any form emerged within the UCCJ. Opponents contended that Expo was being staged as a celebration of Japan's socio-economic success and that it was an attempt to gain the consent of the country to open the way for an economic invasion of its Asian neighbors. It was therefore the responsibility of the church to take a stand against such a move, emphasizing that it was much more important to reach out to those who were suffering as a result of Japan's high-level success. Those in favor of participation contended that, even though social contradictions might exist in Expo '70, it was only natural to witness to the masses who would come to see it. It was important to witness to the ever-present Christ, and there was meaning in having the Protestants and Catholics participate jointly in this project.

After the Sep 1969 meeting of the central committee for the Christian Pavilion, a violent and lengthy dispute erupted at a special UCCJ General Assembly between leaders of the UCCJ and members of the Pavilion Committee on the one side and students, laborers, and some members of the clergy on the other. Opponents staged a protest in front of the Pavilion in Mar 1970, and 14 persons including Christians were arrested. Christians in the Kansai area continued to fight the matter out in the courts until Oct 1976. The issue evolved into a number of major disputes within the UCCJ. The General Assembly and district assemblies in Tokyo, Kyoto, Osaka, and Hyogo Districts could not be held. Controversies over missiology, the representative system of commissions and committees, the confession of faith, and church-state relations erupted. At its Eighteenth General Assembly in Dec 1974, the UCCJ acknowledged its mistake in participating in Expo '70, but disputes and the quest for settlement of related problems continued on for many years.

Bibliography

Hori Mitsuo et al., *Banpaku, toshindai, kyoshi kentei mondai nenpyo, 1967-1976* (Chronology of Expo '70, TUTS, and Ministerial Examination Issues, 1967-1976) (1982). • Phillips, James M., *From the Rising of the Sun: Christians and Society in Contemporary Japan* (1981).

DOHI AKIO

F

Fabricius, Johann Philip

(b. near Frankfurt am Main, Germany, 17 Jan 1911; d. 24 Jul 1791). Fabricius had come to India to work in the (Danish-Halle) Tranquebar* mission in 1740 but, after staying for some time in Tranquebar, he moved over to the mission station at Madras. The Madras mission station was under the Society for the Propagation of Christian Knowledge (SPCK), which also had the support of the Royal Company.

Fabricius was not much acclaimed for his missionary zeal and activities, as some of the Tranquebar missionaries were, but he was known for his literary works. While at Madras, Fabricius undertook the work of a dictionary the likes of which, up till that point, no one had attempted. He completed the English-Tamil, Tamil-English Dictionary in 1779. He also translated German hymns into the Tamil language. He was an excellent scholar of both oral and written Tamil.

Fabricius felt that the previous translation of the New Testament by Ziegenbalg* needed revision, and this resulted in one of his most important works. A patient and diligent worker, Fabricius took several years to complete the revision of the New Testament and finished it in 1766. It was considered far superior to all of its predecessors. Afterwards, he began the much harder job of translating the Old Testament, which he was not able to publish before his death. Nevertheless, he was able to complete several of the Old Testament books before he died. The full work appeared in 1798 and was highly acclaimed both for accuracy and for poetic sensitivities to the Tamil language (see Bible Translation).

The last years of Fabricius's life were a time of tragedy and darkness. He encountered financial difficulties that landed him in prison. His mission successor, Gerricke, was able to secure his release. Fabricius served almost 50 years as a missionary in India.

Bibliography

Samuel, G., *History of the Tranquebar Mission in Tamil, A.D. 1706-1955* (1955). • Fenger, J. Fred, *History of the Tranquebar Mission* (1963). • *India Missionary Records* (London: Religious Tract Society, n.d.). • Neill, Stephen, *A History of Christianity in India, 1707-1858* (1985).

Franklyn J. Balasundaran

Family

In recent times, many Asian countries have attempted to differentiate between Western and Asian cultures; a major point has been that the close-knit family is the basic building block in Asian society. The main non-Christian religions in Asia (Buddhism*, Islam*, and Hinduism*) and the economic systems in the continent have influenced greatly the structure and lifestyle of families. Several decades ago, Asia had largely agricultural and rural populations, as had been the case for ages. The common family structure that fit this context was the extended family or joint family, though this was not the only Asian family structure.

The extended family was patriarchal, patrilocal, and large in size. Male children were preferred. Marriage was usually arranged by the families, and the couples were generally younger than couples today. Changes in Asian society in recent decades have affected many of these characteristics. Das and Bardis's survey of family life in Asia (1978) lists a number of trends that highlight these changes: (1) egalitarian family relations with less segregation and limited subjugation of women to an inferior status; (2) greater individualism and independence; (3) differentiation and specialization of social institutions; (4) urbanization; (5) family planning; (6) social mobility; (7) marital disruption; (8) neglect of and improper care for the elderly; (9) formal education of children; and (10) government influence on family activities.

Industrialization, modernization, and urbanization. In the 1960s, many Asian countries began to see growing industrialization and the related phenomenon of population shifts from rural areas to urban centers. These had significant influences on family life. Urban housing, limited in space and availability, made it difficult for extended families to stay together. This created a shift from extended- family structure to nuclear family, at least in terms of living arrangements. This was compensated for by maintaining a high level of kinship interaction. Nevertheless, the changes also resulted in a greater autonomy of nuclear families and a loosening of tightly arranged extended-family structures. Society also provided more activities designed for the nuclear family.

The changing roles of women. While the traditional role of women as homemakers is still dominant in Asia, significant changes have also taken place. Socioeconomic development has led to a greater number of women entering the workforce. While the proportion of women in the labor force remains low in some Asian Muslim societies (less than one tenth in Pakistan* and Bangladesh*), women form more than one third of the labor force in most Asian nations. Though the earning power of women lags behind that of men, working women are having a greater say in family life. Men in many societies are beginning to help in household duties and in childrearing. In some rapidly developing Asian countries, two-income families engage maids to help with the household chores; many of these domestic workers come from poorer Asian countries. The family lives of both employers and employees are thus affected to varying degrees.

Education. The focus on socioeconomic growth has resulted in greater importance given to education in Asian societies, many of which have traditionally placed a high premium on education. This means that in many situations children are better educated than their parents, leading to a more egalitarian family structure not only between parents and children, but also between husbands and wives, since educational opportunities have also been made available to girls in many cases. Highly educated women have also tended to have smaller families when they marry.

Family planning. More than half the population of the world lives in Asia. The two most populous nations, China and India, share some 35% of the world's population. Given the large populations and rapid population growth, many Asian governments have pushed for family planning as part of their policies. The success of family-planning policies has been mixed in Asia. On one hand, China* is an example of a successful program: the fertility rate, which measures the average number of children born to a woman who has completed her child-bearing years, declined from 5.99 in 1965-70 to 2.36 in 1985-90. Similar dramatic declines are also seen in the rapidly growing economies of East Asia: Hong Kong*, Taiwan*, South Korea*, Singapore*, and Thailand*. This is in part due to strong government measures in the form of public education, incentives, and disincentives. It is also partly due to broad social changes that have taken place in these countries. The necessity of both husband and wife being employed and the rising educational level of women are but two related factors contributing to the phenomenon.

Family-planning policies have been less successful in Muslim and Hindu countries, especially in South Asia and in the Philippines*, where the majority are Roman Catholics*. The reasons are complex, but the more important ones are cultural preferences for large families and a more domestic role for women (South Asian nations), and religious objections to artificial contraception (Philippines). The fertility rate in the Philippines declined from 6.04 in 1970-75 to 4.33 in 1985-90; the figures for Pakistan for the same periods are 7.00 and 6.50.

Better health. Three measures — life expectancies and maternal and infant mortality rates — show a general improvement in the health of Asian people. However, the situation in several South Asian countries (e.g., Nepal*, Pakistan, and Bangladesh*) and others such as Cambodia*, Laos*, and Indonesia* is not as favorable. In general, however, better health means that the population is also greying. This is obvious in countries such as Japan*, where providing for the needs of the elderly is now of critical importance.

Implications for the church. The rapid economic growth in many Asian countries has placed various kinds of stresses on family life and functioning. Two-income families look for a satisfactory child-care arrangement; the provisions are inadequate in many countries. The rising group of elderly people in the population requires urgent measures to ensure that their needs are met in the coming years. The rapid pace of life and changes in lifestyle have often resulted in a loosening of strong family ties and an increasing dissolution of marriages and family structures. In countries with large populations and with perennial problems of corruption, injustice, and poverty, the old issues still remain. Families struggle to survive amidst poverty* and poor health. Overpopulation complicates the problem.

In many Asian countries, there is a new interest in the family. It is the same in Christian circles. While this is good, care has to be taken that the family does not become a new idol. In the Christian faith, the church is more central than the family, for we are called to be a gathered community across ethnic and national boundaries. Given this caution, the church can take action in several areas:

1. Develop a Christian understanding of the family. In the midst of rapid challenges and changes, there is a great need to look into the various aspects of family life and functioning. This should be incorporated into the educational program of the church. There are various issues that need to be looked into: the effects of the economy and government policies on family life, the changing roles of men and women, family values, and the relationship between the family and the church are some examples.

2. Challenge trends which threaten the healthy functioning of families and the satisfactory expression of family relationships. These trends include large changes in the rapidly growing economies, and the issues of pov-

erty and injustice too. Both rapid and sluggish paces in the economy can affect family life negatively.

3. Provide informed and adequate care for families. Pastoral care of families is vital. In recent times, family therapies have mushroomed in the West, and an increasing number are being trained in this area. Courses are beginning to be offered in seminaries. It is important, however, for these various helping processes to be rooted in a sound Asian theological framework. With the increasing need that churches have for seminars and other training programs in family life, the potential is vast.

4. Provide support for struggling families. This can be achieved through counseling and other ways of ministering to families in distress. The points made earlier are pertinent here too.

5. Have a sharper focus on the family. The Asian church has been influenced greatly by the individualistic focus coming from many quarters in the West. This needs to be changed. Evangelism, discipline, pastoral care, and other forms of ministry can include a clearer focus on the family as a recipient and model of ministry. This will affirm the important place which the family has in Asian society, help to deal effectively with the negative influences on healthy family life brought on by socioeconomic changes, and transform Asian family life to fit in with the larger vision of Christian theology and spirituality.

Bibliography

Baker, H. D. R., *Chinese Family and Kinship* (1979). • Das, M. S., and P. D. Bardis, eds., *The Family in Asia* (1978). • Devanandan, P. D., and M. M. Thomas, eds., *The Changing Pattern of Family in India* (1960). • Harriss, John, ed., *The Family: A Social History of the 20th Century* (1992). • Kuo, E. C. Y., and A. Wong, eds., *The Contemporary Family in Singapore* (1979). • Mace, D., and V. Mace, *Marriage: East and West* (1960). • Quiambao, J., *The Asian Family in a Changing Society* (1966).

ROBERT SOLOMON

Far East Broadcasting Company

(FEBC). International, interdenominational radio ministry airing Christian programs across an area where two-thirds of the world's population live (covering Asia, Russia, the Middle East, India*, and Africa).

Far East Broadcasting began when God placed a vision in the hearts of two men, Robert Bowman and John Broger, to begin radio broadcasting to China*. On 20 Dec 1945, with just $1,000 between them, they established FEBC. It was apparent early in the ministry that broadcasting within China would not be possible, so they headed to the Philippines*. Land was very expensive there and living quarters were nearly impossible to find. But a Christian businessman in Manila offered to sell enough land to build not only a radio transmission site, but housing facilities for the staff as well. The organization had no money — only faith that God would provide. The original price for the land — $50,000 — was slashed to $20,000, and, within months, the entire sum was raised. In Sep 1946, licenses to operate two 10,000-watt transmitters were granted. In 1949, a shortwave station was established with enough power to extend programs to China. Those first broadcasts aired just weeks before the Communists took over China and closed the door on traditional Christian missionary work.

From the beginning, it was recognized that nationals were needed for radio broadcasts to minister to their own people. In 1949, a seminar was held in the Philippines for interested Christians from Vietnam*, Myanmar* (Burma), Hong Kong*, Indonesia*, Japan*, Malaysia*, Russia, and Thailand*. They began planning for programs in their respective languages. Ten years later, a sister organization, Feba Radio, was developed and began broadcasting programs to India, Sri Lanka*, Africa, and the Middle East from the Seychelles Islands.

Today, Far East Broadcasting Radio International has a total of 52 stations, studios, and offices in Asia, Africa, the Commonwealth of Independent States, Europe, and North America. Transmitters are located in Saipan, Korea*, the Philippines, and the Seychelles Islands, and 90% of the 1,100 staff are nationals. FEBC airs programs for more than 350 transmitter hours each day in more than 150 languages.

In 1985, FEBC's commitment to spreading the Gospel led the organization to combine efforts with other missionary radio broadcasts "to provide every man, woman and child the opportunity to hear the gospel in a language they can understand." The presidents of FEBC, World Radio Missionary Fellowship (HCJB), SIM International, and Trans World Radio convened to strategize a plan for combining efforts to have the Gospel shared in all megalanguages (those spoken by over one million people). Later, other missionary radio organizations joined them in this commitment to evangelization by radio. The broadcasters divided the remaining unreached language groups and continue making progress toward the goal.

On the average, 84,000 listener responses via letters, faxes, and phone calls arrive every month at FEBC's offices. The international radio ministry has had an impact on millions of lives for Christ. It is difficult to measure, however, the impact that radio broadcasts have had on the growth of Christianity in China in the past 50 years.

The idea of Christian radio as a tool for evangelism was innovative at the time of FEBC's inception, and the radio ministry continues to work today on projects to improve program quality. Current projects include opening new radio stations, building high-efficiency antennas, and converting from analog to digital capabilities for program recording and broadcasting. FEBC has pledged to continue taking "Christ to the World by Radio."

Bibliography

Bowman, Eleanor, *Eyes Beyond the Horizon* (1991).

JIM BOWMAN

Farnham, John Marshall Willoughby

(Fan Yuehan) (b. 1830; d. United States, 1917). North American Presbyterian* missionary.

Farnham and his wife Mary Jane reached China* in 1860 and established the *Qing Xin* (Pure Heart) Church, the first Presbyterian church in Shanghai. He also took in the refugee children of the Taiping Rebellion* and taught them at the *Qingxin Shuyuan* (Lowrie Institute), of which he was principal for 24 years. Mary Jane set up the *Qingxin* Girls' Middle School (later, the Mary Farnham Girls' School). The two schools later became the most prestigious mission schools in Shanghai. With another missionary, Farnham helped establish the *Meihua Shu Guan* (American Presbyterian Mission Press) in Shanghai. In 1878, he resigned from all of his posts with the Presbyterian Church to become secretary of the Chinese Religious Tract Society. He broke off from the Presbyterian Church in 1888 and set up his own chapel.

Farnham compiled one of the earliest Chinese dialect hymnals, the *Shanghai Hymn Book* (1864). In 1891, he established the *Chong Xi Jiao Hui Bao* (Chinese Christian Review) and served as its editor.

China Group

Farquhar, John Nicol

(b. Aberdeen, Scotland, 6 Apr 1861; d. Manchester, England, 17 Jul 1929). Scottish missionary and scholar of comparative religion.

Farquhar was raised in a devout evangelical home and apprenticed as a draper. He entered Aberdeen Grammar School in 1882 and the University of Aberdeen in 1883. He moved to Oxford University in 1885, where he achieved first-class degrees in classical studies in 1887 and 1889. While in Oxford, he was introduced to the study of comparative religion by Max Muller and the professor of Sanskrit, Monier Monier-Williams. He was awarded a doctorate of letters (D.Litt.) by Oxford in 1906 and made a doctor of divinity by the University of Aberdeen.

In Dec 1890, Farquhar sailed for India* as a lay missionary of the London Missionary Society. He served first as a professor in the society's college at Bhowanipur, Calcutta. In 1894, he was approached by Robert P. Wilder to serve with the Young Men's Christian Association* (YMCA), but it was the intervention of John R. Mott which finally brought about an appointment in 1902. He became student secretary of the Indian YMCA with special concern for evangelism among students. He studied Bengali and Sanskrit and produced his first book in 1903 under the pseudonym of Neil Alexander, *Gita and Gospel,* which examined the Bhagavad Gita (later editions of 1906 and 1917 appeared under his own name). He represented the Indian YMCA at World Student Christian Federation (WSCF) conferences in Tokyo (1907), Oxford (1909), and Constantinople (1911). Mott, general secretary of the WSCF, was a personal friend with whom he corresponded and whose support he valued. In 1911, recognizing Farquhar's calling as a writer, Mott secured his appointment to a post created for him — literary secretary to the Indian national council of the YMCA — in which post he remained until his retirement from India and missionary service on grounds of ill health in 1923.

In the view of Nicol Macnicol, fellow missionary in India, Farquhar "found the study of Oriental religions his true vocation." He produced a number of books: *A Primer of Hinduism* (1911), *The Crown of Hinduism* (1913), *Modern Religious Movements in India* (1914), and a final and acclaimed work of reference, *An Outline of the Religious Literature of India* (1920). He also edited a number of series to which other Christian scholars in India contributed. These were The Religious Quest of India series, The Heritage of India series, and The Religious Life of India series. The combined effect of his literary work has been judged to have fundamentally altered the approach of missionaries to non-Christian religions, as he began from a profound acquaintance with Indian literature and philosophy. The most widely known of his works, *The Crown of Hinduism,* put forward his view that Hinduism found its fulfillment in Christianity. This thesis seemed to conservative critics to surrender the unique in Christianity, but "his aim was to show that every earnest desire after the truth which is manifest in Hinduism can be fulfilled only in the revelation of God in Jesus Christ."

After his return to England, Farquhar became professor of comparative religion at the University of Manchester for the last six years of his life.

Bibliography

The Times (obituary) (19 Jul 1929). • *Dictionary of National Biography 1922-30.* • Anderson, Gerald, ed., *Concise Dictionary of the Christian World Mission* (1970). • Sharpe, Eric J., *Not to Destroy but to Fulfil* (1965); *Faith Meets Faith* (1977). • Anderson, Gerald H., et al., eds., *Mission Legacies: Biographical Studies of Leaders of the Modern Missionary Movement* (1994). • Yates, Timothy, *Christian Mission in the Twentieth Century* (1994).

Timothy Yates

Favier, Pierre-Marie-Alphonse

(b. Marsanny-la-Cote, France, 1837; d. Beijing, China, 1905). French vicar apostolic of Beijing during the Boxer Movement.

Favier was consecrated a priest in 1861 and the following year was sent as a Vincentian (see Lazarists) missionary to Beijing. In 1887, he represented the church in negotiating an agreement with the Qing chief magistrate, Li Hong Zhang, to move North Church from Can Chi Kou to Xi Shi Ku. In 1897, Favier was made coadjutor (associate) vicar apostolic and, in 1899, vicar apostolic of Beijing. In 1900, North Church was under siege during the Boxer Movement. Favier and his associate vicar, Stanislas François Jarlin, with the help of 30 French sailors defended the church while waiting for help. When the eight-nation Allied Forces invaded Beijing and relieved the siege of North Church, Favier was involved in negotiations for reparation from China. In 1904, he rebuilt the burnt South Church with compensation paid by China* to the Allied Forces. He wrote many articles on missionary work in China and published a book, *The Story of Church Mission in Beijing.*

Bibliography

Favier, Pierre-Marie, *Peking: Histoire et Description* (1900); *The Heart of Peking: Bishop A. Favier's Diary of the Siege* (1901). • Striet, Robert, ed., *Annales de la Congrégation de la Mission* 70 (1905).

CHINA GROUP, translated by DAVID WU

Federation of Asian Bishops' Conferences

(FABC). *The origin of the federation.* The Federation of Asian Bishops' Conferences took shape during the historic gathering of 180 bishops of Asia in Manila on the occasion of Pope Paul VI's visit to East and Southeast Asia in Nov 1970. This was the first time Asian bishops had come together to share their experiences and to "search for new ways through which we could be of greater and more effective service to our Catholic communities and all the peoples of Asia."

The central area of the bishops' concern was the urgent need for the Asian church to be more truly "the church of the poor," the "church of the young," and "a church in dialogue" with all people of other religious traditions as well as with the cultural traditions of Asia.

The message issued by the bishops at the end of the Manila meeting stressed the importance of cooperation with all people of good will in the search for human development, freedom, justice, and peace, so that the church may "help bind together the new world of Asia as a true family of nations in this part of the earth, linked not only by lines of geography, but by mutual understanding and respect, by the nobler bonds of brotherhood and love." In the first resolution following this message "the Episcopal Conferences here represented are urged to authorize and support a permanent structure for the effective implementation of the decisions of this meeting."

Four months later (18-21 Mar 1971), the presidents of 11 bishops' conferences of Asian countries met in Hong Kong* to establish "a permanent coordinating body for the Episcopal Conferences in Asia." A follow-up committee representing the major areas of South, Southeast, and East Asia was asked to prepare a draft of statutes for a Federation of Asian Bishops' Conferences. Such a draft was sent to the presidents of the conferences in November of 1971.

In Aug 1972, 12 conferences (Bangladesh*, Burma*, India*, Indonesia*, Laos*-Cambodia*, Korea*, Malaysia-Singapore-Brunei, Pakistan, the Philippines*, Republic of China*, Sri Lanka*, Vietnam*) and Hong Kong as an associate member reaffirmed their acceptance of the idea of a federation of Asian bishops' conferences as a sign and instrument of fraternal cooperation and communion. Japan and Thailand expressed hesitation to participate at this stage in the proposed federation.

On 16 Nov of the same year, the statutes were approved by the holy see. In Feb 1973, the presidents of 10 conferences met in Hong Kong in their first formal meeting as the central committee of the FABC. In May 1973, the conference of Thailand joined the federation. The first plenary assembly was held in Taipei, Taiwan*, on 22-27 Apr 1974. All the member conferences, with the exception of Burma, were represented; the Japanese conference sent a bishop-observer and became a full member in Jun 1974.

Organizational and operational structures. The plenary assembly is the highest body; all committees and offices are answerable to it. Its members are the presidents and delegates of the 14 member conferences, the bishops of Hong Kong and Macau, and the representatives of the ecclesiastical jurisdictions of Nepal* and Mongolia. The plenary assembly meets in ordinary session every four years. The direction of the federation is carried out by a central committee comprising the presidents of the member conferences and by a standing committee comprising five bishops elected from different parts of Asia. The principal administrative body of the federation is the central secretariat. Three regional assemblies (East Asia, Southeast Asia, South Asia) act as organs of communication, collaboration, and service to the episcopal conferences.

At the operational level, all activities of the federation are carried out through specialized service agencies that are established by the central committee and function under the central secretariat: the office of human development (OHD), already functioning before 1972; the offices of social communications, education and student chaplaincy, evangelization, and ecumenical* and interreligious affairs, all established in 1972; the office of laity, established in 1986; and the FABC theological advisory commission created in the same year to meet the theological demands of the plenary assemblies and the various offices. The offices consist of a commission of bishops who act as a board of directors and an executive staff. The offices and the theological advisory commission meet once every two years in a joint planning meeting. Each office maintains close links with the related national commissions of the conferences and with the corresponding pontifical councils or commissions in the Vatican.

FABC activities. One of the main activities of the offices is the organization of regional consultations, workshops, colloquia, seminars, and conferences on the challenges confronting Asia and the Asian churches today. Almost 100 meetings of that kind, including 30 Bishops' Institutes for Social Action (BISAs), Interreligious Dialogue* (BIRAs), Lay Apostolate (BILAs), and Missionary Apostolate (BIMAs), have been sponsored and held in different countries by the FABC offices since 1974.

The theological advisory commission has brought out important documents, e.g., "Theses on Interreligious Dialogue — An Essay in Pastoral Theological Reflection," "Theses on the Local Church — A Theological Reflection in the Asian Context," "Asian Perspectives on Church and Politics," and "Towards a Theology of Harmony: Asian Perspectives." One of the major achievements of the theological advisory commission is the 1994 international colloquium on "Being Church in Asia in the Twenty-First Century."

Six plenary assemblies have been held thus far:

- FABC I. Taipei, Taiwan, 22-27 Apr 1974
  — Theme: Evangelization in Modern-Day Asia
- FABC II. Calcutta, India, 19-26 Nov 1978
  — Theme: Prayer — The Life of the Church in Asia
- FABC III. Bangkok, Thailand, 19-29 Oct 1982
  — Theme: The Church — A Community of Faith in Asia
- FABC IV. Tokyo, Japan, 16-25 Sep 1986
  — Theme: The Vocation and Mission of the Laity in the Church and in the World of Asia
- FABC V. Bandung, Indonesia, 17-27 Jul 1990
  — Theme: The Emerging Challenges for the Church in Asia in the 1990s: A Call to Respond
- FABC VI. Manila, Philippines, 10-19 Jan 1995, coinciding with the 25th anniversary of the foundation of FABC
  — Theme: Christian Discipleship in Asia Today: Service to Life

Orientations and impact of the FABC. The basic mode of mission in Asia must be dialogue — dialogue with Asian religions, Asian cultures, and the immense multitude of the poor in Asia. This overarching program of dialogue has been the thematic background of both the pastoral and missionary activity of the local churches of Asia in the past 25 years. It is the dynamic insertion of the Gospel into the life-realities of Asia in a process of humble, loving, and continuous dialogue that the bishops of Asia call "evangelization."

The bishops of Asia have clearly and strongly affirmed, again and again, that "the proclamation of Jesus Christ is the center and primary element of evangelization." They have also made it clear that "the proclamation of Jesus Christ in Asia means, first of all, the witness of Christians and Christian communities to the values of the Kingdom of God," that "the first call to the Churches in Asia is to proclaim Christ through dialogue and deeds," and that it is "in dialogue with Asian peoples and Asian realities that the Church must discern what deeds the Lord wills to be done so that humankind may be gathered together in harmony as his family." It is through this dialogue that the local Christian community becomes "church" and enables itself to be an authentic bearer of the Gospel in its being and life, in its own place and time.

The dialogue and the identification with the poor, in terms of struggle for human rights, liberation, justice, and full human development, are in Asia a task which calls for special attention to the characteristic spiritual and religious vision of Asian peoples. This is a task which must be accomplished ever more increasingly with neighbors of other faiths recognized as true partners in the building up of a truly human community in Asia. Here again, the bishops of Asia have clearly affirmed that "the challenge for the Church is to work for justice and peace along with Christians of other Churches, together with our sisters and brothers of other faiths and with all people of good will, to make the Kingdom of God more visibly present in Asia" (final statement of the FABC's 5th Plenary Assembly, Bandung, 1990).

The FABC documents, and especially the statements of the 4th Plenary Assembly and the Bishops' Institutes for Lay Apostolate, have repeatedly stressed the importance of the laity's active and full participation in the church's life and ministry.

In helping the Asian bishops to grow in mutual knowledge and understanding, to develop ways of fostering among themselves a spirit of solidarity and cooperation, and to move forward in their discernment and action as pastors in their communities, the FABC has contributed to the creation of a greater community of vision, values, and priorities among local Asian churches. It has also enabled Asian bishops to contribute to the ongoing reflection and discernment of churches in other continents, and to the thinking and policies of the central administrative offices of the church.

ALBERT POULET-MATHIS

Federation of Evangelical Churches of India (FECI). Sole national evangelical church body in India* constituted for the purpose of bringing together congregations of the evangelical persuasion.

The Evangelical Fellowship of India took the first step in 1970 by setting up an ad hoc federation with Rev. Pannalall and some other leaders. After some years of negotiation, the federation was officially inaugurated on 4 Nov 1974 with 16 denominations as its founding members. Its purposes are to promote fellowship and unity among evangelical churches, safeguard and promote the historical biblical faith in the life and witness of the church, encourage member churches in evangelism and mission, and encourage sound leadership development for the various ministries of the church. FECI keeps fraternal relationships with other national and international bodies. It presents the united voice of evangelical churches to the government in matters pertaining to their fundamental rights. Member churches hold their own property and conduct their work independently.

The activities of FECI revolve around the central belief that the local church is the basic unit for worship and mission. Currently, FECI assists in maintaining the spiritual life of member churches by arranging conferences for pastors and church leaders, women, and youth, and seminars on public evangelism on both the regional and national levels. FECI also undertakes relief work for the poor in communities where disaster strikes.

FECI has assisted in forming the Evangelical Theological Board with the purpose of bringing together Bible-based evangelical Bible schools, colleges, and seminaries. The board also coordinates and builds up standardized syllabi and teaching programs in theological institutes. FECI invites and makes arrangements for itinerant Bible teachers and evangelists.

The annual general assembly, held at different places on the invitation of member churches, is for fellowship, encouragement, and sharing, in addition to the usual official business and policy-making functions. For effective ministry, the country is divided into eight regions, with all working toward the fulfillment of the central aims of FECI.

Members pay annual fees and give donations for the ministry. FECI seeks to help raise the living standards of church pastors by providing scholarships for their children's education and sponsoring students who wish to go for theological studies.

Presently, 55 evangelical church denominations with 1,600 worshipping groups in 20 states of India are full members. The member churches, in both large cosmopolitan cities and rural areas, include Episcopal, Congregational, Baptist*, Mennonite*, Brethren, Presbyterian*, Pentecostal, Evangelical Quakers, and independent churches. FECI has brought together churches of various doctrinal emphases for a common purpose and fellowship which are unique.

FECI's office is located in Nagpur, with secretaries looking after each department. It has four acres of land and intends to build a conference center with a capacity of 150 for church conferences and seminars. P. T. Chandapilla was the first general secretary. Gabriel Massey joined as associate secretary in 1977 and has been general secretary since 1982. GABRIEL MASSEY

Federation of Independent Chinese Churches

The most influential independent Protestant church in China*.

In 1905, a Shanghai Presbyterian* church pastor, Yu Guo Zhen*, mindful of the crisis of Yi-he-tuan, formed the *Ye Su Jiao Zi Li Hui* (Christian Independent Church). To prevent further cases from arising, he changed the name of his church to the Independent Presbyterian Church. There were other churches outside of Shanghai which took this step as well. In 1910, Yu formed the Federation of Independent Churches with these churches, and he became the first chairman of the federation. In the following year, an official periodical, *Sheng Bao*, was first published. In 1920, the first National Council of Independent Churches was called for, and a constitution was drawn up. Directors were elected, and the name of the federation was now called *Zhong Guo Ye Su Jiao Zi Li Hui Quan Guo Zong Hui* (National Council of China Christian Independent Churches). Yu was appointed lifelong chairman. In 1924, after Yu had retired, he devoted all of his time to the development of the independent church.

In 1929, a building was constructed for the use of the National Council of Independent Churches. At that time, there were about 350 churches under the federation. However, opinions diversified shortly after. In 1933, during the Third National Conference, a statement was made that some previous understandings were mistaken. After this, the federation shrank in size and the successors of Yu could no longer hold all of the churches together. The Fourth National Conference, which was supposed to elect a new group of leaders, was postponed and never held. All of the churches went their own ways, and the federation could exercise control over only 20 churches around Shanghai.

In Feb 1954, the federation held a Three-Self Learning Meeting, and over 40 leaders attended. Xie Yong Qin was elected chairman during the meeting. In 1958, all of the churches from the China Christian Independent Church participated in a nationwide united worship service.

CHINA GROUP

Feliciani, Anthony

(b. Marano, Italy, 4 Oct 1804; d. Dongerkou, Shanxi, China, 18 Mar 1866). Second prefect apostolic of the Hong Kong* Catholic Church (1842-47 and 1850-55).

Feliciani was one of the pioneers of the Catholic Church in Hong Kong. He led the church out of the many troubles caused by the rather unsettled and confused situation of Hong Kong, as well as diligently coordinated the mission work in China*.

Feliciani joined the Order of the Friars Minor (Franciscans*) in 1823 and was sent to Macau in 1833. He came to Hong Kong with T. Joset* from Macau in Mar 1842 and was appointed procurator of the Sacred Congregation for the Propagation of the Faith (see Propaganda Fide) and prefect of Hong Kong on 11 Dec 1842. In Oct 1847 he handed the responsibility of the prefecture to Augustin Forcade. Forcade resigned in Aug 1850, and Feliciani took back the post until 20 Jun 1855, when, under his insistent request to be allowed to go to work on the Chinese mainland, the holy see accepted his resignation.

Feliciani left Hong Kong in Oct 1856 and went to work first in Shandong (1856-59) and then in Shanxi (Hukwang), where he was appointed vicar general and later died, having lived a life of tireless service.

Bibliography

Ricci, J., *Necrologium Fratrum Minorum in Sinis* (1878).

SERGIO TICOZZI

Feminism, Christian

Movement initiated by Christian women for the dignity and liberation of women and for equal participation of women and men in the church and society.

In Asia, Christian women became more conscious of the oppression of women as they gained access to education and worked with other women in the Young Women's Christian Association* (YWCA), the Woman's Christian Temperance Movement, and the Women's Clubs. In the late 19th c., some Christian women in Asia began to challenge deep-seated patriarchal traditions in their culture and male dominance in the church (see Women's Movements). They initiated social reform, literacy* campaigns, and health education for women and advocated changes in marriage and family* structure. Participating in social movements and in the national struggles for independence from colonial rule, they also argued for greater participation of women in ministry and leadership of the church.

A more organized and ecumenical Christian feminist movement emerged in Asia in the late 1970s. Progressive women's groups have been formed in many Asian countries to struggle against economic and political exploitation and sexual discrimination against women. For example, in the Philippines*, a national organization of women's groups, GABRIELA, was organized to promote women's welfare and to fight sex tourism. In Korea*, Christian women's groups struggle for better working conditions for women workers, recompense for women drafted during World War II* to provide sexual services for Japanese soldiers, and the reunification of the country. In Japan*, Christian women are involved in the peace movement and in forming coalitions with other Asian women in fighting sexual exploitation and sex tourism. In Taiwan* and Hong Kong*, Christian women are concerned about the environment, working conditions for women, and women's participation in the political process. Christian women in the Asian subcontinent continue their struggle against poverty*, illiteracy, the dowry, and the caste system. Some of the emerging concerns of Asian Christian women include ecological issues, consumer rights, violence against women, literacy, women's political participation, and their changing roles in the global market economy.

Asian feminist theology developed in the context of women's heightened awareness of their subordinate position in the church and society. Earlier feminist writings of Christian women can be found in church yearbooks, college bulletins, pamphlets, religious journals, and YWCA magazines. Since the early 1980s, Asian Christian women have been creating their own theological networks through the Women's Desk of the Christian Conference of Asia* and the Women's Commission of the Ecumenical Association of Third World Theologians. The Asian women's theological journal *In God's Image* was launched in 1982 by Sun Ai Lee Park, and the Asian Women's Resource Center for Culture and Theology was established in 1988. At the same time, associations of theologically trained women were formed in various countries, including Korea, Taiwan, Indonesia*, India*, and the Philippines. Asian women have met nationally and regionally to discuss patriarchy in the church and society, the relationship between Gospel and culture, feminist biblical interpretation, and collaboration with women of other faith traditions. Some of the important Asian feminist theologians include Marianne Katoppo from Indonesia; Mary John Mananzan, Virginia Fabella, and Elizabeth Tapia from the Philippines; Cho Wha Soon, Chung Hyun Kyung, and Lee Oo Chung from Korea; Kwok Pui-lan from Hong Kong; Hisako Kinukawa from Japan; Nantawan Boonprasat Lewis from Thailand; and Aruna Gnanadason and Stella Baltazar from India.

Since the Bible* is preeminent in church life in Asia, many feminist theological writings focus on reinterpretation of the Bible. Some emphasize women's heritage in the Bible, pointing to Naomi and Ruth, Hannah, Miriam, Deborah, Mary Magdalene, and Mary the mother of Jesus as strong role models. Others have through storytelling, dramatization, and creative performance reclaimed biblical women as subjects with their own thoughts, feelings, and voice. This oral interpretation of the Bible is significant because Asian scriptures and classics have been recited, chanted, and orally transmitted for millennia. Asian feminist theologians have also used insights from socio-political analyses and cultural anthropology to demonstrate the relevance of the Bible to contemporary struggle. Through the process of dialogical imagination, they have related the biblical story to the myths, legends, and folklores of Asia. An emerging approach is to interpret the Bible with the help of cultural studies and postcolonial theories. These various approaches have shown that the Bible is a complex document which must be critically scrutinized through the lens of women's struggles in order to be used as a resource for liberation.

Living in a religiously pluralistic world, when Asian feminist theologians speak about God they are influenced by the religious language and symbolic structure of their cultural environment. They are not so much interested in the abstract debates on the Trinity or the existence of God, but focus on God as the source of life and the sustaining power of the universe. Some feminist theologians have recovered the rich tradition of feminine images of the divine both in the Bible and in Asian religions. They have also challenged the predominant use of male metaphors and images in liturgy, hymns, and sermons in the Asian churches.

Feminist theologians from diverse contexts in Asia have interpreted the life and ministry of Jesus differently. Some have suggested that Jesus is a fully liberated human being who befriended the underdogs of society and transgressed the religious and ethnic boundaries of his time. Some Korean feminist theologians understand Jesus to be a priest of *han,* which is the feeling of woundedness and indignation arising out of experiences of injustice. Several feminist theologians in India speak of Jesus as the embodiment of the feminine and creative principle of the universe, Shakti. Eco-feminist theologians have searched for organic models of Christ that provide alternatives to anthropocentric and androcentric interpretations of Christology.

In the Catholic tradition, Mary has often been presented as a gentle, docile, and obedient mother. But some feminist theologians have reclaimed her as a model of liberated women and true discipleship. As a virgin, she is a self-defining woman, not subject to other human beings; as a mother, she is the giver of life; and as a sister, she stands in solidarity with other oppressed women. She accepts the challenge from God, lives in faith, and helps to found the earliest community of faith. As a co-redeemer in human salvation, Mary has been reinterpreted as a patron of women's persistent fight for dignity and equality.

Although women are the majority in many Asian churches, they are marginalized in the power structures of the church and life of the congregation. Colonial and patriarchal denominational polity, reinforced by indigenous biases and taboos against women, consign them to second-class status. Challenging the churches to live out the teaching that women and men are equal in the life and ministry of the body of Christ, Asian feminist theologians have criticized the church's misogynist teachings and patriarchal models of leadership. Christian women have organized around the issues of ordination of women, prophetic roles for women in religious orders, fuller participation of the laity, and greater representation of women in church synods, conventions, and ecumenical gatherings. They argue that the church must be liberated from the bondage of sexism and begin to recognize the equal partnership of women and men in carrying out God's mission in the world.

A life-affirming, compassionate, and energizing spirituality is emerging in women's groups that struggle against the forces of oppression and death. This ecological and feminist spirituality* celebrates religious and cultural diversity, the interrelatedness of all beings, and the sacredness of the earth. It seeks deeper connection with women's yearnings and hope expressed in Asian popular religions and pays attention to the cries of the indigenous people, the Dalits (see Dalit Movements), minorities, and refugees*. Together with other feminist theologians from the Third World, Asian Christian women want to articulate a liberating spirituality that heals the earth and the suffering of women. Asian feminist theology and spirituality have slowly made inroads in the Asian churches, and their contribution has been recognized in the wider ecumenical movement.

Bibliography

Abraham, Dulcie, et al., eds., *Asian Women Doing Theology* (1987). • Chung, Hyun Kyung, *Struggle to Be the Sun Again: Introducing Asian Women's Theology* (1990). • Fabella, Virginia, and Sun Ai Li Park, eds., *We Dare to Dream: Doing Theology as Asian Women* (1989). • Gnanadason, Aruna, ed., *Toward a Theology of Humanhood: Women's Perspectives* (1986). • Katoppo, Marianne, *Compassionate and Free: An Asian Women's Theology* (1979). • Kinukawa, Hisako, *Women and Jesus in Mark: A Japanese Feminist Perspective* (1994). • Kwok, Pui-lan, *Chinese Women and Christianity, 1860-1927* (1992); *Discovering the Bible in the Non-Biblical World* (1995). • Lee, Oo Chung, et al., eds., *Women of Courage: Asian Women Reading the Bible* (1992). • Mananzan, Mary John, ed., *Women and Religion* (1992).

KWOK PUI-LAN

Feng Yu Xiang

(b. Anhui, China, 1882; d. 1948). "Christian General" of China*.

Feng joined the army when he was a youth. In his early years, he was very critical of Christianity. In 1905, while he was under treatment in a Peking (Beijing) mission hospital, Feng began to show friendliness toward the church. He was baptized in Peking in 1912 and from then on promoted Christianity in the army, using Christian doctrines in his disciplinary measures and recruiting chaplains for the soldiers.

In 1914, Feng was appointed *shizhang* by the government of the North. He later swung his army over to the national government and appointed himself commander-in-chief.

In 1922, Feng started prayer meetings among political figures and was nicknamed the "Christian General." He consistently criticized foreign powers, however, for using Christianity as a pretext to invade China and once fired a chaplain.

In 1927, Feng was the National Revolution Army Second Camp's commander-in-chief. In 1933, he organized the anti-Japanese Alliance Army and was its commander-in-chief as well. In 1936, he became deputy chairman of the Central Army Committee and throughout his term opposed Chiang Kai-shek's dictatorship. In 1946, Feng visited the United States and strongly criticized Chiang for starting the civil war in China. In 1947, the Chinese in America Peace and Democratic Alliance was formed in the USA, and Feng became its chairman. In 1948, while Feng was on his way back to China, his ship caught fire, and he died. CHINA GROUP

Fenwick, Malcolm C.

(b. Toronto, Canada, 1863; d. Wonsan, Korea, 7 Dec 1935). Pioneer missionary who organized the Church of Christ in Korea.

Fenwick was the eleventh son of Archie Fenwick, whose ancestors migrated to Canada from Scotland. In 1889, Fenwick went from Canada to Korea* as an independent missionary with no formal college or seminary education. He did extensive pioneer work and organized the Korean Itinerant Mission. Most of his pioneer mission work was done in and around Wonsan. In 1906, he organized the denomination called the Church of Christ in Korea. Until his death, Fenwick worked from Wonsan throughout the provinces of Chungnam and Kyungbuk.

He was the very first missionary to send out indigenous Korean workers, in this case to both Manchuria and Siberia.

Bibliography

Paik, I. George, *The History of the Protestant Missions in Korea, 1832-1910* (1929). KIN HUH

Ferguson-Davie, Charles James

(b. United Kingdom, 1872; d. Pietermaritzburg, South Africa, 11 Sep 1963). First Anglican* bishop of Singapore*.

Ordained a priest in the Church of England (Manchester, 1898), Ferguson-Davie served as a missionary with the Society for the Propagation of the Gospel (SPG) in India* (Riwari, 1902-7; Rawalpindi, 1907-9) with his wife, Charlotte E. Ferguson-Davie*, a missionary doctor. Until his appointment, the work of the Anglican Church in Singapore, Malaya, and Borneo was under one jurisdiction. From 1909, a separate bishop was appointed for the Borneo territories, and Ferguson-Davie was given charge of Singapore and Peninsular Malaya, together with pastoral oversight of Anglican communities in Thailand* and Indonesia*. This new arrangement greatly facilitated the development of the Anglican mission in the area.

Ferguson-Davie recognized the need for an Asian pastorate if the church was to grow beyond a colonial chaplaincy. During his episcopate, the number of Asian clergy increased from two to 13 (six Tamil, seven Chinese). Mission schools were started in Singapore and Malaya; a medical* mission was opened in Malacca* (1911) and in Singapore (1913), the latter under the guidance of Charlotte Ferguson-Davie. In 1926, St. Nicholas' Home for the Blind was opened in Malacca and continues today to serve the needs of the visually handicapped.

Although Ferguson-Davie had to lead his diocese through World War I and the Great Depression that followed, he succeeded in setting the Anglican Church firmly on the road to Asianization and self-support. He resigned as bishop in 1927, thereafter serving in the diocese of Natal, South Africa, until his death in 1963.

Bibliography

USPG and CMS Archives, Partnership House Library, London. • Loh, Keng Aun, *50 Years of the Anglican Church in Singapore Island: 1909-59* (1963). • *Singapore Diocesan Magazine* (1910-25). FRANK LOMAX

Ferguson-Davie, Charlotte E.

(b. ?; d. South Africa, 24 Mar 1943). Missionary doctor, founder of Anglican* medical* missions in Singapore*.

A medical missionary with the Society for the Propagation of the Gospel (SPG) in India* (Karnal, 1897-1900; Delhi, 1901; Riwari, 1902-6; Rawalpindi, 1907-9), Ferguson-Davie came to Singapore in 1909 with her husband, Charles James Ferguson-Davie*. She opened the first mission clinic in Singapore in 1913 on Bencoolen Street. Under her supervision, this later developed into the St. Andrew's Medical Mission. On 22 May 1923, the 60-bed St. Andrews Mission Hospital was opened to attend to the medical needs of women and children in the crowded Chinatown area of Singapore, where infant and child mortality rates were high. Existing hospital facilities in Singapore were quite inadequate; furthermore, the new hospital with its lady missionary doctors met the needs of many Asian women who refused to see male doctors.

St. Andrew's Mission Hospital was known for the high standard of its training of nurses and midwives and contributed to the development of better medical services in Singapore. Outpatient clinics were opened for prenatal care as well as for the treatment of prevalent venereal diseases. Ferguson-Davie herself continued to act as a consultant physician at the hospital and, until leaving Singapore in 1927, was the guiding light and inspiration for its development.

Bibliography

USPG and CMS Archives, Partnership House Library, London. • *Singapore Diocesan Magazine* (1910-25). • Serene Teo Swee Choon, "A History of the St. Andrew's Mission Hospital" (bachelor's thesis, National University of Singapore) (1988). FRANK LOMAX

Fernando, Solomon

(b. Moratuwa, Sri Lanka, 1849; d. Colombo, Sri Lanka, 1915). Medical doctor and leading Methodist* layman, scholar, and national leader in Sri Lanka*.

Fernando held practically every office open to a layman in the Methodist Church in Ceylon. In 1890, Fernando was circuit steward of Jampettah Street and also the first layman to represent the circuit at the district synod in 1895. He was one of the leading laymen of Ceylon Methodism for many years.

For 25 years, Fernando was director of the Young Men's Christian Association (YMCA); he was also chairman of the executive of the Laymen's Missionary Movement, which was formed in 1912, and a vice president of the Ceylon National Missionary Society, which was formed after the visit of John R. Mott. He was the first Sinhalese layman to be appointed to the local committee of the Wesleyan Methodist Missionary Society in Sri Lanka, which had been dominated by Europeans. One of the patriots of his time, he showed that a devoted Sinhalese Christian could also be an ardent nationalist.

Fernando was president of the Low Country Products Association, a member of the Royal Asiatic Society, and an elected member of the Colombo Municipal Council. In the medical profession, he was highly respected, having at one time been acting president of Ceylon Medical Officers. He was also a lecturer at Ceylon

Medical College. When he was superintendent of jails, he introduced important reforms regarding diet and labor in jails (1912).

He was a strong believer in the mission of the printed page and did much to encourage the dissemination of wholesome literature. He was manager of the Sinhala Christian weekly, *Rivikirana* (first published in Feb 1907).

He was an earnest student of Buddhism*. His lecture on "The Omission of Buddhism," published posthumously in 1918 by W. J. Noble, was a valuable contribution to the subject of Buddhist theism. He was one of the pioneers in Sri Lanka in studying how religious development leads to comprehension and constructive work. In this respect, he was far ahead of his time.

After the riots in 1915, the national leaders of the day, among whom were some prominent Christians, demanded a full investigation by a royal commission into the administration of the country during and after the riots. Fernando spoke at a large gathering in a public hall in Colombo. An Anglican presided; Methodists, Buddhists, and Hindus sat side by side. Fernando delivered the main resolution, demanding justice for the nation. In giving utterance to his feelings, he was profoundly moved, and at the end of his memorable speech collapsed in his chair and died. G. P. V. Somaratna

Figourovsky, Innocent (Innokentii)

(b. 1864; d. 1931). Russian bishop *(episcopos)* of the Orthodox* Church in China*.

Figourovsky arrived in Beijing in 1898 as the archimandrate of the 18th Russian Orthodox mission group to Beijing and did more than his predecessors to develop the Orthodox Church in China. He upgraded preaching and catechism to deepen the knowledge of Chinese Christians, paid attention to youth work by strengthening the school system, expanded social work, and built new mission stations. Most of his efforts were destroyed during the Boxer Rebellion. All the churches except one were burned, in addition to the press and the library. Figourovsky returned to Russia, was consecrated a bishop, and returned to China in 1902. He used the indemnity paid under the Treaty of Xinchou (1901) to rebuild the Orthodox Church in China. In addition to church buildings and cemeteries, a monastery, and a convent, he also set up a dairy, a weaving factory, and a printing press. In 1914, about 800 non-Russian adults and infants were baptized.

Figourovsky took in many exiled Russian officials as clerics in China in the course of the Russian October Revolution. He also smuggled and concealed the coffins of the czar's relatives in Beijing and violated the Soviet-Chinese agreement of 1924, which provided for the return of Russian property to the Soviet regime. In 1922 the Orthodox Mission in Beijing was named the Chinese Eastern Orthodoxy. In 1930 Figourovsky became the patriarch (archbishop) of the Temporary Russian Orthodox Patriarchal Council in Exile.

Bibliography

Latourette, K. S., *A History of the Expansion of Christianity*, Vol. 6 (1945). • Stamoolis, James J., *Eastern Orthodox Mission Theology Today* (1986). China Group

Filipinization Controversy

The term "Filipinization," especially in relation to the struggle of the Filipino clergy for equality with the Spanish friars, was a 19th-c. movement to keep the parishes in the hands of the Filipino clergy.

The first 10 Filipino priests were ordained between 1697 and 1706. This was the brave achievement of a zealous archbishop of Manila, Don Diego Camacho y Avila. Between 1707 and 1723, 34 more Filipino priests were ordained by the Camacho's successor. By 1750 Filipino priests held 142, or nearly one fourth, of the 569 Philippine parishes.

By 1754 two of these Filipino priests were among those singled out by a Spanish Jesuit*, Juan J. Delgado, as men "who, although *indios* ["Indians"], can serve as an example to shame Europeans."

When a subsequent Manila archbishop, Don Basilio Sancho de Santa Justa, quarreled with the Spanish regular orders in 1767 on the question of episcopal visitation, he transferred their parishes to Filipino priests. The archbishop's detractors quipped that "no oarsmen could be found for the coasting vessels, for the archbishop had ordained them all."

Indeed, the idea of Filipino priests was not without its zealous objectors. In 1725 the Spanish Augustinian*, Fray Gaspar de San Agustin, expressed the fear that placing the parishes in the hands of "natives ordained to the priesthood" might only result in "abominations."

Archbishop Sancho's experiment also fared badly, for many of the hastily trained and ordained Filipino priests proved unfit for the noble service entrusted to them. The foibles and misdemeanors of the unworthy ones only lent credibility to the dark prophecy pronounced by de San Agustin half a century earlier. Among the Spaniards, there was always the fear that the intelligent and competent Filipino priests would attract a separatist following.

The expulsion of the Jesuits* in 1768 from all Spanish dominions and the troubles in Europe arising from the French Revolution and the Napoleonic Wars made it difficult for Spain, beginning in 1799, to send new missionaries to the Philippines*. Thus, in the 30 years between 1798 and 1828, only 39 new Franciscans* arrived in the Philippines. Of the Recollects, too, only 18 came between 1800 and 1825. As a result, by about 1822 Filipino priests held some 90 percent of the 1,000 or so parishes and missions in the country, some of these having been in Filipino hands for up to 50 years.

In 1826 a royal decree transferred several curacies held by Filipino priests to the care of the Spanish regulars. In 1837 many Spanish monastics were turned out from their monasteries. In addition, the anticlerical Spanish government disamorticized church lands and suppressed many monasteries between 1833 and 1840.

In that seven-year period of 1833-40, the number of Spanish religious personnel supported by the state plummeted from 175,574 to but 12,736. Many of those excloistered naturally began to look for assignment in the Philippines, especially because by 1830 Spain had lost practically all of her South American colonies.

Thus began the process of transferring many parishes from Filipino to Spanish hands. By 1839, the Filipino secular clergy still held only about 40 percent of the total number of curacies.

The Filipino priests' continued losses of long-held parishes, some for more than 50 years, caused much resentment and restlessness. By the middle of the 19th c., this would lead to the so-called "secularization controversy," or the question of whether the parishes should be administered by the secular clergy, as ordinarily provided for by canon law, or by the regular clergy of the various missionary Spanish orders, a privilege accorded to them by various royal decrees in the past.

But since Filipinos by this time formed the overwhelming bulk of the secular clergy in the Philippines, the issue would soon metamorphose into the "Filipinization controversy."

A new round in the controversy erupted in 1849 when a royal decree handed seven of the 12 parishes in the province of Cavite near Manila over to the Spanish friars. As it appeared to be a calculated move to eliminate Filipino priests in leadership positions, this aroused the most bitter opposition and resentment on the part of the Filipino clergy.

The cause of the Filipino clergy was championed by Pedro Pelaez* (1812-63), a full-blooded Philippine-born Spaniard, who was then secretary to Manila archbishop José Aranguren. Though a most loyal subject of the Spanish Crown, Pelaez was nevertheless specially distinguished by his unflinching support of the Filipino clergy. He defended the dignity and the right to equality of the Filipino clergy and insisted that they be judged on the basis of their own merits, especially since many of them were earning advanced degrees at the University of Santo Tomas in Manila.

In this struggle Pelaez found zealous colleagues in a Filipino priest in Cavite, Mariano Gomez (1799-1872), and in Pelaez's own brilliant student, José Apolonio Burgos (1837-72). Burgos and another young colleague, Jacinto Zamora, were the two curates of the parish of the Manila Cathedral (see Gom-Bur-Za). These champions of Filipino rights brought their clamor to Spain, appealing to the court, lobbying at the Spanish courts, and publishing their cries in the pages of some Madrid newspapers.

A fresh round in the controversy erupted when new royal decrees were issued in 1861 and 1862, partly to compensate the Jesuits who had returned in 1859 and claimed their ancient parishes. The fiercest opponents of the Filipino clergy countered by accusing Pelaez and the Filipino clergy of "separatist" ideas, a fiery issue now that the Philippines represented Spain's largest remaining colony.

Pelaez's sudden and unfortunate demise when the Manila Cathedral crumbled on him in the earthquake of 1863 catapulted to the leadership of the Filipino priests his assistant, Burgos, who in 1868 would earn the doctor of theology degree and in 1871 the doctor of canon law from the University of Santo Tomas.

In the years between 1863 and 1869, what had previously been simply a conflict between the secular and regular clergy was now quickly transformed into a Filipino struggle for racial equality. As Pelaez had done, so Burgos argued from civil and canon law for the rights of the Filipino secular clergy to the parishes, while insisting on the latter's personal and intellectual capacity to merit these high offices.

When the liberal Spanish Revolution of 1868 brought a new governor-general, Carlos Maria de la Torre, to the Philippines in 1869, there arose in Manila an intellectual reformist movement that clamored for reforms and greater liberty. Its lay section, composed of professionals and businessmen, was led by a law professor at the University of Santo Tomas, while the clerical section, composed of the most brilliant Filipino priests, was led by Burgos. Under the influence of their professors, university students at Santo Tomas also organized their own movement, called the *Juventud Escolar Liberal,* which clamored for academic freedom. Many of these students would become leaders of the Filipino Propaganda Movement in later years.

At first de la Torre seemed sympathetic to the reformists. But gradually he came to the view that it was too early for Filipinos to hold the freedoms they were clamoring for. Under de la Torre's successor, Rafael Izquierdo, the so-called "Cavite Mutiny" of 20 Jan 1872 took place. In the wake of this political turmoil, many of the leaders of the reformist movement were exiled overseas, while the three leaders of the Filipino clergy (Burgos, Gomez, and Zamora) were executed on trumped-up charges of leading an attempted rebellion.

The execution of the three priests put an end to the movement toward Filipinization of the parishes. By the early 1870s, the hold of the Filipino priests on the parishes would dip further to but 23 percent of the whole, which by then had risen in number to 792.

By 1895, on the eve of the revolution against Spain, Filipino priests administered only 161, or 20 percent, of the 797 curacies in the country. Some 500 or 600 other Filipino priests at that time served only as coadjutors, mostly to Spanish regulars.

Thus were the roots planted of the religious reform which ultimately led to the formation of the *Iglesia Filipina Independiente* (Philippine Independent Church*). Though it materialized only in 1902, the roots of this movement must be traced back to 1872, or 1863, or even farther.

Bibliography

De la Costa, Horacio, "The Development of the Native Clergy in the Philippines," in *Studies in Philippine Church History,* ed. Gerald H. Anderson (1969). • Santiago, Luciano P. R., "The First Group of Filipino Priests (1698-1706): Biographical Profiles," *Philippine Quarterly of Culture and Society,* Vol. XII (1984). • Brou, A., "Notes sur les origines du clergé philippin," *Revue d'histoire des missions,* Vol. IV (1927). • Schumacher, John N., *Revolutionary Clergy: The Filipino Clergy and the Nationalist Movement, 1850-1903* (1981). T. VALENTINO SITOY, JR.

Filipino Folk Catholicism, Philippines

Faith, understood as an affirmative and committed response to God's offer of life and love, is necessarily embodied and expressed in and through a culture. Culture interprets and incarnates this response. Through the various aspects of a particular culture, such faith is understood and manifested.

Catholicism in the Philippines*, which began in the 16th c., has at present two major forms: official Roman Catholicism* and folk Catholicism. Each understands and expresses the Catholic tradition of Christianity in its own way. While Catholicism in the Philippines is officially Roman in character, Catholic Filipinos in general tend to express their faith according to the patterns of their indigenous, largely cosmic culture. This second form of Catholicism is often referred to as "folk-" or "popular Catholicism." Alternatively, the phenomenon is also called "folk-" or "popular religiosity." These designations derive from the idea that this is the Catholicism of the "folk," or ordinary people (*populus* = people), rather than that of the elite, whether cleric or lay.

Filipino folk Catholicism is a form of religiosity that is rooted in the indigenous culture. Examination of its Catholic expressions reveals underlying cultural patterns of beliefs, values, and customs. The Filipinos' belief in *kapalaran* or *swerte* (fate, destiny), for instance, affects their understanding of God's will. Love for children finds an expression in their devotion to the *Santo Nino,* the child Jesus. And their understanding of Mary is closely linked to the central position of the mother in the Filipino culture.

Because of this, some have looked at folk Catholicism negatively, regarding it as a diluted version of genuine Catholicism. Others have seen in this not only a basic preservation of the culture vis-à-vis the influences of Spain and the United States during their colonial regimes, but also as a concrete example of incarnating Christianity within a specific culture.

Folk Catholicism, given its rootedness in culture, is a habit religiosity. Culture is largely habit since it consists of adopted patterns of thinking and behaving which have been created and developed over a long period of time. The customary or the habitual allows people to hand on values through traditions as well as to internalize such values through repeated realization. Respect for elders, to give an example, is inculcated through the habit of *mano po* in which the hand of an elder is brought to touch the forehead of someone giving respect. Consciousness of solidarity with the beloved dead is fostered not only through annual visits to the cemetery on the first of November, but also through the usual novena for the dead, the commemoration of 40 days, and a year-long mourning by the immediate family. The practice of devotional wiping of the statues of saints both expresses and preserves intuitively the import of body language in communication and in the revelation of deep sentiments.

But precisely because of this rootedness in the culture, folk Catholicism is also largely a form of religiosity which is unreflected upon. Culture is ambivalent, containing both life-giving and death-dealing elements. This ambivalence affects folk Catholicism too. For this reason, Filipino Catholics need to become aware of the strengths and weaknesses of the folk manner of expressing their faith. In becoming aware, they can nurture the former and purify the latter in the light of the Gospel. In this way, folk Catholicism can be a genuine expression of faith that is faithful to both the indigenous culture and the Christian faith.

Bibliography

Boff, Leonardo, "Roman Catholicism: Structure, Health, Pathologies," and "In Favor of Syncretism: The Catholicity of Catholicism," in *Church: Charism and Power* (1985). • De Mesa, José M., *And God Said, "Behala Na!": The Theme of Providence in the Lowland Filipino Context* (1979). • Gorospe, Vitaliano R., *Banahaw: Conversations with a Pilgrim to the Power Mountain* (1992). • Vergote, Antoine, "Folk Catholicism: Its Significance, Value and Ambiguities," *Philippine Studies* 30 (1982).

JOSÉ M. DE MESA

First Church, Chiang Mai, Thailand

Founded 18 Apr 1868, First Church is the oldest church in northern Thailand. It was established by the American Presbyterian* Laos Mission. Daniel McGilvary* and Jonathan Wilson oversaw the church through most of the 19th c. Its first northern Thai member was Nan Inta*, who was baptized in Jan 1869. In Sep 1869, two members were executed by the prince of Chiang Mai, and the five other members fled persecution. Church life came to a halt and recovered only in the late 1870s. In 1878, Nan Inta became the church's first elder. In 1880, the church gave birth to three new churches, marking the beginning of ecclesiastical expansion in northern Thailand. That same year, the church elected three more elders and constituted its first predominantly northern Thai session. Through the 1880s and 1890s, the church experienced steady growth over an extensive geographical area. By

1920, 24 churches had been generated from First Church. Even so, it remained large and included numerous worship centers besides the main building in Chiang Mai. City-based missionaries, assistant pastors, and evangelists itinerating through the rural groups provided pastoral oversight. This centralized model became the dominant style for church leadership and pastoral care among northern Thai churches.

In Aug 1891, the church dedicated its first building designed specifically for worship. In 1894, Howard Campbell arrived in Chiang Mai and soon thereafter assumed pastoral charge of the church. Under his guidance, the church further developed its city-based pastoral care system. By the 1920s, the national team, including as many as four ordained assistant pastors, was doing most of the pastoral work of the church. On 26 May 1929, Banchong Bansiddhi was installed as the church's first senior Thai pastor. By 1930, the church had just over 3,000 members, numbering about one-third of all Thai Protestants. In 1938, Chinese revivalist John Sung* held a series of revival services at First Church that brought new life and enthusiasm. In 1939, a strong supporter of the revival, Boonmee Rungruangwong, became pastor. The period of revival ended in Dec 1941, and the church entered a period of persecution. Its building was seized, and informal worship was maintained at the pastor's home.

After World War II*, First Church's dominant position among northern Thai churches gradually diminished, although it remained the largest church in the Church of Christ in Thailand (CCT). In 1967, it had 1,300 members. Boonyuen Natanath served as pastor from 1957 to 1971. In 1968, the church dedicated its present building. Arun Tongdonmuan served as pastor from 1971 to 1981. Lay leadership played a strong role throughout this era. Pakdee Watanachantrakul became pastor in 1981 and served until 1990. He resumed the pastorate in 1992. The church has remained an important source of ordained and lay leadership for Thai Protestantism. It had about 2,000 members in 1995.

Bibliography

McFarland, George B., ed., *Historical Sketch of Protestant Missions in Siam* (1928). • Swanson, Herbert R., *Khrischak Muang Nua* (1984). • Records of the Laos Mission (microfilm at the Payap University Archives, Chiang Mai, Thailand). • Records of the First District, Church of Christ in Thailand (at the Payap University Archives). • First Church, *Centenary Volume* (1968) (in Thai).

Kummool Chinawong, translated by Herbert R. Swanson

Focolare Movement

The Focolare Movement began in 1943 in Trent, Italy, when, in the midst of the destruction of World War II*, a group of young women gathered around 23-year-old Chiara Lubich. Living and spreading the mutual love proposed by the Gospel opened up the way to deciding what was to be the main aim of the movement: unity. Unity among people, social categories, ages, and races was clearly seen as the ultimate goal to which the whole of humanity is journeying ever more rapidly. The spirituality that developed was to be a spirituality of unity, a way to go to God together, so as to fulfill the testament of Jesus: "That all may be one" (John 17:21). *Focolare,* in fact, means "hearth" or "fireside," where a family would reunite. And it is this invitation to come together, to "love one another as I have loved you" (John 15:12), to bring about the presence of Jesus among people united in his name (Matt. 18:20), that provokes a change in the personal and collective quality of life and proves to be a driving force for unity in the fabric of society.

At first, the spirituality of unity spread within the Catholic Church, the movement being officially approved by Pope John XXIII in 1962 under the name of "Work of Mary." From 1958 on, Christians of other traditions began to come in contact with the Focolare. They felt its spirituality was also for them and that it contributed toward overcoming centuries-old prejudices among Christians. Already in the 1960s, Lubich had meetings with leading figures of other churches, giving rise to a fruitful collaboration toward the unity of all Christians.

In 1981, Lubich was invited to speak about her spiritual experience to over 10,000 Buddhists in Tokyo. Thus began a promising dialogue with people of other religions. Since then, in various countries, the dialogue has extended to involve Jewish people, Hindus, Muslims, Taoists, Sikhs, and animists. The Focolare is a permanent member of the World Conference on Religion and Peace.

The movement is now present in over 180 nations, with an active membership of more than two million, mostly laity. There are many ways to belong to the Focolare, ranging from consecrated people living in small men's and women's communities, called Focolare Centers, to collaboration in its various activities.

The movement moved into Asia on 22 Feb 1966 upon the invitation of Rufino Cardinal Santos, then archbishop of Manila. The first centers were opened in Manila and later in Cebu (1979) and Davao (1987). At the same time, people in other Asian countries came to know the movement. Ever-growing groups living the spirituality of unity brought about the establishment of Focolare Centers in Korea* (Seoul 1969, Taegu 1989), Hong Kong* (1970), Japan* (Tokyo 1976, Nagasaki 1993), Taiwan* (Taipei 1979), India* (Bombay 1980, Goa 1994), Thailand* (Bangkok 1981), Macau (1982), Pakistan* (Rawalpindi 1979, Lahore 1984, Karachi 1986), and Singapore* (1991). In many other countries where centers have not yet been established, large numbers of people are following the spirituality of the movement (Indonesia*, Burma, Bangladesh*, Vietnam*, Laos*, Malaysia, Sri Lanka*, Papua New Guinea).

In 1982, one of the 20 little towns of witness founded by the Focolare around the world was established in Tagaytay, 60 km. south of Manila, with the aim of offering an example of what society could be like if it were transformed by the presence of Christ (Matt. 18:20) through the practice of the new commandment of mutual love (John 15:12). On the Asian continent a special emphasis is placed on interreligious dialogue*, and to this end regular seminars on the great religions are held for the movement's members.

In Asia, there are 29 women's and 22 men's Focolare Centers, 7,700 committed members, 93,000 adherents, and over 460,000 people being influenced by the spiritual unity of the movement. GIACOMO PELLIZZARI

Forcade, Augustine

(b. Versailles, France, 2 Mar 1816; d. Aix-en-Provence, France, 12 Sept 1885). First vicar apostolic of Japan* (1846) and third prefect apostolic of the Hong Kong* Catholic Church (1847-50).

Forcade was ordained a priest in 1839 and joined the Paris Foreign Mission Society* in 1842; he then went to Japan in 1844 and was appointed vicar apostolic of Japan in 1846, being consecrated a bishop in Hong Kong on 21 Feb 1847.

Prevented from returning to Japan, Forcade was also appointed pro-prefect of the Hong Kong Mission and served in this position from 4 Oct 1847 to 24 Aug 1850. In 1848, he invited the Sisters of St. Paul de Chartres* to care for abandoned babies in Hong Kong. Since he was still unable to reach Japan, he resigned from both posts and returned to France. From there he went to Guadalupe as bishop in 1853. In 1861, Forcade was appointed bishop of Nevers, France, and in 1873 archbishop of Aix-en-Provence, where he later died of cholera.

Bibliography

Hong Kong Catholic Church Directory 1995. • Ryan, T., *The Story of a Hundred Years* (1959); *Catholic Guide to Hong Kong* (1962). • Ticozzi, S., *Historical Documents of the Hong Kong Catholic Church* (1983) (in Chinese).

SERGIO TICOZZI

Forman, Charles William

(b. Washington, Kentucky, United States, 3 Mar 1821; d. Lahore, India, 1894). Pioneer Presbyterian* missionary educator in Lahore from 1849 to 1894.

A missionary from the United Presbyterian Church of the United States of America, Forman was born into a family of missionaries who together had contributed over 1,000 years of service to India* and Pakistan*. He was the ninth of 13 children of a well-to-do farmer. With the sudden demise of his father, Forman was obliged to spend the next five years seeking a suitable livelihood, first on the family estate, then in Missouri, and finally back in Kentucky.

Forman's sensitive exposure to the Bible, especially the teachings and prophecies of Christ, and his baptism at the age of 20 were turning points in his life. During his studies at Princeton Theological Seminary, Forman became a member of the Committee on Foreign Missions of the Society of Inquiry Respecting Missions and the General State of Religion. Upon his graduation in 1847, Forman was ordained and sailed for India.

Forman seemed to have a wonderful understanding regarding Christian calling and ministry. He was deeply concerned for the multitudes who did not know and had no means of knowing about God. In his view, the heathen world had greater need for missionaries than did the United States. He felt that someone else could fill his position in America, but not in India. Forman was quite pleased to share this vision with his fellow students at Princeton.

Forman had a strong enthusiasm for spreading English education, which was first fulfilled with the opening of a college in Lahore (Punjab) at the recommendation of the Board of Foreign Missions of the Presbyterian Church in 1865. As the moving spirit behind this venture, Forman naturally became its first principal. Forman's educational philosophy greatly influenced the college and the Punjab, and after his death in 1894 it was named Forman Christian College. As an outstanding educator, Forman was asked to be on every committee on education appointed by the government in Punjab. He served on the education committee in 1863 and 1865, the textbook committee, and the committee for organizing Punjab University College. Later, Forman became a fellow of Punjab University and a participant in the educational conferences of the 1880s and 1890s under the auspices of the Punjab government.

Desiring ardently to maintain the autonomy of mission schools, Forman insisted that the government withdraw from regulating them. In this regard, at the Punjab Missionary Conference he expressed his reservations about the grant-in-aid system to mission schools. Because of various policies to which Forman could not reconcile, he had to run his mission school under constant tension and sometimes in submission to the government demands.

Besides Forman's zeal to educate the people, he also developed sensitivity to their social problems, thinking through the meaning of Christian faith for India. On one occasion, Forman and his colleague Samuel Kellogg had to confront the gripping issue of polygamy. Supporters of polygamy quoted passages from the Old and New Testament. Forman enjoyed engaging in such debates and discussions with learned people of other faiths. In one instance, he engaged in a public controversy with a Muslim at the large school hall at Punjab in the presence of a huge crowd. He held firmly to the Gospel and constantly wrote articles and pamphlets confronting and providing answers to the positions of the "heathens."

In addition to establishing the first missionary society of this area, Forman also constructed a leprosarium in the town of Saharampur for both males and females (see Leprosy Work).

Bibliography

Forman, C. W., "Who Are the Sikhs?" *Foreign Missionary* (Nov 1882); "The Year 1862 at Lahore," *Foreign Missionary* (Oct 1863). • Datta, S. K., ed., *History of the Forman Christian College: Selections from the Records of the College, 1869-1936* (1936). • Pathak, Sushil Madhava, *American Missionaries and Hinduism: A Study of Their Contacts from 1813 to 1910* (1967). • Webster, John, *The Christian Community and Change in 19th Century North India* (1976).

FRANKLYN J. BALASUNDARAN

Foundation Fellowship of Evangelization of Indonesia

(*Yayasan Persekutuan Perkabaran Injil Indonesia,* YPPII). Also known as the Indonesian Missionary Fellowship (IMF).

IMF was incorporated by Petrus Octavianus in 1961 as an independent, interdenominational national body, but it also accepts members from other nations who are integrated into the fellowship with regard to leadership, finances, ministry, and common life.

The goal of IMF is to reach people of all walks of life in the cities and rural areas in Indonesia* and throughout the world, to disciple and include them in God's work. To achieve this goal, IMF has developed a structure with a central council (in Batu-Malang, East Java), two regional councils, six ministry departments, several special commissions, a number of subdepartments, and area representatives throughout Indonesia. IMF bases all of its activities on the four spiritual pillars of holiness, faith, sacrifice, and fellowship.

The organizational structure of IMF allows for a wide range of activities, including evangelistic crusades, seminars, and courses, theological education* (at three accredited seminaries), cross-cultural outreach and world mission, church planting, children and youth ministry, a large annual convention, radio programming, social ministry, printing and publishing, medical* ministry, ministry in public schools, and agricultural ministry.

IMF has sent Indonesian missionaries to Surinam, Pakistan*, Nepal*, and Bangladesh*. It has missionaries currently serving in Brazil, California (United States), Germany, Gambia, India*, Kirgizia, Hong Kong*, Tokyo, Philippines*, and Australia. IMF members also participate in itinerant ministry in various countries, and in congresses and evangelistic consultations worldwide.

Since its founding in 1961, IMF has grown from virtually nothing to being the leading evangelical organization in Indonesia, with a substantial lay staff and property. A large number of churches, including new denominations, have been planted through IMF. About 3,000 graduates from the seminaries of IMF are presently serving in Indonesia and other parts of the world.

IMF has been specially blessed in reaching both government and business executives as well as laypeople through its annual conventions. Today, between 3,000 and 4,000 people from Indonesia and neighboring countries attend the annual IMF missionary conventions.

WAGIYONO SUMARTO

Foundation for Theological Education in South East Asia

(FTE). Successor organization to the Board of Founders of Nanking (now Nanjing) Theological Seminary.

The front page of the *New York Times* for 2 Aug 1930 carried a large headline that the last member of the Wendel family had died, and that their wills had left nearly one hundred million dollars (quickly demonstrated to be radically too high) to five institutions, including Nanking Theological Seminary. Since the assets of the estate consisted of property in Manhattan, it took many years to provide cash to the five institutions.

Regarding the seminary, the will directed, "And the remaining thirty-five equal shares to the 'Board of Foreign Missions of the Methodist Episcopal Church' . . . the income of which is to be used for the maintenance of 'Nankin [*sic*] Theological Seminary.'" By 1938, a little more than $2.5 million had been received from the estate.

The seminary had been created in 1911 through a merger of three smaller schools. Initially, the seminary was sponsored by the Disciples, Presbyterians* North and South, and Methodists* North. In 1912, the Southern Methodists became sponsors of the seminary, and in 1942 the Baptists*.

During the Japanese occupation of coastal China, the seminary carried on its ministry in Shanghai and in Szechuan Province. With the ending of World War II*, the seminary returned to Nanjing. With the liberation of China* by the Communists in 1949, the expatriate members of the seminary faculty were forced to leave China. By 1951, around 10 seminaries from greater China were merged with the seminary, and K. H. Ting* became president of the new Nanjing Union Theological Seminary.

Following the probate of the Wendel will, the board of managers in Nanjing appointed a committee of five to evaluate the possibilities of organizing a New York board for the seminary. On 1 Jun 1932, the managers voted to ask the cooperating churches to form a board of founders in New York. On 23 May 1935, the Board of Foreign Missions of the Methodist Episcopal Church voted to invite the five denominations sponsoring the seminary to a conference to explore the possibility of forming a board for the seminary in New York. Included were the Board of Foreign Missions of the Methodist Episcopal Church, the Board of Foreign Missions of the Presbyterian Church in the USA, the Executive Committee for Foreign Missions of the Presbyterian Church in the US, the United Christian Missionary Society, and the Methodist Episcopal Church, South. On 5 Jun 1937, representatives of the five denominations formed the board of founders.

The founders spent a great deal of energy learning about the circumstances of theological education in

China. Through the Chinese and missionary faculty at the seminary, through studying the *Weigle Report* on theological education in China, and through visits to Nanjing, the founders developed a broad knowledge of theological education in China.

By 1951, it became impossible for the founders to continue a relationship with the seminary, but between 1937 and 1950 they had already provided $1.2 million. Since it was not possible to send funds to Nanjing, the income from the Wendel Fund accumulated. On 26 Nov 1952, the New York Board of Regents approved a change in the founders' charter which made it possible for them to relate to other seminaries in Asia. On 16 Mar 1953, Surrogate George Frankenthaler decreed that the founders could use the income from the Swope-Wendel bequest for theological education in Asia. When Bishop Rajah Manikam (India) communicated to the founders Ting's desire that no organization in the United States use the name of the seminary, the founders changed their name to the FTE.

In Aug 1954, the founders called a "Consultation Regarding Theological Education in Southeast Asia" at Williams Bay, Wisconsin. Since there were a large number of Asians in the US for the general assembly of the World Council of Churches (WCC), it was possible to invite a number of Asians. There were 18 representatives of seven countries in Southeast Asia, and 13 from the US. Representatives from the International Missionary Council (IMC) and the WCC also attended. As a result of the consultation, the founders chose to concentrate on major seminaries in Burma, Thailand*, Taiwan*, Singapore*, Indonesia*, the Philippines*, and Hong Kong*.

One of the recommendations of the participants in the Williams Bay consultation was to call a similar consultation in Southeast Asia. In 1956, the Asian consultation convened in Bangkok. There were 51 delegates from Southeast Asia and nine fraternal delegates from other Asian countries. There were 10 visitors from Asia and 11 from Europe and the US. The consultation agreed to the following plans: to establish a higher theological faculty in Southeast Asia, to organize an Association of Theological Schools and Colleges of Southeast Asia (ATSSEA), to publish a journal of theology for Southeast Asia, and to organize theological study institutes for younger faculty members.

Theological study institutes were held in 1957, 1959, 1960, 1962, and 1963. During the 1957 institute, official action was taken to form ATSSEA. The organization took place in 1959. The first issue of the *Journal of Theology for Southeast Asia,* edited by John Fleming, was published in the summer of 1959.

ATSSEA changed its name to the Association for Theological Education in South East Asia (ATESEA) in the 1980s. By 1996, ATESEA had 75 member seminaries. By the mid-1990s, ATESEA had established a process for accrediting the degree programs of its member schools; established the South East Asia Graduate School of Theology, which grants the degrees of master of theology, doctor of theology, and doctor of pastoral studies, creatively utilizing the faculty of its major seminaries for the degree programs; and continued the publication of the *South East Asia Journal of Theology,* which led in time to the publication of the *Asia Journal of Theology* in cooperation with Northeast and South Asia.

Out of a commitment to have major decisions made in Asia by Asians, the FTE cooperated with ATESEA in the creation of the Joint Regional Planning Commission. After some years of successful decision making in Asia by Asians, the Resource Commission was formed by ATESEA. Now church leaders and seminary presidents from Southeast Asia make the decisions about grants from the FTE for the member schools of ATESEA. Only one consultant from the FTE attends the meetings of the Resource Commission.

When China opened itself to the larger world and the seminary in Nanjing began functioning normally, communication was reestablished between Bishop Ting and the FTE. Initially, the seminary asked the FTE to provide English and Chinese theological works for the library. By the mid-1990s, the relationship between the seminary and the FTE had led to the FTE's publication of the *Chinese Theological Review* and the *Nanjing Theological Journal,* the provision of scholarship assistance for seminary faculty members to receive graduate theological education in Canada and the US, and several grants to help with buildings for the seminary campus, especially a new library.

When the China Christian Council* (CCC) formed its Commission on Theological Education in the 1980s, the FTE began to relate to the commission and the 17 seminaries of the CCC. Through this relationship, the FTE has provided English and Chinese theological books for the students, faculty, and libraries of the seminaries, made grants for the purchase of computers, and provided funds for the training of librarians at the seminaries.

As the FTE looks to the future, it focuses its attention on having decisions about its programs made in Southeast Asia and China. Increasingly, its decision-making role is being turned over to its partners in Southeast Asia and China.

Bibliography

Cartwright, Frank T., *A River of Living Water: A Historical Sketch of Nanking Theological Seminary* (1963).

Marvin D. Hoff

Franciscan Friars Minor

(OFM). The Franciscans owe their origin to St. Francis of Assisi, born of a merchant family in 1181, who in answer to the cross of San Damiano, "Francis, go and repair my church, which is in ruins," set out to build and restore small abandoned churches on the periphery of Assisi. He soon became the leader of a movement which identified with the lepers and the poor. In 1209, Pope Innocent III approved his way of life, and ultimately in 1223, Pope

Franciscan Friars Minor

Honorius III ratified the rule with a papal bull. It was a new order of religious brothers, having no property, living by the work of their hands, and ready to go wherever the Lord called them. It was the first religious order explicitly to invite the brothers to go out as missionaries.

Francis himself set the example and sent his brothers to different places in Europe, and he went to Syria and Egypt and met with the Muslim sultan. In 1219, a missionary province was set up in Syria and Egypt, and by 1263 there were 20 convents spread over the Turkish empire of Constantinople, Greece, Asia Minor, Syria, Palestine, Cyprus, and Egypt. The popes sent the friars as their legates to the Muslim rulers. The friars worked in these areas among Muslims, but because of the difficulties, they turned their attention to the care of Christian slaves, apostates, the holy places, and outreach to the other churches. In 1333, the custody of the Holy Land was established, which has continued till our day with local friars and many missionaries from other provinces of the order.

A second large sphere of influence was the missions to China* and to India*. In 1291, Friar John of Monte Corvino* stayed for a year in Mylapore on his way to Peking (Beijing), where he became the first archbishop in 1294. The friars worked there, and many died in persecutions. In the 18th and 19th cs., when China was open to the West, missionaries came from different countries of Europe and America, and in 1949, when the Communists took over, there were 25 Franciscan dioceses and prefectures. Many friars, local and foreign, were expelled or jailed. Those that remained were brave witnesses to the faith. In recent years, young Chinese friars have once again been entering the order.

In India*, besides John of Monte Corvino, there were St. Thomas of Tolentino, James of Padua, Peter of Siena, and Demetrius of Tiflis, who were martyred near Bombay in 1321. With the vast Portuguese expansion in Asia and the establishment of trading posts, Franciscans also joined in the effort. There were eight friars who accompanied Dom Pedro Alvares Cabral in 1500 to Goa. By 1517, the first Franciscan church was built and a new commissariat was established, which eventually was made into a custody in 1542. In the 17th c., this developed into the two independent provinces of St. Thomas and the Mother of God, with over 500 friars spread all along the coast of India and beyond to Myanmar* (Burma), Malacca*, and Macau. These provinces were dissolved in 1835. In 1925, friars from England came to Bellary, and friars from Holland came to Karachi in 1934. In 1948, the Dutch friars moved to Bangalore. In 1949, a commissariat of India and Pakistan* was set up. In 1958, the commissariat of India was separated from Pakistan. Ultimately in 1985, India became a province and Pakistan a vice-province.

The Portuguese also had their influence in Sri Lanka*, and between 1543 and 1603 there were five friars working there. When the Dutch took over, the friars left but returned in the 1950s for a short time. Because of two diocesan priests who joined in 1960 and 1967, an effort to start the order again was made by the Assisi Province in 1981.

There were friars working in Burma and Bengal in the early 17th c. They were in Arakan, Ava, and Pegu. A Franciscan bishop was appointed to the vicariate apostolic of Arakan, but because of the *Propaganda-padroado** conflicts, this appointment was never enacted. Here too in 1835 the presence of the friars came to an end.

In the 16th c., the Portuguese under Alfonso d'Albuquerque* conquered Malacca, and the friars came along with the traders, soldiers, and settlers. Two Franciscan custodies were established, but when the Dutch came and conquered Malacca, the friars had to leave. In the mid-1900s, the friars returned as military chaplains to the Australian forces and to the prisoners of war. In 1957 (until 1968), a sociological institute was set up in Singapore* to serve as a counterforce to the Communist influence. In 1969, the friars of the Australian province were invited to Singapore. This was the beginning of a new foundation of the order, and in 1991 the custody of Singapore, Malaysia*, and Brunei* was established.

Another important area of Franciscan influence is Indonesia*. In the 14th c., Friar Odoric de Pordenone* and Bishop John of Marignolli* visited Sumatra, Java, and Kalimantan on their way to China. Simultaneous with the Portuguese occupation of Malacca and Macau, and the Spanish conquest of Manila, the Franciscans were engaged in an extensive mission effort. With the arrival of the Dutch and the fall of Malacca, however, the missionary effort came to nought. It was only in 1929 that the friars from the Dutch province came to Jakarta, and a little later to Dutch New Guinea. The war years brought a stop to the work, but after 1945, the friars moved to new areas to set up their houses. In 1983, Indonesia became an independent province.

While the Portuguese were engaged in the area allotted to them by the division of territories, the Spanish friars accompanied their colonizers to the Philippines. In 1576, the custody of St. Gregory the Great of the Philippines* was established in Spain, and the first 15 friars arrived in Manila in 1578. In 1586, it was made into a province. There were tensions among the Spanish friars as they belonged to different Franciscan traditions. Also the friars were not so interested in working among the Muslim population, having had their own long experience of Muslim rule in Spain. They worked hard for the conversion of the Philippines and were interested in moving beyond to China and Japan*. With the 1898 Philippine Revolution, most of the Spanish friars returned to Spain. In 1900, only 70 friars out of 481 remained. By 1905, the center of the province was shifted back to Spain, and the Philippines was reduced to a commissariat and ultimately to a provincial delegation. By 1948, there were only 23 Spanish friars in the Philippines. The situation changed in the 1950s when friars from Italy and the United States entered the country. Gradually, an understanding was reached among the many groups, and the decision was made to work toward an independent Philippine province. This became a reality in 1983.

Friars first arrived in Japan under Peter Baptist, an emissary from the Philippines. With him were other missionaries, Bartholomew Ruiz, Francis de San Miguel, and Gonsalez Garcia. They were given land in Kyoto and cared for the lepers and the sick. They were later martyred, and by 1640 all the friars had died. Even though missionaries were not allowed again until two centuries later, the Japanese Christians kept their faith and welcomed the new missionaries who came toward the end of the 19th c. After the defeat of Japan in 1945, many more missionaries entered Japan. These were eventually merged into one independent province in 1977.

Early work in Vietnam* had little success. The Spanish friars on their way to China opened a house in Hue in 1584. Later a mission from the Philippines was opened in Cochin China in 1719. Italian and German friars followed in the early 19th c. in Cambodia* and Tonkin. This effort ended in 1834.

In the 20th c., the first French friars came to Vietnam and built a friary in 1931. They set up a dependent commissariat in 1928 and spread to other areas in Vietnam. In 1969, Vietnam became an independent commissariat and in 1984 an independent province. While the political change under the Communist regime meant the closing down of some houses, the friars felt it had strengthened their community life and had helped them make clearer options for the poor. In recent years there has been more freedom of movement, and the province is blessed with recruits. Vietnam, which for a long time was in isolation, is once again part of the Franciscan conference of Asia and Oceania.

The Communist takeover of China led to the expulsion of all missionaries and some local Chinese friars. These settled in Taiwan* and Hong Kong*, and the beginnings were laid for a new independent Franciscan entity. Though there were friars earlier in 1633, the real effort of building the order started in 1950. Hong Kong became the center for Bible* research and for translation of the entire Bible into Chinese, especially due to Fr. Allegra. This was completed in 1968. There have been a vast expansion of the church in Taiwan and a regular supply of local recruits. In 1988, Taiwan became an independent province.

Finally, there is the young Franciscan province of Korea*, started only in 1937 with friars from France and Canada. The wars of 1939 and 1950 hindered the development of the order. The year 1955 marks the beginning of a concerted effort to build the order. While friars from different areas of Europe and America came to help, there were also many locals. In 1969 an independent vicariate was established, and in 1987 the independent province of Korea. It is a young and dynamic group and is already sending out its first friars to other areas of the world.

A last foundation is in Thailand*, started in 1985. Recruits are coming in, and there is hope of a new entity growing in this area.

The developments of the church in Asia after Vatican Council II are also having a positive impact on the life of the friars. All the different entities owe their existence and present situations to the efforts of Apollinaris van Leeuwen, former provincial of the Dutch province and later delegate general to the Philippines, Japan, and finally Korea. Noteworthy are the young provinces of India (1985), Pakistan (1985), Korea (1987), Japan (1977), the Philippines (1983), Indonesia (1983), and Taiwan (1988). Asia is a vast continent where, except for the Philippines, Christians form a small minority. Inserted among them are these young provinces, where there is a large group of young and energetic friars, most of them involved in questions of justice and peace and integrity of creation, living among the many people of other faiths and traditions, speaking the message of peace and harmony, and now gradually sending out their own missionaries to other parts of the world.

Bibliography

Iriarte, L., *Franciscan History* (1982). • Moorman, J., *The Franciscan Order: From Its Origins to the Year 1517* (1988). • Ante, O. A., *Contextual Evangelisation in the Philippines* (1991). • Meersman, N. A., *The Ancient Franciscan Provinces in India* (1971). • Dijkstra, O., and L. Mascarenhas, *Dutch Franciscans and Their Missions: India and Pakistan* (1994). • Sweeney, C., *Friars Minor in Japan* (1993). • Flood, D., *Francis of Assisi and the Franciscan Movement* (1980). • Faccio, H. M., *Status descriptionis almae seraphicae provinciae seu custodiae et missionis terrae sanctae* (1951). • *Conspectus Missionum Ordinis Fratrum Minorum* (1951).

Louis Mascarenhas

Franciscan Missionaries of Mary

(FMM). The Franciscan Missionaries of Mary are established in 77 countries and were founded by a French lady, Helen Chopotin (b. 1839; d. 1904). She was later called Mother Mary of the Passion and was a former superior provincial of the Society of Mary Reparatrix in Ootacamund, India*. As a result of deep misunderstandings, she left the society with 20 other sisters in 1876 and went to Rome to obtain permission from Pope Pius IX to live a religious life. The conditions at the time pushed her to found a new institute.

On 6 Jan 1877, authorization was obtained to found the Franciscan Missionaries of Mary, whose preferred aim is to serve in areas where Christ has yet to be known. The sisters celebrate the Eucharist daily and have adopted the Franciscan spirituality of joy, poverty, and simplicity.

The FMM generalate is in Rome, but the first foundation was in India. The sisters spread to China*, Sri Lanka*, Myanmar*, Japan*, the Near East, Pakistan*, the

Philippines*, Indonesia*, Singapore*, Malaysia*, and Korea*.

India. The first FMM community was set up in Ootacamund in 1877. There are now over 100 convents spread over five provinces: Bangalore, Bombay, Delhi, Madras, and Ootacamund. The sisters serve in medical, social, and educational fields.

China. The FMM reached China in 1886 and were the most numerous of the missionary sisters there. Beginning with a boarding school and a hospital at Yantai (Chefoo), they developed their work throughout the country, from Sichuan into Shanxi and beyond the Great Wall into Mongolia and Manchuria. They established dispensaries, orphanages, workrooms, and leprosaria (see Leprosy Work). During the Boxer Uprising, all seven of the FMM sisters in Shanxi were martyred in Jul 1900. They were beatified in Nov 1946. In Nov 1954, Maria Assunta Pallotta was proclaimed "Blessed" for her heroic missionary life, which ended in Shanxi. In 1949, before the Communist takeover, there were about 780 FMM in Shanghai, Hebei, Shandong, Jiansou, Hubei, Hunan, Sichuan, Guangdong, and Shanxi. They had more than 50 schools, 30 hospitals, and 50 clinics under their care. Although all of their flourishing missions were closed with the advent of Communism*, the FMM impact still remains through more humble and hidden activities. Since 1948, the FMM have run a school in Kowloon, Hong Kong*. They also provide pastoral care* and work among the poor.

Macau. The FMM established a Portuguese college and a boarding school in Macau in 1903. The sisters are involved in pastoral, social, and educational activities among the ever-growing population of Chinese from the mainland.

Taiwan. After 1949, there was an exodus of Chinese clergy and religious from mainland China to Taiwan. In 1954, in response to the requests of the local church in Taiwan, the FMM commenced their work among the young educated, the aborigines, and the workers, making contacts through classes, pastoral meetings, and dispensaries. Urbanization and industrialization have presented the FMM in Taiwan with new challenges in their mission.

Sri Lanka. Responding to the need for nurses, the FMM went to Colombo, Sri Lanka, in 1886. Recently, they have focused on evangelization through either direct pastoral work or their presence in a non-Christian milieu. They have penetrated into Polonnaruwa and Mahiyangana and seek to maintain friendly relations in peace and love with the Buddhists. In 1989, there were 20 convents in Sri Lanka.

Myanmar. Since their beginning in Mandalay, where they worked with lepers in 1898, the FMM have extended their work into Bhamo, Chanthaywa, Maymyo, and Yangon (Rangoon), where they spread the Gospel to the poorest.

Pakistan. The FMM arrived as nurses in Lahore in 1912, but the prevailing church law forbade them to study medicine or to assist at births. They sought other avenues of service: setting up schools for the poor, workrooms, home science training, and catechism classes. From Lahore, the FMM spread into the other five dioceses, namely Karachi, Quetta, Rawalpindi, Hyderabad, and Rahimyar Khan.

Philippines. In Dec 1912, 12 FMM sisters reached Manila in response to Bishop Petrelli's request for the FMM to take charge of two schools. Their educational work has extended throughout the country from northwest to northeast and even to the neighboring islands. The sisters have also moved to frontier posts in order to live among the poorest and share in their struggle for justice.

Vietnam. The FMM came to Qui Nhon in 1932 to work among lepers. After World War II, they spread their mission to Vinh and La Qua. After the rise of the Vietnamese Communists, only Qui Hoa allowed the FMMs to remain. They collaborated in the human and social development of the country while continuing their pastoral activities. They focused attention on nonbelievers, because the first aim of their activities is to transmit the message of Christ.

Indonesia. In 1993, six FMM sisters went to Java to take charge of the hospital at Rankasbitung. The FMM have extended their work to Bogor, Serang, Jakarta, Sindanglaya, and Sumatra. They teach in schools, serve the sick, engage in parish work with the young, and live simply in the midst of an Islamic populace. The church in Indonesia presents many evangelistic opportunities.

Singapore. Many exiled missionaries from China came to Singapore in 1953 and involved themselves in educational, social, and pastoral activities. Since 1977, the sisters have sought to live in predominantly Buddhist and Muslim areas.

Malaysia. Four FMM sisters arrived in Jan 1954 to serve the poor villagers in Petaling Jaya and Selangor. The FMM soon extended their mission to Kuala Lumpur, Kuantan, Kuala Terengganu, and Kota Bharu. They run kindergartens, which provide an avenue for dialogue in a Muslim environment and a place for building friendships.

Korea. In 1958, the FMM founded a school in Pusan, which was handed over to the diocese in 1979. FMM sisters, working closely with the local church, continue to train lay teachers in Choki, Seoul, Karibong-dong, San Cheong, Jin Ju, and Mok-dong to ensure sound Christian education. In the latter half of the 20th c., the FMM grew rapidly in Korea.

Present situation. It is necessary to develop an Asian theology and to engage in dialogue with other Asian religions. By the mid-1990s, there were 3,297 FMM members in Asia. The particular challenge facing the FMM varies from country to country. In Japan, Hong Kong, Macau, Taiwan, Singapore, and elsewhere, workers in evangelism must take into consideration the effects of prosperity and consumerism. India, Sri Lanka, Vietnam, mainland China, and Myanmar pose problems arising from poverty* or political systems. The critical question at present is how the FMM can proclaim the Gospel in both developing and developed countries so that the people can easily understand it.

Bibliography

Goyau, Georges, *Valiant Women* (1947).

Andrina Lee and Sabine Fernandez

Franciscan Sisters of the Third Order, Indonesia

The largest group of religious women in Indonesia.

The Franciscan Sisters from Heythuysen (the Netherlands) were the first to arrive in Java. They opened an orphanage in Semarang in 1870 and pioneered education for indigenous girls on the island of Flores (1879; Larantuka) and in the Moluccas* (1905; Langgur, Kei Archipelago). Their most influential school complex was established in Mendut, near the famous Borobudur temple in Central Java (1908-45). Since 1926, Javanese girls have been accepted into the novitiate. Today more than 340 Indonesian sisters of this congregation work on several islands in educational institutions and hospitals and on social and pastoral projects. There are 15 Franciscan congregations active in Indonesia; some form their own provinces and have even surpassed the membership of their mother provinces in the Netherlands or Germany. The Franciscan Missionaries of Mary* (FMM), the largest Franciscan congregation in the world, have run excellent schools (since 1933) but lack novices.

The Congregation of the Sisters of St. Joseph (Amersfort) was founded in 1878 and has been present in Indonesia since 1931, with over 100 members. The Daughters of the Sacred Hearts of Jesus and Mary (Salzkotten; OSF) were founded in 1859 and arrived in Indonesia in 1930, with over 125 members. The Franciscan Missionaries of Mary (FMM), founded in 1877, arrived in 1933 and have over 60 members. The Franciscan Missionary Sisters of St. Anthony (FMA), founded in 1913, arrived in 1931, with nearly 30 members today. The Franciscan Sisters of Mercy (Reute-Sibolga; OSF) were founded in 1849 and arrived in 1964, with nearly 50 members today. The Franciscan Sisters of Penance (Bergen-Sukabumi; OSF), founded in 1838, arrived in 1933 and have over 60 members. The Franciscan Sisters of Penance (Etten-Sambas; OSF) were founded in 1820 and arrived in 1924, now with nearly 100 members. The Franciscan Sisters of Penance and Charity (Roosendaal-Palembang; FSCh), founded in 1845, arrived in 1926 and have over 125 members. The Franciscan Sisters of Penance and Christian Charity (Heythuysen; OSF) were founded in 1835, arrived in 1870, and have nearly 350 members. The Franciscan Sisters of Penance (St. Lucia Bennebroek; SFL) were founded in 1847 and arrived in 1925, with nearly 100 members today. The Franciscan Sisters of St. Elizabeth (Breda; FSE), founded in 1880, arrived in 1925 and have over 75 members. The Franciscan Sisters of the Immaculate Conception of the Blessed Mother of God (FSIC) were founded in 1844, arrived in 1906, and have over 85 members today. The Franciscan Sisters of Martyr St. George (OSF) were founded in 1869 and arrived in 1932, with nearly 150 members today. The Little Sisters of St. Joseph (Heerlen; OSF), founded in 1872, arrived in 1938 and have over 75 members. In total, the orders have over 1,600 members.

Bibliography

Heuken, A., *Ensiklopedi Gereja Katolik,* Vols. II and IV (1994). • N. N., *Buku Peringatan: Genap 150 Tahun Tarekat Suster-suster Franziskus* (1985); *Na Vijfen Twintig Jaar Werken in de Missie van Sambas* (1949).

Adolf Heuken

Franciscans, Secular

The Secular Franciscan Order is an international lay movement living a canonically established and recognized rule of life following the spirit of the Gospel as expressed through the life and teaching of St. Francis of Assisi. The Secular Franciscan Order traces its history, development, and evolution back to the lay penitential movement of the 13th c. in Europe. First known as the Brothers and Sisters of Penance, members of the order lived a simple life based on guidance asked of and given by St. Francis of Assisi, who directed them to live within a loose form of community, yet remain where they were, and to practice various penitential forms, e.g., almsgiving, charitable works, prayers, pilgrimages, support to the churches, etc. As the Friars Minor took on significance in the life and mission of the church, so too did the Brothers and Sisters of Penance. As they sought to enter the contemporary life and mission of the church, they were given various rules beginning with those from Pope Nicholas IV in 1289. Thereafter, they came to be known as the Third Order of St. Francis, with a definitive link to the Friars Minor (First Order) and the Poor Clares (Second Order). In the process of its development, the Third Order of St. Francis evolved into two distinct characters: the Secular and Regular (Religious), each having its own rule of life and history.

From its development to 1978, the Third Order Secular of St. Francis, as it came to be known, established independent entities, mostly under the governance and jurisdiction of one of the branches of the friars (i.e., Friars Minor, Capuchins, Conventuals, and Third Order Regulars). But in response to the call of Vatican Council II to return to the original charism of the founder, the Third Order Secular of St. Francis took on a new, canonically approved rule of life and a new name: the Secular Franciscan Order. The change of name is significant as it not only placed the Secular Franciscans on equal terms with the other members of the Franciscan family, but gave them a centralized and singular structure and organization that are truly their own — secular. In 1995, the Union of the Ministers General of the Four Franciscan Families (the Friars Minor, the Capuchin, the Conventual, and Third Order Regular) was reorganized as the Ministers General of the Franciscan Families, which includes the minister general of the Secular Franciscan Order and the president of the International Conference of the Brothers and Sisters of the Third Order Regular of St. Francis.

The Secular Franciscan Order in Asia, consisting of hundreds of local fraternities, has the largest number of national fraternities worldwide, each including a number of regional fraternities. The recent figures of membership in the national fraternities are impressive: India*, 14,021; Japan*, 1,378; Korea*, 4,777; Philippines*, 2,000; and Vietnam*, 2,091. Hong Kong*, with 175 members, and Taiwan*, with about 150, function as separate national fraternities. Indonesia* and Irian Jaya* have about 200 members, but they have yet to establish themselves as a regional or national fraternity. West Malaysia has several local fraternities and functions like a regional fraternity, although it is not officially connected to any national fraternity. Singapore* and Sabah form a regional fraternity with about 80 members connected to the national fraternity of Oceania. There is at least one local fraternity in Thailand*, Sri Lanka*, and Pakistan*, where there has been no development of a regional or national fraternity.

Before 1978, many separate entities of the Third Order of St. Francis existed. Their local fraternities were established by the Order of the Franciscan Friars, on whom they were dependent: Friars Minor (many varieties before 1900), Capuchins, Conventuals, and the Third Order Regulars. In India, the Capuchins developed provincial fraternities of the Third Order dependent on the provinces of the Capuchins. But the (unwritten) history of the Third Order in India goes back to the arrival of the Portuguese Franciscans in the 1500s. In the Philippines, the history goes back to the arrival of the Spanish Franciscans even earlier. Soon after, Spanish friars from the Philippines introduced the Third Order to Japan, where a number died as martyrs of the faith. In Vietnam, the French Franciscans established local fraternities in the 1800s. The Oblates of Mary Immaculate set up the local fraternity in Colombo, Sri Lanka, early on in the twentieth century. For the rest of Asia, the setting up of local fraternities is fairly recent (from the 1950s to the present).

One could say generally that the Friars Minor and the Capuchins are mainly responsible for establishing local fraternities of the Third Order of St. Francis. The Third Order Regular is beginning to work for the Secular Franciscan Order in Sri Lanka and India, but is not present in any other part of Asia. The Conventuals are present and active with the Secular Franciscans only in Japan and the Philippines. The formal establishment of national and regional fraternities is very recent.

Bibliography

Pazzelli, Raffaele, *St. Francis and the Third Order* (1989). • Iriarte de Aspurz, Lázroo, *Franciscan History: The Three Orders of St. Francis of Assisi,* trans. Patricia Ross (1983).

Michael Goh and Carl Schafer

Fransz, Augustine Leonore

(b. Bodjonegoro, Indonesia, 20 Aug 1907). Ecumenical activist in Indonesia*.

Fransz came from a typical Dutch-Indonesian *(Indo)* background. Unlike many Dutch Eurasians, she chose to stay in Indonesia after the country gained independence from the Dutch and became a citizen. Although she was trained as a lawyer, her whole working life has been dedicated to the Protestant churches in Indonesia, especially the Indonesian Council of Churches (PGI), which she helped found in 1950 (see Communion of Churches, Indonesia).

From 1926 to 1933, Fransz studied at the newly founded Law College in Batavia (Jakarta). During her student years, she was very active in the Student Christian Movement* (SCM). The SCM in Indonesia was initiated by Dr. and Mrs. Van Doorn, who provided spiritual guidance to its members and tried to make them aware of social and political issues. Several of Fransz's friends from those days (Amir Syariffudin, J. Leimena) were active in the national movement and played an important role in the struggle for independence. She participated in the All Asian Student Conference in Citeureup, Indonesia, organized by the World Student Christian Federation in 1933, which made a lasting impression upon her.

After graduating, Fransz worked for the Christian Young Women's Federation, the Indonesian branch of the Young Women's Christian Association* (YWCA), and also for the Student Christian Movement. She spoke to Christian women's groups in many parts of Indonesia. In 1938, she was a member of the Indonesian delegation to the World Missionary Conference in Tambaram. After returning from India*, the delegation joined in the efforts of Indonesian church leaders to found a National Christian Council.

During the Japanese occupation (1942-45), Fransz's work for the Women's Federation was interrupted. She worked for the Protestant Church in Indonesia (GPI) during the war years, making pastoral visits, and continued to serve the church until 1948. A supporter of Indonesia's independence, she was frustrated by the pro-Dutch inclination of many church members and applied to work for the Missionary Consulate, which sent her to lead women's groups in Bali (1948-50).

As she resumed her work for the Women's Federation in 1945, Fransz had the opportunity to attend the Christian Youth Conference in Oslo (1947) and the constituting assembly of the World Council of Churches in Amsterdam (1948). When the Council of Churches in Indonesia (*Dewan Gereja-gereja di Indonesia,* DGI) was instituted in 1950, she served as its assistant secretary, a post she held until 1967, traveling extensively, both at home and abroad. One of her accomplishments in DGI was the founding of a research institute to study the development of the Indonesian churches amidst social changes. She was a staff member of this institute for many years.

Fransz has always shown a special concern for the marginalized people in society. After the war, she worked among displaced persons and, more recently, among political prisoners.

Bibliography

Weber, H. R., *Asia and the Ecumenical Movement, 1895-1961* (1966). • De Jonge, Christiaan, "Mengabdi Gerejaku, Riwayat Hidup Ms Augustine Leonore Fransz," in BPP-PGI, *Pelaku Wancana: Peringatan Dasa Warsa Ms Augustine Leonore Fransz* (1987).

CHRISTIAAN G. F. DE JONGE

Fraser, Alexander Garden

(b. Tallicoultry, United Kingdom, 6 Oct 1873; d. London, 27 Jan 1962). Outstanding Church Missionary Society (CMS) missionary and dynamic principal of Trinity College, Kandy.

Fraser received his education at the Universities of Edinburgh (1890) and Oxford (1893-96). He was originally a Presbyterian* (Church of Scotland) but joined the Anglican* CMS in 1901. He served in Uganda (1901-3) before his arrival in Sri Lanka.

Fraser was principal of Trinity College, Kandy, from 1904 to 1924, serving first as a layman and later as a priest (being ordained in 1912). Thereafter he served in a similar position at Achimota in Ghana (1924-35).

Fraser's ecumenical attitude was visible throughout his career in Sri Lanka*. In 1905, he persuaded two prominent non-Anglicans, John R. Mott (Methodist* layman of the World Student Christian Federation) and Sherwood Eddy (Young Men's Christian Association*), to preach at the Anglican Chapel in Kandy, even though the bishop of Colombo objected.

In 1906, Fraser proposed the establishment of a training college for teachers, which the CMS accepted on principle. This college was finally established in 1914 as a joint venture of the Methodists and Baptists.

One of Fraser's most controversial initiatives was to introduce Sinhalese and Tamil into the school curriculum. This was remarkable, as the renaissance of Sri Lankan languages and culture was in its infancy at this time. Fraser believed that students must master their own language. Because of this commitment, he incurred a good deal of opposition from the CMS. The only support he received was from the government director of public instruction. He also proposed that Sinhalese and Tamil should be eligible as subjects in the Cambridge examinations in the same category as Greek, Latin, and French.

Foreseeing the emerging strength of Buddhism* and Hinduism*, Fraser urged that local Christians be trained to become the leaders of the Christian community. In 1909, the CMS approved Fraser's proposal to admit Sri Lankan clergy as members of the Sri Lanka Conference.

The Trinity College Union for Social Service, founded in 1910, was an expression of Fraser's concerns. In 1910, he had to battle with the Kandyan chiefs for admitting a boy of low caste to the school. In 1915, when the communal riots broke out, he organized the boys into a peacekeeping force and opened Trinity College as a refugee center for Muslims.

In 1919, Fraser published an article in the *Times* of Ceylon agitating for universal franchise. Even radical Sri Lankan leaders, such as Arunachalam, asked for only universal manhood suffrage. Another plan Fraser had for the future of Sri Lanka concerned the University of Ceylon. He proposed that Royal College, Colombo, should be developed into a full university.

By 1916, Fraser's work had brought Trinity College to the front rank of public schools in Sri Lanka. Much of this success was due to his ability to delegate authority to others.

Fraser's significance lies not merely within the compound of Trinity College. His career in Sri Lanka was that of a missionary, although he expressed his views even on government policy matters. His foresight regarding religious and racial cooperation has had a great impact on the history of the island. He was far ahead of many of his contemporaries in the CMS with respect to assessing the capabilities of the Sri Lankan people.

Bibliography

Ward, W. E. F., *Fraser of Trinity and Achimota* (1965).

G. P. V. SOMARATNA

Fraser, Thomas McKenzie

(b. Inverness, 10 Jul 1822; d. Auckland, New Zealand, 10 Aug 1885). First Presbyterian* minister in Singapore*.

Fraser attended Christ's Hospital London as a boy and worked for the Free Church of Scotland newspaper, the *Witness*, in Edinburgh. He obtained his master's degree and was ordained into the Free Church. He was recruited for the Scotch Church in Singapore through a connection with the Singapore firm of Guthries' and arrived in Oct 1856.

The congregation in Singapore used the Missionary Chapel on the corner of Bras Basah Road and North Bridge Road, where Fraser began with two elders and a congregational roll of 37. He had a vision for mission beyond the Scots community and cooperated with Benjamin Keasberry* and the Anglicans*. In 1857, Tan See Boo* from Amoy was appointed as a Chinese catechist. The first meeting of the session minuted the baptism of four converts. Work was also begun among the Chinese at Bukit Timah. Fraser's links with English Presbyterian missionaries in South China* laid the foundation for a connection with the Presbyterian Church of England in 1872. This was shortly before land was obtained for the present church in Orchard Road in 1875.

The family's health was uncertain, so the Frasers moved a number of times. In Dec 1860, he resigned to go to Geelong, Victoria, Australia, where he was twice moderator of the Victoria Assembly and lectured at the Theological Hall. He moved to St. David's, Auckland,

New Zealand, in Aug 1881. These were turbulent years at St. David's, but he brought stable leadership and an improvement in the finances before he unexpectedly died in office. He was remembered as "an accomplished scholar, an able and eloquent preacher, and a faithful pastor."

Bibliography

Elder, J. R., *The History of the Presbyterian Church of New Zealand* (1940). • Greer, Robert M., *A History of the Presbyterian Church in Singapore* (1959). • Johnson, Anne, *The Burning Bush* (1988). • Ryburn, W. M., *St. David's Presbyterian Church, Auckland* (1964).

John Roxborogh

Fraternity of the Queen of the Rosary

(Confreria Reinha Rosari). Oldest Catholic lay organization in Indonesia*.

Established in 1564 in Larantuka (Flores), the Fraternity of the Queen of the Rosary promotes devotion by arranging prayer meetings, novenas, and family rosary prayers. Since the 16th c., it has taken an important part in the very popular celebration of the Holy Week in Larantuka, e.g., the lamentations on Maundy Thursday and the procession with the statue of *Tuan Ma* (Our Lady). Many statues and pictures of the cross, angels, and saints have been preserved in and around Larantuka through the centuries in the custody of the Confreria. Its greatest achievement is keeping the Christian faith through the 18th and early 19th cs. without any contact or support from missionaries. Thanks to the Confreria, there has been an uninterrupted Christian tradition in the former kingdom of Larantuka since the 16th c., the only place in all of Indonesia where this is true.

Bibliography

Petu, P., *Confreria Reinha Rosari: Nusa Tenggara setengah abad karya Misi SVD* (1966).

Adolf Heuken

Freemasonry, Philippines

Secretive organization which has opposed the Catholic Church in the Philippines* in the areas of religion and politics.

Freemasonry assumed its modern political and deistic identity in the early 18th c. The first Masons in the Philippines were Spaniards who established the first lodge in 1856, despite Masonry's having been prohibited since 1812. More important, Filipinos in Spain joined and subsequently founded their own lodges there as part of the Propaganda Movement's mobilization of people and institutions for political reform. Led by Marcelo H. del Pilar, Lodge *Solidaridad,* established in 1889-90, helped inculcate Philippine nationalist goals and promote opposition to the friars who dominated Philippine society. Its membership included most of the leading Filipinos in Spain, including José Rizal. Although Masonry was more of an organized expression of Filipino anticlericalism than its actual cause, Masonic influence on the Propagandists in Spain inhibited the support of Filipino secular clergy for the Propagandists' efforts. The first Filipino lodges in the Philippines, established in 1892, helped fund Lodge *Solidaridad* in addition to clandestinely criticizing the friars in the Philippines.

Masonic rituals and structures probably influenced the revolutionary organization, the Katipunan*, but whereas the latter attracted many members of the lower classes, Masonry remained an institution of wealthy Filipino anticlericals. Masons claim both the founder of the Katipunan, Andres Bonifacio, and the general of the Philippine army and president of the First Philippine Republic, Emilio Aguinaldo*, as their own. At the outbreak of the revolution, Masons and suspected Masons were tortured and deported or executed by Spanish Catholic authorities even though their revolutionary activity was minimal.

During the American colonial era (1898-1941), Masons were able to function publicly, and they continued their opposition to the now-disestablished Catholic Church. They supported some early Protestant efforts as well as the splitting of the Aglipayan Independent Church from Roman Catholicism at the beginning of the century (see Philippine Independent Church). They also lobbied against the Religious Instruction Bill of 1938, which would have facilitated Catholic religious education in public schools.

From 1917 on, when American and Filipino lodges united, Masonry provided transnational social and political bonds linking almost all of the prominent Filipino politicians and many Protestant American colonial administrators. Both groups favored the separation of church and state in the Philippines, effectively to the detriment of the Catholic Church. Important Masons during this period included Manuel Quezon, president of the commonwealth; José Abad Santos, supreme court justice; and General Douglas MacArthur. The Catholic response was most vigorous during the 1930s when young Catholics, the products of reinvigorated Catholic schools, actively engaged Masonic criticism in various popular media, including radio. During the Japanese occupation, such secretive organizations were suspect, and the Japanese raided lodges and removed materials. After the war, Masonry never recovered its significance as a political movement.

In general, it is difficult to distinguish the influence of Masonry per se from that of other fraternal, economic, religious, and political organizations (some formed under Masonic auspices) to which Filipinos, Spaniards, and Americans all belonged.

Bibliography

Causing, Juan, *Freemasonry in the Philippines (1756-1965)* (1969). • Councell, William C., *The Seventy-Fifth Anniversary of Manila Lodge No. 1, 1901-1976: A History of Freemasonry in the Philippines* (1976). • Kalaw,

Teodoro M., *Philippine Masonry: Its Origin, Development and Vicissitudes up to the Present Time (1920)* (1956). • Schumacher, John N., *The Making of a Nation: Essays on Nineteenth-Century Filipino Nationalism* (1991).

David Keck

French, Thomas Valpy

(b. Burton on Trent, England, 1 Jan 1825; d. Muscat, 1891). Missionary to northwest provinces of India (now Pakistan).

Educated at Rugby and University College, Oxford, where he was known for his ability in Latin, and ordained in 1849, French agreed to go to India with the Church Missionary Society (CMS) in 1850. In 1851 he founded St. John's College in Agra for Muslim and Hindu children. His language gifts also facilitated his direct, and at times controversial, preaching in village markets. He also helped found the Derajat Mission in the frontier regions. In 1869 he began training pastors in Lahore and became Anglican bishop there in 1877. He respected Indian literary patterns and encouraged indigenous worship. After retiring to Britain in 1887, in 1891 he accepted the challenge of working for the CMS in Arabia and embarked on a preaching ministry in Muscat. He died after only three months there, but his example helped inspire the formation of the American Arabia Mission.

Bibliography

Kerr, David A., "Thomas Valpy French," in *Biographical Dictionary of Christian Missions,* ed. Gerald H. Anderson (1998). • Stacey, Vivienne, "Thomas Valpy French," in *Mission Legacies: Biographical Studies of Leaders of the Modern Missionary Movement,* ed. Gerald H. Anderson et al. (1994).

John Roxborogh

Friars and the Land Controversy

The word *fraile* (friar) in traditional Spanish usage applied to particular monastic religious orders such as the Dominicans* (Order of Preachers), Franciscans* (Order of Friars Minor), Augustinians* (Order of St. Augustine), and Recollects (Order of Augustinian Recollects). Throughout the Spanish colonial period from the 16th to the 19th cs., friars were sent to evangelize areas in the Philippine archipelago that were assigned to their order. They all used the common strategy of gathering dispersed communities into larger settlements where they eventually set up institutions for education and health care. While the church then considered many aspects of local culture to be idolatrous, it used native languages, imagery, and social structures to support evangelization efforts and sought pastoral solutions to native practices such as polygamy.

The general basis for this mission remained the *Patronato Real* (see *Padroado*), the patronage system in which responsibility for evangelization in the colonies was given by the pope to the Spanish monarchy, but the actual relations of the church with colonial authorities proved to be complex. Dominican Domingo de Salazar*, who appointed the first bishop of Manila in 1579, questioned the Spanish right of conquest over local communities. Under his leadership, the Synod of Manila* (1582-86) condemned abuses by colonial officials such as involvement in the local practice of slavery. When both ecclesiastical and colonial institutions became firmly established from the 17th c. onward, conflicts over jurisdiction became heated. Colonial officials resented the power of the church over the native population in many matters. Religious orders, diocesan clergy, and bishops fought over distribution and control of parishes. This overall atmosphere of conflict among church and colonial authorities, and the resulting deterioration in the quality of pastoral care for the native population, contributed in no small part to the intense controversy surrounding church lands.

All of the friar orders except the Franciscans, and other church entities such as dioceses and the Society of Jesus* (Jesuits), acquired large estates called haciendas through donation, mortgage, or sale from Spanish families. These lands were originally given as royal grants in the 16th and 17th cs. to Spanish *conquistadors* who initially used them for raising cattle. But they remained underdeveloped because their often transient owners were more interested in the commercial possibilities of the galleon trade, and thus more than willing to transfer ownership.

Once in the hands of church entities, haciendas became more profitable enterprises, especially from the late 18th c. onward, when the commercial export of agricultural products began. Cultivation of rice, sugar, and cacao was introduced and better farming methods employed. Because of the vast land area of many haciendas, large portions were leased for a fixed rent to *inquilinos* who then subleased them to sharecroppers *(kasama)* who did the actual farming.

The first controversy involving these estates erupted around Manila in 1745. Those living outside haciendas in Cavite and Tondo (now Rizal Province) revolted because of land boundary disputes and the exemption of hacienda workers from compulsory labor. Since hacienda owners obtained this exemption from the colonial government as a matter of course, the adjacent communities bore the burden of providing the labor demanded by the government. The revolt was resolved with a minimum of military force, thanks to Judge Felipe Calderon y Henriquez, whose commission issued a general amnesty excluding only the leaders of the revolt and provided for a new survey to determine the boundaries of the haciendas.

This political solution, however, failed to address the long-term issues regarding the church lands. While the haciendas contributed to the general development of the areas around them, church ownership of so much cultivated land remained controversial in the context of growing anticolonial sentiment. Moreover, the circumstances and quality of missionary work changed in the 19th c. The later friars were not as dedicated as their earlier counterparts and were often antiliberal as a result of the attacks against the church by liberals in Spain. Hence the friars became the popular symbol for the worst abuses of Spanish colonization during the Philippine Revolution of 1896 and 1898.

Underneath this widespread hatred for the friars lay specific political and economic interests. In the late 19th c., the nationalist campaign of *ilustrados* who were educated in local and European universities increasingly took a strong antifriar stance. Within the haciendas, *inquilinos* had more land under lease and more sharecroppers under their abusive power. Often Chinese mestizos, they had no ethnic ties with the Spanish missionaries and were eager to take full ownership of the haciendas for economic gain. At the bottom rung of the oppressive system in many haciendas were the *kasama,* who saw the friars as absentee owners.

Some religious entities saw the threat to their land properties and transferred ownership to new corporations in which they remained major stockholders. Soon after Spain ceded its former colonies in the 1898 Treaty of Paris*, the American government recognized the political significance of the issues regarding church lands and asked the Second Philippine Commission under William H. Taft to discuss them. Though legitimate ownership by church entities was established, haciendas belonging to the friar congregations were soon sold.

But the root problem of land tenancy was not resolved by the mere sale of church lands, since ownership immediately fell into the hands of the local elite. This problem would once again surface during the turbulent peasant unrest before and after World War II* and continues today because of the absence of comprehensive land reform.

Bibliography

Anderson, Gerald H., ed., *Studies in Philippine Church History* (1969). • Connolly, Michael J., *Church Lands and Peasant Unrest in the Philippines: Agrarian Conflict in 20th-Century Luzon* (1992). • McCoy, Alfred W., and C. de Jesus, eds., *Philippine Social History: Global Trade and Local Transformations* (1982). • Schumacher, John N., *Readings in Philippine Church History* (1979).

Jose Mario C. Francisco

Fryer, John

(b. 1839; d. 1928). English missionary and educator in China*.

Of scanty means, Fryer was baptized into the Anglican* Church when he was in secondary school. He completed his schooling in Humbury, London, in 1860. He reached Hong Kong* in 1861 to tutor at St. Paul's College. In 1863, invited by the Church Missionary Society (CMS), he went to serve in a Chinese government school. In 1865, he left the CMS to set up the Anglo-Chinese College in Shanghai. In 1868, he was concurrently an editor and translator in the Jiangnan Manufacturing Bureau in Shanghai, translating many scientific books. Although he preferred to do mission work in inland China rather than secular work, Fryer was mainly engaged in educational work. He compiled a six-volume collection of Chinese scientific books in 1875 and set up the Chinese Scientific Book Depot in 1885. He helped establish the Institution for the Chinese Blind, and his son George became headmaster of the Fryer School for the Deaf and Dumb.

Fryer was commended twice by the Qing dynasty for his contributions to China. He was appointed a professor of Eastern literature at the University of California in 1896 and continued as an honorary professor after his retirement in 1915. Among his works are *The Educational Dictionary for China* and *Admission of Chinese Students to American Colleges.*

Bibliography

Palmer, Spencer J., *Korea and Christianity: The Problem of Identification with Tradition* (1967). • John Fryer Collection, Archives of the University of California, Berkeley.

China Group

Gale, James Scarth

(b. Ontario, Canada, 19 Feb 1863; d. England, 31 Jan 1937). Canadian Presbyterian* missionary to Korea*, translator, writer, and educator.

Gale graduated from University College, Toronto, in 1884. At a meeting of the Student Volunteer Movement, he was inspired to be a missionary by the preaching of Hudson Taylor*, missionary to China*, and D. L. Moody. In 1888, he was dispatched by the Young Men's Christian Association* (YMCA) of University College, Toronto, as a lay missionary to Korea. He worked as a translator with the Korea Bible Society in Seoul. In 1890, when the YMCA of Toronto was disbanded, he joined the Presbyterian Church of the United States of America (North). He moved to Wonsan, a city in northeastern Korea, and worked with W. L. Swallen, an American Presbyterian missionary. He translated John Bunyan's *Pilgrim's Progress* into Korean and several Korean novels, including *Choonhyang* (Folk Tales) and *Goowunmong* (Nine Dreams on Clouds) into English. He also edited a Korean-English dictionary.

In 1897, Gale went to the United States for his sabbatical and was ordained by the New Albany Presbytery. Returning to Korea, he moved to Seoul in 1899 and founded the Yundong Girls' School (renamed Joengsin Girls' High School) and the Jesus School (renamed Kyungshin Boys' High School). From 1900, he served as a minister at the Yon-dong Presbyterian Church.

Gale was a major interpreter of Korea to the West, with a personal fascination concerning all things Korean. A great church leader, he was elected moderator of the Korean independent presbytery and taught at Presbyterian Theological Seminary in Pyongyang.

Among Gale's many written works are *Korean Grammatical Forms* (1893), *Korean Sketches* (1898), *Korea in Transition* (1909), and *History of the Korean People* (1924). In 1925, he published the Korean Bible*, which was the first private translation in Korea.

Gale joined the staff of the Royal Asiatic Society, Korea branch, until his retirement in 1928, when he moved to England.

Bibliography

Kidok' kio Dae Paik' kwoa Sach'un (The Christian Encyclopedia), Vol. I (1986). • Rhodes, H. A., ed., *History of the Korea Mission of the Presbyterian Church USA, 1885-1934* (1934). • Paik, George L., *The History of Protestant Missions in Korea* (1971). • Rutt, Richard, *James Scarth Gale and His History of the Korean People* (1972). • Ion, A. Hamish, *The Cross and the Rising Sun* (1990). • Anderson, Gerald H., *Biographical Dictionary of Christian Missions* (1998). • Underwood, Lillias H., *Underwood of Korea* (1918). • Underwood, H. G., *The Call of Korea* (1908).

Kim In Soo

Gan Kwee

(b. ?; d. Jakarta, Indonesia, 22 Jun 1901). First Chinese preacher in Indonesia*.

Gan proclaimed the Gospel among the Chinese people in Indonesia, particularly in Java. He came from Amoy in South China, where, as a student of an English missionary, he had become acquainted with Christ and soon confessed Christianity. He entered Batavia (Jakarta) via Singapore* in 1856.

Gan's arrival in Jakarta began a cooperative work with the Society for Internal and External Mission (*Genootschap voor In-en Uitwendige Zending,* GIUZ), which was founded in 1851 in Jakarta. He was invited by GIUZ to be a chief aide to the mission for evangelization among the Chinese in Indonesia, primarily Java. In this enterprise, GIUZ was following the mission philosophy of F. L. Anthing* (1867-83), a Dutch judge in Jakarta who said that proclaiming the Gospel to an ethnic group could be successful only if it was done by a native from that group. Anthing deemed it necessary "to reach the Indonesians and the Chinese with the Gospel by Indonesian and Chinese indigenous preachers."

Gan made many significant evangelistic trips to proclaim the Gospel in numerous centers of Chinese population in Java, but his labors were met with some resistance, even from his own people. His perseverance brought about many new converts in several towns of Java, including Jakarta, Bogor, Cirebon, Semarang, Gresik, Surabaya, and Probolinggo. In 1864, in the city of Cirebon, the family of a Chinese lieutenant, Yoe Ong Pouw, confessed Christianity along with several other Chinese. Meanwhile in Jakarta, all 17 pupils of Gan were baptized in 1868 and became pioneers of the well-known Patekoan Church, which became a congregation of the Indonesian Christian Church in West Java in 1938.

After 16 years of hard labor, Gan changed his methodology of proclaiming the Gospel, choosing to work independently rather than under GIUZ. In 1873, he traveled to Singapore and Taiwan*, returning to Jakarta in 1899 to continue serving the Patekoan Church, where the Gouw Kho family had been serving. On 22 Jun 1901, Gan passed away and was buried in the new graveyard. G. A. W. Geissler, a missionary of the Java Committee, testified that Gan was industrious and full of courage in his service for his Lord. He stood out as a unique phenomenon in the history of Chinese Christians in Indonesia in the second part of the 19th c.

Bibliography

Pouw Boen Giok, *De kerkrechtelijke positie van een ethnisch bepaalde kerk in een ander ethnisch bepaald milieu* (1952). • Panitia Bersama, *Buku Preingatan 100 Tahun Pekaberan Indjil di Patekoan Djakarta, 1868-1968* (1989). • Hartono, Chris, *Gereja di Jawa Barat* (1979).

Chris Hartono

Gandhi, Mohandas Karamchand

(b. Porbandar, Gujarat State, India, 2 Oct 1869; d. New Delhi, India, 1948). Gandhi was born in western India* in a walled town on the Arabian Sea at the edge of the Great Indian Desert. Porbandar was called "The White City" because of its houses built of soft, white stone which hardened when exposed to the elements. It is an appropriate metaphor for Gandhi.

The Gandhis were Vaisyas (third-caste level) of the Modh Bania caste. Their family name originally referred to "dealers in groceries." Later in life, Gandhi was not adverse when pushing a hard bargain to reminding his adversaries rather whimsically that he was after all a *bania,* synonymous with a clever merchant in India.

Gandhi's father was not highly educated, but he was a man of character, impartial, strong-willed, and not afraid to stand up for his rights. Gandhi described his mother, Pitlibai, as saintly. He was the youngest of four children. She heaped great affection upon him.

"Mohan," as Gandhi was called at home, did not regard his record in school as notable. He did refuse to cheat. He lamented the fact that he did not regard good handwriting as important and that he did not gain a better mastery of Sanskrit.

His early marriage at the age of 13 was always a matter of shame for Gandhi. His wife, Kasturbai, though largely illiterate, was a beautiful girl. The Gandhis had four sons: Haridas, Manilal, Ramdas, and Devadas. The general outlines of Gandhi's life are fairly well known. He often said, "My life is my message." Quite exceptionally for an Indian, he wrote an autobiography, *The Story of My Experiments with Truth,* a remarkable document. It gives quite frankly an account of his follies, sins, and the shortcomings of his youth, as well as his personal and religious struggles at home and abroad.

It was as a raw and unpromising young man that Gandhi sailed for England in Sep 1888. He remained there for nearly three years. He enrolled in law at the Inner Temple, London, and engaged also in such studies as French and Latin. He read fairly widely, tasted English life, met prominent leaders, both secular and religious, including Cardinal Manning, Charles Spurgeon, and Joseph Parker. Realizing his ignorance of his own religion, he began to study Hinduism* seriously while in England. Finally, he passed his bar examination and returned to India in Jul 1891.

Back in India, Gandhi was not at all successful. After some months of floundering, he seized upon an opportunity for legal practice in South Africa, where he went in 1893. Though a "slow starter," during his first year in South Africa Gandhi began to hit his stride. Harsh circumstances contributed to this.

In Natal, Gandhi was forcibly ejected from a train, although he possessed a first-class ticket, and was left alone on a winter's night, coatless at the Maritzburg station, all because a white passenger objected to traveling with a "colored man." He pocketed the insult, but in an all-night struggle with himself he decided not to run but to stay and suffer. It was a turning point, the "most creative experience" in his life, as he later termed it. "My active non-violence began from that date." It is strange that he did not develop an intense hatred for the white man, but he did not.

The Maritzburg experience had the most profound influence upon the young Gandhi. In this and similar incidents he showed a stubborn quality of determination and great sensitiveness and pride. His innate timidity was largely overcome. His sense of duty was aroused — a duty to his fellow Indians, whose regular experience was of the same nature as he had tasted. His pride was wounded, but his reaction did not turn inward as resentment but outward with a new sense of social responsibility to relieve the wrongs of his people. Though "justice" was not a frequent word in his vocabulary, he passionately sought economic, social, and political justice for those who were deprived of the same.

With a new orientation, Gandhi needed a cause. He found it in alleviating the harsh lot of his people, which he had now experienced himself. "I then awoke to a sense of my duty; I saw that from the standpoint of self-interest, South Africa was no good to me." He never again lacked a sense of purpose. He gave voice to this through speaking (he was never eloquent) and writing, for he was a lifelong journalist.

Originally Gandhi had intended to stay in South Africa for one year. With a few interruptions, he actually stayed for more than 20 years. Like many other Indians, he discovered his country (and, incidentally, himself) while overseas. South Africa was for him a training ground and laboratory for the more rigorous responsibilities which were to rest upon him in India.

This was the beginning of Gandhi's program of nonviolence. In its formulation, he drew in elements from his family tradition and from Indian religious tradition (especially *ahimsa*), namely, from Hinduism, Jainism, and Buddhism*. To these were added ingredients from Christianity, such as the Sermon on the Mount, and from such Western thinkers as Henry David Thoreau, John Ruskin, and Leo Tolstoy. Mixing these together, he compounded *Satyagraha* (truth force).

In Gandhi's view, there were only two ways of changing human social ills: by violence or by nonviolence. He chose the latter for his essential remedy for India's ills, internal as well as external. Like so many leaders in the field of the spirit, he did not himself formulate ideas in any systematic philosophical manner, though he did expound *Satyagraha* almost incessantly.

Gandhi did not claim any originality for the concept of *Satyagraha*. He felt that soul-force was natural; therefore, it was taken for granted and not often noted in history. He regarded the *rishis* (sages) who discovered the law of suffering as "greater geniuses than Newton."

Gandhi did not like to define *Satyagraha*, partly because he felt that his knowledge of it was ever-growing. He once said, "I have no textbook to consult in time of need, not even the *Gita* which I have called my dictionary. *Satyagraha* is conceived by me as a science in the making." Again, "*Satyagraha* in its essence is nothing but the introduction of truth and gentleness in the political, that is, the national life." "Nonviolence," he once said, "is what St. Paul calls 'love' in 1 Corinthians 13 — plus suffering." This sounds like the cross of Christ.

Gandhi always insisted that *Satyagraha* was not a passive force. "It is essentially an active movement, much more active than the one involving the use of sanguinary weapons. Truth and nonviolence are perhaps the activest weapons you have in the world." He went on to say that while soldiers rest, and fight very little of the time, this internal weapon acts when asleep or awake. By the same token, he asserted that *Satyagraha* was not a negative but a positive force.

This method Gandhi applied with increasing success in South Africa to alleviate the lot of his fellow countrymen there. In 1915, he returned to India and for about one year did not involve himself in politics. Rather, he traveled widely and observed the situation in India with great care. He gradually worked his way into leadership in the nationalist movement (see Nationalism). His predecessors had applied either the polite methods of debating societies or sometimes violent approaches. Gandhi advocated a middle way, a practical, nonviolent method of change.

In the 1920s, Gandhi began his organized campaigns, looking to home rule. He applied increasing pressure during the 1930s and early 1940s, culminating in independence in Aug 1947. His most famous campaign was the Salt March of 1930, the very model of nonviolence. His plans were not limited to protest but always included what he termed "constructive programs" for training and disciplining the masses to assume political responsibility when freedom came.

Along the way, he was given the honorific designation of *Mahatma* (Great Soul). The poet Rabindranath Tagore* is said to have first proposed it. But *Mahatmas* must suffer much. Gandhi was arrested repeatedly and spent years in jail. These experiences he called "my arrest-cure" and used them for study, reflection, and writing. Finally, he paid with his life.

A small flat stone in the garden of Birla House in New Delhi marks the spot where Gandhi fell at the hand of a Hindu assassin on 30 Jan 1948. Inscribed on the stone are two words in Hindi: *He Rama*, "O, God," the phrase on his lips as he died on his way to his regular evening prayer meeting.

Gandhi's contributions were many. He helped to bring freedom to his country and prepared the people for it to a very considerable degree by awakening them, restoring their self-respect and self-confidence, giving them a renewed sense of nationhood. He focused attention to a new degree upon the poor and oppressed of India, taking steps for their relief. He developed a practical, nonviolent mass method of resistance.

Nonviolent, noncooperation campaigns are not restricted to India. The method was used by Vinoba Bhave *(Bhoodan Yajna)* in 1951 and afterward. It was used by Martin Luther King, Jr., and to some degree in South Africa.

Gandhi is rightly called the father of his country, but he also has universal appeal. He continues to stand tall in world history and is a man for the ages.

Bibliography

Fischer, Louis, *Life of Mahatma Gandhi* (1950). • Gandhi, M. K., *An Autobiography: The Story of My Experiments with Truth*, 2nd ed. (1940). • Jones, E. Stanley, *Gandhi: An Interpretation* (1948), republished as *Gandhi, Portrayal of a Friend* (1993). • Mathews, James K., *The Matchless Weapon: Satyagraha* (1989). • Tendulkar, D. G., *Mahatma, Life of Mohandas Karamchand Gandhi*, 8 vols. (1951-54).

JAMES K. MATHEWS

Gaspais, Auguste Ernest

(b. Brittany, France, 1884; d. 1952). French missionary of the Paris Foreign Mission Society (MEP); Vatican representative to the Japanese puppet Manchukuo (Manchu nation) regime.

Gaspais was consecrated a priest on 7 Jul 1907 and in

August was sent by the Paris Foreign Mission Society to do mission work in Dongbei (northeast), China. He became the coadjutor of Ji Lin Diocese in 1920 and bishop in 1923. Following the occupation of Dongbei by the Japanese government and the establishment of the puppet regime of Manchukuo, Gaspais was appointed vicar apostolic by the Vatican, a post he held until Japan's defeat in 1945, when Dongbei was returned to China*. On 1 Mar 1934, Gaspais congratulated the Manchukuo king on his enthronement and on 2 Aug presented the Vatican's letter of friendship to the Manchukuo foreign ministry. Gaspais remained as bishop of Ji Lin until he was imprisoned by the Communists and then deported from China in Dec 1951, when the People's Republic of China was established. He died a year later in France.

Gaspais's two great contributions to the church in China were his mediating role during Japanese occupation and his mediating role regarding Chinese Confucian rites and the church. Gaspais viewed the Chinese rites for Confucius and ancestors as civil rites of respect and not religious in character (see Ancestor Worship). With accompanying letters to that effect from the Chinese ministry of education, he successfully argued his case with the Vatican. In May 1935, the holy see officially permitted, for the first time in 200 years, Christian participation in rendering homage to Confucius and to ancestors.

Bibliography

Minamiki, George, *The Chinese Rites Controversy from the Beginnings to Modern Times* (1985); *Missionaires à Asie*, Vol. 69 (1953).

China Group, translated by David Wu

General Council of the Protestant Evangelical Mission in Korea

The united missionary council established by four mission societies of the Presbyterian* Church (Presbyterian Church in the United States of America, Presbyterian Church in the United States, Australian Presbyterian Church, and Canadian Presbyterian Church) and two of the Methodist* Church (Methodist Episcopal Church and Methodist Episcopal Church, South) in 1905.

Not only was this organization a council of missionaries, but it was a strong expression of the ideal of "One Protestant Church in Korea." Its constitution said, "The purpose of this council is to cooperate in missionary work and finally to organize one evangelical church in Korea." Missionaries in Korea discussed the agenda to establish one church in Korea, and some of them suggested a name — the Church of Christ of Korea. When the Presbyterian Church created the Independent Presbyterian Church in 1910, the discussion discontinued. The council also ceased to meet. It was, however, most significant as a pioneer of the Korean ecumenical movement and the foundation for the Federal Council of Churches in Korea (1924), from which the National Council of Churches of Korea was born.

Among the works of the council was a Bible translation* ministry through the Korea Religious Book and Tract Society, as well as publication of the *Korea Mission Field* (to consolidate Presbyterian and Methodist missionary magazines [1905]), *Christian News* (1906), and a united hymnbook (1908). The council also contributed to educational and medical work, Sunday school ministry, and the Million Souls* for Christ movement.

Lee Duk Joo, translated by Kim In Soo

Gerbillon, Jean-François

(b. Verdun, France, 1654; d. Beijing, China, 1707). French Jesuit* missionary who served in the Qing government of Emperor Kangxi.

Gerbillon was one of five missionaries sent as mathematicians in 1685 to China* by King Louis XIV of France. Arriving in 1688, Gerbillon and Joachin Bouvet* were retained by Kangxi to serve in his government in Beijing, while the other three were sent to Nanjing and elsewhere. Gerbillon studied Chinese and the Manchu language, and the emperor asked him and Bouvet about mathematics and Western philosophy. In 1689, Kangxi sent both Thomas Pereira* and Gerbillon to accompany the emperor legate, Suo E Tu, to negotiate the Treaty of Ni Bu Chu, regarding which Suo E Tu commented, "Accomplishing a task of such magnitude was in fact the contribution of Gerbillon." The five missionaries, the others being Philippus Maria Grimaldi*, Pereira, Antonius Thomas, and Bouvet, were highly trusted by Kangxi, who often accommodated their requests. Indeed, the first church building in Beijing, North Church, was a response to Gerbillon's petition. Gerbillon also went on eight trips to Mongolia and Manchuria as the superior of the French Jesuits in China.

Bibliography

"Lettre du P. Gerbillon," in *Lettres édifiantes et curieuses*, 4 vols., ed. M. L. Aimé-Martin (1843). • Cordier, Henri, "Cinq lettres inédités du Père Gerbillon," *T'oung Pao* 7 (1906); "Observations historiques sur la Grande Tartarie" and "Relations de huit voyages dans la Grande Tartarie de 1688 à 1699," in *Description géographique, historique, chronologique, politique, et physique de l'Empire de la Chine et de la Tartarie chinoise*, 4 vols., ed. Jean-Baptiste du Halde (1735-36). • "Lettre du 30 decembre 1706," in *Relation abrégée de la nouvelle persecution à la Chine*, by Gonzalez de St. Pierre (1712). • Sebes, Joseph S., *The Jesuits and the Sino-Russian Treaty of Nerchinsk (1689): The Diary of Thomas Pereira, S.J.* (1961). • De Thomaz de Bossierre, Yves, *Jean-François Gerbillon, S.J. (1654-1707)* (1994).

China Group, translated by David Wu

Gereja Kristen Protestan di Bali. *See* Bali, Christian Protestant Church in

Gereja Masehi Injili Minahasa, GMIM. *See* Christian Evangelical Church in Minahasa

Ghengis Khan (Chingis Khan)

(1162?-1227). Mongol military ruler who led his people to one of the greatest conquests in world history.

At the time of Ghengis's birth, the Mongol tribes were still very much divided and at war with one another. Ghengis's goal from his early adult years was to unite all of the Mongols under his rule. His father had been killed by the Tartars, and so Ghengis was raised by his mother to be a ruler. She taught him to hunt, fight, and develop the important strategy of forming alliances with trusted friends. This ability to fight and develop alliances of friendships added to his own tolerance of various cultures and peoples and proved to be the mix for world conquest. In his rise to power, Ghengis would form alliances to conquer other tribes, and then he would turn against those whom he had used to procure victory. He defeated the powerful Tartars, the Kereit, the Naiman, and then the Merkid. A great assembly *(khuriltai)* of the united Mongols was held in 1206 in which Ghengis was acknowledged as the single ruler or Khan.

Ghengis continued to extend his influence beyond the Mongol regions, first conquering the Tangurts and then the Xixia. In an effort to control trade routes to the West, Ghengis turned his attention in that direction. In 1219 he moved nearly 200,000 soldiers to central Asia to make war on Shah Ala al-Din Muhammad. The destruction and violence of this six-year campaign is hard to estimate. After turning east and forcing tribute from Korea* and attacking the Jin Kingdom, Ghengis died in 1227 and was burned in *Burkhan Khaldun* (Buddha Cliff) in 1229, along with 40 sacrificed horses and 40 women.

Of special note in Ghengis Khan's reign was his inclusion of all beliefs and cultures. It was a great sign of his authority and power to have all religious leaders represented in his entourage. He sought the advice of Daoists and gave special freedom and encouragement to Nestorian* monks and priests, Muslim clerics, and Buddhist monks. Included even among his wives were women of different ethnic and religious backgrounds. Ghengis also contributed to the development of law in Asia. His *Jasagh,* or Mongol law code, although written for a nomadic people, gave the earliest Mongol laws concerning reasons for capital punishment, laws, and punishments for soldiers, and in addition made clear that all religions were protected and tolerated. This proved to be a brief respite for East Syrian monks, who continued to celebrate their Syriac language liturgy in the shadow of the great Khan.

Bibliography

Rossabi, Morris, "Ghengis Khan," in *Encyclopedia of Asian History* (1988). • Boyle, John Adrew, trans., *History of the World-Conqueror,* 2 Vols. (1958). • Cleaves, Francis Woodman, trans., *The Secret History of the Mongols* (1928). • Grousset, *Conqueror of the World: The Life of Chingis Khan* (1966). • Martin, H. Desmond, *The Rise of Chingis Khan and His Conquest of North China* (1950).

Scott W. Sunquist

Gia Long

(b. Hue, Vietnam, 8 Feb 1762; d. Hue, 1819). Vietnamese founder-emperor of the Nguyen Dynasty (1802-1945); original name Nguyen Phuoc Anh.

Nguyen was a nephew of the last Nguyen lord, Nguyen Phuc Thuan, from the south of Vietnam*, who was killed by his Tay Son rivals. Nguyen Phuoc Anh regained power after long and arduous years of struggle and proclaimed himself Emperor Gia Long, an honorific title, on 1 Jun 1802. The old name of the country Dai Viet was changed to Vietnam. The capital became Phu Xuan (Hue).

In spite of French military help against the Tay Son emperors and the personal assistance of the French bishop Pigneau de Behaine (also known as the bishop of Adran), Gia Long granted the French no favors in state affairs. He, however, did treat the Catholics very well. A seminary was founded at Lai Thieu near Saigon, and Pigneau de Behaine was allowed to visit parishes in the territory under Gia Long's control. Gia Long respected Catholicism but refused the Christian demand to outlaw polygamy and ancestor worship*. Warm relations developed between Gia Long and other French bishops and missionaries in Hue, Nghe An, and Hanoi. Village councils were given an edict not to oblige the Catholics to participate in spirit worship. In line with tradition, the government authorized the repair and building of Buddhist temples and Catholic churches. Although Confucianism* flourished, Buddhism* and Catholicism were tolerated; there was no imperial policy to prohibit them.

In administrative and political terms, Gia Long's rule is seen as successful. The creation of the Nguyen Dynasty code, the *Hoang Viet Luat Le* (Laws and Decrees of Imperial Vietnam), was an important achievement.

Bibliography

Cabaton, A., *Bio-Bibliographie de l'Indochine Française* (1935). • Maybon, L., *Histoire Moderne du pays d'Annam (1592-1820)* (1920). • Ta Van Tai, *The Vietnamese Tradition of Human Rights* (1988).

John G. Kleinen

Gi, Andrew. *See* Ji, Andrew

Gibson, Thomas Campbell

(b. Swatow, China, 29 Sep 1887; d. Edinburgh, Scotland, 30 Dec 1967). English Presbyterian missionary to Swatow and Singapore*.

Sent to Scotland at age three, Gibson attended the

University of Glasgow, where he obtained his master's degree at the United Free Church Theological College. He played golf and rugby and was Student Christian Movement* (SCM) mission secretary. In 1910, he was a steward at the Edinburgh World Missionary Conference, where his father, John Campbell Gibson, chaired the commission on the church on the mission field. Gibson returned to China* as a missionary in 1912. After service in times of civil war, earthquake, and typhoon, in 1919 he joined the Bue-li Theological College in Swatow. In 1922, he married Phyllis Chisholm.

Gibson moved to Singapore in 1932 at a time when it was increasingly difficult for foreign missionaries to work in China and when the Chinese churches in Singapore and Malaya wanted missionary assistance. He also served from 1936 as minister of the Straits Chinese Prinsep Street Congregation. In 1938, he attended the International Missionary Council meeting in Tambaram, India, and was the first secretary of the Malaya Christian Committee of Reference and Counsel.

Interned in Changi Prison from Feb 1942 to 1945, Gibson shared in plans for local theological education and improved relationships between churches and between expatriate and local Christians. After recuperation in England, he returned in Feb 1947 and was involved in the revitalization of Prinsep Street Church and the formation of the Malayan Christian Council and Trinity Theological College. The Gibsons returned to Britain in 1951 and ministered at Haltwhistle until 1965.

Bibliography

Band, Edward, *Working His Purpose Out: The History of the English Presbyterian Mission, 1847-1947* (1948). • *But God: Selected Sermons of the Reverend T. Campbell Gibson*. • Hood, G. A., "The Rev. Thomas Campbell Gibson, MA," *The Presbyterian Church in Singapore and Malaysia: 90th Anniversary of the Church and 70th Anniversary of the Synod, Commemoration Volume* (1970). • *Prinsep St. Presbyterian Church, 1930-1980* (1980).

John Roxborogh

GMIH. *See* Halmahera, the Christian Evangelical Church in

Goh Hood Keng

(b. Singapore, 1886; d. Singapore, 1961). Singapore* Methodist* pastor, evangelist, and writer.

Born into a staunch Buddhist family, Goh and his siblings were required by their parents to bow daily before idols. At the age of seven, Goh was sent to Anglo-Chinese school where, through the chapel services and Bible class, he was confronted by the claims of the Gospel. Before long, he was converted. This antagonized his parents, and for two years he was persecuted. However, his changed life was noted by all, and one day his mother said to him: "Son, I wish you could be a Christian 10 times over." Finishing his education, he stayed on to teach at his alma mater. For 20 years, he remained in this position. His outstanding qualities influenced generations of students, many of whom later became prominent in society.

From the beginning, Goh associated himself with the Middle Road Church (Kampong Kapor Methodist Church). As his preaching gift became recognized, he was invited to speak in the Malay and English services. In 1915, he was ordained a deacon of the church and, four years later, having completed the local preachers' course, he became an elder. He was thus the first Straits-born Chinese to be ordained into the ministry of the Methodist Church. All the while, he supported himself as a teacher. In 1927, he left the teaching profession and became a full-time pastor, a position that he held over the next 25 years. The church had begun in 1896 with just six members and 16 attendees. By the time Goh retired in 1952, it had become the second largest English-speaking Methodist church in Singapore, with over 1,000 members.

A widely read man, Goh spoke and wrote on many subjects: apologetics, ancestor worship*, education, leadership qualities, alcohol, liberal theology, and so on. But evangelism always remained close to his heart. In an article titled "Evangelism: Our Supreme Need," he noted the failure of the church: "If we are honest with ourselves, we must, to our regret, confess that we have all let a great many golden opportunities for soul-winning slip by us. Souls have got beyond our reach and have gone on to perdition while we have been busy here and there with this, that and the other thing, instead of being on our job — winning men to our Master. Think of the thousands of young people who have gone out of our schools, who today never step inside a Christian church." His heart constantly burned for the Lord, and it was not unusual to see dozens of students responding to his messages during chapel services. After his retirement from pastoral work, he continued as Methodist Conference evangelist at large until he died.

Because of his fluency in English and Malay, Goh was offered many job opportunities by the Straits Chinese business community, but he declined them all. To the end, his motto was: "I am happy in the Lord's work. I have one dominating passion: to preach Christ and him crucified. I ask for no great work, I covet no great honor."

Bibliography

Wong Hoon Hee, *The Memoirs of the Late Rev. Goh Hood Keng*.

Bobby Sng Ewe Kong

Gom-Bur-Za

Acronym formed by the first syllables of the surnames of three Filipino priest-martyrs and leaders of the native clergy: Mariano Gomes de los Angeles (b. Santa Cruz, Manila, 2 Aug 1799), José Apolonio Burgos (b. Vigan, Ilosos Sur, 9 Feb 1837), and Jacinto Zamora (b.

Pandacan, Manila, 14 Aug 1835). All three were executed by strangulation *(garrote vil)* in Bagumbayan Field (now Luneta Park, Manila) on 17 Feb 1872 after a summary trial by the council of war in which they were accused of being "instigators and conspirators" of the soldiers' mutiny at the Fort of Cavite on 20 Jan.

Gom-Bur-Za represented a cross-section of Filipino society in the 19th c. Gomes was of Chinese mestizo (Eurasian Filipino) background; Burgos was a *criollo* (a Spaniard born and raised in the country); and Zamora was of Spanish mestizo background. Because of their administrative and academic accomplishments as well as their personal integrity, they emerged as the leaders of the native clergy. Gomes had been pastor of the important parish of Bacoor in the province of Cavite since 1824 and vicar forane of the province since 1844. Burgos had just earned a double doctorate in theology (1868) and canon law (1871) and was one of the two rectors of the Manila Cathedral parish in the walled city (1865). The other rector was Zamora, a bachelor of both canon and civil laws (1858 and 1859).

Gom-Bur-Za sought to uphold the dignity and promote the rights of all their brethren who were the victims of discrimination. Heading the secularization movement, they contributed much and solicited funds to publicize their cause in newspapers and pamphlets in Manila and Madrid. Written by Burgos, the most significant of these works was the "Manifesto to the Noble Spanish Nation, Which the Loyal Filipinos Address in Defense of Their Honor and Loyalty" (1864). Gom-Bur-Za worked on the committee on reforms during the term of the liberal governor-general Carlos M. de la Toree (1869-71). They further encouraged Filipino students in their scholarly pursuits, many of whom proved to be so enthusiastic that the colonial authorities banned Filipinos from acquiring the doctorate in any academic field (1872).

Gomes and Burgos protested their innocence up to the last moment; Zamora had lost his mind in the upheaval. Even today, the Spanish government has still not released the records of their trial. The consensus opinion of Filipino historians is that they were innocent and were made scapegoats for the military mutiny because of their agitation for reforms on behalf of the Filipino clergy.

Far from suppressing Gom-Bur-Za's cause, the Spanish government unwittingly set a larger stage for the nationalist movements, including the Propaganda Movement in Spain (1880-95) and, ultimately, the Philippine Revolution (1896-98), which invoked "Gom-Bur-Za" as their battle cry. To Gom-Bur-Za's memory, the national hero, José Rizal, dedicated his incendiary novel *El Filibusterismo* (The Subversives, 1891). When the Spanish priests left their parishes during the strife, their Filipino coadjutors took over, thus fulfilling one of the goals of Gom-Bur-Za. Partly in reaction to Zamora's fate, his nephew Paulino became a pioneer Filipino Protestant in 1898, and the latter's son, Nicolas, founded *La Iglesia Evangelical Metodista en las Islas Filipinas* (IEMELIF) in 1909.

Bibliography

Artigas y Cuerval, Manuel, *Los Sucesos de 1872* (1911). • Manuel, E. Arsenio, *Dictionary of Philippine Biography,* Vols. I and II (1955, 1970). • Santiago, Luciano P. R., "The Last Will of Padre Mariano Gomes," *Philippine Studies* (1982); "The Filipino Doctors of Ecclesiastical Sciences in the 19th Century," *Philippine Quarterly of Culture & Society* (1985).

LUCIANO P. R. SANTIAGO

Gomes de los Angeles, Mariano. *See* Gom-Bur-Za

Gomes, William Henry

(b. Ceylon, 1827; d. Singapore, 2 Mar 1902). Pioneer missionary amongst the Ibans of Sarawak (1852-72); superintendent of St. Andrew's Church Mission, Singapore* (1872-1902).

Trained for the ministry at Bishop's College, Calcutta, Gomes began mission work amongst the Ibans in Lundu, Sarawak, in 1852 under the auspices of the Society for the Propagation of the Gospel. A gifted linguist, he became fluent in Malay and Iban and translated into Malay a large part of the Book of Common Prayer as well as a life of Christ and more than 130 hymns. At a time when tribal warfare and head-hunting were rife, he established strong Christian congregations along the Lundu River.

Gomes was appointed superintendent of St. Andrew's Church Mission in Singapore in 1872. Working from St. Peter's Church, Stamford Road, he and his team of catechists preached the Gospel in five Chinese dialects as well as in Tamil and Malay. The church premises were also used during the week by Chung Loi Fatt for the school classes which later became St. Andrew's School. Under Gomes's leadership, the mission reached out to the Chinese gambier and pepper planters in Jurong, where St. John's Church was built in 1884. Gomes had a gift for recruiting the right men and training them to teach others. He carried on his ministry to the end, dying in 1902 at the age of 75 years. "Gomes was a true pioneer and his ministry provided the spring-board for the subsequent development of the Anglican Church" (Bobby Sng, *In His Good Time*).

Bibliography

USPG Archives, Rhodes House Library, Oxford. • Loh Keng Aun, *50 Years of the Anglican Church in Singapore Island (1909-1959)* (1963). • Sng, Bobby E. K., *In His Good Time* (1980, 1993).

FRANK LOMAX

Gonsalvez, Jacome

(b. Jun 1676; d. Bolavatta, 17 Jul 1742). Oratorian priest of Konkani origin who provided the Sri Lankan Catholics with religious literature in their own languages.

Gonsalvez arrived in Sri Lanka* in 1706 in the company of another oratorian to assist Joseph Vaz*, who was already serving in the Kandyan kingdom. Of Konkani Brahmin origin, Gonsalvez had received his education at the University of Goa.

Since Gonsalvez's missionary activities carried him to different parts of the island, he had the opportunity to acquaint himself with the manners, customs, vocabulary, and modes of expression of the elite, as well as of the common people. Realizing the difficulties faced by the Roman Catholics* in the Dutch territory because of the prohibition of priests, he made an attempt to equip them with literary material in the vernacular to keep their religious faith alive.

A contemporary document credits Gonsalvez with the authorship of 42 works, 22 in Sinhala, 15 in Tamil, four in Portuguese, and one in Dutch. Some traditions add four more in Sinhala and one more in Tamil. In Sinhala, he wrote both prose and poetry and provided the Catholics with ample material for their instruction and edification. His prose works range over a variety of subjects: holy scripture, theology, hagiography, asceticism, devotions, and apologetics. His best Sinhalese prose works are the *Deva Veda Puranaya,* which is a compendium of holy scripture and Catholic theology; the *Suvisesa Visadhanaya,* a commentary on the Gospel passages read on Sundays and on important feast days; and the *Veda Niti Visarjanaya,* a discourse on the last judgment arranged in dramatic form. Gonsalvez compiled four dictionaries, one of which is a Portuguese-Sinhala-Tamil lexicon.

Gonsalvez introduced the use of drama to teach religion. His style of drama was similar to the Tamil *nadagam* found in South India. The *Raja-tun-kattuwa,* which is the story of the three magi, and the *Mangala Geetaya* are two examples of drama which, following in the path set by the works of Gonsalvez, became popular among the Catholics in the 18th c.

Since Gonsalvez was a musician, he composed in Sinhala a large number of songs to be sung on festive occasions (see Music). The *Ananda Kalippuva* is a poem written to be sung in the traditional *vannam* style.

Although his main stage was in the Sinhala area, Gonsalvez's contribution to Tamil literature* in Sri Lanka is as important. *Christiyani Alayam* (the Christian Treasure House), *Deva Aruiveda Puranam* (a compendium of sacred history), and *Viyakula Pirasangam* (nine sermons on the passion of the Lord) are noteworthy. These books were copied on ollas and sent to the *muhuppus* (lay leaders) of various Catholic congregations.

The activities of Gonsalvez were an inspiration to Catholics in the 18th c. and even later. His contribution to Sinhala literature, drama, and music is remarkable, especially in view of the impact it had on the revival of Sinhala studies in the 19th c.

Bibliography

Perniola, V., *The History of the Catholic Church in Sri Lanka: The Dutch Period,* Vol. 2 (1983). • Don Peter, W. L. A., *Studies in Ceylon Church History* (1963).

G. P. V. SOMARATNA

Gordon, Andrew

(b. Putnam, New York, United States, 17 Sep 1828; d. Philadelphia, Pennsylvania, United States, 13 Aug 1887). Pioneer Presbyterian missionary in Pakistan*.

In 1853 the Associate Presbyterian* Church of North America, meeting in Pittsburgh, decided to send Gordon to begin mission work in India*. Though licensed to preach, Gordon was discouraged from leaving his home country for a foreign land by relatives, friends, and spouse. His wife, however, changed her mind when she was hit in the arm by a bullet. Realizing that she could have lost her life if it had struck her in the heart, she decided she must do something for the Lord. The couple set sail from New York on 28 Sep 1854 with their young daughter and Gordon's younger sister, Elizabeth Gordon, arriving in Calcutta on 13 Feb 1855. They traveled on to Saharanpur and stayed with I. J. Caldwell and his father, A. B. Caldwell, for four months, studying the language, learning and evaluating missionary strategies and efforts, and observing firsthand experienced workers witnessing and distributing literature at a fair. Gordon attended the annual meeting of the Ludhiana Mission of the American Presbyterian Church and gathered much that determined the character of the United Presbyterian Mission.

After consultation with friends, he decided to begin his work in Sialkot on 8 Aug 1855. Leaving his family at Saharanpur, he traveled north to Sialkot, visiting various mission stations en route. He met with some British officers at Sialkot Cantt who encouraged him to build a house and helped raise the funds for it when money from America was delayed. His family joined him in 1856. Two other ordained men and their wives joined them, and the Sialkot Mission was started.

According to Mary Jane Campbell, author of *In the Shadow of the Himalayas,* when Gordon entered Sialkot district there was not a single Christian in the entire population of 640,000. Gordon and his team preached from city to city and village to village, traveling as far as Jhelum and Zafarwal. They also opened schools and orphanages. Gordon baptized a Hindu convert, Ram Bhajan, and another named Chuhrah Johery in 1857. Later others also accepted Christ and many more were baptized.

Through the hard work of Gordon, the first presbytery, named Sialkot, was established. The work grew steadily and a synod was formed that today has 19 presbyteries and is the largest Protestant church in the country.

Bibliography

Gordon, Andrew, *Our India Mission* (1886). • Campbell, Mary Jane, *In the Shadow of the Himalayas* (1942). • Ullah, Barkat, *Saleeb Ke-Alumbardar* (1958). • Jamson, W. N., *The United Presbyterian Story* (1958).

ARTHUR JAMES

Gospel and Cultures

The intrinsic relation between the Gospel of Jesus Christ and cultures has been a central issue in the life of the church from its inception. The day of Pentecost marked the beginning of a dramatic process of the Spirit opening up all languages and cultures as worthy and necessary vehicles of meaningful expression of the story of God's love in Jesus Christ. It also meant a relativization of every cultural expression of the Gospel so that no one particular interpretation can claim to be the exclusive norm of the truth of the Gospel. While the "Jesus story" becomes the "good news" only as it speaks to a particular people and connects with their symbols, addresses their needs, and awakens their creative energies, as the story of "God's love" it can never be identified with any particular expression of it. There is then a double dimension to the relation between the Gospel and cultures, namely, the inaccessibility of the Gospel story apart from its necessary embodiment in a particular culture and yet its transcendence and inexhaustibility over all cultures. The heart of the Christian story, expressed in the words, "the Word became flesh," implies such an intrinsic and double relation.

Cultures are symbolic vehicles by which particular peoples experience and express meaning and organize their social relationships. It is the creative dimension of the human involving the entire way of life shared by a particular people; it is both inherited from the past and yet adapted, or reconstructed, by humans in history. It is the very milieu of human living and not just artifacts such as music* and sculptures. It is basically "a design for living" in terms of which a society adapts itself to its physical and social surroundings. Cultural symbols and social structures mutually imply and exert an impact upon each other.

It is *to* and *within* this complex, dynamic, and changing system of human symbols and power relations that the story of God's love in Christ comes as saving power. Hence the central question that lies at the heart of Christian proclamation is this: How in the encounter of the story of Jesus — always and necessarily embodied in a particular culture — and the story of a particular people, expressed in their cultural symbols, does God's love made manifest in Christ *become the Gospel*, the liberating good news for all.

But time and again in mission history a particular cultural expression of the Gospel has been mistakenly identified with the saving message itself. Further, the colonial might of the Western empires led to an unchallenged belief in the superiority of Western civilization and religion. European culture became the defining measure for all cultures. This led to an unconscious cultural captivity of the Gospel in the West and the enslavement of non-Western cultures and, in many instances in the South, to cultural genocide. Asian countries were no exception. In mission history the examples of Matteo Ricci* in China* and Roberto de Nobili* in India* are often highlighted as early attempts to achieve a more authentic relation between the Gospel and Asian cultures. But, by and large, vestiges of the captivity of the Gospel to a monolithic, Eurocentric culture may be discerned to this day. Even the best examples, until almost a few decades ago, amounted to no more than attempts at "repackaging" European cultural expressions of the Gospel — taken as its unchanging core in cultural idioms of Asia. Whether such attempts were defined as adaptation, translation, or indigenization, they were little more than translations of European cultural expressions of the faith of Western churches. The Gospel became nothing more than a "potted plant" in Asian soil, as D. T. Niles*, a leading Asian theologian, called it.

However, from the turn of the 20th c. there were signs of major changes all over Asia, intensified by a rapid process of renaissance of Asian cultures, struggles for political independence, and the struggle against colonialism* and Western cultural hegemony. In the West, the bankruptcy of the "Christian" culture of Europe was exposed in the two world wars. Further, devolution of church leadership to Asian Christians, local creative theological reflections, and increasingly louder and clearer Asian voices in world ecumenical gatherings all led to an intensive search for local expressions of the Gospel. From the late 1940s to this day, statements of the Christian Conference of Asia and the Catholic Federation of Asian Bishops* have called for a *deeper* and a *two-way* encounter between the Gospel and Asian cultures. The Ecumenical Association of Third World Theologians (EATWOT) provides a significant forum for exchange. Terms such as "contextualization*," mainly among Protestant churches, and "inculturation," primarily among the Roman Catholics, are used to describe the dynamic, two-way relation between the Gospel and culture.

In the encounter between the Gospel and cultures in Asia, there are at least three distinct aspects that stand out. First, religions and cultures in almost all parts of Asia form a single continuum; religions are the soul of Asian cultures. Therefore, the encounter of the Gospel within Asia necessarily involves an encounter with Asian religions, their myths and symbols, and scriptural texts.

Second, there is a new awareness of the critical role of the struggles of the poor and the oppressed within the last four decades. The irruption of the marginalized in Asian history and the cultures of the subaltern introduced many powerful concepts into the Asian Christian theological vocabulary. The movements of the subaltern Minjung* in Korea*, the Dalits* in India, the Burakumin (see Buraku) in Japan*, as well as Asian women everywhere have become critical to the definition of cultures and hence for Asian theological reflection. The production of radical symbols, such as stories, mask dances, and street theater, among the marginalized in Asia has been significant. Therefore, the rootedness of the Gospel in the lives of Asian people means its rootedness in the social movements of Asia's poor that is also predominantly religious. Third, as Asian theologians work primarily within a cosmic religiocultural matrix, link the doctrines of creation and redemption closely and intrinsically. Creation and redemption are not two separate activities of God. Relating creation to redemption in a single continuum leads Asian Christians to assess cultures more positively and to affirm the saving presence of God in them even before the story of Jesus ever reached Asia. Some even speak of the "gospel before the Gospel" to express this perception. They are uncomfortable with those Western theologies whose point of departure is the discontinuity between the Gospel and creation and whose notion of culture is primarily negative. Writings of Asian theologians such as C. S. Song (Taiwan*), Aloysius Pieris (Sri Lanka*), Kosuke Koyama (Japan), Kim Yong Bok (Korea), Chung Hyun Kyung (Korea), and Michael Amaladoss (India) illustrate this sort of radical point of departure in addressing the relation between Gospel and culture in Asia today.

Neither the term "Gospel" nor the term "culture" is referred to in a generic sense, as, for example, H. Richard Niebuhr treated the terms in his classic *Christ and Culture.* Cultures are always specific and therefore plural. Therefore, the approach is inductive and *a posteriori.* Further, if cultures are context-specific and people-centered, they are value-laden and dependent on the symbol-making power of people either in their struggle to liberate themselves or to conserve their status quo. Hence sociopolitical commitments are critical to a redefinition of the Gospel-culture relation. The term "Gospel," too, does not refer only to an unchanging constant but also to the dynamic in which the story of God's love in Jesus *becomes* the good news in the midst of people's struggle for liberation. Neither the Gospel nor culture can be reduced to atomized and disjoined "substances" or essences; rather, they are relational. That is, their reality and meaning are to be found in the interwovenness of people, their social realities, and God's presence in them. Therefore, the processes of inculturation are *integral* and *internal* to the lives of the people; they are not external or merely an intellectual exercise of a few. Further, cultures are not static and unchanging but dynamic; they are not homogenous but multilayered, complex, and increasingly hybrid. Cultures have been described as "webs of meaning" for this very reason. The encounter of the Gospel and Asian cultures, therefore, is also dynamic, multilayered, and pluralist. Liminality characterizes the process of inculturation; hence the process is ambiguous and creative at the same time.

Contemporary Asian discussions on Gospel and cultures address at least four distinct issues in varying degrees. The first issue has to do with the nature of the two-way relationship between the two. For many, not only can a culture open up new avenues for understanding the Gospel; it may also bring to light genuinely new and hitherto undiscovered dimensions. At the same time, like all human cultures, Asian cultures are ambiguous and contain aspects of human sin, and therefore they need to be challenged and transformed by the Gospel. It is critical to hold together the illuminating and enriching power of cultures and the affirming and transforming power of the Gospel. But for others, cultures have only an instrumental value; since they are fallen, the relationship is only one way in which Gospel critiques and transforms cultures. The second issue relates to the role of the Gospel in relation to the structures of Asian societies, particularly to the Asian struggles for cultural identity and community.

"Identity and community" has been an oft-repeated expression in much of the Asian discussion on the Gospel and cultures, as has been the term "people." What, for example, is the shape of a fresh articulation of the Gospel that challenges oppressive forces, whether of a dominant majority culture within or of globalization and neocolonialism from outside Asia? If Asian communities are increasingly torn apart by narrow differences of caste, religion, and language, what is the nature of Christian witness to the Gospel of liberation within Asian cultures?

Third, Asian Christians are addressing the critical issue of the relation between the plurality of religions and cultures and their interrelation. What is the nature of Christian faith, life, and worship that take seriously cultural and religious pluralism?

Finally, as Asian Christians share their life with one another across the plurality of Asian cultures and communicate with Christians in other parts of the world, the relation between the local and global, the contextual and catholic expressions of the Gospel becomes critical. What will be the shape of a crosscultural hermeneutics, which on the one hand takes local cultures and the rich diversity of theological expressions as a gift of the Spirit, and on the other helps promote a common sharing and a unity across cultures? In such a hermeneutic, what may be a possible set of criteria or signs of authenticity in terms of which theological expressions contrary to the spirit of the Gospel may be discerned and critiqued? Further, the question of syncretism is also addressed. Many in Asia argue that the formation of self-identity in general and religious identity in particular is inherently syncretistic. It is part of the process of growth, as is mutation, which may bring into being a radically new reality, a world of meaning. Therefore, as Raymundo Panikkar* advises, the question is not how to avoid syncretism, but what sort of syncretism is Asian theology engaged in; is it positive and life-generating or cancerous and death-dealing? M. M. Thomas has written about a "Christ-centered syncretism."

Asians have just begun making contributions to the discussion on the relation between the Gospel and cultures. The signs on the horizon are rich and augur well for a future when Asian Christians in communion with people out of "every tribe and every nation" will bring to God's throne the heritage of their cultures so that God may be all and in all.

Bibliography

Ariarajah, S. Wesley, *Gospel and Culture: An Ongoing Discussion within the Ecumenical Movement* (1994). •

Duraisingh, Christopher, ed., *Called to One Hope: Gospel in Diverse Cultures* (1998). • Francis, T. Dayanandan, and F. J. Balasundaram, *Asian Expressions of Christian Commitment* (1992). • Kim, Yong-Bock, *Messiah and Minjung* (1992). • Sanneh, Lamin, *Translating the Message: The Missionary Impact on Culture* (1991). • Scherer, James A., and S. B. Bevans, eds., *New Directions in Mission and Evangelization,* Vol. 3: *Faith and Culture* (1999). • Song, C. S., *Tell Us Our Names: Story Theology from an Asian Perspective* (1984). • Yeow, Choo Lak, ed., several volumes in the series Doing Theology with Asian Resources. See particularly *Doing Theology with Cultures of Asia* (1988) and *Theology and Cultures,* Vol. 2 (1995).

CHRISTOPHER DURAISINGH, with contributions from HUANG PO HO

Gospel of Thomas

An early collection of 114 sayings and short narratives attributed to Jesus.

The *Gospel of Thomas* has close relationships with the canonical Gospels and probably preceded them. Known earlier by name and selected citations, the integral Coptic text was discovered in 1945 at Nag Hammadi, where it survived as the second text in Codex II. It was quickly edited with translations. This helped scholars identify fragments of Greek versions and early Christian citations. The Coptic text is a translation of a Greek version. Fragments of three different Greek versions survive. One Greek papyrus manuscript (*P.Oxy.* 1) dates to about 200 C.E. The work is explicitly mentioned by Hippolytus (*Against Heresies* 5.7.20). The dates proposed by scholars for the composition range throughout the 2nd Christian c.

The text explicitly attributes the sayings to Jesus and states that the text is recorded by Didymus Judas Thomas, the traditional twin of Jesus. Thomas, according to the *Acts of Thomas* and to diverse early Christian texts, went to India* as a missionary. There are two contradictory traditions as to where he went in India: the one suggests he went to Cochin/Kerala before dying near modern Madras; the other places his mission in the Indus valley and also places his martyrdom there. It is probable, as has been suggested, that there are reflections of Indian religious traditions in the *Gospel of Thomas.* Its composition is usually placed at Edessa, the capital city of Osrhoene and the traditional site of the relics of Thomas. Certainly the radical asceticism of the *Gospel of Thomas* would have been congruent with religious expectations among early Syrian Christians in the context of Edessa. It has been suggested that the language of composition was Aramaic or Syriac (a dialect of Aramaic), from which it was translated into Greek and Coptic. However, no Syriac text has survived.

Bibliography

Wilson, R. McL., *Studies in the Gospel of Thomas* (1960). • Haenchen, E., *Die Bottschaft des Thomas-Evangelium* (1961). • Ménard, J. E., *L'Évangile selon Thomas* (NHS 5; 1975). Cameron, R., "The Gospel of Thomas," in *The Other Gospels,* ed. R. Cameron (1982). • Layton, B., "The School of St. Thomas," in *The Gnostic Scriptures,* ed. B. Layton (1987). • Meyer, Marvin, *The Gospel of Thomas: The Hidden Sayings of Jesus Translation, with Introduction, Critical Edition of the Coptic Text and Notes* (1992). • De Conink, April D., *Seek to See Him: Ascent and Vision Mysticism in the Gospel of Thomas* (1996). • Loader, William R. G., *Jesus' Attitude towards the law: A Study of the Gospels* (1997). • Patterson, Stephen J., *The Fifth Gospel: The Gospel of Thomas Comes of Age* (1998).

DAVID BUNDY

Gossner, Johannes Evangelista

(b. 1773; d. 1858). The son of a Catholic farmer near Ulm, South Germany, Gossner studied theology in an environment inspired by rationalism and was ordained in 1796. However, during the years he worked as a curate (1796-1803), he entered the circle around Johann Sailer (1751-1832), which emphasized Bible-based preaching and care of souls. This experience brought about a certain openness toward Protestantism. So, in 1802, Gossner was temporarily suspended. But in 1803 he was rehabilitated and appointed a parish priest in Bavaria. In this function, Gossner kept his distance from the institutional church (the hierarchy) and was in close touch with Protestant revivalist groups in Switzerland and Germany. Through these contacts, he became acquainted with mission work outside Europe. In this period, he started his literary activity, which was mainly pastoral in character but included a translation of the New Testament (1815) followed by several explanatory volumes.

By the rising tide of the Catholic Restoration, Gossner was driven out of Bavaria and Germany and even from Russia, where he had worked as an influential preacher in St. Petersburg (1820-24). In 1826, he went over to the Evangelical (Lutheran) Church. From 1829 to 1847, he served as a minister in the Prussian capital, Berlin. As an evangelical pastor, he also experienced difficulties from church leaders. But around him gathered a circle of friends from all layers of society — in Berlin itself and in Germany and abroad.

In Berlin, Gossner became active in the field of home mission and mission abroad. He founded a hospital which was served by a sisterhood he inspired. In 1831, he became a board member of the *Berliner Mission* (founded in 1824). But his old aversion to institutions resulted in his resignation from the board in 1836. In the same year, 12 young men, mostly artisans, came to him to be prepared for a missionary calling. In contrast to the practice of most missionary societies of those times, Gossner had them continue in their professions, teaching them in the evening hours. When they had completed their studies, they were handed over to existing missionary societies. Other groups followed, and in 1842 a new society was officially founded and named the

Gossnersche Missionsgesellschaft, the Gossner Mission Society. Gossner wanted it to have only a minimum of institutionalization. Particularly, the missionary candidates should continue in their professions, receiving instruction in the evening hours. And even on the mission field they should evangelize while earning their own keep in their own professions or by trading. This way, Gossner reasoned, mission work could be less costly and more spontaneous.

The Gossner Mission provided missionaries for Australia (1837), Oceania, Indonesia*, India*, Africa, and America. It assumed a more direct responsibility for two mission fields in India: Bihar (Ganges Valley) and the Adivasi territory in the hill country west of Calcutta (Chota Nagpur). As a consequence of World War I, the Ganges field had to be surrendered to others, but the work among the Adivasi or Kol led to the institution in 1919 of the Gossner Evangelical Lutheran Church of Chota Nagpur and Assam.

Indonesia was the other territory in Asia where Gossner missionaries were active. In close collaboration with the Dutch pastor O. G. Heldring (1804-76), a number of Gossner's pupils were sent to that country as "Christian laborers." J. G. Geissler and C. W. Ottow started missionary work in Irian (1855), which after Geissler's death (1870) was taken over by the *Utrechtsche Zendingsvereniging,* a Dutch society. E. T. Steller (1834-97) and several others Gossnerians revitalized from 1857 the neglected congregations on the Sangir Islands and in that way became the fathers of the *Gereja Masehi Injili Sangir-Talaud,* the Christian Evangelical Church of the Sangir and Talaud Islands (between Celebes and Mindanao). But the work of other Christian laborers in Celebes* and Java led to no tangible results.

Bibliography

Holsten, Walter, *Johannes Evangelista Gossner: Glaube und Gemeinde* (1949). • Kamma, F. C., *"Ajaib di Mata Kita" Masalah komunikasi antara Timur dan Barat dilihat dari sudut pengalaman selama seabad pekabaran Injil di Irian Jaya* (1981). • Reenders, H., *Alternatieve Zending. Ottho Gerhard Heldring (1804-1876) en de verbreiding van het christendom in Nederlands-Indie* (1991).

Th. van den End

Gowing, Peter G.

(b. 1930; d. 1983). American scholar, author, lecturer in the Philippines*.

Gowing received his doctor of theology degree in 1960 in Boston and his doctor of philosophy in 1969 in Syracuse. He was an American church history and religions professor and advocate of Muslim-Christian understanding and relations. Gowing served as a United Church Board for World Mission (UCBWM) fraternal worker and taught at Silliman Divinity School, Philippines, from 1960 to 1971; at Trinity Theological College, Singapore, as South East Asia Graduate School of Theology (SEAGST) regional professor from 1971 to 1974; and then moved to Marawi City in Mindanao to head the Dansalan Research Center.

A man of diverse interests, Gowing was marked by a deep love for teaching, profound scholarship, dynamic preaching ability, earnest friendship, and a witty sense of humor. His introductory letter to Silliman University noted that he and his mission board were "appropriately grateful that I am single." In 1968, he wrote, "It is a great joy to be a teacher — to connect with the minds of other human beings, to learn with and from them. I have a toothache and before long I will have to take courage and seek a dentist. I should be grateful that there are dentists; but for the life of me, I can't figure out why anyone would want to be a dentist when he could be a teacher!"

A prolific writer with articles appearing in many international journals, Gowing is best remembered for his *Mosque and Moro* (1964), *Islands Under the Cross* (1967), and *Mandate in Moroland* (1970).

Bibliography

Sitoy, T. V., Jr., "Peter Gordon Gowing (1930-1983): In Memoriam," *Silliman Journal* XXX.1-2.

T. Valentino Sitoy, Jr.

Great Conference, Shanghai

Greatest Protestant missionary conference held in Shanghai from 25 Apr to 8 May 1907.

During the 1890 missionary conference, the year 1900 was chosen for the next conference. However, several factors led to its delay, and subsequently 1907 was decided upon, as it coincided with the centenary celebration of Protestant mission work in China*. About 1,100 delegates participated in this conference: 361 seats were assigned to mission bodies; 139 delegates were involved in preparatory work, and 604 guests were invited, including 66 delegates representing their headquarters mission board. During the opening ceremony, two chairmen were elected: John C. Gibson and Arthur H. Smith*. There were another eight vice-chairmen and general secretary George H. Bondfield to assist them.

Prior to the conference, 12 topics were selected by consensus, and subcommittees were formed to discuss them. During the conference, the subcommittee chairmen would read their drafts aloud; discussions followed and alterations were made; the final drafts were passed during the conference. The 12 topics included the Chinese church, Chinese pastors, education, evangelistic work, women's work, education for women, Christian literacy* work, ancestor worship*, medical* evangelistic work, the Bible*, cooperation and coordination, and missionaries and natives. During the discussion of the last topic, Shanghai governor Dao Dong Dao Tai, who represented the governor for Kiangsi and Kiangsu, gave a speech pleading that the difference in cultural understanding between China and the Occident not lead to riots and fights. The conference also passed six memoranda and 12 appendices.

Bibliography

Latourette, Kenneth Scott, *A History of Christian Missions in China* (1929).

CHINA GROUP

Grimaldi, Philippus Maria

(b. 1639; d. 1712). Italian Jesuit* missionary who worked in the Qing government during the reign of Emperor Kangxi.

Grimaldi, who joined the Society of Jesus in 1657, arrived in Macau in 1659 and was consecrated a priest. In 1664, following the Tang Ruowang (Schall von Bell*) Affair, all missionaries were confined in Guangzhou. A Dominican* friar known by his Chinese name, Min Ming Wo, escaped in 1669. Grimaldi adopted his name and lived in the same house the Dominican had lived in before. Chinese history differentiates between the two by referring to the escapee as the "true Min Ming Wo" and Grimaldi as "the false Min Ming Wo." In 1671, Kangxi allowed missionaries to return to their respective places and also took into his service those with a good knowledge of calendrical science. Through Ferdinand Verbiest's* recommendation, Grimaldi was assigned to Beijing as his assistant and became his successor (even though he was out of the country) as director of the calendrical bureau when Verbiest died in 1688.

Trusted by Kangxi, Grimaldi accompanied the emperor when he went out to visit his empire in 1683 and 1685 and was sent on a diplomatic mission to Russia in 1687. He returned to Beijing in 1694 and was rewarded by the emperor for his services. Although not directly involved in church mission, Grimaldi's 40 years of service in China* was an important reason for Kangxi's liberal attitude toward church mission in China.

Bibliography

Treadgold, Donald W., *The West in Russia and China: China, 1582-1949* (1973).

CHINA GROUP, translated by DAVID WU

Grooff, Jacobus

(b. ?; d. Surinam, 1852). Apostolic vicar of Batavia (Jakarta) from 1842 to1846 forced by Dutch Governor-General J. J. Rochussen to leave the mission because the bishop claimed the exclusive right to appoint and transfer pastors.

Grooff was apostolic prefect of Surinam (1827-42) before being appointed titular bishop of Canea and first apostolic vicar of Batavia. With four other missionaries, he arrived in Batavia in Apr 1845. In September, he suspended the pastors of Batavia, Semarang, and Surabaya because of their "worldly behavior and non-Catholic opinions." The communities of Semarang and Surabaya protested and rejected the appointed successors, locking the churches and forcing the new priests to return to Batavia. The governor-general accused Grooff of acting "uncolonially" because he suspended the pastors without seeking government approval. Every institution in the colony, churches included, was considered dependent on the government, without whose permission no office could be accepted or changed. Furthermore, no clergyman could conduct a public service (even missionaries passing through to other countries) without prior approval from the colonial authorities.

The bishop protested in the name of freedom of religion, acknowledged five years earlier by the Dutch constitution. The governor-general replied that the constitution had not been made public in the colony. He accused Grooff of trying to make the Catholic Church independent from the government. The bishop politely refused to hand over copies of the documents of suspension and to offer proof that he had the legal right to appoint new pastors in Semarang and Surabaya, regarding his own actions as internal church matters according to canon law and himself as answerable only to the holy see.

At the end of 1845, the government prohibited the four new missionaries from executing any public church activity; the bishop responded by refusing to lift the suspensions even temporarily. Meeting the governor-general officially, Grooff declined to make a decision concerning church matters on pressure from outside the church. The governor-general forbade the bishop to conduct any further church function and ordered him to leave the colony within 14 days. The bishop protested that he had been sent by the pope in consultation with the Dutch king. Convinced that he was only performing his duty, he refused the three days' grace to reconsider his decision. The decision of the governor-general was made public the next day and there were strong reactions. Taking leave from the governor, Grooff and his four priests departed on a ship, leaving only one priest in the whole of the Dutch East Indies (1846), and he was later killed by his homesick Javanese servant in Padang (Sumatra). The suspended priests were quickly deserted by their followers and the government. This struggle for church autonomy came at a very high price.

After returning to the Netherlands, Grooff was rehabilitated and appointed apostolic visitor of Surinam, where he died in 1852. An official agreement between the holy see and the Dutch government in 1847 decided that the apostolic vicar had the right to appoint and transfer pastors, but he ought to inform the governor first and request the government's recognition of the rights and benefits pertaining to their offices. Salaries and expenses for travel were also fixed. Since 1846, the Catholic Church in Indonesia has been free from government interference in its internal affairs. The short, though tough, struggle had proven beneficial to the church.

Bibliography

Van Aerensbergen, A. I., *Chronologisch oversicht* (1934). • Vriens, G., "Wilayah tunggal prefektur-vikariat abad de-

19 dan ke-20," in *Sejarah Gereja Katolik Indonesia* II (1972).
ADOLF HEUKEN

Gurkhali Christians, Myanmar

(Burma). Ethnic Nepali (many of whom are former Gurkha soldiers or descendants of Gurkhas) Christians.

Most of the estimated 250,000 Gurkhali in Myanmar* today immigrated from Nepal* or India* between the 1880s and World War II* and formed settled communities in the hilly tribal areas of Myanmar (Burma). There was extensive Christian mission work in Myanmar until all foreign missionaries were expelled during the 1960s, but the Gurkhali were largely overlooked, and there were only isolated individual conversions, mostly of men who married local Christian tribal women. Since the 1980s, primarily through the burden and personal effort of Gurkhali converts themselves, numerous Gurkhali villages have been evangelized, and Gurkhali congregations and Sunday schools have started in at least five different areas of the country from Yangon to Myitkyina.

As early as 1908, American Baptist* missionaries in Burma had requested Nepali New Testaments and other literature* from the Church of Scotland's Eastern Himalaya Mission in Darjeeling. Their first Gurkhali convert, Lal Singh Basnet, was commissioned as an evangelist among his fellow Gurkhas in 1917, but his efforts lasted only a few years and he returned to India. In the 1960s, George Bahadur became the second known Gurkhali Christian worker, this time in conjunction with the Assembly of God (AOG) Mission in Mogok, but by the 1980s he had given up because of the lack of response. A few years later, a third Gurkhali convert, Harry Bahadur, came forward for ministry with the AOG in Mogok, and after receiving theological training in India he was ordained in 1993.

The 1980s marked a dramatic upswing in the spread of Christianity among Burmese-Gurkhali. The first Nepali-language fellowship had been organized in Yangon by four Gurkhali Christian converts in 1978. B. P. Rai, one of the founders and an ex-Gurkha soldier, established the Gurkha Christian Mission and began annual evangelistic tours throughout Myanmar which have made him the most widely traveled Gurkhali evangelist in the country. Although not ordained until 1994, he served as pastor of a congregation in his home since the baptism of 10 Gurkhali converts in 1980. Another of the founders, Jit Bahadur Limbu, was ordained by the Karen* Baptists in 1980 and serves as pastor of a mixed ethnic church in Mobi, outside of Yangon.

In 1985, the only non-Gurkhali to initiate evangelistic outreach among Gurkhalis, Rev. Dee Zee Daung, a Kachin* Church of Christ pastor, started working among the Gurkhali villages surrounding Maymyo (Pyin-Oo Lwin). The results included several conversions and the establishment of a small congregation. In the meantime, through the initial testimony of a high-caste Gurkhali young man from near Myitkyina (in upper Myanmar) who returned home following his conversion in Bangkok, another Gurkhali congregation was formed. It was taken on by the Myitkyina Zonal Baptist Convention of the Kachin Baptists as the Gurkha Baptist Mission Center, and the first church building for Gurkhalis was built in 1990. Kumar Limbu, sent for theological training by the Kachin Baptists to become their first Gurkhali pastor, graduated in March 1995.

From fewer than 10 Gurkhali Christians in all of Myanmar before 1980, there are now over 300 scattered throughout the country. There are four ordained Gurkhali pastors and several evangelists. The first links with the church in Nepal were made in the early 1990s, and a tenuous flow of much needed Nepali-language materials, expertise, and Christian training opportunities was begun.

Bibliography

Perry, Cindy, "The History of the Expansion of Protestant Christianity among the Nepali Diaspora" (doctoral dissertation, University of Edinburgh, 1994). • Sowards, Genevieve and Erville, eds., *Burma Baptist Chronicle* (1963).
CINDY PERRY

Gützlaff, Karl Friedrich August

(Guo Shi Li) (b. Poland, 1803; d. 1851). First German Lutheran* missionary to China*.

A tailor's son, Gützlaff, or Guo Shi Li, was educated at the school of Johannes Janicke, a Moravian preacher in Berlin. He did further studies at Rotterdam. His interest in China grew after a meeting with Robert Morrison* in England. He sailed to Siam in 1824 as a missionary of the Netherlands Missionary Society (NMS). Within three years, he had translated the Bible* into Thai and had learned the Fujian dialect from the Chinese settlers there. He went to Batavia (Jakarta), Indonesia*, in 1826, where he met Walter Henry Medhurst* and learned Malay and some Chinese dialects. He married Mary Newell, an Englishwoman, at Malacca, Malaysia, in 1829. She died shortly after and left him a considerable inheritance. He married Mary Wanstall, a cousin of Harry Parkes, the future British minister at Beijing, in 1834. The second Mrs. Gützlaff ran a school and a home for the blind in Macau. She died in 1849. Gützlaff's third marriage was to Dorothy Gabriel in England in 1850.

Gützlaff broke off with the NMS in 1828 because they refused to send him to China. He made several trips in the 1830s, sailing along the coast of China, traveling as far north as Tianjin, distributing Christian literature*. He recorded his voyages in *A Journal of Three Voyages along the Coast of China, 1831, 1832 and 1833.* When Morrison died in 1834, Gützlaff replaced him as an interpreter and secretary of the East India Company (EIC) in Guangzhou. While in Macau, Gutzlaff translated the Gospel of John and the Epistles of John into Japanese with the assistance of three Japanese, Otokichi, Kyukichi, and Iwakichi, who were shipwrecked apprentice sailors

Gützlaff, Karl Friedrich August

who drifted to Cape Flattery, Washington, USA. They were sent to Macau by John Mclaughlin of the Hudson Bay Company, a British trading firm. The manuscripts were sent to a printing firm in Singapore*.

Gützlaff was the magistrate of Ningbo in 1841 and Zhenjiang in 1842. He helped the EIC to negotiate the Treaty of Nanjing in 1842 and 1843. Gützlaff then settled in Hong Kong*. Forbidden to enter China by the treaty agreements, Gützlaff formed the Chinese Union in 1844 to employ Chinese evangelists to work in Guangdong. His aim was to have Christian bodies or unions (which would be assisted by their counterpart associations in Europe) in every province. He raised enthusiastic support from Germany through his voluminous writings, but in China, to his disappointment, Gützlaff discovered that many of the Chinese preachers were unconverted opium-smokers and criminals who had duped him by selling the evangelistic literature to the printer, who then resold it to Gützlaff.

Gützlaff died in Hong Kong at age 48 before he could correct the situation, but he was instrumental in attracting other German missionaries to China. His writings on China included the two-volume work *Sketch of Chinese History* and *China Opened.*

Bibliography

Waley, Arthur, *The Opium War Through Chinese Eyes* (1958). • Schlyter, Herman, *Karl Gützlaff als Missionar in China* (1946); *Der China-Missionar Karl Gützlaff und seine Heimatbasis* (1956).

China Group

Haciendas. *See* Friars and the Land Controversy

Hadiwijono, Harun

(b. Wirosari-Grobogan, Central Java, Indonesia, 1915; d. 1983). After he finished his secondary studies, Hadiwijono studied theology in a small theological* school in Yogyakarta until 1941. After that, he rarely ventured out of Yogyakarta. He became a Bible teacher in a Dutch Protestant Mission Hospital. There he also met his wife. In 1946 he was ordained a minister in the Javanese Christian Church of Gondokusuman. In the same year, he started to work as a teacher at Duta Wacana United Theological College until his death at the age of 68. From 1950 to 1952, he continued his theological studies at the Free University, Amsterdam. From 1960 to 1962, he stayed in Serampore, India*, to study Hinduism* and Buddhism*. In 1967, he received his doctorate in theology, from the Free University.

In Indonesia, Hadiwijono is known for his two books, *Man in the Present Javanese Mysticism* and *Iman Kristen.* The first book is his Amsterdam dissertation. He published in Indonesian various chapters of this dissertation, and one of them became a textbook for many seminaries on Javanese Mysticism*. Christians and others have benefited from his thorough knowledge of Javanese mysticism. According to one of his closest students, Rev. Budyanto, in his youth Hadiwijono himself was a follower of *Kebatinan* (Javanese mysticism) but then converted to Christianity under the influence of Rev. Wolterbeek, a missionary whom he regarded highly.

Iman Kristen, which developed from Hadiwijono's lecture notes on dogmatics, runs more than 500 pages and has been through many reprints and editions. Hadiwijono still owes much to the Barthian tradition in this work. The influence of the Dutch Reformed theologian G. Berkouwer can be seen in his dogmatics. In his emphasis on the acts of God rather than his essence, one can detect the influence of the biblical theology movement. Even so, Hadiwijono managed to give the book his own personal flavor, and thus many came to consider *Iman Kristen* as the first contextual work on Protestant theology in Indonesia. However, it is not a contextual work in the strict sense. Although he touched on many aspects of the Indonesian context (Islam, Javanese mysticism, Roman Catholicism*, the Pentecostal* movements), Hadiwijono dealt with them in a critical and often confrontational way.

Although he showed himself a true pupil of the Dutch Reformed tradition, in the course of the years Hadiwijono became more open to new horizons. He was repeatedly elected rector of Duta Wacana (1963-64; 1968-72; 1975-78; 1978-80). Under his leadership, Duta Wacana grew from a small denominational seminary into an ecumenical one supported by 10 churches, including the Mennonites*. He encouraged his students to seek further ways to theologize in Indonesia, with the result that almost all of the lecturers at Duta Wacana are his former students, and Yogyakarta nowadays is regarded as one of the centers of contextual* theology in Indonesia.

In addition to the books mentioned above, Hadiwijono wrote many works on theology and spirituality*, both in Indonesian and Javanese. He also wrote works on both Western and Eastern philosophy, and he preached every Sunday at the Gondokusuman church just across the street from his house in the seminary precinct. Although many regarded him with awe, he remained a very humble person.

Bibliography

Hoekema, A. G., *Denken in dynamisch evenwicht. De wordingsgeschiedenis van de nationale protestantse theologie in Indonesie (ca. 1860-1960),* Series Mission No. 8 (1994) (Indonesian edition: *Berpikir dalam deseimbangan yang dinamis: Sejarah lahirnya teologi Protestan nasional di Indonesia (sekitar 1860-1960)* [1997]) (Thinking in a Dynamic Equilibrium. The Genesis of National Protestant Theology in Indonesia).

E. G. Singgih

Hakka Mission, Taiwan

"Hakka people" refers back to a segment of Han-Chinese who lived during the Sung Dynasty. Hakka people are rightly called sojourners because of the many times they have had to leave their homes and migrate elsewhere. "Hakka" literally means "guest family," probably indicative of how the Hakkas were perceived by other local ethnic groups, that is, as guests or visitors from another province. As a sojourning people, the Hakkas experienced five great migrations from A.D. 317 to the 1800s.

The earliest Hakkas to migrate to Taiwan* were the few who came under Emperor Koxinga, when he fled there from China* at the fall of the Ming Dynasty in 1645. During the reign of Emperor Kangxi (1661-1722), Taiwan came under the administrative authority of the Qing Dynasty. Around 1686-87, the Hakkas began to migrate in large numbers to Taiwan. Through successive migrations from Guangdong Province, the Hakka settled in southern Taiwan, then central Taiwan, and finally in the north of the island.

Today, the largest concentration of the Hakka people in Taiwan is in the north, especially in Taoyuan, Hsinchu, and Mioali counties. There are also significant numbers of Hakka in the southern counties of Pingtung and Kaosiung, as well as in cities like Taipei, Taichung, Kaosiung, Hualien, Taitung, and Nantou. There are three to four million Hakka people, comprising about 15 percent of Taiwan's total population. This makes the Hakka the largest minority group in the country.

Modern Christian mission in Taiwan dates back to 1865 in the south and 1872 in the north. Thomas Barclay (south) and George L. Mackay* (north) are both known to have visited and done early pioneering evangelistic work in Hakka areas. As a result of their work and others who came after them, the Hakka churches in Taiwan before 1945 were all affiliated with the Presbyterian* Church. After the end of World War II*, other Christian denominations came to Taiwan from China, resulting in the presence of more than one church in Hakka towns and some smaller villages.

In 1978, the Hakka churches of Hong Kong*, Malaysia*, Thailand*, and Taiwan organized the World Hakka Evangelistic Association. In 1985, the Bible* Society in Taiwan started translation for a Hakka Bible using the "dynamic equivalence" method. On 8 Aug 1993, the New Testament and Psalms were published.

In 1995, there were about 100 Hakka churches in Taiwan, with 31 congregations within the Presbyterian Church, 52 spread over 11 other Christian denominations, and 17 assembly halls belonging to the Little Flock. The total of about 7,000 Christians was a mere .23 percent of the lower estimate of three million Hakka people in Taiwan, making them the largest unreached people group in the country.

CHEN JOHN CHHONG-FAT

Hall, J. Andrew

(b. 1867; d. 1960). Canadian-born medical missionary to the Philippines*.

The pioneer Protestant medical* missionary in the Philippines, Hall arrived with his wife in 1899 and helped open the Presbyterians' Iloilo mission station. Ordained in 1901, Hall established in that year the first Protestant hospital in the Philippines, introduced modern medicine and sanitation, and helped stamp out a cholera epidemic in Panay Island in 1901-3. He became so popular that, when he would leave Panay for mission business elsewhere, many refused to go to the hospital or even to church until he returned.

The Halls pioneered in nursing education, graduating the first three Filipino nurses in 1909. Moving to Leyte in 1925, Hall rehabilitated Bethany Mission Hospital in Tacloban, concentrated on combating yaws, and healed 18,000 people of this dreadful disease before retiring in 1937.

Bibliography

Laubach, F. C., *People of the Philippines* (1925). • Hall, J. A., and F. O. Smith, *Survey of Medical Missions in the Philippines* (1960). • Kwantes, A. C., *Presbyterian Missionaries in the Philippines* (1989). • Sitoy, T. V., Jr., *Several Springs, One Stream* (1992).

T. VALENTINO SITOY, JR.

Halmahera

(with Ternate). Halmahera is the largest island of the North Moluccas (18,000 sq. km.) with approximately 300,000 inhabitants.

Off the coast of Halmahera are the tiny islands Ternate and Tidore, which in the 15th c. embraced Islam* and became the dominant powers in the region, while most Halmaherans kept to the tribal religion. In 1522, the Portuguese founded a trading post on Ternate and from there brought the Christian faith to Halmahera. The Christian community, which in 1565 was said to number 80,000, suffered from bouts of persecution, which intensified after the Portuguese were defeated by Ternate in 1574. The Dutch, who arrived around 1600, were not interested in saving the remnants of Christianity on Halmahera. Two-and-a-half centuries later, in 1866, the pioneer missionary H. van Dijken (1866-1900) established a mission in the north of the island. Baptism was administered on the profession of personal faith and after years of religious instruction; the converts assembled in a Christian village, Duma, where a Western type of Christianity was practiced. Their numbers were small, but Van Dijken (a former farmer) gained much goodwill for the mission by his agricultural labors. A. Hueting (1896-1915 in Halmahera) used a different method, which led to a rapid growth of Christianity. He was supportive of a mass* movement among the Tobelo tribe, which was seen by missionaries and colonialists as a strike against the Muslim sultan of Ternate. With regard to indigenous culture *(adat*)* Hueting used a selective approach. (See Contextualization.)

The church grew steadily until World War II* but remained dependent on the mission, which did little or nothing to prepare indigenous church leaders and create an organizational framework. The war brought occupation by the Japanese and internment of the Dutch missionaries (1942). The Japanese closed the church buildings, imprisoned a number of native church leaders, and even forbade Christianity, reasoning that it was not in line with Asian culture. Thereupon, a number of Christians founded the independent Protestant Church of Halmahera (GPH), which was recognized by the Japanese, who then reopened the church buildings. However, the Christians on the west coast did not join the GPH. The rift was not healed until 1949, when the *Gereja Masehi Injili di Halmahera* (GMIH) was founded, with a membership of 30,000. By 1965 this number had doubled through natural growth, conversion, and the immigration of Christians from neighboring islands. With the coup d'etat of 1965, when the government pressed the remaining adherents of tribal religions to embrace one of the five permitted religions, there was quick growth by conversion. (See also Christian Evangelical Church in Halmahera.)

Besides the GMIH, there are several smaller Christian communities on Halmahera: Pentecostals*, Baptists*, and Seventh-Day Adventists*. In Ternate, there is a large congregation of the Protestant Church of the Moluccas*. The Roman Catholic* Church has several parishes and a small convent of sisters in Tobelo.

The non-Christian population is mostly Muslim. Owing to the numerous family ties between Christians and Muslims, relations between the two religions are generally harmonious. Ternate has remained predominantly Muslim, while Halmahera is mainly Christian.

Bibliography

Haire, James, *The Character and Theological Struggle of the Church in Halmahera, Indonesia, 1941-1979* (1981). • Magany, M. Th., *Bahtera Injil di Halmahera* (1984). • Fransz, A. L., *Suatu survey mengenai: Gereja Masehi Injili Halmahera* (Benih yang Tumbuh IX) (1976). • Van den End, Th., *Ragi Carita*, 2 Vols. (1993). • *Handbook of Reformed Churches Worldwide* (1999).

H. G. Schuurman

Hamel, Hendrik

(b. Netherlands, 1630; d. 1692). A Dutch crewman who introduced the country of Korea* to the people of Europe through his writings, Hamel was the second known Westerner to come to Korea.

Hamel landed at Quelpart Island (now Chejoo Island, the largest island in Korea, located in the south) with 65 other crewmen after a shipwreck in Jan 1653. He and his company were on the way to Japan to trade. In May 1654, he was sent to Seoul with his company. The Korean government made them serve in the Korean army. Years later, Hamel and other friends were sent to the town of Yeosu, a harbor at the southern tip of Korea.

After spending 13 years in prison, Hamel and eight other friends escaped from their compound and arrived in Nagasaki, Japan, by boat in Sep 1666. Through the Netherlands trade office in Nagasaki, Hamel finally returned to his homeland in Jul 1668. On the basis of his experiences in Korea, Hamel wrote two books: *An Account of the Shipwreck of a Dutch Vessel on the Coast of the Isle of Quelpart* and *The Description of the Kingdom of Korea*. In the first book, he briefly wrote about the story of his shipwreck and prisoner's life in Korea. In the other book, he introduced many aspects of Korea: geography, government, education, industry, agriculture, jurisdiction, currency, taxation, climate, family life, religions, etc. As a result of the publication of the books, many people in Europe became interested in the Orient and read them with much interest.

Hamel was a member of the Dutch Reformed Church, but he never preached the Gospel in Korea. Perhaps he was not interested in missions, or his situation did not permit him to evangelize. Thus, he made no contribution to Christian missions in Korea.

Bibliography

Churchill, J., *A Collection of Voyages and Travels*, 6 vols. (1732). • Lee Byong Do, *A Story of Hamel's Shipwreck* (1954). • *Encyclopedia of Christianity* (in Korea) (1994).

Kim In Soo

Han Kyung Chik

(b. 29 Dec 1902). Han entered O-san High School and was greatly influenced by such national leaders as the elder Lee Seung Hoon, a patriot and founder of the school, and the elder Cho Man Sik, the school's principal. After Han graduated, he entered Soong Sil College (Union Christian College), which was founded by the Presbyterian* Church, United States of America. He went to the United States and studied at Emporia College in Kansas, majoring in liberal arts, from 1925 to 1929. After this, he studied at Princeton Theological Seminary, where he learned both Presbyterian theology and tradition. Upon graduation from the seminary, he discovered he was suffering from tuberculosis and had to spend about three years in a sanatorium in New Mexico, and then in Denver, Colorado. He returned to Korea* in 1932 and became pastor of the Second Presbyterian Church in Sineuju, Pyung-buk.

After Korea's emancipation from Japan*, Han tried to form a political party (the Christian Democratic Party), but the Communist government of Kim Il Sung suppressed it. He fled to South Korea and founded Yong Nak Presbyterian Church with some of his old church members. This church grew rapidly with refugees from North Korea and became the largest Presbyterian church in the world, whose members number around 60,000.

Han became a notable leader not only in the church but also in civil life. He served as moderator of the Korean Presbyterian Church and in many major posts in ecumenical circles. He devoted himself to evangelizing Korea and worked with Bob Pierce, who had organized World Vision* to help refugees* of the Korean War. He also worked with Billy Graham, Bill Bright, and Carl Henry in evangelical activities in Korea.

Han founded several schools through his church and became the chairman of the board of trustees of the Presbyterian Theological Seminary and Soong Sil University.

Han received honorary degrees and prizes from Emporia College (doctor of divinity, 1948), Yonsei University (doctor of divinity, 1956), and Soongjun University (D.Phil., 1977). The Korean government gave him its National Award in 1970, and he received a Templeton Award, a world-famous prize given to religious leaders.

Throughout his life, Han followed a three-point motto: evangelism, education, and social service. His theological position would not be considered radical or fundamentalist; he always tried to follow biblical principles. His sermons were Bible-centered, practical messages related to everyday life, encouraging listeners to practice peace, love, and reconciliation. He was a strong supporter of the ecumenical* movement with an evangelical mind. As a friend described him, he was a successful pastor, broad-minded ecumenist, strong patriot with a Christian spirit, and reformer of the nation.

Bibliography

The Christian Encyclopedia, Vol. XIII (1986). • *History of 25 Years of the Yong Nak Presbyterian Church* (1983). • Hahn Sung-Hong, *Han Kyung Chik Moksaeui Saengewa Sasang* (The Life and Thought of Han Kyung Chik) (1993). RHEE JONG-SUNG, translated by KIM IN SOO

Han Mac Tu

(Nguyen Trong Tri) (b. Dong Hoi, 22 Sep 1912; d. Qui Hoa, 11 Nov 1940). Widely regarded as the most accomplished Vietnamese Catholic poet of the 20th c.

Han was born into a Roman Catholic* family. After his father's death in 1926, his mother sent him to the Christian Brothers Pellerin High School in Hue. But Han soon found the curriculum, especially courses in mathematics and science, utterly at odds with his poetic muse and, over the opposition of his family, dropped out of school.

Already at age 15, under the pen name of Minh Due Thi, Han began composing poems with his older brother Nguyen Ba Nhan. While at Pellerin, under the pen name of Phong Tran, some of his poems were published in newspapers and journals such as *Saigon* and *Phu Nu Tan Van.* Looking for employment, Han Mac Tu went to Saigon in the early 1930s, where he worked for various journals under the pen name of Le Thanh. In 1934, he was appointed to the staff of *Saigon,* then one of the most widely read newspapers in the country, and put in charge of the literature section. He also wrote for *Trong Khue Phong, Dong Duong Tap Chi,* and *Tan Thoi* and once again changed his pen name, this time to Han Mac Tu, by which he is known to posterity.

Toward the end of 1936, Han discovered that he was stricken with leprosy*. Terrified and devastated, he cut off all contacts with his friends and withdrew to Go Boi, a small village some 10 miles from Qui Khon. In addition to physical pains, Han was also emotionally crushed by the abandonment of his girlfriend, Mong Cam, despite her protestations of lifelong fidelity, some six months after the onset of his illness. Fortunately, in 1938, a woman by the name of Le Mai, who had left her family in Thanh Hoa because she did not agree to her arranged marriage and who had corresponded with Han, came to his home, stayed for three months, and surrounded him with unconditional love, admiration, and financial assistance. As his disease worsened, Han was forcibly transported by the health department to the leprosarium in Qui Hoa on 20 Sep 1940, where he died on 11 Nov 1940 at the age of 28.

In his 10-year career as a poet, Han went through a series of noticeable developments. In his youth, he composed his poems in the T'ang poetic tradition, observing its strict conventions. Then, in the 1930s, he took part in the romantic revolution which broke away from staid literary rules and exalted the individual and feelings. This became known as the "new poetry" (his "mad poetry" [*tho dien*], together with Tan Da's "crazy poetry" [*tho ngong*], and Vu Hoang Chuong's "drunk poetry" [*tho say*]). In his romantic period, he published two important collections of poems: *Gai que* (Country Girl, 1936) and *Dau thuong* (Suffering, 1937). Finally, in the last four years of his life and as a result of his fatal illness and isolation, Han developed a new genre, namely, Christian, and more specifically, Roman Catholic poetry.

With his poems of the Catholic period Han achieved his greatest reputation. These poems (which he called *tho dao hanh* [religious-pious poetry] and *tho cau nguyen* [praying poetry]) were published in two collections: *Xuan Nhu Y* (Spring According to Your Wish) and *Thuong Thanh Khi* (Air on High). Of these poems, Han said: "It is only in moments when I suffer in my body and my soul, and especially in moments when I feel myself at peace and purified of all sins, that I am able to write religious and pious poems. Poems of this kind cannot be composed at just any moment." These poems are marked by a deep faith in God and patient acceptance of his illness and graced with biblical allusions. The most famous is the 62-verse poem titled "Ave Maria."

Eighteen days before his death, Han composed in French a poem in praise of the Franciscan Missionary Sisters who took care of the leprosarium: "Angels in heaven, angels of God, angels of peace and joy, bring me a chaplet of flowers./I want to bathe in the sea of glory and love of the Most High/Because, in this lower world, God's miracles bid everyone to keep silent and to be lost in contemplation of the magnificent works of the Most High./Angels in heaven, angels of God, angels of peace and joy, fling up into space roses and lotus flowers, sing melodious songs and perfumed tunes, and fill these women servants of God with blessings, virtues, and happiness."

PETER PHAN

Han Sang Dong

(b. Myungji, Kimhae, Korea, 30 Jul 1901; d. Pusan, Korea, 6 Jan 1976). Korean Presbyterian* minister, evangelist, founder and administrator of Kosin University and Korea Theological Seminary, and founder of the Presbyterian Church in Korea (PCK).

Han was born near Pusan into a Buddhist family in 1901. He converted in 1924 and was baptized in 1925. He entered Presbyterian Theological Seminary, Pyongyang, in 1933 and graduated in 1936; he was ordained the following year.

Han ministered in the churches of Moon Chang of Masan (1937-39), Masanri of Milyang (1939-40), Choryang (1946-51), and Samil of Pusan (1952-73). When the Japanese government forced him to attend Shinto* shrine worship, he organized the anti-shrine movement. He became one of the leaders in the confrontation with Shinto nationalism*. Because of these activities, he was discharged from the moderatorship of Moon Chang Church in 1939, arrested, and imprisoned from 1940 to 1945 in the Pyongyang detention house.

With the defeat of Japan in Aug 1945 at the end of World War II*, Han was released from prison. He became a leader of the church renewal movement in the south of Korea. He founded Korea Theological Seminary in Pusan, which developed into Kosin University. Besides his involvement in theological training, he planted Samil Presbyterian Church in 1952 in Pusan and ministered there until his retirement in 1973. He was also actively involved in national church affairs, emerging as a leader in the formation of the Presbyterian Church in Korea (Kosin) in 1952 and in its later development.

Bibliography

Shin, K. S., *Until the End of the Age: A Biography of the Rev. Han Sang Dong* (1978). • Lee, S. S., et al., eds., *Rev. Han Sang Dong: His Life and Faith* (in Korean) (1985).

SANG GYOO LEE

Han Suk Jin

(b. Euju, northern Korea, 6 Sep 1868; d. 20 Aug 1939). One of the first seven ordained ministers in the Korean Independent Presbytery (1907).

Born into a Confucian* family, Han was baptized in 1891 by Samuel A. Moffett,* one of the pioneering United States Presbyterian* missionaries in Seoul. Moffett appointed Han his assistant and companion in his mission trips to Pyongyang and the northwestern region of Korea. When Han purchased a house for Moffett to open a mission station in Pyongyang, the local magistrate denied them residence and ordered their evacuation. Eventually Han purchased another house and began evangelizing. But in 1894 he was arrested and imprisoned with other Christian believers, and they were tortured for their new faith.

Han graduated from Presbyterian Theological Seminary in Pyongyang as one of the first seven theological students in 1907. In the same year, he was ordained into the ministry. When the Independent Presbytery of Korea was organized in 1907, he was elected secretary. With Kil Sun Joo,* a classmate of his, he drafted the preamble to the first minutes of the Independent Presbytery meeting. Also as a member of the financial committee of the new presbytery, he contributed to the founding of independent Christian churches free from missionary control.

In 1909, Han went to Tokyo, Japan*, and during his three-month stay he opened a church for Korean students in Japan in the Korean YMCA*, which later became the fountainhead of the Korean Independence Movement in 1919. This church is now Korean Union Church in Tokyo.

When Han returned home to Korea in 1910, he helped publish the *Church Herald,* the first Korean- language Presbyterian weekly. In 1911, he began to serve in local churches in Seoul, Masan (on the southeastern seacoast), and Shineuju (on the northwestern tip of Korea). In 1917, Han was elected moderator of the Korea Presbyterian Church and president of the Department of Presbyterian and Methodist* Association. In the same year, he helped found the Federal Council of Christian Churches in Korea. In 1924, the Korea presbytery appointed him chair of the construction committee for the first Korean Christian Retreat Center in the Diamond Mountains on the eastern shores. He devoted most of his remaining life to opening and running the Retreat Center.

Han was known as an advocate for the "Korean church by the Koreans," independent from foreign missionary influence and forming a "United Christian Church of Korea." He was the first minister to tear down the curtain in the middle of the church that separated women and men. He introduced the position of deaconess in the Presbyterian Church and included women in the leadership of local churches.

LEE DUK JOO, translated by DAVID SUH

Hani Motoko

(b. 8 Sep 1873; d. 7 Apr 1957). Japanese educator.

Eldest daughter of the Matsuoka family, samurai of the Nanbu Clan in Hachinohe-i, Aomori Prefecture, Hani, after entering Tokyo First Girls High School, began attending the Akashi-machi Church and was baptized. In 1892, she withdrew from Meiji Girls High School to become a newspaper reporter. In 1901, she married Hani Yoshikazu. She began publishing *Katei no tomo* (Home Friend) in 1903. In 1908, she changed its name and focus to *Fujin no tomo* (Woman's Friend). Her faith was deepened through contact with Uemura Masahisa*, and she began to question the rational ethics of the educated middle class. In 1904, she conceived and published *Kakeibo* (Household Account Book). With the support of readers, she founded *Jiyu Gakuin* (Free School) in 1921, a school free from the requirements of the ministry of education.

Stressing independence, Hani rejected rote learning and noninterventionist (hands-off) education; even in the relatively free education system of the Taisho period, she was a unique presence. In 1931, she founded *Tomo no kai* (Meeting of Friends) from among the readers of *Fujin no tomo*, and this group sponsored exhibitions and lectures, spreading the movement to streamline home life. In 1935, she built a settlement for farmers of the Tohoku region who were suffering financially; in 1938, she founded Beijing Free Life School. Hani Setsuko, an educator and critic, is her eldest daughter. Her writings are collected in *Hani Motoko chosaku shu* (Writings of Hani Motoko), 22 vols. (1970).

Bibliography

Akinaga Yoshiro, *Hani Motoko* (1969). • Saito Michiko, *Hani Motoko no shiso* (The thought of Hani Motoko), in *Onnatachi no kindai* (Women of modern times) (1978).

KANEKO SACHIKO

Helpers of the Holy Souls

Sisterhood founded by Eugénie Smet in Paris in 1856.

Two Helpers nuns arrived in Shanghai in Dec 1867, followed by four more one month later. They built a convent at Xujiahui, Shanghai, and set up branches in Yangjingbang and Hongkou in 1871 and 1893, respectively, with Xujiahui Convent as headquarters. In 1921, the Xujiahui headquarters sent two foreign and four Chinese nuns to Xian County, Hebei, where they set up their fourth branch, and later a fifth branch was opened in Yangzhou, Jiangsu.

The nuns helped the Society of Jesus* to conduct evangelistic activities, ran girls' schools, and engaged in philanthropic works. From the 1870s to the 1940s, the Helpers trained many Chinese nuns for the Shanghai Catholic Church, opened four girls' middle schools and more than 10 primary schools, and ran foundling hospitals, charitable clinics, and handicraft workshops. Of the four middle schools, Xujiahui Girls' Middle School enrolled only Catholic students, and Qiming Girls' Middle School enrolled especially non-Catholics. Both were among the earliest girls' middle schools established in Shanghai.

CHINA GROUP

Henana (Hadisbaia') of Adiabene

(d. ca. 610). After study at the theological school at Nisibis under a certain Moses, Henana was appointed professor at Nisibis*. Soon thereafter, he became convinced that the exegetical and theological traditions of Theodore of Mopsuestia* should be revised in light of the work of John Chrysostom. He also accepted the Creed of Chalcedon. He taught that there were two natures, but only one person and one hypostasis in Jesus Christ. This put him at odds with the faculty, administrators, and students of the theological school at Nisibis. Therefore his appointment was discontinued by Bishop Paul of Nisibis.

Remarkably, Henana was later appointed (572) director of the theological school at Nisibis and survived the efforts of two synods* (585, 596) called to discharge him. His most severe critic was Babai the Great, who wrote a volume titled *The Union in the Incarnation* to counteract the ideas of Henana. The lack of faith of the clergy and bishops led to a split in the school after the publication (580) of its new statutes of governance. Over 300 students left the institution. There were numerous efforts to restore confidence in the theological school, but it never recovered.

Henana was an important author. Among his works were commentaries on the Old and New Testaments, a commentary on the Creed of Nicaea, and numerous homilies. Most of this corpus has been lost. Extant are a treatise on Good Friday, an essay "On the Fast of the Ninevites," and fragments of a biblical commentary (preserved in Išo'dad of Merv*).

Bibliography

Labourt, J., *Le Christianisme dans l'Empire Perse sous la dynastie Sassanide (224-632)* (1904). • Vööbus, Arthur, *The Statutes of the School of Nisibis* (1962); *History of the School of Nisibis* (1965). • Fiey, J.-M., *Jalons pour une histoire de l'Église en Iraq* (1970); *Nisibe: Métropole syriaque orientale et ses suffragants des origins à nos jours* (1977).

DAVID BUNDY

Henriquez, Henry

(b. 1520; d. Punnaikayal, 6 Feb 1600). Successor of Francis Xavier* and first person of the Portuguese Mission of the Catholic Church permanently settled on the coast of India*.

Henriquez belonged to the Society of Jesus* founded by Ignatius of Loyola. He worked on the Pearl Fishery coast in Goa, mainly among the Paravars. On Xavier's order Henriquez started learning Tamil in order to compose a Tamil grammar on the model of the Latin and Greek grammars. His aptitude for language was so extraordinary that he was able to speak Tamil within a year. At the death of Fr. Griminali, Henriquez was appointed as superior of the Pearl Fishery Mission in 1549. As early as 1547, Henriquez had taken charge of Tuticorin and Kombutarei.

Henriquez's special keenness with a sense of absolute sternness was evident in his method of instruction. He was particularly interested in the Christian training of young people. It so happened that on his arrival girls were invited to the catechism classes for the first time. He started instructing the girls in the morning and the boys in the evening. It was also his strict commitment to appoint in every Christian village a teacher of catechism to gather and instruct the children every day. Henriquez scheduled instruction to suit the convenience of the local people. He stipulated the following strict schedule: men on Sundays, women on Saturdays, older women and widows on Fridays, female slaves on Sundays after their masters had returned.

By 1549, Henriquez started selecting Christians for full-time, lifelong Christian service. They brought about remarkable changes among their own people. As a consequence, there were only two Jesuit missionaries left by 1552.

Henriquez's favorite topics were the creation of the world, angels, the incarnation, the Holy Trinity, and the life and death of Christ. Fostering a deeper knowledge of the truths of faith was his priority. For Henriquez, spiritual talks were the chief means of improving the quality of Christian life on the Pearl Fishery coast.

Henry appointed catechists and teachers in each village. Besides paying them, he made sure that the native people were taught the Lord's Prayer, confessions, and creeds in their own tongue. Henriquez even visited and stayed in each village for about one month to explain Christian truths. He vehemently confronted and argued against the errors of idolatry and always saw to it that he engaged constructively with some learned pagans and Muhammadans in public debates. One result of Henriquez's brave and sacrificial investment was the conversion and baptism of a learned yogi at Punnaikayal in 1550. This yogi, who was a native of Vembar, was highly respected by the people. Henriquez's success with the learned yogi by way of exposing the falsehood and unrealistic view of individual rebirth made many Christians believe that the way of Jesus Christ was the only genuine one.

Henriquez was also constantly exposed to the issue of appreciating and utilizing native culture and thought patterns. He seems to have been quite relaxed toward the habits and practices of the local people. Once, on the issue of marriage between relatives, he firmly stated that there can be marriage at the third and fourth degrees of consanguinity. Nor was he too stern about imposing common law upon young believers. He did not want to place a heavy burden on them and thus disciplined them very lightly.

Henriquez relied on three special means for the well-being of Christians: (1) spiritual talks (to devout people); (2) the involvement of lay helpers in mission; and (3) the sacrament of penance. The seminary he opened at Punnaikayal served as the springboard for his missionary activity. From here the best students were sent to the colleges in Goa and Quilo. The opening of a hospital at Punnaikayal was also Henriquez's idea. It was primarily meant for the poor, and ran on the alms of Christians, which were ordered to be collected once per week. Henriquez also made certain that he obtained wine, biscuits, oil, vinegar, and medicines for the sick and the poor.

Henriquez's careful census in 1552 showed that there were 40,000 Christians under his care on the Pearl Fishery coast. Though his work mainly covered the Paravars, he always tried his best to reach out to the Kadayars and Palayars of the coast.

One of Henriquez's contributions was the forming of the "confraternity of charity" with the hope of producting fervent Christians. This confraternity, based on love of God and love of one's neighbor, was almost like a religious society for married people. The fraternity's aim was to live good Christian lives and help others do so. Henriquez laid down some rules in 1578: lead an exemplary life, strive for perfection, help others, care for the sick and poor, visit families and hospitals. Not surprisingly, Muslims and Hindus alike had great respect for Henriquez.

Henriquez spent 53 years teaching catechism, administering sacraments, visiting villages, and writing books. Among his books are a catechism (translation into Tamil of a catechism composed in Portuguese by Fr. Marcos Jorge, S.J.), a shorter catechism (16 pages) by Henriquez along with Fr. Emmanuel of St. Peter, a Tamil grammar, a Tamil-Portuguese dictionary, a booklet for confession, and a Tamil version of *Flos Sanctorum.*

Bibliography

Thekkedath, Joseph, *History of Christianity in India,* Vol. II (1982). • Wicki, J., "P. Henrique Henriques, S.J. (1520-1600)," *Indian Ecclesiastical Studies* 4 (1965) and 5 (1966).

FRANKLYN J. BALASUNDARAN

Henry Martyn Institute

(HMI). Ecumenical Christian organization in Hyderabad, India*, which functions as an expression of the church's ministry of reconciliation.

Named after a dedicated and energetic 19th-c. British missionary, the Henry Martyn School was founded in 1930 with the goal of training missionaries for work among Muslims. In 1959, to reflect a greater accent on research as well as education, it was renamed the Henry Martyn Institute of Islamic Studies and began to shift its focus away from an emphasis on preparing church workers for a ministry of polemics and confrontation to assisting them to engage in a more open dialogue with Muslims and others. The institute's aims and concerns have continued to evolve; they now clearly focus on improving relations between people of different faiths and traditions and encouraging the study of all religions, with a particular emphasis on Islam*. To meet these goals, HMI conducts a broad variety of education, research, and publication programs, as well as promotes active local involvement in work among the poor and in building better relations between communities.

HMI offers three regular programs in the area of education: the master of theology in religions (Islam) degree awarded through the senate of Serampore, an intensive two-week summer course on Islam and interfaith relations, and a two-week winter course in the series Foundations for Reconciliation, which focuses on contemporary and practical issues of peacemaking, conflict resolution, and the ministry of reconciliation.

HMI maintains its own library of more than 15,000 books and periodicals in the area of Islam, Christianity, world religions, and interfaith relations. Hyderabad itself provides another rich resource, with its long-standing traditions of Muslim and Hindu history and culture and the city's many valuable collections of manuscripts and books in Persian, Arabic, Urdu, Telugu, and English.

The institute publishes a quarterly journal, *The Bulletin,* which presents scholarly articles on Islam, Christianity, and other faiths; a semiannual newsletter, *Interaction;* and various booklets and books which focus on Islam, Christianity, and issues of interreligious* concern.

In addition to a program of research and teaching, HMI is also involved in a practical program of interfaith dialogue through the Aman-Shanti ("Peace") Forum. Founded by HMI staff people during the city-wide violence in Dec 1990, the forum draws together people of all religions and traditions to assist in promoting better relations between Hindus and Muslims. This group has worked to assist the victims of riots by helping hospital staff cope with the wounded and dying; bringing food, clothing, and comfort to people dazed by grief, pain, and loss; mobilizing support for day laborers and others who were without food during long periods of curfew; and catalyzing other city-wide attempts to bring relief. After the immediate crisis, the forum continued long-term efforts at peacemaking by bringing local Hindus and Muslims together as a community to help solve common problems and grow in mutual understanding and trust.

ANDREAS D'SOUZA

Hepburn, James Curtis

(b. Milton, Pennsylvania, United States, 13 Mar 1815; d. 21 Sep 1911). Missionary to China* and Japan*.

Hepburn studied at Princeton University, after which he entered the medical school of the University of Pennsylvania, receiving his M.D. degree in 1836. He then earned a master's degree from Princeton University. In 1834, he joined the Presbyterian* Church in the USA (North) in Milton. He married Clara M. Leete in 1840 and went to China as a medical missionary the next year. While in Singapore*, he acquired *Yohane fukuin no den* (The Gospel According to St. John), translated by Karl Friedrich August Gützlaff*, and sent it to the Presbyterian Church mission headquarters. He met Samuel Robbins Brown* at the Morrison Memorial School in Hong Kong*. From 1843, he worked as a medical missionary on Amoy Island, but he and his wife returned to the United States in 1845 due to her poor health.

On 18 Oct 1859, the Hepburns came to Japan and lived at Jobutsu Temple in Kanagawa. Brown arrived in Japan the next November, and they lived together in the temple. Hepburn opened a free medical clinic at Soko Temple but was ordered to close it. He then worked full-time on Japanese language research, focusing on creating an English-Japanese dictionary. In May 1863, he opened a free medical clinic at #39 Yokohama Settlement, and his wife opened an English academy in November. He excelled in the treatment of eye problems, but he also engaged in some internal medicine and surgery. He became widely known when he performed surgery for gangrene on the noted actor Sawamura Tanosuke, an operation recorded even in *Ukiyoe.* A number of well-known persons studied at Mrs. Hepburn's academy, including Hayashi Tadasu, Takahashi Korekiyo, Masuda Takashi (who founded Mitsui Bussan), Miyake Hide (who became surgeon general), and Hattori Ayao.

Eight years after arriving in Japan, Hepburn's Japanese language research culminated in the 1867 compilation and publication of his *Japanese and English Dictionary,* which included an English and Japanese index. As he had come to Japan to do evangelistic work and Bible* translation, early on he and Brown began working together on translating the New Testament. Beginning in Mar 1874, he met with the translating committee at the Brown residence and participated in almost all of the work done by this committee. In 1882, Hepburn was appointed chair of the Old Testament translating committee, working with Guido Herman Verbeck and Philip Kemball Fyson. Concentrating all their energies, they finished the translation in 1887. The $2,000 he received from the sale of the publishing rights to his third edition of the Japanese-English dictionary he donated to Meiji Gakuin, and the Hepburn Building was erected. From 1889 to1891, he served as head of the school.

In 1892 Hepburn built the Yokohama Shiro Church building and published *Seisho jiten* (Bible Dictionary) with Yamamoto Hideteru. On 22 Oct of the same year, he and his wife returned to the United States and resided in East Orange, New Jersey. In 1905, he received an honorary doctor of law degree from Princeton University. In a strange coincidence, the Hepburn Building at Meiji Gakuin burned to the ground the day he died. His wife preceded him in death on 4 Mar 1906 at the age of 88.

Bibliography

Griffis, W. E., *Hepburn of Japan and His Wife and Helpmates: A Life Story of Toil for Christ* (1913). • Yamamoto Hideteru, *Shin Nihon no kaitakusha, J. C. Hebon Hakase* (Dr. J. C. Hepburn, a Pioneer of the New Japan) (1926). • Takaya Michio, ed. and trans., *Hebon shokan shu* (Collected Writings of Hepburn) (1959); *Dokutoru Hebon* (Doctor Hepburn) (1954); *Hebon no tegami* (Hepburn's Letters) (1976).

TAKAYA MICHIO

Hibbard, David Sutherland

(b. 1868; d. 1966). American Presbyterian* missionary, founder of Silliman Institute in the Philippines*.

Hibbard and his wife Laura were pioneer Presbyterian educational missionaries to the Philippines from

1899. After they founded Silliman Institute in 1901, David served as its president for 30 years.

A missionary educator par excellence, Hibbard received a fond tribute from an alumnus in 1929: "In you I have learned many things . . . to love my fellow men; and most of all . . . God and Jesus as my only Savior. I owe you this debt . . . I can never repay you." Another said that Hibbard's friendliness made small men feel, "for the time being, as great as he is."

In awarding him an honorary LL.D. in 1937, the University of the Philippines cited Hibbard as an "educational statesman, moulder of men," and "faithful friend of the Filipinos."

Bibliography

Carson, A. L., *Silliman University (1901-1959)* (1965). • Tiempo, E. K., C. C. Maslog, and T. V. Sitoy, Jr., *Silliman University, 1901-1976* (1977). • Kwantes, A. C., *Presbyterian Missionaries in the Philippines* (1989).

T. Valentino Sitoy, Jr.

Hidden Christians

(Kirishitan No Senpuku). Many Japanese were converted to Christianity by Jesuit* and other missionaries during the 16th and 17th cs. These converts were called Kirishitan*. The Edo Shogunate passed a law forbidding the practice of Christianity in 1612, and the Kirishitans were pursued, arrested, and tortured, especially in 1615-34 (the Genwa through Kan'ei periods). While a number of Kirishitans died a martyr's death as a result, quite a few gave up the teachings of the faith, at least on the surface. Especially in the city of Nagasaki proper, where people were forced to trample on an image of Jesus or a cross or to give up their faith, many felt compelled to renounce their Christianity. They became hidden Christians, joining the Buddhist faith on the surface to camouflage their true beliefs.

Missionary work in Japan* started again when Catholic missionaries returned in 1862, with Oura Catholic Church in Nagasaki being rebuilt in 1865. Bernard Thadee Petitjean, a missionary in the Nagasaki region, came across grandchildren of the Kirishitans. It was not long before more hidden Christians began returning to the church in Urakami (Nagasaki) and other places in Kyushu. These people were called "resurrection Christians." Not all of the hidden Christians, however, returned to the church. Those who chose to remain hidden were soon referred to as "detached Christians," and those who had been called *zencho* (pagans) by the Kirishitans were given the name *kuro* (black), alleged to have come from "cross." In contrast with those who called themselves "old Christians," those who were newly baptized were called "new Christians."

Over the long period of time in which the hidden Christians were concealed, traditional beliefs of Shintoism and Buddhism* and village customs were gradually assimilated into their practices. Some aspects of ancestor worship* also became major pillars of their faith, so that it was changed into a mixture of different religions. Some Shinto and Buddhist beliefs were accepted; the place where ancestors had been martyred became holy ground, and customs and articles left by those who had died were venerated as images of God. The hidden Christians possessed neither doctrine (creed) nor a desire to spread the faith, but a few Christian practices were still visible. The prayers of the Keicho Period (1596-1614) were corruptly pronounced *urassho; Natara* (Christmas) and *Pasuka* (Easter) were observed together with *Osejosai,* which was adapted to the traditional fishing/farming customs. There were remnants of sacramental practice, but these too were changed (e.g., infants drinking baptismal waters).

It was assumed that after the Kan'ei Period (1624-44), the hidden Christians had scattered throughout Japan, and in the latter part of the 17th c., they were considered to be extinct. In 1792, the office for forcing Christians to give up their faith was closed. But beginning with the last days of the Tokugawa Shogunate, when Kirishitans were discovered in Urakami, hidden Christians were found in various places in Kyushu. The majority of them were found in the Hirado and Ikitsukijima areas and Kurosaki (on the Saikai Peninsula), the areas nearest the outer ocean. Those seeking freedom of religion had moved to the Goto Islands. It appears that there were from 50,000 to 80,000 left, and they were organized. Around Hirado and Ikitsukijima pictures of Christ, the Holy Mother, the apostles, and a number of saints had been hung. In the Goto Islands and Kurosaki, manuscripts of the church calendar were found in the form of hanging curtains. The largest organizational structure seems to have comprised groups of five or six homes; there was no larger or more inclusive level. In each group, positions of responsibility were designated: father (leader), teacher (baptizer), and the one in charge of the calendar (designated special celebratory days, etc.). Among the elements of their faith were prayer, baptism, *otempenshiya* (from *penitentia,* "disciplinary training"), faith healing, blessing of newly constructed homes or ships, cleansing of homes, and lucky charms that resembled a rosary or a cross cut from paper.

If hidden Christians returned to the church, all of their positions of responsibility would disappear, as would the fringe benefits. It is presumed that the main factor preventing their return to the church was their fear that all of the articles and traditions they loved and respected would be treated as false idols or superstitions, and they would be forced to give them up. In addition, their religious structure was deeply incorporated into the structure of the village. If they returned to the church, they would be betraying the village and thus break the trust the group had built as they kept their secret through the centuries. All of this made it very difficult for them to return to a Catholic Church which looked very different from their indigenous Christian practices.

Bibliography

Elison, George, *Deus Destroyed* (1973).
SUKENO KENTARO

Higdon, Elmer K.

(b. 1887; d. 1961). American Disciples missionary and pastor in the Philippines*.

The leading Disciples missionary in the Philippines in the first half of the 20th c., Higdon arrived with his wife, Idella, in 1917 and started at Vigan. Moving to Manila in 1919, Higdon became pastor of the Taft Avenue Christian Church, which through his dynamic preaching and church programming drew many professionals and college and high school students.

With his great concern for social issues and zealous advocacy of interchurch union, Higdon was elected president of the Evangelical Union in 1922. He served as executive secretary of the National Christian Council from 1929 to 1935. Higdon subsequently served as secretary of the United Christian Missionary Society. Returning to the Philippines after retirement, he was interim dean of Silliman Divinity School from 1959 until his death.

Bibliography

Higdon, E. K. and I. W., *From Carabao to Clipper* (1941). • Sitoy, T. V., Jr., *Comity and Unity* (1989); *Several Springs, One Stream* (1992). T. VALENTINO SITOY, JR.

Higginbottom, Sam

(b. Manchester, England, 27 Oct 1874; d. New York, 10 Jun 1958). Pioneer agricultural missionary to India*.

At age 20, Higginbottom emigrated to America, where he resumed his education, which had previously been interrupted when family circumstances made it necessary for him to leave school when he was 12. He finished high school at Mt. Hermon, attended Amherst College, and graduated from Princeton Seminary in 1903.

Influenced by D. L. Moody and Robert E. Speer and inspired by the Student Volunteer Movement's call for "the evangelization of the world in this generation," Higginbottom applied to the Presbyterian* Board of Foreign Missions and was sent to India. While teaching economics at the Allahabad Christian College, he became acutely aware of the poverty* of rural people and the struggle of farmers to grow food by traditional agricultural methods. As he considered Jesus' commandment to feed the hungry, he decided that he was being called to teach farmers better ways of growing crops. During a two-year leave, he completed a course in agriculture at Ohio State University. He then returned to India in 1911 and started a school that grew to the 500-acre farm and campus of the Allahabad Agricultural Institute.

Higginbottom required his students to work in the fields to gain practical experience. His faculty's research on soil, seeds, erosion control, irrigation, and fertilizers increased crop yields. He imported American cattle and crossbred them with Indian cows to create a herd that dramatically raised milk production. The Institute's extension department introduced farmers to new methods, while the engineering department produced implements that made cultivation more efficient. A course in home science trained young women to teach nutrition, hygiene, and child care to rural women.

To achieve his goals, Higginbottom overcame formidable obstacles. Financing his projects was difficult, requiring frequent fund-raising trips to America. Recruiting and holding a competent staff of American scientists were not easy, and a rapid turnover of staff slowed the progress of his work. It took years to raise the Institute's academic standards to university levels so that students could earn recognized degrees. Some of his missionary colleagues opposed his efforts on grounds that they lacked a clear evangelical purpose. At one point, they voted to remove Higginbottom and the Institute from the body of the Presbyterian North India Mission.

Higginbottom persisted, however, gaining an international reputation as a practical visionary dedicated to relating the Christian mission to basic human needs. The Indian leader Gandhi* sought his help to improve the condition of India's poor. Several Indian princes employed him as an agricultural advisor. In 1925, the government of India recognized his contributions by awarding him the Kaisar-I-Hind medal for public service. His influence was evident at the 1927 Jerusalem conference of the International Missionary Council, when the council urged its constituency to give greater emphasis to agricultural missions. Princeton, Amherst, and Western Reserve gave him honorary degrees. Affirming the significance of his work, the Presbyterian Church USA elected him moderator of its 1939 general assembly.

Bibliography

Higginbottom, Sam, *The Gospel and the Plow* (1921); *India's Agricultural Problems* (1942); *Sam Higginbottom, Farmer: An Autobiography* (1949). • Hess, Gary R., *Sam Higginbottom of Allahabad* (1967). JOHN BATHGATE

Hindu Cultural Christianity

Christianity expressed in Hindu cultural forms has had great vitality as an idea and has taken on many expressions since the first Jesuit* experiments in the late 16th c. From the days of Roberto de Nobili* (1577-1656), it has been a discussion point, but only a few ever acted with the radicality of de Nobili.

In the modern era, a minority of missionaries and high-caste converts have championed the concept of Hindu cultural Christianity against the mainstream of Christianity in India; the concept often takes the form of "unbaptized believers" remaining in Hindu communities. Serious reflection and action can be traced to the enigmatic Keshub Chunder Sen* (1838-84), who came to prominence soon after joining the Brahmo Samaj* in 1858. The rising tide of Indian nationalism, evidenced in the birth of the Indian National Congress in 1885, forced to the forefront questions regarding the relationship of Christianity and Hindu culture and religion.

Brahmabandhab Upadhyay* (1861-1907) converted to Roman Catholicism* after some years in the Brahmo Samaj*. His attempts at pioneering Hindu cultural Christianity were opposed and suppressed by church authorities with even greater zeal and effectiveness than had been brought against de Nobili centuries earlier. Post–Vatican II Catholicism has developed a dynamic minority of advocates for the inculturation of Christianity to classical Hindu forms, looking to Brahmabandhab as their forerunner and Swami Abhishiktananda (1910-73) as latter-day guru.

Sadhu Sunder Singh* (1889-1929) most strikingly brought the ideal of Christianity in Hindu garb before the minds of Protestants. Leading missionary advocates of the concept, such as C. F. Andrews* (1871-1940) and E. Stanley Jones* (1884-1973), were friends of the Sadhu. The main active expression of the idea is seen in the birth and development of the Protestant Christian ashrams*. Christukula Ashram in Tiruppatur in South India and Christa Seva Sangha Ashram in Pune in western India were started in the 1920s and continue to this day. The vitality of the Christian ashram movement at present lies with the Roman Catholic ashrams, most of which are post–Vatican II but with the forerunner, Shantivanam near Tiruchchirappalli in South India, having started in 1950. A handful of Hindu Christian movements have arisen outside traditional church structures, most strikingly that led by K. Subba Rao (1912-81) in Andhra Pradesh (see Subba Rao Movement).

Powerful advocacy for Dalit* theology has cast a shadow over much of the effort for Hindu cultural Christianity, which is easily painted as Brahminical and as pandering to the prideful oppression which all admit to be present in aspects of the classical Hindu traditions. The problem is the caste structure, which is radically challenged by Dalit theology. The rise of politicized Hindu fundamentalism with its criticism of Westernized Christianity (with goals and motives that are highly suspect among Indian Christians) further complicates discussions at the present time. The eclectic dynamism of classical Hindu cultures, never more evident than at present, ensures that discussions and actions relating to Hindu cultural Christianity are not on the verge of extinction.

Bibliography

Baago, Kaj, *The Movement Around Subba Rao* (1968). • Chenchiah, P., V. Chakkarai, and A. N. Sudarisanam, *Asramas Past & Present* (1941). • Das, Sisir Kumar, *The Shadow of the Cross: Christianity and Hinduism in a Colonial Situation* (1974). • Immanuel, R. D., *The Influence of Hinduism on Indian Christians* (1950). • Mataji, Vandana, ed., *Christian Ashrams: A Movement with a Future?* (1993). • Richard, H. L., ed., *R. C. Das: Evangelical Prophet for Contextual Christianity* (1995). • Sahi, Jyoti, *Stepping Stones: Reflections on the Theology of Indian Christian Culture* (1986). • Thomas, M. M., and P. T. Thomas, *Towards an Indian Christian Theology: Life and Thought of Some Pioneers* (1992).

H. L. RICHARD

Hindu Fundamentalism

Fundamentalism is a modern phenomenon in Hinduism* based on several factors. One significant factor is the political domination Hindus have suffered, first under Muslims and subsequently under Europeans, in particular, the British. Arguably, this long political subordination is responsible for loss of vitality and creativity. When the modern period under British domination began, Hindu culture and civilization were at a very low ebb. However, British rule had a tremendous impact on the Hindu mind.

The British introduction of a new pattern of education had far-reaching significance. This new age broke the intellectual isolation of the Indian mind and saw great interest in the study of Indian religious traditions and culture. Both Orientalists and Christian missionaries engaged in this task. Some of these studies brought Hinduism under severe criticism, which hurt the national pride of Hindus. Some other studies, on the other hand, evoked a sense of great pride in the rediscovered glories of ancient India and the Hindu ethos.

The British period must be critically assessed against this historical background. The enlightened Indian youth were enthusiastic about the new developments, which honored the supremacy of reason over tradition and blind faith, and which fostered a new quest for experimentation and a new concept of social justice and rights. Inspired by the ideas of freedom and democracy, Indian nationalism emerged.

The philanthropic and humanitarian activities of the Christian missions and educators and the reformist policies of the British had a profound impact on Indian society and Hinduism. The success of the Christian missionary enterprise and the resultant growth of the Christian population in India at the expense of Hinduism alarmed Hindu leaders. This challenged some Hindu leaders to brace their nerves to defend their religion against the attacks of its assailants.

Against this general historical background, the emergence of at least two major trends in Hinduism may be identified: first, a trend toward reformation and renaissance, and second, a trend toward militancy and fundamentalism.

Thus, the major factors responsible for the rise of fundamentalism in Hinduism have been the long foreign political domination of the Hindu race; the emergence of the modern period, which brought new education, technologies, and ideologies; nationalism*; the expansion of Orientalism, which produced among Hindus a sense of pride in their national heritage; and the growth of Christianity and Islam* at the expense of Hinduism.

Fundamentalism arose as an answer to the threatening context in which Hinduism found itself during the second half of the 19th c. and the beginning of the 20th c. In evoking ancient history and traditions, modern Hinduism tried to find absolute answers to its current problems — an attempt to return to ancient scriptures and traditions. Even after attaining political independence, this trend not only survived but acquired greater momentum. The partition of India in 1947 on religious grounds and the persistent communal disharmony between Hindus and Muslims contribute to the strength of Hindu fundamentalism.

Additionally, the majority of Hindus believe that the pampered minority communities are overwhelming the majority Hindus and are engaging in "anti-national" and "treacherous" activities. They bemoan the persecution they perceive from these minorities. Finally, the phenomenal success of missionary Hinduism in the so-called Christian West guarantees a long life for Hindu fundamentalism.

Objectives. The chief objective is to defend Hinduism from attack by other religions and alien ideologies. To this end, apologetic writings have been profusely used. The *Shuddhi* program of conversion and reconversion has been successful in this endeavor as well. A second objective is to combat and nullify the challenges posed by missionary religions, such as Christianity and Islam. Hindu fundamentalism wants to check the growth of the foreign religions on the Indian soil. A third goal is the establishment of a Hindu *Rashtra* (nation) in India. This goal is based on the belief that India belongs to Hindus, and Hindu religion belongs to India. The interests of the nation and the religion are inseparable. Hence, the creation of a powerful Hindu nation with Hinduism as state religion demands serious attention. Fourth, there is an expansionist goal, seeking to make the whole world Hindu. The mission is not to reform and progress to the future, but to revive the old and attain the future. Revival of the ancient will mean a glorious future. There is a strong sense of mission, a world to win. In taking up a missionary enterprise, fundamentalists hold the view that they are only turning back to and emulating the example of their ancestors, who are claimed to have traveled all over the world spreading the ideals and values of Hinduism.

Ideological position. The ideological position of Hindu fundamentalism is one of dogmatism, explicit on four levels. First, scriptural dogmatism proclaims that the Vedas alone are true, and all other scriptures are perversions of truth. The Vedas alone command supreme authority. Hence, the call is "Back to the Vedas." Second, religious dogmatism states that Hinduism alone has the answer to all the problems of the world and is the only custodian of true spirituality. Hence, the call is to defend and propagate Hinduism. Third, territorial dogmatism asserts that India alone is the *Dharma Bhoomi* or *Punnya Bhoomi,* the only land of spirituality and virtue. It is the chosen land of God-realization. A birth in India is necessary for final salvation. India alone is the royal nation of the world. By virtue of being the land of perfect spirituality (i.e., Hinduism), India merits the status of the lone princely state in the whole world. And fourth, communal dogmatism believes that Hindus alone are the true sons of the soil. Non-Hindus are enemies, traitors, and saboteurs. This dogmatic position is most clearly expressed in nationalism, which is a religious nationalism. A true Indian is a Hindu and a Hindu alone is a true Indian. This brand of nationalism is uncritically appreciative and defensive of all that is Hindu, and hostile to and suspicious of all that is non-Hindu.

The politicization of Hinduism is one of the by-products of Hindu fundamentalism. This tendency results in communal violence, which is becoming an almost regular feature of Indian social life. Use of force is not only endorsed, but even recommended. This communal dogmatism also expresses itself in the belief that only Hindus are cultured, and others are wicked and full of vice. When Hindus act wickedly, they do so under the debasing influence of uncultured non-Hindus. Hence, the call is to "nationalize" (i.e., to Hinduize all non-Hindu Indians through *Shuddhi*) and then to "Aryanize" (i.e., to civilize the whole world).

Thus, the position of Hindu fundamentalism is an absolutist one: Vedas alone, Hinduism alone, India alone, and Hindus alone. The clarion call is to return to the Vedas and to the past. These prescriptions contain the answers to all the vexing problems of Hindus, India, and the rest of the world. What is therefore expected of Hindus is an aggressive mission. Its tone must not be one of plea or dialogue; it should be one of confrontation, combat, and conquest.

Swami Dayanand Saraswati* (1824-83), the founder of the Arya Samaj*, is said to have sown the seed of Hindu fundamentalism through his dogmatic position on the Vedas and Vedic religion and his hostility toward non-Vedic religions. Swami Vivekananda* (1863-1902), of the Ramakrishna Mission*, made subtle contributions in that he identified spirituality on the one hand with Hindu religion, and Hindu religion on the other hand with India. Bal Gangadhar Tilak (1856-1920) vigorously politicized religion and sacralized politics, and Vir Savakar (1883-1966), called the high priest of Hindu revivalism, further promoted the cause of religious nationalism through the Akhil Bharatiya Hindu Mahasabha. The Rashtriya Swayam Sevak Sangh (RSS), founded by K. B. Hedgewar (1889-1940) and later (1940-73) led by M. S. Golwalkar (popularly called Guruji), and its political wing, the Bharatiya Janata Party (BJP; the erstwhile Jan Sangh), have further enhanced the cause of Hindu fundamentalism. Bal Thackeray's Shivaji cult, called Shiv Sana, founded in Bombay on 19 Jun 1966, and the Vishva Hindu Parishad (VHP), also founded in Bombay on 28 Aug 1964, have taken Hindu chauvinism to threatening proportions.

The offensive posture of Hindu fundamentalism has gradually made the Indian church defensive and apologetic. The religious nationalism of fundamentalists questions the national identity and patriotism of Indian Christians. Evangelism is denounced as an antinational, anticommunal, and subversive program. Christian social service is viewed with suspicion, as are Christian attempts to promote interfaith dialogue. It may be suspected that the antagonistic stance of Hindu fundamentalism has adversely affected the Christian approach to evangelism. A sense of insecurity is gradually emerging among Indian Christians.

On the other hand, the happy fallout of the encounter between Hindu fundamentalism and the Christian church in India is the emergence of a new-found missionary zeal among modern Hindus and their enthusiasm in responding to the social challenges and needs of the time. A remarkable sense of social sensitivity is clearly visible among them. What one needs to be careful about in a fundamentalistic environment is to avoid the danger of fundamentalism begetting fundamentalism. To avoid this, patience and goodwill are imperative.

Bibliography

Baird, Robert D., ed., *Religion in Modern India* (1991). • Gangadharan, K. K., *Sociology of Revivalism* (1974). • Golwalkar, M. S., *Bunch of Thoughts* (1980). • Lele, Jayant K., and Rajendra Vora, eds., *Boeings and Bullock-Carts.* • Mathew, C. V., "Hindu Fundamentalism on the Move," *Areopagus* (1990); "Missionary Hinduism: An Analysis of Missionary Ideologies and Practices of Hinduism in the Modern Period" (unpublished doctoral thesis, Pune) (1990). • Saraswati, Swami D., *Light of Truth* (1984). • Thursby, G. R., *Hindu-Muslim Relations in British India* (1975).

C. V. MATHEW

Hinduism

One of the oldest living religions, with a following of over 500 million people.

The majority of Hindus live in India*, while Nepal* (see final section) has the distinction of being the sole Hindu nation. The word "Hindu" is derived from the name of the river Sindhu (Indus). Hinduism has no founder, no universal prophet, no common creed, and no institutionalized structure. It is now considered to be a fusion of pre-Aryan and Aryan religious elements, the result of a long process of assimilation and evolution. It is more a league of religions than a religion. It is more a culture than a set of doctrines. Hinduism is known for its inclusive, universalistic, and accommodative spirit.

A summary definition of Hinduism is *varnashrama-dharma* — performance of the *dharma* (duties) of the four *varnas* (castes, namely, Brahmin, Kshatriya, Vaishya, and Sudra) and the four *ashramas* (stages of life, namely, *brahmacharya, grihasta, vanaprastha,* and *sanyasa*).

The history of Hinduism is generally divided as follows: Vedic age (2000-600 B.C.E.), the age of protests (600-200 B.C.E.), the age of epics and *puranas* (200 B.C.E.-1000 C.E.), the age of *bhakti* (1000-1750 C.E.), and the modern period (1750 C.E. on). Jainism and Buddhism* are protest movements, while Sikhism is an attempt to reconcile Hinduism and Islam*.

Hindu scriptures are of two categories: *Sruti* and *Smriti* — revelation and truth interpreted. The four *vedas (Rig, Sama, Yajur,* and *Atharva)* constitute the former as the most authoritative scriptures; all the other holy writings constitute the latter. *Mahabharata* and *Ramayana* are the famous epics, the repository of ethical teachings. The *Bhagavad Gita,* a part of the *Mahabharata,* is the best-known scripture, whereas the *Upanishads* are the philosophical writings.

Popular Hinduism, religion at the grassroots level, is highly varied, composite, ritualistic, and colorful with its deities, temples, worship, pilgrimages, and festivals; the *Dassera, Deepavali, Durga Puja,* and *Ganapati* festivals are some of the major ones.

Higher Hinduism is highly philosophical. The *shaddarshanas* (six schools of philosophy) are the *Nyaya, Vaiseshika, Samkhya, Yoga, Purva-mimamsa,* and *Uttaramimamsa.* The last, also called *Vedanta,* has three branches: *Advaita* (monism), *Dvaita* (dualism), and *Vishishtadvaita* (qualified monism), which are propounded by Sankara, Madhva, and Ramanuja respectively.

Brahman, Paramatman, and *Bhagwan* are the three key terms employed to explain "theology" in Hinduism. Brahma, Vishnu, and Shiva constitute the triad, very popular at the grassroots level. Vishnu is believed to have taken *avatars* (incarnations, among whom Ram and Krishna are very popular) for the deliverance of the righteous. The idea of sin varies from age to age, school to school, and from the understanding that it is a personal offense against the gods to a complete denial of the fact of sin. The four goals of life are *dharma* (righteousness), *artha* (material well-being), *kama* (pleasure, especially sexual), and *moksha* (salvation).

Salvation *(moksha* or *mukti)* is the liberation of the soul from the wheel of *karma* and *samsara* (the law of retribution and the transmigration of the soul). Three *margas,* or paths, lead to *moksha: jnana, karma,* and *bhakti,* the paths of knowledge, work, and devotion respectively. These equally good paths compensate for the differences in the aptitude and traits of one and all. *Patanjali's ashtanga yoga* is a spiritual technique or exercise designed to effect the union of the soul with the Supreme Soul.

The history of the early contact between Christianity and Hinduism is enshrouded in mystery, though the church, as per the St. Thomas tradition*, is believed to have been in India for the last two millennia. Until the arrival of Western missionaries, the church in India was largely confined to a few pockets in South India, especially in modern Kerala. Perhaps what can be authentically stated about the ancient Indian church is simply that it did manage to survive and maintain its identity down through the centuries. The Christians found themselves accommodated in the caste structure of Hindu society. In the area of social customs and practices, there were hardly any differences.

It is significant to observe that there is no reference to the Christian community in *Sankaradigvijaya,* the story of Sankara's triumphal encounters with the non-Vedic religions. It is difficult to maintain that Sankara, hailing from Kerala, did not know of the presence of Christians in his native place. One may conclude that at Sankara's time Christianity did not pose a doctrinal or sociological challenge to his faith, nor was it considered competent to do so. Perhaps this was true during the several centuries to follow.

With the arrival of Western missionaries a new era dawned. The 19th century and the early part of the 20th witnessed a significant growth and expansion of the church, which assumed a national status. The Western colonial period also signified the beginning of a new era in Hindu-Christian relationships on the Indian soil. The story of Christian mission under Portuguese rule is largely an unfortunate and sad episode. Having received a royal command to take up a holy war against the wicked enemies of Christ, the Portuguese sailors and missionaries, in their insensitive zeal and fanaticism, committed all kinds of rash acts. Forced conversions took place; several temples were closed and their properties confiscated. There was hardly any serious dialogue between Hinduism and Christianity under the Portuguese. Even the pioneering method of adaptation employed by Roberto de Nobili* (1577-1656) did not evoke any noteworthy response from Hindus. For de Nobili, the difference between Christianity and Hinduism was that of the true religion and the false, and he adopted Hindu style and terminology purely as a method of approach.

Three reasons may explain this absence of ideological encounter in the early years of Western colonialism in India: first, the prolonged conflict and suppression of Hindus under Muslim domination left the Hindu community weak and subdued; second, the negative and insensitively antagonistic attitude of the Westerners toward Hinduism was not helpful in forging any positive contact; third, taking refuge in orthodoxy and conservatism, Hindus insulated themselves against the *mleccha dharma* of the Westerners, and this negative and exclusively dogmatic approach to Christianity discouraged real dialogue.

As more and more colonial powers came to India and large-scale conversions to Christianity took place, and as the Hindu Maratha Empire under Shivaji and the Peshwas boosted the morale of the Hindus, a shift was slowly taking place in Hindu-Christian relationships. Instead of an almost total indifference to Christianity as a religion, a new spirit of resistance emerged among orthodox Hindus. This is what Richard Fox Young identifies as "Resistant Hinduism," a Hindu intellectual opposition. Perhaps this was the Hindu answer to the Christian treatment of Hinduism as a religious and ideological system and not as a culture. Christian interest in Sanskrit and Hindu holy writings enhanced this new spirit of debate and resistance.

Western attitudes to Hinduism were quite varied. Some critically considered it a mass of superstitions and a system of errors and gross idolatry. Others regarded Hindu religion favorably and thought it grand, noble, and sublime. Possibly the former were concerned with the context of the Hindus and the latter with their texts. This might explain what each group found and failed to find in Hinduism. These Western Christian commendations and condemnations significantly enhanced the emergence of reformed and renascent Hinduism, and resistant Hinduism as well. Brahmo Samaj*, Deva Samaj, Prarthana Samaj*, and the Ramakrishna Mission* illustrate the emergence of the former; the *mataparikska* controversy involving John Muir (1810-82) and three Hindu pandits, "The Bombay Debates" in the 1830s between John Wilson* (1804-75) and Hindu pandits, the hostile lectures of Vishnu Bhikaji Gokhale against Christianity (1856-71), and movements such as Dharma Sabha (1830s) and the Madras Hindu Association (1840s) reflect the spirit of the latter. A periodical called *Saddhama-Dipika* was initiated in 1855 to teach Hindu religion and to draw the attention of the people to the hollowness of the religion of the *Padris* (Christian priests). The *Anti-Christian,* published from Calcutta, had the same purpose.

Scholarly Christian missionaries subjected Hinduism to severe theological scrutiny, but at the same time they, without hesitation, made use of Sanskrit and regional languages such as Bengali and Tamil in the propagation of their message. Roberto de Nobili, Constantine Beschi, G. U. Pope, H. A. Popley, the Serampore Trio (including William Carey*), and others consciously developed specialized terminology in these languages for their evangelistic and Bible* translation purposes. It is argued that the careful and extensive use of Hindu words, categories, similes, and metaphors to interpret Christian thought is "an illustration of the positive and creative use of the cultural heritage of India by Christianity." As a result of this diligent "hermeneutical experimentation," an extensive theological vocabulary was readily available for any serious theological discussion or dispute (see Indian Interpretations of Christ). This was a useful tool in the hands of, on one side, Christian missionaries and Orientalists and, on the other, Hindu apologists for theological argumentation and even attack, as evidenced in the *mataparikska* controversy.

Interaction with Hinduism has certainly helped the church to engage in the process of inculturation. The emergence of Indian Christian theology and Dalit* theology, attempts to have indigenized forms of worship and observance of festivals, the impact on Christian literature*, music*, art* and architecture*, dance and drama — all speak volumes in this regard. Christianity and Hindu *bhakti* movements exerted their influence upon each other. There is a strong claim that Christianity decisively influenced the emergence of Hindu *bhakti.* However, this is disputed by most Hindus. The contributions of Narayan Vaman Tilak* in the areas of Christian music and patriotism bear the stamp of Hindu influence. The experiment of Christian ashrams* is another Christian response to Hindu influence in an attempt to be more true to the ethos of Indian soil. The Hindu criticism that the church is too Western and less Indian has also stirred the church in India to take active part in the nation-building process. Another result is the conscious attempt made by the Indian church to liberate itself from the intellectual, structural, and financial dependence upon Western Christianity. E. Stanley Jones's* "round table meetings" with Hindu intellectuals and elite; Acharya Daya Prakash's *Sat Sang* and other activities of the Sat Tal Ashram at Nainital, Uttar Pradesh; the activities of the Kurisumala Ashram in Kerala; *Sneha Badan* in Pune; the Christian Institute for the Study of Religion and Society* (Bangalore); *Ishvani Kendra* (Pune), etc., indicate the positive, appreciative, and dialogical response of Christianity to Hinduism in the modern period.

The Christian influence on Hinduism in modern times may be identified in the emergence of reform movements, renascent movements, development of a strong sense of social commitment and the resultant social services, and emergence of clear missionary ideologies and practices. It is largely due to Christian influences that Hindu thinkers embarked on a conscious program of reinterpreting traditional Hindu concepts and practices in a bid to revitalize Hinduism to face the challenges posed by modern secular and humanistic ideologies, science, and missionary religions such as Christianity and Islam. Efforts are being made to "semiticize" Hinduism, that is, to make it more historical, creedal, dogmatic, and expansive. The Rashtriya Swayamsevak Sangh, Shiv Sena, and the Vishva Hindu Parishad are moves in this direction.

Finally, from earliest times Hindu-Christian relations have always involved the persecution of Christians. Many Christians have had to pay high prices for their conversion to Christ in terms of opposition, hostility, ostracism, physical assault, and some even death. The organized and large-scale persecution of Christians in the northeastern state of Arunachal Pradesh in the 1970s may be the first of its kind in modern India. The tribal Christians there were harassed, terrorized, suppressed, and assaulted. Over 40 places of Christian worship were burned down.

In 1982, there was a fierce clash between Hindus and Christians in Kanyakumari district and elsewhere in Tamil Nadu. This unfortunate episode is known as the Mandaicadu Tragedy. Similarly in Kerala, another South Indian state where almost one-third of the Indian Christian population resides, both communities were on the verge of a clash, which was fortunately averted. This Nilackal Issue generated communal tensions, ill feelings, hostility, and suspicions.

M. B. Niyogi's *Report of the Christian Missionary Activities Enquiry Committee*, Madhya Pradesh, 1956, is highly biased and portrays the Christian missionary enterprise as a subversive antinational program. In 1968, both Madhya Pradesh and Orissa passed anticonversion laws. In 1977, the Supreme Court of India upheld these laws as constitutional. Perhaps receiving inspiration from this verdict, the Arunachal Pradesh legislative assembly passed the Arunachal Pradesh Freedom of Religion Act in 1978. During the Janata rule in 1979, a move led by O. P. Tyagi, an Arya Samajist, to enact a law under the euphemistic title "Freedom of Religion Bill" intended to make religious conversion in India an offense. However, the attempt failed as the government fell. In the 1980s, Christians in the Phulbani tribal district in Orissa came under stiff opposition. Several churches and prayer huts were destroyed. Attempts were also made to reconvert these Christians back to Hinduism. The reconversion of Christians is in fact a national program of modern Hindu missionary activists.

The unsympathetic and critical view of Christianity and its mission in India, the general suspicion of Christian motives in proposing interreligious dialogue* and the consequential Hindu indifference to it, and the modern attempt to promote Hindu religious nationalism are putting considerable pressure on the church in India. Christian attempts to reinterpret their christological, ecclesiological, and missiological understanding using the sympathetic categories of pluralism do not seem to have any appreciable reciprocal effect on the revivalist Hindu attitude toward the church in India.

These incidents and developments may be pointers to a slowly changing situation for Christianity in India. A radical shift in the realm of religious and communal relationships is slowly but steadily taking concrete shape. While in the past the Hindu attitude toward the Christian community had been one of indifference, tolerance, or appreciation, at present one may discern ill feeling, opposition, and animosity in increasing degree. Christians more and more feel themselves a threatened minority in their own homeland. It is heartening to see that the majority of Hindus are very secular and above communalistic prejudices, preferring peaceful coexistence in an atmosphere of mutual respect, goodwill, and confidence. But it must be noted that to unleash communal disharmony and terror does not require the whole majority group to be militant. It needs only a powerful, committed, and zealous band of militant Hindu activists while the majority remain silent or passive. This present trend will continue to be a major theme in Hindu-Christian relations in India.

Nepal. In Nepal*, the only officially Hindu kingdom in the world, Hinduism is the state religion. According to official statistics, 89% of Nepal's population is Hindu, but this figure includes tribal peoples who are now claiming that they are different from Hindus and have their own ancient religious traditions. Hindus in Nepal are more oriented to festivals than religious rites. Rites-oriented Hindus may represent only 1%.

Nepalese Hindus believe that no one can convert to Hinduism from other religions. Hinduism is not just one religion; rather it is a family of religions syncretized under one label. There is no set doctrine. No Hindu gurus can define what Hinduism really is. One is born a Hindu. It is claimed that Hinduism is an ancient traditional religion with a history of about three to four thousand years.

The Aryans, who followed the Vedic scriptures, migrated into India from the northwest. This same group invaded Nepal in about 1500 B.C.E. and introduced many kinds of gods and goddesses. The history of Hinduism in Nepal is vague. Hindu writers do not take care to record dates because of their cyclical view of time. Thus historicity is difficult to define or describe.

Beginning in the 17th c., Catholic fathers occasionally visited Nepal. A small mission to Nepal was established in the 18th c., numerous babies were baptized, and a few adults converted to Christianity, but in 1769 they were all expelled from the country. As one of the last countries in the world to be closed to Christian ministry, Nepal did not reopen again to outside influence until the king regained the throne in 1951. Then Nepali Christians from India began reentering Nepal, along with foreign mission agencies which came to do social development work. Today, with the greater openness to Christian participation and witness in society, Christian churches are becoming firmly rooted in villages and cities across Nepal.

Bibliography

Boyd, Robin, *An Introduction to Indian Christian Theology* (1975). • Brown, David A., *A Guide to Religions* (1991). • Chethimattam, John, *Dialogue in Indian Traditions* (1969). • Devaraja, N. K., *Hinduism and Christianity* (1966). • Immanuel, R. D., *The Influence of Hinduism on Indian Christians* (1950). • Mathew, C. V., "Missionary Hinduism: An Analysis of Missionary Ideologies and Practices of Hinduism in the Modern Period" (unpublished D.Th. thesis, Pune) (1990). • Robinson, Gnana, ed., *Influence of Hinduism on Christianity* (1980). • Young, Richard Fox, *Resistant Hinduism* (1981). • Ahmad Shah, E., *Theology: Christian and Hindu* (1966). • Anderson, Mary M., *The Festivals of Nepal* (1971). • Banerjee, B. N., *Hindu Culture, Custom and Ceremony* (1979). • Frazier, Allie M., ed., *Hinduism* (1969). • Morgan, Kenneth W., *The Religion of Hinduism* (1955). • Sharma, D. S., *Hinduism Through the Ages* (1973).

C. V. MATHEW, with
MANGAL MAN MAHARJAN on Nepal

Hinduism, New Movements

Several new movements sprang up from Hinduism* in the 20th c., especially during the latter half. Several of these, e.g., transcendental meditation (TM), originated in India* but proved to be more popular in the West. Others such as the movement of Sathya Sai Baba are popular within India and in other Asian countries.

TM is associated with Maharishi Mahesh Yogi, born Mahesh Prasad Varma (Warma) in 1911 (or 1918) in Jabalpur (or Uttar Keshi) to a local tax official (or forest ranger) of the *Kshatriya* (warrior) caste. After graduating from the University of Allahabad in 1940 with a degree in physics, Maharishi became the favorite disciple of Guru Dev, a well-known Hindu religious leader who taught him a meditation technique from the Vedas which later came to be known as transcendental meditation. Before his death in 1953, Guru Dev commissioned Maharishi to teach and spread TM in the West. After a period of seclusion, Maharishi began to fulfil his master's wish. He set up the Spiritual Regeneration Movement in India in 1958. In 1959, he traveled to Hawaii, visiting Burma*, Singapore*, and Hong Kong* along the way. From there he also visited San Francisco, Los Angeles, and London, where he founded the International Meditation Society.

Upon his return to India, Maharishi began training TM teachers; the first group, which graduated in 1961, included Beulah Smith, the first American TM teacher. Maharishi went on annual world trips without much success. However, the breakthrough came in 1967 when the popular rock group the Beatles went on retreat with Maharishi in Wales and India and endorsed TM as the answer to human needs. Soon Western celebrities such as the Rolling Stones, Efrem Zimbalist, Jr., Mia Farrow, and Joe Namath followed Maharishi, leading to worldwide fame and a steady income for him. Subsequently, the Beatles and other celebrities withdrew their endorsement of TM, leading to a disastrous American tour by Maharishi, who returned to India disappointed by what he considered to be Western fickleness.

In India, Maharishi concentrated on consolidating his organization, which thrived financially. To escape the scrutiny of the Indian government, he shifted his headquarters in 1970 to Italy, and then to Spain. In 1971, he introduced the Science of Creative Intelligence (which gave a secular and scientific image to TM) and set up the Maharishi International University (MIU) at Fairfield, Iowa, United States. MIU, a four-year liberal arts college, offers bachelor's and master's degrees and is developing Global Television, a program designed to bring TM worldwide through audiovisual technology.

Maharishi announced the World Plan on 8 Jan 1972, which was to spread TM worldwide and to establish 3,600 World Plan centers, each having 1,000 teachers. The World Plan Executive Council was set up at the World Plan Administrative Center in Seelisberg, Switzerland. In the 1970s, TM was taught in public institutions, especially schools and the U.S. Army, using public funds. In 1978, a federal court in New Jersey ruled that TM was a religious practice and thus should not be granted such easy access to public institutions. At about the same time, when enrolment in the basic TM course dropped sharply, the organization introduced the advanced *siddha* program, which made the controversial claim to teach people how to levitate or even fly.

As a technique, TM involves daily meditation using a personal and secret mantra which is given to the individual during the *puja* (worship ceremony) at the basic TM course. This course, lasting fewer than 10 hours spread over a few days, initiates the novice into TM. It is claimed that regular TM enhances one's intelligence, happiness, performance, and health. TM done in groups is also said to produce the "Maharishi effect," a reduction in crime and hospital admissions in the vicinity. Scientific studies show no conclusive evidence. Group TM is also said to purify world consciousness.

In the 1970s, Maharishi announced the World Government of the Age of Enlightenment, which ruled over consciousness and would send "World Governors" to various areas of conflict to achieve world peace. The TM organization publishes literature, including Maharishi's writings, the most well known of which is *The Science of Being and Art of Living.* The movement also has its own magazine, *Creative Intelligence.*

The International Society for Krishna Consciousness (ISKCON) was founded in New York in 1965 by A. C. Bhaktivedanta Swami Prabhupada. Born on 1 Sep 1896 as Abhay Charan De, Bhaktivedanta graduated in 1920 from the University of Calcutta with a degree in English, philosophy, and economics. After working as a manager in a pharmaceutical company for two years, he became the disciple of Bhaktisiddhanta Thakura of the Gaudiya Vaishnava Mission and was initiated by the guru in 1933 into the Caitanya tradition of *bhakti* yoga. Just before his death in 1936, the guru commissioned Bhaktivedanta to carry Krishna Consciousness to the West.

Bhaktivedanta, who was married, produced English-language literature for the mission. He adopted the *vanaprastha* (retired) order in 1954, after which he began translation of the Hindu classic *Srimad Bhagavatam,* which took a decade and three volumes to complete. In 1959, he took *sannyasin* (renounced life), leaving his wife and family. In 1966, at the age of 70, Bhaktivedanta left for New York, where he gathered disciples, set up ISKCON, and began a magazine, *Back to Godhead.* In 1967, he moved to San Francisco and gathered more disciples from the hippie movement. Meanwhile, he continued to publish his books and translations. In 1968, his *Bhagavad-Gita, As It Is* was published. The Bhaktivedanta Book Trust, established in 1972, has published over 60 400-page volumes written by Bhaktivedanta.

ISKCON practice can be traced back to the Vaishnavite devotional tradition of the Bengali saint Chaitanya Mahaprabhu (1486-1534 C.E.), who practiced exclusive devotion toward the Hindu god Krishna. ISKCON followers dress in traditional Hindu attire; the women wear colorful saris while the men wear saffron or white robes. Their heads are shaved, leaving a topknot of hair *(sikha)* signifying their surrender to the spiritual master; and a clay marking *(tilaka)* is applied daily on the forehead and nose to signify the body as the temple of God. In recent times, traditional attire has become optional in conformity with Western culture.

ISKCON promotes the worship of Krishna and the study of the Bhagavad Gita. Chanting of the Krishna mantra *(Hare Krishna, Hare Krishna, Krishna Krishna, Hare Hare, Hare Rama, Hare Rama, Rama Rama, Hare Hare)* is practiced, usually collectively, in the temple or more publicly. The diet is strictly vegetarian, and an ascetic lifestyle is expected.

After Bhaktivedanta's death on 14 Nov 1977, leadership passed to the 20 members of the governing commission appointed by Bhaktivedanta shortly before his death. Of these, 11 were gurus empowered to take disciples. Tensions arose in the leadership, and half the gurus left or were expelled, forming splinter groups. The international headquarters of the movement is at Sridhama Mayapur, West Bengal. ISKCON claims 3,000 initiated members and 500,000 lay members.

Rajneesh Foundation International was established by Bhagwan Rajneesh, who was born on 11 Dec 1931 as Rajneesh Chandra Mohan. He was one of 12 children in a Jain family; his father was a cloth merchant. Rajneesh was said to be a difficult and independent-minded child. He graduated from the University of Jabalpur with a bachelor's degree in 1951 and from the University of Saugar with a master's degree in philosophy in 1957. He claimed that, while a student, he achieved complete enlightenment on 21 Mar 1953, his initial enlightenment having occurred at age seven. While a graduate student, he started teaching at Raipur's Sanskrit College and later at the University of Jabalpur.

A captivating speaker, Rajneesh traveled to speak to various audiences about his experiences. He resigned from his teaching post at the university to become a full-time spiritual guru. Initially, he taught disciples from his Bombay apartment, to which he moved in 1969. In 1970, Westerners began to appear in his group of disciples. He subsequently bought land in Poona to build an ashram (retreat center) in 1974, the same year he founded the Rajneesh Foundation. In the ashram, various therapies (including encounter groups), meditations (including the "dynamic" and *kundalini* varieties), and "experiences" were available. These were often in the form of violent physical exercises (mental and physical injuries were not uncommon) followed by a period of relaxation. Enlightenment was promised through these exercises. Observers have noted the existence of frenzied sexual activities and drug-taking in the *ashram.* Such expressions of personal freedom by Rajneesh's disciples brought about strong disapproval from traditional Hindus. However, Rajneesh's popularity grew in the West, and centers were established in North America, Europe, and Australia.

Before being initiated, Rajneesh's followers are called *shravakas* (sympathetic listeners). After initiation they are called *sannyasins* (or Rajneeshees, neo-*sannyasins,* or orange people). Rajneesh rejected the traditional Hindu understanding of *sannyasi* as the renounced life and instead interpreted it as the right way to life, which included affirming material life.

Sannyasins vow to do four things: wear orange, the color of sunrise; wear a *mala* (a necklace of 108 beads carrying a picture of Rajneesh); use one's new name given at the initiation; and meditate regularly, using five different techniques. *Sannyasins* also celebrate four special days: 21 Mar (Rajneesh's enlightenment day), 6 Jul (Master's Day), 8 Sep ("All Soul Day"), and 11 Dec (Rajneesh's birthday).

A typical day in the ashram begins with the chanting of the *Buddham Sharanam Gatchchami (Buddham Sharanam Goutchami, Sangham Sharanam Gatchchami, Dhammam Sharanam Gatchchami)*, which means: "I go to the feet of the Awakened One, the Commune of the Awakened One, and the Ultimate Truth of the Awakened One." In the morning, disciples attend *satsanq*, which involves meditation and listening to music and taped messages of Rajneesh. In the evenings, disciples attend *darshan*, which is celebrated through dancing and singing and seeks the communion of guru and disciple.

In the summer of 1981, Rajneesh left India suddenly and moved to the United States. He took a vow of silence for three years while his secretary, Ma Anand Sheela, arranged for the purchase of the 64,000-acre Big Muddy Ranch near Antelope, Oregon. Rajneeshis moved to the site to build a commune called Rajneeshpuram. In Jul 1982, some 7,000 Rajneeshis gathered there for a summer festival. In Nov 1982, the organization petitioned for the incorporation of Rajneeshpuram, and in the election in the following month, Rajneeshis won the mayor's office and a majority in the city council of Antelope. While life at Rajneeshpuram was apparently based on doing one's own thing, it became increasingly controlled and authoritarian. The movement became controversial partly as a result of the allegations of free sex and partly as a result of Rajneesh's show of wealth — his followers had given him almost 100 Rolls Royces. In addition, there were charges of immigration fraud. The organization also faced an internal struggle which resulted in Rajneesh denouncing Ma Anand Sheela and calling for the destruction of the book *Rajneeshism*.

In 1985, Rajneesh was expelled from Oregon, and he returned to his ashram in Poona after unsuccessful attempts to establish a commune in several countries. Rajneeshpuram was subsequently dismantled. In Poona, Rajneesh was called "Osho," and he began wearing white rather than orange. Visitors had to have an AIDS-free certificate before being allowed entry into the ashram. Rajneesh died of unspecified causes in 1990.

Sathya Sai Baba was born Sathyanarayana Raju on 23 Nov 1926 at Puttaparthi in the South Indian state of Andhra Pradesh. Stories circulated regarding his birth and childhood. It is said that there were certain omens around the time of his birth, e.g., a cobra was found in the baby's cot, but it did not harm him. At the age of 13, Sathyanarayana is said to have collapsed and was unconscious for several days. Three months after this incident, he claimed to be the incarnation of Sai Baba of Shirdi (1856-1918), a popular Indian guru for whom a temple had been built in Shirdi. Later, he also claimed to be the incarnation *(avatar)* of Krishna, the Hindu god. Following this, Sai Baba left school and began life as a religious guru.

Sai Baba began performing strange feats, such as materializing sacred ash *(vibuti)*, and sometimes Swiss watches, from air. Followers claim that he has the power to heal people who have incurable diseases, raise the dead, and transcend space and time limitations to bless seekers in far-off places and other times. Sai Baba is a charismatic personality and attracts Asians and Westerners who visit his ashram, Prashanti Nilayam, just outside Puttaparthi, to have a *darshan*. He wears saffron robes and a unique hairstyle. Sai Baba has remained largely in India. His followers, however, are found in many countries, especially in Asia. For example, Sai Baba Associations are found in Singapore* and Malaysia*, where there are sizable Indian minority communities. The involvement of prominent professionals in the movement has lent credibility to it. The movement also has become involved in social service, e.g., a temple, the Sai Center, was built in Singapore in 1995, providing among other things a free specialist medical clinic. It is interesting to note that the movement has also begun attracting Chinese followers in these countries. In Singapore, e.g., among the 500 people who attend the weekly *bhajan* at the Sri Srinivasa Perumal Temple, about 25% are Chinese. Among Sai Baba's five registered associations, four attract mostly Chinese.

Sai Baba's teachings are varied, but they include a call to a pure life and surrender to him. The guru-disciple relationship is the key to experiencing this. Devotees can belong to any religious affiliation, for Sai Baba teaches that all religions worship the same Supreme Being. Devotees are expected to live according to the nine codes of conduct and the 10 principles outlined by Sai Baba. The codes include praying daily, meeting for weekly *bhajans*, and loving and serving all. The more important principles include loyalty to one's country, avoiding corruption, and respecting and tolerating all religions. There is also equal emphasis on seeking the powers of Sai Baba for help. Holy ash and other religious artifacts are frequently used in this process. Sai Baba continues to be based at his ashram in Puttaparthi, where a free hospital has been functioning since 1991.

Bibliography

Boa, K., *Cults, World Religions, and You* (1981). • Brooke, R. T., *Riders of the Cosmic Circuit* (1986). • Ebon, M., *Maharishi the Guru* (1968). • Gelberg, S. J., ed., *Hare Krishna, Hare Krishna* (1983). • Melton, J. G., *Encyclopedic Handbook of Cults in America* (1986). • Murphet, H., *Sai Baba: Man of Miracles* (1971). • Rajneesh Foundation International, *An Introduction to Bhap-wan Shree Rajneesh and His Religion* (1983). Robert Solomon

Hmong

Most of the six million Hmong live in China*, but large numbers migrated to Laos* starting in the mid-19th c., and then into North Thailand*, where 90,000-100,000 are scattered over 230 villages, with 8.98% of them claiming to be Christian. Large numbers are also moving to Chiang Mai, the major city of the north, as well as to Bangkok. Because of their cooperation with the American forces against the Pathet Lao in the 1960s and 1970s, thousands of Hmong from Laos migrated to Thailand, and then to Europe and the United States after the war ended in 1975. A few thousand Hmong are found in Myanmar* and Vietnam*.

The Gospel came to the Hmong, both Blue and White, in the early 1950s through the witness of the Overseas Missionary Fellowship (OMF), formerly the China Inland Mission (CIM), which had worked with Hmong since 1896, when James Adam opened a work in Kweichow Province, China.

After all missionaries were expelled from China in 1950, the CIM redeployed its missionaries to other countries in East Asia. Orville Carlson, a seasoned Lisu missionary in both China and Burma, spearheaded the tribal work in North Thailand. In 1951, he was invited to visit the Hmong in Tak Province by Wilf Overgaard, a missionary who had made initial contact with the Hmong. The first Blue Hmong believers came from the village Yellow Creek (Dej Daag). Meanwhile, Ron Rulison was trekking to Blue Hmong villages in Chiangmai Province. In Jul 1953, Otto and Adri Scheuzger moved into Yellow Creek as the first resident missionaries among the Blue Hmong. They made an initial attempt to translate the Bible* and began worship services in August. The Blue Hmong translation was eventually done by a team of missionaries and nationals comprising Barbara Good (Griffiths), Barbara Hey, Mark (Laj Neeb x. Thoj), and Leng (Npuas Leej x. Tsaab).

By Nov 1953, many families were ready to remove the spirit shelf from their homes. The first to do so was Lateng (Laj Teem x. Thoj), followed by Tshang Yi (Chaav Yig x. Thoj). They were the first Hmong believers in Thailand.

The first White Hmong believers were Mblia Tua (Npliaj Tuam x. Xyooj) and family. Finnish missionaries working in Lomsak town made initial contact with the White Hmong. In Jul 1954, Ernie and Mertie Heimbach, who had worked with the Black Hmong in China, took up residence with the White Hmong in Mankhet village, Petchabun Province. Shortly, Don and Kathy Rulison moved into Palm Leaf village. Ernie Heimbach started translation work which was eventually handed over to Doris Whitelock and her national co-workers, Ying (Ntsum Yeeb x. Vaj) in Thailand and Cheng (Tsheej x. Xyooj) in Laos.

Christian work among the Hmong is mainly in Thailand with many subgroups elsewhere in Asia still unreached. The year 1903 saw massive conversions among the Great Flowery Hmong through the work of CIM in western Kweichow Province. United Methodists* were working in Yunnan at about the same time. The Christian and Missionary Alliance (C&MA) had a strong work in Laos until the Communist takeover. Hmong in Myanmar converted as the result of witness by Lisu Christians and have been encouraged by OMF missionaries in Thailand. John Lee (Vam Txoov x. Lis) of the Far East Broadcasting Company* (FEBC) has been much used over recent years to bring a large number of Hmong in Vietnam to Christianity. FEBC has a significant ministry in encouraging the Hmong believers in Asia, particularly in those countries that are closed to traditional missionaries.

Refugees* emigrating to the United States, France, Australia, and French Guiana have established a Hmong church in each of these countries. The Hmong church in the United States is maturing rapidly and showing keen interest in the Hmong church back in Asia. The C&MA has sent three Hmong missionary families to Thailand.

The Hmong Association (*Sib Koom Tes*, SKT) of the Associated Churches of Thailand represents by far the largest grouping of Hmong Protestants in Thailand today. It is subdivided into five districts covering North Thailand. There are believers and churches in 95 villages, with a Christian community of over 4,000. This indigenous group works in close partnership with OMF, Christian Churches of America, and the Great Commission Mission. They also receive encouragement from Hmong Christians overseas, particularly the United States. This grouping of Hmong is able to administrate all its own affairs but still depends on the help of some outside funding. They also have a vision that every village in Thailand should have Christians in it, and some believe that they can have a role in enabling the church to expand across borders to surrounding closed countries.

Other Protestant groups working with the Hmong in Thailand are the Church of Christ of Thailand (CCT), C&MA, the Hope of Thailand Church, as well as other smaller Pentecostal* groups. The Roman Catholics* and Seventh-Day Adventists* have a growing work, and the Jehovah's Witnesses have a small work. Catholic work among the Hmong probably started some decades ago with the Paris Foreign Mission Society* (MEP). J. Mottin studied Hmong culture and began mission work among them in 1973. The Fathers of the Holy Redeemer run a Hmong Center in Chiang Mai and have mission work in Loei and other provinces. There are several dozen Hmong Catholic churches.

Bibliography

FEBC Newsletter (1992). • Kuhn, *Ascent to the Tribes* (1984). • National Statistical Office (of Thailand) Hill Tribe Census (1985-88). • Broomhall, *Some a Hundredfold* (ca. 1920). • OMF International, *North Thailand Roundup* (Jan and Feb 1990). • Xa Moo Zoo, "Thawj Tsaavxwm Le Lug," *Journal of the Associated Churches of Thailand* (Feb 1995).

Frank Schattner and Ronald Renard

Hmyin, U Ba

(b. Thon-ze, Myanmar, 10 Mar 1912; d. Yangon, 7 Sep 1982). Teacher, pastor, church administrator, and pioneer of ecumenical* and youth movements in Myanmar*.

U Ba Hmyin was the preacher at the opening service of the Third Assembly of the World Council of Churches at New Delhi in 1961. The seventh of the nine children of U Ba Pe and Daw May Khin, U Ba Hmyin studied teacher training and taught at the school in Ok-kan town, Tharrawaddy district, southern Myanmar. He later studied at what is now the Myanmar Institute of Christian Theology at Insein. He graduated with distinction and was invited to teach full-time at his alma mater for five kyats per month (approximately one U.S. dollar). At the end of World War II*, together with a few friends, he organized the All Burma Christian Youth League and was its president. The aims of the league, a postwar pioneer ecumenical body, included an increase in the leadership roles of nationals in Christian mission, effective use of youth talent in church work, church-based missions, interchurch and interethnic unity in mission; and higher theological training in the service of missions. Its motto of "service and sacrifice" was subsequently adopted by the Myanmar Baptist* Convention and the Myanmar Institute of Christian Theology, two bodies in which U Ba Hmyin held key posts on different occasions.

After his studies at Yale Divinity School in the United States, U Ba Hmyin returned to serve as secretary of the Myanmar Baptist Churches Union (1952-66) and the Myanmar Baptist Convention (1970-73). On 21 Nov 1953, he married Daw Hnit, a senior teacher at the Baptist Girls' High School, Kemmendine, Yangon, and a national Christian leader. After his marriage, he served many years as the chairperson of the Young Men's Christian Association* and the Myanmar Council of Churches. From 1964 to 1970, he was pastor of Judson Church on the campus of the University of Yangon and was involved with the national Student Christian Movement*. He also served as pastor of the First Baptist Church at Lanmadaw in Yangon. The last church in which he served was the Baptist church at Kemmendine, a model among Burmese-speaking churches. In all he did, U Ba Hmyin served with distinction until his last days.

Kyaw Nyunt

Ho Chi Minh

(b. 19 May (?) 1890; d. 1969). Founder of the Indochina Communist Party and its successor, the Vietminh; president of the Democratic Republic of Vietnam* (North Vietnam) from 1954 to 1969.

Ho's birth name was Nguyen Sinh Cung, but he was also called Nguyen Tat Thanh. After a poor childhood in his native village of Kim Lien, he went to study in Hue. In 1911, under the name of Ba, he left Vietnam, working aboard a French liner. In 1915-17, he lived in London and then went to France, where for six years (1917-23), under the name of Nguyen Ai Quoc (Nguyen the Patriot), he was involved in the French socialist movement; in 1920 he became a founding member of the French Communist Party.

At the end of 1923, Ho went to Moscow to study revolutionary tactics, and in 1924 he took part in the Fifth Congress of the Communist International, where he criticized the French Communist Party for its lukewarm opposition to colonialism* and emphasized the important role of oppressed peasants in revolutions. As a Comintern member, Ho was sent (1925-27) to Canton, a Communist stronghold, and founded a Vietnamese nationalist movement under the name *Thanh Nien Cach Menh Dong Chi Hoi* (*Thanh Nien* for short). In 1927, as General Chiang Kai-shek expelled Communists from Canton, Ho went back to Moscow and, a year later, went to Brussels and Paris and then to Siam (Thailand*), where he spent two years as representative of the Communist International in Southeast Asia.

In 1930, Ho left Siam for Hong Kong*, where he presided over the meeting of the *Thanh Nien,* during which the Indochinese Communist Party was founded. Meanwhile, in Vietnam there were nationalist insurrections against the French, and Ho was condemned to death in absentia by the French government. Arrested in Hong Kong*, Ho escaped to Moscow via Shanghai. In 1935, Ho attended the Seventh Congress of the International in Moscow. In 1938, he returned to China*, and in 1941 went back to Vietnam where, with Vo Nguyen Giap, Pham Van Dong, and five other comrades, he founded the *Viet Nam Doc Lap Dong Minh Hoi* (League for the Independence of Vietnam), known as *Vietminh* for short. About this time he began using the name Ho Chi Minh (He Who Enlightens). Chiang Kai-shek distrusted Ho's Communist sympathies and had him imprisoned in China for 18 months.

In 1945, the Japanese occupied Indochina and eliminated the French government. But on 6 and 9 Aug, the United States dropped atomic bombs on Hiroshima and Nagasaki, forcing Japan* to surrender. Seizing the liberation of Vietnam from both of its enemies, France and Japan, Ho proclaimed on 3 Sep 1945 the independence of the Democratic Republic of Vietnam, of which he became the president. Soon, however, French troops returned, and on 6 Mar 1946 Ho concluded an agreement that permitted the stationing of French troops in northern Vietnam in exchange for French recognition of Vietnam as a "free state" though "part of the Indochinese Federation and the French Union." Differences with the French eventually led to open warfare (1947) which lasted until 1954, culminating in the French defeat at Dien Bien Phu.

On 26 Jul 1954, at the Geneva Conference, an accord signed by France, the Democratic Republic of Vietnam, Great Britain, the Union of Soviet Socialist Republics, and the People's Republic of China (but not by the United States or the Republic of Vietnam) divided Vietnam at the 17th parallel. As a result, some 900,000 people, mostly Catholics, left the North for the South. Ho became the first president of the Democratic Republic of

Vietnam. The accord also provided for general elections to be held in 1956 with the purpose of uniting the two parts, North and South, into one country. South Vietnam, led by Ngo Dinh Diem and backed by the United States, refused to hold the elections. In the meantime, with the assistance of the Soviet Union and China, Ho consolidated his government. Around 1959, Ho began organizing a guerrilla movement (the National Liberation Front or the Viet Cong) in the South with the view to topple the government of the South and reunite the country. During the third congress of the Workers' Party (Lao Dong) in late 1959, Ho ceded his position as the party's secretary-general to Le Duan. He remained chief of state until his death in 1969, and in this capacity functioned as a symbol for the people conveyed by his popular title of "Uncle [bac] Ho."

Ho is often regarded as a Vietnamese nationalist dedicated to the independence of his country against foreign powers such as China, France, and America. While his efforts contributed to the recovery of national independence and reunification, his political alignment with Marxist-Leninist governments and his deeply entrenched Communist ideology, together with the socio-political, economic, and religious policies he sanctioned, have unfortunately marred his undeniable achievements.

Whatever role is assigned to Ho in the history of Vietnam, there is no doubt that Vietnamese Christianity suffered grievously at his hand. His Communist ideology and his repressive anti-religious and especially anti-Catholic measures provoked the exodus of 700,000 northern Catholics to the South in 1954, practically draining the life out of the northern church. From 1954 to Ho's death in 1969 and beyond, severe restrictions were imposed upon the church in North Vietnam. The Catholic Church was unfairly painted as unpatriotic, pro-French, and pro-American. It must be unambiguously pointed out that if Vietnamese Catholics were bitterly opposed to Ho, it was not because of his struggle for national independence (witness the relationship between Ho and Le Huu Tu, bishop of Phat Diem, who was appointed by Ho as Supreme Counselor of his government because of his passionate advocacy for national independence), but because of his allegiance to atheistic Communism which they saw as fundamentally irreconcilable with their faith.

Bibliography

Lacouture, Jean, *Ho Chi Minh: A Political Biography* (1968). • Fenn, Charles, *Ho Chi Minh: A Biographical Introduction* (1973). • Fall, Bernard B., ed., *Ho Chi Minh on Revolution: Selected Writings, 1920-1966* (1967).

Peter C. Phan

Hoa Hao Sect

Variant of Hinayana Buddhism* founded in 1939 by Huynh Phu So (b. 1919) from Hoa Hao village, An Giang Province, Vietnam*.

So's father, believing his sickly son was possessed by a demon, sent him to the Tra Son pagoda near That Son mountain, where he regained his health under the teachings of Master Xom. After his master's death, So returned to his native village. One night amidst a storm, he went into a trance and emerged from it proclaiming himself founder of Hoa Hao (meaning "peaceful and good") Buddhism. He advocated a return to the purity and simplicity of early Buddhism through prayer, meditation, and fasting. With neither temple nor hierarchy, the Hoa Hao prescribes filial piety, love of one's country and fellow human beings, and respect for its founder's Buddhist teachings. In only a few years it attracted about one million adherents.

Though regarded as the Living Buddha by his followers, So was seen by the French as a political agitator. He was placed under house arrest, which only increased his reputation. He moved to Saigon under the protection of the Japanese secret police.

The Hoa Hao opposed both the Communists and the French. In 1946, So created the Democratic Socialist Party, further stressing the difference between the Hoa Hao and the Communists by its clear anticolonial and anti-Communist position. So fell into a trap laid by the Communist-led Vietminh, who arrested and then killed him in Apr 1947.

In Jun 1954, the Hoa Hao reached its peak of influence, controlling most of the territory south and west of Saigon, maintaining private armies, and collecting taxes. In Jun 1955, Ngo Dinh Diem destroyed the Hoa Hao politically and militarily until the coup d'état in Nov 1963. In the late 1960s, many disillusioned nationalist intellectuals from the cities and towns joined the Hoa Hao religious movement. The rise and fall of the Hoa Hao followed a mixed path. It is now neither a political nor a military force. Anthony Do Huu Nghiem

Hobson, Benjamin

(b. Welford, Northamptonshire, England, 1816; d. 1873). Pioneer missionary doctor to China*.

Hobson was the son-in-law of Robert Morrison*, the first Protestant missionary to mainland China. Hobson graduated from the medical school at University College, London, qualified as a doctor, and in 1839 began practice in a clinic of the London Missionary Society (LMS) in Macau, where he became acquainted with Ronghong, whom he recommended to the Morrison Education Society. Ronghong thus became one of the first Chinese students to study in England.

In 1843, Hobson was transferred to take charge of a hospital in Hong Kong*, where Leong Kung Fa* (Liangfa) was evangelizing. The hospital was overwhelmed with patients, necessitating the hiring of many local Chinese. On his return trip to England in 1845, his wife died. Soon afterward he married Robert Morrison's daughter, Rebecca, and returned to the Hong Kong hospital in 1847.

Because of the great demand for medical care, Hobson's great dream was to develop a program for training Chinese in the medical sciences. His dream was delayed by an LMS relocation to Guangzhou in 1848, and then in 1857 he went to work in the Shanghai hospital. In 1859, he returned to England because of illness and never returned to China. He died in England. Hobson nonetheless laid the foundation for medical training in China by publishing treatises in Chinese on anatomy, surgery, obstetrics, and other natural sciences, the most well known being *A Medical Vocabulary in English and Chinese.*

Bibliography

Lockhart, William, *The Medical Missionary in China* (1861). • Wang, K. Chimin, *Lancet and Cross* (1950). • Wang, K. Chimin, and Wu Luh-teh, *History of Chinese Medicine* (1932).

CHINA GROUP

Hodgkin, Henry Theodore

(b. 1877; d. Dublin, 1933). British Quaker missionary to China*.

Born to a Quaker family, Hodgkin received his education in a Quaker school and later was admitted to King's College, Cambridge University, to learn medicine. After his graduation, he worked as a surgeon in London. In 1902, he was involved in the Student Volunteer Movement and came to China in 1905. He was sent by the English Friends' Foreign Missionary Association to Szechwan Chentu for five years. In 1910 he was transferred back to headquarters in London to serve as foreign missions secretary. During his 10-year term, he toured Africa, Asia, and America and witnessed the tragedy of war. Hence in 1915 he founded Wei Ai She and served as chairman until 1920.

In 1921, Hodgkin returned to China and organized Wei Ai She in China, took part in the World Student Christian Federation conference in Peking and the National Christian Conference in Shanghai, and was elected a member of the National Christian Council, which he served until 1929. In that year, he was chosen as Britain's representative to the Pacific Society's conference in Honolulu, at which he spoke in behalf of China. In 1929, he left China for home assignment. After two years of illness, he passed away. Hodgkin wrote many influential books in his lifetime, including *The Christian Revolution: An Essay on the Method of Social Progress* (1923), *Living Issues in China* (1932), and *China in the Family of Nations,* (1928).

Bibliography

Wood, George Herbert, *Henry T. Hodgkin: A Memoir* (1937). • See *The Chinese Recorder.*

CHINA GROUP

Hogan, Walter

American Jesuit* social reformer in the Philippines*.

In the late 1940s, Hogan began working with labor unions in the Philippines, attempting to implement papal social teachings. He attempted to develop a social conscience and initiated projects aimed at social justice. He started the Institute of Social Order (ISO) in 1947. The ISO maintained both a research division which provided social and economic data and a radio broadcast. Hogan believed in the "natural rights" of workers. All employers, he said, had responsibilities to ensure workers' well-being. Hogan was also instrumental in establishing the Federation of Free Workers in 1950. Government officials opposed his work in promoting labor unions; so did the Catholic hierarchy. He was branded a Communist (see Communism). In 1956 Archbishop Santos forbade him from speaking on social matters. Hogan left the Philippines in 1961 and later worked with the Committee for Development of Social Life in Asia, based in Hong Kong*. In the 1960s many of Hogan's initiatives were adopted by the Catholic* Church in the Philippines.

Bibliography

Carroll, John J., "The Philippines: Church of the Crossroads," in Thomas Gannon, ed., *World Catholicism in Transition* (1988). • Fabros, Wilfredo, *The Church and Its Social Involvement in the Philippines, 1930-72* (1988).

FLOYD T. CUNNINGHAM

Hogg, A(lfred) G(eorge)

(b. 1875; d. Bellany, Fife, Scotland, 31 Dec 1954). United Free Church of Scotland educational missionary to India*.

Hogg was educated at George Watson's College and Edinburgh University in Scotland, completing his studies in 1897. He first went to India in 1903 as a lay educational worker, where he taught at Madras Christian College (MCC). His ordination came later (1912), after he had carefully thought out many questions regarding basic issues of the Christian faith. He would always be a careful Christian thinker and theologian, his greatest contributions being to Christian education in India and Hindu-Christian theological awareness. From 1928 to 1930, he served as acting principal of MCC, where he then became principal until 1938.

Hogg's writings were not numerous, but they were significant for the development of Christian thinking about Hinduism* and the broader mission theology of the International Missionary Council (IMC). Although Hogg did not participate much in councils and conferences, the IMC held a major conference in 1938 on the new MCC campus in Tambaram (outside of Madras) that Hogg had helped to relocate. This conference brought him more directly into contact with the contemporary ecumenical* thinking about mission. Hogg's writings reflect his philosophical and theological approaches to understanding central beliefs in Christian theology and Hindu thought. For Hogg, these central beliefs have to do with redemption in Christianity and karma in Hinduism. In 1909 he published a pioneering work with that very title: *Karma and Redemption.* This work was important because it broke away from the dominant Christian approach of the time that viewed the Christian religion as a fulfillment of the goals and aspirations of all other religions. Other books dealing with these same themes followed: *Christ's Message of the Kingdom* (1911), *Redemption from This World* (1922), and *The Christian Message to the Hindu* (long after his return to Scotland, 1947). At the 1938 IMC conference, a debate ensued between the Barthian (or at least dialectical) theologian of mission, Hendrik Kraemer*, and Hogg. Kraemer and the Continental theologians would not allow for any continuity between Hindu religious faith and Christian faith, which was a totally new and discontinuous Word from God. Hogg, on the other hand, had spent his life carefully tracing theological lines concerning some of these central questions, and he found the dialectical approach unsatisfying.

Hogg's students recognized his ability both to listen and to empathize within the Indian context. As one of his students, D. G. Moses, remarked, "He was more than a teacher to his students; he was a real 'guru' in the Indian sense of the term. Many of them came to him sick at heart and palsied in soul, confused by the contrary winds of doctrine that beat upon their lives. To all of them he pointed to the skies and to his own Lord and Master, who was the Bread of Life. To the blight of ultimate meaninglessness in life, he opposed his own blessed Hope in Jesus Christ. . . ."

Soon after the Tambaram conference, Hogg retired back to Scotland, where he was a parish minister until his death.

Bibliography

Sharp, Eric J., *The Theology of A. G. Hogg* (1971); "A. G. Hogg," in *Mission Legacies,* ed. Gerald Anderson (1994). • Moses, D. G., "Alfred George Hogg," *The International Review of Missions* (Jul 1955). • Cox, James L., "Faith and Faiths: The Significance of A. G. Hogg's Missionary Thought for a Theology of Dialogue," *Scottish Journal of Theology,* Vol. 32 (1979).

SCOTT W. SUNQUIST

Holy Cross, Congregation of the

The Holy Cross religious family comprises four distinct congregations: the Congregation of Holy Cross Fathers and Brothers with its generalate in Rome; the Marianites of Holy Cross Sisters with its generalate in Washington, D.C., United States; the sisters of the Congregation of the Holy Cross with its generalate in South Bend, Indiana, United States; and the Congregation of Holy Cross Sisters with its generalate in Montreal, Canada. These four congregations have a common root and founder, and all four have worked and presently work in Asia.

Basil Anthony Mary Moreau was a priest of the diocese of Le Mans in France. In 1835, he was asked to take charge of a small group of brothers, the Brothers of St. Joseph, founded in 1820 by Jacques Dujarie, also of the Le Mans Diocese. Moreau had earlier envisioned forming a group of auxiliary priests to help with the reevangelization of France following the French Revolution. In 1837, he brought these two groups together to form the Congregation of the Holy Cross. In 1841, he founded the Marianite Sisters. The other two communities of sisters grew from the Marianites.

The members of the congregation, in addition to the evangelical vows, took a fourth vow called the Foreign Mission Vow, which stated their willingness to go "anywhere in the world the Superior General may wish to send me." Shortly after the foundation of the congregation, Holy Cross religious were serving in Algeria (1840), the United States (1841), Canada (1847), and Bengal (1853).

The Bengal mission comprised at that time all of present-day Bangladesh*, Assam, and the northern part of Myanmar*. The first group of missionaries settled in the area of Noakhali, and by the end of 1853 four Holy Cross priests, three brothers, and five sisters had arrived in Bengal. Within two years, two of this group had died and two returned home ill. In 1855, two more priests and a sister were sent. Journeying in a small boat from Calcutta to Dhaka, they were caught in a storm, and one of the priests and the sister drowned.

In 1860, Pierre Dufal became the first bishop of Dhaka. By 1876, the congregation felt that it could no longer sustain the mission with personnel and finances. In a few short years, six men had died and seven more had returned home ill. With only six men left to cover this vast territory, the congregation withdrew. In 1888, however, at the urgency of the holy see, Holy Cross returned to Bengal and has served there since.

The congregation's presence in Bengal has been in various ministries, notably education and parochial ministry, and also in development, youth ministry, communications, justice and peace, literacy*, technical training, care of the sick, natural family planning, a pastoral and retreat center, and seminary teaching (see Theological Education).

The only two Catholic colleges in Bangladesh are operated by Holy Cross. Notre Dame College for boys was founded in Dhaka in 1949. Holy Cross College for girls was founded by the sisters in 1950, also in Dhaka. The Holy Cross brothers operate high schools in Chittagong, Barisal, Dhaka (two), Bandura, and Nagari. They also maintain a network of technical schools throughout the country.

Holy Cross began an early mission to the aboriginal, tribal people of Bangladesh, and these now comprise the majority of the Catholics in the country.

Holy Cross personnel began the Credit Union movement in Bangladesh and founded the Christian Organization for Relief and Rehabilitation (CORR), which later became Caritas* Bangladesh. They were also instrumental in the beginning of the Natural Family Planning Movement.

Holy Cross sisters established two local communities of sisters and also many self-help projects for women. They also teach in primary and high schools. The Holy Cross brothers have hostels for students and also run a drug rehabilitation program. In addition, Holy Cross personnel are involved in training programs within their congregation and also in different diocesan seminaries.

The majority of the Holy Cross membership and leadership in Bangladesh are now Bangladeshi. Presently, there are four members of the hierarchy in Bangladesh who are members of the congregation. With independence from the British in 1947, Holy Cross also became involved in India* itself.

The Congregation of the Holy Cross has grown rapidly in India. The Indian Province of Priests is headquartered in Bangalore, Karnataka; and the Indian District of Brothers in Salem, Tamil Nadu. Holy Cross religious work in Tripura, Mizoram, Pune, Kerala, Kadpadi, Meghalaya, Karnataka, Bombay, Bangalore, Salem, and Madras. They are involved in parishes, schools, hostels, student homes, ashrams*, social action, and technical training.

Holy Cross father Theotonius Ganguly was ordained auxiliary bishop of Dhaka in 1960 and became archbishop in 1967, the first Bangladeshi bishop.

One Holy Cross brother has worked in Nepal* for over 20 years. The Sisters of the Holy Cross and the Marianites of Holy Cross have served in India. The Sisters of the Holy Cross served for a period in Bhutan* as well.

While there is still significant foreign Holy Cross presence in Bangladesh, with the growth of the congregation locally, this number is diminishing. The congregation is firmly planted for the future in the churches of Bangladesh and India.

The congregation retains a missionary spirit, serving where there is need within Bangladesh and India. There is reason to presume that, in the future, Bangladeshi Holy Cross religious will serve as missionaries in other lands, as some of the Indian Holy Cross priests have already done.

Bibliography

Clancy, Raymond J., *The Congregation of the Holy Cross in East Bengal, 1853-1953,* 2 vols. (1953). • Goedert, Edmund N., *Holy Cross Priests in the Diocese of Dacca, 1853-1981* (1983). FRANK QUINLIVAN

Holy Rosary Church (Calvary), Thailand

In 1767, the Portuguese Catholics fled Ayutthaya when it fell to the Burmese. A group led by Fr. Corré, a French priest, later established the Santa Cruz Church in Thonburi. Some, however, preferred Portuguese priests and chose to live apart on a deserted piece of land which is the present location of the Calvary Church. They called this site the Holy Rosary Camp, as they had the image of the Mother of the Rosary from Ayutthaya with them. As they had neither church nor priest, they had to worship at the Santa Cruz Church.

A raised wooden church with a large assembly room and a sacristy was built in 1787 on land granted by the king in 1786. A rectory was built beside the church in anticipation of a resident Portuguese priest. The church was named Calvary Church after the crucifix which had been brought from Ayutthaya. A request to the archbishop of Goa for a Portuguese priest was rejected on the grounds that the pope had appointed a French bishop over the area. So the Portuguese Catholics had to be content with the French missionaries.

In 1820, when the Portuguese were allowed to open a consulate, and shortly thereafter an embassy, the Portuguese consul petitioned the Thai king to grant to Portugal the land on which the Holy Rosary Camp was situated. King Rama II issued an edict permitting the Portuguese Catholics to build a church on the property, which in effect made it the property of the Roman Catholic Mission, and not the Portuguese government. Mgr. Florens, the head of the mission, came to exercise pastoral oversight of Calvary Church. The first mass was held on 25 Aug 1822.

The Portuguese community gradually dwindled as many moved elsewhere in search of work and the Chinese moved in to take their place. Occasionally, a Thai priest would come and celebrate mass and the sacraments for believers. In 1837, Fr. Albrand came to live at Calvary Church in order to do evangelistic work with the Chinese. He constructed a large assembly hall of bamboo and thatch for catechumens and Chinese Catholics.

A new building of brick and stone was consecrated on 1 Oct 1839 to replace the now decrepit church built in 1787. It was named the Holy Rosary Church by the coadjutor bishop, Mgr. Pallegoix*, but until the present time its popular name was Calvary Church. In 1858, the king granted the church an adjacent piece of land to enable repairs to be done to the church, which had been damaged by exploding fireworks. A fire on 2 Feb 1864 destroyed the rectory and all records of the church dating back to the time of Fr. Albrand. The present church building was built in 1890 under Fr. Dessalles and consecrated twice on 4 Mar 1891 by Jean-Louis Vey* and again in 1897. René Perros was consecrated bishop on 30 Jan 1910 in a service attended by a representative of King Rama V. The silver jubilee of Calvary Church was celebrated on 1 Oct 1922, and its golden jubilee on 5 Oct 1947.

The first Thai senior pastor of Calvary Church was Huasieng Kitbunchu. Cardinal Michai was the thirteenth senior pastor of Calvary Church. The church building was restored in the 1980s, and on 16 Apr 1987 the church was awarded a certificate by Princess Ratana-racha-suda for its efforts in conservation work.

VICTOR LARQUE, translated by E. JOHN HAMLIN

Holy Spirit Study Center, Hong Kong

The Holy Spirit Study Center is an organ of the Catholic Diocese of Hong Kong, established in 1980 as an expression of its pastoral concern for China* and the church in China. It is a research institute whose primary task is to gather, store, and analyze pertinent data about China that could serve to broaden understanding, increase contacts, and encourage appropriate initiatives. Another task of the center is to assist both China-concerned groups from abroad and delegations from China in their exchanges and visits.

Facilities at the center, which is housed in a wing of the Holy Spirit Seminary College at Aberdeen, include offices for research associates, a library, archives for documentation, and a meeting room.

Publications of the center include *Tripod,* a bilingual and bimonthly periodical of research on religious and social problems in China; *Vox Mundi,* a monthly leaflet in Chinese on Catholic Church world news; "China Bridge," a monthly page on China in the Catholic English weekly *Sunday Examiner* and "God's Love for China," a monthly page in the diocesan Chinese weekly *Kung Kau Po.*

Bibliography

Hong Kong Catholic Church Directory (published annually). • "Hong Kong Holy Spirit Study Center" (pamphlet). • *Tripod,* Nos. 1, 60, 90, 100. Sergio Ticozzi

Home for the Aged Poor, Yangon, Myanmar

In the late 1890s, there lived in Rangoon two young girls united by a bond of friendship that had for its foundation a truly religious spirit of charity. One was Gertrude di Oliveiro, and the other Helen Carr. They were pupils at the same convent school and both were of a mixed parentage that was labeled "Anglo-Indian." These two pious souls grew up together and, from their earliest girlhood days, helped each other in their efforts at succoring the poor. As time went on and they left school, both were attracted to the religious life, but circumstances and perhaps prejudices prevented their joining any congregation of nuns.

Mgr. Bigandet was quick to notice the true worth and piety of these two insignificant-looking little persons and took a special interest in all of their charitable enterprises, watching for an indication of God's design and convinced that they were destined for an unusual career. Di Oliveiro was the dominating character, and Carr seconded and helped her in all her enterprises. When di Oliveiro asked to be admitted as a postulant into the House of the Little Sisters of the Poor, Helen did not join her, and the friends parted company for a while.

Di Oliveiro was admitted into the congregation on trial and passed two years at the Home for the Aged at Calcutta, edifying all around her by her piety and devotion to the old people. Yet the superiors of the congregation decided that it was better to send her home.

Full of regrets, yet submissive to the will of God, this young lady returned to Rangoon and told her story to the good bishop, her friend and benefactor. He consoled her and told her that, if she wished, she and Carr together could try to found a home for the aged in Rangoon, as there was great need there. Joyfully and courageously, the two young women agreed to try, resolving to keep in mind the example of the Little Sisters and to follow out their methods. Bigandet placed at their disposal a small house belonging to the mission, and this they proceeded to furnish in the same way as did the Little Sisters, that is to say, by soliciting alms from door to door. They took in many of the local indigent old persons, and thus the Hospitaler Work of St. Servan was begun anew at Rangoon.

For 10 years, these two courageous young women alone carried on the work. They housed about 30 residents and maintained their home on the same lines of poverty and charity as did the Little Sisters of the Poor, depending on providence for their own sustenance as well as that of those under their care.

During this period, Bigandet died, and in him the two lost a great benefactor. His successor, Mgr. Cardot, was keenly desirous of having the Little Sisters of the Poor come to Rangoon and open a home. He wrote to La Tour, the mother house of the congregation, repeating the request of his predecessor, but without success. At last, in 1898, Cardot had occasion to visit France and made it a point to go to La Tour. He laid the whole case before the superiors of the Little Sisters and was so eloquent in picturing the needs of his flock for such a work of charity in their midst, describing vividly the valiant efforts of the two Anglo-Indian women, that the superiors recognized it was God's will they should go to Rangoon and open a home there. It was decided to send out a band of the congregation to take over the home already opened by di Oliveiro and Carr, and to receive them both into the congregation. On 21 Nov of the same year, the Little Sisters arrived at Rangoon and di Oliveiro and Carr sailed for Europe to enter the novitiate of the Little Sisters at Marino near Rome.

The Home for the Aged was at last established at Rangoon under the care of the Little Sisters of the Poor and was soon filled to capacity. One of their first benefactors was Bishop Cardot who, from his private purse as well as from the mission funds, did all he could to help the foundation from its earliest days. He sold the small house, which Bigandet had placed at the disposal of di Oliveiro, and handed the cash over to the good mother. The vicar general, Rev. Father Luce, made all the arrangements for the purchase of a new property.

World War I and World War II* brought times of trouble, and it was not possible to give alms with the same liberality as before. The Little Sisters understood and, alone with the old people under their care, went gladly without many comforts.

It has been remarked that the Buddhists, both Chinese and Burmese, as well as various other races and creeds, are very sympathetic toward the humanitarian work carried out at the home.

Nationalization of the schools, hospitals, and various

enterprises took place in 1965-66. The Little Sisters were obliged to leave the country, but the home has continued its work under Burmese leadership.

There are still a great number of English-speaking elderly among the residents. Services in the chapel are held alternately in English and Burmese from week to week. Church literature such as missals, holy week manuals, and the lectionary is sorely needed for the spiritual nurture of the home, which has 200 residents. About one-third are Catholic. Many outsiders also attend the services at the chapel, which is considered a semi-public place of worship. Among the benefactors of the home are some Buddhist monks who occasionally help in cash and kind.

Homeland Theology, Taiwan

The theological exploration and exposition of nation-building arising from the peculiar context of Taiwan*.

Taking the Exodus, nation-building, and exiles of Israel in the Hebrew Scriptures as a paradigm, homeland theology reckons that the issues of ethnicity (people), land, power, and God are the main theological themes for the Israelites, the Israelis, and the Taiwanese as well. But, in the Greek Scriptures, the theological focus of nation-building was transformed into community-building *(ecclesia)* in the light of the reign of God proclaimed and realized by Jesus Christ through the power of the Holy Spirit. Thus nation-building coexists with community-building under the reign of God. The global conflicts among nations should be reconciled and redeemed through the sovereignty of God witnessed to by Jesus Christ in calling people to love God and neighbors as themselves.

To deal with the theological motifs of ethnicity, land, power, and God, socio-historical, cultural, and ideological elements in the formation of the Scriptures are entailed in biblical-theological criticism and interpretation. The stories of the people in Taiwan are essential resources for theological deliberation. The story theology developed by C. S. Song is methodologically illuminating for the formation and development of homeland theology.

Asian countries have suffered the consequences of both colonialism* and the Cold War. Ethnic conflicts in Asia and elsewhere today also have theological-political undercurrents. Historically, Taiwan has been dominated successively by several colonial powers in the last four centuries, i.e., the Dutch, Spanish, Ming-Chinese, Qing-Chinese, Japanese, and Kuomintang-Chinese. It has been exploited as an economic and military base by each in turn. Hence, the Taiwanese desire for a homeland with democracy and freedom. The idea of a homeland theology was first suggested by Wang Hsien-Chih when Taiwan was denied its political status by the United States in 1978. Earlier in 1977, the Presbyterian* Church in Taiwan (PCT) had already issued *A Declaration on Human Rights* upholding the universal principle of self-determination. The Taiwanese have dreamed of an independent political identity since the establishment of the Taiwan Democratic Republic on 25 May 1895, when China* ceded Taiwan to Japan*. The PCT's declaration based on human rights bestowed by God became a theological assertion for the Taiwanese vision of "a new and independent country."

The first international symposium on homeland theology was sponsored by the PCT and the Commission on Theological Concerns (CTC) of the Council of Churches in Asia* (CCA) in Sep 1979 in Taipei. Following this, the CTC sponsored the first international symposium on Minjung* theology in Oct 1979 at Seoul. The themes of people, land, power, and God became the main theological foci in Asia after the Taiwan and Korean symposia. In 1989, the CCA held a worldwide mission conference, "Mission of God in the Context of the Suffering and Struggling Peoples of Asia." In 1990, at the ninth assembly of the CCA in Manila, the theme was "Christ Our Peace: Building a Just Society," reflecting the main theological concerns of Taiwan's homeland theology. The First International Symposium (10-17 Mar 1990) on Palestinian liberation theology at Tantur in Israel expounded a theological-political emphasis similar to the homeland theology of Taiwan.

Bibliography

Wang Hsien-Chih, *Collected Essays on Taiwan Homeland Theology,* Vol. I (1988); "Some Perspectives on Theological Education in the Light of Homeland Theology in the Taiwanese Context," *CTC Bulletin,* Vol. 6, Nos. 2 and 3 (Jan-Apr 1986); "Who Are the Taiwanese People? A Theological-Sociohistorical Perspective," *Theology and Church,* Vol. 17, No. 1 (Jun 1986); "The Problem of Religious Fundamentalism in Relation to Ethnicity, Power and Ideology: An Asian Perspective," *The Reformed World,* Vol. 42 (1991). • Dali, Boxing, *The Aboriginal People: Rather Dying than Surrendering* (1995).

WANG HSIEN-CHIH

Hong Hyun Sul

(Harold) (b. 21 Sep 1911; d. 14 Nov 1990). Well-known theological ethicist, theological educator, journalist, and pastor of the Korean Methodist* Church.

Hong did his theological work at Union Theological Seminary in New York from 1929 to 1933, after which he went to Japan* to continue his theological education at Kansai Gakuin College's department of theology until 1936. After his return, he did parish ministry in North Korea and was ordained at the Western Annual Conference in 1938. He taught at John's Bible Institute in Pyongyang before he was appointed professor at the Methodist Theological Seminary in Seoul in 1942. Immediately after his appointment, he expressed his objection to the seminary faculty's political views. Consequently, he was dismissed from his teaching position and was imprisoned.

After the liberation of Korea in 1945, Hong was reinstated in his teaching position at the Methodist Theological Seminary in 1946. During his tenure, he went to Union Theological Seminary and Drew University for two years to do further theological work. Upon his return during the Korean War, he was elected the first president of the Methodist Seminary. He served the seminary as president until his retirement in 1976.

As a Christian ethicist and journalist, Hong initiated a monthly theological journal for church leaders and laypeople, *Kodockkyo Sasang* (The Christian Thought) in 1958.

DAVID SUH, with contributions from LEE DUK JOO; original translated by KIM IN SOO

Hong Kong

Hong Kong comprises Hong Kong Island (29 square miles), Kowloon Peninsula and Stonecutters Island (3.75 square miles), and the New Territories including 236 adjacent islands (365.5 square miles) put under British administration in 1841, 1860, and 1889 respectively. Missionary activity in all three areas began in the early 1840s.

Protestant Church. Hong Kong has long been a center for mission to China. Missionaries met in Hong Kong from 22 Aug to 4 Sep 1843 to produce a better Chinese translation of the Bible*, the Delegates' Version, published in 1855. Issachar Jacob Roberts of the American Baptist* Board of Foreign Missions began work in Hong Kong in 1842, but he soon moved to Guangzhou, where some of the Chinese converts later became leaders of the Taiping* Movement.

There were, however, a number of missionaries who laid the foundations for Christian mission in Hong Kong. John Lewis Shuck, another American Baptist missionary, began the first Protestant congregation in May 1842. Karl Friedrich August Gützlaff* of the Netherlands Missionary Society set up the Chinese Union in 1844 and employed many Chinese to preach and distribute Gospel tracts. The Union attracted the Rhenish, Basel, and Berlin Missionary Societies to send missionaries to Hong Kong and China. James Legge* of the London Missionary Society arrived from Malacca*, Malaysia*, in 1843 and remained for 30 years. He established the Central School, the first government school for Chinese, and the Union Church, from which came the first independent Chinese church in Hong Kong — Tsai Church, led by Wang Yuk-cho, a son of the Basel Mission Chinese preacher Wang Yuen-sum. Legge, a sinologue who later became the first Chinese professor at Oxford University, completed a meticulous translation of *The Chinese Classics* (first edition, Hong Kong, 1860-73). His contemporary, Vincent Stanton, who was appointed the first colonial chaplain in 1843, collected public subscriptions to build St. John's Cathedral, now one of the oldest buildings in Hong Kong, and also started St. Paul's College, a prestigious school today. The Anglican mission began in 1850 with the appointment of George Smith as the first bishop of the Victoria Diocese.

From the 1860s on, there were a noticeable number of prominent Chinese Christians, namely Wong Shing, Wong Fun, Yung Wing, Ho Kai, Tong King-shing, and Wu Ting-fang, all leaders of important Chinese organizations such as the Tung Wah Hospital, members of the legislative council, or champions of social movements, e.g., the campaigns against licensed gambling houses in the 1860s and 1870s. Some, such as Li Hung-zhang, were even invited to serve eminent officials of the Qing Dynasty. Sun Yat-Sen*, father of the Chinese revolution, was baptized during his secondary education in Hong Kong.

Two significant Christian organizations in Hong Kong are the Hong Kong Chinese Christian Churches Union, founded on 8 Apr 1915 to deal with matters relating to the Christian cemetery and later developing other services including medical and senior citizen projects, and the Hong Kong Christian Council, a member of the World Council of Churches established in Jan 1954 and committed to ecumenism and social concerns.

For several years after 1949, there was an influx of Chinese church leaders and missionaries from China* to Hong Kong, resulting in significant church growth. Leung Siu Choh, once the leader of the Young Men's Christian Association* (YMCA) in Guangdong and Shanghai, became the first chairman of the Hong Kong Council of the Church of Christ in China, which registered with the Hong Kong government in 1957. Teng Chih Hui led the Christian Alliance Church and other Chinese Christian communities.

The 1970s saw two significant developments. In 1974, Hong Kong became the headquarters of the Chinese Coordination Center of World Evangelism*, coordinating Chinese churches all over the world. In 1975, the Methodist* Church of Hong Kong was officially created from a union of British and American Methodist missions in Hong Kong.

Today, there are about 260,000 Protestants from more than 50 denominations constituting 950 congregations. Christian contributions to the general welfare in Hong Kong include the Hong Kong Baptist* University, Lingnan College, Chung Chi College of the Chinese University of Hong Kong, 131 secondary schools, 141 primary schools, 143 kindergartens, 3,463 beds in seven hospitals, 24 clinics, and 61 social service organizations.

Roman Catholic Church. The Catholic Church in Hong Kong is as old as the colony itself, since it was established as a mission prefecture on 22 Apr 1841. Its first function was to provide religious services to the Irish soldiers. Its first prefect, Theodore Joset*, soon started to build a church, a residence, and a cemetery, but fatigue and the climate led to his early death in Aug 1842.

Joset was succeeded by Anthony Feliciani* (1842-55, except for the period in which Augustine Forcade* took over, 1847-50). During these years, the building of various institutions continued, including a school, a hospital, and an orphanage for abandoned babies (run by the St. Paul Sisters), while the mission work spread to all the island villages.

After Feliciani's resignation in 1855, Louis Ambrosi* was appointed prefect, and he served in this capacity until his death in 1867. In 1860, under his leadership the prefecture was extended on the Chinese continent to the whole San On District (later Po On). Evangelization work thus spread to the Kowloon, Taipo, Saikung, and Namtau areas. Catholic commitment in education greatly increased with the arrival of the Canossian Sisters in 1860 and the opening of West Point in 1863.

After Ambrosi, the prefecture was entrusted to the Lombardy Seminary for Foreign Missions (later Pontifical Institute for Foreign Missions*, PIME), whose first members had arrived in Hong Kong in 1858. One of them, Timoleon Raimondi, was appointed prefect in Nov 1867. With the progress of the mission work, the prefecture was further enlarged to include Kwai Hsin (Wai Yeung) and Hoi Fung districts, Guangdong; it was raised to a vicariate in 1874. New churches were built in Hong Kong, as well as chapels, mainly in the Saikung area and in the new districts. Education services were improved with the arrival of the Christian Brothers in 1875, who took over the direction of West Point and the Holy Savior's College (renamed St. Joseph's in 1918). In 1877, the first Catholic weekly, *The Hong Kong Catholic Register,* was launched. In 1885, the Paris Foreign Missions Society (MEP) began to operate the Nazareth Press. The present cathedral was blessed in 1888.

After Raimondi's death in Sep 1894, Louis Piazzoli* became vicar apostolic until his death in 1904. His years were marked by the lease of the New Territories to Britain of the New Territories in 1898 and by the almost annual recurrence of the bubonic plague; the mission work continued steadily both in the city and in the inland districts, which gradually grew autonomous.

Dominic Pozzoni* took charge as the third vicar apostolic in 1905 until his death in 1924. He led the church throughout the difficult years of the fall of the Chinese Empire and World War I; thanks to his diligence, this period was characterized by an increase of apostolic zeal, social services to the poor and sick, efforts in the publication sector, and lay associations. He played a major role in the founding of the University of Hong Kong in 1912. In 1922, he divided the local Precious Blood Sisters from the Canossian Sisters and made them autonomous.

In 1926, Henry Valtorta was appointed fourth vicar apostolic. He welcomed other religious orders to work in Hong Kong and created autonomous districts both in the New Territories and inland in the Po On, Wai Yeung, and Hoi Fung areas, providing them with new churches. His concern led to the first Chinese Catholic weekly, *Kung Kau Po,* in 1928. The South China Regional Seminary was opened in Aberdeen in 1931. After the start of the Sino-Japanese War in 1937, subsidies and help for its victims were arranged (see World War II). Unfortunately, all work and activities were disrupted and reduced to a minimum by the Japanese invasion and occupation (1941-45). The post-war reconstruction saw a strong revival of activities in the districts and the churches, activities that were coordinated by the Catholic Center (opened in 1946, it also started an English weekly, the *Sunday Examiner*), as well as the raising of Hong Kong to a diocese in 1946. From the end of the war to the early years of the Communist takeover of mainland China, many religious orders took refuge and started work in Hong Kong, mainly among the large number of refugees. The inland section of the Hong Kong Diocese became inaccessible.

Valtorta died in Sep 1951. His successor, Lawrence Bianchi*, could not be installed as second bishop until Oct 1952, since he was held prisoner by the Communist authorities in Hoi Fung. His years (1952-69) were characterized by a necessarily frantic and even chaotic rhythm of services, both social and religious, to the thousands of refugees* flooding the colony in order to escape either political oppression or natural disasters. Under the sponsorship of the church, chapels for religious activities and centers for the distribution of relief mushroomed in almost every corner, together with schools and colleges to provide education for youngsters. Around them, Christian communities slowly grew up, which later were organized into full parishes. All the Catholic social welfare services were gradually coordinated around a central organization, Caritas–Hong Kong*. The concern for the local needs was paralleled with the new renewal impulse created within the Catholic Church by Vatican Council II (1962-65).

The resignation and departure of Bianchi in 1969 hastened the handing over of responsibility for the diocese to the local clergy. Francis Hsu Chen-Ping* succeeded him as the first Chinese bishop. In order to bring the local church up to the renewal advocated by the Vatican II, he called a diocesan convention (1970-71), which tried to make an overall assessment of all church services. The local church started to reorganize its commitments within Hong Kong society and its relationships with neighboring churches, but unfortunately the bishop died in Apr 1973, followed too soon also by the death of his successor, Peter Lei Wang Kee, in Jul 1974.

John B. Wu Cheng-Chung (made cardinal in 1988) was appointed fifth bishop of Hong Kong in 1975. His main concerns centered on the reorganization of the diocesan institutions and structures and the prudent guidance of the church toward the return of Hong Kong to the mainland in 1997 (this entailed encouraging the political commitment of the Catholics, especially after the signing of the Sino-British Joint Declaration in 1984, and taking various related initiatives). These two concerns were combined in his pastoral letter "March into the Bright Decade: On the Pastoral Commitment of the Catholic Diocese of Hong Kong," issued in 1989 and reassessed in 1994-95 in close cooperation with a large number of others.

In recent years, not a few Chinese Catholics, out of

worry about the future, emigrated to other countries. But, on the other side, a large number of Catholics among the Vietnamese boat people and Filipino domestic helpers came to Hong Kong, requiring special care and services from the church.

The total Catholic Chinese population is about 157,500, divided into 62 parishes with 338 priests, 91 religious brothers, and 599 sisters; there are 272 schools with 290,757 students and 10,678 teachers; in addition, there are 6 hospitals, 17 clinics, 17 child-care centers, 12 homes for the aged, and 13 rehabilitation centers.

Bibliography

Endacott, George B., and Dorothy E. She, *The Diocese of Victoria, Hong Kong: A Hundred Years of Church History, 1849-1949* (1949). • Lau Yuet-sang, *A History of Christianity in Hong Kong* (1941). • Lee Chee-kong, *A Study of Hong Kong Christian Churches* (1987) (in Chinese); *Stories of Churches in Hong Kong* (1992) (in Chinese). • Luk, Bernard H. K., "Custom and Religion," *Hong Kong Report, 1900,* ed. Richard Y. C. Wong and Joseph Y. S. Cheng (1990). • Lo Yin-bin, comp., *A History of Rhenish Mission in China* (1968) (in Chinese). • Smith, Carl T., *Chinese Christians: Elites, Middlemen, and the Church in Hong Kong* (1985). • *Hong Kong Catholic Church Directory 1995* (Yearbook) (1995). • Ticozzi, Sergio, *Historical Documents of the Hong Kong Catholic Church* (1983) (in Chinese). • Ryan, T., *The Story of a Hundred Years* (1959); *Catholic Guide to Hong Kong* (1962).

Timothy Man-kong Wong and Sergio Ticozzi

Hong Kong Catholic Center

One of the best-known Catholic institutions due to its location right in the heart of the busiest district of the city, the Hong Kong Catholic Center was established in 1945 at the close of World War II* to meet the spiritual needs of business people and the armed forces around the central area of Hong Kong. Fathers N. Maestrini and B. Meyer were its founders. Ever since then, the quiet chapel in the midst of business offices has been an attraction for people in this area. Very soon a library, an information desk, a bookshop, and a department for religious articles were set up.

Later the center offered its facilities for the handling of the administration, coordination, and finances of Catholic publications such as the *Sunday Examiner* and *Kung Kao Po* (Chinese Catholic Weekly), and of the Catholic Truth Society (see Literature and Publishing). Because of easy access to its location, the center has hosted diocesan and Catholic laity organizations such as the Liturgical Commission, the Catholic Welfare Committee, the Central Council of Laity, and the Catholic Youth Council.

In 1959, the Catholic Center moved to its present location in the Grand Building under the directorship of Msgr. Vath*, who organized the social welfare program for the diocese which was later developed into the present Caritas–Hong Kong*. In 1978, most of the diocesan and Catholic laity organizations moved to the newly built Catholic Diocesan Center in Caine Road, leaving on Connaught Road Central the chapel, the bookshop, and the department for religious articles, as well as some rooms for meetings and services to the Filipino Catholic community.

Bibliography

Hong Kong Catholic Church Directory (published annually); Ticozzi, Sergio, *Historical Documents of the Hong Kong Catholic Church* (Hong Kong Catholic Diocesan Archives, 1997).

Louis Ha

Hong Kong Catholic Social Concern

Since the beginning of its presence in Hong Kong*, the Catholic Church has always been involved in social services, starting from the care of abandoned babies and the education of children, to assistance of beggars, destitute girls, poor, blind, and old people. These services were carried out by the clergy, religious orders, and lay associations. The assistance of needy families and poor students, organized around the churches, has been done mainly by the Society of St. Vincent de Paul (established in 1863). Educational and social institutions have been run by religious orders, among which the St. Paul de Chartres Sisters* (from 1848), the Canossian Sisters (from 1860), and the Little Sisters of the Poor (from 1923) deserve special mention for their constant and unassuming services to Hong Kong society.

An important role has always been played by the church in assisting the waves of refugees during the entire history of the colony, but especially after World War II* in 1945, the Communist takeover of mainland China* in 1949, and the natural disasters in the 1960s. In these years, the provision of services was, at first, rather disorganized, left to the initiative of individuals, parishes, centers, and hospitals. They were carried out mainly in two sectors: welfare and education. Gradually, a better coordination was required; therefore, for the welfare sector, a Social Welfare Conference of the Catholic Church was established in Dec 1957, which was renamed Caritas–Hong Kong* in 1961. From 1971, due to the decrease of refugees and the improvement of the living standard, Caritas diversified in more specialized services, gradually becoming the only official and central welfare organization of the dioceses, with large subsidies from the government. For the educational sector, the management was first left to the parish and to the religious orders; only since the 1990s has the diocese tried to better centralize it.

On the parish level, lay associations have always carried on their charitable initiatives, and gradually, with the improvement of living conditions, they also started to show concern for other social problems such as workers welfare, resettlement, temporary housing, boat people, and refugees*. On the diocesan level, it was first the

Catholic Youth Council and the Federation of Catholic Students, mainly from 1968 to 1978, that became involved in more politically oriented issues such as the Anti-Corruption Campaign and the nationalistic campaign for Diao Yu Tai Island and for Chinese as the official language (see Nationalism). The concern for sociopolitical issues was continued also by the Justice and Peace Commission, set up in 1977.

Since the signing in 1984 of the Sino-British joint declaration on the future of Hong Kong, direct political concern has made its way mainly through the efforts of the Central Council for the Laity, the Federation of Catholic Students, the Justice and Peace Commission, and the Catholic Institute for Religion and Society (set up in 1985). With the full support of the local hierarchy, they have voiced the Catholic position on many issues, monitoring the process to 1997 and the future of Hong Kong. They have set up social-concern groups in parishes, provided courses for political education, and fostered Catholic political involvement and direct participation in elections. After the Tian'anmen incident of 4 Jun 1989, many Catholic organizations joined hands in organizing support of the patriotic and democratic movement. Cardinal J. B. Wu tried to coordinate and encourage all these social and political initiatives through his pastoral exhortation, "March into the Bright Future," in May 1989, and evaluation of their ongoing implementation.

Bibliography

Wu, John B., "March into the Bright Future" (1989).

Sergio Ticozzi

Hong Xiuquan (Hung Hsiu-Chuan)

(b. Guangdon, China, 1 Jan 1814; d. Nanjing, China, 1 Jun 1864). Chinese revolutionary leader in the "Heavenly King" *(Tian Wang)* of the Taiping Rebellion.

Hong Xiuquan came from a literate Hakka peasant family. He failed the imperial examinations four times. After his second attempt at the examinations in 1836, two preachers, one Chinese and one American (Edwin Stevens), gave him a set of nine pamphlets containing essays and biblical selections, titled "Good Words for Exhorting the Age," written by Lian Fa (see Leong Kung Fa) and published in 1832. He laid them aside after a superficial reading. After his third unsuccessful attempt to succeed in the imperial examinations, Hong fell seriously ill and was plagued by visions. Upon recovery, he resumed work as a village teacher for five or six years. In 1843, frustrated with his fourth failure at passing the examinations, his attention was drawn to Lian Fa's pamphlets through his cousin, Li Jingfang (Ching-fang), who had borrowed them for his own reading and was fascinated by their content. Hong seemed to find illumination for his earlier visions from the pamphlets. He identified God the Father as the venerable old man in his dreams, Jesus as the middle-aged elder brother, and the idols as the demons he saw in his visions. He believed he had received a divine mandate to lead the people. He and Li baptized themselves. They destroyed the idols in Li's home and embarked on their preaching mission. Hong was instrumental in the conversion of his family and two close friends: his cousin Hong Rengan (Jen-kan), nine years his junior, and Feng Yunshan. In 1844 Hong and Feng preached as far as Guangxi.

In 1847 Hong went to Guangzhou to study more Christian doctrine under a Baptist missionary, Issacher J. Roberts. After a few months, Roberts decided against baptizing Hong since he doubted Hong's motives. Hong then proceeded to Guangxi, where he found that Feng, in just two years, had formed a syncretistic religious sect, the *Bai Shangdi Hui* (The Society of the Worshippers of Shangdi), with more than 3,000 followers. In addition to monotheism and baptism, the followers observed religious rites such as the burning of paper containing confessed sins, formal evening and morning prayers and grace, and the consumption of animals sacrificed as part of a marriage, burial, and New Year celebration. Hong was welcomed with reverence as "Master Hung." The increase in Shangdi worshippers led to inevitable hostilities with the Confucian gentry and Manchu authorities.

In January 1851 Hong and his followers set up a new dynasty in Guangxi. Their kingdom was called the "Heavenly Kingdom of Eternal Peace and Prosperity" *(Taiping Tianguo),* and Hong was declared the "Heavenly King" *(Tian Wang).* In March 1853 Hong and his followers captured Nanjing and made it their capital, naming it *Tianjin* (Heavenly Capital). They held the city for more than a decade. Although Hong devoted much time to praying for his kingdom and his palace was run with strict discipline and an insistence on moral education, Hong himself reputedly had 88 wives. Each wife was considered a daughter-in-law of God and the younger sister of the queen. An attempt by Yang Xiuqing (Hsiu-ching), Hong's "East King" *(Tong Wang),* to usurp the throne in 1856 resulted in the deaths of four leaders, which weakened the Taiping Tianguo. Hong died on 1 Jun 1864 during the siege of the city by the Manchu authorities. His 16-year-old son, Hong Tian-kuei-fu, succeeded him on 6 Jun 1864.

Bibliography

Jen Wu-Yen, *The Taiping Revolutionary Movement* (1973). • Spence, Jonathan, *God's Chinese Son: The Taiping Heavenly Kingdom of Hong Xiuquan* (1997).

China Group, translated by Patricia Siew

Hose, George Frederick

(b. England, 1838; d. England, 1922). Anglican* bishop, linguist, and naturalist.

Hose graduated from St. John's College, Cambridge, in 1860. He served two curacies in England and became the colonial chaplain of Malacca* (1868-73) and Singapore (1873-81) and archdeacon of Singapore* (1875-

81). He was appointed bishop of Singapore, Labuan, and Sarawak in 1881.

As bishop, Hose saw the expansion of the English-speaking work mainly in Singapore, Malacca, and Penang. Churches were also established in Butterworth, Taiping, Batu Gajah, Kuala Lumpur, Klang, and Seremban. In Sarawak, he inherited a mission fraught with difficulties, but, with archdeacon A. F. Sharp's assistance, an Asian ministry was established. The diocese became too large for a single bishop, and in Hose's final years plans were made for the eventual formation of two dioceses.

As a naturalist, Hose helped form the Straits branch of the Royal Asiatic Society and became its first president. His knowledge of Malay, gained through pastoral work, gave him great influence among the Straits-born Chinese. It also enabled him to serve as the head reviser of the Malay New Testament. Subsequently, in retirement from the bishopric in 1908, Hose was also instrumental in revising the Malay prayer book, adding to it further translations of many psalms.

Bibliography

Singapore Diocesan Magazine (May 1918 and May 1922). • Saunders, Graham, *Bishops and Brookes* (1992).

Soon Soo Kee

Hough, James

(b. ?; d. ?). Chaplain of the East India Company at Madras; observer of and participant in early Protestant missionary work in India*.

As chaplain at Palamcottah (1816-21), Hough supplied Bibles and prayer books and trained catechists and teachers. He acted as superintendent for the Society for the Promotion of Christian Knowledge (SPCK). He persuaded the Church Missionary Society (CMS) to send Schmid and C. T. E. Rhenius* in 1820 to begin a work in Tinnevelly. Hough was instrumental in transferring the mission work from the SPCK to the Society for the Propagation of the Gospel (SPG) and the CMS, for which he has been labeled the "second father" of the Tinnevelly Mission (incorrectly? C. T. E. Rhenius is usually honored as the second father of the Tinnevelly Church; C. F. Schwarz as its first).

Hough's greatest contribution was as historian of early Protestant missions in India. His four-volume *History of Christianity in India,* published in 1839-45 in London, is an important record of his firsthand observations. In these four volumes, he provides a background of ancient Indian Christian traditions, the arrival of Islam*, and early Roman Catholic* mission in India. More important, however, is his firsthand account of the beginning of the Protestant missions — first, the Danish at Tranquebar, but primarily the English. As an evangelical chaplain, he was directly involved with the SPCK, the SPG, and later, the CMS. His sympathetic portrayal of the arrival of William Carey* and the beginning of the Baptist* Mission in Bengal, as well as details of the London Missionary Society and other new societies, is a salient characteristic of his writing.

In addition to his *History,* Hough wrote an extended *Reply to the Abbé J. A. Dubois.* In 304 pages, he contrasts the Roman Catholic "means" with the Protestant methods and results.

Bibliography

Firth, Cyril Bruce, *An Introduction to Indian Church History* (1961). • Graffe, Hugald, *Tamilnadu in the Nineteenth and Twentieth Centuries,* Vol. IV, Part 2, of the *History of Christianity in India* (1990). • Hough, James, *A History of Christianity in India,* 4 vols. (1839-45); *Reply to the Abbé J. A. Dubois* (1824; originally published at Serampore in the *Friend of India*).

Roger E. Hedlund

House of God, Vietnam. *See* Nha Chua

House, Samuel R(eynolds)

(b. Waterford, New York, United States, 16 Oct 1817; d. United States, 13 Aug 1899). Presbyterian* Church USA missionary who played an important role in the introduction of Western medicine and education in Thailand*.

House graduated from Union College, Schenectady, New York, in 1837 and from the New York College of Physicians and Surgeons in 1845. He arrived in Thailand in 1847 as one of three missionaries sent to reopen the Siam Mission. He served his entire missionary career in Bangkok. House had a scientific background and a scholarly bent which made him a favorite with King Mongkut*, a key figure in Thai modernization. He gave lectures and demonstrations on scientific subjects to royalty and high government officials. By 1852, he abandoned medical* practice as unhelpful to missionary work and took up evangelistic work, primarily tract distribution. In Oct 1852, the mission gave him charge over its education program, and he helped found and obtain pupils for the mission's first permanent boys' school that same year.

While on his first furlough, House married Harriet M. Pettit in 1855 and was ordained in Jan 1856. House played an important part in the conversion of Nai Chune, the first Thai convert to Protestantism, in 1859. He undertook a number of exploratory tours into rural areas, including a famous 1868 trip to Chiang Mai during which he was gored by an elephant and had to sew himself up. The Houses returned to the United States in 1876 on account of her health and resigned from the Siam Mission in 1877.

Bibliography

Feltus, George Haws, *Samuel Reynolds House of Siam* (1924). • Lord, Donald C., *Mo Bradley and Thailand* (1969). • McFarland, George Bradley, ed., *Historical*

Sketch of Protestant Missions in Siam, 1828-1928 (1928). • Wells, Kenneth E., *History of Protestant Work in Thailand, 1828-1958* (1958). HERBERT R. SWANSON

Howell, William

(b. Labuan, 15 Sep 1856; d. Sabu, Sarawak, 17 Sep 1938). Anglican* priest and authority on the Sea Dayak language.

In 1874, Howell was sent to complete his education in England and subsequently trained for the priesthood at St. Augustine's College, Canterbury. He returned to Sarawak in 1878 and was ordained in 1882. A Eurasian, Howell was to spend his whole life in ministry to the Sea Dayaks, often being in sole charge of the Sea Dayak area, namely the Saribas, Krian, and Batang Lupar rivers. His knowledge of the culture and religion of the Sea Dayaks resulted in significant contributions in the *Sarawak Gazette* and *The Chronicle.*

Howell translated parts of the prayer book and the Bible* into the Sea Dayak language and was co-author of the only Sea Dayak dictionary at the time. He has been described as the greatest living authority on the Sea Dayak language in his day.

Bibliography

The Chronicle (Dec 1938). • Saunders, Graham, *Bishops and Brookes* (1992). SOON SOO KEE

Hsi, Pastor. *See* Xi Shengmo

Hsieh Wei

(William Sia, Chia Ui, Sia Hui) (b. Nan Tou, Taiwan, 2 Mar 1916; d. Ming Chen, Nan Tou, 17 Jun 1970). Pastor, preacher, surgeon, and moderator of the Presbyterian* Church in Taiwan* (PCT).

Hsieh studied theology in Taiwan and medicine in Japan* during World War II*. He married a Taiwanese woman who was also studying medicine in Japan. They returned to Nan Tou, took over his father's Ta Tung Clinic in 1946, and were deeply moved by the suffering of the sick and dying, poor and needy, of the mid-mountain regions.

Hsieh was ordained in 1949 into the Nan Tou Presbyterian Church. He volunteered to join the Mennonite* Medical Mobile Clinic in 1950. In 1953, while an assistant resident at Buffalo General Hospital, United States, he decided to build a tuberculosis clinic for the mountain people. With the continuous support of Christian students from America, two Pu Li tuberculosis centers were set up, one for the mountain people (1956-70) and the other for the plains people (1960-70). They later were transformed into the PCT's Hsieh Wei Memorial Youth Camp.

Hsieh's pastoral and medical* work extended beyond Nan Tou County to the mountain and coastal areas. Besides running the Ta Tung Clinic and tuberculosis centers, he devoted one day a week to each of three other medical institutions: the Pu Li Christian Hospital for mountain people (1955-70), where he served as surgeon, preacher, and nursing-school instructor; the Pei Men Mercy Door Clinic at the Great Salt Coast of Tainan County, which was run by the Mustard Seed Mission (1964-70) and where he performed amputations for sufferers of blackfoot disease (much like gangrene, it affects the feet, legs, and hands); and Er Lin Christian Hospital for children suffering from polio (1966-70), which began as a coastal medical mobile clinic and later became a branch of the Chang Hua Christian Hospital, PCT, in Er Lin.

Hsieh was extremely occupied with public, medical, and ecclesiastical commitments. He died in a car crash, probably falling asleep from exhaustion while driving to work at Er Lin Hospital. It was the afternoon after an operation that went past midnight followed by an emergency call at 5:00 A.M. and a morning of clinical work. His last words to his wife before he left for Er Lin were, "Arriving a minute earlier at the hospital is a minute less pain suffered by the patients, and one more patient's life might even be saved." He was known as the Albert Schweitzer of Taiwan and was posthumously awarded a special honor in 1992, the second Taiwan Annual Medical Reward.

Bibliography

The Rev. Dr. Hsieh Wei Memorial Collection (1971). • Moody, Katherine, "Farewell to a Friend," *Outlook* (1970). • Wilson, Kenneth L., *Angel at Her Shoulder* (1964, 1970). CHANG TE-SHIONG (TIU TEK-HIONG)

Hsu Chen. *See* Xu Qian

Hsu Chen-Ping, Francis

(b. Shanghai, 20 Feb 1920; d. Hong Kong, 23 May 1973). Third bishop of the Hong Kong* Catholic Diocese (1969-73) and its first Chinese bishop.

A gifted linguist, a good administrator, and organizer of the local church following the Second Vatican Council, Hsu was born into a Methodist* family in Shanghai and studied at St. John's (1936-40) and Oxford University (1944-47), graduating in English language and literature. While teaching at Nanking Central University, he joined the Catholic Church. In the early 1950s, Hsu took refuge in Hong Kong. From 1955 to 1959, he went to Rome to study philosophy and theology at Beda College, where he was ordained a priest in Mar 1959.

Once back in Hong Kong, Hsu worked mainly in the Catholic Center and was in charge of its administration and that of the Catholic Chinese and English press. He was consecrated auxiliary bishop by L. Bianchi in Oct 1967. After the resignation and departure of Bianchi, he was appointed first administrator and then bishop (27 May 1969) of Hong Kong.

When the Second Vatican Council (1962-65), launched its campaign for renewal, Hsu called a diocesan convention (1970-71) for an overall assessment of the general situation of the local church. He tried to improve Catholic commitment in Hong Kong society and lead the church toward mature relationships with other religious and secular institutions. He died prematurely, preventing him from completing his plans.

Bibliography

Hong Kong Catholic Church Directory 1995. • Ryan, T., *The Story of a Hundred Years* (1959); *Catholic Guide to Hong Kong* (1962). • Ticozzi, S., *Historical Documents of the Hong Kong Catholic Church* (1983) (in Chinese).

SERGIO TICOZZI

Hsu, Paul. *See* Xu Guangqi

Hu Wenyao

(b. Ningbo, Zhejiang, China, 1885; d. 1966). Chinese Catholic patriot.

Hu studied in Belgium on a state scholarship after passing the candidacy examination of Zhejiang in 1908. He earned his doctorate in mathematics from Louvain University, returned to China* in 1913, and taught at Beijing University and Beijing Higher Normal School. He helped set up the science department of Beijing University.

Hu moved to Shanghai in 1921 to serve as dean of studies, later acting principal, of the Sino-French Polytechnic. In 1931, Aurora University of Shanghai, which had been served by French Jesuit* principals, decided to register itself with the Chinese government. In 1932, Hu was appointed principal to facilitate recognition from the national government.

Hu was not baptized until 1942. After the establishment of the Chinese People's Republic, Hu, defying the authorities of the Chinese Catholic Church, supported the government's takeover of Aurora University and was appointed its president. In 1951, together with other nationalists, he initiated the Chinese Catholic Patriotic Assocation*, urging Chinese Catholics to tread the "love New China" path.

Hu was an elected member of the Chinese People's Political Consultative Council in 1952. Since 1954, he was, successively, deputy to the first, second, and third National People's Congress. From 1960 until his death, Hu served as the elected chairperson of the Shanghai Catholic Patriotic Association. CHINA GROUP

Humabon, Rajah of Sugbu

First Filipino to be baptized in 1521.

Humabon, the Rajah of Sugbu (now Cebu City), received Christian baptism when Ferdinand Magellan's* Spanish expedition arrived in Apr 1521. Described as "tattooed in fiery designs of various kinds" and sporting a necklace of great value and earrings set with precious gems, Humabon was apparently the powerful head of a confederacy, his large settlement having trade with various parts of Southeast Asia as far as Ayutthaya, Siam.

Seeking local allies, Magellan convinced Humabon and his followers, some 1,200 individuals in all, to receive baptism. Humabon was christened "Carlos," after Charles I of Spain. Subsequent events, however, showed that the Debuanos apparently missed the religious significance of baptism, thinking it simply a ceremony of political alliance with the Europeans.

Bibliography

Pigafetta, A., *Magellan's Voyage around the World* (1906). • de Argensola, B. A. L., *Conquista de las Islas Malucas* (1891). • "M. Transylvanus," in M. Fernandez de Navarrete, *Colleccion de los Viages y Descubrimientso* (1946). • Sitoy, T. V., Jr., *The Initial Encounter* (1985).

T. VALENTINO SITOY, JR.

Human Development

Since the time of the Industrial Revolution or even earlier, economic development has been the central goal of states and societies. Economic growth has gone hand in hand with technological advancement.

Toward the end of the 1950s-60s there was growing disillusionment over using the Gross National Product (GNP) as a measure of development, because it failed to capture the effect of development on the people. Economists such as Nobel laureate Paul Samuelson developed alternative measures such as net economic growth, which was more accurate than the production-oriented GNP.

In the 1990s, Mahbub-ul-Haq became disillusioned by the World Bank's annual World Development Report and originated the idea of Human Development Indicators (HDI). He gradually refined the HDI to produce the Human Development Report of 1994. The HDI is a composite of three basic indicators of human development: human longevity (measured by life expectancy), human knowledge (measured by a combined estimate of adult literacy and mean years of schooling), and the standard of living (measured by purchasing power, which is based on the per person real gross domestic product adjusted for the local cost of living). Each of these measures is given equal weight in the HDI. The gender- and income-disparity-adjusted HDIs point out a society's sexual bias and an economy's regional, racial, and social biases. Japan*, though in first place, shows a male chauvinism in the gender index. Malaysia* in the 1970s and Thailand* in the 1980s registered the highest degree of progress. For the period from 1960 to 1992, South Korea*, Malaysia, and Thailand were among the top five performers.

Haq's Human Development Index may be viewed as a measure of human happiness based on life expectancy, educational standards, and individual purchasing power. It indicates a country's efforts to meet its people's basic needs: keeping them healthy, raising educational standards, helping them earn the income needed to make choices, and providing adequate housing and habitat.

The UN Conference on Social Development (Mar 1995) also focused on this theme. Critics say that the social dimensions of human development cannot be integrated into the prevalent development process. Social development cannot be planned as a by-product to sustain the market forces driven by the rich nations. Development needs to be redefined.

The Catholic and Protestant churches' understandings of human development in Asia are strongly influenced by the Vatican and the World Council of Churches (WCC) respectively. "The Pastoral Constitution on the Church in the Modern World" (*Gaudium et Spes,* 1965) proposed a concept of human development which underpins the present body of Catholic social teaching. It provided a theology for human development which emphasizes that development is not merely economic development, but also takes into account social, political, and cultural factors. The teachings of this seminal document were developed in the encyclical letters of Pope Paul VI on development of the world's peoples (*Progressio Populorum,* 1967) and Pope John Paul II on the church's social concern (*Sollicitudo Rei Socialis,* SRS, 1987), linking development with justice (1971), peace (1986, 1987), and ecology (1990). Collaboration in the development of the whole person and of every human person is in fact a duty of all toward all and must be shared by the four parts of the world: East and West, North and South (SRS n. 32).

The WCC defines human development as "a process of human liberation in which justice, people's participation, self-reliance, quality of life and meeting of basic human needs are realized through social transformation." Social transformation, it is recognized, has political, economic, ecological, social, and spiritual dimensions.

Liberation is possible mainly through political action, which is essential. However, participation in the political process does not replace a deep sensitivity to the culture of the people. While some particular aspects of culture can hinder change, the ingenuity, cultural creativity, and collective wisdom of the people must be released for them to assume greater responsibility in decision making for social transformation.

The WCC and the Pontifical Commission for Justice and Peace established and jointly sponsored the Committee on Society, Development and Peace (SODEPAX). Its first conference was in Beirut (1968). One of its later meetings was addressed by Gustavo Gutiérrez with material that would be the basis of his book *Theology of Liberation.* Unfortunately, the activities of SODEPAX were discontinued by the Vatican in 1980.

However, even today there is little difference between the Catholic and Protestant churches on the issue of human development linked with justice, peace, and ecology. At the European Ecumenical Assembly in Basel (May 1989), which was jointly sponsored by the Conference of European Churches and the Council of the European (Catholic) Bishops Conference, an inspiring final statement was issued under the title "Peace with Justice for the Whole of Creation." This was followed by the Seoul Convocation (Mar 1990) on the topic "Justice, Peace and the Integrity of Creation" (JPIC), convened by the WCC, with many Catholic individuals and a Vatican delegation participating. This preparation for the WCC General Assembly (Canberra, 1991) replaced the previous theme of a "just, participatory, and sustainable society" as formulated at the fifth WCC General Assembly (Nairobi, 1975).

The experience of the Catholic and Protestant churches in contextualizing human development in Asia has been very similar. Asia, despite its new economic vigor, natural wealth, vast human resources, and rich cultural diversity, is a shabby home to its three billion people, the overwhelming majority of whom are poor. Its massive and widespread poverty* differentiates it from the continents of Europe, North America, and Australia, but relates it to the continents of Africa and South America. Its uniqueness, even among these continents, is its religiousness. It is the cradle of all the world's great religions. The Asian ethos is characterized by economic poverty but cultural wealth. So poverty is not a mere economic concept, nor is religiousness a mere cultural concept. The point at which they coalesce forms the uniqueness of Asia. The genuinely religious person must voluntarily be a poor person, says Sri Lankan theologian Aloysius Pieris. Religion in Asia moderates between excessive wealth and dire poverty. Both extremes are dehumanizing.

Positioned within this reality of Asia, Christianity constitutes a tiny 2.4% of the population. So the concept of human development must be contextualized not merely from an Asian Christian perspective, but also from the perspective of other faiths. In the Asian experience, leaders like Gandhi*, Sukarno*, Mujib-ur-Rehman, Sun Yat-Sen*, and Ho Chi Minh* did not begin with a conceptual definition of human development. They mobilized the people, who were oppressed by the colonizers, into a nationalist liberation movement for independence.

However, two decades of national independence and nation building that coincided with the development decades of the 1950s and 1960s ended in disappointment and frustration. In fact, the plight of the people worsened around 1965, particularly with the intervention of transnational institutions, such as the Asian Development Bank. These institutions restructured the traditional economies. An import orientation moved toward export orientation and participation in the global economy. Rather than produce goods for their own people's basic needs, Asian economies were geared to produce goods for foreign markets or to satisfy the wants of a small local elite. The idealism of the Bandung Conference (1955) had evaporated.

The Asia Ecumenical Consultation on Development (Tokyo, 1970), which was called by the Protestant churches' social-action arm, began searching for a new style of participation in development which could meet the disillusionment after the early enthusiasm for nation building that had characterized the 1950s and 1960s. Community organizing, a new stream of action already emerging in the late 1960s, began to replace economic uplift programs. The Tokyo Conference declared, "The primary focus of church activity in development work should be on the social and community organization of the people for social justice . . . to regain their dignity and help secure justice and dignity for all." The experience of the urban poor in the Philippines, who were following the Saul Alinsky method in their struggle for land to live on, led to the formation of the Asian Committee for Peoples Organisation (ACPO, 1971). It was an ecumenical umbrella organization for training in community organizing in Asia, especially among the urban poor.

Meanwhile, the Asian Catholic bishops were meeting on the occasion of Pope Paul VI's visit (Manila, 1970). The visit initiated the founding of the Federation of Asian Bishops Conference* (FABC). They committed themselves "to the concern for total development of our peoples." This mandate was given to their Office for Human Development (OHD) to implement. Between 1974 and 1986, seven Bishops Institutes for Social Action (BISAs) were held, and national offices of development and of justice and peace were established.

But Asia in the 1970s was characterized by the rise of authoritarian regimes that aimed to protect the economic interests of the local elites and their international backers. Martial law was proclaimed in one country after another: the Philippines* (1972), South Korea (1972), and India* (1975). It was only after 1986, with the people's uprising that overthrew the Marcos dictatorship in the Philippines, that democracy began to be restored in many Asian countries. But at the same time the rapid pace of modernization provoked the rise of religious fundamentalism (see Islamic Fundamentalism) in Asia that was vulnerable to manipulation by vested interest.

The Catholic churches formed a unique response called the Asia Partnership for Human Development (APHD). It consisted of 24 national development offices from Asia, Australia, New Zealand, Europe, and North America. The APHD aimed at funding projects that fostered development, education, and solidarity actions. It also emphasized the role of religion and culture, especially among the marginalized groups. It served youth, fishermen, farmers, women, and indigenous peoples.

The Christian Conference of Asia* (CCA), with the WCC, held an Asia Forum on Justice and Development (Singapore*, Nov 1984) as a follow-up to the Tokyo Conference (1970). It had become more conscious of the need to be in solidarity with the suffering people of Asia — listening to their voices, supporting their struggles, and becoming advocates for them in the process of their own autonomous, authentic development. The Urban-Rural Mission* (URM) section of the CCA developed microlevel support for the marginalized people's struggle. The International Affairs (IA) section dealt with macrolevel issues such as human rights, peace, and justice.

The Asian Cultural (and Religious) Forum on Development (now ACFOD) was launched in 1973 under the ecumenical sponsorship of SODEPAX. It set itself to the tasks of action, dialogue, and mutual support, linking religious and cultural groups in a common endeavor for social justice and development. It sought to break down the barriers built up by millennia of cultural conditioning among the religious, ideological, and cultural blocs of Asia. By including even Marxists, it became a milestone in the history of Asian efforts at development for social change. The underpinning theology for these efforts to emphasize the religious and cultural dimensions of authentic human development was given by the Ecumenical Association of Third World Theologians (EATWOT) at their meeting in Sri Lanka* on the theme "Asia's Struggle for Full Humanity" (Wennappuwa, 1979).

At a joint justice and peace meeting in Thailand (Hua Hin, 1988) between the Forum of Religious Orders for Justice and Peace founded in 1985 and the national Catholic Bishops Offices of Justice, Peace, and Development (started in 1979), the challenge of the hour was articulated. It was declared that there was a need for a new theology and spirituality* to be born in the context of the struggles of the poor in Asia and Oceania. "This theology must be expressed through the religio-cultural traditions of the peoples of our regions, which have enriched us as we have worked with the people in building basic ecclesial communities and basic human communities. It must embrace liberative aspects of different faiths and cultures, the movements for women's liberation, and the struggle to protect nature and life. Each of these in its own way will help us to live and give witness to the Gospel, especially as we work toward harmony and solidarity" (see Women's Movement).

Concern for the poor is central to God's reign on earth. Asian society is characterized by power, privilege, and affluence often at the expense of the poor. This is the antithesis of God's reign. It is not just a matter of improving the situation of the poor, but of directing our cherished world in a direction more in harmony with God's reign on earth. The 1950s and 1960s stressed the economic dimensions of development; the 1970s added the political dimension; the 1980s focused on the religious and cultural dimensions; and the 1990s highlighted the ecological aspects of genuine human development and linked this with concerns for justice.

In the Asian context, the Catholic and Protestant churches gradually came to emphasize the content of liberation in the concept of human development. Not only the economic and political dimensions, but also the religious, cultural, and spiritual dimensions were emphasized, as the marginalized people organized themselves into basic ecclesial or human communities. The ecumenical seminar on the cosmic dimensions of African and Asian spirituality (Colombo, 1992) viewed popular religiosity more positively, while also emphasizing the ecological and feminist dimension of spirituality.

Other efforts at integral human development with strong Christian inspiration and participation, but not organized by the churches, emerged in the 1980s.

The Asian Coalition for Housing Rights (ACHR) brought together representatives of nongovernmental organizations from 10 Asian countries (Bangkok, 1988). It opposed unconditionally all evictions and displacements of people as a denial of their basic human right to permanent shelter.

The Asia-Pacific Conference on Peace and Development (APCPD, Manila, 1988) drew hope from popular movements against nuclear weapons, foreign military bases, onerous debit payments, and environmental destruction. It sought to redefine democracy and development through the participation of workers, peasants, indigenous peoples, women, and other oppressed groups.

The Peoples' Plan for the 21st century (PP21) is a program organized by a broad coalition of nongovernmental organizations and people movements. It is aimed at creating an alternative world through an alliance of hope, and at overcoming the present Northern domination. Its first effort was at the site of one of the greatest disasters of the modern world (Minamata, Japan, 1989). The second effort was in Thailand (Bangkok, 1992). Future efforts are planned in other Asian countries.

Bibliography

CCA News (magazine of the Christian Conference of Asia). • *Info on Human Development* (magazine of the Office for Human Development of the FABC). • Pieris Aloysius, *Towards an Asian Theology of Liberation* (1986). DESMOND DE SOUSA

Huria Kristen Batak Protestant. *See* Batak Protestant Christian Church

Hutchings, Robert Sparke

(b. Dittisham, Devon, 1782; d. Ayer Hitam, Penang, Malaysia, 20 Apr 1827). East India Company Anglican chaplain and pioneer educator in Penang.

Hutchings studied at St. Edmund Hall, Oxford (B.A. 1802, M.A. 1808). In Jun 1813, he was appointed chaplain of the Penang Presidency while remaining rector of Dittisham, Devon, the living he inherited from his father. When he arrived in 1814, his projects included founding a church and the Penang Free School on the principle that it would accept children from all religions and races. The readers and grammars Hutchings wrote for the school remained in use for many years.

In 1816, Hutchings formed the Prince of Wales Island Auxiliary Bible Society* to render the island of Penang "the medium of distributing the Holy Scriptures among the more eastern islands and nations of Asia." He assisted a Major McInnes with revisions of portions of the Malay Bible and late in 1816 took these with him to Calcutta, where he arranged an exchange with the chaplain at Barrackpore. Suffering from indifferent health, he remained for three years working on the proofs for a revised Jawi Malay Bible. While in Bengal, he married the highly spirited Elvira Phipps on 15 May 1818. The substantial St. George's Church was completed during his absence. He returned to Penang in 1820 and in 1825 visited Macau for six months. In 1826, he prepared a report on the Chinese Poor House. His death was attributed to malaria. The Penang Free School continues to honor his memory.

Bibliography

Dumper, Anthony C., *The Church of St. George the Martyr* (1964). • Calcutta Auxiliary Bible Society Reports, 1816-22, in MSS.Ind.Ocn.s.210, Rhodes House, Oxford, with other notes of research by Hutchings' great-grandson Sir Robert Hutchings. JOHN ROXBOROGH

Hwang, Wu-Tong

(Ngg Bu-Tong) (b. South Taiwan, 1909; d. 1995). Taiwanese Presbyterian* Christian leader.

Adopted by the Ngg family, Hwang studied the Confucian classics in Hoklo-Taiwanese during his childhood. The Nggs converted to Christianity in 1915 and dedicated Hwang to serve in church ministry after he suffered a serious illness. He studied at the Presbyterian Middle School and Theological College, both in Tainan, where he received a Western dimension to his education. During his college years, he was once expelled because of impoliteness to teachers caused by his precocity.

Immediately after his theological education, Hwang married Lyim Lann-giokk and was sent in 1932 as a local missionary to serve a remote island church in the Pescadores. He was ordained as a Taulakk pastor in 1937, the year in which there was a full-scale Japanese invasion of China*. From that time on, he had to face the difficult issues of the relationship between church and state in Asia. In 1944, he was transferred to the city to become pastor of the Kagi Church, where he went through the severe bombing of the Pacific War (see World War II).

In 1951, as moderator of the Southern Synod (founded by the English Presbyterian Church), Hwang joined with the Northern Synod (of the Canadian Presbyterian Church) to initiate the formation of the Presbyterian Church in Taiwan (PCT). Hwang served as the first assembly moderator. Then, together with Shoki Coe, principal of Tainan Theological College, he helped to move this denominational island-church into a truly ecumenical* church. In the early 1950s, the PCT joined the World Alliance of Reformed Churches (WARC), the World Council of Churches (WCC), and the East Asia Christian Council/Christian Council of Asia* (EACC/CCA).

From 1951 to 1953, Hwang studied in England. While overseas, he encouraged the PCT to request the New York–based United Board for Higher Education in China to establish a Christian university (Tunghai) in Taiwan. Later, the PCT became the co-founder of this university. In 1954, he presented a paper titled "Taiwan Missions" and initiated the Doubling Movement* (PKU) in celebration of the centenary of Protestant missions on the island. At the Centenary Thanksgiving in 1965, the church consecrated its almost doubled congregations and members. The Kuomintang, realizing the influence of the PCT, often requested that the church preach an anti-communism message, but Hwang always turned down the requests. He believed that evangelization itself was the best tactic against atheistic communism. He retired from the PCT in 1966.

From 1967 to 1972, Hwang was director of the interdenominational Taiwan Christian Service. In 1973, while exiled in New York, he and Shoki Coe in London initiated the Taiwanese Self-Determination Movement in response to his home church's "Statement on Our Nation's Fate." He received an honorary degree in 1987 from his alma mater, Tainan Theological College and Seminary. During his last years, he continued to labor and established the Taiwan Church Archives. He died in his sleep and was buried with a PCT assembly funeral.

Bibliography

Hwang, W. T., *Taiwanese Customs and Legends* (1955). • Hwang, W. T., and C. H. Hsu, *Chronology of the PCT* (1959). • Hwang, W. T., and C. H. Hsu, *Memoir* (1985). • Hwang, C. H. (C. H. Ngg), *Joint Action for Mission in Formosa* (1968). • Tin, J. J., *Dr. Ngg, Bu-tong and His Time* (1994).

JOHN TIN JYI-GIOKK

Hymns (Sambika), Japan

"Hymn" is a general term to describe songs that are used to sing praises to God. In Japan, Christian songs of praise have been sung since the early Kirishitan* period, but since the late 1860s, efforts were made to pull together the different words used to describe them so that gradually they came to be known as *sambika.*

*Roman Catholic**. Five types of religious songs have been compiled as hymns in the Roman Catholic Church. They are *Psalmus, Ordinarium, Liturgia Horarum (Hymnus), Canticum,* and *Cantus Popularis Religiosus.* There have been a number of collections of hymns published by Roman Catholics in Japan, beginning with Father Bernard Thadée Petitjean's *Kirishitan no utai* (Early Christian Songs), which was attached to *Orashiyomarabini oshie* (Chants and Teachings, 1878), and moving on to the *Katorikku seika shu* (Collection of Roman Catholic Sacred Songs) and *Tenrei seika* (Liturgical Sacred Songs).

Generally, the 100-year development can be divided into three periods. Hymnals of the first 50 years (late 1860s to early 1920s) had no music, only words, and the choice of songs in each collection strongly reflected the nationality of the missionary who had put it together. Most of these collections were developed to be used by districts, specific orders of the church, or Catholic schools. This period ended about the time a single collection was developed for the whole country. The bridge to the next period, perhaps it could be called the "quickening period," is reflected in a collection edited by Jean-Maria-Louis Lemareschal, *Seiei* (Sacred Songs, 1883). It was renamed *Nihon seiei* and revised a number of times until the early 1920s. The unifying period that followed began with the publishing of the *Kokyo seika shu* (Collection of Roman Catholic Sacred Songs) in 1933 and ran through the end of World War II until the publishing of *Katorikku seika shu* (Collection of Roman Catholic Hymns) in 1966. The former was the first official hymnal of the church, and its use spread and became firmly established across Japan. The most recent period began after Vatican II when it became possible to perform the mass in the language of each country. A new liturgy in Japanese was created and put into print. Since that time, sacred songs written by Japanese have replaced ones brought from other countries.

Orthodox Church. In the Orthodox Church, as the entire liturgy is sung, all books of liturgy might be called collections of hymns. Nikolai* edited the first materials — *Nisshokeimon* (Liturgy) and *Sho kito shu* (Prayer Book), published in 1877. Other early publications include *Jikakei* (Prayers of the Day), *Hacchokei ryaku* (1884), *Seieihei* (Prayerbook Consisting of Psalms), *Seikyo Hoshin Rei* (1891), and *Hojikei* (Liturgy). In the early 1900s, a two-volume *Hacchokei* of over 1,000 pages was put out. *Saijitsu kei* and *Sanka saikei* (used during Holy Week) were also published.

TAKAHASHI YASUYUKI

Protestant. Protestant hymns were introduced in Japan in 1872. At the Yokohama Missionary Conference that November, James Hamilton Ballagh introduced childlike translations of two hymns, "Jesus Loves Me" and "There Is a Happy Land," which were sung by all present. In 1874, six different collections of hymns translated into Japanese were published in Yokohama, Kobe, and Nagasaki for use in Japanese churches. The first was published for Kobe, Church and consisted of eight songs made into a booklet using woodblock printing. Five of the songs were translated in Yokohama, three in Kobe. In the beginning, each denomination had its own version, and by the 1880s over 100 versions with music had been developed. Contributors who worked independently include Okuno Masatsuna, Henry Loomis (Tokyo-Yokohama area), Matsuyama Takayoshi, Jerome Dean David (Kobe, Congregational), John Carrol Davison, Nagai Eiko (Nagasaki, Tokyo-Yokohama, Methodist*), Nathan Brown (Tokyo-Yokohama, Baptist*). The words of each of the new trans-

Hymns (Sambika), Japan

lations gradually freed themselves from the earliest childish translations. The best of these collections was probably *Shinsen sambika* (Newly Compiled Hymnal, 1888); it had an effect on the literary world, too. The expressions used in *Kirisuto-kyo seika shu* (Sacred Christian Songs, 1884), were very Japanese in nature, making it quickly acceptable.

Early in the 20th c., plans to compile a common hymnal matured, and a hymnal committee prepared and published a *Sambika* (Hymnal) in 1903. The solemnity, grace, and flowing elegance of the words in that hymnal provided the basis for future hymnody in Japan. In the late 1880s and early 1890s, evangelistic hymns had been compiled by the more evangelistic groups; some of those collections include *Sukui no uta* (Salvation Songs, 1897), *Kirisuto-kyo fukuin shoka* (Christian Evangelistic Songs, 1901), and *Ribaibaru shoka* (Revival Songs, 1909). The words of these songs were quite simple, straightforward, and colloquial. A children's hymnal for use in Sunday schools was published in 1923. In answer to the needs of the churches, in 1931 the hymnal committee published a new *Sambika,* and the evangelistic churches put out a *Ribaibaru shoka* by Nakata Ugo in 1932. However, the war began soon after that, and not until after the war was more revision done (see World War II).

In 1954, the hymnal committee of the United Church of Christ in Japan (UCCJ) published a new *Sambika,* and in 1958 the sacred-song editorial committee of the Japan Evangelistic Fellowship put out *Seika.* Both of these collections contain a great variety of songs and unique lyrics. In addition to these, the Anglican* Church of Japan made an agreement with the hymnal committee to publish a joint hymnal, *Kokin seika-shu* (Ancient and Modern Hymns), in 1901. The Lutheran* Church published *Kyokai sambika* (Church Hymns) in 1974. The former included music primarily from England and the United States, while the latter reflected German and Scandinavian influence. All of these hymnals contain translations of hymns mostly from England and the United States. There are still very few hymns written by Japanese, though the percentage is gradually increasing. The words will probably become more colloquial as time goes on. Most of the hymn tunes sound English or American, with a Japanese style of music not yet established in the world of hymnody.

Bibliography

Sakabayashi Isao, *Katorikku tenrei ongaku no rekishi to genjo* (History and Present Situation of Catholic Liturgical Music); *Reihai to ongaku* (Worship and Music) (1978). • *Fukkoku meiji shoki sambika kaisetsu* (Commentary on Hymns of the Early Meiji Period, reissued) (1978).

HARA MEGUMI, JAPANESE DICTIONARY

I

Iakinf. *See* Bichurin, Nikita Yakovlevich

Ibas

(d. 457). Bishop of Edessa (435-49 and 451-57) and a leader of the Persian theological school there.

According to the *Chronicle of Edessa,* Ibas built a new church at Edessa. He translated into Syriac some of the works of Theodore of Mopsuestia*, Theodoret of Cyrus, and Diodore of Tarsus. According to 'Abdisho of Nisibis's *Catalogue of Books,* Ibas was the teacher of Nestorius*. Because of this translation work, his possible role as a teacher of Nestorius, and comments made in a letter to Mari, a bishop in Persia, he was attacked for being "Nestorian*" and deposed by the Robber Synod of Ephesus (449) (see Synods, Early Church). He was restored by the Council of Chalcedon (451) after he condemned Nestorius and Eutychius. However, he was condemned posthumously (553) at the Council of Constantinople. As a result of this condemnation, nothing of the homilies, hymns, and commentaries attributed to him survives.

Bibliography

Acta Conciliorum Oecumenicorum, ed. E. Swartz (1924-40; rev. ed. 1971-). • d'Ales, A., "La lettre d'Ibas à Marès le Persan," *Recherches des sciences religieuses,* Vol. 22 (1932). • Labourt, J., *Le Christianisme dans l'Empire Perse sous la dynastie Sassanide (224-632)* (1904). • Vööbus, Arthur, *The Statutes of the School of Nisibis* (1962); *History of the School of Nisibis* (1965). • De Urbina, Ignatius Ortiz, *Patrologia Syriaca* (2d ed. 1965). • Fiey, J.-M., *Jalons pour une histoire de l'Eglise en Iraq* (1970); *Nisibe: métropole syriaque orientale et ses suffragants des origins à nos jours* (1977). • Gero, S., *Barsauma of Nisibis and Persian Christianity in the Fifth Century* (1981). David Bundy

Ibuka Kajinosuke

(b. 4 Jul 1854; d. 24 Jun 1940). Japanese pastor and educator.

The eldest son of a samurai of the Aizu feudal domain, Ibuka's birth name was Kyokitsu. He studied at his fief's school for sons of samurai. He went with his father to Echigo to participate in the Bishon War but did not join the White Tiger Unit because he was too young. As a result of punitive measures imposed on the defeated Aizu fief, he was forced to pursue his studies in Tokyo, where life was difficult for him. He met Samuel Robbins Brown* in Yokohama and was baptized in Jan 1873.

After completing study at Tokyo United Seminary, Ibuka became a probationary pastor in 1878, a fully ordained pastor in 1879, and pastor of the Kiku-cho branch of Takanawa Church in 1880. He became an associate professor at Tokyo United Seminary and translated a number of the writings of the missionaries. In 1886, he was chosen to serve as one of the Japanese members of the board of trustees of Meiji Gakuin School at the time of its founding and was also in charge of the purchase of land in the process of building Shirogane School. He later became chair of the board of trustees of Meiji Gakuin and was elevated to the position of professor, becoming assistant chancellor of Meiji Gakuin in 1889 under Chancellor James Curtis Hepburn.

The next year, Ibuka went abroad to study at Union Theological Seminary in New York City, majoring in church history. He returned to Japan in Sep 1891, and in November became the second chancellor of Meiji Gakuin. Under his guidance, the school overcame the crisis faced by mission schools during the reactionary time that followed. When the ministry of education issued Order Number Twelve in 1899, the school's leaders protested to the Tokyo ministry of education that it was a violation of the imperial constitution, but they were unable to have it abolished; they were able, however, to maintain their form of Christian education.

Ibuka acted as a mediator between some missionaries and a number of Japanese like Uemura Masahisa*, who considered the autonomy and independence of the Japanese church to be of utmost importance. By avoiding disruptive conflict, he helped Meiji Gakuin to continue its work. As the school grew, he came to feel he could no longer manage its expanded affairs, so he resigned as chancellor, accepted the status of honorary chancellor in 1921, and completely retired in 1924.

As one of the oldest pastors in the Japan Presbyterian*/Reformed Church, Ibuka served it in a number of different capacities, including moderator. He also served as one of the seven Christian representatives in a government-sponsored organization of Christian, Buddhist, and Shinto* bodies for twelve years. Because of his excellent mastery of English, he was active in international organizations such as the World Ecumenical Conference and the International Young Men's Christian Association*. During the Russo-Japanese War, he traveled through Europe and the United States explaining Japan's position. He died after suffering a series of strokes.

Bibliography

Ibuka Kajinosuke to sono jidai (Ibuka Kajinosuke and His Time), 3 vols. (1969-71).

KUDO EIICHI, JAPANESE DICTIONARY

IFES. *See* International Fellowship of Evangelical Students

Iglesia de los Cristianos Filipinos

(Church of Filipino Christians). The *Iglesia de los Cristianos Filipinos* was a nationalist schism led by Gil Domingo in 1913. It was the Presbyterian* counterpart to the Methodists' *Iglesia Evangelica Methodista en las Islas Filipinas,* and the Catholic Church's *Iglesia Filipina Independiente**. Largely limited to southern Luzon, the schism drew away the four largest Presbyterian churches in Cavite Province, a few others in Rizal and Laguna, and some members of the Presbyterian churches of Manila and Cebu. By 1922, some of the schismatics began returning to the main Presbyterian fellowship. The bulk of the Church of Filipino Christians, however, remained as an independent body and, in 1932, merged with other small Presbyterian and Methodist groups to form the United Evangelical Church of Christ in the Philippines (UNIDA).

Bibliography

Roger, J. B., *Forty Years in the Philippines* (1940). • Sitoy, T. V., Jr., *Several Springs, One Stream* (1992).

T. VALENTINO SITOY, JR.

Iglesia Filipina Independiente

(IFI) (Philippine Independent Church [PIC]). Also known as the Aglipayan Church, whose founding is popularly credited to Gregorio Aglipay*.

Dubbed the "remaining tangible result of the Philippine Revolution," IFI was founding through the struggle for filipinization* in the church at the turn to the 20th century. Though the local clergy involved did not intend separation from the Vatican, labor leader Isabelo de los Reyes Sr*. (Don Belong), president of the *Union Obrera Democratica,* proclaimed the founding of IFI on 3 Aug 1902 during a meeting of labor leaders and nominated Aglipay as the first *obispo maximo* (supreme bishop) barely one month after the United States declared the end of the Filipino-American War. Reyes proposed two councils for IFI, a lay and a clergy. Initially, many of the clergy declined their nominations, but when an estimated quarter of the population became adherents of IFI, Aglipay agreed to preside over a meeting of nominated bishops on 1 Oct 1902, thus forming the supreme council, and they adopted a temporary constitution.

Aglipay insisted that IFI was founded by the people because of their desire for liberty. The *Six Fundamental Epistles* (issued intermittently from Sep 1902 until Aug 1903) and the *Doctrina y Reglas Constitucionales* adopted on 28 Oct 1903 stressed that the desire for liberty was in accordance with the will of God and that IFI upheld doctrines similar to the Roman Church*, except those which were nonbiblical. The early songs and prayers of IFI expressed the desire for individual and national liberty. The official prayer book, *Oficio Divino,* was published in 1906; and portions, especially those on the Holy Eucharist and the rites for the various sacraments, were translated into the major languages of the Philippines. In the late 1920s, the leadership, tending toward Unitarianism, revised the *Oficio Divino,* but opposition from the older clergy curtailed implementation of the revisions.

A leadership struggle ensued after Aglipay died in 1940. The older candidate, Santiago Fonacier, was elected successor after the bishops agreed that IFI retain its original doctrines, summed up in the Bacarra Formula, in essence Catholicism minus the pope. Isabelo de los Reyes Jr. was elected secretary-general. In 1946, Santiago Fonacier, ousted in favor of interim *obispo maximo* Gerardo Bayaca, who was replaced by Isabelo de los Reyes Jr. on 1 Sep 1946, opposed the election and was made the leader by his own supporters. In 1955, the supreme court of the Philippines ruled in favor of Reyes Jr. and his group. The losers formed the Independent Church of Filipino Christians (ICFC), but subsequent separations hindered its growth.

In 1946, Reyes Jr. negotiated with the Episcopalians for priest candidates to be trained at St. Andrew's Theological Seminary. In 1947, the general assembly adopted a new Declaration of Faith and Articles of Religion, and a new Constitution and Canons, declaring a return to mainstream Christianity and the doctrines subscribed to at the founding of IFI. The liturgical doctrines of the Filipino Missal and the Filipino Ritual were adopted in 1960. The Concordat of Full Communion with the Protestant Episcopal Church of the United States of America (PECUSA) was enacted in 1961. In 1963, Reyes Jr. became the first chairman of the National Council of Churches in the Philippines (NCCP).

Reyes Jr. was succeeded in the IFI by Macario V. Ga,

who served from 1970 to 1981. In 1976, IFI issued a Statement on Church Mission to recapture the nationalist fervor of the founding days and to arrest the decline in membership. In 1977, during the diamond jubilee celebrations, IFI adopted a new Constitution and Canons allowing radical changes to democratize organizational structures and operational processes, resulting in another leadership struggle in 1981. In 1993, the court of appeals ruled in favor of the proponents of the 1977 Constitution and Canons, which limited the term of the *obispo maximo* to six years without reelection and provided for a surrogate to serve the remainder of his term should he die or be incapacitated while in office.

In 1987, IFI adopted a Statement on Development containing the framework for a comprehensive national program embracing the five areas of education, liturgy and music, faith and witness, justice and service, and ecumenical and international affairs. In 1992, it launched the Decade Agenda to recapture its nationalist heritage in preparation for the centennial celebration in 2002. Presently, it has 35 dioceses in the Philippines and one each in the United States and Canada. Its highest governing body is the general assembly comprising all bishops and representatives from the priests, laypeople, and youth. The interim governing body, the executive commission, also comprises both clergy and laypeople, including youth.

Bibliography

Scott, William Henry, trans., *Doctrine and Constitutional Rules of the Philippine Independent Church* (1982). • Iglesia Filipina Independiente, *Our Heritage, Our Response* (1993). • Whittemore, Lewis Bliss, *Struggle for Freedom: The History of the Philippine Independent Church* (1961). • NCCP, *Church Profiles* (1989).

Apolonio Ranche

Iglesia ni Cristo (INC)

Founded in 1914 by Felix Ysagun Manalo*, the Iglesia ni Kristo, later changed to the Iglesia ni Cristo (INC) to meet changes in the Filipino alphabet, has become one of the larger non-Catholic Christian churches in the Philippines* today. The name, which is Tagalog for "Church of Christ," is a point of honor for its members, who believe that they represent the true faith of Jesus that was lost to apostasy in the first century. Citing Isa 41:2, which speaks of God raising up a leader from the East, the INC believes that its inception in the Philippines was in fulfillment of biblical prophecies and that its founder was "the last messenger of God."

Manalo, who was baptized Roman Catholic* and later converted to Protestantism, failed to attract much attention in the first few decades after the INC's founding. However, after World War II*, with rapid cultural and economic development significantly changing the face of Filipino society, the attractiveness of a highly structured, authoritarian church appealed to many people, and the INC began to increase in number. There are no official figures as to the size of the movement, as the INC will not release any membership data. However, estimates place it at anywhere from three to 10 million worldwide, which would place it above the Jehovah's Witnesses, a Christian sect with similar doctrine. The INC also boasts congregations in at least 70 countries with members from 120 different nationalities represented, although most of its members are former Roman Catholic Filipinos. The INC is presently governed by the Central Administration and consists of several elite members of the church. It is led personally by the son and successor of the founder, Erano Manalo, with the assistance of his righthand man, Eduardo Manalo.

After Felix Manalo traveled to the United States in 1919 to study various Protestant churches, at which time the young INC was struggling with a schism between Manalo and Teogilo Ora, the theology of the sect began to crystallize. Manalo's exposure to churches such as the Seventh-day Adventists* helped shape his developing doctrine. Today the INC teaches, most noticeably, a nontrinitarian theology, asserting that Jesus was not divine, holds to certain dietary restrictions, and rejects Roman Catholic doctrines pertaining to purgatory, the Mass, and the efficacy of baptism performed by non-INC ministers. Its members are required to attend services, performed in the local Filipino dialect, twice a week, and dues are collected from every member based on a graduated scale of income. In keeping with these strict regulations, members of the INC may marry only other members of the church under pain of expulsion. Perhaps the teaching most widely recognized and acknowledged by those outside the INC is that members are instructed which candidate to vote for in political elections, including at times even those outside the Philippines. With the INC's ability to mobilize its members, it represents a formidable voting bloc, a fact not overlooked by aspiring candidates throughout the Philippines. Presently the church publishes two magazines in the Philippines: *Pasugo* and *God's Message.*

Bibliography

Anderson, Gerald H., ed., *Studies in Philippine Church History,* (1969). • Dolan, Ronald E., ed., *Philippines: A Country Study* (1991).

Jeffrey Mann

Immaculate Conception Church, Thailand

First built by Louis Laneau after his consecration in Ayutthaya in 1674 as apostolic vicar of Siam (Thailand*), the Immaculate Conception Church (known as the Conception Church) is located on the banks of the Chao Phaya River just north of the Samorai Temple. In addition to the brick-and-plaster church building, Laneau also built two hospitals, one for men and the other for women, a rectory for priests, living quarters for workmen, and a guesthouse for Catholic inquirers who came to study about the faith.

In 1676, Laneau left the church in the care of Fr. Chandebois, who had arrived in Thailand in 1674 and been assigned as his assistant while studying the Thai language. In 1686, Chandebois was transferred to the College General in Ayutthaya. His successor was Fr. Manuel. When Manuel and most other missionaries were jailed following the 1688 revolution, the Conception Church was left without a priest and was served by only a few catechists sent to instruct the faithful and to perform religious ceremonies. From 1750 to 1755, Fr. Bigot was appointed to oversee the pastoral needs of Conception Church. Bigot was consecrated as a monseigneur in 1755, and the church was again left without a priest until 1762, when Fr. Corre was given oversight of Conception Church and the College General in Ayutthaya.

In 1767, when Ayutthaya fell to the Burmese, Corre, the novices, and some laypeople took refuge in Cambodia. Corre returned in 1769 and established Santa Cruz Church. He was also given oversight of Conception Church.

In 1785, Fr. Langenois, a missionary in Cambodia*, brought some Portuguese Catholics together with their Cambodian servants to Ayutthaya as members of Conception Church. From then on, Conception Church was known as the Cambodian Church. The Cambodian-Portuguese Catholics brought with them a revered carved wooden statue of the Virgin which would be paraded during the procession on feast days.

There were then only two churches in Bangkok — Santa Cruz Church of the Thai Portuguese and Conception Church of the Cambodian Portuguese. Langenois was in charge of both churches until he returned to Cambodia. The priests of Santa Cruz Church then took turns giving pastoral oversight to Conception Church. In 1836, Jean Baptiste Pallegoix* was appointed senior pastor. He built the present church, consecrated on 24 May 1837, and living quarters for priests, which were later pulled down to make room for a school.

The 300th anniversary of Conception Church was celebrated in 1974. The original Conception Church was restored, made into a museum, and commemorated at a ceremony attended by the king.

VICTOR LARQUE, translated by E. JOHN HAMLIN

Imperialism

Some historians have traced imperialism back to the *imperium* of the Greco-Roman world. But "imperialism" itself is a problematic concept, whose meaning has undergone much alteration since its origins in the 1840s. There is no doubt, however, that there have been "imperial" states in every age, in both the East and the West. Since Alexander the Great's incursions into the Middle East and northwestern India in the 4th c. B.C.E., European exploration and expansion in Asia have brought Western and Eastern ideas and institutions in contact with each other. More recently, beginning with the Portuguese and Spanish in the 16th c., successive stages of Western imperialism — Dutch, British, French, German, and American — have intersected periods of Asian history into the 20th c. The 19th and 20th cs. were distinguished by the fact that Asian and African empires were increasingly replaced by Western ones, as the latter established a clear lead in terms of economic, scientific, and military power.

Broadly speaking, Western interest in the acquisition of colonies has been intermittent in modern history. Most European expansion in Asia was weak and tentative until the 18th c. Compared to the great Asiatic empires of the Moghuls in India or the Qing Dynasty in China, European power was relatively insignificant until the Industrial Revolution began to swing the balance in favor of the West. It is historically accurate to describe the period from c. 1700 onward as an age of European expansion, culminating in European preeminence from ca. 1850.

In the early modern era, the Spaniards were uniquely committed to a program of territorial expansion, economic exploitation, conversion to Catholic Christianity, and cultural change. As in their earlier American conquests, the Spanish adventurers were propelled to the Philippines by a curious blend of religious and secular concerns. The Spanish crown, church, *conquistadors,* and colonists all shared an apostolic zeal to spread Christianity throughout the non-European world and a determination to draw all new converts into the political fold of the Hispanic empire. Long before Miguel Lopez de Legaspi's* successful expedition of exploration and colonization was mounted (1565-72), metropolitan authorities in Spain and officials in *Nueva España* (Mexico) viewed the proposed Philippine enterprise — named in honor of King Philip II of Spain — as a concerted effort of soldiers, missionaries, bureaucrats, and merchants to reap their just material or spiritual rewards. Consequently, the white colonial elite of the Philippines, centered in Manila, generally endorsed costly and continuous policies to expand to Sulu, Mindanao, and the northern highlands of Luzon; to utilize the *encomienda** as a means of raising tribute and labor; to impose a system of direct rule throughout the Philippines; and, until the 19th c., to consolidate the resulting political, economic, religious, and territorial gains by resettling the dispersed islanders in hispanicized towns and cities.

The Portuguese seaborne empire in Asia, on the other hand, existed mainly to secure a monopoly on the spice trade. A network of fortified factories developed in Monsoon Asia, buttressing the two great Asian entrepôts that Portugal wrested from Muslim control in the early 16th c. — Malacca* (1511) and Ormuz (1515). The key Portuguese base in South Asia was Goa (captured by d'Albuquerque*, 1510), while Macau (colonized 1557) became the Far Eastern outpost for relations with China and Japan. The Portuguese Jesuit* missionaries who arrived in Goa after 1542 spearheaded the remarkable development of Portuguese missions from c. 1550 to 1750.

The carrot-and-stick approach to winning converts — mass destruction of native temples, harsh laws proscribing the public practice of Hinduism*, Buddhism*, and Islam* in Portuguese-controlled territory, and inducements and incentives that favored converts to Catholicism — produced mass conversions in the 1560s. Yet the net effect of Portuguese imperialism was redistributive rather than transformational: in trade, they skimmed off profits for themselves without radically changing routes, products, or productive techniques; in society and culture, they altered or redirected existing patterns short of actual transformation.

Dutch expansion represented an intermediate stage between the earlier, predatory imperialism of Portugal and the later, more productive imperialism of Britain. Although the Dutch championed free trade in theory, they practiced monopoly extensively, especially regarding the Asian spice trade. As a chartered company, the Dutch East-India Company* (VOC) was a quasi-state organization empowered to wage war, make treaties, conquer, and engage in other non-mercantile business. Dutch dealings with Asian polities were thus characterized by a greater use of force, with at least as much political will and military muscle as the Portuguese had employed before them. In the Banda Islands (1620s) and other parts of the Indonesian archipelago, governors-general such as Coen used techniques based on Portuguese methods of dominating the inter-Asian trade. Conquests and contracts followed. Factories were established in coastal Ceylon (Sri Lanka*), Malabar, Macassar, and Batavia (Jakarta, dominating much of Java). Dutch monopolistic policies were systematically enforced by the draconian *hongi-tochten* (VOC law-enforcement ships). While Dutch imperialism in the East Indies would survive in a more localized form in Indonesia until 1945, the Dutch pattern would serve as a model for future empires, notably Britain, in standing for liberty, opulence, and Protestantism.

With the end of the first British empire in the American colonies (1776-83), British imperialism entered a new, more assertive phase of empire building that shifted its focus eastward. With the Industrial Revolution gathering pace in Britain and the need to secure a natural route of advancement for British capitalism in the first half of the 19th c., British expansion sought to consolidate Britain's lead as a workshop and the banker of the world, to construct a middle-class empire that supplanted the empire of the old colonial system, and to create a cosmopolitan world economy that constituted the basis of a *Pax Britannica.* This was achieved by formal and informal means, whether by annexation or unequal treaties. The defense of key interests in India (the jewel in Britain's imperial crown), coupled with the drive to maintain political and economic stability under British paramount sovereignty, helps to explain how Britain's imperial design was subsequently stretched to include parts of Persia and the Ottoman Empire, Burma, Malaya and Singapore*, northern Borneo (Kalimantan), and China*. Until 1857, the agents and armies of the English East India Company played the leading role in empire building; thereafter, the crown assumed control of the empire. Finally, the gunboats and instruments of British law and order led the banner of British Protestant Christianity into the 20th c. Missions accompanied, but were not necessarily protected by, the Union Jack.

The making of the second French colonial empire (c. 1815-1920) was, by contrast, a product of isolated enterprises and individual initiatives occasionally backed by public opinion. Emperor Napoleon III's colonial escapades in the 1850s did not reflect serious imperialism so much as his desire to boost French prestige and dynastic popularity, and the pull of the forces of circumstance. The establishment of a French protectorate over Cochin China (1857) and the dispatch of French troops to fight in the Chinese campaigns of 1858-69 witness to this. The Catholic missionary program — *la mission civilisatrice* — was probably the most important activity in which France was engaged in Southeast and East Asia. There the French regime often assumed the self-appointed role of protector of Catholic missions and, until the 1860s, adopted missionary interests as a pretext for intervention.

The striving for global mastery among Western imperialistic powers during the 1880s-90s saw the emergence of a German "world policy" *(Weltpolitik).* In the German imperial documents published in the 1880s, Bismarck decreed that the newly established German Reich must stake out her place in the sun so as not to lose out politically or economically to her imperial rivals. In the East, this meant acquiring "concessions" in China (e.g., Kiaochow) and a few islands in the South Pacific. Indeed, the murder of the German Roman Catholic missionaries in Shangtung provided the trigger for the Western scramble for concessions in China in the late 1890s.

The Americans, too, began to pursue their own brand of imperialism in Asia toward the end of the 19th c. At the onset of the Spanish-American War, warships of the United States Navy sank the Spanish fleet in Manila Bay (1898). This spectacular victory galvanized Admiral George Dewey and Presidents McKinley and Theodore Roosevelt. In McKinley's words, "There was nothing left for us to do but to take them all, and to educate the Filipinos, and uplift and civilize them, and by God's grace do the very best we could by them, as our fellow-men for whom Christ died."

Modernization in East Asia would eventually redress the imbalance caused by Western imperialism. China, which failed to modernize in the second half of the 19th c., was progressively carved up into separate imperial spheres of influence. By contrast, three decades after the Meiji Restoration (1868), modern Japanese imperialism triggered off triple intervention by France, Russia, and Germany at the expense of China (1895). The colonial powers participating in the Hague Conference for Peace and Disarmament (1899) then accepted Japan at the conference table as an equal. Subsequently, Japan's victory over Russia in the Russo-Japanese War (1904-5) signalled the first major defeat of a modern European power by a non-Western one. By the early 1940s, Japanese militarism and military occupation had violently dislocated colonial governments and dispelled the mystique of white superiority and the myth of Western supremacy in South and Southeast Asia. It also delivered vital stimulus to indigenous nationalist movements — in India, Burma, Vietnam, Indonesia, the Philippines, Malaya, and Singapore.

Whatever the peculiarities of various forms of imperialism, empire building was produced by the pursuit of national self-interest. The mainspring of action may have been directly economic or strategic, but a multiplicity of other motives usually came into play, whether these were myths of ethnic-cultural superiority or of lost cities of gold and legendary kingdoms, the mandate for civilizing mission, or martial glory. Beyond the modest expectation that the colonies would prove self-sustaining and self-financing, it was often hoped that the benefits accruing to the national government, economy, and society would be mightier yet. In terms of policy objectives alone, the general equation between exploitation and empire appears entirely plausible.

On the other hand, imperialism was uneven in the depth and degree of its impact on the colonized societies. Imperialism was only half the story; indigenous resistance was the other half. Spain's devotion to Catholicism was repeatedly expressed in countless bitter battles with the Muslim Moros of Sulu and Mindanao and in the ongoing efforts of several hundred friars to convert and resettle the Filipinos in permanent Christian communities. In the East Indies, the Java War (1825-30) erupted as a form of Islamic protest against Dutch domination. On the subcontinent, the great Indian Mutiny-Revolt (1857) against the British Raj raised further questions about the burdens and blessings of imperialism. The Philippine Insurrection (1899-1902) against American rule demonstrated how strongly Filipinos wanted independence, even from their American "liberators." Beyond the catastrophe and crisis of two world wars and a depression, the experiences of decolonization, nationalist struggles, end of empire, and the attainment of national independence in many Asian countries persistently illustrate the paradoxes of power. The legacy of imperialism in Asia remains riddled with ambiguities to this day, even as former colonial relationships continue to undergo conversion to more cooperative partnerships among equals.

Bibliography

Boxer, C. R., *The Dutch Seaborne Empire* (1965). • Cady, J. F., *The Roots of French Imperialism in East Asia* (1954). • Neill, S., *Colonialism and Christian Missions* (1966). • Parry, H. H., *The Spanish Seaborne Empire* (1966). • Stanley, B., *The Bible and the Flag* (1990). • Subrahmanyam, S., *The Portuguese Empire in Asia* (1993).

Ernest Chew and Emrys Chew

Independence Movements. *See* Nationalism

India, Churches of North East

North East India* refers to the seven states of Assam, Arunachal Pradesh, Manipur, Meghalaya, Mizoram, Nagaland, and Tripura, which lie to the north and east of Bangladesh and are connected to the rest of the country by a narrow corridor through the northern part of West Bengal. The region is generally mountainous, but its population (31,547,314 in 1991) is concentrated in river valleys and plateaus. The great majority of its indigenous inhabitants are of Mongolian racial stock and belong to more than two hundred ethnic groups, each with its own language and culture. The majority of inhabitants of the plains areas are Hindu, though with large concentrations of Muslims. Traditionally the religions of the numerous hill tribes are primal. Until the advent of the British following the Anglo-Burmese Treaty of Yandabo in 1826, the region had never been connected politically with any major Indian power.

Though Catholic Christians from other parts of India established a few settlements in the region earlier, the history of indigenous Christianity dates from the 19th c. The Serampore Mission (see William Carey) maintained small stations in Guwahati on the Assam plains and Cherrapunji in the Khasi Hills in the early 1830s, but these were turned over to the American Baptist* and Welsh Presbyterian* (then Welsh Calvinistic Methodist Church) missions when they arrived in 1836 and 1841 respectively. During the remainder of the century, these were the major missions working in the North East. Out of their work emerged the two major Protestant churches, the Council of Baptist Churches of North East India (CBCNEI) and the Presbyterian Church of India (PCI).

The pioneer American Baptist missionaries had been sent from their mission in Burma to find a way to reach upper Burma over the hills that separate upper Assam from that region. It was also hoped that they would be able to reach the interior of China* along trade routes through the eastern mountains of Assam. As both these objectives proved impractical, they turned their attention to the Assamese people of the Brahmaputra Valley. They were encouraged by the first baptism of an Assamese, Nidhi Ram, in 1841. Major centers of work came to be established at Sibsagar (upper Assam), Nagaon (central Assam), and Buwahati (lower Assam). The first church was organized in 1845, with branches at the three centers. While the mission made important contributions to the Assamese language and led a movement to prevent the replacement of Assamese with Bengali in the courts and schools of the province, very few Assamese became Christian. This situation changed during the latter part of the century when numbers of Garos from what is today Meghalaya began to become Christian, initially through the work of two young men of that tribe, Omed and Ramkhe. The largest American Baptist

India, Churches of North East

mission center was developed in Tura for the support of the Garo movement. At the same time, numbers of laborers brought into upper Assam from other parts of India, mainly the Chota Nagpur region of Bihar, began to join churches related to the mission. Many of these plains tribes had had contact with Lutheran* and Roman Catholic* missionaries prior to coming to Assam.

The Welsh Presbyterian pioneers began work among the Khasi and Jaintia hill tribes with main centers at Cherrapunji, Shillong, and Jowai. The first Presbyterian church was organized at Nongsawlia, near Cherrapunji, in 1846, when the first Khasis, U Amor and U Rugjon, were baptized. Initially, opposition to Christianity was violent, but gradually the new religion began to be accepted. A well-established church was functioning in that region by the end of the century. A presbytery was formed in 1867, the same year in which the mission established a training school that was to become the first theological seminary in the region.

Though Roman Catholic chaplains visited the region earlier, the first systematic missionary work of that church was begun by German missionaries of the Society of the Divine Savior, popularly called the Salvatorians, in 1890. They established a center in Shillong, but, in addition to their work among the Khasis, they became extensively involved among the tea-garden laborers of upper Assam, many of whom had been connected with the Catholic Church in Chota Nagpur. During the First World War, the German missionaries were interned. Since the British government would not permit them to return, the Salesians* of Don Bosco were assigned responsibility for the region in 1921.

Ninety percent of all the Christians in North East India trace their faith to the work of these three missions. In 1990, 43% of all the Christians of the region were related to the CBCNEI, 26% to the Catholic Church, and 23% to the PCI. The remaining 8% were distributed among a number of small Protestant groups. At the beginning of the 20th c., there were approximately 25,000 Christians in the region, most of whom were located in the present Meghalaya and on the tea gardens of upper Assam.

During the last part of the 19th c., work began in three other areas where major movements to Christianity were to take place. These were Nagaland, Manipur, and Mizoram. Though work among Nagas* had started in the 1870s, significant numbers did not begin to become Christian until the beginning of the 20th c. Similarly, work which began in Manipur and Mizoram during the 1890s resulted in large movements to Christianity among the peoples of those states, but only in the second and third decades of the 20th c.

Assamese evangelists and missionaries connected with the American Baptist mission began work among the Ao Nagas in the 1870s. Progress was difficult. Though in the 1880s there had at one time been almost 400 Naga Christians, in 1895 their numbers were reduced to two. That year a revival began under the leadership of two young men who in turn influenced others of their age group; the movement among the Aos was thereafter irreversible. By the 1920s, there were Christian churches in all the Ao villages and, within 30 years, virtually the entire tribe had adopted the new faith. Through the work of Ao, Assamese, and American Baptist missionaries, the other tribes of Nagaland began to be evangelized from the two major mission centers at Impur and Kohima. Today some 80% of the people of Nagaland are Christian.

Manipur, like Tripura, was a princely state rather than a part of the British-Indian province of Assam, which embraced the rest of the region. Because of his personal friendship with the British political agent in Manipur, an English missionary named William Pettigrew was able to gain entrance to the state in 1894. He was employed by the Arthington Aborigines Mission. Two years later, he joined the American Baptist mission and began work with his wife Alice at Ukhrul in the area inhabited by the Tangkhul Nagas. In 1901, the first baptisms took place. In due course, Christianity spread to other Naga tribes and among the various Zo clans that inhabited the southern and western hills. Today most of the members of the hill tribes are Christian, constituting 35% of the population of the state.

The first missionaries to work among the Mizos* (a Zo people inhabiting the present state of Mizoram) were Herbert Lorrain and F. W. Savidge, also of the Arthington mission. They arrived in 1894, but, when their mission would not maintain them there, they turned over the work to D. E. Jones of the Welsh Presbyterian mission in 1897. The first Mizo Christians, Khuma and Khara, were baptized in 1899, but it was another seven years before significant numbers began to join the movement. This was the result of the first of a series of revival movements that have periodically appeared among Mizo Christians and increasingly come to represent a fusion of Welsh Christianity with traditional cultural forms. By 1930, the entire Mizo tribe had been evangelized, the most rapid conversion of a single tribe to take place in the region. Under an agreement between the two missions, the Welsh Presbyterians worked in the northern part of Mizoram and the British Baptist Missionary Society in the south. Out of their work grew the Mizo Presbyterian Synod of the Presbyterian Church of India and the Mizo Baptist Church.

During the 20th c., the church in Meghalaya grew steadily, as did the educational and medical institutions associated with it. Christians in that state continued to represent a substantial part of the church in the region, but other areas also began to witness rapid growth. The Mizo church grew rapidly, as already indicated, but it represented a single tribe. Much more tribally comprehensive movements began to take place in Manipur and Nagaland. By the last decade of the 20th c., Nagaland tribes such as the Semas, Kyongs, and Chakhesangs were largely Christian, and substantial portions of other major tribes such as the Angamis, Zeliangrongs, and

Konyaks had converted. The structure of the Baptist church in Nagaland was based upon tribal-linguistic associations gathered together under the Nagaland Baptist Church Council. This in turn is a part of the CBCNEI. Similar councils or conventions in Assam, Karbi, Anglong, Manipur, and the Garo Hills of Meghalaya together constitute the CBCNEI which, through the 20th c., was the largest ecclesiastical body in the region.

The Manipur Baptist Convention brought together associations made up of different Naga tribes and Zo dialectical clans. Its churches are concentrated in the hill areas surrounding the central Manipur plateau. Since Indian independence in 1947, there has been more rapid growth of the Christian church in this area than in any other part of the North East.

The 20th c. also saw the Roman Catholic Church becoming increasingly prominent. Prior to 1947, their work was limited by the British government to Meghalaya and the plains of Assam. After 1947, they began to establish a substantial presence in Nagaland and Manipur. An important factor in Catholic growth was the high-standard schools and colleges that they established, beginning in Shillong in Meghalaya. In 1954, they were running 659 educational institutions in the region, including three colleges. By 1990, they operated more than 1,300 institutions, five colleges among them, with an estimated 115,000 students enrolled. This was at a time when the Protestants were scaling down their extensive educational activities. Though at one time they had run the entire educational system in Meghalaya, Nagaland, Mizoram, and the hill areas of Manipur, by 1990 Protestants officially maintained only a little over 1,200 such institutions. While the Catholic expansion was marked by the creation of a number of new dioceses, the center of their ecclesiastical organization in the region remained in the archdiocesan headquarters in Shillong.

Following World War II* and Indian independence, patterns of Christian development changed significantly. The missionary-dominated church and institutional structures were taken over by Indian Christians. The missionaries gradually left the region. By the 1970s most were gone. While the three major Christian denominations remained the CBCNEI, the Catholics, and the PCI, a large number of new church groups began to appear. Many of these were conservative Protestants whose membership comprised persons who had previously belonged to other churches. Some were connected with outside groups, but others were indigenous in origin. Christianity began to spread into areas where there had previously been very few converts, most notably Arunachal Pradesh and Tripura.

Because of the high concentrations of Christians in several of the hill areas, they inevitably became involved in political developments. Political activity after 1947 related both to agitations for the division of the region into the seven states that now exist there and several insurgency movements with the stated goal of complete independence. The majority of Christians supported the state-creation movements, and the governments of the new states of Meghalaya, Nagaland, and Mizoram were controlled by Christians. While many Christians in the areas concerned supported the independence movements and the violent actions associated with them, the churches played a major role in the peace movements that eventually led to peace accords in Nagaland and Mizoram. In fact, those movements were initiated by the churches.

The denominational pattern of missionary work in North East India, as elsewhere, led to the establishment of a Christian community divided into several different church bodies. Denominational differences reinforced linguistic, tribal, and cultural differences that already existed. These have complicated efforts to develop more ecumenical patterns of church life at the regional level. The mainline Protestants established what is now known as the North East India Christian Council (NEICC) in 1937, which provides annual opportunities for church leaders to meet. It has effectively promoted relief programs and runs Union Christian College near Shillong. Relations between Protestants and Catholics have been strained from the beginning. In recent years more positive relationships have developed among lay members of both traditions, especially on occasions when a united voice in dealing with the government was seen as benefiting both. Progress is greatest in the areas the two groups have cohabited the longest — the Assam plains and Meghalaya.

Bibliography

Becker, C., *Early History of the Catholic Missions in Northeast India* (1989). • Becker, D., *History of the Catholic Missions in Northeast India (1890-1915)* (1980). • Downs, Frederick S., *Essays on Christianity in North-East India*, ed. Milton S. Sangma and David R. Syiemlieh (1994). • Downs, Frederick S., *History of Christianity in India*, Vol. V, Part 5; *North East India in the Nineteenth and Twentieth Centuries* (1992). • Karotemprel, Sebastian, ed., *The Catholic Church in Northeast India, 1890-1990* (1993). • Lloyd, J. Meirion, *History of the Church in Mizoram* (1991). • Snaitang, O. L., *Christianity and Social Change in Northeast India* (1993). • Syiemlieh, David, *A Brief History of the Catholic Church in Nagaland* (1990).

Frederick S. Downs

India, Early Christianity in

The origin of Christianity in India* has been the subject of controversy among historians owing to the lack of documentary evidence for the first few centuries. The lack of direct documentary evidence for reconstructing the early history is not a difficulty peculiar to Indian Christianity alone, as to some extent it is true of the Indian people as a whole. As a famous Indian historian has said, "In all Indian literature, there are few professedly historical works." The same is the case with the history of the Christians until the close of the 15th c.

There are two main views among scholars about the origin of Christianity in India. One view holds that Christianity came to India through the work of two apostles, St. Thomas* and St. Bartholomew. The other view would ascribe the arrival of Christianity in India to the enterprise of merchants and missionaries of the East Syrian or Persian Church.

The Indian tradition on the coming of St. Thomas to South India, especially to Malabar, is called the St. Thomas Tradition of the Thomas Christians (see St. Thomas and the Thomas Tradition). We will focus on the aspects of Christianity other than the Thomas tradition, while making pertinent references to this tradition.

The earliest record about the apostolate of St. Thomas in India is the apocryphal work called the *Acts of Judas Thomas**, written in Syriac by the Edessa circle about the turn of the 3rd c. C.E. Besides this, a number of fragmentary passages in the writings of Origen, Eusebius of Caesarea, Rufinus of Aquileia, Socrates, Ephrem* of Nisibis, Gregory Nazianzus, Ambrose, and Jerome speak in unambiguous terms about the Indian apostolate of St. Thomas. Some scholars, such as Bollandist Peeters, do deny outright that St. Thomas ever went to India or any countries of East Asia, but such statements directly contradict those of St. Ephrem. St. Ephrem composed hymns in honor of St. Thomas, whose relics were being venerated in a shrine at Edessa where this great Syrian poet-theologian was living. *The Teaching of the Apostles (Didascalia*)* in Syriac, written in all probability in the early part of the 3rd c., is more comprehensive though it also represents the Edessan tradition: "India and all its own countries and those bordering on it, even to the farther sea, received the apostle's hand of the priesthood from Judas Thomas, who was guide and ruler in the church which he built there."

There is also a view that the apostle Bartholomew came to India. Two ancient testimonies about the alleged apostolate of St. Bartholomew in India are those of Eusebius of Caesarea (early 4th c.) and of St. Jerome (late 4th c.). Both these writers refer to this tradition while speaking about the reported visit of Pantaenus to India in the 2nd c. According to Eusebius, Pantaenus "is said to have gone among the Indians, where a report is that he discovered there the Gospel according to Matthew among some who knew Christ; Bartholomew, one of the Apostles, had preached to them and had left them the writings of Matthew in Hebrew letters which writing they preserved until the aforesaid time." St. Jerome would have that Demetrius, bishop of Alexandria, sent Pantaenus to India, at the request of the legate of that nation. In India, Pantaenus "found that Bartholomew, one of the twelve apostles, had preached the advent of the Lord Jesus according to the Gospel of Matthew, and on his return to Alexandria he brought this with him written in Hebrew characters." Eusebius appears to be not quite sure of the report; Jerome is more categorical. (For the texts, see A. C. Perumalil, *The Apostles in India*, pp. 108-32).

Formerly, the consensus of opinion among scholars was against the apostolate of Bartholomew in India. Beginning with the Bollandist, Fr. Stiltingus, a few have supported his Indian apostolate. But the vast majority were still skeptical about it. Their main argument was that the India of Eusebius and Jerome would have been Ethiopia or Arabia Felix. But two recent studies — one by A. C. Perumalil and the other by G. M. Moraes — have attempted to show otherwise. They hold that the Bombay region on the Konkan coast, a region identified with the ancient town Kalyan, was the field of Bartholomew's missionary activities and his martyrdom. The town of Kalyan, situated as it is at the northeast end of Thana Creek, was an ancient port and is supposed to be the "Kalliana" the traveler Cosmas Indicopleustes* visited in the 6th c. as he reports in his *Christian Typography*. Now according to Pseudo-Sophronius (7th c.), Bartholomew preached to the "Indians who are called Happy," and according to the Greek tradition the apostle went to "India Felix." The word *Kalyan* means "felix" or "happy," and thus it is argued that the Kalyan region came to be known to the foreign writers as "India Felix" and its inhabitants were called the Happy. Scholars such as Perumalil interpret the "India Citerior" of Hieronyman martyrology as western India, and the "India" of the *Passio Bartholomei* (Ante-Nicene Library, Vol. 16) as the Maratha Country (Perumalil, p. 110).

For the apostolate of Bartholomew there is no Indian tradition as we have for St. Thomas. This absence, Moraes would explain, is due to the fact that the history of the Christians of Bartholomew became intermingled with that of the Thomas Christians, who came under the control of the Persian Church. And in the tradition of this church, Bartholomew was associated with Armenia and not with India (Moraes, *A History of Christianity in India from Early Times to St. Francis Xavier*, p. 44). Perumalil, however, thinks that the Bartholomew Christians continued as a separate community until the coming of the Portuguese and then merged with the Christians of Bombay (Perumalil, p. 139).

The South Indian tradition of St. Thomas's arrival is preserved in an oral tradition, and the monument of this tradition is the community of Christians called Thomas Christians, who claim their Christian origins from St. Thomas. The South Indian tradition is usually called the Malabar and the Coromandel tradition, which all historians admit is very ancient.

The Malabar tradition. All written accounts of the Malabar tradition are probably of the post–15th c. period, but the tradition itself is clear, strong, and vital. The tradition comments on the labors of the apostle Thomas at definite places and even with specific families. What may even today be seen and heard in such places as Palayur, Parur, Kokkamangalam, and Niranam cannot be easily dismissed as absolutely legendary since these places, where specific sites and families are pointed out as related to St. Thomas, betray their connections (then) with Hindu worship. The Hindus of Malabar themselves bear traditional testimony to the work of the apostle there.

The Malabar tradition is not contradicted by any other tradition. It has remained the proud patrimony of the Thomas Christians, who have always looked to the region of the Coromandel coast for the tomb of their beloved apostle.

The Coromandel Tradition. Coromandel is a corrupt form of Cholamandalam. It now stands for the southeast coast of India. The tradition of the apostolate of St. Thomas is tied to the Coromandel coast, and it centers on Mylapore (south of present-day Madras), where the apostle's tomb is pointed out; Marco Polo, the Venetian traveler, visited the tomb in ca. 1295. No rival traditions or tombs contradict the present tradition.

The Christians of India and the Church of Persia. Tradition says that the Christians of Malabar on the whole enjoyed peace during the early centuries, that they were highly favored by the local non-Christian rulers, and that Christians from abroad liked to dwell among them.

As to the question of whether there was a local hierarchy for the Thomas Christians, we cannot say anything definite. There is a tradition that St. Thomas conferred priesthood and also high priesthood on the members of certain families, but we have no way to verify this tradition. We know nothing of the early priests or prelates of Malabar.

The original community of Christians in India is alleged to have suffered decline in the course of time. But it was reconstituted and reinvigorated by groups of Christians who came from Persia. It is beyond doubt that some kind of relation between the Christians of India and the church of Persia existed from very early centuries.

The Chronicle of Seert*, an important East Syrian document of the 7th or 8th c., makes reference to a bishop named David, who allegedly evangelized the Indian people between 250 and 300 C.E. And in the list of the bishops who attended the Nicaean Council of 325 is mentioned one John the Persian, who according to the history of Gelasius was bishop of the whole of Persia and greater India.

Many groups of East Syrian Christians are often mentioned as having immigrated to Malabar. Two of them are well known: one is associated with Thomas of Cana (4th c.) and the other with two saintly men, Sapor and Prot (9th/10th c.). The Malabar tradition, whether recorded by the Portuguese or by the local accounts, is always careful to distinguish Thomas the Apostle from Thomas of Cana.

The origin of the division of the Thomas Christian community into two endogamous groups is repeatedly traced to the arrival in Kerala of Thomas of Cana. These groups are known as Southists and Northists. The Southists generally claim that they are descendants of Thomas of Cana. The Northists are said to have been Christians who lived in Malabar both before and after the arrival of Thomas of Cana.

The relations between the church of India and the East Syrian Persian church which started in the 3rd or 4th c. grew to such proportions that the former in the course of time became so dependent on the latter that everything ecclesiastical in India was in effect East Syrian. The community of the Thomas Christians was able to maintain a strong Christian tradition on account of this dependence. At the same time, it must be observed that the varying fortunes of the Persian church affected to some extent the Indian church too.

Eventually, this dependence of the Indian Christian community on the East Syrian church was looked upon by the Portuguese in the 16th c. and by some Western missionaries with suspicion. They accused the Thomas Christians of having fallen into the heresy of Nestorianism*, which the Thomas Christians vehemently deny. This suspicion and the consequent controversy divided the Thomas Christians into various denominations and churches from the 16th c. onward.

Bibliography

Brown, Leslie, *The Indian Christians of St. Thomas.* • Daniel, K. N., *A Brief Sketch of the Church of St. Thomas in Malabar* (1938). • Keay, F. E., *History of the Syrian Church in India* (1938). • Medlycott, G. E., *India and the Apostle St. Thomas.* • Mundadan, A. Mathias, *History of Christianity in India,* Vol. I (1984). • Perumalil, A. C., *The Apostles in India* (1971). • Philip, E. M., *The Indian Church of St. Thomas* (1950). • Podipara, J. Placid, *The Thomas Christians* (1976). • Tisserant, Cardinal Eugène, *Eastern Christianity in India: A History of the Syro-Malabar Church from Earliest Time to the Present Day* (authorized adaptation from the French by E. R. Hambye) (1957). • Yuhanon Mar Thoma, *Christianity in India* (1968).

GEEVARGHESE PANICKER

India Missions Association

(IMA). National federation for all Indian mission organizations working both within and outside India*.

In 2000, there were 121 missions and evangelistic organizations in IMA's membership representing over 15,000 missionaries working in 1,400 locations in India and 10 other countries. Overall, India has over 22,000 missionaries, mostly working within India, but very much cross-culturally. IMA not only provides coordination of the missionary work in India from its headquarters in Madras, but also brings together research centers, training centers, and mission resource groups in cooperative missionary efforts.

IMA also provides training for mission leaders in contextual Indian missiological issues. One of the foci of IMA is unreached peoples. The association has helped to coordinate the efforts to identify and study various groups within India which have not yet been reached with the Christian Gospel. IMA serves as the clearinghouse for churches that wish to adopt and missions that wish to enter a people group.

In 1980, IMA formed a new department, the Indian Institute of Cross-Cultural Communication (IICCC), to help meet the vast Bible translation needs of India. IICCC trains missionaries in Bible* translation skills in cooperation with the Wycliffe Bible Translators. In 2000, under the training and technical supervision of IICCC, Bible translation was going on in over 38 Indian languages which had no scriptures previously.

IMA has sponsored national consultations on evangelism and missions and produces a quarterly publication, *Indian Missions.* The overseas missions department handles the orientation and processing of Indian professionals as tentmakers for overseas missions. The health-care department of IMA networks with about 1,000 committed doctors who have volunteered their services to meet the health-care needs of Indian missionaries. The Missions Standards Cell helps, informs, instructs, and guides the member missions of IMA in their performance standards, accountability, and credibility factors.

EBENEZER SUNDER RAJ

Indian Evangelical Mission

(IEM). In 1954, the Evangelical Fellowship of India (EFI) initiated the indigenous Indian Evangelical Overseas Mission (IEOM) to send Indian missionaries overseas and to support them financially. Although IEOM was involved in the work among overseas Indians in Kenya, Africa, for some time, for various reasons the mission folded.

On 15 Jan 1965, Theodore Williams initiated a meeting at Devlali, Maharashtra, with fellow Indian members of the EFI executive committee to revive missionary interest. Thus the IEM was formed as an indigenous, interdenominational, and evangelical mission.

The objectives of IEM are: (1) to bring "a church among every people and the Gospel to every person"; (2) to challenge Indian Christians to realize their responsibility for world evangelization and to recognize their partnership with other Christians worldwide in fulfilling the task. The motto of IEM, from Isa. 54:2, is "Enlarge . . . stretch forth . . . spare not," resting on the pillars of vision, faith, and sacrifice.

The ministry of IEM includes evangelism, church planting, Bible translation, literacy programs, medical work, teaching, training, literature, and cassette production. It also cooperates with local churches in conducting missionary meetings and conferences to challenge Christians to be involved with missions.

In 1995, IEM was involved with 80 people groups in India and six overseas. It had 266 missionaries, 58 promotional staff, and 44 administrative staff. A monthly magazine, *IEM Outreach,* is produced in 11 Indian languages.

THEODORE SRINIVASAGAM

Indian Independent Church Movements

The Indian Independent Church Movements, also called the "Little Tradition" in South India, are demonstrations of the translatability of the Gospel as well as expressions of an authentic Indian incarnation of Christian faith. These churches of the "Little Tradition" have frequently (and pejoratively) been classed as sects. Historically, attempts were made in Bengal and Madras to produce Indian versions of the faith. In Maharashtra, the Brahmin poet Narayan Vaman Tilak* (1862-1919) brought the richness of the Hindu *bhakti* tradition into the church. Tamil Nadu had its Vedanayagam Sastriyar (1774-1864), Krishna Pillai* (1827-1900), and others who greatly enriched and enculturated the mainstream Christianity of the south. The most radical attempt was the Christo-Samaj and the Church of the New Dispensation of Keshub Chunder Sen* (1838-84), who, however, remained a Hindu. R. C. Das (1908-76) and Sunder Singh* (1889-1929) are examples of individuals who by various means have appropriated the Gospel in an Indian way.

The Small Church Movements, as they are sometimes called (Hollenweger), capture the ethos of these earlier attempts. For the most part, little is known about these movements. In recent decades, a movement around the late Subba Rao (1912-81) attracted the attention of writers (Kaj Baago, Robin Boyd, Sunand Sumithra). More recently, the Bible Mission of Fr. Devadas was the subject of an in-depth study (Solomon Raj). The Bakht Singh* movement has been described in brief, inspirational accounts. Here and there, mention is made of other independent movements in South India. Classification is difficult at this point, but there seem to be three or more types. One distinct category focuses on healing (e.g., Subba Rao and the Bible Mission of Fr. Devadas). Brethren or "baptistic" groups would include the movement around Bakht Singh, numerous local independent assemblies, and several small breakaway denominations in coastal Andhra Pradesh. An example of a Holiness movement is the Laymen's Evangelical Fellowship. But the largest cluster would be numerous indigenous South Indian Pentecostal* fellowships, denominations, and organizations, many of them an outgrowth of the more radical Ceylon Pentecostal Mission.

Statistics are notoriously difficult to obtain for these independent church bodies, but they do represent a vigorous and rapidly expanding section of Christianity in India today. They are a true *indigenous* church movement, in contrast to *indigenized* churches. The distinction is important. Indianization, contextualization*, and indigenization are expressions of the effort to change a nonindigenous church (one of alien origin and pattern) into something more Indian. Hence the Indian rites controversy in which the Catholic Church, as Indian Roman Catholics, resists the de-Latinization of the church. Church union efforts in the Protestant fold have created two nonindigenous amalgamations — the Church of North India and the Church of South India — by a rearrangement of the several European traditions involved.

None of the mainstream denominations (the Great Tradition) is indigenous, including the ancient St. Thomas Syrian Church with its inherited ancient Eastern liturgical traditions. Indigenous Indian Christianity is found in the Little Tradition of the so-called fringe sections, which are largely (not exclusively) of Pentecostal, charismatic, or evangelical origin. Questions of contextualization, adaptation, accommodation, and the cultural transformation of the Christian faith are topics of hot debate in the traditional Catholic, Orthodox, and Protestant denominations — all churches of the Great Tradition in religious studies — whereas cultural incarnation of the faith is a normal expression in churches of the Little Tradition.

Bibliography

Baago, Kaj, *The Movement Around Subba Rao* (1968). • Boyd, Robin, *Introduction to Indian Christian Theology* (1991). • Scott, David C., *Keshub Chunder Sen* (1979). • Solomon Raj, P., *A Christian Folk Religion in India: A Study of the Small Church Movement in Andhra Pradesh, with a Special Reference to the Bible Mission of Devadas* (1986). • Sumithra, Sunand, *Christian Theology from an Indian Perspective* (Bangalore: Theological Book Trust).

ROGER E. HEDLUND

Indian Interpretations of Christ

The variety of interpretations of Christ that have developed in interaction with Hindu concepts and Indian social and historical issues is very complex. Numerous Hindus, Indian Christians, and foreign missionaries have theologized on the person and work of Christ from vastly different perspectives.

Ram Mohun Roy* (1774-1833) was the first Hindu to develop a positive theology of Christ in reaction to the Western orthodoxy of William Carey* and his Serampore colleagues. Roy's position was akin to that of Unitarianism, with emphasis on Christ as a moral and social reformer. A century later, Mahatma Gandhi's* (1869-1948) Christological emphasis was similar, but, rather than the theistic undergirding evident in Roy, the dynamic tensions of Vaishnava theology influenced his portrayal. The historical Jesus was not Gandhi's concern, but rather the ideas he taught and the principles displayed in his nonviolent endeavors for reform. Gandhi's followers were taught to follow the Christ of the Sermon on the Mount.

Ramakrishna* Paramahansa (1836-86), followed by his disciple Swami Vivekananda* (1863-1902), absorbed Christ into a modified *advaitic* worldview. Christ is herein portrayed as an enlightened soul (or as an *avatara,* a manifestation of God) who leads others to enlightenment; but the deepest truth is beyond all names and forms, and so to hold on to Christ is to remain at a lower level of spiritual insight. The philosopher S. Radhakrishnan* (1888-1975) is one of the few Hindu academics to have developed a Christological perspective; he strengthened this concept of the *advaitic* Christ.

Indian Christians have also wrestled with the proper understanding of Jesus Christ in their contexts, and yet the majority of India's churches and individual Christians at present accept orthodox Christological definitions and are without any deep concern for distinctively Indian theological positions.

Advaitic Christ concepts have been developed especially by Roman Catholic* thinkers, starting with Brahmabandhav Upadhyaya (1861-1907). Raimundo Panikkar* (b. 1918) suggested that Christ is the *Ishvara* of classical *advaita* philosophy but later moved beyond this viewpoint toward a theology that Christ fulfills Hinduism*. Similarly, Swami Abhishiktananda (1910-73) moved beyond his published perspective on the *advaitic* Christ; but these writings and concepts have been powerful and influential, and numerous disciples of these masters have contributed to distinctively Indian Christological thought.

Vengal Chakkarai* (1880-1958) from a predominantly orthodox Protestant perspective presented Jesus as *avatara.* His brother-in-law P. Chenchiah* (1886-1959) formed a more radical Christology, with Christ as the new man introducing new humanity. More recent Protestant thinkers have pointed to Christ as liberator from all types of oppression. M. M. Thomas* (1916-96) and S. J. Samartha* (b. 1920) have presented Indian Christologies along this line in contrast with and often opposition to classical Western Christological thought. Numerous Roman Catholic activist theologians are also presenting Christ as liberator, often in acknowledged tension and even conflict with those presenting Christ in terms of *advaita* philosophy.

Into the complexity of this scenario it is necessary to introduce two Hindus who confessed exclusive devotion to Christ, Keshub Chunder Sen* (1838-84) and K. Subba Rao* (1912-81). Despite confessing Christ as supreme guru, neither developed a consistent Christological position. The reality of their devotion to Christ cannot be doubted, yet their works show internal tensions and contradictions as well as development of their ideas. The power of Christ's personality proclaimed in the Hindu context has created some of the most original and diverse Christologies in the past two centuries.

Bibliography

Boyd, Robin, *Indian Christian Theology* (1975). • Chakkarai, V., *Jesus the Avatar* (1932). • Dupuis, J., *Jesus Christ at the Encounter of World Religions* (1991). • Parappally, Jacob, *Emerging Trends in Indian Christology* (1995). • Samartha, S. J., *The Hindu Response to the Unbound Christ* (1974). • Thomas, M. M., *The Acknowledged Christ of the Indian Renaissance* (1969).

H. L. RICHARD

Indian Missionary Society

(IMS). The IMS was founded on 12 Feb 1905 by the Christians of Tirunelveli belonging to the Church Missionary Society (CMS). In its formation, V. S. Azariah*, along with eight clergy and 20 laymen, played a prominent role. It did not happen all of a sudden but in several stages.

First, missionary zeal was kindled in Tirunelveli by the influence of the mission that Thomas Gadgeton Rogland had established in 1859 at Sivakasi, about 75 miles from Tirunelveli.

Second, in the year 1891, men and women joined the Band of Faith and prayed for great things to happen toward the fulfillment of God's promises. In the same year, the Christian students of C. M. College, Tirunelveli (now St. John's College, Palayamkottai), experienced a revival and formed the Christian Brotherhood Association. Yet another society called the Baliar Bhakti Viriti Sangh of Tirunelveli was also born the same year.

Third, in 1897, Thomas Walker of Tirunelveli conducted revival, prayer, and board meetings in several villages.

Fourth, in 1899, Rev. Meyer conducted conventions called Tirunelveli Keswick and organized a Tirunelveli church prayer union. These conventions in towns and villages inspired the Tamil Christians. Thus nationalism*, missionary conferences, and the revivals of Tirunelveli paved the way for the formation of the IMS.

In 1895, Azariah was the first Indian to be appointed secretary of the Young Men's Christian Association* (YMCA). Being the traveling secretary of the YMCA for South India, he visited Jaffna (Ceylon) in 1902 along with Sherwood Eddy, who was then in charge of evangelistic work among students in India. At Jaffna, Azariah found a great missionary zeal among the Jaffna Christians both at their missions home and at Thondi in India. The native Evangelical Society, which was formed in 1832 by Tamils who had migrated to Jaffna, had sent Tamil missionaries to Thondi (near Madurai). Seeing their evangelistic zeal contrasted with the negligence of Tirunelveli Christians at home, Azariah took steps to form a mission society on his return to Tirunelveli.

Motivated by his personal encounter at Jaffna, Azariah gathered some Christians of Tirunelveli soon after his return to India and shared his idea of starting a new missionary society. A constitution drafted on the CMS model was circulated, and a public appeal to assemble at Palayamkottai on 12 Feb 1903 was sent to all Christians who were interested in forming the society. Eight clergy and 20 laymen of Tirunelveli Diocese gathered together and formed the IMS as the native missionary society of all of the CMS churches in Tirunelveli. Thus came into existence the first missionary society formed by Indian Tamil Christians.

The twofold objectives of the IMS were: (1) to develop missionary spirit in the native church, and (2) to spread the Gospel in unevangelized parts outside Tirunelveli district. The threefold principles on which the IMS was founded were: (1) Indian men, (2) Indian money, and (3) Indian management. The first office bearers were A. S. Appasamy* (president), V. S. Azariah (secretary), and J. Anbudaiyan (treasurer).

Bibliography

Asirvatham, Eddy, *Christianity in the Indian Crucible* (1955). • Graham, Carol, *Azariah of Dornakal* (1949). • Harper, Susan Billington, *In the Shadow of the Mahatma: Bishop V. S. Azariah and the Travails of Christianity in British India* (2000). • Hodge, J. Z., *Bishop Azariah of Dornakal* (1946). • Abraham, V. Joseph, *Fifty Years: History of the Indian Missionary Society of Tirunelveli* (1955). • Selwyn, C., "The History of the Indian Missionary Society from 1954-1970" (M.Th. thesis, United Theological College, Bangalore) (1982).

Franklyn J. Balasundaran

Indigenous Religious Congregations

Throughout the centuries, religious groups have been founded and have faded away. Indigenous congregations have been established in mission areas for various reasons, e.g., because the Spirit urged a group of men or women to live a certain calling according to their own cultural heritage; or because the lifestyle of Western congregations was regarded unfitting or felt too foreign for indigenous people to express their vocation (e.g., the Sisters of the Imitation of Christ in Flores, Indonesia, 1935); or because special needs and circumstances required completely new ways of religious life (e.g., the Franciscan Missionaries of Mary* [FMM] in India, 1877); or because members of missionary congregations desired a new kind of apostolate that could not be carried out by the congregation they had entered (e.g., the Sisters of Charity of Mother Teresa* of Calcutta, 1948). Some indigenous congregations started without any connection with Western orders as a response to a need of the region or a call from God, e.g., some of the many congregations founded in India during the 19th c.

The oldest Asian religious are the monks of Syria and Persia, who became wandering missionaries and founded monasteries as far away as China* (7th c.). Their form of Christian order was based on the monastery, and their spirituality was that of the wandering saint. In the 13th c., the Dominicans* set up the semi-autonomous *Fratres peregrinantes* in the Middle East for missions in Asia. Examples of a new kind of dedicated life are the Institutes of Virgins in China (ca. 1740) and the *Domus Dei* in Vietnam* (ca. 1630), both of which greatly strengthened the faithful in times when missionaries had been expelled. In the Philippines*, *beateros,* dedicated women, did apostolic, educational, and charitable work in a new way (since 1684). In China, an apostolic delegate started the *Discipuli Domini,* who, after 1950, spread to different Asian countries.

China. The Congregation of the Disciples of the Lord (CDD) is a community of Chinese priests dedicated to the propagation of the Gospel among Chinese people. It was established in 1927 by the first apostolic delegate in

China, Celso Costantini*. In 1924, he became aware that the more than two million Catholics were served by about 1,100 Chinese and 1,500 foreign pastors and no Chinese bishop. The church in China looked like and was called a foreign religion because many Catholic organizations were led by foreigners. In 1926, Costantini presented six Chinese priests to be consecrated bishops by Pius XI in Rome. He then founded the CDD, which attracted many aspirants.

The new congregation founded Heng Yee High School and Seminary in its motherhouse at Hsuan-Hua. Soon afterward, members of its Beijing (Peking) community studied theology at Fu Jen University. Because during the 20 years between its founding and the Communist takeover there were many civil conflicts and eight years of war against Japan*, the CDD never had more than 100 priests and seminarians, mostly from Northern China. In 1949, the superior general moved to Taipei with a number of priests and seminarians, while others remained in mainland China, facing great obstacles. The future in Taiwan* was hampered by lack of baptisms and recruits. In mainland China, the development of the CDD was understandably slow.

CDD priests who went to Indonesia* opened schools and kindergartens in Pontianak, the St. Joseph Primary and Secondary School in Malang (1949), and a seminary and activity center which can accommodate more than 200 people. The CDD is also in charge of a parish of Jakarta and a new center in Bali* (1993). There are many baptisms and quite a number of seminarians, although few are able to speak Chinese. In response to an invitation from the bishop of Kuala Lumpur, Malaysia, the Bentong Catholic Middle School and the parish were entrusted to the CDD (1957). More than 10 priests were dispatched to this mission, which later founded a community in Malacca* and Petaling Jaya. The Chinese community is especially active in the original Catholic area of Malacca, where many seminarians speak Chinese well. They study philosophy and theology in Taiwan and then return to Malaysia*.

India. More than 200 congregations of religious women have been founded in India, starting with the Sisters of St. Aloysius of Gonzaga in 1750. Most of them were founded during the 19th c., e.g., the Congregation of the Immaculate Heart of Mary in Pondicherry in 1844 and the Ursuline* Franciscan Sisters in 1890. Well known are the Sisters of Charity founded by Mother Teresa in Calcutta.

Because native Indians were for a long time not admitted to religious orders, Pascal da Costa Jeremias persuaded three other priests to found an Indian congregation. They started in the village of Batim (1682) but quickly moved to Goa. The experienced missionary Joseph Vaz* joined them in 1685; soon chosen superior, he persuaded the group to accept the statutes of the Oratory of St. Philip Neri. Though the archbishop of Goa opposed this decision, the Portuguese king and the pope gave their approbation. The Indian Oratorians worked fruitfully in Kerala and Sri Lanka.

Indonesia. In Indonesia the Indigenous Congregation of Sisters was formed mainly because it was not always easy for native girls to accommodate to the way of life of European religious communities and for European sisters to indigenize themselves to the local lifestyle. The first congregations formed included the Sisters of Maria Mediatrix (TMM). Three girls were accepted by J. Aerts*, apostolic vicar of Amboina (Moluccas*) in 1927. They received their religious training from the Daughters of the Mother of the Sacred Heart. During the Japanese occupation (1942-45), the young members had to disperse, but they went on to nurse 150 lepers on the island of Langgur. In 1947, they did their novitiate again to start anew. The Vatican acknowledged their constitution in 1949. By 1993, more than 125 TMM sisters worked in the fields of education, health care, and pastoral service in the Moluccas, New Guinea, Borneo, and Java.

The largest indigenous congregation is the Sisters of the Imitation of Christ (CIJ), with 303 members. They were founded in 1935 by Y. Koeberl on the island of Flores. In the beginning, the Sisters of the Holy Spirit (SSpS) assisted in the formation of novices. Now the CIJ includes 44 convents over many islands of Indonesia.

On the island of Java, P. Willekens* established the *Abdi Dalem Sang Kristus* (Servants of Christ) in 1938. At home in Javanese culture, they spread through most of the Javanese dioceses but also started work in Bali and Borneo. The Servants of the Holy Family started in 1951 on the island of Bangka and run schools in the diocese of Pangkalpinang (Riouw Archipel). From the oldest parish of Indonesia, Larantuka on Flores, come the Daughters of Reinha Rosari ("Queen of the Rosary"), who have grown quickly since 1958, performing apostolic works in several dioceses, especially among the young and the poor. The Society of the Servants of Christ was founded by N. Schneiders in Ujung Pandang in 1958; the brothers work in educational institutions for boys.

Pakistan. There are two indigenous congregations of religious women in Pakistan*: the Franciscan Tertiaries of Lahore and Franciscan Missionaries of Christ the King.

The Franciscan Tertiaries began in Rahmpur with H. E. Dubois, who guided pious young girls to a close imitation of St. Francis and St. Clare of Assisi. The congregation was given diocesan status in 1922, with headquarters at Mariabad after Dubois's death (see Pakistan, Christian Villages in). The sisters teach in schools and care for the sick in dispensaries in Mariabad, Ada, Sangla Hill, Samnabad, Sheikhapura. They work only in the parishes of Lahore. Their novitiate is on Maron Road.

The Franciscan Missionaries of Christ the King were founded in 1937 in Karachi by Salesius Lemmens and Bridgest Sequeira in response to a directive from Rome to found indigenous congregations. This missionary-minded sisterhood engages mainly in instructing children and adults in the rudiments of the faith. From 1942, the sisters have cared for the untainted children of leper parents. Some of their former charges are teachers and paramedical workers today. This congregation has 18 houses in Pakistan spread over four dioceses and also serves in 18 convents in India.

In 1941, St. Francis Convent was opened in the heart of Karachi. Its sisters teach in schools, catechize in different areas, instruct adults, and assist the parish priests in women's ministry. A few helped in the municipal maternity home from 1943 to 1978. They resigned when the roof threatened to cave in. They then founded a new home to care for mentally and physically handicapped boys from Dar-ul-Sakun. St. John's Convent on Drigh Road was started in 1951 to help in parish work and conduct a Bible academy in both Malir Cantt and Natha Khan Goth. In 1960, the sisters took over St. Vincent's Home for the destitute aged, which had been started by the St. Vincent de Paul Society*.

Philippines. Fifty-eight religious congregations for women had been founded in the Philippines* up to 1994, 45 of them between 1970 and 1990, and only three between 1900 and 1940. Between 1565 and 1898 (the Spanish colonial period), no religious congregations were founded for Filipino women. The Spanish colonial church carried on its missionary work in the framework of the *Patronato* Real,* that is, the church in the colonies was under the control of the king of Spain. Only Spanish women born either in Spain or in the Philippines could become religious. Native women were considered racially and culturally inferior and were barred from religious life (see Racism). Besides, the cost of maintaining convents or monasteries was a burden to the king, who did not want a proliferation of religious houses. The small number of Spanish women in the Philippines meant that only the Poor Clares were juridically established as nuns during the whole of the 333-year colonial time.

A subsidiary type of religious life was developed due to these obstacles. This was the *beaterio,* a concept midway between convent and secular life and taken from Spain and Latin America. The term embraced a whole gamut of degrees of religious life from pious women living at home to enclosed, habited women living in community. Four *beaterios* established during the Spanish regime were transformed in the 20th c. into full-fledged religious congregations and exist as such today. Of the four, two were founded by native Filipino women.

The first native *beaterio* was that of the *Beaterio de la Compania de Jesus,* begun in 1684 by Ignacia del Espiritu Santo* and directed by Jesuits*. Their service to their neighbors found expression in the education of young girls and in retreats for adult women. The *beaterio* received temporary approval from Rome in 1931 and definitive approbation in 1948. It was the first indigenous foundation in the Philippines recognized by the pope. It is now known as the Religious of the Virgin Mary* with 628 members in 36 dioceses and in seven countries outside the Philippines.

A second *beaterio,* that of San Sebastian, followed the rules and constitutions laid down for them by the Augustinian Recollects. Founded in 1719 by two Filipina blood sisters, Dionisia and Cecilia Rosa Talampas, it became a congregation of diocesan right in 1929 and of pontifical right in 1970. Its present name is Augustinian Recollect Sisters, with 265 members in 13 dioceses in the Philippines and two in other countries.

Another *beaterio* was founded by Augustinian *beatas* who came from Spain in 1883 to take care of children orphaned by cholera. They were joined a few years later by 10 Filipinas. The group was affiliated with the Augustinian Order in 1902 and continued to follow the observances of the original Spanish members. Recognized by Rome in 1952, they are called the Augustinian Sisters of Our Lady of Consolation, now an all-Filipina congregation.

During the American colonial period (1898-1948), three congregations were founded in the Philippines for Filipino women. The purpose of the congregations founded in the latter part of the 20th c. are varied. Some were founded by bishops for specific tasks in their dioceses, particularly for catechetics, Christian education of youth, and pastoral, liturgical, and social apostolate. Often these groups remain completely linked to the dioceses of origin and at their service. However, some multiply their communities and works into new areas and gradually leave behind their diocesan character.

Some congregations were founded by members of already existing congregations, both native and foreign, and took over some of the features of those congregations; others went through an apprenticeship period, receiving religious and pastoral formation during the early years of the congregation. A few have started as pious unions, with a more secular character.

Of those congregations founded between 1970 and 1990, the majority took traditional names and adopted patterns of conventual life begun in 19th-c. Europe. A small minority reflect the social concerns for justice and for the poor of the Philippine church of that period. Some have focused their efforts on the rural poor, migrant workers, women, and ethnic minorities.

Most indigenous congregations for women have experienced difficulties in their founding years or during periods of transition from the time of the founders to the second generation. Some difficulties emerge because women are often seen as needing to be under the tutelage of the clergy. The majority of the newer congregations suffer from financial difficulties, receiving little or no help from the dioceses and having to work with little remuneration, thus hampering their religious and educational growth, economic stability, and missionary dynamism.

Though the beginnings of these congregations are often very local, some of them have succeeded in going beyond diocesan or national boundaries, with 13 expanding their missions to Asia and Africa and to overseas Filipinos in the West.

The Oblates of Notre Dame (OND) is a Filipina religious community canonically founded by two Oblates of Mary Immaculate* (OMI) missionaries, G. Mongeau and G. Dion, in Cotabato City. The OND is a dynamic response to the pastoral needs and circumstances of the time: the poverty* of the people and the lack of ordained ministers and religious missionaries to reach out to the villages far away. Inspired by the charism of the OMI missionaries, the OND was founded to be partners in evangelizing the poor, with the vision of a well-trained, mobile force of women capable of meeting the needs of the times, intimately anchored in Jesus Christ, and dedicated to the mission of proclaiming the reign of God. As Filipinas of Asian heritage, the OND sisters seek to understand their own people and culture, adapting to a simple, flexible, and pastorally creative lifestyle.

Two teachers from Notre Dame of Siasi, Sulu, pioneered the initial gathering of women (1957). A few years later, recruits increased, and OND personnel were sent to various missions. In 1961, the OND was canonically recognized as a pious union, in 1964 as a society of diocesan right, and in 1987 as a religious institute of pontifical right. The motherhouse and generalate are based in Cotabato City, Mindanao.

After Estrelle Adre and Mary Rose Quijano responded to the founders' vision, the central house was built in Rosary Heights, Cotabato City. From this house young sisters were sent to the missions in the Cotabato area to do catechesis in parishes and assist in the Radio DXMS ministry. In response to the Vatican Council's call for renewal and the need for qualified catechists, the Notre Dame Institute of Sacred Doctrine was established in Cotabato to train professional catechists to be partners in evangelization. In 1971, the first general chapter defined the nature and spirit of the society, mandated a rewriting of the rules and constitutions according to the needs of the time, and elected a new superior general.

At this stage, the sociopolitical and economic conditions of the country were in a critical situation because of the dehumanizing situation brought about by martial law. After the Synod of Bishops in 1971, the Mindanao-Sulu Pastoral Conference consolidated prophetic efforts and formulated a common thrust of building basic Christian communities through education in justice and peace. This has sharpened the sense of being and acting as a local church and evolved a new ecclesiastical paradigm.

Affected by these shifts, the OND eventually emphasized the value of a self-reliant church and the Gospel imperative to change. The growing social consciousness developed more critical and analytical views, but conflicting opinions and ideologies have also created polarizations. Confronted with varied pastoral demands, the communities tried to respond to the needs of the church outside the Cotabato area and later spread to other areas of Mindanao and to the Visayas and Luzon regions. Their primary apostolate is still catechesis in the parishes through school ministries, family life, lay leadership, radio, social services, and dialogue with Muslims.

The 12 years after the second general chapter (1977-89) was a critical period of building bridges between different movements in the society. Inspired by the people's own response to the dehumanizing situation, the OND learned to adopt the concept of conscientization, where education becomes a participative process animating basic Christian communities. This process has allowed the poor to participate actively in becoming church. Participation in mass actions, denouncing the evil deeds that create dehumanizing structures and systems, has resulted in persecutions. This has sharpened the sense of church and prophetic mission. Solidarity with the poor has become one of the significant shifts of emphasis in the OND missionary thrust.

The visit of John Paul II in 1981 challenged the Filipino Catholics to share "their substance, not only the surplus to the foreign missions." This inspired the OND to open a mission in Daru, Papua New Guinea (1982). Some sisters were sent to other mission territories of the dioceses — Golgobip, Bamu, and Tabubil — and to the archdiocese of Port Moresby (1987) to coordinate the programs of lay-leadership training, catechesis, family life, and youth toward building basic ecclesiastical communities in Melanesian culture. They also coordinate the management of the Pastoral Center Sivarai Namona.

The general assembly in 1986 highlighted the role of women religious in the church, the call to prophetic witness through solidarity with the poor, simplicity of lifestyle, and participation in the social transformation process. It reemphasized the original dynamism of being rooted in Christ and a growing sensitivity to the signs of the times so as to become worthy proclaimers of the Good News. OND sisters were sent to Burma (1991), to the diocese of Auki, Solomon Islands, and to Midland, Texas, United States, to do pastoral catechesis (1992).

In 1995, there were 164 professed OND members in 48 communities in the Philippines and in foreign missions. The society is expanding its concerns to the marginalized sectors in society such as the poor peasants, women, children, Muslims, tribal Filipinos, the sick, and the urban poor.

Vietnam. The first semireligious communities in Vietnam* were formed by catechists with the support of Alexandre de Rhodes* (1593-1660). They formed the so-called *Domus Dei,* where all served the church full-time and lived together as a family (because some of them had been expelled by their Buddhist families). The *Domus Dei* adopted the local custom of the *Nha Chua,* a kind of family formed around a Buddhist teacher. Though the catechists were not religious in the strict sense, they shared their belongings and promised to obey their superior. They lived together and studied religion and healing practices. The rules given by de Rhodes (1642) were approved by the synods of Juthia (1664) and Tongking (1670) and by the Congregation for the Propagation of the Faith* in Rome, which recommended the establishment of *Domus Dei* to the bishops in China (1883).

The Congregation of the Mother Coredemptrix (CMC) was founded in 1953 in Bui Chu Diocese, Nam Ha Province, of North Vietnam by Dominic Mary Tran Dinh Thu, a Vietnamese priest. He was a philosophy professor at Ninh Cuong Major Seminary and received a special inspiration to found a congregation to preach the faith to non-Catholics (1941). He quietly gathered volunteers and began to draft a constitution. In 1948, the group was accepted as a pious association by Bishop Ho Ngoc Can. The constitution was officially approved by the holy see in 1952, and the inauguration ceremony, with the first group of 36 novices, was held on 2 Feb 1953 in Bui Chu.

After the 1954 Geneva Conference, which divided Vietnam into the North and South, the congregation migrated to the South, where it quickly spread to the dioceses of Long Xuyen, Saigon, Qui Nhon, Phu Cuong, Xuan Loc, Da Lat, and Phan Thiet. In 1975, the majority of its members emigrated to the United States. They established the US province, which has 103 perpetual professed religious (including 56 priests), 58 temporary professed members, 12 novices, and 30 postulants. Its motherhouse is located in Carthage, Missouri.

The CMC is a clerical congregation whose members dedicate themselves to serving God and people through their vows of chastity, poverty, and obedience. Self-denial, brotherly charity, and consecration to the Immaculate Heart of Mary are the dominant spiritual emphases of the CMC, as is filial love for the pope. Its motto is *Non ministrari, sed ministrare* (Not to be served, but to serve), from Matt. 20:28. The CMC is financially self-reliant, and its activities include running faith centers in non-Catholic regions and evangelization through cultural, educational, and charitable means (see also Daughters of the Cross).

Bibliography

Costantini, Celso, *Con i Missionari in Cina,* Vols. 1 and 2. • The Secretariat of the Chinese Bishops Conference, *Catholic Directory Taiwan ROC* (1994). • Archives of the CDD.

Adolf Heuken, John Liu, St. Philomena's Convent, Amelia Vasquez, Stella-Marie Llerin, John Mary Doan Phu Xuan

Indonesia

Indonesia consists of approximately 13,000 islands on both sides of the equator between the Southeast Asia mainland and Australia. The most important islands are Java, Sumatra, Kalimantan*, and Sulawesi. Important island groups are the Moluccas*, with Ambon and Ceram in the center and Ternate and Halmahera* in the north, and Nusa Tenggara Timur (NTT) with the islands of Flores, Sumba, and Timor*.

The population of approximately 200 million is unevenly distributed between western Indonesia, including Sumatra, Java, and Bali* (85%), and the rest of the country. There are about 300 ethnic groups, with 250 different languages. The Malay language, originally spoken by the coastal people of East Sumatra and Malaya who embraced Islam* at an early stage (1400), and subsequently the lingua franca in the whole archipelago, has been adopted and developed as the official language of Indonesia. There are five religions recognized by the state: Islam, Protestant and Catholic Christianity, Hinduism*, and Buddhism*. Every inhabitant of Indonesia is expected to belong to one of these. These religions constitute 87%, 7%, 3%, 2%, and less than 1%, respectively, of the population. Especially in Java, mystical groups *(kebathinan)* rooted in traditional Javanese culture are influential.

Most Indonesians are of Malay stock. The Malays came from the Asian continent in several waves. In the first centuries c.e., contact with India was established and Hinduism flourished in a number of kingdoms on Java and Sumatra. Contacts with China* were much more transitory. About 1300 c.e., Islam entered Indonesia. It established itself first in Aceh, then in the coastal regions of East Sumatra, Java, and in the North Moluccas (the sultanate of Ternate). In 1525 and 1527, the Hindu kingdoms in the interior of Java collapsed. In the next two centuries, the coastal regions of West Sumatra, Kalimantan, and Sulawesi were Islamized. Only the interior of Sumatra, Kalimantan and Sulawesi, Bali and southeast Indonesia, including Irian, remained outside the Western influence (Islam).

In the meantime, Europeans found their way to Indonesia: first the Portuguese, who in 1511 conquered Malacca* and from 1522 to 1574 had a trade center protected by a fort on Ternate; then the Dutch, who in 1605 established a stronghold on Ambon and in 1619 founded their capital city of Batavia on the ruins of Jakarta (from 1945 onward named Jakarta again). In the next three centuries, the whole of Indonesia gradually came under Dutch rule, but not without fierce resistance in many regions. In the 20th c., a movement for independence came into being. In 1942, the country was occupied by the Japanese (see World War II), but after the capitulation of Japan on 17 Aug 1945, the Republic of Indonesia was proclaimed, with Soekarno (see Sukarno) as president. Until 1949, the Dutch tried to reestablish their authority by military and diplomatic means.

The Republic of Indonesia is founded upon the *Pancasila**, the Five Principles, which include belief in God, humanity, national unity, consultative democracy, and social justice. In one of the first drafts, belief in God was linked to the obligation of Muslims to keep to the law of Islam. But under pressure from the nationalists, this clause was dropped, so Indonesia is neither a Muslim state nor a secular state. The constitution of 1945 gave great powers to the president. Western individualism was rejected as well as Marxism, and a collectivistic "guided" democracy was introduced, modeled upon the structures of village society, and concentrating all political activities in one political party. However, between 1946 and 1959, this *Pancasila* democracy was attacked from three sides. In 1946, it was modified in a pluralistic sense and a number of political parties were founded, including a Protestant (PARKINDO*) and a Catholic party *(Partai Katolik).* The Communists tried to establish a Communist state, first through an armed insurgency (1948) and then through the elections of 1955 and political agitation in the following years. Extreme Muslims established a Muslim state in West Java and South Sulawesi, and the Muslim parties tried to strengthen the influence of Islam in a legal way. In the 1955 elections, these parties received 45% of the vote, and the Communists 15%.

In 1959, Soekarno, with the support of the armed forces, disbanded the constituent assembly formed after 1955 and returned to the constitution of 1945. In the next years, Soekarno incorporated Communism* into the national identity, and Communist influence and agitation increased. Tensions came to a head in Oct 1965. After some generals of the army were murdered, Communism was eliminated both physically and politically. General Suharto became president and a New Order was launched, which stressed economic development using a Western capitalistic model. Politically, however, the country was remodeled on the base of the 1945 constitution. The *Golkar* (functional groups) became the national party. The political parties were forced to merge into *Partai Demokrasi Indonesia* (Indonesian Democratic Party, PDI), *Partai Nasional Indonesia* (Indonesian National Party, PNI [Socialist and Christian parties]), and *Partai Persatuan Pembangunan* (United Party for Development, PPP [Muslims]). All played a marginal role in the state. *Golkar* and PDI include Christians as well as Muslims.

Pancasila remains the nation's foundation to the point that around 1984 all organizations, including the churches, had to recognize *Pancasila* as the only foundation of national life. In the 1970s and 1980s, Christians occupied important posts in the successive cabinets, the bureaucracy, and the armed forces. The Muslims, however, were making up for their previous disadvantage in the fields of education, economics, and politics, the effects making themselves felt in the 1990s. Essential to the New Order was the influence on government by the armed forces, which was based upon the doctrine of *Dwifungsi ABRI,* the dual function of the armed forces. The resignation of President Suharto from office in 1997 and even more so the election of the open-minded Muslim leader, Abdurrahman Wahid, were considered as marking the end of the New Order and the beginning of a more democratic era.

History of Christianity in Indonesia. Possibly from the 7th c. onward, Christian merchants from Persia and India came to Indonesia (North Sumatra, Java?), but they left only very faint traces. In the 16th c., the Portuguese brought Roman Catholicism* to Halmahera, Ambon, and Nusa Tenggara Timur; and in the 17th c. the extreme north of the archipelago was missionized by the Spanish from Manila. This mission was hampered by the subordination of the mission to trade interests.

In 1546, Francis Xavier* brought a fresh missionary spirit, teaching the creed and baptizing. Later he sent several Goanese Jesuits* to the Moluccas who established churches on many of the eastern islands between 1548 and 1568. After 1570, the mission suffered heavily from attacks by Ternate. This Moluccan Mission grew to 150,000 faithful, who suffered from Portuguese officials, Muslim sultans, and Dutch colonialists. The Dutch United East-India Company* (VOC) forced all of them to become Reformed Christians after 1605.

In the Solor Mission, Dominicans* from Goa (since 1556) built strong communities on the islands of Flores, Timor, Solor, and Adonara. Though the lack of missionary personnel and permanent fighting harmed and isolated these remote congregations, they kept their faith and formed the oldest part of the Indonesian Catholic Church (especially the parish and diocese of Larantuka* in eastern Flores). The VOC (1602-1799) forbade Catholic missionaries to enter its territory and suppressed all Catholic missions. Several missionaries and local laypeople died for their faith.

The Dutch East-India Company restricted missionary activities to areas where they served its interests, that is, mainly to East Indonesia. Even there, they were deployed in earnest mostly in areas which were vital to the VOC, such as Ambon and the surrounding islands. Christians were also found on a number of more remote islands, a situation resulting from the Portuguese-Spanish mission or Protestant activities. But these groups were more or less neglected; they had no pastors or church councils and were rarely visited by ministers. The church could do little to improve this situation, as organizationally and logistically it depended completely on the VOC.

In the Moluccas and Jakarta, Justus Heurnius (1624-38) tried to reach out to Moluccans and Chinese in their own language. The complete Bible* was available in Malay in 1733 (New Testament, 1668). In the 18th c., the VOC opened a theological seminary in Jakarta, which existed for only 10 years and, in contrast to its much more long-lived counterpart in Colombo, produced only one indigenous minister. With this one exception, Indonesians could serve only as unordained teacher-preachers without authority to administer the sacraments, or, in some centers, only as members of the church council. As a result, in this period there were no Indonesian pioneers, and no ordained leaders can be named. At the end of the 18th c., there were 55,000 Protestant Christians and a smaller number of Roman Catholics in the archipelago.

In the 19th c., the situation changed. In 1799, the Dutch state took over all assets of the bankrupt VOC. Freedom of religion was proclaimed in 1806 (because a Catholic brother of Napoleon, Louis, became king of Holland). As a consequence, Catholic priests could enter the country again (1808). In 1808, the first Catholic church was officially opened in Batavia (Jakarta), but the few secular priests were able to look after only the Dutch and Indo-European Catholics on Java and Sumatra. Because the first apostolic vicar, Mgr. Grooff*, transferred three pastors without asking permission from the colonial government, he and all priests were expelled from the colony (1846). But a subsequent agreement *(Nota der punten,* 1847) between the crown and the Vatican acknowledged the internal independence of the vicariate.

The existing Protestant congregations were organized into the Protestant Church in the Netherlands Indies, which had no mission work of its own because it was financed by the state, which professed to be neutral in religious matters. However, the way was open to missionaries from the newly formed Protestant missionary bodies. Between 1811 and 1850, a number of English and Americans worked in Java, Sumatra (where two of them were murdered; see Batak Churches*), and West Borneo/ Kalimantan. The first Dutch missionaries of the *Nederlandsch Zendeling Genootschap* (NZG, 1797) were put in charge of the neglected Christian parishes in Java and East Indonesia. After 1830, the Dutch Protestant missions gradually spread out to the neglected Christians in the outer regions, such as North Sulawesi in the Sangir archipelago, which had never been served by resident Protestant ministers or missionaries. At the same time, by the efforts of a number of laypeople, Europeans and Eurasians, the Christian faith first put roots among the Javanese (ca. 1850).

In the meantime, as a result of theological conflicts, a number of new missionary bodies came into being in Holland. These started work in New Guinea (Irian) (1855), North Sumatra (1857), the North Moluccas (Halmahera, 1866), Central Sulawesi (1892), and South Sulawesi (1852/1913/1930). Southern Central Java and Sumba became the mission field of the Calvinist *Gereformeerde Kerk.* In 1836, the German *Rheinische Mission* (RMG) started mission work among the Dayak in South Borneo, and in 1861 the first RMG missionaries arrived in North Sumatra. After World War I, the Basel Mission took over work in Kalimantan from the RMG. These missions stressed the use of tribal languages instead of Malay, aimed at individual conversion, and kept the congregations under close supervision, church independence being postponed until a long nurturing process would result in sufficient Christian maturity. The Salvation Army* came to Indonesia in 1894, the Adventists in 1900, and the American Christian and Missionary Alliance* (C&MA) came in 1930. After working without lasting result in the 19th c., Baptist* missionaries reentered Indonesia in 1952. The Pentecostal* movement was brought in from Europe and America around 1920. In the 20th c., the government allowed the Protestant church to do missionary work in the South Moluccas and Timor.

Among the Protestant pioneers were Joseph Kam* (Ambon, 1815-33), the landowner C. L. Coolen (East Java, 1827-73), L. I. Nommensen* (North Sumatra, 1862-1918), J. L. van Hasselt (New Guinea, 1863-1907), A. C. Kruyt* (Central Sulawesi, 1892-1932), J. H. Neumann (Tanah Karo, North Sumatra, 1900-49), and R. A. Jaffray* (South Sulawesi, 1930-45).

The Catholics concentrated upon work on Flores (1860) and in Central Java (1894), but also had important fields in North Sumatra (1878), West Kalimantan (1885), North Sulawesi (1868), Timor (1883), the Southeast Moluccas (1888), and South New Guinea (1905). Because the few secular priests would never be able to start missions among the indigenous population, Ursuline nuns (1856), Jesuit priests (1859), and Brothers of St. Aloysius (1862) were called in. From their first parish in Surabaya, the Jesuits took over the old parish of Larantuka (1863) and from there quickly reconverted eastern Flores, sent trained religious teachers and catechists to the other parts of the island, and tried to start new missions in western Timor and Sumba. When the Jesuits handed over the vicariate of the Lesser Sunda Islands to the Society of the Divine Word* (SVD) missionaries (1912-19), the congregation had grown from 6,310 to about 27,000 members. Today, the archdioceses of Ende and Kupang and the diocese of Dili form the biggest portion of the Catholic Church in Indonesia (2.45 million, or 46% in 1992).

As the Catholics got a later start than did the Protestants, in most of these territories a certain rivalry developed between Roman Catholic and Protestant missions, which diminished only after 1960. From 1859 until 1902, all mission fields in Indonesia were served by the Jesuits; after 1902, most areas were gradually handed over to other orders and congregations, the Jesuits retaining only the capital city of Batavia (Jakarta*) and the culturally important region of Central Java.

Before the Jesuits handed over all islands outside Java to other orders and congregations (1904-19), they had also inaugurated, besides Flores, the growth of a few indigenous communities at Langgur (Moluccas), Woloan (northern Celebes), Sejiram (western Borneo), Padang, and Medan (Sumatra). The teachers' training schools at Larantuka (1872), Muntilan (1904), and Woloan (1905) produced lay missionaries in great numbers and quality. After Franz van Lith* had succeeded in converting a small group of farmers in Central Java (1904), stronger communities grew in the area of the sultanates of Yogyakarta and Surakarta, supported by many schools, seminaries (1912), hospitals (1919), and novitiates (1922) for local vocations. In the area of the present archdiocese of Semarang, the first lay organizations, periodicals, and native sister congregations (1938) came into being.

Pioneer missionaries among the Catholics were G. Metz (Flores, 1862-85), Le Cocq d'Armandville* (East Indonesia, 1881-96), F. van Lith* (Central Java, 1896-1926), P. Vertenten* (Irian, 1910-25), and F. Cornelissen (Flores, 1925-83).

In colonial times, missionary work was accompanied

by the conviction that Western civilization and Western models of Christianity, and even Western man, were superior. As a consequence, throughout the 19th c. no Indonesians were ordained ministers or priests except by the RMG in North Sumatra (first in 1885). In the Protestant missions, and even more so in the Protestant church, there was a functional hierarchy in which invariably Europeans held the top positions. Almost without exception, Indonesian mission personnel worked as local teacher-preachers, with only a basic education. They served as the (essential) link between the "white" church government and the indigenous church members.

This is not to say that Indonesians received the Gospel only in a passive way. Those who became Christians did so by their own will, consciously, and for their own reasons, which for the most part were not those expected and often assumed by the missionaries. And in many areas, Indonesians played a decisive role in bringing their fellow countrymen to the faith, often without any formal tie to the mission. In North Sumatra, there was the chief Raja Pontas Lumbantobing (ca. 1830-1900); in Java, there were Paulus Tosari (1813-82), Tunggul Wulung (ca. 1803-85), Sadrach* (1840-1924), and many others. Among the tin miners on Bangka Island, the faith was spread by the Catholic doctor Tsen On Nie* from mainland China* (ca. 1785-1871). Others could be named in other regions.

In the 20th c., the situation gradually changed. Between 1878 and 1886, theological* seminaries had been founded in North Sumatra, Java, North Sulawesi, and Ambon. In 1934, a theological academy was established. The Catholics opened their first seminaries in Java in 1911 and in Flores in 1925. A number of Indonesians were ordained, and some of those worked on an equal footing with Europeans. The first Roman Catholic priest of Indonesian descent was ordained in 1926; by 1940 there were 16. A number of churches in North Sumatra, Java, North Sulawesi, and the Moluccas became independent, and the first Indonesian vicar apostolic (bishop) was ordained in 1940.

On the Protestant side, H. Kraemer* (1922-36 in Indonesia) was instrumental in bringing about indigenization. However, European influence remained very strong even in the independent churches, the general idea being that the character, moral soundness, and organizational abilities of the Indonesian Christians still had to be brought up to the European level. In the meantime, the number of Christians grew steadily; in 1941, there were about 1.7 million Protestants and nearly 640,000 Catholics in a population of 60 million.

In 1942, Indonesia was occupied by Japan*. In the confusion of the transition period, there were bouts of persecution by fanatical Muslims in some areas. Christianity was tolerated by the Japanese, and to a certain point protected, even if, among the Dutch-oriented Ambonese, scores of congregation leaders were killed. But the Japanese tried consistently to make the churches into channels for war propaganda and confiscated almost all mission schools and hospitals. The churches were forced to join regional councils of churches *(Kiristokyo Rengokai)* which included Catholics, mainline Protestants, and other Protestant groups. Japanese clergy were sent to Indonesia and, within the narrow margins allowed them, succeeded in providing protection and practical assistance to the churches.

As nearly all foreign missionaries were interned, the war proved that Indonesian Christianity was able to govern itself. A. Soegijapranata*, together with a few Indonesian priests, had to serve the growing Catholic churches between North Sumatra and Flores. A few German and Japanese priests and nuns assisted them. Mgr. Aerts*, 14 missionaries, and many laymen all over the country were killed by the Japanese. After the declaration of independence by Soekarno and Hatta (1945), Mgr. Soegijapranata, Minister I. J. Kasimo*, and many young men fighting in the guerilla army defended their country in various ways. In the first free election (1955), the *Partai Katolik* received two times more votes than the Catholic population. The process of integration into the new situation was smoothed through good relations with President Soekarno, significant contributions in the field of education, health services, social projects, political cooperation, and opposition to Communism.

The declaration of national independence in 1945 also caused quick progress toward church independence. Most Protestant churches which had not been independent before the war became so between 1946 and 1949. After the war of independence, theological education grew quantitatively and qualitatively — Christian universities sprang up in Pematangsiantar, Jakarta, Salatiga, and elsewhere. Leading Indonesian theologians include J. L. Ch. Abineno*, P. D. Latuihamallo*, S. A. E. Nababan*. The laymen T. S. G. Mulia* and T. B. Simatupang* were instrumental in founding and leading the Indonesian Council of Churches. In politics, J. Leimena* and A. M. Tambunan* can be mentioned. The status of the missionaries changed from that of guardians to fraternal workers.

In the Roman Catholic Church, Indonesianization proceeded at a slower pace. A. Soegijapranata became the first Indonesian bishop in 1941. Though a great number of key positions were still held by missionaries, nearly all of whom applied for Indonesian citizenship, the establishment of the hierarchy (1961), the renewal of the liturgy after the Vatican Council (1965), strong growth after the repression of the Communist coup d'état (1965/66), and involvement (though sometimes too careful) in social issues created a favorable situation for an important increase in numbers (1965: 1.68 million; 1985: 4.093 million) and a new vitality of community life, e.g., basic communities in most of the parishes (since 1970), increase of religious literature, groups for prayer and Bible study, Lenten Action (1962), new lay organizations (e.g., *Legio Mariae,* 1951; Marriage Encounter, 1975), marriage preparation courses, and professional and charismatic groups. The daily *Kompas,* the largest newspaper in Southeast Asia, was founded by Catholic ex-seminarians, though since the 1980s it has given up its Christian roots.

After World War II*, the growth of the church accelerated, especially in tribal communities, but, in the aftermath of the 1965 coup d'état, also in Muslim Java. The number of Catholics at present is given as nearly six million (including half a million in East Timor, which became independent in 1999); the number of Protestants is more difficult to estimate but might be put at 12-15 million. Government statistics tend to give higher numbers, because many who have never been baptized in a church have registered themselves as Christians.

The percentage of Christians is highest in the provinces of East Timor (90%), Irian (85%), NTT (75%), and North Sulawesi (55%). Between 25% and 50% are Christian in the Moluccas, North Sumatra, and West Kalimantan; 10-25% in Central Sulawesi, Central and East Kalimantan, and in the capital city of Jakarta; 5-10% in the Autonomous Region of Yogyakarta (Central Java) and South Sulawesi; 3-5% in Central and East Java and Southeast Sulawesi; 1-3% in Sumatra outside North Sumatra and in South Kalimantan; and under 1% in West Java, Bali, and West Nusa Tenggara. Of the total number of Christians, more than 25% live in Java (mostly ethnic Javanese), more than 20% in North Sumatra (mostly Batak), less than 10% in Kalimantan, more than 10% in Sulawesi (mostly Minahasans and Torajans), and 30% in the rest of East Indonesia. Of the Roman Catholics, 35% live on the islands of Flores and Timor, the other concentration areas being Java, West Kalimantan, and North Sumatra.

Present situation. The present situation of the churches is partly determined by their mutual relations and by their relation with government and Islam. Originally, Christianity was planted by the Dutch Reformed. The RMG, which has a mixed Reformed-Lutheran background, brought a Lutheran* strain to North Sumatra; the Dutch Mennonites* founded churches in Central Java; and the Methodists* did so in Sumatra. In 1950, the churches of these denominations founded the Council of Churches in Indonesia (*Dewan* [after 1984, *Persekutuan*] *Gereja-Gereja di Indonesia,* DGI/PGI); in 1994 the membership of the 68 affiliated churches totaled about 10 million, of whom two million were in the Batak churches.

Ecumenism has been fostered by a common Bible* translation (1975), frequent joint meetings at the national level, and a common message on Christmas each year. Since 1966, the Indonesian Bishops' Conference (established in 1925) has often clarified its position on religious (Christian family* life, 1975; seminary education, 1977; abortion, 1990) and public issues (e.g., *Pancasila**, 1985; East Timor general elections).

The 1970s brought some irritations: The minister of religion stopped visas for new missionaries and made it difficult to extend old ones (1978). Catholic Javanese who migrated to Muslim areas on other islands encountered great difficulties in forming communities and building churches, a situation which is becoming even more difficult in the fast-expanding cities of Java. In addition to such harassment from outside the church, the rapid growth since the 1970s has created internal problems: shortage of pastors, lack of indigenous domestic missionaries to replace the foreign ones, loss of apostolic spirit in some lay organizations, difficulties in deepening the faith of the many neophytes, the sharp rise of mixed marriages resulting quite often in apostasy of the Christian spouse.

The visit of John Paul II to five dioceses in Indonesia (1989) strengthened the faithful and their awareness of unity with the universal church. The issue of East Timor, where young people have been massacred (1991, 1999), the accusation of "Christianization by unfair means," and the fear of rising Islamic fundamentalism overshadow the normally peaceful coexistence of different religions. It seems that the Catholic Church of Indonesia in a relatively short time (1863-1980) has achieved self-propelling growth with regard to numbers, an advancing structural organization (new [arch]dioceses between 1989 and 1994), and vigorous life (several diocesan synods since 1989). On the other hand, the increase has slackened since the early 1990s and is lower than the national population growth (1994).

The Indonesian Baptists (ca. 150,000 baptized members) are in part affiliated with the Indonesian Baptist Alliance (*Gabungan Gereja Baptis Indonesia,* GGBI). Most churches issuing from C&MA mission work have united in the *Gereja Kemah Injil Indonesia,* whose six member churches total about 500,000 members, more than half of whom are in Irian Jaya. Between 1930 and 1970, Pentecostalism* went through a number of schisms. In 1979, the Indonesian Pentecostal Council (*Dewan Pentakosta Indonesia,* DPI) was founded. Very tentatively, the combined membership can be put at 1.5-2 million, of whom a relatively large number are of Chinese descent. Adventists (about 200,000) and a number of independent bodies do not belong to any national church council. It should be noted that the lines between the denominations are not rigid. Among the PGI members now are also churches of Baptist, C&MA, and Pentecostal stock. Moreover, since the 1970s an evangelical movement has developed, mainly stimulated from America, which has led to the founding of a number of new church bodies, and of an Indonesian Evangelical Fellowship (*Persekutuan Injili Indonesia,* PII, founded in 1971), which in turn counts many C&MA and Pentecostal churches among its members.

In the 1950s and 1960s, the main ecumenical challenge faced by Indonesian Protestantism was the effort to bring together the DGI member churches into one church body. That effort resulted in the renaming of the "Council" *(Dewan)* to "Association" *(Persekutuan)* in 1984 but did not really change the relation of the member churches. After 1970, a theological reorientation in DGI/PGI circles and the increasing influence of American evangelicalism caused a growing antithesis between evangelicals and ecumenicals, which makes itself felt in evangelization, literature work, and theological education, even if the Indonesian cultural and religious context does not seem to warrant such an American-style antithesis. Besides, the charismatic movement makes itself felt in a number of traditional churches and sometimes generates tensions that threaten to break them up. Relations between Protestants and Catholics, which were strained until the 1960s, have improved.

The relation to the government is partly determined by the Christians' minority position. Because of this, the churches tend to conform to the government policy of the moment, even to the point of making revolution a theological issue in the early 1960s. In 1984-85 all churches and church organizations had to insert into their church order or statutes a formula recognizing *Pancasila* as the sole foundation for the life of the nation. For daily matters, the churches communicate with the government through the ministry of religion *(departemen agama),* which has departments for each of the five recognized religions; the minister is always a Muslim. After Suharto resigned from the presidency in 1997, ideological pressure on religious organizations diminished.

The relation to Islam is uneasy. Islam has long considered Christianity the religion of the Dutch, and Muslim fears that the process of Westernization would bring Christianization in its trail were fueled by the numbers of Muslim youth in Christian schools converting to Christianity in the 1970s and 1980s. Christians tend to suspect the Muslims of striving for an Islamic state and do not appreciate that they have to take a step back now that Muslims are making good their previous disadvantage in education, economics, and politics. In a minority situation, Christians have problems in getting permission for church building; where they are a majority, the Muslim presence may be felt to be ostentatious. In the 1980s, mixed religious education at the state schools was forbidden, and mixed marriages were rendered practically impossible; in this way, important channels for Christianization were cut off. In the late 1990s, hundreds of churches were destroyed or damaged by mobs, mainly on Java, Kalimantan, and Sulawesi; these church burnings, which seem to have been incited by certain people for political purposes, were endorsed by part of the Muslim leadership but condemned by others. During 1999, a religious war raged in the Moluccas, and Christianity was eliminated on several islands. Few Christians have a thorough theological knowledge of Islam, and dialogue has only rarely been practiced. However, since 1945 Christians have earned their legitimate place as members of the nation, and the majority on both sides want to live together in peace.

Bibliography

General History: Ricklefs, M. C., *A History of Modern Indonesia Since c. 1300,* 2nd ed. (1993). • Coolhaas, W. Ph., *A Critical Survey of Studies on Dutch Colonial History,* 2nd ed., rev. G. J. Schutte (1980). • Benda, Harry J., *Japanese Military Occupation in Indonesia: Selected Documents* (1965).

Anthropology: Koentjaraningrat, R. M., *Anthropology in Indonesia: A Bibliographical Review* (1975). • Kennedy, R., T. W. Maretzki, and H. Th. Fischer, *Bibliography of Indonesian Cultures and Peoples* (1962).

Christianity in General: Van den End, Th., *Ragi Carita: Sejarah Gereja-Gereja di Indonesia,* Vol. I (1993), Vol. II (1993) (2nd rev. ed., 1999). • Müller-Krüger, Th., *Der Protestantismus in Indonesien* (1968). • Muskens, M. P. M., *Indonesie, een strijd om nationale identiteit: nationalisten, islamieten, katholieken* (1974). • Muskens, M. P. M., ed., *Sejarah Gereja Katolik Indonesia,* Vols. I-V (1972-74). • Bank, J., *Katholieken en de Indonesische Revolutie* (1984). • Heuken, A., *Ensiklopedi Gereja,* Vols. I-V (1991-95).

Present Situation of Protestant Christianity: Ukur, F., and F. L. Cooley, *Jerih dan Juang; laporan nasional survai menyeluruh gereja di Indonesia* (1979) (abridged ed., Frank L. Cooley, *The Growing Seed: The Christian Church in Indonesia* [1981]). • Cooley, F. L., *Indonesia: Church and Society* (1968) (short bibliography).

The Catholic Church in the 20th C.: Huub, J. W. M., *Boelaars, Indonesianisasi. Het omvormingsproces van de katholieke kerk in Indonesië tot de Indonesische katholieke kerk* (1991).

Batak Churches: Pedersen, P. B., *Batak Blood and Protestant Soul* (1970). • Aritonang, Jan S., *Mission Schools in Batakland (Indonesia), 1861-1940* (1994). • Liddle, R. W., *Ethnicity, Party and National Integration: An Indonesian Case Study* (1970).

Java: Van Akkeren, Philip, *Sri and Christ: A Study of the Indigenous Church in East Java* (1969).

East Borneo: Conley, William, *The Kalimantan Kenyah: A Study of Tribal Conversion in Terms of Dynamic Cultural Themes* (1976).

Ambon: Cooley, Frank, *Altar and Throne in Central Moluccan Society* (1961) (Indonesian edition: *Mimbar dan Takhta* [1987]).

Timor: Peters, G. W., *Indonesia Revival: Focus on Timor* (1973).

Irian: Kamma, F. C., *Ajaib di mata kita,* 3 vols. (1981, 1982, 1994) (Dutch original: *Dit Wonderlijke Werk,* 2 vols. [1977]). • Cornelissen, J. F. L. M., *Pater en Papoea: De ontmoeting van de Missionarissen van het Heilig Hart met de cultuur der Papoea's* (1988).

Halmahera: Hairae, James, *The Character and Theological Struggle of the Church in Halmahera, Indonesia, 1941-79* (1981).

Indonesian Theology: Thomson, Alan, "Theological Publications in Indonesia," *South East Asia Journal of Theology* 15 (1973). • Hoekema, A. H., "Denken in dynamisch evenwicht: De wordingsgeschiedenis van de nationale protestantse theologie in Indonesië (ca. 1860-1960)" (doctoral dissertation, Leiden) (1994).

Bible Translations: Swellengrebel, J. L., *In Leijdecker's*

voetspoor, anderhalve eeuw bijbelvertaling en taalkunde in de Indonesische talen, 2 vols. (1974, 1978).

Church-State Relations: Latuihamallo, P. D., "State, Religion and Ideologies in Indonesia," in M. M. Thomas and M. Abel, *Religion, State and Ideologies in East Asia* (1975).

Christian-Muslim Relations: Gowing, Peter C., "Past and Present Postures in Christian-Muslim Relations in Insular Southeast Asia," *South East Asia Journal of Theology* 18 (1977). • Wawer, W., *Muslime und Christen in der Republik Indonesia* (1974).

Protestant Church: Van den End, Th., *Ragi Carita,* Vol. I, Ch. 18, and Vol. II, Ch. 32 (1980 and 1989). • Locher, G. P. H., *De Kerkorde der Protestantse Kerk in Indonesië* (1948). • *Membelah Khazanah Pelayanan — 390 Tahun Gereja Protestan di Indonesia* (1995). • Ongirwalu, H., *Tata Gereja sebagai Upaya Bertheologia* (unpublished master's thesis). • Van Randwijck, S. C. Graaf, *Handelen en Denken in Dienst der Zending — Oegstgeest 1897-1942* (1981).

Catholic Church: Bishops Office, *Jaarboek 1932-1942; Buku Tahunan/Petunjuk Gereja Katolik 1955-1993.* • LPPS, *Ikhtisar Statistik tentang Gereja Katolik di Indonesia, 1949-1967* (1968). • Bank Penyimpanan Data, *Statistik Tahunan Lembaga/Paroki/Personalia/Sekolah/ Karya Kesehatan Katolik 1981-1990* (ongoing).

General: Van Aernsbergen, A. J., *Chronologisch overzicht van de werksamheden der jezuiten in de missie van Nederlandsch Oost-Indie 1859-1934* (1934) (continued by Fr. Busch, *Chronologisch overzicht (1934-1971)* (1972). • Banawiratna, J. B., *Jesus Sang Guru: Pertemuan Kejawen dengan Injil* (1977). • Bank, J., *Katholieken en de Indonesische Revolutie* (1984). • Hadiwikarta, I., *Himpunan Keputusan MAWI, 1924-1980* (1980). • Haire, James, *The Character and Theological Struggle of the Church in Halmahera, Indonesia, 1941-1979* (1981). • Heuken, A., *Sedjarah Gereja Katolik di Indonesia* (1971); *Ensiklopedi Gereja,* Vols. I-V (1991-95). • Muskens, M. P. M., ed., *Sejarah Gereja Katolik Indonesia,* Vols. I-V (1972-74); *Partner in Nation Building: The Catholic Church in Indonesia* (1979). • Sinaga, B., *Gereja dan Inkulturasi* (1984). • Van der Velden, A., *De Roomsch-Katholieke missie in Nederlandsch Oost-Indië* (1908). • Visser, B., *Onder Portugeesch-Spaanse Vlag: De katholieke missie in Indonesië, 1511-1605* (1925). • Weitjens, J., *De vrijheid der katholieke prediking in Nederlands-Indië van 1900-1940* (1969).

Special Areas: Aster, G., *Morgen is mijn eiland rijk: Vijftig jaren capucijnenmissie op Borneo* (1955); *Een volk ontdekt Christus: De katholieke missie onder de Bataks op Sumatra* (1959). • Coomans, M. C. C., *Evangelisatie en kultuurverandering . . . in Oost-Kalimantan* (1980). • Cornelissen, J. F. L. M., *Pater en Papoea . . .* (1988). • Wessels, C., *De geschiedenis der R.K. missie in Ambon, 1546-1605* (1926).

THOMAS VAN DEN END, with contributions from ADOLF HEUKEN and HENDRIK ONGIRWALU

Indonesia Evangelical Fellowship

(*Persekutuan Injili Indonesia,* PII). Until 1950, almost all Protestant Christians in Indonesia* belonged to churches issuing from Dutch and German missionary bodies. In the years after 1950, American missions became more active in Indonesia, and with them the influence of American forms of evangelicalism made itself felt. A number of evangelical church bodies came into being. In Jul 1971, some evangelical church leaders, among them P. Octavianus and H. L. Senduk, wrote an evangelical confession of faith consisting of seven articles, the first stressing the inerrancy and absolute authority of the Scripture. An Indonesia Evangelical Fellowship (IEF) was founded, which in its first National Congress, held in Apr 1974, included the 1971 confession in its statutes. Among the objectives laid down in the statutes are evangelization, defense of the Gospel truth, coordination of evangelical activities, and assistance to the Indonesian government in realizing national development. The activities planned for 1989-93 included the coordination of mission activities, contacts with government agencies, stimulating the production of theological books, and preparing religious programs for national television. Like all other religious organizations in Indonesia, the PII was persuaded by the government to recognize *Pancasila** (state philosophy) as the only foundation for the life of the state, nation, and society (1985).

Gradually, the IEF opened offices in most Indonesian provinces. The membership of the IEF includes churches and religious organizations, as well as individuals. Among the 51 member churches are the *Gereja Bethel Indonesia* and the *Gereja Kemah Injil Indonesia,* each of which claims a membership of about half a million. In addition, 18 churches are associate members. These 69 churches belong to the evangelical, Pentecostal*, Baptist*, and Wesleyan groups. The IEF is a full member of the Evangelical Fellowship of Asia and the World Evangelical Fellowship. Several leaders of the IEF have a seat on the boards of both organizations.

The IEF takes a critical attitude toward main-stream institutions such as the Indonesian Council of Churches* (PGI) and the theological schools associated with it. However, several member churches of the IEF have also joined the PGI.

Bibliography

Paulus Daun, *Apakah Evangelicalisme itu?* (1986). • Chris Marantika, *Kaum Injili Indonesia Masa Kini.* • *Peta kehidupan dan pelayanan Umat Kristen di Indonesia* (publication of the Direktorat Jenderal Bimbingan Masyarakat Kristen Protestan, Dep. Agama R.I., 1990).

THOMAS VAN DEN END

Indonesian Bishops' Conference

(*Konperensi Waligereja Indonesia,* KWI). Established in 1955 during the first meeting of Indonesian bishops after World War II* at Surabaya, the KWI resumed the tradition of the *Raad van Kerkvoogden* of colonial times (since 1925). The conference, especially its permanent secretariat, became involved in various socio-religious affairs: defending freedom of religion (against colonial restrictions, leftists before 1965, and rightists' infringements after 1970); promoting the social apostolate among workers and landless farmers; and vigorously enacting the renewal of Vatican Council II, especially in the field of liturgy (in the vernacular since 1968) and the ecumenical movement* (common actions with the National Council of Churches against government restrictions in 1974, 1979, and 1981). Family* planning was also an urgent issue dealt with several times (Pastoral Clarification on *Humanae Vitae,* 1968, 1972; letter on respecting human life, 1991).

Current concerns of the conference include accelerating the indigenization process of the clergy, more equal distribution of personnel (1972), and the academic formation of priests in seminaries and lay cadres in 12 Catholic institutions of higher learning (see Colleges and Universities). The secretariat also establishes and maintains good working relations with the central government (particularly with the department of religions), the National Council of Churches (ecumenical Bible* translation, common Christmas messages), and the national bodies of non-Christian religions.

Adolf P. Heuken

Indonesian Christian Intelligence Union

(Persatuan Inteligensia Kristen Indonesia, PIKI*).* PIKI is a gathering body for Christian intellectuals, a continuation of *Gerakan Mahasiswa Kristen Indonesia* (Indonesian Christian Student Movement, GMKI). The goal of this organization, besides deepening the faith of its members and motivating them to strengthen church life, is to prepare a channel for the members' socio-political aspiration, based on their Christian faith and their consciousness as Christ's witnesses.

PIKI was founded in Jakarta* on 19 Dec 1963 in the midst of socio-political unrest in Indonesia arising from the growth of the Communist Party and ideology. The birth of PIKI was motivated by noble ideals to fulfill, maintain, and show responsibility for Indonesian independence, as well as to defend *Pancasila** as the principle and basic ideology of the state. In a relatively short time, PIKI succeeded in founding branches in many provinces, and its members participated in the establishment of some Christian universities (such as Satyawacana University at Salatiga, Central Java, and Paulus University at Ujung Pandang, South Sulawesi).

After the 1960s, PIKI experienced a great decline and has recovered only since 1989. Since that time, its attention and activity have focused on a series of seminars and conferences which discuss national and international issues: Morality, Technology, and Human Resources for the Sake of Ecosystem Integrity (1989); Anticipating the Take-Off Era (a second long-term Indonesian development program, 1989); the Nusantara (Indonesian Archipelago) Concept (1990); Indonesian Culture (1991); Regional Autonomy (1991); Human Resources (1992); and Constructing the Indonesian Nation in the Frame of the Second Long-Term Development, 1994-2019 (1992). These occasions are open gatherings with many speakers and participants who are non-Christians. The aims of such activities are to increase the participation of Indonesian Christian intellectuals in the larger issues faced by their country and to show that Indonesian Christian intellectuals are an integral part of the nation, joined in responsibility to develop and to increase the quality of national life. This enables them to disprove the accusations of certain circles that Indonesian Christians are heirs of a colonial religion and spirit, or merely interested in otherworldly salvation. Such a focus makes PIKI one of the partners of PGI (Communion of Churches of Indonesia* [CCI]), which also has a great interest in national and international issues.

PIKI must today face many serious challenges and handicaps since its recovery. For example, many members face difficulty in gaining career advancements, especially in government office. Thus many Indonesian Christian intellectuals avoid joining the organization. Although in its early beginnings PIKI participated in the development of the embryo of the New Order regime, there is an indication that their current relationship is no longer close. Thus many Christian intellectuals are no longer safe or secure in their positions in political organizations. Meanwhile, Muslim intellectual organizations are making an unyielding effort to plant a strong influence in the ruling political organization. However, the Indonesian government formally supports PIKI's existence and activities and encourages PIKI to work with other intellectual organizations, including the Muslim as well as government institutions.

Bibliography

DPP, PIKI, *Keputusan Kongres Pertama PIKI* (22-24 Jul 1989). • DPP, PIKI, *Laporan Dewan Pimipinan Pusat PIKI kepada Bapak Presiden Republik Indonesia* (1993).

Jan S. Aritonang

Indonesian Christian Youth Movement

(*Gerakan Angkatan Muda Kristen Indonesia,* GAMKI). Formally founded on 23 Apr 1962, GAMKI is actually a merger of two former Christian youth organizations: the Indonesia Christian Youth Union (*Persatuan Pemuda Kristen Indonesia,* PPKI) founded on 4 Nov 1945, and the Ecumenical Christian Youth Council (*Majelis Pemuda Kristen Oikumene,* MPKO) founded 27 Dec 1948.

The origins of PPKI and MPKO may be traced to two interrelated movements, the political-nationalistic struggle for independence from Western colonial rule, and the ecumenical movement striving for church unity and independence from the domination of Western missionary societies. PPKI was formed during a time when Indonesia's new-found independence appeared threatened by the Dutch military's attempt to reannex Indonesia. Together with youth of other religions, PPKI delegates declared their political stand against colonialism at the World Christian Youth Conference in Oslo in Jul 1947. Together with other Christian organizations, PPKI declared its support of *Pancasila** (The Five Principles) as the foundation of the Republic of Indonesia. It did so both at its seventh congress (28-31 Oct 1957) and in a declaration on 27 Nov 1957.

Founded during the Ecumenical Conference of Indonesian Christian Youth (18-28 Dec 1948), MPKO aimed to serve Christian youth work in general and to increase ecumenical consciousness and cooperation both in and outside Indonesia*. Between 1948 and 1950, MPKO was actively involved in the preparation for and formation of the Council of Churches in Indonesia (now the Community of Churches in Indonesia*).

During the consultation (18-23 Apr 1962) that led to the formation of GAMKI, the participants issued a political statement supporting the government's program to regain West Irian (now Irian Jaya) from the Dutch. That statement reflects GAMKI's constitutional goal "to dedicate itself to God by fulfilling its calling in Church, State, and Society." Based on John 17:21, GAMKI aims to deepen the spiritual life of its members, encourage an awareness of and participation in the church's efforts, and nurture the consciousness of being part of one catholic church.

During the turbulent years of 1965-66, GAMKI was actively involved in demonstrations and other action to abolish Communist and Communist-influenced organizations. A number of members died in the struggle. Their support of the Indonesian New Order government was further emphasized when GAMKI signed the Youth Declaration (23 Jul 1973) to found the National Commission of Indonesian Youth *(Komite Nasional Pemuda Indonesia)*, a federation of all youth organizations in Indonesia. A question that arises is the extent to which GAMKI is accepted by the churches. Most Indonesian churches have their own youth organizations, and few join GAMKI. This is because of its pronounced political orientation, often at the expense of its spiritual and ecclesiastical emphases.

Bibliography

Hartono, Chr. T., *Gerakan Ekumenis di Indonesia* (1984). • Ngelow, Z. J., *Kekristenan dan Nationalisme* (1994). • Patmono, S. K., *Gerak Ganda — Sejarah Pergerakan Pemuda Kristen Indonesia* (1988). JAN S. ARITONANG

Indonesian Missionary Fellowship. *See* Foundation Fellowship of Evangelization of Indonesia

Ing Lian Zhi

(b. Beijing, China, 1867; d. 1926). Well-known Catholic in China*.

A Manchu, Ing became interested in Catholicism after reading *Zhu Zhi Qun Zheng* (An Essay on Church Order) by Johann Adam Schall von Bell*. He was also interested in the study of other religions in China. In 1888, Ing became a member of the Catholic Church. In 1901, he was busy preparing the launching of a newspaper called *Da Gong Bao* in Nanjing, and on 17 Jul 1902, the first issue of the paper was published. From that year to 1916, Ing was the main person responsible for the newspaper and the author of many controversial articles published therein. In 1912, along with his friend Ma Xiang Bo, he petitioned the Vatican to open a Catholic university in China. In 1917, he published *Quan Xie Zui Yan*, in which he sharply criticized the haughty attitude of missionaries from foreign countries who despised Chinese Christians. In 1925, he became chairman of the Fu Jen Society, the forerunner of Fu Jen University. He assisted Ben Du Hui in the founding of Fu Jen University.

Bibliography

Boorman, Howard L., ed., *A Biographical Dictionary of Republican China*, Vol. 4 (1974). • Fang Hao, comp., *Ying Lien-chi hsien-sheng jih-chi yi-kao*, 3 vols. (1974). • Hayhoe, Ruth, "A Chinese Catholic Philosophy of Higher Education in Republican China," *Tripod* 48 (Dec 1988). CHINA GROUP, translated by DAVID WU

Innocent IV

(Sinibaldo Fieschi) (b. Genoa, late 12th c.; d. Naples, 7 Dec 1254) Great pope of the Middle Ages known for his conflict with Frederick II, the Inquisition, and concern for Christian missions.

Sinibaldo was the sixth of 10 children born into a rising family in Genoa. He studied at Parma and then at Bologna, where he became proficient in canon law. After passing through many positions in the church in Italy, he was elevated to pope on 25 Jun 1243. Much of his 11-year reign was concerned with solidifying the rule of the papacy and, paradoxically, with relations of the church with those outside the faith and outside Europe. Innocent was the first church leader to recognize that there were "infidels" outside Europe who needed to be reached. He developed the earliest methods and legal protocol for such outreach. In 1254 Innocent sent out John of Plano de Carpine* with a letter to the Great Khan to implore tolerant treatment of Christians in his realm. His purpose was both political, to discourage the further spread of the Mongols to the West, and religious. Innocent also argued for religious tolerance in lands that had varied religious communities, established a permanent Inquisition to keep the church pure (1252), and declared that forced conversions were not to be tolerated.

Bibliography

Podesta, F., *Innocenzo IV* (1928) (in Italian). • Muldoon, James, *Popes, Lawyers and Infidels* (1979). • "Innocent IV," in *New Catholic Encyclopedia.*

SCOTT W. SUNQUIST

Inquisition, Philippines

Institution originally established in medieval times in Spain to be the guardian and protector of the purity of the Roman Catholic* faith.

The Spanish colonization of the Philippines* was essentially a missionary enterprise, and the greatest and most permanent accomplishments of the Spanish colonists were primarily in the field of religion. To understand this, one must bear in mind the unusual relationship between church and state in Spain. There and then, "Spanishness" was virtually synonymous with Catholicism. The papacy in the Vatican granted the crown of Spain complete control over the finances of the national Roman Catholic Church, as well as over the selection of members of the ecclesiastical hierarchy. As a quid pro quo, the Spanish crown accepted the responsibility of spreading the faith and seeing to it that no heretical beliefs or creeds undermined its preeminence in the kingdom. This arrangement brought and sustained unity between the church and state. Their relationship was inextricably intertwined. Spain became a secular, yet a thoroughly theocratic state.

It was inevitable that Spanish colonialism* would bear the imprint of this union. Wherever Spain succeeded in occupying an area, a region, or an island, Spanish *conquistadores* held a sword in one hand and a cross in the other. Friars marched side by side with soldiers. In the case of the Philippine Islands, *Pax Hispanica* was in reality made possible only by *Pax Christi.*

The long rule of Spain in the Philippines may be attributed to the spiritual conquest of that country's indigenous population. Frequently, the friars were the only direct link between the local people and the central government in Manila. Once converted to Roman Catholicism, they had to be prevented from lapsing into their fundamental animism, or from falling under the influence of heretical views (i.e., Lutheranism, Calvinism, and Judaism) brought into the islands either by foreigners or by Castilians, who themselves entered surreptitiously bearing proscribed publications.

Whether the threat to the preeminence of the Catholic faith in the Philippines was real or imaginary, it persuaded the Mexican holy office to extend its authority in the islands. Because the Europeans were not numerous enough, the Inquisition erected did not equal in stature the one founded in the Mexican viceroyalty.

In the Philippines, the Inquisition came under the charge of a commissary, who was directly responsible to the Mexican holy office. Official records indicate that the commissary of the holy office in the bishopric of Manila was appointed in 1583, although episcopal inquisitorial activities were initiated as early as 1572 by the Dominican incumbent, Domingo de Salazar*, bishop of the Philippines, without the knowledge or approval of the tribunal of the Inquisition in Mexico. The commissary's existence in the Philippines represented the absolute and permanent authority of the Mexican tribunal to exercise control over matters affecting church dogmas and to see to it that these dogmas were not corrupted.

Following the precedent excepting the indigenous people of the American mainland from the authority of the holy tribunal, the crown exempted the indigenous people as well as the Chinese in the Philippines from the jurisdiction of the commissary, although the friars who preached the Gospel to the Filipinos zealously guarded them against apostasy. Consequently, the attention of the commissary was directed solely to Spaniards and other foreigners who engaged in practices detrimental to propagating the faith among the indigenous population. The commissary's efforts included searching for censored books that might undermine the influence of the Catholic faith.

Structurally, the office of the commissary of the Mexican Inquisition in Manila was directed by a superintendent-commissary who acted as the superior of the provincial commissaries stationed in major population centers such as Cagayan and Camarines in Luzon, and Cebu and Negros in the Visayas. Among his functionaries were a constable and a notary. The inquisitorial council in Manila was composed of a number of "ministers" serving separately as examiners of published materials, *familiares* (helpers), and *consultores* (counselors). Moreover, the Mexican tribunal always appointed at least three other superintendent-commissaries. The explanation given for this arrangement was that it assured the continuity of the commissary's operations. When one superintendent-commissary died or was removed from office for a given reason, he could be replaced promptly. At any given time, however, only one of the three or four superintendent-commissaries wielded real authority. For the two centuries before the suppression of the Inquisition in 1810, friars of the Dominican* order held the office of superintendent-commissary. The only notable exceptions were Francisco Manrique, an Augustinian, who was the first to serve in that capacity in 1583, and another Augustinian, Diego Munoz, who succeeded him in 1587 and served until his death in 1594. The only interruption of Dominican control of the commissary after that date came during the time of José de Paternina, also an Augustinian, who aroused acrimony by his highhanded tactics while serving in that office during the years 1664-72.

As a procedural weapon, the superintendent-commissary had instructions to conduct his business of detecting violations of the faith and crimes of heresy in utmost secrecy. All other persons, whether accusers or witnesses, likewise had to observe this rule. Violators could expect excommunication, aside from pecuniary or corporal punishments, all at the discretion of the superintendent-commissary. An excommunicated person, however, could request absolution from the superintendent-commissary, which was usually granted so long as the supplicant admitted his guilt. In such cases, he got off with some spiritual penance secretly imposed.

Usually, the superintendent-commissary heard denunciations, meant to be kept secret, in his own residence during the daytime, although he did not preclude night hours when necessary. Since the commissary had instructions not to cause undue inconvenience to witnesses, he sometimes delegated the responsibility of conducting an investigation to the curate or parish priest of the town where the witness lived, whose depositions the commissary's notary duly certified. Refusal by a witness summoned to testify resulted in either excommunication or payment of a fine, or both. To keep track of who received a penalty and who did not, the Inquisition always kept a meticulous record of any investigation. The penalties were meted out in accordance with the social class of the witnesses, as well as in proportion to the gravity of their disobedience.

While the superintendent-commissary heard denunciations from witnesses who testified under oath, he had no authority to make arrests, issue interdicts, or take other measures. Instead, he transmitted denunciations to the holy office in Mexico. These written charges normally started with a statement of the testimony of the first witness. Along with the charges, the statements made, and the evidence given by the witnesses, the superintendent-commissary included pertinent data related to the accused person's birthplace, social class, and properties, if he had any. The Mexican inquisitorial court then held hearings on the charges. In case of crimes of heresy or immorality, the accused was arrested and ordered to be sent to Mexico for trial at his expense.

On the question of sequestration of property, a touchy issue, the superintendent-commissary of the holy office had standing orders to proceed with caution. He was not permitted to confiscate outright the property of a person who was accused of either heresy or bigamy. Rather, the arrested person might entrust his property to a confidant, who in turn took an oath to keep the property intact. Conviction of the accused meant having to return to the Philippines to face just punishment.

Aside from investigating crimes of heresy and immorality, the superintendent-commissary also saw to it that no prohibited books entered the colony. In pursuing this role, he visited all ships arriving in Manila or at Cavite, questioning the ship's commander, master clerk, and passengers, and he inspected the containers where the galleon's cargoes were kept. While on paper great care was taken to keep the individuals involved from suffering unnecessary injustice, the merry-go-round procedures often caused precisely this. By and large, through two centuries of existence, the Philippine Inquisition had no right to arrest or try a person accused of a crime committed within the commissary's jurisdiction. It only communicated to Mexico whatever charges were brought against a person. The Mexican tribunal then ordered the commissary in the Philippines to make the arrest. After the sentence, the accused went back to the Philippines to serve his sentence, usually in the form of imprisonment for a period of at least two years.

Until the abolition of the Inquisition in all of Spain's dominions by the liberal Spanish parliament in 1810, the Mexican tribunal, through its commissary in the Philippines, stood as one of the bulwarks of the faith. It is not fair to say that the Philippine Inquisition contributed nothing to the preservation of the purity of the Catholic faith just because it was a mere arm of the Mexican holy office and limited in power. Rather, it had an unusual restraining effect on the colonists in the islands. As guardian of the faith, the Philippine Inquisition somehow contributed to the successful and lasting Christianization of the Philippines. If the Philippines today can lay claim to being the only Christian country in Asia, its religious impulse and the mind-set of the people being fundamentally Catholic, it is because of this remarkable Spanish achievement.

Bibliography

Bauzon, Leslie E., *Deficit Government: Mexico and the Philippine Situado (1606-1804)* (1981). • Blair, Emma Helen, and James Alexander Robertson, eds., *The Philippine Islands, 1493-1898,* 55 Vols. (1903-7). • Lea, Henry Charles, *The Inquisition in the Spanish Dependencies* (1922). • Medina, José Toribio, *El Tribunal del Santo Oficio de la Inquisicion en las Islas Filipinas* (1899). • Phelan, John Leddy, *The Hispanization of the Philippines: Spanish Aims and Filipino Responses, 1565-1700* (1959).

Leslie Bauzon

Institute for Social Research and Development

(Lambaga Penelitian dan Pembangunan Sasia, LPPS). The Institute for Social Research and Development was established in 1968 by the Indonesian Bishops' Conference in order to activate participation of the Indonesian church in development projects, to coordinate with various foreign funding agencies, and to give advice on how to raise funds and control their proper use. LPPS prepares the national Lenten Action (*Aksi Puasa Pembangunan,* since 1969) and administrates the portion destined for projects on a national level. The Catholic Scholarship Program involving the Bishops' Conference, eight Catholic universities, and student chaplains, is centrally administered by LPPS in Jakarta. The institute provides feasibility studies for social and development projects and evaluation of their implementation. It cooperates with *Caritas* Internationalis* in Rome.

Adolf Heuken

Instructions of 1659

(De Propaganda Fide).* The Congregation of Propaganda saw that its first duty was to acquire a general idea

of the church in the mission territories entrusted to it by Gregory XV and to ask the nuncios, bishops, superiors, and other competent persons for their advice with regard to the best methods for spreading the faith. Francesco Ingoli, the secretary of the Congregation of Propaganda (1622-49), proceeded to use the vast amount of documentation to compose three memoranda on the difficulties encountered by the missionaries in the Far East and the West Indies. He examined the causes of the rather disturbing condition the missions were in at that time and suggested likely remedies to the Congregation. From this work emerged Ingoli's great missionary idea: the formation of a native clergy and the establishment of a native hierarchy.

The program of the Congregation of Propaganda as contained in its decrees and in the numerous instructions of those early years, as well as in the writing of Ingoli, was gradually worked out on the basis of the directives given by Gregory XV and the experience and reflections of Ingoli. A typical document for examination is the Instructions of 1659 to the apostolic vicars of Indochina, entitled *Instructio vicariorum Apostolicorum ad regna Sinarum Tonchini et Cicincinae proficiscentium* and given to François Pallu*, the bishop of Heliopolis; Pierre Lambert de la Motte*, bishop of Berythe; and Ignatius Cotolendi, bishop of Metellopolis. These famous Instructions of 1659 can be divided into three parts:

1. *Antequam discedant* (before setting out). First, in choosing men for the mission the apostolic vicars were to make sure their religious zeal and piety were from God himself. After considering with great diligence, they were to select from among the candidates men of an age and physical health likely to tolerate the hardships. A list of the names, ages, and qualities of the men chosen was to be given to the apostolic nuncio at Paris, so that he could include them in the letter granting the apostolic vicars their appointees. Second, the communication between the apostolic vicars, the Congregation, and the nuncio was to be made more secure, both in the means employed and by trustworthy men who would accept this responsibility and send the letters as safely as possible. They were to set out as quickly and secretly as possible after receiving the instructions from the apostolic nuncio.
2. *In ipso itinere* (on the journey itself). In order to avoid Portuguese regions and places, the men selected for the mission were to take the route through Syria and Mesopotamia (not the one through the Atlantic Ocean and the Cape of Good Hope), and therefore through Persia and the Mongol* kingdoms. They were to write a brief description of the journey and of the regions they traversed and observe also those things that might be pertinent to the propagation of faith and to promoting the salvation of souls and the glory of God. They were also to observe the state of Christianity, the missions, and the missionaries. They were to write all this down and send it to the Congregation of Propaganda.
3. *In ipsa missione* (on the mission itself). First, a native clergy was to be formed; this was the principal reason for setting out. Second, the missionaries were forbidden to become involved in politics or trade. They were instructed to keep their distance from political and business matters and not to undertake the administration of civil affairs. The Congregation of Propaganda had always strictly prohibited such involvement and would continue to prohibit it. If someone slipped into foolishness of this kind, he was to be dismissed from the mission without delay and even expelled in order that there be no harm to God's work. Third, adaptation had to be made to the culture and customs of the people. Concerning this point, the instructions said that the missionaries were neither privately nor publicly to criticize the actions or the practices of the people. They were not to argue harshly or reprehend anything in them, but to instruct them only in the Christian faith, which despises and attacks the rites and customs of no nation, for it is the nature of people to love and value their own things and their own nation. The missionaries were to try to translate the books of the fathers of the church and similar matierals into the native language. Last, spiritual and scientific education were to be set up. Schools were to be established everywhere with the greatest care and diligence for the youth of those regions. These schools were to be free of charge and to teach the Latin language and Christian doctrine, in order that no Catholic would hand his sons over to the other kind of education. At the same time, the missionaries were to recruit for religious vocation those young men who had a pious mind and generous spirit.

The apostolic vicars followed these famous Instructions of 1659, but they could not avoid conflicts with the Portuguese patronage (see Apostolic Vicars and the Congregation of Propaganda).

Bibliography

Archives of the Archdiocese of Bangkok (Thailand).

Surachai Chumsriphan

International Fellowship of Evangelical Students

(IFES). In 1947, 10 national evangelical student movements from North America, Europe, the South Pacific, and Asia formed the International Fellowship of Evangelical Students at Harvard University in Cambridge, Massachusetts, United States. The movements in Europe had been in touch with one another through the International Conference of Evangelical Students that was started by the evangelical Christian student unions in the 1930s. The China* Inter-Varsity Christian Fellowship that was formed soon after World War II* was the youngest and only Asian movement among the founding members of IFES. Today, there are over 120 national movements around the world that are affiliated or closely linked with IFES. In Asia, IFES-related movements are found in Bangladesh*, Hong Kong*, India*, Indonesia*, Japan*, Korea*, Malaysia*, Nepal*, Pakistan*, the Philippines*, Singapore*, Sri Lanka*, Thailand*, and Taiwan* (Republic of China). IFES Asia is divided into two regions: East Asia and South Asia. The two regional offices coordinate regional activities, such as international training conferences for students, graduates, and staff workers.

IFES was formed with a vision for international cooperation among the evangelical and indigenous national student movements. All the member movements are organizationally autonomous and under national leadership. The aim of IFES is to establish student witness on every university and college campus in all nations. These movements share the same missionary vision for the evangelization of the student world and witness to the lordship of Christ in all areas of life. This concern has led many national movements to extend their mission to high school ministry and ministry among graduates and professionals.

In Asia, students have been playing a vital role in their nations, often spearheading independence and revolutionary movements and socio-political changes. Governments are seeing the strategic importance of tertiary education for national development. The university campus is an arena for the clashes of values and ideologies. The IFES movements are facing the constant challenge to be faithful to their calling to proclaim Christ as Savior and to witness to the universal lordship of Christ. Many IFES movements in Asia have been struggling to respond in both theological reflection and practice. Since the 1980s, many Asian university campuses have seen a resurgence of traditional Asian religions as well as the influence of postmodern thinking. The evangelical student movements have been challenged to reflect on and examine what it means to be evangelical in this new religious and intellectual environment.

Bibliography

Johnson, Douglas, ed., *A Brief History of the International Fellowship of Evangelical Students* (1964). • Lowman, Pete, *The Day of His Power: A History of the International Fellowship of Evangelical Students* (1983).

Koichi Ohtawa

International Institute, China

Founded by missionary Gilbert Reid* after he detached himself from the American Presbyterian Mission, the International Institute was established in Peking (Beijing) to cultivate friendliness between Chinese and foreigners, both Christian and non-Christian, by securing the active support of leading Chinese officials and merchants, and also of prominent men in the foreign community. Some have referred to this organization as a mission work among the higher class of China*.

Reid first started his mission work in Shantung, the area around Confucius's homeland, and thus had frequent opportunity to study Confucianism*. He decided to approach the Chinese through Confucius's thinking and then provide them with a better understanding of Christianity. He also supported the reformation of Confucian thought.

Reid changed his usual attire to that of a Chinese scholar and assimilated his hairstyle to look Chinese. He made many friends among the mandarins. As he had the support of the Ching government and foreign embassies, the financial needs of the institute were well taken care of.

During the Yi-he-tuan crisis, the institute's building was badly damaged, so Reid moved it to Shanghai and continued his propagation of "Confucius plus Jesus." Reid was against the revolution of 1911, and he supported Yuen Shi Kai. In 1922, the institute began its periodical *Guo Ji Gong Bao* (International News); though famous scholars were often invited to contribute, the response was not encouraging. After Reid's death, his son took over the position of honorary secretary.

China Group

International Nepal Fellowship

(INF). The roots of the INF go back to November 1936 when two English missionaries, Dr. Lily O'Hanlon and Miss Hilda Steele, arrived in Nautanwa, northern India (on the border of Nepal*), to work among Nepalis. They shared a vision for a band of "valiant men whose hearts God had touched" (1 Sam. 10:26) who would evangelize among their own people. As they waited and prayed for Nepal to open her borders, a group of Nepalis was converted and assembled while medical and education work among Nepalis was established from Nautanwa to Assam. On 22 Feb 1943 the Nepali Evangelistic Band (NEB) was officially registered.

With the revolution of 1951-52 in Nepal came a new openness. The NEB approached the new government of Nepal and was invited to build a hospital. On 18 Nov 1952 six expatriates and five Nepali staff arrived in Pokhara. The hospital they established became known as the Shining Hospital because of the sun's reflection off the metal Quonset huts. David Mukhia*, one of the Nepali members of the band, became pastor of the first Nepali church inside Nepal.

Work expanded, and in 1957 Green Pastures Leprosy Hospital was founded on the outskirts of Pokhara. Throughout the 1960s clinics were established in outlying communities. Then in 1971 it was deemed expedient to change the mission's name to the International Nepal Fellowship.

There had always been a desire to move westward. In 1973 INF was invited to begin leprosy* control work in the western half of Nepal. The work began in Ghorahi in

1973, in Surkhet in 1977, and in Jumla in 1978. In 1986 the first of two large community-health projects began. From its earliest days in Pokhara the mission also had an interest in tuberculosis as one of Nepal's major medical problems. This area of work has grown from a special tuberculosis ward in the Shining Hospital in 1957 to a world-renowned control project covering the whole midwest region of Nepal.

Today INF has programs (hospital assistance, community health, technical services, tuberculosis and leprosy control projects) throughout the west and midwest regions (each region constituting about one-fifth of the country). Drug rehabilitation and AIDS projects are also beginning. All work is in accordance with an agreement with the government which is renegotiated every five years. There are 131 expatriate members and 459 Nepali staff. The foreign staff are from a variety of countries and denominational backgrounds and hold to an evangelical faith.

INF seeks to support and strengthen the Nepali church, and the individual INF members are all involved in Christian fellowships in their area of work.

Bibliography

International Nepal Fellowship, *While Daylight Lasts* (1971); *Serving the People of Nepal for 40 Years: 1952-1992* (1992). • Nepal Evangelistic Band, *From His Hand to Ours.* • O'Hanlon, Lily, and Hilda Steele, *Hills and Valleys.* • O'Hanlon, Lily, *Into Nepal* (1973).

STEVE AISTHORPE

International Religious Research Institute

Research institute investigating new religious movements in Korea.

The International Religious Research Institute was founded by Tak Myung Whan, who had become interested in the rise of various new religious movements, including the Unification Church* of Moon Sun Myung. Through its periodical *Hyundae Chonggyo* (Modern Religions) he exposed various practices and doctrines of new religious movements. Tak was known as the "heretics hunter," and his life was threatened many times before he was assassinated in 1990 by a religious fanatic of a new religious movement. The journal continues to exist under a new team of editors.

DAVID SUH, with contributions from
KIM HEUNG SOO, translated by KIM IN SOO

Interreligious Dialogue

Interreligious dialogue is free, open, friendly exchange among people of different religious traditions. It is primarily a sharing of religious experiences, perceptions, beliefs, and values in an atmosphere of trust and mutual reverence. Partners in dialogue are committed to their respective faiths, yet respectfully welcome mutual sharing. Attentive listening promotes dialogue. Authentic interreligious dialogue is in itself a religious experience since it is God that both partners have come to listen to and encounter. By receiving from each other, each experiences healing and growth, because a new bridge has been set between the two, facilitating the flow of values and insights. Dialogue must be open-ended. Setting preconditions or instrumentalizing for ulterior purposes vitiates dialogue. One has to be ever receptive to the forthcoming insights of the dialogue partner. Dialogue results in the experience of change and growth.

The dynamics of dialogue must be honored. One has to overcome the diffidence that can arise from a fear of one's own faith being exposed to the eyes of the partner. Vulnerability should be accepted as a prerequisite.

Motivating factors. Various factors have ushered in the era of dialogue: first, the growing realization that the world is fast becoming pluri-cultural and multi-religious; second, closer contact between people because of modern means of communication; third, religions that were not originally missionary in nature are now becoming so; and finally, inculturation calls for healthy dialogue with the religio-cultural traditions and values of the people of the world.

There are also some factors internal to the churches which have brought about modern religious dialogue. First, worldwide missionary contact and study of the religions of the world have made dialogue necessary. Second, churches that had been inward-looking for centuries because of the onslaught of rationalism, liberalism, and other challenges have begun to reenter society. Some of the documents emanating from the World Council of Churches, Vatican Council II, and international missionary conferences (e.g., Lambeth, Edinburgh [1910], Tambaram [1938], and New Delhi [1961]) have increasingly acknowledged the values of other religions. Third, significant events such as the Parliament of Religions (Chicago, 1893) and Vatican Council II have contributed greatly to an acceptance of dialogue. The gathering of world religious leaders in Assisi (1986) is further proof that religions are set on a course toward dialogue. And finally, modern biblical scholarship that undertook parallel research into the nature of the many claims of revelation in religions has contributed considerably to an affirmation of the role of religions in the history of salvation. These factors have paved the way for a culture of relationship among religions, and dialogue is its concrete expression.

Types of dialogue. Five types of dialogue are currently identified. First, there is the dialogue of life. People in their diverse life situations mingle freely, relate to each other, and share their joys and sorrows, problems and preoccupations. Celebration of significant events or major festivals promotes mutual interaction. Mixed marriages also contribute to this kind of dialogue.

Second, there is the dialogue of action. Promotion of human rights, restoration of lost or abdicated civic and democratic liberties, working for redress of the grievances of silenced people and freeing them from oppressive structures and powers are among notable projects open to interreligious undertaking. By endeavoring to tap and apply the liberating powers that are available in many religions, dialogue of action strives to enhance the quality of life in societies. Often, relief work for people struck by natural calamities is undertaken at an interreligious level. Joint efforts at safeguarding environmental rights are further areas of dialogue of action.

Third, there is the growing dialogue of religion with the poor and the marginalized. In Asia, Christianity is trying to sever its alliance with its traditional partners (the upper class) and has just begun dialoguing with the marginalized sectors: the Dalits*, tribals, women*, and unorganized labor.

Fourth, dialogue of religious experience. Adherents of different traditions assemble to share their spiritual experiences, quests, obstacles, and breakthroughs. Often enough, the all-pervasive secularism, atheism, or agnosticism prompts believers to share a common platform. Again, specifically religious exercises that are wont to deepen illuminative experiences, such as yoga, mysticism, or prayer, have also become areas for fellowship.

Finally, there is dialogue of theological exchange. Scholars select specific themes, treat them systematically, and contribute to a dialogue venture. This is a major contribution to the dialogue ministry. Probable perils that await the well-intentioned noninitiates can be obviated by attention to the basics in religions and adhesion to an appropriate method. These are helpful steps to prevent dialogue from lapsing into syncretism or superficialities.

Guidelines. First, a believer should guard against the tendency to defend his or her own personal convictions and experiences at any cost. Second, respect for the sentiments and convictions of the other is a fundamental requirement. There should be no preconditions which would interfere with honest dialogue. Third, the integrity of dialogue should not be compromised by hidden or ulterior motives. In Christian circles, interreligious dialogue is often considered a dimension of evangelization. This may be permissible, since the growing Christian sympathy for other religions guarantees the integrity of the religions as well as of the dialogue. Fourth, debates, argumentation, or controversy can damage the very spirit of fraternal dialogue. Fifth, dialogue is not apologetics. The innate desire to defend one's own belief and practice should be checked. Sixth, equality that also respects diversity should be observed. Manifestation of a feeling of superiority can adversely affect the spirit of interreligious dialogue. Finally, self-criticism will further help both partners in the dialogue.

Requirements. First, *inter*religious dialogue is promoted by *intra*religious dialogue. Rigid adhesion to one's religious beliefs and practices, unwillingness to reinterpret them in the light of new insights can lead to atavism. Blind obedience to the uncritically accepted and transmitted can wreck the new culture of religious dialogue. Dialogue within one's own religion can help to preclude the dangers mentioned.

Second, the whole community needs to be prepared. The multi-religious dimension of life in Asia requires early initiation of each community into the dialogue culture. Obviously, catechesis should embody this dialogue culture. Liturgy, administration of the sacraments, and celebration of festivals can also be utilized for educating the community. In other words, there is the need for a spirituality of dialogue. Third, there is the need for a supportive discipline, namely, a sound theology of religions. This is needed to reassure the dialogue partners. Fourth and fifth, sufficient acquaintance with the basics of other religions is greatly helpful to dialogue, as is honest effort to break ingrained traditions and prejudices. This is more difficult where the dialogue partners come from social strata that enjoy particular status or privileges. In Asia, the history of the encounter of religions is a painful one, especially for the minority communities.

The example of Indonesia. Interreligious dialogue in Indonesia was formally started during the late 1960s, in the aftermath of the aborted Communist coup (1965) and the strong recommendation of Vatican Council II (1962-65). Religious tension arose because of (1) different views about the place of religion in the New Order *(Orde Baru);* (2) new laws on marriage (1974), the educational system, and religious courts (1989); (3) several decrees of the minister of religion forbidding common celebration of religious holidays; (4) the establishment of official bodies for dialogue among religious leaders (*Badan Musyawarah antar Umat Beragama,* 1980); (5) the pushing of a policy of "harmony among religions" despite rival missionary activities; and (6) discussion on the human right to choose and change one's religion (1969 onward). Christian leaders and institutions invited Muslim and Hindu leaders and scholars to conduct open and friendly dialogue on different levels. Enthusiastic hopes during the 1970s quickly diminished, but human contacts and trust among many adherents of all the major religions have been established over a long time. Dialogue on solving practical matters (celebration of holidays, common prayer, etc.) proved more successful than dialogue on dogmatic subjects, as did meetings without government involvement. Efforts to implement the Jakarta Charter (1945), which obliges people to fulfill religious obligations by semi-official means, have damaged the atmosphere suitable for dialogue and created suspicion.

The goal of interreligious dialogue. The goal of interreligious dialogue is multiple: first, growth in mutual knowledge and reduction of prejudice, tension, and disharmony; second, mutual enrichment through interreligious interaction; third, enhanced esteem and respect for people devoted to other faiths.

Bibliography

Panikkar, Raimundo, *The Intrareligious Dialogue* (1971). • Hick, John, ed., *Truth and Dialogue in World Religions: Conflicting Truth-Claims* (1974). • Camps, Arnulf, *Partners in Dialogue* (1977). • Irudayaraj, Xavier, ed., *Libera-*

tion and Dialogue (1989). • Arokiasamy, S. J., ed., *Responding to Communalism* (1991); *Communalism in India* (1988). • John, T. K., ed., *Bread and Breath* (1991). • "Dialogue and Proclamation," *Bulletin, Pontificium Consilium pro Dialogo Inter Religiones* XXVI.2 (1991).

T. K. John

INTERSERVE

(International Service Fellowship; formerly known as Bible and Medical Missionary Fellowship). International partnership in cross-cultural mission committed to the proclamation of the Gospel of Jesus Christ in word and deed with five priority ministries: tentmaking ministries, innovative caring, disciple-making, equipping professions, and strategic outreach.

Formed on 28 Sep 1987 as an Indian missionary society, INTERSERVE's beginnings date back to 1852 in Calcutta when a community of single women from England pioneered a ministry across the Indian subcontinent to women and children through education, health care, and compassionate service to orphans, the blind, and the handicapped. For 100 years, it continued as an exclusively women's ministry under the name of Zenana Bible and Medical Mission (ZBMM).

In 1952, its centenary year and five years after Indian independence and the birth of Pakistan, ZBMM opened its doors to men and families; a few years later, the name was changed to Bible and Medical Missionary Fellowship (BMMF).

As BMMF, the fellowship extended its ministries to staffing Christian medical colleges, international schools, and Bible and theological seminaries. It was also involved in theological education by extension programs, literature work, and ministries to students and professional groups. BMMF also pioneered ministries in neighboring countries such as Nepal*, Pakistan*, Afghanistan, Bhutan*, and Bangladesh* and also expanded as far as North Africa. In recent years, INTERSERVE ministries have extended to the Far East, the central Asian republics, and islands of the Indian Ocean.

Pakistan. INTERSERVE work began in the old undivided India*, including schools and colleges in Lahore and Kinnaird College and High School. After partition, the work continued to develop, following the policy initiated in the 1950s of giving up institutions and seconding people to work with churches and organizations in evangelism and Bible teaching, such as the Pakistan Fellowship of Evangelical Students (PFES) and the United Bible Training Center in Gujranwala. A major project in the Sindh was the Christian Caravan Hospital, pioneered by Jock Anderson, Peter Hover, and others, which eventually settled in Kunri.

Nepal. INTERSERVE was one of the mission groups which went into Nepal* as part of the United Mission to Nepal (UMN) in 1954. It has continued to be one of the largest groups within the UMN, currently with 90 partners (missionaries) in Nepal, including those seconded to International Nepal Fellowship* (INF). Mary Cundy and Tom Hale have written about their work in Nepal.

Bangladesh. In 1974, INTERSERVE joined with other agencies to form HEED Bangladesh, a consortium to provide "Health, Education, and Economic Development." INTERSERVE personnel have also been involved in theological* education through the College of Christian Theology in Dhaka.

Afghanistan. INTERSERVE work began in 1968 in Afghanistan as part of the International Assistance Mission (IAM), which in recent years has shown great courage in remaining through the terrible civil wars.

Central Asian Republics (CAR). INTERSERVE started work in the CAR in 1993 and now has 35 partners in strategic positions.

Mongolia. INTERSERVE helped form the Joint Cooperative Services (JCS) in Mongolia* in 1992. In 1995, there were approximately 35 expatriates working with JCS, including eight from INTERSERVE.

China. INTERSERVE started work in China in 1988 and has placed approximately 10 partners there. INTERSERVE works in association with similar agencies to place partners in key locations in western China. Educational and developmental activities focus particularly on the minority groups who belong to the Muslim and Tibetan Buddhist faiths.

Bhutan. INTERSERVE work began in the 1970s in Bhutan with people such as Rachel Pinniger, originally seconded to work with the Leprosy Mission. Recently, INTERSERVE India has placed a tentmaker family in Bhutan.

India. INTERSERVE in India works in partnership with organizations of similar aims to mobilize the professional skills and resources of God's people and mission. It aims to proclaim in word and deed that Jesus Christ is Lord and Savior and is the sufficient answer to every need of humankind. Each member is encouraged to have a strong link with a local church.

As an international fellowship, INTERSERVE now has some 400 partners. Until 1985, the international office was located in Delhi, but because of visa restrictions it was moved to Cyprus. The INTERSERVE family consists of nine national councils and five national committees working together in close partnership under its international council.

Bibliography

Pollock, J. C., *Shadows Fall Apart: The Story of the Zenana Bible and Medical Mission* (1958). • Brown, Bob, *New Bottles* (1996). • Makower, Katherine, *Widening Horizons: The Story of INTERSERVE* (1993).

Lal Nun Tluanga, with Robin Thomson and Linda Bell

Iqbal, Allama Muhammad

(b. Sialkot, Pakistan, 9 Nov 1877; d. Lahore, 21 Apr 1938) Poet-philosopher and Muslim reformer of Pakistan*.

Iqbal's grandfather Shaikh Rafiq left his ancestral village of Looehar after 1857 and came to settle in Sialkot along with his three brothers. Shaikh Nur Muhammad, Iqbal's father, was gifted with native intelligence and natural curiosity. He acquired a reputation as a highly skilled tailor. He obtained his early education from the Mission High School in Sialkot. Sayyid Mir Hasan was his first tutor; he helped him in his early education. Iqbal finished high school in 1892 and received a scholarship from the Scotch Mission College. Mir Hasan encouraged him to continue his education, and consequently, on 5 May 1893, Iqbal entered the college as a first year student, taking courses in liberal arts. Intellectually, Iqbal blossomed at the Scotch Mission College. At home he listened to the discourses of Sayyid Mir Hasan, who cultivated in him a refined taste and a feeling for Persian and Arabic poetry. In 1895 Iqbal completed his second year at the Scotch Mission College in Sialkot. His teachers and parents recognized his talents and encouraged him to pursue higher studies. The same year Iqbal went to Lahore and entered the Government College, which was considered the best institution of higher learning in the subcontinent. He received his bachelor of arts degree in Arabic, English, literature, and philosophy and his master's degree in philosophy. At the early age of 22 Iqbal began to develop a reputation as a poet.

From 1905 to 1908 Iqbal pursued graduate studies in Europe. His thinking was completely changed by this contact with Western civilization. Western society was so different from his own, and he had the opportunity to compare the modes of living and the values he saw in the East and West. He had to develop a rational basis for his beliefs and urged the political and spiritual unity of all Muslim peoples. He tried to reformulate the basic ideas of Islamic theology in the spirit of European philosophy (see Islam). During his three years of residence in Europe, Iqbal composed 24 small poems and lyrics. Although poetry had made him famous in India*, in Europe he began to doubt the usefulness of his being a poet, and he made up his mind to give up poetry. One of his companions, Shaikh Abdul Qadir, whom he met in Europe during his stay there, later became his lifelong friend and convinced him that his poetry had a magnetic quality capable of inspiring a new life in the backward Muslim nation. Sir Thomas (professor of philosophy at the Anglo-Muhammadan College, Aligarh) also agreed with Qadir, and he bowed to their collective judgment. Seven years later, in 1915, Iqbal published his magnum opus, *Asrar-i-Khudi.* He wrote this book in Persian but also composed 150 verses in Urdu.

Iqbal pursued his education in both Britain and Germany. In London, he studied at Lincoln's Inn, in order to qualify at the bar, and at Trinity College, Cambridge. He was enrolled as an undergraduate student to earn a bachelor of arts degree. During this period he obtained permission from the University of Munich, Germany, to submit his doctoral dissertation in philosophy, "The Development of Metaphysics in Persia," to Professor F. Hommel. The university awarded Iqbal the *doctoris philosopiae gradum* on 4 Nov 1907. His dissertation was published in London the following year, and he dedicated it to Professor T. W. Arnold.

The name of Muhammad Iqbal is connected with an important stage in the development of Muslim social thought on the Indo-Pakistan subcontinent, the formative stage of the ideology of Muslim nationalism*. Iqbal's religiophilosophical and sociopolitical views fully reflected the complexity and contradictoriness of the Muslim social strata that were involved in the national liberation movement for the independence of the peoples of colonial India. To a significant extent, this explains Iqbal's tremendous influence on the development of the social thought of the Muslims of colonial India and modern Pakistan. Although Iqbal was never at home in politics, the worsening condition of Muslims at that time drew him into it. In India the 19th c. witnessed the beginning of the Muslim Renaissance led by Sayyid Ahmad Khan's* Aligarh movement. Iqbal fully imbibed this optimistic spirit and participated in the drama of India's political life as a dynamic intellectual leader. In May 1908 he joined the All-India Muslim League and was elected to the executive committee; he was also nominated to a subcommittee to draft the rules and regulations of the British Committee of the Muslim League. Iqbal was the first important public figure to propound the idea from the platform of the Muslim League. Iqbal composed *Darb-i-Kalim* (The Rod of Moses) in 1934-35 and published it in May 1936. This book is Iqbal's only poetic collection on topical, political, and social themes.

Some writers have taken Iqbal to mean that he wanted only a consolidated Muslim unit within the confederation of India, but this is incorrect. A resolution of the All Parties Muslim Conference was a demand for the autonomy of Islam within a free India. It was Iqbal's talent for persuasion that marked him as the founding father of Pakistan. His mission was to persuade the Muslims of the world that their past had been glorious and that there was no reason why their future should not be as well. Iqbal's universal theme is strongly humanistic; his concept of the self involves a plea for respect for one's self and respect for one's fellowship. His poetry reflected the image of his personality and mind. He was against materialism because he believed that it leads to irreligiousness and away from love. But Iqbal believed that profound socioeconomic changes were necessary for the establishment of social justice. His moral and socioethical ideals, sociopolitical ideals, and philosophical views were embodied in his teachings on the reformation of Islam. The basic ideas of these teachings, which sounded forth for the first time in Iqbal's philosophical poems *Asrar-i-Khudi* and *Rumuz-i-Bekhudi,* achieved their ultimate formulation at the end of the 1920s in his lectures on Islam, "The Reconstruction of Religious Thought in Islam," as well as in the philosophical poems *Javaid-Namah* (The Book of Eternity), which Iqbal himself called his swan song. Iqbal was the first to explain the need to reform Islam by citing the progress of the development of social thought, science, and experience. He wanted this reformation in the same way Protestantism did in the West, that is, as a system of universal ethics that included a "national system of ethics." He emphasized that it is the duty of the leaders of the world of Islam today to understand the real meaning of what has happened in Europe and then to move forward with self-control and clear insight into the ultimate aims of Islam as a social policy. This was the one reason why Iqbal presented his philosophical and sociopolitical ideas as part of the doctrine for the reformation of Islam. He had expressed his message clearly in the following stanza in his book, *Darb-i-Kalim* (The Rod of Moses):

> Neither are we Afghans nor Turks,
> nor yet from the lands of Central Asia.
> We belong to the garden, and descend from the same ancestors.
> Forbidden unto us are the distinction of color or race,
> Yes! We are the harvest of a new spring.

With the start of 1938, Iqbal's health sharply deteriorated. Overwhelmed by asthmatic attacks, he steadily grew weaker. Just a few hours before his death, he recited a Persian quatrain from *Hasan Akhtar,*

> The departed melody may or may not come.
> The breeze from Hedjaz may or may not come.
> The days of this *faqir* have come to an end.
> Another wise one may or may not come.

Bibliography

Hafeez, Malik, *Iqbal: Poet-Philosopher of Pakistan* (1971). • Safdar Mohammad, Mir, *Iqbal the Progressive* (1990). • Waheed, Qureshi, *Selections from the Iqbal Review* (1983).

Awais Gill

Irian Jaya

Western half of New Guinea, province of the Republic of Indonesia*, with an area of 460,000 sq. km. (about 22 percent of the total area of the republic).

Until 1949 Irian Jaya belonged to the Netherlands Indies, but after Indonesia became independent the Dutch tried to maintain their hold on Irian, and only in 1963 was the territory surrendered to Indonesia. A mountain range with peaks up to 5,000 m. high runs from west to east; the valleys in between are relatively densely populated, as are the islands in the Cendrawasih Bay and the district around the provincial capital Jayapura in the northeast. In 1996 the population of Irian totaled 2,045,363, of whom 1,154,272 were Protestants (nearly half living in the highlands), 469,681 Roman Catholics* (more than half living in the south), and 414,550 Muslims (the fastest-growing group), other inhabitants being adherents of tribal* religions. Approximately 80 percent belong to the original population, and the others are migrants from other parts of Indonesia — a phenomenon which has resulted in an increase in the Muslim population of Irian.

The original inhabitants of Irian were, and in part still are, adherents to tribal religions. Cargo Cults are an outstanding feature. Of these, the Koreri* movements in the Biak-Numfor culture area have been studied most intensively. Intertribal warfare was, and in some remote areas still is, a common phenomenon. Christianity was introduced into Irian in 1855 by the Gossner* missionaries C. W. Ottow and J. G. Geissler from Berlin. From 1863 on their work was taken over by the Dutch Utrechtsche Zendings Vereeniging (UZV), and from 1951 by the Nederlandse Hervormde Kerk. These bodies worked mainly on the north coast, beginning from the Numfor tribe inhabiting parts of the Cendrawasih Bay area. During the first half-century, progress was slow, owing to the vicious circle of attack and revenge in which the population was caught. After the coastal areas had been pacified by the Dutch, a mass movement toward Christianity started (1907). In 1938 the number of Protestant Christians in the north totaled 80,000. From this mission, in 1956 the Gereja Kristen Injili di Irian Jaya (GKI-Irja) was born, which in 1997 had approximately 625,000 members, mainly on the north coast.

In the meantime, the Roman Catholic Church (RCC) had started work in Irian (1902, after a first start in 1894-96). In 1912 the colonial government, which wished to prevent "double mission," allotted the territory north of the 4°3′ parallel to the UZV and the coastal plain to the south to the mission, in this case the Missionaries of the Sacred Heart* (MSC), who after 1937 were assisted by the Franciscans* (OFM). When the government lifted the ban on "double mission" (in the 1930s), the missions (OFM and MSC) established themselves also in the north. In 1941 there were about 13,000 baptized Catholics in Irian. In 1962 the RCC in Indonesia was given its own hierarchy, but as Irian did not yet belong to Indonesia, only in 1966 was the apostolic vicariate of Merauke in the south converted into an archbishopric, with three suffragan dioceses: Manokwari-Sorong (1966), Jayapura (1967), and Agats-Asmat (1969). At first the bishops were all of Dutch descent; in 1988 an Indonesian (from Java) was appointed bishop of Sorong.

In the 1930s the interior of Irian, where people still lived a Stone Age existence, was "discovered." In 1938 the colonial government allowed the Christian and Missionary Alliance* (C&MA) to start a mission in this territory. At the end of that year, the first C&MA missionaries came to the Paniai region at the western end of the mountain range. Dayak Christians from the C&MA mission field in East Kalimantan were of great help in accomplishing the journey through the dense jungle up from the coast. In 1942 the first Ekari were baptized. In 1943 the Japanese army came in and destroyed all Christian buildings. But the work was resumed in 1946. The change of attitude came when an Ekari evangelist educated at Makassar, Zakheus Pakage, began to preach Christianity. In Apr 1951 people came forward to burn their religious objects. Some of these converts brought the Gospel to their trade contacts among neighboring tribes, which led to group conversions there. In 1952 the Bible school graduated the first Ekari ministers. One of them was among the team that in 1954 began work among the Dani tribe in the Baliem Valley. In the next 25 years, hundreds of little valleys were evangelized. The New Testament was translated into the most important languages, and a national staff was educated which could take over activities in the church, in education, and in medical* care. In 1988 the Gereja Kemah Injil Indonesia Irian Jaya, an autonomous branch of the national Gospel Tabernacle Church of Indonesia, had 59,392 baptized and more than 150,000 unbaptized members, with more than 1,200 national church workers.

Another national church, the Evangelical Church of Irian Jaya (*Gereja Injili Irian Jaya,* GIIJ), was founded in 1976 north and east of the central mountain range by three missionary organizations: the Unevangelized Fields Mission, which was in Irian from 1950; the Asia Pacific Christian Mission; and the Regions Beyond Missionary Union (from 1955). Until 1984 the new church went through a difficult period. The insurrection of the Free Papua Organization *(Organisasi Papua Merdeka,* OPM) against the Indonesian government was accompanied by a pagan reaction. Villages were burned down, old feuds were revived, and many Christians lapsed into pagan customs. In 1986, 200,000 people worshipped in 364 church buildings, which were served by 672 national preachers.

The Australian Baptist* Missionary Society (ABMS) founded its first post in 1956 at Tiom, in the center of the mountain range. In 1976 the work was transferred to an independent church, the Gereja Baptis Irian Jaya (GBIJ), which in 1980 had 110 church buildings attended by 75,000 people.

Two smaller Calvinist churches in Holland also opened mission work in Irian. Since 1956 the Reformed Church* (RC, which in 1944 had seceded from the Reformed Churches in the Netherlands) worked in the Digul area to the southeast. In 1963 the Netherlands Reformed Congregations (NRC) entered the Yali territory east of the Baliem in the central part of the mountain range. The church founded by the RC is named *Gereja-Gereja Reformasi di Indonesia* (Reformed Churches in Indonesia), and that in NRC territory, *Gereja Jemaat Protestan di Irian Jaya* (Protestant Congregations Church in Irian Jaya). These two churches have a little more than 5,000 and 9,000 members respectively.

As for their logistics, the missions working in the interior are served by the Missions Fellowship (1963) and the Mission Aviation Fellowship (1954 in Irian). The RC mission is served by an aviation service of its own. The Roman Catholic Church and the great Protestant denominations in Irian each have a central theological institution of their own in the Jayapura region. The Summer Institute of Linguistics (SIL) works to translate the Bible* into a number of the 250 languages spoken in Irian.

See also Evangelical Christian Church of Irian Jaya.

Bibliography

Giay, B., *Zakheus Pakage and his communities,* (Ph.D. diss., VU, Amsterdam, 1995). • Hayward, D., *The Dani of Irian Jaya: Before and after Conversion* (1980). • *Handbook of Reformed Churches Worldwide* (1999).

THOMAS VAN DEN END

Irwin, Edwin Franklin

(b. Markham, Ontario, Canada, 1888; d. 1966). Pioneer missionary and field administrator of the Christian and Missionary Alliance* (C&MA) to Indochina and Vietnam* for 46 years (1914-60).

Irwin joined the C&MA in his teens and then enrolled at the Missionary Training Institute at Nyack, New York, United States, in 1911. He graduated in 1913, the same year as his fiancée, Marie Morgenthaler (1891-87). While each was single, Frank and Marie were appointed by the C&MA to French Indochina, which in 1911 was opened by R. A. Jaffray* as an extension of the South China* conference. Upon arrival in 1914, they began language study in Tourane (Da Nang), where in later years Marie recalled there had not been even five Evangelical Christians.

In 1915, during World War I, gossipers in the French colony accused missionaries with German surnames of being spies. Because Marie might either be expelled from the country or left alone to live on the same station as Frank Irwin, they were sent to Wuchow, China, to marry, thus avoiding red tape governing the marriage of foreigners under French law.

In Dec 1915 the French government issued a decree prohibiting further Protestant missionary work. The chapels were closed, and only two Canadian couples, the Irwins and William and Grace Cadman*, remained. The Cadmans went to Hanoi to open work in the northern capital in Tonkin, while the Irwins remained in Tourane (Da Nang), the seat of the second largest province of French Indochina. Although the missionary staff had been depleted to two couples, the mission decided that a strong church in an influential city must be established as a base of operation from which to establish churches in outlying areas. These churches would, in turn, follow the same pattern. District missionaries would work alongside the Vietnamese as partners in their endeavors. To facilitate the envisioned church growth, theological training, Scripture translation, and literature preparation were given priority. Thus the Cadmans in Hanoi began translation projects and set up a printing press, while the Irwins began classes for the Tourane Bible Institute in their living room in 1921.

In 1919, when the ban on evangelizing was lifted and

the thatched-roof chapel reopened, the number of converts doubled; it continued to do so every year until there were over 1,000 members in the Tourane church and its outstations.

As the work progressed, Jaffray asked Frank Irwin to become field chairperson of the Indochina mission, which at that time included Vietnam, Cambodia*, Laos*, and East Siam (Thailand*). From then until the 1950s, the chairmanship rotated between Frank and fellow Canadian, David Ivory Jeffrey*. In the 1930s the C&MA divided the mission into separate administrative fields of Vietnam, Cambodia, Laos, East Thailand, and Tribal Vietnam.

Frank Irwin led a mission that was convinced of the necessity of establishing an indigenous and autonomous church that would be self-supporting, self-propagating, and self-governing. He also spearheaded the establishing of a missionary children's school in Dalat, Vietnam, in Jan 1929, which was relocated in 1965 to Thailand and later Penang, Malaysia*.

When Vietnam was occupied by the Japanese in World War II*, out of a desire to show solidarity with Vietnamese Christians, the Irwin family was among 17 C&MA missionaries and 13 children who voluntarily passed up the opportunity to flee Vietnam. They were interned in a prisoner-of-war camp in 1943 in the Mekong delta city of My Tho. Although six of the adults and nine of the children were repatriated after five months, the rest, including the Irwins, with their children, Franklin Jr., and Helen May, remained until the end of the war.

Before Frank and Marie retired from ministry in Vietnam in 1960, all three of their adult children, George, Franklin Jr., and Helen May, and their families had been appointed by the C&MA to Vietnam, where they remained until it was closed to missionary work in 1975.

Frank Irwin worked in harmonious and close cooperation with the national church in evangelism and church planting. Le Van Thai*, the fifth president of the Evangelical Church of Vietnam, was an early convert of the Tourane mission effort and a lifelong colleague in the work of advancing the Evangelical church. Thai said of Irwin: "Although he made many contributions to our lives, the one which we consider the most important, and for which we will never forget him, is that he loved us."

Bibliography

Irwin, E. F., *With Christ in Indo-China* (1937). • Le, Phu Hoang, "A Short History of the Evangelical Church of Vietnam (1911-1965)" (Unpublished dissertation, New York University, 1972), 2 Vols. James F. Lewis

Isaac, Catholicos

(d. 410 C.E.). Catholicos of the East Syrian Church and bishop of Seleucia-Ctesiphon (399-410).

Isaac became Catholicos following the persecution of the Christians in Persia in the last quarter of the 4th c. He reorganized the church and established its role in the Persian Empire. Through his work, with the cooperation of Bishop Maruta of Maipherqat, who served as an intermediary between the Persian church, the Persian government, and the Byzantine government, they were able to gain recognition of the Persian church in the empire from Yezdegerd I*. The Persian church declared its independence from the Byzantine church, and a council was needed to ratify that decision. Isaac's episcopacy was capped by the Council of Seleucia-Ctesiphon (410; see Synods/Councils, Early Asian*), at which this independent status was affirmed. At the council the theological, hierarchical, and territorial structures of the Persian church were established.

Bibliography

Chabot, Jean-Baptiste, *Synodicon Orientale, ou recueil des synodes nestoriens* (1902). • Brun, O., *Das Buch der Synados* (1900). • Labourt, J., *Christianisme dans l'Empire Perse sous la dynastie Sassanide (224-632)* (1904). • Fiey, J.-M., "Les Étapes de la prise en conscience de so identité patriarcale de l'église syrienne orientale," *L'Orient Syrien*, Vol. 12 (1967); *Jalons pour une histoire de l'Eglise en Iraq* (CSCO Subsidia 36; 1970). • Gribomont, J., "La symbole de foi de Séleucie-Ctésiphon (410)," in *A Tribute to Arthur Vööbus*, ed. Robert Fisher (1977). • De Halleux, A., "La symbole des évêques perses au synode de Séleucie-Ctésiphon," in *Erkenntnis und Meinungen*, ed. G. Wiessner (1978). David Bundy

Isabel of Sugbu

First Filipino convert of the Augustinians* in the Philippines*.

The young niece of Rajah Tupas of Sugbu (now Cebu City), Isabel was converted by the Augustinians with the Spaniards' Legazpi expedition of 1565. With her little son and two child-servants, Isabel was apparently sent by her uncle to the Spanish camp as a gesture of goodwill. Being given European clothes and some words about Christianity, she immediately asked to be baptized. As she obviously lacked understanding, the Augustinian prior, Diego de Herrera, decided to instruct her first on what she must believe and hold on to after her baptism.

Through her perseverance, she and the children with her finally reached the stage of baptism. This marked the beginning of Spanish evangelization, subsequently leading to the conversion of most Filipinos.

Bibliography

Coleccion de Documentos Ineditos relativos . . . de Ultramar, 2a. serie (1865). • Sitoy, T. V., Jr., *The Initial Encounter* (1985). T. Valentino Sitoy, Jr.

Ishihara Ken

(b. Hongo, Tokyo, 1 Aug 1882; d. 4 Jul 1976). Japanese scholar of Christian history.

The second son of Ishihara Ryo, Ishihara studied history and philosophy at Tokyo Imperial University. Under the guidance of Raphael von Koeber and Hatono Suite, he undertook the study of Christian history and religious philosophy. In 1914, he translated F. E. D. Schleiermacher's *On Religion (Über die Religion)* and had his first book, *Shukyo tetsugaku* (Philosophy of Religion), published in 1916. After teaching ancient and medieval philosophy at Waseda University and Tokyo Imperial University, he studied in Germany from 1921 to 1923. In 1924, he moved to Tohoku Imperial University, specializing in German mysticism, especially the work of Meister Eckhart, and publishing the results of his work one after another.

Ishihara's work on the history of Christianity in Europe provided a foundation for scholarly studies in Japan*. Some contributions include *Shingakushi* (History of Theology, 1933), *Shinyaku seisho* (The New Testament, 1935), translations of Martin Luther's works, and a history of the Reformation. In 1940, he became president of Tokyo Women's Christian University, and in the midst of the great difficulties being experienced by universities during the war, he continued his research on Luther and Augustine.

The research of Ishihara's later years crystallized into his major works *Kirisuto kyo no genryu* (The Origin of Christianity), *Kirisuto kyo no tenkai* (The Development of Christianity), and *Yoroppa kirisuto kyo shi,* I and II (History of Christianity in Europe, two volumes), all completed by 1972. Each of these works is written from the perspective of searching for the essence of Christianity through history. Another work of note is Ishihara's *Nihon kirisuto kyo shiron* (Historical Theory of Christianity in Japan, 1967), in which he seeks to place Japanese Christianity in the context of world Christianity. An 11-volume collection of his works, *Ishihara Ken chosakushu* (1978-79), is available.

Miyatani Yoshichika, Japanese Dictionary

Ishihara Yoshiro

(b. Dohi Village, Izu District, Shizuoka Prefecture, Japan, 11 Nov 1915; d. 14 Nov 1977). Japanese poet.

Ishihara entered the German section of the foreign trade department at Tokyo Foreign Language University in 1934. After graduating in 1938, he began working for Osaka Gas Company. At this time, he became acquainted with Karl Barth, and in particular with the influence that a book on Fyodor Dostoyevsky by Leo Chestov (1866-1938) had on Barth. Ishihara was baptized by Egon Hessel, a German missionary, at Himematsu Church in Osaka. In 1939 he decided to enter seminary and moved to Tokyo, transferring his church membership to Shinanomachi Church.

Drafted into the army, Ishihara completed the army's Russian language program and in 1941 was assigned to the Kanto District Army Headquarters, where he was attached to intelligence operations. After the war ended, he was arrested by the Russian army in Harbin. In 1949, he was sentenced to 25 years of hard labor by a military tribunal of the Russian army in Siberia. He engaged in forestry, rock quarrying, civil engineering, and railroad construction. He was pardoned on the occasion of Stalin's death in 1953 and returned to Japan via Nachodka. He returned to Shinanomachi Church and began writing poetry.

In 1954, Ishihara first contributed to a poetry magazine, *Bunsho kurabu* (Literary Club). In 1955, he published a poetry bulletin, *Roshinante,* with the help of regular contributors to the magazine. In 1963, he published a collection of his own poems entitled *The Homecoming of Sancho Pansa,* and in 1964 this work won the fourteenth "Mr. H" Award. *Ishihara Yoshiro shishu* (Collected Poems of Ishihara Yoshiro) was published in 1967, and in 1973 he received the eleventh Rekitei Award for his essay collection *Bokyo to umi* (Nostalgia and the Sea). He was highly praised for the way in which these esoteric creations crystallized his experiences in Siberia, reinforced by his reading of Dostoyevsky, Hojo Tamio, and Shiina Rinzo. He died suddenly of acute cardiac insufficiency while taking a bath at his home. *Ishihara Yoshiro zenshu* (The Complete Works of Ishihara Yoshiro) (1979-80) has been published in three volumes.

Bibliography

Anzai Hitoshi, *Ishihara Yoshiro no shi no sekai* (The World of Ishihara Yoshiro's Poetry) (1981).

Takado Kaname

Ishii Juji

(b. Babhara, Kamie Village, Japan, 1865; d. Chausubara, 30 Jan 1914). Social worker.

Born near Takanabe Castle in the Hyuga region of Kyushu, Ishii taught primary school in his hometown. He married Uchino Shinko in 1881 and entered the Okayama Prefectural Medical School to study medicine. Deeply moved by the words of George Müller (1805-98), who worked with orphans, in 1887 Ishii gathered in orphans who were living in Taishi Hall outside the city and started teaching them in a borrowed room of Yuzen Temple. His interest in Christianity deepened, and on 2 Dec 1884, he was baptized at Okayama Church by Kanamori Michitomo. In 1889, in order to put his full energies into working with orphans, he burned his medical books, left medical school, and founded Okayama Orphanage. At the time of the Nobi earthquake (Gifu Prefecture) in 1890, the number of orphans in his care had increased to 169.

To become self-supporting and independent, Ishii obtained wilderness land in Chausubara and helped about 60 orphans put it into cultivation. Many new and imaginative ideas were utilized to better the orphanage, including changing the format from dormitory to family style. A primary and secondary school were established in the orphanage, where the children studied in the evenings. In 1905, a foster-parent program for new babies and infants was started. It has been said that as the number of orphans continued to increase, they suffered from a lack of food, so Ishii many times went without. That same year, because of a major famine in the Tohoku region, the number of orphans exceeded 1,000; in 1909 Ishii moved all of them to the Chausubara Orphanage. Adding the spirit of Ninomiya Sontoku to his Christian faith, he put frugality, saving, and service into practice, striving to make the orphanage self-supporting. In 1907, he opened an office in Osaka (which became the Ishii Memorial Aisen'en Foundation in 1917).

In the meantime, Ishii undertook other causes; in 1902, he founded the Okayama Evangelistic Association to encourage evangelistic work in Okayama Prefecture; in 1907, he and Ishida Sukeyasu planned and organized the East Asian Evangelistic Association, aspiring to create an "East Asian style" of mission work. His wife had died in 1895 of fatigue. He remarried, but later died at Chausubara. His eldest daughter, Tomoko, married the artist Kojima Torajiro in 1913, and her eldest son Koichiro took over his grandfather's work.

Bibliography

Shibata Yoshiyasu, *Ishii Juji no shogai to shiso* (The Life and Thought of Ishii Juji) (1964). TAKENAKA MASAO

Islam

Islam, like Judaism and Christianity, is an Asian religion. But when it crossed the border between Arabia and the Persian Empire, it left the culture of its Semitic roots and had to adjust to new and different cultural contexts.

Expansion beyond Arabia. The first test case arose in the field of jurisdiction. Islamic law, being casuistic in its first period, met with many new problems when the prophet's religion established itself in the Persian Empire. Abu Hanifa (697-767), the great jurist in Kufa, came from a Persian family. He gave great importance to the personal deliberation *(ra'y)* of a lawyer but limited the use of reason to the regulations of *qiyas*, analogy. The legal *madhhab* of the Hanafites, of which he and his immediate disciples are venerated as founders, was adopted later on by Persian and Turk converts and even followed by some of the Shi'ites.

The acceptance of Islam by the Persians was not an easy process. Persian Zoroastrians resisted the new monotheistic faith, but Persian Christians were more appreciative of those who conquered their oppressors. As late as the 10th c. C.E., in many Persian regions Farsi still was the spoken language, although in the field of literature and, naturally, religion, Arabic had replaced Pehlevi (Pahlavi) and had started to become the lingua franca in the empire. Supported by the *shu'ubiyya* movement, which stressed its own cultural values against the predominance and arrogance of the Arabs, some Persians tended to maintain a kind of dualistic worldview inherited from Zoroastrianism* which gave great importance to the might of eternal *zrvan*, or destiny, alongside Allah. These tendencies were attacked as *zindiq* and became a paradigm for heretical movements. Nevertheless, they inspired the development of theology *(Kalam)* and philosophy *(Filsafa)* in Islam.

Besides these intra-Islamic disputes, a last revivalist movement of Zoroastrianism took place which produced a number of literary works of some importance, some of them being apologetic works against Islam. This movement reached its peak at the beginning of the 10th c.

In organizing their state and financial administration and court ceremonies, the Abbasid caliphs, who came to power in 750, continued traditions which had developed under the last Persian dynasty, the Sassanids. This most probably was due to the close relations between the Abbasids and Khorasan; the support of the Khorasanians was decisive for the victory of the Abbasids against the Omayyads, and for many decades they remained the backbone of the military strength of the new dynasty (750-1258).

Islam and the Persians. Thus Islam experienced its first major acculturation when it took over political power in the provinces of the former Persian Empire. Unlike the Byzantine lands, where the Aramaic-Syriac culture became absorbed by Arabic-Islamic traditions and values, the Persian regions absorbed the pure Arabic-Islamic cultural patterns and impressed their own identity on Islam. This development led to a decline of classical Arabic, in which Persian scholars had been outstanding masters, and supported the emergence of different Arabic dialects in the West. This prepared the ground for the development of a new Persian literary language enriched by the influx of many Arabic terms. As the old Pehlevi characters were replaced by the Arabic script, classical Persian-Islamic poetry and fine literature began to develop.

In the eastern border regions of Central Asia (i.e., Sogdia, Khwarizm, the "areas beyond the river," or Transoxania, etc.), the struggle between Islam and other religions (Buddhism*, Manichaeism, Nestorian* Christianity, traditional/ancestral religions, and shamanism*) was much more intensive and led to the rise of a number of heresies. This religious diversity was a mirror of the political situation where regional principalities and tribes had a tradition of fighting for their independence and self-expression. Under the caliphs of Baghdad, these local dynasties could strengthen their position and retain some independence. The Samanids, for instance, ruled from their capital Buchara over Transoxania and Khorasan until the end of the 10th c. When Shi'ite influence on the caliphs became stronger (after the Buyid family took over governmental positions in 945), the eastern vassal states considered themselves as protectors and safeguards of Sunni traditions.

The coming of the Seljuk and the Ottoman sultanate. At the end of the 10th c., the Seljuk (Turk or Turkman) clan began to establish an empire which was to cover most of Iran, thus introducing a very new element in the history of Islam in Asia. The Turks (divided into many nomadic tribal entities which often fought against each other) originated in the areas of Mongolia* and the northern borders of China*, being the western neighbors of the Han. In pre-Islamic times, they had established empires, some of which became vassal states of China, especially during the T'ang Dynasty (618-907), while the western Turks were subdued by the Arabs in 739. Religiously, most of them adhered to shamanic practices or had adopted Buddhism or Manichaeism. Those who later turned to Islam adopted a strong Sunnite, sometimes outspoken anti-Shi'ite attitude, with the Hanafite *madhhab* as legal tradition.

When the influence of the Buyid family declined, the caliph in 1055 invested the Seljuk khan Togril as sultan (virtual ruler), thus legitimizing his rule over Iran and encouraging him to fight against the heresy (of the Shi'ites). His follower Alp Arslan (1063-72) subjugated most of the Asian Islamic countries. One of their most excellent *wezirs* (viziers) was Nizam al-Mulk (1018-92), a Persian from Khorasan who was famous not only for his political skills, but for the educational institutions he established in which scholars like Abu Hamid al-Ghazali (1064-1111) started their careers. As they drove west, the Seljuks established smaller states in Syria, Iraq, and Anatolia.

After Alp Arslan had defeated the Byzantine army in Manzikert (1071), Seljuk influence in Anatolia increased; small Turkish vassal states of the great Seljuk empire emerged and later became somewhat independent emirates. One of them was ruled by Othman (1281-1326), a chieftain whose tribe originated from Merv. Under his successors, more and more of the emirates were conquered, and raids brought them even to the European side of the Bosporus and its hinterland.

When under Sultan Mehmet II "the Conqueror" (al-Fatih, 1451-81) the capital of the Byzantine empire, Constantinople, was taken in 1453, it was obvious that a new empire had emerged. Istanbul became its capital. Mehmet's grandson Selim I (1512-20) conquered Cairo in 1517. Egypt, since 1258 a refuge for displaced, powerless Abbasid caliphs, enjoyed great respect in the Islamic world. After the capture of Cairo, the caliph was brought to Istanbul and surrendered his title to Selim I. Thus the Othmanli (Ottoman) sultanate became the most influential empire in the Islamic world. It remained so until 1922 when Mustafa Kemal "Ataturk" proclaimed Turkey a republic after the defeat of the sultanate in World War I. Two years later, the displaced sultan had to renounce the title of caliph. Ataturk's republic became a laicist state, and a Turkish one as well, in which state and religion were separated strictly, and even in religion all Arabic (non-Turkish) elements were eliminated as far as possible.

Ghazna. The political and military pressure of the Seljuks against Khorazan initiated the decline of the Samanids. One of their Turkish generals fled to the small mountainous kingdom of Ghazna (961) and founded, in the area of today's Afghanistan, a new Muslim kingdom which would become very influential especially for the history of Islam in India. From Ghazna, he and his successors could control the trade routes between Khorasan and the Indus Valley. Since Turkish-Islamic art and culture had not yet developed, and since Arabic was not known by the new rulers of Ghazna, Persian-Islamic culture became dominant and would remain so. During the reign of the greatest sultan, Yamin ad-Daula Mahmud (997-1030), the great mathematician and astronomer al-Biruni (973-1050), who came from Khwarizm, settled in Ghazna, and studied Sanskrit in order to learn more about India. Even the famous Firdauzi (d. ca. 1020) spent some time at this court. From here Islam started to spread into northern India.

At the peak of its power under Sultan Mahmud, Ghaznavid rule extended from western Persia to the Ganges Valley. While the western territories soon were conquered by the Seljuks, Afghanistan, Baluchistan, and the Punjab with northwestern India became the cradle of the later Indo-Islamic culture. This Indo-Islamic culture followed the Persian pattern of Islam, revitalizing, especially in court circles, Sassanid etiquette including the sanctification of the ruler.

The Mongols. A very new situation for Islam in Asia was inaugurated by the raids and devastations of the Mongols. Genghis Khan (d. 1227) himself, although adhering to shamanist* practices, seems to have had a special respect for Nestorian* Christianity, although he encouraged an evenhanded treatment of Muslims and Buddhists as well. Hulagu*, his grandson, however, when conquering Baghdad in 1258, ordered a great massacre especially among the Muslim population, while the Christians were mostly spared. Iraq was devastated, causing a cultural separation between Western Asia (with its centers in Syria and Egypt) and Central and Eastern Asia, where Persian Islam strengthened its dominance.

When around 1260 the Mongol Empire* was divided into four kingdoms, the Mongols in the Ilkhanate (vassal kingdom) of Persia, which was bestowed on Hulagu, turned to Islam gradually. In 1295, the Ilkhan Ghazan, a great-grandson of Hulagu, officially adopted Sunnite Islam; Buddhism* soon disappeared from his kingdom.

Although the Mongols themselves were mainly influenced by the Turkish (and Persian) variety of Sunnite Islam, an edict of religious tolerance issued by Genghis Khan was still honored, resulting in a somewhat evenhanded religious policy. This policy had the effect of allowing the Shi'a to recover and thus prepared its way later to become the national expression of Islam in Persia (Iran).

China. One of the four Mongol kingdoms was China, in which another one of Genghis Khan's grandsons, Kublai Khan, founded the Yuan dynasty (1279-1368) and prepared the way for Islam, especially in the northwestern parts of the Middle Kingdom. Islam, however, had penetrated into China* much earlier, mainly brought by merchants and refugees along the old trade routes in Central Asia. During the Yuan dynasty, it developed to some dominance especially in Yunnan, as is testified by, among others, Marco Polo. The Mongols also used Muslims in governmental and military positions, and Muslims were considered the second highest class in the population, before the Han and the Nan (South Chinese) people.

Naval trading routes had also brought Muslim merchants to the eastern shores of China. Already in pre-Islamic times, Persians — Zoroastrians as well as Nestorian Christians — and probably Arabs had commercial contacts with the T'ang dynasty (618-907) and their capital Changan (Xi'an). In 651, an Arab delegation was received by the emperor, and the spread of the Islamic empire into Central Asia led to an intensification of such diplomatic contacts. They not only intensified already existing relations via the land routes, but they also facilitated trade on the sea routes to India and further to the West, which was mainly in the hands of Persian and Arab Muslims who established their own separate quarters in seaports like Guangzhou (Canton) and Hangzhou. There they were allowed to perform their religious rites and organize their social life according to their own habits.

During the reign of the Sung dynasty (960-1279), the first mosques were allowed to be built, but Muslims were still forbidden to proselytize among the indigenous Chinese. It was only under the Yuan (Mongol) dynasty that a first wave of inculturation took place and was favored by the court. When the Ming dynasty gained power from the Yuan in 1368 and equalized again the rights and social position of the Han Chinese with those of the foreigners, the accommodation was intensified, and intermarriage between Muslims and Han women from noble families was frequent, through Muslim girls were never given to Han Chinese men. These accommodated Muslims became generally known as the Hui (Huihui). Their number and identification with China must have been strong, for Chinese Muslim sailors were allowed to serve in the Ming armada, which in the past had only Han Chinese sailors. This fleet patrolled the Southern Ocean and, under the famous admiral Cheng-Ho, even sailed to Arabia and East Africa, as Ma Huan, Cheng-Ho's translator, narrates (first part of the 15th c.).

The importance of the sea routes. On the sea routes to India, Sri Lanka, and further on to Southeast Asia, the Arab and Persian Muslims continued in the steps of their pre-Islamic ancestors. Their settlements in the southwestern Indian seaports were not exposed to the kind of Turkish-Persian Islam which was cultivated in the North Indian sultanates and their courts, but could maintain much of their Arab identity, expressed in their adherence to the Shafi'i *madhhab* and the maintenance of intensive relations with Baghdad, Yemen, the Hadramaut, Central Arabia, and Egypt. Since most of these merchants settled permanently, they developed special groups among the population, for instance, the Navayat of the Canara coast and the Mappila of Malabar.

The Muslims in these trading communities were most instrumental in spreading Islam to the Southeast Asian and Chinese seaports. This spread intensified in the 13th and 14th cs., when a number of Malayan, Indonesian, and Indochinese coastal communities converted to Islam. Their understanding of Islam maintained a more egalitarian view of society, a characteristic which would prevail in most of the Islamic seaport communities and those Islamic societies which were founded or influenced by them. Where this understanding survived until the last century, it became fertile ground for Islamic reform movements.

India until the Great Moghuls. Indian Islam has both a Turkish background and possible Buddhist elements which contributed to the development of a new Indian court etiquette and religious ideology. The Fatimid rule over Egypt had begun to make its impact on India via the sea routes. The coastal areas around and east of the Persian Gulf up to Gujarat developed their *da'wa* and Isma'ili Shi'ism, which had spread there since 900 from Multan in the area of Sind (situated close to the Indus River, in contrast to al-Hind, which refers to India proper). The Ghaznavid sultans, however, repeatedly fought against them. In 1017, Lahore became the capital of their north Indian province. A military attack by the Ghorides, originating in Afghanistan like the Ghaznavids, devastated northern India. A military slave, Qutbuddin Aibek, proclaimed his independence in 1206 in Lahore and moved to Delhi, making it the capital of his new empire and underlining at the same time that he intended to make his kingdom more "Indian." Already four years earlier, Muslim troops had reached Bengal. A strong inclination toward Sufism, which characterized Aibek and those military slaves who followed him on the throne, facilitated the spread of mystical orders that produced most effective Muslim teachers and missionaries.

After the rise and fall of some kingdoms and sultanates in northern India, Babur, a descendant of the frightful Timur Leng, started in 1526 to build one of the most impressive empires in the history of Islam and of India, that of the great Moghuls, with centers in Lahore, Agra, and Delhi. His grandson Akbar (b. 1542, ruled 1556-1605) incorporated Gujarat, Sind, the Deccan, and other areas into his sultanate. Life at his court was open to poets, people of letters, artists, mystics, and scholars, and in his religious attitude he was very tolerant. His son and heir to the throne, Jehangir, was born in 1569 to a Hindu princess. In 1579, Akbar declared himself to possess infallibility in religious matters.

Jehangir (ruled 1605-27) tried, although without comparable success, to maintain the splendor of his father's court. A clash with the Sikhs was never healed, while, under the influence of his wife Nur Jahan, he was very lenient toward the Shi'a. An opposition group which demanded more support for Sunnite orthodoxy caused political trouble. His son Khusrau Shahjahan is remembered as one of the greatest constructors of the Moghul Dynasty, his most famous edifice being the Taj Mahal in Agra, a mausoleum built for his wife Mumtaz Mahal, who died in 1631 when she gave birth to her fourteenth child. When in 1658 he fell sick, his son Aurangzab (b. 1618, ruled 1659-1707) fought and killed the crown prince. When under his rule religious discipline and orthodox learning according to the Sunnite traditions were favored, religious tensions with the Sikhs and Hindus arose. After his death, the power of the dynasty quickly declined.

In 1757, the British East India Company expanded its rule from Bengal up the Ganges Valley. This stimulated Islamic reformist movements in Delhi. One of the reformers, Shah Waliullah (d. 1763), attacked the "un-Islamic beliefs" which had entered Islam and tried a reform on the basis of a more literal understanding of the sources of Islam.

When the British attacked Islamic educational institutions and the economy declined, a mutiny of Indian soldiers was launched in 1857 with the aim of reinforcing the position of the last Moghul emperor, Bahadur Shah, who had inherited the Moghul throne in 1839. The victorious British, however, pillaged and destroyed Delhi, imitating the patterns which were common in the Orient on such occasions.

The reaction of the Muslims (and Hindus), now under British rule, was twofold. While (Sir) Saiyid Ahmad Khan (1817-98) favored some kind of cooperation with the British and, simultaneously, agitated for a modernization of Islamic education (e.g., the College in Aligarh), others such as Jamaluddin al-Afghani (1839-97) preached the strict difference or even enmity between Islam and the West, including in the fields of science and philosophy which, he asserted, should be derived and developed from Islamic tradition and not imitated from the West.

Another problem was whether or not political cooperation with the Hindus was possible. On this matter, a division of opinion split both groups. While the Indian National Congress (1885) tried to bring both groups to cooperate, members of the Muslim League (1906) favored connections with the caliph in Istanbul as the protector of the legal rights of Muslims.

Some religious scholars who had been educated in the conservative Deoband Institute, such as Abul Kalam Azad and Abul A'la Maudoodi, started to work on the question how the *shari'a,* the traditional Islamic law, could be adapted to present demands in society. Others, such as Muhammad Iqbal (1873-1938), stressed renewing Indian philosophy and poetry, using Urdu in addition to Persian. Iqbal was also a politician, and the idea of creating a separate state for the Muslims, Pakistan, is attributed to him. His friend Ali Jinnah became the first president when that idea, after Indian independence from the British in 1947 and the following civil war, was realized. The Islamic part of Bengal, originally part of this Islamic Republic, separated, however, in 1971 and is known now as Bangladesh*.

Southeast Asia. On their way to China, Muslim merchants from Persia, Arabia, and India had arrived by the 7th c. in the seaports of Southeast Asia. A first Islamic principality, however, does not appear until the 13th c., when the ruler of Pasai, North Sumatra, converted at least some of the inhabitants to the religion of the prophet. He seems to have been under Persian-Shi'ite influence, adhering to the Hanafite *madhhab.* Two centuries later, however, Pasai and other Islamic communities had adopted the Shafi'ite *madhhab,* an indication that South Indian Islam, with its stronger roots in Sunnite traditions, had gained predominance. When in 1413 the ruler of Malacca*, a prince of Sri Vijaya, the great Buddhist maritime empire with its center in South Sumatra which had been destroyed a few decades earlier by the Javanese, turned to Islam, he not only laid the foundations for one of the most influential sultanates in the area, but he also introduced the main elements of the Buddhist court etiquette of Sri Vijaya, which until today are maintained in the Malayan sultanates. After Malacca was conquered by the Portuguese in 1511, the sultanates of Johore, Aceh (North Sumatra), and Brunei* considered themselves as successors of Islamic Malacca. The population, however, was mainly Islamized by teachers from the Sufi traditions.

In Java, Islam spread on two levels: the popular, where mystical teachers *(walis, maulanas)* proved instrumental by founding a kind of boarding school *(pesantren)* in which they introduced their pupils as well as the village populations to the basics of Islam; and the dynastic, which had already been adopted by the first Islamic sultanate in Demak (1478-1546), a dynasty that claimed genealogical relations with the last Hindu empire of Majapahit. This variety of Islam came to its peak in the time of the Mataram Dynasty (from 1581; in 1755 it split, with the help of the Dutch, into two branches: that of Solo, or Surakarta, and that of Yogyakarta). Its greatest ruler, Agung (1613-46), named himself *susuhunan,* an old Javanese title which points to the supposedly supernatural power of its bearer and at the same time stresses its dynastical legitimacy rooted in Majapahit. In 1641, he successfully asked for the title of sultan, which was presented to him by a delegation from Mecca. He added the title of *Kalipatulah (Khalifatu'llah),* thus claiming also a particular relationship with God (usually, the caliphs were called *Khalifatu n-nabi* [representative of the prophet]).

With a view to the strength of pre-Islamic cosmological influences on a Muslim, sociologists differentiate between *santri* and *abangan* Muslims. The *santri* are those who hold more strongly to the international traditions of Islam, Sufi traditions included, while the *abangan* represent a type of Islam where inculturation has progressed much more. Quite often, tensions between the two groups are exploited in the political arena. Since the *abangan* type of Islam is adhered to by the majority of

Indonesian Muslims, the efforts of the *santri* Muslims who tried to establish Indonesia, after its independence (1945), as an Islamic state, met with no success. The *Pancasila** (Five Principles), which became the basic ideology of the Indonesian constitution, gives an equal legal position to the adherents of those religions acknowledged by the government.

In Malaysia*, although closely related to Indonesia in its Islamic history, specific ethnic problems developed. As a result, the Malays are regarded as *bumiputra* (sons of the land), and Islam is the official religion of the state. This should mean that state ceremonies, wherever necessary, are conducted in accordance with Islamic rules, for the head of the state, the *Yang di-Pertuan Agung*, is elected from among the Malayan sultans or rulers. But the people are not obliged to adhere to Islam, except the Malays, who are Muslim by definition, nor are the state institutions and laws based on Islamic fundamentals.

*Cambodia**. Cambodian Muslims are essentially Chams, whose royalty, the Champa, situated in the center of present-day Vietnam*, was destroyed by the Vietnamese in the 15th c. Numerous Malayan immigrants who joined this community took Islam as a means of identification. Although they are not of the Khmer race, Prince Sihanouk called them Khmer Islam. Cambodian Muslims are Sunnite.

In 1975, Muslims in Cambodia numbered 250,000 people grouped in 113 communities. Almost 100,000 of them were massacred by the Khmer Rouge regime, including 93 of the 113 *hakkem*, and more than 270 of the 300 teachers at the schools of the Koran.

Favored by the regime of the Popular Republic of Makpsuchea (1979-89) and aided financially by Indonesia, Saudi Arabia, and Brunei, Islam has seen a rapid rebirth in Cambodia.

See also Religious Nationalism in the Philippines.

Bibliography

Forbes, Andrew D. W., ed., *The Muslims of Thailand*, 2 vols. (1988-89). • Woodward, Mark R., *Islam in Java* (1989). • Esposito, John L., ed., *Islam in Asia* (1987).

OLAF SCHUMANN, with a contribution on Cambodia from FRANÇOIS PONCHAUD

Islam in Indonesia

The first Muslims to appear in the southeast Asian archipelago toward the end of the 7th c. were Persians, Indians, and probably also Arabs from the Hadramaut. They lived in special quarters and later were usually allowed to build small mosques. The first indigenous Muslims most probably were some chieftains ruling in harbor cities in the northern part of Sumatra (Aceh), whose daughters were married to Muslim resident traders. The original inclination to the *Shi'a* had disappeared when the Moroccan traveler Ibn Battuta visited the area in A.D. 1348. Also, the Hanafite legal rite was replaced by the Shafi'ite, which came via India and which accepts to a great extent the continuation of local *adat** (customs).

The most important teachers of Islam among the populace were *walis* or *shaikhs* (sacred men) rooted in *tariqa* or *tarekat* (mystical orders). Their flexible understanding of Islamic doctrine and law facilitated the continuation of specific Indonesian/Malay customs, among them the quasi-religious respect for spiritual and political leaders who are thought to represent the saving powers of the divine lord.

Sumatran and Malay Islam, continuing to a certain extent the Mahayana-Buddhist cultural, political, and religious patterns (including language) of the former Sri Vijaya (Palembang), was strengthened with the foundation of Malacca* in 1403. Its ruler, an aristocratic refugee from Palembang, turned to Islam in 1414. After the Portuguese conquered Malacca in 1511, his descendants preserved Malaccan dynastic traditions at several other Muslim courts on the Peninsula (Johor), North Sumatra, and Borneo.

The Islamization of the Minangkabau (West Sumatra) was initiated by the rulers of Aceh in the 16th c. In the 17th c., *tasauwuf* (Sufism) flourished in Aceh (Hamza Fansura, ar-Raniri). Although it was not established until 1475, by 1478 already the great Hindu empire of Majapahit suffered a heavy, and in the end fatal, blow from this emerging rival. Islam in the harbor cities of northern Java, where it was also adhered to and promulgated by Chinese traders and sailors, maintained a stronger observance of its legal prescriptions, while the holy men preaching in the interior tried to harmonize Islam with the deep-rooted traditional, monistic Javanese worldview. Sultan Agung (ruled 1613-46), the greatest ruler of the Mataram Empire, combined Hindu court traditions with the tasks of an Islamic ruler (sultan), but under his son the *ulama* were persecuted. Kutai, Martapura, and Sukadana in East and South Borneo now came under a strong Javanese-Islamic influence, while in the Moluccas* (Hitu, Ternate, Tidore) and Celebes*, the process of Islamization had already started in the 16th and early 17th (in Makassar) cs.

Islam in Indonesia maintained a basically twofold appearance right through the 19th c. Several instances of heavy conflicts arose between those Muslims who embedded their Islamic worldview in the traditional way of life of their people and those who tended to see in Islam an agent of innovation and restructuring of social life toward the Islamic faith, with its legal prescriptions and social patterns derived from the ideas of the classical *umma*. Instances of such conflicts are the Padri Wars in West Sumatra and the Diponogoro Rebellion in Central Java. Stimulated by returning *hajjis*, who had learned about the emerging reform movements in the Middle East, a growing cultural tension arose toward the end of the 19th c. between the *kaum tua* (the "old," or backward-looking, people) and the *kaum muda*, who started with a reform of the educational system. Later, the *kaum muda* involved themselves in social services, such as

Ahmed Dahlan's *Muhammadiyah* (since 1912), and in politics.

After initiatives taken by Muslim traders in Solo, Central Java, in 1905 *(Syarikat Dagang Islam)* and by young Javanese students, most of them medical students, in Jakarta in 1908 *(Budi Utomo),* the first nationalist movement started under the emblem of Islam in 1911, the *Syarikat Islam.* Under the charismatic leadership of its chairman, H. O. S. Tjokroaminoto (from 1912 to 1934), it combined during its first decade quite different elements, including devout Muslims such as H. Agus Salim and extreme leftists who initiated, after separation from *Syarikat Islam* in 1921, the Indonesian Communist Party. The strong inclination to the goals of Islamic modernism alienated the traditionalist *sunni ulama* (scribes) as well, who separated in early 1926 and established the *Nahdlatul Ulama.* Differences emerged, for example, on the question of limited cooperation with the Dutch colonial government or a strict *hijra* policy.

After the Japanese occupation in early 1942, the *Majelis A'laa Islam Indonesia,* established in 1937 as a consultative body of most of the Indonesian Islamic organizations, was transformed into the *Majelis Syuro Muslimin Indonesia,* or *Masyumi,* to serve as an aide (albeit sometimes obstinate) to the Japanese government. When independence approached, it voiced the opinions of the Islamic politicians who demanded that independent Indonesia be based ideologically on the Islamic *shari'a.* An equally large number of Muslims, gathering around nationalists such as Soekarno* and Muhammad Hatta and supported by the non-Muslims, favored a separation between state and religion. As a compromise, the *Pancasila** was promulgated and finally accepted on 18 Aug 1945, one day after the proclamation of Indonesia's independence.

The struggle for the implementation of an Islamic state, however, was continued on the political field by the Islamic parties under the leadership of a slightly rearranged *Masyumi,* whose leaders (such as Muhammad Natsir) nevertheless cooperated with the national government. Militant groups, however, launched rebellions and tried to establish *Darul-Islam* regions. In the end, all of them failed and were destroyed by the Indonesian army.

The involvement of some leaders of *Masyumi* in regional rebellions against the growing predominance of the Javanese in political and economic positions caused President Soekarno in 1960 to outlaw *Masyumi.* Also, the New Order government under Soeharto, in office officially since 1967, exercised a stiff control of the Islamic parties. In 1973, the four existing parties had to merge into one, the *Parti Persatuan Pembangunan* (Party for Unity and Development). In 1984, the *Nahdlatul Ulama* withdrew and reorganized itself again as a social organization. Like *Muhammadiyah* and other Islamic organizations, but also like the Christian churches, they had to accept *Pancasila* as the "only basis for their social, political, and national life."

During the New Order period, the issue of the relationship between state and religion (Islam) remained on the agenda. After the 1960s, some student leaders tried, in different ways, to develop concepts by which Islam could contribute to, not dominate or determine, the development of a modern cultural, economic, and political orientation of Indonesian society by accepting its pluralistic character. Others, however, saw the future Indonesian society on the lines of international Islamic revivalism. In 1991, protagonists of this movement founded the *Ikatan Cendekiawan Muslimin Indonesia* (Association of Muslim Intellectuals in Indonesia, ICMI). Under the guidance of Dr. Habibie (minister for technology and science and later president), it was sometimes used by the government as a political agency when new members of parliament had to be appointed.

There is an increasing tendency for the government to shape new laws according to Islamic principles, or to separate Muslims in some areas of law from other citizens. This development is observed with growing suspicion by Indonesian constitutionalists who object to compartmentalizing the Indonesian people into (religious) majorities and minorities and demand equality for all Indonesians as citizens, in accordance with the third principle of *Pancasila.* Tensions between Islamic communities and minority communities (Chinese as well as Christian) will continue to flare up into violence in spite of the constitutional stability given through *Pancasila.*

Bibliography

Benda, Harry J., *The Crescent and the Rising Sun* (1958). • Boland, B. J., *The Struggle of Islam in Modern Indonesia* (1971). • Noer, D., *The Modernist Muslim Movement in Indonesia, 1900-1942* (1973). • Hooker, M. B., ed., *Islam in Southeast-East Asia* (1983). • Israeli, Raphel, and Anthony H. Johns, eds., *Islam in Asia,* Vol. II, *Southeast and East Asia* (1984). • Ahmad Ibrahim, Sharon Siddique, and Yasmin Hussain, eds., *Readings on Islam in Southeast Asia* (1985).

OLAF SCHUMANN

Islamic Fundamentalism

Fundamentalism. Fundamentalism is neither a new religious movement (in the technical sense of the term), nor simply a traditional, conservative, or orthodox expression of religious faith and practice. Rather, fundamentalism is a hybrid of both religious modes and it belongs in a category by itself. While fundamentalists claim to be upholding orthodoxy or orthopraxis, and defending age-old religious traditions and time-honored ways of life from erosion, they do so by crafting new methods, formulating new ideologies, and adopting the latest organizational structures and processes. Some of these new methods seem to be in direct violation of the actual historical beliefs, interpretative practices, and moral behaviors of earlier generations, or to be a significant departure from these precedents. Indeed, the fundamentalists find fault with fellow conservative believers who want to conserve the traditions but are not willing to craft new and innovative ways of fighting back against the forces of erosion. At the same time, fundamentalists would reject the suggestion that they are doing something entirely new. A crucial element of their rhetoric is the assertion that their innovative programs are based on the authority of the sacred past, whether the past be represented in a privileged text or tradition, or in the teaching of a charismatic or official leader.

Fundamentalists are not restorationists nor are they marked by a special or distinctive longing for a simpler, less complex world. Yet they are careful to demonstrate the continuity between their programs and teaching and the received wisdom of their religious heritage.

Development in Islamic fundamentalism. Traditional Islam* has been an important reality in Asia. Basically, it is an interiorized religion, heavily influenced by the Sufi mystical path. It is a political quietism that within the Asian context accommodated itself to indigenous practices of piety, devotion to the saints, visitation of tombs, and local customs and rites that have in the course of time come to be regarded as Islamic. A dry legalism affected the study of Shariah, as creative application of the law was no longer permissible, the law being understood as fixed and immutable. Theology has been the study of scholastic writers, not an ongoing reflection on Islamic faith in the light of changing times. Islamic education was carried out in mosques or in the homes of unlicensed teachers who demanded unquestioning acceptance of their teachings. The reformers have one basic principle in common: to renew the Islamic community by reforming it according to the teaching of the Quran, the oral tradition of the Prophet, and the lived experience of the earliest generations of Muslims. In their judgment, the Islamic community's departure from its original spirit and practice is the cause of the weakness of Islamic society.

There are two main tendencies in the revival of the original teachings of Islam. First, the reformers want to go back to the Quran and traditions from the Prophet, to recapture their original spirit. They are aware that the world today is very different from that of the time of the Prophet. They want to discover the Quranic élan and apply its creativity to the changed situations in which Islamic society finds itself today. Second, others, who could be termed fundamentalists, express a nostalgia for the earlier community of believers. They view the first generations of Islam as those who held to the faith, pure and uncorrupted. It was the age when Islam was strong and expanding. They see the early period as a time when religion and state were one both in theory and in practice. Through precise application of the law, they hope to re-create the pristine community. They advocate a return of the kind of Islamic dress prescribed in the Shariah, punishments of offending Muslims, reorganization of financial affairs in accord with Islamic principles, and regulation of the relationship between the Islamic community and others.

When we look for paradigms of this development of Islamic fundamentalism in the Pakistani context, we rediscover that political forces for various reasons fanned fundamentalism for a long time. The government of Zia Ul-Haq* is one classical model, as many fundamentalist ideas were propagated during his time. Strict outward adherence, fasting during *Ramzan* (Ramadan, the month of fasting), the creation of Islamic courts, sidelining the minorities through separate electorates, systematic propaganda against women, encouraging of the Blasphemy Law issue, the enforcement of *Zakat* (the duty of almsgiving in Islam) via banks — all of these are nuances of how the fundamentalist tendency was experienced by the people.

Religious tolerance. As a reaction to the recent past, there is a worldwide reawakening of religion today. In many areas of the world, Pakistan* included, it has taken on radical, even aggressive forms, and because of this has engendered fears in many quarters. However, we must not lose sight of the fact that this widespread return to religion is also an affirmation that spirituality is essential to human existence. It would be a serious mistake to equate the reawakening only with intolerance, for within it is the latent promise of a common search for peace and life together in a global community. At the same time, new religious fervor is often combined with people's deep desire to recover and reassert their ethnic and national identity, to reassert their freedom in a world besieged by globalizing trends. Some of these religious movements provide theological and ideological justification for an exclusivist, defensive, aggressive, nationalistic understanding of the human community.

Globalization through media communication and satellite television is posing a major challenge to Islamic society. Interaction with non-Muslims is a crucial element of this debate. The manner in which the media choose and produce images in turn influences how people look at Islam and creates a shorthand image in the world media, where Islam has come to mean fanaticism, terrorism, and extremism. Muslims have to come to terms with this and prepare a response as to what has to be done with these global images. The non-Muslim has a role to play also. It is a mutual challenge to move from questioning and confrontation toward a common search for regional and even global peace with justice.

ARCHIE DE SOUZA

Islamization

Process by which the public expression of Islamic values and ideals becomes increasingly widespread and authoritative in a society or nation.

Islamization of society begins when the first members of a particular people accept Islam* as their religion. The process of society taking on Islamic values and ideals, however, is a slow one, requiring decades and even centuries, during which the process can endure long periods of inactivity and occasionally encounter setbacks.

In Asia, the process of Islamization has been particularly long and slow. Although Muslim armies had already conquered parts of Central Asia and the Indian subcontinent by the 8th c., and Muslims were present as foreign trading communities in port cities of South and Southeast Asia, there were relatively few conversions from the indigenous populations. The great period of expansion, when many Asian peoples accepted Islam, was the 14th-16th cs.

In the first centuries after conversion, Islamization did not penetrate society to a deep level. Beside their Islamic practices, Asian Muslims often retained traditional rites and customs *(adat*)* that centered on ancestors, holy persons and places, healing procedures, and family organization. Islamization was hampered after the 16th c., when most predominantly Muslim regions in Asia came under non-Muslim (European Christian; Chinese, Burmese, and Thai Buddhist; or Indian Hindu and Sikh) rule.

Reform efforts in the 17th-18th cs., pursued mainly by the *Naqshbandiyya* and *Qadiriyya Sufi* orders, attempted to Islamize society by rooting out customs and practices of non-Islamic origin and by increasing the quality of Islamic education. A second impetus toward Islamization found its inspiration in the 18th- and 19th-c. *Wahhabi* movement of Arab origin. *Wahhabi* views, often brought to Asia by returning *hajjis,* attempted to reorient Islam from being regarded as a personal, mystical path to being understood as an activist, socially oriented program to regulate all of human life according to God's revealed will.

In modern times, most Islamization movements have been based on a conception of Islam as a divinely revealed project to transform society according to the will of Allah. Islamic teaching ought to shape every aspect of human life, from the personal and familial to the social, economic, and political. Muslims should make use of societal structures and organizations to bring this about.

The Islamic way of life, the *shari'a* (see *Shari'a* Law), is elaborated and codified in four major legal traditions. In Asia, the most widespread are the *Hanafi* school in Central Asia and the Indian subcontinent and the *Shafi'i* in Southeast Asia. Islamic prescriptions cover every aspect of life: creed, worship, human relations and business dealings, principles of government, punishments for crimes, family law, and moral instruction.

Muslim approaches to Islamization generally develop one of two lines of thought. In the first, political systems are seen as legitimate and necessary tools for achieving the end of Islamization. The state exists in order to encourage adherence to the *shari'a* and to punish infractions. Certain elements, such as marriage law, inheritance, collection and distribution of the poor tax *(zakât),* maintenance of public endowments *(awqâf),* and punishment for serious crimes (homicide, adultery, blasphemy, sedition) should be regulated by the state. Included within the *shari'a* are norms for the protection and regulation of non-Muslim minorities.

The second view of Islamization either minimizes or rejects the role of the state. According to this view, the state can do no more than demand and judge external conformity; it has no power to change human hearts. True Islamization can occur only when professing Muslims actually begin to live, practice, and internalize the prescriptions of the *shari'a.* Individual Muslims are called to repentance *(tawba)* and to undertake faithfully and freely the Islamic way of life. As more and more Muslims freely practice their faith, a deeper Islamization of society will inevitably take place. Seen in this way, Islamization presumes religious plurality and can be carried out under any form or system of government.

While proponents of the first view concentrate their energies on obtaining and employing political power to enact and execute legislation that would apply *shari'a* prescriptions as civil law, those of the second view work to bring about in Muslims the change of heart necessary if Islam is to be lived according to its original intent. The ongoing dialectic between these two approaches to Islamization constitutes one of the major issues debated today within the Islamic community.

While the goal of a state-supported Islamization is admirable in its intent to bring divine values to bear upon the way society functions and the way people relate to one another, Christians and other non-Muslim minorities find it difficult to reconcile with the pluralist nature of modern Asian societies. In the multireligious context that characterizes Asian societies today, Muslims are but one of several religious groups who claim the duty to profess their faith openly and to influence social, economic, and political realities according to their religious convictions. Just as Muslims have a duty to Islamize society, so Christians are obliged to bring Christian values to bear upon all aspects of human life.

Non-Muslims question whether it is possible for non-Muslim communities to play an active and integral role as full and equal citizens in states guided and shaped by the *shari'a.* While granting that Muslims are entitled to regulate their own affairs in accord with the dictates of their religious beliefs, they would demand convincing guarantees that the civil and religious rights of non-Muslims will be respected in societies guided by the *shari'a.*

Non-Muslims generally find their societal commitments compatible with Muslims who understand Islamization to be a process that must occur within the individual Muslim believer. With these Muslims, they discover they hold many values in common, such as social justice, defense of the poor and oppressed, the promotion of human rights, ethical norms regarding family* life and business practice, and the affirmation of the right of every person to live with dignity and freedom. Most Christians are ready to work together with Muslims to promote these goals.

Christians and other non-Muslims must realize that Islamization is not a passing phenomenon. It is an obligation for Muslims. The question is what kind of

Islamization. Is it one that excludes and marginalizes those outside the Islamic community, or one that welcomes a plurality where each religious group can make its own contribution for the good of the whole?

Bibliography

Enayat, Hamid, *Modern Islamic Political Thought* (1988). • Mitri, Tarik, ed., *Religion, Law, and Society* (1995). • Stowasser, Barbara Freyer, ed., *The Islamic Impulse* (1987). • Al-Faruqi, I. R., *Islamization of Knowledge* (1982). • Rahman, Fazlur, *Islam and Modernity: The Transformation of an Intellectual Tradition* (1982).

THOMAS MICHEL

Iso'dad of Merv

(9th c.). East Syrian, bishop (from 837 C.E.) of the East Syrian Church at Hdatta (in Adiabene).

Iso'dad is best known for his encyclopedic and methodical commentaries on the Bible*. These included textual references and alternative interpretations from numerous earlier writers, including Ephrem* of Syria and Theodore of Mopsuestia. His method was to list the various alternatives and then make his evaluative comments. The resulting commentary is one of the largest on the entire Bible written by one person. It is an essential source for understanding the history of Syriac Christian exegesis and theology. The text has close relationships with the commentaries of Theodore bar Koni and Iso' bar Nun. According to some sources, he was considered a candidate for catholicos in 852 after the death of Abraham II, but due to the influence of his opponent, Theodosius, in the court of the caliph, he was not elected.

Bibliography

Editions:

Old Testament: Van den Eynde, C., ed., *Commentaire d'Iso'dad de Merv sur l'ancien testament* (CSCO 156, 229-30, 303-4, 328-29; 1958-72). • New Testament: Gibson, M. D., ed., *The Commentaries of Isho'dad, Bishop of Hadatha (c. 850 C.E.)* (*Horae Semiticae*, 5-7, 10-11; 1911-1916).

Studies:

Clark, E. G., *The Selected Questions of Isho' Bar Nun on the Pentateuch* (1962). • Brade, L., "Die Herkunft von Prologen in den Paulusbriefexegese des Theodoros bar Konai und Isodad von Merv," *Oriens Christianus*, Vol. 60 (1976). • Van Rompay, L., "Iso' bar Nun and Iso'dad of Merv: New Data for Their Interdependence," *Orientalia Lovaniensia Periodica*, Vol. 8 (1977). • Bundy, D., "The Peshitta of Isaiah 53:9 and the Syrian Commentators," *Oriens Christianus*, Vol. 67 (1983); "The 'Questions and Answers' on Isaiah by Išo' bar Nun," *Orientalia Lovaniensia Periodica*, Vol. 16 (1985). • Molenberg, Cornelia, *The Interpreter Interpreted: Iso' bar Nun's Selected Questions on the Old Testament* (1990).

DAVID BUNDY

Issaraks

A group of armed Cambodians struggling against the French protectorate in Cambodia* between 1945 and 1954; responsible for the destruction of numerous churches.

Taking their name from the Thai word meaning "partisans of liberty," the Issaraks (*Khmer Serey* in Khmer) forged a group of combatants supported by Thailand* against the French presence in and the royal authority of Cambodia. Under their principal leaders, Son Ngoc Thanh, Dap Chhoun, and Prince Norodom Chandarangsey, the Issaraks became particularly active after 1946, following the reconquest of Indochina by France. They united then with the Vietminh, and a number adopted Marxist ideology.

In Aug 1945, the Vietminh burned the seminary and parish buildings of Culas Onieng in Cochin China, which was part of the apostolic vicariate of Cambodia, and imprisoned the French priests. In 1946, following the forced return to the French of the Cambodian provinces of the north (Battambang, Siemreap, and part of Kompong Thom and of Stung Treng) which Thailand had annexed with the aid of Japan* in 1941, the Issaraks and Vietminh attacked several parishes, burning the buildings and killing some 100 Vietnamese Christians in the province of Battambang as well as along the Mekong. A pastor and an elderly priest of the evangelical Church of Siemreap were martyred for their faith.

The Issarak agitation was appeased with the proclamation of independence on 9 Nov 1953 under King Sihanouk. The last Issaraks submitted, following their leader Prince Norodom Chandarangsey.

For the Issaraks, the Vietnamese influence in the church represented the view of the protectorate. A good number of officials and military personnel, whose function it was to defend the Vietnamese Christians, seized the land which had been abandoned by the Vietnamese Christian refugees.

Bibliography

Ponchaud, François, *The Cathedral of the Rice Paddy* (1990).

FRANÇOIS PONCHAUD

J

Jacob Baradaeus

(ca. 500-578). Born in Tella, Syria, the son of a priest, Jacob entered the monastery of Pesilto, near Nisibis*, and became a monk. With another monk, Sargis, he was sent in 527 to Constantinople to intercede for the non-Chalcedonians, where he appears to have come under the protection of the Empress Theodora. He remained in Constantinople for 15 years before apparently being appointed bishop of Edessa, a see which he appears never to have claimed.

According to the sources, Jacob Baradaeus spent the rest of his life reconstituting the hierarchy and priesthood of the Monophysites (later called Jacobites* or West Syrians). The claims of most of the sources are clear overstatements of his activities (100,000 ordinations of clergy are claimed!). Most of his appointments were canonically irregular, and most of those appointed were staunch Monophysites from the monasteries. However, the campaign was effective as he managed to secure the sympathy of the populace and elude the imperial police who were eager to stop his campaign against the Byzantine church. Some of his letters survive and have been edited by J.-B. Chabot as part of the corpus of West Syrian documents *Documenta ad origines monophysitarum illustrandas* (Corpus scriptorum christianorum orientalium 7 [text, 1908] and 103 [translation, 1933].

Bibliography

Pseudo-John of Ephesus, "Vita Baradaei," ed. and trans. E. W. Brooks, *Patrologia Orientalis* 19 (1926). • A. Baumstark, *Geschichte der syrischen Literatur* (1922). • Honigmann, E., *Évêques et évêchés monophysites d'Asie antérieure au VIe siècle* (1951). • Bundy, D., "Jacob Baradaeus: State of Research, A Review of Sources and a New Approach," *Le Muséon* 91 (1978).

DAVID BUNDY

Jacob of Edessa

(ca. 633-708). West Syrian (Jacobite) bishop of Edessa.

Jacob was born in the village of Andiba near Antioch. He studied at Kennišrin with Severus Seboket, focusing on biblical studies. He studied in Alexandria for a time before returning to Antioch, whereupon he was appointed (684) bishop of Edessa.

As bishop of Edessa, Jacob attempted to reform the monasteries and strengthen both the scholarship and the spirituality of the monks. These reform efforts enraged the monastic establishment, and so Jacob remained only four years at Edessa. He then withdrew to the monastery of Mar Jacob of Keysum and then to Eusebona, where he taught Greek and exegesis. Once again, the rigor of his educational requirements and efforts to encourage the students to learn caused problems, and after 11 years he left for Tell Ada'. There he undertook a more accurate translation of the Syriac language Bible* from Greek, perhaps a tacit admission that the clergy and monks were not going to accept his vision of the importance of Greek for theological education. Toward the end of his life, he was reappointed bishop of Edessa. He died on a return trip to Tell Ada' to retrieve some of his books.

Jacob of Edessa was a prolific author. He contributed books on Syriac language and literature, history, theology, philosophy, exegesis, and canon law. He also translated numerous works from Greek into Syriac, the most important of which was probably the collection of 125 homilies of Severus of Antioch. Fragments of his large biblical commentary, a *Commentary on the Hexaemeron*, letters, homilies, essays on ecclesiastical law and liturgy, and a chronicle are extant.

Bibliography

Ortiz de Urbina, I., *Patrologia Syriaca*, 2nd ed. (1965). • Rignell, K. E., ed. and trans., *A Letter from Jacob of Edessa to John the Stylite* (1971); *A Letter from Jacob of Edessa to John the Stylite of Litarb Concerning Ecclesiastical Canons* (1979). • Vööbus, Arthur, "The Discovery of New Cycles of Canons and Resolutions Composed by Jacob of Edessa," *Orientalia christiana periodica* 34 (1968). • Baars, W., "Ein neugefundenes Bruchstück aus der syrischen Bibelrevision des Jakob von Edessa," *Vetus*

Testamentum 18 (1968). • Schlimme, L., "Die Lehre des Jacob von Edessa vom Fall des Teufels," *Oriens Christianus* 61 (1977). • Brock, S. P., "Jacob of Edessa's Discourse on the Myron," *Oriens Christianus* 63 (1979).

DAVID BUNDY

Jacob of Nisibis

(d. 337/338). Jacob of Nisibis became an important model of the good bishop in Syriac literature, and also in Armenia* and in the Latin and Byzantine churches. Perhaps the most important sources are the writings of Ephrem of Syria* (*Hymns of Nisibis* 13-16), who extolled his virtues but unfortunately provided no significant biographical or historical data. According to the Chronicle of Elias of Nisibis (975-1047), Jacob was consecrated bishop in 308/309. According to the Chronicle of Edessa, he was the builder of the first church at Nisibis (ca. 313-20), and a baptistery built beside that church was dedicated to his memory by his successor Vologeses in 359. From various conciliar lists, it is certain that Jacob represented Nisibis at the Council of Nicaea. He was known as an anti-Arian. Works attributed to him by later chronicles and manuscripts, including the homilies of Aphraates, were not written by Jacob. Jacob became a prominent subject in the later hagiographical traditions.

Bibliography

Peeters, P., "La Légende de Saint Jacques de Nisibe," *Analecta Bollandiana* 38 (1920). • Krüger, J., "Jakob von Nisibis in syrischer und armenischer Überliefung," *Le Muséon* 81 (1968). • Fiey, J.-M., "Les Évêques de Nisibe au temps de Saint Ephrem," *Parole de l'Orient* 4 (1973); *Nisibe: métropole syriaque orientale et ses suffragants des origins à nos jours* (1977). • Bundy, D., "Jacob of Nisibis as a Model for the Episcopacy," *Le Muséon* 104 (1991).

DAVID BUNDY

Jacob of Serug

(c. 450–c. 520). Syriac-writing Christian author and bishop.

Jacob was born in Hawra district of Serug. He studied at the School of Edessa during the mid-460s under the Bishop Nonnus*. From 502/3 to 518/19, he served as a clergyperson *(periodeutes)* based in the district of Sarug. When the controversy over Nestorius* began, he sided with Severus of Antioch. However, his adherence to the "monophysite" tradition was often suspect. His letters are important documents for the period.

Jacob was an able poet, as is indicated by the rhythmic homilies preserved in Syriac. Many volumes of his sermons have been published, but the critical problems and issues of authenticity have not been adequately addressed. These homilies suggest that, despite his forays into philosophical theology, he was essentially a biblical theologian. It was this that nourished his irenic spirit and sustained his moderate monophysite position. Because of this reputation, and because of his ability to reconcile persons of differing points of view, he was made bishop of Batna, a small town in the district of Sarug in the region of Osrhoene*. Later Syriac, Armenian, and Arabic Christian writers celebrated his life. Most of these texts are listed in the *Biblioteca Hagiographica Orientalis* (Brussels, 1910).

Bibliography

Bedjan, P., *Homiliae selectae Mar Jacobi Sarugensis,* 5 Vols. (1905-10). • Albert, M., *Homélies contra les juifs par Jacques de Saroug, Patrologia Orientalis,* Vol. 38, No. 1 (1976). • Rilliet, F., *Jacques de Saroug. Six homélies festales en prose, Patrologia Orientalis,* Vol. 43, No. 4 (1986). • Alwan, K., *Jacques de Saroug. Quatre homélies métriques sur la création* (CSCO 508-9). • Olinder, G., *Iacobi Sarugensis, epistolae quoiquot supersunt* (CSCO 110). • Jansma, T., "Encore le Credo de Jacques de Sarug," *L'Orient Syrien,* Vol. 19 (1965); "Die Christologie von Jakob van Sarug," *Le Muséon,* Vol. 77 (1965).

DAVID BUNDY

Jacobite Syrian Orthodox Church, India

The Jacobite Syrian Orthodox Church believes that the Apostle Thomas* is the founder of the church in India*. According to tradition, St. Thomas reached the port of Kodungallore (Kranganoore) in the state of Kerala in 52 C.E. and established the church. He converted many Hindus and Jews to the Christian faith. In the early centuries, there were trade relations between Kerala and the Middle East as is evidenced by excavated Roman coins from the time of Augustus Caesar. According to some traditions, St. Thomas went up to China* and then came again to India. During this second trip, he was killed by fanatics and was buried in Mylapore, south of Madras. On 3 Jul 394, the relics of Thomas were transferred to Edessa. All the Christians in Kerala celebrate 3 Jul as St. Thomas Day.

Relation with the Universal Syrian Orthodox Church of Antioch. The Jacobite Syrian Orthodox Church in India functions as an inseparable part of the Universal Syrian Orthodox Church of Antioch. Though the Christian church was first established in Jerusalem, persecution forced the leaders of the church to leave Jerusalem, and many migrated to Antioch. Paul and Barnabas chose Antioch as the center of their extensive missionary activities. Peter, who gave leadership to the primitive church, also left Jerusalem and came to Antioch because of persecution. Thus in the 1st c., Antioch was the capital of the whole of Christendom, and Peter was its supreme head; even now, Antioch is the capital of the Syrian Orthodox Church; and the patriarch of Antioch, successor of Peter, is the supreme head of the Universal Syrian Orthodox Church. The Jacobite Syrian Orthodox Church in India is the local church under the patriarch of Antioch.

Historical evidences for the relation with the mother church in Antioch. With the first ecumenical council of Nicaea in 325 C.E., the whole of Christendom came under one of the three patriarchates: Rome, Alexandria, or Antioch. The Persian bishop Yuhanon represented India and signed the decisions of the Synod of Nicaea. Accordingly, all the Eastern churches came under the patriarch of Antioch. In 345 C.E., a group of 400 Syrian Christians migrated to Malankara (Kerala) under the leadership of Bishop Joseph and one Thomas of Cana. After their arrival, the Christians in Kerala were called Syrians. According to tradition, the relics of the body of St. Thomas were transferred from India to Edessa in 394 C.E. in keeping with the will of the patriarch of Antioch. Writings of John Chrysostom and Jerome indicate that the Bible* was translated into Indian languages during that time. It is believed that, in the 5th c., there were Indian theological students in the famous Theological Institute of Edessa. And in the historical accounts on Alexandrian patriarchs written by Isidore, it is stated that in the 7th c. the Indian Christians were ruled by the patriarch of Antioch. In 822 C.E., two Syrian bishops, Mar Shabor and Mar Aphrot, reached Kerala with a group of immigrants. They were sent by the patriarch of Antioch. A historical record called the Travancore State Manual indicates that the church in South India was under the patriarch of Antioch in the 10th and 11th cs. Similar evidence suggests that this situation continued in the 13th and 14th cs.

From 1490 to 1599, the church in South India was under bishops from the Nestorian* Church. In 1498, Portuguese navigator Vasco de Gama landed in South India. When the Portuguese arrived, the church in India was ruled by the Nestorian bishops, and there is therefore a tendency among historians to picture the church in India as a Nestorian Church all through the centuries. The Jacobite Syrian Orthodox Church holds the view that the church in India was always part and parcel of the Syrian Orthodox Church except for the period between 1490 and 1599 C.E.

After the Portuguese came to India, Roman Catholic missionaries, priests, and even bishops also arrived. They began to convert the Christians in South India to the Roman Catholic Church*. On 20 Jun 1599, Archbishop Menesis convened the historic meeting called the Synod of Diamper. The Christians in Kerala were then forcefully drawn into the Roman Catholic Church. The church in India had to suffer slavery and persecution under Roman Catholic bishops. In 1650, the leader of the church in India, Archdeacon Thomas, wrote to the patriarch of Antioch to send bishops. The patriarch sent Mar Ahattalla. According to tradition, the Portuguese arrested him and cast him into the ocean. The Christians were incensed and swore an oath in 1653, the Oath at Coonan Cross, to cut all relations with the Roman Catholics and Jesuits*. The leaders of the church then made another request of the patriarch of Antioch, and he sent Mar Gregorios of Jerusalem to Malankara. He arrived in 1665. Mar Gregorios ordained Archdeacon Thomas as bishop. When Thomas assumed charge with the title Mar Thoma I, the church in India once again came under the supreme authority of the patriarch of Antioch, and it became an integral part of the Syrian Orthodox Church, adopting its faith, rituals, liturgy, and traditions as before. The Jacobite Syrian Orthodox Church in India stands firm in this age-old faith and traditions.

The attribute "Jacobite." The Syrian Orthodox Church belongs to the non-Chalcedonian ecclesiastical tradition. The Syrian Orthodox, Coptic Orthodox, Ethiopian Orthodox, Armenian Orthodox, and Indian Orthodox are the five non-Chalcedonian churches. They are also known as the Oriental Orthodox Churches. These five churches do not accept the christological formula of the Tome of Leo passed by the Council of Chalcedon. Therefore the Oriental Orthodox Churches were severely persecuted by the Byzantine and Roman Catholic churches. The persecution of the Syrian Church was so brutal that the church began to decline. But in the middle of the 6th c., a brave bishop named Jacob Baradaeus* gave courage to the Christians and began to revive the church. He traveled far and wide ordaining bishops and priests, and the Syrian Orthodox Church began to thrive again. Knowing the crucial role of Bishop Baradaeus in reviving the Syrian Church, the Byzantine and Roman churches nicknamed the Syrians "Jacobites." Baradaeus, then, is not the founder but the person who revived and saved the church from decline.

The Syriac language. Most of the ancient churches are named after the original language in which their liturgy and other books of worship are written. The Syrian Orthodox Church is known as the Syrian Church because of the Syriac language. Syriac deserves a special status because of its affinity with Aramaic, the mother tongue of Jesus and his disciples. There is a close resemblance between Syriac and Aramaic. Since the language used by Christ was quite similar to Syriac, Syrians claim that Syriac was the language of our Christ and the apostles. By the middle of the 2nd c., Edessa had become the center for the Syriac language. Syriac also played a decisive role in the history of Bible translations. The Syriac Bible *Peshito (Peshitta)* is the official Bible of the Syrian Orthodox Christians. When the Syrian Church was divided because of theological disputes in the 5th c., the language was also divided into West Syriac and East Syriac. The Antiochian Church used West Syriac, and the Nestorian Church used East Syriac.

Theological controversies and misunderstandings. Because the Oriental Orthodox Churches did not accept the christological formula of the Council of Chalcedon, the Byzantine and Roman Catholic churches condemned the Orientals, calling them Monophysites. But the Orientals are not Monophysites, for they condemn not only Monophysitism but also Eutyches, the chief architect of Monophysite teaching. H. B. Biedermann states: "To avoid misunderstanding, it is necessary to explain the term 'Oriental Orthodox Churches.' It refers to those churches which Western ecclesiastical history commonly called, and still erroneously calls, the 'Monophysitic' Churches, i.e., the Coptic, Syrian, Armenian, Ethiopian, and Syro-Indian Churches, to be more precise.

Today they are referred to as 'Oriental Orthodoxy' especially by the World Council of Churches and associate circles, a term increasingly adopted by the ecumenical dialogue in general to distinguish them from the 'Eastern Orthodoxy' of Byzantine tradition."

Faith tradition and practices. The faith traditions and practices of the Syrian Orthodox Church are similar to those of the Universal Syrian Orthodox Church. They comprise mainly faith in the Holy Trinity, the incarnation of the Son of God, the church, the Holy Bible, the traditions of the church, the creed of Nicaea, observation of the sacraments, intercession to St. Mary and to all saints, rites after death and prayer for the departed, daily prayers, lent fasting, observation of Sundays and other feasts, dedication of the church, the three stages of priesthood, the apostolic succession that comes from St. Peter through the holy throne in Antioch, preservation of the apostolic laying on of hands in ordination, infant baptism, the holy cross, the first three ecumenical synods, and the relics of the holy fathers of the church.

Missionary work. The church is highly concerned about the propagation of the Gospel. The Evangelistic Association of the East is a missionary organization that spreads the Gospel in rural and settlement areas. It has already established schools, orphanages, and churches in such areas. Every year, the week of 26-31 Dec is dedicated to the preaching of the Gospel, and during these days an all-Kerala convention is held at Puthencruz. The Servants of the Cross Society* is a similar organization. Spreading the Gospel among Harijans and tribals is their aim. They also try to improve social and economic situations. Conventions are held at diocesan and parish levels. The Syrian Church has also opened a missionary center in North India.

Theological seminary. The Syrian Church has a theological seminary which is affiliated with Serampore University. The seminary provides theological education and training to candidates for the priesthood and gives leadership training to all spiritual organizations of the church. The ecumenical relations and activities of the church are promoted and organized by the seminary.

Spiritual organizations. The Syrian Church also has five official spiritual organizations: the clerical association, the Sunday school association, the youth association, the women's association, and the student movement of India, which aims at the spiritual growth of college students.

Ecumenical relations. The Jacobite Syrian Orthodox Church in India is progressive in regard to ecumenical* relations. In Kerala, theological dialogue is going on between the Catholic Church and the Jacobite Syrian Church. A commission is conducting dialogue with the Mar Thoma Church. The Jacobite Church is helping the Church of the East and the independent Syrian Church in Thozhiyoor. The Jacobite Syrian Church also actively participates in the activities of ecumenical bodies such as the World Council of Churches. An ecumenical secretariat in the church promotes ecumenism and works to improve relationships with other churches. The Jacobite Syrian Church has an open mind regarding ecumenical relations.

Administrative setup. The administration of the Syrian Orthodox Church has been designed in a three-tier system, i.e., the church as a whole, in dioceses, and in parishes as three trusts. The second and third trusts are integral parts of the first but are semiautonomous in temporal matters. Though semiautonomous, the second and third trusts are interdependent and interrelated in spiritual matters and participate in the communion of the one Jacobite Syrian Church.

The church has a democratic system of administration. In all temporal matters, the supreme power is vested in the general body of the church as a whole, which is called the Malankara Syrian Christian Association and meets once every five years. Each diocese has a general body which meets annually. Every parish church also has a general body which meets twice per year. The supreme spiritual authority of the church is vested in the Holy Episcopal Synod. The catholicos of the East is the president of the synod and the head of the Jacobite Syrian Orthodox Church.

Statistics. As a result of internal troubles in 1973, a number of members broke away from the Jacobite Syrian Church and formed the Indian Orthodox (Orthodox Syrian) Church. After the split, the Jacobite Syrian Orthodox Church had about 1.4 million members in and outside Kerala and 625 parish churches.

For the purpose of administration, the church is divided geographically into 11 dioceses, and each diocese is under the charge of a metropolitan. There are also thronal churches directly under the patriarch of Antioch and governed by a bishop delegated by the patriarch. The Evangelistic Association of the East and its parish churches are governed by a metropolitan appointed for that association.

Bibliography

Biedermann, H. B., *An Ecumenical Meeting in the Vienna Dialogue: Five* Pro Oriente *Consultations with Oriental Orthodoxy. Summaries of the Papers,* Booklet No. 2 (1991). • Kaniamparampil, *The Syrian Orthodox Church in India and Its Apostolic Faith* (1989). • Philip, E. M., *The Indian Church of St. Thomas* (1977). • Mar Ignatius Yacob III, H. H., *The Syrian Orthodox* (1985). • Brown, L. W., *The Indian Christians of St. Thomas* (1956). • Babu Paul, D., *Veni, Vidi, Vici: The Story of an Apostolic Visit* (1982); *The Syrian Orthodox Christians of St. Thomas* (1992). • Mathew, Monny A., *History of the Jacobite Syrian Church of India (1972-1980)* (1990). • Geevarghese, D. P. T., *Were the Syrian Christians Nestorians?* (1907).

Adai Jacob

Jaffray, Robert A.

(b. Canada, 1873; d. Pari, Pari, Indonesia, 1945). Outstanding missionary, pioneer, and visionary in Southeast Asia.

Jaffray was born into a prestigious and well-known family, yet he laid these things aside to become God's missionary pioneer in Asia. Trained at A. B. Simpson's Missionary Training Institute in New York, he was ordained and commissioned by the Christian and Missionary Alliance* (C&MA) for South China* in 1896. For 33 years, Wuchow became his home and headquarters for ministry in China, Indochina, and the neighboring islands.

Jaffray started the South China Alliance Press, published the *Bible Magazine* (the C&MA's mission periodical), headed the Wuchow Bible School, spoke at camp meetings, and wrote articles in English and Cantonese.

Early in his ministry in South China, Jaffray was burdened for the 22 million people of Annam (Vietnam*) because they had no Protestant witness. He shared this concern with Simpson, who sanctioned an exploratory trip. Jaffray traveled by boat down the Red River and arrived in Hanoi (Tonkin, North Vietnam). However, as a result of hostility from the people there, he was unsuccessful in establishing a Protestant work.

In 1911, Jaffray led two missionaries to Tourane (Da Nang) in the province of Annam (central Vietnam). They were greeted by Charles Bonnet from the British and Foreign Bible Society* (BFBS) who had conducted limited work there since 1903. Due to ill health, Bonnet was to return to France and the BFBS work relocated to the north in Haiphong. The C&MA purchased Bonnet's house and the first Protestant work was established there.

In 1916, Jaffray became the representative of the Indochina Mission (which included South China Mission). He was responsible for negotiating with the French governor-general to lift the ban and allow Protestant missionaries to work within the prohibited areas. The C&MA missionaries with greater freedom ventured into the northern and central parts of Vietnam, establishing churches in several centers.

In 1928, at the age of 55 and having established work in South China and French Indochina, Jaffray was burdened for the East Indies (Sumatra to New Guinea, South Borneo to the island of Lombok) because they were without Protestant witness. In 1930, despite illness (a heart condition and diabetes) and lack of funds because of the Great Depression, Jaffray, his wife Minnie, and daughter left China and took residence in Makassar (Indonesia). With the help of two colleagues, L. T. Chao and Leland Wang, work was established in Makassar.

Jaffray saw the need for an aircraft to facilitate his ministry, but funds were not forthcoming. In 1939, he inherited some money which was used for the first missionary aircraft. This enhanced travel to the neighboring islands and was greatly used till the Japanese destroyed it in 1942.

As the Japanese occupied many countries in Asia, missionaries were repatriated. Jaffray relocated his missionaries but refused to abandon his people. In 1943, Jaffray, Minnie, and Margaret were interned, although with relative freedom, during which time he wrote extensively. In 1944, Jaffray was taken from his family to a farm in Pari Pari (Indonesia) where eventually he died of ill treatment and starvation in 1945.

Bibliography

Fant, David, Jr., "Robert A. Jaffray," *Alliance Witness* (5 Dec 1973). • King, Louis L., *Missionary Atlas* (1964). • Niklaus, Robert, et al., *All for Jesus* (1986).

Violet B. James

Jainism

Protest movement against Brahminism begun in the 6th c. B.C. in India*.

Jainism never went beyond India as a missionary religion but managed to survive through the centuries. It is the religion of the Jinas, or those who aim to conquer *karma* and *samsara* under the guiding influence of the lives and teachings of the Tirthankaras, as systematized by the educated prince Vardhamana Mahavir (540-468 B.C. or 599-527 B.C.).

There are about three million Jains, almost all in India except for those who migrated to other countries for work and trade. In India, the states of Maharashtra, Gujarat, Rajasthan, and Karnataka are home to almost all the Jains. They are a prosperous and close-knit community with lay and monastic members of both sexes. A high standard of asceticism is prescribed for monks and nuns. The two major sects are the Digambaras (space-clothed) and the Svetambaras (clothed in white). This split occurred in the first century A.D. The entire canon of sacred books was lost by the second century A.D.; however, the Svetambaras had fixed a new canon by the fifth century A.D.

Ahimsa (non-injury), or reverence for life, is the essence of the Jain faith. Everything, even minerals and fire, has life. All forms of life are only different stages in a series of transmigrations caused by *karma*. Higher forms of life are nearer to liberation, getting rid of the *karma* by checking the inflow of fresh *karma* through specific actions and by shedding the past *karma* by austerities and mortification. There is no god to help in this. Following the guidelines given by the Tirthankaras, the soul can be released, which will then attain the infinite states of perception, knowledge, power, and bliss. The attainment of the Three Jewels (right knowledge, right faith, and right conduct) assures the liberation of the soul. As a rigorous ethical system, Jainism is not fatalistic, but in practice it is highly pessimistic. Non-violence, truthfulness, abstention from stealing, charity, and non-attachment are the major vows to be practiced in life. Body, speech, and mind must be kept in perfect control.

The Jains had no temples to begin with, only stupas. Later, temples emerged with images of the Tirthankaras. For Jains, idol worship is "ideal" worship. Today their ways and forms of worship are very close to Hindu worship.

Being a heterodox movement, Jainism had to go through several spells of persecution at the hands of Hindus. Later, they received harsh treatment from Muslims as well. However, the prosperous, enlightened laity of the community always functioned as a strong backbone, especially at times of opposition. The peace-loving Jain community, through their doctrine of *ahimsa* and practice of patience, survived through the centuries even though they never embarked on a conscious and aggressive policy and program of mission.

Given its closeness to Hinduism, the separate existence of Jainism is threatened, and the fear of being absorbed and assimilated into Hinduism is very real. Hindu priests play influential parts in the ceremonies. The Jains have adopted several Hindu social and religious customs. Idolatry has found a place in their worship. Though Mahavir Jain denounced the caste system, the Jain community is not free from caste considerations.

Probably the first encounter between Christianity and Jainism occurred when the European colonialists came to India and established their commercial and political empires. What the Jains saw in these Western Christians (beef-eating, beer-drinking, dancing, and indulgent people) put them off against Christianity, which they considered a foreign religion. Being a non-missionary religion, Jainism could not appreciate the Christian missionary enterprise. While the Western missionary societies had clear approaches to Hinduism*, Islam*, tribal religions, and the Dalits*, they did not take the separate identity of Jainism seriously. Therefore, there was no significant and specific contact between Christianity and Jainism. This is largely true even today.

This does not mean that the two communities did not influence each other. Mrs. Sinclair Stevenson's *Heart of Jainism* (1917) criticized the empty heart of Jainism, that is, its doctrine of *karma* and *samsara* which, she averred, kills all sympathy and human kindness for sufferers. This evoked sharp criticism, and Jain scholars attacked the Christian concept of the just and merciful God. Chapter xix, "Churchianity and the Law of Karma," in the *Encyclopaedia of Jainism* illustrates this ideological encounter. Being a prosperous community, the Jain appropriated the opportunities for Western education in India, and thus in modern times the English-educated Jain generations came under the influence of Western ideologies, philosophies, and values. Christian educational institutions inspired the Jains to start and run their own educational institutions. Christian seminaries have been a model for them in their attempts to train their religious leadership. The Jains have also founded hostels where their students are given religious instruction. Like Christians, Jains too have an extended literature program. Journals such as *The Voice of Ahimsa* (U. P. Aliganj) and *Sraman* (U. P. Varanasi), the Jain *Siddhanta Bhavan* at Arrah, *Parswanath Vidyashram* at Varanasi, and the Jain Mission Society in Bangalore are some examples.

Christian teachings, presence, and missionary enterprise have also inspired the Jains to effect reforms within their religion and to revive their rank and file. More and more young men and women have come forward to take up monastic life and to devote their lives to the cause of Jainism.

The Jains command respect from the Christian community because of their affluence, influence, austerity, and pacifism. The Jains are very appreciative of the life and death of Jesus Christ and his teachings, especially the Sermon on the Mount. They appreciate Christian contributions to nation-building through educational and medical* services, and their patriotic and non-fundamentalistic positions. However, as a religious system Christianity, with its claims and challenges, is still not taken seriously by Jains, perhaps on the ground that it is a foreign religion and that it does not have high regard and respect for the sanctity of life. Turning vegetarian and avoiding the use of alcohol may be the first step Christians can take in helping the Jains remove their prejudices against Christianity and in facilitating fruitful dialogue between the communities.

Bibliography

Daniel, P. S., et al., *Religious Traditions of India* (1988). • De Smet, R., and J. Neuner, eds., *Religious Hinduism* (1968). • Langley, Myrtle, "Respect for All Life: Jainism," in *The World's Religions: A Lion Handbook* (1992). • Nahar, P. C., and K. C. Ghosh, eds., *Encyclopaedia of Jainism* (1988). • Peringamala, José, "Ahimsa as a Point of Departure for Jain-Christian Dialogue," *Bulletin*, Vol. XXV (1990). • Singh, Harbans, and Lal Mani Joshi, *An Introduction to Indian Religions* (1973). • Singh, Hebert Jai, *My Neighbours* (1966). C. V. Mathew

Jakarta

(Batavia, 1619-1942). Capital of Indonesia; see of an apostolic prefect (1807) and vicar (1842); raised to an archdiocese in 1961 comprising the two suffragan dioceses of Bandung (prefecture 1932, diocese 1961) and Bogor (formerly prefecture of Sukabumi, 1948).

In 1522, the Portuguese captain Enrique Leme signed a friendly agreement with the Hindu king of Sunda and planted a *padrao*-stone with a cross on the shore (now in the National Museum). But no Catholic community was allowed to exist in this place for more than 300 years. The Islamic princes of Jayakarta (1527-1619) and the Dutch United East-India Company* (*Verenigde Oost-Indische Compagnie*, VOC ([1619-1792]) forbade all Catholic activities. Notwithstanding the threat of capital punishment, some missionaries passing on their way to the Far East assisted the Catholic *mardijkers* (freed people), former Dutch prisoners from Portuguese territories in India*, Sri Lanka*, and Malacca*, who had been compelled to become members of the Reformed Church. The French Jesuit Alexandre de Rhodes*, deviser of the Vietnamese alphabet, was sentenced to death for celebrating mass with some *mardijkers.* To avoid trouble with France, the Dutch banned him instead, after his belongings were burnt under the gallows (1646).

Because the "black Portuguese" clung so strongly to their old faith, three Protestant churches were built in the 17th c. for the Portuguese-speaking inhabitants of Batavia. The pastors of these churches translated the Bible* into modern Portuguese (1681) and Malay (1733). The descendants of these former Catholic "Portuguese" lost their Christian faith in the beginning of the 19th c. because the official *Indische Kerk* no longer cared about them. During the 18th c., most of the Dutch, Belgian, and German Catholics were visited by priests, who sometimes stayed on in the city illegally for a few years. The VOC was lax, as the officials were too busy making a fortune for themselves. In 1807, King Louis of Holland, brother of Napoleon, granted freedom to all religions.

In 1808, two secular priests arrived in Batavia, obtained a chapel from the governor-general, and started to serve their Dutch and Eurasian flock. When the first bishop, apostolic vicar J. Grooff*, tried to replace three suspended pastors, his actions were regarded as "uncolonial," and, together with his loyal chaplains, he was banned from the colony (1846). After two years without any priest, the new apostolic vicar tried to attract missionaries from religious orders to his vast vicariate, which comprised the whole of present-day Indonesia. Ursuline* nuns arrived in 1856 to start educational work. Three years later Jesuits took over the parishes of Surabaya (1859), Ambarawa (1862, Central Java), and Larantuka* (1863, Flores).

Though the Catholic community in Jakarta remained predominantly Dutch until after World War II*, the indigenous churches in eastern Indonesia and Central Java grew fast (resulting in a constant shrinking of the territory of the vicariate of Jakarta) beginning in 1902, when the Moluccas were handed over to the Missionaries of the Sacred Heart* (MSC). In 1923, all islands outside Java were released from Jakarta to form independent apostolic prefectures or vicariates. Before the Pacific War broke out (1942), the vicariate of Jakarta was confined to the western part of the province of West Java. Its eastern part became the prefecture of Bandung, commissioned to the Crossiers (OSC; 1932). When the apostolic prefecture of Sukabumi was enlarged to form the prefecture of Bogor (1957), the vicariate of Jakarta was reduced to the city and two neighboring districts. In Jakarta, the Jesuits* who took over from the secular priests in 1882 accepted as co-workers both Franciscans* (1929) and Missionaries of the Sacred Heart (1938).

Before 1942, the Catholic educational system had spread its primary schools over most parts of the city and had established a few secondary schools with attached boardinghouses for students. Sisters and brothers engaged primarily in this field. The schools opened the hearts and minds of many Chinese to accept religious instruction and baptism. A Malay parish sprang up on the outskirts (1902) and grew slowly. In 1941, there were reportedly 17,863 Catholics in Jakarta, of whom 1,959 were Indonesians.

During the Japanese occupation, P. Willekens* (1934-52) outwitted the Japanese and stayed on as the "representative of the Vatican." With the help of four priests, a few indigenous sisters, and laypeople, he kept parishes and schools running and helped numerous imprisoned people. Heavy migration to Jakarta after 1945 forced a continuous expansion of diocesan activities.

In 1952, the last Dutch bishop of Jakarta resigned and handed the vicariate over to A. Djajasepoetra, who became its first archbishop in 1961. During Djajasepoetra's time of office (1952-70), the number of faithful grew very fast because of Catholic immigrants from northern Sumatra, Central Java, and the island of Flores, and the natural increase of the local population (about one third of the annual increase is due to adult baptism and another third to child baptism).

The indigenous church of Jakarta then was young, educated, and mobile. Between 1953 and 1961, the number of schools increased from 64 to 101, and the number of pupils from 13,941 to 27,259. Many school buildings were deliberately built on the outskirts; nearly all buildings had to be used for three shifts. In the 1970s, only 38% of the students in Catholic schools were Catholic. Twenty-four new vocational schools were opened before 1975 to enable young people to find work quickly. In spite of this great effort, 45.2% of all Catholic students had to attend non-Catholic schools (1988). To secure their religious instruction, many catechists and teachers of religion had to be trained. An academy for catechetics was opened by the Ursulines in 1970 and later incorporated into the Atma Jaya University (1985). A new government regulation in 1985 required all students to attend religious classes (and from 1989) conducted by teachers approved by the department of religion. After joint protests by the Bishops' Conference and the Council of Churches, private schools were exempted from this regulation to enable them to maintain their own special identity.

The rapid social changes in Jakarta pose a challenge to Christian pastoral care, religious instruction, lay organizations, and family life, which have to adapt continuously in a multireligious and consumeristic society. Issues which continue to concern the church include the poor and unemployed, exploitation of factory workers, squatters ousted by big developers of housing estates, corruption and its effects on all aspects of life, problems of urbanization, the crisis of human values and spirituality, and the lack of recruits to the priesthood and religious life. The church in Jakarta tries to stand on its own feet, to kindle a strong missionary spirit, to become attractive through the daily life of its members, and to be resistant to the temptation of city life and social pressures.

Jakarta, as the capital, is home to a few institutions that contribute toward the development of the church, e.g., the High School of Philosophy, Driyarkara (1969), the Catholic University of Atma Jaya (1960), the Catholic publishers Obor (1951) and Cipta Loka Caraka (1971), the minor seminary Wacana Bhakti (1987), several retreat houses, active national secretariats of *Wanita Katolik** (Catholic Women), Marriage Encounter, *Legio Maria,* and the *Lembaga Daya Dharma* social center (1962), which supports many activities carried out by other foundations or groups involved in the social apostolate.

When Leo Soekoto was ordained archbishop in 1970, there were 20 parishes with more than 70,000 believers. Twenty-five years later, the number of parishes had risen to 48 and believers to over 300,000. There are three equal sources for this growth: migrants, adult conversions, and child baptisms. The aim has been to increase by two parishes each year, but this is impossible because, even though seminaries are full, there is still a lack of priests. Eighteen orders or congregations of priests, three congregations of brothers, and 29 congregations of sisters reside and work in Jakarta.

Bibliography

Van der Velden, J. H., *De Roomsch-Katholieke Missie in Nederlandsch Oost-Indie, 1808-1908* (1908). • *Sinode Keuskupan Agung Jakarta, Menggereja di Jakarta dan sekitarnya pada Tahun 2000* (1990). • Heuken, A., *Ensiklopedi Gereja* II (1992). ADOLF HEUKEN

Jansen, Paul Frederick

(b. 1865; d. 1952). Danish-born American Presbyterian* missionary who worked with lepers in the Philippines*.

Jansen first came to the Philippines in 1898 with the United States Army medical corps, hoping to engage later in leper work. Following his honorable discharge, Jansen married Elizabeth White, an English-born American Christian and Missionary Alliance* missionary. They joined the Philippines Presbyterian Mission in 1902 and worked for a while in Manila.

The Jansens were the pioneer Presbyterian missionaries in Cebu (1902-17) and Batangas (1917-21). Thereafter, they finally had their desire to work with the lepers fulfilled when the Presbyterian Board and the American Mission to Lepers sent them in 1921 as the first resident missionaries in Culion Leper Colony. Receiving assistance from a London evangelical support group called the Culion Leprosy Mission, they stayed in Culion even past retirement in 1933 (see also Leprosy Work).

Bibliography

Rodgers, J. B., *Forty Years in the Philippines* (1940). • "Culion Evangelical Church 75th Anniversary" (souvenir brochure) (1922). • Sitoy, T. V., Jr., *Several Springs, One Stream* (1992). T. VALENTINO SITOY, JR.

Japan

The island nation of Japan is located off the east coast of the Asian continent and stretches approximately 3,000 kilometers from the northeast to the southwest, with a land area slightly larger than Italy or the United Kingdom. This mountainous country uses less than 15% of its land for agriculture. Although the Japanese archipelago includes some 7,000 islands, the population is concentrated on the four main islands of Honshu, Kyushu, Shikoku, and Hokkaido. Close to half of the 125 million Japanese live in the metropolitan areas of Tokyo, Nagoya, and Osaka on the island of Honshu.

Although separated by water, Japan has been deeply influenced by the continental cultures from China* and Korea*. From the 6th c. A.D., many aspects of Chinese culture were brought to Japan by secular and religious scholars and contributed to the overall reshaping of Japanese society. These include the *kanji* writing system, Buddhism*, Confucianism*, science, art, and a centralized system of government. After this influx of Chinese culture Japan's first official history was compiled in the *Nihon shoki* (720) and *Kojiki* (712), works that contain some reliable historical accounts regarding the 5th-6th cs. and mythological traditions regarding Japan's beginnings, the Shinto* cult and pantheon, and Shinto's relation to the imperial household.

Since the late 19th c., Japan has been undergoing a rapid process of modernization. Today the country is recognized as a major industrial and technological power, with a gross national product second only to the United States. At the same time, Japan is a rapidly aging society and has a declining birthrate, a trend which has serious economic and social implications for the near future. Improved health education, diet, and medical care have made Japan's life expectancy one of the highest in the world: 76.36 years for men and 82.84 years for women.

Most scholars agree that the introduction of Christianity to Japan began with the arrival of Francis Xavier* and his Jesuit* colleagues in 1549, though there is some speculation that Nestorian* Christianity may have reached Japan as early as the 13th c. The Roman Catholic* mission began at a time when Japan was a divided country and in the midst of civil wars. In spite of considerable language difficulties, the sustained missionary efforts of the Jesuits, along with the Franciscans* and Dominicans* who arrived later, eventually led to considerable success, particularly in Kyushu and southern Honshu. It is estimated that by 1614 — the year Ieyasu Tokugawa (1542-1616) issued an edict proscribing Christianity — there were 300,000 converts out of a total population of approximately 20 million. The so-called Christian century came to an abrupt end with the unification of Japan under the Tokugawa Shogunate. Government decrees prohibiting Christianity were strictly enforced, European missionaries were expelled, and Japanese converts were systematically persecuted. Christianity continued unofficially for the next two centuries, as the "hidden Christians"* *(Kakure Kirishitan*)* sought to survive in the hostile environment and secretly carried on the faith they had received.

Japan's second encounter with Christianity began in 1859, only six years after Commodore Perry persuaded Japan to open its doors to the West. This too was a time of widespread confusion and chaos. The feudal order was disintegrating rapidly by the end of the Tokugawa period (1603-1868), and the Meiji Restoration government was in the process of building a new order. It was during this difficult transition period that Protestant, Roman Catholic, and Orthodox* missionaries resumed the Christian mission to Japan. Christian missionary efforts began to meet with some success after the Japanese government rescinded the edict prohibiting Christianity in 1873. This initial period of growth for Christian churches ended as the Meiji government stabilized and began to recast a national identity based upon State Shinto and the emperor system. Although churches experienced considerable growth again in the liberal Taisho period (1912-26), particularly among the rapidly growing white-collar class concentrated in urban areas, by the decade of the 1930s Japan had shifted back to authoritarian rule at home, and leaders became preoccupied with mobilizing the masses for military expansion in Asia. In this ultranationalistic environment, church development came to a virtual halt. After varying degrees of resistance to the demands of the state, most churches and Christian institutions survived by gradually accommodating themselves to this nationalistic environment.

With Japan's defeat on 15 Aug 1945 and the enactment of the postwar constitution of Japan (1947), Christian churches found themselves in an entirely new situation. Part of the response to the new situation was the formation of the National Christian Council of Japan (NCCJ, 1948). State Shinto was disestablished and a free-market religious economy was created, which allowed diverse religious groups to compete without government interference for the first time in Japanese history. General MacArthur called for missionary reinforcements to join in building a new Japan. Between 1949 and 1953, over 1,500 missionaries arrived in Japan. While many churches recorded substantial growth in the early postwar period, this growth rate subsided by 1960. In spite of the efforts of over 200 mission societies, representing scores of churches and denominations, as well as the development of a number of independent and indigenous movements, the combined membership stands at roughly one million, which is less than 1% of the total population.

Church statistics taken alone, however, give a misleading picture of the actual role and impact of Christianity in Japanese society. In addition to evangelistic and church development work, many missionaries and Japanese Christians have invested a great deal of time and effort in the fields of education and social welfare. There are close to 2,000 Protestant and Catholic educational institutions — from kindergartens to universities and graduate schools — with a combined enrollment of over 600,000 students. Christians have also played a leadership role in social reform and the development of social welfare institutions. When the Japanese government recognized the services rendered by social welfare organizations in 1926, 22 of the 32 were Christian. Similarly, when in 1956 the government selected four individuals who had rendered distinguished service in the field of social welfare, all four were Christian (J. Ishii*, K. Tomeoka, G. Yamamuro*, and T. Iwasaki).

Inspired by the Christian social vision, many Japanese have also been engaged politically and have worked for the development of a democratic society. I. Abe and T. Katayama*, for example, were founding members of the Social Democratic Party in 1926. In 1947, under the new constitution, Katayama became Japan's first socialist prime minister. During the postwar period, Christians have also been active in various forms of political and social witness on behalf of minorities (such as the Ainu* in Hokkaido and Koreans in Japan) and against resurgent nationalism*.

Even though most Japanese show little interest in church membership, many have a high regard for Christian institutions and the role that Christians have played in the modernization of Japan. There are also some signs that Japanese are more open to Christianity today than in earlier periods. Over the past two decades, average annual Bible* sales have exceeded the total number of Christians. In addition to Bible sales, there are a number of Christian novelists with a significant audience outside the churches. The late Shusaku Endo*, a Roman Catholic novelist, is probably the most widely known both within and outside Japan. One of the most interesting recent trends is the widespread interest in church weddings. Although only 1% of Japanese are Christian, over 30% are choosing to have their wedding conducted in churches or chapels. This suggests that the social stigma once attached to Christianity has declined during the postwar period. Whether this will lead to an increase in the number of Japanese willing to make faith commitments and become involved in the institutional church remains to be seen.

Bibliography

Boxer, Charles Ralph, *The Christian Century in Japan: 1549-1650* (1951). • Breen, John, and Mark Williams, eds., *Japan and Christianity: Impacts and Responses* (1995). • Cary, Otis, *A History of Christianity in Japan*, rev. ed., 2 vols. in 1 (1976). • Drummond, Richard H., *A History of Christianity in Japan* (1971). • Ebisawa Arimichi, ed., *Nihon kirisutokyo rekishi dai jiten* (Historical Dictionary of Christianity in Japan) (1988). • Furuya, Yasuo, ed. and trans., *A History of Japanese Theology* (1997). • Jennes, Joseph, *A History of the Catholic Church in Japan from Its Beginnings to the Early Meiji Era, 1549-1873* (1973). • Kumazawa Yoshinobu and David L. Swain, eds., *Christianity in Japan, 1971-90* (1991). • Lee, Robert, *Stranger in the Land: A Study of the Church in Japan* (1967). • Mullins, Mark R., *Christianity Made in Japan: A Study of Indigenous Movements* (1998). • Phillips,

James M., *From the Rising of the Sun: Christians and Society in Contemporary Japan* (1981). • Reid, David, *New Wine: The Cultural Shaping of Japanese Christianity* (1991). • Yamamori, Tetsunao, *Church Growth in Japan: A Study in the Development of Eight Denominations, 1859-1939* (1974).

MICHIHIKO KUYAMA and MARK R. MULLINS

Japan Evangelical Association

(JEA) *(Nihon Fukuin Domei).* The JEA was founded in Apr 1968 through the merger of three separate organizations with different beginnings and histories but a similar scripturally based faith. The founding members were the Japan Evangelistic Fellowship*, the Japan Protestant Biblical Faith Association, and Missions to Japan, Inc. These scripturally based and genuinely evangelical organizations, while still valuing their own special characteristics, joined together to share the responsibility for preserving and testifying to the historical faith. The objectives of the association are to foster their mutual friendship, provide an avenue for dealing with issues that occur both inside and outside the church, engage in a variety of forms of service, take appropriate measures toward social welfare planning, organize specialized agencies as needed, and cooperate with similar agencies on a worldwide level.

The First Japan Congress on Evangelism was held in Kyoto in 1974 with 1,300 ordained and lay delegates in attendance, holding discussions on the theme of "Japan for Christ." The Second Japan Congress on Evangelism held in Kyoto in 1982 was attended by 2,400 persons coming from inside Japan and from abroad, and it proved to be even more satisfying than the first. A declaration was issued at the end of each of these meetings, and an interpretive manual was published to accompany the second declaration.

Bibliography

Nihon Fujuin Domei, *Habataku Nihon no fujuin-ha* (The Fluttering Evangelistic Denominations in Japan).

OYAMA REIJI, JAPANESE DICTIONARY

Japan Evangelistic Fellowship

(Nihon Fukuin Renmei). Group established in May 1951 primarily by Holiness organizations to promote friendship and mission cooperation and to sponsor evangelistic meetings.

Member organizations include the Japan Church of Jesus Christ, Japan Holiness Church, Japan Free Methodist Church, Japan Nazarene Church, Evangelical Alliance Mission, Christian Brotherhood, Japan Alliance Church, Japan Evangelical Churches Association, Japan Evangelical Band, Japan Rural Mission, Christian Holy Convention, and Japan Christian Layman's League. Some independent churches also belong. This group played a central role in the founding of the Japan Evangelical Association in 1968. The organization has published the hymnal *Seika*, edited by Nakada Ugo.

YAMAZAKI WASHIO, JAPANESE DICTIONARY

Japan, Movement toward Church Union in

Early History. From earliest times, the church has professed in the Apostles' Creed to believe in the "one holy catholic church." However, the division into the Eastern and Western churches and especially the Reformation gave rise to new understandings of doctrine, and an emphasis on faith led Protestant churches to seek greater independence. On top of this, the development of world missions by mission groups from many different nations and races caused the denominations to divide into even smaller bodies.

Even so, churches have been able to see each other's viewpoints as members of one church family. Movements for the reunifying of churches have emerged from time to time. One of these was founded in Japan in Mar 1872, *Nihon Kirisuto Kokai* (Japan Christian Public Society), a church which adopted a Presbyterian-type structure but had no specific denominational connection. It used the doctrine of the Evangelical Alliance, was nondenominational, and sought to be self-supporting, independent, and catholic in nature. The first missionary conference held in Yokohama in Aug 1872 voted to support the principles of this group completely.

However, as early as 1874, other denominational churches were being established by newly arrived missionaries. In opposition to this, already established *kokai* (public society) in the Tokyo-Yokohama and Osaka-Kobe areas again worked to protect the universal spirit of their churches, but those churches related to the American Board of Commissioners for Foreign Missions were dissatisfied with the Presbyterian* type of organization. While they continued to keep the name of *kokai,* they failed to keep its original nature of nondenominationalism.

In contrast, the Presbyterian Church in the United States (North), Reformed Church in America (Dutch), and United Presbyterian Church of Scotland united to form the *Nihon Kirisuto Itchi Kyokai* (Japan Christ Unity Church) in 1877. In January of the next year, churches related to the American Board of Commissioners (Congregational) formed the *Nippon Dendo Kaisha* (Japan Evangelism Association), and then in Apr 1886, they organized the *Nihon Kumiai Kyokai* (Japan Congregational Church) as a church alliance that esteemed self-government, independence, and self-support. About this time, a desire for union of the two churches was kindled. Paralleling the editing of a new hymnal, *Shinsen sambika,* rules and regulations were being drafted in 1888 for the Church of Christ in Japan; in May *Nihon kirisuto kyokai kempo narabini saisoku furoku* (Constitution and Bylaws of the Proposed Church of Christ in Japan) was published; and in November the time for union came about. However, due to inadequate communications be-

Japan, Movement toward Church Union in

tween the two church assemblies in Tokyo and Osaka, opposition to the draft of the constitution arose among those who wielded the power in the Congregational Church, so that for some time the move for union had to be postponed.

In the meantime, representatives of the Methodist* Episcopal Church (South), the Methodist Episcopal Church, USA, and the Methodist Church of Canada met in Nagoya, put forth a proposal for union, and published a joint magazine, *Gokyo* (the Japanese version of *Christian Advocate*). In 1900, they invited the Japan Evangelical Church, the Methodist Protestant Church, USA, and the Church of the United Brethren in Christ to join them. The next year they each elected members to a committee, and in 1902 a basic proposal for union was drafted. However, because the Methodist Protestant Church and the Church of the United Brethren were also discussing the possibility of uniting with the Congregational Church, the Evangelical Church felt the time for union was not yet ripe; only the three original Methodist denominations united to form the Japan Methodist Church in 1907.

Activities to form alliances. There were other movements among the churches besides what has been noted. Beginning with the Bible* translation project in 1872, the ecumenical movement moved forward. The year 1878 was the first year in which elected delegates from each denomination met to talk about mission and to exchange information. At the fourth such gathering in 1885, the Japan Christian Evangelical Alliance was formed. This alliance dissolved in 1906 but was reorganized in 1909, and, in late 1911, eight major denominations came together to form the Japanese Federation of Churches. This alliance reorganized to form the National Christian Council of Japan (NCC) in November 1923.

The yearly meeting of the Missionary Alliance in 1925 voted to consider joining the NCC, and the NCC set up a committee to facilitate the opportunity for church union. Just then they were inspired by news of the forming of the United Church of Canada (Methodist, Presbyterian, and Congregational) and felt the talk of union was peaking. So they went on to issue a basic proposal for the union of various denominations in Japan. The Anglican Church of Japan issued a written appeal to churches across Japan under the name of the Central Committee for the Promotion of Church Union. In 1930, a joint committee composed of representatives from 12 denominations was formed and drew up a tentative draft. However, they were unable to reach an agreement on the use of the word *kokai* and on the problem of apostolic succession.

In Apr 1930, the Japan Congregational Church and the Japan Christian Church merged. A proposal to pursue joint mission was again passed at a meeting of representatives of a number of denominations. Beginning in 1931, lay groups like the Christian Association for Promoting Church Union of All Denominations became active in the movement and put pressure on the NCC. The Oxford Conference on Life and Work held in 1937 also offered a stimulus for Japanese church union.

Ebisawa Arimichi

Formation of the United Church of Christ in Japan. In 1936, a preparatory committee for church union centering on the NCC was formed. In January of the following year, they publicized the constitution of the Church of Christ in Japan *(Nihon Kirisuto Kokai)* and announced that the union would take place in 1940 on the occasion of the legendary 2,600th year of the founding of Japan. It was a time when war threatened, and the Religious Organizations Law had already been enacted in 1939 and gone into effect in Apr 1940. Moreover, the ministry of education was pressuring all Protestant denominations to unite, for it had become almost impossible for individual denominations to exist on their own.

The push toward union was further accentuated by the formation of a nationwide lay movement to commemorate the 2,600th anniversary, and the Association of Christian Schools passed a proposal at their general assembly supporting such a union. At the celebration held at Aoyama Gakuin University on 17 Oct 1940, the Protestant churches announced a comprehensive union. A number of committees worked for the next year making the necessary arrangements, with similar denominations gathering to find commonalties. In the end, 11 blocs were formed which together made one united church; the blocs were designed to preserve the traditions of each group, which actually made the overall union something of an anomaly. The denominational blocs were:

1. Japan Presbyterian Church
2. Japan Methodist Church, Methodist Protestant Church
3. Japan Congregational Christian Church, Japan Church of the United Brethren in Christ, Japan Evangelical Church, Christian Church (Disciples of Christ)
4. Japan Baptist Church
5. Japan Evangelical Lutheran Church
6. Holiness Church (a splinter group following the 1933 split of the Holiness Church; others of the Holiness tradition were placed in bloc 9)
7. Japan Christian Evangelism Church
8. Japan Seika Christian Church
9. Kiyome Church (another group of the Holiness tradition)
10. Japan Independent Christian Church League
11. Salvation Army

The United Church of Christ in Japan (UCCJ) *(Nihon Kirisuto Kyodan)* came into being at its founding convention held on 24-25 Jun 1941 at Fujimicho Church in Tokyo. Most of the Anglican (Episcopal) churches, however, did not join this union, because they were unable to overcome hierarchical and doctrinal differences. After the war, along with the dissolution of the Religious Organizations Act and the coming of missionaries from new denominations to Japan, a number of the smaller denominations left the UCCJ and a variety of newer ones were started; but the larger churches that had been the core of the union, such as the Japan Presbyterian Church, the Japan Methodist Church, and the Japan Congregational Church, remain in the United Church of Christ in Japan.

Bibliography

Miyakoda Tsunetaro, *Nihon kirisuto-kyo godo shiko* (History of Japan's Christian Church Union) (1967). • Inoue Tokichi, ed., *Kyokai godo ni kansuru sanko shiryo* (Reference Materials Related to Church Union) (1931). • National Council of the Church of Japan, *Shokyoha genko seido chosa,* appendix, *Kyokai godo ni kansuru chosa* (Survey of the Present System of Denominations, with Survey of Church Union) (1932). MIYAKODA TSUNETARO

Japanese Overseas Christian Medical Cooperative Service (JOCS)

The JOCS, a modest but very pointed initiative with a branch in Kyoto since 1979, owes its inception to a team of seven Christian students from Kyoto University Medical School who were sent to China* in 1938 to render medical* help to refugees who had become victims of the Japanese invasion of China the year before. This team, on their return, appealed to Christian youth groups at medical schools in Japan* and organized the Japan Youth Medical Association in 1939, which immediately sent yet another team to Wuhu (South of Nanjing), China. When the association received support from the Young Men's Christian Association* (YMCA) in 1942, it opened the Chaotian Hospital on the outskirts of Nanjing, which continued operating through 1945.

After World War II*, the name of the association was changed to Christian Medical Association in Tokyo (1946) and to Japan Christian Medical Association (1948), before it finally became the JOCS (incorporated 1962) in 1960. It sent its first overseas worker to Bandung, Indonesia*, in 1961. An orphanage built in Nepal* in 1970 had to be closed in 1978.

The objectives of the JOCS are defined as: (1) to send medical workers all over Southeast Asia to areas where medical facilities are not available; and (2) to invite students and trainees from these areas for studies in Japan to enable them to provide for effective self-help. In 1964 JOCS joined a short-term medical services program with colleagues from Taiwan*, and since then it has cooperated in exchange programs with Taiwan and Korea* almost every year. Besides this, it has organized study seminars for aspiring overseas workers since 1977.

JAPANESE DICTIONARY

Japanese Shinto Shrine Worship. *See* Shintoism and Christianity in Korea

Java Churches

Christianity has been present on the island of Java at least since the 16th c., and possibly even the 7th c. (Nestorians*). The 16th-c. Portuguese mission made some converts on the northeast coast; the Protestant Dutch (VOC), who drove out the Portuguese and gradually conquered the greater part of Java, established large Christian communities, consisting of Europeans, Eurasians, and Asians from outside Java in the major cities of the north coast. However, they did not bring the Gospel to the indigenous peoples, the Sundanese in West Java and the Javanese in Central and East Java, or even to the people of Chinese descent who, since the 17th c., held a key position in the economy as artisans and traders.

Only in the 19th and 20th cs. did Christianity take root among the Sundanese and the Javanese, the most populous groups in Indonesia, numbering 25 million and 75 million respectively. Besides the churches founded among them by the Dutch Protestant missionary societies, there are now several other churches, such as the Roman Catholic Church and other Protestant churches that originated mainly from the United States, e.g., the Pentecostal* and the Seventh-Day Adventist* churches. Moreover, a number of other churches were founded by migrants from Christianized regions outside Java, such as North Sumatra (the *Huria Kristen Batak Protestan,* HKBP; see Batak), Ambon, Minahasa, and Timor (*Gereja Protestan Indonesia Bahagian Barat,* GPIB). In many places, especially in West Java, these immigrant churches are the largest local Christian communities.

Recent history: mainline Protestants. In the first half of the 19th c., the Dutch colonial government, for political reasons, hindered the newly founded Dutch missionary societies from working among the indigenous population. Not until about 1850 (Central and East Java) or even 1865 (West Java) were these missions allowed to start evangelizing Java proper. In West Java, the Gospel was brought by one Dutch society, and for some time (1905-28) by the Episcopal Methodists* from America. Out of this effort among a thoroughly Islamized population grew a tiny Sundanese church, the *Gereja Kristen Pasundan* (GKP, independent 1934; ca. 30,000 members today), and an overseas Chinese church, the *Gereja Kristen Indonesia Jawa Barat* (GKI-Jabar, independent 1940; 45,000 members today).

In Central and East Java, the missionary situation was far more complicated, even when we leave the Catholic Church and the Protestant churches with a North American background out of the picture. This linguistically and ethnically more or less homogeneous region was evangelized by four, for some time even five, Dutch missions belonging to distinct denominations: Mennonites*, Dutch Reformed, Congregationalists, and conservative Calvinists. This resulted in four distinct Javanese-speaking churches, to which may be added three ethnically Chinese churches that belong to another three denominations.

The total membership of the seven churches is about 550,000.

The strongly Islamic region surrounding Mount Muria, in the northern part of Central Java, was evangelized by the Dutch Mennonites (*Doopsgezinde Zendingsvereniging,* 1851). From this effort originated two churches: the Javanese-speaking *Gereja Injili di Tanah Jawa* (GITJ, independent 1940; 70,000 members in 1998) and the *Gereja Kristen Muria Indonesia* (GKMI, independent 1939 under the name *Tiong Hoa Kie Tok Kauw Hwee Muria;* membership 13,000). Both still cherish their Mennonite heritage, with its distinctive traits such as the avoidance of political and cultural involvement, abstinence from violence, emphasis on the autonomy of local churches, and strict maintenance of church discipline. However, in the war of liberation against the Dutch (1945-49), Mennonite Christians fought together with their fellow countrymen and in this way eliminated the stigma resting on Christianity as the religion of the Dutch oppressors. Unlike the other Chinese churches in Central and East Java, the GKMI did not join the *Gereja Kristen Indonesia,* which was born in 1988 when the three churches of that name in West, Central, and East Java convened in one synod.

The other mission working in northern Central Java was the *Neukirchener Mission,* also known as *Salatiga Zending.* Like the Mennonite mission, it was pietist in character, but it distinguished itself in that the missionaries adhered to "faith mission" principles. The autonomy of the congregation was emphasized, and the mission endeavored to avoid the fortress mentality that had been created by the establishment of "Christian villages" governed by the missionary according to the policy of the Mennonite and East Java missions. The weakness of this pietist mission was that it did next to nothing to prepare the congregations for independence and for a life in the midst of a free and modernizing Indonesia. For a long time after its becoming independent (1937), the church on this mission field, *Gereja Kristen Jawa Tengah Utara* (GKJTU; 20,000 members) suffered from lack of well-educated theological and lay leaders.

Quite different was the policy of the (Neo-)Calvinist mission (*Zending der Gereformeerde Kerken in Nederland,* ZGKN) in South Central Java, where the influence of orthodox Islam* was less felt than in other parts of the islands, and where traditional Javanese culture was still very much alive. It concentrated its efforts upon the great cities and established a network of Dutch-language schools, which after political independence was crowned by a Christian University at Salatiga. After 1945, Javanese Christians from this region played an important part in the Protestant political party of Indonesia, PARKINDO*. Church organization was strictly Presbyterian*; in the church order of the *Gereja Kristen Jawa* (GKJ) (1931), the Heidelberg Catechism was regarded as normative for the interpretation of Scripture. With 225,000 members today (1998), the GKJ is the largest Javanese-speaking Protestant church.

The *Gereja Kristen Jawi Wetan* (East Java Christian Church) grew out of a Dutch Reformed mission which was strongly pedagogical in character, nurturing its converts in so-called Christian villages. Even now the church (150,000 members) is strongest in the countryside. Their denominational differences notwithstanding, the various churches mentioned here are all members of the Indonesian Council of Churches* (PGI).

Other Protestant Bodies. Before World War II*, several missions from America were active on Java: the Methodists (who retired, however, in 1928 to concentrate on Sumatra), the Salvation Army* (1894), Adventists (1909), and Pentecostals* (1921). Of these, the Pentecostal movement was to become the most important. Because of its fragmentation (which was particularly rampant between 1931 and 1971), it is difficult to estimate its membership, but it might be well over one million on Java alone.

Roman Catholic Church. During the 17th and 18th cs., the Catholic Church was practically banished from the Dutch colonial territory. When the mission returned (1808), at first it concentrated on the Eurasians in the coastal cities. Only after 1890 were the first converts from the Javanese won. During most of this period, missionary work was carried out by the Dutch province of the Society of Jesus* (Jesuit Order), which, like its Calvinist counterpart, concentrated on Central Java as the cultural center of Indonesia, and the cities of Yogyakarta and Surakarta (Solo) as the epicenters of Javanese culture. Between 1927 and 1932, the other parts of Java were turned over to the Carmelites* and other religious orders.

The Jesuits founded colleges and theological* seminaries (Mendut and Muntilan near Yogyakarta are among the most famous), and some Jesuits (F. van Lith*) encouraged the Javanese Catholics to engage in politics — even nationalist politics. The first Javanese priest was ordained in 1926; in 1940 a Javanese, Albertus Soegijapranata*, received episcopal rank and was appointed apostolic vicar of Semarang; in 1961, with the establishment of the hierarchy in Indonesia (until then formally still a mission field), he became the first archbishop of Semarang. Catholicism also made headway among the Chinese, especially in West and East Java (Jakarta*, Bandung, Surabaya).

With this background, it is not surprising that after the war Catholics of Javanese and Chinese descent succeeded in establishing a firm foothold in politics and the army (cabinet ministers and prominent army generals), in education (the Catholic schools are famous throughout the country, and there are several Catholic universities), and in the mass media (Indonesia's largest publishing company and the largest daily of the country, even of Southeast Asia, *Kompas,* were both founded by Catholics and still reflect their Catholic background). The primate of the Indonesian church is the archbishop of Semarang, with further sees in Purwokerto, Surabaya, and Malang;

West Java has an archbishop in the national capital, Jakarta, and bishops in Bogor and Bandung.

The Indonesianization of the clergy is making progress. Of the Indonesian monastic congregations founded in the 20th century, several are based in Java. Sendang Sono in Central Java is an important center of pilgrimage*. Several Indonesian orders have been founded, with monasteries and nunneries. At present, the number of Catholics on Java is over one million (only 40,000 in 1940), about one fifth of their total number in the country.

Present situation. Today, the percentage of Christians on Java is one of the lowest in the country, and a large portion of the Christian community consists of people of Chinese descent. Consequently, the churches on this island suffer more from mob violence than do those in other parts of the country. Since 1994, hundreds of church buildings and schools have been destroyed. The total number of Christians in Java, including Jakarta, may be put at 3.5 million, or 3% of the population, of whom about one third belong to the Javanese ethnic entity.

Bibliography

Hartono, Chris, *Gereja di Jawa Barat* (1979). • Van den End, Thomas, *Ragi Carita. Sejarah Gereja di Indonesia,* Vol. I (1980); Vol. II (1998) (3rd ed., with exhaustive bibliography).

CHRIS HARTONO and THOMAS VAN DEN END

Jeffrey, David Ivory (D. I.) and Ruth

(b. 1894 [D. I.] and 1898 [Ruth]; d. 19?? [D. I.] and 1974 [Ruth]). Canadian Christian and Missionary Alliance* (C&MA) missionaries to Vietnam*.

Canadian missionary D. I. Jeffrey arrived in Vietnam in Dec 1918. Two years later, he met Ruth Isabel Goforth, newly arrived from Canada and also an appointee of the C&MA. Ruth was well acquainted with Asia, being the daughter of Jonathan and Rosalind Goforth, famed Canadian Presbyterian missionaries to China. The two were married in Jun 1921 and continued their service until retirement in 1967, completing 46 years of service.

The Jeffreys were sent by the C&MA to its French Indochina mission in Hanoi, which had been opened in 1911 under the auspices of the C&MA's South China Mission. They arrived at a time when the C&MA mission was still in its infancy, with no church organization and few converts. After learning the Vietnamese language, the Jeffreys opened the Tourane (Da Nang) Bible School in an old horse stable in 1921. D. I. served as a teacher for three or four years in a residential program that trained Vietnamese Christian workers for one year before being sent out to distribute Bibles and tracts. After successful field work, the Bible students would return for three years of added study before becoming recognized Christian workers. Invariably, several years of successful pastoral ministry would intervene before the candidate would be recommended for ordination.

In 1927, D. I. was chosen as chairperson of the field. In 1929, he accompanied Paul Gunther to Siam (Thailand*) to open that field for the Alliance. In that same year, he accompanied G. E. Roffe to the Kingdom of Laos* to open mission work in that country. The last leg of the journey in Laos was on horseback over the mountains to Luang Prabang from Vientiane.

Excepting for two years of internment by the Japanese in Mytho, Vietnam (1943-45), Jeffrey alternated with E. F. Irwin in the capacity of chair of the mission. The philosophy of D. I. and other mission leaders was rather progressive for the times. As local church bodies were formed, they became part of a national church administered by the Vietnamese themselves as rapidly as possible. The development of the national church and leadership was constantly a priority goal. The aim was eventually to have everything under the national church. Jeffrey stated: "Self-support was our objective. We did not hire nationals." Small sums of financial assistance were given to get a local church body of believers functioning and self-supporting. Immediately following World War II*, the national church was given considerable financial assistance because of the devastation, but this was withdrawn gradually to return the national church to self-support.

The Jeffreys were always a team while being effective individually as well. They were pioneers in opening the evangelical work among the Vietnamese (Kinh) in the (then) capital city of Hue. Later, when assigned to Saigon, Ruth raised the funds and supervised the construction of the large Vietnamese church building on Galliene (Tran Hung Dao) Boulevard. She was also very active in youth work in Saigon (now Ho Chi Minh City) and launched the publication of *Rang Dong,* a magazine which was very successful in reaching the unchurched youth culture. She also supervised the publication of literature to assist pastors and raised support for translators and secretaries from friends and churches abroad in Canada and the United States.

While D. I. was tied to administration of the mission, Ruth was active in holding short-term Bible schools in Nhatrang and Saigon and carried on extensive church visitation throughout South Vietnam during the 1960s, when the two Vietnams were at war. Any and all kinds of transportation had to be called on to reach her destination.

In 1955, Ruth also began a systematic visitation program in military hospitals, army camps, and prisons in the Saigon area. This work was continued by others, including Canadians Rev. and Mrs. Garth Hunt, who extended the ministry throughout the length and breadth of South Vietnam before reunification under North Vietnam in 1975.

Bibliography

Irwin, E. F., *With Christ in Indo-China* (1937). • Jeffrey, Ruth Goforth, *Amazing Grace: My Life in China and Vietnam* (n.d.). • "Veteran Missionaries Lead Way in Aid

to Cong Hoa Hospital," *World Vision Magazine* (Jan 1966). • Bailey, Anita, "Amazing Grace," *The Alliance Witness* (24 Apr 1974).
JAMES F. LEWIS

Jesuit. *See* Society of Jesus

Jesus Caritas

Universal brotherhood of diocesan priests inspired by the life and example of Charles de Foucauld (1859-1916), who understood the vocation of the priesthood as a vocation of universal brotherhood.

The members of Jesus Caritas, who are called brothers, maintain strong human and spiritual links among themselves, comparable to those of a congregation. They make a personal commitment to follow the way of life and the aspirations of the fraternity, as well as to support the diocesan priests of their respective regions. Jesus Caritas promotes the various diocesan and national efforts to unite diocesan priests in associations and encourages closer exchange of resources and interests among them. The fraternity is ready to share its experiences and the fruits of its search for priestly spirituality with others.

De Foucauld found the unique love of Christ to be a significant binding force calling for constant personal transformation and growth in unity. Hence the fraternity is called Jesus Caritas. To de Foucauld, fearless self-abandonment and a radical commitment to serve others constitute the only way to respond to Christ's love. Adoration of God, sharing and presence among the poor and nonbelievers, friendship and fellowship among priests, and universal communion are the essentials of Jesus Caritas.

The structure of Jesus Caritas is informal, nonhierarchical, and nondirective. Small groups of brothers share, offer support, review their lives, and listen to the Word together. The International Council is responsible for the management and growth of the association. The international, national, and regional officers are elected by the brothers.

In Asia, Jesus Caritas started in the 1970s and is gradually growing. It is present in Bangladesh*, India*, Indonesia*, Pakistan*, and the Philippines*. The Asia brothers still have to find their own ways and means to live the spirit of the association within the key realities and major concerns of Asia: development, human rights, evangelization, and dialogue with believers of other religions.

Bibliography

Emmanuel Asi, *Growing in Discipleship* (1993). • Beurle, Klaus, *Jesus Caritas Asia: Open Hands* (JC-Asia Newsletter).
DIGNA C. DACANAY

Jesus Family

(Yesu Jiating). An indigenous church, the Jesus Family was founded by Jing Dianying (b. Shandong, China, 1890), a converted Buddhist, in 1921 at Mazhuang, Shandong. Jing was converted by Methodist* missionary Nora Dillenbeck while he was teaching her Chinese. She left the Methodist board and helped Jing establish the Jesus Family, staying in the commune for two years until her death from illness. She was buried in Mazhuang.

In 1921, Jing and his wife started a Christian cooperative store dealing in clothing, staple food, and eventually silk weaving to raise funds. Jing also donated the land he had inherited. A chapel was built and farming commenced. In the 1930s, Jing and his companions conducted evangelistic tours all over northern China. During the Sino-Japanese War, the Jesus Family grew in northern and northwestern China. In 1941, there were 140 communities in eight provinces with 6,000 members.

Many donated their homes to the Jesus Family. The organization of each commune or "little home" was patterned after the one in Mazhuang, called the "old home." Each commune was self-sufficient with its own industries (carpentry, bootmaking, bakery, stone masonry, bookbinding, printing, etc.) and farming. There were also schools and kindergartens. The center of each commune was the chapel, and the head of each commune was the Jiachang, or "family head." Members had to agree to donate their possessions and lead simple lives in the commune in submission to the Jiachang. Each day, everyone had to work and attend the several meetings for prayer, singing, fellowship, and the interpretation of dreams.

After the Communist takeover of China, some members were disillusioned by the oppressive organizational structure as well as the suspected corruption and licentiousness of some leaders. Jing was denounced by his own nephew and imprisoned in 1952. He was sentenced to 20 years in prison for alleged links with the Kuomintang. Mazhuang was reorganized and renamed the Beixin Chuang. Other centers either became ordinary churches or were dissolved. In 1958, the various centers were absorbed under the national church unification thrust which stressed united worship of all denominations.

Bibliography

Rees, Vaughan, *The "Jesus Family" in Communist China* (1976). • Whyte, Bob, *Unfinished Encounter* (1988).
CHINA GROUP

Ji, Andrew

(Ji Zhi-wen, or Andrew Gi) (b. Shanghai, China, 1901; d. United States, 13 Feb 1985). Chinese evangelist.

Ji's father died when he was 12. In 1923, while he was studying English at Bethel Secondary School in Shanghai, a China Inland Missionary (CIM) team set up an evangelistic meeting at the school, and Ji repented and was born again. In 1924, he was selected as an officer of the post office in Shanghai. One year later, Wang Tai came to Shanghai for an evangelistic meeting. Ji was deeply touched by Wang's witness and dedication to full-time ministry, so he decided to dedicate himself for life-long, full-time service for the Lord. Ji was baptized by Wang and took upon himself the biblical name of Andrew, indicating his own willingness to bring people to the Lord. At the same time, Ji formed the Bethel Evangelism Team, spreading the Gospel in Shanghai and nearby cities.

In 1926, after being accepted by John Gu, Ji began his official full-time ministerial life. Soon after, Ji was ordained by Rev. Sontas at Bethel Church.

On 10 Jan 1928, Ji married Dorcas Zhang, a colleague on the Bethel Evangelism Team. Thereafter, the Jis began their nationwide evangelistic ministry, bringing tens of thousands of people to Christ. Between 1931 and 1935, Bethel Evangelism Team had reached 133 cities, traveled 50,000 kilometers, conducted 3,385 evangelistic meetings, reached out to nearly half a million people, and brought an estimated 50,000 people to the Lord. These few years of labor had brought about a great revival in China* that would last for the next 12 years.

In 1936, Ji visited the United States for the first time and conducted evangelistic meetings in Los Angeles.

In 1937, Japan* invaded China, and Ji began his ministry of looking after the orphans inside the war zone. One year later, he brought 103 orphans to Hong Kong* for safety.

In 1939, Ji visited the United States for the second time and again conducted evangelistic meetings. He also met Irish evangelist Rev. Owen and invited him to conduct evangelistic meetings in China.

In 1947, Ji rented Da Lu Danching Hall in Shanghai for an evangelistic rally; thereafter he began his worldwide evangelistic campaign on faith. One year later, in 1948, he founded the China Evangelism Association and established a home for orphans in Shanghai.

In 1949, Ji made his third evangelistic visit to the United States. Then, because of the change of political power in China, Ji moved to Hong Kong and conducted evangelistic meetings at Kuai Le Theater; he also set up a publishing venture, sent Paul Shen to begin evangelism in Taiwan, and built an orphanage home, a Bible school, and churches.

In 1950, Ji received an honorary D.Lit. from Oregon Bible Seminary in the United States. The following year, he began his Southeast Asia evangelistic tour, covering countries such as the Philippines*, Indonesia*, Singapore*, and Malaya. In 1952, Ji established the China Evangelism Association in Indonesia, meanwhile building churches, primary and secondary schools, and the South East Asia Bible College, of which Xu Gong-sui became principal, succeeded by Peter Wangso in 1964.

In 1960, Ji established Bethel Bible College in Thailand*, with Lin Pei-yi appointed as principal. That same year, Mrs. Ji moved to the United States to manage the main office there.

In 1967, Ji had an operation in the United States for kidney stones. He soon recovered, but his health was deteriorating. On 20 Oct 1978, Ji retired from the ministry and spent time with his wife in Los Angeles. On 30 Jan 1985, Ji underwent an operation for lung cancer, and he passed away three days later at the age of 85.

Bibliography

Gi, Andrew, *I Was Not Disobedient to the Vision from Heaven* (1968) (in Chinese); *Fifty Years in Ministry to the Lord* (1975) (in Chinese). • *The Father of the Fatherless* (1996) (in Chinese). PETER WONGSO

Jia Ding Conference

(1628). A conference held in the late Ming period in which the Jesuit* missionaries discussed what term they should use for God (Latin: *Deus*).

The conference was held in Jia Ding, presently a suburb of Shanghai. When Jesuit missionaries came to China during the late Ming period, Matteo Ricci* and others used the terms for God found in the Confucian writings: *Tian* and *Shangti*. Nicolo Longobardo* and other Jesuit missionaries opposed this usage and opted instead to use the Chinese transliteration of *Deus*. In order to find agreement on the term to be used, 11 Jesuit missionaries held a meeting in Jia Ding in 1628. The Jesuit superior in Macau, Andreas Palmeiro, presided over the meeting. Nicolas Trigault* and others insisted on the term *Shangti*, but the conference failed to arrive at a mutually accepted term. CHINA GROUP

Jia Yu Ming

(b. 1880; d. 1964). Chinese Christian pastor and theologian.

Originally from Shandongshen, Jia studied in Dengzhou Wenhuiguan in his earlier years. After his graduation in 1901, he entered a seminary of the Presbyterian* Church to receive his education in theology. In 1904, he was ordained as a pastor and went to Yizhou, Shandong, to preach. He went to teach in Nanjing Jinling Seminary in 1915 and then to Tengxian, Shandong, as vice-principal at North China Theological Seminary. In 1921, he started a bulletin, *Ling Guang Magazine*, in Nanjing. He became principal of Jinling Girls' Theological Seminary in 1930. Jia started a Chinese Christian Bible institute in Nanjing in 1936 and became its principal. During World War II*, the school moved to Chongqingshi in Shichuanshen and shifted back to Shanghai after the defeat of the Japanese. In 1948, Jia attended the World Gospel Conference held in Holland and was nominated vice-chairman. In 1954, he was chosen as vice-chairman of the Committee of the Chinese Church Three-Self Patriotic Movement*.

Throughout his life, Jia continued to advocate that Christians focus on gaining knowledge, combined with maintaining a daily quiet time, so that faith and spirituality can be displayed in one's daily life. He authored

Study of Theology, Basic Bible Truth, Total Salvation, and *Saint's Heart Song* (a hymnal). China Group

Jiang Wen Han

(b. 1908; d. 1984). Leader of the Chinese Christian Student Movement* and scholar.

Originally from Hunan, Jiang came into contact with Christianity when he entered the Changsha Young Men's Christian Association* (YMCA) English night school at the age of 12. He was baptized in 1923 at Xinyihui Church. After he graduated from high school, he studied at Yali Institution, Huazhong University, and Jinlu University. After he graduated from university in 1930, he joined the All China YMCA. In 1934, he went to the University of Pennsylvania in the United States to further his studies and received his master's degree in the second year. In 1945, he again went to the United States to study at Columbia University and received his doctoral degree two years later. Each time he returned home, he went back to the YMCA to work, ever making sure that Christian students were aware of the times.

During the resistance against the Japanese in 1937, Jiang was acting secretary for the All China Students Relief Committee. With the outbreak of the Pacific War, he set up student rescue work, adopting the principles of no political or religious discrimination. He also raised funds to help the Tingan Student Sanatorium. In 1949, Jiang was appointed assistant executive secretary of the YMCA National Committee. He became executive secretary of the Association for the Development of Learning in 1955 and of the United Christian Publishing House in 1957.

In 1979, Jiang was employed by the History Research Center of the Shanghai Social Science Institution as a special researcher, carrying out research into the history of Chinese Christianity. Within five years, he wrote books such as *The Ancient Chinese Church and the Jews of Kaifeng* and *The Catholic Jesuits in China During the Ming and Qing Dynasties.* Jiang was one of the initiators of the Chinese Church Three-Self Patriotic Movement* and was chosen as a member when the Committee of the Chinese Church Three-Self Patriotic Movement was established in 1954. He was also nominated as vice-chairman when the China Protestant Association was established in 1980.

Bibliography

Wickeri, Philip, *Seeking the Common Ground* (1988).

China Group

Jiang Zhangchuan

(Z. T. Kaung) (b. Jiangsu, China, Dec 1884; d. 1958). Chinese Methodist* bishop.

Jiang Zhangchuan, or Z. T. Kaung, was the eldest child among four boys and two girls. His father was a wealthy contractor in Shanghai. At age 14, Jiang was sent to a Methodist middle school in Shanghai. Under the influence of a teacher, Clara E. Steger, he became a Christian at age 19, over the protests of his family, who disowned him.

Between 1905 and 1909, Jiang supported himself by teaching and studying at the Anglo-Chinese College in Shanghai. He directed the church school at Moore Memorial Church, which was the largest Protestant congregation in Shanghai, and he preached at neighborhood meetings sponsored by the church. He was one of the first three students in the experimental theology department of Suzhou University. When he graduated in 1912, he became the only person ever to receive a bachelor of divinity degree from Suzhou University. (The theology department merged with Nanjing Theological Seminary in 1913.) During this period, Jiang was reconciled with his family, who were eventually converted to Christianity.

Jiang was ordained in 1912, served as the assistant minister at Moore Memorial Church, and became a full-fledged pastor a year later. Ill from overwork, he was transferred in 1917 to a smaller church in Huzhou, Zhejiang, where he served for three years. In 1921, he was concurrently the presiding elder of the Suzhou district and the chaplain of Suzhou University. He was a trustee of the university (1927-31) and a board member of Nanjing Theological Seminary (1936-40). He was also chairman of the Student Volunteer Movement (1920-30), chairman of the Chinese Home Mission Society founded by Cheng Jingyi* for evangelism in the interior of China, especially in the southwest (1923-41), the head of the Executive Council of the Methodist Episcopal Church (South) (1934-41), and the director of the China Sunday School Union (1937).

In 1923, Jiang became pastor of Allen Memorial Church in Shanghai, whose members included the well-known Sung (Soong) family. Jiang baptized Chiang Kai-shek (Jiang Jie Shi) in October 1930. In the early 1930s, Jiang worked mainly among university students at St. John's in Suzhou. He returned to Shanghai in 1936 to pastor Moore Memorial Church, then the largest Protestant congregation in East Asia. He did a lot of work among the poor and the refugees. In 1941, he was elected the bishop of North China. He was under constant surveillance during the Japanese occupation of North China because of his close ties with the Sung family and Chiang Kai-shek. His diplomatic skill was manifest in his ability to resist the Japanese insistence on a union of the Chinese and Japanese churches. When the Communists came into power, Jiang was among the 19 Protestant leaders who met with Chou En-lai in Beijing in April 1950. He supported the formation of the Three-Self Patriotic Movement*.

Bibliography

Boorman, Howard L., ed., *Biographical Dictionary of Republican China,* Vol. 1 (1967).

China Group

John of Marignolli

(b. Florence, Italy, ?; d. Breslau, 1358 or 1359). Franciscan* and papal emissary to the emperor of China*.

John of Marignolli undertook the last-known Western mission to eastern Asia before the 16th c. The mission was prompted by a group of Alans at Khanbaliq (Beijing), the Mongol capital of China, who, hoping to receive spiritual direction, sent letters to the pope after the death of John of Monte Corvino*. A Franciscan delegation was sent; John was one of them. He left Avignon (where the papal court had its residence at the time) in 1338, traveling by land across Central Asia, together with an enormous war horse (allegedly three-and-a-half meters long and nearly two meters high) sent by the pope as a gift to the emperor.

John reached Khanbaliq in 1342. Later he reported that the Franciscans were received hospitably, that the cathedral and several churches established by Monte Corvino still existed, and that the physical needs of the Franciscans were supplied by the imperial court. In 1345 he left Khanbaliq for Europe, traveling by way of India*; he was plundered of his imperial gifts for the pope in Ceylon but arrived safely in Avignon in 1353. In 1354, John was made bishop of Bisignano. Soon after, he became a royal chaplain of the king of Bohemia, who had been recently confirmed as the Holy Roman Emperor. As royal chaplain, John wrote a Chronicle of Bohemia, containing a report of his travels to Asia.

Bibliography

Emler, I., ed., *Chronicon Bohemiae,* Vol. 3 of *Fontes rerum Bohemicarum* (1882). • Latourette, Kenneth Scott, *A History of the Expansion of Christianity,* Vol. 2 (1938). • *Lexikon für Theologie und Kirche,* Vol. 5 (1960).

CHRISTOPHER OCKER, with contributions from THE CHINA GROUP

John of Monte Corvino

(b. southern Italy, ca. 1247; d. Khanbaliq [Beijing], 1328). Franciscan* missionary to China* and first Roman Catholic* archbishop in Asia.

John of Monte Corvino participated in a Franciscan mission to Persia and Armenia in the early 1280s. In 1289, he returned to Pope Nicholas IV with an official embassy from the Armenian king, Hethum II; the embassy included a Nestorian* bishop born in Khanbaliq, Rabban Sauma. Very satisfied with his work, the pope sent John back to Asia with letters addressed to all Eastern patriarchs and princes.

John first traveled to Armenia and Persia. In 1291, he left the Persian city of Tabriz and continued to India, where he remained for one year, claimed to have won 100 converts, and apparently had some connection with Christians of the Mar Thoma Church. In 1294, he continued to northern China, arriving shortly after the death of Kublai Khan. In 1295, he converted an Ongut Nestorian prince named George to Catholicism, although this proved to be of short-term significance (when George died in 1298, his people returned to Nestorian Christianity). He then made his way to Khanbaliq and received an audience with the great khan, Timur, successor of Kublai. There he presented papal letters and a sermon on the Catholic faith ("but [the Khan] was too far gone in idolatry"). The more immediate objective of this audience, however, was surely not conversion but the acquisition of imperial permission to settle down and preach, which license John received. He remained in Khanbaliq for the rest of his life.

John was not the first Christian in Khanbaliq. A Nestorian community was well established there, including, since 1248, a metropolitan bishop. John regarded the Nestorians as contemptible heretics, and they for their part clearly despised his challenge to their previous monopoly of Christianity in the capital. In spite of rumor mongering and false accusations, John survived imperial investigations. He managed to build a church in the city complete with a tower and three bells (by which he announced masses and the singing of the divine office). He built his residence a stone's throw from the gate of the palace of the great khan. He taught Latin to 40 boys and had them sing the mass and the divine office, which seemed to provide imperial entertainment. The first church was followed by a second, at whose altar John also served. He claimed to have served an additional Armenian church in Khanbaliq, no doubt drawing on his early experience as a missionary.

Letters to the pope and the superiors of the Franciscan Order in 1305 and 1306 led Pope Clement V to make John an archbishop, a position which would allow him to ordain bishops and increase the number of Roman Catholic churches in Asia. Clement named several Franciscans as suffragans and appointed them to consecrate John in 1307. Three of them arrived in 1308 and one more in 1312. This tactic was a departure from Franciscan missions to other places, for example, 14th-c. Bosnia, where the first task was establishing cloisters with churches, from which work in the locality and surrounding region was coordinated, bypassing normal diocesan structures altogether. Such a policy could be effective only where a steady supply of missionaries from the West could be had (which proved difficult enough in Bosnia), and this was not the case in China.

John enjoyed some success. By 1330, there were the two churches in Khanbaliq, including John's metropolitan see, a cathedral, and two Franciscan residences in Zaytun, the port city in southern China, and in Yang Chow. Most converts were from among the ruling Mongols or other foreign peoples. The association of the missionaries with the Mongols meant that, with the rapid decline of the empire and the Chinese national revival in the middle of the 14th c., Nestorian churches as well as those of the new Catholics of China were rapidly destroyed, and Christians seem to have disappeared entirely.

Bibliography

Dawson, Christopher, *Mission to Asia* (1955). • *Großer Historischer Weltatlas,* Part 2: *Mittelalter* (1979). • *Lexikon für Theologie und Kirche,* Vol. 5 (1960). • *New Catholic Encyclopedia,* Vol. 7 (1967). • Wyngaert, Anastasius van den, *Sinica Franciscana,* Vol. 1: *Itinera et Relationes Fratrum Minorum saec. XIII et XIV* (1929). • Moffett, Samuel H., *A History of Christianity in Asia,* Vol. I (1992). CHRISTOPHER OCKER, with contributions from THE CHINA GROUP

John of Plano Carpini

(b. probably at the Tuscan village of Plano del Carpini, c. 1180; d. probably in Italy, 1 Aug 1252). Franciscan* and papal emissary to the Mongolian emperor.

John of Plano Carpini was one of two Franciscans commissioned by Pope Innocent IV in 1245 to visit the court of the Mongolian emperor and convey papal letters to him (the other, Lawrence of Portugal, made it only as far as Breslau). He left the papal court (which at the time was at Lyons) on 16 Apr 1245, traveled through Germany to the still Polish duchy of Silesia, where in Breslau he took on another Franciscan, Benedict the Pole, as translator. With the help of the duke, he proceeded to Kiev, which since 1237 had been within the enormous Mongol territory that now extended from Poland to Korea. Carpini and Benedict were given guides and sent by the Mongols eastward, conveyed from army to army over the Russian steppes to the capital city of the general Batu, who ruled the western Mongol Empire and who at the time kept his winter residence in the city of Sarai.

Batu and his subordinates had devastated Russia, Poland, and Hungary just a few years before; he was believed to pose an immediate military threat to Europe. Batu had the papal letters translated into Mongol and sent the two Franciscans on the arduous journey through the steppes and over the deserts to the imperial capital of Karakorum. They arrived at the imperial camp of Sira Ordu (Superior Court) on 22 Jul 1246, and on 24 Aug joined several thousand envoys from throughout the Eastern world to witness the enthronement of a new emperor, Guyuk Khan. The khan granted them an audience in Nov 1246, provided the Franciscans with his reply to the papal letters, and sent them back to the papal court. They returned through Kiev, Poland, Bohemia, Germany, Liège, and Champagne, keeping records of their travels and discoveries along the way. They reached Lyons and Pope Innocent IV in Nov 1247.

The purpose of the papal embassy was to forestall the continued westward advance of Mongol armies (which had halted only four years before Carpini's embassy). The means at the pope's disposal were only spiritual, in part because of his prolonged conflict with the German emperor, Frederick II, which limited the pope's ability to organize a military campaign out of central Europe. Accordingly, Innocent in two letters to the khan briefly explained the Christian faith and urged conversion. To this Guyuk Khan bluntly noted the absurdity of his becoming "a trembling Nestorian* Christian," the obvious divine favor displayed in Mongol military successes, and the equally evident divine scorn of those who resisted the Mongols since the time of Genghis Khan. He challenged the pope's presumption to speak for God, and he issued the ultimatum that the West promise tribute or suffer the consequences.

Carpini returned not only with Guyuk's letter but also with new information on Mongol history, customs, military preparations, and techniques of warfare, along with incredible tales of central Asian races of dog-faced, hooved men and one-legged, one-armed monsters who moved by turning cartwheels, suicide bombers, and desert earth-dwellers. Unlike subsequent Europeans to travel east (this was the first of four papal missions to the Mongols in the 13th and early 14th cs.), Carpini seemed unimpressed by the Nestorian Christians he encountered. He recorded his observations upon his return in the *Historia mongolorum* (History of the Mongols), which exists in two versions. The better of the two has been translated by Christopher Dawson into English. Carpini's companion, Benedict the Pole, also wrote an account, which survives in two distinct and partial versions.

Bibliography

Dawson, Christopher, *Mission to Asia* (1955). • Guzman, Gregory G., "John of Plano Carpini," *Dictionary of the Middle Ages* (1986). • Painter, George D., "The Tartar Relation," *The Vinland Map and the Tartar Relation* (1995). • Sinor, Denis, "John of Plano Carpini's Return from the Mongols: New Light from a Luxemburg Manuscript," *Journal of the Royal Asiatic Society* (1957). • Wyngaert, Anastasius van den, *Sinica Franciscana,* Vol. 1: *Itinera et Relationes Fratrum Minorum saec. XIII et XIV* (1929).

CHRISTOPHER OCKER and CHINA GROUP

John, Esther

(Qamar Zia) (b. India, 1929; d. Chichawatni, Pakistan, 1960). Christian convert, teacher, and martyr.

Born into a Muslim family, Esther John attended a Christian school from the age of 17. Deeply moved by the example of one of her teachers, she began to read the Bible and underwent a conversion experience. She maintained contact with missionaries when her family moved to Karachi following the formation of Pakistan, though she kept her new faith hidden. When her missionary friend Marian Laugesen was transferred, she persevered in her faith for seven years without other Christian contact, reading her New Testament in secret. In 1955, when her family began to arrange a Muslim marriage for her, she ran away from home.

John found Laugesen in Karachi once more and went to work in an orphanage. When her family renewed pressure for her to marry, she went north to Sahiwal in the Punjab. There she lived and worked in a mission hospital. She was baptized in Dec 1955. Her love of the Bible and sense of vocation led her to enter the United Bible Training Center in 1956. After completing her studies in 1959, she moved to Chichawatni, living with American Presbyterian* missionaries and doing evangelistic work in the surrounding villages. Her family continued to urge her to return home, though at times the pressure to submit to an arranged marriage eased. John wrote that she would return after Christmas if she were allowed to live as a Christian and if no marriage was forced on her. This letter went unanswered. It was unthinkable for a woman in her situation to refuse marriage, but John refused four times.

On 2 Feb 1960, John was found in bed with her skull smashed, having died instantly. Her murder was never solved. She was buried in the Christian cemetery in Sahiwal and was honored with a memorial chapel on the grounds of the hospital where she had worked.

In 1998, a statue of John was dedicated at Westminster Abbey, London, one of 10 statues representing Christian martyrs for the church in the 20th c.

Bibliography

Sokkhdeo, Patrick, "Mission and Conversion in Pakistan: Esther John (Qamar Zia)," in *The Terrible Alternative: Christian Martyrdom in the Twentieth Century,* ed. Andrew Chandler (1998).

Philip Wickeri

John, Griffith

(Yang Ge Fei) (b. Swansea, Wales, 14 Dec 1831; d. 1912). Welsh pioneer missionary and Bible* translator in Central China* with the London Missionary Society (LMS).

John was raised in a godly home; his mother died in his infancy. He delivered his first sermon at age 14 and was nicknamed "the boy preacher." Although a college education was frowned upon by the Christian community at that time, Rev. Elijah Jacob, the new minister of Ebenezer Chapel, John's home church in Swansea, tutored him in preparation for studies at Congregational Brecon College. While at Brecon, John applied to join the LMS in 1853, offering his services for Madagascar. He transferred to Bedford Academy, England, in 1854; while waiting for an opening to Madagascar, he was persuaded to consider China instead. Following his ordination in March 1855, he married Margaret Jane Griffiths (b. Madagascar, 17 Nov 1830; d. Singapore, 1873) in April and arrived in Shanghai in September. Margaret was the daughter of David Griffiths, a founder of the Madagascar Mission. When they arrived, there were 25-30 missionaries of various denominations, both American and European, in Shanghai.

Within a year, John was preaching in Chinese. From Shanghai, he ventured out to other cities (Jiangsu and Zhejiang), preaching and distributing Christian literature. When the Treaty of Tianjin (signed in 1858) made nine more ports accessible, John wrote home to ask for more missionaries and stressed the need to train locals if China was to be evangelized effectively. In July 1860, together with Joseph Edkins*, John Macgowan, and W. N. Hall (d. 1878), he spent a week with the Taiping* rebels in Suzhou to ascertain the character of the movement. He understood the aims of the movement to be the extermination of the Tartars, the abolition of idolatry, and the absolute exclusion of opium*. He was sympathetic to the Taiping cause because of the Christian inclination of its leaders. In December, John obtained an Edict of Religious Toleration from the chief in Nanjing which guaranteed freedom for missionaries to work in the Taiping-occupied territory. The edict became defunct when the Taiping Rebellion collapsed in 1864.

In 1861, John and Robert Wilson (d. 1863) set up the first Protestant missionary residence in Hankou, Hubei. From there, under John's leadership, the LMS reached out to Wuchang (1863) and Hanyang (1867). In 1878, John urged the LMS to send at least two, but preferably four, missionaries to Sichuan. The LMS eventually sent Mr. and Mrs. Wallace Wilson and a Chinese evangelist in 1888. In the 1880s, John made several risky trips to Hunan, a province particularly hostile to foreigners. In answer to his persistent prayer and faith, the province was eventually opened through the work of Hunanese converts, notably Peng Lan-Seng, an evangelist and a native of Changsha, and Wang-Lien King, founder of a church in Hengyang.

John and his wife had three children: Griffith, David, and Mary. In 1860, the eldest, Griffith, was sent home to Wales when he was barely five because of poor health. For the sake of the children's education, they were left in England when the parents sailed for China after their furlough. Mrs. John died en route in 1873. John built the Margaret Memorial Hospital for women at Hankou in 1891 in her honor. The hospital helped remove the prejudice against unmarried women missionaries, a predudice of which John himself was guilty earlier in his missionary life.

In 1874, John married an American, Jeanette Jenkins (b. New York, 26 Jul 1834; d. Hankou, Dec 1885), widow of Benjamin Jenkins, a Methodist missionary. Jeanette worked among the girls and women of Wuchang, teaching, visiting, and supervising their education. She also helped John minister to the foreign merchant sailors. She fell ill and was operated on twice in the United States, first in 1880 and again in 1883. On the way home with Jeanette from the United States in 1881, John addressed the representatives at the Jubilee meetings of the Congregational Union of England and Wales, urging them to send their best to China: "We want men with the three Gs at least — grace, gumption and guts — the best men . . . as for your inferior men, keep them for yourselves."

John founded the Hankou Tract Society in 1876 (renamed the Central China Religious Tract Society in 1884) and served as its president for many years. He also wrote most of the tracts. He was awarded a doctorate by the University of Edinburgh in 1889 for his writings and

Bible translation work. He translated the New Testament into classical Chinese and, later, both the Old and New Testaments into colloquial Chinese.

John played an active part in the first conference of Protestant missionaries in China held in Shanghai in 1877 and organized a conference for native evangelists and deacons in 1891 to equip them for their ministry. In 1904, the Hankou Mission opened a theological institute in a two-story building donated by John. His jubilee in missionary service (1905) was celebrated by many missionary friends and Chinese Christians. Two words which recurred in the tributes to him were "friendship" and "persistence." He fell ill shortly after and retired to be with his sons in the United Kingdom.

Bibliography

Thompson, R. Wardlaw, *Griffith John: The Story of Fifty Years in China* (1906). • John, Griffith, *A Voice from China* (1906). CHINA GROUP

Joint Council of CNI-CSI-Mar Thoma

Tentative name adopted for the union of three churches: the Church of North India (CNI), Church of South India (CSI), and Mar Thoma Church.

During negotiations for the formation of the CNI, there was an understanding that CNI and CSI would consider the possibility of joining together to form one united church for the whole of India. The Mar Thoma Church asked to be included in the negotiations for the wider union on the grounds that it had a long history of close relations with the Anglican Church and was in communion with both CSI and CNI. A Joint Theological Commission of the three churches was appointed to explore the possibility of close cooperation among them.

After several meetings starting in Jan 1975, the Joint Theological Commission recommended the formation of a joint council of the three churches giving expression to their organic oneness, insofar as they were already united in faith and doctrine, had accepted one another's sacraments of baptism and Eucharist, and recognized one another's ordained ministries.

The Joint Council, which was inaugurated at Nagpur on 4 Jul 1978, is presided over by the heads of the three churches, the moderators of the CSI and CNI, and the metropolitan of the Mar Thoma Church. J. Russell Chandran was the first general secretary of the Joint Council. The Joint Council is considered a new model for manifesting the organic oneness of the churches, expressed through conciliar unity. Though it was agreed that the three churches should adopt a common name for the church in which they together belonged, the decision on the name is yet to be made.

However, the Joint Council has initiated several common programs for the churches' mission. The liturgies of the three churches include prayers for the heads of all three churches. The churches also celebrate a festival in thanksgiving for and recognition of the unity among them. J. RUSSELL CHANDRAN

Jones, Eli Stanley

(b. Clarksville, Maryland, United States, 3 Jan 1884; d. Bareilly, North India, 25 Jan 1973). American Methodist* missionary to India*; renowned evangelist and author.

The son of a part-time farmer and a toll collector on the National Turnpike near Washington, D.C., Jones had two brothers and a sister. Apparently his father was not a strong person, and it was his mother who lent strength and stability to the family.

Jones spoke of two conversions, a "horizontal change" on the outside at 15 and an authentic "vertical" one two years later in 1901, when he was radically and enduringly changed on the inside too. This inner conversion was the main theme of his life and ministry. It gave him a sense of reconciliation to God, an at-homeness with himself and others, a new direction, a new personhood, a sense of grace, wholeness, and universal obligations.

Jones gave up his intent to study law and saw his vocation as the Christian ministry. He attended Asbury College, a small Holiness institution in Wilmore, Kentucky, United States, where he received a clear call to missionary service in India. On 13 Oct 1907, he sailed for India as a missionary of the Methodist Episcopal Church and arrived in Bombay on 13 Nov, proceeding immediately to Lucknow, an important Methodist center, to begin service as pastor of the Lal Bagh Church. His electrifying witness attracted hundreds, and many were converted.

In 1911, Jones met Mabel Lossing, a brilliant educator missionary and a Cornish-Dutch Quaker-Methodist. They married and had one child, Eunice. In 1928, he declined his election as bishop of his church. The Joneses moved to Sitapur, 50 miles from Lucknow, which became the center of their service for the next 40 years. They were the district missionaries in charge of education, evangelism, finance, disaster relief, minor medical service, and some editorial work. From Sitapur, he launched out on evangelistic campaigns, eventually covering the whole of India. His health suffered, but he felt divinely delivered from his depression and established a lifelong rigorous preaching schedule for himself.

At the end of World War I, Jones would retreat to the hills during the rainy reason (June to August) to read and study and prepare five Christ- and Gospel-centered lecture-sermons on current topics, which he would deliver week after week in hired public halls on the plains, mostly for non-Christians, under the chairmanship of some local leader. The preaching would be followed by a lengthy question- and-answer period. Then on Saturdays and Sundays, he would preach and teach in the churches of all denominations. He kept up this practice for years, reaching out to every city where the population was above 50,000. In the process, he became acquainted with the leaders of every religious community, as well as the British, and particularly Gandhi*, Tagore*, Nehru*, and a host of other nationalists.

Jones's addresses were later published in book form. In all, he wrote 29 books, many best-sellers. The first, *The Christ of the Indian Road,* published in 1925, established his reputation, and, with some others, was translated into many languages. His devotional book, *The Way,* considered by many to be his most original writing, pushed Tertullian's insight that "the soul is naturally Christian" to new limits. There is a correlation between the writing of the books and Jones's personal religious and social development. The book royalties were donated to evangelistic and other Christian causes, for he was forever helping those in need. With his support, NURMANZIL Psychiatric Center was opened in Lucknow in 1951. Upon his death, his remaining royalties and similar funds from Mrs. Jones became a scholarship endowment fund for the education of hundreds of young persons in India. His books gave him a worldwide reputation, and he became a much sought after speaker and global evangelist. Long before interreligious dialogue* was in vogue, Jones held round-table conferences involving adherents of all religions in India. He wrestled with the problem of human suffering. He was a reconciling agent wherever he went and was even an unofficial go-between for President Roosevelt and the Japanese embassy in Washington, although the effort to forestall the war with Japan was ultimately unsuccessful.

Jones was particularly proud of establishing the Christian ashram* movement. He "baptized" the Hindu ashram (religious retreat), giving a "disciplined group" dimension to his evangelism. In 1930, he founded his first ashram at Sat Tal in the lower Himalayas. Another was situated for a time in the urban setting of Lucknow. Others were established across North America and beyond and sponsored one-week retreats for deepening religious life. The movement has been especially well received in Scandinavia and Japan.

The *Song of Ascents,* published in 1968, is Jones's autobiography. Always Christ-centered, Jones did not believe in retirement but kept up a rigorous schedule even after he suffered a stroke in 1971. In summary, his accomplishments included the incorporation of outcastes, through the Christian movement, into the mainstream of India's life; unifying, through an emphasis on Christ-centeredness, denominations divided by marginal issues of doctrine; making the Christian movement more contextual that is, less Western and alien; and challenging the churches in America to make evangelism an imperative. He was also a pioneer in total evangelism, appealing to the total person, mind, spirit, and body. To him, evangelism was both personal and social, and the kingdom of God, while inward and mystical, was also practical. Jones also presented a practical plan for church union. Of his many books, the most widely sold include *The Christ of the Indian Road* (1925), *Christ of the Round Table* (1928), *Abundant Living* (1942), *The Way* (1946), *Growing Spiritually* (1953), *The Word Became Flesh* (1963), and *Song of Ascents: A Spiritual Autobiography* (1968; reprinted as a festival edition, 1979).

Bibliography

Johnson, Martin Ross, "The Christian Vision of E. Stanley Jones: Missionary, Evangelist, Prophet and Statesman" (doctoral dissertation, Florida State University) (1978). • Taylor, Richard W., "E. Stanley Jones," in Gerald Anderson et al., eds., *Mission Legacies* (1994). • Jones's papers in the archives of Asbury Seminary, Wilmore, Kentucky, United States. • Thomas, C. Chako, "The Work and Thought of Eli Stanley Jones, with Special Reference to India" (doctoral dissertation, University of Iowa) (1955). • Martin, Paul, *The Missionary of the Indian Road: A Theology of Stanley Jones* (Bangalore, 1996).

James K. Mathews

Jones, Francis P.

(b. Dodgeville, Wisconsin, United States, 1890; d. 1975). Missionary to China* of the Methodist Episcopal Church (North).

Jones entered Platteville Teachers' Training College in 1907. In 1911, he went on to Northwestern University and Garrett Evangelical Theological Seminary. Upon graduation, he furthered his studies at the University of Chicago.

Jones came to China (Fukien Hinghwa) in 1915 for mission work. In 1930, during his furlough, he studied at Union Theological Seminary in New York and obtained a master of sacred theology degree. In the same year, upon his return to China, he taught at Nanking University and served on a hymnal committee, which included Bliss Wiant, to produce the final version of *Pu tian song zan* (Hymns of Universal Praise). In 1937, he taught New Testament studies at Nanking Theological Seminary and founded the seminary's school of sacred music. In 1938, Jones started to read for his doctoral degree at Union Theological Seminary. During the Sino-Japanese War, he went to Szechwan Chentu and began work in translating and editing Christian classical literature. The original plan was to produce 54 volumes of classics, but it had to be shelved as a result of political changes.

In 1951, Jones returned to America and taught at Drew Theological Seminary. He also worked as chief editor for *China's News in Brief* for 11 years. He retired in 1960 but continued his translation work with Xu Mu Shi and Xie Fu Ya in the Association of Theological Schools in South East Asia. His translations included works of F. D. E. Schleiermacher and Von Hügel. His contribution was commended as equivalent to that of Kumarajiva, who in the Tang dynasty translated major classical works of Buddhism*.

China Group

Joseph, Tiruchiluvai

(b. India, 1862; d. Kuala Lumpur, 1929). Pioneer pastor and organizer of the Evangelical Lutheran* Church in Malaya.

Joseph was the first pastor sent from India to minister to the growing number of diaspora Tamil Lutherans in Malaya. The Evangelical Lutheran Church in Malaysia and Singapore* (ELCMS) counts Joseph together with German missionaries K. Pamperin and H. Matthe, lay leader A. A. Peter, and Joseph's successor, S. Muthuswami, as its founders.

Joseph was a trained and ordained pastor of the Leipzig Evangelical Lutheran Mission (LELM) in Madras, South India*. LELM work in India was a continuation of mission work started in Tranquebar in 1706 by B. Ziegenbalg* and led to the formation of the independent Tamil Evangelical Lutheran Church on 14 Jan 1919, based in Tiruchirapalli.

In order to take up work among Lutheran Indians in Malaya, Joseph was sent there in 1906. A shop house was rented at No. 5, Scott Road, Kuala Lumpur, and regular services commenced on 30 Jan 1907. A building committee was soon organized, a plot of land purchased, and the Zion Church completed in 1924. This effort was remarkable in the sense that no foreign assistance at all was received.

Joseph appears to have been the principal motivator behind the Zion project; however, he was called back to India before its completion. After retirement, he returned to Malaya, where he stayed until his death in 1929.

Julius D. Paul

Joset, Theodore

(b. Courfaivre, Switzerland, 7 Oct 1804; d. Hong Kong, 5 Aug 1842). First prefect apostolic of the Hong Kong* Catholic Church (1841-42).

Joset was one of the most diligent procurators of the Roman Sacred Congregation for the Propagation of the Faith (SCPF) in the Far East. Foreseeing the bright future of Hong Kong, he took up the heavy responsibility of starting the Catholic Church there.

Joset was a secular priest who was sent by the SCPF to Macau in 1833, first to help its procurator, Raphael Umpierres, and then to succeed him in 1835. On 17 Dec 1839, he was appointed consul general to H. M. Charles Albert, king of Sardinia.

On 22 Apr 1841, Joset was also appointed prefect apostolic of the newly established prefecture of Hong Kong, where he settled on 3 Mar 1842 after being banished from Macau by the Portuguese authorities. He not only diligently carried on his duties as procurator, but also started at once to build the Mission House, arrange for a site and building materials for the church, and level sites for the cemetery, the seminary, and other institutions until his early death. His tomb is located in the Catholic cathedral of Hong Kong.

Bibliography

Hong Kong Catholic Church Directory 1995; Ryan, T., *The Story of a Hundred Years* (1959); *Catholic Guide to Hong Kong* (1962). • Ticozzi, S., *Historical Documents of the Hong Kong Catholic Church* (1983) (in Chinese).

Sergio Ticozzi

Judson, Adoniram

(b. Malden, Massachusetts, United States, 9 Aug 1788; d. on a sea voyage, 12 Apr 1850). Pioneer missionary to Myanmar* (Burma).

After reading a stirring missionary message by a British minister during his study at Andover Theological Seminary in Massachusetts, Judson vowed to be the first foreign missionary from America. He married Ann Hesseltine on 5 Feb 1812 and was ordained and commissioned by the Congregational Church as one of America's first foreign missionaries. The following day, on 18 Feb, Judson and his wife left for India. Through studying the Bible during their long sea voyage to India, the Judsons became convinced of the need for a believer's baptism by immersion. They were both baptized by William Ward* of Serampore in India*. Since the Judsons were no match for the powerful East India Company, their stay in India was short-lived, and they boarded a ship for Myanmar. They arrived at Rangoon on 13 Jul 1813.

The work in Myanmar was then supported by the American Baptists. Like other missionaries, the Judsons first tried to master the Burmese language. As soon as they could speak street Burmese, they built a Burmese *zayat,* the place where people meet for leisure to exchange views and discuss various subjects. A month after the *zayat* was opened, a Burmese Buddhist, Maung Nau, was baptized on 27 Jun 1819. Instead of building a church, the Judsons used the *zayat* as a center for worship and fellowship.

During the second Anglo-Burmese war (1823-26), Judson and four other white men were suspected of being spies and confined to prison. They were severely tortured and given death threats. Because of Ann Judson's unstinting appeals to the guards and Judson's own offer to act as interpreter in peace negotiations with the British, Judson was released on 31 Dec 1825, after nearly one-and-a-half years in prison.

Besides his routine of evangelism and mission, Judson translated the Bible* from the original Hebrew and Greek into the Burmese language. His compilations of an English-Burmese dictionary and a Burmese-English dictionary were greatly appreciated by both the Buddhists and Christians in Burma. Judson's talent for using the Burmese worldview and thought in his evangelization and in the translation of the Bible anticipated the modern theological concept of contextualization*. Because of Judson's honesty and love for the local people, the Burmese king requested him to be his interpreter in negotiations with the British.

It was a great loss and sorrow for Judson that Ann and his daughter died while he was helping finish the negotiations in 1826. His second wife, Sarah Boardman, a 30-year-old widow of a missionary, died in 1845 while en route to the United States on medical leave. Judson married Emily Chubbock in 1846 while he was on a visit in the United States. In Nov 1846, Judson and his bride arrived in Burma. Their happiness in the mission work in Burma, however, did not last long, for Judson died at sea on 12 Apr 1850 and was buried in the waters near the Andaman Islands.

Bibliography

Anderson, Courtney, *To the Golden Shore* (1972). • Judson, Edward, *The Life of Adoniram Judson* (1883). • Maung Shwe Wa, *Burma Baptist Chronicle* (1963).

CUNG LIAN HUP

Justice and Peace Commission

(Idara-e-Amn-o-Insaf, Idara). Idara started out in 1972 as a project of the Pakistan Christian Industrial Service (PCIS), Karachi. PCIS was an ecumenical venture of the Southern Regional Conference and the Roman Catholic Church*. The painstaking spadework was done by Lee Lybarger, a Presbyterian* lay missionary from Cleveland, Ohio, United States. PCIS came into being in 1969. It was akin to the 1950s Industrial Evangelism ministry of the church, functioning under the auspices of the then East Asia Christian Conference (EACC) Urban Industrial Mission (UIM), based in Singapore*.

PCIS focused its attention on improving the lot of workers. It operated an employment service, apprenticeship service, legal service, and business advisory service, and also produced two publications: *PCIS Bulletin* in English and *Jafakash* (The Worker) in Urdu. Both were bimonthlies. By Jul 1993, the activities of the legal service had grown sufficiently to warrant Idara's operating as a separate project.

Chronological development. PCIS functioned from within the premises of the Brookes Memorial Church, Garden Road, Karachi. Its services were available to one and all. Workers, including Muslims, were accustomed to approaching Christian institutions for services traditionally associated with the church. However, they felt a certain reluctance in the domain of legal assistance, suspecting that it perhaps was a new approach for luring them to Christianity. This was another cogent reason for wanting to bifurcate this project.

An office was obtained in 1978 in a commercial high-rise complex fairly close to the PCIS office. It was there that Idara began to sprout forth as an expression of concern and involvement of the local church for marginalized workers. These workers lacked education (the national literacy rate was less than 26%), were ignorant of the law, were ununionized, and lived in settlements that had no real organization.

The sponsors of Idara were the two churches, the Church of Pakistan and the Roman Catholic Church of the diocese of Karachi, headed then by Rt. Rev. Bishop Arne Rudvin and His Eminence Joseph Cordeiro, respectively. The founding members were Clement John, Robert Mendonca, Samuel Xavier, and Hamid Henry. The executive secretary was Arnold Heredia. At first, Idara offered legal redress to aggrieved workers. Courses in labor law that lasted five days to five weeks were periodically conducted so that workers who desired to form unions would be adequately equipped. Those were the years when the Pakistan Peoples Party had just assumed power under its charismatic feudal leader, Zulfiqar Ali Bhutto. He ostensibly gave great freedom to workers and made progressive amendments in the labor policy, so that he could destroy the powerful industrial base of 22 tycoons. Idara assisted workers in forming registered unions. Periodic evening seminars were held to discuss amendments in labor laws. The enthusiasm that evolved resulted in the formation of an Idara Trade Unionists Club, which met on a monthly basis for about one year.

Idara reached out to the most marginalized and discriminated against workers, the sanitation workers (mainly Christians and Hindus of the scheduled class), by visiting their *bustis* (settlements). They were told that they were workers before the law, and any discriminatory treatment could be challenged. Liberal-minded Muslim associates of Idara participated in this socio-political awareness program.

This struggle against discrimination continued. The desire to come to grips with issues such as contracts, denial of safety equipment, and the lack of promotion led to the holding of evening seminars, weekend workshops, and consultations. The first All Pakistan Sanitary Workers Consultation was held on 1-3 Jul 1984.

Gradually, Idara understood how deeply entrenched was the system of discrimination and exploitation of the sanitation workers. This was most evident when sewer cleaners died of poisonous gas. Every year, about two to six municipal workers died of gas poisoning as they stepped, bare-bodied, into the clogged main drains. Idara supported their strikes and provided legal protection and ongoing assistance in the matters of compensation and provision of safety equipment. Yet every time the entrenched union leaders in connivance with the municipal officials diffused the issues by making false promises.

When Idara became autonomous from the PCIS, it took on the responsibility of *Jafakash.* The publication carried educative articles for the target group and write-ups on Idara's activities. As appreciation for *Jafakash* increased, it was turned into a monthly in 1989. Special editions were brought out to mark World Workers Day, International Women's Day, and International Human Rights Day. The journal also carried surveys on mine workers, rural realities, and fisher folk. Copies were

Justice and Peace Commission

mailed gratis to churches, church-related agencies, select trade unions, and Idara associates. The bulk were distributed as educational material at rallies and seminars and to people who visited the office. The production of slides and video programs and a people's drama *Diwar* (Wall) are other examples of endeavors at mass education.

Idara's association with EACC-UIM (changed to Christian Conference of Asia, Urban Rural Mission* [CCA-URM] in 1973) grew with the years. In 1972, two board members attended a URM meeting on grassroots organization. It resulted in giving Idara the impetus to go out into the field. Idara had the opportunity to participate in several training programs, seminars, workshops, and consultations on theology and ideology, urban-rural workers, fisher folk, women workers, child labor, militarization, and transnational corporations, all organized by CCA-URM. Idara sent Muslims to these programs as well. To them, it was an eye-opener that the Asian church was alive and serious about addressing itself to the problems of the workers.

Gradually, Idara's acceptance grew among other trade unions and workers movements, and its publication was accepted as the voice of the Pakistani workers. Whereas in the heyday of the Bhutto regime workers' publications abounded, as Bhutto became autocratic — and eventually when General Zia Ul-Haq took over in Jul 1977 — *Jafakash* remained virtually the only publication of its kind.

Idara has always been conscious that grassroots involvement is at the heart of its mission and ministry. By 1978, the board decided to take on a part-time community organizer (CO) to intensify the involvement of volunteers in tackling problems in the *bustis.* Eventually, two more COs were engaged. Among the problems that the COs tackled: plans to demolish the whole or part of a *busti;* lack of basic amenities; orders converting a coeducational school into a school for boys only; the practice of fish-meal producers to use open land to dry fish and thus pollute the adjoining *busti*'s atmosphere.

The years 1977-89 were years of martial law under Zia. Idara functioned cautiously and under low profile. At one point, there was close surveillance of Idara's activities and publication, and pressures were put on the sponsoring bishops and executive secretary to close Idara down.

Present situation. Since 1980, Idara has expanded its services to reach out to other individuals and groups in Pakistan. Contacts have been deepened in the cities of Hyderabad, Multan, Faisalabad, and Lahore. At Hyderabad, Idara works on an issue-by-issue basis. Idara relates to the Justice & Peace Commission of major religious superiors at Multan. At Faisalabad, Idara supported work among the brick- kiln bonded labor (1987-90 and 1992-93). It has supported the initiatives of Idara-Lahore since 1980.

The number of COs varied from one to five. When there was only one in Oct 1994, Idara commissioned nine new COs. They are engaged in 15 *bustis.*

Idara has continued its involvement with the municipal sanitation workers and has held trade-union and leadership-training workshops for workers from Karachi and Yderabad, following them up with monthly educational seminars. Idara has recently provided legal assistance to the powerloom contract workers of Karachi West and has acquired the services of a labor lawyer. Aggrieved workers from other establishments as well are provided succor. Labor education is further provided through *Jafakash,* which also carries articles on human rights, political and economic analysis, rural and urban problems. *Jafakash* has been placed in stalls all over Pakistan and at about fifty stalls in Karachi alone.

Idara has maintained a liaison with women's nongovernmental organizations (NGOs) and other NGOs related to human rights. In an atmosphere which is being increasingly permeated with sectarian and religious intolerance, Idara has been able to establish working relationships with 33 NGOs in Pakistan. It has a multireligious and ethnic board, committees, and staff, and is free from all bigotry. It continues to identify itself with the downtrodden and their struggles for a new and just society.

Bibliography

Henry, Hamid, "Challenges to URM: A Pakistani Perspective" (unpublished) (1989). • Heredia, Arnold, "Idara-e-Amn-o-Insaf: Half-Yearly Report July-December 1994" (unpublished) (1994). ARNOLD HEREDIA

Jusuto. *See* Takayama Ukon

Kachins

Jinghpaw, more commonly known as Kachins, are a group of people whose population estimates range from 500,000 to as high as 1.5 million. They are scattered across the mountainous intersection of China*, India*, Myanmar*, Thailand*, and Laos*. They are basically Mongolian, but Jinghpaw is their common tongue, although they also speak five other languages — Rawang, Maru, Lashi, Azi, and Lisu — in addition to several dialects of these languages. A fierce, mountain-dwelling agricultural people who use bamboo as their main subsistence, the Kachins practiced slash-and-burn cultivation as they pressed southward, dispossessing other groups. Little is known of the Kachins' origin, but their tradition claims their cradle to be the *Majoi Shingra Bum* (Naturally Flat Mountain), a sort of paradise in the far north (possibly eastern or northeastern Tibet).

The Kachins resisted the British, who annexed Upper Burma (Myanmar) in 1886, and, after 51 years of fierce struggle, they won the right for the Kachin hill areas to be administered separately from the plains. The British recruited Kachins (Chins* and Karens* too) for military police and other army units. During World War II*, the Kachin hill areas were traversed by tens of thousands of Indians, Chinese, British, and other Westerners who were fleeing from the Japanese to Assam and Yunnan. Many Kachins, especially those who served in the military units, evacuated to India with the British forces. They formed the Kachin Resistance Movement, an invaluable help to the British, American, and Chinese forces. An estimated 8,000-10,000 Kachin men and teens engaged in warfare against the Japanese. The Kachins, whose casualty ratio was one Kachin to every 25 Japanese, taught jungle warfare to the Americans. World War II exposed the Kachins to modern technology, increased their sense of identity, and enhanced their political awareness. After World War II, General Aung San sought the cooperation of the Kachins, who mobilized the Shans. This led to the Panglung Agreement and independence from the British. One of the five smaller stars on the flag of Myanmar represents the Kachins.

The Kachins had always known of God *(Karia Kasang)* as the Creator *(Hpan Wa Ningsang)* or the One Who Knows *(Chye Wa Ningchyang)*. They resisted idolatry. They offered sacrifices to the Nat (spirits), but never to God. They believed that God the Creator gave them a book on parchment when creation was completed. But it was baked and eaten by a hungry Kachin on the way home; hence the living word, or the Spirit of God, is always alive in the heart of the Kachins.

American Baptist missionary Eugenio Kincaid met the Kachins in 1837 with the help of a Shan interpreter. In 1858, Karen* Christians in the delta province of Bassein sent missionaries to work with the Kachins, and there were many conversions. The Roman Catholic* Mission, which was formally established by the Paris Foreign Mission Society* (MEP) in 1872, began with the visits of Bishop Bigandet to Bhamo, a major city in Kachin State, in the 1850s and 1860s. The work was subsequently transferred to the Columban fathers, whose first missionary to the Kachins, Patrick Usher, reached Kachin State in 1936. The China Inland Mission (Overseas Missionary Fellowship) started to work with the Kachins in China and came to Myanmar in 1875. The American Baptist Mission Society came in 1877, and the Bible Churchmen Mission Society and the Churches of Christ came in the 1920s. When Ne Win came to power in 1962, the only remaining foreign missionaries were J. Russell Morse, a family of the Churches of Christ who stayed surreptitiously in the Hidden Valley on the China border, and some Columban fathers who stayed until the 1970s.

Ola Hanson arrived in 1890 to improve the translation work begun by William Henry Roberts (who arrived 12 Jan 1879; retired 1914) and others. Among other literature, Hanson completed the Gospel of John in 1895 and the entire Bible* on 11 Aug 1926. He presented the Kachin Holy Bible to Damau Naw on 27 Mar 1927 during the Golden Jubilee celebration. About 90 percent of the Kachins are Christian. Present estimates list about a quarter million Kachin Baptists in more than 200 churches, a small number of other denominations, and about 50,000 Roman Catholics who are found mainly in Myanmar. When Mao Zedong took over China, some Kachins lapsed as Christians, some went underground, and others went to Myanmar. Most of the educated Kachins, including the leaders of the Kachin Independence Movement and its recently deceased director, Brang Seng, are Christian.

At the centennial meeting in 1977, which was attended by more than 100,000 Kachin Baptists, 6,215 people were converted in a single day. Over 35,000 participated in the Lord's Supper. Mission Downward is an outreach project to spread the Gospel throughout Myanmar and to the rest of the world. The Kachin Baptist Convention does mission work among other tribes: the Naga, Wa, Palawng, Shan, Gurkha, Burmese, and Arakanese. There is a Kachin Baptist Fellowship in Pasadena, California, and another at the Tokyo Peace Baptist Church in Nishiwaseda. Tokyo.

Bibliography

Maung Shwe Wa, *Burma Baptist Chronicle* (1963). • Tegenfeldt, Herman G., *Century of Growth: The Kachin Baptist Church of Burma* (1974). • Richardson, Don, *Eternity in Their Heart,* rev. ed. (1984). • Smith, H. W., *Jinghpaw Jubeli Laika* (The Kachin Jubilee) (1928). • Fischer, Edward, *Mission in Burma: The Columban Fathers' Forty-three Years in Kachin Country* (1980). • Nida, Eugene A., ed., *The Book of a Thousand Tongues,* 2nd ed. (1972).

MARAN YAW and Ronald D. Renard

Kafarov, Benedict Petr Ivanovich ("Palladius")

(b. Khazan, 1817; d. 1878). Russian sinologist and archimandrite of the 13th and 15th Orthodox* mission group to Beijing who compiled the Chinese-Russian dictionary.

Kafarov graduated from Kazan Theological Seminary and was ordained and sent to Beijing as a *diakonos* (deacon) of the 12th Orthodox mission group to China. He returned to Russia in 1848, was promoted to *presbyteros,* and returned to China as the archimandrite of the 13th (1849-59) and 15th (1865-78) mission groups. Kafarov provided Chinese military and political intelligence to the Russian government and participated in the Russian armed invasion of northeast China, forcing the Chinese government to sign the Sino-Russian Aihui treaty.

In 1870 he joined the archaeology and ethnology team organized by the Russian Imperial Geographical Institute to investigate the Ussuri area. A gifted linguist, he translated several Chinese and Mongolian texts into Russian and a number of Christian writings into Chinese. He died in 1878 on his way home to Russia. Kafarov wrote scholarly works such as *The Historical Essentials of the Ussuri Area, Travel Notes from Beijing to Manchuria via Hailan Pao, The History of Early Buddhism,* and *The Documents of Early Islam in China.* His best-known work is the Chinese-Russian dictionary, which was completed after his death and published in 1889.

Bibliography

Arkhangelov, S. A., *Nashi zagranichnye missii* (1899).

CHINA GROUP

Kagawa Toyohiko

(b. 10 Jul 1888; d. 23 Apr 1960). Social worker, evangelist.

Son of Kagawa Junichi, Kagawa was head of a shipping agency in Kobe and Sugo Kame. Baptized in Tokushima in 1904 by Harry White Myers, Kagawa later entered the preparatory course for Meiji Gakuin's theology department and then transferred to Kobe Seminary, newly established by the Presbyterian* Church in the United States (South). He graduated from there in 1911. In 1909, he had moved into Kobe's Shinkawa slum district to do evangelism and social service. In 1914, he went to the United States to study at Princeton Theological Seminary, returning to Shinkawa in 1917, where he participated in the labor movement and joined the Yuaikai.

Kagawa provided leadership in labor disputes at the Kawasaki and Mitsubishi Shipyards in Kobe, stressing the need for human liberation of workers. He also took a leading role in the consumers' cooperative and farm cooperative movements, and in 1922 founded the Japan Farmers' Cooperative. He participated in the formative stage of the *Suiheisha* movement (an organization to restore the *Buraku** people to full social rights), but, because of certain discriminatory language in his book *Hinmin shiri no kenkyu* (Research on the Psychology of the Poor), he was censured. Kagawa thereafter separated himself from the *Buraku* liberation movement and its struggle against discrimination.

At the time of the great earthquake in Japan (1923), Kagawa moved to Tokyo and engaged in relief work with colleagues in the Friends of Jesus Society. From that time on, he poured his greatest energy into his religious work, promoting the Farmers' Gospel School and the Kingdom of God Movement and traveling to other countries to preach. In 1940, as an outspoken opponent of war, he was arrested by the Tokyo military police and experienced oppression by the authorities from time to time. Yet he also traveled to sections of Manchuria and China* that were occupied by the Japanese army to do mission work.

After the war, Kagawa continued to participate in a variety of different movements, including the Japan Socialist Party, the Christian Movement for Building of a New Japan, and the World Federalists Movement. During his lifetime, he wrote 150 books and translated 23 others. His most widely read book was the novel *Shisen o koete* (Crossing the Line of Death). At the time of the posthumous publication of his complete works *(Kagawa Toyohiko zenshu)* (1962), consideration was given to deleting the discriminatory language that led to his dropping the *Buraku* cause, but it was decided to retain the original form. The offending words were, however, deleted in the third printing. Kagawa remains one of the best known and respected Christian leaders of modern Japan.

Bibliography

Yokoyama Haruichi, *Kagawa Toyohiko den* (Biography of Kagawa Toyohiko) (1950). • Sumiya Mikio, *Kagawa Toyohiko* (1966). • Kudo Eiichi, *Kirisuto-kyo to buraku mondai* (Christianity and the Buraku Issue) (1983).

KUDO EIICHI

Kalimantan

One of the largest islands of the Malay archipelago.

As a result of the vicissitudes of colonial history, Kalimantan is divided between Malaysia* and Indonesia*. The Indonesian part is 550,000 sq. km.^{2}, or 27% of the total land area of Indonesia, comprising four of the 27 Indonesian provinces: West, Central, South, and East Kalimantan. The population is approximately 11 million. The dense rain forest, which until recently covered most of the island, was the habitat of Dayak tribes; the coastal areas were inhabited by Malays. In West Kalimantan, Chinese immigrants have been numerous for several centuries. In recent years, many migrants from Java and Madura have come to Kalimantan. The coastal Malays embraced Islam* in the 16th and 17th cs.; the Dayak kept to their tribal religion until the 20th c. According to government sources, of the total population of Indonesian Kalimantan, eight million (or approximately 75%) are Muslim; 920,000 (or about 8.5%) are Protestant; and 955,000 (or 9%) are Roman Catholic*. Estimates by the churches themselves are more conservative. Two-thirds of the Christian population live in West Kalimantan.

The first Catholic missionary to Kalimantan, Antonio Ventimiglia, was martyred in 1691; not until two centuries later was the mission resumed in earnest. Initially, it was most successful among the Chinese population of West Kalimantan, where in 1934 the first priest was ordained. In 1961, five episcopal sees were established; by 1993, their number had increased to seven: Pontianak (archbishopric), Sanggau, Ketapang, Sintang, Banjarmasin, Palangkaraya, and Samarinda. As in other parts of Indonesia, the Catholic Church is active in the fields of medical* care and education. The latter includes elementary and secondary schools, as well as professional training (the famous technical school at Pontianak) and lower-level theological education. Socio-economic activities include agricultural training centers.

The Protestant mission first came to Kalimantan in 1835, when J. H. Barnstein of the German *Rheinische Mission* established a mission station at Banjarmasin, South Kalimantan. One hundred years later, the Evangelical Dayak Church *(Gereja Dajak Evangelis,* 1950: *Gereja Kalimantan Evangelis)* was established. In 1997, the membership was 220,000 spread over the whole island. In West Kalimantan, the Dutch Reformed Church in America had a mission in 1839-50, and the Episcopal Methodists* in 1906-28. The latter resulted in an ethnic Chinese church. The Christian and Missionary Alliance* (C&MA), Baptists, and several other missions also founded churches in West Kalimantan. Kalimantan Timur was opened up by the C&MA in 1929. Here the first mission airplane in Indonesia was operated by George E. Fisk (1939). After the war, this church affiliated with the communion of C&MA churches in Indonesia, the *Gereja Kemah Injil Indonesia.*

Christianity in Kalimantan has several distinguishing features. (1) Except for East Kalimantan, there were no early mass conversions. The Dayak trickled into the church, they did not stream into it. Many Dayak adopted Islam, which took a more lenient attitude toward their cultural habits. (2) As in Java (but not in Northern Sumatra), Northern and Central Sulawesi, Nusa Tenggara, and Irian, Christianity has no solid ethnic base in Kalimantan. In the Catholic Church, tensions between Dayak and other members are considerable. (3) Given the slow response of the Dayak to modernization, most Christians in Kalimantan are backward socially and economically, like those in Irian, Nusa Tenggara, and Central Sulawesi, but unlike most other Christian groups in Indonesia. Moreover, because of the low population density, Kalimantan attracts many migrants, the vast majority of whom are Muslim. As in Irian and Nusa Tenggara, both facts combined produce an explosive atmosphere in which it is difficult to distinguish between religious and socio-economic motives. In 1997, serious fighting, in which the army had to intervene, broke out between Christian Dayak and Muslim Madurese in West Kalimantan after the murder of four nuns.

Bibliography

Conley, William, *The Kalimantan Kenyah: A Study of Tribal Conversion in Terms of Dynamic Cultural Themes* (ca. 1976). • Ukur, F., and F. L. Cooley, *Jerih dan Juang; laporan nasional survai menyeluruh gereja di Indonesia* (1979) (abridged ed., Frank L. Cooley, *The Growing Seed: The Christian Church in Indonesia* [1981]). • De Jong, Gerald, "Mission to Borneo," *Historical Society of the Reformed Church in America, Occasional Papers,* No. 1 (1989). • *Missionary Herald* (1835-49). • Humble, Arnold Leon, "Conservative Baptists in Kalimantan Barat" (master's thesis, Fuller Theological Seminary) (1982). • *Handbook of Reformed Churches Worldwide* (1999).

THOMAS VAN DEN END

Kam, Joseph

(b. Den Bosch, Netherlands, Sep 1769; d. Ambon, Indonesia, 18 Jul 1833). Dutch preacher and evangelist in Surabaya and the Moluccas*.

Kam was raised in the Dutch Reformed Church but

was strongly influenced by Moravian pietism as a result of his studies with the Moravian Brethren at Zeist. He was further influenced by British evangelicalism during his continuation of mission studies at Gasport, England. With two other Dutch friends, Kam sailed in 1813 for the East Indies under the support of the London Missionary Society (LMS), not the Netherlands' Missionary Society (*Nederlandsch Zendeling Genootschap*, NZG), arriving at Batavia in 1814.

Kam's work would be wide-ranging (literature, music*, renewal), but most of all his contribution to the church would be through evangelism as he traveled thousands of miles through the eastern islands on his home-crafted vessel. Kam first arrived in the Moluccas in 1815 and was assigned to Amboina at a point in time when the church in the Moluccas was in a low state of affairs, especially with respect to its spiritual life, because of a shortage of ministers since the decline of the Dutch United East-Indies Company (VOC)* in the middle of the 18th c. and the Dutch government's policy of discouraging missionary work among Muslims.

In his effort to restore the spiritual condition of the church in the Moluccas, Kam combined the ideas of pietism (organizing revivals and prayer meetings and praying for evangelism) and the elements of the Reformed Church (the service of preaching and sacrament, application of church discipline, and church organization). The pattern of service he practiced was directly influenced by his earlier experiences both at Den Bosch and Zeist.

Apart from Ambon, Kam's activity was also directed to the congregations in surrounding regions (inside the Moluccas), as well as areas outside the Moluccas, such as Minahasa, Sangir-Talaud (North Celebes), and the island of Timor* (Lesser Sunda). He performed all types of pastoral services in those areas because he was the only minister in the Moluccas then, possibly even in the whole of East Indonesia. During his visits, Kam preached the Gospel, exercised church discipline, served the sacraments, and supervised the teachers' work in schools.

Kam made it a major point to increase the spiritual quality of the church members. This is apparent from the supply of Christian books (Bibles, psalm books, catechisms, and collections of sermons) which he either had printed in his own office or ordered from the outside to be distributed to the congregations that needed them.

The wide area of service and the decline of spiritual life in the Moluccas required more help, so Kam made urgent appeals to the NZG, which sent a number of missionaries to the Moluccas, thereby increasing the speed of reform and the spread of the church to the surrounding areas (Minahasa and Timor).

Until his death, Kam did his utmost to reform the condition of Christianity in the Moluccas and surrounding regions. Through his service, Kam also planted the seed of a church which could preach the Gospel to others in East Indonesia, an essential for church development in the next century. The Protestant Church in the Moluccas (GPM, 1935), the Christian Evangelical Church in Minahasa (1934), and the separated Christian Evangelical Church in Timor (1948) are all indebted to the reformation efforts of Kam one century ago. Kam has been called both the Reformer of the Moluccas and the Apostle of the Moluccas because of his 18 years of evangelistic reformation work there.

Bibliography

Enklaar, I. H., *Joseph Kam, Apostel der Molukken* (1963). • Latourette, K. S., *A History of the Expansion of Christianity*, Vol. V (1978). • Müller-Krüger, Th., *Sedjarah Geredja di Indonesia* (1959). • Van den End, Th., *Ragi Carita* I (1980).

Mesach Tapilatu

Kang Yang Wook

(b. Pyongyang, 1904; d. Jan 1983). Founder of the pro-Communist North Korean Christians Federation.

Kang attended Ju-O University Preparatory College for two years, after which he returned home to study theology at Pyongyang Theological Seminary. As an ordained minister of the Presbyterian* Church, he served in local churches until 1945. After liberation, he supported the pro-Communist politics of Kim Il Sung and was named chairman of the Central Committee of the North Korean Labor Party. Until his death in 1983, he remained a loyal supporter of President Kim.

David Suh, with contributions from Kim Heung Soo, translated by Kim In Soo

Karen, Myanmar

The Karen, one of the major ethnicities in Myanmar, comprise the major groups of Sgaw, Pwo, Pa-O, and Kayah and the minor groups of Paku, western Bwe (with two subgroups: Blimaw, also known as Brek or Bre, and Geba), Padaung, Geko (Gheko), Yinbaw, and others. Most of the Karen are found in the Irrawaddy and Sittang Valleys, from the coast to approximately latitude 10 degrees north, and along the entire length of Tenasserim, from latitude 10 degrees north up through the hills along the Thai border into the Shan plateau as far as latitude 21 degrees north. The Karen did not possess a written language when they migrated into Myanmar; hence the different views on the origin of their various dialects: Sino-Tibetan, Tibeto-Burman, or Mon-Khmer. It is agreed that the Karen languages are monosyllabic and characterized by a peculiar intonation. Thus the word *meh* means "tooth" when pronounced in a high sustained tone and "tail" when pronounced with a heavy falling accent.

There are about four million Karen. The Karen live in compact villages which were formerly surrounded by stockades, a practice still found in some places today. The main structures are houses and granaries, although the latter are sometimes located along trails at some distance from the village. The plains Karen live in Burmese-style houses. The valley villages have houses set on wooden posts with plank floors and walls. Hilltop houses are usually made of bamboo. In both cases, the roofs are made of either grass or leaf thatch. Karen houses are raised above the ground, and longhouses may be raised five or six feet above ground level.

The economy of the Karen entails agriculture, fishing, hunting, gathering, domestic animals, food and stimulants, industrial arts, and trade.

A Karen kin-group consists of persons who are related matrilineally and who participate in certain feasts for ancestral spirits which are barred to non-kin. The leader is the oldest living woman in the line, and, without exception, all her descendants, both male and female, are expected to attend the ancestral feasts lest they be considered malicious.

The young people are given an opportunity to meet members of the opposite sex at events such as weddings and funerals. A young man normally suggests his choice of a girl to his parents, who then arrange for a go-between. The bridegroom gives small gifts to the bride's relatives, and the marriage is finalized at a wedding feast. Monogamy is the rule, and divorce, which may be initiated by either party, is permitted upon the payment of a penalty to the divorced spouse. Concubinage is regarded as a non-formal social liaison. The normal domestic unit is the nuclear family who, among the hill Karen, occupy an apartment in a longhouse. Property is equally shared among the children, although a slightly larger portion goes to the eldest. A widow retains control of the property during her lifetime, but the control ends upon her remarriage.

For years, most Karen have lived under the nominal authority of others: Myanmar (the majority ethnic group), Mons, Shans, Siamese, or British. Among the Karen, however, the most important political unit is the village, headed by a chief who is assisted by a council of elders. The chief leads the village in certain religious rites, and his approval is necessary for an armed raid. The chief and elders also have certain judicial functions. Disgruntled villagers may desert the chief and found a new settlement.

Wealth and age determine status in Karen communities. Occupation is inconsequential because all villagers, including the chief (who receives no tributes), are agriculturists. Wealth is measured by the ownership of horned cattle and bronze drums (however, it is unclear how these are accumulated). In pre-British days, the Karen had slaves who were captured during raids on other Karen villages and ethnic groups. They were treated as household members by the captors and ultimately assimilated into the community.

The main religions of the Karen are Buddhism*, Christianity, paganism, and animism*. However, the traditional religion of the Karen is ethnic or tribal in character, centering on a belief in spirits *(Nat)* and impersonal power that require supplication, propitiation, and manipulation. The Karen believe in the existence of a supernatural creator named *Ywa.* Other supernatural beings include local or nature deities with human characteristics who exercise some control over human events, and the ghosts of those who led evil lives or died unnatural deaths (disease, violence, accidents). Certain ancestral spirits are important in the functioning of matrilineage. Finally, there is also a class of heterogeneous, largely malevolent spirits.

Various theories have been propounded concerning the origin of the Karen. One conjecture is that the Karen left the early cradle of the human race centuries or millennia ago, followed the northern slopes of the Himalayas, or crossed the plains of Tibet, and reached Myanmar via western China. Another account holds that the Karen passed over rivers of sand, which might be the Gobi Desert, and then occupied the lower ranges of the Himalayas in Myanmar and Thailand. Karen oral traditions, unlike those of most primitive races, fail to make a distinct reference to a flood. Therefore, another theory arose that the Karen could have left the cradle of the human race even before the flood. A less plausible theory is that the Karen had had contact with the Nestorian* missionaries or other Christians and derived their ideas from them. The weakness in this theory is that indigenous Karen religious belief lacks a knowledge of Christ. Some early missionaries favored the idea that the Karen belong to the lost tribes of Israel because *Ywa,* their supernatural creator, is phonetically similar to Yahweh. Others argue that the Karen are of Mongolian stock because they are shorter and darker than the Chinese but fairer than the Myanmar and Thai, and because they possess characteristically Mongolian features in their eyes, broad cheekbones, and wide, flat nostrils.

Whatever their origin, the oral traditions of the Karen contain parallels to the biblical creation and fall and the story of a lost book which would, when recovered, bring salvation. All of this seems to have prepared them for the Christian Gospel.

Among missionaries to the Karen, the real pioneers were George Dana Boardman, founder of the Karen mission; Jonathan Wade, who reduced the Karen language to writing; and Francis Mason, translator of the Karen Bible. The first Karen Christian was Ko Tha Byu*, who was baptized by Boardman on 16 May 1828 and who preached among his people in the regions of Tavoy, Mergui, Moulamyine (Moulmein), Yangon, Bassein, and Rakhaing (Arakan) until his death at age 62 on 9 Sep 1840. As other Karen caught the same evangelistic zeal and passion, Christianity spread to other ethnic groups as well: Asho Chins*, Hill Chins, Kachins*, Shans, Lahus, Was, Akhas, Nagas, Kayahs, and others, even in Thailand. The Karen presently form the largest Christian group in Myanmar, with 17 church associations, 1,310 churches, and a total of 197,476 members.

Bibliography

Anderson, Courtney, *To the Golden Shore: The Life of Adoniram Judson* (1987). • Harris, Edward Norman, *A*

Star in the East: An Account of the American Baptist Missions to the Karen of Burma (1920). • Marshall, Harry I., *The Karen People of Burma: A Study in Anthropology and Ethnology* (1922). • Mason, Francis, *The Karen Apostle or Memoir of Ko Tha Byu, the First Karen Convert* (1861). • McLeigh, Alexander, *Christian Progress in Burma* (1929). • Purser, W. C. B., *Christian Mission in Myanmar* (1913). • Trager, Helen G., *Burma Through Alien Eyes* (1966).

Doh Say

Karthak, Robert

(b. Kalimpong, India, 10 Jan 1926). Pastor of Nepali Isai Mandali (Gyaneswor Church), one of the first churches in Kathmandu; founding member of the Nepal Christian Fellowship* (NCF); and father figure to churches throughout Nepal*.

Karthak was born into a Christian family and made a personal decision to follow Christ in 1947. For a number of years, he served as youth leader at Macfarlane Memorial Church in Kalimpong. In early 1956, he came to Kathmandu with a band of young people in answer to God's calling on his life.

Nepal had just opened its door to the outside world, and Christians could now live there. Karthak was set apart for full-time ministry from the time he entered Nepal. He became the first pastor of Nepali Isai Mandali, now known as Gyaneswor Church. Established in 1957, it was one of the first two churches in Kathmandu.

In 1959, Karthak went to London Bible College. He was married upon his return in 1960 and continued to pastor Gyaneswor Church. A founding member of Nepal Christian Fellowship, he served as secretary in 1962 and as president from 1963 through 1978. From 1969, also he served on the formative committee for bringing the Bible Society* into Nepal. He has ministered to churches and people throughout Nepal and been looked to as a kind of elder statesman of the Nepali church, representing Nepali Christians both within the country and internationally. After the restoration of democracy, which resulted in more religious freedom in Nepal, Gyaneswor Church has grown to a membership of over 1,000 baptized adults under Karthak's leadership. The church is now mentoring several smaller churches in various parts of Nepal.

Bibliography

Nepal Church History Project (transcript of a personal interview with Robert Karthak). • Nepal Christian Fellowship historical outline.

Rajendra K. Rongong

Kasatkin, Nikolai (Nikorai)

(Ivan Dmitriyevich) (b. Smolensk, Russia, 14 Aug 1836; d. 16 Feb 1912). First Russian Orthodox* Church missionary to Japan*.

The son of a deacon, Nikolai's birth name was Ivan Dmitriyevich Kasatkin. He went to Smolensk Elementary School and then graduated from Petersburg School of Theology. On 6 Jul 1860, he received the name Nikolai at his initiation (hair-cutting) ceremony; he was ordained a priest on 12 Jul and then went to Japan on 14 Jun 1861 as the priest attached to the Hakodate Consulate. For seven years, he studied the Japanese language, history, culture, religion, and the national traits of the people, after which he began missionary work.

In 1868, Nikolai converted the Shinto priest, Sawabe Takuma. Sawabe was the first fruit for the Orthodox faith in Japan, and he later became the first Japanese priest. In 1869, Nikolai returned to Russia and then came back in 1870 to open official mission work in Japan; he was promoted to archimandrite and became head of the mission work. He moved the center of mission work from Hakodate to Tokyo's Surugadai district in 1872 and opened Denkyo (mission) School and Orthodox Seminary there. On 11 Apr 1880, he was elevated to bishop at a ceremony at Alexander Nefusky Monastery, Holy Trinity Hall, in Petersburg. While in Russia, he was visited by the literary great, Fyodor Mikhailovich Dostoevski. He returned to Japan 24 Feb 1891 and built the Tokyo Cathedral of the Resurrection. He endured great suffering in 1904 because of the Russo-Japanese War. He assigned priests to comfort the over 70,000 Russian prisoners of war who were held in approximately 20 concentration camps around Japan. On 6 Apr 1906, he was promoted to archbishop.

From about 1862, Nikolai worked at translating and publishing many materials, including the Bible*, liturgy, *Hacchkei* (Prayer Book of the Year), *Sanka Saikei* (Prayer Book of Lent), *Gojun Keiryaku* (Prayer Book of Pentecost), *Liturgy for Holy Days, Daily and Monthly Lectionary,* and *Holy Services Liturgy and Lectionary.* In 1901, with the cooperation of Nakai Tsugumaro, he translated and published *Waga Shu Iisusu Harisutosu no Shinyaku* (The New Testament of Our Lord Jesus Christ). He was buried at Yanaka Cemetery. Statistics for the Russian Orthodox Church show 266 churches, 33,017 members, 48 Japanese priests, and 116 preachers at the time of his death. Schools included the Orthodox Seminary, Orthodox Women's Seminary, and Kyoto Orthodox Girls' School. *Seikyo shimpo* (Orthodox News) was only one of a number of regular publications. On 16 Dec 1969, the Russian Orthodox Church bestowed sainthood on Nikolai, making him Bishop, Saint Nikolai.

Bibliography

Mochizuki Kodo, *Nikorai Daishukyo Tsuitoroku* (In Memory of Bishop Nikolai) (1930). • Japan Orthodox Church, ed., *Meiji Bunka to Nikorai* (Meiji Culture and Nikolai) (1969). • *Nihon Seikyo-shi* (History of the Orthodox Church in Japan) (1978). • Nakamura Kennosuke, trans., *Nikorai no mita Bakumatsu Nihon* (The Last Days of the Tokugawa Shogunate as Seen by Nikolai) (1979). • Stamoolis, James, *Eastern Orthodox Mission Theology Today* (1986).

Ushimaru Yasuo

Kasimo, Ignatius Joseph

(b. Yogyakarta, 1900; d. Jakarta, 1986). Served during the Indonesian war of independence (1945-49) as a junior minister and later as minister for the well-being of the people (1947-48) and minister for food supply (1948-49).

Kasimo attended the Catholic Teachers' College in Muntilan (central Java*), where he was baptized. He continued his education at the agricultural academy at Bogor. As co-founder and first chairman of *Perkumpulan Politik Katolik di Djawa* (Catholic Political Association, 1925) and *Persatuan Politik Katolik Indonesia* (Catholic Political Union, since 1930), he became one of the first Catholic politicians of Indonesia. These two prewar organizations became the main political institutions of the indigenous Catholics and later formed the Catholic Party* of Indonesia (1945-73) with other groups. As a member of the *Volksraad* (1931-42), Kasimo had prepared an earlier motion for self-government of Indonesia (1936). As chairman of the Catholic Party, he became a member of parliament (1945-60) after independence. Because the party, together with a Muslim party, rejected President Soekarno's so-called conception of four legs (especially the inclusion of the Communists into the cabinet as the fourth leg), Kasimo had to step down as chairman. Later he became a member of the Advisory Council (DPA) and of the anti-corruption committee (1967).

Throughout his political career, Kasimo kept the principles he learned from Franz van Lith*: simplicity, straightforwardness, and putting the common good before all group interests. In his later years, he worked hard to compensate clients of a private bank that went bankrupt. He had served as a member of the bank's board but had no influence on its business dealings. Today, the Kasimo Foundation educates young leaders for public life.

Bibliography

Heuken, Adolf, *Ensiklopedi: Populer Tentang Gereja Katolik di Indonesia* (1989).

ADOLF HEUKEN

Katayama Tetsu

(b. Tanabe, Wakayama Prefecture, 28 Jul 1887; d. 30 May 1978). Japanese politician.

Katayama graduated from Tokyo University in German law. In 1919, he opened a legal aid society for the needy; in 1926, he helped Abe Iso establish the Social Democratic Party and was named its chief secretary. He was elected to the house of representatives and served for three terms. During his time in office, he appealed for the reduction of military spending by half and was consequently defeated in his bid for reelection in 1942. After this, he helped form the Japan Socialist Party, serving as its chief secretary. In Sep 1946, he was elected party chairman.

In the early postwar time of confusion, Katayama emerged as a leader in the democratization process, and in April of 1947 was reelected in the first general election under the new constitution. His party won the most seats in the diet, and in June he became prime minister under a coalition formed by the Socialist Party, the Democratic Party, and the Nationalist Cooperative Party. He pushed for democratic policies such as the dismantling of the department of home affairs, the establishing of a department of labor, dismantling of the *zaibatsu* (great financial cartels), and child welfare laws. But owing to opposition from both the right and left wings of the Socialist Party and pressure from the occupation forces against the labor offensive, the National Civil Service Law and the National Police Law were enacted, and he was given the derogatory nickname *Guzu Tetsu* (Tinkering Tetsu) by both sides of the opposition. A nonconfidence vote on the supplementary budget proposal forced him to resign after serving for only eight months.

In 1950, Katayama became chairman of the right wing of the Socialist Party, and in 1960 top adviser to the Social Democratic Party at its formation. He retired from the political sphere in 1965.

Katayama was a member of Fujimicho Church, United Church of Christ in Japan. Throughout his political career, he stood for Protestant uprightness, working to protect the constitution and clean up the government, opposing the stationing of American forces in Japan and all moves to reestablish the Japanese military. Beginning in 1954, he chaired the League for the Preservation of the Peace Constitution, and in 1964 he supervised the Ten-Person Committee to Appeal for Constitution Preservation (the new constitution represents Japan's great spiritual revolution), expressing the deep desire that everyone memorize the preamble to the constitution. Even in delirious moments on his deathbed, he repeatedly stated that he was absolutely against war. In his introduction to the *Shorter Bible*, he wrote, "Christianity is truly the religion of the reformers; it provides the motivating power for the establishment of freedom, peace, and democracy."

Katayama's life, based on the Christian faith, was a struggle for preservation of the constitution, peace, and democratization, and even his political opponents lifted high his ideals and showed respect for this ever-forward-moving leader. He was a leader in many organizations, including being chair of the Christian Association for World Federalism, chair of the board of trustees of the Japan Prohibition League, adviser to the Japan-China Cultural Exchange Association, and chair of the Association for Cleaning Up of Politics and Public Elections. Among the books he wrote: *Nihon shakaishugi no tenkai* (Development of Japanese Socialism), *Minshu no kofuku* (Well-being of the People), *Abe Iso den* (Biography of Abe Iso), and an autobiography, *Kaiko to tenbo* (Recollections and Views).

EBISAWA ARIMICHI, JAPANESE DICTIONARY

Katipunan

Filipino secret armed revolutionary movement for independence from Spain.

Founded on 7 Jul 1892 by Andres Bonifacio, the *Kataastaasan Kagalanggalangang Katipunan* (also known as KKK) had over 100,000 members when it was discovered by the Spanish on 19 Aug 1896. The movement led an open revolt on 23 Aug 1896 at Pagadlawin and in 1898 succeeded in ending more than 300 years of Spanish rule in the Philippines.

Bonifacio's decalogue and the Katipunan's code of ethics written by Emilio Jacinto were based on Christian and indigenous values regarding equality and the family. Women were accepted as members, and patriotism and resistance to oppression were regarded as the concrete practice of one's Christian faith. To many Filipino secular priests, the Katipunan's struggle for national independence also included liberating the Philippine church from the *Patronato Real Espanol* and placing it directly under the pope in Rome.

Bibliography

Alvarez, Santiago, *Katipunan and the Revolution* (1993). • Constantino, Renato, *The Philippines: A Past Revisited* (1975). • Ileto, Reynaldo C., *Pasyon and Revolution* (1979). • Reyes, Ed Aurelio C., *Bonifacio: Siya Ba Ay Kilala Ko?* (Bonifacio: Do I know him?) (1995). • Maring, Ester G. and Joel M., *The Philippines* (1973).

TEODORO MAXIMILIANO M. DE MESA

Kattakayam Cherian Mappila

(b. 24 Feb 1859; d. 1 Dec 1931). Prominent Indian Christian poet and writer.

The most prominent Christian poet in Kerala, Kattakayam made enormous contributions in the field of Christian literature. He belonged to an ancient and distinguished family, Pakalomattam, that converted to Christianity from Hindu Brahminism and received baptism from St. Thomas in the 1st c. His parents were Ulhannan and Cicily. His grandfather migrated to Palai in central Kerala and established the Kattakayam family there. His forefathers being farmers, the family became conspicuous by becoming very rich through business.

According to the usual custom, Kattakayam was sent to school at age five and began learning Sanskrit at age 14. His master, Damodaran, was a great scholar as well as a physician. Kattakayam mastered Sanskrit and became proficient in Sanskrit literature. Along with this, he also obtained much knowledge in Ayurveda, but he never used his knowledge of medicine for his livelihood or as a profession.

At age 16, Kattakayam married Mariyamma, who was from a wealthy family, and they had three sons and three daughters. After his father's death, the family responsibilities fell upon him. He dedicated himself to personal cultivation and scholarship. He did not learn English, because English education was not prevalent in those days, but he gained deep knowledge of Christianity and lived as a good Christian, strictly following all the rituals and practices of Roman Catholicism.

Since childhood, Kattakayam had shown inborn skills in writing. Kandathil Varghese Mappila, the founder of Malayala Manorama, encouraged him much in his literary pursuits. They joined together to found the Bhashaposhim Sabha in 1890, which was the first organization of Malayalam writers. *Satyanada Kahalam,* a weekly, began to publish the poems written by Kattakayam. His first drama, *Esther Charithram, was* based on Esther of the Old Testament. He also wrote *Mar Thoma Charithram,* which portrayed the life and ministry of St. Thomas.

The most important work of Kattakayam is *Sree Yesu Vijayam,* which took him eight years to complete. This Christian poetic work covered history from creation to the conversion of the Roman emperor Constantine. Along with his literary contributions, Kattakayam also played a major role in the social and religious realms. Honoring his literary contribution in 1931, the pope awarded him a gold medal and the title Missionary Apostolica.

By 1915, Kattakayam had handed over all the family responsibilities to his sons. He spent the rest of his life in spiritual matters. Toward the end of his life, he fell sick and was completely bedridden. SAMUEL MATHEW

Kau Chang

(Ko Tiong) (b. Chin-chiang, China, ca. 1837; d. Tainan, Taiwan, 16 Sep 1912). First Taiwanese Presbyterian* Christian and first native preacher.

As the first Taiwanese convert of the English Presbyterian mission in Tainan, Kau had a life experience typical of most native converts. He heard the Gospel inadvertently as he passed an evangelistic meeting on his way to seek guidance from the deities in a local temple because of his failed business. The preacher was probably Wu Wun-Swe, an associate preacher from Amoy who accompanied James Laidlaw Maxwell, the first English missionary to Taiwan. Kau was baptized on 12 Aug 1866 together with three native Taiwanese: Tan Che, Tan Ui, and Tan Chheng-Ho. They were baptized by William Sutherland Swanson, an English Presbyterian minister stationed in Amoy who came to Tainan primarily for this purpose.

After his conversion, Kau first served as cook and helper to Maxwell. Then, with his strong faith and enthusiasm for evangelism, he became the first native preacher. In the course of 38 years, he served various churches in virtually every part of the English Mission, spanning across the central, southern, and eastern parts of Taiwan, even including the Pescadores.

Kau's most horrible experience was the persecution of the Pi Tau church on 11 Apr 1868 when he was severely beaten by a frenzied mob and imprisoned by the local authorities for 50 days, partly for his own safety.

The persecution, though originally an anti-Catholic campaign, manifested the typical suspicion of the common Taiwanese people that Christianity was a malicious foreign force which, along with other colonial powers, was trying to impose poisonous control over the minds of the locals. An interesting aspect of this incident was that Kau was imprisoned partially because he confessed that he "was a sinner."

Two months after this incident. Maxwell, together with Hugh Ritchie, the first English Presbyterian minister to Taiwan, wrote a full report, "Violent Persecution in Formosa," to Rutherford Alcock, then English ambassador to China. They asked for his intervention. The outcome was a reparation of 762 silver dollars to Pi Tau church for her loss.

Kau retired in 1904. He resided with his eldest son, Kau Chin-Sheng, in Tainan until his death in 1912. The younger Kau was a teacher at Tainan Theological College, the first Presbyterian seminary in Taiwan. After 1907, he was pastor of Thai Peng Keng Church in Tainan, the first Presbyterian church in Taiwan. Kau Chang raised a distinguished family which, through six generations, has produced many influential leaders in the Taiwanese church and society, including C. M. Kau, the former general secretary of the Presbyterian Church in Taiwan.

Bibliography

Lai, John Yung-hsiang, *Topics on Taiwan Church History,* Series II (1990). • Ng, Bo-kheng, *90 Years' History (1865-1955) of the Thai-Peng-Keng Maxwell Memorial Church, the Presbyterian Church in Taiwan* (1988).

Cheng Yang-en

Kawakami Jotaro

(b. Atago, Tokyo, 3 Jan 1889; d. 3 Dec 1965). Japanese politician.

Kawakami's father, Shintaro, a lumber merchant, became a Christian late in life and was a friend of Tomeoka Kosuke and Honma Shunpei. Jotaro enrolled in Rikkyo Middle School (Rikkyo Gakuin) in 1901 and later sympathized with the opposition to the Russo-Japanese War (1904-5) by such men as Uchimura Kanzo*, Sakai Toshihiko, and Kotoku Shusui. In 1908, he entered First Higher School and loved to read the Bible in his dorm room. He was baptized the following year. A problem developed when he requested that Tokutomi Roka speak on a case of high treason. That speech on "The Prophet of Anathoth" became the model for Jotaro's life.

In 1911, Kawakami entered the law department of Tokyo Imperial University and after graduation served as a lecturer at Rikkyo University. In 1918, he became a professor at Kwansei Gakuin University. He married Sueko, the daughter of Hiraiwa Yoshiyasu. After lecturing at the Laborers School, he joined the Japan Farm Labor Party in 1926. He was elected to the diet at the first regular election in 1928 and became one of the first proletarian representatives ever in Japan. He was defeated twice after that. He served as a lawyer during all this time, but because of poor compensation for his work he fell into poverty. He received support from Kagawa Toyohiko and others.

In 1936 and 1937, with the unified backing of the Proletarian Party, Kawakami was reelected. In 1940, the various political parties were disbanded, but he remained as director of the Imperial Rule Assistance Association. For this, he was purged from public office in 1946. However, in 1951 the purge was rescinded and his status was restored, and the following year he was nominated to chair the right wing of the Socialist Party. In his acceptance speech, he said, "For me, this position is the Cross," a statement which was seen as a manifestion of his faith, and he became known as "Chairman Cross."

A member of the United Church of Christ in Japan's Ginza Church, Kawakami worked to bring about unification of the left and right wings of the Socialist Party. In 1955, he was able to accomplish this and passed on the responsibility of chairperson to Suzuki Mosaburo. About this time, he was wounded by a terrorist. In 1961, he became chairperson again and served for five terms, spanning five years. During this time, he lectured widely around the country, elicting comparisons to the missionary Paul. He collapsed from overwork in May 1965 and died while convalescing at Izu Nirayama. His autobiography, *Watakushi no rirekisho* (My Personal History), was published in 1961.

Bibliography

Japan Socialist Party editor, *Kawakami Jotaro — jujika iincho no hito to shogai* (The Person and Life of Kawakami Jotaro — "Chairman Cross") (1973).

Tanetani Shun'ichi, Japanese Dictionary

Keasberry, Benjamin Peach

(b. Hyderabad, India, 1811; d. Singapore, 6 Sep 1875). Keasberry was born to British parents who moved to Java* in 1814. He was converted while working in Batavia (Jakarta*) and was subsequently employed by Walter Medhurst* of the London Missionary Society (LMS). In 1834, he journeyed to the United States and attended seminary at Andover in Massachusetts. In 1837, he returned to Singapore* as a missionary for the American Board of Commissioners for Foreign Mission (ABCFM). After 1839, he was employed by the LMS. When the LMS closed its mission in 1847, he resisted the pull to China* and stayed in Singapore as an independent missionary.

With the aid of Abdullah bin Abdul Kadir, Keasberry translated into Malay, and printed, textbooks, *The Pilgrim's Progress,* storybooks, and finally a complete New Testament. In 1843, he built the Malay Chapel, now known as the Prinsep Street Presbyterian* Church, and opened a mission among the Chinese. In 1847 or 1848, he established a boarding school for Malay boys, which provided an education and vocational training for orphans. Alongside these boys, a number of Malay princes attended the school, one of whom became the sultan of Johore and another the raja of Kedah. After Keasberry's death the school continued under government sponsorship. His congregations came under the supervision of Presbyterian missionaries after his death and formed the nucleus of the Presbyterian mission in Singapore and Malaya.

In addition to his foundational work in Bible* translation, Keasberry played a critical role in keeping Christian mission to Singapore's indigenous people alive during the period after the departure of ABCFM and LMS missionaries for China, and before the establishment of permanent Presbyterian and Methodist missions in the late 19th c.

Bibliography

Haines, J. H., "A History of Protestant Missions in the Nineteenth Century, 1815-1881" (doctoral dissertation, Princeton Theological Seminary) (1962). • Cook, J. A. B, "A Short Sketch of the Late Rev. B. P. Keasberry," *The Chinese Recorder and Missionary Journal,* Vol. XL (1909).

Robert A. Hunt

Keshub Chunder Sen

(b. Colutolah, Calcutta, 19 Nov 1838; d. 8 Jan 1884). Key figure in early Hindu dialogue with Christianity in India*.

Keshub was the second son of Piari Mohon and Sarada Devei Sen. He was a typical English-educated, Westernized elite of the 19th c. in Bengal. He began to study the Bible and theology with three missionaries, T. H. Burns, the bishop of Calcutta, and James Long.

Unlike Debendranath Tagore, who remained a conservative Hindu, Keshub came much nearer to Christ. He had a deep personal feeling for Christ and sometimes called himself *Jesus Das* (slave of Jesus). He joined the Brahmo Samaj* in 1857. After a breach in the original Brahmo Samaj, he and his followers founded the Brahmo Samaj of India in 1866, introducing elements from many religions to form an eclectic church. He came into prominence in 1866 through his lecture on "Jesus Christ, Europe and Asia." From 1864 on, Keshub had developed a new movement in religion and social reformation which some said was a "semi-alien Christian faith" but which his followers called a "Christocentric Brahmo Samaj." Many regarded him as a Christian, though he never converted. He developed the idea of the New Dispensation of the Spirit and sought to build the Church of the New Dispensation *(Naba Bidhan)* around his own inspiration.

The primary data for Keshub's understanding of Christ and the Trinity are in his famous lecture "That Marvelous Mystery — The Trinity," first delivered in 1882, which represents a mature stage of his thinking. Keshub denied that Christ is God in any ontological sense. His advice was never to say that Christ is the very God of the universe, the Father of all humankind. Christ shows us neither how God can become a human person nor how a human person can become God. Homage to Christ is not the worship of divinity but the worship of humanity. We worship the Father and honor the Son. Christ is not a man-God; on the contrary, Christ is the Father's begotten Son, a child, a creature.

It is to be noted here that Keshub used the term "God-man" for Christ but interpreted it in his own characteristic way. It is identical in meaning with his other term "divine humanity." In divine humanity, the human person remains a human person and God is only superadded to his nature; humanity continues to be humanity, but divinity is engrafted upon it. For Keshub, Christ is divine because he is the incarnation, not of deity, but of "sonship." He is the incarnation of that perfect relationship of love and obedience to God to which every person is called and which God gives according to the measure of a person's openness to him. Christ shows us how we can exalt our humanity by making it more divine, how while retaining our humanity we may still partake more and more of the divine character. It was for this purpose that Christ came into this world.

Keshub admits that through the Son, Jesus Christ, the Father is manifested to humans, but he adds that both ancient Judaism and Hinduism* have sufficiently revealed the Father and that what is unique about Christ is his revelation not of fatherhood but of sonship. We have to appropriate into our lives Christ's pattern of sonship. That is the way to have access to the Father. Christ is also divine humanity because he is the end product of a process of evolution extending from the beginning of creation, through the lower forms of life, right up to the creation of humans. And Christ is the perfection of humanity. Evolution does not stop with Jesus, for he has made it possible for others to become sons of God like him.

Keshub explains the Trinity through the model of a triangle. The apex is the very God Jehovah, the Supreme Brahman of the Vedas. From him comes the Son touching one end of the base of humanity, then running all along the base; he permeates the world, and then by the power of the Holy Spirit drags us degenerated humanity to himself. In the story of salvation, then, divinity coming down to humanity is the Son and divinity carrying humanity up to heaven is the Holy Spirit. After the Son comes the Holy Spirit, who infuses Christ-life into the hearts and souls of all humans, breaking and annihilating the sins and iniquities of the ages and making all humankind partakers of divine life.

Keshub was one of the pioneers who related the Trinity to *Saccidananda.* He related Father, Son, and Holy Spirit to truth, intelligence, and joy; to the still God, the journeying God, and the returning God. In the Trinity, we have three conditions, three manifestations of divinity. Yet there is one God, one substance, amidst three phe-

Khan, Syed Ahmad

nomena. Not three Gods but one. The true Trinity is not three persons, but three functions of the same person.

It is significant to note that in Keshub's Trinity the Father and Spirit hold a special place which is distinguished from the Son's. He calls the Holy Spirit "Savior," but the Son "Brother." The Father is worshipped and prayers can be addressed directly to the Holy Spirit, while the Son is merely honored. What actually incarnated in the Son was not Godhead but sonship. But also, according to Keshub, no adequate definition can be given to God without reference to Jesus Christ, his Son. Moreover, Christ the Son is the unifying factor of all religions and races, and this universal character of Christ is to be brought out by Indian Christology.

Bibliography

Mozoomdar, Pratap Chander, *Keshub Chunder Sen and His Times* (1917); *The Life and Teachings of Keshub Chunder Sen* (1887); *Keshub Chunder Sen's Lectures in India* (1899); *Keshub Chunder Sen in England* (1881). • Scott, David C., ed., *Keshub Chunder Sen: A Selection* (1979). • Parekh, Manilal C., *Brahmarshi Keshub Chunder Sen* (1926). • Ghosh, N., *The Evolution of Navavidhan* (1930). • Sastri, Sivanath, *History of the Brahmo Samaj,* Vol. II (1912). • Borthwick, Meredith, *Keshub Chunder Sen: A Search for Cultural Synthesis* (1978). • Farquhar, J. N., *Modern Religious Movements in India* (1924). • Sarma, O. S., *Studies in the Renaissance of Hinduism in the Nineteenth and Twentieth Centuries* (1944). • Thomas, M. M., *The Acknowledged Christ of the Indian Renaissance* (1967).

K. P. Aleaz and Subhas Adhikary

Khan, Syed Ahmad

(b. Delhi, India, 17 Oct 1817; d. 25 Mar 1898)

Khan's ancestors, both paternal and maternal, were well-respected Muslim leaders. His ancestors came from Arabia and moved first to Herat and then, during the reign of Shahjahan (1628-57), to India*. Even after their arrival in India and up to the reign of Akbar (1805-37) they enjoyed royal titles and dignity.

Khan received his early education from his maternal grandfather, Khan Farid-ud-Din, who was a distinguished scholar. Later he was educated in the Holy Quran, Arabic, and Persian literature and also excelled in history, mathematics, and medicine. Early in his youth Khan was given full liberty of movement within the society of his own class. He was a great thinker and reformer who shaped the destiny of the Muslims of India and galvanized a frustrated mass of people into a nation with a future.

In 1839 Khan was appointed *naib munshi* (assistant clerk) at the commissioner's office at Agra. His connection with Agra (almost 10 years) was quite important in the development of his personality and of his acquaintance with British administration and culture. During this period he developed his skills, as he was at the heart of the new civilization and politics in India. Agra was also an important missionary center. A Roman Catholic* cathedral was built there in 1846, as well as several schools and orphanages. The Church Missionary Society (CMS) was very active in both evangelistic and educational work and established St. John's College in 1850 (see Education). Thus in Agra, Khan became well acquainted with and interested in Western religion, culture, and administration. He acknowledged the administrative and literary superiority of the British, as seen by his acceptance of Western methods of historiography and his unshaken loyalty to the company, but he found that Western culture as a whole was not completely acceptable by the upper-class, official society in which he moved; still it displayed the glitter of the old Mughal center.

Khan possessed great willpower and competency in his work and developed literary tastes that brought him fame in later life. He compiled a pamphlet in Persian, the *Jam-i-Jum,* and a "Transcript and Analysis of the Regulations." Meanwhile, the government published regulations for *munsif* (judge), and Khan passed this examination. In 1841 Hakim Ahsan Ullah Khan recommended in the Mughal court that he be awarded his hereditary titles, and this was readily agreed to with the further appellation of *arid jang.* In 1847 he wrote the first edition of the *Asar-us-Sanadid* (Traces of the Great).

In 1852 Khan wrote and published another piece of history, this time a *Silslat-ul-Mulk* (Series of Kings), in which he claims to record the names and correct dates of 202 rulers of India from Yudhishtar to Queen Victoria, covering a period of 5,000 years. In 1854 Khan brought out an improved second edition of the *Asar-us-Sanadid.* In revising this work, he was helped by Mr. Roberts, collector and magistrate of Shahjahanpur, who suggested the rearrangement of much of the material. Later, in 1861, this book was translated into French by Garcin de Tassy, the famous French Orientalist, and in 1864 Khan was appointed honorary fellow of the Royal Asiatic Society in appreciation for his work.

In Jan 1855 he was transferred to Bijnor (for two years), where (before the mutiny) his interest in historical and religious studies grew. Khan was at Bijnor when the mutiny occurred, and the British considered the mutiny (1857) the outcome of a Muslim conspiracy to reestablish their rule and after the mutiny turned on them "as their real enemies" (see Islam). Khan was called upon to take an active part in the tumult and uproar that took place and was an eyewitness to the misfortunes that befell the British men and women and to the destruction brought about by the civil war between Nawab Mahmud Khan and the Hindus *chaudries* (local leaders). He played his part wisely and bravely, saving 30 British men and women from the hands of the mutineers and looking after the administration of the district until the mutineers defeated him and compelled him to run for his life.

Some of the members of his family perished in the struggle. He was greatly shocked at the destruction of

Muslim families of Delhi and Muradabad, and this left a permanent scar on his sensitive soul. The Muslims, being the chief participants in the war, had to bear the burden of the revengeful policies of the British, whose attitude toward Muslims was by no means fair. The Hindus (see Hinduism) had also participated in the war, yet they had consolidated themselves in such a manner as not to give rise to any suspicions.

The Muslims resisted the English language, and their apathy to it was misunderstood and strengthened suspicions. Khan, therefore, decided to introduce modern history in his school. He stressed the importance of social intercourse between all peoples. He believed that "Friendly relations between the governors and the governed are far more necessary than between individuals." Khan made a great effort first to remove Muslim-Christian hatred, and he succeeded at least in getting favorable results with Muslims and prepared them to learn the English language and Western sciences and later to be loyal to the British.

For better understanding and enhancement in education, he sailed for England on 1 Apr 1869 with his two sons. In England he met the Duke of Argyll, the secretary of state for India, Lord Lawrence, the late governor general, and members of the India Council and of Parliament and discussed with them the political problems of India. In England and Scotland, he visited many important educational institutions and public schools. In his travels, Khan exchanged ideas about educational problems with teachers and professors. He asked for the list of books generally recommended for all classes of students. He also realized not only that books were a predominant factor in promoting quality education but that other factors, such as highly qualified professors, the discipline of school and especially boarding life, social gatherings, and life outside the classroom also play a significant role in an individual's life. His "cultural pilgrimage" to the United Kingdom acquainted him with modern civilization and gave him an awareness of certain social decadence.

Khan reached home on 2 Oct 1870 with great enthusiasm and ambitious programs. He persuaded his friends to join and help him in his mission. In the beginning he faced much opposition and negative response from his country fellows, but he did not give up and kept on struggling for his great mission. Muhsin-ul-Mulk encouraged him at this time in the establishment of the college. He was able to arrange the ceremony for the laying of the foundation stone of the Muhammadan Anglo-Oriental College (MAO) on 8 Jan 1877, the stone being laid by the viceroy, Lord Lytton. Khan took a deep personal interest in the planning and building. At every stage, he saw to it that the fundamental ideas of the movement were given visual expression. Toward the end of 1883, Theodore Beck became the principal of the college. His capabilities, infectious ardor, and generous disposition improved the management and efficiency of the college. This growth continued to the end of Khan's life. The college succeeded in banishing English contempt on the one hand and Muslim fear and pride on the other. It was a liberal education for Europeans and Indians alike, which helped to bring about some reconciliation between the Indians and the British in their approach to culture.

He died after a severe illness and much anxiety at the age of 81. Khan's death created a great vacuum in the Muslims' leadership, and many considered it a national calamity. He was buried on the college premises near the mosque.

Bibliography

Rehmani, Begum, *Sir Syed Ahmad Khan: The Politics of Educational Reform* (1985).

AWAIS GILL

Khin Khin, Katherine

(b. Pyay [Prome], 7 Jul 1909). Burmese writer and educator.

Khin Khin received her education from the American Baptist Mission School (Pyay), St. Mary's Girls' High School, Yangon College, Judson's College, Mortin Lane Teachers' Training School (Moulmein), and the Methodist Girls' High School (Yangon). Fluent in Burmese and English, she wrote articles for magazines and newsletters while she studied at Yangon College. Khin Khin wrote for the magazines *Toe-Teh-Ye* and *Myanmar Ah-Swe* when she was a senior assistant teacher at Eastern Yangon Methodist Girls' and Boys' High School, and when she was a vice-headmistress at Latha St. Mary Girls' High School. From 1942 to 1945, she stayed at Kwanchan-gone Township and worked with the education organization to compile a Burmese dictionary.

Khin Khin served as deputy director in the Ministry of Information in 1945-46. From 1946 to 1964, she was headmistress at St. Mary's Girls' High School, Yangon. She continued to serve another two years after schools were nationalized and then she retired in 1966. As headmistress, she required all boarding students, regardless of religion, to attend morning devotions, which included Bible study. Through the discipline of her school, she shared the Gospel with many students. After her retirement, she served as director of the religious education department of Yangon Diocese, translating volume four of the religious education study guide by Dorothy Louis and making teaching aids for Sunday school classes. In 1970, she served as director of the printing and publication department of the Anglican Church in Myanmar.

Khin Khin took on many leadership roles, including editor of the Christian Literature Society (1941-42); board member of the Young Women's Christian Association* (YWCA) of Yangon; member of the Burmese Women's League Literature Society (1941-48); secretary of the national YWCA, the Yangon YWCA, the Myanmar Women's Council, and Women's Literature Society; member of the Myanmar Council of Churches (1948-92); and member of the Myanmar Bible Society* and the

Yangon Diocese Trust. She continued writing articles for magazines and translating English articles into Burmese for the magazines *Shu-ma-wa* and *Lon-ma-lay*. Her pen name is either Meh Kha Khway or Kha Khway Meh. She was elected for a term to represent Tha-ke-ta Township and participated in the *Pyithu Lutaw* (People's Council) from 1981 to 1985.

A capable, learned, and energetic woman, Khin Khin is completely committed to the welfare of her church and country.

Bibliography

Myanmar Writers and Journalists Association, *News Letter*, No. 5 (in Burmese) (1985). • Holy Cross Theological College, *Golden Jubilee Magazine* (in Burmese) (1985). • Ma Myint Oo, *Lon-ma-lay Magazine* (in Burmese) (1986).

Saw Maung Doe

Khmer Rouge

The Khmer Rouge, so named by Prince Sihanouk in 1967, are Cambodian Communist revolutionaries. They installed the "Democratic Kampuchea" regime which ruled Cambodia from 1975 to 1979. They are responsible for the death of at least two-and-a-half million Cambodians out of a total population of eight million.

The initial cell of the Khmer Rouge consisted of students sent by the French authorities of the Protectorate to pursue their studies in France at the end of the 1940s: Saloth Sar (alias Pol Pot), Ieng Sary, Son Sen, Hu Nim, Hu Youn, Khieu Samphan, Chhum Mum, and Chhum Choeun. Through contact with French students, these Cambodians acquired a Marxist-Leninist ideology in its Stalinist form. Returning home, they attempted to participate in the government of the country, in some cases several months before and in others some years after independence (1953), but Prince Sihanouk refused to share the political power that he monopolized.

In 1960, the Khmer Rouge formed the Pracheachon (Party of the People), the pro-Chinese Cambodian Communist Party of which Saloth Sar (Pol Pot) became secretary general, replacing Tou Samuth, secretary of the Soviet-Vietnamese-aligned Communist Party. After 1962, the royal police pursued the members of the party, accusing them of fomenting unrest among students and in the countryside. Several revolutionaries were imprisoned and executed on Sihanouk's orders. The historic leaders (Pol Pot, Ieng Sary, Nuon Chea, Son Sen) went underground. Khieu Samphan, You Youn, and Hu Nim joined the royal government with the intention of instilling their ideology into the state organisms. In 1967, following a peasant uprising in the region of Battambang for which the Khmer Rouge were held responsible, the three ministers rejoined their old companions in the underground. By 1970, the movement numbered about 3,000 members.

The dismissal of Sihanouk on 18 Mar 1970 was an unexpected opportunity: the Vietcong invaded Cambodia, rounded up all the young men, and formed the Army of National Liberation, which they handed over to the Khmer Rouge. Sihanouk, then in China*, depended on their support against General Lon Nol, who had dismissed him. He invited the peasants to join their ranks. With political and material support from China, the Khmer Rouge gained victory over the troops of Lon Nol in 17 Apr 1975.

The Khmer Rouge emptied all the towns and villages, treating the population as prisoners of war and sending them to work in collective projects, in particular to create a gigantic system of irrigation worthy of the kings of Angkor and an egalitarian rural society. They thought that by this means they could manage to produce three rice harvests during the year. All the intellectuals, the former government officials, and military personnel were killed: "To keep them alive is no profit; to make them disappear is no loss. . . . It is not necessary to be educated to plant rice. The rice paddy is the university," said the Khmer Rouge.

At the end of 1977, the Khmer Rouge began to be rent by internal divisions: Pol Pot and Ta Mok, of the central region, seized power and eliminated the cadres of the five other regions. They plunged into a phobia of espionage and executed their own friends, saying, "It is better to condemn an innocent man than to keep a guilty man alive." They dreamed of reconquering Cochin China, the lower part of Vietnam, called Kampuchea Krom (Lower Cambodia), the cradle of the Khmer race. Incidents of an increasingly bloody nature broke out along the Khmero-Vietnamese frontier. The Vietnamese army made an incursion into Cambodia on 31 Dec 1977 and rounded up 300,000 people to be trained in Vietnam to run the country. On 25 Dec 1978, the Vietnamese army again invaded Cambodia, and on 6 Jan 1979 the Khmer Rouge abandoned Phnom Penh and took refuge in the mountains close to Thailand, then in Thailand itself. Supported by the United States and several Western nations that wanted to counter Soviet expansionism represented by Vietnam, the Khmer Rouge launched anti-Vietnamese guerrilla warfare from 1979 to 1989.

Despite having signed the Paris Accords, the Khmer Rouge refused to lay down their arms or to participate in the elections of 1993. They live in the forest close to Pailin, sell rubies and timber to Thai businessmen, and thus have the means of continuing the war and at the same time sabotaging the reconstruction of the country. Virtually all of the Khmer Rouge today have either died or returned to society.

Bibliography

Ponchaud, François, *Cambodia, Year Zero* (1977). • Pechoux, Christophe, *Les Nouveaux Khmers Rouges*. • Kiernan, Ben, *How Pol Pot Came to Power* (1985). • Beker, Elizabeth, *When the War Is Over* (1986).

François Ponchaud

Khmer Serey. *See* Issaraks

Kil Sun Joo

(b. Anjoo, near Pyongyang, Korea, 15 Mar 1869; d. 26 Nov 1935). Korean Presbyterian* minister, evangelist, and patriot.

Born of a family deeply rooted in traditional Confucianism*, Kil studied Chinese literature from his childhood. He became a successful merchant. He was interested in Taoism* but also sought out truth through other traditional religions. He was never satisfied by these pursuits.

At age 28, Kil was given some Christian literature, including John Bunyan's *Pilgrim's Progress* and a Chinese Bible, by a friend who was converted through the preaching of Samuel A. Moffett*, a Presbyterian missionary at Pyongyang. Kil decided to pray to the Christian God and test his reality. In the midst of his prayer, he heard a voice calling his name. He responded by asking for forgiveness of his sin and salvation for his soul. He was immediately baptized by Graham Lee, a Presbyterian missionary in Pyongyang.

Kil was one of the first seven students to enroll at Presbyterian Theological Seminary established in 1901 in Pyongyang. He graduated in 1907 and was among the first seven Korean ministers ordained by the newly established independent presbytery of Korea, the Jangdauhyun Presbyterian Church in Pyongyang.

Kil played a leading role in the revival of 1907, which began with a Bible conference in Pyongyang. He led many revival meetings throughout the country. He initiated the 4:00 A.M. Daybreak Prayer Meeting, which has become a characteristic feature of the Korean church. In 1912, when the general assembly of the Korean Presbyterian Church was established, he was elected its vice-moderator.

In Mar 1919, Kil was one of the 33 who signed the Declaration of Independence (see Korea Independence Movement of 1919). Imprisoned for two years, he memorized the Book of Revelation and wrote *Malsehak* (Eschatology), which served as the text for his future revival meetings.

Kil read the Old Testament 30 times, the New Testament 100 times, and the book of Revelation 10,200 times. During the 30 years of his ministry, he established 60 churches, delivered 20,000 sermons, baptized 3,000 catechumens, and made 70,000 converts. He also published a novel, *Mansasungchu,* and a collection of sermons, *Kangdabogam.*

Kil fell from the altar and died while leading a revival meeting at the Pyengsu presbytery.

Bibliography

Kil Jin Kyong, *Yongke Kil Sun Joo* (1975); *Yongke Kil Sun Joo Moksa Chujak' jip* (Collection of the Rev. Kil Sun Joo's Writings) (1968). • Kim In Suh, *Kim In Suh Chujak Ch' unjip* (Collection of Kim In Suh's Writings) (1976). • Rhodes, Harry A., *History of the Korea Mission of the Presbyterian Church USA, 1884-1934* (1934).

KIM IN SOO

Kim Chae Choon

(Kim Chae-Jun) (b. North Hamkyung, Korea, 1901; d. 1987). Korean theologian.

Kim completed his studies at Aoyama University (department of theology) in Tokyo (1928) and went on to Princeton Seminary (1929). He was influenced by liberalism and the neo-orthodox theology of Karl Barth and Emil Brunner. Unable to comply with the more conservative theologians at Princeton, he transferred to Western Seminary, where he majored in Old Testament studies (1929-32) and earned a master's degree. He returned home to Korea* and devoted himself to theological education (1939-70). Union College, British Columbia, Canada, conferred on him an honorary doctorate (1958) in recognition of his contributions to theological education in Korea.

An open-minded person, Kim was acquainted with the works of Barth and Brunner, as well as Paul Tillich, Rudolf Bultmann, Reinhold and H. Richard Niebuhr, John Bennett, and Teilhard de Chardin. He translated Richard Niebuhr's *Christ and Culture,* Brunner's *Christianity and Civilization,* and Bennett's *Christian and State.* He was most influenced by Richard Niebuhr and adopted his "transforming Christ" as the model for his theology.

There are five main points in Kim's theology. First, humanity and history must be renewed in Christ through the negating of one's self. He rejected the progressive view of history which sees a socio-cultural progress of the present situation toward an ideal moral and spiritual kingdom. Second, the spirit of Christ is a transforming reality. The Gospel is neither a set of doctrines nor a theological system. It is a dynamic spiritual reality which is active in the Holy Spirit. Third, the kingdom of God is manifested in all human history. There is no separation between the religious and the secular domain, that is, the dichotomy between the natural and supernatural has been overcome. Fourth, the concretization of God's kingdom is a paradox. It is both the work of God's grace through the Holy Spirit and the work of humankind. This common participation is not a simple synergism but a paradoxical theonomy. Fifth, nature and history, tradition and culture, have their own existential meaning in God's creation. Agreeing with Richard Niebuhr's culture-transforming theology, Kim believed in the inherent goodness of God's creation.

Kim rejected both simple materialism and naturalism as well as traditional conservative supernaturalism, that is, the dichotomy of nature and supernature. The essence of the Christian Gospel is the "Word becoming flesh." In other words, heaven and earth are united through the incarnation and have become a creative unity. While heaven is the spiritual work of a supernatural entity, the ultimate concern of the Scriptures is focused on the earth (Matt. 6:10). Kim refuted the Gnostic approach which emphasized the spiritual reality and denounced the created world of nature and history. He looked for a renewal of heaven and earth in God's creation.

Kim's works are collected in 18 volumes published by Hanshin University Press in 1992.

Bibliography

Sang Tack Lee, *Religion and Social Formation in Korea* (1996).

KIM KYOUNG JAE

Kim Ik Doo

(b. Chaeryong, Hwanghae Province, Korea, 1874; d. 14 Oct 1950). Korean Presbyterian* minister and revivalist preacher nicknamed the Billy Sunday of Korea.

The only son of a local scholar, Kim Eungsun, Kim was a model young man until he fell into bad company at age 25. He became notorious for his drinking, gambling, and delight in harassing others, especially Christians. At the age of 27, however, he was converted through a woman missionary. Kim enrolled at the Presbyterian Seminary in Pyongyang in 1906, graduating in 1910, the year of the Million Souls Movement*. He was ordained and served as pastor of the Sinchen Church in Hwanghae Province until 1923.

Kim became a famous evangelist and revivalist throughout the nation. He was elected as moderator of the general assembly of the Presbyterian Church in 1920. His reputation as a faith healer was also reported in the secular dailies. In 1920, Kim was invited to conduct revival meetings by seven churches in Seoul. The Kim Ik Doo Revival had a record attendance of more than 10,000 people.

In all, Kim led 776 revival meetings, preached 28,000 times, established 150 new churches, healed thousands of the sick, and inspired more than 200 to become ministers. It is estimated that more than two million people turned to Christ as a result of his preaching. His healing ministry, however, drew criticism from the Christian and non-Christian communities because there were many who were not cured. As a result, he was ridiculed as crazy and accused of practicing shamanism.

After Korea was liberated from the Japanese, Kim joined the *Kidokkyodo Yonmaeng* (Christian Federation), founded by Kang Yang Uk, the grandfather of Kim Il Sung. In 1949, Kim Ik Doo became moderator of the Christian Federation. In 1950, he was shot and killed by Communist soldiers just as he was pronouncing the benediction toward the end of a daybreak prayer meeting.

Bibliography

Park, Yong Kyu, *An'ak Sangol-han'kook Kiohoe buheung Moksa Kim Ik Doo Chunki* (The Valley of Anak: The Biography of the Revivalist of the Korean Church, the Rev. Kim Ik Doo) (1968). • Clark, Allen D., *A History of the Church in Korea* (1971).

KIM IN SOO

Kim Kyo Shin

(b. Hamheung, South Hamkyung Province, North Korea, 18 Apr 1904; d. 25 Apr 1945). Christian educator, religious journalist, and a leading member of the non-church movement* in Korea.

Kim studied at Hamheung Agricultural School. He went to Japan to study English and later geography. In Apr 1920, he was converted to Christianity and joined the Japanese non-church movement led by Uchimura Kanzo*.

When Kim returned home in 1927, he began teaching in private high schools as well as public schools, such as Kyung Ki and Song Do Boys' high schools. He published a periodical, *Sungsuh Chosun* (The Bible Chosun [Korea]), to propagate the non-church movement, suggesting that the Korean churches return to the Bible instead of the institutional church. In his periodical, he advocated the indigenous nationalist Christian movement over against Japanese and Western influence.

Because of his strong opinions expressed in the journal against Japanese rule, Kim was dismissed from his teaching position and imprisoned in 1941. Publication of his journal was banned. When he was released from prison, he retired to work in a fertilizer factory near his hometown. There he actively involved himself in the labor movement to improve working conditions of factory workers but soon died of typhus.

DAVID SUH, with contributions from
SEO JEONG MIN, translated by KIM IN SOO

King, Louis L.

(b. New Jersey, United States, 1915). Missionary to India* (1947-54) under the Christian and Missionary Alliance* (C&MA); mission executive for India*/Middle East and subsequently vice president of the C&MA for overseas ministries (1954-78); seventh president of the C&MA (1978-87).

King was born on a New Jersey farm to devout Presbyterian* parents. After his conversion he felt the call to ministry and attended the Nyack (New York) Missionary Training Institute, from which he graduated in 1936. Without further formal education, he pastored churches in New York, Illinois, and Nebraska for 10 years; then he and his wife, Esther, sailed for India in 1947. Upon completing studies in the Gujarati language, the Kings started a church in Palanpur, the capital of the state. Working cooperatively with an Indian pastor, Benjamin Bala, they established the first C&MA church in that state.

While on home leave in 1954, King was asked to supervise the work in India/Middle East, and two years later he was elected as the C&MA's vice president of overseas ministries. His vision for making the indigenous church a reality on all C&MA mission fields is one of his enduring accomplishments. His reputation as a missionary statesman, passionate missionary speaker, and effective administrator brought him many distinctions, including two honorary doctorates. He also realized a vision to unite all the overseas C&MA churches in a worldwide fellowship not unlike the World Baptist* Alliance. The first of these gatherings involved a smaller number of representatives but grew into triennial plenary gatherings called the World Alliance Fellowship, attended now by representatives of more than 50 national churches.

Seeking to work amicably and collegially with national church bodies, King pioneered a plan of working agreements between the C&MA of the United States and Canada and the newer national churches that were the fruit of that ministry. The effect was that, beginning in the 1960s, no missionary was appointed to any field without the prior approval and invitation of the national churches. This had positive effects on all the Asian churches of the C&MA, including Vietnam* and Indonesia*, which had grown considerably since 1950.

In the 1960s King became aware of the implications of an urbanizing movement all over the globe and especially in Asia. Whereas the C&MA had been a "hinterland" mission seeking to serve and evangelize the furthest unreached areas of the globe, it now began a strategy to reach the unevangelized urban dweller. Cooperating with national churches, the missions of the C&MA began to strategize, mobilize, and enter the megacities mushrooming across Asia and the world.

King was invited by Euro-American ecumenical* executives to dialogue and present lectures regarding the future of missions in a postcolonial, nationalist world. He became respected as a fierce defender of evangelical theology with its doctrines of the uniqueness of Christ, the irretrievable lostness of the impenitent, and the inescapable duty of the church to evangelize until Christ returned. His public messages, delivered without notes, raised a prophetic voice against institutionalized self-service and galvanized the C&MA and its Asian churches to remain true to their focus on the deeper life, evangelism, and missions.

Bibliography

King, Louis L. "Historical Drift," *The Alliance Life* (13 May 1987). • Niklaus, Robert L., *All for Jesus: God at Work in the Christian and Missionary Alliance* (1986); "From Homestead to Executive Office," *The Alliance Life* (13 May 1987).

James F. Lewis

Kirishitan Evangelism

(Kirishitan Dendo). "Kirishitan Evangelism" is the term given wide currency by Anesaki Masaharu, but "evangelism" is not the word that was used historically. Kirishitan "propagation" in Japan was begun by Francis Xavier*, a Jesuit* missionary who had first gone to India* with a mandate from the king of Portugal. Japan*, however, was not a territory of Portugal, so Xavier's propagation was not part of a Portuguese colonization plan of Christianity and Pepper. He first heard of the situation in Japan from Jorge Alvares and felt a sense of divine calling from his contact with Yajiro (a Japanese criminal residing in Malaya). It is important to note that Xavier made plans for his voyage to Japan without telling the king, and thus, instead of receiving support, he suffered interference from the Portuguese officials. He finally reached Japan on a Chinese pirate ship.

Mission work went forward with particular attention and adaptation to the special conditions present in Japan. Among those who came after Xavier was Francisco Cabral, the head of Jesuit mission work in Japan, who took a more Portuguese orientation. When he and others moved to establish a Japanese church, many of the persons who had assisted the missionaries were estranged. On the other side, the number of people who followed Guecchi-Soldo Organtino, the Italian priest, in the Kansai area increased year by year, something which presented a sense of success greater than that in Kyushu.

When inspector Alessandro Valignano* came to Japan in 1579 and held a meeting on mission work in Japan, the participants established a 21-item plan of action attuned to the situation in Japan. Included were schools for the training of Japanese priests, construction of churches for the Japanese, and translating of the Christian faith into the Japanese culture. Attempting to lay the groundwork for Japanese acceptance of the Gospel, and spurred on by indicators such as *Iezusu-kai nihon kanku jijo tekiyo* (Summary of the Situation in the Japan Area by the Society of Jesus), the Kirishitans achieved greatest success during the decade 1580-90. Hideyoshi, the dictator of Japan, saw the growing number of converts among *daimyo* and military commanders, along with the mobilizing potential of the churches, as more threatening to his absolute rule than were the earlier rebellions of Honganji's monk-soldiers; and so began a persecution of the Kirishitans. In 1587, Hideyoshi issued an order that all Jesuit missionaries be expelled, and persecutions began in Kyoto and Nagasaki. Because of conditions both in and outside of Japan, the eventual outcome was uncertain.

In 1590, Valignano returned to Japan to meet again with leaders there. He reconfirmed the direction of mission work in Japan and gave careful thought to the future, beginning to make use of the printing press he had brought. Thus there appeared to be a return of springtime for the mission work. In view of the peculiar situation present in Japan at the time, Valignano foresaw that having different monastic orders come to Japan to do mission work would only cause a great deal of confusion. With this in mind, he petitioned the pope to give the Jesuit order exclusive rights to do work there. On 28 Jan 1585, Gregory XIII issued an order *(Ex pastolari officio)* to that effect.

However, arguing that the Jesuits were taking too

cautious and self-restraining an attitude toward the work following the expulsion order, the Franciscan and Dominican orders in the Philippines contended that the Jesuits had given up on their mission and pastoral duties, and thus the Japanese believers had been abandoned like lost sheep. Taking advantage of trade negotiations already begun between the Philippines and Japan, Dominican priest Juan Cobo went to Japan as an emissary of the Philippine government, followed in 1593 by Pedro Bautista, a Franciscan* brother. Bautista stayed on to do mission work under the pretext of gathering information about Japan. His action did not necessarily mean he had an understanding of the situation in Japan at the time, and this caused problems, which brought on the martyrdom of 26 believers in Feb 1597. Pope Clement VIII, however, approved passage to Japan via Portugal, and, beginning in 1602, members of the Franciscan, Dominican*, and Augustinian* orders were formally able to do mission work there. In Aug 1608, Pope Paul V issued a papal order removing all restrictions on mission work in Japan.

The new Tokugawa shogunate (government), however, was moving toward a basic policy banning Christianity and suppressing trade with the Spaniards and Portuguese. To counter this, the Franciscan priest Luis Caballero Sotelo set up a plan for doing mission work in the Ou area (northern Honshu), where the Jesuits had not yet done any work. He approached Date Masamune and, while mediating a trade arrangement between the Ouhu Province and Spain, laid plans to set up a diocese for the Franciscan* order. An emissary was sent to Europe regarding setting up the diocese (Keicho Ken'o Shisetsu). However, in Spain and also in Rome, because of information from the Jesuits about Japan, these new developments were received with misgivings, and negotiations suffered because of the cautions being expressed. This was turned into an opportunity, however, as mission work in Ou moved forward. Believers from the Kyoto/Osaka area had been banished to Tsugaru (also in northern Honshu), others had fled from persecution to Ou, and Jesuit priests occasionally traveled north incognito to minister to believers who were in hiding in the mines of Hokkaido, so that, thanks to the persecution, mission work spread throughout the country.

At the same time, pressure from the shogunate became increasingly severe, and from about 1617 into the 1630s, many Christians were martyred, and Japan fast approached the time of its isolation from the outside world. In spite of the martyrs, previously expelled missionaries and some new missionaries continued to slip into Japan. In 1643, this slipping in was brought to a complete halt, and it was announced that the Kirishitan era had ended.

However, plans to rebuild the church of the Japanese martyrs continued, a specific one being the plan in Luzon (Philippines) to sneak the Japanese Kirishitan missionary Kurokawa Juan back into Japan. Meanwhile Giovanni Battista Sidotti, a Jesuit priest, made his way into Japan alone and was subsequently arrested, but, through the interrogation that followed, Arai Hakuseki had his eyes opened to a worldwide vista, causing him to reject the former accusations that the Kirishitans had invaded Japan. This triggered a call for Jesuits stationed in China to influx Japan, and toward the end of the 18th c., a secret religious society was formed in Osaka.

During Japan's first Kirishitan century, fewer than 200 priests came from the four Catholic orders, but the number of those baptized is estimated to run in the hundreds of thousands. In the late 16th c., when they were most prolific, there were about 350,000 believers. At that time the total population of western Japan, where the mission work was carried out, was about 20 million; thus in the 50 years from the beginning of missionary work, about 1.8 percent of the population became believers. Comparing this figure with the percentage of persons who became Christians in the more than 100 years from the resumption of missionary work in 1859 to the present time, one can see how remarkable that conversion rate was.

Bibliography

Anesaki Masaharu, *Kirishitan dendo no kohai* (Rise and Fall of Kirishitan Mission) (1930). • Ebisawa Arimichi, *Nihon kirishitan shi* (History of Japanese Kirishitans) (1966). • Moran, J. F., *The Japanese and the Jesuits: Alessandro Valignano in Sixteenth-Century Japan* (1993).

Ebisawa Arimichi

Kitamori Kazoh

(b. Kumamoto, Japan, 1916; d. Tokyo, 1998). Japanese "pain of God" theologian and Kyodan (United Church of Christ in Japan) Church leader and pastor.

As a high school student, Kitamori was so impressed by Sato Shigehito's paper on Luther that he decided in 1935 to go to Tokyo to attend the Lutheran Theological Seminary. Graduating in 1938, he then enrolled in the department of literature of Kyoto Imperial University, studying with Tanabe Hajime, a disciple of philosopher Nishida Kitaro. He graduated from Kyoto in 1941 (granted the Ph.D. in 1962) and worked as an assistant there until being appointed in 1943 to the Eastern Japan Theological Seminary (subsequently Tokyo Union Theological Seminary). Promoted to full professor in 1949, he taught systematic theology at Tokyo Union until his retirement in 1984. Because of his status as Japan's premier postwar theologian, Kitamori was a major figure in the reorganization of the Kyodan Church, helping to draft its confession of faith. He also pioneered the Kyodan's Chitose Funabashi Church and served as pastor there from 1950 until 1996.

Kitamori's groundbreaking work, *Kami no Itami no Shingaku* (Theology of the Pain of God), was published in 1946. It is one of the few Christian books in Japan's prestigious *Kodansha Gakujutsu Bunko* (Kodansha's Academic Library). The twelfth Japanese edition was published in 1995. *Theology of the Pain of God* has also been translated into English (1965), German (1972), Spanish (1975), Italian (1975), and Korean (1987).

Though he wrote a total of 42 books and numerous articles, Kitamori never abandoned his single-minded devotion to his core theme of the pain of God. As a creative, existential integration of Lutheran theology with a variety of Japanese religious and literary themes, Kitamori's "pain of God" theology repudiates traditional Western views which portray God as incapable of suffering (divine impassibility). The biblical touchstone of Kitamori's theology is Jer 31:20b, which is rendered "My heart is pained" in the *Bungotai* (Japanese Literary Translation). Kitamori said that the essence of God is pain. In Christ, God loves that which must not be loved (humanity) at the cost of allowing his Son to die. The cross of Christ is the place where God enters into a painful inner conflict. There God's pain challenges and ultimately overcomes God's wrath. For Kitamori, the pain of God is the mediating synthesis between God's love and God's justice. Kitamori concluded that Western liberal and dialectical theologies, by overlooking God's pain and focusing on God's love or election, reduce the cross to "an instrument of suffering without teeth."

References to Kitamori have appeared in the writings of a number of Western theologians, including Moltmann, Otto, Solle, Hesselink, Jüngel, Küng, Bohren, and McGrath. Though the general Japanese reading public has shown a consistent interest in Kitamori's "pain of God" theology, its reception has been notably mixed among Japanese Protestant theologians. Japanese Catholic theologians, on the other hand, have been generally more favorable.

Bibliography

Kitamori Kazoh, *Theology of the Pain of God* (1965); *Nihonjin to Seisho* (The Japanese and the Bible) (1995). • Michalson, Carl, *Japanese Contributions to Christian Theology* (1960). • Kumazawa Yoshinobu, *Kitamori Shingaku to wa Nani ka?* (What Is Kitamori Theology?) (1996). • Furuya Yasuo, *A History of Japanese Theology* (1997).

Thomas John Hastings

Koh, Roland Peck Chiang

(b. Sandakan, Sabah, 14 Mar 1908; d. Philadelphia, United States, 6 Oct 1972). First Chinese Anglican* bishop of Malaya (Peninsular Malaysia*).

Koh went to study in Hong Kong* at age 11 and then read commerce at the University of Hong Kong. He did theological studies in China*, England, and America and was honored with doctor of divinity and doctor of law degrees. Converted in Hong Kong, he was ordained a priest by Bishop Roland Hall (Hong Kong) and began to serve as vicar of St. Mary's in 1948.

In 1954, Koh moved to Malaya, which was in a state of emergency (1948-60) because of Communist insurgency. In 1950, thousands of Chinese rural farmers, smallholders, and tin miners had been relocated to barbed villages. An influx of missionaries, expelled from Communist China, were redirected to work in the new villages. Koh's leadership in the Chinese community at Kuala Lumpur led to his appointment and consecration as assistant bishop of Kuala Lumpur on 16 Jun 1958 by the archbishop of Canterbury.

When Malaysia gained its independence from the British on 31 Aug 1957, Bishop Koh was active in forging a national identity for the church and unity among the various races. He was made a "Tan Sri" when the Yang di-Perutan Agong (king) of Malaysia conferred on him the title of Panglima Setia Mahkota (PSM).

On 1 Mar 1965, Koh was enthroned as the second diocesan bishop of Sabah* at the All Saints' Cathedral, Kota Kinabalu. On 7 Apr 1970, he was enthroned as the first bishop of the newly created diocese of West Malaysia at St. Mary's Church, Kuala Lumpur.

Koh's immediate task was to build an autonomous Malaysian church, and he took steps to set up a theological center at Sungei Buloh near Kuala Lumpur in 1972. His sudden death curtailed his vision. He was survived by his wife, Hoh Wai Ying, and four children. Daughter Julia was married to Yong Ping Chung, bishop of Sabah.

Bibliography

Morias, Victor, *Who's Who in Malaysia* (1965). • Roxborogh, John, Robert Hunt, and Lee Kam Hing, eds., *Christianity in Malaysia: A Denominational History* (1992). • *The Anglican News* 1 (Apr 1970) (in Chinese). • *Diocese of Sabah, Silver Jubilee 1962-87.* • Hoh Wai Ying, written notes of Roland Koh, Trinity Theological College (in Chinese).

Lim Cheang Ean

Korea

Korea is a peninsula some 600 miles long, with an average width of 130 miles, precariously located between the empires of China*, Japan*, and Russia. Culturally and linguistically, Koreans are quite different from their near neighbors, and it is commonly believed they are descended from tribes in Siberia. Tradition marks the year 2332 B.C.E. as the date for the country's founding by the mythical ruler Tangun. Chinese civilization was introduced by Kija, who established a colony of scholars, artisans, and craftsmen near Pyongyang in 1122 B.C.E. During the period of the Three Kingdoms (57 B.C.E.–668 C.E.), rival rulers fought for supremacy. United rule came with the establishment of the Silla Dynasty (668-935), which was the golden age of Korean culture and arts. The Silla fell to conquerors from the north in 935, and the latter established the Koryo Dynasty, from which our present word for the country is derived. The Yi Dynasty came to power in 1392, moved the capital to Seoul, and continued in power for the next 500 years. One of the notable achievements of the Yi was the invention of a phonetic alphabet, which brought education within reach of common people.

Because of its location, Korea inevitably became a battleground. In 1592, the Japanese general Hideyoshi laid waste the peninsula until he was defeated by the "turtle boats" (the first ironclad vessels in history) of Admiral Yi Sun Shin. In modern times, two wars have been fought on Korea's soil. The defeat of China in the First Sino-Japanese War* (1894-95) brought an end to China's suzerainty. Then the Russo-Japanese War of 1905 eliminated Russia as a contender for power. Korea became a protectorate of Japan in 1905. Outright annexation came in 1910. Japanese rule sought to destroy all vestiges of Korea's distinctive culture and exploit Korea's resources for world conquest. Independence came at the end of World War II, but peace was short-lived. Korea was divided at the 38th parallel by occupying forces of the United States and Soviet Union. In 1950, Korea was again plunged into war when North Korea launched an all-out attack on South Korea, which was saved by the intervention of the United States and United Nations forces. An uneasy truce was signed in 1953 which has remained in effect until this day.

The religious life of the Korean people has been molded by three faiths: (1) shamanism*, an animistic* faith in which demons and spirits are placated by a shaman who serves as an intermediary with the spirit world; (2) Buddhism*, which was introduced into Korea from China in 372 C.E. and reached its high point of influence during the Silla Dynasty; and (3) the rites, ancestor worship*, and ethical system associated with Confucius, which have influenced all aspects of Korean life. Confucianism* became the state orthodoxy of the Yi Dynasty, which closed its doors to outside influences and became known in the West as the Hermit Nation.

History of Christianity. In 1783, a young Korean scholar named Lee Seung-hoon (Peter Seung-hoon Lee; Yi Song-Hun) accompanied the annual tribute-bearing envoy to Peking, made a study of Christian books which had been translated by the Jesuits*, and was baptized. When he returned to Seoul, he carried some of these books with him and baptized two of his friends, Lee Byok and Kwon Il Shin. The date of their baptism (1784) is considered the beginning of the Catholic faith in Korea. New baptisms occurred and the celebration of the mass was initiated. Concerned about the validity of these rites, the bishop of Peking dispatched a Chinese priest in 1794. Later, responsibility for the infant church was assigned to the Paris Foreign Mission Society*. The first Korean priest, Andrew Kim Tae-goon, was ordained in 1846. It is significant to note that the founding of the Catholic Church in Korea came about by the spontaneous efforts of the Koreans themselves. Missionaries from the West came after an indigenous church had been founded.

Persecution began almost immediately, as Christians were charged with abolishing the practice of ancestor worship. Mass executions of Christians took place in 1791, 1801, 1839, and 1846. French priests continued to enter the country in secret, disguising themselves as Korean mourners, crossing the Yalu on ice, and entering the towns through drain pipes. Most of them were discovered, tortured, and beheaded.

When a Russian war vessel appeared in the Wonsan harbor in 1866, the court reacted with alarm. Fearing the Russians and believing that the Christians were traitors who had asked for the intervention of foreign troops, the vitriolic, anti-Western regent ordered the extermination of all Christians. The number of martyrs during the first 100 years of Catholic history has been estimated as high as 10,000.

The first Protestant to enter the country was R. J. Thomas*, a missionary of the London Missionary Society, who attempted to distribute Chinese Bibles along the coast. In 1866, he accompanied the ill-fated *General Sherman,* an American merchant ship. The ship entered the Taedong River and made a request for trade. This was denied, but the ship continued up the river toward Pyongyang and ran aground. A fight broke out which resulted in the burning of the ship and the extermination of the crew. Thomas perished with the others.

A new day arrived in 1882 with the signing of the Shufelt Treaty, which established diplomatic relations between Korea and the United States. The Korean court believed that a treaty with a Western power would serve as a deterrent to the increasing encroachment of the Japanese. The treaty opened the country to residence by American citizens, but, unlike the "unequal treaties" of China, no mention was made of the propagation of the Christian faith.

Horace N. Allen* (Presbyterian*) arrived in 1884 and was appointed physician to the American legation. It was a most opportune time. A palace coup had just taken place, and a young prince had been gravely wounded. Allen was asked to take charge of the case and nursed his royal patient back to health. In gratitude, the court granted permission for the establishment of a hospital under royal patronage. This was the beginning of missionary medical* work.

The next year, Henry G. Appenzeller* and his wife (Methodist*) and Horace G. Underwood* (Presbyterian) arrived in Seoul. Allen's interpreter was the first Korean Protestant to be baptized. In 1887, the Sae Moon An Presbyterian Church and the Chon Dong Methodist Church were organized.

Converts came from a more distant source. The Scotch missionary John Ross* had begun work among Korean communities along the Yalu River in Manchuria and had made rough translations of some of the Gospels. So Sang-yun, a peddler of Chinese medicines, was converted by Ross and returned home carrying a supply of the Gospel portions. In 1887, he led seven of his friends to Seoul, where they sought out Underwood, requesting baptism. The village of Sorai, from which these men had come, has been honored as the cradle of Protestant Christianity in Korea.

The good news of the Gospel spread rapidly from the beginning. Educational work began with the founding of the Ewha Girls' School by Mary F. Scranton* (Methodist) in 1886 and Pai Chai Boys' School by Underwood in 1887. The circulation of Christian literature in the alphabetized *Han Gul* script became a most effective method of evangelization. An interdenominational Bible* translation committee completed its work on the New Testament in 1900 and on the Old Testament 10 years later. New missionary societies entered the country. Anglicans* and Australian Presbyterians began work in 1890. Southern Presbyterians arrived in 1892 and the Southern Methodists in 1896. The Canadian Presbyterian Mission dates from 1898. The Southern Baptists began work after World War II*. In each mission station, hospitals and schools were begun.

Revivals broke out in 1903 and spread throughout the country (see Korean Revival Movement). In 1907, the Presbyterians graduated the first class at their Pyongyang seminary, ordained the first seven graduates, sent out their first missionaries, and formed the presbytery of all Korea, which became the first and largest Protestant denomination. Christian missions took the lead in national reform movements, promotion of the role of women, and the treatment of leprosy*. The National Christian Council, formed in 1919, served to unite the work of Protestant denominations.

This advance took place in the midst of intense persecution. The Japanese regime singled out the church as the one Korean organization that could block their efforts to stamp out indigenous Korean culture. In 1919, Christians took an active role in the independence* movement and suffered accordingly. In 1935, Christians were forced to worship at the Shinto* shrines, and when Christian schools refused to comply, many were closed. An even harsher time of persecution came in 1950 during the Korean War*, when Christian leaders were singled out for elimination by the Communists. As many as one half of all Protestant pastors were publicly executed or disappeared.

In Korea, Christianity grew much faster than in either Japan or China. Four reasons can be suggested for this: (1) the adoption of the Nevius Methods*, which emphasized self-reliance and minimized the importance of foreign leadership and funds; (2) close cooperation between the various Protestant missions; (3) the fact that the exploitive colonial power in Korea was not the Christian West but Japan, thereby making it patriotic to be a Christian; and (4) The Korean Christians' emphasis on prayer.

Present state of Christianity. The resilience of the Christian movement was again tested during the military regimes of the 1960s and 1970s. Roman Catholics and Protestants alike took part in protesting the denial of human rights and the suppression of democracy. Undoubtedly, these peaceful but persistent protests helped bring about a return to free elections. In 1997, a Roman Catholic layman, Kim Dae-Joon, was elected president of the country.

Today, the Christian movement faces the future with confidence. Twenty-five percent of South Korea's 44 million people are Christian. Christianity has had an impact on every facet of public life. Christian radio stations broadcast the Gospel and have a reputation for honest reporting of the news. Christian chaplains serve in the armed forces. The largest congregation in the world is probably the Full Gospel Church (Pentecostal) in Seoul. Christian universities command the respect of the academic community. Among these are Yonsei University, Ewha Women's University, and the Catholic Segang University. Korean missionaries serve in many countries of the world and look forward with keen anticipation to expanding opportunities for witness and service in Asia and speedy reunion with North Korea.

North Korea since 1950. The division of Korea and the Korean War have brought tragic consequences to the Korean people and the churches in Korea. The joy of liberation from the Japanese occupation of Korea that had lasted nearly half a century was a short-lived experience. The Allied Forces divided Korea into South and North Korea at the infamous 38th parallel. The Russian troops occupied the North, and the United States troops the South. It was meant to be a temporary division but has lasted for half a century.

The Christians in North Korea under the newly established Communist regime faced tremendous challenges as they struggled to be faithful to their convictions as followers of Jesus Christ. Conflicts between Christian ideals and Communist ideologies inevitably pushed the Christians into many confrontations, resulting in persecutions, imprisonment, and even martyrdom. During the Korean War, Christians in North Korea faced the even harsher reality that Christianity was considered a religion of the enemy. Some five million people, mostly Christians, fled from North Korea to South Korea.

There were no signs of Christian community in North Korea after the Korean War until the early 1980s. There were reports of house churches being organized in North Korea in 1983. In 1985, this writer worshipped with Christians in North Korea in house churches in Pyongyang, the capital city of North Korea. The Bible was newly printed, and hymnbooks were printed in 1983 as well.

The Korean Christians Federation (KCF) in North Korea reports that there are some 500 house churches throughout the country, with some 10,000 believers. There are three churches in the capital city of Pyongyang. Bong Su Protestant Church and Chang Choon Catholic Church were built in 1988, and Chil Gol Protestant Church was built in 1990. These churches hold regular worship services on Sundays, with 150-300 believers attending.

There is a theological institute to train pastors for house churches, and there have been increasing opportunities for the leaders of the KCF to meet with church leaders in the United States, Asia, Europe, and other countries around the world. KCF delegations have attended the assemblies of the World Council of Churches in Canberra, Australia, and the World Alliance of Reformed Churches in Hungary in 1987.

Church leaders from North Korea and South Korea have had opportunities to meet together in recent years to discuss their common concerns for peace and reconciliation of divided Korea. The World Council of Churches and the National Council of the Churches of Christ in the United States have sent official delegations to North Korea to meet with church leaders and government officials to further strengthen the Christian communities in North Korea. Billy Graham's visit to North Korea also encouraged Christians in North Korea. There are clear indications that the North Korean government is open to allowing the churches to function officially in the country.

Bibliography

Brown, George Thompson, *Mission to Korea* (1962). • Cho, Kwang, "A Brief History of Catholicism in Korea" (manuscript, n.d.). • Clark, Allen D., *A History of the Church in Korea* (1971). • Clark, Charles Allen, *The Nevius Plan of Mission Work in Korea* (1937). • Hunt, Everett N., Jr., *Protestant Pioneers in Korea* (1980). • Huntley, Martha, *To Start a Work: The Foundations of Protestant Mission in Korea (1884-1919)* (1987). • Kim In Soo, *Protestants and the Formation of Modern Korean Nationalism, 1885-1920: A Study of the Contributions of Horace G. Underwood and Sun Chu Kil* (1996). • Paik, George L., *The History of Protestant Missions in Korea: 1832-1910* (1970). • Rhodes, Harry A., and Archibald Campbell, *History of the Korea Mission, Presbyterian Church in the U.S.A.*, Vol. I, *1884-1934*, Vol. II, *1935-1959* (1965). G. THOMPSON BROWN, with SYNGMAN RHEE on North Korea since 1950

Korea Evangelical Holiness Church

(KEHC). The KEHC began with the formation of a Gospel Mission Hall in 1907 by Chung Bin and Kim Sang Joon in a rented house in downtown Chongro, Seoul. In 1910, in response to the pioneers' request for missionary assistance, John Thomas, a Britisher, became the first missionary and superintendent of the Oriental Missionary Society (OMS) in Korea. Then, the missionary activity of the Gospel Mission Hall came directly under the OMS. On 31 Mar 1911, the Seoul Bible Institute (later the Seoul Theological University) was officially opened for the training of evangelists.

In 1921, the Gospel Mission Hall became the OMS Holiness Church in Korea with a board of directors in place of a superintendent. During World War II*, the imperial Japanese government persecuted Korean churches and expelled all foreign missionaries. The OMS churches suffered and were disbanded. Their buildings were used as factories because of their refusal to comply with Shinto* shrine worship and especially because of their insistence on the second coming of Christ (see Eschatological Movements, Korea).

After national liberation on 15 Aug 1945, a preparatory committee for the reconstruction of the Holiness Church as a new independent denomination was organized with Park Hyun-myung elected as chairman. On 9-11 Nov 1945, the First Reconstructive General Assembly of the KEHC, attended only by Koreans, was held at Seoul Theological Seminary. The Declaration of Reconstruction of the Holiness Church, including the Seven General Principles (the basic guidelines of the church), was read by Park. This established the KEHC as an independent denomination, with the general assembly as the supreme authority. It was Wesleyan-Arminian in theology and Presbyterian* in polity.

When the Korean War* broke out on 25 Jun 1950, the KEHC suffered a great loss of property, lives, and leadership. The superintendent, Park Hyun-myung, and the principal, Lee Kun, were captured by North Korean Communists. Fortunately, with the help of the United Nations and other churches in the world, the KEHC was able to recover some of its leadership and property, enabling continued growth.

A conflict between the parties of the National Council of Churches and the National Association of Evangelicals over the ecumenical movement resulted in a schism at the 15th general assembly in 1960. Despite the KEHC decision to withdraw from both organizations in order to avoid a division at the special general assembly held in 1961, dissension led to a breakaway group, the *Yesung* (Jesus Holiness Church), which held its own assembly in 1962.

The KEHC is the third largest Protestant church in Korea, after the Presbyterian and the Methodist. It has 34 district conferences, including Japan and Europe, nearly 1,900 local churches, and over 700,000 adherents. The overseas mission committee supports over 100 missionaries working in 82 churches in 25 countries. KEHC also governs the Seoul Theological University.

Bibliography

Lee Myung Jik, *A Brief History of the OMS Holiness Church in Korea* (1929). • *Electric Message*, Vol. VII (1908). • Minutes of the General Assembly of the Korea Evangelical Church. • The Constitutions of the Korea Evangelical Holiness Church. KANG KEUN WHAN

Korea, Freedom of Religion in

Historically, Buddhism* (first brought to Korea* from China* in 372 C.E.) was persecuted in Korea until 527 by the Silla (Shilla) Dynasty (ca. 356-935 C.E.). Slowly, Buddhism gained favor and so it was first recognized as the national religion from the middle Silla to the end of the Koryu Dynasty (918-1392 C.E.). The Yi Chosun Dynasty (1392-1910) persecuted Buddhists on the grounds of Buddhism's position against Confucianism*, the state ideology of the dynasty. Buddhists were pushed into the mountain areas for survival, a factor which encouraged the development of monastic Buddhism. In 1784, when the Catholic religion was introduced to Korea by the elite, dissident literati group, the first converts to that faith were persecuted, since they refused to perform the traditional Confucian ritual of ancestor worship and followed vows of celibacy similar to the Buddhist practice. For the Chosun Dynasty, Catholicism and Buddhism were anti-state ideologies and were regarded as anti-social religions to be eradicated.

Under the colonial rule of Japan, all existing institutional religions were under tight control by the government. All of the Buddhist temples and grounds were registered under the National Park Administration Law, and their religious activities were closely watched by the local police. The Japanese government regarded Christianity as the most powerful anti-Japanese nationalist element from the beginning of its colonial rule. The Japanese governors-general approached the American missionaries concerning cooperating with the Japanese to control the politically aggressive Korean churchgoers and Christian elites. In 1910, there was an alleged conspiracy to assassinate the governor-general. The conspiracy was fabricated to eliminate young Christian leaders, and after the March 1st Independence Movement of 1919, religious freedom for Korean Christians was ended. During World War II*, Korean Christians were forced to carry Japanese-language Bibles, and preachers had to preach in Japanese every Sunday. Those clergy and laypeople who opposed Shinto* shrine worship were imprisoned and tortured to death. Students and teachers at Christian schools had to bow to Shinto shrines or they were removed. Many Christian schools were closed.

Liberation came in 1945, and all Korean Christians celebrated not only national freedom but also, and mostly, religious freedom to worship in the Korean language. But for the North Koreans, that freedom of Christian worship was short-lived. The Democratic People's Republic of Korea (DPRK-North Korea), founded separately in 1948, declared in its constitution not only freedom of religion but also equal freedom of propagating critical opinions of religion. Christianity was severely criticized in schools and the public arena, including the government-controlled mass media, and Christian leaders who opposed the pro-government Christians Federation were constantly harassed, arrested, and imprisoned by the authorities before and during the Korean War* (1950-53). The revised constitution of the DPRK dropped the clause regarding the propagation of antireligious opinions. In the 1980s, only one Protestant church and one Catholic church were open for worship. The Christians Federation leaders have been allowed to travel to the outside world and meet with the world Christian communities to discuss the future of Korean reunification and reconciliation.

In the Republic of Korea (South), the constitution guarantees religious freedom along with other basic human rights. However, during the military government of Park Jung Hee (1953-79), almost all human rights were suspended for reasons of national security and economic development. When the Christian community protested against the government's human-rights violations, certain religious activities were severely curtailed and oppressed as religious interference in political affairs. Some religious leaders believed the separation of church and state meant the silence of the church against the government, while others raised their voices against the government's abuse of power and violations of human rights and were arrested and tried on charges of treason and antigovernment activities. During this period, the Christian churches, both Catholic and Protestant, were united in asserting religious freedom to do their mission in the world for the voiceless, poor, and exploited. They believed that religious freedom can be enjoyed when other basic human rights are protected and respected.

David Suh, with contributions from Kim Heung Soo, translated by Kim In Soo

Korea Independence Movement of 1919

In 1919, a popular movement broke out in Korea* which aimed to bring about independence from Japan*. Remarkably, years before Gandhi* and Martin Luther King, Jr., the movement was based on nonviolent principles.

Japan had annexed Korea in 1910. Japanese rule, while benefiting the country in terms of railroads, banking, and commerce, was characterized by police brutality, the suppression of Korean culture, and exploitation of Korean labor and resources.

It could be said that the spark behind the independence movement was the famous Fourteen Points statement which President Woodrow Wilson publicized at the end of World War I. All people were to have the right of "self-determination." Korean patriots took this at face value and began to organize. In spite of the police, spies, and complete control of all the organs of public life, all the planning was done in complete secrecy. A mass demonstration would be held which would dramatize the cause of Korean independence before the world.

Meetings, processions, and demonstrations were planned for all major cities. As one of the last bastions of Korean culture, Protestant mission schools were inevitably involved. Careful instructions were given that this was to be a peaceful demonstration. There were to be no insults, no stone throwing, no looting, no violence. Thousands of Koreans began flocking to Seoul, ostensibly to mourn the anniversary of the last Korean emperor's death. Because the police were growing suspicious, the date was advanced a few days.

Thirty-three men chose martyrdom. They would sign a declaration of independence and proclaim it to the world. One of the first names on the list was that of the nearly blind Kil Sun Chu* (Sun Joo), one of the most revered and respected Presbyterian* leaders in Pyongyang. Of the 33 signers, 15 were Christians, 15 were members of the Chun Do Kyo sect, and three were Buddhists.

On the morning of 1 Mar, these 33 men sat down together at the Pagoda Restaurant in Seoul. After their meal, the declaration was read and dispatched to the governor-general. Then the signers calmly telephoned the police and told them what they had done. The astonished police dispatched the riot vans, but even as the signers were being carried away, thousands began to form in the streets of the principal cities of Korea, shouting *"Mansei, Mansei"* ("10,000 years to the Korean nation"). Schoolchildren and adults alike began to wave the long forbidden Korean flag.

The declaration of independence was a model of restraint, lack of bitterness, and respect for law and order. A few lines give evidence of the strong religious motivation and the influence of the Christian movement: "We herewith proclaim the independence of Korea and liberty of the Korean people. We tell it to the world in witness of the equality of all nations.... We make this proclamation having back of us 5,000 years of history. . . . This is the clear leading of "Hananim" [the term used by the Protestants for God], the moving principle of the present age."

The authorities retaliated with an unrestrained brutality. A reign of terror and violence began that was to cover the whole nation. Since the authorities considered the Christians to be at the bottom of it all, they were singled out for special treatment. Every known pastor in Seoul was jailed. The government also claimed that missionaries had been involved in the plot. Later it was acknowledged that this was not the case. However, once the movement had erupted, the sympathy of the missionaries was clearly on the side of the patriots.

Worldwide public opinion was aroused. Missionaries had been eyewitnesses of atrocities and reported what they had seen. The Federal Council of Churches in America verified the accuracy of the reports and sent an appeal to the Japanese government. Moderate forces in Japan brought more pressure for change. Some reforms were initiated as a newly appointed governor-general took over.

It could be said that the movement resulted in failure in that independence was not achieved. And yet the movement had a far-reaching effect in unifying the Korean people in their national aspirations. Because the leadership of the movement was closely identified with Christianity, Korean patriots came to have a high esteem for the church. The Christian movement in Korea, quite unlike that in China* and Japan, was perceived as an ally of nationalism and not its enemy. This undoubtedly had much to do with the rapid growth of Christianity in subsequent years.

Bibliography

Brown, George Thompson, *Mission to Korea* (1962). • Kim In Soo, *Protestants and the Formation of Modern Korean Nationalism, 1885-1920: A Study of the Contributions of Horace G. Underwood and Sun Chu Kil* (1996). • Kim, John T., *Protestant Church Growth in Korea* (1996).

G. Thompson Brown

Korea Mission of the Japanese Christian Church

Japanese missionary work in Korea* was aimed mainly at Japanese residents. Though there were some efforts to proselytize Koreans, they were largely unsuccessful. The Japanese Presbyterian* and Congregational churches sent their first mission representatives to Korea in 1897. The Japanese Methodist* mission arrived in 1904. They were soon followed by the Holiness, Salvation Army*, Episcopalian, and other missions. Among them, only the Congregationalists made a noticeable effort to work among Koreans, but their work was unfruitful.

In Jul 1912, with the permission and partial support of the governor-general, Terauchi Masatake, the Congregationalists established evangelistic work among Koreans, but both the Koreans and some Japanese Christians suspected the work to be a tool to further Japan's colonial policies. After the March 1st Independence Movement*, even the few Koreans who had joined the church left it. The Congregationalists finally handed over their Korea mission to the Koreans in 1921 and concentrated only on Japanese residents. The Japanese mission in Korea became part of the United Church of Christ in Japan (UCCJ), which was formed in 1940. Kim Seung Tae

Korean Christian Church in Japan

(Zainichi Daikan Kirisuto Kyokai). In 1882, Ii Sujon, a member of the Korean royalty, came to Japan* and met Tsuda Sen, who led him to become a Christian. He was baptized by Yasukawa Toru. He and Henry Loomis, director of the American Bible* Society in Yokohama, translated the New Testament into Korean. Ii also submitted a request to American mission boards to send missionaries to Korea*. In response to that request, a Presbyterian, Horace Grant Underwood* (1859-1916), and a Methodist, Henry Gerhard Appenzeller* (1858-1902), went to Korea to begin mission work there.

While in Tokyo (1882-86), Ii formed a Bible study class and held regular worship. In 1906, the Korean Young Men's Christian Association* in Japan was founded. Besides having youth meetings, they did evangelistic work, especially with foreign students living in Tokyo. Tokyo Church was founded in 1908. The Korean Christian Church in Japan dates its founding to that year.

In 1909, Han Suk Chin, a pastor of the Korean Presbyterian* Church, came to Japan to do evangelistic work. In 1912, the Korean Christian Mission League took over responsibility for mission work in Japan, and the Presbyterian Church and Methodist Church began to send pastors to Japan for three-year terms. After Han completed his term, the Methodists sent O Gi Son to serve. In 1918, churches were started in Kobe and Yokohama; in 1921, the Osaka church; and in the following years, churches were begun in other locations in Japan. In 1927, the Foreign Mission Division of the Presbyterian Church of Canada (PCC) sent Luther Lisgar Young to Japan; working together with others, he helped found a total of 75 churches from Wakkanai in the north to Kyushu in the south

During World War II*, the various Korea-based churches in Japan belonged to the United Church of Christ in Japan (UCCJ); but after the war, they became independent and formed the General Assembly of the Korean Christian Church in Japan (KCCJ), the local churches being divided into four districts (Kanto, Chubu, Kansai, and Seinan). KCCJ presently has a representative on the National Council of Churches in Japan (NCCJ) steering committee and maintains a strong relationship with the UCCJ. Through NCCJ, it is a member of the World Council of Churches, as well as a member of the World Alliance of Reformed Churches. It has a sister relationship with the PCC and receives missionaries from four denominations in Korea: the Jesus Presbyterian Church (United; Tonghap); Jesus Presbyterian Church (Haptong); Christ Presbyterian Church (Presbyterian Church of the Republic of Korea); and the Korean Methodist Church. JAPANESE DICTIONARY

Korean Church Mission to China

The general assembly of the Presbyterian* Church of Korea was formed on 1 Sep 1912. As an expression of its thanksgiving to God for becoming a fully independent organization as a national church, the assembly voted to start a mission to its near neighbor, China*. A thank offering was taken for that purpose, and three volunteers from the graduating class of the seminary, Pak Tai Ro, Sa Pyung Soon, and Kim Yung Hoon, and their wives were commissioned to begin the mission. They departed for China the next year, and the Shandong Mission of the Presbyterian Church USA (PCUSA) transferred to the Koreans a portion of the field in which they had been at work in the vicinity of Laiyang, 100 miles inland of Qingdao (Tsingtao). They were soon joined by a young physician and his wife.

The Koreans began study of the language, which was facilitated by their prior knowledge of the Chinese characters. Within one year, they began to itinerate throughout the countryside, preaching in the marketplaces and holding Bible classes for lay leaders. The PCUSA furnished a building for a medical clinic for the physician, who supported himself from the fees charged. Salaries of the Korean pastors and other expenses were furnished by the church in Korea.

The work was highly successful from the beginning. In 1916, the Korean pastors transferred their membership to the synod of Shandong, to which they then became accountable. In 1923, after 10 years of work, the Korea Shandong Mission reported 591 baptized members, 25 meeting places for worship, and 10 church buildings.

The significance of the Korean mission to the Chinese people is twofold. First, it represents one of the first missions established by Asian Christians to fellow Asians in another country. Because of the advantages of a common culture and similar languages, standards of living, and religious backgrounds, the Korean missionaries were able to identify with the Chinese people in a way that was difficult if not impossible for many North Americans. Second, the Korean missionaries put into practice the method of mission work they had learned in Korea, which was known as the Nevius* Plan. This placed great emphasis on self-support, self-government, and self-propagation. Highly successful in Korea, it was quite different from the traditional way of working in China. Although John L. Nevius had originated this methodology in Shandong, it had not been accepted by his China colleagues. In a sense, it was now reintroduced into China by the Korean missionaries.

The Korean mission in China continued for a total of 44 years through periods of civil strife, war, floods, famine, and revolution. The churches planted were integrated into the Presbyterian Church of China and later into the ecumenical Church of Christ in China. It suffered the same fate as the other foreign missions when the People's Republic of China was established. The last to leave was Pang Chi Il; he returned to Korea in 1957.

Bibliography

Clark, Charles Allen, *The Nevius Plan of Mission Work in Korea* (1937). • *Minutes of the China Council, Presbyterian Church USA* (1914). GEORGE THOMPSON BROWN

Korean Hymnal

First Korean-language hymn book (see also Music).

The Korean Hymnal was introduced by two Methodist missionaries, George Heber Jones (1867-1919) and Louisa C. Rodthweiler (1853-1921), in 1892, about eight years after the coming of resident American Protestant missionaries to Korea*. Until then, Korean believers had to use transliterated Chinese-language hymnbooks. In 1893, the Presbyterian missionary Horace Grant Underwood (1859-1916) published another Korean-language hymnbook for use in worship. Two separate "denominational hymnbooks" were merged and published in a joint edition in 1902. This was the first ecumenical hymnbook in Korea. The joint edition was revised in 1931 as the *New Hymnals.* But the Presbyterians refused to use the 1931 version, and instead created their own version, *New Edition Hymnals;* the Methodists alone used the 1931 edition. In addition, small denominational churches that were introduced into Korea after 1910 published their own hymnbooks.

During Japanese colonial rule, some hymns were prohibited from being sung in church, such as a song written by a Korean Christian and titled "The Beautiful Peninsula of Three Thousand Miles," and songs of praise to the King of kings, or the Lord, on the grounds that they were anti-Japanese and offended the absolute sovereignty of the Japanese divine emperor.

After the liberation of Korea in 1945, various attempts to create ecumenical hymnbooks were made. As the Korean Protestant churches were celebrating the centennial year of 1984, the ecumenical Korean Hymnals Society was formed and published the hymnbook presently used in most of the mainline denominations. It contains 558 songs, mostly Western tunes. Only 26 Korean composers and lyricists are included.

David Suh, with contributions from Seo Jeong Min, translated by Kim In Soo

Korean Revival Movement

The origins of the Korean Revival Movement can be traced to a meeting of Methodist* missionaries for a week of prayer and Bible study at Wonsan Beach in 1903. R. A. Hardie, a medical missionary who had given up his medical practice to concentrate on evangelistic work, led the group, spoke of his own failures and frustrations, and shared how he had become conscious of a new spirit of power. The group experienced a similar period of confession and infilling of the Holy Spirit.

The movement spread across the land as those whose hearts had been moved at Wonsan shared their experiences. In 1904, special evangelistic services were held in Pyongyang by the Presbyterians*. During the morning, systematic house-to-house visitations were held throughout the city. Bible classes and prayer services came in the afternoon. In the evening, the church was filled to overflowing for the preaching service. So many crowded the sanctuary that church members were asked to withdraw to make room for the newcomers. Hundreds of conversions were recorded.

Meetings in Mokpo sponsored by the Southern Presbyterians and led by J. L. Gerdine of the Southern Methodist Mission are described by a participant and are representative of many such meetings held across the land: "As the Spirit [through Mr. Gerdine] took the Word and reasoned of righteousness, and temperance, and judgment, of the sinfulness of sin, and the necessity of cleansing, a deathlike hush fell on all, and it was as if the Word was a scalpel, cutting deep down into men's hearts and laying bare secret sins and hidden cancers of the soul. Then it was that confession of sin poured out of scores of burdened souls, and strong men wept like children. Then, as the yearning love of the Saviour was dwelt upon, a healing balm poured in. Faces shone with new life and light, and the church rang with the hymns of triumph, and men stood six deep, eagerly waiting their turn to testify of blessings received, sins forgiven, differences healed, victory over self, baptism of the Spirit."

The climax of the movement came in 1907 at the Presbyterian men's Bible classes in Pyongyang. All week long, missionaries and Koreans prayed that the meetings then in progress might be a vehicle for revival. At the final service of the meetings, Graham Lee preached and asked for several to lead in prayer. A score of people all began to pray at once. Man after man would rise, confess his sins, break down and weep, and throw himself down to beat the floor with his fists in an agony of conviction. The meeting went on until 2 A.M. with alternate confession, weeping, and praying.

The Pyongyang Pentecost swept through the seminary, which was just then graduating its first class. Missionaries, Korean elders, and lay members alike joined in the confession of sin and the experience of forgiveness. There was no distinction as to region, denomination, or race. One feature of the revivals has become a permanent part of Korean worship experience: all pray their own prayers out loud at the same time. The mingled prayers have the effect of the sound of the falling of many waters.

The revival movement ushered in a period of rapid church growth, which became the formative period of the Christian church in Korea. It was a time of national humiliation and distress for the Korean people. Japan was rapidly taking over control of the country, first as a protectorate (1905) and then by outright annexation (1910). At such a time, the revivals offered individuals a way to achieve dignity and meaning, as the Christian church became the chief organization outside the orbit of Japanese imperialism.

One striking result of the revival movement was its contribution to the unity of the church. The revivals, which had cut across all denominational lines, led to great enthusiasm for uniting the Presbyterian and Methodist churches. In 1905, at a gathering of missionaries from the two denominations, a motion was made and unanimously adopted "that the time is ripe for the establishment of one Korean national church to be called the Church of Christ in Korea." Although organic union never became a reality, close cooperation was achieved through the organization of the General Council of Evangelical Mission in 1905.

Bibliography

Brown, George Thompson, *Mission to Korea* (1962). • Clark, Allen D., *A History of the Church in Korea* (1971). • Clark, Charles Allen, *The Nevius Plan of Mission Work in Korea* (1937). • Rhodes, Harry A., *History of the Korea Mission, Presbyterian Church, USA* (1934).

George Thompson Brown

Korean War

Causes, process, and aftermath. The Korean War broke out on 25 Jun 1950 when the Democratic People's Republic of Korea (North Korea) army crossed the 38th parallel to the south. The 38th parallel was the demarcation line that divided Korea into North and South at the end of World War II* (the Pacific War) when Korea was liberated from 36 years of Japanese colonial occupation (1910-45). The division was agreed upon by the Soviet Union and the United States in order to disarm the surrendering Japanese soldiers in the respective territories and eventually to facilitate a free, independent, and unified Korea.

Series of talks between the Soviet Union and the

United States governments failed to direct the course of reunification. In Dec 1945, the Moscow foreign ministers' meeting of the USSR, US, and Great Britain reached no conclusion. A joint commission met in 1946 and 1947 and resolved to put Korea under joint trusteeship for five years. Both the North and the South protested.

In response to the aspirations of the Korean people for an independent and unified nation, the United Nations General Assembly adopted a resolution to create a temporary commission to conduct and supervise free elections in both sides of Korea. However, the Soviet Union refused to allow the UN commission to enter North Korea to conduct a general election. Only in the South were elections held on 10 May 1948; the elected representatives met on 31 May 1948 to adopt the constitution of the Republic of Korea. The establishment of the Republic of Korea was declared on 15 Aug 1948. Soviet-occupied North Korea followed suit and held an election, thus inaugurating the Democratic People's Republic of Korea (DPRK) in Sep 1948.

On the Korean peninsula, two separate governments were established, but both sides claimed that the other side of the 38th parallel was part of their territory. The two governments were based on distinctively different political ideologies and economic systems. Both governments have been in constant disagreement on the issues of national unification, independence, and basic rights of the people. Not only have the armies of both sides armed themselves against each other, but armed skirmishes and surprise attacks have been rampant. Both sides have sent guerrillas and special forces to spy on and destroy military bases and have helped organize local people for anti-government activities.

With regard to the Korean War, both governments insist that the other is to blame. There is no objective and conclusive evidence as to which side ordered its soldiers to initiate a massive attack across the border. The basic cause of the war was the 38th parallel, which divided the peninsula and the Korean people.

The North Korean army advanced to the south to occupy Seoul, the capital city of the Republic of Korea, and marched through almost all of the southwestern and southeastern parts of Korea. By Sep 1950, after three months' of hard resistance, the South Korean army and the United Nations police force were pushed back to the southeastern tip of the peninsula. In order to rescue the South Korean government, US troops under the command of Douglas MacArthur landed at Inchon, a commercial port near Seoul, behind North Korean lines. In a successful operation the US soldiers pushed the North Korean army back to the north. As the UN forces, including the US and the South Korean armies, reached the northern border between North Korea and China to conclude the war, the Chinese "volunteer" army marched down from China into North Korea and pushed the UN forces back south of the 38th parallel. The Soviets proposed to end the war through truce talks, which began in Jul 1951 and lasted until 27 Jul 1953. Although the South Korean government refused to sign the truce agreement, the war actually ended, and a new demarcation line was drawn approximately along the line of the 38th parallel.

The war casualties in both the North and South were greater than the total number of war casualties during World War II. In the South, 990,000 South Korean soldiers, 40,000 US troops, and 3,000 UN forces lost their lives in combat. In the North, combat casualties were estimated at 510,000 North Korean soldiers and 500,000 Chinese (*The Review of Korean History* [in Korean], by Han Young-Woo, 1997, p. 560). There is no accurate number of civilian casualties during this three-year war period, but unofficial estimates of refugees from the North are some three million. Missing and separated family members may have been nearly 10 million (out of over some 40 million people at the time of the war). Cities, farmlands, and forests were destroyed and devastated.

The Korean War and Christian churches. The division of Korea that led to the devastating armed conflicts between North and South in the Korean War (1950-53) affected all of the Korean people, especially the Christian churches, both Catholic and Protestant. In the Communist North, Christian churches and their members were persecuted overtly by Sunday mandatory meetings and events, such as national and local elections, to block Christians from attending Sunday worship services. Through land reform, the land owners, most of whom were church lay leaders, were expelled from their homes and land; some who resisted the reform were executed. Many clergymen fled to the South with their congregation.

Before the division of Korea, the aggressive Protestant missionary activities in the North had gained many converts to the Christian religion. The center of Christian growth was in the North, and Pyongyang was called the Jerusalem of Korea. World War II statistics showed that Pyongan (where Pyongyang is located) had 29,129 communicant members, while two provinces in the South (Kyunggi, where Seoul is located, and Choongchung) had a combined membership of only 5,714. It is estimated that there were 250,000 Protestants and 50,000 Roman Catholics, and about 2,000 church buildings in North Korea before the division of the peninsula.

After the division, and before the establishment of the Communist North Korean government, some national Christian leaders in the North, such as Yun Ha Young and Han Kyung Jik*, both Presbyterian pastors, organized the Christian Social Democratic Party on 9 Sep 1945. The party dropped the label of "Christian" and became the Korean Social Democratic Party. It was later renamed the *Chosun Minju Dang*, or Korea Democratic Party, to show its ideological distinction from the North Korean government. Before all civilian political activities were banned by the Labor (Communist) Party, the Christian-led Democratic Party attracted the North Korean people and grew to more than 500,000 members within three months. This development was a considerable threat to the Soviet-supported pro-Communists, and violent confrontations between Christians and Communist forces in North Korea increased. The Christian resistance movements were ruthlessly suppressed.

Among the North Korean Christian leaders, there was a small segment of Communist sympathizers who supported the Soviet occupation. With the help of the occupation forces, they formed the Chosun Christians Federation shortly before the general election of 3 Nov 1946 to support the establishment of the Communist regime in the North. The Christians Federation declared its support for the government of Kim Il Sung (who ruled the DPRK from 1948 to 1994) and its nonrecognition of the government of South Korea.

The Christian community in the North was divided. Those who refused to join the pro-North federation were harassed, arrested, and imprisoned. During the Korean War, many non-federation Christian leaders were abducted, and most of them were killed by firing squads of the North Korean army fleeing from the advance of the South Korean and US armies. In South Korea, during the North Korean occupation, Christian leaders were killed or abducted to the North. It has been estimated that 63 pastors were captured and killed in North Korea, and 99 were missing. In the South, some 50 pastors were captured and killed, and 61 Christian lay and clergy leaders were taken to North Korea. About 240 church buildings were destroyed completely, and 705 were severely damaged by North Korean soldiers and US bombing. While the Korean War nearly annihilated the Christian presence in the North, after a great destruction it made possible the rapid growth of Christianity in the South.

Bibliography

Lee Ki-baik, *A New History of Korea,* trans. Edward W. Wagner with Edward J. Shultz (1984). • Kang Wi Jo, *Christ and Caesar in Modern Korea: A History of Christianity and Politics* (1997). • McCann, David R., ed., *Korea Briefing: Toward Reunification* (1997). • Eberstadt, Nicholas, *Korea Approaches Reunification* (1995).

David Suh

Koreri

A form of the Melanesian cargo cult found in the Biak-Numfoor area (northern New Guinea).

More than 40 Koreri movements are known to have arisen in northern New Guinea since the beginning of Christian missions in the area (1855), but they probably existed even before, since they cannot be explained simply as a reaction to the Christian message or to the presence of strangers in general. The largest movement, which flourished from 1938 to 1943 under the leadership of a woman (Angganitha Menufaur), was finally stamped out by the Japanese.

The core of Koreri belief is the myth of the ancestor Manarmakeri, who recaptured the secret of the true nature of things and thus came into possession of the "treasure" and the "food" which the community needs for its ceremonial and economic welfare, and which enables it to put an end to all kinds of suffering, even to death itself. Once a long time ago, Manarmakeri appeared in the guise of an old man, but he was not recognized as the Lord of the Koreri (Utopia), not even when he rejuvenated himself by fire. Therefore, he departed westward, after having promised that he would return one day.

For a time, the arrival of the white man was seen as the return of Manarmakeri and Christian elements were incorporated, but the negative reaction of missions and government caused the movements to manifest themselves as resistance against all foreign presence. Thus the so-called syncretistic character of the movements is only of secondary importance. Also the poverty of the indigenous population as compared to the affluence in which the strangers lived led to a shift of expectations: the Utopia expected was the arrival of ships with Western goods. Features of the Koreri movements, which are to be interpreted as reactions against the negative aspects of life, are the emergence of a *konoor,* a herald of the returning messiah; the discontinuation of daily routine; and the performance of rituals intended to hasten the return of Manarmakeri, especially dancing night and day. The failure of Utopia to materialize will lead to disillusionment with the *konoor* who started the movement, but the belief in Koreri remains and will become manifest on another occasion.

In other parts of western New Guinea (Irian Jaya), as in the rest of Melanesia, similar movements have arisen. These are based on different myths, but all of them have as common elements the Utopia, lost by foolish behavior toward one of the ancestors but still present somewhere outside the reach of the living, and a savior who will return from there. Here, too, until recently the reaction of Christian missions, Catholic and Protestant, has been predominantly negative.

Bibliography

Kamma, F. C., *Koreri: Messianic Movements in the Biak-Numfoor Culture Area* (1972). • Strelan, John G., *Search for Salvation: Studies in the History and Theology of Cargo Cults* (1977). • Strelan, John G., and Jan A. Godschalk, *Kargoisme di Melanesia. Suatu Studi tentang Sejarah dan Teologi Kultus kargo* (1989) (updated Indonesian edition of the previous volume).

Thomas van den End

Kozaki Hiromichi

(b. Kumamoto, Japan, 17 May 1856; d. Tokyo, 26 Feb 1938). Japanese pastor and educator.

Kozaki was one of the first participants in the educational program of the *Kumamoto Eigakko* (English School) directed by Captain Leroy L. Janes, a Civil War officer, who taught the Bible in addition to liberal arts to young people from samurai background. A unique religious experience among these students led to the formation of the Kumamoto Band, a supportive fellowship. Baptized by Janes, Kozaki and with others moved to Kyoto in order to study at Doshisha, a Christian school established by Joseph H. Neesima*. Upon his graduation from Doshisha in 1879, Kozaki served churches in Miyazaki and Tokyo and organized the Tokyo Young Men's Christian Association*, for which he published *Rokugo Magazine*. In 1882, he organized Tokyo First Christian Church, later called Reinanzaka Church, which became a bastion of the Japan Congregational Church (JCC).

While taking initiatives in planning and publishing Christian periodicals, Kozaki became president of Doshisha upon the death of Neesima in 1890 and served in that position until 1897. From 1898 to 1931, he served as pastor of Reinanzaka Church. While he exerted distinguished leadership in the JCC, his leadership also extended to ecumenical circles as well as to the promotion of overseas missions, such as work in Micronesia, Hawaii, and the West Coast of the United States.

Kozaki's leadership quality was marked by tolerance and genuine interest in the religious orientation of other Christians. This enabled him to play a constructive role in cooperative ventures among churches in Japan. He was influential not only in organizational matters but in the realm of thought and theological insights. He represented Japan at international conferences of the World Sunday School Association and the International Missionary Council.

Bibliography

Kozaki Hiromichi, *Reminiscences of Seventy Years* (1933).

ROBERT MIKIO FUKADA

Kraemer, Hendrik

(b. Amsterdam, 17 May 1888; d. Driebergen, Holland, 11 Nov 1965). Major figure in the Protestant mission in Indonesia* and worldwide ecumenical* leader.

Kraemer became an orphan at the age of nine and was then raised in an orphanage of the Netherlands Reformed Church in Amsterdam. He decided to become a missionary and enrolled in the Netherlands Missionary School in Rotterdam (1905-11). Because of his linguistic abilities, it was suggested that he become a Bible* translator for the Netherlands Bible Society*. After making up for the secondary education he had not received, he studied Oriental languages with the famous Islamic scholar C. Snouck Hurgronje at the University of Leyden in 1911. In the meantime, he was active in the Student Christian Movement*. In 1919 he married, and in 1922 he received his doctoral degree. (The University of Utrecht awarded him an honorary doctorate in theology in 1936.)

After studying Islam* in Cairo (1921-22), Kraemer arrived in Indonesia, where he worked for the Netherlands Bible Society on the island of Java* from 1922 to 1937. His task was a novel one: he was to advise Bible translators and missionaries about the religious, cultural, and political awakening of the Indonesian peoples. He studied the changes in Javanese society extensively and sympathetically. He saw the Indonesian national movement in the context of rising nationalism* in Asia. The revival of Islam in Java he connected with similar developments elsewhere in the Islamic world. The whole awakening of Java was, in his view, the result of a growing self-consciousness visible among many colonized peoples at that time. He succeeded in initiating contacts with various kinds of indigenous groups (e.g., Muslims, with whom he discussed matters of faith). He urged missionaries to pay more attention to what was happening among Indonesian Muslims and wrote a book about Islam, which was, however, considered dangerous by the colonial government and hence banned. His review articles about the Indonesian press were widely read, even in Dutch government circles, although some government officials and fellow missionaries found him suspect because of his openness toward the national movement and his critical remarks about Dutch colonialism*.

During his first term, Kraemer lived in Yogyakarta, Central Java, and then moved to Malang, East Java (1926), where, together with B. M. Schuurman, he taught at the newly established theological seminary, *Bale Wiyata* (House of Religious Education), a school which gave much attention to Javanese culture. By then, Kraemer was renowned for his knowledge and experience, and his advice was often sought when new situations emerged. At the end of his first term, he was asked to visit regions outside Java and to give advice regarding the future of the Christian congregations there. In his reports (*From Missionfield to Independent Church*, 1958), he pleaded for a reorganization of the colonial Protestant Church responsible for these congregations and suggested that autonomous indigenous churches be instituted in the various parts of Eastern Indonesia (Minahasa, the Moluccas*, and Timor*).

After attending the World Missionary Conference in Jerusalem (1928), Kraemer became even more aware of the urgency to establish independent churches in the mission field. He considered it wrong to wait until the Indonesian Christians were ready by the standards of the missionaries to lead their own churches. The Indonesians should form their own churches, with the missionaries as advisers. During his second term, together with other missionaries, he led the Protestant churches of East and West Java to independence.

In 1932, Kraemer was involved in the struggle between the government and the mission to Bali*. The government wanted to preserve the original Hindu culture on this island by prohibiting missionary activities, but Kraemer defended the right of the churches to propagate the Gospel, stating that it was useless to try to protect the Balinese people from foreign influences. He saw the task of the church as helping the Balinese people face modern times. The island then became a mission field of the newly established East Javanese Christian Church.

Kraemer was a strong supporter of good theological training for Indonesian ministers. Together with others, he took the initiative to establish theological education of a higher academic level to train ministers for the newly instituted Protestant churches in a national and ecumenical context. In 1934, a theological seminary was founded in Bogor, which was soon moved to Jakarta *(Sekolah Tinggi Teologia).* Kraemer was the first chairman of its board of directors.

When on furlough in Holland, Kraemer was asked by the International Missionary Council to write a book about the missionary task of the church and the relation between Christianity and other religions. The result was *The Christian Message in a Non-Christian World,* presented to the World Missionary Conference at Tambaram, Madras (1938). In the meantime, he was asked to become professor of religions at the University of Leyden. When he accepted this invitation, his career in Asia came to an end.

During his years in Holland (1935-47) Kraemer was deeply involved in efforts to reorganize the Netherlands Reformed Church and to make this church aware of its missionary task. Between 1945 and 1950, he tried to convince his compatriots that the Indonesian people had the right to demand and receive independence. In 1947, he became the first director of the Ecumenical Institute of the World Council of Churches in Bossey, Switzerland, where he worked from 1948 to 1956. In 1956-57, he was visiting professor at Union Theological Seminary, New York, after which he retired.

In retirement, Kraemer remained active and continued to write (e.g., *The Theology of Laity,* 1958). Though a layman all his life, without formal theological training (he called his relationship to theology an "eternal engagement," never leading to a marriage), Kraemer exercised an immense theological influence on the mission in Indonesia, the Netherlands Reformed Church, and the international ecumenical movement. Through his books *Religion and the Christian Faith* (1956) and *World Cultures and World Religions: The Coming Dialogue* (1960), he also contributed to the development of dialogue between people of different faiths (see Interreligious Dialogue).

Bibliography

Hallencreutz, C. F., *Kraemer Towards Tambaram: A Study in Hendrik Kraemer's Missionary Approach* (1966). • Spindler, M. R., "Introduction," in M. Dirkzwager, *Hendrik Kraemer: Bibliografie en Archief* (1988). • Potter, Philip A., "The WCC and the World of Religions and Cultures: Kraemer in Retrospect," *Ecumenical Review* 41.1 (1989). • Neill, S., et al., eds., *Concise Dictionary of Christian World Mission* (1971). • Lossky, N., et al., *Dictionary of the Ecumenical Movement* (1991).

Christiaan G. F. de Jonge

Krishna Pillai, H. A.

(b. Tirunelveli District, India, 23 Apr 1827; d. 1900). Indian Christian poet.

Krishna Pillai read many of the Tamil classics and gained much knowledge of Tamil literature. He worked as a Tamil pandit and read Tamil scriptures. His friend Dhanakoti explained salvation to him, and later he was baptized as Henry Alfred (H. A.). As a Christian, he continued his study of and commitment to Tamil poetic thought.

Krishna Pallai was not a technical theologian, so his theology was very much that of the evangelical missionaries with whom he came into contact in his early days as a Christian. He was called the Protestant Beschi and the Christian Kambar for his epic *Rakshanya-Yatrikam* (Pilgrimage for Salvation), published in 1894. Taking his style from Kambar and his substance from Bunyan's *Pilgrim's Progress,* he wrote another book, the *Rakshanya Manoharam* (The Beauty of Salvation), a substantial Tamil-language work of great beauty on the Christian religion.

Bibliography

Appasamy, A. J., *Tamil Christian Poet* (1966). • Boyd, R. H. S., *An Introduction to Indian Christian Theology* (1991). • Firth, Cyril Bruce, *An Introduction to Indian Church History* (1961). • Grafe, Hugold, *History of Christianity in India,* Vol. IV, Part 11 (1990). Vibin John

Kruyt, Albertus Christian

(b. Surabaya, 10 Oct 1869; d. The Hague, 19 Jan 1949). Dutch missionary pioneer to Central Celebes*, Indonesia*.

Kruyt was a member of the famous Kruyt family that contributed many missionaries to Indonesia (especially East Java and Central Celebes, also Minahasa and the Karo Batak region in Sumatra). The son of a missionary in Mojowarno, East Java, Kruyt decided to become a missionary too and received his education at the seminary of the Netherlands Missionary Society in Rotterdam (1884-89). In 1890, he married Johanna Moulijn.

It was decided that Kruyt, together with a delegate of the Netherlands Bible Society, would initiate missionary work in the Poso region, Central Celebes. The delegate chosen by the Bible Society was N. Adriani*, with whom Kruyt formed an exemplary missionary team until Adriani died in 1926. In 1890, the Kruyts set out for Indonesia. After an orientation in Gorontalo, North Celebes (1891-92), Kruyt moved to Central Celebes to start the missionary work that would occupy him until his repatriation in 1932. In 1895, he and his wife were joined by Dr. and Mrs. Adriani.

Kruyt was convinced that the Gospel could be preached effectively to people only if the missionary knew their language and customs thoroughly. Living among the peoples of Central Celebes, he started to learn their language and to study their religious and cultural life. By learning and exploring, he acquired an enormous amount of anthropological and ethnological knowledge, which made him an internationally renowned scholar. The theories he developed about the religious and spiritual life of tribal societies were for a time considered authoritative. His emphasis on the historical development of cultures from low, or primitive, to high, or more spiritual, showed the influence of evolutionary thinking. The results of both his and Adriani's research into the peoples of Central Celebes were gathered in three volumes, titled *De Bare'e-sprekende Toradja's van Midden-Celebes* ("The Bare'e-speaking Torajas of Central Celebes, 1912-14; 2nd rev. ed., 1950-51). Kruyt wrote numerous other books and articles.

For Kruyt, research was indispensable to his work as a missionary. In his opinion, the Gospel had to be preached to the people within the context of their own society and culture in order to avoid the disintegrating effects of Christianization seen elsewhere. Becoming a Christian should not mean a disruption of the traditional structure of society or a replacement of one's own culture by European culture. He rejected the confrontational approach to other cultures and religions which were often labelled heathen.

The so-called sociological missionary method that Kruyt developed as an alternative together with Adriani became very influential, e.g., for the mission among the related Toraja peoples in South Celebes. He believed that by avoiding derogatory remarks about tribal religion and studying it sincerely, the missionary can bring about an encounter with the Gospel which transforms the spiritual life of the people from within. According to this method, too, the missionary approaches the people as a community. The decision to become Christian should be taken together when a whole community is ready. Accordingly, baptizing individuals ought to be avoided because it tends to isolate them from the community; baptizing groups is preferred.

Kruyt recognized the role of the traditional leaders in the process of becoming Christians, and afterwards he tried to give them a prominent role in the life of the congregations. According to the principle that the order of the church had to respect the traditional social order, children of slaves *(em)* were not allowed, for some time, to take the training for missionary teachers. In order to avoid alienation of the people from their cultural roots, efforts were made to preserve the para-Christian customs which did not conflict with Christian values and to transform into Christian customs the ones that did.

Following his missionary ideas, Kruyt patiently lived and worked among the people until Christmas 1909, when the time came to baptize the first group of Christians. In the course of years, the work steadily expanded. The number of missionary workers, both indigenous and Dutch, grew. Among them was Kruyt's own son, Johannes (1893-1978), who joined the mission in Central Celebes in 1916. Only after World War II* was an independent church instituted in this region, the Christian Church of Central Celebes (1947).

Although linguistic research and Bible* translation had been left to Adriani, Kruyt became directly involved in this too after Adriani died. He translated the books of the New Testament not yet translated by Adriani and, together with Mrs. Adriani, revised the existing parts, resulting in a complete printed New Testament in the Bare'e language (known as Pamona in Central Celebes) in 1935.

In 1932, Kruyt retired as a missionary, but back in the Netherlands, he remained very active publishing books and articles about the peoples of Central Celebes. In 1898, he became a corresponding member of the Royal Netherlands Academy of Sciences, and in 1933 a full member. Although he never had a formal university education, being mainly self-taught, the University of Utrecht awarded him an honorary doctorate in theology in 1913. After repatriation, he also became a member of the board of the Royal Institute for Linguistics and Anthropology (1933-46) and of the Netherlands Missionary Society.

Together with N. Adriani, Kruyt laid the foundation of a new approach in the Dutch missionary enterprise from the beginning of the 20th c. The way they explored together the religion, culture, and language of the peoples of Central Celebes became a paradigm for contemporary and later missionaries.

Bibliography

Latourette, K. S., *A History of the Expansion of Christianity,* Vol. V, 6th ed. (1978). • Brouwer, K. J., *Dr. Albertus Kruyt: Dienaar der Toradja's* (1951). • *Biografisch Lexicon voor de Geschiedenis van het Nederlandse Protestantisme* I (1978). Christiaan G. F. de Jonge

Kubushiro Ochimi

(b. Kumamoto Prefecture, Japan, 16 Dec 1882; d. 23 Oct 1972). Women's movement* leader.

Kubushiro was the eldest daughter of Okubo Shinjiro and Otowa; her uncles included Tokutomi Soho and Tokutomi Roka, her mother's younger brothers. After graduating from Joshi Gakuin High School, she studied at the Pacific School of Religion in the United States, married Kubushiro Naokatsu, and lived in Seattle, Washington. They returned to Japan in 1913, and, after living in Takamatsu for a time, moved to Tokyo, where they jointly founded Tokyo Citizen's Church.

Immediately following this, Kubushiro's husband died. At the urging of Moriya Azuma, she joined the Japan Woman's Christian Temperance Union (JWCTU) in 1916. From the start she worked with Hayashi Utako on the problem of the Tobita red-light district in Osaka, but their work ended in failure. From this experience, they painfully learned that in order to combat licensed prostitution, women had to have the right to vote. So Kubishiro became active in the women's suffrage movement, serving as director in charge of the general affairs of the association working to bring about women's suffrage. In the movement to abolish prostitution, the purification (clean-up) committee joined with the Alliance for the Abolition of Prostitution.

After World War II*, Kubishiro ran for the diet but was defeated. She then returned to the JWCTU, and in 1956 mobilized the power of many women's organizations to get the Prostitution Prohibition Law approved. Having traveled abroad in 1928 and 1938 to attend the World Conference on Mission and Evangelism, she later made a number of other trips to observe firsthand the prostitution situation in different countries, including China, which she visited as the leader of a group of representative Japanese women at China's invitation in 1957. From 1962 to 1971, she was president of the JWCTU and served as its honorary president afterward. In 1966, at the age of 83, she passed the United Church of Christ in Japan ordination examination. Her autobiography, *Haisho hitosuji* (Single-Mindedly — Prostitution Abolition), was published in 1973. TAKAHASHI KIKUE

Kudat

Northernmost town on the island of Borneo, first capital of the British North Borneo Chartered Company during 1881-84 when it ruled Sabah (formerly North Borneo), and birthplace of two local denominations related to the Basel Missionary Society (BMS), namely, the Basel Christian Church of Malaysia (BCCM) and the Protestant Church in Sabah (PCS).

BCCM was formed on 4 Apr 1883 when 14 Hakka families, 96 persons in all, were recruited by the chartered company to open up its newly acquired territory; they landed at Kudat. This was the first group of Hakka Christian refugees resettled by Rudolph Lechler (one of the first two BMS missionaries to China) and Walter Medhurst*, who was also commissioned by the company to import Chinese laborers. The church is one of the pillar religious organizations in the modernization of Sabah.

PCS was the result when BCCM urged its last BMS missionary, H. Bienz, to initiate a mission to the Rungus tribes in Kudat in 1951. Accompanied by BCCM interpreters, Bienz began evangelism and laid the groundwork. In 1952, BMS sent its first missionary to the Rungus, Heinrich Honeggar, who had formerly worked among the tribal peoples in Kalimantan, Indonesia, to spearhead the mission. BMS was commissioned to transliterate the Rungus' spoken language into a written form using the Roman alphabet.

Kudat is noted for extensive interdenominational cooperation and fellowship among the various churches, including the Roman Catholic Church*, subsequent to Islamization* and the persecution of Christians by the Muslim-dominated regimes from 1970 to 1985. Aspiring to set up a sultanate in Sabah, the then chief minister, Mustapha Harun, coerced the people to embrace Islam*. Foreign missionaries were expelled and strong indigenous Christian leaders jailed. In 1983, Petrus Joannes de Wit, an outspoken Roman Catholic priest, was found murdered. All the churches put up a united front for survival against the common threat. This ecumenical cooperation is exemplary in the region.

Bibliography

Basel Christian Church of Malaysia Centenary Magazine, 1882-1982. CHONG TET LOI

Koung, Z. T. *See* Jiang Zhangchuan

Kupang

Catholic archdiocese (since 1989) on the island of Timor*, Indonesia, which forms a church province with the suffragan dioceses of Atambua (1936) and Weetebula (1959).

Though situated in a mostly Protestant area, Kupang was chosen as the seat of the archdiocese because the town is the capital of the administrative province of Nusa Tenggara Timur. Most of the Catholics live in the diocese of Atambua, where they form 92.5% of the population. The evangelization was started among the Belu tribe in 1883 by Jesuits* and continued by the Society of the Divine Word* (SVD) since 1913, when the whole congregation reached just about 3,000 faithful. By 1936, they had grown to 42,000, and by 1992 to 348,000. This rapid conversion may be due to the old Dominican* Mission of the 16th and 17th cs. in this area, though it never penetrated very far from the shore. The enormous growth was aided by a steady increase of missionaries, priests and sisters, and lay teachers. Even today, 62% of all schools are run by diocesan foundations.

In the diocese of Kupang itself (1967), the growth started after 1965, when the government, afraid of Communists, demanded that every citizen be a member of a recognized religion. On the island of Sumba (Weetebula), the mission was started in 1889 by Jesuit missionaries, but it was given up after 1898 because of a shortage of personnel. A new start in the 1920s created bad feelings among Protestant preachers who regarded the island as their territory. German Redemptorist* missionaries took over from the SVD fathers in 1957. The congregation has grown steadily since, though hindered by polygamy and a staunch Islamic population on the neighboring island of Sumbawa, where only two parishes could be established. Under an Indonesian bishop, the diocese comprises roughly 20,000 faithful in 12 parishes. ADOLF HEUKEN

Kyaw Than, U

(b. Pakokku, Myanmar, 17 Dec 1923). Lay ecumenical* leader and professor in Myanmar*.

U Kyaw Than was the associate general secretary of

Kyaw Than, U

the World Student Christian Federation (WSCF) from 1950 to 1956. In this capacity, he traveled to universities in Europe, the United Kingdom, North America, Australia, and New Zealand, but he concentrated on the ecumenical leadership training of undergraduates in Asia. A delegate of the Burma Baptist Convention, he was elected to the central committee of the World Council of Churches by the assembly at Nairobi in 1975, and later to the executive committee, serving until 1992. U Kyaw Than was chairperson of the history working group of WSCF, producing a centenary publication edited by Philip Potter. His main concerns are mission in unity and the Christian's role in the university.

After graduating with honors from the University of Yangon, he served on its faculty while earning his master's degree. In 1981 he was conferred a D.D. degree in church history by the senate of the South East Asia Graduate School of Theology (SEAGST). In 1956 he succeeded the late Bishop R. E. Manikam as the joint East Asia secretary of the International Missionary Council and the World Council of Churches. He organized the East Asia Christian Conference (EACC, now the Christian Conference of Asia*) that was held at Prapat, Indonesia*, the following year. At the EACC inaugural assembly in Kuala Lumpur, Malaysia*, in 1959, U Kyaw Than was elected associate general secretary. In 1968 he succeeded D. T. Niles* as general secretary and held the post until 1974, one year after the fifth assembly in Singapore*.

A visiting professor of mission at Yale Divinity School, United States, from 1974 to 1976), U Kyaw Than's services were later shared with the Vancouver School of Theology, Canada, for one year before he became the William Paton Fellow at Selly Oak Colleges in Birmingham, United Kingdom. He returned to Myanmar in 1978 to teach in theological* schools on Seminary Hill, Insein, until 1984. He was appointed director of the Training Institute for Christian Participation in National Development (TICPIND) by the National Council of Churches, and his target is the development of the Chins, an ethnic minority in the northwestern border region of Myanmar. Since Oct 1984, U Kyaw Than has been serving at the Mahidol University, Thailand, the University of Oregon, United States, and Lutheran* School of Theology, Chicago, Illinois, United States. The Evangelical Lutheran Church in America supported him while he was on a Fulbright program in the United States. U Kyaw Than is now involved with Buddhist-Christian relations.

Bibliography

Kyaw Than, U, *Joint Labourers in Hope* (1973); *Witnesses Together* (1959); *The Common Evangelistic Task of the Church* (1957); *Hpoont pyo ye nint ka-rit-yan* (Christians in development) (in Myanmese) (1984); *Athin-daw I tha-U Kyaw Thana* (The mission of the church) (in Myanmese) (1983).

KYAW NYUNT

L

La Salle Brothers

(Brothers of the Christian Schools). Congregation of religious educators (Latin, *Fratres Scholarum Christianarum)* founded in 1682 by Jean-Baptiste de la Salle, a French priest from Rheims. He was canonized by the Roman Catholic Church* in 1900 as a saint and named the patron of all Catholic teachers by Pius XII in 1950.

The La Salle Brothers were originally from Europe (Ireland, France, Germany, Czechoslovakia, Hungary) and the United States (then also considered a missionary territory, originally manned by brothers from Ireland and France). When they first came to Asia in 1852, they established in Singapore* a foundation known as St. Joseph's Institution. This foundation was the first in Asia. From Singapore, the brothers branched out to different countries: Penang, Malaysia* (1852), Sri Lanka* (1867), Myanmar* (1860), Hong Kong* (1875), and the Philippines* (1911). They also established a foundation in the territory of Australia in 1905.

The pre–World War II* period saw the schools of the brothers, both primary and secondary, flourish under the British educational system. Coming separately from France, the brothers also established foundations in French Indochina, initially in Vietnam* in 1865 and later in Cambodia* in 1905. In the French system, schools were established up to the baccalaureate.

The primary purpose of these schools was evangelization or the Christian education of youth, especially the poor, in accordance with the goals of the congregation's founding mission. In many of these institutions, except for the one in the Philippines, the majority of the students were non-Christians, including a majority of Buddhists in Vietnam and Sri Lanka and a substantial minority of Muslims in Malaysia.

The brothers' schools, entirely for boys, acquired the merited reputation of being excellent schools within the givens and assumptions of the colonial system. The ultimate test in those days, at least in the British Empire, was success in the final examinations. The schools thus became centers for the propagation of the English language and the training of intellectual elites (from all religions and social classes, since the French- and British-type schools were state-subsidized). From among these schools of the pre-war period arose leaders of their respective societies who assumed key roles in government upon the attainment of independence after World War II.

The post–World War II period saw the movement of Australian brothers to New Zealand (1953) and Papua New Guinea (1946) and of Sri Lankan brothers to India* (1961) and Pakistan* (1959). The same period saw expansion in the number of schools from the pressure of population growth and the desires of newly independent countries, which valued education as an instrument of social development.

Numerous schools were founded in Hong Kong*, the Philippines, Singapore, Malaysia, and Thailand (by missionaries from Vietnam and Europe who established the first school in 1951). A change in government system in Myanmar slowed down the progress of the brothers there. The war in Indochina decimated the numbers of brothers although some went to France and the United States. The lone foundation in Cambodia was closed by the Pol Pot government. After independence, a *bumiputra* nationalist movement in Malaysia placed a premium on the "children of the soil." Because they could not really evangelize among the Muslims, the brothers had instead concentrated their work in the early period among the Chinese and the Tamils. Laws in West Malaysia favoring the Islamic majority and the Islamization of the country have made the continuation of these schools doubtful, especially in view of the decrease in the number of brothers after the sociological changes which followed Vatican II (1962-65).

Religious congregations including the Brothers of the Christian Schools are presently in the process of "re-founding" themselves by looking back at their past and "re-engineering" religious structures for future work among youth and for apostolic works of education in Asia in the 21st century. In this re-founding, the brothers have taken cognizance of some of their past shortcomings: they did not indigenize education rapidly enough, but continued the status quo of elitist colonial education (even in the propagation of the English language); they did not move to develop the indigenous national languages as media of instruction; and in effect they were accused of perpetuating colonialism* and being neutral if not negative toward the rapid movements of nationalization. In the process, too, especially since fewer young members have joined the congregation in the past 30 years, some of the remaining brothers have become identified with the conservative element in the church in spite of the changes brought about by Vatican II; they are perceived as reactionary and as having lost their nerve in attempting to make their education relevant to the present.

The brothers, much diminished in number and new membership, continue their work in Asia under a set of parameters dictated by political, economic, and social changes. Many of the societies where they work continue to be non-Christian but value education more than ever. In developed city-states such as Hong Kong and Singapore, the need for foreign manpower in education is less. However, in countries still developing, such as Indonesia and the Philippines, and in a country that is rapidly developing and trying to multiply its educational services to keep up with demand, such as Thailand, and in countries newly recovering from war, such as Vietnam, the need for technical and qualified manpower at all levels continues.

Bibliography

Gonzalez, Andrew, *The Brothers in Asia* (1982). • Towey, John, *Irish de La Salle Brothers in Christian Education* (1980).

Andrew Gonzalez

Labor Movement (Rodo Undo), Japan

The labor movement in Japan was strongly influenced by Christianity from its inception until the early 1920s. When the modern labor movement began around the end of the 19th c., one of the main leaders was Katayama* Sen, who had studied at Andover Theological School. A number of other people who supported the movement from the sidelines, including Shimada Saburo, were also Christians. Most of the leaders of the largest labor dispute to occur during the Meiji period, a dispute involving railway engineers, were Christian. After the dispute Ishida Rokujiro and others formed the Reform Japan Railways Group, which emphasized the ethics of union members and also initiated a temperance program.

Labor unions that were organized during this period declined rather quickly, but some groups restarted not long after 1910. The Yuaikai, for example, was founded by Suzuki Bunji, a secretary of the Unitarian Hiromichikai. Meetings of the Yuaikai were held at the Iikan, a building administered by the Unitarians. When this group became more like a labor union, Matsuoka Komakichi became its secretary under President Suzuki.

However, the person who most influenced the Japanese labor movement after World War I was Kagawa* Toyohiko. Kagawa, urged on by laborers, became the leader of the Kansai Alliance Group and thus became the theoretical leader of the new labor-emancipation movement that emerged from the Yuaikai into the Japan Federation of Labor Unions. Because of his influence, a large number of the leaders became Christians. Because of the defeat he suffered in the horrendous labor dispute at Kawasaki Shipbuilding, however, Kagawa stepped back from the front lines of the labor movement, and the relationship between labor unions and the Christian church soon dwindled to almost nothing.

As the labor movement escalated after World War II*, the involvement of Christians was evident in various areas. The relationship between the two can be observed in the answer Takano Minoru, a leader in the labor world, gave to a question about what he expected from the Christian church: "Don't get in our way!" he said.

Bibliography

Sumiya Mikio, *Nihon rodo undo-shi* (History of Japan's Labor Movement) (1966); *Nihon no shakai shiso* (Thought of Japanese Society) (1968).

Sumiya Mikio, Japanese Dictionary

Labor Unions, Indonesia

J. Djikstra, secretary to the then apostolic vicar of Semarang, A. Soegijapranata* (archbishop in 1961), tried to find work for the unemployed who were seeking help from the cathedral parish of Semarang (Central Java); but many became members of the Communist-led union (SOBSI) after finding employment. To counter this undesirable effect, a local *Ikatan Buruh Pancasila* (*Pancasila** Workers' Union) was established (1954). Representatives of workers, and later (landless) farmers, from various parts of the Semarang vicariate met at the Girisonta retreat house to discuss a constitution for a union based on "social justice which is inspired by belief in God," and acknowledging human rights and free relationship with workers of all nations; but these values were rejected by the strong leftist organizations. After the formation of a basic ideology, different national unions for workers (1957), farmers, fishermen (1958), and nurses (1959) were set up with a general secretariat, *Biro Sosial Pancasila,* in Semarang. This office started educating cadres and distributing relevant information (*Bulletin Sadhana,* 1972). The unions chose the name *Pancasila* to stress their national, nondenominational, and antiatheist attitude.

Soegijapranata, elected chairman of the Social Committee of the Bishops' Conference, supported these unions. He inspired them with the spirit of the social teachings of the church. But the *Pancasila* Unions did not regard themselves as Catholic organizations nor as part of the Catholic Front under the leadership of *Partai Katolik*, for 90% of their ordinary members were not Catholics. The workers' and farmers' unions had strongholds in Central Java and Lampong (southern Sumatra), the fishermen on the islands of Flores* and Bangka. The Communists persuaded President Sukarno* to dissolve all social organizations that were not active in at least 20 of the 27 provinces of Indonesia (1960). The unions of *Ikatan Pancasila* met the requirement and could not be dissolved.

In 1973, after the leftist threat was crushed by a bloody retaliation following the Communist coup d'etat (1965), the unions of *Ikatan Pancasila*, like all others, were forced to join the official All Indonesian Workers' Federation (FBSI). This spelled the end of the independent labor movement because the key positions of all FBSI subdivisions were in the hands of the government-controlled GOLKAR. Many members could not accept this fusion and left the unions. Some of the former leaders and cadres of *Ikatan Pancasila* established non-governmental organizations to improve the situation of factory laborers, fishermen, household servants, and small farmers. ADOLF HEUKEN

Labuan

An island situated at the southwesterly end of Sabah, facing the Menumbuk and Kuala Penyu coastal area.

Taken on 24 Dec 1846 by G. R. Mundy in the name of Queen Victoria of Britain, the island of Labuan became part of the Straits Settlement Administration before being transferred to the British North Borneo Chartered Company and administered as part of the North Borneo territories from 1889 to 1906.

The Anglican* Church (1850) and the Catholic Church (1855) were the first to establish themselves in Labuan. In the Anglican Church the Cathedral of St. Savior, was the seat of Francis McDougall*, bishop of Labuan and Sarawak. Don Carlos Cuarteron, a Spanish Catholic friar, received permission from the Catholic Congregation of the Propagation of the Faith in Rome to spread the Gospel in Labuan and Borneo. Labuan was designated a prefecture with Cuarteron as prefect apostolic of Labuan and Borneo Mission. By 1857, there were 70 Catholics in Labuan. The island was used by the Catholic Church as the base for mission activities in Borneo proper, especially in North Borneo where work was started in 1857.

Cuarteron continued to use Labuan as the main base for mission work. But with the lack of personnel, the result was not good, and by 1881 the number of Catholics in Labuan had declined to 20. Cuarteron's work was passed on to the Mill Hill Mission under Thomas Jackson, who, in addition to the vision of maintaining Labuan's position as the center for missionary works in North Borneo, had plans to build a school and a seminary to train priests. The scant population and the isolation of Labuan from North Borneo and the major trade routes precluded these plans from materializing.

The number of Christians fluctuated but never grew substantially. At the beginning of the Japanese occupation, there remained only two churches in Labuan, one Anglican and the other Catholic. The two church buildings were burned down during the war.

Although the Basel Mission had sent a Chinese pastor by the name of Yap Hen Moo to minister to the Chinese coal miners as early as the late 19th c., the Basel Church in Labuan did not officially start until Dec 1979.

Ever since becoming a federal territory in 1984, Labuan has developed. The Malaysian* government's effort in promoting Labuan's status as an off-shore investment center promises to make Labuan an important island with a larger population, which will open up more avenues for churches to develop there.

Bibliography

Saunders, Graham, *Bishops and Brookes: The Anglican Mission and the Brooke Raj in Sarawak, 1848-1941* (1992). DANNY WONG TZE-KEN

Lahu

The approximately 600,000 Lahu peoples speak Tibeto-Burman languages and inhabit China*, Burma*, Thailand*, and Laos*. A small number (5,000) reside in Vietnam*. The Lahu comprise two main groups: the larger Black Lahu (75%) and the Yellow Lahu; there are also subgroups, e.g., the Lahu Nyi and Lahu Na are Black groups. There are also a few thousand Lahu who are neither Black nor Yellow. Over half of the Lahu live in the Yunnan province of China, from where they began to migrate southward, mainly to the Kengtung area of Burma, in the 19th c. Since 1962, many have fled to Thailand, where they now number more than 50,000.

Traditionally, the Lahu believe in a supreme being and creator, *Gui Sha*, and other spirits. Calling themselves *bon ya* (children of blessing), the Lahu devote much time to seeking blessing. Perhaps this accounts for the many Lahu who have become Christians, especially in Kengtung State and Thailand.

The American Baptist* Mission in Kengtung started work with the Lahu in the early 20th c. The pioneers in this work were H. H. Tilbe, who devised a Lahu script, and the Young family. By 1950, an estimated 28,000, mainly Black Lahu, were Christian. Many Lahu, especially Christians, fled the political unrest in Burma after Ne Win came to power in 1962. The Lahu Baptist Convention claims that almost all the Black Lahu, and more than half the entire Lahu population in Thailand, are Christian. Little is known of Christianity among the Lahu outside Thailand except that in 1994 a Lahu Baptist Church in Kengtung was holding regular services, and that a handful of Lahu in China, Laos, and Vietnam are Christian.

Bibliography

Lewis, Paul and Elaine, *Peoples of the Golden Triangle* (1984). • Sowards, Genevieve and Erville, eds., *Burma Baptist Chronicle* (1963). RONALD RENARD

Laimleckhoven, Godefroid Xavier de

(b. 1707; d. 1787). Jesuit* missionary who entered the interior of China* during the reign of Emperor Qian Lung (Qing Dynasty).

Laimleckhoven joined the Society of Jesus in 1722. In 1735, after becoming a priest, he traveled from Vienna to Lisbon, preparing himself for China. He arrived in Macau in 1738. He studied mathematics with the intention of working in the calendrical bureau, but, after arriving in Macau, the plan was changed: he slipped into the interior of China, adopting the same Chinese name (Nan Huai Ren) as had Ferdinand Verbiest when he worked for the Qing government during the reign of Kangxi.

Laimleckhoven was consecrated bishop of Macau in 1756. He returned to China's interior and moved from place to place, living in a small boat. He went to Jiangnan in 1760, disguised himself as a farmer, and did clandestine mission work in Shanghai and Suzhou, often hearing confessions and conducting mass in the early morning. In his later years, he lived in the Christian village of Pu Dong Jin. In 1784, he wrote *Zhao Shi Tang Gui,* a book on religious discipline to govern the religious life of the church members. Despite the government's prohibition of Christianity, some areas in Jiangnan continued to be a haven for Christians; this was undoubtedly the result of Laimleckhoven's clandestine mission work, which continued for more than 40 years. CHINA GROUP

Lallave, Manrique Alonso

(b. 1839; d. 1889). Spanish Dominican* missionary who became a Presbyterian* pastor; Bible* translator.

Lallave was the first Protestant Bible agent to attempt to open a depot in Manila (1889). While yet a Dominican* in 1861-71, Lallave had served in Pangasinan. When the liberal Spanish revolutionary government of 1868-71 allowed friars to leave their order, Lallave and three fellow Dominicans applied for this dispensation. But a less liberal Philippine governor having been appointed, they were instead haled before their own order's tribunal and subsequently deported to Spain.

In 1872, Lallave turned Protestant and served as a Presbyterian* pastor in Madrid and Seville. At the same time, he joined Freemasonry. He also married and raised a family. In 1889, the British and Foreign Bible Society* sent him and F. P. Castells to Manila with boxes of Spanish Bibles and Pangasinan Gospels that Lallave himself had earlier translated. Shortly after arrival, however, Lallave died of a sudden mysterious illness.

Bibliography

Ocio y Viana, H. M., *Compendio de la Reseña de los Religiosos de la Provincia del Santisimo Rosario de Filipinas* (1895). • Alonso, Esther, "Spanish Friar and Evangelist in the Philippines," *Missionary Herald* XCV (1899). • Abrines, L. Frau, and R. Arus Arderiu, *Diccionario Enciclopedico de la Masoneria,* Supplemento 23 (1957). • Sitoy, T. V., Jr., "An Aborted Spanish Protestant Mission to the Philippines," *Silliman Journal* XV.3 (1968). T. VALENTINO SITOY, JR.

Lam Ka Tseung, Domingos

(b. Hong Kong, 9 Apr 1928). First Chinese bishop of Macau.

Ordained a priest in Dec 1953 after his literary and theological studies in Macau's St. Joseph's Seminary, Lam taught in the local seminary and then worked as editor of the *Revue Aurora* from 1955 to 1958, when he was appointed parish priest of Taipa Island. In 1962 he was sent to Singapore* to work in St. Joseph's parish and to edit the publication *Rally.*

Lam returned to Macau in 1973 and was appointed rector of St. Joseph's Seminary in Oct 1974 and vicar general in 1976. Keen on educational services, he reorganized the Catholic schools for greater effectiveness. As pastor to the Chinese, he set up 11 centers for catechetical formation, promoted the establishment of several lay associations, especially among the students, and revitalized the diocesan publications.

Consecrated auxiliary bishop in 1987, Lam succeeded A. R. da Costa on 7 Oct 1988, when the latter resigned his bishopric. He continued the policies of his predecessor and also saw to the restoration of ancient buildings, among them the Bishop's Palace (1993), the Cathedral Center (1994), the complex of St. Joseph's Seminary (1991-94), and the Curia Archives with the diocesan historical treasures.

A knowledgeable and jovial man, one of Lam's key concerns was the preparation of the church for the return of Macau to China in 1999. SERGIO TICOZZI

Lamont, Archibald

(b. Port Bannantyne, Bute, Scotland, 14 Sep 1864; d. Durban, South Africa, 27 Nov 1933). Presbyterian* missionary who pioneered continuing education for Chinese working men in Singapore* from 1890 to 1897; activist against racial discrimination against blacks and Indians in South Africa.

The son of Alexander Lamont and Sarah Graham, Lamont obtained a master's degree from the University of Glasgow in 1888. On 15 Dec 1889, he was ordained by the presbytery of Glasgow and inducted as a missionary of the Presbyterian Church of England at Singapore. After he had studied Chinese for a few months in Amoy, he began to conduct Hokkien services in Neil Road and various preaching halls in Singapore and Malaya. As he became more interested in education, he gave up the preaching halls and transferred his Hokkien-speaking congregation to Un Sam Guan, his former tutor in Amoy.

In 1891, Lamont began the Singapore Chinese Educational Institute in his own home to fit young Chinese men for the responsibilities of leadership. On 25 Apr 1892, the institute was reconstituted under Tan Teck Soon (chairman), Lim Koon Tye (honorary secretary), and Tan Guan Hon (treasurer). Evening classes in English and Chinese history and literature, mathematics, and shorthand were started in a classroom of the Raffles Institution.

In 1893, Lamont bought the Eastern School, River Valley Road, which had been founded in 1890 as an Anglo-Chinese government grant-in-aid school but was threatened with closure due to mismanagement. He merged it with his own evening classes under the English Presbyterian Mission. The enrollment soon rose to 400 students; later, the school moved to more commodious premises on Club Street.

In 1894, Lamont coauthored, with Tan Teck Soon, an English novel, *Bright Celestials.* His other publications include *Heights of Hell, South Africa in Mars,* and articles in various periodicals, including "The Social Cancer," which was the subject of a libel action.

In 1893, Lamont married Henrietta Williams Bell, and they had a son on 21 Feb 1900.

In 1896, the English Presbyterian Mission withdrew its support for the Eastern School to concentrate on work in China*. Lamont resigned on 16 Nov 1897 and, in 1898, was called to the pastoral charge of the Free Church congregation at Dailly, Ayrshire, Scotland. H. Rankin succeeded him as principal of the Eastern School, which closed permanently on 31 Oct 1902.

During his period in the United Kingdom, Lamont served in various other churches: St. Paul's North Shields, presbytery of Newcastle (27 Feb 1902 to 4 Dec 1906); the congregation at Wembley, presbytery of London North (18 Jan 1907 to 30 Mar 1908); and Wardie United Free Church (1908-11).

In 1910, Lamont visited his sister in Adelaide, South Africa, and became a permanent resident in that country in 1912. His first ministry was in Tarkastad where he met and married his second wife, Beatrice McEwan, the daughter of a Scottish immigrant, who bore him three sons. Lamont was installed as minister of St. Ninians, Greyville, Durban, in 1916. He became a city councillor but, because of his stand against racial discrimination, most white Durban residents found him too liberal in his views. He was defeated in both provincial and parliamentary elections in 1927 and 1929. His election as Durban's mayor in 1929 came as a surprise. He was defeated in his bid for a fourth term as mayor, but the white workers of Durban elected him a member of the provincial council for Greyville in 1932. In recognition of his efforts to improve the conditions of the black people, a new Umlazi black township was named Lamontville in his honor.

Lamont was buried in Durban in 1933.

Bibliography

Greer, Robert M., *A History of the Presbyterian Church in Singapore* (1959). • Moore, Donald and Joanna, *The First 150 Years of Singapore* (1969). • Mouton, F. A., "Eerwaarde Archibald Lamont — Kampvegter Vir die Minderbevoorregte," *Historia* 34.1 (May 1989). • Song Ong Siong, *One Hundred Years History of the Chinese in Singapore* (1902).

Anne Johnson

Laneau, Louis

(b. Mondoubleau [Loir-et-Cher], France, 31 May 1637; d. Juthia, Thailand, 16 Mar 1696).

Laneau was studying at the Sorbonne when he first came into contact with the Paris Foreign Mission Society* (MEP) and dedicated his life to its service. He left Paris in Sep 1661 and sailed from Marseilles on 2 Jan 1662 with Mgr. Pallu* and eight other missionaries and auxiliaries. He arrived in Siam on 27 Jan 1664 and was almost at once put in charge of the college founded by Lambert de la Motte*. He quickly became proficient in Siamese and was even able to write in that language (at the request of King Phra-Narai) explanations concerning the mysteries of the Christian faith, the apostles, evangelists, the principal founders of the religious orders, the last times, and more. Having read these explanations, the king invited Laneau to have religious discussions with him and communicated the substance of these discussions to several of the prominent mandarins. The king's brother likewise had conversations with Laneau on the same subjects.

In Apr 1671, Laneau made an expedition to Phitsanulok, situated about 80 leagues north of Juthia. There he baptized six or seven dead infants, and a number of the inhabitants promised to convert to Christianity. Obliged to return to Juthia several weeks later, he was not able to follow up this attempt at evangelization. On his return, he had a hospice built near the college, where he cared for the sick and saw some conversions.

Appointed bishop of Metellopolis in 1673 and vicar apostolic of Nanking and Siam, Laneau was consecrated at Juthia on 25 Mar 1674 and straightaway took up residence in Bangkok. He obtained a plot of land from the king and built on it a church dedicated to the Immaculate Conception. There he organized a parish comprising, for the greater part, Portuguese expelled from Cambodia*. In 1676, he made a second expedition to Phitsanulok and stationed a missionary there by the name of Pierre Langlois. In 1679 or 1680, he transferred the college or general seminary to a property given him by the king. It was situated to the northwest near Juthia in a place called Mahapram, on the banks of a stream of the same name which flows into the Mei-nam.

On 3 Apr 1680, Laneau was given jurisdiction over

Japan*, but he was never able to go there. On 24 Nov 1681, he was appointed administrator general of the missions of Siam, Tonkin, and Cochin China. In 1682, he visited the last-named mission by way of the Nha-trang River and reached Fai-fo, where he consecrated Mahot as bishop of Bide and held a synod.

On his return to Siam, Laneau built at Juthia a church which was consecrated on 25 Mar 1685 in honor of St. Joseph. About this time, the abbot of Choisy described him thus: "A tall man of noble appearance, although he is only 45 years old he looks more like 60. Twenty-four years in the mission field do not give you a fresh complexion!"

A catastrophe ruined all of the hopes of the French and the missionaries. A mandarin named Pitra-cha, hostile to foreigners, had their protector, the chief minister Phaulcon, assassinated, removed the king, and mounted the throne. Conflict erupted between the Siamese and the French, the latter being obliged to withdraw; but against their word the French took the mandarins hostage. Laneau did everything to prevent this regrettable act, clearly foreseeing the consequences.

The French paid no attention to this wise advice, and the bishop bore the anger of the Siamese, who insulted him, trapped and imprisoned him with several of his priests, together with French officers and soldiers, and pillaged all the buildings of the mission in Juthia. During his imprisonment, Laneau wrote part of the work *De deificatione justorum,* printed for the first time in 1887. He was set free in 1690, and in the following year the college was returned to him with little more than the walls remaining. There the missionaries, students, and some French, totaling 113 persons, gathered. Laneau took advantage of this peaceful interlude to request and obtain the release of the French prisoners.

Difficulties caused by the opposition of the Portuguese were less severe than during the episcopate of de la Motte*; several, however, had to be referred to Rome. On 22 Oct 1696, Pope Innocent XII addressed a letter to Laneau titled *Cum sicut ad (Jus Pont. De Prop. Fid.* II, p. 161). This letter confirmed the orders of Clement X and, on pain of excommunication, prohibited the archbishop of Goa and other ordinaries of the Indies from obstructing the administration of the vicars apostolic.

Several days before his death, Laneau dictated a letter for the cardinals of the Congregation of the Propaganda but would not sign it until he had received the last sacraments. Possibly with knowledge of this letter, Pope Innocent XII addressed a eulogy to him on 6 Jan 1697. By this time, the bishop had been dead for 10 months. He was interred in the church at Juthia, his principal virtues being mortification, humility, love of souls, and hard work.

Concerning the various works of which he was author, the letter that announced Laneau's death said: "He translated into Siamese catechisms for children and for persons more advanced in the knowledge of our holy mysteries, an explanation of the sacraments and the right disposition to receive them, two dictionaries, one in Siamese, the other Balli and Latin, a collection of prayers to be recited aloud during Mass, and instructions on this adorable Sacrifice."

Bibliography

Memoirs of the MEP, trans. Frank Lomax.

Frank Lomax

Langheim, Henry W.

(b. 1871; d. 1957). American Presbyterian* medical missionary who built Silliman Mission Hospital in the Philippines*.

Langheim, the second Protestant medical missionary in the Philippines, and his wife, Ruth, came as Presbyterian missionaries to Dumaguete, Negros Oriental, in 1901. Being the first man equipped with modern medical* training in Negros Oriental, Langheim, with permission from the Presbyterian board, was co-opted as government provincial health officer in 1901-6. He effectively combated cholera (1901-3) and supervised anti-smallpox vaccination for 95,000 persons, representing 95 percent of the provincial population (in 1905-6). A nurse, Ruth trained medical helpers and substituted for her husband in his absence.

From his government salary, Langheim built the Silliman Mission Hospital in 1903, which he developed during the following 15 years into the chief medical center in Negros Oriental. It also represented an important contributing factor to the rapid growth of Protestantism in the region.

Bibliography

Laubach, F. C., *People of the Philippines* (1925). • Hall, J. A., and F. O. Smith, *Survey of Medical Missions in the Philippines* (1960). • Kwantes, A. C., *Presbyterian Missionaries in the Philippines* (1989).

T. Valentino Sitoy, Jr.

Lao Religion

The Lao make up only 45% of the population of Laos*; in fact, many more ethnic Lao live in northeast Thailand than do in Laos. The Lao are known as *Theravada* Buddhists*, but the tapestry of Lao religiosity goes far beyond a simple outline of Buddhist metaphysics. S. J. Tambiah describes the complex of Lao religious belief in terms of four kinds of rituals.

First there are rituals performed by Buddhist monks which procure merit for laypeople or the village as a whole. Monks provide merit for the community by maintaining and reinforcing Buddhist metaphysics and moral standards outlined in the four noble truths and the eightfold path. Buddhist rituals normally occur during festivals which follow the pattern of the agricultural cycle and lunar year, on the four lunar-month sabbaths, and in the daily routine of the monks, such as begging for food.

Second, there are guardian-spirit rituals which function to ensure that these spirits will protect and bless the individual and the community. The *nak* serpent spirit is especially important because it provides the rain so badly needed for rice cultivation. The fluid nature of these categories can be seen in that, when a Buddhist novice is ordained a monk, holy water is poured through the mouth of a *nak* image onto the head of the new monk.

The third kind of ritual is known as the *sukhwan* rituals. They are perhaps the most important rituals for the Lao. These ceremonies, like those for the guardian spirits, are performed by laypeople with little or no participation from the monks. The monks often carry out merit-making rituals before *sukhwan* and guardian-spirit rituals, but do not actually get involved in praying and offering gifts to spirits. The spirit world is part of the suffering of existence that they are attempting to escape. The Lao believe that people have two basic spirits, the *khwan* and the *vinjan*. The *vinjan* is the spirit which holds the essence of life and leaves the body only at death. But the *khwan* is a spirit essence which can leave a person during periods of illness, emotional stress, transition, or travel. In the ritual, prayers call the *khwan* spirit back. A string tied to the wrist attaches one's *khwan* spirit to the individual in order to ensure well-being and balance in personal and community life.

Fourth, evil-spirit rituals deal with taboo behaviors and unexplained evil in life. Lay specialists are often paid a fee to perform complicated and occasionally bizarre rituals in order to restore to wholeness the person being afflicted by an evil spirit.

The Christian Gospel can be effectively communicated to Lao people after a foundational understanding of a personal, loving God and of the biblical concept of sin has been built. In communicating the Gospel to Lao people, relationships must be kept in the forefront. One of the strongest aspects of Lao culture is the high value it places on relationships. This can be a formidable obstacle for Christian witness, but it can also be a means by which the Gospel can spread.

Finally, Christian witness must take into account the issue of spiritual power in the lives of Lao people. Certainly for many Lao converts to Christianity the power of Christ over the spiritual world is one of the most attractive aspects of the Gospel. Yet Christians must be careful that Jesus does not simply become one more spirit to pray to for the needs and wants of this life.

Bibliography

Hardon, John A., *Religions of the Orient* (1970). • Lester, Robert C., *Theravada Buddhism in Southeast Asia* (1973). • Tambiah, S. J., *Buddhism and the Spirit Cult in North-east Thailand* (1970). • Terwiel, B. J., *Monks and Magic* (1979).

Laos

Tucked away in the foothills of the Himalayan Mountains, landlocked Laos shares borders with Thailand*, Myanmar* (Burma), China*, Vietnam*, and Cambodia*. Although the Mekong River runs more than a thousand kilometers through Laos into Cambodia, it does not provide navigable waters to the sea. Both the geographical isolation and 30 years of the Indochina War have allowed Laos' four-and-a-half million people to keep most of their traditional cultures.

Though sparsely populated, Laos possesses 119 different ethno-linguist groups. The Lao break up the mosaic into three distinct social categories: the Highland Lao (14%), the Midland Lao (36%), and the Lowland Lao (50%). Since the 14th century, Lowland Lao have dominated politically and economically. They are followed in influence by the Highland groups, particularly the Hmong. The Midland Lao groups are last socially and economically; some of them are being assimilated into Lowland Lao culture.

The Lao monarchy was formed in 1353, and, although Laos was often a vassal state of neighboring kingdoms, the monarchy governed until the French colonial period in 1893. After World War II, a Lao independence movement sprang up which eventually forced France to grant Laos its freedom in 1953. From the start of the Lao Kingdom until the coming to power of the Communists in 1975, *Theravada* Buddhism* was the state religion. Even now the government sees Buddhism* as the only legitimate Lao religion.

The Lao People's Revolutionary Party was formed in 1955 by former members of the Indochinese Communist Party. Twenty years later the party gained complete control of Laos, and the country was renamed the Lao People's Democratic Republic (Lao PDR). During the party's first 12 years in power, more than 10 percent of the then three million people fled as refugees.

The drive toward complete socialism was abandoned in 1986 with the adoption of the new economic policy. The new policy allows for private enterprise and foreign investment in a free market economy. Today socialism is rarely mentioned as a goal while nationalism*, with an emphasis on traditional Lao Buddhist values, is on the rise. Nevertheless, the party remains in firm control. The effect of the new economic policy has been significant in urban areas. Regardless, the Lao PDR remains one of the poorest countries in the world. The annual average per capita income is about $200, the infant mortality rate is among the highest in Asia, and life expectancy is less than 50 years of age.

Roman Catholic Church. The first Christian mission to Laos was attempted in 1642 by the Jesuit* Jean de Leria. He stayed for five years before pressure from Buddhist monks forced him to leave. There was then a period of over 200 years when there was no known Christian contact.

The next Western attempt to reach Laos was initiated by Mgr. Miche, apostolic vicar of Cambodia, who in 1858 entrusted to P. Ausoleil and P. Triaire this difficult task of bringing the Gospel to the Laotians. He instructed them to found the first station at Luang Phra

Bang, having heard about this province from the people. Luang Phra Bang was situated in the north of Laos and was a long way from Cambodia. The missionaries had decided to go there via Bangkok. After a very long and difficult journey, they arrived at Luang Phra Bang. Unfortunately, three of the servants who had accompanied them contracted the terrible forest fever; two died, while Triaire also got the same fever and died not long after. Ausoleil, therefore, had to return to Bangkok.

In 1870, during the Vatican Council, the cardinal prefect of the Congregation of Propaganda proposed to Mgr. Dupond to take Laos under his jurisdiction and to evangelize it. Dupond accepted the task, but his death in 1872 prevented him from accomplishing it. P. Martin, as the superior of the mission, also mentioned sending missionaries to Laos in accordance with the will of Dupond, saying that Jean-Louis Vey*, who was in France for health reasons, would be the right person to make the decision about this project. The directors of the Paris Foreign Mission Society* (MEP) could ask Vey about the matter.

As apostolic vicar, Vey initiated the first step by charging P. Prodhomme and P. Perraux to open the new mission in the Laotian province. Prodhomme recorded that the two missionaries began their adventure, passing through the so-called Dong Phraya Fai, the dangerous forest full of fever, and settling down at Kengkoi, where a great number of Laotians were living. The mission was doing quite well, even though the enterprise of evangelization was not without problems, e.g., forest fever and the shortage of material resources and personnel.

In the first year of the mission, Prodhomme and Perraux founded a Christian community with 40 baptized Laotians. This encouraging result caused Vey to be so curious that he decided to make a visit to this new community on 1 Jan 1877. By the end of 1880, the zeal and perseverance of the two missionaries resulted in 250-300 Christians and catechumens. Vey decided to continue this work, but he realized that Kengkoi could not be the center of the mission, since it was too far from the Laotian provinces. Most Laotians, in fact, were living in the northeast of Siam, not in the north around Kengkoi, so it would be much better to send the missionaries to this part of Siam in order to survey possibilities for the new mission. Morever, the governor of Ubon, situated in the northeast of Siam, invited the missionaries to settle in his province.

So on 2 Jan 1881, Vey officially announced that Prodhomme and Xavier Guego were being sent to Ubon to begin the new mission in Laos. They left Bangkok on 12 Jan 1881 with a catechist and some assistants. After a long and difficult journey of 102 days, they arrived at Ubon on Easter Sunday, 24 Apr 1881.

With the permission of the governor, Prodhomme and Guego were able to buy a piece of land that had been abandoned because it was supposedly haunted by wicked spirits. With great curiosity, the Laotians came in number to see them, so the missionaries took advantage of the opportunity by preaching the Gospel to them. The arrival of the missionaries caused dissatisfaction and anxiety among the slave traders. They felt that the missionaries could be an obstacle by liberating slaves and informing the authorities in Bangkok about their activities. The slave traders, therefore, made the false charge that the missionaries had also come to practice slave trading. This charge could not be sustained, since it was contrary to what the Laotians had seen of the missionaries, who had accused the slave traders before the tribunal and had liberated slaves. Conversions began, and Christian communities were founded and grew year by year. In 1883, Vey reported to Paris that the missionaries were planning to settle in Laos, having surveyed the topography up to Wiengchan. He had appealed several times to the councils of the MEP, asking for whatever help was needed to sustain evangelization in Laos, as the Congregation of Propaganda had instructed him to throw all his resources into this mission.

The number of Christians and catechumens was growing quite rapidly. In 1885, there were 485 Christians and more than 1,500 catechumens, and in 1888 there were 648 Christians and more than 4,500 catechumens.

Although there was some gradual progress of Roman Catholic work in Laos, persecution was always a threat. In 1878 Catholic fathers pioneered again in northeastern Laos, but the mission came to a tragic end with the martyrdom of 12 priests in 1884 and five more in 1889. In the French colonial period, the most successful Catholic efforts were in southern Laos.

Vey continued to support the mission of Laos as much as he could. Every year, some missionaries from Laos had to go to Bangkok to report on their mission and to take back all the necessary resources, such as foodstuffs, supplies, salaries for the catechists, financial support for the mission, and also the new missionaries to Laos. Certainly, the personnel were not sufficient for the new growing mission, but they were one of the most important factors that led to its success.

The separation of the mission of Laos from the mission of Siam and the elevation of the mission of Laos to a new vicariate were Vey's ideas. There were several motivating factors: (1) Vey realized that divine providence was preparing the way, since the princes who were governing the Laotian provinces were no longer the enemies of the mission. (2) Communication between the Laotian provinces and Bangkok, the center of the mission, was very difficult, since the mission of Siam was vast and the missionaries had to travel there by the Mekong River, which cost them time and difficulties. Vey thought that, as a new vicariate, the mission of Laos could contact Paris directly via Saigon. (3) The mission of Siam could not sustain the new mission because Siam also needed more personnel and material resources for work which was growing quite fast. (4) The progress of the mission of Laos was reason enough to propose to Rome the creation of a new vicariate. In fact, Vey gave the total number of Christians in Laos as 7,000, counting those who occupied the region of Bassac to Nongkai.

Vey proposed the matter to Paris in 1896. The councils of the MEP seemed to agree. The directors of the MEP sent letters to the apostolic vicars of Oriental Cochin China, Occidental Cochin China, northern Tongking, southern Tongking, Occidental Tonking, and Cambodia, asking for their opinions on the boundary of the new mission of Laos. All the apostolic vicars of these regions cooperated immediately and sent their opinions on the subject to Paris. Vey also proposed that the Congregation of Propaganda establish the mission of Laos as an apostolic vicariate.

In Dec 1897, Paris informed Vey that the Congregation was quite ready to separate the mission of Laos from the mission of Siam. On 17 Jan 1898, the missionaries who were working in Laos were invited to vote for the first apostolic vicar of Laos.

In the 20th c., the approach of the Roman Catholic Church changed. Most all exploratory work came from the south through Bangkok. Major cities to the east of the Mekong River were the focus of missionary activities which concentrated on educational and medical* work. By 1967, there were over 30,000 Catholics; 27 primary schools and three secondary schools were run by the Roman Catholic Church.

In 1975, a number of Catholic properties were confiscated by the government when the Communists took control. After the new economic policy was initiated, some Catholic churches were refurbished, and a new training school for village girls opened in Vientiane. The Catholic Church is organized into four vicariates overseen by three bishops. There are 16 other ordained priests, seven of whom were ordained after 1975. There are roughly 35 thousand Catholics, of which the largest group is Midland Lao, followed by Lowland Lao. The most pressing issues for Catholics are a lack of religious freedom, the training of the laity for ministry, and the need to rekindle a deep spirituality.

Protestant Church. The first Protestant missionary to Laos was Presbyterian Daniel McGilvary*. He made several trips to Laos between 1872 and 1898 from Chiang Mai, Thailand. In 1902, Gabriel Contesse began the work of the Swiss Brethren in southern Laos. Mission work in the north would not start until the arrival in 1929 of G. Edward Roffe from the Christian & Missionary Alliance*.

Just before the Communist takeover in 1975, all foreign missionaries left Laos. At the time, both the northern and southern churches were self-governing, having worked together for many years toward a smooth merger into the Lao Evangelical Church (LEC). Except for a couple of Seventh-Day Adventist* congregations, the LEC is the only Protestant church in the Lao PDR.

In 1975, when the Communists took control, the Gospel had not yet penetrated the dominant Lowland Lao society. Today, Khamu Christians in the north outnumber Hmong, and significant numbers of Lowland Lao people are entering the church, even from the growing urban middle class. In the south there has been good growth among Midland and Lowland Lao Christians as well. While many of the first-generation Christians were social outcasts, this stigma is now being eliminated. The acceptance of Christian belief is due in part to the number of Christians who have become local officials and the excellent reputation of a prominent Lao Christian doctor. The major issues facing the LEC are the lack of religious freedom and the lack of trained clergy and lay leaders (there are only four ordained pastors for 228 churches). In spite of these difficulties, the LEC has grown from an estimated 17,000 in 1975 to roughly 32,000 today. This is even more notable when we remember that large numbers of Christians left the country after "liberation."

The Lao constitution calls for freedom of religious belief, but Christians have been singled out for harassment since the Communists took power. Generally, Christians are allowed to meet for worship, instruction, and prayer meetings, but problems may arise with the government when too many new Christians enter the church. In 1993 relations between the LEC and the government were becoming almost cordial, but late in 1994 an effort was made to close churches in several provinces. In some areas, Protestants and Catholics were pressured to sign affidavits renouncing the church and promising not to share their religious beliefs with others. Some 40 LEC churches were torn down or converted into schools. Christian literature was confiscated, and at least 18 Christians were arrested and held without trial. While hampered by restricted religious freedom, an insufficient number of trained clergy, and a membership with little economic clout, the church in Laos is growing and slowly making itself felt in Lao society, perhaps for the very first time.

Bibliography

Andrianoff, David, "Daniel McGilvary and Early Protestant Missionary Outreach into Laos" (unpublished paper) (1991). • Brown, MacAlister, and Joseph J. Zasloff, *Apprentice Revolutionaries: The Communist Movement in Laos, 1930-1985* (1986). • Chazee, Laurent, *Atlas des Ethnies et des Sous-Ethnies du Laos* (1995). • Decorvet, Jeanne, and Georges Rochat, *L'Appel du Laos* (1946). • Dommen, Arthur, *Laos: Keystone of Indochina* (1985). • Gunn, Geoffrey C., *Political Struggles in Laos: 1930-1954* (1988). • Roffe, G. Edward, "Laos," in *The Church in Asia*, ed. Donald E. Hoke (1975). • Lao Christian Service, *Life After Liberation* (1987). • Stuart-Fox, Martin, *Laos: Politics, Economics and Society* (1986).

SURACHAI CHUMSRIPHAN on the Roman Catholic Church

Larantuka

Small town in east Flores* and the oldest parish in Indonesia* (1550).

In 1951, Larantuka was the apostolic vicariate. By 1961, the diocese had 220,700 Catholics in 31 parishes (1991) entrusted to the Society of the Divine Word* (SVD) missionaries.

Goanese and Portuguese Dominicans* started missions in East Indonesia during the middle of the 16th c. In spite of strong resistance from Muslim villages and later from the Dutch United East-India Company* (*Verenigde Oost-Indische Compagnie,* VOC), the so-called Solor* Mission developed rapidly (1598 — 25,000 faithful; 1606 — 50,000). A fort built by the mission to protect the priests and the congregation in Lohayong on Solor Island was conquered and destroyed by heavy artillery of the VOC (1613). Seven missionaries with hundreds of faithful and some Portuguese soldiers fled to Larantuka, which became the center of missionary activity in eastern Flores. Though rarely visited by priests from Dili (Timor*), the people of Larantuka kept their faith through centuries, mainly because of the sodality of the *Confreria Reinha Rosari* (1564), which still organizes prayer meetings as well as popular processions and celebrations during Holy Week and Easter.

Since 1860, the mission has been resumed by secular and Jesuit* missionaries among the remaining 3,335 "old Catholics." After initial suspicion was overcome and Franciscan* sisters (from Heythuisen, 1879) took over the schools, nearly all from east Flores converted because of the groundwork of the Portuguese missionaries. The graduates from the teachers' training college of Larantuka became pioneers of the mission in central and western Flores in the beginning of the 20th c.

The Jesuits eventually handed over the mission to SVD fathers (1917) who, with new manpower, expanded their activity to the surrounding islands. The indigenous congregations of the Daughters of the Queen of the Rosary (founded 1958) and Followers of Jesus (CIJ) have strengthened and partially taken over the work of the Sisters of Servants of the Holy Spirit (SSpS; in Flores since 1925). Many faithful and religious from the diocese of Larantuka are staunch promoters of Christianity throughout the country. Seasonal workers migrate to East Malaysia, where they encounter difficulties because of their religion.

Adolf Heuken

Larena, Demetrio

(b. 1857; d. 1916). Church leader and first Filipino governor of Negros Oriental, Philippines*.

An advocate of modern education and progress, Larena served as governor of Negros Oriental from 1901 to 1906 under the American regime. In his first year of administration, his province boasted 51 public schools with 7,000 pupils and 22 American and 109 Filipino teachers. This represented a substantial increase over the previous Spanish educational system which, in 1892, had 5,215 pupils and 23 teachers. Larena convinced the American Presbyterian* missionaries in 1901 to build what is now Silliman University in Dumaguete, the provincial capital.

The chief Philippine Independent Church* leader in Negros Oriental, Larena turned Protestant in 1907, remaining faithful to his death. He was the first elder of Bais Evangelical Church in his hometown (1909) and the first Filipino trustee of Silliman Institute (1910).

Bibliography

"D. Larena," *Sixth Annual Report of the Philippine Commission* (1906). • Hibbard, D. S., *The First Quarter: A Brief History of Silliman Institute* (1926). • Rodgers, J. B., *Forty Years in the Philippines* (1940).

T. Valentino Sitoy, Jr.

Latuihamallo, Peter Dominggus

(b. Mamasa, Indonesia, 15 Aug 1918). Indonesian theologian, scholar, and professor.

After completing his first theological degree at the Hoogere Theologische School (HTS), Jakarta, in 1948, Latuihamallo was ordained a minister of the Protestant Church in the Moluccas* (GPM) in Ambon. His knowledge of Dutch, English, French, and German helped him in his theological studies, and especially in anthropology and sociology, which were entrance requirements for further studies in Christian ethics in particular and theology in general. Better known as a theologian than a church minister, he was appointed the first Indonesian professor at HTS after he had obtained his doctorate from Union Theological Seminary, New York, United States. He was also appointed several times as rector of HTS, while continuing to teach ethics.

Latuihamallo had a close relationship with Islamic leaders, having once studied in an Islamic college (1945), an experience which broadened his understanding of Islamic doctrines, e.g., the oneness of God *(Tauhid).* His association with Muslims also gave him the opportunity to correct their misconceptions of Christian doctrines, e.g., the doctrine of the Trinity, which the Muslims perceived to be tritheism. Latuihamallo realized that ethics is closely related to other fields because it is relevant to the morality of human action. In a pluralistic community, he was in favor of, and attended, interreligious dialogues* on ethics at the national and international level, e.g., in Broumana, Lebanon (1971).

Latuihamallo saw the church as a dynamic, creative, and responsible partner of the state in social reform for the betterment of its community. Through his lectures, he called on Christians to participate in national development to reform society and to guarantee a stable future. He was instrumental in bringing about cooperation between the Indonesian and Dutch governments, especially with regard to the problem of Moluccans living in the Netherlands. He was awarded the medal of Commander in the Order of Orange-Nassau by the Dutch queen, Juliana, when she visited Jakarta in 1971.

Latuihamallo served as chairman of *Dewan Gereja-*

gereja di Indonesia (Indonesian Council of Churches*, DGI) from 1979 to 1984 and as chairman of the Association for Theological Education in South East Asia (ATESEA), as well as being a Protestant representative in the Indonesian state legislative body.

Bibliography

Darmaputera, E., ed., *Konteks Berteologi di Indonesia — Buku Penghormatan untuk HUT ke-70 Prof. Dr. P. D. Latuihamallo* (1990). • Latuihamallo, P. D., ed., *Kewarganegaraan Yang Bertanggungjawab — Mengenang Dr. J. Leimena* (1980). • Simatupang, T. B., ed., *Disuruh ke Dalam Dunia, Tugas Kita Dalam Negara Pancasila Yang Membangun* (1973). • Thomas, M. M., ed., *Religion, State and Ideologies in East Asia* (1965). MESACH TAPILATU

Laubach, Frank C.

(b. 1884; d. 1970). Leading pioneer of the contemporary adult-literacy movement.

Laubach and his wife, Effa Seely, arrived in the Philippines* in 1915 as missionaries of the American Board and began new work in Cagayan, Misamis (now Cagayan de Oro City). With his new ideas, Laubach immediately won the friendship and admiration of the leading townspeople and the high school students. When the Cagayan Evangelical Church was organized in 1917, 90% of its members were young students. After brief service as seminary dean in Manila (1924-26), the Laubachs moved to Dansalan, Lanao, for Christian work among the Muslim Maranaws.

In 1930, Laubach began missionary work among the Maranaw people of the Philippines. He found that even the most impoverished people can master the written and spoken word. He discovered the potential of volunteers, as newly literate Maranaws taught adult learners through a one-to-one instructional program known as "Each One Teach One" (The Laubach Method). He demonstrated that literacy is an effective means of positive community change.

Over the next 40 years, Laubach visited 103 countries bringing literacy to the "silent billion." He and his team did literacy work worldwide in 315 languages. With local literacy workers, his teams tirelessly field-tested instructional materials and techniques, searching for effective methods of teaching illiterates. A prolific writer and accomplished speaker, he wrote 40 books on prayer, literacy, justice, and world peace.

In 1955, Laubach founded Laubach Literacy International. He said, "A literate person is not only an illiterate person who has learned to read and write, he is another person. He is different. To promote literacy is to change man's conscience by changing his relation to his environment. It is an undertaking on the same plane as the recognition and incarnation of fundamental human rights."

The *Frank C. Laubach Heritage Collection* is a four-book set containing selections from Laubach's best-known books. This collection preserves Laubach's works for succeeding generations of readers, offering comprehensive background information on his experiences and philosophy.

Bibliography

Frank C. Laubach Heritage Collection (New Readers Press, P.O. Box 888, Syracuse, N.Y. 13210-0888). • Laubach, F. C., *People of the Philippines* (1925); *Seven Thousand Emeralds* (1929). • Sitoy, T. V., Jr., *Several Springs, One Stream* (1992).

ROBERT F. RICE and T. Valentino Sitoy, Jr.

Lausanne Congress on World Evangelism

(LCWE). The International Congress on World Evangelism in Lausanne, Switzerland, in Jul 1974 was the result of the vision and initiative of American evangelist Billy Graham. Twenty-seven hundred participants attended from all over the world, and nearly every evangelical denomination and parachurch group was represented. Approximately 50% were from the Two-Thirds World.

The congress took place soon after the World Council of Churches (WCC) Division of World Mission and Evangelism meeting in Bangkok, where powerful voices had called for a moratorium on all forms of evangelization. The congress, under the banner "Let the earth hear his voice," provided a platform for evangelicals to declare that evangelism is at the heart of the church's mission. At the congress, there were devotional Bible studies each morning, which were followed by presentations on 14 theological issues confronting modern evangelization. These papers had been distributed prior to the congress, and most participants had responded to the issues before they reached Lausanne. All the issues were significant, but with the passing of time two stand out.

First, the concept of a people group as a key to evangelization was discussed and studied. This presentation by Donald McGavran of Fuller Theological Seminary (Pasadena, California, United States) was seminal. The human race was depicted as a "magnificent and intricate mosaic"; the aim of evangelization is to plant a church in each piece of this mosaic. In this address McGavran made the church in the West aware of the growth of the church in Africa and Asia with the emergence of new missionary societies which had great potential for world evangelization.

Second, the whole notion of social responsibility in the mission of the church was a major theme. It came through two papers: "Evangelization and the Word" by René Padilla of Argentina, and "Evangelization and Man's Search for Freedom, Justice and Fulfilment" by Samuel Escobar, also from South America but working in Canada. Both of these addresses created extensive discussion by noting that the American way of life had influenced much of evangelicalism with a consequent loss of a prophetic role in society. Overall, the congress was overwhelming in its support for a fresh awareness that the Gospel sometimes comes in the setting of an alien culture. There were some participants who had little involvement with questions of justice and who thought such an involvement was a deflection from their evangelistic call. However, the conclusion was uncompromising: "Although reconciliation with man is not reconciliation with God, nor is social action evangelism, nor is political liberation salvation, nevertheless we affirm that evangelism and socio-political involvement are both parts of our Christian duty."

The congress also left an enduring legacy in a covenant consisting of 15 clauses. It was endorsed by almost all of the participants, and it quickly became an influential statement on mission and evangelization used throughout the world for all kinds of cooperative endeavors. The covenant stressed the authority of the Bible, placed social justice among the purposes of the church's mission, emphasized the urgency of the evangelistic task, and linked mission with the world's problems. It stressed the role of the Holy Spirit and confirmed the belief in the second coming of Christ. The single most important outcome of the congress, the covenant became a basis for fellowship and cooperation in world evangelization. Over the years it has provided a working program and a theological framework for evangelism.

The congress also supported the formation of a committee to promote world evangelization. Its first chairman was Billy Graham and successive chairmen were A. J. Dain, Leighton Ford, J. R. Reid, and Fergus Macdonald. Committee members represent geographical regions as well as church and parachurch groups. The task of the LCWE committee is to promote world evangelization, and in order to do this it has established four working groups: intercession, strategy, communication, and theology.

The Lausanne movement does not have a formal membership. Those who wish to join it do so by simply supporting it. However, the LCWE committee members sign the Lausanne Covenant each time they meet. From the beginning, the LCWE has sought to cooperate with all those who can subscribe to the covenant. The intercessory working group publishes material for prayer and promotes Pentecost Sunday as a day of prayer for the unreached. The strategy working group, in association with World Vision's* research arm (Mission Advanced Research and Communications Center, MARC), publishes yearly handbooks on the status of world evangelization, promotes a creative program on urban evangelization led by Ray Bakke of Chicago, and cosponsors many projects which study ways to reach unreached people groups. The communication group encourages evangelism with press releases, a quarterly journal on world evangelization, and the publication of small Lausanne Occasional Papers which highlight issues related to evangelization. The theology working group (often in cooperation with the theology unit of the World Evangelical Fellowship) regularly holds consultations, and the papers are subsequently published. The topics covered include Gospel and Culture, Simple Lifestyle, the Relationship between Evangelism and Social Justice, Evangelism and the Holy Spirit, Conversion and Evangelism, and Modernity.

In 1974, the LCWE appointed Gottfried Osei Mensah of Nairobi, Kenya, as a minister at large. He became a familiar figure at conferences around the world as he encouraged a fresh commitment to evangelism. He was followed by others, including Tom Houston of the City Temple, London.

Soon after the 1974 congress, a national congress on evangelism was held in Africa. This was quickly followed by other national conferences and consultations. These were not controlled by the LCWE committee, but were an important part of the LCWE movement. One of the most active local groups was based in Hong Kong* and known as the Chinese Christian Consultation on World Evangelization* (CCCOWE). It was established in 1976. By regular publications, it highlighted the spiritual needs of the Chinese people throughout the world with special emphasis on those groups who have not been reached with the Gospel. Another group who had their genesis in Lausanne focused on Jewish evangelism. They met regularly, held conferences, and promoted the Gospel amongst Jewish people. It is virtually impossible to ascertain all of the activities that have been generated by Lausanne initiatives. In Europe, 25 new organizations or missions were started. In India*, 400 Christian leaders met in 1976 at Devali to plan further on evangelization. In 1978, 350 leaders from Asian countries met in Singapore* for a Lausanne leadership conference on evangelism.

The first major conference held under the auspices of the LCWE committee took place in Pattaya, Thailand*, in 1980. It was designed to be a working conference that produced strategies to reach unreached people groups. The findings were then published as Lausanne Occasional Papers. Later, under the auspices of the intercessory working group, a prayer assembly was held in Seoul, Korea*, where Christians from all around the world gathered to pray for world evangelization.

The 1974 congress was followed by a second major congress in Manila in 1989. The congress was planned under the leadership of Thomas Wang of Hong Kong* and the United States. Evangelicals from what had been the Union of Soviet Socialist Republics attended, symbolizing the dramatic political changes which were taking place. The congress's theme was "Proclaim Christ Until He Comes." It gave encouragement to evangelization, pinpointed the uniqueness of Christ as the most contentious issue in contemporary evangelism, and highlighted modernity as the prevailing cultural environment which made evangelism difficult. At the conclusion of the congress, the Manila Manifesto was issued as a concise statement of the deliberations, but it did not replace the 1974 covenant.

Overall, 173 countries were represented at the Manila Congress; 50% of the delegates were under the age of 45. Networks of Christians became responsible for particular subjects; resulted in 45 "tracks" and 425 different workshops. Some of the tracks continued to interact after the congress had ended, the most notable being A.D. 2000, which developed a life of its own. No longer responsible to the LCWE, it began to coordinate Christians throughout the world to engage in fresh evangelistic planning. Bible studies were led by John Stott of the United Kingdom, Ajith Fernando of Sri Lanka, and David Penman of Australia. The major addresses took up the theme of the whole church, the whole Gospel, and the whole world.

In Stuttgart, Germany, in Feb 1994, the LCWE radically changed its structure. The determinant for representation moved from geography to a commitment to cooperate in world evangelization. The committee was made smaller, and its office was moved from Charlotte, North Carolina, United States, to Oslo, Norway. In 1974 there were no other evangelical organizations committed to world evangelization. This had changed over 20 years, the LCWE having played a significant role in influencing other bodies that now had a commitment to world evangelization. Financial support ceased to come mostly from North America, and the various national groups committed to the movement met its financial needs. At a time when sections of the church were faltering in the evangelistic task, the LCWE committee provided an entity which underlined that, without evangelism, the church perishes.

Bibliography

The Lausanne Covenant. • *Let the Earth Hear His Voice,* ed. J. D. Douglas (1975). • *Proclaim Christ Until He Comes,* ed. J. D. Douglas (1990). • *World Evangelization Magazine* (Akersgate 68, 0180, Oslo, Norway). • Lausanne Occasional Papers. • *The Future of World Evangelization — The Lausanne Movement,* ed. E. Dayton and S. Wilson (1984). • Wells, David F., *Turning to God* (1989); *God the Evangelist* (1987).

JOHN R. REID

Lawa

(Lava; Lua). Indigenous tribe in Thailand numbering approximately 20,000 and speaking a Mon-Khmer-related language.

Many Lawa have become assimilated into the northern Thai culture and no longer consider themselves Lawa. There are various dialects among those still speaking Lawa. The eastern part of the tribe had Buddhist temples and was deeply involved in Buddhist practices for many years. The western part was strongly animistic until the last ten to fifteen years, during which time the Buddhist clergy and laity have made a major effort to build temples and introduce Buddhist practices into the villages. The elaborate system of spirit ceremonies and appeasement by animal sacrifice has lessened, but in both parts of the tribe animistic beliefs still persist. No doubt, the oppressive system of spirit sacrifices caused the western Lawa to be more open to Christianity, and it is in the West that the church has developed.

The Lawa are loyal and helpful in their family* relationships. Polygamy is not usually practiced, and divorce is rare. Though the culture is based on individual ownership, and there are extremes of wealth and poverty, all work to help others, creating a sense of community responsibility. These qualities have been a help in building a stable church. The Lawa have a deep sense of the need for "home," though increasing numbers of young people are going to the cities for employment. Recent economic developments include the planting of passion fruit, cabbages, and other vegetables for cash crops. The resulting increase in wealth has changed the outward form of life of the Lawa (roads, electricity, motorized vehicles, etc.). Villages tend to be large, a fact which has helped support growing churches.

The Lawa's first contact with Christianity was through Sgaw Karen* Christians living near them. The first convert was a woman who in the 1930s went to a hospital in Chiang Mai to seek help for her leprosy*. Later, her brother and a few others believed when Presbyterian* missionaries made a few trips into the area. However, during the war years, contact was broken off, and the believers returned to animism.

In 1954, New Tribes Mission (NTM) sent Eugene Nelson and Charles Week into the Lawa area. No other mission was working there at the time. After learning the basics of the language, Nelson and Week itinerated in the villages, and in 1956 the first believers were baptized. The first church was established in the village of La-up in Maesarieng district of Maehongson Province.

In 1957, Don and Janet Schlatter began literacy work, which was a fruitful ministry as the Lawa were open to learning to read in their own language. Songbooks, health tracts, and other literature were produced for the growing church in La-up and neighboring villages. The first edition of the Lawa New Testament was published by the United Bible Society (UBS) in 1971.

By 1981, there were believers in seven villages. This number increased to 15 by 1994. In seven of these, local elders managed the local churches and carried out regular teaching, communion services, weddings, funerals, etc. The Lawa churches organized themselves into a group of associated churches with a body of men to oversee the appointment of new elders and care for workers, both full- and part-time, and arrange for the twice yearly conferences. Some of the younger people received more formal training at the Bible training center at Phayao or Bangkok Bible College, but most of the training was carried out on a local level.

Roman Catholic missionaries came into some of the villages in the 1970s but had not learned the Lawa language. Approximately 200-300 Lawa have become Catholics. Fewer than 20 joined a charismatic group in Maesarieng, where they worship in Thai. Most of the Christian Lawa belong to the group started by NTM. In 1990, they voted to join the Associated Churches of

Thailand, which is made up of Overseas Missionary Fellowship–related churches. The Lawa group has, however, kept its original emphasis of being self-supporting, self-governing, and self-propagating. They have built their own churches, paid their own evangelists, and made their own decisions. They wrote a constitution in 1990. The number of baptized believers is over 1,000.

Though NTM missionaries lived in the eastern part of the tribe for over 10 years and learned that dialect well, no one believed, and there are no longer any missionaries living there.

In 1986, parts of the Old Testament were published, and work is in progress on the translation of the complete Old Testament. A revised edition of the New Testament was published by the Thai Bible Society.

Don Schlatter

Lazarists (Vincentians)

Philippines. Known in the Philippines* as *Padres Paúles* or Vincentians, the Lazarists (Congregation of the Mission) were founded by Vincent de Paul in France in 1625 primarily for the evangelization of small towns and villages and for the training of the clergy, especially in seminaries. From Paris, they spread to different parts of Europe, the Americas, and even Africa.

The *Paúles* came to the Philippines by way of Spain. After years of delay, on 22 Jul 1862, Gregorio Velasco and Ildefonso Moral, together with lay brothers Romualdo Lopez and Gregorio Perez, all from the Spanish province of the order, finally arrived in Manila. Through the Spanish provincial superior, Ramon Sanz, this first mission was established during the term of Jean Baptiste Etienne, the order's fourteenth superior general (1843-74), who also approved the opening of the Philippine mission of 15 Daughters of Charity* (DC), a congregation founded likewise by Vincent de Paul.

From the start, the *Paúles* undertook the direction of diocesan seminaries. The first, Manila's San Carlos Seminary (1862), was soon followed by those of Nueva Caceres-Naga (1865), Cebu (1867), Jaro (1869), and Nueva Segovia-Vigan (1870). After the Philippine revolution for independence (1898-1902), the *Paúles* established other seminaries in Calbayog (1905), San Pablo (1914), Lipa (1931), Bacolod (1946), and Sorsogon (1956). For over 100 years, this has been the principal ministry of the *Paúles,* resulting in a large majority (more than 75% at one point) of Vincentian alumni among the diocesan clergy in the Philippines. Moreover, since the seminaries of Cebu, Naga, and Jaro became in the 1880s also centers of learning *(seminario-colegios)* for both aspirants to the priesthood and extern students, Vincentian influence was also felt among civic leaders, the most notable of whom was Sergio Osmena, former president of the Philippines.

Through these years, the *Paúles* were also involved in the direction of the DCs and other Vincentian-related organizations, such as the Ladies of Charity, the Society of St. Vincent de Paul, the Legion of Mary, and the Children of Mary.

Establishment of the Philippine province. In Dec 1871, 10 years after the arrival of the first Vincentians, the Philippine mission was canonically made a distinct province of the congregation. First called the the Province of Manila, from 1894 it took the name of the Province of the Philippines. The number of missionaries grew steadily; from the four pioneers of 1862 it increased to 46 in 1871 and then averaged in the fifties. Although considered autonomous from Spain, the Philippine province depended largely on personnel from the mother province. Recruitment of native candidates for the order did not materialize until 1935, when two aspirants entered the novitiate, one of whom became the first Filipino Vincentian bishop, Teotimo Pacis. In 1950, a seminary on the secondary level was established in Polo (Bulacan) for the training of the order's own candidates, and in 1963, the cornerstone was laid for the new novitiate in Angono (Rizal). Two other houses of formation were subsequently established (1979, 1985) in Tandang Sora (Quezon City) for college and theology students.

Present situation. Like most congregations throughout the Catholic world, the Vincentians of the Philippine province felt and experienced the winds of change in the 1960s and 1970s. It was during these decades that they gradually turned over to the diocesan clergy the direction of seminaries, particularly the theological seminaries in Naga and Jaro. As of 1995, only the Cebu theology seminary remained under the administration of the Vincentians.

The Vincentians are also engaged in seven parishes, two educational institutions including a university, and two mission posts in Thailand* and Japan*. Evangelistic work is conducted through popular village missions and the formation of basic ecclesiastical communities.

China. After the suppression of the Jesuits*, Louis XVI gave their China* mission to the Lazarists in 1783. The Lazarists (two Chinese and three Europeans) had worked in Sichuan and Beijing from the late 17th c. Portuguese Lazarists went to Macau in 1785. The new mission territory was vast, comprising the provinces of Mongolia, Hebei, Sichuan, and Jiangxi. The mission also included the work of the Jesuits at the imperial court. The French Revolution (1789) and the reign of Napoleon (1799-1815) prevented the Lazarists from sending significant manpower until after 1830, by which time the link with the court had been broken and there were no further requests from the emperor. The last European missionary to work at the imperial court was a Portuguese Lazarist, Gaetano Pires Pereira (1763-1838). In 1840, Jean Gabriel Perboyre*, who worked in Hubei Province, was executed in Wuchang (Sichuan). He was the first foreign missionary in China to be canonized.

The Opium* War treaties and particularly the French treaties of 1858 and 1860 were of immense importance to the mission. As a consequence of these treaties, the

French government undertook the protection of Catholic missionaries and their converts. The Lazarists took full advantage of their government's support to further their aims, building churches, seminaries, and orphanages. The Daughters of Charity, a sister community of the congregation, came to China in 1850. During this period, the ecclesiastical divisions were reorganized with much of the territory given to other orders. The Lazarists retained sections of Hebei in the north, including Beijing and Tianjin, as well as Jiangxi and Zhejiang in the south.

The Boxer Uprising (1900) destroyed much of the work of the previous 50 years, making it difficult for the Lazarist authorities to accept the radical opinions of their recently arrived Belgian confrere Vincent Lebbe*, who, sensing the new mood of patriotism in China, advocated both the sinification of the church and renunciation of the French protectorate. After World War I, Irish, Italian, Dutch, Polish, Spanish, and American Lazarists began arriving in China, further weakening allegiance to the protectorate. In time, Lebbe's ideas became widely accepted, and in 1926 the first six Chinese bishops were ordained. Three were educated in Lazarist seminaries. Two of them were Lazarists, Soun Melchior and Hou Joseph.

Despite the Civil and Sino-Japanese Wars, the community continued to expand until the expulsion of foreign missionaries and the suppression of religious communities in the early 1950s. In 1951, small groups of Chinese, Dutch, and American Lazarists began working in Taiwan*. In 1987, the Lazarists' province of China was created from these missions.

Bibliography

Coste, P., *The Life and Work of St. Vincent de Paul* (1952). • Dela Goza, R., and J. M. Cavanna, *Vincentians in the Philippines, 1862-1982* (1985). • Ferreux, Octave, "Histoire de la Congrégation de la Mission en Chine (1699-1950)," *Annales de la Mission* (1963). • Poole, Stafford, *A History of the Congregation of the Mission (1645-1843)* (1973). • Van den Brandt, J., *Les Lazaristes en Chine, 1697-1935* (1936). • Baptizer, J., *A History of the Christian Missions in China* (1929).

Manuel Ginete and Joseph Loftus

Le Huu Tu

(b. Di Loan, Quang Tri, 20 Oct 1896; d. Saigon, 24 Apr 1967). Second Vietnamese bishop of Phat Diem and nationalist political leader.

Tu was a prominent religious and political figure who played a key role between the French colonialists and the Communist regime during the years of conflict (1945-54). He created an independent administration popularly known as "The Republic of Mgr. Tu," and under his guidance Phat Diem flourished. After the Geneva agreements (May-July 1954), he led an exodus of Catholics to South Vietnam and thus helped establish the non-Communist regime of Ngo Dinh Diem in the South.

An abbot from the contemplative order Citeaux in Chau Son, Tu was elected as successor to the first Vietnamese bishop, Nguyen ba Tong. Because he was respected by both French and Vietnamese politicians, his consecration in 1945 was attended by important people like Pham van Dong, Vo Ngyen Giap, and Vinh Thuy (ex-emperor Bao Dai*). Relations between Bishop Tu and Ho Chi Minh were initially based on a common enthusiasm for nationalism*. When President Ho invited Tu to be his "supreme counselor," the latter apprised the president, "As long as you fight for the independence of Vietnam, I shall always be at your side; but if you wish our country to become Communist, I shall always fight against you."

In the autumn of 1946, after Ho Chi Minh eliminated many nationalist opponents, Tu used local troops to organize a nationalist, non-Communist regime, the *Cong-giao Cuu-quoc* (Catholic Association for National Salvation). When freedom of the press was suppressed, the only non-Communist nationalist newspapers were the *Nhiem Vu* and *Tieng Keu*, both published in Phat Diem. After the Communists attacked the episcopal see of Phat Diem on 15 Oct 1949, Tu and another nationalist, Bishop Pham Ngoc Chi, openly supported the Bao Dai government and fought against the Communists after five years of ambiguous relations. A further decisive consideration was the Vietminh's close association with Communist China* and Russia.

In the midst of political tumult, Tu was nevertheless able to build up his diocese. He was the first bishop to elect a Vietnamese priest, Luca Ly, to be the general vicar. He also sent young seminarians and sisters abroad to study, and many among them eventually became important pillars (bishops and professors) of the Vietnamese church. He opened primary and secondary schools in Phat Diem for 3,000 students and initiated two organizations, *Hung Tam* (Heroic Heart) and *Dung Chi* (Strong Will). An outstanding leader during a critical period in the history of Vietnam, Tu provided an alternative for non-Communist nationalists during the French-Vietminh War.

Bibliography

Gheddo, Piero, *The Cross and the Bo-Tree* (1970). • Doan doc Thu and Xuan Huy, *Giam Muc Le Huu Tu va Phat Diem* (1973).

Vu kim Chinh

Lebbe, Frederic Vincent

(Lei Ming Yuan) (b. Gent, Belgium, 19 Aug 1877; d. Chongqing, China, 24 Jun 1940). Vincentian missionary priest to China and promoter of local Catholic bishops and local churches.

On 6 Nov 1895, Lebbe joined the Congregation of the Mission (Vincentians) in Paris. In Mar 1901, he arrived in Beijing, where he was ordained a priest on 28 Oct of the same year. In 1920, he was sent to Europe to care for Chinese students. On 28 Oct 1926, he witnessed the first

Chinese bishops being ordained in Rome. In 1927, Lebbe returned to China to continue his work under Bishop Sun of Anguo.

Baptized Frederic, Lebbe chose to be confirmed Vincent out of admiration for St. Vincent de Paul. His father was Belgian, but his family had deep roots in France and England. During his youth, he lived and was educated both in France and in Belgium.

From his formative years on, Lebbe looked at the world through his deep faith and had a keen interest in the modern trends of his time. He saw the need for and possibility of reconciliation between the church and modern society. At the time, he was an enthusiastic champion of French culture.

When he first arrived in China, Lebbe discovered another cultural world as refined as the one he had left behind in Europe. He saw the need for the church and the Gospel* to enter deeply into the local culture. Being always the first to practice what he preached, he tried to live up to this vision and to become as Chinese as possible. He took the Chinese name of Lei Ming Yuan (thunder singing in the distance), by which he later became widely known in China.

At first, Lebbe was sent by his bishop to preach the Gospel in the villages of Hobei Province, then in the city of Tianjin, which he did with considerable success. He adopted a Chinese style of living and, whenever the cause was just, sided with the Chinese. He had a deep knowledge of the Chinese language and customs and established good relations with the local authorities. He started a daily newspaper that gave Christian views on national events. It soon became the most widely read newspaper in northern China.

During these years, Lebbe understood that the church in China could not become Chinese unless it was under the direction of the Chinese. As this was very much against the accepted ideas of the time, he met with strong and painful opposition.

In 1920, Lebbe was sent to Europe to evangelize the flow of Chinese students in search of modern knowledge, a work to which he dedicated himself entirely. Being in Europe gave him a chance to meet higher church authorities, including the pope, and to promote his vision of the church in China, a vision which was very much in line with Rome's thinking.

On 28 Oct 1926, the first six Chinese bishops were consecrated in Rome by the pope himself. Lebbe returned to China to work under Bishop Sun in a countryside diocese. Before leaving Europe, he established a seminary that would train European priests for the service of the Chinese bishops: the Society of the Auxiliaries of the Missions. Later he also encouraged the foundation of a group of European women missionaries: *Auxiliaires Féminines Internationales Catholiques.*

Under the Chinese bishop, Lebbe continued to follow the vision of bringing the Gospel into the life of the local people. He founded two Chinese congregations, the Little Brothers of St. John the Baptist and the Little Sisters of St. Theresa of the Child Jesus, in order to have dedicated men and women sharing the life of the people and working side by side with them in the fields and in their homes. With regret, he left the Vincentians to become the superior of the Little Brothers. He also became a Chinese citizen.

When the Sino-Japanese War started, Lebbe raised volunteers around a core group of Little Brothers and Sisters and established the first ambulance corps for the Chinese armies. They took care of wounded soldiers on the battlefield.

On being imprisoned by the Communist armies, Lebbe's health deteriorated. After his liberation, he was brought to Chongqing, where he died. The government of the Republic of China published a decree in his honor. According to Cardinal Leo Suénens, Lebbe's vision and life together constituted one of the roots of the Second Vatican Council.

Bibliography

Lebbe, Vincent, *En Chine, il y a du nouveau* (1930). • De Jaegher, Raymond, *Father Lebbe: A Modern Apostle* (1950). • Leclerc, Jacques, *Thunder in the Distance: The Life of Père Lebbe,* trans. George Lamb (1958). • Levaux, Léopold, *Le Père Lebbe: Apôtre de la chine moderne* (1948). • Soetens, Claude, *Inventaire des Archives Vincent Lebbe* (1982); *Recueil des Archives Vincent Lebbe,* 4 vols. (1982-84). • Thoreau, Vincent, *Le tonnerre qui chante au loin* (1990). PETER MERTEN and HUGH O'DONNEL

Lechler, Rudolf

(Li Li-ji) (b. Württemberg, Germany, 1824; d. 1908). Missionary to China* sent by the Basel Mission.

Born into a pastor's family, Lechler was confirmed at age 18 and intended to go into business. He became an apprentice in a company, where he served for four years. Because of a serious illness, he felt he had to heed God's call and entered the Basel Missionary Training School in Switzerland in 1844. Two years later, he felt called to China and was commissioned to preach around the Swatow area of Guangdong, becoming the first resident Basel missionary to China.

Soon Lechler found that China was not open enough, and his team, including Swedish-born colleague T. Hamberg, was often harassed by government officials and civilians alike. In 1852, they were obliged to leave the area, but by then he had mastered the Hakka dialect, so he insisted on remaining to work in the Hakka region. This brought him into contact with the Hakka-initiated Taiping Rebellion*. In 1856, the Second Opium* War broke out, and Lechler retreated to Hong Kong*, where he worked at St. Paul's College. He was home on furlough from 1858 to 1861.

When Lechler returned to China, he became general secretary of the Basel Mission in China, a position he held for some 40 years. He was especially friendly toward China and its people, and on several occasions he refuted spiteful remarks about China. He was a solid and conscientious worker, frequently penetrating into the small islands along the coast with his preaching and healing. After returning to Germany in 1889, he cared for the sick, lonely, and elderly in his native land and was awarded the Württemberg government medal. In addition to editing *Collected Works on China,* he compiled a Hakka-Chinese dictionary (with Hamberg) and a Chinese hymnal.

CHINA GROUP, translated by LENA LAU

Lee Kuan Yew

(b. Singapore, 16 Sep 1923). Builder and first prime minister of modern Singapore*.

Lee's political career is almost coterminous with modern Singapore and his name synonymous with the city-state. A third-generation Chinese born in British Singapore, Lee always thought in terms of Singapore and Singapore's interest. From his early days at Raffles Institution until his time at Cambridge, where he topped the law examinations with double first honors in 1949, Lee had been a brilliant scholar. After qualifying as a barrister-at-law in London in 1950, he returned to Singapore to begin his legal practice and political career as adviser to several government employees' unions. Having succeeded in building a broad support base which included the educated Chinese and the Communists, Lee formally inaugurated the People's Action Party in 1954, which marked the beginning of his eventful struggle for Singapore's independence from British rule.

After winning a decisive election in 1959, Lee formed the first government of self-rule and became its prime minister at the age of 35. A vital referendum in 1962 led to the merger of Singapore with Malaya in the following year. But Singapore was painfully forced out of the federation on 9 Aug 1965 to become an independent nation. This was largely due to the political conflict between Lee's island-state (Chinese majority) and the Muslim-dominated central Malay government led by Tunku Abdul Rahman.

After the separation, Lee's leadership was seriously challenged. Yet he managed to transform a former British colony of migrants of very diverse ethnico-religio-cultural backgrounds into one of Asia's most formidable economic powerhouses in the course of some 20 years, a most remarkable achievement that even his fiercest critics have to admit. On 28 Nov 1990, Lee voluntarily handed over the premiership to Goh Chok Tong, having served in that capacity for 31 years. He remained in the cabinet as senior minister.

Lee's style of governance is often characterized as authoritarian and paternalistic, favoring consultation rather than confrontation, discouraging organized dissent, and valuing closely monitored feedback. But what ultimately mattered to Lee and his supporters was that the system be efficient, clean, and pragmatic.

In a multi-religious nation where religion is a most sensitive issue, Lee's government was firmly committed to the maintenance of religious harmony; it would not allow the mixing of religion with politics. Groups that seemed to threaten that harmony were outlawed (Jehovah's Witnesses, Children of God). Although never a very religious person himself, the aging Lee seemed to be quite well disposed toward religions of the Confucian-Taoist-Buddhist tradition. At the same time he appeared to be increasingly critical of some of the most cherished ideals and established socio-political institutions of the Christian West, such as freedom, democracy, human rights, welfare, and the media. He is gradually being recognized as an ardent apologist for Asian, especially Confucian, values and a firm believer in the ultimate triumph of the East over the West economically, politically, and culturally.

Bibliography

Chew, Ernest C. T., and Edwin Lee, eds., *A History of Singapore* (1991). • Lianhe Zaobao, *Lee Kuan Yew: A Pictorial Biography* (1994). • Josey, Alex, *Lee Kuan Yew* (1968); *Lee Kuan Yew,* Vol. II (1980). • Sng, Bobby E. K., *In His Good Time,* 2nd ed. (1993).

CHOONG CHEE PANG

Lee Myung Jik

(b. Seoul, Korea, 2 Dec 1890; d. Seoul, 30 Mar 1973). Representative leader of the Korea Evangelical Holiness Church* (KEHC).

Lee contributed much to the development of the KEHC through a lifelong service of teaching, writing, preaching, and church administration. After completing his studies at the Tokyo Bible Institute of the Oriental Missionary Society (OMS), he returned to Korea to work as an evangelist in 1911 and was ordained in 1914 as one of the first four ministers of the KEHC. He taught at Seoul Bible Institute (later, Seoul Theological University) from 1917 until his retirement, when he was made its president emeritus.

Lee was the first and long-serving editor of *Whal Chun* (Living Water), the official magazine of the OMS Holiness Church, which was first published in 1922. He contributed many articles himself. In 1935, he became the first Korean principal of Seoul Bible Institute. He was imprisoned by the Japanese government during World War II* for advocating the doctrine of the second coming of Jesus Christ. In 1951, he again assumed leadership of Seoul Theological Seminary after the principal, Lee Kun, was captured and taken to North Korea by the Communists during the Korean War*. He received a doctor of divinity degree from Azusa College (Azusa University), Los Angeles, California, United States, in 1958 for his services to the KEHC. He remained as principal when the government upgraded the seminary to a university in 1959. He wrote many books, including *The History of Four Thousand Years in the Old Testament.*

Bibliography

Lee Chung Young, *A History of Korea Evangelical Holiness Church* (1970).

KANG KEUN WHAN

Lee Soo Jung

(b. South Chulla Province, 1842; d. 28 May 1886). One of the pioneer translators of the Bible* into Korean script.

Accompanying an observation team of envoys to Japan in 1882, Lee studied Western knowledge and taught the Korean language at Tokyo Foreign Language School. He studied agricultural science with Tsuda Sen, a Japanese agriculturalist who introduced Lee to Christianity. On 29 Apr 1883, he was baptized by a Japanese pastor in the presence of an American Presbyterian* missionary, G. W. Knox. A representative of the American Bible Society, H. Loomis, persuaded Lee to translate the Bible into Korean. First he transliterated the Chinese characters into Korean script so that the Koreans could read the Chinese Bible. Later in 1885, he translated the Gospel of Mark into the Korean script for use by the general public. The first American missionaries to Korea, the Underwoods* and the Appenzellers*, learned the Korean language from Lee, and carried his Korean translation to Korea. Back in Korea in 1886, he was executed for unknown political reasons.

David Suh, with contributions from Seo Jeong Min, translated by Kim In Soo

Lee Sung Bong

(b. Kangdong, Pyungnam, Korea, 4 Jul 1909; d. 2 Aug 1965). Revivalist of the Korea Evangelical Holiness Church* (KEHC).

Lee started a church of the KEHC in Suwon in 1928 after his graduation from the Seoul Bible Institute. A handsome, healthy man blessed with a clear voice and spiritual passion, he traveled even to Manchuria and Japan* to preach at many revival meetings. His message was focused on the fourfold gospel of regeneration, holiness, divine healing, and the second coming of Christ. He proclaimed, "The second coming of our Lord is near; if you do not repent, you, your family, and your nation shall perish."

Lee was imprisoned by the Japanese during World War II* but resumed his revival movement after the war ended in 1945. In 1954, he organized the Immanuel Special Unit as a jubilee evangelistic band of the KEHC and took it with him for a year to 70 areas around the country for revival meetings. In 1958, he started a campaign to expand the church and held 408 revival meetings with the Immanuel Special Unit.

Lee's preaching challenged, comforted, and encouraged Korean Christians and others, especially when they were suffering during the Japanese domination and the Korean War*.

Bibliography

Lee Chung Young, *A History of Korea Evangelical Holiness Church* (1970).

Kang Keun Whan

Lee Yong Do

(b. Keum-Chun, Whang-Hae-Do, Korea, 6 Apr 1901; d. Won-San, 2 Oct 1933). Methodist* pastor and a leading revivalist of Korea* in the early 1930s.

Lee's Christian pilgrimage began early under the influence of his mother, who was known as a pious woman of prayer. Deeply concerned about the national crisis and loss of political freedom during his teenage years, Lee became actively involved in the nationalist movement, participating in the March 1st Independence Movement* (1919). Because of his political activity, Lee was imprisoned four times for over three years; therefore it took nine years (1915-24) for him to finish high school (Han-Young Suhwon-Korean-Anglo School). Persuaded by Wasson, principal of Song-Do High School, Lee enrolled in Hyup-Sung Theological School (Union Methodist Theological Seminary) in 1924. It was at Hyup-Sung that his lifetime friendship with Lee Ho Bin and Lee Whan Shin first developed.

Wrestling with the tension between his nationalistic zeal and the demand of Christian faith by the school, Lee developed a new passion for Sunday school education, an area in which he manifested great giftedness in poetry writing, drama, storytelling, and music. In the winter of 1925, Lee took a leave of absence from school in order to recuperate from tuberculosis in Kang Dong. Here Lee had his first decisive "Aldersgate" experience while he was leading a revival meeting at a local church after an all-night prayer. Lee burst into weeping as he read Scripture, and with him the whole congregation wept. This was a decisive experience for Lee; his health was restored as he went about preaching with new zeal.

At his graduation in Jan 1928, Lee was installed as a pastor at Tong-Chun Methodist Church. Here Lee met prayer partner Park Jae Bong and became increasingly converted to the life of deepening piety, fasting, and praying at the mountain. Lee was also shaped as a political and religious reformer through his mystical experiences in the Holy Spirit and of expelling demons. Soon after his ordination in the Methodist Conference on 28 Sep 1930, Lee devoted himself to the nationwide revival movement.

As a voice crying out in the wilderness for repentance, prayer, and love, Lee called for a reform of the church through spiritual renewal. He anxiously hoped the Holy Spirit would breathe pentecostal* vitality and passion into the Korean church. Lee was keenly conscious of the struggles of the Korean church in the 1930s, a church which had been depressed by political, social, and ecclesiastical hardships and frustrations. Lee lamented the lack of prayer, repentance, praise, thanksgiving, passion, joy, love, and responsibility. He remarked that the failure lay in the church's "not receiving the Holy Spirit." Lee felt that the missionaries' fundamentalistic, Western, Protestant orthodoxy was powerless or indifferent to the ultimate questions asked by Korean people in their own existential context. The missionaries' one-sided emphasis on biblicism and creedal dogmatism was a form of institutional captivity which turned the church away from the urgency of the present realities. The facts that great crowds were gathered and the fire of revival spread imply that Lee's message provided what the historical time required and what people yearned for. His sermons that challenged mere religious rituals offered without spirit and truth aroused strong suspicion among Presbyterians* that Lee was advocating a non-church movement (see Non-Church Principle). Lee's prophetic voice for church reform was a challenge to most established orders and principles, and consequently caused uneasy feelings.

Voluntary prayer circles gathered after Lee's revivals. His charismatic stress on the fullness of the Spirit and mystical union with Christ, his free-style revivalism (i.e., weeping, emotionalism, various manifestations of gifts, ecstasies), the subjectivity of experience, and his criticism directed toward ecclesial corruption resulted in restrictions and opposition from many Protestant evangelicals. Presbyterian churches passed resolutions in 1931 and 1932 to forbid Lee's revivals at their churches and finally branded Lee a heretic in 1933. The Methodist Conference also suspended Lee (he was posthumously reinstated to the Methodist Conference in 1997).

At the same time that Lee's ecclesial conflicts from misunderstandings deepened, so did his personal suffering from illness. His struggle with tuberculosis worsened to the extent that he had to withdraw from all activities to recuperate in Won-San (1933). Although Lee himself made it clear that he did not want to see a new church arise because of a church split, he painfully permitted his name to be used as the first president of the Cho-Sun Jesus Church (Jun 1933), a new assembly that had been gathered by Lee Ho Bin, Paik Nam Joo, Han Joon Myung, and others who had been expelled from the mainline churches. Just four months later, Lee died of tuberculosis. Jesus Church had over 20 assemblies after Lee's death, forming an indigenous charismatic* community.

Lee's emphasis on prayer, experiential faith, and the fullness of the Holy Spirit was a shift from the Protestant missionaries' emphasis on correct doctrine. Lee favored reading Saint Francis, Thomas à Kempis, Tolstoy, and Sunder Singh*, an indication of his concern with perfection as perfect love. Lee is often referred to as the Meister Eckhart of Korea because of his primary concern with the mystical piety of self-denial and yieldedness, mystical union with Christ, self-giving love, imitation of Christ.

Lee's *theologia experimentalis* sought to bring together the union with God through prayer and the self-giving love and humility of Christ. Lee's thoughts had a more dynamic and less speculative understanding of the mystical union than did German mysticism, as he integrated mystical faith with the imperative of love. Thus he rejected the separation of contemplative piety from the life of love: faith, prayer, and love were inseparable. The highest stage of faith is loving God and neighbors, and in this loving is the mystery of being one with God. The core of Christian faith is in a concrete living in imitation of Christ. Christ is incarnated where his life is lived out. God is not to be sought somewhere outside of us but within us.

Lee's mystical union occurs in our imitation of Christ through actual suffering with Christ. Lee's *Passion Mysticism* adopted the nuptial metaphors used by the Christian mystics and the language of the Song of Songs and John to describe the mystical union with the suffering Christ. In his preaching, Lee was more concerned with the suffering Christ than with the exalted Lord. Lee's call was to suffer with the suffering *han*-ridden Korean people. Lee's undifferentiated love was present when he extended his hand, beyond theological differences, to embrace those denounced by the church even though this resulted in his own rejection by the orthodox.

Lee's legacy is *Semeon*, meaning "it is meet and right to be silent." Lee lived a short life of crisis moments, being loved as well as rejected by many. Like "a lonely wild flower," Lee silently wanted to "take up the cross, following the pattern of Christ." Lee's mystical piety can be understood as an expression of the struggles of the Korean people in their historical context to find new meaning and freedom and to form a shared community through prayer and mystical experience.

SUNJA KWOCK, with contributions from LEE DUK JOO

Legge, James

(b. Huntly, Scotland, 1814; d. 1897). Scottish Congregational missionary of the London Missionary Society (LMS) and sinologist.

The son of a prosperous businessman who belonged to an independent, mission-minded chapel, Legge was educated at Aberdeen University and Highbury Congregational College. He was sent by the LMS to Malacca* in 1839 to head the Anglo-Chinese College; this was part of the LMS strategy to reach China by reaching the Chinese diaspora. In 1843, the college, renamed the Anglo-Chinese Theological Seminary, was moved to Hong Kong*, where Legge was principal until 1856. Legge also served as pastor of Union Church in Hong Kong for several years. From 1860, Legge translated Chinese classics with the help of scholars such as Wang Tao and wrote tracts and articles on Christianity. While in Hong Kong, Legge became a central figure in the debate over the proper term for God in Chinese. Legge defended the term *Shong Di.* In matters of Chinese philosophy and thought, Legge was second to none in the 19th c. His appreciation of Confucian thought and appropriation of natural theology to explain the truths found in the Chinese classics often brought Legge into conflict with the Protestant community in China*.

After his return to England in 1873, Legge was appointed to the chair of Chinese studies by Oxford University in 1876, where he served until his death in 1897. He received a D.D. diploma from the University of New

York in 1843 and an honorary doctorate from Aberdeen University in 1870. His publictions include his major work, *The Chinese Classics* (7 vols.), as well as *The Life and Teaching of Confucius, The Life and Teaching of Mencius, The Religions of China: Confucianism and Taoism Described and Compared with Christianity,* and *Travel of Fah-hien.*

Bibliography

Neill, Stephen, Gerald Anderson, and John Goodwin, eds., *The Concise Dictionary of World Mission* (1971). • Legge, Helen Edith, *James Legge: Missionary and Scholar* (1905). • Pfister, Lauren, and Norman Girardot, *The Whole Duty of Man: James Legge and the Victorian Translation of China.* • Wylie, Alexander, *Memorials of Protestant Missionaries to the Chinese* (1867). • Wong Man-kong, *James Legge: A Pioneer at the Crossroads of East and West* (1996).

CHINA GROUP

Lei Ming Yuan. *See* Lebbe, Frederic Vincent

Leimena, Johannes

(b. Ambon, 6 Mar 1905; d. Jakarta, 6 Mar 1977). Indonesian Christian statesman and ecumenical leader.

Johannes Leimena was a leader of nationalistic Indonesian Christian students before World War II*, chairman of the Indonesian Christian Party, a leader in the Council of Churches of Indonesia*, and a cabinet minister.

As young orphan, Leimena went with his uncle, a teacher, to Java. He finished senior high school in Batavia (Jakarta), entered the indigenous medical college, and graduated in 1930. In 1939, he obtained his doctorate in medicine with a dissertation on liver function. From his student years, Leimena took an active part in the *Jong Ambon,* a nationalistic Moluccan youth organization, became leader of the Christian student organization *CSV op Java,* and developed a thorough understanding of the realities of colonialism*, Indonesian nationalism*, and the ecumenical movement*. Leimena was one of the Indonesian youth leaders at the time who made an important breakthrough in the history of Christianity in Indonesia: he reconciled the Christian faith with a nationalistic attitude when many of the Christian intellectuals had lost their faith in the church and left it to take part in the national struggle. Under his leadership, *CSV op Java* hosted the Australasian Conference of the World Student Christian Fellowship in Citeureup, Bogor, in Sep 1933.

Leimena worked as a physician in a mission hospital in Bandung. He married R. Tjitjih Prawiradilaga in 1933, and they were blessed with four daughters and four sons. In the early months of the Japanese occupation, Leimena was imprisoned by the Japanese military commander because of his connection to mission personnel, but he was released six months later after he successfully cured the Kempetai commandant of malaria. Then he was appointed to run a small hospital in Tangerang, near Jakarta.

Leimena cultivated good relationships with the nationalist youth in Jakarta and the officers of *Pembela Tanah Air* (Fatherland Protectors, PETA, an Indonesian military corps organized by the Japanese) in Tangerang. In Sep 1945, some weeks after Indonesian independence was proclaimed, Leimena took a key role in crushing a radical leftist rebellion which tried to proclaim the Soviet Republic in Indonesia.

Leimena was one of the leaders of the Indonesian Christian Political Party (PARKINDO) when it was established in 1945. He became its chairman (1950-59), then an adviser (1959-73). He became a member of the Indonesian Democratic Party's (PDI) central advisory council after PARKINDO was fused into the party. Leimena was PARKINDO's representative in various cabinets. In the first decade of Indonesian independence (1946-56), Leimena was appointed health minister. He was also a member of parliament (1956-59), the prime minister's deputy (1959-66), seven times acting president, and a member of the supreme advisory council (1968-73).

Alongside national politics, Leimena also maintained his prewar commitment to the church, serving as a leader in the National Council of Churches (vice-chairman, 1950-64; honorary chairman, 1964-77). He referred to this blend of Christian faith and nationalism as "responsible citizenship," explaining it as a citizenship with responsibility to both God and fellow citizens. The exercise of power — political, economic, cultural, social, or military — must always be done responsibly toward God and toward the neighbor whose life is affected, directly or indirectly, by its use.

Leimena was a supporter of President Sukarno's controversial ideas launched in 1964 on the parallel between the goal of Indonesia's revolution and that of the Christian religion. His support was based on his conviction that Sukarno* was the only guarantee of national unity at that time and the belief that the church, motivated by love, ought to be involved in the struggle for freedom, truth, justice, and national unity.

Bibliography

Leirissa, R. Z., "Biografi Dr. J. Leimena," in P. D. Latuihamallo et al., eds., *Kewarganegaraan yang Bertanggungjawab* (Responsible Citizenship) (1980).

ZAKARIA J. NGELOW

Lek Talyong

(b. Bangkok, Thailand, 22 Jan 1900; d. 18 Sep 1980). Important leader in the Thai Protestant church after World War II*.

Lek Talyong received his education at Bangkok Christian College (BCC), where he became a teacher in 1918. He studied in the Philippines* and, after his return to

Thailand*, was the assistant head teacher of a government school until 1935. He served as treasurer of the Church of Christ in Thailand (CCT) from its founding in 1934 until 1941 and then as moderator of the general assembly of the CCT in 1941-42. He resigned that position, however, when the government required teachers in government schools to accept Buddhism*. At that time, he was also in charge of religious activities in a government university dormitory. After World War II, he rejoined the CCT and was its general secretary from 1951 to 1958. At various times, he also served as the business manager of BCC, the business manager of Bangkok Christian Hospital, and the director of the CCT's department of education.

Lek Talyong married Karunradt Wintien in 1927. They had five children. An ordained clergyman, Lek Talyong was also active in working with the CCT's First Church, Samray, and in various service and ministry projects in the Christian community. He provided the CCT with important leadership during the period when it was taking over more responsibility from missionary organizations.

Bibliography

Pongudom, Prasit, *History of the Church of Christ in Thailand* (1984) (in Thai). • *Lek Talyong Memorial Volume* (1980). • Papers of Lek Talyong, Payap University Archives, Chiang Mai, Thailand.

PRASIT PONGUDOM, translated by HERBERT R. SWANSON

Lembaga Biblika Indonesia

(The Biblical Institute of Indonesia, LBI). Catholic Bible society in Indonesia founded in 1956 by Franciscan* friars in Jakarta.

In 1971, the LBI became an official agency of the Indonesia Bishops' Conference and a member of the World Catholic Federation for Biblical Apostolate (Stuttgart). Together with the Protestant *Lembaga Akitab Indonesia* (LAI), LBI finished an ecumenical translation of the entire Bible* (including the deuterocanonical/apocryphal books) in 1975. This edition was distributed by both agencies along with the *Good News for Modern Man*, an ecumenical translation of the New Testament in an easily understood Indonesian language (1977/1980). The ecumenical editions were published with the imprints of both Bible societies and financed by the Indonesian government. Because they use common Indonesian words such as *Allah* (God), *nabi* (prophet), and *kurban* (sacrifice), they may not be distributed in Malaysia*, which claims such words as exclusively Muslim, though some are Arab-loaned words from ancient Hebrew.

LBI plays an important role in the Catholic community by promoting Bible groups and discussions, publishing commentaries and written courses, and organizing Bible weeks and exhibitions. ADOLF HEUKEN

Leones, Juan

(b. Bauang, La Union, Philippines, 27 Dec 1885; d. Manila, 23 Apr 1935). First Filipino home missionary (1909) among the Sigay and Kalingas in the Philippines*.

Leones was converted in 1908 and suffered for his faith, losing his inheritance, his parents' affection, and his fiancée's love. He resigned from government service to become an evangelist of the United Brethren to the partly christianized Bago mountain people of Sigay, La Union, in 1909 and won 41 converts within a year. After seminary studies and ordination in 1914, Leones returned to the Bagos and played a part in the conversion of all of them within four years. In 1919 he started a new mission among the Kalingas, baptizing some 400, including one leading chieftain, within the first four years. His dedication and commitment served as a shining example for later home missionaries.

Bibliography

Laubach, F. C., *People of the Philippines* (1925). • Roberts, W. N., *The Filipino Church* (1936).

T. VALENTINO SITOY, JR.

Leong Chi Hing, Andrew

(b. Nam Hoi, 1837; d. Hong Kong, 15 May 1920). One of the first local priests of the Hong Kong* Catholic Church who, in his long life, was a visible link with the church's beginnings in the colony.

Leong's family left their village in Guangdong and emigrated to Hong Kong after the British takeover in 1841. In 1850, Leong entered the local seminary together with his uncle Mark Leong (?-1904) and, after his philosophical and theological studies, was ordained a priest on 24 Apr 1862.

Leong was soon assigned to work in the inland districts, first in Sun On (Po On), and later in Kwai Hsin (Wai Yeung) and Hoi Fung, where he spread the Gospel with great zeal and prudence, gaining the respect of everyone. His linguistic gifts helped him to master the Hakka, Hoklo, and Mandarin languages.

In 1898, Leong was recalled to Hong Kong and entrusted with the care of the Chinese Catholic community and associations of the city. In 1912, he celebrated his golden jubilee and received from the holy father the title of "apostolic missionary" as an official appreciation for his missionary commitment.

On 18 May 1920, the day of Leong's funeral, the *Hong Kong Telegraph* wrote: "Possessed of an active and cheerful disposition, and endowed with great tact and common sense, he proved to be a most valuable auxiliary and a wise counselor in the work of the propagation of faith."

Bibliography

Ryan, T., *The Story of a Hundred Years* (1959).

SERGIO TICOZZI

Leong Kung Fa

(b. 1787; d. 1855). First Protestant Chinese convert, also known as Ah Fah, Liang Fa, and Liang Ah-Fa.

Leong was born near Canton and came from a poor family. Having little education, he learned to cut wooden blocks for printing. In 1815, he accompanied William Milne* to Malacca*, where his skill as a printer was put to good use. The next year, Leong was converted and baptized by Milne on 3 Nov. Together they produced the *Monthly Chinese Magazine,* which sought to promote the cause of Christianity. This magazine was printed for seven years. In 1819, Leong returned to China* and distributed Gospel tracts. For this he was arrested and given 30 blows with a bamboo cane. He was released only after Robert Morrison* intervened. He then returned to Malacca.

After Milne's death, Leong returned to China and worked alongside Morrison. In 1823, he helped print the first complete Chinese Bible*, which had been jointly translated by Morrison and Milne. The London Missionary Society (LMS) appointed him a native evangelist, an office to which he was later ordained by Morrison in 1827. He wrote many tracts, one of which was called "Good Words to Admonish the World." It was said to have influenced Hong Xiuquan*, the leader of the Taiping Rebellion*. His other writings included various expositions of Scripture passages and Christian beliefs, one on Chinese religion, and another on his experiences. He traveled extensively in Kwangtung Province, preaching and distributing tracts by the thousands. He had a special interest in candidates who came to Canton to sit for the triennial literary examination. Through his ministry, a number of candidates were converted, some of whom became his fellow workers.

Being a Christian worker in 19th-c. China was not without costs. The imperial edict against the conversion of Chinese and the printing and distribution of Christian literature was still in force. In 1834, the authorities apprehended a number of Leong's colleagues, one of whom was severely beaten and another put to death. Careful inquiries pointed to Leong as a leader of evangelistic activities among the Chinese. The several attempts made to arrest him kept him on the run. Finally, he escaped by fleeing to Singapore*. Of his many travails, he wrote: "I call to mind that all who preach the Gospel of our Lord Jesus must suffer persecution; and though I cannot equal the patience of Paul or Job, I desire to imitate the ancient saints, and keep my heart in peace."

In 1839, after the persecution had abated, Leong returned to China. The end of the First Opium War and the signing of the Treaty of Nanking (1842) opened up a new chapter in Chinese evangelism. Despite little progress, Leong continued in steadfastly proclaiming the Gospel to his countrymen. In 1848, he assisted at the LMS hospital in Canton and pastored a small church of some 30 believers. By the time he died, Protestant Christian work among the Chinese had become firmly established.

Bibliography

Medhurst, Walter H., *China: Its State and Prospects* (1838). • Wylie, Alexander, *Memorials of Protestant Missionaries in China* (1867). • Lovett, Richard, *The History of the London Missionary Society, 1795-1895,* Vol. 2 (1899). • Harrison, Brian, *Waiting for China* (1979).

BOBBY SNG EWE KONG

Leontiev, Maxim

(b. ?; d. Beijing, 1698). First Russian Orthodox priest in China*.

Leontiev (Father Maksim Leont'ev), the parish priest of 500 Russian frontiersmen of a fortress in Albazin, was among the 69 captives of the Qing troops when they recaptured the border area of Siberia in 1683. Emperor Kangxi allowed the captives to practice their religion and gave them a Buddhist temple for their worship, which subsequently became the Nikolskii Church *(Olo-su-pei kuan).* The church was embellished in 1685 with icons, including a picture of St. Nicholas, and with church plates taken from the razed Church of the Resurrection in Albazin. It was renamed St. Sophia Church about a decade later. Peter the Great encouraged Leontiev's mission and understood it as a welcome outpost to economic and political expansion, a vision that was never realized. Emperor Kangxi also offered a seventh grade official post to Leontiev, who served in China for 27 years until his death in Beijing.

Bibliography

Stamoolis, James J., *Eastern Orthodox Mission Theology Today* (1986).

CHINA GROUP

Leprosy Work

Leprosy work in Asia represents a distinctive fusion of medical*, biblical, colonial, and missiological histories. From the late 19th c. through much of the 20th, ministries with lepers were a crucial focal point for missionary activity and Christian service.

Leprosy is a contagious, chronic disease caused by the *microbacterium leprae.* Though Armauer Hansen discovered this bacillus in the 1870s, many aspects of the disease — its transmission and its unpredictable, often lengthy incubation period — remain a mystery even today. Such uncertainties about the disease exacerbated people's fears of contagion and increased the stigma of "lepers." Although patients with this disease have fought a long battle against this term and prefer to be called Hansenites, this article retains the traditional terminology because of the biblical, historical, and social importance of the stigmatized term. While today most scholars argue that the leprosy mentioned in the Bible was not the disease produced by the *microbacterium leprae,* many leprosy workers over the last two centuries have viewed their efforts as imitations of Jesus' own healings and as fulfillments of his command to "cleanse the lepers" (Matt. 10:8).

Leprosy, once widespread in Europe, had largely disappeared from most of the continent by the Reformation. The disease remained endemic to most of Asia, however, which at the beginning of the 20th c. still had several million lepers. From the 16th c., when European Christians began to establish colonies and missions, they were appalled at what they discovered. Words such as "fetid," "squalor," and "pus" occur frequently in missionary accounts, as do the phrases "lost toes" and "deformed faces." Massacres of lepers by Indians and Chinese were commonly reported, though not as frequently as simple descriptions of begging lepers living in hovels or cemeteries. While some Asian rulers had made occasional provisions for segregating lepers, Christians came to see their work with the "unfortunates" as part of a distinctive Christian vocation, one which would demonstrate the unique transforming compassion of the religion. In general, while conversion was not required of lepers seeking treatment in leprosaria or treatment centers administered by Christians, missionaries promoted the Gospel and wrote home of the happiness Christianity had brought to lepers' lives.

From the 16th to the mid-19th c., the forms of Christian leprosy work in Asia were either ad hoc responses to the presence of lepers within colonies (e.g., San Lazaro Hospital in the Philippines*) or part of a distinctive missionary outreach (as with the Franciscans* in Japan*). While there had been many local examples of Christians responding to the needs of lepers, concerted leprosy work began in 1874 with the formation in Dublin of the Mission to Lepers in India* (later the Mission to Lepers) under the leadership of Wellesley Bailey. Its efforts benefited from the much publicized death of Father Damien in 1889 in Hawaii's Molokai leprosarium, which aroused great concern for leprosy patients and support for effective control and treatment. The mission's initial goals were to provide material support, medical treatment, and the solace of the Gospel. As hopes for an effective treatment emerged at the beginning of the 20th c., promoting efforts to cure patients also became part of the work. While the mission to lepers remained the most important institution of its kind in the United Kingdom, it helped foster the establishment of similar missions in America, China*, Japan, the Philippines, and elsewhere. By the late 1930s, for example, the American Mission to Lepers was providing support to 56 stations in Asia (105 stations worldwide). The vitality of the Asian leprosy missions indicates the extent to which Asian Christians responded to the call of Christ and to the needs of their neighbors.

Leprosy work also engaged many diverse institutions, both local and international, and many different Christian vocations. Protestant mission boards in Europe and America supported missionaries ministering to lepers, and dozens of Catholic religious orders assumed responsibilities as chaplains and nurses. (While denominational and national rivalries sometimes interfered with concerted leprosy work, ecumenism and cooperation have on the whole been characteristic of the enterprise.) In different ways, the Red Cross, the Young Men's Christian Association*, the Salvation Army*, as well as the Boy Scouts and Girl Scouts became involved through prayers, donations, and extensive, well-organized fund-raising strategies. Women have been active both as founders and leaders of leprosaria (e.g., Mary Reed at Chandag Heights in the foothills of the Himalayas, and thousands of nuns and laywomen serving as nurses throughout Asia) and as administrators and fund-raisers (e.g., Charlotte Pim, a cofounder of the Mission to Lepers). Christian doctors could also fulfill their vocations through participation in non-religious medical associations, such as the International Leprosy Association and the World Health Organization.

Physical and spiritual ministries with lepers were conducted in dispensaries, clinics, leprosy wings in hospitals, and leper colonies. In the first half of the 20th c. especially, the last option was often chosen in order to provide shelter for outcasts as well as to segregate the infectious. A central element of many such leprosaria and treatment centers was teaching basic reading and writing, both so that the Gospel could be more readily transmitted and so that vocational and technical training might be provided for patients. Many leprosy stations produced strong Christian congregations. A message of work and self-support was preached to help provide dignity to scorned outcasts, to meet the material needs of patients, and to prepare those cured for gainful employment afterwards. Recognizing the need for services on much greater scales, however, leprosy workers also lobbied governments to provide humane legislation and funding for medical treatment.

Recurring issues for leprosaria included how to address leper sexuality (some institutions required sterilization before marriage), how to care for the noninfected children of lepers (the children were often placed in orphanages because of their higher susceptibility to the disease), and how to provide care and sustenance to severely impaired people. Funding for the construction of buildings and infrastructure maintenance were also concerns. Consistently, medical missionaries reported that they were able to assist only a fraction of the lepers in their areas, in many cases having to turn away very sick patients for lack of food and facilities. Because of tight budgets and limited resources, leprosy work has been particularly susceptible to wartime disruptions. Occupying armies have cut off much-needed supplies (as the Japanese did to Culion in the Philippines); medical resources and personnel have been diverted to front lines; and missionaries have been attacked (Communists killed doctors and missionaries at Ban Me Thuot in Vietnam).

Christians were active in leprosy work in almost every country in Asia (establishing, for example, important leprosaria in Chiang Mai in Thailand* and Kwang-ju in

Korea*, as well as the Kentung colony in Burma). Such efforts preceded and fostered similar ventures in Africa and South America. Of the work in Asia, the medical and missionary enterprises in India, China, Japan, and the Philippines were the most important. Leprosy missions in India*, in particular, produced several notable figures (such as Bailey and Reed), and their fame helped to generate support for leprosy work throughout the world. The most recent example is Mother Teresa* and her Missionaries of Charity. From their initial work with five lepers in 1957, they had by 1990 established 25 leprosy rehabilitation centers and 96 mobile leprosy clinics worldwide. As with India, the frequency with which missions encountered lepers in China led to many efforts to establish homes and provide care. Of these many institutions, the Maryknoll leprosarium led by Father Sweeney at Sunwui was one of the most famous, both because of the high quality of care provided and because of Sweeney's heroic efforts to feed and shelter the lepers during World War II*.

In Japan, the anti-Christian persecutions of the early 17th c. destroyed the early Franciscan and Jesuit* centers for treating lepers, but some Japanese Christians brought lepers into their own homes, and in some cases priests were hidden among them. With the reopening of the country in the 19th c., missionaries again established leprosaria. In the first decade of the 20th century, the Japanese government under the patronage of Empress Teimei established extensive leprosy centers and trained medical personnel. The activism of Japanese Christians helped prompt this notable government interest in systematic medical care for lepers.

The Culion leprosarium in the Philippines, founded by the United States colonial government in 1906, became by the 1930s the largest leprosarium in the world, having upwards of 7,000 lepers and serving as a major research center. From the beginning, Jesuits served as chaplains and the Sisters of St. Paul des Chartres as nurses. In most other countries, segregation in a leper colony was voluntary (though often a practical necessity). By contrast, the American colonial government sought to enforce a strict policy of isolation in an (unsuccessful) effort to eradicate leprosy from the islands. In the Philippines as elsewhere, the end of colonial rule and changes in medical practices led Asian governments generally to concentrate more on outpatient treatments than on leper colonies.

Since the 1980s and the development of effective multi-drug therapies that readily cure patients, the greatest emphasis has been on making these medicines widely available. While there remains a need for sustained leprosy work, the need is no longer as acute and the prospects are no longer as uncertain as they were a century ago. While medical missionaries were the most prominent laborers in this vineyard, the enormous amount of Christian energy dedicated worldwide to research, local leprosy committees, fund-raising, sermons, and prayers indicates that leprosy work in Asia engaged the whole body of Christ.

Bibliography

Burgess, Perry, *Born of Those Years: An Autobiography* (1951). • Chapman, Ronald Fettes, *Leonard Wood and Leprosy in the Philippines: The Culion Leper Colony, 1921-27* (1982). • Miller, A. Donald, *An Inn Called Welcome: The Story of the Mission to Lepers, 1874-1917* (1965) • Thomas, Howard Elsworth, *A Study of Leprosy Colony Policies* (1947).

David Keck

Levavaseur, Gervais

(b. Diocese of Sees, France, 1730; d. Cochin China, 1777). Paris Foreign Mission Society* (MEP) priest and pioneer of the mission working among Khmers in Cambodia*.

Levavaseur was the first missionary assigned exclusively to the apostolate attached to the Khmers. He laid the foundation for and created the first instruments of the missionary work of future centuries by developing seminarians and religious leaders and by producing relevant literary work.

Levavaseur arrived in Cambodia on 15 May 1768. Four months later, he was installed in the region of Kompson Thom. With the help of some Buddhist monks, he studied the Khmer writing and language. Some years later, he translated the principal prayers and a beginner's catechism into the Khmer language. He compiled a Khmer-Latin dictionary, which was translated into French around 1850 by Mgr. Miche. This served as the basis for all of the linguists of the 19th and 20th cs.

Around 1770, Levavaseur was charged by Mgr. Piquel, bishop of Cambodia, with the creation of a "little school," a regional school for the preparation of future priests. For young Khmer Portuguese girls, Levavaseur founded in the same way a religious congregation, a branch of the Lovers of the Cross* created in Siam in the preceding century by Pierre Lambert de la Motte*.

Levavaseur's personal journal is a mine of information as much about the history of missions as about the political and cultural context of the epoch in Cambodia.

François Ponchaud

Li Bo Yu

(b. Huxian, Shaanxi, 1908; d. 1980). Chinese Catholic bishop of Zhouzhi Diocese, China.

Li was born into a poor peasant family who were devout adherents of the Catholic faith. He left home in 1920 to seek a monastic life and was consecrated a priest in 1933. From 1935 to 1938, Li studied at Beijing's Furen University (the Catholic University of Peking), after which he engaged in pastoral work in various counties including Zhouzhi, Huxian, Xinping, and Wugong. After liberation, he immediately expressed his support for the

Chinese Communist Party and the People's Government. In 1950, he attended the first Conference of Personages of Various Circles of Zhouxian as a representative of the religious circles. In 1951, appointed superintendent bishop, he urged all Catholic believers to participate in land reform and the campaign for resisting U.S. aggression and aiding Korea. He was regarded as an outstanding patriot within the Chinese Catholic Church.

In 1956, Li attended the Chinese Catholic Patriotic Association Sponsors' Conference in Beijing. He addressed the First Representative Conference of the Chinese Catholic Church in 1957 on "The Present Situation of the Patriotic Movement of the Chinese Catholic Church and Its Future Tasks." He was concurrently vice-chairperson of the Chinese Catholic Patriotic Association and chairperson of Shaanxi Provincial Catholic Patriotic Association. During the Cultural Revolution, he was framed and imprisoned for five years. He was rehabilitated in 1978. He died two years later from illness. On 26 Feb 1990, the tenth anniversary of his death, a memorial service was held in his native town by the Shaanxi Provincial Catholic. CHINA GROUP

Li Deng Hui

(b. Batavia, Java, 1873; d. 1947). Chinese Christian activist and educator.

Li accepted Christ at the age of 14 when he was studying at a Christian school in Singapore*. In 1892, he went to the United States to study and graduated with a bachelor's degree from Yale University (1899). He knew many different languages. In 1901, he began to build schools in Batavia and then went to Shanghai in 1905. He initiated the To Use Education to Arouse the Nation program and the World Chinese Students Federation, which began by encouraging students to be patriotic. He motivated students to boycott American goods when the United States passed legislation prohibiting Chinese laborers.

In 1906, Li taught German and Latin in Fudan Public School and later served there as dean of students. In 1912, he became head of the English department of Zhonghua Publishing House. He became principal of Fudan that year as well. In 1917, when Fudan became a university, Li went to Nanyang twice to raise funding. On his return he improved the school facilities and also began to accept female students. He contributed greatly to the development of Fudan.

During the war of resistance against Japan*, Fudan moved; Li remained in Shanghai to set up Shiyan Secondary School. Li loved his country and loved teaching. During the Washington Peace Conference in 1921, he set up the National Peoples' Diplomatic Support Committee to fight against all the powers that were infringing upon China's rights. Li was also a committee member and vice-chairman of the Education Association of the Chinese Protestant Church and the Association of the All China Protestant Church. In 1931, he served as chairman of the Christian Flood Relief Committee. When he became chairman of the Chinese People's Committee Against Opium in 1935, he wrote about and exposed the illegal dealings of public officials. Li was also chosen to be a member of the United States Geographical Society.

CHINA GROUP

Li Matou. *See* Ricci, Matteo

Li Rong Fang

(b. Hopei, China, 1887; d. 1965). Chinese Christian writer and university professor.

Li graduated from Peking (Beijing) University in 1911 and obtained a master of arts degree in 1913. He furthered his studies at the University of Chicago in 1914. Three years later, he returned to China*. He taught at Yenching University from 1921 to 1928 as an Old Testament professor. After the graduate school of religion separated from the university, Li served as dean of Yenching Graduate School of Religion. In 1928, he studied at King's College, London University, and returned to China the following year. From 1929 on, Li served on the faculty of Yenching Graduate School of Religion. He taught courses in Bible literature, Old Testament doctrine, church management, and worship. His many writings in Chinese include *Guide to Old Testament Study, Introduction to Old Testament Literature, Teachings of the Psalms,* and *The Prophet Jeremiah: His Life and Teachings.* His writings in English include *Fragments Excavated in Palestine* and *Apocrypha and Pseudepigrapha.*

CHINA GROUP

Li Wenyu

(b. Pudong, Shanghai, 1840; d. 1911). Chinese Jesuit* and well-known writer.

Li was born into the West Li family of Tangmu Qiao, Pudong, where Catholicism continued to be propagated by faithful adherents and new Jesuit missionaries who returned to Jiangnan (south of the Yangtze River) after Emperor Yongzheng's ban on Catholicism was lifted. Li was baptized as an infant and was taught the rudiments of Catholicism from childhood.

In 1852, Li was admitted to Sheng Yi Na Jue (St. Ignatius) public school in Xujiahui, Shanghai. In 1862, he joined the Xujiahui Society of Jesus and was among the first to enter the newly established junior college of the Shanghai Society of Jesus. Li was consecrated a priest in 1869 and set out to preach the Gospel in 1871, beginning with Songjiang, Nanhui, Qingpu, and then Anhui. Between 1875 and 1878, he taught at the monastery in Dongjiadu, Shanghai.

In 1879, when *Yi Wen Lu,* the first newspaper of the Shanghai Catholic Church, was launched, Li returned to Xujiahui to serve as editor in chief. He was also editor in chief of *Sheng Xin Bao* (Sacred Heart Newspaper), founded in 1887. The two newspapers carried many articles on Catholicism and Li's personal comments on current events. Among the books Li wrote, edited, or translated are *Li Ku* (A Well of Truths), a defense of Catholicism; *Mo Jing Ji* (A Treasure of Writing), which comprises a collection of the writings of Wu Yushan, the first Chinese Jesuit priest in Jiangnan; and *Xin Jing Yi Yi* (An Interpretation on the New Testament). Li, who headed the literary work in the Chinese Catholic Church for 32 years, was highly esteemed by Chinese Catholic intellectuals. CHINA GROUP

Li Zhizao

(Li Chih-tsao) (b. Renhe, Hangzhou, China, 1565; d. 1630). Only high-ranking Chinese intellectual baptized by Matteo Ricci*, and one of the "three pillars" of the early Catholic Church in China*.

Li was one of the Chinese officials who willingly learned European astronomy, geography, mathematics, and Catholic doctrines from Matteo Ricci. Baptized Liang (Leon) by Ricci, Li converted to Catholicism upon the earnest persuasion of the critically ill Ricci one month before the latter's death (May 1610). Upon conversion, Li helped missionaries spread the Gospel to his native home and sheltered them during precarious times when they came under suspicion and were rejected by other Chinese officials. He helped the missionaries with their translation work by polishing up their Chinese and did some writing himself to propagate Catholicism. Li, Xu Guangqi*, and Yang Tingjun* are considered the three pillars of the early Chinese Catholic Church.

Bibliography

"Li Chih-tsao," in *Eminent Chinese of the Ch'ing Period*, ed. A. Hummel (1943-44). • Peterson, Willard J., "Why Did They Become Christians? Yang T'ing-yun, Li Chih-tsao, and Hsu Kuang-ch'i," in *East Meets West: The Jesuits in China, 1582-1773*, ed. C. Ronan and B. Oh (1988). • Standaert, N., *Yang Tingyun: Confucian and Christian in Late Ming China* (1988). CHINA GROUP

Liang Ah Fah. *See* Leong Kung Fa

Lindvall, Alfred

(b. 1881; d. 1958). Swedish Salvation Army* (SA) pioneer in the Philippines*.

Alfred Lindvall and his wife, Agness, arrived in the Philippines in 1937. They had already served 36 years in South America, including several years as territorial commanders. In the Philippines, Lindvall engaged in evangelistic work; and, beginning with San Nicolas Market, Manila, within two years the SA had opened 15 centers. Because of their bands and drums, these halls attracted much public attention. In 1938, Lindvall began a cadets training center, which moved to Baguio in 1941. In the meantime, additional SA workers and Filipino converts expanded the work into the provinces. The Lindvalls remained in the Philippines during World War II*, though their activities were curtailed. Immediately following the war, the SA began relief efforts. The Lindvalls retired in 1946, and the SA work in the Philippines came under the direction of the United States corps.

Bibliography

Coutts, Frederick, *The Better Fight: The History of the Salvation Army*, Vol. VI, *1914-46* (1973). • Sanders, Robert F., *Sinimula Ng Panginoon (Pioneered by God): History of the Salvation Army in the Philippines* (1979).

FLOYD T. CUNNINGHAM

Lingayats

Religious group in India constituting a classless society combining several castes.

The word *lingayat* can mean "one who wears the *linga*." An alternative label, *Vira-Saiva*, may be translated "a staunch Saivite." The movement took shape at what is now called Basava Kalyana ca. C.E. 1160. Basava, the founder of the movement, was born to a Saivite Brahmin family at Bagevadi in Bijapura District ca. C.E. 1106. At the age of eight, when he was to be invested with the sacred thread, he refused, saying that he was a worshipper of Siva and Siva only, and the *upanayana* ceremony would involve him in the worship of the sun and other traditional customs. This piety and firmness of purpose were accepted by his parents. Later, as the minister of the Kalyana Kingdom, he would propagate his faith in Siva through the whole region of northern Karnataka. Basava made popular the renewed Saiva faith, not only by his high position in the palace, but by a series of miracles such as the feeding of a multitude, healing the sick, and restoring the dead to life. He is now deified as the reincarnation of Siva's servant Nandi and called *Basavesvara*.

It should be noted that the *linga* has no phallic significance for the *lingayat*, but is only the supreme object of devotion; it is the sign of the god Siva. Because Siva is without form, the *linga* has been bestowed as an object of worship. It removes all impurities. Although the ultimate goal of the *Vira-Saiva* is the merging of the soul with the Supreme *(Sivadvaita)*, it begins with a belief in the distinctness of the soul from God. In the spiritual pilgrimage, there are six halting places of the soul *(shatshala)*. In his hall of religious experience *(Anubhava mantapa)*, Basava had actually erected a throne or staircase of six steps to illustrate these spiritual stages, namely *bhakta, mahesvara, prasada, pranalingi, sarana*, and *aikya*. Before reaching the first stage, God is viewed as personal. The conception of the personality of God vanishes when the individual soul mounts the first step. At this stage, an attempt is first made by the individual to realize the Supreme Reality, and this continues in succeeding stages. The distinctness of the soul apparent in the first step goes on decreasing as it rises higher and higher, vanishing completely in the fifth step, where the individual soul is totally surrendered to God. In the sixth step, there are complete union and identification of the individual soul with Siva.

The eight coverings *(ashtavarana)* or aids of faith which separate the *Vira-Saivas* from other people are *guru, linga, jangama, padodaka, prasada, mantra, vibhuti,* and *rudraksha.* They worship the first three, partake of the next two, and gain inner purity through the last three. The *guru* makes the disciple a new creation through *lingadiksha* (initiation through presenting a *linga*); *jangama* is the preacher of the faith. The *padodaka* is the water in which the *guru's* feet are washed, and the *prasada* is the food of which he partakes. The *mantra,* a five-syllable formula (called *Sivaya*), purifies the soul. The *vibhuti* (sacred ashes) rubbed on the body portrays the pure mind of Siva. The *rudraksha,* an angular berry serving as beads for counting prayers, represents Siva's eyes or gaze and is believed to remove all sin.

The five rules of conduct *(panchachara)* of the *lingayats* are *lingachara, sadachara, sivachara, ganachara,* and *brutyachara. Lingachara* means that after *lingadiksha* no god other than Siva should be worshipped. *Sadachara* is not only one's own personal good conduct, but the good conduct of family and community. To offer wealth, strength, and goodwill to others regardless of caste is *sivachara.* Ganachara means loyalty to one's own community and not allowing Siva to be ill spoken of. *Brutyachara* is the devotee's conduct as a selfless servant of Siva.

The *Vira-Saiva* religious literature is called *vachana sahitya.* The *Lingayat* reforms are directed against Vedic and sacerdotal traditions. Different caste groups, as well as men and women, are treated as equal. The dead are buried in a *padmasana* posture with the *linga* in the palm. No *sraddha* ceremony is performed, and the idea of reincarnation is rejected. At childbirth and at the age of eight, the *guru* performs the eightfold ceremony.

Bibliography

Nandinath, S. C., *A Hand Book of Virasaivism* (1942). • Malledevaru, H. P., *Essentials of Virasaivism* (1973). • Ishwaran, K., *Religion & Society among the Lingayats of South India* (1983). • Parvathamma, C., *Sociological Essays on Veerasaivism* (1972). • Sargant, N. C., *The Lingayats: The Vira-Saiva Religion* (1963). • Desai, P. B., *Basavesvar and His Times* (1968). • Krishna Rao, A. N., *Virasaiva Literature & Culture* (1943). • Murty, M. R. Srinivas, *The Essence of Vacana Dhama* (1946). • Tipperudrasvami, H., *Virasaiva Religion in Vacanas* (1969). • *The Cultural Heritage of India,* Vol. IV (1956). • Sakhare, M. R., *History and Philosophy of Lingayat Religion* (1942).

K. P. ALEAZ

Lisus, Myanmar

The Lisus are a Lolo race. Linguistically and culturally related to the Lahu and Akha, the Lisus can be found widely in the Shan State, Kachin State, and in the Mogok township. They belong to various churches.

Lisu Christian Church of Myanmar (LCCM). In about 1920, missionaries from China Inland Mission (CIM; Overseas Missionary Fellowship) came to Myanmar to evangelize among the Lisu animists. The LCCM became a member of the Myanmar Council of Churches in 1970. The LCCM used to focus its ministry on the Lahu, Wa, and Chinese, but they now include the Hmong nationals. The church also assisted the Lhaovo Baptist* Church through Mr. Samuyepha, who had ministered to the Lhaovo since 1935, Mr. Joel, and Mr. Thethiyu in 1938, and David Fish, who focused on teaching. A prominent leader of LCCM, Fish founded the education center in Lashio (1972), which taught more than 700 Lisu children between 1972 and 1988, with a few progressing to high school and even the university. Fish also helped establish a mission center in Myintgyina around 1980 and founded new villages for people in remote areas.

Lisu Baptist Church (LBC). The LBC began in 1906 and owed its development to the foreign missionaries serving the Kachins, Shans, Pa-Os, and Burmans. The Mogok Lisu Baptist Church applied to be affiliated with the Myanmar Baptist Convention (MBC) in 1973 and was accepted in 1977. The Lisu Baptist churches in the Shan and Kachin States merged with the Mogok Lisu Church and formed the LBC. This merger was accepted by the MBC in 1983. The activities of the LBC include the promotion of evangelism and church growth, the upgrading of the Bible school, and social work such as rehabilitation programs, clinics, educational centers, and the provision of jobs.

Lisu Assemblies of God (AG). Yang Paul, a Chinese, started the AG ministry in Myanmar. He learned the Lisu language in 1928 and, with the help of three Lisu traders, arrived at Chiladee village, Putao township, on 20 Jul 1931. Under his leadership the AG mission flourished among the Lisus first and then among other nationals. Clifford Morrison came around 1939 and continued the mission work until 1960. The priority of the Lisu AG, which has done mission work among the Nagas from 1966, is soul winning.

Churches of Christ. Founded by J. Russell Morse in 1933, the Churches of Christ is based mainly in Putao. Morse and his family preached Christ, did social work amongst the Lisu and the Tawang, established schools, dispensed medicine, provided farm tractors, and gave other kinds of aid to church members. More government officials are members of this church than of any other Lisu church. The Morses were the only missionaries to do social work among the Lisus. Other church leaders performed social work within their respective churches.

The Roman Catholic Mission to the Lisu began approximately in 1960, when priests brought Lisu children from the villages to the Roman Catholic* Mission in Namtu for training and some schooling.

The Bhamo Lisu Baptists owe much to Tong Wu (b. 1874; d. 15 Jan 1959), who promoted education and economics among them. He built a school in the village of Dawabya, Bhamo region, and brought in teachers for the Lisu children. He bought farms for the poor and provided them with work.

The Lisu alphabet was introduced by J. O. Fraser, who translated some portions of the Bible. His work in translation was continued by A. B. Cooke and Crane, among others. Cooke, in particular, did much literature work for the Lisus. All Lisu churches use the same Bible. The LCCM and the Churches of Christ share the same hymnbook. The LBC and the Lisu AG have developed their own hymnbooks.

Bibliography

Enriquez, C. M., *Races of Burma* (1933). • Fish, David, *A Short History of LCCM.*

NU SAR

Literacy

The desperate need for Christian literacy ministry in Asia today may be seen in statistics indicating that, although over 90% of the Asian population has the entire Bible* translated and printed in their language, and over 95% have the New Testament or at least one of the Gospels printed in their language, less than half of the population can read Scripture.

In the 20th c., Frank Charles Laubach* (1884-1970) led the way in promoting literacy in Asia; accordingly, he has been called the apostle of literacy. He wrote almost 100 books, large and small, and helped develop literacy primers in 315 languages during his 40 years of literacy work around the world. Laubach was a world literacy pioneer who started the "Each One Teach One" method in the Philippines*, serving as a missionary there from 1915 to 1941. In 1930, he adapted the Roman alphabet to the Maranao language of the Muslims in Mindanao and devised a picture-word-syllable method for teaching adults to read. They began to teach one another, and the "Each One Teach One" literacy method was born.

By 1935, Laubach had responded to calls from missionaries in Malaysia*, Indonesia*, Ceylon (Sri Lanka*), and India*. During the final 35 years of his life, he visited virtually every country in Asia except China* and Japan*, helping missions and governments to communicate in nearly 200 languages of Asia. In 1960, Laubach wrote: "The most bruised people on this planet, the naked, the hungry, the fallen among thieves, the sick, the imprisoned in mind and soul, are the 1,200 million illiterates. . . . At least a billion are virtual slaves . . . hungry, driven, diseased, afraid of educated men in this world and demons in the next." This description is even more appropriate today as the number of illiterates in Asia has increased by many millions.

Two major literacy efforts current in Asia today are those of the Summer Institute of Linguistics (SIL) and Literacy & Evangelism International (LEI, known in Asia as Literacy International). SIL's work in literacy is just one component of a broader program of linguistic research, language development, and practical assistance. The primary focus of this work is the lesser-known languages of the region, where literacy rates commonly approach zero in the mother tongue and 5-20% in some other language.

The vast majority of SIL's work in Asia has been in the Philippines* and in Vietnam*. Work has also been done in a number of other Asian countries with Indonesia, Malaysia, and Thailand being the most notable of these. Work has been completed in 43 languages and continues in another 219. Technical assistance has been provided to other agencies working in another 102 languages throughout Asia.

In objective perspective, SIL works in languages spoken by less than 3% of the Asian population; worldwide, SIL has translated and printed New Testaments in languages spoken by fewer than 1,000 people.

LEI has developed adult literacy primers mostly in the major languages of Asia. The distinctive of LEI literacy primers is their Bible content, beginning usually by Lesson 12 and continuing through 60 to 90 lessons. The last 26 lessons have as reading material 26 short Bible condensations, from Genesis to Revelation.

The largest publisher of literacy materials in Asia today (nearly one million LEI literacy primers) is Scripture Ministries of India in Madras. They began with Hindi and Telegu and then 10 major languages. Between 1987 and 1994, over 8,000 new churches were planted in India as a result of literacy classes using Bible-content primers. In addition, "the Literacy ministry continues to touch thousands of lives and homes, transforming many to the glory of God. The Model Literacy Zones, in 50 areas, target a 4-year program to bring total literacy and spiritual, physical, and social uplift."

Current government literacy statistics are often padded. The United Nations Educational, Scientific and Cultural Organization (UNESCO) overlooks this government padding. Though the United States pegs its literacy rate at 93%, a figure of 80% functional literacy is consistently given by reliable pollsters such as Harris. UNESCO reports Iraqi literacy going from 10% to 90% between 1984 and 1994. Another example of misleading statistics is seen in Pakistan: "In a literacy rate officially pegged at 27%, the share of people who are capable of writing more than just their own name is probably only 10% — among females less than half that" (*Time,* 17 Apr 1995). The World Bank's *Far Eastern Economic Review, Asia 1995 Yearbook* gives "regional performance figures" for 16 countries of Asia. The figure for Pakistan is 65% adult illiteracy, and for females it is 79%. These padded statistics on Pakistan are typical of other Asian nations.

Governments have been largely unsuccessful in developing literacy programs, because volunteer tutors are essential for any successful literacy program. Those programs with strong Christian motivation have provided volunteers for viable literacy solutions. Bible-content primers in Pakistan begin with Old Testament stories. In

Book 3, the last in the series, and with due notice on the front cover, Jesus is presented as Son of God and Savior.

Non-readers comprise the vast majority of the peoples yet to be reached with the Gospel. A tribal man in India had been paying 80 rupees monthly interest on a loan of 20 rupees. He saw the love of Jesus in the literacy program that made him aware of the exploitation.

Strategic current uses of literacy programs in Asia may be seen in northern Iraq (Kurdistan) and in India. Among the Muslim Kurds in northern Iraq, a missionary and a former Kurdish guerrilla leader, a poet who desires his people to turn to Christ, believe adult literacy is the best way to reach the Kurds. A Bible-content Kurdi primer series in Roman script is being prepared for 12 new believers who are to be trained for literacy ministry. Another exemplary use of literacy as a bridge for Christian witness is seen in the ministry of Anand Chaudhari, Rajasthan Bible Institute, Jaipur, India. By 1995, out of 1,000 literacy classes conducted throughout northern India by his students, 500 have, with purposeful planning, become churches in Hindu and tribal communities. In addition, Operation Mobilization in India has newly trained its slum workers, from Bombay to Calcutta, to use Bible-content literacy primers in Hindi, Tamil, Telegu, and Bengali.

Bibliography

The Frank C. Laubach Heritage Collection (1990). • *A Guide for Bible-Content Adult Literacy Primer Construction.*

ROBERT F. RICE

Literature and Publishing

Since the earliest accounts of the life of Jesus, writing and publishing have been the lifeblood of Christian existence. Asia, with the ancient tradition of written communication, has produced great works of Christian literature in its many cultural contexts. The Asian regions of Korea* and China* invented movable types some 700 years before Gutenberg. The Chinese, being pioneers in using movable types, were also the first to manufacture paper. It was no coincidence, then, that the oldest continuing "newspaper" was the court gazette at Peking, which disappeared only in the early 20th c. The art of printing from negative reliefs was known in China around 594 C.E. and from there spread along the caravan routes to the West, where taking impressions from wooden blocks became quite common. However, the early printers followed the prevailing style of the scribes for the simple reason that the reading public was familiar with it. Thus the invention of printing did not revolutionize the production of books. Individual patrons valued the manuscript book and often despised the printed product. In fact, it was the art of the book binder that won over connoisseurs to printed books. The educated urban classes provided the best markets, and printing presses sprang up at all the flourishing centers of international trade. Governments and churches, especially the monastic orders, provided patronage. The Jesuits*, for instance, brought the first modern printing press into India in 1550.

India. In 1556 Jesuit priests set up a press in Portuguese Goa and printed books in Latin and Portuguese. Later they printed books in Tamil and other Indian languages. Unfortunately, this was followed by a break in publishing activity in India. In any history of early printing and publishing in India, names such as the Baptist Mission Press, the Diocesan Press, Basel Mission Press, the Wesley Press, and the American Mission Press will figure prominently. Between 1801 and 1832 the Serampore Mission Press single-handedly published 212,000 volumes in 50 languages. Christian publishing for Protestants began in Tranquebar*, where the Danish missionaries Ziegenbalg* and Plutschau* arrived in 1706. They handprinted the first copies of the Gospels and Acts in Tamil by 1709. By 1713 five books were printed in Portuguese and one in Tamil, and copies of the New Testament followed in 1715 (see Bible Translation).

In 1948, under Fr. James Stuart (first secretary of the Society for the Promotion of Christian Knowledge [SPCK] in India), the publishing house as we know it today grew up. It has published books ranging from Christian theology to Indology in English as well as books in Indian languages. In 1859 it became a registered autonomous body under the name Indian Society for Promoting Christian Knowledge (ISPCK).

In 1751 the Diocesan Press was set up. It was a great help to the societies which preceded the Christian Literature Society (CLS). Later in the 19th c., the fastest-growing line of Christian publications was school textbooks. The CLS was engaged in this work for over a century. The SPCK organized committees in different cities for publishing in the regional languages. The Methodist Publishing House and the Tract and Book Societies in Allahabad and western India were set up and published in Hindi, Hindustani, Roman Urdu, and Marathi.

In the case of other regional languages in India, publishing was next done in the Malayalam language. The first Malayalam book was printed in 1772 in Rome. A New Testament was printed in Bombay in 1811. The Church Mission Society (CMS) Press was established in Kottayam, Kerala, in 1821. The first ecumenical effort in Christian publishing in Malayalam was the formation of the Malayalam Christian Literature Committee at Tiruvalla, Kerala, in 1925. Later this merged with the CLS in 1952. Other Protestant agencies doing publishing in Malayalam now are the Evangelical Literature Service and the Living Literature Center in Kottayam.

The Roman Catholic Church* operates a number of publishing houses in Kerala. The important ones are the Deepika Book House, Jyoti Book House, Janatha Book Stall, and Prakasham Publications. Today almost all of the organizations, institutions, and churches have their own publications. Some of the recent publishers include the Theological Book Trust (TBT). Launched in 1986 with the title Kingdom Concerns, TBT is a new Asian

Christian publishing house located in Bangalore. The North East Association of Theological Schools, Board of Theological Education of the Senate of Serampore College, and Association for Theological Education in South East Asia* (ATESEA) together publish the *Asia Journal of Theology*. *AJT* is a quarterly publication printed in Bangalore. The Deepika Educational Trust, Madras, publishes *Dharma Deepika: A South Asian Journal of Missiological Research*. The Dharma Research Association, Bangalore, publishes *Journal of Dharma*, an international quarterly of world religions. *Theology for Our Times* (started 1994) is a journal annually published by the Indian School of Ecumenical Theology. *Bangalore Theological Forum* is a quarterly published by the Division of Research and Post-Graduate Studies of the United Theological College, Bangalore. *Vidyajyoti: Journal of Theological Reflection* is published by Vidyajyoti Educational and Welfare Society (VIEWS), Delhi.

Sri Lanka. During the Portuguese period (1505-1658) the Roman Catholics made a great impact on Ceylon. Even at this early period, Ceylonese Catholics contributed to Christian literature. The most prominent among them was Alagiyavanna Mohottala, who wrote a number of Sinhala poetical works. Among them, "Kustantinu Hatana" is highly regarded as a Sinhala poem. The Dutch period (1638-1796) is significant for the preparation of Christian writings in Sri Lanka. Scripture and other Christian materials were translated into Sinhala and Tamil for use in school. The printing press set up in Colombo in 1732 published many of these documents. During the British period Christians retained the monopoly on printing and publishing until 1862. The Bible Society* (1812) was mostly devoted to the publication of the Scriptures in the vernacular. The Wesleyan Mission Press (1815), the Church Missionary Society Press (1823), and the Baptist Mission Press (1841) were the first Protestant printing establishments. The Roman Catholics set up Gnanarthapradipaya Press in Colombo in 1869. The American missionaries assembled their first press in Jaffna in 1818. The establishment of the Religious Tract Society in 1840 was important since it undertook to publish Christian literature other than the Scriptures.

The Roman Catholic Sinhala Weekly, Gnanarthapradipaya (1866), *the English Weekly Catholic Messenger* (1869), and the *Tamil Satiyaveda Patukavalan* (1878) are newspapers that have continued to this day. Among the Protestant publications, *Udaya Tarakei* (1841) and *Ilankie Nesan* (1948) in Tamil and *Lanka Nidhanaya* (1839), *Uragala* (1844), and *Vivecakaya* (1846) in Sinhala are noteworthy. The first Baptist missionary, James Chater, published a Sinhalese grammar and a lexicon (1817). Benjamin Clough published a two-volume Sinhala-English (1818) and English-Sinhala dictionary (1822). This was later enhanced and edited by Charles Carter of the Baptist Mission (1862). M. Winslow's *A Comprehensive Tamil and English Dictionary of High and Low Tamil* (1862) and Peter Percival's *Tamil Dictionary* have followed the model of dictionaries in the European languages.

Hong Kong. The first Catholic newspaper, published by the Hong Kong Catholic Press in 1877, was the *Hong Kong Catholic Register*. It was followed by the *Religião e Patria*, published in 1914 in Portuguese by J. Pereira. *The Rock*, published in English by the Catholic Union and the Catholic Men's Club in 1920, lasted for 18 years. The Chinese Catholic dailies *Chung Wo Yat Po* and *Chung Wo Evening News* lasted for only two years, from 1930 to 1931. At present the Hong Kong Catholic Diocese publishes two weeklies, *Kung Kao Po* in Chinese and the *Sunday Examiner* in English. *Kung Kao Po*, established in 1928 by A. Granelli, has the largest circulation among the Chinese Catholic weeklies. Its English counterpart, the *Sunday Examiner*, was established in 1946 by Fr. Maestrini. Today the Hong Kong Catholic Diocese is also engaged in the press and publication sector through other organs, such as the Catholic Truth Society, the Diocesan Audio-Visual Center, the Social Communications Office, the Holy Spirit Study Center, which publishes *Tripod*, and so on. Other Catholic organizations committed to this sector but operating outside the responsibility of the Diocese include the East Asia Catholic Press Association, Union of Catholic Asian News (UCA News), Vox Amica Press, Xavier Publishing Association, New City Press, and Le Graine de Seneve Company.

Indonesia. The effort to provide Christian literature in Indonesia began soon after the arrival of the first Roman Catholics (early 16th c.). Earliest literature generally consisted in translations of Portuguese and Latin religious instructions into Malay. Concerned about the inefficiency in producing Christian literature, several groups decided to build a common Christian publishing house in the 1930s. Missionary personnel and Indonesian Christians agreed to found a commission on literature, which was called *Noodlectuurcommissie van kerk en Zending* (Emergency Commission on Literature of the Church and Mission). Since 1950, along with the formation of the Council of Churches in Indonesia (CCI, now Communion of Churches in Indonesia*), that commission became a permanent institution with the name *Badan Penerbit Kristen* (BPK; Christian Publishing House). This publishing house built a special partnership with CCI, which continues today. Since the 1970s BPK has used a new name, *BPK Gunung Mulia* (BPK-GM). BPK-GM has a "twin sister," *Taman Pustaka Kristen* (TPK; Christian Publishing Garden). *Gunung Mulia's* main concern is to fulfill the needs of the churches and Christian people in central Java*. Mainly for Bible* translation, publishing, and distribution, Lembaga Alkitab Indonesia (LAI; Indonesian Bible Society) was established as a successor to some of the foreign Bible and missionary societies. At present BPK-GK is the largest Protestant publishing company in Indonesia. It has published more than 2,000 titles, most of them in Indonesian. Besides other publishing houses, some Christian universities and seminaries have opened their own

Literature and Publishing

publishing departments. Recently, *Yayasan Musik Gereja* (Church Music Foundation) developed its publishing department to publish hymnals and books on church music*.

There are around 50 publishing companies in Indonesia. Modern Roman Catholic publishing began with the foundation of Kanisius Printing and Publishing (1922) in Yogyakarta and Arnoldus Press (1925; now *Nusa Inda)* in Ende* (Flores). After independence (1945), other institutions such as Obor (1951; Jakarta) and Cipta Loka Caraka (CLC; 1970) expanded the scope of publications. CLC, founded by Fr. Adolf Heuken, S.J., has published several series of pocket books and encyclopedias used by people of different Christian denominations in Indonesia and eastern Malaysia. An *Encyclopedia of the Church (Ensiklopedi Gereja),* five volumes in full color, is in print, the first book of its kind in Bahasa Indonesia. *Life* (started as *Kerkelijik Weekblad),* an Indonesian Catholic weekly, has been published by the archdiocese of Jakarta since 1946.

China. The very first printing press in China was the London Missionary Society (LMS) Press, founded in 1818. In 1847 the LMS commissioned Alexander Wylie* to go to Shanghai to take charge of the printing press. Its main task was to print the "Delegates Version" of the New and Old Testaments, which had just been completed. The China Alliance Press was set up by Robert Alexander Jaffray* in Kwangsi Wucknow in 1911. He also founded *Bible News (Sheng Jing Bao),* a periodical that is published every two months. In 1951 both the Christian and Missionary Alliance* (C&MA) and the China Alliance Press moved to Hong Kong to continue work. Signs of the Times Publishing House is the publishing house of the Seventh-day Adventists*. In 1905, Miller set up a press at Shang-tsai-hsien at Honan and printed *Fu Yin Xuan Bao* in Mandarin. In 1909 the monthly paper was renamed *Shi Zhao Yue Bao I** (Signs of the Times; monthly). It ceased operation in Jun 1951. The China Sunday School Society dates back to 1907. When the Missionary Conference at Shanghai was held, a committee was formed to promote Sunday-school education. Three years later, in Apr 1910, *Zhong-guo-zhu-ri-xue-hui* (China Sunday School Committee) was registered. In 1924 the organization was renamed *Zhong-guo-zhu-ri-xue-he-hui* (China Sunday School Society). Later, in Dec 1956, with three other Christian publishing organizations, they formed the China Christian Union Publication Society. The China Baptist Publication Society was first named Baptist Publication Society and was set up by Southern Baptist Convention missionaries. At the end of 1956, China Baptist Publication Society was merged with three other publication societies into the China Christian Union Publication Society. Christian Literature Society for China was founded in Shanghai in 1887 with the aim of transferring the knowledge of the Occident to China. At the end of 1956 the society merged with three other Christian publishers and formed the China Christian Union Publication Society; it ceased its own operation in 1957. The society had published over 2,000 books.

Beijing Beitang Press was set up by the Lazarists* near the church, Beitang, in Beijing. They produced three books, two Latin elementary grammar books and one Latin-Chinese dictionary. Beitang Press had produced four million books by 1946. Shanghai Catholic Guangoi Press is the publishing organ of the Shanghai Diocese; it was founded in 1984 and is the largest Catholic press. The first issue of the quarterly *Collection of Catholicism Study Material* was published in Dec 1985. By Oct 1994 35 issues of the quarterly review had been published.

In 1868 J. Young Allen* published a weekly paper, *Jiao Hui Xin Bao* (The Church News). In 1875 this periodical was renamed *Wan Kuo Kung Pao* (Review of the Times), but it discontinued in 1883. In 1889 the Society for the Diffusion of Christian and General Knowledge (SDCGKC) published *Wan Kuo Kung Pao. Wen She* Christian Literature Association was inaugurated in Mar 1925 and published the first issue of *Wen She Yue Kan* by October. However, the publication was discontinued in Jun 1928. *Association Progress* was the official publication of the Youth Association; it was first published in Shanghai in Mar 1917. After 150 issues, it was discontinued in Feb 1932. *Chinese Monthly* was first published by Anglo-Chinese College in Malacca* (1815) and was the pioneer in Chinese periodicals. This periodical lasted from 1815 to 1821, and seven volumes were printed during these seven years. *Nu Duo,* a women's magazine, was published by the Christian Literature Society for China in Shanghai. Its first issue was printed in 1912. The publication was discontinued in Feb 1951. The SDCGKC in Shanghai published *The Chinese Christian Review* beginning in 1891. Publication of the magazine ceased in early 1917. In 1902 *Zhen Guang Yue Bao* (True Light Monthly) was inaugurated in Canton; it was later changed to *Zhen Guang Za Zhi.* From Jul 1926 the magazine was published in Shanghai, the last issue appearing in Dec 1941. *Truth and Life* was a combination of *Zhen Li Zhou Kan* (Truth Weekly) and *Sheng Ming Yue Kan* (Life Monthly). They published a magazine called *Zhen Li Yu Sheng Ming* (Truth and Life) beginning in Mar 1926. *Fu Yin Zhong* was the official publication of the Chinese Home Missionary Society. It was published from 1919 to 1955. *Xie Jin* was an official periodical of the National Christian Council. It was founded in 1943 in Chungking. Before its last issue in Apr 1951, a total of nine volumes had been published. *Tien Feng* was founded by Wu Yao Zong in Szechwan, Chentu, in Feb 1945. At present it is the official periodical of the Chinese Christian Three-Self Patriotic Movement* and China Christian Council*. *China for Christ* was first published in Shanghai on 10 Jan 1920. From 10 Oct 1922 (issue No. 25), it became the official periodical of the National Christian Council of China. It stopped at issue No. 200 in 1941. *Fu You Bao* (Happy Childhood Magazine) was the first children's magazine in Chinese. The distribution work was handled by the

China Sunday School Association and was taken over by the Literature Society in 1929.

Korea. Although Korean* Christian publications got a relatively late start, the variety and number of its publications are among the greatest in Asia. The first resident missionaries arrived in the 1880s and immediately began publication. The Korean Tract Society was established in 1889 as a combined Methodist and Presbyterian work for the promotion of Christian publications. Under the leadership of J. Heron, H. G. Underwood*, and F. Olinger, this society's first book publication was *Seong Gyo Choal Li* (Salient Doctrines of Christianity). Other books were soon published to aid in evangelistic work in Korea. The society broadened to include the Salvation Army and later the Holiness Church and was renamed The Christian Literature Society of Korea (CLSK).

The earliest periodical publication, *Korean Repository,* was published at Trilingual Press and was started by Olinger to provide monthly updates on information about Korea mission work. In 1901 H. B. Hulbert began the monthly *The Korea Review* (Presbyterian), and in 1904 *The Korea Methodist* began publication. These were combined and published as *The Korean Mission Field* until 1941. The Anglicans published *The Morning Calm* from 1890 to 1939, again for the purpose of communication about mission work in Korea.

The first Korean Christian journal was the *Bible and Church Monthly,* published by Methodists beginning in 1901. Other denominational publications soon followed: *Grace and Truth* (Plymouth Brethren, 1904), *Kyung Hyag-Jap Ji* (Roman Catholic, 1906), and *Three Angels' Message* (Adventist, 1910). The first theological journals were *Theological World* (Methodist, 1916), *Theological Review* (Presbyterian, 1918), and *Living Water* (Oriental Missionary Society, 1921).

Both Methodists and Presbyterians began the publication of newspapers in Korea in 1897. Henry Appenzeller* began publication of *The Christian Advocate* on 2 Feb, and Horace Underwood first produced *The Christian News* on 1 Apr. In Jul 1907 the two papers combined and became known as *The Christian News* (renamed *The Christian Herald* in 1907 and then restarted as *The Christian Messenger* from 1915 to 1937). During Japanese rule in Korea, publications had great difficulty; censorship was constant and publications ceased and were restarted. The Japanese, for example, suppressed *The Christian Messenger* frequently because of its anti-government articles. The Japanese softened their policy somewhat, professing "cultural rule" that permitted more freedom of speech. Therefore, many magazines were founded and many theological positions found expression during the 1920s: *The Chosen People* (1919), *Young Man* (1921), *New Life* (1923), *Sunday School* (1925), *Rural Life* (1929), *Bible and Chosen* (1927), *Spirit and Truth* (1928), and many others. By the 1930s, the Japanese conquest in Asia (beginning in China) was intensifying and censorship again increased. Not until after the Pacific War did publications again proliferate.

The CLSK began periodic publications for children *(New Friends,* 1952), for women *(New Home,* 1948), for pastors *(Christian Thought,* 1957), and for home worship *(The Upper Room).* Many other Christian publications have been at the forefront of political protest and the struggle for justice in Korea. It is estimated that about 2.2 million volumes a year are produced by the CLSK in Korea.

Thailand. The first printing press was introduced into Siam in 1796 by Msgr. Garnault. The book *Khamson Christang* (Christian Catechism) was printed the same year. This printing press was founded in the Santa Cruz Church at Thonburi. But it was Msgr. Pallegoix* who officially founded the Catholic Press of Assumption in 1838. The Assumption Press had been directed by Msgr. Vey* when he arrived in Bangkok in 1865. He wrote to Msgr. Dupond, who was in Rome at that moment, that he was publishing *Vie de Saints* in the Siamese language and that he needed the necessary instruments for the press in Bangkok. Vey was a strong advocate for Christian Thai publications. In 1904 he published *Phra Evangelico* (the Gospels), two volumes of meditations on the Gospels, and numerous prayer books, catechisms, and school books. Protestant publications in Thailand, pioneered by Dr. Bradley*, have been limited because of the small Christian readership.

Japan. In 1913 22 mission board cooperated to organize the *Nihon Kirisuto-Kyo Kobun Kyokai,* one of the forerunners of the Christian Literature Society of Japan. Earlier in 1907, when the three Methodist denominations united in Japan, they formed the publishing house of the Japan Methodist Church. In 1926 this group united with *Nihon Kirisuto-kyo Kobun Kyokai* and became the Christian Literature Society of Japan *(Kyo Bun Kwan).* In 1944 it merged with Shinkyo (Protestant) Publishing Company. By 1985, its one hundredth year, the *Kyo Bun Kwan* had published approximately 1,200 books. Ten Protestant groups joined into one corporation on 5 Oct 1944 in Tokyo and formed *Shinkyo Shuoppan Sha.* It was not until after the war that the publishing activity of *Shinkyo Shuppansha* got under way. It published over 1,400 academic and religious works. In Jan 1954, two monthly publications, *Kirisuto-Kyo Bunka* (Christian Culture) and *Fukuin To Jidai* (The Gospel and the Times), were begun, and these were combined into one, *Fukuin To Sekai* (The Gospel and the World) in Apr 1954. *Japan Christian Quarterly* was started in Oct 1893 and was published regularly until Dec 1925. Publication was suspended during the Pacific War (1942-50) but was resumed in the summer of 1951. In 1992 it became a yearly publication and was renamed the *Japan Christian Review.*

Iwaya Sazanami and Kurushima Takehiko made outstanding contributions to oral children's stories in their early period; they took children's literature that had been under the control of adults and freed it to stand by itself, thus making it truly literature for children. Wakamatsu Shizuko was the first Japanese to translate Western children's stories into Japanese. Her translations of "Little Lord Fauntleroy" and other stories appeared in *Jogaku Zasshi* (Girls Magazine). Deserving special mention is *Tetsu No Kutsu* (Iron Shoes; 1920) a solid, exciting story of faith by poet Yamamura Bocho, published serially in *Otogi No Sekai* (Fairytale World). From the mid-1920s to the early 1930s, two popular writers of children's literature, Oshikawa Shunryo and Sasaki Kuni, were active contributors to the magazine *Shonen Kurabu* (Boys' Club). The works of such writers as Nobe Shitenma, Muraoka Hanako, and Uesawa Kenji in *Shokoshi* (Small Children of Light; Kyo Bun Kwan Publishers) and *Kodomo No Tomo* (Children's Friend) are worthy of note. *Nihon Kirisuto-Kyo Jido Bungaku Zenshu* (Complete Collection of Japanese Christian Children's Literature) in 15 regular volumes and two additional volumes, was produced between 1982 and 1985. *Japan Christian Activity News* is a monthly (quarterly since 1933) English newsletter published by the National Christian Council in Japan.

Modern Catholic publications began in Japan in 1881 with the publication of *Kokyo Banjo* (Catholic News), and *Seikyo Zasshi* (Magazine of Sacred Teachings). The first novel appeared in serial form in *Kokyo Zasshi* beginning in Oct 1890. The first original novel came out in 1891, after the periodical *Koe* (Voice) had appeared, but *Koe* did not become a literary publication until after 1901. After 1919 *Koe* concentrated on spiritual training. Replacing it was the more literary journal *Katorikku* (Catholic News; Dec 1920). The first purely literary Catholic magazine was *Zozo* (Creation; 1934-40). Later, *Gendai Katorikku Bungei Sosho* (Modern Catholic Literary Library; 1942-44) was notable for its promotion of the Catholic cultural movement through times of rapid change and deprivation.

Conclusion. Christians have pioneered in almost every country in Asia, both in periodical production (both Roman Catholic and Protestant) and in vernacular production. As a result, literacy became an issue on a mass level and Asian societies were exposed to Christian and Western ideas — ideas that were often confused. Although there is still a great deal of Western Christian literature in Asia, today Asian Christian literature crosses political boundaries. Indonesian literature is read in Malaysia, Chinese books pass between countries in Asia, and English-language literature from the Philippines or India is read in seminaries throughout Asia.

Bibliography

Eapen, K. E., "The Role of the Book," in *Christian Publishing: The Indian Experience,* ed. Jane R. Caleb (1984). • Natarajan, S., *A History of the Press in India* (1962). • Isreel, Samuel, "Indian Publishing," in *Christian Publishing: The Indian Experience,* ed. Jane R. Caleb (1984). • Koilpillai, Victor, "Trends and Problems in Christian Book Publishing in India," in *Christian Publishing: The Indian Experience,* ed. Jane R. Caleb (1984). • Caleb, Jane R., "Publisher's Clinic," in *Christian Publishing: The Indian Experience,* ed. Jane R. Caleb (1984). • Philip, T. M., "Regional Book Publishing and Distribution," in *Christian Publishing: The Indian Experience,* ed. Jane R. Caleb (1984).

Imti Samuel Longkumer

Little Brothers of Jesus

Religious order founded in Algeria in 1933 and inspired by the example of Charles de Foucauld (see Little Sisters of Jesus).

Living in small communities called "fraternities," each comprising two or three brothers, the Little Brothers live their contemplative life by sharing in the social conditions of those without status or influence in society. Manual work constitutes their principal source of livelihood, and household chores, eucharistic celebrations, regular prayer, and sharing with neighbors form their daily life.

Some of the brothers may be called to be priests for the sacramental life of the community. A number of fraternities in a country or continent area comprise a region, with a regional head. The central fraternity, called the "general fraternity," located in London, United Kingdom, comprises a prior and three assistants.

The fraternities in Asia are found in Pakistan* (founded in 1954), among Muslim workers first in Quetta, then in Karachi; in Vietnam* (1954), among workers first in Saigon, then in Cantho (1957); in Japan* (1956), among workers in Kawasaki, then in Tsuruga and Nagoya; in India* (1964), in a Hindu-Christian village in Alampoundi, then in Bangalore; in Hong Kong* (1969); in Seoul, Korea* (1970); and in Manila, Philippines* (1977). A fraternity existed in Jaffna, Sri Lanka*, among Hindu-Christians from 1955 to 1959.

All the fraternities are international, with Little Brothers of the country living with others from countries in Asia and Europe.

Bibliography

Carretto, Carlo, *Letters from the Desert* (1972); *In Search of the Beyond* (1975); *The God Who Comes* (1975). • Voillaume, René, *The Need for Contemplation* (1972); *Source of Life: The Eucharist and Christian Living* (1975).

Bernard Jagueneau

Little Brothers of St. John the Baptist

First Chinese religious order.

In 1928, Vincent Lebbe* (Lei Ming Yuan), a Belgian Vincentian missionary priest in Ankuo, China*, founded the Little Brothers of St. John the Baptist. Two years earlier, Pope Pius XI, convinced by Lebbe, had ordained the first six native Chinese bishops. Lebbe believed that "China belongs to the Chinese, and the Chinese belong to Christ." If the church wanted to be rooted in China, it should let the native bishops and priests run their own church. Therefore Lebbe founded a native Chinese religious community. From the beginning, the members of the Little Brothers increased rapidly, and they soon spread into north China into the provinces of Hebei, Shan Hsi, San Hsi, Hsin Chiang, and Gan Su. They were invited into these provinces by the newly ordained Chinese bishops, since many foreign missionaries had left the dioceses.

During the Sino-Japanese War, which began in 1936, Lebbe led the Little Brothers and many lay Catholics to serve as rescue and medical teams in the battlefields in order to prove the loyalty and patriotism of the Chinese Catholic Church and to change the common perception of the Catholic Church as a foreign religion. Lebbe died on 24 Jun 1940 during the war and was buried in Chung Ching with government recognition and honor for his patriotic service to the country. Cao Li-Shan took Lebbe's place as "head of the family."

In 1945, after World War II*, the Little Brothers returned home from the battlefield to help rebuild their country. Civil war with the Communist armies under Mao Tse-tung broke out. The Little Brothers' community of over 200 members was scattered throughout China. Thirteen of them under Alexander Tsao went to Hong Kong*. The bishop of Hong Kong, Laurentius Bianchi, sent the Little Brothers to serve the mainland refugees in Tiao Kin Lin refugee camp. There they established a church, two schools, and two clinics.

In 1954, Tsao led four Little Brothers to Taiwan* and founded a parish in the Taipei diocese at Ching Mei. In 1957, Bishop William Kupfer invited the Little Brothers to the Taichung diocese, where they established their religious house.

In 1964, at the request of Raymond De Jaegher, the Little Brothers went to Saigon, Vietnam*, to take over two schools, the Free Pacific English School and the Ming Yuan Chinese School, which they ran with great success until the Vietnamese Communists took over Saigon in 1975. After that, some Little Brothers fled to the United States where they opened two religious houses, mission centers, and schools in the diocese of Brooklyn and in the archdiocese of Los Angeles to care for the Chinese and Vietnamese immigrants.

Today, the headquarters of the congregation is located in the diocese of Taichung, Taiwan, where they operate Viator Junior and Senior High School, a novitiate, and a large parish in Taichung city.

Outside mainland China, there are 60 Little Brothers; in mainland China, there are over 30. The number of Little Brothers both in and outside mainland China is gradually increasing.

The Little Brothers follow their patron saint, John the Baptist, as the herald of Christ who prepared the way for the Lord. Lebbe had a strong personality and expected each of the Little Brothers to have one too. Therefore he reminded them what our Lord had to say regarding the times of John the Baptist: "Since John the Baptist up to this present time, the kingdom of heaven has been subjected to violence, and the violent are taking it by storm" (Matt. 11:12).

The Little Brothers live a monastic life and a missionary life as well. They follow Lebbe's spirituality embodied in three principles: total sacrifice, true love for the people, and constant joy. They seek to practice Lebbe's teachings on how to live the life of the Beatitudes.

The congregation has three distinct charisms: the first is a family style of life, which means all members, ordained priests included, call one another brother, love one another as one family, and have equal rights. The second charism is inculturation. This means that liturgy, theological thought and expression, architecture, and lifestyle should be integrated into the Oriental culture and civilization (see Contextualization). The third charism is modernization — the congregation should be an up-to-date community and follow the renewal spirit of the Second Vatican Council, the *aggiornamento* principle. The Little Brothers strive to help undeveloped countries improve their citizens' quality of life. Evangelization, education, and social development are the primary fields of their work.

Stanislaus Su, with contributions from
John B. Thu Tran and the China Group

Little Flock

(Jidutu Juhui Cu). The Little Flock is an indigenous Chinese church started by Watchman Ni (1903-72; see Watchman Nee*) in Fuzhou in 1922. In China, Little Flock assemblies spread to Shandong, Jiangsu, Zhejiang, and Fujian. Although the concept of denominations is denounced and each local church is supposedly independent, in reality Shanghai serves as the headquarters of the different assemblies. There are no clerical orders, and members are addressed as brothers and sisters. Although everyone may participate in preaching, fellowship, and the breaking of bread, female Christians must cover their heads as a sign of submission to authority. The church does not observe Christian festivals such as Christmas or Easter or display symbols such as crosses.

Ni launched the Little Flock in Shanghai in 1928, and membership increased rapidly, in part because of Ni's prolific writing. He produced the periodicals *Revival, The Christian,* and *Preaching Notes,* as well as the three-volume book *The Spiritual Man* (1928) and *The Normal Christian Church Life (Concerning Our Missions)* (1940). Christians from other churches were asked to leave their denominations and join the Little Flock. In the 1930s and 1940s, the Little Flock was helped financially by the English Brethren Church.

In 1947, Ni and 27 fellow workers met in Fuzhou and decided on a different approach to evangelism. The practice in use till then had been the Antioch Principle, that is, the sending of apostles to new places, but the new approach would be the Jerusalem Principle, or the dispersion of believers, either voluntarily or because of persecution, to unevangelized areas where they would settle and begin new churches. The approach had already been used by Witness Lee (Li Changshou) in Yantai in 1933, when 70 families migrated to Shanxi and 30 families to the northeast. The result of their work was the establishment of 40 assemblies in Shanxi. The migration approach was adopted in Shanghai in the 1950s. The motto was "China for Christ in Five Years."

In 1948, Ni and his right-hand man, Witness Lee of Yantai Juhui Cu, popularized the Hand Over movement: church members were encouraged to surrender their business, property, and investments to the local church. With the wealth thus amassed, a regional training center for workers was established just outside Fuzhou. In 1950, Witness Lee introduced the Little Flock to Taiwan*. Assemblies are also found in Hong Kong*, the Philippines*, and Singapore*.

In 1952, during the period of the Three-Self Reform Movement, Ni and the Little Flock were accused of being corrupt capitalists. Ni's resistance to the confiscation of the property in Fuzhou was regarded as counterrevolutionary. Ni was arrested, imprisoned, and died in a work camp in 1972. In 1956, four leaders of the Little Flock in Shanghai were also arrested. The Little Flock organization itself was not considered counterrevolutionary, and it became part of the Three-Self Patriotic Movement. In 1958, most of the Little Flock assemblies supported the national church unification program, but some resisted and retained their distinctive worship.

The Gospel Bookroom, which was founded by Watchman Ni in Fuzhou, moved to Shanghai in 1927. The main activity of the Bookroom was to publish the works of Watchman Ni. Its publications were distributed to other assemblies. In 1948, it had a shopfront to sell its publications to the general public. It closed in 1950 when the Shanghai Assembly became part of the church unification program.

Bibliography

Whyte, Bob, *Unfinished Encounter* (1988). • Covell, Ralph, *Confucius, Buddha, and the Christ: A History of the Gospel in Chinese* (1986). • Kinnear, Angus I., *Against the Tide: The Story of Watchman Nee* (1973).

China Group

Little Sisters of Jesus

Religious order belonging to the spiritual family of Charles de Foucauld (1858-1916) and founded by Little Sister Magdeleine (1898-1989), 8 Sep 1939, in Algiers.

Charles de Foucauld (b. Strasbourg, France, 15 Sep 1858) entered the military academy of St. Cyr, where he lost his faith. Dismissed for indiscipline at the start of his military career and reinstated in the same year, he was sent with his regiment to Algeria. He left the army and in Jun 1883, disguised as a Jewish rabbi, went to Morocco, which was then closed to foreigners. While there, he was struck by the Muslims' simple and deep faith in God.

Returning to France on 28 Oct 1886, de Foucauld underwent a conversion, made a pilgrimage to the Holy Land, and then entered the Trappist* Monastery in France. He left the monastery on 23 Jun 1897. He desired to follow the hidden life of Jesus and spent the next three years as a servant at the Poor Clares* monastery in Nazareth.

On return to France, de Foucauld was ordained a priest. Seeking people unreached by the Gospel, he established his first fraternity at Beni Abbes, Algeria, near the Moroccan border. On 11 Aug 1905, he settled among the Tuaregs at Tamanrasset in the Hoggar, where he died on 1 Dec 1916.

In defining his vocation and mission, de Foucauld spoke of Nazareth as the place God chose to live as a poor man among humankind, working, praying, and making friends. De Foucauld lived a contemplative life expressed by the adoration of the Eucharist. His experience of God brought him close to his neighbors; and, in humble friendship and love, he welcomed all as brother or sister to his house, which he called a "fraternity."

In the footsteps of de Foucauld, Little Sister Magdeleine wanted to translate God's love for each one into everyday living and to go to minorities and outcasts. "I thought it was only a matter of my founding, in the Sahara, a very small congregation of nomad Little Sisters who would live under the tent for a part of the year. Then on 26 July 1946, I had the certainty, like a great light which overwhelms you, that the Little Sisters must spread throughout the world and become universal." On 16 Aug 1946, Magdeleine founded the first worker fraternity in Marseilles, France. In 1949, a fraternity joined a group of gypsies in their caravan. There was also an adoration fraternity in Beni Abbes, Algeria, where de Foucauld had begun his life of prayer and hospitality. In 1950, the Little Sisters put up their tent in the desert in El Abiodh, Algeria, and also established a foundation at Tamanrasset, where de Foucauld lived for 11 years and died.

Following the desire of de Foucauld, who said, "For the spreading of the Gospel, I am ready to go to the ends of the earth and to live until the last day of judgment," Father René Voillaume, founder of the Little Brothers of Jesus*, and Sister Magdeleine, accompanied by Sister Jeanne, went around the continents to spread the fraternity.

In 1953, the Little Sisters began work in Asia with an adoration fraternity near the Ganges River in Varanasi, India*, and another in Trivandrum, Kerala, among the Syro-Malankar Christians. In the same year, a community was also set up in Saigon and another among the mountain people in N'kaot, with a novitiate in Dalat, Vietnam*. The Little Sisters have survived the changes of regimes in Vietnam.

Fraternities have been founded in Korea*, among people suffering from Hansen's disease (leprosy*); in Japan*, where there are an adoration community facing the Russian island of Sakhalin and a fraternity among the Hi Sabetsu Buraku people; in Macau, where the adoration fraternity is near the border of the People's Republic of China; and in Hong Kong*, where the Little

Sisters lived among fishermen in their sampans. A group went to Colombo, Sri Lanka*, while another fraternity was founded in Bangalore, India. In Karachi, Pakistan*, and Kabul, Afghanistan, fraternities were begun among Muslims. In the 1970s, another community was founded among Christian minorities in Multan, Pakistan. The Little Sisters went to the Philippines in 1976 upon the invitation of Bishop Bienvenido Tudtud to establish a presence among the Muslims in Iligan diocese.

Most of the foundations have continued up to the present. There are now regional houses and houses of formation in Korea, India, Japan, and the Philippines. There are six fraternities in Korea, including a presence among factory workers in Taegu, and among people working in the garbage-dumping area in Nanzido. There are also six fraternities in India, among which are a fraternity in a slum area in Bombay and another among migrants and factory workers in Hosur. There are likewise six fraternities in Japan, one among the prostitutes in Ikebukuro. A fraternity was recently founded in Hiroshima. In the Philippines, the Iligan fraternity is temporarily closed, but a new one was opened among slum dwellers in Quezon City. In Hong Kong, there are a regional house, a house for refugees in Saikung, and another among workers in Aberdeen. The fraternity in Macau is among poor refugees.

In 1994, there were 1,400 Little Sisters from 64 nations in 60 regions and 280 fraternities around the world. About 130 Little Sisters are in Asia, living in approximately 30 fraternities; most of them already with native members. Their motto is "Unity in love, leaven in the dough, smile in the world."

Bibliography

Cry the Gospel with Your Life (1978). • Spink, Kathryn, *Call of the Desert* (1993). • Voillaume, René, *Seeds of the Desert* (1954). Marguerite Louise of Jesus

Liu Cho Wan, Anthony

(b. Sheung Tak, Guangdong, China, 1866; d. Sheung Tak, 3 Mar 1923). One of the most prominent local priests of the Hong Kong* Catholic Church and official translator of the church.

Liu entered the local seminary in 1886 for his philosophical and theological studies. After two years of pastoral practice in Hoi Fung District, he was ordained a priest on 1 Nov 1894. He was assigned back to Hoi Fung, where, according to a witness, "he worked humble and happy among many tribulations and fights, bringing to the troubled hearts the evangelical patience." He was always on the move, ever ready to visit even faraway villages on foot and satisfied with very little food. In 1910, he was recalled to Hong Kong, having won intense admiration from all those who knew him; they would remember him for a long time to come.

In Hong Kong, Liu helped at Rosary Church in Kowloon and, later, in the direction of the West Point St. Louis Orphanage. A man of exceptional learning and a gifted linguist, his advice was constantly sought, and family disputes were often referred to him. Because of his wisdom, experience, and acknowledged fairness, his decisions were invariably accepted as final.

Liu died in 1923 while staying in his native village, but his body was brought back to and buried in the Catholic cemetery in Happy Valley at the insistent request of Hong Kong Catholics.

Bibliography

Ryan, T., *The Story of a Hundred Years* (1959).

Sergio Ticozzi

Liu Huan Liming

(b. Anhui, China, 1897; d. 1970). Chinese Christian woman activist.

Liu was an influential woman among Christians in China*. She lost her father at a tender age and was much influenced by her Christian school. In 1911, she gained entrance to the Knowles College in Jiangxi, and, in 1914, she received a scholarship to study at Northwestern University in the United States. She returned to China in 1920 and was involved with the women's movement*. She headed the China Christian Women's Regulation Society *(Zhonghua Jidujiao Funu Jiezi Xiehui)* in 1921 and was also editor of the monthly *Temperance.* In 1926, she organized the China Ladies in Politics Association *(Zhonghua Nuzi Canzhen Hui)* and was elected its chairperson. In 1937, she led the organization in its resistance against the Japanese invasion of China.

After her husband, Liu Shenen, principal of Jianghu University, was murdered by a traitor, Liu went to Sichuan and became engaged in welfare work for women and children. She was known for her outspokenness. When the war ended, she returned to Shanghai and joined the China Human Rights Committee in 1946. After the establishment of the Republic of China, she was a committee member of the Chinese People's Political Consultative Conference and the vice-chairperson of the United National Women's Regulation Society. She was also an executive committee member of the National Young Women's Christian Association* (YWCA). She died as a result of intense persecution during the Cultural Revolution. She authored many books, one of which is *China Women's Movement.* China Group

Liu Ting Fang

(b. Chekiang, China, 1891; d. New Mexico, United States, 1947). Chinese Christian scholar and hymn writer.

After graduating from St. John's University in Shanghai, Liu left for the United States, where he studied at the University of Georgia, Columbia University, Union Theological Seminary (New York), and Yale University. He majored in psychology, philosophy, and theology. He made excellent grades and won many scholarships. Liu taught religious education at Union Theological Seminary in 1918 and was elected a member of the American Church History Society and a council member of the Religious Education Assocation.

Liu returned to China* in 1920 and became principal of Peking (Beijing) Teacher's Training College. He also taught psychology at Peking University and theology at Yenching University School of Theology.

During the period 1921-26, Liu was appointed dean of Yenching Graduate School of Religion. He went to the USA in 1926 and lectured at Yale and Hartford Theological Seminaries. In 1927, he represented the Chinese Church at the Lausanne meeting of Faith and Order.

After returning to China in 1928, Liu taught at Yenching and Chinghua Universities. Some time later, he resigned from Chinghua and taught mainly in Yenching University's psychology and religious education departments. When the National Christian Council was formed, Liu became one of the council members. From 1933 to 1935, he served as an executive council member. In addition, he was chairman of the China Christian Education Council (1925-28), the China Christian Religious Education Council (1931-34), the committee that edited the hymnbook *Pu Tian Song Zan* (Hymns of Universal Praise) (1932), and chief editor of *The Life* (1920-24), *The Truth* (1924), and *Truth and Life* (1928 on).

Liu went to the USA during the Sino-Japanese War. He was given an honorary doctorate by Middlebury College and an S.T.D. by Oberlin Theological College.

Liu's articles include "Discussions on the Problems of the China Church," "Revival Movement," "The Church and the Student Movement," "The Responsibility of the Missionary in a New Cultural Movement," and "The Psychology of Learning Chinese."

Bibliography

Cha Shih-chieh, *Concise Biographies of Important Chinese Christians* (1982). • West, Philip, *Yenching University and Sino-Western Relations, 1916-1952* (1976). • Lam Wing-hung, *Chinese Theology in Construction* (1983).

China Group

Liu Zhanern

(Herman Liu) (b. Hanyang, Hubei, China, 1896; d. Shanghai, 7 Apr 1938). Chinese Baptist* layman, educator, and civic leader.

Liu received his primary and secondary education in mission schools and became a Christian. He graduated from Suzhou University (Tongwu) in 1918 and went on a scholarship to the United States where he received a master's degree from the University of Chicago and a doctorate from Teachers College, Columbia University. He returned to China in 1922 and served as education secretary of the national Young Men's Christian Association* (YMCA) for six years. In 1926, he was chief delegate from China to the world YMCA conference in Finland. He took the opportunity to observe the educational systems in Europe.

In 1928, Liu was appointed president of the University of Shanghai (formerly Shanghai Baptist College). Liu assumed this position at a politically difficult time when private schools were required to be registered with the national government and the teaching of religion was curtailed. When the Japanese invaded Manchuria and Shanghai in 1931 and 1932, patriotic students disrupted learning at the universities in protest. When the Sino-Japanese War broke out in 1937, Liu moved the university to the International Settlement so that it could continue to function. Under his decade of leadership, the university grew and gained academic recognition.

Liu traveled much and made several trips to the United States. In 1929, he attended the World Education Conference in Geneva. In 1933, he was in Banff, Canada, for the conference of the Chinese Institute of Pacific Relations, of which he was a founding member. He also visited, along with E. Stanley Jones* and others, major American cities to promote interest in overseas missions.

Liu played a key role in the organization of the Chinese Baptist Alliance in 1930 and spearheaded the Forward Movement. He was also a primary figure at the Baptist convention in Jiangsu. He was a member of the National Christian Council (NCC), the Council of Higher Education of Christian Colleges, the China Christian Association, the War Relief Committee of the NCC, and the International Red Cross.

With the outbreak of the Sino-Japanese War in 1937, Liu organized an anti-enemy committee and was appointed by Hollington Tong, vice-minister of information, to try to persuade the United States to support China against the Japanese. He was assassinated, most likely by Japanese agents, in Shanghai on 7 Apr 1938.

Liu's wife, Wang Li-ming, who was from Anhui, was a supporter of the Women's Christian Temperance Union. Becoming increasingly critical of the Kuomintang, she attended the Chinese People's Political Consultative Conference as a delegate from the China Democratic League. She later served as a leader of the China Women's Federation.

In 1985, Liu was declared a revolutionary martyr by the People's Republic of China.

Bibliography

Boorman, Howard L., ed., *Biographical Dictionary of Republican China* 7 (1968).

China Group

Lockhart, William

(b. Liverpool, England, 1811; d. England, 29 Apr 1896). Pioneer missionary doctor.

Lockhart studied at the Meath College of Medicine in Dublin, becoming a fellow of the Royal College of Surgeons of England in 1834. He went to Canton in 1838, having been sent by the London Missionary Society (LMS) to help Peter Parker*, who had opened an ophthalmic hospital in 1835. Lockhart moved to take charge of a hospital in Macau in 1839. He was then dispatched to Batavia (Jakarta*) and returned in 1840 to begin medical work in Zhousan after the British occupied the island during the First Opium War. In 1843, he accompanied Walter Medhurst* to Shanghai and established the Shangdong Road Hospital. In 1852, Lockhart treated the wounded of the Small Sword Uprising, which was closely related to the Taiping Rebellion*. When the French colonial army moved to suppress the Small Sword Society, Lockhart volunteered to enter the city and lure them to surrender.

Lockhart went to Beijing in 1861 as a medical officer in the American embassy and established a hospital in the city. He retired from service in China* in 1867 and opened a private practice in England, where he died. He was commended by the British consul, Sir H. S. Parkes, for his political and missionary contribution in China. His writings include *The Medical Missionary in China* and *Notes on Peking and Its Neighbourhood.*

Bibliography

MacGillivray, Donald, *A Century of Protestant Missions in China, 1807-1907* (1979) • "Medical Missions at Home and Abroad" (monthly publication of the Medical Missionary Association, London). China Group

Lokayato. *See* Carvaka (Lokayato) Philosophy

Longobardo, Nicolo

(Lung Huamin) (b. 1559; d. Beijing, 11 Dec 1654). Longest-serving Jesuit* missionary in China* during the late Ming and early Qing Dynasties.

Longobardo arrived at Shaozhou from Macau in 1591 and served as Lazarus Cattaneo's* assistant, taking charge of the Shaozhou residence when Cattaneo went north the following year. Longobardo preached in the countryside, winning many converts among the villagers. In 1610, Matteo Ricci* summoned him to Beijing, and, when Ricci died, Longobardo succeeded him.

Longobardo was among a minority of Jesuit missionaries who objected to Ricci's adoption of *Tian* and *Shangdi* (terms found in the Confucian classics) as translations for the Latin *Deus* (God). After magistrate Shen Que filed a complaint in 1616, the missionaries were in danger, and Longobardo hid in the home of Yang Tingjun in Hangzhou. In 1622, the authorities of the Society of Jesus in Macau relieved him of his leadership post and replaced him with Giovanni Aroccia. As a missionary of ordinary status, Longobardo moved in and out of Beijing to places about 10 days' journey from Beijing, preaching the Roman Catholic* faith. From 1636, he preached in various places in Chanting, including Jinn, Tain, Qingzhou, and Wanan. He was still giving sermons at the Southern Cathedral when he was nearing 90. He died at age 95, having worked about 58 years in China. Upon news of his death, Emperor Shunzhi sent government officials to attend his funeral and donated 300 taels of silver for his burial expenses.

Bibliography

Treadgold, Donald W., *The West in Russia and China: China, 1582-1949* (1973). • Vath, Alfons, *Johann Adam Schall von Bell S.J. (1592-1666)* (1991). • Bertuccioli, G., "La figura e l'opera di Nicolo Longobardo," *Scienziati sciliani gesuiti in Cina nel secolo* (1985). • Goodrich, L. Carrington, *Dictionary of Ming Biography, 1386-1644* (1976). China Group

Lovers of the Cross

(Amantes de la Croix). Indigenous Catholic religious congregation of women.

Although the Lovers of the Cross in Asia was first formally established in Thailand* in 1667, its beginnings in Vietnam* may be traced back to 1640, when Christianity was banned by Lord Trinh Trang. Three young women from the Đong parish went to the capital to confess their faith, but upon their arrival, they discovered that Trinh Trang had reversed his decision. They returned home and decided to live together at Bái Vàng Village, Hanoi Diocese, Hà Tây Province, to encourage one another to do good works. They gradually persuaded other women to join them. Although Bái Vàng village did not have its own religious house until 300 years later, the Bái Vàng Convent is considered the pioneer house of the Lovers of the Cross in Vietnam.

In 1670, Pierre Lambert de la Motte*, who had been appointed vicar apostolic of Cochin China* in 1659, visited Tonkin on behalf of François Pallu*, who was on his way to Europe. In keeping with the objective of developing indigenous Catholic leadership, de la Motte established a local congregation for women at Kiên Lao Village, Bùi Chu Diocese, Nam Hà. The first two to profess their vows at a ceremony presided over by de la Motte in Pho Hien, Hung Yen Province, were Agnes and Paula. Others followed. The sisters were called Lovers of the Cross, and they were charged with teaching the catechism to young girls, evangelizing women and attending to their maladies, and baptizing infants (including those of non-Christian parents) in danger of death. In Vietnam, they served as a potent auxiliary force in mission work.

In 1671, de la Motte established a convent in the home of a pious Christian Annamese widow named Lucia Ky in Quang-ngai Province. Others were later established in other Paris Foreign Mission Society* (MEP) missions, even in Siam, Burma, and China.

An 18th-c. MEP missionary in Tonkin, Joseph Pavec, noted that many young girls forced by their parents to participate in superstitious ceremonies or to marry non-Christian youths (or those they did not love) joined the Lovers of the Cross and "consecrated themselves to God to avoid these dangers." By ca. 1750, they numbered about 500, of whom some 70-85% were in Vietnam. One hundred years later, the figure for Tonkin alone had risen to 673.

The Lovers of the Cross contributed more than their full share to the roll of Vietnamese martyrs. In the persecution of 1857-62, about 100 of them perished, while 80 of their convents were destroyed and all 2,000 residents therein dispersed. In the final outburst of persecution in 1885, another 270 were martyred along with some 24,000 other Christians in the vicariate of East Cochin China (Qui-nhon) alone. Vietnamese statistics showed there were 772 Lovers of the Cross in 1898.

In Vietnam, after the 1954 Geneva Conference, a large number of the sisters migrated to the South and effected mission work. The addition of new sisters in 1957 helped the older congregation in the North perform their apostolic work. In the South, the situation was more favorable, and the congregation was able to make better progress. In 1994, there were 3,224 professed Lovers of the Cross, 293 novices, and 2,268 postulants in Vietnam.

Bibliography

Launay, A. C., *Histoire Générale de la Société des Missions-Étrangères,* Vols. I and II (1894); *Mémorial de la Société des Missions-Étrangères,* Vol. II (1916). • Piolet, J. B., *Les Missions Catholiques Françaises au XIXe Siècle,* Vol. II (1903). • De Frondeville, H., "Pierre Lambert de la Motte, Évêque de Beryte (1624-1679)," *Revue d'Histoire des Missions* I (1924).

VALENTINO SITOY and ANNA PHAM THI THUC

Lozano, Balbino

(b. ?; d. 1907). Filipino Protestant martyr.

From Santander, Cebu, Lozano was a Filipino Protestant martyred by fanatics on 15 Dec 1907. The Santander Presbyterians*, then numbering about 45, had built a chapel scheduled for dedication on that day. The local Catholic* curate, one of the few Spanish priests then remaining in the country, acted out of a paranoid fear that the Protestants were going to kill him and burn his church.

As the court later established, the priest led 300 armed men in attacking the Protestants. Lozano, being the first man they encountered, was lanced to death. Found guilty, the priest and five others were sentenced to long prison terms. After the case was appealed, the Philippine supreme court upheld the convictions and sentences in 1909. The priest died in prison.

Bibliography

"The United States vs. Silverio Perez, et al.," *Philippine Reports XIII: Report of the Philippine Commission to the Secretary of War* (1908). • Sotto, A. C., *Mga Handuman sa Akong Tinuhoan* (1954). • Sitoy, T. V., Jr., *Several Springs, One Stream* (1992).

T. VALENTINO SITOY, JR.

Lu Bo Hong

(b. Shanghai, China, 1875; d. 1937). Well-known Catholic in China.

Lu was born into a family that had remained staunchly Catholic since their conversion in the Ming period. Devoted to his faith since his youth, Lu was highly regarded by the church. In 1913, when Catholic Action in China was founded, Lu was elected its president. In 1935, the organization held its first representative meeting, and he was elected presiding chairman. In 1936, Pope Pius XI conferred on Lu the honor of *la dignité de camérier de cape et d'épée.*

In 1912, Lu founded St. Joseph's Hospice. In 1924, 1926, and 1935 respectively, he founded Sacred Heart Hospital, St. Joseph's Hospital in Song Jiang, and Shanghai Mercy Hospital for the mentally ill. Lu also founded a junior high school. In 1922, he became the manager of the Chinese Electric Company and in 1924 took over the Water and Electric Company. In 1925, he founded the Wuxhing Iron and Steel Company; in 1928, Lu became general manager of the Nanto Water Company. In 1929, he founded Da Cheng Shipping Company. When war broke out following the Lu Gou Bridge Affair, Lu moved to the French territory. On 30 Dec 1937, he was found murdered. The authorities in the French territory failed to arrest the culprit, and so the case has remained unresolved.

CHINA GROUP

Lu Hao-dong

(b. 1868; d. 1895). Chinese Christian and anti-Qing revolutionary.

A native of Guangdong Province, Lu was born into a merchant's family in the neighborhood of Sun Yet-yet-sun's home. In 1883 he first received from Sun aspects of Euro-American culture and democratic revolutionary ideologies and determined to get rid of all ill-founded customs. In November of the same year, he destroyed idols in the Northern Precincts of the Village Temples and was pursued by the wealthy landlords. He escaped to Hong Kong, where he was baptized into the Christian church. Later he went to study at the Shanghai Telegraphic School. Upon graduation he became a translator at the Shanghai Telegraphic Office, later becoming its chief.

He returned to Guangdong in 1890 and traveled between Guangdong and Hong Kong to assist with Sun's revolutionary activities. In 1894 he drafted the petition letter to Li Hung-zhang and also traveled north with Sun to Tien-tsin for the petition. The trip achieved nothing, and they returned unhappily to Hong Kong, where they organized the Revive China Society, which was officially inaugurated in February 1895. Lu designed the Revolutionary Army's official flag, which depicted a white sun against a blue sky. An action date was set for October, but word went out unexpectedly. While Lu was preparing to destroy the party's membership list, he fell into enemy hands at his office. He was executed on November of the same year. Sun called Lu "the first person to have been martyred for the Republican Revolution in China."

CHINA GROUP

Luering, H. L. Emil

(b. Dolmenhorst, Oldenburg, 9 Dec 1863; d. Frankfurt, 14 Oct 1937). German Methodist* pioneer missionary to Malaysia*.

Luering came to Singapore* in 1889 after having studied the natural sciences, theology, and philology at the Universities of Zurich and Strassburg. This stood him in good stead as he became an expert in local culture and had the rare gift of speaking many of the languages of the Malay Peninsula.

In 1890, in a pioneering effort, Luering was sent to Sarawak to lay the foundations for missionary work among the Dayaks, who at that time were hostile to foreigners. From 1891 to 1907, he worked mainly among the Chinese in Singapore, Johor, Ipoh, Sitiawan, and Penang. While in Ipoh, he was commissioned by the British colonial government to visit China* and encourage Chinese immigrants to settle in Malaysia. The fact that Foochow Chinese communities are presently found in Sitiawan and Sibu is attributed to his initiatives.

Luering was also the first to take an interest in the Orang Asli in Perak. He studied their language and culture and paved the way for missionary work to begin in the 1930s.

In 1909, Luering returned to Germany, where he spent 25 years of his life teaching in the Methodist seminary in Frankfurt. While there, he cofounded the Frankfurt Society of Oriental Languages and thereby was instrumental in creating scholarly interest in the languages of the Malay Peninsula. His unfinished memoirs provide a valuable chronicle of the early missionary experiences of the Methodists in Malaysia at the beginning of the 20th c.

Luering stands out as a fine example of a missionary who took a keen and genuine interest in the culture and languages of the local people.

Bibliography

Luering, Emil, "The Sakai Dialect of the Ulu Kampar, Perak," *JSBRAS* 25 (1901); *Wundersame Wege* (Nürnberg, 1922). • Somner, Carl Ernst, "Wundersame Wege zum 100 Geburtstag Dr. Emil Luerings," *Evangelist* (1963).

HERMEN SHASTRI

Lumentut, Agustina

(b. Rampi, Sulawesi, 10 Feb 1937). First Indonesian woman moderator of a national church body.

Lumentut was the third of 12 children. Her parents moved from Minahasa to assist Dutch missionaries in Central Sulawesi in the 1930s. World War II*, the Japanese occupation, and the convulsions of the newly independent nation brought tumult to her growing years, during which her pastor father became her model.

At 17 Lumentut was accepted for ministry training. Though father was a key leader in the Christian Church in Central Sulawesi (GKST), which held its first synod in 1947, she battled poverty*, loneliness, and mockery as the only woman in her class. However, a Dutch professor encouraged her to continue, and a vision of the prophet Amos fired her imagination and paced her future ministry.

Lumentut became internationally known for her love of truth and justice, her effectiveness as a mediator, and her understanding of development as a God-given mandate. Her vision to enrich the lives of all led her to become a champion of the poor and underprivileged. Her ideas on community development balanced preaching and teaching with the fight to create a social climate which would enable people to progress out of poverty. She studied in Australia, India, and at Trinity Theological College, Singapore*.

Nationwide recognition came during the 1980s, when Lumentut was elected vice–general secretary of the Indonesia Communion of Churches (PGI). As the first woman member of the church's national executive, she worked for unity and servant leadership. In charge of the women's desk, she strove to enable women to play their part in ministry at all levels as lay leaders and pastors.

The 1990s saw Lumentut elected moderator of the Central Sulawesi Christian Church for two four-year periods, the first woman in Indonesia to hold such a post. She was also a member of the Central Committee of the World Council of Churches. After retirement she continued as ambassador at large for the national church. In 1998, she addressed Pope John Paul II and the Synod of Asian Bishops representing the Christian Conference of Asia*. She called for dialogue, noting that "among women also are found the gifts and graces of those who may appropriately be ordained to pastoral and sacramental ministry." Therefore "the church must order its life to be able to receive such gifts and graces."

Bibliography

Kirk, Margaret, *Let Justice Flow* (1997).

MARGARET KIRK

Luntungan, Rein Markus

(b. Karegesan, North Celebes, Indonesia, 10 Nov 1907; d. Jakarta, 10 Jun 1979). Minahasan church and ecumenical leader in Indonesia*.

Luntungan was one of four Minahasan students sent by Rev. Wenas to receive a higher theological education at the Theological Seminary in Bogor. While studying, he was chosen as a member of the Indonesian delegation to the International Missionary Council's conference at Tambaram, Madras, in 1938. Ordained in 1940, he served as director of the School of Native Pastors in Minahasa, secretary of the Christian Council of East Indonesia, moderator of the Protestant Church in Indonesia, and pastor of several congregations in Minahasa and Jakarta. He was also one of the founders of the Indonesian Council of Churches* (*Dewan gereja-gereja di Indonesia,* DGI). He spent his last years of service (1968-79) as the moderator of the Evangelical Christian Church in Minahasa* (GMIM).

As secretary of the Christian Council of East Indonesia, Luntungan warned the churches, especially in the eastern part of the country, against the general tendency to strengthen the tribal churches, for it would threaten the ecumenical movement developing in Indonesia. He also paid much attention to the development of youth in the church. After World War II, he understood that the youth of the churches in Indonesia faced sudden social changes even as they realized their potential power in labor and political movements. The church needed to guide these young people spiritually by coordinating the various youth movements arising from nationalism and by providing an umbrella institution through which they could fill their yearnings. The Conference of Church Youth Leaders held in Makassar (now Ujung Pandang) on 28-29 Feb 1948 accepted his opinions. This conference was significant in the ecumenical history of Indonesia as it was the first step for Indonesian Christian youth in making international connections with other Christian youth. As a result of this conference, the churches, particularly in the eastern part of Indonesia, were motivated to build youth centers as meeting places where Christian youth could come to meditate and to receive spiritual guidance.

Luntungan had the theological conviction that a person who knows the truth also has a responsibility to execute justice, which is seen as action, something which can be done to liberate society from poverty*, ignorance, and underdevelopment. Christians, therefore, have to administrate the diaconia of God in developing education, health care, agriculture, and other fields. The church must be an initiator, activator, and innovator in society, because Jesus Christ is the renewer in the development of God's world. Luntungan taught the Minahasan church to give much attention to educating the next generation. He said, "If you want to enjoy the fruit of your work as soon as possible, plant corn or rice; if you want to reap a richer but later harvest, plant cloves of coconut. But if you want fruit of eternal value, plant human lives."

Bibliography

Holtrop, P. N., *Selaku Perintis Jalan* (1982). • *Sepuluh Tahun dalam Kenanga Pendita Rein Markus Luntungan 1907-1979* (1989).

Arnold Parengkuan

Luo Wen Zao

(b. 1616; d. 1691). First Chinese bishop of the Catholic church in China*.

A native of Fuan, Fujian Province, Luo became one of the earliest members of the Catholic Church when he was baptized on 24 Sep 1633 after the preaching of two missionaries, a Spanish Dominican* and a Franciscan*, in his hometown. When the missionaries in Fujian were evicted to Macau in 1638, Luo followed. In the following six years, Luo went twice to Manila, studying Latin, Spanish, and philosophy at St. Thomas College on his second trip. His first application to join the Dominican order was rejected, and he was sent back to help a Dominican missionary. His second application in 1650 was accepted. He returned to continue his studies in Manila and was ordained on 4 Jul 1654, becoming China's first native Dominican priest. He was sent to do mission work in Fujian.

When the Johann Adam Schall von Bell* (Tang Ruo Wang) Affair broke out in 1664, all missionaries were deported to Guangzhou. Luo, being Chinese, had greater mobility and was left in charge of all mission work in Fujian. For the next six or seven years before the missionaries were allowed to leave Guangzhou, he visited Fujian, Zehjiang, Jiangxi, Guangdong, Shanxi, Shandong, Hunan, Sichuan, Jiangnan, and Zhili. The only Chinese priest then, he was commended by the Dominican missionaries to Pope Clement X, who made him a bishop. He was consecrated by an Italian missionary bishop, Bernadino delle Chiesa, in Guangzhou Franciscan Church on 8 Apr 1685.

After his consecration, Luo went to Hangzhou, then Nanjing, where he used the Jesuit* headquarters for his Jiangnan church administration. He visited Hangzhou and Shanghai often, and on 1 Aug 1688, he ordained three Chinese priests: Wu Yu Shan, Wan Qi Yuan, and Liu Wen De. On 10 Apr 1690, Pope Alexander VIII established the two dioceses of Beijing and Nanjing. Luo was appointed bishop of Nanjing diocese, but he died within one year of his appointment.

Bibliography

Biermann, Benno M., *Die Anfänge der neueren Dominikanermission in China* (1927). • Launay, A. C. *Histoire générale de la Société des Missions-Étrangères* (1894). • Moule, A. C., "The Life of Gregorio Lopez," *New China Review* 1 (1919).

China Group, translated by David Wu

Lutheran Church

Lutheran churches can be found in most Asian countries today, and like most of the other mainline churches here, they, too, trace their roots to early European and North American mission work. For instance, Bartholomew Ziegenbalg's* (1683-1719; Danish-Halle Mission) arrival in India* in 1706 marked the beginning of Lutheranism in Asia. Lutheranism first appeared in China* in 1831 when German minister Karl Gützlaff* (1803-51) touched Chinese soil. (Gützlaff was initially sent to Asia by the Dutch Missionary Society in 1823.) The first emissaries of the Rhenish Mission (Barmen) came to the

Batak country of Indonesia* in 1861. And James A. B. Scherer of the United Synod of the South (an antecedent of the Evangelical Lutheran Church in America) reached Tokyo in 1892.

According to the Lutheran World Federation (LWF), there are more than 50 Lutheran churches in 19 Asian countries, totaling nearly five million members. They are divided here into the following four groups:

- China area: Hong Kong*, Taiwan*
- East Asia: Japan*, Korea*, Philippines*
- Indian subcontinent: Bangladesh*, Myanmar*, India, Nepal*, Sri Lanka*
- Southeast Asia: Indonesia, Malaysia*/Singapore*, Thailand*

China area. In 1847 the Rhenish Mission (RM) and Basel Mission (BM) each sent two missionaries to China, thus marking the beginning of Lutheran mission work among the Chinese. The first American Lutheran missionary to China, Daniel Nelsen (1853-1926), arrived in 1890. A year later the Norwegian Lutheran Mission (NLM) would send the first group of Norwegian missionaries to China.

During the 1920s and 1930s — the height of Lutheran activity in China — no fewer than 30 Lutheran mission societies and 600 Lutheran missionaries were stationed here. By the end of 1949, when the Communist Revolution took place, 16 of these mission groups, together with the churches they founded, had joined the Lutheran Church of China (LCC), a nationwide union church established in 1920. According to its final report in the spring of 1951, the LCC, a charter member of the LWF since 1947, had 103,054 baptized members, including 83,126 communicants, along with 727 congregations, 180 ordained pastors, and 1,001 evangelists and Bible women.

During the 1950s the Lutheran church disappeared as Chinese churches entered the so-called postdenominational era. Yet Lutheranism did not vanish from the Chinese people. New Lutheran churches were established in Chinese communities outside mainland China, in places such as Hong Kong, Taiwan, Singapore, and Malaysia, by Chinese workers and missionaries who had previously labored in China. Today there are approximately 100,000 Chinese-speaking Lutherans around the world, including 42,000 in Hong Kong, 13,500 in Taiwan, 40,000 in Malaysia and Singapore, and 5,000 in North America, Europe, and Australia.

Hong Kong. There are seven autonomous Lutheran churches in Hong Kong, with 156 congregations and 42,000 members altogether. These churches are:

- The Chinese Rhenish Church, Hong Kong Synod (CRC), with 11,528 members, has been a member of the LWF since 1974. The CRC was officially established as a church in 1951 and is closely related to the RM, which began its China mission in 1847.
- The Evangelical Lutheran Church of Hong Kong (ELCHK), with 12,840 members, was established in 1954 by eight American and Scandinavian mission bodies that had previously labored in China and began mission work in Hong Kong in 1949. The ELCHK has been an LWF member since 1957.
- The Hong Kong and Macau Lutheran Church (HKMLC) has 2,145 members and was established in 1978 by the Norwegian Lutheran Mission, which began work here in 1949. The HKMLC joined the LWF in 1994.
- The Lutheran Church, Hong Kong Synod (LCHKS), with 8,100 members, was established in 1974 by the Lutheran Church–Missouri Synod (LC-MS), which started work in Hong Kong in 1949. The LCHKS joined the LWF in 1979 but withdrew in 1989.
- The South Asia Lutheran Evangelical Mission (SALEM), with 500 members, was established in 1977 by the Lutheran Church–Wisconsin Synod.
- The South Guangdong Lutheran Church, with 300 members, was established by the Breklum Mission in 1975. The mission began in Hong Kong in 1962.
- The Tsung Tsin Mission, Hong Kong (TTM), with 7,000 members, was established in 1952. It is closely related to the BM, which began its China mission in 1847. The TTM joined the LWF in 1974.
- The Christian Mission to Buddhists (CMB), founded in 1922 by Norwegian missionary Karl L. Reichelt (1877-1952) in Nanjing before moving to Hong Kong in 1930, has ceased to be a church as such, though it continues to serve Chinese churches as a study center for Chinese religion and culture.

Taiwan. There are six Lutheran churches in Taiwan totaling 134 congregations and 13,500 members. They are:

- The China Evangelical Lutheran Church (CELC), with 2,621 members, was established in 1966; the LC-MS began mission work in 1951.
- The China Lutheran Gospel Church (CLGC), with 225 members, was established in 1961; the Norwegian Evangelical Lutheran Free Church (NELFC) began mission work in 1954.
- The Chinese Lutheran Brethren Church (CLBC), with 2,300 members, was established in 1956; its mission was begun by the Church of the Lutheran Brethren, USA (CLB), in 1951.
- The Lutheran Church of ROC (LCROC), with 1,200 members, was established in 1956; its mission was begun by the NLM in 1952, and it joined the LWF in 1995.
- The Taiwan Lutheran Church (TLC), with 5,473 members, was established in 1954 by seven American and Scandinavian missions that had previously worked in China (1950). The TLC joined the LWF in 1960.
- The Lutheran Church of Taiwan (LCT), with 1,578 members and established in 1974, was begun by the Finnish Missionary Society (FMS) in 1956; it joined the LWF in 1984.

East Asia. Lutheran work began in East Asia at the

end of the 19th c., first in Japan (1893), then in the Philippines (1946), and later in South Korea (1958).

Japan. There are five Lutheran churches in Japan with a total membership of 32,500:

- The Japan Evangelical Lutheran Church (JELC), with 22,170 members, was established in 1922. It was begun by United Synod of the South, USA (1893), and joined the LWF in 1952.
- The Japan Lutheran Brethren Church (JLBC), with 1,256 members, was established in 1979. It was begun by the CLB (1949) and joined the LWF in 1979.
- The Japan Lutheran Church (JLC), with 3,059 members, was established in 1968 by the LC-MS (1948).
- The Kinki Evangelical Lutheran Church (KELC), with 2,549 members, was established in 1961. It was begun by the Norwegian Missionary Society (NMS) and the NELFC (1950) and joined the LWF in 1976.
- The West Japan Evangelical Lutheran Church (WJELC), with 3,466 members, was established in 1962 by the NLM (1949).

Korea. Lutheran mission in Korea did not begin until 1958, although the first Protestant appeal occurred in 1832, when Karl Gützlaff, the German Lutheran pioneer missionary to China, tried to deliver a Bible* to the Korean royal court.

The Lutheran Church in Korea (LCK), with 3,065 members, was established in 1971 by the LC-MS (1958) and joined the LWF in 1972.

Philippines. The only Lutheran church in this Catholic-dominated country is the Lutheran Church in the Philippines (LCP), with 25,000 members. It was established in 1957 by the LC-MS (1946) and joined the LWF in 1973.

Indian subcontinent. Lutheran churches are found in five countries in this area, but, aside from those in India, they are all very small.

Bangladesh. There are two Lutheran churches in Bangladesh:

- The Bangladesh Lutheran Church (BLC), with 2,700 members, was established in 1981 by the Danish Santal Mission (1979) and joined the LWF in 1986.
- The Bangladesh Northern Evangelical Lutheran Church (BNELC), with 8,603 members, was established in 1968 by the Norwegian Santal Mission.

India. India is not only the place where Asian Lutheranism began back in 1706, but it is also where 26% of the nearly five million Asian Lutherans live. The nine Lutheran churches here, all LWF members, have almost 1.3 million members combined. The United Evangelical Lutheran Churches in India (UELCI), established in 1975, serve as the India national committee of the LWF.

The Andhra Evangelical Lutheran Church (AELC) has 400,000 members and was established 1927. Its mission was begun by what is known today as the Evangelical Lutheran Church in America (ELCA) in 1842; it joined the LWF in 1950.

The Arcot Lutheran Church (ALC) has 34,000 members and was established in 1913. Its mission was begun by the Danish Missionary Society (DMS) in 1863, and it joined the LWF in 1961.

The Evangelical Lutheran Church in Madhya Pradesh (ELCMP) has 13,090 members. Established 1949, its mission was begun by the Swedish Evangelical Mission (1877). It joined the LWF in 1950.

The Gossner Evangelical Lutheran Church in Chotanagpur and Assam (GELC) is the first fully self-governing and property-owning Protestant church in India. It has 354,432 members and was established in 1919. Its mission was begun by four missionaries sent from Berlin in 1844 by Johannes Evangelista Gossner (1773-1858). It joined the LWF in 1950.

The India Evangelical Lutheran Church (IELC) has 56,493 members; its mission was begun by the LC-MS (1895), and it joined the LWF in 1970.

The Jeypore Evangelical Lutheran Church (JELC), with 140,000 members, was established in 1928. It was begun by the Schleswig-Holstein Evangelical Lutheran Mission (SHELM) in 1882 and joined the LWF in 1950.

The Northern Evangelical Lutheran Church (NELC), with 73,000 members, was established in 1950. Its mission was begun in 1867 by two former German Gossner Society missionaries, Hans Peter Boerresen (1825-1901), a Dane, and Lars Olsen Skrefsrud* (1840-1910), a Norwegian. It joined the LWF in 1950.

The South Andhra Lutheran Church (SALC), with 31,155 members, was established in 1945. Its mission was begun by the German Lutheran Hermannsburg Mission (1865), and it joined the LWF in 1952.

The Tamil Evangelical Lutheran Church (TELC) has 103,000 members and was established in 1919. It was begun by the Danish-Halle Mission, the oldest Protestant mission in India (1706). It joined the LWF in 1947.

Myanmar (Burma). The Evangelical Lutheran Church in Myanmar (ELCM) is the only Lutheran church in Burma, embracing two former Indian congregations (Tamil and Telugu) plus Burmese- and English-speaking members. It has 1,500 members and was established in 1978. It was begun by the German Leipzig Mission (1878) and the Indian TELC and AELC. It joined the LWF in 1978.

Nepal. The NELC in India has opened a number of congregations among Indians, mainly Santals, in certain districts of Nepal.

Sri Lanka. The Lanka Lutheran Church (LLC) was begun in 1927 by Indian pastors of the IELC as part of the LC-MS mission in South India. It has seven congregations and 685 members.

Southeast Asia. Over half of the nearly five million Asian Lutherans live in the four countries making up this area (Indonesia, Malaysia, Singapore, and Thailand), and about 96.5 percent of these are in Indonesia.

Indonesia. There are eight Lutheran churches in Indonesia, all of them members of the LWF. The vast majority of the 2.4 million Indonesian Lutherans live in the province of Sumatra and were started by the German Rhenish (not specifically Lutheran) Mission (RM).

The Batak* Christian Community Church (GPKB) has 2,000 members and was established in 1927, when the GPKB broke with her mother church, the HKBP. It is closely related to the United Evangelical Mission (VEM) of Germany and the Lutheran Church of Australia (LCA). It joined the LWF in 1972.

The Christian Protestant Angkola Church (GKPA), with 28,006 members, was established in 1974, when it separated from its mother church, the HKBP. It is related to the VEM and joined the LWF in 1977.

The Christian Protestant Church in Indonesia (GKPI) has 255,801 members. It was established in 1964, when it separated from the HKBP. It is related to the VEM and joined the LWF in 1975.

The Indonesia Lutheran Church (HKI), with 255,601 members, was established in 1927, when it withdrew from the HKBP. It is related to the ELCA and the Evangelical Church of Westphalia in Germany. It joined the LWF in 1970.

The Indonesia Christian Lutheran Church (GKLI) has 16,895 members. It declared independence from the HKBP in 1965 and joined the LWF in 1970.

The Protestant Christian Batak Church (HKBP) is the largest Lutheran church in Asia and the mother church of all other Indonesian Lutheran churches. It has 1,559,478 members and was established in 1930. It was begun by the RM (1861) and joined the LWF in 1952.

The Protestant Christian Church in Mentawai (GKPM) has 22,326 members. It was established in 1973, when independence was granted by the HKBP. Its mission work was begun by the RM in 1901, and it joined the LWF in 1984.

The Simalungun Protestant Christian Church (GKPS) has 187,834 members. Its mission was begun by the RM in 1903, and it gained independence from the HKBP in 1963. It joined the LWF in 1967.

Malaysia/Singapore. The Lutheran churches in these two countries are often grouped together due to their close geographical and historical background. There are four Lutheran churches here — two in Malaysia alone and two in both Malaysia and Singapore.

The Basel Christian Church in Malaysia (BCCM) has 45,000 members (including 32,000 Chinese-speaking and 13,000 Malay-speaking). It was established in 1925 by Hakka-speaking Christians arriving from China in 1882. BM support began in 1902; it joined the LWF in 1979.

The Evangelical Lutheran Church in Malaysia and Singapore (ELCMS) has 3,000 members. It was begun in the later part of the 19th c. by Tamil Indians immigrating to the Malay Peninsula. Established in 1907, it is supported by the TELC in India and the Church of Sweden Mission. It joined the LWF in 1968.

The Lutheran Church in Malaysia and Singapore (LCMS), with 6,764 members, was established in 1963. It was begun by a corps of international workers coordinated by the ELCA in 1953. It joined the LWF in 1971. Beginning in 1998, the LCMS became two independent churches: the Lutheran Church in Malaysia and the Lutheran Church in Singapore.

The Protestant Church in Sabah (PCS), with 30,000 members, was established in 1966. It was began by the BM and BCCM in 1953 and joined the LWF in 1995.

Thailand. Although the first Protestant missionary to arrive in Thailand (Karl Gützlaff in 1828) was a Lutheran, there was no Lutheran church in Thailand until a century and a half later.

The Evangelical Lutheran Church in Thailand (ELCT), with 2,150 members, was established in 1994. It was begun by the NMS, along with the FMS, ELCHK, and LCMS (1976). It joined the LWF in 1994.

Compared with Lutheran churches in Europe, North America, and Africa, the Lutheran church in Asia is relatively small, but it is a growing church. Between 1987 and 1997 membership increased by 25 percent — from about four million to nearly five million. The LWF has played an important role in the development of life and work in these churches and has carried out various social and relief projects in Asian countries besides the 19 mentioned above, such as Bhutan*, Pakistan*.

Bibliography

Bachmann, Theodore, *Lutheran Churches in the World: A Handbook* (1977). • Bachmann, Theodore, and Mercia Brenne Bachmann, *Lutheran Churches in the World: A Handbook* (1989). • Burgess, Andrew S., ed., *Lutheran World Missions* (1954). • Hsiao, Andrew, *A Brief History of the Chinese Lutheran Churches* (1998). • Ji Wong-Yong, *A History of Lutheranism in Korea: A Personal Account* (1988). • Sangeetha Rao, K., *Heritage, Achievement and Hope for the Future: A Research Survey of Lutheran Churches in India* (1982). • Tokuzen, Yoshikayu, *Japan Evangelical Lutheran Church in Mission from 1893-1993.*

Andrew Hsiao, with contributions from
Tokuzen Yoshikazu, J. Raplan Hutauruk,
and the China Group

M

Ma Xiang Po

(b. 1840; d. 1939). Well-known Chinese Catholic patriot.

A native of Dan Yang, Jiangsu Province, Ma left his home in 1852 for Shanghai and enrolled at Xu Hui High School. He joined the Society of Jesus* in 1862 and was ordained a priest in 1870. He devoted himself to the mission work in places like Ningkuo and Xuzhou, and others. From 1872 to 1874, he was in charge of Xu Hui High School. In Dec 1876, Ma voluntarily left the Society of Jesus, and, for the next 20 years, he was active in politics, holding several responsible positions. In 1901, he withdrew and lived quietly in Xu Jia Hui. In 1903, he founded Zhendan University, and in 1905, with other prominent people, founded Fudan University, serving as its first president.

In 1911, Ma resumed his involvement in politics but again withdrew to Xu Jia Hui from 1920 to 1936. When Japan occupied the northeastern part of China, Ma published several articles urging the people to rise up against the Japanese. His great influence upon the public established him as an "old patriot." He went to Nanjing in the winter of 1936 and was appointed a member of the Chinese government the following year. He moved to Guilin when the Japanese launched a massive invasion of China, and in 1938, when Guilin became dangerous, he attempted to move on to Kunming. Physically weakened, he died in Vietnam in 1939 while en route to Kunming. He wanted news about the war in China even on his deathbed. The People's Liberation Army took back his body from Vietnam and buried it in Shanghai. His tomb was destroyed during the Cultural Revolution; but in 1984, on the forty-fifth anniversary of his death, the city council of Shanghai rebuilt his grave and moved it to the Garden of Song Qing Ling. Several of his religious articles are available in Fan Hao's collection of his writings.

China Group, translated by David Wu

Ma Zuchang

(b. Guangzhou, Honan Province, China, 1279; d. Guangzhou, 1338). Ma's ancestors, who were of the Unggud tribe, for generations lived at Tianshan of Jingzhou (Puzi village, Siziwang Qi Xichang, Inner Mongolia Province) and were East Syrian (Nestorian*) Christians. His great-great-grandfather, Xilijishi, had served the Jin Dynasty as a military administrative assistant or *Bing ma panguan.* Xilijishi's descendants took the word *ma* (horse) from his official title to be their surname.

Zuchang's great-grandfather, Ma Yuehe, was a minister of rites. His father, Jun, was an associate administrator of Zhangzhou Circuit and settled in Guangzhou. Zuchang studied very hard from the time of his youth. When he grew up, he studied under a Confucian scholar, Zhang Xuste, who praised Zuchang's ability. During the Yuan and Song Dynasties, the imperial court operated under the examination system. Zuchang passed his examinations, ranking first in both the regular civil-service and the metropolitan examinations. In the palace examination, he placed second. He subsequently served as investigating censor, academician awaiting instructions, minister of rites, vice-censor in chief of Jiangnan, and deputy palace secretary at the bureau of military affairs. During his time in office, he never feared powerful and corrupt officials in the court but presented his complaints against them to the grand councillor Temuder. He also suggested to the imperial court that it set up military schools to train military recruiters.

Though Ma came from a family that had been Nestorian Christians for generations, he was well versed in Confucian studies. He was also gifted in writing prose and poetry. An emperor of the Yuan Dynasty praised him as the only great Confucian scholar in China. He edited the *Records of the Emperor* and authored *Great Teachings of Huangtu, A Brief Record of Chenghua, Golden Advices to Various Emperors,* and *A Brief Account of Ten Thousand Autumns.*

In the fourth year of the reign of Zhiyuan, Zuchang died at the age of 59. He was posthumously conferred the titles Honan assistant director of the right, senior military protector, and duke of Wei Prefecture.

China Group, translated by David Chng

Macau (Catholic Church)

When the Portuguese established their first settlement off the coast of South China* in Macau in 1553, there were traders and priests among them. They expected it to become a bastion of Christianity as well as an important trading port for the Far East, and, accordingly, they called it the "City of the Name of God, Macau."

Since the early 16th c., traders and missionaries had started to travel in the area. In 1521 Alvaro Margalhães may have been the first Portuguese Catholic priest to set foot on Chinese soil. In 1542 another pioneer, Estevão Nogueira, lived in Ningpo as the vicar of a Catholic community of 1,200 Portuguese, while in 1552 Francis Xavier*, coming from Japan* with the intention of entering China, died on Shangchuan Island, just south of Macau. In the 1560s, after the Portuguese consolidated their position in the Pearl River delta, more Jesuit* missionaries, from Goa and Malacca*, came to the region to carry out Xavier's dream.

In 1567 Bishop Melchior Carneiro was delegated by the pope to exercise his episcopal ministry in China and Japan. In 1569 he established the Santa Casa da Misericordia (Holy House of Mercy), a charitable association, and opened a hospital for the poor, later known as St. Raphael's Hospital, and the Leper Asylum (see Leprosy Work) of St. Lazarus.

The Diocese of Macau was formally established on 23 Jan 1576, covering the whole of the Far East, including Indochina, China, Mongolia*, Japan, and Korea*. In Macau there were then about 5,000 Catholics. However, because of the political conflicts due to the union of the thrones of Portugal and Spain, the situation there remained unstable until 1690.

Meanwhile, the Jesuits started the Mother of God (or St. Paul's) public school (operating already in 1565), which was made into a university college — the first in Asia — in 1594. In 1584, under the directives of A. Valignano* (1538-1606), M. Ricci* (1552-1610) and F. M. Ruggieri* (1545-1607) succeeded in entering and working in China. In 1579 the Franciscans* arrived, followed by the Augustinians* in 1586 and the Dominicans* in 1587. In 1588, with the establishment of Funai diocese, Japan was separated from Macau. In 1602 the building of the Mother of God's Church (popularly known as St. Paul's) was started, and the church was solemnly consecrated in Dec 1603.

In the second half of the 17th c., the Holy See established the autonomous vicariates covering almost the whole Chinese Empire, Mongolia (then known as Tartaria), Korea, and Indochina, thus reducing the immense area of the original Macau diocese. In 1690 Beijing and Nanjing were also established as autonomous Portuguese dioceses, while Macau was given back Guangxi, Guangdong, Hainan, and Tonkin (the latter only until 1696).

With the arrival of bishop João de Casal* in 1692, the political situation became stable. However, within the church, the Rites Controversy (see Ancestor Worship) was creating divisions and bad feelings among members of different religious orders. In 1705 the papal delegate C. T. Maillard de Tournon* arrived in Macau, after having been expelled from China because he did not meet with the favor of the emperor. These disagreements raised conflicts and brought persecution of Chinese Catholics in Macau, with the expulsion of the Augustinians in 1712 and the prohibition of preaching to the Chinese in 1746.

Meanwhile, in 1728 St. Joseph's Seminary-College was founded by the Jesuits for the training of missionaries for China and local students. In 1762 all Jesuits were banned from Macau. St. Paul's College was closed and then used as army barracks, while in 1784 the responsibility of St. Joseph's Seminary was taken up by the Lazarists*.

In 1834 all religious orders were banned in Portugal and in its colonies, resulting in Macau's complete loss of control over the China missions. In 1835 a fire destroyed the Mother of God Church, together with the adjacent St. Paul's College; only the church's façade remains, and it has become the symbol of Macau.

In 1841 the prefecture of Hong Kong* was established and detached from Macau, followed by Zhaoqing in 1848 and Guangdong and Guangxi in 1858. However, in 1866 the missions of Singapore* and Malacca were handed over to Macau by Goa. In 1908, following the 1903 agreement with the ecclesiastical authorities of Guangzhou, Macau exchanged the responsibility of Hainan Island with the area of Zhaoqing. In 1940 the Timor mission, with the establishment of the diocese of Dili, was cut off from Macau too, but it did not become practically autonomous until 1945.

During the Sino-Japanese War Macau was a place of refuge, attracting many people from the mainland. After World War II* and the Communist (see Communism) takeover in China, it again registered a strong influx of refugees. The church tried its best to provide relief and medical and educational facilities. Meanwhile, from 1955 its inland territories of Zhaoqing and Zhongshan became practically inaccessible.

In 1967, as a consequence of the Cultural Revolution in China, riots and disorder also broke out in Macau, forcing crowds of people to escape to Hong Kong or elsewhere; among them were many Catholics. In 1976 the victory of the Socialist party in Portugal raised great political uncertainty for the future of Macau, but fortunately both society and church recovered quickly. However, they again had to face a large number of refugees from the mainland. In order to provide for their spiritual needs, several pastoral centers were opened and put into operation, some of them specializing in youth services. These became the basis for evangelization work and religious formation.

On 1 Jul 1981 Macau handed back to the local hierarchies the parishes it had in Singapore and Malacca. After the start of negotiations between China and Portugal regarding the future of Macau, in 1985 Bishop Arquiminio da Costa* was invited by the Chinese government for an official visit. From 1988 Macau diocese had its first local Chinese bishop, Domingo Lam Ka Tseung*, who continued to encourage pastoral and evangelizing work in the parishes through a better arrangement of personnel and duties. As a member of the committee that drafted the basic law of the special administrative region, he also had to take up the responsibility to prepare the church for the return of Macau to China in 1999.

Present situation. Out of a population of 420,000 inhabitants, Macau has 22,129 resident Catholics (plus 13,043 out of the territory), with 89 priests (45 secular and 34 religious), eight brothers, and 153 nuns. The male religious orders working in Macau include the Jesuits (SJ), from 1562, now with eight priests and two brothers, working in schools; the Salesians* of Don Bosco (SDB), from 1906, now with 17 priests and six brothers, engaged in educational and social work; the Paulist Fathers (SSP), from 1987, now with three priests working in mass media and parishes; the Comboni Missionaries of the Heart of Jesus (Verona Fathers, MCCJ), from 1993, now with three priests working in pastoral work; one Redemptorist* Father (CSSR), from 1989, working with the mute and deaf; and one Camillian* Father, from 1982, engaged in spiritual formation.

The female religious orders operating in Macau include the Canossian Daughters of Charity (FDCC), from 1873, now with 22 sisters working in schools and with the aged; the Franciscan Missionaries of Mary* (Franciscan Sisters, FMM), from 1903, now with 46 sisters engaged in educational and pastoral work; the Missionary Sisters of Our Lady of Angels (MNDA), from 1929, now with five sisters engaged in education; the Daughters of Mary Help of Christians (Salesian* Sisters, FMA), from 1945, now with 17 sisters working in schools; the Precious Blood Sisters* (SPB), from 1946, now with eight sisters engaged in educational and medical work; the Dominican* Sisters (OP), from 1949, now with eight sisters working in schools and child care; the Fraternity of the Little Sisters of Jesus* (IJ), from 1956, now with two sisters sharing the conditions of the poor people; the Sisters of Our Lady of Perpetual Help (MPS), from 1956, now with eight sisters working with children and youth; the Daughters of St. Paul* (FSP), from 1959, now with five sisters working in book distribution and mass media; the Good Shepherd Sisters (RGS), from 1975, now with four sisters working with girls from problem families; the Sisters of Charity (MCA), from 1981, now with six sisters working with girls from problem families; the Maryknoll* Sisters (MM), from 1982, now with four sisters working in pastoral work and with the aged; the Sisters of St. Anna (HCSA), from 1987, now with 18 sisters engaged in the care of the aged and sick.

Other religious associations present in Macau include Opus Dei*, from 1989, with one priest and two volunteers; the Focolare* Movement, from 1983, now with three men and four women; the Little Brethren of Mary (IM), from 1986, now with six members; and the Volunteers Association of Don Bosco, from 1960, now with 11 members, engaged in catechetical and pastoral work.

There are 130 lay associations with 5,446 members; six parishes (the Cathedral, St. Lawrence, St. Anthony, St. Lazarus, Our Lady of Fatima, and Our Lady of Carmel in Taipa); three missions and 20 other churches or chapels; and 11 pastoral centers. There are also 35 educational institutions with 40,800 students, and Catholic social services are carried out by 25 charitable institutions.

The church in Macau is gradually becoming fully Chinese, although it still has to take care of about 9,000 Portuguese-speaking Catholics. Macau has been called the Rome of the Far East and the mother of missions in Asia. Indeed, it has played a central role in the spread of the Christian faith in the area, and it is still called to continue its bridge role, mainly with the church in China.

Bibliography

Texeira, M., *Macau e sua Diocese,* 16 Vols. (1940-77). • Basto da Silva, B., *Cronologia da Historia de Macau,* 2 Vols. (1992, 1993). • Rego, A. de Silva, *Les Missions Portuguaises, Agencia Geral do Utramar, Lisboa* (1958). • Montalto de Jesus, C. A., *Históric Macao* (1902; 2d ed. 1926; facsimile reprint 1984). SERGIO TICOZZI

Macau — Social Welfare Services (Catholic)

The social concern of the Macau Catholic Church started with the establishment of a charitable association, the Santa Casa da Misericordia (Holy House of Mercy), a hospital for the poor later known as St. Raphael's Hospital, and the Leper Asylum of St. Lazarus under the leadership of Mgr. Melchior Carneiro (1516-83) soon after his arrival in 1568 (see Leprosy).

Over the years, this tradition of social welfare has diversified to include care for abandoned babies, instruction of youths, refugees*, children, and the aged. More than 1,400 scholarships were awarded to needy students in 1994.

At the diocesan level, the Macau Caritas, member of Caritas* Internationalis (founded 13 Nov 1975 to better plan and coordinate services), provides training for disabled drivers, assistance and four homes for the aged, services to teenagers, hospital care and three homes for the handicapped, and two children's homes for unwanted babies (see Medical Work).

The two main social service institutions run by secular missionaries or religious orders have been the Secretariat for the Diocesan Services of Social Assistance (established in 1961 under the sponsorship of the USA Catholic Relief Services), which ceased to function in 1993, and the Ricci Social Services Center, started in 1952 for the benefit of refugees but now engaged in the care of the aged, family education, rehabilitation, and telephone counseling.

By 1995 the Catholic Church in Macau operated 35 educational institutions, two providing tertiary courses,

17 providing secondary schooling, 29 providing primary schooling, and 23 offering pre-primary programs. Five institutions offer commercial diplomas. The church also runs 25 charitable institutions: two children's homes, eight creches, six homes for the aged, three dispensaries, four student hostels, and two homes for girls from problem families.

Bibliography

Directorio Catolico de Macau (1995). SERGIO TICOZZI

MacGillivray, Donald

(Ji Lifei) (b. Ontario, Canada, 1862; d. London, 1931). Canadian Presbyterian* missionary who worked for 40 years in China*.

MacGillivray was the son of Scottish immigrants who were poor but devout Christians. A brilliant scholar, he was awarded a scholarship to study classical literature at the University of Toronto. He was ordained after his graduation and went to China in 1888 under the Canadian Presbyterian Mission, serving first as an itinerant preacher in Henan. He then went to Shanghai as an editor with the *Tongwen Shuhui,* later the Christian Literature Society (CLS), and eventually became its general secretary (1921). He raised a great deal of money in Canada for the CLS before resigning in 1929 because of ill health. He went to convalesce in Tunbridge Wells, England, and died in London in May 1931. His best-known works include *A Mandarin-Romanized Dictionary of China* and *A Century of Protestant Missions in China, 1807-1907.*

Bibliography

Barr, Patt, *To China with Love* (1972). • Brown, Margaret, *MacGillivray of Shanghai* (1968). • *Chinese Recorder* 62 (1931). CHINA GROUP, translated by PATRICIA SIEW

Mackay, George Leslie

(b. Canada, 21 Mar 1844; d. Tamsui, Taiwan, 2 Jun 1901). First foreign missionary sent by the Canadian Presbyterian* Church (CPC).

While still a teenager, Mackay decided to become a foreign missionary, having been inspired by William C. Burns, the great missionary to China*. In 1870, after his graduation from the University of Toronto and Princeton Theological Seminary, he revealed his intention to become a missionary to Rev. MacLaren, convener of the Foreign Mission Committee of the CPC. As the committee was not ready for this a new undertaking, Mackay went instead to Edinburgh for further evangelistic studies, especially under Alexander Duff*. On 14 Jun 1871, having heard Mackay's eloquent plea, the general assembly of the CPC decided to send him to the foreign field, preferably China.

Mackay left Canada on 19 Oct 1871, arriving one month later at the English Presbyterian mission of Swatow, China. He set out for Takaw (now Kau-Hsiong) in Formosa (Taiwan) at the end of the year. After obtaining an elementary knowledge of the customs, ethos, and language of the Taiwanese people from the English missionaries, he decided to go north and work where "the name of Christ has not been mentioned."

On 9 Mar 1872, in the company of Hugh Ritchie and Matthew Dickson, Mackay arrived in Tamsui, the principal site of the northern mission. He stated upon arrival: "One look toward the north, another toward the south, another far inland to the dark green hills, and I was content. There came to me a calm, clear, prophetic assurance that here would be my home, and Something said to me, 'This is the land.'"

Mackay began his missionary work in harsh conditions, living alone in a strange and hostile environment, learning Taiwanese from neighboring children, facing antagonistic mobs, curing sick yet reserved people, discussing faith issues with both local gentry and common folk, and recruiting native workers. On 9 Feb 1873, he baptized Giam Chheng-hoa, Gou Khoan-ju, Ong Tiong-chui, Lim Kek, and Lim Poe. Before his first furlough in 1880, he concentrated his labor along the Tamsui River and around the Taipei Basin, working predominantly among the Han settlers. After 1884, when the Sino-French War brought persecution to the northern church, he shifted to the northeastern coast, working primarily among the Kavalan aborigines.

In more than 30 years of labor, Mackay won 2,400 believers, established single-handedly 60 churches with affiliated clinics, built the Mackay Mission Hospital, and founded a women's school and Oxford College, forerunner of Taiwan Theological College and Seminary and Tamsui College, and trained 60 native pastors to assist in his work. Everywhere he went, he would bring "white medical water" (quinine plus lemon juice) for the cure of malaria and forceps for tooth extraction. He claimed, "No part of my preparatory training proved more practically helpful than the medical studies pursued in Toronto and New York."

Mackay married a Taiwanese, Tium Chhong-beng. His love for Taiwan is best summed up in words he wrote during his second furlough in Canada: "Far Formosa is dear to my heart. On that island the best of my years have been spent. There the interest of my life has been centered. . . . There I hope to spend what remains of my life, and when my day of service is over I should like to find a resting-place within sound of its surf and under the shade of its waving bamboo." He was an energetic, enthusiastic, and dedicated person who lived by his own motto: "Rather burn out than rust out!"

Bibliography

Mackay, George Leslie, *From Far Formosa* (1895). • Keith, Marian, *The Black-Bearded Barbarian: Mackay of Formosa* (1930). • MacKay, R. P., *Life of George Leslie Mackay, DD, 1844-1901* (1913). CHENG YANG-EN

Magellan, Ferdinand

(b. Portugal, ca. 1480; d. Mactan, 26 Apr 1521). Born of lesser provincial nobility as Fernao de Magalhaes, Magellan entered the Portuguese royal service as a page at court. In 1505, he went to East Africa and served in the Portuguese navy, which was in constant combat. Magellan rendered eight years of distinguished service as an admiral. Nevertheless, he was sent back to Portugal without any recognition. Angered by the king's refusal to grant him a promotion, Magellan transferred allegiance to Spain in 1518 and became Fernando de Magallanes, a subject of King Charles I.

Treaty of Tordesillas. The 1494 Treaty of Tordesillas was an agreement between Portugal and Spain that created a longitudinal demarcation of the earth. The area west of this line was for Spanish exploration, and the area east for Portuguese explorers.

Originally, Magellan's information and calculations led him to believe that the Spice Islands (the Moluccas*) lay to the east. However, the Spanish interpretation of the treaty calculated that the Moluccas lay to the west of the demarcation line, falling into their territorial sphere. Given this situation, Magellan's ambition to lead an expedition to the Moluccas was revived.

The expedition. King Charles I outfitted five ships with about 250 men under Magellan's command as captain-general. In Sep 1519, Magellan set sail with his armada from the port of Seville on a voyage of discovery.

The armada sailed southwesterly toward the continent of South America, where they made tentative explorations and replenished their supplies. In Oct 1520, having probed the eastern coast of South America, Magellan sailed through the southern strait for 38 days and reached calm, open water by November, calling it the Pacific Ocean.

Magellan's voyage proved to be turbulent as well. His expedition was fraught with starvation, illnesses, and dissension and mutiny, mostly brought about by the crew's sense of uncertainty and the distrust between the Spanish and Portuguese men. Magellan sailed form the Pacific with a reduced fleet of three ships (the result of desertion and shipwreck) but remained undaunted in his quest to find a new route to the Moluccas. On 6 Mar 1521, after sailing for three months and 20 days, they came upon the island of Guam, where they were able to replenish their supplies once more. Wary of the hostility and treachery exhibited by the natives, Magellan sailed further and landed on what is now the Philippine island of Samar on 16 Mar 1521. Magellan and his crew later established a settlement in the neighboring island of Cebu.

Magellan was welcomed by friendly natives led by their king, and an alliance was formed. He soon learned that not only was this island rich in gold and spices, but it was also ideally located for the exploration of neighboring islands. More important, he believed that the natives should be taught and converted to the Catholic faith. In a one-month's stay, Magellan converted the people of Cebu, led by their king and queen. He then urged the king of Cebu to have the neighboring chiefs convert to Christianity and be subject to his rule, whereupon they would be considered vassals of the benevolent Spanish crown and governed by Magellan himself. Those who refused were to be dealt with by force of arms. All the neighboring chiefs agreed, with the exception of Lapulapu, chief of the island of Mactan. Learning of his refusal, Magellan plotted to storm his village and bring Lapulapu to submission. He gathered about 60 men and sailed for Mactan. Magellan ordered only 49 of his men to disembark and attack. They were met by Lapulapu and about 3,000 of his men armed and ready. Magellan and his men were overcome. At dawn on 26 Apr 1521, after giving the order for retreat to his men, Magellan was slain by the villagers of Mactan.

Mistrust had been sown between the natives and Magellan's men. Fearing treachery, the Spaniards boarded their ships and sailed for home. On 8 Sep 1552, only the battered ship *Victoria* found its way back to Spain, with Juan Sebastian del Cano at the helm and 17 other survivors. Del Cano had sailed westerly from the Philippines toward the Indian Ocean and around the Cape of Good Hope, completing the first circumnavigation of the world.

Bibliography

Agoncillo, Teodoro A., and Milagros C. Guerrero, *History of the Filipino People* (1977). • Blair, Emma, and James Robertson, eds., *The Philippine Islands, 1493-1898,* 55 vols. (1902-9). • De la Costa, Horacio, *Readings in Philippine History* (1992). • *The Philippines: Pigafetta's Story of Their Discovery by Magellan* (translated from early French manuscripts, researched and commented on by Rodrigue Levesque) (1980).

José Mario C. Francisco

Mai Hoa

Legendary 16th-c. Christian princess in Vietnam*.

According to legend, Princess Mai Hoa, elder sister of King Le The Tong (1573-99), for whom she was regent, became acquainted with one of the missionaries who came to visit the court. The missionary's name was Fr. Ordonnez de Cevallos, whom she first met in 1591. His intelligence and handsome appearance led to her falling in love and wishing to marry him, despite his having made a vow to live a single and chaste life during his priesthood.

Cevallos explained that, as a man devoted to God, he was forbidden to marry, and he then proceeded to teach Mai Hoa about love for God. She proved content to devote her life to performing charitable activities for the people. Early on, she agreed to be baptized (1591) as a Christian and accepted Mary as her sponsor, which explains her name change to Mai Hoa (Mary Flower).

Mai Hoa raised money to build a convent in the area of An Truong, ancient capital of the Les, which today lies

Maitrichit Chinese Baptist Church

in the territory of the villages of An Truon, Lam Son, Quang Thi, Van Lai, and Phuc Lap, located on the left side of the Chu River toward the dam of Bai Thuong in Thanh Hoa Province. In 1942, there still remained a few vestiges of the former earthen fortress and royal palace. This piece of land was about one kilometer wide and three kilometers long. A village called Da-To (Christ) was found there; it may have been established by Princess Mai Hoa, who became superior of the convent. Next to the village, there is a worship base where some broken pieces of porcelain remain. This could be the location of the former chapel or convent. In the same area, there is a well called Da-To. These evidences discovered by Rev. Poncet could prove a historical core to the story about Princess Mai Hoa, although there is still debate as to its historicity.

Bibliography

Cevallos, Ordonnez de, *Historia y viage del mundo* (1615). • Du Caillaut, Romanet, *De la Veracité d'Ordonnez de Cevallos* (1916). • Phan Phat Huon, *Viet Nam Giao Su Tap* I (1998).

ANTHONY DO HUU NGHIEM

Maitrichit Chinese Baptist Church

Founded on 1 Jul 1837 as the world's first Protestant Chinese church, Maitrichit Chinese Baptist Church has been variously known as Wat Kok (Island Temple) Church and Chinese Baptist Church. It is strategically located amidst the Swatow Chinese of Bangkok, Thailand. In 1935, the church moved to Maitrichit Street, from which it derived its current name.

Pioneer evangelization began in Siam (Thailand) in 1828. Karl Gützlaff* baptized the first Chinese convert, Boon Ty. Rev. John and Eliza Jones, of the American Baptist Foreign Missionary Society (ABFMS), began Chinese worship and a school in 1833. On 8 Dec 1833, Boon Ty was rebaptized (by immersion) with two new Chinese converts. Boon Ty assisted the educational work and led 30 believers in worship. In 1835, Rev. William Dean* relieved Jones, preached to 50 on Sundays, baptized three more, and later began theology classes.

After the church was organized (1837), Boon Ty and three others either lapsed into opium* addiction or died, yet the membership gradually increased. Dean and two members, Tang Tui and Koe Bak, left in 1842 to establish the China Baptist Mission in Hong Kong. The small church continually addressed problems of illiteracy, child slavery, and the prevalent opium trade as this immigrant Chinese community struggled out of poverty* to create a mercantile sector in Siamese society.

Out of evangelistic fervor in 1860, the church formed a Society for Diffusion of the Religion of Jesus. Coupled with Dean's return in 1865, it helped the church to grow impressively. Chinese Baptists in Thailand claimed 500 members, did significant educational work under partial royal patronage, spun off one Siamese and five Chinese churches, and set up a program of theological training, eventually placing six ordained preachers in pastorates. Violent opposition in 1882-84 from a secret Chinese labor organization (the Red Letter Society) impaired Chinese Christianity in Siam, but by the time of Dean's retirement in 1884 the Christians had managed to consolidate their position.

Without Dean, theological* training regressed, as did the activity and membership of the church. After the Baptists left Siam in 1893, the church faltered and depended upon Ling Tong Baptist Convention for pastoral leadership and on American Presbyterians (the Fullers and Siegles) to do pan-Chinese evangelistic outreach around Bangkok.

Attempts to retain traditional rural Chinese values and culture were discouraging. Rural pastors were brought in from China*. Pastor Tieh led some members in a cultural revival (1926) by living on a rural rubber plantation, which was later sold. Its Long-hoo-Niam (Farmer's Ideal) Church moved at that time and was renamed Hua Khu Chae Church. Voices such as that of Rev. A. F. Groesbeck (ABFMS) clamored for training of indigenous urban Chinese leaders in Siam but to no avail.

Rev. Jacob Lim, the church's first self-supported pastor, brought the John Sung* revivals to Thailand in the 1930s. Allied bombing after 1941 forced out all but some elderly members. After the Japanese surrender in 1945, attendance grew, and the ministries of youth, music, and education again flourished.

Maitrichit Church joined the 7th District (Chinese) of the Church of Christ in Thailand (CCT) from its inception in 1934, with the guarantee of local church self-government. In 1954, however, the 7th District created a policy requiring that any baptism by immersion be preapproved by the district. So Maitrichit and its surviving daughter church, Hua Khun Chae, declared independence for five years, creating a new 12th District (Chinese Baptist) by 1959.

Aggressive religious and educational ministries such as Bethel Bible Institute (founded in 1962) contributed to the growth of the church from 200 members (1948) to 801 (1976). The Maitrichit Church Mission Society was formed in 1978. By 1987 Maitrichit had grown to 1,182 members and had planted most of the 28 churches in the 12th District. It was also a charter member of the Thailand Baptist Convention and the Chinese Congress on World Evangelism.

Bibliography

ABFMS, Records of the American Baptist Foreign Mission Society (Chiang Mai, Thailand). • Hervey, G. Winfred, *The Story of Baptist Missions in Foreign Lands* (1886). • Kho, Samuel, *150 Years of Thankfulness: A History of the Maitrichit Chinese Baptist Church, 1837-1987* (1987). • Smith, Alexander Garnett, *A History of Baptist Missions in Thailand* (1980).

DONALD S. PERSONS

Malacca

(Melaka). This city on the west coast of the Malay Peninsula was founded around 1400 by Paramesvara, a Malay prince who found refuge there from dominance by the Javanese Majapahit kingdom. It was ideally located to provide water and provisions for Chinese and Indian traders waiting for the changing monsoon winds which allowed East-West trade. By exercising political and military hegemony over rival port towns in the region, Malacca, under a succession of Malay sultans, became an important trade center. In 1511, the city was conquered by the Portuguese under Alfonso d'Albuquerque*, and a church was built in 1515. Portuguese sea power soon gave it a virtual monopoly in both the China-India trade and the spice trade with Europe. The Dutch broke the Portuguese monopoly with their conquest of Malacca in 1641, and the 1824 Anglo-Dutch treaty left the administration of the city in the hands of the British. By that time, its role as a center of trade was diminishing in the face of competition from Singapore* and Penang in the British Straits Settlements and Batavia (Jakarta) in the Dutch East Indies.

Malacca became the home of Francis Xavier* in 1545, but he left in disappointment, having failed to gain local support for further missionary activities. In 1557, the town was made a diocese and by 1613 had five churches and a Catholic community of over 7,000. Within a few years of the Dutch conquest in 1641, Roman Catholic religious activities were forbidden in the town. The Dutch did not encourage a Protestant alternative, so the Christian community was much reduced. Dutch missionary activity in the region, when it finally began, was based in the Indonesian archipelago, and the only remnant of Dutch Christianity in Malacca is the Dutch Reformed architecture of Christ Church, now used by an Anglican congregation.

Robert Morrison* and William Milne* established the Anglo-Chinese College in Malacca in 1815 as a means of both reaching local Chinese and preparing missionaries and missionary publications for the hoped-for opening of China. London Missionary Society (LMS) missionaries also prepared translations of Bible* books and other Christian literature in the Malay language and had a long association with Abdullah bin Abdul Kadir (Munshi Abdullah), a Malacca native. This association influenced the development of Malay literature, as missionary publications of Abdullah's work introduced vibrant colloquial writing into a literature previously dominated by stylized court language. Abdullah, for his part, influenced the use of Malay by several generations of missionary translators, including Benjamin Keasberry* and William Shellabear*. With the removal of the LMS from Malacca in 1843, the city's importance as either a missionary or Christian center languished.

Bibliography

Teixeira, Manuel, *The Portuguese Missions in Malacca and Singapore, 1511-1958* (1963). • Harrison, Brian, *Waiting for China: The Anglo-Chinese College at Malacca, 1818-1843* (1979). • *Christianity in Malaysia*, ed. Lee Kam Hing, Robert Hunt, and John Roxborogh (1992).

ROBERT HUNT

Malahay, Restituto C. and Enrique C.

(b. 1873 and 1877, respectively; d. 1965 and 1960, respectively). Filipino siblings, evangelists, and Presbyterian* ministers in the Philippines.

The Malahay brothers were from the landed Malahay clan of Guihulngan, Negros Oriental, Philippines, which since the early 1900s had contributed many lay and clerical leaders to the evangelical church. Numbered among the first students of Silliman* Institute in 1901, the brothers were baptized on 26 Oct 1902 as the first Protestant converts in Negros Oriental. In 1905, Presbyterian missionaries baptized the entire Malahay clan in Guihulngan, a total of 175 individuals who formed the nucleus of what soon became the largest Protestant local church in the Philippines, numbering up to 15,000 in the early 1930s (before daughter congregations separated).

In 1905, the Malahay brothers began preaching as volunteer student evangelists in towns near Dumaguete. Restituto was ordained in 1909 as the first Presbyterian minister in Negros Oriental. That same year, he became the first pastor of the Guihulngan Evangelical Church and concurrently the first Filipino stated clerk of the Cebu Presbytery. Enrique was ordained in 1912 and subsequently became pastor of Jimalalud Evangelical Church. Both brothers served their respective congregations for about half a century, exerting great influence on Protestantism in northern Negros Oriental.

Bibliography

69th Annual Presbyterian Board Report (1906). • "The Pioneers," *Philippine Presbyterian* VI (Apr 1915). • Magtolis, C. M., Jr., *Protestantism in Guihulngan: 1901-1959* (1980). • Sitoy, T. V., Jr., *Several Springs, One Stream* (1992).

T. VALENTINO SITOY, JR.

Malankara Orthodox Church, Mission Board

Statutory body of the church to promote the cause of mission.

Malankara Orthodox Church, having its apostolic origins from St. Thomas, was a fully indigenous church until the 16th c. Its emphasis was on witnessing through high morals and selfless service in the sociopolitical life of the vast non-Christian majority in the southern part of India. From the 16th c. on, the church was faced with the challenges of Western ecclesiology and mission, the result of its subjugation by the Roman Catholic* missionary bishop Alexis de Menezis. The subsequent turmoil in the history of this church, especially because of the ecclesiastical dominance of outside churches (Protestants: Anglican Church*; Syrians: West Syrian Church of Antioch), made the church ineffective in mission.

It was only in the 19th c. that the educated leaders of the church began to think about missionary activities among the non-Christians. In 1888, a missionary society, the *Threesaishubaho Sanghom*, was started in the state of Malabar, and branches were established in many places. In 1892, a meeting of the priests from Kollam, Thumpamon, and Niram emphasized the immediate urgency of mission under the auspices of the church. The great saint Mar Gregorios of Parumala organized a program of uplifting and preaching the Gospel to the backward classes. Bishop Patros Mar Osthathios, one of the metropolitans of the Malankara Church, founded the Society of the Servants of the Cross on 27 Sep 1924. Within half a century, this society had baptized 30,000 people. There were also the Paurastya Suvishesha Sanghom (established 1924), the outside Kerala diocesan mission (established 1930), the Thumpamon diocesan mission (established 1935), the St. Paul's Suvishesha Sanghom (established 1953), the Andamans Mission (established 1964), and the Bhilai Mission (established 1972).

Projects such as the Marriage Assistance Fund (MAF), Sick Aid Foundation (SAF), and the House Building Aid Fund (HBAF) were started by M. V. George (later Metropolitan Geevarghese Mar Osthathios*). The Yacharam Boys Village at Andhra Pradesh, India, which took care of the non-leper children of leper parents, and several other boys' homes were in need of consolidation and central support. These projects and programs were coordinated when the episcopal synod of the Malankara Orthodox Church decided to establish a mission board.

The mission board was constituted in 1978 with the following objectives: to consolidate the missionary activities already started by various agencies and individuals in the Malankara Orthodox Church; to decide the priorities in the missionary agenda of the church; to administer and monitor the observance of, and collections relating to, Mission Sunday (the first Sunday in July, when the church specially remembers the first missionary of the Church of India, the apostle Thomas*); to organize various programs for the internal mission; and to effectively carry out the external mission.

The mission board is also responsible for the Mission Training Center at Mavelikkara, Kerala, India, which is engaged in recruiting and training full-time, non-clerical mission workers. In addition, the board, which is also called the Malankara Orthodox Mission Society, is now coordinating the activities of various boys' and girls' villages and children's homes. It has also launched a program to start *balavadis* (nurseries for children) in all the villages of India where none as yet exists.

Jacob Kurian

Malankara Orthodox Monastic Orders

The Malankara Orthodox Church has monastic orders for men and women. There are more than 15 monasteries and 10 convents. The monks and nuns take vows of poverty, chastity, and obedience. The Order of Imitation of Christ (OIC) was started in 1918 at the Bethany Ashram, Perunad, Ranni. The Order of the Congregation of Sacred Transfiguration (CST) at Mount Tabor Dayara, Pathanapuram, was started in 1920. Various other orders followed: Mar Kuriakose Dayara (Mylapra, Pathanamthitta); Bethlehem Ashram (Chengamanadu, Kottarakkara); Holy Trinity Ashram (Angady, Ranni); St. Paul's Ashram (Puthuppady, Calicut); Mount Carmel Ashram (East Kallada, Quilon); Mount Horeb Ashram (Sasthamkotta); St. Thomas Ashram (Sooranad); St. George Mount Ashram (Chayalode, Adoor); Bethany Convent (Perunad, Pathanamthitta); Mount Tabor Convent (Pathanapuram); St. Mary's Convent (Othera); Bethlehem St. Mary's Convent (Kizhakkambalam); St. Mary's Convent (Adoor); Nazareth Convent (Kadambanad South); Basalel Convent (Sooranad); St. Mary Magdalene Convent (Kunnamkulam); and St. Paul's Sisterhood (Puthuppady).

Jacob Kurian

Malankara Syrian Christian Association

Highest body in the administration of the Malankara Orthodox Syrian Church*.

The Malankara Syrian Christian Association has a membership of 3,000 people. Every parish is represented in this forum by one priest and two laypersons. According to the constitution of the Malankara Orthodox Church, the Malankara Syrian Christian Association should meet to elect the catholicos and the Malankara metropolitan, the bishops, the trustees, and members of the managing committee. Also, the association is responsible for any amendment to the constitution. This association is probably the largest ecclesiastical assembly in the world directly linked with the administration of a church.

Jacob Kurian

Malaysia

Malaysia is strategically located at one of the major crossroads in Asia. West Malaysia, or Peninsular Malaysia, is situated at the southernmost tip of the continent of Asia. East Malaysia, comprising the states of Sabah and Sarawak, is situated across the South China Sea on the island of Borneo bordering Kalimantan* in Indonesia*. Malaysia has a total land area of 329,749 square kilometers.

Peninsular Malaysia, formerly called Malaya, was carved up and ruled by several Malay sultanates as early as the 14th c. Malacca* became an important trading post for vessels plying between Europe, India, and China. The Portuguese captured Malacca in 1511 and ruled it for over a century. The Dutch took over and ruled from 1641 until it was handed over to the British in 1795. The latter had been ruling Penang since 1786. Malaya, which included Singapore* at that time, gained independence from the British in 1957. A few days after gaining independence herself, Singapore, together with Sabah and Sarawak, joined the Federation of Malaya in 1963 to form Malaysia. Singapore left in 1965 to become an independent republic.

Malaysia is a secular democracy modeled after the British parliamentary system. It has a constitutional monarchy represented by the *agung* (king) as its figurehead. The governance of the nation is carried out by the prime minister and a federal cabinet. A rapidly industrializing society, Malaysia practices a free-market economy, although stringent control is exercised in a number of areas by the federal government. Besides being endowed with vast natural resources, Malaysia is also one of the world's largest producers of palm oil and rubber.

The Malaysian constitution states that "Islam is the religion of the (Malaysian) Federation but other religions may be practised in peace and harmony in any part of the Federation." The drafters of the constitution, as well as the nation's founding fathers, made it clear that having Islam as the official religion of the country does not mean that Malaysia is an Islamic state. The constitution also provides for every person the right to profess, practice, and propagate one's faith, but such propagation may be restricted by law among persons professing the religion of Islam. In other words, religious freedom, including freedom for all minority groups, is guaranteed in the Malaysian constitution.

Malaysia has a population of 22 million. The major ethnic groups are the Malays, forming 47% of the population, the Chinese, 25%, and the Indians, 7%. There are over 80 native people groups in Malaysia; and principal among them are the Ibans (540,000), Dusuns (250,000), and Bajaus (230,000). Malay is the national language of the country, although English as a second language is commonly used in commerce and industry. The use of Mandarin is largely confined to the Chinese community, as is Tamil to the Indian community.

The Malays are, by law, defined as Muslims and therefore practice Islam. Fifty-eight percent of the total population profess the Islamic faith; 26% practice a mixture of Buddhism, Taoism, Confucianism, and spiritism; 8% Christianity; and 7% Hinduism.

Nestorian* Christians en route to China through the Straits of Malacca in the 7th c. may have provided the earliest contacts with Christianity. Catholic diplomats, travelers, and priests also made use of the Straits of Malacca in their journeys to China during the Middle Ages. Nestorian and Armenian Christians (see Armenia) from what is today Eastern Turkey were resident in Malacca as traders during the Malay sultanate of the 15th c. The full impact of Christianity was brought by the arrival of the Portuguese, Dutch, and British colonizers.

Soon after the Portuguese capture of Malacca in 1511, Alfonso Martinez, a Catholic Franciscan, arrived to become the first parish priest of Malacca. His colleague, Duarte Coelho, built the first church in the country, St. Paul's Church in Malacca, in 1521. The Franciscans* were the precursors of the Roman Catholic mission. Francis Xavier*, the well-known Catholic Jesuit* priest, assumed responsibility of St. Paul's Church in 1545 for a brief period. The Dutch Reformed Church built Christ Church, Malacca, the first Protestant church in Malaysia, in 1753. This was handed over to the Anglicans in 1838. Benjamin Keasberry* of the London Missionary Society carried out a faithful ministry among the Malays and the Malay-speaking Chinese during this time. Francis Thomas McDougall* established Anglican work in Sarawak in 1847; Charles Moir a Presbyterian, labored in Penang (1851); and John Chapman, who was with the Brethren, also labored in Penang (1860). The Basel Mission (Lutheran) started work in Sabah (1882), as did the Methodists in Peninsular Malaysia through James Thoburn* and William Oldham* (1885).

Major missions that worked in Malaysia include the Franciscans, Jesuits, the La Salle*, Marist*, and Gabriel Brothers, the Daughters of St. Paul*, Sisters of the Holy Infant Jesus, and Good Shepherd Sisters on the Catholic front. Among Protestant missions were the London Missionary Society (1815), the Anglican Society for the Propagation of the Gospel (1856), the Methodist mission (1885), Lutheran missions from Germany, Norway, Sweden, and Switzerland (1882), Seventh-Day Adventist mission (1911), Borneo Evangelical Mission (1928), and the Overseas Missionary Fellowship (1953). Missions focusing on student work include the Scripture Union (1961), International Fellowship of Evangelical Students* (1962), the Navigators (1966), Campus Crusade for Christ (1968), Inter-school Christ's Ambassadors (1970), and Chi Alpha (1975).

The Pangkor Treaty between the British and the Malay sultans in 1874 recognized the latter as head of the religion of Islam and Malay customs and culture. This meant that Malays were to be considered Muslims, and hence little missionary work was carried out among them. During the emergency from 1948 to 1960, missionaries from China were encouraged to work in the "New Villages" created to resettle Chinese squatters (see Communism). In 1963, the government introduced an indigenization policy for the church under which all foreign priests and Christian workers can work only 10 years. The result, after some initial difficulties, has been the total indigenization of church leadership today. A 1974 government policy which offered mission school teachers the option to be civil servants has resulted in the church's losing her fundamental influence over her schools.

The early days of Christianity were largely focused on chaplaincy work among the Portuguese and later the British. The Catholic College General, which operated in Penang from 1809 to 1983, provided a significant base for Catholic church leadership in Malaysia. Anglican* work, which first started in 1847, enjoyed the favor of the British colonial government; and this continued to make steady inroads in both urban and rural areas. Methodist* work started in 1885 and was initially concentrated in a few pockets around the country.

Besides establishing churches, the Catholic and Methodist missions, and to a lesser extent the Anglican,

Basel, and Brethren missions, established outstanding schools. The Catholics, the Salvation Army*, and the Adventist mission also served the community well through their welfare homes, clinics, and hospitals. Over the years, these ministries have resulted in significant numbers being added to the church. In the last two decades, a greater emphasis on evangelism and charismatic* renewal have brought significant growth to the church.

Of an estimated 1.75 million Christians today, slightly less than 50% are Roman Catholics. The Orthodox Church, both the Mar Thoma and Syrian traditions, constitute a tiny fraction of one percent. Of the 50% who are Protestants, the largest three denominations are the Anglican, with 170,000; the *Sidang Injil Borneo* (Evangelical Church of Borneo), with 155,000; and the Methodist, with 130,000. Other significant denominations include the Basel Christian Church in Sabah (45,000), Seventh-Day Adventist (38,000), Assemblies of God (35,000), and the Protestant Church of Sabah (30,000). Smaller denominations include the Presbyterian*, Baptist*, Full Gospel Assembly, Lutheran* Church in Malaysia and Singapore, Christian Brethren, and the Evangelical Lutheran Church of Malaysia and Singapore.

The major Christian population is concentrated in Sabah and Sarawak, with some native groups such as the Kadazan, Dusun, Lun Bawang, and Kelabit almost totally Christian. Significant numbers are also found among the Chinese, Indians, and the *orang asli* (aborigines) in Peninsular Malaysia. Except for Sabah and Sarawak, Christians are largely found in urban centers. There are fewer Christians in the northern states of Kedah and Perlis and the east coast states of Kelantan, Trengganu, and Pahang.

The 1991 Population and Housing Census showed that the church had grown by about 12.5% in the preceding 10 years. More churches have been planted in the last decade (1990s), and even greater growth has taken place. Many churches today are led by high-caliber people, and there is an increasing level of cooperation across denominations. Evangelism and missions are increasingly emphasized, and there is a greater robustness of faith. Many denominations, including the Catholic Church, are experiencing renewal.

Bibliography

Hunt, R., K. H. Lee, and W. J. Roxborogh, eds., *Christianity in Malaysia — A Denominational History* (1992). • Ho, D. K. C., "The Church in Malaysia," in *Church in Asia Today,* ed. S. Athyal (1996); "Into the 21st Century: Challenges Facing the Church in Malaysia," in *Christian Reflections within an Emerging Industrialized Society,* ed. Thu En Yu et al. (1998). • Roxborogh, W. J., *A Short Introduction to Malaysian Church History,* rev. ed. (1989). • Koh, P., *Freedom of Religion in Malaysia — The Legal Dimension* (1987). • Muzaffar, C., *Islamic Resurgence in Malaysia* (1987). • *Information Malaysia Year Book 1998* (1998). Daniel K. C. Ho

Manalo, Felix

(b. Taguig, Rizal, 10 May 1886; d. Philippines, 12 Apr 1963). Filipino founder of the *Iglesia ni Kristo** (Church of Christ) in the Philippines*.

From Taguig, Rizal, Philippines, Manalo had little formal education but possessed a talent for leadership. Deeply curious about spiritual things, Manalo, a Catholic, went through a pilgrimage of faith, first among the messianic, nationalist Colorum sect of Mount Banahaw, and in 1904-13, as evangelist successively of the Methodists*, Presbyterians*, Disciples, and, by 1911, Seventh-day Adventists*. When a mutual break occurred with the Adventists in 1913, Manalo founded his own church in 1914, a cohesive and nationalist organization.

Manalo taught a unitarian theology and that he himself was the "angel of the East" in Rev 7:2. Slow in growth before 1945, the *Iglesia ni Kristo* thereafter increased rapidly to about 1.5 million in 1980.

Bibliography

Tuggy, A. L., *The Philippine Church* (1971). • Clymer, K. J., *Protestant Missionaries in the Philippines, 1898-1900* (1986). T. Valentino Sitoy, Jr.

Manikan, Braulio

(b. 1870; d. Capiz, 1928). First Filipino Baptist* evangelist, Bible* translator (into Ilonggo), and senator in the Philippines*.

From Ibajay, Aklan, Manikan was an ex-Catholic seminarian converted in Spain about 1897 through the Swedish Baptist missionary, Erick Lund. Becoming fast friends, the two collaborated in translating into Ilonggo the Gospel of Mark, which was published by the British and Foreign Bible Society in Madrid in 1900.

When the American Baptists sent Lund as their first missionary to the Philippines in 1900, Manikan came home with him and subsequently became the Baptists' foremost evangelist in Panay and western Negros. When Lund left the Philippines for the United States in 1912, he gave Manikan the major responsibility of overseeing the Baptist Mission's evangelistic work. Manikan became so popular, however, that he was elected Philippine senator in 1916.

Bibliography

Briggs, C. N., *The Progressing Philippines* (1913). • Laubach, F. C., *People of the Philippines* (1925). • Nelson, L. A., "Dr. Erick Lund, First Baptist Missionary in Iloilo" (unpublished manuscript). T. Valentino Sitoy, Jr.

Mar Gregorios Orthodox Christian Students' Movement

(MGOCSM). Organization for enriching fellowship, spirituality, and social commitment among students in India.

The MGOCSM was originally started as the Syrian

Students' Conference on 1 Jan 1908. The late Vattasseril Geevarghese Mar Dionysius, metropolitan of Malankara, provided leadership for the starting of the students' movement. In 1960 the movement adopted its present name.

MGOCSM has branches in high schools and at various arts, science, and professional colleges. Regular get-togethers for Bible study, prayer, and fellowship are the most important feature of the movement. The annual conference is an occasion for deeper and wider interaction among students in a spirit of prayer and fellowship.

MGOCSM of India attained a high reputation during the leadership of metropolitan Philipos Mar Theophilos. Student centers at Kottayam Trivandrum and Alwaye, the medical and engineering ancillaries, bookshops, orientation programs, arts competitions, and audiovisual projects, etc., are some of the most successful features of MGOCSM. The movement has also entered into the broader fellowship of the worldwide Orthodox Students Fraternity (Syndesmos). Its headquarters is located in Kottayam, Kerala. JACOB KURIAN

Mar Thoma, Abraham

(b. Kallooppara, Central Travancore, 1880; d. 1947). Metropolitan of the Mar Thoma Church of Malabar (1944-47).

Mar Thoma was consecrated bishop in 1917. He was called the great Christian missionary of India* by E. Stanley Jones*. He was instrumental in extending the mission activities of the church into the farthest regions of India. He gave shape to the Voluntary Evangelists' Association with a view to encouraging each member of the church to be a Christian activist. For three decades, he was a powerful speaker at the Maramon Convention and was president of the National Missionary Society for a few years.

In the struggle for national integration, the metropolitan opposed the move by Dewan Sir C. P. Rama Swamy Iyer to keep the princely province of Travancore out of the union of India. In this connection, the metropolitan made significant political addresses in the capital city of Trivandrum. Further, he convened an emergency meeting of the church council to register the protest of the church.

Mar Thoma's life was marked by simplicity, devotion in the context of ashram* centers, and strong verbal protests against autocratic isolationists. In a eulogy delivered on the demise of the metropolitan, Pattom A. Thanu Pillai, who was to become the first chief minister of Travancore, spoke on the valuable contributions of the metropolitan and categorized him over and against the bishops of other churches who were subservient to the isolationists. The metropolitan occupies a unique position in the political history of the province of Travancore. A. T. PHILIP

Mar Thoma, Juhanon

(b. Ayroor, Central Travancore). Metropolitan of the Mar Thoma Church of Malabar (1947-76).

Mar Thoma was consecrated a bishop in 1937 and metropolitan in 1947. He was consciously committed to leading the church in the new socio-political situation in independent India. His social and political views impressed the people. Early in his tenure of office, however, he had to brave the winds of internal dissension which led to the eventual separation of the St. Thomas Evangelical Church.

The metropolitan's Bhu-Bhavan Dan movement, which made rehabilitation facilities available to the landless, was welcomed and endorsed by the state government. His treatise on Communism*, which was sent to the parishes in a circular, and his warning to Christians and the upper classes reveal the spirit of discontent in the social transition of India. He suggested political alternatives involving the leftist and rightist parties in the local democratic setup. During the period of political emergency imposed by Indira Gandhi, the metropolitan vehemently informed her of the negative consequences it would involve. In fact, the prime minister had issued an order to arrest the metropolitan. However, after being advised by the chief minister of Kerala and other progressive forces, the arrest warrant was canceled.

The metropolitan was an ecumenical activist. He led the opening worship of the New Delhi General Assembly of the World Council of Churches (WCC) in 1961. Jawaharlal Nehru, the prime minister of India, then addressed the gathering. For a time, the metropolitan served as vice-president of the WCC. M. M. Thomas*, Indian theologian and ecumenist, was guided and greatly encouraged by the metropolitan at the beginning of his career. A. T. PHILIP

Mara Evangelical Church

The Mara Evangelical Church was founded in 1907 by Reginald Arthur Lorrain, an English Baptist from London. Originally named the Lakher Mara Church, it became the Lakher (Mara) Independent Evangelical Church in 1960, with the consent of the missionaries. After 1961, it was decided to hold the general assembly annually, and in 1967 the name was changed to the Mara Independent Evangelical Church, with headquarters in Saikao, India.

In 1970, the Mara Independent Evangelical Church of Burma split into the Mara Independent Evangelical Church and the Mara Independent Church. In 1987, they reunited to form the Mara Evangelical Church.

The Mara Evangelical Church initiated cross-cultural missionary activities in 1937, sending three missionaries to the Mru and Vakung (animistic tribes in the Rakhine), but evangelistic work had begun among neighboring Khamis as early as the 1920s. However, there is no record of any conversion, and the missionaries were forced to leave Rakhine during World War II*. Because of a lack of funds, missionary work to the Khami did not resume until 1966, but it has now expanded to include the people of Dai (Lemro Chin), Mru, Vakung, and Rakhine.

In 1985, the Evangelical Mission of Myanmar was officially established. In 1993, there were 29 missionaries and 26 native workers serving 31 churches, 4,062 believers, and 10 schools. The goal of the mission is to found 40 indigenous churches and to make them missionary churches by the year 2005. The Evangelical Mission encourages participation by other churches.

Joseph M. Zalei

Marantika, Simon

(b. Kuralele, Moluccas, 16 Nov 1909; d. Jakarta, 24 Sep 1989). Indonesian preacher and ecumenical* leader.

Marantika was one of the Indonesian preachers who took over the leadership of the church from the Europeans after the Japanese occupation of Indonesia at the beginning of 1942. After graduating from the Hoogere Theologische School (HTS), Jakarta, in 1940, he was ordained as a minister of the Protestant Church in the Moluccas (GPM) in the same year.

Marantika's role as a leader began during the period of the Japanese occupation in the Moluccas* (Feb 1942). In Oct 1942, he was appointed moderator by the GPM synod, a position he held until the Japanese capitulation (1942-46). He was a church figure whom the Japanese administration could accept and dialogue with. It was not an easy task, because the Japanese suspected Christians and their leaders of being accomplices to the Dutch. Still Marantika was appointed vice-chairman of the ecumenical organization the *Ambon-Syu Kiristokyo Rengokai* (Fellowship of Christian Churches in Ambon), formed by the Japanese administration, and comprising GPM, the Roman Catholics*, the Pentecostal* churches, the Seventh-Day Adventists*, and the Salvation Army*.

Marantika was both a leader and a shepherd for the GPM congregations. Through his pastoral writings in the newspaper *Sinar Matahari,* published in Ambon, he took care of the congregations who were experiencing difficulty, helping them get clothing and food and alleviating the oppression of the Japanese administration. In the midst of the suffering, Marantika admonished the members of the church to fulfill their calling (service, fellowship, and witness), even though it might mean a great sacrifice. At the same time he urged Christians to abandon the past attitudes of dependence upon others (the Dutch government and its church) and to try to meet their own needs through self-support. He stressed that the church should be completely self-supporting.

Marantika was also known as an activist for the ecumenical movement. In 1947, he attended the International Christian Youth Congress in Oslo, Norway, as chairman of the Union of Christian Youth in the Moluccas. In the same year, he was also appointed chairman of the Christian Council in East Indonesia.

Because of his reputation as a leader and his activities in the ecumenical movement, both inside and outside GPM, Marantika was appointed general secretary of *Dewan Gereja-gereja di Indonesia* (Council of Churches in Indonesia*, DGI). Apart from settling the internal problems of the churches, he was also involved in regional and international ecumenical activities (Christian Conference of Asia* [CCA], World Council of Churches [WCC], and World Alliance of Reformed Churches [WARC]). He was at one time vice-chairman of the East Asia Council of Churches (EACC, now CCA) and a member of the Division of Inter-Church Aid and Service to Refugees (of the WCC). After retiring as general secretary (1967), he was entrusted with a few duties by the EACC, e.g., secretary of the evangelism commission (1967-71) and director of the Program of Mutual Action for Mission (1971-78).

Bibliography

Mailoa, Derek, *Riwayat Hidup Singkat Ds. Simon Marantika* (1989). • Tanamal, Peter, *Gerakan Pemuda Kristen Dalam Gereja Protestan Maluku* (1972). • Marantika, Simon, *Bersama GPM Melintasi Masa Pendudukan Jepang di Maluku 1942-1945* (1989).

Mesach Tapilatu

Marcionites and Marcion

(d. ca. 154). The Marcionites were a group named after their founder, Marcion, one of the most influential Christian theologians of the 2nd c. He was born in Sinope, a port on the Black Sea in the Roman province of Pontus (part of modern-day Turkey) in Asia Minor. Little is known about his life other than that he was apparently the son of a bishop and heir to a shipping company with trading connections that extended from India* to North Africa and Italy. According to early Western Christian heresy specialists such as Justin Martyr, Irenaeus of Lyon, and Tertullian, he was for a time a member of the church of Rome where he came under the influence of a theologian by the name of Cerdo, who was accused of having gnostic beliefs. The story is that he was excommunicated in 144 C.E., but that story may be based on efforts of his detractors to discredit him.

What is certain is that Marcion and his followers founded churches all over the Roman Empire as well as within the independent Asian kingdoms of Osrhoene* and Commagene and the Roman-controlled provinces of Syria. This network of churches was provided with a copy of the scriptural canon established by Marcion, which included the Gospel according to Luke and the genuine Epistles of Paul; the Epistle to the Hebrews and the Pastoral epistles were not included. These churches became a formidable social force in western Asia until the establishment of imperial Byzantine Christianity in the region at the end of the 4th c. It is possible that many Marcionites joined the Manichaean tradition during the 4th c. They were a prominent presence along the trading routes to the east of Antioch. There is a large anti-

Marcionite corpus in early Syriac literature including Bardaisan*, the *Pseudo-Ephremian Commentary on the Lucan Parables,* Adamantius *(The Correct Faith in God),* and the hymns and prose refutations of Ephrem of Syria*.

According to the information provided by his enemies, Marcion and the Marcionites believed that there was a radical disjunction between the Old and New Testaments, and therefore between the God of the Hebrew Bible and the God of Jesus Christ. He found the image of God revealed in the Hebrew Bible to be one of incompetence, evil, and anger. Through his incompetence, this creator allowed evil to enter the world. All of the imperfections of the creation, including those exhibited in humanity, are the result of the incompetence of the creator. Marcion did not consider Jesus to be the Messiah anticipated by the Hebrew Bible. He understood the Hebrew Bible to anticipate that the advent of the Messiah would result in a positive social and political transformation and the restoration of Judaism. Such was certainly not the case with Jesus Christ.

Marcion rejected the Hebrew Bible as relevant for Christian faith but accepted it as a reliable record of the history of Judaism. Unlike the Jewish and Christian interpreters who used allegory to resolve problems of content and taste, Marcion apparently insisted upon reading the texts literally, as one would the Greek historians. The rules and regulations of the Hebrew Bible were deemed of no import for the Christian tradition. This approach to biblical interpretation may well have encouraged the more historical and analogical exegesis of the Christian theologians in Asia and Asia Minor. In these contexts, the exegetical styles of the Western and African churches, based on the Greek interpretative methods for dealing with classical Greek literature, did not become popular.

Marcion understood that the Messiah was a universal Savior through whom the entire universe would be redeemed. As such, he was not to be limited by relationships to Judaism and to matter. Matter was considered evil, and therefore Marcion was probably docetic, that is, he believed that Jesus appeared to be born of Mary but probably was not. Contrary to the Alexandrian and Syriac theologians, Marcion would therefore not have accepted the Platonic idea of the presence of God in each person. He did, however, according to Ephrem of Syria, have a developmental understanding of salvation that was to be worked out, with the assistance of God, as humans moved back toward reunion with God.

Marcion's works are largely lost. Described by the Western and Byzantine imperial churches as heretical, his works were not preserved. Among the lost works is one titled *Antitheses* in which Marcion articulated his understanding of the Bible and of the church. This volume apparently circulated widely in Marcionite circles.

Bibliography

Texts: Justin Martyr, *1st Apology* 26; Irenaeus, *Against Heresies* 1.27. • Tertullian, ed. and trans. E. Evans, *Adversus Marcionem* (1972). • Mitchell, C. W., E. A. Bevan, and F. C. Burkitt, eds. and trans., *St. Ephraem, Prose Refutations* (1912, 1921). • Adamantius, *De recta in deum fide.*

Secondary Literature: Bundy, D., "Marcion and Marcionites in Early Syriac Christianity," *Le Muséon,* tome 101 (1988); "The Pseudo-Ephremian Anti-Marcionite Commentary on the Lucan Parables," *Le Muséon,* tome 103 (1990) • Drijvers, H. J. W., "Marcionism in Syria: Principles, Problems, and Polemics," *Second Century* (1987-88); "Christ as Warrior and Merchant: Aspects of Marcion's Christology," *Studia Patristica* 21 (1989). • Hoffman, R. J., *Marcion: On the Restitution of Christianity: An Essay on the Development of Radical Paulinist Theology in the Second Century* (1984). • Wilson, D. S., "Reconsidering Marcion's Gospel," *Journal of Biblical Literature* 108 (1989). • Wilson, R. S., *Marcion: A Study of a Second- Century Heretic* (1933). • Wilson, S. G., "Marcion and the Jews," *Anti-Judaism in Early Christianity,* ed. S. G. Wilson (1986). David Bundy

Marist Brothers

Roman Catholic specialists in the field of mission education.

The Marist congregation was founded in 1817 by French priest Marcellin Champagnat. Its members do not receive sacerdotal ordination. In 1891, at the request of the apostolic vicar of Beijing, six brothers came to Nantang. Five more came to Shanghai in 1893 to help the Jesuit* fathers at St. Francis Xavier's College. Two years later, the number of brothers in Shanghai increased to 13, and they took over the administration of the college. In 1898, they opened schools in Hankao and Wuchang, where three brothers from the Shanghai community taught in the municipal Franco-Chinese School. In the five years 1901-5, they started schools in Kwanzhou, Chunqieng, Zhifu, Chuntou, Ningbo, Nanchang, and Weihuifu. In 1909, the Franco-Chinese School situated in the French concession in Shanghai was entrusted to them by both the Jesuits and the authorities.

In addition to schools, the Marist Brothers set up their provincial house, juniorates, and novitiate on the outskirts of Beijing* to ensure good administration and the training of future members from among the Chinese. In 1946, the Marist Chinese province counted 239 members in China, with 97 Chinese. Other nationalities included French, British, German, Hungarian, Portuguese, Swiss, and Irish. They had more than 21 secondary and primary schools under their care, rendering great service to the Chinese and the church in China.

China Group, translated by Dufresse Chang

Marks, John Ebenezer

(b. London, 4 Jun 1832; d. ca. 15 Oct 1915). English educator, priest, and missionary to Myanmar*.

Sent by the Society for the Propagation of the Gospel

(SPG) as a lay educator, Marks left for Moulmein in Dec 1859 and arrived in May 1860. He was ordained a deacon on All Saints' Day 1863 and transferred to Yangon where, with the help of Col. Sir Arthur P. Phayre, he started a school in "The Cottage" with money collected within five days. By the end of 1864, there were 220 boys, and the school was transferred to "Woodland" under the name of St. John's College. In 1869, 13 acres of land were purchased, and the college stands today as testimony to Marks's leadership and dedication.

With the exception of a small mixed school in Moulmein, there were no educational facilities for the poor and destitute. So Marks started the Diocesan Orphanage for boys within the walls of St. John's College.

In 1863, Marks met Thonzay Mintha, a son of King Mindon, in Yangon, and was granted permission by the bishop of Calcutta to establish schools in Mandalay. In 1869, he opened a school built at King Mindon's expense. Among his students were nine princes. King Mindon also built a church at Marks's request. It was consecrated in 1873 by Bishop Milman of Calcutta. Queen Victoria donated a font.

Marks retired in 1895 but continued tireless work in establishing missionary schools for the benefit of both Christians and non-Christians in Myanmar. He was also responsible for translating a part of the Prayer Book into Burmese. In 1879, Archbishop Tait awarded him the Lambeth degree of D.D. in recognition of his services to the church. In 1898, the Marks Memorial Fund was set up, first as a pension and, after his death, as a scholarship for university students.

Of Marks it was said that "it was not so much his educational or missionary activity that secured him this prominence. It was the influence of his own personality. He had a perfect genius for forming and keeping friendships with all classes and races." His contribution to education in Myanmar was comparable to Adoniram Judson's evangelistic work.

Bibliography

Marks, John Ebenezer, *Forty Years in Burma* (1917). • Chen, Paul A., *The Christian Church History* (1988).

SAW MAUNG DOE

Marques, Pero

(b. Nagasaki; fl. 1614-73; d. Cambodia[?], 1673). Japanese Jesuit* exiled to Macau* in 1614.

Marques was born to a Portuguese father and a Japanese mother. After being exiled, he labored among Japanese Christian exiles in the Khmer kingdom in 1616 and in the Annamese port of Faifo (Hoi An) from 1617 to 1619. Marques was the companion of Italian Jesuit Father Christoforo Borri in Annam from 1625 to 1627. Knowing the Vietnamese language, he also accompanied Father Alexandre de Rhodes* in opening a new mission in Tonkin in 1627.

Warmly received at the Trinh court, de Rhodes and Marques laid the foundations for Christianity in Tonkin. During their first year in Hanoi, they won some 1,200 converts. Marques returned to Macau in 1628 and in 1633-35 served as a pioneer missionary on the island of Hainan with a Chinese lay Jesuit from Macau, Brother K'iu Liang-pin (1561-ca. 1635), also known as Domingo Mendes.

Marques was back in Annam in 1652-73, being one of five Jesuits there. When the MEP (Paris Foreign Mission Society*) missionary Father Louis Chevreuil arrived in 1665, he found Marques and another old, sickly Jesuit in a Christian village of 40 persons in Lower Cambodia. Marques died in 1673 during a new outbreak of Khmer-Annamese conflict.

Marques had a brother, also a Jesuit exile, named Father Francisco Marques, who with others tried to reenter Japan in 1643, but was captured and kept under detention until his death in 1651.

Bibliography

Launay, A. C., *Histoire Générale de la Société des Missions-Étrangères,* Vol. I (1894). • Brou, A., "Les Statistiques dans les anciennes Missions," *Revue d'Histoire des Missions,* Vol. III (1929). • Pfister, A., *Notices . . . sur les Jésuites de l'Ancienne Mission de Chine,* Vol. I (1932). • Le Than Khoi, *Le Viet-Nam* (1955). • Texeira, M., *Portuguese Missions in Malacca and Singapore,* Vol. I (1961).

T. VALENTINO SITOY, JR.

Marshman, Hannah

(b. Bristol, England, 13 May 1767; d. Serampore, India, 5 Mar 1847). First woman missionary in India*.

Marshman was the wife of Joshua Marshman, the closest associate of William Carey*, the father of modern English missions in the East. Carey and other English Baptists founded the Baptist Missionary Society in England in 1792. In 1793, Carey and John Thomas came to Bengal and settled in the north. In 1799, the second group of Baptist missionaries, including Joshua and Hannah Marshman, arrived in Bengal and took shelter in the Danish settlement Serampore. Carey joined them and founded the Serampore Mission on 10 Jan 1800. Serampore took a pioneering role in spreading Christianity in Eastern countries.

Strangely, the Marshmans have received little attention from Baptist historians although the development of church history in North India is highly indebted to them. According to historian George Smith, Hannah Marshman was the first woman missionary to India, a fact that has not been officially recognized.

The missionary societies of Great Britain, in their formative stages, were adverse to women's participation in missionary work. Yet many zealous wives, without due recognition, shared the responsibilities of their missionary husbands. The Baptist women led in this respect, and Hannah Marshman was among the forerunners.

When Hannah came to India, women were subjected

to various inhuman practices, deprived of human rights, and imprisoned in ignorance. Hannah dedicated her life to the poor and distressed women of Bengal, who would turn to her for advice and relief in emergencies.

Hannah played a major part in organizing and developing the Serampore Mission. She took upon herself the role of leader of the Mission Union and earned money for the mission by maintaining a girls' boarding school. She worked among the local families and took in a number of orphans and destitutes. Serampore had a pioneering role in introducing female education in Bengal. Hannah played the leading part in this program when she started the Mission Girls' School in 1821. She died after serving 47 years in Serampore.

Bibliography

Chatterjee, Sunil Kumar, *Hannah Marshman (The First Woman Missionary in India)* (1987).

SUNIL KUMAR CHATTERJEE

Marshman, Joshua

(b. Westbury Leigh, Williston, England, 20 Apr 1768; d. Serampore, India, Dec 1837). Early English Baptist missionary to India*.

Marshman's father, John, was a weaver, a man of fervent piety, and his mother was a woman of superior mental gifts, as well as of deep spirituality. When Marshman was 15, a bookseller from Holborn, who was a former resident of Westbury Leigh, proposed to John Marshman that his son come to the metropolis to help in his shop. Joshua, who was passionately fond of reading, soon found himself in a congenial atmosphere, but his duties left him little time for leisure. The drudgery of walking the streets several hours each day and carrying heavy packages of books soon became nearly intolerable.

At the end of five months, Joshua returned to his rural home and took his place at his father's loom. He now had time for reading and before reaching 18 years of age had read more than 500 books. He found little sympathy for his thirst after knowledge among his acquaintances. When he sought admission into the church, he met with the objection that he had too much head knowledge of religion to have much heart knowledge of its truths.

In 1791, Marshman married Hannah Shephard, a lady who possessed in an eminent degree those qualities of heart and mind which fitted her to be the helpmate to her husband. Three years after their marriage, he accepted the position of master of a school in Broadmead, Bristol, and there he labored successfully for five years. Reading with ever-increasing interest the accounts of the mission work in India and the spiritual needs that vast field had, he resolved to offer his service to the Baptist Missionary Society. He was accepted and made hasty preparations to join the party of William Ward*, Charles Grant, and Brunsdon, who were about to set sail for India. After a voyage of five months, the vessel came to anchor on 5 Oct 1799. Captain Wickes sent the mission party in his boat to Serampore. Two members of the party, Grant and Brunsdon, men of great zeal and much promise, died soon thereafter.

On their arrival, the Danish governor, Colonel Bie, gave the strangers all the help in his power and gladly consented to the establishment of a mission in the settlement of Serampore. It was decided that Ward, who had a Danish passport, should visit William Carey* at Mudnabatty and invite him to establish in Serampore a mission embracing various types of mission work. The proposal met with Carey's approval and on 10 Jan 1800 he took up residence in Serampore.

The missionaries decided to live together and to dine at a common table. A house on a walled plot of ground was purchased near the riverside. In May, the Marshmans opened two boarding schools, having in view not only the education of children and youth, but also a means by which to support the mission work. These schools became the most popular and remunerative establishments of their kind in the region. Hannah Marshman*, who was known as the first woman missionary to India not only gave invaluable aid to the schools, in the home, and among the little band of Christians, but exerted a good influence in non-Christian circles as well.

In Apr 1800, the first Christian marriage from among the converts was solemnized, the bride being the daughter of Mr. Krishna, a carpenter, and the bridegroom the son of one of the first Brahmin converts. In Oct, the first death in the Christian community occurred. Marshman, who was at the time alone in Serampore, determined to take the opportunity to loosen the bonds of caste. A plain coffin was made and covered with white muslin. A Brahmin convert and a Muslim convert lifted the coffin and bore it to the cemetery. The deceased had belonged to a low caste before his conversion, and the sight of his being thus honored in burial was a lesson not easily or readily forgotten.

In Jun 1811, Brown University followed its compliment to Carey by conferring upon Marshman the honorary degree of doctor of divinity. In the summer of 1818, an English monthly periodical titled *Friend of India* was started by Marshman. The very first issue of this new periodical contained a critical essay on the burning of widows, a custom that urgently needed reform.

In the early years of the 1820s, Hannah Marshman suffered from ill health and was obliged to return to England. For 20 long years, she had toiled incessantly, allowing herself no respite from exacting cares and duties. In one of the letters sent to his wife while she was in England, Marshman wrote, "In a recent examination of our affairs we found that we had been able to contribute more than 40,000 pounds (nearly $200,000) to the work of the Serampore Mission, besides supporting our families. This filled me with joy."

In Mar 1823, Ward died. After his death Marshman wrote, "This is to be a most awful tremendous stroke and I have no way left but that of looking upward for help. I feel the loss of Mr. Ward as a counselor beyond everything."

In the beginning of 1826, Marshman made his first and only return visit to England. He reached his native village on a Sabbath morning and made his way at once to the old meeting-house, feeling almost a boy again when he heard himself addressed as Joshua. In the interests of the cause of the mission, Marshman visited the main cities of England and Scotland, where he spoke strongly of the needs of India, and even the need to "take all Asia for Christ." But he was homesick for India and rejoiced when his health was sufficiently restored to permit him to return. Marshman embarked for India on 19 Feb 1829 and reached Serampore on 19 May.

Marshman was the strongest polemicist of the Serampore Trio, a most vocal defender both of the Baptist mission and of the Christian faith. He lived the longest and even began the huge task of translating the Bible* into Chinese while residing in India.

The death of Carey, his beloved colleague, was a heavy blow to Marshman, which was followed by another tragedy. His youngest daughter had married Lieutenant Havelock (later Sir Henry Havelock). Mrs. Havelock was in the bungalow with her children when fire broke out in the night, and the Havelocks' youngest child was killed. The news of the death of his grandchild devastated Marshman; he was seldom afterward seen to smile.

A few days before his death, Marshman asked to be carried to the chapel at the hour of the weekly prayer meeting and placed in the midst of the congregation. There in a firm voice he sang a hymn that had often been used by his colleagues and himself during times of trial and difficulty.

Marshman passed away on the morning of 5 Dec 1837. Hannah Marshman died in Mar 1847 at the advanced age of 80. Both were buried in the consecrated acre in Serampore which encloses the mortal remains of this devoted band of missionaries who made the Serampore station famous in the annals of mission history. On one occasion, a dignitary from the Church of England remarked that, though there had been but a few men sent to Serampore, they were giants.

Bibliography

Potts, E. Daniel, *British Baptist Missionaries in India (1793-1837)* (1967). • Carey, Eustace, *Memoir of William Carey, D.D.* (1836). • Hopper, J. J. M., *Bible Translation in India, Pakistan, Ceylon* (1963). • Holcomb, H. Helen, *Men of Might in India Mission* (1901). • Laird, M. A., *Missionaries and Education in Bengal, 1793-1837* (OUP, 1972). • Sachchidananda, Bhattacharya, *A Dictionary of Indian History* (1962). Franklyn J. Balasundaran

Martin, Samuel

(b. 1839; d. 1910). Missionary preacher and evangelist known as the "Father of the Churas."

After graduating from Jefferson College, Canonsburg, Pennsylvania, USA, in 1861, Martin spent a year studying theology at the Steubenville Presbytery. He interrupted his studies to enlist with the Volunteer Infantry, 90th Regiment of Ohio, rising to the rank of first lieutenant. He resigned from the army in the summer of 1863 to resume theological studies at Allegheny Seminary (Pittsburgh, Pennsylvania). He did his third and fourth year of theological studies at a seminary in Xenia, Ohio. He was given the license to preach in the summer of 1865. In May 1866, he was appointed to the India mission by the General Assembly in Allegheny. He married Lydia Lucretia Mossman on 27 Sept 1866 and immediately proceeded to Philadelphia to begin the six-month voyage to India.

The couple spent 20 years preaching and teaching in India. They were the first to bring in the Ditts*, an outcast group who eventually became the backbone of the Punjab Church. The Martins championed self-support and pioneered mass movements*. He obtained land from the government to establish colonies for native Christians, an outstanding example being the Village Martinpur in District Sheikhupura of the Punjab (see Pakistan, Christian Villages). Martin himself baptized over 7,000 converts, concentrating in the areas of Zafarwal, Sialkot, and Pasrur, and working among people of both low and high castes (the Megs, Churas, Brahmins and Muslims). Among his protégés were leaders like Thakur Dass. Martin was affectionately called *Churean da Pir* (Father of the Churas). He emphasized education and taught skills to men and women to enable them to earn a living.

The Martins had five daughters and two sons. Three daughters became career missionaries in the Sialkot Mission. The independent Punjab Synod was organized before Martin's death.

Bibliography

Ballantyne, Agnes L., *The Samuel Martin Family* (1955). • Martin, E. Josephine, *An Evaluation of Dr. Samuel Martin's Life and Work in India* (1928). • Nisar, Julius I., "The History of the U.P. Church in Pakistan" (B.Th. research paper submitted to Gujranwala Theological Seminary, 1990). • Campbell, Mary Jane, *In the Shadow of the Himalayas* (1942). Arthur James

Martin, W(illiam) A(lexander) P(arsons)

(Ding Wei Liang) (b. Indiana, USA, 1827; d. Beijing, 1916). Author, educator, and American Presbyterian missionary to China.

The son of a preacher, Martin has been described as "the foremost American in China" and a "pioneer of modern state education in China." He graduated from Indiana University in 1846 and New Albany Theological Seminary (Indiana) in 1849. Ten days after graduating, he married Jan VanSant, and together they sailed for China on 23 Nov 1849. Four sons were born in China.

From 1850 to 1859, the Martins were based in

Ningbo. Martin publicly sought support from his government for the Taiping* Heavenly Kingdom, a revolt against the Manchu regime. In 1858, he was an interpreter for William B. Reed in the negotiations of the Treaty of Tianjin. After a furlough and a year in Shanghai, Martin went to Beijing in 1863, where he founded the Presbyterian Mission. In 1864, he became professor of English at the Tong Wen Guan (Interpreters College or College of Foreign Languages), which was established in Beijing in 1862 to train interpreters to help China in her negotiations with foreigners. By 1862, Martin had translated Henry Wheaton's *Elements of International Law* (written in 1836) for the benefit of the Chinese. He returned to the United States in 1867, did advanced work in international law and political economy, and earned his doctorate from Indiana University. He returned to China in 1869 to become president of Tong Wen Guan, where he expanded the eight-year curriculum to include international law and science. The college marked the beginning of Western education in China. In 1902, it was absorbed into the Imperial University.

Martin presented a controversial paper on the issue of Chinese ancestral rites at the 1890 General Missionary Conference in Shanghai. He made a distinction between cultural forms and religious content and suggested that kneeling and bowing before ancestors were not idolatrous acts. His views were strongly opposed by Hudson Taylor* and rejected by the majority at the conference.

Martin's evangelistic strategy was to work for mass conversions. He was convinced that whole families or communities should be baptized "as soon as they committed themselves to a better doctrine," even though they had little understanding of the new faith. The catalyst for mass baptism would be the conversion of the head of the family or community, with teaching and training to follow baptism. As the number of true converts grew, they would exert "an irresistible influence upon the community to which they belong."

Martin was deeply disappointed during the siege of Beijing by the Boxers: "From my 30 years of teaching international law they [the Chinese] had learned that the lives of Ambassadors were not to be held sacred." In 1900, he became president of Imperial University, founded in 1898. From 1902 to 1905, he was president of the University of Wuchang. He rejoined the Presbyterian Mission in 1911 but was mainly engaged in literary work from 1906 until his death in Beijing in 1916. Among the books he wrote in Chinese: *Tiantao Suyuan* (Evidences of Christianity), *Tiantao Hechiao* (Christianity and Other Creeds), and *Kowu Jumen* (Natural Philosophy, 7 vols.).

Bibliography

Anderson, Gerald H., et al., eds., *Mission Legacies* (1994). • Covell, Ralph, *W. A. P. Martin, Pioneer of Progress in China* (1978).

China Group

Martinez, Josefa Jara

(b. 1894; d. 1987). Filipino pioneer social worker and educator.

Martinez was an outstanding Filipino Protestant civic leader. After her studies in the United States, she worked for the Philippine Commission on Public Welfare (1921-34) and was the first Filipino executive secretary of the Associated Charities of Manila under the American Red Cross. She was a founder of women's clubs, *puericulture* centers, and the first national institution for homeless children. She also organized the Women's Civic Assembly of the Philippines*, the Community Chest of Greater Manila, and the Philippine Council of Welfare Agencies. She served as first president of the Philippine Social Workers Association and the first director of the School of Social Work, Philippine Women's University. A United Nations social work adviser in Guatemala and Mexico in 1956-64, she thereafter headed various Philippine service agencies.

Awards given Martinez included an honorary L.H.D. (Silliman* University, 1953); Legion of Honor Award (Philippine Armed Forces, 1954); Award of Merit (Philippine Social Workers Association, 1966); Gold Vision Triangle Award (Philippine Young Women's Christian Association* [YWCA], 1965); and Social Worker of the Year Award (Philippine Professional Regulatory Commission, 1978).

A woman of deep Christian faith and unwavering commitment to service, Martinez was an ordained elder and women's auxiliary president (1926-29) of the United Church of Manila, as well as president (1930-34) and then executive secretary (1934-46) of the Manila YWCA. Her readiness to serve was passed on to her children, including Amelita M. Ramos, wife of Philippine president Fidel V. Ramos.

Bibliography

Philippine YWCA Magazine (Jan-Mar 1987). • Sitoy, T. V., Jr., *Comity and Unity* (1989).

T. Valentino Sitoy, Jr.

Martini, Martino

(b. Trent, Italy, 1614; d. Hangchow, China, 1661). Italian Jesuit* missionary in Hangzhou in the early period of the Qing Dynasty.

Martini arrived in China* in 1643 when the Ming Dynasty was threatened and the country was in great turmoil. He had to move from place to place until 1646, when he settled in Hangzhou. By 1648, he had baptized 250 new converts. In 1650, the Jesuits, upon learning about the Dominican* and Franciscan* complaint to the Vatican against them regarding the veneration of Confucius and paying homage to ancestors, sent Martini to Rome to defend their position and to appeal against the Vatican injunction forbidding such practices. Martini arrived in Rome in 1654 and successfully brought Pope Alexander VII over to the Jesuit position.

In 1657, Martini sailed from Lisbon and returned to Hangzhou. In 1659, he built a church near Tian Shui Bridge, completing it in two years. He had a vast knowledge of Chinese geography and history and wrote, in Latin, *The New Atlas of China, The History of Ancient China,* and *The Record of Tartar War,* which were all published in Europe and hence available to only a few Chinese.

Bibliography

Martini, Martino, *De bello tartarico in Sinis historia* (1654); *Novus Atlas Sinosis* (1655/1981); *Sinicae historiae decas prima* (1658). • Demarchi, Franco, and Riccardo Scartezzini, eds., *Martino Martini, Umanista scienziato nella cina del secolo XVII* (1995). • Melis, G., ed., *Martino Martini: Geografo, Cartografo, Storico, Teologo* (1983).

CHINA GROUP, translated by DAVID WU

Maryknoll

Maryknoll, or the Catholic Foreign Mission Society of America, was founded in the United States in 1911 for the purpose of sending young American Catholics to foreign missions. Up until 1908, America herself was considered missionary territory by the Vatican and received missionaries from the Catholic countries of Europe. The two priest founders of Maryknoll, James Anthony Walsh and Thomas Frederick Price, felt the time had come for the American Catholic Church to take up its missionary responsibilities. Maryknoll would undertake the missionary work entrusted to it by the holy see with the objective of training an indigenous clergy who in due time would take over the running of the local church from the foreign missionary. For this reason, Maryknoll does not accept indigenous recruits into its own society. Rather, it directs them to their own local dioceses.

Maryknoll today comprises three missionary entities: the Maryknoll Fathers and Brothers, the Maryknoll Sisters, and the Maryknoll Association of the Faithful (lay missionaries). The foundress of the Maryknoll Sisters was Mary Rogers, associated from the beginning with James A. Walsh in the editing of the mission publication *The Field Afar.* The foundation date for the sisters congregation is 14 Feb 1920. Having been informally associated with Maryknoll's work since 1975, the laity formally established their own association on 15 Aug 1994.

Approval for establishing the society came first of all from the American bishops on 27 Apr 1911, and then from Pope Pius X on 29 Jun 1911, the latter date being considered by the Fathers and Brothers as their foundation day. In their application to Rome for permission to start Maryknoll, the founders expressed a preference for missions in China*. The Catholic Foreign Mission Society of America was incorporated under that title in New York State on 30 Apr 1912. Walsh was chosen as the first superior of the society, and he purchased a 93-acre farm in Ossining, New York, to serve as a seminary (Maryknoll headquarters to this day). The seminary opened its doors on 21 Sep 1912. The hill overlooking the Hudson River on which the seminary was built was called Mary's Knoll. Gradually the name Maryknoll came to be applied to the society as a whole. Today, one often sees the initials MM, meaning Maryknoll Missioner, after a Maryknoller's name.

China. After six years of preparation, the first group of Maryknoll missionaries, four priests, left New York for China in Sep 1918. Arrangements had been made between Walsh and Canton bishop J. B. de Guébriant of the Paris Foreign Mission Society* (MEP) to permit the Maryknollers to work in his vicariate until they could establish their own mission. The four members of that first group were co-founder Thomas F. Price, Francis X. Ford, Bernard F. Meyer, and James Edward Walsh (the middle name distinguishes him from co-founder James Anthony Walsh). The Maryknollers arrived in Canton in Nov 1918, just in time to celebrate with the French missionaries the armistice ending World War I. Their first place of residence in China was the town of Yangjiang on the coast in southwestern Guangdong Province, where they spent the first year studying Cantonese and learning mission methods.

After five years, in 1924, southwest Guangdong was separated from the vicariate of Canton and given to the charge of Maryknoll. Since the center of this first Maryknoll mission was the town of Jiangmen, the territory was called Jiangmen Prefecture. James E. Walsh, who would be the last foreign missionary to leave China in 1970, was appointed first prefect by Rome. Foreign missionary personnel in the prefecture in 1924 comprised 24 priests, three brothers, and 23 sisters. Catholics numbered 6,333. James E. Walsh was consecrated a bishop in May 1927 on Shangchuan Island, famous as the place where St. Francis Xavier* died in 1552.

During the 1920s and 1930s, as more Maryknollers arrived in China, the MEP missionaries turned over more of their territory to them. Eventually, in addition to Jiangmen, four other mission territories came under Maryknoll's supervision. These were Jiaying (present-day Meixian, in 1925) in northeast Guangdong Province, Wuzhou (1930) and Guilin (1938) in Guangxi Province, and Fushun (1932) in Liaoning Province. The first leaders (some of whom were later ordained bishops and their prefectures raised to the status of dioceses) were Ford in Jiaying, Meyer in Wuzhou, John Romaniello in Guilin, and Raymond Lane in Fushun.

Thus by the early 1950s, when Catholic ecclesiastical jurisdictions numbered 144 in China (20 archdioceses, 79 dioceses, and 45 prefectures), Maryknoll supervised five of them. From 1918 to 1949, a total of 237 priests, 173 sisters, 14 brothers, and two lay people (medical doctors) served as Maryknoll missionaries in China. In addition to preaching the Gospel and establishing churches, the Maryknollers were involved in educational and medical* works. In their five missions, they administered about 70 primary schools and some 50 clinics and dispensaries. The total number of Catholics in the five China Maryknoll missions in 1949 was about 67,000.

Hong Kong. Prior to the 1950s, the only institution the Maryknoll Fathers had in Hong Kong* was a business office, the purpose of which was to provide logistical support for the missionaries up-country in China. It was located at first on Austin Road in Kowloon and later in Stanley, where a centerhouse was built in 1935. Unlike the Fathers, the Maryknoll Sisters, who came to Hong Kong in 1921, took up apostolic work in the colony itself. They established the Maryknoll Convent School in Kowloon in 1925 and later the Maryknoll Sisters School on Bluepool Road on Hong Kong Island. They also built Our Lady of Maryknoll Hospital in Wongtaisin in 1961 and staff it to the present day.

After the expulsion of foreign missionaries from mainland China in the early 1950s, the Fathers became actively engaged in apostolic work in Hong Kong. In early 1952, Msgr. Riganti, chancellor of the Hong Kong diocese, assigned four refugee areas to the pastoral care of the Maryknoll Fathers. These were Tung Tao Tsuen, Kowloontsai, Ngautaukok, and Chai Wan. In addition to evangelization work, the Maryknollers started schools, most notably Maryknoll Fathers School in 1957, Maryknoll Technical School in 1966, and Kwun Tong Maryknoll College in 1970. Today, Maryknoll has 27 priests, two brothers, and 28 sisters doing church work in Hong Kong.

Taiwan. Maryknoll began work in the Taichung area of Taiwan* in 1951. Under the leadership of William Kupfer, the Maryknollers took up the study of the Taiwanese dialect for the purpose of evangelization in the three counties of Taichung, Nantou, and Changhua, which made up the Taichung prefecture under their care. In 1952, the Maryknollers were assigned to Miaoli County of the Hsinchu diocese, where the Jiaying missionaries from the mainland could use their Hakka dialect. William Kupfer was consecrated as the first bishop of the Taichung diocese in 1962; he retired in favor of a Chinese bishop in 1986. Today, there are 30 Maryknoll Fathers and 12 Maryknoll Sisters stationed on Taiwan, mostly involved in parish catechetical work.

Korea. Maryknoll's mission work in Korea* began in 1923 with the arrival of Patrick Byrne in Seoul. In 1927, Byrne was appointed the first prefect apostolic of Pyongyang in what today is North Korea. John Morris took Byrne's place as prefect in 1930. In 1939, William O'Shea was consecrated first bishop of the vicariate of Pyongyang, having been appointed prefect the previous year. O'Shea consecrated the Korean priest Francis Hong Yong-ho as his successor on 29 Jun 1944. After World War II*, Maryknollers returned in greater numbers to Korea. Byrne, as Rome's representative in Korea, was consecrated a bishop on 14 Jun 1949 in the Seoul Cathedral. Captured by the North Korean army after their invasion of the South on 25 Jun 1950, Byrne eventually died in a North Korean prison camp on 25 Nov 1950.

In 1958, Rome established the Cheong Ju vicariate, appointing Maryknoller James Pardy as the first bishop (consecrated 16 Sep 1958). In 1961, Rome established the vicariate of Inchon and appointed Maryknoller William McNaughton as first bishop (consecrated 24 Aug 1961). In 1969, Bishop Pardy resigned as bishop of Cheong Ju in favor of a Korean bishop, Nicholas Cheong. During the 1950s, the Maryknoll Sisters established a hospital in Pusan, to which refugees from the North flocked for treatment. Today, the approximately 30 Maryknoll priests in Korea are mainly involved in parish ministry.

Japan. Maryknoll formally began missionary work in Japan* in 1933. In 1937, Maryknoll was entrusted with the care of the Kyoto prefecture apostolic, and Patrick Byrne, who had served in Korea, was appointed prefect apostolic. In 1941, Byrne turned leadership of the prefecture over to Msgr. Paul Furuya. In 1946, Maryknollers began to return to Japan. In those years following World War II, Leopold Tibesar started the Ginza parish in the Mitsukoshi Department Store, where many of the future leaders of the Catholic Church in Tokyo were baptized. In 1954, Maryknoll accepted a mission territory in Hokkaido. In addition to parish work, Maryknollers became involved in various specialized apostolates, e.g., the Good Shepherd Movement for mass communications, justice and peace work, community development centers for the marginalized, and more recently setting up centers for alcoholism and drug rehabilitation. Twenty-eight Maryknoll priests and brothers work in Japan.

Philippines. Maryknoll formally began its work in the Philippines* in 1926 with the assignment of James Drought. The Maryknoll Sisters also arrived in 1926 and began a school in Malabon, which later developed into the nationally known Maryknoll College. From the 1920s to the 1940s, many Maryknoll Sisters arrived in the Philippines to do medical and educational work. The Fathers did not arrive in any large numbers until the China missions were closed to them in the early 1950s. Maryknollers from China at first took up parish work on the island of Luzon in 1952. From there they moved in 1958 to Davao, in Mindanao, because of the perceived greater need. They were led by Joseph Regan, the local Maryknoll superior, who was ordained bishop of Tagum in 1962. An average of six or seven Maryknoll Fathers arrived annually for the next 10 years.

From the 1960s to the 1980s Maryknollers staffed an ever-growing number of parishes in Davao, built schools and parish centers, started catechetical training and lay leadership programs, and established a social action center, a radio station, a seminary, a hospital, and a language school. Youth programs, the *cursillo,* farmers' organizations, credit unions and cooperatives, and the basic ecclesial communities were promoted on both the local and national levels. Above all, indigenous vocations of both men and women flourished. In fact, Maryknoll is best known in the Philippines for its Tagum Contribution, namely the establishment of a fully mature church with local personnel in positions of leadership, and with its own resources. Bishop Joseph Regan turned the Tagum diocese over to a Filipino bishop in 1980. There are now about 20 Maryknoll men and 15 Maryknoll sisters serving in various apostolates throughout the country.

In line with the missionary purpose of transferring leadership of local churches over to indigenous bishops and priests, Maryknollers began to leave their traditional Asian missions in the 1970s and 1980s to look for new mission commitments in other countries of Asia. They now have a small presence in each of the following countries: Indonesia* (1973), Bangladesh* (1975), Nepal* (1977), Thailand* (1982), Cambodia* (1989), and Vietnam* (1992).

Bibliography

The Catholic University of America, "Maryknoll Missioners" and "Maryknoll Sisters," *New Catholic Encyclopedia* (1967). • Wiest, Jean-Paul, *Maryknoll in China: A History, 1918-1955* (1988). • Kroeger, James, *Living Mission* (1994).

PETER J. BARRY

Mass Movements, Pakistan

The term "mass movements" describes a set of phenomena that were active in the northern Indian subcontinent, especially in the Punjab, in the 1800s and up to the 1930s (specifically, between 1870 and 1891). No precise beginning or end of the movements can be designated. They were by and large leaderless and produced no particularly prominent personages. They simply began to happen. Those who were part of the movements belonged to what are now known as the scheduled castes or the *Chuhra* (one level above what in India are known as the Dalits*). Hindu society regarded them as outcasts, unfit for any religious practice and not even permitted to enter a Hindu temple or shrine. The foci of the movements were the three major egalitarian religions of the subcontinent: Sikhism, Islam, and Christianity. Those who became Sikhs began to be known as the *Chhote* Sikh; those who became Muslims were known as *Musali;* those who became Christians were known as either *Nasari* or *Isai.*

Contemporary and subsequent commentators on the movements fail to find common ground concerning the motives that inspired them. Some have seen them as a public revolt against the caste system as such. Others consider that the basic attraction was that Sikhism, Islam, and Christianity teach that human beings are equal under God. Some Catholic and Protestant commentators have suggested that the movements were an expression of the fundamental monotheism and oppression of the lower- caste people. One of the key elements in the various mass movements was the appearance of local evangelists preaching to their own people. Missionaries were not the catalysts in these movements. Catholic commentators have also noted an unusual lack of doctrinal motivation in the first "converts." Acceptance of Christianity had for them the character of a declaration of allegiance. This allegiance was general and not tied to any specific group of Christians. Missionaries did not notice this quality at first and were disappointed at the apparent ease with which the *Nasari* ignored the differences between the Catholic, Anglican*, Lutheran*, Presbyterian*, and evangelical churches. A central plank of the convictions of the first converts seems to have been their desire to become People of the Book. They were very dedicated to Holy Scripture.

This doctrinal uncertainty might explain the lack of acceptance granted by Islam and Sikhism to the *Musali* and the *Chhote* Sikh. Christian churches strove, however, to integrate the *Nasari* into the Christian community. The descendants of the *Nasari* now form an integral, important, and influential part of the Christian communities in the north of the Indian subcontinent.

Bibliography

Latourette, K., *History of the Expansion of Christianity,* Vol. 7. • Macaire, Fr., "Les Conversions en Masse au Punjab," *Kerk en Missie, Analecta Ordinis Minorum Capucinorum* (1925), and materials concerning Fr. Constant Lievens, SJ, of Chota Nagpur. • Stock, Frederick and Margaret, *People Movements in the Punjab.*

JOHN ROONEY

McCormick Hospital

First modern hospital in northern Thailand (Chiang Mai).

McCormick Hospital grew out of Presbyterian* missionary medical work begun in 1872 by Charles Vrooman (1841-82), the first Western-trained doctor in northern Thailand. It was officially established in 1887 by James Cary and called the American Mission Hospital. James McKean (1860-1949) arrived in 1890 and, under his direction, the hospital became a growing, stable institution used by an increasing number of patients. McCormick Hospital advanced even further through the work of Edwin C. Cort (1879-1949), who first joined its staff in 1908. Cort oversaw the building of a new hospital complex on a new site, which was completed in 1925. He renamed the hospital after Mrs. Cyrus McCormick, who helped fund this expansion. In 1929, Prince Mahidol, a doctor and the younger brother of the king, added to the hospital's prestige by practicing medicine there for a brief period.

During World War II*, the Thai government seized the hospital and renamed it, but then turned it back over to the American Presbyterian Mission at the end of the war. Cort returned in 1946 and remained director until 1949, when he retired. McCormick is still one of the leading hospitals of northern Thailand. In 1992, King Bhumibol officially opened the rebuilt Mahidol Building, named in honor of his father. McCormick Hospital has played a leading role in the introduction of the advanced technologies of Western medicine into northern Thailand.

Bibliography

McFarland, George B., *Historical Sketch of Protestant Missions in Siam, 1828-1928* (1928). • Prasit Pongudom, *History of the Church of Christ in Thailand* (1984) (in Thai). • Presbyterian Church USA, *Records of the Siam Mission* (microfilm copy, Payap University Archives, Chiang Mai, Thailand). Onukun Konkaew

McDougall, Francis Thomas

(b. Sydenham, 30 Jun 1817; d. Nov 1886). Pioneer medical missionary and first Anglican bishop in Borneo.

McDougall's father and grandfather were soldiers in the East India Company, and he spent his childhood in Malta and Corfu. He trained as a surgeon in London (M.R.C.S. 1839, F.R.C.S. 1854) and studied at Magdalen College, Oxford (B.A. 1844, M.A. 1845). He married Harriette Bunyon in 1843. At the request of Rajah James Brooke*, they agreed to go to Sarawak along with W. B. Wright and his wife. Brooke reassured the Dyaks that their religion was not under threat, and it was intended that the mission would have a civilizing effect. In Jun 1848, the party arrived in Kuching, where they purchased land for building and started a dispensary downstairs in their combined quarters. The Wrights resigned early, but others gradually joined the mission especially after the visit of Bishop Wilson of Calcutta for the consecration of St. Thomas Church in 1851. The Society for the Propagation of the Gospel (SPG) took over support in 1853, and churches were built in Banting, Lundu, and Quop. McDougall became bishop of Labuan* in 1855 and of Sarawak in 1856. A synod of clergy was first held in 1864.

McDougall survived a Chinese revolt in 1857, but his enthusiastic role in an attack on "pirates" in 1862 brought controversy. His relationship with the rajah was complicated by a succession dispute in 1863. Despite an evangelical background and broad sympathies, he was uncomfortable with theological debate and is remembered more as a doctor and sailor than as a missionary. Rough in dress and in language, he was an impetuous personality well described as "a rollicking mixture of Bishop, Surgeon and Sea-Captain." His ministry secured the future of the Anglican* Church into an era when other denominations were granted access and the connection with the government became less direct. The McDougalls finally left Sarawak in 1867. In 1868, he became vicar of Godmanchester. His translation of the Book of Common Prayer into Malay was published in 1858, and his Malay catechism appeared in 1868. Harriette's sensitive descriptions of their adventurous life in Sarawak have remained in print.

Bibliography

Saunders, Graham Edward, *Bishops and Brookes: The Anglican Mission and the Brooke Raj in Sarawak, 1848-1941* (1992). • Taylor, Brian, *The Anglican Church in Borneo, 1848-1962* (1983). • Thompson, H. P., *Into All Lands: The History of the Society for the Propagation of the Gospel in Foreign Parts, 1701-1950* (1951). John Roxborogh

McFarland, Samuel G.

(b. Smith Township, Pennsylvania, United States, 11 Dec 1830; d. United States, 1897). Presbyterian* Church USA missionary educator who played an important role in the introduction of Western education into Thailand*.

McFarland graduated from Washington and Jefferson College in 1857 and from Western Theological Seminary in 1860. He married Jane Hays in 1860 and arrived in Siam in Sep 1860. They participated in opening the Phet Buri Station, the first Protestant missionary station outside of Bangkok, in 1861. McFarland founded a boys' school in Phet Buri, while his wife began a girls' vocational school there.

In 1865, McFarland published an English-Thai dictionary which went through several editions, last revised in 1890. In 1876, he published the first Thai hymnal containing notes. McFarland also translated a number of books of the Bible* and wrote or translated several theological works. His evangelistic work led to the establishment of the Bangkabun Church, the first Protestant rural church in Siam, in 1878.

At the invitation of the Thai government, McFarland resigned from the Siam Mission in 1878 to establish a Western-style school, the Suan Anand School, for princes and sons of nobility in 1879. The school was one of the government's first experiments in Western-style education; it grew fairly rapidly and expanded its base to include a wider class of students. The school was closed in 1892, and McFarland thereafter worked for the textbook department of the foreign ministry, where he prepared a number of texts for government schools. He retired to the United States in 1896.

Bibliography

McFarland, George Bradley, ed., *Historical Sketch of Protestant Missions in Siam, 1828-1928* (1928); Wyatt, David K., "Samuel McFarland and Early Educational Modernization in Thailand, 1877-1895," *Felicitation Volumes of Southeast-Asian Studies* (1965).

Herbert R. Swanson

McGilvary, Daniel

(b. Moore County, North Carolina, United States, 16 May 1828; d. 22 Aug 1911, Chiang Mai, Thailand). Presbyterian* Church USA (PCUSA) missionary who played an important role in the expansion of Protestantism into northern Thailand*.

Born of Scottish immigrant parents, McGilvary had a largely informal education. He taught school until he entered Princeton Theological Seminary in 1853, graduating in 1856, and returning to North Carolina to pastor two rural churches. He was ordained in 1857. He arrived in Thailand in 1858 as a member of the Bangkok Station, Siam Mission, PCUSA, and married Sophia Royce Bradley in 1860. In 1861, the McGilvarys participated in the opening of the Phet Buri Station, the first Protestant missionary station outside of Bangkok. In 1868, the McGilvary family moved to Chiang Mai, the chief city of Thailand's northern dependencies, and founded a new Presbyterian mission, the Laos Mission.

The McGilvarys worked alone for one year and were responsible for the conversion of six men by early 1869. A persecution of these Christians in Sep 1869 led to the execution of two, the scattering of the others, and the threatened closure of the Laos Mission. McGilvary's perseverance prevented the lapse of Protestant work in northern Thailand. From 1870 until about 1890, McGilvary was the unofficial leader of the Laos Mission and took charge of expanding its work, including establishing several rural Christian communities which became important Christian centers. In 1878, he played a leading role in obtaining the so-called Edict of Religious Toleration* from the Thai central government. This gave certain civil rights to northern Thai converts. The events surrounding that achievement also marked a step in expansion of the central government's power into northern Siam.

McGilvary made a number of exploratory tours beginning in the 1870s and going as far as the Shan States in Burma* and Yunnan Province in southern China* in the 1890s. Those tours laid the groundwork for the eventual establishment of mission stations in Lampang, Phrae, Nan, and Chiang Rai in northern Thailand, and the Presbyterian Kengtung Station in Burma. McGilvary's tours inspired the Laos Mission with the vision of a greater mission to the Thai peoples of China and French Indochina, which vision dominated mission work until the 1920s.

McGilvary is credited with introducing Western medicine into northern Siam. He supported theological training for northern Thai evangelists and pastors, and he played an important role in promoting mission boarding-school education, particularly for women. He also promoted literacy* among the northern Thai. As the Laos Mission expanded in the late 1880s, McGilvary became a father figure and honored role model for the mission. Though playing a less active role in mission decision-making, he continued active evangelistic work, including visiting established Christian groups, until his death on 22 Aug 1911 in Chiang Mai. Throughout his life, his colleagues and the general public held McGilvary in great esteem, and businesses and government offices in Chiang Mai were officially closed in mourning on the day of his death.

Bibliography

McGilvary, Daniel, *A Half Century Among the Siamese and Lao* (1912). • McFarland, George Bradley, ed., *Historical Sketch of Protestant Missions in Siam, 1828-1928* (1928). • Wells, Kenneth E., *History of Protestant Work in Thailand, 1828-1958* (1958). • Smith, Alex G., *Siamese Gold* (1981). • Swanson, Herbert R., *Krischak Muang Nua: A Study in Northern Thai Church History* (1984).

HERBERT R. SWANSON

McKean, James W.

(b. Scotch Grove, Iowa, United States, 10 Mar 1860; d. Long Beach, California, United States, 9 Feb 1949). Presbyterian* Church USA missionary who founded Thailand's first leprosarium.

McKean studied at Lennox College, Iowa, and received his M.D. degree from the Bellevue Medical College, New York City, in 1882. He married Laura B. Willson in 1889 and began missionary work at the mission hospital in Chiang Mai, Thailand, the same year. McKean developed the hospital, later named McCormick Hospital, into a large, relatively modern facility. He built its first permanent building and its first permanent operating room, and in 1904 established a medical laboratory which produced the smallpox vaccine and other medicines. He developed a large network of rural evangelists who did vaccinations and first aid in rural areas. McKean is credited with having helped popularize public health measures in northern Siam. He also served as personal physician to the local ruling princes of Chiang Mai. In 1908 he founded the first leprosarium in Thailand, later known as McKean Leprosarium, and he oversaw its expansion into a major center for treating leprosy* under royal patronage, using the most modern methods of treatment then available. Most of the leprosarium's patients converted to Christianity and later established numerous leper churches throughout northern Thailand. McKean retired in 1931. Throughout his career, McKean emphasized the evangelistic importance of medical missions.

Bibliography

McFarland, George Bradley, ed., *Historical Sketch of Protestant Missions in Siam, 1828-1928* (1928). • McKean, James W., "Leprosy in Siam," *Siam: General and Medical Features* (1930).

HERBERT R. SWANSON

McKinley, William

(b. Niles, Ohio, United States, 29 Jan 1843; d. Buffalo, New York, United States, 14 Sep 1901). American president.

A Republican, McKinley was a former congressman and governor of Ohio. He was elected president in 1896 and again in 1900 and assassinated in 1901. McKinley was an astute politician urged on by strong imperialist factions in the United States. A Methodist*, McKinley agreed to the accession of the Philippines* after prayer. He believed himself duty-bound to "civilize" and "Christianize" the Philippines. While the American public was divided on the accession issue, McKinley followed those who believed that it was "manifest destiny" for the United States to expand its interests in East Asia, and that the United States should share in the "white man's burden" to both civilize and evangelize the darker-skinned races. Expansionists justified their position by appeals to social Darwinism, but McKinley saw the world situation in more providential terms. The annexation opened the doors to aggressive and immediate American Protestant missionary advance into the country and to the pursuit of perfectionist and progressive social engineering goals for Philippine society under American tutelage.

Bibliography

Olcott, Charles S., *William McKinley*, 2 vols. (1916). • Gould, Lewis L., *The Presidency of William McKinley* (1980). FLOYD T. CUNNINGHAM

Medan

Capital of North Sumatra Province and seat of a Catholic archbishop (1961).

In 1941, the apostolic vicar of Padang moved to Medan because mission among the Batak tribes was gradually being allowed after long disputes with the colonial government since 1928. The mission proved successful. The Catholic congregation grew from 2,915 faithful in 1912 to over 400,000 in the 1990s. Pope John Paul II was well received in 1989 by the native archbishop A. G. Pius Datubara in this mainly Christian province in Indonesia. The oldest and largest church is the *Huria Kristen Batak Protestan* (HKBP; see Bataks*), with about three million members.

In the archdiocese of Medan, which today comprises the suffragan dioceses of Sibolga, Palembang, Tanjungkarang, and Pangkalpinang, Franciscans* from Goa served Asian and European traders from 1668 to 1788. Because the sultan of Aceh had strongly forbidden any conversion from Islam*, evangelization was difficult among the Acehnese. During the 1870s, European planters in Sumatra were served once a year by a traveling Dutch priest from Batavia/Jakarta. For a few years toward the end of the 19th c., Fr. Wennecker opened a station in Medan and studied both the Batak language and Keling to serve contract workers from South India. Capuchin* missionaries took over from the Jesuits* a group of 4,200 Catholics (mainly Europeans) in 1912. They wanted to drop this unpromising mission in 1917 but had no permission from Rome.

During the 1820s Catholic communities grew first among the Chinese in Padang on the west coast of Sumatra. There were also good mission schools run by religious sisters and brothers among the small hill tribe of the Pasemah in the mountains of Dempo. After many difficulties among Chinese tin workers on the island of Bangka, a mission was begun by Paul Tsen On Ngie shortly after he had been baptized in Penang (1827).

Catholic mission in Batak country itself was forbidden on the basis of paragraph 123 (117) of the *Reglement op het belied der Regeering van Nederlandsch-Indie (Indische Staatsregeling)* as a "double mission." Since the coming of L. I. Nommensen* (1861), the Protestant Batak Church of the *Rheinische Missiongesellschaft* grew fast among the Toba and Simulungun Bataks. But after 1926, many Bataks who moved to Medan became Catholics, though the Capuchins did not encourage them to do so because contact could not continue to be maintained once they moved back again. The Catholic Bataks themselves tried to get permission to run Catholic schools in Batavia (Jakarta). Opposition by Protestant ministers and pamphlets against Roman Catholicism made the Bataks even more curious. The government slowly lifted the ban (1928, Sibolga; 1933, Tapanuli; 1939, Nias) because, among other reasons, it hoped Catholic schools would ease its school budget during the years of worldwide economic depression. Catholic schools, convents, and parishes were slowly established and served 18,000 faithful before the Pacific War started (1942).

During the Japanese occupation (1942-45) and the war for independence (1945-49), the Catholic communities were served by local catechists and sporadic visits of Javanese priests. All Dutch missionaries were detained by the Japanese. When the troubles were finally over, Catholics had grown to more than 35,000 faithful. New missionaries from China, some expelled by the Communists (1952), especially Italian Xavierians (SX) and German/Swiss Capuchins, reinforced those who survived the wars. New parishes and mission posts opened, schools were repaired and multiplied, and sisters and brothers opened hospitals, polyclinics, and secondary schools. In 1955, a minor seminary was established in Pematangsiantar, completed by a major seminary (1956) in Parapat which later (1967) moved to Pematangsiantar too, where it was incorporated into the Catholic University of St. Thomas (established in 1984). Many religious societies opened novitiates in the 1950s and 1960s to hasten indigenization of church personnel.

Mission in the autonomous area of Aceh, which belongs to the archdiocese of Medan, is virtually impossible. Even Catholic and Protestant Batak residents in southern Aceh are not allowed to celebrate their liturgy or pray in common. Churches built in the 1980s have been burned down several times. ADOLF HEUKEN

Medhurst, Walter Henry

(b. London, 29 Apr 1796; d. England, 24 Jan 1857). English missionary who worked in Malacca*, Penang, Batavia (Jakarta), and China*.

Medhurst became an apprentice in a printing firm in Gloucester at age 14. In 1816, under the London Missionary Society (LMS), he left England for Madras, India*. He went to Malacca a year later to help William Milne* set up a printing press and was also ordained that same year. His 40-year career as an LMS missionary extended far beyond Malacca and involved him in many activities other than printing.

In his three years in Malacca (Jun 1817 to Sept 1820) and one-and-a-half years in Penang (Sept 1820 to Jan 1822), Medhurst was involved in the printing and distribution of tracts and Scripture portions. In 1819 alone, 54,950 tracts, Scripture portions, and books were printed by his press and distributed to neighboring countries.

Medhurst had gone to Malacca intending to "labor for the benefit of China." To this end, he learned the Chinese language and the Hokkien dialect. As soon as he was able, he began preaching and teaching in Chinese and Hokkien, and writing tracts on a variety of subjects. In 1820, he compiled and printed a vocabulary of Hokkien words.

In Jan 1822, Medhurst went to Batavia where he labored among Chinese immigrants for 21 years. He devoted much time to the printing and distribution of tracts and Scripture portions, as well as to preaching and teaching. Using Chinese and Hokkien, he conversed with the locals about the Gospel in their shops, in the marketplaces, and on street corners. In 1823 he completed a Hokkien-English dictionary. He also learned Malay and wrote and printed books in the Malay language.

Medhurst undertook several exploratory trips to different parts of the Malayan Peninsula, Borneo, Java, and Bali* to assess the possibility of mission work in those places. In Aug 1835, he went on a voyage of observation along the northeast coast of China with Rev. E. Stevens, an American Congregational missionary. On this voyage he confirmed that the coastal areas of China were accessible for the distribution of tracts and Scripture portions.

Upon the signing of the Treaty of Nanking in 1843, Medhurst left Batavia for China, arriving in Shanghai on 22 Dec 1843. In Shanghai, he got the printing press into operation and began printing and distributing Christian literature. In Jun 1847, Medhurst was appointed a member of the committee to revise the Chinese version of the New Testament, a revision that was completed in Jul 1850. In 1851, Medhurst, together with Milne, John Stronach*, and James Legge*, began the revision of the Chinese version of the Old Testament, which was completed two years later (see Bible Translation).

Medhurst's contribution lies in the printing and distribution of Christian literature, the compilation of Chinese-English and English-Chinese dictionaries, and the revision of the Chinese Bible. He also wrote books on Java and China and numerous pamphlets on Chinese dialects and philological questions, especially on the rendering of the divine names in Chinese. All of these facilitated the work of missionaries who worked among the Chinese in Southeast Asia and in China. The Medhurst College in Shanghai was named in his memory in 1904.

Bibliography

Latourette, K. S., *A History of Christian Missions in China* (1975). • Sng, Bobby E. K., *In His Good Time* (1980, 1993). • Medhurst, W. H., *China: Its State and Prospects* (1838).

Eileen Poh

Medical Mission Sisters

(MMS). Catholic religious mission founded in 1925 by Anna Dengel as a pious union, the Society of Catholic Medical Missionaries, to serve the sick and suffering throughout the world.

An Austrian medical doctor, Dengel was inspired by Dr. Agnes McLaren (b. 4 Jul 1837; d. 17 Apr 1913), a Scottish Presbyterian* suffragette who became a Catholic in 1898 and worked among the poor in Edinburgh. Moved by the plight of Muslim women forbidden to see male doctors, McLaren started the St. Catherine's Hospital for Women in Rawalpindi in 1909. She wanted the hospital work to be managed by a women's religious order, but several appeals to the authorities were unsuccessful as canon law then forbade the practice of medicine by those who had taken public vows.

Dengel, whose medical studies were sponsored by McLaren, took charge of the hospital in 1928. In 1936, approval was granted for the pious union to become a religious congregation, the MMS. In 1959, MMS came under the direct jurisdiction of the Congregation for the Propagation of the Faith*, and medical work was encouraged.

In 1995, there were over 700 MMS, of whom almost half were Asians, serving more than two-and-a-half million people in 20 countries. There were 235 Indian sisters, 30 Indonesians, three Pakistanis, and 45 Filipinos. Most were stationed in Asian countries, although some were serving in Europe, North America, Latin America, and Africa.

The sisters take a vow to live a simple, celibate life in solidarity with one another and with all who cherish life. They seek to bring wholeness to others through healing in love.

Bibliography

Alvarez-Morelos, Trining, "Healers of the Soul and Body," *Philippines Weekly Women's Magazine* (26 Aug 1960). • Dengel, Anna, "The Work of Medical Mission Sisters in India-Pakistan," *The Medical Woman's Journal* (Sep 1942). • Rhomberg, Hans-Peter, *Anna Dengel* (1992).

Victorina de la Paz

Medical Missionary Society in China (MMSC)

The MMSC was founded at Canton (Guangzhou) in 1838, mainly on the initiative of the surgeon of the British East India Company, Thomas R. Colledge, and two American missionaries, Elijah Coleman Bridgman* and Peter Parker*, from the American Board of Commissioners of Foreign Missions, Boston, Massachusetts. It aimed at giving continuity to what had been temporarily run free clinics for poor Chinese in Canton and Macau*. The MMSC began to raise funds and recruit qualified staff to practice Western medicine, while at the same time witnessing to the Gospel "until permitted to publish openly and without restraint the truth of the gospel" (as it was phrased in one of its founding documents).

Later the MMSC took up logistic responsibilities for the coordination of medical* work in the whole of China* for the various mission boards that started coming in significant numbers only after the Treaty of Tientsin (1858).

While it can rightly be claimed that the MMSC succeeded in reaching its aim of propagating the idea of medical missions in Europe and North America, the society was superseded in professional importance by the China Medical Missionary Association*, founded in Shanghai in 1886, and steadily lost its dominant influence, recognizable in the change of its name to the Canton Medical Missionary Society (up to 1925).

Bibliography

The Medical Missionary Society in China: Address with Minutes of Proceedings (1838). • Thomson, J. C., "Semi-Centennial of the Medical Missionary Society," *The China Medical Missionary Journal*, Vol. 2, No. 3 (1887). • Parker, P., *Statements Respecting Hospitals in China* (1842). China Group

Medical Work

The idea of medical missions in its technical sense was conceived in Protestant circles in Asia in the early 19th c. as the result of their unsuccessful missionary encounter with China*, then rigidly sealed off from any foreign contact — politically, economically, and religiously. In the widely read diaries about his various journeys along the Chinese coast, Karl Gützlaff* (1803-51), German by birth and first serving the Dutch Missionary Society in Bintang and later the British legation at Singapore*, advocated the employment of medical work in the service of the Gospel, meaning the dispensing of drugs and distributing of tracts. According to him, it was only in this combination that the xenophobic Chinese would seek contact with nonnationals, and thus China could be opened to the Gospel. A couple of years later, in 1838, the Medical Missionary Society in China* (MMSC) was founded in Canton (Guangzhou) by physicians, missionaries, and businessmen from North America, Britain, India, and China, not all of them Christians. The aim was twofold: "to encourage the practice of [scientific] medicine among the Chinese" and to "advance the cause of mission," as the respective minutes state. While the idea was spread globally by prudent public relations, the press, and personal agents, the twofold goal proved to be crucial, as the first medical missionary and well-known advocate of the MMSC, Peter Parker* (1804-88), immediately recognized. Churches suspected doctrinal aberrations, the home boards wanted to make medicine a means to an end, and the missionary physicians had to safeguard their medical responsibility for the suffering people — conflicts that remain today.

China was the heartland of medical missions. It was here that various methods of medical missionary service were practiced first, such as dispensary work, itineration, hospitals for different genders and diseases, asylums for the lepers (see Leprosy Work), the insane, and opium addicts (see Opium), production of medical literature and journals, study of indigenous ways of treatment, and academic medical education. The most remarkable contribution in this regard was the Peking Union Medical College, founded in 1906 and taken over by the Rockefeller Foundation in 1915. It was in China, too, that most hospitals were built and that most of the doctors (male and female), nurses, and assistants were stationed. While the numbers of medical missions' institutions and personnel multiplied with the onset of the 20th c., the situation changed dramatically in 1949, when all missionaries had to leave the country and Christian medical institutions had to close down or be nationalized.

For medical missionary work, pre-1947 *India** was next in importance to China and has held a prominent place ever since. The work commenced in the British provinces in 1864 (W. J. Elmslie of the Church Missionary Society [CMS], London, at Srinagar, Cashmere) and added female medical missions (Clara Swain*, 1834-1910, the first woman medical missionary, from 1870 working in Bareilly, Uttar Pradesh). Women medical missionaries added a new feature to the medical missionary enterprise, gaining access both to the women's quarters (*zenanas* and harems) and to the children. This proved of vital importance for their social and educational uplift and contributed significantly to the emancipation of women in all of Asia. Centers of the work were West Bengal (part of which is now Bangladesh*, with links to Burma/Myanmar*) and the Madras Presidency, with Vellore, now the location of the largest medical missionary institution — the Christian Medical College and Hospital (CMCH), a teaching hospital with 1,500 beds and a faculty of over 580 offering degree programs in 77 departments attended by 620 graduate and postgraduate students with special emphasis on rural and public health ministries. Another center was the Northwest Frontier Province (most of which is now Pakistan*), where the CMS had a "chain" of mission hospitals (Quetta, Dera Ghazi Khan, Dera Ismail Khan, Tank, Bannu, Peshawar, and Srinagar) along the frontier to Afghanistan and where, in Rawalpindi, Anna Dengel's Medical Mission Sisters started their work among women in the 20th c. (see below on Pakistan). In the Punjab, Ludhiana became the site of the North Indian School of Medicine for Christian Women, founded in 1894 by Edith Brown, which now is the Christian Medical College Ludhiana. Finally, Miraj in the Bombay Presidency needs to be mentioned, where the American Presbyterians founded the Miraj Medical School (1892-1953). In all, there were more than 300 medical missionary stations in India at the turn of the century, looked after by 200 missionary physicians, 111 of whom were women. Catholic medical work came in much later.

Women medical missionaries played a dominant role in *Ceylon/Sri Lanka** as well. Nine of them and one male colleague worked among the Buddhist Singalese in the south.

Indonesia. The Protestant Medical ministry was pioneered in Indonesia* in the last two decades of the 19th c. In 1882 A. Kruyt* of the Dutch Missionary Fellowship *(Nederlands Zendingsgenootschap),* who assisted his father's missionary work in Mojowarno in rural East Java*, began treating local villagers and founded a clinic and a hospital that treated close to 4,000 patients in 1895. In 1889 a clinic was opened near the governor-general's palace in Jakarta because there was no institutional health care in the city. From 1890 to 1900, the *Rheinische Missions Gesellschaft* had a missionary doctor in the field in Irian Jaya. They also opened a clinic among the Batak* people in Pearadja in North Sumatra in 1900 and a hospital in 1901. The Mission of the Reformed Churches in The Netherlands began its work in Central Java, where J. G. Scheurer opened a clinic in 1897 (Yogyakarta). Around the same time the Reformed churches began medical mission work on the eastern island of Sumba.

True to its original purpose, the hospital in Mojowarno is still functioning as a rural Christian hospital under the *Gereja Kristen Jawi Wetan* (the East Javanese Christian Church), and the Kruyt tradition has continued with F. Kruyt, a woman doctor who decided to remain in Indonesia after Indonesian independence and who until recently served as director of the Protestant hospital Mardi Santosa in Surabaya. The clinic opened in Jakarta and grew into the Queen Emma Hospital, now Cikini Hospital, officially governed by the Communion of Children in Indonesia. The Batak churches now operate a hospital in Balige in North Sumatra. The Yogyakarta clinic grew into Petronella Hospital but became a government hospital during the Japanese occupation and as Bethesda Hospital is now the largest Protestant health-care facility in Indonesia. Its former director, Guno Samekto, was the chairperson of the Indonesian Christian Association for Health Services (PELKESI) from its inception in 1983 in Balige until 1992. Bethesda Hospital is a member of YAKKUM, the health-care association of the Javanese Christian Church (GKJ). The *Gereja Masehi Injili Minihasa* runs Bethesda Hospital in Tomohon, Northern Sulawesi.

The Sundanese Christian Church, although small in numbers in this predominantly Muslim region, operates its own hospital in Bandung, as do the Seventh-day Adventists*. The Salvation Army*, which started its work in the villages of Central Java in 1894, currently operates 20 hospitals and health posts, as well as a number of social welfare institutions. One of their largest hospitals is in Palu on Sulawesi*.

Christian medical professionals in Indonesia now respond to the challenge of finding a balance between the pursuit of excellence in high-cost specialized medicine and low-cost service to the poor. A number of the hospitals mentioned above are known regionally for sophisticated services. At the same time many new health-care posts in rural areas and urban *kampungs* are established by Christian health-care organizations. One of the priorities PELKESI has set for itself is the training and provision of primary health care for poor communities. Several of the Christian hospitals are equipped with active, rural community development units.

The medical mission work of the Roman Catholic Church* is more centrally administered and is concentrated in the predominantly Roman Catholic areas of Indonesia, such as Flores and East Timor*. However, in almost every major city a high-quality Roman Catholic hospital can be found. Three of the most well known are the Carolus Hospital in Jakarta (established in 1919), the Borromeus Hospital in Bandung (1921), and the Panti Rapih Hospital in Yogyakarta (1929). All three are run under the auspices of the sisters of Carolus-Borromeus*. The Roman Catholic counterpart of PELKESI is PERDHAKI. Cooperation between Protestant and Roman Catholic health-care institutions is increasing, especially in the field of pastoral care* and counseling.

Medical missions were instrumental in gaining access to *Korea** because, after the successful treatment of Prince Min Yok Ik by H. N. Allan* (Northern Presbyterian Mission, United States) in 1884, permission for Christian missionary activities was granted. Centers of medical missionary work were Seoul, with five hospitals, and P'yongyang (at least up to 1950/53). What today is the Yonsei University College of Medicine in Seoul is an offspring of what had been the Severance Union Medical College set up by medical missionaries in 1904.

In *Japan** the situation was somewhat different, because Western medicine had already been introduced by the government, so that medical missions did not play such an important pioneering role as they did in other parts of Asia. Only a few hospitals were built at Tokyo, Osaka, and Kobe in the 19th c., St. Luke's International Medical Center at Tokyo being in operation up to the present (see Japanese Overseas Christian Medical Cooperative Service).

While the recognition medical missionaries received in *Siam/Thailand** is demonstrated by the fact that they were officially put in charge of smallpox vaccination by the government, their work remained marginal, as was the case in *Laos** too (see McKean, James W.). In both countries the first Western medical procedures (vaccinations, operations) were performed by missionaries. Fifteen medical missionaries were working in 10 stations at various places in these countries by the end of the 19th c., whereas in *Burma/Myanmar** (see below on Myanmar) the American Baptist Missionary Union ran not fewer than 17 medical stations at the same time.

Medical missionary work in *Vietnam**, *Cambodia**, the *Philippines**, and the British Straits Settlements (1826-1946), especially in *Malaysia** and *Singapore**, was present by the end of last century too, but it did not play an important pioneering role. The medical work of Protestant and especially of Catholic missions developed extensively during the 20th c., but is slowly giving preference to primary health care nowadays instead of concentrating on institutionalized hospital work, as was done in the medical mission work of old. At present many of the older medical clinics and major hospitals have been nationalized, while newer pioneering medical work continues (e.g., Nepal*, Cambodia*).

Medical work in *Myanmar (Burma)* has undergone significant changes from its beginnings up to the present — changes not in its basic motivations, but in its ways and means of dispensation. Striving for healing and caring for the needy in a mood of disinterested benevolence is still seen as a genuine witness to the Gospel. While during the colonial era Christian medical work could be equated with hospital work, the focus today is in accordance with the World Health Organization's (WHO) *Alma Ata* declaration (1978) on primary health-care measures and community-based activities (PHC). Thus there is a sober-minded reappraisal of traditional medicine, once categorically rejected as simply superstitious. Today nearly all the hospitals erstwhile built and maintained by mission agencies have been fully integrated into the government health-care provision scheme by nationalization during the 1960s. Most of their charity programs, however, are still managed and entertained by church missions: for instance, the care of the blind, deaf and dumb, lepers (Leprosy Hospital at Moulmein, once under the directorship of Saw Wah Htoo, now under the auspices of the Myanmar Christian Leprosy Mission), the aged, drug addicts, and HIV+/AIDS sufferers.

Historically, the American Baptists (American Baptist Foreign Mission Society; see Baptists*) were the first to introduce medical missions into Myanmar. Their physician was Jonathan Price, who also attended to King Bagyidaw. Geographically, Baptist medical work was concentrated in the Shan states (northeast), where at least 18 doctors, both foreign and indigenous, served from 1890 on. They established hospitals in Hsipaw (by M. B. Kirk Patrick), and Mongnai, Kengtung, and Namkharn (by Gordon Seagrave*) and opened numerous dispensaries, including Rest Haven, a sanitarium for recuperating tuberculosis patients. Medical work in the Chin Hills (west) was started by Dr. and Mrs. E. N. East in 1902, followed by J. G. Wooden until 1915. The Baptists also provided medical services in the Kachin Hills in the north at Bawn Wang and Machyang Baw from 1951 to 1958. In Lower Burma, their main medical work centered around a small hospital opened by Susan Haswell in 1880, with Ellen Mitchell as its first woman missionary doctor, and Shaw Lu, son of one of Adoniram Judson's* early Mon converts, becoming her assistant. A new hospital had to be built in 1917, with Martha J. Gifford as its first doctor, and a nurses' training school got started with the help of Mon nurse Ma Hla Yin; this school received government recognition in 1924. Baptist medical work in Yangon (Rangoon) began with J. Dawson, who provided his services in a building on Merchant Street and treated many injured in the earthquake of 1855. In 1882 he was invited by Lady Dufferin, wife of the viceroy of India, to open a women's hospital (which eventually became the Dufferin Maternity Hospital) and run a nurses' training school of which Daw Saw Sa, Myanmar's pioneer woman medical doctor and surgeon, became the first superintendent. An offspring of the Baptist missionary work is the self-supporting Kayin Baptist Mission Society, established in 1912, which in 1975 started a Fellowship for the Blind with Integrated Training Schools in Yangon and Myitkyina under the leadership of the blind U Thein Lwin.

The first health-care institution of the Anglican* mission (Society for the Propagation of the Gospel, SPG) was a school for the blind, founded in 1914 by W. C. Purser, followed in 1920 by a school for the deaf and dumb, for which Mary Chapman was responsible. Both of these schools are still functioning, while the hospitals and dispensaries initiated by Farrant Russel in Mandalay (1921), Maingkwan (1930), and Mohnyin (1931) are no longer operating. Quite some time later, the Upper Myanmar Methodists* opened a hospital and outreach center in Tahan which is still in operation, while the corresponding projects of the Lower Myanmar Methodists (church clinics, distribution of milk powder, and nutrition classes) are now being discontinued.

The Seventh-day Adventist* Mission built a 60-bed hospital in 1947 providing specialist services, with a school of nursing added in 1953 under the supervision of Harriet Dinsmore and Petra Sukau. In 1965 this became the Government Eye, Ear, Nose, and Throat Hospital.

The Roman Catholic Mission also did successful medical missions work in the Yangon (Rangoon) area, especially in its Bishop Bigandet Home and Hospital for Lepers founded in 1896 by the *Mission Étrangères de Paris* (MEP; see Paris Foreign Mission Society*). Part of it has become an orthopedic clinic under government auspices, while the attached Home for the Aged is still managed by compassionate, dedicated sisters who care for the elderly and homeless.

The Myanmar Council of Churches (MCC) is today the agency that coordinates most of Christian medical work in the country. Formed first as the Burma Representative Council of Missions in 1914, it now counts 12 member churches, 16 corresponding local/regional Christian councils, and seven cooperating bodies. The MCC works through five units, all having health concerns and programs: the ecumenism and missions department has care and counseling training and services; the Urban Rural Mission* is active in health-education programs and runs a clinic with outreach services in the Singaung Gyi village; the service and development department had a 10-year integrated development project with a strong focus on primary health care, transferring responsibility for further development to the regional councils; and the nurture and development unit, which incorporates women's work, youth, and university Christian work, stressing the health information aspect. One of the more recent health-care projects of the MCC

Medical Work

is the Preventive Education and AIDS Caring Environment (PEACE) Project in high-risk areas, which includes the training of pastors, church leaders, youth, women leaders, and workers of other nongovernmental organizations (NGOs) for the care and counseling of HIV/AIDS sufferers, home care, peer education, and support services. The youth department of the largest MCC-affiliated group, the Myanmar Baptist Convention, has a drug rehabilitation program; and its Christian education department (1992) launched Project Hope for AIDS education (with a strong biblical emphasis), and its women's department organizes programs on care for and counseling of HIV victims as well as courses on nutrition and malaria prevention.

Among other cooperating bodies of the MCC, the Young Men's Christian Associations* (YMCA) and Young Women's Christian Associations* (YWCA) engage actively in health education, sports, and fitness activities and offer a Sick Companion Course stressing compassionate caring in a program that is very similar to that of training for qualifying nurse aides.

Independent of the MCC is the medical and charitable work of the Young Crusaders, who, besides maintaining a leper mission in Mayankyaung village and an orphanage, have a variety of rehabilitation programs for drug addicts and alcoholics that are supplemented by income-generating activities and courses on theology, the latter being compulsory for all participants.

Finally, the Myanmar Christian Health Workers' Services Association is a professional organization and successor to the former Burma Christian Medical Relief Society (BCMRS; 1951), founded by Daw Saw Sa, U Thaung Tin, and U San Ba in cooperation with the Baptist, Anglican, and Methodist medical missionaries. It maintained a 25-bed hospital and a nurses' training school, with Drs. Rajan, Ba Than Chain, Daw Khin Si, and Daw Nyein May on the staff. Today the aims of the Myanmar Christian Health Workers' Services Association are the spiritual nurturing of health-care personnel, the launching of service and development projects, the training and awarding of scholarships to outstanding students and nurses, the dissemination of health practices, and the provision of emergency services in cases of natural disasters or whenever the nation demands it.

Catholic medical work in *Pakistan* began taking shape in the 1890s, when a central concern of the church in then North India was the medical care of women and children, who at that time had hardly any access to professional medical help. This concern was stimulated by admiration for the work of the Protestant Zenana missions — that branch of missions, especial medical missionary work, done by women for women in the women's quarters of China and South Asia, where males were not permitted to enter. The first attempt to found a hospital for women was at Lahore in 1895, when the government asked the mission to take over responsibility for the city's asylum for insane women. The next initiative was taken by the Mill Hill Missionaries* (MHM) in Rawalpindi, who worked with Agnes McLaren (1837-1913) to bring about St. Catherine's Hospital in 1909. This hospital was administered by a local committee and financed by donations mainly from Europe via a support agency in London known as The Acton Group.

In 1927 St. Catherine's was replaced by the first Holy Family Hospital under the responsibility of the Austrian physician Anna Dengel (1892-1980), member and founder of the Society of Catholic Medical Missionaries (SCMM) in Washington, D.C., United States (1924), in order to provide stability for the work and permit its extension. Dengel wanted the SCMM to be a religious congregation, which at that time demanded a substantial change in canon law because this strictly forbade medical practice for priests and members of religious orders. She constantly pressed her matter to the Curia, and, in Feb 1936, the instruction *Constans ac sedula* was promulgated, permitting and encouraging the religious to engage in medical and caring activities. This led to an expansion of Catholic medical work worldwide. After World War II* and the coming about of the Islamic Republic of Pakistan (1947), Catholic medical work went in a number of new directions prompted by various needs.

Today the Catholic Church in Pakistan staffs and manages 11 hospitals, with the Society of Catholic Medical Missionaries, the Daughters of the Cross*, the Franciscan Missionaries of Mary*, the St. John of God Sisters, the Sisters of Mercy*, and the Medical Helpers of Würzburg, Germany, as the main sisterhoods working therein. The church also established a number of rural dispensaries and small-town clinics, with a limited number of beds, especially for maternity and nursing care, and it entertains various outreach health-care services and clinics. There is a strong emphasis on leprosy control coordinated nationwide by Dr. Pfau of the Daughters of the Heart of Mary from the Marie Adelaide Leprosy Centre in Karachi. Care of the aged is provided by five homes for the aged in Karachi and Lahore. Three institutes, known as *Dar-ul-Sukun,* are dedicated to the care of the mentally handicapped; one home at Okara is for blind children; and four institutes in Karachi, Rawalpindi, and Faisalabad care for children with physical handicaps (the Rawalpindi institution is attached to St. Joseph's Hospice, founded in 1964 by Frank O'Leary, the first in a series of hospices around the world known as Hospice International). In addition, the diocese of Rawalpindi runs a drug rehabilitation service at Peshawar that grew from James van der Klugt's response to the needs of young victims of the drug traffic in the 1970s, many of whom were stranded in Peshawar on their return from Afghanistan in search of cheap drugs.

Bibliography

Balme, H., *China and Modern Medicine: A Study in Medical Missionary Development* (1921). • Stauffer, M. T., *The Christian Occupation of China* (1922). • Balfour, M. I., and R. Young, *The Work of Medical Women in India*

(1929). • Browne, S. G., F. Davey, and W. A. R. Thomson, eds., *Heralds of Health* (1985). • Bowers, J. Z., *Western Medical Pioneers in Feudal Japan* (1970). • Grundmann, C. H., *Sent to Heal! The Emergence and Development of Medical Missions in the 19th Century* (1999); *Journal of the Christian Medical Association of India,* Nagpur/New quarterly paper.

Indonesia

Dake, W. J. L., *Het medische werk van de zending in Nederlands-Indie* (1972). • De Jong, C. G. F., *Geschiedenis van de Nederlandse zending op Zuid-Sulawesi 1852-1966* (1995); *De Gereformeerde Zending in Midden-Java 1931-1975* (1997). • Van den End, T., *Ragi Carita,* Vols. 4 and 5.

Myanmar

Seagrave, Gordon S., *The Life of a Burma Surgeon* (1961; reprinted 1990); *Tales of a Waste-Basket Surgeon* (1944); *My Hospital in the Hills* (1955). • Reed, K. L., and R. O. Ballon, *Bamboo-Hospital: The Story of a Missionary Family in Burma* (1961). • Beaver, R. Pierce, *American Protestant Women in World Mission* (1980). • Lippard, W. B., *The Ministry of Healing: A Study of Medical Missionary Endeavor on Baptist Foreign Mission Fields* (1920). • Maung Shwe Wa, *Burma Baptist Chronicle* (1963).

Pakistan

Burton, K., *According to the Pattern: The Story of Dr. Agnes McLaren and the Society of Catholic Medical Missionaries* (1946). • Dengel, A., *Mission for Samaritans: A Survey of Achievements and Opportunities in the Field of Catholic Medical Missions* (1945). • *Ecclesiae Instituta Valetudini Fovendae Toto Orbe Terrarum Index* (1986).

Christoffer H. Grundmann, with Aart M. van Beek (Indonesia), Sein May Chit (Myanmar), and John Rooney (Pakistan)

Melaka. *See* Malacca

Mennonites

Mennonite engagement in Asia began when the Dutch Mennonite Missionary Society (DMMS) sent Pieter Jansz to Indonesia* in 1851. Jansz settled in north-central Java, laying the foundation for what became the *Gereja Injili di Tanah Jawa* (GITJ). In 1871 the DMMS founded a mission in Sumatra. Nearly 50 years of labor yielded meager results, and the work was turned over to the Lutheran* Batak Christian Church in 1931. In 1920 an indigenous movement among Chinese people in north-central Java led by Tee Siem Tat resulted in the formation of the *Gereja Kristen Muria Indonesia* (GKMI), which forged a spiritual relationship with the DMMS but no formal organizational affiliation.

In 1948 the Mennonite Central Committee (MCC), a relief and service agency of North American Mennonites, entered Indonesia to assist the war-devastated Mennonites in north-central Java. In addition to assisting the churches in Java, MCC subsequently sent development teams to Timor, Halmahera, Sumatra, and Sulawesi. GKMI organized *Pengutusan Injil dan Pelayanan Kasih* (PIPKA, Board of Mission and Service) in 1965. In addition to a series of church development and service projects in various parts of Indonesia, it cooperated with two North American agencies, Mennonite Brethren Missions/Services (MBM/S) and Eastern Mennonite Missions (EMM), in certain projects. PIPKA, with assistance from EMM, extended its ministry to Singapore* in 1990.

Mennonite Brethren missionaries from Russia arrived in India* in 1890 and began working in association with the Baptists* in the Hyderabad, A.P., area. From this work grew the Mennonite Brethren Church of India. Responding to the 1898-99 famine in India, the Mennonite Board of Missions (MBM) began work in the area of Dhamtari, M.P., in 1899, which led to the founding of the Mennonite Church in India in 1912.

In 1940 the MBM sent missionaries from M.P. to Bihar Province. The MBM joined other missions in founding the United Mission to Nepal* (UMN) in 1954. The MCC appointed workers to serve with the UMN from 1957. In 1900 the General Conference Mennonite Church Board of Missions (GCMCMB) sent missionaries to Champa and Jagdeshpur, M.P. In 1913 the Brethren in Christ Board of Missions (BIC) established a mission in the region of Saharsa, Bihar. In the 1980s the BIC extended their witness to Orissa Province and into Nepal. The MCC has done relief and development work continuously in India, Pakistan*, and Bangladesh* since World War II*. The MBM/S has sponsored ministry in Pakistan since 1981, including a church development team made up of Japanese and North American workers. The MBM, MBM/S, and MCC have participated in the International Assistance Mission to Afghanistan since its founding in the 1970s.

Mennonites began working in China* in the 1890s under the auspices of a variety of mission agencies. In 1901 H. C. and Nellie Bartel went to China with the Houlding Mission, an independent mission. In 1905 they separated from Houlding and began a work that in 1913 became the China Mennonite Mission Society, with programs in Szechwan-Kansu and Shantung-Honan provinces. In 1914 the GCMCMB assumed responsibility for work begun in 1909 by Henry and Maria Brown in Hopeh Province. In 1919 the MBM/S took over the work begun in 1911 by F. J. Wiens among the Hakkas in Fukien Province. In 1947 the Mennonite Board of Missions sent five missionaries to start a mission in Szechwan Province. All Mennonite work in China was ended with the coming to power of the Communists in 1949. The MCC initiated relief programs in Hong Kong* and Taiwan* in the early 1950s. The General Conference Mennonites took over the program in Taiwan in 1954. The mission continued building up a large medical program along with planting a network of churches. Eastern Mennonite Missions entered Hong Kong in 1965. The

Commission on Overseas Mission (CIM; successor to GCMCMB) joined the EMM in Hong Kong in 1974. In 1996 the ministry was extended to Macau*. In 1980 a group of Mennonite program agencies established the China Educational Exchange to sponsor the placement of teachers of English in China and the training of Chinese in the teaching of English in Mennonite colleges in North America.

The MCC began working in Vietnam* in 1954, and EMM in 1957. The MCC concentrated on relief and medical* work; the EMM evangelized and founded churches. Cooperating with the Evangelical Church of Vietnam (ECVN), the MCC helped to develop the Evangelical Clinic in Nha Trang (1960) and the ECVN Bible Institute in Nha Trang. These efforts were suspended in 1975 when the North Vietnamese won the war (see Vietnam War), but they were resumed in the 1990s. The MCC continued working with war refugees in Cambodia*, Laos*, and Thailand*. In the 1990s the EMM launched a church-planting ministry in Thailand.

During World War II*, the MCC sent a contingent of workers to the Philippines* to establish a medical and relief project. This was phased out in the early 1950s. In 1971 a group of churches in the Philippines, subsequently calling themselves Philippines Mennonite Missions Now, invited the EMM to send missionaries to assist them in leadership training. By this time the MCC had also returned to the Philippines to do development work.

For several years following the end of World War II in 1945, the MCC engaged in relief work in the Osaka area in Japan*. Four mission boards began working in Japan during this period: MBM/S (Osaka); MBM (Hokkaido); GCMCMB (Miyazaki); and BIC (Yamaguchi). Later the MBM, GCMCMB, and BIC, following their Japanese members who moved for reasons of education and employment, established several centers in Tokyo. Although Mennonite/BIC membership in Japan has remained small, these churches have used their considerable financial resources to participate in a variety of international projects.

In response to conditions resulting from the Korean War*, in 1953 the MCC began a relief program. Later the work was expanded to include a vocational school for war orphans and development. This program was phased out in 1970. In the 1990s, in response to Korean appeals for collaboration in the area of discipleship and peace witness, the COM has appointed workers to Korea*.

In 1990 the MBM joined other Christian agencies in forming a cooperative program in Mongolia* and has had workers there since then.

Mennonite and Brethren in Christ baptized (adult) membership in Asia stands at 157,075: Hong Kong/China, 90; India, 87,466; Indonesia, 62,723; Japan, 3,450; Philippines, 1,494; Singapore, 16; Taiwan, 1,494; and Vietnam, 115.

Bibliography

Dyck, C. J., *An Introduction to Mennonite History* (3d rev. ed. 1993). • Horsch, James E., ed., *Mennonite Yearbook and Directory, 1997* (1997). • Shenk, Wilbert R., ed., *Mission Focus: Current Issues* (1980). • Klassen, James R., *Jimshoes in Vietnam* (1986). • Martin, Earl S., *Reaching the Other Side* (1978).

Wilbert R. Shenk, with contributions from Luke S. Martin (Vietnam) and Charles Christano (Indonesia)

Merauke

District capital of southern Irian Jaya (western New Guinea) which in 1966 became the center of an archdiocese with the suffragan dioceses of Agats, Jayapura, and Sorong-Manokwari.

In 1892 and 1896, Jesuit* missionaries paid short visits to the northern coast of Dutch New Guinea in order to test the possibility of opening a mission on this island. Nearly a decade later, the Missionaries of the Sacred Heart* (MSC), who had taken over the Moluccas* and New Guinea from the Jesuits (1902), stationed four missionaries in Merauke (1905) "to promote the native population." They made contacts with cannibal tribes, studied their languages and customs, and compiled grammars and dictionaries. They urged the authorities to curb headhunting, cannibalism, and frequent tribal wars. An additional problem was that hunters of the precious birds of paradise *(Cenderawasih)*, brought venereal diseases through intercourse with young women (a custom of *otiv bambari*), which would have almost destroyed the Marind-anim tribe if not for the work of Fr. Vertenten*, who set up medical and educational facilities in special villages. The Spanish influenza of 1918 killed 18% of the Marind-anim. Only with special government subsidies was the mission able to help them.

In 1922, some indigenous people were ready to be baptized. Courses for carpenters were offered, and wooden houses, schools, and chapels erected. Teachers from the Kei Archipelago fit well into this difficult area and made it possible to expand evangelization to the west (Mimika, 1926) and the north (Fak-fak, 1929). During the 1930s, unhealthy competition between Protestant and Catholic mission workers aroused ill feelings on both sides. A line of separation was drawn by the colonial authorities, which resulted in a more Protestant north (Jayapura) and a Catholic south (Merauke).

Thanks to the Daughters of the Heart of Mary (since 1928) and religious brothers and lay teachers from the Kei Islands, the mission grew steadily. In 1937, the northern part of New Guinea was handed over to Franciscan* missionaries, who operated from Hollandia (Jayapura). During World War II*, young men of the Muyu tribe were able to replace the Kei teachers, who could no longer leave their Japanese-occupied islands.

After World War II, the mission opened a Catholic

training college for village teachers in Merauke (1949), a technical school (1953) with extension courses in various skills (repair of cars, electronics, building), and a nursing school. In 1950, New Guinea was separated from the Moluccas and formed the vicariate of Merauke (MSC), which was later divided into the prefectures of Hollandia (1954) and Sorong-Manokwari and the diocese of Agats. Evangelization made great progress with the help of catechists from the Muyu tribe. Primary schools and polyclinics were established in strategic villages. In 1951, religious sisters opened the first novitiate; a seminary was established in 1956, and advanced courses for teachers followed in 1963. The religious brothers went to the villages to persuade the people to give up their nomadic existence, to start planting vegetables and coconut and rubber trees, and to begin digging fish ponds.

Pastoral care* in New Guinea has always been difficult because communication over a vast area has to be done without ready transportation. Around 1958, cargo-cult (see Koreri) madness infected the southern parts of the area. Since 1989, the Antonius Foundation has given special instructions to help villages upgrade their agriculture so as not to be completely outdone by the better-prepared immigrants from Java, Flores, and Timor*.

The diocese of Merauke comprises roughly 110,000 Catholics in 26 parishes, each with several stations run by laymen. Native priests and deacons are educated at the theological seminary of Pineleng (Manado, Northern Celebes). In all four dioceses of Irian Jaya, experiments in the inculturation of liturgy and preaching have been carried out since the 1970s (see Contextualization). The education of indigenous clergy and lay leaders ("lay deacons") has been given special attention in preparation for an indigenous church in a few years' time. At present, "domestic" missionaries from Flores and Java assist by replacing the rapidly decreasing number of foreign missionaries.

Bibliography

Muskens, M. P. M., ed., *Sejarah Gereja Katolik Indonesia,* Vol. IIIa (1974). • Haripranata, H., *Carita Sejarah Gereja Katolik di KEI dan di IRIAN BARAT* (n.d.). • Cornelissen, J. F. L. M., *Pater en Papoea* (1988). Adolf Heuken

Methodism

Methodism is a Protestant denomination that separated from the Church of England in the eighteenth century. The Holy Club, made up of students of Oxford University and guided by John and Charles Wesley, practiced a pietistic faith in which they adhered to strict religious precepts, doing theological research and living ascetic lifestyles. The name came from a joke about their methodical discipline. In 1738, John, having experienced a complete Christian conversion, had a cleansing of the spirit and began to lead a life of spiritual reawakening. Because he was unqualified to expound in Church of England churches, the next April he began street preaching. The first Methodist building was erected in Bristol, and the first annual meeting was held in 1744. Wesley and his followers had no intention of withdrawing from the Church of England; however, in 1784, they established articles of faith, and, in 1797, were officially recognized as an independent church by the Church of England. With this the whole world became their parish, with work extending beyond England to the United States and Canada.

In 1737, the Wesleys had gone to the Georgia Colony (in North America) to do mission work, but this was a failure. In 1760, Robert Strawridge became the first missionary; and when the first annual American conference was held in Philadelphia, there were over 100 churches. They overcame difficulties encountered at the time of the American Revolution, and the Methodist Episcopal Church, USA, was officially instituted at the Baltimore annual conference in 1784. The Wesley Methodist Church withdrew in 1843 over differences on the slavery issue, and in 1845 with the North/South split, the Methodist Episcopal Church, South, was organized. The Methodist Protestant Church, rejecting the episcopal structure, had been organized in 1828 and rejoined at the time of the merger in Kansas City, Missouri, in 1939 to form the Methodist Church.

Methodism in Asia had a complex beginning. Methodist missionaries came to Asia from both a divided church in the United States (USA), as well as from the United Kingdom (UK), and thus brought varying traditions of Methodist polity, theology, and liturgy. The Methodist Episcopal Church (MEC) in the USA was the first to send missionaries to China, followed by missionaries from the MEC South (MES), and then the Wesleyan Methodists of the UK in 1853. Similarly fragmented efforts characterized Methodist missions in India* (beginning in 1856), Japan* (1873), and Korea* (1885).

One result of the fragmentation was a division of resources, often deplored by the missionaries themselves, who overcame the situation with unofficial cooperation, but a century later the different traditions served to provide the newly independent Methodist churches with several choices to develop their own polities and official worship resources. Thus Chinese churches found it congenial to use the order for holy communion from the MES even though their founders came from the MEC, while Malaysians preferred the British Wesleyan tradition to that of their MEC founders. The exact influence of this eventual confluence of traditions has yet to be studied fully, because until recently studies on mission history tended to focus more on the founding of institutions (and thus the missionaries who almost always managed them) than on local congregations and the largely local clergy serving the second generation of Methodists throughout Asia.

The founding of schools, hospitals, and publishing houses constituted the backbone of Methodist mission strategy in the 19th and early 20th cs. Unfortunately, the few studies on their relationship to the development of common Christian life raise more questions than answers. For example, it has been shown that Methodist schools in Malaysia* helped to ensure that an elite minority of English speakers would dominate a church whose membership was largely Tamil- or Chinese-speaking. It would be intriguing to know how the institutional outreach to India's civil servants related to the mass movements of Methodism among the Dalits*, or how Methodist colleges shaped the social structure of the church in China.

The legacies of the institutional mission strategy are ambivalent. Most institutions were self-supporting, and in the case of schools and publishing houses generated considerable revenue for missionary salaries. These characteristics, however, linked them with the colonial establishment and its economic order, thus affecting their social witness. As Bishop Thoburn* (of India and Malaysia) pointed out in the 1890s, the opium* which the missionaries so hated directly financed the Methodist schools.

Methodist institutions were also a problematic legacy in some places after national independence was achieved (see Nationalism). In Malaysia, Indonesia, Myanmar, and China, for example, the social services around which the Methodists built much of their witness were taken over by national governments whose resources dwarfed those of the churches. Even today in these countries and others, Methodist churches are still seeking for a new mission stategy. In India and Borneo, the maintenance of such institutions by the local church has resulted in a continuing financial dependence on the United States or a drain on resources needed elsewhere.

The role of key leaders such as James Thoburn, William Taylor*, and Henry Appenzeller* has long been recognized. Less noted are the efforts of equally significant Asian preachers and leaders. Although the contribution of some Asian Methodist leaders has been sufficiently documented, still lacking is a methodology for comparing missionary understanding and theories (which are relatively well known) with the practice and preaching of the churches (also documented), and with what is known about local cultures, in order to discern the distinctive contribution of Asians in shaping their church. To illustrate, while Methodist missionaries in Malaysia focused on the spiritual task of evangelism among Tamil immigrant workers, Tamil pastors such as Samuel Abraham (in early-20th-c. Malaysia) showed an equal or greater concern to protect the rights of the workers and to create means of social advancement. In this Samuel Abraham was a pioneer, and he set the tone for the Tamil missionary outreach quite independently of any missionary leadership.

In both India and Malaysia, many pastors are critical of their inherited role as teacher/pastors and are working out contextually relevant models. The style of worship and preaching of the early-20th-c. Methodist churches in China and India also shows a strongly indigenous character independent of Western missionary influence. There has also been a lack of appreciation for the contribution of non-Methodist Asian leaders upon the Methodist movement; for example, the renowned revivalist John Sung*, although not a Methodist, influenced greatly the Methodist movement in Indonesia*, Malaysia, and Singapore in the 20th c. Preachers born a generation after his death are still imitating his style.

The contributions of strong Methodist individuals such as James Thoburn and James Hoover were not alway unmixed blessings. Thoburn, whose influence spread from India to the Philippines*, was biased against indigenous language schools and believed in using expatriate churches to finance local missions. His policies resulted in the still-existing divisions in Southeast Asia between the middle-class English-educated Christians and those of the poorer classes who spoke only indigenous languages, for the English-speaking churches had developed independently of the Tamil-, Chinese-, Malay-, and Batak-speaking churches. James Hoover, pioneer leader of the Chinese Methodists in Sarawak, was racially prejudiced against the indigenous peoples of Borneo. Similar prejudice remains a problem today. Missionaries are the children of their age, and the social, cultural, and racial biases of their time and society reflect upon their missionary enterprises. More study needs to be done on how the receiving cultural and social situations shaped the input of Methodist missionary attitudes and teaching in Asia.

It must also be noted that the development of the Methodist movement cannot be separated from the religious, economic, and political movements which shaped the different Asian societies. Communist rule in China has led to the kind of ecumenism which made the Chinese Methodist movement, now part of the China Christian Council*, postdenominational. Nationalism* and a desire for autonomy in the Philippines resulted in at least two branches of the Methodist movement: the Evangelical Methodist Church in the Philippines (IEMELIF) and the independent Philippine Methodist Church. The Holiness movement strongly influenced missionaries and Asian church leaders in India and Malaysia even when it degenerated into Sabbatarianism and temperance. And the boom of the rubber industry in Southeast Asia after 1910 helped make the Chinese churches of Malaysia and Sumatra (many of whose members owned rubber plantations) rich even as it sparked the creation of laboring-class Tamil churches comprising immigrant rubber tappers.

A challenging task is to identify the different factors which shaped Methodism in the different Asian countries: social, cultural, economic, political, ideological, historical, and individuals. Only with more detailed study can we discover whether there is such an entity as Asian Methodism. Some areas to be further explored for a better understanding of the Methodist movement in Asia, for example, are an analysis of Tamil hymnody to uncover dominant theological themes, and an examination and comparison of preaching among the different Chinese dialect groups to understand the interactive influences as Christians attempt to make the Gospel of Jesus Christ relevant to the people of a particular setting.

China. Initially, three Wesleyan mission boards of the United States sent missionaries to China, namely the Methodist Episcopal Church, Methodist Episcopal Church (South), and Methodist Protestant Church. The Methodist Episcopal Church and the Methodist Episcopal Church (South) had separated because of the growing tensions between the northern and southern sections of the United States over slavery. In Mar 1940, over 100 delegates representing these three missions came to Shanghai for a conference, and an official resolution of union was passed. The new name was fixed as the Methodist Church in China, the top hierarchy being the Central Conference Executive Committee, and the headquarters operating in Shanghai.

The mission in China was divided into four bishops' dioceses: North China (with the three annual conferences of North China, Shantung, and Zhang Jia Kou); West China (with the Szechwan annual conference); South China (with the three annual conferences of Foochow, Hinghwa, and Iongbing); and East China (with the three annual conferences of East China, Kiangsi, and Central China). Two Chinese and two missionaries were elected as the four bishops. After 1950, the Central Conference Executive Committee was chaired by Bishop Jiang Chang Chua. In 1958, the Methodist Church in China began to emphasize nationwide united worship.

The United Methodist Church Mission (UMC), China, was formed in the 20th c. by three English missionary societies: the Methodist New Connexion Missionary Society (MNCMS), the Methodist Free Church Mission (MFCM), and the Bible Christian Methodist Mission (BCMM). In 1860, J. Innocent (MNCMS) and a companion had arrived in Shanghai intending to make it a missionary stronghold, but they were thwarted by the Taiping* Heavenly Kingdom. They went instead to Tianjin, a commercial port, to preach in the English and French concessions. Later, they went to Shanxi and Mongolia. Hu Ngen-ti, Innocent's Chinese assistant, returned to his hometown in Laoling County, Shandong, and preached with success. The Gospel soon spread to Yongxin, Huimin, Zhanhua, and Binzhou Counties in the Yellow River Delta. Some Chinese Christians were ordained as pastors, and Shandong became another mission field.

Without the consent of MFCM, W. R. Fuller and others chose to do mission work in Ningpuo, Zhejiang, eventually developing the work in other coastal cities such as Zhenhai, Xiangsan, and Shipu, and building a hospital in Ningpuo. One of the missionaries, Galpin, translated the Bible* into the Ningpuo vernacular. In 1876, R. Inkermann was appointed to preach in Wenzhou, in the south of Zhejiang, when the area was opened. UMC later extended the work to places such as Huangyan, Lishui, and Youngjia and founded a hospital in 1900.

In 1885, upon the advice of James Hudson Taylor* (China Inland Mission, CIM), T. E. Vanstone (BCMM) decided to work in the southeast of Yunnan. The following year, he extended toward Zhaotang; and from 1905, working with the CIM, he went to Anishun, Shimenkan, and other places in Guizhou. Many among the converts were from minority groups such as the Miaozu and Yizu.

The Wesleyan Methodist Missionary Society, China (WMMS), an English mission, worked mainly in Hubei, Hunan, Guangdong, and Guangxi in China. In 1852, the Wesleyan Methodist Conference dispatched J. Cox to Guangzhou, but his work was impeded by the outbreak of the Second Opium War in 1856. Cox spent some months in Singapore and then returned to England for furlough. He went back to China and opened up WMMS work in Hankou in 1862 after a meeting in Nanjing (Jan 1862) with a rebel chief whom he knew. He was convinced that the rebels, though Christian, would oppose Christian missions.

Cox cooperated with Griffith John* (London Missionary Society, LMS), with whom he stayed until he found his own premises a few months later, and agreed that LMS would work in the Changjiang River basin and WMMS in the Han River basin. In 1865, Cox was joined by W. Scarborough, known for his collection of Chinese proverbs (retired to England in 1885), and David Hill (d. 18 Apr 1896), who succeeded Scarborough in 1885. Hill expanded the ministry of WMMS through charitable works: flood and famine relief and ministry to the blind. W. A. Cornaby, who reached China in 1885, edited the *Chinese Christian Review* and the *Chinese Weekly* while stationed in Hanyang.

WMMS entered Hunan in 1896, covering Pingjiang and Liuyang to the northeast of Changsha and Paoching and Linling in the south of the province.

The field in Guangzhou was actually opened in 1852 by an independent missionary, G. Piercy, who ministered to British soldiers in Guangzhou and Hong Kong while studying the Chinese language. He was subsequently recognized by the WMMS and supplied with additional workers. The field included Xinhui and Shaoguan. J. J. Macdonald, a medical doctor (killed by pirates in 1906), was sent to Wuzhou in the neighboring province, Guangxi, when it was opened as a treaty port in 1898, but apart from some medical work, WMMS did not make much headway in that region.

India. Methodism stemming from the American branch was a relative latecomer to India. The British branch started earlier in the 19th c. The former began work in North India in 1856. For some years, the Methodist Episcopal Church had planned this initiative, but candidates to launch the effort were sparse. Many declined the opportunity. Finally, the task was accepted by William Butler, a preacher of the New England Conference. Born in Ireland in 1818, he had come to the United

States in 1850. Butler had waited for others to accept the invitation to India; but since no one came forward, he offered himself. He was given wide discretionary power both in his work and in the selection of a location.

The Butlers sailed immediately for India, arriving in Calcutta on 25 Sep 1856. They chose as their field an area which was entirely unoccupied by missionaries. It covered much of what is now Uttar Pradesh. The Butlers desired to start work in Lucknow, but no housing was available. So they proceeded to Bareilly, which became the birthplace of Indian Methodism in Dec 1856. On the way, Butler secured as a helper a preacher from the Presbyterians* in Allahabad, Joel Janvier, the first Indian Methodist preacher. The first Methodist services in English and Hindustani were held on Sunday, 25 Feb 1857.

Hardly had work begun before the Sepoy Mutiny of 1857 broke out in May. With the insurgents at the doors, Janvier was preaching on the text: "Fear not, little flock, for it is the Father's good pleasure to give you the kingdom." Since then, this text has been a symbol and rallying cry of Indian Methodism. The Butlers a few days earlier had barely escaped with their lives to the mountains at Naini Tal, where they remained for months. All other missionaries in that part of India were killed. Butler was assumed to be dead also, but somehow he escaped.

Meanwhile, two other families had sailed and were eventually met by Butler in Agra, where the party sang the doxology under the dome of the Taj Mahal. Work could not be started again until late in 1858. The next year, the missionary group was further reinforced by the families of James M. Thoburn and Edwin W. Parker, both of whom later became bishops of the church.

William Butler did not himself gain mastery of the language but laid plans and cared for business details so that the others would be free for the actual work of evangelism. In fact, the success of the early mission was due not only to Butler but in large measure to the remarkable caliber of his colleagues.

The first convert responding to the preaching of J. L. Humphreys was a Muslim named Zahur-ul-Haqq. He later became a preacher and in 1882 the first Indian district superintendent.

The first church was dedicated in Naini Tal in Oct 1858. The first institution was an orphanage, founded the same year in Lucknow for children whose parents were killed in the mutiny. A printing press started operations in 1861. Humphreys studied medicine during his first furlough, and upon his return to the field in 1867 started training Indian girls to assist him. An industrial school was launched in 1868. Bareilly Seminary was started in 1870. The church paper, *The Indian Witness*, appeared the following year. The missionary statesman Thoburn was later to say, "The best missionary policy is that which avails itself of every agency out of which anything good can be wrought."

The India Mission Conference was established in 1864. This later became the North India Conference. As years went by, this work extended to 13 annual (or regional) conferences in nine different language areas.

Originally, the Methodist field was restricted to an area of what is now Uttar Pradesh, north of the Ganges. In 1870 a global evangelist, William Taylor*, came to India and spent four years evangelizing among English-speaking peoples. Taylor influenced Thoburn, and together they broke out of the narrower confines of North India to the wider countryside. Both men were expansionists.

Thoburn, whom John R. Mott called the greatest missionary strategist of the century, launched American Methodism in Burma, in Malaya, and finally in the Philippines*. In 1954, Methodists led the way in Christian witness in Nepal*. After independence in 1947, Methodists in Pakistan separated from Indian Methodists and are now united as part of the Church of Pakistan.

Meanwhile, Methodist women had begun their work in India in 1870 with two prominent leaders. One was Isabella Thoburn*, an educator and sister of James Thoburn. She was the moving force in establishing the deaconess movement in India and a school for girls which eventually bore her name, Isabella Thoburn College, the first college for women in all of Asia. Associated with her was Clara Swain*, the first female doctor of any missionary society and founder in Bareilly of the first hospital for women in Asia. Women, both missionaries and nationals, have always enjoyed prominence in Indian Methodism.

Methodism was deeply committed to evangelism. At least 80% of the Protestants of India are estimated to be of depressed-class origin. The means by which they came into the church was by mass movements*. For from the early days, whole caste groups in certain areas responded to the preaching of the first Catholic missionaries. Beginning in the early 1800s, a similar development took place in several Protestant fields in South India. The story of this whole development is simply told by J. Waskom Pickett, who studies the process thoroughly in his book *Christ's Way to India's Heart.*

The mass movements followed the natural social organization of the people — along caste lines. Often, all the people of a particular depressed class living in one village would enter the church. Their baptism was preceded usually by a period of instruction in basic Christian beliefs and practices. The movement would spread from village to village as the word was shared with relatives or fellows of the same caste nearby.

Once the church was scattered widely in villages. This is still true, but many have drifted toward the cities. Strong laypeople make up the membership in urban churches. They are now entirely self-supporting in their pastoral ministry and help in rural areas as well. The members are loyal Indian citizens and take their rightful place in their free nation. Since 1956, all of the bishops have been Indian nationals.

Indonesia. The first person who wanted to spread Methodism to Indonesia*, especially to Java, was

Thomas Coke, the righthand man of John Wesley. However, he did not reach Java, for on 3 May 1814, he was found dead in his cabin and buried in the Indian Ocean.

In 1905, the Methodists from America who had been working in Singapore and Malaysia since 1885 wanted to expand to Indonesia. There were three places where the Methodist missions started their work. On 20 Feb 1905, John Russel Denyes was assigned by the Malaysia Annual Conference to open the work in Java. On 5 Nov 1905, a congregation was organized in Bogor. On 1 Jul 1906, the first Methodist school was started in Bogor. In a short time, work was expanded to Batavia (Jakarta) and into adjacent areas.

In May 1905, Soloman Pakianathan (a Tamil preacher) arrived in Medan*. He was sent by G. F. Pykett (district superintendent in Penang) to supervise a private school owned by Hong Teen, a young Baba Chinese who had been a student in the Methodist Anglo-Chinese School in Penang. Now the door was opened for the Methodist mission to start evangelism within the school, and Pakianathan took control. He held religious services in English and promptly organized a Sunday school class for young English-speaking Chinese. This was the embryo of the congregation in Medan.

On 2 Feb 1906, C. M. Worthington was appointed to open the Methodist work in Pontianak, West Borneo, especially among the Chinese people.

In 1907, the work of the Methodists in Indonesia was organized into one district, and Denyes was promoted to district superintendent. In 1908, Pakianathan was transferred from Medan to Palembang to start the Methodist work there. On 1 May 1908, a Methodist school was established through which the door for evangelism was opened. In 1909, work began in Bangka; in 1911, Mark Freeman, a Methodist missionary, moved there.

In 1919, the whole work of Methodism in Indonesia was organized as a mission conference named (Netherlands Indies Mission Conference) with around 2,000 members, 30 congregations, and 14 pastors (nine missionaries and five native). In the same year, a hospital was established in Tjisarua, which is surrounded by Sundanese villages.

In 1921, the work among the Batak people in the interior of Asahan, Sumatra, commenced. This work was started in response to a request from Tuan Nagari Manurung, a village chief who had written a letter to W. F. Oldham* in Singapore 11 years earlier. Lamsana Lumbantobing, the first Indonesian to be ordained by the Methodist Church, was appointed to Asahan. Besides evangelizing the Toba Batak in the Pardembanan jungle, he also conducted Sunday services for the Christian Bataks who had migrated from Tapanuli to East Sumatra to work as clerks and plantation workers. Most of them had become Christians through the endeavors of the Rhenish Mission, which had been working there since the 1860s.

In 1925, the work in North Sumatra became the North Sumatra Mission Conference, distinct from the Netherlands Indies Mission Conference.

In the 1930s, the Methodist mission withdrew from Java and West Borneo to concentrate its work in Sumatra because of a lack of funds during the depression. But Methodist work in Sumatra was very uncertain. There were a number of missionaries who departed and did not return. Support from America was greatly decreased, and the exchange on the American dollar was unfavorable. Fortunately, two new missionaries were added. Both Ragnar Alm and Egon Ostrom were from Sweden. Ostrom worked among the Chinese and Alm among the Batak (Toba).

During World War II*, the American missionaries were evacuated. Both Ostrom and Alm, being from a neutral country, were permitted to remain. Ostrum was killed in Tebing Tingi because a young extremist suspected him of being a spy for the enemy. Alm then fled for safety. During the war, the responsibilities of the Methodist mission in Sumatra were shouldered by native ministers, Luther Hutabarat, David Hutabarat, and Yap Un Han. Many of the church's workers withdrew at that time, causing a shortage.

After the war was over, the congregations and schools were reactivated. Alm returned after three years on leave, and new missionaries were added: Per Eric Lager, J. Wesley Day, Gusta Rabbinate, Geoffrey Senior, and E. E. Dixon, etc.

In the 1950s, there were great migrations of the Batak people from Tapanuli to East Sumatra. They were forced by poverty* to leave Batakland and attracted by the plantation lands abandoned by the Dutch. Many new congregations were organized, but there were no workers available. In 1953, Alm opened a school for Batak pastors in Kisaran, Asahan, to train four supply pastors. At the same place, in 1956, Alm also opened a one-term pastoral training school for Bataks. The graduates of this school became the leaders of the Batak congregations. Among the Chinese churches, there was a lack of workers, so in 1954, the Chinese district started a Bible school for Chinese in Medan. Dixon was the first principal of this school.

In 1964, the Methodist Church of Indonesia become an autonomous church. The political confrontation between Indonesia and Malaysia was the main reason for this action. It was very difficult for the Methodist Church in Indonesia to be led by an American bishop whose headquarters was in Singapore. Wismar Panggaboan was elected as the first leader of the church. At that time there were 22,000 members and 21 pastors (five were missionaries). A group of discontented pastors and members separated to form a new church named the Free Methodist Church in Indonesia. In 1964, the Methodist Church of Indonesia expanded its work to Java.

In 1969, the first General Conference was held in Medan. The conference decided that the church should have a bishop instead of a chairman. Johanes Gultom was elected to lead the church, and in 1973 he was reelected for a second four-year term. During his leadership, the organization of the church was consolidated. The Book of Discipline was issued for the first time in 1973, and in 1977 Hennanus Sitorus was elected bishop. There were 33,000 members, 50 pastors, and 101 supply pastors at that time. In 1981, Sitorus was reelected for a second four-year term, during which time the Methodist Church of Indonesia promoted its evangelism especially among the Karo Batak in Sumatra. Mass baptisms were conducted several times. After this eight-year period, the membership numbered around 60,000.

In 1985, the General Conference again elected Gultom bishop, but he passed away after two years. A special session of the General Conference was held in Jan 1988, and Hamonangan Panggaboan was elected bishop. At the General Conference in 1989, he was reelected. During his term, a relationship between the Methodist Church in Indonesia and the Korean Methodist Church developed, and many church buildings were financed by the Korean Methodist Church.

At the General Conference in Bogor, 13-17 Oct 1993, H. Sitorus was elected bishop. There were at the time about 76,980 members, 113 pastors, 115 supply pastors, 238 congregations, and 155 mission posts. There are two annual conferences and 10 districts within the Methodist Church. Around 70% of the members are Batak, 20% are Chinese, and the rest are from various ethnic groups.

Japan. The Methodist movement that began in England in the 18th c. developed into an influential organization in the United States. From there the Methodist Episcopal Church, began missionary work in China in 1847. Robert Samuel Maclay labored in Wenzhou doing both educational and evangelistic work. Learning of the impending opening to Japan* in 1853, he recommended to the Home Mission Board that a mission to Japan be launched. When he returned to the US on furlough in 1871, he promoted this idea in the mission magazine. In November of the next year, Maclay was appointed superintendent of the Japan Mission; Julius Soper, Merriman Colbert Harris, and John Carrol Davison were assigned as missionaries; and later Irvin Henry Correll, who was serving in China, was reassigned to the Japan Mission.

Just as the prohibition of Christianity was lifted (1873), the American missionaries arrived in Yokohama, where they stayed from July through August of that year. They welcomed William L. Harris, the bishop of China, on 8 Aug to oversee the organizing of the Japan District at a meeting in Maclay's home. They set up four circuits (Yokohama, Edo [later Tokyo], Nagasaki, and Hakodate), with Maclay and Correll in Yokohama, Soper in Tokyo, Harris in Hakodate, and Davison in Nagasaki. On 28 Aug 1884, the Japan Annual Conference was established with eight districts: East Tokyo, West Tokyo, North Tokyo, Yokohama, North Yokohama, Nagasaki, Hokkaido, and Northern Honshu. In 1899, the church decided to form a conference in Kyushu; when it was organized in 1904, the church had two conferences. Mission work in Okinawa began in 1892, and work with the Japanese in Korea was started in 1904. Among the following leaders who were raised in the Methodist Church were Honda Yoitsu, Yamaga Hatanoshin, Bessho Umenosuke, Ishizaka Kameji, Yoshioka Seimei, Abe Yoshimune, and Muto Takeshi. When the church merged in 1907 with two other Methodist churches, it had 77 churches, 30 preaching points, and approximately 7,000 members.

On 30 Jun 1873, about two weeks after the missionaries of the Methodist Episcopal Church, USA, arrived in Yokohama, Davidson Macdonald and George Cochran, missionaries of the Methodist Church of Canada, also landed in Yokohama. Their language teachers, Makino Eikichi and his servant Yasutomi Kiyohiko, were seekers, and in April of the following year, the first baptism in Japan by Methodists occurred at the Cochran home. Maclay and Correll of the US church also attended. In October, Suzuki Kiichi and his wife were baptized by Correll. The Canadian Mission first established its roots in Tokyo and Shizuoka, where Cochran got to know Nakamura Masanao. They made their headquarters at Dojinsha, an English and Chinese tutorial school in Koishikawa. Macdonald became acquainted with a former shogun's vassal in Shizuoka, Ebara Soroku.

In Sep 1876, George Marsden Meacham and Charles Samuel Eby arrived, and their area of work became the Japan District of the Toronto Conference, under the name Japan Methodist Church, with three areas — Tokyo, Shizuoka, and Yamanashi (the latter included Nagano and Kanazawa). In 1889, the church organized the Japan Conference. In addition to Nakamura and Ebara, Japanese who were converted by the Canadian Mission included Hiraiwa Yoshiyasu, Yamaji Aizan, and Takagi Mizutaro. It is also important to take note of the *Chuo Kaido* (Central Tabernacle), the Self-Supporting Band, and the Home Mission Society of the Japan Methodist Church. At the time of the three churches merging, there were 29 congregations (four self-supporting), 20 preaching points, and about 3,300 church members.

The Methodist Episcopal Church, South, came a bit later, when in July 1886 James William Lambuth and Oscar Adolphus Dukes arrived to work in Kobe. On 17 Sep, a founding ceremony was held for the Japan Southern Methodist Church, and in November, Walter Russel Lambuth arrived. With Kobe as the center, they concentrated their work on Kansai and Shikoku, and the next year Samuel Hayman Wainright began working in Oita. The mission field extended east to include Osaka, Wakayama, and Kyoto; in Jul 1892, the Japan Conference of the Southern Methodist Church was organized. Uzaki Kogoro, Hori Minekitsu, Kugimiya Tokio, Akazawa Motozo, and Hinohara Zensuke became leaders in this church. At the time of the 1907 merger, it had 37 churches (17 self-supporting), 74 preaching points, and about 5,400 church members.

These Methodist churches put much effort into educational work. The Methodist Episcopal Church started *Aoyama Gakuin* (school), *Chinzei Gakuin, Fukuoka Jo Gakuin* (girls school), *Iai Jo Gakko, To Gijuku,* and

Hirosaki Gakuin. The Canadian Methodist Church founded *Toyo Eiwa Jo Gakuin, Shizuoka Eiwa Jo Gakuin,* and others. The Methodist Episcopal Church, South, established *Hiroshima Jo Gakuin, Lambuth Jo Gakuin* (Seiwa College), *Palmore Gakuin,* and *Kwansei Gakuin.* They also put emphasis on publishing, establishing a number of different publishing concerns, which eventually became the *Kyo Bun Kwan* (Christian Literature Society of Japan).

Earlier, in 1883, the three Methodist churches had begun a movement to unite their groups, because they felt that in a new mission field such as Japan, it was important to work together. In 1887, a proposal was drawn up and forwarded to their North American home churches for approval, which did not come easily. So in 1891, with Yamaji Aizan as main writer, they put together *Go kyo* (Keeping the Faith) as a regular publication of the three churches. In 1900, they reached out to other denominations such as the Japan Methodist Protestant Church, the Japan Evangelical Church, and the Japan Church of the United Brethren in Christ, in hopes of bringing about a large-scale merger. The annual conference meetings of the three original denominations voted in favor of the merger, but the Methodist Protestant and Brethren Churches were also being approached about merging with the Japan Congregational Church, and voices from the evangelical churches indicated that such talk was premature. In the end, the three Methodist churches merged and moved toward becoming a self-supporting, independent church. In 1906, Honda Yoitsu went to the US to negotiate this move with the mother churches. On 22 May 1907, the founding general conference for the Japan Methodist Church was held at *Aoyama Gakuin.* Honda was elected the first bishop of the church; he was followed by Hiraiwa, Uzaki, Akazawa, and Kugimiya. The sixth bishop was Abe Yoshimune. Abe was elected chairman of the executive committee of the National Christian Council of Japan and did extensive study and consultation on a proposal for major unification of the church in response to needs at that time. In 1941, the Japan Methodist Church joined the Japan Presbyterian Church, Japan Congregational Church, and others to form the United Church of Christ in Japan. The Methodists have continued to play a central role in this group since the war.

Korea. Before missionaries came to Korea, the Bible* had already been translated into Korean in Manchuria and Japan. Korean colporteurs brought it into Korea secretly and distributed it, so baptismal candidates appeared. To address this situation, the Korean Christians requested that American and European churches send missionaries. In answer, the American Methodist Church dispatched missionaries to Korea.

In Sep 1883, Young-Ick Min, a member of the Korean embassy, traveled to America. He met John Goucher and requested the establishment of hospitals and schools in Korea. Goucher approached the Board of Foreign Missions of the Methodist Episcopal Church in New York about the matter. Meanwhile, Goucher charged Robert Maclay, a missionary residing in Japan, to research the missionary situation in Korea. Maclay came to Korea and requested permission from the Korean government (through the American embassy) to conduct mission activity. Emperor KoJong granted the request, but permitted the mission to found only schools and hospitals.

The Board of Foreign Missions of the Methodist Episcopal Church appointed H. G. Appenzeller*, W. B. Scranton*, and Mrs. M. F. Scranton (Scranton's mother), who were sent to Korea in 1885. They started a full-scale missionary work through the schools and hospitals established. Because Korean standards of living, society, politics, and economics were difficult in the late 19th c., the Korean response was very positive. The first Korean Methodists were converted in Manchuria, and they acted as colporteurs, selling Scripture portions in northern Korea. The first wave of these included Choi Sung-Kyun and his co-workers, the students of Paichai Boys' School and Ewha Girls' School. Appenzeller baptized Korean Methodists on 24 Jul 1887 and founded the first Methodist church, Bethel Chapel, at Chung-Dong on 9 Oct 1887. Since that time, the church has grown through the ministries of Korean colporteurs, and evangelists (both male and female).

In the late 19th c., Korea was in a state of social confusion. During this time, the Donghak farmers revolution, the Sino-Japanese War (1894), and Queen Min's murder by the Japanese (1895) occurred. Nevertheless, many people joined the church. A number of intellectuals converted in jail after the Independent Club Trial (1899).

Meanwhile, Yoon Chi-ho had joined the Methodist Episcopal Church. After the failure of the Kapshin-Chungbyun political revolt (1884), Yoon studied abroad, going through China to America. After he finished his studies at Vanderbilt University, he came back to Korea in 1894. Taking up official employment, he also made a request to the Board of Foreign Missions of the Methodist Episcopal Church, South. In response, the Methodist Episcopal Church sent Chinese missionaries, Bishop Hendrix, and Rev. G. Reid to Korea and surveyed the possibility of a Korean mission. In 1895, Reid settled in Seoul and started mission work. After that, the Methodist Episcopal Church sent Campbell and Collyer to Korea, and they joined with the evangelical movements.

In the first stage, the Korean Methodist Church was divided into two regions, North and South, but they cooperated with each other in the management of the theological seminary, Bible classes, and the women's edification movement. After the 1 Mar Independence Movement (1919), they made an effort to form one Methodist church in Korea. The two sides organized a Committee on Church Benevolence and began confidential talks toward union. They agreed to the elementary principles for union and requested permission from the mother church in the USA. The Methodist Episcopal Church agreed to the union in 1928, and the Methodist

Episcopal Church, South, in 1930. As a result, church bishops, missionaries, and Korean leaders from both churches gathered and formed the Joint Committee on Methodist Unification to organize the Korean Methodist Church.They then selected the Doctrinal Statement of the Korean Methodist Church and the Social Creed, as well as elected the first superintendent, Ryang Ju-Sam.

The Korean Methodist Church took an active part in national resistance movements against the Japanese colonialists, such as the 105 Mem Sagun (Conspiracy Case, 1911) and the 1 Mar Independence Movement. Many Methodist pastors and laymen who participated were imprisoned as a result. In addition, Nam Kung Uck and Choe Yong-Shin demonstrated against the Japanese by leading the agricultural improvement movement.

In the late period of Japanese rule, Japan strengthened its religious control, creating a crisis for the Korean Methodist Church. Bishop Chung Chun-Su organized the pro-Japanese church, *Hyukshin Kyodan* (Renovational Church). Immediately, many pastors and laymen opposed it, so some were put in jail and others were excommunicated. At that time, an ordained deaconess Choi In-Kyu of Tong-Chun Church, the evangelist Kwon Won-Ho, and pastor Kang Chong-Keun were martyred.

After emancipation, the Korean Methodist Church began the rebuilding process. Following the Korean War*, the church split, but the two sides later reunited. After that, as Korean Methodists fully dedicated themselves to evangelical outreach, many people came to the church; there were 4,300 churches and 1,289,242 church members in 1993. Especially after the 1960s, the Methodist Church was concerned about industrial and farm mission. It eagerly participated in social movements and the democratic struggle during the time of the military regime, so many pastors and students were again imprisoned.

Since 1991, through movements such as Seven Thousand Churches and Two Million Church Members, Korean Methodists have sought to increase the membership of the church and its influence in society. Meanwhile, they have endeavored to fix in people's minds the mission ideas of national union and world peace.

Lower Myanmar. In lower Myanmar the Methodists began as the Methodist English Church. With about 60 members it was started in 1879 by James M. Thoburn (who later became bishop) and F. E. Goodwin, who came from Calcutta at the invitation of Christian sympathizers in Yangon (Rangoon). Helped by R. E. Carter, who had arrived from America a few days earlier, they began with a fortnight of evangelistic meetings held in the Baptist church and the town hall. The church building was completed in 1880 with a parsonage for J. E. Robinson (later bishop), who succeeded Carter in that same year.

The first missionary of the Women's Foreign Missionary Society (WFMS) to Myanmar was Ellen Warner, who arrived in 1881 and established an English Girls' School on Lewis Street the following year. An orphanage was opened in 1887 in connection with the English Girls' School. In 1883, a Seaman's Rest was opened in a rented house.

Under the Bengal Conference of 1888, the Burma District included Malaysia until the Malaysia Mission was established in 1889. In 1892, the Burma, Calcutta, and Tirhoot Districts of the Bengal Conference were consolidated into the Bengal-Burma Conference, and the rest into the North-West India Conference. The Bengal-Burma Conference met in Yangon (Rangoon) in Feb 1895. The first Burma Mission Conference, chaired by Bishop F. W. Warne, was held in Feb 1901 with A. T. Leonard as general secretary. The Women's Conference, organized at the same time, comprised Fannie Perkins, Charlotte Illingworth, S. S. Turrell, Luella Rigby, and the wives of the missionaries. In Feb 1908, the Central Conference for Southern Asia and the All-India Epworth League Convention were held in Yangon. The Burma Mission District Conference was divided into the Burmese, or Barmar (for Barmar work), and Rangoon Yanon (all other languages), Districts in 1916. The conference was further divided into four districts in 1920: Barmar, Chinese, English, and Indian. The English and Barmar Districts were led by the missionaries; the Chinese and Indian work were also partly led by them.

Schools were established in about 20 cities and villages within the first 25 years; new converts and Myanmar ministers came mainly from these schools. The Epworth League also influenced and trained many young people to be missions-minded.

After World War II*, some missionaries returned to Myanmar to help reconstruct the work. The 43rd session of the annual conference was held in Oct 1946, chaired by C. D. Rockey, with U Ba Ohn as general secretary, and new leaders were trained. Church developments were affected by the changed political policy of 2 Mar 1962. There were suggestions by missionaries of both denominations that the Episcopal and the Wesleyan Methodist Church in Myanmar should unite. Meetings were held, but nothing materialized.

On 8 May 1964, Hobart B. Amstutz, the last American bishop in Burma, sent a telegram to say that the general conference had approved the autonomy of the Methodist Church of the Union of Burma (Lower Burma). The 62nd annual conference (5-10 Oct 1964), chaired by H. B. Amstutz with Henry Ang as general secretary, elected Lin Si Sin, the Chinese district superintendent and a Myanmar citizen, as the first national bishop. There were then 24 national ministerial workers serving 13 churches and 13 Gospel centers.

All foreign missionaries had left Myanmar by May 1966. Four high schools, four middle schools, and nine primary schools were nationalized in 1964 and 1965. There were 1,295 baptized children and 1,645 full members in 1965.

The church became more steady and mature under the leadership of the second bishop, U Hla Sein, a Barmar minister, from 1969 to 1980. The Methodist centenary was celebrated on 23-25 Nov 1979.

The Barmar mission started mainly through schools and social work in the cities and the rural areas. In 1892, a Barmar girls' school was opened in Yangon, and Barmar work was started in Thongwa. In 1893, a Christian agricultural project was begun on the Myitcho Canal, north of Pegu. The work in Pegu was officially established in 1894. In 1896, 100 acres of land was secured at Thandaung for an orphanage. The Twanti mission was started in 1903. In 1904, the Barmar Boys' School in Yangon and a school at Syriam opened. The first indigenous minister, U Pe Tun, was accepted on a trial basis in 1904. He was followed by U Po Myint, U Mo Khin, U David, and U Po Sein.

After World War II, much of the Barmar mission work could not be reorganized. Union Christian High School was established by the American Baptists and Methodists in Yangon in 1947. Another joint venture with the American Baptists was the Methodist Kingswood School at Kalaw in 1948. The Burmese Social Center on 46th Street, Yangon, was opened in 1950. The Burmese Methodist Church struggled amidst staunch Buddhists and a growing Baptist Church. Presently, there are eight churches and three Gospel centers in the Barmar District.

Chinese work in Myanmar began with a Chinese Methodist evangelist from Vancouver, Canada, who arrived in Yangon in 1895. Working with another Christian from China, he baptized three Chinese that year. Several home churches were formed as more Christians came from China. In 1901, there were 55 members. As the worshippers increased, they were allowed the use of the Methodist Church on Lewis Street. The first Western missionary to the Chinese was C. J. Soelberg, who arrived in 1913. In 1917, a Chinese kindergarten was started by the WFMS in a rented house on 22nd Street. It developed into the Anglo-Chinese Girls' School. An old bungalow at the corner of Canal and 19th Streets was purchased in 1917 for the Chinese church and the Anglo-Chinese Boys' School. John Sung* was invited to preach at evangelistic meetings, and seven Gospel teams evangelized throughout Yangon City.

Another prewar Chinese church was in Pegu, 50 miles from Yangon. Tan Kim Sein (d. 1906) arrived from China in 1904 and, working with five other Chinese Christians, visited nearby cities and began holding worship services. He also established ties with the Yangon Chinese community on 22nd Street. A Chinese school was opened in a rented house in Pegu in 1914. A timber building erected in 1915 served as a church (upper floor) and the Chinese school (ground floor). World War II (1941-45) scattered the believers; after the war, worship services were held in houses as the Pegu church building had been destroyed (rebuilt in 1950).

The Rangoon building was reclaimed in 1945. Under Mark Lim, the church was reorganized and the school reopened. Under the leadership of Lin Si Sin from the United Church of South China, who was invited by the Yangon Chinese Church in 1949, a Mandarin-speaking church was organized in Kamayut, a suburb of Yangon, in 1956. In 1958, a Gospel team of seven visited the Chinese congregations in nine cities in northern Myanmar. Four groups came under Methodist care: Kyaukme, Mandalay, Maymyo, and Namhsan. The church then developed northward. The political watershed of 1962 resulted in a lack of Chinese-speaking pastors to serve the growing congregations. On 1 Nov 1992, an interdenominational Chinese Christian Preachers Training Center was opened under the leadership of Grace Tan. There are presently 12 Chinese churches and three Gospel centers.

Work among Indians in Myanmar began with the first Methodist English Church, which took care of Tamil and Telugu believers. A boys' school for the Indians was opened in 1883, and a mission center was opened in Toungoo to serve the English and the Indian people in 1886. Work among the Tamils began in 1893 and among the Hindustani in 1913 at Pegu. A Telugu girls' school was opened on Lewis Street, Yangon, in 1904. In 1921, W. W. Bell was appointed the first full-time missionary in Indian work. In 1928, the Rangoon Telugu Church was organized, with E. John as the first pastor. Many Indians returned to India after the political changes of 1962. Presently, there are only three Indian churches and one Gospel center.

In the Lower Myanmar Conference, there are altogether 19 ordained pastors and five supply pastors serving 24 churches and seven Gospel centers. There are 2,097 full members and 1,119 baptized children.

Upper Myanmar. The Methodist Church in Upper Myanmar grew through the work of missionaries appointed to Myanmar in 1887 by the Wesleyan Methodist Conference in the United Kingdom. Joseph H. Bateson and W. Ripley Winston arrived in Mandalay in early 1887. Winston started a school in a rented house near the center of Mandalay. The first three converts, Pho Chway, Maung Khin, and Pho Choong, were baptized in Mandalay on the first Sunday of Dec 1888. Winston also erected the Home for Lepers in Mandalay in 1891 (see Leprosy Work).

In 1966, there were 54 men and 25 women missionaries. All the mission schools and the Home for Lepers were then nationalized by the revolutionary government, which had come into power on 2 Mar 1962. When the Methodist Church became autonomous in 1964, U Ba Ohn was elected the first indigenous conference president, and the church had three districts: Mandalay, Tahan, and Maingdaungphai. There are today six districts (the three new ones being Falam, Haka, and Tamu), with a total community of 39,629.

Evangelistic work is supported by personal gifts, collections, and pledges. The Tahan and Falam Districts have opened home mission fields among the Dai in the Mindat and Kanpetlet areas. It is expected that Mindat and Kanpetlet will become a new district, with about 5,000 community members.

The Tahan District worked among the Asho Chin in Magway division in 1990, and within three years formed

11 new societies with a total community of 207 new converts. The Tahan District also opened the Tahan Wesley Clinic on 15 Jan 1987 and the Letpanchaung Wesley Clinic on 5 Jan 1992. Three doctors and a number of nurses treat a daily average of 330 patients, of whom 250 are outpatients.

The Tamu District works among the Khumi Chin in the Paletwa area, and the Maingdaungphai District among the Shan and Naga hill tribes. The Mandalay District works among the Yinnet tribe in Southern Shan State.

The conference encourages higher theological education* and training. In 1988, the Methodist Theological Training Institute was upgraded, becoming the Myanmar Theological College, an interdenominational institution.

Philippines. The arrival of Methodism must be seen in the context of the Philippine Revolution of 1896. For more than three centuries, Protestantism was banned in the Philippines. Spanish colonialism had a policy that the Roman Catholic Church* was the only religion of the state, and officially it reigned supreme in the islands. Located at a crossroads for travel, where the Pacific Ocean meets the China Sea, the 7,100 islands of the Philippines became, for the West, a place where Asian cultures and Western pragmatism blended. On 2 Mar 1899, after the Philippines was ceded to the United States by Spain (Treaty of Paris, 10 Dec 1898), James Thoburn of the Methodist Episcopal Church visited the Philippines to look at the possibilities of starting mission work in the country. On 4 Apr 1910, the first officially appointed missionaries arrived. They were Thomas Martin and Jones Maclaughlin.

Methodism pioneered mission and evangelism largely through student work (dormitories, among them Hugh Wilson Hall, and the Central Student Center on T. M. Kalaw Street), hospitals (Mary Johnston Hospital in Tondo), and education (Harris Memorial College and Wesleyan University, and, in joint effort with the Presbyterians, the Philippine Christian University). Its largest parish churches are located in metro Manila, among them the Knox Memorial Church, Central Student Church, and Good Samaritan Church.

Methodism has also been active in ecumenical* ventures, such as the National Council of Churches in the Philippines, and was among the pioneering churches that joined with the Presbyterian Church in establishing a common seminary, Union Theological Seminary, now in Dasmarinas, Cavite. A member of the World Methodist Council, Philippine Methodism has counted among its members several prominent Filipinos, including a Philippine supreme court justice, a cabinet officer, and several high-ranking military officers.

There is today a groundswell of demand for autonomy from the United States Methodists, as the bishops' salaries are still paid by the American Methodist Church. Younger clergy demand autonomy as a step toward asserting selfhood, self-determination, and independence from American Methodism. The debate is still unsettled, with the older clergy battling to maintain ties (including financial aid) with US Methodism.

Today, there are almost half a million adult members. The vision of being the biggest Protestant denomination by the twenty-first century while facing many handicaps was realized, as witnessed by the burgeoning growth of local churches. This growth averaged one new local church per week throughout the Philippines. Strong in the Wesleyan tradition of mission and evangelism, Philippine Methodism is slowly but surely catching up with the rapid population growth (estimated at 2.3% of the 65 million Filipinos).

By increasing their giving for ministers' pensions, salaries, and other emoluments, the Methodists have surpassed other denominations in tithing and church support. The episcopal sees are served by three bishops: Manila and the southern Luzon area, Mindanao and Visayas, and the Baguio area and northern Luzon. A fourth episcopal diocese may be needed.

Iglesia Evangelica Metodista en las Islas Filipinas (IEMELIF, Evangelical Methodist Church in the Philippines) is the product of a nationalist schism in 1909 led by Nicolas Zamora*, the first Filipino ordained Protestant minister. Believing that Filipino churches should be governed by Filipinos themselves, Zamora led into schism four out of nine members of the Methodists' annual conference, 25 out of 121 local preachers, and about 1,500 out of some 30,000 church members. After Zamora's death, a few groups separated from the IEMELIF, though these merged in 1932 with other small evangelical groups. In 1948, a small IEMELIF segment joined the United Church of Christ in the Philippines, but the main body remained intact (about 112,000 members in 1995) and is a member of the National Council of Churches in the Philippines.

Like the IEMELIF in 1909, the Philippine Methodist Church is the result of a schism in 1933 from the Methodist Episcopal Church on nationalist grounds. Reacting to what they considered high-handedness on the part of the mother American church, Cipriano Navarro, Melquiades Q. Gamboa, and Samuel W. Stagg carried into schism 27 ordained ministers, some deaconesses and Bible women, and about one sixth of the entire Methodist church membership. Their movement was supported by five American missionaries. The resultant Philippine Methodist Church was especially strong in Manila and in Pangasinan Province. In 1948, the Philippine Methodist Church, under the leadership of Roberto P. Songco, joined two other denominations in forming the United Church of Christ in the Philippines.

Sri Lanka. The Methodist Church, which established the third English missionary Society in Sri Lanka during the 19th c., constitutes one of the most prominent Protestant groups in the country today. The original mission was headed by Thomas Coke and seven others. They set sail on 13 Dec 1813 and arrived on the island on 29 Jun 1814. Coke died on the voyage. Upon their arrival the missionaries started work in Jaffna, Batticaloa (for Tamils and Matara), and Galle and Colombo (for Sinhalese).

In 1819, the Methodists divided Sri Lanka into two districts, the North and the South. The Tamil-speaking area in the North and East came under the jurisdiction of the North Ceylon District. The rest of the island, mainly Sinhalese-speaking, was brought under the South District.

The Methodist mission produced some outstanding ministers during the first half of the 19th c. Among the chairmen of the North District, Peter Percival (1837-51) was a Tamil scholar and educator, and J. Kilnes (1860-75) was a proponent of self-support and self-government for the church. In the south, D. J. Gogerly (1838-62) is credited with pioneer research into Buddhist philosophy, which was hardly known among the Europeans at that time. In fact, his polemics led to the Buddhist-Christian controversies. He was followed by R. S. Hardy, another Buddhist scholar.

Between 1870 and 1900, the Methodists followed the government and the Anglicans in opening schools of a high standard, including Wesley College, Colombo; Richmond College, Galle; Kingswood College, Kandy; Central College, Jaffna; and the Methodist College for Girls, Colombo. An increasing number of educational missionaries arrived in Sri Lanka, many of whom had a profound influence on their pupils. From 1885 to 1905, industrial schools for destitute children made a great impact on the country. The Methodists were also involved in medical* work among mothers, and Bible women were trained to assist them.

In the early 20th c., there was an increased emphasis on the schools, though evangelism was still the primary objective. Changing theological convictions, however, led to more liberal attitudes regarding Buddhism* and Hinduism*. There was also a movement toward increased responsibility for Sri Lankans. Since many missionaries left during World War II, this movement accelerated.

In 1950 the North and South Districts were combined into a single district. Its first chairman was a Sri Lankan, S. G. Mendis. The British Methodist Conference transferred full authority in 1964 to an autonomous Sri Lanka Conference. F. S. de Silva became the first president.

Since 1940 the Methodist Church has been negotiating a church-union scheme with the Anglicans, Baptists, Presbyterians, and the Jaffna Diocese of the Church of South India on the basis of a historic episcopate. Although church union has not come about, the Methodists have contributed to cooperation between the churches in the National Council of Churches and several other ecumenical bodies. The Center for Religion and Society opened in 1951, specializing in Buddhist studies and interfaith dialogue (see Interreligious Dialogue).

The Methodist Church has taken an impartial stand on the question of national unity and the idea of self-determination for minorities. In 1983, the chairman of the Methodist Church, Soma Perera, was swift to condemn terrorist acts on both sides of the ethnic strife. As seen in the allocation of personnel in leadership positions, the Methodist Church has remained an example of Sinhala-Tamil unity.

The Methodist Church suffered with other Christian denominations as a result of the takeover of the schools by the government in 1960. Although there was a temporary decline, in the recent past there have been real evangelism and conversion among both Sinhalese and Tamils.

Bibliography

Badley, Brenton T., *Visions and Victories in Hindustan* (1931). • Hollister, John N., *The Centenary of the Methodist Church in Southern Asia* (1956). • Mathews, James K., *South of the Himalayas* (1955). • Mead, Frank S., *Handbook of Denominations,* 6th ed. (1980). • Akagawa Motozo, *Mesojisuto kyokai* (Methodist Church), *Sakai Chokichi, "Nihon mifu kyokai"* (Japan Methodist Protestant Church), *Nihon shukyo koza* (Lectures on Japanese Religion) 13 (1935). • Spencer, D. S., *Journal of the First General Conference of the Japan Methodist Church* (1907). • Yamaga Hatanoshin, *Godo mesojisuto kyokai shoshi* (United Methodist Church Magazine) (1923); *Kuranaga Takashi Kanada mesojisuto nihon dendo gaishi* (General History of the Canadian Methodist Church's Mission in Japan) (1937); *Nakamura Kinji, Nanmi senkyo go-ju-nen shi* (Fifty-year History of Southern Methodism) (1936). • Krummel, John W., *Missionary Work of the Methodist Episcopal Church, USA, in Tokyo during the Early Meiji Period* (1982). • Coplestone, J. T., *History of Methodist Mission,* Vol. IV (1973). • Doraisamy, T. R., *The March of Methodism* (1982). • Means, N. T., *Malaysia Mosaic* (1935). • Brooks, E. N., *Java and Its Challenge* (1917). • Ward, W. T., *Sunlight and Shadow of Missionary Life* (1915). • Diffendorfen, R. E., ed., *The World Service of the Methodist Episcopal Church* (1923). • Alejandro, D. D., *From Darkness to Light* (1968). • Anderson, G. H., et al., *Studies in Philippine Church History* (1965). • Deats, R., *History of Methodism in the Philippines* (1978). • Jenkins, H. L., *Methodism World Wide* (1982). • *Journal of Philippines Annual Conference* (1990, 1991, 1992). • Nabong, Juan, "Rediscovering Our Ancient Heritage," speech in the IEMELIF Cathedral (1959). • Wellington, E., "The Central Conference of the Methodist Church" (Commission of Mission Overseas, mimeograph, 1960-65). • Laubach, F. C., *People of the Philippines* (1925). • Gutierrez, M., "The IEMELIF — First Indigenous Church in the Philippines," *Philippine Christian Advance* II (Apr 1950). • Deats, R. L., *The Story of Philippine Methodism in the Philippines* (1964). • Gowing, P. G., *Islands Under the Cross* (1967). • Sitoy, T. V., Jr., *Several Springs, One Stream* (1992). • Harwood, H. J., *Conference Journal* (1925). • Beadon, G. R., *Conference Journal* (1954). • Ang, Henry, *Conference Journal* (1965, 1966). • Tan, Grace, *Conference Journal* (1979);

Methodist Autonomous Church, Silver Jubilee (1990). • Hla Sein, *Methodist Centenary History* (1979). • Chen Su Yung, *The Call of Macedonia* (1958). • *Conference Minutes* (1992). • *Diamond Jubilee Souvenir 1927-1987* (1986). • Daw Mi Mi, "Methodism in Myanmar" (typed manuscript, 1988); *The Upper Myanmar Methodist Centenary Book* (1987). • *The Tahan District Synod Minutes* (1992). • Small, W. J. T., *The History of the Methodist Church in Ceylon* (1970). • Harmon, Nolan B., ed., *The Encyclopedia of World Methodism* (1974). • *The Christian Encyclopedia* (1986). • Lee, Sung Sam, *Hankuk Kamrikyohoe-sa* (History of the Methodist Church in Korea) (1986).

Robert Hunt, China Group, James K. Mathews, Richard Daulay, Sasaki Tadakazu, Miyakoda Tsunetaro, Sawada Yasunobu, Lee Duk Joo (translated by Kim In Soo), Grace Tan, Lal Pan Liana, Salvador D. Eduarte, T. Valentino Sitoy, G. P. V. Somaratna

Mezzabarba, Carlo Ambrogio

(b. 1685; d. 1741). Second papal legate sent to China* during the reign of Emperor Kangxi.

In 1715, Pope Clement XI reiterated the prohibition of ancestor worship* and the veneration of Confucius in the Apostolic Constitution *Ex illa die.* To ensure compliance, the pope sent Mezzabarba as a special legate to China to complete the work begun by Charles Thomas Maillard de Tournon* in 1705 and 1706. Mezzabarba reached Lisbon in 1719, journeyed on to China the following year, and was granted an audience with Emperor Kangxi on 31 Dec 1720. Mezzabarba met with the emperor several times. On 17 Jan 1721, Kangxi ordered the missionaries in Beijing to translate *Ex illa die* into Chinese, and the following day, having read the translation, issued the following instruction which was conveyed to Mezzabarba: "From now on, there is no need to have Westerners doing mission in China. It is all right to stop them." On 21 Jan, Kangxi jailed Pedrini, who was doing translation work for Mezzabarba. On 1 Mar 1721, Mezzabarba, who sensed constant surveillance, bade Kangxi farewell and left China two days later as he felt he could not accomplish his mission.

Mezzabarba left for Macau*, where he stayed for six months. From Macau, he sent out an eight-point agreement on Chinese rites. These eight points he communicated to the missionaries in China with the instructions that they never be translated into Chinese. Near the end of 1721, Mezzabarba, with the remains of Cardinal de Tournon, returned to Rome via Brazil and Portugal. Before he died, he was given the title patriarch of Alexandria.

Bibliography

Rosso, Antonio Sisto, *Apostolic Legations to China of the Eighteenth Century* (1948). • Rule, Paul, *K'ung-tzu on Confucius: The Jesuit Interpretation of Confucianism* (1986) • Ross, Andrew C., *A Vision Betrayed* (1994).

China Group, translated by David Wu

Miche, Jean-Claude

(b. diocese of St. Die, France, 1805; d. 1873). Member of the Paris Foreign Mission Society* (MEP) and first apostolic vicar of Cambodia*.

Friend of the kings of Cambodia — and the Founder of Modern Cambodia, as historians call him — Miche exercised a particularly important influence in the process of establishing the French Protectorate of Cambodia. Arriving in Siam in 1837, Miche learned the Cambodian language and aligned himself with Cambodian prince Ang Duong, who was in mandatory residence at the court of Bangkok. Miche was then sent to Battambang but had to flee to Malaua because of the destruction of the city. He was then assigned to the apostolate of the Montagnard* tribes of Cochin China. Condemned to death by the Vietnamese authorities, he was rescued by the arrival of a French ship.

Prince Ang Duong was then placed by the court of Bangkok on the throne of Cambodia, a country under the protectorate of Siam. He contrived to make Miche come to the court of Andong, its capital, so he would have an intermediary to ask France for support. Named bishop coadjutor of the apostolic vicariate of Cochin China in 1848, Miche was given the vicariate of Cambodia and Laos* in 1850 when the vicariate of Cochin China was divided. Miche thus became apostolic vicar of Cambodia.

Aware of the political role the king of Cambodia would like to have played, Miche accepted only the role of translating the letters of the king. He showed himself rather hostile to those arriving from France, refusing in 1859 even to translate a royal missal proposing to conclude a military alliance with the French troops. After the death of King Ang Duong in 1860, Miche asked Catholics to take arms in favor of Norodom, the new king, against his brother, who was contesting the ascension. Miche also rallied the Muslim Chams in favor of the crown. After victory, he asked Siam to repatriate King Norodom (a refugee to Siam) and reinstate in Cambodia the sword of gold and the sacred lance, emblems of the royal power. By this move, Miche joined the French military authorities in convincing King Norodom to establish a protectorate under France. Article 15 of the treaty signed in 1863 accorded total freedom to the missionaries.

Miche asked that the apostolic vicariate of Cochin China of 1850 be revised. The vicariate of Cambodia of that time included two countries, Cambodia and Laos, whose population practiced *Theravada* Buddhism* and were judged impenetrable to Christianity. In contrast, converts in Cochin China were numerous. Miche asked that Laos be detached from his vicariate, but he wished to retain the three provinces of Basse–Cochin China, situated to the west of the Mekong (Chau Doc, Vinh Long,

Soc Trany), "in order to find a kernel to form some Christian Annamites." The Congregation of Propaganda responded favorably to this demand in 1870. Miche's request seriously weakened the apostolate attached to the Cambodians: progressively, all of the mission's attention was oriented toward the Annamite (Vietnamese) groups of Cochin China at the expense of the Khmer people, whose missionary personnel were losing hope of conversion. The installation of the French protectorate, favoring the Vietnamese presence in Cambodia, was disastrous for the mission, diverting the interest of the church from the Khmer. It appeared to the Khmer for several centuries that the church embodied colonialism* and was an enemy of the state.

Bibliography

Ponchaud, François, *The Cathedral of the Rice Paddy* (1990).

FRANÇOIS PONCHAUD

Middleton, Thomas Fanshaw

(b. Kedleston, Derbyshire, England, 1759; d. 1822). First Anglican bishop in India* after the diocese of Calcutta was established.

Middleton was from a noble family, his father being a rector. He studied at Pembroke College, Cambridge, and was awarded a doctorate for his treatise on the Greek article in 1811. He was ordained in 1792 and held a number of positions before being appointed vicar of St. Pancras in 1811. Three years later, he was consecrated the first bishop of Calcutta, which constituted a vast diocese covering all of the territories of the East India Company. When he was appointed bishop of India, he was 55 years old and was serving as archdeacon of Harringdon.

Before coming to India, Middleton had connections with the work there through his support of the India Society for the Propagation of Christian Knowledge (ISPCK). Middleton was aware of the vastness of his diocese and the task ahead of him. He was assisted by three archdeacons from Bombay, Madras, and Calcutta. In strengthening his work, he undertook two important visits to them. One of the great merits of Middleton's administration was that he set himself diligently to make himself acquainted with all the affairs of his vast diocese.

In his first trip, Middleton visited several mission stations in the Madras Presidency and moved on to Travancore and Cochin. This helped acquaint him with the old Syrian church of Malabar, where the Church Missionary Society (CMS) missionaries had already started the "mission of help." His visit helped strengthen the relationship between the Syrians and the CMS missionaries. In the same year, he extended his visit to Colombo as well. This lengthy tour opened Middleton's eyes both to the enormity of his task and to the actual conditions in which it had to be accomplished.

In 1819, Middleton took a second tour of visits to the same stations. During his visit to Colombo, he ordained not only a Sinhalese who had studied in England, but also Christian David, who was from Tamil Nadu and was working among the Tamils in Ceylon.

Middleton did not reject any of the colonial support he could get as a bishop. He traveled with a considerable array of chaplains, secretaries, servants, and even a contingent of armed men, the total being in the neighborhood of 300 persons.

While in Calcutta, Middleton had opportunities to meet with Raja Ram Mohun Roy*, founder of the Brahmo Samaj*. Middleton tried to convert Mohun Roy to Christianity, but Mohun Roy interpreted the approaches of Middleton as a bribe to become a Christian. Middleton's book *Letters to a Learned Hindu* contains their interviews. Middleton was disappointed not to see his dream of Mohun Roy becoming the leader of the Indian Church realized. But the learned men of Calcutta at that time understood missionaries as an extension of colonial rule. In addition, the Hindu Renaissance gave them an opportunity to safeguard their own religious claims against the missionaries' offensive methods of preaching and their claims of superiority.

One of Middleton's early concerns was to establish a missionary college. In founding such an institution, he had four purposes: (1) to train native and other Christian youth in the doctrines and discipline of the church in order for them to become preachers, catechists, and schoolmasters; (2) to give English education to young Hindus and Muslims, under the assumption that the propagation of English knowledge in India would be conducive to the progress of civilization and Christianity; (3) to promote translation of the Scriptures and the liturgy and to improve books and tracts; and (4) to make a home for missionaries upon their first arrival in India. These intentions seem to reflect the colonial attitude. He had not intended to produce leaders for the Indian church, but only catechists, missionaries, and schoolteachers. He expected their education to promote the spread of Christianity.

The foundation stone for the missionary college was laid on 20 Dec 1820; it opened in 1824. The majority of students were missionaries' sons or were from the Anglo-Indian community. But this institution could not survive for long, and it did not realize Middleton's hopes. From the middle of the century until 1917 it was lost sight of; only in 1917 did it again become a theological center for Indian students.

Middleton has not been universally acclaimed as India's first Anglican bishop. Yet he proved to be a devoted and conscientious bishop who laid foundations on which later bishops could build. Middleton himself was anxious to bring about many of the changes introduced by his successors.

Bibliography

Gibbs, M. G., *The Anglican Church in India, 1600-1970* (1972). • Neill, Stephen, *A History of Christianity in In-*

dia, 1707-1858 (1985). • Firth, C. B., *An Introduction to Indian Church History* (1976).

FRANKLYN J. BALASUNDARAN

Mieng, Doan Van

(b. Vietnam, 1 Jan 1914; d. Saigon, Vietnam, 19 Dec 1994). Professor at Nhatrang Bible Institute, district superintendent, and president of the Evangelical Church of Vietnam* (1960-75).

Mieng studied at the Nhatrang Bible College and eventually became one of its lecturers (1956-60). In 1960, he was elected president of the Evangelical Church of Vietnam (ECVN), a position he held until 1975 (the year of the Communist takeover). His home was looted by the French army on two occasions. He was brutally beaten and his wife almost killed. In spite of these sufferings, he continued relentlessly to preach and teach the Bible*.

Mieng believed the promises in the Bible and modeled his life after that of the biblical patriarch Abraham, a man of faith. At the peak of the Vietnam War*, Mieng prayed that God would allow him to remain in Vietnam. When the Communists gained control in 1975, Mieng resolutely stayed behind even though the mission pleaded with him to leave Saigon for his own safety.

Mieng suffered under the hands of the Communists. As vice-president of the ECVN, he continued to preach and pastor the displaced church. His sermon notes, which became the main source of encouragement to hundreds of people, were circulated to pastors. Mieng died on 19 Dec 1994, two weeks before his eighty-first birthday. He left a great and lasting impact on his people and the church.

Bibliography

Chanh, D. T., "Memorial Service of Rev. Doan Van Mieng," Kingsgrove Vietnamese Church, Australia (15 Jan 1995). • Cowles, H. Robert, comp., *Operation Heartbeat* (1976). • Doan Van Mieng, "I Believe God for Vietnam," *Alliance Witness* (28 May 1969). VIOLET JAMES

Mill Hill Missionaries

(MHM). The society known as the Mill Hill Missionaries, properly called St. Joseph's Society for Foreign Missions, was founded by Herbert A. Vaughan at Mill Hill, London, in Mar 1866. The simple aim of the society was to preach the Gospel in foreign lands.

The society's first involvement in Asia came in 1875 when it was invited by Bishop John Fennelly to take responsibility for the Telegu-speaking missions in the apostolic vicariate of Madras. In 1879, Rome directed that priests of the society be sent as chaplains to the British troops on the northwest frontier of India* who were engaged in the current Afghan war. The Roman authorities confidently assumed that the British intended to annex Afghanistan. The society was promised a prefecture apostolic in the newly opened territory. But the British did not annex Afghanistan, so the projected prefecture did not materialize. In 1882, the MHM in Afghanistan were reassigned. In 1886, however, the MHM were invited back to the northwest. They were charged with the care of the missions in the newly established prefecture apostolic of Kashmir and Kafiristan. This comprised the territory between Afghanistan and Little Tibet.

In 1881, Thomas Jackson was withdrawn from the Afghanistan mission to lead the first group of MHM to the island of Borneo. The territory which was their responsibility comprised what is now the states of Sarawak, Sabah, and Brunei*. In 1906, the first band of eight MHM arrived to work in the archdiocese of Jaro, Philippines*. The MHM are still active in all these mission areas, where, since 1875, more than 600 MHM priests and brothers have labored.

Madras involvement started with the Telegu missions but soon spread also to the Tamil-speaking stations in Madras city itself. A consistent theme of this work has been the training of local clergy through St. Joseph's Seminary, Nellore; St. John's Major Seminary, Nellore; and St. John's Regional Major Seminary, Hyderabad. To cope with the special demands of the caste system, the MHM established four indigenous* religious congregations. The Sisters of St. Anne of Phiringipuram were set up to serve Telegu women of caste. The Fatima Sisters were established to handle the needs of non-caste Telegu women. The Franciscan* Sisters of St. Joseph were founded to serve non-caste Tamil-speaking women. The congregation of the Little Brothers of St. Francis was founded to do for the young men what the sisters were doing for the women. The sisters are still in operation, but the brothers' congregation became moribund in the 1930s. In 1905, the Sisters of Jesus, Mary, and Joseph were brought in to provide medical care for women. This was in addition to the normal work of evangelization, pastoral care, and education. The four dioceses that now cover the original Mill Hill missions are fully self-sufficient with local personnel. The MHM now in India concentrate on work among the depressed classes.

The mission in the north of India took on three special responsibilities: chaplaincy to the army, the development of education (both academic and industrial), and special needs in medical* care. The mission was the birthplace of the Society of Catholic Medical Missionaries and of the movement known as Hospice International. Recently, MHM have been involved in new initiatives. Members have moved into the tribal apostolate in Sind. A new indigenous religious congregation, the Missionaries of St. Thomas, has been established to provide outreach into the remote areas of the northwest frontier province. After the establishment of Pakistan, the western section of the mission became the diocese of Islamabad-Rawalpindi, and the eastern section, in India, became the prefecture apostolic of Kashmir and Jammu. India's immigration policies made it difficult to continue staffing this mission, so, in the late 1970s, it was transferred to the care of the Capuchins* of Kerala.

The Borneo missions were conducted in circumstances of great hardship. The methods applied have been broadly traditional, and the results have been very good. Sound, vibrant Catholic communities, comprising one archdiocese and five suffragan sees, have been established. The Church in Sabah is probably unique in that its dioceses are governed by a parliamentary system. The MHM are well known in this region for their social and educational work. Individual MHM have made solid contributions to our knowledge of the ethnology, anthropology, and linguistic richness of the region. The 1970s was a period of trauma for the mission in Sabah. It saw the expulsion of most of its missionaries. A good number of those expelled were redeployed for service in Pontianak, Indonesia*, and then in West Irian.

Involvement in the Philippines was a response to the chaos that had come upon the church with the Philippine revolution, the departure of the friars, the takeover of the country by the Americans, and the land reforms of Governor Taft. The task of the missionaries was to rebuild the Catholic community and heal the rift that had come about through the Aglipayan* schism. The MHM followed a policy of improving education and social services. The work of rebuilding the structures of the local church has been painstaking but rewarding.

India and the Philippines are now considered to be suitable areas of recruitment for the MHM. A number of Indians either have already been accepted as full members of the society or have elected to become temporary associate members. JOHN ROONEY

Millenarianism, Philippines

Derived from the word "millennium," millenarianism is based on the prophecy about the return of Jesus Christ to earth after one thousand years. Millenarians do not believe in direct human and political action in order to change their social and economic conditions. Rather, they believe in, and wait for, divine intervention, such as the second coming of Christ, to realize their aspiration to a good life. They prepare themselves for providential happenings by living religiously, piously, and prayerfully. Though not ideologically revolutionary, millenarianism is nevertheless a form of protest by the poor that reflects their withdrawal from society and their hope and expectation for deliverance from poverty* via divine intervention. It is a sign of their disaffection with existing social conditions.

Millenarianism has been common in the Philippines* both historically and in contemporary times. One of the best-studied historical millenarian groups is the *Cofradia de San José* (Brotherhood of Saint Joseph) founded by Apolinario de la Cruz* in 1831. It was popular among Tagalog Christians in 19th-c. colonial Philippines in the Banahaw mountain area, especially in Lucban, Tayabas Province, south of Manila. De la Cruz sought recognition for his confraternity from the Spanish ecclesiastical authorities, who unfortunately misunderstood the aims and nature of the sizable movement and subjected it to military suppression in 1841. The *Cofradia* assumed an apocalyptic character, its members comparing their suffering under the Spanish regime to the passion of Jesus Christ.

Another millenarian group was the *Dios Buhawi* on Negros Island during the 1880s. It was headed by Ponciano Elopre, who fashioned himself as *Dios* (God) *Buhawi* (a great whirling force, e.g., a cyclone). He believed that he alone could save the world from eternal perdition and prophesied that the world would be deluged (though he did not say when) and that those who did not believe in him would perish. He had a large following among the impoverished and embittered sugarcane plantation laborers on Negros Island. The Spanish authorities used the civil guard to track him down and violently suppressed the group during a series of military operations (1888-89) in Siaton town.

Yet another group was the *Babaylan**, founded and led by Dionisio Sigobela, or Papa Isio, who styled himself as the pope of *Babaylanism.* A carryover from the pre-Hispanic religious tradition adhering to fundamental animism, *Babaylanism* had as its leaders priests or priestesses, called *Babaylanes,* who were accorded much honor and influence in the indigenous society. Though the influence and power of the *Babaylanes* were diminished by the Spanish missionaries and by centuries of the evangelistic labor of Roman Catholicism, *Babaylanism* could not be eradicated.

Papa Isio was popular among the downtrodden sugarcane workers on Negros Island because he exuded a supernatural aura, convincing his followers that he was chosen by Jesus Christ to liberate them from foreign rule, return them to their simple rustic existence and pre-Hispanic religious beliefs, and revive their old system of communal land ownership.

Babaylanism survived into the early years of American colonial rule. The colonial Philippine constabulary, led by John R. White, undertook a series of military campaigns against the movement, culminating in attacks on Papa Isio's headquarters at Mansalanao on top of Canlaon Mountain. He was captured on 6 Aug 1907. His death sentence was commuted to life imprisonment because the American authorities considered him mentally disordered. He died in the Bilibid Prison in Manila. According to oral history in Negros Occidental, many followers of *Babaylanism* in towns such as Kabancalan and Ilog, in an ironic twist, embraced the fundamental Baptist faith brought by American Protestant missionaries.

Millenarian groups had tragic endings because the central government viewed them as a military problem instead of looking into the fundamental causes of their disaffection with existing realities in colonial society. Yet millenarianism flourishes today. The mystical mountain of Banahaw continues to draw believers. Two better-known groups are *Tatlong Persona Solo Dios* (Three Persons One God) and *Ciudad Mistica* (Mystical City). The former was founded in 1936 by Agapito Ilustrissimo, a onetime commander of the *Pulahan* (a Visayan peasant rebel group in the early 20th c.). It is presently led by *Suprema* José Ilustre, Agapito's son. The latter was founded by Bernarda Batacan shortly after 1910. Its leaders have all been women, and its incumbent *suprema* is Isabel Suarez, who is admirably intelligent and authoritative. Both of these groups see themselves as pure expressions of Filipino indigenous religion *(tall na Filipino)* and firmly believe that the world is about to end. They are opposed to foreign religions (such as Roman Catholicism). Millenarians regard Banahaw Mountain as the New Jerusalem where the second coming of Christ will occur.

Perhaps the largest contemporary millenarian group is the Philippine Benevolent Missionaries Association (PBMA), founded in 1956 by the charismatic itinerant divine healer Ruben Edera Ecleo. He operated in northern Mindanao and attracted tens of thousands of followers. During the 1960s and 1970s, Mindanao was plunged into ethnic conflict aggravated by lawless bands, private armies, and military deserters. Ecleo invited those who had become refugees in their own land to San José in Dinagat Island, where they could build houses and plant crops on his family's land and fish in the sea fronting his property. San José grew from six hamlets to a municipality of 50,000 people. The PBMA now claims a membership of over two million nationwide. Its annual May convention attracts tens of thousands to San José Mountain. Huge concrete letters on the mountain spell out HOLY LAND and overlook the sea.

The PBMA has three categories of members identified by their rings: blue for the rank and file; red for monitors who ensure that members do not deviate from the teachings of PBMA; and white for select members with healing powers. When Ecleo died in 1989, his followers initially expected him to return at 3:00 A.M. on 18 May 2000, but they have revised the year to 2015. They expect this to be the day of the last judgment, when only PBMA members will be saved from the end of the world.

Bibliography

Bauzon, Leslie E., "Modern Millenarianism in the Philippines and the State: Focus on Negros, 1857-1927," in Kingsley M. de Silva, ed., *Sectarianism and the Secular State* (2000). • Cullamar, Evelyn T., "Babaylanism in the Negros, 1896-1907" (master's thesis, Ateneo de Manila University) (1975). • Hart, Donn V., "Buhawi of the Visayas: The Revitalization Process and Legend in the Philippines," in Mario D. Zamora, ed., *Studies in Philippine Anthropology* (1967). • Ikehata, Setsuho, "Popular Catholicism in the Nineteenth-Century Philippines: The Case of the Cofradia de San José," in *Reading Southeast Asia (Translation of Contemporary Japanese Scholarship on Southeast Asia)* (1987). • Almeda, Luz S., "The Spiritual Associations in Surigao del Norte: Their Socio-Economic, Political, Educational and Religious Implications" (doctoral dissertation, San Nicolas College) (1992).

LESLIE E. BAUZON

Million Souls Movement

First nationwide evangelistic undertaking by the Korean church to win a million souls for Jesus in 1910.

On 12 Jul 1909, three Southern Methodist* missionaries at Songdo (Kaesung), feeling that the enthusiasm for the 1907 revival was beginning to wane, isolated themselves for one week of prayer and Bible study. Following this, 10 missionaries of that mission and five Korean church leaders went to a temple in the mountains for a few days of prayer and a conference. After earnest prayer, they experienced an indescribable outpouring of the Holy Spirit upon them. These men were led to pray for a million new converts throughout Korea during the coming year and proposed this to the general council of missions in September, which adopted the goal. Sunday, 20 Mar 1910, was set aside as a day of prayer for one million souls.

To win one million souls for Jesus was a bold attempt, especially considering that there were only 8,000 baptized members and about 200,000 people who were connected with the Christian church at the time. Nevertheless, Christian workers, both missionaries and Koreans, young and old, men and women, all made strenuous efforts to make this a goal a reality. "Two particular methods of work are worthy of mention. One was the distribution of Christian literature. Many millions of tracts and 700,000 Gospels of Mark were distributed and given out with an urgent call to accept Jesus as Savior. Nearly every home was visited and daily prayer was offered for this work by thousands of Christians. The second was the custom of contributing days for evangelistic work. The Korean farmers did not have much ready money to give to employ evangelists. Neither were there many evangelists who could be employed. Therefore a custom had grown up whereby a person would contribute one day or two days or a week or more of his/her time, promising to go to some place away from his/her own village and there to preach to the unsaved. It was reported that over 100,000 days of preaching had been contributed; men and women going from house to house to tell people about Christ. . . . This meant, of course, far more than the money equivalent of preaching time, for it meant that many men were at work for Christ, instead of only a few paid workers. It is a method that might well be revived today" (Clark 1971:172).

The results of the Million Souls Movement were not as great as had been hoped for. However, all are agreed that the movement was wonderfully beneficial. Coming at the time of the annexation of Korea to Japan, the gloom in many Korean hearts was partly dispelled by finding a new hope. "Although the increase in the years since has not been so marked, the gains of those revival years have never been lost" (Rhodes 1934:287-88).

Bibliography

Clark, Allen D., *A History of the Korean Church* (1971/1986). • Reed, C. F., "1,000,000 Souls This Year," *Korea Mission Field*, Vol. V, No. 11 (1909). • Rhodes, Harry A., ed., *History of the Korean Mission: Presbyterian Church U.S.A., 1884-1934* (1934). • Underwood, Lillias H., ed., *Korea Mission Field,* Vol. VI, No. 1 (1 Jan 1911).

TIMOTHY KIHO PARK

Milne, William

(b. Kennethmont, Aberdeenshire, Scotland, Apr 1785; d. Melaka, 2 Jun 1822). Pioneer Protestant missionary to Southeast Asia.

Milne attended Congregational churches in Huntly and Aberdeen known for their strong missionary interest. He studied at Marischal College, Aberdeen, in 1806-7 and then at Gosport as a London Missionary Society (LMS) candidate for China*. He was ordained in Jul 1812, married Rachel Cowie the next month, and in September left to join Robert Morrison* in Canton.

Arriving in Macau* in Jul 1813, Milne was immediately asked to leave. He was also denied the right of remaining long in Canton. Under Morrison's direction, in Feb 1814 he was sent out to distribute tracts and see where a Chinese and Malay college might be located. He returned from Java and Melaka (Malacca*) convinced that Melaka would be a suitable site. He and his family moved there in May 1815, began teaching, and set up a printing press. In 1818, the foundation stone of the Anglo-Chinese College was laid by the departing English governor, Major Farquhar. The Chinese-style building was completed in 1820, and Milne was the first principal.

Melaka provided a relatively secure environment. For two years, Milne helped out with the Dutch church (Christ Church, where he is now commemorated), but his calling was first of all to the Chinese, and then the Malays. Milne was taught Malay by the Muslim teacher Munshi Abdullah, with whom he and Rachel developed a mutually respectful relationship.

Milne's writings reveal sensitivity to the difficulties of relating to the Malay and Chinese worlds. Despite the number of LMS missionaries sent to join the Ultra-Ganges Mission, success proved more elusive in evangelism than in printing and education. The material published in English, Chinese, and Malay forms an important part of the early history of printing in the region.

Milne served as editor of a monthly magazine in Chinese (1815-21) and the quite substantial *Indo-Chinese Gleaner* (1817-22). Of his many tracts, "Two Friends," a dialogue between Zhang, a Christian, and Yuan, an unbeliever, was widely used and revised by others. Shortly before his death, Milne completed the Chinese Old Testament in collaboration with Morrison. In 1820, the University of Glasgow awarded Milne an honorary D.D. degree. His son, William Charles Milne, later served with the LMS in China.

The mission was adversely affected by the brevity of the lives of Milne and others (Rachel died in 1819), by the understandable difficulty of deciding whether to concentrate on Malay or on Chinese ministry, and by uncertainty over which of the three Straits Settlements (Penang, Melaka, or Singapore*) should be the focus. Relationships among the missionaries were not always straightforward. If the immediate legacy was not very great, Milne, along with Morrison, deserves attention for his deliberate sense of strategy (which at times left the LMS unsure who was setting policy), his sensitive attitude to other religions, and his commitment to mutual education as the foundation of Christian mission.

Bibliography

Bays, Daniel. H., "Christian Tracts: *The Two Friends,*" in *Christianity in China,* ed. S. W. Barnett and J. K. Fairbank (1985). • Doran, Christine, "'A Fine Sphere for Female Usefulness': Missionary Women in the Straits Settlements, 1815-45," *Journal of the Malaysian Branch of the Royal Asiatic Society* 69.1 (1996). • Harrison, B., *Waiting for China* (1979). • O'Sullivan, Leona, "The London Missionary Society: A Written Record," *Journal of the Malaysian Branch of the Royal Asiatic Society* 57.2 (1984). • Milne, William, *Retrospect of the First Ten Years of the Protestant Mission to China (Now in Connection with the Malay)* (1820).

JOHN ROXBOROGH

Minh Mang

(b. Saigon, 25 May 1792; d. Hue, 20 Jan 1841). Second emperor of the Nguyen Dynasty; original name Nguyen Phuoc Chi Dam, but ruled under the name Minh Mang (the Right Dynasty) from 1820 to 1841.

Minh Mang resisted Western culture and promoted Confucianist morals. He disapproved of Christianity because of the Catholics' refusal to participate in ancestor worship and their alleged disloyalty to the emperor. Missionaries and their followers were heavily persecuted after 1825. Internal rebellion, even from direct subordinates such as the viceroy Le Van Duyet in Saigon, and the external threat of French intervention hurt the cause of the Catholic missions and their followers. To conserve Confucian values and traditions, state security arrested and executed several French, Spanish, and Filipino priests who worked in Vietnam*. Vietnamese priests and their followers were also persecuted. Attempts to reassure the French king Louis Philippe that the Catholics had nothing to fear as long as they obeyed Vietnamese laws and customs were frustrated by the Society of Foreign Missions. A delegation sent to France for this purpose and headed by Phan Thanh Gian returned to Vietnam unsuccessful in 1840.

Minh Mang's interest in education led him to reestablish the national college in Hue *(Quoc Tu Giam).* Under his reign, the mandarin examination system was refined. Literature and art were promoted.

Bibliography

Cabaton, A., *Bio-Bibliographie de l'Indochine Française* (1935). • Ta Van Tai, *The Vietnamese Tradition of Human Rights* (1988).

JOHN G. KLEINEN

Minahasa. *See* Christian Evangelical Church in Minahasa, The (GMIH)

Minjung Theology

Indigeneous Korean theology which emerged in South Korea* during the 1970s largely as a result of the experiences of the people who were involved in the Korean human rights movement and in the mission of the church with the lower echelon of Korean society, namely, the *minjung*.

Minjung Theology is a Christian theology of the people, for the people, and by the people. In May 1973, one year following the declaration of martial law in South Korea, the term "Minjung Theology" was first used when a group of leading clergymen and theologians of the Korean Church issued the "Theological Declaration of Korean Christians, 1973," a protest against the ruthless and oppressive government of Park Chung Hee. This development in Asian theology in the particular context of South Korea inspired theologians from 17 Asian countries ranging from India to Japan to hold a theological consultation, sponsored by the Christian Conference of Asia* (CCA) and organized by the Theological Commission of the National Council of Churches in Korea on 22-24 Oct 1979. This consultation attempted to have a thorough discussion of Minjung Theology in order to formulate a clearly defined theology of the *minjung*.

The Minjung. Minjung is a Korean word, but it is a combination of two Chinese characters, *min* and *jung*. *Min* may be translated as "people" and *jung* as "the mass." Thus, *minjung* means literally "the mass of the people," or "mass," or just the "people." But the translation into English of *minjung* as "people" does not do justice to the word. It has a more encompassing meaning that refers to the people who are politically oppressed, economically deprived, exploited and therefore poor, socially alienated, and culturally and religiously repressed or discriminated against. It refers to the people who are weak and powerless in terms of input into and influence on political, economic, and social policies and events.

In order to understand better the word *minjung*, there is a need to ask who the *minjung* are. The *minjung* are present where there are sociocultural alienation, economic exploitation, and political repression. A woman is *minjung* when she is dominated by a man, by her family, or by sociocultural structures and factors. An ethnic group is *minjung* when it is politically and economically discriminated against by a powerful ruling race, as in a colonial situation. When the intellectuals are suppressed for using their creative and critical abilities against rulers and the powerful on behalf of the oppressed, then they too belong to the *minjung*. Workers and farmers are *minjung* when they are exploited, whether they are aware of it or not. They are *minjung* when their needs, demands, and basic human rights are ignored and crushed down by ruling powers.

The historical roots of Minjung Theology. The roots of Minjung Theology are grounded in the historical experiences of the oppressed people of Korea to the same degree as is Korean Christianity. Indeed, they lie as far back as the period when Protestant Christianity entered Korea.

Protestant Christianity entered Korea at the end of the 19th c. with the arrival of American missionaries in the country. Finding that the *Hangul*, the vernacular script, was despised and neglected, these missionaries studied seriously the Korean language and used it to communicate to the people. They actively pursued the translation of the Bible* and other literary works into the vernacular Korean language. The oppressed groups in Korea quickly read and studied the Bible, with its language of salvation and liberation of oppressed people. Thus the *minjung* character of early Korean Protestantism is very evident because the medium of the missionaries' message was the language of the lower-class people rather than the elite Yangban language, which consisted of Chinese characters. Moreover, because of persecution by the Confucian establishment, Korean Christianity spread among the lower echelon of Korean society. Korean Protestantism had its main constituency among the *minjung* of Korea.

The Japanese victories in the Sino-Japanese War (1894-95) and in the Russo-Japanese War (1904-5) and the secret treaty of Taft-Katsura between Japan* and the United States gave Japan absolute hegemony over the Korean people. Japan forced a protectorate upon Korea in 1905. The Korean people virtually lost their independence, as Japan forcefully controlled the Korean nation by means of military power. This led to the annexation of Korea as a territory of Japan in 1910. The annexation abolished the Korean government and established a military colonial government system. The religious forces, including Protestant Christianity and the Tonghak* *(Ch'ondokyo)*, were suppressed and became targets for a colonial cultural policy.

The Korean people were forced to participate in emperor worship, regarding the Japanese emperor as a god. They were subjugated to an assimilation policy which forced them to become Japanese in body and soul, and at the same time they were required to serve the Japanese as their masters. Their language was taken away. Their political rights were non-existent, and their economic resources were exploited to serve the Japanese in Japan. Simply put, the Koreans were as completely enslaved as the Israelites in ancient Egypt.

In this historical situation, it was natural for Korean Protestantism to identify with the Korean people in their national aspirations for political reform, social and economic development, cultural enlightenment, and above all, for national independence. In its early period, Korean Protestant Christianity participated in peoples' movements, such as the Independence Club activities (1895-97), the Righteous Army movement (a resistance movement from 1906 to 1909), and the Shinminhoe movement (New Society, 1906-10), as well as in evangelistic activities.

Korean Christianity responded to the aspirations and struggle of the Korean *minjung*. Christian participation was biblically inspired, transcending the official teaching (dogma) of the churches and the official policy of the separation of religion and politics. The participation of Korean Christians in the March 1st Independence Movement of 1919 made a decisive historical connection with the destiny of the Korean people under Japanese colonialism*. Churches became special targets of Japanese military reprisals: 47 churches were burned down, and hundreds of Christians perished in demonstrations, while thousands, including women, were subjected to imprisonment and torture. This is recognized by Minjung Theology as an exodus event for the Korean people.

A few points should be made here: (1) The stories of the suffering servant and crucifixion were connected with the suffering of the Korean people. The Korean *minjung* churches were able to relate to the suffering of the Korean *minjung* under Japanese colonialism. (2) The Messianic hope for a new age and a new future provided a language of hope among the Korean people, who suffered from despair under Japanese military rule. The *Ch'ondokyo* (Religion of the Heavenly Way — Tonghak), popular Buddhism*, and Korean folk religions played similar roles, whereas official Confucianism was regarded as obsolete. Christianity was able to connect its language of Messianic hope with the aspirations of the Korean people. (3) The Christian God of peace and justice became part of the traditional Korean theodicy as the Korean people struggled for justice and liberation against Japanese imperialism. This experience of the Korean Christian movement is at the root of Minjung Theology.

With the defeat of Japan in World War II* on 15 Aug 1945 came liberation for the Korean people. Unfortunately, this independence was not absolute, for the Korean people had to endure another experience of oppression. The rivalry between the two superpowers, the United States and the former Soviet Union, divided Korea and its people into two opposing sides. With the US force in the south and the former Soviet Union in the north, the two camps became deadlocked over the type of government Korea should have. The territorial division drove the Korean peninsula into an extreme state of tension, which ultimately led to the Korean War* from 25 Jun 1950 until a ceasefire was signed on 25 Jul 1953. The churches in the north were completely destroyed physically and ecclesiastically, and thousands migrated to the south. In the north, the Christian community confronted the Communist regime; and in the south, the Christian community colluded with the corrupt dictatorial regime of Syngman Rhee, who ruled Korea from 1948 to 1960. Having turned Korea into a virtual police state, Syngman was able to maintain his government in power through repression of the people and US support.

Given the experiences of the Korean people from Japanese colonial rule up to the dictatorial regime of Park Chung Hee (1960s and 1970s), Korean theologians made efforts to concretize their theology. They were fully aware of the *minjung's* call for action which would lead to liberation, and which could be pursued with the *minjung's* own strength. The poem "Hear Our Cry!" by Chi Ha Kim was a desperate protest against the ruthless dictatorship of the Park regime. It made clear that the people were not crying for food alone; they also needed freedom, dignity, justice, and the right of participation.

For the first time in Korean history, an anti-system movement began to materialize during the oppressive rule of Park in the 1970s. Christians in South Korea heard the cry of the living Christ in the cry of the *minjung*. It moved forward with new momentum in May 1973 with the issuance of the "Theological Declaration of Korean Christians, 1973," which vividly depicted the life of Christians under the dictatorial regime, outlined the course they should take in resisting injustice and political repression, and confessed the faith which impelled them to struggle for the Korean *minjung*. In this context, Minjung Theology emerged as a Korean political theology, and the Christian community catalyzed similar movements in society at large.

The conclusion of the "Theological Declaration of Korean Christians, 1973" states:

> "Jesus the Messiah, our Lord, lived and dwelt among the oppressed, poverty-stricken, and sick in Judea. He boldly confronted Pontius Pilate, a representative of the Roman Empire, and he was crucified while witnessing to the truth. He has risen from the dead, releasing the power to transform and set the people free.
>
> "We resolve that we will follow the footsteps of our Lord, living among our oppressed and poor people, standing against political oppression, and participating in the transformation of history, for this is the only way to the Messianic Kingdom."

Besides this declaration, the "Declaration of Human Rights in Korea" by the Korea National Council of Churches (1974), the "Declaration of Conscience" by Bishop Daniel Tji (1974), the "Theological Statement of Korean Christians" signed by 66 leaders of churches and seminaries (1974), and the "Declaration for the Restoration of Democracy" signed by 12 church leaders (1976) all show clearly that Korean Christianity is seeking to be a church for and of the *minjung*.

Minjung Theology in the 1970s and 1980s. The birth of Minjung Theology in the 1970s, which emerged out of the anti-dictatorship movement, is popularly known as First Generation Minjung Theology. The chief representatives of the First Generation Theology are Nam-Dong Suh, Byung Mu Ahn, Yong-Bock Kim, Young-Hak Hyun, Dong-Whan Moon, and David Kwang-Sun Suh. The First Generation Minjung Theology provided the framework for later development in the midst of the Revolutionary Democratic Movement in the 1980s. This particular development is called Second Generation Minjung Theology.

Although there are theological differences among the First Generation theologians, they hold consistently to the major contents and basis of Minjung Theology. First, it is a presupposition that the *minjung* are the subjects of God's redemptive history. Minjung Theology has resulted from grasping God's revelation as it has appeared in the struggle of life. The *minjung* bear the historical burdens that beset human societies. The sustenance of human life, the creative process in cultural life, the transforming dynamics of the social and political process are fundamentally based upon the endurance and struggle of the *minjung*. Therefore, they are the subjects not merely of real historical understanding, but of real history-making. In a world divided into two parts, God accomplishes his redemptive work through the *minjung*. The *minjung* express their suffering and yearning via a special language known as *han*, the phenomenon of storytelling, and mask-dances.

Second, the insight that the *minjung* are the subjects of history is developed into a theological concept that is able to relate the unity of Scripture and the reality of the *minjung*. This is the so-called confluence of two stories or overcoming of subject-object duality. Jesus Christ and the *minjung* are not separated but are always associated with each other. The question of who Jesus Christ is is very much dependent upon the question of who the *minjung* are. The two questions are interdependent. According to Yong-Bock Kim, in Minjung Theology there is an affirmation that the Messiah is of the *minjung* and the *minjung* are of the Messiah, and the two cannot exist without each other. After his analysis of the words *ochlos* and *laos* in the Gospel of Mark, Ahn Byung Mu states that Jesus always stood on the side of the *minjung* — the oppressed, the aggrieved, and the weak. According to Ahn, Mark used the term *ochlos* to refer to a social, historical class. The word *laos*, on the other hand, is used to refer to a national and religious group. In Minjung Theology, Jesus is truly part of the *minjung*, and not just "for" the *minjung*. Jesus is the personification of the *minjung*, their symbol (David Kwang-Sun Suh).

Third, it is a fundamental principle in Minjung Theology that the social biography (or story) of the *minjung* reveals who they are in their persons and in their corporate body. Suffering and struggle are their prime realities, which are directly related to the reality of power. The reality of power is just as complex as the experiences of the *minjung*. The experience of the *minjung* and the reality of power must each be understood as a whole. For this, there is a need to hear again the stories in the Gospels, this time on the basis of the stories in the *minjung* social biography. This social biography is simply the story of the *minjung*, a drama in which the antagonist (power) and the protagonist create events and sequences of events unfolding in interaction with the ecological environment, with socioeconomic structures. The emotions of anger and joy are expressed in the story. The social biography describes the experiences of the people in a holistic, integrated way, including the objective conditions of their life as well as their subjective experiences. It arises out of the people's self-expression and self-communication of their own sufferings and hopes throughout the generations. Thus Minjung Theology moves out of the confines of biblical theological language, which has been filtered through Western civilization. In terms of etymology, *han* is a psychological word that denotes the feeling of suffering experienced by a person who has been repressed either by himself or by the oppression of others. According to Suh, such a feeling of helpless suffering and oppression is at the heart of the biography of the individual Korean. And this feeling of *han* is also a collective feeling in the social biography of the oppressed *minjung* of Korea.

Fourth, the revelation of God does not appear beyond space and time but in the field of human history. This is the substructure of revelation. Since human history is concerned with the material world, when the material world is grasped, the substructure of revelation is rightly understood. Thus there is a connection between theological cognition and social scientific cognition.

The Second Generation Minjung Theology of the 1980s. The Second Generation Minjung Theology attempted to overcome the limitations of the First Generation Minjung Theology. It was brought about by a social movement after the Kwangju Minjung Struggle in 1980. In May 1980, Doo Whan Chun sent troops to the southwest city of Kwangju to crush a revolt; about 200 people were killed. It was later proven that this Kwangju Minjung Struggle was not a response to any social upheaval, but a power play resulting from conflict among the generals and ruling class. This power-play struggle called for a refinement of the First Generation Minjung Theology. First, the Minjung Theology of the 1970s was seen as too ambiguous, nonscientific, and unable to incorporate the changes in the *minjung* movement in the 1980s. Second, although the First Generation Minjung Theology emphasized practice, it failed to show any reasonable progress, having fallen into the mode of sentimental, private practice.

The Second Generation Minjung Theology developed by trying to draw a relationship between the scientific worldview of Marxism and the Christian faith. In the process, it criticized the dialogue between western Christianity and Marxism, and thus turned to Latin American theology.

There was a suggestion that Minjung Theology must be developed into a more general theology corresponding to the Christian faith's traditions (Jae-Soon Park, Jin-Han Suh). The church was viewed as Minjung Theology's special field, and traditional theological themes were reinterpreted.

The task of Minjung Theology. In the 1990s, there was a sudden change unparalleled in Korean history. In 1987, there was the democratization movement, and in the 1990s the democratic government emerged. Worldwide socialism broke down and world capitalism emerged. These changes challenged Minjung Theology anew. Some argue that Minjung Theology now is of no use because the meaning of the word *minjung* has changed. On the other hand, it is held that Minjung Theology should now focus on, for example, the unification of North Korea and South Korea and globalization of the Korean *minjung* environment. It must also accomplish tasks related to other real situations, theology of religion, feminist theology (see Feminism), and similar theologies.

Bibliography

Ahn Byung Mu, *Minjung Sinhak Ijagi* (Story of Minjung Theology) (1987). • Yong-Bock Kim, ed., *Minjung Theology* (1981). • Yong-Bock Kim, *Messiah and Minjung* (1992). • Young-Jin Min, *Hankuk Minjung Sinhakeui Jomyong* (Reflection of the Korean Minjung Theology) (1984). • Changwon Suh, *A Formulation of Minjung Theology* (1990). • David Kwang-Sun Suh, *The Korean Minjung in Christ* (1991). • Lee Jung Yowng, ed., *An Emerging Theology in World Perspective: Commentary on Korean Minjung Theology* (1988).

Yong-Bock Kim, with contributions from Choi Hyeong-Mook, translated by Kim In Soo

Missionaries of the Holy Family

(*Missionarii Sacrae Familiae,* MSF). Founded by Jean Berthier in Grave, Netherlands, in 1895 to give older men and those with little financial means the opportunity to study for the priesthood.

The MSF accepted mission work in hardship areas, e.g., Greenland, the tropical forests of the Amazon (Brazil), and, since 1926, Eastern Borneo (Kalimantan*) in the diocese of Banjarmasin. The two Indonesian provinces also run the new dioceses of Samarinda (1961) and Palangkaraya (1994). Some of the 93 members work in Java (Semarang, 1932, and Jakarta*). The central administration of the whole congregation (963 members in 1988) is situated in Rome. Adolf Heuken

Missionaries of the Sacred Heart, Indonesia

(MSC). Missionary society that took over a part of the Jesuit* mission (1902) that covered all of the Dutch East-Indies (1854-1902).

The whole Moluccan archipelago and Dutch New Guinea (Irian Jaya) were handed over to the MSC fathers (1904) at Langgur on the Kei Islands. With new manpower, MSC started work the following year in Merauke (New Guinea) and in 1919 in the flourishing mission of Minahasa and the whole of Sulawesi (Celebes). Four dioceses of Indonesia are entrusted to MSC: Ambonia (1902), Merauke (1905), Manado (1919), and Purwokerto (Java, 1927). In 1961, the Indonesian MSC formed its own province, with its headquarters in Jakarta, minor seminaries in Kakaskasen, Langgur, and Saumlaki, a novitiate in Kebumen (Java), and a major seminary in Pineleng (North Celebes). About 265 members of the Sacred Heart Mission work in Indonesia.

Adolf Heuken

Missionary Sisters of the Immaculate Conception

(MIC). The Institute of the Missionary Sisters of the Immaculate Conception was founded in Côte-des-Neiges (Montreal, Canada) in 1902 by Délia Tétreault (Mother Marie-du-Saint-Esprit). In 1908 she was visited by Bishop Jean-Marie Mérel of Canton, China*, to whom Archbishop Paul Bruchesi of Montreal had offered the help of the first Canadian missionary congregation.

Mainland China: Southeast (1909-52), Northeast (1927-53). Six sisters arrived in Canton on 7 Oct 1909. They began at once attending to the works for which they were needed. From 1938 to 1951, at the request of civil authorities, they headed the Fong Tsun Psychiatric Hospital in Canton. They left this city in 1951. In response to various appeals, the MICs also worked at the Shek Lung leper colony (1913-52), Tsungming (1928-48), Tsung Shing and Tong Shan (1929-31), Suchow (1934-48), and Shameen (1949-52).

Another group of MICs went to Manchuria: Leao Yuan Sien (1927-51), Pamientcheng (1929-47), Fakou (1930-47), Taonan (1931-43), Szepingkai (1931-53), Tong Leao (1932-47), Paitchengtze (1933-53), and Koungtchouling (1933-47).

One hundred forty-three MIC sisters worked in northern and southern China. In every place, they suffered hardship brought about by the war between China and Japan, World War II*, and the Communist invasions; they were finally expelled. One Chinese MIC did remain on the mainland until Jun 1980.

Philippines (1921-present). At the prompting of a Chinese physician who had known the MICs in Canton, Archbishop J. O'Doherty of Manila requested the foundress to send sisters to take charge of the Chinese General Hospital of Manila. The MICs worked in this hospital from 1921 to 1939.

In 1935, the MICs began working among the youth of Manila and the suburbs. They run two schools there: the Immaculate Conception Academy (Greenhills) and the Immaculate Conception Academy of Manila (Gagalanguin). In Mindanao, they have operated the Immaculate Heart of Mary Academy in Mati since 1947, a Students' Center that opened in 1952, a house of retreats, and various pastoral services in Malita (1981). They opened a novitiate in Baguio in 1955. In two areas of Mindoro, they promote holistic education among the tribal population. A few assignments are carried out sporadically in response to specific needs, especially among the most destitute of Filipino society, and in fulfillment of the MIC commitment to evangelization and social justice.

Japan (1926-present). A request by the Canadian Franciscans in Kyushu led the Canadian MICs to Naze in

1926 and to Kagoshima in 1928. As their projects proved impossible to realize, the foundress recalled her missionaries (1933-34).

Meanwhile, the Canadian Dominicans*, having opened missions in northern Japan*, welcomed the MICs to Koriyama in 1930. In 1934, the sisters settled in Aizu Wakamatsu, also of Fukushima Ken. Today they operate a school in each of these two places: the Xaverio School and the Aizu Wakamatsu Xaverio School.

During World War II, the sisters were placed under house arrest in their convent from 1941 to 1943. After being returned to Canada at that time, they went back to their houses in Japan in 1946. In 1949, they opened a kindergarten in Tokyo, then a dormitory for students and an MIC novitiate; from 1957 to 1992, they headed an orphanage in Koriyama, and in 1994, they opened a house in Yumoto (Iwaki) for parish ministry.

Hong Kong (1928-present). In 1927, the order to leave China and quickly find temporary accommodation forced the MICs to take refuge in Hong Kong* for a while. The foundress later asked the local bishop for the authorization to keep a permanent residence there. This is how the primary Anglo-Chinese school of Tak Sun began in Kowloon in 1928. From 1941 to 1943, the sisters were held, and then stayed voluntarily, at Camp Stanley; finally they returned to Canada. Invited back by the bishop after the war, they returned in 1947 and reorganized the Tak Sun School in another building of Kowloon. After being transformed and enlarged, the work of Tak Sun was handed over to a Catholic corporation in Jul 1993.

The educational work of the MICs has continued in Kowloon, benefiting thousands of pupils at the school campus of Tak Mong since 1953 and at the secondary school of Tak Oi since 1970. Moreover, the MICs provide various pastoral ministries and services to migrant workers.

Taiwan (1954-present). Through the apostolic administrator, the Canadian Jesuits* who had been missionaries in Suchow invited the MICs expelled from China to come to Taiwan. The first group settled in Kuanhsi in Aug 1954. There is still a kindergarten in this place, and the MICs are involved in evangelization and Christian education.

The MICs also worked in Shih Kuang Tse (1955-86), Suao (1958-71), Hsinchu (1964-71), and Nan Ao (1966-80). They left these works to respond to other needs of the church as the state was able by now to carry on the services that had been initiated.

A house was established in Taipei in 1956, and another in 1985, for the pastoral and evangelizing activities of the local church.

Present situation. The MIC currently has 19 houses in Asia, with 119 members: 52 in the Philippines, 30 in Japan, 22 in Taiwan, and 15 in Hong Kong. As they are a missionary institute, there are exchanges of personnel with the MICs of Africa and the Americas.

Among Asian-born MICs, 71 are from the Philippines, 15 from Japan, six from Hong Kong, seven from Taiwan, and eight from China. Recruitment is easier in the Philippines, as it is a Catholic country. Note that the MICs are still drawn to China, which was their first field of apostolate; today, they work in this country in various professions. On occasions, some of them take part in major Asian Catholic ecumenical, social, and religious conferences and assemblies. Everywhere, the MICs live out the charism of their foundress as missionaries of thanksgiving in the manner of Mary.

Bibliography

"The M.I.C.s in Asia," *The Precursor* (75th Anniversary Issue), No. 1 (1977). • Pana, Vivencia, "Inculturation of the Spirituality of Thanksgiving," *Tambara,* Vol. VII (Dec 1990). • Lao, Christine Veloso, *A Chronicle of Grace* (1996). • "Brief History of the Congregation of the Missionary Sisters of the Immaculate Conception and of the Origin of the Quebec Foreign Mission Society," MIC Archives (unpublished, 1971).

GEORGETTE BARRETTE, translated by ANTOINETTE KINLOUGH

Miyahira Shusho

(Hidemasa) (b. Okinawa, Japan, 1904; d. 26 Dec 1976). Miyahira was known as Shusho in Indonesia; in Japan*, his personal name was Hidemasa, the difference reflecting the way the character in question is pronounced. Miyahira became a member of the Oriental Missionary Society, which was a branch of the Holiness Church in America. In 1927, he finished his theological education at the Seisho Gakuin in Tokyo. In the same year, he left for the Netherlands Indies (Indonesia). Until 1929, he worked as an evangelist in the Minahasa area (North Sulawesi), supporting himself by trading.

In 1929, Miyahara joined the Salvation Army* (SA). He was trained at the SA school in Bandung (West Java) and afterward worked in the SA lepers' hospital, Semaroen, in Surabaya (East Java). When he heard that Kagawa Toyohiko* was about to visit the Netherlands Indies, Miyahira started working among the Japanese in Surabaya (1935). In those years, the Japanese citizens in Java numbered about 7,000-8,000, and among them Christians were relatively numerous, but there was no Christian ministry available for them. Through Miyahira's labors, on 5 Jan 1936 the first Japanese congregation in Java was established in Surabaya. Miyahira left the SA, obtained the official permit from the Netherlands Indies government which was needed to carry on a full-time ministry among the Japanese in East Java, and on 24 Apr 1938 was ordained a minister of the Holiness Church. However, only six months later Miyahira was expelled by the Dutch government, which suspected him of spying for the Japanese military.

In Mar 1942, Miyahira returned to Indonesia as a navy officer aboard a Japanese warship. He became the secretary of the Japanese governor of East Indonesia in

Macassar (Sulawesi), and until Dec 1942 headed the office for religious affairs of the Japanese administration. In that capacity he did much to protect the Indonesian Christians from vexations and intrigues at the hands of other groups and from suspicions on the part of the Japanese authorities. He ordained several ministers and provided money to build churches. In the second half of 1943, he lost his position, but his work was carried on by several other Japanese pastors.

After the war, Miyahira visited the churches in independent Indonesia several times. He was engaged in mission work in Sulawesi and Kalimantan*. He died on his way back to the church in Kalimantan after receiving medical treatment in Japan. Today his name is honored by Indonesian Christians.

Bibliography

Miyahira, Shusho Hidemasa, *Shinsho no shitaggatha* (Following my vocation) (1980) (English version: *My Activity in Celebes During the War*). • Van den End, Thomas, "Tana Toraja," *Doc.* 177 (Dutch edition), *Resp.* 154 (Indonesian edition). • Pandeirot-Lengkong, Beatrix B. B., "The Protestant Churches and the Missionary Fields During the Japanese Occupation in Indonesia 1942-1945, in the Japanese Navy Controlled Areas: A Bibliographical Survey" (doctoral dissertation, South East Asia Graduate School of Theology) (1996) (in Indonesian).

THOMAS VAN DEN END

Mizo

Literally translated "highlander," Mizo has two basic meanings. First, it is a generic term describing all the tribes living in the Indian states of Assam, Manipur, Mizoram, and Tripura, as well as Bangladesh* and Myanmar*, who claim to have originated in a mythical place called Chhinlung; they speak very closely related dialects of the Tibeto-Burman family of languages and have almost identical cultures. Such tribes include, among others, the Bawm in Bangladesh; the Halam groups in Tripura and Assam; the Kuk-Thado groups in Manipur and Assam; the Lusei, Lai, and Mara groups in Mizoram; and the Chin or Zomi groups in Myanmar. Second, Mizo means the inhabitants of Mizoram ("land of the Mizo"), especially those who speak the Lusei or Duhlian dialect. Mizoram is a state of the Republic of India that covers a hilly terrace of 21,087 square kilometers; it is flanked by Bangladesh and Tripura in the west, Myanmar in the east and south, and Assam and Manipur in the north. Most of the Mizo groups have a high percentage of Christians, and the rest are fast becoming Christian. This article deals with the Mizo in Mizoram.

Oral traditions present an obscure picture of the past. Historians believe that the Mizo were a part of a great wave of the Mongolian race spilling over into eastern and southern Asia centuries ago. After many years of wandering, they came to western Myanmar around the 7th c. A.D. and dwelt there for about 10 centuries.

The Mizo were pushed westward in their search for safer pastures, which often led to clashes among themselves and war with the neighboring tribes. This resulted in the development of the system of chieftainship in the late 15th c. By the time they crossed the Tiau River in the 18th c. and settled down in present-day Mizoram, the traditional system of village administration had been perfected. Similar to the Greek city-states, each village was ruled by a chief whose responsibility was to defend the village, lead the men on looting and head-hunting forays, allocate lands for cultivation, settle all disputes, feed and care for the poor, and offer shelter to anyone seeking refuge. The chief was assisted by a council of elders. The other village functionaries were the village crier, the blacksmith, and the priest, all appointed by the chief and remunerated in terms of rice and meat. The chieftainship (abolished in 1954) was hereditary, being passed on to the eldest son.

The Mizo were animists, recognizing one supreme being called Pathian, but offering sacrifices to avert the anger of the many evil spirits believed to dwell in streams, hills, trees, or anything out of the ordinary. They also believed that the soul went either to *pialral,* their version of a paradise, or *mithi khua,* the abode of the dead. The former was open only to those who qualified by either killing a specified number of wild animals or giving several costly ceremonial public feasts.

The Mizo had three annual festivals, the *Mim kut, Chapchar kut,* and *Pawl kut,* each associated with particular agricultural activities. They loved to sing and dance, having a number of community dances which were expressions of their gay, carefree spirit and which corresponded with their agricultural, hunting, and fighting activities. Festivals and ceremonies were accompanied by rituals, singing, and dancing, during which *Zu* (rice beer) flowed freely.

A gregarious and close-knit society, the Mizo have evolved some principles of self-help and cooperation to meet social obligations and responsibilities. Construction of village paths, water holes, and other public utilities was accomplished through voluntary community work known as *hnatlang.* Every family was expected to contribute labor for the welfare of the community and to participate in *hnatlang.*

The Mizo developed a unique code of conduct called *tlawmngaihna* that basically stands for selfless service for others. It is a compelling moral force that requires a person to be hospitable, kind, unselfish, courageous, and helpful to others. In war or peace, in dealing with individuals or in day-to-day public life, this spirit guides civic life.

For about a century, the Mizo were content to settle into their seminomadic and warlike life, hardly known to the outside world except to their immediate neighbors, who avoided the fierce head-hunters. The British administered the land from 1891 to 1947. By abolishing inter-village war and head-hunting and other social evils, by enacting legislature alien to them, and introducing different economic and value systems, the traditional Mizo lifestyle was drastically altered. Mizoram, then Lushai Hills, became a part of Assam, administered by a superintendent. Lushai Hills became Mizo District in 1954; that developed into the Union Territory of Mizoram in 1971, and on 30 Jun 1986 Mizoram became the twenty-third state of the Republic of India*.

The first Christian missionary who visited Mizoram was William Williams, a missionary to the Khasi of Meghalaya. Williams came from the Welsh Calvinistic Methodist Church, later called the Presbyterian* Church of Wales. He stayed for only a few days in 1891. On 11 Jan 1894, two missionaries of the Arthington Aborigines Mission, F. W. Savidge and J. H. Lorrain, arrived at Aizawl, capital of Mizoram. They developed a Mizo alphabet following the Roman scripts, thus reducing the Mizo language into written form for the first time. The two pioneers were replaced by D. E. Jones, a Welsh Presbyterian missionary, in 1898. He was soon joined by Edwin Rolands.

The two pioneers, Savidge and Lorrain, returned to southern Mizoram in 1903 as missionaries of the Baptist* Missionary Society (BMS). Mizoram was then divided into two mission fields: the much larger northern part fell to the Welsh Presbyterian mission with Aizawl as its headquarters, and the southern part to the BMS with Serkawn as its headquarters.

In 1907, R. A. Lorrain, the brother of J. H. Lorrain, established an independent Lakher Pioneer Mission to work among the Mara in the southernmost part of Mizoram. The three missions worked side by side, observing strict comity with mutual harmony and cooperation. The result was the establishment of three churches, namely, the Presbyterian Church of Mizoram, the Baptist Church of Mizoram, and the Mara* Evangelical Church.

Other groups, such as Roman Catholic* (1916), the Salvation Army* (1925), Seventh-Day Adventists* (1941), and the United Pentecostal* Church (1949), ministered to dissident Christians. The evangelization of Mizo in Mizoram was completed by 1950. During the last few decades, numerous indigenous sects have arisen, making the number of different Christian groups over 80 at last count.

In 1995, Christians made up over 85% of the total population of 689,756 in Mizoram. Non-Christians in Mizoram are non-Mizo. The literacy rate is 82%, the second highest among the states of India.

The churches in Mizoram are active in mission outreach. The Presbyterian Church, with a membership of 300,613, supports 789 missionaries on 21% of its total budget. The Baptist Church with its membership of 81,532 supports 438 missionaries on 47.70% of its total budget. Altogether the churches in Mizoram supported about 1,500 missionaries in 1994.

Bibliography

Hrangkhuma, F., *Mizo Transformational Change* (1989). • Hminga, C. L., *The Life and Witness of the Church in Mizoram* (1987). • Ray, A. C., *Mizoram Dynamic of Change* (1982). • Lloyd, J. M., *History of the Church in Mizoram* (1991). • Chapman, E. and M. Clark, *Mizo Miracle* (1968). • Thanga, L. B., *The Mizos: A Study in Racial Personality* (1978). • Lalthangliana, B., *Mizo History in Burma* (1980). • McCall, A. G., *Lushai Chrysalis* (1977).

FANAI HRANGKHUMA

Moffett, Samuel Austin

(b. Madison, Indiana, United States, 25 Jan 1864; d. Monrovia, California, United States, 24 Oct 1939). American Presbyterian missionary to Korea*.

Moffett studied at Hanover College, majoring in chemistry, and received his master of science degree in 1885. He furthered his studies in Chicago at McCormick Theological Seminary, where he received his basic theological degree in 1888. After graduating from seminary, he was appointed as a missionary to Korea by the Presbyterian Church (North).

Moffett arrived in the port city of Chemulpo on 25 Jan 1890. After several trips to the northern part of Korea, he decided to work in Pyengyang (Pyongyang), becoming the first Protestant missionary to take up long-term residence in inland Korea.

Moffett faced many difficulties as he began his mission work. On one occasion, as he was preaching, he was hit by a stone which was thrown by a young man who later became a theological student at Presbyterian Theological Seminary, which was founded by Moffett. That young man was Rhee Gipoong, who was one of the first seven ministers of the Korean Presbyterian Church and who was later dispatched to Cheju Island at the southern tip of the Korean peninsula.

When Moffett first reached Pyongyang, there was not a single Christian; by the time he retired as a missionary, there were over 1,000 churches in the area.

One of Moffett's important contributions was the founding of Presbyterian Theological Seminary, which he served for more than 20 years as president. The seminary began in 1901 as a theology class for two young men, Kim Jongsub and Bang Gichang. Two years later, the Presbyterian Council in Korea decided to start a seminary in Pyongyang and recognized Moffett's theological class as that seminary. In 1918 Moffett became the second president of Soongsil College (now Soongsil University), which traces its beginnings to a class for boys started in 1898 by his college and seminary classmate William Baird. With Baird, Moffett also founded the Soongeui Girls' School (now Soongeui Women's Junior College, Middle and High School), which, along with Soongsil University has since relocated from Pyengyang to Seoul.

In 1907, Moffett was elected moderator of the first presbytery of the Korean Presbyterian Church. In 1910, he represented the Presbyterian Church in Korea at the Edinburgh Missionary Conference. In 1919, he was elected moderator of the general assembly of the church.

When the Independence Movement* broke out in 1919, Moffett helped the Christian leaders and demonstrators. He also strove to report the brutality of the Japanese army and policemen to the world. His opposition to the Japanese imposition of Shinto* shrine worship resulted in the closure of the seminary, as well as the Soongsil and Soongeui Schools. He was forced out of Korea by the Japanese in 1936. He returned to America for medical treatment and died three years later.

Moffett adopted the Nevius* method (the Three-Self Principle) in his work. For his constant zeal to extend the missionary frontiers, he was called "The Looking-up-the-Road Man."

Two of Moffett's five sons also became missionaries to Korea. His third son, Samuel Hugh Moffett, was a professor at Presbyterian Theological Seminary until he retired in 1981. In 1963, the government of the Republic of Korea posthumously honored Moffett with the National Merit Award for his contributions to the country.

Bibliography

Lee Jong Hyeong, "Samuel Austin Moffett: His Life and Work in the Development of the Presbyterian Church of Korea, 1890-1936" (Ph.D. diss., Union Theological Seminary, Virginia, United States) (1983). • Rhodes, H. A., ed., *History of the Korea Mission of the Presbyterian Church in the U.S.A., 1884-1934* (1934). • Paik, George L., *The History of Protestant Missions in Korea, 1832-1910* (1971).

KIM IN SOO

Moluccan Mission

Mission of the Jesuit provinces of Cochin and Manila in the 16th and 17th cs. in the Moluccas. See Indonesia*.

Moluccas

The churches in the Moluccas include the Protestant Church in the Moluccas (Reformed), the Christian Evangelical Church in Halmahera (also Reformed), the Roman Catholic Church*, several Pentecostal churches, the Seventh-Day Adventist Church, the Salvation Army*, and several evangelical churches.

The Protestant Church in the Moluccas (Gereja Protestan Maluku, GPM). GPM, which became an independent church on 6 Sep 1935, belongs to the Reformed church family. Its long history may be divided into five periods: first, the period of the Portuguese mission (1540-1605); second, the period of the Dutch United East-India Company* (*Verenigde Oost-Indische Compagnie,* VOC, 1605-1800)*; third, the period of the Netherlands Missionary Society (*Nederlandsch Zendeling Genootschap,* NZG, 1800-1815); fourth, the state church of the Indies (*Gereja Protestan di Indonesia,* GPI, 1815-1935); and fifth, the period of the Protestant Church in the Moluccas (1935-present).

In the Portuguese period, Roman Catholic missionaries came to the Moluccas. They began in the Central Moluccas when Antonio Galvao, the Portuguese governor, occupied Amboina in 1538. From the arrival of Francis Xavier* (1546), Christianity began to develop in the Moluccas. Through the missionary activity of Xavier and others, the people in the islands of Ambon, Lease (Saparua, Haruku, and Nusalaut), and Ceram received the Catholic faith. The method used was to organize general education for children and catechetical education for adults which would end in mass baptisms. By 1569, the number of Christians in Ambon, Lease, and Ceram rose to 47,000. But the number suddenly declined after the Muslim sultan of Ternate, Hairun, was killed in 1570 by the Portuguese administrator; the result was an intense opposition led by Hairun's son, Babullah, which caused much suffering for both the Portuguese and Moluccan Christians. The number of Christians in the Central Moluccas declined suddenly to 25,000, and then to 16,000 in 1605.

The period of the VOC began when the Dutch conquered the Portuguese fortress in Amboina on 23 Feb 1605; four days later, on 27 Feb, they conducted the first Protestant baptisms in Amboina. This date is recognized as the anniversary of the establishment of the Protestant Church in Indonesia. The early development of Protestantism in the Moluccas was mainly in the Central Moluccas, i.e., in Ambon, Lease, and Ceram. The adherents of Roman Catholicism were gradually declared Protestant by the VOC administrator. From 1635, Protestantism was introduced to the Southeast Moluccas (the islands of Kei, Aru, Tanimbar, and Kisar) and the North Moluccas (the islands of Bacan and Obi). Both European ministers and Moluccan religious teachers helped establish churches in these new areas. By the end of the 18th c., Christianity had spread to most of the Moluccan archipelago, with the church having a total membership of about 50,000 people. This encouraging development began to wane in both quantity and quality as the VOC declined and church subsidies were limited to existing congregations.

Between 1800 and 1935, both NZG and GPI made every effort to reform the church in the Moluccas. The work of Joseph Kam* (b. 1769; d. 1833) was especially important in two areas. First, the training of Moluccan schoolteachers and church officials became a priority, and several schools were successively opened, namely the School for Christian Teachers (Ambon, 1835), the Theological School (STOVIL, Ambon, 1885), and two schools for religious teachers (Ambon, 1827, and Tual, 1828). Second, the Moluccan congregations were given the right to choose their own church board. Both of these developments, deliberately or otherwise, created conditions leading to an independent church. In Aug 1935, the colonial Protestant church was separated from the government, and on 6 Sep, the GPI congregations in the Moluccas received a new status as the independent Protestant Church in the Moluccas (*Gereja Protestant Maluku,* GPM), although financially it was still fully dependent upon GPI.

Since autonomy in 1935, GPM has faced some challenges and seen encouraging developments. The first challenge occurred during the Japanese military occupation (1942-45), when there was a shortage of food and clothing, and GPM members were persecuted by the Japanese military administrator, with 80 ministers and 83 religious teachers killed by the *Kempetai,* the Japanese military police. In the midst of the suffering, however, there was a positive development: the GPM congregations led by S. Marantika* sought to be completely self-supporting, both in finances and leadership.

The second challenge followed in the first two decades of Indonesian independence (1945-65). Financially, the GPM struggled to survive because the government of the Netherlands Indies stopped subsidies in 1950. Other internal problems were caused by poorly organized leadership and administration. In addition, social, political, and economic problems of the nation (e.g., the rebellion of the Republic of the South Moluccas, and inflation) affected the GPM. Under the leadership of Th. P. Pattiasina*, the GPM issued a "Message of Repentance" *(Pesan Tobat)* in the synod assembly of 1960. All church officials and members confessed disobedience and showed their willingness to be reformed by the Word and the Holy Spirit to accomplish the task of the church in the midst of rapid social changes. The assembly planned a reformation in many fields of ministry, such as theological education, liturgy, church doctrine, and church organization. The church reformation went along smoothly because it coincided with reformations by the government (national development). The positive results of the reformation showed in the financial and personal contributions of GPM members to the church.

Since the 1930s, the GPM has shown interest in ecumenical* issues. In 1938, W. H. Tutuarima (acting moderator of the GPM) attended the conference of the International Missionary Council (IMC) in Madras. The GPM has also sent delegations to the assemblies of the World Council of Churches (WCC) since 1948 (Amsterdam) and is a member of the Communion of Churches in Indonesia (PGI; since its founding in 1950), the Christian Conference of Asia* (CCA; since 1957), the WCC (since 1948), and the World Alliance of Reformed Churches (WARC; since the 1970s).

The GPM represents the entire Moluccas archipelago except the island of Halmahera*. The main base of the church is in the Central Moluccas (Ambon, Lease, Ceram, and Buru) and in the Southeast Moluccas (Kei, Aru, Tanimbar, and Kisar). The synod office of the church is in Amboina (Ambon City). The GPM comprises 26 presbyteries and 796 congregations, with over 460 ministers and religious teachers and nearly 550,000 church members. The GPM has a university, the *Universitas Kristen Indonesia* (Indonesian Christian University in the Moluccas, UKIM), with four faculties (theology, economics, technology, and social and political sciences).

The Christian Evangelical Church in Halmahera. The mission which first evangelized Halmahera was the Utrecht Mission Union (UZV, Netherlands) in Jul 1866. At that time, Halmahera Island was under the influence of the Islamic sultan of Ternate. The center of mission activity was in Duma, a village located on the shore of Galela Lake. Playing an important role in the process of Christianization in Halmahera was H. van Dijken, an evangelist and agricultural specialist who worked mainly in the villages around the lake from 1866 to 1900. He baptized the first Halmaheran in Jul 1874. The other missionary who helped organize the church of Halmahera was A. Hueting, who worked mainly in Tobelo from 1915 to 1930. When Hueting started his work, there was a concurrent movement to embrace Christianity amongst the Tobelo ethnic group in reaction to the sultan of Ternate's decree to exile their leader, Hangaji. As a result of the work of van Dijken, Hueting, and later missionaries, the number of Christians increased yearly until there were 15,000 in 1942.

During the Japanese military occupation (1942-45), the Christians in Halmahera suffered greatly. All the European and Ambonese officials were arrested, and services could not be conducted because of the shortage of ministers and the destruction of many church buildings by the Allied Forces' offensive.

After World War II*, the church in Halmahera was led again by missionaries of the Netherlands Reformed Church (NHK, *Nederlands Hervormde Kerk*). On 6 Jun 1949, the independent Christian Evangelical Church in Halmahera (*Gereja Masehi Injili Halmahera,* GMIH) was formed, and local leadership began to replace the European missionaries.

The GMIH is very active in the ecumenical movement*, being a member of the Communion of Churches in Indonesia* in the Moluccan Region (PGIW Maluku), the PGI, CCA, WCC, and WARC. The main bases of the GMIH are in the more densely populated areas of North Halmahera (Galela and Tobelo) and Morotai (North Moluccas). Its synod office is in Tobelo where there is a theological seminary (formed in 1968, first in Ternate). The GMIH has 15 coordinators of territory service (KPW, the same level as presbyteries) in the whole of Halmahera and Morotai Islands, 315 congregations, and 105 ministers and religious teachers. The church has nearly 135,000 members.

The Roman Catholic Church. The Catholic Church in the Moluccas began with the arrival of the Portuguese at the beginning of the 16th c. Until 1565, this church had thousands of members in the North and South Moluccas who had been converted in mass baptisms, Francis Xavier being one of the most notable pioneers. But after the murder of Sultan Hairun by the Portuguese administrator in 1570, the Catholic Church gradually disappeared from the Moluccas.

The church in the Moluccas began to grow again at the end of the 19th c. when the government of the East Indies showed a neutral attitude toward all religions and denominations in Indonesia. The first areas for mission were the Kei and Tanimbar islands, and the target groups were the adherents of tribal religions. The first baptism in Kei was held in 1889, and in Tanimbar, 1913. The base of mission activities was first in Langgur (Kei) and then in Amboina. In 1925, a pastor living in Amboina began to organize the mission activities on Ceram and Buru Islands. Now Catholics are concentrated in the Kei and Tanimbar Islands and Amboina. Members of the Catholic Church can also be found in the Central Moluccas (Ceram and Buru) and the North Moluccas (Halmahera, Ternate, Bacan, Obi, etc.). Roman Catholics number about 75,000. The office of the Amboina bishopric is in Amboina.

The Seventh-Day Adventist Church, Salvation Army, Pentecostal Churches, and Evangelical Churches. A number of other churches entered the Moluccas (Amboina) at the beginning of the 20th c. The Adventists came in 1921, the Salvation Army* and the Pentecostal* churches (e.g., the Assemblies of God, the Bethel Full Gospel Church) after the 1930s, and the evangelical churches (the Holy Word Christian Church, the Word of God Church, etc.) since the 1960s. In general, the central offices of these churches are in Amboina. The total membership is about 25,000.

Ecumenical cooperation among the churches in the Moluccas began during the Japanese occupation, when an ecumenical board, the *Ambon-Syu Kiristokyo Rengakai,* was formed by the Japanese administrator. Today ecumenical relations are instrumental in the development of an ecumenical consciousness among the members of these churches. Since the 1960s, a number of ecumenical boards have been formed, e.g., the Communion of Churches in Indonesia in the Moluccan Region (PGIW Maluku), the Council of the Pentecostal Churches in Indonesia (DPI), and the Communion of Evangelical Churches in Indonesia (PII). PGIW Maluku consists of churches from various denominational backgrounds, e.g., the Protestant Church in the Moluccas (Reformed), the Christian Evangelical Church in Halmahera (Calvinist), some Pentecostal churches (the Bethel Full Gospel Church, the Bethel Indonesian Church), and the Salvation Army. The DPI includes 13 Pentecostal churches, and the PII 11 evangelical churches. Ecumenical cooperation among the churches is visible in the attendance of members of all the churches during celebrations of Christian holidays.

Statistics from the department of religions in the Moluccan area indicate that there are 34 Protestant churches in the Moluccas, with 1,686 permanent congregations and 142 in the process of formation; 1,854 ministers; 340 religious teachers; and 687,000 members. The number of Catholics is 75,000. Christians comprise 45% of the entire population of 1,700,000 in the Moluccas.

Bibliography

Abineno, J. L. Ch., *Sejarah Apostolat di Indonesia* I (1978). • Van den End, Th., *Ragi Carita* 2 (1989). • Chauvel, R., *Nationalists, Soldiers and Separatists* (1990). • Müller-Krüger, Th., *Sedjarah Geredja di Indonesia* (1989). • Latourette, K. S., *A History of the Expansion of Christianity,* Vols. 3 & 5 (1978 and 1980). • *Handbook of Reformed Churches Worldwide* (1999).

Mesach Tapilatu

Mongkut, King

(Rama IV) (b. 18 Oct 1804; d. 1 Oct 1868). Fourth king of Thailand's Ratanakosin Era, son of King Rama II and Princess Boonrod (later, Queen Sri Suriyendra).

Mongkut received a palace education and then entered the Buddhist monkhood in 1824. In 1829, he founded the historically significant reformist Thammayutika sect, which sought to reintroduce the practices of the Buddha into modern Thai religion. Mongkut initiated this reform partly in response to missionary attacks on traditional Buddhism*. While still a monk, he also undertook the study of French, English, history, and various scientific subjects with both Catholic and Protestant missionaries. He read widely and acquired an insightful knowledge of world events.

Mongkut became king in 1851, and he immediately brought to an end the severe restrictions his predecessor had placed on missionary work, thus opening the door for the expansion of Christian missionary institutions and evangelism. Mongkut was a liberal and undertook the modernization of Thailand* in various fields. He opened up the nation to Western trade through treaties with European nations and the United States. He promoted the study of Western knowledge as well as military modernization, and he dispensed with numerous old traditions. His reign marked the beginning of an era of significant social transition in Thailand, and he is still known as the Father of Reform.

Western missionaries saw Mongkut's reign as a new era of hope for Christian expansion. Mongkut gave land to the missionaries to build their stations, allowed them full freedom to evangelize, and counted missionaries such as Dan Beach Bradley* as his advisers and friends. He allowed Protestant missionary women to teach the women of his palace. He also strongly encouraged the popularization of missionary medicine and printing. He allowed the missionaries to establish stations outside of Bangkok and particularly gave permission in 1866 for the founding of a Presbyterian* station in Chiang Mai, a northern Thai dependency.

Mongkut pursued a policy which accepted the missionaries as important sources of Western learning, but he strongly and publicly criticized their religion and affirmed the reasonableness and correctness of Buddhism. He channeled missionary efforts so that they became a source of controlled social change without successfully Christianizing Thailand. His reign thus marked a major shift in the Christian missionary role in Thailand, one which both opened doors and set directions for the development of Christian missions for the rest of the 19th c.

Bibliography

"Mongkut," *Thai Encyclopedia. Royal Institute Edition, 1960-61* (1960-61) (in Thai). • McFarland, George B., *The Historical Sketch of Protestant Missions in Siam, 1828-1928* (1928). • Ophat Sawikul, *The Father of Reform* (1991) (in Thai). • Moffat, Abbot Low, *Mongkut the King of Siam* (1968). • Griswold, A. B., "King Mongkut in Perspective," selected articles from the *Siam Society Journal*, Vol. IV (1959). • Wyatt, David K., *Thailand: A Short History* (1984).

Prasit Pongudom

Mongolia

Formerly the Mongolian People's Republic (MPR), Mongolia lies between China* and Russia. Although roughly the size of Western Europe, Mongolia numbers only 2.5 million people, a quarter living in the capital, Ulan Bator. There are four main Mongol ethnic groupings. Mongolia is approximately 80% Khalka. The Buriats live predominantly in Buriatia in Siberian Russia. The Kalmucks live in the Volga River valley in Russia. Various tribes live in China's Inner Mongolia, Gansu and Xinjiang Provinces.

The Mongol chieftain Temujin united several warring central Asian tribes and was proclaimed Genghis Khan* in 1206. He and his sons undertook a devastating military campaign which expanded the Mongol frontier east to the Chinese coast, south to Burma (Myanmar*), and west into Persia and Hungary. Kublai Khan shifted the Mongol capital from Karakorum to Da-tu (modern Beijing), becoming the first of the Chinese Yuan emperors (r. 1280-94). The rise of the Ming Dynasty from 1368 forced the Mongols back to their original pasturelands in Central Asia. Various uprisings in the following centuries failed to produce another Mongol state until 1911, when the Manchu were thrown out of Urga (modern Ulan Bator). Mongolia then maintained a precarious political independence until aligning itself with Soviet Russia in 1924. In 1990, Communism collapsed, and a parliamentary democracy was constituted and free-market economics embraced.

The underlying worldview of the Mongols is shamanism*, but Tibetan Buddhism*, which Kublai introduced, remains the dominant religion. Atheism is a legacy of Soviet-style Communism. Today shamanism, Buddhism, and Islam* (acknowledging a Khazak minority) are the three official religions, but the law also affirms freedom to practice the religion of one's choice.

Mongolia's Christian history started when the East Syrian Christian (Nestorian*) Kerait tribe was incorporated into Genghis's growing empire. The intermarriage of Christian Keraits and the house of Genghis continued for 200 years to ensure Kerait allegiance. Many Keraits were literate in the Uighur-Syriac script, which had spread through Central Asia from use of the Syriac Bible*. Genghis approved this script for record keeping. Literate Christian Keraits were therefore appointed to key government posts and effectually administered the Mongol Empire. This ancient script has evolved into the current *mongol bichig* script, a direct result of the introduction of the Syriac Bible into Central Asia.

Christian history amongst the Mongols can roughly be broken into five periods:

1. *The Pre-Mongol Era* (635-1206; from the arrival of the Persian Christians to the rise of Genghis Khan). East Syrian Christianity became established in centers along the Silk Road. Rumors of a large Christian population under Prester John circulated throughout Europe, arising probably from knowledge of the Christian Kerait chieftain Unc Khan.
2. *The Mongol Era* (1206-1368). Papal envoys, mainly Franciscan, shuttled between Europe and Mongol Asia, often with mixed political and evangelistic agendas. John of Plano Carpini*, William of Rubruck*, and John of Montecorvino* are names that dominate this period. Montecorvino lived 30 years in Da-tu, where he translated the NT and Psalms into Mongolian.
3. *The Post-Mongol Era* (1368-1765). Mongolia was a vassal province of Ming (1368-1644) and then Manchu China (1644-1911); no Christian contact with the Mongols is known from this period.
4. *The Pre-Modern Era* (1765-1991). The Moravians established themselves at Sarepta, near modern Volgograd, to evangelize the Kalmucks, and they founded a small congregation. The London Missionary Society (LMS) worked in Buriatia between 1817 and 1840 and translated the first complete Mongolian Bible. The LMS also established a work in Inner Mongolia. The Swedish Mongol Mission (now the Evangelical East Asia Mission) ran a medical clinic in Urga between 1919 and 1924. It also established three centers in Inner Mongolia and planted a viable Mongol church there. The Scandinavian Alliance Mission (now The Evangelical Alliance Mission) entered Mongolia in 1895, but suffered heavy losses during the Boxer Uprising of 1900. Subsequently, many new missions located themselves at the strategic border town of Kalgan (modern Zhang-jia-kou). A Catholic work was initiated by the Lazarists* in 1834, then continued under the Belgian order of the *Congregatio Immaculati Cordis Mariae* (CICM: Scheut Fathers*) from 1865. This Catholic work (schools, farming, and literature) centered on the Ordos region of Inner Mongolia. All missionaries left Inner Mongolia by the mid-1950s because of the rise of Communism*. A revision of the LMS New Testament was published in 1952.
5. *The Modern Era* (from 1991). The modern Mongolian church is the result of several coinciding factors. With the establishment of a democratic parliamentary system, an open-door policy followed. A modern Khalka translation of the NT had been published in 1990 by the United Bible Societies* and was ready for immediate shipment to Mongolia. Several

Mongols who had been converted in Eastern Europe returned to Mongolia in 1991, and Western Christians began arriving later that year.

Half a dozen churches were established by the end of 1992. By the end of 1994, there were about 3,000 Christians, and by the end of 2000 over 30,000, mainly in Ulan Bator, but also with significant numbers in Erdenet, Darhan, and most provincial centers. There is now a Christian presence (family, home group, or church) in every province of Mongolia. Evangelism and church planting have been priorities, along with leadership training. The law requires that all religious groups must register with the government, and most Ulan Bator congregations have done so.

The CICM established a papal embassy and mission in Ulan Bator in 1992 at the invitation of the Mongolian government, and now has a growing congregation. Several Protestant churches are solely under Mongolian leadership, growing rapidly with outreach programs to the Chinese, Russian, and Khazaks, as well as ongoing evangelism amongst their own people. Current initiatives include development projects, a new Bible translation, localized leadership training, and the establishment of the Mongolian Evangelical Coalition, which consists of Mongolian Christian leaders.

Bibliography

Athyal, S., ed., *The Church in Asia Today* (1996). • Bawden, C. R., *Shamans, Lamas and Evangelicals* (1985). • Dawson, C., ed., *Mission to Asia* (1966). • Hoke, D. E., ed., *The Church in Asia* (1975). • Lovett, R., *James Gilmour of Mongolia* (1895). • Moffett, S. H., *A History of Christianity in Asia,* Vol. I: *Beginnings to 1500* (1992). • Mortenson, V., *God Made it Grow* (1994). • Verhelst, D., et al., *CICM Missionaries, Past and Present, 1862-1987* (1995).

Hugh P. Kemp

Montagnards

In the 1950s, French colonialists began regular use of the word "Montagnard" for the more than 60 ethnic minorities who inhabit Vietnam's high valleys and plateaus and spill over, in lesser numbers, into Cambodia* and Laos*. They constitute an estimated 8% of the Socialist Republic of Vietnam's (SRV) 75,030,000 population. Additional minorities include Khmers, Chinese, and Chams, which raises the total minority population to around 13%.

Now called "national minorities" (informally *nguoi Thuong Du*) by the SRV, Montagnards are not a homogeneous people, but a racial and ethnic mix coming from both Malayo-Polynesian and Mongoloid ancestry. Prior to 1900, a combination of factors including impenetrable mountain terrain and the absence of political or economic pressures isolated the Montagnard tribes from each other and their Vietnamese lowland neighbors, who called them savages *(moi)* and regarded them as inferiors.

An 1170 Sanskrit inscription at a Cham temple in Nhatrang includes the word *Randaiy* (Rhade) and seems to be the first historical reference to the Montagnards. The aftermath of the 20th century's Indochina wars with the Japanese, French, and Americans increasingly forced Montagnards into the broader society but also resulted in massive dislocation, disruption of livelihood, loss of life, and land takeovers.

Montagnards in the southern two-thirds of the highlands (the Annam Cordillera; Truong Son) include the Rhade (200,000), who live around Banmethuot; the Jarai (242,000), who comprise seven distinct subgroups in the environs of Pleiku; the Bahnar (140,000) near Kontum; and the Koho (107,600) with subgroups in the Dalat area. The Jarai, who were granted autonomy under the French, resisted assimilation by the South Vietnamese government in the 1960s and led an insurgent movement called FULRO (French acronym: United Front for the Liberation of Oppressed Peoples), which was joined by others but is now defunct.

In the highland provinces north and west of the Red River Delta bordering China* and Laos are found the largest groups: the Tay (also Tho; 1,190,400), the Thai (Black and White [so-called because of the color of women's blouses]; 1,040,500); the Muong (914,000); the Nung (706,000); the Hmong (Meo; 558,100) who since 1850 have arrived from South China; and the Man (Dao, Yao; 474,000). As a group, the northern Montagnards have assimilated more of the Sino-Vietnamese culture than have the others.

Animistic* beliefs prevail among the Montagnards; their world includes both good and evil spirits that must be dealt with by ritual and shamans (see Shamanism). Seemingly modeled on the Chinese netherworld, a spiritual bureaucracy governs the unseen world and must be placated to cope with evil, harm, disease, and death. Children are protected by amulets against evil spirits, and crops are guaranteed by offerings at the time of planting and harvest.

Gerald Hickey says, "There is a similarity in the format of ceremonies performed in conjunction with religious beliefs and practices" (*Sons,* p. 26). Animal sacrifice has been widespread. If a water buffalo is sacrificed by the Jarai, it is slowly killed by being first tethered to a stake, then its rear leg tendons are cut, after which comes a lethal blow to the neck by men who dance around it brandishing sabers and spears. A feast follows as villagers consume the offerings of food, meat, and rice alcohol to the rhythmic accompaniment of unique hammered brass gongs.

Like some others, the Hmong of North Vietnam and Laos employ shamans, who as masters of the spirits secure the release of a soul held in the grip of disease or death. Through trance and the assistance of his tutelary spirit, the shaman intervenes with the malevolent spirits who may require payment of money or sacrifice. Upon death, mortuary rites last a minimum of three days, while the deceased is guided on his journey to the other world by sacrifices, rituals, and the song of a reed instrument.

The future of the Montagnard way of life is in some question. Slash-and-burn agriculture and excessive logging have resulted in deforestation, erosion, the floods of 1991 and 1992 in Son La and Lai Chau Provinces, and further loss of traditional Montagnard land holdings. It is estimated that between 1940 and 1990, one half of the forests were cut down. As of 1968, more than half (1.9 million) of the 2.8 million nomadic cultivators had been resettled.

In 1979, the SRV reported large-scale settlement of 57,000 North Vietnamese on tribal lands in Lam Dong Province. In 1989, the Vietnamese Politburo adopted measures for the further economic development of traditional Montagnard lands with the apparent intent to integrate Montagnards into the majority Vietnamese population. The illiteracy rate of Montagnards is estimated at 80-90% (compared to 12% for the general population), even though the SRV claims almost all minorities read and write in both the official and their native language. Vietnamese is the medium of instruction wherever schools are available.

Bibliography

Dutt, Ashok K., ed., *Southeast Asia: Realm of Contrasts* (1985). • Gergerson, Marilyn, and Dorothy Thomas, *Notes from Indochina on Ethnic Minority Cultures* (1980). • Hickey, Gerald Cannon, *Sons of the Mountains* (1982). • Hockings, Paul, ed., *Encyclopedia of World Cultures* (1993). • *Human Rights in Developing Countries Yearbook 1993* (1993). • Keyfitz, Keith, and Wilhelm Flieger, *World Population Growth and Aging: Demographic Trends in the Late Twentieth Century* (1990). • Whitfield, Danny J., *Historical and Cultural Dictionary of Vietnam,* Vol. 7 *of Historical and Cultural Dictionaries of Asia,* (1976). • *World Directory of Minorities.*

James F. Lewis

Mooler Theh

(b. Morkohder, Myanmar, 15 Sep 1905; d. Taunggyi, Myanmar, 5 Apr 1993). Teacher, preacher, and evangelist in Myanmar*.

Mooler Theh studied at Tuongoo Paku School up to the seventh grade and then moved to Ko Tha Byu* High School, Bassein. He passed the tenth grade there in 1924 and entered Judson College at Rangoon. Being poor, he was granted free tuition and board in exchange for working at the school. After two years in college, he entered the Burma Divinity School (Myanmar Institute of Theology) at Insein and graduated with a bachelor of theology degree in 1931. The principal of the school, V. M. Dyer, was particularly enthusiastic about Gospel team evangelism. During the four years Mooler Theh attended the school, Dyer and his students carried out evangelistic campaigns all over Burma, went to India* three times, to Thailand* twice, and to Singapore* and Indonesia* once. These evangelism trips made a deep impression on Mooler Theh's future work.

In 1931, H. I. Marshall asked Mooler Theh to join the teaching staff of Karen Theological Seminary at Insein. That he did and, in fact, served there effectively and faithfully until his death in 1993. It was a great opportunity to instruct many young men and women and mold them to become worthy witnesses for Christ. He did not limit himself to teaching but, during the holidays and whenever he was available, organized Gospel team trips to many ethnic groups throughout the country, baptizing a large number of these diverse peoples. He was also requested by the Burma Divinity School to help teach part-time there, and he willingly did so until his last days.

A tribute in the introduction to Mooler Theh's autobiographical notes and anecdotes (1988) reads: "I have known Thra [meaning 'teacher,' 'minister,' 'preacher,' or 'reverend' in Karen] Mooler since my days at the Burma Divinity School during 1950 to 1954 as a teacher as well as a friend. He was always accessible for help and guidance as I prepared myself for the ministry. His major field was evangelism and, as usual, he never spared himself, whether it was teaching in the classroom or traveling with Gospel teams. He has a tremendous zeal for winning souls, and this passionate concern has carried him throughout the far corners of Burma and even beyond. Not surprisingly, he is well known, loved, and respected by the Karens* and also by many among the other racial or minority groups in Burma. . . . His dedication to evangelism coupled with his wonderful sense of humor can be a forceful spiritual uplift for his hearers and coworkers."

Mooler Theh was not an intellectual giant or a sophisticated individual. He was modest and humble, and he did great things for God in his own simple and unassuming ways. One day, when he and his friends were on a Gospel team campaign trip to Kayah State, his closest friend, Peter Hla, asked him, "You speak only the simplest sentences, and yet your sermons are appreciated and useful to your listeners; they are also crazy about your skits and one-act plays. What is your secret?" He responded by saying that there was no secret, but that it might have been like this: "There is no value in a 0 (zero). However, if it is placed behind 1 (one), together they become 10 (ten). Now zero has attained some value. I consider myself to be nothing. I am a '0,' and God is a big '1.' I place myself right behind God and can achieve a slight usefulness."

Bibliography

Kyaw Dwe, Clifford, "Thra Mooler Theh (Teacher and Evangelist)," Introduction to Mooler Theh, *Autobiographical Notes and Anecdotes* (1988).

Clifford Kyaw Dwe

Moon, Sun Myung. *See* Unification Church, Korea

Moralde, Agripina N.

(b. 1893; d. 1977). First Filipino woman evangelist in Bicol and second ordained Protestant woman minister in the Philippines*.

Converted through Policarpo Pelgone* about 1910, Moralde and her colleagues Geronima Solano, Dolores Maravillas, and Apolonia Dino ably demonstrated women's ability to do church work. These women often served as pioneer evangelists and went on preaching tours by themselves throughout the Bicol Peninsula.

Beginning in 1915, Moralde served as manager and youth worker in the Presbyterian* dormitories at Albay. There she exerted a powerful influence on students, many of whom later became outstanding leaders of the church, such as Bishop Leonardo G. Dia and the ministers Crispin Faune and Getulio Erandio. She was ordained in 1937. Moralde continued church work well beyond retirement age.

Bibliography

Tabios, A. D., J. P. Cruz, and M. G. Pejo, *The Evangelical Church in the Bicol Region: A Brief History* (1974). • Sitoy, T. V., Jr., *Several Springs, One Stream* (1992).

T. Valentino Sitoy, Jr.

Morris, J. Glenn

(b. Atlanta, Georgia, United States, 30 Jan 1915). American missionary founder and first president of Thailand Baptist Theological Seminary (TBTS).

Morris was one of the early missionaries to Thailand* appointed by the Foreign Mission Board (FMB) of the Southern Baptist* Convention (SBC), United States. He graduated from Mercer University in 1940 with a bachelor's degree and from Southern Baptist Theological Seminary in Louisville, Kentucky, with a master of theology degree in 1944 and a doctor of theology degree in 1946.

Morris and his wife, Polly Love Morris, were appointed by the FMB in 1946 to serve in China*. In 1947, after a year at Yale University School of Chinese Studies, Morris went to China, where he served in theological education from 1947 to 1950 in the cities of Beijing, Tsingtao, and Shanghai.

In 1951, Morris was reassigned to Thailand and arrived in Bangkok on 1 Mar 1952 with his wife and son, Glenn, Jr., to serve as pastor of Grace Baptist Church. He held this post for about 20 years. He was instrumental in the establishment of TBTS, which opened in Bangkok in Oct 1952. Morris served as president of TBTS until 1972, when a Thai leader assumed the presidency. He then served as teacher, academic dean, and treasurer until his transfer to Hong Kong in 1983.

During Morris's tenure in Thailand, the seminary, which began in rented facilities, moved into new permanent buildings in Bangkok's Toong Mahamek area in 1961. The curriculum was developed on four different levels, the highest being master of theology. TBTS established a working relationship with Asia Baptist Graduate Theological Seminary, headquartered in Hong Kong*.

In Hong Kong, Morris served as a teacher at Hong Kong Baptist Theological Seminary until his retirement in 1987, at which time he moved to Jackson, Mississippi, United States.

Ann Fox

Morrison, Robert

(b. Northumberland, England, 1782; d. Guangzhou, China, 1 Aug 1834). First Protestant missionary to China*.

Of Scottish parentage, Morrison was converted in his teens when he was an apprentice shoemaker to his father. He joined the Presbyterian* Church (1798) and studied theology, astronomy, and medicine at Hoxton College. He also acquired a rudimentary knowledge of Chinese in London and prepared for missionary work at the Missionary Academy in Gosport, Hampshire. He joined the London Missionary Society (LMS) in 1804 and was sent to study medicine, Chinese, and astronomy in London. Morrison was ordained in June of 1807 and set sail for Guangzhou in Sep 1807 via New York because of the hostility of the East India Company (EIC) toward missions.

In Guangzhou Morrison improved his Chinese with the help of two Chinese Catholics. From 1809 until his death, he worked as an interpreter for the EIC in order to secure his presence in Guangzhou. He also served as an interpreter for the unsuccessful diplomatic mission of Lord Amherst in Beijing in 1815. Though Morrison considered himself primarily a missionary, he was regarded as a representative of both the British trading company and government, a situation in which he experienced much tension, but which gave him legal status on Chinese soil.

Morrison was largely responsible for the establishment of the Anglo-Chinese School in Malacca*, Malaysia*, which was started in 1818. His vision was for a cross-cultural institution which would promote mutual respect. The building was completed in 1820, with William Milne* in charge. Unfortunately, the student population did not comprise the intended number of European students and Chinese from the educated or official classes. The students were mainly Chinese whose ultimate goal was to conduct business deals with foreigners. The curriculum was relegated to the elementary grades. In the first 15 years of the school, however, 40 students completed their education, and 15 students were baptized. Milne died in 1822, and the school was moved to Hong Kong in 1842.

Morrison concentrated on literary work. With Milne's help, he translated the Bible*, finishing by 1819. His Chinese dictionary (1815-23) became the standard work for many years. He also translated the shorter catechism of the Church of Scotland and part of the prayer book of the Church of England. In addition, he wrote pamphlets.

On a visit home in 1824, Morrison, by then well known, sought to stimulate British interest in missions and in the study of Eastern languages. In China, however, Morrison made few converts. Prior to his death, he and his colleagues had baptized only 10 Chinese. The first person baptized by Morrison was Tsae A-ko in July 1814. In 1823, Morrison ordained Leong Kung Fa*. Morrison died at Guangzhou on 1 Aug 1934 and was buried in Macau*. He was a man of vision and integrity.

Bibliography

Latourette, K. S., *A History of Christian Missions in China* (1929). • Morrison, Eliza Armstrong, comp., *Memoirs of the Life and Labours of Robert Morrison, D.D.*, 2 vols. (1839). • Broomhall, Marshall, *Robert Morrison a Master Builder* (1924). • Rubinstein, Murray A., *The Origins of the Anglo-American Missionary Enterprise in China, 1807-1840* (1996). China Group

Mosher, Governeur Frank

(b. Stapleton, New York, United States, 28 Oct 1871; d. 19 Jul 1941). Second Episcopal bishop of the Philippines*.

Mosher was serving as bishop of Shanghai in China* prior to his election to the Philippine Missionary District in 1920. He followed strictly the policy of Bishop Brent* of not doing aggressive proselytizing among the already Christian Filipinos. His administration was more of nurturing and strengthening the already established mission churches. The only expansions made during his tenure were the establishment of St. Paul's Mission in Balbalasang, Kalinga Apayao, in 1925, and of St. Francis of Assisi Mission in Upi, Maguindanao, in 1927.

A long-lasting contribution of Mosher's to the church was the establishment of St. Andrew's Training School (SATS) for the ordained and lay ministry of the church in 1932. Though its operation was disrupted by World War II*, SATS was able to graduate the first three Filipino clergy before its transfer to Cathedral Heights in Quezon City in 1947.

Mosher retired from the Philippines in 1940 because of poor health.

Bibliography

Journal of the Annual Convocation of the Missionary District of the Philippine Islands (1921-40).

Edward P. Malecdan

Mouly, Joseph Martial

(b. 1807; d. 1868). French missionary of the Vincentian Order and bishop to China* and Mongolia; first vicariate appointed in the former Apostolic Vicariate of Northern Zhi Li (Hebei/Chihli).

In 1833, at the age of 26, Mouly left France. He arrived in Macau* in 1834. In 1835 Mouly left Macau and disguised himself in order to enter into China's inland. He succeeded in getting into a Christian village in the north, Xi Wan Zi. In 1870 Rome restructured the Diocese of Beijing, which was established in the late 17th c. A new diocese of Shandong and a diocese of Mongolia were created. Mouly was appointed to be the vicariate of Mongolia. In July 1842 Mouly went to the province of Shan Xi, where he was consecrated by Joachin Sallveti, a Franciscan* who was there doing clandestine mission work.

The Diocese of Beijing was divided into the Vicariate Apostolic of North Zhi Li, Southeast Zhi Li and Southwest Zhi Li. Mouly was made the vicariate of North Zhi Li. The vicariate apostolic of North Zhi Li was later to become the Diocese of Beijing. However, at the time Mouly was not yet able to enter Beijing. In October 1860, when the British and French allied soldiers entered Beijing, Mouly accompanied them. Through the intervention of French representative Gros and French army commander Montaulan, the Qing government returned the now closed South Church and two churches that have been confiscated, North Church and East Church, to Mouly. From then on, it was no longer necessary for Mouly to continue clandestine mission activity that had gone on for 20 years.

Now Mouly appeared in public as the vicariate of North Zhi Li. He first lived in the South Church and later moved to the North Church. Early in 1867, the new cathedral in Beijing, which he built, was completed. The work of the Catholic mission, which was terminated when the Qing government discontinued the service of missionaries in the calendrical work, was again resumed under Mouly's leadership. Mouly was a strong French nationalist who relied on French political protection for his work, yet he is an important figure in organizing the structure of the Roman Catholic Church* in China.

Bibliography

Charbonnier, Jean, *Histoire des Chrétiens de Chine* (1992). • Thomas, Antoine, *Histoire de la Mission de Pekin*, Vol. 2 (1933). China Group

Mozoomdar, Pratap Chander

(b. 1840; d. 1905). Indian theist, faithful follower of Keshub Chunder Sen*, author.

Mozoomdar succeeded Keshub in the leadership of the Brahmo Samaj*. His best-known books are *The Life and Teachings of Keshub Chunder Sen* and *The Oriental Christ.* His other writings include *Aids to Moral Character, The Silent Pastor, Asheesh* (in Bengali), and *The Spirit of God.* He came nearest to Keshub in his discipleship of Jesus Christ in the Church of the New Dispensation *(Naba Bidhan).*

The Oriental Christ elucidates the understanding of Jesus Christ as divine humanity which Mozoomdar learned from Keshub. He pictures Christ in the framework of Oriental patterns of thought and spirituality. The Eastern Christ is an incarnation of unbounded love and grace; the Western Christ is an incarnation of theology, formalism, and ethical and physical force.

Christ as the Son of God was the manifestation of divine character in humanity. Only the Eternal himself can reveal his character in relation to humans. That character descended into Christ for the enlightenment, conversion, regeneration, and adoption of all people, and hence Christ is simultaneously Son of God and Son of Man. Christ revealed the true relation between God and human persons. Christ taught not only humanity, but also divinity through humanity, realizing the spirit of God in himself. We can think of God at one level as humanlike because we humans have the image of God in ourselves. Knowing Christ's humanity and ourselves in relation to it is therefore to know God himself as he is related to us without losing the mystery of his transcendent being.

The cross is the symbol of God's will ruling all the events of human life; it brings victory over nature, sorrow, want, and death. The substance of resurrection is the spirit of God with whom we commune every day. God has created us because he loves us, because we are necessities in the economy of his nature; the divine humanity of Christ crowns this marvelous structure of the human person. The indispensable necessity for Christ is the necessity for the creation of all things, the evolution and progress of all things, the perfection of things from the imperfect. God is all in all, and Christ is his spiritual manifestation only as the type ever growing into perfection. Still Jesus Christ is unique because he completes all other partial and local incarnations, he makes for a truly spiritual and universal incarnation of the spirit, and he provides an everlasting model of the divine order of humanity; he is "the type of humanity."

According to Mozoomdar, Christ has not only risen, but returned as he had promised in the Holy Spirit. Therefore, the Brahmo Samaj declares the dispensation of the spirit, making possible an unceasing succession of divine humanity. The function of the Son shall never cease: the consummation of creation is interpreted as his second coming. According to Mozoomdar, the Spirit of God is active in the creative process, illuminates the triune nature of God, constitutes the basis for the oneness of humanity and the destiny of humans, and provides a proper framework to interpret the meaning of Christ. Mozoomdar criticized the Christian church for relegating the Holy Spirit to the margins and thus perverting its theology into a Christo-monism.

Bibliography

Mozoomdar, P. C., *The Faith and Progress of the Brahmo Samaj,* 2nd ed. (1934); *Keshub Chunder Sen and His Times* (1917); *Lectures in America and Other Papers,* 2nd ed. (1955); *The Oriental Christ,* 2nd ed. (1933); *The Spirit of God,* 2nd ed. (1918); *The Life and Teachings of Keshub Chunder Sen,* 3rd ed. (1931). • Thomas, M. M., *The Acknowledged Christ of the Indian Renaissance* (1969). • Ghosh, N., *The Evolution of Navavidhan* (1930). • Sastri, Sivanath, *History of the Brahmo Samaj,* Vol. II (1912). • *The New Dispensation and the Sadharan Brahmo Samaj* (1881). • *Slokasangraha: A Compilation of Theistic Texts* (1904).

K. P. Aleaz

Mukhdi Akbar

Mystical movement in Selayar Island, South Sulawesi.

The Igma "religion" Binanga Benteng (after 1945 called the Mukhdi Akbar Movement) was founded between 1912 and 1918 by Haji Abdul Gani Daeng Manrapi Ibn Rakhman (ca. 1846-1922). Gani was born in Batangmata (North Selayar) but eventually moved to a small fishing hamlet to the southwest called Binanga Benteng.

On his several trips to the Middle East, Gani was deeply influenced by both Sufism and the modernist and reformist spirit which prevailed within Islam at the end of the 19th c. and which to a large extent was dominated by the Egyptian reformer Muhammad 'Abduh (1849-1905). 'Abduh's low opinion of the Eastern Islamic way of life, his emphasis on reason and a relatively open attitude toward modern Western movements, technology, and science, became typical of Gani as well. Both he and 'Abduh were rationalists; they held that obtained knowledge and revealed religious truths are not incompatible with each other and that human reason is an indispensable tool for understanding divine truths. However, reason alone is not enough. It has to be supplemented by intuition, as revelation to Gani was intuitive knowledge of Allah and an intuitive feeling where happiness can be found, in this world and in the next. Gani's concern was the internalization of the religious life, and he juxtaposed this with formal observance of the Islamic law and the code of duties. As in most *tariqah,* the most important task of the religious leaders was the moral education of the faithful, whereas the initiated elite did not need dogmas or laws.

The primary written sources which still exist have their origin in the apocalyptic and mystical experiences of Gani's disciples, among whom Haji Muhammad Yusuf (d. 1948) and Sumatra-born Ince Abdul Rahim were prominent. These documents use the Selayarese language. The most important is a kind of synopsis given by Gani to several of his disciples as a "declaration of the truth." It granted them the right to be gurus.

Mukhdi Akbar is essentially a reformist, mystical, and apocalyptic movement existing on the fringes of Islam. Some articles of ancient Sufism have been preserved, e.g., the doctrine of the Light of Muhammad. Although in past centuries these articles were found throughout Indonesian Islam, by now they have largely vanished elsewhere. These beliefs, then, are not unique in South Sulawesi, but have roots that go deep into Middle Eastern theology for well over 1,000 years. Both elements, the apocalyptic and the mystical, are interwoven and difficult to disentangle as they tend to express the same feelings and anxieties on different levels.

In addition, the reformist spirit that in a certain sense

is common to all mystical movements manifests itself in the early writings of Mukhdi Akbar. They criticized the religious practices and beliefs, including mystical practices, which prevailed within Islam on Selayar Island (and South Sulawesi in general) at the beginning of the twentieth century. These practices and beliefs were considered too closely associated with the popular world of magic and superstition.

The movement was formally banned by the Indonesian government in 1966; thereafter many members converted to Christianity.

Bibliography

De Jonge, Christiaan G. F., *Geesten, Goden en Getuigen. Geschiedenis van de nederlandse Zending onder Buginezen en Makassaren in Zuid-Sulawesi (Indonesia)* (1991).

CHRISTIAAN DE JONGE

Mukhia, David

(b. Kurseong, Darjeeling District India, 4 Jan 1901; d. Pokhara, Nepal, Jan 1991). Pioneer Nepali evangelist on the border of Nepal and in Assam, first pastor in Nepal* and first chairman of Nepal Christian Fellowship*; persecuted for his faith.

Mukhia's parents immigrated from Nepal to Darjeeling, where they worked for missionaries of the Scottish Presbyterian* Mission and became Christians. According to his testimony, he was "born again" on 25 Dec 1920. Both his parents died when he was small. He was brought up by an uncle, took teacher's training in Kalimpong, then taught school and did preaching on the side at Sukhia Pokhri, a town bordering eastern Nepal.

In 1930 Mukhia was called to work alongside Dr. Cecil Duncan as an evangelist and dispensary helper at the Raxaul Medical Mission on the southern border of Nepal. For over 20 years he did pioneer evangelism among Nepalis in India. He was married in 1935 to Premi Gurung. In 1940 they moved from Raxaul to Nautanwa, another border town further west, to work with the Nepali Evangelist Band (NEB). In 1942 they were sent east to Shillong in Assam, which also had a large Nepali population. Extensive evangelistic tours were made, a one-room Nepali school was started, and a small Nepali church established. On 10 Jan 1943 the NEB missionaries ordained Mukhia at a special nondenominational ceremony in Calcutta.

When Nepal opened up and the NEB was invited to start medical work in Pokhara, the Mukhias joined the team. They entered Nepal in 1953, and a congregation was established in Pokhara under Mukhia's guidance. A small thatch-roofed church was dedicated in 1955, the first Protestant church building in Nepal. At the first meeting of the Nepal Christian Fellowship in 1960, Mukhia was elected chairman. But the following year he and his family were forced to cross the border back into India at Nautanwa when a warrant was issued for his arrest in Nepal following his performing a baptism ceremony in Tansen. He continued to minister from there until he was able to return to Pokhara in 1969, when he again took up full-time preaching and pastoral duties. He died at the age of 90 in Pokhara. His wife remained there.

Bibliography

Nepal Church History Project, transcript of personal interviews with David and Premi Mukhia (1986). • Perry, Cindy, *A Biographical History of the Church in Nepal* (1993).

RAJENDRA K. RONGONG

Mulia, Todung Sutan Gunung

(b. Padang Sidempuan, North Sumatra, 21 Jan 1896; d. Amsterdam, 11 Nov 1966). Indonesian churchman, educator, and politician.

Mulia was one of the greatest Indonesian churchmen, despite never having attained a formal theological education. He was instrumental in the development of the ecumenical* movement in Indonesia*, as well as in education and in politics.

Mulia did his middle and higher education in the Netherlands (teacher's diploma, 1917; master of law, 1932; doctor of letters and philosophy, 1933). Beginning in 1917, he served as a teacher in several towns in Indonesia. Meanwhile, because of his expertise in education, from 1922 to 1927 (and then in 1935-42), he was appointed a member of the *Volksraad* (People's Council), the embryo of parliament created by the Dutch colonial government. During his second term of membership in the *Volksraad,* he founded the indigenous Indonesian Christian Party, the embryo of PARKINDO.

The resurgence of nationalism* in Asia generally, and in Indonesia particularly, influenced and colored Mulia's struggles in each endeavor. It also influenced his dissertation, *Het Primitieve Denken in de Moderne Wetenschap* (The Primitive Thinking in Modern Science), which he defended at Leiden University in 1933. In this work he declared that the mental ability of the Eastern nations (including Indonesia), which were often called primitive peoples by the West, was not of a lower quality than that of the Western modern nations. His ideas and struggles were supported as well as influenced by Hendrik Kraemer*, a Dutch churchman and theologian who rendered much help in promoting self-supporting Indonesian churches.

Mulia began his activity in church circles in Batavia (Jakarta) in 1922. He not only served his Batak* church (HKBP), but he also contributed to missions and cooperative church bodies, activities which led to their growth thereafter. Because of his church leadership and high degree of education, he was appointed as the only indigenous Indonesian delegate to the International Missionary Conference in Jerusalem in 1928. This experience gave him more encouragement to fight for the independence of Indonesian churches from Western missionary paternalism. European missionaries, especially from the *Rheinische Missionsgesellschaft* (Rhenish Mission Society), which had founded the HKBP, were not supportive of this idea.

During the revolution for the independence of the Republic of Indonesia (1945-49), while holding various important posts in government office (e.g., minister of education and culture), Mulia was actively preparing an ecumenical body for the Indonesian churches. When the Council (now Communion) of Churches in Indonesia was founded on 25 May 1950, Mulia was chosen to be the first general chairman; he served until 1960. Concurrently, he was chosen general chairman of the Institution for Theological Education in Indonesia (the executor of the Jakarta Theological Seminary) and chairman of the board of the Indonesian Bible* Society. He also helped to found Indonesia Christian University.

In the midst of his very busy schedule, Mulia wrote some textbooks in Indonesian: *India: A History of Its Political and National Movement* (1949); *United Nations Organization* (1952); and (with K. A. H. Hidding) *Encyclopedia Indonesia* (three volumes). However, in church circles he expressed his ideas orally rather than in written form.

Mulia's expertise in a wide field of knowledge (he was called an encyclopedist) and his integrity as a scientist, politician, educator, and churchman, led to his being awarded an honorary doctorate from the Free University of Amsterdam on 20 Oct 1966, just three weeks before his death.

Bibliography

Aritonang, Jan S., *Pemikiran dan Pelayanan TSG Mulia di bidang Kegerejaan/Oikumene* (working paper on T. S. G. Mulia Memorial Lecture) (1989). • *Ensiklopedia Indonesia*, Vol. IV (1983). • Ngelow, Z. J., *The Transformation of Nationalism* (1992) • Verkuyl, J., *Gedenken en Verwachten* (1983).

Jan S. Aritonang

Muntilan

Small town in Central Java regarded as the "Bethlehem of Java."

The first group of Javanese converts was baptized by Franz van Lith* at the Sendangsono spring in 1904. A school complex from primary level to teachers' training college and vocational schools formed the elite of Indonesia's first generation of Catholics, who occupied important positions in church and society from the 1940s. Many priests, bishops, teachers, university professors, state officials, and military leaders received their first training at Muntilan. During the war of independence, fanatic religious groups burned part of the school complex and killed indigenous and foreign missionaries.

Adolf Heuken

Murray, William

(b. United Kingdom, 1864; d. Scotland, 25 Aug 1946). Presbyterian* missionary minister in Malaya and Singapore.

Murray served from 1902 to 1936 as a missionary of the foreign missions committee of the Presbyterian Church of England and was very active in religious and social work, especially among youths in Singapore. He was awarded the Order of the British Empire on 6 Jun 1936.

Murray was ordained at Crook County, Durham, ministering there from 1887 to 1893. He served in St. Andrew's Presbyterian Church, Penang, from 1893 to 1899 using the Masonic Temple on Northam Street for worship while preparations were being made to build a new church. There he learned the Malay language and baptized his language teacher into the Christian faith.

Murray returned to Southeast Asia in 1902 as minister of the Prinsep Street Presbyterian Church, Singapore, serving Malay-speaking Straits Chinese. Although conversions were few, he built up the work among youths, some of whom later became outstanding citizens. The first company of the Boys' Brigade was formed in 1930.

In 1908, Murray inaugurated a reading club in English language and literature as a new section of the Chinese Christian Association and later a dramatic section and a debating society. He raised funds for a new church building, which was completed in 1931. He was also active in synod affairs. He retired to Scotland on 15 Feb 1936.

Bibliography

Hood, G. A., *The Presbyterian Church in Singapore, 1881-1981: 100th Anniversary Commemoration Volume* (1982). • Tan Kek Tiam, *Prinsep Street Presbyterian Church, 1930-1980* (1980). • Song Ong Siang, *One Hundred Years' History of the Chinese in Singapore* (1902).

Anne Johnson

Music, Asian Christian

The term "Christian music" denotes music that is used in church, particularly in worship*. Asian Christian music in general includes instrumental music and choral music. Instrumental music in the church employs reed organ, piano, electronic organ, or more recently pipe organ in Japan*, Korea*, Hong Kong*, and Taiwan*, and guitars in the Philippines*, gamelan orchestra in Indonesia*, Khaen ensemble in Thailand*, and harmonium, tabla, sitar, or tamboura in the Indian subcontinent. These instruments play preludes and postludes, accompany congregational singing, and occasionally are used for recitals or concerts. Some portable instruments are employed for outdoor evangelistic meetings.

Keyboard instruments are used to play mostly Western music, but they are also capable of playing some new Asian compositions. Other Asian instruments are used to play the traditional hymns or certain new repertoires specially composed for the church. Being more flexible, guitars are used for both Asian and Western repertoires. They are particularly popular among young people.

Choral music represents the core of Christian music

in that it includes congregational hymn singing and choral anthems. Hymns are the main concern of this article. Given the diversity of countries, cultures, peoples, and churches, there is no such thing as "Asian" Christian music. "Asian" in this context can refer only to the geographical region of Asia or to certain general aspects of Asian culture. From a practical point of view, this subject may be divided into three categories: (1) ancient Asian hymns and lyrics; (2) hymns of Western origins, or written by Asians in a Western style; and (3) hymns composed by Asian Christians during the last three decades.

Ancient Asian Hymns. Christian music is closely related to the history of Christian missions in Asia. We therefore must trace the early days of mission in different Asian countries in order to understand this subject.

The Nestorian* priest Alopen went to China in 635 C.E. A hymn of praise written during this time is one of the oldest extant Christian hymns. This being the golden age of the Chinese arts (the Tang Dynasty [618-907]), one can assume that the tune must have been composed by a Chinese Christian of that time. Historical documents also indicate that over 30,000 people were converted by the Nestorians during the Mongol Kingdom of the 13th c. There is little doubt that they composed their own hymns. Unfortunately, no musical notations from that period are extant.

The Mar Thoma* Church in South India, which claims its origin directly from St. Thomas*, one of the disciples of Jesus, inherited some Christian music from the Syrian Orthodox* tradition. But in general, Indian Christians have, from the early period of mission, been composing their own hymns, which they call lyrics. They have thousands of lyrics, mostly still in oral tradition. The Marathi hymnal preserves but a small portion of this rich treasure. The tremendous wealth of Karnatic hymns of South India deserves serious research. Christians in Pakistan* have, from the early part of the 20th century, been singing the whole book of the Psalms using their folk melodies, but very little of this tradition is known outside of the country. Here lies another treasure of Christian heritage. Since Bangladesh*, Sri Lanka*, and Nepal* all belong to the Indian cultural area, their musical traditions and practices are somewhat similar. To some extent, they also share some hymns.

The first Western Protestant missionary to Japan, Jonathan Goble, arrived there in 1860. He was a strong advocate of encouraging the Japanese to adapt folk melodies and to use the *shambisen* (plucked lute) and *koto* (zither) for accompanying hymn singing. Although the Russian Orthodox Church and its liturgies and songs were introduced in 1872, a Japanese Christian of that time recorded that 70% of its hymns were taken from Japanese folk *(yookyoku)* tradition, and 20% from theatrical *(gidayu)* repertoires. Only 10% were from the "strange" Russian tradition.

From these examples we can see that, during the early missionary movement, there were efforts to encourage the use of native melodies. But gradually Asian Christians began to accept, assimilate, and feel at home with Western Christian music, and they eventually gave up their own music almost totally.

Western-Influenced Hymns. In the history of mission, churches in Asia have accepted Western musical traditions, especially those of the 19th-c. gospel variety. This Western gospel-song tradition, traditional European works (including those of Palestrina, Bach, Handel, Vivaldi, Beethoven, Brahms, and Mendelssohn), and, to a lesser degree, the contemporary works of Vaughan Williams, Stravinsky, Britten, Tippett, and Rutter, have formed the major part of Asian Christian music until today, especially in the Philippines and Northeast Asia. The rather limited statistics in the chart on page 571, which are drawn from the writer's personal collection of hymnals, give a general indication of the numbers of hymns written by native people.

In general, since Western music has dominated most Asian churches since the 19th c., Asian Christians have internalized Western music and begun to imitate Western styles, especially those of gospel songs. As a result, a great majority of Asian church music has sounded like Western music. We may name this an imitation period. The end of World War II and the birth the nationalism* brought in a new era of Asian identity. There were more conscious efforts to utilize native materials, yet they were mixed with Western harmony. This was a syncretistic period, one in which there was an awareness of identity, yet a borrowing of Western harmonic language. It was not until the last three decades that more Asians began to dig into their own roots and experiment with combining the raw materials with their own traditional music. This was the search-and-experimentation period. Many new hymns have been published; Thailand and Cambodia deserve special attention here.

Cambodia has produced a large number of new hymns, many of which were printed in Australia by refugees. It is worth mentioning that many of the tunes are of folk origin and have become very popular among the people within and outside of Cambodia. Christians in Udon Thani, northeast Thailand, have composed many new hymns to be accompanied by their traditional folk instruments. They have also created new liturgies and adapted symbols from their own context. Nothing was borrowed or copied from the West.

Asian hymns of the last three decades. For a closer look at Asian Christian music, we should examine two publications by the Christian Conference of Asia* (CCA; East Asia Christian Conference until 1973). The *EACC Hymnal,* published in 1964, was a landmark in the history of Christian music in Asia. This hymnal contained 97 Asian and 100 Western hymns. It was the first time Asian hymns went across country boundaries and became available at ecumenical and international gatherings. Although some of the hymns exhibited ethnic Asian features, many of them belonged to the first two periods, the imitation and syncretistic.

The publication of *Sound the Bamboo: CCA Hymnal*

Native Compositions in Asian Hymnals

Country	*Hymnal*	*Year*	*Total Hymns*	*Native Texts*	*Native Music*
Korea	Chan Yong Ka	1894	117	7	0
	Han Yong Chan Sung Ka	1984	558	17	7
	Chanyong Chanyong	1991	140	140	140
India	Sacred Hymns (Marathi)	1930	682	382+	382+
	Tamil Christian Lyrics	1932	100	100	100
Pakistan	Zabur	1900s	Complete Psalter		All
Japan	Sambika	1931	604		24
	Sambika	1954	567	51	41 (arr.)
	Sambika II	1967	259	22	22
	Tomo ni Utaoo	1976	50	24	24
(Okinawa)	Ryukyu Sambika	1992	70 + 35	5 + 35	8 + 35
China	Putian Songzan	1936	550	62 (23 by missionaries)	72
	Zanmei Shi	1985	400 + 42	102	102
(Overseas)	Huaren Shengsong	1992	123	123	123
Taiwan	Seng-si	1926	92	10	10
	Seng-si	1964	522	109	32
	Hakka Hymns and Anthems	1985	80	80	80
Thailand	CCT Hymnal	1985	304	14	17
Cambodia	Kampuchean Hymnal	1985	206		200+
Philippines	Ang Pilipino Himnal	1985	112+50	112	112
	Imnaryong Pilipino	1990	106		84
	Alawiton Sa Pagtoo	1974	355	109	137
Indonesia	Kidung Jamaat	1984	478		100+
	Kidung Ceria	1987	400		100+
	Nyanyikanlah Kidung Baru	1991	230		157+
Malaysia	CCM Hymnal No. 1	1986	24	24	24

1990 (SB), however, went beyond these limitations. This new hymnal contains 280 hymns in 38 languages from 22 Asian countries. Most of the hymns were recorded and transcribed from native worship services or were specially written for the hymnal. Many were typical popular hymns in their respective countries. Although one can still find works that belong to the first two periods, many are experimental in that old materials are treated with new harmonic skills either grown out of the native tradition or acquired from international musicianship. Not only does this collection represent the third period of search and experimentation, it also shows the dawn of a new era and promise of mature Asian Christian music.

The musical styles of Asian hymns. Although it is impossible to describe all of the different styles of Christian music in Asia, we may be able to get a general impression by describing the characteristics of some of it. Most traditional Asian music is monophonic — a single melodic line made up of individual pitches, their ornamentation, timbre, and rhythm. Harmony, with the exception of some folk traditions, such as the Japanese *gagaku,* Indonesian gamelan, and the multipart tribal music of Taiwan, is absent. However, because of missionary influence and the Western educational system, most Asian musical cultures have been affected, in varying degrees, by Western harmonic practice. In analyzing the music of Asian hymns, therefore, both monophonic and harmonic aspects must be considered.

1. *The beauty in Asian monophony.* Some of the most typical and beautiful Asian hymns are monophonic. The beauty is generally found in the unique features of the indigenous styles: unique quality of timbre and vocal production; peculiar attack and decay; the minute detail of microtones and ornaments, particular idioms, motifs, melodic shapes, and progressions; rhythmic tension and relief; intrinsic unity between text and tune; and special instrumental effects. None of these characteristics can be adequately conveyed by signs, notations, or words. All these songs are beautiful in their own right. Those outside of the culture or unfamiliar with the particular styles may find it difficult to comprehend or appreciate their beauty and value. Hence any attempt to alter or harmonize them might impair their beauty and integrity. Some of them represent the best of the ethnic styles and defy any arrangement or "improvement."

2. *Rhythmic features.* Rhythm in general is less com-

Figure 1

Scale	Initial Note	Final Note	Time Signature	Country	SB #
C D E	C	D	Free time	Papua New Guinea	4
C D E	E	C	4/4	Myanmar	61
Four-tone scale:					
A C D E	A	A	3/4	Taiwan	5

Figure 2

Mode	Scale	Initial Note	Final Note	Time	Country	SB #
G (sol)	G A C D E	G	G	2/4	China	80
A (la)	A C D E G	E	A	6/8	Korea	245
C (do)	C D E G A	E	G	4&6	Philippines	102
D (re)	D E G A C	A	D	4/4	Japan	242

Figure 3

Scale	Initial Note	Final Note	Time	Country	SB #
E F G B C	B	E	4/4	Indonesia	201
E F A B D	E	A	3/4	Japan	189

plex in East Asia than in South Asia. The polyphonic stratification of the Balinese gamelan and the Indian tabla (a set of two drums) accompaniment probably represent the highest rhythmic density in Asian music, even though the melody may be very simple.

No single description of a particular rhythm or rhythmic character can represent the general quality of rhythm in a given country, let alone that of Asia. We have, however, identified a few rhythmic features which are prevalent within certain cultures and may provide us pictures of its unique character. For instance, triplets formed by an eighth note, then a quarter note are popular among the Kurukh of India, the Burmese, and the Koreans. But they all vary in their own way. The Kurukh use two pairs of such triplets to lead to quarter notes or other values, as seen in *Puna Binko* (SB 133). This is further reinforced by the drum.

The effect is an almost constant alternation between two rhythmic patterns. When singing a series of eighth notes, the Burmese are fond of shortening the first of the two. This is quite prominent in their folk tradition, as exhibited in *Phaya Sin* (SB 57). Compound complex time marks one of the most typical rhythms of Korean folk traditions. They use the same pattern as above but reversed immediately, showing very strong syncopations and rhythmic vitality. These two sets of patterns are frequently reversed again with variations. *Hon Shin* (SB 75) and *Choo-Soo* (25) are two fine examples.

Another feature of Asian rhythm is the complex rhythmic accompaniment of the tabla. Although we realize its important role in almost all Indian music, we regret that due to its enormous complexity and the highly specialized skill required for performance, the tabla accompaniment for hymns from the Indian subcontinent has not been notated. I would refer to "This Earth" (SB 276) to show how the composer uses an additive rhythm of 3+4 in the entire piece. It is very refreshing to feel such a rhythm after singing familiar songs in regular duple, triple, or quadruple time.

3. *Scales and melodic characters.* A scale, or the consecutive enumeration of pitches that make up a melody, is an integral determinant of musical style. A style of music may be classified by the number of scale degrees and their intervallic relationships.

Songs with only three notes may create interesting and beautiful music. Both *Aso Aso* (SB 4) and *Falam Chin* (61) are in the C D E scale, but they vary in the use of initial and final note (see Figure 1 above).

The *anhemitonic penta,* or five-tone scale without half steps, is more common in Northeast Asia or the countries using the Chinese system (China, Korea, Japan, and Taiwan), but is also found in Thailand, Vietnam, and the Philippines (see Figure 2 above). Although some songs may employ the pitches in the same G A C D E or C D E G A groupings, emphasis of a certain pitch hierarchy differentiates them from one mode to another.

The *hemitonic penta,* or five-tone scale with half steps, is popular in Japan and Indonesia (see Figure 3 above). The first example is set in the Indonesian *pelog* scale, which features one large gap and two small intervals. The Japanese *in* scale shows more variety: a minor second, a major third, and a minor third. While the description contrasting Japanese *in* and Javanese *pelog* may seem subtle, the ear will perceive instantly the differences and the country of origin.

Hymns written in a diatonic scale but with a flattened seventh degree, C D E F G A Bb C, such as *Thevaram* (SB 10) from Sri Lanka, are quite popular in the Indian subcontinent. A changing fourth degree is also common in this region. For example, "Why, O Lord?" (SB 251) from India uses *fa* when descending to *mi* or *re,* but *fa#* ascending to *sol.* This example shows one aspect of *raga,* an organizing principle of Indian melodies.

The Indian octave is divided equally into 22 *srutis,* i.e., microtonal intervals. The actual sizes of intervals in a given *raga* depend on the number of *srutis* employed. Furthermore, the melodic intervals may change in ascending or descending. Unfortunately, no Western musical vocabulary can adequately describe the minute, subtle tonal arrangements found in *raga;* hence the terms scale, mode, ornamentation, melodic shape, and mood are needed to explain the phenomena meanings of *raga.* Hymns employing the *raga* concept constitute a rich resource still awaiting serious study and analysis.

4. *Harmonic practices.* Most Asian hymn melodies either are written in Western idioms or are adaptations of existing folk tunes or imitations of traditional styles. There are also new innovations which, bypassing ethnic features and boundaries, are integrated into international styles. Among all these, one feature prevails: Asian composers can hardly resist the fascination of harmonizing their melodies.

a. *Adopted Western harmony.* Some Asians have so adopted European musical styles and harmony into their repertoire that they have become part of their own national style. They have cultivated a built-in instinct to harmonize any song with three chords: tonic, dominant, and subdominant. Such practices can be found in all parts of Indonesia as well as among the Maoris of New Zealand, the Tongans, and the Tahitians. All of these groups, however, have developed certain characters of their own. The Maori (see SB 60) and the Tahitians (SB 74) have adopted the Western harmonic language as is, but their vocal production, which is known as open-throat singing, is uniquely their own. The Tongans have added a strong contrapuntal bass part, resulting in an antiphonal leader-chorus effect (SB 247). The Ambonese (SB 7) and the Batak people (Sumatra) have adopted the European chorus, but some of them prefer to drop the bass part, resulting in three- part choruses. In Burmese choral singing, only tonic and supertonic chords are utilized, most of them in second inversion.

b. *Indigenous/Ethnic harmony.* The indigenous harmonic practices of the tribal people of Taiwan include the contrapuntal harmony of *Ami* (SB 99), the sectional canon of *Puyuma* (SB 96), the reiterated drone of *Paiwan* (SB 182), the double-third singing of *Bunun* (SB 190), and the parallel fourths of *Saisiat* (SB 121).

c. *Contextual harmony.* In contextual harmony, the harmonic techniques may grow out of the native melodic material, be borrowed from other Asian traditions, or be the composer's innovations. Examples from various countries reveal the emerging Asian styles:

1. Chinese: The lyrical melody is complemented by the use of imitative counterpoint and occasional heterophony, as seen in "Holy Night" (SB 10).
2. Indonesian: The Indonesian gamelan music is organized in a colotomic structure, in which the music is marked off into "temporal units according to the entrance of specific instruments in a specific order at specific times" (William Malm: *Music Culture of the Pacific, the Near East and Asia,* 1977, p. 43). *Tondo* (SB 202) is a piano reduction of a simplified gamelan version. The main melody is outlined in octaves by the *saron* (metalophones), while the *bonang* (kettle gongs) anticipate and decorate the melody in a Javanese way. A new hymn (*Lagu Kasih,* SB 203), accompanied in Javanese *kacapi* (zither) style, may open our ears to this enchanting melody.
3. Japanese: An example from the *gagaku* music, *Tokyo* (SB 242) is set in series of fourths and fifths and other free figurations in the alto. And in *Kamitakata* (SB 27) we see voices paired in parallel fourths and fifths.
4. Korean: In *Choo-Soo* (SB 245) typical Korean rhythms and melodic idioms are harmonized in parallel fourths and fifths with *changgo* (drum) accompaniment.
5. Filipino: Characteristics of Filipino music include triple meter, minor modes, and a sudden switch to the tonic major in the refrain or in the second half of the song (e.g., SB 278, *Ilaw*).

Love for the guitar and *banduria* (like a mandolin) can be seen in all varieties of music (SB 82, *Caturong Na Nonoy*).

d. *Contemporary international styles.* Both melodic and harmonic styles may show certain traits of Asian cultures, but be interpreted with contemporary techniques, resulting in styles which are neither Asian nor Western (*Toytoy,* SB 160; "Lullaby," SB 277). The music is complex, striking, and haunting.

The Hunger Carol (SB 144, "Smoky Mountains") employs Indonesian gamelan techniques, where the *bonang* (kettle gongs) play the figures anticipating, imitating, or echoing the main melody, with the lower part punctuating like *kenong* or *kempul.* Although the feeling of the accompaniment is similar to that of a gamelan or *kacapi,* the texture and harmonic effect are no longer purely Indonesian.

In *Chhun Bin* (SB 224), the Indian *Bhairav raga* (C D♭ E F G A♭ B C) is paired with the additive rhythm of 3 + 2 + 2 to express the mysterious yet truly human character of the Holy Spirit. The accompaniment, which is neither Indian nor Western, uses different figures to convey such mystery.

After decades of experimentation, Asian composers have begun to employ principles which not only maintain the character of Asian melodies, but also embrace its beauty through the appropriate use of writing in parts. They have begun to utilize traditional and contemporary musical languages to communicate the meanings of the Gospel to modern people. Theologically, they have found ways to confess their faith to Asians as well as to peoples in other parts of the world.

See also Center of Church Music.

Bibliography

Rak Phra Jao and Rao Pen Tha, *The Love of God Sets Us Free: A Collection of New Thai Hymns*, AILM Collection of Asian Church Music, No. 14 (1989). • *Sound the Bamboo: CCA Hymnal 1990.* • Ka Goa Siong-chan, *Teach Us to Praise: In Search for Contextual Church Music* (1992).

I-TO LOH

Myanmar

(Burma). Officially the Union of Myanmar, and known as Burma before the change of name in 1989, Myanmar has a physical landscape consisting of a central plain, a horseshoe curve of hilly areas in the west, north, and east, and a coastal strip extending southward like a tail.

Within Myanmar's 261,228 sq. mi., there is a diversity of languages and ethnic groups. The Bamars, who occupy the central plain, are the ethnic majority (69%). Many of the ethnic minorities live in the hilly areas. The Shans (8.5%), Kayins (6.2%), Rakhines (4.5%), Mons (2.4%), Chins (2.2%), Kachins (1.4%), and Kayahs (0.4%) have been given political recognition by having constituent states of the union named after them.

The great majority of the people (89.4%) are *Theravada* Buddhists, with Christians (4.9%), Muslims (3.9%), animists (1.2%), and Hindus (0.5%) as religious minorities. Buddhism* permeates Myanmar society and culture. Social life is regulated by a Buddhist calendar of activities, and art, architecture, and most literature (before the 19th c.) have been inspired by Buddhism.

Urban civilization first developed in the 1st c. and reached a high level at Bagan (Pagan; 11th-13th cs.). After three wars in the 19th c., Myanmar fell under British rule, regaining independence on 4 Jan 1948. After independence, Myanmar went through the phases of parliamentary democracy (1948-62), military government (1962-74), an East-bloc-type socialist government (1974-88), and again a military government. Yangon (Rangoon) is the capital, and Mandalay, the last capital of the Myanmar kings, is the second largest city.

The first Christian missionary to Myanmar, a French Franciscan named Pierre Bonfer, arrived in Thanlyin, the principal seaport, in 1554. He learned Mon, the local language, and attempted to proselytize among the people. Failing in his efforts, he left in 1557.

In 1559, a Portuguese mercenary, Filipe de Britto, took advantage of a confused political situation and established himself as ruler of Thanlyin. The Jesuit* missionaries who arrived in Thanlyin made a number of converts, the most famous of whom was Natshinnaung, ruler of Toungoo and eminent poet. The Myanmar king of Inwa captured Thanlyin in 1613 and resettled its Christian population in a number of villages in northern Myanmar. Known as *bayingyis* (from the Arabic *feringhi,* denoting the Franks or Europeans), these Christians served as royal musketeers and gunners.

The Italian Barnabite Order started a mission in 1721 to care for the *bayingyi* communities, with Sigismondo Calchi* and Giuseppe Vittoni as its first missionaries. The status of the mission was raised in 1741 when Pio Gallizia was appointed bishop and vicar general. The Barnabites established schools and a seminary, but their most outstanding achievement was their literary work in the Myanmar language and their printing on the press of the Congregation of Propaganda the first Myanmar books: a language primer and an exposition of Christian doctrines in 1776, a prayer book and a catechism in 1785.

The first Protestant missionaries arrived in Yangon, which had suceeded Thanlyin as the principal port, in Dec 1807. They were Chater and Felix Carey*, sent by the English Baptist* mission in Serampore, India. Chater left Myanmar in 1812 to establish a Baptist* mission in Sri Lanka*, and Carey, who had gained access to the Myanmar court by his skill in smallpox vaccination, resigned from the mission in 1814 to enter the service of the court. The work of the Baptist mission was soon taken over by the American Baptists.

Adoniram Judson*, the first American Baptist missionary, arrived in Yangon in Jul 1813. In early 1817, on a press donated by the Serampore mission, he printed two tracts in the Myanmar language — one written by himself, the other by his wife, Ann — representing the first use of the printing press in Myanmar. The Baptists went on to make the printing and distribution of religious tracts an important part of their work.

Three wars between Myanmar and the British in the 19th c. resulted in British acquisition of parts of Myanmar in 1826 and 1852 and final annexation in 1885. The Catholics continued to maintain a mission in the Myanmar kingdom, with responsibility taken successively by the Congregation of Propaganda in 1829, the Oblates of Turin in 1840, and the Paris Foreign Mission Society* (MEP) in 1856. With the Myanmar court trying to modernize the kingdom and establish relations with the continent of Europe to stave off the British threat, members of the mission such as Paolo Abbona of the Oblates and Paul Ambrose Bigandet of the Paris Society enjoyed favor at the court.

The Protestants found greater freedom in Myanmar under British rule. The Baptists (A. Judson) printed the Myanmar Bible* in 1840 and made many converts by creating a script and literature for the Kayins (Karen), as well as employing Kayin assistants as teachers and itinerant preachers. Anglican chaplains arrived with the British troops and administrators, and the diocese of Yangon was established in 1877, with Jonathan Holt Titcomb as the first bishop. The Anglican mission was sustained by the Society for the Propagation of the Gospel, which sent its first missionary to Mawlamyine in 1854. Its most distinguished missionary, Jonathan Ebenezer Marks*, founded a boys' school, St. John's College, in Yangon in 1863. On the invitation of the Myanmar court, Marks started a school in Mandalay in 1869 that was attended by royal princes, including Thibaw, Myanmar's last king.

A Methodist Episcopal mission was started in Yangon in 1878 by James Thoburn*, and a Wesleyan Methodist mission in Mandalay in 1886.

The various missions were prominent in educational work in Myanmar under colonial rule, fulfilling a need of the new middle class which could not be satisfied by the traditional monastic education and a parsimonious colonial government. The Catholics maintained such schools as St. Paul's High School in Yangon, which attracted the Myanmar social elite, while the Baptists provided an extensive school system as well as Judson College, a constituent part of the University of Yangon founded in 1920.

The missions were also active in social work, particularly among the handicapped and underprivileged, establishing hospitals, leprosaria, schools for the blind and deaf, and orphanages. An agricultural extension work also introduced new breeds and strains and organized peasants in a cooperative.

Under colonial rule, the missions made many converts among the ethnic minorities. Consequently, a division along ethnic, religious, and cultural lines developed between the Christian ethnic minorities and the Buddhist Bamar (Burmese) majority. The division sharpened as the nationalist movement developed on a basis of Buddhist traditionalism. The nationalists looked on the Christians as Western in outlook and pro-British in political sympathy.

After independence in 1948, a widespread insurgency developed into which the ethnic minorities were drawn, creating a difficult situation for the churches. Also, despite the provision in the constitution for religious toleration, Buddhism was made the state religion in 1960.

The military government which came to power in 1962 suspended the provision making Buddhism the state religion but, as part of its socialist program, nationalized the Christian schools, expelled all foreign missionaries, and restricted relationships with the outside world. For over two decades, the churches were thrown on their own resources; they were forced to curtail their programs, but they also developed a strong national leadership and a spirit of self-help. The succeeding socialist government continued the policies of the military government after 1974, but the new military government which came to power in 1988 took new initiatives and created new conditions.

In the contemporary situation, Christianity in Myanmar remains a minority religion and a religion of ethnic minorities. Through a number of cease-fire agreements concluded in the 1990s, the insurgency involving the ethnic minorities has largely come to an end. The hilly areas are receiving priority in the government's policies of development, as well as in programs of international assistance. The churches are therefore finding fresh opportunities in their work among the ethnic minorities.

Elsewhere, the churches find a problem in establishing a satisfactory relationship with Buddhism. On the one hand is the cultural divide between Christians and Buddhists first created in the early days of the missions, when Christian communities were kept aloof from their social and cultural environment to better preserve their Christian identity. On the other is the continuing effort to create a Myanmar national identity in terms of the majority religion and traditional culture.

In facing up to the opportunities and challenges of their contemporary situation, the churches find strength in the further development of their own resources, as well as in the reestablishment and strengthening of their international ties of Christian fellowship.

See also Baptists.

Bibliography

Burma Baptist Chronicle (1963). • Cady, John F., *A History of Modern Burma* (1958). • Central Statistical Organization, *Statistical Yearbook 1997.* • *An Outline of the History of the Catholic Burmese Mission* (1887). • Purser, W. C. B., *Christian Missions in Burma* (1913).

Tun Aung Chain

Myanmar — Christian Development Work

Italian and French Catholic missionaries arrived in Burma in 1692, followed by the American Baptists* (ABM) in 1817. The Anglican* Mission (SPG) from England and the Methodist* Episcopal Church of America missionaries arrived in 1854, and finally the Wesleyan Methodists came in 1885.

When the missionaries arrived, Buddhism* was strongly rooted and the Myanmar (Burmese) kings did not tolerate the ethnic Burmese becoming Christian converts. Their belief was, "To be a good Burmese, one must be a Buddhist." However, a few became Christians but retained their national-mindedness and ethnic dress.

During the 19th c., three Anglo-Burmese wars were waged (1824-26, 1852-54, and 1885-86). When the Suez Canal was opened in 1869, the opportunity arose to trade Burma's rice crop in the European market. The British made arrangements to bring in moneylenders and laborers to establish the work. The British also planned to trade with China*, and thus a river route from the Irrawaddy to Bhamo and then onwards to cross the mountains of west China was explored.

Missionary activities in Myanmar. As the territories of the Myanmar king gradually came under British rule, the propagation of the Gospel with social welfare and development work by the missionaries spread from lower Burma to the hilly regions. Achievements included development of the Burmese and other ethnic alphabets, translation, literature*, and publications; mission schools, a college, schools for the blind and deaf, and technological and agricultural schools; hospitals, dispensaries, leprosy hospitals, and rehabilitation centers; and orphanages, a home for the aged, a girls' home, and social welfare programs. Prominent Catholic missionaries in Bible* translation and literacy* work were Carrapiet, Di Amato, De Britto, and Bishop Paul

Myanmar — Christian Development Work

Bigandet. Writings on special subjects such as geology and zoology appeared in Burmese.

In 1819, Adoniram Judson*, the Baptist missionary, first labored to help form the Burmese alphabet. In 1840, the complete Bible had been translated into Burmese. The Judson Dictionary (English to Burmese and Burmese to English) was completed in 1843 and is still widely used today. Other missionaries produced ethnic literary works for the Sgaw and Pwo Karen*, Mon, Kachin*, Chins*, Lahu*, and Wa, and translated the Bible into various ethnic languages. The Catholics established primary schools (160), middle schools (85), high schools (29), and a college.

In 1820, the first Baptist Mission day school and first coeducational school in Myanmar was started by Ma Min Lay (an ethnic Burmese), making education possible for girls, who were not permitted to study along with boys at the monastery. In 1826, Mrs. Jonathan Wade started a boarding schools for girls. As mission work grew among the Karens, day schools and boarding schools increased in number. Schools for other racial groups also began to be established.

In 1834, Cephas Bennett of Mission Press in Moulmein helped establish the first Government English School. Between 1860 and 1905, the Anglican missionaries started mission schools in the lower and middle parts of Myanmar. In Rangoon, St. John's College was opened, and Anglican missionary John Ebenezer Marks* taught the nine sons of King Mindon and those of his ministers. Methodist missionaries established well-disciplined mission schools during the early part of this period.

Up until 1871, the highest education available in Myanmar was high school. The Karens requested a college education that would be recognized by Calcutta University. So in 1872, the High School Department was founded as a new college; it was renamed Rangoon Baptist College in 1909.

In 1877, Lady Dufferin, wife of the viceroy of India, opened the Women's Hospital and the Nurses Training School in Rangoon. Dr. Douglas, a missionary, was put in charge. In 1893, a special Teachers' Training School was opened to produce teachers who could teach both English and Burmese.

Leprosy* work was started by the Catholic, Methodist, and Baptist missionaries in 1898, and leprosy hospitals were soon opened. Susan Haswell (ABM) started the hospital in Moulmein. It was never nationalized by the government and is today one of the best homes and hospitals for leprosy patients in Myanmar. The ABM also started a mission to the blind.

John R. Mott, general secretary of the World Student Christian Federation (WSCF), visited Burma in 1913 and encouraged students and missionaries to further the ecumenical movement. The next year, in 1914, the Burma Representative Council of Mission (BRCM) was formed for unity and cooperation among the denominational churches and foreign missionary groups. The Anglican Blind School was also formed, the Baptists having handed over this work to the Anglicans. Rev. Pursur built the Blind School in Rangoon by expanding St. Michael's School building. His successor, William Henry Jackson, introduced Braille in Myanmar in 1917. Vocation and craft workshops were also arranged for the blind.

The Pyinmana Agricultural School, formally established in 1923 for the development projects of the rural and hilly regions, had begun in 1915 with Brayton Case's* agricultural demonstration programs around the Pyinmana and Myingyan areas. One of the agricultural products, the "Bo Case" bean, was listed in the daily radio market quotations. The Myaungmya Sgaw Karen Baptist Convention established the Yedwinyegan Agricultural School with the help of the Pyinmana Agricultural School.

In 1916, the educational authorities in Myanmar founded the University of Rangoon, and the Rangoon Baptist College became a constituent college in the new university. Four years later, in 1920, Mary Chapman, a Bible Church missionary, formed the Anglican Deaf School, which has become the Mary Chapman Training College for Teachers and School for the Deaf, under the umbrella of the Church of the Province of Myanmar (Anglican), a member of the Myanmar Christian Council (MCC). In the same year, Rangoon Baptist College was renamed Judson College. The British government paid half of the construction costs of Judson College, and John D. Rockefeller also made contributions. The college was completed in 1934, and Hla Bu* was its first national principal. The BRCM formed a technical and agricultural committee that year as well. Student uprisings at the University of Rangoon in 1920 mobilized Buddhists and Marxists.

To encourage more participation of national delegates from the National Christian Council, the International Missionary Council laid down new policies at its meeting in 1921. As a consequence, in 1923 the BRCM became the Christian Council in Burma (CCB).

In 1930, heavy taxes and the collapse of the world rice market led many small farmers into heavy debt and ruin at the hands of the English banks and Indian moneylenders, generating anticolonial sentiments. The nationalist movement arose, led by the Gandhi*-inspired Buddhist monk U Ottama (see Nationalism). The CCB changed the name of its agricultural committee to the "rural construction committee," which included Brayton Case and many national leaders. Agricultural demonstration centers were opened in 1939 near Taunggyi and in Pansai near the China* border for the benefit of mountain farmers in the northern and southern regions.

World War II and its aftermath.* From 1941 to 1945 Burma was occupied by the Japanese military. When World War II broke out, the Burma Independence Army (BIA) was formed by a group of military anticolonialists under the leadership of socialist Aung San. Some members of the BIA belonged to the Burma Communist Party (BCP) and joined the Japanese to fight the British. With British support, various ethnic groups (the Karen,

Myanmar — Christian Development Work

Kachin, and Chin were mainly Christian) organized guerrillas to fight the Japanese.

The war resulted in much destruction, and Christians were suspected of being pro-British. Their villages and churches were burned, many schools were closed, and the undamaged villages were crowded with refugees.

The rural construction committee worked right up to the outbreak of the war. Their activities included visits to the rural areas as they sought to improve farming and agricultural land use, encourage rural pastors to be more interested in development programs, guide rural youths to attend cottage industry and agricultural schools, distribute good seedlings, and cooperate with the rural construction programs of Judson College to improve health and education.

In 1948, Burma gained independence and there was political turmoil. The ethnic groups rose up in arms. The BCP led another armed insurrection, Chinese Kuomintang forces marched into Shan State, and many churches found themselves in territory controlled by the Union Military Police and Communists. Life was difficult for the Christians. At this time, the CCB changed its name to the Burma Christian Council (BCC) and formed a relief and rehabilitation committee, which sponsored two extensive agricultural projects, one in the Irrawaddy Delta at the Pwo Karen village of Alesu, and the other, the Nantma-lat Agricultural Project, in a valley in Shan State northwest of Taunggyi.

In 1949, the Pyinmana area fell into the hands of the BCP. When the government regained control, the Pyinmana Agricultural School was run by the government with the cooperation of the Ford Foundation. The next year, in 1950, the Judson College campus was taken over by the government and later amalgamated with the government college into a single university. This college helped develop many leaders for the churches, mission schools, community, government departments, and private professions. There were over 100 Christian personnel working in the University of Rangoon in 1963.

In 1959, the National Church Loan Fund (ECLOF) was started. During the period 1959-94, the ECLOF provided 254 loans for church buildings. There were few problems with arrears. Starting in 1977, ECLOF also provided loans for development projects such as fisheries, agriculture, and special fund-raisings. The loans were suspended after 1985 because many development projects failed due to lack of understanding of development theory, inexperience, lack of skills, poor management, weakness in supervision, insincerity and dishonesty, the unstable political situation, and the lack of training.

In 1962, political turmoil in Burma intensified. National leaders were in conflict, insurrection was gaining momentum, and ethnic groups desired federal state autonomy. Tensions also arose over the issue of Buddhism* as the state religion. The economy worsened, and the army seized power, vowing to establish a socialist state. In 1963, banks, the rice industry (which contributed 70 percent of foreign exchange earnings), trade (largely controlled by Indians), mission schools, hospitals, and private firms were nationalized.

In 1966, all foreign missionaries had to leave the country. The BCC was reconstituted as the Burma Council of Churches. The relief and reconstruction committee became the Christian Service Board (CSB) and had the following functions: emergency relief work, rehabilitation, rural development (agriculture, livestock farming, fisheries, road and bridge construction, water supply projects, etc.), and special pilot projects such as the 10-year Integrated Development Project (selecting a specific poor village and enabling its people to achieve their comprehensive development project themselves within 10 years).

In 1973-74, the Burmese Way to Socialism was established, and the 20-year Socialist Economy Plan was implemented. Separation of religion and state was enacted in the constitution, and the socio-economic and political agenda was dictated by one-party rule.

On 4 Aug 1975, the Myanmar Christian Fellowship of the Blind (MCFB), led by U Thein Lwin with a 13-member committee, was formed. Under the Self-Supporting Karen Baptist Mission Society (SSKBMS) — a member of the Myanmar Council of Churches (MCC) since 1981 — it carries out all-around development projects today.

U Kyaw Than introduced an experimental development plan in 1977 with the blessings of the BCC/CSB. Called the Training Institute for Christian Participation in National Development (TICPIND), it was particularly successful in the Chin* State and continued through 1984.

In 1985, the Myanmar Baptist Mission formed its own rural development committee at its headquarters and also formed development committees among its language and regional groups in order to implement all-around development in their areas. The year 1986 made the distribution of educational literature and training programs on human development a priority.

In 1988, a mass demonstration for democracy* in Myanmar moved the political system toward a multi-party arrangement. Today, Myanmar still struggles to achieve a genuine democratic state and market economy. Foreign and national entrepreneurs and their companies are on the rise in Myanmar. Hotels, tourism, and modern city development are greatly encouraged. At the same time, negotiations are being made for a ceasefire with the insurrection groups. The total development of the border areas, trade, roads, and communications is a priority.

In 1990, the Myanmar Leprosy Mission became an interdenominational organization. Two years later, in 1992, the SSKBMS formed a development committee, and its community-based health care and rural-youth development programs are now being carried out in the mission fields.

In 1994 the MCC was reorganized, and the CSB became the Service and Development Unit (SDU). An ecumenical forum was held by the SDU on 15-17 Jun, resulting in the following MCC-SDU resolutions: to consider the environmental degradation and deforestation in development concerns; to revive and promote development projects suspended in 1985; to encourage sloping cultivation for mountain farmers; to encourage integrated development projects in hilly regions and remote rural areas; to promote vocational skills and technical training; to safeguard farmers' lands and promote reclamation projects through the initiative of the local people; to establish a service fund for emergencies and communicable diseases such as AIDS; and to promote rehabilitation programs for the physically handicapped. Similarly, the Lisu* Christian churches also formed a development committee and are now planning to implement sloping cultivation for their people instead of slash-and-burn cultivation in the hilly regions.

In Mar 1995, the Mara* Evangelical Church formed its development committee and planned to make an extension of a waterway for smooth communication and irrigation.

Summary. The long civil war negatively affected Myanmar's development and impoverished its people, especially those living in the hilly regions. The MCC, with 12 member churches and a majority membership from the racial groups in the hilly regions, aims, through the SDU, to promote coordination and cooperation among its constituent churches, each of which has its own social service and development programs. The SDU encourages MCC members to organize specific development committees at their respective headquarters and down to regional and local levels.

Bibliography

Yu, Maung B. C., *Life of Brayton Charles Case* (1951). • Khin, U Ba, *Foreign Missionary Organization in Burma* (1963). • Wa, Maung Shwe, et al., *Burma Baptist Chronicle* (1963). • Hman, Nyi Win, *MCC-CSB Development Program & Preliminary Evaluation Case Study* (1986). • Paw, Naw Lah Yu, *History of the SSKBMS* (1990). • *Third World Guide* (1991/92). • Myatt, Amarylla, *The Mary Chapman Training College for Teachers and School for the Deaf* (1993). • Reports of the MCC-SDU.

MARIP JA NAW

Mysticism, Javanese

Phenomenon in modern Indonesia* bearing the character of a religious movement with adherents from all walks of life, from peasants to professors and from privates to generals, and including both men and women; found mainly among the Javanese, which is the largest ethnic group in Indonesia (65-70 million).

The adherents of Javanese mysticism have formed numerous organizations with a wide variety of characteristics, from informal, esoteric (and thus almost anonymous) groups to formal, modern, and exoteric groups with professional national leadership (e.g., the Association for Unity [PANGESTU], *Sapta Darma* [Seven Holy Duties], and *Sumarah* [Submission, i.e. to God's will]). Some of them have an international organization (*Susila Budi Darma* [roughly, High-minded Morals, SUBUD]), holding regular conventions promoting consolidation and spreading propaganda. The total number of such organizations is over 400.

The beginning of the numerical growth of Javanese mystics occurred in the early 1950s, when the young Republic of Indonesia entered the post-independence era, an era of social, economic, and political consolidation. The post-war atmosphere was full of turmoil and insecurities, demoralization, and misconduct; it was a survival period of the Indonesian Revolution. Many people were dissatisfied with the role of the five recognized religions in Indonesia (Islam*, Protestantism*, Hinduism*, Roman Catholicism*, and Buddhism*), which they felt were unable to contribute effectively to the process of nation- and character-building. Thus new initiatives sprang up from among non-formal religious circles which claimed to be able to offer alternatives or supplementary methods to lead the people to attain better lives, both materially and spiritually.

Present-day Javanese mysticism has its roots in the religious traditions of the Javanese. Ancestor worship*, which includes the concept of the heavenly origin of the ancestors, animism*, and dynamism, provides the basic understanding of matter-spirit, the visible-invisible relations. The Hindu (Saiva-Shiddanta) and Buddhist (Mahayana) religions came to Java beginning in the 5th c. A.D. and lived together in peaceful coexistence, since both had very strong mystical leanings. In the period of the Majapahit Kingdom (1293-1528), people's interest in the mystical life rose, indicated by the composition of mystical treatises, among them *Dharmasunya* (1418) and *Nirathaprakreta* (1459) in the Old Javanese language. Later, *Dewa Ruci* was composed, using Middle Javanese and containing a pre-Islamic Hindu mystical teaching, which is widely popular even to the present day.

Islam came to Java in the 15th c. Not only orthodox Islam was introduced, but also mystical Islam, as represented in the writing of Syams al Din of Pasai and Hamzah of Pansur, both from North Sumatra. Their influence surfaced later in the mystical literature of Java, such as *Suluk Sukarsa.* In the 18th c., court poets in Surakarta rewrote in Modern Javanese many classical mystical treatises, e.g., *Dharmasunya* and *Dewa Ruci Jarwa.* In the 19th c., *Serat Wirid* was composed by Ranggawarsita, another well-known court poet of Surakarta. Later, Mangkunegara IV, a poetry-loving duke of Surakarta, composed *Wedhatama.* Both writings contain Javanese mystical teaching as developed in that period. Twentieth-century Java inherited this mystical background and became the fertile nursery for a large number of mystical groups which came into being after the birth of the Republic of Indonesia (1945).

Main Tenets. In Javanese mysticism, mystical union

between the individual and God is the supreme goal of life. It is a reunion of the human spirit with God the Spirit, of servant with master, a reunion of spirits of the same nature. God's Spirit as the source of life is described as a great ocean or an immeasurably huge body of water. The human spirit is like a small drop of water, limited in size and individualized. The human spirit has to return to the great ocean, a return of a prince to the king's palace. Here Javanese mysticism, like other mystical movements, adopts the principles of emanation and monism that dominate its thought pattern.

Spirit-matter dualism is another basic idea in the system. The spirit-matter dualism here is less radical than the dualism of the gnostics or the Manichaeans of the 2nd-3rd c. A.D. in the Roman and Persian Empires. Macrocosm and microcosm as manifestations of matter are regarded as negative. The human spirit is imprisoned in the body and tightly bound by human passions. The spirit or human authentic self must seek to control the dynamics of all passions through proper and thorough exercises (fasting, meditating) until reaching mastery. A parable often used to illustrate this is the driver of a coach drawn by four horses. He must master and coordinate the four horses so that he can safely usher the dear passenger to the final destination.

The liberation of the spirit is essentially a liberation from the dominance of matter. By this mystical liberation, the spirit is freed from captivity and enters its authentic spiritual abode for good. Liberation can be accomplished within one's lifetime, or at the moment of one's death, or after a series of reincarnations.

Most mystics maintain a very high standard of morality. Temptations from the material world, e.g., in the form of greed, envy, and sexual lust, must be highly guarded against. The law of *karma,* or good works, is basically the key to self-liberation.

The Javanese mystics are not against religions. They openly recognize religions as revelations of God. Since many religions are too busy with formalities (rituals, religious services, organization, canon law, etc.), the mystics claim that their teachings emphasize not the outer shell as do religions, but the inner seed, which is the most important. Many mystics blame the failure of religious education to maintain high moral standards on the followers, and for that reason they offer alternatives. In several cases, this attitude ignites a negative reaction from the leaders of formal religions, who suppress the mystical groups, regarding them as dangerous enemies. As a result, the mystical groups in Indonesia are administratively coordinated by the department of education and culture, and not by the department of religious affairs.

The role of the mystical teacher, who is usually regarded as the bearer of the true revelation from God, is central to Javanese mystical spirituality. In some cases, fanciful personal ideas of the teacher, which may be highly subjective and unreasonable, are accepted without any question by the followers. At times, this leads to chaotic social conduct or amorality. Libertinism, as practiced by Marcus the Gnostic (a follower of Valentinus, the great gnostic teacher of the 2nd c.) in deceiving female followers to participate in the rite of mystical union, leads to adultery. Similar incidents are sometimes reported in the modern period concerning some Javanese mystical teachers. A teacher was arrested because, on the basis of a vision, he summoned his followers to kill a person believed to be the incarnation of an evil spirit. High subjectivity in esoteric circles becomes a possible source of much trouble. Yet these incidents must be regarded as extraordinary rather than the general rule.

Bibliography

Bavinck, J. H., *Christus en de Mystiek van net Oosten* (1934). • Hadiwijono, H., *Man in the Present Javanese Mysticism* (1967). • Poerbatjaraka, R. M. Ng., *Kapustakan Djawa* (1952). • Sopater, Sularso, *Inti Ajaran Aliran Valentinian dan Inti Ajaran Aliran Pangestu* (1983).

Sularso Sopater

Nababan, Soritua Albert Ernst

(b. Siborongborong, Indonesia, 24 May 1933). Batak* theologian and ecumenical church leader.

The son of a teaching couple, Nababan went to public school during the Dutch colonial period. He entered the Theological Seminary in Jakarta (STT) in 1956, the period of independence in Indonesia*. He continued his theological studies at Ruperto Carola University (Heidelberg, Germany) and obtained his doctor of theology degree in 1962. After his return from Germany, he focused his ministry on ecumenical* institutions at the national and Asian regional levels and on international movements (World Council of Churches [WCC] and Lutheran World Federation [LWF]).

Nababan was one of the church leaders who helped develop the Council of Churches in Indonesia (DGI, now PGI). He was elected general secretary of DGI in 1967 and served until 1989. He was chairperson of PGI from 1984 to 1989. Under his leadership, at its 10th General Assembly (1984) in Ambon, the PGI accepted *Pancasila** as the basis for living in the society, nation, and state of Indonesia.

An ecumenical leader at the regional, national, and international levels, Nababan also led his home church as the *ephorus* of the Batak Protestant Christian Church (HKBP) (1987-92). In serving the church and society, he proved himself capable in church management. Unfortunately, he did not produce much in writing. As a pastor and theologian, Nababan persuaded Christians to be sensitive to the dangers of materialism, consumerism, and individualism. He called the churches of Indonesia to take an active role in building the nation so that they would not be left behind as the country entered the era of industrialization.

Bibliography

Nababan, S. A. E., *Kyriosbekenntnis und Mission bei Paulus: Eine exegetische Untersuchung zu Römerbrief 14 and 15* (doctoral dissertation) (1962). • Simatupang, T. B., "Dynamics for Creative Maturity," in G. H. Anderson, *Asian Voices in Christian Theology* (1976).

J. Raplan Hutauruk

Nagaland Missionary Movement

(NMM). A mission department of the Nagaland Baptist Church Council (NBCC), established in 1937 in Bayavu Hill, Kohima; the highest body of the Baptist* Church in the state.

As a constituent member of the Council of Baptist Churches in North East India (CBCNEI), NBCC is linked to the North East India Christian Council, the Asian Baptist Federation, and the Baptist World Alliance.

Begun as a home mission, the NMM received its present name when churches had been established among all the Nagas and the work expanded to other unreached peoples. Its work includes surveying mission fields, planting churches, training missionaries, and networking with other mission agencies.

Workers are now found in Uttar Pradesh, Bihar, Sikkim, the Indo-Bhutan border (West Bengal and Assam), Arunachal Pradesh, Golaghat, and the North Cachar Hills districts of Assam, Orissa, Andhra Pradesh, the Andaman Islands, Maharashtra, Nepal*, and Myanmar*. There are also chaplains working in 11 major cities and in the Christian Medical Hospital, Vellore. Currently, there are 26 cross-cultural missionaries and 80 evangelists ministering in 20 mission fields. NMM celebrated its silver jubilee in Nov 1994. Rev. Pongsing

Nagas

India is a nation of tribes having as many as 465 distinctive groups. Among the major classifications: the Himalayan tribes (some major tribes found in North India are the Bhotia, Tharu, Raji, Santal, Munda, Oraon, Ho, Chero, Kharia, Gujas, Gaddi, Kanura, and Bakrawai); tribes found in the North East (Adi, Assamese Bora, Gangte, Garo, Hallam, Hmar, Jantia, Karbi, Khamti,

Khasi, Komren, Mao, Maran, Mishmi, Nagas, Nokte, Paite, Riang, Simte, Tangsa, Thadu, Tiddim, Tripuri, Vaphei, and Wancho); Central tribes (Baiga, Bathudi, Bhil, Bhumij, Gond, Kawar, Khond, Koi, Kora, Lodha, Santal, Saharia, and Saora); Western tribes (Bhil, Damor, Dhanka, Dhodia, Dubla, Gamit, Garasia, Kali, Kathodi, Kokna, Koli-Mahadev, Korka, Kunbi, Mina, Thakur, and Varli); Southern tribes (Ilrular, Kamara, Kerumans, Koya, Kuruba, Malayali, Peniyan, Pulayan Marati, Sugalis, Yanadis, Yarukulas, Savaras, Toda, Valmiki, and Yerava); and Island tribes (Andamanese, Jarwa, Necobanese, Onge, and Shompen).

Common cultural characteristics of tribes in India include their binding and accessibility to each other (in, e.g., food collection, trapping, hunting, and pastoralism). They observe ritual and ceremonial practices in connection with death, fetishes, and supernatural fear. The Dominance of superstition is another common phenomenon among the tribal societies.

Tribes in India are all considered low-class and untouchable (Dalits*), resulting in a spirit of depression due to social oppression. They suffer deprivation of many social, political, and economic rights and privileges. Exploitation by landlords and moneylenders is not an uncommon problem, particularly in the central and western regions. Sharp conflict and tension between the high-class and low-class (called *Adivasi* in Central India) are daily affairs, especially in Bihar and Madhya Pradesh States today.

Rapid social change is observed among tribal communities, as many are becoming educated and assuming higher social positions. Tribal affairs are now self-governed in most regions; for example, the tribal states in North East India.

Another spectacular change among Indian tribals is the new openness and receptivity to Christian faith in recent decades. Their hearts and minds are open to seeking a supernatural security and reality which can pervade their present condition of depression. Furthermore, they look for a power that can deliver them from the slavery of the caste system and offer them an opportunity for social equality. That the Creator God of the Christian faith is on the side of suffering people presents a great opportunity.

The Nagas are a distinct tribe in Southeast Asia living in Nagaland (North East India) and northwest Myanmar. In India, Nagaland is a political state covering hardly one-third of the tribe. Actually, the Nagas spread across the entire North East (Arunachal, Assam, and Manipur) of India and northwest of Myanmar (Great Nagaland).

The Nagas are a mountainous Tibeto-Burmese family of Mongoloid stock having a distinct culture. Elwin traces their origin back to the northwest part of China*. They migrated during the conflict between the Chinese and Tartars in the 13th and 14th cs. Anthropologically, the Nagas are related to Himalayans, Burmese, Japanese, Thai, Malaysian, Filipinos, Polynesians, and Melanesians (Bareh 1970:19).

The tribe comprises as many as 38 subtribes (Anal, Angami, Ao, Chakhesang, Chang, Chin, Chothe, Damsa, Haimi, Htangram, Kalyon, Kenyu, Khampti, Khiamngan, Komren, Konyak, Kuli, Lamkang, Lotha, Mao, Maran, Maring, Mayon, Mongsang, Nokte, Para, Phom, Pochury, Poumai, Rengma, Rangpan, Singpho, Tankhul, Tansa, Thangal, Wancho, Yimcho, and Zemei). They number over three million and cover an area of 30,000 square miles ranging from the Assam Valley in the west to the Chindwin River in the east.

The Nagas are a non-caste, classless, autonomous, and free hill-dwelling people. In early history, they were a headhunting and warring tribe. Religiously animistic, they worship spirits and immediate gods, yet recognize an invisible and supernatural creator. Idols and temples are unknown to them. Generally, the Nagas are described as a sociable and hospitable people, humorous and genial in nature, honest, brave, reciprocal, and hardworking.

World War II*, education, and Christian missions have opened up the Naga worldview. Modern times have led them to seek spiritual protection and security under a supreme power and authority. They have begun to be more aware of present realities and to see the world beyond their boundaries.

The Nagas are a tribe where Christian mission has had a resounding impact. They have caught the attention of the world by their unique response to Christianity. A spectacular church growth movement that took place in the late 1970s and 1980s is considered a miracle of modern mission. Christianity is the basic factor in the drastic change of the tribe's entire outlook.

As early as 1872, Christianity had penetrated into the headhunting tribe through an American Baptist missionary, E. W. Clark*. The American Baptists proceeded to press further into the land of the tribe with the Gospel. The early converts began to evangelize their fellow tribesmen in the hills. In a series of later evangelistic movements, the entire tribe embraced Christianity. In the 1990s, 90% of the total population of over one million in Nagaland were Christians.

Several factors contributed to this phenomenal change. When the Nagas discovered that many of their monotheistic exercises were similar to those in the Old Testament, their consciences were awakened. When they were exposed to World War II and had to struggle politically with the government of India in the mid-1940s, they began seeking a sovereign God. When their headmen turned to Christ, the entire community was attracted to Christianity. Also, when they recognized that the true God is stronger than the natural objects they believed to possess spirits, they began to believe the Gospel. Nagas today are involved in mission outreach throughout India and the surrounding countries.

Bibliography

Alemchiba, M., *A Brief Historical Account of Nagaland* (1970). • Bareh, H., *Gazetteer of India: Nagaland District*

Gazetteers (1970). • Barkata, S., *Tribes of Assam* (1969). • Dozo, P., *Cross over Nagaland* (1992). • Elwin, V., *The Nagas in the Nineteenth Century* (1969). • Hodson, T. C., *The Naga Tribes of Manipur* (1911). • Hutton, J. H., *The Angami Nagas* (1921). • Latourette, K. S., *A History of Christianity*, Vol. II, *Reformation to the Present* (1975). • Major, V. K., *Nagaland in Transition* (1967). • Maxwell, Neville, and George Anthony, *Indian and Naga* (1973). • Neill, Stephen, *The Story of the Christian Church in India and Pakistan* (1970). • Philip, P. T., *The Growth of Baptist Churches in Nagaland* (1976).

P. DOZO

Namgung Hyuk

(b. Seoul, 1 Jul 1882; d. ?). Presbyterian* minister, theologian, and first Korean professor at Presbyterian Theological Seminary in Pyongyang.

Namgung served as general secretary of the National Council of Churches in Korea* after the emancipation from Japanese occupation. He was kidnapped by the Communists during the Korean War* in 1950 and taken to North Korea. It is uncertain how or when he died.

After finishing his studies at the Methodist*-run Baejae School, Namgung worked at the custom house for a while and then taught English at Soongil High School, established and run by Presbyterian* missionaries. His students included Kim Seongsoo, who became vice president under President Rhee Syngman, and Kim Byungro, who became the first chief justice of the supreme court.

Namgung married a Christian and converted to Christianity in 1917 under her influence. Deciding to become a minister, he entered Presbyterian Theological Seminary and graduated in 1921. He did further studies at Princeton Theological Seminary, United States (1924, Master of Theology), and Union Theological Seminary, Virginia, United States (1927, Doctor of Divinity). He was the first Korean to hold a Doctor of Divinity degree. He taught at Presbyterian Theological Seminary upon his return to Korea. He did some Bible* translation, wrote Bible commentaries, and was also editor of the theological magazine *Sinhakjinam*, published by Presbyterian Theological Seminary.

In 1932, Namgung was elected moderator of the general assembly of the Presbyterian Church. When the seminary was forced to close by the Japanese government in 1938, Namgung fled to Shanghai and remained there until Korea's emancipation. Devoting himself to the ecumenical movement, he became general secretary of the National Council of Churches in Korea in 1946. There was no further news of him after his capture by the Communists.

Bibliography

Kidok' kio Dae Paik' kwoa Sach' un (The Christian Encyclopedia), Vol. III (1986). • Min Kyong Bae, *Hankook Kidok' kiohoe-sa* (Handbook of the Korean Church) (1993). • Rhodes, Harry A., *History of the Korea Mission of the Presbyterian Church USA, 1884-1934* (1934).

KIM IN SOO

Nan Inta

(b. Chiang Mai Province, Thailand, 1804; d. northern Thailand, 27 Aug 1882). First baptized Christian convert in northern Thailand* and first ordained northern Thai elder.

Nan Inta, baptized by Daniel McGilvary* of the Presbyterian* Laos Mission, taught the northern Thai to missionaries, wrote Christian tracts, and worked as an evangelistic assistant. Prior to his conversion, he studied for the Buddhist monkhood and served as abbot of a temple. His Buddhist studies earned him the honorific title *nan*. His wife's name was Chunpeng.

When the McGilvarys, the first foreign missionaries to northern Thailand, arrived in 1867, Nan Inta began to visit them frequently and gained a knowledge of Christianity. He resisted conversion, however, until McGilvary correctly predicted a solar eclipse for 17 Aug 1868, which convinced Nan Inta that traditional Buddhist cosmology was incorrect. He was baptized on 3 Jan 1869. In Sep 1869, Nan Inta fled from persecution in Chiang Mai when two converts were murdered. In 1871, he resumed an active Christian life, and in 1873 the Siam presbytery took him under its care for preparation for ordained ministry. On 1 May 1875, the First Presbyterian Church of Chiang Mai ordained him an elder, and the following year his wife and children converted to Christianity. In 1878, Nan Inta's daughter, Kham Tip, wanted to marry a young man who was training for the ministry, but influential relatives insisted the ceremony follow northern Thai animistic traditions. The Laos Mission appealed to the king of Thailand for redress, and the king's viceroy in Chiang Mai issued the so-called Edict of Toleration* on 8 Oct 1878.

On 4 Jul 1880, the Laos Mission founded the Bethlehem Church, the first rural church in northern Thailand, in Sarapee District. Nan Inta's family and another family formed the core of this church, with Nan Inta serving as leader and first elder. In May 1882, he moved to the area of the Mae Dok Daeng Church, the second rural church in the north, where he died. In 1904, the Laos Mission reported that all of his more than 70 living descendants were Christians. He was the founder of the Intaphun family, a significant family in northern Thai church history.

Bibliography

Curtis, Lillian Johnson, *The Laos of North Siam* (1903). • McFarland, George B., ed., *Historical Sketch of Protestant Mission in Siam, 1828-1928* (1928). • McGilvary, Daniel, *A Half Century Among the Siamese and the Lao* (1912). • Swanson, Herbert R., *Krischak Muang Nua* (1994). • Wells, Kenneth E., *History of Protestant Work in Thailand, 1828-1958* (1958).

PRASIT PONGUDOM, translated
by HERBERT R. SWANSON

Nantang

(Church of the Immaculate Conception). The oldest Catholic church in China*, situated near Xuanwumen in Beijing.

In 1650, Emperor Shunzhi donated to his tutor, J. Adam Schall von Bell*, a plot of land east of a small chapel built by Matteo Ricci* (1552-1610). Schall built a church on it, which was named Xitang when a second church (Tongtang) was built to its east. Its name changed to Nantang after a third church (Beitang) was built to its north. It served as a residence for Jesuits (see Society of Jesus) and, when the Jesuit order was dissolved, Portuguese Lazarists* employed by the imperial court. The church closed around 1830 when the Qing court ceased to employ missionaries as astronomers. At the intervention of the French, the church was returned to the Catholics in Oct 1860, when the Anglo-French forces entered Beijing. The church was destroyed during the Boxer Rebellion and later rebuilt from the indemnity paid.

China Group, translated by Dufresse Chang

National Christian Conference, China, 1913

A National Christian Conference was held in Shanghai on 11-14 Mar 1913. Out of 120 delegates, one-third were Chinese. The dual goals of the conference were, first, to respond to the call of the Edinburgh Missionary Conference 1910 to promote the world Christian movement in China*; and, second, to study the situation of the church in China after 1911.

Prior to the conference, the chairman of the continuation committee of the Edinburgh Missionary Conference, John R. Mott, came to China and held a series of preparatory meetings in various areas. He became the chairman of the National Christian Conference. During the conference, a China Continuation Committee was formed, and this became the first Protestant interdenominational organization in China. The China Continuation Committee decided to devote itself to a comprehensive survey of mission work in China, and the outcome was the publication of a voluminous study, *Christian Occupation of China.*

The conference also stressed the relationship between mission bodies and Chinese churches and pastors. The majority of the delegates agreed that Chinese church leaders were capable and rich in their spirituality; however, there was still a need for foreign missionaries to stay on and help the Chinese churches. China Group

National Christian Conference, China, 1922

The theme for the 1922 conference was "The Chinese Church." It was held in Shanghai on 2-11 May 1922. There were 1,025 delegates; this was the first time the Chinese delegates (568) exceeded foreigners (457). Cheng Jing Yi was elected chairman. The purpose of the conference was to reduce the responsibilities of foreign missionaries and to promote the goals of self-government, self-support, and self-propagation of the Chinese church.

Five topics were prepared in advance for discussion at the Conference: (1) the existing situation of Christianity in China; (2) the future ministry of the church; (3) letters to fellow Christians and Chinese nationals; (4) church leaders; and (5) coordination and cooperation between churches. Other issues covered included evangelism, education, medical work, literature work, industry and economics, and women. During the conference, the National Christian Council was founded with the aim of promoting union among the churches and indigenization. Ten resolutions were passed during the conference.

Bibliography

Rankin, Milledge Thereon, *A Critical Examination of the National Christian Council of China* (1928). • Callahan, Paul E., "Christianity and Revolution as Seen in the National Christian Council of China," *Papers on China* (East Asian Research Center, Harvard University) (1951). • Rawlinson, F., Helen Thoburn, and D. MacGillivray, *The Chinese Church 1922 National Christian Conference* (1922). China Group

National Christian Conference, China, 1954

After the inauguration of the new China, all the denominations of the Protestant Church in China were invited to the National Christian Conference of 1954 (22 Jul-6 Aug). There were 247 representatives from 62 churches and organizations. The task of this conference was to conclude the work of the Three-Self Movement* during the previous four years, to confirm future strategy and principles, to unite all the churches, and to form a committee to lead the Chinese Christian Anti-Imperialism Three-Self Patriotic Movement. Bishop Chen Jian Zhen reported on the preparation of the committee, and Wu Yao Zong reported on the movement's four years of work. The conference then adopted four resolutions, a letter to fellow Christians, and the constitution of the Chinese Christian Three-Self Patriotic Movement committee; it also elected 139 committee members.

China Group

National Conference of Bishops of the Chinese Catholic Church

The only conference of bishops in the history of the Chinese Catholic Church.

Held in Shanghai on 12 Jun 1924 and presided over by the papal legate, Celso Constantini*, the conference was attended by 48 of the total 62 bishops in China. Only two of the bishops were Chinese, having been newly appointed. More than 30 others, including the heads of various orders, attended as non-voting members. The conference was held in the main hall of the Yangjingbang Catholic Church; the opening and closing ceremonies were held in the Xujiahui Catholic Church. The votes on the proposals presented were kept secret. Some of the 861 rules concerning Catholicism in China were not made public until 12 Jun 1929, five years after the conference.

CHINA GROUP

Nationalism

The roots of modern nationalism have been traced by some scholars to 18th-c. Western Europe and North America — in particular, to the American colonists who justified their separation from the regime of George III, as well as to the French revolutionary upheavals of the period. These events were closely linked with the emergence of the concept of popular sovereignty, the growth of secularism, the decline of older religious and feudal loyalties, and the spread of urbanization, industrialization, and improved communications.

But the word "nationalism" itself was not widely used, nor was rigorous analysis attempted of the nature of nationalism until the 19th c. — the age par excellence of European nationalism. It was in 19th c. Europe that "nationalism" was first used to distinguish peoples or communities differentiated by language, religion, culture, and physical appearance. It was also the grounds for arguing that these peoples, or "nations," should be the basis of sovereign states. The reshaping of the modern European world in the 18th and 19th cs. led to the belief that the Europeanization and modernization that accompanied the Western advances into Asia that began in the 16th c. and reached their zenith in the 19th would inspire similar nationalisms of the European type.

The Eurocentric bias implicit in this view, however, obscures the possibility of nationalism developing autonomously in other parts of the world, outside the European milieu, and in terms other than that of its European stereotypes. To suggest, for instance, that there was no idea of nation or national consciousness in Asia prior to the period of Western dominance would hardly seem accurate. As Wang Gungwu argues, there was indeed a national consciousness often "related to differences in language and aspects of culture as well as dynastic interests and some idea of territorial rights," even if it was not expressed in terms of the modern European nation-state. Indeed, nationalism of the European sort may not provide a suitable model for Asian polities, especially in Southeast Asia, where a profusion of groups distinguished by race, language, religion, and culture are intermingled within a single territorial unit and are more likely to lead to what A. D. Smith calls "ethnic nationalism." This is especially notable in areas where territorial borders embrace culturally distinct groups, as in the case of the Muslims of southern Thailand* and the southern Philippines*, and in the minority non-Myanmar and non-Buddhist communities in Myanmar*.

By and large, however, the ascendancy of nationalism in the Asian context should be seen against the background of colonialism* and belongs more to what Smith calls "territorial nationalism" or "nationalisms without nations." In such cases there are an identifiable territorial unit and an administrative apparatus, but the people concerned are not culturally homogenous. The main aim of the nationalist movement is to "take over the alien's political machinery and adopt his administrative unit as the basis of the projected 'nation.'" But while ethnic nationalism was often subsumed by the demands of forging a unified territorial nationalism during the anti-colonial struggle, fears of cultural submergence and the retreat into communal insecurity frequently produced a divisive ethnic nationalism upon independence.

In Asia, the growth of nationalism was to a large extent of the territorial kind and lay largely in its reaction against foreign domination. The series of Western advances into Asia from the 16th to the 18th cs., and especially their hegemony of the region by the 19th and early 20th cs., together with the emergence of Japanese imperialism by the first half of the 20th c., spurred the Asian rulers and elites, initially, and the masses, subsequently, to react against that dominance. Japan's defeat of Russia in 1904-5 provided some encouragement to Asian nationalism, but its own advance into Korea* (1894), Manchuria (1931-32), and China* (from 1937), a by-product of the welding of Japanese nationalism, also established Japan* as the new Asian hegemonist and the bane of Chinese nationalism.

But nationalism itself is not necessarily synonymous with anti-colonialism. Not all Asian anti-colonial groups or polities turned to nationalism in defense against Western imperialism. Some anti-colonial movements could be galvanized as much by a transcendent religion such as Islam* or by a transnational ideology such as Marxism, both of which are inimical to nationalism. Thailand, for example, never found the need to fan the flames of nationalism, preferring instead the path of diplomatic compromises to ensure its independence. Others such as China and Japan, while never colonized by the West, turned to nationalism, unlike Thailand, in preemptive self-defense. Still others, such as Cambodia* and Malaya, found much difficulty in invoking nationalism successfully in their anti-colonial struggle. In the face of imperial solidarity and willingness to resort to repressive force, there were few successes for the nationalists, however resolute their determination. It took World War II*, and the unleashing of the new forces it inspired, to bring about the dismantling of the colonial edifice.

The perception that the Bible* and the flag went hand in hand in the history of Western imperialism in Asia had unfortunate consequences for the relationship between Christianity and Asian nationalism. Insofar as Christianity was seen as the ideological agent of its patron and ally, European imperialism, it became an enemy of Asian nationalism. The manner in which Christianity was introduced into Asia — in C. R. Boxer's words, by "a mixture of carrot-and-stick methods, in which the stick sometimes predominated" — further fuelled its oppressive image in the eyes of Asians. Often, discriminatory and coercive laws were enacted, as in the early Portuguese-controlled territories in Asia during the 16th c., particularly along the west coast of India and in Ceylon, that prohibited the public practice of Hinduism*, Buddhism*, and Islam and favored converts to Christianity at the expense of non-converts. "If they did not actually force people to become Christians at the point of the sword," observes Boxer, "[they] made it very difficult for them to be anything else."

In the Philippines*, the record of Spanish colonial and ecclesiastical rule was no less notorious and contributed to the growth of Philippine nationalism against Spain and the church. In China, the influx of both Catholic and Protestant missionaries in the aftermath of China's enforced opening after the wars of 1839-42 and 1858, and the occupation of Beijing in 1860, further confirmed in Chinese minds the negative perception of Christianity as a foreign religion backed by gunboats, and of Christian missionaries as the ideological arm of foreign aggression. Like their Chinese cousins, Vietnamese leaders also regarded the missionaries as agents of a subversive movement. An imperial edict in 1825 charged the "perverse religion of the European" with "corrupting the hearts of men" — a fear perhaps not entirely unfounded, as French missionaries proved that they were some of the foremost advocates of a more interventionist policy in Vietnam's internal affairs in the late 19th c.

Apart from foreign missionaries, local converts to Christianity were also viewed with suspicion by indigenous nationalists — and not unjustifiably so. In Burma, the minority Christian-led Karens supported British rule and pacification efforts during the 1880s and had little sympathy for Burmese nationalism. During World War II, while the Burmese nationalists initially co-operated with the Japanese, the Karens aided the Allies.

Where they could, Asian polities took steps to circumscribe the spread of Christianity and the influence of Christian missionaries within their domains. Some expelled foreign missionaries and banned Christianity, as China did in 1724 after an ecclesiastical catastrophe, the rites controversy (see Ancestor Worship) which pitted the pope in Rome against the emperor of China. Others wielded the weapon of terror from time to time. In 1597, 26 Christians were crucified at Nagasaki during the reign of the regent Toyotomi Hideyoshi. In Vietnam, seven missionaries were executed between 1837 and 1838. During the persecutions of 1839, 1846, and 1866 in Korea, more than 2,000 Catholics were killed. Thousands of Chinese Christians and about 250 foreigners, mainly missionaries, perished in the anti-foreign and anti-Christian Boxer Uprising of 1900 in China.

But Christianity was not always an enemy of Asian nationalism. At times, it was also an ally. Hong Xiuquan*, the rebel leader of the anti-Manchu Taiping* movement (1851-64) in China, was apparently inspired by the Old Testament story of how a chosen few with God's help had rebelled against oppression. Sun Yat-Sen*, a Christian, led the 1911 revolution that brought an end to alien Manchu rule. Sun had this to say about the impact of his Christian beliefs on his revolutionary zeal: "Men say that the revolution originated with me. . . . But where did the idea of the revolution come from? It came because from my youth I have had intercourse with foreign missionaries. Those from Europe and America with whom I associated put the ideals of freedom and liberty into my heart." Though unpersuaded by Christianity, the Indian nationalist leader Mohandas Gandhi* was deeply impressed by the teachings of Jesus in the New Testament and found in them an important source for the development of his technique of non-violent resistance, or *satygraha.* Christian political parties were also useful allies in the nationalist struggle. In Indonesia, for instance, Protestant parties such as *Partai Kaum Masehi Indonesia* (1930) and *Partai Kristen Indonesia* (1945), and Catholic parties such as *Perhimpunan Politik Katolik Indonesia* (1931) and *Persatuan Katolik Republik Indonesia* (1945) all contributed to the nationalist cause during the colonial period.

Indonesia. Indonesian nationalism developed as a struggle for independence from Dutch colonialism* and at the same time as a movement to unite Indonesia as a nation. The course of Indonesian nationalism began in the first and second decades of the 20th c. as an ethnic or regional cultural movement. On 20 May 1908, *Boedi Oetomo,* the first modern organization established among and for the development of the Javanese, was formed. This date is now celebrated as National Awakening Day. Similar organizations were formed among different ethnic groups. Subsequently, nationalism developed as a religio-economic movement in Sarekat Islam and then became a politico-ideological movement in the 1920s, especially under radical Communism.

As a political movement, Indonesian nationalism divided into two wings: the non-cooperative wing, which radically mobilized people to end colonial power, and the cooperative wing, which struggled within the *Volksraad,* a semi-parliament formed in 1917 to function as adviser to the colonial government. Radicalism in the nationalistic movement under Communism* and later in organizations coordinated by Dr. Sukarno* in the 1920s was answered by the colonial government's supervision and curtailment of nationalistic activities in the next decade. The efforts of the nationalists in the *Volksraad* came to a dead end with the government's rejection of even the moderate wishes of the nationalists. The situation was put to an end by World War II and the Japanese occupation of Indonesia (1942).

A small group of Indonesian Christians living in cities (especially in Java) had a role in the nationalistic movements. They were involved in the ethnic nationalistic groups with their social, economic, and cultural emphases, as well as in the more political-ideological groups. Most of them took the conservative way of cooperation with the colonial government. With an eye to the formation of the *Volksraad,* some European Christians in Indonesia formed a Christian political party. Some Indonesian Christians and groups (the Javanese *Partai Kaoem Christen,* the Ambonese *Christelijke Ambonsche Volksbond, Persatuan Minahasa,* and some Bataks) joined this pro–colonial government political party. The Indonesians were organized into an indigenous branch in 1926, and in 1930 tried, but failed, to form an independent Indonesian Christian political party (*Partai Kaoem Masehi Indonesia,* PKMI). They supported the idea of Indonesian independence under the guardianship of, and in union with, the Netherlands. T. S. G. Mulia, F. Laoh, J. Soselisa, and R. M. Notosoetarso were the leaders of these conservative Christians. G. S. S. J. Ratulangie can be put in this category, but in the late 1930s he became a radical. Some other progressive Christians, such as A. J. Patty and Amir Sjarifuddin, joined radical nationalists in the non-religious organizations.

A Protestant Christian group that maintained Christian idealism and supported the progressive nationalistic movement arose among the young people and students. Their new horizon was a credit to the efforts of tutors such as B. M. Schuurman, H. Kraemer*, C. L. van Doorn, and J. M. J. Schepper. They oriented the younger generation toward positive involvement in the nationalistic movement. The *CSV op Java* (Christian Students Union in Java) developed a Christian outlook that stressed participation in the national life as well as an ecumenical attitude toward international affairs. Out of this circle emerged prominent Indonesian Christian politicians such as J. Leimena and A. M. Tambunan.

The Christian politicians of both the conservative and radical wings fought for religious freedom, an absolute necessity for upholding national unity, given the reality of Indonesian pluralism. The formulation of *Pancasila** the state ideology that made pluralism possible but was not itself a religious ideology, was in part a result of the Christian politicians' rejection of an Islamic ideological concept.

More widely than in the politico-ideological sphere, the nationalistic attitude of Protestant Christians in Indonesia was expressed in the ecumenical* movement. Indonesian churches became a church of Indonesians and for Indonesians in their unity and diversity. The forms of the churches as ethnic or regional institutionalized the idea of ecumenical concern for the nation in its diversity and unity.

The Japanese occupation of Indonesia lasted only a short time but brought with it basic changes and gave particular opportunities for the development of Indonesian nationalism. A preparatory committee that was set up when the Japanese began to experience defeats succeeded in planning the formation of an independent Indonesian nation. The committee meetings revealed that there were two different views concerning the basis of an independent Indonesian nation. Secular nationalists confronted Islamic nationalists. The first group insisted on a secular state that acknowledged the place of religions, but the Muslim groups struggled for an Islamic state. The agreement that was achieved in the end was a state that acknowledges God but not as a religious state. Independent Indonesia would be based on *Pancasila,* the five principles of the oneness of God, a just and civilized humanity, Indonesian unity, democracy in accord with wisdom determined by consultation and representation, and social justice for all Indonesian people.

After the Japanese surrendered to the Allies, the leaders of the nationalistic movement proclaimed Indonesian independence on 17 Aug 1945 in Jakarta. There followed the Indonesian revolution to defend that independence from the Dutch intention to recolonize Indonesia both by diplomacy and by armed force. Indonesians successfully defended their independence, and the Dutch government acknowledged Indonesian sovereignty on 27 Dec 1949.

In the present era of independence, Indonesian nationalism works as a motivating spirit for nation building and development and actively promotes a just and peaceful world.

Myanmar (Burma). Nationalism in Myanmar developed in the first half of the 20th c. as the Burmese sought independence from British colonial rule. The independence movement in Myanmar had its origin in a number of Buddhist societies formed for the social enhancement of the Myanmar people, the most important of which was the Young Men's Buddhist Association (YMBA) founded in Yangon in 1906. The YMBA movement soon spread, and a general council of YMBAs and allied associations was established in 1910, with annual conferences from 1911 onwards. The first major clash between the YMBA and the British colonial government came in 1916-17 over the issue of wearing shoes in religious precincts.

In 1920, the general council changed its name to the General Council of Burmese Associations (GCBA) and unsuccessfully opposed the establishment of the University of Rangoon (Yangon) as an elitist institution. Students went on strike in December 1920. Subsequently, a system of national schools was established. The GCBA also protested the exclusion of Myanmar from the constitutional advance extended to India by the Government of India Act of 1919 and succeeded in obtaining it in 1923. However, the GCBA was divided between those who accepted limited representation and those who rejected it. There was further division in the GCBA in the late 1920s, but the independence movement which had begun as an urban middle-class movement had already extended to other sectors of Myanmar society. Buddhist monks became an active political force; and, under the impact of the Great Depression, a peasant rebellion led by Saya San, a former GCBA organizer, broke out in 1930-31.

A new political group, the Dobama ("We Burmans") Association, was formed in 1930. Its members adopted the title *thakin* (master), a term of address used for British colonial rulers. The Dobama movement spread widely and convened its first conference in 1935. As socialist ideas filtered into Myanmar, the Dobama movement split into socialist and traditionalist wings in 1938. Dobama-sponsored oil-field strikes in 1938 culminated in a mass upheaval in 1939, commonly referred to as the Revolution of the Myanmar Era 1300. With the outbreak of war in Europe in 1939, the Dobama developed an underground movement, made contact with the Japanese army, and arranged military training for a group of young men, the Thirty Comrades, who formed the nucleus of the Burma Independence Army (BIA) established in December 1941. The BIA, later reorganized as the Burma Defence Army (BDA), fought against the British in cooperation with the Japanese. Disillusionment with the Japanese led to the clandestine formation of the Anti-Fascist Organization (AFO) in August 1944, in which the BDA was joined by the Socialists and Communists, outgrowths of the socialist wing of the Dobama. They launched an armed resistance against the Japanese on 27 Mar 1945.

After the war, the AFO, renamed the Anti-Fascist People's Freedom League (AFPFL), emerged as the principal force of the independence movement. Its leader, Aung San, arrived at an understanding with the British government on the steps required for independence in the Aung San–Attlee Agreement of January 1947. He also came to terms with the Shan, Kachin, and Chin ethnic minorities in the Panglong Agreement of 12 Feb 1947. Aung San and six colleagues were assassinated on 19 Jul 1947, but the move toward independence was continued by his successor, Thakin Nu. Myanmar gained independence on 4 Jan 1948.

The independence movement was influenced in its earliest phase by Christian institutions and thinking, especially in relating religion to social improvement, but the nationalists' view of Christianity as the religion of the colonial rulers, the emphasis on Buddhism in defining the Myanmar national identity, and the commitment of Christians, influenced by Western missionaries, to law and order resulted in the exclusion of Christians from the independence movement in the 1920s and 1930s. It was only in the final phase, with the secularist outlook of Aung San and the AFPFL, that the efforts to build a national consensus involved Christian participation. Generally, the independence movement created division between Myanmar Buddhists and Christians.

Sri Lanka. The unique culture of Sri Lankan Tamils took on a distinctiveness as a result of their immigration to the island from diverse regions of India*. They migrated to the island in various waves beginning in pre-Christian times. In fact, many features of Sri Lankan Tamil culture stand in sharp contrast to mainland Tamil customs. This is because they lived in close proximity to the Sinhalese Buddhist civilization. By the 13th c., in the wake of the collapse of the Sinhalese civilization, a Tamil Hindu kingdom arose in the Jaffna Peninsula. This kingdom continued until it was subdued by the Portuguese in 1619. Under the Portuguese (1619-58) and the Dutch (1658-1796), the Tamils were treated as a separate ethnic entity and were administered separately within the colonial administrations in Sri Lanka.

British rule (1796-1948) centralized the administration of the island in 1833. The Jaffna area is generally considered to have had the finest system of English-language schools in all of Asia during the 19th c. Therefore the educational standards of the Sri Lankan Tamils, especially those in Jaffna, were far superior to the rest of the country.

In response to the tide of Christian conversions, a Hindu religious leader, Arumuga Navalar*, reformulated Hinduism in Jaffna in order to meet the challenge of Christian missionaries. Tamil language and culture underwent a revival as a result. The Tamils and Sinhalese cooperated in the national struggle for independence. However, the situation changed after independence.

With the electoral victory of S. W. R. D. Bandaranaike in 1956, Sinhalese was declared the only official language. Tension over the language issue led to riots in 1958. Soon after the riots, Bandaranaike and S. J. V. Chelvanayagam signed a pact offering concessions to the Tamils in the Tamil areas. However, the pact was unilaterally revoked by the government because of the pressure from Sinhala extremists. Tamil leaders since then have treated the government in Colombo as untrustworthy when it comes to Tamil grievances.

The imposition of the language policy led to quotas for placement in universities and government employment. The unemployed Tamil youth became radicalized and formed youth organizations, one of which was the Tamil New Tigers, to demand a separate state for Tamils. In 1974, Tamil political parties unified and called for the creation of a Tamil state in the northern and eastern provinces. In 1976, they formed the Tamil United Front to demand a separate and independent state to be called Eelam. The Tamil youths rejected the moderate politicians' program of action and began a wave of violent assassinations. Thereafter, all militant groups subscribed to the notion of Eelam on principle. The extent of the Tamil Eelam, however, varied from one political group to another. Nevertheless, there was an agreement among them that the northern and eastern provinces should form the Tamil homeland.

Political unrest escalated in the 1980s as groups representing the Tamil minority moved toward organized insurgency. Tamil bases were built up in jungle areas of the northern and eastern parts of the island. Increasingly, the southern Indian state of Tamil Nadu gave official and unofficial support. The Liberation Tigers of Tamil Eelam (LTTE) constituted the strongest threat, but there were competing groups which were sometimes hostile to each other.

The Sri Lankan government responded to the unrest by deploying forces to the north and east. In July 1983, extensive organized anti-Tamil riots took place in Colombo and elsewhere. The riots created a movement of refugees within the island and from Sri Lanka to Tamil

Nadu. Therefore, Sri Lankan Tamil nationalists received sympathy and support in South India.

The Sri Lankan president, Jayawardene, after prolonged negotiations, signed an accord with the Indian government on 29 Jul 1987 with a view to achieving peace in the country. The Indian government provided a peacekeeping force (IPKF) to enforce the conditions of the accord, which called for an autonomous indigenous Tamil region within a united Sri Lanka. The Sri Lankan government, LTTE, and IPKF, however, disagreed over the implementation of the accord. The LTTE began an offensive against the IPKF, which was trying to disarm them. The Premadasa government negotiated a withdrawal of the IPKF which was completed in March 1990; six months later the LTTE launched an offensive against the Sri Lankan government forces.

With the departure of the IPKF, the LTTE gained dominance over the Tamil area by eliminating the opposing militant groups. When the LTTE resumed military operations in 1991 against government security forces, they were the unrivaled leaders of the Tamil Eelam. They have resorted to military operations as well as guerrilla tactics to achieve their aim. They have claimed responsibility for many political murders. De facto administration of the northern peninsula and some parts of the eastern province has fallen into the hands of the LTTE.

After the election victory of the Kumaratunga government in Jan 1994, there was a truce between the LTTE and the security forces. With the failure to settle the issues by negotiations, however, military actions resumed in March 1995.

Christians form a minority among the Sri Lankan Tamils. Nevertheless, the church has taken a sympathetic view toward the nationalist aspirations of the Sri Lankan Tamils. The church has condemned the acts of violence on both sides and reiterated the need for peaceful negotiations.

See also Religious Nationalism in the Philippines.

Bibliography

Boxer, C. R., *The Portuguese Seaborne Empire, 1415-1825* (1969). • Deats, Richard L., *Nationalism and Christianity in the Philippines* (1967). • Escoto, Salvador P., "The Ecclesiastical Controversy of 1767-1776: A Catalyst of Philippine Nationalism," *Journal of Asian History* 10 (1976). • Fukui, H., ed., *Political Parties of Asia and the Pacific* (1985). • Kohn, Hans, "Nationalism," in *International Encyclopedia of the Social Sciences,* Vol. 11, ed. David L. Sills (1968). • Lutz, Jessie Gregory, *Chinese Politics and Christian Missions: The Anti-Christian Movements of 1920-28* (1988). • Mews, Stuart, ed., *Religion in Politics: A World Guide* (1989). • Neill, Stephen C., "Christianity in Asia," in *The Encyclopedia of Religion,* Vol. 3, ed. Mircea Eliade (1987). • Sharman, Lyon, *Sun Yat-sen: His Life and Its Meaning* (1965). • Smith, A. D., *Theories of Nationalism* (1971). • Smith, A. D., ed., *Nationalist Movements* (1976). • Stanley, Brian, *The Bible and the Flag: Protestant Missions and British Imperialism in the Nineteenth and Twentieth Centuries* (1990). • Tiwari, K. N., *World Religions and Gandhi* (1988). • Wang Gungwu, "Nationalism in Asia," in *Nationalism: The Nature and Evolution of an Idea,* ed. Eugene Kmenka (1973). • Ngelow, Zakaria J., "Transformation of Nationalism: A Study on the Encounter of Protestant Christianity and National Movement in Indonesia, 1900-1950" (Ph.D. diss., South East Asia Graduate School of Theology) (1992). • Cady, John F., *A History of Modern Burma* (1958). • Maung Maung, *From Sangha to Laity: Nationalist Movements of Burma, 1920-1940* (1980). • Trager, Frank N., *Burma: From Kingdom to Republic* (1966). • Bose, S., *States, Nations, Sovereignty: Sri Lanka, India and the Tamil Eelam Movement* (1994). • De Silva, K. M., *Managing Ethnic Tensions in Multiethnic Societies: Sri Lanka, 1880-1985* (1986). • Wilson, A. J., *S. J. V. Chelvanayagam and the Crisis of Ceylon Tamil Nationalism* (1994).

ALBERT LAU, ZAKARIA J. NGELOW, HANSON TADAW, and G. P. V. SOMARATNA

Navalar, Arumuga

(b. 18 Dec 1822; d. 10 Dec 1879). Hindu reformer in the 19th c. whose contribution to the Tamil language and Saivism sparked a revival of Hinduism* in Jaffna.

Navalar was born into a Vellalar family with several Tamil scholars in its ancestry. His father was a Tamil playwright, physician, and author of several Tamil medical works. First educated in traditional Hindu temples, Navalar later studied at the Methodist English school in Jaffna where he came under the influence of Rev. Peter Percival (d. 1875). In 1842 Percival invited him to participate in Bible* translation because he knew Tamil and Sanskrit. Navalar read the available Bible commentaries and other biblical works in order to translate precisely, acquiring a mastery of Christianity which later proved useful in his Hindu polemics. He also adopted the methods of the missionaries as he spread Hinduism.

Navalar then studied the Saiva Siddhanta in Tamil and the Saivagamas in Sanskrit to redress the neglect of his own religion. In 1845 he gathered a group of young Tamil scholars and taught them Tamil literature and Saivism. In 1847 he turned to preaching, selecting the Vasanta Mandapam of the Siva temple at Vannarpannai as the site of his work. He lectured on Friday evenings, urging his hearers to practice what they heard in his sermons. Many underwent the *Saiva Deeksha* (initiation), gave up meat, became regular temple-goers, and adopted *Saiva-acharam* (modes of conduct appropriate for Saivites). He soon extended his sphere of activity, preaching in the neighboring villages, establishing schools, and providing funds. He adopted the missionaries' educational methods and in 1870 started an English school in Jaffna.

Navalar also employed other methods to resist the spread of Christianity in Jaffna. He wrote books such as *Uppirapotam* (Radiant Wisdom) and *Caivatusanapari-*

karam (Annihilation of Enemies against Saivism) to counter arguments against Hinduism. His *Yalpanasamayanilai* (State of Religion in Jaffna) criticized the practices of the missionaries and their converts. He renovated a number of Hindu temples, among them the Siva temples at Keerimalei and Thiruketeesvaram, which date back to a time even before the arrival of the Portuguese.

Navalar also devoted his attention to abuses within the Hindu temples, condemning the practice of temple dancing and the slaughter of goats on the Hindu festival days. He criticized the Saiva priests for neglecting the letter of the Agamas.

Navalar set up a printing press and printed several Tamil books, replacing the practice of manually copying manuscripts on palmyra leaves. Regarding his contribution to the Tamil language as a service to his religion, he wrote a book on Tamil grammar and made a significant contribution to Tamil literature when he adapted the prose style of writing for Hindu literature. By adopting many of the practices of the Christian missionaries, Navalar was able to organize a countermovement to stem the success of Christian evangelism and revitalize Hinduism; this made him a national hero in Sri Lanka.

Bibliography

Young, R. F., and S. Jebanesan, *The Bible Trembled: The Hindu-Christian Controversies of Nineteenth-Century Ceylon* (1995).

G. P. V. Somaratna

Nee, Watchman

(Nee To-sheng) (b. Swatow, China, 4 Nov 1903; d. 1 Jun 1972). Founder of the Local Church movement (Little Flock*) in China*.

"I want nothing for myself; I want everything for the Lord." These words of Watchman Nee can be regarded as the motto of his life and ministry. The Local Church movement which he founded also spread overseas, especially after the establishment of the Communist regime in 1949. Through his itinerant preaching and voluminous literature work, Nee greatly influenced the conservative wing of the Chinese church. The theological vocabulary he formulated has become an important ingredient in today's Chinese theology. For almost 20 years, he was imprisoned by the Chinese government, but he kept his faith until his death.

Born in Swatow, Nee was called *Shu-tsu,* which means "declare your ancestors' merits." Later, he was renamed *Tosheng,* which is the sound produced when a time-watcher hits the bamboo gong at night. Shortly after his birth, his parents returned to Foochow, where Nee received his early education in Chinese classical studies. In 1916, he entered junior high school at the Anglican* Trinity College, which was run by the Church Missionary Society. However, religious activities at school did not interest Nee, whose sensitive mind was absorbed in the events of the day. Subsequent to the formation of the Republic in 1912 under the leadership of Sun Yat-Sen*, China moved into a period of intellectual revolution commonly called the May Fourth Movement (1915-23). This was a time when traditional Confucianism* was criticized for its alleged inability to modernize the country and Western learning was introduced as a viable means to build the young nation.

Nee's conversion came in Apr 1920 after he attended a Gospel meeting of Dora Yu, a Methodist evangelist. Disenchanted with Anglican doctrine and liturgy, Nee spent a year at Yu's Bible school in Shanghai, where he received basic training in Christian living. He was deeply influenced by Margaret E. Barber, a British missionary who introduced him to the Holiness literature of writers such as T. Austin-Sparks, Jessie Penn-Lewis, D. M. Panton, Andrew Murray, and F. B. Meyer. Part of Nee's inspiration for Christian service came from the Keswick Movement and the Welsh Revival (1904-5). He also became familiar with the Brethren Movement through the writings of J. N. Darby, George Müller, William Kelly, and C. A. Coates. He also studied the lives of significant Christian leaders, including Martin Luther, John Knox, Jonathan Edwards, John Wesley, George Whitefield, David Brainerd, John Henry Newman, D. L. Moody, Charles Finney, and C. H. Spurgeon.

Nee began his literature ministry in 1923 by editing *Revival,* a devotional magazine for free distribution. In 1926, he published *The Christian,* which succeeded *Revival* and gained wide circulation in only a few years. At age 25, during a period of serious illness, Nee wrote his first major book, *The Spiritual Man,* an exhaustive analysis of human psychology from a biblical perspective that seeks to explain the whole process of spiritual formation. These early efforts laid the theological foundation for his future career.

The Chinese indigenous church movement was gaining momentum during the 1920s. Many church leaders attempted to develop an independent, nondenominational church suited to the cultural and ethnic characteristics of the Chinese people. Nee's Local Church was a unique model in this broad movement. It began in 1927 with a small household gathering in Shanghai. This group multiplied quickly, and many local churches were founded. To the threefold ideal of self-propagating, self-governing, and self-supporting, Nee added the principle of locality, i.e., there is only one true church in each city. Such exclusiveness in defining ecclesial boundaries was controversial to Nee's contemporaries. Nee had a team of fellow workers, including Witness Lee, Simon Meek, and Faithful Luke. Through their ministries, local churches were planted in many cities in Southeast Asia.

Nee's theological outlook was influenced by the Brethren tradition. For a time, he had contact with the Exclusive Brethren in London. In 1933, he was invited to visit the Brethren communities in England and the United States. However, this relationship was later severed because their principle for Christian fellowship was too restrictive and their emphasis on perfection in Christ too excessive for Nee.

In the 1930s, Nee was briefly exposed to the Pentecostal* movement through the ministry of Elizabeth Fischbacher of China Inland Mission. He did not speak in tongues and reacted to what he deemed as excessive on the part of the charismatic groups. In 1938, he attended the Keswick Convention, and during his European tour he gave a series of talks on Romans 5-8. Based on this lecture series, his book *The Normal Christian Life* presented his theology derived from *The Spiritual Man* and mingled with insights gleaned from the Keswick tradition and Brethrenism.

After Pearl Harbor, Japanese occupation of China's eastern seaboard jeopardized the economy of the country. This affected the financial condition of Nee's movement. In 1942, Nee decided to help his brother George in his pharmaceutical company in order to raise money for his fellow workers in the ministry. But he was misunderstood and criticized. The elders at the Shanghai assembly forbade him to preach until he gave up his secular job. As founder of the movement, such rejection was a heavy blow to Nee and caused him to revise his ecclesiology regarding the structure of authority.

Subsequent to the Sino-Japanese War, Nee published several books on ecclesiology, including *The Orthodoxy of the Church, Authority and Obedience,* and *On Church Affairs.* In 1947, Nee consigned all his business assets to the church and was restored to his former senior position. His new ecclesiology was summarized in the Jerusalem Principle, which limited the power of the elders in the local assemblies, placed the whole movement under central control, and launched a program of evangelism by dispatching a host of workers to unreached areas. As a result, his movement continued to prosper at the eve of the Communist takeover of the mainland. By 1949, there were over 700 local churches with a combined membership of 70,000.

When the Communists came to power in 1949, the Christian Church in China struggled for survival. Any form of imperialism in the church was to be purified; and, under these circumstances, the Local Church movement was doomed. Nee himself was arrested in Manchuria in Apr 1952 on charges of corrupt business practices. Four years later, in a public trial in Shanghai, he was found guilty on political and moral grounds and was sentenced to 15 years in prison. Some of his churches joined the Three-Self Patriotic Movement*; others went underground.

In 1950, during a visit to Hong Kong*, Nee had been begged by Witness Lee not to return to Shanghai. Nee refused and said, "I do not care for my life. If the house is crashing down, I have children inside and must support it, if need be with my head." Nee's love for God's church surpassed that for his own life.

Nee bestowed on the Christian church the legacy of a spiritual theology based on a trichotomy of the human constitution — body, soul, and spirit. Salvation for him lay in the restoration of communication between God's Spirit and the human spirit. He regarded sanctification as the lifelong process of the spirit's controlling the soul and the soul's directing the body. In the Christian life the spirit constantly walks in step with the Holy Spirit and in the light of Scripture. Nee considered the local church the most congenial environment for the cultivation of such spirituality.

Bibliography

Lam Wing-hung, *The Spiritual Theology of Watchman Nee* (1985). • Nee, Watchman, *The Spiritual Man* (1968); *The Normal Christian Life* (1968). • Kinnear, Angus I., *Against the Tide: The Story of Watchman Nee* (1973). • Robert, Dana, *Understanding Watchman Nee* (1980).

Lam Wing-hung

Neesima Jo(seph Hardy)

(b. Edo [Tokyo], Japan, 12 Feb 1843; d. 23 Jan 1890). Founder of Doshisha University.

Born in the Edo residence of the Annaka domain as the eldest son of Tamiji (secretary of the Annaka Clan) and Tomi, Neesima's childhood name was Shichigosanta, and his posthumous name was Keikan. While studying in the United States, he went by the name Joseph Hardy Neesima. At one time, he also used the name Yozefu (Joseph), but mostly he used Jo. He celebrated his coming of age in 1857 and served as an assistant to his father, studying mathematics and navigation at the Warship Training Center in Tsukiji from 1860 to 1863. In 1863, he switched his language study from Dutch to English.

Feeling a pull to the United States and Christianity, Neesima read *Mi Renp-shi ryaku* (History and Geography of the US) by Elijah Coleman Bridgman and a Chinese version of the Bible. In Jun 1864, he left Japan from Hakodate on an American ship and arrived in Boston in Jun 1865. With the help of the ship's captain, Alpheus Hardy, and his wife, Neesima enrolled at Phillips Academy. On 31 Dec 1866, he was baptized at the church affiliated with Andover Theological School. In Sep 1867, he enrolled at Amherst College, graduating in Jul 1870 with a bachelor of science degree. He then proceeded to Andover Theological School, and in Jul 1874 graduated from a special course. From Mar 1872 until Sep 1873, during the time he was studying at Andover, he was a member of the Iwakura Mission, heading an investigation of educational systems in the United States and Europe. On 24 Sep 1874, he was ordained at Mount Vernon Church in Boston and received an appointment as a missionary associate of the American Board of Commissioners for Foreign Missions (ABCFM). He attended the yearly meeting of the ABCFM in Rutland, Vermont, appealing for help to build a Christian school in Japan.

After receiving support, Neesima returned to Japan following a 10-year absence. On 29 Nov 1875, with the help of the adviser of Kyoto Prefecture, Yamamoto Kakuma, and ABCFM missionary Jerome Dean Davis, he founded Doshisha English School. In Jan 1876, he married Yamamoto's daughter Yaeko (Neesima Yae). In Apr 1877, he opened a girls school and in Nov 1887 Doshisha Hospital, Kyoto Nursing School, and Toka School (a branch of Doshisha in Sendai). In Nov 1888, he announced to all of Japan his intention to build Doshisha University, appealing to all of Japan's citizens for help. Because of the great effort he gave to this project, he fell ill at Oiso, Kanagawa Prefecture, and died there. A 10-volume collection of his writings, *Neesima Jo Zenshu,* was published beginning in 1983.

Bibliography

Davis, J. D., *Neesima Jo Sensei den* (Biography of Professor Neesima Jo), trans. Murata Tsutomu and Matsuura Masayasu (1891); *Neesima Jo no Shogai* (The Life of Neesima Jo), trans. Kitagaki Soji (1977). • Hardy, *Life and Letters of Joseph Hardy Neesima, 1891* (1980). • Wada Yoichi, *Neesima Jo* (1973). • Uoki Tadakazu, *Neesima Jo — Hhito to Shiso* (Neesima Jo — The Man and His Thought) (1950). SUGII MATSURO

Nehru, Jawaharlal

(b. Allahabad, India, 14 Nov 1889; d. New Delhi, 27 May 1964). Indian nationalist politician and independent India's first prime minister.

Nehru was born into the privileged world of India's English-educated, professional elite, under British imperial rule. He was educated at home, then in England at Harrow School and Trinity College, Cambridge, and studied law in London. After World War I, he became involved in the Indian nationalist movement against British rule. His mentor and close friend was Mahatma Gandhi*, and his participation in Gandhi's campaigns of nonviolent civil disobedience led him to several lengthy prison sentences. He became a prominent member of the nationalist party, the Indian National Congress, and was groomed by Gandhi to be his heir, although he was far more radical than were most other leading congressmen.

When India gained independence in 1947, Nehru became her first prime minister and retained that position until his death, as the Congress Party won each election held during his lifetime, not least because of his immense popularity and public standing. He also became a prominent international figure, calling for a nonalignment position during the Cold War and enabling the restructuring of the British Commonwealth in a period of decolonization. He married in 1916, but his wife died in 1936, leaving him with one daughter, Indira, who was born in 1917. She later became a forceful and controversial prime minister of India and mother of another Indian prime minister, Rajiv Gandhi.

Nehru entered politics to forward a vision of a new India, not because of a love of politics or for personal profit or aggrandizement. He was a radical but democratic socialist who wished to replace British imperialism with freedom for India, which he hoped would in turn enable a democratic India to dismantle its hierarchical, agrarian social structures and build both a strong industrial economy and a more egalitarian society. Although he was born a Hindu, his father, a dominant influence in his life, was hardly orthodox, and he himself was agnostic in belief. He was also deeply critical of the way religious traditions and structures could serve vested interests and inhibit what he saw as essential social change. In the case of India, he was particularly anxious that the so-called Untouchables at the base of Hindu society and India's women should be relieved of age-old discrimination justified by religion, and freed to play a rightful role as citizens. He also believed that the new India should become a secular state, recognizing and treating equally India's major religious traditions, not just the Hindu traditions of the majority, but also the beliefs and practices of India's religious minorities, including Muslims, Christians, Sikhs, and Parsis. In maintaining this vision, he argued against those who believed that the Indian nation was essentially Hindu in its cultural origins and identity. But he also argued with Muslims, who contended that India was made up of two nations, one Hindu and one Muslim, each of which was entitled to a national homeland when independence came. In an interview in 1946 with a London Catholic newspaper, he insisted that Christians should have no fear for their religious freedom when India gained independence and that they were an integral part of India with long traditions: "They form one of the many enriching elements in the country's cultural and spiritual life. In a country where there are so many creeds we must learn to be tolerant."

Nehru as prime minister was crucial to the future of Christianity in India. His ideals and political influence were expressed in the new constitution of 1949, which proclaimed that India was a secular state in which equal citizenship was guaranteed to people of all religions and that freedom of religion was one of its citizens' fundamental rights. However, in practice religious minorities were fearful at the time of independence because of the fierce sense of Hindu and Muslim "communalism" generated as British power waned. There was a bloody toll as the country was partitioned into India and Pakistan*. Minorities looked to Nehru as guardian of their rights when Hindu politicians complained of the "foreign hand" (either Pakistani or Western) in India. Nehru insisted publicly that Muslims and Christians should be made to feel equal and not be harassed, though inevitably he could not prevent discrimination and harassment at the local level on a daily basis. In 1952, he wrote to the premiers of each state within the Indian union specifically condemning any harassment of Christians. Aware that many Christian converts came from deeply impoverished backgrounds, he added that he wished Indians were as prepared to serve them as were foreign missionaries.

Perhaps inevitably, the foreign missionary presence was a most sensitive issue in the aftermath of the politi-

Neill, Stephen Charles

cal struggle for independence from foreign rule and the partition of the country on religious lines. Nehru did not himself like evangelical activity, but he was generous in his commendation of the social service which many missionaries rendered to the most vulnerable and weak members of society. He personally did not think that India had anything to fear from missionaries' religious activity, considering how few converts there had been even in the period of British rule. However, he was firm that there were some sensitive areas, particularly in border regions, where foreigners might have to be excluded. In particular, there was the northeast border region, where Naga and Mizo tribal peoples had converted to Christianity in large numbers and were, during the 1950s, engaged in struggles for separate political status. Where he felt the integrity of the Indian union was at stake, he had no hesitation in restricting the foreign missionary presence in 1953. He refused to countenance tribal demands for political autonomy, and armed force was used to suppress them.

Since Nehru's death, national and local politics have suggested how vulnerable Christians can be in areas where they are poor converts, as well as how powerful a role Nehru played in holding together India's many religious communities with his secular tolerance.

Bibliography

Nehru, Jawaharlal, *An Autobiography* (1946). • Gopal, S., *Jawaharlal Nehru: A Biography,* 3 Vols. (1975-84). • Brown, Judith M., *Nehru* (1999). • Brass, P., *The Politics of India since Independence* (1990). JUDITH M. BROWN

Neill, Stephen Charles

(b. Edinburgh, Scotland, 31 Dec 1900; d. Oxford, England, 20 Jul 1984). Anglican churchman, biblical scholar, and historian of Indian Christianity.

Born in Britain to medical* missionaries, Neill lived two years as a child in India. He was educated at Dean Close School in Cheltenham and Trinity College, Cambridge, and returned to India* in 1924 with his parents to serve with the Bible Churchmen's Society, a split from the Anglican Church Missionary Society (CMS). They located in the Tirunelveli region (also known as Tinnevelly) and resided in Amy Carmichael's compound at Dohnavur. Tensions arose between the strong-willed Carmichael and the newcomers; within six months the elder Neills had left, and in late 1925 Stephen departed as well. The differences between Neill and Carmichael have never been clarified, and he omits this phase of his life in his autobiography. The animosities were so deep that she severed her mission's connection with the diocese of Tinnevelly when Neill was named its bishop.

Within a few months, Neill had gained a sufficient knowledge of Tamil to begin itinerant work on his own. He established a pattern that he would follow during his two decades of missionary life in India — learning the language of the region in which he ministered; placing strong emphasis on evangelism, literature work (providing catechists, teachers, and lay workers with notes and simple books in their own language), vernacular theological education, and spiritual development; and fostering an ecumenical spirit. For him gospel, mission, and church all went together. He also became known for his organizational skills, prodigious literary output, theological acumen, and readiness to speak his mind.

After the break with Carmichael, Neill found work with the help of the CMS/Anglican contacts he had made in Cambridge, and in 1926 he was ordained a deacon in the (Anglican*) Church of India, Burma (Myanmar), and Ceylon (Sri Lanka*). The following year he took up a fellowship at Trinity College, Cambridge, and after ordination as a priest in 1928 returned to India under the auspices of the CMS. He served as principal of Alwaye Christian College in Travancore and in 1930 was appointed warden of Tirumaraiyur, a theological college in Tirunelveli that trained Indians in direct evangelism. In 1935, he was named to the General Council of the Church of India, Burma, and Ceylon, where he learned how to function in a large-scale church organization. He took part in the 1938 Madras conference of the International Missionary Council, chairing the section "On the Training of the Ministry," and served as an Anglican delegate to the Joint Committee on Church Union in South India, activities which enhanced his ecumenical vision.

In Jan 1939, Neill was consecrated bishop of Tinnevelly, at the time the youngest bishop in the Anglican communion, where he proved to be a hard-working, driven person who brooked no opposition from the British authorities or indigenous churchmen. In 1944, his health broke, and Archbishop Foss Westcott ordered him sent home to England for medical treatment. What actually precipitated the crisis is a matter of contention, but recognizing that little chance existed for further advancement in the Church of England, he resigned his position in Tinnevelly, although he retained the title of bishop.

Neill, who never married, spent the remainder of his life in travel, writing, lecturing, and ecumenical work. He taught for a year at Cambridge, served three years with the World Council of Churches, ran a publishing venture (World Christian Books), and in 1962 was appointed professor of missions at the University of Hamburg, Germany. Retiring in 1967, he then went to Nairobi, Kenya, to direct the department of religious studies at University College. During his last years he lived in Oxford, where he completed two volumes of *A History of Christianity in India* (1984, 1985).

As Neill had a global reputation, he taught or lectured at universities and seminaries in many countries. He had knowledge of the biblical and classical languages as well as several modern European and Indian languages, and he was the author, co-author, or editor of 65 books, as well as innumerable essays, reviews, addresses, and sermons. His most notable works were in church history, ecumenics, and missions, such as *Anglicanism* (1958,

1977), *A History of the Ecumenical Movement, 1517-1948* (edited with Ruth Rouse, 1954), *A History of Christian Missions* (1964), and *Colonialism and Christian Missions* (1966).

Neill's life ambition was to write a general history of the spread of Christianity in South Asia. He addressed some aspects of this subject in his first historical book, *Builders of the Indian Church* (1934), which focused on the activities of prominent Christians through the centuries, and he related the account of Christian development in more detail in *The Story of the Christian Church in India and Pakistan* (1970). However, he was able to deliver only two volumes of his magnum opus to Cambridge University Press before his death. The first volume carried the story to 1707, and the second covered the period 1707-1858. Although it is a work of great erudition, with dozens of pages of notes and bibliographies covering many languages, marked by fairness and generosity to individuals and points of view both Christian and non-Christian, in fact the time had passed when a lone individual could carry out a task so massive as writing the full story of Christianity in the subcontinent. Since the 1960s, numerous scholars from the West and India had engaged in a far-reaching reinterpretation of Indian history, and much of the research was unknown to Neill, who relied heavily on traditional primary and secondary sources for his work. Contemporary critics regarded it as a history written in the traditional, somewhat paternalistic missionary style and as essentially an apologia for both Western missionaries and British rule in India. Scholarship in Indian Christianity has advanced far beyond Neill's work, which remains unfinished.

Bibliography

Jackson, Eleanor C., ed., *God's Apprentice: The Autobiography of Bishop Stephen Neill* (1991); "The Continuing Legacy of Stephen Neill," *International Bulletin of Missionary Research* 19 (Apr 1995). • Lamb, Christopher, "The Legacy of Stephen Neill," *International Bulletin of Missionary Research* 11 (Apr 1987). • Pierard, Richard V., "Stephen Neill," in *Historians of the Christian Tradition*, ed. Michael Bauman and Martin I. Klauber (1995).

Richard V. Pierard

Nepal

A small country about 500 miles long and 100 miles wide, Nepal (population 20,188,000) is sandwiched between China* (Tibet) and India*. Except for a narrow strip of low-lying plains along the southern border and temperate valleys interspersed in the middle hills, the country is entirely mountainous and has few natural resources. Nepal opened its doors to the outside world in 1951 following the overthrow of the Ranas, who had ruled Nepal as a private fiefdom for over 100 years, and the restoration of King Tribhuvan to the throne. Desperately needed development programs were begun, and Christian missions were welcomed to help in the process, particularly in the areas of health and education.

A brief experiment with parliamentary democracy ended in 1961 with a return to one-party rule headed by the Hindu monarch. The ban on political parties was not lifted until April 1990. A new constitution was adopted in November of that year, and parliament was elected the following year. The Nepal Congress government fell in July 1994, and in elections the following November the Communist Party received the mandate of the people to form a new government.

Although officially a Hindu kingdom, Nepal is a mosaic of diverse cultures, languages, ethnic groups, and religious practices. Government religious statistics (89% Hindu, 7% Buddhist, 3.5% Muslim) are suspect to many scholars, especially in view of the rising ethnic consciousness and assertiveness by Buddhists and other minorities.

Nepal's first known contact with Christianity came through the periodic travels of Jesuit* and then Capuchin* missionaries seeking to get into Tibet during the early 1600s. A Capuchin mission was established in Nepal in 1715, and the work extended to the three city-kingdoms of Kathmandu, Bhadgaon, and Patan over the next 50 years, during which two churches were built. But in 1769 the small group of missionaries and Nepali Christians were forced into exile across the border in India. Following this, Nepal was firmly closed to Christianity for over 180 years.

However, as a result of extensive Nepali emigration during the oppressive Rana regime, many Nepalis came into contact with Western missionaries across the border in India. A thriving Nepali church took root through the efforts of the Church of Scotland's Eastern Himalayan Mission in Darjeeling, Kalimpong, and Sikkim from the 1870s onward. In building on the earlier work of William Carey's* team in Serampore, the Nepali Bible was translated and revised, with Rev. Ganga Prasad Pradhan* serving over 30 years as the primary Nepali translator. Other missions worked and prayed for Nepal's opening along its southern border, notably at Rupaidhia (Assembly of God), Nautanwa (Nepali Evangelistic Band, NEB), and Raxaul (Regions Beyond Missionary Union); the NEB extended their work into Assam and established a Nepali church in Shillong led by Pastor David Mukhia*.

Following Nepal's cautious opening to the outside world in 1951, Nepali Christians converted in India began to make their way into Nepal, many alongside Western missions which were invited by his majesty's government, notably the Nepal Evangelistic Band (later International Nepal Fellowship) to Pokhara, the United Mission to Nepal* (UMN) to Tansen, Bhaktapur, and Kathmandu, and a few years later the Leprosy* Mission to a site just outside the Kathmandu Valley. The first resident missionary of the modern era was the Jesuit father Marshall Moral, who moved to Kathmandu in January 1951 and started St. Xavier's School by the following July. The missions were limited to development activities by their agreements with the government and have never received visas for church-related work. This left the way open for the development of the church in Nepal under indigenous leadership, with the moral support and Christian presence of the missions.

The first church in Nepal (1955) was built at Ram Ghat, Pokhara, by the Nepali members of the NEB under the leadership of Pastor David Mukhia, and on the land of one of their early evangelists, Buddhi Sagar Gautam. Col. Nararaj Shamsher, who had been converted and baptized across the border in Raxaul, returned and opened his home for the first Christian worship services in Kathmandu in 1953, led by a team of three men from the Mar Thoma Church of South India. Tir Bahadur Dewan of East Nepal returned in 1954 and became pastor of the first church in Bhaktapur, while Pastor Robert Karthak* (who became a kind of father figure within the emerging church) and a team of young people from Kalimpong entered Nepal in 1955 and pioneered Byaneswor Church in Kathmandu. To the west, Barnabas Rai had been crossing occasionally from Rupaidhia into Nepalganj since the 1940s, where he moved permanently with his co-worker John Singh in 1953.

Two significant events marked the turning of the first decade of the church in Nepal: in 1959, the first meeting of what became the Nepal Christian Fellowship* (NCF) brought together the few Christians scattered across the country and aided in the formation of churches; and in 1960 the first major court case was brought against Christians, as a result of which Pastor Prem Pradhan* spent four-and-a-half years in prison for his faith. Until the early 1970s, the church was marked by slow growth, counting about 500 Nepali Christians, 30 congregations, three church buildings, and six to eight pastors. Court cases and societal opposition continued. NCF took the lead in providing short-term Bible teaching, leadership training, formation of the Bible Society*, and the first Bible school in Nepal.

With the calling of a national referendum in 1980 and a short period of relative religious freedom, the Good News Festival was held in Kathmandu in the spring, the first publicly advertised evangelistic meetings. This was followed by a six-week, country-wide, literature-evangelistic campaign called Target '80, a cooperative effort of NCF, the Bible Society in Nepal, and Nepal Campus Crusade for Christ; most of the churches were involved. By 1985 the number of Christians in Nepal was estimated at nearly 25,000, mostly Protestant, but also with a growing Catholic community under Nepali leadership. Father Antu Sharma SJ was made the Ecclesiastical Superior of Nepal in 1984. Major Protestant groups of churches now include the Assemblies of God Nepal, Agape Fellowship, the Evangelical Christian Fellowship of Nepal, and the Evangelical Christian Alliance of Nepal (mostly Four-Square Churches), in addition to the NCF (now called National Churches Fellowship of Nepal), each with its own Bible school.

The surge in evangelism and Christian conversions was accompanied by an increased number of legal cases against Christians, including one which went to the Supreme Court and ended in six-year sentences against three Christian leaders for "propagating Christianity in ways injurious to Hindu religion." However, the restoration of democracy in 1990 ushered in a new period of relative religious freedom and emphasis on human rights; all religious prisoners were granted amnesty, and pending cases were dismissed. Nepal's 1991 census figures numbered Nepali Christians at over 30,000, but current estimates by church leaders place the figure at over 330,000. The largest numbers are among tribal groups such as the Rai and Tamang, although Christians can now be found among each of the more than 60 language groups of Nepal and in each of the 75 districts.

Bibliography

Burgyone, Samuel, and Jonathan Lindell, "Nepal," in *The Church in Asia*, ed. Donald Hoke (1975). • Metzler, Edgar, "UMN: A Case Study in Wholistic Ministry" (Asia Consultation on Wholistic Ministry) (Nov 1994). • Perry, Cindy, *A Biographical History of the Church in Nepal* (1993).

CINDY PERRY

Nepal Christian Fellowship

(NCF). Since the introduction of Protestant Christianity into Nepal*, new Christian converts have identified themselves as Christians, with no denominational linkage. This was the policy both of the mission which entered Nepal at the invitation of the government to do development work in the early 1950s and of individual Nepali and Indian Christians who entered at about the same time (mostly from Darjeeling and Sikkim). No foreign denominations were to be introduced in Nepal. As the church slowly took root and fellowships were started in various centers, however, there was a growing awareness of the need of the scattered Christians to gather into a united fellowship. With the encouragement of Ernest Oliver, executive secretary of the United Mission to Nepal*, a meeting was held in an old house of Bhaktapur in 1959. A total of 30 Christians from various parts of Nepal met for the first time and decided to form a fellowship for all Nepali Christians in Nepal. The Nepal Christian Fellowship (NCF) was to aid in the formation of local churches and to meet annually to help coordinate Christian work in Nepal.

NCF's annual gatherings gave the growing young indigenous churches encouragement and a sense of solidarity in the face of increasing persecution beginning in 1960. The formation of NCF as a loose fellowship of churches helped to avoid the introduction of denominations into Nepal and allowed the churches to mature in an indigenous manner. Gradually NCF took on the role of providing leadership training. Evangelists were hired and annual regional conferences organized to provide Bible* teaching for the growing number of new Christians. A constitution and basis of faith were approved in 1980.

NCF, now called National Churches Fellowship of Nepal (NCFN), became a member of the Evangelical Fellowship of Asia and of the World Evangelical Fellowship* in 1988. It is estimated that 30% of Nepal's total population of 20 million people have heard the Gospel, approximately 330,000 (1%) are Christians, and about 1,500 churches and fellowship groups exist countrywide. NCFN has set a goal of reaching the whole nation with the Gospel and of establishing at least 8,000 churches, in joint cooperation and partnership with individual churches, church groups, parachurch organizations, and various missions and mission agencies.

Bibliography

Lindell, Jonathan, *Nepal and the Gospel of God* (1979).

SIMON PANDEY

Nepal, Law and Freedom of Religion in

Except for a brief period in the mid-1700s when there was a Catholic mission in the Kathmandu Valley, Nepal* was closed to Christianity until the 1950s. Even then, the law of the land was designed to protect Hinduism*, and conversion "of anyone of Hindu race" to "foreign religions, such as Christianity or Islam," was expressly forbidden. With the revision of the Mulki Ain (National Law Code) in 1963, this was slightly changed so that it was a crime not only to convert Hindus, but also "to disrupt the traditional religion of the Hindu community in Nepal." Personal conversion carried a penalty of one year's imprisonment; it was three years for attempting to convert another, six years for actually converting another, and expulsion from the country of any foreign national engaged in such activities. Where conversion was effected, it was to be "invalidated, and such a person shall remain in his Hindu religion." When the law was again revised in 1992, the penalty for personal conversion was removed. In the 1962 Constitution of Nepal, and again in the new 1990 Constitution, the fundamental right of every person "to profess his own religion as handed down from ancient times" was affirmed, but not the right of conversion. However, in 1990 the right of every religious community "to maintain its independent existence" and "to manage and protect its religious sites and trusts" was defined.

Since the arrest of three men in Nepalganj in 1958, at least 400 Nepali Christians have suffered terms of imprisonment for their faith. In the most widely known early case, nine men and women were arrested in 1960 at a baptism in Tansen; eight served a one-year term, and Pastor Prem Pradhan was sentenced to six years, of which he served four and was then given a pardon by the king. Harassment and sometimes torture by local officials have forced many to renounce Christianity. Raids and closure of Christian meetings, threats and severe social pressure were not unusual. In 1976 both Operation Mobilization and the Summer Institute of Linguistics personnel were ordered out of the country. In spite of this, the church took root and the number of national Christians grew from fewer than 10 in the early 1950s to over 25,000 in the 1980s.

With the change of government and the advent of democracy in 1990, a new emphasis on human rights and a new spirit of freedom began to prevail. Thirty people serving jail sentences on conversion-related charges and nearly another 200 with cases pending in different courts were all granted amnesty. Thus in the 1990s churches began to experience greater freedom than ever; large public meetings began to be publicized and held, and local Christian radio programs broadcast. Despite sporadic harassment and some new legal cases, Nepali Christians are enjoying the greatest religious freedom they have had in centuries. This is reflected in ever-expanding Christian activities, growth of the churches, and increasing involvement in the social-development sphere. However, the law concerning the right of every religious denomination to maintain its independent existence has still not been fully implemented. No Christian organization has yet been allowed to register using the term "Christian" in its title.

Bibliography

Metzler, Edgar, *Guidelines for Religious Activities of Expatriate Christians* (1994). • Perry, Cindy, *The History of the Expansion of Protestant Christianity among the Nepali Diaspora* (1994). • Shah, Rishikesh, *Politics in Nepal, 1980-1990* (1990). • *Himal*, Vol. 6.5 (1993).

G. JACOBS BLESSON

Nestorian Church (East Syrian Church)

Commonly called the Nestorian church, the "Church of the East" developed, for the most part, outside of the Roman Empire in Persia and further east in Asia. Their identification with Nestorius*, bishop of Constantinople (and later exiled heretic), has to do with their christological formulations. Both Nestorius and the Church of the East sought to protect the two natures in Christ after the incarnation in opposition to monophysites, who claimed that after the incarnation there was one nature in Jesus Christ. This "dyophysite" theology was condemned, and Nestorius was deposed by the controversial Council of Ephesus (431).

The dyophysite theology of the Church of the East can be traced to the early theological tradition from Antioch. The Antiochene school tended to be more literal in its exegesis, as opposed to the highly allegorical interpretations that developed in Alexandria, Egypt. There was a direct line in the development of theology in Asia in the first centuries of the Common Era. The writings of Diodore of Tarsus (d. 393?) and Theodore of Mospuestia* (ca. 350-428), along with the philosophy of Aristotle, were translated into Syriac in the early centuries, providing a basic orientation to theological development for the monasteries, churches, and theological schools that developed in Persia, India*, and along the Silk Route. Theodore was Nestorius's teacher, so he passed on the same exegetical approach and christological concerns. Although the Western churches have, since 431, identified "Nestorianism" as a heresy, in fact the theology is nearly identical with that of Chalcedon (451), and Nestorius himself felt vindicated when, in exile, he heard of the decisions of the council.

Once the theology of the Church of the East was condemned by the other churches (monophysites as well as the "Orthodox"), it was easier for these Asian churches to establish their own identity as Persian churches. Thus both the political and ecclesiastical developments of the 3rd through 6th cs. created an Asian church with an identity that became less and less "Roman." This Asian church not only developed its own theology but also different views on marriage, spirituality, worship, and liturgy; it spoke a different language; and it developed its own monastic and theological schools. The Church of the East suffered great persecutions under the Sasanian Empire of Persia (beginning 226 C.E.) but continued to preach to its Zoroastrian* and pagan neighbors and planted both monasteries and churches from Persia to the Pacific.

Nestorianism in China. Reliable evidence indicates that China's first contact with Christianity was through Nestorian *(Jing Jiao)* missionaries (see China). In 1625, during excavation work for a building in Shaanxi, the Xian Monument was unearthed. Identified as a "Nestorian" relic by the Jesuits*, it is a black stone approximately 10 feet high, four feet wide, and a foot thick with more than 1,756 Chinese characters and 70 Syrian words inscribed on one surface. The monument indicates that it was erected in 781. The inscriptions briefly describe Nestorian doctrines and trace the beginning of the Nestorian Church in China. Included is a long list of the names of Persian or Syrian missionaries. The inscriptions were composed by bishop Jing Jing (Adam), who is believed to be the son of Issu (Persian name, Yazdbozid), a Nestorian secular priest who had come from north Afghanistan (Balkh) and was a general in the Chinese army. Jing Jing helped a Buddhist scholar to translate the Buddhist *sutras* into Chinese, which could possibly explain the Buddhist terminology found on the Xian Monument.

According to the inscriptions, the Nestorian monk Alopen, from Syria (Da Jin), arrived in the capital city of Changan in 635. He was escorted by Duke Fang Xuenling, with a guard of honor, to an audience with Tang Emperor Tai Zong (626-49), who invited him into the imperial library and asked him to translate the Bible* into Chinese. The emperor allowed a monastery housing 21 monks to be built in the capital and, as a gesture of honor, allowed his portrait to be placed in it. Emperor Gao Zong (649-83), son of Tai Zong, bestowed on Alopen the title of "great patron and spiritual lord of the empire." It is uncertain whether the title was only honorific or whether Alopen had been appointed an archbishop by the Nestorian patriarch in Seleucia-Ctesiphon, Persia.

With the exception of Empress Wu (690-705), who favored Buddhism at the expense of the Nestorians and Manichaens, the early Tang emperors were tolerant toward the Nestorian Church, which they referred to as the *Jing Jiao* (the luminous or illustrious religion). It was also called the Messiah religion. Under Emperor Xuan Zong (712-56), new missionaries came from Persia in 744. In 745 the Chinese officially referred to the faith as the "Syrian religion *(Da Jin)*." During the An Lushan rebellion (755-57), Issu won favor for the church when he helped suppress the insurrection. Issu was also noted for his benevolence to the poor and the sick. From the documents discovered in 1907 in the Dunhuang caves on the Old Silk Route, Bishop Jin Jing, well versed in Chinese and a prolific translator, had evidently translated the Gospels, portions of Acts, Paul's Epistles, and the Psalms. He also translated the Syriac "Gloria in Excelsis Deo."

The tide turned against the church in the 9th c. under Emperor Wu Zong (840-46). He was a staunch Daoist, and all foreign religions suffered. He began by persecuting the Manicheans in 843, and he passed a second edict in 845 that decreed the closure of Buddhist, Zoroastrian, and Nestorian temples and monasteries. Monks, nuns, and priests were forced to return to secular life and pay taxes. Foreign personnel were expelled. By the 10th c. Christianity was practically extinct in the Chinese Empire.

The Nestorian mission returned to the Chinese Empire in the 13th c. under the Mongol rulers, who set up the Yuan dynasty. (This dynasty is officially dated 1280-1368 by the Chinese, although Khubilai Khan was ruler of most of China by 1260. Mongol history dates the dynasty to Genghis Khan in 1206.) The Yuan rulers were tolerant of all religions. Nestorian missionaries from China had earlier brought Christianity to the tribes in Central Asia and Xinjinang. The Uighurs, Naimans, Onguts, and many Mongols had become Christians. Khubilai Khan's mother, Princess Sorocan (Sorkatani), belonged to a Christian tribe, the Kerait, which was converted en masse in the 11th c. In 1235 there were a Nestorian church and a theological school in Khanbaliq (Beijing), the Mongol capital. Khanbaliq became the seat of a metropolitan see. By 1289 Khubilai had established a special office, the *Zongfu*, to look after Nestorian affairs. According to the Archbishop of Soltania, there were more than 30,000 wealthy Nestorians in China by 1330. The *History of the Yuan* recorded that there were 72 Nestorian churches in China between 1289 and 1320. The *Topography of Zhenjiang District* recorded that there were 23 Christian families with 166 members and 109 slaves in Zhenjiang, Jiangsu. They were referred to as "alien residents." Mar Sargis, a Christian doctor from Samarkand who was appointed governor by Khubilai in 1277, built six monasteries in Zhenjiang and one in Hangzhou.

When the Yuan dynasty fell to the Mings, the Nestorian Church once again disappeared from the Chinese Empire.

Bibliography

Burkitt, F. C., *Early Eastern Christianity* (1904). • Fiey, J.-M., *Jalons pour une historie de l'eglise en Iraq* (1970); *Communautes Syriaques en Iran et Iraq des origins a 1552* (1969). • Chabot, J.-B., ed. and trans., *Synodicon orientale our Recueil de synods nestoriens* (1902). • Drijvers, Han J. W., *East of Antioch: Forces and Structures in the Development of Early Syriac Theology* (1984). • Labourt, J., *Le Christianisme dans l'empire Perse sous la dynastie Perse* (1904). • Vine, A. R., *The Nestorian Churches* (1937). • Wigram, W. A., *An Introduction to the History of the Assyrian Church; or the Church of the Sassanid Persian Empire, 100-640 A.D.* (1910). • Moffett, Samuel Hugh, *Christianity in Asia*, Vol. I: *Beginnings to 1500* (1992). • Cary-Elwes, Columba, *China and the Cross* (1957). • Lee Shu Keung, *The Cross and the Lotus* (1971). • Covell, Ralph, *Confucius, Buddha and Christ* (1986). • Saeki, P. Y., *The Nestorian Monument in China* (1916). • Moule, A. C., *Christians in China before the Year 1550* (reprinted 1972). • Foster, J., *The Church of the Tang Dynasty* (1939).

SCOTT W. SUNQUIST and THE CHINA GROUP

Nestorian Church, China

(Jing Jiao) The Nestorians (more accurately, East Syrian Christians) were followers of Archbishop Nestorius* of Constantinople, student of Theodore of Mopsuestia*. They were condemned as heretics by the Roman Catholic Church* at the controversial Council of Ephesus in 431 for emphasizing the two distinct persons in Christ, one human and the other divine. The condemnation was based on their rejecting the term "Mother of God" and preferring instead "Mother of Christ" for the Virgin Mary.

Reliable evidence indicates that China's first contact with Christianity was through East Syrian missionaries. In 1625, during excavation work at a building in Shaanxi, the Xian Monument was unearthed. Identified as a Nestorian relic by the Jesuits*, it is a black stone approximately 10 feet high, four feet wide, and a foot thick with more than 1,756 Chinese characters and 70 Syrian words inscribed on one surface. The monument indicates it was erected in 781. The inscriptions briefly describe Nestorian doctrines and trace the beginning of the Nestorian Church in China. Included is a long list of the names of Persian or Syrian missionaries. The inscriptions were composed by Bishop Jing Jing (Adam), who is believed to be the son of Issu (Persian name, Yazdbozid), a Nestorian secular priest who had come from north Afghanistan (Balkh) and was a general in the Chinese army. Jing Jing helped a Buddhist scholar to translate the Buddhist sutras into Chinese, a factor which could possibly explain the Buddhist terminology found on the Xian Monument.

According to the inscriptions, the Nestorian monk Alopen, from Syria (Da Jin), arrived in the capital city of Changan in 635. He was escorted by Duke Fang Xuenling, with a guard of honor, to an audience with Tang emperor Tai Zong (626-49), who invited him into the imperial library and asked him to translate the Bible* into Chinese. The emperor allowed a monastery housing 21 monks to be built in the capital and, as a gesture of honor, permitted his portrait to be placed in it. Emperor Gao Zong (649-83), son of Tai Zong, bestowed upon Alopen the title of "great patron and spiritual lord of the empire." It is uncertain whether the title was only honorific or whether Alopen had been appointed an archbishop by the Nestorian patriarch in Seleucia-Ctesiphon, Persia.

With the exception of Empress Wu (690-705), who favored Buddhism* at the expense of the Nestorians and Manichaeans*, the early Tang emperors were tolerant toward the Nestorian Church, which they referred to as the *Jing Jiao* (the luminous or illustrious religion). It was also called the Messiah religion. Under Emperor Xuan Zong (712-56), new missionaries came from Persia in 744. In 745, the Chinese officially referred to the faith as the Syrian religion *(Da Jin)*. During the An Lushan rebellion (755-57), Issu won favor for the church by helping suppress the insurrection. Issu was also noted for his benevolence to the poor and the sick. Documents discovered in 1907 in the Dunhuang caves on the Old Silk Route indicate that Bishop Jin Jing, well versed in Chinese and a prolific translator, had translated the Gospels, portions of Acts, Paul's Epistles, and the Psalms. He also translated the Syriac "Gloria in Excelsis Deo."

The tide turned against the church in the 9th c. under Emperor Wu Zong (840-46). He was a staunch Taoist (see Taoism), and all foreign religions suffered. He began by persecuting the Manichaeans in 843 and passed a second edict in 845 which decreed the closure of Buddhist, Zoroastrian*, and Nestorian temples and monasteries. Monks, nuns, and priests were forced to return to secular life and pay taxes. Foreign personnel were expelled. By the 10th c., Christianity was practically extinct in the Chinese Empire.

The Nestorian mission returned to the Chinese empire in the 13th c. under the Mongol* rulers, who set up the Yuan Dynasty. (This dynasty is officially dated 1280-1368 by the Chinese, although Kublai Khan was ruler of most of China by 1260. Mongol history dates the dynasty to Genghis Khan in 1206.) The Yuan rulers were tolerant of all religions. Nestorian missionaries from China had earlier brought Christianity to the tribes in Central Asia and Xinjinang. The Uighurs, Naimans, Onguts, and many Mongols had become Christians. Kublai Khan's mother, Princess Sorocan (Sorkatani), belonged to a Christian tribe, the Kerait, which was converted en masse in the 11th c. In 1235, there were a Nestorian church and a theological school in Khanbaliq (Beijing), the Mongol capital. Khanbaliq became the seat of a metropolitan see. By 1289, Kublai had established a special office, the *Zongfu,* to look after Nestorian affairs. According to the archbishop of Soltania, there were more than 30,000 wealthy Nestorians in China by 1330. The *History of the Yuan* recorded that there were 72 Nestorian churches in China between 1289 and 1320. The *Topography of Zhenjiang District* recorded that there were 23 Christian families with 166 members and 109 slaves in Zhenjiang, Jiangsu. They were referred to as alien residents. Mar Sargis, a Christian doctor from Samarkand who was appointed governor by Kublai in 1277, built six monasteries in Zhenjiang and one in Hangzhou.

When the Yuan Dynasty fell to the Mings, the Nestorian Church once again disappeared from the Chinese Empire.

Bibliography

Moffett, Samuel Hugh, *Christianity in Asia,* Vol. I, *Beginnings to 1500* (1992). • Cary-Elwes, Columba, *China and the Cross* (1957). • Lee Shu Keung, *The Cross and the Lotus* (1971). • Covell, Ralph, *Confucius, Buddha and Christ* (1986). • Labourt, J., *Le Christianisme dans l'empire perse sous la dynastie sassanide* (1904). • Saeki, P. Y., *The Nestorian Monument in China* (1916). • Moule, A. C., *Christians in China before the Year 1550* (1972). • Foster, J., *The Church of the Tang Dynasty* (1939).

China Group

Nestorian Monument. *See* Nestorian Church (East Syrian Church); Nestorian Church, China

Nestorius

(b. ca. 381; d. Upper Egypt, ca. 451). Bishop, theologian, and preacher.

Originally from Germanicia in Syria Euphratensis, Nestorius entered a monastery in Antioch, where he developed a theology along the Antiochene school pattern. It is very likely that he studied under Theodore of Mopsuestia*. Nestorius became well known because of his preaching, and so in 428 he was consecrated bishop of Constantinople at the insistence of Theodosius II in spite of the opposition of local church leaders. Wanting to identify himself immediately with what he understood to be the orthodox school, Nestorius began preaching against various heresies. One "heresy" Nestorius identified was the use of the term *theotokos* ("God-bearer") for Mary. Nestorius reasoned that Mary did not carry within her "God," but she bore the human Jesus, so she could be called *anthropotokos* or *Christotokos.* Nestorius was concerned to prevent the humanity and divinity of Jesus from becoming confused. He reasoned that theological statements must be clear in expressing that Jesus was fully human and fully divine, but these two natures *(ousiai)* must be kept distinct in the one person *(prosopon).* When he preached against the use of the commonly accepted *theotokos,* in support of the emperor's chaplain, Anastasius, a great and violent controversy erupted in the capital. In the midst of a period of increasing devotion to the mother of Jesus, Nestorius not only alienated the masses but also many church leaders, who then enlisted Cyril, the patriarch of Alexandria (412-44). Cyril, a product of the more Neoplatonic and allegorical tradition of Alexandria, was a formidable foe. Both bishops were involved in a struggle, not only for personal authority but also for the supremacy of their own school's teaching over the See of Constantinople. Who would control the important see at the center of the empire? Concern for worldly power clouded the concern for theological clarity.

In Aug of 430, Pope Celestine of Rome condemned Nestorius's teachings. Nestorius was given 10 days to retract teachings that had brought 12 anathemas against him. The emperor called a general council to meet in Ephesus in Jun 431. The council deposed Nestorius, the emperor accepted the ruling, and Nestorius was returned to his monastery in Antioch. In 435 his books were all condemned, and in 436 he was banished to Upper Egypt, where he died after some 15 years. Later historians have evaluated Nestorius's reaction to *theotokos* as rather strong, if not extreme, but at the same time his theology of Jesus was misrepresented by Cyril and other detractors.

Of special concern to the church in Asia is the connection between the banishment of Nestorius and the dyophysite ("two nature") doctrine and the spread of churches loyal to this school in Persia. These East Syrian churches are often misnamed "Nestorian"* by Western churches.

Bibliography

Driver, G. R., and L. Hodgson, eds. and trans., *Nestorius: The Bazaar of Heracleides* (1925). • Bethune-Baker, J. F., *Nestorius and His Teaching* (1908). • Loofas, F., *Nestorius and His place in the History of Christian Doctrine* (1914). • Turner, H. E. W., "Nestorius Reconsidered," *Studia Patristica,* Vol. 13 (1975).

Scott W. Sunquist

Nevius Methods

The early missionaries to Korea* felt a need for advice on mission strategy from a more experienced missionary. They approached the board of foreign missions of their home churches, which arranged for John L. Nevius* (1829-93) to go to Korea. Nevius had graduated from Princeton Theological Seminary in 1854 and worked as a missionary in China for many years. He wrote a number of articles on mission strategy for the *Chinese Recorder,* a missionary magazine.

Nevius arrived in Korea in Jun 1890 and stayed for two weeks. He lectured on the methods of mission work and the planting and development of missionary churches to the Federal Council of Protestant Evangelical Missionaries. His basic principles may be summed up as the Three-Self principles: self-support, self-government, and self-propagation. He insisted that the Korean Church should not depend on other churches.

In regard to methodology, Nevius advised that each convert ought to be a witness for Christ in his or her respective chosen field and area of work and that each one should be self-supporting. A church should be developed only to the extent that the local converts will be able to manage and support it on their own. Whenever and wherever possible, the church ought to set aside the better-qualified personnel for evangelistic work among their neighbors. Church buildings should be designed, built, and financed by the local Christian communities without depending on foreign funds.

In his book *The Korean Church and the Nevius Methods,* C. A. Clark provides an exposition of the Nevius Plan as it applied to Korea. Mission growth was achieved through wide itineration for personal evangelism. Self-propagation was achieved through the "layering method": each individual Christian learned from someone more qualified and taught another learner. Self-government was evident in that each group had its own chosen unpaid leaders and each circuit its own paid helpers who would later yield to pastors. Self-support was practiced when local believers provided for their own chapels, and each group, as soon as it was founded, contributed toward the salary of the circuit helper.

Group leaders and circuit helpers guided believers in systematic Bible study. Strict discipline was enforced by the application of biblical penalties. There were cooperation and union with other bodies or at least territorial divisions and noninterference in the policies of churches in other regions. There was a spirit of general helpfulness in the economic life of the people.

The Nevius Principles helped the Korean church to grow rapidly and also to form early on a Korean Christian culture and mind. Within only 20 years of the arrival of the first Protestant missionaries, a Korean presbytery was founded, with the majority of leadership being Korean.

Bibliography

Clark, C. A., *The Korean Church and the Nevius Methods* (1930). • Rhodes, H. A., ed., *History of the Korea Mission of the Presbyterian Church U.S.A., 1884-1934* (1934). • Paik, George L., *The History of Protestant Missions in Korea, 1832-1910* (1971). • Min Kyoung Bae, *Hankook Kidok' kiohoe-sa* (History of the Korean Church) (1993). • Underwood, H. G., *The Call of Korea* (1908).

Kim In Soo

Nevius, John Livingston

(b. Seneca, New York, 1829; d. Yantai, China, 1893). American missionary of the Presbyterian Church USA (North) to China*; evangelist, teacher, and author.

Nevius lost his father as an infant. He lived with his grandparents as a teenager and attended the Dutch Reformed Church in Ovid, New York, with his grandfather. After studying at the Ovid Academy for seven years, he entered Union College, Schenectady, New York, as a sophomore in 1845. He graduated in 1848 and headed for Georgia the following year to "seek his fortune," much to the disappointment of his mother. Thirteen months after his arrival, however, he decided to enter the ministry. He enrolled at Princeton Theological Seminary in 1850, and was accepted by the Board of Missions as a candidate for China in 1853.

In that same year he was also ordained and married to Helen Coan. They left from Boston and arrived in Ningbo, Zhejiang, in the spring of 1854, where Nevius was able to preach and teach in Chinese after one year. His wife returned home in 1856 because of ill health. She rejoined him in 1858 when, because of rebel activity, they sought refuge in Japan for eight months.

After the Tianjin Treaty (1860), Nevius decided to move his operations to Yantai (Chefoo), Shandong. Nevius and his wife returned to the United States in 1864. He received his doctorate in theology from Union College and returned to China in 1869 to teach at the new theological school in Hangzhou.

After the Tianjin massacre (1870), the couple moved to Yantai. Between 1872 and 1881, Nevius visited 60 preaching points in Shandong on horseback until a famine in 1877 provided an opportunity for relief work and penetration into the Shandong hinterland. Nevius bought an orchard, introduced new varieties of fruit, and helped improve local species. Poor health again forced his wife to return home in 1879, and Nevius followed in 1880.

Returning to China in 1882, Nevius resumed his itinerant ministry, usually with another missionary. Every summer he led a Bible school in his home for 30 to 40 men from the rural areas. He taught five hours daily. At the Second Decennial Missionary Conference in Shanghai* (1890), Nevius was invited to speak on his missionary method. On his way home for furlough, he stopped in Korea for two weeks and shared his method with the Presbyterian missionaries there. They adopted his method as mission policy, and new missionaries had to pass an examination based on his booklet.

The Nevius Method.* The approach of Nevius may be summed up as the Three-Self Principles: self-support, self-government, and self-propagation. The key is for each convert to become a witness for Christ in his or her respective chosen field and area of work. Each believer is both a teacher of someone and a learner from someone better qualified. The "layering method" that Nevius invented means that each group of believers, under the care of unpaid leaders, contributes toward the salary of a circuit helper who trains them in systematic Bible studies. The circuit helper later yields to a pastor. Circuit training is conducted to produce district, provincial, and national leaders. Churches should be designed, built, and financed by the locals themselves, with no dependence on foreign funds for pastors. Discipline is enforced by the application of biblical penalties. Nevius stressed cooperation and union with other bodies or at least territorial divisions and noninterference in lawsuits or similar matters. He advocated a spirit of general helpfulness in the economic life of the people. The adoption of the Nevius method helped the churches in Korea* to grow rapidly and retain their Korean identity.

Nevius died of a heart attack in Yantai at age 64. His writings included a commentary on the Gospel of St. Mark, *China and the Chinese, Methods of Mission Work,* and *Demon Possession and Allied Themes.*

Bibliography

Anderson, Gerald H., et al., eds., *Mission Legacies* (1994). • Clark, C. A., *The Korean Church and the Nevius Methods* (1930). • Rhodes, H. A., ed., *History of the Korea Mission Presbyterian Church U.S.A., 1884-1934* (1934). • Paik, George L., *The History of Protestant Missions in Korea, 1832-1910* (1971). • Min Kyoung Bae, *Hankook Kidok' kiohoe-sa* (History of the Korean Church) (1993). • Underwood, H. G., *The Call of Korea* (1908). • Chao, Samuel H., *John Livingston Nevius, 1829-1893: A Historical Study of His Life and Methods* (1996).

Kim In Soo and the China Group

New Religious Movements. *See* Cults

Newbigin, (James Edward) Lesslie

(b. 8 Dec 1909; d. 30 Jan 1998). Leader during the middle and latter part of the 20th c. in the Asian church, in the ecumenical* movement, and in serious theological reflection on the church's mission.

After his ordination and missionary commissioning in 1936 by the Church of Scotland (though English by birth and education), Newbigin served for almost four decades in India*. Upon his arrival there, he quickly became one of the architects of the church union that resulted in the Church of South India* (CSI) (1947). One of his earliest books, *The Reunion of the Church: A Defence of the South India Scheme,* gave a theological rationale for the visible unity of the church, a theme which became characteristic in his extensive work within ecumenical circles. That book led to his more complete ecclesiological work, *The Household of God* (1953). Numerous articles on the theme of unity (e.g., "What Is a 'Local Church Truly United'?" and "The Form and Structure of the Visible Unity of the Church") illustrate his influence on the language of ecumenical debate, especially during the 1960s and 1970s.

When the new CSI elected its first bishops in 1947, Newbigin was among them. He served first as bishop of Ramnad-Madurai (1947-59) and later as bishop of Madras (1965-74). From 1959 until 1965, he was seconded by the CSI to the International Missionary Council (IMC) (1959-61) and the World Council of Churches (WCC) (1961-65). During those years, he guided the integration of the IMC into the WCC and served as the first director of the Division (later Commission) of World Mission and Evangelism, which was formed at the WCC New Delhi Assembly in 1961.

Upon his retirement from service in India in 1974, Newbigin returned to England and again took up membership in the United Reformed Church, serving as its moderator in 1978-79. He taught ecumenics and the theology of mission at Selly Oak Colleges from 1974 to 1979, during which time his most important articulation of a theology of mission *(The Open Secret)* was written. From the early 1980s until his death in 1998, he was the guiding force behind The Gospel and Our Culture movement in Britain and other Western societies, fostering for the churches of the West a sense of the missionary encounter of the Gospel with their own culture.

Newbigin was a prodigious author, publishing hundreds of articles and more than 30 books. Among them, some that are lesser known outside of India may be the most significant. Western readers became very familiar with *A South India Diary* (1951) and *The Good Shepherd* (1974), which made vivid his work as pastor and then as pastor to pastors. Lesser known are works addressing the Indian audience: *Sin and Salvation* (1956), a catechesis of sorts, two-thirds of it written in Tamil and the remainder in English, published in both languages; *The Holy Spirit and the Church* (1972), addresses given at a convention in Madras; and *Christ Our Eternal Contemporary* (1968) and *Journey into Joy* (1972), each representing lectures given at the Christian Medical College at Vellore to a mixed group of Christian and Hindu staff and students. Here the character of Newbigin's own evangelizing is perhaps most evident.

The religiously plural — albeit largely Hindu — setting of India shaped the way Newbigin would later engage the religiously plural (he would say dominantly "pagan") societies of the West. His personal engagement in dialogue with Hindu scholars, reading and discussing alternately the Gospel of John and the Upanishads, led both to his commentary on that Gospel *(The Light Has Come)* and to the approach articulated in the much republished article "The Basis, Purpose and Manner of Interreligious Dialogue." In the West, he encouraged missionary dialogue as the needed style for witness, a style maintaining "proper confidence" in the "uniqueness of Jesus Christ" while remaining open to the surprises and conversions the Spirit continues to bring. His books *Foolishness to the Greeks* (1986) and *The Gospel in a Pluralist Society* (1989) initiated a broad movement toward a new missional vision among the churches of the West.

Newbigin's major contribution was to articulate a rationale for mission in the culturally and religiously plural world of the late 20th c. and to ground it in the biblical account of the character, actions, and purposes of God. In that, he has been an apologist for the Gospel, providing a way to believe it within a postmodern context, and for the Christian mission, providing confidence for giving witness to the unique revelation of God in Christ.

Bibliography

Newbigin, Lesslie, *The Household of God* (1953); *Honest Religion for Secular Man* (1966); *The Open Secret: Sketches for a Missionary Theology* (1978); *Unfinished Agenda: An Autobiography* (1985); *Foolishness to the Greeks: The Gospel and Western Culture* (1986); *The Gospel in a Pluralist Society* (1989). • Hunsberger, George R., *Bearing the Witness of the Spirit: Lesslie Newbigin's Theology of Cultural Plurality* (1998).

George R. Hunsberger

Ng Chiong Hui

(Chang Hue Hwang, Shoki Coe) (b. Chiong-hoa, Taiwan, 20 Aug 1914; d. England, 27 Oct 1988). Pioneer Taiwanese theologian recognized worldwide as a scholar, ecumenical leader, and theological educator.

A third-generation Christian in Taiwan*, Ng was the son of a Christian preacher and one of the few Taiwanese students in his time to receive an overseas education. He studied philosophy at Tokyo University (1934-37) and theology at Westminster College, England (1938-41). He returned from England with his English wife after World War II*, when Taiwan was liberated from 50 years of Japanese imperial rule, only to face a new dictatorial regime under the Kuomintang from China. In the so-called 2/28 Incident (28 Feb 1947), more than 20,000 Taiwanese elite were either massacred by Chinese nationalists or ended up missing without a trace. Under this hardship Ng was the first Taiwanese to be appointed principal of Tainan Theological College by the southern synod of the Presbyterian* Church in Taiwan since the founding of the college in 1865. During the Japanese occupation, the college had been forced to close for eight years.

Ng served as principal from 1947 to 1965, during which time he was elected twice as the moderator of the Presbyterian Church in Taiwan (PCT). In 1965, when the church celebrated its centenary, Ng dedicated the fruitful missionary result of the Doubling Movement* (PKU). He also accepted the invitation of the World Council of Churches (WCC) to join the Theological Education Fund (TEF, 1965-79), and later he became director of the TEF.

One of Ng's most significant contributions in theological education was his proposition on the methodology of contextualization* for Third World theologies. He advocated a shift from the static concept of indigenization to the dynamic process of contextualization*, that is, an interaction between the text and the context. He explained: "By Contextuality we mean the wrestling with God's word in such a way that the power of the incarnation, which is the divine form of contextualization, can enable us to follow his steps to contextualize" (*Theological Education* 11 [1974]). He stated that the task of theological education is threefold: Christian formation, theological formation, and ministerial formation. During his term in the TEF, he and other Asian church leaders worked together to form the regional association for theological education in Asia and also established the South East Asia Graduate School of Theology (SEAGST) to develop further the concept of contextualization.

When Taiwan was expelled from the United Nations, the Presbyterian Church in Taiwan issued a statement in 1971 which insisted that the future of Taiwan should be determined by its own inhabitants and which demanded a democratic reform of its political system. Ng and three other Taiwanese exiles, Ng Bu Tong, Lim Chong Gi, and Song Choan Seng*, organized the Formosa Christians for Self-Determination to support the position of the Presbyterian Church in Taiwan vis-à-vis the government. Though started outside Taiwan, the self-determination movement had an enormous impact on political developments in Taiwan and was also significant to later efforts in constructing contextual theology in Taiwan.

Exiled for 22 years, Ng was granted permission to return in the summer of 1987 through the efforts of the Presbyterian Church in Taiwan. Ng saw himself as a lecturer, not a writer. His active participation in theological education, church ministry, and the democratic political movement demonstrated that he was a theologian of praxis, faithfully practicing the concept of contextualization throughout his life.

Bibliography

Ng Chiong Hui, *The Oral Biography of Ng Chiong Hui* (1990) (in Chinese). • Shoki Coe, *Recollections and Reflections*, 2nd ed. (1993). • World Council of Churches, *Dictionary of the Ecumenical Movement* (1991).

Huang Po Ho

Ng Ho Lee

(b. 1888; d. 1979). Ng first came to Singapore* in 1913 to take up a teaching post. He joined the Anglican St. Andrew's Mission in 1916 as a catechist-in-training (part-time) at the invitation of catechist Dong Bing Seng* and others. Moving on to China*, he spent a year at a seminary in Kulangsu, Fukien. He was then made a deacon in 1924 and posted to St. Paul's Church, Penang. He returned to Singapore in 1926 and was ordained the first Hokkien-speaking priest in 1927. He served the Hokkien congregation at St. Peter's Church, Stamford Road, as well as St. John's Church, Jurong. When the Hokkien- and Foochow-speaking congregations at St. Peter's moved to a new site because of government requisition of the land and formed the Holy Trinity Church, Ng continued as the priest in charge of the Hokkien-speaking congregation until his retirement in 1956.

Bibliography

Sng, Bobby E. K., *In His Good Time* (1993).

John Chew

Ngo Dinh Diem

(b. Hue, Vietnam, 1901; d. Nov 1963). Catholic president of South Vietnam killed in a coup d'état.

The third son of Ngo Dinh Kha, a high-ranking official in the court of Hue, Diem graduated from the Hue School of the Mandarinate and became governor of Phan Thiet Province. Known for his integrity, competence, intelligence, and patriotism, he was appointed minister of the interior in May 1933 and head of the secretariat of the committee for reforms set up by Bao Dai. He resigned in September, as his efforts were undermined by the French and their allies at the court of Hue. He went to the United States, where he lived mainly in Boston, Massachusetts, learning, reading, and praying with the Maryknoll* Mission.

On 11 Mar 1945, Bao Dai* invited Diem to form a nationalist government, but the invitation was not answered. Either it did not clear the Japanese-controlled communication service, or Diem chose not to reply. Diem, believed to have been helped by the Kempetai (Japanese security police) when the Japanese were in authority, no longer trusted the Japanese.

On 28 Feb 1946, the French high commissioner to Indochina, Admiral D'Argenlieu (a Carmelite monk and a Gaullist), approached Diem, who replied with conditions unacceptable to the Frenchman. There was no way the civil services and the French government would admit Diem as the nationalist leader of a united Vietnam*. Earlier, Diem had been arrested by the Vietminh and exposed to the peril of disease and hunger in the northern mountains. He was later taken to Hanoi, where Ho Chi Minh tried to persuade him to enter the government. Although Diem refused, Ho thought it would be politically wise to set him free.

Diem was present at many of the 1947-48 negotiations with the French for a political solution toward the independence of Vietnam. In Feb 1948, Diem called for an assembly of nationalist leaders, including those of various sects and other religious groups, and representatives of the provincial governments in the South, to discuss in Saigon the conditions for further negotiations with France. But on 22 Mar, M. Bollaert, a radical socialist parliamentarian who replaced D'Argenlieu as high commissioner, categorically rejected the dominion status regarded by Diem as necessary for the success of an anti-Communist government in Vietnam.

In Jun 1949, Diem rejected an offer to become prime minister because "the national aspirations of the Vietnamese people will be satisfied only when our nation enjoys the same political status as India* and Pakistan."* In Jun 1954, the French agreed to Diem being the premier of South Vietnam, and he assumed office one week later in Saigon, forming his new government on 7 Jul 1954 and facing the daunting task of devising a workable political apparatus, reviving the national economy, resettling some 900,000 refugees from the North, and bringing order and stability to a country near socio-economic collapse.

By early Oct 1955, Diem had effectively extended his authority by neutralizing the dissident sects and groups. The referendum of 23 Oct 1955 made him the president of the new Republic of Vietnam, but he was confronted by the Communists, who formed the National Front for the Liberation of South Vietnam in Dec 1960. His difficulties were compounded by widespread civil disturbances, especially by Buddhist groups who regarded Diem's policies as anti-Buddhist and discriminatory. His government was accused of being dictatorial, nepotic, and suppressive. The fact, however, was that there were secret negotiations going on between Diem and Communist representatives for a gradual reunification of Vietnam without the intervention of foreign powers. This political maneuver led to a coup d'état by the nationalists, aided by the Americans, on 1 Nov 1963, which resulted in Diem's violent death.

Anthony Do Huu Nghiem

Ngo Dinh Thuc

(b. Phu Cam, Hue, Thue Thien Province, Vietnam, 6 Oct 1897; d. Europe, 1995). Archbishop of Hue, elder brother of South Vietnamese president Ngo Dinh Diem*.

Ngo's father, Ngo Dinh Kha, a minister at the imperial court of Hue, had studied at the Roman Catholic seminary in Penang. Thuc enrolled at Hue Pellerin College, run by the La Salle Brothers*. He continued at An Ninh minor seminary and Phu Xuan major seminary in the diocese of Hue. In 1919, Bishop Allys sent him to study in Rome, where he earned his doctor of theology and philosophy degree. After his ordination as priest in 1925, he did one year of doctoral studies in ecclesiastical law at the Apollinary University and went on to study literature at the Catholic Institute of Paris.

Thuc returned to Hue in 1929 to teach at Sacred Heart School and, two years later, became a professor at Phu Xuan major seminary. In 1935, he became director of both Hue Providence School and *Sacerdos Indochinensis* monthly magazine. He was also consecrated bishop of Vinh Long diocese, which had 40 priests and 40,000 believers. Twenty-two years later, he was made archbishop of Hue until reunification in Apr 1975, when he was exiled. In exile and until his death, he traveled between Rome and Paris.

The promotion of Dinh Diem to the presidency of South Vietnam in the 1950s and Dinh Thuc's personal involvement in politics and secular affairs gave rise to scandal. Though before his death Thuc repented of some wrongdoing in his episcopal life, he and his family continue to be more condemned than praised for their actions in secular and spiritual matters.

Bibliography

Tran anh Dung, *Hang Giao Pham Cong Giao Viet Nam (1960-1995)* (1996). • Truong Ba Can, *Cong Giao Viet Nam sau qua trinh 50 nam* (1995).

Anthony Do Huu Nghiem

Nguyen Ba Tong

(b. Go Cong, Saigon, 7 Aug 1868; d. Phat Diem, 11 Jul 1949). First Vietnamese Catholic bishop after more than 300 years of mission work in Vietnam*.

A South Vietnamese with 18 years experience as a parish priest and 19 years as the secretary of the diocese of Saigon when elected to be a bishop in North Vietnam, Nguyen Ba Tong was an important symbol of unification between the politically divided North and South. An excellent pastor who wanted "to live and to die" with his flocks, he guided the diocese of Phat Diem in the tradition of Cu Sau (Tran van Luc*) to become one of the most important dioceses in Vietnam.

Following a decree by Pope Pius XI on 7 May 1932 to entrust the highest office in Vietnam to a local, Nguyen Ba Tong was ordained on 11 Jun 1933 by the pope himself at St. Peter's Cathedral in Rome. On 20 Oct 1945, he was made bishop of Phat Diem after two years as vice-bishop. Keen on "Vietnamizing" the Catholic Church, he developed the minor seminary Phuc Nhac and the major seminary Thuong Kiem to provide the necessary manpower for the future. He restored the Sisters of the Cross, initiated by his predecessor Alexandre Marcou (Thanh), as a diocesan order with an important role in every parish. Convinced of the importance of prayer in mission, he invited the contemplative orders from Hue to form new houses, e.g., the Carmelite Sisters in Tri Chinh and Citeaux in Chau Son. His successor, Bishop Le Huu Tu, was the abbot of Chau Son.

Under Nguyen, pastoral care extended beyond the confines of the church. He built the dike, Kim Tung, to prevent flooding and to gain more land for cultivation. He also built the first theater, Nam Thanh, where some of his plays, such as "Jesus' Passion" *(Tuong Thuong Kho),* were performed because he believed it was important to foster culture. This innovative passion play is still performed during Holy Week in many South Vietnamese parishes.

Bibliography

Nguyen Trong, *Les Origines du Clergé Vietnamien* (1959). • Phan Phat Huon, *Vietnam Giao Su* (1962).

Vu Kim Chinh

Nguyen Trong Tri. *See* Han Mac Tu

Nguyen Truong To

(b. Nghe-an Province, Vietnam, ca. 1830; d. 1871). Vietnamese scholar and advocate of Westernization.

Nguyen was born into a Catholic family and studied the Confucian classics at a young age with local scholars. Since Catholics were not allowed to take the Confucian civil service examinations, he found employment teaching Chinese at the La Xoai Catholic Seminary, where he came to the attention of French missionaries sent by the Foreign Mission Society, under whom he began studying Western languages and academic disciplines.

During the French invasions of Vietnam* that began in 1858, Vietnamese Catholics and European missionaries were suspected of aiding the French, so Nguyen fled the country briefly, traveling to the Foreign Mission Society's seminaries in Hong Kong* and elsewhere in Asia, where he deepened his knowledge of Western studies and languages.

Returning to Vietnam in 1861, Nguyen served the French navy in occupied southern Vietnam and contributed as translator and interpreter to the negotiations that resulted in the Treaty of Saigon (1862), according to which Vietnam agreed to cede southern Vietnamese territory, pay an indemnity, and make other concessions to France. Nguyen later regretted his cooperation with the French. He recommended to the Vietnamese emperor in Hue that the Nguyen Dynasty maintain peaceful relations with the French colonial regime installed in Saigon after 1862 while strengthening itself through Westernizing reforms.

Between 1863 and 1871, the year of his death, Nguyen sent to the Hue court more than 15 reform petitions. *Giao Mon Luan* (On Religious Sects), Mar 1863, defended the role of Vietnamese Catholics during the conquest and advocated religious freedom in Vietnam. *Thien Ha Dai The Luan* (On the World Situation), Mar-Apr 1863, argued that Vietnam had no alternative to peaceful relations with France in the short run. *Ngoi Vua la Quy; Chuc Quan la Trong* (Precious is the Throne; Respected is the Official), May 1866, advocated political and administrative reforms; *Ke Hoach Gay Nen Nhan Tai* (A Plan for Creating Men of Talent), Sep 1866, urged Western studies for training a new Vietnamese elite; and *Te Cap Bat Dieu* (Eight Urgent Matters), Nov 1867, urged reform in eight areas, including defense, education, the legal system, and fiscal policy.

While many contemporary Vietnamese scholars and officials considered all Catholic Vietnamese to be guilty of pro-French collaboration, Nguyen argued that it was possible for Vietnamese Catholics to be good Christians as well as loyal subjects of their Confucian monarch. The reigning emperor, Tu-duc, was impressed with Nguyen's learning and convinced of his sincere desire to help Vietnam regain full independence. The emperor received Nguyen's petitions, invited him to court on several occasions, and called on him for state service, notably in Jan 1867, when Nguyen and several officials were sent to France to purchase modern machinery and books and to hire French experts to come to Vietnam as instructors. Despite such evidence of imperial approbation, ultimately Nguyen's status as a Christian, his wartime contacts with the French, and his advocacy of potentially far-reaching Western-influenced transformations in Vietnamese society caused Vietnam's elite, including the emperor, to reject his suggestions for reform, which therefore had little direct impact.

Nguyen remains an important figure in the history of

Asian Christianity because he was one of the first Vietnamese to confront the question of traditional Vietnam's administrative and technological backwardness vis-à-vis the West and to formulate a program of reforms to remedy the situation. He was also one of the first to grapple with the thorny question of whether the political loyalties of Asian Christians rested with their traditional non-Christian rulers, who were often hostile to Christianity, or with the Western powers, which were Christian but often, as in the French case, imperialistic.

Bibliography

Boudarel, Georges, "Une lettre catholique qui fait un problème: Nguyen Truong To," in *Catholicisme et sociétés asiatiques,* ed. Alain Forest and Yoshiharu Tsuboi (1988). • DeFrancis, John, *Colonialism and Language Policy in Vietnam* (1977). • McLeod, Mark W., "Nguyen Truong To: A Catholic Reformer at Emperor Tu-duc's Court," *Journal of Southeast Asian Studies* 25, No. 2 (1994). • Nguyen The Anh, "Traditionalisme et Reformisme à la cour de Hue dans la seconde moitié du XIXe siècle," in *Histoire de l'Asie de Sud-est: révoltes, réformes, révolutions,* ed. Pierre Brocheux (1981). • Truong Ba Can, *Nguyen Truong To: con nguoi va di thao* (1988).

MARK W. MCLEOD

Nguyen Van Binh

(b. Saigon, 1 Sep 1910; d. 1995). Vietnamese archbishop.

When Paul Nguyen Van Binh terminated his elementary course at Taberd, the famous school run by the Brothers of the Christian Doctrine, he was admitted into the minor seminary of St. Joseph of the Saigon Vicariate. In 1932 he was sent for study to the Institute of the Propaganda Fide* in Rome and was ordained a priest there on 27 Mar 1937.

Due to his physical state, he had to return home in 1938. Isidore Dumortier, bishop of Saigon, nominated him to the post of vicar of Duc Hoa. In 1942 he quit Duc Hoa to be a teacher at the minor seminary and chaplain of the elementary and high school at Taberd. This was during the time that the patriotism of the Vietnamese people, who were under French rule, rose up and stimulated some priests such as Nguyen Ba Luat to join the National Liberation Front in 1946. In such political circumstances, Nguyen took orders from his ecclesiastic superior in 1948 to go to Cau Dar, a remote, rustic parish in the northwest of the vicariate that actually belongs to Da Lat Vicariate. In the meantime, Jean Cassaigne replaced Dumortier as bishop of Saigon.

In 1955 Cassaigne offered him the chair of professor at the major seminary, but some months later he became bishop of Can Tho, an immense vicariate newly erected in the plain of the giant Mekong River. From that time, the 46-year-old bishop traveled almost every day from Can Tho to various locations within his vicariate, such as Chau Doc, Rach Gia, Ha Tien, Soc Trang Bac Lieu, and Camau, to help the local people as well as the 1954 refugees in their spiritual and material need. Many of their complex problems, both juridical, social, and religious, could not have been solved smoothly without Nguyen's active collaboration.

On 24 Nov 1960, he was appointed archbishop of Saigon to replace Bishop Simon Nguyen Hoa Hien, who moved to Da Lat Diocese. He developed a good relationship with the government of President Ngo Dinh Diem*. From 1963 to 1975, the archbishop faced up to the extremist Buddhists led by Thich Tri Quang and the progressive Catholics led by Truong ba Can, both of whom were supported by the Communists inside and outside of the country. The purpose of the Buddhist struggle was clear: to make Buddhism* the national religion of Vietnam*. The archbishop played the role of moderator in the at-times armed conflict between Buddhists and Catholics in Saigon.

From 1975 to his death in 1995, Nguyen was surrounded by the national priests who, under the command of the Communists, interfered in his ecclesiastic administration. When he passed away, Nguyen left an archdiocese dominated by Communist perspectives.

Bibliography

Le ngoc Bich, *Cac Giam Muc Mot Thoi Da Qua* (1933-95). • Gheddo, Piero, *Catholics et Bouddhistes au Vietnam* (1968). • Phan phat Huon, *Viet Nam Giao Su Quyen II* (1962). • Tran anh Dung, *Hang giao Pham Coong Giao Viet Nam (1960-95)* (1996). • Truong Ba Can, *Duc Tong Giam muc Phao lo Nguyen van Binh* (1995).

PHAN PHAT HUON

Nha Chua

("House of God"). Vietnamese name of the celibate lay brotherhood of catechists organized by Father Alexandre de Rhodes* in ca. 1641.

Previously, indigenous catechists in the Vietnamese Catholic missions were generally married men living with their families. To approximate the Catholic priesthood, de Rhodes carefully selected and trained a group of unmarried men, whom he organized into the *nha chua.* After passing through two lower grades, members publicly took the three vows of celibacy, poverty, and obedience to the head catechist appointed by de Rhodes. The members lived a common life, all alms and gifts received from the faithful going into a common fund. They were also given rudimentary instruction in medicine, in effect making them rural health workers.

The *nha chua,* who numbered more than 100 by 1653, served as the cohesive force behind the strong organization into which the Jesuits* had gathered their Vietnamese converts. Along with Christian literature*, it was the *nha chua* which enabled the Vietnamese Christian communities to hold out even in the most dire of circumstances and persecutions from the late 17th to the 19th centuries.

Bibliography

S. Neill, *A History of Christian Missions* (1966). • Seumois, A., in *New Catholic Encyclopedia* (1967), Vol. III. • Phan, Peter, *Mission and Catechesis: Alexandre de Rhodes and Inculturation in Seventeenth-Century Vietnam* (1998). T. Valentino Sitoy, Jr.

Nichiren/Soka Gakkai

Term referring to both a Japanese Buddhist tradition (sect) and to Nichiren Daishonin (1222-82), the person who first elaborated its teachings.

The Nichiren form of Buddhism*, unlike many other traditions in Japan*, has no Chinese, Korean, or Indian antecedents. Although Nichiren initially studied in a temple belonging to the Tendai sect, his studies led him to the conviction that the Lotus Sutra *(Hokkekyo)* was the ultimate expression of the teaching of Buddha. He taught that salvation could be achieved by simply reciting the name of the Lotus Sutra with the formula *Nam Myoho Renge Kyo* (homage to the Sutra of the Lotus of True Law).

Nichiren was extremely critical of existing Buddhist schools and established his own single-practice sect. He became known for his exclusive claim for the truth of the Lotus Sutra and his view that other schools of Buddhism (Zen and Pure Land) were in error and were undermining the health of the nation. In spite of persecution, Nichiren gathered a number of followers, and the new Buddhist tradition became firmly established. Over the centuries, this tradition evolved into several different sects, which not only worshipped the Lotus Sutra, but also venerated Nichiren as the Buddha for the age of *mappo* (the "last days" of the Buddhist law), a time of social decay when all other religions have become misguided.

The teaching of Nichiren is most widely known today from the activities of *Soka Gakkai* (Society for the Creation of Value), a lay religious movement affiliated with the Nichiren Shoshu sect, founded in 1930 by Tsunesaburo Makiguchi (1871-1944) and Josei Toda (1900-1956). During the first two decades, membership growth was minimal because of government restrictions and persecution during wartime. Makiguchi, in fact, died in 1944 while serving a prison term for violating the Peace Preservation Law. Toda revived the movement after the war ended, and rapid membership growth accompanied the major population shift from rural to urban areas as Japan was rebuilt. During the early postwar years, *Soka Gakkai* was often the target of criticism for its aggressive proselytizing activities, characterized as *shakubuku* (smash and flatten).

The next phase of development softened some of the rough edges of the movement. Daisaku Ikeda, the third president, helped to create a more positive public image by stressing education, peace activities, and interreligious dialogue*. Over the years, *Soka Gakkai* has established its own private school system, which includes a university, has sponsored numerous conferences and publications, and raised funds for many humanitarian causes around the world. *Soka Gakkai* now reports a membership of 17 million, with religious activities based in 1,000 centers throughout the country. While outside observers have estimated that probably only three or four million are active members, it still represents the most powerful religious movement in contemporary Japan. In 1975, Soka Gakkai International (SGI) was established to spread the teachings of Nichiren outside Japan. Today, SGI has an organizational presence in 76 countries and claims a membership of 1.26 million drawn from 115 countries.

For most of its history, *Soka Gakkai* was a lay religious movement belonging to the Nichiren Shoshu sect. In 1991, however, after years of conflict between President Ikeda and the priestly hierarchy, *Soka Gakkai* was issued a notice of excommunication by the headquarters. *Soka Gakkai* members and lay leaders are now learning to conduct the rituals and ceremonies that once were considered the responsibility of ordained Nichiren Shoshu priests.

Soka Gakkai is widely known for its involvement in politics. According to official representatives, *Soka Gakkai* became involved politically to protect religious freedom and stem political corruption. Such activities were also an attempt to put into practice Nichiren's teaching as summarized in the phrase *rissho ankoku,* which means to establish true Buddhism and on this basis reform the country and make it secure.

Soka Gakkai first became involved in local politics in the mid-1950s, electing a member to Tokyo's prefectural assembly and 33 others to various ward assemblies. The following decade, it became directly involved in national politics, creating the *Komeito* (Clean Government Party) in 1964, with an agenda to reform politics and work for world peace. It quickly grew to become the third largest political party in the national diet.

In 1970, *Komeito* legally separated from its religious sponsor, but almost all of the party's candidates and supporters have been *Soka Gakkai* members. The story of *Soka Gakkai*'s involvements in national politics through *Komeito* has been one of political compromise. In spite of high ideals, some candidates have been unable to resist the bribery and corruption that permeate so much of Japanese electoral politics. In Dec 1994, *Komeito* was dissolved, with many of its former members joining the New Frontier Party *(Shinshinto)*. *Soka Gakkai* representatives have indicated that they will no longer support one political party but will consider the strengths of each individual candidate in future elections.

Bibliography

Fujii, Manabu, "Nichiren," in *Shapers of Japanese Buddhism,* ed. Yusen Kashiwahara and Koyu Sonoda (1994). • Inoue, Nobutaka, et al., eds., *Shinshukyo jiten* (Dictionary of the New Religions) (1990). • Metraux, Daniel,

"The Dispute Between the *Soka Gakkai* and the Nichiren Shoshu Priesthood," *Japanese Journal of Religious Studies,* Vol. 19, No. 4 (1992). • McFarland, H. Neill, *The Rush Hour of the Gods: A Study of New Religious Movements in Japan* (1967). • Shimazono Susumu, "The Expansion of Japan's New Religions into Foreign Cultures," and Shupe, Anson, "Soka Gakkai and the Slippery Slope from Militancy to Accommodation," in *Religion & Society in Modern Japan,* ed. Mark R. Mullins et al. (1993). • Watanabe, Shoko, *Japanese Buddhism: A Critical Appraisal* (1964).

MARK R. MULLINS

Nikolai. *See* Kasatkin, Nikolai (Nikorai)

Niles, Daniel Thambyrajah

(b. Tellipallai, Sri Lanka, 8 May 1908; d. Vellore, India, 17 Jul 1970). Internationally famous ecumenical* leader and Methodist theologian; teacher, evangelist, and pastor.

Niles was the son of a well-known lawyer and the grandson of a pastor and poet. He studied at the United Theological College, Bangalore (1929-33). In 1936, he began his service as a Methodist* minister in Jaffna. He was the principal of Jaffna Central College (1953-61), chairman of the Methodist Conference of Northern Sri Lanka (1954-64), chairman of the Northern District Synod (1964-68), and president of the Sri Lanka Methodist Conference from 1968 until his death in 1970. He communicated equally fluently in Sinhala, Tamil, and English and therefore became a link between the various ethnic groups in Sri Lanka.

In addition to his responsibilities in the Methodist Church, Niles was active in ecumenical organizations in Sri Lanka and abroad. In 1933, he associated with the Student Volunteer Movement*. In 1938, he attended the International Missionary Council conference at Tambaram. This conference brought him into close contact with Hendrik Kraemer*. He served as general secretary of the National Christian Council of Sri Lanka (1941-45) and was one of the initial members of the negotiating committee for church union in Sri Lanka when it was set up in 1945.

Niles preached the opening service at the World Council of Churches (WCC) organizing session in Amsterdam in 1948 and at its 1968 assembly in Uppsala, Sweden. He was chairman of the WCC's youth department (1953-59), and in 1968 he was elected one of the six presidents of the WCC, in addition to being the executive secretary of its department of evangelism (1959-70).

Niles was among the founding members of the East Asia Christian Conference (EACC) and served as its general secretary (1957-68) and chairman (1968-70). The EACC (now CCA, Christian Conference of Asia*) hymnal, for which he wrote a large number of English verse translations of Asian hymns, is still popular.

Niles was also involved in interreligious dialogue*, especially with Hinduism* and Buddhism*. His book *Buddhism and the Claims of Christ* (1967) uses Buddhist idioms to explain Christian beliefs. His contribution to Sinhalese and Tamil relationships was seen during his tenure as the chairman of the Methodist Conference of Sri Lanka.

Niles's writings dealt with important moral issues and were translated during his lifetime into Sinhala and Tamil. In addition to pursuing a wide range of public activities, Niles authored several books. Noteworthy among them are *That They May Have Life* (1952), *Upon the Earth* (1962), which was regarded as the best statement at the time on mission theology and strategy, and *A Testament of Faith* (1972).

In recognition of his distinguished service as both a theological writer and an administrator in the world church, Niles was awarded honorary doctorates of divinity by Budapest University and Serampore College.

Bibliography

Neill, S. C., *Brothers of the Faith* (1960). • Small, W. J. T., *A History of the Methodist Church in Ceylon* (1970).

G. P. V. SOMARATNA

Nisibis, School of

Ancient theological school of the East Syrian (Nestorian*) church.

Nisibis was a town (present-day Nusaybin, Turkey) located on a busy trade route linking Antioch and the Mediterranean world with India* and the Seres (China*). Its location brought both trade and new ideas. The earliest Christian communities in Nisibis are difficult to date but may be as early as the time of Addai*, the apostle of Edessa. Ephrem* identifies the first bishop as Jacob (Mar Yoqub; bishop 308-38), who is credited with founding a theological school (the predecessor of the School of Nisibis) and who attended the Council of Nicea.

The school itself was not founded in Nisibis until the next century, possibly 471, when Bishop Barsaume of Nisibis convinced the great theologian Narasai* (399-502), who had to flee Edessa, to become the interpreter of a new school in Persia. This important decision helped to ensure that Persian theology would be dominated by the dyophysite, East Syrian tradition. What this also meant is that a school would be founded for training Persian Christians who would become the missionaries and bishops from Nisibis to India and to old Cathay (China). After Narsai's leadership, the school continued to grow in numbers of students, organization, and influence. In 567 Henana of Adiabene (d. 609?) came to Nisibis and challenged the theology of the school. He was repudiated, but returned in 573 as director of the school, teaching his "errors." This controversy weakened the school and reflected in a religious sphere what was going on in the political sphere in the struggle of the Byzantines and Persians over the hearts of the citizens of Nisibis. At the time of the Arab invasions in the mid-7th c., controversies were still present, although Babai the Great (supervisor of the convents) had done much to consolidate Nestorian theology. Thus for nearly two centuries this "School of the Persians" was a dominant influence in early Asian theology outside the Roman Empire.

The school itself was primarily concerned with the proper interpretation of Scripture according to the Antiochene tradition. The Psalms were to be memorized, and all the students were to take the foundational courses in biblical interpretation given by the head of the school. Thus the principal of the school was always called "The Interpreter" (possibly as a reminder of Theodore of Mopsuestia, who is "The Interpreter" of the dyophysite tradition). Monks and priests in training had to know only three theologians: Diodore, Theodore of Mopsuestia, and Nestorius. In the sermons of Narsai we can see the preoccupation with teaching the full divinity and full humanity of Jesus, but with equal clarity the separation of the two is affirmed and opponents (Cyril of Alexandra) condemned. The school was under the authority of the local bishop, who is given credit for penning the guidelines or statutes of the school. These "Statutes of the School of Nisibis" help us to see what type of community was envisioned and what types of theological and personal problems the students encountered. At its height in the early 6th c., the School of Nisibis had over 1,000 students.

Bibliography

Gero, Stephen, *Barsauma of Nisibis and Persian Christianity in the Fifth Century* (1981). • Scher, A., ed. and trans., *Barhadsabba, Cause de la fondation des ecoles* (1907). • Vööbus, A., *History of the School of Nisibis* (1965); *The Statutes of the School of Nisibis* (1962).

SCOTT W. SUNQUIST

Nitobe Inazo

(b. Morioka, 1 Sep 1862; d. Victoria, Canada, 15 Oct 1933). Japanese educator; member of the Imperial Academy and the House of Peers; representative on the *Izokuin.*

The child of Jokun Jujiro, a magistrate of the Nambu domain, Nitobe was adopted by his grandfather, Ota Tokitoshi, and bore the name Ota from the age of 10 to 28. In 1877, he entered Sapporo Agricultural School in the second class of students at that school. The same year, under the influence of William Smith Clark, he signed the Covenant of Believers in Jesus. The next year, he was baptized by Merriman Colbert Harris. In 1884, he left Tokyo University to study in the United States at Johns Hopkins University. Soon after his arrival, he attended a Quaker meeting and joined the Baltimore Friends. In 1887, he moved to Germany to study agricultural administration and economics at Bonn, Berlin, and Halle Universities. In 1891, he married Nitobe Mariko (in Elkinton) and returned to Japan to teach at Sapporo Agricultural School. Later, he served as an engineer for the governor-general of Taiwan, part-time professor at Kyoto Imperial University, principal of the First High School (1906), professor in the law faculty of Tokyo Imperial University (1913), and the first chancellor of Tokyo Women's Christian University. As an educator, he had a great influence on the character of his students. In 1920, he became assistant director of the League of Nations office, where he worked on the international level as a bridge across the Pacific Ocean.

One of Nitobe's most widely read books, *Bushido* (The Way of the Samurai, 1899), explained the ethics and morality of the Japanese people as related to the virtues of *Bushido.* Introduced widely outside of Japan, it helped foreigners to better understand the Japanese. Nitobe followed the Quaker style, putting more emphasis on the light of God as experienced in each person's heart than on church and creeds. He felt that Christ was a sorrowful man and Christianity a sorrowful religion. In response to the many sorrows of people's lives, we must have compassion for and sympathize with them as we relate to them with an abundant heart.

While attending the Investigative Conference on Issues in the Pacific as leader of the delegation from Japan, Nitobe died in Victoria Canada. *Nitobe Inazo zenshu,* a 16-volume set of his complete writings, is available.

Bibliography

Ishii Mitsuru, *Nitobe Inazo den* (Biography of Nitobe Inazo) (1934). • Maeda Tamon and Takagi Yasaka, eds., *Nitobe Hakasei tsuito shu* (In Memory of Dr. Nitobe) (1936). • Yanaihara Tadao, *Uchimura Kanzo to Nitobe Inazo* (Uchimura Kanzo and Nitobe Inazo) (1948). • Matsukuma Toshiko, *Nitobe Inazo* (1969). • Tokyo Women's Christian University Nitobe Inazo Research Group, eds., *Nitobe Inazo kenkyu* (Research on Nitobe Inazo) (1969). • Takeda Kiyoko, "*Nitobe Inazo — dentoteki kachi no kakushin to sengo minshushugi no ne*" (Nitobe Inazo — Reform of Traditional Values and Roots of Postwar Democracy), in Ogawa Keiji, ed., *Nihonjin to Kirisuto kyo* (The Japanese and Christianity) (1973). • Sato Masahiro, *Nitobe Inazo shogai to shiso* (Life and Thought of Nitobe Inazo) (1980).

UNUMA YUKO, JAPANESE DICTIONARY

Noble, Robert Turlington

(b. Frisby, England, 1809; d. Masulipatnam, India, 17 Oct 1865). Greek scholar, education pioneer in the Andhra area, India*.

Noble was noted for his critical knowledge of the Greek texts of the New Testament. He received ordination as a clergyman of the Church of England and on 8 Mar 1841 took final leave of his native land on the ship *Robarts* bound for Madras. He reached Masulipatnam, his field of mission, by the end of October. The chief city of the district, Masulipatnam then had a population of over 50,000.

Masulipatnam had for more than two generations

been under the English government. But up to that time little had been done for the spiritual or intellectual uplifting of the people. Masulipatnam was regarded simply as a military station of the East India Company's government and headquarters of the civil administration in Telugu country.

Noble pioneered educational work in the Andhra area. He started (1843) and ran an English-language school for children of the middle classes and higher castes in which Christian Scriptures formed the basis of moral and intellectual learning. Many of the students became converts and church leaders, the first being baptized in 1852 and then ordained in 1864. Twenty-four years later, the school became Noble College.

Bibliography

Noble, John, *A Memoir of the Rev. Robert Turlington Noble, Missionary to the Telugu People in South India* (1866).

A. T. Philip

Nommensen, Ludwig Ingwer

(b. Nordstrand, Germany, 6 Feb 1834; d. Sigumpar-Laguboti, Indonesia, 23 May 1918). German missionary pioneer among the Bataks* in Sumatra, Indonesia*, and lifelong leader of the German Mission and the Batak Church (1862-1918).

Nommensen was one of the missionaries sent out by the German Rhenish Mission (*Rheinische Missionsgesellschaft*, RMG) in Wuppertal-Barmen. An interest in proclaiming the Gospel to non-believers had led him to enroll in the Rhenish mission seminary at Wuppertal-Barmen in 1857. In 1862, he arrived on the island of Sumatra, where the Batak people lived. He remained there until he died in 1918, leaving only on four occasions for furloughs in Germany (1880-81, 1892, 1905, and 1912). During his long service in Batak land, he saw great changes among the Batak people as a result of the Gospel. Many of the Bataks converted from their traditional religion to Christianity. By 1918, the northern territory of the Batak land (where most of the Toba Bataks lived) had witnessed construction of church buildings, schools, and hospitals sponsored by the Rhenish Mission in Sumatra.

Three new mission stations were initiated by Nommensen. In 1864, he started with the valley of Silindung, where he met with great difficulties from the Bataks, who still adhered to the traditional religion (ancestor* worship). Although his faith was severely tested, he remained, and the following year some of the local Bataks were converted. Initially, the converts had to leave their villages and live together with Nommensen in *Huta Dame* (Village of Peace) because of persecution from their fellow Bataks, but mass conversion of the villagers one year later enabled the converts to remain in their own villages. In 1883, Nommensen moved to Laguboti, a village near Lake Toba. In 1890, he moved on to Sigumpar. Together with some other missionaries, he planned a new mission field here. In comparison with his first experience in Silindung, Nommensen faced less difficulty in the new mission field. In 1903, Nommensen and other missionaries reached Simalungun land, a region heavily influenced by Islam*.

From the start, Nommensen organized the local congregants to become self-reliant. In 1867, he drew up a church order that guided all aspects of ecclesial life, such as liturgy, Christian ethics, and church leadership (involving the work of elders, deacons, and Sunday school teachers). After 15 years, in 1881, when 5,188 Bataks had been baptized, Nommensen, together with missionary Koedding, implemented a hierarchical church structure for the Batak church, rising from the congregational level to the central headquarters. The highest position was the *ephorus*, whose responsibilities included heading the missionary task and developing the daily life of the church.

To nurture the new converts in the Christian faith, Nommensen translated Luther's Small Catechism (1874) and the New Testament (1874) into Batak (Toba). In 1904, at age 70, he was conferred an honorary doctor of theology degree by the University of Bonn (Germany) for his efforts. In 1911, at age 77, he was honored as an officer of the Dutch Order of Orange-Nassau.

During his long service, Nommensen was twice widowed. In 1887, his wife and their four children died. His second wife, whom he married in 1892, died in 1902, leaving him with three children. At the time of his death, there were 180,000 members of the Batak church, with 34 Batak pastors and 788 teacher-preachers.

In Nommensen's honor, the new Batak Christian university, located in Pematang Siantar and Medan, North Sumatra, was named Nommensen University in 1954. His pioneering spirit and leadership skills were a unique contribution, playing a special role in the spread of Christianity among the Bataks (Angkola, Toba, Simalungun, and Pakpak Dairi). A church body he organized, the *Huria Kristen Batak Protestan* (HKBP), is today one of the largest churches in Asia (over three million).

Nommensen left to the Batak congregations a pietistic theology in the tradition of the Western church. This legacy has not led to narrow denominationalism and confessionalism. Thus, the Batak church (HKBP) is prepared to enter the new era, the ecumenical* life of Asian Christianity. After 56 years of service, Nommensen left the Batak church with the continuing struggle to find its own Christian expression in the context of Batak culture. Nommensen was a patriarchal missionary figure full of love, compassion, and dedication, taking a pastoral approach with everyone he met.

Bibliography

Schreiner, Lother, "Ludwig Nommensen Studies — A Review," *Missions Studies*, Vol. IX.2, 18 (1992). • Pierard, Richard V., "Nommensen, Ludwig Ingwer (1834-1918)," in *The New International Dictionary of the Christian Church* (1978). • Menzel, Gustav, *Ein Reiskorn auf der Strasse: Ludwig I. Nommensen, "Apostel der Batak"* (1984).

J. Raplan Hutauruk

Non-Church Principle

(Mukyokai Shugi). Form of Christianity promoted by Uchimura Kanzo*.

Repulsed by the denominationalism of the missionaries and by friction within the church, influenced by the Quakers, and reflecting the nationalism of his time, Uchimura evolved his own evangelistic interpretation of Christianity, and, around 1900, he began strongly advocating his beliefs. Centering his faith solely on the saving grace of Christ's sacrifice, he felt that church structures, an ordained ministry, and even the sacraments of baptism and communion were completely unnecessary.

The term *Mukyokai* (non-church) first appeared in an article written by Uchimura: "Kirisuto shinto no nagusame" (Consolation for Christian Believers), in *Tokyo dokuritsu zasshi* (Tokyo Independence Magazine, 15 Jun 1899). *Mukyokai shugi* (non-church principle) first appeared in the third issue of the magazine *Mukyokai* that was launched in Mar 1901. Uchimura himself was not completely opposed to the church. In the inaugural issue of the magazine, *Mukyokai* was explained as a "church for believers with no church." In *Seisho no kenkyu* 85 (Biblical Study), Uchimura wrote, "With the advance of *Mukyokai,* it should become a church." In fact, Uchimura himself baptized a few people. However, his disciples interpreted the Non-Church Principle much more radically as a strong denial of church.

Uchimura's overall belief system could be described as non-church. Whatever his followers may have said, he viewed the church of God *(ecclesia)* as a gathering of those who were called by God. Using Uchimura's Bible study group as a model, Fujii Takeshi, Azegami Kenzo, Tsukamoto Toraji, Yanaihara Tadao, Sakaeda Yoshitaka, Ishihara Hyoe, and Masaike Jin each organized independent groups; at the present time, a large number of such groups continue to meet around the country.

Bibliography

Sekine Masao, *Mukyokai kirisutokyo* (Non-Church Christianity) (1949). • Ishihara Hyoe, *Mukyokaishi* (History of Non-Church) (1950). • Tsukamoto Toraji, *Watakushi no mukyokaishugi* (My Non-Church Principle) (1962). • Iwakuma Nao, *Mukyokai shugi to wa nani ka* (What Is the Non-Church Principle?) (1967). • Caldarola, Carlo, *Uchimura Kanzo to mukyokai* (Uchimura Kanzo and Non-Church) (1978) (English version: *Christianity: The Japanese Way* [1979]). • Miura Hiroshi, *The Life and Thought of Kanzo Uchimura* (1996).

Suzuki Norihisa

Nonnus of Nisibis

(late 8th- 9th c.). West Syrian theologian; one of the earliest Christian writers to use the Arabic language for original compositions.

Nothing is known of Nonnus of Nisibis's early life or death date. The earliest reference to him is in the record of a debate with the Chalcedonian theologian Theodore Abu Qurrah about 812-13 C.E. While he was still young, this debate took place before an Armenian prince at the request of the bishop of Tagrit. The latest reference to Nonnus records his participation in the Armenian Council of Sirakawan in 862 C.E. A multicultural context is reflected in the preservation of his writings. These are found in Georgian, Armenian, Syriac, and Arabic.

Perhaps Nonnus's most important contribution is his *Commentary on John.* First written in Arabic, it is extant only in Armenian. It preserves a wide number of exegetical traditions from earlier biblical commentators and demonstrates the originality of Nonnus's thought. Also important is the *Apologetic Treatise,* which endeavors to clarify the differences in the theological commitments held by various parties of the Christian community in the 9th-c. west Asian context. Other surviving texts include the *Treatise Against Thomas of Marga,* a letter to a correspondent whose name is lost, and a letter to a monk known only as John. These are sufficient to establish Nonnus as an important Asian Christian writer.

Bibliography

Mariès, L., "Un Commentaire sur l'Évangile de saint Jean, rédigé en arabe (circa 840), par Nonnus (Nana) de Nisibe, conservé dans une traduction Arménienne," *Revue des études arméniennes* 1 (1920-21). • Graf, G., *Geschichte der arabischen christlichen Literatur* II (1947). • A. Van Roey, *Nonnus de Nisibe: Traité apologétique. Étude, texte et traduction* (1948). • Bundy, D., "The Commentary of Nonnus of Nisibis on the Prologue of John," *Orientalia Christiana Analecta* 218 (1982).

David Bundy

Northern Cathedral

(Beitang) (the Savior's Church) (Xi Si Ku Catholic Church). A bishop's cathedral of the Beijing Catholic Church first built in the 17th c. in north Beijing and relocated to Xi Si Ku in the 19th c.

In 1699, Emperor Kangxi was cured of malaria with quinine supplied by the French Jesuit missionaries staying in the Southern Cathedral. In appreciation, he granted them a residence at Xianmen in the imperial city, which they remodeled into the Savior's Chapel. Shortly thereafter, upon the request of François Gerbillon* and others, Kangxi granted them a plot of land beside their residence on which they built a larger church, the Savior's Church, commonly referred to as the Northern Cathedral.

In 1801, the Jesuits* in Beijing were replaced by French Lazarists* who took up residence in the Northern Cathedral. When the Qing regime stopped using missionaries for calendrical work, the Northern Cathedral was left vacant until 1827. It was later confiscated and demolished. The capture of Beijing by Anglo-French allied forces in 1860 resulted in the Sino-French Treaty. This agreement returned the Northern Cathedral and other confiscated churches to their rightful owners. Under the care of Bishop Mouly, a French Lazarist who entered Beijing with the allied forces, the Northern Cathedral was restored and became a bishop's cathedral. In 1887, the Empress Dowager Chixi decided to enlarge her imperial courtyard and closed the surrounding vicinity (including the Northern Cathedral) to outsiders. Negotiations were held between Qing foreign minister Li Hongzhang and church representative Pierre-Marie-Alphonse Favier, a French Lazarist, to build a larger church (seating capacity 2,000) at Xi Si Ku.

During the Boxer Uprising, the eight-nation allied forces battled to capture the strategic cathedral. During the Cultural Revolution, the cathedral was again destroyed. The Beijing People's Municipal Government returned the property to the Catholic Church in Feb 1985. After beginning work the following May, the Beijing Patriotic Association restored it within six months.

China Group

Noyen, Petrus

(b. 1870; d. 1921). Founder of the Society of the Divine Word* (SVD) mission of the Lesser Sunda Islands (eastern Indonesia) in 1912.

Prior to his work in Indonesia*, Noyen worked as a missionary in Shantung, China* (1894-1910). He strategically transferred the center of the Divine Word mission from the mainly Catholic area of eastern Flores (1915) to Ende in the center of the island and rushed missionaries and teachers to western and central Flores, where animists were looking for a respected religion. The rapid growth of the church confirmed his foresight. With the exception of a few pockets of Muslims in Ende* and on the western coast of Manggarai in the diocese of Ruteng, Flores is today the "Catholic island" of Indonesia.

Bibliography

Vroeklage, B. A. G., *Petrus Noyen: Eerste Apostolische Prefect der Kl. S Soenda-Eilanden N.O.I.* (1930).

Adolf Heuken

Nuclear Weapons, Movement against

(Gensuibaku Kinshi Undo). News reports of the horrors of the atomic bombings of Hiroshima and Nagasaki were strictly controlled by the Allied Occupation Forces so that their full extent was hidden from the public. When the Fukuryu Naru No. 5 was covered with nuclear fallout from the H-bomb test at Bikini Atoll in 1954, a signature campaign to stop all nuclear testing was launched. Over 20 million signatures had been collected by the time the first World Conference Against Atomic and Hydrogen Bombs was held in 1955, and the Japan Council Against Atomic and Hydrogen Bombs *(Gensuikyo)* was formed.

An annual world conference held every summer served as the axis around which other grassroots peace movements coalesced, yielding a movement with influence of international proportions. At the same time, China-USSR antagonism and Socialist Party–Communist Party rivalry infected the movement. Dispute over whether the 1963 Limited Test- Ban Treaty applied to *all* or only *some* (capitalist) countries caused a gigantic rift in the antinuclear movement. The 1963 world conference ended in a two-way split. By 1965, the split became formalized into the Japan* *Council* Against Nuclear Weapons *(Gensuikyo)* and the Japan *Congress* Against Nuclear Weapons *(Gensuikin),* and this split proved permanent. Grassroots representatives who wanted them to get back together persuaded the preparations committee for the 1977 and later conferences to include members from both sides, and united World Peace Conferences were held. But in 1984, a change in the officers and objectives of *Gensuikyo* led to irreconcilable quarreling in the preparations committee.

From the beginning in 1954, Christians participated in the antinuclear movement through regional *Gensuikyo,* labor, peace, women's, and youth organizations. In 1957, they began making active contributions when a member of the Japan Women's Christian Temperance Union and a director of the Christian Peace Association became directors of the Japan Council *(Gensuikyo).* When the danger of a split arose, Christian groups, along with Nihonzan Myohoji, Jinrui Aizenkai, and others, held World Religionist Peace Conferences in 1961 and 1964. The Japan Religionists Peace Association was founded, and it worked with the Japan Confederation of A-bomb and H-bomb Sufferers Organizations, regional *Gensuikyo,* and grassroots organizations to promote unity and progress in the movement. A minister who was a member of the Hiroshima Christian Peace Association became the leader of a people's march for peace.

Iijima Munetaka, Japanese Dictionary

Nunes, Carneiro Leitao Melchior

(b. Coimbra, Portugal, ca. 1516; d. Macau, 19 Aug 1583). First rector of the Jesuit College at Evora, Portugal, and first bishop delegate of the holy see to exercise his episcopal ministry in the Far East (from 1568 to 1581), becoming one of the main pioneers of the Catholic Church in Macau*.

Nunes joined the Society of Jesus* (Jesuits) in 1543. In 1555 he was appointed bishop of Nicaea and was consecrated bishop at Goa in 1560. In 1567 Pope Pius V sent him to the Far East to exercise his episcopal ministry in China* and Japan*. He arrived in Macau in 1568 and soon helped to set up the *Senado* (Town Council). In the following year, he established the *Santa Casa da Misericordia* (Holy House of Mercy), a charitable association which founded the present St. Raphael's Hospital, the Leper Asylum of St. Lazarus, and an orphanage.

Nunes tried to open missions in mainland China. He went to Canton twice in 1576, but it was only in 1584 that the mission was finally established through the work of Frs. A. Valignano* (1538-1606), M. Ruggieri* (1545-

1607), and M. Ricci* (1552-1610). In 1579, he welcomed to Macau the first Franciscan* fathers and in the following year he ordained five Jesuit priests. He retired in 1581, when the first appointed bishop of Macau, Leonardo Fernando de Sa (?-1587), arrived.

Bibliography

Texeira, M., *Macau e sua Diocese,* Vol. 2 (1940).

SERGIO TICOZZI

Nusa Tenggara, East

(Lesser Sunda Islands, Eastern Half). East Nusa Tenggara is one of the provinces in Indonesia* and consists of 556 islands with an area of 47,349 sq. kms. It has a population of over 3.3 million, with a population density of 70 persons per sq. km. This province is known as a Christian province because the majority of the people are Christian. It is, however, also the poorest province. There are 1,777,972 Roman Catholics, 1,035,704 Protestants, 286,515 Muslims, 9,701 Hindus, 249 Buddhists, and 189,859 animists.

Christianity was first brought to the region by the Portuguese in the 16th c. In 1556, Dominican* Antonio Taveira baptized 5,000 persons in Timor (see Dili) and many people in Flores. Unfortunately there was no pastoral care. It was only in 1561 that three Dominican missionaries were sent to Solor* Island, namely Antonio da Cruz, Simao das Chagas, and Brother Alexio. The Portuguese built a fortress on Solor Island to protect themselves and a number of native Christians against attacks by Muslims from Java. Catholicism quickly spread into the surrounding area so that by 1599 there were 100,000 Catholics. Solor and Larantuka* (a town on Flores Island; see Ende*) became the headquarters of the Catholic Church in the 16th c.

In 1613, the Dutch United East-India Company* (*Verenigde Oost-Indische Compagnie,* VOC) wrested control of Solor Island from the Portuguese. The attack was led by Apollonius Scotte. A few soldiers were stationed on the island. The others moved on to conquer Timor Island as well. In Kupang, the VOC built a fortress called Fort Concordia which became the center of Protestant Christianity in Timor during the period of VOC domination. Solor Island was abandoned by the VOC in 1630 because it was no longer profitable for their trade. The Dominican missionaries continued to work there until 1862, when they were replaced by the Jesuits*, who expanded their area of activity into Sumba Island but had to abandon it because of an Indo-Dutch government law that forbade two mission bodies working in the same area. In 1913, the Jesuit mission was taken over by the Society of the Divine Word* (SVD), which still operates today, except in Sumba Island, which was given to the Redemptorists* (CSSR).

The Catholic mission opened schools and hospitals and developed the community. The SVD set up a seminary, the Institute for Higher Learning for Catholic Philosophy, in Ledalero-Maumere, Flores, and a university, the Catholic University Wydia Mandira in Kupang, in Timor.

The Protestant church is represented by denominations such as Presbyterian*, Pentecostal*, Adventist, and the Salvation Army*. The largest Protestant churches in the area are the Evangelical Christian Church in Timor (*Gereja Masehi Injili di Timor,* GMIT) and the Sumba Christian Church (*Gereja Kristen Sumba,* GKS). The membership of other denominations is small.

GKS is the result of the evangelistic work of several mission agencies from Holland — the *Nederlandsche Gereformeerd Zendingsvereniging* (NGZV), 1881-84; the *Zending der Christelijke Gereformeerd Kerk* (ZchGK), 1884-96; the *Zending der Gereformeerd Kerken in Nederland* (ZGKN), 1896-1947; and several congregations of the *Nederlandse Zendelingsvereniging* (NZG) in Sumba. The later congregations consist of Christians from Sawu Island who were relocated by the Indo-Dutch government in the 1860s. The work of GKS is in Sumba, an island with a population of about 450,000.

The NGZV started mission work in Sumba in 1881 with the arrival of J. J. van Alpen. In 1884, they handed over their work to the ZchGK, which sent two more missionaries, W. Pos and C. de Bruijn, in addition to van Alpen. Evangelistic work among the Sumbanese produced little. The missionaries worked only among the congregations of people from Sawu until the ZGKN took over in 1896. Their work was unsuccessful because the situation in Sumba was not safe, there were animosity toward the white people and a strong adherence to *marapu* (tribal religious belief), and the missionaries were not sufficiently trained.

The missionary work of the ZGKN slowly showed better results, with the first Sumbanese baptized in 1915. The success of the ZGKN could be attributed to several factors. First, there were relatively more security and peace. Prior to the establishment of Indo-Dutch authority in the region in 1901, there were internecine wars between the local kings and active slave trading. By 1912, the Indo-Dutch government was able to bring peace to the land and stop slave trading. Second, the missionaries were better trained, with knowledge of medical* skills, the local language, customs, and culture, and they were thus better able to provide medical care and to evangelize and preach to the people in the Sumba language. L Onvlee translated the Bible* and a hymnal into the Sumba language with the help of a native Christian, Umbu Hina Kapita. Third, natives were involved in evangelism so that people were reached through methods that were more meaningful to their culture. To help the missionaries, a training institution was started in 1924 to equip local Christians to become lay preachers. Fourth, there was a more comprehensive approach in evangelism. The mission established schools, hospitals, and other ministries to improve the lives of the people. In 1913, the Indo-Dutch government gave the ZGKN a monopoly on opening schools on Sumba Island.

Japanese soldiers occupied Sumba Island in Mar 1942. All the Dutch missionaries were arrested and taken to Ujung Pandang* (Sulawesi). The Christians were suspected of being Dutch spies, and Hapu Mbay became the first native Christian martyr in Sumba. At the beginning of the occupation, church services were prohibited, and representatives of the Japanese forces were present at various church meetings. But after the Japanese were defeated in the Pacific War, they were more restrained toward the Christians. In spite of the difficult situation, about 500 were baptized during the Japanese occupation. The congregations were served by native Bible teachers and a native pastor, Herman Mete Malo. Attempts to form an independent church were started at this time.

After the Japanese surrender, the Dutch missionaries returned to Sumba in 1946. Attempts to form an independent church were renewed, and the GKS declared itself independent on 13 Jan 1947. It grew rapidly under the leadership of native preachers who endeavored to contextualize* the Gospel in the Sumba culture to make it less foreign to the people. Church architecture (see Art and Architecture) followed the design of Sumba houses, and the symbol of the church became a horse rather than a cross, because Sumba is the largest producer of horses in Indonesia. Mbaha Ratubandju, a pastor, labored on the contextualization issue.

Presently, the church is divided into 14 districts with 412 congregations and a total membership of 169,180 served by 77 pastors and 458 lay preachers. The GKS is very active in reaching out to animists, and many animists have joined the church through mass baptism (see Animism).

The GKS participates in various ecumenical* activities. Working together with the GMIT, it established a theological school of higher learning in Kupang, which later became the Christian University, *Artha Wachana.* At the national level, the GKS was a founding member of the Indonesian Council of Churches (*Dewan Gereja-gereja di Indonesia,* DGI). Internationally, the GKS is a member of the Reformed Ecumenical Synod (RES) and the World Alliance of Reformed Churches (WARC), and it continues to maintain a working relationship with the *Gereformeerde Kerken* in the Netherlands.

Bibliography

Dicker, Gordon, *Pengabaran Injil di Pulau Timor* (1960) (published as a stencil, Kupang, 1975). • Brookes, G. F., "Spirit Movements in Timor: A Survey" (master's thesis, Melbourne College of Divinity) (1977). • Noach, M. A., *Langkah Pertama. Suatu tinjauan terhadap periode 25 tahun G.M.I.T., 1947-1972* (published as a stencil, Kupang, 1972). • Peters, George W., *Indonesia Revival: Focus on Timor* (1973).

On the Christian Church of Sumba: Van den End, Th., *Gereformeerde Zending op Sumba 1859-1972. Een bronnenpublicatie* (1987) (Indonesian edition: *Sumber-sumber Zending tentang Sejarah Gereja di Sumba 1859-1972* [1996]). • Kapita, Oe. H., *Sedjarah Pergumulan Indjil di Sumba* (1955); Sumba dalam jangkauan zaman (1976).

On the Catholic Church in Nusa Tenggara: Haripranata, H., *Ceritera Sejarah Gereja Katolik Suimba dan Sumbawa* (1984). • Piskaty, K., and J. Riberu, *Nusa-tenggara, setengah abad karya SVD 1913-1963* (1966) (translation from a German original); *Sejarah Gereja Katolik Indonesia,* Vol. IIIb (1974). F. D. WELLEM

Oblates of Mary Immaculate

(OMI). In Jan 1816, Charles-Joseph-Eugene de Mazenod (bishop of Marseilles from 1837 until his death in 1861; beatified in 1975; canonized on 3 Dec 1995) founded a mission-preaching society at Aix-en-Provence, France. Its purpose was to preach parish missions to the people of small towns and country areas of Provence that were not being reached by the church's ordinary ministry. This society was made up of diocesan priests; by 1824 it had become a religious community with vows. On 17 Feb 1826, Pope Leo XII formally approved this society as a religious congregation with the title of Missionary Oblates of Mary Immaculate.

From the outset, the ambition of this group of mission preachers was to go forth into the "vast expanse of the whole earth." A resolution to accept foreign missions as soon as possible was passed by the 1831 general chapter. This became a reality in 1841 when a first group of Oblate missionaries left for Canada. One year later, they had gone to England and Ireland. Jaffna in Sri Lanka* was their foothold in Asia beginning in 1847.

While still in the seminary of St. Sulpice in Paris, de Mazenod debated with others whether it was better to go as a missionary to China* or to remain as a mission preacher in France. When Pope Pius VII in 1814 favored the latter, de Mazenod opted to remain in France. On 8 Aug 1847, he agreed to send his Oblates in response to a request from Bishop Orazio Bettachini of Jaffna.

In Sri Lanka the Oblates preached missions, were put in charge of or founded parishes, founded schools and other training centers, and contributed to the formation of the diocesan clergy and to studies on the social situation in Sri Lanka and elsewhere in Asia. Several Oblates became bishops in Sri Lanka (in Jaffna) and elsewhere. An Oblate was archbishop of Colombo from 1883 (Charles Bonjean) until 1976, when Archbishop Cardinal Thomas Cooray, the Oblates' third cardinal, resigned. As the Oblates in Sri Lanka grew in number, they were able to found other missions in Asia: India* (Madras, Bangalore, 1967), Pakistan* (Multan, Karachi, 1970), and Bangladesh* (Sylhet, 1973).

In 1933 the Oblates accepted missions in Laos* (area of Vientiane and Luang-Prabang). The original group came mostly from France, and they were joined by confreres from Italy in 1955. In 1966 a mission in Thailand* was founded from Laos. The Thailand mission still exists as a delegation directly under the Oblate general administration. Due to the political developments in Laos, the Oblates (five of whom were killed and others went missing) were expelled in 1975. Only one Oblate remains in Laos today, a native Laotian who is vicar apostolic of Vientiane.

In 1939 Oblates from the United States began missionary work in the Philippines* (Mindanao and Sulu). During the war with the Japanese, three were killed and 15 were imprisoned. The Oblates did parish ministry, opened a network of schools (the Notre Dame schools and colleges), became involved in the means of social communications (newspapers and radio), and established their own houses of formation. Several of them have become bishops. They also founded a mission in Hong Kong* in 1966.

Oblates from the United States founded missions in Japan* in 1948. Besides manning their own houses of formation, these Oblates are engaged in parish ministry and in a variety of "first evangelization" endeavors.

The last major Oblate foundations in Asia date from 1977: in Indonesia* (especially French and Italian Oblates expelled from Laos as well as Australians) and Tahiti (Oblates from the United States mostly).

There are over 570 Oblates in Asia, including 437 priests, 33 brothers, and 103 seminarians; eight are bishops (two archibshops, four bishops, two retired).

Bibliography

Levasseur, Donat, *A History of the Missionary Oblates of Mary Immaculate*, Vol. I, 1815-98; Vol. II, 1898-1985, trans. John Rheidt and Aloysius Kedl (1985, 1989). • Boudens, Robrecht, *Catholic Missionaries in a British*

Colony, Success and Failures in Ceylon, 1796-1893 (1979). • Lawrence, Joseph-Claude, *Work and Working of the Archdiocese of Colombo in Ceylon (1947-1970)* (1970). • Mongeau, Gérard, *Notre Dame Banner: Story of the Oblates of Mary Immaculate in the Philippines* (1983).

Aloysius Kedl

Oblates of Notre Dame. *See* Indigenous Religious Congregations

Odes of Solomon

Early Christian hymnbook (late 1st to late 2nd c.) used in western Asia.

The *Odes of Solomon* were first discovered by J. R. Harris in the Syriac language in 1907 and published in English in 1909 (and 1911). Forty were titled "Odes" and 18 "Songs of Solomon." Much has been written on the *Odes* this century, mainly among German scholars trying to locate the place, time, and theology of their composition. There is still no consensus, but it appears that they were originally composed in Syriac in a community in or near Edessa that was influenced much by Johannine theology. Some early commentators speculated about a gnostic or dualistic origin for the *Odes*, but recently it has been noted that they are clearly Christian, but from a different context from most early Christian literature. They are clearly trinitarian, they speak about God the creator, they have a good deal of baptismal imagery, they are very dependent upon the Old Testament, and they recognize that salvation has come through Christ who was killed and then raised from the dead. The *Odes* were apparently used in worship and often have Christ speak in the first person or in a dialogue. They have a clear missionary concern (the word going out into all the world) but never mention Jesus specifically.

Bibliography

Charlesworth, J. H., *The Odes of Solomon* (Syriac with English translation and notes) (1978); *The First Christian Handbook: The Odes of Solomon* (1992). • Drijvers, H. J. W., "Odes of Solomon," in *East of Antioch* (1984). • Hamman, A., *Les Odes de Salomon* (1981). Harris, J. R., and A. Mingana, eds., *The Odes and Psalms of Solomon*, 2 Vols. (1916-20). • Lattke, M., *Die Oden Salomos in ihrer Bedeutung für NT und Gnosis*, 4 Vols. (1979-86). • Pierre, M. J., and J. M. Martin, eds. and trans., *Les Odes de Salomon* (1994).

Scott W. Sunquist

Odoric of Pordenone

(de Portu Naono, Odoricus) (b. unknown; d. 14 Jan 1331). Italian Franciscan who went to China* as a tourist during the Yuan dynasty.

De Pordenone left Italy between 1314 and 1318, passing Sumatra, Java, and Borneo in 1321 on his journey to China, but he said nothing about Christians in these places. He reached China in 1322 and toured Guangzhou, Qhuanzhou, Fuzhou, Hangzhou, Yangzhou, and Beijing. His longest stay (three years) was in Beijing, where he helped Montecorvino* preach the Gospel. In 1330 he returned to Italy by way of Hetao, Shanxi, Gansu, and Xizang (Tibet). Before his death he dictated, under the instruction of the head of the Franciscan* Order, an account of all he had seen and heard during a decade of travel in the East. In the compiled book *(Chronica compendioca a mundi exordio ad finem firme Pontificatus Ionnis XXII)*, de Pordenone mentioned the favored treatment Montecorvino received from the Yuan emperor and the piety and discipline of Catholic converts.

Bibliography

Yule, Henry, *Cathay and the Way Thither: Being a Collection of Medieval Notices of China*, rev. Henri Cordier (1925, 1926).

China Group

Ogilby, Lyman Cunningham

Fourth and last American bishop of the Philippine Episcopal Church (PEC).

Ogilby was consecrated suffragan bishop of the Episcopal Church (see Anglicans) on 2 Feb 1953 and installed diocesan bishop in 1957. It was during his time that Filipinization and the move toward autonomy in the PEC slowly gained momentum. The move to autonomy, the bishop said, "should be steady and sure." At the same time the bishop strengthened the education ministry of the church by the establishment of Trinity College of Quezon City in 1962 (see Education). The college was to be operated jointly by both the Philippine Independent Church (PIC) and the Philippine Episcopal churches.

Ogilby resigned as bishop of the district on 1 May 1967 to give the leadership of the church to the Filipinos.

Bibliography

Journal of the Annual Convocation of the Missionary District of the Philippine Islands (1957-66).

Edward P. Malecdan

Oh Keung Sun

(b. Sagok-myon, Kongjoo-koon, Chung-nam, Korea, 4 Oct 1878; d. Seoul, Korea, 18 May 1963). Pioneer of medical* education and social work in Korea*.

The first son of Oh In Mook, Oh studied Chinese literature in his hometown and entered Paijae School in Seoul, which was founded by Henry Appenzeller*, an American Methodist missionary to Korea. While in school, he joined the Independent Club and was elected general secretary. The Korean government later ordered the dissolution of the club and arrested all of its staff members. Oh escaped to his native town and hid himself in the home of Rev. Steadman, an American Baptist* missionary. Oh was baptized and became a Christian.

Olcott, Henry Steel

With the help of the missionaries, Oh went to the United States to study in 1902. He entered the medical school in Louisville, Kentucky, and graduated in 1907. After finishing his training, he was appointed a medical missionary to Korea of the Presbyterian* Church in the United States (Southern). In 1908 he returned to Korea and became head of the Jesus Hospital in Koonsan-city, Chun Book. When he was in Koonsan, he founded Anrak School in 1908 and Youngmyong Middle School in 1909. He moved to Kwangjoo, Mokpo, and finally settled in Seoul.

In Mar 1912 he received an invitation from the president of Severance Medical School and Hospital to teach. He accepted the offer and was installed as the first Korean professor of the school. He taught anatomy, physiology, pathology, and dermatology.

He had much concern for orphans and so founded *Kiong-sung Boyookwon* (Seoul Orphanage) for orphans in 1919. In 1924 he organized the Institute for the Study of Contagious Diseases of Seoul, and in 1928 the Institute of the Anti-Tuberculosis of Severance. In 1931 he founded *Keungsung Yangnowon* (Seoul Senior Citizens House), the first senior citizens' home in Korea. In the same year, he became the second president of the Severance Medical School and Hospital.

Oh was conferred an honorary doctor of medicine by Central University and an honorary juris doctor from Louisville University, his alma mater, in 1934. In 1942 he retired as president of the school and hospital and was named president emeritus.

In 1946 Oh was recommended to be president of the board of the Association of Social Work and was awarded a medal by the Korean government for his contribution to social services. He was also decorated by Severance Medical School, the city of Seoul, Kiongko Province, and the government again.

On 18 May 1963, Oh died, and the funeral ceremony was held at Severance Medical School and Hospital. On Independence Day, 15 Aug 1963, the government awarded him the Supreme Medal of the Government posthumously. He had two sons and three daughters. His first son became minister of the department of health and society of the Korean government.

Bibliography

Haekwan, *Oh, Keung San* (1977). • Lee You Bok, "Oh Keung Sun," *Severance Kioouhoebo* (1934). • Cho, T. S., "Doctor Kung Sun Oh, a Pioneer of Western Medicine in Korea," *Yonsei Medical Journal* (1963). • *Encyclopedia of Christianity (of Korea)* (1994).

KIM IN SOO

Olcott, Henry Steel

(b. Orange, New Jersey, 2 Aug 1832; d. Adayar, Madras, 17 Feb 1907). Founder of the Theosophical Society and advocate of the Buddhist revival in Sri Lanka.

The Theosophical Society was founded in 1875 with Helena Petrovna Blavatsky, William Q. Judge, and others in New York. Olcott became its president. He, with Blavatsky, visited India* in 1878. He settled there in 1879 and in 1882 established the headquarters of the Theosophical Society at Adayar, Madras.

His first contact with Sri Lanka* was made in 1874 when he heard about the Buddhist-Christian debate at Panadura (1873). Thereafter he corresponded with several Buddhist monks in Sri Lanka before his first visit to the island in 1880. When he first arrived in Galle, the leading Buddhist monks of the country gave him a tumultuous welcome, and thereafter he observed *pan sil* (five precepts) and officially embraced Buddhism*.

Olcott came to the rescue of the Sinhala Buddhists when they were put into a disadvantageous position after the Colombo riot of 1883. He made a visit to England to present the case of the Sinhala Buddhists before the colonial government.

The first branch of the Theosophical Society in Sri Lanka was established in 1880. In 1881 Olcott urged the Buddhists in Sri Lanka to establish their own schools. Within a decade, three English colleges and over 250 vernacular schools were established. Olcott assisted them by recruiting teachers from Europe and America.

Olcott was keen to equip the Sinhala Buddhists with modern religious organizational structures. The Young Men's Buddhist Association (1885), Buddhist Sunday schools (1885), a Buddhist catechism (1881), a Buddhist flag (1885), and Buddhist carols (1885) are some of the innovations which owe their origin to Olcott.

Buddhists did not initially understand the difference between theosophy and Buddhism. The realization of this difference later created a rift between Olcott and some prominent Buddhist monks on Sri Lanka.

In 1889, on a visit to Japan, he persuaded the Japanese to enter into cordial relations with Sri Lankan Buddhists for the first time in history. On several occasions during his visits to Sri Lanka, he tried, without success, to get the various Buddhist sects on the island to unite.

Olcott edited the *Theosophists* (1888-1907) from Adayar. His *Buddhist Catechism* (1881) had a great impact on the Buddhist revival in Sri Lanka. It was translated into 22 languages during his lifetime.

Olcott's contribution to Hinduism* is as important in India, where he spent most of his time and located his headquarters. In recognition of his services toward the revival of Hindu philosophy in India, Taranath Tarka Vachaspoti, a well-known pundit in Calcutta, conferred on him the sacred thread of Brahmin caste and adopted him into his *gotra*. Because of the Theosophical Society's stance on the universal brotherhood of humanity, his international headquarters at Adayar became one of the few places in colonial India where all races, faiths, and religions could live together. The schools he opened for pariahs in India became a liberating force.

Olcott is revered by the Sinhala Buddhists for his contribution he made to the enhancement of their culture. He is respected as a national hero, despite the fact that he was an American, because he accelerated the tempo of the Buddhist revival.

Bibliography

Olcott, H. S., *Old Diary Leaves,* 3 Vols. (Madras, 1895, 1899, 1903).

G. P. V. SOMARATNA

Oldham, William Fitzjames

(b. Bangalore, South India, 15 Dec 1854; d. Los Angeles, United States, 27 Mar 1937). Founder of Methodism* in Singapore* and Malaysia*; missionary "beloved of three continents," having served in India*, Singapore, Malaysia, the Philippines*, America, and South America.

The son of a British army officer, Oldham was educated at Madras Christian College. He served for a time as a government engineer and surveyor. Following his conversion and call to the ministry, Oldham proceeded to America to complete college and theological training. Then on their way to India, by a remarkable synchronization of events, Oldham and his wife Maria were met by Bishop Thoburn* at the harbor in Bombay and were told of their appointment to Singapore. The Oldhams always regarded the appointments of the church as God's will.

Thoburn accompanied Oldham, and the party was met by Charles Phillips, an ex-Wesleyan, who had written of the need in Singapore earlier. Singapore was regarded as central to the Malay Peninsula and the islands around, including the Philippines.

Within a short time, the nucleus of the first Methodist church in Singapore came into being. Oldham had the foresight and courage to remain in Singapore as the first resident Methodist missionary pastor. The growth of the Methodist Church was then slow but sure. By December 1885, sufficient funds had been collected for the church to erect its first premises at Coleman Street. Wesley Church was later erected in 1909 at Fort Canning, where it still stands as a mother symbol of Singapore's Methodism.

The education of the young also presented the Methodist missions with a great opportunity for service and outreach, and Oldham was not slow in seizing it. The Anglo-Chinese School began on 1 Mar 1886 at a rented shop house in Amoy Street. With the continued dedication and undaunted spirit of the Oldhams and the cooperation of other missionary workers, it is little wonder that the school quickly gained public acceptance and won recognition for its academic standards.

Apart from preaching five times each week in English and Tamil, Oldham also taught between five to eight hours a day in the rapidly expanding school. Thus he steadfastly continued as superintendent of the Methodist Mission until failing health compelled him to return to the United States in 1889, where he lectured on missions in a Wesleyan university and pastored a local church in Columbus, Ohio.

It has been said of Oldham that there was probably no other person of his years who had a wider acquaintance with missionary history and conditions of that era. Among his several achievements were the establishment of one of the most widely respected and influential educational systems in the region, mission among girls and women, and medical* work. With the missions' help, different churches were established along linguistic lines. Methodists, led by Oldham, were also heavily involved in legislative and social action against the evils of alcohol, tobacco, and opium* addiction at that time. Even years later, in 1904, when Oldham returned to the East as missionary bishop for the region, he was appointed to a government opium commission to investigate and help eradicate the antisocial menace of the drug. He therefore had great influence, directly and indirectly, on the fabric of society in developing Singapore, many effects of which still remain today.

In the United States, Oldham became secretary of the Methodist Board of Foreign Missions and, in 1916, was appointed general superintendent of the Methodist work in South America, a post he held for the next 12 years. He was to visit Singapore for the last time in Jan 1936 at the age of 81, to participate in the weeklong jubilee celebrations of the founding work he had established in Singapore. One unexpected but wonderful event that occurred during that time proved to be a fitting final tribute to this man who gave his life to God.

An elderly Chinese man watching the historical pageant which was part of the festivities was the sole surviving member of that group of 30 whom Oldham had addressed 50 years earlier at the Celestial Reasoning Association. As the Chinese sage watched the drama unfold, his soul was deeply stirred, and two days later his old friend, the aged bishop, baptized him into the fold in a moving ceremony at Wesley Church.

Oldham died in the United States on Easter Day 1937.

Bibliography

Doraisamy, T. R., *The March of Methodism* (1982); *Oldham Called of God* (1979). • Wong, Lana, *By My Spirit.*

HO CHEE SIN

Omar I. *See* Umar I

Ong Van Huyen

(b. North Annam, 15 Jan 1901; d. ?). Classical scholar, general secretary of the Evangelical Church of Vietnam* (ECVN), and president of the Theological and Bible Institute in Nha Trang.

Ong was born into a very prestigious and high- ranking family, his great-grandfather having served as minister of the military in the Annamese empire. He studied Chinese, Vietnamese, and French and, after completing his studies with high honors, became a teacher.

During this period, he became a Christian and had a keen desire to study the Bible. He indicated his desire to enroll in the Tourane Bible School (Nha Trang Theological and Bible Institute), which had been recently established (1921). Ong was not accepted as a student because he looked too young. (In a culture that revered age, youthfulness was not an asset.) But the teacher allowed him to audit some courses for the year. Meanwhile, his wife became a Christian and demonstrated change in her life.

In 1922 Ong was officially accepted as a student but was made to study three years (instead of two) and then do a two-year practicum to plant a church. A church was established and a building was constructed in the southern delta area.

Upon graduation in 1928, Ong returned to the southern delta to start another church in Can Tho. Within a short time, the dean of the Bible school invited him to teach New Testament and Vietnamese. He continued in this ministry for almost five decades, becoming an outstanding lecturer in homiletics. He never forsook his pastoral responsibilities throughout this time and became active in the ECVN, becoming its general secretary, a post he held for 30 years.

During the Japanese Occupation in 1942, all foreign missionaries were interned and later repatriated. Ong assumed leadership at the school until it was temporarily shut down by the Japanese. In 1948, when the missionaries returned, Ong worked as a dean with the missionaries until 1960 when he became the only dean. The school moved to Nha Trang and was called Nha Trang Theological and Bible Institute. Ong was made president of the institute, a title he held until the Communists shut it down in 1976.

Ong has left an indelible mark on the ECVN through the excellent training of pastors who continue to have an impact on Vietnam despite repression by the current government.

Bibliography

Cowles, H. Robert, comp., *Operation Heartbeat* (1976). • James, Violet B., "American Protestant Missions and the Vietnamese War" (Ph.D. diss., University of Aberdeen, 1989). • Sutherland, Spenser T., "Vietnam's Remarkable Mr. Huyen," *Alliance Witness* (26 May 1971).

VIOLET JAMES

Opium

Narcotic derivative of the sap of the Eurasian poppy *(Papaver somniferum).*

Use of, and trade in, opium has taken place in Asia since antiquity but became an organized industry only in the wake of European colonialism*. The intentional development of a market for opium in Asia by European merchants from the early 18th c. on had deleterious social effects throughout the region, particularly in China*. The creation of hundreds of thousands of new addicts weakened societies, as did the vast increase in smuggling and, along with it, the spread of corruption and the undermining of local and national political authorities. The opium trade was closely associated with early Protestant mission efforts, not least through the involvement of Robert Morrison* and Charles Gützlaff*, who distributed Bibles and Christian literature* while serving as translators on ships smuggling opium into China.

The opium industry was initially developed in India*, where the taxable sale of opium was used to help finance the operations of the British East India Company. Realizing the detrimental effects of opium in its base of operations, the company sought export markets to replace Indian consumption. In 1685 the company gained access to the China market through the single open port of Canton (Guanzhou) and began to trade English and Indian goods for Chinese silk and tea. The value of company exports from China soon exceeded the value of goods the Chinese would purchase, since restrictions on foreign traders insured that the Chinese market was largely unaware of the industrial products Europe had to offer. Initially, the imbalance was made up with payments to China in silver from India. In the late 18th c., the company and her European rivals sought to redress the trade balance by illegally importing Indian opium into China through independent agents called "country traders." This strategy proved so successful that the overall balance of trade shifted in favor of the company and its European agents, which used the excess revenues to further finance their operations in India. Where European colonial powers extended their control over Asian governments, as in Malaysia* and the Netherlands East Indies, revenue was derived from licensing fees paid by opium dealers. In the Straits Settlements of Malaysia, this accounted for over 50 percent of government revenues during the 19th c.

In China, by the 19th c., the illegal import of opium was creating intolerable social pressures, as both the corruption and the draining of silver from the economy created political instability. In 1838-39 an imperial commission under Lin Tse-Hsu made progress in stopping the illegal trade, and in 1839 vessels containing 20,000 chests of opium were burned in the Canton harbor. This action, while a legal exercise of Chinese sovereignty, greatly damaged British commercial interests and provoked the Opium War of 1839-42. As victors, Britain imposed the Treaty of Nanking on China, which opened Chinese ports to foreign trade and missionaries. Similar provisions were later extended to other foreign powers. A second conflict broke out in 1856 over the Chinese seizure of an opium cargo at Canton and resulted in wider concessions to European trade. Missionary entrance to China was predicated on the treaties which arose from these events and was thus the direct result, in fact and in the Chinese mind, of the spread of trade in narcotics by the Western powers.

While efforts to suppress the opium trade in China were thwarted by British military intervention, a growing antiopium campaign was being mounted in Europe, India, and the Straits Settlements by missionaries and others aware of its tragic human toll. In the early 20th c., local antiopium sentiment, often aligned with nationalist sympathies, grew throughout Asia, particularly among the overseas Chinese, who were the primary consumers of opium outside of India. As a result of these pressures, an opium commission was appointed in 1894 to investigate opium use in India. Heavily weighted to business interests, it found nothing undesirable in the system of licensed trade. In 1907 an international commission was set up to investigate the opium trade in East Asia. Pressure on Britain to join came from the United States and other countries which had banned or restricted opium in their territories. A similar commission was set up on a local basis in British Malaya. The immediate effect of these commissions, and pressure from the Chinese government on Great Britain, by far the largest supplier, was a restriction on the sale of opium across Asia. By the advent of World War II*, opium no longer played an important role in funding colonial governments or in redressing trade imbalances, and the trade was outlawed. However, neither the large addict population nor the economic needs of the opium suppliers were fully considered in these decisions. Opium was replaced in Asian markets by two other poppy derivatives, morphine and heroin, both of which were easier to smuggle and whose profits were, since they were outlawed, not subject to government taxes.

See also Chinese People's Committee against Opium.

Bibliography

Hsu, Immanuel C. Y., *The Rise of Modern China* (1970) • Owen, David E., *British Opium Policy in India and China* (1968). • Cheng, U Wen, "Opium in the Straits Settlements," *Journal of Southeast Asian History*, Vol. 2, No. 1 (1961). ROBERT HUNT

Opus Dei

Personal prelature of the Roman Catholic Church* with the pastoral mission of spreading, in all spheres of society, a deep awareness of the universal call to holiness and the apostolate in the fulfillment of one's ordinary professional work.

Opus Dei (Latin for "God's work") was founded in Madrid, Spain, on 2 Oct 1928 by Blessed Josemaria Escriva de Balaguer, an Aragonese priest, whose published works in various languages include: *The Way* (over 4 million copies sold), *Christ Is Passing By, Friends of God, The Way of the Cross, The Furrow, The Forge,* and *Holy Rosary.*

Escriva's message was a spiritual revolution that brought Christian spirituality to secular life. "There is no other way," he said. "Either we learn to find Our Lord in ordinary everyday life, or else we shall never find him."

Historical background. Escriva founded Opus Dei when he was 26 and guided and inspired its growth for 47 years. He moved to Rome in 1946, where he lived and worked until his death on 26 Jun 1975, by which time Opus Dei had spread to five continents with over 60,000 members of 80 nationalities. He brought nearly 1,000 professional men to the priesthood. The holy see established Opus Dei as a personal prelature on 28 Nov 1982.

Beatified on 17 May 1992, Escriva also founded the Priestly Society of the Holy Cross in 1943, which is united to the prelature of Opus Dei, whose aim is to provide spiritual and ascetic guidance to secular priests, leading them to sanctify their ministry and to remain always at the disposition of their bishop and the needs of the diocese.

Escriva was succeeded by Bishop Alvaro del Portillo, his closest collaborator, who lived with him for 44 years. Del Portillo died on 23 Mar 1994 in Rome, after making a pilgrimage to the Holy Land. He was succeeded by Msgr. Javier Echevarria, appointed prelate by Pope John Paul II on 20 Apr 1994 and consecrated bishop in Jan 1995. The central offices of Opus Dei are located in Rome.

Opus Dei (officially, Prelature of the Holy Cross and Opus Dei) is a personal prelature of international scope. It is not a religious order or secular institute. The members do not take vows. Its juridical status likewise differentiates it from movements, lay associations, or groups. The figure of the personal prelature was introduced into the legislation of the church by Vatican II.

Opus Dei serves the local church by providing the ongoing spiritual and intellectual formation of its faithful and their friends who, like leaven in the mass, encourage others to seek Christ through their word and example. The prelate maintains relationships with the territorial ecclesiastical authorities in order to carry out this specific task within the church.

Opus Dei in Asia. Opus Dei started apostolic work in the Philippines* in 1964 when two young Filipinos, who joined the institution in the United States, returned to Manila and set up the Maynilad Cultural Center in the Singalong District. Today there are more than 40 centers of Opus Dei in Metro Manila, Laguna, Batangas, Cebu, Iloilo, Bacolod, and Davao. Apostolic activities are held in major cities of the country.

Opus Dei in the Philippines has a number of corporate apostolic undertakings, such as the Makiling Conference Center in Calamba, Laguna; the Center for Research and Communication (CRC) in Pasig; the Punlaan School in San Juan; and the Anihan Rural Development Center in Calamba, Laguna.

The corporate projects are relatively few compared to the various apostolic initiatives organized by members working with their friends or colleagues with the aim of giving Christian formation in all sectors of society. Southridge and Woodrose Schools in Alabang are examples of these initiatives. Others are the EDUCHILD courses on parenting, the Theological Centrum for seminarians and priests, nursery schools, and youth clubs. Many such initiatives are for the less privileged in society, such as the Southridge Night School, the Dagatan Family Farm School in Batangas, the DUALTECH

Orthodox Church

Training Center for technical workers, and the Center for Industrial Technology and Enterprise (CITE) in Cebu, whose students are all on full scholarship.

Escriva and his successor prelates have constantly pushed for apostolic expansion to spread the Christian message and lay spirituality in and from the Philippines. From humble beginnings in Singalong, Manila, Opus Dei now has centers in Hong Kong*, Taiwan*, Singapore*, and Macau*.

Its activities are addressed to people from all walks of life: men and women, students and professionals, intellectuals, farmers, and manual workers, rich and poor. The activities include retreats, doctrinal talks, courses on spirituality, recollections, and spiritual direction, as well as cultural, professional, and sports activities all geared to prepare men and women to give Christian testimony in their respective environments and stimulate others to live out evangelical values.

Membership in Opus Dei. The majority of Opus Dei members are married and are called supernumeraries. A relatively small number, called numeraries and associates, commit themselves to remain single to give more time to the formation of the other members and to the various apostolic activities of the prelature.

Opus Dei is basically for laypeople who see membership as a calling from God, a divine vocation. Members do not carry distinguishing marks or insignias. Priests of the prelature, constituting only 2 percent of the members, come from the ranks of the numeraries and associates who have completed their civil and ecclesiastical studies and attend to the pastoral needs of its faithful.

Opus Dei maintains no political or social platforms other than the moral norms emitted by the Catholic Church regarding such issues.

Bibliography

Escriva, Josemaria, *The Way* (1983). • Berglar, Peter, *Opus Dei, Life and Works of Blessed Josemaria Escriva* (1994). • Fuenmayor, Gomez Iglesias, Illanes, *The Canonical Pathway of Opus Dei* (1994). • Le Tourneau, *All about Opus Dei* (1989).

CONOR DONNELLY

Orthodox Church

Orthodox churches, those churches of the East with historic patriarchs centered in Alexandria, Jerusalem, and Antioch (and later autocephalous churches and their daughter churches in communion with them) have had only limited influence in the development of Christianity in Asia (outside of Russia), further to the East, in the modern period (see the Jacobite Syrian Orthodox Church* and the Malankara Orthodox Church).

China. While there were occasional contacts between the Russian Orthodox and the Chinese, including the employment of Russians who were nominally Orthodox, the first sustained missionary work was the result of a Chinese military victory in 1683. In the area of Siberia claimed by both Russia and China*, a Cossack exploration party was captured and taken to Peking (Beijing). Given the choice of prison or imperial service, they joined the military establishment defending a section of the city wall. Maxim Leontiev*, the parish priest of the fortress of Albazin, was among those seized. He was given an old Buddhist temple as a church to minister to the Russians in imperial service. In 1686 Albazin fell to the Chinese, and some of its Cossack defenders chose to serve the Chinese emperor. The Russians took Chinese wives but nevertheless remained Orthodox. In 1692 some Chinese were baptized, including one of Mandarin rank.

In spite of the unusual beginnings, some in Russia saw this as an opportunity for the advancement of the Christian faith. Peter the Great proposed sending an entire delegation, his motives being more political than evangelistic. To the Chinese, the Russian priests were Chinese civil servants, while the Russian Orthodox Church considered them missionaries. Their status as civil servants continued until 1737, with the mission supported by the Chinese government until 1858. The archimandrite, head of the mission, was the Russian ambassador to Peking as well as a Chinese civil servant. All diplomatic relations between Russia and China were conducted through the Peking monastery.

The religious work of the Russians was primarily confined to preserving the faith of the Albazin descendants, their government wanting to be sure that the missionaries studied Oriental languages to serve as a liaison with the Chinese court. It is the judgment of Eastern Orthodox scholars that for two centuries the Orthodox missionaries did no real missionary activity but engaged in scientific research and writing and regrettably took no advantage of favorable circumstances to spread their faith. It was only after 1858 that missionary work commenced with the separation of the diplomatic legation from the mission. Isaias Polikin, a monk, was able to establish a Christian community at Dun-Dinan, but his efforts at creating an indigenous clergy did not bear fruit until 1884, when a native Chinese was ordained to the priesthood.

Missionary work moved forward under Innocent Figourovsky*, who had four definite aims for the mission: (1) Christian education for the Chinese by upgrading preaching and catechism; (2) youth ministry by strengthening the school system; (3) publishing (he printed a Russian-Chinese dictionary); and (4) social services and evangelization. The Boxer Rebellion was a severe setback. All churches but one were burned; the press and library also were lost. While considerably smaller, the Orthodox had a greater loss in proportion to their total numbers than did either the Roman Catholics or the Protestants.

Figourovsky returned to China after the rebellion as a bishop and used the compensation for the losses incurred to rebuild the mission. A master of innovation, he transformed railway cars into chapels and schools to minister to the 80,000 Orthodox in Manchuria, many of whom worked for the railroad. Fifteen of his 34 workers were artisans and technicians. In spite of striking growth in the early years of the 20th c., the Orthodox remained a minority church in China.

The Russian Revolution brought change as funds were cut off and mission stations closed. Conversely, immigration of White Russians settling in Manchuria added greatly to the Orthodox presence in China. The Diocese of Harbin became a center of Orthodoxy even under Japanese occupation, an Orthodox university and theological seminary being founded there. However, emigration from Russia slowed up the work of the Orthodox mission because of (1) hesitancy to engage in proselytizing in a host country; (2) absorption of clergy ministering to the needs of refugees*; and (3) lack of missionary vision that furthered a ghetto mentality. Prior to the Pacific War, there were five Orthodox parishes in China: Beijing, Tianjin, Shanghai, Harbin, and Xinjiang.

The Communist (see Communism) victory on the mainland led to the Orthodox Church of China having a Chinese bishop, Simon Du, in 1950 and becoming autonomous in 1957. In that same year Basil Yau Fu-An was consecrated bishop of Beijing. Figures published in 1961 estimated 20,000 Orthodox believers. The Cultural Revolution of 1966 caused the closing of all places of worship, and current estimates show fewer than 10,000 Orthodox in China.

Korea. Late in the 19th c., some Korean emigrants in Russia became Orthodox, returned to their country, and established a mission in Jul of 1897. However, the Korean government would not grant Russian missionaries permission to enter Korea*. The political ambition of Russia coupled with Japan's desire to keep Russian influence out of Korea no doubt added to the problem. After waiting two years at the border town of Novokievsk, they returned to St. Petersburg. Visas were granted after prolonged negotiations, and the first resident missionaries arrived in Korea in 1900.

Archimandrite Chrysanthe Scetkovskij ministered to Orthodox Koreans and evangelized. When the necessity for a Korean translation of the liturgy, catechism, and ordinary prayers became apparent, he applied for assistance to Figourovsky in China, but the Boxer Rebellion prevented such cooperation. Translation work was abandoned, and missionary effort was put into establishing a school.

The Russo-Japanese War* halted all mission work as Korea was unable to remain neutral, and Russian missionaries were forced to leave. After the war the mission returned under a new head, Archimandrite Paul Ivanovsky, whose six years of leadership proved the most successful for the mission. Many works were translated, including the entire collection of liturgical books, and the first Korean was ordained to the priesthood. However, the Russian Revolution in 1917 meant an end to missionary funds.

The difficult history of the Korean people has affected the Orthodox Church there. During the Japanese occupation the church came under the supervision of the diocese of Japan*. During the Korean War* Alexios Kim, the Korean priest, was captured and exiled. Providentially, chaplains accompanying the Greek Expeditionary Force took over the services, allowing the church to continue. At present there is a small Orthodox community in Korea with some young Koreans trained in Athens. The priest of the Seoul congregation in the late 1970s was Daniel Na, a graduate of Holy Cross School of Theology in Massachusetts, United States.

Japan. The arrival in 1861 of Nicholas Kassatkin* (1836-1912) in Hakodate as chaplain to the Russian consulate in Japan was the beginning of Orthodox missionary work. He engaged in language study and met with Japanese who were interested in Christian teaching. Because of the political situation, conditions favored change even though it was illegal to convert. In Apr 1868 he was able to baptize his first converts, who took Christian names, becoming Paul Sawabe, John Sakai, and Jacob Urano.

Kassatkin decided to commence a regular Orthodox mission and traveled to Russia to submit his plans before the Holy Synod. The rules he constructed to govern the mission specified that the new converts evangelize. This principle accounts for the success of the work in Japan since there were never more than four foreign workers during the entire history of the Orthodox Church in Japan.

Refusing a bishopric in Peking (Beijing), Kassatkin returned to Japan in Feb 1871. Early in 1872 he purchased land overlooking Tokyo, where he established a school and later built the Cathedral of the Resurrection, known by the Japanese as *Nicolai-Do* (House of Nicholas). Some converts were imprisoned, but official persecution ended with a decree on 10 Feb 1873 ordering the removal of anti-Christian edicts from public notice boards.

The Great Synod met biennially with lay delegates from every congregation to decide on the business of individual congregations and the Japanese church as a whole. In 1875 Sawabe was ordained to the priesthood and Sakai ordained as deacon. The number of Japanese priests rose steadily, with 34 more evangelists ordained by 1890.

Nicholas remained in Japan during the Russo-Japanese War, though he withdrew from public services since the liturgy required the celebrant to pray for the armed forces of the nation. Church growth was slowed by the war even though the war enabled Japanese priests to minister to 73,000 Russian prisoners of war. In return the prisoners constructed several chapels for the church. In 1906 Kassatkin was promoted to archbishop, and in 1911 he celebrated 50 years of missionary service. When he died on 16 Feb 1912, the Japanese Orthodox Church had a membership of 33,017 organized in 266 congregations and served by 35 Japanese priests, 22 deacons, and 106 catechists.

The Cathedral of the Resurrection, destroyed by the earthquake of 1923, was rebuilt through the sacrificial giving of the Japanese. World events arose so that, in 1940, the church, compelled by the Japanese government to prepare a new constitution, was forced to declare its independence from Moscow. After World War II* the church submitted to the jurisdiction of the North American Metropolitanate rather than return to Moscow's jurisdiction. When the North American Metropolitanate became the autocephalous Orthodox Church of America, the Japanese Orthodox Church retained its autonomous status under the Patriarchate of Moscow.

Bibliography

Caruso, Igor A., "Missions Orthodoxes en Coree," *Irenikon,* Vol. 11 (1934). • Cary, Otis, *Roman Catholic and Greek Orthodox Missions,* Vol. 1 of *A History of Christianity in Japan* (1909). • Drummond, Richard H., *A History of Christianity in Japan* (1971). • Hale, Charles R., *Missions of the Russian Church in China and Japan* (repr. ed. 1975). • Latourette, Kenneth Scott, *A History of Christian Missions in China* (1929). • Stamoolis, James J., *Eastern Orthodox Mission Theology Today* (repr. ed. 1992). • Widmer, Eric, *The Russian Ecclesiastical Mission in Peking during the Eighteenth Century* (1976).

James J. Stamoolis, with contributions from the China Group

Osias, Camilo O.

(b. Bacnotan, La Union, 23 Mar 1889; d. Manila, 1976). Filipino educator, author, statesman, and lay church leader.

A former Catholic seminarian, Osias was first drawn to the Protestant missionaries through his curiosity about the Bible* and his desire to learn English. He was converted and joined the United Brethren in 1904.

After studying in the United States on a government scholarship (1905-10), he rose quickly from supervising teacher to the first Filipino superintendent of schools. He became assistant director of education in 1917 and served as president of the National University (1921-41), Philippine senator (1925-29), and later Philippine resident commissioner in Washington, D.C. (1929-35). As a delegate to the Philippine Constitutional Convention in 1934, an assemblyman in 1938, and a senator in 1965, he consistently defended religious freedom and the separation of church and state.

Zealous for church union (see Ecumenical Movement), Osias was the prime mover behind the organization in 1924 of the United Church of Manila.

Bibliography

Laubach, F. C., *People of the Philippines* (1925). • Roberts, W. N., *The Filipino Church* (1936). • Galang, Z. M., *Encyclopaedia of the Philippines,* Vol. 9 (1936). • United Church of Manila, *Golden Jubilee Book* (1974). • Sitoy, T. V., Jr., *Several Springs, One Stream* (1992).

T. Valentino Sitoy, Jr.

Osorio, Adriano Reyes y

(b. ?; d. mid-1930s). First Filipino Presbyterian* evangelist, "the Apostle of Antique."

Osorio and his wife became Protestants while in Spain in the 1890s. When American Presbyterian* missionaries came to Osorio's native Iloilo City in 1900, he became their ready evangelist. Intelligent, highly cultured, and eloquent, he was instrumental in the early organization of the Presbyterian Church of Iloilo in Sep 1900. By 1901 Osorio was conducting 16 regular weekly services with an aggregate attendance of about 1,000.

In 1902 Osorio convinced several villages in Antique province to become Protestant en masse. Ordained the second Filipino Presbyterian minister in 1905, Osorio served as pastor of Culasi Evangelical Church until his retirement in 1916. Culasi became a strong Protestant center, with nearly half the Panay Presbyterians coming from its immediate environs by 1918.

Bibliography

The Assembly Herald (Presbyterian), Vol. 5 (Jul 1901), Vol. 12 (Jul 1906). • *65th Annual Presbyterian Board Report* (1902). • Rodgers, J. B., *Forty Years in the Philippines* (1940). • Sitoy, T. V., Jr., *Several Springs, One Stream* (1992).

T. Valentino Sitoy, Jr.

Osrhoene

Independent Syrian (some sources say Parthian or Arab) kingdom between Roman territory, Commagene, Adiabene*, and Persian territory, and then a Roman/Byzantine province.

The kingdom was founded ca. 130 B.C.E. and was incorporated as a Roman province probably in 214 C.E. but perhaps as late as 240 C.E. The capital of Osrhoene was Edessa. Its wealth was derived from its position on the trade routes that ran east of Antioch toward China* and India*. The name Osrhoene is probably a Syriac phrase which means "ten eyes," a reference to the 10 hills that constituted the old city. The area remained contested between the Roman and Persian Empires until the Arab invasions of the 7th c. The other early name for the city, Urfa, is attested in early Near Eastern sources.

The Christian tradition for the early period is difficult to map with certainty. According to Eusebius, the correspondence between Jesus and Abgar* reproduced by Eusebius demonstrated the early founding of Christianity. While that correspondence is certainly inauthentic, it is probable that versions of Christianity arrived in Edessa during the 1st c. The early Addai* and Thomas* traditions are difficult to accept as authentic in their present forms, as authentic on the basis of extant information. According to the independent witness of Julius

Africanus, the theologian Bardaisan* was part of the royal entourage at Edessa in about 196 C.E. The *Chronicle of Edessa* records that in 312, a flood destroyed the Christian church, and that after Nicaea, at which Edessa was represented, a church with a cemetery was constructed. Hints of conflict between the various Christian- and Jewish-related religious traditions in 4th c. Edessa can be seen in the writings of Ephrem* of Syria, who, according to tradition, moved to Edessa after Nisibis was surrendered to the Persians in 363 C.E. During the late 4th and early 5th c. a theological school flourished at Edessa. Because of internal conflicts and competing theological commitments, as well as pressure from the competing Byzantine and Persian governments, it became necessary to divide the institution. Therefore, in the 5th c. the East Syrians (the so-called Nestorians*) left the city to establish the theological school, sometimes called a university, in Nisibis*.

During the Crusades, Edessa was occupied by a Crusader force that established an independent state known as the County of Edessa. This was eventually destroyed by Turkish and Mongol* forces, but the occupation proved disastrous for the local Christians, who were often blamed by the Islamic majority population for the deeds of the western European Christians who made up the occupying forces. Edessa is now again known as Urfa and is located in southeastern Turkey.

Bibliography

Bundy, D., "The Life of Abercius: Its Significance for Early Syriac Christianity," *Second Century* 7 (1989-90); "Christianity in Syria," *Anchor Bible Dictionary* 1 (1992). • Dillemann, L., *Haute Mésopotamie orientale et pays adjacents* (1962). • Drijvers, H. J. W., *Bardaisan of Edessa* (1966); *East of Antioch* (1984). • Jansma, T., *Natuur, Lot en Vrijheid: Bardesanes, de filosoof der Arameërs en zijn images* (1969). • Phillips, G., *The Doctrine of Addai* (1876). • Segal, J. B., *Edessa the Blessed City* (1970). • Teixidor, J., *Bardesane d'Édesse: la première philosophie syriaque* (1992).

David Bundy

Osthathios, Mar Geevarghese

(b. Mavelikkara, 9 Dec 1918). Prominent Indian mission-theologian and social worker.

Mar Osthathios, bishop of the Malankara Orthodox Syrian Church, is widely known as M. V. George. After his theological education at Jabalpur and in America, he became a professor at the Orthodox Seminary. He started many institutions and service programs, including St. Paul's Mission Training Center at Mavelikkara, Marriage Assistance Foundations, Sick Aid Foundation, St. Paul's Ashram and Boys' Home at Puthuppady, and Mar Gregorios Boys' Home at Yacharam. He authored about 30 books, some of which have been translated into German. His *Theology of a Classless Society* has drawn the attention of mission-thinkers, especially because it eloquently argues that the model for human sharing is found in the Holy Trinity. Mar Osthathios was also engaged in a massive project running the *balavadis* (nurseries) in the villages of North India. Jacob Kurian

Osthathios, Patros

(b. northern Kerala, 1886; d. 2 Feb 1968). First Christian leader in Kerala to initiate programs for the benefit of the low castes.

Osthathios was born into an ancient Syrian Christian family. As a student, he wrote and spoke against the untouchability and social discrimination practiced by the high castes. Known as M. P. Patros, he was the first educational secretary appointed by the king of Cochin to initiate educational programs for low-caste people. He took part in the famous solidarity demonstration at Vaikom to plead for the rights of low-caste people in Kerala. Later he became a deacon, priest, and bishop of the Malankara Orthodox Church. He believed he had a twofold calling: (1) to lead a movement pleading for the indigenous character of the church, especially emphasizing worship in the local language; (2) to lead a missionary movement to work among low-caste and outcaste people.

He put on *kavi* robes and traveled extensively on foot, living on the same bare subsistence level as the poor. He supported the vernacular movement. Osthathios founded the Society of the Servants of the Cross* on 14 Sep 1924 to work among low-class people and baptized about 25,000 non-Christian Dalits*. He had a typical Indian style of visiting the people, helping them, and conducting prayer meetings. Upon his death, he was buried at Carmel Dayara, Kandanad, Mulanthuruthy.

Jacob Kurian

P

Pacific War. *See* World War II

Padroado

Abbreviated form of *Padroado Real* of the Portuguese, or the *Patronato Real* of the Castillians, standing for the "crown patronage" of the missionary expansion.

Padroado had its origin during the Iberian wars of *Reconquista* in the peninsula and northern Africa and then became a religious accompaniment of the discoveries and overseas expansion of the Iberian powers. The encirclement of European Christendom by Islamic forces and the loss of adherents of the papacy due to reformation in northern and central Europe produced a convergence of interests and made mutual dependence of the papacy and the Catholic kingdoms of western Europe a timely necessity. From it emerged the system of crown patronage *(Padroado/Patronato)* that was initially favorable for all concerned, but an early decline of the Portuguese political and military presence in the East made it a liability for the papacy and for the interests of the church in Asia at large. Both Castille (Spain) and Portugal provided the geographic knowledge, personnel, and material means for the expansion of the church overseas.

Padroado, or "patronage," was not only a form of ecclesiastical benefice and royal patronage but also a contract between the church and the state, a form of church-state relationship in which the state played an active role in the administration and support of the church. It developed extensively in the colonial empires of Portugal and Spain. Papal grants were its foundation, but it was extended through the centuries by the unilateral action of the state, since this patronage was vigorously defended by both Portugal and Spain. Two kinds of rights were assigned to the patron, namely, *jus praesentandi* (which entitled the patron to appoint someone to the ecclesiastical benefice, whether as bishop, parish priest, abbot, etc.) and *jus honorifica.*

Christianity throughout Europe had, in part, developed by means of this system of patronage. In the 15th c., Portuguese patronage was extended overseas by the popes, as the building of churches and the formation and maintenance of missionaries entailed enormous expenses. The Order of Christ, established in Portugal in 1319, first received this right of patronage. As the administrators of the Order of Christ were members of the royal family, the overseas patronage became known as the royal patronage. Playing an important role in the destiny of Portugal was Henry the Navigator, one of the sons of John I, king of Portugal (1385-1433), born at Porto on 4 Mar 1394. In 1415 Henry took the city of Ceuta, on the North African coast, and this marked the beginning of a new era of Portuguese exploits in maritime discovery. Henry worked out a grand strategy to take Western Christendom to the Indian Ocean.

Pope Martin V (1417-31) started a long list of graces and privileges, granted by the church to the Portuguese overseas patronage, in his bull *Sane Charissimus* of 4 Apr 1418. In view of his work for the cause of the faith, which included the conversion of African Negroes, Pope Nicholas V (1447-55), with the bull *Romanus Pontifex* of 8 Jan 1455, and Pope Callistus III (1455-58), with the bull *Inter Caetera* of 13 Mar 1456, bestowed on Henry special privileges.

King John II (1481-95), after the death of Henry, took up the work again, and with great zeal. But during this period, Spain contemporaneously emerged as a strong Catholic political power and allied itself closely with the papacy. It is significant that Rome used the term *catholicissimus* (most Catholic) to address the king of Spain. Upon the return of Christopher Columbus from his first trip to America, Ferdinand and Isabella immediately asked Pope Alexander VI (1492-1503) for documents affirming their right to the recently discovered territory and investing them with the extent of jurisdiction similar to that formerly conferred on the kings of Portugal. It was an opinion, as ancient perhaps as the Crusades, that the pope, as vicar of Christ, had competent authority to dispose of all countries inhabited by heathen nations, in favor of Christian potentates or Christian kings. In their application to the holy see, they were careful to represent their own discoveries as in no way interfering with the rights formerly conceded by it to their neighbors. They proposed wider services on their part for the propagation of the faith, which they affirmed to be the principal motive of their present operations.

On 3 May 1493, Alexander VI published the bull *Inter Caetera* in which he, of his own and certain knowledge and with his plenitude of apostolic power, confirmed these rights for them in the possession of all lands discovered, or thereafter to be discovered by them, in the western ocean. This gave the same rights of jurisdiction formerly conceded to the kings of Portugal. To avoid rivalry between the powers and to avoid any misunderstanding with the Portuguese, the pope drew a line of demarcation between Spanish and Portuguese zones of exploration in the New World, a hundred leagues west of the Azores and Cape Verde Islands.

That which lay to the west was to belong to Spain; that to the east to Portugal. Other bulls followed: *Piis Fidelium* of 25 Jun 1493, granting vicarial power to appoint the missionaries who were to go to the Indies, and various privileges to these and to the natives of the lands discovered; *Inter Caetera* of 28 Jun 1493, broader than the bull of the same name, with some variations but with the same intent; *Eximiae Devotionis* of 2 Jul 1493, granting *pleno jure* all the privileges that the Portuguese enjoyed; and *Dudum Siquidem* of 25 Sep 1493, which annulled the previous concessions and made a new general grant, unconditional and unlimited and broader so as to include India*.

Since the papal line of demarcation cooped up their enterprises within narrow limits and favored Spain, the Portuguese complained and contended that the line should be removed 370 leagues west of the Cape Verde Islands instead of just 100. By the Treaty of Tordesillas on 7 Jun 1494, the line was moved 370 leagues to the west, and thus Brazil was acknowledged as Portuguese responsibility.

At length Pope Alexander VI, by the brief *Cum Sicut Magestas* of 26 Mar 1500, again confirmed and decreed that the apostolic commissar for the newly discovered lands would be appointed by the Portuguese king. Since the rights acquired by the king over the territories of the Indies were not clarified, the grant of general patronage was issued again during the papacy of Julius II (1503-13). The bull *Universalis Ecclesiae* of 28 Jul 1508 gave the rulers of Portugal the right in perpetuity to grant permission for the construction of churches and to propose persons for the offices and benefices of the cathedrals, collegiate churches, monasteries, and other institutions for religious services. It stipulated that presentations for benefices decreed in consistory were to be made to the pope and to the rest of the bishops.

Pope Leo X (1513-21) issued the bull *Cum Fidei Constantiam* of 7 Jun 1514, restoring all jurisdiction to the Order of Christ. At the same time, the pope, by another bull, *Pro Excellenti Praemanentia* of 12 Jun 1514, erected the diocese of Funchal in the Madeira Islands, and to this were attached India and Brazil. Moreover, Pope Leo X confirmed the rights of patronage in different documents, especially in *Praecelsae Devotionis* of 3 Nov 1514, which confirmed all the privileges conceded by Nicholas V and Sixtus IV. These privileges were extended to the unknown lands.

The right of presenting the candidate for bishop was reserved for the crown of Portugal, while the presentation of candidates for other ecclesiastical posts was the privilege of the administrator of the Order of Christ. Pope Paul III (1534-49), by the bull *Aequum Reputamus* of 3 Nov 1534, erected the diocese of Goa, the patronage of which was given to the Portuguese crown. In this bull we find a clear definition of the Portuguese patronage, or *Padroado.* According to this definition, the right of presenting to the pope a suitable candidate for the bishopric, as well as the right of presenting to the bishop candidates for the four dignities, canonicates, and benefices, was given to the king. The king on his part was bound to provide for the necessities of the diocese: payment of the ecclesiastical officials; building and repairing churches, chapels, and monasteries; and providing them with necessary articles for divine worship.

It is interesting to note that these two nations, Spain and Portugal, were still continuing, more or less, in the political and religious spirit of the Middle Ages. With their strong attachment to the papacy and to the idea of the universal Christian republic, they became the instruments for the expansion of the church in the newly discovered countries.

As the administration of the Order of Christ was incorporated in the Portuguese crown, the right of patronage too was thus incorporated. This was confirmed by the papal bull *Praeclara charissimi* of Paul III, dated 30 Dec 1551. In 1558 Paul IV raised the diocese of Goa to metropolitan status, with the suffragan dioceses of Cochin and Malacca*. In 1575 Gregory XIII erected the diocese of Macau*, including under its jurisdiction China*, Japan*, and other adjacent islands. In 1558 the diocese of Funay was created by Sixtus V, including the Japanese province of Bungo and other territories and islands of Japan, as a suffragan of Goa archdiocese. In 1580 Portugal fell under the Spanish crown and remained thus up to 1640, when a national revolution reestablished a Portuguese dynasty on the throne. In this period (1580-1640), something new happened within the church organization. The Congregation for the Propagation of the Faith (Propaganda Fide*) was established in 1622, taking command of all mission work, having ordered the missionaries by "the instructions" to evangelize the lands other than those already under *Padroado.* By 1640, after the victory of the Portuguese revolution, relations between the two missionary bodies were seriously undermined, and the Portuguese *Padroado* had been greatly reduced in Asia.

Under Spanish pressures, the holy see did not recognize John IV as legitimate king of Portugal until 28 years later. In the meantime, the sees on the Continent and overseas were not filled when vacant. The French too had entered the fray under Louis XIV, and the Jesuit Alexandre de Rhodes* sought to promote French national interests in the East by founding the *Société des Missions Étrangères* (Paris Foreign Mission Society*) under the aegis of Propaganda Fide in 1658. Vicars apostolic were sent directly by Propaganda Fide, but with instructions to be prudent and not to interfere unduly with the jurisdiction of the *Padroado.* But since no exact notions of geography were available, clashes were unavoidable. The holy see tended to support the vicars apostolic while trying to do justice to Portuguese claims. It was often an impossible task, and the more visible trend was to limit the Portuguese *Padroado* to territories under its effective political control. Still, in 1690 Alexander VIII created two new *Padroado* dioceses, those of Peking (Beijing) and Nanking (Nanjing). These areas were earlier under the diocese of Macau. However, under Pope Innocent XIII some territories were put under vicars apostolic and taken out of the *Padroado* jurisdiction. Siam (Thailand*) was such a case, as were Tonkin and Cochin China (under French missionaries). These regions were detached from Malacca (see the following section on Siam). The political situation in Portugal during these extended periods of diplomatic isolation from the Vatican only made matters worse.

The Society of Jesus (Jesuits*) had been a strong pillar of the Portuguese *Padroado* in the East. The persecution of the Jesuits in Portugal (1759), France (1762), and Spain (1767), and the suppression of the Society by Clement XIV under the pressure of the Bourbon kings on 21 Jul 1773, further weakened the Portuguese *Padroado* missions. The Goan native clergy did a magnificent job in sustaining the network of missions as best they could. The native Congregation of Oratorians, led by the Goan priest Joseph Vaz*, was particularly notable in its achievements in Ceylon (Sri Lanka) following the expulsion of Portuguese European missionaries by the Dutch, and in Goa following the suppression of the Jesuits. Unfortunately, the native clerics seldom got the recognition they deserved. On the contrary, the colonial discrimination made them victims of bad propaganda. It is not surprising that native priests in Goa (1787) and in the Philippines* (1872) led unsuccessful political revolts to end the racial discrimination within the colonial church structures. Much earlier, the first ever vicar apostolic of Propaganda Fide, D. Matheus de Castro, a Goan native, fought bitterly the racial discrimination of the white regular clergy in Goa and even conspired with the neighboring Muslim rulers of Bijapur and the Dutch at Vingurl to expel the Portuguese from Goa in 1654.

The climate generated by the reforms of Pombal, and later by the French Revolution (ca. 1789) and liberalism in Portugal, further contributed to deterioration of church-state relations. Antichurch legislation of liberal governments in Portugal in the 1830s led to the severance of diplomatic relations with the Vatican until 1841. Under this climate, *Padroado* did little for the upkeep of its missions, making it necessary for Propaganda Fide to step in more actively, creating its vicariates in Calcutta and Madras in 1834 and in Pondicherry and Ceylon in 1836. Several Portuguese dioceses remained vacant: Goa since 1831, Cranganore since 1823, Cochin since 1822, and Mylapore since 1820.

In 1838, after consulting three important theologians, the holy see issued the bull *Multa Praeclare* (24 Apr), which was a first major blow to the jurisdiction of the *Padroado.* It transferred the missions of St. Thome of Mylapore to the Madras Vicariate, missions of Cranganore and Cochin to the Verapoly Vicariate, and those of Malacca to Ava and Pegu. This step, without sufficient tact and without the consent of the Portuguese crown, was unacceptable to *Padroado* and led to a violent exchange of writings from either side. The bull had not touched the jurisdiction of Goa Archdiocese, and this led to serious conflict of double jurisdiction with the vicar apostolic Bishop Hartmann in Bombay, resulting in intervention by the Vatican with *Probe Nostis* and the so-called Goan Schism. The Portuguese parliament declared four Goan priests, condemned by the Vatican for siding with the *Padroado* cause in the Bombay Vicariate, as national heroes in 1853. The archbishop of Goa, D. José Maria da Silva Torres, who was too truculent on the issue, was recalled to Portugal, and a more practical and mutually acceptable solution was sought through a concordat between Portugal and the holy see in 1857. It respected the Portuguese *Padroado* in Goa, Cochin, Mylapore, and Malacca and ordered a demarcation of the jurisdiction of Goa before a ratification of the concordat in 1860. This process did not really take place, and Pius IX suggested a revision of the concordat, to which Portugal reluctantly agreed in 1871; but it was not worked out until 23 Jun 1886 under Leo XIII. *Padroado* was reduced to Goa with the diocese of Daman, the titular diocese of Cranganore, and the dioceses of Cochin, St. Thomas of Mylapore, Malacca, and Macau. This set to rest the problems from outside. In India, the local national hierarchy could finally emerge. In recognition of its historic services to the church, the holy see granted to the Goa Archdiocese the honorific title of patriarchate.

But the new threat for the *Padroado* came from within, from the Portuguese republicans, after 1910. Relations with the Vatican were again interrupted until 1918. The republicans sought to end *Padroado,* but, after hearing the views of its representatives in India, no action was taken. The church ties were considered beneficial for Portuguese national interests in territories outside Portuguese jurisdiction in India. The positive attitude was rewarded by the Vatican after the restoration of diplomatic relations by granting cardinalate to Lisbon in 1923. In 1928-29 new agreements took place: Daman Diocese was suppressed, and Bombay would be alternately under Portuguese and British candidates.

When Salazar came to power and instituted the so-called *Estado Novo* in Portugal, he sought to retain what could be maintained of the *Padroado*. The Concordat of 1940 recognized semi-*Padroado* rights, and following the independence of India in 1947, Portugal signed a fresh accord with the Vatican in 1950 renouncing the right to present candidates to the dioceses of Mangalore, Quilon, Trichinopoly, Cochin, St. Thome, and Bombay, and also freeing itself from all responsibilities for the maintenance of those churches. In 1953, also, some missions that had earlier depended on Goa were transferred to local bishops. The Goa Archdiocese was reduced to Goa, Daman, and Diu, which came under Indian occupation in 1961. Only in 1974, after the fall of the Salazar regime, did the new rulers of Portugal officially renounce *Padroado* rights in India. Only then could the Vatican raise the native administrator apostolic of Goa, Raul N. Gonsalves, to the dignity of archbishop and patriarch. Macau then remained as the last vestige of *Padroado* under Portuguese rule.

Siam, Padroado, *and apostolic vicars.* The Jesuit mission of Siam was part of the province of Japan and hence depended on the provincial who was residing at Macau. The influence of *Padroado* extended over this part of the world, with jurisdiction of the diocese of Goa, Malacca, and Macau. However, it is well known also that, instead of supporting the missions, the *Padroado* system had become a hindrance. Missionaries of other countries, members of various religious orders, were allowed to work only under the conditions of *Padroado* and also in limited numbers.

After the Council of Trent, the holy see became more and more conscious of its duty to direct missionary work instead of leaving it to the Spanish and Portuguese *Padroado*. In 1622 the Congregation of Propaganda Fide was officially established, and in 1658, through the initiative of Jesuit Alexander de Rhodes, Missions Étrangères de Paris (MEP) was founded.

Jean de Bourges recorded that Lambert de la Motte*, himself, and Fr. Dédier left Marseilles on 27 Nov 1660 for Cochin China, but, in order not to pass the mission lands under the *Padroado*, as the instruction of Propaganda Fide had said, they took the route passing Persia. They arrived at Tenesserim on 19 May 1662. Here de la Motte met Fr. Cardoza, a Portuguese Jesuit in charge of two parishes there, who treated them with great hospitality. Cardoza invited the bishop to celebrate the sacrament of confirmation for the Christians in his parish. They left Tenesserim on 30 Jun 1662 and arrived at Ayutthaya on 22 Aug 1662; initially they stayed in the Portuguese settlement.

The news of the arrival of the bishop spread throughout the Portuguese settlement, and most of the Catholics came to greet and congratulate him with joy according to the custom of the country. However, it was very difficult not to admit his rights to superiority. Soon the bishop noticed the poor spiritual condition of the place, and this made them decide to stay on their own. Moreover, the situation was rather bad, as Launay describes.

In fact, two or three weeks after their arrival, Fr. Fragoso, a Dominican* and an official of the inquisition of Goa, called the bishop to be present in the procession at the tribunal, but he did not go. The archbishop of Goa also called him to Goa, but he did not go there either, since the apostolic vicar was not under the Portuguese *Padroado*.

Nationality was not the cause of the violent opposition that was to develop between the missionaries of the *Padroado* and the apostolic vicar. Among the Jesuits and other religious groups was already, in addition to the Portuguese, a mixture of nationalities many of whom occupied important positions. Rather, the cause was the fact that the French missionaries had been sent by Propaganda Fide to break the monopoly of the mission in this part of the world that came under the Portuguese *Padroado*.

The first victim of this opposition was de Rhodes, because he had initiated the foundation of the MEP. When he wanted to go back to the missions, his Jesuit superior did not dare allow him to return to any that depended on the *Padroado*. In 1654, at the age of 64, he was sent to Persia, where he died four years later, having worked so successfully that the Shah attended his funeral.

In fact, the *Padroado* meant there was no distinction between church and state. The archbishop of Goa, as well as any missionary, even non-Portuguese who depended on the *Padroado*, looked on the newcomers as intruders and usurpers of the legitimate religious authority.

On 27 Jan 1664, the other apostolic vicar, François Pallu*, arrived at Ayutthaya together with Fr. Laneau*, Fr. Hainques, Fr. Brindeau, and a lay assistant, De Chameson-Foissy. Lambert and Pallu agreed that Siam, with its policy of religious tolerance, was the most convenient base for their persecuted missions of Cochin China, Tonkin, and China. So they asked Rome for jurisdiction over Siam. After a long consideration of this request, Rome approved it in 1669 by the brief *Cum Sicut* of 4 Jun 1669 and *Speculatores* of 13 Sep 1669, insisting only that the peace they enjoyed in Siam should not let them forget their more important missions. On 25 Mar 1674, Laneau was nominated bishop of Metelopolis and apostolic vicar of Siam; he was consecrated by Lambert and Pallu.

The transferred jurisdiction of the Siam mission from the head of the Malacca Diocese to the apostolic vicar did not stop opposition to the *Padroado*. On the contrary, it grew even more embittered. Notwithstanding all the orders coming from Rome between 1673 and 1674 (three bulls and four other constitutions were issued to support the authority of the apostolic vicar), the *Padroado* declared them null and void, since they contradicted the privileges of the *Padroado*.

According to Launay, Bartolomeo da Costa and Joao de Abreu, both Jesuits, created the most serious opposition against Lambert. It seemed that there was a sign of reconciliation when the Portuguese and the Jesuits accepted the French missionaries' invitation to support them at the first annual festival of the mission on St. Joseph's Day, but the reconciliation was not permanent. On the third and last visit to Siam in 1682, Bishop Pallu brought with him the text of the famous oath the pope ordered his vicars to administer to every priest in his diocese, acknowledging the sole right of Rome to dispatch missions and requiring all priests to obtain the vicar's sanction before officiating. This order placed the Portuguese and Jesuits in Siam definitely under the control of the French bishop in Ayutthaya, and so it was not gladly accepted.

The priests under the *Padroado* in Siam protested to the apostolic vicar that they were ready to submit to the orders of Rome as soon as the Jesuits, who were the most important group of *Padroado* missionaries, had made their submission, since the apostolic vicar exerted pressure and threatened to excommunicate them if they did not submit.

They also added that it was right and proper for the Jesuits to lead the way by reason of the influence they enjoyed both in court circles and over the masses, as this influence rendered them better able both to gain approval for those who took the oath and to obtain remission of the threatened sanctions. So the Jesuits in Siam were responsible for the insubordination of others. Propaganda Fide began to exert pressure on the Jesuits, which explains the series of papal fulminations and other hard treatment inflicted upon the Society in Rome. The Jesuit general in Rome found himself between the anvil of *Padroado* and the hammer of Propaganda Fide. If he were to force the Jesuits in Siam, Tonkin, and Cochin China to submit to the apostolic vicars, he would provoke a reaction of the Portuguese government, which would affect all the other Jesuit missions depending on the *Padroado*.

The general of the Society delayed until 1674 before issuing orders that all the Jesuits should submit themselves to the apostolic vicars. At last, on 10 Oct 1681, by the order of the general, the Jesuits in Siam made their submission to the apostolic vicar.

Among the Jesuits in Siam, J. B. Maldonado made the most sincere submission. He arrived at Siam for the first time in 1673 and had stayed there for 11 years. On 21 Jul 1684 he sailed for Macau, being in charge of a mystery mission for the king of Siam. He was absent for three years. In 1687 he returned to Siam, and then left for Europe in 1691.

At first he was very opposed to the apostolic vicars, but after observing the policy of the popes about the mission and authority of the apostolic vicars, he submitted to them together with his companion, Manuel Soares. Bishop Laneau wrote in his letter dated 17 Jun 1691 that Manuel Soares entirely agreed with Maldonado, even though he was a Portuguese.

It is noteworthy that, during the persecution of 1688-91, the French church and college were destroyed and the French missionaries were put in prison, which, for the most part, did not sadden the Portuguese. Only the Jesuits showed sincere sympathy for them and tried to help them in various ways.

In 1691 the Jesuit visitor Aleixo Coelho arrived at Ayutthaya from Macau. He appointed Antonio Diaz as the new superior and ordered Maldonado to return to Macau. In 1696 Maldonado was sent to Cambodia, where he died in 1699.

Bibliography

Bullarium Patronatus Portugalliae regum in ecclesiis Africae, Asiae atque Oceaniae, 4 Vols. (1868-79). • Da Silva Rego, A., *O Padroado Português no Oriente e a sua Historiografia (1838-1950)* (1978). • Boxer, C. R., *The Church Militant and Iberian Expansion, 1440-1770* (1978). • De Souza, Teotonio R., "The Portuguese in Asia and Their Church Patronage," in *Western Colonialism in Asia and Christianity,* ed. M. D. David (1988).

Teotonio R. de Souza and
Surachai Chumsriphan

Paik, George L.

(Paik Lak-Joon) (b. Jung Joo, Pyenbguk Province, Korea, 9 Mar 1895; d. 13 Jan 1985) Presbyterian* pastor, historian, educator, administrator, and politician.

Paik graduated from Sing-seung Middle School and moved to China*, where he studied for three years at the Sin-won school in Tianjin. After he graduated, he went to the United States and entered Park College in Missouri, majoring in history. At Princeton Theological Seminary he studied theology and received his master's degree. He received his doctoral degree from Yale University, where he majored in Korean church history. He was ordained in the Kansas Presbytery in the United States in 1927 and transferred to the Korean Presbyterian Church. He served at Dae-hyun Presbyterian Church in Seoul and as a professor in Yon-hee Technical School (now Yonsei University). During the Japanese regime, Paik worked for the native literature movement with Chung In Bo and contributed much to forming a branch for studying Korean classic literature.

After emancipation in 1945, Paik helped reestablish Yon-hee College (which had been confiscated by the Japanese government) as a university and became its first president. Retiring from that post, he became chairman of the board of trustees and served as president emeritus.

Paik served many years in various areas as a politician. When the Korean War* broke out in 1950, he was named by President Syngman Rhee as minister of education and contributed to keeping education going under the difficult conditions of the war. Resigning two years later, he was elected chairman of the Educational Council of Seoul City and chairman of the Korean Educational Council. He also contributed much to nongovern-

Pakistan

mental diplomacy through his work in the Society of the World University Service and the United Nations Educational, Scientific and Cultural Organization (UNESCO). Paik was also elected speaker of the senate of the Korean parliament until it was dissolved by Park Jung Hee's military coup in 1960.

His most valuable contributions were in the area of education. He contributed to unifying Yon-hee University and Severance Hospital and Medical School in 1957 and became the first president of Yonsei University, from which he retired in 1961. He created the Society of Korean Church History with those who taught the subject at various seminaries and universities.

In 1931 Paik contributed to the creation of the Institute for the Study of Korean History *(Jindanhakhoe)*, the Society of Korean Popular Customs, and the Society of Administration of Korea. He was a fellow of the Royal Historical Society (1938). He received an honorary doctor of divinity from Park College in 1948 and an honorary doctor of humanities from Springfield College in 1954, and he was also named to receive the Medal of New York University. The Korean government gave him a National *Mugoonghwa* Decoration.

Paik published many books, including his doctoral dissertation at Yale, *The History of Protestant Missions in Korea, 1832-1910* (1973); *A Cultural History of the World* (1956); *A Short Biography of H. G. Underwood* (1934); *Korean Education and the National Spirit* (1954); *Present Situation and Ideal of Korea* (1963); *My View of Life* (1971); and more. He also wrote numerous articles in many magazines, periodicals, and newspapers.

Bibliography

The Christian Encyclopedia, Vol. VII (1982). • *Memorial Lecture of Dr. Yong-je Paik, Lak-joon* (1992).

Kim In Soo

Pakistan

Pakistan, the "country of the pure" (*pak* means "pure" in Urdu), stretches from the Arabian Sea in the south to the world's highest mountains, the Karakoram, Hindu Kush, Himalayas, and Pamirs, in the north, bordering on China*. To the west lie Iran and Afghanistan, and to the east India*. The Indus River forms Pakistan's axis and, with four tributaries, drains Pakistan's mountainous north, creating the fertile Indus Valley, which is crisscrossed by the largest irrigation scheme in the world.

Pakistan's Muslim majority obtained separate nationhood at India's independence from British rule in 1947 and has since seen an alternation of army and civilian governments, with yet another military takeover in Oct 1999. Pakistan officially became the Islamic Republic of Pakistan in 1973 under Zulfikar Bhutto, and since 1988 has been pursuing the policy of the increasing Islamization* of the country, despite the *shari'a* being in direct conflict with Pakistan's constitution. About 95 percent of the population is Muslim, 2.5 percent Christian, and 1.5 percent Hindu, plus Ahmadyyans and others.

The official language of Pakistan is Urdu, yet 70% of the people understand or speak Punjabi, the language belonging to the five-rivers basin, the Punjab. Pakistan's six major languages and an additional 62 local dialects witness to Pakistan's 6,000-year-old history and the resultant rich cultural patterns still prevalent today, though with the coming of Islam*, these have been colored with Islamic values and traditions.

Christian beginnings. There have been three periods of Christian development in Pakistan: (1) the West Asian period from 45-1000 C.E.; (2) the first Roman Catholic missions from the mid 16th to the 18th c.; and (3) the modern Protestant and Roman Catholic missions from the 19th c.

The Acts of St. Thomas*, an apocryphal Gospel written in Edessa between 180 and 400 C.E., describes St. Thomas's ministry in Taxila, Punjab, and the conversion of Gondaphorus, Taxila's Parthian king. A clear preoccupation with the fabulous and with miracles, as well as its insistence on sexual continence even within marriage, initially denied the Acts any claim to historicity. However, its credibility began to increase with the discovery of 744 coins in the Taxila area, as far as Jammu, bearing Gondaphorus's name. A later inscription, the *Takht-I-Bahi,* testifies to Gondaphorus's accession to the throne and also to his death about 55 C.E.

The *Didascalia Apostolorum**, a sober Christian manual, mentions Christian communities east of Persia during the first centuries, as does Eusebius, the 4th c. church historian. The Metropolitan diocese of Riv Ardushir in southeast Persia has had the oversight of churches, including those in Baluchistan, after 424 C.E. and is verified by the *Synodicon Orientale,* covering the period from 410 to 600 C.E. (see Synods/Councils, Early Asian).

When Islam expanded across Persia and entered the Sindh with the conquests of Muhammed bin Qasim in 712, tens of thousands of Christians were dispersed and thousands forced to accept Islam, with many escaping into India and Kurdistan.

Before 1000 C.E., Christian communities in Thatta, on the river Indus/Sindh, venerated St. Thomas as the founder of their church, calling themselves Sons of Thomas or Barthemai. An inner group of the specially enlightened acted as guardians of books and relics believed to be from apostolic times.

When the Portuguese established themselves in southwest India in 1510, Babur, the descendent of Genghis Khan*, entered northwest India from Afghanistan and founded the Moghul Empire. By 1580, Jesuit fathers had followed Akbar's invitation to come to Lahore. Akbar established his trading station in Thatta to evade Portuguese control, with the Portuguese following suit. Both the Carmelites* and the Augustinians* were invited to provide religious care.

At first Jesuit* missions had little success, yet a third mission arrived in 1594, and by 1597 Lahore boasted a fairly large church comprising Portuguese, Armenians, and Hindustanis. A royal announcement procured toleration for Christianity and also permission for conversion. Yet political disagreements between the Portuguese in Goa and the Moghul government were followed by the closure of churches in Lahore and Agra, the discontinuation of state funds for priests, and the migration of Lahore's Christian community to Agra.

Neither Akbar nor his son Jehangir embraced Christianity as many missionaries had hoped. Under Shah Jehan, persecutions intensified, and during Aurangzeb's reign, all schools teaching non-Muslim religions had to close.

Before 1813, European traders had come to India for financial exploits, with the British East India Company (BEIC) being especially hostile to missionary efforts. Despite this, it became the very agent for Henry Martyn's* chaplaincy service in South Asia and his translations of the New Testament into Urdu, Persian, Hindi, and also Arabic (see Bible Translation). A new era of toleration for pastors and missionaries began with Lord Minto's Charter of 1813. New laws were passed by W. Bentinck to abolish Hindu customs such as *sati, thagu* (human sacrifice), and infanticide of baby girls.

When the East India Company's charter came up for renewal before the British government in 1833, a clause was added that opened up India to missionary enterprise without restriction. Thus the Roman Catholic Church* reestablished mission work in the Sindh in 1842, and the Anglican* Church in 1850. The annexation of the Punjab in 1849 opened up further areas for missionary work. The first new Protestant missions to India were the following: the American and United Presbyterian* missions, the Church Missionary Society (CMS), and the Church of Scotland, which agreed to a comity arrangement in 1862.

BEIC rule ceased with the suppression of the Indian Mutiny in 1857, followed by a proclamation by Queen Victoria declaring religious freedom to all Indians under the law. Much Anglican work concentrated initially on urban evangelism, with special outreach to the young, literate, and high-caste individuals, distributing Gospel tracts and opening up institutions. Yet converts were few in number and suffered much hardship and great dislocation.

The great response to the Gospel from the depressed Hindu classes during the two great people movements* in northwest India overturned the assumption most missions had held that winning the upper classes was a better strategy than attempting to win the lower. The Megs, a lower Hindu caste, were the first to start turning to Christ after 1859. Yet in 1884 conversions stopped suddenly due to delayed baptism and the failure to open schools for the new converts' children and to give systematic religious instruction to the new converts. By 1908, over 22,000 Megs had returned to Hinduism*.

The conversion of the Chuhras, another landless Hindu labor class and considered untouchable, reached its height between 1905 and 1930, with hundreds and thousands of Chuhras turning to Christ. The Chuhras' ready response to the Gospel in the United Presbyterian Mission convinced other missions such as the American Reformed Presbyterian, the Church of Scotland, the Salvation Army*, the United Methodist* Church of the United States, as well as the various missions of the Anglican Church, to join in this work among lower castes.

With the exception of the RC Church, the Brethren churches, and Pentecostal* groups, all other missions kept to comity arrangements (see Ecumenical Movement). However, large cities such as Lahore, Karachi, Peshawar, Rawalpindi, Multan, and Hyderabad were open to all churches.

At partition in 1947, the Methodist mission area was cut, with the larger portion going to India and many believers migrating to join their families there. After 1947 the American Presbyterian Church became the Lahore Church Council, but not until 1993 did it merge with the United Presbyterian Church to form the present-day Presbyterian Church of Pakistan. A further union of great importance took place in 1970 when the Anglican Church of Pakistan, the Methodist Church, the Pakistan Lutheran Church, and the Sialkot Church Council joined to become the second-largest denomination, the Church of Pakistan.

Early missionary methods. Bible translation, bazaar preaching and itinerant work, religious debates, literacy* and reading rooms, education* (from village schools to prestigious colleges), medical* work (hospitals and clinics), *Zenana* (women's) work (e.g., Zenana Bible and Medical Missions) were all early missionary methods. As in most areas of Asia, pioneering medical, translation, literacy, and educational work was initiated by early missionaries and laid the foundation for later movements of independence.

Protestant pioneers. Andrew Gordon* (b. United States, 1828) served with the United Presbyterian Church of North America in Sialkot. He emphasized preaching and distributing books and in 1857 opened an orphanage. Gordon led an educated Hindu and an outcast Chuhra to the Lord, the result being the beginning of the Chuhra movement. In 1858 nine Hindus and one Muslim were baptized. Two schools opened, one in Gujranwala and one in Sialkot. Gordon also opened an industrial school to teach men to manufacture soap, oil, candles, and more, and to teach women sewing.

Charles W. Foreman* (b. 1821; d. 1894) emphasized Christian schools as means of spreading the Gospel. In Gujrat, Gujranwala, and Rawalpindi, he supervised government schools and became the first deputy director of the Regional School Directory of the Punjab. He maintained an evangelistic ministry of distributing material printed through the Bible and Tract Society and opened schools, colleges, and dispensaries. Foreman Christian College, opened in 1862, offered education to thousands, with many rising to leadership positions both in the church and in the government.

Thomas Hunter (d. 1857) was martyred during the Indian Mutiny. He was a Church of Scotland missionary to Bombay and Sialkot and an itinerant preacher who emphasized language acquisition (both Urdu and Punjabi). During the Indian Mutiny, Hunter was shot first, and then his wife and children were slaughtered.

The Indian pioneer Ditt* was illiterate, lame, and not too attractive. He bought and sold hides and was a member of the Chuhra outcaste. Ditt insisted on immediate baptism after conversion, and, despite social pressure and ostracism, returned to live with his own people and witnessed faithfully, leading first his wife, two children, and a neighbor to the Lord, and later on four more people. After 11 years the number had risen to 500, and after 1875 the Chuhra movement began.

I. D. Shahbaz* (b. 1895; d. 1916) was a gifted Indian poet who paraphrased all of the Psalms in Punjabi and set them to local tunes, which had immediate appeal to the simplest villager due to their familiar tune and rhythmic patterns. They were easily memorized and are to this day favorites in Punjabi worship.

Christianity in Pakistan today. The 1994 census revealed that 95 percent of the members of the Church of Pakistan are descendents of those who were born Hindu and became Christians during the Chuhra movement between 1880 and 1930. The other 5 percent are descendants of individual converts from Muslim, Caste Hindu, and the European communities.

The government census held in 1999 shows that Christians number four million, or about 2.5 percent of the population, with 51 percent of them belonging to the RC Church. Eighty percent of all Christians reside in the Punjab, and the majority of Christians in the other three provinces are Punjabis who have settled there.

Compared with the fragmentary nature of Protestantism, the monolithic structure of the RC Church has given birth to a vast range of ministries, with educational services being in the lead. By 1982 the RC Church was running 552 educational institutions. Stability and economic benefits are offered through CARITAS* and Catholic Relief Services. After education, health services take second position, with hospitals being run in six of the major cities in Pakistan. Of further importance is preventative medicine, with mobile units and dispensary programs.

Roman Catholic ministries. Especially during the last 15 years, social welfare work has taken on greater importance. NGOs (CARITAS) championing of human rights, the National Commission for Justice and Peace, and women's issues (offering help also to Muslim women) have all given new identity to what it means to be a Christian.

Part of the new social awareness among Catholics has meant greater concern for the following: justice, peace, and human development; working against depressive structures (e.g., bonded labor); foundation of Christian villages*; housing schemes; formation and training of laity and lay leadership through pastoral centers, seminaries, and exposure programs; publication of literature* on social and religious matters; dialogue for social harmony and interfaith cooperation, aid to refugees (and rehabilitation [from Afghanistan, Iran, Iraq/Kurds, Sudan, the former USSR]); and evangelistic missions to tribal people near Hyderabad, Multan, and among those in bonded labor.

The Roman Catholic Church of Pakistan is divided into eight dioceses, their main thrust being church and church-planting work, especially in the Hyderabad Diocese, which conducts outreach to the Hindu tribes. In the Lahore Diocese, schools have increased in number from three in 1980 to 22 in 1999, and congregations from four to 18.

CHAP, the Christian Hospital Association of Pakistan, is responsible for a total of 60 hospitals, including those of the Church of Pakistan and of other denominations. Islamabad has an effective Church of Pakistan Health Care Network, running a total of 48 clinics.

Further Church of Pakistan ministries include: church planting, institutions for special-needs children, Human Rights Commission and Commission for Peace and Justice, and a women's desk (vocational centers and a range of programs for the empowerment of women). Pakistan invites members from NGOs or parachurch organizations to help create awareness in health, hygiene, sanitation, population planning, HIV/AIDS and drug rehabilitation programs, legal aid services, and also small loan schemes.

Other denominations and missions active in church work and planting include: Presbyterian Church of Pakistan, Salvation Army, Associate Reformed Presbyterian Church, Free Gospel Assemblies, and the Brethren churches. Many of these churches run primary and secondary schools, medical institutions, clinics, dispensaries, bookrooms, Christian literature programs *(MASIHI ISHAT KHANA),* the Open Theological Seminary (theological education by extension classes), Bible training institutes (22), and several seminaries.

Parachurch organizations include: Operation Mobilization, Scripture Union, Pakistan Fellowship of Evangelical Students (see International Fellowship of Evangelical Students), Pakistan Bible Correspondence School, Gospel Recording Ministries, and others.

In the late 1990s, Pakistan's literacy* rate was still less than 35 percent. While school attendance at the primary level has recently been made compulsory, budget allocation for education is so low that facilities are often woefully inadequate, with children of the poor missing out.

No provision is made for Christian students in government schools to receive Christian religious instruction, yet Islamyat and Pakistan studies are compulsory for all. There have been claims that government census figures are falsified to keep financial grants to minority communities to a minimum, thus hindering their social advancement and opportunities to influence matters of concern to the majority community.

While the 1949 Objectives Resolution for Pakistan's

new constitution had stated that adequate provision shall be made for the minorities freely to profess and practice their religion and develop their cultures, in the 1973 constitution the word "freely" was omitted. In 1977 General Zia-ul-Haq* initiated the process of Islamization with the Eighth Amendment, which introduced separate electorates for the minorities. Thus Christians were given the right to elect their representatives to the provincial and national levels, but for many years not to local government.

Even on national issues the voice of the minorities often goes unheard. Non-Muslims may not become prime minister or president of Pakistan. The doors to government jobs are closed to Christians; the army, air force, and navy enforce strict quota systems, and the upper ranks are closed to non-Muslims.

Apostasy from Islam carries the death sentence, and the Law of Evidence demands the witness of two Christian men for that of one Muslim, the witness of a woman being half that of a man, and that of a Christian woman being half again of that.

The Law of Blasphemy, Article 295 B and C, is responsible in large part for the increasing division between Pakistan's majority and minority communities and for paralyzing Pakistan's minorities from responsible action in society. Desecration of the Holy Koran or of places of worship carries a sentence of life imprisonment, and blasphemy of the Prophet of Islam capital punishment. False accusations have led to trials, and in recent history Pakistan has seen a mushrooming of such cases, yet with courts finding it difficult to produce any evidence to convict those accused.

Bibliography

Foster, J., *To All Nations, Christian Expansion from 1700 to Today* (1960); *God Has No Favorites* (1968). • Miller, B., *Praying Hide* (1943). • Mughal, D., ed., *A Christian Church in Pakistan: A Vision for the 21st Century* (1997). • Rooney, J., ed., *St. Thomas and Taxila, A Symposium on St. Thomas* (1988); *Symphony on Sands,* Pakistan Christian Church History Monograph, no. 6 (1988). • Stock, F., and M. Stock, *People Movements in the Punjab* (1975). • Thomson, A., "New Movements," *Church History 3, Reform: Rationalism: Revolution, ISG Study Guide 14* (1976).

Ilse Berner

Pakistan, Christian Villages in

The first Christian villages began to appear in the area now called Pakistan* (then, still India*) in the mid-1890s. Their inspiration goes back, however, to the establishment in 1760 of the village of Chuhari in the then kingdom of Betiah, south of Nepal. The Capuchins* were the pioneers of Pakistan's Christian villages. Their first aim was to create enclaves where Catholic life might be lived to the full. A secondary aim was to find settlements for orphans under Capuchin care. Between 1895 and 1906, the yearly average of these orphans amounted to more than 300, reaching a peak of 424 in 1900. To settle these orphans, four large villages were established: Maryamabad, Khushpur, Anthonyabad, and Francisabad. The smallest, Maryamabad, covered one square mile; the largest, Francisabad, 10 square miles. At the same time, the Mill Hill* Missionaries established Yussufpur, near Rawalpindi, as a settlement for artisans and market gardeners. The 1919 flu epidemic wiped out the population of Yussufpur.

In 1938, the Dutch Franciscans* started a small village near Hyderabad, Sindh, called St. Isidore. It is now known by its nickname, Padri-Jo-Goth. Development was halted in 1942 during the Hur revolt. Padri-Jo-Goth was granted an indemnity of 400 acres as part of the Hur peace settlement. This holding was extended later to 1,200 acres.

In 1948, the government of Pakistan granted six tracts of land for Christian villages, three to the Protestants and three to the Catholics. Thus the Mill Hill Missionaries built the villages of Josephabad and Mariakhel, and the Italian Dominicans* established Loreto. The Protestant villages did not do well. Two of them, Amritnagar and what is now called Fatimapur, more or less converted to Catholicism.

Catholic priorities turned then to the provision of low-cost housing colonies in towns, inspired by Karachi's Catholic colonies. Many Christian housing associations burgeoned alongside the officially sponsored church colonies. It is difficult to say how many of these are now active.

John Rooney

Pal, Krishna

(b. Burra Gram, India, 1764; d. Calcutta, 1822). First convert of the Serampore mission, first Indian missionary to his own people, and composer of the first Bengali hymn.

Pal was born to Hindu parents Shri Mooluckchan Pal and Nulita. Early in his adulthood Pal became a disciple of the Mulpara Gossian, and later the Khurta Bhoja sect. He became a guru himself, making others his disciples, and remained in this position for 16 years. He was married to Rasso, who bore him four daughters. They settled in the suburbs of Serampore.

Pal's first encounter with the Gospel occurred on the day he met John Thomas, William Ward*, and Brunsden. In 1800 he was converted to Christianity and, on 28 Dec of the same year, was baptized by William Carey* in the Hooghly River. Pal's first act after his baptism was to build a place for worship. This was the first missionary chapel in Bengal. He worked under the direct supervision of the missionaries until 1803. In the following year, he was sent to Calcutta as a full-time missionary, where he ministered for about five years. After his retirement from missionary work, he continued to preach and teach the Gospel in different parts of the country: Sylhet, Cutwa, Burbhoom, and Berhampore. He then resided at English Bazaar near Malda for six years, where he made frequent visits to all the surrounding villages. In 1816 Pal returned to Calcutta, where he eventually died of cholera.

Bibliography

Paul, R. D., *Changed Lives* (1968). • Smith, George, *The Life of William Carey* (1935). • Stanley, Brian, *The History of the Baptist Missionary Society, 1792-1922* (1992).

HENKHOLUN DOUNGEL

Palaez, Pedro Pablo

(b. Pagsanjan, Laguna, 29 Jun 1812; d. Manila, 3 Jun 1863). Leader of the Filipino clergy, church administrator, writer, and teacher.

Palaez was one of the first Filipino priests to take up the common cause of the native clergy. During the Spanish regime, there was a polarization of the priesthood in the colony. The Spanish priests belonged to religious orders, which rarely admitted Filipino priests, and served as the parish priests of the towns. The native priests, on the other hand, were relegated to coadjutorships. The few parishes which had been administered by Filipino priests were further reduced by a series of royal decrees in the 19th c. which ordered them to turn over their parishes to Spanish priests. Palaez spearheaded the campaign for the secularization of the parishes which, in effect, meant the Filipinization of the parishes. The situation had racial overtones. Although Palaez was a *criollo* (a Spaniard born in the colony, considered inferior to a *peninsular,* a Spaniard born in Spain), he identified himself completely with native Filipinos. His baptismal godfather was a Filipino secular priest. In his various writings and correspondence with government and church officials, including the papal nuncio to Spain, Palaez vigorously defended the rights of Filipino priests, vouched for their integrity and competence irrespective of their racial background, and identified the outstanding ones among them.

He graduated as STD at the University of Santo Tomas in 1844 together with two other native priests, Don Mariano Garcia, an *indio* (a Spanish term for Malay Filipinos), and Don Ignacio Ponce de Leon, a Spanish *mestizo* (Eurasian Filipino). He taught theology and philosophy in his alma mater and the College of San Jose to the next generation of Filipino priest-scholars, whom he encouraged in their studies.

In 1844 he began to ascend in the Manila cathedral chapter until he became its treasurer, the position he held when he was killed in the great earthquake of 1863. He was appointed secretary of the archdiocese in 1845, and served until his resignation in 1850. The chapter elected him as *vicar capitular* (equivalent to acting archbishop) after the death of Archbishop Jose Aranguren (1861-62). He coedited *El Catolico Filipino,* the first religious newspaper in the Philippines (1861-62).

Upon his death, the leadership of the Filipino clergy fell to his longtime collaborator, Don Mariano Gomes, and his former students Jose A. Burgos and Don Jacinto Zamora (see GOM-BUR-ZA).

Bibliography

Archives of the Archdiocese of Manila, "Credentiales del Dr. Don Pedro Pablo Palaez," *Libro del Gobierno Eclesiastico* (1853 and 1862). • Santiago, Luciano P. R., "The Filipino Doctors of Ecclesiastical Sciences in the 19th Century," *Philippine Quarterly of Culture and Society* (1985). • Zaide, Gregorio F., *Great Filipinos in History* (1970).

LUCIANO P. R. SANTIAGO

Palladius. *See* Kafarov, Benedict Petr Ivanovich ("Palladius")

Pallegoix, Jean Baptiste

(b. Combertault, Côte-d'Or, 24 Oct 1805; d. Bangkok, 18 Jun 1862). Pallegoix entered the major seminary of Dijon when he was 17 and later was sent to teach the fourth year in the minor seminary of Servières. During his 1826 vacation, he composed "An Abridged Life of St. Francis Xavier,"* of which only a few copies were printed at the time, but it was later reprinted. On 17 Feb 1827, he entered the Major Seminary of the Foreign Missions and was ordained a priest on 31 May 1828.

He left for Siam on the following 31 Aug, sailing from Le Havre. After spending several months in Macau*, he proceeded to Singapore* and reached Bangkok toward the middle of 1830. As soon as he had gained a rudimentary knowledge of Siamese, he went to oversee the Christian Mission in Juthia, which he found to be materially and morally in a dismal state. It was at that time that he conceived the project of constructing a church on the ruins of that built by the first vicars apostolic. Pallegoix was put in charge of the parish of Holy Cross in Bangkok; he built a church which was dedicated on 1 Sep 1835 and replaced a "low, damp shed with an altar which had become a den of snakes." Soon after he began the construction of the Church of the Immaculate Conception, dedicated on 24 May 1837.

In 1835 Pallegoix was appointed pro-vicar. By virtue of a letter of 3 Jun 1836, he was chosen to be coadjutor by Msgr. Courvezy, who, on 3 Jun 1838, consecrated him at Bangkok as bishop of Mallos. From this period, as the division of the Siam mission was under consideration, it was decided that Courvezy should reside in Singapore and Pallegoix remain in Bangkok, in which city the new bishop at once began the Calvary Church (Our Lady of the Rosary), which was replaced in 1890 by a more beautiful building. The original piece of land was said to have formerly belonged to Portuguese Christians, and the consul of Portugal claimed it as the property of his nation. The Siamese government replied that it had been given to the Roman Catholic mission. The bishop then reinstalled and enlarged a printing press, which proved very useful not only for his vicariate but also for Cochin

China because it possessed Roman characters accented according to the method of the Annam missionaries.

In 1841 Pallegoix founded a seminary-college in Siam because the king prohibited students from traveling to Penang to study. On 10 Sep of that year, Siam was divided into two vicariates apostolic: one was officially given the name of East Siam and continued to be called Siam; the other was West Siam, better known as the Peninsula of Malacca*.

The part governed by Pallegoix, Siam, comprised at that time about 4,300 Christians made up as follows: in Bangkok, 1,700 Annamites in the parish of St. Francis Xavier, 700 Portuguese-Cambodians in the parish of the Immaculate Conception; 500 Portuguese-Siamese in Holy Cross and 500 at Calvary; 100 at Juthia; 800 Annamites at Chanthaboun. To have the complete total, one must add Catholics dispersed through the kingdom. There were five indigenous priests, several catechists, and some 20 Annamite religious.

In 1843 the prelate made a pastoral tour on the Tha Chin River, sailing up from Nakhon Xaisi, and he sent two missionaries, J. B. Grandiean and J. B. Vachal, on an expedition to the north. In 1844 he realized his long-cherished project of building a church at Juthia. In 1845 he built a dwelling fit for a bishop's house, which had previously been only a thatched hut. The years 1848 and 1849 were marked by the establishment at Bangkok of a convent of Annamite religious and by the construction of a new seminary-college.

During 1849 cholera decimated the population of Bangkok, and it was then that something took place which affected the mission quite profoundly. In July the king sent to the bishop an embassy demanding animals for the king. The missionaries consulted by the vicar apostolic concluded that the king, following Siamese ideas, wanted to foster these animals in order to preserve his own life. Consequently, to give them to him was to cooperate in an act tainted with superstition, and this must be refused. The bishop, who depended on the goodwill of the prince and held the opposite view, nevertheless accepted in practice the advice of his collaborators and conveyed his refusal to the king. The latter, greatly annoyed that his royal word had been questioned, ordered all Catholic buildings to be destroyed. Pallegoix then decided to follow his own feelings and presented animals to the king, and the indigenous priests also offered similar presents. The king revoked the more severe of his orders but expelled the missionaries who had opposed the gifts, eight in all. The affair was made known to Rome, which supported the bishop. The king died in 1851, and his successor, Mongkut*, a friend of Pallegoix for more than 15 years, gave permission for the missionaries to return to Siam, declared that he would exempt Christians from all superstitious acts, wrote personally to the bishop promising him his protection, sent him presents, and on 28 Feb 1852 granted him a very solemn audience. He thus repaired the evil committed by his predecessor and gave peace to the mission and the apostolic workers. Having learned of his good disposition, Pope Pius IX, by his letter *Pergrata Nobis* of 20 Dec 1852, addressed his thanks to the king. He thanked him again on 7 Oct 1861 by the letter *Summa Quidem*.

In 1853 Pallegoix came to France, bringing with him two young Siamese and carrying the manuscripts of his Siamese-Latin-French-English dictionary and of his work "Description of the Thai or Siam Kingdom." He had an audience with Napoleon III and the empress and obtained authorization to have his dictionary printed by the royal printing press. He then proceeded to Rome, and in Feb 1855 made his way back to Siam bearing presents for the king from the pope and the French emperor.

In 1858 Mongkut, in reparation for wrong done to the mission, gave to the parish of Calvary a small property which extended the church land up to the Mei-nam and considerably augmented its value. King Mongkut expressed the wish that his good friend Pallegoix be given the most solemn of funeral rites.

From the Memoirs of the MEP,
translated by CANON FRANK LOMAX

Pallu, François

(b. Tours, France, 30 Aug 1626; d. Moyang, China, 29 Oct 1684). Primary founder of the Paris Foreign Mission Society* (MEP) and vicar apostolic of southwest China*.

Pallu, whose father (Etienne Pallu) was a lawyer and mayor, was made a canon of St. Martin's in his youth. In Paris, Pallu became acquainted with Alexandre de Rhodes*, who was recruiting workers for the mission field in Tonkin and Cochin China. Upon the recommendation of Rhodes* in 1653, and with the influence of friends such as Pierre Lambert de la Motte* and the duchess of Aiguillon, Pallu was eventually appointed by Pope Alexander VII in 1658 as titular bishop of Heliopolis and vicar apostolic of Tonkin, Laos*, and southwest China. Although the king of Portugal protested that this was an infringement upon Portuguese responsibilities, the appointment was upheld by Alexander VII.

The MEP grew out of Pallu's conviction that secular priests would be more effective than regular priests in helping to establish the Christian church in non-European lands. Secular priests, free from subordination to religious orders, would be more adaptable in training and developing a native church leadership, which would make Christianity more acceptable to the locals in eastern and southern Asia. The MEP was made possible in part by the unqualified support of many individuals, such as Bernard de St. Theresa, the bishop of Babylon, and the Order of the Holy Eucharist. Pallu set up a seminary in Paris to recruit and train secular priests. Leaving Paris on 8 Nov 1661 with nine other missionaries, he sailed from Marseilles on 2 Jan 1662 and, after passing through Persia, Oman, and India*, arrived at Ayutthaya, capital of Siam (Thailand*) in 1664 with Louis Laneau*, Pierre Brindeau, Louis Chevreuil, and Antoine Hainques. The other five had died during the journey. In Siam

Pallu met de la Motte, the vicar-general of Cochin China. They discussed the missionary project in Vietnam*, which was regionally divided into north and south. Pallu formulated the *Instructiones ad Munera Apostolica* and decided to join forces with de la Motte.

Desiring a real missionary congregation, Pallu recommended that all missionaries come under the leadership of one general superior; take the vows of poverty, chastity and obedience; meditate three hours and fast daily; abstain from drinking alcohol; and sleep on the ground. He advised the French missionaries to live in charitable harmony with their Portuguese counterparts, and he worked toward good relations with the Jesuits*. During Lent of 1664, the Portuguese and French missionaries met for a common procession.

Unable to enter Tonkin because of the prohibition against Christianity, Pallu returned to Europe in 1667 to report to Pope Clement IX and to sort out the problem of spiritual authority in Tonkin and Siam. He persuaded the pope to confer religious authority over the whole of Siam to the French bishops (Papal Bull of 4 Jul 1669), who would have the right to control all missionaries desiring to work in Vietnam (Bull of 13 Sep 1669). In addition, the catechists serving as assistants to the missionaries would also come under the authority of the bishops. Pallu, however, failed to obtain the statute of missionary congregation for MEP.

In 1670, after sending a missionary named Sevin to Rome to coordinate matters on his behalf, Pallu returned to Asia. In 1673 he appointed Louis Laneau to be vicar apostolic of Siam and Nanking. Pallu, Lambert, and Laneau, in full regalia, were granted an audience with King Narai of Siam on 18 Oct 1673, on which occasion they presented letters from Pope Clement IX and King Louis XIV.

In mid-1674 Pallu sailed for China*, but a storm diverted him to the Philippines*, where he was arrested by the Spanish on suspicion of being a spy and imprisoned for three months. He was then escorted to Madrid via the Pacific Ocean, Mexico, and the Atlantic Ocean. Upon the request of Louis XIV, the Spanish released him from Madrid, and he returned to Rome in 1677. The Portuguese continued to challenge the authority of the French bishops. Pallu relinquished his post as administrator of Tonkin in 1679. In 1680 he was appointed the head of all China missions and vicar apostolic of Fujian. Pallu went to Paris in 1680 but failed to gain a personal audience with Louis XIV. However, Louis later agreed to allow all French missionaries to take the vow of obedience to the bishops.

Pallu returned to Thailand in 1681 with financial aid for the missionaries there. In 1683, on his way to China, he was captured by Ming soldiers and taken to Formosa (Taiwan*), where he was imprisoned for several months. He eventually reached Fujian on 27 Jan 1684 and died in Moyang later that year. In 1912 his body was removed to Nazareth in Hong Kong.

Anthony Do Huu Nghiem, with contributions from the MEP Memoir, translated by E. John Hamlin

Pancasila

State foundation and national ideology of the Republic of Indonesia*.

Pancasila means literally "the five principles" (Sanskrit), these principles being the belief in: (1) the One almighty lordship; (2) a just and civilized humanity; (3) the unity of Indonesia; (4) (the principle of) peoplehood guided by the wisdom of deliberation and representation; and (5) social justice for the whole people of Indonesia.

In the country, however, beyond its official status and wording, *Pancasila* is largely believed to be the most important symbol of Indonesia's national identity as she pursues modernity. *Pancasila* serves to guide the value system and way of life of Indonesians as well as being Indonesia's key to maintaining unity amid its immense diversity.

Historically, *Pancasila* was first introduced by Sukarno* (Soekarno) in his speech before the Investigating Body for the Preparation for an Independent Indonesia on 1 Jun 1945, albeit in different order and wording. Sukarno's speech was intended to break through a deadlock in which the members of the body could not agree whether the future independent Indonesia would be a secular state based on nationalism or a religious state based on Islam. A revised version of Sukarno's proposal was accepted unanimously, namely, that the independent state of Indonesia would be neither a secular nor a religious state, but a "*Pancasila* state."

This inclusive and "neither-nor" approach (namely, the "*Pancasila* approach") has been seen by many as a typical "wise and smart" Indonesian way of reaching and maintaining harmony by avoiding potential conflicts. In fact, it is primarily because of this kind of spirit, and not because of the formal and rather vague analytical meaning of the five principles, that *Pancasila* has been successful, at least so far, as the foundation of Indonesia's unity. "The Five Principles," according to T. B. Simatupang*, "are wide enough an umbrella for everybody. Nobody has anything against them; people can accept them; we can all live together under them." The core spirit of *Pancasila* is thus its inclusive and nondiscriminatory approach toward plurality. Because of *Pancasila,* it is peculiar that although Indonesia has the largest Muslim community in the world, it is not an Islamic state and Islam is not the state religion. In the *Pancasila* state, Indonesia acknowledges Islam*, Protestantism, Roman Catholicism, Hinduism*, and Buddhism* (first principle).

The *Pancasila* state has another peculiarity with regard to the relationship between state and religion. On the one hand, separation between state and religion is maintained in the sense that one is not to be subordinate to the other. On the other hand, this does not mean absolute separation. Although the state has no right to intervene in the internal affairs of any religion, it has the responsibility to help develop all the five religions. At the same time, although any of the five religions has no right to be directly involved in state affairs, The Broad Outlines of the State Policy say that ". . . all religions have the full, continual, and collective responsibility for establishing the basic spiritual, ethical, and moral framework of the national development" — hence its constitutional role in state affairs.

The Indonesian churches faced a difficult situation in 1985 when a law was ratified obliging all social organizations, these included, to put in their constitutions "*Pancasila* as the sole basis" of their organizations. The National Council of Churches and the Bishops' Conference of Indonesia, on behalf of the Indonesian churches, expressed their objection because this would be in direct contradiction to the very nature of the church as a universal body of Christ. After a long struggle, however, an agreement was finally reached in 1987 whereby the churches as organized bodies regard Jesus Christ as the foundation of their faith and life, whereas *Pancasila* is the only basis for activities in the society and the state.

With regard to the interreligious relationship, *Pancasila* promotes both the principle of religious harmony and religious freedom. Emphasis naturally is given to the so-called threefold religious harmony, namely, harmony between religious organizations and the government, harmony among the religious organizations themselves, and internal harmony within the religious organizations. Insofar as religious freedom and religious harmony are concerned, where religious freedom may not endanger religious harmony, and on the other hand religious harmony may not reduce religious freedom, these two principles are, on the practical level, still very difficult to reconcile, but Indonesia cannot do without them if she wants to maintain her unity.

Bibliography

Darmaputera, Eka, *Pancasila and the Search for Identity and Modernity in Indonesian Society* (1988). • Geertz, Clifford, ed., *Old Societies and New States* (1963). • *P-4: The Guide to the Living and the Practice of Pancasila and GBHN, The Broad Outlines of the State Policy* (1978). • Sidjabat, T. B., and Walter Bonar, *Religious Tolerance and the Christian Faith* (1965). • Simatupang, Tahi Bonar, "This Is My Country," *International Review of Mission,* Vol. 67, No. 251 (Jul 1974). • Van der Kroef, J. M., "Pancasila," in *Indonesia in the Modern World,* Part 11 (1956).

EKA DARMAPUTERA

Pan-China Catholic Evangelization Committee.

See Catholic Central Bureau

Paniqui Assembly

A meeting of 26 Filipino priests in 1899 to discuss church affairs during a time of political and ecclesiastical turbulence.

Initiated by Gregorio Aglipay* and convened on 23 Oct 1889 at Paniqui, Tarlac, the Paniqui Assembly adopted the Provisional Ordinances of the Philippine Church, believing that the end of Spanish sovereignty also meant the end of *Patronato* Real Espanol.* They did not, however, intend to break from the Vatican. Canon Nine stated that the canons adopted would be nullified as soon as there were properly designated bishops to govern the dioceses.

The ordinances provided for a council comprising delegates, chosen by the military vicar of each diocese, who would elect the president, who would in turn select the secretary. The council would establish the administrative and financial rules of the church, while the president, who would also serve as military vicar-general with the mandate to enforce canonical laws during times of crisis, would see to their implementation. Aglipay, whose appointment as military vicar-general by President Emilio Aguinaldo* on 20 Oct 1898 led to his excommunication in May 1899, was elected to the post again.

Bibliography

Achutegui and Bernard, *Religious Revolution in the Philippines,* Vols. I-IV (1960, 1966, 1971, 1972). • Agoncillo and Guerrero, *History of the Filipino People* (1987). • Scott, W. Henry, *Aglipay before Aglipayanism* (1987).

APOLONIO M. RANCHE

Pantoja, Didace de

(b. Spain, 1571; d. Macau, Jan 1618). Spanish Jesuit* missionary to China* during the late Ming period.

Pantoja's original destination was Japan*. He arrived in Macau* in 1599, where Matteo Ricci* had established a mission center for Nanjing and was planning another trip to Beijing. The Nanjing mission base needed help, so Pantoja's mission destination was diverted to China. Pantoja first came to Nanjing and in 1600 accompanied Ricci to Beijing. This time Ricci succeeded in presenting his gifts to the emperor, Wan Li, of which the emperor most appreciated the clock and a Western musical instrument, which Ricci taught the court musician to play for him. Following the establishment of a mission center in Beijing, Pantoja helped Ricci in his work there, teaching new believers the doctrine of the church. In 1605 Pantoja started to preach in several villages, resulting in the baptism of about a dozen new members. The following year he baptized another 13 members. This was the beginning of the Catholic mission to reach the villages outside the city of Beijing.

Pantoja was masterful in the use of the Chinese language. In 1614 he published a doctrinal book, *Seven Victories,* to which the Chinese intelligentsia responded as favorably as they had toward Ricci's book *The Meaning of the Teaching of Heaven.* Yang Ting Jun, a well-known Christian, and several non-Christian scholars wrote the preface for the book. In 1616, as a result of the accusation made by Chinese magistrate Shen Que against missionaries, Pantoja and three other missionaries were deported to Macau, where Pantoja died two years later.

Bibliography

Mungello, D. E., *The Forgotten Christians of Hangzhou* (1994). • Vath, Alfons, *Johann Adam Schall von Bell, S.J. (1592-1666)* (1991). • Goodrich, L. Carrington, *Dictionary of Ming Biography, 1386-1644* (1976).

China Group

Parekh, Manilal C.

(b. Rajkot, Gujarat, 1885; d. 1967). Parekh was born in a Jain home and was introduced to Hindu Vaisnava Bhakti by his father. A serious illness (tuberculosis) prompted him to progress from Jainism* to theism. He came under the influence of the writings of Keshub Chunder Sen* and served for some years as a *pracaraka* of the Church of the New Dispensation in Sindh and Bombay. The next stage in his pilgrimage was his growing interest in Christ, toward whom Keshub had so firmly pointed. Parekh's tuberculosis gave him opportunity for study and reflection. He studied the Bible and the Vacanamrit of Swami Narayana, the famous Gujarati Vaisnava religious and social reformer of the early 19th c. The study of Vaisnava Bhakti led him beyond the rationalism of the Brahmo Samaj* to the conviction that God becomes incarnate, and this belief in turn pointed him to the Christ of whom he read in the New Testament.

Parekh was baptized in the Anglican* Church in Bombay in 1918. He considered baptism only a spiritual matter. He became disillusioned with the Westernization of the Indian Christian community and wanted a Hindu church of Christ free from Western influence. He felt strongly that the new disciples of Christ should remain within their own community, witnessing from there. He drew a clear distinction between evangelism, i.e., proclamation of the Gospel to individuals, and proselytism, by which he meant mass conversion by dubious means. Like Brahmabandhav Upadhyaya (1861-1907) of Bengal, he made a distinction between *samaja dharma* (the social aspect of religion) and *moksa dharma* (the spiritual aspect of religion). In his view, Christianity should be *moksa dharma* only.

Concerned about only the spiritual dimension of religion, Parekh held that Jesus' teachings carried the idea of the kingdom from the socio-political plane to the spiritual, and the new kingdom which Jesus inaugurated is a spiritual rather than a secular one. *A Hindu's Portrait of Jesus Christ* points to this spiritual aspect. Jesus abides in us now in spirit, and this spirit of Christ becomes for every disciple a bond of unity between oneself and God the Father on the one hand, and fellow disciples on the other. A Hindu can arrive at such a spiritual experience while still remaining a Hindu; there is no need to become a Christian.

By the end of the 1930s, Parekh came to the final stage of his spiritual pilgrimages, namely *Bhagavata Dharma*. He conceived *Bhagavata Dharma* as a universal personal religion of devotion in which Christian devotion is one element among others — perhaps the central and organizing element. He used the term to describe a religion of personal *bhakti* which is seen at its clearest in Christianity and Vaisnavism, but is also seen in all other theistic faiths. His bitter experiences in both the Brahmo Samaj and the Christian church had eventually brought him to the conclusion that change of religion is undesirable since it tends to lead to exclusiveness and communalism. For the new harmony which he was evolving, he wanted a name which avoided the implication that one particular tradition had a monopoly on the truth, and this he found in *Bhagavata Dharma.*

Bibliography

Parekh, Manilal C., *A Hindu's Portrait of Jesus Christ* (1953); *Christian Proselytism in India — A Great and Growing Menace* (1947); *Sri Vallabhacharya* (1943); *The Gospel of Zoroaster* (1939); *Sri Swami Narayan* (1936); *The Brahma Samaj* (1929); *Rajarshi Ram Mohan Roy* (1927); *Brahmarshi Keshub Chunder Sen* (1926); *Mahatma Gandhi* (with R. M. Gray) (1922); *From Brahmo Samaj to Christianity* (1919); "Mr. Gandhi and Religion," *Young Man of India* (May 1924); "The Spiritual Significance and Value of Baptism," *NCC* [National Council of Churches] *Review* (Sep 1924); "Our Objectives," *National Missionary Intelligencer* (Feb 1926); "The Christian Religion and the Jains," *NCC Review* (Mar 1926); "Keshub Chunder Sen: His Relation to Christianity," *International Review of Mission* (Jan 1928); "Our Cultural Heritage," in *An Indian Approach to India*, ed. M. Stauffer (1928); "A Meditation," *NCC Review* (Apr 1928); "The Ideal Missionary," *Christa Seva Sangha Review* (May 1931). • Boyd, R. O. S., ed., *Manilal C. Parekh, 1885-1967; Dhanjibhai Fakirbhai, 1895-1967: A Selection with Introductions* (1974).

K. P. Aleaz

Paris Foreign Missions Society (MEP)

Founded by French priests and laypeople in 1660 and approved by the Holy See in 1664, the MEP is an institute of apostolic life comprised of priests who dedicate their whole lives to serve the growth of local churches, mainly in Asia. They started with a *Séminaire des Missions étrangères.* The word "Paris" was added when other societies of the same type were created in Europe and America.

Françis Pallu* and Peter Lambert de la Motte*, the two main founders, were appointed apostolic vicars (bishops sent by the pope on a mission) in Jul 1658. They left for the Far East with a few companions in the following years. They first settled in Siam (Thailand*), Tonkin, and Cochin China (North and South Vietnam*). Pallu was the first to reach China* in 1684. He died a few months later in Fujian Province.

Their enterprise responded to three main desires: (1) zealous priests and laypeople in France did not want to leave to religious societies alone the care of spreading the Gospel to the ends of the world; (2) the new Congregation of Propaganda (Propaganda Fide*) founded in Rome in 1622 wanted to take direct charge of evangelization to escape the "patronage" of the worldly powers of Spain and Portugal; (3) the Portuguese Jesuit* Alexandre de Rhodes*, who had ministered in Vietnam and suffered persecution, advocated the need to appoint local priests and bishops if the church was to survive and develop in Asia.

Before they left Europe, clear "Instructions" were given to the apostolic vicars by the Congregation of Propaganda: to create a local clergy as numerous and well trained as possible; to adapt to local traditions while avoiding involvement in political affairs; and to refer to Rome all important issues, particularly for consecrating a bishop.

Training Asian ministers. Pallu strongly supported the nomination of Gregory Luo Wenzao* as the first Dominican* bishop, while his companions founded a seminary in Ayutthaya near Bangkok. Many priests from Southeast Asia and later from China were trained there. One of the better known was Andrew Lee, who became the outstanding apostle of Sichuan Province in 18th-c. China. Due to persecutions, the seminary had to move to Malaya, where it became what is now the Penang General College. Over 1,000 priests and 70 bishops had graduated from this college when it celebrated its 300th anniversary in 1964.

Besides opening seminaries in various parts of Asia, the French missionaries also nurtured female vocations to consecrated life. They soon understood the need for women to be the apostles of women in the context of the local traditions hostile to men and women mixing together. As early as 1667, the Lovers of the Cross* were founded in Siam and later developed in Vietnam. In 18th-c. China, the French missionaries made official the institution of "Virgins." Saint Martin Moye, a missionary in Sichuan, entrusted these dedicated women with the education of girls and the instruction of female catechumens. At a time when priests were very few and often repressed by civil authorities, much attention also was given to the formation of catechists and community leaders. They instructed people in the faith, ensured that converts lived the Christian way, and conducted prayer services on Sundays. A number of catechists and virgins died for the faith and were later given the titles of "Blessed" or even of "Saint" by the Holy See.

Pastoral care. Aiming at the formation of pastors and being close to the local people in their own way of life, the French missionaries paid particular attention to catechetical instruction, proper administration of the sacraments, and moral conduct inspired by the Gospel. From the early years of their presence in Asia, they held church synods with the local converts. At the first synod, which took place in Siam in 1664, Pallu defined his famous set of "directives to the missionaries." The synod of Sichuan, convened in Chongqing by Bishop Dufresse in 1803, was attended by some 15 Chinese priests; it produced basic guidelines for pastoral ministry in China. At that time the use of Latin was required in the Catholic liturgy. But an earlier concern of the missionaries had been to obtain from Rome special permission to use Chinese. St. Paul, they argued, had been a Jew with the Jews, and a Greek with the Greeks; besides, Pope Paul V had already granted an authorization in 1615. But despite their repeated demands, Latin was finally imposed by Rome, with the argument that Chinese priests could be good at learning Latin and that by doing so they would have access to theological sources and would not feel inferior to their Western colleagues. The rule was maintained until 1965, when local languages were authorized by Vatican Council II. While the official liturgy was maintained in Latin, the missionaries managed to produce a large number of books of prayer and spirituality in Asian languages. Dealing with the "Chinese rites" (see Ancestor Worship), however, MEP missionaries departed from the tolerance exercised by the Jesuits. With the Dominican and Franciscan* missionaries preaching among the farmers in the southern provinces, they saw that ancestor worship was mixed with the cult of local deities and condemned it as superstitious. Maigrot de Crissey issued a mandate forbidding the practice of Chinese rites in his Fujian diocese. The interdict was later extended by Rome to the whole of China and lands of Chinese civilization such as Korea* and Vietnam.

Pioneers in many Asian lands. While their spiritual and pastoral orientations were well established in the 17th and 18th cs., the MEP fathers were few in number and almost disappeared at the time of the French Revolution. After the Napoleonic era, however, they benefited from a new passion for mission ventures in romantic and colonial France. For example, from the end of the 18th c. up to 1990, the MEP was the only Roman Catholic mission society to work in Cambodia*. Martyrdom in Asian lands inspired generous young men. Catholics in France also learned to support missions financially. The MEP priest Chaumont, exiled in England during the revolution, learned from the Anabaptists that small donations from the faithful could produce large amounts of money.

This idea led to the foundation of a fully fledged organization in Lyon in 1822: the Propagation of the Faith, with its bulletin, the *Annals.* Vocations to mission in Asia steadily increased in the MEP Society: 50 in 1830, 185 in 1850, and 343 in 1870. Toward 1910, MEP missionaries in Asia numbered 1,400. As the MEP priests were ever growing in number, they were entrusted with more and more missions by the Congregation of Propaganda: Japan* and Korea in 1831, Manchuria in 1838, Malaysia* as separate from Siam in 1841, Tibet in 1846, South China (Guangdong, Guangxi, and Hainan) in 1848, Burma (Myanmar*) in 1855, and Laos* as separate from Siam in 1899. Meanwhile, they retained the care of their earlier missions in South India and in the southwestern provinces of China (Sichuan, Guizhou, and Yunnan). The intervention of colonial powers in the Far East affected mission growth in a rather ambiguous way. The

French protectorate in China served the apostolate of the MEP and other missionary societies, but it aroused hostility in a large part of the population. Blessed Chapdelaine was martyred in Guangxi and Blessed J. P. Néel was beheaded in Guizhou. With the Boxer upheaval in 1900, many missions were destroyed. Msgr. Guillon, bishop of Moukden (Shenyang), was killed in his cathedral.

The MEP mother house in Paris preciously keeps a *Salle des martyrs* where relics of those who died for the faith are displayed. One of these martyrs, St. Teophane Vénard, was a source of inspiration to St. Theresa of the infant Jesus, the young Carmelite* sister who became a patron saint of the missions. Three bishops and seven priests of the Foreign Missions were canonized by the pope in Seoul in 1984, together with 94 Korean martyrs. Again in Rome (1988), two bishops and eight MEP priests were canonized together with 11 Spanish Dominicans and 96 Vietnamese martyrs. In China and Korea, MEP bishops surrendered themselves to the police with a view to saving the lives of the faithful, often quoting the words of the Gospel: "The good shepherd gives his life for his sheep."

Cultural exchanges. Focusing on evangelization among the poorer people in the provinces, MEP missionaries generally did not mix much with the local intellectuals. But being familiar with the people in remote areas, they contributed to local developments in agriculture, public works, and medical care. Moreover, some missionaries collected a wealth of data in botany, geology, ethnography, linguistics, and regional history which proved to be an invaluable source of information about Asia. Grammars, dictionaries, and other works were published at the MEP printing press of Nazareth in Hong Kong. A thesis was written by P. Fournier under the title *La contribution des missionnaires français au progrès des sciences naturelles au XIXe siècle* (1932). Other works include P. E. Favre's *Malay Grammar,* L. Gibert's over 1,000-page *Dictionnaire historique et géographique de la Mandchourie,* Fr. Lamasse's books in sinology, and Gervais Levavasseur's* *Cambodian-Latin Dictionary* (ca. 1770).

The mid-20th-c. great turn. From the end of World War I on, with the growth of nationalism* in Asia, some MEP directors understood the winds of change and hastened the takeover of Asian dioceses by Asian bishops. Msgr. de Guébriant, apostolic visitor in China, channeled the message to Rome together with the Lazarist* Vincent Lebbe*. Six Chinese bishops were consecrated in Rome in 1926, thus fulfilling the earlier purpose of the MEP founders, which had long been delayed for various reasons. After World War II*, political events precipitated the withdrawal of foreign apostolic vicars and the takeover by Asian bishops. Some 100 dioceses earlier organized in Asia by the MEP are now run by Asian bishops. Under them, nearly 250 MEP missionaries, generally aging, still offer their pastoral help, often as assistants under local parish priests. After the establishment of Communist regimes in China, Vietnam, Cambodia, and Laos, MEP missionaries had to withdraw from these countries. Some were given new missions in Taiwan* (Hualien), Indonesia*, Mauritius, Madagascar, and New Caledonia. Others made good use of their knowledge of Asian languages to serve Asian migrants in France and other countries. A few have recently gone back to Cambodia.

Despite the lack of priestly vocations in France, a few young men still join the MEP Society. Their urge to serve the Gospel is enriched with a better perception of the values contained in the Asian cultural and religious tradition.

The many works concerning the MEP can be consulted in their archives, 128 Rue du Bac, Paris 75007, tel. 33.1.44 39 10 40 and in their *Bibliothèque asiatique,* 28 rue de Babylone, Paris 75007, tel. 33.1.45 49 42 34.

Bibliography

Guennou, Jean, *Missions étrangères de Paris* (1984). • Ponchaud, François, *The Cathedral of the Rice Paddy* (1990). • Rollin, Vincent, *History of Missions in Cambodia, 1555-1967* (1968). • Pianet, J., *History of Missions in Cambodia, 1552-1852* (1929). • Launay, A., *History of Missions in Cochinchina, 1658-1823* (1924-25).

JEAN CHARBONNIER

Park Hyun Myung

(b. 1903; d. ?). Key leader of the Korea Evangelical Holiness Church* (KEHC) who guided it to become an independent denomination.

After his graduation from Seoul Bible Institute (now Seoul Theological University) in 1925, Park served for several years as an evangelist of the Seoul Tongnimmon Holiness Church. In 1927, after his ordination, he accepted an invitation by the Tokyo Korean Holiness Church and served as its pastor for six years. While in Tokyo he attended lectures at universities and, upon returning to Korea* in 1934, became a professor at Seoul Bible Institute, teaching church history until his arrest by the Japanese police during the disbanding trials of the KEHC. He was so severely tortured that he was released from prison because of his poor physical condition.

After the war ended in 1945, Park was elected chairman of the Preparatory Committee for Reconstruction of the Holiness Church, and, in the reconstructive general assembly held at Seoul Theological College (9-11 Nov 1945), he successfully led the conference to establish the KEHC as a new independent denomination. He was elected its first superintendent, a post he held four times. As superintendent, he visited the United States to solicit help for the development of the KEHC. Deeply concerned about the ecumenical movement, he led the KEHC to join the National Council of Churches of Korea. On 10 Aug 1950, during the Korean War*, both he and Lee Kun (principal of Seoul Theological University) were arrested and sent to North Korea by the Communists.

An independent, broad-minded man of firm faith and strict character, Park has two sons and two daughters. His eldest son is Park Sang Jung, who served in the World Council of Churches in Geneva and was a general secretary of the Christian Conference of Asia, and is presently director in the Christian Institute for the Study of Justice and Development in Korea.

Bibliography

Lee Chu Young, *A History of Holiness Church* (1970). • Oh Young Pil, *Story of Trials of Holiness Church* (1971).

KANG KEUN WHAN

Parker, Peter

(b. Framingham, Massachusetts, United States, 1804; d. 1888). American Presbyterian* and the first Protestant medical* missionary to China*; diplomat.

Parker was educated at Amherst College, studied theology and medicine at Yale University, and was ordained a Presbyterian minister in Philadelphia before he was sent by the American Board (ABCFM) to Guangzhou, China, in 1834. After leaving Guangzhou, he proceeded to Singapore* for one year to study Chinese but returned the next year and set up the Ophthalmic Hospital, which soon became a general hospital and dispensary. In 1837 he went to Japan to provide instruction on smallpox vaccination. In Feb 1838 Parker, together with E. C. Bridgman, T. R. Colledge, G. T. Lay, and W. Jardine, founded the Medical Missionary Society* in Canton, China, to promote evangelism through medical care. Chinese hostility caused by the First Opium* War (1839-42) resulted in a temporary closure of the hospital, causing Parker to leave China. He traveled throughout Europe and the United States on furlough, raising money and prayers for his Medical Missionary Society. He returned to Guangzhou in 1842 with his bride, Harriet Webster, and reopened the Ophthalmic Hospital.

Drawn increasingly into diplomatic work, Parker, together with Bridgman, assisted ambassador Caleb Cushing in 1844 in negotiating a treaty between China and the United States. As a result of strained relations with ABCFM secretary Rufus Anderson, Parker resigned from his mission board in 1845 and was appointed by President Tyler as secretary and interpreter to the American legation in China. Ill health forced his return to America in 1855. He went back to China again as the United States commissioner and helped revise the earlier treaty, resulting in the Treaty of 1858. He returned to the United States again and was active in the American Evangelical Alliance. He was chairperson of the Yale Alumni Association and regent of the Smithsonian Institution. He wrote several books on medical work in China.

Bibliography

Parker, Peter, *Statements respecting Hospitals in China* (1841). • Glick, Edward V., *Peter Parker and the Opening of China* (1973). • Harvey, Samuel C., "Peter Parker: Initiator of Modern Medicine in China," *Yale Journal of Biology and Medicine,* Vol. 8, No. 3 (1936). • Latourette, Kenneth Scott, "Peter Parker: Missionary and Diplomat," *Yale Journal of Biology and Medicine,* Vol. 8, No. 3 (1936). • Stevens, B., and W. Fisher Markwich, *The Life, Letters, and Journals of the Rev. and Hon. Peter Parker, M.D.* (reprint 1972). • Brown, G. Thompson, *Earthen Vessels and Transcendent Power* (1997). • Parker's personal diaries, along with some of his correspondence and sermons, Yale Medical Historical Library, New Haven, Connecticut, United States. • Parker's correspondence with the ABCFM, Houghton Library, Harvard University, Cambridge, Massachusetts, United States.

CHINA GROUP

PARKINDO

(Partai Kristen Indonesia). Christian Political Party (1945-73) initially founded as the National Christian Party (PKN) by Basuki Probowinoto and others three months after the Indonesian proclamation of independence.

W. Z. Johannes was chosen as interim chairman of PARKINDO, which held its first congress on 6-7 Dec 1945 in Surakarta. At this congress a constitution was agreed on and a new executive committee appointed under the chairmanship of Probowinoto, with A. M. Tambunan* as secretary. A Christian party in North Sumatra, *Partai Kristen Indonesia* (the "Indonesian Christian Party," PARKI), founded by Jasmen Saragih* (d. 1968) and Melanchton Siregar, combined with PARKINDO in 1947. The basis of PARKINDO was "The Bible as the Word of the Lord." Its aim to defend the Republic of Indonesia and to help the government achieve world peace and implement justice reflected concern over Dutch efforts to recolonize Indonesia, with likely armed conflict. PARKINDO's strong support for Indonesian independence contrasted with the attitude of Protestant Christian political parties such as Christelijk Staatkundige Partij (CSP), Partai Kaum Christen (PKC), and Partai Kaum Masehi Indonesia (PKMI).

PARKINDO's basic principle, essentially theocratic and developed in political and Christian student circles since the 1920s, was stated by Probowinoto as follows: "The glorification of the Lord's Name is the ultimate aim of all creatures and all human efforts including the field of politics. Christian politics is not only directed at worldly gain. For Christian politics, the measure of greatness is not the worldly results obtained, but whether in all of its efforts the party promotes, defends and carries out the fundamentals of the Word of the Lord." During its quarter-century history, PARKINDO had been a channel for the political aspirations of Indonesian Protestant Christians who composed 8-10 percent of the population. PARKINDO endeavored to safeguard religious minorities against discrimination by emphasizing religious freedom and monitoring developments adverse to religious tolerance.

Under the dual leadership of J. Leimena* and A. M.

Tambunan, PARKINDO supported and defended *Pancasila** as the basis for the nation. PARKINDO's endorsement by Protestant Christians was made clear at the first general election held in 1955, when it obtained about 30 percent (1,044,325 votes out of 3,471,283) of the Protestant Christian vote. It had a ministerial representative in almost every cabinet, including T. S. G. Mulia*, J. Leimena, W. J. Rumambi*, and M. Putuhena. Leimena was acting president several times. There were also PARKINDO representatives in various national bodies such as the People's Council (DPR), the People's Assembly (MPR), and the Dewan Pertimbangan Agung (DPA; one of the highest councils of the Indonesian state).

In 1973 there was a restructuring of political parties in Indonesia coinciding with the New Order era. PARKINDO merged with several other parties to become the Indonesia Democratic Party (PDI, *Partai Demokrasi Indonesia*). Thus ended the political party based on Protestant Christian principles. But Protestant Christians were still able to channel their political aspirations via the channels provided in the (new) political arrangement.

Bibliography

Sidjabat, W. B., ed., *Partisipasi Kristen dalam Nation Building di Indonesia* (1968). • Simorangkir, J. C. T., *Manuscript Sejarah Parkindo* (1989).

Zakaria J. Ngelow

Parmalim

Syncretistic movement of North Sumatran Toba-Batak people.

The Parmalim sect began as a nativistic messianic Batak* sect closely associated with Si Singamangaraja, the great priest-king of the Bataks who was regarded as the living manifestation of the deity. The religion developed around 1880 under the leadership of Guru Somalaing, a high-ranking *datu* at the court of Si Singamangaraja. From 1889 until 1891, Guru Somalaing acted as guide to an Italian botanist named Elio Modigliani. From this contact it seems many Mariological concepts were introduced into Parmalim worship and theology.

Basically, the Parmalim creed is animist (see Animism), with specific reference to Si Singamangaraja, together with several Muslim elements, although it is highly debatable whether or not Si Singamangaraja XII was ever a Muslim. After his death in 1907 in a battle against the Dutch, the movement took a highly nationalistic turn and also resulted in a new movement called *"pagudamdam"* or *"parhudamdan,"* based on the worship of Si Singamangaraja.

Congruent with most Batak belief, Parmalim is monotheistic — minimizing the likelihood of Hindu influence — and based on a belief in *tondi* or, in Karo, *tendi* ("soul-power" or, "the soul of the living human being"). There are many other deities and spirits with which one relates, but there is one high God. The *mangupa tondi* rite to recall the wandering *tondi* consists of beating drums, offering sacrifices of chickens to the deities and the spirits, requesting the *tondi* to return home, and sprinkling rice on the head of the deprived person holding a feast. A person lives in perpetual servitude to his or her *tondi*, and it must at all times be honored. Batak belief in a high God and the soul helped in the understanding of Christianity, but its strong nationalistic and ethnic identity made early communication very difficult.

Bibliography

Pederson, *Batak Blood and Protestant Soul* (1970). • Warneck, Johannes, *Die Religion der Batak* (1908). • Tobing, Ph. O. L., *The Structure of Toba-Batak Belief in the High God* (1963).

Sixtus Hiddin Situmorang

Pastoral Care and Counseling

Pastoral ministry in Asian churches is as old as the church in Asia. The process of caring for people and helping them in times of trouble is located not only in Christian ministry but also in Asian culture and society. Pastoral care, therefore, as practiced in Asia, has been the product of forms of pastoral care defined by Western missionaries and churches (imbibed by Asian churches through the process of church planting and theological* education), and also Asian cultural and social factors which have shaped pastoral care through cultural paradigms, forms, expectations, and patterns. Pastoral care in many parts of Asia has retained the traditional form of pastoral ministry from "cradle to grave," with the pastor playing a directive and authoritative role.

The modern pastoral care and counseling (PCC) movement, which began in the United States in the early decades of the 20th c., is also increasingly influential in many parts of Asia. This has been due both to the increasing number of pastors and others who are studying pastoral counseling in the United States, and also to the growing popularity of books in this area among Asian Christians. In recent times, PCC has also been influenced by the charismatic* movement, with an emphasis on deliverance ministry and inner healing. Many of the books dealing with these areas come from the West.

The following is an account of the developments in some Asian countries which have been influenced by the modern PCC movement.

Japan. One of the first Asian countries to be exposed to modern pastoral counseling, Japan* was visited by American educators and psychologists such as W. P. Lloyd (1951) and Carl Rogers (1952), resulting in great interest and the development of school and vocational counseling. In the church, W. P. Browning, an American missionary, began offering courses in pastoral counseling at Tokyo Union Theological Seminary in 1953. Subsequently, some Japanese pastors returning from studies in the United States began teaching pastoral counseling at other seminaries.

A significant event was the formation of the Japan Institute of Pastoral Care (JIPC) on 1 Feb 1963. As a result, the first weeklong clinical pastoral training was held in 1964, with American Paul Johnson as a guest. This became an annual event until the student riots in the early 1970s. JIPC started publishing its own journal, *Bokkai Shinri* (Pastoral Psychology), in Jul 1981, which was subsequently replaced by a newsletter.

Another development was the establishment of Counseling centers: Kansai Pastoral Counseling Center in Kobe (1972), and Growth Counseling Center and Christian Counseling Center in Tokyo (early 1980s). Meanwhile, many basic books in the field were translated into Japanese. Following the Second Asian Conference on Pastoral Care and Counseling (ACPCC) in Tokyo in Jul 1984, the Pastoral Care and Counseling Association of Japan was formed and promises to have a growing impact on the churches.

South Korea. Courses in pastoral counseling were first offered at the Methodist Seminary in Seoul in 1956. Clinical pastoral education (CPE) was provided initially by Joseph Cahil from 1978 to 1980 at the department of theology and graduate school of Yonsei University in cooperation with Severance Hospital. Meanwhile, pastors returning from pastoral counseling studies in the United States began teaching the subject in various seminaries. The Catholic Church also opened the Catholic Welfare Center in Myong Dong Cathedral in Seoul, providing free medical, legal, and youth counseling services. St. Mary's Hospital, well known for its hospice ministry, attracted many pastors who were interested in this aspect of pastoral care.

Taiwan. A counseling room was set up in 1962 at the Mackay Memorial Hospital, and this program, supported by the chief psychiatrist of Taiwan University Medical School, was officially approved in 1967. The hospital also set up the Taiwan Lifeline Service, a telephone counseling service staffed by volunteers. A family counseling center began functioning in Taipei in 1971 and was later incorporated into the counseling service offered at Mackay Hospital. At this time, Peter Hsian Chih Shih returned from a year's study in the United States and set up a CPE program at Changhua Christian Hospital in 1967. This program was structured as a six-week course offered six times per year the following year. A supervision course began to be offered in 1977, and by 1986 it became a three-year program. Meanwhile, the Taiwan CPE Association was formed in 1975, centered around Mackay, Changhua, and Catholic Hospitals. Pastoral counseling has gradually become an important subject in seminary education. Taiwan Theological School began offering a master's program in pastoral counseling in 1970, led by Theodore Cole.

Indonesia. Pastors returning from studies in the United States began teaching PCC in several seminaries in Indonesia*. At the Universitas Kristen Satya Wacana, bachelor of divinity students may choose to major in pastoral counseling. Basic counseling books have been translated into Bahasa Indonesia. The Fifth Asian ACPCC was held in Bali in Aug 1993, and this was a boost for the movement in Indonesia.

Thailand. No formal CPE program existed in Thailand* until recently. Presently, CPE programs are being offered at McCormick Hospital in Chiang Mai, Bangkok Sanitarium, and Bangkok Christian Hospital.

The above countries do not use English as a major language, and this has affected the spread in them of the modern PCC movement to some extent.

Philippines. Albert Dalton was appointed in 1964 as chaplain at St. Luke's Hospital in Quezon City by the Episcopal Church in the United States. In April the following year, the Philippine Association for Clinical Pastoral Care (PACPC) was constituted, followed by an experimental CPE program in which Narciso Dumalagan, who was later to succeed Dalton, participated. In 1966 the first fully accredited CPE program was offered at St. Luke's, which became the first fully accredited CPE center outside the United States Dumalagan succeeded Dalton as executive director of PACPC in 1969. Soon more CPE centers were established in some hospitals. The first parish-based CPE center was set up at Santo Tomas parish in Tagum, Davao, in 1973 under the supervision of Jerry Peters.

In Feb 1981 the PACPC was replaced by the Clinical Pastoral Care Association of the Philippines (CPCAP), comprising 10 institutions, and in 1982 CPCAP was renamed the Pastoral Care Foundation (PCF) of the Philippines. The first ACPCC was held in Jun 1982 in Metro Manila and was attended by 86 participants from 16 countries. (The fourth conference was also held in Manila in Jul 1989.) PCF has its headquarters at St. Luke's Hospital. At present there are nine CPE centers located in hospitals and parishes. PCC has become a required part of the theological curriculum of most seminaries in the Philippines.

Singapore. Gunnar Teilman, a Methodist minister, led in the formation of the Churches Counseling Center (CCC) in 1966. Some courses in counseling were offered. In 1969, a related 24-hour telephone counseling service, the Samaritans of Singapore (SOS), was launched under the directorship of Teilman. The Clinical Pastoral Care Association (CPC) in Singapore was formed in Feb 1974, and CPE, with an initial group of six clergy, was started by Albert Dalton, in conjunction with the CCC. This CPE training program was shifted to Mt. Alvernia Hospital under the supervision of some Methodist ministers and Catholic sisters in 1983. Ngoei Foong Nghian succeeded Dalton as executive secretary/director of CPC in 1977, serving until 1986 when Frans De Ridder took over. The Dutch pastoral psychologist Heije Faber visited Singapore in Apr-May 1982 to conduct various training sessions. The CCC, renamed Counseling and Care Center in 1976, continues to provide counseling services and counselor training (including marriage and family therapy and pastoral counseling) under the leadership (since 1990) of its director, Anthony Yeo.

There is a growing interest in PCC in the churches,

with many pastors seeking to specialize in this area. Churches have also set up counseling centers, some of them dealing with specific problem areas such as family life, drug addiction, and sexual problems. The seminaries include PCC in their curriculum. Trinity Theological College offers an M.Min. program and an M.Th. program in pastoral theology built around PCC.

Malaysia. Though there are no formal CPE programs in Malaysia*, PCC is being taught at the major seminaries. Some Christian counseling centers have also been functioning for some years. This includes, in some cases, telephone counseling for those going through a crisis.

India. In 1969 Frank Lake, a British missionary and doctor and founder of the clinical theology movement, was instrumental in setting up the Christian Counseling Center in Vellore by the Church of South India*. Under the present leadership of Director B. J. Prashantham, the center continues to offer counseling and training services. It also publishes literature and books in counseling. The center uses both Western and Asian approaches to counseling.

A similar counseling center, the Institute for Counseling and Personal Growth, was started at the Free Church in New Delhi by Salim Sharif in 1978. The center has explored methods of preventive counseling in the context of poverty*, social pathology, and social injustice. Carlos and Saroj Welch started a program in 1980 called *Vyakti Vikas Karayakaram* (Program for Personal Growth), which aims to help clergy deal with problems in their personal lives and pastoral ministries.

PCC has gained steady recognition as part of the curriculum in several seminaries. United Theological College in Bangalore began offering an M.Th. in pastoral counseling in 1976. The third ACPCC was held in New Delhi in 1986.

Sri Lanka. Theodore Perera, influenced by Frank Lake, started a program called the *Deva Suva Sevawa* (Divine Healing Ministry) in 1971, which aims to bring healing to the whole person, body, mind, and soul.

PCC has been in Asia for some time. Mention has already been made concerning the ACPCCs, which are linked to the international conferences on pastoral care and counseling. Attempts are being made to make PCC more Asian in character, but significant progress has yet to be made in this.

Bibliography

Augsburger, D. W., *Pastoral Counseling across Cultures* (1986). • Choi, P., *Counseling: A New Frontier in Asia* (1980). • Dumalagan, N. C., et al., eds., *Pastoral Care and Counseling in Asia: Its Needs and Concerns* (1983). • Espino, J. M., *Ministry to the Aging in Changing Asian Family Values* (1989). • Hunter, R., ed., *Dictionary of Pastoral Care and Counseling* (1990). • Prashantham, B. J., *Indian Case Studies in Therapeutic Counseling* (1978).

Robert Solomon

Patalinghug, George B.

Filipino evangelist and pastor.

Converted in 1903, Patalinghug served as a volunteer evangelist in Dumaguete and other nearby towns of the Negros Oriental at the beginning of 1904 while he was still at Silliman* Institute. In 1907 he helped in opening the Protestant mission on Siquijor Island. On completion of his studies, Patalinghug and a colleague were sent as the first evangelists to Bohol, where they labored for about three years beginning in 1908. Following his seminary studies in Manila, Patalinghug was ordained in 1916. For 38 years (1916-54), he served as pastor of the Fuente Osmena Evangelical Church (subsequently renamed Bradford Memorial Church) in Cebu City. It was probably the longest unbroken pastorate in any Protestant local church in the Philippines. During this period Bradford rose to become one of the strongest Protestant local churches in the country.

Bibliography

70th Annual Presbyterian Board Report (1907). • *The Philippine Presbyterian,* Vol. 1 (Jul 1910). • Sitoy, T. V., Jr., *Several Springs, One Stream* (1992).

T. Valentino Sitoy, Jr.

Patianom, Harnald Dingang

(b. Mengkatip, Central Kalimantan, Indonesia, 29 Oct 1902; d. 12 Dec 1987). First indigenous Dayak evangelist.

In 1918 Patianom passed an examination for minor government officials, earning a promotion in 1920 in the government office in Buntok, Central Kalimantan*, where he served until 1924. From 1924 to 1926, he followed a course for evangelists, and during a missionary conference (1926) in Banjarmasin (South Kalimantan), he was elected and dedicated as the first indigenous (Dayak) evangelist, stationed in Buntok.

In 1928 he was transferred to Banjarmasin, where he studied at the theological seminary from 1932 to 1935. On 5 Apr 1935, during the general synod for the inauguration of the Evangelical Dayak Church in Kuala Kapuas, Central Kalimantan, he and four colleagues were ordained as the first Dayak pastors of the church. He was stationed in Benangin, of the church district Muara Teweh, Barito, Central Kalimantan, until 1943, when he was transferred to Banjarmasin, where he served in various capacities until his death.

During the Japanese occupation, the Japanese authority decreed new church leadership for the Dayaks (see World War II). Of the eight committee members, only one was an ordained minister, namely Patianom, who was appointed vice president. He provided the spiritual leadership that guided the church during this critical period. Through his pastoral circulars, he encouraged local pastors, evangelists, elders, teachers, and deacons to be faithful in their ministries. In one letter, he urged them "to obey God rather than men" (Acts 5:29), an important encouragement at a time when there were many attempts to influence the church to be unfaithful to her calling.

A conference for all church workers was held (12-20 Jun 1944) for the first time in Banjarmasin. Although most of the time was spent listening to Japanese propaganda, Patianom insisted that the afternoons (3:00-5:00 p.m.) be reserved for church affairs, such as the problems of worship*, evangelization, finances, etc. The afternoon sessions provided opportunity for the sharing of information and experiences. Through his leadership, four evangelists were ordained as assistant pastors at the end of the conference.

After the war, a general synod was held in Banjarmasin (17-23 Feb 1946), where Patianom was elected president of the church. He proposed changing its name from the Evangelical Dayak Church to the Evangelical Kalimantan Church, the reason being that the Dayak Church should become a church for all people in Kalimantan, not only a tribal church. It took four years before the general synod accepted it (1950).

In his paper he wrote, "The change of the name from Dayak to Kalimantan is of basic principle, for there was no reason to discriminate Christians who are in Kalimantan. This general synod opens a new door for all Christians in Kalimantan. . . ." For Patianom, the church exists not for her own sake but for the world's sake, and in this case for the sake of all people in Kalimantan. The change of the name emphasized the missionary responsibility of the church to all in Kalimantan and put into practice the doctrine of the church as "one holy catholic church."

Patianom was president of the church until 1954. He was also the director of the Theological Seminary in Banjarmasin (1948-60). He understood the necessity of sound theological education for the church to cope with the revolutionary new situation. In 1946 he reopened the old theological seminary, closed since 1937, and two years later became its director. Under his leadership, the seminary became central in the life of the church, for the young church cadres were recruited from it.

Patianom was also known nationally for his involvement in the formation of the Council of Churches in Indonesia* (PGI). He represented Kalimantan in the preparatory meeting in 1949 in Jakarta. The idea of ecumenism further motivated him to change the name of the Dayak Church to the Kalimantan Church (see Ecumenical Movement).

He served as chairman of the Banjarmasin district (1 May 1966–31 Dec 1968) and was advisor to the board of synod from 1954 until his death.

Bibliography

Witschi, Hermann, *Christus siegt. Geschichte der Dajak-Mission auf Borneo* (1942). • Ukur, Fridolin, *Tuaiannja sungguh banjak. Sedjarah 25 tahun Geredja Kalimantan Evangelis dan 125 tahun Pekabaran Indjil di Kalimantan* (1960). FRIDOLIN UKUR

Paton, William

(b. London, England, 1886; d. 1943). British Presbyterian* missionary to India* and pioneer of the modern ecumenical* movement.

Paton was educated at Archbishop Whitgift School Croydon, at Pembroke College, Oxford, and at Westminster College, Cambridge. According to Paton's own account, in the early months of 1905 he was converted to a "living faith." His context for Christian growth and ministry, as it was for many in the early 20th c., was the Student Christian Movement* (SCM) and its missionary components of the Young Men's Christian Association* (YMCA) and the Student Volunteer Movement (SVM). In 1911, Paton married Grace Mackenzie MacDonald (who later left the Presbyterian Church for the Anglican* Church, and then left the Anglican Church, becoming a Roman Catholic in 1936). Paton's earliest ministry was with the SCM, where he helped strengthen the work at Cambridge when it had been severely weakened by the founding of the Cambridge Intercollegiate Christian Union (CICCU). Paton then became the men's candidates' secretary for England's SVM, but his strong pacifist position in a time of war (a position that changed in light of Hitler's Germany) became a legal issue, so he left for India in 1916. In the midst of political and theological issues, Paton managed to publish an important book that identified his fundamental concern in ministry: *Jesus Christ and the World's Religions*, published in 1916, with over 50,000 copies sold. Paton, now an ordained Presbyterian, became a YMCA traveling secretary in India. He returned from India for two years (1918-20) and then was called back to India to serve as the first secretary of the National Christian Council of India (see Ecumenical Movement). He served in this capacity from 1922 to 1926, helping in the development of Christian unity and indigenous Indian evangelism.

In 1926 Paton was called to succeed J. H. Oldham as secretary for the International Missionary Council. It was in this, the broadest ecumenical stage, that Paton would have the greatest impact on church life in the 20th c. For the next 17 years, Paton would be a key leader in the formation of the World Council of Church (WCC), outlining responsible Christian action in society, but always preaching Jesus Christ from pulpits, on the radio, and in his writings.

Bibliography

Jackson, E. M., *Red Tape and the Gospel: A Study of the Significance of the Ecumenical Missionary Struggle of Dr. William Paton* (1980). • Sinclair, Margaret, *William Paton: A Biography* (1949). SCOTT W. SUNQUIST

Patronato. *See* Padroado

Pattiasina, Thomas Paulus

(b. Booi, Moluccas, 17 May 1916; d. Ambon, 19 Dec 1979). Indonesian theologian, nationalist, and ecumenical* leader.

Pattiasina graduated from Hoogere Theologische School (HTS, the Theological College), Jakarta, in 1941 and was ordained a minister by the Protestant Church in Jakarta in 1943.

After World War II*, he took part in the national revolution together with the pro-Republic people of the Moluccas* in order to defend the independence proclaimed on 17 Aug 1945. From March to June 1946, he served as head of the vice governor's office in Yogyakarta. He became a minister of the Protestant Church in the Moluccas (GPM) in Jun 1946 but was relieved of his duties in 1948 because he was deemed too involved in the national struggle. After the transfer of sovereignty to Indonesia, he was appointed again as minister of the GPM (1954). As a nationalist, he did not agree with Moluccan politicians who tried to separate themselves from the Indonesian government by forming the Republic of the South Moluccas in Apr 1950. From 1965 to 1978, he occupied the position of moderator of the synod. As a leader, he was listened to by both civil and military personnel, especially in the Moluccas.

He initiated the framing of a theological basis for the GPM organization (church order, church law, etc.) and was one of the few GPM ministers who, since the 1950s, affirmed that the duty of the church is both in religious and nonreligious fields (social, political, economic, cultural, etc.). His most important contribution for GPM was the proclamation of *Pesan Tobat* (The Message of Repentance) in 1940 as a basis for the reformation of the GPM to fulfill the duties of fellowship, service, and witness. He strongly emphasized the autonomy of the church, especially with regard to funds and human resources.

Pattiasina also paid attention to the importance of evangelism, which he saw as the main duty of the church that ought not to be neglected, but which should be conducted with a full sense of responsibility, as in congregational worship. Congregation members must develop a consciousness of their evangelistic duty in life, and this has to be taught from childhood. In 1956 Pattiasina formed the *Tunas Pekabaran Injuil* (School of Evangelization, TPI), whose aim was to organize worship services and give its members, the Sunday school children of the congregations of GPM, an understanding of evangelism and the opportunity for involvement in evangelistic activities such as collecting clothes, books (school textbooks, magazines), and food (rice) to be sent to the mission field.

Pattiasina was one of the GPM leaders who suggested the involvement of GPM in ecumenical activities on the local, national (Communion of Churches in Indonesia* [PGI]), regional (Christian Conference of Asia* [CCA]), and worldwide (World Council of Churches [WCC] and World Alliance of Reformed Churches [WARC]) levels. As moderator of the GPM synod, he sponsored the formation of the Common Union of Churches in the Moluccas area (PGIW Maluku) in 1967.

Bibliography

Rajawane, A. N., "Pesan Tobat dan Maknanya Bagi Pembangunan Jemaat," in *Materi Pembinan Umat* (1989). • Van den End, Thomas, *Ragi Carita,* Vol. 2 (1989). • Chauvel, R., *Nationalists, Soldiers, and Separatists* (1990).

Mesach Tapilatu

Paul, K. T.

(b. Salem, South India, 24 Mar 1876; d. 11 Apr 1931). Tamil Christian statesman in India*.

Paul's father, a Tamil Christian, was a government official in Salem. After graduating from the Madras Christian College, Paul studied law and entered government employment. Sometime later, however, he became headmaster of the Arcot Mission School in Pungannur, and after that a history tutor at Madras Christian College.

Paul and his peers, who were drawn from many parts of India, participated in founding the National Missionary Society (NMS) in 1905 at Serampore (West Bengal), whose purpose was the propagation of the Gospel and the indigenization of the church. Between them, V. S. Azariah* and Paul provided the NMS with strong leadership. Azariah took responsibility for the mission in Dornakal in 1909, and Paul became general secretary of NMS and made it a nationwide evangelistic agency. Many newly formed Christian ashrams* and several Indian missionary societies joined in.

From 1912 to 1913, Paul accompanied John R. Mott throughout India. He was appointed one of the national secretaries of the Young Men's Christian Association* (YMCA), and in 1914 became general secretary. In this period Paul developed a program for rural construction, the promotion of cooperation, and adult education. Under him the YMCA had a team of dynamic thinkers, including L. P. Larsen, J. N. Farquhar*, and S. K. Datta, who gave intellectual Christian leadership to the educated classes. Their literary output was also considerable.

Paul was also active in the South Indian United Church (SIUC) and took part in the Tranquebar Conference, which started the negotiations for church union in South India. He remained a committee member until his death. He was moderator of the SIUC from 1925 to 1927 and was also a vice president of the World's Student Christian Federation (WSC) from 1926 to 1928. In 1928 he was an active participant in the Jerusalem meeting of the International Missionary Council. He authored the book *British Connections with India.*

After serving the NMS for seven years and the national YMCA for 18, he gave up his job to give himself more fully to public service. He opposed separate communical electorates for Christians in the legislature, and he argued his case against it not only because of his commitment to national unity in a religiously pluralistic society but also out of his conviction that the mission of the church was to be a servant community among all communities of India. He represented the Indian Christian community at the Round Table Conference in London in 1930 to resolve the deadlock in British-Indian relations.

Paul died at the age of 55. He was one of the first Christian statesmen of India and produced a theology of the church and the church's mission in the context of the developing nationalism* of a religiously pluralistic society.

Bibliography

David, M. D., *The YMCA and the Making of Modern India* (1994). • Rouse, Ruth, *The World's Student Christian Federation* (1948). • Thomas, M. M., and P. T. Thomas, *Towards an Indian Christian Theology* (1992).

LALFAKZUALA

Paulos, Gregorios

(b. Tripunithura, Kerala, India, 9 Aug 1922). Philosopher, thinker, theologian, and author.

Paul Varghese (Gregorios Paulos) was at one time a journalist and a workers' union leader. After a term of service in Ethiopia and theological education at Princeton, he became associated with the work of Aluva Fellowship House, Orthodox* Seminary, the Student Christian Movement* (SCM), and the Mar Gregorios Orthodox Christian Students' Movement* (MGOCSM). One of his major contributions has been to the World Council of Churches, which he has served in various capacities, such as associate general secretary and president. He has also been the principal and chief architect of the Orthodox Theological Seminary, Kottayam.

Gregorios Paulos earned his doctorate from Serampore University, in addition to many honorary doctorates conferred on him by various centers of international repute. A bishop of the Malankara Orthodox Syrian Church*, an effective leader of interreligious* and peace movements, and a powerful author, he is a unique personality. His ability to communicate effectively in scientific and philosophical discussions is widely appreciated. A versatile genius of comprehensive and analytic perception, he has produced works critically evaluating the cultural and philosophical roots of the West and the East with a special interest in searching for an integral view. Among his voluminous writings are *Joy of Freedom, Cosmic Man, Human Presence, Science for Sane Societies, Enlightenment East and West,* and *A Light Too Bright.*

JACOB KURIAN

Pe Maung Tin, U

(b. Yangon, 24 Apr 1888; d. Yangon, 22 Mar 1973). Christian layperson, Pali scholar, and educator in Myanmar*.

U Pe Maung Tin, whose name is synonymous with Myanmese literature, was the first national professor of Pali language at the University of Yangon. An Anglican*, he was the fifth child of U Pe and Daw Myaing. He graduated with a bachelor of arts degree from the University of Rangoon in 1909 and a master of arts degree from the University of Calcutta in 1911. He was the youngest professor in Myanmar in 1912. U Pe Maung Tin was referred to as "M. A. Maung Tin" or "Pali Maung Tin" because of his knowledge of Buddhism*, Pali, and Myanmese literature. He obtained his D.Lit. degree from Oxford University and proceeded to Paris for further studies. Highly regarded by his Western colleagues, he was close friends with professors J. S. Furnival and Luce. The latter subsequently married his sister, who became well known as Daw Tee Tee Luce for her work with waifs and strays. Mrs. Rhys David of the Pali Text Society in London and scholar-priests depended on his knowledge. He was appointed a member of the Indian Education Service, Myanmar being part of British India* in his time. He was also professor of Oriental studies and was honored by the Pali Text Society for his translation of the *Visuddhi Magga,* the Pali canons, into English. In 1930 he donated to the Pali Text Society the thousand pounds sterling awarded to him by King Mongkut of Thailand*. Against opposition from his Western peers, he established the Burmese literature* department at the University of Rangoon and served as its professor. He became principal of the university in 1936.

U Pe Maung Tin was a prodigious writer, and his works, such as a Burmese grammar, selections of Burmese prose, a history of Burmese literature, and the *Visuddhi Magga,* are still used as references. Many did not realize that he was a Christian and thought he was a former Buddhist monk because of his knowledge of Buddhism. He was a leader of the Christian Literature Society of the Burma Council of Churches. He was invited by the University of Chicago, United States, to serve as visiting professor.

Bibliography

Ma Lay Lon, *Pe Maung Tin or Father Longlife,* Vols. I and II.

KYAW NYUNT

Peace Movement (Heiwa Undo), Japan

That the Christian idea of peace in ancient times was absolute nonviolence is clear. Because of this, many believers and priests were martyred. In 313, after Christianity had been officially recognized, the responsibility of Roman citizens to serve in the military was born, and the "just war" concept slowly emerged. Leaders of the Reformation affirmed this stance, first articulated by Augustine. Near the end of the Middle Ages, citizens' movements such as the Peace of God movement appeared; after the Reformation, in opposition to the tragedy of religious wars, ideas for peace were reborn in a number of sects, including the Mennonites, the Baptists, and the Religious Society of Friends (Quakers). From this background came a number of different Christian antiwar peace movements in reaction to the two world wars in the 20th c.

In Japan in 1885, the Quakers propagated their thoughts about peace, and a magazine, *Heiwa* (Peace), was published in 1892-93. Uchimura Kanzo*, who came under this influence while studying in the United States, took an antiwar position in relation to the Russo-Japanese War, and such men as Kashiwagi Gien supported it. Kagawa Toyohiko* urged the labor union movement to form an antiwar peace movement, but he was unable to maintain an uncompromising stance during World War II*. Akashi Junzo and others of *Todaisha* (Watchtower Society) suffered cruel punishment for their antiwar stance. The position of the Non-Church Movement group is not clear, but men like Asami Sensaku were arrested because of their pacifism.

After the war, a variety of peace movements were born in the Christian world, though many were silenced by the tension stemming from the Korean War*. The Christian Peace Association* *(Kirisuto-sha heiwa no kai)* was born at this time to express clearly their desire for peace. In Feb 1951 a Call for Peace was issued by Asano Junichi*, Omura Isamu, Inoue Yoshio, Kiramori Kazoh, Sekine Masao, and others. In Kyoto, Shimizu Yoshiki, Muto Kazuo, Watanabe Nobuo, and others organized. Other peace groups were formed elsewhere in the country. An organization for information exchange among Christian peace groups was established in Mar 1953 that included absolute pacifists such as Masaike Jin, Ishihara Hyoe, and Sekiya Masahiko. In 1954, when the Japanese antinuclear movement was born, the Christian Peace Association was a founding member, and in 1960 it was a central member of the opposition to the Japan–United States Security Treaty and actively promoted the proclamation issued by the United Church of Christ in Japan. In Apr 1964, when the Japan Christian Peace Association was founded as an alliance of peace groups across the country, opposition to the basic characteristics of the movement emerged. People who had attended the All-Christian Peace Conference in Prague, Czechoslovakia, in Jun 1961 promoted peace movements, and to help them work together the All-Japan Christian Peace Conference was organized in Sep 1962. At their second meeting, they voted to oppose the Vietnam War*, setting up the Emergency Conference of Christians for Peace in Vietnam. At the third meeting in Mar 1969, the structure for domestic and international solidarity was set, and its purpose was clarified. After this, a number of people participated in the Religious Bodies Peace Conference, which was related to the Japan Communist Party. Also, in different parts of the country the peace movement went forward with groups taking up issues related to the constitutionality of the self-defense forces and the movement to renationalize Yasukuni Shrine.

Bibliography

Morioka Iwao, "Kirisuto-sha heiwa no kai no ayumi" (The course of the Christian Peace Association), *Gekkan kirisuto* (Christ monthly), Vol. 8 (1961). • Inoue Yoshio, *Kirisuto-sha heiwa undo no sengo ni-ju-nen* (Twenty Years in the Christian Peace Movement after the War), Vol. 8 (1965).

Ogawa Keiji, Japanese Dictionary

Pelgone, Policarpo

Filipino Presbyterian* minister and Philippine* army colonel.

An outstanding early Filipino Presbyterian minister in the Bicol region of Luzon, Pelgone was a former Catholic* seminarian and later a Philippine army colonel during the Philippine revolution against Spain in 1896-97. He turned Protestant about 1909 under the influence of Julian Bertumen*, another former Catholic seminarian who had given him a Latin Bible* to read. Pelgone, a persuasive speaker, converted many men and women among the Bicol intelligentsia who later became outstanding Protestant leaders, notably Agripina Moralde*.

Following in his footsteps, his daughters Jael and Noemi also became outstanding national church leaders.

Bibliography

Tabios, A. B., J. P. Cruz, and M. G. Pejo, *The Evangelical Church in the Bicol Region: A Brief History* (1974). • Sitoy, T. V., Jr., *Several Springs, One Stream* (1992).

T. Valentino Sitoy, Jr.

Pentecostalism

An evangelical restorationist movement that emphasizes the baptism and gifts of the Holy Spirit for the life and mission of the church and indigenous forms of worship and church structure.

The landscape of modern Pentecostalism includes: (1) "Classical Pentecostals," those believers attending denominational or independent churches that highlight classical Pentecostal doctrines — divine healing through the atonement of Christ, premillennial eschatology, and especially the function of speaking in tongues as a vital evidence of Spirit baptism; (2) "Neo-Pentecostals" or "Charismatics" from the mainline Protestant churches, the Roman Catholic* Church, and the Orthodox* churches who have experienced or promote the charismatic gifts; (3) Neocharismatics and indigenous groups, often called the "Third Wave," which includes the "New Apostolic Reformation churches" that have underscored the importance of "signs and wonders" in ministry (Acts 5:12), and, notably in the latter, the return of the apostolic and prophetic offices (Eph 4:11).

Notwithstanding these Western categories, classical Pentecostal churches in Asia reflect more diversity in beliefs and practices than their Euro-American counterparts by focusing more attention on the broader range of Pentecostal phenomena. Due to the belief that the Holy Spirit confers gifts and callings directly upon believers apart from ecclesiastical institutions, Pentecostalism has easily been contextualized (see Contextualization), as in the case of the Indian Pentecostal Church of God and the Pentecostal Mission (formerly Ceylon Pentecostal Mission) in India* and Sri Lanka*; the Pentecostal Church of Indonesia* (GPI); Japan* Bible Church; True Jesus Churches of China* and Taiwan*; and Church of the Living God in the Philippines*.

Since the Old Testament prophet Joel predicted that the "daughters" and "maidservants," as well as the "sons" and male servants, would prophesy in the end times (Joel 2:28-29; Acts 2:17 [AV]), women* have played influential roles, particularly in Korea* and Singapore*. In many places of Asia, Pentecostal spirituality has appealed to marginalized populations (e.g., lower castes in India; Lisu people of Myanmar*; Overseas Chinese in Indonesia and Malaysia*). However, in recent decades it has also attracted the middle classes and occasionally wealthy persons, obvious in the membership of the large Yoido Full Gospel Church in Seoul, Korea, Trinity Christian Centre in Singapore, and many other congregations from India to Korea.

Since the charismatic* movement receives treatment elsewhere, the following essay focuses primarily on classical Pentecostalism and includes (1) 19th-c. precedents; (2) beginnings of modern Pentecostalism; (3) missionaries to Asia; and (4) bibliography.

19th-c. Precedents. Reports of revival movements in Asia in the 19th c. sometimes contained descriptions of Pentecostal-like phenomena: visions, dreams, prophecies, miracles, persons falling prostrate, and in rare instances speaking in tongues. Participants sought the "outpouring" of the Holy Spirit for holy living and empowerment to evangelize. News of revivals in the United States and the United Kingdom in 1857-60 inspired similar happenings in British India, China, Japan, Australia, and the Pacific islands, among other places. Controversial movements arose in South India in Tirunelveli (1860-65), led in part by John Christian Aroolappen, and in Travancore (1873-81) by Justus Joseph. Belief in the dispensational premillennial teachings of the Christian Brethren and appearances of Pentecostal phenomena marked both. Nevertheless, apart from these in India, such movements generally tended to be local and on a small scale.

These developments did not always occur as a result of events in the West. In some cases, unusual happenings accompanied the ministries of missionaries and national believers as they evangelized and established churches. Rhenish missionaries in Sumatra reported that conversions increased as a result of Batak* believers experiencing dreams, revelations, and visions. In missionary accounts that resembled the "signs" that were to follow the preaching of the Gospel according to Mark 16:18, opponents poisoned the food of certain missionaries (e.g., Ludwig Ingwer Nommensen*), but without success. An indigenous Christian movement with charismatic dimensions guided by Sadrach Surapranata* flourished in Central Java and established contacts with the followers of Edward Irving in the United Kingdom and the Netherlands. Extraordinary incidents also characterized the evangelization of the Karens* in Myanmar. Claims to miraculous physical healings and exorcisms of evil spirits in China followed the work of Chinese ministers such as Hsi Shengmo* (Pastor Hsi), who worked closely with the China Inland Mission, and various missionaries, including those of the Christian and Missionary Alliance*. John L. Nevius* and other Presbyterian* missionaries exorcised demons. Another Presbyterian, Jonathan Goforth, played a leading role in the 1908 revival in Manchuria that exhibited Pentecostal expressions.

Notable revivals, frequently marked by Pentecostal-like phenomena, arose shortly after the turn of the 20th c. in India, China, Manchuria, Japan, and Korea. Stories of the Welsh Revival (1904-5) sparked their emergence, though social and cultural factors contributed to their appeal as well. Along with the attention placed on confession and repentance, these awakenings displayed the intense desire of Christians for indigenous leadership and worship forms, reflecting varying degrees of dissatisfaction with the ecclesiastical structures and liturgies imported from the West. The revival of 1905-6 in India significantly prepared the churches for the nation's independence in l947 through the subsequent increase in indigenous leaders and Indian identification. Revival in Presbyterian and Methodist* circles in Korea in 1906-10 reinforced the indigenous makeup of the churches and forged a sizable Christian presence in the nation.

Thus, by the time the first Pentecostal missionaries arrived in Asia from the United States in 1907, Pentecostal-like movements and expressions had appeared for almost half a century in various places. These precedents have relevance for understanding contemporary Pentecostal churches and the ongoing charismatic renewal of other Asian churches.

Beginnings of modern Pentecostalism. The roots of Pentecostalism become visible in the 19th-c. holiness movement, evangelical healing movement, and the mounting popularity of premillennial teachings among evangelicals. Wesleyan-holiness and "Higher Life" (Keswickian) advocates defined baptism in the Holy Spirit as a postconversion experience intended for every believer. To the Wesleyans, it brought sanctifying grace; to Higher Life believers, it offered "full consecration" to empower Christians for witness. Many of these "radical evangelicals" also anticipated that miraculous "signs and wonders" (Acts 5:12) would accompany Gospel proclamation in the evangelization of the world just as they had in the period of the early church. By the 1880s, some speculated that God might even confer unlearned languages (Mark 16:17) on missionaries to expedite Gospel preaching, enabling them to bypass the nuisance of language school.

Due to the popular nature of early Pentecostalism, the movement had almost as many "founders" as revival centers. Historians trace the origins to North American revivals in Topeka, Kansas (1901), Fargo, North Dakota (1904), Houston, Texas (1905-6), Zion, Illinois (1906-7), the Azusa Street Revival in Los Angeles, California (1906-9), and the many others that followed in their wake in Chicago, Illinois; Dunn, North Carolina; Spokane, Washington; Memphis, Tennessee; Nyack, New York.; Cleveland, Ohio.; and Toronto, Canada. Influential revivals in Europe occurred in Oslo, Norway; Stockholm, Sweden; Sunderland, United Kingdom; and Amsterdam, Holland.

The leader of the Topeka revival, Charles F. Parham, stamped the hallmark of classical Pentecostal theology by claiming that speaking in tongues (understood to be unlearned human languages) represented indispensable evidence of Spirit baptism. This bestowal from the Holy Spirit would then linguistically equip the initiated to evangelize the world quickly in the "last days" (Acts 2:4, 17). William J. Seymour, an African-American and understudy of Parham who shared the latter's millennial urgency and belief in Spirit baptism, shepherded the interracial and intercultural Azusa Street Revival. Azusa notably accentuated the outpouring of the Holy Spirit upon the poor and oppressed (e.g., Americans of African and Hispanic descent) and the reconciliation of the races as fundamental to the work of the Spirit. The publication of the *Apostolic Faith* magazine (1906-8) and the subsequent travels of the persons who visited the revival greatly contributed to making the Pentecostal movement worldwide in scope.

Despite the better-known North American origins, Pentecostalism in southern Asia evolved independently in the summer of 1906, in part under the leadership of the former Methodist missionary Minnie F. Abrams. Holiness influence and expectancy of the imminent premillennial return of Christ among missionaries and Indian believers on the subcontinent encouraged the awakening that had begun in the preceding year and had swept through many Protestant mission stations. The occurrences of tongues beginning in Jul 1906 in Mumbai (Bombay) simply added the most unusual feature to the long list of paranormal phenomena that had characterized the revival from its outbreak in the Khassia Hills of northeast India. Abrams and other missionaries from established mission agencies stressed the importance of tongues (understood as simply unknown languages to the speakers and auditors) as an important evidence of Spirit baptism. Yet, unlike the Pentecostal missionaries who arrived from America in 1907, they did not insist on tongues as an absolute requirement; neither did they consider it as a substitute for formal language training.

By the end of the decade, most Pentecostals had dropped the notion of the utility of tongues for preaching. Although they were still viewed as potentially recognizable languages of humans or of angels (1 Cor 13:1), believers uttered them during times of intense prayer. From this perspective, prayer in tongues constituted an experiential dynamic from which one derived spiritual power.

Missionaries to Asia. The Pentecostal missionary diaspora from Euro-America began in 1904, when two women traveled from a revival in Fargo, North Dakota, to South Africa. However, the larger expansion commenced in 1906-7 with Pentecostals going to the traditional sites of Protestant mission endeavor: Africa, the Middle East, British India, Southeast Asia, China, Japan, and Korea. By 1910 at least 200 Pentecostals served as missionaries. Key pioneers in Asia included Alfred G. and Lillian Garr (1907); George E. Berg (1908); Esther B. Harvey (1913); and Robert F. Cook (1913) in India; Thomas J. McIntosh (1907); E. May Law (1907); Alfred and Lillian Garr (1907); Arie and Elsje Kok (1910); and Robert and Aimee Semple [McPherson] (1910) in China; Johann Thiessen (1921) and William Bernard (1922) in Indonesia; Folke Boberg (1922) in Inner Mongolia*; Martin L. Ryan (1907) and Carl F. Juergensen (1913) in Japan; Mary C. Rumsey (1928) in Korea; Nikolai and Martta Poysti (1923) in Manchuria; J. Clifford and Levada Morrison (1929) in Myanmar; Benjamin H. and Cordelia Caudle (1926) in the Philippines; Walter H. Clifford (1921) in Sri Lanka; and Verner and Hanna Porkka Raasina (1946) in Thailand. Veteran missionaries sometimes joined the Pentecostal movement; from the Christian and Missionary Alliance came William W. Simpson (1912) and Victor G. Plymire (1920) in China and Tibet, respectively. Max Wood Moorhead (Young Men's Christian Association*) in Sri Lanka, and Maud Orlebar (Young Women's Christian Association*) and Susan C. Easton (Woman's Union Missionary Society of America for Heathen Lands) in India became Pentecostals in 1907.

These and the missionaries who succeeded them made long-term contributions to Asian Christianity through their activities in church planting, education, and charitable enterprises. Their legacies are easily found in the Pentecostal denominations that emerged from their ministries. Almost from the inauguration of Pentecostal missions, however, indigenous Pentecostal congregations and organizations began to take shape for various reasons, as in the case of the founding of the True Jesus Church in Beijing, China, in 1917.

The first Pentecostal agency to send personnel to Asia (especially China) was the Pentecostal Missionary Union, founded in the United Kingdom in 1909 under the leadership of Cecil H. Polhill and modeled after the China Inland Mission. Later agencies included the Assemblies of God (United States; 1914), International Pentecostal Holiness Church (1915), Evangelization Society of the Pittsburgh Bible Institute (1920), Dutch Pentecostal Missionary Society (1920), Pentecostal Assemblies of Canada (1925), Finnish Free Foreign Mission (1927), International Church of the Foursquare Gospel (1927), and Velbert (Germany) Mission (1931), as well as missionaries from the congregationally based Scandinavian Pentecostal churches.

Much study remains to be done on Pentecostalism in Asia since a survey of the expansion, beliefs, and practices of Pentecostals has yet to be written. Nevertheless, the growing number of monographs, particularly by younger Asian scholars, reflects encouraging progress.

Bibliography

General

Ahonen, Lauri, *Missions Growth: A Case Study on Finnish Free Foreign Mission* (1984). • Burgess, Stanley M., ed., *New International Dictionary of Pentecostal and Charismatic Movements* (2000). • Conn, Charles W., *Where the Saints Have Trod: A History of Church of God Missions* (1959). • Dempster, Murray W., Byron D. Klaus, and Douglas Petersen, eds., *The Globalization of Pentecostalism: A Religion Made to Travel* (1999). • Yeol Soo Eim, "The Worldwide Expansion of the Foursquare Church" (D.Miss. dissertation, Fuller Theological Seminary, 1986). • Gee, Donald, *Wind and Flame* (1967). • Goff, James R., Jr., *Fields White unto Harvest: Charles F. Parham and the Missionary Origins of Pentecostalism* (1988). • Hollenweger, Walter J., *Pentecostalism: Origins and Developments Worldwide* (1997). • Ma Wonsuk and Robert P. Menzies, eds., *Pentecostalism in Context* (1997). • McGee, Gary B., *This Gospel Shall Be Preached: A History and Theology of Assemblies of God Foreign Missions to 1959* (1986, 1989); • Miller, Thomas William, *Canadian Pentecostals: A History of the Pentecostal Assemblies of Canada* (1994). • Orr, J. Edwin, *Evangelical Awakenings in Eastern Asia* (1975). • Synan, Vinson, *The Holiness-Pentecostal Tradition: Charismatic Movements in the Twentieth Century* (1997). • Van der Laan, Cornelis, *Sectarian against His Will: Gerrit Roelof Polman and the Birth of Pentecostalism in the Netherlands* (1991).

China

Bays, Daniel H., ed., *Christianity in China: From the Eighteenth Century to the Present* (1996); "Indigenous Protestant Churches in China, 1900-1937: A Pentecostal Case Study," in *Indigenous Responses to Western Christianity,* ed. Steven Kaplan (1995); "The Protestant Missionary Establishment and the Pentecostal Movement," in *Pentecostal Currents in American Protestantism,* ed. Edith L. Blumhofer, Russell P. Spittler, and Grant A. Wacker (1999). • Crawford, Mary K., *The Shantung Revival* (1933). • Hocken, Peter, "Cecil H. Polhill: Pentecostal Layman," *Pneuma: The Journal of the Society for Pentecostal Studies,* Vol. 10 (Fall 1988). • Hunter, Alan, and Kim-Kwong Chan, *Protestantism in Contemporary China* (1993). • Johannesson, Jan-Endy, *Dokumentation av Svensk Pingstmission I Kina* (Documentation on Swedish Pentecostal missions in China) (1992). • Law, E. May, *Pentecostal Mission Work in South China* (ca. 1916). • Taylor, Mrs. Howard [Geraldine Taylor], *Pastor Hsi* (1900).

East Timor

Peters, George W., *Indonesia: Focus on Timor* (1973). • Trompf, G. W. , ed., *Cargo Cults and Millenarian Movements* (1990).

India

Abrams, Minnie F., *The Baptism of the Holy Ghost and Fire* (1906). • Kurundamannil, Joseph Chakko, "Yuomayam: A Messianic Movement in Kerala, India" (D.Miss. dissertation, Fuller Theological Seminary, 1978). • Lang, G. H., *The History and Diaries of an Indian Christian (J. C. Aroolappen)* (1939). • McGee, Gary B., "Pentecostal Phenomena and Revivals in India: Implications for Indigenous Church Leadership," *IBMR,* Vol. 20 (Jul 1996); "'Latter Rain' Falling in the East: Early-Twentieth-Century Pentecostalism in India and the Debate over Speaking in Tongues," *Church History,* Vol. 68 (Sep 1999). • Orr, J. Edwin, *Evangelical Awakenings in India* (1970). • Pothen, Abraham Thottumkal, "Indigenous Cross-cultural Missions in India and Their Contribution to Church Growth: With Special Emphasis on Pentecostal-Charismatic Missions" (Ph.D. dissertation, Fuller Theological Seminary, 1990).

Indonesia

Cooley, F. L., *The Growing Seed: The Christian Church in Indonesia* (1978). • Partonadi, Sutarman Soediman, *Sadrach's Community and Its Contextual Roots* (1990). • Tapilatu, M., *Gereja-gereja Pentakosta de Indonesia* ("Pentecostal Churches of Indonesia") (1982). • Warneck, J., *The Living Christ and Dying Heathenism* (1909).

Japan

Mitama ni michibikarete — nihon asenburi kyodan soritsu san-ju-nen-shi (Led by the Spirit: Thirty-year history of the Japan Assemblies of God Church) (1979).

Korea

Mullins, Mark R., "The Empire Strikes Back: Korean Pentecostal Mission to Japan," in *Charismatic Christianity as a Global Culture,* ed. Karla Poewe (1994). • Boo-Woong Yoo, *Korean Pentecostalism: Its History and Theology* (1988). • Hong Young-gi, "The Backgrounds and Characteristics of the Charismatic Mega-churches in Korea," *Asian Journal of Pentecostal Studies,* Vol. 3 (Jan 2000).

Mongolia

Boberg, Folke, *Mongoliet som Missionsfält* ("Mongolia as a Mission Field") (1946).

Myanmar

Chin Kua Khai, "Dynamics of Renewal: A Historical Movement among the Zomi in Myanmar" (Ph.D. dissertation, Fuller Theological Seminary, 1999). • Mason, Francis, *The Karen Apostle, or Memoir of Ko Thah Byu* (1884).

Philippines

Esperanza, Trinidad Cabanilla, "The Assemblies of God in the Philippines" (M.R.E. thesis, Fuller Theological Seminary, 1965). • Montgomery, Jim, *Fire in the Philippines* (1975).

Singapore

Abeysekera, Fred G., *History of the Assemblies of God in Singapore, 1928-1992* (1992).

Sri Lanka

Somaratna, G. P. V., *The Origins of the Pentecostal Move-*

ment in Sri Lanka (1995); *Walter H. Clifford: The Apostle of Pentecostalism in Sri Lanka* (1995).

Taiwan

Rubinstein, Murray A., *The Protestant Community of Modern Taiwan: Mission, Seminary, and Church* (1991).

Thailand

Shaffer, Ervin E., *Under the Shade of the Coconut Palms: Missions-Thailand* (n.d.). • Smith, Alex G., *Siamese Gold: A History of Church Growth in Thailand: An Interpretive Analysis, 1816-1982* (1981).

Vietnam

Steinkamp, Orrel N., *The Holy Spirit in Vietnam* (1973).

GARY B. MCGEE

Perboyre, Jean Gabriel

(b. Montgesty, France, 6 Jan 1802; d. Wuhan, China, 11 Sep 1840). Vincentian missionary priest to China* and martyr.

Perboyre was born into a French peasant family in which six of the eight children either became priests or entered religious life. Their paternal uncle, Jacques, a Vincentian priest who had an underground ministry during the French Revolution, established, when peace returned, a minor seminary at Montauban, where his nephews studied. Perboyre completed his secondary education in two and a half years, decided to become a priest, and made his novitiate at Montauban. He longed for the China mission after receiving news of the martyrdom of Francis Regis Clet, a Vincentian priest, in China toward the end of 1820.

After his ordination as a priest on 23 Sep 1826, he became the professor of the major seminary of Saint Flour in Auvergne. Then he successfully reorganized the minor seminary at Montauban. In 1832 he was appointed a novice director in Paris.

In spite of poor health, Perboyre succeeded in persuading the superior general to let him go to China to take the place of his younger brother, Louis, also a Vincentian priest, who died in Java in 1831 while en route to China. Leaving Le Havre on 21 May 1835, he arrived in Macau* on 29 Aug, studied Chinese for a few months with the Portuguese Vincentians before departing for his mission in Hunan on 19 Dec 1835, and arrived at Nan Yang Fou toward the end of 1836, after a long, exhausting journey, to join three Chinese Vincentians, Fathers Sung, Pei, and Wang. He continued to study Chinese, fell seriously ill, but recovered to work alongside the Chinese confreres throughout 1837.

Sent to Hubei in the beginning of 1838, he settled at Tchai Yuen Keou, where there was a small but fervent Christian community, and worked until the autumn of 1839 when a persecution of Christians was directed by the viceroy of Wuhan. On 15 Sep 1839, Perboyre, hiding in the woods, was betrayed and apprehended. He underwent a yearlong trial and was tortured and passed from one tribunal to another until he appeared before the viceroy himself. This is remarkably similar to the experience of Jesus, and during this time he composed an inspiring prayer beginning "O my Divine Savior! Transform me into yourself. . . ." He died on Friday, 11 Sep 1840, hung on a cross-shaped gibbet in the company of bandits.

Perboyre, by his saintly life and death, continues to inspire missionary zeal in many Vincentians.

Bibliography

Sylvestre, A., *La vie de Jean Gabriel Perboyre* (1994). • De Montgesty, G., *Two Vincentian Martyrs* (1953).

ANDRE SYLVESTRE

Pereira, Thomas

(b. 1645; d. 1708). Portuguese Jesuit* missionary serving the Qing government of Emperor Kangxi.

Pereira, who learned music from childhood, left Europe for Goa in 1666 and arrived in Macau* in 1672, moving on to Beijing when Ferdinand Verbiest* recommended him to Emperor Kangxi, who was interested in Western music. Pereira produced teaching materials in Chinese and taught craftsmen to make various musical instruments, which he used to teach Kangxi two or three songs. When Philippus Maria Grimaldi* went to Russia in 1687, Pereira took his place as assistant to Verbiest. In 1689 Kangxi assigned Pereira and François Gerbillon* (1654-1707) to accompany the emperor legate, Suo E Tu, to Ni Bu Chu to negotiate the Sino-Russia Treaty (the Treaty of Ni Bu Chu). The emperor was pleased with the outcome of the treaty, and in 1690, when Pereira went to the palace to bid the emperor farewell before his visit to the provinces, Kangxi inquired about the missionaries and churches in his itinerary. On his trip to the south, the emperor met the missionaries and sent his officers to the churches with monetary gifts. In 1693 Pereira wrote a long letter to the emperor regarding a Jesuit missionary facing difficulty in Hangzhou. In response, Kangxi issued an injunction allowing the propagation of Christianity in China. By 1700 there were approximately 300,000 Christians in China. Undoubtedly Pereira, together with Grimaldi and Gerbillon, contributed greatly toward the spread of Christianity in China in this period.

Bibliography

Treadgold, Donald W., *The West in Russia and China: China, 1582-1949* (1973). • Väth, Alfons, *Johann Adam Schall von Bell, S.J. (1592-1666)* (1991).

CHINA GROUP, translated by DAVID WU

Perez, Asuncion Arriola

(b. 1893; d. 1967). Filipino social worker, patriot, and church lay leader.

Perez studied social work in the United States and was a university teacher in Manila when the great Tondo fire of 1923 moved her to quit teaching and join Josefa Jara-Martinez* in working for the poor and homeless. As executive secretary of the Associated Charities of Manila, she successfully waged a campaign for a governmental law requiring fire safeguards and implementation of health rules and sanitation in building permits. She organized an unemployment council, which later became the National Relief Administration. In 1935 she became the sole female member of the National Security Board and of a special commission to revise the Philippine Labor Code. In 1941 she became director of public welfare. During World War II*, she and her husband joined the Filipino guerrillas and conducted espionage activities. She eventually received the rank of colonel. Both she and her husband were captured in 1944; she was later released, but her husband was executed by the Japanese.

In 1945 she resumed her government work in social welfare, and in 1948 she became a member of the Philippine president's cabinet, the first women in such a position. That same year she was elected chairperson of UNICEF. She was one of the first women to hold such a high position in the United Nations.

A devout Christian, she took important leadership positions in the Methodist* Church, serving for many years from 1948 as chairperson of the Bethel Girls' High School in Manila and from 1954 to 1964 as president of what is now the Philippine Wesleyan University.

Bibliography

Higdon, E. K., and I. W. Higdon, *From Carabao to Clipper* (1941). • Quiambao, E. C., "Asuncion Perez, Social Worker," in J. V. de Guzman et al., *Women of Distinction: Biographical Essays on Outstanding Filipina Women* (1967). • Sitoy, T. V., Jr., *Comity and Unity* (1989).

T. Valentino Sitoy, Jr.

Perez, Francisco

(b. Tenesserim, 1643; d. Faifo, 29 Sep 1728). First Asian Catholic prelate in Vietnam* (1692-1728).

Bishop Francisco Perez was born in Tenesserim and was a Filipino-Thai, described by a French source as "d'un père manillois, et d'une mère siamois" [of a Manilan father and a Siamese mother]. A former student at the *Missions Étrangères de Paris* (MEP, Paris Foreign Mission Society*) seminary at Mahapram, near Ayutthaya, Perez was ordained a priest at Ayutthaya on 31 Mar 1668, and in 1674 was placed in charge of a missionary district in Tenesserim. In response to a Roman Propaganda Fide request in 1687 for nominations of Asian priests to the episcopate, Bishop Louis Laneau, vicar apostolic of Siam since 1673, submitted his name to Cardinal Altieri, prefect of the Propaganda. In 1691 Perez was named new vicar apostolic of Cochin China and was consecrated that same year by Bishop Laneau. Perez held his post faithfully till his death at Faifo on 29 Sep 1728.

Interestingly enough, Perez was a contemporary of the first Chinese Catholic prelate, Bishop Lo Wen-Tsao* (Gregorio Lopez), O.P. (1611-91), vicar apostolic of Nanking in 1674 and bishop of Nanking from 1690 till his death.

Bibliography

Launay, A. C., *Mémorial de la Société des Missions Étrangères* (Paris).

T. Valentino Sitoy, Jr.

Periyar, Rationalist Movement of

E. V. Ramaswamy Naickar (b. Erode, 1879; d. 1973; also known as EVR and Periyar) was brought up as a businessman and was destined to lead the struggle for Tamil cultural nationalism*. As a young man, he was at first a wandering *sannyasin* in Benares and later became a leader of the Congress Party until 1925. In 1926 he participated in the non-Brahmin conference at Madurai, which brought him into contact with the Justice Party. EVR soon founded the Self-Respect Movement, a social-action group aimed at eradicating untouchability and caste. The Self-Respect Movement stood for the negation of God, religion, Brahmins, as well as Mahatma Gandhi* and his congress. During this period he was arrested several times for leading public agitations. In 1937 he led the first anti-Hindi agitation and was elected president of the Justice Party. Since 1939 he stood for the ideal "*Dravida Nadu* for Dravidian people." In 1944 at Salem, EVR officially transformed the Justice Party into the mass organization Dravida Kazhagam (DK). Despite the demand for *Dravidanadu*, the emphasis of the DK was more on social reform than political activity. Especially important to the movement was widow remarriage and intercaste marriages.

In 1949 EVR's young lieutenant, C. N. Annadurai, broke away to found the Dravida Munnetra Kazhagam (DMK). In 1952 EVR led a major anti-Hindi movement, tarring over the Hindi names on Tamil Nadu's railway platforms. In 1953 he broke images of the god Vinayaka (Ganesh) to demonstrate his opposition to superstition. He opposed Rajaji's caste-based education program but later supported Congress when the Nadar Kamaraj became the leader. He burned the national flag in 1955 and the India* constitution in 1957, opposing the North Aryan–dominated central government. In the 1960s EVR burned pictures of the god Rama because he saw the *Ramayana* as a record of an imperialistic war by northerners against southerners. When the DMK came to power in Tamil Nadu in 1967, there was reconciliation with the DK, and statues of EVR were erected in several places, all with the following inscription: "He who created God is a fool, he who propagates God is a scoundrel and he who worships God is a barbarian." In 1971 EVR organized in Salem an Eradication of Superstition Conference at which images of Rama were beaten and other Hindu deities were obscenely portrayed.

EVR often reiterated that no Brahmin can be for equality and justice, as caste distinction is prescribed by the Vedas, Shastras, Puranas, and Ithihasas. Even

Krishna, the philosophical god of the Hindus, proclaimed that he created the four *varnas,* and this compels a Dravidian to be an atheist. Politically, this anti-Aryanism led to the demand for *Dravidanadu.* EVR, however, had a soft spot for Buddha for advocating reason. According to him, if God is beyond human knowledge, and something that exists only when believed in, there is not much sense in such a contention. The person who invented God can be forgiven because he was a fool and did it out of ignorance. He assumed there must be a cause for the creation and that cause was God, but in his view, religion and scripture are not like that. The inventors of these have invented absolute falsehood. They have classified and organized religion only in order to cheat and threaten people. All religionists are equally opposed to reform and enlightenment; the superstition and exploitation of the priests can be destroyed only by atheism.

At the end of his life, EVR organized a Conference for the Eradication of Social Degradation of the Tamils. The relevance of this great leader of the Tamils lies in the fact that, through his efforts, the oppressed were made aware of their downtroddenness and came to realize that this degradation is human-made and hence alterable through struggle.

Bibliography

Ramaswamy, E. V., *Dear Youths; God and Man; Hindu Festivals; March toward Peace, Prosperity, and Progress; Rational Thinking; Rural Development* (1983); *Materialism* (1984). • Veeramani, K., *Periyar and His Ideology* (1983); *The D.K.: What It Stands For* (1983). • Joseph, P., *The Dravidian Problem in the South Indian Cultural Complex* (1972). • Ryerson, Charles A., *Regionalism and Religion: The Tamil Renaissance and Popular Hinduism* (1988).

K. P. Aleaz

Persekutuan Gereja-Gereja di Indonesia, PGI. *See* Communion of Churches, Indonesia (CCI)

Pfander, Karl Gottlieb

(b. Waiblingen, Saxony, Germany, 1803; d. England, 1866). German scholar of and apologete to Islam*.

Raised in a pietist family in Saxony, Pfander attended the Moravian Academy at Stuttgart, where he was greatly influenced by the work of the Basel Mission. He gave himself to missionary work at the age of 17, entering the Basel Mission training school where he studied the Bible, manual trade, finance, Arabic, and the Koran. In 1825 Pfander was ordained in the Lutheran* Church and began his work in Karabagh, Armenia*. His work was among the two-thirds majority who were Muslim.

Pfander studied Persian, traveled to Iran and Baghdad, studied the works of Henry Martyn, and began writing tracts for Muslims in Persian. It was Pfander's belief that Muslims would respond to the clear teachings of Scripture if they were given the opportunity.

Pfander's major work, the *Mizan-al haqq* ("Balance of Truth" or "Roads to the Truth," 1829), has been translated into many languages and is still a classic in the debate between Christianity and Islam. In this work he defends the truthfulness of the Bible against the prevailing view of textual corruption taught by Muslims. Two of his other works are also particularly noteworthy: *Miftar Al Asrar* (Key to the Secrets, 1844) and *Tariq al Hayyat* (The Way of Life).

These works carried public disputation with the learned men of Islam to a high level of competence and won a number of converts by the excellence of the author's presentation of the Christian faith.

After nearly three years of transition, Pfander transferred to work with the Church Missionary Society (CMS) in 1840. He is worthily described as the greatest of all missionaries to Mohammedans, serving the CMS for 25 years, during which he worked in an exclusively Muslim area in Peshawar on the northwest frontier.

It is probable that Pfander influenced Sir William Muir, the learned and pious ruler of the Northwestern Provinces and later principal of Edinburgh University, to write his four-volume *Life of Mahomet* with a view to provide missionaries with weapons in their difficult spiritual warfare with Islam. Understandably, later CMS attempts to communicate Christian faith to Muslims gained their strength from the contributions of Pfander and Muir.

Bibliography

Bennett, Clinton, "The Legacy of Karl Gottlieb Pfander," *IBMR,* Vol. 20 (1996). • Powell, Avril, "Maulana Rahmat Allah Kairanawi and Muslim-Christian Controversy in India in the Mid-Nineteenth Century," *Journal of the Royal Asiatic Society* (1975-76). • Zwemer, S. M., "Karl Gottlieb Pfander," *Moslem World,* Vol. 31 (3 July 1941).

A. T. Philip

PGI. *See* Communion of Churches, Indonesia (CCI)

Pham Ngoc Chi

(b. Ton Dao Village, Kim Son District, Ninh Binh Province [Phat Diem Diocese], Vietnam, 14 May 1909; d. Da Nang, 1990). Vietnamese Catholic educator and bishop.

Pham entered the probatorium at Ba Lang in 1920, then the minor seminary at Phuc Nhac, after which he was sent to Rome for further studies in 1927. He continued to study law at Paris University (1935) after his ordination as a priest on 23 Dec 1933, and returned to be a professor at Phat Diem major seminary, later becoming its vice-director, then director. On 5 Aug 1950, he became bishop of Bui Chu Diocese, where he reorganized the pastoral*, educational, and social activities and sent seminarians abroad for training. The number of seminarians increased, and he founded a number of diocesan congregations, such as the Coredemptrix*, Dominican* Sisters, Lovers* of the Holy Cross, Hospital Brothers of St. John of God, and Auxiliary Fathers to the Mission.

In 1954 he was appointed minister in charge of the clergy seeking refuge in the South by Nuncio Dooley. Many churches, schools, and hospitals were built and many volunteers and social workers were recruited in his effort to reintegrate the refugees* into the South. On 5 Jan 1957 he was assigned as apostolic delegate to the Catholic Action* in the Council of Bishops, South Vietnam, which emphasizes evangelization by every layperson in the individual's social environment.

Chi was nominated bishop of Qui Nhon on 5 Jul 1957. His final pastoral ministry was in the Da Nang Diocese. When Vietnam* was reunited under the Communist regime in 1975, he was placed under house arrest from May that year until his death.

Bibliography

Tra Kieu, *A Catholic Parish in the South of Da Nang, Province of Quang Nam* (n.d.). • Le Ngoc Bich, *Cac vi Giam Muc mot tho i da qua* (1933-95). • Phan Phat Huon, *Viet Nam Giao Su Tap* II (1962).

ANTHONY DO HUU NGHIEM

Phaulkon, Constantine

(b. Custode, Cephanlonie, Greece, 1648; d. Lawo [Lop Buri], Thailand, 5 Jun 1688). An expatriate who played an important role and exercised considerable influence in the royal administration of Siam (Thailand*) during the reign of King Narai the Great (Phra Narai Maharaj).

The story of Phaulkon's life has been written from different points of view, depending on whether the writer benefitted or felt harmed by him. Even the story of his birth has been variously reported.

Phaulkon's original name was Hierachy, which may be translated "Hawk" or "Falcon." When he received his first communion, he received a new name, Constantine Hierachy. Nothing certain is known about his parents. Written testimony from the priest De Beze, who was close to him, asserted that his parents were Greek and that an ancestor of his mother was once governor of Venice.

When he was 10 years old, he left his parents to seek his fortune aboard an English merchant ship. Later he journeyed to India* in the employ of George White, who changed his name to Phaulkon, which also means "Hawk" or "Falcon."

Phaulkon was intelligent and a quick learner. In his time at sea, he was able to master the skills of navigation so as to be employed as an able-bodied seaman. When he returned to Europe, he signed on with a ship going to Bantam on Java of present-day Indonesia*. There he was employed by a British company. One day a fire broke out in the business office. Everyone fled to save their lives except Phaulkon, who risked his life to extinguish the fire.

With the substantial reward he received for his heroism, he returned to the employ of George White, who was by then a partner of Richard Burnaby, and traveled aboard a merchant ship to Ayutthaya, Siam.

Later he purchased his own ship and loaded on merchandise from Ayutthaya to market on his own. Unfortunately the ship was wrecked twice: the first time in the Strait of Malacca, and the second time at Nakorn Sri Thammaraj (on the southwestern coast of the Gulf of Siam, or Thailand). This discouraged him from engaging in seaborne trading.

He then borrowed a sum of money from the East India Company office in Ayutthaya and deposited it with Okya Kosa Tibodi Lek. This led to his employment by Lek in the government merchandise storage depot. The exact year of his acceptance into royal government service is unknown; however, the first record of his name is dated 8 Feb 1674, where it is noted that he had returned from Louvo and reported the gift of a book by Msgr. Lambert to King Narai. This indicates that he was already working in the government office and that he was about 26 years of age. Phaulkon worked in this capacity long enough to gain the approval and satisfaction of Lek, who helped him gain an audience with His Majesty King Narai. He was accepted in the service of the king and achieved royal approval so that he was given the title Okluang Sura Songkhram. He was assigned supervision of the royal vessel and management of exports for sale abroad. When Kora Kosa Tibodi died, Phaulkon was promoted to the rank of Okprha Ritikamhang Phakdi Srisrenthatasena, serving as assistant to the port authority.

Phaulkon fell in love with a Japanese woman of partly Portuguese descent named Dona Marie Guyomar de Pina. She was a virtuous and strict Catholic woman. He had formerly been Catholic, but when he had come into the employ of an Englishman, he converted to Protestantism to be like his employer. Now he converted back to Catholicism and was baptized by Jesuit* priest Antoine Thomas on 2 May 1682. Two or three days later, he married Marie Guyomar. They had two sons: George, born 1684, and Juan, who died 11 Jan 1688, a few months before Phaulkon lost power.

Phaulkon began to play his important role with the arrival of the royal French ambassador Chevalier de Chaumont in Ayutthaya on 22 Sep 1685. Phaulkon was appointed deputy of King Narai in negotiations on protocol for welcoming and dealing with this state visitor who had brought a gift from King Louis XIV. When Msgr. Laneau translated the greeting and petition of de Chaumont to King Narai into Portuguese, Phaulkon served as interpreter, translating it into Siamese, and presented the greeting and petition to King Narai. In addition, Phaulkon acted as Siam's representative in signing the treaty between France and Siam. The treaty was of benefit both for the proclamation of Catholic Christianity in Siam and for the development of trade between France and Siam. Thus the second delegation from France, led by de la Loubere and arriving on 27 Sep 1687, brought a royal medal of Saint Michael from King Louis XIV, which was presented to Phaulkon on 23 Nov 1687. Phaulkon was given the title of Chevalier of Saint Michael, which is the equivalent of nobility in France. In addition, Louis XIV sent a picture of himself framed in gold and studded with jewels, with the words "Be faithful to me," a coin of high value and a statement of royal intention to care for Phaulkon's son in the royal palace. At that time Phaulkon was raised in rank with the title of Okya Vichaien and given the duties of the "Samuh Nayoke."

At this point it is clear that Phaulkon had succeeded well both in high rank, with attendant responsibilities given to him by the royal government, as well as personally. However, he had aroused the hatred of some Siamese and foreigners due to the favor he had received from King Narai, as well as his great influence and substantial wealth. His aid to missionary efforts toward the conversion of King Narai to Catholicism, his support of their labors in spreading Catholicism in Siam, and his influence favoring the development of trade with France aroused the hatred of Buddhist monks, Siamese nobility, civil servants, and Siamese people in general. They were afraid that Siam would become a colony of France. Consequently, on 18 May 1688 Phra Petracha fomented a revolution in the palace at Lop Buri. Phaulkon was arrested, imprisoned, and cruelly tortured. On 5 June 1688, he was executed at the Sak Monastery (wat) on the banks of Chupson Lake in the city of Lawo (Lop Buri). Before his death, he gave the Medal of Saint Michael, two silver crosses, and his crucifix to the guard who led him from the prison, with instruction that he give them to his son George.

At the time of his execution, Phaulkon was 40 years of age. A scant seven months after he received the rank of Okya Vichaien and the office of Samuh Nayoke, Fr. De Beze, who was close to Phaulkon and had received his last confession, reported that before the executioner administered the axe, Phaulkon knelt for a long moment of prayer, and he wished to proclaim with complete certainty and openly before the face of God, where he would soon present himself, that he died with pure heart, innocent of the charges brought against him by Phra Petracha; that he had acted in the best interests of King Narai; and that he tried to make it possible for the king to approach the true throne of God. Only Phaulkon himself would know the truth of his words.

Bibliography

Launay, Adrien, *History of the Siam Mission, 1662-1811* (1920). • Court Records of King Narai (1963). • Anamwat, Tanorm, *History of Thailand from Prehistoric Times to the Fall of Ayuthya* (1979). • Drans, Jean, and Henri Bernard, *Memorandum of Father De Beze on the Life of Constance Phaulkon* (1947). • Gomlabudr, T., trans., Bangkok Archive description of the journey of Fr. Dachard to Siam (1974). • Sukpanich, Kajorn, *Okya Vichaiyen and Foreign Affairs during the Reign of King Narai* (1963).

SURACHAI CHUMSRIPHAN, translated by JOHN HAMLIN

Philippine Independent Church. *See* Iglesia Filipina Independiente

Philippines

Christians in the Philippines, who comprise 94 percent of its 76 million inhabitants, account for nearly half of the total Christian population of Asia from Korea* and Japan* to Lebanon and Jordan. How this came about must be attributed to the particular way that the Filipinos responded to the Christian faith since it was first preached to them in the 16th c.

Although Christianity, in its Nestorian* form, had come early to East Asia, certainly by 635 C.E. in China*, the Christian faith arrived in what is now the Philippines only with the coming of the first Spanish expedition in 1521. In fact, Islam* antedated Christianity in the Philippines by at least 150 years. By 1565 Islam had advanced as far north as the Manila Bay area, though the arrival of Christianity would push it back southward, a line of stalemate between the two faiths being ultimately drawn in southern Mindanao and southern Palawan.

The Magellan* expedition of 1521 had baptized a few thousand on the island of Cebu. The Portuguese coming from the Moluccas* added to this number a few hundred more along the eastern and northeastern coasts of Mindanao in 1539. But the first permanent conversions of Filipinos took place only with the arrival of the Spanish expedition of Miguel de Legazpi* in 1565. Conversion was at first slow. Up to 1570 only about 100 on the island of Cebu, and most of these children at the point of death, had been baptized by the Augustinians* who accompanied Legazpi.

The pace of conversions, however, began to accelerate after 1572, when Legazpi moved his capital to Manila. The coming of the Franciscans* in 1578 signaled the arrival of more Spanish missionary orders. The Jesuits* followed in 1581, the Dominicans* in 1587, and the Recollects in 1606. Manila had become a missionary bishopric by 1580, with the Dominican Fray Domingo de Salazar* as the first bishop of Manila. In 1595 Manila was raised to an archdiocese, with three suffragan sees in Cebu (for the Visayas and Mindanao), Nueva Caceres (for southeastern Luzon), and Nueva Segovia (for northern Luzon).

In 1594 the Philippines was partitioned into separate spheres of mission responsibility among the various Spanish missionary orders. The Augustinians, who had come first, held on to their missions in Cebu, Panay, and the Tagalog and Pampango regions in Luzon. The Franciscans took responsibility for the Bicol Peninsula and the lake area of what is now Laguna de Bay. The Dominicans were given the provinces of Bataan, Pangasinan, Zambales, and northern Luzon. On the other hand, the Jesuits were given the islands of Bohol, Leyte, Samar, and a few other places in northern and western Mindanao. When the Recollects arrived in 1606 after all the choice mission stations had been apportioned to the other missionary orders, they were assigned to several noncontiguous territories in various parts of the archipelago.

The Catholic faith brought by the Spanish missionaries in the 16th c. was marked by a crusading spirit, which was partly in reaction to losses to Protestantism in northwestern Europe and partly to their surprising discovery that Islam had antedated them in the Philippines. Undoubtedly, most of the earlier conversions of Filipinos were due to Spanish zeal, though probably even more instrumental was the Filipinos' discovery that Christianity in its Catholic form was congenial with traditional Filipino animistic religion (see Animism). Indeed, the structure and the worldview of pre-Christian Filipino religion dovetailed with those of Catholicism. Moreover, the healing powers attributed to baptism and the belief that Christian ceremonials and symbols were effective against the dreaded evil spirits drew masses of Filipinos to the new faith.

This was both a blessing and a curse. On the one hand, it made Christianity easily understandable and acceptable to the Filipinos. Yet, on the other hand, the new converts were for a long time assailed by the tendency to continue to hold on to those aspects of their old heathen faith, which they did not find inconsistent with Christianity.

In the beginning, resistance to conversion was posed by the newly islamized people of the Manila Bay area or by traditional animists elsewhere. Revolts with definitely anti-Christian overtones raged in the Tagalog provinces around the Manila Bay area in 1574, in the Ilocos and Cagayan in northern Luzon in 1589 and 1596, in Bohol and Leyte in 1622, and in Caraga in northeastern Mindanao in 1630.

The quarter of a century between 1595 and 1620 saw some of the most determined efforts of the various missionary orders to win to Christian allegiance as many of the Filipinos as possible under Spanish control. By about 1620, nearly half the Filipinos subject to Spanish rule had been converted, though mostly nominally. The conversion of the other half would take the better part of the next 275 years or so of Spanish rule. It can safely be said, however, that by about 1700 all coastal and lowland Filipinos, except in those southern territories under the strong sway of Islam, had been baptized.

Beginning in 1701, the new century witnessed a fresh burst of missionary zeal on the part of the various missionary orders. A number of *misiones vivas* ("active missions") were launched that year for the conversion of the mountaineers in northern and southeastern Luzon and in the other larger islands of the archipelago. Nearly 150 years later a fresh burst of missionary zeal arose in 1848 and 1849, in northern Mindanao, eastern Negros, and northern Luzon.

The Filipinos had always been an inherently religious people. The gradual Filipino acceptance of Christianity as their new communal faith was reflected in the role that religion played in the various anti-Spanish revolts since the beginning.

In the first century of Spanish rule, anti-Spanish Filipino revolts generally rejected Christianity and sought a return either to Islam or to pre-Spanish animism. But beginning about 1650, it was increasingly seen that Filipinos generally held on to their new Christian faith even while in rebellion against Spain. By about 1745, when agrarian revolts arose in many places around Manila, there was evidence that the Filipinos had begun to appeal to the highest ideals of the Christian faith in their struggle against justice and Spanish oppression and misrule.

By the 19th c., Christianity, which had now indigenized in a Filipino garb, became the moving spiritual force in the Filipinos' pursuit of their most ardent aspirations for freedom and a better life.

The popular *pasyon* (story in verse form of the sufferings and redemptive work of Jesus Christ) increasingly became a vehicle for expressing Filipino aspirations. The afflictions of Jesus Christ, the Son of God, who assumed in his person the role of the Suffering Servant of the Lord (Isa 53:1-12), tended to give meaning to the Filipinos' own tribulations and misery.

It was not difficult for Filipinos to find similarities between certain particularly hated Spaniards and those *pasyon* characters who had opposed Jesus Christ and condemned him to death on the cross, and who had the capacity and means to bribe people into silence regarding the fact of the resurrection by offering gold, silver, wealth, jobs, and high positions.

On the other hand, the followers of Jesus Christ in the *pasyon* were poor and lowly folk, devoid of education and worthless by the world's standards. Yet it was from among them that the Beloved Master chose his first 12 disciples and commissioned them to proclaim his teachings and perform astonishing feats for all the world to see. There was never any doubt that Jesus' disciples were the same sort of men and women as the Filipinos of the time.

Appeal to the highest ideals of the Christian faith became stronger yet by the mid-19th c. as the Filipinos' struggle for human dignity and freedom intensified. The *Kartilya* (or Primer) of the revolutionary society of the Katipunan* was permeated throughout by Christian ideals. Thus its eighth article stated: "Defend the oppressed; fight the oppressor"; while the last and twelfth article enjoined: "Whatever you do not want done to your wife, daughter, or sister, do not do to another's."

Thus religion played a major role in the Philippine revolution against Spain and later in the subsequent struggle against the United States. Indeed, the lasting and most important legacy that Spain gave to the Philippines was the Christian faith in its Catholic form.

Up to the close of the 333-year Spanish regime, which ended only in 1898, the only form of Christianity allowed in the Philippines was the Catholicism of the Spanish people. Although under the influence of liberalism Spain itself had allowed the free entry of Protestant missions into its own borders since 1869, this religious tolerance was never extended to its Philippine colony throughout the Spanish regime. An attempt by Spanish Protestants to open a mission in Manila in 1889, and a fresh bid by London Missionary Society missionaries in 1892, were both nipped in the bud by the Spanish authorities.

Thus it was not until the United States wrested the Philippines from Spanish control in 1898 that Protestants were free to enter. Indeed, the Philippines and Vietnam* were the last East Asian countries to be opened to Protestant missions.

The first regular Protestant missions that opened work in the Philippines were those of the United Presbyterians* and the Methodist* Episcopals* in 1898, the American Baptists* in 1900, the United Brethren and the Disciples in 1901, and the Congregationalists (American Board) in 1902. The Seventh-day Adventists* came in 1906. On the basis of the work of individual volunteers since 1900, the Christian and Missionary Alliance* also opened their own Philippine mission in 1908. All these were evangelical groups that had been strongly influenced by 19th-c. evangelicalism in the United States. On the other hand, the Protestant Episcopal Church also started its own Philippine mission in 1901.

The evangelical missions that came to the Philippines were generally influenced strongly by the principle of comity and cooperation in missions. Thus, in 1901 the so-called "Evangelical Union of the Philippine Islands" was organized to institutionalize this principle. The chief objectives of the Evangelical Union were to encourage cooperation among the various mission groups and to seek to form only one Protestant Church for the entire country. The Evangelical Union divided the entire country into separate spheres of work among the various missions and adopted a common name, *La Iglesia Evangelica* (The Evangelical Church), for all Protestant churches.

Thus out of the Evangelical Union has emerged the present conciliar movement for cooperation represented by the National Council of Churches in the Philippines and the organic union of at least four major denominational strains represented by the United Church of Christ in the Philippines.

From the very beginning, Protestantism was identified with the United States (see Colonialism). This was as much a bane as a boon to Protestantism. At first, many Filipino intellectuals who were active in the rebellion against Spain examined Protestant principles out of curiosity. Those who continued the nationalist struggle, this time against America, tended to reject it outright. Those who saw in America a symbol of industrial progress and a new world order identified Protestantism with modernization and Westernization. Those who had been disillusioned with the Catholicism of the Spanish, for whatever reason, generally drifted toward Protestantism.

In places where anti-American sentiments had ceased, Protestantism quickly gained ground in the first few years. But many Filipinos found American Protestantism too rational and liturgically dry. It was not surprising, then, that with the rise under Gregorio Aglipay* in 1902 of the *Iglesia Filipina Independiente** (Philippine Independent Church), which retained Catholicism but was marked by intense Filipino nationalism*, many of those earlier attracted to Protestantism found in the Aglipayan movement a more suitable religious alternative.

Aglipayanism and Protestantism had always gone hand in hand. After the Philippine Independent Church lost a major court battle on the question of church properties to the Catholic Church in 1907, many Aglipayans returned to Catholicism, though a good number crossed over to Protestantism altogether.

In a predominantly Catholic country, Protestantism in the Philippines has generally placed strong emphasis on the Christ-centeredness of the faith, the efficacy of Christ's work of salvation without the need for other intercessors, and ethical living according to scriptural standards.

Like the Catholic Church which had its schism in the Philippine Independent Church, the various Protestant churches in the Philippines were likewise assailed with schism basically on nationalist grounds. The best representatives of these break-away movements were the *Iglesia Evangelica Metodista en las Islas Filipinas* (IEMELIF, Evangelical Methodist Church in the Philippine Islands), a 1909 schism from the mother Methodist Episcopal Church; and various other smaller Presbyterian or Methodist schisms which in 1932 came together under the name *Iglesia Evangelica Unida de Cristo* (UNIDA). Of the indigenous, independent evangelical groups, the largest is the *Iglesia ni Kristo**, founded in 1913 by Felix Manalo*.

In the immediate postwar period, however, the most salient characteristic of Protestantism in the Philippines was the advent of many new and oftentimes small Protestant missions. Many of these were refugee missions that had been driven out of China* by the Communist takeover of that country. A good number of them, moreover, were generally conservative and evangelical. Among them may be mentioned the Southern Baptists, the Free Methodists, the Christian Reformed Church, various kinds of Pentecostals*, Holiness groups, Churches of God, Churches of Christ, and so on.

Generally zealous in evangelism, their coming changed the complexion of Philippine Protestantism altogether. By the 1990s the total membership of these postwar groups had exceeded that of the earlier-arrived Protestant missions combined.

The participation of the Catholic Church in the modern Ecumenical* Movement following Vatican Council II has brought about a fresh and refreshing atmosphere in Catholic-Protestant relations in the Philippines. This development was generally initiated by the leadership of both groups, to which the members, from each side, responded with a fair degree of enthusiasm.

But perhaps even more far reaching in terms of bringing about closer inter-church understanding and cooperation in the Philippines is the rise of the Charismatic* Movement, involving Catholics, Protestants, and the Aglipayan-Episcopal quarter in the Philippines. In a way, the Charismatic Movement, for Catholics, is a rediscovery of those evangelical elements in historic Christianity that Protestants had found valuable in expressing their evangelical sentiments.

Out of the Philippines' 76 million citizens, 94 percent are Christians. The rest are Muslims (4.6 percent) and adherents of other faiths.

In the national census of 1990, 82.9 percent of the population identified themselves as Roman Catholics. Current estimates would regard about 10 percent of them as active participants in the Charismatic Movement. The Philippine Independent Church in 1990 numbered 2.6 percent, and *Iglesia ni Kristo* 2.3 percent. Protestants at that time accounted for 5.79 percent of the total population; more than half of them were members of conservative evangelical groups that entered the country after 1945.

The Charismatic Movement has tended to blur the traditional distinctions among denominations. Some Filipino Christian groups still identify themselves as Protestant or Catholic but are little concerned about their denominational identity, while others tend to drop altogether traditional denominational trappings. With so many Filipino Christians from various denominational groups able to join together in prayer, speaking the same religious language and praying in the same way, there is bound to be an increasing recognition of oneness and fellowship in Christ, the one common Lord and Master.

Bibliography

Deats, Richard L., *Nationalism and Christianity in the Philippines* (1967). • Gowing, Peter G., *Islands under the Cross: The Story of the Church in the Philippines* (1967). • Sitoy, T. Valentino, Jr., *Comity and Unity: Ardent Aspirations of Six Decades of Protestantism in the Philippines (1901-1961)* (1989). • Tuggy, Leonard, *The Philippine Church: Growth in a Changing Society* (1971).

T. Valentino Sitoy, Jr.

Philippines, Martial Law

Martial law was officially imposed on the Philippines* by President Ferdinand E. Marcos on 21 Sep 1972 with Proclamation 1081. Grave danger of a violent overthrow of the government by the Communist New People's Army and serious rebellion which were affecting the economy, the schooling of students, and the administration of justice were cited as reasons for this decision. This imposition of martial law, which signaled the beginning of a "New Society," was officially intended not only to restore law and order in the midst of widespread unrest, but also to reform the social, economic, and political institutions of the country.

Marcos, whose second and final four-year term under the 1935 constitution would have ended in Dec 1973, explicitly stated that the imposition of martial law was not a military takeover. Public officials were to continue with their duties and government offices with their functions, but in the spirit of "a new and reformed society." Dubbed as "constitutional authoritarianism," the martial law regime was described by Marcos as less totalitarian than democratic since its ultimate aim was "the reinstatement of individual and national freedom." Marcos, who ruled by decree, insisted that martial law was intended to be only "an interlude to a new society."

At the time when martial law was declared, the constitutional convention was in its final stage of drafting a new constitution. On 20 Oct 1972, this convention, which was dominated by pro-Marcos forces, adopted an article providing for a change from the presidential system of government to a parliamentary one. Under this provision not only would all presidential orders and decrees issued under martial law become part of the law of the land, but during the transition the president would continue to rule by combining the powers vested in him under the 1935 constitution and the executive powers vested in the office of prime minister under the newly drafted constitution. This move virtually ensured Marcos's continuation in power even after the expiration of his term of office in 1973. Four years later, a referendum, the regime's preferred way to make legal changes, made the suspension of democracy permanent by giving the president the power to suspend the legislature and to rule indefinitely by decree. But the Marcos administration was largely dependent on the military for the enforcement of presidential decrees.

The immediate impact of martial law included the restoration of peace and order, the dismantling of private armies, and the construction of roads and buildings as well as increased economic and social benefits. These changes were in the beginning generally popular, despite a wait-and-see attitude. Increasingly, however, the "smiling martial law" came to be seen by many as a totalitarian regime with scant regard for human rights. Politics began and ended with Marcos. The moral implications of this political situation became a point of conflict and disunity among the Catholic bishops of this predominantly Catholic country, while the political system itself was condemned by national and international organizations.

Most members of the Catholic Bishops' Conference of the Philippines (CBCP), the national organization of all Catholic bishops in the country, gave indirect approval to martial law in its first years. A minority of 17 bishops and 17 religious superiors of the Association of the Major Religious Superiors in the Philippines (AMRSP), however, took exception to this stand. They issued a less supportive statement which included open criticism of some of the first actions of the government. Progressively, they would dissociate themselves from the majority of the Catholic hierarchy and press the CBCP to take a stand denouncing the injustices committed under martial law.

By 1974, the position of the CBCP had shifted from noncritical involvement to critical noninvolvement. It asked for a reduction in the period of martial law and a return to constitutional government. But not until 1977 did the bishops, because of a perceived religious repression, take a common stand against the martial law regime. In a joint pastoral letter, the CBCP strongly attacked the excesses of the martial law regime and lamented religious repression.

In upholding the principle of the separation of church and state, the National Council of Churches in the Philippines (NCCP), which represents some 10 percent of the Filipino Christians, never openly challenged the government. But while these churches acknowledged their responsibility to cooperate with the state, they also specified that such responsibility would entail rational criticism and prophetic judgment. This position notwithstanding, outspoken pastors were detained, the NCCP offices were searched, and workers who were members of cultural minorities were harassed.

Most outspoken in questioning the constitutional legitimacy of the martial law regime was the Civil Liberties Union of the Philippines. Organized in 1938 for the purpose of achieving complete political, economic, and cultural independence for the Philippines and protecting and enhancing the dignity and freedom of every Filipino, the group was in the forefront of many legal actions related to martial law.

The long-repressed resentment against martial law after 20 years of one-man rule, the United States' threat to withdraw economic and military aid in the absence of legitimate elections, and the loss of all credibility of the government in the socio-economic field forced Marcos to call for immediate elections in Feb 1986. The widow of a slain senator, Corazon Aquino, decided to run for president against Marcos.

In response to the call for elections, the CBCP promulgated a series of letters which called for participation and vigilance in the coming elections. But the AMRSP and various church groups maintained that the freedom to vote or not to vote according to one's conscience remained a viable alternative. Church-related groups such as the National Ecumenical Forum for Church Response (NEFCR) and the Church Office for International Relations and News Analysis Network (CONTAK) opted for boycott, the position also taken by the Communist Party of the Philippines (CPF), the National Democratic Front (NDF), and many of the cause-oriented groups.

As it turned out, the elections were widely considered to be unparalleled in the amount of fraud despite the efforts of the National Movement for Free Elections (NAMFREL), a volunteer movement organized to ensure free and honest elections. In their post-election statement, the CBCP strongly condemned the many irregularities which had occurred, saying that "a government that assumes or retains power through fraudulent means has no moral basis." To the bishops "such an access to power [was] tantamount to a forcible seizure and [could] not command the allegiance of the citizenry." The people were therefore morally obliged to make the government correct such evil. This declaration was unprecedented in the Catholic Church in two ways: it was the first time that the bishops of a nation, in an official act, condemned its government as morally illegitimate and hence unworthy of citizenry allegiance; and it was the first time that the church, through its leaders, endorsed a revolution before, and not after, the fact.

In a post-election statement of condemnation, the NCCP and the Philippine Independent Church* (PIC) called the massive vote-buying, ballot snatching, harassment, and terrorism "acts of subversion against the sovereign will of the people and an insult to the honor and dignity of the nation." The United Church of Christ in the Philippines (UCCP) not only condemned the conduct of the elections but also summoned its people "to engage in protests against injustice, dishonesty, and unrighteousness among which the call for disobedience is a possibility."

The civil disobedience which became the rallying cry of Aquino to protest the elections and to claim the victory that was rightfully hers spread like wildfire. It was supported by the churches, cause-oriented groups, and even by young officers who wanted reform within the ranks of the military. Days later, there was a military revolt led by Marcos's defense minister and the deputy chief of the armed forces of the Philippines. When thousands of people from all walks of life intervened as human buffer zones at Epifanio de los Santos Avenue, the two warring military groups were prevented from shooting it out, leading to the defeat of the forces loyal to Marcos. With the military toppling Marcos and "people power" ousting him, the martial law regime came to its end.

Bibliography

Vreeland, Nena, Geoffrey Hurwitz, Peter Just, Philip Moeller, and R. S. Shinn, *Area Handbook for the Philippines,* 2nd ed. (1976). • "The Philippines: Five Years of Martial Law," *Pro Mundi Vita: Dossiers* (May-Jun 1977). • "Church and State in the Philippines," *Pro Mundi Vita: Dossiers* (Oct 1981). • "People's Movements," *Pro Mundi Vita: Dossiers* (Apr 1982). • "People Power and Kilowatts: The Unfinished Revolution in the Philippines," *Pro Mundi Vita: Dossiers* (Feb-Mar 1986).

Jose M. de Mesa

Philippines, Mission Society of

Diocesan Filipino clerical mission society and Missionary Society of Apostolic Life.

Popularly known as Fil-Mission, the society's official or statutory name is Mission Society of the Philippines (MSP). A Missionary Society of Apostolic Life has a particular focus on mission. Its threefold contribution to mission would be: (1) *ad gentes* (to those who have not yet heard the salvific and liberating Good News of Jesus Christ); (2) *ad exteros* (to people outside their own cultural and language group and nation); and (3) *ad vitam* (meaning devoting themselves to a lifelong commitment to this unique form of missionary witness).

The Catholic Bishops Conference of the Philippines, on the fourth centenary of the evangelization of the Philippine* Islands (1565-1965), organized the MSP "to express in the concrete our gratitude to God for the gift of our faith." The MSP was founded as a special contribution of the Filipino church to mission in Asia and the Pacific.

The pioneering group consisted of some priests from the different dioceses who volunteered to become members of the MSP. They were the first sent to Thailand* and Indonesia*. At the same time, the formation plan for missionary priests was conceived.

In May 1966 the construction of the seminary in Tayud Consolacion, Cebu, began and, after a year, was ready for the school year 1967-68. The seminary temporarily closed down due to lack of personnel and financial constraints in 1970 but was rehabilitated and now serves as a training ground for newly accepted seminarians for their spirituality formation year.

In 1988 the MSP council decided to move to Makati from Pasay City. From then to 1994, the house served as both office and home to the MSP priests who held special positions in the Philippines. In 1995 the central office moved to Pope Pius Catholic Center, and the house now only serves as home for the MSP council, returning missionaries, and those waiting to be sent to foreign mission fields.

With a vision and mission that "the gift of faith [be] lived and shared for Him by all, especially the peoples of Asia," MSP today has 60 full-fledged members and five associate members (diocesan priests who volunteered for mission for three years), with five mission stations in Asia — Hong Kong*, Taiwan*, Thailand, South Korea*, and Japan* — and three in Oceania — Papua New Guinea, the Solomon Islands, and New Zealand. In the Philippines, it has three parishes, one each in the three big island groups, Luzon, the Visayas, and Mindanao.

The Associate Membership Program was established by the MSP in order to accommodate Filipino diocesan priests "who feel the stirring of the missionary vocation." Priests who want to join the program may temporarily commit three years of their lives in the foreign mission apostolate, after which they can go back to their home diocese.

The Fil-Mission Auxiliary Association (FMAA) is a nationwide, parish-based Catholic lay and religious organization committed to the propagation of missionary consciousness among the Filipino faithful. Any Catholic man or woman of good moral standing in the community, 25 years or older, and willing to show exemplary dedication and a high level of commitment may join the FMAA. This is in concordance with Fil-Mission's commitment to lay participation in the mission of the church.

The MSP has also included youth in its family. Young people from 13 to 24 may join the Filipino Youth with a Mission (FYM). The FYM has the following objectives: (1) to spiritually form the young people with the Word of God and the Catholic doctrines in order to become better witnesses of Christ; (2) to support the Filipino missionaries through prayers; (3) to promote mission in their own families, parishes, schools, and communities; and (4) to profess sincere commitment to becoming agents of evangelization.

In addition, MSP maintains strong bonds with an affiliated lay mission group, the Philippine Catholic Lay Mission.

Bibliography

Banaag Ng Misyong Pilipino (Jul 1998 Special Edition). • *World Mission,* Vol. 10, No. 9 (Oct 1998).

Josefina Tondo

Phillips, Charles

(b. England, 1935; d. 1904). Active layman instrumental in founding Wesley Methodist Church, Singapore*; superintendent of Sailor's Home.

While in the army, Phillips was sent to Singapore* in 1864. In 1872 he was appointed superintendent of the Sailor's Home, a post he held until his death in 1904. A devoted and active Christian layman, he was sensitive to the needs of the church and its new mission fields. He helped the Brethren's Sunday School and the Anglican*, Presybterian*, and later Methodist* churches. His keen observation of the needs of young people led him to establish the Christian Institute, a center providing a host of recreational and religious activities for youngsters. In 1883 he asked Bishop J. M. Thoburn* of India* to establish a Methodist mission in Singapore after he had learned of the exciting Methodist work in India. Two years later, on 7 Feb 1885, Bishop Thoburn and the first group of Methodist missionaries set foot in Singapore, and almost immediately a series of evening meetings was set up, resulting in the nucleus of the first Methodist church, named the English Church. This was the predecessor of the present Wesley Methodist Church. Phillips handed over his Christian Institute to the Methodists, thus further strenghtening their mission. In Bishop William Oldham's* words, Phillips was indeed "the true father of Methodism in Singapore."

Bibliography

Sng, Bobby E. K., *In His Good Time* (1980, 1993).
SYMOND KOCK

Phillips, Jeremiah

(b. 1812; d. United States, 1879). Free Will Baptist missionary from America; first translator of the Bible* into the Santal language, which he reduced to writing using the Bengali script.

Phillips and his wife were among the first appointees of the Free Will Baptist* Foreign Mission Society, organized in 1832 in Maine for sending missionaries to India* at the invitation of General Baptist missionaries from England working in Orissa. Phillips served at Sambalpur, Cuttack, Balasore, and Jellasore, and later at Midnapore in Bengal.

Phillips produced a grammar and dictionary and translated the Gospels and other Bible portions into Santali. His journal for 10 Nov 1855 recorded: "Have today completed the translation of the Gospel of Luke in Santal. This and the book of Genesis, together with 20 chapters of Exodus, I have translated since returning from Balasore near the end of March last." The report in the *Calcutta Christian Observer* also mentions the printing of a Santal primer, an introduction to Santal grammar and vocabulary, the Gospel of Matthew, and one or two tracts.

Phillips also began village Santal schools, which he staffed with Santal teachers. Santal response resulted in village transformation. Later, at Midnapore in Bengal, a Bible school was established and named the Phillips Memorial Bible School in honor of Phillips, who had laid the foundation of the Bengal-Orissa Baptist Mission among the Bengalis, Oriyas, and Santals. After 44 years in India, Phillips returned to America. The merger of Free Will Baptists with Northern Baptists in 1911 brought the oversight of the mission to the American Baptist Foreign Mission Society (ABFMS) and the Women's ABFMS.

Bibliography

"Phillips, Jeremiah," in *The Encyclopedia of Missions*, ed. Edwin Munsell Bliss (1891). • Peggs, James, *A History of the General Baptist Mission* (1846). • Torbet, Robert G., *Venture of Faith: The Story of the American Baptist Foreign Mission Society and the Women's American Baptist Foreign Mission Society 1814-1954* (1955). • *Calcutta Christian Observer* (1855, 1865). • *Calcutta Missionary Herald* (1840, 1841).
ROGER E. HEDLUND

Philoxenos of Mabbugh

(ca. 440-523). Philoxenos (Akhsenaya) was born in Persia and received his education at the theological* school of Edessa. In that context he became, theologically, a West Syrian and a primary theologian of that tradition. He was consecrated (485 C.E.) bishop of Mabbugh (Hieropolis) in Syria, where he became an influential writer and church politician. His involvement in intrigues in Constantinople led to his arrest and exile in 519. He died in 523.

His literary production was significant and written only in Syriac. Among his writings were commentaries on the Gospels of John (prologue), Matthew, and Luke. Large collections of homilies, liturgical texts, and some letters survive. He also commissioned and led a new translation of the Scriptures in an effort to achieve a Syriac version that more accurately reflected the Byzantine biblical text tradition. A catalogue of his writings (including extant manuscript references), together with a study of relevant biographical material and an introduction to his theology, was established by André de Halleux, *Philoxène de Mabbog: sa vie, ses écrits, sa théologie* (1963).

Bibliography

Budge, E. A. W., ed. and trans., *Philoxenos of Mabbug: Discourses*, 2 Vols. (1893-94). • Vaschalde, ed. and trans., *Three Letters of Philoxenos of Mabbogh* (1902); *Philoxenos: De Trinitate et Incarnatione*, CSCO 9, 10 (1907). • De Halleux, *Philoxène: Lettre aux moines de Senoun*, CSCO 231, 232 (1963); *Philoxène: Commentaire du Prologue johannique*, CSCO 380, 381 (1977). • Watt, John, *Commentary of Philoxenos on Matthew and Luke*, CSCO 292-93 (1977).
DAVID BUNDY

Phule, Jotirao Govindrao

(b. 1827; d. 1890). Indian "Mahatma" who opposed the caste system.

Although the exact month and date of Phule's birth is not known, his followers celebrated his sixtieth birthday on 11 May 1888, when they also conferred on him the title Mahatma. His father, Govindrao, and mother, Chimnabai, belonged to a community known as the Mali, which was considered a lower caste by the Brahmins of upper caste.

Phule's mother died when he was about one year old. His father sent him to school, and after his primary education in 1841 he was admitted into a Christian high school at Poona, where he made a few good friends from the so-called upper castes. Phule completed his secondary education in 1847.

In 1848 an incident occurred which left a lifelong imprint upon his inner psyche. He was invited to attend the marriage of a Brahmin friend. But as he joined the marriage procession, the relatives of the bridegroom, knowing that he belonged to a low caste, insulted and abused him. He returned to his home with tears in his eyes and related the incident to his father. Perhaps this was the experience which led him to pen "A person who has sustained an injury to his body alone will know what physical pain is." After the incident, he made a lifelong decision not only to oppose the caste system but also to make all efforts to facilitate the uplifting of all of the oppressed low castes.

Phule made every effort to bring unity among all the non-Brahmins, particularly the Shudras (touchable low caste) and Ati-Shudras (untouchable low caste), both of which he fully believed were from the same bloodline. He asserted also that these are the original inhabitants of today's India* and the so-called upper castes, including the Aryan Brahmins, came to India from outside as invaders and interlopers. Phule is indeed the first Indian and low-caste revolutionary thinker who attempted to reinterpret history from below. Through reinterpreting history and demythologizing the Hindu scripture, he tried to lay down the ideological basis for the unity of the non-Brahmins, as well as for building a new identity of their own. He started an organization in 1873, the *Satya Shodhak Samaj* (Truth-Seeking Society). His main teachings, which later became the teachings of the Samaj, maintained that there was no divine sanction (as stated in the Hindu Brahmanic scripture) for the caste system.

According to Phule, the humanly created Hindu Brahmanic myths and scriptural texts were the main sources of crushing the basic human rights of Shudras and Ati-Shudras. He also questioned the universality of the Vedas and other Hindu scriptures because their study was not opened to all. He saw education as the main agent of change in human life.

According to Phule, the lack of education was responsible for all the problems of Shudras and Ati-Shudras. He opened the first school for girls in 1848. In 1851 he opened a school for children of the untouchables. At a later stage, he added more schools and worked together with his wife in these schools.

Besides education, Phule also favored a radical change in some of the other Hindu Brahmanical social and religious practices. He strongly supported the remarriage of widows. Hindu widows, particularly the younger ones, were exploited by the Brahmins sexually. Phule opened a widows' house for them in his own home.

Finally, through reinterpreting human history, Phule tried to identify historical personalities who struggled against the oppression suffered by the low caste, personalities such as King Bali, Gautama Buddha, and Jesus Christ. According to Phule, Bali was a pre-Aryan king whose kingdom extended over almost all of present India, and he was a friend of the downtrodden. Bali was killed by a Brahmin invader. To Phule, there was a prophecy regarding the second advent of Bali which was found in the words that Dalit* women in Maharashtra used to say: "May Bali's Kingdom come." The mission of the second Bali will be to emancipate "the depressed, oppressed and weak." This prophecy he saw fulfilled in the coming of Jesus Christ into the world. Phule's own words in this regard were, "Thus the prophecy of our venerable old ladies, 'May Bali's Kingdom come,' seems to have materialized (partially). When that Baliraja (Jesus Christ) was crucified by a few wicked *desperados,* a great movement of liberation was set in motion in Europe, and scores of people became his followers (embraced his teachings) and they strove ceaselessly to establish His Kingdom on earth in consonance with the dictates of our Creator."

Bibliography

Phule, Jotirao Govindrao, "Slavery (in the Civilised British Government under the Cloak of Brahmanism)," in *Collected Works of Mahatma Jotirao Phule,* Vol. I, trans. P. G. Patil (1991). • Patil, P. G., trans., "Selections," in *Collected Works of Mahatma Jotirao Phule,* Vol. II (1992). • Keer, Dhananjay, *Jotirao Phooley — Father of the Indian Social Revolution* (1974). • O'Hanlon, Rosalind, *Caste, Conflict, and Ideology — Mahatma Jotirao Phule and Low Caste Protest in Nineteenth-Century Western India* (1985).

James Massey

Piazzoli, Louis

(b. Alzano, Italy, 12 May 1845; d. Milan, Italy, 26 Dec 1904). Second vicar apostolic of Hong Kong* Catholic Church (1985-1904).

Piazzoli first pioneered missions in the mainland section of the Hong Kong Catholic Vicariate and was later a very pastoral and zealous bishop. He joined the Lombardy Seminary for Foreign Missions (later, the Pontifical Institute for Foreign Missions) in 1868 and arrived in Hong Kong in 1869. He worked first in Chinese inland areas, which, with the central residence at Saikung, covered Po On, Kwai Hsin (later Waiyeung), and Hoi Fung Districts of Guangdong Province. Always on the move from village to village, he consistently showed concern and care for his people.

Piazzoli was recalled to work in the urban area in 1892, where his zeal won him the admiration of the whole community, especially during the outburst of the plague in 1894.

After the death of T. Raimondi, he was appointed by the holy see as vicar apostolic of Hong Kong on 11 Jan 1895 and consecrated bishop the following 19 May. He was a vigilant and understanding pastor, taking care of his administrative and pastoral duties with diligence. Many, including government officials, sought his opinions in various matters. Because of the serious deterioration of his health, he left Hong Kong in Aug 1904, with the hope that his native air could be of some help. However, he died not long after his arrival in Italy.

Bibliography

Notice Biographique de Louis Marie Piazzoli, Vicaire Apostolique de Hong Kong (1906). • B. M., *Mons. Luigi M. Piazzoli* (1942).

Sergio Ticozzi

Pickett, Jarrell Waskom

(b. northeast Texas, United States, 1890; d. Boston, Massachusetts, United States, 1981). Missionary in India*; bishop of the Methodist* Episcopal Church; director of

India's Mass* Movement Study under the National Christian Council of India, Burma, and Ceylon.

Pickett wrote many books, mainly in the area of mission studies, and contributed literarily to the Mass Movement Study. Among the important works he undertook is *Christ's Way to India's Heart,* a study of six years in the mission field to bring about "factual data about the mass movements to Christianity which have developed in many parts of India and in the light of these data to examine critically the policies and programmes of the churches and missions." Another of his works is *Christian Mass Movements in India: A Study with Recommendations.* This is a long volume with 15 chapters wherein he deals with many different aspects of mass movements in India. The above works show Pickett's interest in both the people and work of Christian missions.

Christian Mass Movements in India is a noteworthy work wherein the author deals with Indian religions and the fundamental groups of Hinduism and Islam* in relation to Christian missions. Pickett argues that mass conversion is as important as individual conversion because the people converted to Christianity in mass movements lived as social units more than as individuals. For them, decisions were often made collectively rather than individually.

Instead of "mass movements," Pickett chose to use the term "group movements" to explain the conversion of the "depressed classes" in large number. He said, "nowhere in India have the people turned to Christ 'en masse'" (*Mass Movements in India,* p. 21). He argued that, during the time of the so-called mass movements, people converted only within a group where people accepted the Christian religion. Group decisions were important for these groups. In modern times, historians refer to these movements as "people's movements" rather than "mass movements" or "group movements."

Bibliography

Warner, Gertrude L., *Moving Missions* (1938). • Pickett, J. Waskom, *Christian Mass Movements in India* (1933); *Christ's Way to India's Heart* (Lucknow, n.d.); *Christian Missions in Mid-India: A Study of Nine Areas with Special Reference to Mass Movements* (1938). • Badley, Brenston, *Visions and Victories in Hindustan* (1931). • Gray, G. F. S., *The Anglican Communion, A Brief Sketch* (1958). • Yonge, C. M., *Pioneers and Founders, or Recent Workers in the Mission Press* (1871). • Paul, Rajaiah, *Triumphs of His Grace* (1907). FRANKLYN J. BALASUNDARAN

PIME. *See* Pontifical Institute for Foreign Missions

Pitakanon, Boonkrong

(b. Uttaradit Province, Thailand, 16 Jul 1925; d. Bangkok, 15 Oct 1994). Pitakanon was the firstborn son of a non-Christian family. Due to poor health, he could not fulfill his ambition to be a doctor, so he studied law at Thammasart University. But World War II* broke out just one year before he finished his bachelor's degree, and again poor health prevented him from taking one final examination. He was sent to a Christian hospital in Chiang Mai Province and found the Lord there.

From 1952 to 1953, he assisted Richard S. Buker in his ministry with lepers. Inspired by Phil 3:8, he dedicated himself for full-time ministry and completed the course of study in the Christian and Missionary Alliance Bible school in Khon Kaen Province.

He served as pastor of Cholburi Baptist Church (1959-66) and Immanuel Baptist Church (1966-70 and 1975-85; retired). While pastor of Immanuel, he also served for many years as chairman of the Thailand Baptist Churches Association. From the time of his retirement from Immanuel until his death, he served as visiting preacher, teacher, and honored committee member of many Christian institutions and churches.

From 1970 to 1974, he also served as general secretary of the Thailand Bible* Society and was among the founders of the Thailand Protestant Coordinating Committee, a joint committee of the major Protestant denominations in the country.

Although suffering from cancer, he continued to preach, teach, and train young Christian leaders, making disciples in many parts of the country, as his health permitted, until the very end of his life.

RAK-A-RAM PITAKANON and EU-A-REE PITAKANON

Plutschau, Henry

(b. Wesenburg, Germany, 1677; d. Germany, 1752). One of the founders of the Tranquebar mission in India*.

Plutschau had come to India along with Bartholomew Ziegenbalg* on 6 Jul 1706. Before coming, Plutschau, a German Lutheran, was ordained by the Danish church, as they were sent by the king of Denmark.

Scant information exists about Plutschau alone, as more importance was given to Ziegenbalg. Missionary Stephen Neill* wrote contrasting remarks about the two men, saying that Ziegenbalg was "gifted, intense, emotional, impetuous, wholly dedicated to the work that he had in mind throughout his missionary career. He had to contend with endless difficulties, but even his most ardent admirers are trained to admit that for a number of these difficulties he himself was responsible." Plutschau, he writes, "was in a very different mold. [He was] six years older than his colleague. Sober, rather slow, he was cut to be an admirable follower, but not a leader. The two worked well together in mutual confidence and fellowship."

Plutschau was given very little attention by historians, and Ziegenbalg seemed to have been the dominating personality of the two.

Bibliography

Neill, Stephen, *A History of Christianity in India, 1707-1858* (1985). • Firth, C. B., *An Introduction to Indian*

Church History (1976). • Gibbs, M. Q., *The Anglican Church in India, 1600-1970.*

Franklyn J. Balasundaran

Po, San Crombie

(b. Bassein, Myanmar, 4 Oct 1870; d. Bassein, Myanmar, 7 Jun 1946). Apologist for the Karen* and lay missionary of Bassein-Myaungmya Baptist* Mission.

San C. Po lived with his parents at Kozu, near Bassein, until he was 10 years old, when he was sent to Bassein to study at Ko* Tha Byu Memorial Hall. The principal, Dr. Nichols, liked the intelligent, disciplined, and promising Karen lad.

In May 1886, San C. Po and Nichols left Burma (Myanmar*) for the United States. He enrolled at Colgate Academy in Hamilton, New York. During his three-year term of study there, San C. Po distinguished himself as a prizewinner in elocution. After graduating from the academy, he accompanied Hugh Stevenson to his hometown, where he met Crombie, a graduate of Albany Medical College (AMC). San C. Po made up his mind to study medicine at AMC, and Crombie was happy to be his preceptor and benefactor. Crombie eventually gave San C. Po his middle name. San C. Po was admitted to AMC in the fall of 1890 and was granted free tuition. Struggling through with sleepless nights and much worry, he finally graduated, together with 66 other young men, in 1893.

He succeeded in applying for a job but was asked to return home by Dr. Nichols, who cabled him, "Proceed home; passage money; New York Bank." In May 1894 San C. Po headed for home. He arrived first at Rangoon (Yangon) and then proceeded to Bassein, where he started to work as a private practitioner. A year later he joined the army medical service and was appointed resident medical officer in Bassein. He had been there for more than six years when R. Castor took charge of the Bassein Civil Hospital. Castor was abusive in language and high-handed in dealing with his staff. San C. Po clashed with him and tendered his resignation. He returned to private practice in Bassein in 1902.

From 1902 to 1912, San C. Po worked mostly with public welfare in the Bassein district, especially in the area of preventive measures against the plague and cholera. He was awarded a Delhi Durbar Medal in 1911 for his humanitarian service. In 1916-17 he was nominated for membership in the Myanmar Legislative Council (MLC) and served in it until 1923. He helped the Karen people by presenting their grievances to the authorities and defending their cases against wrong accusations and false information. From 1925 to 1926, he was president of the All-Burma Karen National Association. During his tenure in office, he was awarded a Commander of Order of British Empire (CBE). In 1933 he was made a knight bachelor by the king. After the separation of Burma from India*, a new government was introduced, and the legislative council was replaced by the senate and the house of representatives. San C. Po was then nominated a senator, and he remained in this capacity until the British government evacuated Burma in 1942. During the Japanese regime, San C. Po had a hard time working for peace between Burmese and Karens in the Bassein and Myaungmya areas. He also had tactfully to maintain an understanding between the Japanese and the Karens, as the former looked upon the latter as pro-British. In his later years, San C. Po's ambition was to see Burma become a free country where indigenous races would live in harmony and contribute their united efforts in building up a strong nation.

San C. Po was a member of the Bassein Sgaw-Karen Baptist Church and participated actively in its ministry. In 1933 he was elected a lay missionary in charge of the Bassein-Myaungmya field in place of Dr. Nichols, who died in America. He was not a pulpiteer but made good speeches at social functions. Wealth and fame did not prevent him from recognizing and mixing freely with the poor and needy. Equal status for all was a principle in his social intercourse. His professional career took him among many people of other denominations, where his pleasant nature and broad outlook were greatly appreciated. His social traits and personality were summed up by the remarks of a coworker: "He is a man who makes you feel better after seeing him." In short, San C. Po did not preach Christianity, but he lived it, particularly as a medical* doctor and social worker. He tried his best to be a good neighbor and to be loving and kind. He did not confine his services to Christian circles but served everyone at large.

Bibliography

Po, San C., *Burma and the Karens* (1928); *The Karen Pioneer* (unpublished autobiography, ca. 1941-45).

Clifford Kyaw Dwe

Poblete, Pascual H.

(b. 1857; d. 1921). Filipino nationalist, journalist, and Bible translator.

From Naic, Cavite, Philippines, Poblete founded five newspapers from 1888 to 1893. He was arrested in 1896 by the Spanish authorities because of his fierce nationalist views and was sent as a prisoner to Barcelona (see Nationalism). He was released in 1898. Poblete met a Bible agent for the British Foreign Bible* Society, R. C. Walker, in Madrid and was commissioned to translate into Tagalog the Gospels and Acts, which were published that same year in Madrid.

Beginning on 7 May 1899, the first Presbyterian* religious services in Manila were held in Poblete's home and continued for months. Though deeply sympathetic to Protestantism, Poblete, who founded the Nationalist Party in 1901, could not countenance a church under foreign missionaries. Instead, in 1902 he assisted his good friends Isabelo de los Reyes* and Gregorio Aglipay* in organizing the Iglesia Filipina Independiente* (IFI).

Bibliography

Laubach, F. C., *People of the Philippines* (1925). • Galang, Z. M., *Encyclopedia of the Philippines* III, 3rd ed. (1950). • Rodgers, J. B., *Forty Years in the Philippines* (1940). • DECS, *Duyan ng Magiting* (1989).

T. Valentino Sitoy, Jr.

Poe-ka-Untong. *See* Doubling Movement

Pontianak

Seat of the Catholic metropolitan bishop for the church province of Borneo comprising the dioceses of Banjarmasin (1938), Sintang (1948), Ketapang (1954), Samarinda (1955), Sanggau (1968), and Palangkaraya (1993).

Since the 1870s, a missionary from Batavia (Jakarta*) has regularly visited the Chinese and Dutch Catholics in the western part of Borneo. The first church, erected in 1873, in Singkawang had 250 members and was served for a short time by a Jesuit* missionary (1873-79). Mission among the indigenous Daya tribes in the interior of the island around the mission post of Sejiram was attempted between 1890 and 1898. In 1905 the Jesuits handed over the Borneo mission to the Capuchins*, who started with five missionaries and were assisted by Franciscan sisters* (SFIC) the following year. Different schools in Nyarumkop (near Singkawang) became the first center of learning for Daya and Chinese children (1916). Three years after Pontianak had been raised from an apostolic prefecture (1905) to an apostolic vicariate (1918), the mission in eastern Borneo was handed over to the Missionaries of the Holy Family (MSF, 1921). From four parishes close to the western coast and from Sejiram in the interior, the "Father of the Borneo mission," Pacificus Bos* (1918-33), tried hard to establish mission posts among the Daya tribes of the interior, which was covered by dense woods and accessible only by rivers. The hard work of prewar missionaries prepared the fast growth of nearly all dioceses in Borneo after 1950.

Up to the Pacific War* (1942), the Catholic community of Borneo grew to 10,000 faithful. The congregation of the archdiocese of Pontianak (1961) consists mainly of two ethnic groups: indigenous Daya of the interior and Chinese of the western coastal region and cities. Though the area of the archdiocese of Pontianak shrank from 553,000 sq. km. (1905) to only 42,000 sq. km. (1968), the church itself grew from only 500 to 136,315 Catholics (1992), and in the whole of Borneo to nearly 450,000 members. The lack of priests and physical distance among the churches led to the formation of *Badan Pimpinan Umat Katolik* (Leaders Council of the Catholic Community), which organizes liturgical services, administers the sacraments, and provides social assistance to the poor. Indigenous clergy and religious of different orders and congregations serve the seven dioceses of the Indonesian part of the world's largest island.

Adolf Heuken

Pontifical Institute for Foreign Missions

(Pontificium Institutum Missionum Exterarum, PIME). The PIME was constituted by Pope Pius XI in 1926 by unifying two existing, similar institutions, namely, the Lombardy Seminary for Foreign Missions in Milan and the Pontifical Seminary of the Holy Apostles Peter and Paul for Foreign Missions in Rome. The former was founded in 1850 by the bishops of Lombardy, under the initiative of Angelo Ramazzotti (1800-1861), while the latter was founded in 1871 by Peter Avanzini (1832-74), sponsored by Pope Pius IX himself. Both seminaries were the expression of the deep concern of the Italian bishops for the evangelization of mission countries by sending their own diocesan personnel directly.

The PIME, under unified leadership, took charge of all the missions entrusted to the previous seminaries, both of which were quite committed to Asia. The Lombardy Seminary, after a first missionary attempt in Micronesia in 1852-55 (present Papua New Guinea), had started to work in the vicariate of Hyderabad (1854) in central Bengal (1855), Hong Kong* (1858), East Burma (1868), and Henan, China* (1869), while the Pontifical Seminary of Rome had worked in South Shaanxi, China (1885).

The PIME fathers arrived in 1854 at Hyderabad, which was entrusted to them from 1870. The work has been mainly among the Telegu-speaking population. This vicariate was raised to a diocese in 1886. In 1927 the Bellary area was cut off from Hyderabad and entrusted to the Franciscans*. A further cut was made in 1933 with the establishment of the vicariate of Bezwada (present Vijayawada, diocese in 1937). From Hyderabad was separated the diocese of Warangal in 1952, which gave rise to the dioceses of Nalgonda in 1976 and Khamman in 1988. From Vijayawada, the dicoese of Eluru was divided in 1976. At present, in India, the PIME members are working under local bishops in Bombay, Nalgonda, Vijayawada, Warangal, Khamman, Eluru, Kurnool, and Jalpaiguri.

In 1855 the PIME started work in the Central Bengal Mission. It was established into an independent prefecture with Krishnagar as its center in 1870, which was raised to a diocese in 1886. Bhutan was ceded to the vicariate of Tibet in 1886, while Assam was given to the Salvatorian Fathers in 1889. The missionary work has been carried out mainly among Anglo-Indians and Bengals. Since 1902, evangelization was spread beyond the Ganges among the local tribes, mainly Mundari, Santal, Oraon, Pahari, and Mahali. In 1927 the Krishnagar Diocese was divided, and the PIME retained responsibility for the less developed area, established as the diocese of Dinajpur.

After the political division between India* and Pakistan*, the area of the Dinajpur Diocese (which remained in India) was divided into the diocese of Jalpaiguri and the prefecture of Malda in 1952 (the latter was absorbed by the Dumka Diocese in 1962), while the area belonging to East Pakistan was divided into the dioceses of Dinajpur and Jessore (present Khulna). The diocese of Rajshahi was cut off from the former in 1990. Today the PIME members are working under local bishops in the dioceses of Dhaka, Dinajpur, Rajshahi, and Chittagong.

In 1867 the East Burma Mission welcomed the first PIME fathers, who settled in Toungoo Prefecture in 1868, which was raised into vicariate in 1888. Missionary work has been carried out mainly among the ethnic groups of Karens*, Kachins*, Shans, Kayahs, Prés, Padaungs, Akhas, and Was. In 1927 there was a first division with the establishment of the prefecture of Kengtung. In 1955, both Toungoo and Kengtung became dioceses: from the former, the Taunggyi Diocese was separated in 1961 and the Loikaw Diocese in 1988, while from the latter the prefecture of Lashio in 1975 (diocese in 1990). The PIME members were drastically reduced in number by the government policy of nationalization and expulsion of foreign personnel in 1966. Only a few of them work under the local bishops in Taunggyi and Loikaw today.

The Henan Vicariate in China was entrusted to the PIME in 1869, with its center at Nanyang. In 1882 the North Henan Vicariate was cut off and made autonomous, with its center first at Xiaozhuang and then at Weihui. In 1906 the South Henan gave rise to the West Henan Prefecture, centered at Zhengzhou and entrusted to the Xaverian Fathers. In 1916 the South Henan was again divided by establishing the East Henan Vicariate, with its center at Kaifeng. Further divisions were made in 1927, 1928, and 1933 with the establishment of the prefectures of Xinyang, entrusted to the Divine Word Fathers* (SVD); of Guide, given to the Augustinian Recollects; and of Zhumadian, taken over by the Chinese clergy, respectively. The North Henan Vicariate ceded to the Divine Word Fathers the prefecture of Xinxiang in 1936.

The South Shaanxi Vicariate in China was established in 1887 and divided into Hanzhong Vicariate and Xing'an (Ankang) Prefecture in 1928, with the PIME retaining responsibility for the former.

In 1946, when the Catholic hierarchy in China was established and all vicariates were raised into dioceses, the PIME fathers were responsible for three of them — Kaifeng, Nanyang, and Weihui (Anyang) — until their expulsion by the Communist government in the early 1950s (see Communism).

The Hong Kong Prefecture, established in 1841, saw the arrival of the first PIME fathers in 1858, to whom it was entrusted in 1867. It was made a vicariate in 1874 and a diocese in 1946. In 1968 the responsibility of Hong Kong was handed over to the local clergy, and today the PIME fathers work under Chinese bishops.

More recently, the PIME's commitment to Asia was further expressed by taking up evangelization work under the local bishops in Japan* (1950, in the dioceses of Osaka, Tokyo, Fukuoka, and Yokohama), the Philippines* (1968, in the dioceses of Manila, Kidapawan, Pagadian, Ipil, and Dipolog), Thailand* (1972, in Bangkok and Chiang Mai), Taiwan* (1986, in Kao-hsiung), and Cambodia* (1990, in Phnom Penh). In 1992 the PIME also opened the Euntes Asian Center in Zamboanga, Philippines, to provide missionary formation training to Asian religious leaders and operators.

At present, the PIME members also are working in other continents: they started in Africa in 1936 (in Ethiopia from 1936 to 1943, Guinea-Bissau from 1946, Ivory Coast from 1972, and Cameroun from 1967); Brazil in 1946; the United States in 1947; and Papua New Guinea in1981 (Alotau and Vanimo Dioceses). The PIME's total membership is around 600.

Bibliography

Tragella, G. B., *Le Missioni Estere di Milano,* 3 Vols. (1950, 1959, 1963). • Brambilla, G., *Il Pontificio Istituto delle Missioni Estere e le Sue Missioni,* 5 Vols. (1943). • Gheddo, P., *PIME, una proposta per la missione* (1989).

SERGIO TICOZZI

Poor Clares

The Poor Clares (officially known as the Order of Saint Clare or the Order of the Poor Sisters) is a congregation of religious women founded by Francis of Assisi in 1212. They are wholly dedicated to the contemplative life, professing observance of the Gospel, either according to the rule confirmed by Innocent IV in 1253 or by Urban IV in 1263.

The Poor Clares have been in existence in Central Asia since the rise of the Mongol* Empire. However, it was during the 17th c. that they began to flourish in other parts of Asia.

The first Poor Clare to reach the Far East was Jeronima de la Asuncion of Toledo, Spain. With the permission of both civil and ecclesiastical authorities in Spain and the Philippines*, and upon the proper authorization of the holy see, she established the first monastery in Manila on 31 Oct 1621. In addition, a monastery was established in Macau*, China*, on 4 Nov 1633, which was eventually closed in 1875.

In other parts of Asia, monasteries were established in the 1930s in Pegu, Myanmar* (17 Jun 1932), from Besancon, France; Dacca, Bangladesh* (13 Oct 1933; transferred to Mymensingh in 1968), from Cleveland, United States; Sunda, Java (9 Dec 1934; transferred to Pacet, Sindanglaja, in 1948), from Amerzondern, Netherlands; Vinh, Vietnam* (19 Nov 1935), from Roubaix, France; Bang Pong, Rajaburi, Thailand* (1936), from Florence, Italy; and Singkawang, Borneo (8 Dec 1937), from Duivendrecht, Holland.

The Japanese invasions in East Asia changed the

course of many Poor Clares' lives. Those in Burma fled to India*, establishing the first monastery in Alwaye, Kerala, on 29 Nov 1942, giving rise later to those in Panakahalli, Talavadi (8 Sep 1971), and Dudhani, Bihar (13 Feb 1978).

The monastery in the Philippines was bombed on 22 Feb 1945, killing 10 Poor Clares. The survivors transferred later to Quezon City on 20 Feb 1950. From this, other monasteries arose in other parts of the country: Sariaya, Quezon (19 Jun 1957); Calbayog City, Samar (16 Jan 1965); Guagua, Pampanga (29 Jun 1968); San Pablo, Laguna (28 May 1973; transferred to Cabuyao in 1975); Consolacion, Cebu (29 Sep 1975); Lamitan, Basilan (26 Oct 1986); Maria, Siquijor (15 Apr 1986; revitalized in 1990); Josefina, Zamboanga del Sur (25 Nov 1989); Balanga, Bataan (5 Feb 1989); Kidapawan, North Cotabato (2 Feb 1990); Lopez, Quezon (10 Feb 1990); Sorsogon, Sorsogon (28 Jun 1990); Gamu, Isabela (9 Jan 1991); Naval, Leyte (9 Apr 1991); Mondragon, Northern Samar (20 Oct 1991); Iguig, Cagayan (9 Apr 1992); Cantilan, Surigao del Sur (25 Oct 1992); and Bolinao, Pangasinan (27 Jun 1993).

The Poor Clares in Vietnam sought asylum in France on 30 Dec 1950. They returned from exile on 27 Sep 1972 and settled in Thu Duc, Saigon.

Postwar Asia saw the establishment of the first Adoration monastery in Quilon, Kerala (31 May 1946), from Dacca, Bangladesh, which later gave rise to others in India: Kotagiri, Nilgiris (31 Sep 1958); Celacombu, Kerala (15 Oct 1973); Nagercoil, Tamil Nadu (19 Mar 1974); Vellore, Madras (10 Aug 1979); Gnanapuram, Visakhapatnam (7 Dec 1986); Sherthallai, Kerala (25 Mar 1987); Eluru, Andhra Pradesh (8 May 1987); Milagres, Mangalore (27 May 1992); and Mahuva, Gujarat (15 Oct 1993).

The first monastery in Japan was established from Valleyfield, Canada, on 23 Aug 1947 in Hchioji-shi, Tokyo, from which arose those of Nishinomiya, Hyogo (1950), and Joetshi-shi, Niigata (1987).

During the succeeding decades, others arose in Tewattee, Ragama, Sri Lanka* (8 Jun 1953), from York, England, and in Hiroshima, Japan (1951; transferred to Fukuoka in 1961), from Cleveland, United States.

In the 1960s, new ones included those in Kiryu-shi, Gumma-ken, Japan (1 Mar 1961), from Boston, Massachusetts, United States, and in Rawalpindi, Pakistan (1966), from Dacca, Bangladesh, which was eventually closed.

More monasteries were established during the last three decades, including that in Taipei, Taiwan (25 Mar 1971), from Belgium, which was closed a decade later. This was followed in Yenshui, Tainan (30 Nov 1990), from Cabuyao, Philippines.

Others were established in Thailand, such as in Bang Seng Arun Thabsake (10 Mar 1972), Udon Thani, Udon Thani (2 Feb 1979), and during the last two decades in Sampran, Nakon Phathon (29 Nov 1984); Phanom, Surat Thani (29 May 1988); Thare, Sakon Nakhon (26 Dec 1985); and Ban Dung, Udon Thani (22 Aug 1990).

In South Korea*, the first monastery was established in Hallim, Cheju (1972), from Minneapolis, Minnesota, United States. Others followed in Irishi, Jeonlabug (8 May 1984), from Augsburg, Germany, and in Inchon-kun, Kyonggi (18 May 1994), from Nocera Inferiore, Italy.

In Indonesia, other monasteries were established in Gamping, Yogyakarta (10 Aug 1974), from Pacet; Gunungsitoli, Sumatra (26 Jul 1976), from Senden, Germany; Sikeben, Bandar Baru (23 Aug 1992), from Gunungsitoli; and Sarikan, Kecamatan Toho (15 Aug 1992), from Singkawang.

The first Capuchin* Sacramentine Poor Clare monastery was established in Quezon City, Philippines (22 Dec 1979; transferred to Lipa City, Batangas, in 1981), from Mexico; followed later in Laoag City, Ilocos Norte (25 Aug 1991).

At present, there are 62 Poor Clares monasteries in Asia, with the largest number in the Philippines (19) and India (13).

Bibliography

Curia Generale, *CTC Communion and Communication* (1987-95). • Fraine, Mary David, *Clarion Call: Eight Centuries of Franciscan Poor Clare Life* (1993). • Omaechevarria, Ignacio, *The Poor Clares across the Centuries,* trans. from Spanish by Mary Edgar Meyer (1977). • Ruano, Pedro, et al., *400 Years (1578-1978) Franciscans in the Philippines* (1979); *Jeronima de la Asuncion: Poor Clares First Woman Missionary to the Philippines* (1993).

Amelia de Ntra. Sra. de Guadalupe

Positive Faith Team, Korea

(PFT). A short-lived organization, the PFT was formed in 1932 under the leadership of Hugh H. Cynn. It comprised missionaries, clergy, and non-Christians disillusioned with the authoritarianism and conservatism of Korean Protestantism.

The general ethos of the PFT was expressed in a five-point declaration and a 21-point program for improving lives. The five points were: (1) a faith in God revealed in Jesus, nature, and history; (2) the need to overcome evil; (3) gender equality and the right to enjoy liberty responsibly; (4) a preference for altruism over greed; (5) the need for society to provide equality and security and to meet the economic and cultural needs of its people. The 21 points of the program include such desiderata as a clean body, diligence, patriotism, group loyalty, protection of the weak and poor, elimination of obsolete customs, and the abolition of early marriage.

The PFT was regarded with suspicion by both the Japanese police and the Protestant church. The former was wary that it might engage in independence activities; the latter regarded it as a challenge to the status quo. By 1935 the PFT had been aborted. Kim Seung Tae

Poukombo

(b. En, Cambodia, ?; d. 1867). Instigator of the second revolt against the French Protectorate in Cambodia*, the church, and Christians.

At the request of King Norodom (1862-1904), a protectorate treaty was signed between Cambodia and France in Jul 1863. Beginning in 1864, the Achar Sua, a member of the royal family, fomented a revolt against the French presence.

In 1865, with this revolt scarcely subdued, Poukombo, of the Rhade minority, who was passing himself off as a Khmer prince, attacked the provinces of Kratie, Banam, Ondoing, and Lompong Thom and led an armed struggle against the occupants. He was supported in these attacks both by the Buddhist monks and local peasants. Two years later he was surrounded by French troops and was beheaded in Dec 1867.

Several Christian communities (Moat Krasas, Ponhea Lu, and Banam) were targets of the rebels: villages and churches were burned, Jean Baptist Barreau was assassinated as he finished celebrating the Eucharist in his parish of Moat Krasas, and two Cambodian Christians of that same parish were martyred.

Barreau saw in this revolt a wish "to destroy the religion as far as the complete extermination of the Christian name of the country," and yet the insurrection of Poukombo was first of all a nationalist revolt which knew how to utilize the popular dissatisfaction against foreigners, French, and Vietnamese. The close relations between the church and the royal power, linked to the French "protectors," were doubtless the source of this anti-Christian violence. The concession by the king and the protectorate authorities of several lands to the church had given rise to profound local resentments. Moreover, the church in many communities was a foreign church, not of the French, but of the Vietnamese — the "detested strangers."

This theme of violence against Christians and foreigners continued into the 20th c. During the revolt of 1905 against the French Protectorate, Fr. Guyomar was assassinated, several churches were burned, and numerous Vietnamese Christians were massacred; in 1946 the Issaraks* did the same. General Lon Nol, in 1970, destroyed some 40 churches and killed a good number of Vietnamese Christians in order to seal national unity against the Vietcong aggressor. François Ponchaud

Poverty

The English word "poverty" (from the 12th c. Latin *pauperts* and the Old French *poverte*), simply defined, means the "state of being poor," but like many other words, it carries a web of meanings associated with that definition. In present-day discourse, "poverty" is linked intimately to the conceptual notions and indicators of "social inequality," "progress," and "development" (and its correlates, "developed," "developing," and "underdeveloped") in modern nation-states. With an estimated population of three billion, Asia has nation-states that range from among the wealthiest to the poorest in the world, according to conventional economic indicators, i.e., per capita gross national product (GNP).

"Poverty" semantically and experientially covers a variety of states and conditions about which various peoples, embedded in their respective religions and cultures, do not necessarily have equivalent perceptions and evaluations. Further, "the poor" are not necessarily the antithesis of "the rich." Among many others, it includes people who have been excluded from their own community; people who are abandoned, humiliated, or suffering from sickness; the hungry; those who lack protection; and those who are deprived of their social status or sources of livelihood. Thus material poverty is one of a host of circumstances connoting the general condition of "lack," "deficiency of," and "being deprived of."

In many Asian cultures, abundant material possessions, prosperity, longevity, good health, education, belonging to a particular ethnic or social group, and the abundance of offspring are some indicators of "the good life." Ontological explanations for this are often attributed to correct living according to a culture's respective religious and ethical tenets in the present time or in previous lives. Within various local cultural practices are also found symmetrical and asymmetrical interdependencies between different social and economic groups that allow a circulation of gifts and services around its social body (e.g., *jajmani* in India).

"Voluntary poverty," the religious and ethical ideal of the renunciation of possessions and status for a life of meditation and/or service, is also practiced in various religious traditions in Asia.

In recent decades, however, commentators have drawn attention to the unparalleled global nature of modern capitalism and the damaging effects it has on local economies, cultural beliefs and practices, and the environment.

Debates on poverty and development. Theorists generally agree that, with the shift from a nomadic or agricultural condition to cities and commerce, the expansion of a mercantile economy, and the monetization of society, "the poor" became defined in terms of what "the rich" could possess, that is, money, property, and influence. Prevailing notions that "poverty" is a result of idleness, laziness, or certain inherent cultural traits (and hence efforts to alleviate poverty would be counterproductive) have been largely debunked. However, the analytical problem of defining "poverty" continues to be unresolved, and lively debates about the whole range of assumptions that go into what makes "adequate standards of living" and the indicators to be taken into account to determine the "poverty line" are not uncommon in all streams of the social sciences.

In this century, two definitions of "poverty" have dominated perceptions of the economic and social development of Asian nation-states. The first is inspired by the pioneering systematic work of Charles Booth and

Benjamin Rowntree in late 19th and early 20th c. England. Usually termed the "absolute poverty" or "subsistence" approach, this model computes the minimum level of income necessary to sustain life by ascertaining the cost of food sufficient to meet the average nutritional needs of each adult and child within a family, with an additional allowance for basic clothing, fuel, and rent included. Families living below this total income figure are said to be living in poverty.

The second approach, pioneered by Peter Townsend in the 1970s, argues that the concept of "basic needs" is a matter of social definition. Consequently, when people find that, through lack of income, they are excluded from basic participation in society, they experience "relative poverty." In other words, while they may have more than enough income to sustain life, their quality of life could be much lower when compared to the rest of the community in which they are embedded.

Both perspectives are manifested in the policies and strategies of Asian governments and international aid agencies. The first development decade (1960-70), for instance, saw many government policy makers viewing the eradication of poverty in terms of a rising GNP in which "trickle-down" benefits would reach the masses. By the 1970s, when it became clear that prioritizing industrial growth and commercializing agriculture did not automatically lead to improving the conditions of "the poor," this growth-oriented approach shifted into the "basic needs strategy," which gave more attention to meeting the "basic needs" and social needs (health, education, human rights, participation in social life) through employment and political involvement. At the same time, direct assistance was given to those who were "absolutely poor."

The 1980s is known as the "structural adjustment policies" (SAP) decade. During this period, the International Monetary Fund (IMF) encouraged governments to embark on austerity measures which included, among others, eliminating subsidies and protectionism, reducing government expenditures (especially welfare expenditures), privatizing state enterprises and liberalizing markets with the belief that the conditions of Third World debt would be alleviated. However, detractors observe that these policies have also produced a drastic decline in food subsidies and an increase in inflation, resulting in much hardship for a significantly expanded pool of "the poor," with the weakening of social safety nets.

A publication of the World Commission on Environment and Development, *Our Common Future* (the "Brundtland Report," 1987), stressed the intensification and interdependence of ecological and economic crises and made a strong plea for the principle of "sustainable development" — economic development that seeks to meet the needs and aspirations of the present development without compromising the ability to meet those of the future. Thus, not only is there a populist critique of neoliberal economic development, there is now the added component of ecological perspectives in conceptualizing about the generation of wealth.

The Social Summit in Copenhagen (1995) is indicative of renewed international attempts in addressing the ramifications of an alarming gulf not only between "rich" and "poor" nations but also between the "haves" and "have-nots" within each nation-state.

Christianity, poverty, and development in Asia. Contemporary Asian Christians continue to draw from a number of sources for their thinking and response to "poverty" — biblical texts, Western church history, modern debates about poverty and development — as well as from their own local social and political histories and experiences.

Traditional Christian thinking on "poverty" can trace its roots to Jewish thought, which regarded "poverty" as a misfortune and not a virtue. Based on the belief that "the poor" would never entirely disappear in human history (Deut 15:11), the giving of charity (almsgiving) to "the poor" and needy is considered a duty. Various legislative pieces and provisions in the Old Testament, as they developed over the centuries, give a sense of how this is further embodied in community structures and ritual practices. Usury is forbidden (Exod 22:25, 27); "the poor" have access to the produce of the land during harvests (Deut 24:19-21; Lev 19:9-10); "the poor" and foreigners are included in community festivals (Deut 16:11, 14); tithes are allotted to them (Deut 14:28-29); and individual properties are automatically returned in the year of Jubilee (Lev 25).

Another strand in the Old Testament contrasts the humble spirituality of "the poor" with the arrogance and self-sufficiency of the materially rich. The authors of certain of the Psalms (e.g., 49, 73), Proverbs (14:31; 17:5), and the book of Job, for instance, identify "the poor" with "the godly" and as being in God's favor.

These themes recur in the texts of the New Testament. The early church, comprising a wide cross section of various social classes and ethnic groups, with "the poor" and marginalized in greater numbers, and inspired by the lifestyle and teachings of Jesus of Nazareth, makes a number of references to these early experiments in resource sharing and reallocation (e.g., Acts 2:44-45; James 5:1-6; Rom 15:26-27).

Christians consider Jesus of Nazareth as embodying the ideal "poor man" (2 Cor 8:9; cf. Phil 2:4-11). His sayings with regard to the tension between an allegiance to wealth and possessions, on one hand, and to God, on the other (e.g., Matt 6:24; Luke 4:14-21; 12:22-34; 21:1-4), have been variously interpreted by Christians throughout the centuries. At one pole are individuals and groups who advocate a complete renunciation of private property and the institution of having possessions in common; at the other is a belief that wealth, power, and prosperity are the rightful signs of God's blessings for a true Christian, but one must cultivate an indifference to them.

Charity (almsgiving), relief, and medical* work for

"the poor" have been distinctive features of Christian missions throughout the centuries, regardless of doctrinal and theological differences, and the missions to Asia were no different. However, these social* concerns are often juxtaposed with or placed subservient to the preaching of the Gospel in order to win converts to the Christian faith. From the mid-1950s on, churches and church-related agencies became more engaged in a combination of social analysis, theological reflection, and social activism to tackle the ill-effects of rapid industrialization, urbanization, and economic development in Asia. Theologians and laypersons within the Roman Catholic Church* and a number of Protestant churches began to speak of an integral aspect of proclaiming the Gospel in terms of the "humanization" of unjust structures and "liberation" from an exploitative type of human development imposed by economically rich countries. Various organizations and projects set up among the urban and rural poor are attempts to give shape to the notion of a "development from below," or in more recent years based on the principle of "empowerment."

The Roman Catholic Federation of Asian Bishops' Conferences* (FABC) in the first Bishops' Institute for Social Action (BISA) institutionalized this mood when they recognized the need for not merely "working for the poor, as it were from the outside or from above, like a beneficent institution or an administrative agency," but also "working with the poor and being with them in order to learn from their real needs and aspirations" (*For All the Peoples of Asia,* Vol. 2, p. 346). This "Church of the Poor" is epitomized as being faithful to the spirit of the Gospel in the light of the two salient realities that characterize the majority of peoples in Asia — "poverty" and "religiosity."

Similar pastoral concerns are discernible in the ecumenical organizations, the Christian Conference of Asia* particularly, through the Urban Industrial Mission (later changed to Urban Rural Mission*). Over the years a corpus of "hands-on" literature has grown out of the numerous training programs for community organizers and pastors, and on the whole these works are critical of *laissez-faire* capitalistic and elitist development, which are seen as inimical to the concerns of "the poor." The question of whether the church should continue to remain satisfied with merely treating the symptoms of injustice and inequity, rather than addressing the underlying causes, characterizes this posture.

Generally, churches and parachurch organizations coming from the evangelical and independent streams are cautious about this kind of Christian social activism. The reasons are varied and nuanced, but they take issue with an alleged idiosyncratic interpretation of the Scriptures and the influence of an atheistic social philosophy, Marxism, in its descriptive analysis. Further, it is argued that tackling the problems of "poverty" and "development" are not central to the identity and mission of the church, although social concerns should be high on every church's agenda.

Bibliography

For All the Peoples of Asia. The Church in Asia: Asian Bishops' Statements on Mission, Community, and Ministry, Vols. 1 and 2 (1984, 1987). • Sachs, Wolfgang, ed., *The Development Dictionary: A Guide to Knowledge as Power* (1992).

YEOH SENG GUAN

Pozzoni, Dominic

(b. Paderno d'Adda, Italy, 21 Dec 1861; d. Hong Kong, 20 Feb 1924). Third vicar apostolic of Hong Kong* Catholic Church (1905-24).

Pozzoni was a pioneer missionary in the inland districts of the Hong Kong Vicariate and one of its most diligent bishops. He joined the Lombardy Seminary for Foreign Missions (later, the Pontifical Institute for Foreign Missions) in 1882 and arrived in Hong Kong in 1885. In early 1886 he was assigned to the inland districts, with Saikung as its center, first to help and then to succeed L. Piazzoli* when the latter was recalled to the city in 1892.

Being assigned to a large area, he had to travel almost continuously within the Po On, Kwei Hsin (later Waiyeung), and Hoi Fung Districts. In May 1904 he was summoned to the city to assist Msgr. Piazzoli, who was seriously ill, and to accompany him back to Italy. After the death of the latter, Pozzoni returned to Hong Kong in Jan 1905, where he was appointed vicar apostolic and was consecrated bishop in the following October.

As bishop, he took care of his flock with diligence, making several pastoral visits even to the remotest parts of the vicariate, as well as fostering spiritual life among the urban Catholic communities and associations. He played an important role in setting up Hong Kong University in 1912 and carefully led the church through the difficult years of World War I.

After a final pastoral visit to the Saikung District in Dec 1923, Pozzoni suffered a heart attack, the aftereffects of which resulted in his death the following February. His funeral represented a solemn show of respect and affection for him by the whole colony of Hong Kong.

Bibliography

The Rock, Bishop Pozzoni Memorial Number (Mar 1924). • Germani, F., *Domenico Pozzoni, Vescovo-Vicario Ap. di Hong Kong* (1991).

SERGIO TICOZZI

Pradhan, Ganga Prasad

(b. Kathmandu, 4 Jul 1851; d. Darjeeling, India, 28 Mar 1932). Early Nepali Protestant church leader and scholar.

Pradhan was the second Nepali convert of the Church of Scotland's Eastern Himalayan Mission and one of the first ordained Nepali ministers. He translated the Bible* into the Nepali language, developed Christian literature* and primary-level textbooks in the Nepali language, and started the first Nepali-language newspaper in Darjeeling.

Pradhan went to Darjeeling with his parents on 26 May 1861 at the age of 10. Separated from his parents, he began to work at a tea estate at a tender age, where he came into contact with Scottish missionaries. He had little formal schooling but did a great deal of self-study and later became a teacher.

In January of 1875 he was baptized in Allahabad, to which he had traveled on foot because of opposition from the Hindu Nepali community in Darjeeling. He married a former Roman Catholic* nun, Elizabeth Rai, and began to work as an itinerant preacher and translator of the Nepali Bible. He produced rough drafts in Nepali for the entire Old and New Testaments and was made an honorary foreign member of the British and Foreign Bible Society in 1914. He also concentrated on producing Christian literature and primary-level school textbooks, and by the 1920s had produced a total of 24 books and booklets in Nepali. He also became proprietor of the Gorkha Press in 1901.

Pradhan was appointed an elder of St. Columba's Church, Darjeeling, in 1900 and was ordained as pastor of the same in 1901. As a founding member of the Gorkha Mission (to Nepal), Pradhan and his family sought to emigrate as Christians to his birthplace of Kathmandu, Nepal, in 1913, but they were denied permission to stay and had to return to Darjeeling. He composed several Christian songs, one of which was a popular prayer-song for "opening the door of salvation to the *Gorkhalis*" (Nepalis).

Pradhan died at the age of 91 in Darjeeling.

Bibliography

Sangati, Vol. 7/8 (1975). • Perry, Cindy, *A Biographical History of the Church in Nepal* (1993).

RAJENDRA K. RONGONG

Prarthana Samaj

(Prayer Society). Theistic society formed in 1867 in Bombay, India*, under the influence of Keshub Chunder Sen* of the *Brahmo Samaj** and John Wilson* of the Church of Scotland and led by Atmaram Pandurang (1823-98).

The aims of the *Prarthana Samaj* were weekly theistic worship and social reform. Keshub's second visit to Bombay in 1868 strengthened the organization considerably. In 1870 the first marriage according to the theistic rites took place, and at about the same time R. G. Bhandarkar and M. G. Ranade joined the *samaj*. In 1872 P. C. Mozoomdar* from Calcutta spent six months in Bombay building up the congregation, starting night schools for working people, and beginning the journal of the *samaj*, the *Subodh Patrika*.

In 1874 Dayanand Saraswati* came to Bombay, but his ideas about the Vedas prevented the *Prarthana Samaj* from following him. He founded the *Arya Samaj** the following year. A little later there was a proposal to change the name of *Prarthana Samaj* to the Bombay *Brahmo Samaj*, but on account of the dissensions in the *Brahmo Samaj* in Calcutta, the Bombay leaders were not in favor of identifying themselves with it. Pandita Ramabai*, who had not yet become a Christian, did valuable work among the women of the *samaj* in 1882-83.

The declared objectives of the *samaj* at its founding were the disapproval of the caste system, the introduction of widow marriage, the encouragement of women's education, and the abolition of child marriage. *The Prarthana Samaj Report, 1911-1912* presents the cardinal principles of faith as follows: (1) God is the creator of this universe. He is the only true God; there is no other God beside him. He is eternal, spiritual, infinite, the store of all good, all joy, without parts, without form, one without a second, the ruler of all, all-pervading, omniscient, almighty, merciful, all-holy, and the savior of sinners. (2) His worship alone leads to happiness in this world and the next. (3) Love and reverence for him, an exclusive faith in him, praying and singing to him spiritually with these feelings, and doing the things pleasing to him constitute his true worship. (4) To worship and pray to images and other created objects is not a true mode of divine adoration. (5) God does not incarnate himself, and there is no one book that has been directly revealed by God or is wholly infallible. (6) All men are his children; therefore they should behave toward each other as brethren without distinction. This is pleasing to God and constitutes man's duty.

Beliefs of the *samaj* were the same as those held by the *Sadharan Brahmo Samaj*. If theistic worship is the first interest of the *samaj*, social reform has always held the next place. The religious activities of the *samaj* included Sunday services, Sunday school, the Young Theists' Union, the Anniversaries, the work of a few missionaries, the Postal Mission, and the *Subodh Patrika*. There were night schools for working people, a free reading room and library, and a ladies' association for spreading instruction and culture among women and girls. It should be noted that there had never been amongst the members of the *Prarthana Samaj* the rigid exclusion of idolatry, nor was the breaking of caste a necessary condition of membership. The movement did not spread widely, as it had only one or two missionaries. Several societies, originally connected with *Prarthana Samaj*, later called themselves the *Brahmo Samaj*. The *Prarthana Samaj* did not produce much literature.

Under Ranade's able guidance, the *Prarthana Samaj* avoided some of the errors of the *Brahmo Samaj* of Bengal. It did not cut itself off from the parent Hindu community and form a separate sect. Ranade was anxious to point out that the theism of the *Brahmo Samaj* and the *Prarthana Samaj* was nothing new and that it was organically related to the older theism of Hinduism*. According to him, the *Prarthana Samaj* only continued the religious tradition of the *bhakti* saints of Maharashtra such as Jnanadev, Eknath, Namdev, Tukaram, and Ramdas.

Today India has gradually accepted almost all the items of the social reform program that the *Prarthana Samaj* and *Brahmo Samaj* stood for, but not their religious doctrines, preferring instead plurality of theological expression. By insisting on a formless God and rejecting the doctrine of *Avataras,* the *Prarthana Samaj* did away with the principle of mediation between the finite and the infinite and reopened the yawing gulf between God and creation. Moreover, that pure theism cannot grow without allegiance to an authority and without posing a religious cannon of its own is proven by Ranade's theological work in 39 articles, titled *A Theist's Confession of Faith.*

Bibliography

Sastri, Sivanath, *History of the Brahmo Samaj,* Vol. II (1912). • Ranade, Mahadev Govind, *Religious and Social Reform,* comp. Kolaskar (1902). • *The Speeches and Writings of Sir. N. G. Chandavarkar* (1911). • Shinde, V. R., *The Theistic Directory* (1912). • *Prarthana Samaj Report, 1911-1912.* • Farquhar, J. N., *Modern Religious Movements in India* (1924). • Sarma, D. S., *Studies in the Renaissance of Hinduism in the Nineteenth and Twentieth Centuries* (1933).

K. P. Aleaz

Pratipasen, Esther

(b. Bangkok, 17 May 1844; d. Bangkok, 1929). First Thai woman to become a Protestant Christian.

Adopted at age nine and named Esther by Dr. and Mrs. Stephen Mattoon, a missionary couple to Thailand*, Pratipasen had the opportunity to study nursing for three years in the United States. She accepted Christ upon her return to Bangkok, joined a church in 1860, and thus became the first Thai woman Christian.

A reputable midwife who assisted at the birth of Queen Rambaibarni in 1904 and cared for the infant queen, her popularity in Thai homes and palaces provided many opportunities for sharing the Gospel. She taught many children to read the Thai language and together with her husband translated John Bunyan's *Pilgrim's Progress* into Thai.

Bibliography

Wells, Kenneth E., *History of Protestant Work in Thailand, 1928-1958* (1958). • McFarland, George Bradley, ed., *Historical Sketch of Protestant Missions in Siam, 1828-1928* (1928). • Pintadoung, Thanom, *The Grace of God in the Time of the Rama Dynasty* (1982).

Matana Pratipasen

Pratipasen, Taud

(Archan Todd) (b. Bangkok, 27 Jul 1910; d. Bangkok, 29 Mar 1984). Thai evangelist and scholar.

Pratipasen began his ministry as an interpreter with the Southern Baptist* Mission in Thailand. After his graduation from Thailand Baptist Theological Seminary (TBTS) in 1956, he worked as a teacher in that school as well as a church planter and pastor.

In 1972 he was selected as the first Thai principal of TBTS and served until his retirement in 1976. Under his leadership the seminary expanded and student enrollment doubled. He wrote a book, *Man's Philosophy and God's Truth.* He also translated at least 10 books for the Textbook Committee of TBTS, including books on archaeology, Christian doctrine, history and the Bible, both volumes of *Halley's Bible Handbook,* and W. T. Conner's classic, *Christian Doctrine.*

Well versed in Thai language and culture and a zealous evangelist who preached and witnessed in many areas of Thailand, working either with a group or alone, Pratipasen was able to communicate the Gospel to highly educated Thai Buddhists, one of whom became a well-known pastor in Bangkok. He is best remembered for his thoroughness as a teacher and fearless zeal as an evangelist.

Bibliography

Fortieth Anniversary Celebration of the Thailand Baptist Theological Seminary (Bangkok, 1992).

Matana Pratipasen

Prautch, Arthur W.

Missionary, merchant, colporteur, and first American Methodist Episcopal local preacher in the Philippines.

A former American Methodist* missionary in India* (1884-87), Prautch came with his wife to Manila in Dec 1898 as a cattle and lumber merchant. He started preaching soon after his arrival and was duly licensed in 1899. That same year he held Protestant services in Catholic* churches that were deserted by the Spanish friars in Manila. He was credited with discovering the preaching talents of Nicolas Zamora* and as a team began a Protestant preaching ministry that was marked by antifriar rhetoric.

In 1901 Prautch helped to organize the Federal Party. In 1902 he wrote the first public defense of Gregorio Aglipay's* Iglesia Filipina Independiente* (IFI) in the *Manila Times.* A close friend of Aglipay, Prautch served for many years as an American Bible Society colporteur in IFI.

Bibliography

Laubach, F. C., *People of the Philippines* (1925). • Stuntz, H. C., *The Philippines and the Far East* (1904). • Deats, R. L., "Nicolas Zamora: Religious Nationalist," in G. H. Anderson, ed., *Studies in Philippine Church History* (1969). • Sitoy, T. V., Jr., *Several Springs, One Stream* (1992). • Copplestone, J. Tremayne, *History of Methodist Missions,* Vol. 4 (1973).

T. Valentino Sitoy, Jr.

Prayer. *See* Daybreak Prayer Meeting

Prayer House Movement

Prayer houses in Korea* are located deep in the mountain areas for individual meditation and prayer. The Korean Prayer House Movement began in the critical times of Japanese colonial rule, when believers felt the need for escape from the world for prayer and meditation. It was a kind of Protestant monastic movement. After the liberation of Korea, a number of revival movement leaders built prayer retreat houses deep in the mountains, to which vast numbers of believers flocked for revival meetings which included speaking in tongues and faith healings. The mountain site prayer house movement grew after the Korean War*. These places became the birthplaces of new religious movements, most of which are a mixture of Christian practice and indigenous religious teachings. Presently, prayer houses are used as spiritual retreat centers and for revival meetings. Some prayer houses are used for caring and healing of the terminally and mentally ill.

David Suh, with contributions from
Seo Jeong Min, translated by Kim In Soo

Presbyterian and Reformed Churches

Those Protestant churches whose origins are related to the mission work of churches in this tradition or who have come to regard the Calvinist tradition as an important part of their identity.

Presbyterian and Reformed churches are found in most parts of Asia today. They include churches who relate to presbyterian government by elders and ministers and those whose historic links are through missions which were culturally linked to national Presbyterian churches, such as those in Scotland and the Netherlands, or to churches which derive from migration of those peoples, such as the Reformed Church in America. They include many churches which have united with other traditions, and now also include churches emerging from the mission work of Asian churches. The mission work of the London Missionary Society (LMS), now the Council for World Mission (CWM), is an important part of the story.

The CWM and the World Alliance of Reformed Churches (WARC) are networks which help provide international contacts. Bilateral relationships between some Asian and some Western Presbyterian churches have been important links for support. They also facilitate the return to the West of a Gospel which has sometimes retained a less self-conscious wholism of world-view and mission than that of the older churches. Whether Western Presbyterian churches will allow themselves to be challenged by the Asian contribution to world Presbyterianism remains to be seen.

Presbyterianism has not been unaffected by its encounter with Asia. Classic formulations of Reformed theology have provided security for many seeking a comprehensive understanding of the mind of God. Others have distanced themselves from statements such as the Westminster Confession which appeared more as foreign points of distinctiveness relevant to the mission than as a benefit to the church of either universal or contextual statements of belief. Despite exceptions, contextual theologies appear to be treated with some nervousness yet continue as a process which is driven by the resilience of local culture, whether or not the activity is owned and moderated by the church. Some notable Asian theologians are Presbyterian, including C. S. Song and K. Koyama*. Presbyterian missionaries whose articulated theology has been strongly influenced by their experience of the Asian church include Lesslie Newbigin* in Madras and Hendrik Kraemer* in Indonesia. It is striking that the subject of John Hersey's missionary novel, *The Call*, John Treadup, was an American Presbyterian in China.

Presbyterian mission was often associated with a commitment to higher education (see Colleges and Universities). This was not unique, but it was important. Education represented a broader basis for support among the sending churches than would have otherwise been possible. It helped grow a church of people who identified with Western education, frequently in English, as a route to nation building. It could also mean a difficulty in identifying directly with the poor and other marginalized groups. Yet Presbyterian missions were frequently happy to embrace ideals such as the Three-Self Movement and the Nevius Method*, which stressed the autonomy and responsibility of the national church. The relatively democratic structures of Presbyterianism provided scope for local leadership to take responsibility. Presbyterianism also proved adaptable to Confucian values, a factor which has contributed to its growth in Chinese and Korean societies.

In these situations, it has not been easy to cope with cultural diversity other than by the formation of separate Presbyterian churches, and the participation of youth in leadership can appear countercultural. As in the West, women have in places been able to exercise significant leaership, but this has seldom been easy. Ecumenism has sometimes been driven by local needs and resulted in participation in significant union schemes. In other places, it has been a source of suspicion and appeared as a foreign solution to a foreign problem.

Presbyterianism came to Asia in the 17th c. with the Dutch in Sri Lanka*, Indonesia*, the Malay Peninsula, and Taiwan*. Later Scottish and English Presbyterians were traders, soldiers, and members of mission societies and church missions in India*, Malaya, Singapore*, and China*. American Presbyterians were missionaries in India, Thailand*, China, Japan*, Korea*, and the Philippines*. Australian Presbyterians had a mission in Korea, and New Zealand Presbyterians have worked with the China Inland Mission (now Overseas Missionary Fel-

Presbyterian and Reformed Churches

lowship) and through their own mission board in Canton, Malaya, Singapore, and Indonesia.

From the early 19th c., a common pattern was to combine itinerant evangelism and medicine with education and a commitment to the formation of independent national churches. In the 20th c., comity sometimes has led to shared arrangements for theological* education (Bangkok Institute of Theology; Trinity Theological College, Singapore) and participation in union churches (Church of Christ in Thailand, CCT; United Church of Christ in the Philippines, UCCP; Church of South India, CSI; etc.). Migration and mission have seen the spread of Taiwanese and particularly Korean Presbyterianism elsewhere in Asia and to many parts of the world. International networks include the CWM and the WARC. Ecumenical involvement has been a common but not universal feature, and sometimes an occasion for controversy.

South Asia: Pakistan. American Presbyterian missions began in Lahore in 1849 and Sialkot in 1854. The Church of Scotland arrived in 1857. Mass movements* of depressed classes changed the focus of mission from the 1870s, but there was still involvement in higher education, and Gujranwala Theological College was founded in 1877. In 1904 the missions joined the Presbyterian Church of North India, and in due course most became part of the Church of Pakistan* in 1970.

India. Presbyterian work in India began with expatriate Scottish communities and Scots and American missions. After 1813 the East India Company provided for Church of Scotland chaplains and churches in Calcutta, Madras, and Bombay. The first chaplain, James Bryce, laid the foundation for wider involvement among soldiers and traders and mission among Hindus. The Scottish Missionary Society sent a missionary in 1823. John Wilson* and his wife, Margaret, in Bombay from 1829, Alexander Duff* in Calcutta from 1830, and John Anderson in Madras from 1837 were pioneers of higher education. American Presbyterians arrived in the 1830s, including in Ludhiana and Allahabad. The Farrukhabad Mission was the foundation of American Presbyterian work in Uttar Pradesh and responded to mass movements among low-caste communities. Work in Maharashtra was taken over from the American Board of Commissioners for Foreign Missions (ABCFM) in 1870. Mission included village itineration, medical and agricultural work, and education. There was concern for rural development and for the situation of women.

The northern churches formed the Presbyterian Church in India in 1904, which in 1924 became part of the United Church of North India and, in 1970, the Church of North India*. In the south, Scottish missions had an educational focus based on Madras Christian College. Presbyterian churches joined the South India United Church and, in 1947, became part of the Church of South India*. In Assam in the northeast, the Presbyterian Church of India remains a distinct church.

Bangladesh. The Church of Bangladesh, formed in 1970, includes Presbyterians and others who were formerly part of the Church of Pakistan. It has links with Reformed churches in the Netherlands.

Sri Lanka. The Dutch Reformed Church dates from 1642. As the religion of the colonial government, its membership reached about 400,000 before the end of Dutch rule in 1796. Under the British, Church of Scotland chaplains were present from 1830 and the Dutch and Scottish Presbyterians united in 1882. Membership has since dropped to about 5,000 through migration and reversion to Catholicism and other faiths.

Southeast Asia. Myanmar. The Presbyterian Church of Myanmar is concentrated in the Chin Hills and on the lowlands close to the border with India. It grew out of revival in the 1930s among Lushai Presbyterians in Northeast India and their migration from Assam, particularly after World War II*. It has some 30,000 members and sends missionaries to other states in Myanmar.

Thailand. The Presbyterian Church is now part of the Church of Christ in Thailand (CCT). American Presbyterians sent their first missionaries in 1838 (see Dan McGilvary*, Samuel McFarland*, and James McKean), and work was centered on Chiang Mai and Bangkok. In 1934 the churches joined with others to form the Church of Christ in Siam, which became the CCT in 1939. Missionaries left or were repatriated during World War II, and some churches experienced persecution. After the war there was rapid growth. By 1957 the Presbyterian Church of the USA had dissolved its mission into the CCT, which still has a large number of churches of Presbyterian background.

Malaysia. Presbyterianism came with the Dutch conquest of Melaka (Malacca*) in 1641, but the community was still small by the 19th c. Later, English-speaking churches developed with British involvement in Ipoh, Kuala Lumpur, and Penang, and Chinese churches expanded north from Singapore and Johor. In the 1950s, missionaries relocated from China and served as a bridge between the two streams. An English Speaking Presbytery was formed by 1990. St. Andrew's, Kuala Lumpur, still maintains an expatriate ministry. There is a small Indian work and some outreach in Sarawak.

Singapore. English- and Chinese-speaking streams were associated with the respective expatriate communities, and there was a strong component of Straits Chinese families. The Scots community called its first minister in 1856, and the Presbyterian Church of England missionary J. A. B. Cook* arrived in 1882 to lead the Chinese mission. Migration and other links with Christians in South China and the work of the Presbyterian Church of England Mission were important. Presbyterians have been involved in primary and secondary schools, but their leadership came late and was less important than in other regions of Asia. The Bible Presbyterian Church has been influenced by the teaching of Carl McIntyre and the work of John Sung*, causing a split which today continues, with both churches maintaining growth and leadership in missionary work in Asia.

Indonesia. The Dutch United East India Company* (*Vereenigde Oost-Indishe Compagnie,* or VOC) was formed in 1605, expanding Dutch influence which supplanted the Portuguese, Spanish, and English in the region. The Reformed church was the only officially accepted religion and began by taking over (often forcibly) Catholic congregations (freedom of religion was only allowed from 1807). Mission work was carefully controlled. The Reformed character of the church remained strong, though some of the missionary societies which began work after the government took over from the VOC in 1800 were more broadly evangelical. Not until 1935 was the church separated from the government. Reformed confessions remain widely accepted, and churches are often regional. Many of a Presbyterian character are associated with the Gereja Protestan Indonesia* (GPI), which held its first plenary synod in 1936 (see Indonesia* for regional churches). By 1993 the membership was some nine million. Most larger Protestant churches are members of the WARC, and some are also members of the Reformed Ecumenical Synod.

Philippines. Within weeks of the American sinking of the Spanish fleet off Manila on 1 May 1898, American Presbyterians decided to enter the Philippines. James Rodgers arrived in Apr 1899, and a church was established by 1900. Comity arrangements among Protestants were made in 1901 as part of an evangelical union. Comity was remarkable until it inevitably broke down with increasing mobility, theological diversity, and the rise of independent churches. Presbyterians were allocated Luzon, south of Manila, and part of the western Visayas. As part of the United Evangelical Church of the Philippines (formed in 1929), in 1948 they helped form the United Church of Christ. Educational involvement included Silliman Institute (1899), later Silliman* University, and Union Theological Seminary (1907). The Philippines Christian Reformed Church was founded in 1961, and the Korean Evangelical Presbyterian Mission founded four local congregations by 1983 and convened a presbytery in 1987.

Northeast Asia: China. Presbyterians were among the early LMS (see Robert Morrison) and ABCFM missionaries from Britain and America, and mission was supported by some among the trading community in Canton, including David Olyphant. The Presbyterian Mission Press, established in Macau* in 1844, then located in Ningbo and Shanghai from 1860, was a major source of Christian and general literature*. The English Presbyterian Mission was active in Xiamen (Amoy) from 1851, along with the Reformed Church of America, and in Shantou (Swatow) from 1856. American missionaries were successful in Shandong Province from 1862, and in Manchuria the United Presbyterian Church of Scotland and the Irish Presbyterians had a presence from 1869. By 1907 there were 12 Presbyterian missions in China from England, Scotland, Ireland, Canada, the United States, and New Zealand, and presbyteries and synods had been established in a number of areas. The Presbyterian Church of China was formed that year. In 1927 it became part of the Church of Christ in China (see China Christian Council).

Strategy and experience saw development from medical* clinics to teaching hospitals, and from local schools to colleges* and universities. Three-self ideals were not always easy to realize, but patterns established by John Campbell Gibson, John Nevius*, and Calvin Mateer were important. Many, such as W. A. P. Martin* and James Legge*, gained great respect for Chinese culture and at the same time became committed to sharing the best of their own, though this was not always well understood. Congregations associated with Presbyterian mission have largely flowed into the China Christian Council and have sought to work within the framework of the Three-Self Patriotic Movement*. Though formal links were broken after 1950, some Presbyterian forms and emphases remain. Presbyterians overseas have related to the Amity Foundation* and personally to different parts of the church in China.

Taiwan. The Dutch presence on Formosa in the 17th c. included pastoral work in Sinckan by Georgius Candidus from 1627 to 1639. The Presbyterian Church of England Mission worked in the south from 1865 and Canadian Presbyterians in the north from 1871. A North Formosa Presbytery was formed in 1904 and the Taiwan Synod in 1912. There is distinct work among Hakka peoples, native Taiwanese tribal peoples, and Chinese nationalists fleeing the mainland with the fall of China to the Communists in 1949. The Presbyterian Church has represented a social conscience and been subject to government pressure, often because of her primary concern for Taiwanese nationals and oppressed minorities.

Japan. Missionaries from the major American Presbyterian groups began work following the 1854 Japanese-American treaty, beginning with the arrival of James Hepburn* and his wife Clara from the PCUSA in 1859. The PCUS began at Kochi on Shikoku in 1855, the Reformed Church in America (RCA) in Nagasaki in 1859, and the Cumberland Presbyterian Church in Osaka from 1876. The Yokohama Kaigan Church was established in 1872 and the Japan Christian United Church (Presbyterian) in 1877. Scottish missions contributed to medical work from 1874 to 1900. A theological seminary was started in Kobe in 1907 and a Women's Christian College in 1918. The famous Christian social reformer Toyohiko Kagawa* was a graduate of Kobe and then of the Presbyterian seminary in Princeton in the United States. Under the Religious Organizations Law (1939), the Japan Presbyterian Church, with 30 other denominations, became part of the United Church of Christ in Japan *(Nihon Kirisuto Kyodan)* in 1941. After the law was abolished in 1945, some left in 1951 to form the Japan Christian Reformed Church.

Korea. Presbyterian involvement spread from Manchuria. Dr. Horace and Frances Allen* of the PCUSA moved from Shanghai in 1884 and began medical work. Horace Underwood* of the Reformed Church arrived the following year. A Presbyterian Council was created in 1889, and Presbyterians from Canada, the United States, and Australia were active from the early 1900s, but response was slow before revival from about 1903 to 1910. The methods of John Nevius* proved invaluable in establishing norms of Bible study and witness among laypeople. The Union Presbyterian Church in Korea held its first general assembly in 1912. Protestant comity arrangements were important at an early stage. The biggest difficulties faced by Christians in general were those caused by Japanese occupation and debates over compulsory Shinto worship. Christian work was strongest in the north before World War II* and the Soviet occupation. The Presbyterian churches and missions jointly operated a theological seminary (Presbyterian Theological Seminary, started by Samuel A. Moffett* in P'yongyang in 1901), Bible schools, hospitals, schools, and colleges. Severance Medical College and Hospital grew out of Allen's early work, and in particular gained a high reputation.

The Korean War* caused enormous suffering, and the ongoing division of the country is a source of tension. In this situation, the church in South Korea has grown rapidly. Presbyterians continue to form one of the major denominational groups but are split into over 120 different Presbyterian churches. Korean Christians show a dedicated spirituality and a high commitment to global mission.

Bibliography

"American Presbyterians in India/Pakistan 150 Years," *Journal of Presbyterian History,* Vol. 62, No. 3 (1984). • Brown, G. Thompson, *Earthen Vessels and Transcendent Power: American Presbyterians in China, 1837-1952* (1997). • De Jong, Gerald F., *The Reformed Church in China, 1842-1951* (1992). • Heuser, Frederick J., *A Guide to Foreign Missionary Manuscripts in the Presbyterian Historical Society* (1988). • Hewat, E. G. K., *Vision and Achievement, 1796-1956: A History of the Foreign Missions of the Churches United in the Church of Scotland* (1960). • Stock, Frederick, and Margaret Stock, *People Movements in the Punjab with Special Reference to the United Presbyterian Church* (1975). • Walls, Andrew F., "Missions," in *Dictionary of Scottish Church History and Theology,* ed. Nigel M. de S. Cameron (1993).

John Roxborogh

Presbyterian Church in Taiwan, Confession of Faith and Public Statements

Initially, the Presbyterian* Church in Taiwan* (PCT) accepted the Apostles' Creed, the Nicene Creed, and the Westminster Confession as their rule of faith. But rapid change brought about by industrialization and economic development in Taiwan and the uncertain national and international political situation which threatened basic human rights and the future of Taiwan led the PCT to issue several public statements which were based on their theological reflection on faith in the Taiwanese context. These statements caused serious tension between the PCT and the ruling government, as well as other church denominations and PCT members. The PCT deliberated on two questions: Who is Lord? and, For what purpose does the church exist? After seven years, it revised its confession of faith in 1985.

The *Statement of Our National Fate* (29 Dec 1971) was issued when President Nixon of the United States was about to visit China. It was intended to oppose powerful nations making unilateral decisions for their own benefit at the expense of smaller nations such as Taiwan. It maintained the God-ordained right, affirmed by the United Nations charter, of all people to determine their own destiny.

Our Appeal Concerning the Bible, the Church and the Nation (18 Nov 1975) declared: "In order to save the nation in this time of crisis we in the church must be really united so that we can fulfill our responsibility to promote justice, liberty and peace. Then the church may be worthy to be called a servant of Christ for these times." The church proposed that the government preserve the freedom of religious faith guaranteed to the people in the constitution, help overcome Taiwan's isolation in foreign relations, establish a relationship of mutual trust and confidence with the church, work toward the reconciliation and cooperation of all people in Taiwan, and preserve the human rights and welfare of the people. The statement also urged the church to express its concern for justice, promote unity and a better understanding of its faith, strive for independence, establish ecumenical ties, and be more concerned about world problems.

The *Declaration on Human Rights* (16 Aug 1977) was an appeal to all countries concerned, especially the United States, and to Christian churches worldwide to take effective steps to help Taiwan, under threat of an invasion from Communist China, to achieve independence and freedom. Mass media distortion of facts and an attack on the church resulted in the departure of many members from the PCT and the imprisonment of the general secretary, C. M. Kao, three years later. In 1978, the general assembly appointed the Faith and Order committee to draft a new confession of faith, which was finalized and approved by the general assembly on 11 Apr 1985.

A Public Statement on the Sovereignty of Taiwan (20 Aug 1991) proclaimed that Taiwan is an independent, sovereign country, separate from China. It categorically affirmed a new Taiwanese constitution, using the official name "Taiwan." It proclaimed United Nations recognition and membership and sought a new relationship with China based on mutual recognition and respect.

Hsu Hsin-Te

Presentation of the Blessed Virgin Mary

(PBVM). International congregation ministering in 25 countries and officially known as the Congregation of the Union of the Presentation of the Blessed Virgin Mary.

The PBVM was founded by Irishwoman Nano Nagle on Christmas Eve 1775 in Cork, Ireland, in response to the need to provide deprived children with education. The order was named the Congregation of the Presentation of the Blessed Virgin Mary in 1805. Although Nano's work began on a small scale, her vision was universal: "For I can assure you, my schools are beginning to be of service to a great many parts of the world. . . . If I could be of service in saving souls in any part of the globe, I would willingly do all in my power."

Presentation sisters first arrived in Asia in 1842 in response to Archbishop Carew's request in 1840 for Irish nuns to render help to the neglected children of the Catholic troops (mainly Irish) of the British Army stationed in India*. The pioneer sisters were Mother Francis Xavier Curran from Rahan, three professed sisters from Maynooth, and a young postulant from Kilkenny. They were joined by two experienced senior sisters from Maynooth a year later. The sisters began teaching in a building the archbishop purchased for them from the East India Company. Presently there are more than 10 Presentation schools in Madras alone, and many more throughout India. In Asia, India has the strongest Presentation group with 145 perpetually professed sisters, and they have extended their work to Zambia.

From Madras, the sisters were sent to Rawalpindi in 1895 to teach the children of the British and Irish military personnel. The pioneers were Mother Ignatius McDermot and Srs. Evangelist Coastworth and Xavier Lonergan. They started a school in Oct 1895 with three children, and in less than six months' time the number had increased to 40. Reinforcements came from Ireland as the number kept increasing. Gradually, educational opportunities were extended to non-British children. Through their untiring efforts, the sisters were able to overcome the initial reluctance to send girls to school. Presently there are 11 Presentation convents in Pakistan*: two in Rawalpindi, and one each in Peshawar, Murree, Sargodha, Josephabad, Jhelum, Wah, Risalpur, Swat, and Tando Allahyar in Sindh.

In addition to schools and informal education, the sisters also provide pastoral* care when needed. In rural Josephabad, they run a dispensary, providing health care to women and infants. In Sargodha, they run centers to provide informal education and to enable women to learn income-generating skills. In Sindh, the sisters work mainly with the tribal people, providing health and pastoral care and helping them to acquire literacy.

Responding to the requests of two Redemptorists, Jerry and John O'Donnell, Presentation sisters from Ireland went to the Philippines* (Himamaylan, Negros Occidental) in 1960. Pioneered by Sisters Baptist Kearns, Carmel Claxton, Annunciata Hayes, and Regina Keyes, Presentation convents are presently found in Binalbagan, Cebu, and Caibiran.

In 1976, in light of Vatican Council II, the Presentation congregations in Pakistan, India, and the Philippines joined with other Presentation groups to form the Union of the Sisters of the Blessed Virgin Mary. The Presentation sisters in Asia reach out to the needy, irrespective of class or creed, and strive daily to grow in solidarity with the poor and to stand with them in their struggle for justice and human dignity.

Bibliography

Letters of Nano Nagle (2) (1769). • General Chapter, *Our Way of Life* (1986). • Murphy, Mariam, *Pakistan Presentation Story* (1988). • Pires, Lisa, et al., *Celebrating 150 Years of PBVM Presence in India, 1842-1992* (1992). • Annals of the Presentation Sisters of the Philippines Region.

CATHERINE SARDAR

Propaganda Fide Congregation

(Congregation for the Evangelization of Peoples, since Vatican II). The Propaganda Fide Congregation was founded by Pope Gregory XV in Jan 1622 (papal Bull issued 22 Jun 1622) as a special Roman dicastery for the spiritual direction of the evangelization of peoples. It was not something that came about overnight. Already toward the end of the 13th c., Ramón Lull (1235-1315) from Catalonia had suggested to the pope that a missionary center be established in Rome, because, in his opinion, the spread of the faith was the principal and constant concern of the church. The conferring of missionary patronage (see *Padroado*) on the kings of Portugal and Spain, with the obligation to spread the Catholic faith in their recently discovered overseas countries and to organize missionary activity, seemed to dispense with the need for a missionary center in Rome. The disadvantages of this system, however, soon became obvious: it limited the influence of the popes in evangelization and, above all, was confusing missionary activity with politics, nationalism*, and colonialism*. After some popes in the 1500s failed to separate again the spread of the faith from politics and colonialism, due to the opposition of the missionary patronage kings, Gregory XV succeeded in founding a permanent missionary dicastery, whose members today are cardinals and bishops and whose staff is comprised of an international personnel. The pope gave it three sweeping tasks to accomplish: the propagation of the faith, the preservation of the Catholic faith (that is to say, the organization and provision of pastoral care* for Catholic families in the diaspora — for that reason also parts of Europe, America, and the Near East were, in the past, under jurisdiction of this congregation), and finally, dialogue with other Christian churches for the purpose of reestablishing Christian unity. It was evident that the separation of Christian churches was the most serious obstacle to evangelization. Today these latter functions are the responsibility of other curial dicasteries and of the bishops' conferences (see Federation of Asian Bishops' Conference).

The main points, therefore, of the congregation's missionary program were: separation of missionary work from colonial politics; the exclusion of every form of interference by the temporal powers in missionary concern; sending out well-qualified and trained missionaries (see Apostolic Vicars); the formation of indigenous priests; the consecration of native bishops; and adaptation to the customs and practices of the peoples. With regard to this latter point, the congregation, in an instruction written in 1659 (see Instructions of 1659)to its apostolic vicars and missionaries in the Far East, said: "Beware of forcing the people to change their way of life, their customs and traditions, as long as these are not in open contradiction to religion and good morals. Is there anything more foolish than to transplant France, Spain, Italy, or any other European country (that is to say its customs and practices) to China! That is not what you should bring to them, but the faith which neither despises nor rejects the lifestyle of any people or their customs as long as they are not evil in themselves, but rather desires their preservation and promotion." It was not the congregation's fault that, despite these clear directives, the disastrous Chinese Rites Controversy developed. This rites controversy was finally resolved by a new instruction of the congregation in 1939 (see Ancestor Worship).

Another priority of the congregation's missionary program and work was to establish, as rapidly as possible, an ecclesiastical hierarchy, appointing local bishops and thus forming local churches. This was, however, hindered until the concordat of 1886 with Portugal by the missionary patronage of this power, who claimed spiritual jurisdiction over the entire continents of Asia and Africa.

From its very beginnings, the congregation recommended in its decrees the study of languages as an indispensable means for missionaries in their work of evangelization. Therefore, they needed books, grammars, dictionaries, and especially Bibles*, catechisms, and liturgical books. As early as 1627, the congregation founded its own polyglot printing press, which rendered great services to local languages and their development. In 1909 it was fused with the Vatican polyglot printing press. In the same year a college for the formation of missionaries, especially from missionary countries, was founded in Rome, and it took the name of Pope Urban VIII: Collegio Urbano.

The duties, competence, and territories of the congregation have undergone a number of changes in the course of the centuries. Dialogue with Orthodox*, Protestants, and Anglicans*, with a view to restoring church unity, and the pastoral* care of Catholics in the diaspora of separated churches have passed into the jurisdiction of the congregation for the Oriental churches, which was originally an offshoot of the Propaganda Fide Congregation, to the Pontifical council for promoting Christian unity, and the local episcopal conferences. A new definition of the congregation's territorial competence was introduced with the curial reforms of 1908.

It is also within the competence of the congregation to regulate and coordinate throughout the world both missionary work itself and missionary cooperation. This last activity of missionary cooperation and missionary animation is carried out mainly through four missionary societies.

See also Instructions of 1659.

Bibliography

Menzel, C., *Historia Congregationis Cardinalium de Propaganda Fide quam brevi compendio explicatam eruditorum iudicio exponit . . .* (1721). • Mejer, O., *Die Propaganda, ihre Provinzen und ihr Recht. Mit besonderer Rücksicht auf Deutschland dargestellt von . . .* (1852). • Trede, Th., *Die Propaganda Fide in Rom, ihre Geschichte und ihre Bedeutung* (1884). • Regatillo, E. F., *Tercer Centenario de la Propaganda Fide, in: El Siglo de las Misiones IX* (1922). • Otaduy, E. M., *Alma Mater. La Sgda. Congr. de Propaganda Fide* (1928). • Roy, E., *Le ministère pontifical des missions: La Sacrée Congrégation de la Propagande* (1944). • Metzler, J., ed., *Sacrée Congregationis de Propaganda Fide memoria rerum. 350 Years in the Service of the Missions, 1622-1972,* 3 Vols. (1971-76).

Josef Metzler

Puang Akkapin

(b. 23 May 1892; d. 19 May 1963). Key figure in the Church of Christ in Thailand (CCT) before and after World War II*.

Born to Luang A. Natchanopakarn and Phan, Puang suffered through a difficult youth, in part because his father died when he was eight. He converted to Christianity in 1915 and then studied at the Presbyterian Siam Mission's Theological Training School in Phet Buri. He subsequently engaged in evangelism in Phet Buri. In 1922 he married Ngern Sapudom. He continued to do evangelism until 1931, when he became pastor of the Khunanukul Church in Pitsanuloke for two years. He then carried out private evangelism and became a leader in the CCT's prewar revivalistic-evangelistic movement fostered by John Sung* and others. In 1946 the CCT general assembly elected him moderator. In that office he traveled extensively, conducting local church revivals and promoting evangelism. He attempted to reintroduce the prewar revival movement and, in doing so, had a great impact on CCT directions in the 1950s. He took a leading role in the integration of the American Presbyterian* Mission into the CCT and the creation of permanent structures for CCT ministry. Under his leadership, the CCT built its first office building in 1954. While moderator, he also served as director of the CCT's evangelism department. His term as moderator ended in 1958, five years before he died.

Bibliography

Tongkham Puntupong, "The Life of Rev. Puang Akkapin" (in Thai), *Church News,* Vol. 16 (Aug 1963) • Samrit Wongsung, *Teacher without a Degree* (in Thai) (1970). •

Records of the American Presbyterian Mission (Payap University Archives, Chiang Mai, Thailand).

PRASIT PONGUDOM, translated by HERBERT R. SWANSON

Pule, Herman. *See* De la Cruz, Apolinario

Punjab Catholic Truth Society

In 1869 a group of English Catholic laymen established in London the Catholic Truth Society (CTS) as a means of producing inexpensive tracts responding to attacks on the church, which were common at the time. In 1910 the Capuchin* missionaries established a section of this organization at Lahore with the name Punjab Catholic Truth Society. It was used as a means of producing and distributing Catholic literature* in Urdu and Punjabi. A group of dedicated workers kept the organization active for many years. These were Francis Hadiri, M. B. Utarid, and the Capuchin fathers Lievin, Victor, Vincent, and Vitalis. The Punjab CTS was able to reissue the Urdu works of Bishops Hartmann and Pezzoni, the New Testament in Urdu, the four Gospels in Punjabi, translations of the *Imitation of Christ,* prayer books, missals, and a host of smaller pamphlets which were translations of the CTS's London publications. In line with the London policy of the time, these tended to be of a rather confrontational nature. After the Second World War, the Punjab CTS continued, but rather fitfully, until it was replaced by other means of publication. JOHN ROONEY

Qi Qing Cai

(b. Shantung, China, 1909; d. 1990). Chinese pastor.

Qi studied at the University of Shanghai and Shantung Baptist Theological College (SBTC) from 1931 to 1935. In 1947 he completed his doctorate in theology in the United States. After graduating from SBTC, Qi served as pastor of Shanghai Baptist Grace Church for 54 years. He served as chairman of the National Baptist Union, managing director of the China Baptist Book Room, vice managing director of the University of Shanghai, and managing director for a number of Christian schools since the 1940s. Qi was devoted to theological* education, and he founded Grace Volunteers Theological College. He served as vice principal of China Baptist Theological College and Shanghai Devotion Seminary for several years.

After the inauguration of the New China (1948), Qi served as the representative for the Shanghai People's Representatives Council. He was also elected six times as a member of the Shanghai People's Political Consultative Council from 1954 to 1985. In the 1980s, Qi was also made director of Nanjing Union Theological Seminary and managing director of East China Theological Seminary.

Qi supported the Three-Self Patriotic Movement* and was one of the 40 people who signed the "Three-Self Manifesto." He served as a council member of the National Three-Self Patriotic Movement Committee since 1954 and was elected its vice chairman in 1980. In 1981, when the Shanghai Protestant Church Committee was formed, Qi was elected its first chairman. In 1985 he was voted as the honorable chairman. His sermons have been edited and compiled in "Sermons of Pastor Qi Qing Cai."

China Group

Qingpu Case of Missioners

Early legal case involving missioners that took place at Qingpu, not far from Shanghai.

When Shanghai was opened as a port to foreigners, the treaty stated that "foreigners are confined to areas which are a day's distance from the port, and should not stay overnight (away from the port)." On 8 Mar 1848, three missionaries of the London Missionary Society — Walter Henry Medhurst, William Muirhead, and William Lockhart*, ignoring this restriction, left Shanghai to distribute tracts. When the tracts were handed out, there was confusion and violence. Lockhart's staff confronted the sailors crowded around him, and the sailors fought back and causing injuries to the missionaries. The British consul at Shanghai, Rutherford Alcock, intended to end the trouble, but he made the situation worse by using navy vessels to stop Chinese vessels carrying food supplies. The Qing (Ching) dynasty was under great pressure to act. It first captured the 10 sailors and displayed them as prisoners in the marketplace. It then paid an indemnity of 300 liang, and finally it sacked the official *Su-song-tai-dao-xian-ling.* This, then, was the first incident in which a mandarin was sacked in a missioner's case.

China Group

Qu Tai Su

(b. 1549; d.?). Well-known Catholic in China during the Ming period.

A native of Changshu, Jiangsu Province, and born into a non-Christian intellectual family, Qu took 15 years to become a Christian. He met Matteo Ricci* in Shaozhou in 1590 and spent about two years learning European mathematics and astronomy, as well as Christianity, from him. Qu admired Ricci, and although he helped Ricci time and again when Ricci encountered difficulties, Qu did not become a Christian until 1605, when he was baptized by Joannes de Rocha and given the Christian name Ignatius. He brought his 14-year-old son to learn the teachings of the church from de Rocha as well, and when Qu died, his son went to Hangzhou in 1623 and invited Julio Aleni* to Changshu. Thus Christianity entered Qu's home village through the initiative of his son.

China Group

Quoc Ngu

Romanized Vietnamese alphabet devised ca. 1634 by the Jesuit* fathers Gaspar de Amaral (1594-1646) and Antonio de Barbosa.

An important cultural innovation, this romanized script was first employed in a Vietnamese dictionary the two fathers had prepared for their colleagues. Alexandre de Rhodes*, S.J., subsequently perfected the system of transcription, adding diacritical marks and signs to indicate the varying tonal characteristics of Vietnamese words. Later Jesuits succeeded in persuading the Vietnamese rulers to adopt *quoc ngu* as the national script.

A truly revolutionary innovation, the *quoc ngu* enabled missionaries to write Christian literature* for their converts in the vernacular, obviating the tedious process for the latter to learn Chinese.

It was soon after the development of this script that there followed the first great wave of conversions in Vietnam*. From 1600 to 1630, the number of Christians rose from but a few thousand to 94,000 in Tongking and 30,000 in Annam. In large measure the *quoc ngu* was responsible for the amazing French Catholic missionary success in Vietnam (nearly 528,000 Christians in 1898), which at that time was second only to the achievements of the Spanish in the Philippines.

Bibliography

Buttinger, J., *The Smaller Dragon: Vietnam* (1958). • Von Pastor, L. F., *History of the Popes,* Vol. XXIX (1951).

T. Valentino Sitoy, Jr.

Rabbula

(d. 435 C.E). Born in Calcis to a pagan father and Christian mother, Rabbula converted to Christianity about 400 C.E. He was consecrated bishop of Edessa (411/12–435). As bishop, he led a bloody campaign against the Jews, pagans, and those considered heretics, destroying at least four pagan temples and a synagogue. Rabbula also destroyed at least 400 copies of the *Diatessaron,* the Gospel harmony developed by Tatian* that had served for centuries as the Gospel of the Syriac church, and replaced it with the separate Gospels in the Syriac *Peshitta* version, which he may have commissioned. His inflexible administrative style and harsh treatment of those with whom he disagreed won him many enemies. He did, however, organize food relief for the poor and built an infirmary for the care of the sick. He also apparently codified the monastic rules and established strict guidelines for the lifestyle of clergy, monks, and laity.

The theologians of Edessa had normally been partisans of the East Syrian tradition that revered the teachings of Diodore of Tarsus and Theodore of Mopsuestia*. At the Council of Ephesus (431), Rabbula continued this tradition by refusing to condemn Theodore and Nestorius*. However, he changed his mind and became an enthusiastic and doctrinaire supporter of the politics and theological positions of Cyril of Alexandria. He then banned from Edessa the writings of Theodore and Nestorius. This put him even more at odds with significant segments of his clergy. His contentious and doctrinaire approach to issues destroyed the academic leadership role of Edessa and can be said to have permanently divided the Syrian church.

Bibliography

Black, M., "Rabbula of Edessa and the Peshitta," *BJRL,* Vol. 33 (1951). • Blum, G. G., *Rabbula von Edessa,* CSCO 300 (1969). • Peeters, P., "La Vie de Rabbula, évêque d'Edesse," *Recherches d'histoire et de philologie orientale* (1951). • Vööbus, *Syriac and Arabic Documents regarding Legislation relating to Syriac Asceticism* (1960).

David Bundy

Racism

Attitudes derogatory to a particular ethnic group based on assumptions of the negative characteristics of that group and corresponding assumptions about the superiority of one's own; and practices based on such attitudes, leading to discrimination against members of that particular ethnic group.

Discrimination, in both contemporary societies and historically, has taken many forms. What is specific to racism is, as its name suggests, the emphasis on racial characteristics of the discriminated group — typically skin color and other phenotypical characteristics — but also often including what are actually cultural characteristics, such as forms of behavior, language, habits, and cultures.

This makes the concept of racism controversial in two ways: first, as a mechanism of negative discrimination, and second, because of its dependence on the scientifically shaky and much disputed notion of race. Despite its common usage as a term to denote a population sharing physical features, often a common culture, and thought to have evolved through a real or imagined shared historical process, there is no agreed definition of the term, which evolved largely out of 19th c. Darwinian disputes. Today its most accurate usage, if it is to be used at all, is to describe a human population with certain gene frequencies. All human races in this sense are statistical averages — that is, groups who share certain genes to a higher degree than do other groups who have a slightly different distribution of genetic characteristics. All such human groups share genes with other populations — there is no "pure" race, due to centuries of mingling through intermarriage, conquest, migration, and colonialism. Races were often confused with or identified with ethnicities, identities based partly on common physical characteristics but more particularly on shared culture, history, and often geography, with culture here usually including a language and very often a religion.

The notion of racism, then, is based on very uncertain scientific grounds — the notion of race itself being unclear and there being no clear evidence of any systematic differences between human populations in terms of such characteristics as intelligence, artistic creativity, adaptability to environment, martial skills, or other indices favored by those who wish to discriminate in terms of race. Racism, it should be stressed, is not simply the description of differences between human groups — the Japanese and the Jews clearly differ in many cultural and phenotypical respects, for example — but the attribution of negative characteristics to certain groups on the basis of race. This process is akin to stereotyping: the isolation of specific individual characteristics which are then generalized as being typical of that group as a whole and are also frequently derogatory.

It is sometimes thought that racism is a peculiarly Western disease, but examination of historical and contemporary Asian societies shows that this is not the case, even though patterns of racism and its social and religious sources may be different in some cases. This can be seen clearly when it is recognized that the very historical identity of many Asian nations is defined in terms of superior race ("us") versus barbarian races ("them") beyond the boundaries of the civilized community. The process of state formation in both China* and Japan* illustrates this — China with its self-definition as the "middle kingdom," and Japan through its premodern policy of excluding foreigners and maintaining the "purity" of the Japanese race and culture.

Historically, racist attitudes and practices in Asia can be broadly grouped into three periods: indigenous precolonial racism, racist patterns developing as a direct result of colonialism*, and postcolonial contemporary racism. The three often still interact, with ideas inherited from the colonial era, for example, continuing to influence contemporary attitudes deeply. Patterns of ethnic relations in Malaysia*, for instance, are structured by the patterns set up during the period of British colonialism.

Indigenous precolonial racism tended to take several characteristic forms — racism based on economic segregation, on religious differentiation, or on concepts of racial hierarchy. In the first group fell discriminatory practices based on the separation and exclusion of certain groups identified racially and confined to certain kinds of often menial tasks. There are parallels here with the position of Jews in medieval Europe, but Asian examples would include the Burakumin of Japan (see Baraku) or practices of slavery in premodern northern Thailand* or in China, especially in Yunnan and Szechuan, where tribal peoples were often slaves of Han Chinese or, in some cases, of other tribes. The second group would include such examples as anti-Muslim stereotyping in Hindu-dominated areas of India*, where there is an association, even if an illegitimate one, of race and religion. The third case can be found in many premodern Asian societies which were ethnically plural. Thus Mogul Indians (of Persian origin) ranked higher in the ethnic hierarchy than Hindu Indians — the indigenous population, in fact — in precolonial North India, and both ranked higher than members of the numerous and widely scattered tribal communities. Such ranking becomes racism when the members of the disadvantaged groups are stereotyped, excluded from access to power and social resources, and often treated as scapegoats for problems in the wider society for which they were in no way responsible.

Despite these kinds of examples, there is substantial evidence that, on the whole, much of precolonial Asia was relatively free of racism. Other forms of discrimination of course existed, but stereotyping based specifically on racial characteristics tended to be less frequent, as evidenced by rates of intermarriage (Thais and Cambodians, Arabs and Malays, Chinese and Manchus, and so on), borrowing of cultural traits (Vietnamese and Chinese), and religious conversions, which often implied joining a new ethnic community (even today to convert to Islam in Malaysia is to *masok Melayu* — to "enter Malaydom"). Slavery and attitudes of racial and cultural superiority did exist, but extreme forms of racism were relatively rare. This situation was changed dramatically by colonialism, which had many effects on racial patterns: it introduced new racial hierarchies, promoted unprecedented migration of peoples, created new political and economic structures, generated numerous new stereotypes — for example, of the Asian as being somehow simultaneously lazy, exotic, erotic, and untrustworthy — and reflected in art, literature, political attitudes, and social practices something the Palestinian-American scholar Edward Said has collectively characterized as "Orientalism."

Racism in the colonial context tended to take certain forms, including the exclusion of Asians from colonial institutions such as government, clubs, higher education, or senior roles in the economic or political bureaucracies; Asians were also excluded socially (no intermarriage and little significant social intercourse) and a middleman class was created to mediate between the colonists and the natives (Peranakan Chinese in Malaya and Singapore*, "Indos" or Eurasians in Indonesia). In addition, racial division was encouraged by the establishment of religious segregation, unequal access to the new colonial legal system, and new patterns and hierarchies of work; and by the British plantation system in Malaya, its French equivalent in Indochina, and the Dutch "Culture System" of agricultural production in the Dutch East Indies. New racial groups were introduced to work these new systems — Chinese throughout Southeast Asia, Tamils to Malayan plantations, Punjabis to the railways and police forces of colonial Southeast Asia, Koreans to Japan, and even Japanese to Malaya and to regions far beyond (Hawaii, California, Peru, and Brazil). Colonial languages took precedence over indigenous ones, and preferment in the colonial civil services or in education required mastery of these foreign tongues. The novels of the distinguished Indonesian writer Pramoedya Ananta Toer vividly portray the ambiguities and anguishes, the social exclusions and humiliations that deeply marked the young subjects of these colonial regimes.

While objectively colonialism may have brought benefits, it cannot be denied that it was racist in nature. It not only created entirely new ethnically based social structures — such as those of Malaysia and Singapore — but it also created racist patterns in education, health care, work, the distribution of wealth, and other areas, which in some cases still perpetuate themselves in current patterns or are only just now being overcome in the independent nations of Asia. Unfortunately, nationalism* itself — the successor to colonialism — has often been racist, turning to the stereotyping and exclusion of its own ethnic minorities or adopting policies on immigration that favor some and exclude others.

The contemporary situation illustrates that the evils of racism are far from over throughout Asia. This can be seen by looking at four examples. First, ethnic conflict, whether based on political (e.g., desire for independence), economic, or racial grounds, has not disappeared. And such conflict, being ethnic, requires the demonization of the Other, leading not only to fresh forms of discriminatory practice, but also to brutality of a kind rarely found in nonracial conflict. Sri Lanka*, which appeared to be a model developing South Asian society, has since come to the verge of disintegration because of such conflict. Cambodia* has seen violence against its own long-resident Vietnamese community, and Burma and Assam have experienced decades of racial strife, in both cases approaching the proportions of civil war.

Second, all Asian societies are actually plural, even those that constantly emphasize their homogeneity, such as Japan and Thailand*. All contain minorities, often valued during times of economic growth but easy targets of discrimination when things turn bad. Japan, for instance, despite its major advances on almost all other fronts, still has a major problem in coming to terms with its large Korean (and, for that matter, its much smaller Chinese and Indian) minority, which is still treated in a discriminatory way regarding marriage, employment, and education. Racism, especially when based on visible differences, is an easy way to create scapegoats and, given the inherent plurality of modern Asian societies, is likely to remain a potential danger and source of social conflict, especially when allied with (as it is in Japan) ultraconservative politics, which employs a myth of origin and racial purity as an ideology for promoting exclusion.

Third, a major trend in Asia today is the migration of peoples, whether for work or as political or economic refugees. Indonesians flock to Malaysia; Thai workers staff the construction sites of Singapore; Hong Kong has a huge community of Filipinas working as domestic servants or in the entertainment industry; Japan has a massive number of illegal foreign workers from the Middle East, Taiwan, Korea, and Southeast Asia. The presence of such new minorities — often illegally in the country, usually cut off from its language and culture but physically visible — is threatening to the local society. Rising crime rates in Japan have come to be associated with the presence of foreigners; Filipinas in Hong Kong, many of them deeply religious and in respectable domestic work, are widely stereotyped as prostitutes. Racism in such settings takes two forms. One is outright discrimination against such minorities — exclusion from political or social participation, denial of fair wages and human rights — characteristic actually of colonialism. The other is the social construction of stereotypes, which in turn influence behavior. Southeast Asians in Japan find it harder to rent housing than do Caucasians, for example; non-Japanese Asian women are assumed to be prostitutes; the honesty and trustworthiness of all foreigners is questioned. Outright racial discrimination can be identified and fought with legal, political, social, religious, and scientific weapons. More subtle stereotyping and its representation in the media, literature, and so forth is harder to combat, as it is more insidious and pervasive, and hence damaging, in its effects.

Fourth, new forms of racism constantly appear: it is a dynamic and volatile process. One of the newest forms is so-called "scientific racism" based on ideas largely culled from a small number of Western sociobiologists. The most common form of this phenomenon, which has appeared in many places, including Japan, China, Singapore, and Malaysia, is the argument that genes are the determinant of intelligence, and that there is a strong correlation between race and intelligence. According to this argument, some races are just better endowed naturally than others. Education and improving the environment will do little to enhance intelligence. The races thus favored deserve special privileges to complement their natural superiority. What is interesting about such arguments is their widespread distribution throughout the region, their quite open racism, and their attempt to base themselves on "scientific" evidence which is highly questionable and fiercely disputed. Nevertheless, the presence of such forms should alert us to the ever fresh and apparently better-founded ways in which racism can reappear — in this case as ideology masquerading as science.

The problem of racism is not likely to disappear. Historically, Christianity has often been implicated in the creation of racist attitudes — in patterns of religious exclusion based on race, especially during the colonial period, through patterns of nonindigenization and missionary policy. The environment has now changed in many ways. While Christianity clearly does not deny ethnic and cultural difference, its ideological basis is the subordination of those differences to a higher unity. The result historically in Asia was often the promotion of forms of access and empowerment not available within colonial or precolonial state systems. For example, the provision of education to local girls in Myanmar*, China, India, Malaya, and Singapore; the creation of health care facilities for ethnic minorities in South and East Asia; opposition to unfair labor practices and feudal social structures in the Philippines; and translating and recording of vernacular languages have all been part of this social mission. Today in Japan, it is Christians who are at the forefront of efforts to secure human rights, medical* care, and fair wages for foreign workers, including the illegal ones whose dignity as human beings is eroded. And this essentially is the key to overcoming racism — the celebration of diversity, recognition of the fundamental genetic unity of the human species, and the centrality of human dignity as a mirror of the divine, against which image any racism is a basic spiritual insult, a scientific error, and a diminution of the self who expresses the prejudice.

Bibliography

Leng, Chee Heng, and Chan Chee Khoon, eds., *Designer Genes: I.Q., Ideology, and Biology* (1984). • Yoshonobu, Kumazawa, and David L. Swain, eds., *Christianity in Japan, 1971-1990* (1991). • Said, Edward, *Orientalism* (1985). • Sigler, J., ed., *International Handbook on Race and Race Relations* (1987). • Watson, James L., ed., *Asian and African Systems of Slavery* (1980). JOHN CLAMMER

Radio. *See* Christian Broadcasting System (CBS), Korea; Far East Broadcasting Company

Raffles, Thomas Stamford

(b. 1781; d. 1826). British Indies administrator and founder of the port of Singapore*.

The founding of Singapore as a free port, independent of the authority of the Muslim Sultanate of Johore and freely accessible to both Protestant and Catholic missionaries, opened the door for Christian missionary activity throughout the archipelago, and particularly to the Chinese. It remains a strategic center of missionary activity in Asia even today. Its founder, Thomas Raffles, entered the service of the British East Indies Company at an early age and distinguished himself through self-study and the mastery of several Malayan languages. After service in Penang, and under Lord Minto in Malacca* and Java, Raffles controlled much of Java and Sumatra on behalf of the company from 1811 to 1816. His efforts at reform were not appreciated, and in 1816 he returned to London, out of favor with the company. On his return to Asia a year later, he convinced Lord Hastings of the need for vigorous action to secure British trade through Southeast Asia. In 1819 he landed on Singapore Island and established a British port through a treaty with the Sultanate of Johore-Riau. In 1823 and 1824 he reorganized the administration of the port and secured Dutch recognition of Britain's claims to it. Ill health forced his return to England before his death in 1826.

Bibliography

Wurtzburg, C. E., *Raffles of the Eastern Isles,* ed. Clifford Witting (1954). • Sng, Bobby E. K., *In His Good Time* (1993). ROBERT A. HUNT

Rajanubhab, Prince Damrong

(b. 21 Jun 1862; d. 1943). Thai king, son of Rama IV; reformer.

Born to King Mongkut* (Rama IV) and Princess Choom, Prince Damrong played a leading role in expanding the authority of and modernizing the Thai nation-state. His traditional palace education included exposure to missionary and other Western writings, and he also studied English, which he polished through frequent discussions with Protestant missionaries. From 1889 until 1892 he served as minister-designate of the Ministry of Public Instruction. He participated in the founding of the Suan Anan School, headed by Rev. Samuel G. McFarland*, as a model for Westernizing traditional Thai education. He also founded the first public school in Thailand*.

Damrong held the office of minister of the interior from 1892 until 1926, during which time he reformed local and regional governmental administration. His reform and modernization of the Thai state frequently paralleled European and American missionary efforts to introduce Western methods and technologies, particularly in education and medicine. Damrong used the missionaries to promote social change; he supported the expansion of their work and allowed them full freedom to evangelize in Thailand. He used his authority, however, to prevent them from openly attacking Buddhism* in their evangelism.

Damrong continued in public service until 1932, when a coup d'etat forced him to move to Penang. He resided there until 1942, when he returned to Bangkok, where he died the following year. Among his other accomplishments, Damrong initiated the modern study of Thai history, and he remains known as the "Father of Thai Historiography."

Bibliography

Damrong Rajanubhab, H. R. H. Prince, *Memories* (in Thai) (1968). • McFarland, George B., ed., "Introductory Chapter," in *The Historical Sketch of Protestant Missions in Siam, 1828-1928* (1928). • "The Introduction of Western Culture in Siam," *Journal of the Siam Society,* Vol. 2 (Oct 1926). • Praphun Trenarong, *The Life and Work of Prince Damrong Rajanubhab* (in Thai) (1973). • "Damrong Rajanubhab. H. R. H. Prince," *The Thai Encyclopedia,* Royal Institute edition (in Thai) (1960-61). • Wyatt, David K., *Thailand: A Short History* (1984).

PRASIT PONGUDOM, translated by HERBERT R. SWANSON

Rama IV. *See* Mongkut, King

Ramabai, Pandita

(b. 23 Apr 1858; d. 1922). Champion of women's rights in India* and pioneer in women's education and social* reform.

Ramabai was born in an ashram* located in a jungle, the Gangamula Forest in the Western Ghats. Her father, Anant Shastri Dongree, was an "orthodox reformer." By the age of 16, Ramabai had lost both parents, an elder sister, and a brother. After her brother's death, she was married in Jun 1880 to Bepin Behart Medhavi, and they had a daughter, Manorama, in Apr 1881. Ramabai's husband died of cholera after a brief illness in Feb 1882. Thereafter she decided to devote the rest of her life to the uplifting of women.

She founded the Aryan Mahila Samaj for the emancipation of women in India. Long before she came to Poona in 1882, Ramabai no longer believed in her ancestral faith. It was then that Christianity provided the kind of faith she needed. She was particularly impressed by the Christian concept of a personal God as the God of love. She was baptized with her daughter on 29 Sep 1883. In 1887 she published a book, *The High Caste Hindu Women.* She also founded the Saradha Sadan in Bombay on 11 Mar 1889. In 1898 Ramabai founded the Mukti Sadan at Kedgaon. In 1919 she had bestowed on her the royal Kaisar-O-Hind gold medal.

Bibliography

Krishnarudongree, Rajesh, *A Life of Faith and Prayer* (1969). • Macnicol, Nicol, *Builders of Modern India* (1930). • Sengupta, Padmini, *Pandita Ramabai — Her Life and Work* (1970). • Shah, A. B., *The Letters and Correspondence of Pandita Ramabai* (1977).

P. Raja Jeya Singh

Ramakrishna Mission

Outstanding Hindu renascent movement which represents a successful attempt to synthesize the mystical and practical aspects of religion (see Hinduism, New Movements).

Founded by Swami Vivekananda* in Calcutta in May 1897 for the dissemination of Hindu spirituality and for social service, the mission is named after Vivekananda's illustrious guru Sri Ramakrishna Paramahamsa (ca. 1836-86), who remains the inspiring source of its teachings and practices. The mission also incorporates the activities of the Ramakrishna Math ("order") founded in 1899 as centers of monks devoted to the teaching of Ramakrishna's precepts. The three major aims of the mission are: training of monks who would work for the spiritual and physical welfare of the masses; promotion of industry and art; and propagation of Vedantic teachings.

As an international organization, the mission has its branches (about 150) in various countries. The Belur Math near Calcutta functions as the headquarters. Administration is largely in the hands of monks. The four areas of its work are education, health, relief projects, and religio-cultural activities. Recognizing education as a powerful means to bring about religious and social change, the mission runs many schools and colleges for boys and girls as well. It also runs dispensaries and hospitals. Relief work has a significant place in its activities. In the field of religious and cultural activities, the mission conducts special classes and lectures on Hindu religion, runs libraries and reading rooms, and publishes religious books and periodicals. More than 750 disciplined and dedicated monks and many lay workers and part-time volunteers are responsible for the success of the mission. General secretary Swami Gambirananda says the mission is the first step in uplifting the masses, educating women, rebuilding India*, and regenerating the world on the basis of Hindu spirituality.

The mission is faithful to the spirit of Hindu religion in its totality, both to the beliefs and practices of the masses at the grassroots level and also to the reflective philosophies of the enlightened. Its basic tenets appear to be pluralistic: the realization of God is the essence of religion; all religions are the same; all religions lead to the same goal, namely, the experience of divinity. Hence, it overtly denounces conversion from one religion to another.

Emerging in the context of growing nationalism* and sustained Christian mission in colonial India, the mission has done a yeoman's service to the defense and renaissance of Hinduism. The mission is committed to a worldwide Vedantic mission, and in this it may be considered an Eastern "counterattack" on the West. Prior to the explosion of guruism, it was the Ramakrishna Mission that had done much to spread a knowledge of Hindu spirituality outside India. Through its concerted social service, it has successfully countered the Western criticism of Hindu religion as an "otherworldly" religion. Christ is highly revered in the mission as a great messenger and divine incarnation. Like Buddhahood, Christhood is the perfect ideal of humans. However, its understanding of Christ and Christianity is quite different from that of the traditional Christian understanding. Vivekananda's understanding of Christ, which the mission faithfully adheres to, is in terms of the principle of Vedanta, where the historical Jesus is unimportant as long as the idea of Christhood is recognized.

In the light of its pluralistic approach to religion, the mission does not seem to be appreciative of Christian missionary enterprise. However, its own missionary and social activities are modeled after Christian missionary ideologies and practices.

Bibliography

Gambirananda, Swami, *History of Ramakrishna Math and Mission* (1983). • Baird, Robert D., ed., *Religion in Modern India* (1981). • Mathew, C. V., *Neo-Hinduism: A Missionary Religion* (1987). • Purohit, B. R., *Hindu Revivalism and Indian Nationalism* (1965). • Sarma, D. S., *Hinduism through the Ages* (1973). • Thomas, M. M., *The Acknowledged Christ of the Indian Renaissance* (1976).

C. V. Mathew

Ramaswamy, E. V. *See* Periyar, Rationalist Movement of

Raux, Nicolas Joseph

(b. 1754; d. 1801). French Vincentian missionary (CM) who went to China* during the reign of Emperor Qianlong of the Qing dynasty.

In 1773, following the dissolution of the Society of Jesus*, the French king, Louis XVI, sent Raux and two other missionaries to China. They departed France on 25 Aug 1783, arriving in Guangzhou on 29 Aug 1874. They traveled north on 7 Feb 1785, arriving in Beijing on 29 Apr. The emperor met them and assigned Raux, who devoted his time to learning Chinese and the Manchu language, to do translation work. In 1788, following the death of the Jesuit Joseph d'Esphinha, Raux was appointed to replace him as chief of the Calendrical Bureau. Raux also conducted clandestine mission activities. He presided over the North Church, conducting elaborate masses on important days in the church calendar, and established several schools where Christians could learn the teachings of the church. He also established a monastery to train Chinese priests.

Bibliography

Latourette, Kenneth Scott, *A History of Christian Mission in China* (1929).

China Group, translated by David Wu

Rawlinson, Frank Joseph

(Le Lingsheng) (b. England, 1871; d. 1937). American missionary to China*.

The son of a Plymouth Brethren preacher, Rawlinson was an Anglican* in his early years. Without much schooling, he migrated to America at age 18, working as a carpenter and a fireman. After 1891 he studied at Bucknell College and Rochester Theological Seminary. He received United States citizenship in 1900. Sent by the foreign mission board of the Southern Baptist* Convention, he reached Shanghai in 1902 to serve as a school principal and founded the second Baptist church, the predecessor of Huai En Church in Shanghai. In the course of 35 years, Rawlinson returned to the United States twice to obtain his master's degree from Columbia University and his doctor of divinity degree from Union Theological Seminary. He resigned from his Baptist post in 1912 to become editor of the monthly *Chinese Recorder and Missionary Journal,* owned by the Mission Press and first published in May 1865 with S. L. Baldwin* as editor. Rawlinson held this position until his death during a Japanese bombing raid in 1937.

Rawlinson switched his Baptist membership and joined the mission board of the Congregational Church in 1916. He was active in interdenominational work, participating in the drafting of the constitution of the National Council of Churches (NCC) of China and serving on its executive committee and other permanent committees. He wrote many articles on the problems of education and workers in China, was director of the Department of Chinese Schools of the Shanghai Municipal Council, and chairman of the board of directors of the Shanghai American Boys' School. Included among his works are "Chinese Ideas of the Supreme Being" and "Naturalization of Christianity in China."

Bibliography

MacGillivray, Donald, *A Century of Protestant Missions in China, 1807-1907* (1979). • Rawlinson, John Long, *Rawlinson, The Recorder, and China's Revolution: A Topical Biography of Frank Joseph Rawlinson, 1871-1937* (1990).

China Group

Real Situado, Philippines

A phrase originally used in the Philippines* to signify the proceeds raised by the galleon trade levied in Acapulco and then returned to the Philippines; later came to mean the subsidy or appropriation from the Mexican treasury to help the Philippines make up its chronic deficit.

The Spanish colony in the Philippines existed as a mere appendage of the viceroyalty of Mexico, which exercised jurisdictional control over the civil, ecclesiastical, and fiscal affairs of the Philippines. Specifically, the insular colony endured fiscal dependence on the Mexican viceroyalty as a part of the Spanish seaborne empire. The reason for the nearly complete reliance of the islands on the silver supplied by the viceregal treasury of Mexico, at the Spanish crown's orders, is found in their inability to produce adequate income to meet their finances. This inability to raise enough money from purely local sources of revenue was compounded by borrowing and malfeasance. The result was a 250-year fiscal nightmare for the Spanish administration in the Philippines, for the viceregal authorities of Mexico, and for the Castilian crown in Madrid. The Philippine treasury did not just incur chronic and recurrent deficits by having more expenditures than revenue; it was also in a deeper state of perennial bankruptcy.

Precisely to ensure the economic survival of the Philippine colony, the Spaniards initiated the galleon trade via the transpacific route in 1567 from Manila to Acapulco and back to Manila. This trading system was founded on the theory that, without it, the Spanish colonial establishment in the archipelago could not possibly endure. Thus, the hope was that the galleon trade would ensure the sustenance and prosperity of the islands. The Manila settlers got the exclusive right to ship merchandise from Asia, mainly Chinese silk fabrics which were bought insatiably by the Mexicans, to the port of Acapulco. The profits of this trade went back to the Philippine traders. The customs tax and other customs proceeds collected in Acapulco were rebated to the Manila treasury, not deposited in the viceregal treasury in Mexico City. The income produced by this trading system was to ensure the continued existence of the Philippine colony.

The Philippine *situado,* which was constituted solely from the rebates from Mexico, had none of the characteristics of a pure and outright subsidy. However, even the income from the galleon trade proved inadequate to meet the expenses of the insular treasury. The idea of making the galleon trade pay the expenses of the Philippines went unrealized and unfulfilled, with the colony's revenue always falling short of enabling the islands' treasury to succeed in balancing its budget. It was for this reason that Spain, through the Mexican treasury, had to establish a standing fund from which the Philippine *situado* as subsidy, whether whole or half-subsidy, could be drawn. Thus the meaning of the Philippine *situado* was transformed from galleon-trade income to subsidy or appropriation from the Mexican treasury to help the Philippines make up its chronic deficit.

Since this constant deficit continued until 1800, the Philippines became a heavy financial burden on Spain. The Spanish crown was therefore forced to order its more affluent American colony, Mexico, to send annually to the islands what is now firmly established as the Philippine *situado,* or subsidy, to aid the Philippines and enable the government of the archipelago to implement Spanish imperial policies both within the islands and outside of them.

After 1687 the Philippine *situado* was fixed at 250,000 pesos per annum, although the amount actually reaching Manila varied according to what was added or subtracted in Mexico City. Despite obstacles such as stormy seas, shipwrecks, or the lurking Dutch and British sea dogs, the Mexican silver kept flowing into the archipelago as a matter of compelling economic necessity.

Specifically, the Philippine *situado* went to meet a variety of needs. When Spain sought the realization of the ambitions for hegemony in Asia, the *situado* was used to finance relief and expeditionary forces to the Moluccas*, which the Spaniards held until 1662. A protracted conflict with the Dutch, who also coveted the Moluccas and the Philippines, accompanied this venture into the Spice Islands. Just as expensive as the outfitting of expeditions to the Moluccas was the military necessity of building forts and garrisons, not only to combat the Dutch threat, and later the British threat, but also to fight the unpacified Philippine inhabitants, especially the Muslim Filipinos (Moros), who resisted Spanish aggression and sovereignty in the colony.

Aside from defense expenditures, the *situado* was used in paying the salaries and gratuities of all military, governmental, and ecclesiastical personnel. This payment of salaries was a necessary incentive to induce all personnel to remain in the islands as well as to reward them for their services. And of course, the *situado* was employed for the construction of ships to guarantee the comings and goings of the Acapulco galleons. The money for the purchase of the supplies for the Philippines, and the pay of the men recruited in Mexico for military service in the archipelago, likewise came from the *situado,* as did the money for the provisions of the galleons while crossing the Pacific Ocean. In short, the *situado* was employed for the conquest of Asia and, when that failed, for the preservation of the islands.

In the end, it was the Christianization of the Philippines that became the greatest achievement of the Spaniards, with the ecclesiastical hierarchy dominating virtually every facet of the colonization of the Philippines, and the political administration merely complementing the missionary effort. The Augustinian*, Dominican*, Jesuit*, and Franciscan* Orders, as the pioneers in the evangelical labor among the Filipinos, each maintained a friary or community in Manila. Each received quite sizable grants by royal decree from the Philippine *real situado,* or royal subsidy, from Mexico. The allotments were employed primarily to cover the living expenses of the archbishop, bishops, suffragans, curates, and acolytes of the various bishoprics of the islands; to cover the needs of the individual religious groups and their respective convents; to build, repair, and maintain sanctuaries such as the Manila Cathedral; and even for the specific purpose of regularly purchasing and transporting from Spain barrels of wine for the celebration of the masses by priests and friars working for the propagation of the faith among the Philippine population.

The Mexican *situado* to the Philippines was formally abolished in 1804, although by some communication breakdown somewhere along the line between Spain and Mexico, the subsidy continued to arrive in Manila until the last galleon cleared the waters of Acapulco in 1815. Philippine contacts with Mexico were subsequently severed when the Mexicans dislodged direct Spanish authority in their country, thus making the viceroyalty into a republic in 1821. Thus the Spaniards lasted in the Philippines as long as they did because of the Mexican *situado.* And because of the Mexican *situado,* the Spanish program of colonization and its consequent Christianization of the Filipinos was to a large degree realized and fulfilled.

Bibliography

Bauzon, Leslie E., *Deficit Government: Mexico and the Philippine Situado, 1606-1804* (1981). • Bourne, Edward Gaylord, "The Philippine *Situado* from the Treasury of New Spain," *American Historical Review,* Vol. 10 (Jan 1905). • LeRoy, James A., "The Philippine *'Situado'* from the Treasury of New Spain," *American Historical Review,* Vol. 10 (Jul 1905); Vol. 11 (Apr 1906). • Schurz, William Lytle, "The Philippine *Situado,*" *Hispanic American Historical Review,* Vol. 1 (Nov 1918). • *The Manila Galleon* (1939).

Leslie E. Bauzon

Reconstruction Church

Movement of Korean Christian leaders who opposed the Japanese orders to pay respect to Shinto* shrines and survived the Japanese persecution and prison terms in

1945 when Korea* was liberated at the end of World War II*.

The group of ministers and lay leaders who were released from prison, including Han Sang Dong* (1901-76), Lee Ki Sun (1876-1950), Choe Duk Ji, and Cho Su Ok, demanded the reform of the Korean churches which had obeyed the Japanese orders to worship the Japanese idols. Some attacked the church leaders who bowed down to the Japanese Shinto shrines, and some destroyed the church buildings whose ministers had defiled the church by idol worship. The leaders of the movement formed the Central Committee for the Reconstruction Church in 1948 near the southeastern port city of Pusan. This was further developed into the General Assembly of the Reconstruction Church in 1952. The movement later became Koryu Presbyterian Church, prominent in the southeastern part of Korea (see Japanese Shinto Shrine Worship and Korean Christianity).

Bibliography

Choi, J. K., *A History of Christian Reconstruction Movement in Korea* (in Korean) (1956).

David Suh, with contributions from Sang Gyoo Lee

Redemptorists

(Congregation of the Most Holy Redeemer, CSSR). The Redemptorists are also known as the Baclaran Fathers, after the small fishing village of Baclaran outside Manila where the National Shrine of Our Lady of Perpetual Help stands. Built in 1953, largely from the weekly donations of the devotees, this fitting monument to the Filipinos' ardent love for Mary draws an estimated 100,000 Marian devotees every Wednesday the whole year round. The shrine is cared for by the Redemptorists. But the assignation of the Redemptorists in the Philippines as the "Baclaran Fathers," although understandable, is nonetheless inaccurate: they do not all live and serve only at the Marian shrine in Baclaran, nor is their ministry confined to promoting the popular Baclaran Marian devotion.

The Redemptorists, founded by St. Alphonsus Maria di Liguori at Scola, Italy (1732), first came to the islands at that crucial period when the Philippine church was very young and had been struggling to stay alive. The expulsion of numerous Spanish friars by the Americans, the new colonial rulers, caused a massive shortage of priests to minister to the people.

So the task was cut out clearly for the first band of Irish Redemptorists who landed in Opon, Cebu, of the southern Philippines in Jun 1906: to protect, nourish, and further spread the seed of Catholicism among the natives. And they were soon on the road toward accomplishing this mission.

From their monasteries, the Redemptorists set out to distant towns and villages not easily accessible to the local priests. There they would stay for one to two weeks at a time, visiting every home, instructing the people in the basic tenets of the Catholic faith, warning those who would persist in their sinful ways, but offering God's compassion and forgiveness to those who responded to his call.

At home the missioners ministered to the people who came to their monasteries. In time it became necessary to enlarge their private chapels to accommodate the people's increasing demands. They were also often called upon to conduct spiritual retreats for priests and other religious, as well as to serve in schools run by the latter.

In the early 1960s, radical changes in the pastoral approach of the Redemptorists were occasioned by their deepening involvement in the people's struggle for justice and peace. Christian community-building became a primary concern in Redemptorist preaching and mission work. Partnership with Redemptorist lay coworkers is also a new priority among them.

Thus it was that the congregation and its ministry spread and developed. Through the years, many Filipino vocations have joined their ranks. Presently, the Redemptorists operate from 11 mission centers spread over the three major islands of the Philippines. While the vice province of Manila (comprising the units in Luzon) remains juridically under the Australian Province, the vice province of Cebu (comprising the units in the southern Philippines) became a province in 1996.

Bibliography

Boland, Samuel J., *Spreading the Net — the Redemptorists in Luzon (1911-1982)* (for private circulation only. Baclaran, Paranaque, Philippines) (1982). • Baily, Michael, *Small Net in a Big Sea — The Redemptorists in the Philippines (1905-1929)* (1978).

Ben Moraleda

Reformed. *See* Presbyterian and Reformed Churches

Refugees

Central to the memory of the Jewish people and fundamental to their identity as a people was the historical experience of the Exodus. At that time, the Jews who had migrated to Egypt found themselves cruelly oppressed by the pharaohs. God intervened on their behalf, and under the leadership of Moses they made their exodus from Egypt. At that point in time, they were the early refugees who sought asylum in a place to which God had directed them. Their security in the new land lay in the covenant relationship they shared with God.

This experience has been transmitted from generation to generation in the history of people up to our present times. In Christianity we are confronted with a synthetic view of life that respects and upholds the human person, as well as promotes a recognition and observance of people's rights and freedoms, by individuals, communities, societies, and states. In this light the displaced person — the refugee, the asylum seeker, the mi-

Refugees in Asia
(from the U.N. World Refugee Survey, 1999)

Bangladesh
- Rohingya (50,000)
- Chin (3,000), from Myanmar
- Bihari (230,000), from Pakistan
- Chakma (40,000), from India

Burma/Myanmar
- 500,000 (1 million internally displaced in Burma)

Cambodia
- Over 22,000 internally displaced

China
- Vietnamese (281,000), from Vietnam
- Laos (1,000)
- Kachin ("Thaisands"), from Burma (no exact count)
- North Korea (over 100,000)

India
- Tibet (China) (110,000)
- Sri Lanka (110,000) (Tamils)
- Burma (40,000)
- Afghanistan (16,000)
- Bhutan (15,000)
- 520,000 internally displaced (350,000 Kashmiris)

Indonesia
- Over 10,000 internally displaced from East Timor, Acch, Irian Jaya, and ethnic Chinese

Iran (more refugees than any country in the world)
- Afghans (1.4 million)
- Iraqis (531,000)

Japan
- Over 1,000

Nepal
- Over 1,000, from Bhutan
- Tibet (3,100)

North Korea
- Over 100,000, to China for food

Pakistan
- Afghans (1.2 million)
- Kashmir (15,000)

Philippines
- Over 1,000, foreign
- 122,000 internally displaced
- (45,000 in Malaysia)

Sri Lanka
- 560,000 internally displaced
- (110,000 ethnic Tamils in India)

Thailand
- Burma (350,000), Karen, Shan, and Mon ethnic groups
- Cambodia (36,000)
- Laos (11,300)

Vietnam
- Cambodia (15,000)

grant — merits a special place. This has also been expressed in legalistic terms by the United Nations charter for refugees and displaced persons.

Analyzing the signs of the times in Asia, we realize that the reason we have so many displaced people — people on the move, without a home and without a land — is basically because there are two strong social categories in all our areas: the oppressor and the oppressed. Structured inequality (political, social, religious, economic), expressed in discriminatory laws, institutions, and practices, has led people to seek asylum elsewhere. Our refugees or displaced persons have been victims of several forms of repressive measures: detentions, trials, killings, torture, bannings, propaganda, states of emergency, and other desperate and tyrannical methods.

Working together for the common good of all people calls for an analysis of what the oppressed are going through. Wherever refugees or displaced persons are to be found in Asia, the symptoms of suffering seem similar. To begin with, the refugee goes through a state of humiliation.

Humiliation starts as a prejudice (racial, ethnic, national, religious, cultural, or political). One becomes a nobody, a nonperson in his/her own land. This uproots people from their homes, sometimes from land they owned for generations or from sacred places where their ancestors were buried, and makes them refugees. They find themselves dumped in damp, dirty places where there are no jobs and no land to work on. As workers, they are either unemployed, underemployed, or have no regular income at all. They speak of starvation wages, of being cheated and robbed. Punishment becomes their lot when they step out of line. They are mercilessly kicked, whipped, teargassed, wounded, raped, killed, petrol-bombed, burned, and imprisoned. There is evidence of indescribable horrors of torture all over Asia.

Our response to this suffering humanity in all its naked reality is first to be conscious of our sin in the suffering faces of our refugees. We have to bring them that message of hope by reaching out to them, to restore their credibility in humanity, by being open to all, minority or majority groups on a sociological level, by acknowledging their diversity of cultures and teaching them to be subjects of their own histories. This better future, however painful and hard, is a must for the churches in Asia, to restore that covenant relationship with our people.

Today in Asia there are refugees from economic oppression (job seekers from South and Southeast Asia), political oppression (from Vietnam*, China*, Cambodia*, Laos*, Myanmar*), and religious and ethnic oppression (Pakistan*, Myanmar, Cambodia, Afghanistan). Christian communities, which themselves are often very poor in Asia, seek to identify with refugees and meet basic human needs (see Racism).

Cambodian refugees. During the regime of the Khmer Rouge (1975-78), approximately 50,000 Cambodians took refuge in Thailand* and 150,000 in Vietnam. After the Vietnamese army seized power and occupied the country (1979-89), almost half the population left for Thailand. The greatest number went in search of food or seeds; then they returned to the country. Others preferred to remain in Thailand, where they have progressively chosen to migrate to the West.

Around 300,000 Cambodian refugees have been accepted in friendly countries (United States: 180,000; France: 60,000; Canada: 15,000; Australia: 15,000; etc.). Nearly 350,000 others lived for a dozen years in camps before being repatriated to Cambodia, according to the terms of the Paris agreement of 23 Oct 1991.

The church, both Protestant and Roman Catholic*, has been particularly present and active in those camps. Until 1979, only Robert Venet of the Foreign Missions Society of Paris* (MEP) visited the refugees, took them news and money, and facilitated contacts with embassies. Through the refugees, he was able to gather some information about the Christians remaining in the country. After 1979, when the presence of the refugees became a political issue, as a humane base for justifying the maintenance of the siege of Cambodia to the Khmer Rouge, the churches and the nongovernmental organizations (NGOs) surged.

The Catholic Office for Emergency Relief and Refugees (COERR) of Thailand officially permitted the presence of diverse Catholic NGOs in the camps and coordinated their work. The majority of those dispensed services would be useful then in their return to their country. One would notice more particularly the presence of the Jesuit* Refugees Service (JRS).

More than 1,000 Cambodian refugees discovered a new dimension in their lives: the traditional structures of life having been destroyed, they were more open to the Christian faith.

At the time of their return to Cambodia (after 1993), much against their will, these repatriated people had numerous difficulties in reentering: they had no land or money, were suspected of being foreign agents, and many went to be members of disinherited neighborhoods.

The repatriated Catholics had, for their part, some difficulty in entering the ecclesiastical groups, which were highly organized. In addition, the political climate was one of extreme suspicion. Nevertheless, those who managed that first difficulty gave new breath to the old community, which had been cut off from the outside for more than 15 years and knew little about the general evolution of the world.

Bibliography

Pastoral Care of Migrants and Refugees in Asia (1992). • *Muslim and Christian Perspectives and Practices* (1991). • *Working with Refugee Women* (1989). • *World Refugee Survey* (1994). • *The Many Faces of Women Migrants.* Cormack, Dan, *Killing Fields, Living Fields* (1997). • Ponchaud, François, *Cathedral of the Rice Paddy* (1990). • Chandler, David P., *A History of Cambodia,* 2nd ed. (1993). Archie d'Souza and François Ponchaud

Reid, Gilbert

(b. New York, 1857; d. Shanghai, 1927). American Presbyterian* missionary to China*.

Reid's ancestors were from Scotland, and his father was a clergyman. During his school days at Hamilton College, Reid had an admiration for Chinese Confucian culture. He graduated from Union Theological Seminary, New York, in 1882. In that same year, he was sent to China by the American Presbyterian Mission. He first arrived in Shanghai and was sent to Shantung for mission work, where he gained more opportunity to understand Confucianism*. During his furlough in 1892, he proposed an outreach to scholars and officials, but he met with objections from the mission board. Thus he formed a new board, the Mission to the Higher Classes in China (MHCC).

Two years later he returned to China independent of mission bodies and made friends among the royal family, such as Gong Qin-Wang. He was also employed by the London *Times* as a journalist and wrote articles in support of reformation. In 1897 the MHCC was renamed *Shang Xian Tang* (International Institute) in Peking (Beijing). However, the outbreak of the Boxer Rebellion* halted the activities, and the institution had to start all over again in Shanghai in 1903. Reid was principal of the institution and published *Shang Xian Tang Ji Shi* (All about the International Institute). His idea of "Confucius plus Jesus" was welcomed by the Qing government.

After the revolution in 1911, Reid showed empathy to Yuen Shi Kai's restoration of the dynasty. In 1917 he was appointed director of the *Peking Post* and was later exiled by the government because of his interference in China's internal affairs. In 1921 he returned to China and restored the International Institute and issued *Guo Ji Gong Bao* (International News). As he took a hostile stand toward the movement of 30 May, the International Institute hence acquired a bad name and Reid was depressed until his death.

Bibliography

Reid, Gilbert, *Glances at China* (1892); *China, Captive or Free? A Study of China's Entanglements* (1921); *A Chris-*

tian Appreciation of Other Faiths (1921); *The Siege of Peking* (1900). • Tsou Mingteh, "Christian Missionary as Confucian Intellectual: Gilbert Reid (1857-1927) and the Reform Movement in the Late Qing," in *Christianity in China from the Eighteenth Century to the Present,* ed. Daniel H. Bays (1996). • "Gilbert Reid's Biographical Record" is located at the Presbyterian Historial Society, Philadelphia, Pennsylvania. CHINA GROUP

Relics of Japanese Catholic Martyrs, Macau

Remains of the 188 martyrs killed between 1587 and 1614 in Japan*.

Some of the remains of the 188 martyrs killed between 1587 and 1614 at Yamaguchi, Kyushu, Nagasaki, etc., were brought to Macau* in the 1620s to 1630s by Japanese Catholics who took refuge there from persecution. This was intended to eliminate for centuries all public evidence of the Catholic faith in Japan.

On their arrival in Macau, the bones of the martyrs were placed in a chapel of the Church of the Mother of God (popularly known as St. Paul's). In 1806 the bishop of Macau opened the boxes and identified the bones, making up a list of 59 people. These remains almost perished in the fire of 1935. They had been kept in cases with detailed labels, but these were burned in the fire and the bones were later mixed with those of martyrs from Vietnam*.

The remains were then moved, first to the Church of St. Anthony and later to the Cathedral's Blessed Sacrament Chapel, where they remained until 1974, when they were transferred to St. Francis Xavier School on Coloane Island. In Sep 1976 they were enshrined in the Chapel of St. Francis Xavier there.

In 1991 Japanese experts examined the bones and managed to identify some of them. According to the wishes of Nagasaki Catholics, the relics of some of the martyrs were brought back to Japan on 20 Jan 1995 by Macau's bishop, D. Lam, in three reliquaries. Two of these were put in St. Philip's Cathedral, next to the Martyrs Monument in Nagasaki, and the third was put in the local bishop's house.

The bones, which remain in Macau, are intended to be placed for public veneration in a special crypt located in the museum which will be set up under the pavement of St. Paul's ruins.

Bibliography

Reliquias dos Martires do Japao (1995). • Davies, Shaan, *Macau Miscellany* (1992). SERGIO TICOZZI

Religious Affairs Committee

(RAC). National organization of the Chinese Catholic Church formed during the Representative Assembly of the Chinese Catholic Church in Jun 1980.

The aims of the RAC were to carry on the tasks of church building and preaching, guiding believers in obeying the Lord's commandments, adhering to the principles of independence and democratic management, holding consultations and making decisions regarding important religious matters, and developing international relations based on equality, goodwill, and mutual respect. RACs at the provincial and municipal levels were subsequently organized.

In addition to the RAC, the other two national bodies of the Chinese Catholic Church are the Patriotic Association (PA) and the Bishops' Deputation. In Sep 1992 a resolution was passed at the Fifth Representative Assembly to subordinate the RAC under the Bishops' Deputation, thus leaving the Chinese Catholic Church with two national bodies. CHINA GROUP

Religious Congregations, Indigenous. *See* Indigenous Religious Congregations

Religious Nationalism in the Philippines

There are three ways of understanding Filipino religious nationalism*. First, it can be understood to mean devotion to the interests of one's nation through religion as the unifying principle of nationhood. Advocates of religious nationalism in this respect believe that national advancement and independence can only be attained and sustained on the basis of linking religion and the nation-state and that this nation-state can only be construed in terms of religion or faith as its defining characteristic. This contrasts sharply with secular nationalism, which is understood as devotion to the interests of one's nation in economic and political terms in accordance with the people's free will, not God's will.

Religious nationalism, in the sense used above, exists in the form of Islamic nationalism in the southern Philippines. The seeds of Islamic nationalism and Muslim Filipino separatism began as early as the Spanish colonial period. Iberian colonial advance into the Philippines resulted in the religion of the colonizers, namely, Christianity, being imposed upon the colonized. This is unique in the modern period of Southeast Asia. However, Islam* preceded Christianity in the Philippines by a century and a half. In the southern islands in particular, it has deep roots. Under fundamental Islam, religion, culture, politics, and society are of one fabric. The Islamized southern islands became a world apart from the Christianized world of the northern Philippines. Consequently, the Muslim Filipinos developed a sense of separate identity from, rather than a shared identity with, the Christian Filipinos. The Muslims regarded the Christian-dominated government in Manila as foreign, *gobierno al sarwang.* This separatism was fueled by the typecasting of Muslims by Christians as inferior and fearsome, which ignored the rich culture and creativity of Muslim Filipinos. The outbreak of the Muslim secessionist rebellion, a protracted struggle that continues to this day, became the inevitable outcome of centuries of neglect by the central government and prejudice engendered by overzealous and intolerant Christian missionaries. A breakaway group of the Moro National Liberation Front called *Abu Sayyaf*, or "Bearer of the Sword," is particularly dedicated to the principles of Islamic fundamentalism.

Second, religious nationalism can be understood in the Philippines in terms of the establishment of indigenous or homegrown churches, although the religion involved is still of foreign provenance, namely, Christianity. Nevertheless, the establishment of these indigenous churches in the Philippines is viewed as a manifestation of Filipino religious nationalism in modern times. There are three prominent expressions of Filipino religious nationalism understood in this context. They are: (1) the *Iglesia Filipina Independiente** (IFI), or the Philippine Independent Church (PIC), also known as the Aglipayan Church, established in 1902; (2) the *Iglesia Evangelica Metodista en las Islas Filipinas* (IEMELIF), or the Evangelical Methodist Church in the Philippine Islands, organized in 1909; and (3) the *Iglesia Ni Cristo**, or Church of Christ, founded by Felix Manolo Ysagun (1886-1963) in 1911 and registered in 1914.

Third, Filipino religious nationalism is understood not only in terms of the establishment of homegrown churches, but more crucially in terms of a pure indigenousness in religious belief, *or taal na Filipino,* a religious belief that is purely Filipino in content and origin. The mystical mountain of Banahaw in the southern Tagalog region is one place among many others all over the Philippines where religious groups looking at themselves as pure expressions of Filipino indigenousness in religion can be found. Two of the better-known Banahaw sects today are *Tatlong Persona Solo Dios,* or "Three Persons One God," founded on 27 Aug 1936 by Agapito Ilustrissimo, a former commander of the Visayan peasant rebels known as the Pulahanes, and whose present *supremo* is Jose Ilustre, Agapito's son; and *Ciudad Mistica,* or "Mystical City," founded by a woman, Bernarda Batacan, shortly after 1910. The latter's leaders have all been women, and its incumbent *suprema* is Isabel Suarez.

Both groups, based respectively in Kinabuhayan and Santa Lucia, municipality of Dolores in Quezon Province, are very nationalistic in orientation. Stopping short of venerating Jose P. Rizal, the Filipino national hero, they regard him as a great representative of the Malay race. Some cults actually venerate Rizal, such as the *Watawat ng Lahi,* or "Standard of the Race." The ritual hymn of the Tatlong Persona Solo Dios sounds like the Philippine national anthem.

Many of the believers of Tatlong Persona Solo Dios and the Ciudad Mistica descended from Filipinos who resisted Spanish colonial aggression and fled to the Banahaw mountain to avoid owing homage to foreign rulers. By escaping to the mountain, they were branded by the Spaniards as *tulisanes,* or "bandits." *Suprema* Isabel Suarez, however, insists that her forebears and those of the Ciudad Mistica flock were not bandits — just people wishing to be free from colonial subjection. The Spaniards did often stereotype those who did not want to be part of the colonial order as outlaws, subversives, and troublemakers.

The Banahaw sects invariably refer to the "Voice" coming from the mountain. This voice guides them in their daily conduct morally and spiritually. Aside from the voice, they speak of the "Eye" which provided illumination from above to their ancestors through the darkness during the colonial period and which continues to provide them not only with illumination but with enlightenment as well. These beliefs reinforce their claim of being the true manifestations of "Filipino-ness" in religion. They are against foreign religions, such as Roman Catholicism, which is why the latter is attacking the Banahaw sects with "tongues of fire." There is no mutual tolerance, much less harmony, between the Banahaw sects and the Roman Catholic Church.

In summary, Filipino religious nationalism has taken three forms: (1) one of religion as the unifying and defining characteristic of the nation-state; (2) one of churches that are homegrown or established in the Philippines after breaking away from their mother churches; and (3) one of sects claiming to be absolute demonstrations of Filipino religiosity.

Bibliography

Bauzon, Kenneth E., *Liberalism and the Quest for Islamic Identity in the Philippines* (1991); "Modern Millenarianism in the Philippines and the State: Focus on Negros, 1857-1927," in *Sectarianism and the Secular State,* ed. Kingsley M. de Silva • Juergensmeyer, Mark, "The Future of the Secular State," in *Sectarianism and the Secular State,* ed. Kingsley M. de Silva • Meimban, Adriel Obar, "Religious Nationalism: The Role of Indigenous Churches" (lecture delivered at New Era College, Diliman, Quezon City, 1994); "A Historical Analysis of the Iglesia Ni Cristo: Christianity in the Far East, Philippine Islands Since 1914" (paper delivered at the 13th Conference of the International Association of Historians of Asia, Sophia University, Tokyo, 4-9 Sep 1994). • Maring, Ester G., and Joel M. Maring, *The Philippines* (1973).

Leslie E. Bauzon

Religious of the Sacred Heart

(RSCJ). Roman Catholic* religious congregation of women.

The RSCJ was founded in Paris in 1800 by Madeleine Sophie Barat (1779-1865) for the Christian education of girls after the French Revolution. It grew rapidly in numbers and in educational and religious influence in Europe and North America. During the lifetime of the foundress, 111 houses were founded in Europe, North and South America, and North Africa. A foremost missionary, Rose Philippine Duchesne, pioneered in the education of girls in St. Charles, Missouri, United States, from which the congregation spread to different states, establishing schools and colleges for women.

Recognized for their educational philosophy and pedagogy, particularly as described in *Education of Catholic Girls* by Janet Stuart (superior general from 1911 to 1914), the RSCJ received requests for foundations from many countries.

With the closure of 47 houses and the expulsion of the RSCJ from France at the time of the Third French Republic, new houses were founded in New Zealand and Australia, eventually leading to the establishment of the congregation in Asia. From Japan (founded in 1908), the congregation spread to China in 1926, Korea in 1956, Taiwan in 1960, and the Philippines in 1969. The congregation in India was founded from England in 1939. RSCJs are also working in Indonesia and among the Chinese.

Prior to Vatican II, the congregation was semi-contemplative, educating girls and women within convent premises according to a basic humanistic philosophy of education, with a uniform curriculum throughout the world. Today, considerable autonomy is allowed each province, and strong unity is created through frequent international meetings and regular communication. Its spirituality focuses on "union and conformity" with the heart of Jesus.

Japan. In 1908 the first convent and school in Japan* were founded by a group of RSCJs from Australia headed by Amelie Salmon. It came as a response to the appeal of Pope Pius X to the superior general in Rome to help provide Christian education* in Japan. The first schools were intended for the education of upper-class Japanese girls and some foreigners living in Tokyo. Four other similar foundations were made in Japan: Obayashi (near Osaka) in 1923; Shibuya, Tokyo, in 1948; Susono near Mt. Fuji in 1952; and Sapporo in 1963. Shibuya was the site of the University of the Sacred Heart, which has been a leader in Catholic higher education for women in Japan.

Foundations established after Vatican II, with its thrust of openness to the world and particularly to the world of the poor, shifted emphasis. Cloister, which had prevented the religious from going out of their compounds, was dissolved, and religious were now free to minister to the needier and poorer elements of Japanese society.

In 1967 a small community was begun in Amakusa in Hondo, an island near Nagasaki, to work among old Japanese Christians in a completely new way — in small institutions not owned by the congregation, in the parish, government school, and parochial kindergarten.

Other communities that opened followed this pattern: Nagoya in 1971 and three other houses in Tokyo: Adachi (1986), Sanya (1990), and Wakamiya (1991).

Works have also diversified. Aside from the traditional, established schools, some religious have gone into retreat and spiritual direction, counseling, and social service, particularly among day laborers, migrants, and alcoholics.

China. The foundation in China* was made from Japan and was led by Conchita Nourry. An international school and elementary and secondary Chinese schools were established in 1926 inside the French concession in Shanghai. In 1937 Aurora College for Women, affiliated with the Jesuit* Aurora University, was founded.

During World War I, the school compound became a concentration camp, and the college was turned into a Red Cross hospital. Life returned to normal until the gradual takeover by the Communists. In 1951 the schools were completely closed.

Korea. The foundation in Korea* in 1956 was a response to the call for the reconstruction of society needed after the Korean War*. The Korean and international schools in Seoul were opened the following year, and Sacred Heart College for Women began in 1964. Two small, makeshift schools for the poor were also set up. An evening school for religious women of different congregations was begun to provide them with an educational basis for their life and ministries. The number of RSCJs grew rapidly, as did the rest of the Korean church.

Most of the expansion in apostolic works in Korea took place in the capital city of Seoul, but ministries have been diversified to include parochial involvement and ministry with industrial workers. Outside Seoul, the religious have worked in a mining village as pastoral workers and nurses. Difficulties in personnel and finance necessitated the merger of the liberal arts college with two other institutions of higher learning in Seoul, leading to the establishment of the Catholic University of Korea.

Taiwan. A continuity of the work of Chinese RSCJs with their own people was sought in Taipei, leading to the foundation of a middle school in 1960 and an elementary school in 1964. An international school was built in 1966 and closed in 1971. Similarly, a college was built in 1967 but was closed in 1972.

Outside the work in schools, the religious have worked in other educational and social service agencies, teaching and counseling, and more recently, with migrant workers.

Philippines. The Philippines* marks a clear departure from previous RSCJ foundations. The religious opted in 1969 not to establish their own schools but instead to enter into already existing institutions and agencies. A diversity of ministries with the thrust for justice in solidarity with the poor characterizes the congregation in the Philippines. The religious are in campus ministry, political education, teaching and administration, pastoral work, community-based projects for the rural poor, ministry with industrial laborers, and counseling.

Indonesia. In 1984 an RSCJ was appointed to explore the needs of the country that the congregation could respond to. Although the perceived needs seem to be in more remote parts of the country, due to difficulties in obtaining resident visas for work in remote areas, the five

RSCJs who have worked in Indonesia* have had to work in institutions of higher learning in Jakarta.

India. The congregation went to India* in 1939 from England in response to the archbishop of Bombay's appeal to start a college for both Catholic and Muslim girls. Today, Sophia College, with its reputation for high academic standards and innovative methods, has provided space on its campus for a polytechnic, a school for mentally retarded children, and a training course for nursery school teachers.

A school was opened in Bangalore in 1948 but was handed over to another congregation in 1972 to allow the RSCJs to move toward the underprivileged, particularly in North India, and to enter into the ashram* movement.

Insertion among the poor began in 1961 with the foundation of a high school for the girls of the scheduled caste in Haregaon in Maharashtra. Later, in other villages in Maharashtra, other RSCJ communities were formed in an effort to improve the level of education and monitor the health needs in these villages. Similar communities were established in villages in Bihar for the uplifting of small children, school dropouts, and women. Work has begun in Torpa near Ranchi among tribal girls.

The RSCJs in India pioneered in the ashram movement by reopening an abandoned ashram in Pune in 1972 and later opening another at the foothills of the Himalayas, where both Christians and non-Christians from different countries have gathered.

Bibliography

Williams, Margaret, *The Society of the Sacred Heart* (1968); *The History of the Far East Province* (1973).

AMELIA VASQUEZ

Religious of the Virgin Mary

(RVM). The first indigenous congregation of religious women in the Philippines, the RVM was founded in 1684 in Intramuros, Manila, by Ignacia del Espiritu Santo* (1663-1748), a Filipino-Chinese *mestiza* from Binondo. During the Spanish colonial era in which Ignacia lived, no native woman could aspire to the religious life. The existing *beaterio* was open only to Spanish women.

When her parents wanted her to marry, the 21-year-old Ignacia adopted the spiritual exercises of St. Ignatius under the direction of Paul Klein (1650-1717). Having decided thereafter to "remain in the service of the Divine Majesty and live by the sweat of her brow," she left home, supported herself by needlework, and lived a life of prayer and penance. A community was formed when several women, attracted by her way of life, joined her. They lived in poverty* and sometimes had to beg for food. They were called Beatas de la Compañia de Jesus because they frequented the church of St. Ignatius and received spiritual direction from the Jesuit* Fathers. The name was changed to Compañia de la Beatas de la Virgen Maria (1912) and to Congregacion de Religiosas de la Virgen Maria (1932).

The community grew, and a set of rules and regular time order were drawn up for them. The *beatas* were known for their devotion, humility, application to work, and spiritual exercises. They accepted native, *mestiza,* and Spanish girls as boarders, taught them sewing and other skills, and formed them in Christian faith and life.

The 1726 constitutions presented by Ignacia to the archdiocesan office were approved in 1732. After her death (10 Sep 1748), King Ferdinand VI's decree of royal protection (25 Nov 1755) officially acknowledged the *beaterio* but explicitly defined it as a secular association. A royal decree (1761) ordered the *beaterio* to be placed under the direct supervision of the governor-general, and some parts of the constitutions that suggested religious life were to be changed.

The *beatas* were not officially religious but continued to live their "religious" life in the spirit of the original foundation. The archbishop of Manila recognized their status and, together with other churchmen, supported the *beaterio* and its retreat works. The *beatas* were placed under the guidance of the archbishop of Manila when they lost their Jesuit confessors and spiritual directors because of the Jesuit expulsion from the Philippines (1768-1859). They continued their apostolic endeavors, mainly retreats for women and the education of young girls.

When the Jesuits returned and established missions in Mindanao, they appealed to the *beatas* for assistance. Three new members of the *beaterio* responded and left for Mindanao (1875). They looked after young girls ransomed from slavery, while the Jesuits took care of the *beatas'* religious and spiritual formation. Soon *beaterios* were opened in Dapitan, Dipolog, Zamboanga, and Butuan (1880-96). The *beatas* distinguished themselves in the education of young girls.

The Spanish-American War led to the end of the Spanish colonial rule in the Philippines. The Mindanao *beatas* returned to Manila (1900) and were reunited with the Manila *beatas.* Since an episcopal mandate (1875) decreed that any *beata* who volunteered to go to Mindanao had to give up all rights to return to the mother house, the *beatas* petitioned for reorganization and the amendment of their constitutions. These were achieved in their first general chapter (1902). Since then, several schools were opened and other fields of apostolate were started throughout the country. The congregation was canonically erected (1906) and became an institute of pontifical right (1948) with the definitive approbation of its constitutions.

The first RVM missions outside the Philippines were opened in Sacramento, California (1959), Honolulu, Hawaii (1971), and Indonesia* (1977). Several mission houses were started in Papua New Guinea (1980), Rome (1980), and Ghana, West Africa (1982). Recent foundations include Islamabad, Pakistan* (1992), Papua New Guinea (1994), and Pago Pago, American Samoa (1995).

The RVMs, who number over 650, serve God in different fields of apostolate (schools, dormitories, retreats, seminaries, social ministry, formation, and special ministries) in several parts of the Philippines, Asia, Africa, Europe, and the United States. Education is their main apostolate. The RVMs manage 78 schools, eight of which are in foreign missions. They also serve through the dormitory and retreat apostolates and are strengthening their social and pastoral ministries. True to the spirit of the foundress, they also help in the formation of native religious communities in Africa.

Bibliography

Ferraris, Maria Rita, *From Beaterio to Congregation* (1975); *Beaterios for Native Women in Colonial Philippines* (1987). • Foronda, Marcelino, *Mother Ignacia and Her Beaterio* (1964); *Landmarks in RVM History* (1981).

Maria Anicia Co

Revivalism, Indonesia

Spiritual awakening produced by the Holy Spirit working among Christians in the church which results in genuine repentance; striving for holy living; love for God, fellow Christians, and fellow human beings; and enthusiasm for evangelism and missions often marked by signs and wonders.

In its relatively short history, Indonesian Christianity has experienced at least five particular revivals in accordance with the above definition. Those revivals are as follows.

Pietistic revival. Protestant Christianity came to Indonesia together with the Dutch United East India Company*, which ousted the Portuguese in 1605. However, early Indonesian Christianity was weak, evangelization was not seriously done, and Christians were not zealous. The pietistic movement in Europe changed the whole Indonesian scene. This movement influenced some European Christians, who formed several mission organizations that had a great interest in evangelism and making new converts in Indonesia*. Those organizations were Nederlands Zendeling Genootschap (NZG), Rheinische Missionsgesellschaft (RMG), and Basel Mission (BM). NZG came in 1814, its first missionaries being Joseph Kam* (who was actually sent by the London Missionary Society), Bruckner, and Super. Kam was stationed in Ambon, Bruckner in Central Java, and Super in Jakarta. RMG came in the 1830s. L. I. Nommensen* worked in North Sumatra with the people of Tapanuli; Barnstein, Becker, Huppert, and Kruismann evangelized Kalimantan*; and Colen and Emde worked in East Java. BM came in the beginning of the 1920s and worked in Kalimantan. Wherever they went, churches were planted and mass conversions took place. One of the most outstanding examples of this was the Nias Revival, which extended from 1916 until the mid-1920s. It began when a man was touched by the Word of God and repented. He made restitution with someone he had sinned against. This deed touched many people, and mass repentance and conversion spread all over Nias Island. Pietistic revival resulted in the forming of many national churches.

Pentecostal revival. Pentecostal* teachings were introduced in Indonesia by Bethel Temple Mission from Seattle, Washington, United States. Its first missionaries, Groesbeck and Van Claveren, arrived in Bali* in 1921. They stayed only one year, and their work was unsuccessful due to local rejection and government restrictions. In 1922 they left Bali for Surabaya. After cooperating with Bon Van Evangelisme, an existing evangelistic agency, these men were given permission to spread Pentecostal teachings in Java. Van Cleveren went to Lawang, Groesbeck to Cepu, and each traveled in East and Central Java. They preached the Foursquare Gospel: Jesus as lord and savior; Jesus as healer; Jesus as the baptizer of the Holy Spirit; and Jesus as the coming king. Their work in East and Central Java was successful. Revival took place, and the first Pentecostal worship was held in Cepu in 1922. It was testified that the worshippers were filled with the Holy Spirit and spoke in other tongues. The first Pentecostal mission was not only making new converts, but also training new workers with unusual zeal and enthusiasm. These new local workers spread Pentecostal teachings throughout Indonesia, and they claimed marked revivals, signs, and wonders. This revivalistic phenomenon continues in Indonesia, and Pentecostals have become one of the larger Christian groups in Indonesia.

Evangelical revival. This revival was sparked by the work of evangelist John Sung* from Fukien, China*. Sung was one of the most powerful Chinese evangelists of his time. He was greatly used by God to revive and rejuvenate churches. He preached the gospel of salvation and love. When Sung came to Surabaya in 1939, his first meetings were held during the daytime when people were at work, but the church was always full. People closed their stores and businesses to come to Sung's meetings. They learned some unconventional teaching, such as praying contemporaneously and loudly, singing short choruses, and crying for their personal sins. Wherever he went and wherever he preached, people were convicted of their sins and repented. They came forward, cried for their sins, and knelt down before the altar and prayed for forgiveness. Besides preaching for revival, Sung also helped local congregations form evangelistic bands. The people were trained to witness and evangelize. They were divided into groups with three people each. They carried flags and tracts and witnessed to their relatives, friends, and neighbors. This activity produced tremendous church growth, especially among the Chinese. Many people also left their businesses or work to be full-time servants of God. Sung's revival movement had a lasting impact in Chinese churches in Indonesia.

Charismatic revival. The modern charismatic* movement was started in the early 1960s in the United States. It can be termed the neo-Pentecostal movement because of its similarities with classical Pentecostalism in its stress on experience, action, and behavior, and also in its emphasis on speaking in tongues, healings, and some other miraculous gifts of the Holy Spirit. In Indonesia, this movement began in the middle of the 1960s, being brought to the country by charismatic American Episcopal missionaries. One of the most notable persons was the missionary Stubb. He stayed at Lawang, East Java, and from there spread charismatic teaching to other regions of Indonesia. He trained workers for that purpose. Full Gospel Business Men's Fellowship helped speed the spread of this movement; many professionals, artists, and businesspeople came to be Christians through the work of the charismatics. The impact of this movement is still being felt today. The charismatic revivalistic group has also become one of the largest Christian groups in Indonesia.

Second evangelical revival. The second evangelical revival began in the 1960s, but the way leading to this revival had been paved by the ministries of many parties in the 1950s and early 1960s. They were Leland Wang, Andrew Gih*, Tsao She Kuang, and Detmar Scheunemann. The work of Southern Baptist* Mission, Overseas Missionary Fellowship* (OMF), Wesleyan mission agencies, and World Evangelical Fellowship* with its Indonesian counterparts also made a significant contribution to the second evangelical revival. During the 1960s and on through the early 1990s, many new converts were added to the existing churches, new churches were planted, and church growth took place like never before in Indonesia. The zeal for evangelism was rekindled and strengthened. One of the most outstanding events of this period was the Timor* Revival in 1965. Signs and wonders also followed this revival, but the emphasis was still repentance and regeneration. Many intellectuals, businesspeople, and countless others were also brought to the church from the 1970s through the early 1990s. The most promising aspect of this period was the sharpening of young people's spiritual awareness. Revivals have helped Indonesian churches grow, and this has been due to the combined efforts of the Pentecostals, charismatics, and evangelicals.

Bibliography

Douglas, J. D., *New 20th Century Encyclopedia of Religious Knowledge* (1991). • Hartono, S. H., *Pietism in Europe and Its Influence in Indonesia* (1974). • Naipospos, P. S., *John Sung: God's Torch in Asia* (n.d.). • Peters, G. W., *Indonesia Revival* (1973). • Talumewo, S. H., *History of Pentecostalism* (1988). • Van den End, *Indonesian Church History*, 2 Vols. (1993).

Petrus Pamudji

Revolution of 1688

In the 17th c., Siam was opening itself to Western countries. All foreigners were welcomed by the king, Narai. This policy was provided to counterbalance the influence of these countries, because the period of maritime discovery was also the period of colonization. Also during this time, Siam was at war with Burma, Chiang Mai, and Cambodia*; the relationship with foreign countries helped guarantee the security of Siam.

Narai's positive attitude toward foreigners caused Constantine Phaulkon*, Guy Tachard*, and even Louis XIV to nurture false hopes of converting both the king and the country to Christianity. It is well known that the king of France took a lively interest in helping convert the king of Siam. Phaulkon was greatly embarrassed when Ambassador Chaumont insisted that the object for which the king of France had commissioned him was to obtain the conversion of the Siamese king.

Phaulkon himself realized that such conversion could not be obtained immediately, because it would cause rebellion in the country; Msgr. Laneau* also considered the demand for the king's conversion to be premature. Tachard was nevertheless anxious about establishing the Catholic religion in Siam. He would have had little difficulty persuading Phaulkon that the Jesuits* were the very people to give effect to this purpose, owing to the supremacy of their influence at that period over Louis XIV.

In fact, the king had never considered converting to Christianity. Clearly what King Narai had done for foreigners, and especially for missionaries, emanated from the political situation and was for political reasons. This misunderstanding led missionary activities to disastrous results when the famous Revolution of 1688 occurred. Phra Phetracha took power of Siam, and an anti-French attitude spread over the country. In short, the misreading of Siam's motives in foreign diplomacy led to a disaster both for French foreign relations and for missionary activity (see also Nationalism).

Surachai Chumsriphan

Reyes, Isabelo de los, Sr.

(b. Vigan, Ilocos Sur, Philippines, 6 Jul 1864; d. 10 Oct 1938). Labor and religious leader, newspaperman and patriot, and cofounder of *Iglesia Filipina Independiente** (IFI), popularly known as Don Belong.

Reyes studied at the Vigan Seminary and graduated from the University of Santo Toma in 1883 and the Notarial in 1887. He started writing for the press when he was 16 and founded *El Ilocano* (1889) and *El Municipio Filipino* (1894). In 1890, he became editor of *La Lectura Popular.* A prolific writer, his works included *Ilocanadas: Articulos varios sobre Etnologia; Historia y Costumbres del Pais; Las Islas Visayas en la Epoca de la Conquista;* and *Historia de Filipinas,* Vol. I. In addition, he was a businessman, a commercial agent, exporter, publisher, printer, and property owner in Manila, Tarlac, and Pangasinan.

Arrested in Dec 1896 on suspicion of subversion, Reyes was deported to Spain. He was released in 1898, when he was employed by the Overseas Ministry in Madrid. He continued his business endeavors, wrote for the Spanish press, translated the Gospels of Luke and John into Ilocano for the British Bible Society*, and published *La Sensacional Memoria sobre la Revolucion Filipina en 1896-1897, La Religion del "Kapitunan" Filipinas: Independencia y Revolucion!* and the fortnightly *Filipinas ante Europa.* He returned to the Philippines in Oct 1901 to resume journalism. He joined Pacual Poblete's *El Grito del Pueblo* and in 1902 founded the *Union Obrera Democratica* and co founded the IFI. He was jailed for labor agitation. In 1903-4, he published two fortnightlies: *La Iglesia Filipina Independiente: Revista Catolica* and *La Redencion del Obrero.* He was also one of the founders of the Republican Party of the Philippines (1905).

Reyes went to Spain in 1906 on business and to do research for the major liturgical, theological, and constitutional works of the IFI, such as the *Oficio Divino.* He returned in 1909 and published *La Religion Antigua de los Filipinos.* From 1912 to 1919, he was a councilor in Manila. In 1922, he was elected senator for Ilocos but suffered a stroke in 1929 and retired from politics. Thrice widowed, his 27 children included his junior namesake, who was *Obispo Maximo* of IFI for 25 years.

Bibliography

Llanes, Jose L., *Isabelo de los Reyes* (1949). • Scott, William Henry, *Cracks in the Parchment Curtain* (1982).

William Henry Scott

Rhee Seung Man

(Syngman Rhee) (b. 26 Mar 1875; d. Hawaii, United States, 19 Jul 1965). First president of the Republic of Korea* (South).

Rhee was an exiled independence fighter until he returned home in 1945 to assume the presidency of South Korea, which he did on 15 Aug 1948.

One of the first graduates of Pae Jae High School (founded by American missionaries), Rhee was deeply involved in the Korean newspapers, through which he advocated the enlightenment of the people and the independence of the nation (see Nationalism). As a progressive political activist, he participated in the Independence Club and the Ten Thousand People's Congress to protest against the Japanese advance to Korea and to advocate the reform of the old royal dynasty. When the Japanese-controlled royal court disbanded the Independence Club, Rhee was imprisoned with other nationalist leaders for nearly six years. In prison he read the Bible and was converted to Christianity.

After his prison term, he taught as principal of Sang Dong Youth Academy, a mission school, before studying politics at Georgetown and Princeton Universities in the United States, receiving a doctorate from the latter. Upon his return home in 1910, he was an active participant in youth movements such as the Young Men's Christian Association* (YMCA), of which he was one of the leading members. He decided to take an exile in Hawaii at the conclusion of the Japanese annexation of Korea in order to organize the independence movement in exile.

In 1919, when the Korean government in exile was formed in Shanghai, China, he was elected first as prime minister and later as president. Rhee worked hard to show the world that Koreans wanted an independent, sovereign nation through his diplomatic activities in the United States. But he had to wait until the Japanese were defeated in the Pacific War in 1945, upon which he returned home at age 70 to begin his political activity. Rhee's conservative, pro-American, and anti-Communist party won the general election of 1948 and formed a parliament that elected Rhee as the first president of the Republic of Korea (South).

He continued to serve as president during the Korean War*, and in the refugee assembly he was reelected for a second term, which ran until 1956. The constitution was changed to allow him to run for a third term, and he led the country as president until 1960. As he ran for a fourth term of office, the presidential election was rigged, and the students in major universities and high schools hit the streets to demonstrate against Rhee and demand his resignation. This was called the April 19, 1960, Student Democratic Revolution, in which hundreds of students in front of the presidential palace were killed by police shooting. Rhee apologized for the tragic incident and resigned his presidency.

Once again he was exiled to Hawaii, where he died in 1965. Until his death, he was a devout member of the Korean Methodist* Church, and while he was in Korea he attended Jung Dong Methodist Church in Seoul.

David Suh, with contributions from
Seo Jeong Min, translated by Kim In Soo

Rhenius, Charles T. E.

(b. Fortress Gravdens, Province of West Prussia, 5 Nov 1790; d. Palamcotta, India, 5 Jun 1838). Missionary to India* and one of first modern missionaries.

Rhenius occupied the foremost position among missionaries, not only in Tinnevely, where he labored from 1820 to 1838, but in southern India during the whole of his Indian life. He was one of the ablest, most clear-sighted, practical, and zealous missionaries that India has ever seen. A man of great administrative skill and fervent missionary zeal, Rhenius was an excellent preacher and a keen scholar in the vernacular. He was one of the hardest and most continuous workers with which India has been blessed.

Rhenius's father, an officer in the Prussian army, died when Rhenius was six years old. Until the age of 14, he remained at home in the care of his mother. When he was 17, he went to live with a childless uncle.

A missionary publication turned his thoughts toward foreign missions. In 1810 Rhenius entered a seminary in Berlin established to prepare young men to enter missionary work. But his mother was shocked when she heard that he wanted to be a missionary and was against his going overseas.

Rhenius was ordained in Berlin as a minister of the

Lutheran Church, the established church of Prussia, on 12 Aug 1812. He spent more than a year in England, a portion of this time under the roof of Rev. Thomas Scott, which further prepared him for the work he expected to enter into.

On 4 Feb 1814, Rhenius left London for Portsmouth and then for India as an appointed missionary. He reached Madras on 4 Jul. On 20 Jul he left Madras for Tranquebar* and remained until 9 Jan the following year, studying the language.

Rhenius went to Madras as the Church Missionary Society (CMS) missionary, under whose auspices he was laboring, desirous of establishing a mission at the capital of southern India. He settled in Madras and began practicing the vernacular.

He opened a school for boys, and instruction of young people became a very important part of his mission work. He introduced portions of Scripture as reading lessons. Having great talent in foreign languages, he was asked to revise the Tamil Scriptures. In 1817 the number of schools had increased, and he prepared his Tamil grammar for use in these normal schools. Meanwhile, the government had given permission to the church to form Tamil congregations. But the Hindus opposed the government, and this permission was withdrawn.

In 1818 Rhenius organized a society comprising Christians of all classes, Europeans, and natives of India called the Religious Tract Society of Madras, marking the beginning of his enterprises. After spending six years in Madras, Rhenius was appointed to a new field in the province of Tinnevelly.

Included in this new province was Palamcotta, the headquarters of the provincial government. Rhenius was requested by the missionaries of Tanjore to pastor the church established by his own society; about 10,000 people were enrolled under his pastoral care. He preached the Gospel not only in large towns but also in the surrounding villages and in the schools he established. He continued translating the Scripture into Tamil and also prepared a harmony of the Gospels, a work which has been used in South India. Rhenius also revised *India Pilgrim.* He founded training centers to equip people as catechists and teachers. At Tinnevelly, as in Madras, a religious tract association was formed, and Rhenius made a list of the villages in which there were Christians. In 90 villages, there were 838 families and more than 3,000 souls. On 3 Jan 1826, the foundation stone of the house of worship was laid in Palamcotta, and on 26 Jun it was dedicated to the worship of God. The number of schools was increased, and there was a good relationship between the parent church and converts from the outlying villages.

In 1832 there was a great drought and famine, as well as an outbreak of cholera. To foster the spirit of self-help, a poor fund was established to help the Christian congregation. Rhenius moved like an angel of mercy; enterprising, bold, and talented, he collected a good sum to help the people.

The Native Philanthropic Society was founded to help the poorer Christian natives in their temporal affairs, such as acquiring land and building schools and prayer houses. A Friend-In-Need Society was founded to care for its own poor. A Widow's Fund Society for relieving needy widows of catechists and schoolmasters was also established. In 1835 a Native Missionary Society, one of the earliest Asian mission societies, was organized for the maintenance of catechists who were sent outside the province. In the course of time, Rhenius, as a Lutheran* clergyman, naturally desired to ordain the men he had trained according to the order of the Lutheran Church, but the Society for the Propagation of the Gospel (SPG) refused. As a consequence of this interference, he left Tinnevely in hopes of establishing an independent mission elsewhere. He left the property he had acquired to the CMS.

He formed a new society and continued his literary labors, finding peculiar pleasure in the translation of the Scriptures into Tamil. He also completed his Tamil grammar. His cares during the whole of his missionary career had been heavy, and his labor unremitting. Since he entered India as a missionary in the summer of 1814, he had not left the country even for one day.

Rhenius died at the age of 48, having spent fully half his life in India. He was carried to his grave with great lamentation. His body rests in a quiet area in the church where he was working in Palamcotta.

Rhenius's Tamil writings may be looked upon as a legacy of no mean value to the Christian church of South India. More important, Rhenius opposed the observance of caste practices. When Hindu parents opposed the idea of making their children sit alongside and dine with Dalit* children and threatened to withdraw their children from the hostels, Rhenius pleaded with them for understanding. When they refused to oblige, he promptly ordered the closure of the hostel. Such was the man and his courage to take a stand.

Bibliography

Holcomb, Helen H., *Men of Might in India Missions: The Leaders and Their Epochs* (1901). • Mason, Caroline, *Lux Christ: An Outline Study of India* (1903). • Pickett, J. Waskom, *Christ's Way to India's Heart.*

FRANKLYN J. BALASUNDARAN

Rhodes, Alexandre de

(b. Avignon, France [see below for date]; d. Persia [Iran], 5 Nov 1660). French Jesuit* missionary who contributed to the development of the Vietnamese national script; linguist; author.

When Rhodes was born in France, it was then a papal state. There is some uncertainty about his date of birth. His birth record no longer extant, some historians put his birth on 15 Mar 1591, but according to Rhodes's own memoirs, he could have been born in 1593. His family was well connected with the Jesuits, his grandfather having donated to the Society of Jesus a piece of land in Cavaillon.

In 1612 Rhodes entered the Jesuit novitiate of St. Andrew at the Quirinal, Rome, with the desire to be a missionary to Japan*. After four years of theological studies, he was ordained to the priesthood, and in 1618 he was allowed by his superior general to go to the mission in the Far East. During the months before his departure, Rhodes deepened his knowledge of mathematics and astronomy, which would serve him well later in his missionary work. He sailed for Macau* on 4 Apr 1616 with five companions on the *Saint Theresa* via Barcelona, Lisbon, and Goa.

After a two-year stay in Goa (three months after his arrival, Rhodes fell seriously ill and was sent to the island of Salsette to recuperate), Rhodes received orders to leave for Japan. On 12 Apr 1622 he resumed his voyage, visiting Cochin, Ceylon (Sri Lanka*), Negapatam (Nagapattinam), Malacca*, and China* on the way. Rhodes arrived in Macau on 29 Mar 1623, intending to go to Japan later. Here he stayed at his order's famous Saint Paul College to study Japanese. However, as Japan had just expelled missionaries and began persecuting Christians, Rhodes's superiors sent him in Dec 1624 to what was known then as Cochinchina, or the "Inner Part" *(Đang Trong),* to reinforce his confreres who had begun missionary work there in 1615.

It is helpful to understand the geopolitical situation of Vietnam* at the time Rhodes began missionary work there. The reigning dynasty was the "Later Lê Dynasty" (so named to distinguish it from the "Former Lê Dynasty" of 980-1009). The Later Lê Dynasty was inaugurated in 1428 by Lê Loi, who assumed the name of Lê Th i Tô after liberating the country from the domination of the Ming dynasty and renamed the country from *Đai Ngu* to *Đai Viet* (Rhodes referred to the country as Annam). The Later Lê Dynasty officially ended in 1788 with its last king, Lê Chieu Thong, but already in 1527 power was wrested from it by the Mac dynasty, which ruled from 1527 to 1592. In 1532 two families, the Trinh and the Nguyen, rose up to defend the Later Lê Dynasty against the Mac dynasty and forced the latter to withdraw to the northernmost part of the country bordering China (Cao Bang). But the Lê kings were nothing more than puppets, and real power was in the hands of the Trinh and Nguyen families. Soon rivalries arose between the two families, the Trinh dominating the north (which Rhodes referred to as Tonkin and often called *Đang Ngoai,* the "Outer Part") and the Nguyen the south (which Rhodes referred to as Cochinchina and often called *Đang Trong,* the "Inner Part," which consisted of three provinces: Quang Binh, Thuan Hoa, and Quang Nam, now the central part of Vietnam. This "Cochinchina" differs from the later Cochin China, which was the French colony. In fact, the French referred to the north as Tonkin, the center as Annam, and the south as Cochin China.)

The war between the Trinh and the Nguyen began in 1627, the very year Rhodes went to Tonkin (indeed, he met the Trinh lord and his army on their way to war against the south), and lasted until 1672 without victory for either side. The country was divided into two parts, with the river Giang as the border, until it was reunified by King Gia Long of the Nguyen family in 1802; he named the country Vietnam. The rivalry between the north and the south complicated the work of missionaries, as one side often expelled them on the charge of spying for the other or used them to obtain merchandise and military wares from their countrymen, especially the Portuguese.

Mission in Tonkin. Christianity first arrived in Tonkin in 1583 with a group of missionaries, among whom was Bartholomeo Ruiz, who left in 1586 for Manila. The first Jesuits to be sent to the north were the Italian priest Giuliano Baldinotti and the Japanese lay brother Giulio del Piano. They arrived on 7 Mar 1626 to begin missionary work. They were warmly welcomed by Lord Trinh Trang, but Baldinotti left on 18 Aug of the same year because he did not know the Vietnamese language and also because his task was only to explore whether the conditions were favorable for missionary work. Following his report the Jesuit superior, Benedito de Mattos, decided to send Rhodes and Pedro Marquez* to Tonkin (to be replaced by himself and Antonio de Torres, who both arrived in Cochinchina in 1627). To avoid arousing the suspicion of Lord Trinh Trang, who disliked the Portuguese because of their dealings with the Nguyen, he had them return first to Macau and then sail for Tonkin on a ship of Portuguese traders. They arrived at Cua Bang port, Thanh Hoa, on the feast of St. Joseph, 17 Mar 1627. They stayed and preached there for 15 days and succeeded in converting many people, among whom was a magician who was harassed by demons even though he had 25 altars erected in their honor. He approached Rhodes for help, whereupon Rhodes gave him a crucifix and told him to remove all the altars and sprinkle the house with holy water. Freed from demonic disturbances, the magician asked for baptism.

Meanwhile, Lord Trinh Trang, who was organizing his first war against the Nguyen, sent word to the Portuguese traders that he would like to meet them. The two missionaries left Cua Bang for Hanoi to meet the lord; after a few days they met him, his fleet of 224 ships, his 300 elephants, and his army of more than 200,000 soldiers on their way to the south. The Portuguese merchants offered the lord gifts and arms for his military expedition, whereas the missionaries presented him with religious articles. The lord ordered them to wait for him near Thanh Hoa until his return from the war, and the missionaries stayed there for two months and converted more than 200 people. Lord Trinh Trang returned in defeat, and the missionaries joined him on his way back to Hanoi. Rhodes then gave him a copy of Euclid's geometry in Chinese and attempted to preach the faith to the lord, but he remained indifferent. The missionaries arrived in Hanoi on 2 Jul 1627 and were given a house near the lord's palace. Among the many who came to listen to their preaching was the lord's sister, who converted and took the name of Catherine. She was instrumental in converting her mother and 17 other people in her family. From Christmas 1627 to Easter 1628, 500 people were baptized, many of whom belonged to the nobility. After conversion, the men renounced their concubines, thus angering them and their guardians, who began accusing the missionaries of being magicians capable of killing with their breath. Trinh Trang gave credence to their accusations and grew cold toward the missionaries.

During this difficult time, a lunar eclipse was about to occur. According to popular belief, an eclipse is caused by the sun or the moon being eaten by a dragon. To relieve the pains of the sun or the moon, an order was given to shoot, ring bells, and beat drums and other instruments in the belief that such din would scare the dragon to cough up the heavenly bodies it was devouring. Rhodes's knowledge of astronomy stood him in good stead. He impressed Trinh Trang with his explanation and prediction of the lunar eclipse and regained the lord's favored treatment for the missionaries.

Missionizing was done apace, and by Trinity Sunday in 1628 there were 1,600 Christians. Once again these conversions aroused hatred for the missionaries. Since they had baptized many dying people, they were accused of killing them. Furthermore, one Buddhist monk accused them of conspiring with the Mac dynasty to topple the Trinh and even of planning to burn Hanoi. Trinh Trang again issued an edict forbidding the new religion. The missionaries were to be confined to their house, with guards keeping watch to prevent the faithful from coming to see them. After 15 days, Rhodes got out of the house and began visiting the faithful in secret. During this time a captain and his family converted, and Rhodes gave him the name of Ignatius. Rhodes divided the city into seven districts; each district had a chapel where the faithful gathered to worship, listen to the Bible and the lives of the saints, and say their daily prayers.

One of Trinh Trang's intentions in allowing missionaries to stay in his country was to attract Portuguese traders. Because many Portuguese ships were sunk near Hai Nam and no merchandise was brought to Hanoi, the lord was disappointed and angry at the missionaries and asked them if they wanted to go back to China. They said they would leave after the Portuguese ships had arrived. At the beginning of 1629, when no Portuguese ship showed up, the lord ordered Rhodes and Marquez to leave for Cochinchina, though he did give them as parting gifts 20 ounces of gold and several meters of cloth. About 500 faithful bade them farewell. In Mar 1629 they sailed for Thanh Hoa (where two years earlier they had been left to wait for the lord's return from the war in the south), then for Nghe An. Upon arriving at Cochinchina, they did not want to cross the border for fear of being charged as spies for the Trinh by the Nguyen lord, Nguyen Sai. They remained at Bo Chinh, where they baptized 25 people, and then went back to Nghe An. Here they were able to predict a solar eclipse on 25 Aug 1629 to the governor of the province, who treated them favorably because he believed that, if these men knew the secrets of the natural heaven, they would also know those of the supernatural heaven. Their preaching brought 600 people to the faith.

In the meantine, they learned that a Portuguese priest, Gasparo d'Amaral, and a Japanese priest, Saito Paolo, were arriving in Hanoi, so they went to meet them. Lord Trinh Trang, hearing that a Portuguese ship had arrived, sent word to the captain and his sailors that he would like to see them, without the missionaries. He was told that, unless the missionaries were allowed to enter, they would not come. So Rhodes and his companion were able to go back to Hanoi. But they could not remain there long because the lord once again ordered them to leave. Hearing of their banishment, the faithful came for confession during five days and nights. On 5 Jun 1630 Rhodes, Marquez, d'Amaral, and Saito Paolo boarded the ship for Cua Bang port, but not before they had baptized 22 more people. Here ended Rhodes's mission in the north; in three years he and his companions succeeded in building a church of more than 5,000 people.

The organization of catechists. Another lasting accomplishment of Rhodes was his organization of lay catechists first in the north, and later in Cochinchina. Indeed, the extraordinary success of his preaching rendered the collaboration of lay catechists a necessity. The need for collaborators had been discussed at the first assembly of Jesuit missionaries in 1625 at Hai Pho in which Rhodes took part. Their superiors in Macau* thought the organization of collaborators should be disbanded and that local people should not be employed for the work of mission. On the contrary, the missionaries saw the necessity and usefulness of having local people as collaborators, especially in the preparation of catechumens, because they knew the language and were familiar with the native customs. Their assistance was compared to the feet of missionaries which went where the missionaries were either unable or forbidden to go. They were, so to speak, the missionaries' eyes and ears to detect unfavorable reactions to Christianity.

In 1627, when he was first missionizing in the north and was faced with the rapidly increasing number of conversions, Rhodes made use of educated converts such as Buddhist monks and Confucianist teachers to assist him in catechesis. In the north he discovered that families had the good custom of sending their young children to Buddhist monks at monasteries or to Confucianist teachers to be formed intellectually and morally. Christians too wanted to have their children live with missionaries and be educated by them. The four young men chosen by Rhodes were Francis, Andrew, Anthony, and Ignatius. Francis, a Buddhist monk for 17 years and the first Vietnamese Christian to be martyred (in 1630 or

1631), was baptized on the feast of St. Francis Xavier and hence named after the saint. He wanted to live and work with Rhodes and was assigned the task of copying the catechetical lessons and teaching them to others. In 1629 Andrew brought to Rhodes 112 catechumens, whom he had taught the faith, to be baptized. His zeal and piety so impressed Rhodes that he enlisted him as catechist. Anthony was 30 years old at his conversion and resigned from his military service to work for Rhodes. Ignatius was a cavalry captain and, after his conversion, helped Rhodes teach and baptize 600 catechumens in 1629 at Nghe An.

When he was deported to Cochinchina in Mar 1629, Rhodes took with him Ignatius and Anthony, leaving behind Francis and Andrew to take care of the faithful in Hanoi. However, Rhodes was concerned that a more stable organization of catechists be established to help the church during the missionaries' absence. After he, his companions, and his catechists returned to Hanoi on the Portuguese ship shortly after their banishment to Cochinchina in 1629, and before their final departure in Jun 1630, Rhodes had the idea of having the four catechists take vows as religious. During the last mass before their departure, in a solemn ceremony, the catechists swore on their knees, with their hands on the Bible, that they would remain celibate until the return of the missionaries, that they would not keep for their private use whatever money or gifts were given by the faithful, and that they would obey the leader appointed by Rhodes. Ignatius was appointed their leader, and Rhodes wrote down a few rules for them to observe during his absence.

The catechists trained some 100 other catechists. When Gasparo d'Amaral returned after a 10-month absence to Hanoi in the spring of 1630, he found they had established 20 new churches and baptized 3,340 catechumens.

Mission in Cochinchina. Rhodes returned to Macau in 1630 and remained for 10 years, until Feb 1640, when his superior Antonio Ruben sent him back to Cochinchina. After his arrival at Hai Pho, he was introduced by the city governor, a Japanese he had befriended, to the new Nguyen lord, Cong Thuong Vuong (who had succeeded Sai Vuong in 1636), to whom he presented several gifts. At Hue he stayed at the house of Minh Duc Vuong Th i Phi, a concubine of Lord Nguyen Hoang (the grandfather of Lord Cong Thuong Vuong), whom Jesuit Di Pina had baptized and given the name of Mary Magdalene. Rhodes remained at Hue for 35 days and baptized 94 people, among whom were one Buddhist monk and three members of the lord's family.

After visiting Thuan Hoa Province, Rhodes came back to Hai Pho. The governor of Quang Nam then decided to expel missionaries, so in Sep 1640 Rhodes left for Macau but returned with Benedetto de Mattos on 17 Dec 1640 to Cua Han, from where he visited the provinces of Quang Nam, Binh Dinh, and Phu Yen and baptized 1,305 people. The governor of Quang Nam issued an edict expelling Rhodes and de Mattos. In Jul 1641 the missionaries left for Manila on the way to Macau. At the end of Jan 1642, Rhodes came back to Hai Pho and immediately went to Hue to offer gifts to Lord Cong Thuong Vuong, including some watches. The lord was pleased. During the day Rhodes taught the lord mathematics, and at night he preached. Soon, however, the lord expelled him from Hue; Rhodes came back to Cua Han, where he hid during the day and preached during the night. During this time he trained many collaborators such as catechists Andrew, Ignatius, and Vincent.

After two years of clandestine activities, Rhodes was advised by the Portuguese to leave the country. Before he went back to Macau in Sep 1643, Rhodes gathered 10 catechists and had them take religious vows, as he had done in Tonkin. During his absence the catechists baptized 293 dying people. After a short stay in Macau, Rhodes once again returned to Cochinchina in Jan 1644. He met the catechists at Cua Han, and together with them went to Hue to offer gifts to the lord. On this occasion he baptized 200 people, among whom were a military officer and his family and many soldiers. Again in Sep 1644 he was ordered to leave the country. After boarding a Portuguese ship, Rhodes and nine catechists disembarked in secret and came back to land. Rhodes sent Ignatius to the northern provinces of Cochinchina, whereas he visited its southern provinces. As they were passing through Quy Nhon, Rhodes and his companions were arrested but later released by the presiding officer. To mislead the authorities, the faithful spread the rumor that Rhodes had left for Europe; meanwhile he hid in the house of a widow and continued his ministry, traveling around undetected. On 26 Dec 1644, as he was listening to confession on a boat, he was arrested, but once again the lord ordered him released. Rhodes left Qui Nhon for Hai Pho on 15 Feb 1645. From there he went to Cua Han, Hue, and the province of Quang Binh. On the way he was arrested together with nine faithful (among whom were catechists Ignatius and Vincent, who were later martyred); they were brought back to the capital, where the lord decided this time to have him killed. He was spared death by the intervention of a court official, but was ordered to be expelled and was imprisoned in Hai Pho while waiting for a Portuguese ship. While in prison, a Japanese Christian regularly brought Rhodes a ladder he used to climb over the prison wall at night and go out to minister to the faithful and then climb back into the prison in the early morning. He did this for 22 days and baptized 92 people.

On 3 Jul 1645, Rhodes boarded the ship for Macau. An official recited the edict of expulsion and threatened with death any ship captain who would bring him back into the country. Here ended Rhodes's four years of clandestine mission in Cochinchina, with four expulsions from the country. Three years in the north and four years in the south allowed him to create a vibrant church. Soon the church would be tested by persecution. Among his close collaborators, three were martyred: Andrew of Phu Yen (1644), whose death was witnessed and recorded by Rhodes himself, and Ignatius and Vincent in 1645, after Rhodes had left the country.

Lobbying for the establishment of a hierarchy in Vietnam. Rhodes left Macau on 20 Dec 1645, sailing to India en route to Lisbon. On 14 Jan 1646, he landed in Malacca, a former prosperous Portuguese port which had fallen to the Dutch in 1642. Rhodes, who had visited Malacca 23 years earlier, was saddened by the suppression of the Catholic Church by the Protestant Dutch. From Malacca he boarded a Dutch ship for Batavia, where he was jailed for two months because he was found saying mass in the house of a Portuguese.

After three years of adventurous travel, Rhodes arrived in Rome on 27 Jun 1649. Realizing that, with the decline of the Portuguese in the East, Catholic mission in Vietnam would lose a major support, Rhodes devised plans to strengthen it. At the time, the church in Tonkin belonged to the diocese of Macau in China, and that of Cochinchina to the diocese of Malacca in Malaysia, both located in Portuguese colonies. In his first report to the Congregation for Missions (Propaganda Fide*) on 2 Aug 1650, he pointed out that there were 300,000 faithful in Vietnam, with an average annual increase of 15,000. Pastoral care of that population would require at least 300 missionary priests from Europe, a number both hard to obtain and which would also create opposition from the governments of Tonkin and Cochinchina. The best solution would be to create a native hierarchy, beginning with the ordination to the priesthood of catechists who had met the requisite conditions. Anticipating objections to his proposal from the Portuguese crown and also because of the relative youth of the church in Vietnam, Rhodes suggested that the holy see appoint bishops as apostolic vicars under its direct authority and emphasized that the willingness of the church in Vietnam to suffer martyrdom provided proof of its maturity. On 1 Aug 1651, Propaganda Fide proposed to Pope Innocent X that he send a patriarch, two or three archbishops, and 12 bishops to Vietnam. The pope thought the measure premature, and Rhodes's proposal went unheeded. In May 1652, Rhodes wrote a second report, similar to the first, and sent it directly to the pope, emphasizing that the Vietnamese church had suffered martyrdom and that there were well-prepared candidates for the priesthood among the 100 catechists he had trained. On 30 Jul, Propaganda Fide met with the pope and decided to send a visitor to Vietnam to inspect the situation. The pope considered Rhodes the best candidate to be the bishop in Annam, but Rhodes declined the nomination, not because he was barred from seeking episcopal honors as a Jesuit, but because his expulsion prohibited his return to Vietnam. Instead, he was made head of the Vietnamese mission and was charged with recruiting missionaries for it.

On 11 Sep 1652 he left Rome for France, where he contacted several Jesuits, among whom were 20 novices who volunteered for mission. He also recruited priests who were Jesuit alumni and who belonged to the association, Société des Bons Amis. Three among them, François Pallu*, François Laval, and Bernard Piquet, were judged worthy candidates for the episcopacy. On 7 Mar 1653, Rhodes submitted their names to Propaganda Fide. Unfortunately, Rhodes's project was opposed by the Portuguese crown, which had received from the holy see since the 16th c. the right to nominate bishops in the lands they discovered (the *Padroado* system). But it was supported by the French hierarchy, especially by Saint Vincent de Paul and the archbishop of Rheims. In Aug 1658, Pope Alexander VII appointed François Pallu (founder of the Missions Étrangères de Paris) as bishop of Tonkin and Lambert de la Motte* as bishop of Cochinchina. As for Rhodes, his superiors, under pressure from the Portuguese crown, sent him as missionary to Persia. On 16 Nov 1654, he left Marseilles for Persia and died there on 5 Nov 1660.

Rhodes's contributions to the Vietnamese culture. In addition to his missionary accomplishments, Rhodes has left an extraordinarily important legacy to the Vietnamese culture, that is, his contribution to the formation of the national script which had been devised by a number of Italian and Portuguese missionaries. Rhodes himself was a highly gifted linguist, fluent in some 13 languages. The national script, in contrast to the Nom (Nam) script, uses the Roman alphabet and diacritical marks to distinguish various tones of the Vietnamese language. Invented in the early part of the 17th c. and improved during 150 years by missionaries for the use of Catholics, the Roman script was recognized as the national script on 6 Apr 1878 in Cochinchina, effective on 1 Jan 1882 and later in Tonkin.

In 1651 Propaganda Fide published *Rhodes's Cathechismus pro iis qui volunt suscipere baptismum in octo dies divisus* (Catechism Divided into Eight Days for Those Who Want to Receive Baptism). This 324-page bilingual text (Latin and Vietnamese in Roman script) is the oldest extant prose work in the Vietnamese language. As Rhodes informed us, this work had been in circulation in Vietnam in manuscript form since 1624, and in composing it, he had availed himself of the assistance of the natives, especially the catechists.

In the same year, Propaganda Fide also published Rhodes's 500-page *Dictionarium Annamiticum Lusitanum et Latinum* (Vietnamese Portuguese and Latin Dictionary). In preparing this dictionary, Rhodes made use of the dictionary of Gaspar d'Amaral, *Annamiticum-Lusitanum,* and that of Antonio Barbosa, *Lusitanum-Annamiticum.* Appended to the dictionary is Rhodes's essay on the grammar of the Vietnamese language, *Linguae Annamiticae seu Tonchinensis brevis declaratio,* an eight-chapter monograph with separate pagination. In recognition of Rhodes's permanent contribution to the language and culture of Vietnam, the government celebrated the third centenary of his arrival in Tonkin in 1927 and of his death in 1961.

Bibliography

Rhodes, Alexandre de, *Histoire du Royaume de Tunquin et des grands progrès que la prédication de l'évangile y a fait en la conversion des infidèles. Depuis l'année 1627 jusques à l'année 1646* (1651); *Relation des progrès de la foi du royaume de la Cochinchine vers les derniers quartiers du Levant* (1652); *La glorieuse mort d'André Catéchiste de la Cochinchine qui a le premier versé son sang pour la querelle de Jésus-Christ en cette nouvelle Eglise* (1653); *Divers voyages et missions du P. Alexandre de Rhodes en la Chine et autres royaumes del'Orient, avec son retour en Europe par la Perse et l'Arménie* (1653); *Sommaire des divers voyages et missions apostoliques du R. P. Alexandre de Rhodes de la Compagnie de Jésus, à la Chine, et autres Royaumes de l'Orient avec son retour de la Chine à Rome. Depuis l'année 1618 jusques à l'année 1653* (1653). • Phan, Peter C., *Mission and Catechesis: Alexandre de Rhodes and Inculturation in Seventeenth-Century Vietnam* (1998). PETER C. PHAN

Riberi, Antonio

(b. 1897; d. Dec 1967). Vatican representative to China* (1946-49) and Taiwan* (1953-59).

A native of Monaco, Riberi was consecrated a priest in 1922, and from 1925 he worked as a diplomat for the church. In 1934 he was assigned as Vatican representative to East Africa and consecrated an archbishop. He traveled extensively in East Africa but was unable to return because war broke out in Europe at the time he went to make a report to the pope. At Christmas time of 1942, he brought greetings from the pope to the American and British troops held in the concentration camp in Italy. On 6 Jul 1946, the Vatican decided to establish an embassy in China. Riberi, appointed consul, arrived in Shanghai on 14 Dec. He presented his credentials to President Jiang Jie Shi (Chiang Kai-shek) in Nanjing on 28 Dec and expressed the hope that Jiang would defeat the Communist Party of China. In 1949, when the People's Republic of China was established, Riberi remained in Nanjing as an ordinary citizen of Monaco but continued to function privately as the Vatican's consul and a leader of the Chinese Catholic Church. He implemented Pope Pius XII's policy toward China forbidding Chinese Catholics to support the new government. In Mar 1951, when the coadjutor of Nanjing, Li Wei Guang, and priests, nuns, and 793 church members expressed their support of the new government, Riberi sent letters of opposition to bishops in the various dioceses. He was expelled from China in Sep 1952 but stayed in Hong Kong* for 13 months. He went to Taiwan in Oct 1953, established diplomatic ties between the Vatican and Taiwan in November, and became the Vatican's consul to Taiwan with a consulate in Taipei. He left Taiwan in 1959 and became the Vatican's ambassador to Ireland. In Jun 1967 he was made a cardinal.

Bibliography

Wiest, Jean-Paul, *Maryknoll in China* (1988).

CHINA GROUP, translated by DAVID WU

Ricci, Matteo

(b. Macerata, Italy, 16 Oct 1552; d. Beijing, 11 May 1610). Pioneer Jesuit* missionary to China* and advocate of the Jesuits' missionary method of accommodation who became the religious and cultural bridge for all subsequent Catholic Christian endeavor in that country.

After studying law in Rome, Ricci entered the Society of Jesus in 1571 and embarked in its training program for missionaries. Very shortly thereafter, he entered into his scholastic endeavor at the Roman College, where he studied theology, mathematics, science, and a broad range of ethical subjects. Particularly was he introduced to Stoic moral philosophy. For Ricci and his Jesuit colleagues, this humanistic learning system, as well as the emerging physical sciences, was the foundation for the Christian faith and the revelation of Jesus Christ.

Beginning in May 1577, he spent nine months at the University of Coimbra learning Portuguese and receiving further grounding in Aristotelian and Thomistic thought. This educational background became the basis for the Western learning which Ricci and other Jesuits introduced to China. Ricci left Lisbon on 24 Mar 1578 and spent four years in Goa, where he taught, continued his study of theology, and tried to regain his health. While in Goa he was consecrated a priest on 26 Jul 1580. Alessandro Valignano*, visitor and vicar-general for the Jesuits in India, assigned Ricci and Michele Ruggieri*, an Italian Jesuit colleague, to the China mission in 1582. He also greatly influenced Ricci by his theory and practice of accommodation growing out of his experience in Japan (see Contextualization).

In 1580 Ricci reached Macau* and immediately began studying the Chinese language and script. In 1583 Ricci and Ruggieri obtained permission from the governor-general of Guangdong and Guangxi Provinces in China to reside in the city of Zhaoqing (Chao Ch'ing), a few miles north of Guangzhou (Canton). Initially the two missionaries dressed in the gray robes of Buddhist monks, assuming that this would gain them the respect of the people. Gradually Ricci learned that these religious figures were despised in society and gave him little access to the scholarly class whose influence he desired. Ten years later, after political pressure caused Ricci to move to Shaozhou, he changed his garb to that of the Confucian* literati. In 1584 Ricci drew a world map with China in the center, a map which was greatly respected and widely distributed in China.

To identify with the elite of China meant much more than external dress. The missionaries had to avoid studiously any criticism of Confucius, the patron saint of the literati. They had to be ostentatious in their display of learning in order to meet the expectations of literate and illiterate alike, who felt that letters and science must be of high repute in Europe, and that these men were surely some of the best representatives of that learning. Ricci's European educational background in astronomy, mathematics, science, and philosophy prepared him well for this role. At the same time, he was not patronizing in his attitudes. He did not refuse, for example, to perform the "bowing" ceremonies that later Protestants were loath to observe. When asked why he was in China, Ricci's usual reply was that he had come as an ignorant barbarian to learn from China's fine teaching.

Ricci's goal was to reach Beijing (Peking) and to be able to influence the emperor and other officials to receive the Christian faith. After Ruggieri's departure in 1588, the governor of Zhanqing, Liu Jiezal, forced Ricci to leave. He proceeded to Shaozhou but with Beijing as his hoped-for destination. During his sojourn, he engaged in learned conversations with scholars on many religious and philosophical topics, such as human nature; demonstrated his scientific learning; and began to write materials that would help the faith penetrate Chinese culture.

In Shaozhou, Ricci was visited by Qu Rukei, who was drawn by Ricci's reputation. Ricci imparted some knowledge of European mathematics and explained Catholicism to him. Qu advised Ricci to don the silk robes of the Chinese literati. After six years each in Zhaoqing and Shaozhou, there were still not many converts. In 1595 Ricci sought a chance to leave Shaozhou and set up residences in Nanchang and Nanjing. He did preaching by means of scientific learning. While he continued with his Chinese studies, he introduced the Chinese to Western philosophy and science. In 1598 Ricci failed to secure a meeting with the Chinese emperor in Beijing. His second attempt in 1600, however, came to a successful conclusion. The gifts he carried to Beijing to be presented to the emperor included a striking clock, a harpsichord, an album of world maps, a portrait of the Heavenly Lord, a portrait of the Madonna, a cross, etc. Among all the gifts, the clock and the harpsichord were most treasured by the Wanli emperor. With the tacit consent of the emperor, Ricci was finally able to reside in Beijing and establish his residence there. This marked a turning point in the history of his missionary work in inland China, because, in the subsequent 10 years, he realized much greater successes than he had in the previous 17.

Ricci became friends with several important scholars and government officials, including the grand secretary Xu Guangxi*, who became a Christian. The method of cultural accommodation he and his Jesuit companions implemented aimed first at proving that no irreconcilable differences existed between Chinese culture and the Christian message, and second at dressing up this message as much as possible in Chinese garb. The prevalent view among the Jesuits of honors rendered to Confucius as nonreligious ceremonies and of ancestor veneration as nonsuperstitious acts led sadly to the Rites Controversy (see Ancestor Worship).

One of Ricci's first efforts at this accommodation was to publish a tract on friendship, a subject of extreme importance and interest to the Chinese, for whom friendship and human relationships rank above other virtues. Of equal importance to this small booklet was Ricci's own modeling of friendship. He was more than a scholar — he was a remarkable human being whose life of friendship, humility, and love demonstrated the faith of which he wrote. Many have noted that even when nearing death, his willingness to be hospitable to many visitors to the very end meant that he was a martyr to friendship.

Among the scientific works which Ricci, with help from two scholars, Xu Guangqi and Li Zhizao*, translated into Chinese, none was more important than Euclid's *Elements of Geometry.*

Another major effort made by Ricci was a series of 25 tracts on diverse moral questions and ways that people might control their evil tendencies. This kind of publication, referred to by the Chinese as "opinions" or "sentences," was cast in a form familiar to them (see Literature and Publishing).

The most important of Ricci's original works was undoubtedly *Tianzhu Shiyi* (The True Idea of God). Prepared as a preevangelistic work for non-Christians rather than for converts, this book — finally approved in 1603 when its author was 52 years old — was an apologetic for the Christian faith and represented nine years of Ricci's life. For many of the elite, it was the Gospel in Chinese for late Ming and early Qing (1644-1911) China, because it spoke directly to the contemporary Chinese context.

Two assumptions guided Ricci in writing this significant book. First, the Chinese mind needed to be approached by way of "natural law," the theory that human beings are able to reason from human nature and from the nature of the universe to the existence and nature of God and the kind of moral life pleasing to God. Ricci's second assumption was that contemporary neo-Confucian thought, originating some 400 years before Ricci and filled with many metaphysical ideas coming from Buddhism* and Taoism*, was a perversion of the traditional Confucian legacy dating back to Mencius, Confucius himself, and even to the revered sage-kings of ancient Chinese history. Ricci believed that this tradition had an awareness of a supreme deity and was derived from the teaching of early Jewish missionaries who made their way to China after the flood that covered the earth in the days of Noah. In short, Ricci believed that theological and moral truth could be found in the ancient Chinese writings and, when clarified, purified, elevated, and supplemented by a more direct biblical revelation, could serve as the Gospel in Chinese.

Many criticisms have been leveled at Ricci's views and his work from that time until now. He has been faulted for his views on Confucianism, for his forcing of Christian truth into unacceptable Chinese forms, for his failure to include more specific Christian truth, and for his lack of understanding of Buddhism and Taoism. Notwithstanding the accuracy of many of these evaluations, his landmark effort has continued to have significance as the first bridge in East-West communication and understanding.

The True Idea of God included many subjects of interest to non-Christian inquirers. Among these were the existence of a supreme being, creation, providence, human nature, the nature of the human soul, the world of demons, transmigration, the existence of heaven and hell, a defense of celibacy within the Catholic Church leadership, and a very short section on God's sending of Jesus into the world to be the Savior.

With Ricci's death in 1610 in Beijing, the first period of the Jesuit mission in China came to an end. Many Chinese scholars became Christians during his lifetime, and hundreds of converts were also made by Ricci's Jesuit colleagues in many places in the countryside as well. Ricci was buried with the emperor's sanction in Beijing in a plot belonging to a eunuch of the court. His tomb remains in Beijing today. His Chinese name — Li Matou — is the best-known name of missionaries who have served in China among both Christian and non-Christian Chinese.

Bibliography

Cronin, Vincent, *The Wise Man from the West* (1955). • Criveller, Gianni, *Preaching Christ in Late Ming China* (1997). • Tacchi-Venturi, P., ed., *Opere Storiche del P. Matteo Ricci, S.J.*, 2 Vols. (1911-13). • *Tripod* (journal published by Holy Spirit Study Center, Hong Kong), special issue on Matteo Ricci (1982). • Maletesta, Edward J., *The Society of Jesus and China: A Historical-Theological Essay* (1997). • Gallagher, Louis, *China in the Sixteenth Century: The Journals of Matteo Ricci* (1953). • Latourette, Kenneth Scott, *A History of Christian Missions in China* (1966). • Ross, Andrew C., *A Vision Betrayed: The Jesuits in Japan and China, 1542-1742* (1994).

Ralph R. Covell, with contributions from
Jean-Paul Wiest and the China Group

Richard, Timothy

(b. Caermarthenshire, Wales, 1845; d. Golders Green, Wales, 17 Apr 1919). English Baptist* missionary to China* known for his attempts to adapt the Christian faith to Chinese culture and for his work in literature*, relief, and reform.

Born into the home of a devout Welsh farmer, Richard was converted during the great Scottish revival in 1860. While studying at Haverfordwest Theological College in Pembrokeshire, he resolved to go to China. He sought to join the China Inland Mission (CIM) but was referred to the Baptist Missionary Society (BMS). He sailed for China under its auspices in 1869 and began his work in Yantai, Shandong (Shantung), in 1870. Seven of his BMS colleagues either died or were forced by illness to return home in the next several years. As a result, he as the lone survivor of the mission moved in 1875 from the coast to Tsingchou (now Weifang), farther west in the province. One reason this location appealed to him was because there were many religious and moral sects in the area whose adherents were seeking something "higher" than was to be found in the three Chinese religions. These, he believed, were the types of people on whom missionaries should focus in their evangelism rather than preaching indiscriminately to the masses.

When famine set in in 1876, he, along with John Nevius*, a Presbyterian colleague, worked with Chinese officials in distributing aid to the victims. When Richard heard that conditions in Shanxi Province were worse than anywhere, he traveled there to help. He was able to get funds from the China Relief Committee and organized extensive relief work in Taiyuan and adjoining cities with the aid of local officials. Due to his tireless efforts in meeting the needs of so many suffering people, Richard became known as the trailblazer in famine relief. This in turn commended the Christian faith to many seekers and helped open Shanxi to Protestant mission work and to modern education.

In his relief efforts as well as in his subsequent work in China, Richard took care to relate well to local and provincial officials and to promote friendly relations with the higher classes. Even at this early stage of his ministry, Richard also went out of his way to make friends with Roman Catholics* and adherents of non-Christian faiths, since he believed that they too were working for the welfare of China.

After 15 years in Shandong and Shanxi, Richard returned to England with his wife and four young daughters. There he urged the BMS board to consider a proposal of united missionary effort that would establish a high-class college in each of the 18 provincial capitals of China. This, in his view, would enable many of the higher classes to become Christian and thus influence their fellow countrymen. His board, accustomed to more traditional means of mission work emphasizing direct evangelism among the masses, did not accept his proposal.

Upon his return to his colleagues in Shanxi, Richard found that many suspected his orthodoxy and were no longer able to work with him. After short periods of time in Shandong and Beijing (Peking), he and his family moved to Shanghai in 1891. There he became director of what became known as the Christian Literature Society (CLS). This society, under his direction, published periodicals, books, and pamphlets which showed the relationship of education and religion to many aspects of Chinese life. It also sponsored lectures, museums, and reading rooms with literature that related to the enlightenment of China. The best known of the journals was the *Review of the Times (Wanguo Gongbao)*. Richard's translation of Mackenzie's *History of the Nineteenth Century* had a circulation of one million copies.

As a result of these educational and literary efforts, Richard and his colleagues became well known among

Chinese officials. This led to their attempt to submit a memorial to the *Zongli Yamen* (Foreign Affairs Office), and to the emperor issuing an edict that would reaffirm religious liberty and ban the many types of slander being published against the Christian faith. From 1898 to 1900, many Chinese reformers, such as Liang Qichao, Kang Yuwei, Zhang Zhidong, and Li Hongzhang, sought to institute changes in the Chinese government system and society. Richard and his missionary friends, including Young J. Allen*, Gilbert Reid*, and W. A. P. Martin*, exercised great personal influence upon these men and their ideas. Ultimately, this reform movement failed to make specific changes, but these reform concepts continued to influence official thinking.

After the tragic Boxer Rebellion resulted in the death of many Catholic and Protestant Christians, Richard proposed to Governor Ceng of Shanxi Province that the provincial government make reparations which would be used to establish in Taiyuan Shanxi University, a secular school that would include both Western and Chinese learning.

For the remainder of his life and ministry, Richard used literature, contacts with government officials, and relations with many religious groups to advocate his basic thesis: the Gospel could be regarded as a means of saving the soul of each individual or as a means of saving the nation through the collective efforts of regenerated souls. Many of his colleagues did not object to this; they did wonder whether his concept of faith and regeneration was the same as theirs, or whether he had departed from his original faith in order to accommodate to Chinese indigenous religions. Hudson Taylor* was particularly critical, believing that the "Shanxi spirit," as he labeled Richard's beliefs, had led many of his CIM missionaries to resign from the mission and return to England or to join other mission agencies where they adopted Richard's views.

Where Richard differed most from his missionary colleagues was in his view of Buddhism*. He found great affinity between the Christian faith and two Buddhist scripture portions: the *Lotus Scripture* of the Tian Tai school and *The Awakening of Faith* of the Pure Land School. Believing it was impossible for God to have left all but Jews and Christians without any knowledge of his salvation, he affirmed that the *Lotus Scripture* was God's revelation for Asia. It was indeed the "Gospel in Chinese."

Why did Richard believe this? To him this small Buddhist book embodied the best of Mahayana Buddhism that had been brought into China and eventually into Korea* and Japan*. He found there the God who is both transcendent and immanent; salvation by faith rather than by works; a deep sense of compassion for the world, comparable to the kingdom of God; and the reality of the Messiah who had come to bless all humankind.

Richard's argument was partly historical and partly theological. He was convinced that when the apostle Thomas* traveled to India*, he had direct personal contact with Ashvagosha, a Buddhist saint who had written *The Awakening of Faith.* Thomas had taught him the truth of the Gospel, which caused him to transform the works-oriented Hinayana Buddhism into its grace-oriented Mahayana form. Theologically, Richard used a specific Buddhist term, *Zhenru,* as equivalent to the idea of Messiah. Most scholars have criticized Richard's views as being pure speculation and fancy.

Despite his attempts to find Gospel truth in Buddhism and his more tolerant views on the ancestral rites, Timothy Richard stands out as one of the better-known and admired Protestant missionaries to China.

Bibliography

Broomhall, A. J., *It Is Not Death to Die!,* book 7, *Hudson Taylor and China's Open Century* (1989). • Covell, Ralph, *Confucius, the Buddha, and Christ* (1986). • Latourette, Kenneth, *A History of Christian Missions in China* (1966). • Richard, Timothy, *Forty-five Years in China* (1916); *Conversion by the Million in China* (1907). • Soothill, W. E., *Timothy Richard of China* (1924).

Ralph R. Covell, with contributions from the China Group

Rites Controversy. *See* Ancestor Worship

Robinson, Philip and Elisa

(Philip: b. England, 1831; d. Kilburn, England, 1886). When he was 14 years of age, Philip Robinson came to a personal conversion while at school in Oxford. He soon began teaching in Sunday school. At age 19 he migrated to Melbourne, Australia, but in 1857 moved to Singapore* to work in a commercial firm. The following year he and a colleague launched a new firm which soon became Robinson and Company, located in what is now Raffles Place, Singapore. This became and has remained one of the largest commercial enterprises in Singapore.

Robinson and his wife, Elisa, were a devout couple brought up in the Brethren tradition. They held simple gatherings for Christian fellowship regularly in their home. However, in his annual report to the church, Robinson wrote, "A few believers who had been led to see the duty as well as the privilege of assembling together on the first day of the week after the manner of the earliest churches planted by the apostles, viz., for the breaking of bread and Christian worship, were meeting together privately for these religious exercises. Seeing however that such a gathering . . . could not be a sufficient witness for Jesus in showing forth his death to others . . . they were led to seek the opening of a place for public worship where these desiderata could be enjoyed." And so, in 1864 Robinson and six other believers rented a room in Bencoolen Street and inaugurated the Brethren movement in Singapore. The meetings in the "Mission Room" consisted of worship services, the breaking of bread, Bible studies, and a Sunday school. During the first 15 months, there were 15 baptisms in the Brethren tradition of total immersion. Conviction that this was the right biblical way of baptism led others, including some Western missionaries, to join the Brethren.

In 1866 a new meeting place was opened in Bras Basah Road to accommodate the growing congregation and was named Bethesda Chapel. In his annual report, Robinson declared that the Brethren "would desire not to pass lightly over the claims of the perishing heathen in their neighborhood." As a result, the Chinese Gospel Hall meetings were begun in 1866, with a former Presbyterian catechist, Tan See Boo*, as leader. Tan brought with him great ability in the Chinese ministry.

In 1882, with the assistance of friends in England, Robinson built a house for the accommodation of visiting missionaries. Dr. Bobby Sng described Robinson as one of the Christian laymen who "did much good for the Gospel by the clarity of their Christian testimony and their selfless labors."

We know very little about Elisa Robinson except that in all things she shared her husband's interests. They had a son, Stamford Raffles Robinson, and a daughter, Blanche Robinson.

Philip Robinson had played an active and decisive part in the early years of the Brethren of Singapore. On 19 Aug 1883, it is recorded that he preached for the last time at the evening meeting of the Bethesda assembly.

Bibliography

Sng, Bobby E. K., *In His Good Time* (1980, 1993). • Finlay, M. H., *The Story of One Hundred Years of the Lord's Blessing* (1964).

FRANK LOMAX

Rodrigues de San Pedro, Augustin. *See* El Padre Capitan

Rodrigo, Michael

(b. 30 Jun 1927; d. 10 Nov 1987). Roman Catholic* priest who suffered martyrdom at the hands of terrorists in southern Sri Lanka*.

Rodrigo served as a professor at the National Seminary at Ampitiya for 16 years (1952-68). He was regarded as the leader of liturgical renewal in the Roman Catholic Church in Sri Lanka in the 1960s. When he returned from his doctoral studies at the Institute Catholique de Paris in 1973, he held many revolutionary views, which often disagreed with the official position of the Roman Catholic Church. His dress also differed from the traditional Roman Catholic clerical dress. Since he was not able to teach at the National Seminary, he taught at Aquinas College, Colombo, for a few months in 1973.

The bishop of Badulla, Leo Nanayakkara, invited him to serve in his diocese. He was able to put some of his new ideas into practice there and later became director of the Sewaka Sarana, the seminary of the Badulla Diocese. The seminary underwent changes during this period, since he introduced some non–Roman Catholic methods to the teaching curriculum. He encouraged the seminarians to spend time with villagers in order to learn the problems of the people. His desire was to take the seminary to the rural setting. Since the bishop was not willing to accede to that request, he decided to open an ashram* in Buttala, which he named *Subaseth Gedara* (House of Blessing). The community dressed and lived like the rural people. Men wore the sarong and shirt, while women wore the cloth and jacket.

During this period Rodrigo took part in the activities of the villagers. During the year of 1986, he mingled with the people, participating in the activities of the village. He established a *pintaliya* (traditional meritorious water pot), free first aid, and free nursery education. The Subaseth Gedara trained a choir of Buddhist children of the village to sing *Wesak Bhakti Geeta* (Buddhist carols). Within a short time the Subaseth Gedara was accepted as a part of the village.

He also introduced a procedure to get a reasonable price for the produce of the villagers. The marginalized people in the area received a visible uplifting during the short time he served in the village.

Rodrigo wrote a number of books and articles for publication in international journals and books. He also contributed to the Sinhala newspapers and journals regularly. The tremendous amount of work done at the time is reflected, to some extent, not only in the writings but also in other creative contributions such as slides, posters, etc. His work was not welcomed in the mainstream of the church; neither did he receive the approval of the village elite. He received several death threats from those who did not favor his program of action.

On 10 Nov 1987, during the height of the Jathika Vimukthi Perumuna uprising in Sri Lanka, Rodrigo was gunned down by an assassin while celebrating mass at Subaseth Gedara. He is still remembered in the forums of interreligious* dialogue for his maxim, "Only after a dialogue of life is there dialogue of prayer, and then of religious experience."

Bibliography

Michael Rodrigo Memorial Issue, Dialogue, n.s., Vol. 15, Nos. 1, 2, 3 (1988).

G. P. V. SOMARATNA

Roman Catholic Church

Asia is a vast geographical area characterized by great ethnic, cultural, economic, and political diversity. Ethnic communities have settled in their lands for centuries, and different nations have been shaped by the religious traditions of Hinduism*, Buddhism*, Confucianism*, and Islam*. Enormous wealth and massive poverty* coexist within and between countries. Political structures ranging from ancient monarchies to recent Communist* and democratic governments face the impact of growing urbanization and modern technology. This diversity has led to both interdependence and conflict throughout Asia's history.

Within this vast and diverse region, Catholic Christianity constitutes a small minority — roughly 2 to 3 percent of the total population. Nevertheless, it remains an abiding presence because of its long history, established institutions, and social involvement.

The origins of the Catholic Church in different parts of Asia were linked with each other because many missionaries traveled and worked in different areas. Foremost among them is Jesuit* Francis Xavier*, who arrived in Goa in 1543, traveled to Malacca, the Moluccas*, and Japan*, and died in Sancian Island off the Chinese mainland. Different religious groups such as the *Missions Étrangères de Paris* (Paris Foreign Missions*, MEP) dispatched their members throughout the region.

Underlying this apostolic zeal was a common historical framework for evangelization. Though Eastern Christianity came to Asia much earlier, the Latin church undertook systematic missionary work in conjunction with European exploration, colonization, and commerce. Its juridical foundations in Portuguese and Spanish territories lay within the patronage (see *Padroado*) system, wherein the king received the pope's mandate for evangelization in exchange for certain rights or privileges over church administration and personnel. While patronage provided material resources and bureaucratic support, missionary work often became entangled with political interests. In territories outside the patronage system, missionaries dealt with powerful trading companies of other European nations. Thus the church often established its first communities in areas under Western control and used foreign political and economic power for protection. Only rarely was it directly critical of colonial governance or economic exploitation.

The church's association with European power shaped native attitudes toward Christianity. Some local rulers welcomed or barred missionaries because of their desire for or aversion to political alliance and Western knowledge. As a result, the church was often drawn into power struggles between and among Western nations and the local elite.

Related to but distinct from this political framework was the common perspective that other religions and cultures were erroneous and inferior. Such a perspective prevented missionaries from adapting to local contexts defined by ancient cultures and religious traditions and bringing Christianity closer to Asian peoples and their cultures. This failure is best symbolized in the Chinese Rites Controversy (see Ancestor Worship) that ended in the condemnation of Jesuit Matteo Ricci's* acceptance of rites honoring, but not worshipping, ancestors.

In spite of its association with Western power and negative perspective on local cultures and religions, the church was able to contribute to the general development of groups and communities. Though unconcerned with what today would be called "inculturation" (see Contextualization), missionaries preserved and at times developed local language, literature, and culture simply because they had to use them for evangelization. Missionaries generally produced the first linguistic texts and cultural studies of some local communities.

Moreover, though often silent on direct political issues, the church tried to help alleviate the plight of the poor. The status of marginal groups such as mountain tribes improved because of the church's concern for them. After the initial period of establishing missions, the church built an extensive network of educational, medical*, and social institutions across Asia, some of which survive to the present day.

The core of the Christian story in Asia, however, lies in the blood of many canonized and common martyrs. Throughout this story were continuous persecutions at the hands of Western, local, and regional powers for reasons religious and otherwise. But countless Christians, such as the famous martyrs of Nagasaki (see Kirishitan Evangelism), the victims of the Shin-yu executions in Korea*, and the obscure Filipino Chinese Lorenzo Ruiz, offered their lives for the faith they considered their own. This basic story is told in different forms in each of the following countries.

India. According to tradition, the Apostle Thomas (see Thomas Traditions) brought Christianity to India*. Then followed settlements of Christian merchants from Syria from the 4th to the 9th cs. In the midst of the Hindu majority and an increasing Islamic presence, these communities survived especially around Kerala until missionaries from the Latin church arrived.

While a short-lived mission in Mylapore existed at the end of the 13th c., Roman Catholicism took root only with the coming of the Portuguese and other Europeans in the 16th c. Following his arrival at the Christian center of Goa in 1542, Xavier proceeded to minister among the Pavaras and to establish structures for continuing growth.

Relations between Syrian and Latin Christianity proved difficult because of long-standing differences in liturgical practice, theological tradition, and language. Syrian Christians were put under Latin jurisdiction through the 1599 synod at Diamper. But after 54 years under Latin bishops, they proclaimed their independence in the Coonan Cross Declaration and renewed ties with the ancient church in Antioch. Some Syrian Christians returned shortly to Latin jurisdiction and were officially constituted as the Syro-Malabar Church after 230 years under Latin jurisdiction. A fraction of those who split from the Latin church eventually entered into communion with the Holy See in 1930 and were recognized as the Syro-Malankara Church.

Latin missionary efforts continued through religious orders. The Franciscans* and Dominicans* worked under the Portuguese patronage system, reaching enclaves of Portuguese influence such as Bassein, Bombay, and Malabar. But during the 17th c., the Propaganda Fide Congregation* of the Vatican began sending other religious, particularly Carmelites*, Theatines, and Capuchins*, to evangelize areas under the control of other European trading companies.

Roman Catholic Church

Aside from these areas under European influence, missionaries went wherever they were welcome, such as to Madurai in the south and Bengal in the north. In 1594 the Jesuits went to the Mogul court. Robert de Nobili* arrived in 1606 and brought a new perspective to evangelization by adapting native culture. He spoke and dressed like the Hindu high caste and studied the riches of their thought. But with this as the exception rather than the rule, Latin Christianity was slow in integrating with local culture and developing local personnel, though a Brahman Oratorian from Goa, Matthew de Castro*, was consecrated first Indian apostolic vicar in 1637.

Evangelization suffered during the 18th c. as a result of conflicts outside and within the church. Trade competition intensified among the European companies, some of which did not allow church ministry within their territories. The British East India Company gained dominance until the 1857 Sepoy mutiny. This power struggle aggravated issues of ecclesiastical jurisdiction between those within the Portuguese patronage system and those working through the Propaganda Fide, most of whom were non-Portuguese. This continuing rivalry led to conflict and even rioting. In 1886, Pope Leo XIII established the episcopal hierarchy in India, limiting the power of the Portuguese monarchy until its official end in 1928.

By the first quarter of the 19th c., Latin missionary activity received new impetus with the coming of more personnel from religious orders, especially of women, and the restored Jesuit order. Missionaries spread everywhere to minister to settlements of migrant workers in the expanding trade industry and to communities of aborigines, especially in the Chota-Nagpur district. Their early involvement in education and medical care (see Medical Work) laid the foundations for an extensive Catholic presence in these areas to the present day.

Church activity continued throughout the disruptions of the two world wars. The church was not involved in the struggle for independence as a consequence of its historical ties with colonial powers. Nevertheless, its leadership became local in membership and perspective. The Catholic Bishops' Conference* was founded in 1944, and the first plenary council of India held in Bangalore in 1950.

Sri Lanka. Because evangelization and European colonization came together in the 16th c., Christianity became entangled with political rivalries among local rulers and between European nations. In the mainland, it was caught in the struggle between King Bhuvanekabahu and his brother. The king refused Christianity for fear of the Buddhists, but he welcomed the Franciscans* to Kotte in 1543 in exchange for Portuguese support. His grandson-successor, Dharmapala*, became a Christian, transferred Buddhist properties to the Franciscans, and handed his kingdom to the Portuguese before his death. The Catholic Church flourished then as part of the diocese of Goa and later Cochin. Jesuits, Dominicans, and Augustinians* came in the early years of the 17th c.

In 1658 the Dutch ousted the Portuguese and forced the Dutch Reformed Church on Catholics. Joseph Vaz*, an Indian priest from Goa, came in 1687 to minister secretly to the remaining Catholics. The Buddhist kings of Kandy permitted evangelization of other areas. After the British overthrew the Dutch in 1796, the church enjoyed religious freedom. European missionaries, mostly from religious orders, began work in education and social development.

In 1834 Sri Lanka* was eventually constituted as a separate apostolic vicariate, with an Indian Oratian missionary, Vincente do Rosayro, as its first bishop. In 1887 the episcopal hierarchy was established, with Colombo as an archdiocese and Jaffna and Kandy as suffragan dioceses. Christopher Bonjean, a French Oblate* and former bishop in Jaffna and Colombo, became Colombo's first bishop. The number of indigenous clergy and religious increased in time, and Thomas Cooray became the first Sri Lankan archbishop in 1947 and cardinal in 1960. Today about one in 16 Sri Lankans are Catholic.

China. Changing attitudes of political rulers mark the history of Christianity in China*. "Nestorian"* Christianity from Persia flourished from the 7th to the 9th cs. until persecutions obliterated it. Only under the more open Yuan dynasty (1280-1368) would the next mission take place. Giovanni da Montecorvino*, an Italian Franciscan who arrived in Beijing in 1294, translated Christian texts into Mongolian at the emperor's request and became Beijing's archbishop in 1307. Catholicism disappeared with the collapse of the Yuan dynasty.

The arrival of the Portuguese in the 16th c. brought new missionaries. Among them were Alvaro Margahhaes in 1521 and Estevao Nogueira in 1542. The Jesuits founded St. Paul's school in 1565, which became the first university college in Asia in 1584. Institutions for the care of the poor and lepers (see Leprosy Work) were set up. By 1576 Macau* had been formally established as a diocese with jurisdiction over China, Indochina, Mongolia*, Japan*, and Korea*. Other religious orders followed: Franciscans in 1579, Augustinians in 1586, and Dominicans in 1587.

Missionary work flourished during the late Ming and early Qing dynasties from the late 16th c. Controversy over the Chinese rites honoring ancestors* erupted within the church. Jesuit Matteo Ricci studied Chinese culture and judged these rites not to be contrary to the Christian faith. But church leaders disagreed and banned them until the early 20th c. This fueled the conflict between Emperor Kangxi* and papal legate C. T. Maillard de Tournon*, who was later expelled from China.

Franciscans came to Fujian Province in 1631. By the end of the Ming dynasty in 1644, Catholicism had penetrated 13 provinces, and some court members had become converts. Other Jesuits, such as Johann Adam Schall von Bell* and Ferdinand Verbiest*, tried to preach the Christian message through humanistic and scientific learning. Aware of the Confucian tradition of the court, they produced maps and calendars and taught painting and languages. With the arrival of Bishop João de Casal in 1692, the political situation had become stable. St. Joseph's Seminary was founded in 1728 for both missionaries and Chinese Catholics.

Nevertheless, antiforeign sentiment remained and took an anti-Christian turn, especially during the turbulence of 19th-c. China. From the time of the first Opium* War in 1840, Christian missionaries used their colonial status to protect their interests. The British occupation of Hong Kong* provided the church with a new center for missionary activity. Originally a mission prefecture, it extended its coverage to San Po, Kowloon, and Kwai Hsin. Because of its freedom, it was able to open many schools, especially with the arrival of the Canossian* Sisters in 1860, and to engage in social work and publishing Christian texts.

The 1900 Boxer Uprising intensified antiforeign sentiment. Foreigners and Christians used the Beijing Cathedral as their refuge. After World War I and the Bolshevik revolution, Chinese intellectuals increasingly despised Christianity because of its association with foreigners. An exception was Vincent Lebbe*, a Catholic missionary who championed Chinese patriotism and became a Chinese citizen. Though six Chinese bishops were consecrated in 1926, the development of local Chinese leadership came too late. Most bishops were still foreign at the time of the 1949 revolution.

There remains a significant number of Catholics, who share much in common but are divided in their attitude toward the Communist government. Some belong to the government-sanctioned Chinese Catholic Patriotic Association*, and others do not.

Japan. Christianity came to Japan* when conflicts between rival feudal lords were common across the nation in the 16th c. Thus missionaries had to deal with changing powers in order to evangelize. Xavier was allowed to begin a mission at Kagoshima in 1548 but could not proceed to the capital in Kyoto. His successors were able to expand the mission to other parts of north Kyushu and Kyoto. This expansion was made possible with the conversion of feudal lords, such as Sumitada Omura, and the favor of Nobunaga Oda, who assumed power in Kyoto in 1568. During his reign Jesuit missions expanded rapidly as a result of the policy of adaptation proposed by Jesuit visitor Alessandro Valignano*. In 1584 Hideyoshi Toyotomi assumed power and soon promulgated an edict expelling missionaries. He ordered the execution of 26 Christians in 1597.

The subsequent and long-lasting Tokogawa shogunate carried out more extensive and brutal persecutions. Missionaries and lay Christians, including children, were tortured and killed. This led to the Shimabara rebellion by Christians in 1637. As a result, even European traders were closely watched and later expelled. At the beginning of the 18th c., Jesuit Giovanni Batista Disoti, who came from the Philippines*, was arrested and died in prison. Catholicism survived secretly around Nagasaki and in northern Kyushu villages without priests for over two centuries.

With a weakened shogunate and pressure from the Western powers in the 19th c., the country gradually opened its doors to foreigners. Theodore Augustin Forcade* of the MEP opened a mission at Naha in 1844, and Grudence Seraphim Girard at Tokyo in 1859. Though proselytizing in Japanese was still officially forbidden, evangelization proceeded with the building of the first church in Yokohama in 1862 and in Nagasaki in 1864. Japanese Catholics in hiding soon came forward. The Meiji government cracked down on them once more, executing more than 200 until the prohibition of Christianity was revoked in 1873.

The church grew rapidly with the end of persecution. In 1885 the Oura church was built in Nagasaki and vicariates established. The first church conference decided to establish the episcopal hierarchy and set up three dioceses (Hakidate, Osaka, and Nagasaki) and the Tokyo metropolitan. In 1896 the Tokyo conference promulgated a set of national church rules.

While the MEP continued to play a key role, new religious orders came to work in new areas, such as education and social welfare. Religious orders for native women (e.g., the Sisters of the Visitation) were established, and the number of native religious and priests increased. With all bishops Japanese, the Japan Catholic Church received approval under the Religious Organizations Law.

Following the devastation of World War II*, the church embarked on the reconstruction of buildings and revival of church life. Formal relations between the Vatican and the Japanese government were established. In 1960 Archbishop Doi became Japan's first cardinal, and in 1966 the Catholic Bishops' Conference was formally organized.

Korea. From the late 16th c. on, many attempts to evangelize in Korea* were undertaken from Catholic settlements in Japan, China, and the Philippines. With the Japanese invasion of Korea in 1592 came many lay catechists. Thousands of Koreans were taken back to Japan as prisoners and converted. Many ended up as Christian martyrs on Japanese soil. Catholic literature from China was known before the baptism of Peter Yi Sung-hun, a Korean diplomat in Beijing. Upon his return in 1784 he baptized others, one of whom was a noble named Yu Hang-gom, who preached in Honam (Henan) region. The expanding community elevated 10 people to act as clergy since foreign missionaries were prohibited. Upon learning of their error, they secretly brought in a Chinese priest, Chu Mun-mo, to minister to some 4,000 Catholics. Thus the earliest Catholic communities were indigenous* Christian groups started through the witness of Japanese soldiers and Chinese Christian literature.

While the presence of some prominent leaders among the Catholics earlier ensured some freedom, the queen regent of young King Sun-jo ordered the great Shin-yu persecution in 1801. More than 300 Catholics, including Yu-Hang-gom, were martyred, while the survivors hid in the mountains. The main offense of the Christians seemed to have been refusal to conduct the ancestor rites as required by law.

In spite of the persecutions, priests from Beijing came from 1811 on, and, by order of the pope, the French MEP in 1828. The number of Catholics continued to grow even when local rulers used the threat of persecution to destroy their political enemies. Bishop Simeon-François Berneux established a seminary in the secluded mountains of Paeron-san. The first Korean priest, St. Andrew Kim Tai-kon (Dae-gun), was martyred in 1846.

Political threats from Western powers made local rulers more suspicious of Catholics. During the latter half of the 19th c., China and Japan competed with these powers for political and economic influence over Korea. Thus, in 1866 the Great Persecution of French missionaries and thousands of Korean Catholics took place at Pyung Jin (1866-71). Missionary work remained undeterred, with a common mission policy drawn up in 1868. Preparation of Korean clergy was resumed, social work undertaken by religious sisters, and religious literature published. A treaty with France in 1886 gave Catholics extraterritorial status. A seminary ordained its first 10 graduates in 1896. The erection of Yakhyon Church in 1893 and Seoul Cathedral in 1898 symbolized the growth of the church. The Catholic Church remained rural until after 1945.

While turbulent for the Korean nation, the period of Japanese colonization (1910-45) did not hinder the expansion of the church. Catholics in Korea did not rally strongly against Japanese colonial rule (1905-45). Friction over Shinto* and ancestral rites was resolved in the 1930s by an agreement between Japan and the Vatican defining the rites as "civil," not "religious." German missionary Benedictines* arrived in 1909 and founded an abbey near Wonsan. American Maryknoll* Fathers began work in northwest Korea in 1923, and Maryknoll Sisters came in 1924. German Benedictine Sisters arrived in 1925, and Columban* Fathers in 1933. Franciscan Fathers also arrived in the mid-1930s, as did Columban Sisters.

In 1945 there were an estimated 183,000 Catholics in both North and South Korea. By 1949 South Korea had 157,668 Catholics, but the Communists had suppressed the church in the North.

After the Korean War*, conversions increased and institutions flourished: Hyosong Women's College began in Taegu in 1952; Catholic Medical College in Seoul in 1954; American Jesuits started coeducational Sogang College, also in Seoul, in 1960, which became a university in 1970; and the Religious of the Sacred Heart* began Sacred Heart College for Women in Ch'unchon in 1964. A second regional seminary was founded in Kwangju in 1962 to accommodate a large influx of priestly vocations.

The Korean hierarchy was formally established also in 1962, and the nine vicariates apostolic were raised to the rank of dioceses and archdioceses. Archbishop Stephen Kim Su-hwan of Seoul was made a cardinal in 1969. A nationally respected voice for justice and peace, Kim retired as archbishop in 1998, replaced by Cheong Jin-seok.

A Catholic, Chang Myon, opposed President Syngman Rhee* in the 1960 election. Chang became prime minister after the student uprising of 1960 but was overthrown by a coup d'etat in 1961. Resistance to President Park Chung-hee's authoritarian rule coalesced in liberal religious quarters throughout the 1960s, culminating in the imprisonment of the bishop of Wonju, Daniel Tji Hak-soon, in 1974. Another Catholic opposition figure jailed at that time, Kim Dae-jung, became president in 1998 after democracy was established.

In 1984 Pope John Paul II visited Korea to preside at the canonization of 103 martyrs of the 19th-c. persecutions. Seoul was the site for the 44th International Eucharistic Congress in 1989.

Clergy and religious became increasingly native, but the split of Korea into the Communist North and the democratic South remains a difficult challenge to the church today.

Thailand. The ancient capital of Ayutthaya was the center of missionary efforts in Thailand* beginning in 1567 by Dominicans and continued in 1607 by Jesuits, who established their own church and school. The MEP missionaries thus found a thriving Christian community there in 1662. Two years later they were granted jurisdiction over Siam, which became their mission base for Cochin China, Tonkin, and China because of its policy of religious tolerance.

The mission at Siam grew during the long and prosperous period of King Narai the Great (1657-88), who welcomed foreigners, especially the French. François Pallu* organized the Synod of Ayutthaya* in 1664, and Lambert de la Motte* founded the College General and the first hospital. In spite of this freedom, which lasted until the fall of Ayutthaya in 1767, the number of Siamese Christians remained small.

After the Revolution of 1688*, King Phra Phetrajam became hostile to the French and persecuted Christians until 1691, when he returned the seminary. Further persecution took place during the reign of King Taisra (1709-33), who forbade missionaries to use the Thai and Pali languages for evangelization.

The situation of the church changed with the coming of a new dynasty in 1782. King Rama I, hoping to begin negotiations for an alliance with foreign countries and to promote trade with these countries as before, sent for the missionaries expelled by his predecessor, King Taksin. In 1802 the number of Christians was estimated to be only 1,500, and in 1811 about 3,000.

In 1827 Pope Leo XII put Singapore* under the jurisdiction of the apostolic vicar of Siam. But in 1841, because of the increasing number of Catholics and missionaries, the ecclesiastical region of Malaya was separated from Siam, establishing the Mission of Oriental Siam. Under the leadership of Jean-Louis Vey* (1875-1909), the church included 23,000 Christians and established many schools. His successor, Msgr. Perros (1909-47), sent missionaries to the North and all regions previously unreached.

Vietnam. While Christianity is believed to have begun in the early 16th c. in Vietnam*, sustained missionary work was established by the first half of the 17th c. through the Jesuits. Most prominent among them was the French Alexandre de Rhodes*, who brought many to the church and formed lay catechists. Moreover, he studied local culture and devised a Latin script for Vietnamese in which he wrote pioneering linguistic and Christian texts.

Missionary work expanded rapidly in the following two centuries in spite of its many serious difficulties. Tension between rulers from the North and South hindered the work of missionaries, who were suspected of spying by both and, at the same time, were used as mediators to obtain equipment from the Portuguese. As in other Asian countries, there were conflicts between early Portuguese missionaries under the patronage system and later ones who were mostly French and belonged to the MEP. The consequences of the Chinese Rites Controversy affected the church in Vietnam. Bishop Alexander (d. 1738) excommunicated Flory, who, like Ricci in China, held that these rites honoring the dead were not idolatrous. Though the church reversed its policy against the rites in 1939, this policy's implementation in Vietnam took place only in 1964. But the last and most serious challenge to the church throughout its history was numerous persecutions, resulting in the death of some 130,000, including bishops, priests, and catechists. The reigns of Minh Mang, Thieu Tri, and Tu Duc during most of the 19th c. proved most difficult for the church, even though an 1862 treaty put South Vietnam under French rule.

Nevertheless, the church continued to grow in number and scope. It has been able to establish an effective network in education and social work. But new problems arose after the country's division by the 1954 Geneva Accord into the North under the Communist regime and the South under a pro-Western government. In the North the church's educational and social institutions were confiscated and its activities limited to sacramental celebrations and pious devotions. While the church in the South retained its many educational and social development institutions, it had to cope with the massive influx of Catholics from the North. With the reunification of Vietnam in 1976, the church continues its ministry in a context marked by strong political currents.

Indonesia. In the early 14th c., when Franciscan missionaries visited the harbors of Sumatra and Java*, they found remnants of Eastern (Persian, Indian, and Arab traders) communities dating to the 7th c. Succeeding missions in the 16th c. came from the Portuguese centers such as Goa to the Moluccas*. From 1546 Jesuits including Xavier worked in Ambon and Halmahera*, and Franciscans and Augustinians followed shortly. Their ministry had expanded well beyond Malacca by 1570.

Church growth was hindered from 1605, when the Dutch East India Company (VOC) suppressed all Catholic missions in their territories. This powerful trading company pressured Catholics to become members of the Dutch Reformed Church, and Catholic missionaries and laypeople who resisted were martyred. However, through the 17th and 18th cs., Catholic ministry was continued by the Franciscans among the Aceh in Sumatra, the Theatines in South Kalimantan*, and the Dominicans in the southeastern islands of Flores and Timor*.

With religious freedom granted by King Louis Napoleon of Holland in 1806, the first apostolic prefecture was officially opened in what is now known as Jakarta* (Batavia). An 1847 agreement between the Dutch government and the Vatican acknowledged the internal independence of the church. Religious orders opened schools in Jakarta and Surabaya, and Dutch missionaries worked among the European and Chinese Catholics in Java and the Bataks in Sumatra. Jesuits in Surabaya expanded their missionary activities by sending trained religious teachers and catechists to Flores and beyond. Toward the beginning of the 20th c., the church succeeded in organizing local communities, such as the Javanese mission of Jesuit F. van Lith*, and establishing schools, seminaries, hospitals, and novitiates. Because of the expansion, new ecclesiastical territories were created.

During the Japanese occupation (1942-45), nearly all missionaries were detained and many Christians killed. But after the 1945 declaration of independence, smooth relations between the Catholic church and President Sukarno's government allowed the church to make significant contributions in education and health care.

Philippines. In 1565 the first Spanish missionaries settled in Cebu, one of the many islands of the only Asian country with an overwhelming Catholic majority. Though within the framework of Spanish patronage, initial evangelization here differed from that in Latin America because of the impact of Bartolomé de las Casas on the church in Spain. Like de las Casas, who strongly criticized the manner of evangelization in the New World, Augustinian Martin de Rada complained against Spanish exploitation of the natives. Missionaries also used the vernacular rather than Spanish and produced the first grammars and dictionaries of the now romanized local languages. Early texts, such as Franciscan Juan de Oliver's catechism and Dominican Francisco Blancas de San José's sermons, indicate that, while they condemned much of native culture as pagan, they used whatever was helpful for preaching the Gospel.

Evangelization spread rapidly to different areas with the coming of other religious orders — Franciscans in 1577, Jesuits in 1581, Dominicans in 1587, and Recollects in 1606. By 1598 an archdiocese was established in Manila, the seat of colonial government, and dioceses in Cebu, Nueva Caceres, and Nueva Segovia. Missionaries succeeded because they coopted local leaders to help in organizing towns where small dispersed communities *(barangays)* settled. Aside from teaching Christian doctrine, they brought new methods of farming and imported crops such as Indian corn and cacao. Formal education started with the founding of schools — Colegio de Manila in 1596 and Colegio de San Jose in 1601 by the Jesuits, and Colegio de Santo Tomas in 1623.

The church began to face serious external and internal obstacles in the 17th and 18th cs. Muslims in Meguindanao defeated Spanish forces in 1596 and thus closed southern Mindanao to the church. Through most of the colonial period, Muslim groups conducted raids on Christian settlements in the Visayas, Luzon, and northern Mindanao to capture slaves. Jurisdictional conflicts endemic to the patronage system occurred among religious personnel and between ecclesiastical and civil authorities. One such conflict had disastrous effects on the development of the native clergy: Archbishop Diego Camacho ordained ill-prepared candidates in the early 18th c.

In spite of these conflicts, Catholicism managed to grow. Religious orders opened hospitals and other charitable institutions and continued to send missionaries to China, Tonkin, and the Marianas Islands. Ignacia del Espiritu Santo*, a Chinese *mestiza,* began a *beaterio,* a community for single women, which developed into the Religious of the Virgin Mary*. But of greater import than these was the deepening appropriation of Catholicism by the local people. Whatever the church brought, such as the passion narrative and feasts of saints, the locals transformed and incorporated into their own ethos.

The church's situation deteriorated in the 19th c. because the clergy was fewer and less qualified. This aggravated the anti-Spanish sentiment caused by abuses of Spanish civil officials. Two threads of anti-colonial sentiment — popular uprisings such as Hermano Pule's in 1842 on the one hand, and the Propaganda Movement of the educational elite on the other — came together in the revolutions of 1896 and 1898. The Catholic Church was sharply divided, but there was significant religious participation in the events leading to the revolution. Aside from the masses, who often saw their struggle in religious terms, some of the native clergy offered their lives for the nationalist cause and took part in the revolution. Others under the leadership of Gregorio Aglipay* broke away to form the Philippine Independent Church*.

The church floundered in the aftermath of the revolution and upon the arrival of American imperialism. It had to rebuild its institutions and regain its composure. New religious orders with American or English-speaking members, such as the Christian Brothers and Sisters of St. Paul, aided in the reconstruction. By the outbreak of World War II, the church had an extensive network of modern schools and health-care institutions, but it was just beginning to address the festering problem of injustice to peasants and labor.

Roman Catholic Church Today. The second half of the 20th c. witnessed many profound changes across Asia, such as the 1949 victory of the Chinese revolution; the divisions into India and Pakistan*, North and South Korea, and North and South Vietnam; and the independence of Indonesia*, the Philippines, Malaysia, and Singapore. Effects of the more recent wars in Vietnam, Laos*, and Cambodia* spread beyond their borders. No less extensive than these political developments is the growing impact of rapid urbanization, modern technology, and economic interdependence on people's lives in the region. Traditional rural cultures can no longer be isolated because of electronic communication.

The historic Vatican Council II enabled the Catholic Church to face these monumental changes better. Its call to read "the signs of the times" and "to make the joys and sorrows of the world" its own led to the aggiornamento that Catholic Christianity needed and desired.

In Asia, as elsewhere, this renewal meant facing modernity as well as rediscovering Christian foundations. Sunday congregations now celebrated the Eucharist in their own tongues, and laypeople participated not only in rites but in other tasks of the church as well. The Bible*, previously available to clerics only, provided new life to Catholic worship, spirituality, and practice. Conferences of church leaders were not limited to internal matters, and relations with other Christian churches improved.

But more crucial for Asia was the shift in the church's view of mission. Expressed as "integral evangelization" or in other analogous terms, this view recognized concern for all dimensions of personal and social life as essential to Christianity. Catholic individuals and groups throughout the region became involved in social issues and collaborated with other religious and secular entities. In 1972 the Catholic and Anglican Bishops' Council of Japan issued the statement "Gospel to Society." The Catholic office for emergency relief and refugees and the Jesuit refugee service based in Thailand initiated ministries for the victims of war in Vietnam and Cambodia. Though speaking to a minority, the Catholic Bishops' Conference of Indonesia has consistently addressed social concerns in its pastoral letters. All levels of the Catholic Church in the Philippines contributed to the downfall of the Marcos dictatorship in 1986.

The Federation of Asian Bishops' Conferences* (FABC), established in 1970 in the spirit of Vatican Council II, best describes the tasks of the church for the future. It invites the church in Asia to engage in dialogue with culture, other religions, and the poor. The task of inculturation requires both respect for and evangelization of all cultures. Encounter with other religions means sharing each other's gifts from God through word and life. Solidarity with the poor demands living the faith that does justice. This triple dialogue can only be realized through a pastoral strategy that forms basic communities and empowers the laity.

This challenge to the church in the new millennium is in continuity with its history in Asia. It is nothing less than a call to transform itself from a church in Asia to a church of Asia.

Bibliography

General

Athyal, Saphir P., *The Church in Asia Today: Challenges and Opportunities* (1996). • Clark, Francis X., *An Introduction to the Catholic Church of Asia* (1987). • Karotemprel, Sebastian, *Heralds of the Gospel in Asia* (1998). • Rosales, Gaudencio, and C. G. Arevalo, eds., *For All the Peoples of Asia: FABC Documents from 1970-1991* (1992). • Eilers, Franz-Josef, *For All the Peoples of Asia: FABC Documents from 1992-1996* (1997).

India

Neill, Stephen Charles, *The Story of the Christian Church in India and Pakistan* (1970). • Perumalil, H. C., and E. R. Hambye, eds., *Christianity in India: A History in Ecumenical Perspective.*

Japan

Fujita, Neil S., *Japan's Encounter with Christianity: The Catholic Mission in Pre-Modern Japan* (1991). • Laures, Johannes, *The Catholic Church in Japan: A Short History* (1962).

Korea

Biernatzki, William E., Luke Im Jin-chang, and Anselm Min Kyoung-suk, *Korean Catholicism in the 1970s: A Christian Community Comes of Age* (1975). • Catholic Conference of Korea, *Statistics of the Catholic Church in Korea* (1997) (in Korean). • Dallet, Charles, *Histoire de l'église de Corée* (History of the Church of Korea), 2 Vols. (1874). • Kim, Chang-mun, and Chung Jae-sun, *Catholic Korea, Yesterday and Today* (1964). • Kim, Chi-ha, *The Gold-Crowned Jesus and Other Writings* (1978). • Moon, Kyu-hyon, *Hanguk chonju kyohoe sa* (A history of the Korean Catholic Church), 2 Vols. (1994). • *Pro Munda Vita: Centrum Informationis,* "Korea: Perspectives on the Church in Modernizing South Korea," No. 39 (1971). • Ruiz de Medina, Juan, *Origenes de la Iglesia Catolica Coreana desde 1566 hasta 1784* (Origins of the Korean Catholic Church from 1566 to 1784) (1986). • Grayson, James Huntly, *Early Buddhism and Christianity in Korea: A Study in the Implantation of Religion* (1985).

Indonesia

The Documentation-Information Department, *The Catholic Church in Indonesia* (1975). • Muskens, M. P. M., *Partner in Nation Building: The Catholic Church in Indonesia* (1979).

Philippines

Anderson, Gerald H., *Studies in Philippine Church History* (1969). • De la Costa, H., and John N. Schumacher, eds., *Church and State: The Philippine Experience* (1976). • Ileto, Reynaldo, *Pasyon and Revolution: Popular Movements in the Philippines, 1840-1910* (1979). • Rafael, Vicente L., *Contracting Colonialism: Translation and Christian Conversion in Tagalog Society under Early Spanish Rule* (1988). • Schumacher, John N., *Readings in Philippine Church History* (1979). • Tuggy, Arthur Leonard, *The Philippine Church: Growth in a Changing Society* (1971).

José Mario C. Francisco, with contributions from W. L. A. Don Peter (Sri Lanka), the China Group (China), translated by Dufresse Chang, Sergio Ticozzi (Hong Kong), Matsumura Sugakazu (Japan), William E. Biernatzki (Korea), Surachai Chumsriphan (Thailand), Peter C. Phan (Vietnam), Adolf Heuken (Indonesia), and José M. de Mesa (Philippines)

Ross, John

(b. Ross-shire, Scotland, 1841; d. Scotland, 1915). Scottish pioneer missionary in Manchuria and translator of the New Testament (NT) into Korean.

Ross was educated at Glasgow University (1865-69) and was a pastor in Scotland before his appointment by the United Presbyterian Church (later the United Free Church) in 1872. Upon his arrival in China* his wife died, but he worked hard with great success in his language study and in 1873 delivered his first sermon in Chinese. His concern was to reach unreached areas in Manchuria. Beginning in 1874, Ross's base for his itineration was Mukden (Shenyang). His strategy involved careful study of and empathy with the culture, sure knowledge of the language, and concentration upon the major population centers. In addition to being concerned for frontier areas of Manchuria, Ross also began to learn about Korea* through traders who came to Manchuria. At this time Korea was still closed to foreign workers and diplomats, so Ross began his study of the language through Koreans in Manchuria. In 1874 he began work on an English-Korean primer with a Korean trader named Yi Eung-Chan. By 1875 the first Korean Protestants were baptized by Ross — four of his language helpers. With the aid of his brother-in-law, John McIntyre, Ross used his dictionary and Korean helper to begin translating the NT. In 1882 Luke and John were published and a Korean grammar was published, and these were followed by the complete New Testament in 1887 (Ross Version; see also Bible Translation). One of his helpers, Suh Sang Yoon, was sent into Korea as a colporteur to sell Bible portions as early as 1883 (Protestant missionaries did not enter the "hermit kingdom" until 1884). In 1887, with the whole New Testament completed, Ross himself traveled to Korea for the first time, where the first Presbyterian* church was being established (Seoul).

Ross was not only a student of languages, an area in which he was naturally gifted, but also of the Confucian* cultures of East Asia. His approach to Chinese rites (see Ancestor Worship) was closer to that of the Jesuits* than of the Dominicans*. In 1879 he also produced the first history of Korea in the English language. Ross witnessed one of the amazing beginnings of a modern church in

Asia where villages were turning to Christianity before a missionary was present in the country. All of the earliest Protestant evangelistic work was done by Koreans.

Because of ill health, Ross returned to Scotland in 1910, where he continued to research and write until his death.

Bibliography

Grayson, James H., *John Ross: First Missionary to Korea* (1982) (in Korean). • Kim, Y. S., *The Ross Version and Korean Protestantism* (in Korean), trans. into English by Allen Clark. • Ross, John, *Chinese Foreign Policy* (1877); *History of Korea: Ancient and Modern* (1879); *The Manchus* (1880); *Mission Methods in Manchuria* (1903). • Some of Ross's letters and materials are available in the National Library of Scotland and at the National Bible Society of Scotland. SCOTT W. SUNQUIST

Roy, Ram Mohun

(b. Radhanagar, Burdwan District, Bengal, 22 May 1772 or 1774; d. England, 27 Sep 1833). Father of modern India and founder of the Brahmo Samaj*, which challenged fundamental Christian doctrines.

Ram Mohun learned Bengali and Persian in his own native village and was later sent to Patna to master Persian and Arabic. It was his Islamic studies at Patna that made him entertain early in life a strong prejudice against idol worship. The first 30 years of his life were obscure, but it is certain that in 1803 he published his first book, *Tuhfat-ul-Muwahhidin* (A Gift to Monotheists), written in Persian with an Arabic preface. It was a protest against idolatry and superstition in all religions and an attempt to found a universal religion based on the unity of the godhead. From 1809 to 1815, he studied English and Indian religions in Rangpur. In 1815 he settled in Calcutta, where he devoted himself to the publication of the Vedanta texts, the agitation for religious and social reform, and the defense of Hinduism* against the attacks of Christian missionaries. In 1815-19 he published his *Abridgement of Vedanta;* translations of the Kena, Isa, Mudaka, and Katha Upanishads; two papers defending Hindu theism and two *Conferences (Dialogues) on Sati.* He began an agitation for the abolition of *sati (setee)* and for religious reform, writing tracts and petitions against it and organizing vigilance committees to ensure that no force was employed whenever there was a case of *sati.* In some cases he himself went to the Calcutta burning grounds and tried to prevent the rite by his earnest persuasion. He persisted in his effort until the inhuman rite was abolished by law by Lord William Bentinck in 1829.

Ram Mohun supported the introduction of scientific and English education in India. In 1816 he and David Hare initiated the planning of an institution for the education of Hindu children, and in 1817 the Hindu College, which later became Presidency College, was founded. He also established his own English school, the Anglo-Hindu School, to provide free instruction for Hindu boys. In 1823 he wrote a letter to Lord Amherst, the governor-general, setting forth in forceful language his views on the educational needs of the country. He pleaded for a scientific system of education rather than Sanskrit education. In 1830, when Alexander Duff* opened a school, he supported his venture.

Ram Mohun was as great a champion of the freedom of the press as he was of Western education. He supported the editor of the *Calcutta Journal* against the government in 1823. He himself started two journals, the *Samvad Kaumudi,* a Bengali weekly, in 1821, and *Mirati-ul-Akhbar,* a Persian weekly, in 1822. He was also associated for some time with the *Bengal Herald,* started in 1829.

The greatest objective of Ram Mohun's life was to save the people of his country from the evils of Puranic Hinduism and draw their attention to the original purity of the teaching of Vedanta. In 1828 he founded the Brahmo Samaj*. Earlier, in 1815 in Calcutta, he had established a society, the Atmiya Sabha, which held weekly meetings during which sacred texts from the Upanishads were expounded and hymns composed by himself and his friends were sung. These meetings discontinued after 1819. In 1821 he formed another association, the Calcutta Unitarian Society, with both Indian and European members, but it did not prove a success. He then thought of establishing a purely indigenous institution for the worship of the one true God. He gathered like-minded friends and started the Brahmo Samaj on 20 Aug 1828. Prince Dwarakanath Tagore (father of Debendranath) was one of the chief supporters. The weekly *samaj* meetings included the chanting of the Upanishads followed by explanations of Vedantic passages, a sermon in Bengali, and the singing of hymns.

In 1830 the orthodox opponents of Ram Mohun, led by Radha Kanto Deb, organized a revival association, the Dharma Sabha, which published the *Samachar Chandrika.* Controversy between the Brahma Sabha (popular name of Brahmo Samaj) and the Dharma Sabha raged in the pages of the *Samvad Kaumudi* and the *Samachar Chandrika.*

From 1820 to1823, Ram Mohun was engaged in a controversy with the Christian missionaries of Serampore on the fundamentals of Christianity which started with the publication of his book *The Precepts of Jesus, The Guide to Peace and Happiness,* in which he tried to separate the moral teachings of Jesus from the "historical" and miraculous accounts given in the Gospels. In the Marshman*–Ram Mohun Roy controversy, he denied that Jesus is Jehovah God and rejected the Christian doctrines of the Trinity and atonement, and influenced a trinitarian missionary, William Adam, to become a Unitarian Christian.

Ram Mohun had three fundamental ideas in his Brahmo religion: (1) a monotheistic faith in the unity of God inspired by Islam*; (2) morality as the essence of true religion which is opposed to polytheism and idolatrous worship; and (3) religion should hold only to beliefs which are reasonable and thus avoid superstition and unnecessary mysteries and miracles. He claimed objectivity in approaching the truths of Christianity. The appeal of Jesus Christ to him was primarily to his ethics and monotheism.

He separated the teachings of Jesus from the historical events of his life, death, and resurrection and their biblical interpretation. He regarded Jesus the Son as inferior to the Father because the Son was always dependent and subject; there was only the unity of will, and not the identity of being, between Jesus and God; the mediator and Messiah was only the firstborn of all creatures. He held the opinion that the necessity of the cross for righteousness cannot be seen in any passage pronounced by Jesus and that it was a later interpretation by the apostles in the context of the Jewish religion of sacrifices. Today we have to recover the meaning of Jesus Christ in a spiritual sense, i.e., in moral and rational terms. The blessings of pardon are always available from the merciful Father through repentance. For Ram Mohun, the Holy Spirit was synonymous with the prevailing influence of God; the Council of Nicaea may have favored the irrational doctrine of the Trinity as an accommodation to the polytheism to which the Gentile converts were accustomed.

In 1830 Ram Mohun left for England where, before his death, he argued the case of the ex-Delhi emperor, Abu-nasar Muin-ud-din Akbar; saw that the appeal against the abolition of *sati* was defeated; contributed his view on the renewal of the company's charter; saw the reform bill passed; and had the opportunity to visit France.

Bibliography

Collett, Sophia Dobson, *Life and Letters of Raja Ram Mohun Roy,* ed. Hem Chandra Sarkar (1914). • Bhosh, Jogendra Chunder, and Eshan Chunder Bose, eds., *The English Works of Raja Ram Mohun Roy* (1906; reprinted 1978). • *Raja Ram Mohun Roy — His Life, Writings, and Speeches* (1925). • *The Complete Works of Raja Ram Mohun Roy, Sanskrit and Bengali* (1880). • *The Father of Modern India,* Commemoration Volume of Ram Mohun Roy Centenary (1933). • Farquhar, J. N., *Modern Religious Movements in India* (1924). • Sarma, D. S., *Studies in the Renaissance of Hinduism in the Nineteenth and Twentieth Centuries* (1944). • Banerji, Brajendranath Sajanikanta Das, ed., *Rama Mohana Granthavali* (1952). • Killingley, Dermot H., *The Only True God. Works on Religion by Ram Mohun Roy. Selected and Translated from Bengali and Sanskrit* (1982); *Ram Mohun Roy in Hindu and Christian Tradition: The Teape Lectures, 1990* (1993). • Thomas, M. M., *The Acknowledged Christ of the Indian Renaissance* (1969).

K. P. Aleaz

Royola, Pedro F.

Second Filipino Protestant missionary to Hawaii and pastor of the first Filipino congregation in the United States.

Royola was ordained in 1914 by the Cebu Presbytery of the Evangelical Church in the Philippine* Islands (Independent Presbyterian*). After briefly serving churches in Bohol and Negros Oriental, he left in 1916 to join Simeon Ygloria as the second Filipino Protestant missionary in Hawaii. After eight years among Filipino plantation workers, Royola moved to the United States mainland and organized the Filipino Presbyterian congregation in Salinas, California. It was the first Filipino congregation in the United States. He served as its first pastor and stayed until 1931. Returning to the Philippines, Royola affiliated with the United Evangelical Church, which was his last post before retirement as pastor of Dumaguete (1945-54).

Bibliography

Laubach, F. C., *People of the Philippines* (1925). • *Minutes, 4th UCCP General Assembly* (1954). • Sitoy, T. V., Jr., *Several Springs, One Stream* (1992).

T. Valentino Sitoy, Jr.

Ruggieri, Michele

(b. Spinazzola, Italy, 1543; d. Salerno, Italy, 1607). First Jesuit* missionary in China* in the late Ming dynasty.

Ruggieri, who had been a civil lawyer in Naples, joined the Society of Jesus in 1572 and was assigned to preach the Gospel in India* in 1576. From Rome he went to Lisbon, where he was ordained a priest (1578), and together with Matteo Ricci* and other Jesuits, he arrived in Goa on 13 Sep 1578. Soon Valignano, the superior of all Jesuit missions in Asia, assigned Ruggieri to Macau* to study Chinese language and culture in anticipation of entering interior China. In 1581, taking advantage of the opportunity provided Portuguese businessmen in Macau to trade in Guangzhou every spring and autumn, Ruggieri entered Guangzhou and became acquainted with a few local officials. In Dec 1582, after he carried gifts, including Western clocks, unknown in China then, and paid his respects to Chen Rui, governor of Zhaoqing, he was housed in the Buddhist Tian Ning Temple. Expressing willingness to become a Chinese subject, he wore the robe of a Buddhist monk. He returned to Macau several months later when Governor Chen left his post. When a new governor was appointed, Ruggieri was invited to Zhaoqing. He arrived with Ricci on 10 Sep 1583, and with the magistrate's permission, they built the first Society of Jesus residence in China, the Celestial Fairy Temple. Ruggieri raised funds for its construction among the Portuguese businessmen in Macau. Ruggieri lived on Zhaoqing for five years, during which time he traveled to Shaoxing in Zhejiang, Builin in Guangxi, and elsewhere. In 1584 he published the first Chinese book on Catholic doctrines, *The True Account of the Lord of Heaven.* Ruggieri felt it necessary for the pope to send an emissary to the Chinese emperor to obtain his approval to preach Christianity in China. He requested, and finally obtained, Valignano's consent to be sent to Rome for this mission. In 1588 he left Zhaoqing for Macau, from which he sailed back to Europe. Pope Sixtus V had just died and was succeeded by several new popes. In poor health and seeing no hope for a papal emissary to China, Ruggieri did not return to China before he died.

Bibliography

D'Elia, Pasquale M., ed., *Fonti Ricciare* (1942-1949) I:147, 174-77, 264. • Dunne, George H., *Generations of Giants* (1962). • Ross, Andrew C., *The Jesuits in Japan and China, 1342-1742* (1994).

JEAN-PAUL WIEST and THE CHINA GROUP

Rumainum, Filip J. S.

(b. Numfoor, West New Guinea [Irian Jaya], 1914; d. Jan 1968). Rumainum's father, the teacher-preacher Willem Rumainum, was kidnapped by pirates from Biak in his youth (ca. 1900), but was ransomed by a Christian native. Subsequently, he was sent to Java, where he was educated in the Depok Seminary near Jakarta. Afterwards, Willem Rumainum became a missionary in his native island, Numfoor. His son, Filip, frequented the teacher training school at Miei (1928-34), which was headed by the very able missionary I. S. Kijne (1923-58 in Irian). After taking his certificate, he was sent to Ambon, where he followed a course in agriculture. For six years he led an agricultural education center of the mission and then became a teacher-preacher. After the war, in Mar 1947, he led the Irianese delegation to the Conference of Malino, where the Christian Council of Eastern Indonesia* was founded. In 1948 he was sent to Timor* to the Theological Seminary for Eastern Indonesia. After his return to Irian in 1952, he was ordained a minister, the first Irianese minister to have received a regular theological education, and became chairman of the Biak-Numfoor church district, with 34,000 Christians.

In 1956 the church of Irian became fully independent under the name of Gereja Kristen Irian Jaya*. Rumainum became its first chairman and remained in this capacity until his sudden death. As a leader of the church, he gained the respect of all of the tribes represented in the church membership, but he also distinguished himself by his administrative abilities. These were eventful years for the people and church of Irian, as in 1962 the Dutch colonial rule over the region came to an end, and after an interregnum under the auspices of the United Nations, Irian became a province of the Republic of Indonesia. In those years, Rumainum provided the leadership which enabled the church to remain loyal to the government and at the same time become the one Irianese-led organization where the people of Irian found a safe haven.

THOMAS VAN DEN END

Rumambi, Wilhelm Johanis

(b. Tompaso, North Celebes, Indonesia, 7 Apr 1916; d. Jakarta, 22 Jan 1984). Minahasan pastor, ecumenical* leader, and politician.

Rumambi studied at the Theological Seminary in Bogor, later in Jakarta (1934-40), and was ordained in 1940. In his career as a pastor, he worked in several congregations in Minahasa. During the Japanese occupation, the Christian Evangelical Church in Minahasa* (GMIM) allowed him to serve in the office of religious affairs in Manado. Thereafter he became head of a department which administered school affairs in his church. When Indonesia was still politically unstable and the country remained divided into several tribal areas, Rumambi became a representative of the Minahasan church for a conference of missionaries held in Jakarta from 10 to 20 Aug 1945. After this conference, he came into contact with a friend from the Moluccas* and Timor and prepared a similar conference for the churches in the eastern part of Indonesia*. His church sent him to Makassar to prepare for the conference in 1947, where he was elected general secretary of the Christian council in the eastern part of Indonesia. In this position Rumambi gave much attention to the problems of unity among the churches in Indonesia, many of which were scattered over several islands throughout Indonesia. He clearly saw this process of unity as the will of the Lord. His experiences at the Whitby conference of the International Missionary Council (IMC) in 1947 and as a participant of the Joint Commission of East Asia in Manila in 1948 enabled him to realize this vision.

Rumambi contributed much to the formation of the Indonesian Council of Churches* (*Dewan gereja-gereja di Indonesia,* DGI). Together with T. Sihombing from Sumatra and B. Probowinoto from Java, he wrote a proposal and provided schemes for a committee to look into the development of the Council of Christian Churches. His proposals were significant in the formation of church unity. Thus it was natural that he should be elected the first general secretary of the council. As soon as he took on this role, he conducted visitations to the local churches in the different regions, realizing that it was better to make direct contact with churches than to communicate through letters. Although the larger ecumenical movement influenced the process of church unity in Indonesia, this influence was not seen as determinative. This process was aroused first by the experiences of the local churches since World War II, then through the Japanese occupation, and consequently during the period the Indonesian nation struggled for its independence. In this connection, Rumambi also strongly felt that church unity in Indonesia was not to be used for acquiring worldly power or to build an omnipotent church.

In 1956 Rumambi entered politics. With approval from his church in Minahasa, he was elected a member of the constituent assembly. Between 1959 and 1966, President Sukarno* appointed him to a number of government posts, his last position being minister of information. After government service, he returned to Christian service as the secretary of the Commission of

Church and Society of the Indonesian Council of Churches (ICC). From 1974 to 1983, he worked as general secretary of the Indonesian Bible Society. While holding this post, he asked the Roman Catholic leaders to work together with the Protestants. He remained an honorary chairman of the ICC until his death in 1984.

Bibliography

Holtrop, P. N., *Selaku Perintis Jalan* (1982). • Hartono, Chris, *Gerakan Ekumenis di Indonesia* (1984). • *Berita Oikumene* (Feb 1984). • *Wending*, Jaargang 4 (Mei 1949).

ARNOLD PARENGKUAN

Rural Evangelism (Noson Dendo), Japan

Rural evangelism in Japan includes four general categories: evangelism of farm families, evangelism in areas that are primarily agricultural, evangelism in small towns that serve as the economic bases for farming communities, and evangelism that takes into account Japan's basically agricultural social and psychological background.

During the Kirishitan* Period, feudal lords *(daimyo)* were the target of evangelization because they had control of their areas, and Christian influence would then spread quickly to the peasantry. Among the hidden Christians who were later forced into hiding by severe persecution were many farmers, and their customs and habits included a number of adaptations reflecting a Christian influence on their lifestyles. Protestant rural evangelism can be divided into three periods: the Meiji-Taisho Era (1868-1926), the early Showa Era (1926-45), and the late Showa Era (1945-present). Two-thirds of all the churches in the first period were rural, but because of the rise of nationalism and the modernization of society, they suffered a rapid decline. In the second period, Gospel schools for rural people and small farming village churches were active, and rural evangelism was first carried out with much intentionality. The third period, after World War II*, began with the enthusiastic belief that Japan's recovery would originate in rural areas. With support from foreign churches, evangelistic work was done on a grand scale, but along with rapid urbanization, changes in society, and the return of nationalism*, internal factors such as local churches' movement toward becoming self-supporting were passed along to the rural churches, causing them to decline. Even so, rural evangelism was enthusiastically engaged in as a central evangelistic issue in Japan. Something that continues to be important in all areas of Japanese society is the strength of community and the symbolic meaning of traditional values and life; evangelism is done by exploring how these can go together, as in 1 Cor 9:23 (to share in its blessings).

Bibliography

Sumiya Mikio, *Nihon no shakai shiso — kindaika to kirisuto-kyo* (Japanese social thought — modernization and Christianity) (1968). • Kikuchi Yoshiya, Kibo Toshi, *Kyokai to dendoken* (The church and larger parish evangelism) (1962).

SHIMIZU KEIZO, JAPANESE DICTIONARY

Ryang Ju Sam

(b. Yongkang, South Pyunan Province, North Korea, 25 Jan 1879; d. 1950?). Methodist* pastor, first bishop of the Korean Methodist Church, and educator.

In 1902 Ryang went to China* to study at the Anglo-Chinese College in Shanghai, a mission school run by the Methodist Episcopal Church, South. There he was baptized. After his graduation he went to San Francisco, California, where he founded a Korean-American Methodist church in Dec 1906, the oldest Korean-American church in the United States. He also published a Korean magazine, *Dae Do* (The Great Way), to enlighten the Korean immigrant population.

In order to advance his theological education, Ryang attended Vanderbilt University Divinity School (1910-12) and Yale Divinity School (1912-13). Upon his return to Korea*, he was appointed a professor at Union Methodist Theological Seminary. In 1908 he was appointed director of the celebration event of the centennial year of the foreign mission of the Americn Methodist Episcopal Church. He served as minister of Chongkyo Methodist Church in Seoul for two years and organized the mission board in the Methodist Church to begin mission work for Koreans in Manchuria.

When the northern and southern Methodist mission bodies became united, the Korean Methodist Church was born. Ryang was eleted the first superintendent (bishop) of the Korean annual conference. He served in that position for eight years. After liberation in 1945, he was appointed president of the Red Cross, Korea, in 1949. During the Korean War*, the invading North Korean military agents kidnapped him to the north. He is listed as a missing person from the war.

DAVID SUH, with contributions from
LEE DUK JOO, translated by KIM IN SOO

Ryburn, Horace W.

(b. Erwin, Tennessee, United States, 1 Jun 1911; d. United States, 1 Mar 1993). Presbyterian* missionary who played a central role in integrating Presbyterian missionary work into the Church of Christ in Thailand (CCT).

Ryburn, who graduated from Davidson College (1932) and Princeton Theological Seminary (1937), was ordained in 1937. He then served as a Presbyterian missionary in Chiang Mai, Thailand, from 1938 until Dec 1941. He married Mary Turner in 1942. In 1947 he became field administrator of the American Presbyterian Mission (APM) in Thailand. Ryburn oversaw the reestablishment of the APM after World War II* and the subsequent process that led to the integration of the APM into the CCT in 1957. This was a milestone in the emergence of the CCT as a fully independent church body. Ryburn assumed the position of Presbyterian field representative and continued to play a predominant role in CCT missionary policy and activities. In 1972 he assumed the position of CCT ecumenical secretary as a way to further reduce his leadership role. His retirement in 1976 marked the end of a strong missionary presence in the CCT. Ryburn was active in foreign community affairs in Bangkok and was an influential voice in Presbyterian missions.

Bibliography

Interview with Horace Ryburn (Payap University Archives, Chiang Mai, Thailand). • Presbyterian Church USA, *Records of the American Presbyterian Mission* (Payap University Archives, Chiang Mai, Thailand).

KUMMOOL CHINAWONG, translated by HERBERT R. SWANSON

S

Sabah Anglican Interior Mission

(SAIM). Originally known as the North Borneo Interior Mission, SAIM was officially launched on 6 Jan 1958 when the mission in Tongud on the Kinabatangan River was opened with the purpose of reaching the indigenous peoples living in the upper reaches of the Kinabatangan and Labuk Rivers. The idea of a Gospel outreach to the people of the interior had been promoted two years earlier by an English surveyor, Bruce Sandilands. Frank Lomax of St. Michael and All Angels, Sandakan, followed up Sandilands's call, and a report was prepared after several field trips to the area.

The mission was started with a school and a medical* station; from the outset, the main financial support came from the Anglican* parishes in the coastal towns of Sabah. It was from this that SAIM came into being as an organization. The first group of workers were five Iban* missionaries from the churches in Sarawak, including Andrew Kiri, Arnold Puntang, Lawrence Lawin, Francis Krie, and Joseph Majang, together with an English nurse, Wendy Gray, and an Australian teacher, Joan Goodricke. A two-way radio connecting Sandakan and Tongud was set up to ensure communication between the two places (a letter took at least one week to arrive). Communications between the various interior stations were maintained by boats along the rivers. Between 1960 and 1965, SAIM expanded its work by setting up three medical clinics at Tongud, Telupid, and Segama. A new school was opened in Segama and an agricultural farm in Tongud.

SAIM was initially administered by Rev. Lomax. As the work grew, a council and an executive committee were formed with a full-time coordinator sent out by the Society for the Propagation of the Gospel (SPG). By the late 1960s, SAIM encountered numerous problems, including the absence of a full-time coordinator after 1965 and a hostile attitude (by the then state government) to foreign missionaries. SAIM suffered a setback when many foreign missionaries were asked to leave, and the clinic and the agricultural farm, not yet self-supporting, had to be closed.

In 1973 the future of SAIM was discussed, and a decision was made to carry on the work with the emphasis shifted from practical mission to evangelistic work. A Bible* school was started to train lay workers among the indigenous peoples, and translation of the Gospels and the Epistles into local languages was sped up. SAIM continued to grow after 1975, with new stations at Penangah and Beluran. All the missionaries participating in the work of SAIM are now Malaysian, including many new theologically trained young Kadazan and Chinese missionaries. From the first eight converts baptized at Tongud in 1958, the Anglican Church of the Interior had grown by 1995 to around 17,000 Christians and now has its own evangelist training center, the Valley of Blessing, at Telupid, Labuk, directed by a veteran of the mission, Fred David.

Danny Wong Tze-Ken and Frank Lomax

Sadrach, Surapranata

(Kiai) (b. Jepara, Central Java, Indonesia, 1835; d. Karangjasa, Central Java, Indonesia, 14 Nov 1924). Charismatic Javanese pioneer evangelist in Central Java*.

Sadrach's great achievements in mission work were in communicating the Gospel and developing a Christian community along the lines of the Javanese context of the 19th c. This typical, uniquely indigenous Christian community manifested itself through its organization, leadership, teaching, and traditions. Originally, organization was not a concern of Sadrach's community, and stress was placed rather on personal relationships and fellowship between the *guru* (religious teacher) and the *murid* (disciple), as in the Javanese *paguron* (Javanese discipleship system). Although the Reformed* church model of organization was introduced by Dutch missionary J. Wilhelm, it did not change the basic Javanese pattern. Sadrach still functioned as *guru* and *kiai* (an honorary title for a religious leader) and remained the decisive figure in the community. Sadrach's community was basically rural in character, and church officials were not paid. Worship and liturgy were flexible. Javanese customs and rites concerning pregnancy, childbirth, circumcision, marriage, death, land cultivation, farming, harvest, etc., were selectively Christianized to make them appropriate for the community. The features of Sadrach's Christian community were uniquely Javanese.

But this caused Sadrach to come into conflict with the Dutch missionaries. Problems arose because of a fundamental difference in sociocultural and political contexts between the Javanese and the Dutch. Two kinds of accusations were made against Sadrach and his community by the Dutch missionaries. The first consisted in unfounded charges based on rumors and innuendoes that were uncritically accepted and propagated by missionaries due either to their lack of knowledge and understanding of the Javanese culture or to vested political and personal interests. The second type of accusation was based on theological and missiological issues arising from the missionaries' orthodox view of Western Christianity as the single norm by which Javanese Christianity must be measured and to which Javanese Christianity conformed. The accusations covered four major themes: Sadrach's authority and central position in the community were considered contrary to Calvinistic principles; the understanding and proclamation of Christ as *ratu adil* (just and righteous king) and *panutan* (exemplary figure) were seen as being contrary to the nature of Christ as the incarnation of God; proclaiming the Gospel as *ngelmu* (knowledge) was considered contrary to the teaching of salvation by faith and grace alone as explained in the Scriptures; and the preservation of Javanese *adat* (traditions) in Sadrach's community was adjudged contrary to the Christian teaching on rebirth and new life in Christ.

In summary, Sadrach developed a style of leadership and form of Christian community that were rooted in and inspired by traditional Javanese values and customs. But whereas he and his community viewed their achievements as the communication of the Gospel relevant to the Javanese soul, the Dutch missionaries viewed them as compromise, syncretism, and falsehood.

Bibliography

Adriaanse, L., *Sadrach's Kring* (1899). • Lion Cachet, F., *Een jaar op reis in dienst der Zending* (1896). • Quarles van Ufford, P., "Why Don't You Sit Down?" in *Man, Meaning, and History* (1980). • Partonadi, Sutarman S., *Sadrach's Community and Its Contextual Roots* (1988, 1990).

SUTARMAN S. PARTONADI

Sailer, Randolph C.

(b. Philadelphia, Pennsylvania, United States; d. 1981). Missionary of the Presbyterian* Church in the United States of America (North) to China.

Sailer received a Christian education since his youth. He graduated from Princeton University in 1919 and was president of the Student Volunteer Band. He obtained a master's degree from Columbia University in 1922 and a doctorate the following year. At the same time, he took courses at Union Theological Seminary, New York. He came to China* in 1923 and taught in Yenching University. He had been dean of the psychology and education departments.

Sailer served as chairman of Yenching University Christian Fellowship for many years and supported students who had financial difficulty by his own means. During the Sino-Japanese War, members of anti-Japanese organizations frequently took cover in his residence. During the civil war in China, he helped those students who supported the Communist Party escape from the Nationalist Party's persecution and helped them in transporting medicine to the Liberated Area.

In 1951 Sailer left China and returned to the United States. In later years he taught in Pakistan* at Forman Christian College. He retired in 1963. In 1973 he was invited to China for an official visit and was welcomed officially by the government. Zhou En Lai commended him as a "friend of the Chinese people." After he returned to the United States, he wrote an article, "Ten Suggestions for Working to Understand China and America Better," and served as president of the Washington America-China Friendship Association. After his death, Beijing University held a memorial service in his honor. Both the *China Daily* and *Beijing Weekly* ran articles in remembrance of Sailer. CHINA GROUP

St. Andrew's Church Mission, Singapore

On Pentecost Sunday 1856, a sermon was preached to the mainly British congregation of St. Andrew's Church by the residency chaplain, William Humphrey, exhorting them to accept responsibility for a planned evangelistic campaign in Singapore*. As a direct result, the St. Andrew's Church Mission was formed on 25 Jun 1856; Tamil and Chinese catechists were appointed, and in 1862, the Society for the Propagation of the Gospel (SPG) commissioned Edward Venn to be superintendent of the mission. By this time, the mission had 70 Tamil and Chinese converts.

The work of the mission expanded further with the appointment in 1872 of William Henry Gomes*, a gifted linguist from Ceylon (Sri Lanka*) who had worked in Borneo and Malacca*. Under his leadership, St. Peter's Mission Chapel was opened on Stamford Road in 1875 and St. John's Church, Jurong, in 1884. By this time the mission was working in the Hokkien, Tamil, and Malay languages. After the death of Gomes in 1902, R. Richards was appointed superintendent of the mission. Two mission catechists, Dong Bing Seng* (Foochow) and Chan Wing Tsuen (Cantonese), together with D. S. Ponniah (Tamil), became the first Asian clergy to be ordained in the diocese. Under Richards's able leadership (1902-34), more Asian clergy were ordained and work was extended to other dialect groups. Today, St. Matthew's (Cantonese), Christ Church (Tamil), and Holy Trinity (Hokkien/Foochow), as well as St. Andrew's School, owe their origins to the mission.

Before the outbreak of World War II*, the mission had effectively created an Asian Anglican* church in Singapore.

Bibliography

USPG Archives, Partnership House Library, London. • Swindell, F. G., *A Short History of St. Andrew's Cathedral, Singapore* (1929). • Loh Keng Aun, *50 Years of the Anglican Church in Singapore Island (1909-1959)* (1963). • Sng, Bobby E. K., *In His Good Time* (1980, 1993).

Frank Lomax

St. Joseph, Church of

(Ayutthaya, Thailand*). The first temporary building of the Church of St. Joseph was erected in 1666 as part of a settlement, the St. Joseph Settlement, in Ayutthaya established by Lambert de la Motte* on land granted by King Narai*. The settlement included a school and dormitory for novices and a residence for priests. A small hospital was added in 1669 with Louis Laneau* as the doctor.

From 1679 the church in Ayutthaya served as the center for all Catholic mission work in the Far East. In 1685 Laneau, the apostolic vicar of Siam, built a new church building of brick. It was consecrated and commended to the care of St. Joseph.

The church suffered during the religious persecution that followed the death of King Pra Narai in 1688. The Burmese invasion of 1767 completely destroyed the St. Joseph Settlement and dispersed the Catholics. The bishop himself, missionaries, and Portuguese priests under his care were taken captive to Burma*. A group under Fr. Corre fled to Cambodia*. Thai Catholics of Portuguese descent escaped to Bangkok. Vietnamese Catholics were scattered among villages around Ayutthaya. Land belonging to the Catholics was claimed by others.

In 1830 Fr. Pallegoix* visited Ayutthaya to assess the situation. He bought some of the land around the old church building and encouraged the dispersed Vietnamese Catholics to reestablish the Catholic village. Fr. Albert was commissioned to rebuild St. Joseph's Church in 1835. He pastored the 200 or so Catholics until 1851.

His successor, Fr. Larnaudie, constructed a sugar factory to provide a means of livelihood for the church members. Fr. Perreaux, appointed priest in 1872, was shocked to see the pitiful ruins of the original church and its small successor commissioned by Pallegoix. He bought back much of the former church land to build a temporary wooden church, pulled down the church commissioned by Pallegoix, and built a new church on the foundations of the original one. The remains of the 13 missionaries buried a century earlier were discovered during the excavation to lay the foundation. The cornerstone of the church was dedicated on 21 Nov 1883 by Jean-Louis Vey*, who came with 16 other missionaries, but the construction was hampered by a lack of funds.

Perreaux opened St. Joseph in 1884 to educate the children of Catholics, using the "church language," that is, Romanized Thai. The temporary building was burnt in 1888, and the new church was dedicated on 19 Mar 1891. Repairs were made to the church in 1948 and 1966. A new roof was made for the 300th anniversary of the church in Apr 1969.

Victor Larque, translated by E. John Hamlin

St. Joseph's Institution

Oldest Roman* Catholic school in Singapore*, conducted since 1852 by the Brothers of the Christian Schools, also known as La Salle Brothers*.

At the request of Jean Beurel* (of the Paris Foreign Mission; MEP*) for dedicated missionary teachers competent to teach in English, four French and two Irish Brothers were assigned to establish schools in the Straits settlements of Singapore and Penang.

The *Singapore Free Press* of 22 Jun 1848 quoted Beurel's aspirations: "English, French, Chinese, Malay, Mathematics, Book-keeping, Drawing, etc., will be taught. It will be open to everyone whatever his religion. Non-Catholics will not be required to attend instruction in the Catholic religion unless their parents want them to do so. The Masters will always watch carefully over the morals of all the students."

As more missionaries arrived, the Brothers opened schools at the bishops' request in India* (1859), Burma* (1860), Ceylon (Sri Lanka*) and Indochina (1866), Hong Kong (1875), and the Philippines (1910).

In 1933 St. Joseph's established St. Patrick's as an affiliated primary and secondary school with boarding facilities. In 1938 it took over St. Anthony's Boys' School, and in the 1950s it built feeder primary schools: De La Salle School, St. Michael's, and St. Stephen's. The enrollment of these schools varies between 1,000 and 1,500. Approximately 30 percent are Catholics, 10 percent other Christians, 30 percent Buddhists, 5 percent Muslims, 5 percent Hindus, and 20 percent others.

The Brothers no longer depend on missionaries from overseas. Increasingly they depend on lay colleagues, many of whom come from their schools and have Christian views of life and education.

Bibliography

Brown, Francis, *La Salle — Malaysia, Singapore, 1852-1952* (1959). • *A Sign of Faith, La Salle Brothers' 300 Years, 1680-1980* (available from the La Salle Brothers).

Brother Patrick

St. Joseph's Society for Foreign Missions. *See* Mill Hill Missionaries

St. Paul de Chartres, Thailand

Second Catholic order to arrive in Thailand*; founded in 1696 by a French parish priest, Louis Chauvet.

When the order of St. Paul de Chartres was granted its final approbation in 1949, it had already established its work in Vietnam*, China*, Japan*, Thailand, Laos*, the Philippines*, Africa, France, Belgium, Switzerland, the West Indies, and Canada. In 1963 the order went to the USA.

Seven sisters of St. Paul de Chartres arrived on 24 Apr 1898 from Saigon at the invitation of Msgr. Jean-Louis Vey*, of the Paris* Foreign Mission (MEP), to work at the St. Louis Hospital and to do administrative work in Bangkok schools. The governor of Indochina was so impressed with their diligence, patience, and efficiency that he awarded them a gold medal on 20 May 1899.

In 1900 there were 13 nuns at work in Thailand. Fr. D'Hondt requested them to assist in training the local nuns of the Lovers of the Cross*, or *Amantes de la Croix,* now called Sisters of the Sacred Heart, in Bangkok. Sr. Henriette was appointed for the task. In 1901 Mother Donatienne was chosen as the mother superior.

The sisters of St. Paul de Chartres decided to shift their educational work to Thailand when their school in Saigon was bombed in 1903. They established two schools, the Assumption Convent (1905), their first school in Thailand, and the Santa Cruz Convent (1906). Mother Saint-Xavier was the first principal of the Assumption. She arrived in Bangkok on 8 Mar 1904 with two other sisters, Agnes de Saint-Paul and Angelique. They were joined by Sisters Anselme, Marie-Blanche, and Mathilde de Saint-Paul in June. While the two schools were under construction, the sisters stayed at the St. Louis Hospital. They studied Thai and taught French, English, and Portuguese. They also helped in the hospital when a smallpox epidemic broke out.

In 1907, when the Sisters of the Holy Infant Jesus returned to Malaysia*, Msgr. Vey handed their school, the Holy Infant Jesus Convent in Bangkok, to the St. Paul de Chartres, who made it their headquarters and renamed the school the St. Joseph Convent. (The present headquarters is in Bangna.) Two nuns were sent in 1907, and four more in 1909, to help with the school at Wat Kalwar (now Kularb Wattana School). The school was handed over to the Ursulines* in 1924.

In 1909 the sisters helped in the school of the Church of St. Paul in Petburi and also continued their welfare work with orphans and infants. In 1913 they assisted in the school of the Bang Nok Kwaek Church. In 1914 they opened a hospital for leprosy* patients. They opened the St. Francis Xavier* Convent School in 1925, and in 1926 an indigenous novitiate was opened at the St. Joseph Convent to train local girls who desired to join the order of St. Paul de Chartres.

Initially the sisters had to support themselves and raise funds by growing vegetables, baking bread, and sewing. It was not long before they earned the sympathy and respect of the people. A palace official gave annual gifts to the school. In 1947 the MEP relinquished the St. Paul de Chartres in Thailand to the direct care of their headquarters in Chartres, France. The novitiate was moved to the St. Joseph Convent in Bangna in 1973.

In 1976 the sisters assisted in the social welfare and refugee work of the diocese of Udon Thani among Laotian refugees in Nong Khai Province. They also worked with orphans in Pattaya. In 1978 they helped with the evangelistic station in Udon Thani.

Over the years, the sisters of St. Paul de Chartres have made significant contributions to Thailand in education, hospital, and social welfare work.

ORASA CHAOWCHIN, translated by E. JOHN HAMLIN

St. Paul's Ruins, Macau

Remains of a public school founded by the Jesuits (see Society of Jesus) in the early 1560s.

Soon after arriving and settling in Macau* in the early 1560s, the Jesuits opened and ran the Mother of God's, or St. Paul's, Public School (already operating by 1565). From 1574, the school received a government subsidy of 1,000 cruzados.

In 1577 the school had 150 students, among whom were the missionaries who were studying the Chinese language and culture. In 1584, after M. Ruggieri* (1545-1607) and M. Ricci* (1552-1610) succeeded to enter and work in the Chinese empire, the number of missionaries at the school increased to 12 out of 200 students.

On 1 Dec 1594 the school was made into a university college, the first in Asia, and it began awarding degrees in theology and the arts in 1597. In 1601, 59 Jesuits were teaching and studying humanities and languages there.

In the following year, on the site of a chapel destroyed by the fire beside the college, the Mother of God's Church (popularly known as St. Paul's) was started, and its main structures were finished in 1603. The façade of carved stone was built by local craftsmen and Japanese Christians (exiled in the 1620s) under the direction of the Italian Jesuit Carlo Spinola (martyred in Japan* in 1622) between 1610 and 1644.

When the Jesuits were expelled from Macau in 1762, St. Paul's College was closed and later turned into army barracks until a fire destroyed it completely in 1935. The church's walls were not consumed by the fire, but they were later torn down due to the danger of collapse. Only the façade was saved, and it still rises in four colonnaded tiers, with their carved symbols and statues, around the Virgin Mary, "Mother of God," whose statue is placed in a niche on the third row and surrounded by roses and lilies. St. Paul's façade has become the symbol of Macau. Recently, restoration works have been started with the purpose of turning the entire complex into a museum of history.

Bibliography

Valente, M. R., *Igrejas de Macau* (1993).

SERGIO TICOZZI

St. Thomas and the Thomas Tradition

St. Thomas and the Thomas Tradition

The Thomas Christians are those who claim their Christian origin from the apostle Thomas. Formerly, there were Thomas Christians in several parts of India* and also in Persia, but only those of the southwest coast of India have come down to the present day. They alone are the subject of this article and are meant by the term "Thomas Christians."

The Thomas Christians (Syrian Christians) of India hold the establishment of their church by St. Thomas almost as an article of faith. They claim that St. Thomas came to India in 52 C.E.

There are two views among scholars about the origin of Christianity in India. According to one, the foundation of Christianity in India was laid by St. Thomas, the apostle, or even, as some would hold, by two apostles, viz., St. Thomas and St. Bartholomew. The other view would ascribe the arrival of Christianity in India to the enterprise of merchants and missionaries of the East Syrian or Persian church. Such a position is held by all who deny the apostolate of St. Thomas in any part of India. Those who propound the apostolic origin do not deny the role of the East Syrian church in reinforcing Indian Christianity.

The earliest record about the apostolate of Thomas is the *Apocryphal Acts of Judas Thomas,* written in Syriac in the Edessan circle about the turn of the 3rd c. C.E. Even though this work is apocryphal, several scholars find in it a historical nucleus that represents the late 1st or 2nd c. tradition about the apostolate of St. Thomas in India. Besides, a number of fragmentary passages in other writings of the 3rd, 4th, and following centuries speak about the apostolate of St. Thomas. From the 4th c. onward, the major churches are unanimous in their witness to the tradition.

Many others, drawing their inferences from the *Acts of Judas Thomas,* have lent their support to the view that St. Thomas preached in northwest India. An important group of scholars consider the South Indian tradition more reliable than the *Acts.* They give greater importance to the South Indian apostolate in view of the living tradition of the community of St. Thomas Christians of Kerala and the tomb of Thomas at Mylapore.

In support of the early Christianization of North India, we do not possess any actual vestiges as we do for South India. The South Indian claim to the apostolate of St. Thomas is supported by two monuments: the community of St. Thomas Christians, with their living tradition, and the tomb of Mylapore, which is definitely identified as the burial place of St. Thomas at least from the 14th c. onward.

The Indian tradition of the establishment of the church by St. Thomas in Kerala was handed down from generation to generation by word of mouth among the Christians of St. Thomas and to some extent among their non-Christian neighbors. According to the Indian tradition, St. Thomas came by sea and first landed at Cranganore in about 52 C.E. He converted high-caste Hindu families in Cranganore, Palayur, Quilon, and some other places. He crossed over to Cathay (China*?) and preached the Gospel and returned to India, where he organized the Christians of Malabar and erected a few public places of worship. Then he moved to the Coromandel (east coast of South India) and suffered martyrdom on or near a place which is now called Little Mount. His body was brought to the town of Mylapore and was buried in a holy shrine he had built.

This tradition is made up of the elements of the traditions prevalent in Malabar, Mylapore, or Coromandal and the East Syrian Church. Some details of this combined tradition may be found in a few songs (popular among the Thomas Christians) such as *Rebban Pattu (Thomma Parvam),* the *Veeradyan Pattu,* the *Margam kali pattu,* etc. It is likely that a few of these songs were taken from manuscripts handed down from family to family.

In the 16th c., the Portuguese came to know that the Christians of St. Thomas had in their possession not only songs but also written records that commemorated the life, work, death, etc., of St. Thomas. But most of these records were destroyed after the Synod of Diamper in 1599. Some of the Hindu accounts on the origins of Kerala (Keralolpathy) and a Tamil account about Kandappa Raja contain allusions to St. Thomas and his works.

The following summary of the song *Reban Pattu* gives an idea of the tradition prevailing among the Thomas Christians:

"Thomas the apostle coming from Arabia landed in Malankara (Cranganore) in the year 50 A.D. in the month of *Dhanu* (December/January). After a short stay here, he proceeded to Mailapuram (Mylapore) and from there went on to China. Coming back to Mailapuram port, he sailed to Malankara, being invited by the king of Tiruvanchikulam (in the Cranganore area) and founded seven churches there: in Cranganore, Kollam, Chayal, Niranam, Kokamangalam, Kottakkayal, and Palayur.

"In 59 A.D., in the month of *Kanni* (September/October), he was called back to Mailapuram by the king, who imprisoned the apostle because he had given to the poor the money the king had entrusted to him for building a palace for him. But the king's brother died at that time and was brought back to life, and he revealed himself to the king of the heavenly palace. Thomas thereupon was set free and the king, along with 700 non-believers, received baptism.

"After a stay of two and a half years in Mailapuram, the apostle returned to Malabar and worked there and converted many to Christianity. The apostle ordained priests and consecrated bishops in Malabar. In the year 69 A.D., he departed from there to the land of the Tamils.

"Back in Mailapuram in the year 72 A.D., on the third day of the month of *Karkadakam* (July), the apostle met on his way to the Little Mount some Brahmins going for a sacrifice to the temple of the goddess Kali. They wanted him to take part in their worship; he, however, with the sign of the cross, destroyed the temple, and the Brahmins in their fury pierced him with a lance. With a prayer on his lips, the apostle gave up his spirit on a rock in the forest near the shore of the sea and his soul flew up to heaven in the form of a white dove accompanied by angels, and in a vision he promised his help to all those who prayed at his tomb."

This tradition is clearly influenced by the account of the *Acts of Judas Thomas* and also by the East Syrian tradition.

Oral tradition. Some Christian families traditionally trace their Christianity from the apostle. The tenacity of these claims before the coming of the Portuguese (in the 16th c.) makes it difficult to discredit them. These families claim to have been converted from the Brahmins of Kerala. Some of them remember many details about their origins and still point out the original place and houses of residence. A few even have a number of palm-leaf documents in their private archives which, they think, contain all the details about their origin. Some of the most important of these families are: Pakalomattam, Sankarapuri, Kalli, Kalikav, Koyikkam, Madeipur, Muttodal, Nedumpally, Panakkamattam, Kottakali, etc. Certain of these families have a succession of priests, and each of the priests regards himself as the next of his family, counting from the first, who is believed to have been ordained by St. Thomas.

There is a rich tradition related to many of the old churches and communities. The best known of these is that of Palayur Church, not far from Cranganore. The Christian church of Palayur stands in a compound where there are seen remnants of Hindu worship such as a tank, a well for drawing water for sacrifice, the round stone with which this well was covered, etc. The Brahmins in the neighborhood of Palayur, which their ancestors cursed and left, called it "cursed place." Both the Christian and Hindu traditions say that, when St. Thomas converted some Brahmins there, the rest ran away to a nearby locality.

The tomb of Mylapore and St. Thomas. The name Mylapore means the "town of the peacocks." It is a famous town on the eastern coast of South India. This coast is known in history as Coromandel, derived from Cholamandalam, the country of the Cholas. St. Thomas's tomb is situated in Mylapore.

Some scholars are of the opinion that the story of the tomb is a "barefaced impostor" made up by the Portuguese. Others argue that this is not so, since the story of the death and burial of Thomas in India was known even before the coming of the Portuguese. No other place in India other than Mylapore claimed to be the place where St. Thomas underwent martyrdom and was buried. So one may reasonably be convinced of the authenticity of the tomb. Scholars such as Mathias Mundadan are of the opinion that the argument of convergence of western tradition and the native Indian tradition appears to be reasonable enough to confirm the age-old belief of the local St. Thomas Christians, viz., that their origin as Christians is from the mission of St. Thomas the apostle.

Bibliography

Brown, Leslie, *The Indian Christians of St. Thomas* (B I Publishers, New Delhi). • Daniel, K. N., *A Brief Sketch of the Church of St. Thomas in Malabar* (1938). • Keay, F. E., *History of the Syrian Church in India* (1938). • Mundadan, A. Mathias, *History of Christianity in India*, Vol. I (1984). • Perumalil, A. C., *The Apostles in India* (1971). • Philip, E. M., *The Indian Church of St. Thomas* (1950). • Podipara, J. Placid, *The Thomas Christians* (1976). • Tisserant, Cardinal Eugene, *Eastern Christianity in India: A History of the Syro-Malabar Church from Earliest Times to the Present Day* (authorized adaptation from the French by E. R. Hambye) (1957). • Yuhanon Mar Thoma, *Christianity in India* (1968).

GEEVARGHESE PANICKER

St. Thomas Evangelical Church of India (STECI). The STECI was inaugurated on 26 Jan 1961 at Tiruvalla, Kerala, South India*. Twenty-five thousand people were present when the declaration of the new church was read and unanimously passed.

The formation of a new church was inevitable because of struggles in the Mar Thoma Syrian Church of Malabar for nearly 14 years. After Metropolitan Abraham Mar Thoma* passed away, the low-church evangelical wing (the majority of the church) was left without episcopal care. The new metropolitan, Juhanon Mar Thoma*, whose theological and doctrinal views paralleled those of the Orthodox Syrian Church of Malabar, passed his high-church position on to the evangelical Mar Thoma Church. This eventuated in his giving a public declaration and a court affidavit changing the Reformed Mar Thoma teaching to the Jacobite Syrian teaching and his excommunicating four leading evangelical priests of the Mar Thoma Church, namely, P. I. Mathai, John Varghese, C. M. Varghese, and K. O. John. This, along with the litigatory processes of K. N. Daniel (a lay theological* teacher in the Mar Thoma Church) to safeguard the Reformed teaching of the church, precipitated the formation of the STECI (see Presbyterian and Reformed Churches). Thus nearly 80 priests and 25,000 lay members of the Mar Thoma Church came out to form the STECI.

On STECI's inaugural day, two bishops were consecrated, K. N. Oommen and John Varghese. Five years later, after Varghese's death, certain internal dissensions and problems set in in the new church. This dogged the church for decades and disengaged the vigorous movement the church was to be.

The various church boards, however, encompassing evangelism, Sunday school work, women's* work, and youth work, provided leadership to keep the STECI going. A central, annual, weeklong convention of the church at Tiruvalla around every 26 Jan gave continuous impetus to growth.

The church spread throughout Kerala, in almost all

the main cities and states of India, and even into all the Arabian Gulf states and North America. In all these places outside Kerala, the STECI's spread was related to the migration of STECI members. Presently there are 208 parishes and nearly 50 presbyters with 100 full-time lay workers in the church.

The church is largely confined to the Christians originating from Kerala of the diaspora of the Syrian Christians. They are primarily Malayalam-speaking, but they reach out to non-Christians both from the Malayalam and non-Malayalam people-groups. They have an active and vigorous missionary program.

At present, the church is stabilized around 12,000 members. STECI's original founders returned to the mother church, and many left for more free church traditions. On the whole, the outlook of the present church is progressive and positive in a land where 96 percent of the population is still non-Christian.

P. T. CHANDAPILLA

Salesians

(Salesians of Don Bosco or Society of St. Francis de Sales). Religious order founded by John Bosco (1815-88) in Turin, Italy.

Bosco's work with street children in 1841 gave birth to the Salesian order. Eighteen years later, on 13 Dec 1859, he founded a society unique in the history of religious orders — the Society of St. Francis of Sales, composed of the ranks of the boys who grew up with him. The order was approved by the Catholic Church on 1 Mar 1869, with the education of poor young people as its main aim.

In 1906 the Salesians came to India* and Macau*, from where they spread to the whole of East Asia. The Salesian diocese of *China**, which included Macau, Hong Kong, mainland China, and Taiwan*, was officially inaugurated on 28 May 1926. It now has 140 members working in vocational centers, grammar schools, young teens' centers, halfway hostels for youth, and publishing houses, as well as engaging in evangelistic work in local churches.

The original Chinese name of the society was "Salesians of St. Francis," but because this foreign name sounded awkward to Chinese ears at the time, in addition to not being very meaningful, it was changed to "The Salesians" in 1928 in accordance with the aims and spirit of the order. Since the canonization of Bosco in 1934, his surname was added, making the official name "The Salesians of Don Bosco."

Similar humble beginnings marked the commencement of the order's work in the *Philippines**. The uncertainty the Salesians found themselves in, with the fall of the mainland China into Communist hands, led the superiors headquartered in Turin to develop a fallback position in case the worst may yet occur to the expatriated missionaries in Hong Kong. The order's Japanese confreres offered their houses for this eventuality, but fresh opportunities opened up in Vietnam* and the Philippines.

Carlo Braga, superior of the order in China, began to look into new placements in the Philippine Islands. The year 1950 saw a sea of correspondence between Braga and Turin. He reported his visit to the islands in March of the same year, recounting his meeting with the apostolic delegate, Egidio Vagnozzi, and the archbishop of Manila, Gabriel Reyes. He was surprised to learn about the presence of a school named after St. John Bosco in Tarlac. Founded in 1947 by a U.S. Army chaplain, James Wilson, it eventually became the first official presence of the order when it was turned over to Anthony Di Falco on 15 Sep 1951. Months later, Braga sent Guido D'Amore, John de Reggi, and John Monchiero to Victorias, Negros Occidental, to supervise the construction of a school being built by the Victorias Milling Company. Its owner, Don Miguel Ossorio, insisted that the Salesians initiate their work in the Philippines by setting up a specialized school that would train youth in technical skills.

In 1953 Braga followed these pioneering works with agreements with the archbishop of Manila and the archibishop of Cebu. Msgr. Reyes leased the old diocesan seminary in Mandaluyong, where today stands a college of engineering. In Cebu, Dona Maria Aboitiz, matriarch of a giant shipping company, introduced the Salesians to Julio Rosales, who blessed her initiative with a letter she carried by hand to Turin officially requesting that the order take charge of the Cebu Boys' Town, established by the city government in 1949 after the Flanagan concept. Attilio Boscariol and Lorenzo Nardin entered the premises on 24 Feb 1954. Similarly, the Ayala family of Makati, through its planner, Col. Joseph McMicking, gave a six-hectare parcel of land for another technical school. Finally in 1958, the De Leons of Pampanga gave their generous offer of land for the order's sixth school in the span of five years.

Before long the Salesians became noted for the technical training of the young, which the government has recognized as the order's most important contribution to the development of the nation. In fact, a Filipino Salesian priest, Precioso Cantillas, holds the important post of president of the Philippine Association of Private Technical Institutions (PAPTI) and is a board member of the government-organized Technical Education Skills Development Authority (TESDA). Both agencies look into the development of the technical education program that should power the country to industrialization.

In 1968, in line with the redimensioning requested by Vatican II on religious institutes, the order made a preferential option for the poor. Thus Don Bosco Youth Center was established in the most notorious slum area of the country, Tondo. The order returned to the original idea of the founder: to be in the midst of the poor and uplift them socioeconomically and morally. The provincial chapter of 1969 broadened this option when it opened all of its existing technical schools to nonpaying, out-of-school youth for a one-year training program.

On 22 Dec 1967, the order celebrated the ordination of its first Filipino priest, Leo Drona, who, 20 years later, became the first Filipino Salesian bishop. In fact, the growth of Filipino vocations warranted that these be nurtured in the local setting. In 1963 the studentate of philosophy was opened in Canlubang, Laguna, and in 1973 the theologate at the Don Bosco Center of Studies in Paranaque. Affiliated since 1987 with the Salesian Pontifical University (UPS) in Rome, the latter is open to other religious orders that wish their students to obtain a bachelor's degree in theology.

Given the preparation of its ever growing number of confreres, the order expanded its apostolic presence with parishes, a publishing house with a printing press, retreat houses, a hostel for university students, and centers for street children. The order's commitment to youth ministry gained recognition from the conference of bishops when it called on the order to man the secretariat of the Episcopal Commission on Youth (ECY) in 1989. This commission took charge of the World Youth Day celebration in Manila, 10-15 Jan 1995.

Missionary work became a feature when, in 1972, Filipino Salesians went to help their confreres in *Thailand**. In 1980 a station was established in Araimiri in the Gulf Province of *Papua New Guinea* and a year later one in Badili in the capital of Port Moresby. Organized for the school dropouts who could not pursue further studies in high school and college, the national government has recognized the value of this work by awarding a special diploma to graduates. In 1985, upon the request of the superiors in Rome, missionaries were sent to *East Timor,* where a fledgling group of Salesians found it hard to sustain the missions earlier established by the order's Portuguese province due to Portugal's cessation of exercise of political right over the area in 1975.

Finally, on 30 May 1992, the single province that had existed canonically since 12 Aug 1963 was divided into two. To date, there are 412 priests and lay brothers working in 25 houses in the north and 20 in the south, including the mission stations found in the delegations of Papua New Guinea, under the Manila Province, and of East Timor, under the Cebu Province.

With a median age of 34 years old, the order looks brightly to the future, knowing that with a developing and young country like the Philippines, where 60 percent of the population is 24 years old and below, the work among the young, especially the poorest, will always require from the order all the initiative and creativity it can muster.

Bibliography

Tassinari, Vasco, *Don Braga, l'uomo che ebbe tre patrie* (1990). • Santos, Emiliano, *Don Bosco Philippines, Silver Jubilee* (1976).

Francis Gustilo, with a contribution on China by the China Group, translated by Lena Lau

Salvation Army

The Salvation Army (SA) is more of an international charity organization than a Protestant denomination. It was founded by William and Catherine Booth of the Wesleyan Methodist Missionary Society in the United Kingdom in 1865. It embraced a faith similar to that of the Protestant churches; however, the SA ruled out all sacraments normally performed by other churches. The SA serves people from lower classes of society by providing necessities and doing evangelism. It adopted the hierarchy system of the army: the highest level of organization is called "headquarters," and the top-ranked person is called "chief commander." The gospel hymns used by the SA are tunes of pop songs matched with simple religious lyrics; brass instruments are often used to lead the songs. Because of the SA's involvement in providing needy service in World War I, the SA was finally accepted with other world Christian organizations.

India. Frederick Booth-Tucker, of the Indian Civil Service, commenced SA work in Bombay in Sep 1882. The adoption of Indian food, dress, and customs gave the mission ready access to the people, especially in the villages. In addition to evangelistic work, the SA inaugurated various social services for the relief of distress caused by famine, flood, and epidemic. It provided educational facilities at the elementary and secondary levels for the lower classes, as well as vocational training. In 1888 a home for ex-prisoners opened in Bombay, and medical work began at Nagercoil in 1893. At present the SA operates 10 hospitals and a number of clinics, 44 children's homes, 140 schools, and 94 social institutions (providing care for the handicapped, elderly, destitute, and blind). These programs and 1,200 corps (churches) are administered by 3,200 officers, with the support of 200,000 soldiers (adult members).

Pakistan. Work began in Lahore in 1883, when this country was part of India* (becoming a separate SA territory after partition in 1947). The SA has over 36,000 soldiers, with operations in the Punjab, Karachi, and Islamabad areas. The 110 corps, seven social service institutions, and four schools are administered by 271 officers.

Bangladesh. SA presence in Bangladesh* began with cyclone relief activity in 1970. Growth in evangelistic and social work followed. A large medical program operates in the Jessore area, which includes HIV/AIDS counseling services. Eleven corps, two social service institutions, 11 schools, and 13 medical units are served by 26 officers and more than 600 soldiers.

Sri Lanka. William Gladwin began SA ministry in Sri Lanka* in Jan 1883. In 1888 John Lyons opened a home for ex-prisoners in Columbo at the request of the governor of Ceylon. Current social outreach programs include children's homes, hostels, clinics, and community and day-care centers. 146 officers also minister in 41 corps with a membership of over 2,900.

Myanmar (Burma). In Jan 1915 Ruben Moss arrived to open a women's rescue home, a juvenile prisoner's home, and a corps. Success with the rehabilitation of young delinquents resulted in the SA being entrusted with the care of other criminals. By 1928 there were corps representing four language groups (Burmese, Telugu, Tamil, and English). At the outbreak of World War II*, there were 27 officers, 127 soldiers, seven corps, and three social institutions in Myanmar*. The work was reestablished after the war by Clayson Thomas and seven Burmese officers. After 1965 reentry visas for foreigners were no longer issued, resulting in a totally indigenous leadership of the mission.

Singapore/Malaysia. In May 1935 SA work began in Singapore*. It spread to Penang in 1938, Malacca* and Ipoh in 1940, Kuching in 1950, Kuala Lumpur in 1966, and Kota Kinabalu in 1996. Together with Myanmar*, Singapore and Malaysia* form an SA command comprising 80 officers and 1,400 soldiers serving in 37 corps, 13 social service institutions (including homes for children, the aged, the mentally handicapped, and those undergoing alcoholic rehabilitation), nine kindergartens, and 10 day-care centers.

Indonesia. Adolf van Emmerik and Jacob Brouwer commenced SA work in Indonesia* in 1894. In 1898 the SA in Java came under Australian command (until 1905), led by F. Cumming, with headquarters in Semarang. Operations were extended to Ambon, Bali*, Kalimantan* Timur*, Sulawesi, Sumatra, and Timor Kupang, and a network of medical* and social services was begun. In 1910 there were 60 officers, 22 corps, five schools, and eight social institutions in Indonesia. Despite its official dissolution during World War II, the SA was reestablished and has grown under Indonesian national leadership to 499 officers, 170 corps, 97 schools, and 44 social institutions.

Philippines. Salvationist John Milsaps arrived in Manila in 1898 as a chaplain during the Spanish-American War, unofficially beginning SA work there. In the 1930s Filipinos who had been converted through contact with the SA in Hawaii returned home, commencing meetings in Panay, Luzon, Cebu, and Mindanao islands. In Jun 1937 Alfred Lindvall officially inaugurated the work. SA operations were suppressed by the Japanese in 1942, but after cessation of hostilities in 1946, 14 corps were found to be intact. Current operations involve 190 officers and more than 4,100 soldiers ministering in 69 corps, two children's homes, dormitories for students and working women, 43 social service centers (including nutrition and literacy programs), 22 childcare learning centers, and three medical clinics.

Japan. In Sep 1895 a group of 14 officers led by Edward Wright arrived to establish the SA in Japan*, seeking to adapt their message and methods to Japanese culture. Such cross-cultural adaptation was facilitated by the leadership and literary influence of the first Japanese officer, Gunpei Yamamuro*, whose *Common People's Gospel* sold over three million copies. Under Henry Bullard, the SA gained national recognition in 1900 by successfully challenging legalized prostitution. SA social evangelism resulted in rapid growth in numbers and influence, with 147 corps, 512 officers, and 25 social welfare institutions by the mid-1930s. The SA responded to the many needs felt by the poor as a result of industrialization and gained governmental support for relief efforts during times of famine (1906, 1932) and earthquake (1923). Forced to cut ties with international headquarters in 1940, the SA was dissolved by government action in 1943, only to be reestablished after World War II. Current operations by 187 officers and 3,776 soldiers include 51 corps, two hospitals, and 21 social service institutions (including homes for children, the elderly, girls on probation, alcoholic rehabilitation centers, and day nurseries).

Korea. Work commenced on the Korean peninsula in Aug 1908 under the leadership of Robert Hoggard, with rapid growth in members (2,500 by 1914). Although the Korean SA continued to advance in subsequent decades (100 corps by 1940), tensions with Japan eventually led to the suppression of official operations. SA work was reestablished in 1946 under the leadership of Herbert Lord, and, although very successful, half of its corps was cut off as a result of the partitioning of the country following the Korean War*. 568 officers and 38,104 soldiers currently serve in 213 corps, 17 social service institutions, and several educational centers and day-care facilities.

China. In 1906 an SA women's rescue home opened in Dalny, Manchuria. The first corps followed in 1909. In Dec 1915 Charles Rothwell and William Salter arrived in Beijing to open the SA work. In the following years over 50 international officers arrived as missionary reinforcements. Operating from its headquarters in Beijing, the SA began training Chinese officers in 1918. Subsequently, SA work extended throughout China's provinces, opening corps, clinics, orphanages, feeding centers, homeless shelters, and vocational training homes for ex-prisoners. There were 90 corps with some 3,000 soldiers by the 1930s. Relief work also increased among refugees dislocated by Japan's expansion into China*. In 1939 the SA had 13 refugee camps in operation in Tientsin, Beijing, and Shanghai, sheltering 114,000 persons, distributing nearly 19 million meals, and providing medical treatment for over 200,000 patients. By 1941 there were 260 officers at work in China (212 of whom were Chinese), ministering in 82 corps and 26 social service centers. Suppressed during World War II, the SA was officially reestablished in Sep 1945. With the rise of the Communist regime in 1949, SA work was at first stifled, and then suppressed by 1951. In recent years, however, the SA's China Development Department has funded a center for rehabilitation medicine, a drinking water improvement project, the rebuilding of primary schools and orphanages, post-flood relief, and a child sponsorship program.

Hong Kong. Mission work began among the non-Chinese population with the establishment of a seaman's home in 1898. In Mar 1930 the SA opened women's work in the crown colony, at government request, under the direction of Dorothy Brazier and Doris Lemon. In 1939 Hong Kong became the administrative center for the Army's work in China, later to be moved to Kowloon. Officers number 42, with 1,688 soldiers serving in 19 corps, six schools, seven kindergartens, and 60 social service centers (including homes for children, the elderly, and handicapped persons).

Taiwan. Following pioneer work by Yasowo Segawa in 1928, corps were established in Taipei, Taiching, Keelung, Tainan, and Takao. The early mission was primarily among Japanese nationals living on the island, but in 1936 a Formosan officer was appointed to serve his own people. Banned during World War II, SA operations in Taiwan* were reestablished in Oct 1965 by George Lancashire. Formerly linked administratively with Hong Kong*, Taiwan became a separate SA command in Jan 1997. Five corps are served by 10 officers and 106 soldiers.

Bibliography

Wiggins, Arch, *History of the SA,* Vol. 4: *1886-1904* (1964) and Vol. 5: *1904-14* (1968). • Coutts, Frederick, *The Better Fight: History of the SA,* Vol. 6: *1914-46* (1973); *Weapons of Goodwill: History of the SA,* Vol. 7: *1946-77* (1986). • *Salvation Army Yearbook: 1998* (1997).

R. David Rightmire, with contributions from the China Group, Captain Thangvella, and Petrus Soedjarno

Samartha, Stanley Jedidiah

(b. Karkal, Karnataka, 7 Oct 1920). Indian Christian theologian, ecumenist, and writer active in interreligious dialogue.

Samartha completed his theological studies at United Theological College (UTC), Bangalore. After a period of work as a pastor, he became a lecturer in Bangalore. He then obtained his master's of theology and STM degrees and was appointed principal at Bangalore Seminary. In 1958 he took his doctoral degree at Hartford Seminary, and in 1960 he became professor of history of religions and philosophy, as well as the first director of the department of research and postgraduate studies, at UTC. In 1966 he became principal of Serampore College. In 1971 he became the first director of the World Council of Churches' subunit on dialogue. Samartha is presently a consultant of the Christian Institute for the Study of Religion and Society* (CISRS) and visiting professor at UTC.

As a well-known writer in India*, Samartha's writings appear in many journals in India and abroad. Among his books are: *The Hindu Response to the Unbound Christ* (1974); *Courage for Dialogue* (1981); *The Lordship of Christ and Religious Pluralism* (1981); *The Search for New Hermeneutics in Asian Christian Theology* (1987); and *One Christ; Many Religions* (1991). He has also edited many books. Among Samartha's many theological contributions are a pioneering work in the methodology of biblical interpretation and a revised Christology in theocentric perspective, both with special reference to the multireligious context in Asia. These represent his most significant contributions in this area. Regarding the interpretation of the so-called "exclusive" passages of the Bible*, Samartha says: ". . . one possible way of responding to these texts is to accept them as expressions of commitment within a particular community of faith without extending their authority beyond its boundaries. The hermeneutical question would then be not what to do with these texts, but how to relate them to each other in the life of the larger community" ("In Search of a Revised Christology: A Response to Paul Kmitter," *Current Dialogue,* Dec 1991, p. 31).

Samartha pleads for a Christology from below instead of a Christology from above. He prefers the paradigm of a "bullock-cart" to a "helicopter" in Christology (*One Christ; Many Religions,* 1991). Samartha's "revised" Christology went to the extent of saying that Jesus Christ is divine but he was not ontologically the same as God: "Jesus Christ is divine because he is human. He is human because he is divine. . . . This is not to deny the divinity of Jesus Christ confessed by the believing community but to reject the notion that Jesus of Nazareth is ontologically the same as God" (*One Christ; Many Religions,* pp. 103-33).

Jacob Kurian

Sambiasi, Francisco

(Bi Fangji) (b. 1582; d. Guangzhou, China, 1649). Italian Jesuit* missionary.

Sambiasi arrived in Macau* in 1610, originally en route to Japan. In 1617 he entered inland China* after propagating the faith in Shanghai, Kaifeng, Nanjing, Changsu, Hua'an, and elsewhere, and baptizing over 1,000 converts. He also collaborated with Xu Guangqi* (by dictating while Xu took notes) on a book, *Ling Yan Li Suo,* a theological work expounding abstruse theories on the soul (*anima* in Latin). He arrived in Guangzhou toward the end of the Ming dynasty and, ordered by Emperor Yongli, accompanied Pang Tianghou to Macau to obtain the aid of 300 Portuguese soldiers and artillery, proceeding to assist the fighting in Guilin. In return, Sambiasi was allowed to build a church in Guangzhou, and completed it before the Qing troops sacked the city in 1647. Sambiasi was wounded but rescued by a Qing soldier, a former Jesuit brother. He died two years later at age 67 and was buried in Macau.

Bibliography

Treadgold, Donald W., *The West in Russia and China: China, 1582-1949* (1973). • Vath, Alfons, *Johann Adam Schall von Bell, S.J. (1592-1666)* (1991). • Goodrich, L. Carrington, *Dictionary of Ming Biography, 1386-1644* (1976).

China Group

Samray Church, Thailand

First church of the Siam Mission of the Presbyterian* Church USA in Thailand*, founded 31 Aug 1847.

Stephen Mattoon served as the first pastor of the Church in Samray, and Presbyterian missionaries provided its pastoral care until the end of the 19th c. Quakieng, a Chinese immigrant and the first Asian member, joined in Sep 1849. In 1857, the mission moved its work and the church to a new location — Samray in Thonburi. The first ethnic Thai member, Nai Chune, joined in 1859. The congregation dedicated its first chapel on 25 May 1861 and ordained its first Thai elder in 1867.

The church grew steadily throughout the 19th c. and remained the leading church of the Siam Mission. In 1896, the Siam Presbytery ordained Yuen Tieng-Yok* (1850-1927) as its first Thai pastor, making it the first Presbyterian congregation to achieve self-rule and self-support. He remained pastor until his death in 1927. In 1903, the congregation experienced a crisis when the Siam Mission moved the Bangkok Boys' School, a strong pillar of the church, to a new location. The church survived and in 1910 completed a new church building. From 1927 on, elders led the church until it called its next pastor, Thongsuk Mungkaraphun, in 1935. He served only two years, and the church did not call another pastor until 1979, when Thongsuk returned to serve as pastor until 1984.

Bibliography

McFarland, George B., *Historical Sketch of Protestant Missions in Siam, 1828-1928* (1928). • Prasit Pongudom, "Notes on a Christian: Kru Yuen Tieng-Yok," *Church News* 57 (July 1988) (in Thai); *History of the Church of Christ in Thailand* (1984) (in Thai). • Presbyterian Church USA, *Records of the Siam Mission* (microfilm copy at the Payap University Archives, Chiang Mai, Thailand). • Yuen Tieng-Yok, *Autobiography of Yuen Tieng-Yok* (1928) (in Thai).

CHEEWIN MUNGKARAPHUN, translated by HERBERT R. SWANSON

Samuel, V. C.

(b. Omalloor, Pathanamthitta, 6 Apr 1912). Indian theologian and authority on Chalcedonian christological issues.

Samuel acquired proficiency in Syriac and did his doctoral studies at Yale University, concentrating on the christological issues in the 5th c. His finding and arguments in favor of the theological orthodoxy of the non-Chalcedonians remain unchallenged. He was associated with the work of the Christian Institute for the Study of Religion and Society* (CISRS). Much of his time was spent in teaching at various theological colleges: Serampore College, Holy Trinity Theological College (Ethiopia), United Theological College (Bangalore), and Orthodox Theological Seminary (Kottayam). He was the editor of the *Indian Journal of Theology* for some time. Among his important writings are *Yesu Christu Aru?*, *The Council of Chalcedon Re-examined*, *Itheru Indian Sabhayo*, and *Truth Triumphs*. A recognized consultant at various world conferences and ecumenical* dialogues, his two main concerns are summarized by his biographer, Sunny Kulathakkal: "He was keen, in the first place, to promote the principle that the Church in India* should be really Indian. Out of this concern he had a deep interest in comparing the roots the historic faith with the religious heritage of Hinduism*. Secondly, he realized that the chain of apostolic origins by Indian Syrian Christianity does not tally with its present standing either as part of the Roman Catholic Church* or as that of the Antiochene Syrian Church" (*Orthodox Identity in India*, p. 17).

Bibliography

Kuriakose, M. K., ed., *Orthodox Identity in India: Essays in Honour of V. C. Samuel* (1988).

JACOB KURIAN

San Lone, Victor

(b. Insein, Myanmar, 23 Jan 1930; d. 1985). Born to Saw Po Hlaing and Naw Caroline, San Lone passed his matriculation in 1949 and became a student at Yangon University. During his first year of study there, the Karen* insurrection broke out at Insein, and he joined the Karen National Defense Organization (KNDO). He was captured and put into prison for one year.

San Lone earned his bachelor of arts degree in 1955 and began work as a teacher at Union High School, where he later served as principal. He taught until 1963. He began theological studies, gaining the bachelor of religious education degree at the Myanmar* Institute of Theology in 1974 and the master of theology from South East Asia Graduate School of Theology in 1977.

San Lone served as a faculty member of Karen Baptist* Theological Institute and lecturer at the Myanmar Institute of Theology. He served as general secretary for the Burma Baptist Convention from 1973 to 1984. He participated in the ecumenical* movement within and outside of Myanmar. He was president of the Myanmar Council of Churches and also served on the General Committee of the Christian Conference of Asia.

ANNA MAY SAY PA

Sandjaja, Richardus

(b. ?; d. 1948?). Parish priest of Muntilan and Magelang (Central Java*).

Sandjaja replaced eight Jesuits* murdered by a gang of fanatical Muslim youths in 1945. He taught moral theology at Muntilan Seminary. On the night of 20 Dec 1948, he and Jesuit Brother M. A. Bouwens were tricked into attending a meeting of the local Laskar Hisbullah branch of Muntilan to discuss the effects of a Dutch military attack on the area. Instead, both were abducted and murdered. Their mutilated bodies were discovered two years later, excavated, and buried with a ceremony attended by hundreds of Boy Scouts and air force officers.

ADOLF HEUKEN

Santa Cruz Church (Kudichin), Thon Buri, Thailand

The beginnings of Santa Cruz Church in Thon Buri may be traced to 1767, when the Burmese army invaded Ayutthaya and caused Portuguese Catholics there to flee. Fr. Corre led a group to seek refuge in Cambodia*. He returned to Bangkok with his flock after Taksin liberated the Thais and was crowned king in Thon Buri in 1769. Corre attempted to gather the scattered remnants of Catholics of Ayutthaya, who were mostly the Portuguese and their descendants.

King Taksin contributed funds to the refugees and a boat for their use. He also promised them land to build a church. Corre named the piece of land in Thon Buri the Santa Cruz Camp in honor of the Day of the Glorious Cross, 14 Sep 1769. A small temporary church was built on 25 May 1770 and named the Santa Cruz Church. The members were mainly Portuguese.

When Corre died in 1773, there were only three priests available: Msgr. Le Bon, Msgr. Garnault, and Fr. Coude. From 1773 to 1779, they took turns giving pastoral care to the Santa Cruz congregation. In 1779 King Taksin expelled all missionaries from Thailand*. Le Bon died on Goa in 1780. Coude, an evangelist in Phuket and two other places, was appointed chief of the Siam Mission in 1782.

In the same year the newly crowned King Puttajodpha invited Coude to return to Bangkok immediately to see to the pastoral needs of the congregation of Santa Cruz. Coude could not leave Phuket because of the many converts there who needed instruction. The king then arranged for a Portuguese missionary from Macau*, Fr. Francisco, a Dominican*, to oversee Santa Cruz Church. The Catholics from the Holy Rosary Church chose to join Santa Cruz Church so that they would not be under either a French or a Thai priest.

When Coude arrived from Bangkok for his appointment as head of the mission, he received mixed reactions. Most at Santa Cruz Church were very happy to see him, but some opposed him, just as members of the Holy Rosary Church had done. In the face of this division of opinion, Francisco returned to Macau in 1785. Even though many delegations were sent to Macau, no more Portuguese came to Bangkok. Ultimately, the situation calmed down and became normal again.

Fr. Willemin was given charge of Santa Cruz Church from Coude's death in 1785 until 1788. Garnault then entrusted Santa Cruz Church to Fr. Florens, who was also given oversight of Chantaburi Church. In 1794 Garnault took up permanent residence in Bangkok. He gathered all the novices together and had them live in the novice residence at Santa Cruz Church. He was senior pastor of the church, principal of the novices academy, and head of the mission.

In 1794 Garnault set up a printing press brought from Penang. Later on, the press moved to Ascension College. Garnault and Florens gave pastoral care and oversight to Santa Cruz Church. In 1801 Florens became senior pastor and served both the Santa Cruz and Chantaburi churches until 1810. At this time, Frs. Rabeau, Pascal, and Jeremias assisted him.

In 1834 Msgr. Courvezy assigned to Fr. Pallegoix* the responsibility of building a new Santa Cruz Church, which was consecrated on 1 Sep 1835.

In 1913 Fr. Guillaume Kin da Cruz was senior pastor of Santa Cruz Church. He demolished the old church, which was falling down, and began construction of a new building. The cornerstone was laid on 8 Apr 1913, and the completed, beautiful structure was consecrated on 17 Sep 1916. Guillaume also purchased beautiful stained glass reproductions of the 14 stations of the cross for the instruction of the faithful. In addition, he purchased a carillon with 16 chimes.

On 16 Jan 1949, the members celebrated the silver jubilee of his ordination to the priesthood and the golden anniversary of his appointment as senior pastor of Santa Cruz Church. At the same time the members put up a memorial monument to him and placed it near the rectory. He died in 1955 at Santa Cruz and was buried there in the church that he himself had built.

On 13 Nov 1966, Fr. Anselme organized a celebration of the 50th anniversary of the building of the third structure.

The Santa Cruz Church had alternating Thai and French pastors from the *Mission Étrangères de Paris**. They brought great progress to the members in both material and spiritual matters.

VICTOR LARQUE, translated by E. JOHN HAMLIN

Santa Maria, Fray Antonio Caballero de

Spanish Franciscan* who, with confrere Fray Antonio del Puerto, preached for six months at the Annamese capital of Hue in 1645. These two were the chief Franciscan opponents of the China* Jesuits in what exploded into the "Chinese rites controversy."*

With some Spanish Franciscan nuns (Poor Clares*) expelled by the Portuguese, Santa Maria and del Puerto were sailing from Macau for Manila when their vessel was blown by storms to Tourane. There they were arrested and brought to Hue. Eager to open trade relations with Manila, Nguyen Phuc-lan, of Hue, welcomed them. Within six months, the two Franciscans converted and baptized 2,000 persons, including 50 members of the royal household. Among the latter was one christened Stephen, who was a learned Buddhist priest and cousin to the Nguyen ruler.

But when the Franciscans denounced Vietnam's*

Confucian* traditions, this triggered great indignation at the Nguyen court, leading to the immediate expulsion of all European missionaries and the martyrdom of many Annamese Christians, including Stephen and two of the Jesuits' catechists (see Vietnam).

Bibliography

De Huerta, F., *Estado . . . Histórico-Religioso de la Santa; Apóstolica Provincia de S. Gregorio Magno . . . de las Islas Filipinas* (1865). • Rhodes, A., *Divers voyages et missions* (1884). • Pfister, A., *Notices . . . sur les Jésuites de L'Ancienne Mission de Chine*, Vol. I (1932-34). • Buttinger, J., *The Smaller Dragon: Vietnam* (1958).

T. Valentino Sitoy, Jr.

Šapûr I (239-70)

The son and successor of Ardašîr I*, Šapûr I continued the Persian efforts to dominate northern Mesopotamia. The first campaign was in 241 and may have reached the outskirts of Antioch. The second campaign was either in 253 or in 256 (probably), which resulted in the conquest of Antioch, Cappadocia, and Cilicia. The third campaign against the Romans took place in 260; during it the Roman Emperor Valerian was captured. During and after these campaigns Šapûr I imported into Persian territory thousands of Christians (Greek, Syriac, Armenian). These deportees he established in villages, and he used them to teach Western technologies to Persians and to produce goods. Along with the workers came priests and bishops. The Christians reinforced the Christian groups that had been in Persian lands for some time. It is probable that the bishop of Antioch, Demetrianus, was among the deportees.

Šapûr I was also a protector and promoter of Mani. During this period Manichaeism established itself throughout the Persian Empire and became a tradition with which to be reckoned within the Roman Empire.

Bibliography

Scher, Addai, ed., *Chronique de Séert, Patrologia Orientalis*, Vol. IV, No. 1 (1908). • Peeters, P., "St. Démétrianus, évêque de Antioche?" *Analecta Bollandiana*, 43 (1924). • Labourt, J., *Le Christianisme dans l'Empire Perse sous la dynastie Sassanide (224-632)* (1904). • Sprengling, M., ed., *Third Century Iran: Sapor and Kartir* (1953). • Frye, Richard N., *The Heritage of Persia* (1963). • *Atti del Convegno internazionale sul Tema: la Persia nel Medioevo; Roma, 31 marzo–5 aprile 1970* (1971). • Chaumont, M. L., *La Christianisation de l'Empire Iranian des origines au grandes persécutions du IV e siècle* (CSCO 499; Subsidia 80; 1988). • Winter, E., *Die sâsânidisch-römischen Friedenverträge des 3. Jahrhundert n. Chr. — ein Beitrag zum Verständnis der aussenpolitischen Beziehung zwischen den beiden Grossmächten* (1988).

David Bundy

Šapûr II (308/9-379)

Šapûr II continued Persian efforts to control northern Mesopotamia. His early efforts to take Nisibis were frustrated, according to tradition, by Bishop Jacob of Nisibis*. However, the city of Nisibis was surrendered to Šapûr II by the Byzantine Emperor Jovian after the death of Emperor Julian (361-63).

Under Šapûr II the most severe persecution of Christians in Persia was undertaken, led by the Zoroastrian clergy and supported by the state. These persecutions are well documented in martyr narratives dating from the reign of Šapûr II (see Zoroastrianism).

Bibliography

Assemani, S. E., *Acta Sanctorum Martyrum Orientalium et Occidentalium* (1748; repr. 1970). • Labourt, J., *Le Christianisme dans l'Empire Perse sous la dynastie Sassanide (224-632)* (1904). • Sprengling, M., ed., *Third Century Iran: Sapor and Kartir* (1953). • Frye, Richard N., *The Heritage of Persia* (1963). • Wiessner, G., *Zur Märtyrerüberlieferung aus der Christenfolgung Schapurs II* (*Untersuchungen qur syrischen Literaturgeschichte*, 1; *Abhandlungen der Akademie der Wissenschaften in Göttingen. Philologisch-historische Klasse*, Vol. 67; 1967). • *Atti del Convegno internazionale sul Tema: la Persia nel Medioevo; Roma, 31 marzo–5 aprile 1970* (1971). • Chaumont, M. L., *La Christianisation de l'Empire Iranian des origines au grandes persécutions du IV e siècle* (CSCO 499; Subsidia 80; 1988).

David Bundy

Saragih, J. Wismar

(b. Raya, North Sumatra District of Indonesia, Sep 1888; d. Pematangsiantar, North Sumatra, 7 Mar 1968). Local pioneer missionary teacher to the Simalungun-Bataks; author and translator.

A devoted missionary to the Simalungun, Saragih cared about the development of his own ethnic group. His main approach to his people was "Gospel and progress," combining the preaching of the Gospel with the teaching of secular knowledge.

Born of a royal family with 12 slaves in a feudal society, Saragih experienced many civil wars and often had to flee to another village for safety, but this did not hinder him from studying his own language. The mission school in his area, which opened in 1907, awakened him to modern education and opened his heart to Christ. He was baptized on 11 Sep 1910.

He was given permission to continue studying (1911-15) at the teacher-school *(zending-kweekschool)*. He prepared himself as a teacher in his local context, seeing education as a means to evangelize. To him, the aim of education is to lead his people to Christ and to make them rich, smart, respectful, and honest.

J. Warneck*, a German missionary, encouraged Saragih to study more in order to become a priest. This created the opportunity for Saragih to lead movements for evangelization. On 2 Sep 1928, Saragih formed an advisory committee *(Komite na ra Marpodah)* to publish brochures, a magazine for laypeople, and evangelistic tracts. Saragih attempted to compile a dictionary of his Simalungun language. Voorhoeve, a Dutch linguist, said that Saragih was the first local person in all *Nederland-Indie* (Dutch East Indies) to compile such a work. Saragih wrote about 30 books on church life and general topics for laypeople. He also translated the New Testament into Simalungun.

The advisory committee influenced Simalungun Christians to initiate the Action Committee *(Kongsi Laita)*, a massive movement to evangelize the Simalungun. An important slogan of the movement was, "Anybody who talks to his fellow more than five minutes should begin to talk about Jesus Christ!"

During the Japanese occupation (1942-45), Saragih and his fellow workers started a movement, Learning to Become Witnesses for Christ *(Paraguru saksi ni Kristus)*, similar to a catechesis for laity. When questioned by the Japanese military, they explained that their movement was similar to the work of Toyohiko Kagawa* (an active social worker, author, and evangelist in Japan*).

In 1964 Saragih was among those who campaigned for an autonomous church. Prior to 1964, the Simalungun community was absorbed by another neighboring ethnic church, the Batak* Toba Church (HKBP). Saragih desired the freedom to use the Simalungun language in church instead of Batak Toba.

Bibliography

Pederson, F. D., *Darah Batak dan Jiwa Protestan* (Batak Blood and Protestant Soul) (1975). • Saragih, J. Wismar, *Marsinalsal* (an autobiography) (1977).

Martin Lukito Sinaga

Saraswati, Dayanand

(b. Kathiawar, Gujarat, 1824; d. Ajmer, 30 Oct 1883). Father of modern Hindu revivalism, outstanding reformer and missionary, and founder of the *Arya Samaj**.

Mulshankar (the premonastic name of Swami Dayanand Saraswati) was born in a Shaivite Brahmin family and received traditional instructions. At 14 he began to oppose image worship. At 24 he took *sannyasa* (life of renunciation) and came to be known as Dayanand Saraswati. Having studied under the famous Vedic scholar Swami Virjanand, he dedicated the rest of his life to preaching the infallibility of the Vedas, reforming and defending Hindu religion, reforming Indian society, and opposing the false teachings of Christianity, Islam*, Brahmanism, and other non-Vedic religions.

In 1875 he founded the *Arya Samaj*, the pioneer revivalist movement that set the pace for the growth and development of religious nationalism* that later changed the course of the history of India*. In the same year he also published his magnum opus, *Satyartha Prakash*, a revised edition of which appeared in 1884. Chapter 13 is an examination of Christ and Christianity, and both are discredited. Dayanand argues that the world would be better off without such an ensnaring and superstitious faith as Christianity. In 1877 he visited Punjab and began his successful mission there by preventing two Hindus in Ludhiana from becoming Christians. Touring and lecturing all over North India, he established branches of the *samaj* in many places, and soon the movement became a strong mass movement, though the Brahmin orthodoxy opposed Dayanand and his teachings. His use of Hindi, the language of the masses, contributed greatly to the movement's success. In 1880 he founded a society called *Paropakarini Sabha* (renewed in 1883), which spearheaded the missionary task of the *samaj*.

Later, seeing the leading role that the *samaj* played in defending Hindus and their religion against missionary religions such as Islam and Christianity, the Hindu orthodoxy accepted the *samaj* as authentically Hindu and eulogized Dayanand as "the Savior of Hinduism," "the Luther of India," and "the regenerator of *Aryavarta*."

Dayanand was a great reformer and attempted to cleanse Hindu religion and society of evils such as image worship, polytheism, and superstitious beliefs and practices such as pilgrimage, child marriage, untouchability, and the oppression of women*. His was a clarion call to get back to the roots of the Vedas. As a revivalist teaching that the Vedas and Vedic religion alone are true, he inspired fellow Hindus to embark on a worldwide mission of promoting Vedic religion and countering the challenges of Islamic and Christian missionary enterprise. He successfully led the reconversion program *(shuddhi)* and Hindu solidarity *(sanghatan)*. He labored to uplift the depressed classes and integrate them into the mainstream of Hindu society.

As a nationalist, he wanted to promote the cause of national independence by initiating the ideology of religious nationalism and Hindi as the national language. However, his strongly negative, unipolar approach to nonvedic religions and non-Hindu communities has done great damage to the cause of communal harmony in India, as evidenced in the long-drawn-out conflicts between his followers and Muslims in India.

Dayanand attempted to remold Hindu religion after the pattern of the Semitic missionary religions. He gave it a holy book (the Vedas), a creed (the Ten Principles of the *samaj*), a fellowship of committed members (the *Arya Samaj*), an inspiring slogan ("back to the Vedas"), and a missionary organization (the *Paropakarini Sabha*). Among the ideologues of modern Hindu renaissance, Dayanand stands out as a towering personality. In Dayanand and his movement, Christianity finds a sharp critic and a strong opponent, especially to its missionary program.

Bibliography

Andrews, C. F., *The Renaissance in India: Its Missionary Aspect* (1913). • Baird, Robert D., ed., *Religion in Modern India* (1981). • De Smet and J. Neuner, eds., *Religious*

Hinduism (1968). • Garg, Ganga Ram, ed., *World Perspectives on Swami Dayananda Saraswati* (1984). • Jordens, J. T. F., *Dayananda Saraswati: His Life and Ideas* (1978). • Mathew, C. V., *Neo-Hinduism: A Missionary Religion* (1987). • Rai, Laipat, *The Arya Samaj* (1915).

C. V. MATHEW

Sarvodaya Movement. *See* Bhave, Vinoba

Sauma, Rabbane. *See* Yaballah III

Sawada Miki

(b. Hongo, Tokyo, 19 Sep 1901; d. Spain, 12 May 1980). Social worker, member of the Anglican* Church of Japan* *(Nippon Seikokai).*

Eldest daughter of Iwasaki Hisaya of Mitsubishi Zaibatsu (Financial Group), Sawada attended kindergarten, elementary division, and junior high division of Tokyo Girls' Normal School. Fearing she would be influenced by her Christian school friends, her family forced her to leave the school in 1916. She was then given a very strict education at home. In Jul 1922 she married a diplomat, Sawada Renzo, and in December of that year accompanied him first to Argentina and then to Beijing, London, Paris, and New York. In England she was deeply impressed by a visit to an orphanage, the Doctor Barnard's Home. During World War II*, she worked as head of the Relief Society for Second-Generation Japanese living in Japan. After the war, she was enraged to find the dead bodies of infants born of Japanese mothers and occupation-forces fathers in the ditches and on the back streets of the city, and once when driving in a car she came upon an abandoned mixed-blood baby's body and felt called to become a mother to these children. In 1947 she founded the Elizabeth Sanders Home in Oiso and became directly involved in raising the children who came there. She devoted herself completely to managing this home. As the children matured, she established the Stephano School for them on the same premises. She also built a church and called an Anglican priest to serve as chaplain to tell the children about God. Almost every year she traveled to the United States and Europe to collect funds for the home. In 1962 she built the St. Stephen's Settlement on land in the Amazon basin in Brazil so that the grown children might move there to live a free life. She died suddenly while traveling in Spain. She wrote *Kuro hada to shiroi kokoro* (Black Skin and White Heart) in 1963. She collected relics of the Kirishitan* era and wrote *Ozora no kyoen* (Banquet in the Sky) in 1941 and *Kirishitan ibutsu shu* (Early Christian Relics) in 1959.

Bibliography

Kosakai Sumi, *Kore wa anata no haha* (This is your mother) (1982).

MATSUDAIRA KORETARO, JAPANESE DICTIONARY

Schall von Bell, Johann Adam

(b. 1 May 1592; d. 15 Aug 1666). German Jesuit* missionary with mathematical and calendrical expertise who served at the Ming and Qing courts in Beijing.

A native of Cologne, Germany, Schall studied at the German College in Rome. He entered the Society of Jesus* there in 1611 and later was a student of theology at the Roman College. As a volunteer for the China* mission, he arrived in Macau in 1618 and spent the next two years studying Chinese. At one point he assisted in defending the city against the Dutch invasion.

In 1623 Schall found himself at the Bureau of Astronomy in Beijing, where he assisted Xu Guangqi* (1562-1633) in reforming the Chinese calendar. From 1627 to 1630, he was a missionary in Xi'an, Shaanxi Province. Johann Terentius Schreck (Deng Yuha, 1576-1630), a Jesuit astronomer and a personal friend of Galileo, died less than a year after he arrived at the court in Beijing. Xu recommended that Schall and Giacomo Rho (Luo Yage, 1592-1638) replace him.

After the death of Rho, Schall labored alone in continuing the reform of the calendar, although Muslim and Chinese astronomers opposed the imperial sanction of the new methods. Besides making astronomical instruments, he directed a foundry for 20 cannons that were used to defend Beijing against the Manchus. Schall befriended and eventually baptized an elderly court eunuch named Joseph. This in turn led to the conversion of 10 more eunuchs. When Schall presented to the emperor an album of the life of Christ, several princesses were allowed to view it. Joseph explained its significance to them, and, when they sought to become converts, he baptized them with Schall's permission. By 1640, 50 imperial concubines and more than 40 eunuchs had followed the same path. At the end of the reign of the Ming dynasty in 1644, there were perhaps 150,000 Chinese Catholics.

The Qing government that overthrew the Ming dynasty as a result of the Manchu invasion of Beijing allowed Schall to retain the mission compound. The regent, Dorgon (1612-50), named Schall director of the Bureau of Astronomy. After Dorgon's death, the Shunzhi emperor (1638-61) ascended the throne. He admired Schall, often visited him in ordinary clothes, and called him *mafa,* the Manchu equivalent of "grandfather." In 1650 Schall got imperial permission to build the Nantang (South Church); the stele inscription is extant in the wall surrounding the later church building of that name. With his additional honorary titles, Schall was the protector of the Catholic missions so that local officials tolerated the presence of missionaries throughout China. The emperor later turned to Buddhism*, but with his death on 5 Feb 1661, Schall's status was less secure. Four regents headed the government following the death of the Kangxi emperor (r. 1662-1722).

On 20 Apr 1664, Shall suffered partial paralysis that impaired his limbs and speech. Six months later, Yang Guangxian (1597-1669), whose periodic complaints to the Board of Rites about Schall since 1660 had largely been ignored, charged Schall, his two immediate assistants, and five Catholic Chinese astronomers with errors in their calculations and with selecting an inauspicious date in 1658 for the burial of a prince, the son of the Shunzhi emperor, and his favorite concubine. Yang also claimed that the missionaries poisoned the minds of the people with false ideas and plotted the overthrow of the state. Yang's charges led to the imprisonment of Shall, his assistants, and the astronomers in the bureau whom Yang named as well as the other three Jesuits in Beijing (Ferdinand Verbiest*, Nan Huairen, 1623-88; Ludovico Buglio, Li Leisi, 1606-82; and Gabriel Magalhaes, An Wensi, 1610-77). In early Jan 1665, the 25 Jesuits, four Dominicans*, and one Franciscan* in the provinces were ordered to be remanded to Beijing. All churches were closed.

Schall endured prolonged interrogations by several tribunals. Even the accurate calculation of a solar eclipse by Verbiest on Schall's behalf in a contest with the Chinese and Muslim astronomers using their own systems did not lead to the prisoners' release. Schall and the others Yang listed were sentenced to death by dismemberment. An imperial edict of Apr 1665 spared Schall's life but ordered the council to deliberate on the punishment for him and the others. Some officials viewed the subsequent earthquake in Beijing and the fire in the imperial palace as signs of heaven's displeasure with the verdict. The council remained adamant and ordered Schall and his immediate assistants to be flogged, imprisoned, and banished, but the others were to be dismembered. However, an edict of 17 May 1665 pardoned and released Schall and his assistants, but the five Chinese astronomers were executed. Moreover, the missionaries in the capital, except those appointed to the court, were expelled to Guangzhou (Canton) in September. In 1671 they were allowed to return to their mission stations in the interior.

Schall died a year after his release and was buried near the grave of Matteo Ricci* (1552-1610). Schall's tombstone is one of the more than 60 that are located in the recently restored *Li Madou mu* (Matteo Ricci cemetery) in Beijing. After the Kangxi emperor took direct control of the government in 1667, Verbiest asked that a commission reopen Schall's case. The emperor approved its recommendation that the name, titles, and ranks of Schall be restored.

Bibliography

Schall von Bell, Johann Adam, *Chongyi tang ri ji suibi* (Sketches of famous Christian saints presented in the Tongyi Church) (1637); *Jincheng shuxiang* (The image of the Savior); *Zhenfu xunchuan* (Eight beatitudes), also titled *Zhenfu jingdian* (The Gospel of the Eight Beatitudes); *Zhuzhi qunzheng* (Divine providence proved by several ways) (1629); *Zhujiao yuanqi* (Beginning and progress of the Christian teaching), 4 Vols. (1643). • Attwater, Rachel, *Adam Schall: A Jesuit at the Court of China* (1962). • Bernard, Henri, *L'Encyclopedie astronomique du Père Schall. La reforme du calendrier chinois sous l'influence de Calvius, de Galilee et de Kepler,* Monumenta Serica, Vol. 3 (1938). • *International Conference in Memory of the 400th Anniversary of the Birth of Johann Adam Schall von Bell and the Historiography of the Catholic Church in China* (1992). • Malek, R., ed., *Western Learning and Christianity in China: The Contribution and Impact of Johann Adam Schall von Bell (1592-1666)* (1998). • Pfister, L., *Notices biographiques et bibliographiques sur les Jesuites de l'ancienne mission de Chine,* 2 Vols. (1932-34; reprinted 1971 and 1975). • Vath, A., *Johann Adam Schall von Bell. Missionar in China, Kaiserlicher Astronom und Ratgeber am Hofe von Peking, 1592-1666* (1933; reprinted 1911).

John W. Witek

Schereschewsky, Samuel Isaac Joseph

(b. Lithuania, 1831; d. Tokyo, 1906). American Episcopal missionary and bishop to China*.

The son of Orthodox Jewish parents, Schereschewsky was reared in the Jewish faith and given an excellent education. He went to Germany, training to be a rabbi, at age 19 and enrolled in Breslan University two years later. During his studies, he came into contact with British missionaries of the Society for Promoting Christianity among the Jews. In 1854 he was baptized in a Baptist* church and furthered his studies at Western Theological Seminary (Presbyterian*) in Pittsburgh, Pennsylvania. In 1858 he switched to the Episcopal Church and transferred to study at General Theological Seminary in New York. In 1859 he was sent to Shanghai for mission work and was ordained as an elder the following year.

For the next decade, he involved himself in the British troops' exploratory work of the Yangtze River, served as the Chinese secretary in the United States embassy, and also visited the descendants of Jewish people in Henan. His mission work was mainly related to the translation of the Bible* into Chinese and Mongolian and the translation of the Church of England *Prayer Book* into Chinese. These translations were later published by the Bible Society* of the United States.

In 1871 he returned to the United States and became a United States citizen in 1875. He was consecrated a bishop in 1877 at Grace Church in New York City and returned to China as bishop of the Shanghai Diocese. Two of his most enduring works are the establishment of St. John's College and St. Mary's Girls' College.

At age 52 he was stricken with paralysis as the result of sunstroke, and he resigned from his episcopate in 1883. After his retirement and despite his having to type with only one finger, he continued to devote his energy to the revision of the translation of the Bible in simple Wenli. His translation was regarded as the best translation before the He-He-Ben version was published in 1919. He also edited a dictionary in Mongolian.

Bibliography

Eber, Irene, *The Jewish Bishop and the Chinese Bible: S. I. J. Schereschewsky, 1831-1906* (1999). • Muller, James Arthur, *Apostle of China: Samuel Isaac Joseph Schereschewsky* (1937). CHINA GROUP

Scheut Fathers

(CICM). The Congregation of the Immaculate Heart of Mary (*Congregatio Immaculati Cordis Mariae,* CICM) was founded by Theophile Verbist, a Belgian diocesan priest (1823-68). Appointed national director of the Work of the Holy Childhood in 1860, he showed great dedication, with special concern for missionary work among the Chinese. In order to reach out to the Chinese people and the many abandoned infants, Verbist, together with his first companions, founded a missionary congregation. Its statutes were approved in 1862. Shortly after, the first group established residence at Scheut, near Brussels (which explains the popular name "Missionaries of Scheut" or "Scheut Fathers"). The official founder's day of the congregation is 28 Nov 1862. The founder left for China* with an initial group on 25 Aug 1865, and he died in Inner Mongolia* on 23 Feb 1868.

Pope Pius IX, hearing about the premature death of Verbist, spoke the prophetic words: "Man drops down when his hour has come, but God does not let his work perish." The congregation grew quickly, and gradually other mission territories were entrusted to the Scheut Fathers: Zaire (Belgian Congo, 1888); Philippines* (1907); Singapore* (1931); Indonesia* (1937); United States (1946); Japan* (1947); Haiti, Guatemala, Hong Kong, and Taiwan* (1953); Dominican Republic (1958); Brazil (1963); Cameroun (1966); Zambia/Senegal (1976); Nigeria (1977); Mexico (1979); Chad (1990); and Mongolia (1992).

From the beginning, the Scheut Fathers counted Dutch members in their ranks, and a few Chinese were accepted as well. It would take the missionary institute until the 1950s before a real breakthrough in internationalization came about. Originally the missionaries wanted to dedicate all their efforts to the building up of the local clergy, and yet as a matter of policy, no local candidates were accepted as members. In the early 1950s, however, members from the Belgian Congo (Zaire) and the Philippines were accepted. At present, the institute fosters the missionary charism in all its locations. In addition to Zaire and the Philippines, a promising formation program for future missionaries is on its way in Indonesia. Others have followed suit.

This turn of events transformed the Scheut Fathers into an international religious institute that is exclusively missionary. The overall membership almost reached 2,000, but today there are about 1,350 members.

China. China was the first mission of CICM, and therefore the Scheut Fathers, even into the 20th c., were identified only with China. CICM work started in Xiwanzi, then extended to Inner Mongolia, which CICM took over from the Lazarists*. Later Scheut missionaries worked in Gansu, Ningxia, Xinjiang, Shanxi, and Jehol Provinces. From 1865 to 1955, after the Communist takeover, 680 Scheut Fathers were sent to China. Two-hundred fifty of them died and are buried in China. As did their founder, more than 100 of them died very young of typhoid fever. In 1930 the outgoing superior general, Joseph Rutten, discovered a vaccine developed by a Polish doctor that proved successful against the fever.

The work of CICM in China consisted mainly in opening catechumenates, orphanages, schools, and seminaries. The land in areas such as Ordos and North Shaanxi was dry, and so the farmers were poor. Brigands and looting soldiers made the whole region unsafe. The CICM missionaries initiated projects of irrigation on land bought from the landlords in order to help the poor farmers. They surrounded the villages in the whole region with walls to defend their people. During the Boxer Rebellion, however, many of these villages were invaded by the Boxers; thousands of Catholics in the Inner Mongolia region as well as several CICM missionaries died as martyrs.

Several CICM missionaries undertook research on Mongolian and Chinese languages, culture, and traditions, expressing Christian teaching in Chinese-styled paintings. In 1948 the Verbiest* Academy in Beijing was started to continue this work.

All CICM missionaries, except one Chinese confrere, were expelled from China after the Communist takeover. Some left China after undergoing torture and spending years in jail. CICM then opened missions respectively in Hong Kong, Taiwan, and Singapore. In the early 1980s, when China opened up again, CICM launched its China Program. This was realized mainly through the Ferdinand Verbiest Foundation, a joint venture of CICM and the Catholic University of Leuven. The foundation promotes academic research — mainly history — and cooperation with China in the fields of pastoral work, human development, and cultural exchange.

Philippines. Early in the 20th c., the apostolic delegate Agius and Bishop Dougherty of Nova Segovia (Vigan) appealed to the CICM (Scheut) Fathers to send missionaries to the Philippines on account of the huge number of Catholics left without priests after most of the Spanish priests had returned to Spain. Due to the CICM charism to bring the Gospel to those who have never heard it, after some hesitation a first group of nine was sent in 1907. They were sent to the Montanosa (North Luzon), where the local people were still almost all tribal religionists. Later they also took care of the neglected Catholics in other areas, but the history of conversion of the Igorots in Montanosa reads as an epic. With very limited resources, new mission stations were opened, schools started, and charitable institutes developed. Colleges were founded, and two of them, St. Louis in Baguio and St. Mary's in Bayombong, were recognized as universities.

Today, some 139 mission stations, churches, formation houses, and other entities are under the care of CICM missioners. Statistics cannot convey the full extent of the CICM results in Montanosa. Some 400 missionaries have been sent during the last 90 years, and at present, some 185 are active. Special attention has been devoted to the formation of the local clergy, through minor seminaries and also through management of the Major Seminary of Manila and other seminaries. Scholarly confreres have specialized in linguistics, anthropology, and folklore studies, with special attention to cultural research among the pygmies *(Negritos)*.

During the early 1950s, the first Filipino members were welcomed in the institute and, from 1965 on, sent to other missions all over the world. More than 100 Filipino confreres have been sent. They work side by side with their Belgian, Dutch, Zairean, Indonesian, and Latin American brothers, bearing witness to the international brotherhood and the universality of the kingdom.

The Asian Social Institute (ASI) was founded by Fr. Senden of CICM. The Maryhill School of Theology (MST), where many religious congregations of men and women and several dioceses send their trainees, is another ministry of the CICM that offers courses for laypeople. At present, over 500 students are enrolled at MST, which has a central concern for the missionary dimension of the church.

Indonesia. In 1937 the CICM was entrusted in Indonesia with the apostolic prefecture of Makassar (now Ujung Pandang). During the early days, Dutch members of CICM were sent there. The local people, staunchly Muslim, were not open to conversion. CICM has worked mostly with the ethnic Chinese, the Toraja people from the animistic mountain region, and transmigrants from other regions.

Within three years of the end of World War II* 18 new missionaries arrived in Indonesia, but new hope was dashed by political upheaval. The Darul Islam* movement made the whole region unsafe. For several years the government did not allow Dutch nationals to enter Indonesia. As a result, CICM sent Belgian members to help out in the fast-growing mission.

With the new order under President Suharto in 1965, a new era opened with a stable government and economic growth. This was a time of national unity and greater openness to the Christian faith, and so both Catholic and Protestant churches prospered.

In 1979 the first local candidates in Indonesia were accepted, and the formation program has been growing ever since. Between eight and 12 candidates are accepted annually. The ordained members work today in Brazil, the United States, and the Philippines.

CICM also started an agricultural school (Makale-Toraja) and a school for catechists which trains lay leaders.

Singapore. Scheut Fathers bought a property in Singapore in 1931 that served as a religious center and a guest house. After CICM members were expelled from China, some of them settled in Singapore. The bishop in Ninghsia became the apostolic vicar of the diaspora Chinese. In that capacity, the bishop visited and preached to countless communities of Chinese all over the world. He was also instrumental in bringing religious instruction courses to Singapore.

After China's turn to Communism*, some Scheut members were assigned to Hong Kong. Two apostolates were engaged in schoolwork, including catechetical programs in the schools, and parish work with a strong emphasis on spreading the Good News.

A social center (Po Yin) was also set up in the Yao Tung Estate. In the 1980s, as China was opening up more and more, Hong Kong became increasingly important for Christian work, and so the Scheut Fathers were engaged in studying mission history in order to prepare for future ministry.

Taiwan. In Taiwan, some Scheut Fathers exiled from China were moved to Taipei, especially in the Wari Hua District. Very soon Maryknoll missionaries in Taichung called upon them to take responsibility for the minor seminary and to start a training center for male catechists.

In northern Taiwan, more parishes were accepted among the local Taiwanese-speaking people. Evangelization in Taiwan was accelerated for a short time when American relief services were distributed via the different churches. When this stopped in the mid-1960s, conversions dropped off, and this has been the case to the present. Scheut Fathers in Taiwan have been among the few groups of foreign missionaries who work primarily among local Taiwanese (*tiok-kien*–speaking people).

The Scheut Fathers established two primary schools, one with a famous music department, but both with special programs for the mentally retarded. In the heart of Taipei, the CICM helped develop the Taiwan Pastoral Center and also various counseling centers. In the late 1980s, the Scheut Fathers transferred much of their work to the local church.

Japan. The CICM mission in Japan started in 1947. Several young missionaries were sent for specialized studies in a variety of disciplines: education, sociology, missiology, comparative religions, linguistics, etc. CICM is active in four dioceses: Tokyo, Osaka, Hiroshima, and Nagoya. They started parishes and pioneered in team ministry, showing great creativity in their attempts to establish contacts with the Japanese people. Many started kindergartens in the hope of reaching out to parents via their children, while others taught foreign languages.

Soon the church buildings in Japan became "wedding halls." Non-Christians who wanted a church wedding were allowed to have their marriages blessed in the church, provided they attended at least three preparatory sessions on the Christian understanding of marrriage.

CICM started its own high school in Himeji and Oriens and an institute for religious research. CICM also started the only Catholic correspondence course for religion in Osaka. They also pioneered YCW (Young Catholic Workers*) and special outreach to refugees from Indochina.

Conversions in the Christian sense of the word are scarce in Japan, with about 60 Scheut Fathers in the country. In 1989 the first African (Zaire) members were sent to Japan, followed by Filipinos and Indonesians, starting a new chapter of the CICM work in Japan.

FRANS DE RIDDER

Schwartz, Christian Friedrich

(b. Sonnenberg, Neumark, Prussia, 22? Oct 1726; d. Thanjavur, India, 13 Feb 1798). Lutheran* missionary, educator, diplomat, and statesman.

The son of a humble tradesman, whose devout wife allegedly dedicated the child to the Lord before her premature death, Schwartz was confirmed in a pietistic personal faith by the local pastor and received a grammar school education. While he was studying in nearby Küstrin, his teacher inspired him with stories of the Royal Danish Mission in Tranquebar*, India*, and the writings of August Hermann Francke, whose charitable institution in Halle was the major force behind this outreach. In 1746 Schwartz enrolled at Halle University and lived at the Francke Foundation. He had already learned Hebrew, Greek, Latin, and English, and now he was instructed in Enlightenment thought, theology, mathematics, and the natural sciences. He caught the eye of Benjamin Schultze (1689-1760), a Halle-trained missionary who had recently returned from South India, and he enlisted Schwartz's help in preparing a new Tamil Bible* translation and recommended his appointment to the Danish mission. Ordained in Copenhagen on 17 Sep 1749, Schwartz went first to London and then to India, arriving in Tranquebar in Jul 1750 at the age of 23. He would never return to Europe.

A gifted linguist, Schwartz mastered several major Indian languages as well as Persian and Portuguese. Following the principles he learned at Halle, he ministered among the local congregations in the Tranquebar region by preaching, establishing schools, and training indigenous pastor-teachers (catechists) to spread the Gospel message. As conflicts among the British, French, and various Indian rulers tore at the fabric of society, Schwartz was inexorably drawn into politics. In 1762, at the request of some Tranquebar Christians, he went to Trichy (also known as Trichinopoly; now Tiruchirapalli) to minister to them and other Indians and soldiers of the British garrison. In 1763 he began serving Mohammed Ali, the *nawab* of Carnatic (then under British "protection") as a military chaplain, and in return the prince gave him a large sum of money to found schools, including a special one for "orphans" of soldiers. In 1765-66 the British commander funded the building of Christ Church in the city and established schools for Tamil- and English-speakers. As he was now under British jurisdiction, he amicably transferred his missionary connection to the Society for the Propagation of Christian Knowledge in 1767, while retaining his Lutheran orientation. A year later the East India Company appointed him chaplain of Trichy, with a £100 annual salary, most of which he diverted to local missionary projects. From this time on he usually spelled his name Swartz.

When a conflict erupted between the *nawab* and the rajah of Tanjore (today Thanjavur), Schwartz engaged in various relief efforts on behalf of the poor and suffering in Tanjore and in 1778 relocated there permanently. The British authorities asked him in 1779 to undertake a peace mission to Hyder Ali, ruler of Mysore, and in 1783-84 he made a second embassy to the king's successor, Tippu Sultan. Although these diplomatic efforts had limited success, they reflected both the deep confidence the Indian rulers had in his integrity and his own concern for peace and expanding opportunities for preaching the Gospel. In Tanjore, the dying rajah Tulaji in 1787 named his 10-year-old cousin Serfoji as his heir and begged Schwartz to be his guardian. He refused at first, but when the British allowed a rival, Amar Singh, to take the throne, he oversaw the boy's protection and eventual confirmation as maharajah of Tanjore. Serfogi II became an enlightened ruler, thanks to the teaching he had received from Schwartz, the "rajah-guru."

He developed the first program for a system of public high schools for Maratha Brahman youths, one that had the support of both the regional rajahs and the East India Company. The curriculum combined biblical and Christian texts with the principles and sciences of the Enlightenment, English literature, and European philosophy and prepared the students for civil service positions in the Madras presidency. Another achievement in Tanjore was the introduction of smallpox vaccination in 1794. He also mentored Vedanayaka Sastri (1774-1864), the first important Christian poet to write in Tamil.

Schwartz laid the foundation for the largest Protestant community in India when in 1778 he went to Tirunelveli to baptize the children of some Europeans. There he met and eventually baptized a Maratha Brahman widow named Clorinda from Palamcottah (now Palayamkottai), and she endowed the first church building in the city in 1785. He sent his trusted catechist and evangelist Sathiyanadan (Satyanathan; c. 1753-1815) to serve as its pastor-teacher. On 26 Dec 1790 Schwartz and the Tanjore missionaries ordained him, and a few years later he became a leading light in the evangelization of the lowly Shanar community, one of the earliest mass* movements of Christianity in modern India.

Some historical questions still need further clarification. They include Schwartz's attitude toward caste, his confessional stance (Lutheran vis-à-vis Anglican), his relationship to Roman Catholics, the importance of celibacy for his career (he allegedly refused to accept a bride sent from Germany), and a critical appraisal of his role in British expansionism in India.

Bibliography

Frykenberg, Robert Eric, "The Legacy of Christian Friedrich Schwartz," *International Bulletin of Missionary Research*, Vol. 23 (Jul 1999). • Germann, Wilhelm,

Missionar Christian Friedrich Schwartz (1870). • Jeyaraj, Daniel, ed., *Christian Frederick Schwartz: His Contributions to South India* (1999). • Lehmann, Arno, *Es begann in Tranquebar* (1955). • Pearson, Hugh, *Memoir of the Life and Correspondence of the Reverend Christian Frederick Swartz,* 2 Vols. (1834-39). RICHARD V. PIERARD

Scott, William Henry

(b. Detroit, Michigan, United States, 10 Jul 1921; d. Quezon City, Philippines, 4 Oct 1993). American Episcopal lay missionary in the Philippines*, teacher, and author.

Separated from the United States Navy while in China* shortly after World War II* Scott was hired by Randall Norton in 1946 to teach English courses at St. John's University Middle School in Shanghai. One of the many foreigners forced to leave China during the civil war and the subsequent Communist victory in 1949, he enrolled at Yale University, where he finished his bachelor of arts degree under the U.S. Veterans' "study now, pay later" program. He later earned his master's degree from Columbia University and then his doctoral degree from the University of Santo Tomas in Manila, Philippines.

Scott was appointed by the Episcopal Church in the United States of America (ECUSA) as a lay missionary to the Philippines in 1953. He was assigned to teach English and history at St. Mary's High School in Sagada, Mountain Province. In 1963, two years after the signing of the Concordat Relationship between the ECUSA and the Philippine Independent Church* (PIC), Scott was loaned to the PIC to become director of the Aglipay* Institute in Laoag, Ilocos Norte. Three years later he moved to Manila, where he pursued his doctoral studies and received his doctoral degree in 1968. After this he taught at Trinity College of Quezon City, the University of Santo Tomas, the University of the Philippines, and St. Andrew's Theological Seminary (SATS), also in Quezon City. His teaching ministry included a stint with Silliman University* in Dumaguete City.

When martial law was declared on 21 Sep 1972, Scott was arrested and incarcerated. He was not given any work assignments after his acquittal and was eventually released from prison in 1973. Scott was advised by the church leaders to "rest." Therefore he went to Sagada, where he spent his time writing. In 1975 he published one of his scholarly books, titled *The Discovery of the Igorots.*

He returned to teaching in Jun 1978 and was appointed professor of church history by Robert Hibbs, dean at SATS. Scott introduced the teaching of Philippine church history courses at the seminary.

In Jun 1981 he traveled back to the United States for study and research through the invitation of the Ford Foundation. He returned to the Philippines in 1983 and resigned from SATS to devote more time to writing and to give an opportunity to Filipinos interested in teaching there.

In Sep 1993 Scott went to Manila from Sagada for a medical checkup and to follow up on the publication of a book he had just written. He died the following month at St. Luke's Medical Center in Quezon City. He was buried in Sagada in a coffin made of local pinewood, as he had wished.

Bibliography

Conklin, Harold C., "A Bibliography of William Henry Scott," *Pilipinas: A Journal of Philippine Studies,* No. 22 (Spring 1994). • Owen, Norman G., "William Henry Scott: The Man and His Work," *Philippine Studies Newsletter* (Oct 1993–Mar 1994). EDWARD P. MALECDAN

Scranton, Mary Fletcher

(b. 9 Dec 1832; d. 8 Oct 1909). First female missionary of the Methodist* Episcopal Church sent to Korea*.

Scranton was accompanied by her doctor son, William Benton Scranton*, and his newly wed wife. She purchased an estate of a Korean aristocrat near the American legation in Seoul and opened a modern school for girls in her own living quarters in May 1885, about one month after her arrival in Korea. No students showed up until one year later, when a young woman covered herself up and came at night to Scranton's house to study English, desiring to become an interpreter for Queen Min. From this one unknown student, what is now Ewha School has grown to become a prestigious girls high school and Ewha Women's University with some 20,000 women — the largest all-women's university in the world. The name Ewha, meaning "pear blossoms," was given by Queen Min because the property the Scrantons purchased was on a pear orchard at the time. Besides her work as the first principal of Ewha Hakdang ("School"), she organized the Association of Methodist Women and promoted Bible* studies among church women.

Bibliography

Fifty Years of Light: Women's Foreign Missionary Society of the Methodist Episcopal Church (1938). • Hillman, Mary, *Korea Mission Field,* Vol. 6, No. 1 (1910). DAVID SUH

Scranton, William Benton

(b. New Haven, Connecticut, United States, 5 May 1858; d. Kobe, Japan, Mar 1922). One of the first medical* missionaries of the Methodist* Episcopal Church sent to Korea*.

Scranton graduated from Yale University in 1878 and New York Medical College in 1882. After his marriage, he opened a private clinic in Cleveland, Ohio. When he was diagnosed with a serious disease, he volunteered to go to Korea and accompanied his wife and widowed mother, Mary Fletcher Scranton*, arriving in 1885.

As his mother opened the first modern girls school in their newly purchased house in Seoul, he opened a clinic for women who were afraid of going to the Western hospital just opened by the royal court, known as a place only for men. He opened medical clinics for Korean women, one of which is now Ewha Women's University Medical School Hospital near the East Gate of Seoul.

After the accidental death of his fellow missionary H. G. Appenzeller* in 1902, he took up the administrative duties of the mission agency in Korea. Scranton was an evangelist and Bible* translator as well as a medical doctor. He translated all of Romans and parts of Genesis, Exodus, Psalms, and James as part of the Korean Bible Translation Committee. However, he left the Methodist mission for the Anglican* Church because of some disagreements with the mission board at home. For some years after 1907, he worked as a medical doctor in an American-operated gold mine in Unsan, North Korea, before he went to Kobe, Japan.

Bibliography

Hunt, Everett N., Jr., *Protestant Pioneers in Korea* (1980). • Huntley, Martha, *To Start a Work: The Foundations of Protestant Mission in Korea: 1884-1919* (1987). • Paik, L. George, *The History of Protestant Missions in Korea, 1832-1910* (1929/1970).

David Suh, with contributions from Lee Duk Joo, translated by Kim In Soo

Scripture Union and Children's Special Service Mission (SU and CSSM), India

Organization working among children and young people in evangelism, growth in Christian life, and witness.

As early as 1881, missionaries and British merchants published cards and SU readings in English and Bengali. By 1884 the cards were available in seven Indian languages. Today there are nearly 40,000 annual volumes of Bible* reading notes in English, Hindi, Tamil, Malayalam, Oriya, and Kannada. The Bible Society* of India* publishes cards with SU readings for those unable to buy the notes.

Bernard Herklots from England actually started the ministry in 1896 but returned home in 1899. By default, Roderic Thomas Archibald, who reached India in 1901 and served for 45 years, is considered the founder of SU and CSSM in India. He was succeeded by Cecil M. Johnston (1947-72), John Jacob (1973-86), and presently Gnanaraja. The work now serves 11 language areas in India.

In Jun 1907 the first Indian worker, Babu Rakhal Chandra Biswas, was appointed in Bengal. Today there are 41 field staff and 16 office staff. The staff run meetings in schools, churches, hostels, etc., using various media (visual aids, skits, and music). In addition, follow-up is done through the weekly Inter-School Christian Fellowship, or "SU clubs," where the regular and systematic teaching of God's Word is emphasized. Other activities include vacation Bible schools, camps, and one-day retreats. There is a 10-acre camp center by the beach at Mahabalipuram, a tourist center near Madras. The headquarters, formerly at Allahabad (1948-60), Chengannur (1961-68), and Tiruvalia (1968-87), is now in Madras.

SU and CSSM is not only a nursery of the church winning children to Christ, but also a training ground for Christian workers. It also paved the way for church union in bringing together workers of different denominations, especially in the early part of the century when church union was unknown. SU notes encourage personal meditation and family worship in the midst of rapid social changes.

Bibliography

Sylvester, Nigel, *God's Word in a Young World* (1984). • Pollock, J. C., *The Good Seed* (1959).

D. Stephen Abraham

Scudder, Ida Sophia

(b. Ranipet, Madras Presidency, 1870; d. 1960). Missionary doctor and founder of the medical college at Vellore in South India*.

Scudder's father, John Scudder, served as a medical* doctor in the North Arcot Mission of the (Dutch) Reformed* Church of America. Ida Scudder returned to India on a short-term visit to be near her sick mother. The deplorable conditions of women during childbirth and their refusal to allow male doctors to examine them touched her. So she returned to the United States and trained to become a medical doctor herself. She began her medical practice in 1899 and in 1900 opened a hospital at Vellore. Later she began a nursing school in 1918 with funds raised in America. The school started on a secure financial basis and eventually had the support of 40 missions. The majority of its students were women, but by the 1950s a substantial minority were men.

The school is connected with a hospital and has several roadside bus clinics. Its staff comes from four continents, and it is an outstanding interdenominational Christian institution in Asia.

Bibliography

Douglas, J. D., *Dictionary of the Christian Church* (Grand Rapids: Zondervan, 1974/78). • Barfour, Margaret I., and Ruth Young Humphrey Milford, *The Work of Medical Women in India* (1929).

Roselyn Serto

Seagrave, Gordon Stifler

(b. Rangoon, 13 Mar 1897; d. Redlands, California, United States, 28 Mar 1965). Medical* doctor, missionary, and founder of a nursing school and a hospital in Namkham, Myanmar*.

Among the many medical missionaries to Burma,

Seagrave was the most lionized. He spent most of his life in a village called Namkham in the northern Shan State of Burma. Born to a missionary couple of the American Baptist Mission in Burma, he grew up in a mixed culture of Burmese, Karen*, and English. His desire to become a medical missionary to the rural areas motivated him to study at Johns Hopkins University in the United States. He married Marion Grace Morse in 1920, graduated in 1921, and returned to Burma with his wife and baby in 1922.

Seagrave then began his medical missionary work under the American Baptist* Foreign Mission Board at Namkham with a wastebasketful of surgical instruments salvaged from his university training. He is known to many throughout the world as the "Burma Surgeon." Knowing that he could not handle the Karen patients around the Namkham area alone, he began to train local Karen women to help him in his hospital and during his tours to the surrounding areas. In order to have better facilities for both the patients and the workers in the hospital, Seagrave began to build new buildings out of cobblestones with his own hands. His family, his friends, workers at the hospitals, and even the nurses helped him finish the buildings of the hospital, including the nurses' home.

Through the years, Seagrave trained many native women — Karen, Shan, Kachin*, and a half-dozen other races — to be nurses, and their abilities astonished all who came to know them. So great was the reputation of Seagrave's kindhearted deeds that even the Buddhist girls enthusiastically joined his nursing school and lived together with the Christians at the nurses' home in Namkham.

During World War II*, Seagrave was commissioned by the United States Medical Corps. He and his nurses joined other units in India*. After the war they returned to Namkham and rebuilt the hospitals damaged by the war. His benevolent work for the local people was so appreciated that a former president of the Union of Burma, Sao Shew Thaike, his wife, and the ambassador of the United States to Burma, Mr. Sebald, and his wife, visited him to see his humanitarian work in Namkham in 1954.

Due to his association with and love for the local tribes, the government suspected him of being a traitor and jailed him for treason in 1950 for almost seven months. Four lawyers, a Burmese, an English, an Indian, and a Sino-Burman, defended him without fee. He was warmly welcomed back by the people in Namkham after his release. His death at the age of 68 was a great loss.

Bibliography

Seagrave, Gordon S., *Burma Surgeon* (1943); *My Hospital in the Hills* (1955). • Newhall, Sue M., *The Devil in God's Old Man* (1969).

Cung Lian Hup

Secularization

Refers to the declining influence of religion on modern society, supposedly an inevitable outcome of modernization.

The characteristics of modern societies are industrialization, use of high technology, greater economic development, more literacy*, a comprehensive educational system, urbanization, and a powerful, bureaucratic state. Modern societies seek to apply reason to all areas of life. Traditional societies, in contrast, are usually agrarian, use simple technology, have a nearly subsistence economy, rely on oral tradition, orient education to the tasks of survival, and are governed by religious values, *adat**, and the elders. By these definitions, Asia is clearly in transition between the two kinds of societies, with the modern parts still strongly influenced by their close traditional roots.

Many Asian leaders hope that the intellectual tools and technology of the modern world can be adopted while the religious and cultural traditions of their countries can prevent the moral problems of many modern (mostly Western) societies. Thus a critical question is whether religion can survive the onslaught of modernity.

Most theories of modernization assume a process of secularization. Secularization can have several different meanings, the most common being the decline or disappearance of religion as a result of modernization. In the 19th c., many scholars viewed secularization as an inevitable result of the growth of rationality. Social evolution was thought to be sweeping away superstition. This attitude is still common in most major Western universities. Karl Marx saw religion as false consciousness, an ideological tool used by the powerful to control the oppressed masses. Sigmund Freud, on the other hand, considered religion an infantile neurosis, the projection of an idealized and feared father figure into the heavens. Both thought religion would wither away as society became more rational and just. Even classic sociologists such as Max Weber, Emile Durkheim, and Ferdinand Toennies, who saw religion as a positive source of meaning and values in traditional societies, believed it could not survive the rationalizing impact of modernity.

Theories of secularization have had their greatest impact in Asian countries influenced by Marxism. Secularization in China*, for example, was not seen as only a logical result of increasing rationality, but was taken as a political policy and a desirable social goal. Religion was to be eradicated as part of the creation of a modern, socialized society. In spite of nearly 50 years of religious persecution, religion is currently resurgent in China.

Religion is an assumed reality in most Asian countries. Theories of secularization have influence primarily in indirect form, as students absorb the antireligious or secular assumptions of much Western university education. For example, all Indonesians officially believe in God — by law. If secularization is a danger to most Asians, it is probably not in the form of atheism or even agnosticism. The spiritual world is still close to the experience of many Asians. But nominal belief is already common. It may in part stem from the rationalizing influence of modern life.

Secularization

There is empirical evidence for the decline of traditional religion in western European countries. Ironically, religion is resurgent in the formerly Communist countries which tried the hardest to wipe it out. But the major blow to theories about the inevitable decline of religion in modern societies comes from the United States. Between 1880 and 1960, church membership in the United States grew from 20 to 63 percent! Since the 1960s, traditional church membership has declined, but evangelical* and Pentecostal* churches have mushroomed. Non-Christian religions and nontraditional religious practices are also flourishing. Those who still argue that modernization brings an inevitable decline of religion have a very hard time explaining the American situation.

Secularization may also mean the displacement of religion from the center of the life of a community to its periphery. Traditional societies have very strong religious institutions that play a role in every area of life. Modernization is accompanied by differentiation and specialization. The complexity of modern life requires that more and more different institutions, each ruled by a highly trained elite, take over smaller and smaller areas of life. As "secular" institutions proliferate, religious institutions are pushed more and more to the side. Instead of being central to all of life, they become just one area among many. Instead of competing with government for supremacy (as the religious leader competes with the village head), religion becomes an optional activity for one's free time. Religion is a matter of free choice and is confined to feelings and private life in contrast to the pragmatic rationality of the "real world."

The compartmentalization of religion to the realm of feelings and private life is a major problem for Asian Christians. Some Asian countries have a strongly entrenched state religion, such as Buddhism* in Thailand* or Islam* in Malaysia*. Indonesia* includes general belief in God at the heart of the national ideology. Religion is included in all areas of public life. Political, military, and business leaders all reinforce the centrality of religion in the life of the nation. Even in strongly materialistic (Confucian*-influenced) Asian cities such as Seoul, Tokyo, Taipei, Hong Kong, and Singapore*, religion is a strong force in public and private life. Asians may be more likely to change their religion than to lose it altogether.

Nevertheless, the compartmentalization of religion into a separate sphere is a likely effect of modernization in Asia. Religion is unlikely to be banned from public life, as in the West. Christians and others will participate in formal, public expressions of their religion, but in the everyday life of academia, business, and government, their faith may be irrelevant. Many Asians are uncritical of Western science. Belief in objective rationality seems to leave no room for religious values in professional life. Technical or instrumental reason, uninfluenced by subjective bias, is assumed to be the modern way to address the real problems of life. Contradictions between Christian values and the demands of government, business, or science are solved by compartmentalization. Christian values or beliefs are not doubted; they are simply ignored when it comes to practical life. Business is conducted by the "laws" of business, science by the methods of science, and political or bureaucratic relationships by the pragmatics of power relationships.

A third meaning of secularization is the process by which government and other institutions take over many of the values and functions that used to belong to religion. Instead of religion being the source of ethics and moral practice, leadership in these areas is taken over by government and other institutions. In the West, this process is best seen in the practices of the welfare state. No longer do communities of believers, in obedience to their faith, take care of the poor, the sick, the orphans, and the aged. Instead it is done by large institutions and the government. The values and practices of the church are now taken care of by the insurance industry, welfare, social security, old-age homes, and orphanages. Some writers, such as Talcott Parsons, see this as a positive development. The social values of religion are now adopted by the whole society and professionalized. Others see it as just another example of the marginalization of religion and the depersonalization of care.

Most of the social security, protection, and welfare that Asians experience is based in their own ethnic and religious communities. This compares favorably with the depersonalized institutions of the West, which are often run on a profit motive. As social problems become larger, it is inevitable that government and private industry will step in, if for no other reason than to discourage social unrest. While this may be appropriate in some cases, government bureaucracies are not only impersonal, they are often inefficient and vulnerable to corruption.

The ideologies of nationalism* and development, two of the strongest symbols of modernity, threaten to take over the functions of religion in Asian societies. National pride, a valuable means of uniting highly diverse societies around common goals, has proven most effective in freeing Asian societies from colonial domination, but it becomes a form of idolatry when religion is treated as a tool to further national goals and passionate loyalty to the nation takes the place of real worship of God alone.

Secularization is seen also in the tendency of Asians to put their faith in the economic policies of development. While the church may continue its charitable activities, real hope for achieving a just and prosperous society is located in rational economic plans, investment, the World Bank, and large corporations. Religion loses its prophetic function of criticizing wealth and power and may become a legitimator of economic power. National "development" often sacrifices the well-being of poor people and traditional cultures for the enrichment of an elite through business. One of the most dangerous and destructive forms of secularization in the 20th c. is what Jurgen Habermas calls "the colonization of the lifeworld by money and power." Capitalism and bureaucracy are two extremely powerful structures by which money and power take over what rightly belongs to God. Secularization of this type is a form of idolatry.

Secularization is sometimes identified with a change in the way people look at the world. Instead of viewing the world with awe and a sense of mystery, as a dwelling place of God's power and presence, modern culture approaches the world "rationally," pragmatically, and as a source of resources and enjoyment. Modern science seeks to understand, manipulate, and dominate the natural world. The earth is viewed instrumentally, as something to be used for the benefit of humanity, rather than as a sacred creation to be approached with reverence. Activists in the environmental movement have sometimes blamed Christianity for this attitude, which has led to a world-threatening ecological crisis. But the real cause is a secularizing modern culture that has enthroned utilitarian reason as the god of a mechanistic world.

It is commonplace in Asia to decry the influx of Western sexual values, individualism, and materialism through television and film. These are indeed serious concerns. But less recognized, and far more serious, is the inundation of a technological way of thinking that lies at the heart of modern culture. One of the most passionate and comprehensive critiques of this "modern" way of thinking was written in 1954 by a French sociologist and theologian named Jacques Ellul, who drew a distinction between technologies per se and the mentality, or worldview, or ethos that makes them possible in the modern world. Ellul calls this ethos "technique," explaining it as the totality of methods rationally arrived at and having absolute efficiency in every field of activity. Technique is the scientific process, or "modern" way of thinking, that makes technology possible. It is a way of thinking that subordinates all values to the value of efficiency and utility.

On the one hand, traditional Asian cultures believe the power of God inhabits the natural world. Belief in spirits, *jinns, nats,* and other supernatural beings from the spiritual world that indwell trees and rocks and rivers is common, not only in local animistic* religions, but also among most of the followers of the world religions. Offerings, meditations, and prayers are often made to these beings, even by political, economic, and military leaders. Most Asians seem far from Max Weber's "disenchantment of the world" or Ellul's rule of technique. On the other hand, when it comes to development projects, factories, industry, and transportation, most Asian countries place economic priorities above protection of the environment. It is, however, debatable whether modern, utilitarian rationalism is the primary cause of an attitude of unconcern for the natural environment.

Finally, secularization sometimes refers to the conformity of religion to the world. In itself, this is not a product of modern culture. Even in New Testament days the apostle Paul had to warn his readers not to be conformed to the world. But in modern culture, when religion becomes worldly, it usually means it becomes modern. The major characteristics of modern culture become the characteristics of the church. On the one hand, this may be considered a positive kind of contextualization*. There are many valuable elements of modern culture. Modern churches that use rational methods, stress individual dignity, and go through a process of differentiation and specialization of functions may be very effective in certain contexts. The danger is that negative characteristics of modern culture will be uncritically accepted as the modern, or even the scientific, way to "manage" a church.

Since Christianity is a minority religion in many Asian countries, with little influence on public life, the temptation is to compromise with those in power in order not to lose any more of an already diminishing influence on society. This is reinforced by Asian cultural values of harmony and suppression of conflict. Compromise and retreat is the best way to deal with the powerful. The safety of the religious institutions depends on the protection of the powerful.

Secularization as conformity to the world is best tested by how faithful Christians are in their practices. Are Christian business leaders different from non-Christians? Are they less materialistic, more honest, more fair to their employees, more conscientious about the value of their products and services to society, more concerned about the environment, more ready to sacrifice their own interests for the good of others, more concerned about justice than profits, etc.? How do Christians deal with power conflicts, corrupt bureaucracies, persecution, dishonest employers, labor unrest, racial discrimination, family violence, etc.? These and many more ethical questions may be a more telling measure of how far modern secularization has pressed the church into the mold of the world than church attendance or theological affirmations. In the face of negative pressures of secularization, Asian Christians need to learn resistance to the culture of modernity as well as adaptation to its positive elements.

Bibliography

Baum, Gregory, *Religion and Alienation* (1975). • Bellah, Robert N., *Beyond Belief* (1970). • Berger, Peter, *The Sacred Canopy* (1969). • Childress, James F., "Secularization," in *The Westminster Dictionary of Christian Ethics,* ed. James F. Childress and John Macquarrie (1986). • Ellul, Jacques, *The Technological Society* (1964). • Toennies, Ferdinand, *Community and Society* (1957). • Toulmin, Stephen, *Cosmopolis: The Hidden Agenda of Modernity* (1990). • Weber, Max, *The Protestant Ethic and the Spirit of Capitalism* (1958). • Wilson, Bryon, *Religion in Secular Society* (1969). • Wuthnow, Robert, *Rediscovering the Sacred* (1992). BERNARD T. ADENEY

Seda, Frans

(b. 1926). Chairman of *Partai Katolik* (Catholic Party), Indonesia*, in 1961 and successively minister of plantations (1964-66), agriculture (1966), finance (1966-68), and communications (1968-73).

Seda came from the island of Flores and studied at the Xaverius College in Muntilan, Central Java*, to become a teacher. As a student, he participated in national youth organizations and political and military actions during the war of independence (1945-49). He studied economics at the High School for Economics in Tilburg, Netherlands (1950-56). In 1961 he was made vice chairman of the Catholic Party and was sent on a secret mission to the Netherlands to make the Dutch government accept the Bunker Plan (1963) to prevent new fighting in New Guinea. During his time as minister in different governments under Presidents Sukarno* and Suharto, and as ambassador to Belgium and Luxembourg and to the European Common Market (1973-78), he cofounded the Catholic University Atma Maya in Jakarta (1962) and also the predecessor of the present Association of Catholic Institutes of Higher Education (APTIK), *Majelis Perguruan Tinggi Katolik* (1966). Besides taking an active part in various national business associations, Seda was also involved in the establishment of the daily *Kompas,* now the largest newspaper in Indonesia, and the Institute of Management Education and Training (LPPM) in Jakarta. He organized the national celebration to commemorate 450 years of the Catholic Church in Indonesia (1984) and the closing ceremony of the National Marian Year in Maumere, Flores (1988). He also organized the visit of Pope John Paul II to Indonesia (1989). He was a member of the Papal Commission, *Iustitia et Pax,* in Rome (1984-89).

Bibliography

Universitas Katolik Atma Jaya, ed., *Frans Seda — Ad multos annos* (1992).

Adolf Heuken

Seitz, Paul

(b. Le Havre, Rouen, France, 1906; d. France, 1992). Founder of an orphanage, the Town of Christ the King; bishop of Kontum Diocese in Vietnam*.

Seitz was a Boy Scout when he was drafted into the French army to serve in Maroc. After his military service, he completed his secondary schooling and entered the seminary of the Paris Foreign Mission Society* (MEP). In 1955 he was sent to Hanoi, where he assisted Vicar Villebouet at a parish and was also a chaplain for both French and Vietnamese youth. His concern for street children and orphans led him to build an orphanage at a former military camp in Ba Vi. In 1946, for security, the orphanage moved to a suburb in Hanoi and was named the Town of Christ the King.

Seitz was nominated superior of the MEP in North Vietnam on 15 Feb 1952 and, four months later, became the bishop of Kontum Diocese, in the middle of West Highland, central Vietnam. Strategically located, Kontum was inhabited mainly by ethnic minorities, of whom 20,000 were Catholics and only 6,000 capital ethnic (Vietnamese). Problems arose because of the massive migration of the northerners moving south of the 17th parallel. By 1957 there were 35,000 capital ethnic Catholics and 30,000 ethnic minority Catholics. In 1959, under the leadership of Seitz, Kontum had 94 priests (59 Vietnamese, 25 French), five congregations for women*, one for men, four high schools, and 44 elementary schools run by the Catholic Church. Seitz was not allowed to remain in Vietnam, so, after May 1975, he returned to France.

Anthony Do Huu Nghiem

Semarang

Capital of the province of Central Java* and seat of a Catholic archbishop (1961; apostolic vicariate, 1940).

The church province of Semarang comprises the dioceses of Malang (1961; Ocarm; apostolic prefecture, 1927), Purwokerto (1961; MSF; apostolic prefecture, 1932), and Surabaya (1961; Lazarist* Fathers; apostolic prefecture, 1928). For decades the parishes of Surabaya (1810) and Semarang (1808) looked after only the Dutch and Indo-European Catholics of Eastern and Central Java. Several attempts at the end of the 19th c. to preach the Gospel among the Javanese population in and south of Semarang did not succeed. After years of studying the Javanese language and customs and living among the villagers of Muntilan, Franz van Lith* was able to baptize 171 people in the mountains of Kalibawang (1904). By creating an outstanding system of education and carefully selecting the students, a small but apostolic-minded group of young Catholic teachers and educated laypeople was formed in the colleges of Muntilan (since 1904) and Mendut (1908; for girls). With the help of the Franciscan* Sisters of the Heythuizen (since 1870 in Semarang), the Brothers of Aloysius (1911), and the Brothers of the Immaculate Conception of Mary (FIC, 1920), an excellent network of schools was developed throughout Central Java.

The mission in the province of East Java was looked after by the Lazarist Fathers in Surabaya (1923) and by the Discalced Carmelites* in Malang (1923). Both cities became centers of active Catholic communities and many educational and health institutions.

During the 1930s, Indonesian Catholics increased, doubling their size in 1942 (30,460 Javanese Catholics), and outnumbered the Dutch. The rapid growth of the church was accompanied by the erection of important institutions in Central Java: *Katolika Wandawa* was the first charitable organization (1914), *Wanita Katolik* the first women's organization (1923), and *Pakempalan Politik Katolik Djawi* (1923) the embryo of the future Catholic Party. Since 1928, catechists began to be formed in special courses. Just before the outbreak of the Pacific War, Albertus Soegijapranata* was appointed the first Indonesian bishop to head the newly erected vicariate apostolic of Semarang. With a small group of Javanese priests, sisters, and brothers, the church not only stood on its feet but grew steadily in numbers during the difficult time of the Japanese occupation, when all Dutch church personnel were interned in concentration camps. After recovering from heavy losses of personnel and buildings, new projects were started from the 1950s: a teacher training college, *Sanata Dharma,* in Yogyakarta (1955; university since 1993); a farming school, *Taman Tani,* in Salatiga (1965); a technical school, *Kolese S. Mikael,* in Surakarta (1967); and an academy for carpenters, joiners, and cabinetmakers, *Kebon Kayu,* in Semarang (1970).

The major seminary S. Paulus (1936) became a theological faculty by state (1961) and papal law (1984); the catechetical academy *Pradnyawidya* (1971) provided secondary education for catechists and teachers of religion. Both institutions are located in Yogyakarta.

During Justinus Cardinal Darmojuwono's time of office (1964-83), the Catholic community grew from 78,543 (1960) to 301,345 members. It now numbers almost half a million among a population of 31 million (1994). Thousands from animistic* and mystical Javanese groups (*kebatinan;* see Mysticism, Javanese*) became Christians after 1965, after an aborted Communist *coup d'etat,* when every citizen had to be a member of one of the five "acknowledged" religions. Vocations to religious life and the priesthood are strong, and, at minor and major seminaries, novitiates of both sexes from many congregations are well supported. The Roncalli Institute in Salatiga (1968) promotes the spiritual formation of different religious congregations for women; several retreat houses (e.g., in Ungaran, Klaten, Yogyakarta) cater to the rising spiritual and religious needs of the faithful in the archdiocese; the Soegijapranata Foundation coordinates and promotes charity and social work among the poor. Archbishop Darmaatmadja was promoted to the cardinalate by Pope John Paul II (1994), who visited the diocese in 1989.

ADOLF HEUKEN

Sendangsono

Most popular place for pilgrimage for Indonesian Catholics, situated in the Kalibawang Mountains of southern central Java*.

In the water of a fountain (a *sendang* — Javanese) under the roof of a *sono* tree frequented by Buddhist monks of the renowned Borobudur Temple compound (9th c.), 171 Javanese villagers from this mountain area were baptized on 14 Dec 1904 by Franz van Lith*. This event is considered the birth of the Catholic Church in Java, which now has about one million members.

In the valley around the fountain are bamboo huts, chapels (1920), stations of the cross (1958), and other facilities for pilgrims, who come from all over Indonesia* to pray for the intercession of Mary Mother of Christ. The place is also popular with non-Christians because of its serenity and quietness, suited for meditation and prayer.

ADOLF HEUKEN

Seoul Central Holiness Church

(SCHC). Mother church of the Korea* Evangelical Holiness Church* (KEHC).

The SCHC began on 30 May 1907 as Gospel Mission Hall with premises in the downtown area of Chongno, Seoul. It was rented by two pioneer evangelists, Chung Bin and Kim Sang Joon, who had studied at Tokyo Bible Institute of the Oriental Missionary Society (OMS). They proclaimed the Fourfold Gospel of regeneration, holiness, divine healing, and the second coming of Jesus Christ. In 1910 they requested the OMS for help, and the missionary work of the Gospel Mission Hall came under the direct supervision of the OMS. In 1912 Mrs. C. E. (Lettie) Cowman, one of the five founders of the OMS, donated a new building, the Mukyodong Gospel Mission Hall, in Mukyodong, Chongno.

Though intended originally as a parachurch organization (preaching the Fourfold Gospel at night and leading converts to established denominational churches in the day), the need to follow up with an increasing number of converts led to the establishment of a church in 1921. The OMS Gospel Mission Hall became the Korea OMS Holiness Church. It played a central role in the development of the Holiness Church in Korea, and Mukyodong became the Mukyodong Holiness Church. On 29 Dec 1932, the OMS churches were closed and used as factories by the Japanese.

The church was reopened on 29 Aug 1948, after the liberation of Korea in 1945. It was renamed Seoul Central Holiness Church, in keeping with the vision to become the central church of the KEHC. In 1957 the church celebrated its 50th anniversary with a new building, the Jubilee Memorial Building. Under the leadership of Senior Pastor Lee Man Shin (since 1974), the church moved to larger, new premises on the east side of downtown beside *Tongdaemoon* (East Gate). With about 10,000 congregations, Central Church is presently the largest church of the KEHC.

Bibliography

Lee Chun Young, *History of Holiness Church* (1971). • *Whal Chun* (Living water) (KEHC, Seoul). • *History of 70 Years of the Central Holiness Church* (1978).

KAN KEUN WHAN

Seven Martyrs of Thailand

The seven martyrs of Thailand* are seven Christians of *Wat Mae Phra-tai-tas* (Church of the Holy Mother of the Redeemer) in the village *(moo ban)* Songkhon, presently situated in Mukdahan Province. Their names are: Philip Siphong Onpitak, a teacher; Sister Agnes Phila Thipsuk; Sister Lucia Khambang; Agatha Phutta Vongvai; Cecilia Butsi Vongvai; Bibiana Khampai Vongvai; and Maria Phon Vongvai. They chose to witness to their faith in the Lord Jesus Christ by their death, enduring oppression, persecution, and torture rather than abandoning their faith.

During the war in Indochina toward the end of 1940, Thailand demanded that France return some territory along the Mae Klong River. Negotiations were fruitless. Fierce conflict broke out along the border. Thai people were very angry with France and French people. France, the French, and the Catholic religion were seen as enemies of Thailand. Because French missionaries had been spreading the Catholic faith in the area since the Ayutthaya period, Thai Catholics were persecuted, discriminated against, and subjected to violence in order to force them to abandon their Catholic faith and become Buddhists. French missionaries were expelled from pastoral positions in churches in several provinces and forced to travel to Bangkok, where they had to live together in a single location. Catholic churches and schools were closed. Thai Christians were left with no one to depend on, no priests to give them pastoral care. Some missionaries, priests, and ordinands were treated violently.

Because there were no priests in charge in Songkhon village, Catholics were vigorously pressed to give up their faith. However, their strong *Khru Yai* (head teacher), Philip Siphong Onpitak of the parochial school, and two sisters gave them pastoral care and strengthened the faith of all Catholics. Khru Siphong carried out the duties of a priest. On Sundays he rang the bell to summon all the faithful to worship and charged the people not to abandon their faith. His activities were under constant police surveillance. He was hated and was the first one to be eliminated. He knew this well, as he said at one time, "I will no doubt have to die because of this."

Khru Siphong was murdered on 16 Dec 1940. Some police brought him a forged letter purporting to be from a county official requesting Khru Siphong to come and meet him. Khru Siphong made the mistake of believing that the letter was genuine and went with the police. Along the way, one of the police shot him to death, following which the police destroyed all evidence, dug a pit, and buried him.

Following the murder of Khru Siphong, people in Songkhon village were too frightened to declare openly that they were Catholics. Some gave up their faith altogether, but a large group maintained their faith under the guidance of Sisters Agnes Phila and Lucia Khambang. Police placed all kinds of obstacles in their way in hopes of cutting the faithful off from their leadership, thus easing the task of pressing them to give up their faith. One day the village headman called a meeting to announce a decision by the county official that all those holding to the Catholic faith should profess the Buddhist faith. He said that the Catholic faith would be eradicated from Bankhon. Serious consequences, including death, would follow for any who failed to obey.

This was at Christmas time. Silence and fear dominated Bankhon. No Christmas mass could be held in the church, as had been done each year. However, these two sisters led the faithful in prayer and song as they remembered the birth of the holy child. Sister Agnes Phila wrote a letter to the county official with this message: "These people will never give up the Catholic faith, which is the true religion, to embrace Buddhism* as ordered by the government. Even though we may be falsely accused of unfaithfulness to the government, they are willing to give up their lives for God, but will never give up their God." On 26 Dec 1940, the police took both sisters, and the Catholics who were willing to give up their lives for their faith, to the church cemetery. Along the way, they alternated praying and singing. At the cemetery they knelt down and prayed together. Then the police shot all six of them to death. They were buried in the cemetery of the Church of the Holy Mother of the Redeemer in Bankhon.

On 26 Dec 1986, the bodies of the seven martyrs were taken from their graves and moved to the new Church of the Holy Mother of the Redeemer to await naming as martyrs. On 26 Oct 1989, Pope John Paul II, in the Basilica of St. Peter in Rome, named these seven as martyrs, models of faith in Christ, and an honor to the Catholic Church in Thailand.

Surachai Chumsriphan, translated by E. John Hamlin

Seventh-day Adventists

The name Seventh-day Adventist (SDA) denotes that the church accepts the Second Coming (Second Advent) of Jesus Christ as the Blessed Hope and the grand climax of the Gospel. His coming will be literal, personal, visible, imminent, and worldwide. When he returns, the righteous dead will be resurrected and together with the righteous living will be glorified and taken to heaven, but the unrighteous dead will be annihilated. Also, the name "Seventh-day" denotes that the church accepts that the great principles of God's law are embodied in the Ten Commandments and exemplified in the life of Christ. They express God's love, will, and purposes concerning human conduct and relationships to God and humankind. These precepts are the basis of God's covenant with His people and the standard in God's judgment. The beneficent Creator, after six literal days of creation, rested on the seventh day and instituted the sabbath for all people as a memorial of creation. The fourth commandment of God's unchangeable law requires the observance of this seventh-day sabbath as the day of rest, worship, and ministry in harmony with the teaching and practice of Jesus, the Lord of the sabbath. The sabbath is also a symbol of our redemption in Christ, a sign of our sanctification, a token of our allegiance, and a foretaste of our eternal future in God's kingdom. The sabbath is God's perpetual sign of the eternal covenant between God and God's people. Joyful observance of this holy time lasts from evening to evening, sunset to sunset (Friday to Saturday), in a celebration of God's creative and redemptive acts (Gen 2:1-3; Exod 20:1-17; Deut 5:6-21; Isa 56:5, 6; 58:13, 14; Matt 5:17-20; 12:1-12; Heb 4:1-11).

The church accepts the following 27 fundamental doctrines as taught in the Bible: (1) the Holy Scriptures;

(2) the Trinity; (3) God the Father; (4) God the Son; (5) God the Holy Spirit; (6) Creation; (7) the Nature of Man; (8) the Great Controversy between Satan and Christ; (9) the Life, Death, and Resurrection of Christ; (10) the Experience of Salvation; (11) the Church; (12) the Remnant and Its Mission; (13) Unity in the Body of Christ; (14) Baptism by Immersion; (15) the Lord's Supper with Footwashing prior to It; (16) Spiritual Gifts and Ministries; (17) the Gift of Prophecy as Manifested in the Works and Ministry of Ellen G. White; (18) the Law of God; (19) the Sabbath; (20) Stewardship; (21) Christian Behavior; (22) Marriage and Family; (23) Christ's Ministry in the Heavenly Sanctuary; (24) the Second Coming of Christ; (25) the Death and Resurrection of Man; (26) the Millennium and the End of Sin; and (27) the New Earth (see *Seventh-day Adventist Yearbook,* 1995, pp. 5-8).

Organizational structure. In 1922, the present organizational structure for the worldwide Seventh-day Adventist Church was developed. The highest in the hierarchy is the general conference (GC) with its current headquarters in Silver Springs, Maryland. The world is divided into 13 divisions. These divisions are further subdivided into union conferences or union missions that oversee the work of the conferences, missions, or sections. (The only difference between the missions/sections and the conferences is that, in order to achieve conference status, the organization has to become financially and in manpower independent from the higher organization.) These sections in turn supervise the work of the local churches through the local church pastors.

The SDA churches in Asia are found in three divisions: The Asia-Pacific Division (APD), comprising Bangladesh*, Brunei*, Hong Kong*, Indo-China, Indonesia*, Japan*, Korea*, Macau*, Malaysia*, the Philippines*, Singapore*, Sri Lanka*, Thailand*, and Taiwan*; the Southern Asia Division (SAD), comprising India*; and the Trans-European Division (TED), comprising Pakistan*. No organizational structure of the church exists in China* today, but programs for missions are under the South China Island Union Mission (SCIUM) sited in Hong Kong, formerly known as the Far Eastern Division (FED).

Former and present divisions of Asia. A division in Asia known as the "Asiatic Division" (AD) existed in 1909, when a vice president of the GC was appointed to oversee it, although it had never been formally organized up to that time. Its territorial jurisdiction comprised China, India, Japan, Korea, the Malay Peninsula, the Philippine* Islands, and the Straits Settlements. It ceased to exist after 1918, when the India Union Mission (IUM) and the Australasian Union conference came under the supervision of J. E. Fulton, the former president of the AD, and the Far Eastern section (East Asian Union, the North China Union, the South China Union, and the Philippine Union) was placed under I. H. Evans, with headquarters in Shanghai. In 1919 the Far Eastern section became the FED.

The IUM was first organized in 1910, and it became a part of the AD from 1915 to 1918. In 1919 it was reorganized as a separate union, and then in 1920 it became the SAD. A further reorganization of its territorial jurisdiction was carried out in 1986, with Pakistan under the TED.

The China Division (CD) was formed in 1930, when the mission work was separated from the FED and it had jurisdiction over Hong Kong and Macau. After the change of government in 1949, a provisional committee of the division was in charge of the work of nationals. The main division committee operated from Hong Kong and supervised the territory, but not under the mainland government. On 1 Jan 1950 the provisional committee became the CD, and territories not under the mainland government together with Hong Kong and Macau became the SCIUM under the control of the FED.

Resources for the development of the SDA Church in Asia. The SDA Church in Asia started with three resources: (1) laypeople relocating to the territory; (2) colporteurs entering the territory selling and distributing religious books and magazines; and (3) missionaries sent by the established church organization. The GC voted to form the Missionary Society of SDAs in 1869 for that purpose.

China, Hong Kong, and Macau. Overcoming the odds of being considered too old (65 years at the time), Abram La Rue went to Hong Kong as an independent colporteur. In 1888 he began a seamen's mission for the sailors who came to Hong Kong. He entered Canton the same year, and in 1889 he went to Shanghai colporteuring. Although he did not know Chinese, he befriended a Chinese man who worked in the colonial court of Hong Kong and later translated his tracts into Chinese. In 1898 the church voted officially to open mission work in China. J. N. Anderson and family, together with Ida Thompson (Mrs. Anderson's sister), arrived in Hong Kong in Feb 1902. Ida Thompson started an English school for Chinese children. The first baptism in Hong Kong conducted by Anderson comprised converts of La Rue.

In Dec 1902 Edwin H. Wilbur and his wife (both nurses) went to Canton, becoming the first permanent SDA workers in mainland China. On 15 Feb 1903 the first SDA church was organized with eight members. In Apr 1903 Anderson moved to Canton, which became the headquarters for China's work.

In 1904 Timothy Tay convinced Keh Ngo-pit, a Chinese Protestant minister, of the SDA message, and together they converted T. K. Ang, another Christian leader. In 1906 Anderson ordained Keh Ngo-pit to the SDA ministry at Amoy.

The first general meeting of the workers in China was held from 10 to 20 Feb 1907 with W. W. Prescott from the GC. Through this meeting the China Mission was organized into three local missions: Kwangtung, Honan, and Fukian, with headquarters at Shanghai.

In 1909 the second meeting of workers convened in

Shanghai and the China Union Mission (CUM) was formed with six mission fields. In 1912 CUM was dissolved, and the missions were placed directly under the AD. A further reorganization took place in 1917 when the work of China was divided into two Unions: North China Union Conference (Chekiang, Anhwei, Kiangsu, Shantung, Honan, Hupeh, Hunan, Kiangsi, and Szechwan) and South China Union Conference (Fukian, Kwangtung, and Kwangsi). In 1918, with the dissolving of the AD, China came under the Far Eastern section, which was later called the FED. The union conferences of China were also discontinued, but the organized mission work persisted under union missions.

In 1930 China was separated from the FED and, together with Hong Kong and Macau, formed the CD, with H. W. Miller as its first president. After 1950, when the present government took over, however, the mission work in China was not officially maintained by the GC, and contacts with the church within China were loosely maintained by the SCIUM, whose headquarters is in Hong Kong. (No official organizational structure exists in China today.)

Borneo, Brunei, Malaysia, and Singapore. The first SDA to visit Singapore may well have been La Rue as well. H. B. Meyers, a convert from India, came to Singapore in 1900, and he worked there for 5 1/2 months. The next SDA worker to visit Singapore was E. H. Gates from Australia. He baptized a young soldier on 9 Mar 1902. On 28 Oct 1904 G. F. Jones and his wife and Robert Caldwell from Australia began further pioneer work in Singapore and Malaysia (Malay Peninsula and the Dutch East Indies). In 1905 the Malaysian Mission was formed with G. F. Jones as superintendent and R. W. Munson as secretary. Singapore served as headquarters. The first church building was dedicated in Aug 1909 in Singapore.

Evangelistic work was started in Kuala Lumpur, the Malay Peninsula, by R. P. Montgomery in 1911. He was succeeded by A. R. Duckworth from Singapore. By 1914 the first SDA church in Malaya was organized with 12 members at Kuala Lumpur. The Federated Malay States Mission was organized that same year.

In 1931 the Singapore Mission was merged with the Malay States Mission to form the West Malaysia and Singapore Mission. In 1988 the West Malaysia and Singapore Mission was bifurcated into the SDA Church of Peninsular Malaysia and the SDA Mission of Singapore.

East Malaysia (part of Borneo) was also believed to have been entered by La Rue sometime between 1888 and 1903. The next visit was by a Chinese colporteur from Singapore in 1909. In Jun 1913 R. P. Montgomery and his wife went from Singapore and established an office in Sandakan, then capital of North Borneo. On 1 Jan 1914 seven Chinese were baptized. The next year L. B. Mershon became director of the mission, and he moved the headquarters to Kota Kinabalu (Jesselton). Later the headquarters was moved to Tamparuli, which remains as headquarters of the Sabah Mission today.

Phang Soon Siew went to Kuching, Sarawak, in 1915 as a colporteur. When R. P. Montgomery was refused permission to stay in Sarawak by the reigning rajah, a dentist, S. M. Tan, set up a clinic in Kuching. In 1916 another layman, C. M. Lee, opened a photography studio in Kuching. Evangelistic efforts were carried out by these two laymen. Upon the death of the rajah, Sir Charles V. Brooke*, his successor, proclaimed religious liberty, thus making it possible for the church to evangelize publicly.

The North Sarawak Mission, which was formed in 1934, had territorial jurisdiction over Brunei, with Gus Youngberg as overseer. In Feb 1936 Sarawak and Brunei were united under one organization, the Sarawak Mission (SM). The North Borneo Mission (NBM), formed in 1913, remained as it was until 1 Jan 1956, when it merged with the SM to form the Borneo-Brunei-Sarawak Mission.

In 1961, in another reorganization, the NBM became the SDA Church of North Borneo, later known as the SDA Church of Sabah and presently called the Sabah Mission of SDAs. The mission of Sarawak was officially designated as the SDA Church of Sarawak and is presently called Sarawak Mission of SDAs, which also oversees the work in Brunei*.

Bangladesh, India, Myanmar, Pakistan, and Sri Lanka. Tradition has it that the work started when William Lenker and A. T. Stroup, two colporteurs from America, landed in Madras and began selling SDA Christian literature to the people in 1893. However, from Lenker's writing, it appears that Anna P. Gordon had been teaching SDA doctrines in India prior to his arrival in Madras in 1893. The first mission appointee was Georgia Burrus (later known as Georgia Burgess), a Bible instructor from America who arrived in Calcutta on 23 Jan 1895. In Nov 1895, Dores A. Robinson and Martha May Taylor arrived in Calcutta and opened the regular SDA Mission. The SDA publishing work began in 1896, as did the medical work started for middle-class Hindus. An orphanage was established in Jul 1896.

In late 1898 or early 1899, the first SDA mission station in the Indian countryside was opened at Karmatar. A church school for English-speaking children was opened in Calcutta that same year. From 1900 to 1910, SDA work continued to grow rapidly. The entire mission work was administered directly as a detached mission by the GC and, for a brief period, by the Asiatic division. In 1910 a reorganization of the Indian SDA work was carried out along language lines. The India Union Mission was formed, with J. L. Shaw as the first superintendent, and included the following missions: Bengali (Bengali-, Oriya-, Santali-, and Assamese-language areas); North Indian (Hindustani-, Bihari-, Rajastahni-, Punjabi-, and Sindhi-language areas); South India (Tamil-, Telegu-, Kanarese-, Malayalam-, and Singahalese-language areas); Western India (Marathi- and Gujarati-language areas); and Burma.

Colporteurs from India entered Bangladesh during the late 19th c. Lal Gopal Mookerjee, a descendant of William Carey's first convert from India, opened the first

Seventh-day Adventists

mission station at Gopalganj, Bangladesh, in 1906 with his own funds and effort. In 1909 A. G. Watson, an Anglo-Indian, was placed in charge of the station, while Mookerjee went to Calcutta to develop city work. In late 1909 J. C. Little was assigned to that mission field, and by early 1910 the first SDA church was organized.

In 1910 the Bengali Mission was formed under IUM, with its headquarters in Calcutta. Bangladesh was under this mission. L. G. Mookerjee, A. G. Watson, W. A. Barlow, and W. W. Miller were assigned to work in Bangladesh under the supervision of W. R. French. In 1915 L. G. Burgess succeeded French; in 1919 Burgess was succeeded by L. G. Mookerjee; and in 1986, Bangladesh became part of the FED.

In Myanmar (Burma), Herbert B. Meyers, a convert from Calcutta, India, and A. G. Watson entered the country as colporteurs in 1902. Through their efforts, Daw May and her brother, Maung Maung, joined the SDA church. Maung Maung became a self-supporting worker. In 1904 the SDA church began to raise funds to support a permanent worker. Maung Maung attended the general meeting of the SDA workers in India, where he pleaded for a worker to be sent to the country. Heber H. Votaw was sent from India, and in 1905 the Burma Mission was established. Medical work* was pioneered by L. F. Hansen, and in 1907 Ollie Oberholtzer started permanent medical work in Moulmein. She also worked among the Shans in the interior. The first SDA church was organized in 1907 in Rangoon with 23 members.

In 1919 the Burma Union was organized into the following missions: the Irrawaddy Delta, the Rangoon and Upper Burma, and the Tenasserim. When World War II* came to Burma, the missionaries were forced to leave the country. Many of the Anglo-Indian members also left the country, leaving behind Burmese workers, who were severely persecuted. After the war missionaries returned and evangelistic, publishing, educational, and medical work began again. Young people were sent to Spicer Memorial College in India for training. In 1960 the Burma Union Bible Seminary was opened, with W. W. Christensen as principal. In 1938 the Burma Union (presently known as Myanmar Union Mission [MUM]) was reorganized and came under the jurisdiction of the FED.

In Pakistan Anna Knight, a black American, canvassed in 1901. By 1909 A. C. E. Johnston reported that he had a Bible study group in Karachi. In 1913 S. A. Wellman converted S. Samuels, who was instrumental in starting much of the work in Punjab. When the Northwest India Mission was organized in 1914, V. L. Mann started medical work at Chuharkana, and F. H. Loasby spearheaded evangelistic work.

In 1919 the Punjab Mission was organized under the Northwest India Union Mission, and in 1937 it was reorganized as the Punjab Local Mission Field. In 1949 it became the Pakistan Union Section. Another reorganization took place after the Indo-Pakistan war of Dec 1971, when the East Pakistan Section (Bangladesh) became inaccessible to the Pakistan Union leadership. The East Pakistan Section became the Bangladesh Section, placed directly under the SAD. The Pakistan Union Section came directly under the TED.

La Rue was probably the first SDA to have visited Sri Lanka (1888 and 1903). In 1904 Harry Armstrong and G. K. Owen evangelized in Colombo. Armstrong's first convert was Tussaint, his landlord. R. W. Yeoman canvassed on the island at the same time. It was in 1916 that the SDA church had its first national worker, S. J. Thambipillai, baptized through the effort of T. S. Nayagampillai, an Indian layman. The first church was organized in 1922, shortly after the arrival of H. A. Hansen, who was superintendent of the work on the island. The first two Sinhalese converts *cum* workers were Don Edmond Wijesingha and his brother, Don Edward Wijesingha.

Originally, Sri Lanka belonged to the South Tamil Mission, and on 12 Dec 1922 the Ceylon Mission was organized. In 1923 a mission school was established. The Ceylon Union was organized in 1950. In 1986 Sri Lanka (the former Ceylon Union) was put under the FED.

Indochina. Fred L. Pickett with his wife, Ada, were the first SDA workers to enter Cambodia (Jan 1930). When they were refused permission to build a church by the government, they established a church of 32 Cambodians at Tinh Bien, in the territory of Vietnam. Two Cambodians were recruited to assist him: Eng Pheng and Svay Sas.

The French Indochina Mission was organized in 1937, with Pickett as the first president. Robert Brenz and his family came to assist the work in Phnom Penh in the same year. During World War II, the Japanese forced the missionaries to flee to Vietnam, and SDA work remained dormant until after the war.

In 1953 Tran Tran, a colporteur, started the work again with three converts baptized by W. K. Sam from Vietnam. In Oct 1957 Ralph and Beatrice Neall arrived in Cambodia. With the assistance of Giang Tu Minh, on 1 Nov 1958 the first church was organized with 11 charter members. The church received government recognition in 1959.

Political unrest in 1965 dealt another blow to SDA work in Cambodia, but it was revived again by Johann C. R. Adam, who arrived from Indonesia in 1970. On 17 Apr 1971 services were resumed in the restored church building. However, as of 6 Mar 1975 the work again was halted by the invasion of the Khmer Rouge*. Even though the SDA church was not officially functioning, SDA work has never completely ceased to exist in Cambodia. In 1991 official SDA work in Cambodia was restarted by the Southeast Asia Union Mission (SAUM), mainly through the efforts of the Adventist Development and Relief Agency (ADRA), and in Dec 1992 Dan Walters was sent officially to oversee the work.

SDA work in Laos* was initiated in 1939 by Nguyen Tan Vang, a Vietnamese colporteur, who sold literature in French, Vietnamese, and Chinese. The first official missionaries were Dick and Jean Hall, who arrived in 1957 from Ubol, Thailand. Together with a Lao native, Mun Lamsri, Hall built a church building in Namtha. When the Pathet Lao came in 1961, SDA work continued through the laity. Although the work at Namtha was apparently halted, work among the Laotians persisted in Chiengkong.

In 1963 two Meo (H'mong*) converts from Chiengkong began work among their own people in northern Thailand. Information on the progress of the denomination was sporadic; however, the work was carried on faithfully by converts. In 1967 a record of three persons was baptized in Vientiane. Angel Biton and his wife Nenita, from the Philippines, were sent as missionaries to Vientiane. Sixteen believers welcomed the couple. The Bitons were replaced by Sophon Jaiguar and his wife in 1973.

In 1974 Dick Hall revisited Namtha and baptized 16 Meo believers, and the first official church was organized with 74 baptized members. The Vientiane church building was dedicated on 28 Sep 1975. The denomination was officially recognized by the government in 1979; however, missionaries were not permitted to work in the country. The work was supervised by the Thailand Mission.

Doung Thien Thi, an SDA, entered Vietnam to sell books, but he had to leave the country because of immigration problems. The second known contact, Tan Kia Ou, went into Haiphong and Hanoi selling books during the summer of 1920. The work was finally established when R. H. Wentland arrived in Saigon in 1929.

By 1937 a mission was established with five churches and 250 members, with F. L. Pickett as superintendent. On 1 Sep 1937 R. H. Rowlett established a training school in Saigon. This became the Vietnam Adventist Publishing House. During World War II the missionaries were evacuated. After World War II Vietnam entered into civil war; it became a divided nation in 1954. In 1955 large-scale medical work began with the opening of the Saigon Adventist Hospital. Official SDA work was again closed to the outside world when the Communists took over in 1975, but the church remained alive in the hands of many Vietnamese who remained behind.

Indonesia. Adventism, which first came to Asia in 1888, made its way into Indonesia in 1900. The American Methodist minister, Ralph Waldo Munson, who had worked in Burma and Thailand, was won for Adventism after having been cured of a serious illness in an Adventist hospital in America. He asked to be sent to Southeast Asia, and in 1900 he arrived in Padang on the west coast of Sumatra. As the colonial government permitted only one society to work in a given area and more promising fields were already occupied by other missions, Munson had to content himself with Padang and its Muslim population. However, the Adventist message was initially brought to the partly christianized Bataklands by Munson's first native convert, Immanuel Siregar, a son of the first Batak to convert to Christianity (in 1861). After some years in Medan, on the east coast of Sumatra, Munson moved to West Java (1909), where he established churches in Sukabumi and Jakarta. In the meantime, missionaries from Australia, among them sister Petra Tunheim, started work in East Java. In 1920 Adventism was brought to the Minahasa* region (North Celebes) by Samuel Rantung and M. E. Direja (first baptisms, 1921), and in the following year to Ambon by a pensioned soldier who had become an evangelist on Java (first baptisms, 1922). Batak* converts brought Adventism to Borneo. In 1929 there were seven "missions" in Indonesia: East Java (1913), West Java (1913), North Sumatra (1917), Celebes (1923), Batakland (1927), Ambon (1929), and South Sumatra (1929). Of these, the first two and the last were in Muslim territory, and the other four in largely christianized areas. Until then the Adventist mission in the Netherlands Indies had been a part of the Malayan Union, Far Eastern division, but in 1929 it was organized into a separate Netherlands East Indies Union and transferred to the Central European division, because it was supposed that German and Dutch missionaries could work more efficiently in the Netherlands Indies than their American colleagues. At that time there were about 60 churches with a membership of nearly 3,000. The church ran 16 schools with an enrollment of 1,509 pupils. In the same year the Netherlands East Indies Training School, later to become Indonesia Union College and now called Indonesia Adventist University, was opened in Cimindi near Bandung, West Java.

In 1938, as a consequence of political and economic developments in Europe, the Union was reconnected with the Far Eastern division. But World War II brought many difficulties. In 1940 the German missionaries were interned by the Dutch, and in 1942 the Dutch workers in turn were imprisoned by the Japanese. A number of churches were closed, transfer of membership from one denomination to another was forbidden, and several Indonesian workers were tortured by the Kempeitai. However, even under these circumstances the church continued to grow; in 1946 membership stood at over 6,000. In accordance with the political changes taking place, in 1947 the name was changed from *Het Advent Zendingsgenootschap in Nederlandsch Oost-Indië* to Indonesia Union Mission of Seventh-day Adventists. In the following years, more schools were opened, in line with the national education policy making elementary education compulsory, and hospitals were founded in Bandung (1950) and Medan (1969). Colportage and publishing work, which had been started by Petra Tunheim, had had its center in Bandung since 1929, where in 1954 the publishing house, printing establishment, and book depot were accommodated in a new building, which was later substantially enlarged. The political unrest that began in the 1950s had a favorable effect on the growth of Adventism. Especially in Java and South Sumatra, many were won over from the Muslim community. At the same time Adventism spread to other regions, such as Central Celebes and Timor, where Christianity had already been introduced by other denominations. In 1964, when membership had reached 22,968 in 385 churches, the Indonesia Union was divided into the West Indonesia Union and the East Indonesia Union. In 1970, when the government advised church groups to have national leaders, Nelson G. Hutauruk became president of the former and Anton Waworundeng of the latter.

In the mid-1990s Adventists in Indonesia numbered approximately 150,000 members (more or less evenly divided between the West and the East Indonesia Union) in more than 950 churches. Besides ordained ministers (nearly 100), the churches are served by credentialed missionaries and literature missionaries, elders, deacons, treasurers, Bible school leaders, and leaders of the evangelistic effort, all of whom are elected by church members. Each church sends a delegate to the district conference as well as to the Union conference, which meets every four years. The GA elects the Union board. The Union in turn sends delegates to the Far Eastern division conference and to the general conference in Washington, which is the central organ of the Seventh-day Adventist Church.

Japan. Japanese work began when La Rue entered Yokohama and Kobe in the spring of 1889 selling Christian literature. The first SDA workers sent to Japan were W. C. Grainger and T. H. Okohira in 1896. Among the first four Japanese baptized was Hide Kuniya, who was later ordained to the ministry. The first church was organized in Tokyo on 4 Jun 1899 with 13 members. F. W. Field was sent in 1901 to be superintendent of the mission field. The first sanitarium was opened on 1 Jun 1903 in Kobe. In 1914 a publishing house was established. By 1917 SDA work was organized into the Japan conference, with B. P. Hoffman as president. This conference was reorganized in 1919 at the AD committee meeting held in Shanghai to form the Japan Union Mission. Due to the government's suspicion of foreigners, the SDA church in Japan was dissolved in 1943. On 20 Sep of that year, the Japanese government imprisoned 36 leaders and six laymen. After the war, General Douglas MacArthur released the political prisoners, which included many SDA workers. Properties belonging to the church were returned. F. R. Millard became the first postwar president of the Japan Union Mission on 18 Nov 1945.

Korea. In May 1904 a Korean, Lee Ung Hyun, who was passing through Kobe, Japan, en route to Hawaii, was attracted by a signboard, made by a Japanese pastor, that read in Chinese, "The Seventh-day Adventist Church." As a result of Bible studies, especially on Jesus' Second Coming, the sabbath, and baptism, he embraced Seventh-Day Adventism and was baptized together with a Korean companion, Son Heung Jo. Lee continued his trip to Hawaii, while Son returned to Korea. On the ship home, Son imparted his faith to Im Ki Pan, a Korean returning from Hawaii. Im and Son began to spread the new faith and sent a plea for missionaries. In August Hide Kunia, a Japanese pastor, and F. W. Field, the Japan mission director, visited Korea. In 1905 there were four churches with 140 sabbath-keepers in northwestern Korea. W. R. Smith from the United States arrived to fill the need for a resident missionary.

In Jan 1907 Mini Scharffenberg arrived from America. Later in the year two missionaries started a worker's training course. In 1908 Riloy Russel and his wife arrived in Sooan to set up a clinic in the school. In 1909 publishing work began. The monthly magazine *Shi Jo* (Signs of the Times), the oldest Christian magazine in Korea, was first published in 1910.

In 1909 the church center moved from Soonan to Seoul, a small city in northwestern Korea. Seventh-day Adventism grew rapidly until World War II, when the American missionaries left Korea in the spring of 1941. More than 40 leaders of the Korean Seventh-day church were arrested by the Japanese police; four were tortured and died. In 1943 the church was disbanded by the Japanese colonial government. Because of suppression and persecution, many workers and members fled to the mountains. At the close of the war (15 Aug 1945), they came out of hiding and were active in evangelism, establishing schools, a publishing house, and hospitals until 1950, when North Korea invaded South Korea. The end of the Korean War* saw rapid growth of the church from 7,000 (before the war) to over 16,000 members. Elementary schools increased from two to 26 and academies from one to eight. Before the Korean War there was only a worker's training institution. After the war there were two high schools and a junior college, and two hospitals instead of one.

The welfare services of the Korean Seventh-day Adventists were appreciated especially during the Korean War. At present there are approximately 550 churches with over 116,000 members and 587 ministerial workers; 10 elementary schools with a total enrollment of over 2,700; eight junior academies with over 2,600 enrolled; seven senior academies with nearly 3,200 enrolled; one university and two colleges with nearly 2,700 students altogether; 16 language institutes; two hospitals with 706 beds; one publishing house; and three food factories.

Philippines. In 1905 G. A. Irwin, president of the Australian Union conference, visited the Philippines en route to the GC, where he recommended that the church enter the territory with colporteurs. Upon his recommendation, R. A. Caldwell from Australia went to the Philippines during that same year. The next year J. L. McElhany and his wife started their work in April, mainly with the Americans in Manila. In Dec 1908 L. V. Finster began the work among Filipinos. By 1911 the first church was organized in Santa Ana with 18 members.

Many other missionaries came to work in the territory: E. M. Adams (1911: Manila and Iloilo), Floyd Ashbaugh (1911: Panay, Guimaras), C. Fattebert (1913: Cebu), R. E. Hay (1913: Ilocanos, Northern Luzon), W. E. Lanier (1913: Pasay, Manila), and R. Stewart (1913:

Cebu). The first church school to be established was at Jaro, Iloilo. Today the greatest amount of SDA educational work (a total of 219 schools and colleges) in Asia is in the Philippines.

The publishing work started in the backyard of the Finsters' home in 1913. H. A. Hall opened a dispensary at Malate in Jul 1928.

Thailand. SDA work in Thailand was started by R. A. Caldwell and G. F. Jones, who were colporteuring in Southeast Asia when they entered Thailand in 1906. Subsequently others followed: Phang Yin Hee from Singapore; Ezra Longway and his wife, who came in Dec 1918; and F. A. Pratt, who arrived in Bangkok on 28 Feb 1919. Pratt became the first director of the Thailand Mission, and he was instrumental in converting Pleng Vitiamyalaksana, the first Thai convert. Pleng became the pioneer and administrator of the medical work with R. F. Waddell in 1937.

By 1951 the Bangkok Sanitarium and Hospital (known today as the Bangkok Adventist Hospital) was opened. A nursing school was started in 1941, but it closed down because of World War II. It was reopened in Jul 1947, and a new building was added. In 1986 the school of nursing was incorporated into the newly established liberal arts college, Mission College.

Taiwan. Between 1907 and 1912 T. S. Yang from Fukien, China, came to Taiwan to canvass. Japanese colporteurs joined him. However, organized work occurred only in Mar 1934, when Nagao Wachi and his family were sent there by the Japan Mission. Nagao left Taiwan in 1942, and Kiomitsu Hatada succeeded him. World War II closed the door to SDA work, and Hatada was imprisoned.

After World War II B. S. Lin was commissioned to lead the work in Taiwan. He arrived on 14 Apr 1948. The Taiwan Mission was reorganized in 1949. When mainland China fell into the hands of Chinese Communists, missionaries came to Taiwan, and mission funds were also diverted to the island.

Bibliography

Rajaoman Nainggolan, "Indonesia," in *Light Dawns over Asia: Adventism's Story in the Far Eastern Division, 1888-1988,* ed. Gil G. Fernandez (1990). • Oh Man-Kyu, *The History of Seventh-Day Adventists* (1988). • Lee Young Lin, *A Study on Korean Seventh-Day Adventists History* (1966). • *Seventh-Day Adventist Yearbook.*

PHOON CHEK YAT, THOMAS VAN DEN END, and OH MAN-KYU

Severance Hospital

The oldest, largest, and best-known hospital in Korea*.

Named after its benefactor, Louis H. Severance, a businessman from Ohio, United States, Severance Hospital was started by Christian missionaries. It is attached to Yonsei University.

The hospital began with the *Kwanghaewon* (House of Extended Grace) clinic established with governmental permission by Horace N. Allen* in 1885. J. W. Heron, A. T. Ellers, and O. R. Avison were Allen's medical* colleagues in the clinic. In 1886 the authorities granted permission to begin a medical class with 16 students. In 1899 Avison became the first principal of the medical school. In 1906 Esther L. Shields began to train nurses at the school.

In Sep 1904 a modern building was built through the donation of Louis H. Severance, and the clinic became a general hospital. Medical classes were started at the hospital in Mar 1905. The hospital continued to grow with the continuing support of the Severance family and the union missionary work in Korea.

During the Japanese occupation, the hospital was renamed the Associate Hospital of the Asahi Medical Professional School. Its name reverted to Severance Hospital after Korea's liberation. Even though its building and equipment were destroyed during the Korean War, the hospital treated more than 10,000 patients.

The hospital was merged with Yonhee University in 1957 to form Yonsei University, because the two institutions shared a similar mission ideology. Two subsidiary hospitals are Yong Dong Severance Hospital in Seoul and Won Zoo Christian Hospital in Kang Won Province.

Bibliography

Rhodes, H. A., ed., *History of the Korea Mission of the Presbyterian Church USA, 1884-1934* (1934). • Rhodes, H. A., and A. Campbell, eds., *History of the Korean Mission of the Presbyterian Church USA, 1935-1950* (1984). • Min Kyong Bae, *Hankook Kidok'kiohoe-sa* (History of the Korean Church), new rev. ed. (1993). • Moffett, Samuel H., *The Christians of Korea* (1962). KIM IN SOO

Shah, Gyani

(b. Palpa, Nepal, 1923). One of the early converts from within Nepal*; trained as a nurse; captain in the Nepalese Army; female leader in the early Kathmandu church from the mid-1950s; has done pioneering work since 1970 at Tikapur, western Nepal.

Related to the Nepalese royalty, Shah hails from western Nepal. She was a devout Hindu* who did pilgrimage of the four religious places *(Char Dham Tirtha)* when she was 17 years old, but she had no peace in her mind. Her first contact with a Christian was in the person of Dr. K. Harbord, a missionary from India* who visited her uncle, the Nepalese governor of Palpa at the time.

Shah left home one day to become a yogi, but in 1941 she ended up penniless at a mission hospital in Patna, India, where they gave her work. She was baptized into the Christian faith two years later, did a year of Bible* training, then studied nursing and midwifery and took a post in Jasidih, where she hoped to settle down. But she was diagnosed with tuberculosis, a fatal disease at that time, and so she was sent to the hill station of Almorah for treatment. The fever persisted for a year and a half until a Tibetan Christian doctor at the hospital challenged her with these words: "Shah, there is bound to be something between you and God. You must accept it and confess it. This may be the reason for your sickness. Only then can you be healed." She tried to ignore this advice, as she thought it related to her returning to Nepal, and she did not want to go. But she later made the decision to go back to Nepal, and said, "When I made that decision with determination, from the next day all my fever disappeared." She entered Nepal in 1953 to live and work as a Christian nurse, first working with the Nepal Evangelistic Band in Pokhara, then with the United Mission to Nepal* in Kathmandu. Later she served for 10 years as matron of the military hospital and was finally recommended for promotion to the rank of major, but because she would have had to participate in Hindu ceremonies, she forfeited the promotion and retired as a captain.

Shah played a prominent role in the establishment of the first churches in Kathmandu. One of the first three national Christians to reside in Kathmandu, she helped lay the foundation for the first church building at Putali Sadak and served on the first church committee of Nepali Isai Mandali (later Gyaneswor Church). Her home in Sanepa later housed a branch of Gyaneswor Church.

Following her retirement from the military hospital and as a single woman in her fifties, she pioneered a Christian outreach among the Tharu people around Tikapur, a remote, undeveloped area of western Nepal. She started the first local medical* work and helped establish the first school and Tikapur Church, which now mentors other churches in the area.

Bibliography

Nepal Church History Project (transcript of personal interview with Gyani Shah) (1986). • Perry, Cindy, *A Biographical History of the Church in Nepal* (1993).

Rajendra K. Rongong

Shamanism

Practice of attaining ecstasy through the work of a shaman.

Shaman defined. Eliade defined the shaman as "a master of ecstasy," who is distinguished from other individuals in the clan not by his possessing a power or a guardian spirit, but by his ecstatic experience. Shamanism is therefore defined as a technique of ecstasy.

Etymologically, "ecstasy" means the state of "being carried outside of oneself" (soul out of body). The reports of shamans, or people close to them the world over, including in the Philippines*, indicate that, in ecstasy, the soul of the shaman is absent from his body, which may be lying rigidly on a mat on the floor or ground. Generally, although there are exceptions, the shaman in ecstasy is conscious. He hears and sees spirits and follows their lead and counsel. In ecstasy the shaman is neither possessed (although there are also exceptions) nor indwelt by the spirits as a medium. Rather, in ecstasy the shaman possesses his helping spirits, he operates aided and supported by their magical powers. Ecstasy and trance are synonymous.

A shaman experiences ecstasy during his journeys to: (1) the sky to meet the heavenly god face-to-face in order to present an offering on behalf of the community; (2) the underworld or elsewhere in the universe, either in search of the soul of the sick person which has gone astray, usually being decoyed by deceased relatives, or in order to accompany the soul of the dead to the land of the spirits in order to learn broader and deeper truths by conversing with these higher beings.

In India*, shamanism consists in a special relation to a tutelary spirit who takes hold of the shaman as its medium or enters into him, investing him with higher knowledge and powers — above all with dominion over other spirits.

In China*, most shamans are women*. They are called *wu*. Shamanism is characterized by the descent of an intelligent *shen* into a person. Ecstasy, described as "magical flight," "ascent to heaven," or "mystical journey," is the cause of the incarnation of the *shen*, and not its result. Because the *wu* is able to "rise to higher spheres and descend into the lower," the intelligent *shen* descends into him. However, the "descent of the *shen*" very soon gives rise to many parallel experiences that finally fade into the mass of "possessions."

Some scholars believe that the *wu* was preceded by the shaman hooded with a bearskin. The "bearskin-masked dancing shaman" belongs to the magic of the hunt, in which men played the leading part. This seems to confirm the existence of male shamanism in protohistorical times. Nonetheless, Chinese *wuism* dominated religious life prior to the preeminence of Confucianism* and Buddhism*.

The shamanism practiced in Japan* today is rather different from that found in North Asia and Siberia. It is primarily a technique of possession by ghosts and is practiced almost exclusively by women. The principal functions of Japanese shamans are: (1) to summon a dead person's soul from the beyond *(shinikushi)* or the soul of a living person from far away *(ikikuchi);* (2) to prophesy success or failure for the client *(kamikuchi);* (3) to expel diseases or other evils and practice religious purification; (4) to ask God for cures of particular diseases; and (5) to give information on lost objects.

Many Japanese shamanesses are blind from birth. They are taught for three to seven years by an accredited shamaness, after which the candidate is married to her tutelary god. Mystical marriages of shamanesses to their tutelary gods are documented even in the Kojiki and Nihongi. The shamaness is often called spirit-woman and is herself venerated as divine. Spirit-women gods and certain rituals pertaining to them can be compared with the characteristic feature of matriarchy: female rulers of territorial estates, female heads of families, matrilocal marriages, visitor marriage, matriarchal clan with clan exogamy, etc.

In Korea*, shamanism is documented as early as the Han period. Male shamans wear women's dress. Female shamans outnumber males. The origins of shamanism may include southern elements. There are stag horns on the shaman's head-dress of the Han period, indicating relations with the stag cult of the ancient Turks. The cult of stags is typical of hunter and nomad cultures, and female shamans do not seem to play much of a role there. The dominance of shamanesses in Korea may be the result of a deterioration of traditional shamanism or influence from the south. Today, women are the initiation masters even of men.

The studies of Jung Young Lee tell us that Korean shamanism, historically, is the protest of women against sexual repression in a male-dominated society. According to Lee, shamanism did attempt to modernize society (Lee 1980, 30). Today, the *mudang*, or female shaman, in Korea is the initiator even of the male shaman. The *mudang* specializes in summoning the souls of the dead so that reconciliation between the deceased and the living can be effected. The *mudang* is quite creative in her rites. According to Daniel Kister, the *mudang* has much to offer: a life of lowly self-sacrifice and devoted service; a dynamic spirituality of God's active presence; insight into, and sympathy for, the problems of others; and an ability to help people laugh and play in the presence of the gods (Kister 1995).

In the Philippines, shamanism is still very much alive. The 17th c. missionaries who wrote about the neophyte shaman among the Bisayas told of her climbing a *balete* tree to hold her meetings with the *diwata* (Alcina 1960, 216-17). In northern Luzon, in the Bisayas, and in Mindanao, female shamans were well known. A male shaman, Agapito Ilustre, was the founder of a Christian religious sect centered in *Barangay Kinabuhayan* (resurrection) on Mt. Banahaw in southern Luzon. Agapito began as a *pulahan* (a red-band-wearing rebel) in the last quarter of the 19th and the first quarter of the 20th c. (Marasigan 1985, 12). The very name portrays its Christian character: *Samahanáng Tatlong Persona Solo Dios* (An Association of Three Persons One God). It holds four sacraments: baptism, confirmation, holy orders, and matrimony. Although the *supremo* (supreme head) is a male (he is the son of old Agapito), their priests are all women, perhaps underscoring the possible matriarchal character of early Filipino religious leadership. They have no eucharistic liturgy. Their "mass" is really the liturgy of the word with ritualistic dancing, prayers, and hymns. The *Samahan* pay close attention to the Voice which speaks to them. Marasigan interprets the Voice, not merely as an external physical sound, but essentially as an interior experience of a believing community (Marasigan 1985, 13, 23). Today in the Philippines, shamans-in-the-making are still attracted to the *balete,* which they climb. And in Tawi-tawi, Sulu, Arlo Nimmo, a Swedish anthropologist, reported a female shaman, Laisiha, who flew one night to Borneo in search of a grandson whom the evil spirits had decoyed to Borneo.

For Central and North Asia, where shamanism first crystallized into an autonomous and specific complex (Eliade 1972, 504), the initiation of the *Avam Samoyed* contains certain exemplary themes which help us understand shamanistic belief. In this initiation, the novice encounters several divine figures (the Lady of the Waters, the Lord of the Underworld, the Lady of the Animals) before he is brought by his animal guides to the "Center of the World," on top of the Cosmic Mountain, where the World Tree grew and the Universal Lord is found. From the World Tree, by the will of the Universal Lord, he receives the wood with which to make his drum. Some demonic beings teach him the nature of diseases and their cures. In the end, another demonic being cuts his body into pieces, boils it, and exchanges it for better organs (ibid., 42).

The other major Asiatic area where shamanism is practiced is Indonesia* and Malaysia*. In these two regions the original autochthonous religious complex, which lay at the base of shamanism, was enriched and modified from other higher cultures: the central and northern area by Buddhism* and Lamaism, and the Indonesian area by India and other southern influences. In the latter Asiatic region, the focus is on the motif of the Cosmic Tree as it relates to other shamanic themes: the Center, the Axis of the World, the hole in the vault of the sky, and the motif of shamanic ascent to the sky, along with belief in the Supreme Being living in the sky and with whom mankind in the paradisal time was on familiar terms so that men could easily reach him by climbing a tree, rope, ladder, or vine. After a ritual fault on the part of humanity, the Supreme Being withdrew to the highest heaven, thus becoming a *deus oteosus,* without a calendar of cults. As a result of this, humanity in general could no longer contact him except through prayer and sacrifice. But still a few select and privileged individuals — the shamans, heroes, and initiates — could reach the Supreme Being.

The initiation in the *Avam Samoyed* comprises three stages: first, the separation (the novice has smallpox or disease and is brought to the middle of the sea); second, the transition (when, for example, he encounters the master of diseases and is instructed in cures and special healing); third, he ascends to the Center of the World, where he meets the Lord of the earth and visits the Cosmic Tree on which are perched peoples from various lands. He is instructed to make an instrument from the branch of the Cosmic Tree and is also instructed in the art of shamanizing. He sees his body mutilated and his flesh stripped from his bones. He is minced and boiled in a cauldron. He is given a new set of organs for sight and hearing, so that he can practice his profession. His head is forged on an anvil by the blacksmith, the anvil on which the best shamans are forged. He now shamanizes indefatigably. It seems as though the initiation lasts for years, but the transition and incorporation can be phased out at even longer intervals.

For Indonesian and Malaysian shamanism, the idea of "Center" is very important, being found in the most primitive cultures. The myths of Central Asia tell that the Center is situated in the North, which corresponds to the Center of the Sky. The North is understood to be the Center through the whole Asian area from India to Siberia. The Semang of the Malay Peninsula believe in a Supreme God, Ta Pedun; the Pahang Negrito believe in Bonsu, who lives above the seven levels of the sky with his brother Tang.

Communication between earth and heaven happened in *illo tempore* (primordial time) by some physical means (rainbow, bridge, stair, vine, cord, chain of arrows, mountain) which are variants of the World Tree or the *Axis Mundi.* The symbolism of the Cosmic Tree implies the idea of the "Center of the World," a point where the three cosmic zones meet.

The *tadu* or *bajasa* of *Bare e Toradia* in Zulawesi climbs the rainbow to the house of Pue de Songe, Supreme God, and brings back the patient's soul. Her ecstatic capacities are not limited to journeys to the sky or about the earth, for in the great funerary festival (the *Mompemate*), the *bajasa* leads the soul of the dead to the land of the beyond.

The World Tree is found in every Dayak village or house. The tree, represented by seven branches, symbolizes the World Axis and the road to the sky because a similar World Tree is always found in the Indonesian ship of the dead, which is believed to bring the dead to the celestial beyond. The tree, represented with six branches (seven, including the tufted top), with the sun and moon on either side, sometimes takes the form of a lance decorated with the same symbols that serve to designate the shaman's ladder, which he climbs to the sky to bring back the patient's fugitive soul. The tree-lance-ladder on the ships of the dead is only a replica of the miraculous tree that stands in the beyond and to which all souls come in their journey to God *(Devata Sangiang).* The Indonesian shamans (Sakai, Kubu, and Dayak) also have a tree they climb to reach the world of spirits in seeking the patient's soul.

The Bataks* derive their religious ideas mainly from India, believing in a three-region universe: the sky (with seven stories where the gods dwell), the earth (occupied by humans), and the underworld (home of the dead).

In their mythology, the Ngadju Dayak of South Borneo are cosmologically dualistic. However, the World Tree is prior to the dualism, representing the cosmos in its totality. It symbolizes the unification of the two supreme divinities.

The world was created as a result of the conflict between the two polar principles: the feminine (cosmologically lower, symbolized by water and snake) and the masculine (the upper region; the bird). In the struggle, the World Tree is destroyed, but only temporarily. It becomes the archetype of all creative human activity. The World Tree is destroyed only that it may be reborn.

The mythology of the Ngadju Dayak expresses also the ancient cosmological schema of the hierogamy between heaven and earth, as well as the symbolism of complementary opposites: bird-snake; the dualistic structure of the ancient lunar mythologies (opposition between contraries; alternate destructions and creations and the eternal return).

Christian response to shamanism. It would appear from the long presence of Christian missionaries that Christianity and shamanism had been partners for some time in Asia: Orthodox Christianity with Central and North Asian shamanism, as well as with shamanism in middle and southern Indian tribes, and Roman* and Anglo Christianity in other parts of India. There was also a long coextistence with other Christian denominations, including Roman Catholicism in Australia, Japan*, Korea, China, Southeast Asia, Indonesia, and especially the Philippines.

While Christianity cannot agree with the basic polytheism of shamanism, still there are many points in which the two can find common ground. Essential to all shamanic initiation is the need for the shaman-to-be to die to his or her previous self in order to be reborn to a new and higher life. Eliade termed this the principle of the "paschal mystery," which, in the history of religion, found its most perfect example in the passion, death, and resurrection of Jesus Christ.

Then, too, the shamanic respect of creation as a whole finds a sympathetic note in Christianity's respect for the earth rooted in the creation narrative, and finding fulfillment in the "New Creation." Shamanism also finds a sympathetic note in Christianity's cosmic view of the earth, which is much earlier than the chthonian. It was born with humanity's experience of the manifestations of the sacred in the world. For the world is not only symbolic. It is even sacramental of God's attributes: his majesty is revealed in the trees and the mountains; his eternity in the sweep of the seas and oceans; his solidity in the impenetrability of rocks and boulders; his infinite creativity in the prolific productivity of the earth. We need this conviction today in our concern for the integrity of ecology and creation.

Finally, vital to primitive shamanic thought is the intimate unity of heaven and earth originally imaged by humanity's easy commerce with the sky and how, after the fall, at least the shaman and some privileged human beings could still contact the sky. The intercessory role of Christian saints is hereby pointed out for today's Christians.

Bibliography

Alcina, Francisco, *Historia de las Islas Bisayas* (Muñoz text, Part 1, Books 3 and 4; preliminary translation by Paul S. Lietz, Philippine Studies Program, mimeographed, Chicago, 1960). • Eliade, Mircea, *Zalmoxis: The Vanishing God* (1972). • Kister, Daniel, "Korean Shamanism," *Landas, Journal of Loyola School of Theology,* Vol. 8, No. 1 (Jan 1995). • Lee, Jung Young, "Korean Shamanism and Sexual Repression," *Asian and Pacific Quarterly of Cultural and Social Affairs,* Vol. 12, No. 1 (Spring 1980). • Marasigan, Vicente, *A Banahaw Guru: Symbolic Deeds of Agapito Illustrisimo* (1985). • Nimmo, Arlo N., "The Shaman in Sulu," *Asian and Pacific Quarterly of Cultural and Social Affairs,* Vol. 8, No. 4 (Summer 1975). • Demetrio, Francisco, and Marcelino Panis, Jr., *Respect the Earth* (1990).

FRANCISCO R. DEMETRIO

Shanghai Bishop's Diocese

The Shanghai Bishop's Diocese includes about 100,000 believers. Formed in 1946, it grew from the Jiangnan Vicar Apostolic Diocese (or Jiangnan Mission) established by the papacy of Rome in 1856 under the charge of the Provincial Society of Jesus of Paris, France. The Jiangnan Diocese was divided into the Jiangsu vicar apostolic diocese under the French Jesuits* and the Anhui vicar apostolic diocese under a Spanish Jesuit missionary. The Jiangsu Diocese developed the three vicar apostolic dioceses of Haimen (1926), Xuzhou (1931), and Nanjing (1934), thus forming the Shanghai vicar apostolic diocese, which became the Shanghai Bishop's Diocese in 1946. In 1949 the diocese split into three, the Suzhou Bishop's Diocese and the Superintendent's Dioceses of Yangzhou and Haizhou. After the founding of the Chinese People's Republic, the Catholics in Shanghai launched the anti-imperialist Patriotic Movement. In 1960 Friar Zhang Jiashu* (d. 1988) was elected bishop at the First Representative Conference of the Shanghai Catholic church. During the Cultural Revolution, the Shanghai Diocese suffered. It was only in 1978 that church buildings were successively returned and church activities could resume. The Xieshan Monastery was reopened in 1982, and a training class was started to recruit nuns. The sale of religious articles (icons, rosaries, etc.) and the publication of religious materials also resumed.

CHINA GROUP

Shanghai Catholic Intelligentsia Association

Intellectual circle of Catholics founded in 1986 in Shanghai with the aim of uniting Catholics to serve the society, glorify God, and love the country and to engage in the four modernizations leading to the unification of China*.

The immediate undertakings of the association were to mobilize the Shanghai Catholic intelligentsia to organize technical, legal, cultural, health, art, religion, and philosophy conferences; develop travel, entertainment, and friendship-fostering activities; begin social services such as medical* care, legal consultation for higher studies, and information exchange; assist the Shanghai Diocese in receiving Catholic visitors both from other parts of China and from abroad; facilitate the coming of lecturers from abroad, Hong Kong, Macau*, and Taiwan* for cultural and technical exchange and consultation; and organize pilgrimages and tours for its members.

The association has had three changes of board executives since its founding. In 1994 the general assembly agreed to the election of 57 executives, five of whom live overseas. Under the able leadership of Chu Zhong-gan, elected chairman for three successive terms over the past 10 years, the association has achieved excellent results in the realization of its aims and the development of its activities. Originally located at the Chuengqiengnanlu Catholic Church, the association now operates from the Juilu Christ the King Church.

CHINA GROUP, translated by DUFRESSE CHANG

Shanghai Missionary Conference, 1877

First missionary conference that included all the denominations and mission bodies in China*.

The conference took place from 10 to 24 May and drew 122 missionaries representing 19 mission bodies and four missionaries independent of any mission body. The idea of having all the missionaries come together was developed when several Presbyterian* missionaries took their vacation in Chefoo in the summer of 1874. The agenda was to include mission strategies and discuss topics of common interest to various mission bodies. Letters were circulated to seek opinions and agreement. A seven-person preparatory committee was then formed and had its first meeting in Shanghai on 25 Dec 1875. After making all the necessary considerations, invitations were sent out for a conference to be held in May 1877.

Robert Nelson and Carstairs Douglas* were appointed chairmen of the conference, and 19 subcommittees were named. General affairs were taken care of by William Muirhead, Alexander Williamson, and Calvin Wilson Mateer. Topics of discussion covered mission strategies, mission methods, medical* services, education, women*, literature* and publications, self-support of local churches, training of local pastors, Christianity and Chinese culture, and more. Twenty resolutions were passed, and six reports made by subcommittees were accepted. Another 14 subcommittees were appointed to continue further work. Out of these, the one that took charge of literary and statistical work was later named the Committee of School Textbooks and made enormous contributions to Protestants' literary and publication works. This committee later developed into the Christian Literature Society for China *(Guang-xue-hui).*

Bibliography

Records of the General Conference of the Protestant Missionaries of China, Held at Shanghai, 10-24 May, 1877 (1877).

CHINA GROUP

Shanghai, Second Decennial Conference at

With David Hill and John Livingstone Nevius* as chairmen, the conference was held from 7 to 20 May 1890.

Four-hundred forty-five missionaries (including several Chinese delegates) representing 36 mission bodies and 18 missionaries independent of mission bodies participated in this conference. Nineteen subcommittees submitted a total of 16 reports. Nine resolutions were passed during the conference, and 15 standing committees were formed thereafter. As compared with the first conference in 1877, mission strategies, mission methods, translation and circulation of the Bible*, training of local pastors, and cultural issues and customs (especially on ancestor* worship) continued to be of common interest. New topics included opium* trading and addiction, publication of school textbooks, mission work with minority groups, nurseries, special schools for the blind and deaf, etc. During the conference, cooperation and coordination between denominations and mission bodies was stressed.

China Group

Shari'a Law

Islamic way of life which encompasses every aspect of the life of the Muslim; commonly used to refer to the totality of religious prescriptions binding upon Muslims.

The *shari'a* has two foundational bases: the Qur'an and the sunna. Muslims hold the Qur'an to be the revealed word of God and hence the most sacred source of Islamic legislation. The sunna is the collection of sayings, deeds, and judgments of the prophet Muhammad found in the compilations of *hadith* reports going back to Muhammad. For Sunni Muslims (more than 90 percent of the world's Muslims), the sunna, together with the Qur'an, is the basis of Islamic belief and practice. Shi'a Muslims posit a third legal foundation, the teachings of the imams, the line of first descendants of Muhammad whom Shi'a regard as infallible teachers.

In addition to its revealed (Qur'an) and prophetic (sunna) sources, two secondary sources of the *shari'a* are generally recognized: the communitarian and the rational. A *hadith* from Muhammad stating that the Muslim community will never agree on an error forms the basis for community consensus *(ijma')* regarded as a principle of law. The rational basis covers a vast literature of jurisprudence *(fiqh)* which determines, for example, whether a particular *hadith* is to be taken restrictively or broadly, whether certain traditions abrogate earlier ones, and the use of analogical reasoning to determine the application of the *shari'a* to new situations outside the scope of 7th c. Arabia. After the 10th c., most of the Sunni Islamic world accepted the doctrine of *taqliel* (imitation), which asserted that all valid interpretations of the sources of the law had been made and that future generations would need only find and apply the correct interpretation to their situation. Today more and more Muslims believe in *ijtihad* (independent reasoning on the sources of *shari'a*), by which well-informed Muslims, after conscientious study and reflection, can make decisions regarding controverted issues of law.

The *shari'a* encompasses far more than belief and ritual. In addition to creed *('aqîdah)* and worship *('ibâdah)*, the *shari'a* includes prescriptions regarding marriage, divorce, and inheritance; human relations and proper behavior in matters of diet, dress, and gender interaction; business affairs *(mu'âmalât)* and instructions on banking, lending, and the management of benefices; principles of government, prescribed punishments *(hudûd)*, and moral instruction *(akhlâq)*.

In Sunni Islam*, the *shari'a* is elaborated and codified in four major legal traditions *(madhab*, pl. *madhâhib)*, all of which are mutually recognized and acceptable. In principle, a Sunni Muslim may follow the judgment of any of the four schools. Shi'a Muslims have their own codification of the *shari'a*.

Islamic jurisprudence classifies human acts into five categories: obligatory, recommended, indifferent, reprehensible, and forbidden. Obligatory prescriptions include the performance of the pillars of Islam (profession of faith, daily prayer, Ramadan fast, poor tax, and pilgrimage to Mecca). Recommended practices include a vast range of acts of worship, daily behavior, and business ethics. Reprehensible acts such as divorce, while not strictly forbidden, are strongly discouraged. Forbidden acts include serious crimes such as homicide, adultery, and blasphemy, as well as offenses such as the eating of pork and the consumption of alcohol.

Christians recognize the right of Muslims to regulate their lives according to religious principles and thus accept the comprehensive role that the *shari'a* plays in the organization of their lives as believers. Christians are concerned, however, that civil application of the *shari'a* can affect adversely the rights and duties of non-Muslims.

Christians in Asia hold that, according to modern principles of citizenship, all groups in society are accorded the right of public expression of their faith, and all groups have an equal responsibility to contribute to the formation of that society. Muslim movements that argue for the civil application of the *shari'a* as the cornerstone of the Islamization* of society would seem to violate that principle.

The *shari'a* regulates not only internal affairs of Muslims but also matters of interreligious relations (e.g., marriages between Muslims and non-Muslims, court testimony of non-Muslims, and the construction of non-Muslim places of worship) and those affecting society as a whole (e.g., dress codes, systems of banking and interest-taking, and prescribed punishments). When Muslims, even as a majority, impose their religious prescriptions on those outside the community, it creates a hierarchy of citizenry that results in restrictions on the rights of non-Muslims and ultimately in their marginalization. Christians hold that just laws, democratically enacted and impartially executed, offer a sounder basis for respecting the dignity and civil rights of all citizens.

Bibliography

Coulson, N. J., *History of Islamic Law* (1964/78). • Schacht, Joseph, *An Introduction to Islamic Law*, Vols. I and II (1964/96). • Anderson, Norman, *Islam in the Modern World* (1990). • Maudogdi, Sayyid Abul Ala, *Towards Understanding Islam* (1954). • Rahman, Fazlur, *Islam and Modernity, The Transformation of an Intellectual Tradition* (1982). • Mitri, Tarik, ed., *Religion, Law, and Society* (1995). THOMAS MICHEL

Sharp, Arthur Frederick

(b. England, 1866; d. England, 24 Jan 1960). Pioneer of Chinese missions and tractarianism in Sarawak (1889-1911).

Sharp was a missionary with the Society for the Propagation of the Gospel (SPG). Prior to his appointment as vicar of Kuching (1898) and archdeacon of Sarawak (from 1900), Sharp was assistant chaplain of the cathedral and principal of St. Andrew's House in the diocese of Singapore* (1892). When Sharp arrived in Sarawak, the work of the Anglican* Mission was at an ebb, with a declining number of missionaries and low morale.

Without neglecting the Dayak ministry, Sharp began developing the Chinese ministry through evangelistic meetings and the appointments of Chinese Anglican leaders. He also encouraged Chinese cultural developments through the Chinese Institute, established in 1907, and the removal of social barriers between European missionaries and Chinese Christians. In the process, Sharp helped develop a truly Asian church.

A tractarian, Sharp introduced and strengthened Anglo-Catholicism in worship and liturgy, which became the established ecclesiastical tradition in the Sarawak church. He also helped establish the Borneo Mission Association (BMA) in 1909 to garner home support for the mission in Sarawak. Upon his return to England in 1911, he remained a keen supporter of the Sarawak church through the BMA for many years as its secretary.

Bibliography

Sharp, A. F., *The Wings of the Morning* (1954). • Saunders, Graham, *Bishops and Brookes* (1992). • *The Chronicle*, Vol. 20 (Nov 1930); Vol. 36 (Mar 1960).

SOON SOO KEE

She Shan

(Basilica of Notre Dame). Pilgrimage destination situated on top of She Shan in Songjiang County near Shanghai, with Mary as patron.

The Basilica of Notre Dame was built in 1871, demolished in 1925, and then rebuilt over 10 years to twice its original size in order to accommodate 2,000 people. In May (the month of Mary for Catholics), pilgrims throng here from the nearby villages and city, and, in the last decade, from Hong Kong, Macau, Taiwan, and elsewhere.

The church and its surroundings were taken over by other units during the Cultural Revolution but returned to the Shanghai Diocese in Mar 1981 when the Shanghai Municipality implemented a policy of religious freedom. Extensive repairs were made with government and other assistance. A regional seminary was established in Oct 1982 for the six provinces in Eastern China and Shanghai Municipality. The seminary building was completed in Nov 1986.

DUFRESSE CHANG

Shee, Rebecca

(b. Toungoo, Myanmar, 17 Jan 1912; d. Loikaw, Myanmar, 16 Nov 1991). Evangelist in Myanmar* and Thailand* and the first ordained Kayin woman.

Shee was a pioneer leader among the Kayin people in Myanmar, having served as a nurse, mother for orphans, teacher, evangelist, training coordinator, chairperson, and ordained minister.

After finishing her schooling at Paku Christian High School at Toungoo, Shee joined the divinity school (now Myanmar Institute of Theology) at Seminary Hill, Insein, in 1936 and was awarded the bachelor of theology degree in 1940. She then joined the nursing schools at Namkhan and Mawlamyaing, where she was awarded certificates for midwifery and nursing. She then served faithfully among the tribal people in Gawgaligyi, as a nurse at the mission hospital and then as a house mother in an orphanage, even though she was unmarried. She was an outstanding leader in every sense because of her bravery, kindness, humility, cheerfulness, perseverance, undivided love, and dedicated life.

Shee was the first woman evangelist sent by the Kayin Baptist* Convention of Myanmar to work among the Karens* of Thailand. She and two other friends from Myanmar opened a Bible* school for the Karens in Thailand at Baw Keow in 1958 to provide Christian nurture and leadership development for the young people there. The school has become the Center for Uplift of Hill Tribes, which is located at Chiang Mai, Thailand. Shee was also among the first sent by the Myanmar Baptist Convention to organize women's* leadership training courses at Chiang Mai in 1962.

The major part of Shee's involvement in the ministry was within the context of the Kayin Baptist Convention. She served as its only woman evangelist for more than 20 years (1959-83), and also as its coordinator for women's work for several years. She was even elected chairperson of the Myanmar Baptist Convention for a couple of years.

On 30 Dec 1978, Shee became the first Sgaw-Kayin woman to be ordained by the Kayin Baptist Convention at its Phu Than Byu 150th Jubilee Celebrations at Tavoy. She was the only woman among the 17 ordinands. Her tireless service for Christ and her undivided attention to the total ministry of the church proved to be an inspiration for many Kayin Baptist young women. The status of Christian women was upgraded, and they enjoyed greater freedom and gained respect in their work. Women themselves understood their roles and assumed prominent and responsible positions in solidarity with men.

Shee was loved and respected by all. Her varied and

diversified services were greatly appreciated not only by the Kayin Baptists but also by the Christians of Myanmar. A worship service in her honor was conducted by the Kayin Baptist Convention Women's Society on 26 Feb 1983. She was commended as follows: "From the time you followed our Lord Jesus Christ and did His work, you did it wholeheartedly and happily. You never talked about salary but trusted in the Lord fully for sustenance. You were the best follower of Christ and you had given all your talents, which God had given you, in ministering to the needs of God's people. Among all our women, you were unique and special. You served the Lord unstintingly. Even though you had only one eye, that did not slow you down and become a drawback for you to go all out for God. You were always energetic, enthusiastic and enterprising in carrying out all the responsibilities given you. Not only that, you went the second mile in everything you did. Words are insufficient with which to honor you."

Although Shee retired from full-time work in 1983 because of old age, she remained a faithful and dedicated leader until her death on 16 Nov 1991.

Bibliography

Nyo Kwee Tha, "Rev. Rebecca Shee, the First Ordained Woman of Sgaw-Kayin Baptist Church" (research paper, Myanmar) (1994). • Shee, Rebecca, *The Life of Rebecca Shee* (1986).

Clifford Kyaw Dwe

Sheffield, D. Z.

(b. ?; d. Pei-tai-ho, China, 1 Jul 1913). American missionary to China* and educator.

Sheffield took part in the American Civil War and belonged to the northern (Union) side. After the war, he went to seminary and graduated in 1867. He was sent by the American Board of Commissioners for Foreign Missions (ABCFM) to China and arrived in the north of Tungchow in 1867. Sheffield mastered the Chinese language so well that he could preach fluently in Chinese within a few years. He acted as a translator for John R. Mott* whenever he came to China for visits. He was later put in charge of the revision of the Bible* in Mandarin and Wenli.

When Sheffield arrived in northern Tungchow, there was a newly opened school, which he further developed into the famous *Lu He Nan Shu* (Lu He Boys' School). Many years later, the school developed into *Lu He Shu Yuan* (Lu He High School), North China Union College, and he saw these developments through in the capacity of principal.

Sheffield was much more than an administrator and teacher in these schools. He also compiled textbooks on history, systematic theology, political economics, moral theology, psychology, political science, and other topics. These texts were adopted by other schools as well. In 1913 he went to Pei-tai-ho for a rest, where he suffered his second stroke and passed away.

China Group

Shellabear, William Girdlestone

(b. England, ca. 1862; d. United States, ca. 1947). Pioneer of the Methodist* mission to the Malays.

One of few missionaries to the ethnic Malays, Shellabear is best known for his literary and translation work which helped to revitalize the Malay language. His linguistic proficiency and genuine devotion to mission work among the Malays enabled him to produce much Malay literature*, notably, *Malay Proverbs, New Testament, Old Testament,* and *English-Malay Dictionary.* He did tracting and made house-to-house visitations. With others, he started street meetings, held friendly discussions on Islam* and Christianity, and conducted Malay services in a rented shop house on Arab Street, Singapore*.

Shellabear inaugurated (1890) the Methodist efforts to evangelize the Malays. He first arrived in Singapore (1887) as a captain of the British Royal Engineers, being enlisted in a company of Malay soldiers. At first, Shellabear attended the Church of England services at the cathedral, but finding no opportunity to get acquainted with any missionary, he soon found his way into the Methodist Church, where he became acquainted with William Oldham*. It was Shellabear's exposure to the Malay soldiers and his observation of the church's general apathy toward Malay work that drew his interest to mission among the Malays.

In 1891 the Methodist Mission engaged Pang Yan Whatt, a Chinese Christian from Borneo, to work alongside Shellabear at the printing press. The former, who could recite and read Arabic characters fluently, was also to become a valiant and faithful preacher to the Malays. From 1904 to 1909, Shellabear was assisted by a native in the translation of the Bible* into Malay. Shellabear moved to Malacca* (1904), believing that the language used in that part of the Malay Peninsula was better. Among his few converts in Singapore was a Malay man, Haji Abdul Shukor, who was baptized and renamed Andreas.

Apart from his achievement in publishing Malay literature and translation work, Shellabear's efforts to evangelize the Malays did not make any significant breakthroughs among the Malay community, whose unrelenting resistance to Christian mission work is not unknown. In 1920, ill health forced him to leave Singapore for the United States.

Bibliography

Shellabear, W. G., *The Life of the Rev. W. G. Shellabear, D.D.;* "The Gospel for Malays," *Moslem World,* Vol. 34 (1946). • Sng, Bobby E. K., *In His Good Time* (1980, 1993).

Paul Russ Satari

Shen Ti Lan

(b. Kiangsu, China, 1899; d. 1976). Shen graduated from Soochow University in 1922 and was baptized a Christian while still in school. He was a young man when the historic May Fourth Movement and North Advancement took place, and these had a great impact on him. He decided to devote his life to nurturing young people who favored democracy and progress.

Shen became principal of Mai-lun Middle School in 1931 and worked there for the next two decades. In the later part of the anti-Japanese war, he went to Chungking and taught in Yenching and Soochow Universities. He also went to Great Britain and the United States to develop an understanding of these countries' educational systems.

Shen served as chairman of the Young Men's Christian Association* (YMCA) at Soochow University. In 1922 he participated in the World's Christian Student Federation Conference in Peking and became a staff member of the YMCA at the national level after his graduation. In 1927 he founded the China Christian Student Movement Preparatory Committee together with other Christians.

Shen was very active in the anti-Japanese and democracy movements and participated in the Shanghai People Save China* Committee, as well as other patriotic activities. He took part in the *Bao Wei Zhong Guo Da Tong Meng* (Protect China Alliance), which was founded by Song Qing Ling. In 1951 he joined *Zhong Guo Min Zhu Tong Meng* (China Democratic Alliance), becoming a central committee member. After Shen returned from inland to Shanghai in 1946, he continued as principal of Mai-lun Middle School and also taught at St. John's University. In Sep 1949 he represented the education sector at the National Political Consultation Meeting. He was elected a committee member from the first to the fourth meetings. He was also a committee member of the Shanghai Political Consultation Meeting from its second to fourth meetings. He signed the "Three-Self Manifesto" in Jul 1950 to show his support for the self-governing, self-supporting, self-propagating movement of the Protestant church in China. CHINA GROUP

Shen Zigao

(b. Shanghai, 1895; d. 1982). Nationalist and Chinese Anglican* bishop.

Shen studied the arts and theology at St. John's University in Shanghai, founded by Bishop Schereschewsky* in 1872. Between 1917 and 1934, he pastored the Nanjing Anglican Church. He also studied theology at Oxford and Cambridge Universities in England. In 1934 he received his doctorate in theology from St. John's University and was sent to the county of Xiaxi to preside over the mission field founded by the Chinese Anglican Church. The aim was to develop the diocese into a self-supporting one. The church was involved in the war of resistance against the Japanese. Shen was associated with political activists such as Zhou Enlai, Ju De, and others. He was forced to leave Xiaxi for Sichuan in the latter part of the war.

He took up a teaching post at the Huaxi Theology Institute. In 1946 he was the secretary of the Chinese Anglican Church Institute and also dean of the Shanghai Central Theology Institute. He also taught at Nanjing Union Theological Seminary, which was set up in 1952. He retired in 1958 and settled in Shanghai.

In 1954 he was elected a committee member of the national Three-Self Patriotic Movement. He was a consultant to the China Christian Hymns Committee before his death in 1982. Shen was an advocate for the indigenization of the church and encouraged the adaptation of traditional Chinese music* and art* in the church. CHINA GROUP

Shi Mei Yi

(Mary Stone) (b. Jiangxi, China, 1 May 1873; d. Pasadena, California, 1954). Chinese medical* missionary.

Shi (also known as Mary Stone, a name she adopted while studying in the United States) was the daughter of a Methodist pastor in Jiujiang, Jiangxi. Her mother was a school principal. Defying tradition, her parents refused to bind her feet. Her mother taught her the Chinese classics and Christian literature*. Her father, impressed by the work of American medical missionary Dr. Kate Bushnell, decided that she should become a doctor. Shi studied at the Rulison-Fish Memorial School in Jiujiang for 10 years under Gertrude Howe, a Methodist* from Lansing, Michigan. In 1892 she left for the United States with Howe and studied medicine at the University of Michigan. She graduated in 1896 together with another Chinese, Kang Cheng (Ida Kahn), the first two Chinese women doctors trained in the United States. They returned to China* as medical missionaries of the Women's* Foreign Missionary Society of the Methodist Church and set up practice at Jiujiang. In the first 10 months, Stone and her associates treated more than 2,300 outpatients and made almost 300 house calls. Their one-room hospital was always filled.

During the Boxer Uprising in 1900, Stone lost her father, causing both her and Kahn to seek refuge in Japan*. They returned in 1901 and formally opened the Danforth Memorial Hospital, a 95-bed, 15-room hospital donated by I. N. Danforth of Chicago in memory of his wife. Stone was superintendent. Kahn left in 1903 to set up a medical center in Nanchang.

In 1907, Stone herself underwent surgery in Chicago. She took this as an opportunity to raise funds for her hospital. During busy periods, Stone's hospital was treating almost 5,000 patients per month. She supervised the training of more than 500 Chinese nurses during her tenure in Jiujiang and translated training manuals and textbooks for their use. In addition, she supervised a home for cripples and adopted four boys.

A Rockefeller Foundation scholarship enabled her to do postgraduate work at Johns Hopkins University from 1918 to 1919. Her sister, Phoebe, also a doctor and a graduate of Johns Hopkins, took charge of the Danforth Hospital in her absence.

Upon her return to China in 1920, Stone decided to leave the Methodist Board of Missions. She left with 20 staff and students who set up the Shanghai Bethel Mission in a rented house with the assistance of Jennie V. Hughes, an American missionary. In fewer than 10 years, the Bethel Mission had developed a hospital, primary and secondary schools, an evangelistic training department, and an orphanage. In 1930 a missionary from Hebei bequeathed her farm and orchard to the mission. Bethel Crusades were organized in more than 20 cities in 1930, and the mission even went overseas.

From 1920 until the Japanese invasion in 1937, Bethel was well known for its training program for nurses. Stone conducted Bible* classes for the nurses, intending to produce nurse-evangelists. The Japanese invasion forced Bethel members to move inland and to Hong Kong, resulting in new Bethel churches. Stone went to the United States to raise support for the Mission. She returned to Shanghai after the Japanese surrender but spent her last years in Pasadena, California, where she died at the age of 82. In 1948 the Bethel hospital built a surgery ward in her honor. The Bethel churches on the mainland became part of a national unified church in 1958. A pacesetter, Stone was the first Chinese Christian woman to be ordained in central China, the first president of the Women's Christian Temperance Union in China, and a member of the China continuations committee of the National Missionary Conference.

Bibliography

Boorman, Howard L., ed., *Biographical Dictionary of Republican China,* Vol. 3 (1970).

CHINA GROUP

Shiina Rinzo

(Otsubo Noboru) (b. Shikamagun, Sosa Village, Hyogo Prefecture, 1 Oct 1911; d. 28 Mar 1973). Japanese author.

Shiina left home in 1926 because of disharmony between his parents and withdrew from the third year at Himeji Junior High School. While working at a variety of jobs (fruit store clerk, apprentice cook, delivery boy), he studied for and passed the entrance exam for a vocational school. In 1929 he became an apprentice conductor of Ujigawa Railways (present-day San'in Railway) and organized a cell for the Japanese Communist Party. In 1931, all such workers were summarily arrested, and in 1932 he was sentenced to four years in prison. In 1933 he appealed for conversion of his sentence and had it changed to a three-year suspended sentence. Afterwards, he was followed around by special higher police. He changed jobs many times and had his eyes opened by readings of Nietzsche and Dostoyevsky. In 1939 he joined a literary circled called *Sosaku* (creation) and began publishing novels. He made his debut in the literary world in 1947 with *Shinya no shuen* (Midnight Banquet) and *Omoki nagare no maka ni* (In the Midst of a Serious Current). In 1948 he produced *Ein naru josho* (Preface to Eternity), and in 1949 *Sono hi made* (Until That Day), becoming Japan's* premier existentialist writer. As such, he was a standard-bearer among postwar writers. In 1950, in desperation, he was baptized at Akaiwa Sakae's Uehara Church. In 1952 he wrote *Kaiko* (Unexpected Meeting), and in 1955 *Utsukushii onna* (Beautiful Woman). The next year he received an Artist Commendation from the Japanese minister of education. He also wrote plays, scenarios, and television dramas. He presided over the Protestant literary group *Tane no Kai* (seed group). *Choekinin no kokuhatsu* (Accusation of the Prisoner), written in 1969, was his final masterpiece. He died of heart disease and aneurysms, an illness that he had had since 1957. His funeral was held at Mitaka Church (Ishijima Saburo, pastor), where he had transferred his membership in 1966. A complete collection of his works (24 volumes), *Shiina Rinzo zenshu,* was published from 1970 to 1979.

Bibliography

Saito Suehiro, *Shiina Rinzo,* 2 Vols. (1984). • Takado Kaname, *Shiina Rinzo Ron* (Theory of Shiina Rinzo) (11 Jan 1978); *Fukuin to sekai* (The Gospel and the world) (8 Apr 1979).

TAKADO KANAME, JAPANESE DICTIONARY

Shin Suk Koo

(b. Chungju, North Chung Chung Province, South Korea, 3 May 1875; d. 10 Oct 1950). One of the 33 original signatories of Korea's* Declaration of Independence on 1 Mar 1919, which triggered the nationwide anti-Japanese independence movement.

Shin accepted Christianity in 1907 with an ardent desire to save the troubled nation which was under Japanese occupation. Before he was ordained into the Methodist* ministry in 1917, he served as an evangelist in Kaesung and Choonchun as a vigorous nationalist preacher (see Nationalism).

He was imprisoned for two and a half years because of his leadership in the independence movement. He served as a parish minister in various city churches in North Korea and led an opposition to the Japanese Shinto* shrine worship. He was arrested again for this.

After liberation in 1945, he joined the other Christian leaders in North Korea in opposing the North Korean Communist Party. On 1 Mar 1946, he was to speak on behalf of the Communist Party, exposing the "failures" of the movement, but he spoke instead about the "success" of the movement as a nonviolent people's movement against Japanese colonialism*. He was arrested by the North Korean security force on the spot. In 1948 he was arrested again as one of the organizers of the Christian Democratic Party, an opposition party to the North Korean Labor Party which established the Democratic People's Republic of Korea (DPRK, North).

In the wake of the Korean War*, he was arrested again. His body was found in the outskirts of P'yongyang when the United States and South Korean troops advanced to the city in Oct 1950.

DAVID SUH, with contributions from LEE DUK JOO, translated by KIM IN SOO

Shintoism and Christianity in Korea

Shinto was based on the ancient Japanese mythology of the Yamato people who lived in the central part of Japan*. The mythology taught that Izanaginomikoto and Izanaminomikoto, two primeval deities, descended from the heavenly world on a floating bridge and created the Japanese isles by stirring the sea below.

The two deities landed on the newly created land and created more deities. In the process of creating the fire-god, the female deity, Izanaminomikoto, died and descended to the underworld. With the hope of returning her to the heavenly world, the male deity, Izanaginomikoto, traced her. It was dark and the male deity lit the light with his comb in his head. The female deity was dark, swallowed up with worms, and she was ashamed. She became angry and chased the male deity. The male deity was afraid and separated from her, blocking her entrance to heaven with a large rock. Then the heavenly world was ruled by the sun goddess. The sun goddess sent her great-great-grandson to rule the divinely created land of Japan. Thus Shinto mythology taught that Japan was created by a divine creator and was to be ruled by descendants of the deities as emperors of Japan.

Shinto is the traditional folk religion of Japan, drawing from animism*, shamanism*, phallic worship, and ancestor* worship centered around village shrines. However, it was made the state religion in the early years of the Meiji Restoration after 1868 and identified closely with Japanese foreign policies and national life until 1945. Wherever the Japanese governed, Shinto shrines were built and worship and obeisance to the shrines were imposed. Such impositions and the governmental orders to visit Shinto shrines and pay obeisance to Shinto deities became a serious issue with Christians not only in colonies but also within Japan itself.

Shinto worship under Japanese occupation. It was a trial for Koreans to maintain their national identity under the Japanese policy of assimilation through the forced use of the Japanese language in schools as well as in public. In the wake of the Japanese invasion into China* in the early 1930s, the Japanese government forced Koreans to change their family names to the Japanese style. At the same time, the Japanese imperial government ordered all Korean students on all levels to attend the Japanese Shinto ceremonies and pay their respects to the shrine, giving three deep bows and three hand claps. The Christian mission schools protested the orders and refused to send their students to the mountain shrine sites. In defiance of the Japanese threats, some American missionaries closed down the schools and left Korea*. Korean teachers reopened the schools and followed the government orders to send the students to the shrines.

The Korean Christian leaders faced the most trying time when the Japanese authorities forced them to pay respects to the Shinto shrines in public ceremonies. Individual clergymen and elders of the church protested and refused to do this on religious grounds. However, at the general assembly of the Presbyterian* Church in 1935, the church delegates adopted a resolution that Shinto shrine worship was not a violation of the first two of the Ten Commandments and that it was a civil act of respect toward the Japanese empire and the spirits of the nation.

In protest, some Korean pastors left the country for China and went into exile, but some organized a nationwide protest movement. The leaders of the resistance movement called on all the churches of Korea to: (1) refuse to perform shrine worship at all costs; (2) refuse to send children to schools that practiced shrine worship; (3) refuse to attend churches that practiced shrine worship; (4) worship in house churches; and (5) organize a network of protesters.

The leading members were harassed, threatened, and arrested by Japanese authorities. Chu Ki Chul died in prison on 20 Apr 1944. For the shrine protest incident, some 2,000 Christians were arrested, some 200 churches were closed down, and 50 people are known to have been martyred in prison. It was not only a protest movement on the grounds of the Christian faith, but also a political movement of anti-Japanese nationalism*.

After the liberation of 1945, those imprisoned because of involvement in the antishrine worship movement were released. They initiated the "reconstruction" movement of the Korean church that had defiled itself by the idol worship of Japanese shrines. They demanded the repentance of all participating pastors and elders of the church and the suspension of all of their ministerial duties for three months, as well as other items, in order to cleanse the polluted Korean churches. The participating ministers refused the demands on the grounds that they suffered as much as those who were imprisoned by keeping the churches going under the most difficult of circumstances. The reconstruction group formed a separate Presbyterian denomination under the name of Koryu, which flourishes in the southeastern part of South Korea.

Bibliography

Anesaki Masaharu, *Religious Life of the Japanese People* (1961). • Earhart, H. Byron, *Japanese Religion: Unity and Diversity* (1975). • Holtom, D. C., *Modern Japan and Shinto Nationalism* (1943). • Kitagawa, Joseph M., *Religion in Japanese History* (1966). • Clark, Allen D., *A History of the Church in Korea* (1971/1986).

WI JO KANG and DAVID SUH, with contributions from KIM IN SOO and KIM SEUNG TAE

Shoki Coe. *See* Ng Chiong Hui

Sibu Christian Settlement

In 1900 a Methodist* entrepreneur in Foochow named Wong Nai Siong was moved by the abject poverty of Chinese farmers, scraping out a living on minute plots of land. He was inspired by the history of the *Mayflower* Pilgrims sailing to North America to found a new colony. Rajah Charles Brooke*, governor of the independent colony of Sarawak on the west coast of the island of Borneo, undertook to provide land for 1,000 settlers from China*. The land granted was on the Rejang River in Sarawak, and Wong lost no time in selecting his settlers from amongst the Methodist Christian farmers of Fukien Province.

In Dec 1901 the settlers arrived on the Rejang. The plan was that the colony should be self-sufficient after the first crop of rice, but the first three crops failed; a number of the settlers managed to work their way back to China, and less than 500 of the original number were left. The rajah gave grants and Wong committed his whole life savings to helping the farmers.

The superintendent of the Singapore* District of the Methodist Episcopal Church visited Sibu (chief town of the Rejang area) in 1902 and again the following year. The result was the appointment in 1903 of J. M. Hoover as missionary in charge of the settlement; at the same time, Brooke put Hoover in sole charge of the communal development of the settlement. From then on, both the agricultural life and the church life of the community began to prosper.

In 1909 the district superintendent reported on his three-day tour of six churches in the Sibu District and inspection of acres of rice, rubber, and pepper. On the river side, a rice mill had been built which "was a boon to the whole countryside." He described the colony as in every sense Christian, and Rev. and Mrs. Hoover as "the ministers, educators, physicians, magistrates, and general viceroys of the whole enterprise." By the year 1926, the settlement had grown to more than 10,000 farmers, and some 30,000 acres were under cultivation. There were 23 churches and over 1,000 children in the schools. A visitor to the colony in 1936 reported rubber holdings on both sides of the river, each holding extending four or five miles along the river, with a Methodist church and school in each area. He described Hoover as a "household word" in Sarawak; many of the projects that contributed to the prosperity of the region, such as the sawmill and the ice plant, were initiated by Hoover.

By 1936 the Methodist mission in Sibu was so well developed that an international "Summer School of Theology" was held there in that year, attended by 40 pastors. In 1951, when Sibu celebrated the jubilee of the Methodist settlement, there were already 50 churches, 12 preaching stations with 12,864 baptized members, 25 full-time pastors and Bible* women*, and 60 affiliated schools.

Bibliography

The Malaysia Message (Feb 1909, Aug 1926, Aug/Sep 1936). • *Minutes of the Malaysia Conference of the Methodist Episcopal Church* (1903). • Sng, Bobby E. K., *In His Good Time* (1980, 1993).

Frank Lomax

Sidjabat, Walter Bonar

(b. Tigaras, North Sumatra, 19 Oct 1931; d. 2 Feb 1987). Indonesian theologian.

During his life, Sidjabat was well known as an activist in the Christian youth and student movements. He was also an expert in science and in the theology of religions, becoming especially known as an exponent for the contextualization* of theology in Indonesia*.

When he was a student at the Jakarta Theological Seminary from 1950 to 1955, Sidjabat was an activist and a leader of various Christian youth and student organizations. He was even appointed chairman of the central board of the Indonesian Student Christian Movement*. He developed these activities at an international level, which included the Young Men's Christian Association* (YMCA), while he was studying at Princeton Theological Seminary from 1956 to 1960.

Sidjabat's dissertation, *Religious Tolerance and the Christian Faith,* showed his expertise in the science and theology of religions and led him to well-deserved positions in several universities and institutions, including a professorship at his alma mater, Jakarta Theological Seminary. He held this position until the end of his life. He is well known as a promoter of interfaith dialogue, especially between Christians and Muslims (see Interreligious Dialogue). As he emphasized in his dissertation, although the Christian's and Muslim's understanding of God differs, this need not hinder them from cooperating in the development of the Indonesian nation, since they share a common history and a common task.

Sidjabat was also active in many ecumenical organizations, serving as assistant professor at the Ecumenical Institute of the World Council of Churches (WCC) in Bossey, Switzerland (1960), secretary of the Research Institute of the Communion of Churches of Indonesia (CCI, 1960-72), and member of the Faith and Order Commission of the WCC (1975-86).

All of these occasions gave him opportunity to realize his obsession, namely, to show that theology in Indonesia is not merely imported from the West but has developed roots and been engaged in the pluralistic Indonesian soil, while at the same time remaining faithful to its foundation, the Word of God. This obsession he expressed in a speech titled "The Relevant Word of God in the Indigenization of Theology in Indonesia" (1965). In this connection he was active, compiling and publishing writings that show the participation of Christians in all fields of the nation's life, such as *Our Present Calling in Indonesia* (1964) and *Christian Participation in Nation Building* (1968). The same motivation drove him to promote Christian publishing and magazines (see Literature and Publishing).

Sidjabat combined his experience as a student

trooper during the revolutionary era (1945-49) in his homeland and his admiration for the struggle of the people there with his enthusiasm for the indigenization of theology in his great work, *Ahu Si Singamangaraja* (The Legendary Figure Si Singamangaraja, 1982). The vision, enthusiasm, and hard work he showed during his life stimulated the interest of many in the church and in theological* education, leading to the development of both contextual theology (see Contextualization) and interfaith dialogue.

Bibliography

Sidjabat, W. B., "The Exposition of the Gospel and Law in the Realm of the Muslims in Indonesia" (M.Th. thesis, Princeton Theological Seminary, 1957); *Religious Tolerance and the Christian Faith* (1965). • Yayasan Bina Darma, *Senerai Kumpulan Beberapa Tulisan Prof. Dr. W. B. Sidjabat,* (unpublished anthology for W. B. Sidjabat Memorial Lecture, Salatiga, 1988).

Jan S. Aritonang

Sihombing, Justin

(b. Pangaribuan, Indonesia, 1890; d. Pematangsiantar, Indonesia, 1979). Teacher-preacher, pastor, and church leader of the Batak* church (HKBP).

Sihombing was a son of a traditional Batak physician who still adhered to the traditional Batak religion (ancestor* worship). When Justin was seven years old, he studied at the first elementary school built by the missionaries in Pangaribuan, a village in North Sumatra. After he finished his studies, the local missionary, Mr. Meis, appointed him assistant teacher in the same school. Based on his ability and seriousness of service, he prepared to be a teacher and continued his studies at the Seminary of Sipoholon near Tarutung (1908-12). As a mission teacher (similar to a teacher-preacher), he was placed in his home village. Later he was selected for theological* training in the same seminary (1923-25).

As an evangelist and pastor (1925-28), he worked to understand the lives and difficulties of the local people and the church members that lived far from the centers of the German missionaries. He also worked among the Bataks who migrated from Batakland and lived among other Indonesian tribes, the majority of whom are Muslim. Sihombing also worked in Medan, the largest city in North Sumatra. Medan was the center for the Dutch colonial* government and the economic center of Sumatra. As a local non-European pastor, he was the first Batak pastor entrusted with a parish. Until 1942, parish pastors had been German missionaries (the European pastors). Sihombing was also the first Batak pastor that was appointed a district president (*praeses,* a pastor leading a district). At that time, the German mission fields and the Batak church were divided into several districts.

At the beginning of the national movement in Indonesia, Sihombing was elected the *ephorus* (the highest position) of HKBP. He held that position for five terms (1942-62), retiring in 1962, when he was appointed special lecturer at the Faculty of Theology of HKBP Nommensen* University in Pematangsiantar, where he served until 1972 (82 years old).

During his leadership as *ephorus,* he reestablished a good relationship with the German Mission Society (RMG) in Germany. At the same time, he also joined the ecumenical* movement at the national and international levels. He was the main author of the confession of faith of the HKBP, which was the basis for HKBP to join the Lutheran* World Federation (LWF) in 1952. He was honored by the University of Bonn, Germany, with an honorary doctorate in theology in 1951 for his successful leadership during a difficult period in Indonesia* (the Dutch colonial rulers suspected him of being pro-German while, during the Japanese occupation [1942-45], he was suspected of being pro-Dutch).

During his service in the church, Sihombing dedicated his ministry to pastoral visits to the congregations that were spreading outside of Tapanuli. He was not a prolific author, but he did write on the history of the HKBP, on preparation for pastoral ministry, and on life after death.

For many people in Indonesia, Sihombing is well known as an important church leader who led the largest Protestant church in Indonesia, even in Asia.

Bibliography

Sianipar, F. H., *Barita ni Ompu I Dr. Justin Sihombing* (1978).

J. Raplan Hutauruk

Sikhism

At less than 500 years old, Sikhism was founded by Guru Nanak (1469-1539) and originated in the "land of five rivers," i.e., Punjab (now part of India* and Pakistan*). Largely an ethnic religion, its adherents constitute the majority community in Punjab, though large numbers of them are found elsewhere in India and abroad. There are over 15 million Sikhs in the world.

Sikh means "disciple," one who believes in God as the true guru whose word has come to humanity through 10 historical figures, who are also treated as gurus. A Sikh also believes in the guruship of the Sikh community and that of the sacred scriptures, *Guru Granth Saheb,* which has adorned the guruship since the death of Guru Gobind Singh in 1708. The *(Adi) Granth,* compiled by the fifth guru, Arjun, contains the teachings, prayers, and hymns of early gurus and reformers. Gurmukhi is the official and sacred language of the Sikhs. Sikh religion revolves around the Sacred Book. Sikh temples (*gurudwaras,* of which the most famous is the Golden Temple in Amritsar) are the nerve centers of the sacred and secular aspects of Sikh life.

Gradually, the Sikhs grew in number and developed features that distinguished them from Hindus and Muslims. In an attempt to contain the growth of the Sikh community, the Muslim rulers of Delhi subjected them to persecution, in which two of their gurus, Arjun and Tegh Bahadur, suffered martyrdom. This compelled them to transform into a powerful martial people.

Guru Gobind Singh founded the Khalsa, the Sikh brotherhood of the initiated who wear "five K's": *kesh* (uncut hair), *kanga* (comb), *kara* (iron bangle), *kachah* (shorts), and *kirpan* (sword). The initiated receive the new name Singh, meaning "lion."

What the Sikhs believe is a harmony of Hindu and Muslim teachings. They believe in strict monotheism. God is popularly known by three names: Hari, Sat Guru, and Sat Nam. True worship* is singing praises and meditating on his name. They do not believe in the incarnation of God who is eternal and formless and whose will is supreme. Image worship, pilgrimage, and asceticism are useless. The world, created by God for his purposes, is transitory, and one should not attach oneself to the illusionary world. Humans, whose essence contains a part of God, are created to please the creator. They are subject to *karma* and transmigration. Sikhism stands for casteless society and the brotherhood of humanity and respects the dignity and equality of women. Salvation is submission to the will of God, to have a love union with God. An intense devotional relationship of worship is the means to achieve it. Reunion with God is the destiny of human beings.

Until the Western missionaries came in the 19th c., there were no Christian churches in the Punjab, though there is a tradition that the apostle Thomas preached in the Punjab region (see St. Thomas Evangelical Church of India). The history of the church in Punjab begins with the arrival of the American missionary John C. Lowrie in Nov 1834 and the founding of the Ludhiana Mission of the Presbyterian* Church. This was followed by many others, such as Methodist*, Baptist, *Anglican*, and Salvation Army* missions. Evangelism, education, and medical* mission were the major concerns of the missions. Forman* Christian College in Lahore (1864), Kinnaird College for women, also in Lahore (1913), Gordon College in Rawalpindi, Murray College in Sialkot (1889), Edwards College at Peshawar (1900), Baring Christian College at Batala (1944), Christian Medical College (School, at the time) for women* at Ludhiana (1894) founded by a member of the Plymouth Brethren, Dr. Edith Brown, and others were the leading educational institutions. John Newton, James Wilson, James Campbell, Edith Brown, John Hyde, Henry D. Griswold, J. S. Barr, and S. Martin were some of the early leading missionaries. Nattu, a high caste convert, and Ditt*, an outcaste convert, were two leading nationals who worked for the expansion of the church.

The total Christian population in Punjab numbered only 3,796 in 1881 (almost all the converts during the early years of missionary work were from the upper castes). But thereafter, due to mass movements from Dalit groups such as Chuhras, Meghs, and Chamars, there was a rapid rise in the Christian population. In 1901 it rose to 37,980, and in 1921 to 375,031.

The converts were primarily from Hindu and outcaste backgrounds, with some Muslim converts, but the response from the Sikh community was largely negligible. This is true even in present times. There are about 225,000 Christians in Indian Punjab as per the census of 1991, of whom 90 percent are of Dalit origin. Christianity has not been very successful in making serious inroads into Sikhism in its evangelistic efforts. Converts from Sikhism do not form a significant group. The most famous Sikh convert is the late Sadhu Sunder Singh*. In present times, it is Bhakt Singh, founder of the Bhakt Singh Assembly, who is quite influential in Andhra Pradesh and Tamil Nadu. Even these have failed to penetrate the Sikh community, and they are popular not in Punjab but elsewhere.

The prosperous and close-knit Sikh community, which practices brotherhood in a commendable manner, has been successful in withstanding the pressure from Christian missions. Their martial spirit and aggressive political agenda and total commitment to the Shalsa have effectively insulated their eclectic religion from Christian evangelistic efforts. There has been competition between Sikh and Christian missionary enterprises in winning converts from the scheduled castes.

This does not mean that Christianity did not exert any influence on the Sikh community and their religion. The Christian educational and medical institutions have been a great inspiration in the formation of similar Sikh institutions. Christian educational institutions also produced outstanding and enlightened Sikh leaders. The starting of the Khalsa Young Men's Association, Khalsa Tract Society, Sikh Education Conference, Khalsa Students' Club, etc., was due to the influence of parallel Christian organizations.

Sikh and Christian communities in Punjab have maintained cordial relationships. It is noteworthy that even during times of heightened Sikh militancy, Christians have not been subjected to any harassment. The Christian Institute of Sikh Studies under the auspices of Baring Union Christian College, Batala, is a point of meeting for dialogue and united religious and social activities. During the riots that preceded the partition of India in 1947, the Christian community rendered great assistance to the victims, and the Sikhs are grateful. In the context of confusion created by militancy and political turmoil, there is an unprecedented openness among Sikhs to the message of the Christian Gospel. The majority of Punjabi Christians are still predominantly illiterate and very poor, and they need to enhance their socioeconomic status before they can expect the Sikh community to take them on parity and initiate a process for better understanding, interaction, and joint endeavors.

Bibliography

Campbell, Ernest Y., "The Church in the Punjab," in *Three Studies of North Indian Churches,* ed. Victor E. W. Hayward (1966). • Davies, Douglas, "Religion of the Gurus: The Sikh Faith," in *The World's Religions. A Lion*

Handbook (1992). • McMullen, Clarence O., et al., *The Amritsar Diocese* (1973). • *Religion and Society*, Vol. 38, No. 2 (Jun 1991). • Singh, Harbans, and Lal M. Joshi, *An Introduction to Indian Religions* (1973). • Singh, Herbert Jai, *My Neighbors* (1966). • Zachariah, Aleyamma, *Modern Religious and Secular Movements in India* (1992).

C. V. Mathew

Silliman University

Established in Dumaguete in the province of Negros Oriental as the Silliman Institute, this mission-founded school has been recognized as the major educational institution in the central Philippines* for much of its history. The school was founded reluctantly, as American Presbyterian* missionaries, newly arrived in the Philippines after Spain ceded its former colony to the United States in Dec 1898, hoped to focus on mission tasks rather than educational ones. But when the philanthropist Horace B. Silliman offered $1,000 in gold to the Board of Foreign Missions of the Presbyterian Church of the USA for an "industrial school," the missionaries were urged to select a suitable location, to purchase land, and to open a school that would be called "Silliman Institute."

David S. Hibbard and his wife Laura, pioneer Presbyterian missionaries, officially began Silliman Institute classes on 28 Aug 1901 when they met a group of 15 (or perhaps 16) boys, aged 12 to 16. Its student body quickly grew, and six months after lessons began there were more than 100 boys, ranging from 8 to 24 years of age. Soon the Silliman Institute offered a wide range of courses, from beginners' English to pre-college courses. Vocational training was added in 1904 when Charles A. Glunz, an able and dedicated instructor, joined the growing institution.

In 1910 the Silliman Institute received government recognition and the authority to confer degrees. This year saw the school's first graduates, a group of three young men. The first woman graduate received her degree in 1914. In time more women enrolled at Silliman until, some 40 years later, the ratio of women students to men students was about equal. As the decades passed, Silliman Institute expanded its student body, curriculum, property, and buildings. In Mar 1938 the institute was given university status, and in Jun 1938 Silliman University opened its doors to 1,123 students.

From its beginning, Silliman University featured religious instruction. Bible* study and chapel services were essential parts of its education. The Presbyterian annual mission report of 1932 indicates that about 2,500 students, approximately three-fourths of all students, had joined the church since the founding of the school.

Soon after World War II*, its government became independent from the church; gradually, Filipinos took the place of missionaries on both the board of trustees and the faculty. Five members of the United Church of the Philippines, founded in 1948 by Presbyterian and other ecumenical Protestants, form one-third of the board of trustees.

Today Silliman University remains a major institution in the Philippines. The school has a student body of more than 10,000, and Bible courses are still required of all students. Silliman University is well known nationally for its marine biology department, while its students in the fields of nursing, certified public accounting, and engineering regularly earn special recognition.

Bibliography

Hibbard, D. S., *The First Quarter: A Brief History of Silliman Institute during the First Twenty-five Years of Its Existence* (1926). • Kwantes, A. C., *Presbyterian Missionaries in the Philippines: Conduits of Social Change (1899-1909)* (1989). • Tiempo, E. K., C. C. Maslog, and T. V. Sitoy, Jr., *Silliman University, 1901-1976* (1977).

Anne C. Kwantes

Simatupang, Tahi Bonar

(Pak Sim) (b. Sidikalang, 28 Jan 1920; d. Jakarta, 1 Jan 1990). Indonesian military and ecumenical* leader.

Simatupang was one of the first generation of top leaders in the Indonesian army. Retired at a relatively young age, he joined the ecumenical movement, holding high positions in the Council of Churches in Indonesia*, Christian Conference of Asia*, and World Council of Churches, where he was acknowledged as an ecumenical thinker.

He attended elementary school in Pematangsiantar (1927-34) and junior high in Tarutung, where he also learned his Christian catechism under E. Verwiebe, a German missionary. Young Simatupang went to a Christian school in Jakarta for senior high (1937-40). There he took an active part in the Batak* church youth organization. He thought of becoming a physician, but after the Netherlands was occupied by Germany, he entered the military academy opened in Bandung because he wanted to prove untrue the Dutch myth that Indonesians could not build a modern army to defeat the Netherlands because of their small physical stature. He rose to the rank of officer, but his career with the Netherland-Indies army (KNIL) ended with the Japanese occupation. He was imprisoned for some months and released as a civilian.

During the Japanese occupation, which he expected to be short-lived, Simatupang prepared himself for the future of the new Indonesia, broadening his knowledge by studying Indonesian history, language, and culture in the national library (known as *Gedung Gajah*). Then, disguised as a Japanese-language bookseller, he traveled around the cities of Java* to gauge the situation and attitude of the people under Japanese occupation. Together with some Batak friends, he studied ideologies and revolutions from secondhand books purchased in the market. He made contact with Sutan Sjahrir, who led an underground resistance to Japan*, and moved to Bandung to meet his colleagues from the military academy (A. H. Nasution and A. E. Kawilarang), where they formed a study group to develop their military knowledge.

Simatupang's preparations proved useful in his commitment to an independent Indonesia. Together with some ex-officers of KNIL and PETA, he helped Oerip Sumohardjo build the Indonesian army (TNI). The task was made more difficult in a time of armed confrontation between the newly independent Indonesia and the Netherlands. The Indonesian army took a major role in the double strategy of Indonesia against the Netherlands: diplomacy and war. Simatupang represented TNI in the Indonesian diplomatic delegations. His major success, after the Linggadjati Conference agreed to form a United Indonesian Republic (RIS), was to replace, against the wishes of the Dutch, the Netherlands-Indies army with the TNI.

In 1950 he was appointed *Kepala Staf Angkatan Perang* (KSAP), the Armed Forces Staff Commander. He tried to develop a professional army to avoid the fate that befell countries that came under military rule and had democracy abolished after obtaining their independence through armed struggle. He met with the opposition, including those from President Sukarno. An incident on 17 Oct 1952 between military leaders and Sukarno marked the beginning of the turning point in Simatupang's military career. His position as KSAP was abolished and he was retired in 1959. Though aware of developments against himself, he continued to serve the army by developing military doctrine and cadres through his lectures in the Army Staff Command Training (SSKAD) and Military Law Academy (AHM).

Upon retirement from the army, Simatupang devoted himself to the ecumenical movement. He equipped himself in Bossey by studying the theological* works of Karl Barth, Reinhold Niebuhr, and others. He acknowledged that his thinking was influenced by three Karls, i.e., Carl von Clausewitz (on military strategy), Karl Marx (on revolution), and Karl Barth (on theology). His main contribution to the ecumenical movement in Indonesia was in the formulation of principles and strategies regarding churches' responsibility toward the Indonesian people and society. Together with other DGI leaders, Simatupang formulated a positive, creative, critical, and realistic approach toward national life and ideas. The church has to accept positively, develop creatively, judge critically, and think realistically on national issues. The Indonesian Council (now Communion) of Churches institutionalized the National Conference on Church and Society, which in 1976 proposed the implementation of *Pancasila* for national development. The People's Congress of 1984 accepted the guidelines, and in 1988 *Pancasila* became a national philosophy. Simatupang also contributed to the development of interreligious harmony in Indonesia, especially by confronting activities intended to limit or upset religious life in the nation.

Simatupang wrote books and many articles on military, political, and church matters. His collected articles are in *Iman Kristen dan Pancasila* (Christian Faith and *Pancasila*, 1984) and *Dari Revolusi ke Pembangunan* (From Revolution to Development, 1987). His autobiography, *Membuktikan Ketidakbenaran Suatu Mitos* (Proving the Falseness of a Myth), was published posthumously in 1991. His experience in the Indonesian Revolution is recorded in *Report from Banaran* (1st ed., 1960).

Bibliography

Kasenda, Peter, "T. B. Simatupang: Pejuang, Prajurit dan Pemikir" (T. B. Simatupang: Warrior, soldier and thinker), *Prisma*, Vol. 2 (1991). • Simatupang, T. B., "The Situation and Challenge of the Christian Mission in Indonesia Today," *South East Asia Journal of Theology*, Vol. 10, No. 4 (1969); "Kurzer Ruckblick auf die Geschichte der christlichen Kirche in Indonesien," in *Indonesiens verantwortliche Gesellschaft*, ed. Rolf Italiaander (1976); "Dynamics for Creative Maturity," in *Asian Voices in Christian Theology*, ed. Gerald H. Anderson (1976); "Doing Theology in Indonesia Today," *CTC Bulletin*, Vol. 3, No. 2 (1982); *Gelebte Theologie in Indonesien, zur gesellschaftlichen Verantwortung der Christen* (1992).

Zakaria J. Ngelow

Simon, K. V.

(b. Edayaranmula, India, 7 Feb 1873; d. 20 Feb 1944). Indian Christian poet, writer, and preacher.

In the latter half of the 19th c., a series of reform activities started among the Malankara Christians in which Simon, the great Malayalam poet, played a very significant role. He may be rightly called the Martin Luther of Kerala, because he raised his voice against the evils in the traditional Christian communities.

The son of Varghese and Kochupennu, Simon was brought up in a strict Christian atmosphere with moderate financial comfort and security. His father was well versed in the Itihasah and Puranas. His brother taught him Sanskrit, Tamil, and English. These favorable circumstances and intense encouragement from the family circle boosted his innate faculties.

Even at age six, Simon spent much time reading. He acquired sound knowledge of history, literature, religion, and the Bible*. He showed a great interest in poetry, and at age seven began writing poems in Malayalam and Sanskrit. He acquired knowledge of Greek, Hebrew, Syriac, Kannada, Telugu, and Tamil. Attracted to bhajans (traditional Hindu songs), he wrote a number of Christian bhajans and began to sing in public.

In 1890, Simon became a schoolteacher at his alma mater. After four years, he became its headmaster. In 1895, he attended the revival meetings conducted by V. D. David and accepted Christ as his Savior. He then resigned to train for full-time Christian ministry. In 1900, he married Rahelamma, who was always an encouragement to him. They had one daughter.

In 1902, Simon took up work in the ministry.

Through his eloquent and powerful sermons, he challenged the traditional Christian communities. His firm stance for the cause of reformation forced the leaders of the church to take action against him, and finally in 1915 he was excommunicated from the Mar Thoma Church*.

After a short while, Simon was able to gather a group of like-minded people and organized the *Malankara Viyojitha Sabha.* He started publishing a magazine under the auspices of this movement. In 1919, they decided to merge with the Brethren Church.

Simon was a strong advocate of social reform and criticized a number of social evils. His sermons were apologetic in nature. It was his contribution to Malayalam literature, especially in poetry, that earned him his fame. His most famous work is an epic, *Vedaviharam,* based on the book of Genesis. He had the desire to put the complete Bible into poetic form, but did not succeed in completing this task. Simon also wrote books on history and apologetics, as well as Bible commentaries. *Good Samaritan* is another of his notable works.

Simon traveled widely in South India to do Christian ministry. In 1943, he became sick and was bedridden for a short period. He died shortly thereafter from rheumatic fever. SAMUEL MATHEW

Singapore

A small island-state situated at the crossroads of Southeast Asia, with Malaysia*, Brunei*, and Indonesia* as its immediate neighbors. Until it became independent in 1965, Singapore was always a part of larger political entities, such as the Melaka and Johor Sultanates, the British and Japanese empires, and the Malaysian federation.

As a British colony, it became a plural society where Asians and Europeans met mainly in the marketplace and created a vibrant *entrepot* trade and a dynamic port city. It was invaded and occupied by the Japanese during World War II*, reclaimed by the British, and became a self-governing state in 1959 and a constituent state of Malaysia in 1963-65.

Government and economy. The People's Action Party (PAP) has been the governing party since 1959, under the premiership of Lee Kuan Yew (1959-90) and Goh Chok Tong (1990-present). Singapore is a democratic republic with an elected president and unicameral parliament, with a dominant party and limited opposition. The government has been the mainspring of rapid economic development through the involvement of multinationals alongside local industrial and commercial enterprises, and heavy public investment in infrastructure and human resources, education, health, public housing, and defense, resulting in high standards of living and per capita incomes (over 85 percent own their own homes).

Religion and society. The government is secular in outlook and takes an evenhanded approach to peoples of various (or no) religions. It passed the Religious Harmony Act in 1991 to maintain religious tolerance and respect and to minimize religious interference in politics.

According to the 1995 General Household Survey, based on 2.5 million residents aged 10 years and above, 85.5 percent professed some religious faith or belief. Of those surveyed, Buddhists, Taoists, and other Chinese sectarians formed 53.8 percent; Muslims (mainly Malays), 14.9 percent (see Buddhism*, Taoism*, and Islam); Christians (mainly Chinese), 12.9 percent; and Hindus (mainly Indians), 3.3 percent (see Hinduism). There are also small communities of Jews, Sikhs, and Baha'is.

The resident population of Singapore totals more than 3.2 million. It comprises Chinese (77.2 percent), Malays (14.1 percent), Indians (7.4 percent), and persons of other ethnic groups (1.3 percent). Nationhood and nation-building policies have produced social cohesion and a distinct national identity.

There are four official languages — Malay, Chinese (Mandarin), Tamil, and English — with Malay the national language and English the language of administration. The general literacy rate is over 92 percent.

History of Christianity in Singapore: 19th c. origins. With the establishment of a British settlement in Singapore by Stamford Raffles* in 1819, Protestant and Roman* Catholic missions began work among the European residents and then the Asians. The earliest Protestant groups to arrive were the London Missionary Society (LMS), the American Board of Commissioners for Foreign Missions, and the Church Missionary Society. The first Roman Catholic chapel was built in 1831; an Armenian church followed in 1835; the Anglican* St. Andrew's Church (now a cathedral) was consecrated in 1838; and the Malay Chapel (the forerunner of Presbyterian* churches) for local Malay-speaking Chinese was started by former LMS missionary Benjamin Keasberry* in 1843. English merchant Philip Robinson formed the first Christian Brethren congregation in 1864, and Anglo-American Methodist* missionaries from India*, William Oldham* and James Thoburn*, founded the Methodist Church in 1885. The Roman Catholics, Anglicans, Methodists, and Presbyterians set up mission schools whose graduates later provided significant indigenous leadership for both church and state.

20th-c. church growth. Western missionary impulse and initiative led to the founding of several more denominations: the Seventh-day* Adventists (1908), Assemblies of God (1933), Salvation* Army (1935), Southern Baptists* (1950), United Lutheran* Church of America (1952), and Church of Christ (1956). Asian Christians set up Syrian Christian and Chinese Baptist churches in the 1930s, and after the Pacific War several largely indigenous denominations were founded: the Bible*-Presbyterian Church (1950), the Bible Church (1958), Evangelical Free Church (1959), and Christian Nationals' Evangelism Commission (1960).

Alongside these young churches, several new evangelical parachurch organizations started ministries among students in schools, colleges, and universities, notably the Inter-Varsity Christian Fellowship (1952), Youth for Christ (1957), Scripture Union's Inter-School Christian Fellowship (1958), and Fellowship of Evangelical Students (1959). The Graduates' Christian Fellowship commenced its witness to professionals in 1955. In addition to the "mainline" Trinity Theological College, several more conservative Bible colleges and seminaries were started.

With the closure of mainland China* to foreign missions, the Overseas Missionary Fellowship of the China Inland Mission (OMF) established its international base in Singapore in 1951. The OMF assisted in the birth and growth of several churches and training institutions, including the Bible Church, Singapore Bible College, Discipleship Training Center, and Asian Missionary Training Institute (now the Asian Cross-Cultural Training Institute).

There was a steady increase of membership in the Catholic Church and in older Protestant denominations (united in the Malayan, now National, Council of Churches), and more rapid growth in the younger churches. Between 1970 and 1978, the number of Protestant congregations rose from 186 to 261. While Catholics outnumbered Protestants in 1970, the situation was reversed in 1980; the number of Catholics had grown by 11,000, and Protestants by nearly 74,000. The Navigators and Campus Crusade for Christ joined the Inter-Varsity Christian Fellowship and Catholic Students' Society in campus and other ministries.

In the 1970s and 1980s, many older denominations experienced charismatic* renewal, while independent charismatic churches were formed and flourished. The movement's leaders included the Anglican bishop Joshua Chiu Ban-It* and his successor, Moses Tay. Fundamental and evangelical churches also grew. The Singapore Billy Graham Crusade in 1978 provided the impetus for the formation in 1980 of the Evangelical Fellowship of Singapore (EFOS), comprising both churches and parachurch organizations. Several Crusade committee members, including its Brethren chairman Benjamin Chew, constituted the EFOS Council. The Singapore Center for Evangelism and Mission was also set up in 1980, reflecting growing concern for evangelistic outreach and overseas missionary service.

According to the census that year, about 9.9 percent of the resident population aged 10 and above were professing Christians (Catholic and Protestant). The proportion of Christians in 1990 increased to 12.5 percent (285,282). Significantly, among Singaporeans with tertiary education, over 30 percent were professing Christians (in the 1980 and 1990 census reports) — a testimony to faithful sowing, planting, and nurturing over the years.

Christians are involved in many areas of social welfare and community service. In addition to mission schools and community hospitals, they play an active part in youth counseling, prison and drug rehabilitation ministries, and various charitable institutions. The Singapore Council of Social Service and the Community Chest were led for many years by a Catholic layman, Ee Peng Liang. There is a higher percentage of Christians in parliament than their proportion in the population.

Bibliography

Foo, S. L., and S. Balachandrer, eds., *Singapore 1998* (1998). • Chew, Ernest, and Edwin Lee, eds., *A History of Singapore* (1991). • Doraisamy, T. R., *Forever Beginning: 100 Years of Methodism in Singapore,* 2 Vols. (1985-86). • Hinton, Keith, *Growing Churches Singapore Style* (1985). • Sng, Bobby E. K., *In His Good Time: The Story of the Church in Singapore, 1819-1992* (1993). • Turnbull, C. M., *A History of Singapore, 1819-1988* (1989). • Wong, James, *Singapore: The Church in the Midst of Social Change* (1973).

ERNEST CHEW CHIN-TIONG

Sino-Japanese War, 1894-1895

In the 19th c., Korea* was politically dominated by China*. By the second half of the century, Korea was of growing strategic and economic interest to Japan*, whose program of modernization had given it a renewed interest in both international affairs and the Korean iron and coal deposits, which were so crucial for industrialization. In 1875 Japan forced Korea to open its doors to international trade and to declare itself independent from the Chinese in its foreign policy. In 1885 Japan's involvement in Korean political reform movements almost provoked war with China; a war was averted by a treaty in which China pledged not to station troops in Korea. By 1894 Japan was more militarily confident. After the brutal suppression of Korean reform movements by the Chinese and the subsequent stationing of Chinese troops in Korea, Japan declared war on China on 1 Aug 1894. Japan's newly modernized military was able, by Mar 1895, to control most of Shantung and Manchuria, as well as all sea access to Beijing. China was forced to seek a peace treaty. In the end, it recognized Korean independence and ceded Formosa and the Pescadores to Japan, as well as giving a large indemnity to Japan and recognizing Japanese trading rights in parts of China.

Both northern China and Korea were subject to much greater foreign influence after the Sino-Japanese War, and with this, missionary influence increased. This was particularly important in Korea, where missionaries had been able to reside only since the 1880s. The war also seems to have led many Chinese and Koreans to reflect on the reasons for their national weakness. In Korea in particular, the number of converts increased sharply after 1894. At the same time, the humiliation of foreign domination, even if it meant independence from China for Korea, sparked internal reform movements sharply inimical to Western domination and sympathetic to the Communist movement taking shape in Russia (see Communism). The war also spurred Russia into greater involvement in the region as it protected its own strategic interests. Korea, whose internal political developments were of such interest to Japan and China in the late 19th c., remains a focal point of both strategic and ideological struggle in East Asia.

Bibliography

Hall, John Whitney, *Japan from Prehistory to Modern Times* (1970). • Hsu, Immanuel C. Y., *The Rise of Modern China* (1970). • Fairbank, John King, *China: A New History* (1992).

ROBERT A. HUNT

Sisters of Providence of Portieux, Cambodia

Installed in 1875 in the Cochin Chinese part of the apostolic vicariate of Phnom Penh (and in 1881 at Phnom Penh), the Sisters of Providence of Portieux constructed a nursery, a hospital, and later an orphanage and a home for the elderly according to the practice of the period. In 1905 they created similar works at Battambang, second city of the realm. Their charitable action in service to the most destitute has left a lasting memory, mentioned even in the nation's official schoolbooks.

After Cambodia* achieved independence, the sisters constructed a boarding house for 80 young girls at Kep on the coast. Their secondary school in Phnom Penh received more than 1,400 pupils, the majority of whom came from the Cambodian bourgeoisie, with a great majority of Vietnamese and Chinese (see Vietnam and China). The solid human and intellectual training, religious instruction, and contacts with teachers became the privileged ways of the apostolate.

In 1970 the Sisters of Providence of Cambodia numbered about 200, of whom scarcely nine were Cambodian. After the expulsion of the Vietnamese from Cambodia, only 49 nuns remained in the country, of whom nine were Khmer, five Chinese, 20 Vietnamese, and seven French. In 1975 the French sisters were expelled and the others sent to collective work projects. Three Khmer sisters and a dozen Vietnamese were executed by the Khmer* Rouge. In 1995 nine the nuns of Providence, including four Cambodians, were present in Cambodia.

Bibliography

Brown, Mary Borromeo, *History of the Sisters of Providence of Saint Mary-of-the-Woods* (1949). • Logan, Eugenia, *History of the Sisters of Providence*, Vol. II (1978). • Madden, Mary Roger, *The Path Marked Out: History of the Sisters of Providence of Saint Mary-of-the-Woods*, Vol. III (1991). • Mitchell, Penny Blaker, *Mother Theodore Guerin, A Woman for Our Time* (1998). • Wolf, Ann Collette, *Against All Odds: Sisters of Providence Mission to the Chinese* (1990).

FRANÇOIS PONCHAUD

Sisters of the Precious Blood

Hong Kong diocesan congregation of Chinese sisters whose vocation is to spread the Gospel among their Chinese compatriots.

The foundation of the Precious Blood congregation closely followed the development of the diocese of Hong Kong. It began as a third order (tertiaries) of the Canossian Daughters* of Charity in Hong Kong, an Italian missionary congregation whose policy is to recruit young local women to assist them in their work, to meet the missionary needs of the diocese. The local community, comprising laypeople and young women who freely offer themselves completely to God, was called the Canossian Tertiaries of Precious Blood Sisters. Those so inclined may join the community life of the Canossian Sisters, following a simple rule of life in accordance with the Canossian spirit.

In 1842 Antonio Feliciani succeeded Theodore Joset as prefect apostolic in Hong Kong. He suggested to the holy see that the missionary work in Hong Kong be entrusted to the Pontifical Foreign Missions Institute of Milan (PIME)*. On 12 Apr 1860, Fr. Burghignoli brought six Italian Canossian Sisters to Hong Kong, including Lucia Cupis, the assistant superior general and mistress of novices, who became the first superior of the Hong Kong region. They founded an English school and an orphanage for Chinese children. Unfamiliar with the local language and customs, the sisters, with the permission of the then prefect apostolic, Louis Ambrosi*, recruited two young Chinese to assist them in their work, Magdalen Tam and Anne Tam, who were formally accepted at a reception ceremony on 1 Aug 1861. They received their habit and began their novitiate on 11 Nov 1862. On 25 Dec 1863, they pronounced their first vows and became the first Canossian Tertiaries. Their habit is similar to the Canossian Sisters except for the color and the shape of the bonnet.

Concerned about future contribution of the Chinese sisters, the Hong Kong Vicariate decided to found a local congregation, with the rule of the tertiaries as a basis. In 1861, when in Italy to discuss the affairs of the diocese, Fr. Raimondi raised the question of the rule and obtained the pope's permission to found the congregation. In 1874, in Rome for his consecration as bishop, he again discussed the tertiaries' rule and constitutions with the pope. In 1890 he decided that the Canossian Tertiaries' constitutions should be the rule of life of the Tertiary Sisters.

Between 1904 and 1905, Dominic Pozzoni* brought from Italy the constitutions of the Precious Blood Sisters and translated them into Chinese after his consecration as bishop in 1905. He permitted the Chinese Canossian Sisters to adopt the translated version in 1912, naming it the "Constitution of the Precious Blood Sisters of Charity."

The Canossian Tertiaries remained under the authority of the Canossian superior until 1922, when they became an independent congregation of Chinese sisters after the apostolic letter *Maximum Illud* (1919) of Pope Benedict XV, which stressed three main points: (1) the local church should have local bishops; (2) local culture should be respected; and (3) religion and politics should be kept separate. Because of language problems, the superior appointed Magdalen Tam as facilitator of communication between the Chinese and the Italian sisters. She was also responsible for the care of the Chinese sisters, reading the rule and giving instructions. After her death, Clara Tam succeeded her. She later became the first superior of the Precious Blood congregation.

The tertiaries taught in a school, worked in an orphanage, or went out in pairs to evangelize in nearby villages Po On, Hoi Fung, Waiyeung, Sai Kung, and others. They did similar work when they became an independent congregation with 36 sisters and seven novices. In 1924 they opened Tak Ching Girls' School and Tak Ying Girls' School, followed by other schools later, including the Chi To Primary School.

Initially, the local congregation had financial problems. They had to work hard to supplement their allowances from the bishops' curia. Bishop Pozzoni and some priests helped obtain temporary housing and land on which to build a convent in Sai Wan Ho. On 7 Jun 1929, Bishop Henry P. Valtorta, in accordance with Vatican letter no. 1792/29, officially announced the establishment of the Congregation of the Precious Blood in the vicariate apostolic of Hong Kong. At the same time, the Congregation for the Propagation of the Faith granted Valtorta the authority to recognize retroactively the vows already taken. On 27 Jun 1929, the sisters moved to the present mother house on Un Chau Street in Kowloon. On 1 Jul 1929, Valtorta blessed the new convent. Eighteen days later Pope Pius XI declared the Precious Blood a local congregation. MARIA GORETTI LAU

Sitiawan Christian Settlement

A successful Methodist* experiment in Christian settlement in Sibu, Sarawak (see Sibu Christian Settlement), inspired a similar endeavor on the Malay Peninsula. H. L. E. Luering*, Methodist missionary at Ipoh, was approached by the Government Protector of Chinese in the state of Perak, on the west coast of Malaysia*, to go to China* and bring down a number of Christian Chinese settlers. The instability of the Chinese population in Perak at that time, with its chronic imbalance of males (roughly 4:1) and attendant problems of immorality, was a strong reason for this project. The government undertook to pay the passage of 500 families, each to be given three acres of land; the authorities would also support the colonists for the first six months, by which time their gardens were expected to bear fruit. The center of the new colony was to be Sitiawan, about 60 miles from Taping and Ipoh.

In 1903 Luering proceeded to Foochow, China, and selected 500 farmers from the Foochow District of the Methodist Church to migrate to Perak. Unfortunate delays in the survey work necessitated makeshift arrangements for the settlers on their arrival. They were surrounded by dense jungle in which wild elephants, tigers, panthers, and reptiles abounded. Some immigrants ran away in fear, others died of malaria, but the rest settled on their blocks of land (some 2,500 acres in all) and eked out a meager existence by planting sweet potatoes and rearing pigs for the market in Penang. Sunday services and prayer meetings had been held from the very beginning of the settlement, and, as the immigrants became more successful and prosperous in their agricultural efforts, they built their own church.

In the early days, Luering was assisted by William G. Shellabear* in the formation of the colony. Later, B. F. Van Dyke was appointed resident missionary and is especially remembered for founding the orphanage at Sitiawan. A pastor, Huong Paw Seng, came from China to minister to the Foochow congregation. In the meantime, rubber seeds, originally from Kew Gardens, London, had been planted in Sitiawan, and eventually the settlers, for whom rubber was an unknown crop, were persuaded to plant rubber in their holdings. This became the source of their later prosperity; by 1905, over 20,000 rubber trees had been planted. In 1928 the New Pioneer Church was dedicated in Kampong Koh in memory of the early pioneers of the Sitiawan settlement. In that year also, the Anglo-Chinese School, opened in 1912, reached an enrollment of 300 boys.

By the time the settlement celebrated its jubilee year in 1953, eight churches had been established and new congregations were coming up. Sitiawan remained an important Methodist Church center from which later generations of Christians spread the Gospel to other parts of Southeast Asia.

Bibliography

Annual Report of the Missionary Society of the Methodist Episcopal Church (1905, 1909). • *Minutes of the Malaysia Conference of the Methodist Episcopal Church* (1906). • *The Malaysia Message* (Sep 1921, Mar 1928). • Sng, Bobby E. K., *In His Good Time* (1980, 1993).

FRANK LOMAX

Sjarifuddin, Amir

(b. Medan, Sumatra, 27 May 1907; d. Ngalihan, Solo, Indonesia, Dec 1949). Fighter for the independence movement, politician, lawyer, and lay theologian; first minister of information in Indonesia*, minister of defense, and prime minister; only Christian to occupy the highest ministerial position in mainly Muslim Indonesia (see Islam).

Sjarifuddin grew up in a devout Muslim family but became Christian as a result of his high school education in Holland and his association with members of the Student Christian Movement* (SCM) in Jakarta. He studied law in Jakarta and was active in the Indonesian nationalistic movement (see Nationalism). In his political involvement, he did not join the various Christian parties but chose instead to be active in politics that were socialistic and revolutionary in character. Sjarifuddin believed it would not be possible to overthrow the Dutch colonial power and bring changes to the existing colonial structure through parties that were Christian based, because the Christian party was dominated by Dutch Christians who were not revolutionary enough and whose loyalty was to the Dutch colonial government, and also because Christians in Indonesia were a small minority (see Colonialism). Thus he believed Christians should join parties that were more nationalistic in orientation and try to influence them from within with their Christian ideals.

In his struggle for Indonesian independence, Sjarifuddin was inspired by the biblical books of Amos, Jeremiah, and Isaiah. He saw that the social conditions in Indonesia during the period of Dutch occupation were similar to the social situation of Israel during the 8th and 9th cs. B.C.E., characterized by injustice and oppression of the people by those in authority, which could only be ended through a social revolution. The Dutch government, perceiving Sjarifuddin as a dangerous enemy, jailed him, but he was later released through the help of his friend J. M. Schepper.

Sjarifuddin was also antifascist. During the Japanese occupation, he organized an underground movement to fight the Japanese (see Japan). He was accused of spying for the Dutch, was arrested and condemned to death, but the sentence was later commuted to life imprisonment. Sjarifuddin was still in jail in Malang, East Java*, when Indonesia declared her independence.

At the first constituted Indonesian cabinet, Sjarifuddin served as minister of information (1945). In 1948 he was made prime minister and was concurrently minister of defense. When he stepped down as prime minister in 1949, he opposed the government. He joined forces with the Indonesian Communist Party and rebelled against the government (see Communism). He was later executed by the government without due process of law.

Sjarifuddin was also a pioneer in the ecumenical* movement and a lay theologian in Indonesia. Throughout his life, he remained faithful to his church and his Christian faith. He preached often and even conducted choirs. During the Japanese occupation, he was asked to be the advisor of the Christian Unity Movement in Jakarta, comprising various Christian groups and initiated by the Japanese to garner support for their war effort. The movement later changed its name to the Organization for the Preparation of Christian Unity, and Sjarifuddin served as its chairman. Comprising 37 denominations in the Jakarta area, the organization dealt with internal quarrels between churches and was able to stop the atrocities of the Japanese and the Muslims against Christians. This body played a significant role in bringing unity among Christians in the Jakarta region.

Bibliography

Willem, F. D., *Mr. Amir Sjarifuddin, tempatnya dalam kekristenan dan dalam perjuangan kemerdekaan Indonesia* (1982). • Verkuyl, J., *Gedenken en verwachten. Memoires* (1983).

F. D. WELLEM

Skrefsrud, Lars Olsen

(b. Gudbrandsdalen, Norway, 4 Feb 1840; d. 11 Dec 1910). Scandinavian Lutheran* missionary, first of the Gossner Mission (1863-65) and then of the Nordic Santal Mission of India* for 40 years, and social reformer.

Skrefsrud lived almost half a century among the Santals. He and H. P. Boerresen, a Danish missionary, had to leave the Gossner Mission Society due to controversy with some senior missionaries. It was at this time that they met F. C. Johnson, the Baptist* missionary who was working among the Santals. The union of this trio led to the founding of the Ebenezer Mission to the Santals in 1857, establishing their work under the name of the Indian Home Mission (IHM) to the Santals. Later, in 1910, the official name of the mission was changed to the Santal Mission of the Northern Churches (SMNC).

The Santals are one of the largest aboriginal tribes of India, scattered over a wide area in Bihar, Orissa, West Bengal, Bangladesh*, and Assam, the majority living in Bihar. The mission was located in Genogaria, a village in the southeast of the Santal Parganas District.

Skrefsrud was the fifth child of a poor tenant farmer. His opportunity for formal education was very limited. He attended an ambulatory school between the ages of eight and 12, and also a Sunday school course in Lillehammer where secular subjects were taught.

Deeply influenced by the bad company he kept, Skrefsrud faced imprisonment for his misdeeds at Lillehammer and in Kristiania from Jun 1858 to 12 Oct 1861. Later, he was able to see this as a gateway to a new life. His mother, who belonged to the so-called Hangean Friends, a lay movement within the church of Norway, inspired Skrefsrud and made a deep impression on him in his childhood. Skrefsrud realized he was a sinner in a meeting of a Hangean preacher, Martinius Fremstad, an experience he later admitted was like "a new cloth put into an old garment." After much struggle, he joined the Gossner Mission Society. His conversion and missionary calling changed his life entirely, and as a missionary he was far ahead of his time.

At the time of Skrefsrud's arrival in Santal Parganas, the Santals were in a state of disintegration. Skrefsrud intervened in the internal fighting and disputes among the Santals. Personal experience had given him the conviction that even the most fallen person could be raised and restored to a new life. He felt himself to be the chosen instrument of a higher power, guided to the Santals to effect their spiritual transformation and social advancement.

Through Skrefsrud's rebaptism on 5 Apr 1868 at Calcutta, he was able to bring himself and the work he represented into a new relationship with the Baptists. In 1874, while in England, he consented to do deputation work for the Baptist Missionary Society (BMS). As a result of these meetings, he brought substantial funds back with him to India from Baptist churches in England. But his changed view in regard to baptism opened the way for him to be ordained in the Lutheran church. This took place on 26 Jul 1882 in Kristiania during his visit to Europe in 1881-83.

Skrefsrud influenced the organizations and development of the Santal church to a great extent. He wanted to establish a "Santal church in a Santal form" and often criticized those missionaries who tried to transplant a European form of Christianity. His efforts to form a national societal church had two basic characteristics: (1) a simple form for church organization contextualizing the simple principles of the apostolic church and molded as far as possible in conformity with the Santal sociocultural institutions; and (2) a positive understanding of the national character and customs of the people, emphasizing the social equality between Christians and non-Christians. Skrefsrud earnestly tried to let Christianity take a Santal form and consciously tried to allow the people, as far as possible, to retain their innocent customs. Converts were allowed to retain their old names, and in worship services the Santal national instrument and the drum were used.

Skrefsrud stressed the need for regular church order because, as early as 1874, the mission had won many converts through the mass movement in 1873-74. Pastors were assigned to look after the spiritual well-being of the people, and the elders' duty was to guard the local congregation. Older men of some experience and influence were appointed traveling elders. They received a small remuneration and traveled constantly, with their central residence remaining at Ebenezer. Three or four hundred workers, pastors, catechists, teachers, elders, and women workers, paid and unpaid, met on the last Sunday in the month. This monthly workers' meeting became a permanent institution, and regular communion services were held at the main station once each week. In all of these, Skrefsrud stressed the difference in the categories of service between the secular and the spiritual leaders and workers.

In 1877, after the break with the BMS, it became important and necessary for Skrefsrud and Boerresen to find a doctrinal basis for their mission that would be acceptable to all the different sectors of their supporters. Later they found the expression "Evangelical Protestant Mission" to suit their purpose and used it in the trust deed.

Though Skrefsrud had engaged himself in too many practical and administrative matters, he was a high-quality preacher too. For him, presenting the Word of God meant "presenting the food in their homely plates." He would not recognize any other means of conversion than the simple preaching of the Gospel, though he invariably made education the sequel to conversion. He loved to use similes taken from the life of the Santals, and it was noted that his preaching related to the Santal traditions. For instance, he often made allusions to the monotheistic notion of God as expressed in their traditions of Thakur as creator and preserver.

Skrefsrud's linguistic talent was tremendous and became legendary. He spoke 42 languages. His literary work can be classified into works of linguistic, religious, and social importance.

Skrefsrud's Santal grammar was a great step forward, laying the foundation for all later works on this language. It was regarded as a standard book of the highest quality. His linguistic works on Santali had for him a specific purpose: that of preparing himself for translating the Holy Scriptures into Santali. He had the New Testament Santali translation ready by 1880, and a part of the Old Testament as well (see Bible Translation).

Skrefsrud also made use of tunes sung at the different Santal festival and social occasions. His original hymns, based mainly on Scripture texts, were inspired and practical for proclaiming the Gospel. Being familiar with the tunes, non-Christians took readily to the hymns, and in this way certain Christian teachings were spread far into the Santal villages.

Skrefsrud could not avoid coming into contact with the social problems of the people among whom he was working, and so his social reform encompassed a wide field. Skrefsrud's active hands and involvement in questioning the readministration of Santal Parganas during 1871 and 1872 brought about great change toward peace and a well-functioning government. This also led to the Santal Parganas land settlement. In addition to being a staunch social reformer, Skrefsrud served as a nonofficial adviser to the government officers, and some lieutenant governors took his advice on many questions.

Skrefsrud also took a very active part in checking the Kherwars movement, which, as it grew, became an anti-Christian movement. Although he attended to all kinds of social matters among the Santals, he looked upon the Kherwars as a disturbing element to the peaceful social uplifting of the Santals.

Skrefsrud also fought against intemperance, encouraged education, established a Christian colony in Assam, and launched many other movements for the welfare of the people. In Jan 1909 he had a stroke, and two months later another. He died the following year.

Skrefsrud's books and publications include: (1) two editions of the hymnbook (in Santal); (2) *Girja Puthi* (1885), a church handbook containing the order of service together with the translation of the Sunday Gospel pericopes and the history of the passion of Christ; (3) a translation of Luther's *Small Catechism* (1885); (4) a translation of Volrath Vogt's *Bible Story Book* (1886); and (5) *Hor Hopionren Pera* (The Friend of Santals), a monthly Santal paper started in Apr 1890 that continued until Oct 1904.

Bibliography

Hodne, Olav, *L. O. Skrefsrud: Missionary and Social Reformer among the Santals of Santa Parganas, 1867-1881* (1966); *Santalen* (newspaper, 1886); *Eighteenth Annual Report* and *Fiftieth Annual Report* (on the Baptist mission to the Santals) (1867, 1868).

FRANKLYN J. BALASUNDARAN

Smith, Arthur Henderson (Ming En-bo)

(b. Vernon, Connecticut, 1845; d. California, 1932). American Board of Commissioners for Foreign Missions (ABCFM) missionary to China*.

After graduation from Beloit College at age 22, Smith furthered his studies at Union Seminary in New York (1870). In 1872, after marriage to Emma Jane Dickenson (1871), he was ordained a Congregational pastor and was sent to Tientsin, China, for mission work. In 1877 he was assigned the task of relieving famine in Shantung, and the mission work of the ABCFM was extended thereafter. This experience made clear for Smith the need to focus all mission work in China on the poor and hungry. In 1885 he began writing for Shanghai's *Zi Lin Xi Bao* (The North China Daily News and Herald) and published two works: *Chinese Civilization* and *Chinese Characteristics.* He also was a regular contributor to the *China Mail* (Hong Kong), *Chinese Recorder, Celestial Empire* (Shanghai), and *International Review of Missions.* These informed readers of the tradition of China and the present situation in China. From then on, Smith was called a China expert.

During the Boxer Rebellion*, Smith was trapped in Beijing (Peking). This experience became the foundation for his two-volume work *China in Convulsion* (1901). After the rebellion, Smith proposed that the Occident should use forces to suppress rebellion. In 1906, when he met the president of the United States, Theodore Roosevelt, he suggested that the American government refund to China's government part of the Indemnity of 1900, the result being that China could develop her education and encourage students to study in America. After this event, he wrote numerous articles in Christian journals stating that "it is the opportunity and responsibility of the USA to promote healthy development of China."

After World War I, Smith retired in America. When he passed away in 1932, the State Department of the United States sent a telegraph to his family commending him for making many suggestions that were beneficial to the United States in her relations with China.

Bibliography

Smith, Arthur H., *Chinese Characteristics* (1890); *Village Life in China* (1899); *Proverbs and Common Sayings from the Chinese* (1888); *Rex Christus: An Outline Study of China* (1903); *China in Convulsion; The Uplift of China* (1907); *China and America Today* (1907); *A Manual for Young Missionaries to China* (1918). • Hayford, Charles W., "Chinese and American Characteristics: Arthur H. Smith and His China Book," in *Christianity in China: Early Protestant Missionary Writings,* ed. Suzanne Wilson Barnet and John King Fairbank (1985); *Missionary Herald,* Vol. 120 (1924); Vol. 121 (1925); Vol. 129 (1933). • Pappas, Theodore D., "Arthur Henderson Smith and the American Mission in China," *Wisconsin Magazine of History,* Vol. 70 (1987).

China Group

Smith, George

(b. Wellington Somerset, England, 1815; d. 1871). Church Missionary Society (CMS) missionary and first English bishop in China*.

Smith was ordained after his master of arts studies at Oxford University. A member of the CMS, he went to China with Thomas McClatchie in 1844 to survey for suitable mission fields. His first exploratory visit took him to Hong Kong, Guangzhou, and Macau*. In May 1846 he went to Shanghai and Ningbo and decided that Ningbo would be suitable for a missionary center. He also explored Fuzhou and Xiamen. Ill health forced his return to England, where he was conferred an honorary doctorate in theology. In 1849 he was consecrated bishop of Victoria, Hong Kong, with jurisdiction over all English clergy in China. He developed St. Paul's College in 1847 from a class for boys started by Vincent Stanton, a colonial chaplain, and he brought a group of missionaries with him to Hong Kong in 1850. During the Taiping Rebellion*, a cannonball struck the church building in Shanghai in which Smith was speaking. After the ratification of the Treaty of Tianjin in 1860, which opened up inland China to missionary work, Smith tried unsuccessfully to persuade the CMS to send more personnel to reinforce the six missionaries in China (three in Ningbo, two in Shanghai, and one in Fuzhou). In 1863 he ordained Dzaw Gang-lac, his first Chinese deacon in Shanghai.

In 1860 Smith's wife established the Diocesan Native Female Training School in Hong Kong. The school aimed at training teachers and suitably educated spouses for the male converts of St. Paul's College. Smith retired to England in 1864, where he remained until his death.

Bibliography

Smith, George, *A Narrative of an Exploratory Visit . . . to Hong Kong and Chusan . . . 1844, 1845, 1846* (1857); *Our National Relations with China* (1857); *The Jews of Kai-Fung-Foo.* • Latourette, Kenneth Scott, *A History of Christian Missions in China* (1929). • Murray, Jocelyn, *Proclaim the Good News* (1985). • Stock, Eugene, *History of the Church Missionary Society* (1889). • Yates, Yimothy E., *Venn and Victorian Bishops Abroad* (1978).

China Group

Social Action, Roman Catholic

Organized, coordinated effort to effect concrete changes in society toward a greater measure of justice, focusing on every area in which injustice operates (e.g., unjust labor conditions, rural and urban poverty, infringements of human rights).

The complexities of modern society, e.g., aggressive industrialization, laissez-faire economic development, repressive political regimes, the negative effects of technological modernization, all cause serious imbalances and fissures in the social order. These social problems cannot be solved by private charity. They demand organized, coordinated efforts at different levels — local, national, and international — to effect needed structural and institutional changes in order to produce greater justice for all. Each of these efforts is called social action. They endeavor to affect the causes of social problems and not just alleviate their symptoms, which is the role of charitable works.

The Catholic Church has always engaged in charitable works. But as a whole, it was slow to act in the area of social injustice. A major reason was that disruptions in the social order were accepted as unavoidable, historical accidents which should be alleviated by numerous initiatives of charity. One of the earliest Catholic social reformers to influence Catholics in Asia was the French professor Fredric Ozanam (1813-53), founder of the St. Vincent de Paul Society. His method of alleviating the sufferings of the poor, by personal service to them in their homes, anticipated some of the methods of modern social work. His lectures expounded a social doctrine that foreshadowed Pope Leo XIII's social encyclical in 1891.

Catholic social doctrine based on sources such as Scripture and tradition has always upheld the primacy of the sacredness and dignity of every human person made in the image and likeness of God. To render service to the victims of indignity caused by the defects and disorders of existing society is the universal basis of Catholic social action. Moreover, the consciousness that Jesus Christ has identified himself in a special way with the victims of injustice makes serving them a test of one's discipleship (Matt. 25:31-46).

But this universal Catholic social doctrine has to be applied in new and creative ways to the social problems produced by the constant changes in different societies. The resultant Catholic social teachings are contained in the social encyclical letters of the popes. The social encyclicals from Pope Leo XIII on the "Condition of the Working Class" (*Rerum Novarum,* 1891) to Pope John Paul II's "Hundred Years Later" (*Centesimus Annus,* 1991) on the global significance of the collapse of Communism in 1989 provide a distinctive Catholic approach to contemporary social problems.

However, understanding the relevance of papal social teaching to a local situation implies a hermeneutical exercise on the part of the local church. Pope Paul VI emphasized, "It is up to the Christian communities to analyze with objectivity the situation which is proper to their own country, to shed on it the light of the gospel's unalterable words, and to draw principles of reflection, norms of judgement, and directives for action from the social teaching of the church" ("Call to Action," *Octogesimo Adveniens,* 1971).

Vatican Council II (1962-65) provided the modern foundation for Catholic social action in Asia. The Pastoral Constitution on the Church in the Modern World (*Gaudium et Spes,* 1965) spells out the Catholic Church's social mission in theological terms. The "social question" becomes a "theological question" about the self-identity of the church and her relationship with the world.

The Church sees herself in the midst of human society as a visible sign of the already existing intimate union with God that is shared by the whole human family. Its mission is to transform the human family from within as a leaven and a kind of soul for human society. For the "earthly and heavenly city [to] penetrate each other . . . is accessible to faith alone." The Church believes that only God, whom she struggles to serve, meets the longings of the human heart for liberation from all bondage, which is ultimately caused by sin — personal sin as well as sinful structures which create widespread violations of human dignity and rights. She is also painfully aware that Christ's Gospel of human liberation may be better practiced in certain sectors of society than in the church. So she both speaks and listens to the world.

The role of the Church in the sphere of culture is not to be bound exclusively to any particular culture, but to renew and transform every culture from within. In the economic, social, and political spheres, her role is more to provide enlightenment and spiritual energy for temporal tasks than to draw up a blueprint for the social order.

The next 10 years (1965-75) spawned some extraordinary documents of crucial significance to social action in the Catholic Church in Asia. The most notable was "Justice in the World" (1971), produced by the synod of bishops, that made social action an integral part of the Church's social mission. Action on behalf of justice and participation in the transformation of the world are constitutive dimensions of the preaching of the Gospel, or, in other words, of the Church's mission for the redemption of the human race and its liberation from every oppressive situation. Pope Paul VI wrote three encyclicals that crystallized the Church's consciousness of its social mission. In the "Development of the Peoples" (*Progressio Populorum,* 1967), he emphasized that the whole human person and all human persons are the central focus of development even as "the social question has become worldwide." In a "Call to Action" (*Octogesimo Adveniens,* 1971), he recognizes that many new social problems have emerged that are extremely difficult to resolve. However, despite these difficulties, Christians must become involved in the process of social reform as their response to the demands of the Gospel. In "Evangelization in the Modern World" (*Evangelii Nuntiandi,* 1975), he links the Church's mission of evangelization with liberation as "a constitutive part, not only of preaching the Gospel, but also of upsetting, through the power of the Gospel, humankind's criteria of judgement."

Social action is now seen as a ministry of justice because the gifts of grace and charity demand, as an essential element in their fulfillment, a recognition of the dignity and rights of our neighbors. Two meetings in Asia reflected on 100 years of Catholic social teaching. The colloquium of the Asian bishops' Office for Human Development and the seminar of the Asian Center for Prog-

Social Action, Roman Catholic

ress of Peoples (ACCP, Mar 1992) — a regional grassroots network — were both critical of the lack of an Asian perspective in Catholic social teaching. The Eurocentric perspective can be corrected only by "a new inductive methodology beginning from Asian praxis," asserted ACCP.

There was some early evidence of Catholic social action in Asia. Jesuit (see Society of Jesus) missionary Walter Hogan organized a social action network in Asia called Socio-Economic Life in Asia (SELA) in 1959. It expanded into the Bureau of Asian Affairs (BAA) a decade later. In India*, a diocesan priest, Fr. Vadakkan, led a struggle against peasant eviction and landlordism in Kerala in 1961, despite widespread opposition from the bishops.

A major reason for the cautiousness of the Catholic Church in the field of injustice, despite the social teachings of the popes, was that in practically every Asian country the church was established by foreign missionaries as a colonial transplant from above, not an indigenous growth from below. The foreign missionaries collaborated closely with the colonial officials to alleviate the distressing effects of colonization on the poor through numerous institutions such as orphanages, schools, and hospitals (see Colonialism). But the causes of poverty created by colonization itself were never addressed. The indigenous clergy and laity accepted the colonial mind-set and hardly joined the independence struggles.

However, a landmark date for Catholic social action in Asia was 1965. It was the ending of Vatican II, the year the Indochina war escalated and Mao launched the Cultural Revolution in China (see Communism). The first Priests' Institute for Social Action (PISA) organized an Asian movement of priests under the initiative of SELA. With it, social action entered the mainstream of the Catholic social apostolate. It ignited a series of events in social action extending into the next three decades.

PISA brought together many scattered initiatives of Catholic inspiration that were germinating: farmers and workers movements, a federation of free farmers, a federation of Asian trade unions, research and training centers, an Asian social institute (Manila) and Indian social institute (New Delhi), and an institute of social order (Manila).

The next major event was the Baguio Colloquy (1969) organized in Asia by the German Catholic funding agency *Misereor.* Inspired by the success of PISA, it recommended the establishment of a regional office to motivate, encourage, and coordinate the social action efforts within the Catholic Church in Asia. This became a reality in 1972 as the Office for Human Development (OHD) of the Federation of Asian Bishops' Conferences* (FABC).

Social action in the Catholic Church in Asia began to emerge at two distinct levels after 1965. At the grassroots level, movements of Catholic activists became more discernible. These movements were among workers, university and school students, intellectuals, priests, sisters, and religious orders of men and women. The workers joined the Young Christian Workers* (YCW) movement inspired by Belgian priest (later cardinal) Joseph Cardign to act in their working milieu. The school students followed similar inspiration to found the Young Christian Students (YCS) movement. By the late 1960s the International Movement of Catholic Students (IMCS) began discussing topics like "Christianity in the Asian Revolution" and "From Social Service to Structural Reform of Society." Catholic intellectuals formed the International Catholic Movement for Intellectual and Cultural Affairs (ICMICA). The religious orders of women formed the Asian service center for religious women, now called Asian Meeting of Religious (AMOR). Religious orders of men and women formed the Asia-Oceania Forum of Religious for Justice and Peace (1985) that grew into the International Forum of Religious for Global Solidarity (IFRGS, 1993). All these were federations of local, national, and transnational organizations of Catholic men and women.

At the level of the hierarchy, the FABC was formed. It resolved at its initial meeting in Manila (1970) to commit itself more truly, in Asia and with Asians, to become the church of the poor. This mandate was given to its OHD, which conducted seven Bishops' Institutes for Social Action (BISA, 1974-86), numerous Asian Institutes for Social Action (AISA, 1987-91), and has now initiated a program of Faith Encounters in Social Action (FEISA, 1994) to emphasize the interreligious dimension of social action. The OHD also coordinated the justice and peace network of the FABC from 1979, out of which emerged Hotline, a human rights network to meet urgent appeals, and the now autonomous Committee of Asian Women (CAW), an Asian women workers' network. Both have their secretariats in Hong Kong*. OHD joined the Christian Conference of Asia* (CCA) to form an ecumenical community-organizing network called Asian Committee for Peoples Organization (ACPO, 1971).

Two seminars by Canon Houtart on religion and development (Bangalore, 1973, and Baguio, 1975) have had widespread impact in Asia by analyzing the negative role of religion in supporting exploitative structures on the one hand and looking after the victims of exploitation on the other.

Another ecumenical venture of OHD and CCA was the Ecumenical Coalition on Third World Tourism (ECTWT, 1982), organized to address issues of injustice in tourism in the Third World.

The Catholic Church in Asia has been wary of social activism because of the fear of the infiltration of Communism* and its atheistic ideology. Brazilian Archbishop Helder Camara's remark is pertinent to Asia, where Mother Teresa is venerated as a saint: "When I feed the poor, they call me a saint; when I ask why they are poor, they call me a communist."

The social question is now also a spiritual question. There are two possible starting points for living out one's faith in the heart of the world. The first is to fix one's gaze on God and strive to translate into daily life one's logic of faith. The other begins with the joys and sufferings of people and traces a path from them to God. However, it is not easy to find the point of equilibrium between an active and involved faith and a prayerful and contemplative life. The Caritas* International's seminar toward a spirituality of social action (Bangalore, 1980) attempted to articulate an adequate spirituality.

Serious tensions, evident particularly among the young, have arisen between the so-called spiritual Catholics who are considered not sufficiently mindful of the social dimension of the Gospel, and the socially committed Catholics who risk emptying the risen Christ from the Gospel. One group wishes the church to be neutral in sociopolitical matters and confine itself to purely religious matters of converting individuals to Christ, so that they may subsequently assume their responsibility in sociopolitical matters. The other group regards human advancement and cultural, economic, and political liberation as an integral dimension of the Gospel.

A spectrum of responses emerge from these two views of spirituality*. One response is that questions of social justice and political power lie outside the scope of the church. Only when economic and political questions touch the individual Christian's interior life and conscience or when the rights of the church as an institution are infringed upon should the church respond. A second response sees social realities such as poverty*, deprivation, oppression, and suffering as God's will. They provide the Christian with occasions for either meritorious endurance or virtuous generosity. A third response chooses to address poverty, misery, and suffering by providing relief and undertaking emergency measures, but not addressing the causes. The fourth response identifies the root cause of poverty, misery, and suffering as backwardness. It seeks to introduce new technology into industry, agriculture, and communications to achieve maximum efficiency. While this response helps some who gain control over the technology, it further impoverishes others who are marginal to the modernization process. The Green Revolution and foreign aid are good examples of this response. The fifth response comes from those individual Christians and groups who are struggling for structural change. It is their conviction that the present economic, political, and cultural structures must be replaced by new structures that are not exploitative at all or at least less exploitative.

Bibliography

Digan, Parig, *Churches in Contestation* (1984). • Dorr, Donald, *The Social Justice Agenda* (1991).

Desmond de Sousa

Social Ethics (Shakai Rinri), Japan

The way a person lives in relation to society.

In Christianity, salvation is not something based on moral actions, but rather on God's grace through Jesus Christ. Anyone who has been saved by God's grace will strive to do good works. Actions done in answer to God's grace are not limited to neighborly relations but apply also to the fields of politics, business, and society.

Christianity of the early Meiji Period encouraged ethical thinking, with its emphasis on monogamy, temperance, and hard work; moderation and honesty were seen as virtues. Confucian ethics provided the groundwork for the acceptance of these ethics (see Confucianism). It is important to note that Kozaki Hiromichi*, in his book *Seikyo shinron* (New Theory of Religion and Politics), written in 1886, gave a Christian critique of the controlling structure of the emperor system with the emperor at the top. Neesima Jo* advocated the development of persons with dignity to support one's country, pushing for their participation in that structure. From its beginnings, Christianity has promoted the education of girls and women*, exerting efforts to raise the social position of women in society. In 1886 the Japan Women's Christian Temperance Union was founded, emphasizing temperance, abolition of prostitution, and peace, initiating a movement to respect the rights of women. Yamamuro Gumpei of the Salvation* Army also emphasized temperance and the abolition of prostitution, extending himself to abolishing the red-light districts. Ishii Juji* and Tomeoka Kosuke, both Christians, were modern-day pioneers in social work who fought hard for universal human rights.

In the late 19th c., Japan's modernization took a nationalistic path centered on the emperor system and soon acquired an ultranationalistic tinge (see Nationalism). Christianity as a whole became incorporated into this national structure, but a few Christians stood firm in their faith, carrying out their Christian social responsibility. The first group included Uchimura Kanzo* and those influenced by him. Guided by Scripture, they opposed the absolutization of all things and emphasized pacifism. The Uchimura Kanzo Disrespect Incident and his antiwar stance at the time of the Russo-Japanese War are specific actions reflecting this. Later, in 1936, one of Uchimura's disciples, Yanaihara Tadao, wrote *Minzoku to heiwa* (Ethnicity and Peace); another, Nambara Shigeru, published *Kokka to shukyo* (The State and Religion) in 1942. Both spoke out against absolutizing the nation. The second wave included Yoshino Sakuzo, Nakajima Shigeru, and Imanaka Tsugumaro. These men were influenced by Ebina Danjo; theologically, they took a liberal stance, but in their social ethics they sought mediation with politics, and from the 1920s to the early 1930s they defended democracy, criticizing the elevation of the nation-state above all else. The nation-state should exist for the social welfare of its people, they said. The third group was made up of Abe Iso, Murai Tomoyoshi, Kishimoto Nobuta, and Suzuki Bunji, all of Unitarian thinking, who took a critical stance against the estrangement of humanity found in capitalistic society. They emphasized socialism from a broadly Christian standpoint. Their liberal stance caused them to be isolated from the church, but Kashiwagi Gien, remaining in the church as a pastor and standing on an evangelistic faith, continued to push for socialism and pacifism.

In the fourth group we could include those Christians who underwent great persecution during the war because they refused to compromise their faith. One group of them included Akashi Junzo (who refused military service) and the Holiness group who, from an eschatological stance, remained loyal to Christ even though it meant enduring terrible suffering. Their faith was a simple one, but it gave them the strength to stand up against the absolutization of the emperor and the state. The fifth group, largely the established church, lost the energy it had had in the mid-19th c. and gradually became a bourgeois organization; upon entering the 20th c., they gradually adjusted to the nationalistic fervor of the times and were mobilized on the side of the state during the war. In the 1930s, Kagawa Toyohiko*, Sugiyama Motojiro, and others founded the Agricultural Cooperative Union; under the leadership of Nakajima Shigeru and others, socialistic Christian ideals were brought forward, but with the introduction of dialectic theology their liberal standpoint underwent a critical examination in the quest to find a relationship between Christianity and Japan's* nationalistic thought. After World War II*, when theologians like John C. Bennett and Emil Brunner came to Japan, theological interest in Christian ethics deepened, and issues of peace, labor, occupation, marriage, and gender were examined anew. Since the latter half of the 1960s, different churches have dealt with issues such as Christians' war responsibility, the Yasukuni* Shrine, and human rights, as the social responsibility of Christians has been explored.

Bibliography

Dohi Akio, *Nihon purotesutanto kirisutokyo shi* (History of Japanese Protestant Christianity) (1980). • Kudo Eiichi, *Shakai undo to kirisutokyo* (Social movements and Christianity) (1972); *Kirisutokyo to buraku mondai* (Christianity and the Buraku issue) (1983). • Sumiya Mikio, *Nihon shihon shugo to kirisutokyo* (Japanese capitalism and Christianity) (1962); *Gendai nihon to kirisutokyo* (Modern Japan and Christianity) (1962). • Sumiya Mikio, ed., *Nihon in okeru kirisutokyo to shakai mondai* (Christianity in Japan and social issues) (1963). • Doshisha University Humanities Research Office, eds., *Nihon no kindaika to kirisutokyo* (Modernization of Japan and Christianity) (1973). • Tomura Masahiro, ed., *Jinja mondai to kirisutokyo* (The shrine problem and Christianity) (1976). • Nakajima Shigeru, *Shakaiteki kirisutokyo gairon* (Introduction to socialistic Christianity) (1928). • Shimada Keiichiro, *Fukuin to shakai* (The Gospel and society) (1971). • Kumano Yoshitaka, *Nihon kirisutokyo shingaku shisoshi* (The history of Japanese Christian theological thought) (1968). • Morioka Iwao and Sasahara, *Kirisutokyo no senso sekinin* (Christian war responsibility) (1974). • NCC-CCRAI, *Ajia no shukyo to sabetsu* (Asian religions and discrimination) (1984). • Franklin, Samuel H., *Kirisutokyo shakai ronri gairon* (Introduction to Christian social ethics) (1964).

TAKANAKA MASAO, JAPANESE DICTIONARY

Socialism (Shakai Shugi), Japan

A way of thinking that seeks to realize its goals by parliamentary means, direct action, or even violent revolution, seeking social resolution of the class inequalities inherent in the capitalist method of distribution of products.

With the rise of Japanese capitalism came the organizing of the Socialism Study Group in Oct 1898 and the Socialist Association in Jan 1900 that called for the abolition of armaments and the hierarchical system, the turning of privately owned land into public land, the holding of regular elections, and the dismantling of the House of Peers. These groups organized the Social People's Party and then had it banned that same day. The beginnings of the socialist movement are deeply indebted to Christian socialists such as Murai Tomoyoshia, Abe Iso, Katayama Sen, Kinoshita Naoe, Ishikawa Sanshiro, Nishikawa Kojiro, and Kawakame Kiyoshi, who saw the equality of humanity before God and love of the neighbor as basic Christian beliefs. In Nov 1903 two materialistic socialists, Kotoku Shusui and Sakai Toshihiko, speaking out against the Russo-Japanese War and for socialism, formed the *Heiminsha* (Society of Commoners) and began publishing a weekly newspaper, *Heimin shimbun* (Nov 1903 to Jan 1905). The Christian socialists lent their cooperation to this effort; pastors and laypeople from rural areas also supported it; promoters also emerged. In Oct 1905, after the breakup of *Heiminsha*, Kinoshita Abe and Ishikawa stated their arguments in the publications *Shin kigen* ("New Era," Nov 1905 to Nov 1906) and then *Sekai fujin* ("Woman of the World," Jan 1907 to Jul 1909). In contrast to the severe anarchistic methods used by Kotoku and others (owing to the severe pressure they were under), these men were generally more parliamentary policy-oriented in what they said. In the end, most of them finally withdrew from the movement.

The creation of capitalistic monopolies stimulated by World War I caused a push for the restructuring of the society and the expansion and intensification of the labor movement. Kagawa Toyohiko*, leading the *Yuaikai So Domei* (a nationwide labor movement), spoke out for guild socialism, but syndicalism took over the leadership of the movement, so Kagawa withdrew. With the labor union and farmers' union as parent groups, a proletarian movement emerged with Christians like Abe, Katayama Tetsu, and Kawakami Jotaro as active members. After the war, the various factions joined and, calling for socialistic policies, formed the Japan* Socialist Party. These men became party leaders, but whether a theoretical connection between Christianity and socialism was ever confirmed is not clear.

Bibliography

Matsuzawa Koyo, *Nihon shakai shugi no shiso* (Japanese socialist thought) (1973).

DOHI AKIO, JAPANESE DICTIONARY

Society of Jesus

(Jesuits, SJ). The Society of Jesus was founded by St. Ignatius Loyola in Paris in 1534. The new order was approved by Pope Paul III in 1540 in the bull *Regimini Militantis Ecclesiae.* From the start, it was an order concerned both for reform and education in the church ("Spiritual Exercises") as well as missionary outreach in Asia and Europe. One of Loyola's first six companions was St. Francis Xavier*, who was the first missionary of the post-Reformation era to reach the East Indies and Japan*. By 1600 the Jesuits had over 8,500 members serving in five continents.

The Jesuit presence and contribution to Asia through the centuries begins with the high-profile arrival of the first Jesuit, St. Francis Xavier. He was a cofounder of the Society of Jesus in Goa on 6 May 1542 as a missionary of the Portuguese *Padroado**, a Jesuit superior, and the papal nuncio to the East Indies (from the Cape of Good Hope to China* and Japan). Xavier sallied back and forth from his base at Goa, visiting and laboring at the Fishery Coast of South India*, Malacca*, the Moluccas*, and even Japan. Xavier and his successors did not admit any locals into the Society but took initiatives to utilize their talents. A significant contribution of the Jesuit presence in Asia was Xavier's establishment of a "school of native boys" at St. Paul's in Goa, which trained African and Asian boys as catechists and even ordained them as secular clergy to assist the white missionaries. In 1563 the school had 645 students. Later the number rose to 800. It was a significant step in recognizing the importance of vernacular languages and cultures for missionary work. In fact, Xavier's insight into the importance of local cultures became the foundation for all modern missions. Xavier's successors in India and elsewhere in Asia have made fundamental contributions to vernacular languages with the publication of grammars, vocabularies, and religious literature that has fostered the cultural growth of Asian people. The Jesuits Henrique Henriques*, Thomas Stephens, Diogo Ribeiro, Karel Prykrill, John Ernst Hanxleden, Angelo Maffei, Joseph Beschi, and John Baptist Hoffman are some of the outstanding contributors to different Indian languages, since they introduced the first printing press in Asia in 1556. The work of Robert De Nobili* in India, Matteo Ricci* in China, João Rodrigues Tçuzzu in Japan, and Pedro Chirino in the Philippines* is already well known internationally. This tradition of Jesuit linguistic contribution continues in every country where the Jesuits are active and maintain educational establishments.

It was from Goa that the Jesuits fanned out to the rest of Asia. By 1600 they had 69 houses staffed by 464 Jesuits, including 310 in India, Malacca, the Moluccas, and Ethiopia. The remainder were in Japan and China. After 1601, new administrative provinces came into existence, starting with the province of Cochin. Japan and China followed suit. These continued to depend on revenues from Goa and the properties the Jesuits owned in the Portuguese province of the North, with its capital at Bassein (north of Goa). In Goa the Jesuits were asked by the government to administer the Royal Hospital, which cared largely for the sick passengers who arrived after long and painful voyages from Lisbon and elsewhere. The Jesuits have administered the hospital since 1579. A Jesuit brother, Gaspar Antonio, became well known for his invention of "cordial stones," which were sought after as antidotes for poisoning. They brought in large revenues to the Jesuits at St. Paul's College.

The Jesuits combined normal religious missionary activity with diplomatic missions when the need arose. The Moghul emperor Akbar had Jesuits residing at his court of Fatehpur-Sikri (Agra). They continued there during the terms of his successors, who outlived by a few years the suppression of the Society of Jesus by Pombal in Portugal and its outposts overseas in 1759. Though the Jesuits soon realized the futility of their efforts in the Moghul court to achieve the conversion of the emperors, they continued to be useful political informants for the Portuguese viceroys in Goa.

Their high sense of discipline and militancy, with a centrally controlled organization that allowed significant leeway for individual creativity, was largely responsible for their rapid missionary success in the wake of the establishment of the Portuguese *Estado da India.* However, even Xavier was not always above human blindness. While taking initiative to utilize local talent, neither he nor his successors could think of admitting Asians (excepting Japanese, who were considered white) into the Society of Jesus until after the suppression of the Old Society. Ironically, their illusions about Japan came almost to nought in their own lifetimes, while India can today boast the third-largest ethnic group of Jesuits in the world, nearing 3,000. The relics of Xavier in India continue to witness to this phenomenal growth.

At the time of the suppression of the Society by the authorities of Portugal, France, and Spain (the Bourbon rulers), actions that were later confirmed by the papacy, the Jesuits had earned as much praise as hatred. Their ability to finance their activity had raised many questions and aroused much envy. They had also angered most other religious orders by their "airs of superiority." The last official historian of the Old Society, Julio Cesare Cordara, described two causes for the suppression of the Society: natural (human hatred and malice) and supernatural (God's design). He believed that the Almighty had permitted it as a punishment for the Jesuits' sin, namely, the "subtle vice of pride, from which God shrank back." The Society was restored in 1814 for almost the same reason that it was initially established — to back up a beleaguered papacy. It did not take the papacy long to realize what it had lost with the suppression of the Society. Some people were inclined to see this restoration as part of the wider process taking place in Europe with the Congress of Vienna, and therefore a reactionary development to it. The restored Society of Jesus has served in the new dispensation of European imperialism in Asia with its network of educational and charitable works. If the numerically insignificant Christian minority in Asia is looked upon with respect, it is due in some measure to the educational contribution of about 5,000 Jesuits in Asia (1992).

Bibliography

Wessels, C., *Early Jesuit Travellers in Central Asia, 1603-1721* (1924). • Correia-Afonso, John, *Jesuit Letters and Indian History* (1955). • De Souza, Teotonio R., ed., *Jesuits in India: In Historical Perspective* (1992); *Discoveries, Missionary Expansion, and Asian Cultures* (1994). • Costello, M. Joseph, trans., *The Letters and Instructions of Francis Xavier* (1992).

China. The Jesuit Francis Xavier, sent by both Pope Paul III and St. Ignatius of Loyola, traveled to India and then Japan, arriving at the isolated island of Shangchuan near the coast of Guangzhou in 1552. He died there without setting foot on the mainland because of the severe maritime restrictions. Though Xavier is referred to as the "Apostle of the Orient," the pioneer of modern Chinese mission is another Jesuit missionary, Matteo Ricci* (1552-1610). He was one of the few missionaries who had gained access to China and was accepted because of his linguistic and scientific abilities. He set up the early homes for other Jesuit missionaries in Zhaoqing, Shaozhou, Nanchang, Nanjing, and Beijing (Peking). The Jesuits were the only missionaries in China between the 1580s and 1620s. Other congregations, such as the Franciscans*, Dominicans*, Augustinians*, and Paris Foreign Mission Society* (MEP) arrived in China after 1630 or thereabouts. The Jesuits remained the most numerous, numbering 59 of a total of 103 missionaries at the beginning of the 18th c., and they served the royal court with their expertise in science and technology: calendar, mapping, music, medicine, etc. The persecution started during the reign of Emperor Yongzheng, who ascended the throne in 1723, and it continued during the reign of his successor, Qianlong, who ascended the throne in 1736. Propagation was forbidden, the Society of Jesus was dissolved, and the remaining Jesuits in Beijing were later replaced by Lazarists* from France and Portugal. Bishop Laimleckhoven*, who died in hiding near Poudon in 1787, was the last Jesuit in China until 1842, when Jesuits once again returned to China after the Society was restored in 1814. Propaganda Fide* established the Jian-nan pontifical diocese and entrusted its administration to the Jesuits, who arrived in considerable numbers to run seminaries, schools, printing establishments, churches, observatories, and museums. Local Chinese were admitted into the Society from 1867. In 1949 there were six dioceses run by the Jesuits: Shanghai, Xianxian, Anqing, Bangfu, Yuanhu, and Jiengxian, with 800 missionaries, both foreign and indigenous.

China Group, translated by Dufresse Chang

Indonesia. Francis Xavier worked for two years (1545-47) in the Moluccas, sending newly arriving Jesuits to its deserted Christian villages. He visited the islands of Ambon, Ternate, and Morotai, thus laying the groundwork for the beginning of the Jesuit Moluccan Mission* (1545-1666).

Though a few Jesuits tried to serve the few Catholics in the Dutch Indies, they were unable to do much permanent work. In Macassar they looked after the Portuguese refugees from Malacca (1646-68), and in Batavia (Jakarta) they secretly visited the Mardjikers, former Portuguese and Catholic Indians sent as slaves to Batavia and freed after formally converting to the Reformed Church (see Presbyterian and Reformed Churches). Aegidius d'Abreu* was killed in Jakarta, and A. de Rhodes* was sentenced to death but was released and deported from under the gallows (1646). Only Governor-General Maetsuyker, who studied at a Jesuit college in Belgium, protected Jesuits against the protests of the (Reformed) Church Council. He and J. F. A. d'Almeida, the first translator of the Bible* into Portuguese, were accused of being crypto-Jesuits.

In 1859 two Jesuits invited by the apostolic vicar of Batavia took over the parishes of Semarang and Surabaya on the island of Java*. Due to new arrivals, they settled also on eastern Flores, in Larantuka (1862), Maumere (1873), Sikka (1884), and Timor* (Atapupu, 1883). Thanks to the Dominican missions of the 16th c., the church in eastern Flores grew quickly and was handed over to Society of the Divine Word* (SVD) missionaries (1919). Health care services (smallpox injections), schools, and riding missionaries made Flores a Catholic island. Minahasa (northern Celebes*), the Kei Archipelago (Moluccas), and western Borneo were other Jesuit mission fields. These were transferred to other missionary orders in the early 20th c.

Since the first decade of this century, the Jesuits concentrated on Java and finally on Central Java only. After several failures, Franz van Lith*, who spent years studying the Javanese language and culture, was able to baptize the first large group of village people in Sendangsono (1904). By building a network of schools and some teacher training colleges and by carefully selecting pupils, well-trained and engaged lay apostles have fully supported the evangelization since the late 1920s. Candidates for the novitiate and the major seminary were accepted in the 1920s. In 1926 the first Javanese Jesuit was ordained, and in 1940 A. Soegijapranata* became the first Indonesian bishop. Most of the Dutch Jesuits suffered in Japanese concentration camps. Ten Indonesian and Dutch Jesuits were murdered by religious fanatics during the struggle for independence (Magelang 1945, Muntilan 1948). Since the 1950s, the Jesuits have concentrated their work on the apostolic vicariates of Jakarta and Semarang. Besides slowly handing over many parishes to the growing number of secular priests, the Society has put more and more of its members to work at secondary and vocational schools, retreat houses (Giri Sonta and Sangkal Putung in Central Java, Civita in Jakarta), lay leadership training courses and literature*, mass media, and social works (Catholic trade union: *Ikatan Pancasila;* political prisoners on the island of Burn; Vietnamese refugees on Galang Island, SODEPAXI secretariat). A (vice)province of its own (1971), many of Central Java's 246 members (1992) work in centers for catechetical education, focusing on pastoral and spiritual care and church-music* development; in agricultural schools, focusing on training courses for social and managerial cadres; and in minor and major seminaries for several dioceses. Since 1992, the Jesuit missions of Singapore*, Malaysia*, and Thailand* have joined with those of the Indonesian province with the hope of providing missionaries in the future, because they can no longer be expected to come from Western countries. International coordination among Asian Jesuits is fostered and coordinated by the Bureau of Asian Affairs in Manila (since 1968).

Bibliography

Van Aernsbergens, A. I., *Chronologisch Oversicht (1859-1934)* (1934). • Heuken, A., *Ensiklopedi Gereja IV* (1994). • Jacobs, H., *The Jesuit Makassar Documents* (1988). • Vriens, G., *Sejarah Gereja Katolik Indonesia,* Vol. II (1972). • Wessels, C., *De geschiedenis der Katholieke Missie in Ambon 1546-1605* (1926). Adolf Heuken

Thailand. Balthasar Sequeira was the first Jesuit in Siam (Thailand). He left San Tomé in Sep 1606, arriving at Mergui-Tenasserim around December or January, and finally at Ayutthaya or Odia during the Holy Week of 1607 (between 19 and 26 Mar).

Sequeira first left Lisbon on 24 Mar 1578 with the annual fleet to India. He said his first mass on 12 Mar 1579 at San Roque together with his 13 companions, who included Matteo Ricci.

After 30 years in India, Sequeira was sent by his provincial to respond to a request from King Ekatot-Sarot to renew relations with Siam. Sequeira was quite old then, but he was the only person available at that time. He stayed two and a half years in Siam, fell sick at the end of 1609, and desired to return to either Goa or Cochin. He died en route in the city of Piple. The missionary who accompanied him to Siam was a Franciscan, Andre Pereira, of whom little is known.

Soon other Jesuits followed: Pedro Morejón, a Spaniard 63 years of age; Antonio Francesco Cardim, a Portuguese; and Romano Nixi, a Japanese Jesuit. They left Macau* on 13 Dec 1625. After a short stay in Manila, they left in Feb 1626 and arrived at Ayutthaya in March. Cardim passed through Siam on his way to Laos*. Morejón's arrival in Siam was slightly more complicated.

Morejón was the nephew of the archbishop of Toledo and the viceroy's confessor. In 1625 he went to Malacca, from where he decided to go to Siam while waiting for an opportunity to go to Japan. He arrived at Ligor and was informed by Antonio Gonzalves Cavalleiro, a Portuguese and a friend of the Society, about the possibilities of the mission in Siam and also about some recent trouble between the Spaniards from the Philippines and the Siamese. The *Sargento Mayor,* D. Fernando de Silva, had taken hold of a Dutch ship in the Menam River, and the Siamese king had given orders for the arrest of de Silva and his men. In the ensuing battle, some Spaniards were killed and about 30 of them were imprisoned.

Morejón decided to change his plans and returned to Macau instead, but with his heart still set on Japan. The governor of the Philippines wrote to the superior in Macau, who then agreed to send Morejón to Siam to secure the release of the imprisoned Spaniards. Morejón's mission was successful, and he returned to Manila with the released prisoners.

Marini recorded that Morejón and Cardim built the first residence in Siam, most probably in the Japanese settlement at Ayutthaya. Cardim also mentioned the residence when he said that Nixi took care of the Japanese in the beautiful church they had built.

After the departure of Morejón for Manila, Giulio Cesare Margico, an Italian, was sent to Ayutthaya as the new superior. He arrived in Aug 1627, bringing with him a letter from the governor of the Philippines to the king of Siam expressing satisfaction at the happy solution of the Spaniard incident. But in the beginning of 1628, the Spaniards started a new war of piracy against Siamese trade, capturing and burning a few of the Siamese ships and thus arousing Siamese wrath against Margico. Cardim believed the Siamese threatened to burn Margico alive. King Songtham set Margico free, but the hostility of the people forced the Jesuits to curtail their activities.

Cardim went to Manila. Margico and Nixi, betrayed by a Christian, were arrested and imprisoned. The Japanese were able to gain Nixi's freedom. He went to Macau and then to Cambodia*, where he died in 1630. Margico died in prison in 1630, poisoned by his traitor. The Society of Jesus then discontinued its residence in Siam.

The second advent of Jesuits in Siam came just a few years later. Joao Marai Leria arrived in 1639 and left in 1641 for Laos, his real destination. Giovanni Filippo de Marini arrived on 15 Feb 1642 and left in 1643 for Japan. Thomas Valguanera, a Sicilian, arrived from Macau and remained until 1670, when he was appointed visitor of the Japanese and Chinese province. He returned to Siam on 23 Mar 1675 and died there on 19 Jan 1677.

Valguanera first came to Siam with Francisco Rivas, who stopped on his way to Cochin China. The Japanese Christians in Siam had urgently requested pastoral care from one or two Jesuits.

A Portuguese pilot, Sebastiao Andrés, who arrived at Ayutthaya at about the same time as Valguanera, had asked to be admitted into the Society as a coadjutor brother. He died seven months later and left property valued at 14,000 *Scudi Romani* to the Society for the foundation of a college. Valguanera built a residence and a church in the Portuguese settlement, just across the river from the Japanese settlement, and in 1656 he was nominated the first superior. In 1666 there was a school at the residence.

After the residence was built, Valguanera then built the college in accordance with the will of Sebastiao Andrés. It was named the College of San Salvador.

Besides the construction of new forts in different towns, King Narai also ordered Valguanera to build the new royal residence at Lop Buri. King Narai was so pleased with Valguanera that he gave him a new and better church to replace his first church, which was accidentally burned in 1658. The king also permitted Valguanera the freedom to do missionary work in Siam. Usually the king never permitted foreigners to accompany him; Valguanera was an exception.

In his *Un Missionario Assorino: Tommaso dei Conti Valguarnera S.J. (1609-1677)*, Giovanni Gnolfo describes the Jesuit approach in Asia as one of enculturation: Matteo Ricci in China, De Nobili in India, and Valguanera in Goa, Macau, and Siam. Valguanera also did some religious writing in the Siamese language.

From 1655 to 1709, about 30 Jesuits passed through the residence. Nineteen were Portuguese, one Belgian, one Polish, one Japanese, and four French. About 16 were either en route to China or were expelled from nearby missions. The actual members of the residence were rarely more than four. Usually there were only two. At the beginning of the 18th c., only Gaspar da Costa* remained. For a year or two after his death in 1709, no Jesuits resided there.

During the Ratanakosin Period, the Jesuits came to reside and work in Siam again (in 1954). Presently they are involved in the care and development of student life and scholarship of Catholic university students. They have a center at Xavier Hall in Bangkok and at Seven Fountains in Chiang Mai. VORAYUTH KITBAMRUNG

Society of the Divine Word

(SVD). The SVD was founded in Steyl, Holland, on 8 Sep 1875 by Blessed Arnold Janssen (1837-1909). A simple priest from the diocese of Munster, Germany, Janssen challenged his fellow German Catholics to involve themselves in the missionary work of the church. Because of von Bismarck's *Kulturkampf* then raging in Germany, Janssen established his first mission house — in effect, the first Catholic mission seminary of Germany — in Steyl, a Dutch town by the German border. From the start, Janssen had spoken out clearly "against all forms of nationalism* in missionary activity." As the SVD constitution states: the Divine Word missionaries "work first and foremost where the Gospel has not been preached at all or only insufficiently and where the local church is not viable on its own."

Like that of preceding missionary orders, Janssen's sight was set on that vast land of high culture and teeming millions, *China**. The first SVD missionaries sent from Steyl were the Bavarian father (later bishop) John Baptist Anzer and the Italo-Austrian father (declared blessed in 1975) Joseph Freinademetz. The two took over South Shantung mission from the Franciscans* in 1882. Eventually, two SVD mission centers were established, one in Taikia and the other in Kao-mi. At the outbreak of the Sino-Japanese* War in 1937, both centers counted 157 SVD priests, 10 of them native Chinese. The fast-rising port city of Tsingtao was turned over to the SVDs in 1898 when the German expeditionary forces occupied the city. After World War I, when German missionaries could no longer return either to Mozambique or Togo, or even to New Guinea, the SVDs acquired the South Honan Vicariate. Ten years later, American SVDs took over a new mission in North Honan. In 1922 the SVDs went farther toward northwest China: Sinkiang, Ch'ing-hai, and West Kansu, an immense, partly desert territory of more than three million square kilometers and 8,000 Catholics.

The SVDs came to Peking in 1933 on the invitation of the Vatican. *Fu Jen* (Catholic University of Peking) was founded by American Benedictines in the 1920s as a university along American lines. The Benedictines* requested that the SVD take over the institution of learning. The SVD superior general accepted the offer, convinced that "the university furthers the work of the mission in a most effective way, and it is in tune with the charism of our founder."

With the coming of the Communists (see Communism), the SVD missionaries of all nationalities, including the Chinese, had to leave China. A sizeable number of them, including Thomas Cardinal Tien, an SVD and the first Chinese cardinal, crossed over to *Taiwan** in 1954 and settled at the prefecture of Chiai, the southwest portion of the island. Fu Jen was also transferred, this time as a joint venture of the SVDs, the diocesan clergy, Jesuits (see Society of Jesus), and Holy Spirit Missionary Sisters. It has 5,000 college students, only one percent of them Catholics. Attached to the SVD China Province is the Hong Kong District, with its 19 members. The society still counts a dozen confreres in mainland China.

The first three SVD missionaries reached *Japan** in 1907. They started in Akita, diocese of Niigata, in which territory 14 mission stations rose between 1924 and 1934, each with its own church, parochial house, and kindergarten. Similar foundations were established in Tokyo, Nagoya, and Nagasaki. It is in the field of higher education that SVD Japan found an efficacious missionary apostolate. After World War II*, when Japan became more open to foreigners and foreign religious, Nanzan (Catholic) University was established in 1949 with all the encouragement of Rome. Language and local culture rendered conversions slow and far between. By the

1990s, the SVD missionaries had 15,000 Catholics under their spiritual care. Recruitment of indigenous* vocations began as early as 1920, when priestly candidates were sent for formation to Rome, Steyl, and Vienna. In Tajimi, an hour away from Nagoya, the SVD community received its first Japanese brother novices. Then a minor seminary was set up in Nagasaki, and in 1950 a scholasticate in Nagoya, where the SVD theology students now stay while taking up theological* studies at Nanzan University.

The coming of the Americans and the consequent cessation of the Spanish *Patronato Real*, the birth of the schismatic Philippine Independent Church, and the severe shortage of native priests gravely altered the situation of the Catholic Church in the Philippines*. In response to Rome's appeal, which was sent to modern non-Spanish missionary congregations in Europe, Janssen sent a trusted SVD missionary from New Guinea to visit the Philippines. Two years later, in 1909, the first SVD missionaries arrived in Manila. They were assigned to the mountainous province of Abra in the diocese of Nueva Segovia. In 1922 the SVDs took over Lubang Island, then in 1937 the whole island-province of Mindoro. Going south, they opened a mission in 1972 in Agusan del Sur, and the year following another mission in the diocese of Surigao, both areas in the large island of Mindanao. Although their preoccupation was mainly pastoral in maintaining the faith of baptized Filipino Catholics, the SVDs did frontier work among non-Christian tribal minorities in Abra (the Tingguians), Mindoro (the Mangyans), and Agusan (the Manobos). The society founded not only mission schools but also colleges and two universities in urban Catholic centers. The school apostolate of the Philippine SVDs (1994: 63,000 pupils and students) aims both at improving the quality of the Catholic faith and at training future lay leaders. In the early 1960s, the SVDs were running two major and six minor college/seminaries with 1,200 students for the priesthood. The first SVD seminary, Christ the King Mission Seminary, was established in 1934 in present Quezon City. The philosophy and theology departments were transferred to Divine Word Seminary, Tagaytay City, which also accepts diocesan and non-SVD seminarians. In 1980, it was preparing 350 seminarians for the priesthood. As of 1994 Tagaytay counted 120 SVD alumni presently working in foreign lands.

In *Indonesia**, the SVD took over the Lesser Sunda Islands from the Jesuits in 1913. Fr. Noyen* became the first apostolic prefect of the entire area east of Bali, though Flores was handed over by the Jesuits later (1920) because of the lack of personnel after the war. At its beginning, the new prefecture had about 30,000 Catholics living on Flores and another 3,000 on Timor*. Noyen chose Ende* in central Flores as his mission center, far from the established Jesuit missions in Larantuka and Sikka in the east. From Ende, he moved quickly to the west after the arrival of new missionaries from the former German colony of Togo (Africa). Within three decades, Flores became the "Catholic island" of Indonesia. In 1933 a novitiate was opened in Todabelu to receive local candidates for the SVD. A minor seminary was established in 1926, followed by a major seminary in 1935 at Ledalero, now the largest seminary in Indonesia. At the time of the silver jubilee (1938), the SVD Lesser Sunda missions had increased tenfold to 300,000 Catholics served by 107 SVD missionaries.

In May 1940, 62 German and Austrian missionaries were detained by the Dutch authorities; 18 of them drowned when the MS *van Imhoff*, on its way to India*, was hit by Japanese bombs off the island of Nias. Two years later, all Dutch missionaries were detained by the Japanese; 22 of them died in concentration camps. In 1941 the first Florenese seminarians were ordained priests. They, together with Msgr. Leven, a German-born nationalized Dutch citizen, six old Dutch missionaries, and four Japanese priests, continued the fundamental services and prepared people for baptism throughout the war. Thus the church of Flores not only survived but grew in number.

After the war, new SVD missionaries arrived. Western Timor (1948) and Bali*-Lombok (1950) became independent SVD apostolic prefectures. A number of SVD anthropologists studied the customs *(adat*)*, languages, and religions of East Indonesia. Their published research has helped missionaries preach the Gospel more meaningfully. Social developments were promoted throughout Flores (bridges, roads, wells, planting of trees, dispensaries, etc.). With financial help and advice from Catholic funding agencies, specialized local institutions (headed by SVD fathers), and working with different government agencies ("Flores Plan"), the SVD fathers promoted social welfare, education, and primary health care throughout the island. In 1961 the dioceses of Ende, Larantuka, Ruteng, Atambua, and Denpasar (followed by Kupang in 1967) were established and entrusted to SVD bishops.

Because the Serikat Sabda Allah (SVD) is a missionary congregation, many of its Indonesian members have been sent from the Catholic areas of Flores and Timor to other parts of Indonesia, e.g., to Jakarta* (1953), Irian* Jaya (1969), Surabaya (1970), and Kalimantan* (1982), and also to foreign missions in Malagasy, Papua New Guinea, Taiwan*, and Zaire. There are four SVD provinces in Indonesia with a total of 489 professed members and 461 students and novices (1993).

India received its first SVD missionaries only in 1931. The district, which was to become the prefecture of Indore, lies in the heart of India with a surrounding population of 39 million Hindus and two million Muslims (see Hinduism, Islam). The SVDs labor among the untouchables. There are 22 SVD districts under an SVD bishop, 108 fathers, and 25 lay brothers. As conversion in the traditional way to the Catholic religion in this predominantly Hindu land is very difficult, prayer and dialogue centers have been established (see Interreligious Dialogue). After over 60 years of SVD presence in six dioceses, Catholics number 366,000.

In 1948 the SVDs moved toward the east into the state of Orissa, in what are now the ecclesiastical jurisdictions of Sambalpur, Rourkela, and Cuttack — Bhubaneshwar — all three under SVD Indian bishops. The original five main stations located south of Ranchi, which were offered by the Jesuits in 1946, were already a flourishing mission of 50,000 Catholics. Thirty years later, the number increased threefold. Special attention was given to the missionary work among the aborigines and untouchables. Another foundation (1949) was started in Bombay, this time a parish in the great metropolis. Besides two parishes, the SVDs run an urban development center, the *Gyan Ashram* (founded by Fr. Proksch), and the Institute of Indian Culture. Already before World War II*, an official concern for the recruitment of native vocations was aired. Only in 1951, however, were the first Indian novices accepted. Vocations come largely from southwest India, in particular, Kerala, which claims to have the highest literacy rate of all states and the highest concentration of Catholics. It is at the Jesuit-run pontifical central seminary in Pune, near Bombay, where SVD theology students complete their ecclesiastical studies. Also in Pune, the SVDs run a missiological institute, *Ishvani Kendra,* in cooperation with priests and sisters of other religious orders. It stresses the importance of theologico-missiological questions which must be confronted in missionary work in India. Eighty young Indian SVDs are working in other SVD missions: Papua New Guinea, Africa, Taiwan, Philippines.

SVD presence in *Korea** started only in 1984. SVD confreres, eight in all, conduct a parish and a formation house for future SVD members. The SVD mission in Korea formerly belonged to SVD Japan Province but has recently become an independent region.

In 1994 the SVD counted a worldwide membership of 5,366 professed and 337 novices. Of its 20 bishops in Asia, 16 are native-born. The membership in Europe, and partly in America, is decreasing in absolute terms as well as in percentage. The growth is manifestly in Asia, which makes up 40 percent (2,276 members/novices). It was providential that Janssen did not found a national German foreign mission society. During the world wars, for example, American SVDs were acceptable in areas where German SVDs were not, and vice versa. Where today countries such as India and Indonesia do not allow foreign missionaries to enter, local SVDs make up for the lack of personnel. From the very start, tribal minorities were a chief concern of the SVDs. A phenomenon has risen in which SVD missionaries from the Two-Thirds World are found in other Two-Thirds World countries. In a five-year period (1988-93), India, Indonesia, and the Philippines sent 423 priests and brothers to foreign missions. As soon as possible, the society recruited native candidates, and in areas such as the Philippines and Indonesia helped in the development of the diocesan clergy.

Bibliography

Report to the General Chapter of 1994: Of the Superior General and of the Generalate Officials. • *Report to the General Chapter of 1994: The Provinces and Regions of the Society of the Divine Word in Asia-Pacific.* • Bornemann, Fritz, *Arnold Janssen, Founder of Three Missionary Congregations* (1975). • *Arnold Janssen: gestern und heute* (1989). • Bornemann Fritz, et al., *A History of the Divine Word Missionaries* (1981). • Muller, Karl, *The Renewal Chapters of the Society of the Divine Word* (1982). • *SVD Catalogus 1994.* • *SVD Word in the World* (1990-91, 1992-93, 1993-94). • Petu, Piet, *Nusa Tenggara, Setengah abad karya misi SVD (1913-1963)* (1966). • Tennien, M., and T. Sato, *I Remember Flores* (1957). • Heuken, A., *Ensiklopedi Gereja* III (1994).

ANTOLIN V. UY, with ADOLF HEUKENON Indonesia

Society of the Servants of the Cross

Malankara* Orthodox Mission Society for work among the Dalits* of India*.

Established on 14 Sep 1924 by M. P. Patros, the objective of this society was the social, economic, and spiritual uplifting of Dalit Christians. The volunteers of the society work on self-employment and house-building projects, educational aid, and spiritual nourishment of Dalit Christians who have joined the Malankara Orthodox Church. About 75,000 people benefit from the society's work. New clothes are distributed to the people during the annual visits of the Gospel team.

The society has about 20 centers for regional coordination. The annual get-together is a festive occasion to review the solidarity among Dalit Christians. Recently, the society has started running a house for the aged. The headquarters of the society is at Carmel Dayara, Kandanad, Mulanthuruthy. JACOB KURIAN

Socio-Pastoral Institute

(SPI). National ecumenical* federation of regional and subregional centers open to the religio-cultural heritage of Asia, and global and ecological consciousness, and oriented to the church of the poor.

Conceptualized in 1979 and set up in 1980 as a "training and service institute for church people (bishops, clergy, religious and lay persons) who feel concerned about the situation and would like to contribute their share to the process of social transformation," SPI "is a response to the need for a more systematic educational program among church people to develop a critical consciousness in favor of the grassroots." It was founded by a small group of people brought together by the common vision of "a society struggling to become a truly human society in the Kingdom of God." SPI has tried to develop a common methodology from the sharing of various tools of analysis; of group communication, action, and organization; of hermeneutics, pedagogy, etc. It is envisioned as a service for church people as individuals or as organizations in their efforts to contribute their share as a people of faith in the process of transforming Philippine* society.

SPI recognizes that people live in a situation of worsening crisis, especially in the developing and Two-Thirds World countries of Asia and the Pacific. There is widespread economic deprivation, political confusion, cultural alienation, ecological destruction, and domination by the connivance of the foreign and local powers compounded by the presence of a fragmented church and multireligious reality. However, amidst this situation it also sees that there is a determined struggle of the people for true freedom and liberation. SPI stands in solidarity with the people in their quest for true freedom and liberation.

SPI participates in creating conditions for the self-transformation of persons, communities, churches, society, and the care of creation. It assists in the formation and training of, and renders services to, socio-pastoral agents and local church communities for the care, nurturing, and growth of the emerging church of the poor toward the integrity of humanity and creation.

The more specific objectives of the institute are reflected in the three programs it runs: (1) Theology in Philippine Context (an effort to delve more deeply into the biblical and theological* foundations, inspirations, and motivations for Christian involvement in social transformation in the Philippines); (2) Pastoral Sociology (an attempt to use the tools of social analysis and organization to make church people and church-related bodies more responsive and effective in their participation in the social process); and (3) Faith and Ideology (a response to the dilemma being faced by church people vis-à-vis the various conflicting ideologies present in Philippine society).

SPI derives its unique character from the threefold perspective of its programs: ecumenical, Asian, and regional. The SPI board is ecumenical in its composition and adheres to its ecumenical character in the lineup of resource persons and seminar participants. In addition, the Clergy-Laity Formation Program (CLFP) collaborates with SPI. SPI is also a member institute of the Association of Christian Institutes for Social Concern in Asia (ACISCA). Both organizations are ecumenical; the latter is Asian in scope. These threefold perspectives and approaches to Two-Thirds World and Asian realities make SPI relevant to the needs of the Philippine local church and all the local churches of Asia.

Bibliography

"Vision, Mission, Goal Statement Resolution, Socio-Pastoral Institute National Assembly" (18-22 Feb 1992), Daroca Training Center, Villa, Iloilo City.

JOSEFINA TONDO

Soedarmo, Raden

(b. Surakarta, 4 Aug 1914; d. Salatiga, 10 Dec 1991). Systematic theologian and seminary professor; first-generation Javanese Christian.

Born into a non-Christian family, Soedarmo was the son of a court musician in the palace of the king of Surakarta. His father was open-minded enough to allow him to study in a Christian school, where he accepted Christ and was baptized on 14 Feb 1933. After his secondary education, he studied theology at the Free Reformed University of Amsterdam and completed his doctoral program in 1957. He married Ali Margaretha Aten, a Dutch woman, and they had six children.

From 1949 to 1955, Soedarmo taught dogmatics at Yogyakarta Reformed Theological* Seminary. In 1955 he moved to Jakarta to become a professor of systematic theology at Jakarta (Union) Theological Seminary, where he served until his retirement in 1978. He was president of the seminary for two terms.

Soedarmo represented the conservative wing of the Reformed family in Indonesia (see Presbyterian and Reformed Churches), as well as in international circles. He published *Ikhtisar Dogmatika* (Dogmatics in Outline), a study handbook for his students, which has been reprinted eight times (1992). He also published *Kamus Istilah Teologia* (Dictionary of Theological Terms), reprinted five times, and five other books, mainly in theology but also on practical topics. In addition, he translated many commentaries for use in Indonesia.

Inspired by Abraham Kuyper, he channeled his sociopolitical concerns through the *Parti Kristen Indonesia* (Indonesian Christian Party) to voice his Christian witness in the political life of his country, but he left the party when it merged with others to form the Indonesian Democratic Party.

Soedarmo was a founding member of the foundation that published *Sinar Harapan* (Ray of Hope), an evening daily, as a Christian contribution via mass media for the building up of society. He taught philosophy in Indonesian universities and, as a member of the board of trustees of the huge Indonesian Christian University in Jakarta, helped formulate its motto, "To serve and not be served."

For several terms he was a voluntary member of the executive board of the Council of Churches in Indonesia, where he tried to impart the best of the Reformed tradition and enrich the national Christian effort in the common search for church unity. He also served on the interim committee of the Reformed Ecumenical* Synod (Reformed Ecumenical Council in 1988), representing Asian member churches. After his retirement from Jakarta Theological Seminary, he served as a pastor in Salatiga, Central Java*, for about 10 years until his ailing body forced him into total retirement from active service and responsibilities.

SULARSO SOPATER

Soegijapranata, Albertus

(b. Soerakarta, 1896; d. Steyl, Netherlands, 6 Jul 1963). First Indonesian bishop (1940) and later archbishop of Semarang (1961).

Born to Islam*-*Abangan* parents, Soegijapranata asked to be baptized during his studies at the teachers training school in Muntilan. He had private tuition in Latin and Greek because he wanted to become a Jesuit (see Society of Jesus). Franz van Lith* paid special attention to the talented young man, who at first refused even to think about becoming a Christian. In 1920 he started his noviceship in the Netherlands under the guidance of P. Willekens, who in 1940 asked the Vatican to make Soegijapranata bishop of that part of his vicariate, which was situated in Central Java*. Prior to this appointment, Soegijapranata was a parish priest, spiritual adviser to different organizations of the lay apostolate, and editor of *Swara Tama,* a magazine for social action.

Soegijapranata was the only Catholic bishop who could move freely during the Japanese occupation. With 11 native Jesuits, he ran the dioceses and supported regions devoid of clergy when all Dutch missionaries were imprisoned by the Japanese occupation forces (1942-45). During the struggle for independence (1945-49), he mediated between fighting groups to avoid bloodshed, and between the new republic and Dutch politicians. In order to make his stand clear to everyone, he left Semarang, occupied by the Dutch, and resided in Yogyakarta, temporary capital of the republic. He explained the resistance of his people and their right for independence in foreign newspapers. In Yogyakarta, he befriended President Sukarno* and his family.

Soegijapranata was broad-minded and mixed easily with people of different national, political, and religious backgrounds. He asked his flock to support the republic and its cause without hating other people. "A hundred percent Catholic, and a hundred percent Indonesian!" became his motto in national matters. He reminded politicians to keep ethical standards in their dealings and to put common interest above that of their own groups.

After years of occupation and the struggle for independence, the Catholic community of his diocese needed spiritual renewal and integration into the life of the new country. Stressing the importance of *Pancasila* as the unifying ideology of the vast archipelago, he gave strength and guidelines to the laypeople working in the social, political, and educational fields. He supported the trade unions, development projects, and teachers training institutions in his diocese. He defended church institutions against attacks from the left and right and gave new spirit to those who had difficulty adjusting to the new situation.

After taking part in the first session of Vatican Council II, he went to the Netherlands for medical treatment and died in a convent of the Sisters of Divine Providence, who also worked in his diocese. Soegijapranata and I. J. Kasimo* are regarded as the pioneers of integration of the Catholic community into the new Republic of Indonesia. President Sukarno posthumously raised his first Indonesian army bishop to the rank of general and national hero.

Bibliography

Moeryantini, H., *Mgr. Albertus Soegijapranata SJ* (1975). • Bank, J., *Katholieken en de Indonesische Revolutie* (1983). • Heuken, A., *Ensiklopedi Gereja* IV (1994).

Adolf Heuken

Soka Gakkai. *See* Nichiren/Soka Gakkai

Solarte, Paulino

Evangelist and second Filipino ordained by the Presbytery of Manila.

A native of Iloilo City, Solarte was one of the earliest Presbyterian* converts, won to Christ in 1901 through the preaching of evangelist Adriano R. Osorio*. A fiery and eloquent speaker. Solarte himself soon became an assistant to the Presbyterian missionaries. As evangelist, he labored in Iloilo and its immediate environs. He served as the chief leader of the Iloilo Evangelical Church beginning in 1902, after Osorio concentrated his labors in Antique Province. At the beginning of 1906 that church engaged Solarte as their lay pastor. Because Solarte's service was effective, the Presbytery of Manila ordained him that year as the second Presbyterian minister in Panay, after Osorio. Solarte remained pastor of the Iloilo Evangelical Church until he was succeeded by Jose Moleta in 1912.

Bibliography

69th Annual Presbyterian Board Report (1906). • Sitoy, T. V., Jr., *Several Springs, One Stream* (1992).

T. Valentino Sitoy, Jr.

Solor Mission

Mission of the Goanese Dominicans* from the 16th to the 18th cs. in the Lesser Sunda Islands of eastern Indonesia. See Indonesia*. Adolf Heuken

Song Choan-Seng

(b. Tainan, Taiwan, 19 Oct 1929). Taiwanese theologian, former president of Tainan Theological College and Seminary, a pioneer of Asian theology, and a founder of the Programme for Theology and Cultures in Asia (PTCA); the guru of story theology.

Since 1985, Song has served as professor of theology and Asian cultures at Pacific School of Religion and on the faculty of the Graduate Theological Union in Berkeley, California. He also serves the South East Asian Graduate School of Theology as regional professor of theology.

The son of a worker of the Taiwan* Church Press of the Presbyterian* Church in Taiwan (PCT), Song graduated from the department of philosophy of the National Taiwan University in 1954. He earned his first theological* degree from the University of Edinburgh, Scotland, in 1958 and returned to Taiwan to teach Old Testament at Tainan Theological College. Later he moved to the field of systematic theology and earned his Ph.D. from Union Theological Seminary, New York. He returned to Taiwan in 1964 and resumed teaching at Tainan Theological College.

Although influenced by Western theologians such as

T. F. Torrance and Karl Barth, Song in his inaugural address as president of Tainan Theological College, Oct 1965, advocated a "theology of the incarnation," emphasizing "renewal of theology" and the Christian faith "in the light of God's Word and the needs of the world." He said: "Whether in an industrial society or rural community, if a minister does not know how to, or is unwilling to, pick up a hammer, lift a spade with workers and farmers and toil with them, the words he says on Sunday from the pulpit may become sounding brass and tinkling cymbal." Thinking from the context and situation of the people became and has been his way of doing theology. As president of a theological college, he was also very much involved in the New Century Mission Movement of the PCT and was appointed chairperson of its coordination center.

In Oct 1970 Song went to the United States. In Dec 1971 the PCT issued its first public statement, the *Statement on Our National Fate.* In Dec 1972 Song, together with Shoki Coe (Hwang Chang-Hui), Hwang Wu-Tong*, and Lin Tsung-Yi, initiated a movement in North America called Taiwanese Christians for Self-Determination in response to the PCT's statement. The movement mobilized the Taiwanese people "to assert their human rights of self-determination for the future of Taiwan and to promote the cause of self-determination in the international community of nations." He was editor of *Chhut-thau-thin* ("raising the head above the sky," meaning liberation), the occasional journal of that movement. Song, by all accounts, is one of the great contributors who promoted and popularized the political culture of self-determination and democracy not only inside Taiwan but also outside it.

From Jan 1971 to Aug 1973, Song was the secretary for Asian ministries of the General Programme Council of the Reformed Church in America. In Sep 1973 he accepted an invitation to become associate director of the secretariat of the Faith and Order Commission, World Council of Churches (WCC). Worldwide experiences enriched and deepened his critical theological reflection, especially in the field of the Gospel* and culture. In *Christian Mission in Reconstruction: An Asian Analysis,* Song advocates a new perspective on mission, emphasizing the importance of understanding Christian mission not only from God's salvation, or redemption, but also from God's creation. He stresses that "culture as a whole is none other than the manifestation of God's creative power translated into actual forms and events." Christian mission "consists in an effort to search for and appreciate different shapes which the cultural dynamic of creation takes in different cultural and historical contexts." He also perceives histories as a continuation of God's creation. In this way, he takes culture and history very seriously in his theology. His theology is a "third-eye theology," or a "theology from the womb of Asia." He emphasizes that "the frontiers of our theology must move from the history of Israel and history of Christianity in the West to the history in which we are involved in Asia."

Beginning in 1983, Song and Asian theological leaders such as Masao Takenaka* (Doshisha, Kyoto, Japan*) and Yeow Choo-Lak (Association for Theological Education in South East Asia) conducted theological seminars and workshops that developed into the PTCA in 1987. More than 300 Asian theologians and church leaders have participated in efforts to do theology with Asian resources. To him, culture is the matrix or womb of theology, i.e., "the totality of life is the raw material of theology," and cultures are endowed with theological significance.

In 1994 Song completed his three-volume *Cross in the Lotus World (Jesus, the Crucified People; Jesus and the Reign of God;* and *Jesus in the Power of the Spirit).* In a recent article he reflects on his own theological journey: "For me theology is like story-telling." The title of his above-mentioned trilogy expresses clearly what he seeks to do: "a theological effort [is an effort] to understand Christian faith in the part of the world not dominated by Christianity." The five stages toward a theological reconstruction in the multicultural world he suggested are as follows: (1) "Asking a fundamental question," such as "the possibility that God may be working also outside the church"; (2) the story of Jesus as the story of suffering people is the key to unlocking the mystery surrounding God; (3) the reign of God provides the link between stories of Jesus and stories of different cultures; Asian Christians must discern the stories of God's reign in Asia and realize how God is speaking to them; (4) identifying a theological problem: "With the story of Jesus as the story of God's Reign and with the stories of people in Asia that reflect the story of God's Reign, we return to the Christian church, to its faith and theology and look at it with a new eye"; (5) Jesus and stories of people: "As the story of Jesus and stories from Asia interpenetrate each other, a theological space is also opened for the stories of Hebrew Scripture. Stories from other parts of the world also come into play. What takes place is a theological feast of stories — the story of Jesus, stories from Asia, stories in Hebrew Scripture, and stories from the rest of the world, told as stories of God's Reign."

As early as 1965, Song proposed a *theologia viatorum* (theology on the way) to his colleagues at Tainan Theological College, and his own theological journey continues.

Bibliography

Song Choan-Seng, *Christian Mission in Reconstruction: An Asian Analysis* (1977); *Tell Us Our Names: Story Theology from an Asian Perspective* (1984).

CHEN NAN JOU

Song Hoot Kiam

(b. 1830; d. 1900). Founder of the oldest family of Straits Chinese Christians in Singapore*.

Born in Malacca*, Song studied at the London Missionary Society Anglo-Chinese College. When the college was moved to Hong Kong in 1843, he went with the principal, James Legge*, to continue his studies. Two years later, on home leave, Legge brought Song and two other Chinese boys to Scotland, where they studied in a parish school. All three boys were converted and baptized in the Congregational church from which William Milne* had come. They were also presented to Queen Victoria. Song returned to Singapore in 1849. He taught briefly, but in 1853 he joined the P & O Steamship Company, where he served as cashier until he retired in 1895. When Song returned from Scotland, his parents arranged a marriage for him with a non-Christian girl. His refusal to marry her earned him the displeasure of his parents. Instead, he chose Yeo Choon Neo, a former student of Chinese Girls' School (of Sophia Cooke* fame). After her death, Song married Phan Fung Lean of Penang. Their eldest son, Song Ong Siang, later became a prominent lawyer and was a leading figure on the local scene.

Song worked alongside Benjamin Keasberry* and was for many decades a key figure in the Malay Chapel; the oldest Straits Chinese church, it is today known as Prinsep Street Presbyterian* Church. His fine melodious voice made him a natural choice in leading congregational singing. He preached from the pulpit both in English and Malay. His own parents and a number of young men were led to Christ by him. Two of them, Tan Kong Wee and Tan Boon Chin, later became his sons-in-law, and they were in much demand as lay preachers both in the church as well as in prison work. Another convert, Foo Tong Quee, took up business and became a leader in the Hylam community.

When he died, Song was survived by nine daughters and five sons. The *Straits Chinese Magazine* paid him a tribute, noting that "he was neither rich nor great, but he was a specimen of the best type of the Chinese character. Sober, persevering and conservative, he was a mighty rock to his large family. . . . He toiled on quietly, and in hope and faith, raised up sons and daughters to worship God, and to work for the kingdom of heaven" (Dec 1900).

Bibliography

Cook, J. A. Bethune, *Sunny Singapore* (1907). • Song Ong Siang, *One Hundred Years' History of the Chinese in Singapore* (1923).

Bobby Sng Ewe Kong

Song Ong Siang

(b. 1871; d. 1941). Singaporean lawyer, church elder, community leader, and writer.

Eldest son of Song Hoot Kiam* and Phan Fung Lean, Song studied in Singapore* at Raffles* Institution and briefly at Christian Brothers' School (now St. Joseph's Institution). A brilliant student, he finished his studies at the top of his class and was awarded the Queen's Scholarship. In 1888 he proceeded to England to study law, first at Middle Temple and then at Cambridge. This he did with distinction, winning more scholarships and awards. Five years later he was called to the bar. Returning to Singapore, he and another schoolmate, also a Queen's scholar, started a legal firm. Over the next four decades he was to play an active role in community service, seeking to uplift the welfare of the Straits Chinese and to promote female education. In 1894 he produced the first Romanized Malay-language newspaper, *Bitang Timor.* However, due to poor support, it survived for less than one year. Three years later, together with another prominent leader named Lim Boon Keng, he began the *Straits Chinese Magazine,* which ran for 11 years. He also helped found the Singapore Chinese Girls' School, Chinese Philomathic Society, Straits Chinese British Association, and Chinese Volunteer Corps (where he rose to the rank of captain). He became a nominated member of the legislative council and was knighted by King George V in 1936, the first Chinese in Singapore and Malaya to receive such an honor. His monumental 600-page book, *One Hundred Years' History of the Chinese in Singapore,* covers the period 1819-1919 and was published in 1923. It remains an invaluable work of reference.

Song belonged to the oldest Straits Chinese church in Singapore, now known as the Prinsep Street Presbyterian* Church. He remained a devout Christian and served as church elder for many years. He sang in the choir, edited the church magazine, and occasionally preached from the pulpit. The Chinese Christian Association, formed in 1889 to encourage members to take a Christian view of life and service, received his lifelong support. Although its regular activities were held at Song's own church, its doors were open to all. Through its fortnightly lectures, Bible* classes, debates, reading facilities, and music and drama presentations, many young Christians were helped and a number came to the faith.

Bibliography

Cook, J. A. Bethune, *Sunny Singapore* (1907). • Song Ong Siang, *One Hundred Years' History of the Chinese in Singapore* (1923). • Prinsep Street Presbyterian Church, *150 Years of Faithfulness, 1843-1993.*

Bobby Sng Ewe Kong

Sook Phongnoi

(b. Petchaburi, Thailand, 15 Oct 1906; d. Bangkok, Thailand, 1 Jun 1972). Thai pastor and evangelist.

Sook was one of the early local ministers recognized as a godly and influential worker in the church in Thailand*. He traveled widely throughout Thailand, carrying with him the Gospel of Jesus Christ.

Sook was a catalyst in encouraging the expansion of the Thai church after World War II*. He crossed denominational lines by assisting in the ministries of most missions that started their work in Thailand after the war, e.g., the Southern Baptists*, Overseas Missionary Fellowship, Christian and Missionary Alliance* (C&MA), Full Gospel Churches of Canada, and others.

His loving, friendly, and supportive attitude toward both local and foreign ministers won him their hearts. He was a humble servant of God who brought many to Christ. In 1969 he founded the Union of the Evangelical Christian Churches of Thailand with the purpose of evangelizing the Thais. It was later renamed the Evangelical Fellowship of Thailand (EFT) and accepted by the Thai government as a legal religious organization apart from the Catholic Church and Churches of Christ in Thailand. Sook reluctantly agreed to be its first chairman. Highly respected, he was referred to as "our loving Barnabas."

Born into a pious Buddhist family, Sook's father was an artisan who made altars for Buddhist temples (see Buddhism). Sook attended a Christian boys school with an anti-Christian attitude, but after he was struck with a near-fatal disease and was lovingly cared for by Paul Eakin*, a Presbyterian* missionary, he was impressed by the love of Christ seen in this missionary and was converted during his high school years. After high school, he dedicated his life to the Lord and was one of the first students of McGilvary* Bible* College. He was married to his wife of 43 years on 4 Mar 1929. After his graduation in 1930, he took his wife to Bangkok and ministered for seven years in the second district of the Church of Christ. After this he moved south to the province of Trang and served there for another seven years before going to Nakornsrithummarat, where he pastored for another 10 years. His strong emphasis on zealous prayer, trust in the power of the Holy Spirit, and Bible study brought about revival in many Thai churches.

When World War II* broke out, Japanese troops captured Thailand (see Japan). The Thai government had no choice but to ally with the Japanese, resulting in the emergence of an anti-Christian movement in which missionaries and local Christians were eventually persecuted. Sook was arrested and accused of being a traitor and a pro-American activist. He was handcuffed and sent to jail. Defending himself against the charge, he was able to gain his freedom after 33 days in jail.

In 1951 Sook received a scholarship to continue theological training for one year at San Francisco Theological Seminary in California, United States. Once again, he was separated from his family. He returned to serve with the Far East Broadcasting Company* in pioneering the first Thai Christian radio ministry. The programs were recorded on tape in Bangkok and sent to Manila to be broadcast until the Thai government allowed them to be broadcast from various local stations in Thailand. Sook served in this area of ministry until the last day of his life. He traveled extensively all over the country as an evangelist, preacher, and Bible teacher in numerous churches and revival meetings.

He composed several indigenous Christian songs, which were sung in Thai churches across the country. He also took part in translating many popular English hymns into Thai.

Bibliography

Churin Thoptang, Charun Rattanaputra, Thummada Phongnoi, et al., *Loving Barnabas* (1975).

THANAPORN THUMSUCHARITKUL

Soreh Presbyterian Church

First Protestant Church in Korea*.

Soreh Presbyterian Church* is located at Songchun-ri, Daesu-meyn, Jangyon-kun, in Hwanghae Province. It was founded by Suh Sang Yun and his brother Kyung Cho, who were from Uiju, on the banks of the Yalu River in North P'yongan. Suh was selling ginseng in Manchuria in 1878 when he fell ill and was cared for by John McIntyre, a Scottish Presbyterian missionary. Suh was then employed by McIntyre to help him with his Korean language study and Bible* translation work. In the process, Suh and his brother, who visited him in Mukden, were both converted. Suh was baptized by McIntyre's brother-in-law, John Ross* (d. 1915), in Manchuria. In 1882 the Korean translations of the Gospels of Luke and John were completed.

Suh returned to Korea in 1883 with the printed Korean translation. His preaching and distribution of the Korean Gospel translation was reported to the officials. To escape arrest, Suh fled to Soreh, where his uncle lived, and initiated a congregation. The consensus is that the church was started in 1883. Although there were many converts, there were no ministers until the arrival of the missionaries to Korea.

In 1886 Suh brought his brother Kyung Cho and two other young men to Seoul to meet Horace Underwood*, who baptized them in 1887. Underwood also went to Soreh and baptized many in the town.

In 1895 the Christians in Soreh built a new church building, raising their own funds, without any foreign assistance. It was the first Protestant church built and funded by the Koreans themselves.

Bibliography

Min Kyoung Bae, *Hankook Kidok'kiohoe-sa* (History of the Korean church), new rev. ed. (1993). • Paik, George L., *The History of Protestant Missions in Korea* (1971). • Clark, Allen D., *A History of the Church in Korea* (1971/1986).

KIM IN SOO

Sotto, Angel Costada

(b. 1885; d. 1978). Filipino pioneer evangelist in Negros Oriental, preacher, and pastor.

One of the first two Presbyterian* evangelists in Cebu in 1903, Sotto belonged to the famous Sotto family of Cebu City, who were the local leaders of the Philippine Independent Church*. Sotto was sent as a pioneer evangelist to Negros Oriental in 1904. He employed his talents as a dynamic preacher, fierce controversialist, poet, writer, and playwright to advance the work. From 1905 to 1912, Sotto preached in Dumaguete, Valencia, Sibulan, Amlan, Tanjay, Bais, Guihulngan, and Siquijor Island. Ordained by the Cebu Presbytery in 1912, Sotto became the first pastor of the newly organized Tanjay Evangelical Church, serving until 1917.

Loaned by the Presbyterian Mission to the American Board Mission in northern Mindanao, Sotto spent the rest of his ministerial career as pastor of Dipolog, Cagayan, and Baliangao.

Bibliography

Sotto, A. D., *Mga Handumanan sa Akong Tinuhoan* (1954). • Sitoy, T. V., Jr., *Several Springs, One Stream* (1992). T. Valentino Sitoy, Jr.

Souvignet, Henri-Emmanuel

(b. Monistrol, France, 25 Dec 1855; d. Phu Ly, Vietnam, 18 Mar 1943). Missionary for the *Mission Étrangères de Paris**; studious author sympathetic to the Vietnamese.

Souvignet departed for Indochina in Nov 1882, where he worked at Ke So and other mission stations in the midlands of northern Vietnam*. From the 1890s to 1943, Souvignet lived in Phy Ly, south of Hanoi in the province of Ha Duong, located in the heart of the Red River delta. His encyclopedic works on the language, history, and culture of Vietnam are characterized by his serious attempt to abstain from pejorative and racist remarks about the conquered Vietnamese population.

Although Souvignet never developed a scientifically coherent perspective on the society in which he lived for so many years, his works are still outstanding. Unlike his colleague in Hue, Leopold-Michel Cadiere*, Souvignet was a man with a mission who hoped to offer his French countrymen a "key" in order to open up the field of "morality of the Annamese" and to give them "the secret of loving these people in better understanding," according to his introduction in *Varietes Tonkinoises,* his best-known book (1903). A study of the land situation of the district of Kim Son shows an early interest in the consequences of the colonization for the Vietnamese population (1905, p. 553). A second part of *Varietes Tonkinoises* appeared in 1922, this time totally devoted to the Vietnamese language.

Bibliography

Souvignet, H. E., *Varietes Tonkinoises* (1903, published under the pseudonym A-B = RP Souvignet and Dronet). • "Regime foncier du huyen de Kim Son," *Revue Indochinoise* (1905). John G. Kleinen

Spirituality, Christian

For the Christian, spirituality means being attuned to the Holy Spirit and acting in the Spirit under the Spirit's guidance. Humans are not pure spirits but incarnate persons. They do have a spirit, but that spirit must always live and act within the context of a human existence, except for those rare moments of true transcendence when, like St. Paul, they do not know whether they are in the body or out of the body (2 Cor. 12:2). The goal of Christian spirituality is union with God and with all others in God in love. Spirituality is a way of coming to integration, of gaining freedom to be who one is as a human person re-created in Jesus Christ, and acting in accordance with that reality. Spirituality is then lived within a cultural context and is (and should be) deeply influenced by it.

The coming of Christian faith to Asia. According to the story, one of the Lord's Twelve, St. Thomas*, first brought the faith to the southern shores of India*. The site of his martyrdom and his tomb are held in veneration. Historically, missionaries came from Syria in the 4th c., first Nestorians* from eastern Syria and then Monophysites from western Syria. Not only geographically but culturally these Syrians were closer to India than were the later Western missionaries; they gave birth to an indigenous liturgy and spirituality that endure till today. It was also Syrian and Persian Christians walking across Asia who first brought the faith to China* in the 7th or 8th c.

Christ Jesus shared his revelation in simple Semitic terms with stories, images, and parables that arose out of his own Jewish culture. The very first Christians had a spirituality very similar to their fellow Jews, yet one profoundly transformed by the ever-present risen Lord and his new commandment to love as he loves. A long struggle of over six centuries sought to find the way to transmit Jesus' revelation using adequate Greco-Roman philosophical concepts. Once established, this conceptional terminology became normative. Through the succeeding centuries in most of the world, it was virtually necessary to become a Greco-Roman in one's thinking in order to embrace Christianity. In addition, missionaries from Western Christianity usually came to Asia in the company of colonizing forces who sought to use conversion to Christianity as an aid to colonization. Thus the converts were required to abandon their own culture and accept that of the colonizing Christian country.

Adaptation, nativization, and contextualization* were part of the earliest history of the church. The philosophy of Greece and Rome and the use of their languages for the liturgy as well as the "baptism" of many of the feasts and symbols found among the indigenous peoples were a part of this. This enculturation continued in eastern European countries with Christian missionaries such as St. Cyril and St. Methodius playing an important role in the actual ongoing development of the native culture.

Early Roman Catholic attempts to develop Asian spirituality. An initial breakthrough within the Western Christian missionary outreach to Asia came with the courageous and extraordinarily brilliant undertakings of Matteo Ricci* (d.1610), a priest of the Society of Jesus*

(Jesuits). His superior, Alessandro Valignano*, had a profound appreciation of Chinese culture and moral values and was convinced of the possibility of their being integrated into Christianity. He totally supported Ricci's efforts. At first, Ricci sought to adapt Buddhist ways, but then he saw that the way to reach the influential persons in China was through the scholarly traditions of Confucianism* and Taoism*. Proving himself a consummate scholar — his tomb continued to be held in honor even through the whole course of the Communist era — he presented Christianity as the fulfillment of the profound mysticism of Lao Tzu (600 B.C.E.) and the intense humanism of Confucius (551-479 B.C.E.), bringing them together through the mystery of the incarnation and the incorporation of the Christian into Christ. He reinterpreted the cult of ancestors, which was so central to Chinese piety, in the light of the command to honor parents and the church's traditional veneration of saints (see Ancestor Worship). In general, he sought to distinguish clearly between rites which were expressions of civil piety and those which were part of a religious cult incompatible with Christian belief.

Earlier, Francis Xavier* (d. 1552), another outstanding Jesuit missionary, in the course of his brief but very successful missionary efforts in Japan*, found that it was necessary to adapt to the local culture in order to get a hearing. His work and that of his coworkers and immediate followers were almost totally eradicated by long and fierce persecution.

In India, Roberto de Nobili* (d. 1656), emulating Ricci, departed from the general practice of the Portuguese missions and adopted the saffron dress, clogs, vegetarian diet of the *sannyasi,* and mark on the forehead with santal paste which denoted the teacher. He allowed his Brahmin converts to continue to wear the thread that marked their caste as well as the *kudumi* (single plait of hair). Thus he opened the way for members of all castes to enter into the church. De Nobili was convinced that the whole person needed to embrace Christ, and Christ needed to enter into the whole of life, not just the lofty aspects such as art, music, philosophy, and ritual, but also the everyday things like food, clothing, and ornamentation. "All things are yours, and you are Christ's, and Christ is God's" (1 Cor. 3:23). Concerning the many rites and religious invocations of the Hindus, he changed their intentions and preserved them quite in keeping with the most ancient tradition of the church.

Unfortunately, a long controversy ensued in regard to these adaptations. While Pope Gregory XV initially decided in favor of this wise move toward enculturation, in the end the illusion of the superiority of European culture along with the forces of colonization won out, and these early attempts by Western missionaries at adaptation were generally abandoned by the end of the 17th c. This closed attitude was reinforced by a developing Protestant theology that held that nature was essentially corrupted, and therefore all that was "pagan" — anything that belonged to religions that did not live by the Judeo-Christian revelation — was corrupt; any accommodation was a compromise with error. In the succeeding centuries, it became the general practice for Christian missionaries to look upon Hinduism*, Buddhism*, and Confucianism* indiscriminately as pagan religions to be totally shunned and to demand that their converts abandon completely everything associated with their previous religious experience, adopting the practices of the Christian West in their place. This attitude no doubt was in large part responsible for the fact that those centuries of missionary activity bore mixed results. This was very different from the attitude set forth by Vatican Council II:

"Men and women look to the various religions for answers to those profound mysteries of the human condition which today even as in olden times deeply stir the human heart. . . . Religions together with the advancement of culture have struggled to reply to these same questions with more refined concepts and in more highly developed language. Thus in Hinduism men and women contemplate the divine mystery and express it through an unspent fruitfulness of myths and through searching philosophical inquiry. They seek release from the anguish of our condition through ascetic practices or deep meditation or a loving, trusting flight toward God. Buddhism in its multiple forms acknowledges the radical insufficiency of this shifting world. It teaches a path by which men and women with a devout and confident spirit can either reach a state of absolute freedom or attain supreme enlightenment by their own efforts or by higher assistance. Likewise other religions to be found everywhere strive variously to answer the restless searchings of the human heart by proposing 'ways' which consist of teachings, rules of life and sacred ceremonies. The Catholic Church rejects nothing which is true and holy in these religions. It looks with sincere respect upon those ways of conduct and of life. . . . Acknowledge, preserve and promote the spiritual and moral goods found among these men and women as well as the values in their society and culture" *(Nostra aetate,* 2).

Roman Catholic monasticism. Almost all major world religions have at their heart an identifiable monastic group: men and women who dedicate their lives totally to living the deeper spiritual dimensions of their religious beliefs. As consciousness reawakened in the 20th c. as to the need for enculturation, it is not surprising to find that these men and women took the lead in developing an Asiatic spirituality. Their way of life not only afforded them the time needed for the necessary study, but also the opportunity for the depth of spiritual experience that is absolutely essential for developing an authentic spirituality. In doing this, they were already fulfilling a mandate of Vatican Council II:

"Working to plant the Church and thoroughly enriched with the treasures of mysticism adorning the Church's religious tradition, religious communities should strive to give expression to these treasures and to hand them on in a manner harmonious with the nature and the genius of each nation. Let them reflect attentively on how Christian religious life may be able to assimilate the ascetic and contemplative traditions whose seeds were sometimes already planted by God in ancient cultures prior to the preaching of the gospel" (*Ad gentes,* 18).

The council did not fail to note that this was actually the case: "Worthy of special mention are the various projects aimed at helping the contemplative life take root. . . . All are striving to work out a genuine adaptation to local conditions" (*Ad gentes,* 18).

Roman Catholic Spirituality in India. A far-seeing French priest, Abbé Jules Monchanin, came to India in 1939. His desire was that what is deepest in Christianity might be grafted onto what is deepest in India. In 1950, with a French Benedictine, Father Henri Le Saux, who took the name Abishiktananda ("Bliss of Christ"), he started Saccidananda Ashram (see Ashram Movement) on the banks of the Kavery, the sacred river of the south, near Kulitalai. It was their intention to identify themselves with the Hindu quest for God as being *(sat),* knowledge *(cit),* and bliss *(ananda),* and to relate this quest with their own experience of God in Christ in the mystery of the Trinity. Monchanin, who took the name Prama Arabi Ananda ("Bliss of the Supreme Spirit"), was convinced that the Hindu experience of the Atman, the ground alike of being and of consciousness as the "one without a second," and the Christian experience of God as a trinity of persons, are complementary truths. Within the depths of the one, there is revealed a communion of knowledge and love which does not destroy but perfects the unity of the one being. But to discover this point of unity in the two traditions, it is necessary to ascend to the source of both traditions, the point at which they originally burst forth and took shape before they had hardened into systems. This was the task that Monchanin set for himself: "to rethink everything in the light of theology and to rethink theology through mysticism." With the passing of these two founders the spiritual development of Saccidananda Ashram was very strongly carried forward by another Benedictine, who came from England, Dom Bede Griffiths. Dom Bede became known throughout the English-speaking world for his writings on "the marriage of the East and the West" in the spiritual search.

In 1956, a Cistercian* monk from Scourmont Abbey in Belgium, Father Francis Mahieu, arrived in Kerala, inspired with a call to revive the monastic tradition of the ancient Syrian church in India while assimilating as much as possible the spiritual heritage of India, with its ascetic and contemplative traditions, and a Gandhian vision regarding the economy of the community. Kerala, while keeping many of its own characteristics, was no longer so isolated from the general currents of Indian Hindu culture. Mahieu found it remarkable how, at least in some instances, spiritual experiences in altogether different cultural and religious traditions came to be expressed in almost identical terms while preserving their own proper features. The ashram he founded, Kurisumala near Vagamon, Kottayam, not only adopted the clothing and postures of the Indian *sannyasi,* but also incorporated into the community prayer "seeds of the word" found in the sacred books of India — both those seeds which give witness to spiritual experiences similar to those recorded in the Bible, and those which reveal the search for God as it is found among the Hindus.

De Nobili found a worthy follower in a native Indian Jesuit, Father Ignatius Hirudayam, who founded a city ashram, Aikiya Alayam, in Madras in 1965. While the emphasis here was much more academic in comparison with Saccidananda and Kurisumala, and while the ashram became an important center for dialogue, the liturgies celebrated at Aikiya Alayam and the spiritual practices of the center truly reflected the Indian culture.

Students and seekers have come from all parts of India to these ashrams. The ashrams have been truly a leaven in the life of the church in India and have inspired similar efforts on the part of women as well as men in other parts of the country. The assimilation of Indian symbols, colors, smells, gestures, and postures into the essentially Christian rituals and meditation practice has made these expressions of Christian spirituality more attractive and acceptable to the average Indian and has opened the way for Indians to enter into the deeper similarities and the completing fullness of Christianity. Of the various limbs of yoga, it is *hatha* yoga, with its bodily training, integration, and attention to the breath, that has been most widely incorporated into Christian meditation practice. Some of the techniques of *jana* yoga have also been found very useful to Christians, especially the use of mantras, which Christians take from the Bible.

Roman Catholic spirituality in Japan. In Japan*, the lead has been taken by priests coming from outside and has been mostly in the area of Zen, which has in fact exercised significant influence on Japanese culture. Not surprisingly, it was the Quakers who opened the Christians' dialogue with Japanese Zen Buddhism. Two Jesuits, E. Lasalle and William Johnston, forged ahead with the practice of a Christian Zen. And Japanese Dominican Fr. Oshida (who has much to do with the training of the future leadership of the church of Japan) and Jesuit Fr. Kadowaki have done much to bring Zen practice into the heart of Japanese Christian communities. Primitive Christian chants are easily integrated into Zen practice, e.g., *Kyrie eleison.* Where *koans* (enigmatic statements, the pondering of which helps break the hold of the rational mind) are used, they can be drawn from the Christian New Testament, e.g., "I live, now not I but Christ lives in me" (Gal. 2:20).

Zen, which fosters a state of consciousness that sees into the essence of things, brings about inner purification and liberation from systems and conceptual thinking. This opens the way for the Holy Spirit to act in the Christian through his gifts. The practice and attitudes of Zen are used as a way of deepening the level of one's Christian faith, inspiring not just contemplation but the gentle, smiling compassion of the Boddhisattva. The ways of coming to sense one's "Buddha nature," as it is expressed in *Mahayana* Buddhism, are used by Christians to help them cultivate in faith their Christ-consciousness.

The renewal of the contemplative dimension of Christianity with practices coming from the Desert Fathers of the first centuries and the spiritual masters of the Middle Ages, practices which are being made widely available through Centering Prayer, the Contemplative Outreach, and the Christian Meditation Movement, has encouraged these parallel efforts to develop an enculturated contemplative spirituality within the Christian communities of Asia. Thomas Merton, one of the most significant spiritual teachers of the 20th c., who spent the last days of his life in Asia (Thailand), did much to authenticate the work of these pioneers. Officially, the Roman Catholic Church* set its seal on the development of an authentic Asian spirituality through the teachings of Vatican Council II: "Whatever truth and grace are to be found among the nations, as a sort of secret presence of God, this activity frees from all taint of evil and restores to Christ its maker . . . and so whatever good is found to be sown in the hearts and minds of men and women or in the rites and cultures peculiar to various peoples is not lost" (*Ad gentes,* 9). This activity is fostered by the ongoing guidance of the Secretariat for World Religions.

It is seen as essential to stand steady in the stream of one's own tradition while being open to humbly accept and incorporate what is good and valuable in other cultural and religious traditions.

Roman Catholic spirituality in other countries. Ricci found a worthy successor in a fellow Jesuit Fr. Pierre Teilhard de Chardin, who brought the same kind of genius to his work in China. Teilhard, like Ricci, was a far-seeing man. His gaze carried him beyond national and ethnic cultures to the time when they would necessarily come together to form one world culture. His was a vast cosmic vision, yet he promoted a spirituality that meshes well with contemporary valuations of nature, science, and technology, affirming the values of work, invention, learning, and recreation. He would have found more response in India with a kindred spirit such as Sri Aurabindo Ghose, who clearly saw all human activity as inherently religious. Teilhard's advanced ideas met a check similar to Ricci's and had to wait until Vatican Council II before their influence could permeate the more institutional church and foster certain dimensions of an authentic Asian spirituality. But widespread and fierce persecution devastated the church in China and also sought to destroy the traditional culture of the people through the frenzied Cultural Revolution. In survival mode, Chinese Christians have clung to spiritual ways taken directly from the Bible with little that is properly Chinese.

In Thailand, where monasticism is expected to be a part of everyone's life, at least for a time, and the national culture is thoroughly identified with Buddhism, the small Christian minority has largely stood apart and preserved the spirituality brought by the missionaries. This is generally true in all the Asian countries where Christians are a small and to some extent fearful minority. Things have taken a decided shift in Korea in recent decades, where the church has been intensely engaged in expansion and at the same time strongly devoted to prayer and contemplation.

Muslim countries offer a different kind of challenge to indigenization of Christian spirituality. Careful discernment is necessary to sort out what is truly part of the national and ethnic culture of the people and what comes from the religious culture of Islam. This does not mean that Christians cannot celebrate what they have in common with Islam* and Islamic spirituality, but still relatively little has been done along these lines.

The Philippines stand uniquely as the Christian country of Asia. For centuries, a Spanish Catholicism has been forming the culture. Even the native Apostolic Church takes its spirit from this Western spirituality. This is not to say that there are no hues in the spirituality of the Filipino Christians that are proper to them, but they are not readily identified as Asian.

In general, it must be said that Christian spirituality in Asia is in transition as Western forms recede and truly Asian approaches develop, mostly in minority contexts. The need for enculturation or indigenization is now more widely understood and accepted and is beginning to be realized, especially in India and to some extent in Japan.

Protestant spirituality in Asia. Any study of Asian Protestant spirituality must first take into consideration a major divide in Protestant religious consciousness. The division may be understood in terms of the difference between traditional and modern thought (although it is often inappropriately identified as the East-West divide).

It is not the case that Asian Christians are not aware of the need to express their faith in an authentically Asian way; rather, this issue is subsumed under a more basic consideration: On what epistemological basis can an authentic Christian spirituality be expressed in Asia?

Conservative Christians have tended to base their contextualization* efforts on a more or less traditional conception of God. An example may be seen in the symposium "God in Asian Contexts." Here the preferred method of contextualization is the translation model, since the main concern is to render the biblical norm in a form suitable to the social and religious context. The effectiveness of this approach is everywhere apparent, as evidenced by the phenomenal growth of conservative churches in Asia. The reason may lie in the fact that evangelical Christianity shares a similar worldview with the folk religions of Asia. It presupposes a level of interchange between the human and the divine which folk religionists can readily understand. Such a spirituality, however, has tended to be less concerned with the sociopolitical context. A case in point — perhaps a rather extreme case — is the spirituality of Watchman Nee*.

The more liberally oriented Protestant Christians, on the other hand, have sought to develop a spirituality where God is encountered within the sociopolitical matrix. The epistemological basis is usually in terms of the cosmic Christ (Raimundo Pannikar*, S. J. Samartha*, and others) or, more recently, in terms of process thought. Here, the Moltmannian conception of God as immanent transcendence has been found to be particularly attractive. The ensuing spirituality is almost invariably understood to be a spirituality of liberation. Spirituality denotes a dynamic inner quality of life, such as a certain attitude of honesty, fidelity, and willingness toward the real (Sobrino). For many, the context of political and economic oppression demands a critical spiritual response sustained by hope. This must be so if the negative reality is to be overcome by the larger positive reality.

This response takes many forms. In Korea, it is expressed in the combat spirituality of Minjung*. For the Indian theologian M. M. Thomas*, it is embodied in the concept of humanization. Thomas sees certain aspects of the modernization process in Asia as a spiritual awakening in which both Christians and non-Christians can participate. In this respect, Christian spirituality has much in common with the aspiration of secular humanism. Some would call the latter secular spirituality.

But a common thread that runs through Asian Protestant spirituality is the central role given to the incarnation. It provides the main paradigm for both evangelical and liberal Protestants for their spirituality of engagement.

Bibliography

Abishiktananda (Henri Le Saux), *Prayer* (1973). • Acharya, Francis, *Prayer with the Harp of the Spirit: The Prayer of Asian Churches,* 4 vols. (1983). • Chan, Simon, *Spiritual Theology* (1998). • Dechanet, J. M., *Christian Yoga* (1960). • Graham, Aelred, *Zen Catholicism* (1963). • Griffiths, Bede, *Return to the Center* (1977). • Johnston, William, *Christian Zen* (1971); *The Still Point: Reflections on Christian Mysticism* (1977). • Kadowaki, J. K., *Zen and the Bible* (1987). • Merton, Thomas, *Mystics and Zen Masters* (1967). • Vadakkekara, C. M., ed., *Prayer and Contemplation* (1980). • Viyagappa, Ignatius, ed., *In Spirit and In Truth: Essays Dedicated to Fr. Ignatius Hirudayam, S.J.* (1985). • Weber, J. G., ed., *In Quest of the Absolute: The Life and Work of Jules Monchanin,* Cistercian Studies Series, Vol. 51 (1977). • Fabella, Virginia, Peter K. H. Lee, and David Kwong-suh Suh, eds., *Asian Christian Spirituality* (1992). • Nacpil, Emerito P., and Douglas J. Elwood, eds., *The Human and the Holy* (1978). • Ro, Bong Rin, and Mark C. Albrecht, eds., *God in Asian Contexts: Communicating the God of the Bible in Asia* (1988). • Sobrino, Jon, *Spirituality of Liberation* (1988). • Thomas, M. M., *The Christian Response to the Asian Revolution* (1967).

BASIL PENNINGTON, with SIMON CHAN on Protestant Spirituality

Sri Lanka

The Democratic Socialist Republic of Sri Lanka, formerly Ceylon, which is an island nation in the Indian Ocean off the southeastern coast of the Indian subcontinent, is a member of the Commonwealth of Nations. It is separated from India* by the Palk Strait and Gulf of Mannar. The island is somewhat teardrop in shape, with its pinnacle in the north. The maximum length from north to south is about 440 km. (about 273 miles); the width is about 220 km. (about 137 miles). The total area of Sri Lanka is 65,610 sq. km. (25,332 sq. miles). The administrative capital of Sri Lanka is Sri Jayavardhanapura; Colombo is the commercial capital and largest city.

Sri Lanka became an independent member of the Commonwealth in 1948. Prime Minister Solomon W. R. D. Bandaranaike dominated Sri Lankan politics until his assassination in 1959. His wife, Sirimavo Bandaranaike, succeeded him, but her radical socialist policies created opposition, and she lost the 1965 elections. Reelected in 1970, she ruled until defeated in the 1977 elections by the conservative United National Party, led by J. R. Jayawardene. The latter, who became president in 1978, reduced state control of the economy and focused development efforts on rural projects. He was reelected to a six-year term in 1982. Ranasinghe Premadasa of the ruling United National Party succeeded him in office. The next government was formed by the Sri Lanka Peoples' Party under the leadership of Chandrika Kumaratunga in 1994.

Since the promulgation of a new constitution in 1978, Sri Lanka has had a strong presidential system of government. The cabinet is responsible to the elected parliament. The court system is extensive, and Sri Lankan law is based on a complex mixture of English, Roman-Dutch, and customary law.

The chief of state and head of government of Sri Lanka is the president, who is elected directly to a term of six years. The president appoints the prime minister and members of the cabinet and may dismiss parliament at will. According to the 1978 Sri Lanka constitution, the unicameral parliament is the "legislative power of the people." The 225 members of parliament are elected directly by a system of proportional representation.

Sri Lanka's economy is predominantly based on agriculture. Most of the citizens are subsistence farmers who make a living by growing rice on their small plots. A large export trade in tea, rubber, and coconuts is the dominant commercial activity. Foreign exchange also comes from the domestic and skilled labor provided to oil-rich countries in the Middle East.

The majority Buddhists' well-being falls within the responsibility of the government. The interests of ethnic minorities are generally looked after by their own political parties. Muslims, while being represented in the national political parties, have had their own Muslim Congress since 1982. The welfare of each major religion is looked after by a ministry at government level. Therefore the ministries of Buddhism*, Hinduism*, and Islam* attend to the needs of these religions. Christianity, on the other hand, has no ministry of its own because denominational differences prevent it from being represented by one body. However, the ministry of cultural affairs deals with issues relevant to the Christian religion.

Except for a very small number of European descendants, almost all Sri Lankans are the descendants of migrants from India. The two major racial groups differ ethnically, linguistically, and in religion. The Sinhalese, 74 percent of the population, speak Sinhalese and are Buddhists. The Tamil (18 percent), who are concentrated in the north, speak Tamil and are Hindus. Small numbers of Tamil-speaking Muslims (7 percent), burghers of Dutch and Portuguese descent, Malays, and Europeans make up the remainder. The Sinhalese and Tamils observe caste distinctions, which are often important in politics. Sinhalese was the sole official language from 1956 to 1987, and since 1987 Sinhalese and Tamil have been official languages, with English as the link language. English is spoken by about 10 percent of the population and is commonly used in government. The most serious problem facing the country is the long-standing civil war, with ethnic overtones, which turned increasingly violent after 1983 and disrupted the economy. Some sections of Tamils have claimed that they have been discriminated against since independence, and militant Tamils demanded a separate Tamil state in the mostly Tamil Northern Province and the ethnically mixed Eastern Province.

History. Sri Lanka's first settlers were probably those Mesolithic Age proto-Austroloid ethnic groups who migrated from the Indian subcontinent. These settlers were absorbed by the Indo-Europeans who arrived from North India in the 6th c. B.C.E. and developed into the Sinhalese. The Tamils migrated from South India over a long period from about the 1st c. B.C.E. Buddhism was introduced to the island in the 3rd c. B.C.E. The classical Sinhalese civilization was nourished by Buddhism and South Indian influence. The first Europeans to arrive in Sri Lanka were the Portuguese, who ruled some parts of the country from 1505 to 1658. Next came the Dutch (1638-1796), and finally the British (1796-1948). The independent Sinhalese kingdom was annexed by the British in 1815.

There are legends that connect Christianity in Sri Lanka to the evangelism of the apostle Thomas (see St. Thomas and the Thomas Tradition). Some archaeological evidence found in the North Central Province shows that Christians were a powerful minority in the 6th c. and 7th c., but these communities died out. The present form of Christianity, however, began with the arrival of the first Franciscan* missionaries in 1542, Jesuits (1602; see Society of Jesus), Augustinians* (1604), and Dominicans* (1605) in the Portuguese period. The Dutch who took over the Portuguese territory introduced the Reformed (see Presbyterian and Reformed Churches) faith while trying to suppress Roman* Catholicism. The Indian Oratorians secretly served the Roman Catholics during the Dutch period. In the 19th c., the British allowed open competition for religious activities. The Bible* was available in Tamil beginning in 1708, and in Sinhalese beginning in 1722. The Ceylon auxiliary of the British and Foreign Bible Society (see Bible Societies), which was inaugurated in 1812, began revising the Sinhalese Bible in 1813. The work of the Tamil Bible was assigned to the Madras auxiliary.

In the period of British rule, the Roman Catholic and Dutch Reformed churches continued to function, while the new missionary bodies such as the Baptists* (1812), Wesleyan Methodists* (1814), American Board of Commissioners for Foreign Missions (1816), and Church Missionary Society (1818) set up schools, hospitals, printing establishments, and churches to evangelize the country. The Salvation Army* (1883), Seventh-day Adventists* (1904), and Assemblies of God (1923) were other important missions in Sri Lanka in the first half of the 20th c. The Roman Catholic Church received new vigor with the arrival of new European missionaries beginning in 1842. The dioceses of Colombo (1845) and Jaffna (1847) were the first two bishoprics to be set up. In 1886 the Roman Catholic hierarchy was organized under an archbishop resident in Colombo. Today there are 11 dioceses with over one million Catholics. The Ceylon Pentecostal Mission, founded in 1924, is a Sri Lankan Christian organization with missions in America, France, England, India, and Malaysia*. There has been a proliferation of independent and foreign-affiliated missions since the 1960s.

The leadership of the church gradually came into the hands of the national leaders beginning in the 1930s. The Roman Catholics had their first Sinhalese bishop in 1939. The first Sinhalese Anglican* bishop was appointed in 1945. Today the Christian church is in complete control of the national leadership.

Sri Lanka's independence was a turning point in the history of Christianity. The Buddhist majority, which came to power under democratic elections, brought with it Buddhist sentiments to reduce the influence of Christians in the country. Therefore, in 1956 Christian nuns were prohibited from working in government hospitals. In 1961 the denominational schools were taken over by the government. Since 1966, there have been some unsuccessful attempts to introduce legislation making it difficult for people to convert to another religion. The constitutions in 1972 and 1978 made Buddhism the religion of the government while tolerating other religions.

During the 1980s, new Christian groups developed in Sri Lanka. Most of them were Pentecostal* and charismatic* sects which believe in the literal interpretation of the Scripture. These groups have received inspiration from the Christian bodies in America, Korea*, and more recently, Singapore*. They are even more divided than the traditional churches, which failed to be united after repeated attempts of church union similar to that in South India. The new churches have taken Christianity to almost every village in Sri Lanka. They have made converts from Buddhists, Muslims, intellectuals, and ordinary people. The majority of the leaders of these churches are themselves converts from other religions.

Current state of Christianity. Christians form a beleaguered minority in Sri Lanka today. The traditional churches have lost their numbers and privilege since independence. Growth is seen only in the newly emerging fundamentalist and Pentecostal churches. The liberal and inclusive forms of Christian faith supported by many in traditional churches have seen a reduction of their own numbers.

The following statistics, taken from the government department of statistics (1997), show a breakdown of religious affiliations in the country:

Roman Catholics	1,005,609
Dutch Reformed	1,700
Church of Ceylon (Anglican)	33,147
Wesleyan Methodists	28,471
Church of South India (formerly ABCFM)	5,000
Church of Foursquare Gospel	6,187
Assemblies of God	19,880
Others (Approximately)	25,000

Christians are equally divided among the two major ethnic groups, Sinhalese and Tamil. Nevertheless, there is mutual cooperation among them in spite of ethnic rivalries in the country at large.

Of the 25 administrative districts of the country, Christians form the majority only in the Chillaw District. They also form a major percentage in Gampaha and Colombo Districts. Most of the Protestants are concentrated in the cities of Colombo, Jaffna, and Kandy. However, Christians are found in all parts of the country due to the activities of new independent churches. Reliable statistics pertaining to these numbers are not available.

The Christian church began the process of indigenization in the 1960s. Services and education are conducted in the Sinhalese and Tamil languages, although a few churches in cities continue to hold services in English. Christianity has been accepted as a national religion despite occasional criticism of the Buddhists, who do not want their members to be converted to Christianity. So far, people of all walks of life have given their life to Christ because of personal experiences with him.

Bibliography

De Silva, C. R., *Sri Lanka: A Survey* (1988). • De Silva, K. M., *A History of Sri Lanka* (1990). • Somaratna, G. P. V., *The Events of Christian History in Sri Lanka* (1997).

G. P. V. Somaratna

Sri Mo Wichai

(b. Chiang Mai, Thailand, 16 Jan 1868; d. 19 Apr 1938). Important figure in the development of northern Thai Protestantism.

Born to Nan Sriwichai and Wandee Wichai, Sri Mo was baptized in 1880. In 1889 he became one of the first northern Thai to travel to the United States. His letters from the United States, later published, constituted one of the earliest sources of information on the West printed in northern Thai. Upon his return, he became an evangelist with the Chiang Mai Station of the Presbyterian* Laos* Mission (northern Thailand*). He married Kham Baw Chaiwan, and they had nine children. He was ordained an elder in 1893 and a clergy in 1910. He served as an assistant pastor of First Church, Chiang Mai, the "mother church" of northern Thai Protestantism. He was a senior member of the church's pastoral-evangelistic team and oversaw work with its numerous rural groups. On occasion, Sri Mo served as acting senior pastor. In 1913 he became a part-time instructor at the mission's Theological* Training School, later the McGilvary* Theological Seminary. In later years he devoted much of his energy to the seminary. Sri Mo served as moderator of the North Laos Presbytery in 1910 and was elected the first moderator of the first district of the newly established Church of Christ in Siam in 1934. Sri Mo was widely recognized as the northern Thai church's most important figure and a leader in the gradual "nationalization" of Thai Protestantism.

Bibliography

Boonserm Satraphai, *Sri Mo, The First Person to Go to America* (in Thai) (1980). • McFarland, George B., ed., *Historical Sketch of Protestant Missions in Siam* (1928). • Swanson, Herbert R., *Krischak Muang Nua* (1984).

Kummool Chinawong, translated by Herbert R. Swanson

Staunton, John Armitage

(b. Adrian, Michigan, 14 Apr 1864; d. 24 May 1944). Episcopal Church pioneer missionary to the pagan Igorot Filipinos of Sagada, Mountain Province, Philippines*.

Appointed missionary to the Philippine District in 1901, Staunton was an Anglo-Catholic Episcopal priest whose personal devotion was founded on the Blessed Sacrament and the Blessed Virgin Mary. He established a church, Saint Mary the Virgin, in Sagada in 1904. He introduced services similar to those of the Roman* Catholic Church, including the elaborate processions of the statues, especially the Virgin Mary's; the strict observance of confession before receiving Holy Communion; the withholding of the chalice from the laity; and the carrying of the reserved sacraments to the sick members of the congregation. Staunton would spend 15 minutes praying before the reserved sacraments in the Roman Catholic church before proceeding to the Episcopal church each time he visited the Bontoc mission, which was 18 kilometers west of Sagada. Likewise, in Manila (1904-8) he attended services at the Roman Catholic cathedral instead of the Episcopal cathedral, whose rector was an evangelical.

During the early 1920s, financial support from the Episcopal Church in America was reduced drastically, and it affected the vast industrialization projects started by Staunton in Sagada. The National Council had to turn down requests from Staunton because of large deficits ($950,000) in 1923. Disappointed, Staunton recommended that the Sagada mission be handed over to the Roman Catholics, after which he submitted his resignation (Dec 1924), which was immediately accepted by Bishop Mosher and the National Council. Staunton and his wife, Maria, left the Philippines on 23 Feb 1925. On 22 Sep 1930, he renounced his allegiance to the Episcopal Church. He was ordained a Roman Catholic priest in Sep 1933 at the age of 69.

Bibliography

Scott, William Henry, *Staunton of Sagada: Christian Civilizer* (1962). • *The Growth of a Mission: Sagada, 1904-1922* (1922). • *Sagada Mission Today: 1930* (1930).

FLOYD T. CUNNINGHAM

Stebbins, I. R.

(b. 1894; d. 1971); Mary Hartman Stebbins (b. Norway, 1892; d. 1964). American pioneer missionaries of the Christian and Missionary Alliance* (C&MA) to Indochina.

Arriving in Tonkin, Vietnam*, on 2 Nov 1918, Stebbins began French- and Vietnamese-language study in Saigon with John Olson, a recent immigrant to the United States from Norway. Mary Hartman (1892-1964), who traveled by ship and arrived in Indochina at the same time as Stebbins, was to become his wife on 23 Mar 1920 in a ceremony at the American Consulate in Canton, South China*. Six of their adult children also served in Asia as missionaries. Harriette married George Irwin, son of Franklin and Marie Irwin*, and served in Vietnam until 1975. Ruth married Ed Thompson and served with the C&MA first in Cambodia* and later in Vietnam, where they were killed on 1 Feb 1968 during the Tet Offensive in an attack on the mission compound in Banmethuot. Elizabeth married Floyd Gibbs and served with the C&MA in the Philippines*. George married Jackie Masters and served with Overseas Crusades in Vietnam for four years. Anne and David Moore served with the C&MA in Indonesia*. Thomas married Donna Stadsklev, daughter of C&MA missionaries to Ivory Coast, and served in Vietnam from 1956 to 1975.

Stebbins was present at the baptism of the first Protestant Vietnamese convert, Mr. Lang, who became his associate and language teacher. An early encouragement in their work came from Mr. Pethie, who was manager of the Standard Oil Company and vice-consul for the American government.

After language study, the Stebbinses moved to Tourane (Da Nang) in 1920 and did evangelism alongside Vietnamese converts Mr. Hou, Mr. Khanh, and student-preacher Mr. Thua. Among the most significant of the converts of Stebbins's ministry is Mr. Lieu, a well-known actor and scholar of Chinese classics. Before his conversion, Lieu sought to embarrass the missionaries by asking questions drawn from the Chinese classics. But after several weeks of attempting to show that the Confucian classics were superior, Lieu embraced the Gospel and became the most effective witness throughout central and southern Vietnam.

From Tourane the Stebbinses went to Sadec for two-and-a-half years, the native place of their language teacher, Mr. Lang. Rumors spread that inquirers would receive $20 if they converted. While this was not true, the effect was to draw attention to the new religion and raise interest. The Stebbinses' first converts, Mr. and Mrs. Ngo and his mother and relatives, formed the nucleus of a new evangelical church in Sadec. He was also instrumental in starting the Evangelical Church of Vietnam (ECVN) at Cao Lanh when the mayor, Mr. Xa-Hanh, became a believer, along with several other prominent businessmen. Other mission stations were opened at the same time by colleagues Herbert Jackson, who went to Cantho, and Rev. Grupe, who went to Chau Doc assisted by the converted actor, Lieu.

The Stebbinses moved from Sadec to Saigon and then to Vinh Long (80 miles from Saigon) in the delta. At Vinh Long, the Stebbinses worked with a new student-preacher, Mr. Huyen, who was to become the seventh president of the ECVN. Prior to World War II*, the Stebbinses moved to Hue, where their many contacts with French colonial administrators and the Vietnamese bureaucracy proved of great benefit in starting churches in the area. The family of nine returned to the United States in 1941 to escape World War II. In 1949 Rev. and Mrs. Stebbins returned to Vietnam alone. During the next five years Rev. Stebbins opened three new churches in Saigon, driven by the vision of reaching the new urban masses. This opened the eyes of national church leaders, who at first doubted that a major city could support more than one evangelical church. After a year of furlough, the Stebbinses returned to Hue, where they held evangelistic meetings in a large tent provided by Christian friends in the United States. Until their retirement in 1960, they taught English classes in their home and thus witnessed to many university students, professionals, businessmen, and government workers.

Bibliography

Le, Phu Hoang, "A Short History of the Evangelical Church of Vietnam (1911-1965)" (Unpublished dissertation, New York University, 1972), 2 Vols. • Stebbins, I. R. "To The Regions Beyond" (Unpublished manuscript, 1961).

JAMES F. LEWIS

Sterrett, Thomas Norton

(b. Urumia, Persia, 10 Nov 1912; d. Nyack, New York, USA, 10 Feb 1978). American missionary, Bible* scholar, and musician.

In 1938 Sterrett received a bachelor of arts degree in biblical education from Columbia Bible College, and a bachelor of arts from Wheaton College. In 1940 he did postgraduate work at Dallas Theological Seminary and received his master of theology and doctor of theology degrees.

He married Eloise Fain on 10 Jun 1938 and arrived in India* the next year. He was in Uttar Pradesh (UP) for 14 years. The couple's children, Anne (b. 26 Nov 1942) and Gerald (b. 14 Feb 1945), were born in Kanpur, UP.

From 1939 to 1948, Sterrett worked with the Independent Board for Presbyterian* Foreign Mission in Kanpur. From 1949 to 1953, he was with the Canadian Presbyterian Mission as principal and teacher at Bundelkhand Bible School, Jhansi, UP.

By 1954 Sterrett was in India as representative of the International Fellowship of Evangelical Students (IFES)*. From 1954 onward he was based in Madras with the ministry of the Union of Evangelical Students of India (UESI)*, which was formed that year. First he became a UESI staff worker, but from 1956 he was able to induct full-time Indian workers into this national movement.

In 1975 the Sterretts returned to the United States, where he founded a discipleship training center in Nyack, New York, with the Inter-Varsity Christian Fellowship. There he died in 1978.

Sterrett was a musician, well accomplished in piano, organ, trumpet, accordion, and other instruments. He is remembered as a clear and convincing Bible teacher for students in the Indian subcontinent. His book, *How to Understand the Bible,* has been widely used not only in India but throughout the world.

Bibliography

Sterrett, Barbara Jo, personal letter, 4 Jan 1994. • Sterrett, Anne, fax letter of 5 Feb 1994. • Personal memories of writer.

P. T. Chandapilla

Stockwell, F. Olin and Esther

(b. Oklahoma and Korea, 14 Dec 1900 and 20 Mar 1900 respectively; Esther: d. Denver, Colorado, 16 Oct 1992). American missionaries to China* and Singapore*.

Olin served as pastor in his home state of Oklahoma immediately after his marriage to Esther on 20 Jun 1924. In 1929 they went as Methodist* missionaries to Foochow, China, and in 1939 to Chengdu. During this period, Olin served as an effective missionary preacher while Esther taught music* in church-related colleges. They returned to the United States on furlough in 1941, and Esther earned a master of music degree in Chicago. Olin returned to China* during World War II*, and Esther rejoined him in 1946.

In 1950 Olin was arrested by the Chinese Communist government and was imprisoned in Chungking for two years. There he wrote some meditations or devotional talks with only the help of Moffatt's translation of the New Testament. He also wrote about his experiences on the margins in an anthology of modern poetry, calling it *With God in Red China.*

Olin and Esther came to Singapore at the end of the missionary exodus from China occasioned by the new Communist government and the hatred engendered by the Korean War*. They were "missionary refugees" welcomed on to the Trinity Theological College faculty, where they remained for 12 years (1955-67).

Esther taught English and music (piano and organ), and kept her home open to students and friends. Olin had one message, which he preached repeatedly, namely, that a strong church demanded well-trained pastors. He said, "Our march toward a self-governing, self-supporting, and self-propagating church depended on trained leadership, and that leadership we could produce at Trinity."

The Stockwells showed faithfulness and courage in China. Teaching in two languages in Singapore, they manifested a consuming desire to train Christian leadership for the churches of Southeast Asia.

Bibliography

Stockwell, F. Olin, *With God in Red China* (1953); *Meditations from a Prison Cell* (1954).

Ho Chee Sin

Stone, Mary. *See* Shi Mei Yi

Stronach, Alexander

(b. Edinburgh, Scotland, 15 Apr 1800; d. London, 6 Feb 1879). London Missionary Society (LMS) missionary in Penang, Singapore*, and Xiamen (Amoy).

After a time as an evangelist with the Irish Evangelical Society, Stronach married Eliza Clark, was ordained in 1837, and was appointed by the LMS to Singapore along with his younger brother John. He and Eliza moved to Penang in 1839, where he was involved with preaching and schools. He visited Hong Kong in Aug 1843 for the LMS Conference of Missionaries and the Convention of Missionaries on Bible* translation. After returning to Penang and then to Singapore in 1844, he oversaw the closure of the LMS mission there, sharing in the view that mission to China* at that time needed to be based in China itself. In 1846 he reestablished the Melaka (Malacca*) printing press in Hong Kong and then joined his brother John in Amoy. They were appreciated as preachers and missionary colleagues. With Eliza, Alexander also ran a boarding school from 1850 to 1860. He wrote booklets entitled *Glory of Christ* and *Grace of Jesus,* as well as 37 of the 85 hymns in the Amoy hymnbook, which he compiled in 1857.

Bibliography

Wylie, Alexander, *Memorials of Protestant Missionaries to the Chinese* (1867).

John Roxborogh

Stronach, John

(Shi Dun Li) (b. Edinburgh, Scotland, 7 Mar 1810; d. Philadelphia, Pennsylvania, United States, 30 Oct 1888). London Missionary Society (LMS) missionary in Singapore* and Xiamen (Amoy) and Bible* translator.

Stronach studied at Edinburgh University and the Glasgow Theological* Academy. He married Margaret Ralston in Jan 1834. With his brother Alexander, he arrived in Singapore in Mar 1838. He became a secretary of the Singapore Tract and Book Society, assisted in English services, worked on a Malay New Testament, and encouraged a Malay girls' school run by Margaret. In Aug 1843, he was in Hong Kong to attend the LMS Conference of Missionaries and the Convention of Missionaries on Bible translation. From 1844, he and Margaret pioneered LMS work in Amoy, but she died in 1846 while returning to England for her health.

From 1847 to 1850, Stronach was based in Shanghai and involved with Walter Medhurst*, William Charles Milne (son of William Milne*), Elijah Bridgeman, and Bishop Boone in the Delegates' Translation of the New Testament. After disputes over the word to be used for God in the Old Testament, he joined Medhurst and Milne to work on their own version, produced in 1853. He and Medhurst also translated the Bible into colloquial Mandarin. He returned to Amoy, where he was based until 1876. He married Lucretia Brown in Philadelphia in 1878 and retired from the mission. He was remembered for his good humor, speaking and apologetic gifts, idiomatic Amoy, and place in the history of the Chinese Bible.

Bibliography

Wylie, Alexander, *Memorials of Protestant Missionaries to the Chinese* (1867).

John Roxborogh, with contributions from the China Group

Stuart, John Leighton

(b. Hangchow, China, 1876; d. 1962). Missionary to China* of the (Southern) Presbyterian* Church in the United States, educator, and diplomat.

Born into a Presbyterian missionary family in China, Stuart went to America to study in 1887. He attended a public school in Alabama and was a good student. He graduated form Hampden-Sydney College in 1896 and taught for three years before entering Union Theological Seminary, New York. In 1902, upon his graduation, he was ordained as a pastor.

Stuart returned to China in 1904 and worked in Hangchow. Four years later, he was posted to Nanking (Nanjing) Theological* Seminary, where he taught until 1919. While there he wrote an introductory book on Greek in Chinese and compiled the *Greek-Chinese Dictionary of the New Testament.* When Yenching University was founded in 1919 (from the union of Peking University, North China Union College, and North China Union Women's* College), he was named principal, a post which was changed to dean of studies 10 years later. Stuart devoted almost 30 years of his life to the development of Yenching University and showed his full support for academic freedom. He also developed the first school of journalism in China and formed Harvard-Yenching Institute of Chinese Studies, which enabled Yenching to develop Chinese studies to the best standards of any purely Chinese institution. The links of Yenching with Harvard and Princeton made Yenching the premier private university in China.

In 1946 Stuart was appointed United States ambassador to China. During his term in office, he supported the nationalist government's outbreak of civil war and hence opposed the revolution of the China Communist Party (see Communism). Stuart was called back to America in Aug 1949. He suffered a severe stroke at the end of that year. He died 13 years later.

Bibliography

Stuart, John Leighton, *New Commentary to the Book of Revelation; Greek Learning; Fifty Years in China: The Memoirs of John Leighton Stuart, Missionary and Ambassador* (1954). • Edwards, Dwight, *Yenching University* (1959). • Lutz, Jessie G., *China and the Christian Colleges, 1850-1950* (1971). • Shaw, Yu-ming, *An American Missionary in China: John Leighton Stuart and Chinese-American Relations* (1992). • West, Philip, *Yenching University and Sino-Western Relations, 1916-1952* (1976).

China Group

Student Christian Movement

(SCM). Its diverse, pluralistic cultures and the quest for truth has always inspired the birth of new movements in Asia. Since the 1870s, this rich Asian context paved the way for the emergence of autonomous and self-determining student movements. In fact, the history of SCM goes back to the formation of the World Student Christian Federation (WSCF) on 17 Aug 1895 in Vadstena, Sweden, with the vision and mission of "the evangelization of the world in this generation." With this motto, John R. Mott*, one of the founding members of WSCF, traveled throughout Asia to inspire students to start the Student Christian Movement in Asia. In this way, students and faculty in academic communities pioneered the modern missionary and ecumenical* movement in Asia. After World War II*, SCMs took a radical approach which was influenced by liberation, feminist, ecological, and contextual theologies to empower students for social transformation. Presently, 16 national Student Christian Movements exist in Asia. These SCMs include Australia, New Zealand, and the Pacific because they became an integral part of Asia.

The aims of SCM could be summarized as follows, though each movement has its own goals: to call its members to faith in God, Christ, and the Holy Spirit according to the Scriptures, and to discipleship within the life and mission of the church; to help members grow in the Christian life through prayer, study of the Bible*, and participation in the worship* and witness of the church; to help members witness to Jesus Christ in the academic community; to bring members into fellowship with one another in mutual service and to support efforts to serve all students in their need; to help members strive for peace and justice in and among nations; to help members work for the manifestation of the unity of the church; and to help members be servants and messengers of the "reign of God" throughout the world.

The Student Christian Movement in Japan* played a vital role in the formation of the ecumenical student movement both at the national and global levels. As early as 1870, a student association called Believers in Jesus was launched, followed by the student Young Men's Christian Association* (YMCA) in 1888. In 1901, the Japan city YMCA alliance was set up and was merged with the student YMCA alliance in 1903 to become the National Council of YMCAs of Japan.

The SCM also exists in India*, Pakistan*, Sri Lanka* (Ceylon), and Bangladesh*. Members from the academic community and theological* and church leaders from undivided India and Ceylon came together to start the Student Christian Association of India and Ceylon in 1912 in Serampore, West Bengal, India. Though Myanmar* (Burma) joined the movement in 1920, political changes toward separate nationhood in Pakistan prompted Sri Lanka, Bangladesh, India, and Myanmar to form their own autonomous movements. SCM of India became the second-largest movement in Asia, next to Indonesia*, with creative local, regional, and national activities. This movement played a significant role in the freedom struggle in the 1940s and protested against central control in the 1970s. Over 100 college and university units focus on social justice, peace, and creation, including gender, *dalit**, indigenous people, human rights, ecological concerns, and biblical and theological foundations for the social gospel.

In 1955, SCM of Sri Lanka adapted its own constitution and programs and became autonomous. It was very active in high schools, colleges, and universities and contributed to ecumenical leadership. Due to various factors, including ethnic conflict, this movement became weak. The SCMs in Pakistan and Bangladesh are not very strong due to the religious context. However, these SCMs are active in a few cities among college students, teachers, and church leaders in organizing Bible studies and social work. The history of the Myanmar SCM has the same roots as the SCMs in the subcontinent. Though government restrictions have hampered the movement's involvement at national, regional, and interregional events, it is still doing Bible study, fellowship meetings, and social work.

Since 1896, the China* SCM has been active among high school and college students. In 1910 Ting Limeiyi set up many China student resolution groups. By 1922 its membership reached 30,000. The Chinese delegation proposed to have an independent movement at the 11th World Student Christian Alliance Congress in 1922 in Peking (Beijing), and this laid the foundation for the China Christian Student Movement Planning Committee in 1927. This movement was gradually drawn into the powerful current of the national student movement. Later, in 1939, the national Christian Inter-Varsity society was established. During the war, the society was not able to continue its activities, and soon it disappeared forever.

The Indonesian SCM began in the 1920s when the chaplaincy organized activities for students on campus. On 28 Dec 1932, the *Christelijke Studenten Vereeninging op Java* (CSV) was founded. In 1945, after Indonesia became independent, the *Perhimpunan Mahasiswa Kristen Indonesia* (PMKI) was created to continue CSV's work. On 9 Feb 1950, *Gerakan Mahasiswa Kristen Indonesia* (GMKI) was established from a fusion of the CSV and the PMKI. This movement was committed to attaining the ideals of "a deep-rooted faith, a high level of intellect, and a strong sense of service." This movement became the largest in the world, with 50,000 members focusing on a wide range of contemporary issues.

The SCM of Hong Kong has its origins in the 1920s, but many Chinese intellectuals opposed Christian activities, seeing them as an instrument of colonialism*. Though it was reestablished after 1949, it disappeared again in the 1970s and was then restarted in 1981 as a city group. The SCM of Singapore* was started in 1939 as part of SCM Malaya and became autonomous in 1965, organizing social work and protesting the war in Vietnam*. In early 1987, the movement was accused of being part of a Marxist plot to overthrow the government. Since then, it has maintained a low profile but has remained committed to supporting student activities. The SCM of Malaysia* was started in 1939 and was active among seminarians, church youth, and high school students. Due to various factors, this movement is inactive. The SCM of Thailand* was established in 1951 and became strong with many activities in the 1960s and 1970s, but it later disappeared due to political reasons. The SCM was again started in the mid-1990s to continue some limited activities. The SCM in Taiwan* began in 1954 when the first student center was opened for students of the Presbyterian* Church of Taiwan. The SCM there focuses on concern for the aborigines, environmental protection, human rights, and the nationhood of Taiwan.

In the 1960s, the Korean Student Christian Federation (KSCF) was active in social development and moved into active struggle against the Yushin dictatorship, supporting democracy demonstrations. Due to the emergency measure of the government in the mid-1970s, KSCF was forced to go underground. KSCF consolidated in the 1980s and is focusing on contemporary issues, including reunification of the Koreas*. The SCM of the Philippines* was established in 1960 and went underground in response to Marcos's crackdown on academic organizations. The SCM immersed itself amongst the poor and peasants and fought for their dignity.

During the 1950s, a split took place in the SCMs between a group emphasizing personal salvation and one that laid a stronger emphasis on the social gospel with an openness to ecumenism. Though this trend marked a decline in membership, many movements continued to prepare ecumenical* leadership for Asian churches. Most of the movements were consolidated during the last quarter of this century. The SCMs have been enrolling over 90,000 every year in Asia and the Pacific, which continuously stands as the largest SCM in the world. The SCM in Asia-Pacific is recommitted to engaging Christian students in issues of justice, peace, and creation.

Bibliography

WSCF, *Life of the Movements of World Student Christian Federation* (1992). • Potter, Philip, "Celebrating God's Faithfulness: The WSCF as a Community of Memory," *WSCF Journal* (Dec 1995). • Ledger, Christine, "World Student Christian Federation," in *The Dictionary of the Ecumenical Movement* (1991). • De Dietrich, Suzanne, *World Student Christian Federation: 50 Years of History, 1895-1945,* trans. Audrey Abrecht (1946). • Carino, Feliciano V., "Current Intellectual, Ideological and Spiritual Climate," *Ecumenical Student Ministry in Asia-Pacific* (1995). • Engel, Frank, *Living in a World Community: An East Asian Experience of the World Student Christian Federation, 1931-1961* (1995). • Potter, Philip, and Thomas Wieser, *Seeking and Serving the Truth: The First Hundred Years of the World Student Christian Federation* (1997). Daniel Peter and Shin Seung Min

Student Organizations, Catholic. *See* Catholic University Students Organization (Indonesia)

Students. *See* International Fellowship of Evangelical Students; Student Christian Movement; Union of Evangelical Students of India

Studium Biblicum

Bible* study institution set up by the Franciscans in China*.

First set up in Beijing, the Studium Biblicum moved to Hong Kong under the leadership of Gabriel Allegra (1907-76). Its purpose was to carry on the translation of the entire Bible into Chinese.

Allegra was sent to Beijing in 1941 for this purpose, and in Aug 1945 he succeeded in holding the official inauguration of the Studium Biblicum on the premises of the Catholic Fujen University. In 1946 the Chinese translation of the first book, the Psalms, was published, followed by that of two other Wisdom books in 1947.

But the political situation in Beijing was unstable. After some changes of residence, the Studium Biblicum, with its members, was permanently transferred to Hong Kong in 1948, where in 10 years the entire Old Testament and the four Gospels were published. The text plus commentary totaled 7,500 pages.

The translation and commentary work continued for almost another decade. Finally, in 1968 the one-volume Chinese Catholic Bible was published and in 1969 a copy could be presented to Pope Paul VI.

The work of the Studium Biblicum has continued with the publication of Bible-related works, such as the commentaries, a Bible dictionary (1975), books and periodicals, and with the organization of courses and conferences on Bible topics.

Bibliography

Gozzo, S. M., *Memorie Autogiografiche del P. Gabriele M. Allegra, OFM* (in Italian) (1986). Sergio Ticozzi

Stuntz, Clyde B(ronson)

(b. La Grande, Iowa, United States, 8 Oct 1886; d. Monroe, Louisiana, United States, Dec 1965). Methodist* missionary to Pakistan*.

Stuntz was the son of missionary bishop Homer Clyde Stuntz (1858-1924) and Estelle Clark Stuntz. His early years were spent in India* (Calcutta and Bombay/Mumbai) and Manila, Philippines*. He studied at Cornell University, graduated from Wesleyan University (1910), and later studied at Columbia University (master of arts in Sanskrit, 1913) and Drew Theological Seminary (bachelor of divinity, 1913). In 1913 he married Florence (Sally) Ada Watters and was appointed in that same year as a pastor in Farley, Iowa (1913-15). In 1915, the Stuntzes accepted an appointment for Clyde to pastor the Thoburn Church in Calcutta, and so they set sail on 20 Nov 1915. Because European conflicts spread to India, the Stuntzes requested a move from Germanic areas of Calcutta and were subsequently sent to Lahore. Stuntz's early success with Indian languages continued as he mastered Urdu, Punjabi, and Gurmukhi within a few years.

One of Stuntz's greatest concerns in this new area was the treatment and even the safety of large numbers of outcastes who were becoming Christian. They were often denied homes and land, and Stuntz began to consider how these oppressed people could continue to live in their own country. At the same time the British government began programs of irrigation and canal work to bring water to the dryer areas of present-day Pakistan. The method Stuntz devised was to procure sites (near irrigation areas) for villages where whole Christian communities could move and begin a new life. These villages, called *chaks,* at first were given numbers for identification, and later they were named. Stuntzabad was the first such name given. Quickly, villages like Stuntzabad developed health-care centers, high schools, and even post offices.

With the partition in 1947, Stuntz's ministry suddenly changed. Muslims were migrating, in the midst of great violence, to East and West Pakistan, and Hindus (and Sikhs) were migrating to India. The Stuntzes began to organize transportation for the pilgrims by providing free busing. For his sacrificial service to Pakistan, Stuntz was later decorated by the Pakistani government. From 1951 to 1952, Stuntz moved from his rural work to begin a Methodist work in Karachi and then Lahore (1952-56). Throughout his time in Pakistan, Stuntz was remarkable for his recognition of villagers — there were thousands he could call by name — and his unselfish work in providing for the basic needs of the oppressed poor. The Stuntzes returned to the United States in 1956, and nine years later he died.

Bibliography

Encyclopedia of World Methodism.

SCOTT W. SUNQUIST

Subba Rao, Kalagara

(b. ca. 1912; d. 9 May 1981)

Subba Rao was born into a Kamma ("clean" caste) agricultural family in the Godavari district of Andhra Pradesh, India*. At 16 years of age, he was sent to Calcutta and earned a B.A. degree with first class honors at City College, Calcutta, in 1930. In 1935, he completed his B.T. degree and took a teaching job in Andhra. He married Srimatti Nagendramma in 1937. In 1939, in relation to his writing and lecturing on the war, he was awarded the title Rao Saheb. He was an atheist opposed to religion and especially to *sadhus* and priests. He was living a reckless life, and since his impertinent ways ruined his health, he retired to Munipalle for rest.

In this situation in 1942, he had a vision of Christ. His health was restored, but the full implications of his life-changing vision only gradually emerged. To his own surprise, he realized that when he invoked the name of Jesus, healings occurred. He acknowledged that there was power in the name of Christ and began to minister to those who sought help. The chronology of these events is not at all clear. How long the silent period lasted, when the open healing ministry developed, and how and when Christian contacts began cannot be stated with certainty. Christians quite naturally expected this devotee of Christ to be baptized. This proved a major point of contention between Subba Rao and Christians for the rest of his life. Subba Rao would not be baptized, and he regularly and vehemently taught that baptism is just one more senseless ceremony.

Strikingly, the published writings of Subba Rao are almost entirely attacks on the church. Even some of his poems, published as devotional hymns, are in fact attacks on the church and Christianity. By 1958 Subba Rao was conducting healing meetings in Hyderabad. The full extent of his ministry is hard to determine, but he touched hundreds of thousands, and some estimate that up to 10,000 people (mostly Hindus) recognized him as their guru. Today meetings continue on the pattern Subba Rao developed: the singing of his 34 *bhajans* and some traditional Christian songs, a brief reading from the New Testament, and then the laying on of hands and healing. It is claimed that about 20 groups are meeting in various places, mostly in Andhra Pradesh. On the anniversary of Subba Rao's death, a large crowd assembles in Munipalle, and at Christmas a similarly sizable function is held in Vijayawada.

Subba Rao remained a faithful devotee and servant of Christ within the Hindu community until his death. A small memorial shrine was built behind the prayer hall in Munipalle, and flowers are placed there daily on Subba Rao's grave. Statues and pictures of Subba Rao are present, but there is not the slightest hint of any worship being offered to him. People are still turning to Jesus Christ through the ongoing ministry of the disciples of Subba Rao, but clearly the dynamic force of the movement could not survive Subba Rao's demise.

Bibliography

Airen, C. D., *Kalagara Subba Rao, The Mystic of Munipalle* (n.d.). • Baago, Kaj, *The Movement around Subba Rao* (1968). • Rao, K. Subba, *Gurudev! Where Can I Get So Many Millstones?* (n.d.). • Richard, H. L., ed., *Free from the Madness of Religions: The Life, Ministry and Hymns of K. Subba Rao of Andhra Pradesh* (forthcoming). • Thyagaraju, A. F., *Subba Rao: The Man and His Message* (1971).

H. L. RICHARD

Suh Nam-Dong

(b. Chulla Province, Korea, 1918; d. 1984). Proponent of Minjung* theology and first president of both the Korean Christian Professors' Association and the Association for Korean Theological* Studies.

Suh studied at Doshisha, Japan* (bachelor's degree, 1941), and Emmanuel College, Canada (bachelor of divinity, master of theology, 1956). He taught at Hanshin University (1952-62) and Yonsei University (1962-75). He was dismissed as a professor in 1975 and imprisoned because of his defiance of the military dictatorship. In prison he came to understand the significance of the *minjung* (the "masses"). He started at this time to publish articles on Minjung theology.

In 1984 Suh was awarded an honorary doctorate by Victoria University, Canada, in recognition of his contribution toward the sociopolitical Minjung theology in Korea* and Asia. Nicknamed "The Antenna of the Korean Theological World" by his Korean contemporaries, Suh was quick in acquainting Korean Christians with the development of theological trends in the world. He was familiar with Western theology and was influenced by Rudolf Bultmann, Paul Tillich, the Niebuhr brothers, Dietrich Bonhoeffer, Teilhard de Chardin, Carl G. Jung, and Mircea Eliade. In the mid-1960s, Suh delivered a paper titled "The Present Christ" at the North-East Asian

Theological Association held in Tokyo. Suh was at that time immersed in the secular theology of Bonhoeffer and Friedrich Gogarten. His paper contained some seeds of thought for his future interest in Minjung theology. Suh argued that if the present church does not recognize the coming Christ in the face of a suffering brother, then it repeats the religious failure of the Hebrew people.

Minjung theology saw the face of God and Christ in the real experience of the suffering *minjung* (Matt 25:31-46). Suh believed that the living God and resurrected Christ are not confined to the tradition of the past or the Scriptures, but are found in the soul and body of the suffering *minjung*. He considered Western theological systems and doctrines stumbling blocks to an encounter with Christ. He therefore suggested a radical turn in the orientation of theological paradigms. He insisted that the task of Korean Minjung theology is to testify to the confluence of the *minjung* tradition in Korean history and the *minjung* tradition in Christianity in the *missio Dei* of the Korean church. He saw it as necessary to participate in contemporary sociopolitical events and to interpret them theologically, because they are God's intervention in history and the work of the Holy Spirit. To do so, one needs to maintain the two *minjung* traditions. He called this approach the "pneumatological historical interpretation" and contrasted it with the traditional christological interpretation. He did not regard the two approaches as contradictory. Rather, he deemed them to be complementary, but he gave greater emphasis to the pneumatological interpretation. In the traditional interpretation, Jesus of Nazareth redeems the individual from sin. The pneumatological interpretation asserts that the individual imitates the life of Christ and re-creates in his life the events of the historical Jesus. Suh maintained that the traditional interpretation of biblical paradigms such as the Exodus and the Crucifixion-Resurrection is limited when focused only on the religious interpretation of the events and neglects the sociopolitical thrust. Though Minjung theology is a theology of the *han* (the unutterable forbearance of unjust suffering), Suh emphasized that it is not Communism*.

Bibliography

Kim Yong Bock, ed., *Minjung Theology, People as the Subjects of History* (1981). KIM KYOUNG JAE

Sukarno

(b. Surabaya, 6 May 1901; d. 1970). First president of the Indonesian Republic (1945-66) who proclaimed the independence of Indonesia*.

Sukarno came into contact with different Christian politicians struggling for independence during the years of the "national awakening" *(kebankitan nasional)* before the Pacific War. During his exile to Flores (1933-37), he entertained good relations with the Dutch Society of the Divine Word* (SVD) missionaries at Ende* and learned several chapters of the Bible* by heart. Throughout his presidency, he showed a positive attitude to Christian churches and never regarded them as related to the colonial or imperialist powers. He protected the lawful interests of Christian minority groups, appointed Christians to high offices in the government, and had good personal relations with several churchmen. His later leanings to the left did not alienate him from the Christians of his country, though they tried to distract him from this dangerous leftist course.

Bibliography

Adams, C., *Sukarno, An Autobiography* (1965). • *Ensiklopedi Nasional Indonesia* XV (1991). ADOLF HEUKEN

Sulawesi

The Protestant churches in Central, South, and Southeast Sulawesi include both members and nonmembers of the Indonesian Communion of Churches* (*Persekutuan Gereja-gereja di Indonesia*, PGI). Member churches of PGI cover the majority of Christians in the region, typically organized as ethnic and/or regional churches. In Central Sulawesi, the members of PGI are the Indonesian Protestant Church of Toli-toli (*Gereja Protestan Indonesia Buol Toli-toli*, GPIBT); the Indonesian Protestant Church of Donggala (*Gereja Protestan Indonesia di Donggala*, GPID); the Central Sulawesi Christian Church (*Gereja Kristen Sulawesi Tengah*, GKST); and the Christian Church of Luwuk Banggai (*Gereja Kristen di Luwuk Banggai*, GKLB). They are linked by the General Synod of Churches in North and Central Sulawesi *(Sinode Am Gereja-gereja Sulawesi Utara/Tengah)*, a regional ecumenical* body based in Manado. The non-PGI churches include several Pentecostal* churches, the Salvation Army*, and the Seventh-day Adventists*.

GPIBT was formed in 1965. It originated with Christian migrants from North Sulawesi (the Minahasans and the Sangirese) and was initially fostered by the Christian Evangelical Church of Minahasa (*Gereja Masehi Injili Minahasa*, GMIM). The church has about 10,000 members.

The GPID was organized in 1965 by GMIM and GKST. In addition to migrants from North Sulawesi, church members include the indigenous Kulawi people of the Palu Valley and the To Seko, refugees from South Sulawesi who fled the Muslim persecution in the 1950s. Later members include Christian transmigrants from the island of Bali*. The church has about 23,000 members.

GKST is also a multi-ethnic church of Pamona, Mori, Badak, and other ethnicities in Central Sulawesi. GKST was formed in 1947 from a Dutch mission, the *Nederlandsch Zendeling Genootschap* (NZG), which was begun in 1891 by two famous missionaries, A. C. Kruyt* (1869-1949) and N. Adriani* (1865-1926). The membership numbers more than 108,000, and it is the largest church in Central Sulawesi. As a territorial church, its congregations are found only in Central Sulawesi.

The GKLB was organized in 1966 and was initially part of the GKST. The members now number around 70,000 indigenous people of the Luwuk Peninsula and the Banggai Islands. There are also some migrants.

In South Sulawesi, PGI member churches are the Toraja Mamasa Church (*Gereja Toraja Mamasa,* GTM); the Toraja Church *(Gereja Toraja);* the Indonesian Protestant Church of Luwu (*Gereja Protestan Indonesia Luwu,* GPIL); and the Christian Church of South Sulawesi (*Gereja Kristen di Sulawesi Selatan,* GKSS). There are also some congregations of the Jakarta-based Protestant Church of Western Indonesia *(Gereja Protestan di Indonesia bagian Barat,* GPIB). The non-PGI denominations in South Sulawesi are the same as those in Central Sulawesi, with the addition of some Chinese churches.

The GTM, formed in 1947, is the fruit of a Dutch mission, the *Zending van de Christelijk Gereformeerde Kerken* (ZCGK), in Mamasa, Pitu Ulunna Salu, and the Mamuju highlands. The ZCGK took over these mission fields in 1928 from the Protestant Church of the Netherland Indies *(Indische Kerk),* which had worked there since 1913. GTM congregations, with a membership of about 75,000, have spread to a few sites in South Sulawesi. Departing from its mission tradition, the GTM has for some years ordained women as church ministers. In 1980, some schismatic congregations in the Mamuju region formed the Protestant Church of South Sulawesi (*Gereja Protestan di Sulawesi Selatan,* GPSS).

The Toraja Church was formed in 1947 from the work of another Dutch mission, the *Gereformeerde Zendingsbond* (GZB), which began in 1913. The ethnic church has spread to other regions in Indonesia through the migration of Torajanese Christians. The total membership is about 250,000. The church struggles with lay education and faces the problem of a resurgence of pre-Christian traditions as Toraja develops into a cultural tourist center.

The GPIL, formed in 1966 as a result of a schism in the Toraja Church, comprises Christians from the multi-ethnic community in the Luwu region. Its congregations, found also in Ujung Pandang and Jakarta*, have a total membership of about 7,000.

The GKSS was founded in 1966 in the midst of Buginese and Makassarese Muslim societies. Evangelism among these two ethnicities dates back to the Portuguese period of the 16th c. but met with little success. In the 1930s, some opportunities for missions opened in areas worked by the *Indische Kerk* and the Reformed Church from Surabaya, but the small congregations suffered persecution from Muslim rebels troubling South and Southeast Sulawesi during the 1950s and early 1960s. The church membership, including Christian migrants from other regions, numbers about 5,000.

Only one member church of PGI, the Protestant Church of Southeast Sulawesi (*Gereja Protestan Sulawesi Tenggara,* GEPSULTRA), is in Southeast Sulawesi, but there are some GPIB congregations and various non-PGI congregations.

GEPSULTRA was formed in 1957 through the long and difficult labor of a Dutch mission, the *Nederlandsch Zendings Vereniging* (NZV). The congregations in this region also suffered persecution from the Muslim rebels in the late 1950s and early 1960s. Besides the indigenous Tolaki and Moronene, membership of the church now consists of Torajanese migrants and transmigrants from Java and Bali. The membership numbers 19,000. GEPSULTRA has supported rural reconstruction by developing a "rural theology."

Most of the churches and congregations in South and Southeast Sulawesi are linked by the regional ecumenical body based in Ujung Pandang, the Indonesia Communion of Churches in the South and Southeast Sulawesi Region *(Persekutuan Gereja-gereja di Indonesia Wilayah Sulawesi Selatan dan Tenggara,* PGIW Sulselra).

Bibliography

Van den End, Th., *Ragi Carita* 2 (1989). • *Handbook of Reformed Churches Worldwide* (1999).

Zakaria J. Ngelow

Sun Myung Moon. *See* Unification Church, Korea

Sun Yat-Sen

(b. Guangdong, China, 12 Nov 1866; d. Mar 1925). Chinese Christian revolutionary and leader of the Kuomintang.

Sun Yat-Sen, Japanese pseudonym Nakayama Sho and popularly referred to as Chong-Shan (the Chinese pronunciation of his Japanese alias), came from a family of farmers, although his father worked for some years as a tailor in Macau*. At age six, Sun was taught the Chinese classics at a village school, but in 1879 he was sent to join his brother in Hawaii, where he studied at Iolani College in Honolulu, run by the Church of England. He returned to China* after his graduation in 1882 but was expelled from his native village because he broke a finger off one of the village temple idols.

He went to Hong Kong in 1883 and enrolled at the Queen's College in 1884. He was baptized by Charles R. Hager, an American Methodist* missionary, and returned to his native village for an arranged marriage to Lu Mu-Chen (b. 1867; d. 1952). They had two daughters and a son. He married a second wife, Soong Ching-ling, in Tokyo on 25 Oct 1914, giving rise to controversy and adverse comment, especially among the Christian community.

In 1886 Sun studied at a medical school in Canton that was attached to the Pok Chai Hospital, the oldest Western hospital in China. It was run by John G. Kerr. In 1887 Sun enrolled at the newly established medical school of the Alice Memorial Hospital in Hong Kong, where he was supervised by the dean, James Cantlie. He graduated in 1892 and set up practice in Hong Kong in 1893.

While studying in Canton and Hong Kong, Sun came into contact with young radicals and anti-imperialists. In 1894 Sun presented a proposal for reform to the governor of Hebei, but it was ignored. Disappointed, Sun went to Hawaii and started the *Hsing-chung-hui* (Revive China Society, RCS). In Jan 1895 he joined forces with the Fu-jen Society in Hong Kong organized by Yang Chu-yun in 1892. Sun then went to Canton to recruit soldiers for a revolt in that city, but the plot was discovered one day before its planned occurrence. Sun escaped, taking refuge in Japan* for the next 16 years. In 1896 Sun went to England to visit the retired Dr. Cantlie and was arrested by the Chinese legation at Portland Place on 11 Oct. His release was secured with the help of Cantlie, who prevailed on the British authorities. The incident boosted Sun to international fame. He wrote about this experience in *Kidnapped in London* (1897).

Sun returned to Japan in 1897 and plotted new revolts against the Manchus. An attempted revolt in Huichow, 150 miles east of Canton, failed for lack of ammunition. Between 1903 and 1905, Sun attempted to increase the membership of the RCS by recruiting in Southeast Asia, England, and Europe. He returned to Tokyo in 1905 and was elected director of Tung-meng-hui, an amalgamation of his RCS and the Hua-hsing-hui, an association of Chinese political refugees and the radical student organizations in Japan. The propaganda organ of the Tung-meng-hui was the *Min Pao.* After several failed uprisings and the banning of the *Min Pao* by Japan, Sun decided to go to the United States, where he was able to raise considerable support for the Tung-meng-hui.

While traveling by train in the USA from Denver to Kansas City, Sun read about the revolution in Wuchang, Hubei, on 10 Oct 1911. He returned to China and was elected president of the provisional government of the Republic of China in Nanjing in Dec 1911. In Mar 1912 he relinquished the presidency to Yuan Shih-kai, who in return appointed Sun director of railway development in September. Yuan dismissed him in Jul 1913 when Sun publicly denounced him.

In Aug 1912 Sun was elected director of the Kuomintang, a federation of the Tung-meng-hui and four smaller parties: the United Republican Party, the People's Progressive Party, the Progressive Republican Party, and the People's Public Party. The acrimonious tension between Yuan Shih-kai and the Kuomintang led to the assassination of Sun Chiao-jen, a Kuomintang activist. Sun again sought asylum in Tokyo after a failed attempt to overthrow Yuan. He reorganized the Kuomintang and returned to China in Apr 1916, when Yuan's defeat seemed imminent. After Yuan's death on 16 Jun, Sun spent much time writing and trying to protect the Republican Constitution of 1912. He reorganized the Kuomintang in 1923 with the aim of uniting China under his revolutionary program. Sun's "Three People's Principles" of nationalism*, democracy, and the people's livelihood formed the party manifesto. Disappointed when the Western powers and Japan refused to help, Sun aligned the Kuomintang with the Soviet Union and the Chinese Communist Party. In 1923 Sun invited the Comintern to help him reorganize the Kuomintang. After the completion of the reorganization in 1924, the Kuomintang became a more disciplined pyramidal organization with a structure similar to the Russian Communist Party. Opposition to the inclusion of Communists led to friction within the Kuomintang leadership.

Sun died of liver cancer in Beijing while negotiating with leaders of the northern government on 12 Mar 1925. He was given a private Christian funeral service on 19 Mar at the chapel next to the Beijing Union Medical College. He was then given a state funeral, and his body was laid to rest at a temple in the Western Hills. In 1929, Sun's coffin was transferred to a marble mausoleum on Tzu-chin-shan, near the tomb of the first Ming emperor. He was declared the *kuo-fu* (father of the republic) by the national government on 1 Apr 1940.

Sun received the nickname *Sun Ta-pao* (Big Gun Sun) because of his exaggerated announcements of military expeditions and the many abortive military attempts. Sun was nevertheless respected as a man of honesty, sincerity, integrity, and selfless devotion to his country.

Bibliography

Boorman, Howard L., *Biographical Dictionary of Republican China,* Vol. III (1970). • Cantlie, James, *Sun Yat Sen and the Awakening of China* (1912). • Fairbank, John King, *China, A New History* (1992).

CHINA GROUP

Sun Yuan Hua

(b. 1581; d. 1632). Well-known Chinese during the late Ming period converted through the influence of Xu Guangqi*.

Sun went to the city of Shun Tian to sit for the government examinations in 1606. Failing, he remained in the city and lived in the house of Xu, who was at that time translating *The Principle of Calculus* with Matteo Ricci*. Sun studied European mathematics with Xu and learned directly from the missionaries Ricci, Didace de Pantoja*, and Sabbatino de Ursis*. Influenced by them, he was baptized Ignatius in 1621 in Beijing. He went to the home of Yang Ting Jun in Hangzhou and invited the missionaries Lazarus Cattaneo* and Semedo to start mission work in his hometown, Jiading, Zhejiang (Shanghai). He built a church and more than 10 houses for the missionaries. In 1628, Jesuit (see Society of Jesus) missionaries in China* held a meeting in Jiading to discuss the use of the Latin word for God, *Deus.* The four Chinese Catholics who attended were Sun, Xu, Li Zhi Zao, and Yang Ting Jun. Sun wrote an introductory preface for Alphonsus Vagnoni's* book on church doctrine.

Sun was knowledgeable about the deployment of Western cannons and was the governor of Denglai in

1630. During a period of internal turmoil and border unrest, Sun was taken hostage when Dengzhou was captured by the enemy, and, when the government troops recaptured the place, Sun was imprisoned in Beijing and condemned to death. Johann Adam Schall von Bell* (Tang Tuowang), a Jesuit missionary working in the calendrical bureau, disguised himself as a charcoal merchant and administered him the sacraments of penance.

Bibliography

Ross, Andrew C., *A Vision Betrayed* (1994).

China Group, translated by David Wu

Sunder Singh

(b. Punjab, 3 Sep 1889; d. 1929). Indian Christian mystic, evangelist, and author.

Sunder Singh was the first to show the world how the Gospel of Jesus Christ is reflected in unchanged purity on the Indian soil. He represents a simple, childlike, and yet clear and spiritual religious faith based entirely upon the New Testament, expressed in an Indian spirituality.

Sunder Singh was the youngest son of Sirdar Sher Singh, a Sikh by descent and a wealthy landowner in Punjab. His mother was a gifted Hindu lady and a faithful exponent of her religion who encouraged him to seek peace of soul and to love religion. Her prayer was that Sunder should become a *sadhu* (holy man). As a child, he learned the Bhagavad Gita by heart. Though Sunder Singh understood that peace of mind is the greatest treasure on earth, he could not find this peace from any source.

Sunder Singh studied in a mission school. With much prejudice about Christianity, he refused to read the Bible* in the daily lessons and went to the extent of burning the New Testament. He began to undergo a struggle of mind. The unrest of heart increased until one day he got up early in the morning and began to pray, "If there is a God at all, He would reveal Himself to me and show me the way of salvation, and end this unrest of my soul." After his prayer he saw a light shining in the room, and in that light appeared the living Christ. He heard a voice, "Why do you persecute me? See I have died on the cross for you and for the whole world."

This vision of Christ which he saw on 19 Dec 1904 made a profound difference in his life. His heart was filled with inexpressible joy and peace, and from that day he became an ardent disciple of Christ and sought to proclaim his message far and wide. Later, on 3 Sep 1905, he was baptized in St. Thomas* Church at Simla.

Having committed his life to Christ, Sunder Singh chose the path of the cross and decided to bear the cross at all costs. This meant severe persecution and opposition from family circles. On one occasion his relatives wanted to kill him by mixing poison in his food, but God gave him a miraculous escape.

To show that he was no longer a Sikh, he cut off his long hair, distributed all his possessions to the poor, and began the life of a Christian *sadhu*. Clad in a saffron robe and a turban, he went on evangelistic tours throughout India*. His greatest joy was to serve and suffer for Jesus, whose love he felt so deeply. For years he walked on the slopes of the Himalayas in his incessant ministry of preaching the Gospel, encountering many hardships from the climate, robbers, steep narrow roads, and persecution. He visited many parts of Punjab and Jammu and Kashmir and then proceeded farther to Baluchistan and Afghanistan. He soon came to be known as the "apostle of the bleeding feet." Meanwhile he spent eight months in St. John's Divinity School at Lahore, but he found this too confining. He did not want to limit his ministry to any particular denomination. As a wandering *sadhu*, he could carry the message of Jesus Christ to all churches and to all people of other faiths.

He had the burden to take the Gospel to Tibet, which was closed to missionary activity. Between 1908 and 1929 he made no fewer than 20 risky trips to that country, enduring severe hardships, including imprisonment, which he gladly accepted. Between 1918 and 1919 he visited southern India, Sri Lanka*, Myanmar* (Burma), and Malaysia*. He also made visits to Britain, America, and Australia in 1920, and several European countries in 1922. During his visits, Sunder Singh challenged the churches in the West to abandon their materialistic outlook. During his second trip to Europe, he also visited important places in the Holy Land.

Sunder Singh often expressed his desire to die as a martyr. Owing to hectic travels and crowded programs for an extended period, his health began to suffer. He had heart attacks, troubled eyesight, ulcers, and several other complications which compelled him to confine himself to his residence at Sabathu. Due to his physical weakness, he avoided long journeys. He spent time in prayer, meditation, correspondence, and literary work.

On 18 Apr 1929, he started for Tibet and never returned. Apart from his regular correspondence with friends all over the world, he also wrote seven books: *At the Master's Feet* (1922), *Reality and Religion* (1923), *Search after Reality* (1924), *Spiritual Life* (1925), *Spiritual World* (1926), *Real Life* (1927), and *With and without Christ* (1928).

Since the day of his conversion, Sunder Singh endeavored to follow Christ and made every effort to imitate his life of prayer and meditation. He organized his devotional life of prayer and meditation along the pattern set by Jesus. Christ-centeredness was prominent in his life and ministry. He had a number of visions in which great truths were revealed to him. The life and teachings of Sunder Singh are of great importance to the Christian community. His interpretation of Christianity with the mystical insights gained from the religious heritage of India is of paramount significance. His life and ministry are a challenge to rethink and reorganize patterns of Christian spirituality for southern and central Asia.

Bibliography

Appasamy, A. J., *Sunder Singh: A Biography* (1958). • Parker, Rebecca, *Sadhu Sunder Singh: Called of God,* 6th ed. (1927). • Sharpe, Eric J., "The Legacy of Sadhu Sunder Singh," *IBMR,* Vol. 14 (1990): 161-67.

Samuel Mathew

Sung, John

(Song Shangjie) (b. Fujian, China, 27 Sep 1901; d. 18 Aug 1944). Chinese revivalist.

A modern-day John the Baptist, Sung's fearless and tireless ministry in China* and Southeast Asia has resulted in thousands of conversions as well as revival in the life of churches he visited.

The sixth child and fourth son of Sung Xue Lien, a Methodist* pastor, Sung was named Zhu En ("God's grace") at birth because he was the first child born after his mother's conversion. Following custom, he took on a new name, Shangjie ("noble and frugal"), when he grew older. He was known as the "little pastor" because he assisted his father in preaching and distributing tracts.

After completing high school in China, Sung furthered his studies at Ohio Wesleyan University, USA, where he graduated with honors in 1923. He was given free tuition, but he had to work for his board. While working on his master's degree in chemistry at Ohio State University, he was elected president of the International Students' Association and was also a member of the International League for Peace. Declining attractive offers from several institutions after his doctoral studies, he enrolled at Union Theological Seminary in New York in the fall of 1926. In 1927 he was warded for six months at Bloomingdale Hospital because seminary authorities were concerned about his mental stability; Sung's life was dramatically changed after attending a revival meeting in New York. During his hospitalization, he read through the Bible* 40 times. Upon discharge, he stayed with Rollin H. Walker, his former teacher from Ohio Wesleyan University, until October, when he returned to China. In early 1928, he was reluctantly married to his betrothed, Yu Chin Hua. They had three girls and two boys. In addition to their Chinese names, they were given the names of the books in the Pentateuch, except for the youngest, who was named Joshua instead of Deuteronomy.

Sung taught chemistry and Bible three days a week at the Methodist Christian High School in Fujian to help send his younger brother through college. He spent the rest of the week in evangelistic activities. He was labeled a counterrevolutionary by the Kuomintang, who were displeased by his objection to the ceremonial bowing before the portrait of Sun Yat-sen. Sung considered the act idolatrous. A timely resignation from the school prevented his arrest. A marked man, he became an itinerant preacher. He visited the smaller towns and villages, attracting a following of young evangelists who had been recently converted when the Bethel Band from Shanghai visited Fujian in May 1928. The band was led by Andrew Gih* and a converted Jew, Joseph Flacks.

In 1930 Sung was appointed by the Methodist bishop of Fuse to study the literacy and mass education experiment initiated by James Yen at Beijing. Although impressed by the literacy movement, Sung doubted its spiritual benefit. He shortened his intended monthlong stay in Beijing to two days and traveled to Shanghai. He met with Mary Stone (Shi Mei Yi*) and Jenny Hughes, the founders of the Bethel Mission. While awaiting a ship to return to Fujian, he accepted an invitation to Nanchang from William E. Schubert of the Methodist Episcopal Mission. Together with a Chinese colleague, he had been praying for 50 days for a revival. Sung considered Nanchang a turning point in his ministry, for it was a prelude to his revival ministry.

From 1931 to 1933, Sung joined Andrew Gih's Bethel Worldwide Evangelistic Band (WEB) and, together with Frank Ling, Philip Lee, and Lincoln Nieh, ministered in northeastern, northern, and southern China. On one occasion, Sung accepted personal invitations and separated from the rest of the team to minister on his own. In spite of the uncertain conditions caused by the Japanese invasion, which in 1932 necessitated the move of the Bethel Mission into the International Settlement for safety, the WEB team insisted on proceeding with the Bethel Short Term Bible School in Shanghai. Sung, as chief editor, insisted on the continued publication of the Bethel magazine, *Guide to Holiness.* Through Andrew Gih, Sung learned that the Bethel leaders were unhappy that he did not teach the eradication of sin and faulted him with attracting converts to himself. They also suspected him of pocketing gifts meant for the mission. Sung denied the latter and decided to let time disprove the veracity of the former. He disagreed with the doctrine of eradication, stressing instead the work of the Holy Spirit in mortifying the deeds of the flesh. While the WEB was staying with Marcus Cheng at Changsha, Gih received a telegram from the Bethel Mission which contained instructions to disband the WEB. Sung went on to Hengyang where a letter awaited him. It requested him to relocate his family, who were then with the Bethel Mission in Shanghai. He became an independent missionary. By 1934, Sung had become a well-known preacher in both northern and southern China.

Between Jun 1935 and Dec 1939, Sung made several visits to Chinese churches in Indonesia*, Malaysia*, the Philippines*, Taiwan*, Thailand*, and, most of all, Singapore*, which he visited seven times. Before World War II*, there were an estimated 10 million Chinese in Southeast Asia and five million in Taiwan (then Formosa), mainly emigrants from Fujian and Guangdong. Inevitably, the fame of John Sung would spread to these people. His reputation was such that, for example, in Surabaya, Java*, the local Chinese business community closed their shops for one week to attend his meetings from morning till evening. As in China, thousands were converted, many were healed through prayer,

Christian lives were revived, and churches were given fresh spiritual vitality. Everywhere he went, he formed evangelistic bands that went out to preach regularly. One such group of his converts was known still to be meeting in Penang in the early 1990s. He also left behind groups that met regularly for prayer and Bible study for the sustenance of spiritual life. The Chin Lien Bible School (now Seminary) was founded in Singapore on 14 May 1937 by one of his assistants, Leona Wu, to train Sung's converts for ministry. Even today, many Chinese Christians, including some very eminent retired Christian leaders, still trace their Christian conversions and/or commitments to Sung's work in Southeast Asia. Sung is one of the greatest evangelists of the modern period of church history.

From 1940 until his death, Sung remained in China, suffering from cancer and tuberculosis. He spent his time mainly in prayer, Bible study, and correspondence. He died on 18 Aug 1844 surrounded by friends and relatives. His funeral, which was attended by about 300 people, was conducted by another renowned Chinese preacher, Wang Ming-tao*. Sung was buried in Xiangshan ("Fragrant Hills"), or the Western Hills of Beijing.

Bibliography

Lyall, Leslie T., *A Biography of John Sung* (1961). • Schubert, William E., *I Remember John Sung* (1976). • Tow, Timothy, *John Sung My Teacher* (1985).

IRENE TAY, HWA YUNG, and THE CHINA GROUP

Sung Revivals in Southeast Asia

It is estimated that, before World War II*, some 10 million Chinese lived in Southeast Asia and another five million lived in Taiwan (Formosa). Most were emigrants from Fujien and Guangdong (the two southern coastal provinces of China) and maintained close ties with their motherland. The revivals in China under John Sung* inevitably spilled over to these people. Between Jun 1935 and Dec 1939, Sung made a number of visits to the Chinese churches in Indonesia*, Malaysia*, the Philippines*, Taiwan*, Thailand*, and, most of all, Singapore*, where he ministered seven times.

Sung's impact on the region was similar to that which he made on the churches in China. The local Chinese business community in Surabaya, Java*, closed their shops for one week to attend his meetings from morning till evening. This is merely one example evidencing his far-reaching reputation. During the revivals, thousands were converted to Christianity, many were healed through prayer, Christian lives were revived, and churches were given fresh spiritual vitality.

Everywhere he went, Sung formed evangelistic bands which went out to preach regularly. One such group of his converts was known to be still meeting in Penang in the 1990s; another also continued to meet at Jubilee Presbyterian Church in Singapore. Sung also left behind groups which met regularly for prayer and Bible study for the sustenance of spiritual life. In Singapore, the Chin Lien Bible School (now Seminary) was founded on 14 May 1937 by one of his assistants, Leona Wu, to train Sung's converts for the ministry.

Even today, there can still be found many Chinese Christians, including some very eminent retired Christian leaders, who trace their Christian conversions and commitments to Sung's work in Southeast Asia. His ministry can rightly be described as apostolic, and he was possibly the most effective evangelist of the 20th c.

Bibliography

Lyall, Leslie T., *John Sung, Flame for God in the Far East* (1954). • Schubert, William E., *I Remember John Sung* (1976). • Tow, Timothy, *John Sung My Teacher* (1985).

HWA YUNG

Suzuki Masahisa

(b. Chiba Prefecture, Japan, 7 Aug 1912; d. 14 Jul 1969). Japanese pastor.

Baptized by Mitsuoka Kyuuma at Japan* Methodist* Chuen Church in Feb 1929, Suzuki graduated from the theology department of Aoyama Gakuin. He served the Japan Methodist Himonya and Kamedo churches. During the time he was chief editor of the Methodist paper *Nihon mesojisuto jiho* (Japan Methodist Times), he criticized the opportunistic nationalism* of the church leaders and introduced articles on Karl Barth and the German Confessing Church in opposition to the war. In 1941, when the United Church of Christ in Japan (UCCJ) came into existence, he became a minister of the UCCJ and pastored the Hongo Chuo Church and Komagome Nishi Katamachi Church. He was known for his fine preaching. He also held a number of national-level church positions, including chair of the UCCJ Mission Research Institute, chair of the Commission on Evangelism, executive committee member, and moderator of the general assembly, working diligently in each position for the structural renewal of the UCCJ. On Easter Sunday in Mar 1967, as the UCCJ moderator, he issued the "Confession of War Responsibility" of the UCCJ. He also worked hard to see the realization of union between the UCCJ and the United Church of Christ in Okinawa*, as well as the building of Seireien, a nursing home for orphaned elderly A-bomb survivors. At the Fifteenth General Assembly of the UCCJ in 1968, the moderator's proposal to support the construction of a Christian pavilion at the 1970 World Exposition (Expo '70*) to be held in Osaka was passed. This gave rise to a movement opposing the Christian Pavilion, which exploded into a very serious situation. Soon after the assembly, Suzuki fell ill. Possessed of great powers to put the Gospel into compelling and concise terms and metaphors, skillful, and blessed with lucid historical, theological*, and humanistic insights, he had a great effect on the youth of his day, and many theology students flocked to his church. His major literary works include: *Temote* *zen-go-sho, Tetosu-sho* (I and II Timothy, Titus), 1952; Barth's *Kirisuto-kyo rinri I-IV* (Christian Ethics, I-IV), 1955; *Shinko to jiyu no tegami — Garateyabito e no tegami kokai* (Lectures on Galatians — the Faith and Freedom Letter), 1965; *Kirisuto-kyo no gendai-teki shimei* (The Present-Day Calling of Christianity), 1969; *Shuyo, mikuni o — shu no inori to sekkyo* (Thy Kingdom Come — Lord's Prayer and Sermon), 1969; *Kami no kuni no otozure — Maruko fukuin-sho kokai* (Lectures on Mark — Coming of God's Kingdom), 1969; *Suzuki Masahisa sekkyo-shu* (Collection of the Sermons of Suzuki Masahisa), 1969; *Suzuki Masahisa chosaku shu, I-IV* (The Works of Suzuki Masahisa, I-IV), 1980.

Bibliography

Nihon mesojisuto jiho (Japan Methodist Times,) 2398-2478 (1938). • *Toki ni kanatte — Suzuki Masahisa bokushi tsuito bunshu* (Equal to the times — collection of eulogies to Suzuki Masahisa), (1969). • Yoda Shunsaku, *Kirisuto-kyo no shonin-tachi — teiko ni ikiru 4 "Suzuki Masahisa"* (Christian witnesses — living in protest 4 "Suzuki Masahisa") (1974).

Yoda Shunsaku

Swain, Clara

(b. 1834; d. Castile, New York, United States, 1910). First woman missionary doctor in the world.

Responding to an urgent plea for a woman doctor in India*, Swain became one of the first two missionaries sent out in 1869 by the newly formed Women's* Foreign Missionary Society (WFMS) of the Methodist* Episcopal Church. In Bareilly, North India, she began work on the morning of her arrival and was soon so swamped with patients that a hospital became an imperative.

The coming of WFMS to India provided a new stimulus for work by and for women. A Mogul ruler, the nawab of Rampur, though an opponent of Christianity, was so impressed by her work that he donated a tract of 40 acres, including a palatial residence, for her use. In 1872 this became the first women's hospital in Asia. Other buildings followed the first units in the fine modern medical center which bears her name. After two terms at Bareilly, Swain became a physician in the palace of the rajah of Khetri in 1885, where she labored to bring healing and the Gospel to an area untouched by Christianity.

She spent her last years in Castile, New York, United States, returning to India only once in 1906 for the 50th jubilee of Indian Methodists. She died at age 76.

Bibliography

Balfour, Margaret I., and Ruth Young, *The Work of Medical Women in India* (1929). • Barclay, Wade Crawford, *The Methodist Episcopal Church,* Vol. III (1957). • Neill, Stephen, Gerald H. Anderson, and John Goodwin, *Concise Dictionary of the Christian World Mission* (1970). • Tucker, Ruth A., *Guardians of the Great Commission* (1988).

Samson Samuel

Syncretistic Movements

Syncretism is usually understood as a combination of elements from two or more religious traditions, ideologies, or value systems. In the social sciences, this is a neutral and objective term that is used to describe the mixing of religions as a result of culture contact. In theological* and missiological circles, however, it is generally used as a pejorative term to designate movements that are regarded as heretical or sub-Christian. Representatives of established or mission churches frequently regard adaptation or selective adoption of their traditions by local peoples as "unauthorized religious productions" and illegitimate forms of religious synthesis. The legitimate cultural reshaping of Christianity is referred to as the "inculturation" or "contextualization"* of the Gospel, though most social scientists would also include these cultural adapations as examples of syncretism.

The term "syncretistic movements" refers to a wide range of new religions that emerged as a result of the interaction between transplanted Western Christianity and local religious traditions in the diverse cultural contexts of Asia and Africa. As Farquhar concisely explained, with reference to movements in India*: "The old religions are the soil from which the modern movements spring; while it will be found that the seed has, in the main, been sown by missions." Barrett (1997) reports that there are over 15,000 religions or religious movements in the world today. This figure is probably too small, since several hundred new religions have been documented in Japan* alone. He also points out that two or three new non-Christian religions are formed every day. Most of these new religions would be regarded as syncretistic movements.

Syncretistic movements are complex phenomena that vary widely due to the interaction of a number of factors, including the cultural and religious diversity of the receiving society (plural religious traditions, classes, ethnic groups, regional differences), the pluralism of Christian traditions transplanted by the mission churches (Reformed theology, Pentecostalism*, dispensationalism, Unitarianism), the diverse Christian traditions within the Judeo-Christian Scriptures (the Old Testament and expressions of Jewish Christianity, Hellenistic Christianity, and early Catholicism within the New Testament). Most movements are initiated by charismatic* founders, who creatively adapt beliefs and practices from local traditions and combine them in unique ways with elements drawn from the Bible* or Christianity. In the Asian context, these founders draw from a vast reservoir of beliefs and practices related to tribal or folk religious traditions, Hinduism*, Buddhism*, Confucianism*, Taoism*, Shintoism*, and the ancestor* cult. The religious experiences of founders and their unique combination of indigenous and exogenous elements provides the foundation for the development of these new movements.

Representative movements in Asia that have been shaped by or have borrowed elements from Christianity include the Brahmo Samaj*, established in India (1828);

the God Worshippers Society *(Pai Shang-ti Hui)*, established in China* (1847); the Heavenly Virtue Holy Church *(T'ien Te Sheng Hui)*, also organized in China (1920) and later successful in Hong Kong and among the Chinese diaspora in Malaysia*; the Religion of the Heavenly Way *(Chondogyo)*, established in Korea* (1860); and Cao Dai*, or the Cao Daist Missionary Church, established in Vietnam* (1919). These and many other new religions throughout Asia find a place for Jesus Christ (along with other spirits and deities) or incorporate beliefs or ideas from the Judeo-Christian tradition, but they usually claim to be establishing a new path that transcends the established religions of both East and West. Tensokokyo, a Japanese messianic movement founded in 1948, for example, does not use the Bible in worship or teaching, but its sacred text is permeated by biblical themes and ideas (particularly from Genesis and Revelation). The movement regards its founder as the manifestation of the second coming of Christ and the future Buddha (Maitreya), thus superseding both Buddhism and Christianity.

Of particular concern in the field of Asian Christianity are those movements that claim to be authentic expressions of Christianity, though independent of the authority of the mission churches. These indigenous movements often reject much in the creeds and traditions of established Western churches. Their own theology is newly crafted by interpreting the Bible in light of native culture without the authoritative guidance of ecumenical* creeds. One such movement is the Holy Spirit Association for the Unification of World Christianity*, founded in Korea by Sun Myung Moon in 1954. This controversial missionary movement has spread outside of Korea, particularly in Japan and the United States, and is usually regarded as heretical by the established churches because of its messianic claims for its founder. Many other movements, however, are identifiably Christian in spite of their rejection of missionary instruction and control. They often represent serious attempts to understand the Christian faith in light of local cultural traditions and concerns and, as experiments in inculturation, have much to teach the mission churches. Turner's study of independent churches in Africa reminds us that these younger churches are "movements" and are still in the process of development. Most movements pass through several stages and in time may be accepted as member churches in various national councils and the World Council of Churches (the Kimbanguist movement, for example). This suggests that dialogue between established churches and new indigenous movements in Asia is an important missiological task (see Interreligious Dialogue).

Bibliography

Barrett, David B., ed., *World Christian Encyclopedia* (1982); "Annual Statistical Table on Global Mission: 1997," *International Bulletin of Missionary Research,* Vol. 21, No. 1 (1997). • Farquhar, J. N., *Modern Religious Movements in India* (1919). • Gort, Jerald D., et al., eds., *Dialogue and Syncretism: An Interdisciplinary Approach* (1989). • Hexham, Irving, and Karla Poewe, *New Religions as Global Cultures* (1997). • Mullins, Mark R., *Christianity Made in Japan: A Study of Indigenous Movements* (1998). • Steward, Charles, and Rosalind Shaw, eds., *Syncretism/Anti-Syncretism: The Politics of Religious Synthesis* (1994). • Turner, Harold W., *Religious Innovation in Africa* (1979).

MARK R. MULLINS

Synod of Ayutthaya, 1664

When the French missionaries arrived at Ayutthaya, they were welcomed by 10 Portuguese priests and one Spanish priest whom they found serving a Christian community estimated at 2,000 souls. The 11 priests included four Jesuits (see Society of Jesus), two Dominicans*, two Franciscans*, and three secular priests. According to the French missionaries, the situation of mission was quite poor.

With the arrival of François Pallu*, two bishops, five priests, and one lay assistant organized an assembly called the Synod of 1664 at Ayutthaya. Their names were Lambert de la Motte*, Pallu, Deydier, Chevreul, Hainques, Brindeau, Laneau*, and de Chamesson. The synod was dominated by de la Motte, and the sessions can be summarized as follows:

Apostolic spirituality. They were scandalized by the behavior of the missionaries whom they met in Ayutthaya, since these missionaries, according to them, did not follow the principles of the mission or of their vocation. They planned also to institute an apostolic congregation composed of three orders: the bishops, priests, and lay assistants; the women*; and the people who lived in the world, or a type of secular order.

The instructions to the missionaries. They decided to publish "The Instructions to the Apostolic Vicars" given by Propaganda Fide*. For the reason of practicality, they issued "The Instructions to the Missionaries," consisting of 10 chapters, which gave instructions on all areas of missionary life.

The erection of a seminary. De la Motte had made the program come true when he founded the seminary in 1665. This first establishment in the Far East was placed under the protection of St. Joseph. It received young people who seemed to have the qualities and virtues required for the priesthood. This was the first office indicated by Rome. In addition, many families of the court sent their children to learn European language and sciences, and the king paid for the children of the mandarins. Pascal M. D'Elia recorded that "On account of the small number of the missionaries and of persecutions, the first assembly of Bishops and missionaries of the Society decided in 1664, that a general seminary should be opened for all oriental youths of good hope who might come from the different kingdoms of the Far East, such as India*, China*, Annam, Tonkin, Cambodia*, Cochinchina and Japan*." The first general seminary for mission lands was opened in Ayutthaya. Two years after the first ordination of some native priests in Ayutthaya (1669), Cardinal Barberini, prefect of Propaganda Fide, congratulated de la Motte: "What your grace wrote to us, about the ordination of native priests, their normal qualities, their zeal and works, has filled us with joy; therefore we exhort you in the Lord to make all possible efforts to increase the number of good natives worthy of being ordained priests" (*Revue illustree de l'Exposition Vaticane* [Rome, 1925], p. 99).

During 1682, 39 seminarians were trained there, 11 from Tonkin, eight from Cochin China, three from Manila, one from Bengal, three from Siam, and one from China. Others were of Portuguese, Peguan, or Japanese descent. In 1686, by the intervention of Constantine Phaulkon*, the college was moved to Ayutthaya. Phaulkon, with the consent of Laneau, paid for all the expenses of construction, but later it was moved to Mahapram again. The college continued to exist until the fall of Ayutthaya in 1767. It was founded again at Hondat in Cambodia, then at Virampatnam in India until 1808, and then at Penang.

In 1670, after de la Motte had visited Tonkin during the absence of Pallu, he came back to Ayutthaya and founded the female congregation which he had intended, according to the program. In fact, he had already founded this kind of congregation in Tonkin; thus, he named the congregation similarly: *Amantes de la Croix* (Lovers of the Cross*).

Bibliography

Revue illustree de l'Exposition Vaticane (1925). • Chumsriphan, Surachai, *The Great Role of Jean-Louis Vey, Apostolic Vicar of Siam (1875-1909), in the Church History of Thailand during the Reformation Period of King Rama V, the Great (1868-1910)* (1990).

Surachai Chumsriphan

Synod of Manila

Assembly held in the diocese of Manila, Philippines*, in 1582.

Organized by the first bishop of Manila, Domingo de Salazar* (1579-94), the synod's participants came from the Augustinian*, Franciscan*, and Jesuit (see Society of Jesus) Orders, as well as the secular clergy and laity.

The synod was held in response to the many problems that surfaced during the gradual spread of Spanish colonial rule (starting in 1565) in the various islands. These difficulties became more manifest during the governorship of Gonzalo Ronquillo de Penalosa (1580-83). The Augustinians, the first missionaries in the Philippines, pointed out the following unjust acts committed against the Filipino locals by the Spanish *conquistadores:* thievery, indiscriminate killing, slavery, provocation of conflicts, heavy taxation through the *encomiendas* (an *encomienda* refers to the power to collect tribute from a designated number of natives in a given territory), and price fixing of the goods that the natives were forced to sell to the Spaniards, resulting in scarcity and want.

Born in 1521, de Salazar joined the Dominicans* in 1546 and later served as a missionary in the Americas. In Mexico he was influenced by the ideas of another Dominican, Bartolome de las Casas, a vocal critic of Spanish excesses in the New World and a fervent supporter of native American rights. De Salazar was consecrated bishop of Manila in 1579 and soon thereafter journeyed to the Philippines with several other missionaries. Upon his arrival in Manila in 1581, he immediately realized the need for the clergy to formulate a common response to Spanish abuses in the archipelago using the principles set down by Catholic moral theology. As a consequence, the 1582 synod clarified key issues concerning the conquest and evangelization of the Philippines and made strongly worded directives to the Spanish lay community in the archipelago.

In brief, the synod issued the following recommendations, statements, or decisions during the deliberations: the prohibition of slavery in accordance with the *cedula,* or decree, of Philip II; the need for the governor of the colony to study and vigorously enforce the royal laws and ordinances in order to ensure justice for the locals; the justification for the conquest of the Philippines on the basis of the spiritual authority granted to the Spanish monarchy by the papacy; the lawful use of sovereignty in the archipelago; the correction of abuses and the restitution that should be made to the Filipinos by the Spaniards; the duties of the Spaniard who was assigned an *encomienda;* the possibility of providing native Filipinos with responsibilities in local government; the duties of other classes of people living in the colony; and the teaching of catechism in the local Philippine languages instead of Spanish. The Jesuit Alonso Sanchez, a confidant and shipboard companion of de Salazar, played a key role in the proceedings as an official theologian and canonist and also synod secretary.

The 1582 Synod of Manila produced mixed results. In order to avoid paying restitution, some of the Spaniards stopped going to confession because of the synod's decree that compensation to the natives must precede any absolution. Nevertheless, the Spaniards eventually made restitution either individually or through a common fund for the benefit of the poor or victims of disasters. The synod's decisions also caused rifts between the church and the Spanish lay community. Moreover, the abuses that the synod set out to condemn continued in the subsequent decades and centuries. In 1591 de Salazar himself returned to Spain to petition the Spanish monarch directly for reforms. He died in 1594.

Nevertheless, the synod provided a clear justification for Spanish rule in the archipelago, but only within a spiritual context, i.e., the spread of the Gospel to non-Christians. In addition, the assembly also equated the payment of tribute with requisite obligations, such as justice, defense, religious instruction, and even paternal care for the locals. More important, it established the principles or guidelines that the clergy would use to denounce future abuses in the Philippines. The synod also linked Christianization with the promotion of justice, an idea that is a prominent feature of Catholic teachings in the second half of the 20th c. Furthermore, the synod prescribed the most effective method for proselytizing among natives in the Philippines, i.e., the use of the local languages instead of Spanish in spreading Christianity. Because of these actions taken at such a critical juncture, the 1582 Synod of Manila thereby established a more solid foundation for the Catholic Church in the Philippines (see Roman Catholic Church).

Bibliography

Anderson, Gerald H., ed., *Studies in Philippine Church History* (1969). • Bernad, Miguel A., *The Christianization of the Philippines: Problems and Perspectives* (1972). • De la Costa, Horacio, *The Jesuits in the Philippines: 1581-1768* (1961). • Fernandez, Pablo, *History of the Church in the Philippines (1521-1898)* (1979). • Schumacher, John N., "The Manila Synodal Tradition: A Brief History," *Philippine Studies*, Vol. 27 (Third Quarter 1979).

JOSELITO N. FORNIER

Synod of Tonkin, First

Convoked by Bishop Pierre Lambert de la Motte* (1624-79) of the *Mission Étrangères de Paris* (MEP, Paris Foreign Mission Society*) and vicar apostolic of Cochin China, on 14 Feb 1670 at the Christian village of Dinh-hien in Nam-Dinh Province.

On this occasion, the first seven Tonkinese were ordained to the Catholic priesthood, namely, Martin Vat*, Anthony Van Huc, Philip Nhum, Simon Kien, James Van Chu, Leo Thu, and Vitellus Tri. Lambert also conferred minor orders on 10 other catechists and gave the tonsure to another 20. The First Synod of Tonkin passed 33 canons, the most important being the reorganization of the parishes of Tonkin into nine ecclesiastical districts.

Bibliography

Launay, A. C., *Histoire générale de la Société des Missons Étrangères*, Vol. I (1894). • De Frondeville, H., "Pierre Lambert de la Motte, Évèque de Beryte (1624-1679)," *Revue d'Histoire des Missions*, Vol. 1 (1924).

T. VALENTINO SITOY, JR.

Synods/Councils, Early Asian

From the 4th c., synods and councils became decision-making bodies for the Syriac-language church that stretched from Antioch to China*. These meetings, primarily of bishops, occurred in two areas, West Syria and East Syria. Both used the occasions to denounce the theological mentors* of the other as well as to set social and ecclesiastical policy.

The compilation of East Syrian church council documents was undertaken about 800 C.E. at the instruction of the patriarch Timothy I. This text was edited, with a French translation, by Jean-Baptiste Chabot, and is titled *Synodicon Orientale, ou recueil des synodes nestoriens* (Paris, 1902). The most important councils of the Persian church were the following.

Seleucia-Ctesiphon (325). Under the presidency of Papa bar 'Aggai, this synod met and apparently deposed Papa. The synod is known from various sources, but even its date is uncertain. No records have survived, if indeed there were records kept.

Council of Seleucia-Ctesiphon (399/400). This council met under the presidency of Maruta of Maipherqat and ratified the negotiations that temporarily stopped the persecution of Christians in Persia. It also elected Isaac as bishop and catholicos of Seleucia-Ctesiphon.

Council of Seleucia-Ctesiphon (410). Sometimes inappropriately called the Council of Isaac, this gathering approved a creed (not that of Nicaea) and a text thought by the participants to be the Canons of Nicaea. At the encouragement of Maruta of Maipherqat, coconvenor of the council, the church was reorganized and then declared its independence from the Byzantine Church and from the bishop of Antioch.

Council of Dadišo' (420). The catholicos called this council at Marktabta' of Tayyaye' (not Seleucia-Ctesiphon) to clarify his own role in the Persian church. The council affirmed the primacy of the bishop of Seleucia-Ctesiphon and reaffirmed the independence of the Persian church from that of the Byzantine Empire.

Council of Seleucia-Ctesiphon (486). Sometimes called the Council of Acacius (Aqaq), this council confirmed the nullification of the Synod of Bet Lapat held by his rival Barsauma*, adopted a creed, affirmed classical East Syrian theology, asserted the authority of the bishops over the monks, and limited celibacy to the monks. It also reaffirmed the independence of the Persian church from Byzantium.

Council of Seleucia-Ctesiphon (786/87). Under the leadership of the convener Timothy I, this council condemned the perfectionistic theology and spirituality of Joseph Hazzaya and John of Apamea, among others.

The West Syrian synodicon was edited by Arthur Vööbus, *The Synodicon in the West Syrian Tradition*, CSCO 367, 375 (1975, 1976).

Bibliography

Brun, O., *Das Buch der Synhados* (1990). • Labourt, J., *Le Christianisme dan l'Empire Perse sous la dynastie Sassanide* (1904). • Fiey, J.-M., "Les Étapes de la prise en conscience de so identité patriarcale de l'église syrienne orientale," *L'Orient Syrien*, Vol. 12 (1967); *Jalons pour une histoire de l'Eglise en Iraq*, CSCO Subsidia 36 (1970). • Gribomont, J., "La symbole de foi de Séleucie-Ctésiphon (410)," in *A Tribute to Arthur Vööbus*, ed. Robert Fisher (1977). • De Halleux, A., "La symbole des évêques perses au synode de Séleucie-Ctésiphon," in *Erkenntnis und Meinungen*, ed. G. Wiessner (1978). • Gero, S., *Barsauma of Nisibis and Persian Christianity in the Fifth Century* (1981).

DAVID BUNDY

Taberd, J. L.

(b. ca. 1787; d. Calcutta, India, 31 Jul 1840). French missionary of the Paris Foreign Mission Society* (MEP) to Cochin China and India*.

Taberd arrived in Cochin China in 1820 at the age of 33, where he was appointed vicar apostolic. He was driven out of Cochin China and passed through Penang on his way to Calcutta. In Calcutta he hoped to use the Baptist* Mission Press to publish his Vietnamese dictionary. For two years he stayed as the guest of John Clark Marshman*. While in India, he was appointed vicar general of Bengal (1838), but 22 months later he died.

Taberd was so well loved by his host in Calcutta that Marshman wrote his biography, titling it *The Friend of India.* In the book Taberd is praised both for his work in India and his great knowledge of literature, medicine, languages, world history, laws, cultures, and the religions of Cochin China. Scott W. Sunquist

Tachard, Guy

(b. Angouleme, Guyene Province, French Guiana, 7 Apr 1651; d. Chandernagor, Bengal, India, 21 Oct 1712). French Catholic priest, knowledgeable mathematician, and one of six early Jesuits (see Society of Jesus) sent to work in Siam (Thailand*) and China.

Before he was sent to Siam, Tachard had just returned from the American colonies. He had gone there with Maréchal d'Estrée and remained from 1680 until 1684, a total of four years. He worked there both as a teacher and a diplomat.

Tachard arrived in Siam for the first time on 23 Sep 1685 as part of a diplomatic mission under the leadership of Chevalier de Chaumont, the ambassador. The mission included five other Jesuits, and it brought a message from King Louis XIV to King Narai*. One purpose of this mission was to convince King Narai to convert to Christianity. Tachard had a good enough knowledge of Portuguese to act as translator for de Chaumont's mission.

Tachard met and became close to Constantine Phaulkon*, a Greek noble who had entered the royal service of King Narai. Phaulkon had gained the confidence of King Narai and obtained considerable political influence. Tachard returned to France with a Siamese diplomatic mission which had Okphra Visutsunthon as its ambassador. In Dec 1685, Tachard received a request from Phaulkon to pay his respects to the pope and present him with various gifts.

Tachard returned to Siam with the Siamese mission for his second visit. They were accompanied by a second French mission, which had De La Loubére as its ambassador. They arrived 27 Sep 1687.

At the advice of Phaulkon, King Narai appointed Tachard as his special ambassador to carry a royal letter and gifts for Louis XIV and Pope Innocent XI in Rome. This special mission include three Thai nobles and two Tonkinese teachers. It left from Ayutthaya on 3 Jan 1688. Tachard presided over the presentation of King Narai's letter and gifts to the pope in Rome. Before they returned to Siam, this special mission paid a second visit to the pope. In honor of both audiences, the Vatican had two special coins struck, one side picturing Pope Innocent XI and the other picturing Tachard and the three Siamese nobles. In addition, the pope commissioned Carlo Maratta, a well-known artist, to paint the portraits of the special mission.

Tachard then returned to Siam for his third visit. King Phra Petracha had succeeded to the throne, and Tachard waited on the king with the letter from Louis XIV that had originally been intended for King Narai (originally written in 1687). This audience took place on 29 Jan 1689.

Tachard played an important role in Thai and Thai Catholic history. He introduced both mathematical and astronomical knowledge into Siam, and each time he visited the country he kept a travel diary. That diary contains accounts of evangelistic work, important religious events, political happenings, and general social conditions of the Siamese people. These records very much assist the Thai today to know their own country, its conditions, and customs in that era. They are a useful aid to the study of both Thai history and the history of Thai Catholicism.

Tachard's travel diary was published in two volumes, the title of the first volume being *Voyage de Siam des Péres Jesuites, Envoyez par le Roy aux Indes & a la Chine avec leurs Observations, Astronomiques; et leur Remarques de Physique de Geographic, d'Hydrographic, & d'Histoire.* This volume contains an account of Tachard's first visit. It records various observations of natural science, geography, and astronomy. It was of great value in expanding European knowledge of the arts, humanities, and science. It also provided information that enhanced the safety of sea travel.

The second volume was titled *Second Voyage du Père Tachard et des Jesuites Envoyez par le Roy au Royaume de Siam contenant diverses Remarques d'Histoire, de Physique, de Geographic & d' Astronomie.* It documents Tachard's second visit to Siam, including events taking place at that time.

Besides penning these two volumes, Tachard also cooperated with Bouhours and Gaudin as well as others in preparing a two-volume French-Latin and Latin-French dictionary. It was published in Paris in 1689.

After Tachard left Siam in 1699, he returned to India* and gave his life over to building up the Jesuit order there. His attempts to resurrect the Jesuit work in India, however, did not meet with success, and he finally died in the city of Chandernagor in Bengal.

Concerning Tachard's personality, various opinions are given both by those who knew him personally and by those who later studied his documents and books. He is thus portrayed in both a favorable and not-so-favorable light, as can be seen by the following examples.

Père de la Chaise, Louis XIV's confessor, had great respect for Tachard, especially because in difficult times or in the face of opposition he never became discouraged. Rather, he had the wisdom to deal with obstacles and was an untiring worker. When he set his mind to do something, he persevered until he accomplished what he had set out to do.

M. Lucien Lanier, author of *Étude Historique sur les Relations de la France et du Royaume de Siam de 1662 a 1703,* commented on Tachard's nature: "He is a person of firm resolve, and if he seems to soften at times it's only an outward appearance when he faces fantastic difficulties. He is a person who is resilient and able to give good advice. He doesn't become discouraged nor does he tire in his work. He's not willing to retreat from the goals he feels he must obtain. He's also an outstanding expert in covering up, and quite capable in cutting down or turning traitor on a person in order to fix his own mistakes or recover power he's lost."

Whether he is viewed in a positive or an unfavorable light, Tachard still possessed many good qualities. His usefulness to others has continued down to the present.

SURACHAI CHUMSRIPHAN, translated by HERBERT SWANSON

Taiping Rebellion

One of the revolutionary attempts against the Ch'ing (Qing) dynasty in the 19th c.

The Taiping movement founded a small kingdom in China* that lasted for 14 years. The rise of Taiping Heavenly Kingdom was closely related to Christian missionary work in southern China during the late Ch'ing period. Its leader, Hung Hsiu-chaun (Hong Xiuquan)*, first came into contact with Christianity in 1836 through an evangelical tract, *Chuan shih liang yen* (Good Words for Exhorting the Age), which was written by the first Chinese Protestant preacher, Liang Afa*. In 1843, Hung claimed he had received a vision and established the God-worshipping Society in Kwangtung Province. In Apr 1844 Hung and Feng Yun-shan went to Kwangsi Province to preach his new religion and seek followers.

Hung's religious and political ideology was different from traditional Christianity but was more capable of fulfilling the needs and political expectations of the rural population than was Confucianism*. On 11 Jan 1851, the revolution broke out in Chin-tien, Kwangsi Province; the Taiping Heavenly Kingdom was founded. The name of the kingdom means the heavenly kingdom comes to earth; it borrows from the biblical concept of the coming of the kingdom of God. The revolution aimed to overthrow the corrupt and oppressive Qing government and introduce peace and harmony.

After the kingdom was established, the number of followers of the movement increased steadily; the oppressed peasants, especially the Hakka, responded to the hope offered. In Sep 1851, Hung adopted a new calendar, established a government structure, and prohibited the owning of private property. Moreover, he invested Yang Hsiu-ching (Yang Xiuqing) as the eastern king, Hsiao Chao-kuei as the western king, Feng Yun-shan as the southern king, Wei Chang-hui as the northern king, and Shih Ta-kai (Dakai) as the assistant king (Wing King). All of them were under the command of Hung, the heavenly king. In 1852 the Taipings took Yuen-chou, Hanyang, Hankou, and Wuchang. In Mar 1853 they captured Nanking, which became the capital of the kingdom and was named the Heavenly Capital. In May the Taipings launched their military operations to the west and north. The operation to the north nearly reached Peking and Tientsin. The operation to the west took Anhing, Kiukiang, and Wuchang. The Qing empire was in a very dangerous situation, however, for the initial success was followed by a series of murders and massacres among the kings in 1856. A total of 20,000 people were killed, including Yang, his family, and his followers and the northern king, Wei. Afterwards, Shih, whose wife and children were slaughtered by Wei and his general Qin, entered Nanjing to a hero's welcome (Dec 1856). Wuchang, Chenkiang, and Kiukiang fell, and Nanking was besieged.

In 1858 Hung promoted some able generals, such as Li Hsiu-cheng as the loyal king and Ch'en Yu-cheng as the Ying king, and invested his cousin Hung Jen-kan as the Kan Wang. Hung Jen-kan proclaimed "Tzu-cheng hsin-pien." It advocated that the kingdom implement political reforms, learn Western scientific techniques, and develop the economy. Though these measures restrengthened the kingdom, the Qing government gained the upper hand in the coming military actions. Hsiang-chun (the Hsiang army), Huai-chun (the Huai army), and the Western-equipped Chang-shun-chun, which were trained by Tseng Kuo-fan, Li Hung-chang, and the Western nations respectively, formed a great force to combat the Taipings. Soochow and Hangchow fell in 1863 and 1864, respectively. In Jul 1864, the fall of the Heavenly Capital marked the end of the Heavenly Kingdom.

The Taiping movement started as a Christian-influenced religious movement with elements also from Chinese writings, but it ended as a revolutionary movement. The movement itself was an attempt to institute political, social, and cultural reform. Moreover, it may be counted as a pioneer of the coming rural revolutionary movements in China. In this aspect, it showed one of the implications of the spread of Christianity in China.

Bibliography

Spence, Jonathan, *God's Chinese Son: The Taiping Heavenly Kingdom of Hong Xiuquan* (1996). • Jen Yu-wen, *Taiping Tianguo quanshi* (Complete history of the Taiping), 3 Vols (1962). • Boardman, Eugene Powers, *Christian Influence upon the Ideology of the Taiping Rebellion, 1851-1864* (1952). • Fairbank, John K., ed., *Cambridge History of China,* Vol. 10, pt. 1, *Late Ching, 1800-1911* (1978). • Chin Yu-fu, *Taiping Tianguo shiliao* (Historical material on the Taiping) (1955). • Guo Tingyi, *Taiping Tianguo shishi rizhi* (Daily record of events in the Taiping), 2 Vols. (1946/1976). • Guo Yisheng, *Taiping Tianguo lishi ditu ji* (Historical atlas of the Taiping Heavenly Kingdom) (1989). • Franz, Michael, and Chang Chung-li, *The Taiping Rebellion: History and Documents,* 3 Vols. (1971). • *Taiping Tianguo yinshu* (Facsimile reproductions of Taiping texts), 20 Vols. (1961). • Teng Ssu-yu, *Historiography of the Taiping Rebellion* (1962). • Wang Qincheng, *Taiping Tianguo de wenxian he lishi* (The sources and history of the Taiping) (1993).

Lee Chee Kong

Taiwan

Formerly Formosa ("beautiful island"), Taiwan is located between the Philippines* and Japan*, 100 miles off the coast of China. For thousands of years the aborigines had lived undisturbed on this island, until settlers and privateers from China* and Japan began to arrive and occupy certain parts of the island in the 16th c.

In Aug 1624, Dutch troops occupied southern Taiwan and became its first sovereign regime. Under the chartered system of the Dutch East-India Company* (VOC), this colonial rule lasted for 38 years. In 1626 Spanish troops came to occupy northern Taiwan but were expelled by the Dutch in 1642.

In Feb 1662 the Dutch were defeated by Cheng Chheng-kung (Koxinga), a defeated general of the late Ming dynasty in China. The Chengs established the first independent Han kingdom in Taiwan, lasting three generations. They recruited massive Han settlers from the southeastern part of China, primarily from the Hakka-speaking area of Kwantung Province and the Hoklo-speaking region of the southern Fukien Province, whose descendants eventually became the majority population in Taiwan. This regime attempted to "restore the Ming Dynasty in China," did not identify with the island, and was destroyed in Aug 1683 by Qing troops led by Shih-lang, a defecting general from Koxinga's camp.

On 27 May 1684, Taiwan was designated a prefecture of Fukien Province, marking the beginning of Chinese rule. The following two centuries saw a number of small- and large-scale insurgencies and counterrebellions. In 1895 Japan defeated the Qing dynasty, and Taiwan was ceded under the Shimonoseki Treaty (see Sino-Japanese War).

Resenting the Qing decision, the people of Taiwan established the independent Republic of Formosa, but it collapsed within a few months of the arrival of the Japanese. The Taiwanese suffered political oppression and cultural discrimination during 50 years of Japanese colonial rule. Ironically, Taiwanese society was also modernized in the process, for the discriminatory educational system introduced them to modern science, medicine, and democracy. Meanwhile, resistance movements persisted, some violent (1895-1915) and others nonviolent (1915-45).

At the end of World War II*, the allies conceded Taiwan's "return to China," as the Cairo Declaration (1943) was deemed a clandestine agreement between Chiang Kai-shek and Western leaders. The representative body of the Chinese regime, headed by Chen Yi, arrived on 25 Oct 1945. The corrupt administration and concomitant extreme economic inflation, along with the "conqueror" mentality of the Chinese occupation troops, led to the infamous "February 28 Incident" against Chen Yi and his regime, which resulted in the death of an estimated 20,000 Taiwanese, mostly intellectuals and elites.

In 1949 the Nationalist regime was defeated by the Chinese Communist Party and expelled from China. For more than 35 years since, Taiwan has been forced to serve as the refuge of the Republic of China (ROC) and the base for its future "restoration of China." In 1971 the People's Republic of China was admitted to the United Nations, and the membership of the Republic of China was terminated.

On 10 Dec 1979, the "Formosa Magazine Event" (or "Kao-Hsiong Incident") signalled a new era, beginning with the indictment for treason of dozens of opposition leaders and the arrest of several Presbyterian* ministers (including C. M. Kao) and laypersons. This led to the formation of the Democratic Progessive Party on 28 Sept

1986, heralding "partisan politics" in Taiwan. In 1987 martial law, which had lasted 38 years, was finally lifted. For the first time, Taiwanese were able to elect representatives of congress and the legislative body in 1991 and 1992, the provincial governor of Taiwan and the majors of Taipei and Kao-Hsiong in 1994, and the president in 1996.

The government of Taiwan is becoming more indigenized and democratized. The economic system in general remains capitalistic but state-dominated. Taiwanese society consists primarily of four ethnic groups: the Hoklo people (73.3 percent), the Hakka people (12 percent), the aborigines (1.7 percent), and the "mainlanders" (13 percent). The majority (75-80 percent) of the population, especially the Han people, are affiliated with Buddhism*, Taoism*, or folk beliefs, the last being a mixture of Buddhism, Taoism, Confucianism*, folklore, and animistic beliefs. Christians, including Protestants and Catholics, constitute 2-3 percent of the entire population. However, the ratio among the younger and more modernized generations may vary greatly.

History of Christianity in Taiwan. Christianity in Taiwan can be traced back to the Dutch and Spanish mission in the 1620s. Starting in 1627, the Dutch Reformed Church (through the VOC) sent about 30 ministers, including Georgius Candidius, Robertus Junius, Simon van Breen, Daniel Gravius, and Antonius Hambroek, and many mission associates to evangelize the aborigines. From 1626 onward, the Spanish Catholic Church, predominantly the Dominicans* and Franciscans*, sent about 40 missionaries to Taiwan, most notably Bartolomé Martinez, Jacinto Esquivel, and Teodoro Quiros. However, because their primary mission goals were China and Japan, their impact on northern Taiwan was insignificant. After the expulsion of both regimes, all traces of these two missions were largely dissipated within half a century.

The missionary enterprise began for the second time in the 1860s, initiated by the "Great Missionary Movement" of the West and occasioned by the Tien-chin Treaty between the Qing government of China and foreign imperial powers in 1858, which entailed the opening of several seaports (including Keelung, Tamsui, and Takao) and ensured the freedom of evangelism in those areas.

On 18 May 1859, Dominican fathers Fernando Sainz and Angel Bufurull, along with three Han catechists from Amoy, came to Takao and established a church in Ban-Kim-Chng. This marked the beginning of the "Restoration of Mission." Facing antagonism from the Taiwanese people and competition from Protestant missionaries, the Dominicans adopted a "qualitative" approach to mission until the end of World War II, because "undue haste in baptizing half-instructed or uninstructed souls would only be so much wasted effort since most of them would invariably revert to their pagan practices."

In Sep 1860, Carstairs Douglas* and H. L. Mackenzie* of the English Presbyterian mission in Amoy came to northern Taiwan and discovered that the Amoy dialect was prevalent in Taiwan. Douglas urged his church to start a new mission in Taiwan, preferably a medical* ministry. On 29 May 1865, James L. Maxwell, accompanied by Douglas and three Han associates, came to Takao and began his medical mission in Hu-sian (now Tainan) on 16 Jun (a date designated as a commemorative day by the Presbyterian Church in Taiwan [PCT]), but local resistance soon forced a return to Takao. On 12 Aug 1866, four Han believers — Ko Tiong, Tan Che, Tan Ui, Tan Chheng-Ho — were baptized by W. S. Swanson from Amoy, the firstfruits of the English Presbyterian mission.

Several missionaries followed soon after Maxwell. Hugh Ritchie, the first Presbyterian minister to Taiwan, evangelized among various ethnic groups. William Campbell, a church historian, edited a comprehensive Taiwanese dictionary and initiated ministries to the Pescadores and among the blind and the deaf. Thomas Barclay founded the Tainan Theological College (1876) and the Taiwan Church Press (1884), helped organize the first southern presbytery (1896), and single-handedly translated the entire Romanized Taiwanese Bible*.

On 9 Mar 1872, George Leslie Mackay of the Canadian Presbyterian Church arrived in Tamsui and began his 30-year ministry in northern Taiwan. On 9 Feb 1873, he baptized five Han believers, Giam Chheng-hoa, Gou Khoan-ju, Ong Tiong-chui, Lim Kek, and Lim Poe. He single-handedly established the groundwork of the northern Presbyterian mission: the Mackay Memorial Hospital, the Oxford College, the Women's* School, 60 churches with affiliated clinics, and 60 native preachers. He was succeeded by William Gauld, who, with the cooperation of local leaders, built many beautiful churches, helped organize the first northern presbytery (1914), and fostered the formation of the Taiwan Synod (1912), the forerunner of the PCT.

The antiforeign mentality of the Taiwanese people resulted in various afflictions and persecutions for missionaries and local converts, such as the assaults on Revs. Campbell, Barclay, and Mackay; the martyrdom of Chuang Chheng-Feng; the harassment of Pi-tau Church in 1868; and the great persecution of northern churches during the Sino-French War in 1884. In the midst of such a difficult situation, the Presbyterians endured in their faith and testified to the Reformed spirit of "burned but never consumed" *(Nec tamen consumebatur).* On the other hand, early Presbyterian missionaries also adopted a more contextualized approach to mission, engaging in medical, educational, and social services in addition to evangelism. Some of the more prominent missionaries in these fields included David Landsborough, Marjorie Learner, Campbell Moody, George Ede, Edward Band, George W. Mackay, and G. Gushue Taylor.

From 1915 onward, while Taiwan was under Japanese rule, some local leaders (notably Gou Hi-eng) began to advance the missionary principle of "self-support, self-government, and self-propagation." Missionaries had in fact begun to ordain native ministers as early as 1895 in the north (Giam Chheng-hoa and Tan Hoe) and 1899 in the south (Phoan Beng-chu and Lau Bo-khun), but it was only when all the Western missionaries were expelled by the Japanese government in the early 1940s that the Taiwanese church was forced to become autonomous, a process spanning several decades.

In the 1940s, with the outbreak of the Pacific War, the Japanese government began the so-called "royal citizen movement" to Japanize the Taiwanese people and to enforce Shintoism*, in association with Japanese emperor worship and military patriotism. The Taiwanese churches, like the German churches during the World War II, were forced to choose between God and Tienno (the Japanese emperor) and faced the challenge of "confessing the Lordship of Christ." Some individual Christians and churches yielded to the pressure; others did not. As a result, seminaries, church schools, hospitals, and many churches were either closed or confiscated up until the end of the war. Most pastors were sent for "spiritual formation," a process of patriotic indoctrination and brainwashing by the Japanese authorities. This experience of church-state confrontation is both humiliating and revealing.

Under the Japanese "segregated" policy, two missionaries, Mr. Inoye from Japan and N. P. Yates from Canada, began to work among the aborigines. Meanwhile, James Dickson and his wife encouraged and trained several aborigines, such as Chi-wong, Dowai, Kao Tien-wong, and Hsu Nan-mien, to evangelize among their own people. The rapid growth of the aboriginal churches, partially owing to the efforts of Revs. Loh Sian-chhun, Ou Bun-ti, Kho Iu-chai, and Chng Sian-bo, immediately following Japanese rule was hailed as "the miracle of the 20th c." In 1947 Yu-shan Theological* College was established to train aboriginal preachers.

Up to the end of World War II, except for some small Japanese churches, the PCT was the only significant Protestant missionary force in Taiwan. In the late 1940s, however, with the defeat of Chiang Kai-shek and his Nationalist Party and the subsequent transfer of his regime to Taiwan, other denominations came, including the Methodists*, the Southern Baptists*, the Lutherans*, and the Anglicans*. Minor churches, such as the Mennonites*, Holiness Church, Assemblies of God, and Seventh-day Adventists*, and Chinese indigenous churches such as the True Jesus Church, Little Flock*, New Testament Church, and other independent churches, all seized the opportunity to evangelize among refugees at a critical time (see Indigenous Congregations). The PCT also launched a series of evangelistic movements, significantly the Doubling Movement (1954-64) and the New Century Mission Movement (1965-70). In general, all churches grew considerably until 1965 when the shift of *zeitgeist* resulted in a degree of stagnation. For the purpose of interchurch coordination, the major denominations formed the National Council of Churches in Taiwan.

On the other hand, from the 1970s onward, the political future of Taiwan has become a paramount concern and a divisive issue. The PCT, in the belief that the future of Taiwan is an integral part of the salvific mission of God, issued three statements in the 1970s, calling for social and political reform, proposing the right of the Taiwanese people to self-determination, and expressing the hope for a "new and independent country." Other churches disagreed and criticized the PCT. To some degree, conflicting political ideologies and contrasting attitudes toward the current Nationalist regime and its China policy continue to alienate the churches from one other.

Christianity in Taiwan is presently experiencing steady growth in comparison with population growth. However, the rapidly changing and intensely challenging situation of Taiwan also marks the beginning of another complicated yet critical era for Christianity in Taiwan.

Bibliography

Cheng, Lien-min, ed., *A Centennial History of the Presbyterian Church of Formosa, 1865-1965* (1965). • Fernandez, Pablo, *One Hundred Years of Dominican Apostolate in Formosa* (1959). • Ong, Ioktek, *Taiwan: A History of Anguish and Struggle* (1979). • Tong, Hollington K., *Christianity in Taiwan: A History* (1961).

Cheng Yang En

Taizé Community, Asia

Monastic community founded by Brother Roger in 1940 in France, comprising both Roman* Catholics and Protestants of different backgrounds.

There are about 100 brothers from 25 countries seeking to live out a "parable" of reconciliation, leading a simple life, earning their own living, and sharing with others through their own work. For Taizé, reconciliation also involves close identification with those who suffer. Toward the end of the 1960s, small groups of brothers began living among the poorest in different parts of Asia such as Hong Kong, Calcutta, Seoul, and Bangladesh*. Today they also work with tribal minorities, the student world, the arts, prisoners, and street children, and they help promote elementary schooling.

Since the late 1950s, an increasing number of young people worldwide have visited the village of Taizé to pray and deepen their faith and commitment, including hundreds of young Asians, often sent by their churches, who stay for several months.

Upon the invitation of Asian church leaders, Taizé collaborates with the national youth commissions and ministry teams in practically every country in Asia. Several large international gatherings were held (Madras, 1985 and 1988; Manila, 1991), in addition to an ever-continuing series of smaller meetings, prayers, and retreats, to encourage the young people in their commitments and to foster communion within the body of Christ and throughout the human family.

The music of Taizé is sung in more than 15 Asian languages. For World Youth Day 1995, Taizé songs in Tagalog were used for prayer in the Philippines*.

Brother Roger, whose writings are translated into many Asian languages, has coauthored three books with the late Mother Teresa* of Calcutta. In 1974 he became the second recipient of the Templeton Prize. In 1988 he was awarded the United Nations Education, Science and Culture Organization's (UNESCO) prize for peace education.

Bibliography

Gonzalez-Balado, José Luis, *The Story of Taize* (1977). • Spirik, Kathryn, *A Universal Heart: The Life and Vision of Brother Roger of Taizé.* TAIZÉ COMMUNITY

Takakura Tokutaro

(b. Ayabe, Kyoto Prefecture, Japan, 23 Apr 1885; d. 3 Apr 1934). Japanese theologian and pastor.

After completing study at the Fourth High School, Takakura went on to the Department of German Law of Tokyo Imperial University and, under the influence of Uemura Masahisa*, was baptized. After this, he decided to enter seminary, left Tokyo University, and entered Tokyo Union Theological* Seminary. After graduating, he assisted Uemura at Fujimicho Church as an evangelist and then pastored the Kyoto Yoshida Church and Sapporo Kita Ichijo Church. In 1918 he returned to Tokyo to become a professor at Tokyo Shingakusha. From there he went to England and studied at Edinburgh, Oxford, and Cambridge, returning to Japan* in 1924. He immediately started a church in his home in Okubo, which later became Tyoama Church. While teaching at Tokyo Shingakusha, he also pastored this church.

The next year, after Uemura's death, he became president of Tokyo Shingakusha. This school merged with the theology department of Meiji Gakuin, and when Japan Theological Seminary was started, he became head of the faculty and, later, president. A number of the members of Fujimicho Church transferred their membership to Tyoama Church, and this church became Shinanomachi Church. He also helped form *Hukuin-Doshi-Kai* (Evangelical Friends Society), and they began publishing *Fujuin to gendai* (The Gospel and Today) as a beginning of their movement to bring reform to the church.

However, his demanding schedule took a toll on his health, and extreme fatigue threw him into deep depression, which caused him to take his own life. As a young man, he suffered with problems of identity and approached the Christian faith as a way to deal with these. He received salvation in the faith, but his relationship to culture was a problem for him (see Gospel and Culture).

In England he studied under J. Paterson and enjoyed reading Peter Taylor Forsyth, Friedrich von Hugel (1852-1925), and Ernst Troeltsch, but he was especially influenced by Forsyth and adopted that theological standpoint. After returning to Japan, he spoke strongly for a Gospel-centered Christianity and, as such, opposed the social* action–centered faith. He became one of the first Japanese to introduce the neo-orthodoxy of Karl Barth to Japan.

Before studying in England, he wrote *Oncho no Okoku* (Kingdom of Grace) in 1921. Later he wrote *Oncho no shinjitsu* (Truth of Grace) in 1925, *Oncho to Shomei* (Grace and Life's Calling) in 1926, and *Fukuinteki Kirisuto-kyo* (Gospel Christianity) in 1927. He advocated Christianity as a religion of grace and gave to the not yet mature Christian faith in Japan a theological self-awareness. The complete works of Takakura, *Takakura zenshu,* were published in 10 volumes in 1936-37, and a five-volume set of his works, *Takakura Tokutaro Chosaku-shu,* was published in 1964. SATO TOSHIO

Takayama Ukon

(b. Settsu, Japan, ca. 1552; d. Manila, 5 Feb 1615). Typical Christian *daimyo* (feudal lord); spiritual name, Jusuto.

Takayama was the eldest son of Takayama Hidanokami. Baptized in Sawa Yamato in 1564 by Lorenco, he was a follower of Wata Koremasa at Settsu Akutagawa Castle. But when Koremasa was killed in battle, Ukon attacked Koremasa's son and became a follower of Araki Murashige, and subsequently the head of Takatsuki Castle with a stipend of 20,000 *koku* (4.95 bushels of rice). He built a church on this land, contributed to the building of Kyoto Namban-ji Temple (Kyoto South Europe Church), and worked to convert the citizens in his domain. In 1578 his lord (Araki Murashige) turned his back on Oda Nobunaga, an action that resulted in Takatsuki Castle being attacked by both of their armies. Pushed to the edge of disaster, he was almost forced to surrender, but somehow he managed to survive. In 1581, when Alessandro Valignano* visited Gokinai, he was received at Takatsuki and celebrated Easter there on a grand scale. The next year, at the Battle of Yamazaki after the change at Honnoji Temple in Kyoto, he achieved military successes. Azuchi Seminario, first located in Azuchi, was moved to Takatsuki. After this, he served as a general for Toyotomi Hideyoshi and was on the battlefront when they conquered Kameyama Castle, also fighting at Shizugatake and Komakiyama. In 1585 he participated in the conquest of Negoro; however, on 15 Oct of that year, he was transferred by Hideyoshi to Harima Akashi. Because he also had a residence in Osaka, he came and went at Osaka Castle often, and thus exercised much influence on officers and soldiers there. In 1587 he joined the forces in Kyushu but was expelled by Hideyoshi on 24 Jul of that year. After going into hiding for a short time on Shdoshima Island, he went to the Konishi's domain in Higo and visited the associate head of the Jesuit Order in Kazusa (see Society of Jesus). He became the retainer of Maeda Toshiie and helped to eradicate Odawara. After Toshiie's demise, he worked for his heir,

Maeda Toshinaga, and, while raising his reputation as *chajin* (one of seven famous tea servers of Riky), he devoted his energies to spreading the Christian Gospel. In 1614 he was expelled from Nagasaki by Tokugawa Ieyasu and went to Manila, where he was well received as a model of Japanese Christianity, but very soon he became ill and died.

Bibliography

Johannes Laures, *Takayama Ukon no shogai — shoki nihon kirisuto-kyo shi* (The life of Takayama Ukon — early Christianity in Japan) (1948); *Takayama Ukon no kenkyu to shiryo* (Research and historical records of Takayama Ukon) (1949). Ebisawa Arimichi, *Takayama Ukon* (1958). MATSUDA KIICHI

Takenaka Masao

(b. Beijing, 6 Sep 1925). Japanese ethicist, theological* educator, and ecumenical* leader.

Takenaka has been one of the most significant contributors to a variety of ecumenical movements and programs not only in Japan but on the international scene, while serving as a professor of Christian ethics and sociology of religion at Doshisha University in Kyoto from 1955 to 1996. He was educated at Kyoto University (in economics), Doshisha University (in theology), and Yale University (in social ethics), where he received his Ph.D. in 1954.

Takenaka has been in great demand as a lecturer, and his participation in ecumenical programs includes a theme lecture at the Third Assembly of the World Council of Churches in New Delhi, the John R. Mott Memorial Lecture of the East Asia Christian Conference (EACC), the Burns Memorial Lecture at Knox College (New Zealand), and the Karnahan Lecture at Union Theological Seminary in Buenos Aires. He served as visiting professor at Union Theological Seminary, New York; Yale University; and Harvard University.

Takenaka played an important role in promoting experimental ministries in urban-industrial areas in Japan in the 1950s and 1960s and elsewhere in Asia. He served as the chairperson of the Committee of the Witness of the Laity, EACC, 1959-67; the Urban Industrial Mission* of the EACC, 1968-73; the Urban Industrial Mission of the World Council of Churches, 1968-75; and as a member of the Theological Education Fund Committee, 1971-77. He continued from his student days to be an influential leader in the Student Christian Movement* and in the World Student Christian Federation. In addition to holding administrative positions at Doshisha University as dean of the School of Theology and as director of the Center for American Studies, he has served as chair of the board of Nishijin Community Center, the Asian Christian Art Association, the Program of Theology and Culture in Asia, and Nippon Christian Academy.

Takenaka's research and writing have covered a wide range of subjects from ethical concern for Christian witness to Christian expressions through art*. He has also written social biographical studies on relatively unknown personalities and their imaginative work for indigenous expression of the Gospel message.

Takenaka has been a pioneer in frontier ministries in Japan both in establishing the theological ground and in providing practical leadership, always based upon ecumenical concern and imaginative vision. His work has affected Christian circles not only in Japan but in the international arena of Christian mission.

In addition to numerous publications in the Japanese language, his books in English include *Reconciliation and Renewal in Japan* (1957); *Christian Art in Asia* (1975); *God Is Rice: Asian Culture and Christian Faith* (1986); *Cross and Circle* (1990); and *The Bible through Asian Eyes* (1991). ROBERT MIKIO FUKADA

Tambunan, A. M.

(b. Tarutung, North Sumatra, 1911; d. 1970). Prominent member of the Indonesian parliament, the Christian party, PARKINDO, and the Council of Churches in Indonesia*.

Tambunan studied law in Jakarta, assisted the Dutch mission consuls, and became active in the ecumenical* movement. He was a member of the Lutheran Batak* (HKBP) church. He gained prominence as a leader in the church and government after 1945.

From 1967 to 1970, Tambunan served as minister of social affairs. He received honorary degrees from St. Olaf College, Northfield, Minnesota, United States, and Temple College, Chattanooga, Tennessee, United States. He wrote several articles on religion and politics in which he urged his fellow Christians not to stand aside, but to participate in a responsible way in the political life of the young republic. Yet he kept a critical attitude toward the government. Hence he did not really come to the fore until after the Sukarno* period. In several contributions, Tambunan emphasized the social responsibility which churches have within society. Tambunan was a sincere and stimulating example of a layperson who, during the last decade of colonialism* and the first decades of independence, gave guidance to the Indonesian churches.

Bibliography

"Die Stellung des Laien in der H.K.B.P.," in Hans de Kleine (Hrsg), *Ist . . . gemacht zu seinem Volk." 100 Jahre Batakkirche* (1961). • Speeches of Tambunan as minister of social affairs plus a short biography, *Bahasa Indonesia*, 4 Vols. (1969, 1970). ALLEN G. HOEKEMA

Tanada, Lorenzo M.

(b. Tayabas, 10 Aug 1898; d. Quezon City, 28 May 1992). Filipino patriot, nationalist, defender of human rights, and peace advocate.

Tanada, or Ka Tanny, was one of the few modern-day Filipino patriots. After fighting in World War II*, he and his organization, the Civil Liberties Union, sought neither United States recognition nor any reward for their efforts, which they considered a duty to their country. He consistently asserted the dignity of the people and the sovereignty of the nation, maintaining that nationalism* was the "primal virtue of the citizen." In the Cold War period, his stance was labeled communistic, yet he was reelected four times as senator (1947-71). Despite his advanced age, he stood at the front line against the Marcos dictatorship and the United States bases, and he triumphed. He was a rallying force and inspiration for many church people, and he was heartened by the growing nationalism among clerics and nuns.

Bibliography

Constantino, Renato, ed., *The Essential Tanada* (1989). • Maramag, Ileana, ed., *Nationalism: A Summons to Greatness* (1965). TEODORO MAXIMILIANO M. DE MESA

Taoism

One of the most ancient Chinese religio-philosophical traditions.

Though its origin is often attributed to Lao Tzu, the Taoist movement is now generally thought to have existed centuries before him. According to Ssu-ma Chien's *Historical Records (Shi Chi)* (late 2nd c. B.C.E.), Lao Tzu was a senior contemporary of Confucius (K'ung Tzu), who lived in the 6th c. B.C.E. Lao Tzu's family name was Li, his given name Erh, and he was also known as Tan. *Lao* means old, and *Tzu* is a title of respect for gentlemen in ancient China*; literally, Lao Tzu is "the old master." A native of the state of Ch'u in southern Hunan, Lao Tzu was reputed to have instructed Confucius in ceremonies. A 5,000-character book, *Lao Tzu,* later known as the *Tao Te Ching,* on the significance of *Tao* (way) and *Te* (individual power) was named after him and is essential for an analysis of his philosophy, even though some words or sentences were added by later editors or writers.

Taoism is essentially a Chinese entity. Its relation to Christianity can be traced back to the T'ang dynasty (618-906 C.E.) when Christianity was first introduced to China by Syrian monks in 635. Syrian Christianity, which flourished in the T'ang capital Changan from 635 to around 845, made some remarkable and ingenious attempts to "contextualize"* Christianity by using familiar Taoist, Confucianist, and Buddhist terms and concepts. All subsequent Christian missions to China have to relate to Taoism on both the philosophical-mystical and religious-popular levels.

The earliest occurrence of the word "Taoism" (*Tao Chia* or "Taoist school") is found in *Historical Records,* in which Taoism was equated with the Huang Lao school, named after Huang Ti ("Yellow Emperor"), the earliest legendary king and common ancestor of the Chinese, and Lao Tzu. The Huang Lao school, which emerged in the 4th-3rd c. B.C.E. in the middle Warring States period, was fashionable in the 2nd c. B.C.E. during the Han dynasty. The meaning of the word "Taoism," however, has since become rather complicated. In the 3rd c. C.E., when another Taoist branch (*Hsuan Hsueh,* "mystical learning") was flourishing, Taoism was associated with Lao Tzu and Chuang Tzu rather than the Yellow Emperor. Modern Chinese scholars recognize two forms of Taoism: Taoist philosophy *(Tao Chia)* and Taoist religion *(Tao Chiao).* Taoist philosophy competed with Confucianism* and legalism from the 5th through the 2nd cs. B.C.E. Taoist religion is that unique Chinese organized indigenous movement which was included, with Buddhism* and Confucianism after the 3rd c. C.E., among the "three teachings."

Central to the philosophical and religious teaching of Taoism is the concept of Tao, literally "way." Tao is often extended from its metaphysical root to imply a moral or sociopolitical principle by which the individual persons and society are governed. Lao Tzu was perhaps the first Chinese intellectual to develop a concise system of metaphysics based on the concept of Tao.

He gave an almost totally new meaning to Tao in the *Tao Te Ching* by establishing it as the original source of the universe metaphysically: "Tao produced the One, the One produced the Two, the Two produced the Three, and the Three produced the ten thousand things" (ch. 42). Tao is the prime source, the One is the primordial being, or the Chaos; the Two indicates *yin* (the negative or the feminine) and *yang* (the positive or the masculine); the Three are *yin, yang,* and their unity. Tao determines all things, or everything depends on it: "The great Way is broad, reaching left as well as right. Myriad creatures depend on it for life yet it does not turn away from them" (ch. 34); "Myriad creatures all revere the Way" (ch. 51). Lao Tzu believed that the Tao is universal and that everything will develop or transform perfectly according to Tao. It also, therefore, included the way of universal process and the highest principle. This is Lao Tzu's simple ontology.

Tao is mysterious: "We look at it and do not see it. . . . We listen to it and do not hear. . . . We touch it and do not find it. . . . Infinite and boundless, it cannot be given any name" (ch. 14). We cannot understand Tao by our senses or our reason, but it is a real being. Tao is beyond the capacity of ordinary knowledge and the human intellect, but people can reach or gain Tao by intuition: "The pursuit of learning is to increase day after day. The pursuit of Tao is to decrease day after day" (ch. 48). "One may see Tao of Heaven without looking through the windows" (ch. 47). The Tao functions spontaneously, without any will or purpose: "Man models himself on earth, Earth on heaven, Heaven on Tao, and Tao on spontaneity" (ch. 25). Tao "accomplishes its tasks, but does not claim credit for it. It clothes and feeds all things but does not claim to be master over them. Always without desires, it may be called the small. All things come to it and it does not master them; hence it may be called the Great" (ch. 34). Tao functions totally through natural processes and emerges from natural processes, hence it is not like a creator who creates the world through will and purpose. According to Confucianism, Tao is a general principle of politics and morality and Te is individual virtue or character. However, for Lao Tzu, Tao is the ultimate reality and the general principle of the universe, and Te is the localization of Tao. Te is the individual principle of everything and everybody. It is significant to note that the Chinese character for Tao has been advisedly used to translate the Greek word *logos* in the "Union Version" of the Chinese Bible* and other translations.

Lao Tzu's philosophy is paradoxical. Everything contains opposite sides, and each side depends on the other: "Being and non-being produce each other; Difficult and easy complete each other; Long and short contrast each other. . . . Front and back follow each other. Therefore the sage manages affairs without action (*wu-wei,* literally 'no behavior' or 'doing nothing'), and spreads doctrines without words" (ch. 2). *Wu-wei,* however, does not mean absolute nonaction; rather, it is the negation or restriction of human action, particularly social activities. There are a number of gradations in the Taoist theories of *wu-wei:* as nonbehavior or doing nothing; as taking as little action as possible; as taking no action for the spontaneous transformation of things; and as taking action according to objective conditions and the nature of things, namely, acting naturally.

Lao Tzu believed that *wu-wei* can lead to a peaceful and harmonious society: "The more cunning and skill man possesses, the more vicious things will appear. The more laws and orders are made prominent, the more thieves and robbers there will be. Therefore the sage says: I take no action and the people of themselves are transformed. . . . I engage in no activity and the people of themselves become prosperous" (ch. 57). The opposite of *wu-wei* is *yu-wei,* or taking action. Here cunning and skill, laws and orders belong to *yu-wei,* which causes vicious actions, thieves, and robbers; in contrast, *wu-wei* brings prosperity, harmony, and peace. About *we-wei,* Lao Tzu coined a famous paradoxical phrase: *Wu-wei erh wu-pu-wei,* "do nothing and nothing is left undone." He said, "No action is undertaken, and yet nothing is left undone. An empire is often brought to one who undertakes no activity. If one undertakes activity, he is not qualified to win the empire" (ch. 48).

Another important concept related to *wu-wei* is *tzu-jan,* "spontaneity" or "being natural." The Tao is natural, and all things in the world should develop spontaneously. Unnatural effort must finally fail. The belief that the universe and social life will develop spontaneously is the foundation of the theory of *wu-wei,* as well as of Taoist philosophy. The Taoist ideal society is a primitive community with a natural, harmonious, and simple life, and exists without war and competition.

It was obviously difficult for the religious populace in ancient China to find satisfaction in philosophical Taoism. They thus found solace in religious Taoism, although philosophy and religion are interrelated. For example, Taoist philosophers were both thought of as the founders of Taoist religion and revered as gods in its polytheistic system. The earliest Taoist religious book, the *Classic of the Great Peace (T'ai-ping Ching),* and other classics were claimed to have been originally handed down by Lao Tzu. To compete with Buddhism, later Taoists even said that Lao Tzu had been the instructor of Sakyamuni. Many noble titles were conferred on Lao Tzu, e.g., "Saint Ancestor Great Tao Mysterious Primary Emperor." Clearly, Lao Tzu was considered a divinity in the Taoist religion, as were other Taoist philosophers such as Chuang Tzu and Lieh Tzu.

The classics of Taoist philosophers were also revered as sacred texts of the Taoist religion. The *Tao Te Ching* was referred to as the "Great Upper Mysterious Primary Emperor Tao Te True Classic," the *Chuang Tzu* as the "Southern Chinese True Classic," the *Lieh Tzu* as "Vacant Empty Ultimate Virtue True Classic," and the *Wen Tzu* as "Mastering of the Mystery True Classic." Taoist religion also borrowed many concepts and ideas from Taoist philosophy, such as the Tao material or vital force *(Ch'i),* heaven *(t'ien),* individual power *(te),* spontaneity *(tzu-jan),* nonaction *(wu-wei),* sitting and forgetting *(tso-wang),* and pure person *(chen-jen).* Words or ideas from the *Lao Tzu* and *Chuang Tzu* are frequently found in Taoist religious texts, such as the *Classic of the Great Peace, The Master Who Embraces Simplicity (Pao P'u Tzu),* and later books.

However, a comprehensive investigation of Taoist religion reveals that it is possible to overemphasize the connections between Taoist religion and philosophy. Some religious Taoists do not regard Taoist philosophers as the most important thinkers or as gods. There are many historical figures, legendary heroes, ancient and contemporary emperors, scholars, and generals woven into the polytheistic system of Taoist religion. The more Taoist religion matured, the less the significance of Taoist philosophers as deities, the fundamental reason being that Taoist philosophers concentrate on spiritual transcendence whereas religious Taoists seek physical immortality. Taoist philosophers do not think it necessary to pursue a long life: "The reason I have great trouble is that I have a body. When I no longer have a body, what trouble have I?" (*Tao Te Ching,* ch. 13). Chapter 75 added, "It is only those who do not seek after life who are wiser in valuing life." Chuang Tzu said, "The True Man of ancient times knew nothing of loving life, knew nothing of hating death" and "Life and death are fated — constant as the succession of dark and dawn. . . . Man can do nothing about it." The founders of philosophical Taoism advocated transcendence as the answer to man's impotence over life and death. Although there are vague references to long life in the *Tao Te Ching* and *Chuang Tzu,* no Taoist philosopher has focused on longevity and immortality. In contrast, Taoist religion emphasizes the possibility and importance of immortality.

Philosophical and religious Taoism differ in their attitudes toward society's rules. The former is antitraditional and transcends common values. Both Lao Tzu and

Chuang Tzu criticized rulers and the political and moral theory of Confucianism, believing that society would be better off without ruler, law, or morality. Religious Taoists, however, respect rulers and Confucianism. For example, the religious Taoist Ko Hung (283-343 C.E.) said, "The people who want to be immortals must have loyalty for the ruler and filial piety for parents . . . as the basic principle." He also wrote the "outer chapters" to develop Confucianism. K'ou Ch'ien Chih, another important religious Taoist, said that a Taoist should also learn Confucianism and help the emperor govern the world. Taoist religion pays much more attention to the present and practical interests than Taoist philosophy. In general, philosophical Taoism is more individualistic and critical; Taoist religion is more social and practical. Hence religious Taoists endowed philosophical terms such as *Tao, te,* and *wu-wei* with meanings of their own.

A major strength of Taoism is its adaptability. Over time, it has incorporated Confucianist and Buddhist beliefs and practices and is difficult to distinguish from folk religion in its practice of sorcery and fortune-telling, physiognomy and geomancy.

In Korea, where the folk religion bears a similarity to the Taoist tradition, Taoism, with emphases on immortality, exorcisms, and talismans, was popular from the 7th c. throughout the Koguryo, Paekche, and Silla kingdoms of Korea*, surviving better than Buddhism when Korea opted for Confucianism in the 14th c. It continues to exert its influence in modern Korea because of its successful adaptation to popular shamanism*. In Japan*, contrary to the popular belief that Shintoism* is purely indigenous, Taoist ideas of *yin* and *yang* and the Five Agents were already present in early Japanese works such as the *Kojiki* (The Ancient Chronicle); and the Shinto veneration of sacred objects (sword, bronze mirror) resembles Taoist rituals. Taoist influences in Japan, however, are perhaps more implicit and diffused than in Korea.

Inasmuch as Taoism has influenced Chinese Buddhism, religious Taoism itself has been transformed by Buddhism in the beliefs in transmigration, heavens and hells, and the adoption of a pantheon of deities and bodhisattvas. Although diametrically opposed in some basic beliefs and practices, Confucianism and Taoism are sometimes allied against Buddhist competition. Though Confucian rationalism is incompatible with much of religious Taoism, yet some religiously inclined Confucianists do find Taoism well suited to their personal needs. The recent policy of liberalization in mainland China has led to a revival of Taoism in the form of popular practices such as Ch'i-kung and Kung-fu and other physical and mental exercises and therapies.

Taoism is popular among Chinese everywhere; in Taiwan*, Hong Kong, and Southeast Asia, Taoism permeates their daily lives and is evident in the folk religions and calendrical festivals. Even the sophisticated urban dwellers are attracted to geomancy *(feng-shui).*

Taoism has long been a challenge to Christian mission in Asia and will continue to be in the foreseeable future. Taoist-Christian dialogue in the philosophical-mystical realm, especially on *Tao* and nature *(tzu-jan),* can be very meaningful and promising. One is inclined to think that the Taoist preception of *Tao* is even more profound than the Greek understanding of the *Logos,* and by implication closer to the biblical position. However, on the religious-popular front, there seems to be very little room for meaningful dialogue. For much of the popular Taoist beliefs and practices would naturally and perhaps justifiably be regarded as "superstitious" from the Christian perspective. Being increasingly conscious of this "image" problem, educated and mission-minded Taoist leaders in different places are trying very hard to "intellectualize" their beliefs and practices in order to make them intellectually more respectable and attractive, particularly to the young and educated. In view of the current interest in religion among Chinese everywhere, competition for potential "converts" between Taoism, Buddhism, and Christianity is likely to continue and escalate. If the image problem of popular Taoism is that of "superstition," the Christian stigma is one of "foreignness," i.e., that Christianity came to Asia via Western missions, although it actually originated in West Asia. However, being Asian or Chinese does not necessarily make a religion, whether Taoist or Christian, more appealing, because young and educated Asians are increasingly more cosmopolitan in their outlook. For Christianity, it is vital that it maintain its universal and yet unique character which is at the heart of the Gospel of Jesus Christ.

Bibliography

Liu Xiaogan, "Taoism," in *Our Religions,* ed. Arvind Sharma (1993). • Chen Gu-ying, *A Commentary on Lao-Tzu* (1993). • Küng, Hans, and Julia Ching, *Christianity and Chinese Religions* (1989). CHOONG CHEE PANG

Tatian

(2nd c.). Tatian was born in Syria (perhaps Adiabene or Palmyra) but went to the Mediterranean area, perhaps to Athens, where he studied rhetoric. He traveled to Rome, where he met Justin Martyr and may have become a Christian. Later he returned to Syria, where he founded a school.

His most influential composition was the *Diatessaron.* This was a harmony of the four Gospels intended to respond to the pagan criticism that the four sometimes disagree on details of Jesus' life and ministry. This single interpretation highlighted the ascetic aspects of Jesus' teaching. It became the Gospel of choice among the Syriac Christians and remained so until its copies were destroyed by Rabbula in the 5th c. It is extant in translations ranging from Persian and Arabic to Old Dutch. The oldest fragment found in Mesopotamia, at Dura Europos, is in Greek and dates from the early 3rd c. That the fragment is in Greek demonstrates that the text was circulated in Greek, as well as Syriac, from the earliest period. A full commentary on the text by Ephrem* the Syrian (ca. 306-73) survives in both Syriac and Armenian. The *Diatessaron* is very important for New Testament textual criticism.

The other surviving Tatian writing is *Oration to the Greeks.* This text is a full-scale critique of Graeco-Roman religion and society as well as an apologetic for Christian perspectives. The other writings known to early Christian historians have been lost, including *Perfection according to the Savior* and *On Morals.* It is unclear whether a volume titled *Those Who Have Propounded Ideas about God* was ever completed.

Bibliography

Eusebius, *Church History* 4.16.7; 4.16.29; and 5.13.6. • Hogg, H. W., "The *Diatessaron* of Tatian," ANF 10. • Whittaker, M., *Tatian: Oratio ad Graecos,* Oxford Early Christian Texts (1982). • McCarthy, C., *St. Ephrem's Commentary on Tatian's Diatessaron: An English Translation of the Chester Beatty Syriac Ms. 709* (1993). • Hawthorne, G. F., "Tatian and His Discourse to the Greeks," *Harvard Theological Review,* Vol. 57 (1964). • Quispel, G., *Tatian and the Gospel of Thomas* (1975). • Petersen. W., *Tatian's Diatessaron: Its Creation, Dissemination, Significance, and History in Scholarship* (1994).

David Bundy

Tay Sek Tin

(b. Fukien Province, China, 1872; d. Singapore, 1944). Alias Tay Peng Ting, Tay became a Christian at the age of 13. His heart to spread the Gospel caused him to join the London Missionary Society (LMS) theological* class in Amoy. In 1897, because of ill health, he decided to move to Singapore* with its warmer climate. There he joined Archibald Lamont*, an English Presbyterian* missionary with the Hokkien Church. Soon he was invited to become pastor of the Prinsep Street Presbyterian Church and, with Lamont, began to plan new churches, first in Paya Lebar in 1903, Spiritual Grace Church in 1905, then a church at Seletar in 1908. He had the distinction of being the first Chinese-ordained minister in the synod of the Singapore-Malaya Presbyterian Church.

Tay also pastored a new church opened in Tanjong Pagar in 1904 which was eventually to become the Jubilee Presbyterian Church of Outram Road. The Tanjong Pagar premises reflected the interests and influence of Tay: there was a book room for the sale of good Chinese literature as well as a reading room (to replace the earlier one started by Tay in Cross Street), a meeting place for discussion of Chinese affairs (known as Su Po Sia), as well as the headquarters of the Christian Endeavor movement. He was involved in many other projects for the Chinese community such as the Chinese Young Men's Christian Association* (YMCA), which he declared was to be "for all Chinese young men of good character, whether professing the Christian faith or not."

Tay also helped raise thousands of dollars to provide medication for opium* addicts. He was a prime mover in establishing the Opium Refuge, the *Khai Eng So,* in 1906. However, his ill health continued to plague him and, in 1912, he resigned from the post of minister of the church in Tanjong Pagar. Even then he continued to play an active part in church development, particularly in the founding of Zion Presbyterian Church and Choon Guan School in 1923. He died in 1944.

The substantial testimonial to Tay in the *90th and 70th Anniversary Commemorative Volume of the Presbyterian Church in Singapore and Malaya* records that he played a significant part in the establishment of the Presbyterian church in Singapore and Malaya. The churches he founded were self-supporting, both in terms of finance and human resources. His contribution to society was considerable both in the field of education (schools and kindergartens) and in welfare agencies such as the Anti-Opium Council and the Chinese YMCA.

Bibliography

Bethune Cook, J. A., *Sunny Singapore* (1907). • Sng, Bobby E. K., *In His Good Time* (1980, 1993). • *90th and 70th Anniversary Commemorative Volume of the Presbyterian Church in Singapore and Malaya* (1970).

Frank Lomax

Taylor, James Hudson

(b. Yorkshire, England, 21 May 1832; d. Changshu, Hunan, China, 1905). English missionary pioneer and founder of China* Inland Mission (CIM, now Overseas Missionary Fellowship).

Taylor was the firstborn of James and Amelia Taylor, a devout and generous Methodist* couple. James Taylor, Sr., was a local preacher, druggist, mathematician, and honest businessman. Amelia was the daughter of a Methodist minister. Keen interest in the Chinese led the senior Taylor to make a prenatal dedication of his firstborn as a missionary to China. Because of delicate health, James, Jr., was largely schooled at home, learning Hebrew from his father when he was barely four.

At 14, Taylor worked at a local bank. A transforming spiritual experience at age 17 convinced him that he was destined to do missionary work in China. He began to prepare himself by gathering information on the country. He gained experience by visiting the poor and sick and helping in evangelistic meetings. Two-thirds of his meager income went to charity, teaching him to live in the faith that God would provide for all his needs. He tried to gain some medical* and surgical knowledge by attaching himself to a physician in Hull and going to London for more training.

He interrupted his medical studies to leave for China in Sep 1853 under the Chinese Evangelization Society (CES). When he reached Shanghai, the city was suffering from civil war between the imperialists and some local rebels. Staying in rented quarters, he mastered sufficient Chinese to begin visiting and preaching in the nearby villages dressed as a Chinese, either alone or with another missionary. He started a dispensary on an island off Shanghai and worked closely with the older William Burns, an English Presbyterian whom he regarded as a spiritual father.

In 1856 Taylor moved to Ningbo and resigned from the poorly managed CES. At age 25 he married the 21-year-old Maria Dyer, an orphan of missionary parents. The threat of tuberculosis in 1860 forced Taylor to rest in England. He completed his medical studies in 1862 and also revised a translation of the New Testament into colloquial Ningbo. On Sunday, 25 Jun 1865, while recuperating in Brighton, he agonized over the sight of Christians worshipping in comfort while millions were perishing in China. His spiritual struggle led to the formation of the nondenominational China Inland Mission. The organization's purpose was to preach the Gospel to as many Chinese as possible, especially in the interior regions that were still unreached by other Protestant agencies.

Taylor returned to China in May 1866 with his wife, four children, another married couple, five single men, and nine single women on the ship *Lammermuir.* Some of the crew were converted during the long, perilous journey. Although Taylor wanted two recruits for each of the 11 unreached provinces and two for Mongolia*, the party initially settled in Ningbo and worked in the other cities of Zhejiang before expanding to other provinces. They met with difficulties and discouragements. The Taylors lost a child not long after their arrival.

In 1868 Taylor and his party were driven out of Yangchow, a city north of Shanghai, and funds for the CIM fell off. Before 1870, Taylor lost his wife and two other children. Taylor himself fell ill and had to return to England because the CIM home director, W. T. Berger, was unable to carry on with the demanding responsibilities. In London, Taylor married Miss J. E. Faulding, who happened to travel home for furlough on the same steamer as Taylor. They returned to China in 1872.

Taylor returned to England in 1874 following the death of Miss Batchley, secretary of the CIM. A fall suffered earlier when he was traveling up the Yangtze led to an enforced five-month bed rest in London. Taylor continued to direct the CIM from his bed, recruiting 18 men for China. In 1881 he prayed for 70 new missionaries (42 men and 28 women), and in 1886, 100 more. Among his recruits were the "Cambridge Seven," who left for China in 1885. In 1890, at the second gathering of Protestant missionaries in Shanghai, Taylor recommended the recruitment of 1,000 new missionaries in the ensuing five years. After China's defeat by Japan* in 1895, Taylor asked for even more missionaries.

Taylor traveled to North America, Scandinavia, Australia, and New Zealand as the CIM became better known. In 1889 he helped establish a CIM center in North America. His writings also inspired the formation of mission groups in Germany that cooperated with the CIM. Taylor remained director of the CIM until 1902.

He spent his later years in Switzerland. During the Boxer Uprising, 79 CIM missionaries and their children died. Taylor, unable to be in China because of his health, advised the mission to show the Chinese "the meekness and gentleness" of Christ and not to claim any reparations, even when offered. He made his 11th and last visit to China in 1905. He died after addressing Chinese Christians in Changsha, Hunan, the last province to allow the residence of Protestant missionaries.

Taylor was a man ahead of his time in his ecumenical* outlook. A good administrator, a pioneer, a kind, loving, and humble person, his contribution to the proclamation of the Gospel in China is impossible to measure, for the CIM survived beyond his death. Taylor continues to be an inspiration to many today.

Bibliography

Latourette, K. S., *These Sought a Country* (1950). • Anderson, Gerald H., et al., eds., *Mission Legacies* (1994). • Taylor, Dr., and Mrs. Howard Taylor, *Hudson Taylor and the China Inland Mission* (1918). • Broomhall, A. J., *Hudson Taylor and China's Open Century,* 7 vols. (1989). • Christie, Vance, "Hudson Taylor: Founder, China Inland Mission" (1999). China Group

Taylor, William

(b. Rockbridge County, Virginia, United States, 1821; d. United States, 1902). American Methodist* missionary in India* (1870-75).

Taylor was converted in rural Virginia and entered the Methodist ministry as an itinerant preacher. From 1849 until his retirement in 1896, he served as a Methodist missionary, and from 1884 as a missionary bishop.

More than any other individual, Taylor was responsible for the worldwide spread of Methodism beyond Europe and America. He had already ministered in California, Australia, New Zealand, the West Indies, South Africa, and Sri Lanka* before he came to India in 1870. He spent four years in India, first in Lucknow with James Thoburn*, then in other areas including Bombay, Pune, Calcutta, Madras, and Bangalore. The Methodist ministry expanded under him.

His method was to conduct revival meetings. Along with Thoburn and other Methodist leaders, Taylor was a "holiness" preacher whose ministry resulted in thousands reportedly "saved and sanctified." A spiritual awakening was said to have resulted in moral and spiritual transformations. Another result was that Methodist churches were organized in Bombay, Calcutta, and other cities, and eventually all of India was divided into regional Methodist conferences.

Taylor believed in a model of local autonomy of self-supporting churches, a policy which brought him into conflict with the mission board. In India, the expansion of Methodism throughout the subcontinent meant a violation of comity rules, resulting in further controversy and conflict. When the mission board refused to send the missionaries Taylor requested, Taylor recruited them himself.

Holiness advocates generally supported Taylor in his conflict with the mission board. At the height of the conflict, Taylor wrote a book titled *Pauline Methods of Missionary Work,* in which he presented his mission theory. Taylor was an inspiration to well-known Methodist missionaries in India, including the Thoburns, E. Stanley Jones*, J. Waskom Pickett*, E. A. Seamands, and others.

In addition to his influence in the Methodist Church, Taylor and his missionary principles had a great impact on the Holiness Movement as well as upon the more recent worldwide Pentecostal* movement.

Bibliography

Bundy, David, "The Legacy of William Taylor," *International Bulletin of Missionary Research,* Vol. 18, No. 4 (Oct 1994). • Glover, Robert H., *The Progress of World-Wide Missions* (revised) (1960). • Latourette, Kenneth Scott, "The Great Century in Northern Africa and in Asia," in *History of the Expansion of Christianity,* Vol. VI (1944).

Roger Hedlund

Telok Ayer Chinese Methodist Church

The oldest Chinese-speaking Methodist* congregation in Singapore*.

In 1885 the South India Conference of the Methodist Episcopal Church sent William F. Oldham* and James Miller Thoburn* as pioneer missionaries to start the Methodist work in Singapore. As a result of their evangelistic meetings, an English Methodist church (Wesley Methodist Church) was started in 1885. The following year, in response to the eagerness of the Chinese to learn the English language, Oldham founded the Oldham Mission School, which later became the Anglo Chinese School. In 1889 Benjamin R. West, a missionary doctor, was appointed to start the Chinese work. He rented a house on Upper Nanking Street to practice medicine. He conducted two services on Sunday and preached in Malay. His sermons were translated into the Hokkien dialect. In 1893 H. L. E. Luering* succeeded West. With the help of Bible* women from Amoy, China, the congregation grew from 40 in 1891 to 170 in 1894.

In 1901 W. G. Shellabear* was appointed to head the Chinese work. Under him, two congregations were formed, one Foochow-speaking group pastored by Ling Ching Mi, and the other Hokkien-speaking, pastored by Lau Seng Chong. In 1905 the church premises were moved to No. 12, Japan* Street (Boon Tat Street), and in 1913 to Telok Ayer Street.

Between 1909 and 1913, the church grew and needed more space. F. H. Sullivan paid $3,600 for land to set up the Methodist Mission Center at the junction of Telok Ayer Street and Cecil Street. More land was bought in 1921, and a three-story building was built. The foundation stone was laid by Bishop G. H. Bickley in 1924, and on 11 Jan 1925 Bishop Titus Lowe dedicated the completed sanctuary. The design has both Chinese and Western influences, appealing to the migrant Chinese. The sanctuary has a rectangular main body sitting on arched colonnades, with an open pavilion on the roof that is carved with the traditional Chinese motif at the front of the building. In 1989 the church was made a national heritage monument by the Singapore government.

In 1935 John Sung*, the well-known Chinese evangelist, conducted revival meetings at the church. Sung's meetings brought great growth to many churches, especially the Chinese-speaking churches in the region.

In 1941, when Singapore fell into Japanese hands, the church was used as a refuge sanctuary for about 300 people. Under the leadership of Hong Han Keng, the church was able to continue its weekly services and offered help to many who suffered during the war years.

In the 1960s, the church spawned two other congregations, one in Telok Blangah and one in Queenstown. These churches are now autonomous. Telok Ayer Chinese Methodist Church celebrated its 100th anniversary in 1989. Currently it holds services in Hokkien, Mandarin, and English, with a total membership of 1,300.

David C. Wu

Temengong, Basil

(b. Betong, Sarawak, Malaysia, 11 Oct 1918; d. Simunjan, Sarawak, Malaysia, 22 Sep 1984). First Iban bishop of the Anglican* Church in Sarawak.

Temengong became the first Sarawakian and the first Iban to be made bishop of the Anglican diocese of Kuching and Brunei* when he was consecrated on 6 Dec 1968. Under his episcopacy, the Anglican Church in Sarawak made great strides toward complete indigenization.

He was active on the ecumenical* scene and served as chairman of the Council of Churches of East Asia (1979-83), vice president of the Council of Churches of Malaysia* (1981-82), and chairman of the Association of Churches in Sarawak (from 1983 until his death).

Temengong trained at the Bishop's College in Calcutta, was ordained deacon by Bishop Tarafdar on 16 Nov 1941, and served as assistant chaplain at St. Thomas, Calcutta. After his ordination as priest (11 Apr 1943), he was stationed at Asansol from 1943 to 1946. He had his postordination training at St. Augustine's College, Canterbury, spending some time with the Community of the Resurrection at Mirfield and serving at the parish of All Saints, London.

Temengong was made canon of Borneo in 1960 and archdeacon of Kuching in 1963. In recognition of his service to the mission and the country, he was conferred the state award, the Panglima Negara Bintang Sarawak, which carried the title *Datuk* by the governor of Sarawak.

Bibliography

Taylor, Brian, *The Anglican Church in Borneo, 1884-1962* (1983). AERIES SUMPING JINGAN

Teodoro, Toribio M.

(b. 1887; d. ?). Filipino philanthropist and lay church leader.

Teodoro was the son of a poor farmer and became an industrialist through earnest toil. A working student at age 12, he was employed in a cigar factory and later worked as a leather cutter in an uncle's slipper factory. In 1910, with his small savings, he started a slipper shop which became the Ang Tibay Shoe Factory, the largest shoe and slipper factory in East Asia in 1922.

A Presbyterian* since his youth, Teodoro followed the 1913 nationalist schism of the *Iglesia Evangelica de los Cristianos Filipinos.* Inspired by the idea of church union, Teodoro initiated the move toward the formation of the United Evangelical Church of Christ (UNIDA), which made him its honorary president for life (see Ecumenical Movement).

Bibliography

Galang, Z. M., *Encyclopedia of the Philippines,* Vol. 9 (1936). • Sitoy, T. V., Jr., *Several Springs, One Stream* (1992). T. VALENTINO SITOY, JR.

Tep Im Sotha, Paul

(b. Phnom Penh, 1934; d. Mai, 1975). Prefect apostolic of Battambang; first Cambodian apostolic prefect.

Tep Im was born to a Khmer father and a mother who was a French-Vietnamese half-caste. His father was one of the founders of Scouting in Cambodia*. At age 13, young Paul was sent to a Scout jamboree in Moisian, France. During that jamboree, he expressed the desire to become a priest. He was then sent to the seminary at Montpellier where he completed his secondary studies, then to the seminary of Paris at Issy-les-Moulineaux. Ordained a priest in 1959 in the Cathedral of Paris, he went on to pursue studies at the Angelica University of Rome, where he completed a master's degree studying the first foreign missionaries to Cambodia.

Upon returning to his country, Tep Im was named vicar in his native parish. Besides his parish activities, he recruited from time to time some intellectuals to a group called "Roman Peace." Several of these intellectuals later became Khmer Rouge* officers.

In 1968 the Saint-Siege decided to confer a part of the responsibilities for directing the Church of Cambodia to the Cambodians. Tep Im was named apostolic prefect of Battambang. There again he was not content with limiting his work to Christians only, and he became a professor of philosophy. He surprised the traditional faithful by having scenes of the life of Jesus painted in the center of the church of Battambang in the style of the representations of the Buddha in the pagodas.

In Mar 1975, while on a trip to Europe, he suddenly decided to return to Cambodia to be near his people in a test that seemed imminent. With the arrival of the Khmer Rouge at Battambang on 24 Apr 1975, he tried to escape to the Thai border. Some days later, he was arrested and executed in the place called Spean Youn, in the commune of Bat Trang, district of Mongkolborey.

Bibliography

Ponchaud, François, *The Cathedral of the Rice Paddy* (1990). FRANÇOIS PONCHAUD

Teresa, Mother

(b. Skopje, Yugoslavia, 27 Aug 1910; d. Calcutta, India, 2 Sep 1997). Founder of the Missionaries of Charity, India*.

Mother Teresa was born Agnes Gonxha Bojaxhiu, the youngest of three children of Nikola and Dranfile Bojaxhiu. Their hometown of Skopje was a political pawn between Macedonia and Yugoslavia and was part of Yugoslavia when Agnes was born. The natives were of Albanian origin.

Agnes's father owned a prosperous construction business and was respected as a community leader. His political involvement, seeking to gain greater recognition for Albanians, led to his death by poisoning by rival groups. Agnes's mother had no interest in politics. A devout Catholic, she was mindful of her children's religious upbringing. Skopje had no Catholic schools; therefore the children had to receive their education in a public school. At their mother's insistence, they attended religious classes at a nearby parish church every day after school.

It was at this center that Agnes was exposed to mission work. A letter sent by Brother Anthony from his mission in Darjeeling, India, particularly interested her. Consumed by an overpowering desire to devote her future years to mission work, she apprised her mother of her intentions. An above-average student, Agnes delighted in tutoring those showing less aptitude at their lessons. Since teaching came naturally to her, she sought to join an order dedicated primarily to the spread of education. The Loreto Order in Ireland had several schools in India, a country Agnes was drawn to.

On 29 Nov 1928, at the age of 18, Agnes joined the Loreto sisters at their convent in Rathfarnham in Dublin, Ireland. On 6 Jan 1929, she was sent to India to begin her novitiate in Darjeeling, a city situated in the hills of the Himalayan mountain range. On 24 May 1931, after completing two years as a novice, Agnes took her first vows. She chose to call herself Teresa in memory of Teresa of Lisieux in her native Skopje. In 1937 Agnes, now Teresa, took her final vow in Loreto, Darjeeling. She was sent to St. Mary's Convent in Calcutta to teach history and geography. St. Mary's is one of six branches of schools in

Calcutta run by the Loreto Order, Loreto House at 7 Middleton Row being the main center.

In 1939 World War II* broke out, and India, being a colony of the British Empire, became automatically involved. Calcutta became the base for troops fighting the Japanese. Thousands of acres of farmland were torched to prevent the Japanese gaining control of them. Calcutta streets were thronged with homeless refugees. The starving and the dead and dying were everywhere. The misery of the people was further augmented when, in 1946, riots broke out between Hindus and Muslims leading to the great massacre. Eventually it led to India being partitioned and Pakistan* created. Hindus from the newly created Muslim Pakistan fled to India, adding to the throng of refugees in Calcutta. It was this scene that greatly disturbed Teresa. She found it difficult to continue the relatively comfortable life within the walls of the convent with so much suffering outside its gates.

On 10 Sep 1946, Teresa was on her way to Darjeeling to attend a religious retreat. At every station where the train stopped, she saw hordes of emaciated refugees stretching out their arms begging for food. She distinctly heard an inner voice saying, "I was hungry and you gave me no food, naked, and you did not clothe me," and then again, "Inasmuch as you did not do it to one of these, you did not do it to me." Teresa took this to be a clear message from God. She called it "the day of decision."

On her return from Darjeeling, she sought an audience with Ferdinand Perier, archbishop of the Catholic diocese of Calcutta. She pleaded that she had a second call, to give up Loreto and serve Christ in the slums among the poorest of the poor. She referred to the poor as Christ in disguise. The archbishop refused. Teresa submitted to his wishes and continued teaching. At the same time, she took to visiting the poor in the worst slums with the help of Father Henry, who worked in the area.

After two years, Teresa appealed to the archbishop again, who was not convinced of her devotion and dedication. He helped her seek permission of Pope Pius XII. In her letter, Teresa requested that she be allowed to live cloistered among the poorest of the poor with no protection of her order and with only God to guide her. On 12 Apr 1948, the pope granted Teresa permission to form the new order, provided she could get 10 new novices within two years.

Teresa immediately left for Patna in Bihar state, some 300 miles from Calcutta. There she took a crash course in medicine at Patna Holy Family Hospital, a Catholic medical school under the directorship of Mother Denegal. Adopting the native dress *sari,* made of a coarse fabric, white with a blue border, she set the stamp on an order soon to be recognized and identified the world over.

On 21 Dec 1948, after a training period of three months, Teresa returned to Calcutta and immediately opened her first slum work center in Motijheel Street. She also took Indian citizenship. With Fr. Henry's help, and through the generosity of Michael Gomes, a local donor, Teresa found a home and workplace on 14 Creek Lane. She was also joined by her first nun, Subhashini Das, a former pupil from St. Mary's Convent. Later known as Sister Agnes, she became Teresa's right hand. Within a few months, 11 others followed. Teresa was now qualified to establish her new order.

In 1950 the pope granted recognition to the new order, the Missionaries of Charity. The nuns of the new order were put through an extended period of training and trial and had to take the vows of poverty, chastity, obedience, and charity. The majority of Teresa's nuns were Indian. On 26 Mar 1969, the International Association of Co-workers of Mother Teresa was affiliated on a formal basis with the Missionaries of Charity. Within months she was invited to open centers in several countries. Many women from foreign lands joined her order and wore the same garb as the Indian nuns. Ann Blakie is the head of the International Co-workers. Teresa's mission has no income, no fund-raising programs, no grants, and no church maintenance. It is run solely on donations and on charity. Her belief was that "God is a friend of silence. We preach Christ without preaching" — in short, with acts, not with words. She said, "In my work, I belong to the world. In my heart, I belong to Christ."

On 22 Aug 1952, Mother Teresa's first center of mission work was opened. It was devoted to the care of the dying destitute. She picked them up from the streets and housed them in a most unlikely place — in an annex to the Kali temple. Pilgrims who came to worship Kali, the patron Hindu goddess of Calcutta, were housed here. She named the place *Nirmal Hriday* (the place of pure heart).

Mother Teresa moved her headquarters to 54A Lower Circular Road. In 1955, *Shishu Bhavan,* a home for abandoned children, was opened. People from India as well as from foreign countries have adopted children from this center. Mother Teresa kept in touch with the progress of these children. In 1957 she started to work with lepers (see Leprosy Work). In 1965 *Shanti Nagar* (city of peace), a cluster of houses for the lepers she had been tending for some time, was opened. In Calcutta itself, she cared for 17,000 lepers. There are mobile clinics as well, 60 in the city itself. With the help of the Indian government, Mother Teresa was able to treat and care for over 50,000 lepers in the whole of India.

In 1963 a new branch of mission work was opened for men, the Brothers of Charity, under the leadership of Brother Andrew. In 1968 Mother Teresa was asked to open centers outside of India, the first being in the slums of Rome. In 1970 a convent was opened in London to train novices from Europe and America. In 1971 a center was opened in Belfast, Ireland, and another in the Bronx, New York, United States.

By 1986 the Missionary Sisters and Brothers of Charity had over 3,000 sisters and more than 400 brothers in India and across the world from Venezuela to Taiwan*, as well as over 150,000 co-workers. They have houses in 87 countries.

Recognition of Mother Teresa's work in the form of awards has poured in from all over the world. To name just a few, these include: Pope John XXIII Price for Peace, awarded by the Vatican (1971); John F. Kennedy Award (1971); Ceres Medal, awarded by the United Nations Food and Agricultural Organization in recognition of her work with the hungry and poor (1975); Nobel Prize for Peace (1979); Bharat Ratna ("Jewel of India"), awarded by the government of India (1980).

Bibliography

Mother Teresa, *My Life for the Poor* (1985). • Egan, Eileen, *The Spirit and the Work* (1965). • Watson, Jeanne D., *Teresa of Calcutta* (1984). • Muggeridge, Malcolm, *Something Beautiful for God* (1971). • Doig, Desmond, *Mother Teresa, Her People and Her Work* (1976). • Douglas, J. D., "Mother Teresa," in *Encyclopedia of Religious Knowledge,* 2nd ed. (1991). • Menachery, George, *Encyclopedia of India* (1973). SUJATA BANERJEE

Teresian Association

(TA). The TA was founded in Spain by a Spanish diocesan priest, Pedro Poveda, in 1911, during a time of social and religious unrest in Europe. In Spain this unrest manifested itself in an outpouring of anticlericalism culminating in the assassination of many church people. One of them was Poveda, who was executed shortly after the outbreak of the Spanish Civil War in 1936. The task to continue the association fell on Josefa Segovia, first president of the association, who had worked closely with the founder from the initial stages.

Named after the active contemplative St. Teresa of Jesus, the TA was approved by Rome as a Primary Pious Union in 1924. Its specific field is education and culture, and it is now present in 28 countries. The members, laypeople with no external distinguishing trait, aim to live like the first Christians, fully inserted in temporal structures in order to transform them from within. There are two types of commitments. Those who constitute the Primary Association are fully dedicated to the fulfillment of the mission and the realization of the TA, and those who constitute the Cooperative Associations carry out the mission according to their specific characteristics. Upon joining the association, they begin their formation where they are and continue their status in society, be they professionals or students.

In 1948 five Teresians prepared to go to mainland China*. Impeded by the Chinese Revolution, two of these members went to the Philippines* in 1950. The TA was among the first to go to the Philippines as a lay group with canonical status in the church. Already in 1954, a small residence was opened for students, later to grow into the TA university student center in Manila. In 1956 the TA established its first foothold outside Manila, with a residence for university students in Iloilo City, where students live in a family atmosphere and are formed for a more meaningful presence in society. Poveda Learning Center in Quezon City, a primary and secondary school, began to function in 1960. The school implements the particular educational style of Poveda, who was honored by the United Nations Education, Science and Culture Organization (UNESCO) in 1974 as educator and humanist. The TA expanded its activities and presence in the 1960s and 1970s to the cities of Cebu, Bacolod, and Davao, and in the 1980s to Cagayan de Oro. In all these centers, activities continue up to the present.

Aside from presence in these educational and sociocultural centers, members fulfill their mission in many varied areas that have to do with human development such as medicine, mass communication, research, teacher training, social outreach, and the arts.

In the 1950s, the bishop of Osaka, Japan*, Msgr. Taguchi, expressed his wishes to Segovia to have some Teresians in his diocese. In 1957 contacts were made with Fr. Arrupe and some Jesuits (see Society of Jesus) regarding the possibility of TA presence in Japan. In Feb 1959 two members arrived in Nagoya to study Japanese. In April of the same year, they were invited by the Society of the Divine Word* (SVD) Fathers to teach at Nanzan University. In 1967, with the opening of Veranda House, a residence for university students, the TA made a more visible presence. This residence closed in 1982 when the SVD Fathers asked the TA to take charge of another residence with larger capacity, Maria House. In 1966 the TA initiated its presence in Tokyo. Members taught at Sophia University and Seisen International School and later began work with migrant workers.

Impelled by the missionary spirit and invited by the then bishop of the diocese of Tainan, Msgr. Lokuang, who had known the association in Rome, the TA sent the first two members to Taiwan* in Nov 1963. They started studying Chinese and, two years later, assumed several catechetical activities aside from teaching. In 1969 the Teresian University Residence was inaugurated, and it has been much appreciated since then for its atmosphere of mutual trust, respect, and joy. In 1968 some members went to Taipei. As in Tainan, they initiated their presence in the university. In later years, members started to work in media and women's issues, with migrant workers and Taiwan aborigines.

The TA presence in India* became a reality in 1973. Members attended to educative and social development programs, training teachers in rural areas and giving special attention to handicapped children.

In these countries, which are seats of Buddhism* and other Asian religions, witnessing to Gospel values is primarily lived in the manner of "salt of the earth." Special attention is given to the study of the language and culture of the country to uncover the seeds of Christianity in these cultures.

The lay character of the TA members facilitates expansion. Like anyone else, members take their places in both private and public sectors through their professions and occupations. The presence of members within state structures is a principal characteristic of the TA.

Because of the flowering of vocations to the TA from the 1950s to the 1970s among the young in Catholic Philippines, it is there that the TA is "rooted in the Orient." In Japan, India, and Taiwan, where Christians form a very minimal number, the association still has a foreign face because native vocations are few.

Bibliography

Institucion Teresiana, ed., *Statutes of the Teresian Association* (1992). • Gonzalez, Encarnacion, *Pedro Poveda, His Life and His Times* (1993). • TA Information Bureau, ed., *Teresian Association* (1992). PILAR FERRER

Ternate. *See* Halmahera

Terrenz, Johann

(Joannes Terrentius) (b. 1576; d. 13 May 1630). First Jesuit (see Society of Jesus) missionary to help the Ming court revise the Chinese calendar.

A German, Terrenz was a learned Jesuit scholar who reached China* in the late Ming period. He was already highly regarded for his scientific knowledge in 1611. When he heard that Nicolas Trigault's* purpose in returning to Europe was to take expert mathematicians to help China, he immediately volunteered and did much preparatory work for revising the Chinese calendar. He left for China with Trigault in 1618, arrived in Macau* in 1620, and moved inland one year later. He first studied Chinese in Jiading, proceeding later to Hangzhou, where he stayed at Li Zhizao's* home and completed the Chinese translation of the two-volume *Introduction to the Human Body.* While in Beijing, he translated into Chinese (dictating while Wang Zheng took notes) the three-volume *Graphic Illustration of Wonderful Implements.* After the enthronement of Emperor Chongzheng, he employed Jesuit almanac specialists to correct the errors in the Ming calendar. In 1629 Terrenz, recommended by Xu Guangqi*, was engaged by the emperor to revise the calendar. He died of illness shortly after this appointment.

Bibliography

Ross, Andrew C., *A Vision Betrayed* (1994). • Vath, Alfons, *Johann Adam Schall von Bell, S.J. (1592-1666)* (1991). • Beckman, J., "Die Heimat des Chinamissionars P. Johannes Terrentius (Schreck) S.J.," *Zeitschrift fur Missions- und Religionswissenschaft,* Vol. 23 (1967). • Goodrich, L. Carrington, *Dictionary of Ming Biography, 1386-1644* (1976). • Iannaccone, I., "Johann Schreck (Terrentius): scienziato, linceo, gesuita e missionario nell'impero dei Ming," *Asia Orientale,* Vol. 5, No. 6 (1987). CHINA GROUP

Tha Byu, Ko

(b. Bassein, Myanmar, ca. 1778; d. Sandoway, Myanmar, 9 Sep 1840). First Kayin Baptist Christian and ardent evangelist and missionary.

Born in U Twa village near Bassein, Ko Tha Byu lived with his parents until he was 15. He was then a "wicked and ungovernable boy," and when he left his parents he became a robber and a murderer. According to his own confessions, he murdered no fewer than 30 of his fellow countrymen. Heavily in debt, he was sold as a slave in the Moulmein bazaar and bought by Shwe Be, a Burmese Christian and disciple of Adoniram Judson* (the first American Baptist* missionary to Myanmar*). Shwe Be tried to teach him but made little progress. Later, Judson took charge of him and taught him to read and write.

In the 22 Apr 1827 entry in his journal, Judson recorded, "Maung Tha Byu, a poor man belonging to Maung Shwe Be" ("Maung" being the usual prefix to a Burman man's name until he has reached more mature years, when it is changed to "Ko"). Judson described Tha Byu as "a Karen by race, imperfectly acquainted with the Burmese language, and possessed of very ordinary ability. He has been about us several months and we hope that his mind, which is exceedingly dark and ignorant, has begun to discern the excellency of the religion of Christ." Judson recorded that Tha Byu had "a diabolical temper," but after much prayer and hard work there was a breakthrough.

After he had been taught the Christian doctrines. Tha Byu applied for membership in the then small Burmese church of Moulmein. The matter was postponed a while, and later he accompanied George Dana Boardman (the first American Baptist missionary to the Karens of Burma) to Tavoy, where he was baptized on 16 May 1828. From the day of his baptism to the day of his death, he never slackened his labors in preaching Christ in places where the Gospel had never been heard, from Tavoy to Thailand*, from Martaban to the borders of Chiang Mai, from Rangoon to Arakan. Tha Byu became a faithful and successful missionary, a distinguished instrument in the hands of God to arouse the attention of the Karen race to Christianity. And though he was the first of his race to be baptized, he lived to see hundreds upon hundreds follow in his steps, in whose conversion he had played a significant part.

After his baptism, Tha Byu asked for permission to go and tell the little he knew to his Karen friends. After hearing Tha Byu, people traveled two days or more to visit teacher Boardman in Tavoy and learn more of Christianity. Tha Byu was an unceasing and tireless pioneer preacher, an itinerant evangelist. A contemporary mission worker said of him, "Ko Tha Byu was an ignorant man; yet he did more good than all of us, for God was with him." He was never ordained. "He was not adapted for the pastoral office," cryptically remarked Francis Mason, the first translator of the Bible* into Karen.

Rheumatism and blindness stopped Tha Byu's itinerancy. In Feb 1840, he accompanied Rev. Abbott and his family (the first missionaries to the Karens of Bassein) to Sandoway. On arrival, he was sent to a small Karen village nearby, where he remained until his death on 9 Sep 1840. No mound marks his grave, but the eternal mountains are his monument, and the Christian villages upon the hillsides are his epitaph.

God fully and richly blessed Tha Byu's ministry. After 12 years (1828-40) of his labor, there were 1,270 members belonging to the Karen Baptist churches, scattered over a large area in dozens of villages. To the last, he did not have one anxious thought about his future. When he was asked, his usual reply was, "God will preserve me."

Bibliography

Mason, Francis, *Ko Tha Byu, the First Karen Christian* (1983). • Ya Ba Toh Loh, *Memoir of Saw Ko Tha Byu* (in Karen) (1950). Clifford Kyaw Dwe

Thai, Le Van

(b. Da Nang, Vietnam*, 1899; d. United States, 1985). Early Vietnamese convert to Christianity, pioneer evangelist, urban pastor, spiritual mentor, and fifth president (1942-60) of the Evangelical Church of Vietnam (ECVN; also *Tin Lanh),* established through missionary efforts of the Christian and Missionary Alliance* (C&MA).

Thai was born into a poor family of nine. As a youth he and his friends threw stones and caused disturbances during evangelistic meetings in Da Nang held by pioneer C&MA missionaries. He was converted in 1920 and felt called to preach. After two years of training at the Tourane Bible Institute (established in 1921), he was appointed student pastor (1924-25) to Hoi-An at the mouth of the Song Cai River valley. He evangelized throughout that province, establishing churches in at least six villages. He subsequently returned and graduated from the Bible Institute and then served during 1926 in My Tho south of Saigon (now Ho Chi Minh City), where more than 500 came to Christ, thus laying the foundation for one of the strongest churches in the ECVN at the time. He was appointed to Hanoi (capital of Tonkin) in 1928, where his energetic preaching resulted in a thriving church. His evangelistic efforts were sometimes opposed by the French on the grounds of the treaties of 1874 and 1884, which forbade propagating religion except by Buddhists and Catholics. Once in the village of Gia Thuong, Bac Ninh Province, Thai was ordered to be arrested, but, since the village chief had become a new convert, the arrest was never made.

Thai attributed his success, in part, to the prior work of missionaries William and Grace Cadman*. Grace led the project to translate the Scriptures from Hebrew and Greek into Vietnamese. William assisted through the production and printing of literature and hymnbooks, thus providing the tools for church expansion. The lifelong friendship of the trio contributed significantly to a respectful and amiable relationship between mission and church through the years. Thai continued as a pastor in Hanoi until 1932, when he was elected superintendent of the northern district consisting of Tonkin and Thanh Hoa provinces in north-central Vietnam. His leadership led to the establishment of 30 churches in the region of Tonkin (Hanoi) before World War II*.

Thai was elected by the ECVN to consecutive terms as president from 1942 to 1960. He served his church at a crucial time in the history of Vietnam that was stressed by French colonial rule, Japanese occupation during World War II, and the subsequent struggle by contending Communist* and nationalist factions for independence from the French. From 1944 to 1945, northern Vietnam was decimated by the worst famine in her history, made worse yet by strategic bombing of the Japanese by American aircraft. Almost two million Vietnamese perished. In spite of these difficult times, all of the ECVN churches became self-supporting by 1945.

During the war of independence from the French (1945-54), Thai led the ECVN to reaffirm an earlier principle adopted by the 1928 ECVN constitution, Article VIII, Section 1, which stated that the church and its ministers would "not discuss politics or other matters outside the purpose of this organization." This policy opposing political engagement either on the side of the Communist guerillas or the French set the pattern for the *Tin Lanh* movement to remain apolitical and thus focus on evangelism and church planting. However, the effect was that both the Vietminh and French held them in suspicion, and not a few preachers and Christians were imprisoned and executed by both sides. "Under his direction, the ECVN had stabilized its economic situation after the great exodus of 1954-56, the mission drastically reduced mission subsidies to local churches and launched an aggressive program of evangelism which resulted in the doubling of church membership between 1954 and 1960."

While Thai was president, the national church took its first steps to become involved in social service. With a gift to the ECVN from the estate of W. C. Cadman, Thai supervised the establishment of an orphanage on 18 coastal acres north of Nha Trang. It opened in Sep 1953 and later added a primary school, a junior high school, and vocational classes. After his resignation in 1960, he traveled as a nationwide evangelist, and from 1973 to 1975 he cooperated with Le Hoang Phu to develop the Theological Education by Extension (TEE) program. His writing ministry contributed devotional books and training manuals for young preachers. In 1975 he immigrated to the United States, where he died in 1985. Though largely self-educated, Thai was one of the most prolific writers, effective speakers, and influential leaders in the history of the ECVN.

Bibliography

Irwin, E. F. *With Christ in Indo China* (1937). *Thong Cong ("Fellowship")* (1985). • Le Van Thai, *Bon Muoi Sau Nam Chuc Vu* (My forty-six years of ministry) (1960). • Le Phu Hoang, "A Short History of the Evangelical

Church of Vietnam (1911-1965)" (Unpublished dissertation, New York University, 1972), 2 Vols.

James F. Lewis

Thailand

Thailand is a moderately sized nation located in Southeast Asia with an area of 513,115 square kilometers and borders of a total length of about 8,000 miles. It is bounded on the west by the Union of Myanmar*; on the north, northeast, and east by Laos*; on the southeast by Cambodia*; and on the south by Malaysia*. Thailand is divided into four regions — north, northeast, central, and south — and 75 provinces, with a total population of over 60,000,000. The population includes several ethnic groups, of which the Thai are the largest. The two other largest ethnic groups are the Chinese, who have a long history in Thailand, and the Malays (mostly Muslim), located primarily in the south. Smaller ethnic groups include hill tribal peoples and peoples living along Thailand's borders. Central Thai is the official language, with numerous local dialects and other ethnic languages in use.

History. Historians hold to one of two theories concerning the origins of the Thai nation. The long-standing theory claims that the Thai people originated in northern and central China* and slowly immigrated southward from about 4,000 B.C.E., arriving in Indochina in the 13th c. Archeological and other more recent historical evidence, however, has led to a second theory which argues that the Thai people originated in modern-day Thailand and expanded from there into the Shan States, northern Vietnam*, southern China, and northeast India*.

Modern Thai history begins with the establishment of the Kingdom of Sukhothai in 1238. King Ramkhamhaeng (reigned 1279?-98) was the most important of the Sukhothai kings and inventor of the Thai alphabet. After his reign, Sukhothai fell into decline and the Kingdom of Ayutthaya replaced it as the foremost Thai state from 1350 until 1767, when the Burmese destroyed the city of Ayutthaya. The Ayutthaya era played a major part in creating Thai social, economic, and political patterns. Its so-called "feudal" system, officially created in 1654, remained generally in force until the 20th c. Western contact with Thailand also began in the Ayutthaya era, beginning with the Portuguese in the 16th c. After the fall of Ayutthaya, a nobleman named Taksin fled the destruction of the city, gathered forces, forced the Burmese out of Ayutthaya, and reestablished the Thai state. He reigned as king from 1767 to 1782, when he was assassinated and replaced by King Phutthayotfa Chulalok, or Rama I of the Chakri dynasty. Rama I moved the capital to Bangkok.

During the Sukhothai and Ayutthaya eras, a second major Thai kingdom also played a major role in the life of the Thai people, namely, the northern Lan Na Kingdom, with its capital at Chiang Mai. Founded in 1296, the Lan Na Kingdom developed a high culture until it fell under the Burmese from 1558 to 1774. The northern states, which had composed the Lan Na Kingdom, ousted the Burmese with the help of King Taksin and, as a result, gave allegiance to him and then to the Chakri kings. In the 20th c. those states were merged into the Thai state.

The Bangkok Era opened a period of renewal, recovery, and development into a modern nation state. It also marked an era of renewed contact with the West. The reign of Rama IV, King Mongkut* (1851-68), initiated the modernization of Thailand and the opening of the nation to the West, particularly Great Britain. In this era, Stephen Mattoon, an American Presbyterian* missionary, served as the American consul in Bangkok. The reign of Rama V, King Chulalongkorn* (1868-1911), initiated an era of political and social reform that included the establishment of a Western-style bureaucracy, the centralization of power, and the end of debt slavery and "serfdom." Such things as Western education and modern public utilities were first introduced during his reign. The movement toward reform climaxed in 1932 with a revolutionary takeover that established a constitutional monarchy. During the ensuing years, Thailand experienced numerous military coups until Oct 1973, when student and popular demonstrations pushed the nation more firmly toward democracy. Military intervention in politics continued, however, until May 1992, when further public demonstrations led to the emergence of a more democratic constitutional monarchy. Thailand is a developing nation with a mixed agricultural and industrial economy. It is the stated policy of the government to turn Thailand into a "newly industrialized country" (NIC).

Religion. Buddhism* is the national religion of Thailand, but freedom of religion is legally and constitutionally guaranteed. Although Thailand has followed a broad-minded policy regarding other religions, it remains committed to preserving Buddhism and follows a policy that effectively limits the expansion of other religions. The general populace sometimes shows a negative attitude toward other religions, such as viewing Christianity as an anti-Buddhist foreigners' religion.

History of Christianity in Thailand. Although there may have been a few Christians in what is now Thailand as early as the 14th or 15th c., the first Western missionaries to reach the Kingdom of Ayutthaya were the Portuguese Dominican* missionaries Jeronimo da Cruz and Sebastiao de Canto, who arrived in Ayutthaya in 1567. Other missionaries joined them, but the mission came to an end when the Burmese seized Ayutthaya in 1569 and executed the Christian missionaries. Franciscan* missionaries entered the country in 1585 and established work that continued until the fall of Ayutthaya in 1767. The first Jesuit* missionary reached Ayutthaya in 1607, but the Jesuits did not establish a permanent presence there until 1655. In spite of serious divisions among various Catholic missionaries in Thailand during the late

17th c., the work there prospered under the reign of King Narai (1656-88). The mission erected a seminary (College General) to serve several countries in East Asia in Ayutthaya in 1665, and the mission ordained the first Thai priests and opened the first hospital in the country in 1669. The seminary continued in existence until the fall of Ayutthaya. By the year 1674, Catholics numbered some 600 converts. Eventually mission and church work became embroiled in political intrigue having to do with the expansion of French power and the role of a "Greek adventurer," Constantine Phaulkon*. Matters came to a head in 1688, and the Catholics suffered a period of persecution until 1691. Missionaries had been quite hopeful that King Narai would convert, but this was probably never a possibility. A much longer period of persecution began during the reign of King Thai Sa (1709-33) and continued into the 1740s. Thai Catholicism suffered with the fall of Ayutthaya, and eventually King Taksin (1768-82) ordered all Catholic missionaries to leave the country. French missionaries returned to Thailand in 1784 at the invitation of Rama I.

In 1785 there were 413 Siamese Catholics of Portuguese origin at the Santa Cruz church in Thonburi, 379 Cambodian Catholics at the Immaculate Conception church in Samsen district, as well as 580 Annamite Catholics. In 1802 the total number of Christians of the vicariate was estimated to be about 2,500, and in 1811 still only about 3,000. It may be noted that during the time of Msgr. Garnault (1786-1811), the restoration of the mission was begun. In 1827 the decree of Pope Leo XII gave ecclesiastical jurisdiction over Singapore* to the apostolic vicar of Siam. Propaganda Fide* confirmed this jurisdiction over Singapore to the apostolic vicar of Siam on 12 May 1834. In 1835 about 1,500 Annamite Christians, fleeing from persecution, settled in Samsen and requested asylum from Bangkok. This became the origin of the St. Francis Xavier* church in Samsen.

Because of the increasing number of Catholics and missionaries, Msgr. Courvezy (1834-41) asked Rome to nominate a coadjutor bishop, and in 1838 M. Pallegoix* was nominated and consecrated bishop on 3 Jul. By the brief *Universi Dominici* of 10 Sep 1841, Rome separated the ecclesiastical region of Malaysia from the Mission of Siam, establishing the Mission of Oriental Siam comprising the kingdom of Siam and Laos, and the Mission of Occidental Siam consisting of the Malayan Peninsula, the island of Sumatra, and southern Burma (Myanmar). Pallegoix was the apostolic vicar of Oriental Siam, and Courvezy the apostolic vicar of Occidental Siam.

Msgr. Dupond's* (1865-72) annual report of 1867 gives us the general view of the situation of the mission as follows: the number of Christians was 8,000, baptism of the Siamese 667, and baptism of children 257. Since Dupond was full of zeal and could speak Siamese as well as two Chinese dialects, he gave great exposure to the mission among the Chinese and Siamese. He built eight new churches for these new Christian communities, and the older places were also quickly developed. When he died on 15 Dec 1872, he left the mission of Siam composed of 10, 000 Christians, 20 European missionaries, and eight local priests. Expansion began seriously during the period of Msgr. Jean-Louis Vey* (1875-1909). The masterpiece of his works was the evangelization carried out in Laos, where he had initiated the spreading of the Good News by sending P. Prodhomme and P. Xavier Guego to begin the new mission on 2 Jan 1881. Finally, Pope Leo XIII erected the apostolic vicariate of Laos on 4 May 1899, and P. Cuaz was nominated apostolic vicar of Laos on 24 May 1899. Under the direction of Vey, who had governed the mission for 34 years, the mission of Siam progressed greatly in various ways. In 1909, the last year of Vey's episcopacy, the mission of Siam included 23,600 Christians and 57 churches and chapels, with 79 Christian communities, 59 seminarians, 44 missionaries, 21 local priests, 17 religious men, 123 religious women, 21 catechists, three colleges with 861 pupils, 62 schools with 2,692 pupils, and one hospital.

The mission had anticipated the needs of modern times and cooperation in the countrywide reformation initiated by King Rama IV and King Rama V. A printing press had been set up quite early. In 1885 P. Colombet founded the first modern Catholic school in Bangkok, Assumption College. It was placed under the care of the Brothers of St. Gabriel when they arrived in 1901 following Vey's invitation. The Sisters of St. Paul de Chartres* came to Siam even before the Brothers of St. Gabriel (1898) to take care of and direct St. Louis Hospital (which Vey had just founded) and to take responsibility for the formation of the native religious women, a task that had been revived at Samsen, the so-called *Amantes de la Croix* (Lovers of the Cross*) community.

From time to time, Vey mentioned the project of evangelization in the northwest of Siam, close to Burma, since the central west already possessed several stations. However, the circumstances, necessary resources, and required personnel for these enterprises had never been at his disposal to undertake the evangelization. During the time of Msgr. Perros (1909-47), his successor, the spread of the Catholic mission prospered more than previously. Missionaries were sent to fulfill his projects in the north and northwest in Chiengmai, Chiengrai, and Lampang. They also advanced to Nakornratchasima. As a result, it can now be said that the Catholic religion has spread to all parts of Siam. During the 20th c. the mission of Siam followed the slow but uninterrupted progress of the other missions. The southwest part of the country became an independent mission in 1930. This was the apostolic vicariate of Ratchaburi under the care of the Salesian* priests. It became an apostolic prefecture on 28 May 1934. Then it was erected an apostolic vicariate on 3 Apr 1941. Ratchaburi was finally erected a diocese on 18 Dec 1965. The Chanthaburi apostolic vicariate was established on 18 Oct 1944 and was also erected a diocese on 18 Dec 1965. The apostolic prefecture of Chiengmai was erected in 1960 and was also erected a diocese on 18 Dec 1965.

During the 20th c., many other religious congregations, both men and women, came to work in Thailand: Ursulines* of the Roman Union, Carmelites*, Salesians, Sisters of Mary Help of the Christians, Capuchin* Sisters, Redemptorists*, Camillian* Fathers, Fathers of Betharam, De La Salle Brothers*, Stigmatines, Jesuits, Sisters of Holy Infant Jesus*, S.A.M. Fathers, and Oblates* of Mary Immaculate, in addition to the various Thai congregations of sisters in each diocese.

On 18 Dec 1965 the two ecclesiastical provinces of Bangkok and Thare Nongseng were created, giving Thailand its first archbishops. The Church took on responsibility for refugees* from Vietnam*, Cambodia, Laos, and Burma beginning in the late 1960s. The church in Thailand assisted the government in relieving and helping refugees by organizing the Catholic Office for Emergency Relief and Refugees (COERR, 1975). These many efforts are aimed at protecting the moral values of life and facing the urgent problems created by the influx of refugees from Indochina.

On 10 and 11 May 1984, Pope John Paul II came to Thailand for a short visit; this gave a wonderful opportunity to all the faithful to welcome him and to see and closely feel his presence.

Protestant missionaries, meanwhile, first entered Thailand in 1828, when Jacob Tomlin and Karl Gützlaff* arrived in Bangkok in the name of the London Missionary Society (LMS). They remained for only a brief time. Permanent missionary work began with the arrival of American Baptist* missionaries in 1833 and the American Board of Commissioners for Foreign Missions (ABCFM) in 1834. The Baptist mission established the first Protestant church in Thailand, a Chinese immigrant congregation, in 1837. The most influential Protestant missionary of the 19th c., Dan Beach Bradley* of the ABCFM, arrived in 1835. American Presbyterian work received a permanent footing in 1847. In 1850 Bradley returned from a furlough to take up work under the American Missionary Association, an American abolitionist organization, after he had withdrawn from the ABCFM for theological reasons. As the other Protestant missions dwindled, the Presbyterian Siam Mission grew slowly. In 1861 it established a station in Phet Buri, and in 1867 Daniel and Sophia McGilvary* founded a station in Chiang Mai, which became the Laos Mission (located in northern Siam). The new mission founded the Chiang Mai Church in 1868. Political tensions with the local prince led to the execution of two converts in 1869 and slowed work for a decade. In 1878 the Siamese royal commissioner in Chiang Mai issued the "Edict of Toleration," which granted the Christians freedom to practice their religion. In 1889 the Laos Presbytery (founded in 1885) ordained Kru Nanta as the first Presbyterian clergy in Thailand. In the same year the Laos Mission established the first formal theological institution in Thailand, the Evangelists' Training School in Chiang Mai. An experiment in creating a system of pastoral care in the mid-1890s ended in failure and led to a hiatus in ordaining northern Thais as pastors. Meanwhile, the Siam Presbytery (founded 1858) ordained Yuen Tieng-Yok as pastor of Samray Church in 1896, the first Thai pastor in a church under the Siam Mission.

Baptist work had come to a standstill before 1900 after a period of expansion among Chinese immigrants from the 1850s through the 1880s under the leadership of William Dean (retired 1884). Work among the Thai was closed down by 1868, and little Chinese work continued after China "opened" for mission work in the 1850s. The last Baptist missionary left the field in 1893, but the mission left behind a strong church in Bangkok (the first Baptist church in East Asia and the first Protestant church among Chinese), which later became known as the Maitrichit* Church. At the same time, other Protestant missionary bodies appeared in Thailand. Although not a mission as such, the American Bible Society* (see also Bible Translation*) had long contributed financially to the work in Thailand. In 1889 it appointed John Carrington as its first foreign secretary in Thailand. The British Disciples of Christ first established a station in 1903, which they later moved to Nakhon Pathom in 1906. The Seventh-day Adventists* started work in Bangkok in 1918. The Christian & Missionary Alliance* established work in the northeast, the last region to be evangelized by Protestant missionaries, in 1929. The two Presbyterian missions remained the dominant Protestant presence, however. Between 1885 and 1910 they established permanent stations in Lampang (1885), Phrae (1893), Nan (1895), Chiang Rai (1896), Pitsanuloke (1899), Nakhon Sri Tammarat (1900), and Trang (1910). They also created a system of boarding schools and local schools that contributed to the development of Western education, as well as hospitals and clinics, which played an important role in the introduction of Western medicine into Thailand. Even before 1900 the ABCFM, Baptist, and Presbyterian printing presses contributed to the rise of modern printing and the modernization of the Thai language. Missionaries produced dictionaries, grammars, newspapers, and a variety of published materials. The Laos Mission established Thailand's first Protestant seminary in 1912, which was renamed McGilvary Theological Seminary in 1923. In 1920 the two Presbyterian missions united as the American Presbyterian Mission in Siam (APM). That event gave impetus to a growing movement to found a national, ecumenical church (see Ecumenical Movement); and the Church of Christ in Siam held its first general assembly in Apr 1934. The prewar era closed out with the growing influence of revivalism, especially among the Chinese churches in Bangkok. That influence culminated in the revivals of John Sung* in 1938 and 1939. These revivals had a strong impact on churches throughout Thailand. Rising nationalism*, however, was leading to greater persecution of Christians; and Thailand's entry into World War II* as a Japanese ally forced the Western missionaries to flee and led to the closure of churches and Christian institutions in many parts of the country.

The allied victory in 1945 led to the reestablishment of Presbyterian work, the revival of the Church of Christ in Thailand (CCT), and the entry of numerous new missionary groups, including Asian mission groups. These included the Worldwide Evangelistic Crusade (1947), the Finnish Free Foreign Mission (1947), the Southern Baptist Mission (1949), the Overseas Missionary Fellowship (1951), the New Tribes Mission (1951), and the American Baptist Mission (later Thailand Baptist Missionary Fellowship), which reentered Thailand in 1952. The Presbyterian Church in Korea (KIM) mission took up work in 1956, and the Church of South India* sent a missionary couple in 1959. The rapid expansion in the number of missionary groups, most of which did not affiliate with the CCT, eventually led to the formation of the Evangelical Fellowship of Thailand in 1970, which by 1979 numbered 40 mission groups and 105 churches. Meanwhile, the APM in 1957 took the unprecedented step of dissolving itself into the CCT. The Disciples Mission took the same step in 1961. The CCT also grew, and by 1980 included 198 churches, 79 organized groups, and nearly 29,000 communicant members. While the newer missions emphasized evangelism, Protestantism became actively engaged in social development work, pioneered by the APM in the late 1940s and later augmented by World Vision* and other agencies as well.

The postwar mission expansion continued into the 1980s and led to the opening of Protestant work in nearly every corner of Thailand. Evangelism met its greatest success among tribal peoples. The Karen* Baptist Convention (founded 1954), for example, number over 14,000 communicant members. Protestant theological education also grew, with over 18 seminaries and Bible schools. The 1980s also saw the rapid growth of Pentecostal* churches, such as the Hope of Bangkok Church and the Rom Klao Church. Korean missions, too, had a major impact on the thinking of Thai Protestants. Missionary influence remained generally strong, although greatly reduced in the CCT. By the late 1990s the CCT had 424 churches, 118 organized groups, and about 55,500 members.

Bibliography

McFarland, George, *Historical Sketch of Protestant Missions in Siam, 1828-1928* (1928). • Pongudom, Prasit, *History of the Church of Christ in Thailand* (1984) (in Thai). • Smith, Alex G., *Siamese Gold: A History of Church Growth in Thailand* (1982). • Swanson, Herbert R., *Krischak Muang Nua: A Study in Northern Thai Church History* (1984). • Wells, Kenneth E., *History of Protestant Work in Thailand, 1828-1958* (1958). • *Documenta Indica* I, *Documenta Indica* II, ed. J. Wicki (*Monumenta Historia Societas Jesu,* 1948/50). • Tamtai, B., "Portuguese, the First Farang Contacting with Thai: 470 years of Friendship between Siam and Portugal" (in Thai), in *Silapa Watanatham (Art and Culture* monthly magazine), Vol. V, No. 9 (Jul 1984). • Burnay, J., "Notes Chronologiques sur les Missions Jésuits Du Siam au XVII Siècle," in *Archivum Historicum Societatis Jesu,* Vol. XXII (1953). • Hutchinson, E. W., *1688 Revolution in Siam: The Memoir of Father de Beze, S.J.* (1968). • Launay, A., *Histoire de la Mission de Siam* (1920); *Siam et les Missionaires Francais* (1896). • Surachai Chumsriphan, *The Great Role of Jean-Louis Vey, Apostolic Vicar of Siam (1875-1909)* (1990).

Prasit Pongudom, Herbert R. Swanson, and Surachai Chumsriphan

Thailand Baptist Mission Fellowship (TBMF)

Originally founded in 1952 as the American Baptist* Mission (ABM) in Thailand*.

The ABM took up work among Chinese churches in Bangkok and with tribal peoples in northern Thailand. In 1955, it officially affiliated with the Church of Christ in Thailand (CCT). In the 1950s and 1960s, it opened schools, dormitories, clinics, and hospitals in remote areas. In 1961, it participated in the opening of the Kwai River Mission, Sangklaburi. After an era of rapid expansion in the 1960s, the ABM entered a period of retrenchment in the 1970s. In 1974 the American Baptist Church and the Australian Baptist Missionary Society reformed the ABM as the TBMF. The Baptist Union of Sweden joined the TBMF that same year. Associated with the TBMF were the Thailand Karen* Baptist Convention and the Thailand Lahu* Baptist Convention, as well as the 12th District (Chinese) of the CCT. The TBMF has its headquarters in Chiang Mai and has official relations with several other Baptist missionary groups besides its original three member groups. In recent years, it has encouraged its associated churches to join the CCT, and as of 1995, five CCT districts originated in ABM-TBMF work. The TBMF has emphasized tribal and urban community development, as well as evangelism.

Bibliography

Records of the TBMF (Payap University Archives, Chiang Mai, Thailand), *The Thailand Tattler.*

Herbert R. Swanson

Thailand, Roman Catholic Church

(Siam). The first Catholic missionaries who came to Siam were probably the chaplains of the Portuguese ships in the 16th c. which were sent to Ayutthaya bringing the officers of Portugal to enter into relations with Siam, but there are no documents to confirm this hypothesis.

There is a written history prepared by the foreigners stating that in 1544 Antonio de Paiva, a Portuguese, had traveled to Ayutthaya in the time of Phra Jairaja and was afforded an audience and conversation about religion with the king. The king was converted and baptized, being given the Portuguese name Dom Joao; however, no person or evidence can confirm this claim. The first missionary who mentioned Siam in writings about his missionary task was St. Francis Xavier*, who mentioned it in his four letters written from Sancian, although his real purpose was to go to China*.

There is no record of any resident missionary in Siam before 1567. Written sources indicate that the first two missionaries were Friar Jéronimo da Cruz and Sebastiao da Canto, both Dominicans. They arrived at Ayutthaya in 1567 and were given a residence befitting them in one of the best locations of the city. Da Cruz and two new missionaries were killed by the Burmese in 1569. Next arrived the Franciscans* (1582-1767), whose missionary work in Siam is still unknown to us.

The first Jesuit who came to Siam was Balthasar Segueira. He arrived at Ayutthaya or Odia during Holy Week of 1607 (16-26 Mar). The Jesuits had their own residence, school, college, and church. Their missionary works were recorded by the missionaries.

All the missionaries mentioned above were sent to Siam under the *Padroado** system. The setting up of the Sacred Congregation De Propaganda Fide* on 6 Jan 1622 was an event of major importance in the history of the church, and especially in the history of the mission. Propaganda Fide sent three apostolic vicars, Msgrs. François Pallu*, Pierre Lambert de la Motte*, and Ignatius Cotolendi, to carry on the missionary work in China and Indochina. However, they could not avoid the conflicts resulting from the Portuguese patronage in these regions.

On 22 Aug 1662 de la Motte, M. Jean De Bourges, and M. Dedier arrived in Ayutthaya. They were the first missionaries of the newly established Missions Étrangères de Paris* (MEP). On 27 Jan 1664 the other apostolic vicar, Pallu, and L. Laneau, M. Haingues, M. Brindeau, and a lay assistant, M. De Chameson-Foissy, arrived in Siam. De la Motte and Pallu had the same opinion that Siam, with its policy of religious tolerance, was the most convenient base for their persecuted missions of Cochin China, Tonkin, and China. Therefore they asked Rome for jurisdiction over Siam. It was very difficult for the missionaries of *Padroado* to accept the rights to superiority of these apostolic vicars, making conflict and controversy between the *Padroado* and apostolic vicars inevitable. After long consideration of the request, Rome approved it in 1669 by the bull *Speculatores.* On 13 Sep 1674, Laneau was nominated apostolic vicar of Siam and was consecrated by de la Motte and Pallu.

When the French missionaries arrived in Ayutthaya in 1662, they were welcomed by one Spanish and 10 Portuguese priests, whom they found serving a Christian community estimated at 2,000 souls.

With the arrival of Pallu, two bishops, five priests, and one lay assistant organized an assembly, the so-called Synod of Ayutthaya 1664*. The sessions can be summarized as follows:

1. They planned to institute an apostolic congregation composed of three orders, and this congregation would be named the congregation of Amateurs de la Croix de Jesus Christ (Lovers of the Cross of Jesus Christ*).
2. They decided to publish the instructions to the apostolic vicars given by Propaganda Fide. They also issued "Instructions to the Missionaries."
3. They agreed to the erection of a seminary.

Undoubtedly, the growth of the Mission of Siam was evident during the long and prosperous period of King Narai the Great (1657-88), who opened the country to foreigners and gave liberty to the missionaries to preach the Gospel. Narai desired to base his reliance on France and to withdraw from the influence of the Dutch powers. At the same time, the French influence in this part of the world strengthened the role of the missionaries and the progress of evangelization.

By 1665 de la Motte had made the program of the synod come true when he founded the College General in Ayutthaya.

In 1669 the first hospital was founded by de la Motte and was supervised by Laneau. Besides Ayutthaya, the missionaries preached the Gospel in other places such as Phitsanulok, Lop Buri, Samkhok, and Bangkok. In 1674 there were about 600 Siamese Catholics. It was in this year that the Church of the Immaculate Conception* in Samsen District of Bangkok was built. The Christians of other nationalities (Portuguese, Annamite, and Japanese) were more numerous. In fact, the missionaries had been working from this period until the fall of Ayutthaya in 1767, but the fruit of their evangelization was indeed very small.

Narai's attitude toward Christianity made Constantine Phaulkon*, Guy Tachard*, a Jesuit priest, and even King Louis XIV misunderstand that there was hope of converting both the king and the whole country to Christianity. This led to disaster for the missionary activities when the famous Revolution of 1688* occurred. With an anti-French attitude, Phra Phetraja, the new king, persecuted all the Christians. The situation of the mission became better in 1691 when the king gave the seminary back to Laneau. Another persecution occurred during the reign of King Taisra (1709-33). The missionaries were forbidden to leave the capital, and they were forbidden to use the Thai and Pali languages in their teaching of religion. Moreover, the end of 1743 and the beginning of 1744 saw further persecution. Besides these difficulties, Christianity was affected by the invasion of Burma and the fall of Ayutthaya in 1767.

With the advent of the present dynasty in 1782, the situation of the mission improved gradually. Yet the situation of the Catholic mission at the end of the 18th c. was not so favorable, since an expulsion of the missionaries took place by the order of King Taksin (1768-82). King Rama I (1782-1809) sent for the missionaries because he wished to begin negotiations for an alliance with foreign countries and promote trade with these countries, as had been done before. In 1785 there were 413 Siamese Catholics of Portuguese origin at the Santa

Cruz Church in Thon Buri, 379 Cambodian Catholics at the Immaculate Conception Church in Samsen District, as well as 580 Annamite Catholics. A. Launay described the general situation of the Mission of Siam in the beginning of the 19th c., stating that in 1802 the total number of Christians of the vicariate was estimated to be about 2,500, and in 1811 about 3,000.

It may be noted that during the time of Msgr. Garnault (1786-1811), the restoration of the mission was begun. In 1827 the decree of Pope Leo XII gave ecclesiastical jurisdiction over Singapore* to the apostolic vicar of Siam. Propaganda Fide confirmed this jurisdiction on 12 May 1834. In 1835 about 1,500 Annamite Christians fleeing persecution settled in Samsen and asked for asylum from Bangkok. This was the origin of the St. Francis Xavier Church in Samsen.

Because of the increasing number of Catholics and missionaries, Msgr. Courvezy (1834-41) asked Rome to nominate a coadjutor bishop, and M. Pallegoix* was nominated and consecrated bishop on 3 Jul 1838. By the brief *Universi Dominici* of 10 Sep 1841, Rome separated the ecclesiastical region of Malaysia* from the Mission of Siam, establishing the Mission of Oriental Siam, comprising the kingdom of Siam and Laos, and the Mission of Occidental Siam, which consisted of the Malayan Peninsula, the island of Sumatra, and southern Burma. Pallegoix was apostolic vicar of Oriental Siam, and Courvezy was apostolic vicar of Occidental Siam.

A very famous and outstanding person during the 19th c. in the Mission of Siam was Pallegoix (1841-62), whose fame spread far beyond the borders of Siam. He had a brilliant mind and deep knowledge of science, mathematics, and languages. He acquired a very deep knowledge of the Siamese and Pali languages. He was the author of the well-known Thai-Latin-French-English dictionary, the first such fundamental work for the Thai language. While he was at the Immaculate Conception Church, he learned Pali from Prince Mongkut*, who had entered the monkhood at Wat Rajathivas near his church. Mongkut in turn took Latin lessons from him.

The annual report of 1867 of Msgr. Dupond (1865-72) gives the general view of the situation of the mission as follows: the number of Christians was 8,000; baptism of the Siamese, 667; baptism of children, 257. Since Dupond was full of zeal and could speak Siamese as well as two Chinese dialects, he gave great exposure to the mission among the Chinese and the Siamese. He built eight new churches for these new Christian communities, and the older places were also quickly developed. When he died on 15 Dec 1872, he left a Mission of Siam composed of 10,000 Christians, 20 European missionaries, and eight native priests.

During the period of Msgr. Jean-Louis Vey* (1875-1909), a period of expansion began seriously. The masterpiece of his work was the evangelization carried out in Laos*, where he had initiated the spreading of the Good News by sending P. Prodhomme and P. Xavier Guego to begin the new mission on 2 Jan 1881. Pope Leo XIII finally erected the apostolic vicariate of Laos on 4 May 1899, and P. Cuaz was nominated apostolic vicar of Laos on 24 May 1899. Under the direction of Vey, who had governed the mission for 34 years, the Mission of Siam progressed greatly in various ways. In 1909, the last year of Vey's episcopacy, it included 23,600 Christians and 57 churches and chapels, with 79 Christian communities, 59 seminarians, 44 missionaries, 21 native priests, 17 religious men, 123 religious women, 21 catechists, three colleges with 861 pupils, 62 schools with 2,692 pupils, and one hospital.

The mission had envisioned the needs of modern times and cooperated in the country's reformation initiated by Kings Rama IV* and Rama V*. A printing press had been set up quite early. In 1885 P. Colombet founded the first modern Catholic school in Bangkok, the Assumption College. It was placed under the care of the Brothers of St. Gabriel when they arrived in 1901, following Vey's invitation. The Sisters of St. Paul de Chartres* came to Siam even before the Brothers of St. Gabriel, that is, in 1898, to take care of and direct St. Louis Hospital, which Vey had just founded, and also to take responsibility for the formation of the native religious women which had been revived at Samsen, the so-called Amantes de la Croix community.

From time to time Vey mentioned the project of evangelization in the northwest of Siam, close to Burma, since the central west already possessed several stations. However, neither the circumstances, necessary resources, nor required personnel for these enterprises had ever been at his disposal to undertake the evangelization. During the time of Msgr. Perros (1909-47), his successor, the spread of the Catholic mission prospered more than it had previously. Missionaries were sent to accomplish his projects in the northwest, in Chiengmai, Chiengrai, and Lampang. They advanced also to Nakhon Ratchasima. As a result, it can now be said that Catholic religion has spread to all parts of Siam.

During the 20th c., the Mission of Siam followed the slow but uninterrupted progress of the other missions. The southwest part of the country became an independent mission in 1930. This was the apostolic vicariate of Ratchaburi under the care of the Salesian* priests. It became an apostolic prefecture on 28 May 1934, then an apostolic vicariate on 3 Apr 1941. Ratchaburi was finally erected a diocese on 18 Dec 1965. The Chantaburi apostolic vicariate was established on 18 Oct 1944 and was also erected a diocese on 18 Dec 1965. The apostolic prefecture of Chiengmai was erected in 1960 and was also erected a diocese on 18 Dec 1965.

During the 20th c., many other religious congregations, both men and women, came to work in Siam, now known as Thailand, "the land of the free people." They include, among others, Ursulines* of the Roman Union, Carmelites*, Salesians*, Sisters of Mary Help of the Christians, Capuchin* Sisters, Redemptorists*, Camillian* Fathers, Fathers of Betharam, De La Salle Brothers*, Stigmatines, Jesuits, Sisters of the Holy Infant Jesus, Oblates of Mary Immaculate, and various Thai congregations of sisters in each diocese.

Since the Catholic Church in Thailand had increased through the zealous labor of the bishops and missionaries, and since indications were that greater growth would occur in the future, the Sacred Congregation of Propaganda Fide judged that the time was ripe to establish the Sacred Hierarchy in Thailand. Strong support was also given by two former apostolic delegates to Thailand, namely, the Right Reverend Monsignors John Gordon and Angelo Pedroni. Therefore, on 18 Dec 1965, the two ecclesiastical provinces of Bangkok and Thare-Nongaseng were created, giving the country of Thailand its first archbishops.

1. The Metropolitan Church of Bangkok (formerly an apostolic vicariate), with its cathedral dedicated to the Assumption of the Blessed Virgin Mary.

2. The Ecclesiastical Province of Thare-Nongaseng, which was created by the bull *Qui in Fastigio* of 18 Dec 1965. Its cathedral is consecrated to St. Michael the Archangel.

In 1973 Archbishop Joseph Kiamsun Nittayo of Bangkok resigned for reasons of health and old age. His successor was Archbishop Michael Michai Kitbunchu, who later, on 2 Feb 1983, was nominated by His Holiness Pope John Paul II to become the first cardinal of Thailand.

At that time, great political and social changes were taking place, especially in the capital city of Bangkok. As a consequence, the church felt an increase in its responsibilities and a need for the expansion of its numerous and varied activities, especially in the fields of welfare and social development. The church also took on responsibility for the refugees from Vietnam*, Cambodia*, Laos, and Myanmar*. The church in Thailand assisted the government by organizing the Catholic Office for Emergency Relief and Refugees (COERR) beginning in 1975. The many efforts of the COERR are aimed at protecting the moral values of life and facing the urgent problems created by the influx of refugees* from Indochina.

In 1984, on 10 and 11 May, His Holiness Pope John Paul II came for a short visit to Thailand; this gave a wonderful opportunity to all the faithful to welcome him and to see and closely feel his presence.

In the remote village areas, Thailand is facing great poverty* and poor education and public health facilities, with the consequent increase in problems caused by a shifting and emigrant working population, including a rise in the problem of prostitution. Furthermore, the rapid spread of materialistic progress and modern technology has not allowed adequate time for the population to adapt itself properly to these new changes (see Secularization).

Today in the 10 dioceses of Thailand, the various responsibilities of the 10 bishops are well coordinated through the regular meetings of the Episcopal Conference. The whole population of Thailand is around 61 million (statistic of 2000), but the Catholic population is under 300,000 (or only about 0.5 percent). Thailand has been called "The Land of Smiles." In fact, in spite of the presence of various religions in the country, all people live in peace and harmony. And so in a true spirit of friendship, the Catholic Church continues to collaborate in the spiritual and social development of the country.

Bibliography

Zubillaga, P. F., *Cartas Y Escritos de San Francisco Javier* (1953). • Walz, A., *Compendium Historiae Ordinis Praedicatorium* (1948). • Da Silva, A., *Documentacao para a Historia das Mssoes do Padroado Portugues do Oriente* (1952). • Burnay, J., "Notes Chronologiques sur les Missions Jésuits du Siam au XVII Siècle," in *Archivum Historicum Societatis Jesu* XXII (1953). • Launay, A., *Documents Historiques* (1920); *Histoire de La Mission de Siam* (1920). • Guennou, J., *Missions Etrangeres de Paris* (1986). • Hutchinson, E. W., *1688 Revolution in Siam: The Memoir of Father de Beze, S.J.* (1968). • *Archives des Missions Etrangères de Paris, Siam,* Vol. 894 (1867). • *Archives of the Archdiocese of Bangkok,* "Vey," "Records," "Letters," "Documents of Dioceses," and "Annual Reports."

Surachai Chumsriphan

Theodore of Mopsuestia

(ca. 350-428). Theologian, bishop, student of Diodore, and teacher of Nestorius*.

Little is known of Theodore's life. He was a student of Libanius (a pagan rhetoretician) and Diodore of Tarsus. He was the bishop of Mopsuestia from 392 until 428 and led both in pastoral care and theological controversy. His teachings and homilies were foundational in the theological development of the Church of the East (see Nestorian* Church). Even though Theodore is known to have been a strong defender of the Councils of Nicea (325) and Constantinople (381), against the teachings of Apollinarius and Arius, his teachings were eventually condemned by the Second Council of Constantinople (553). Theodore's theology can be gleaned from his (extant) "Controversy with the Macedonians" and his catechetical homilies (both in Syriac). These writings have a special concern to keep the two natures in Christ distinct, and their weakness, as that of the writings of his student Nestorius, is how there is any unity in this one *prosōpon* (person). Nestorius, and later Narsai*, would continue this theological tradition in Persia and, through their students, transport it to China*.

Bibliography

Swete, H. B., *Theodori episcopi Mopsuesteni in epistulas B. Pauli commentarii,* 2 Vols. (1880-82). • Devresse, R., *Essai sur Theodore de Mopsueste* (1948). • Mingana, A., *Woodbrooke Studies,* Vols. 5 and 6 (1932, 1933). • Greer, R. A., *Theodore of Mopsuestia: Exegete and Theologian*

(1961). • Norris, R. A., *Manhood and Christ: A Study in the Christology of Theodore of Mopsuestia* (1963).

SCOTT W. SUNQUIST

Theological Education

Theological education in Asia followed the development of Christianity in the region: West and East Syrian monasteries, Roman Catholic* orders, Protestant missionaries, local expressions of faith, and Asian mission within Asia. Some trained local leadership from the start; for others that came later, particularly if missionaries were leaving. The earliest Asian school outside the Roman Empire, the "School of the Persians" in Nisibis began educating Persian monks and priests for pastoral and missionary work in the 5th c. The curriculum was centered around biblical exegesis and liturgy. Most theological training was monastic; it took place at such centers as Mosul, Arbela, and Karka of Beth Selokh.

Beginning in the 16th c., some Catholic orders sought to develop the local priesthood and recruit and train catechists from an early stage. The first generation of Protestant missionary societies focused on Bible* translation and evangelism. Ordination was a matter of fitness for leadership whether or not there was training. Anglicans*, Presbyterians*, and Methodists* were more involved in education as a mission to the larger society than as a training base for evangelists or ordained clergy. Church of Scotland schools in India* had some high-caste converts who received ordination, but theological education tended to follow that of other forms of tertiary education, and for Protestants generally this was a largely postwar development. A significant exception was the strategic use of Bible schools by the Christian and Missionary Alliance* and some Pentecostal* churches where leadership training, evangelism, and church planting took place together.

Western ministry standards were not always relevant, and so local accreditation networks laid a foundation for contextual curricula. The theology of Western liberalism may have been transmitted to a generation of leaders but has had little relevance in a multireligious society. However, its social concern is something evangelicals have only recently regained. Its interest in contextual theology (see Contextualization) provided tools that everyone needed for Christian theology to take root in Asia. Conservative Western Christianity related better to Asian spiritual realities but was also capable of exporting Western concerns that were less relevent.

An appreciation of contextual and holistic theology and its implications for theological education has become more acceptable over time, but as elsewhere the visions of the seminary and the felt needs of congregations are not easily aligned. It is one thing for the aim of theological education to shift from Western norms to those that are local as well as more genuinely universal, but quite another for owners and leaders to follow.

South Asia. Theological institutions in Bangladesh* include Aizawl Theological College, the College of Christian Theology in Bangladesh, National Major Seminary, JNB Memorial Baptist Training Institute, and St. Andrew's Theological College.

There are over 120 institutions from various denominational, cultural, regional, and linguistic backgrounds in India*. Included among these are 18 major Roman Catholic seminaries. The earliest seminary for training clergy in South Asia was the Seminary of the Holy Faith (later St. Paul's College), founded by a Portuguese diocesan priest, Diego da Barba, in 1541. In the next year its work was taken over by the Jesuits*. The oldest Protestant institution is Serampore College. Founded in 1818 by William Carey*, Joshua Marshman*, and William Ward*, the college offers secular subjects in addition to theological studies. The Senate of Serampore College was established in 1918 to provide accreditation for Protestant and Orthodox* institutions. The senate has a membership of 40 seminaries, most of which are denominational but one of which is Union Biblical Seminary (UBS). Founded in 1953 by 11 mission groups, including the Evangelical Fellowship of India, by 1994 the UBS Association comprised more than 20 churches, missions, and Christian organizations.

Before 1980 theological education for most Nepali Christians meant going to India, though the Assemblies of God had a discipleship training center in Kathmandu. The Nepal Bible Ashram (NBA), established in 1981 by the United Mission to Nepal and the International Nepal Fellowship, was forced to close in 1983. The low literacy* rate in Nepal* (about 24 percent) is a difficulty. The 1990 constitution forbids proselytism but allows the registration of religious bodies. Other theological institutions include Nepal Ebenezer Bible College (1992) and the Nepal Great Commission Training Center, but new theological study centers continue to open in an effort to keep pace with rapid church growth.

Prior to 1877, Protestant missionaries in Pakistan* personally trained converts to become pastors and teachers. Candidates for the Catholic priesthood were sent either to Indian seminaries or to Kandy, Sri Lanka*. In 1877 the Punjab Synod of the Presbyterian Church of North America established the first Protestant seminary. Other churches, such as the Associate Reformed Presbyterian Church, Associate Presbyterian Church, Scotch Presbyterians, Methodists, and Anglicans, followed suit. Protestant theological schools in Pakistan today include Gujranwala Theological Seminary, Faith Theological Seminary, United Bible Training Center (for women only), Lahore Bible Institute, Open Theological Seminary, FGA Bible Institute, Hyderabad Bible Institute, Zarepath Bible School, Sada-e Pakistan Bible School, Pakistan Bible School, Kalam Seminary, St. Thomas Theological School, and the Presbyterian Seminary. Christ the King, the first Catholic seminary, was established in 1958 by Dutch Franciscans in Karachi. Church Foundation Seminars and the Pakistan Bible Correspondence School in Faisalabad also provide theological education. The

Multan Pastoral Center and the Christian Study Center, Rawalpindi, engage in Asian cultural and ecumenical studies.

Theological education in Sri Lanka* dates from the 16th c., when Franciscan* missionaries set up monasteries. St. Anthony's College at Mutwal was one of the finest colleges in Sri Lanka during the Portuguese period. The Jesuits came in 1602 and introduced an organized system of theological education in the Portuguese language. The Dutch in the 17th c. (beginning in 1642 in Galle) introduced Calvinism and curbed Roman Catholicism. They set up seminaries in Jaffna (1690) and Colombo (1685) for Sinhala and Tamil preachers, and promising students were sent overseas for higher training. This practice was continued under British rule. Theological education during the colonial period favored the upper classes but began to take on a more local character after the Colebrooke Reforms in 1832. The Anglicans, Methodists, Baptists*, Assemblies of God, and the Ceylon Pentecostal Movement have established their own theological institutions. Independence in 1948 saw further proliferation of schools, especially with the growth of independent churches. Theological institutions were opened by the Fellowship of Free Churches (Lanka Bible College, 1974), Calvary Church in Colombo (Institute of Christian Education, 1984), the Church of the Foursquare Gospel (1987), the United Pentecostal Church (1988), and the Dutch Reformed Church. The Theological College of Sri Lanka (1963) was a joint venture of Anglican, Methodist, and Baptist churches. Sinhala and Tamil began to be used as media of instruction. Although Western influence is still evident, attempts are being made toward contextualization*.

Southeast Asia. The standardization and promotion of theological education in Southeast Asia was greatly aided by the founding of the Association for Theological Education in South East Asia (ATESEA) in 1957. Based in Singapore*, ATESEA has grown in membership to 70 institutions spread over 13 countries. Functions include publishing the *Asia Journal of Theology* and occasional papers, accreditation services, regional planning, and faculty development. ATESEA operates the South East Asia Graduate School of Theology (SEAGST), begun in 1966 to grant postgraduate degrees, by combining the faculty and other resources of regional seminaries.

Theological education in Indonesia* was rejected by the mother church in Holland in the 17th c. because it was thought that theological studies could be undertaken only in the West. A Protestant seminary was set up in Batavia in 1745, but it closed after 10 years. The idea of theology as a Western discipline modified only gradually during the 20th c. Some mission bodies established schools to train teachers for the dual role of school and church teacher. When the government tightened regulations, training was focused solely on church ministry. This action led to the opening of an ecumenical* seminary in 1878 at Depok and the first minor Catholic seminary in 1911 at Muntilan. With the expansion of the church, the move toward church self-government, and the difficulty for foreign missionaries to obtain work permits, the number of institutions increased. This accelerated after independence in 1945. Today the Catholic Church has 31 minor seminaries and 10 major seminaries, as well as a number of lay training academies. Protestant institutions number over 100 schools. Many of these are members of *Perhimpunan Sekolah-Sekolah Teologi di Indonesia* (PERSETIA). A Consortium of Theology and Theological Education was formed in 1992 by the department of religious affairs.

In 1808 the Roman Catholic College General moved to Penang, Malaysia, from Thailand*, and until recently it has served as the major seminary for the region. As the church in Asia developed, dioceses opened their own seminaries. In East Malaysia* three minor seminaries were set up, but they were discontinued in the 1970s. Presently all Catholic priests in Malaysia are trained in Penang and at St. Peter's College (1951) in Kuching.

Protestant theological education began in Malaysia* with Methodist missionaries, who established a theological school in Penang in 1898. It moved to Singapore in 1902 and was the precursor to Trinity Theological College (1948). Other institutions include Baptist Theological Seminary (1954), Bible College of Malaysia (1960), House of Epiphany (1952), Methodist Theological School (1954), Malaysia Evangelical College (1972), Malaysia Bible Seminary (1978), *Seminari Theoloji Malaysia* (1979), and *Seminari Theoloji Sabah* (1988). Smaller denominational schools have also been established in the postwar period to train rural pastors and laity. These include *Sidang Injil Borneo* schools in East Malaysia and those in West Malaysia run by Pentecostal* and Charismatic* churches.

In the 18th c. a Roman Catholic seminary was established at Monhla in Upper Myanmar* with the help of missionaries from Thailand. In Lower Myanmar the College of St. John produced not only ecclesiastical leaders and missionaries but also engineers, physicians, and pilots. Protestant theological education was initiated by American Baptist missionaries in 1840, when E. L. Abbot opened a school in Thandwe to train converts. This developed into a mission school for pastors and teachers. Presently some 13 theological institutions exist in Myanmar, including a major Roman Catholic seminary in Yangon and three Baptist seminaries in Insein Hill in Yangon. Other, smaller Methodist, Anglican, Presbyterian, and Pentecostal institutions are all members of the Myanmar Council of Churches and cooperate in faculty training and library development.

Theological education in Singapore* began in 1902 when the Methodist Theological School in Penang was relocated and renamed the Jean Hamilton Training School. A parallel school for women, later named Eveland Seminary, was set up in 1901. These merged in 1948 to become Trinity Theological College, the first major ecumenical theological college in Malaysia and Singapore. The college is a founding member of ATESEA and a founding participating school of SEAGST and now offers its own graduate programs for training faculty throughout Asia. The Singapore Theological Seminary (later renamed Singapore Bible College) was established by the Union of Chinese Christian Churches in 1952 with the assistance of the Christian Nationals' Evangelism Commission (CNEC) and the Overseas Missionary Fellowship (OMF). It became the first institution in Southeast Asia to be accredited by the Asia Theological Association (ATA).

In 1662 two French Catholic priests, François Pallu* and Lambert de la Motte*, opened the College General at Bang Pla Het, Thailand*, on land granted by His Majesty Pra Narai. Students came from Siam, Tonkin (North Vietnam), Cochin China (South Vietnam), and China*. The staff and students suffered many difficulties: poverty, harsh climate, makeshift dwellings, hostility, expulsions, arson, looting, destruction, war, civil unrest, persecution, captivity, slavery, and hard labor. These hardships resulted in several relocations within Siam, and eventually in 1808 to Malaya. In 1972 *Lux Mundi* was established south of Bangkok for the training of Thai priests.

The oldest Protestant theological institution in Thailand is the McGilvary Faculty of Theology of Payap University (MFT), which began in 1889 as the Evangelistic Training School. Founded by the Laos* Mission of the Presbyterian Church, USA, it gave instruction in English; classes were taught entirely by missionaries. MFT's first Thai president took office in 1975. Other Protestant theological institutions in Thailand include Bangkok Institute of Theology (started in 1941 as a Bible training center by Chao Wei Chen from China), Thailand Baptist Theological Seminary (established in 1952 by the Foreign Mission Board of the Southern Baptist Convention, USA, with the sponsorship of the Thailand Baptist Mission and the Thailand Baptist Churches Association), Bangkok Bible College and Seminary (opened in 1971 by missionaries and Thai Christians), Lutheran* Institute of Theological Education (1986), and Thailand Evangelical Seminary.

The first Catholic seminary was opened in Vietnam* in 1666, just six years after Alexandre de Rhodes'* death. Until the 1950s the Christian and Missionary Alliance (C&MA) was the only Protestant mission; in keeping with its policy, it started a Bible school almost immediately in Da Nang in 1921. This became the main theological institution for the Evangelical Church of Vietnam (ECVN). It continued under the authority of the C&MA until 1960, when it moved to Nha Trang as the Nha Trang Bible and Theological Institute (NBTI). Although there were setbacks, NBTI continued to expand. After 1975 the influence continues through the ministry of its graduates. A Catholic theological institution is the Vien Dai-Hoc Da Lat Faculty of Theology at the College Pontifical Saint Pie X.

East Asia. During the late 19th and early 20th cs., a number of regional Protestant seminaries were established in China*. The Sheng Dao Guan (Methodist), Presbyterian Academy, and Ji-du-hui Bible School merged in 1910 and later became the Nanking Theological Seminary. In 1952 seminaries in East and North China merged, forming what would be named Nanjing Union Theological Seminary. By 1954 there were four surviving Protestant seminaries in China: Nanjing (a union of 11 theological institutions), Yenching or Beijing (a union of 11 theological institutions), Canton (a union of Anglican, Church of Christ in China, and Methodist schools), and Chung King (started by the China Inland Mission). Today there are 17 regional Protestant seminaries in China and Mongolia*. It is not known how many smaller unofficial seminaries and Bible colleges exist.

The Beijing Sacerdotal College was founded for the education of priests. Higher training was provided at Furen (Fujen) Catholic University. The Sacerdotal College was abolished in 1950 when the central ministry of education took over management of Furen University. The Catholic Church maintains several major seminaries established in the 1980s when the church regained vitality. They include Beijing Diocese Major Seminary (1981), China Catholic Theology (1983), Hebei Catholic Theological College (1984), Inner Mongolia Diocesan Seminary (1985), Shanxi Catholic Theological College (1985), Shenyang Catholic Theological College (1983), Sichuan Catholic Theology College (1984), and Chongnan Catholic Theology College.

Catholics set up a local seminary in Hong Kong* in 1846. Named Immaculate Conception Seminary in 1888, it closed during the Japanese occupation was relocated in 1949, and was inaugurated as Holy Spirit Seminary in 1957. The Regional Seminary for South China was opened in 1931. Students came mainly from Hong Kong, Guangzhou, Jianmen, Jiaying, Guilin, Santou, and Wuzhou. The administration and teaching were entrusted to Irish Jesuits. After 1949 students came from as far as Northeast China. When students from China could no longer come, the seminary closed in 1964. The Holy Spirit Seminary College then became the major seminary for Hong Kong and Macau. Today Holy Spirit Seminary College is an ecclesiastical university.

There are some 13 Protestant institutions in Hong Kong that serve various denominations, including the Evangelical Church, Assemblies of God, Baptists, Christian and Missionary Alliance, Church of Christ, Evangelical Free Church, Hong Kong Evangelical Church, Methodists, Rhenish Church, Swatow Church, Tsung Tsim Mission, Adventists (see Seventh-day Adventists), Anglicans, and Lutherans.

In the 16th c. the Council of Trent ordered each diocese to establish a seminary, and so Funai College was opened in 1580 in Japan*. Promising students were sent to Europe for higher training. The college closed in 1587 when the Jesuits were expelled. However, in 1593 a one-year course was set up for practical and systematic theology, and another school was started in 1601 in Nagasaki.

The next phase of theological education in Japan was

not until the mid-1800s, when Roman Catholic, Orthodox*, and Protestant seminaries were established. For many reasons, including natural disasters, war, riots, financial problems, ecumenism, and government policy, development was complicated and involved numerous relocations, mergers, separations, growth, and closure. Many seminaries have been incorporated into universities as departments of theology. Catholic seminaries were established by the Paris Foreign Missionary Society* (MEP), *Compagnie des Petres de Saint Sulpice,* the Cistercians*, Franciscans*, Dominicans*, Salesians*, and Jesuits*. Many of these became incorporated into the School of Theology at Sophia University. The Orthodox Church founded Denkyo School in the 1870s. It later divided into the Orthodox Seminary and the Orthodox Seminary for Women. Other Orthodox theological institutions were established but closed during World War II*. After the war, the Orthodox Seminary reopened in 1954 as the Tokyo School of Theology.

Protestant theological education was first conducted in missionary homes. Seminaries were opened by the *Nihon Kirisuto Kokai,* Japan Presbyterian Church, Japan Congregational Church, American Board of Commissioners for Foreign Missions, Japan Methodist Church, Protestant Episcopal Church in the United States of America, Church of England, Northern Baptist Church, Southern Baptist Church, Lutheran Church, Reformed Church in America, Holiness Church, Free Methodists, Salvation Army*, Assemblies of God, Foreign Christian Missionaries of the Christian Church (Disciples of Christ), and Nazarenes. When the United Church of Christ in Japan was founded in 1941, 15 seminaries and departments of theology merged to form three seminaries. In accordance with the new education system after World War II*, these merged in 1949 to become Tokyo Union Theological Seminary.

There are now some 24 theological institutions affiliated with one or more of the following: Japan Association of Theological Education, Japan Evangelical Seminary Association, North East Asia Association of Theological Schools (NEAATS), and the ATA.

In 1888 Henry Appenzeller*, the first Methodist missionary to Korea*, undertook the training of three students. This small group became the more structured "Theological Class" in 1893, and later the Methodist Theological Seminary. It trained both men and women. The Seoul Theological College was founded in 1911 by the Korea Evangelical Holiness Church in cooperation with the Oriental Missionary Society (OMS). The Presbyterian College and Theological Seminary began in 1901 in the home of Samuel A. Moffett*. Presbyterian theological schools include three institutions for the study of Calvinist thought: the Korean Association of Calvin Studies (1964), the Institute of Calvinistic Studies in Korea (1985), and the Korea Association of Calvin Studies (1987).

During the Japanese occupation, seminaries that refused to comply with Shinto* worship were closed. Those in the South were reopened after the war, but in North Korea all seminaries disappeared after the Communist (see Communism) takeover (see Korean War). In South Korea, theological institutions increased. Some evolved into universities. The Institute of Advanced Christian Studies was established in 1988 to respond to issues facing the Korean church. Institutions such as the Methodist Theological Seminary and the theology department of Hanshin University are involved in indigenous theology. The Korea Association of Accredited Theological Schools (KAATS) was formed in 1965 with nine member-schools: College of Theology, United Graduate School of Theology at Yonsei University, Presbyterian Theological Seminary, Methodist Theological Seminary, Seoul Theological Seminary, Hankuk Theological Seminary, Daejun Mokwon Theological Seminary, Samyook Union (College) Theological Seminary, and St. Michael's Theological Seminary. By 1995 KAATS had 31 member-institutions and cooperated with organizations such as NEEATS, ATESEA, World Conference of Associations of Theological Institutions (WOCATI), and the World Council of Churches Program on Theological Education (WCC-PTE).

St. Joseph's Seminary College was opened in Macau in 1728 by Jesuits to train personnel for China. After they were expelled in 1762, the administration of the seminary was taken over by the Lazarists*, who remained until 1854. The Jesuits returned from 1862 to 1871. In 1928 the Seminary College again returned to Jesuit hands, but in 1939 the administration passed to diocesan clergy. The college was closed in 1972, when the Chinese Cultural Revolution overflowed into Macau. In recent years the seminary complex has been restored.

Roman Catholic theological education in the Philippines* was a very late development. Most of the church leaders were friars trained in Spain. With the advent of American imperialism in 1898, theological education fragmented but also rapidly expanded with the numerous Protestant groups that entered. From the six seminaries in existence after World War II (Union, St. Andrew's, Philippine Baptist, Laoag College of Theology, Silliman*, and Central Philippine), Protestant theological institutions are said to have grown to over 300 schools. The Philippine Association of Bible and Theological Schools (PABATS) has a membership of 98, 12 of which are fully accredited. Founded in 1968, PABATS includes activities such as accreditation, conferences to address issues of Philippine theological education, consultation services, and publishing.

In 1872 the Canadian Presbyterian George Mackay* initiated a training program which eventually became Taiwan* Theological College and Seminary (TTCS). English Presbyterians established Tainan Theological College (TTC) in 1876. Foreign missionaries were deported in World War II, and the Japanese Kiristo Kyodan took over TTCS and appointed a Japanese president. TTC was closed down, but after the war TTC and TTCS returned to the Presbyterian Church in Taiwan (PCT). The PCT opened the Presbyterian Bible College (1952) as a lay training institution and Yu-San Theological College (1957) for tribal church workers. There are also institutions established by the Lutheran Church, Free Methodist Church of China, Taiwan Holiness Church, Taiwan Baptist Convention, and the Congregation for Catholic Education.

Bibliography

South Asia

Kanagaraynam, Donald J., *Education for Christian Ministries in Sri Lanka* (1978). • *The History of Serampore College* (1967). • *The Story of Serampore and Its College* (1961).

Southeast Asia

Indonesia

Baan, A. G., *Ichtisar Statistik ttg Gereja Katolik, 1947-1967* (1968). • Boelaars, H., *Indonesianisasi* (1991). • Muller-Kruger, Th., *Der Protestantimus in Indonesien,* (1968). • Van den End, T., *Ragi Carita I* (1980); *Ragi Carita II* (1989). • Yang, Liem Khiem, "Sekolah Tinggi Theologia Jakarta dan Studi Theologia di Indonesia," in *Tabah Melangkah,* ed. Sri Wismaody Wahono et al. (1984).

Malaysia

Destombes, Paul, *"Un Seminaire de Paris," Bulletin MEP* (1934). • Guennou, Jean, *Missions Étrangères de Paris* (1986). • Hunt, Robert, et al., eds., *Christianity in Malaysia: A Denominational History* (1992). • Launay, Adrien, *Historie Générale de la Société des Missions Étrangères,* Vol. 3 (1894). • Sng, Bobby E. K., *In His Good Time* (1980).

Thailand

McFarland, George Bradley, ed., *Historical Sketch of Protestant Missions in Siam, 1828-1928* (1928). • Swanson, Herbert R., *Krischak Muang Nua* (1984).

Vietnam

James, Violet, "American Protestant Missions and the Vietnam War," Ph.D. thesis, University of Aberdeen (1989).

East Asia

Hong Kong

50th Anniversary: Regional Seminary for South China, Holy Spirit Seminary, 1931-1981 (1981). • *Hong Kong Catholic Church Directory.*

Japan

Tokushu naichi shingakko no shi (Special collection, History of Japanese theological schools), Inter Nos. 2 (1941). • Hecken, J. van, *The Catholic Church in Japan since 1859,* rev. J. van Hoydenck (1963). • *Nihon kirisutokyo kyoiku shi* (History of Christian education in Japan) (1977). • *Nihon seikyokai 1970-1980* (Japan Orthodox Church) (1980). • Tadataro, Matsudaira, "Seikokai shingakuin shi" (History of Anglican seminaries), *Shingaku no koe* (Voices of theology), Vol. 3, No. 1 (1956). • *Uemura Masahisa to sono jidai* (Uemura Masahisa and his times) (1938). • Yasuo, Ushimaru, *Nihon seikyo shi* (History of the Japan Orthodox Church) (1978).

Korea

Lee Myung Jik, *Brief History of OMS Holiness Church* (1929). • *The Materials of Theological Educational Institutions in Korea* (1995). • Lee Sung-Sam, *Kamirikyowa sinhaksaehakkio* (The Methodist Church and the Theological Seminary).

General

Allen, Yorke, *A Seminary Survey* (1960). • Gilmore, Alec, comp., *An International Directory of Theological Colleges, 1997* (1996).

Compiled by Christabel Wong Lee May; edited by Christabel Wong Lee May and John Roxborough (see List of Contributors in the front of this volume)

Thoburn, Isabella

(b. 1840; d. Lucknow, 1901). First missionary of the Women's* Foreign Missionary Society of the Methodist* Church.

Thoburn arrived in India* in 1870 and immediately went to Lucknow, her home for 31 years, where she threw herself wholeheartedly into a plan for the Christian education of the girls and young women. To Thoburn, education was related to the whole of life. It concerned attitudes, conduct, and the development of personality. Lucknow became the center of Zenana schools.

She saw her little day school of six pupils, which was started in a room in a crowded bazaar, develop into a boarding school, a high school, a college for women, and later the Isabella Thoburn College. She realized her ideal of a Christian college for Indian and Eurasian, Hindu, Muslim, Mohammedan, and Christian women in which religious prejudice and racial pride were transcended.

Thoburn also founded the Girls' High School (Kanpur) in 1874 and helped establish the Wellesby School for Girls in Naini Tal (1891). She was the editor of the *Rafiqi Niswen* (The Woman Friends) some years and the author of *The Life of Phoebe Rowe.*

Her guiding principle in all her work was the conviction that only the love of Christ enthroned in the heart of the individual and the spirit of Christ ruling a person's conduct would prove sufficient to overcome prejudice, contempt, bitterness, and hatred. She died of Asiatic cholera.

Bibliography

Barclay, Wade Crawford, *History of Methodist Missions* (1957). • Tucker, Ruth A., *Guardians of the Great Commission* (1988).

Blessy Mathews

Thoburn, James M.

(b. St. Clairsville, Ohio, USA, 1836; d. Pennsylvania, USA, 1922). After graduating from Allegheny College in Ohio, Thoburn arrived in India* in 1859 as a missionary of the Missionary Society of the Methodist* Episcopal Church of the United States. By 1870 he had established a reputation as a powerful evangelist with a strong desire for the territorial expansion of Methodism in India. In that year, he invited William Taylor* to conduct evangelistic campaigns in India. With the success of these meetings in forming new congregations, Thoburn became an enthusiastic advocate for Taylor's idea of developing a network of missionary churches whose ministry would be financed by the their local European and Anglo-Indian congregations. He moved his own ministry to South India, where Methodists could expand unhindered by comity agreements, and in 1876 a self-supporting South India Annual Conference had been formed. Upon being made a "missionary bishop" in 1888, he became one of the last and greatest of this independent breed. Thoburn challenged men and women to set up self-supporting ministries, and from Calcutta to Manila he encouraged the development of congregations and institutions which could pay the way for mission work without relying entirely on aid from the United States. Yet he would also work with the Methodist Mission Society when it could provide resources for expansion, and in the 1890s he worked to bring his missionaries into its more secure salary structure.

In 1878 Thoburn initiated work in Rangoon (Yangon), characteristically using his success in Calcutta as a jumping-off point for eastward expansion. In 1886 he personally initiated a self-supporting congregation in Singapore* and used that growing base to bring Methodism to the Dutch East Indies, Malaya, and the Philippines*. Ever an entrepreneur, Thoburn did not hesitate to accept grants for Methodist schools from Singapore's colonial government, even while waging an active campaign against the sale of opium*, which financed those grants. His years in India had also given him a wide view of Methodist resources, and he recruited missionaries from Britain, Germany, India, Sri Lanka*, and China* to found congregations in Southeast Asia. In the late 1890s, he took advantage of US victories in the Philippines to establish Methodism in the Philippines, pushing the idea as the patriotic Christian response to God's providential freeing of the Filipinos from the twin tyrannies of Spanish rule and Catholicism.

Thoburn helped found the *Lucknow Witness (India Witness)* and encouraged women in mission work, beginning with his sister Isabella Thoburn*, who later founded a college for women in Lucknow.

In 1908 Thoburn was forced to retire to the USA in ill health but was able to attend the Edinburgh Conference in 1910.

Bibliography

Barclay, W. C., *History of Methodist Missions*, Vol. III (1957). • Copplestone, J. Tremayne, *History of Methodist Missions*, Vol. IV (1949). • Oldham, William, *Thoburn — Called of God* (1918).

ROBERT HUNT

Thomas, M(adathiparampil) M(ammen)

(b. Kavungumprayar, Kerala, India, 15 May 1916; d. 3 Dec 1996). Lay Indian theologian, moderator of the World Council of Churches (WCC), scholar, author, and ecumenical* leader.

Thomas was born in South India* into a middle-class Mar* Thoma Christian home. As a boy, he attended an elementary school run by a Christian mission. From 1931 to 1935, he attended college in Trivandrum and graduated with a bachelor's degree in chemistry. While at college, he participated in the activities of the Student Christian Movement* (SCM), the Mar Thoma Youth's Union, and an informal prayer meeting in the city. After his graduation in 1935, he taught in the Asram High School at Perumbavoor in Kerala. Then in 1937 he joined a Christian institute at Alleppey, where he dialogued with people of other religions while remaining faithful to the centrality of Christ. His guru was Sadhu K. I. Mathia, who instilled in him both a love for nonconformity regarding the church and society and a commitment to interreligious* dialogue. During the following three years, 1938-41, he experimented with social work projects in Trivandrum (he started *Deenabala Bhavan*, a home for the rehabilitation of street boys managed under the interreligious council; initiated the Beggar Relief Committee in cooperation with the Trivandrum City Corporation; and was involved in the formation of the Kerala Youth Christian Council of Action [YCCA]). During this period, he also studied Gandhism, his first ideology, and Marxism. He worked to relate the centrality of Christ to Marxism. His insight was that the cross of Christ was like the Gandhian *Sathyagraha* (a political fast) and that Christ, through this *Sathyagraha* on the cross, would have created strife in the community — strife against injustice and low morality. With Br. Keithan, he also studied the works of Reinhold Niebuhr, Hendrik Kraemer, John MacMurray, V. A. Demand, C. H. Dodd, Nicolas Berdyayev, Christopher Dawson, and others. While working full time with the YCCA in Christavashram (an ashram* in Kerala), he simultaneously applied for Christian ordination and membership in the Communist Party. He was rejected by both. He also organized the short-lived National Christian Youth Council and accepted the principles of Marxist politics while rejecting Marxism as a total interpretation of reality. During the period 1943-45, he was invited to lead SCM programs in Madras. Later, from 1945 to 1958, he served as secretary of the Youth Department of the Mar Thoma Church. From 1947 to 1975, his services took on an international tone. From 1947 to 1952, he served on the staff of the World Student Christian Federation. During this time, he participated in different conferences organized under the auspices of the WCC. From 1948 on, there was a shift in his theology, as he felt his Christian obligation was to follow the Marxian

Thomas, M(adathiparampil) M(ammen)

technique within the framework of democracy wherever possible. From 1949 onward, he affirmed the universal Lordship of Christ as the basis of Christian concern in politics and society. His papers, sermons, and lectures presented during this time on various occasions are presented in his *Theology of Contemporary Ecumenism.* During the early 1950s, Thomas worked with P. D. Devanandan* as a coeditor, and in 1957 they cofounded the Christian Institute for the Study of Religion and Society (CISRS) based in Bangalore. Devanandan was director and Thomas was associate director. In 1961 Thomas served as chairman of the Church and Society Working Committee, and in 1966 he chaired the sessions of the Third World Conference on Church and Society in Geneva. In 1969 his wife was called to glory, and Thomas had to deal existentially with suffering and death. From 1962 to 1976, he gave able leadership to CISRS as its director. He retired from the WCC in 1975 when his term ended, after which he returned to his hometown in Kerala to consolidate his theology with a biblical perspective. After his retirement, he was appointed governor of Nagaland, a northeastern state of India, from 1990 to 1992. As governor, he criticized the emergency principles of Prime Minister Indira Gandhi just as he had done earlier through articles in the *Telegraph.* He also published 13 books in his mother tongue, Malayalam, by 1986. He lectured in various seminaries and universities as a visiting professor and led the Christian Conference of Asia* (CCA) delegation to China* in 1983.

For Thomas, theology is dynamic and is a result of the process of action and reflection, rather than a static and systematic framework from the Bible*. That was why he founded the Action and Reflection Groups. However, his theology included the biblical themes of creation, the fall, and redemption, as well as resurrection and new creation. Creation is dynamic and progressive; God created out of nothing, while we are given freedom and the responsibility to be creative with this creation. All of the events of history are the creative acts of God, including the incarnation, as well as the acts of the revolutionary movement in Asia.

Under the influence of Gandhism, Thomas saw sin as ignorance and basically believed in the goodness of man. However, he later moved to a more traditional view in which man is totally dependent on God, although he wants to be independent and like God.

Jesus Christ is the only Savior. While different movements could be tools in God's providence, they cannot be tools of redemption. Redemption has socio-cosmic dimensions. Salvation is the organic unity of all: the fulfillment of creation, restoration of all relations, forgiveness, the end of all alienation, and striving toward humanization. The cross meant God's identification of Christ with suffering humanity. The suffering of the cross is comparable to *Sathyagraha,* where through nonviolence we bring a societal struggle. The cross leads to the brokenness of our self-righteousness. At the cross we see our commonness of sin and the forgiveness of God. Spirituality is combatting the oppressive forces, whether of the church or of the state, in order to help people see the value of fellow humans. Resurrection is the hope that this commitment to the cross will lead to the fulfillment of what was promised at creation: the promise of life.

Thomas acknowledged that the West has had both a positive and a negative impact on Asian life. The positive influence includes the value of the individual person, the understanding of the dynamics of history, the respect for political movements and their struggle for freedom, and the linear view of history moving toward a goal. Historical theology leads people to a search for purpose and meaning. This search leads them to a decision for or against Christ in every movement of any nation, because the questions they ask are related to God, humanity, and the world. All these trends are deemed as a preparation for the Gospel. The negative influences of Western culture are idols — ancient gods and modern gods such as materialism and rationalism — arrogance and self-righteousness, fear of the future, and concern for success, all of which cause inhuman manipulations. Because of these weaknesses, the impact of the West, which otherwise was good, could not be realized by Asia.

In evaluating political ideology, socialism, or capitalism, Thomas provides these guidelines: (1) Since Christians are a part of society before and after they are "born again," they need to adopt a political and social ideology. (2) The Gospel is above any ideology, and so it can judge ideologies as well as redeem them. (3) Christians need to choose what fits best in their situation. The guiding principle is that which minimizes evil and that which maximizes good. (4) Even though socialism is better suited to Asia than capitalism, it should not become an ideology. (5) One's selection of these ideologies does not determine one's relationship with Jesus Christ. (6) The ideological differences should not be described in terms of holy-unholy or heaven-hell, since they are not pure black-and-white systems of thought and practice.

According to Thomas, the church should not withdraw from the world under the pretext of pure spirituality, revivalism, or pietism. Instead it should withdraw from the world in order to reenter the world with Christ. Second, the church should not muster religious groups against the secular and revolutionary movements of different communities.

Thomas also welcomes the spirit of the Indian renaissance among the Hindus who, in the past, were influenced by the Christian West. This explains why he defends the Hindu leaders and discounts Christians as naïve in his widely known book *The Acknowledged Christ of the Indian Renaissance.* While welcoming this revolutionary ferment, the church must evaluate the strategies employed in the revolution and use them with discretion. In China, the church should provide a moral and religious foundation to society. The judgment and forgiveness through Christ must be proclaimed in Asia through prophetic ministry. Knowledge of the ideological and political conflicts must be acknowledged, along with the limitations of Marxism and the revolutionary protests. Marxism is idolatry since it demands total allegiance. Revolutionary protests might become tyrannical and self-righteous if the cross of Christ does not justify the protesters. For Thomas, the *diakonia* services should be changed to prophetic ministry and organize adequate political education for the church and responsible citizenship to a larger community that would include women's* status and role, family welfare, and responsible population growth. The lay workers should be helped to solve their problems in the light of Christian revelation. The church should also change from church-oriented to world-oriented patterns of living. Bible* study should be related to action in the cultural and social environment, and Christian education should be geared to the whole people of God for the ministry in the world. Confessions of faith, unlike in the West, must be in terms of churches' response to the revolution. To confess Christ is to point to him wherever he is at work. The struggle for justice leads to strife, so the action should include the gift of Christ to live by the grace of God.

Bibliography

Thomas, M. M., *The Man and His Legacy* (1997); *The Acknowledged Christ of the Indian Renaissance* (1969); *My Ecumenical Journey; Towards a Theology of Contemporary Ecumenism* (1978). • Philip, T. M., *The Encounter between Theology and Ideology: An Exploration into the Communicative Theology of M. M. Thomas* (1986). • (The bibliography of M. M. Thomas runs 77 pages in Heilke T. Wolters.) KUCHIPUDI CLEMENT

Thomas, Robert Jermain

(b. Rhayada, Wales, England, 7 Sep 1840; d. Pyeng Yang, Korea, 2 Sep 1866). First Protestant martyr in Korea*.

Thomas was the son of a minister of the Congregational Church. After graduating from New College in London in 1865, he applied to be a missionary to China* and was appointed by the London Missionary Society (LMS). He was ordained in his hometown church in Jun 1863 and married Caroline Godfrey two weeks after his ordination.

Thomas and his wife arrived in Shanghai and began mission work with Muirhead, the chief of the mission station. But Thomas not only got into trouble with Muirhead, but his wife also died suddenly. He went through hard times and decided that he could not continue his mission work, so he submitted his resignation to the LMS in Dec 1864.

For a while, Thomas worked as an interpreter for the Chinese customs but returned to work as a missionary on the advice of A. Williamson, a missionary of the Scotland Bible Society (see Bible Societies) who worked in Manchuria. By chance, Thomas met two Korean Catholics who had escaped from severe persecution by the Korean government. Hearing the story of their persecution, Thomas felt strongly that he should preach the Gospel to the Korean people. In 1865 Thomas heard that a ship was going to the west coast of Korea to trade. He was able to get aboard and reached Jajari, a small island off the coast. He spent two and a half months there, preaching the Gospel and learning the Korean language from the natives. He planned to go to Seoul, the capital city, but had to return to Peking (Beijing) due to a shipwreck.

In 1866 he again had a chance to go to Korea aboard the *General Sherman,* an American trade ship. The captain of the ship asked Thomas to be the guide and preacher of the ship, and he agreed. The *General Sherman* arrived at Juyoungpo, a small port on the west coast of Korea, on 16 Aug, and the ship continued to sail into the inner land. She sailed up to the Taedong River near the city of Pyeng Yang (P'yongyang), the largest town of northern Korea.

The Korean officers told the crewmen that the Korean government did not trade with foreign nations except China and asked them to leave immediately. The ship, however, sailed up the river, and the Korean soldiers and people began throwing stones and firing their guns. A fight between them and the crewmen ensued. At last, the ship was fired upon, and the crew jumped into the river and swam to land; Korean soldiers then killed them with swords. Thomas also jumped into the river with several Chinese Bibles* in his arms. Just before a soldier thrust his sword into him, Thomas gave the Bible to the soldier and was killed.

Thomas was the first and last martyr in Korean Protestant mission history. The general assembly of the Presbyterian* Church of Korea built the Thomas Memorial Chapel at the spot of his martyrdom in 1932. The T-shaped chapel was built according to the first letter of his name.

Bibliography

Lovett, R., *The History of the London Missionary Society, 1785-1895* (1899). • "The Record of the Rev. Robert Jermain Thomas," in *The Congregational Year Book, 1860, 1866, 1885* (London Missionary Society, Livingstone House). • Oh, M. W., *Two Visits of the Rev. R. J. Thomas to Korea* (1933). • Kim In Soo, *A History of Christianity in Korea* (1994). • *Encyclopedia of Christianity (of Korea)* (1994). KIM IN SOO

Thomsen, Claudius Henry

(b. Holstein, Denmark, 1782; d. ?). First principal missionary pioneer to the Malays in Malaya and Singapore*.

One of a few known missionaries who sought to reach the ethnic Malay, Thomsen typifies much of 19th c. Protestant mission work in terms of theology and methodology: literature*, translation work, and the educational enterprise tempered with evangelism.

Attached to the London Missionary Society (LMS), Thomsen arrived in Malacca* in 1815. While there, he baptized two Malay converts to Christianity, thus indicating that no matter how difficult it was to convert these

Malay-Muslims, it was never an impossibility. In 1822 he moved to Singapore, and within the next six months established a Malay school for 20 to 30 pupils and began erecting a Malay chapel. His zeal and efforts to reach the Malays were noted by Stamford Raffles*, the founder of modern-day Singapore.

He devoted considerable energy to publishing tracts and translation work in Malay after studying the language for six years, but his language instructor, Munshi Abdullah, said these works were unintelligible and misleading to the Malays. Thomsen's limited proficiency of Malay, his lack of understanding and appreciation of Malay culture, and the meager personnel support from the LMS combined to frustrate many of his efforts to evangelize the Malays.

In 1830, some 30 to 50 Malays reportedly attended the preaching services at the Malay chapel. Opposition from Muslim leaders led to the closure of the Malay school, and chapel attendance declined to 10 or 12 Malays in the following year. When Thomsen departed Singapore in 1834, it was reported that there were no known Malay Christians left; presumably all reverted to Islam*.

Bibliography

Abdul Kadir, Abdulla Bin, *The Hikayat Abdullah* (1969). • Lovett, Richard, *The History of the London Missionary Society, 1795-1895* (1899). • *Report of the Directors to the Twenty-ninth General Meeting of the London Missionary Society on 15 May 1823* (1823). • Sng, Bobby E. K., *In His Good Time* (1980, 1993). • Milner, C., "Notes on C. H. Thomsen: Missionary to the Malay," *Indonesia Circle*, No. 25 (Jun 1981).

Paul Russ Satari

Three-Self Patriotic Movement

The Three-Self Patriotic Movement of Protestant Churches in China (TSPM) was formally established in 1954 at the First National Christian Conference in Beijing. Its aim, stated in the revised 1997 constitution, is to "serve as the patriotic and church-loving organization of Chinese Christians . . . to lead Christians to love the nation and the church, to safeguard the independence of the church, to strengthen unity within the church, and to serve the aim of making the Chinese Church well run."

Together with the China Christian Council* (CCC), the TSPM is the national organizational expression of Protestant Christians in China. The two are said to function as "two hands of one body," with the relationship based on "co-operation and differentiation of function." While the TSPM undertakes patriotic education and relationships with the government, the CCC is concerned with the ecclesiastical affairs of Protestant churches in China*. The committees of both national bodies are elected at the National Christian Conference, which meets every five years. The church monthly, *Tian Feng*, is published jointly by the TSPM and CCC.

Historically the TSPM grew out of efforts to make the Chinese church independent of Western mission boards, on the basis of the Three-Self principle of self-government, self-support, and self-propagation. This idea was originally formulated in the 19th c. by Henry Venn*, Rufus Anderson, and John Nevius*, but it was not taken up systematically by Chinese Christians until the late 1940s. In the early years after the establishment of the People's Republic of China in 1949, meetings with Communist government officials, the promulgation of the "Christian Manifesto," struggles involving prominent Christian leaders, and the movement to support China's entry into the Korean War* served as formative influences on the organization of the TSPM. The TSPM was disbanded in 1966 and was not reorganized until 1980.

One of the most often cited achievements of the TSPM following the Cultural Revolution (1966-1976) was to change the foreign image of Christianity in China and promote unity among Chinese Christians. However, many Chinese Protestants continue to oppose the TSPM for a variety of theological, ecclesiastical, and political reasons. In recent years, the emphasis has been shifted from "three-self" to "three-well," that is, doing well the tasks set out in the Three-Self principle and seeing to it that the church is well run.

The TSPM is based in Shanghai. Y. T. Wu* was the first chairperson, followed by K. H. Ting*, who served from 1980 to 1997. Guanzong Luo was elected to succeed him at the Sixth National Christian Conference in 1997. Three-Self associations can be found in most provinces, autonomous regions, and municipalities and in some cities and towns.

Bibliography

Wickeri, Philip L., *Seeking the Common Ground: Protestant Christianity, the Three-Self Movement and China's United Front* (1988). • *Chinese Theological Review*, 1985-present.

Philip Wickeri, with contributions from Shen De Rong

Tia Danday

Illiterate Filipino Presbyterian* convert who opened mission work in Guinobatan, Philippines*.

Tia ("Auntie") Danday, an old and unlettered itinerant vendor of odds and ends, was among the first Presbyterian converts in 1904 in Legazpi City in the Bicol Peninsula. Though illiterate, she began her work in the nearby town of Guinobatan. Aside from distributing free tracts to all she met and simply repeating aloud the Bible* verses she had learned from the Presbyterian missionary Roy Brown within the hearing of people in the marketplace in Guinobatan, she was able in 1906 to win 23 new believers, whom she later brought to Brown for baptism.

Bibliography

70th Annual Presbyterian Board Report (1907). • Tabios, A. D., J. P. Cruz, and M. G. Pejo, *The Evangelical Church in the Bicol Region* (1974). • Sitoy, T. V., Jr., *Several Springs, One Stream* (1992). T. VALENTINO SITOY, JR.

Tianjin Religious Affair

Concerns the burning of a church in Tianjin, China*, and the killing of Catholic missionaries.

In 1860, during the Second Opium* War, Tianjin was occupied by British and French allied forces. Following the war, the French took over the ancient palace of Tianjin by force and used it as their embassy. In 1869 Cheverier, a missionary, built the Notre Dame des Vitroires Catholic Church. In the summer of 1870, the rumor spread that the church was involved in kidnapping and selling children. On 21 Jun the local magistrate brought the kidnapper to the church to investigate the matter and was stopped by the French consul, Henry Fontanier. The crowd that had gathered in front of the church sent delegates to meet the French consul. Carrying a gun, Fontanier unsuccessfully sought help from the commerce officer, Chong Hou. As he was returning to the embassy, he met a Chinese officer, Liu Jie, and sought his help. Liu refused to help and walked away. Fontanier shot Liu and injured some of his followers, enraging the crowd, who then beat Fontanier and his secretary to death. The riot resulted in the deaths of 20 people, including French embassy personnel, priests, and nuns. The Catholic Church, the French embassy, the orphanage, and other buildings were burned to the ground. The French representative to China, Rochechonart, filed a complaint with the Chinese government and made several demands. The Chinese government rejected the demand that the two Chinese officers, Zhang Guang Zao and Liu Jie, pay with their lives. In September an agreement was reached. The officers Zhang and Liu were demoted to conscripted soldiers, the 20 persons deemed responsible for the affair were given the death penalty, another 25 were made soldiers, and a generous compensation was paid to the French government.

Bibliography

Brown, G. Thompson, *Earthen Vessels and Transcendent Power* (1997). CHINA GROUP

Tilak, N(arayan) V(aman)

(b. Karazgaon, India, ca. 1862; d. Bombay, 9 May 1919). Strikingly influential poet with indigenous Christian ideas.

Tilak was a well-known poet in the Marathi language and came from a scholarly and orthodox Brahmin family. He found caste regulations unconvincing and became an adventurous seeker after truth. After reading the New Testament, Tilak found Jesus an irresistibly attractive personality. With further study of Christian literature*, he accepted Christ publicly through baptism, because he stood out as the ideal man, the personification of divine love, with unfailing faith in himself for identification with God, which finally led to the great sacrifice of suffering on the cross. It filled him with great appreciation for the power of Jesus and the effectiveness of prayer.

In Tilak's mind, Christian teachings began to interact with ideas from other religions of India*, especially Hinduism*. His poetic skills visualized God as "home of all trust," "father and mother," "inseparable companion," and "existent in all things." His relationship with Christ transformed itself into a deep experience of reality. "Christ is life of all that is." Christ became manifested as "the soul's rest," "the gracious tenant of the heart," "brother and friend," "the king," "the transforming presence," "the mother guru" with a charming smile and indulging love, "the crucified" reaching the climax of love and spiritual ecstasy in the *bhakti* (devotion) dimension, and "the lord of yoga" culminating in an ultimate union.

Tilak earnestly believed that Christianity in India should interact with the devotional ideas of Hindu saints such as Namdev, Tukaram, and Dayaneshwar for enriching spiritual life. He referred to himself as "the elected Tukaram for Maharashtra," a "Tukaram and St. Paul blended together." He felt that Indian Christians should utilize the rich religious literature of India, its music and musical instruments, and *bhajans* (devotional songs) in place of the dominating organ music and Western tunes. He believed ideas about prayer, such as *pratasmaran* (morning prayer) and *manaspuja* (mental worship), could be successfully adapted. He also experimented with the concept of a Christian *sannyasi* (mendicant) who was not a *vairagi* (detached from all passions) but an *anuragi* (deeply attached to Christian love). He developed the idea of *durbar* (place of royal audience) of God and Christian *ashram** (hermitage) where believers, without distinction of caste, color, or creed, could gather as children of God for worship and spiritual nourishment. He believed that Christianity does not stand in opposition to other religions and that an open attitude is appropriate in a pluralistic society.

Tilak was far ahead of his time and continued his experimentation in spite of opposition from some missionaries and fellow Christians. His life and works belied their apprehension that Indianization leads to de-Christianization. Tilak's poetic genius created excellent Christian devotional hymns, *abhangs* (lyrical poems), and *Christayan* (stories of Christ set in the poetic form of *Ramayana,* the popular Hindu epic). The need for promoting indigenous Christian ideas is still relevant in the multireligious societies of Asia, and Tilak's model of interfaith interaction was pioneering and is still inspiring today.

Bibliography

Tilak, N. V., *Bhaktiniranjana* (Nasik, n.d.). • Tilak, A. D., ed., *Abhanganjali* (1959). • Uzagare, B. K., ed., *Tilakanchi Kavita* (1951). • Winslow, J. C., *Narayan Vaman Tilak* (1923). • Jacob, P. S., *The Experimental Response of N. V. Tilak* (1979). PLAMTHODATHIL S. JACOB

Timor. *See* Evangelical Christian Church of Timor

Timpuyog Misionera Filipina

(TMF) (Philippine Missionary Society). First Protestant missionary society in the Philippines*.

With an Ilocano name, the TMF was organized by the United Brethren Annual Conference in 1912. Directed by five Filipinos and two American missionaries, its chief objective was to send Filipino missionaries to the remaining parts of the country not yet evangelized. Half of its finances came from the United Brethren Mission, and half from the local churches, particularly from 15 percent of their annual budgets and special offerings every first Sunday of each month.

The special field of the TMF was the neighboring Mountain Province, starting in Benguet in 1915, Ifugao shortly afterwards, and Kalinga in 1919. Much of the Protestant success in this area was due to the work of this missionary society.

Bibliography

Laubach, F. C., *People of the Philippines* (1925). • Roberts, W. N., *The Filipino Church* (1936). • Sitoy, T. V., Jr., *Several Springs, One Stream* (1922).

T. Valentino Sitoy, Jr.

Ting Li-mei. *See* Ding Limei

Ting, K. H.

(Ding Guangxun) (b. Shanghai, China, 20 Sep 1915). President, China Christian Council* (CCC), retired; chairperson, National Committee of the Chinese Christian Three-Self Patriotic Movement of the Protestant Churches in China (TSPM), retired; principal, Nanjing Union Theological* Seminary; president, Amity* Foundation; church leader and theologian.

Born in China's* most cosmopolitan city, Ting grew up in a middle-class Christian family. His grandfather was an Anglican* priest, and his father a banker. But the greatest influence in his early life was his mother, a devout Christian, who inspired and supported her son through her example and prayers until her death at the age of 101.

Ting received a bachelor of arts degree from St. John's University in Shanghai in 1937 and a bachelor of divinity degree from its school of theology in 1942. In the same year, he was ordained to the Anglican diaconate and priesthood and married Siu-may Kuo (d. 1995). They had two sons. Ting was consecrated bishop of the Anglican diocese of Chekiang (Zhejiang) in 1955.

Ting's experience in wartime China (1937-45) convinced him of the necessity of involvement in the struggle for national salvation and freedom from foreign domination. After service in the Young Men's Christian Association* (YMCA) and a pastorate in the Community Church in occupied Shanghai, Ting went to Canada to serve as mission secretary for the Student Christian Movement* in 1946. In 1948 he received a master of arts in religious education from Union Theological Seminary in New York and moved to Geneva to work as mission secretary for the World Student Christian Federation.

In 1951, against the advice of many friends overseas, Ting returned to China, committed to support the program of the newly established Communist government and identify with the TSPM. This was at the time of the Korean War*, when foreign missionaries were being expelled and Chinese churches were severing their connections with Christians overseas. Ting served for a brief time as general secretary of the Christian Literature Society (1952-53), before becoming principal of the newly established Nanjing Union Theological Seminary in 1953.

In the 1950s and early 1960s, Ting was active in the TSPM and became a well-known interpreter of the Chinese revolution in the Western world. He was convinced that Christians could and should work together with socialists. As principal of Nanjing Union Theological Seminary, he also played a constructive role as a theologian and church leader.

Ting lost all his church and political positions at the start of the Cultural Revolution (1966), when he was compelled to become part of a political study group together with others who were in disfavor. He again came into public view in the early 1970s and met with a few overseas visitors.

At the end of the Cultural Revolution era (1966-76), Ting emerged as the preeminent leader of China's Protestant Christians and headed both the newly organized CCC (1981) and the reestablished TSPM. After that, he traveled widely and met with church leaders all over the world. In 1991 he led the CCC delegation to Canberra when it joined the World Council of Churches. By this time, Ting had become a significant voice for the interests of the church on a national level in China, using his positions with the National People's Congress and the Chinese People's Political Consultative Conference to promote greater religious freedom. Ting retired from his church positions in 1997, although he continues to be active in theological writing and political life.

Ting is China's best-known theologian. His abiding concern has been the encompassing love of God, stressing the continuity between creation and redemption, the cosmic Christ, and the role of Christians in society.

Under Ting's leadership, Christianity in China has assumed a higher profile than at any time in its history. Despite criticism of him in some conservative church circles, his contribution to the reemergence of church life and the opening of China to the outside world in the 1980s and 1990s is widely recognized. As both theologian and churchman, Ting has promoted reconciliation between church and society, Christian and non-Christian, China and the world. This will be his enduring legacy to Christians in China and the church universal.

Bibliography

Ting, K. H., *Selected Writings* (1999). • "A Tribute to K. H. Ting on His Eightieth Birthday," *Chinese Theological Review,* Vol. 10 (1995). • Ting, K. H., *No Longer Strangers: Selected Writings of K. H. Ting,* with introduction by editor Ray Whitehead (1989). • Wickeri, Janice, ed., *Love Never Ends* (2000). PHILIP WICKERI

Ting, K. K. (Bishop). *See* Ding Guangxun

Tomita Mitsuru

(b. Ehime Prefecture, Japan, 3 Nov 1883; d. 15 Jan 1961). Pastor and first moderator of the United Church of Christ in Japan (UCCJ).

Tomita was baptized by Robert Eugenius McAlpine, missionary of the Presbyterian* Church in the United States (South), at Kinjo Church (Japan* Presbyterian Church). After studying for three years in the theology department of Meiji Gakuin, he transferred to the newly founded Kobe Seminary and graduated in its first graduating class. While a student, he was drafted for the Russo-Japanese War. He was ordained as a minister in the Japan Presbyterian Church in 1911 and, after pastoring Tokushima Church, studied at Princeton University. He returned to Japan in 1920 and became pastor of Shiba Church, where he pastored for the rest of his life. He continued to adhere to the strong evangelistic faith of the Presbyterian Church (South), but he also carried on the tradition of the orthodox conservative theology of the "North." He centered his ministry in preaching and, at the morning and evening worship services on Sundays, always centered his sermons on Bible* interpretation. While in the Japan Presbyterian Church, he served as moderator of the Tokyo District, moderator of the synod, and chair of the Mission Commission. During that time, he also served as moderator of the National Church of Christ in Japan and also chair of the Kingdom of God Movement Central Committee. When the UCCJ was founded in 1941, he had a central role in the planning and preparation, being elected moderator for two terms. During this time, he fought hard against outside pressure from the government and the military, as he struggled to protect the Japanese church. After the war, he continued to serve on the executive committee and as chair of the commission on missions. He worked to keep the UCCJ together, and even as various denominations withdrew from the UCCJ, he continued to believe that its founding was the providence of God and worked for a coming together within the church, pushing for the independence and self-reliance of the Japanese church. When the Christian schools were having great difficulties, he served as chair of the board of trustees of such schools as Japan Seminary and its successor, Tokyo Union Theological School; Meiji Gakuin; and Kinjo Gakuin. A compilation of his sermons, *Maruko ni yoru Funuinsho* (Gospel of Mark), was published in 1942. INAGAKI NORIKO, JAPANESE DICTIONARY

Tondo Conspiracy

(1588-89). In 1587, five native chiefs of Manila — Martin Panga, governor of Tondo; Agustin de Legaspi*, former governor of Tondo; Gabriel Tuambacan; Francisco Acta; and his son, Pitongatan — met while in prison, where they were being held under various charges. After their release, they met with other chiefs for three consecutive days, where they plotted against the Spanish authorities who had taken everything they had. They planned to help any enemy of Spain who would attack Manila.

The chiefs were set to conspire. De Legaspi and the rest reportedly sent some shields, arquebuses, and weapons to Japan* and Borneo, warning them to fortify themselves against Spain, which had intentions of going there.

Later, de Legaspi befriended the Japanese captain Joan Gayo, who arrived in Manila. Through an interpreter, de Legaspi made a pact with Joan Gayo, who agreed to come to Manila with soldiers from Japan under the pretext of peace and commerce, but he and his troops were to help the chiefs in the attack against the Spaniards. When all was over, de Legaspi was to be appointed king and collect tribute from the natives, to be divided between him and the Japanese. This pact was agreed upon in the presence of other chiefs involved in the conspiracy.

In Feb 1588, an English pirate ship sailed through the islands and plundered the ship *Santana,* forcing the chiefs to make preparations in case of an attack against Manila. A few days later, Estevan Taes, chief of Culacan, came to Tondo to meet with Martin Panga. Both decided that, since the English did not attack, they should gather all the rebel chiefs for a meeting in Tondo to discuss further plans of revolt against the Spaniards. This meeting, however, did not materialize.

Consequently, de Legaspi and Panga called for a meeting in Tondo with the other chiefs, where they agreed that Magat Salamat, Agustin Manuguito, and Joan Banal were to go to the Calamianes and advise the Borneans to attack. From Borneo, Magat Salamat would proceed to Cuyo Island and persuade Chief Sumaelob to join the Borneans in the attack.

The plan was that, when the fleet from Borneo reached the port of Cavite, the Spaniards would call upon the local chiefs for help, and the latter would then have the opportunity to seize the houses of the Spaniards and fortify themselves. If the Spaniards took refuge in the fortress, the native soldiers, who outnumbered the Spaniards, would pursue them. The Borneans were in the process of building seven galleys and other warships for the plot.

On 26 Oct 1588, Governor Santiago de Vera discovered that local chiefs of Manila were holding secret meetings. The governor began making inquiries and summoning witnesses. Details and information regarding the conspiracy were revealed to him.

A week into de Vera's investigation, on 4 Nov 1588, Captain Pedro Sarmiento arrived in Manila from the Calamianes, informing the governor that he left behind three local chiefs of Tondo: Magat Salamat, Agustin Manuguito, and Joan Banal. The servant and chief of Sarmiento's *encomienda*, Antonio Surabao, testified that the three local chiefs went to Borneo to persuade its king to join forces with the chiefs of Jolo and Sumaelob, chief of Cuyo, who had a combined strength of 2,000 men. They even persuaded Surabao to join, and he feigned agreement to avoid any suspicions. Surabao also informed Sarmiento that Amarlangagui, the chief of Baibai in Manila, revealed that "all the chiefs of this neighborhood (Manila) had plotted and conspired with the Borneans" to rebel against the king of Spain. De Vera immediately issued orders for the arrest of the plotters.

While on Cuyo Island, where he met with Sumaelob, Magat Salamat was arrested. Other arrests followed, and all were tried and found guilty. The conspiracy leaders, de Legaspi and Panga, were meted the most harsh sentence of being "dragged and hanged; their heads were to be cut off . . ." as a warning against the crime. The rest were sentenced to years of exile and the payment of gold, and their properties were confiscated for the royal treasury and judicial expenses.

The Tondo Conspiracy is considered one of the early revolts against Spain and a precursor of the Katipunan*.

José Mario C. Francisco

Tonghak Movement

The *Tonghak* (eastern learning), in contradistinction to *Sohak* (western learning), was "an eclectic, religious, anti-foreign system that developed into a political reform movement against the corruption and oppression of the officials" (Rhodes 1934:42). The Tonghak movement began with Choe Chei-Woo, a Korean scholar, as leader. In making a mosaic of scriptures, the Tonghak Bible*, called the *Tong Kyong Dae Chun* (Great Canon of the East), Choe took the five relations from Confucianism*, the law of heart-cleansing from Buddhism*, the law of cleansing the body of moral and natural filth from Taoism*, the use of charms and the practice of magic from shamanism*, and last of all, monotheism from Christianity, doing away with the images and adopting the Catholic practice of the use of candles in worship. As a political movement, it "changed the history of Asia, made one nation, and unmade another, and radically influenced the development of all the great powers of the world" (Speer 1904:366).

Under the control of the pro-Chinese reactionaries in the regime of Emperor Kojong, the body politic of the Korean government was perceived as "rotten to the core." The selling and buying of government positions was widely practiced, and one who purchased an official position generally reimbursed the seller by extortion. Local and national governments increased tax levies until they reached three to four times the legal rate. The discontented people could no longer remain silent. Chon Pong-jun raised a peasant army in the south and marched on the capital professing loyalty to the king but death to the corrupt officials. In order to check their movement, King Kojong appealed to China* for help. This became the immediate cause of the Sino-Japanese War*, which broke out in 1894.

"The leaders of the movement, particularly Chon Pong-jun, were inspired by the traditional Confucian ideal of realizing the 'Way of the Sages,' not by any vision of a modern popular democratic society. But the Tonghak peasant army was infused with a strong patriotic ardor, a burning desire to protect the nation from foreign aggression, and with the egalitarian dream of abolishing the *yangban* class system. The Tonghak peasant movement, an incipient form of modern nationalism*, had the potential to develop into a full-fledged social revolution, if only foreign intervention had not brought it so abruptly to an end" (Eckert 1990:221).

The discontented people were antiforeign and, incidentally, anti-Christian, because in their eyes the vices of Korean officials were due to the corruption of good morals by contact with foreigners. The Protestant missionaries in Korea*, however, had gained a strong foothold even before the Tonghak revival and uprising of 1894. The conditions of discontent out of which the Tonghak movement arose were favorable to consideration of the message of Christianity. Missionaries were mixed in their attitude toward the Tonghaks. At least one missionary, Samuel A. Moffett*, allowed the use of a church building for a Tonghak rally, while discouraging their use of violence to bring about social change. And when the Tonghak movement failed, it left multitudes more ready than ever to listen to the missionaries. They had been taught the folly of worshipping spirits and the necessity of worshipping God only (Paik 1970:260).

Bibliography

Eckert, Carter J., Lee Ki-baik, Lew Young Ick, Michael Robinson, and Edward W. Wagner, *Korea Old and New: A History.* (1990). • Paik, George L., *The History of Protestant Missions in Korea, 1832-1910* (1970). • Rhodes, Harry A., *History of the Korea Mission of the Presbyterian Church USA, 1884-1934* (1934). • Speer, Robert E., *Missions and Modern History* (1904). • Clark, Allen D., *A History of the Church in Korea* (1971/1986).

Timothy Kiho Park, with contributions from Kim In Soo

Tordesillas, Treaty of. *See* Magellan, Ferdinand

Traditional Religion, Myanmar

Traditional religion in Myanmar* is the worship of spirits called *Nat.* These are the spirits of the sun, moon, sky, earth, water, fire, and rain, among others. The natural world is personified and propitiated through sacrificial rites performed by shamans (see Shamanism). As an agricultural society, the people of Myanmar depend on the regularity of the cycle of nature and thus offer sacrifices to ensure fertility and prosperity. Traditional religion also includes the worship of ancestral spirits (see Ancestor Worship).

Among the Burmese, the majority ethnic group, there is a belief in a main pantheon comprising 37 chief spirits (spirits of former kings, heroes, or ordinary men and women) headed by Thakyamin. Burmese believe that someone who was admired and honored in life becomes a spirit in death. Likewise, someone who dies an unnatural death, e.g., through murder or an accident, also becomes a spirit. Sacrifices can be offered to them for help or mediation. An example is Maung Tint De, a blacksmith famed for his strength and his exceptionally beautiful sister. King Thele-Kyaung of Pagan made Maung Tint De's sister his queen but killed Maung Tint De because he feared his strength and popularity. The sister committed suicide at the news of her brother's death. Both are believed to have become the Mahagiri spirits and are still worshipped at Mount Popa in an annual spirit festival.

Minority ethnic groups are also spirit worshippers. The Kachins* worship spirits of nature such as heaven (Ma-dai), moon (Shar-Tar), thunder (Mu-Shan), storm (Bong-Pwe), wind (En-Bong), cloud (Swam-Mwai), thunderstorm (Me-Phrat), rain (Marang), and sun (gyan). Some spirits are benevolent, e.g., Pone-nat, the guardian of the traditions, and Dane-nu and Dane-Wah, the spirits who guard women in labor. Others are evil spirits: Ju-tone harms fishermen and hunters, Saut-pee harms women in labor, and Sart-wah causes accidents and death. Each Kachin family offers sacrifices at altars inside the house of the ancestral spirits of parents, grandparents, and great-grandparents. An ancestral spirit, U-ma, from whom originated the first ancestor of the Kachin chiefs, the Duwas, is honored at a special festival.

The Karens* worship traditional spirits called Duwai, Aung-Kwai, Aung Saw Klo, and Pu-Pa-Doe, to whom they offer sacrifices in season. At Aung-Kwai spirit feasts, the family gathers for worship and sacrifice to the ancestral spirits, praying for forgiveness of sins and blessing for the future. The Kayahs worship spirits called Kay-nat, Ta-Proot, and Kee-soe nat. The main annual sacrifice is to the spirit called Ku-Bo-toe for rain. The Chins worship and offer sacrifice to spirits (Doi) such as Ko-Zin. En-doi are spirits who control the affairs inside the house, namely, the spirits of parents, grandparents, and other ancestors. Yearly sacrifices are made also to Gum-doi, the spirits of land and forest, on whom the Chins depend for their livelihood.

For some minorities, there is a high deity above the spirits. The Kachins know him as Karai-Kasang, the immortal, all-knowing creator of humankind. No sacrifices are offered to him, nor is he worshipped, except in times of extreme need. The Karens believe in Ywa, who created the whole world, including men and women. There is also another deity, Mu-Kaw-Le, who tries to destroy all the good work of Ywa. Since the arrival of Mu-Kaw-Le, Ywa has left humans to their own devices. However, Karens believe that Ywa will come back to effect reconciliation. The Chins also believe in a harmless high deity called Pathian. The Lushai (Mizo) believe in the existence of one supreme god, and the Kyonak Nagas recognize a supreme deity of a highly personal character who is more associated with the sky than the earth.

Spirit shrines are built in houses and yards, under trees, near rivers, and in the forest. Flower offerings are made daily. An individual can organize a spirit feast. Shamans or priests set up shrines and offer coconuts, bananas, and strong drinks to invoke the spirits. Music is played to induce possession of priests and devotees. At such feasts, women or *natkadaws* (spirit wives), believed to be married to the spirits, become possessed and, in their trance, divine the will of the spirits.

Famous spirit festivals draw mammoth crowds annually. The Taung-Pyone festival is held in honor of two Hindu brothers, Shwe-Pyin-Gyi and Shwe-Pyin-Lav, heroes in the court of King Anawratha (1044-73) who were put to death for insubordination and are now worshipped as major spirits. During the festival, there is much music, dancing, and divination through shamans and *natkadaws.* The worshippers wash the images of the two brothers and put them on small rafts and float them down the river while chanting prayers for blessings. The annual festivals are usually related to the agricultural year. The most important are the festivals of paddy sowing and harvest. Shamans usually lead the festival dance and sacrifices, although others may also lead, as in the Karen Aung-Kwai feast where the mother officiates.

The Kachins believe that, after death, the spirit goes to Su-Gar, the abode of all spirits, including that of parents and grandparents. The Kayahs believe that all the dead go to the silver mountain at De Maw Soe. The Karens also believe there is a land of the dead and some, probably because of Buddhist influence, also believe in reincarnation. The Chins usually build shrines for the spirits of the dead to reside in.

Although Buddhism* is the religion of the majority in Myanmar, spirit worship still permeates the land. Spirit shrines are found outside monasteries, near pagoda precincts, and in homes. All Myanmese believe that spirits have existed since the beginning of time and will continue to exist as long as there is life on earth. Christians, on the other hand, remove their places of *Nat* worship upon baptism. Those Myanmese who were not also Buddhists (most tribal peoples) have converted at a much faster rate to Christianity (see Karen, Kachin).

Bibliography

Myanmar Socialist Programme Party Central Committee Headquarters, *Custom and Culture of the Indigenous Peoples of Myanmar* (1975). • Htin Aung, *Folk Elements in Burmese Buddhism* (1967). • Po Kya, *Thirty-seven Nats* (in Burmese). • Spiro, M. E., *Burmese Supernaturalism* (1967). • Temple, R. C., *Animism, Thirty-seven Nats* (1960). SAW DANIEL

Tran Van Luc

(Cu Sau) (b. My Quan, Thanh Hoa; d. Phat Diem, 6 Jul 1899). Outstanding Vietnamese clergyman and architect of the cathedral Phat Diem (North Vietnam*).

Originally named Peter Tran van Huu, Tran was an extraordinary priest who was able to harmonize politics and religion with his pastoral and diplomatic skills and successfully bridged Eastern and Western cultures in both architecture (see Art and Architecture) and literary works.

He learned the old literature* (in Chinese characters) before adopting the clerical formation (in French and Latin), first in Vinh Tri (1840-50) and then in Ke Non (1855-58). At the end of his formation, persecution led to the dispersion of the seminary. He surrendered himself to rescue the rector of the seminary, Vice Bishop Jeantet. He was interrogated and jailed in Lang Son, the province at the Chinese frontier where he earned the lifelong nickname Cu Sau ("the deacon") because of his merciful nature and pastoral ability (Luc also means Sau). He was highly esteemed by the provincial, who trusted him to teach his children. In 1860, when Le Phung and company threatened to invade North Vietnam and surrounded Lang Son, the provincial depended on Cu Sau to lead the military in repelling the invaders back to Chinese territory. He was then allowed to do mission work freely in North Vietnam. In 1873 he successfully mediated in a conflict between the French colonialists and the Vietnamese authority. In 1886 he was made "delegate" for three provinces — Thanh Hoa, Nghe An, and Ha Tinh — by the royal authority, but he declaimed the office after 35 days. King Thanh Thai conferred on him the *Le Bo Thuong Thu* (1899), and King Khai Dinh posthumously conferred on him *Nam Tuoc Phat Diem* in 1925. The French gave him two titles, *Chevalier de la Region d'Honneur* (1884) and *Officier de la Region d'Honneur* (1887).

Tran is best known for his pastoral work in Phat Diem (35 years) and the cathedral, a blend of Eastern and Western architecture which took 20 years to build (1871-91). He also composed scholarly poems in the old literary style and popular poems reflecting Catholic doctrine or moral life. The "Song of Piety," with 1088 verses, explains the reciprocal relationships between parents and children.

Alias Père Six, Tran was both a churchman and a patriot. His skill in integrating the spirit of Christianity with the Vietnamese arts and poems made him a model in enculturation.

Bibliography

Olichon, *Le Père Six, Curé et Baron de Phat Diem* (1935). • Tran cong Hoan, *Tien su Cu Sau Tran Luc, Lm Nam Tuo Phat Diem* (1963). VU KIM CHINH

Tranquebar

In 1612 the Dutch showed their interest in advancing toward the East. The Danes had also planned to establish a company at Copenhagen with a view toward having trade and commercial contacts with India*. The first vessel of Denmark arrived on the Coromandel Coast in 1616 and was soon followed by many other vessels. The victory of these merchants motivated them to establish a settlement on the coast for the protection and convenience of their goods and ships and for the development of their trade and commerce. The raja of Tanjore allowed them to lease the town of Tranquebar, which included five miles of land on the coast of Coromandel. Along with the capital Tranquebar, 15 other villages originally belonged to Tanjore's kingdom. The Tanjore king was one of the tributaries to the Great Mogul. He received an annual tribute from the Danes but had no authority over the governance of Tranquebar, which was entirely controlled and managed by Danes. At Tranquebar, the Danes established their Danish trading colony in 1620. Since then, Tranquebar has been a possession of the Danes, but they were paying rent to the king of Tanjore at the rate of 3,111 rupees per year.

The word "Tranquebar" can be translated "village of waves" or "song of the waves," because at Tranquebar the waves sing a very special tune. It is one of the four cradles of Christian missions in India. Here the first Protestant mission was started by the Royal Danish Mission with German missionaries Bartholomew Ziegenbalg* and Henry Plutschau* on 9 Jul 1706, the day they arrived. It was financed by the Church of England through the Society for the Propagation of the Gospel (SPG). James Lynch, the first Methodist* missionary to India, landed in India in 1816, and he first made a pilgrimage to Tranquebar to pay homage at the graves of the great pioneers and pledged himself to the service of India. The result was the establishment of a flourishing South India Province of the Methodist Church. The Society for the Propagation of Christian Knowledge (SPCK) was so moved by the laboring efforts of the Tranquebar missionaries that they decided to provide financial assistance to their work in the Tanjore and Trichy areas.

The work of the London Missionary Society (LMS) in establishing the Travancore mission also had its allegiance to Tranquebar. It was to Tranquebar that Vedamanickam, a Travancore pilgrim to Chidambaram, went in search of a Christian teacher for his people, and the result was that the German Ringeltaube (1770-1816) promised to go there. It was at Tranquebar that the first LMS missionaries from England landed and spent some time preparing for work in other places. It was to Tranquebar that a new convert and former clerk of Tippu Sultan's army went to receive instructions and fellowship. Tranquebar seemed to have had a magnetic attraction. Tranquebar also became a base for the early Christian missionaries, as they were not officially allowed to work in British East India Company territory. However, this problem was solved in 1813 when the charter was renewed. This good news gave the impetus for missionary enthusiasm, which led to the formation of a number of missionary societies such as the LMS (1795), the Scottish Missionary Society (1796), and the Church Missionary Society (CMS) (1799). It was at Tranquebar that 33 Christian leaders (mostly Indians) met and issued a passionate appeal for Christian union which came to be known as the Tranquebar Manifesto.

It is a strange coincidence that there was a special significance to the room where the first meeting was held. During the early days of the missionary work of Ziegenbalg and Plutschau in Tranquebar, they became unpopular with the Danish authorities and were imprisoned in a cell for 40 days. It was in that cell that Bishop V. S. Azariah* led the 1919 pioneers of the Church of South India (CSI) Union movement to pledge not to leave the room until clear guidance was shown to them. It was at Tranquebar that leaders of various churches had the special opportunity of learning from the experiences of emerging nationalism* and evangelistic fervor to transform Western church history and to shape the destiny of the emerging church of the East.

In 1919 two conferences were held at Tranquebar. The first (29-30 Apr) was organized on behalf of the Evangelical Forward Movement, and 65 ministers attended representing four different churches: Anglican*, South India Union Church (SIUC), Wesleyan, and the Church of Sweden. The theme was "Personal Evangelism: The Greatest Work of the World." The second conference was the Tranquebar Conference on Church Unity, at which seven Anglican and 26 SIUC representatives were present. Although it was an Indian conference, two Europeans (Sherwood Eddy and Herbert Arthur Popley) helped a great deal with drafting the manifesto. Azariah was the convener of the conference. The main theme of the conference was based on the unity of the church as given in John 17:21. Azariah, who dominated the discussion, pressed the matter of Episcopal ordination, which a few SIUC representatives were not happy to accept. Eddy tried to reconcile the differences and was able to help with framing the manifesto, incorporating the three main forms of government of the Episcopalian, Presbyterian*, and Congregational churches. A resolution known as the Tranquebar Manifesto was presented by Azariah, V. Santiago, and Meshach Peter with the help of Eddy and Popley.

The Tranquebar Manifesto basically endorsed the Lambeth Quadrilateral. The acceptance of the historic episcopate did not stipulate any particular theory on episcopacy. This idea was brought out by Eddy on several occasions after the Madras meeting. The references to the three elements (Congregational, Presbyterian, and Episcopalian), reconstruction after the war, and the critical situation in India were new items in the manifesto.

Bibliography

Samuel, G., *History of the Tranquebar Mission* (in Tamil) (1955). • George, K. M., *Church of South India: Negotiations towards Union, 1919-1947* (1977). • Lehmann, E. Arno, *It Began at Tranquebar* (1956). • Sandegren, J. Frederick, *The Song of Tranquebar* (1955). • Fenger, J. Frederick, *History of the Tranquebar Missions* (1863).

FRANKLYN J. BALASUNDARAN

Transcendental Meditation. *See* Hinduism, New Movements

Trappists

Officially the Cistercians* of the Strict Observance, the Trappists are a Catholic contemplative order following the Rule of St. Benedict. Cistercians were founded in 1098 at Citeaux, France, by 21 monks including their abbot, St. Robert of Molesme.

*China**. Trappists first arrived in Asia in 1883. At the request of Bishop Delaplace of Beijing, four monks with their superior, Ephrem Seignol, came from France and founded Yang Kia Ping, Our Lady of Consolation Abbey, west of Beijing. Vocations flourished. This abbey, in turn, opened a new monastery, Our Lady of Joy, Liesse, at Tchengtingfu. Both communities were dispersed by the Communists in 1947. Thirty-three monks were martyred for their faith. Consolation remains dispersed. Joy has been relocated on Lan Tao Island, Hong Kong, by the courageous efforts of Paulinus Lee. A group of young women, following the Trappist way of life, formed a community near Beijing, Our Lady of the Rosary, in 1993.

*Taiwan**. Bishop William Kupfer, of the Taichung Diocese, invited Lan Tao (Our Lady of Joy) and New Clairvaux Abbey, United States, to found a Trappist community jointly. Clement Kong and Regis King arrived in 1984 to begin Holy Mother of God Monastery at Shuili.

*Japan**. Bernard Favre, first abbot of Yang Kia Ping, China, personally brought about the arrival of Trappist monks and Trappistine nuns. He arranged for nine European monks to establish Our Lady of Phare, Hokkaido, in 1896 and for eight nuns from Ubexy, France, to establish Tenshien, Our Lady of the Angels, Hakodate, in 1898. Phare founded Annunciation Monastery, Oita (1980). Tenshien founded Nishinomiya Osaka (1935) and Imari (1953). Nishinomiya founded the convents of Nasu (1954) and Miyako (1981).

*Indonesia**. Dutch Trappists arriving from the abbey of Koningshoeven, Tilburg, founded the first contemplative abbey in central Java*, Rawaseneng, in 1953. Rawaseneng prospered with vocations and was raised to an independent abbey in 1978. Rawaseneng opened a second monastery, Larantuka (1995), on the island of Flores. In 1987 Trappistine nuns came from Vitorchiano, Italy, to establish a convent in Gedono, Central Java.

South Korea. Since the 1970s, vocations from Korea* were accepted into the community of Tenshien, Japan. After their formation, these sisters, with some Japanese nuns, returned to Korea in 1987 to establish the convent of Sujong in the diocese of Masan.

Philippines.* Pedro Lazo, a Filipino monk of Mepkin Abbey, United States, returned in 1972 with five American monks to begin the first contemplative abbey in this country on Guimaras Island. This abbey had many vocations and has sent some monks to assist other communities. In 1993 the abbey of Vitorchiano, Italy, established a second convent in Asia, Matutum, in the diocese of Marbel, South Cotabato.

India. Francis Mahieu, a Trappist monk from Scourmont, Belgium, went to India* in 1955 to join Fr. Le Saux (Abhishiktananda). In 1956, with Bede Griffiths, he founded an ashram* in Tiruvalla, later transferred to Kurisumal (1958). This community of 22 Indian monks was incorporated as an abbey into the Trappist Order on 9 Jul 1998.

Bibliography

Lekai, Louis J., *The Cistercians, Ideals and Reality* (1977). • Merton, Thomas, *The Waters of Siloe* (1949). • Jen, Stanislaus, *History of Our Lady of Consolation, Yang Kia Ping* (1978); *History of Our Lady of Joy* (1978) (both printed privately and available from Lantao Monastery).

THOMAS X. DAVIS

Treaty of Paris, 1898

Signed on 10 Dec 1898 in Paris, the treaty concluded the war between the United States and Spain. Spain was compelled to cede to the United States countries under Spanish sovereignty, including the Philippine* Islands, for which the United States paid Spain $20,000,000. The Vatican exacted $7,227,000 worth of gold from Washington as settlement for 403,713 hectares of friars' land, most of which had been held for centuries. The treaty completely ignored the victory of the Philippine revolution over Spain and the declaration of independence by the Filipinos on 12 Jun 1898 in Kawite, Cavite. The Catholic Church chose to protect its own interests first and aligned itself with the new colonial power. The treaty opened the Philippines to the influx of American Protestant missionaries.

Bibliography

Agoncillo, Teodoro A., *History of the Filipino People* (1990). • Constantino, Renato, *The Philippines: A Past Revisited* (1975). • Foreman, John, *The Philippine Islands* (1906).

TEODORO MAXIMILIANO M. DE MESA

Tribal Work, Vietnam

Evangelization among Vietnam's* highland minorities may be dated from 1770 when Roman* Catholics missionized briefly among the Stieng of the central highlands. Records also show that a few other tribals from northeastern Cambodia* were baptized.

A church among the Bahnar began after 1849 when French Catholic priests fled into the central highlands to escape persecution by the Nguyen emperor Minh Mang (1820-40). The early history of the Bahnar mission at Kontum is closely associated with Father Pierre Dourisboure, who labored there from 1850 to 1885. In 100 years, the mission increased from 900 (1865) to 12,000 (1908) to 25,255 (1949). Other Catholic missions were established at tribal population centers across the country, but most successfully in the central highlands.

The Protestant mission to the mountain tribes began in the 1920s as a joint endeavor of the Christian and Missionary Alliance* (C&MA) mission and the Vietnamese church established by it, the Evangelical Church of Vietnam* (ECVN; *Tin Lanh*). In 1929 missionaries began evangelizing in the highlands: J. J. Van Hine among the Tho in Lan Son, Herbert Jackson among the Koho in Dalat, and Gordon Smith among the Rhade in Banmethuot. Scores of ethnic Vietnamese clergy also joined with expatriate C&MA missionaries to evangelize other tribal groups, including the Bru, Chru, Chrau, Jeh, Katu, Mnong, Pacoh, Roglai, and Stieng.

Institutions of compassion and education were established throughout the highlands both north and south, and especially by the Catholics in the south. These included Bible* schools and seminaries, hospitals, clinics, leprosaria (Bahnar, Koho, Rhade; see Leprosy Work), and elementary and secondary schools. Vocational technical schools were also established, such as the Chilamasre Vocational Technical School near Dalat, named after four subgroups of Koho (Chil, La, Ma, and Sre), which operated until 1975.

Three staffers of the Banmethuot Leprosarium were abducted by the Vietcong in 1962 — Ardel Vietti, Archie Mitchell, and Dan Gerber, who were never seen again. Other missionary tragedies followed in 1968 when missionaries Ed and Ruth Thompson, Theo Ziemer, Ruth Wilting, and Carolyn Griswold were killed during the Tet offensive. Hank Blood and Betty Olsen were taken into the jungle and did not return.

Linguistic work by pioneering missionaries and Christian linguists included dictionaries and Scripture translations by Dourisboure (Bahnar, 1885), Dournes (Koho, Bahnar), Cassaigne (Koho, 1936), Evans (Koho New Testament), and Thomas (Chrau New Testament). After 1950, Wycliffe Bible* Translators and the Summer Institute of Linguistics (USA) produced some of the first language learning materials and Scripture portions in several Montagnard dialects.

The Vietnamese War of Independence with the French and Japanese slowed mission advance and stopped most missionary activity in the north after the

1954 Paris Peace Accord, which divided Vietnam into north and south. In 1954 the highland Protestant Christians numbered 3,000 in 162 villages led by 117 tribal pastors and 31 American and 21 Vietnamese missionaries. They numbered 21,241 believers in 16 tribes by 1965.

Highland minority churches suffered greatly throughout the years of the War of Independence (1954) and the Vietnam War* until the Communist takeover in 1975. Since 1975, tribal Christians have experienced more restrictions on the practice of their religion than their majority Vietnamese fellow believers. Reports of forced church closings and pressures of many kinds have been received outside Vietnam. Some improvement is known to have occurred in the urban areas, but rural churches continue to have difficulties.

Church statistics since 1975 are unreliable, but there are reports of both advances and declines. Since 1989, many converts among the Hmong of northern Vietnam have been reported. Other significant increases are believed to have occurred among the Bahnar, Hmong, Jarai, Chrau, Central Mnong, Koho, Rhade, Stieng, and Yao. Tribes least evangelized include: the Muong (914,000), Nung (706,000), Tay (1,190,400), Black and White Thai (1,040,500), and Yao/Man (474,000).

Bibliography

Dourisboure, Pierre, and Christian Simonnet, *Vietnam: Mission on the Grand Plateaus* (1967). • Dowdy, Homer, *The Bamboo Cross* (1964). • Hickey, Gerald Canon, *Free in the Forest: Ethnohistory of the Vietnamese Central Highlands, 1954-1976* (1982); *Sons of the Mountains: Ethnohistory of the Vietnamese Central Highlands to 1954* (1982). • Le Hoang Phu, "A Short History of the Evangelical Church of Viet Nam (1911-1965)," 2 Vols. (Ph.D. diss., New York University, 1972). James F. Lewis

Trigault, Nicolas

(b. 1577; d. 1628). Belgian Jesuit (see Society of Jesus) missionary to China* in the late Ming period.

Trigault came to Nanjing from Macau* in the spring of 1611. In 1612 he was summoned to Rome to report on the mission in China. He arrived in Rome in 1614. En route to Rome and during his stay there, he translated Matteo Ricci's* journal on China from Italian into Latin, adding some material to it. The book was published in 1615. Trigault secured permission from the pope to use Chinese for mass and to dispense with the requirement of taking off the hat during mass.

From Rome, Trigault traveled to Italy, France, Germany, Belgium, and Lisbon in Feb 1618. In April of the same year, he set out to return to China with 22 missionaries. In Jul 1620, Trigault arrived in Macau with 7,000 books from the West. Of the 22 missioners that started out with him, 12 died en route or after their arrival in Goa due to illness; six stayed in India* because of physical weakness; and only four arrived in Macau. Three of the remaining four later made significant contributions in changing the Chinese calendar to the Western-style calendar: Johann Terrenz*, Jacques Rho, and Johann Adam Schall von Bell*. After Trigault returned to China, he and Semedo visited Nanchang, Jianchang, and Shaozhou, where they inspected the mission points. Trigault also went to Kaifeng, Shanxi, and Shaanxi on a preaching mission. During the later part of his life, he settled in Hangzhou and devoted his time to writing, mainly in Latin. His main Chinese writing, *Xi Ru Er Mu Zi* (Vocabulary by Tones for Europeans), comprises three volumes. The first deals with the Chinese language and characters, the second with the Chinese characters arranged according to their tones, and the third with the list of Chinese characters arranged according to their strokes, providing their tonal pronunciation using the Western alphabet. The purpose of these volumes was to facilitate the education of missionaries.

Bibliography

Trigault, Nicolas, *De Christiana expeditione apud sinas suscepta a Soc. Jesu ex. P. M. Ricci commentariis libri* V (1605); *Vita Gasparis Barzei Belgae e Societate Iesu B. Xaverii in India Socii* (1610); *China in the Sixteenth Century: The Journals of Matteo Ricci, 1583-1610,* trans. Louis Gallagher (1953); *De Christianis apud Japonius triumphis* (1623); *Xinru ermu zi* (Vocabulary by tones for Europeans), 3 Vols. (1926). • Dunne, G., *Generation of Giants* (1962). • Polgar, L., *Bibliographie sur l'histoire de la Compagnie de Jesu, 1901-1980,* Vol. 3, Part 3 (1990). • Vath, Alfons, *Johann Adam Schall von Bell, S.J. (1592-1666)* (1991). • Bernard, H., "Un portrait de Nicolas Trigault dessine par Rubens?" *Archivum Historicum Societatis Jesu,* Vol. 22 (1953). • Dehaisnes, C., *Vie du P. Nicolas Trigault* (1862). • Goodrich, L. Carrington, *Dictionary of Ming Biography, 1386-1644* (1976).

China Group

Trinh Nhu Khue

(b. Trang Due village, Duy Tien District, Ha Nam Province, 11 Dec 1889; d. Nov 1978). First cardinal of the Church of Vietnam* who served for 21 years after reunification in 1975.

The eldest in a family with two brothers and four sisters, Trinh Nhu Khue was baptized as Joseph Mary. At age six, he served as a choirboy in a church in Cat Lai. About two years later, he entered the minor seminary of St. Peter in Hoang Nguyen. Ten years later, he went to the Ham Long parish in Hanoi to assist Rev. Pepaulis, who sent him to study at the Puginier school. After the probationary years, he studied theology, philosophy, and other disciplines at the major seminary.

After his ordination as a priest, he was sent as a curate to Khoan Vi, then as a seminary teacher (1933-40) to Hoang Nguyen. In the Ham Long parish he assisted Rev. Pepaulis, and during World War II* he spent much time taking care of the war victims and praying for them.

When Pepaulis returned to France, Khue became the vicar in 1947 and promoted the Legio Mariae movement.

On 15 Aug 1950, Khue became the first Vietnamese bishop of the Hanoi Diocese. He emphasized the veneration of Our Lady Mary, the respect of the Saint-Sacrament, and the education of the clergy for, he said, "Seminary is the eyeball of the bishop." He moved the diocesan seminaries and his family to the South when the country was split into the North and South, but he himself remained behind. In 1960 Hanoi became an archdiocese, and he was appointed archbishop in Jun 1963, assisted by the vice bishop of Hanoi, Joseph Mary Trinh Van Can. Khue died two years after his appointment as cardinal (1976). DO HUU NGHIEM

Trollope, Mark Napier

(b. London, England, 1862; d. 1930). Anglican* missionary and bishop in Korea*.

Educated at Lancing College and New College, Oxford, Trollope was sent by the Church of England to Korea in 1890. A careful student of language and culture, Trollope took six years to study Korean in Seoul before beginning a pioneering work on Kangwha Island. Under his leadership, the first Korean Anglicans were baptized there. After 11 years in Korea (1901), Trollope returned to England, where he carried on pastoral work in London.

In 1911, with his good knowledge of Korean culture and language, he was called back to be the first Anglican bishop in Korea. Trollope led the Anglicans to a neutral political position (unlike many of the denominations in Korea) regarding nationalism* in the midst of increasing oppression by the Japanese. In the 1920s Trollope led in the building of St. Mary and St. Nicholas Anglican Church (completed in 1925), which is a Byzantine-style cathedral.

Bibliography

Trollope, Constance, *Mark Napier Trollope: Bishop in Corea, 1911-1930* (1936). SCOTT W. SUNQUIST

Tsen On-Nie, Paul

(b. 1795; d. 1871). One of the first lay apostles of Indonesia*.

Baptized in Penang, Malaysia*, in 1827, Tsen settled on the island of Bangka (Riau) in 1828, where he worked as a doctor and on his own initiative taught catechism and prayer to the Chinese coolies of the tin mines. When he learned of a Catholic bishop in Batavia (Jakarta), he sent him news about this small group of believers. In 1849 a missionary was sent to Bangka. Fifty disciples were baptized immediately and 24 more in 1851. In 1854 a permanent mission post was opened with 176 Chinese Catholics, the first parish among non-Dutch Catholics in Indonesia.

Bibliography

Van Aernsbergen, A. J., *Chronologisch Oversicht* (1934).
ADOLF HEUKEN

Tsen, Philip Lindel. *See* Zheng Hefu (Philip Lindsel Tsen)

Tu Duc

(b. Hue, Vietnam, 22 Sep 1829; d. 19 Jul 1883). Anti-Catholic fourth emperor (1848-83) of Nguyen dynasty (1802-1945).

Tu Duc's original name was Nguyen Phuoc Hoang Nham, but he ruled under the honorific name Minh Mang ("self-morality"). Although very cultured and educated, he issued several edicts to persecute Vietnamese and French Catholics. Though the edicts were not strictly observed in many parts of the country, Tu Duc's intentions and policies were used by the French as a reason to invade Vietnam*. A combined French-Spanish force bombarded Da Nang in 1858, took the city, and occupied Saigon several months later. After admirals Charner and Bonard started to conquer the southern part of Vietnam, Tu Duc sent a delegation to negotiate a peace treaty, which was concluded in 1862. A Vietnamese priest, Dang Duc Tuan, was part of the delegation that negotiated with the French. After three provinces were ceded to the French in 1862, more freedom was granted to Catholics. The French started to spread Catholicism, fomenting a religious war between Vietnamese Christians and non-Christians.

Tu Duc's reign has been characterized as stormy, caused by pro-Catholic and anti-Catholic rebellions. Persecutions took place, but their extent was widely overstated. Realistic sources put the total number of victims as 25 European missionaries, 300 Vietnamese priests, and an estimated 30,000 followers between 1848 and 1860. A nationalist movement, the Van Than, composed of Confucianist mandarins, threatened to use the Catholics as a scapegoat for the lost territories of Vietnam. In spite of this internal threat, Tu Duc continued his tolerant policy, motivated to reform Vietnam. In 1864, for example, the Catholic priest Nguyen Hoang worked in Hue to teach and translate Western books. Nevertheless, Tu Duc lost three more provinces to France in 1874. After the invasion of Hanoi a year before (1873), the whole of northern Vietnam, called Tonkin, became a French protectorate, followed by central Vietnam in 1883. Tu Duc's young successor, Ham Nghi, who ascended the throne a year later, became a symbol of Vietnamese resistance against the French and fomented a monarchistic movement (called Can Vuong) with strong nationalist overtones. Catholic villages became an easy target for the rebellious troops. In the province of Quang Tri, for example, thousands of Catholics were killed after the order was given to *binh tay, sat ta* (chase away the

Westerners, kill the Catholics). After Ham Nghi was dethroned and captured (Dec 1887) and subsequently exiled to Algeria, the movement died down. In some cases, the French used loyalist mandarins to pacify the central part of Vietnam. The southern-born Catholic Tran Ba Loc and his troops, composed of militant Catholics, earned a grisly reputation in this regard.

Bibliography

Nguyen The Anh, *Economy and Society in Nguyen Vietnam* (in Vietnamese) (1971). • Tsuboi, Y., *L'empire vietnamien face a la France et a la Chine* (1987).

JOHN G. KLEINEN

Tupas, Rajah of Sugbu

A Filipino, Rajah Tupas of Sugbu (now Cebu City) waged nightly guerrilla attacks for three months against the Spaniards' Legazpi expedition when they arrived in Apr 1565. Eventually, however, the Spaniards' incessant raids for buried treasure on the Sugbuanons' sacred burial grounds and their seizure of highborn hostages forced Tupas and his chiefs to capitulate the following July.

Although some Sugbuanons had been baptized since 1565, Tupas held out against pressure to turn Christian, giving one excuse after another. On 21 Mar 1568, Tupas and his son and heir, Rajah Pisuncan, were baptized by the Augustinian* Fray Diego de Herrera.

Bibliography

Collecion de Documentos Ineditos relativos . . . de Ultramar, 2a. serie III. • Rodriquez, I. T., *Historie de la Provincia Agustiniana . . . de Filipinas* I. • Sitoy, T. V., Jr., *The Initial Encounter* (1985).

T. VALENTINO SITOY, JR.

Turner, E. Stanton

(b. Iowa, United States, 1887; d. ?). American missionary serving the Young Men's Christian Association* (YMCA) in the Philippines*.

Turner attended Grinnell and Oberlin Colleges. J. R. Mott of the YMCA sent Turner to the Philippines in 1915, where Turner served as secretary of student work (1915-18) and general secretary (1918-41) of the YMCA. He retired from YMCA work in the Philippines in 1952.

Turner continued policies that welcomed Roman Catholics* and even Muslims (see Islam) into YMCA membership and secured support for the YMCA from leading Filipino politicians and financiers. He purposely avoided using the YMCA as a Protestant means of evangelism and was proud that in all of his years in the Philippines he never asked anyone to change church affiliations. His policies, endorsed by Mott, promoted "interconfessionalism." Nevertheless, the Catholic hierarchy accused the YMCA of having a "de-Catholicizing" influence, while Methodists (see Methodism) accused it of "selling out" to Roman Catholicism. Turner promoted the increasing role of Filipinos in positions of leadership in the YMCA. He was interred during the war with Japan and was succeeded as general secretary by Domingo Bascara.

Bibliography

Turner, E. S., *Nation Building* (1965). • Hopkins, Howard C., *John R. Mott* (1979).

FLOYD T. CUNNINGHAM

Uchimura Kanzo
(b. Edo [Tokyo], 23 Mar 1861; d. 28 Mar 1930). Independent Japanese evangelist.

The eldest son of Uchimura Yoshiyuki, a retainer of the Takasaki feudal clan, Uchimura went from the Tokyo English School to Sapporo Agricultural School in 1877. Nitobe Inazo and Miyabe Kingo were his classmates. He was baptized by Merriman Colbert Harris, a Methodist* missionary from the United States, on 2 Jun 1878. He graduated from the school in 1881 and became an official in the governmental program to develop Hokkaido. He was instrumental in the founding of the Sapporo Young Men's Christian Association* and Sapporo Independent Church. He left Sapporo in 1883 to teach at Gakunosha and work in the Department of Agriculture and Commerce. In November of the following year, he went to Elwyn, Pennsylvania, United States, where he worked as a male nurse at a facility for mentally retarded children. In Sep 1885, he entered Amherst College as a special student, where he was greatly influenced by Julius Hawley Seelye, the college president, and experienced a conversion. He graduated from Amherst in 1887 and studied at Hartford Seminary until January of the following year, returning to Japan in May. In September he assumed the position of head teacher at Hokuetsu Gakkan in Niigata but returned to Tokyo in December because of a conflict with school management and missionaries. After that, he taught at a number of places, including Toyo Eiwa School and Suisan Denshujo (school). He became a part-time teacher at First Advanced High School in 1890 but was relieved of his duties there in January of the following year for an incident of disrespect against the Tenno Emperor. After teaching at Teisei Gakkan in Osaka and Kumamoto English School, he moved to Kyoto in 1893.

His name as a writer became known through his books and magazine articles. In 1893 he published *Kirisuto shinto no i Nagusame,* (Comfort for the Christian Believer) and *Kyuan roku* (Record of a Search for Peace); in 1894, *Dendo no seishin* (Spirit of Mission Work), *Chirigakuko* (Treatise on Geography), and *Japan and the Japanese;* in 1895, *How I Became a Christian* and many magazine articles, especially in *Kokumin no tomo* (The Citizen's Friend). From Sep 1896, he worked at Nagoya Eiwa School (forerunner of Nagoya Gakuin), and in 1897 he moved to Tokyo to serve as editor in chief of the English column of the daily newspaper *Yorozuchoho.* That year he also published *Kosei e no Saidaiibutsu* (The Best Bequest to Future Generations) and *Aigin* (Song of Love). In May 1898 he quit the magazine job and in June started a new magazine, *Tokyo dokuritsu zasshi* (Tokyo Independence Magazine), serving as its editor in chief. This magazine ceased to exist in Jul 1900; in September he founded another, *Seisho no kenkyu* (Biblical Study). Together with this work, he served as a guest contributor to *Chohosha.* For three years, from the summer of that year, he held a summer seminar. About that time, he also began to lead a Bible class in his home. Some of the people who participated in this class were Shiga Naoya, Osanai Kaoru, Oga Ichiro, and Kurahashi Sozo. From Mar 1901 to Aug 1902, he published *Mukyokai* (Nonchurch*). He also worked with Kuroiwa Ruiko, Kotoku Shusui, and Sakai Toshihiko in the protest movement against copper mine poisoning in Ashio. These men founded the *Shakaikairyo Dantai Risodan* (Organization for the Betterment of Society). In 1903 he took an antiwar stance against the mounting prowar feeling at the beginning of the Russo-Japanese War, and because *Chohosha* had taken a prowar stance, he resigned from that magazine. After this, his life centered around his weekly Sunday Bible class and publication of *Seisho no kenkyu.*

Together with Nakata Juji and Kimura Seimatsu, he started the Awaiting the Second Coming of Christ Movement. From 1921, he gave 60 continuous lectures on the book of Romans to several hundred listeners. In 1924 he issued a strong protest to the anti-Japanese bill issued by the United States. In 1926 he started the English publication, *The Japan Christian Intelligencer.* In it, as his two favorite words ("Jesus" and "Japan") illustrate, he advocated nationalism* or a flourishing spirit of independence and Christianity; holding on to an evangelistic faith, he spoke out for *Mukyokai* (Nonchurch Movement), his own original type of Christianity. Because of this work, his influence was felt by a great number of people. He had a wide effect not only on Japanese Christianity, but also on other religions, scholarship, thought, education, and literature. Two of his books, *How I Became a Christian* and *Japan and the Japanese,* were translated into a number of European languages, and he received considerable attention from Europe, too. Beginning in 1932, his works were published by Iwanami Shoten in 20 volumes; in 1981-84, 40 more volumes were published. Kyobunkwan published a total of 50 volumes of his works, including *Shinko chosaku* (Works on Faith), *Seisho chukai* (Bible Commentaries), *Nikki shokan* (Diary and Letters), *Eibun chosaku* (His Works in English). Uchimura is one of the most influential and original Christian thinkers in Asia.

Bibliography

Hiroshi, Miara, *The Life and Thought of Kanzo Uchimura, 1861-1930* (1996). SUZUKI NORIHISA

Uemura Masahisa

(b. Shiba Ward, Tokyo, 15 Jan 1858; d. Tokyo, 8 Jan 1925). Japanese pastor, theologian.

The eldest son of Tojuiro and Tei, Uemura's birth name was Michitaro (one explanation says he was born in the home of his mother in Chiba Prefecture). The Uemura family was a 2,500 *koku* (one *koku* equals 4.96 bushels) retainer of the *shogun,* but they fell into bankruptcy at the time of the Meiji Restoration. He came into contact with Christianity when he went to Tokyo to study at Shubunkan and the preparatory school run by James Hamilton Ballagh. In Jun 1873 he was baptized at the Yokohama Public Church by Ballagh. His parents and younger brothers were also baptized later. Soon he decided to become an evangelist, studying at Brown Preparatory School and Icchi Shin Gakko (United Seminary). He was ordained in 1880 and became the pastor of Shitaya (Toshimagaoka) Church. In 1887 he established the church that would later become Fujimicho Church and served as pastor there for the rest of his life. As an evangelist, his work included: (1) forming evangelical churches; (2) building up an acceptance of a theological way of thinking and the related training of evangelists; and (3) participation in written campaigns in opposition to society.

In a life of faith that began in the Public Church and moved to the Japan Presbyterian* Church, he provided directional leadership to bring the Christian churches together and help them become self-supporting and independent, based on an evangelical faith (Jesus Christ as the Son of God incarnate, offering redemption through his death on the cross; and the resurrection).

Defying the influence of liberalism, he, as a professor at Meiji Gakuin, worked to solidify a faith with the above doctrine as its core. In addition, as one of the founders of Tokyo Shingakusha (seminary), he took on the responsibility of the theological education and training of evangelists.

Through his own publications such as *Nihon hyoron* (Japanese Criticism), *Fukuin shuho* (The Good News Weekly, forerunner of *Fukuin shimpo,* and others, he engaged in a wide range of literary criticism on such subjects as politics, society, education, and religion. His contributions in the areas of Bible* translation (into Japanese), hymn editing, literary criticism, and English literature are also of note.

His health was greatly damaged because of the strenuous effort he put into the reconstruction of Fujimicho Church and Tokyo Shingakusha after they were devastated by the Great Earthquake of Kanto (1923). He died suddenly at his home in Kashiwagi, Tokyo. A list of his written works include *Shinri ippan* (One and All Part of Truth), 1884; *Fukuin Michishirube* (A Guide to the Gospel) 1885; *Uemura zensho* (The Complete Works of Uemura), 8 vols., 1931-34; *Uemura Masahisa chosakushu* (The Works of Uemura Masahisa), 7 vols., 1966-67.

Bibliography

Saba Wataru, ed., *Uemura Masahisa to sono jidai* (Uemura Masahisa and that period), 8 vols. (1937-76). • Takeda Kiyoko, "Uemura Masahisa ni okeru atarashii 'jiga' no kakuritsu" (Establishment of the new "self" in Uemura Masahisa), *Ningenkan no sokoku* (1959). • Sumiya Mikio, "Uemura Masahisa to nihon no kirisuto-kyo" (Uemura Masahisa and Japanese Christianity), *Chuo koron* (1965). • Ouchi Saburo, "Kindai nihon shiso shijo no Uemura Masahisa" (Uemura Masahisa in the history of modern Japanese thought), *Fukuin to sekai* (1965). • Kyogoku Junichi, *Uemura Masahisa, sono hito to shiso* (Uemura Masahisa, the man and his thought) (1966). • Ishihara Ken, "Uemura Masahisa no shogai to rosen" (The life and path of Uemura Masahisa), *Kirisuto-kyo shiron* (Christian thought) (1967). • Kumano Yoshitaka, "Uemura Masahisa ni okeru tatakai no shingaku" (Uemura Masahisa's theology of conflict), *Nihon kirisuto-kyo shingaku shisoshi* (The history of Christian theological thought) (1968). • Ouchi Saburo, "Uemura Masahisa no shiso kisoron" (The foundation of Uemura Masahisa's thought), *Tohoku Daigaku Nihon bunka kenkyujo kenkyu hokoku* (Report of research on Japanese culture, from Tohoku Imperial University) (1975). • Kato Tsuneaki, "Uemura Masahisa," *Nihon no sekkyokatachi* (Japanese preachers) (1972). • Tashiro Kazuhisa, "Uemura Masahisa ni okeru shingaku shiso" (Theological thought of Uemura Masahisa), *Nihon shisoshi kenkyu* (Research on the history of Japanese thought) (1975). UNUMA HIROKO

Uemura Tamaki

(b. 24 Aug 1890; d. 26 May 1982). Pastor of the Presbyterian* Church of Christ in Japan (UCCJ), consultant for establishment of the World Federation of Nations.

Uemura was born the third daughter of Uemura Masahisa* and Sueno. After attending morning prayer services with Watanabe Sadako (later the wife of Ishihara Ken) for approximately one year, she was baptized by Uemura Masahisa* at Fujimicho Church on 16 Apr 1905. She graduated from Joshi Gakuin Girls School in 1910. In 1911 she went to the United States to study medicine but soon realized that she was not suited for medicine. She changed her major to philosophy and graduated from Wellesley College in Jun 1915. She taught at Tsuda College and Joshi Gakuin Girls School and then was college dean of *Jiyu Gakuen* (Freedom School) until 1925. In 1917 she married Kawado Shuzo, but he died of lung cancer in Jun 1919. She was influenced to become an evangelist by the death of both her younger sister, Sayo (who began studying for the ministry) in 1920, and her father, Masahisa, in 1925. In September of that year, she went to England to study at Edinburgh New College and the theological department of Edinburgh College, returning to Japan in Dec 1929. Beginning in Sep 1930, she served as an instructor at Tokyo Women's Christian University, Tokyo Union Theological Seminary, and Tokyo Seikei Girls School. From October of that same year, she began leading a Bible study class at her Kashiwagi home, and the next year she joined the Japan Presbyterian Church's Kashiwagi Church as its leader.

On 19 Apr 1934 (22 years before women's ordination was permitted in the U.S. Presbyterian Church), Uemura was ordained a pastor of the Japan Presbyterian Church at its national assembly. In Oct 1934, the Kashiwagi church building was dedicated, and, three years later, a celebration to recognize the establishment of the church and to install her as pastor was held. From 1937 to 1938, she actively protested the government-general of Taiwan's attempt to close the Christian schools and went there to serve as principal of the Tainan Presbyterian Girls' School. During these years, she was active in the Young Women's Christian Association* (YWCA) of Japan, serving on the executive committee beginning in 1922, as chair of the religious education committee in 1931, as vice president from 1931, being elected president in 1937, and serving as honorary president from 1961. In addition to her work in the YWCA of Japan, she made a valuable contribution to the development of the World YWCA, serving as vice president from 1938 to 1951. In 1946, at the invitation of the Women's Division of the Presbyterian Church in the United States, she went on a speaking tour of the United States as a private citizen and emissary for peace, with persons from such countries as China* and the Philippines*. The opportunities she had during this time to meet with these persons made her realize keenly the pain that was caused by Japan's invasion of their countries. The church building where she served was destroyed by fire during the war and rebuilt in 1947. In 1948 she became a member of the National Public Safety Commission. In 1951 she left the UCCJ, joining the Japan Presbyterian Church in Tokyo. She retired from the pastorate in Apr 1973.

In 1950 she went to the United States with Hiratsuka Raicho, Gauntlett Tsune, Jodai Tano, and Nogami Yaeko to appeal to Secretary of State John Foster Dulles for the establishment of peace and an overall peace treaty. In 1955 she and Shimonaka Yasaburo, Maeda Tamon, Kaya Seiji, Yukawa Hideki, Hiratsuka, and Jodai joined together to form the Seven Member Committee for World Peace. This committee spoke out and worked actively against many different international issues, including nuclear testing, the Berlin crisis, the Cuban missile crisis, the introduction of U.S. nuclear submarines into Japanese ports, and U.S. bombing of North Vietnam. Her writings include a collection of sermons, *Kitare yuke* (Coming and Going), 1961; *Asa no Hikari Ueyori* (From the Heaven Morning Light Comes), 1973; and a three-volume set including the above two plus an autobiography, *Watakushi no ayunda michi* (The Path I've Walked), which was published in 1985 under the title of *Uemura Tamaki chosaku shu.*

Bibliography

Imamura Takeo, ed., *Uemura Tamaki Sensei no jidai* (The times of Uemura Tamaki) (1987).

JAPANESE DICTIONARY

Ujung Pandang

Formerly Makassar in southern Celebes; seat of a Catholic metropolitan bishop (1961), whose province includes the suffragan diocese of Amboina (Missionaries of the Sacred Heart [MSC]; apostolic prefecture of Nederlands Nieuw-Guinee since 1902) and Manado (MSC; Apostolic Prefecture of Celebes since 1920).

Before 1545, local rajas asked for priests from Malacca*, but only the missionary V. Viegas worked among them for three years (1545-48). Southern Celebes was Islamized in the late 16th c., but the sultans of Makassar treated the Portuguese missionaries well. Portuguese missionaries, with another 3,000 Portuguese, fled to Ujung Pandang after Malacca fell into Dutch hands (1641). Franciscans*, Dominicans*, and Jesuits* served the community without difficulty until the Dutch forced the sultan to expel them from his territory (1661). Some went to Larantuka (Flores) and the Solor mission.

Between 1888 and 1895, Jesuit missionaries from Surabaya visited the Kei archipelago, Kessewooi, and Watubela Island in the Moluccas in order to find a suitable mission field. Other promising parts were closed by the colonial government on the grounds of avoiding *dubbele zending* (double mission) in the same area. On the island of Langgur (Kei), a small group of converts offered the hope of planting a church by means of simple village schools (1889). The first wooden church was built in Langgur in 1893. In 1904 the Missionaries of the Sacred Heart* (MSC) took over the small community of 1,170 faithful and 17 chapels that were served regularly from the parish of Langgur, which had a real church and a school with a boarding house. Because of the increase in missionaries, the establishment of new posts on the islands of Tanimbar and Yamdena, and growth in the number of indigenous Christians (more than 12,000 faithful), the prefecture (1904) was raised in 1920 to the apostolic vicariate of Nederlands Nieuw-Guinee, with its own bishop, comprising the Moluccas* and Dutch New Guinea.

Before the Japanese forces occupied the Moluccas (1942), there were 31,500 Catholics in the archipelago. Secondary education (1931) and a hospital (1928) had been opened on the island of Tual (Kei); young people had been accepted as seminarians and religious brothers and sisters. But most mission institutions were destroyed by the Japanese. The bishop, J. Aerts, and 12 Dutch missionaries were accused of spying and shot dead; 25 missionaries died in camps or while trying to flee to unoccupied territory. The Protestant church experienced the same brutal treatment by the occupation forces. But catechists and religious teachers strengthened the faithful.

In northern Celebes, former Manadonese soldiers of the Dutch forces who had become Catholics in Central Java asked for a Catholic priest (1868). Because the colonial resident regarded Minahassa as an exclusively Protestant mission field, visiting Catholic priests from Batavia (Jakarta) or Surabaya encountered difficulty and much restriction. But in 1886 a parish priest was allowed to reside permanently in Manado. He built chapels, trained catechists, and invited the Sisters of Jesus, Maria, and Joseph (JMJ) to establish a school (1898), which was only allowed to accept pupils after 1909. In 1907 the community reached more than 8,000 members; a teachers training school was opened (1905), and a monthly magazine published (1909). In 1920 the Jesuits handed the mission to the MSC. At the same time, the mission was raised to the apostolic prefecture of the Celebes*, with 11,100 faithful. Before the Pacific War reached the island (1942), many parishes had been established in Minahassa and a few outside this mainly Christianized area. In 1937 the prefecture was divided into the apostolic vicariate of Manado (MSC) and the apostolic prefecture of Makassar/Ujung Pandang, which was entrusted to the Belgian Scheut Fathers* (CICM). During the war, Japanese secular priests sporadically served the deserted parishes and strengthened the catechists and religious lay leaders in their difficult tasks. The young church did not fall but grew in numbers and inner strength.

After war (1945), revolution (1945-49), and several local uprisings in the Moluccas (Republik Maluku Selatan), and in southern Celebes (Darul Islam), evangelization resumed and intensified. Indigenous clergy (since 1944) and members of different religious congregations took over and filled many posts because the church spread quickly. Church membership in the province of Ujung Pandang increased from 61,712 in 1942 to nearly 373,000 in 1993.

Because of historical development, most Catholics in the church province of Ujung Pandang live in the larger cities (Ujung Pandang, Manado, Ambon) and on the Kei archipelago, in Minahassa, and in the central part of Celebes (Toraja). Many migrate to Jakarta and other large cities in Java. Steady growth is supported by schools on all levels, apostolic lay organizations, and growing numbers of religious sisters who increasingly take over mission posts and even parishes. Several minor seminaries and a major seminary in Pineleng (1954, Minahassa) educate the local clergy. All three dioceses are headed by indigenous bishops (since 1993). ADOLF HEUKEN

Ulay, Maria

(early 17th c.). Pious Filipino woman.

Ulay (or Uray) was the daughter of Pedro Manuel Manook, chief of Dapitan, Zamboango, and granddaughter of Datu Pagbuaya, the Bohol chieftain who in 1563 led the migration of 800 families to Dapitan following the disastrous Portuguese-Ternatan raid earlier that year. Manook's family (apparently including Maria as a child) and followers were baptized in 1609 by Pedro de Acuna (1573-1643).

Ulay had been married to Gonzalo Maglinti, but, upon his death, she relinquished her property and right of succession to her children and devoted herself to a life of prayer and meditation. Her request to join the Franciscan* Poor Clares nunnery in Manila (established in 1621) was refused because she was an *india.*

Remaining in Dapitan under the Jesuits'* tutelage, she lived a semiconventional life which involved a fixed daily schedule of attendance at mass, prayer, meditation, examination of conscience, the Rosary, and other devotions, as well as weekly confession. She also wove and sewed ecclesiastical vestments and altar linens for the local Jesuit church.

The appellation "Uray," a variant of the Cebuano term *ulay* (virgin), was probably either an honorific title or else indicative of her singular devotion to the Virgin Mary. Though not mentioned, she probably had a number of young women who joined her for various lengths of time in this life of devotion. She flourished between 1609 and 1621.

Bibliography

Combes, F., *Historia de Mindanao, Jolo y sus adyacentes* (1667), Bks. 1 and 2 (1897). • del Costa, H., *The Jesuits in the Philippines (1581-1768)* (1961). • Sitoy, T. V., Jr., *The Initial Encounter* (1985). T. VALENTINO SITOY, JR.

Umar I

(Omar I; 'Umar Ibn al-Khattab) (b. ca. 586, Mecca, Arabia [now in Saudi Arabia]; d. 3 Nov 644, Medina, Arabia). Second successor to Muhammad as leader of the Muslims, after Abu Bakar, and first to use the title "Commander of the Faithful."

Under Umar, Muslim armies extended Islamic reign significantly into non-Muslim and non-Arab lands. He laid down the first, and enduring, guidelines for Muslim administration of these conquered territories, including the founding of military centers which would grow into true Islamic cities, the registration of those owed military pensions, the creation of the office of *qadi,* as well as mandating certain religious observances. His reign is particularly important to non-Muslim groups living under Islamic political systems, as his first treaties with non-Muslims established the principle of religious tolerance for non-Muslims, the maintenance of distinctive non-Muslim private and family law under Muslim rule, the obligation of non-Muslims to support the Muslim state through taxes in place of active participation in its military expansion, and the primacy of Muslim law and administration over local traditions and customs in cases of conflict. Later expansions and elaboration of Umar's original treaties led to much harsher treatment of non-Muslim minorities but continued to be known as the "Covenant of Omar,"* drawing their authority from Umar's unique position as one of the first four Muslim leaders.

Bibliography

Moffett, Samuel Hugh, *A History of Christianity in Asia,* Vol. I (1992). • *Shorter Encyclopedia of Islam,* ed. H. A. R. Gibb and J. H. Kramers (1961).

ROBERT HUNT

Umayyad Caliphate

(656-750). The Umayyads were a merchant family of the Quraysh tribe which grew to prominence as administrators under Muhammad and his first three successors, Abu Bakar, Umar*, and Uthman. During the civil war which occurred after Uthman's death in 656, a member of the family, Mu'awiyah, then governor of Syria, defeated 'Ali, Muhammad's son-in-law, and established himself as caliph. Before his death, Mu'awiyah succeeded in having tribal leaders give an oath of allegiance to his son Yazid I and thus established a principle of hereditary succession. Notwithstanding civil wars and intertribal conflicts, the Umayyads would rule most of the Islamic world until 750, when the last Umayyad, Marwan II, was defeated by forces loyal to Abu al-'Abbas as-Saffah, who founded the 'Abbasid dynasty.

Under the Umayyad caliphate, Muslim forces extended Islamic rule west into North Africa and Spain, east into northwestern India and Central Asia, and north into much of modern-day Turkey. Although initially dependent on existing Byzantine and Persian administrative structures, they undertook an intensive program of Arabization which spread both the language and Arab administration into newly conquered lands.

Umayyad expansion, particularly in its attacks on Constantinople (669-78) and southern France (halted at Poitiers in 732), led to extended conflict with Christian nations and rulers. These conflicts between Eastern and Western empires, which date from the wars between Greek and Persia and extend into the period of the Crusades, the modern colonial era, and even the struggles for economic independence by the oil-producing Islamic states, may be seen as an enduring struggle to control the complementary natural resources of East and West, as well as trade between them. However, the religious dimension to this pattern of conflict, which was introduced during the period of Umayyad expansion and continued during the Crusades, deeply intertwined Christian-Muslim relations with political and economic conflicts between competing empires. This led to increased Muslim suspicions of the Christian minority within Islamic territories and harsher treatment by Muslim rulers, which was reciprocated in the Christian West.

Bibliography

Moffett, Samuel Hugh, *A History of Christianity in Asia,* Vol. I (1992). • Hitti, Philip K., *A History of the Arabs* (1970).

ROBERT HUNT

Unbaptized Believers. *See* Hindu Cultural Christianity

Underwood, Horace Grant

(Won Doo Woo) (b. London, 1859; d. Atlantic City, New Jersey, United States, Oct 1916). First ordained missionary from the Presbyterian* Church of the United States (North) to Korea* in 1885.

The fourth son of John Underwood, a scientist, inventor, and deeply committed Christian, Underwood migrated with his family to the United States in 1872 and settled in New Jersey. Underwood graduated from New York University in 1881 and continued further studies at the Dutch Reformed Theological Seminary in New Brunswick, New Jersey. He was ordained by the Dutch Reformed Church. Initially interested in serving in India, Underwood's interest in Korea was aroused through an address given to students at the seminary by A. Oltsman from the Reformed Church Mission in Japan. He graduated from the seminary in 1884 and joined the presbytery of New Jersey. On 24 Jan 1885, Underwood reached Yokohama, Japan*, where he observed missionary work, taught English, and learned some Korean. He left on the steamer *Tsuruga Maru* and arrived at Chemulpo (Inch'on), Korea, on 5 Apr 1885.

In Apr 1886, he taught chemistry and physics to a medical class at the Kwanghaewon, the first modern hospital, run by Horace N. Allen*, another U.S. Presbyterian missionary. In July Underwood secretly baptized No Tohsa, Allen's language teacher and the first Protestant to be baptized in Korea. Also in 1886, he opened an orphan school, which later became Kyung Sin School. In Nov 1887, Underwood organized the first church in Korea, the Saimoonan, with 14 members meeting in his home in Chong Dong, Seoul. He and some colleagues formed the Bible* Translation Committee, which was responsible for the new Korean translation of the New Testament (1900) and the Old Testament (1910). Underwood also founded the Christian Literature Society and edited and published the first hymnbook, *Chan Yang Ga,* in 1893.

Notable among his contributions was the founding of Yonhee College ("Chosen Christian College"), which grew out of Kyung Sin School in 1915. Yonhee College merged with the Severance Hospital and Medical School in 1957 to form Yonsei University.

Underwood married Lillias Horton, a medical missionary in Korea, and they had a son, H. H. Underwood. Horace exhausted himself in establishing Yonhee University and died in Atlantic City, New Jersey, in 1916. He was awarded the Tae Geuk Medal by Emperor Kojong of the Old Choson Dynasty. He was posthumously awarded the President's Decoration by the Korean government in 1963. Four generations of the Underwood family served in Korea. The Saimoonan Presbyterian Church in Seoul erected a memorial monument for Underwood in 1927, which was forcibly dug out by the Japanese police in 1942 when all American missionaries were forced out of Korea.

Bibliography

Underwood, Horace Grant, *The Religions of Eastern Asia* (1910); *The Call of Korea: Political, Social, Religious* (1908). • Rhodes, Harry A., ed., *History of the Korea Mission: Presbyterian Church U.S.A., 1884-1934* (1934). • Hunt, Everett N., Jr., *Protestant Pioneers in Korea* (1980). • Grayson, James Huntley, *Early Buddhism and Christianity in Korea: A Study in the Explanation of Religion* (1985). • Underwood, Lillias H., *Fifteen Years Among the Topnots* (1904); *Underwood of Korea* (1918). • Anderson, Gerald, ed., *Biographical Dictionary of Christian Mission* (1998). KIM IN SOO

Unification Church, Korea

Religious organization founded by Moon Sun Myung in 1954.

The official name of the Unification Church is the Holy Spirit Association for the Unification of World Christianity. Moon was born in North Korea* in 1920. He studied in Kyungsung Commercial-Technical High School in Seoul and later went to Japan to study at Technical High School, which was attached to Waseda University. After liberation, he became interested in religion and made himself a preacher in the Christian church in P'yongyang.

During the Korean War*, he began to organize the Unification Church and reached out aggressively to young people during this time of confusion and desperation. He preached that Seoul, Korea, would be where the last things would happen, for it is the center of salvation of the world. Moon proclaimed himself to be the second Jesus who was going to complete the unfinished work of Christ. In 1957 Moon's theologians and theorists of his "doctrines" published *The Divine Principle,* in which he insisted that the Christian Scriptures were incomplete, as the work of Jesus was incomplete. The cause of the fall was sexual corruption, in which people inherit the blood of Satan through sexual desire. Therefore, human sexual activities must be cleansed by a pure form of marriage. Jesus' work was incomplete due to his celibacy, and Moon's work is to unify all humankind in marriage by his own physical and symbolic initiation. He performs wedding ceremonies for hundreds and thousands of young couples from all over the world who have never known each other prior to their marriage but whose marriages have been arranged by matchmaking church authorities. In the 1970s, young people all over the world were fascinated by this Asian religion and joined Moon's church, selling chewing gum and flowers for the cause.

The Unification Church is basically a secretive sectarian religious organization, and no official membership is disclosed. It has had close contact with military governments and business sectors of the wealthiest nations of the world. During the Cold War, Moon advocated a staunch anti-Communist position and received support from the anti-Communist military regime of Korea and elsewhere. After the fall of the Communist world, he reached out to the former Soviet Union, China, and now the North Korean Communist government.

The National Council of Churches of Korea made investigative studies of Moon's church and its doctrines and came close to condemning the church as heretical, but it merely pointed out some of the incompatible elements over against the teachings of the Bible and Christian tradition. The National Council of Christian Churches of the United States of America also made an extensive study of Moon's organization and its activities in the United States, and, respecting the basic human rights of religious freedom, the study document informed interested individuals of the basic tenets and practices of the Unification Church. There were a number of attempts of the Unification Church to join the World Council of Churches, with no apparent success due to fundamental differences over Christology.

The Unification Church runs prestigious educational institutions for young people in Korea, has opened medical schools and hospitals in China* for overseas Koreans, and operates a theological school in New York State. Moon's church publishes daily newspapers not only in Korea but in the United States and Japan*. From time to time, it organizes a worldwide international scholars' peace conference in Seoul and other metropolitan centers and invites world-renowned academicians and theologians, including Nobel Prize winners, to highlight the church's involvement in world politics.

Bibliography

Yamamoto, J. Isamu, "Unification Church (Moonies)," in *A Guide to Cults and New Religious Movements,* ed. Ronald Enroth (1983). • Wi Jo Kang, "The Influence of the Unification Church in the USA," *Missiology,* Vol. 3, No. 3

(Jul 1975). • Choi Synduck, *Shinheoung Jongkyo Jipdan-ui Kwanhan Bikyo Yungu* (A comparative study on the new religions in Korea) (1965). • Park Young-Kwan, *The Unification Church* (1980). • Song Yong-jo, "The Holy Spirit and Mission" (Ph.D. diss., Fuller Theological Seminary, 1981). DAVID SUH, with contributions from KIM HEUNG SOO, translated by KIM IN SOO

Union of Evangelical Students of India

(UESI). Weekly Friday prayer meetings in 1949 by a group of college students at the home of Professor Hannington Enoch at 190 Poonamallee High Road, Madras, South India, convinced the professor that God was encouraging him to raise a student movement emphasizing salvation through the atoning work of Christ on the cross and to build up students through God's Word. Almost simultaneously, little prayer groups of students with similar faith and conviction met in Vellore and Coimbatore. The merger of these three groups at a retreat near Vellore gave birth to the UESI in 1954.

The faithful prayer of Christians in India* and overseas was vital for raising an evangelical witness. Stirrings toward actual organization were found among students themselves. Some criticized Enoch that this movement was funded from the West, a criticism UESI's founding fathers felt that time would disprove. They adopted a strong financial clause in the constitution that UESI would look to God alone in faith and prayer for the supply of all needs, that no membership fee would be charged, nor would appeals be made to the general public for funds. UESI formulated four aims to give purpose and direction to the activities of campus groups, called Evangelical Unions (EUs) and Inter Collegiate Evangelical Unions (ICEUs), now numbering 220. The *raison d'etre* of UESI is evangelism, followed by a focus on fellowship among believing students and raising a testimony on campus and through missions. Distinctives of UESI include student initiative, an interdenominational stance, the autonomy of EUs, and financial independence.

David C. C. Watson from the United Kingdom; T. N. Sterrett* from the United States; John Moody from Australia; P. T. Chandapilla, the first Indian staff worker and general secretary; and D. Jeyapaul and H. S. Ponnuraj, student pioneers, laid the foundation for student ministry in the 1950s.

The first All-India Camp in Bangarapet (Karnataka) in 1957 aided expansion of the national work. P. C. Varghese and P. Sathkeerthi Rao, then staff workers, pioneered student and graduate work in the 1960s, and Evangelical Graduate Fellowships (EGFs) were formed in several states.

People called of God came, leaving their lucrative employment, and kept joining UESI from the early 1960s, trusting only in God for all their needs. Basic minimum consolidated salary (BCMS) became the mode of salary disbursement from the 1970s. This is a need-based system aiming for equal distribution of finances on a monthly basis. Salary is not based on seniority or qualifications.

In the Indian context, women must be reached only by women. When taboos and social restrictions regarding women prevailed in India, God raised women to work with UESI from the 1960s. To begin with, wives of full-time staff workers and friends of UESI pioneered among women students. Then three Canadians — Mary Beaton, Alison Miller, and Jean Palmquist — joined the staff. Indian lady staff workers joined from 1967 to pioneer and consolidate the work.

The 20th Anniversary National Conference in 1974 was a landmark for UESI, diversifying the movement's expansion. Professional associate groups such as the Evangelical Medical Fellowship of India (EMFI), Evangelical Teachers' Fellowship of India (ETFI), and Evangelical Professionals' Fellowship of India (EPFI) were formed.

The UESI national office is located at 10 Millers Road, Madras 600 010 (Tamil Nadu). As work expanded, UESI faced problems of coordination and communication. The principle of decentralization was discussed and introduced. The North East Region (seven states) and five other states have been decentralized. This has facilitated the speedy expansion of work within states, more graduate support, use of regional language in camps and conferences, and autonomy of the states under the UESI umbrella. Work is now established in all states in India except in Jammu and Kashmir, Himachal Pradesh, and Sikkim. The official organ of the UESI is the English language bimonthly, *Our Link.*

UESI encourages members to be actively involved in their local churches. Several graduates, trained and nurtured by UESI, are full-time Christian ministers in India and abroad. Some are on the UESI staff team.

A hallmark of UESI ministry is the small cell-group meeting for prayer and Bible study led by students on college campuses and at hostels. Personal evangelism by students is emphasized. Quality and not quantity has been UESI's slogan. Hundreds of students from other faiths have come to know Christ through personal work, cell groups, and camps. They face expulsion from home and college as well as other forms of persecution. One student was denied his college scholarship. Discipleship costs in India, and many pay the price.

Some EUs were born in graduates' homes. Graduates' involvement and support form the backbone of the ministry. UESI was affiliated in 1959 with the International Fellowship of Evangelical Students* (IFES), which has over 130 member national movements.

India has 190 universities, about 8,000 colleges, and a student population of eight million. After 40 years of ministry, 27 staff couples, six single staff workers at the national level, several state staff workers, and hundreds of graduates and students find the task an uphill one still. What began as one little cell has now a myriad of shoots like the Indian banyan tree.

Bibliography

UESI Publication Trust, *The Spreading Flame* (1994).

PREMA FENN

United Mission to Nepal

(UMN). The United Mission to Nepal (UMN) was established as an interdenominational mission on 5 Mar 1954 at a meeting in Nagpur, India*. In Sep 1954 a constitution was adopted and eight missions were approved as charter members: Regions Beyond Missionary Union, Church of Scotland Mission, American Presbyterian* Church, Methodist* Church in Southern Asia, Zenana Bible and Medical Mission (now INTERSERVE), World Mission Prayer League, Swedish Baptist Mission, and the United Christian Missionary Society.

Over four decades later, UMN members number 39 from 16 countries, representing a wide diversity of denominations and mission organizations. Twelve are from Asian countries: India, the Philippines, Australia, New Zealand, Japan, and Korea.

Mission agencies, informally linked together in the Nepal Border Fellowship, had been working with Nepalis in the border areas for years prior to the opening of the country in 1951. In May 1953, after several medical missionaries had accompanied ornithologist Bob Fleming on bird expeditions to Nepal, an official government invitation was extended to establish a hospital at Tansen, the main town in west-central Nepal, and maternity welfare clinics in the Kathmandu Valley.

Later, medical work spread to four hospitals with associated community health, nutrition, and mental health programs and a nursing school. As Nepal had almost no infrastructure for development, UMN was asked to work in other areas. Schools were established and vocational training and nonformal education started. In the 1960s UMN began to work in industrial development, a unique approach which set up private companies to help develop Nepali infrastructure. In this approach, poor rural communities are assisted in skill development and organization to improve their quality of life.

The purpose of UMN has always been "to minister to the needs of the people of Nepal in the name and spirit of Christ and to make Him known by word and deed, thereby strengthening the universal Church in its total ministry." The agreement with the Hindu-dominated government prohibited UMN expatriates from "proselytizing," which was interpreted as "the attempt to convert by coercion or the offer of material inducement."

Expatriate Christians participate fully in the life of local fellowships but do not take official leadership positions. By mutual agreement, the local churches and the mission had separate organizations, partly as a result of government policy. This had the side effect of providing opportunity for a truly indigenous church. In addition to the personal contributions of expatriate missionaries, UMN has been able to cooperate with the churches in scholarships for Christian youth, linking local church needs with outside resources, and assisting local church-sponsored social service organizations registered with the government. By expressing God's love in development service and the sharing of their personal faith, the missionaries attempt to express a holistic ministry and witness.

The second purpose of UMN has always been to "train the people of Nepal in professional skills and leadership." The number of expatriate missionaries has decreased, but in 2001 they still totaled about 150 in approved-visa posts, along with spouses and children. Over 2,000 Nepali staff serve in the various projects and related agencies. As UMN moved into its fifth decade, its vision focused on enabling Nepali communities and organizations, including the church, to carry forward spiritual transformation in Nepal.

Bibliography

Lindell, Jonathan, *Nepal and the Gospel of God* (1979). • Metzler, Edgar, "United Mission to Nepal, a Case Study in Wholistic Ministry," *Wholistic Ministry* (1995). • Poppe, Joy, *A Time to Embrace* (1993).

EDGAR METZLER

United Theological College (UTC), Bangalore

First ecumenical theological college in the world, founded by representatives of different churches.

UTC was founded in 1910, the same year as the World Missionary Conference in Edinburgh, Scotland. The concern which led to the decision to establish UTC was the same as that behind the plan for the missionary conference, namely, the commitment to manifest the oneness of the church.

UTC was inaugurated a few months earlier than the Edinburgh conference. Speaking at the golden jubilee celebration of the college in 1960, Eric W. Nielsen of the Theological Education Fund observed that the history of UTC is coterminous with the history of the ecumenical movement.

UTC had its origins at a meeting held at Kodaikanal, a hill station in South India, in Jun 1906. The meeting had been called by J. Duthie, a missionary of the London Missionary Society (LMS) serving in South Travancore. A person who attended this meeting said, "we had nothing but felt need, and a dream." In order to make his dream of an ecumenical theological college a reality, Duthie had called together representatives of four missionary societies working in South India and Ceylon. J. H. Wickhoff of the American Arcot Mission was the first president of the governing council of the college. In 1911 Bernard Lucas drafted the constitution and rules and regulations of the college. The theological basis of the college was defined as "the doctrines held in common by the evangelical churches of Christendom." It was also Lucas who, in 1912, suggested the motto, "Not to be served, but to serve."

It was Duthie's vision to have a theological college which was "something different" with a "broader outlook" and a commitment to meeting "the intellectual and social demands" of the Indian people. The aim of the college was defined as training "a higher class of Agents for work as Pastors, Evangelists and theological teachers."

The first principal of the college was L. P. Larsen of the Danish Missionary Society. He described the objective of the college as providing a "sound theological education." From the beginning, it was the concern of the college to develop Indian leadership and an authentically Indian character for the church.

At the first valedictory address given to the first group of graduates in 1913, G. E. Philips spoke of three distinctive features of the college which have been maintained all through the history of UTC, namely, the oneness in Christ, intellectual excellence, and practical religious service.

It was in 1912 that the 17 Miller's Road property was purchased and the two foundation stones for the library and the chapel were laid by John R. Mott and R. T. Horton, respectively.

In Aug 1910 (the year UTC was established), the members of the college (both faculty and students) formed the Carey Society, named after the great missionary William Carey*. All the extracurricular programs of the college were organized by this society. The Carey Society was affiliated with the Student Christian Movement* and for many years gave leadership to the movement in Karnataka.

In 1911 the South India Missionary Language School was located on the college campus. This reflected Larsen's conviction that it was good for young missionaries to become acquainted with those being trained for the ministry. In 1963, it was integrated with the college as the department of Indian languages.

Another institution located at the college and closely linked with it is the Young Men's Christian Association* (YMCA) Training School. It was another of Larsen's convictions that ministerial training and the training of YMCA secretaries were closely related. This relationship goes back to 1913. World War I interrupted the YMCA training program. After the end of World War II*, the school was reopened at UTC.

The concern of the college for relating the Gospel to other religious faiths and to different issues of society led to the formation of the Christian Institute of Religion and Society (CISRS). The first director of the CISRS was P. D. Devavandan*, who had been a member of the faculty at UTC.

Soon after the senate of Serampore College was established for coordinating theological education in South Asia, UTC was affiliated with it in 1919.

In the early years, theological education at UTC was at the bachelor of divinity level, but with the demands for more advanced levels the college developed master's and doctoral levels. The college has played an important role not only in equipping men and women for the ordained ministry but also for the training of lay men and women for different ministries in the church.

Bibliography

Chandran, J. R., ed., *Fifty Years of Service* (1960); *To Serve, Not to Be Served* (1985). J. Russell Chandran

Ursulines

The Ursulines, founded by Angela Merici (1474?–1540) in Brescia, northern Italy, in 1535, were originally a company of young virgins living in their own homes — this at a time when the only courses open to young women were marriage or religious life within an enclosed monastic framework. The Council of Trent (1545-63) basically changed the structure of the order, but the apostolic drive remained, finding its outlet in the education of young women and in missionary impetus like that of Blessed Mary of the Incarnation, who made the foundation in Quebec, Canada, in 1639 from the convent of Tours, France. Some brief indication of the spread of the order is necessary to understand the roots of Ursulines in Asia.

Canadian Union of Ursulines. Quebec, Canada, was the first place the Ursulines settled for evangelization, and from this fertile ground came the foundations of the Ursulines in China* (1922) and Japan* (1936).

Tildonk Ursulines. Founded by the Abbe Lambertz in the Brabant, Belgium, the first group adopted the constitutions of the Ursulines of Bordeaux (1832), but without solemn vows or papal enclosure. The Ursulines in Indonesia* (1856) and India* (1903) are founded from the congregation of Tildonk.

Roman Union of Ursulines. The Roman Union of the Order of St. Ursula was created at the request of Pope Leo XIII on 28 Nov 1900. According to the last statistics available, there were 3,718 Roman Union Ursulines in 259 communities spread over 29 countries and 134 dioceses. The Ursulines in Thailand* are founded from the Roman Union.

Indonesia. In 1855, after a law prohibiting missionary work had been abolished by the East Indian government, seven Ursulines from Sittard and Maaseyk in Holland set out for present-day Indonesia, a land composed of over 13,000 islands with a population 86 percent Muslim, arriving there on 7 Feb 1856. They had been invited by Msgr. Vranken, bishop of Batavia (now Jakarta). Under the leadership of Ursula Meertens and with the assistance of Vranken, a house was founded first in Noordwijk, Batavia (1856), then a school for girls (1861) and a house in Veltevreden, and another in Surabaya (1863). Other houses were later opened in Bandung (1906), Madiun (1914), Malang (1920), and Bogor (1962). The work of the sisters at first was mainly among the Dutch colonists, especially in educating the Dutch children for whom no other provision had been made. By 1929, after many of the houses had entered the Roman Union beginning with Noordwijk in 1906, the sisters decided to devote themselves more intensively to the young Indonesians. By 1939 the Indonesian houses had been erected into a vice province of the Roman Union, a move which proved a blessing during the Japanese occupation of the country when the missionaries were interned and the Indonesian sisters struggled to keep the educational works alive. From 1965, after the Second Vatican Council favored enculturation, vocations increased dramatically. Indonesian Ursulines now number 274, of whom 230 are Asian, in 25 communities in many parts of the country, including Timor*, Timur, and Irian Jaya*. In Jun 1989, two other groups (a lay group called Kerabat Santa Angela and another, Ursulin Sekulir) affiliated with the Federation of the Company of Saint Ursula were founded to promote Ursuline apostolate among the laity.

India. Through the intervention of Msgr. Meulemann, archbishop of Calcutta, who desired to find another religious order to take over work in the tribal area of Chota Nagpur in Bihar Province from the Loreto Sisters, who were having to withdraw, four sisters from Tildonk, Belgium, arrived in Ranchi, Bihar, on 13 Jan 1903. While they made efforts to learn the local language, they were greatly helped by the Daughters of St. Anne, a native congregation with whom they worked. From the beginning, the Ursulines concentrated their efforts on the poorest and most needy among the tribal peoples, mainly in a wide variety of educational works. From 1919, tribal young women from Bihar Province were admitted into the order, then others from Kerala in the south, Madya Pradesh, and Mysore. Their work now includes not only education at all levels but also medical* services in hospitals and clinics, and catechesis. They number over 450 religious in more than 54 communities spread over Bihar and Madya Pradesh, up to Nagaland, Assam, and West Bengal. Because of the vast distances covered by these Ursulines, they were divided in 1994 into two provinces and a regional group.

China. On 22 Jul 1922, three Ursulines, Marie du Rosaire Audit, Marie de L'incarnation Guay, and Marie de la Croix Davis, from the Canadian community of Stanstead, founded from Quebec in 1884, landed in Swatow (present-day Shantou) in Guangdong Province, China. They immediately set about beginning the works of the Holy Childhood, founding an orphanage and a primary school. In 1923 they received an indult of affiliation to the Roman Union, dependent on the province of the north of France, and were joined by other Ursulines of various nationalities, enabling them to found before 1930 another primary school in Chao Chou Fu and a congregation of Chinese virgins in Hopo. By 1933, the Chinese mission was joined with that of Thailand* as one Asian entity, while in 1947 a wider grouping with Indonesia came into being. This was largely due to the entry into the order of Chinese postulants as early as 1929 and the increase of missionaries. The outbreak of the Japanese War did not completely stop the increase of educational works. Classes were opened in Stella Matutina High School, Swatow, in 1937, but the arrival of Communism*; the expulsion of missionaries; the imprisonment of the principal of Stella Maris, Marie Augustin Zing; and the return of the other Chinese sisters to their villages closed down the works in China by 1952. In 1958 the entry into the order of young Chinese from Swatow (through France) and the United States made possible a foundation in Hualien, Taiwan* (then Formosa), under the leadership of Ursula Blot. The apostolic stress was still on education both in Hualien and later (1964) in Kao-hsiung, except for the foundation of the Institute of Saint Martha for aboriginal girls by Msgr. Verineux, of which Blot was the first superior general. In 1972 a foundation was made in Taipei. Taiwan became the province of China of the Roman Union in 1984, while the Institute of Saint Martha received its first native superior in the same year. Ursulines in Taiwan are now engaged not only in education but also in parish work, spiritual leadership, youth work, and work for the Chinese bishops' conference. They number 23 sisters in three communities, with one working in the Philippines* and another in Hong Kong. All but three are Chinese. On 27 Jan 1995, eight laypersons made their commitment to the Friends of Angela, an informal lay association founded in 1991 to promote spiritual life among the members and Ursuline educational apostolate.

Thailand. The Ursulines have been in Thailand since 1924. Four sisters from Belgium, Yugoslavia, and France, previously destined for China, were "re-routed" in mid-ocean and disembarked in Bangkok not really knowing what they were destined for there. They settled in the parish of Calvary, opening a poor school. In 1928, with increased numbers from Holland, Italy, France, Belgium, and the United States, Mater Dei School, Bangkok, was opened. In 1932 the sisters were able to open Regina Coeli in Chiengmai, northern Thailand. In 1955 the Thai province opened another school in one of the poorer sections of Bangkok, Regina Mundi, better known by its Thai name of *Vasuvedi*. In 1964, with the cooperation of the Jesuits, a student center and hostel were opened in Chiengmai to serve the needs of the student population there, while in 1965 in Bangkok, the National Catechetical Center and Sister Formation Institute were established under the initiative of Theodore Hahnenfeld. Yet another project, this time in social development, was put in hand in 1974 in Chombung, diocese of Rat Buri. It has been followed by others in recent years. The province of Thailand numbers some 45 sisters, of whom 25 are Thai, living in six communities. From belonging first to the province of the north of France, then being joined with Indonesia in 1938, the mission became a province in 1955 and received its first Thai provincial, Mary Joseph Dardanaranda, at that time. Leadership is now almost all Thai.

Japan. The province of Japan* was founded by three

Ursulines from Quebec on 15 Oct 1936. Against a historical background of religious persecution from the time of Paul Miki and his companions, crucified in Nagasaki on 5 Feb 1597, up to the end of the 19th c., the three Canadians settled in Sendai after living for 10 months with the Dominican sisters of Tsunogorocho. A further three Ursulines arrived in Sep 1937, and three more in 1939, enabling the completion of the school in 1940. Beginning in 1941, various sisters were interned for the duration of the war, but in 1948 a second foundation was made by the Canadian Ursulines of Rimouski (founded from Quebec in 1906). They settled in Hachinohe, opening a school there. In Sep 1953, the three Canadian provinces formed the Canadian Union, thus allowing for union among the Ursulines in Japan too. The two missions were united in dependence on the province of Quebec until they became a separate province in Jul 1975. By then there was a small foundation in Yagi, diocese of Kyoto, and another in Tokyo (1972). The year 1993 saw the foundation from Japan of a community and novitiate in Mati, Davao Oriental, Philippines. There are nearly 70 Ursulines in Japan. Leadership is almost all Japanese.

Bibliography

Rio, Marie-Benedicte, *History and Spirituality of the Ursulines* (1992). • NN, *Gedenkboek van de Religieuzen der Rom. Unie op Java* (1935). • Lembaga Pendidikan S. Ursula, *Mengenang "Santa Ursula"* (1983).

Ellen Mary Mylod

Vagnoni, Alphonsus

(b. 1566; d. 1640). First Italian Jesuit* missionary in Shanxi, China*.

Vagnoni arrived in Macau in 1605 and moved on to Nanjing. In 1616 he was the first missionary to be imprisoned when the Chinese magistrate, Shen Que of Nanjing, filed charges against missionaries. In 1617 Vagnoni and Alvare de Semedo were deported to Macau*. Semedo reentered China by changing his Chinese name. Vagnoni followed suit, changing his Chinese name from Wang Feng Xiao to Gao Yi Zhi. In 1625 Vagnoni was invited to Jiangzhou by Han Lin, a well-known scholar in Shanxi who was greatly influenced by Xu Guangqi*. With the help of Han and another man of high standing who was converted in Beijing, Vagnoni was able to baptize 200 people in the first year, including 60 from the educated class. He baptized 500 in the second year. By 1630 Vagnoni had baptized 2,000 people. Vagnoni remained for a long time in Jiangzhou and preached in other places as well. When he died, the church numbered 8,000. Vagnoni wrote several Chinese books on the teaching of the Catholic Church and education, including *A Brief Explanation of Church Doctrine, The Life of Holy Mother,* and *The Life of Saints in the Catholic Church,* which were all published in Jiangzhou.

Bibliography

Latourette, Kenneth Scott, *A History of Christian Missions in China* (1929). • Vath, Alfons, *Johann Adam Schall von Bell, S.J. (1592-1666)* (1991).

China Group

Valignano, Alessandro

(b. 1538; d. 1606). Italian missionary and visitor to the East for the Society of Jesus (Jesuits*).

Valignano came from an Italian noble family. He obtained his doctorate of law at the University of Padua before he was 20. Joining the Society of Jesus in 1566, he was appointed Visitor to the Eastern Missions of the Society of Jesus in 1573. Leading a team of about 40 Jesuits, he sailed from Lisbon on 23 Mar 1574, arriving in Goa on 6 Sep. In 1578, on his way to Japan*, Valignano stopped in Macau* for 10 months, making a study of conditions in China*. He concluded that Jesuit missionaries entering inland China should be "Sinicized" and learn the Chinese language and script. It was a landmark decision which influenced Jesuit policy in China. In 1583 Ruggieri* and Matteo Ricci* succeeded in getting into inland China and established the first residence of the Jesuit mission in Zhaoqing (Guangzhou, a city west of Canton). Valignano continued his journey to Japan, where he personally conducted evangelistic meetings and supported the adaptation of mission work to Japanese culture. He returned to Macau again and approved of Ricci and the other Jesuits who dressed as literati and studied Confucian philosophy in an attempt to create a Chinese Christianity. Illness prevented him from making a tour of the various Jesuit residences in China. He died in Macau on 20 Jan 1606. In his journals, Matteo Ricci attributed the founding of the Catholic Church in China to him.

Bibliography

Dunne, George H., *Generation of Giants* (1962). • Dehergne, Joseph, *Repertoire des Jesuites de Chine de 1552 a 1800* (1973). • Moran, J. F., *The Japanese and the Jesuits, Alessandro Valignano in Sixteenth Century Japan* (1993). • Ross, Andrew C., *A Vision Betrayed: The Jesuits in Japan and China, 1542-1742* (1994). • Schütte, J. F., *Valignano's Mission Principles for Japan* (1980).

China Group

Van Bik, David

(b. Chin Hills, Myanmar, 28 Jul 1926). Christian educator and translator in Myanmar*.

Van Bik was born the son of Chawn Tur, a pioneer preacher whose zeal led him to different villages to proclaim his faith in Christ. He died when Van Bik was ten years old, leaving bleak prospects for his widow and four children, especially in the area of education.

When Van Bik passed the fourth standard, a Karen* Christian, the subinspector of schools for the Chin* Hills who was also his father's mentor, offered to help him study at the only high school in Chin Hills, the Government High School in Falam. He studied there for three years until the outbreak of World War II*, when all educational institutions in Myanmar were closed. He also worked under the British government.

Van Bik resigned from government service in 1945 to study at the Presbyterian* Theological College in Cherra Poonjee, Assam, India* (where he completed a three-year theological training), and in the Serampore College matriculation courses in 1949. He returned the same year and taught for two years in the Chin Bible Training School in Hakha, Chin Hills, started by American Baptist* missionaries Robert G. Johnson and his wife in 1948.

Van Bik continued his theological studies at the Burma Divinity School (Myanmar Institute of Theology) in Insein and graduated with a bachelor of theology degree in 1955. He resumed teaching at the Chin Bible Training School until 1957, when he was ordained to the Gospel ministry at the Zomi (Chin) Baptist Convention meetings in Bualkhua, which coincided with the fiftieth anniversary celebration of the first conversion in that area.

In 1957 he studied for a master of arts degree at the Berkeley Baptist Divinity School (American Baptist Seminary of the West) in Berkeley, California, USA, returning in 1959 to serve as principal of the Zomi Theological Seminary in Falam (the former Chin Bible Training School in Hakha) until 1963.

When the military gained power in Myanmar in Mar 1962, it was evident that the days of the missionaries were numbered. The urgent need to translate the Bible into the Chin language led Van Bik to resign from the seminary to become a full-time Bible* translator. He worked with Robert G. Johnson mainly on the Old Testament until all missionaries were expelled midway through 1966. Continuing alone, Van Bik completed the Old Testament in 1972 and the New Testament in 1976.

Though the manuscripts were ready in early 1977, there were no facilities for printing them in Myanmar. Travel both within and outside of Myanmar was restricted and dangerous, and the borders were virtually closed. Anyone might be subjected to a body search without warning. Nevertheless, through the courtesy of the Bible Society* of India*, upon the request of the United Bible Societies, 10,000 copies (financed by the International Ministries of the American Baptist Churches, USA) were printed and brought into the Chin Hills in 1979. These were distributed within one year, leading to a second printing of 5,000 copies and a third of 10,000 copies.

Van Bik translated seven other books into the Chin language and wrote an English-Chin dictionary, Bible commentaries (1 and 2 John, Ephesians, Hebrews, Luke, Acts, and Daniel), as well as books on the Holy Spirit and the Pentecostal movement.

In 1990 the Chin Christians opened a Christian College in Hakha, Chin State, with Van Bik as principal. On 21 May 1994, the American Baptist Seminary of the West conferred on him an honorary doctor of divinity degree.

Sang Awr

Van Lith, Franz G. I. M.

(b. Oirskot, Netherlands, 1863; d. Semarang, Central Java, 1926). Founder of Javanese Catholicism in Central Java and advocate of cultural evangelism.

Van Lith entered the Jesuit* novitiate in Holland in 1881. After ordination, he was sent to do mission work in Java in 1896. Convinced the Gospel could be preached successfully only if the missionary knew the language, customs, and ways of thinking of the people, he settled in the small town of Muntilan (Central Java) to live among the Javanese.

In 1904, van Lith baptized 194 villagers in Sendangsono* in mountainous Kalibawang. This is regarded as the start of the Catholic Church among the Javanese. In the same year, he opened a primary school in Muntilan, followed by several secondary schools, a teacher training college (1906), and a minor seminary (1911). His former pupil, Mgr. Soegijapranata*, said that van Lith "trained us to become people aware of their dignity, who could achieve something on their own, ready to sacrifice and to defend their rights and that of their religion."

In 1918, van Lith was appointed a member of the Education Council *(Onderwijsraad),* where he defended the importance of the Javanese language in education. As a member of the Commission for the Revision of the Political Structure of Netherlands India *(Herzienings-Commissie),* he questioned the Dutch majority in the Consultative Parliament *(Volksraad).* Because he attacked colonialism* by justifying Javanese rights to independence, the Dutch ambassador at the Vatican denounced him "as a very dangerous person." His article in the Dutch magazine *Studien,* "The Policy of the Netherlands in Respect to Netherlands India" (1922), became the inspiration for young Catholic Javanese to start political training and actions. For health reasons, he had to go on leave (1920-24). Upon his return to Java, he started several schools in Semarang. He died two years later. Many of his students later occupied important positions in the church, society, and government.

Bibliography

Van Rijckevorsel, L., *Pastoor Francisco van Lith SJ: De Stichter van de Missie in Midden-Java 1863-1926* (1952). • Van Klinken, Gerry, "Power, Symbol and the Catholic Mission in Java: The Biography of Frans van Lith S.J.," *Documentatieblad voor de Geschiedenis van de Nederlandse Zending en Overzeese Kerken* 4 (1997).

Adolf Heuken

Vat, Martin

(fl. 1670). One of the first seven Tonkinese catechists ordained to the Catholic priesthood.

Vat was ordained on 14 Feb 1670 by Bishop Pierre Lambert de la Motte* (1624-79) of the *Missions Étrangères de Paris* (MEP, Paris Foreign Mission Society*) and vicar apostolic of Cochin China, on the occasion of the First Synod of Tonkin held at the Christian village of Dinh-hien in Nam Dinh Province. The other six priests were Anthony Van Huc, Philip Nhum, Simon Kien, James Van Chu, Leo Thu, and Vitellus Tri.

Vat was 66 years old and the leading Tonkinese priest of his time. In a 12-month period in 1666-67, he and another catechist converted and baptized 3,000 new Christians in the provinces of Nghe-Ane and Buchinh. Some 1,500 of these, especially those of the villages of Ke-nam and Ke-song, were baptized by Vat's own hands.

Bibliography

Launay, A. C., *Histoire Generale de la Societe des Missions-Etrangeres* (1894). • De Frondeville, H., "Pierre Lambert de la Motte, Eveque de Beryte (1624-1679)," *Revue d'Histoire des Missions,* Vol. 1 (1924).

T. Valentino Sitoy, Jr.

Vath, Charles

(b. Niederlahnstein, Germany, 12 Oct 1909; d. Kraneuchal, Germany, 18 Aug 1974). Director of the Hong Kong Catholic Center, founder and president of Caritas*–Hong Kong (1953-68), and president of Caritas Internationalis (1972-74).

After his studies, Vath was sent by his firm (Bayer) to China* in the 1920s as a businessman. There he gained experience and success in Shanghai, Guangzhou, and other cities. In 1948 he resigned from his business career and joined the Beda College in Rome for his philosophical and theological studies, where he was ordained a priest in Mar 1952. In the same year, he returned to Hong Kong* and was appointed director of the Catholic Center.

Vath supervised all of the center's activities with care, finding the present permanent location in the Grand Building. In Jul 1953 he started an emergency assistance scheme, which gradually grew into Caritas–Hong Kong. In Jan 1961 he was honored with the title of monsignor.

In the same year, he left the directorship of the Catholic Center to become bishop's delegate for all the cultural, social, and charitable services of the diocese, as president of Caritas–Hong Kong. He not only enlarged the services of Caritas in many social fields with the help of local resources (contributing to its rapid growth), but also, being the Far Eastern representative of Misereor, the German Catholic bishops' social aid agency, he had to be always on the move to examine and control its several projects, despite his intermittently ill health.

In 1968 Vath was asked to take up the responsibilities of Misereor all over the world. When he returned to Germany, Caritas was an organization well established, managed by competent personnel, and much appreciated by all the people of Hong Kong.

In 1972 he was elected president of Caritas Internationalis, a post he kept until he succumbed to cancer in 1974.

Bibliography

Caritas-Hong Kong, 40 Years of Partnership in Love and Service (1993).

Sergio Ticozzi

Vaz, Joseph

(b. Goa, 21 Apr 1651; d. Kandy, 16 Jan 1711). Known as the "saint" and "apostle" of Sri Lanka*.

Vaz was born to a Brahmin family in Konkan. He received his theological education at the Dominican* Academy of St. Thomas Aquinas in Goa and was ordained in 1676. Hearing of the difficulties that the Catholics faced in Sri Lanka under the Dutch, he desired to go there. Before visiting the island, he served three years as superior of the Kanara mission (1681-84). On his return to Goa, he joined the Oratorians, then just recently established. He soon became the congregation's superior.

In 1686, accompanying a lay brother, he arrived in Jaffna disguising himself as a beggar. He secretly ministered to the Catholics on the Jaffna Peninsula. On many occasions, the people who attended masses he offered were punished by the Dutch authorities.

After one year's work in Jaffna, Vaz went to Vanni and, from there, to Puttalam. Since this town was in the domain of the king of Kandy, he was able to minister to the Catholics there and slip incognito into the predominantly Catholic town of Chilaw in the Dutch territory. He remained in Puttalam for 18 months.

Vaz proceeded to Kandy and was taken prisoner as a Portuguese spy. He utilized the time in prison to learn the Sinhala language. When he was freed one year later, he was able to converse with the people in that language. Eventually he won the confidence of the king of Kandy. The king not only allowed him to preach in Kandy, but also gave him permission to visit the Dutch territory.

Vaz could mingle with the Sri Lankan population without being noticed by the Dutch authorities. This was an advantage the European priests lacked. For nearly 10 years, Vaz was the only priest on the island. Therefore he appointed lay leaders known as *muhuppu* (native wardens) and *annavi* (catechists) to care for the religious needs of the Catholics in the Dutch territory. The bishop of Cochin appointed him vicar-general of Sri Lanka in 1699. Two Oratorians arrived in the same year to join his band. The priests instructed the people faithfully. When Vaz had a sufficient number of priests, he sent them to visit the Catholics at least once a year.

All the Oratorian priests lived in poverty*. They received neither stipends nor subsidies. Vaz laid the foundation for nearly one-and-a-half centuries of Oratorian ministry in Sri Lanka. Because of his efforts, the Roman

Catholic* religion survived the repression of the Dutch for over a century.

The remarkable spread of the faith made the Catholic Church consider conferring ecclesiastical honors upon Vaz. But he managed to resist. By the time he died, he was revered for his holiness of life, and there were more than 70,000 people who openly professed the Catholic faith in Sri Lanka. When the pope visited Sri Lanka in 1995, Vaz was canonized as the saint of Sri Lanka.

Bibliography

Perera, S. G., *Historical Sketches* (1939). • Perniola, V., *The Catholic Church in Sri Lanka; The Dutch Period*, Vol. I (1983).

G. P. V. Somaratna

Venn, Henry

(b. Clapham, England, 10 Feb 1796; d. Mortlake, England, 13 Jan 1873). Anglican evangelical missionary statesman and administrator.

Venn was brought up in Clapham, where his father, John, was vicar of Holy Trinity, the church attended by the members of the "Clapham sect," as William Wilberforce, Henry Thornton, and others were known. His grandfather, also Henry, had been a leading figure in the evangelical revival and a well-known preacher, highly regarded by his grandson, who compiled a volume of his life and letters in 1834. Venn was educated at Queens' College, Cambridge. In 1819 he became a fellow of the college and was ordained a deacon. After serving as a curate in the City of London and tutor at his old college, through the influence of Wilberforce he was appointed to St. John's, Drypool, Hull. There he married Martha Sykes in 1829. After Hull (1827-34), he returned to London as incumbent of St. John's, Holloway (1834-46), one important reason being his wish to resume his work with the Church Missionary Society (CMS), begun when he was a curate in 1828. After the loss of his wife in 1840, Venn assumed the work of the CMS as honorary secretary, effectively chief executive of this influential and extensive Victorian multinational agency, to which he devoted the rest of his working life (1841-72).

Venn's period was one of the growth of the British Emipre and, with it, the development of the Church of England into the Anglican Communion. He was influential in achieving recognition for the voluntary society (CMS) by the episcopate, and he set out his understanding of the relationship in a document which became normative for the society, the appendix to the 39th Report of 1838. Nevertheless, he found himself in dispute with the evangelical bishop of Calcutta, Daniel Wilson, and with the first bishop in New Zealand, G. A. Selwyn. At home, Venn faced the exaltation of the episcopacy associated with J. H. Newman and the Tractarian movement at Oxford, which also resulted in the idea of "missionary bishops," bishops understood as leaders of missionary work and advocated by Wilberforce's son, Samuel, a high churchman and bishop of Oxford. Venn, by contrast, viewed bishops as the "crown" of the church's building, not its foundation, to be introduced after initial evangelism and church planting. His wish was for an indigenous episcopate, as in the case of the African Samuel Crowther (consecrated in 1864), and failing this, at least pastors fluent in the language of the people, such as W. A. Russell, consecrated for North China in 1872.

As a missionary strategist, Venn laid great emphasis on the planting of the indigenous "native" church. He set out his views in three memoranda, in 1851, 1861, and 1866. It was to occur by a movement from below, small cells or "companies" coalescing into larger groupings which would become the "Native Pastorate Church." Such churches would be "self-governing, self-supporting, and self-extending," a three-self formula which Venn shared with his contemporary, Rufus Anderson of the American Board of Foreign Commissioners (see Nevius Method). The first native pastorate church was set up in Sierra Leone in 1861, but Venn's ideas were influential also in India*. His ultimate intention was expressed in the term "the *euthanasia* of the mission," whereby expatriate missionaries would give way to indigenous leadership. He also held the view that the missionary had a different calling, as an evangelist, to that of the pastor, a role better fulfilled by indigenous clergy.

In addition to his work for the CMS, which was onerous and has been estimated to have involved him in a correspondence of some 6,000 letters, many of great length and complexity, Venn acted as editor of the *Christian Observer* (1868-72). Apart from his work on the life of his grandfather, he also wrote a study of the great Roman Catholic* missionary Francis Xavier* in 1862. He was created a prebendary of St. Paul's Cathedral, and a bust of him can be found in its crypt.

Bibliography

Knight, W., *Memoir of the Reverend H. Venn* (1880). • Stock, E., *History of the Church Missionary Society* (1899). • Shenk, W. R., *Henry Venn — Missionary Statesman* (1983). • Warren, M. A. C., *To Apply the Gospel: Selections from the Writings of Henry Venn* (1971). • Williams, E. P., *The Ideal of the Self-Governing Church* (1990). • Yates, Timothy E., *Venn and Victorian Bishops Abroad* (1978). • Anderson, G. H., et al., eds., *Mission Legacies: Biographical Studies of Leaders of the Modern Missionary Movement* (1994).

Timothy Yates

Verbiest, Ferdinand

(Nan Huairen) (b. Pitthem, Belgium, 1623; d. 1688). Belgian Jesuit* missionary who served China* in calendrical matters during the reign of Kangxi, Qing dynasty.

Verbiest studied mathematics and astronomy at the Louvain University after joining the Society of Jesus. In 1657 he accompanied Martinus Martini*, a Jesuit missionary returning to China, and arrived in Macau* in 1658. Verbiest first worked in Xi'an, Shaanxi Province, when he entered China. In 1660 he went to Beijing to assist Johann Adam Schall von Bell* and was imprisoned with him in 1664 following the "Tang Ruowang Affair" (opposition to Western methods and science led by Chinese astronomers). Verbiest energetically defended Schall, who was finally released in May 1665 upon the intervention of the empress but who died in 1666. In 1668 the Kangxi emperor again placed calendrical matters under the charge of missionaries, and, being the most familiar with calendrical work of the three Jesuit missionaries in Beijing, Verbiest was appointed to succeed Shall as chief director of the astronomical bureau. The excellence of Verbiest's work is seen in the six huge bronze calendrical instruments he designed and made, currently preserved in Beijing. In 1674 and 1680, he was ordered to make cannons.

Kangxi greatly appreciated Verbiest and made much use of him. He learned Western science from him and accorded him various titles, the highest being the First Officer in the Work Department, the only Jesuit to be conferred such honor by the Qing court. Verbiest successfully pleaded the cause of the missionaries who were deported to Guangzhou after the Tang Ruowang Affair, and they were allowed to return to their respective places of work and reopen their churches. Verbiest served as director of the Calendrical Bureau for 20 years and was instrumental in helping new missionaries entering China. He recommended the Jesuits Claudio Grimaldi and Thome Pereira to become his assistants. In addition to materials on calendrical matters and science, Verbiest also published religious books in Chinese, among them *Discourse on the Fundamental Teachings of the Church* and *Discourse on Good and Evil*. Verbiest wrote and dispatched important essays to Jesuits in Europe defending the need for more missionaries while at the same time encouraging the training of indigenous clergy. Verbiest's grave and those of Matteo Ricci*, Schall, and other Jesuit missionaries have been restored and are located in the Zhalan Cemetery in Beijing.

Bibliography

Dehergne, Joseph, *Repertoire de Jesuites de Chine de 1552 a 1800* (1973). • Pfister, Louis, *Notices biographiques et bibliographiques sur les Jesuites de l'ancienne mission de Chine* (1932-34), pp. 338-62. • Witek, J., ed., *Ferdinand Verbiest (1628-1688): Jesuit Missionary, Scientist, Engineer, and Diplomat* (1994). • "Ferdinand Verbiest, His Life and Work," *Proceedings of the International Conference on F. Verbiest* (1988). • Bosmans, H., "Les ecrits Chinois de Verbiest," *Revue des Questions Scientifiques*, Vol. 74 (1913). • Blondeau, R. A., *Ferdinand Verbiest: als Oost en West elkaar ontmoeten* (1983). • Libbrecht, U., *Ferdinand Verbiest* (1988).

China Group, translated by David Wu

Verenigde Oost-Indische Compagnie. *See* Dutch United East-India Company

Verkuyl, Johannes

(b. Nieuw-Vennep, Holland, 16 Jan 1908; d. 27 Jan 2001). Dutch missionary to Indonesia* and professor in missiology.

Verkuyl came from a large farmer's family who were members of the Reformed Church in Netherland. From 1927 to 1932, he studied theology at the Free University of Amsterdam (founded by Kuyper). Through his membership in the Dutch Student Christian Movement*, he came in contact with people outside the circle of his own church, e.g., Hendrik Kraemer*, who influenced him much when he became a student pastor and a missionary. After graduating, he married M. M. van den Heuvel (d. 1983) and became a minister (Laren, Holland, 1932-36).

In 1934 he was asked to become a part-time student pastor for Asian students, mainly Indonesians and Chinese, studying at the various institutes of higher education in the Netherlands. He accepted and worked among these students, at first part time (1935-36) and then full time (1937-39). He himself considered this work preparation for missionary service in Indonesia, which he had already decided to pursue at an early stage of his career as a minister. Although his main task was to minister to Christian students, he also had contacts with non-Christian Asians, with whom dialogues were organized. Already during those years, he was aware of the "colonial problem." He wrote in favor of Indonesia's independence and participated in an action to promote the revision of the Dutch-Indonesian colonial relation (Sutardjo-petition for an Indonesian parliament).

In 1938 Verkuyl decided to accept a calling to become a missionary minister in Indonesia. As part of his preparation, he studied missiology with J. H. Bavinck at the Free University of Amsterdam and received the equivalent of a master's degree in 1939, less than two weeks before the family set sail for Indonesia. There Verkuyl became a missionary minister of the Christian Churches of Java, grown out of the missionary work of the Reformed Churches in the Netherlands. He was stationed in Purwokerto and served the churches in the Banyumas region, Central Java (1940-42).

After the Japanese invasion and occupation of the Netherlands Indies, Verkuyl, like all other citizens of Allied nations, was interned, but he continued to participate in the various church activities and pastoral work organized in the camp. During discussion about the future, the idea of the Inter-Church Literature Service was conceived, which was implemented after the war by Verkuyl. Another outcome of prison discussion was a study group, dubbed the Verkuyl group, after the war, which became a strong advocate of Indonesian independence.

After the Japanese capitulation, Verkuyl and his family settled in Jakarta, where he became a minister of the Javanese churches. During the struggle for independence, he dedicated himself to what he called in his Memoirs, "the service of reconciliation." In spite of the fact that most members of his church in the Netherlands and the political party affiliated with it favored continuation of the colonial relation, he pleaded in brochures and lectures for recognition of the independence of Indonesia and the reconciliation of the Dutch and Indonesian nations. In 1946 the Netherlands Indies government sent him to the Netherlands to explain the nature of the Indonesian struggle and to plead for a peaceful solution.

In May 1947, Verkuyl participated in the Kwitang Conference in Jakarta with representatives of the Dutch missions and the Protestant churches in Indonesia to formulate the new relationship of equality between the churches in Indonesia and Holland, giving Indonesian churches the prerogative to decide on the assistance they wished to receive from their partners overseas. After the conference, the Verkuyl family left for furlough in Holland, where he wrote his doctoral dissertation about religious freedom under Bavinck and received his degree in 1948.

In 1946 an emergency committee was instituted to set up a center for Christian literature, an idea conceived during internment. It grew to become the Christian Publishing Company *(Badan Penerbit Kristen)* in 1950 and is the present Gunung Mulia. Apart from publishing work (1945-62), Verkuyl also taught at the Jakarta Theological Seminary as a part-time lecturer from 1946 to 1949, a full-time lecturer on behalf of the Javanese Christian churches from 1949 to 1954, a full professor specializing in Christian ethics from 1954 to 1962, and at the Christian University of Indonesia. As a lecturer, he published extensively in several fields of theology (about 30 books, including a six-volume handbook on Christian ethics, which is still in use).

In 1963 Verkuyl retired as a missionary and returned to Holland, where he became the general secretary of the Netherlands Missionary Council (1963-68). From 1965 until his retirement in 1978, he was a professor in missiology at the Free University of Amsterdam. The handbook he wrote on missiology was translated into English (*Contemporary Missiology: An Introduction,* 1978). He became an opponent of apartheid in South Africa. He also protested against nuclear arms, even though his freedom from internment had been related to the use of atomic bombs to defeat Japan.

Verkuyl has consistently emphasized the *missio politica oecumenica,* the ecumenical and political mission of the church in society. He has written extensively on all kinds of social, political, and spiritual issues, such as Marxism (a subject studied since his Indonesian years) and, recently, the new cults (especially New Age). He combines a strong conviction about the absolute necessity of proclaiming Christ and an awareness of the developments in churches and society. In Indonesia, he is remembered for his contribution to the development of social thought in the Protestant churches.

Bibliography

Baarda, T., et al., eds., *Zending op weg naar de toekomst: Essays aangeboden aan Prof. Dr. J. Verkuyl* (1978). • Tan, T. H., *The Attitude of Dutch Protestant Missions toward Indonesian Nationalism, 1945-1949* (thesis, Princeton, 1967). • Verkuyl, J., *Gedenken en verwachten: Memoires* (1983), summarized by the author (especially ch. 20) in *International Bulletin of Missionary Research,* Vol. 10 (1986).

CHRISTAAN DE JONGE, with contributions from PIETER N. HOLTROP

Vertenten, Petrus

(d. 1938). Belgian missionary who served in Okaba (1910-15) and Merauke (1915-25) in southern New Guinea and saved the Marind tribe of Papua New Guinea from extinction; wrote the first Dutch-Marind dictionary with H. Geurtjens and drew the first map of southern New Guinea.

Adventurers from Queensland hunting for birds of paradise (1914-22) brought venereal disease and Spanish influenza (1920) to the Marinds, who, having no resistance, died in large numbers. In 1900, there were 20,000 Marinds; by 1920, only 9,000 were left. The hunters also caused the Marinds to resort to alcohol. They drank as a means of combating the spreading disease. They also organized big feasts where, according to their custom, alcohol was consumed to overcome the mental depression arising from their belief that the many deaths were the result of the new prohibition on head-hunting. Handing out medicine did not change the situation. Therefore, Vertenten, then the only missionary living among the Marinds, wrote several articles to attract the attention of the public and the government to the plight of this remote area. Only after a social democratic member of the second chamber in Den Haag intervened was Vertenten called to Jakarta to explain the situation.

Several doctors identified the venereal disease (1922). The mission built 12 schools in model villages to isolate uninfected Marinds. In 1922 the first Marind adults were baptized. The tribe was saved from extinction.

In 1924 Vertenten accompanied a group of officials needing his advice on how to persuade the Jahrag tribe in the Digoel area to give up cannibalism. His simple advice was to make them breed chickens and pigs. It worked. In the early 1930s, Vertenten and H. Guertjens had to defend their method of saving the Marinds against the accusations of German ethnologist Dr. Wirtz, who wanted the people left unchanged as an interesting object for further ethnological studies.

Bibliography

Cornelissen, I. F. L. M., *Pater en Papoea* (1988) (contains a bibliography of articles and books written by Vertenten).

ADOLF HEUKEN

Vey, Jean-Louis

(b. Araules, near Issingeaux Haute-Loire, France, 6 Jan 1840; d. ?). Vey's parents were peasants and good Christians and gave him his first education. Having manifested his great ability to study, he took his first Latin lessons from the school of the commune. His teacher found that he could study Latin with extraordinary facility. Attentive to his study, he also appreciated the games and could play very well. Unfortunately, he lost one of his eyes playing these games and, as a result, could not see clearly. This physical defect did not affect his intellectual ability. Having noticed the rapid progress of his student, his personal tutor advised his father to send him to the minor seminary of Monistrol in the diocese of Puy. The only obstacle to this plan was his defective eye.

The bishop of Puy, who later visited the commune for some days to administer the sacrament of confirmation, observed that young Vey had great talents and said: "envoyez le vite au petit Séminaire, on verra plus tard" [send him immediately to the minor seminary, and we'll see later]. His premeditation and his decision were praiseworthy. At the seminary of Monistrol, the masters admired Vey, for he was a serious and brilliant student. Later the grand vicar of the diocese asked him to be admitted as an aspirant in the seminary of the Paris Foreign Missions Society* (MEP). He decided to do so and entered the MEP on 5 Oct 1862, to the great regret of his friends and his masters, who saw his departure as the loss of a good subject for the diocese. At Rue de Bac in Paris, Vey, dominated by his vocation, paid all of his attention to developing the necessary elements for the mission in the future. Finally he was ordained priest on 10 Jun 1865.

He received his destination for the mission: Siam. For his departure at Lyon, his parents came to see their son for the last time. They kindly gave him up for the service of God and encouraged him for his mission. Vey departed for Siam on 14 Jul 1865 and arrived there in September, having been welcomed by Msgr. Dupond*, newly consecrated bishop of Azoth, and eight other missionaries.

P. Clémenceau, who had directed the seminary of the mission and also ministered to some Christian families at the place called Assumption for many years, died in January of the preceding year, and no one had replaced him. Dupond did not hesitate to entrust this office to the zeal of Vey. Noticing the high qualifications of this young missionary, he entrusted to him the direction of the seminary and the press of the mission which, with the residence of the bishop, were at that time the only institutions set up in the Assumption quarters.

He devoted his first years to learning the Siamese language. Having observed that knowing only this language was not sufficient for him to work with the Buddhists, he continued to deepen his language skills by learning Pali, which could give him the root and etymology of the words. He succeeded so well that, after Bishop Pallegoix* (who had composed *Dictionarium Linguae Thai sive Siamensis interpretatione Latina, Gallica et Anglica*, published in 1854 in Paris), he may be said to have been the best scholar among foreigners who have lived in Siam.

Dupond departed for Rome and left the direction of the mission to one of his missionaries, who also soon left. Vey was too young to take over and had only been in the mission for four years. So Dupond entrusted the direction of the mission to P. Martin, one of the older missionaries, and gave him the title of superior of the mission.

But Martin was too old to consider the difficult affairs of the missionaries, and so quite often Vey would step in and provide badly needed counsel and advice. In light of this situation, Vey was in fact promoted by Dupond, but the irregularity of the appointment required the Propaganda Fide to step in.

After investigating the story, Rome decided to wait until the temper and melancholy of the missionaries was calmed. Martin seemed to know Rome's intention.

Vey arrived in Bangkok from France in Jan 1874 and was appointed procurer of the mission. Finally, Pope Pius IX nominated Vey apostolic vicar of Siam, bishop *in partibus* of Geraza, on 14 Jul 1875.

Under the direction of Vey, who governed the mission for 34 years, the mission of Siam progressed in different ways. In examining Vey's annual report, one finds that he mentioned the new stations and the new churches or chapels which were established and founded almost every year. In his annual report of 1877, he said that the success of this year was due to the experiences of the year before, and, because of the newly baptized Christians who lived in Bangkok, two chapels were established.

At Chantaburi, a new Christian community was also established in a village where some Chinese Christians were living; meanwhile the missionaries were going to found the new community at Ban Kacha, a village full of Chinese families.

In the province of Ratchaburi at Donkabuang, a native priest who was in charge "est parvenu a avoir un terrain et bâtir un 'rong' servant d'eglise et de catechumenate" [came to have a piece of land and to build a small building to serve as church and house for the catechists].

The most glorious and magnificent church of Ayutthaya, St. Joseph's, was also rebuilt through Vey's initiative. Before the destruction of Ayutthaya in 1767, the mission of Siam possessed a strong, beautiful church dedicated to St. Joseph. The mission of Siam was considered by all the first mission of the MEP, and this church was the first center.

Under the supervision of P. Perraux, the church was rebuilt in 1883 and fully completed in 1891. In 1890 Vey reported to Paris that four stations were founded in the different provinces of Siam.

Up to the year 1907, he still mentioned some new Christian communities which were recently founded. In 1873, when Dupond left the mission of Siam, there were 10,000 Christians, 22 churches and chapels, 49 seminarians, six native priests, and 16 catechists. But in 1909, the last year of Vey's episcopacy, the mission of Siam had 23,600 Christians, 57 churches and chapels with 79

Christian communities, 59 seminarians, 44 missionaries, 21 native priests, 17 religious men, 123 religious women, 21 catechists, three colleges with 861 pupils, 62 schools with 2,692 pupils, and one hospital.

Bibliography

Chumsriphan, Surachai, *The Great Role of Jean-Louis Vey, Apostolic Vicar of Siam (1875-1909), in the Church History of Thailand during the Reformation Period of King Rama V, the Great (1868-1910)* (1990).

Surachai Chumsriphan

Vietnam

The Socialist Republic of Vietnam covers 332,600 sq. km. (128,400 sq. mi.) in southeast Asia. The country is bordered on the west by Cambodia* and Laos,* on the north by China,* and on the south by the China Sea. The two principal geographic regions, the Red River delta in the north and the Mekong River delta in the south, are connected by a narrow, mountainous strip. The principal cities are Hanoi (the capital) in the north, Hue (the former imperial city) in the center, and Ho Chi Minh (formerly Saigon) in the south. In the years between 1975 and 1995, the population more than doubled from 33 to 73 million. The population is rather homogeneous, with 85 percent being Vietnamese, but there are significant numbers of tribal (see Tribal Work*) peoples, such as the Nung and the Hmong, in the highlands. There are also over one million ethnic Chinese, who are located mostly in Cho Lon, a part of Ho Chi Minh City. Religiously, the greater part of the Vietnamese population is Confucian (see Confucianism*). Other major groups include Buddhists (see Buddhism*), who comprise an estimated eight million members; 4,800,000 Catholics; 600,000 Protestants of various denominations; and 3,000,000 Caodaists (see Caodaism), a local religion centered in Tay Ninh.

Roman Catholic Christianity. Christianity appears to have entered Vietnam in the first decades of the 16th c. An edict of 1663 mentions that, in 1533, under the reign of King Le Trang Ton, there was a rescript proscribing the "Da-to (= Christian) religion" which mentioned a certain I-Ni-Khu, a Westerner (probably a priest) who, by way of the sea, had secretly entered the Ninh Cuong, Quan Anh, and Tra Lu villages in North Vietnam to preach the new religion. The first convert might have been Do Hung Vien, the son of a court official by the name of Do Bieu under King Le Anh Ton (1556-73). In 1628 a Spanish priest and world traveler, Ordonnez de Cevallos, published a memoir wherein he reported having baptized Princess Mai Hoa* and even Lord Nguyen Hoang. Generally, historians attach little credence to Ordonnez's tales, especially his baptizing Lord Nguyen Hoang. In 1550 the Dominican* priest Gaspar de Santa Cruz left Malacca* (Malaysia*) to missionize Cambodia* and, on his way, stopped in Ha Tien, South Vietnam. In 1580 two other Dominican priests, Luis de Fonseca and Gregoire de la Motte, also came from Malacca to missionize in Quang Nam, in central Vietnam. In 1583 four Franciscan* priests — Diego d' Oropesa, Bartolomeo Ruiz, Pedro Ortiz, Francisco de Montila — and four lay brothers came from the Philippines* to missionize in the North. The missionary enterprise was strengthened by the arrival in 1615 of Jesuits* Francesco Buzomi, Diego Carvalho, and three lay brothers at Han seaport, in Quang Nam.

From 1615 to 1659 the bulk of missionary work was carried out by the Jesuits, of whom the most famous was the French Alexandre de Rhodes* (1591-1660). De Rhodes arrived in central Vietnam (then known as Cochin China, not to be confused with South Vietnam, also called Cochin China by the French in the 19th c., central Vietnam being called Annam) in Dec 1624; after a few months of language study, he was sent with Pêro Marques to the north (Tonkin), arriving there on 19 Mar 1627. After almost four years of highly successful mission, he was expelled from the country, went back to Macau* in 1630, remained there for 10 years, and in 1640 came back to Cochin China. For five years, during which he was expelled four times, de Rhodes conducted clandestine missionary activities. On 3 Jul 1645 de Rhodes was expelled from Vietnam for good. De Rhodes's extraordinary accomplishments do not consist only in the huge number of conversions he brought about; they also include three long-lasting achievements. First, he set up an organization of lay catechists, of whom two were later martyred, to assist him in the evangelizing work and to guide the church during the missionaries' absence. Second, after 1645 he went to Rome to lobby for the establishment of a hierarchy in Vietnam; as a result of his tenacious efforts in the face of fierce opposition by the Portuguese crown, in 1658 Pope Alexander VII appointed François Pallu* bishop of Tonkin and Lambert de la Motte* bishop of Cochin China. Third, he was the leading contributor to the romanizing of the Vietnamese script, using the Roman alphabet and diacritical marks to distinguish the various tones of the Vietnamese language, and authored several works in Vietnamese.

Missionary work in the next two centuries, though highly successful, met with grave difficulties. Some of these stemmed from the political situation of the country at the time. When Christianity first came to Vietnam, the reigning dynasty was the Hau Le, i.e., "Later Le" dynasty (so named to distinguish it from the Tien Le, i.e., "Earlier Le" dynasty of 980-1009). The Later Le dynasty was inaugurated in 1428 by Le Loi, who assumed the name of Le Thai To after liberating the country from the domination of the Ming dynasty. It officially ended in 1788 with its last king, Le Chieu Thong, but already in 1527 power was wrested from it by the Mac dynasty, which ruled from 1527 to 1592. In 1532, two clans, the Trinh and the Nguyen, rose up to defend the Later Le dynasty against the Mac dynasty. But the Le kings were nothing more than puppets, and the real power was in the hands of the Trinh and Nguyen. Soon rivalries divided the two clans, the former dominating the North, and the latter the South (which at the time included only three central provinces, i.e., Quang Binh, Thuan Hoa, and Quang Nam). Military conflicts between the two families erupted in 1627, the very year de Rhodes went to the North, and lasted off and on for 45 years with seven wars until 1672, without victory for either side. The country was divided into two parts, with the river Giang as the dividing line, until it was reunified in 1802 by King Gia Long of the Nguyen clan, who named the country Vietnam. The rivalry between the North and the South greatly complicated the work of missionaries since each side, especially the Trinh clan, suspected them to be spies for the other and, when convenient, used them as mediators to obtain merchandise and military wares from their countrymen, especially the Portuguese.

The second source of severe problems for the mission in Vietnam was the *padroado** system, initiated in 1494 by Pope Alexander VI, whereby it was agreed that lands discovered by Portugal in Asia and Africa would belong to the Portuguese crown and that no missionary could enter them without its prior permission. At the time the church in Tonkin belonged to the diocese of Macau in China, and the church of Cochin China to the diocese of Malacca in Malaysia, both located in Portuguese colonies. After de Rhodes had succeeded in having French bishops appointed to the two Vietnamese dioceses and having them placed under the authority of the Propaganda Fide Congregation* (founded in 1622 by Pope Gregory XV), friction was created between the earlier missionaries, mostly Spanish Jesuits and Dominicans under Portuguese authority, and the later missionaries, who were mostly French and belonged to the Paris Foreign Mission Society* (MEP), a society recently founded by Bishop Pallu. The jurisdictional dispute between these two groups of missionaries did much harm to the missionary enterprise.

The third source of problems was what has been referred to as the Rites Controversy (see Ancestor Worship). As is well known, this controversy began in China with the so-called Chinese Rites dispute during which the Dominicans, the Fransciscans, and the French missionaries succeeded in having the Jesuits' more liberal attitude toward the practices of offering sacrifices to Confucius and the ancestors rejected and in having these rituals condemned as superstitions. In 1710 Pope Clement XI ratified the Holy Office's 1704 decree condemning these practices, and in 1715 he enjoined an oath of obedience on all concerned, to which all the Jesuits complied. Pope Benedict XIV renewed the condemnation, insisting on the absolute rejection of the Chinese rites in his bull *Ex Quo Singulari* (1742). The Chinese Rites controversy, of course, had repercussions for Vietnam. Bishop Alexander (d. 1738) excommunicated Flory, the superior of the French missionaries in South Vietnam, for allowing these rites. In 1739 Pope Clement XIII sent Bishop Achards de la Baume to Vietnam to bring about harmony in this matter. In 1939, the Propaganda Fide Congregation issued an instruction, *Plane compertum est*, recognizing that the Chinese rites were not religious in character and declaring them to be expressions of devotion and respect toward national heroes and of filial piety toward ancestors, and therefore permitted to Catholics. Only in 1964 was this policy applied in Vietnam.

The last and most severe challenge to the infant church was the numerous persecutions perpetrated against its members by various Vietnamese rulers. It is estimated that 30,000 were killed under the rule of the Trinh clan in the North and under the rule of the Nguyen clan and the Tay Son family in the South during the 17th and 18th cs.; that 40,000 were killed under the reign of three emperors, i.e., Minh Mang (1820-40), Thieu Tri (1841-47), and Tu Duc (1848-83); and that 60,000 were killed by the Van Than movement (1864-85). Of these 130,000 killed for the faith, eight were bishops, more than 200 priests, 340 catechists, and 270 members of the Lovers of the Cross* society, a Vietnamese female religious congregation founded by de La Motte. In 1988 Pope John Paul II canonized 117 of these martyrs.

In spite of these severe difficulties, the church expanded rapidly. In 1933 the first Vietnamese bishop, Nguyen Ba Tong, was consecrated. In 1934 the first Indochinese council was held in Hanoi with the participation of 20 bishops, five religious superiors, and 21 priests, and its policies had extensive implications for the life of the church. Unfortunately, no sooner had the church begun its expansion than the country was engulfed in the independence war against colonialist France, and the 1954 Geneva Accord divided Vietnam into two parts, the North under the Communist regime and the South under a democratic and pro-Western government (see Vietnam War). As a result of the partition, 900,000 Vietnamese, of whom 700,000 were Catholic, fled the North, thereby dramatically swelling the Catholic population of the South. After the exodus, in the 10 northern dioceses there were seven bishops and 327 priests left to serve some 831,500 Catholics. In contrast, in the South, according to the statistics provided by the Propaganda Fide, there were 1,100,000 Catholics, 67,854 catechumens, 254 seminarians, 1,672 catechists, and 1,264 priests in 1957. To commemorate the 300th anniversary (1659-1959) of the establishment of the first two dioceses in Vietnam and to mark the growth into maturity of the church, a national Marian Congress was celebrated in Saigon on 17 Feb 1959 under the presidency of Cardinal Gregorio Agagianian, Prefect of the Propaganda Fide.

On 8 Dec 1960, with the constitution *Venerabilium Nostrorum* issued on 24 Nov 1960, Pope John XXIII established the Vietnamese hierarchy, dividing the church into three ecclesiastical provinces — Hanoi, Hue, and Saigon — with 20 ordinaries, and no longer simply apostolic vicars. Thus, after 400 years of mission, the Vietnamese Catholic Church became a full-fledged church with its own hierarchy.

The church in the North since 1954. Cut off from the

church in the South and the Church of Rome for almost 21 years (1954-75), persecuted by the Communist government, and devastated by the departure of a great number of clergy and laity in 1954, the church in the North barely survived. With its educational and social institutions confiscated by the government and its clergy practically under house arrest, the church limited its activities to sacramental celebrations and pious devotions. It could not benefit from the great reforms instituted by Vatican Council II (1962-65). Even now, there is at least one diocese without a bishop and several with a severe shortage of clergy (e.g., one diocese with only three priests). In the 1990s the government adopted a more open policy toward the church. It allowed one seminary to function in the archdiocese of Hanoi and one for the dioceses of Vinh and Thanh Hoa. In 1994 the government permitted the transfer of Bishop Nguyen Son Um, formerly bishop of Da Lat (in the South), to the diocese of Thanh Hoa, which had been *sede vacante* since 1990.

The church in the South until 1975. Compared with the church in the North, the church in the South was in a far more favorable situation. Not only did it benefit from the massive influx of Catholics in 1954, but it also enjoyed 20 years of freedom (1955-75) that fortunately coincided with a period of extensive renewal in the Catholic Church. The church in the South was making rapid gains; in 1959 it had 1,226,310 Catholics, 1,342 native priests, 715 brothers, and 3,776 sisters. In addition, it exercised an extensive influence on the society at large through its numerous first-rate educational, health-care, and social institutions. A Catholic university was founded in 1957 in Da Lat, and a pontifical theological faculty was established in 1958 in the same city.

The church in the South since 1975. When Communist North Vietnam conquered the South in 1975 and when the country was reunified in the following year, the Catholic Church faced a severe challenge. All its educational and social institutions were confiscated, and almost all its religious organizations were disbanded, from the committees of the Vietnamese Episcopal Conference to parish councils. Hundreds of priests were sent to "reeducation centers," and Archbishop Nguyen Van Thuan was imprisoned and then placed under house arrest. Though regular sacramental celebrations were allowed, permission was required for religious activities with numerous participants. The government restricted the number of priestly ordinations and interfered with the appointment of bishops. For example, Archbishop Nguyen Van Thuan was prevented from succeeding Archbishop Nguyen Van Binh (d. Jun 1995) in the Ho Chi Minh archdiocese; in the meantime Bishop Huynh Cong Nghi had been appointed apostolic administrator of the archdiocese but was not allowed to assume office.

Since 1988, however, the Communist government has adopted a more relaxed attitude toward religious institutions. Six seminaries were allowed to reopen: in Hanoi, Vinh-Thanh, Nha Trang, Ho Chi Minh, Can Tho, and Hue. The number of seminarians grew so large that in Oct 1993 the Vietnamese Episcopal Conference requested the opening of two more seminaries in the dioceses of Xuan Loc and Thai Binh. Besides these official seminaries, there are several underground centers where thousands of seminarians are being trained. The lack of qualified professors is drastic, and the level of academic preparation is far from satisfactory. Recently the government permitted a few priests to go to France and Rome for higher studies. With the victory of the Communists in 1975, all important Catholic educational establishments were either nationalized or shut down. Many books, documents, archives in libraries, diocesan chanceries, religious houses, and private homes were burned for fear of harboring incriminating evidence. The library of the Vietnamese Episcopal Conference located in Ho Chi Minh City was as good as destroyed. Fortunately, the libraries of St. Pius X Pontifical Faculty in Da Lat and of St. Joseph Seminary of Ho Chi Minh Archdiocese have been preserved in relatively good condition.

Since the late 1980s, restrictions on the publication of religious works have been eased. Works on the Bible,* theology, spirituality*, liturgy, and liturgical music* have appeared. Of special note are new translations of the *Liturgy of the Hours* and the *Roman Missal.* Deserving praise is a modern translation of the New Testament with scholarly introductions and notes, the fruit of 20 years of labor by a team of 14 translators. Thirty-thousand copies of this 1,299-page volume, published in Aug 1994, sold out immediately. The translation of the Old Testament has also been completed. In addition, the translation of the new *Catechism of the Catholic Church* sold out.

Protestant Church/Evangelical Church of Vietnam (ECVN). The ECVN, better known as *Tin Lanh* or "Good News" Church, was the work of the Christian and Missionary Alliance* (C&MA). The need for a Protestant witness in this French-controlled peninsula called Indochina (Vietnam, Laos*, and Cambodia*) was first noted by A. B. Simpson in his missionary magazine in 1887. This challenge was pursued by Robert A. Jaffray* while he was stationed in South China in 1889. Due to the hostility of both the Vietnamese and the French, the mission was unsuccessful.

In 1911 Jaffray landed in Tourane (Da Nang), central Vietnam. There he found the representative of the British and Foreign Bible Society (BFBS), who had distributed portions of the Gospel in Chinese and French among the Vietnamese. As the BFBS was relocating its center to Hai Phong in the North, its property was sold to the C&MA. The C&MA commenced its work in Tourane and spread to Hai Phong and Hanoi in the north and Saigon and My Tho in the south. The mission strategy was to learn the vernacular, translate the Bible into spoken languages, distribute Bible portions to the villagers, and preach the Gospel.

A Bible school was established in 1921 in Tourane to train the Vietnamese to preach the Gospel to the people in their own languages in areas inaccessible to missionaries. This was the most important contribution of the C&MA ministry. The Bible school was patterned after Simpson's Missionary Training Institute in Nyack, New York. The main objective was to give the national Christians a thorough education in the Bible so that they could evangelize the whole of Indochina and hasten the return of Jesus (a reflection of Simpson's ecclesiology linked to eschatology).

From one member in 1911, the church grew to 4,115 baptized members in 1927. That same year saw the formation of the Evangelical Church of Indochina (called the Evangelical Church of Vietnam in 1950). The missionaries taught the Christians to support their own workers, and at an early stage many of the churches became self-supporting. Wherever the church was not self-supporting, it was governed by the mission. At a time when the people had strong antiforeign feelings because of French colonial rule, the national leaders believed that self-support was the route to independence and self-government.

In 1938 Chinese evangelist John Sung* visited Vietnam, leaving an indelible mark on the people and the church. His preaching was followed by outstanding revivals, adding more than 1,000 members to the church. Sung introduced a method of evangelism called "witnessing bands," comprising new believers who were sent out in teams to distribute literature and invite people to Christian meetings.

The Vietnamese in the Mekong delta and central Annam were particularly responsive to the Gospel, but work in Tonkin was slow and unproductive. The greatest response, however, was in the South in My Tho and Can Tho, where large numbers of people, even entire villages, became Christians. By 1940 there were 123 churches, 86 of which were fully self-supporting.

By the end of World War II*, all the churches were self-supporting. As the work was successful among the Vietnamese, the missionaries sought to reach out to the tribal peoples scattered in the central highlands of Vietnam, Laos, and Siam (Thailand*). These one-and-a-half million people spoke over 30 different languages and dialects. In the mid-1950s, the C&MA established two main Bible schools for the tribes, one in Da Lat and the other in Banmethuot. There was also a short-term program for laypersons in Pleiku. The Da Lat school trained workers for the Koho tribe and the minorities living in that vicinity. Banmethuot served the Raday, Jarai, and Muong tribes.

The Koho tribe was the most responsive to Christianity. It comprised one third of all the tribes in Da Lat province. In 1955 the Koho church had 1,500 baptized members and 4,100 followers. By 1965 there were 3,551 baptized members and 12,625 followers.

The Stieng tribe, relatively unreached despite missionary efforts since 1953, experienced a revival in which entire villages became Christians.

By 1974 the Tribes Church totaled 45,000 Christians, with a strong church in all the major groups. This was significant in that while the tribes made up only 16 percent of the population of South Vietnam, they comprised 33 percent of the ECVN. Only six tribes with a total of 50,000 people were without a church in their communities.

The wars in Vietnam affected the ECVN physically and financially, but it did come of age, bringing to birth a core of able C&MA Vietnam leaders and a strong Vietnamese church. Men such as Le Van Thai* (president of the ECVN during the three wars, 1941 to 1960); Ong Van Huyen* (dean of Nha Trang Bible and Theological Institute and secretary of the ECVN); and Doan Van Mieng* (president of the ECVN, 1961-75) were some of the outstanding leaders. Throughout the War of Independence (1945-54) and the Vietnam War* (1959-75), the church adopted a policy of noninterference in politics. It believed that every Christian must be a good citizen and serve his country but underscored the church's task as spiritual, i.e., to preach the Gospel of Jesus Christ. But this distinction was never clarified in the individual's mind. This lack of precision caused the church much suffering and bloodshed. Neither the Vietminh (Communist) nor the French understood on which side the Christians stood.

In 1954, when Vietnam was divided into the Communist North and the American Vietnamese South, both the C&MA and the ECVN identified with the American military presence in the South. The 1,000 Protestant refugees who moved south were absorbed into the Evangelical Church of South Vietnam. The rest of the Protestants who refused to move south remained as the ECVN, with no missionary assistance or church affiliation with the South.

The C&MA cooperated with the American and South Vietnamese governments in creating a peaceful environment in the South for the extension of its spiritual mission. Some of the missionaries believed that since South and Central Vietnam were more receptive to Christianity, this division might even be providential.

Between 1955 and 1965, the C&MA and the ECVN joined in a two-pronged strategy to reopen churches closed during the war and consolidate the existing churches for evangelism and church planting. The presence of thousands of refugees and the American presence in South Vietnam led to a profusion of Protestant missions after 1955. The C&MA, the sole Protestant mission since 1911, and its offspring, the ECVN, were challenged by other Protestant missions and denominations. Many of these missions did not share the same philosophy as the C&MA, nor did they see their role in South Vietnam as solely spiritual. Numerous organizations responded to the refugee situation by extending physical and social relief as their primary obligation. The ECVN was in a dilemma.

For more than 45 years, it had believed that the ultimate goal of the church was spiritual and that it must not be distracted by any other option. But new organizations were actively involved in social and educational projects that seemed viable options for the church. As the war escalated (1960-69), the ECVN saw the need to identify with the social and physical needs of the people in order to make the Christian message authentic.

The leprosarium (see Leprosy Work*) in Banmethuot, a joint project of the C&MA and the ECVN, was later assisted by the Mennonite Central Committee (MCC). By 1965 the hospital was treating 170 patients, with 41 clinics in surrounding villages and a total of 5,532 patients. A new hospital was opened in Pleiku, a joint venture between the ECVN and the MCC.

The church also established two primary schools for the tribes in Da Lat and a high school in Nha Trang. In 1966 the church cooperated with a multidimensional organization called the Vietnamese Christian Service, with the MCC taking leadership. The church's involvement in social and educational programs was a source of concern for the C&MA, as it believed there was a definite decline in spiritual and evangelistic zeal. The mission assisted the church in radio work (see Far East Broadcasting Association*), as this was primarily a spiritual ministry. In 1975, when the North liberated the South, the ECVN was broadcasting the Christian message in Southeast Asia 62 times each week.

The Vietnamese Christians suffered heavy losses throughout the protracted war, but the church continued to grow. By 1975 there were 510 churches with 54,000 baptized members; 276 Bible students at Nha Trang; 900 laypeople trained by theological training by extension, and an able president at the helm of the ECVN. In 1975 all the missionaries were repatriated and reassigned new fields. Four Mennonites* remained for about one year before they, too, left the country with hundreds of Vietnamese. All the pastors who remained were ordered by the new government to help rebuild the country. The Bible Institute was shut down. Doan Van Mieng, the church's president, and 500 pastors were given the option of leaving the country, but they chose to remain with their people. One hundred evangelical churches were closed and 90 pastors sent to reeducation camps. Three pastors were executed in 1978.

Ninety-nine percent of the tribes churches were closed, and their pastors sent to reeducation camps. One church leader reported that the church in North Vietnam numbered 13,000 and the church in the South, 130,000. The government expressed the desire to have one Protestant church for Vietnam, but the ECVN resisted the government's efforts for unification and paid heavily for it. There is evidence of a revival in several places in Vietnam, resulting in numerous conversions. Thousands of cell groups and Bible study groups are scattered throughout the country, and the numbers are increasing daily.

Prospects. Despite external difficulties, the Vietnamese Church, both Catholic and Protestant, is vibrant and growing. With regard to percentages, Vietnam has the second largest number of Catholics in Asia, after the Philippines. The number of Catholics is estimated at a little less than five million (about 6 percent of the total population [see below]), and the number of Protestants at just over 600,000.

- Hanoi: total population, 30,424,000; Catholics, 1,769,000; female religious, 983; active priests, 197; Catholics per priest, 8,980
- Hue: total population, 9,700,000; Catholics, 515,542; male religious, 122; female religious, 1,840; active priests, 256; Catholics per priest, 1,939
- Ho Chi Minh: total population, 23,162,000; Catholics, 2,057,334; male religious, 683; female religious, 3,929; active priests, 914; Catholics per priest, 2,251
- Total for Vietnam: total population, 63,286,000; Catholics, 4,800,000; male religious, 805; female religious, 6,752; active priests, 1,377; Catholics per priest, 3,153

Bibliography

Du Caillaut, Romanet, *Essai sur les origines du Christianisme au Tonkin et dans les autres pays anamites* (1915). • Cadière, Léopold, *Résumé histoire Annam* (1911). • Launay, Adrien, *Histoire de la mission en Cochinchine, 1658-1823: Documents historiques I (1658-1728); Documents historiques II (1728-1771); Documents historiques III (1771-1823)* (1924). • James, Violet, "American Protestant Missions and the Vietnam War" (Ph.D. dissertation, University of Aberdeen) (1989). • Taylor, Keith Welles, *The Birth of Vietnam* (1983). • Williams, Michael G., *Vietnam at the Crossroads* (1992). • Karnow, Stanley, *Vietnam: A History* (1984). • Phan, Peter, *Mission and Catechesis: Alexandre de Rhodes and Inculturation in Sixteenth-Century Vietnam* (1998).

Peter C. Phan and Violet James

Vietnam War

Twenty-year long armed struggle (1955-75) between the Democratic Republic of Vietnam* (Communist North Vietnam) and the Republic of Vietnam (South Vietnam) during which the United States (U.S.), Union of Soviet Socialist Republics (USSR), and China* were directly or indirectly involved and which concluded with the victory of Communist North Vietnam and the reunification of the country under the name of the Socialist Republic of Vietnam.

The Vietnam War was the consequence of French colonialism*. In 1858-59, a Franco-Spanish fleet attacked Tourane (Da Nang) and then Saigon. Subsequently, France annexed the three provinces of Cochin-China, the southernmost part of Vietnam, and then in 1867 it annexed three other provinces. In 1874, France and Vietnam signed a treaty which recognized French possession of all Cochin-China and permitted the French to trade in Tonkin. In 1884, France imposed a treaty whereby the entire Vietnamese empire was made into a "protectorate." By 1885, Cochinchina (the South) was a directly administered colony, while Tonkin (the North) and Annam (the center) were protectorates to which in 1887 Cambodia* and in 1893 Laos* were added to form the *Union Indochinoise*.

Before 1900, opposition to French domination took the form of sporadic local uprisings; only in the 1930s did it become a national movement for independence. In 1930, the Indochinese Communist Party was established in Hong Kong*, and in 1941 Ho Chi Minh founded the *Viet Nam Doc Lap Dong Minh Hoi* ("League for the Independence of Vietnam"), known as *Viet Minh* for short, which became openly Communist in the mid-1950s. During World War II*, the Japanese deposed the French administration and disarmed its forces. In 1945, at Japan's behest, Emperor Bao Dai* revoked the Franco-Vietnamese 1874 and 1884 treaties and proclaimed the independence of Tonkin, Annam, and Cochinchina. After the Japanese surrender, the Viet Minh quickly gained control of the country, and on 2 Sep 1945 Ho Chi Minh*, as president of the new Provisional Government, read the declaration of independence which marked the birth of the Democratic Republic of Vietnam.

After World War II, with the cooperation of the British, the French succeeded in regaining control of South Vietnam and subsequently of much of Vietnam, but the struggle for independence continued, despite repeated attempts by the French to suppress insurrection. In May 1954, with Chinese military assistance, the Viet Minh inflicted a decisive defeat on the French army at Dien Bien Phu, resulting in the end of French rule in Vietnam. In May 1954, an international conference on Indochina was held in Geneva, and an accord signed by France, the Democratic Republic of Vietnam, Great Britain, the USSR, and the People's Republic of China (but not the U.S. or the Republic of Vietnam) divided Vietnam into two parts at the 17th parallel, with the stipulation that free elections would be held in 1956 with the aim to reunify North and South Vietnam under a single popularly elected government. As a result of the Geneva accords, almost 130,000 people moved to the North, while some 900,000 (mostly Roman Catholics) moved to the South.

In Dec 1954, South Vietnam achieved complete sovereignty from France. With the backing of the U.S., Ngo Dinh Diem*, a strongly anti-French and anti-Communist Roman Catholic, became prime minister and then president of the Republic of Vietnam in 1956. Diem rejected the Geneva-stipulated popular election to reunify the country and began building the South into an independent, separate state. His efforts to stabilize the political situation of the South, initially surprisingly successful, were jeopardized by the guerrilla warfare conducted by the Communists (the Viet Cong). The Diem government requested and received the help of American military advisors and materiel to fight against the Viet Cong, and President John F. Kennedy sent more non-combat military personnel after the North Vietnamese unified the South Vietnamese Communists into an organization called the National Liberation Front (NLF) in Dec 1960. By the end of 1962, the number of military advisors in South Vietnam reached 11,000, and they were authorized to engage in combat if fired upon. However, the war against the Viet Cong was unsuccessful, and popular dissatisfaction against the Diem government, especially against his family, grew. In Nov 1963, with the tacit approval of the United States, a coup was carried out against Diem during which Diem and his controversial brother Nhu were killed. A series of unstable administrations followed in quick succession, and the political instability facilitated the military successes of the NLF.

Meanwhile, in the North, the Democratic Republic of Vietnam, under Ho Chi Minh's leadership, underwent a political and social revolution in the Communist mold. A controversial land reform in 1953-56, the purpose of which was to eliminate the class of landlords and rich peasants and to redistribute the land, had an estimated 15,000 people killed. This reform was followed in 1959-60 by an equally disastrous movement to establish cooperatives. Politically, as mentioned above, in 1960 North Vietnam decided to support the NLF to overthrow the government of the South.

An incident in 1964 provoked a deeper commitment of the U.S. to the war in Vietnam. On 2 Aug, North Vietnamese patrol boats fired on the U.S. destroyer *Maddox* in the Gulf of Tonkin. As a result, President Johnson succeeded in obtaining virtually unrestricted authority from the U.S. Congress to conduct war in Vietnam. The number of U.S. forces in Vietnam increased from 23,000 in 1965 to more than 500,000 by Mar 1968. To reinforce the NLF, North Vietnam sent its regular troops to the South and relied increasingly on aid from China and the United Soviet Socialist Republic. In Mar 1965, the U.S. began bombing the North in retaliation fro the Viet Cong's attacks on U.S. bases.

A measure of political stability returned to South Vietnam when in 1967 Nguyen Van Thieu and Nguyen Cao Ky were elected president and vice-president, respectively. On 30 Jan 1968, during the Tet (New Year) celebrations, the North Vietnamese and the Viet Cong launched a massive offensive with the hope that the general populace would join them in overthrowing the government. It was a total miscalculation and the NLF suffered heavy casualties, with some 33,000 Viet Cong killed. Though a complete military defeat, the Tet offensive achieved a strategic political victory because it convinced the American public that the Vietnam War could not be won as quickly and easily as the U.S. government claimed. Questions were also raised about the morality of U.S. participation in a war that began to be seen merely as a Vietnamese civil war. Sentiment against U.S. participation in the war was expressed in peace marches, demonstrations, and acts of civil disobedience. In Oct 1968, President Johnson ordered a total halt to the bombing of North Vietnam, and the U.S. and Hanoi agreed to begin preliminary peace talks in Paris, in which South Vietnam eventually agreed to participate in direct negotiation with the NLF and North Vietnam.

After Richard Nixon became president in 1969, he

began withdrawing U.S. troops from Vietnam and instituted a program of "Vietnamization," whereby the Army of the Republic of Vietnam (ARVN) would assume all responsibility for the defense of the country. In 1970, the Vietnam War expanded as the U.S. and ARVN troops crossed over into Cambodia in order to destroy North Vietnamese sanctuaries and staging areas and U.S. planes bombed northern Laos. These events prompted further antiwar demonstrations in the U.S. In Mar 1972, the North Vietnamese invaded the northernmost part of South Vietnam, and President Nixon ordered the mining of Haiphong and other North Vietnamese ports and an intense bombing of the North.

Meanwhile, the Paris peace talks continued, and on 27 Jan 1973 an agreement was reached by the U.S. North Vietnam, South Vietnam, and the NLF. It was stipulated that a cease-fire would take effect immediately, all U.S. forces would be withdrawn and all its bases dismantled, all prisoners of war would be released, an international force would keep the peace, the South Vietnamese would have the right to determine their future, and the North Vietnamese forces remain in the South but would not be reinforced. In Jul 1973, the U.S. Congress made any further U.S. military action in Indo-China illegal.

In spite of the Paris Accords, the war between the North and South continued unabated, with the ARVN significantly weakened by the U.S. drastic cut in military aid in Aug 1974. Meanwhile, the North was preparing for a full-scale and final invasion of the South. In Jan 1975, the North Vietnamese captured the province of Phuoc Long, about 60 miles north of Saigon. In March, they invaded the central highlands and controlled Hue and Da Nang and advanced southwards along the coast. When President Thieu ordered the withdrawal of all the ARVN from the central highlands and the two northernmost provinces, general panic followed, and the retreating armies disintegrated. In April, the Communists threatened Saigon. On 21 Apr, Thieu resigned, to be succeeded for a few days by his vice-president and then by General Duong Van Minh. On 30 Apr, the South Vietnamese government surrendered unconditionally to the Communists.

Thus the 20-year war ended. On 2 Jul 1976, the country was officially united as the Socialist Republic of Vietnam, with the capital in Hanoi. Saigon was renamed Ho Chi Minh City. Besides astronomical material loss, the human cost of the Vietnam War was tragic. More than 1,000,000 civilians on both sides were killed; some 225,000 of the ARVN and some 900,000 Viet Cong and North Vietnamese were killed. Some 50,000 Americans lost their lives. Several hundred thousand South Vietnamese emigrated, mainly to the U.S.

The Vietnam War affected Vietnamese Christianity (predominantly Roman Catholic) in profound and lasting ways. First, it provoked the exodus of 700,000 North Vietnamese Catholics to the South in 1954-55. This exodus practically emptied a majority of northern dioceses of both their clergy and laity, robbing them of vitality, a disaster from which they have not yet fully recovered even today. At the same time, it created huge ecclesiastical problems for the church in the South, which lacked requisite resources to absorb in a very short time the sudden influx of immigrants. In fact, northern Catholics tended to congregate together in parishes of their own, served by their own clergy, and thus maintaining a quasi-independent existence from the church of the South. Second, the war instilled in many Catholics a bitter hatred of Communism and Communists which blinded them to possibilities of collaboration with their ideological enemies for the welfare of their country and for a peaceful resolution of the conflict, even after the Second Vatican advocated such a collaboration. Third, with the presence of Americans, the Protestants were afforded the opportunity for significant expansion in the country. Fourth, the defeat of South Vietnam occasioned another exodus of a large number of Catholics, both clergy and laity, mostly to the United States, thereby depriving the Vietnamese Church of its vital members. Finally, the eventual victory of the Communists and their control over the entire country allowed them to impose anti-religious (especially anti-Christian) policies which are still in vigor at the present time, though in significantly relaxed form.

Bibliography

Brazier, Chris, *Vietnam: The Price of Peace* (1992). • Karnow, Stanley, *Vietnam: A History* (1984). • McNamara, Robert S., *In Retrospect: The Tragedy and Lessons of Vietnam* (1995). • Smith, Ralph, *An International History of the Vietnam War, Vol. I: Revolution Versus Containment, 1955-61* (1983); *Vol. II: The Struggle for South-East Asia, 1961-65* (1985); *Vol. III: Making of a United War, 1965-66* (1990). • Schulzinger, Robert D., *A Time for War: The United States and Vietnam, 1941-1975* (1997).

Peter C. Phan

Vietnamese in Cambodia

The history of the Catholic Church in the last two centuries has been strongly influenced by the presence of Vietnamese immigrants in Cambodia*. The significant proportion of Christian Vietnamese in the church has seriously handicapped the mission to the Khmers.

Khmers and Vietnamese belong to two entirely different and opposing cultural eras. The Khmers belong to the Indian cultural era, are *Theravada* Buddhists, and are an oral rather than a literary civilization, the majority being peasants, soldiers, or civil servants. The Vietnamese belong to the Chinese cultural era and practice ancestor* worship and Mahayana Buddhism*; theirs is a literary civilization, and in Cambodia they are artisans, merchants, and fishermen. At least since the 17th c., relations between the two peoples have been marked by war, annexation of the southern provinces of Cambodia by Vietnam, and even annexation of the whole country between 1840 and 1845, provoking a veiled hostility universally shared by the Khmer people against the Vietnamese "devourers of land." The French Protectorate (1863-1953) stirred up this opposition by using Vietnamese nationals as civil servants in their administration of Cambodia.

In Apr 1970, the racial hatred exploded in the assassination of at least 4,000 Vietnamese nationals and the expulsion of 250,000 others. In 1973 and 1975, the Khmer Rouge expelled Vietnamese living in the "liberated zones," then after 1978 executed those who remained there. From 1979 to 1989, the Vietnamese military occupation of Cambodia favored the arrival of new Vietnamese settlers and exacerbated again Khmer nationalism*.

In 1921 the Vietnamese community had risen to 6.6 percent of the whole population of Cambodia and to 25.9 percent of that of Phnom Penh. In 1970, it consisted of about 400,000 members, or 5 percent of the whole country. Today, a rough estimate of the Vietnamese population of Cambodia is between 400,000 and 800,000, or between 4 percent and 8 percent of a total population estimated at around 10 million.

The presence of about 50 Vietnamese Christians (Cochin-Chinese) near Phnom Penh was recorded as early as 1665. For two centuries, the Vietnamese presence in the church posed few problems; the proportion of Vietnamese residents in the church and in the Cambodian population remained limited. The persecution of Christians in 1858 and 1862 during the reign of Emperor Tu Duc set in motion the departure of Cochin-Chinese Catholics for Cambodia.

The foreign missionaries saw in the immigration of Vietnamese Christians a chance to plant the Christian faith in Cambodia. Moreover, until 1850 Cochin China and Cambodia formed one single vicariate apostolic. In 1850 Msgr. Miche*, appointed bishop of Cambodia and Laos, repeatedly requested that the provinces of Lower Cochin China situated to the west of the Mekong (Chau Doc and Hatien) form once again part of his vicariate, thus enabling "the mission to revive." This was granted in 1870. From then on, there was a shift of the infrastructure of the vicariate toward Cochin China, where Christians were more numerous. From 1869 to 1884, Vietnamese immigrants created more than 20 important parishes in Cambodia. This massive presence of Vietnamese Christians in the church progressively turned the attention of the missionaries away from the Khmer people. From that time, for the Khmers, Catholic and Vietnamese became synonymous and worthy of the same execration. It is therefore not surprising that the churches became the favorite targets of popular revolts (1865, 1885, 1946, 1970, etc.).

After 1902, conscious of this obstacle to the evangelization of the Khmers, a majority of the missionaries sought a return to the situation of 1850. Only one year after independence (1955), the vicariate of Phnom Penh was confined to Cambodian territory. In 1970 the Catholic Church comprised 65,000 Christians, of whom 60,000 were Vietnamese. Even though in 1968 Msgr. Ramousse had decided on the Khmerization of the liturgy as a tangible sign of enculturization, the weight of the Vietnamese remained very heavy.

From Apr 1970, following the deposition of Prince Sihanouk, pogroms and assassinations of numerous Vietnamese and the expulsion of the greater part of them deprived the church of most of its faithful. It was more than decimated. Despite the sufferings and the traumas caused by these events, this was an unhappy yet unique occasion in the long history of the church for the small number of Khmer Christians to take the place which should always have been theirs. But the coming to power of the Khmer Rouge* in 1975 was a disaster which destroyed this new missionary initiative.

After the proclamation of freedom of religion on 4 Apr 1990 and the rebirth of the Catholic Church in Cambodia, episcopal orientation in matters pastoral drew its lessons from the past. Vietnamese Christians were asked to make an effort to learn the Cambodian language and to involve themselves in the social life of the country; in a word, Vietnamese Christians were asked to be missionaries.

In 2000, the number of Vietnamese Christians in Cambodia was estimated at 18,000, still three times the number of Cambodian Christians.

François Ponchaud

Vincentians. *See* Lazarists (Vincentians)

Vivekananda, Swami

(b. Calcutta, 12 Jan 1863; d. Belur Math, 4 Jul 1902). Modern Hindu thinker and organizer, world-renowned missionary monk, and founder of the Ramakrishna* Mission.

Narendranath Datta (Swami Vivekananda's premonastic name) had a traditional pious Hindu upbringing. Having studied at Presidency College and the Scottish Church College, he came under the influence of Western rationalism and humanism. As an active member of the Brahmo Samaj*, he considered the true way of serving God as doing good to humanity. Since 1881, he had come under the life-transforming influence of Sri Ramakrishna Paramahamsa. As his most illustrious disciple, Vivekananda vigorously carried out the mission entrusted to him. As a wandering monk, he toured all over India, after which he dedicated his life for the service of "Mother India" in Kanyakumari. He ably represented Hindu religion at the Parliament of Religions in Chicago in 1893, and swayed it to a considerable extent as "the man of the parliament."

Vivekananda conducted two missionary journeys, to America and Europe, and established branches of the Vedanta Society at various centers for the propagation of Hindu spirituality. In 1897 he founded the Association of Ramakrishna Mission and, in 1899, the Ramakrishna Math (monastic order) for carrying out religious, cultural, and social services. He died of asthma and diabetes.

Vivekananda's mission was successful. He was able to propagate Hindu spirituality in the West and even to convert many to it, the most notable being Margaret Noble, popularly known as Sister Nivedita. He instilled a new sense of pride in the hearts of Hindus by exposing the heritage and glory of India's past. While denouncing religious fanaticism, he dreamt of a spiritual conquest of the West by India. He proposed an international exchange, the West exporting its science and technology to the East and the latter exporting its superior spirituality to the West. He preached an East-West synthesis. He stood for radical transformation of Indian society and opposed the practice of untouchability and discrimination of women. He inspired the cause of nationalism* and the political struggle for Indian independence. He ably synthesized the mystical and practical aspects of religion in his mission. Vivekananda's mission has been so comprehensive and inclusive that many strands of people, such as nationalists, militants, reformers, revivalists, pluralists, and exclusivists, equally regard him as their source of inspiration.

Vivekananda presented Vedantic spirituality as the quintessence of practical and true spirituality which is universal and tolerant. His evolutionary theory of religion ably placed all other religions, including Christianity, below the Advaita Vedanta, which according to him was the highest and final stage of religious experience. This was of paramount significance to Hindu religion at a time when it was severely attacked by some Christian missionaries through their preaching and literary activities. Though theoretically opposed to interreligious conversion, he endorsed the practicality and necessity of *shuddhi* rite (reconversion to the Hindu fold). He was probably constrained in this by the then nationalistic tempo.

Vivekananda was an able organizer, as testified by the very successful Ramakrishna Mission. It has been acknowledged that he was greatly influenced by Jesus Christ's example in organizing a band of disciples to continue his mission. Through reforms and reinterpretation of Hindu concepts in light of modern scientific knowledge, Vivekananda was able to revitalize Hindu religion to face the challenges of modern times.

Bibliography

Baird, Robert D., ed., *Religion in Modern India* (1981). • *The Complete Works of Swami Vivekananda,* 8 Vols. (Calcutta). • Chaudhuri, S. K. R., *Swami Vivekananda: The Man and His Mission* (1966). • Datta, B., *Patriot and Prophet* (1954). • Mathew, C. V., *Neo-Hinduism: A Missionary Religion* (1987). • Sarma, D. S., *Hinduism through the Ages* (1973).

C. V. Mathew

Walanda-Maramis, Maria

(b. Kema, North Celebes, Indonesia, 1 Dec 1872; d. Manado, 22 Apr 1924). Minahasan advocate for women's rights.

Walanda-Maramis was not satisfied with the judicial system in Minahasa, especially in regard to the oppression of women in society. In Minahasan society, the woman's place was in the kitchen, and women were destined to become wives and mothers. Moreover, a woman in the early 20th c. could not choose a husband for herself. Her father provided money for her brothers' education but not for hers. Walanda-Maramis could not accept these inequalities. She believed that God created men and women equal, and she thus rebelled against the unfair customs and traditions in her society.

According to Walanda-Maramis, a family depends on a mother not only for basic household chores but also for the upbringing and education of the children. Therefore, girls must also be educated and trained in order to have a developed and stable society.

She shared these ideas with her friends and sent articles regarding women's rights and responsibilities to newspapers. *Percintaan Ibu Kepada Anak Temurunnya* (PIKAT) — (The Love of a Mother toward Her Children and Descendants) — can be considered the theme of her life. This phrase became the name of the organization she founded which later expanded to many regions in Indonesia.

Bibliography

Matuli-Walanda, A. P., *Ibu Walanda-Maramis: Pejuang Wanita Minahasa* (1983). • Lely, T. P., "Maria Walanda-Maramis: Pahlawan Wanit Pendiri PIKAT," *Maesaan,* No. 7 (Jan 1992). • *Sejarah Setengah Abad Pergerakan Wanita Indonesia* (1978). • Manus, M. B. P., *Maria Walanda-Maramis* (1982).

Arnold Parengkuan

Walandouw, Theodora

(b. Semarang, Indonesia, 21 Jul 1919). Indonesian Christian woman politician.

Walandouw was for a long time active in the *Kongres Wanita Indonesia* (Indonesian Women's Congress, KOWANI), an organization of women at the national level, and was its treasurer from 1948 to 1958. In 1949, when Indonesia's political future was uncertain, she helped initiate and coordinate the Women's Conference at Yogyakarta. The eastern part of Indonesia still formed the state of Eastern Indonesia, and Yogyakarta was the center of the government of the Indonesian Republic. In this conference, women from different parts of Indonesia discussed their fights, duties, and roles in realizing full freedom for the people of the country. Walandouw was elected treasurer of the contact board for the Indonesian Women's Congress. As a member of the congress committee in 1950, she shared in discussing the issue of a marriage ordinance to protect women's rights and appealed to all women's organizations in Indonesia to study the place of women in marriage, especially in the traditional and religious laws. In this organization, she not only struggled for the rights and responsibility of women, but also expressed her opinion on other political issues regarding both internal affairs and foreign affairs. She was the representative member of the Indonesian Christian Women's Association (a part of PARKINDO*) in the film censorship committee from 1950 to 1960. As a Christian woman in the KOWANI, she was trusted to administrate the department of medical* and family* welfare. She was a member of the Indonesian delegation to the Meeting of ASEAN Women Leaders and International Women's Year Post Conference held in Jakarta on 11-12 Dec 1975. Because of her active involvement in politics, she was elected a member of the Indonesian Legislative Assembly in 1977, a position she held until 1982 (see also Feminism; Women's Movement).

Bibliography

Sejarah Setengah Abad Pergerakan Wanita Indonesia (1978). • Simorangkir, J. T. C., *Manuscript Sejarah Parkindo* (1989). • Roeder, O. G., *Who's Who in Indonesia* (1971).

Arnold Parengkuan

Walsh, Pakenham

(b. ?; d. 10 Jan 1959). Irish Anglican* bishop, principal of Bishop's College, Calcutta, and founder of Christushishyasram.

Walsh was a true scholar, an inspiring speaker, and a learned writer. After retiring from his post as principal at Bishop's College, he and his wife became very much attached to the Malankara Orthodox Church. With the cooperation of some members of this church, he started the Christushishyasram at Thadagom, Coimbatore. This ashram* was a new experiment to integrate monastic ideals and family* life in the cultural setup of India* and within the spiritual renewal of the Eucharist. Walsh and his wife donated all their properties and savings to the ashram, which they had already given to the Malankara Orthodox Church.

Walsh's books on church history and the Eucharist are well known. He was also an ardent lover of peace and struggled hard to bring unity between the two factions of the church in India. Both he and his wife were buried at the Christushishyasram*. JACOB KURIAN

Wang Liangzuo

(b. Guangyuan Xian, Sichuan, 1920; d. ?). Pioneer in the anti-imperialist and patriotic movements of the Chinese Catholic Church.

Wang made plans to enter the monastery of the Chengdu Diocese at age 10 and was consecrated a priest in 1948. He did pastoral work in his hometown, where Catholicism had already existed for more than two centuries, and was loved and highly esteemed. After the establishment of the Chinese People's Republic, he sponsored the anti-imperialist and patriotic movements of the Chinese Catholic Church. On 30 Nov 1950, Wang and more than 500 converts, under the direction of his church and diocese, issued a declaration advocating "severing all relations with the imperialists" and "establishing a new church on the principle of self-government, self-support, and self-propagation." Other churches emulated the move.

Wang was one of the sponsors of the Chinese Catholic Church. In 1957 the Chinese Catholic Patriotic Association* (CPA) was officially inaugurated, and Wang was elected a member of its standing committee.

On 16 Dec 1957, the Chengdu Diocese convened a meeting in Chengdu attended by over 100 delegates from 35 cities and counties in Sichuan and took the lead in implementing the resolution of the First Representative Meeting (1957) of the Chinese Catholic Church toward independence and self-government. They chose their own bishop, Li Xitang, who was consecrated in Jul 1958 in the Chengdu Pinganjie Cathedral by Bishop Wang Wencheng of the Nanchang Diocese. Wang was appointed chief of the advisory and consultative councils. In 1980 he was chosen vice chairperson of the Chinese CPA. Concurrently, he was also the chairperson of the Sichuan CPA, a member of the standing committee of the Sichuan Provincial People's Congress, and a member of the Sixth and Seventh Chinese People's Political Consultative Councils. CHINA GROUP

Wang Ming-tao

(b. 1900; d. 28 Jul 1991). Chinese pastor widely recognized as one of the most influential figures in the Chinese church who worked to build an indigenous church upon the principles of self-propagation, self-government, and self-support.

The Chinese world into which Wang was born in 1900 suffered from much sociopolitical turmoil. Since the middle of the 19th c., the Ch'ing Dynasty had been incompetent to deal with successive foreign aggressions and civil rebellions. Eventually, in 1911, under the leadership of Sun Yat-sen*, the Republican government replaced the dynasty, and China* emerged as a new nation in international politics. However, because of internal divisions provoked by local warlords and external aggression by foreign powers, the country was far from being united. The weakness of the nation was blamed on traditional Confucianism due to its alleged inability to modernize Chinese society. The quest for wealth and power precipitated an intellectual revolution, called the May Fourth Movement (1915-1923), which emphasized science and democracy as the means to build the young nation. These developments greatly affected the sensitive mind of Wang Ming-tao.

Educated and baptized in the church run by the London Missionary Society in Peking, Wang grew up in a conservative Christian background. Like most young intellectuals of his generation, he felt the obligation to participate in the task of national salvation. He did not aspire to be a Christian minister, partly because pastors received low salaries and were not greatly respected. But in 1918, threatened by a serious illness, he promised God he would give up politics for the Christian ministry if he could survive. Wang did recover and was faithful to his promise.

From the mid-1920s on, Wang labored to build an indigenous church upon the threefold principle of self-propagation, self-government, and self-support (in that order). His church began in a household gathering in Peking where a few people came for Bible study, prayer, and fellowship. This group grew, and in 1937 the Christian Tabernacle — the name of Wang's church — was constructed. Visible spirituality was the criterion for membership; this kept the size of his congregation small. In 1949, when mainland China came under Communist rule, the Christian Tabernacle had a membership of only about 570.

Several features characterized Wang's church. Simplicity in Christian life and service were emphasized to the extent that anything not mentioned in the Bible should not be done. There were no traditional liturgy, no choir, no offering bags, and no celebration of Christmas. Wang received no theological* education and believed that both Scripture and the Holy Spirit were adequate in the making of God's servant. His preaching was practical and powerful, and throughout his itinerant ministry he unreservedly attacked the worldliness of Christians and the apostasy of the churches. It was his ideal that he should become a model for Chinese pastors and the Christian Tabernacle, a model church.

Doctrinal purity was given first priority in Wang's ministry. He did not often invite outside speakers to his pulpit lest erroneous doctrines be taught to his congregation. For the same reason, not many contributors were welcomed in his quarterly magazine, *Spiritual Food,* which enjoyed a wide circulation. In both preaching and writing, he was a strong opponent of theological liberalism that was gaining popularity in some denominations in China in the 1920s, thanks to the transplantation of the controversy between liberals and fundamentalists in American churches by missionaries.

Ever since Wang had abandoned his political ambition for a total commitment to the Gospel cause in China, he took a firm stand against any form of political involvement. He believed that only the Gospel could save his own kinsmen from sin and corruption. The church must be separated from the state because of the functional differences between the two. This principle of separation was closely followed in Wang's response to the political situations in the 1940s and 1950s.

During the Sino-Japanese War (1937-1945), Peking fell under the control of the Japanese army, which sought to control the churches of North China. Wang was invited to join the Japanese-led Chinese Christian Federation of North China, but he declined on the ground that the Christian Tabernacle was already an indigenous church, not pro-Britain or pro-America. He kept a coffin in his house for the possible consequence of his stance: receiving the death penalty. Indeed, his refusal incensed the Japanese authority, which, however, took no action against him. This amazing turn of events, interpreted by Wang as divine protection, perpetuated his view of political non-involvement and strengthened his willingness to be a martyr. Undoubtedly this prepared him for another crisis in the 1950s.

When the Communists came to power in 1949, the Christian church in China faced the problem of survival under an atheist government. In order to purify the church of "imperialism" and establish complete independence, all foreign missionaries were asked to leave the country. And Chinese Christians were instructed to render their contribution to the socialist reconstruction of the nation. Under the guidance of the Communist Party, the Three-Self Patriotic Movement* (TSPM) was organized to direct the nationwide Christian church (see Communism).

Confronted with the unfavorable religious policy implemented by the TSPM, Wang continued to stay away from politics and refused to give in. Such nonconformity was hardly acceptable to the new regime and led to his imprisonment in the summer of 1955. In the following year, he signed a confession and was released. But afterward Wang was exceedingly sorry for what he had done and thought he had betrayed the Lord. He revoked the previous confessions and was in jail again until Dec 1979.

In 1979, China entered into a new era of Four Modernizations under the leadership of Teng Hsiao-ping. A more tolerant religious policy was adopted which brought about Wang's release. During the 1980s, Wang and his wife lived in Shanghai, welcomed visitors to their home, and shared their experience of suffering for Christ.

The central doctrine of Wang's theology was regeneration in Christ, upon which Christianity stands or falls. Whereas the liberals preached an earthly kingdom of God to be established through human effort, and whereas the Communists envisioned a utopia through revolution, Wang affirmed that only a changed person through genuine rebirth could change society. This teaching has significantly affected the Chinese church today in its outlook on world mission and social involvement.

Bibliography

Wang Ming-tao, *Treasuries of Wang Ming-tao,* 7 Vols., ed. C. C. Wang (1976-78). • Lam Wing-hung, *Wang Ming-tao and the Chinese Church* (1982). • Leslie, Lyall, *Three of China's Mighty Men* (1973).

Lam Wing-hung (taken from "Wang Ming-tao," by Lam Wing-hung, in *Ambassadors for Christ: Distinguished Representatives of the Message throughout the World,* ed. John D. Woodbridge [Moody Press, 1994]. Used by permission.)

Wang Zheng

(b. 1521; d. 1644). Well-known Chinese Catholic in the late Ming period.

A native of Jingyang, Shanxi, Wang passed the highest government examinations in 1622 when he was more than 50 years old. Closely associated with missionaries, Wang brought Western physics, mechanical engineering, and other fields into China*. He was baptized in Beijing and took on the name Philip. In his *Biographies of Chinese Catholics,* well-known Chinese Catholic historian Fang Hao claimed that Wang was probably baptized around the time he met Didace de Pantoja* in Beijing in the winter of 1621 or 1622. Wang knew Nicolas Trigault* and Johann (Joannes) Terrenz*. In 1624, because of his mother's death, he resigned from his position and returned to his village. In 1625 he invited Trigault to his hometown, which marked the beginning of Christianity in Shanxi. Wang learned Latin from Trigault, helped him complete his book *Xi Ru Er Mu Zi* (Materials for Western Scholars), intended to help missionaries learn Chinese by using Latin for the Chinese pronunciation, and wrote a long preface for the book. Wang returned to Beijing in the winter of 1626 and, in 1627, together with Terrenz, translated *Yuan Xi Qi Qi Tu Shuo Lu Zui* (Western Instruments Pictorial Illustrated), a book introducing Western physics and mechanical engineering which had great influence in Chinese academic circles. In 1944, on the 300th anniversary of his death, the *Truth Magazine* of Chongqing published a commemorative issue with articles honoring Wang as one of five distinguished scholars. CHINA GROUP, translated by DAVID WU

Wang Zhenting (C. T. Wang)

(b. Zhejiang, China, 25 Jul 1882; d. Hong Kong, 1961). Chinese Christian politician, businessman, and diplomat.

The son of a Methodist* pastor, Wang studied at the local schools in Fenghua near Ningbo, Zhejiang, and mission schools in Shanghai, Jiangsu, before entering the Anglo-Chinese College in Tianjin in 1895. He matriculated at the preparatory school of Peiyang University at age 14, but left his studies during the Boxer Uprising in 1900 to teach at the Anglo-Chinese College. He then taught at the Provincial High School at Changsha, Hunan, until 1905, when he went to study in Japan and became the secretary of the Chinese Young Men's Christian Association* (YMCA) in Tokyo. He continued his studies in the United States at the University of Michigan in 1907 and then transferred to Yale University in 1908. He returned to China in 1911 and served as secretary of the YMCA in Shanghai.

After the 10 Oct 1911 revolt at Wuchang, Wang was appointed a representative of Hubei to the Hankou Conference to organize a provisional national government. In 1913 he was appointed vice speaker of the Senate in Beijing. He was also the representative of the Kuomintang in Beijing. After Sun Yat-sen's* public criticism of Yuan Shi Kai in 1913, Wang left Beijing for Shanghai. He then became general secretary of the national YMCA while also acting as governor of the 81st District of Rotary International.

Wang was among the five Chinese delegates sent to the Paris Peace Conference (1919-20). They prevented the transfer of Shandong to Japan*, insisting on its return to China*. Wang returned to Shanghai in 1920 to concentrate on business enterprises. He was president of China College in Beijing from 1921 to the 1940s. In 1922 Wang was appointed minister of foreign affairs in Beijing, where he was acting premier for one month (mid-Dec 1922 to mid-Jan 1923). In 1924 he negotiated two agreements with the Russians on China's behalf, but both were repudiated by the Chinese cabinet.

From 1928 to 1931, Wang was foreign minister of the national government. He resigned after an almost fatal attack by students angry at the government's failure to retaliate when the Japanese invaded Shenyang (Mukden) in Sep 1931. He went to the United States as the Chinese ambassador from 1936 to 1938. He then went to Hong Kong*, where he helped the Bank of Communications relocate some of its assets to Manila, Philippines*. He returned from Hong Kong and retired to Chongqing, Sichuan. In 1944, the same year of his wife's death, Wang was appointed chairman of the Executive for Yuan's war crimes investigation commission. He remarried in 1946. After the Communist takeover of China, he returned to Hong Kong, where he worked as chairman of the board of directors for the Pacific Insurance Company.

Bibliography

Boorman, Howard L., ed., *Biographical Dictionary of Republican China,* Vol. III (1970). CHINA GROUP

Wang Zhiming

(b. Yunnan, China, 1908; d. 1973). Christian pastor and martyr.

Little is known of Wang's childhood and youth. He grew up in Wuding County in the mountains of Yunnan Province, where he attended Christian schools, and as a young man he taught in a similar school for over a decade. Later he became an evangelist and was eventually elected chairman of the Sapushan Church Council in Wuding in 1944, becoming general superintendent of all ethnic minority churches in Wuding and Lequan Counties in 1949. He was ordained a pastor in 1951 or 1952.

Among the Miao, an ethnic group known as the Hmong in other parts of Southeast Asia, Christianity was very strong. Their shared faith, the result of Western missionary activity in the early 20th c., helped shape an ethnic identity among what was an impoverished and weak community.

After 1949, Wang responded positively to overtures of cooperation with the new government of the People's Republic of China. He supported the Chinese Christian Patriotic Three-Self Movement* and was even named a model worker. But with the outbreak of the "Anti-Rightist Movement" in 1958, Wang refused to denounce landlords and former missionaries and counseled forbearance to Miao Christians. As a result, he increasingly ran into political difficulties.

During the Cultural Revolution, Wuding County became a focal point of attacks on religion. Wang was declared a counterrevolutionary and made an object of criticism by the Red Guards. Twenty-one Christian leaders, among them Wang Zhiming, were imprisoned in Wuding between 1969 and 1973. He was sentenced to death in 1973 and executed at a mass rally in December of that year. Christian protests immediately afterwards threw the rally into confusion, demonstrating that the attempt to eradicate religion in Wuding was a failure.

As part of the government's efforts to correct the wrongs of the Cultural Revolution, Wang was posthumously rehabilitated and his family given compensation. In 1981, a memorial was erected near his home, the only monument thus far in China known to commemorate a Christian executed for his faith during that turbulent era.

In 1998, a statue of Wang was dedicated at Westminster Abbey, London, one of 10 statues representing the continuing importance of Christian martyrdom for the church in the 20th c.

Bibliography

Wickeri, Philip L., "The Abolition of Religion in Yunnan: Wang Zhiming," in *The Terrible Alternative: Christian Martyrdom in the Twentieth Century,* ed. Andrew Chandler (1998). PHILIP WICKERI

Wanita Katolik

(Catholic Women's Organization, Indonesia). The oldest existing Catholic lay apostolic organization in Indonesia*.

Founded by Baroness Maria Suryadi Darmoseputro Sasraningrat (1924) in Yogyakarta, *Wanita Katolik* spread rapidly among women teachers, wives of government officials, and workers in factories owned by Catholics in Central Java. In 1934, it became a member of the International Union of Roman Catholic Women. After a ban by the Japanese military authorities (1942) and a short liaison with the Catholic Party* (until 1949), *Wanita Katolik* started anew, forming branches all over Indonesia in the early 1950s. Cooperating with local Marian sodalities, it emphasized the spiritual formation of its members, family* apostolate, girls' education, and charity. It fights for the emancipation of women in society and amendments to the law, being especially active in this regard before the enactment of the marriage law of 1974, which still puts women in a position inferior to men. *Wanita Katolik* takes an active part in the Congress of Indonesian Women (KOWANI) and the World Union of Catholic Women's Organizations (1975). (See also Feminism; Women's Movements.) ADOLF HEUKEN

Ward, William

(b. Derby, England, 20 Oct 1769; d. Serampore, 7 Mar 1823). The "Printer Preacher" of India.

While completing the necessary arrangements to go to India as a missionary, William Carey* said the following to a young printer and newspaper editor in 1793: "If the Lord bless us, we shall want a person of your business, to enable us to print the Scriptures. I hope you will come after us." Later, on 13 Oct 1799, the printer arrived on Indian soil in Serampore as a missionary. He was none other than William Ward, who became one of the "Serampore Trio" along with Carey and Joshua Marshman*.

Ward was born to John Ward, a carpenter and builder. Ward lost his father at an early age and was brought up by his mother, a woman of rare intelligence and ardent piety and an attendant in the ministry of the Methodists. In his childhood, Ward was known for his sobriety and thoughtfulness. While his friends spent their time in recreation, Ward devoted his time to reading. He never neglected an opportunity for mental improvement. On leaving school, he was placed as an apprentice with Mr. Drury, who headed a large printing establishment in the town. Due to his constant reading and attempts at composition, he gradually acquired great fluency and command of language. As a writer, he was able to express himself with great clarity and facility. He even began to edit a journal on behalf of Mr. Drury. The *Derby Mercury* became one of the most influential papers in the county. Thus his apprenticeship in the printing establishment made him an eminent journalist and an efficient printer by trade.

In 1796 he was baptized at Hull by Mr. Pendered and began devoting his time to communicating the divine truth to his fellow countrymen, renouncing all interest in politics and journalism. He began to make diligent preparations for the work of preaching the Gospel. While preparing himself for the ministry, a member of the Baptist Missionary Society came in search of laborers to join Carey in India, and Ward offered himself as a missionary. Ward and Marshman, along with other missionaries, sailed for India, and in Oct 1799 they reached Calcutta after a voyage of nearly five months. Since they were opposed by the East Indian Company, they established themselves at the Danish settlement of Serampore, where the Danish governor, Colonel Bie, extended all help within his power in the establishment of a mission. At Serampore they were joined by Carey and Thomas, who had preceded them to India. Soon after Ward's arrival, printing commenced at Serampore in late 1799. Ward undertook the entire responsibility for the work of printing. Using a wooden press Carey had brought from Malda, Ward began printing Carey's New Testament in Bengali; on 18 Mar 1800 he printed the first page of the New Testament, which he gave to Carey. On 7 Feb 1801, the last page of the Bengali New Testament was issued from the press. Ward worked the 19 presses with great diligence in the printing of the Scriptures and tracts. With the combined efforts of Carey and Ward, the work of giving the Bible* to the people proceeded with astonishing rapidity. Ward had established printing to such an extent that, by 1832, portions or all of the Christian Scriptures in 44 languages and dialects had been issued from the Serampore press.

In 1812, a fire destroyed the 200-foot-long printing house. The whole establishment was thus destroyed, with all the 12 fonts of Indian type, stores of books, printed sheets, papers, and more. Instead of being disheartened over the loss, Ward recovered the melted typemetal from the ruins and began casting the type at once. Within two weeks, he was able to print the Scriptures in one language, and in hardly two months' time the fonts of type were so far restored that printing was resumed on a large scale.

Ward was not merely a printer but also a writer and historian of the mission. Among his most commendable writings are: *The Account of the Writings, Religion, and Manners of the Hindoos,* a massive book of four volumes;

Reflections for Every Day in the Year; and his "Farewell Letters."

As a missionary, Ward was very much concerned about the training of the more advanced college youth for missionary duties. He established an auxiliary missionary society among native Christians and also started a religious magazine in Bengali. He was reckoned by far the best preacher at Serampore.

Ward was generally distinguished by an amiable and affectionate disposition. He possessed an excellent aptitude for business and had great clarity of perception. He had vast knowledge of the character and habits of the natives, spoke Bengali with the ease and fluency of a native, and hence was able to have a powerful influence over the people.

Ward continued with his writing for 20 years, which caused his health to deteriorate gradually. He returned to England for rest in 1819 but was back again at his post in Serampore in 1821.

Sixteen months after his return to India, in 1823, Ward was stricken with cholera of a virulent type and passed away after laboring together with Carey and Marshman for 23 years as if one soul animated all three.

Bibliography

Holcomb, H. Helen, *Men of Might in India Mission* (1901). • Marshman, J. Clark, *The Life and Times of Carey, Marshman, and Ward,* Vols. I and II (1859). • Daniel, F. Potts, *British Baptist Missionaries in India* (1793-1837) (1967). • "Ward, William," in *The Encyclopaedia of Missions,* 2nd ed. (1904). • Younge, C. M., *Pioneers and Founders or Recent Workers in the Mission Field* (1871).

Franklyn J. Balasundaran

Warneck, Gustav

(b. Naumburg, Germany, 6 Mar 1834; d. Halle, Germany, 26 Dec 1910). German scholar and founder of the science of missions.

As a pastor and theologian, Warneck first served a congregation and then became a mission inspector of the Rheinish Mission Society in Wuppertal-Barmen, Germany (1871-77). His practical experience helped him understand the problems faced by the various missionary societies. He continued dealing with missionary problems in a scientific manner and then produced a systematic treatise on this matter. He was the first to think and write about this subject dogmatically. Through his studies, missiology became an official field of theology at universities in Germany and then throughout Europe and North America. Warneck was the first person to receive an official appointment to the chair of missionary science. As an extraordinary professor at the University of Halle, he taught *Missionslehre* (theory of missions) from 1896 to 1908. His inaugural lecture was "Mission's Right to Citizenship in the Organism of Theological Science" (1897). Until the end of his life, he never stopped working on missiology and taking the initiative to help various missionary societies and German regional churches in theory and practice of mission and missiology.

In 1874 Warneck founded a scientific missionary journal, *Allgemeine Missionszeitschrift (AMZ),* in which articles on missionary topics were published. For a similar purpose, in 1879, the Mission Conference of Saxony was established. This conference became a model for the other provinces in Germany. These mission conferences provided opportunity for German pastors to discuss missionary topics and problems and to find closer fellowship. In 1885 the German Protestant Committee was founded as an organized expression of cooperation among the missionary societies and the German churches. This was all the vision of Gustav Warneck. His contribution can be seen also in the continental missionary conferences. His article that was sent to the Centenary Conference of Foreign Missions held in London in 1888 gave a clear vision for an international missionary agency which would coordinate all Protestant missionary activities. The foundation of the International Missionary Council in 1921 can be regarded as the realization of his vision.

His various writings included *Pauli Bekehrung, eine Apologie des Christentums* (Paul's Conversion, An Apology of Christendom, 1870), *Das Studium der Mission auf der Universität* (The Study of Mission at University, 1877), *Moderne Mission und Kultur* (Modern Mission and Culture, 1879), *Abriss einer Geschichte der Protestantischen Missionen* (Sketch of the History of Protestant Missions, 1882-1910), and his important book *Evangelische Missionslehre* (Theory of Missions), which appeared in five volumes (1892 and 1903). Warneck put all his ideas in this three-part book with its subtitle, "An Attempt at a Theory of Missions." This book can be understood as his pioneering work in acquiring for missiology a place in theological education. In his book *Sketch of the History of Protestant Missions,* Warneck suggested incorporating the history of missions within the biblical disciplines and the study of mission proper within the framework of practical theology. He insisted that church history is part of missiology.

Warneck's systematic missiology paid special attention to the ecclesiastical basis of mission because the historical developments in the mission field were coincident with his theory on Christianizing the nations *(Volkscristianisierung).* This can be seen in the developments of the German missionary activities among the Bataks* in Indonesia (1861-1940), where the Batak folk church was growing. Warneck was well informed about the Batak mission through his son, Johannes Warneck*.

Bibliography

Holsten, W., "Gustav Warneck," in *Concise Dictionary of the Christian World Mission* (1971). • Verkuyl, J., *Contemporary Missiology, An Introduction* (1987). • Lehman, A., *Gustav Warneck* (1962).

J. Raplan Hutauruk

Warneck, Johannes

(b. Dommitzsch, Germany, 4 Mar 1867; d. Bad Salzuflen, Germany, 1 Sep 1944). German missionary pioneer among the Bataks* in Sumatra, Indonesia*, and a missiologist.

Warneck was one of the first generation of German Rheinish missionaries who worked in the Rheinish mission field in Sumatra. He first worked from 1892 to 1906 and then continued from 1920 to 1932. After his first missionary stint, he was appointed to the Rheinish Mission staff in Wuppertal-Barmen, and then as a lecturer for missiology at Bethel Theological School. After his second period of service in Sumatra, he returned to Germany and led the Rheinish Mission Society from 1932 to 1937.

He opened the first mission station in Nainggolan on the island of Samosir (1892) and then took over the Rheinish mission station at Balige near Lake Toba (1894-1906). In 1896 he taught at the seminary for teacher-preachers *(gurus)* and pastors *(pandita)* in the Silidung Valley (Pansurnapitu). From 1898, he led the seminary, moving it to the other edge of the valley (Sipoholon). He revised its curriculum and produced textbooks (church history and world history) and NT commentaries. During his second term, he led the Rheinish Mission and the Batak church in Sumatra. He succeeded the late I. L. Nommensen* as *ephorus* and reorganized the Batak church. Each congregation could elect its own *kerkraad* (church council) from among the indigenous workers (the teacher-preachers and pastors), elders, and some influential members of the congregation. Each congregation was autonomous from the council but still under the authority of the missionary stationed in the "main congregation." The main reorganization can be seen in his concept of a new constitution which was accepted by the general synod of the Batak church in 1929 and enacted in 1930. The Batak church was renamed the Huria Kristen Batak Protestant* (HKBP) and was legally recognized by the Dutch government as an independent church body in 1931. The *ephorus* was still appointed by the leader of the Rheinish Mission in Germany.

During his ministry in Germany, Warneck produced brochures and books on the Batak mission field for missionary friends in Europe. His missiological study concentrated on the language, literature, and beliefs of the Bataks. In 1906 he wrote a Batak-German dictionary, and in 1909 *Dei Religion der Batak.* As a result of his research, he wrote *Die Lebenskraefte des Evangeliums: Missionserfahrungen innerhalb des animistischen Heidentums* (2nd ed., 1908). Its English translation, *The Living Christ and Dying Heathenism: The Experiences of a Missionary in Animistic Heathendom,* was published in 1909, with a second edition in 1954. He described the religious evolution of "animist" peoples from a psychological perspective. His other scholarly work was *Paulus im Lichte der heutigen Heidenmission* (1913; Paul in Light of Today's Mission to the Heathen).

Bibliography

Flender, W., *Warneck, Johannes* (1962). • Schreiner, Lothar, "Warneck, Johannes (1867-1944)," in *Concise Dictionary of Christian World Mission* (1971).

J. Raplan Hutauruk

Wenas, Albertus Zacharias Runturambi

(b. Tombatu, North Celebes, Indonesia, 28 Oct 1897; d. Tomohon, 11 Oct 1967). Minahasan pastor and pioneer for an independent church in Minahasa*.

The first native leader of the Minahasan Church, Wenas was educated in the School for Native Pastors in Minahasa and at the Missionary College in Rotterdam, later in Oegstgeest, Netherlands. His departure to the Netherlands in 1915 was supported by people from a number of Minahasan congregations. At the time, there were signs of dissension between the teachers and pastors of the church. The people in Minahasa yearned for a new vitality in the life of the church. A few years later, after his return, he found the people in Minahasa influenced by the national movement (see Nationalism). In this situation he struggled for an independent church in Minahasa.

The situation in Minahasa at this time was colored by controversy over how an independent church should be founded. What should its relationship be with the Netherlands Missionary Society (which was still working in the schools of the church), and how should it relate with the Protestant Church in Indonesia (PGI*), which administered the church in Minahasa? Wenas faced the tensions arising from this issue and decided that the time had come to build a self-supporting church which did not depend on the mission board. It meant that the church in Minahasa must keep close ties with the Protestant Church in Indonesia.

Wenas devoted himself to developing the life of the church in Minahasa. He lived during difficult times: the colonial domination (see Colonialism), the Japanese occupation (see World War II), and the civil war in Minahasa. In the 1930s, when the Evangelical Christian Church in Minahasa was still part of the PGI, the structure of the church was based on a hierarchical system. Yet Wenas, as the director of the School for Native Pastors in Minahasa, did not fully obey the orders of the executive board of the church in fulfilling his duty. He did his best for the development of the school and mobilized all the congregations in Minahasa to support the school financially. For him, this was a way to prepare the congregations for a self-supporting church. He sent four young men to the newly instituted Theological Seminary in Bogor (West Java) to become leaders and urged them to complete their studies before returning to Minahasa. He also struggled for equal rights for all church workers, especially those administrating the sacraments. In connection with this, he wished that all the local churches had native leaders.

During the Japanese occupation, Wenas served as the moderator of the Evangelical Christian Church in

Minahasa. This was the first time a native pastor in Minahasa led the church. He bravely faced struggles with the Japanese administration. When the Japanese government asked him to deliver a speech for a groundbreaking ceremony for the war victims of the Japanese Navy, Wenas said: "We Christians must firstly keep in mind the monument of Christ in Golgotha." During the civil war in Minahasa, Wenas was chosen by President Sukarno* as a member of the Supreme Advisory Council in 1959. He rejected this honor and chose to serve the children of Minahasa who were in trouble. He took the initiative to bridge the gap between the rebel army and the government in Jakarta.

Wenas can also be called the founder of the Bethesda Hospital in Tomohon. In addition, he gave much effort to social work, especially as the director of the orphanage in Tomohon. He was one of the pastors in North Celebes who initiated the ecumenical movement in this territory.

Bibliography

Ds A. Z. R. Wenas (1879-1967) Pelajan Geredja di Minahasa (1969). • Lintong, D. M., *Ds A. Z. R. Wenas: Ketua Sinode GMIM 1942-1967* (1978). • *33 Tahun PGIW Sulutteng* (1988). • Van den End, Th., *Ragi Carita* Vol. 2 (1989).

ARNOLD PARENGKUAN

White, Elizabeth

(b. 1869; d. ?). English-born Christian and Missionary Alliance* (C&MA) pioneer missionary to the Philippines* and wife of Paul Frederick Jansen.

With previous missionary service in Spain, Venezuela, and the western Catskill Mountains in New York, United States, White came to the Philippines in 1900 as a single woman and the first officially appointed C&MA missionary there. Finding no justification for opening specifically C&MA work in a field where larger missions had already been established, White attached herself to the Philippine Presbyterian* Mission. Her excellent command of Spanish made her a valuable colleague.

After she and Paul Frederick Jansen married in 1901, they officially joined the Presbyterian Mission. They pioneered in Cebu in 1902, then moved to Batangas in 1917 and to the Culion Leper Colony in 1921, where they continued as independent missionaries after retirement in 1935.

Bibliography

Christian and Missionary Alliance Report (1901-2). • Laubach, F. C., *People of the Philippines* (1925). • Sitoy, T. V., Jr., *Several Springs, One Stream* (1992).

T. VALENTINO SITOY, JR.

White, W. C.

(Huai Lu Guang) (b. England, 1873; d. 1960). Canadian Anglican* missionary to China*.

White migrated to Canada with his family in 1881. After graduating from high school, he worked in the Young Men's Christian Association* (YMCA). In 1894 he enrolled in Wycliffe Bible College and audited in a medical* school. In 1896 he was ordained as a deacon in Toronto. The following year, he was sent by the Church Missionary Society as a missionary to the northern part of Fukien, China. He took on the Chinese name of Lu Guang, which means "walking toward light." He adopted the same outfit and hairstyle as the Chinese and performed dental work to approach the Chinese.

In 1899 White was ordained a pastor and was deeply impressed by the Chinese culture. In 1909 he was consecrated a bishop and returned to Honan to start a new missionary district. He supported the indigenization of the Chinese church and commented that property that belonged to the mission board should be under the Chinese bishop's control. In 1929 White consecrated Chinese pastor Zheng He Fu* as assistant bishop and, five years later, installed him as bishop.

During the warlord time, White was involved in resolving a conflict at Honan. While China suffered drought, he took up famine relief work in Honan and was commended by the locals and government officials. White had once been the agent for the Ontario Royal Museum, and he purchased a few thousand pieces of ancient Chinese crafts from Honan. During the years 1929-31, the purchase sum amounted to more than C$90,000, and the most precious collection included inscriptions on bone tortoise shells of the Shang dynasty as well as Bronze Age items. White was also interested in collecting the remains of Jews who resided in Kaifeng, and these collections were later shipped to the University of Cincinnati in the United States.

In 1934 White retired from the mission field and took a teaching post at Toronto University. He taught the archaeology of China and was head of the Far East Collection of the Royal Museum. In 1946 he paid another visit to China for one year.

Bibliography

White, W. C., *Luo Yang Gu Mu Lao* (The excavation at Luo Yang Caves); *Zhong Guo Si Miao Bi Hua* (Wall drawing of China temples); *Zhongguo You-Tai-Ren* (Jews in China); *Zhongguo Qing Tong Qi Wne Hua* (Bronze Age civilization of China). • Austin, Alvyn J., *Saving China* (1986).

CHINA GROUP

Wickremasinghe, Cyril Lakshman

(b. Kurunegala, Sri Lanka, 25 Mar 1927; d. Colombo, 23 Oct 1983). Church of Ceylon bishop of Kurunegala and promoter of ecumenism and interreligious dialogue*.

Wickremasinghe was the son of the first minister of agriculture in the state council of Sri Lanka*. After his initial education at Royal College, Colombo, he studied at the University of Ceylon, obtaining a first-class bachelor's degree in economics in 1948. He attended Keble College, Oxford, to read for the D.Litt. degree but discontinued his studies because of his intention to accept the call for the service of God. He graduated from Ely Theological College in 1951. In 1952 he was ordained a deacon in Colombo, and in 1953, a priest in London. He served at All Saints Poplar in the United Kingdom from 1952 to 1955. Upon his return to Sri Lanka, he served at the Church of Ceylon cathedral in Colombo (1956-58) and as university chaplain at Peradeniya (1958-62).

Wickremasinghe was consecrated bishop of the Kurunegala Diocese on 16 Dec 1962 and served in that capacity until his death. He continued the process of indigenization in the diocese which was begun by his predecessor, Lakdasa de Mel. He maintained a cordial relationship with the leading Buddhist monks of the country. He made an impact on the Anglican* Bishops' Conference at Lambeth held in 1968, insisting on the necessity to hold such meetings in Third World countries.

Wickremasinghe made a serious attempt to bring about a united Protestant church in Sri Lanka with the cooperation of the Methodists* and Baptists*. In 1974 his attempt was about to be realized when a lawsuit was brought against the unification scheme by some members of the Anglican Church. He also collaborated with Buddhists and Hindus in national reconciliation efforts when ethnic problems struck the country in 1977. He was instrumental in setting up the department of Christian civilization at the University of Kelaniya.

Wickremasinghe was actively engaged in interdenominational cooperation in Sri Lanka. He encouraged Yohan Devananda to set up an ashram* at Ibbagamuwa in the diocese of Kurunegala. He was instrumental in founding the Christian Workers Federation in 1972. From 1977 to 1983 he served as a peacemaker between Tamil militants and the government of Sri Lanka. He was accepted as an impartial national leader by both parties. He remained celibate until his death.

G. P. V. Somaratna

Wilhelm, Richard

(Wei Li Xian) (b. Tübingen, Germany, 1873; d. 1930). German Allgemeiner Evangelisch Protestantischer missionary and Chinese studies scholar.

Wilhelm studied in Bashehui Theological Seminary in 1894. Three years later he was sent to Tsingtau, Shandong. He was sympathetic toward the courageous fight of the Chinese against the Baguolianjunin in 1900 and felt that it was a boost to the Chinese cultural spirit. In the bloody incident after the Germans occupied Jiaozhou and forcibly built the Jiaoji Railway, Wilhelm led doctors to rescue the injured people. He also set up Lixian Institution and Tsingtau Institute, which emphasized the passing on of technology.

Wilhelm was very interested in Chinese culture, especially Confucianism*. He formed the *Zunkongwenshe* in 1913 and specially converted his tennis court into a Chinese *Gujicangshulou.* There were a total of 30,000 old books. In his 20 years in China, he translated many Chinese classics as well as poetry, history, and novels. He was the literary consultant to the German embassy. In 1924 he returned home and taught Chinese studies at Frankfurt University and obtained an honorary doctorate. He also started the Chinese Institution in Frankfort and Munich, which was named *Weida de Deyizhi Zhongguoren.* His famous works include *Zhongguo Wenming Jianshi, Shiyong Zhongguo Changshi, Zhongguo Jingshen,* and others. Wilhelm's two sons also became Chinese studies scholars and taught at Beijing University.

China Group

Willekins, Petrus Johannes

(b. 1881; d. 1971). Last Dutch apostolic vicar of Batavia (Jakarta) (1934-52).

Willekins served as a visitor of the Jesuit* provinces of Madura (southern India), Hungary, and England. He established the first major seminary in Indonesia* in Muntilan (1936). He founded the indigenous* congregation of the sisters of Abdi Dalem Sang Kristus (1938). Willekins pushed Rome to nominate the first Javanese as apostolic vicar of Semarang (1940). He fought with colonial authorities for the opening of many village schools, opposed the Japanese authorities after proclaiming himself Vatican delegate (1942-45), and worked after his resignation as instructor of young Jesuit priests in Giri Sonta (Central Java, 1952-63).

Bibliography

Bank, J., *Katholieken en de Indonesische Revolutie* (1984).

Adolf Heuken

William of Rubroek (Rubruck/Rubruquis)

(b. Rubroek, in French Flanders, between 1215 and 1230; d. ? after 1258). Franciscan* missionary to the Mongols.

Very little is known of William's life apart from his travels to the Mongol court and his recorded observations made for King Louis IX of France. William joined the Franciscans as one of the early second-generation friars and traveled to the Holy Land around the year 1248. Somehow William became friends with the king of France, in part because of the king's favor toward and shared spirituality of the friars. Thus, when William began his missionary journey to the Mongols, he did so with the king's blessing, accompanied by one of the king's clerks, Gosset. His journey seems to have been both to preach to and provide pastoral care for German prisoners of the Mongols, as well as to make contact with other Christians and preach to the Mongols themselves. His greatest contribution seems to have been his realistic appraisal of Mongol power and politics and his detailed description of the geography and people he encountered. William had very little respect for the East Syrian (Nestorian*) priests and monks he encountered. He goes on at length about the drunkenness of the priests and their ignorance of their own theology and language of worship (Syriac). He even questions why they do not have the body of Jesus on their crosses.

Bibliography

Jackson, Peter, and David Morgan, eds. and trans., *The Mission of Friar William of Rubruck: His Journey to the Court of the Great Khan Mongke, 1253-1255* (1990).

Scott W. Sunquist

Williams, Samuel Wells

(b. Utica, New York, 22 Sep 1812; d. New Haven, Connecticut, United States, 16 Feb 1884). American missionary in China*, sinologue, linguist, and diplomat.

Williams graduated from the Rensselaer Institute in Troy, New York, in 1832 with a major in geology. When only 20 years of age, he was appointed a missionary with the American Board of Commissioners for Foreign Missions to serve as superintendent of the mission press in Guangzhou (Canton). Arriving in Guangzhou in 1833, he worked as editor of the *Chinese Repository*, an important periodical in English commenced the year before by Elijah Bridgman of the same mission.

From 1845 to 1848 Williams was in the United States, where he married Sarah Walworth and also compiled his best-known work, *The Middle Kingdom*, from lectures given to many audiences. From the honoraria received from his lectures, he was able to buy from Berlin a font of moveable Chinese type. Also during this time in the United States, he received from Union College the degree of LL.D. From a trip made to Japan in 1837 in a vain attempt to return some shipwrecked Japanese seamen to their homes, he learned Japanese, translated the Gospel of Matthew and Genesis for them, and led them to accept the Christian faith as they lived in his home in Canton. Later, in 1853-54, he served as interpreter for the Perry expedition to Japan. His account of this trip, *Journal of the Perry Expedition to Japan, 1843-1854*, was published in 1910.

Williams's experience as an interpreter led to his appointment to diplomatic service with the United States State Department. In 1857 he was secretary of the United States legation in Japan. Along with William Reed, he helped negotiate with China the treaty of Tientsin (Tianjin) in 1858. After two years in the United States from 1860 to 1862, where he lectured widely, he returned to China to serve as secretary of the United States legation in Peking (Beijing) until 1876. While holding this post, he finished writing in 1874 *A Syllabic Dictionary of the Chinese Language*, a book on which he had worked for 11 years.

In 1877 Williams returned to New Haven, where he was appointed professor of Chinese language and literature at Yale University. In 1883, aided by his son, Frederick Williams, he revised and enlarged his *Middle Kingdom*, the best work extant on Chinese government, geography, religion, and social life. In 1881 the senior Williams was elected the president of the American Bible Society.

Bibliography

Latourette, Kenneth S., *A History of Christian Missions in China* (1966). • Williams, Frederick Wells, *The Life and Letters of Samuel Wells Williams, LL.D.* (1889).

Ralph R. Covell, with contributions from the China Group

Wilson, John

(b. Lauder in Berwickshire, England, 1804; d. "The Cliff," near Bombay, India, 1 Dec 1875). Scottish missionary to India* of the Scottish Missionary Society (SMS).

At the age of 14, Wilson was sent to Edinburgh to prepare for the ministry. During his studies he became increasingly interested in missionary work and even founded (22 Dec 1825) the Edinburgh Association of Theological Students in Aid of the Diffusion of the Gospel. In 1828 he published *The Life of John Eliot, the Apostle of the Indians.* His attention was redirected from the North American Indians to India when he began tutoring the sons of Sir John Rose and Alexander Walker, who had worked in India. Wilson signed on with the Scottish Missionary Society and took time to study medicine (1827-28) at Edinburgh before getting married (to Margaret Bayne of Greenock), becoming licensed to preach, and then sailing for Bombay. John and Margaret arrived in Bombay in 1829 and immediately began learning about the culture (studying Marathi) and pioneering mission work in west India. Bombay would be, for over four decades, his base for ministry, and scholarship would be his vocation.

Before the end of the first year (27 Dec) Margaret had begun the first Western school for Indian girls (the first of seven such schools in seven years) and by the end of their second year John was preaching in Marathi, had formed a local Presbyterian* church, and had founded the first Christian periodical in India *(Oriental Christian Spectator)*. After founding other schools for boys, Wilson founded a coeducational college (29 Mar 1832) that placed special emphasis on the education of women and education in local languages (Marathi, Gujarathi, Hindustani, Portuguese, Persian, Arabic, and Sanskrit). In light of some differences with the SMS, Wilson and others transferred to the Church of Scotland. He continued to develop his college, nonetheless, which was first called Ambrolie English School and was later named Wilson College.

Another area of Wilson's ministry in India was with educated Indian scholars. Wilson would engage in courteous public discussion with Hindus, Muslims, and Parsis, and his knowledge of and respect for other religions and cultures opened many doors for ministry. At the same time, such contact brought on conflict, as many students expressed an interest in becoming Christian. In 1839 the college was reduced from 284 to 50 students because of religious conflict over the conversion of some Parsi students (see Zoroastrianism). By the end of his ministry in India, Wilson could count hundreds who had become Christians, at least in part through his witness.

Bibliography

Stephen, Leslie, and Sidney Lee, eds., "Wilson, John," in *The Dictionary of National Biography,* Vol. 21. • Smith, George, *The Life of John Wilson* (1879). • Wilson, John, *A Memoir of Mrs. Margaret Wilson* (1838).

Scott W. Sunquist

Wilson, John Leonard

(b. Durham, England, 23 Nov 1897; d. Yorkshire, England, 18 Aug 1970). Anglican* bishop interned during World War II*; ecumenical* leader.

Wilson was trained at Queen's College, Oxford, and Wycliffe Hall. He went to Cairo in 1928 under the auspices of the Church Missionary Society, but his self-confessed modernist view on the virgin birth terminated his appointment in 1929. He then became dean of St. John's Cathedral and archdeacon of Hong Kong* from 1938 to 1941. He was subsequently consecrated bishop of Singapore* in Hong Kong on 22 Jul 1941 amidst some resignations in the Singapore Diocese because of his modernist views.

Singapore surrendered to the Japanese in Feb 1942. For one year, Wilson was free to help with the physical and spiritual needs of the suffering, but he was eventually interned and tortured. Wilson, however, found that the experience of torture awakened in him the reality of the Christian faith he confessed. Prior to his internment he arranged for the diocese to function with Asian priests, with D. D. Chelliah* in charge of diocesan affairs, and also for interdenominational services to be held. During his interment, he agreed with Bishop Amstutz of the Methodist church and Mr. Gibson* of the Presbyterian* church for the need to promote closer cooperation among Christians. The war ended in 1945, and this vision was realized in 1948 when a united training college (Trinity Theological College) for church workers and clergy was founded and the Malayan Christian Council was formed with Bishop Wilson as chairman and Bishop Amstutz as secretary.

Wilson resigned as bishop of Singapore in 1949 and continued his ministry in England.

Bibliography

The Courier (Sep 1970). • McKay, Roy, *John Leonard Wilson Confessor for the Faith* (1973).

Soon Soo Kee

Winslow, J(ohn) C(opley)

(b. England, 1882; d. England, 1974). Society for the Propagation of the Gospel (SPG) missionary to India* and pioneer of the Christian ashram* movement.

Winslow was born, raised, and educated in England. Under the auspices of the SPG, he went to India in 1914. His work, from his earliest years, was marked by a concern for issues of justice, racial equality, nationalism* (he was a supporter of Gandhi*), and spiritual formation in the Indian context. In 1921 he pioneered a Christian ashram with a small community of seven Marathi men and women. This ashram, *Christa Seva Sangha,* was first established in Miri but later (1922) moved to Poone (Pune). Following the establishment of the ashram, Winslow penned a book about spiritual life in India named after the ashram, *Christa Seva Sangha.* This concern for Indian Christian spiritual life is reflected in other books by Winslow: *Christian Yoga* (1923), *The Indian Mystic* (1926), and *Eucharist in India* (1920). He also wrote a "Liturgy for India," which became part of the Indian version of the *Book of Common Prayer.* Winslow was also fascinated by the poetry and person of Narayan Vaman Tilak*. He provided translations of Tilak's poetry and wrote works about him.

Winslow's concern for an indigenized (see Contextualization) Christian faith brought him close to C. F. Andrews*, but it also produced great frustrations. In 1934 he left his beloved India and his ashram in light of the strong movements toward a more Western-style approach. In England he worked with the Moral Rearmament Movement but continued his concern for spirituality, founding Lee Abbey and Fellowship in Devon. Winslow returned to India, visiting Pune at the age of 91, and then died a few months later in England.

Bibliography

Noreen, Barbara, *Crossroads of the Spirit* (1994). • See Winslow's reports and papers in the SPG files at Rhodes House Library, Oxford, England, and papers on the *Christa Seva Sangha* at Bishop's College, Calcutta, India.

Scott W. Sunquist

Wolfe, Leslie

American Disciples missionary to the Philippines* who was conservative and controversial.

A zealous "restorationist" Disciples missionary, Wolfe arrived with his wife in 1907 for a stormy, 35-year career in the Philippines. Wolfe was the Disciples' leading missionary in Manila and its immediate environs and was largely responsible for organizing the work that produced a third of all Filipino Disciples.

Fiercely conservative in theology, Wolfe frequently clashed with colleagues in his own mission. He considered their theology "liberal." Disagreeing even with the United Christian Missionary Society, Wolfe led all the Tagalog Disciples of southern Luzon into a schism in 1926, calling themselves "Churches of Christ."

The Ilocano Disciples of northern Luzon joined the United Church of Christ in the Philippines in 1948, but Wolfe's followers did not do so until 1962.

Bibliography

Maxey, M., *History of the Philippine Mission of the Churches of Christ* (1973). • Sitoy, T. V., Jr., *Several Springs, One Stream* (1992). T. VALENTINO SITOY, JR.

Women's Christian Temperance Union, Japan

(Nihon Kirisuto-kyo Fujin Kyofukai) (JWCTU). Women's organization with an office located in Tokyo, Shinjuku Ward, Hyakunin-cho 2-chome.

When Mary Clement Leavitt, a special envoy from the World Women's Christian Temperance Union, came to Japan in 1886, 56 Christians living in Tokyo gathered to form the Tokyo Women's Christian Temperance Union (WCTU). Yajima Kajiko was elected its first president. The WCTU was the first women's organization in Japan. In 1893 a national structure was formed, and it became the Japan WCTU. A list of past presidents includes: Yajima, Ushioda Chisaeko, Kozaki Chiyo, Hayashi Utako, Gauntlett Tsune, Sawano Kuni, and Kubushiro Ochimi. Since its inception, the JWCTU has been based on the Christian faith and worked toward three basic objectives — world peace, chastity, and temperance — while taking leadership in social reform and in organized volunteer service for women's movements. It has exerted its efforts for the abolition of prostitution, temperance, women's suffrage, and peace, contributing much to each effort. Some of the results include the revision of civil and criminal law (petition for monogamy) in 1888; the presentation of two white papers on the control of foreign prostitutes to a council of elderly statesmen (adopted in 1921); a law prohibiting smoking by minors passed by the diet; and rules controlling prostitution officially announced in 1900. In 1929 they collected 180,000 signatures on a disarmament petition; in 1950 a law prohibiting the consumption of alcoholic beverages by children and teenagers was passed; and laws prohibiting prostitution (1956) and unruly conduct in public by inebriated persons (1961) were passed. In addition to being instrumental in getting these bills passed, the JWCTU also worked against the nationalization of Yasukuni Shrine, for the elimination of Turkish baths, and against prostitution tourism. The organization took action on issues appropriate to the times as it strove for respect of human rights, a lasting peace, and the prevention of war. It has been committed to sending delegates to World WCTU conventions and other international conventions related to women and peace issues. It has opened city organizations around the country and a national office in Tokyo for communication and administration. It is affiliated with the World WCTU. Some practical projects it has accomplished include a dormitory for women, another for women students (Jiai Dormitory), a social welfare foundation, Kobe Women's Dormitory, Osaka Women's Home, Tokushima Children's Home, Kochi Student Dorm, Kure Jiai Dorm, Kamoshima Hikari Nursery for Infants, and a regular publication, *Fujin shinpo* (Women's News).

Bibliography

Nihon kirisuto-kyo fujin kyofukai go-ju-nen-shi (Fifty-year history of JWCTU) (1936). • "Fujin kyofukai soritsu kyuju-nen kinen-go" (Ninetieth anniversary of the founding of WCTU), *Fujin no tomo* (Woman's friend) (1976). • *Nihon kirisuto-kyo fujin kyofukai hyakunen-shi* (One-hundred-year history of the JWCTU) (1986).

EBISAWA CHIEKO

Women's Movement, Philippines

Before the Spanish colonization of the Philippines, the *mujer indigena* of the precolonial society enjoyed an egalitarian status. Women had the same freedom of movement and opportunities for economic and political activities as men. In the religious sphere, women were the *babaylan** (priestesses) who celebrated the important rituals for the community. The Spanish friars and colonizers were shocked by women's freedom and the lack of "feminine" values typical of Spanish women of the 15th c., and so they resolved to domesticate women through education and religion. They succeeded to a large extent, but Filipino women have retained the collective memory of their equality and freedom, which today inspires them in their movement for emancipation.

Throughout the Spanish regime there were women who distinguished themselves as patriots, poets, and revolutionaries. There were some initial efforts at organization among women belonging to the secret revolutionary organization; among the upper class, who organized a Masonic lodge for women; and among the women of Malolos, who clamored for higher formal education for women.

More organizations were formed during the American period (1898–1946). These may be classified into three categories. First, there were political organizations aimed at obtaining women's suffrage, the education of women regarding political matters, and Philippine independence (e.g., *Asociacion Feminista Ilonga,* 1906; National Federation of Women's Clubs, 1922; the *Liga Nacional de Damas Filipinas,* 1922; and the Women's Civic Assembly of the Philippines, 1946). One organization, the Philippine Women's League for Peace, was established to help the pacification drive of the Americans. Second, there were social service and civic organizations aimed at labor and prison reforms, welfare and social services, and campaigns against prostitution, gambling, and drinking (e.g., the Women's Red Cross Association, 1898; *Asociacion Feminista de Filipinas,* 1905; the Girl Scouts of the Philippines; and the Society for the Advancement of Women, 1912). Third, religious organizations specified religious purposes in addition to social services (e.g., the Catholic Women's League and the Young Women's Christian Association*).

These early women's organizations were not feminist

in the modern understanding of the word, even if one or two bore the name "feminists" (see Feminism). There was no analysis of gender relations, no questioning of women's stereotyped roles, and no agenda for change. Their activities were reformist rather than emancipatory. Some were even used by colonial powers as well as by male political leaders.

The first organization of women to raise the issue of women's liberation was the *Malayang Kilusan ng Bagong Kababaihan* (MAKIBAKA), or "Free Movement of New Women," founded in 1970. After the declaration of martial law in 1972, the organization had to go underground. There was a lull in women's organizations until about 1978, when other feminist groups were established. Among the first were the PILIPINA (Organization of Pilipina Women's Vision of Philippine Society), SAMAKANA *(Samakan ng Malayang Kababaihang Nagkakaisa),* Center for Women Resources (CWR), and the KMK (an association of women workers). After the assassination of Benigno Aquino in 1983, women's organizations mushroomed. Some were expressly feminist, and others were political protest groups that were not expressly feminist. Among these were the KABAPA *(Katipunan ng Bagong Pilipina),* Concerned Women of the Philippines, AWARE (Association of Women for Action and Research), and WOMB (Women for Ouster of Marcos Boycott).

In 1984 the Center for Women Resources took the initiative in convening the women's groups and women's desks in a consultation that would discuss and determine the characteristics of a Third World women's movement. In that meeting there was a consensus that the women's movement in the Philippines was a constitutive dimension of the struggle for societal transformation, not only in its objective but in the process of change. The participants also agreed to form a federation called GABRIELA, after Gabriela Silang, a female patriot executed by the Spaniards.

Presently, GABRIELA is the widest network of Philippine women's organizations, with 400 member organizations and 50,000 individual members, 95 percent of whom are grassroots women. Its main strategies include organization, mobilization, education, feminist scholarship, legal actions, women's actions for women's welfare, cultural strategies, and international solidarity.

In the mid-1980s, women's studies developed in some colleges and universities in the Philippines. Feminist educators in these schools formed the Women's Studies Association of the Philippines (WSAP).

Within this context of women's struggle for fuller humanity in the Philippines (which is 85 percent Catholic) arose the concern about the role of religion in the perpetuation and justification of women's subordination and oppression. In 1978 the Philippine Association of Theologically Trained Women (PATH-TWO) was formed, which later became the Association of Women in Theology (AWIT). In 1983, with the formation of the Women's Commission of Ecumenical Association of Women in the Philippines (EATWOT: Ecumenical Association of Third World Theologians), feminist theologizing started in earnest among the Filipino EATWOT members. For the last two decades, they have initiated theological reflection and publication in national, regional, and intercontinental conferences and international dialogues.

Bibliography

Fabella, Virginia, *Beyond Bonding: A Third World Women's Theological Journey* (1993). • Mananzan, Mary John, *The Woman Question in the Philippines* (1991). • Santos, Aida, "Do Women Really Hold Up the Sky?" in *Essays on Women,* rev. ed., ed. Mary John Mananzan (1991).

MARY JOHN MANANZAN

Women's Movements

The church women's groups of each denomination in every country were formed much earlier than the national or regional Christian women's organizations or movements. These church women's groups were organized mainly for fellowship, prayer, and worship; to raise funds for evangelization and charity work; and to provide service for the domestic affairs of the church.

Asian Church Women's Conference (ACWC). Women leaders from Asia who attended the assembly of the Presbyterian* women (Presbyterian Church in the United States of America [PCUSA]) in 1956 at Purdue University and Stony Point in New York, USA, discussed the need to know each other's situation as Asian women; to establish ecumenical* fellowship among the church women for encouragement; and to assist in leadership development. This led to the formation of the ACWC in Nov 1958 in Hong Kong*. The meeting resolved to hold the ACWC every four years to promote the Fellowship of the Least Coin and to prepare the Circle of Prayer Booklet to be used in conjunction with the Least Coin project.

The ACWC works with church women's groups in 16 countries, transcending culture, creed, color, and race, helping Asian women become more capable of discovering themselves, realizing their gifts and potential, and enabling them in the struggle toward the creation of a society of peace and justice.

Fellowship of the Least Coin (FLC). A movement of prayer for peace and reconciliation of Christian women, the FLC was conceived and founded by Shanti Solomon of India, who was part of the Pacific Mission Team organized by Margaret Shannon on behalf of the PCUSA. The team consisted of seven women from different countries traveling through Asia in Sep 1956. While the team went to Korea, Solomon remained in Manila reflecting on the experiences of the team's travel and how to overcome barriers governments set up to keep women apart. Upon the team's return, she suggested that prayer could transcend every national boundary. Her challenge to the Christian women of Asia and the women from the PCUSA was to combine their efforts and resources and launch an international project of justice, peace, and reconciliation in which every Christian woman could participate, regardless of her economic status. This was accepted by the team as an expression of their Christian unity and solidarity with suffering humanity and with women of every nation. Every time a woman prayed, she was to set aside a "least coin" of her currency.

The ACWC and FLC developed close relationships with the EACC, now the Christian Conference of Asia* (CCA), when they were inaugurated. The fund was kept by the EACC until 1970. At the fourth assembly of the ACWC in 1970, Solomon was named executive secretary of the FLC and the ACWC. In 1979, at the executive committee meeting of the ACWC in Manila, it was decided to separate the FLC and ACWC accounts. The autonomous FLC, with its own constitution and guidelines, became an international prayer movement, with its fund administered by the International Committee for the Fellowship of the Least Coin (ICFLC). The FLC Fund provides grants each year for not fewer than 40 projects all over the world. The ICFLC comprises women representatives from regional and world bodies.

World Day of Prayer (WDP). Another worldwide movement of which the Asian Christian women have been so much a part is the World Day of Prayer, initiated and carried out by women from some countries in Africa, Asia, the Caribbean, Europe, Latin America, the Middle East, North America, and the Pacific. WDP (the first Friday of March) is a movement bringing together women of various races, cultures, and traditions in closer fellowship, understanding, and action throughout the year. The International Committee for the World Day of Prayer was formed in 1967 to plan and promote the WDP movement and celebrations and to provide coordination of the national WDP committees in sharing experiences and preparing materials for WDP for each year. More than 170 countries participate in the WDP.

Christian Conference of Asia (CCA) — Women's Concerns. In their early years, the FLC and ACWC were assisted by the CCA, a regional ecumenical body with 15 national councils and 103 churches from 16 Asian countries. The CCA works closely with the World Council of Churches (WCC), other regional ecumenical conferences of churches, and world professional and ecumenical organizations.

At the CCA Sixth Assembly (Penang, Malaysia*, 1977), the issue of women's participation in all aspects of church ministry and decision-making bodies was raised. This led to the consultation on women's concerns and theology in Hong Kong (Aug 1978), which recommended the CCA do study, research, and theological reflection on the major issues identified and organize, with local and regional initiatives, leadership training courses for women. The seventh assembly of the CCA (Bangalore, 1981) decided to constitute the committee for women's concerns and to appoint a full-time executive staff to bring women's concerns and issues into the life of the church and to ensure adequate attention to women's issues during CCA meetings.

A series of workshops was conducted on a subregional and national basis, in collaboration with the women's groups of the National Council of Churches, to empower ecumenical leadership among women in Asia under the theme "Working Together towards a New Community." The objectives were: to enhance the full participation of women in all aspects of church ministry at the local, national, and regional levels; to understand the concept and to seek models of partnership from the biblical and theological perspectives; to affirm and exercise inclusive leadership and collective decision making through participatory methods and various forms of art in dealing with conflicts, problems, and issues.

Several workshops organized jointly with other CCA program desks to understand and explore models of partnership and to seek ways of dealing with pressing community issues were: Gender Partnership (Youth and Women's Concerns), Partnership of Women and Men in God's Mission (Evangelism and Mission and Women's Concerns), Gender and Development (Development and Service and Women's Concerns), Women and Beijing: Churches' Response (Urban-Rural Mission [URM] and Women's Concerns).

Women's Concerns also organized workshops and conferences on specific issues in collaboration with regional bodies such as the Asian Women's Resource Center for Culture and Theology (AWRC); the World Student Christian Federation, Asia/Pacific region (see Student Christian Movement); the Asian Migrant Center; the Asian Women Human Rights Council; and the Women's Team of the WCC.

The Emerging Asian Women's Theology. The Asian woman' s experience of pain and suffering is the starting point of theologizing from women's perspectives. The emerging Asian women's theology is a contextual theology. Since the 1970s, women theologians in Asia have felt the need to do theology in the Asian context, inclusively and distinctively from women's viewpoint. These women have been involved in the two Asian women theological networks, namely, the AWRC and the Women's Commission of the Ecumenical Association of Third World Theologians (EATWOT). The popular women's or feminist* movement has also challenged the church women to broaden their concerns and reread the Bible from their own experience.

The effort at theologizing from women's perspectives was first manifested in the journal *In God's Image (IGI),* a forum for Asian women to express their suffering and joy, struggle for liberation, aspirations, and theological reflection in various creative forms. The journal speaks of Asian women's reality. It encourages women to be in solidarity with one another in the struggle for full humanity. The founding editor of *IGI,* Sun Ai Lee-Park, prepared the first issue in Dec 1982 with the cooperation of a few friends working in the CCA office in Singapore*.

In Nov 1987, Asian women theologians from 16

countries met in Singapore and strongly affirmed the need to have an Asian women's resource center with the objectives of forming a community of Asian women engaged in theology and ministry and encouraging them to articulate Asian women's contextual theology.

In Sep 1988, the AWRC was inaugurated at the coordinating team meeting in Hong Kong. It was decided that the AWRC should undertake the responsibility of publishing *IGI* and that the editor of *IGI* should also be the coordinator of AWRC. Yvonne Dahlin of the Church of Sweden Mission worked as an organizer for both the AWRC and *IGI*. The AWRC was based in Hong Kong until Jul 1991, when the office was moved to Seoul. At present, the AWRC is functioning from Kuala Lumpur, Malaysia.

The Women's Commission of EATWOT, formed in 1983, sought to rework some of the main theological themes from third world women's perspectives. The motive and theological basis of the Women's Commission is well summed up by Virginia Fabella: "Asian women cannot speak of religion and cultures without speaking of poverty* and multiple oppressions. Neither can they speak of liberation from poverty* and oppression without speaking of 'spiritual' liberations."

Bibliography

A History of the Asian Church Women's Conference, pp. 15-21, and ACWC Pamphlet. • Circle of Prayer, *40th Anniversary Special Volume, 1956-1996.* • *World Day of Prayer International Committee 1995 Quadrennial Meeting Report.* • *CCA Penang to Bangalore* (1977-81); *CCA Bangalore to Seoul Report* (1981-85); *History of CCA* (1957-95). • *In God's Image* (Sep 1987); Vol. 10, No. 1 (1991); Vol. 11, No. 4 (1992). • *We Dare to Dream* (1985); *Doing Theology as Asian Women* (1989). • AWRC and EATWOT Women's Commission in Asia. Esther Byu

Woods, Robert W.

(Robin) (b. United Kingdom, 14 Feb 1914; d. 20 Oct 1997). Archdeacon of Singapore* and vicar of St. Andrew's Cathedral, Singapore (1951-58).

Woods's ministry at the Anglican* cathedral in Singapore in the immediate postwar era ushered in a new and vigorous stage of development for the Anglican Church in Singapore and Malaya. He pursued a policy of planting churches in the new suburbs of Singapore with considerable success. Under his leadership, independence and self-support were fostered amongst the new congregations so that they no longer saw themselves as mere extensions of the cathedral. As archdeacon, Woods took special interest in the new villages set up during the Communist insurgency in Malaya (see Communism).

A north transept was built onto the cathedral in 1952 to provide facilities for parish and diocesan meetings and administration. With an eye to the future, Woods purchased land on which mission schools were later built. In cooperation with Methodist* and Presbyterian* church leaders, and with the help of ex-China missionaries, he promoted Anglican involvement in Trinity Theological College (founded in 1948) as a training ground for future pastors and leaders of the church in Singapore and Malaya. The Anglican contribution was enhanced by the opening of St. Peter's Hall in 1954.

The administrative ability and pastoral care which Woods brought to Singapore were to further distinguish his subsequent ministry in England as archdeacon of Sheffield, dean of Windsor, and bishop of Worcester. He left behind in Singapore a much expanded Anglican Church firmly rooted in local society and able to function well in the newly independent nation.

Bibliography

Woods, Robin, *Robin Woods, An Autobiography* (1986). • USPG Archives, Partnership House Library London. • Loh Keng Aun, *50 Years of the Anglican Church in Singapore Island (1909-1959)* (1963). Frank Lomax

World Christian Women Regulate Society

The World Christian Women Regulate Society was founded in the United States in 1882. The Chinese Christian Women Regulate Society was organized by members in China* and was set up in Shanghai in 1921. Its objective is to promote a high standard of living, advocate equal rights for both sexes, protect a mother's love and children, and show concern for world peace, the human race, and humanitarian aid. Participants are mostly Christian women of the middle- and upper-income groups.

The first chairperson of the society was a well-known woman doctor, Shi Meiyue, with the chief executive being Fu Yunmei. The society operated from an office in Shanghai. By 1922 there were 82 branches of the society in China. The society's headquarters includes departments devoted to protecting women, children, international peace, morality, etc. In 1921 a women's institute for child rearing was established in Shanghai. It took in homeless persons, female beggars, maids, and abandoned women and provided them with a place to live as well as training in various skills. The Shanghai Ladies Apartment was set up in 1932, providing working women and female university students with a second home. The society also established a ladies' home economics school, which serves as a women's vocational high school. The quarterly *Regulation* was published in 1922. In addition, *Regulation Collection, China Women's Movement,* and other books were also published.

China Group

World Evangelical Fellowship

(WEF). Continuation of the international Evangelical Alliance formed in 1846 in London.

Reconstructed as the WEF in 1951 at Woudschoten, the Netherlands, the organization now represents Evangelical Alliances, or Fellowships, in 105 countries and six regional associations, embracing approximately 150 million evangelical Christians and representing an estimated 600,000 churches. The threefold purpose of the WEF is the furtherance of the Gospel (Phil 1:12), the defense and confirmation of the Gospel (Phil 1:7), and fellowship in the Gospel (Phil 1:5). The 1951 founding conference reaffirmed the seven points of the Statement of Faith of the Evangelical Alliance (1846), a statement that is widely used by churches and mission agencies today. The current mission statement as outlined in the Singapore Covenant (1994) begins: "The World Evangelical Fellowship and member organisations exist to establish and help regional and national evangelical Alliances, empower and mobilise local churches and Christian organisations to disciple the nations for Christ."

In order to strengthen the autonomous national and regional bodies, the WEF maintains a low-profile structure with an international office in Singapore. A general assembly is held every four to six years. Membership in national bodies is open to individuals, local churches, mission agencies, and national churches. WEF maintains a close working relationship to the Lausanne Committee for World Evangelization and the more recent AD 2000 and Beyond movement, which is an associate member of WEF.

As an evangelical movement with focus on evangelism and church planting, church enrichment, global missions, social action, and religious liberty, the WEF is having a greater impact on Asian churches than is generally acknowledged. At present, national fellowships function in Bangladesh*, Cambodia*, India*, Indonesia*, Israel, Japan*, Korea*, Malaysia*, Myanmar*, Nepal*, Pakistan*, Philippines*, Singapore*, Sri Lanka*, Taiwan*, and Thailand*. Each works with the regional body, the Evangelical Fellowship of Asia. One of the earliest and stronger of fellowships is the Evangelical Fellowship of India* (EFI, 1951), representing 24 denominations, 20 independent congregations, 75 agencies and institutions, and 3,000 individual members. The EFI holds an annual conference and sponsors commissions and departments in the areas of Christian education, theology, revival and evangelism, and women's concerns. Its missionary arm, the India Evangelical Mission* (1965), sponsors 450 cross-cultural missionaries. The EFI Committee on Relief (EFICOR) is one of the largest relief and development agencies in India. EFI has had a major role in the development of the Union Biblical Seminary in Pune, the largest theological college affiliated to Serampore. The Evangelical Fellowship of Asia (1983) has sponsored two Asia Mission Congresses (1990 in Korea and 1997 in Thailand). It sponsored the Asia Church Consultation in Indonesia (1994).

In addition to the work of national alliances and fellowships, the WEF-sponsored international commissions have had a significant impact on the Asian churches directly and indirectly. The Missions Commission has sponsored several research projects, encouraged self-supporting (tent-making) missionaries, and maintains an extensive publishing program. The first director of the commission was Chun Chae Ok of Ewha Women's University in Seoul, Korea, a former missionary to Pakistan. The number of cross-cultural missionaries from Asia, Africa, and Latin America now exceed those coming from Western countries.

The WEF Theological Commission has had a significant impact on Asian theological colleges and churches. It was founded as the Theological Assistance Programme (TAP) after the fifth general assembly of the WEF (1968), with Bruce Nicholls as the theological coordinator. It was developed into a full commission in 1975 with Byang Kato of Nigeria as the first chairman and Bruce Nicholls as executive director (1975-86). In 1971, TAP was a partner in launching TAP-Asia. In 1974 it became the autonomous Asia Theological Association (ATA), with Bong Rin Ro of Korea as executive director and Saphir Athyal as chairman. Under Bong Ro, the ATA has developed a network of theological schools and initiated Theological Education by Extension (TEE) in 1971, an accrediting association (1976), and the Asia Graduate School of Theology (1980s) for master's and doctoral studies in the Asian context. It was a catalyst for two research centers (Seoul 1973, New Delhi 1974). ATA has published regular newsletters, monographs, and books. It holds a conference every two to four years.

Under the editorship of Bruce Nicholls, the WEF Theological Commission launched *Theological News* in 1969 (a global newsletter), the *Evangelical Review of Theology* in 1977 (a theological journal), and a monograph series, and has published symposia of many task forces and consultations. The Theological Commission sponsored the global consultation "The Nature and Mission of the Church" (1983) in Wheaton, Illinois, United States. The Theological Commission has jointly sponsored, with the Lausanne Congress on World Evangelization*, consultations on simple lifestyle, evangelism and social responsibility, the work of the Holy Spirit, and conversion; a consultation with the WCC: "The Use of the Bible" (1976); and dialogues with the Roman Catholic Church* (1993 and 1997). Many theological colleges in Asia have benefited from its scholarship fund. The Theological Commission developed the International Council of Accrediting Agencies 1980 (ICAA), renamed the International Council for Evangelical Theological Education 1996 (ICETE).

The WEF affiliate Interchurch Relief and Development Association (IRDA) has been a catalyst in developing national evangelical relief and development agencies in many Asian countries, supported by TEAR Fund in several Western countries and World Relief Commission in the United States.

The WEF Religious Liberty Commission defends the rights of Christian minorities and persecuted believers, especially in eastern Europe, North Africa, and Asia. It emphasizes religious freedom as the foundation of all other freedoms in society and organizes protests to governments in cases of abuse.

The Commission on Women's Concerns (1984) focuses on the role of the family*, on the abuse of women and children, and on biblical social and sexual ethics. Its Asian counterpart is the Women's Ministries for the Evangelical Fellowship of Asia.

The recently formed Youth Commission (1992) encourages the formation of Youth Commissions in national fellowships and regional associations.

The effectiveness of WEF has been its emphasis on the priority of prayer, spiritual renewal, and discipleship; its emphasis on personal piety and integrity in relationships and finance; and its commitment to the essentials of the historic evangelical faith. It gives priority to the local church, to global missions, and to compassionate service to the poor and oppressed. It seeks to integrate evangelism and church planting with the whole of Christ's mission in the world, adopting a servant role to the churches in Asia and working for the coming of Christ's kingdom on earth.

Bibliography

Fuller, W. Harold, *People of the Mandate: The Story of the World Evangelical Fellowship* (1996). • Howard, David M., *The Dream That Would Not Die* (1986). • Waldron, Scott, ed., *Serving Our Generation: Evangelical Strategies for the 80s* (1980). • WEF Theological Commission, *Evangelical Review of Theology*, ed. Bruce J. Nicholls (1977-present) (published quarterly since 1977).

BRUCE J. NICHOLLS

World Spiritual Food Evangelistic Meeting/Rally

The World Spiritual Food Evangelistic Meeting/Rally (WSFEM) sprang up to form a separate Chinese Christian denomination in the 1940s. It was founded by Zao Shiguang, who came to the Christian faith in his school days. After graduating from high school, Zao assisted the Shanghai Christian and Missionary Alliance* (C&MA) "Truth Abiding Hall" *(Shouzhen Tang)* in their evangelism.

In 1932 Zao was ordained by the Far East branch of the C&MA. In 1936 he was sent twice, on a mission to India* and on another to Southeast Asia by Di Fuming, South Asia Region director of the C&MA. In 1941 Zao returned to Shanghai and resigned from the Truth Abiding Hall. He then organized the Southeast Asia Evangelical Committee, preparing to return to Southeast Asia. Unfortunately, the Pacific War broke out, forcing Zao to remain in Shanghai. While there, he published the monthly periodical *Spiritual Food* and set up the Spiritual Food Hall. Toward the end of the War of Resistance against Japanese Aggression, Zao built many Spiritual Food Halls while evangelizing in Jiangsu, Zejiang, and other provinces. In addition, he built primary and secondary schools, an orphanage, homes for the aged, seminaries, etc. He published the *Inspiration Lecture Notes, Song of Songs, Spiritual Food Hymns,* and more. All were well received. After establishing the independent denomination, Zao continued to sponsor and organize the WSFEM. In May 1946 the WSFEM held its first national conference in Shanghai. Zao was elected chairman. At the second national conference in Sep 1949, he was elected lifelong chairman, but Zao had already left the country with his family. In 1958, each and every Spiritual Food Hall on the continent participated in a joint worship service.

CHINA GROUP

World Vision

International Christian relief and development organization.

Originating in China* and Korea*, World Vision's work now touches the lives of more than 73 million people in nearly 100 nations. Its inspiration came in 1947 when Bob Pierce, World Vision's founder and first president, came face-to-face with the need of White Jade, an abandoned girl in the Chinese city of Xiamen. Pierce, an evangelist and war corespondent, pledged $5 per month to feed, clothe, and teach the child.

In Korea three years later, he enlarged his idea by founding World Vision, an organization that would care for Korea War* orphans by appealing to North Americans to sponsor them. By 1999, World Vision donors were sponsoring nearly 1.4 million children worldwide. Many of them are in poorer Asian countries such as India*, Bangladesh*, Indonesia*, Myanmar*, and the Philippines*.

World Vision's mission is: "To follow our Lord and Savior Jesus Christ in working with the poor and oppressed to promote human transformation, seek justice and bear witness to the good news of the Kingdom of God." World Vision raises funds and does relief and development work in 21 nations in Asia. It has provided emergency food and relief supplies to the victims of floods, typhoons, and cyclones in Bangladesh, India, China, and Papua New Guinea. It has responded to refugees and other victims of war and civil strife in Cambodia*, Laos*, Thailand*, Sri Lanka*, Myanmar, and Vietnam. In 1996-97, World Vision set up six noodle factories in North Korea to provide 60,000 meals per day for children and the elderly faced with starvation.

While World Vision responds to disasters, its emphasis is on development projects that help poor people achieve self-sustenance and justice. In the South Asia region, for example, World Vision has focused on education, health care, and micro-enterprise projects that lessen the possibility of children being sold into labor or prostitution. In Thailand and Myanmar, World Vision operates programs for street children and AIDS education. In Cambodia, Vietnam, and Laos, projects emphasize land-mine awareness and agricultural rehabilitation. In Bangladesh and India, where more than 100,000 children are sponsored, the organization has focused on public health and income-generating projects that lead to safer, economically-viable communities. In Indonesia, which felt the brunt of the 1998-99 Asian economic crisis, World Vision instituted food-for-work programs that gave thousands of poor families both jobs and rice.

Pierce expanded World Vision's work in Asia through missionary contacts and evangelism services. Its work in Taiwan, for example, began in the early 1950s in collaboration with a Presbyterian* missionary couple. World Vision–sponsored pastors' conferences in the Philippines (1955), Indonesia (1957), Burma (1958), Thailand (1959), and Sri Lanka (1969) introduced those countries to the organization's mission and work.

In the 1960s, World Vision's focus broadened from orphans to include impoverished children and emergency relief to the victims of war or natural disasters. In the 1970s, the organization reexamined its approach to assistance, recognizing that the sponsorship model did not adequately address the root causes of hunger and poverty. In addition to sponsors, World Vision began seeking business and government resources. It expanded its focus from the child to the community, endeavoring to bring about long-term self-sufficiency.

As a result of the Vietnam War*, World Vision undertook large-scale relief efforts. With its boat, *Seasweep*, it rescued thousands of Vietnamese boat people from the South China Sea. In 1970, World Vision was the first nongovernmental agency to respond to Cambodia's appeal for help. Stanley Mooneyham, World Vision president at the time, led a convoy of trucks loaded with $100,000 worth of medicine through hostile territory into Phnom Penh. In 1972 he conducted the first evangelistic crusade ever held in that country and opened the nation's first Christian pediatric hospital.

The war eventually forced World Vision to close its operations temporarily in Cambodia, Laos, and Vietnam. The Khmer Rouge* executed Minh Tien Voan, World Vision Cambodia's deputy director, and turned the hospital into a torture and execution center. Eventually, World Vision was able to resume operations in Southeast Asia. Elsewhere in Asia, it began permanent work in Mongolia* (1995), North Korea (1995), mainland China (1987), and Malaysia* (1997).

In the 1990s, World Vision began a more concerted effort to provide a voice for the poor and marginalized of Asia and elsewhere. Through its advocacy efforts, it brought international attention to issues such as the plight of child laborers in South Asia, the killing and injuring of innocent people by land mines in Southeast Asia, and the lot of the poor as a result of the Asian economic crisis.

Celebrating its 50th anniversary, World Vision reemphasized both its focus on children and its Christian witness in Asia. It sees the child as central to transformational development in the community. At the same time, the motivation for its work remains its desire to manifest Christ's word and truth.

Bibliography

Irvine, Graeme, *Best Things in the World Times: An Insider's View of World Vision* (1996). • Yamamori, Tetsunao, Bryant L. Myers, and David Conner, eds., *Serving with the Poor in Asia* (1995). John McCoy

World War II

World War II and the Japanese conquests profoundly affected Christianity in Asia. The impact was both negative and positive. On the one hand, Christians in Japan* proper and the areas under Japanese rule suffered greatly. Congregational life and evangelistic, educational, and social ministries were disrupted, church properties were destroyed in the bombings and fighting, Christians were harassed, imprisoned, or martyred, and international missionary work ceased. On the other hand, the Japanese occupation broke the back of Western imperialism and forced Asian Christians to draw upon their own physical and spiritual resources for survival. Out of the trauma of war and occupation emerged an independent and vibrant indigenous church.

War in Asia: The first phase, 1931-41. Japan had expansionistic designs in East Asia since the 1890s (Korea*), and these were a source of ongoing tension with the other great powers. When Western leaders condemned the Japanese invasion of Manchuria in 1931, attack on Shanghai in 1932, and creation of the puppet state Manchukuo, they responded by withdrawing from the League of Nations. In Jul 1937 its soldiers clashed with Chinese troops outside of Peking (Beijing), and an all-out war ensued. In the ensuing months, Japanese forces captured the major cities of China, including Nanking (Nanjing), the capital of Chiang Kai-shek's Kuomintang or Nationalist regime, where they brutally massacred thousands of people. Chiang moved his government to the safety of Chungking (Chongqing) in Szechwan (Sichuan) Province and sought to organize resistance. His Communist rivals did likewise from their strongholds in the north. The Japanese military operations soon bogged down, and their control did not extend much beyond the urban areas. The government of their client, Wang Ching-wei, a disaffected former associate of Chiang, gained no international recognition. In Nov 1938 the Japanese announced the "Greater East Asia Co-Prosperity Sphere," a scarcely veiled scheme for economic and cultural hegemony, and utilized such slogans as the "New Order in Asia" and "Asia for the Asians" to win support in the region.

In the areas under military rule, they allowed foreign missionaries to continue working, although many of them chose to return home. Those who remained, particularly American missionaries, strongly condemned the war in China*, as they had done in 1931-32. In books, articles, and letters, they sought to influence world opinion by accusing the Japanese of violating international agreements and committing atrocities. In

Sep 1938 a group led by Frank Price of Nanjing Theological Seminary created the China Information Service, whose bulletin documented the military's misdeeds, criticized United States neutrality legislation, and called for an embargo against Japan. Congregationalist Walter Judd, who served in the occupied area, was so concerned about the moral irresponsibility of the pacifist and isolationist clergy and churchgoing public in America to the plight of China that he resigned his post in 1938, returned home, and gave over 1,400 speeches warning of Japanese aggression.

On the other hand, missionaries in Japan suggested that the Japanese were not as satanic as the friends of China were making them out to be, and that every indication of American opposition to Japan merely increased the hostility to them and made it more difficult for Christians there. United States measures against Japan would only drive it into the arms of the Axis powers. Baptist* William Axling insisted that the West was responsible for Japanese expansionism by closing the door to immigration and setting up trade barriers against its goods. The West wanted to dominate China and exclude Japan from the area, and blocked Japanese efforts for a peaceful solution.

This attitude reflected the larger problem that faced Christians in Japan. Christianity there appealed mainly to members of the middle class, who tended to identify with the establishment and affirmed their country's nationalist aspirations. Thus in the matter of participation in state Shinto* rites, most Christians were eager to be regarded both as good citizens and members of a "mainline" religion, and they readily accepted the argument that shrine attendance was not an act of worship but an expression of patriotism and loyalty. The National Christian Council on various occasions declared its support of the government and willingness to help correct public opinion toward Japan overseas. However, a few courageous voices of criticism were heard. Christian scholar Tadao Yanaihara lost his post at Tokyo Imperial University in 1937 for criticizing the Manchuria policy, and the noted evangelist and social reformer Toyohiko Kagawa* was arrested twice in 1940 because of peace activism and apologizing to China for Japan's actions. The American-educated Kagawa also in Aug 1939 and again in Sep 1941 publicly called upon Christians on both sides of the Pacific to help avert a break between the two countries.

Being members of a supranational church, the Roman Catholics* easily adjusted their position to go along with national policy, but things were more difficult for Protestants because of their long-standing links with Britain and North America, the homeland of most of the 1,000 missionaries serving in Japan. In spite of their affirmations of loyalty, Japanese Protestants from 1937 on were subjected to close police scrutiny and pressure to reduce their Western ties. The regime also objected to such doctrines as divine sovereignty and the kingdom of God (which made God greater than the emperor), and the second coming of Christ (the Japanese emperor would not reign forever). Although the imperial constitution guaranteed freedom of religious belief, the Diet in 1939 passed a Religious Bodies Law that regularized government controls over these bodies. It required every religious organization to obtain recognition from the ministry of education, which in turn would guarantee them legal security and immunity from unwarranted interference by local police and petty officials. Then the government announced on 12 Jun 1940 that a denomination must have a minimum of 50 congregations and 5,000 members to receive approval. Because so few bodies were that large, church leaders began exploring the possibility of union, an idea long favored by Protestant ecumenists (see Ecumenical Movement). A further impulse to this was a police action in August against the Salvation Army* that charged the group with espionage because of its British connection.

In the ensuing negotiations, the churches agreed to total financial self-support, full autonomy in matters of ownership and administration, and the formation of one ecclesiastical body. This would satisfy the regime's misgivings about the Protestants' Western ties. Some 34 denominations united in the new Church of Christ in Japan (CCJ; *Nihon Kirisuto Kyodan)* at its founding general assembly on 24-25 Jun 1941, and the government approved its charter in November. Not joining were the Seventh-day Adventists*, Jehovah's Witnesses, and a portion of the Episcopal Church. Within this curious body, the various denominations kept a sense of identity through the existence of 11 "blocs" where traditional creeds and forms of worship were maintained, while the overall structure was monolithic with all authority concentrated in a director, former Presbyterian* minister Mitsuru Tomita*. At the same time, all but a handful of missionaries returned to their homelands. The attempt to impose state Shinto on Korean Christians met with more resistance, although the Catholics accommodated to the policy. The Methodist* and Presbyterian churches finally yielded to the intense pressure and recognized shrine attendance, but a government effort in 1939 to force an organic union of all Christian denominations met with little success.

Police surveillance of the churches intensified, and any activities of which the regime disapproved became excuses for imprisoning church leaders and expelling missionaries. In 1940-41, almost all missionaries were evacuated.

Christians in Japan's other colony, Taiwan*, were treated in the same manner. Attendance at Shinto shrines was mandatory, Christianity was seen as subversive because of Western ties, Christian school curricula controls were made more nationalistic, all church properties were placed under local (i.e., Japanese) control to avoid confiscation, missionaries were forced to leave, and the Japanese Christian church functioned as the protector of the Taiwanese ones. In China, the Nanjing authorities allowed Japan's Protestant mission society, the East Asia Mission (originally founded in 1932 to work in Manchuria), to send clergy to work with their Chinese counterparts and encourage a union of Protestant churches. The regime expected the churches to govern themselves and live without foreign funds and personnel. This way they would play a role in the Japanese program of de-Westernization and through the spirit of Christ become good citizens of the New Order in East Asia.

The outbreak of war in Europe complicated the picture. Japan joined the Axis alliance although retaining its non-aggression treaty with the Soviet Union, and it pressured Vichy France to allow stationing troops in Indochina. However, since the French administration remained intact, the Roman Catholic* churches were generally left alone until late in the war. After the German conquest of Holland, the colonial administration in the Dutch East Indies interned the German missionaries there (see Indonesia). This meant that the Lutheran* Batak* churches in Sumatra* had to function completely independent of European direction, which prepared them well for survival under the later Japanese occupation. The German Mennonite* work among the Chinese at Kelet, Java, became the independent Muria Christian Church.

The Dutch Mennonites also reorganized their mission stations as churches. Then, as relations between Japan and the United States rapidly deteriorated, two noteworthy Christian initiatives occurred. One was that of the "John Doe Associates," a complicated effort at personal diplomacy involving Fr. John M. Drought and his superior, Bishop James E. Walsh, veteran China missionaries and leaders of the Catholic Foreign Mission Society of America at Maryknoll*, and two well-connected people in Japan. Although they acted as couriers and carried messages between high officials in both governments, they could not gain acceptance of a plan that might have prevented war because the Americans were adamant that Japan had to withdraw from China. The other was the sending of a Christian delegation to America in a last-ditch attempt to gain a mutual understanding between the two countries. The National Christian Council in Japan and the Federal Council of Churches and International Missionary Council in the United States organized the conference that took place in Riverside, California, in Apr 1941. Among the Japanese churchmen present were Dr. Kagawa, Methodist bishop Yoshimune Abe, educator Michi Kawai, and Congregationalist layperson and member of parliament, Tsunejiro Tsuyama. The delegates then scattered across the country, speaking to various church groups, and regathered in Atlantic City, New Jersey, to confer with representatives of over 30 mission boards and agencies. Resulting from the meetings was a decision by American missionary administrators to appoint a study committee to rethink mission-church relationships. A return visit by American church figures was planned, but the outbreak of war rendered this impossible.

The Pacific War, 1941-45. The surprise attack on Pearl Harbor, Hong Kong*, the Philippine* Islands, and Malaya on 7-8 Dec 1941 brought Asia into the global conflict. The Japanese quickly neutralized Thailand* through a protectorate and in the next six months seized Burma (Myanmar*), Malaya, Singapore*, the Dutch East Indies, the Philippines, and a portion of the Aleutian Islands, and in their vast new empire set out to implement the principles of the Greater East Asia Co-Prosperity Sphere. They courted indigenous leaders in the Philippines, Indochina, Thailand, Burma, Malaya, Indonesia*, and Singapore, which they generously renamed Syonan — Light of the South. They encouraged cooperation among Muslims and Indians, backed the Free India movement of S. C. Bose, and portrayed the war as a collaborative effort of Asians against Western imperialism.

The juggernaut was halted in mid-1942 only after spectacular Allied naval victories in the Coral Sea and off Midway Island, and a long, bitter campaign of capturing Pacific islands ensued until the Japanese homeland was within aerial range. The Americans subjected its cities to incessant bombing and prepared for a massive invasion, but the dropping of the atomic bombs forced the imperial regime to capitulate on 14-15 Aug 1945. Japanese forces on the Asia mainland and in Indonesia surrendered within the next month, a United States army of occupation took over the country, and reconstruction began.

For Christians, the war years were a continuing time of trial. Missionaries and Western laypersons were interned, and some were repatriated in two exchanges that occurred in 1942-43. Others were placed in such notorious internment camps as the University of Santo Tomas in Manila, Camp Stanley in Hong Kong, and Changi in Singapore. For a time, Western civilians in the area of China under Wang Ching-wei's collaborationist regime were allowed some freedom of movement, but in response to the United States' policy of interning Japanese-Americans permission was given in early 1943 to round up and incarcerate all Westerners still at large. The treatment that civilians in occupied areas received depended on the caprice of local commanders. One of the most egregious examples of missionary martyrdom occurred in the Philippines. In Apr 1942, the American Baptist missionaries on the island of Panay fled to a mountain retreat, which they called "Hopevale." Japanese soldiers eventually found the place and in cold blood executed the entire group of 12 people, including the women and a child.

In Japan, Christians were expected to give unreserved support to the war effort. The CCJ was reorganized and the bloc system eliminated, and the director saw that it gave undeviating obedience to every government directive. Church members called on families of soldiers and cared for their needs, and they raised money to pay for airplanes. Christians participated in the marches to the Shinto shrines. Prayers for victory were said, and sermons were directed toward helping the war effort. A Bureau of Indoctrination ordered Protestant thinkers to harmonize the ancient spiritual bases of the Japanese people with Christian doctrines, show how the Christian revelation came from the peculiar genius of the Japanese people, and teach the spiritual virtue of Asian expansion. It forced the united church to revise its doctrines and bring them in line with state Shinto. Several thousand people were jailed for alleged disloyal sentiments. The unregistered churches were dissolved and their properties confiscated. The Russian Orthodox* Church was not registered and shrank to a quarter of its prewar size. Roman Catholics reorganized under the Religious Bodies Law as a totally autonomous body called the "Japan Catholic Church" and were left alone.

Christians in Korea* were severely persecuted and their churches put under political control. After years of pressure, in Jul 1945 all Protestant churches were ordered to abolish their denominational distinctions and unite in a Korean-Japanese Christian Church. Following this, 3,000 Christians were arrested and 50 died in prison. Many others were slated to be killed in the event of a Japanese defeat, but the surrender came too quickly. In Taiwan, rural churches and Christians among the mountain tribal peoples were singled out for particularly harsh treatment. The CCJ official Y. Abe was sent to Wang's China in 1942 to shepherd the nascent church union there. Those who accepted this church believed they were manipulating the occupation state to their advantage, and such a body could better withstand improper state influence than loosely cooperating denominations. In Singapore and Malaya, a Federation of Christian Churches was created in Jun 1942 with the approval of the Japanese authorities, but it was suspended in early 1943 when they feared that it might become a united front against the occupying forces. In Indonesia, the Japanese interned Western missionaries, and about one third of the Protestants and one tenth of the Catholics were killed or died from hunger or disease. They sought to involve the whole population in the war effort and did not persecute Indonesian Christians as such except in the Moluccas* and New Guinea, where scores of congregation leaders were suspected of being pro-Dutch and were killed. Churches were used as channels of propaganda for the Greater East Asia Co-Prosperity Sphere, and they were forced to join regional councils of churches that included both Protestants and Catholics. The military government took over all Christian schools and modeled them on the Japanese pattern, and church meetings required permission. A number of Japanese ministers and priests were sent to give guidance to Indonesian Christians, and they, along with some Japanese Christian officers and civil servants, did much to protect the local believers. The Batak HKBP church chose one of its own people to be its bishop *(ephorus)*, a position that a German missionary had always held before.

Japan overran the Philippine Islands in a few weeks and interned all American missionaries as nationals of a "hostile" nation. As part of the program to win over the Filipinos to the Greater East Asia Co-Prosperity Sphere, the "Religious Section" came with the invasion forces. Its task was to undermine all confidence in America and bring the Philippine churches into line with the Japanese ones. It comprised 26 priests and ministers, with the Catholic unit led by the bishop of Osaka and the Protestant one by several men who had been educated in the United States and who now belonged to the CCJ. Headquartered in Manila, it set out to coordinate religious activities in the island and see that the churches helped rather than hindered the occupation.

Ecumenists had made considerable progress in the prewar years toward closer cooperation and even church union with the Presbyterian-Congregationalist merger in 1929 (United Evangelical Church) and the formation of a cooperative Philippine Federation of Evangelical Churches in 1938. The Religious Section ignored the existing PFEC and on 10 Oct 1942 created another agency that would include all Protestants: The Federation of Evangelical Churches in the Philippines. Chosen as its president was Enrique C. Sobrepeña*, a prominent United Evangelical Church minister. In Apr 1943 the Filipino leaders decided to try to create a united church in hopes that it would be less subject to direct control by the Japanese, and in October the Federation's executive committee decreed its dissolution and reconstitution as the new Evangelical Church in the Philippines. Eleven churches refused to be a part of this, and only five groups were present at its inaugural general assembly in Apr 1944. When Japanese rule ended in Feb 1945, both the United Church and the Federation fell apart and the prewar PFEC was restored. There was bitter recrimination against those church leaders who were suspected of being overly cooperative with the occupation authorities — Sobrepeña himself was tried by a military court but acquitted — and the cause of church union in the Philippines was dealt a severe setback.

Aftermath. The losses due to the war were enormous. For example, of the 1,800 Protestant church buildings in Japan before the war, 540 were destroyed in the bombings and 200 more were dismantled or dynamited to keep fires from spreading. Approximately one-half of the Protestants were without church homes. At least 120 pastors were imprisoned during the war, and several died in jail. In the Philippines, an estimated 80 percent of all church properties were destroyed, mostly in the process of liberation. In Manila alone, 47 churches were in ruins and the Episcopal church lost 90 percent of its buildings, while 257 Roman Catholic priests and members of religious orders were dead. The losses of church records and historical materials were incalculable.

The wartime demoralization of the clergy and congregations and the compromises many Christians made with Japanese Shinto and the occupation authorities had a baneful effect on the church. This was clearly recognized in the Confession of War Responsibility* that the Church of Christ in Japan issued in 1967. It says the "CCJ was formed largely because of the Religious Bodies

Law, and the church as the 'light of the world' and the 'salt of the earth' should not have acted in concert with the war effort; yet it approved of the war, supported it, and neglected its calling to serve as a watchman for the nation. The CCJ seeks the forgiveness of God, of Asian neighbors, and of the Japanese people for mistakes committed at the time of its formation and during the war years, and asks for God's help and guidance so that it might never repeat its errors." This confession is the only one of its kind issued by a religious body in Japan after World War II.

The war contributed to the advance of Christian missions. Many of the young men and women who served in the American armed forces in the Pacific received their first exposure to Asian societies and were stimulated to return as missionaries. Servicemen in the Philippines actually engaged in evangelistic endeavors in their free time, and new missionary societies arose from their efforts, such as the Far Eastern Gospel Crusade (now SEND, International). General Douglas MacArthur's open invitation to send missionaries to help in the reconstruction of occupied Japan further encouraged this sense of evangelical awareness.

However, the most significant impact of the war is how it forced the Asian church into a state of independence that it had not experienced before. The cutting off of Western mission funds made it become self-supporting, the removal of foreign missionaries compelled it to become self-propagating, and the newly gained responsibilities of leadership encouraged it to become self-governing.

Churches and Christians also learned to work together in the struggle against Japanese imperialism and simply to survive in the most adverse of circumstances. World War II was a critical factor in the maturation of the church.

Bibliography

Brook, Timothy, "Toward Independence: Christianity in China under the Japanese Occupation, 1937-1945," in *Christianity in China from the Eighteenth Century to the Present,* ed. Daniel H. Bays (1996). • Craft, Stephen C., "Peacemakers in China: American Missionaries and the Sino-Japanese War, 1937-1941," *Journal of Church and State,* Vol. 41 (Summer 1999). • Drummond, Richard H., *A History of Christianity in Japan* (1971). • Iglehart, Charles W., *A Century of Protestant Christianity in Japan* (1959). • Ion, A. Hamish, *The Cross in the Dark Valley: The Canadian Protestant Missionary Movement in the Japanese Empire, 1931-1945* (1999). • Iriye, Akira, *The Origins of the Second World War in Asia and the Pacific* (1987). • Lee Kun Sam, *The Christian Confrontation with Shinto Nationalism* (1966). • Pederson, Paul, *Batak Blood and Protestant Soul* (1970). • Pierard, Richard V., "Pax Americana and the Evangelical Missionary Advance," in *Earthen Vessels: American Evangelicals and Foreign Missions, 1880-1980,* ed. J. A. Carpenter and W. R. Shenk (1990). • Sitoy, T. V., *Several Springs, One Stream: The United Church of Christ in the Philippines* (1992).

RICHARD V. PIERARD

Wu Jingxiong

(b. Yinxian, Zhejiang, 1900; d. 1986). Second envoy to the Vatican appointed by the Republic of China*.

A doctor of law, Wu was once the head of the department of law of Dongwu University (Suzhou University) and a member of the Legislative Yuan of the Kuomintang government. He attended the San Francisco Conference as an advisor to the Chinese delegation and helped translate the United Nations Charter. Originally a Protestant, he converted to Roman Catholicism after a stay with a Catholic professor of law at Aurora University in Shanghai in the winter of 1937, when he had occasion to read a brief biography of St. Theresa and several other well-known works on Catholic doctrine. He was baptized by President Cai Er Meng (Germain) of Aurora University. Not long after, his entire family became converts. In Dec 1946, accompanied by his family, Wu went to Rome as the envoy of the Kuomintang government, which had unilaterally sent its first envoy, Xi Shoukang, to establish diplomatic ties with the Vatican in July.

In Feb 1949, Wu received a telegraph from President Sun Ke of the Executive Yuan to "return home for consultation." Soon after, he resigned from his post as envoy and spent his remaining 30 years living and working abroad.

CHINA GROUP

Wu Lei-ch'uan

(b. Hangzhou, Zhejiang, 1870; d. Beijing, 1944). Chinese Christian scholar.

At age 23, Wu passed the provincial examination of the civil service exams, and in 1898 he became a metropolitan graduate. Soon afterward, he was appointed to the Hanlin Academy. He acted as supervisor of Zhi-jiang Provincial College between 1906 and 1909, becoming director of Hanlin Academy in 1910. After the Xin-Hai Revolution, he became chief secretary in the education department of the Bei-Yang government in Beijing between 1912 and 1925 and acted as the department's chief spokesperson from 1925 to 1926. From 1924, he taught courses on Christianity and Confucianism* at Yenching University. In 1926 he resigned his post at the education department to become a professor at Yenching and was made its vice chancellor shortly afterward. From 1920 to 1929, he acted as deputy director of the education department in the Republican Government. From Aug 1929, he was registrar at Yenching University. He wrote *Christianity and Chinese Culture.*

Bibliography

Ng Lee-ming, *Christianity and Social Change in China* (1981). • Cha Shih-chieh, *Concise Biographies of Important Chinese Christians* (1983). • West, Philip, "Christianity and Nationalism: The Career of Wu Lei-ch'uan at Yenching University," in *The Missionary Enterprise in China and America*, ed. John K. Fairbank (1974).

China Group, translated by Lena Lau

Wu Yaozong

(Wu Yao-Tsung or Y. T. Wu) (b. Guangzhou, China, 1893; d. 1979). Chinese leader of the Three-Self Movement*.

Wu, who studied at the Customs College in Beijing from 1908 to 1913, worked for seven years with the Chinese Customs Office at Guangzhou, Yingkou, and Beijing. He became a Christian in 1920 and was baptized by Rowland Cross, an American missionary in Beijing.

Wu studied at Union Theological Seminary in New York in 1924 and enrolled as a graduate student at Columbia University in 1925. He received his master's degree in 1927. After returning to China*, he involved himself in the student division of the Young Men's Christian Association* (YMCA). In 1932 he was appointed chief editor of the Association Press in Shanghai, where he wrote and translated much material. Wu was a member of the Fellowship of Reconciliation in China and remained a pacifist until the Japanese invasion. He spoke at the World Committee of the YMCA, the executive committee of the World Student Christian Federation, and the Oxford Conference in 1937. Following this trip, he decided to further his studies at Union Theological Seminary, where he was influenced by the thoughts of Reinhold Niebuhr. He attended the Madras Conference of the International Missionary Council in 1938.

His increasing disenchantment with the Kuomintang was matched by a growing interest in Marxism. In 1947, after attending the World Conference of Christian Youth in Oslo, Norway, in July and the World Alliance Meeting of the YMCA in Edinburgh, Scotland, in August, he wrote "The Present-Day Tragedy of Christianity" for the *Tien Feng*. In this work, he accused Protestantism of nurturing capitalism. The angry reaction from *Tien Feng* sponsors like the Christian Literature Society forced Wu to resign as editor of the paper. In Jul 1949 he wrote an article criticizing missionary work and accusing the British and Americans of using the Chinese Christian church to achieve their imperialistic ambitions. He argued that Protestantism must reform itself by separation from capitalism if it was to survive the inevitable progress of society toward socialism. Otherwise, the demise of capitalism would be the death of Protestantism.

In 1950 he started the Three-Self Reform Movement, which began with a Christian manifesto signed by 40 prominent Chinese Christians. The objective of the manifesto was basically to obtain the cooperation of the churches in the achievement of the Communist ideal of national self-sufficiency. In Apr 1951, Premier Chou Enlai met with the Christian leaders to create a 25-man Preparatory Council with Wu as the head. The national conference was held in Jul 1954 in Beijing, where Wu emphasized the "Love-Country Love-Church" spirit. The Three-Self Movement was officially established, thus placing the official church under the direct influence of the Communist regime. In 1961 Wu became president of the National Conference of Christian Churches in China.

Wu held several key posts in the Republic. He was also president of the Nanking Theological Seminary and moderator of the Church of Christ in China. He and his wife, a physician named Yang Su-lan, had two children, a son and a daughter. Wu was a controversial figure among Christians because of his efforts in relating Christianity to Marxism (see Communism).

Bibliography

Boorman, L. Howard, ed., *Biographical Dictionary of Republican China*, Vol. 3 (1970). • *Documents of the Three-Self Movement* (compiled by the National Council of the Churches of Christ in the USA, 1963). • Wickeri, Philip, *Seeking the Common Ground* (1988). • Xu Rulei, "True Israelite," *Chinese Theological Review*, Vol. 6 (1990). • Ng Lee-ming, "A Study of Y. T. Wu," *Ching Feng*, Vol. 15 (1972).

China Group

Wu Yi Fang

(b. Hupeh, China, 1893; d. 1985). Female Christian educator in China*.

Wu received her education in Hangchow, Shanghai, Soochow, and elsewhere. She entered Jinling Girls' College (arts and sciences) in 1916 and graduated two years later. Since beginning her teaching career at Peking (Beijing) Women's Training School in 1918, she devoted her entire life to education.

In 1922 Wu received a scholarship to attend the University of Michigan (United States) for further study. She earned her doctorate in biology in 1928. Afterward, she returned to China and was appointed the first principal of Jinling College for Girls, where she served for 28 years. Beginning in 1981, she was honorary principal of Nanjing Teachers Training University, education minister of Jiangsu Province, assistant provincial governor of Jiangsu, representative of the National People Representatives Conference, vice chair of the National Women's Union, and provincial government vice chair of Jiangsu. Wu was also honorary chair of the Amity Foundation*.

After Wu was baptized in 1918, she took John 1:1 as the foundation stone of her faith. She was often invited to students summer and winter camps as a speaker. She was one of 40 people who signed the "Three-Self Manifesto." In 1954 she became vice chair of the Chinese Christian Three-Self Patriotic Movement* Committee for the first and second meetings. In 1980 she was elected its honorary chair.

Wu remained a patriot all her life and was very active during the anti-Japanese war. In 1943 she was one of six professors who visited the USA to seek support from the nongovernment sector. In 1945 she was the official delegate of China who participated in the drawing up of the United Nations constitution. In 1979 she was awarded the Sophia Prize by the University of Michigan and was well commended by the chancellor as an extraordinary woman in education and politics. CHINA GROUP

Wu Yushan

(b. Changsu, China, 1632; d. 1718). First Chinese priest of the Society of Jesus* in Jiangnan, China, and well-known artist whose work depicted mountains and waters in the Qing dynasty.

Wu often went to the Xing Fu Buddhist convent in Suzhou during his middle-age years and was a close friend of monk Mo Yong, but from 1675 on he was inclined toward Catholicism through his contact with Jesuit missionaries Lu Rima (Franciscus de Rougemont), Bai Yingli (Phillippe Couplet), and others. He was converted and christened Ximan Sawulue (Simon Xaverius). In 1681 Couplet was recalled to Europe. Wu intended to go with him, but his plans did not materialize when they reached Macau*. Wu remained in Macau for five months and returned to his hometown in the summer of 1682. He returned to Macau in the winter and joined the Society of Jesus. He was over 50 years old when he began to study Latin and other required courses for the priesthood. He was consecrated a priest on 1 Aug 1688 in Nanjing by Chinese bishop Lo Wenzao*. His first pastoral assignment was in Shanghai. In 1691 he was put in charge of the religious affairs of the Jiading Catholic Church.

Wu died at age 86 after serving 30 years as a priest. He composed many poems reflecting his own preaching career and religious feelings, which are collected in an anthology, *San Yi Ji.* His sermons from 15 Aug 1696 to 25 Dec 1697 and other religious activities were compiled by Zhao Lun, a convert in Jiading, in a book, *Kou Duo* (Record of Word and Deeds), the first collection of sermons by a Chinese priest.

Bibliography

Chaves, Jonathan, *Singing of the Source: Nature and God in the Poetry of the Chinese Painter Wu Li* (1993). • Chen Yuan, "Wu-Yu-shan: In Commemoration of the 250th Anniversary of His Ordination to the Priesthood in the Society of Jesus," *Monumenta Serica,* Vol. 3 (1938). • Chou K'ang-hsieh, ed., *Wu Yu-shan (Li) yen-chiu lun-chi* (reprint of 11 articles on Wu Li plus three new articles) (1971). • Lippe, A., "A Christian Chinese Painter: Wu Li (1632-1718)," *Metropolitan Museum of Art Bulletin,* Vol. 11 (1952). • Tchang, M., and P. de Prunele, *Le Pere Siomon a Cunha, S.J. (Ou Li Yu-chan), L'homme et l'oevre artistique* (1914). CHINA GROUP

Wuhan Convent

Chinese Catholic religious convent situated in the city of Wuhan (see also Xieshan Monastery).

After over two years of preparation, the convent opened its doors on 14 Jul 1985 with 20 aspirants: 14 postulants and six who were called to enter the novitiate to become novices on the day of inauguration. According to the rules set by the convent, the aspirants need two years to complete their postulancy. The novitiate also lasts two years. Only those who complete two years of novitiate can make their first vows to become full-fledged sisters.

During postulance and the novitiate, the trainees devote half the day to attending classes and the other half to acquiring practical skills.

The convent continues to train new sisters for the Wuhan Diocese. Some of these graduated from rehabilitation or health-care classes, some took up accounting, some typewriting Chinese, and others tailoring, embroidery, weaving, and electronic organ playing. All of them possess a specific skill to fulfill the functions of a modern Catholic Chinese sister.

In 1993 the convent recruited 20 more aspirants. There are also over 10 sisters who belong to the advanced-age group living in the same convent.

CHINA GROUP

Wylie, Alexander

(b. London, England, 1815; d. Feb 1889). British missionary to China* and sinologist.

Wylie first entered China in Aug 1847 when he was 31 years old. His first job was as director of the mission press set up by the London Missionary Society in Shanghai. He returned to Britain in 1860 and was later sent by the British and Foreign Bible Society to China. In 1877 he returned to Britain due to his poor eyesight. In 1883 he suffered from a stroke, which debilitated him until his death six years later.

In 1848 Wylie married a missionary who had worked in South Africa. The following year, they had a daughter, but his wife passed away after giving birth. From that point on, his full attention was on his literary work. Wylie's work included publishing *Liu He Cong Tan,* editing the *Chinese Recorder,* and being involved in setting up the Asian Culture Council North American Branch.

Wylie was a remarkable linguist and a voluminous writer. He acquired the French, Russian, German, Manchu, and Mongol languages while in charge of the press. He translated *Qing Yuan Ke Meng* (Dictionary of Mongol) into English and wrote *Zhong guo Wen Xian Ji Lue* (Notes on Chinese Literature). He also translated many mathematics books into Chinese. Wylie's voluminous collection of both Chinese and English books was later donated to the Asia Culture Library and became the foundation of the library's collection.

Bibliography

Wylie, Alexander, *Memorials of Protestant Missionaries to the Chinese* (1867). • Cordier, Henri, "The Life and Labours of Alexander Wylie . . . A Memoir," *Journal of the Royal Asiatic Society of Great Britain and Ireland,* n.s., Vol. 19 (1887). CHINA GROUP

Xavier, Francis

(b. Aragon, Spain, 7 Apr 1506; d. Shangchuan, an island off the Canton coast of China, 3 Dec 1552). Spanish Jesuit*, one of the founding members of the Society of Jesus, who introduced Christianity to Japan* and established its first Christian mission.

Xavier was the sixth and last child of Doña Maria de Azpilqueta y Aznarez de Sada and Juan de Jassu y Atondo of Navarre. During his university studies in Paris, he met Iñigo (Ignatius), a Basque nobleman from Loyola. In due course, Xavier and a little band of university students gathered around Ignatius, forming the nucleus of a new religious order, the Society of Jesus. After securing his doctorate as a distinguished student, Xavier worked as a college professor for a short while before proceeding to Italy, where he served as secretary to Ignatius in Rome. In answer to a request that came to Ignatius from King John III of Portugal, Xavier was sent to India* to preach the Gospel.

Appointed apostolic nuncio to Asia, Xavier sailed from Lisbon on 7 Apr 1541 and reached Goa on 6 May 1542. Xavier spent a total of 19 months in Goa, interspersed with extended periods of ministry elsewhere. Six months after his arrival, on 15 Sep, he sailed to the Fishery Coast in southeast India, 150 leagues away, where he was welcomed by the *Paravas,* the pearl-divers of a low caste, of whom some 20,000 had already embraced Christianity six or seven years earlier. In the year he spent with the *Paravas,* Xavier translated the first principles of the Christian faith into Tamil, with the help of three seminarians who accompanied him from Goa, and composed a sermon on what it meant to be a Christian. He moved farther south to stay four months at the capital, Tuticorin, where he wrote that his arm ached and his voice became hoarse because of the countless baptisms. He remained in Tamil Nadu until Sep 1543, went to Goa in mid-November with a high-ranking Portuguese official, Martim Affonso, returned to Tamil Nadu in December, and made brief visits to Cannanore and Cochin.

He went to Manappad and journeyed on foot to the villages on Cape Comorin and beyond, tolerating great physical pain and suffering. He was well loved, especially by children, who called him *Periya Padre* (Great Father). In Travancore, in exchange for Portuguese military support for the local ruler, he baptized more than 10,000 people among the Macaus within a month. He also secured financial assistance from the local ruler, Rama Varma, to build churches for the converts in 1544. In the same year, Xavier also promoted Portuguese military intervention to replace a deposed ruler of Jaffna in exchange for facilities to introduce Christianity in that region.

In one of his many bold letters to King John II of Portugal, he wrote from Cochin on 20 Jan 1545: "I hear voices from India rising to heaven with the complaint that Your Highness is dealing stingily with them since only a small portion of the abundant revenues which enrich your treasury from here is being given by Your Highness to alleviate its very serious spiritual needs."

In 1549 Xavier was appointed the first provincial of the Society of Jesus in Goa, and so much of his time was taken up with the administration of the Colégio de Santa Fé (which the Jesuits inherited in 1551), the installation of Jesuits from Portugal working in India, and voluminous correspondence. Xavier's letters were later compiled as the two-volume *Epistolae S. Francisci Xaverii Aliaque ejus Scripta* by historians Geog Schürhammer and Josef Wicki (Monumenta Historica Societatis Jesu [Rome: 1944, 1945]).

During his short sojourn in Goa, Xavier attended to prisoners and to the sick and dying in the hospital. He preached to the simple folk and the neglected youth. In spite of his efforts in India, Xavier was convinced that Christianity would not outlive missionaries in India. He wrote to Ignatius of Loyola that he saw "no way of perpetuating our Society through the Indians, natives of the land; and that Christianity will last among them for as long as shall last and live we who are here, or those whom you may send from there." He then became acquainted with Tabarija, former sultan of Ternate and half brother of Sultan Hairun. Tabarija had become a Christian and told him about the deserted Christians in the Moluccas*.

In early 1545, Xavier heard rumors that two kings in southern Celebes had been baptized and asked for missionaries to instruct their peoples. After a pilgrimage to the tomb of St. Thomas* the apostle in Mylapore, Xavier sailed to Malacca*, where he stayed till Dec 1545. He fought hard against the immorality of the Portuguese, with their numerous Malay concubines and slave girls. He succeeded in a kind of reformation of this rich city, while trying hard to learn a bit of Malay. Francis's example of a simple, holy, and hardworking life gave him an irresistible power over the hearts of others, even non-Christians. Bad news from Macassar brought Xavier to the Christian village of Hatiwi in Ambon in Feb 1546.

On Ambon and the other islands of the Moluccas Xavier was going to visit, he tried to persuade the Portuguese to give up their vices. He gave religious instructions to baptize many islanders, using eager young boys as his interpreters and catechists. Hearing about the abandoned Christians on Morotai and northern Halmahera, he sailed to Ternate, where he was liked by Christians and Muslims alike. He composed songs telling the salvation history, arranged religious instruction courses, and looked after the sick and dying. On his daring journey to Morotai in an open *cora-cora* (rowing boat), he strengthened the Christian villagers and converted many. He promised to send Jesuit priests to these faraway islands. This became the start of the Jesuit Moluccan Mission (1545-1666). In 1547 Xavier was back in Malacca with a few native boys who were sent to Goa to study at St. Paul's Seminary, established by Xavier as "a school of native boys" from Africa and Asia. In Malacca, Francis encouraged the defenders of the city, who were about to surrender to the combined armies of the sultans of Aceh, Johore, and Bintang. Here he also met Yajir (Yajiro), a Japanese fugitive, whom he baptized in Goa the following year and who convinced Xavier that Japan* was ripe for evangelization.

The prospect of introducing Christianity to Japan aroused Xavier's enthusiasm. Together with two other Spanish Jesuits, Cosme de Torres and Juan Fernandez, and with Yajir as interpreter, Xavier arrived in Kagoshima on 15 Aug 1549. The local ruler received the missionaries cordially and granted them permission to preach, in the hopes that their presence would attract the Portuguese ships and lucrative trade.

With Yajir's help, Xavier compiled a simple catechism in Japanese. This proved an embarrassment for the mission, since Yajir's use of Buddhist terminology led to the misconception that the religion the missionaries taught was actually a sect of Buddhism. Xavier thus changed his approach away from adaptation to the local culture by insisting that all religious terminology remain untranslated.

During this first stage of the mission, 100 people, including Yajir's own family, received baptism. A year later, Xavier left these new converts in Yajir's care while he traveled to Kyoto, the capital of the empire. Xavier's goal was to obtain permission to preach throughout the whole country. To do this he sought an audience with the emperor.

Along the way, Xavier visited Hirado and Yamaguchi in 1550, and after a strenuous journey he finally reached his destination. Denied an audience with Emperor Go-Nara, a figurehead rather than a powerful sovereign, Xavier decided not to prolong his visit. He had learned another lesson, but this time in favor of contextualization*. Apostolic poverty was unattractive to the Japanese, and henceforth Xavier decided it was crucial both to dress well and to bring expensive gifts on official visits.

Unable to speak Japanese well, Xavier relied on Juan Fernández, who was proficient in the language, and two talented Japanese — Bernard, who accompanied him on his travels throughout Japan, and a blind minstrel, Brother Laurenço. Xavier was given permission to preach, and the number of Christians grew steadily to several hundred.

From his discussions with the Buddhist clergy, Xavier gathered that Christianity would be more appealing if it entered Japan via China*, as had previous cultural innovations such as Buddhism and the writing system. Reasoning that the conversion of China would likewise be imitated by the Japanese, Xavier departed for China in 1551. He died on the small island of Sancian before reaching the mainland.

Bibliography

Schurhammer, Georg, *Francis Xavier: His Life, His Times*, Vols. I-IV (1982). Brodrick, James, *Saint Francis Xavier, 1506-1552* (1952).

CHRISTAL K. WHELAN, ADOLF HEUKEN, and CARLOS MERCÊS DE MELO, with contributions from TEOTONIO DE SOUZA

Xi Lin Religious Affair

(Xi Lin Jiao An). This affair arose when the Chinese government executed Auguste Chapdelaine, a French missionary. In 1852 Chapdelaine was doing clandestine missionary work in the province of Guangxi, where it was forbidden. He was arrested four years later in the district of Xi Lin, together with 25 Chinese Catholics. In 1856 the local government of Xi Lin sentenced to death the missionary and two of the 25 believers, a man named Bei Man and a woman, Cao Gui Ying. The French government, on the pretext of this incident, and the British government, on another pretext, jointly launched an attack against China in what is known as the Second Opium* War.

CHINA GROUP

Xi Shengmo

(Pastor Xi) (b. Western Zhang Village, Shanxi, China, 1835; d. Western Zhang Village, Shanxi, China, 19 Feb

1896). Well-known Chinese evangelist, pastor, hymn composer, and founder of opium* refuges.

Xi, whose birth name was Xi Liaozhih, was a Confucian scholar who in 1851 passed his BA, the first of three literary degrees. Xi came from a family of medical doctors who were familiar with traditional Chinese medical prescriptions. This gave him an interest in attaining immortality and led him into Daoism* and a sect called the Golden Pill, a sister group of the White Lotus society. Missionaries like Timothy Richard* believed that this group had elements of the Christian faith passed down to them by Nestorian* Christianity after its demise in China in the middle of the 19th c.

With the end of the severe Shanxi famine in 1879, a British Methodist missionary, David Hill, and Timothy Richard conducted a unique type of literature evangelism at the time of the triennial examinations in Taiyuan. Believing that public preaching was not appropriate at this time in China, they offered prizes for the best literary essays on Christian themes. Couched in Buddhist terminology such as "The Regulation of the Heart," the essays sought to lead scholars to examine the Christian faith. Xi wrote a winning essay, went reluctantly to get this prize from Hill, and became his assistant in writing literary tracts and translating the New Testament. Within two months, he became a Christian and accepted Hill's help in breaking his addiction to opium. This was done through dependence on the Holy Spirit and through Hill's use of the traditional missionary medicine — probably morphine. When this victory over opium was won, Xi changed his name to Shengmo, meaning "overcomer of demons." After Hill returned to Hankow, Xi was baptized in Nov 1880 at Pingyang by J. C. Turner, missionary with the China Inland Mission (CIM).

Following his conversion, Xi manifested gifts of leadership for ministry and began to organize a community of believers with characteristics resembling both a Christian church and a Christian sect. He had previously worked in the magistrate's office and had a sense of political power. As he saw situations where Christians were being persecuted, he agitated for treaty rights which guaranteed protection to converts. This made him so *non grata* to the government that it took away his literary degree, but later, upon missionary intervention, it was reinstated.

With obvious gifts in evangelism, Xi soon had worshipping groups in 27 villages. One of his favorite methods was exorcism, accompanied both by prayer and fasting. Exorcism was not then practiced extensively either by Chinese leaders or missionaries. The first to benefit from this was Xi's wife, who seemed to be deranged and had fits of uncontrollable rage.

Because of his background in medicine and his theological convictions, Xi also believed strongly in healing and practiced it in his ministry. Since he had been helped to overcome his debilitating opium addiction, Xi was instrumental, with CIM financial help, in establishing as many as 50 opium refuges, radiating in all directions from the center near Pingyang. These centers were run by reformed addicts who had come through his system, first as patients, then as converts, evangelists, and assistant refuge keepers. When they became apprentices, they were trained personally by Xi. After they had completed this process, Xi sent them out with his own specially prepared pills to find places where addiction was strong to establish centers and evangelize. Churches established as a result of the outreach by opium refuges were made up largely of recovered addicts.

One of the largest of these centers was at Hongtong, thirty miles north of Pingyang. Each fall, hundreds gathered for conference meetings that were usually followed by a mass baptism, conducted both by Xi and Dixon Hoste, who, more than other missionaries, was able over a 10-year period to have a useful, but subordinate, relationship with Xi. Ten miles away at Xi's home in Western Chang Village, Xi developed a utopian community called Middle Eden, where he worshipped and ministered together with family members, 50 or 60 disciples, and many recovering opium addicts. Many of the hymns used in churches and the opium refuges were composed by Xi, who also had unusual gifts in music. These were published as *Xi Shengmo Hymns* by the Shanghai Presbyterian* Press in 1912.

Xi was an independent, strong-willed man. For the most part, he was respectful in his relationships with missionaries, although many noted that he frequently manifested an antiforeign attitude. Not all agreed with his charismatic emphasis, his desire for control, nor his use of opium refuges as the principal method in his evangelism. He had a high sense of his own identity. Hudson Taylor* recognized this and in 1886 ordained him virtually as a bishop over this section of the work in Shanxi. Three groups of missionaries — the seven CIM missionaries known as the Cambridge Seven, CIM single women, and CIM missionaries from Scandinavia — worked under Xi's direction in Shanxi. This decision, unprecedented at this stage of missionary history, reflected Taylor's conviction that missionaries were merely the "scaffolding" in the building of an indigenous Chinese church. It is also testimony to the unusual stature of this converted opium addict, who was an instrument in leading thousands of addicts to faith in Christ and in helping develop one of the largest group of churches in China.

Bibliography

Austin, Alvyn James, "Pilgrims and Strangers: The China Inland Mission in Britain, Canada, the United States and China 1865-1900" (Ph.D. diss., York University, North York, Ontario, 1996). • Broomhall, A. J., *Assault on the Nine,* Book 6:1875-87 of *Hudson Taylor and China's Open Century* (1988). • Latourette, Kenneth Scott, *A History of Christian Missions in China* (1966). • Taylor, Mrs. Howard, *Pastor Hsi: Confucian Scholar and Christian* (1900).

RALPH R. COVELL, with contributions from THE CHINA GROUP, translated by PATRICIA SIEW

Xie Fu Ya
(b. Chekiang, China, 1892; d. Canton, China, 18 Aug 1991). Chinese Christian scholar and writer.

Xie graduated in 1912 from Tokyo Tong-wen College and in 1916 from Tokyo St. Paul's College. He served in the Young Men's Christian Association* (YMCA) from 1917 to 1925. Xie went to the United States for further study in 1925 and enrolled at the University of Chicago. The following year, he transferred to Harvard University.

Xie returned to China in 1927 and became a lecturer at Lingnan University School of Philosophy. After the anti-Japanese war, he went to Nanking (Nanjing) and taught at Nanking University. Xie left for Hong Kong* in 1949.

In 1958 he went to the USA and translated many important Christian books into Chinese. In later years he went back to China and resided in Canton. His writings include *Education for Personality, A Philosophy of Religion, Chinese Ethical Idea, Reflections on America, A Philosophy of Life, Individual Gospel, Outline of Christianity,* and others. CHINA GROUP

Xie Hong Lai
(H. L. Zia) (b. Zhejiang, China, 1873; d. 1916). Influential Chinese Protestant writer and publicist; director of publications for the Young Men's Christian Association* (YMCA) in China.

The eldest of the seven children of a Presbyterian* minister, Xie was taught the Confucian classics as a child. In 1892 he enrolled at the Buffington Institute (later Suzhou University), a school established by the Methodists*. After graduating in 1895, he taught physics and chemistry at the Anglo-Chinese College in Shanghai, another forerunner of Suzhou University. He developed and compiled science teaching materials. In 1900 he worked part time with the Commercial Press in Shanghai, editing and translating textbooks on science, mathematics, and geography. In 1904 he joined the YMCA full time, serving as secretary of the national committee and director of the publications department. His writings were of a high literary standard yet easy enough for the average reader to understand. He contracted tuberculosis in 1907, spent several months in the mountains of Colorado in 1909, and returned to recuperate in the mountains of Jiangxi, during which time he wrote *Consumption: Its Nature, Prevention, and Cure.* Aware of impending death, he moved to Hangzhou, where he continued to work as editor in chief of the YMCA Association Press. In 1914 he prepared the Bible study leaders and directed the follow-up program in Hangzhou for the meetings of Sherwood Eddy of the World Student Christian Movement. He initiated the informal Fortnightly Club in Hangzhou to provide a forum for the intelligentsia and professionals to discuss philosophical and ethical issues.

In the course of his career, Xie produced more than 200 books, pamphlets, and articles in Chinese and English. He also compiled the first edition of the YMCA hymnbook and was responsible for publicizing the YMCA throughout China. Xie was so highly respected that more than 20 memorial services were held in his honor when he died at age 43.

Bibliography

Boorman, Howard L., ed., *Biographical Dictionary of Republican China,* Vol. 2 (1968). CHINA GROUP

Xieshan Monastery
First monastery established since the Chinese Catholic Church gained independence and self-government (see also Wuhan Convent).

Established in Oct 1982, Xieshan Monastery, located in Xieshan, Songjiang County, Shanghai Municipality, is run by a board of directors comprising mainly the leaders of the Catholic churches of Shanghai Municipality, Jiangsu, Zhejiang, and Anhui. Three more provinces (Shandong, Jiangxi, and Fujian) joined in 1983, and the recruits increased from 34 to 62. A new building completed in Sep 1986 increased the accommodation capacity to 200, making Xieshan the largest monastery of the Chinese Catholic Church. Departing from the old system, which required 10 years of training for a recruit to become a priest, Xieshan shortened the training to four to six years (recruits take philosophy for one to two years and theology for three to four years) and added courses on politics and patriotism. Between 1982 and 1992, Xieshan Monastery trained 98 new priests.

CHINA GROUP

Xin Jia Po Hua Wen Ji Du Jiao Lian He Hui. *See* 11th Union of Chinese-Speaking Christian Churches of Singapore

Xu Bao Qian
(b. Chekiang, China, 1892; d. 1944). Chinese Christian leader in education.

Xu studied at the Peking (Beijing) School of Custom from 1910 to 1915 and became a Christian during this time. After graduation he served in the Young Men's Christian Association* (YMCA) from 1915 to 1920. Later he went to the United States for further study at Union Theological Seminary (New York) and Columbia University. He majored in theology and philosophy.

Xu returned to the YMCA in 1924 and became executive secretary of the Christian School Association at the same time. He taught at Yenching University School of Philosophy as a vice professor from 1926 to 1927 and from 1927 on was also in charge of the school of philosophy.

Xu took up the post of secretary of Wei-ai-she in 1929. In 1930 he became a research staff member of the World YMCA and a regional staff member of the World

Student Christian Federation. In 1937 he went to Shanghai and became a publication staff member of the YMCA. During the later part of the anti-Japanese war, he went inland and continued with literature work. He was director of Zai-she, a Christian Literature Worker's volunteer organization.

Xu died in a car accident while on his way to Chungking. Xu's publications include *Religious Experience Talk* and others. CHINA GROUP

Xu Guangqi

(Hsu Kuang-ch'i, Paul Hsu) (b. Shanghai, 1562; d. Shanghai, 1633). Grand minister of the Ming dynasty and significant member of the Catholic Church who contributed much to the propagation of Christianity during the late Ming period.

In 1596 Xu was introduced to Catholicism when he met the Jesuit Lazzaro Cattaneo* in Guangzhou, and in 1600 he visited Matteo Ricci* in Nanjing. He visited the Nanjing compound again in 1603 to learn Christian doctrines and was baptized "Paul" by the Jesuit missionary Joao de Rocha. In 1604 he sat for the highest examinations in the country and was appointed to the Hanlin Academy. He became a high-ranking government magistrate in Beijing, having studied mathematics under Ricci, and jointly translated *The Principles of Calculus*, as well as books on hydraulics, geography, and astronomy. In 1607 Xu invited Cattaneo to Shanghai. He built a small church beside his home. In about two years, mainly through the persuasion of Xu, there were 200 new members. When Xu returned to Beijing in 1610, Ricci had died of illness. Xu moved to Tianjin and continued to learn European science from Sabbatino De Ursis and other Jesuit missionaries.

In 1616, when the magistrate Shen Que of Nanjing wrote to Emperor Wan Li to complain about the missionaries, accusing the Jesuits of harboring wrong motives in China and requesting their expulsion, Xu wrote a beautifully crafted, lengthy letter in their defense which became classic reading for Chinese Catholics. He stated the Jesuits were "the disciples of the holy sage, their way is right, discipline strict, knowledge vast, understanding deep, hearts pure, opinion firm, and in their own country, they excelled above most people." He noted that the doctrine of the Catholic religion they preached has "serving God as its foundation, saving souls as its goal, practicing love and kindness as its method, changing evil to good as its way, repentance as its discipline, blessing in heaven as the reward of doing good, eternal punishment in hell for doing evil, that all their teaching and precepts are the best according to both the principle of heaven and humankind, helping people to do good and shun evil with sincerity." Xu also suggested the way to accommodate the missionaries and how the Chinese magistrates should govern them. Xu's brief received the imperial stamp "noted." The influence of his letter was reflected in the fact that no action was taken by Emperor Wan Li following the submission of Shen Que's first brief. (Of the 13 Jesuit missionaries in various localities, only four were deported to Macau* and nine were able to escape harm mainly because of their defense by Xu, Li Zhizao*, and Yang Tingjun*.)

On 21 Jun 1629, when the Calendrical Bureau of China failed to predict the exact date of an eclipse, Emperor Chong Zhen decided to revise the calendar and entrusted Xu with the task. He was assisted in correctly predicting the eclipse and revising the calendar by three missionaries trained in calendrical matters: Johann Terrenz* (Deng Yuhan), Giacomo Rho (Lo Yage), and Johann Adam Schall von Bell* (Tang Ruowang). Xu also helped the missionaries translate Christian books. Among the many writings and articles Xu left behind was the *Encyclopaedia of Agriculture*. In 1933 and 1983, academicians in China and the Chinese Catholic Church held various memorial services and published commemorative books in his honor. Xu was buried in Xujiahui in Shanghai Nandan. In 1983, 350 years after his death, the local government erected a marble statue in front of his grave and opened a park named after him, the Guangqi Garden.

Bibliography

Xu's collected writings are found in Hsu Xuang-ch'i, *Zending Xu wending gongji* (1933). • Dunne, George H., *Generations of Giants* (1962), pp. 98-100, 208-15, 222-25. • Standaert, Nicholas, *Yang Tingyun: Confucian and Christian in Late Ming China* (1988), pp. 35-37, 92-94. • Xi Zezong, *Xu Guangqi Yanjiu lunwenji* (collected essays on Xu) (1986).

CHINA GROUP, translated by DAVID WU

Xu Qian

(Hsu Chien) (b. Jiangxi, China, 26 Jun 1871; d. Hong Kong, Sep 1940). Chinese scholar and reformer of the judiciary system in China*.

Xu was born in Jiangxi but raised in Anhui. When Xu was four, his father died, leaving him to help support the family by teaching as he studied for the imperial examinations. He ranked eighth in the second-division examinations. From 1905 to 1907, he studied law and government at the Jin Shi Guan, predecessor of the law college of Beijing University. He was appointed a Hanlin compiler in 1907. As head of the Law Codification Bureau of the Ministry of Justice, he modernized the judiciary system and laid the foundation for an independent judiciary in China.

Xu was appointed a judge in Beijing in 1908 and represented China at the Eighth International Conference on Prison Reform in Washington, D.C., in 1910. He visited Russia, Europe, and England, and then returned to China after the Oct 1911 revolt in Wuchang. He resigned from office and organized the Guomin Gongjin Hui at Tianjin with his younger brother, Xu Sun. They advocated a federal republic with a centralized legislature and judiciary and a decentralized executive administration. The Guomin Gongjin Hui merged with the Tong-menghui in 1912 to form the Kuomintang. Xu went to join the staff of Sun Yat-Sen* at Shanghai, where he practiced law for three years. Xu vowed to become a Christian if his prayers for President Yuan Shih-kai's death were answered. After Yuan died in Jun 1916, Xu joined the Anglican* Church.

Xu returned to Beijing to take office as vice minister of justice in 1916. He resigned in May 1917 after President Li Yuanhong, Yuan's successor, ignored his advice not to dissolve the parliament. He again went to Shanghai.

While in Beijing, Xu had been elected president of the General Association for Religious Freedom, a united effort of different religions to lobby for the guarantee of religious freedom in the national constitution that was being drafted at that time. In 1917, Xu was appointed secretary-general of Generalissimo Sun Yat-Sen's military government at Guangzhou. He then became minister of justice in Guangzhou in Sep 1918. In that same year, Xu was chosen leader of the National Salvation Movement, a joint effort of Chinese and foreign Protestants. In 1919 Xu attended the Paris Peace Conference as an unofficial observer. He opposed the Treaty of Versailles because it was uncertain regarding the return of Shandong to China.

After returning to China, Xu was briefly chief editor of the Catholic *Yishibao,* published in Beijing and Tianjin. He resigned in May 1920 to serve as intermediary between Feng Yuxiang, the Christian general, and Sun Yat-Sen. In May 1921, Xu was appointed head of the supreme court in Guangzhou.

Xu founded a newspaper, the *Ping Jih Pao,* in Shanghai in 1924. He also established the Fa-cheng Tahsueh school of law and government. While Feng Yuxiang's army occupied Beijing (Oct 1924 to Apr 1926), Xu was adviser to Feng and was appointed chancellor of the Sino-Russian University in 1925. He was elected to the Central Executive Committee of the Kuomintang in Jan 1926.

In Apr 1927, Chiang Kai-shek, leader of the right-wing Kuomintang, began a purge of Communists in areas under his control. Xu was on his wanted list because of his left-wing associations. Feng also began a purge of Communists in Henan in Jul 1927. A week later, the Kuomintang faction in Wuhan broke off their ties with the Communists. Xu thus found himself under suspicion from the two factions of the Kuomintang and the Communists. He retired from public life in Sep 1927 and settled in Kowloon, Hong Kong.

Xu, together with the Nationalist dissidents of Chiang Kai-shek's regime, set up a rival government in Fujian in 1933. Xu returned to Hong Kong* after it collapsed in 1934. Following the outbreak of the Sino-Japanese War in 1937, Xu was in the National Defense Council in Nanjing. He went to Hong Kong for surgery in 1939 and died there in Sep 1940.

The twice-married Xu (he was widowed in 1920) had two sons and three daughters. His widow, Shen I-pin, from Zhejiang, published a collection of his poems in 1943. Xu had written on a variety of subjects, including law, religion, calligraphy, and economics.

Bibliography

Boorman, Howard L., ed., *Biographical Dictionary of Republican China,* Vol. 2 (1968).

CHINA GROUP

Xujiahui Observatory

Located in Xujiahui, Shanghai, China, the Xujiahui Observatory was first set in three single-story houses by French Jesuits* in 1873. In 1880, a top floor was added to the houses and two wings were attached. A new building was constructed in 1892, and the observatory was moved into it in 1901. It had four departments: astronomy, magnetic gas, meteorology, and seismology. The department of astronomy later moved to She Shan, and the department of magnetic gas to Lujiabang, Kunshan. The observatory was headed successively by Jesuits Colombel, Dechevres, Chevalier, Froc, and Gerzi. Its main task was to make meteorologic observation and forecasts. Gerzi headed the observatory for 36 years (1894-1931). Froc's success with typhoon forecasts in the Far Eastern sea earned him the title "Father of the Typhoon" and several medals from the authorities of the French Concession of Shanghai and the French government. After the birth of New China, the Shanghai People's Government took over control of this observatory.

CHINA GROUP

Yaballah III

(b. Kuoseng, China, 1244; d. 1317). Patriarch of the East Syrian Church.

Of Mongol descent, Yaballah entered a monastery near Beijing, China*. After three years' novitiate, he received the tonsure from the archbishop Nestorius. He studied there in the theological school under the tutelege of a certain Rabban Sauma and was later ordained as a priest.

Rabban Sauma and Markos decided to go on a pilgrimage to Jerusalem. When they arrived at Maragha, Markos was consecrated metropolitan bishop of China (ca. 1280). Two years later (1282), he was elected patriarch of the East Syrian Church. Barhebraeus* informs us that he knew no Syriac, but his abilities in the language of the Mongols was more important. Together with the Mongol Il-Khan, he sent his old teacher Rabban Sauma to Paris on a mission to explore cooperation and peace between the Mongols and the Western powers. Mar Yaballah III guided the church through the tumultuous reigns of eight Mongol Khans of the Il-Khanate of Persia. He died, probably on 13 Nov 1317. Shortly after his death, his biography was written in Persian. It survives in a Syriac translation.

Bibliography

Bedjan, Paul, ed., *Histoire de Mar Jab-Allah, Patriarche, et de Raban Sauma* (1895). • Budge, E. A. W., *The Chronography of Bar Hebraeus,* 2 Vols. (1932). David Bundy

Yagi Jukichi

(b. Sakai Village, western Tokyo suburbs, 9 Feb 1898; d. 26 Oct 1927). Japanese poet.

The second son in a farming family, Yagi attended the Kamakura Methodist* Church, while studying at the Kamakura Normal School and in an English Bible class at Koishikawa Gospel Church, when he advanced to the Tokyo High Normal School. He was baptized by Tominaga Tokuma of Komagome Christian Group on 2 Mar 1919, but he left this group about two months later, probably because he was influenced by the Non-Church* Movement of Uchimura Kanzo*. When he graduated in the spring of 1921, he became an English teacher at Mikage Normal School in Hyogo Prefecture. In Jul 1922, he married Shimada Tomi. From about this time, he began to concentrate on writing poetry and sought to blend his poetry and his faith. In Aug 1925, he published his first collection, titled *Aki no hitomi* (A Look at Autumn). After this, his poems appeared in different publications, including *Nihon shijin* (Japan's Poets). In the spring of 1925, he transferred to the Chiba prefectural school, Higashi Kasai Junior High School, and lived in Chiyoda Village, Kashiwa. In 1926, however, he was diagnosed with second-stage tuberculosis and had to be hospitalized. He spent about a year at temporary quarters in Chigasaki fighting the disease. A second collection of poetry that he had compiled, *Mazushiki shinto* (The Poor Believer), was published posthumously in Feb 1928. A number of other collections have been published, so that he has become a religious poet of acknowledged originality. In 1982, *Yagi Jukichi zenshu* (The Complete Works of Yagi Jukichi) was published in three volumes. Excerpts from his poetry display the joining of simplicity with local customs and experiences of the common person. "I want to think of Christ/like one lone tree/like a stream.// Bring your hands together/go away washed clean/what a marvelous world/what a blessed world."

Bibliography

Seki Shigeru, *Yagi Jukichi — shi to shogai to shinko* (Yagi Jukichi — poetry, life, and faith) (1965). • Tanaka Kiyomitsu, *Shijin Yagi Jukichi* (The poet, Yagi Jukichi) (1969). Sato Yasumasa

Yamamuro Gunpei

(b. Okayama Prefecture, Japan, 22 Sep 1872; d. 13 Mar 1940). Commander in chief of the Japan Salvation Army*.

Yamamuro's parents were very poor farmers, and early in his life Yamamuro was adopted out. But because he was not able to persuade his adoptive parents to let him go to school, he ran away from home to Tokyo and became a printer. He taught himself, but one day he encountered street-side evangelism and entered the faith. He entered Tsukiji Mission School and in 1889 met Niijima Jo* at the first summer school sponsored by the Doshisha. In September he entered the Doshisha but found study there extremely difficult. At the time of the 1891 earthquake, he assisted Ishii Juji's relief efforts with orphans, helping collect contributions. Eventually he quit school over worries about his faith and stayed near Ishii, where he heard of the opening of the Salvation Army in Japan. He entered in Dec 1895. The following January, he became the Salvation Army's first Japanese officer. A purifying experience helped him resolve his faith anxieties. In 1899 he married Sato Keiko. He wrote a simple explanation of Christianity titled *Heimin no fujuin* (The Gospel for the Common Person). In 1900 he began a movement to abolish prostitution and was injured in a skirmish in the red-light district, which aroused sympathy and support for the Salvation Army's work. In 1906, the year after the Russo-Japanese War ended, he set up an employment desk as a way of confronting the economic depression. The next year, when the World Commander in Chief General William Booth came to Japan, Yamamuro was his translator, and his excellent translation generated a great deal of enthusiasm all around the country. When Booth left Japan in 1907, Yamamuro was appointed chief secretary of the Japan Salvation Army, and he became Japan commander. His work as a pioneer in many different fields is noteworthy. In 1909 he began the "charity kettle" movement. In 1912 the Salvation Army Booth Memorial Hospital was opened, and in 1916 a tuberculosis sanatorium was opened. In 1922 he pioneered a movement to combat child abuse. In addition, he worked in a variety of ways to protect the human rights of all in such areas as antiprostitution, relief for areas with poor agricultural harvests, relief for victims of the Great Kanto Earthquake (1923), and protection against trafficking of people. As a result, people came to refer both to Yamamuro's Salvation Army and Salvation Army's Yamamuro. He died of acute pneumonia. On the cloth that covered his coffin were embroidered the words "victory" and "triumphal return." In 1926 he wrote *Kyuseigun ryakushi* (Short History of the Salvation Army).

Bibliography

Akimoto Mitaro, *Yamamuro no shogai* (The life of Yamamuro) (1951). • Yamamuro Buho, *Yamamuro Gunpei kaiso shu* (Collection of Yamamuro Gunpei's Memories) (1965). • Miyoshi Akira, *Yamamuro Gunpei*, 1971.

TAKAMICHI MOTOI, JAPANESE DICTIONARY

Yan Yongjing

(Yen Yung-Kiung) (b. Shanghai, Jiangsu, China, 1838; d. 1898). Chinese Episcopalian professor, pastor, and translator.

Yan (Y. K. Yen) first studied at a school founded by William J. Boone*. At age 14, he was brought to the United States, where he graduated with honors from Kenyon College in Ohio in 1861. He returned to China in 1862 during the American Civil War and worked as a translator for a foreign company in Shandong while serving as a volunteer preacher at the Church of Our Savior in Shanghai. In 1866 he served at the Anglican* church in Wuchang, Hubei, and was ordained a priest in 1870. He was responsible for the planning and building of Boone School in Wuchang. He returned to Shanghai in 1878 to help in the planning and development of St. John's College (founded in 1879). While serving as dean of the school for eight years, he taught mathematics and natural philosophy. From 1887 to 1898, Yan pastored the Church of Our Savior.

Yan and his wife were the only two Chinese at the third General Missionary Conference held in Shanghai in May 1890. Yan urged missionaries to "adopt a Chinese mode of life" and not to be overbearing in manner. A controversial issue at the conference was ancestor* worship. Yan opposed any compromise, explaining that he did not even have pictures of his parents in his house lest non-Christians misinterpret the act as idolatry. He went to England in 1894 as a representative of the Chinese church and urged the British to ban opium*. Yan and some others built a garden for the Chinese because the British forbade them to enter their garden in the British settlement.

Yan translated many books during his lifetime, including one on educational theory as well as many Christian books. He and his wife had five sons and a daughter, all educated either in the United States or in England. One of his sons, Huiqing (W. W. Yen), was a scholar and an ambassador to the Soviet Union from 1933 to 1936.

CHINA GROUP, translated by PATRICIA SIEW

Yang Sida

(b. Puxian, Guangdong, 1901; d. 1963). Chinese patriot, editor, and writer.

Yang was converted and baptized when studying in Shanghai. He earned his doctorate in medicine from Paris University, France. He was teaching at Aurora University when Shanghai was liberated in 1949, and was the first Catholic in the university to cooperate with the Chinese Communist Party. In Jan 1951, when the People's Government took over the administration of Aurora University, he was the first to support the move and accept government appointments, assuming the posts of dean of studies and the head of the medical college, positions formerly occupied by foreigners. In the autumn of 1952, Aurora University was renamed Shanghai Second

Medical College, and Yang was appointed its vice president. In 1956 he attended the conference sponsoring the formation of the Chinese Catholic Patriotic Association. In 1957, at the First Representative Conference of the Chinese Catholic Church, his speech was entitled "The Question of the Relations between the Chinese Catholic Church and the Vatican." His speech influenced the formation of the Chinese Catholic Patriotic Association, and he was elected the vice chairman of the new national body. He was proficient in English and French, and used them to counter negative ideas foreigners had about China's achievements and religious policy.

In the medical field, he edited and wrote over 50 academic theses, including those on hygiene, forensic medicine, phototherapy, and human anatomy. In 1959 he was elected a member of the standing committee of the Third Chinese People's Political Consultative Council.

China Group

Yang Tingjun

(b. Hangzhou, 1557; d. 1627). Famous Chinese Catholic in the late Ming dynasty, a convert from Buddhism*.

Yang was one of the officials in Beijing who had contact with Matteo Ricci* after the latter's arrival in 1601, but he did not convert to Catholicism until after Ricci's death. In 1611 Yang returned to Hangzhou to offer condolences to his good friend, Li Zhizao*, whose father had died. There he met two missionaries, Lazarus Cattaneo* and Nicolas Trigault*, guests of Li. Yang invited them to stay at his house, desiring to learn about Catholic doctrine and baptism. Yang, however, had concubines and therefore could not be received into the Roman Catholic Church. Though at first resistant, Yang, admonished by Li, eventually gave up his concubines and was baptized "Michel" by Cattaneo.

Yang persuaded his parents, wife, and children to become converts and established the first Catholic church in Hangzhou. In 1616 and 1622, when missionaries met with opposition and their lives were endangered, Yang sheltered them in his home.

Yang authored *Dai Yi Bian* (An Answer to Doubtful Questions), an exposition of Catholic doctrines and a defense of Catholicism. Yang was one of the "three pillars" of the early Chinese Catholic Church, the other two being Xu Guangqi* and Li Zhizao. China Group

Yapsutco, Julia Sotto

(b. ca. 1885; d. 1942). First Protestant Filipino woman ordained in the Philippines*.

Yapsutco belonged to the illustrious Sotto family of writers and politicians of Cebu City and was the sister of the Philippine senators Vincente and Filemon Sotto. Through the influence of her cousin Angel Sotto*, she turned Protestant and was responsible for the conversion of her husband, Luis, a former town mayor. After his ordination in 1920, he became pastor of Dipolog. On her husband's death in 1926, Yapsutco became an evangelist and organized the Iligan Evangelical Church in 1931. Ordained on 9 May 1936 by the Northern Mindanao District Conference of the United Evangelical Church (UEC), she remained pastor of Iligan until 1938, when she became president of the UEC National Women's Association.

Bibliography

Sotto, A. C., *Mga Handumanan sa Akong Tinuhoan* (1954). • Sitoy, T. V., Jr., *Several Springs, One Stream* (1992). T. Valentino Sitoy, Jr.

Yashiro Hinsuke

(b. Hakodate, Aoyanagi-cho, Japan, 3 Mar 1900; d. 10 Oct 1970). Japanese Anglican* priest.

The second son of Anglican priest Yashiro Kinnojo and Yoshiko, Yashiro was baptized on 27 May 1900 by the priest Walter Andrews. He was confirmed by Bishop Andrews on 5 Sep 1915. After serving as an assistant to the priest for a time, he entered Rikkyo University. In 1920 he crossed over to Ch'ing-tao in China*, and after experiencing something like a "Kierkegaardian earthquake," he returned to Japan*. In 1925 he was ordained a deacon by Samuel Heaslett, and in 1927 he was ordained a priest. In the fall of that year, he went to England to study, returning to Japan in late 1932. The next year he became priest of St. Michael's Church in Kobe. On 29 Sep 1942, he was consecrated bishop of the Kobe Diocese. During World War II*, he devoted his energies to preserving the Anglican Church of Japan (NSKK) from military and special police pressure to force it to join the other Christian denominations. After the war, he conducted services to facilitate the return to the NSKK of churches that had earlier joined the United Church of Christ in Japan, working especially hard for the reestablishment of the NSKK and the rebuilding of schools and churches that had been destroyed by fire. After the war, he was the first ordinary citizen to receive permission from the government to travel abroad when he attended the Lambeth Conference in England. On his return trip to Japan, he visited many countries in search of international aid. He served as chair of the boards of trustees of a number of NSKK-related schools, including Shoin Women's University, Momoyama School, Rikkyo University, and St. Luke's School of Nursing, establishing a number of kindergartens and nursery schools, in addition to the above schools. In 1959 he presided over the centennial celebration of Anglican mission work in Japan. He was on the steering committee of the Wider Episcopal Fellowship and played an important role in the Anglican Communion. He became ill while engaged in preparations for the 1968 Lambeth Conference and died.

Bibliography

Yashiro Kinichi and Yamaguchi Kosaku, *Kaiso no Yashiro Hinsuke* (Memoirs of Yashiro Hinsuke) (1976); *Momo-*

yama gakuin kyuju nen shi (Ninety-year history of Momoyama School) (1974). • Yashiro Hinsuke, *Mikaeru no tomo* (Friend of Michael's).

Toma Shigeyoshi, Japanese Dictionary

Yasukuni Shrine Issue

(Yasukuni Jinja Mondai). Issue related to the attempt to return this shrine, which had been privatized by a Shinto directive after the Pacific War, to national government administration and funding.

This action began in 1952 when the Japan Bereaved Families' Public Welfare League (known as the Japan Association for the Bereaved Families of the War Dead, beginning in 1953), at their Fourth General Meeting, voted to appeal for subsidizing pilgrimages to Yasukuni Shrine with government funds. In 1967, a bill by Murakami calling for the nationalization of the shrine was brought before the national parliament. National Foundation Day was celebrated that year for the first time. This signaled the beginning of the "Yasukuni Era." This issue has gone through two different phases: working for the passage of a nationalization bill through parliament, and after that the approval of formal shrine visits by the emperor. On 30 Jun 1969, the day after the 100th anniversary of the shrine's founding, the Yasukuni Shrine Bill was introduced to the sixty-first session of the national parliament, having been signed by 241 members of the Liberal Democratic Party (LDP), but was defeated. It was introduced to every session after that through 1974, and defeated each time. In 1975, a courtesy bill was prepared but never introduced. The group for defending and preserving the national shrine next took a completely different approach, by working for the nationalization in stages. In 1976 the group established the "Group to Honor the Spirits of the Fallen Heroes," and from 1978 various local assemblies called for official visits to Yasukuni Shrine. In 1981 the joint-visit group of parliament members was formed. A memorial day for those who had died in the war was established in 1982, and Prime Minister Suzuki Zenko made what amounted to an official visit to the shrine after saying, "I won't say if my visit is personal or official." Next came Prime Minister Nakasone, who introduced the "Final Settlement of Accounts for Post-War Politics" as his banner, and in Jul 1983 he directed a study of the constitutionality of making official visits to Yasukuni Shrine. In November the results of the LDP Small Committee on the Yasukuni Shrine Issue were compiled, and in 1984 conversations were held on the possibility of the cabinet making an official visit, with a constitutionality report being issued in Aug 1985. With this in hand, Prime Minister Nakasone prepared to make the first official visit by a national leader on 15 Aug. However, the cries of protest from countries in Asia were so vigorous that he was forced to cancel his plans "for the good of the country." Because Japan became a major political power during Nakasone's time, the Japanese people's conscience regarding war crimes was questioned. The opposition movement shifted from preventing nationalization to protesting official visits. A number of battles over unconstitutionality were waged in the courts: Tsu City's groundbreaking ceremony, the refusal of enshrinement of a self-defense forces' officer by his Christian wife, Minoo City's monument to the war dead, lottery fees, and the giving-of-grain festival. The Peace Survivors' Group was born out of contact with the Association of Bereaved Christian Families (in Asahikawa, 1982; Tachikawa, 1986; and Shizuoka, 1987). The "Freedom of Religion" issue thus confronts the Japanese emperor system head-on, and calls for a new approach to the root of this problem (see also Shinto Shrine).

Bibliography

National Parliament Library Investigative Bureau, *Yasukuni jinja mondai shiryoshu* (Collection of documents on the Yasukuni Shrine Issue) (1976). • Japan Survivors' Group, *Eirei to tomo ni san-ju-nen — yasukuni jinja kokka-i goji undo no ayumi* (Thirty years together with the spirits of the war dead — the journey of the group for defending and maintaining the nation) (1976). • Murakami Shigeyoshi, *Kokka shinto* (National Shinto) (1970); *Irei to shokon* (Repose and invocation of the spirits of the dead") (1974). • Tomura Masahiro, *Yasukuni toso* (The Yasukuni fight) (1970).

Tomura Masahiro, Japanese Dictionary

Yates, Matthew Tyson

(b. Wake County, North Carolina, USA, 8 Jan 1819; d. Shanghai, China, 1888). Pioneer Southern Baptist* missionary in China.

Yates was the son of a godly farmer who opened his home to preachers of all denominations. Young Yates was baptized at a church camp-meeting in 1836. At age 19, he used his earnings from teaching vocal music and money provided by his home church to attend college at Wake Forest Academy and College in North Carolina. He married Eliza Moring (1821-94) on 26 Apr 1847. He and his wife sailed from Boston as missionaries of the Foreign Mission Board, Richmond, Virginia, arriving in Shanghai via Hong Kong* in Sep 1846.

As unexpected arrivals, they slept on the parlor floor of Bishop William Boone's* overcrowded house. A fellow missionary helped them find a place to live — an unfurnished, rat-infested, former pawnbroking establishment. They hired a Chinese servant who spoke no English and began learning Chinese from him. Poor eyesight forced Yates to learn Chinese by mingling with the people. He soon acquired fluency of the language, enabling him to begin preaching locally and also outside Shanghai. Between 1853 and 1856, Shanghai was beset with civil unrest inspired by the Taiping Rebellion*. The Little Sword Society, a branch of the Triad Society, had captured the walled city of Shanghai for a year and a half in 1853-54. Yates helped the American commissioner

Humphrey Marshall to rescue Wu Tianzhang, the Qing customs superintendent, from capture by the rebels. Yates's house, although in the line of fire, was ideally situated as an intelligence center, and he supplied information on the uprising to Marshall and the *North China Good News.*

Poor health forced Yates to take a furlough in 1857. Shortly after his return to China, the American Civil War broke out and his home mission was unable to support him. Yates had to support his family and himself by working as an interpreter for the municipal council of the foreign community and the United States Consulate.

At the 1871 Shanghai Missionary Conference, Yates stressed that, in order for there to be a strong native church, membership must be based on genuine conversion and not on wealth or status. Converts must see themselves as disciples of Jesus and not of the missionary. Yates was in favor of converts memorizing Scripture in their own native language.

In the 1870s, when he had lost his voice from constant preaching, Yates was for a time the American vice consul general in Shanghai. He used his emoluments to build chapels and develop mission work. After regaining his voice, he returned to full-time missionary work. A later affliction requiring nine surgical operations led him to concentrate on Bible* translation work.

Yates spent 41 years in Shanghai and died at age 69. The Old North Gate Baptist Church was built during his time. He wrote books on ancestral worship* and the Taiping Rebellion, as well as a language book for missionaries, *First Lessons in Chinese.* The Yates Memorial Hall and a girls middle school in Shanghai were named after him. In Suzhou, a middle school was also named in his honor.

Bibliography

Speer, Robert E., *Servants of the King* (1914). • Bryan, F. Catherine, *At the Gates: The Life Story of Matthew Tyson and Eliza Moring Yates* (1949). China Group

Yen, Y. K. *See* Yan Yongjing

Yesu Jiating. *See* Jesus Family

Yezdegerd I (Yazdegerd or Yzdkrt)

(5th c.). Persian emperor from 399 to 420.

Yezdegerd was the Persian emperor of the Sasanian dynasty during a critical time in the development of the Syrian church in Persia. He has been given the title "the Persian Constantine" because of his more favorable treatment of Christians after years of severe persecution. During his reign the persecution begun under Shapur II* was terminated and, similar to the time of Constantine a century earlier in the West, Christians were once again given freedom to worship and to rebuild church buildings that had been destroyed. For his leniency toward Christians, he was labeled by his Zoroastrian citizens "Yezdegerd the Sinful" and the "friend of Jews." The second title was given because, according to tradition, he married a Jewish woman, Šōšan-doxt (or Gasyan duxt), the daughter of a Jewish exilarch (probably Kahana I). Yezdegerd's wife, the queen, helped in the establishment of colonies for Jews in Šōš (Sashar), Šōštar (Shuster), and Gai (Ispahan). In addition, Yezdegerd had at least one other high-ranking Jew in his court who was probably a cousin of the queen.

The *Acts of the Synod of Mar Isaac* (410) enumerates a list of beneficent acts toward the Christians, preceded by the statement, "By the will of God who disposed the heart of Yezdegerd, King of kings, to enact all types of good works he has written. . . ." It continues, "He ordained that all through his empire the churches destroyed by his ancestors should be magnificently rebuilt, overturned altars should be diligently repaired, those who had been tried for God by chains and blows should regain their freedom, and presbyters and rectors, with all their communities, should be without fear and without risk." Once again, like Constantine, it was the emperor ("king of kings") who called this synod to help the church reorganize and encouraged that they remain in good fellowship with the church of the West. His concern for good relations with the Byzantine empire was shown in his sending a legate who was a bishop, Jahaballaha.

Bibliography

Chabot, J. B., *Synodicon orientale* (1902). • Fiey, J.-M., *Jalons pour une histoire de l'église en Iraq* (1970).

Scott W. Sunquist

Ygloria, Simeon

(b. 1884; d. 1922). First Filipino overseas missionary.

Ygloria of Lucban, Tayabas, went to Hawaii for mission work. A Philippine constabulary noncommissioned officer when he was converted in 1906, he joined the Silliman Student Church. Ygloria had a gift for languages, speaking Tagalog, Cebuano, Ilongo, Bicol, Ilocano, Spanish, English, and later, Portuguese, Japanese, and Hawaiian Kanaka. He was at Union Theological Seminary (Manila) when he heard of a call for an evangelist among the tens of thousands of Filipino sugar plantation workers in Hawaii.

Upon ordination in 1913, Ygloria was sent to Honolulu. With his linguistic skills, Ygloria easily made many connections. Though his congregations were frequently moving, in 1916 he organized a Filipino church in Ewa with an initial 149 members. Overworked, Ygloria's health deteriorated, and he died in his late thirties.

Bibliography

Wright, G. W., "The Story of Simon," *The Philippine Presbyterian,* Vol. 8 (Apr 1917). • Laubach, F. C., *People of the Philippines* (1925). T. Valentino Sitoy, Jr.

Yoido Full Gospel Church

Largest Pentecostal* church in the world, located on the small island of Yoido in the middle of metropolitan Seoul, Korea.

With an estimated membership of 500,000, the church was first organized by a young pastor. Cho Yonggi, and his mother-in-law, Choi Ja Sil, and a small number of followers gathered in a tent installed in the refugee squatter area on the outskirts of Seoul. It was one year after the end of the Korean War*, and the devastated families gathered together to pray for the strength to rebuild their broken homes and businesses.

The message was simple: Cho advocated that Christian faith has to do with praying for the "three-beat blessings" of health, wealth, and success. When Cho and his mother-in-law began speaking in tongues and healing the sick by simply praying, the tent church was filled with war refugees*, the poor, and those devastated by the war. The church was moved into a new building in the western part of the city in 1958. In 1973 the Full Gospel Church completed the construction of its new sanctuary in the present location. A dome-shaped, grand structure which houses some 20,000 people, it is situated in the heart of the island beside the National Assembly Hall. Every Sunday, in six different services, some 100,000 people come to worship and to hear Cho preach. His sermons are broadcast on television and radio simultaneously and relayed to 12 different places in the city for people not able to attend.

The Full Gospel Church on Yoido Island is the center of the Korean Pentecostal church movement. The church publishes various magazines and tracts for the Bible study "cell" groups which meet weekly outside the church. It has a research center for the Pentecostal movement called the International Theological Research Institute. The Full Gospel Ministry-Theology Seminary was established in 1983 to educate clergy for the movement. The church operates numerous monastery-like prayer house retreat centers for revival meetings, individual prayers, and meditation, as well as faith healings. In recent years, the church has built low-income housing for the poor, elderly, and needy. In 1995, it opened Sonshin College, a four-year humanities and arts college in a southern suburb of Seoul.

David Suh, with contributions from
Lee Duk Joo, translated by Kim In Soo

Young Christian Workers

(YCW). Begun as a Catholic movement in Belgium by Cardinal Joseph Cardijn (1882-1967).

Cardijn grew up in a working-class family and witnessed the exploitation suffered by his own father and other workers. As a young priest and director of social action for the Brussels area in 1915, he started to organize workers and train young people in order to help them attain self-dignity, human and spiritual growth, as well as the improvement of their living and working conditions. YCW groups were started and held their first National Congress in 1925.

In 1927 the movement spread to France. By the early 1930s, YCW groups and contacts had spread to Switzerland, Spain, the Netherlands, Portugal, Denmark, Poland, and Yugoslavia. In 1932 the movement spread to Africa, starting from the then Belgian Congo, and to Canada and Colombia. By 1935, the YCW had spread to Asia, starting in Vietnam*, and then on to Australia.

The first international coordination was established in 1931, followed by the First World Congress in 1935 and the first international secretariat and bureau in 1945. The International Young Christian Workers (IYCW) was thus born. It obtained full official recognition in 1957 through the celebration of its First World Assembly in Rome, with the adoption of its manifesto and statutes as well as the election of its international executive committee.

As for the spreading of YCW in Asia, from Vietnam (where later it was abolished) it extended to India* in 1946, Sri Lanka* and the Philippines* in 1947, Japan* in 1949, Hong Kong* in 1957, Taiwan* in 1958, etc. At present, it is operating in 17 Asian countries, and it has initiated contacts with four other nations, namely, Vietnam, Malaysia*, Bangladesh*, and China*.

Since the 1940s, some coordination has been established with followers of other world religions and, since the 1950s, with the World Council of Churches. Today the IYCW is involved in organizing workers of all major religions (Muslim, Hindu, Buddhist, Christian) and even those with no religious affiliation.

The YCW is concerned with the formation and welfare of young workers, both male and female, with the objectives of fostering their self-dignity and maturity, both as members of society and as Christians. The IYCW Manifesto reads: "We must form a new youth to build together a new world. A world no longer built on exploitation, ignorance, violence, war, but a world founded on respect for the person, the family, society and the world human community." Their practical methods are: "By the young workers, with the young workers and for the young workers," "serving, educating and representing the young workers," "see, judge and act: education through action."

YCW branches are usually set up in local parishes or institutions and coordinated on the diocesan level, and take part in the international movement of the IYCW.

Bibliography

Aubert, R., M. Fievez, and J. Meert, *Cardijn* (1992). • *IYCW 40th Anniversary, 1957-1997* (1997). • O'Sullivan, H., *Making Monday the Best Day of the Week* (1997). • *YCW International Bulletin.*

Sergio Ticozzi and Tu Hui Yao

Young Men's Christian Association (YMCA)/ Young Women's Christian Association (YWCA)

The YMCA was founded by 22-year-old George Williams in London in 1844. This occurred in the era of the Industrial Revolution, which saw the increasing movement of young men from the rural areas of the country into the major industrializing cities. Founded to house newly arrived urban youths in Christian hostels, which provided a wide range of services from spiritual development to educational, social, and recreational programs, the YMCA grew rapidly and soon spread across the country. In the following year, 1845, YMCAs were started in Switzerland, the United States, France, Canada, Germany, and the Netherlands.

By 1855, the first World Conference of YMCAs in Paris instituted the World Alliance of YMCAs and adopted a mission statement henceforth known as the Paris Basis. The Paris Basis states: "The Young Men's Christian Associations seek to unite those young men who, regarding Jesus Christ as their God and Saviour according to the holy Scriptures, desire to be his disciples. . . ."

In 1875 the World YMCA Week of Prayer was created. The Week of Prayer begins on every second Sunday of November, and each local YMCA takes time to pray and recover the sense of the YMCA's vision and mission. In 1878, a permanent headquarters of the World Alliance was established in Geneva.

In 1880 the International Committee of YMCAs in the USA and Canada began missionary work in Asia, South America, and Europe. The first Asian YMCAs were started by missionaries in Japan*, China*, and India*, with Tokyo's first YMCA opening in 1880. From 1895 to 1914, John R. Mott visited Asia extensively in his travels in his capacity as national secretary of the World Student Christian Federation and the Intercollegiate YMCA of the USA and Canada. He was particularly influential in initiating and organizing missionary and local leadership to found YMCAs in Asia.

Generally speaking, the YMCAs in Asia developed at a different pace in different countries with different emphases and agendas. In most Asian countries, the YMCA took root in rural areas and engaged in the social concerns of agrarian communities, participating in rural development work, education, and socioeconomic programs, and sometimes in the political concerns of different communities. Vocational training for the masses and Christian welfare services for the young, elderly, and disabled characterized most YMCA programs in Asia.

In countries under colonial rule, the city YMCAs essentially grew rather rapidly with the development of educational, sports, and social programs. In many countries, the leadership of the YMCA was instrumental in the development of the Boys Brigade and Boy Scouts movements. In many cases, the YMCAs pioneered sporting events and introduced new sporting activities into Asia. This was in line with the YMCA's philosophy and emphasis on the development of individuals in the totality of body, mind, and spirit, as symbolized by the Y's inverted equilateral triangle.

The indigenization and further development of YMCA work for many Asian countries accelerated after World War II*. The disruption due to the war and the evacuation of foreign leadership left a vacuum, and local leaders began to seek an indigenous approach to YMCA work in their own countries. The formation of the Asia Alliance of YMCAs (AAY) in 1949 and the eventual establishment of Chinese or local YMCAs, in contrast to colonial YMCA movements, can only be understood in the context of decolonization and independence movements in Asia (see Nationalism).

As the YMCA has been an international youth movement with worldwide affiliations, international relations are promoted between various YMCAs in Asia through twinning programs and youth camps, as well as exchange programs. The first World Alliance Conference held in Asia was in 1937 in Mysore, India. The general assemblies of AAY are held every four years, while the conference of national general secretaries and other regional workshops are scheduled more frequently. A brief outline of YMCA programs in Asia includes the following.

Rural reconstruction. Asian YMCAs started as organizations for urban youth but saw tasks of development predominantly in villages and rural areas stricken by poverty*. Thus YMCAs started rural services and self-help development for whole villages. The development of cooperative banks is one example. In Southeast Asia and East Asia, environmental workshops have been a recent developmental program designed to educate rural communities about environmentally friendly agricultural methods, as well as to develop more sustainable economic development in local contexts.

Education and literature ministries. Most YMCAs were involved in the publication of books, newspapers, and magazines. The first project of the YMCA in Japan was the establishment of a publishing company for the periodical the *Cosmos* in 1880. In China the YMCA magazine *Youth* was started in 1906, and was renamed *Youth Progression* after it merged in 1917 with another publication in the spirit of the intellectual climate of that time. Literacy* projects were common, and education programs were started to help youth, who had to work during the day, acquire new skills and knowledge, as well as a basic education to prepare for a better future. Programs ranged from vocational skills training, such as secretarial training and domestic helpers programs, to business administration and foreign languages, sports, and physical education, etc.

Social programs. The YMCA emphasizes social fellowship and cultural exchanges among youth from different countries to promote goodwill and confidence. This was the necessary condition for direct Christian witness in largely non-Christian Asian settings. Aggressive evangelism has not been the YMCA's approach, but rather a gradual process through social involvement which touches both the educated leadership and the illiterate masses. In Singapore* the YMCA was the first to introduce nonalcoholic and smoke-free disco dancing in the 1970s, and the YMCA continues to be a front-runner in reaching youth who have dropped out of school.

Health and wellness programs. A firm believer in the value of physical training and sporting activities to restore health and revitalize the spirit of youth, the YMCA has been ahead of its time in pioneering sporting and camping programs. The game of basketball was invented by the YMCA, and annual festivals of sports and sports camps are regular features of many YMCAs in Asia.

Community development and welfare programs. At the risk of appearing humanistic and political, the YMCA in Asia has been participating in the struggle for human rights and social justice on behalf of the poor, oppressed, elderly, and disabled in many countries. YMCA child care and student centers, youth drop-ins, and camps for the disabled are some of the familiar programs which have been well received in many Asian countries. Throughout its history, the YMCA has been innovative and farsighted in the development of community and social services to promote and develop lasting communities.

Ecumenical cooperation. The YMCAs in Asia were ecumenical* pioneers, with Christians from different denominations participating in wide collaboration in social service and reform movements and other projects to meet the challenge of real needs. Many cooperative projects carried out by the YMCA were initiated by Christians but executed by people who did not actually confess Christ as Lord and Savior. In 1988, A. Vassilaqui became the first Roman Catholic* president of the World Alliance of YMCAs. In 1991, for the first time in its history, the World Alliance elected J. W. Casey, a Roman Catholic, as secretary general.

Spiritual life and Christian emphasis. In some Asian countries, the YMCA continues to work toward developing the spiritual life of youth and to nurture in them a greater knowledge of Jesus Christ and the kingdom of God. In many Asian YMCAs, the Christian identity has been weakened as social action has replaced rather than augmented spiritual formation.

The YMCA continues to grow as a voluntary youth movement with international affiliations and constituent members from all social backgrounds, creeds, races, and nationalities. The flowering of the YMCA in Asia may be due to several factors. First, the YMCA's participation in the social and political concerns of the population has served as a channel for Asian Christians to express the desire for Christian unity beyond denominational, racial, and national barriers. With its wide range of programs, the YMCA provides an effective avenue for Christian participation in the social and political questions of the day.

Second, the YMCA has penetrated into the nonreligious arena, where church and mission could not go (e.g., the sociopolitical arena). Asian YMCAs have served effectively as halfway houses between the church and the world, providing Christian leaven in public opinion and courageous criticism of oppressive traditional ways of life in Asia, pointing society to new possibilities and a new vision of life. Because it is not a church but a Christian agency dedicated to community and voluntary welfare services with rich resources and experience, the YMCA enjoys a unique position of acceptance and collaboration with governmental agencies, even in some restricted-access countries.

Third, the YMCA provided indigenous leadership in an era when church and mission were largely dominated by foreign experts and missionaries. In this way, many gifted lay Christian leaders found that, through the YMCA, they were able to use their gifts and abilities in direct Christian service. For instance, Seijiro Niwa, the first national general secretary of the YMCA in Japan (1903), was a Japanese, as was Y. Honda, the first Japanese chairman of the National YMCA Committee (1903). Similarly, all members of the Chinese YMCA Board were locals by 1907, with C. T. Wang (Wang Zhenting*) as the first Chinese national general secretary (1912). The Korean YMCA was completely indigenous from its inception in Jun 1922. Thus the YMCA has benefited and continues to benefit from having prominent, indigenous lay leadership and initiative in the manifestation of Christian unity. The YMCA continues to attract lay Christian leaders into its board and staff.

The YWCA is also a worldwide movement rooted in the Christian faith. The preamble of the constitution of the World YWCA states that it "Recogniz(es) the equal value in God's sight of all human beings, without distinction of race, nationality, class, or religion, and seek(s) to promote understanding and cooperation between people of different nations, races, and groups." The YWCA originated in London with a Prayer Union started by Emma Roberts in 1855. A bit later, during the Crimean War, when Florence Nightingale recruited nurses, Mary Kinnaird set up a home for nurses and called it the YWCA; this is the origin of the name. These two organizations merged in 1877 and became the YWCA of Great Britain. Following this, YWCAs were founded in other countries, and the World YWCA was organized in 1894.

China. The YMCA was established in China by missionaries who set up schools. In 1885, two neighboring mission schools, those of Fuzhou and Peking, started a youth society in their schools. In 1898 the North America YMCA sent a delegate to China as its first general secretary. He set up the City Youth Association and the National Youth Council. The first Chinese chief executive was the Shanghai Youth Association's Cao Xuegeng, the Shanghai YMCA having been started on 1 Jun 1900.

The YMCA in China organized youth activities and social welfare programs within the China Christian Circle. Participants were mostly non-Christian, and the content of its activities was not religious. It promoted literacy, entertainment, sports, and friendship among youth and adults.

At present, most major provinces in China have a YMCA. In the past, the YMCA was financially dependent upon the North American YMCA. After the Republic of China was established, the YMCA became completely independent in its management of finances. The national headquarters set up the China National YMCA in Shanghai. Its first publication was the *Youth Association Magazine*, renamed *Youth* in 1906. In 1917 *Youth* merged with *Progress* and was renamed *Youth Progression*. The publication ceased in 1932.

The characteristics of the YWCA in China are similar to those of the YMCA. The YWCA organizes activities beneficial for women in society, such as child-care centers and women's hostels. The earliest YWCA originated from a Christian girls-school young ladies' association in 1890, founded by a missionary (Si Tuer) in Hangzhou. In 1899 the China National Youth Association Society appointed some Eastern and Western women, who gathered together and set up the Chinese National Young Women's Society Planning Committee. In 1903 the World YWCA sent Martha Berninger (Bei Ninge) to Shanghai to serve as China's first YWCA secretary. She set up their office and at the same time organized the women's rally and other activities. When China's YWCA joined the World YWCA in 1905, the first general secretaries were, successively, A. E. Paddock, Grace Coppock, and Rosalee Venable. School and city YWCAs were established, with the Shanghai YWCA being the earliest (1908) and now serving as headquarters of the national council of YWCAs in China.

At present, there is a YMCA in every major city of China. During the Chinese revolution, the YWCA in Shanghai was especially known for its ladies physical education program and labor movement. The *Young Women's Paper* was published by the YWCA national society in 1917. Due to the political situation at that time, the publication was interrupted. In 1932, it changed its name to the *Woman's Voice*, a monthly publication. The publication was interrupted by World War II; it was resumed in 1942 but ceased in 1948.

Japan. The National Committee of YMCAs in Japan works for cooperation between and development of the many YMCAs. This national-level mutual cooperation has been in existence from the early days. For example, in an 1882 memorandum addressed to Uchimura Kanzo* and Miyabe Kingo, the Sapporo YMCA offered money to publish the *Rikugo zasshi* (Cosmos Magazine) and wrote that they would do everything possible to assist their affiliated organizations. In 1887 the Japan YMCA was organized, with Iwamoto Yoshiharu, Yamaga Hatanoshin, Terasawa Kyukichi, and Honma Shigeyoshi as liaison secretaries. The organized movement really began with the first summer camp program. At the fourth summer camp (in 1892), the name was changed to the National Committee of YMCAs, and the organization began to publish *Seinenkai geppo* (Youth Association Monthly) to support the YMCAs. The organizations that led to the present-day structure include the Alliance of Japan Student Christian Associations, founded when John R. Mott was in Japan, and the Japan Alliance of City YMCAs. Both were present at the fifteenth summer camp, and they merged to form the National Committee of YMCAs in Japan. Persons related to the YMCA include Honda Yoitsu, Ibuka Kajinosuke, Motoda Sakunoshin, Sasamori Uichiro, Uchigasaki Tojiro, Watanabe Nobu, Hirasawakinji, Terasawa, Miyagawa Tsuneteru, Kozaki Hiromichi, Alexander Durham Hail, and Jerome Dean Davis. The objectives as stated in the first constitution were to: (1) plan for the unified association of YMCAs; (2) promote the establishment of YMCAs in all regions of Japan; (3) spread Christianity to youth; (4) cultivate the spiritual life of youth, encourage in them a spirit of service, encourage the development of mind, body, and spirit; and (5) spread the kingdom of Christ. There has been no change in these objectives, but they have come through a number of transitions and now use the shortened basic objective and motto of all YMCAs around the world, as stated in the Paris Basis: "That All May Become One" (John 17:21). The national committee does not have programs like the local organizations do. However, as a national activity it sponsors a summer camp, has undertaken a national cooperative mission program, and promotes the ecumenical* movement. It too was forced to join the United Church of Christ in Japan under the wartime Religious Organizations Law in 1942, but immediately after the war it regained its independent status. It has issued a number of periodical publications, including: *Nihon gakusei kirisuto-kyo seinenkai* (YMCA Student Christian Associations), *Nihon no seinen* (Japanese Young Men), *Kirisuto-kyo kodan* (Christian Rostrum), and *Kaitakusha* (The Pioneer). At the present time, there are 30 city YMCAs and 36 student YMCAs affiliated with the national association.

In Japan, an organizing committee for the YWCA was set up in 1901 with such women as Tsuda Umeko, Hirano Hamako, and Kozaki Chiyo as members. They were joined in 1904 by Kawai Michi and published *Meiji no joshi* ("Women of Meiji," later renamed *Joshi seinen kai*, "Young Women's World"). In 1905, these women opened an office in A. Caroline Macdonald's home, and on 25 Nov of that year the inaugural ceremony of the Tokyo YWCA was held at the home of Okuma Shigenobu. At that time, their activities centered primarily around women students, for whom they held summer camps and provided dormitories. The YWCA of Japan joined the World YWCA the following year. During the Taisho Period (1912-25), it engaged in activities called for by the times, such as relief activities in Siberia and disarmament. It also began staff training activities. The Yokohama YWCA was started in 1913, the Osaka and Kobe YWCAs in 1918, and the Kyoto YWCA in 1920. In Oct 1925, the first national assembly was held. The YWCA operated residences, organized recreational activities such as camps, opened facilities for working women, and organized the Labor Survey Division, with an office in Nagoya that studied and surveyed the actual conditions of women laborers. Tsujikawa Cho was head of this program. The YWCA was forced to merge with the United Church of Christ in Japan in 1941 by the ministry of education, and toward the end of World War II*, local YWCA buildings were expropriated, bringing all activities to a virtual halt. The publication of *Joshi seinen kai* was also halted in Mar 1944. At the first executive committee meeting after the war, the leaders decided to rebuild, and they began with assistance from abroad. The work of the YWCA of Japan since the war has been characterized by a decision to be socially responsible, with the goal of preserving human rights, defending the constitution, and participating in the antinuclear movement. In 1982, there were 24 local YWCAs and 30 campus YWCAs in Christian junior and senior high schools. In Mar 1946, the YWCA published *Josei shinbun* (Women's Paper), and in 1950 they began publishing the official organ, *YWCA*.

Myanmar. According to available records, the YMCA in Myanmar started in 1894 at Yangon (Rangoon). Myanmar, under British administration, was part of an Indian empire that comprised India* (including Pakistan* and Bangladesh*), Burma, and Ceylon. Until World War II, the YMCA in Myanmar existed only in Yangon and Mandalay. The Yangon YMCA functioned as a British YMCA, an Indian YMCA, and a Burmese YMCA (mainly a hostel operation for students). It had social, recreational, and hostel facilities. The Mandalay YMCA was mainly concerned with social activities.

Almost all of the facilities of the YMCA in Myanmar were destroyed in the Pacific War, except for the Lammadaw hostel building which, though severely damaged, was repaired with the help of local and international donors and the assistance of fraternal secretaries who came with the army units which reoccupied the country.

With the assistance of the YMCAs of North America and the Baptist* mission, the Union Hall School building, located at the corner of Bo Aung Gyaw Street and Mahabandoola Street, was acquired, and YMCA activities were reorganized in Yangon with two buildings, one of which was a hostel for students and workers who had no accommodation in Yangon.

In 1951 the National Council of YMCAs of Myanmar was instituted with indigenous leadership. In 1953 it became a member of the World Alliance of YMCAs. It is also a member of the Asia Alliance of YMCAs. Meanwhile YMCAs were organized in the district towns of Mandalay, Moulmein, Myitkyina, Maymyo, and Taunggyi. The Rangoon YMCA remained the main place for YMCA activities, and it received the services of fraternal secretaries from North America. The new YMCA building at 263 Mahabandoola Street, Yangon, completed in 1965, is now the center of YMCA activities. It also houses the offices of the Myanmar Council of Churches and the National Council of YMCAs in Myanmar.

Though the activities of the YMCA in Myanmar were curtailed with the establishment of the military government in Mar 1962, the number of YMCAs has increased to 11: Yangon, Mandalay, Pyin Oo Lwin (Maymyo), Taunggyi, Myitkyina, Kalemyo, Tahan, Haka, Moegaung, Bago (Pegu), and Yezin.

The programs of YMCAs of Myanmar include religious programs; sports and recreational activities; outreach programs at the satellite towns of Yangon, Mandalay, and Myitkyina; hostels and tourist facilities at Yangon and Myitkyina; educational programs (especially languages classes in English, Japanese, and Thai); nursery training; computer technology; vocational training (carpentry, plumbing, sewing, economy stoves, basic electrical equipment repairs, masonry, beauty parlor, cane work); health clinics; and programs in response to the needs of local YMCA communities.

The National Council of YMCAs of Myanmar has its own constitution and meets triennially. There is a board which meets annually and an executive committee which meets monthly. The total membership is over 17,000.

In 1891 Emily Kinnaird, daughter of one of the founders of the YWCA in Great Britain, attempted to establish the YWCA in Myanmar. But this effort was not successful until 1899, when Agnes Hill, then general secretary of the India National Committee, visited Yangon and held meetings at the home of a Presbyterian pastor, which were attended mainly by foreigners.

In 1900 the YWCA of Yangon was officially recognized as a branch of the India National Committee, which was affiliated with the World YWCA. Under the leadership of Dr. Cote (president) and Miss Lindsay (general secretary), the YWCA building on Bogalay Bazaar Street, where it still stands today, was dedicated in 1902. In 1907, a holiday home for work-weary members was set up in Thandaung. It was moved to Kalaw in 1919.

During World War II, the YWCA building was used as a nightclub. A membership reunion was held at the end of the war in Dec 1945. The YWCA was rehabilitated and reestablished with the help of foreign donations.

In May 1950, the Myanmar YWCA became independent of the National Committee of India, as decided at the quadrennial conference held in Bombay. In Oct 1951, the National YWCA of Myanmar became an affiliate of the World YWCA. Presently, the YWCA of Myanmar has seven local associations. Eighty percent of its members are Christian. Buddhists, Muslims, and Hindus participate as associate members.

The triangular logo of the YWCA symbolizes body, mind, and spirit. The purpose of the YWCA is therefore to nurture, train, and build up the lives of young people in the areas mentioned, with a Christian emphasis. Leadership training to maximize resources to meet the changing needs of the community is an especially important emphasis. Its motto is "By Love Serve One Another." The Myanmar YWCA has developed its own contextually applicable constitution, and the services it renders to various communities have been highly valued and have inspired many. Its rallying motivation is "Together we can make a difference . . . Towards the Future."

Pakistan. The YWCA in Pakistan was established in 1950 after it separated from the combined YWCA of India, Pakistan, Burma, and Ceylon. Before then, the YWCA of the Indian subcontinent had established a local association at Lahore and Karachi, the key motivation being Christian concern for women and girls. The primary policy of the YWCA was to provide Christian ministry for women and girls irrespective of "color, class, or creed."

The YWCAs in Karachi and Lahore played a key role in the rehabilitation of the refugees* from India in 1947. The newly formed All Pakistan Women's Association (APWA) asked the secretary of the YWCA of Karachi to act as a consultant on a working committee to set up hostels. The YWCA of Karachi has also set up community centers for refugees in Korangi and North Karachi, running clinics, primary schools, and adult literacy centers. The YWCA of Lahore worked with the refugee centers located near the border areas. It also set up one of the first secretarial schools in Pakistan.

In the 1950s, Ms. Elfving visited various cities in Pakistan, and different Y groups were started. However, only Rawalpindi developed to meet the criteria for affiliation with the YWCA (1952). A hostel for working women was started in a rented building, and thus, when the capital shifted to the twin city of Islamabad a few years later, a great need was met. Later, the YWCAs of Sialkot and Peshawar were established.

Elfving organized the national office, temporarily located at the YWCA of Lahore. Later, a holiday home was started in Murree, and in the summer months the national office was located there. The national councils met in Murree and developed a constitution. The work of the associations was evaluated, and the major priorities for the coming years were selected. Various staff members and volunteers were trained as leaders in different international organizations and by the World YWCA leadership programs.

The associations faced new challenges both with the rapidly changing political climate and with the sudden changes in leadership. Large sections of the expatriate community left the country, and other trained and experienced leaders either migrated or retired from active work in the YWCA.

From 1968 to 1991, as finances diminished, the national council decided to work without staff, and the national presidents doubled up as honorary national general secretaries as well. In 1992, a separate national office was set up at the present location, 62 K, Model Town, Lahore. The staff comprises a general secretary; a secretary for development, who is also the coordinator of Young Women's Programs for the National YWCA; a part-time accountant; and two service staff. The work of the YWCA includes hostels and education, both formal and nonformal. Although the emphasis has been on primary and vocational training, the YWCA has moved more into nonformal education, providing a variety of skills ranging from language to music, arts, and crafts.

In 1995, Women in Development became a major program. The different social work and literacy* centers of the associations are developing into community centers. The literacy course tackles major issues, such as health, the environment, and the status of women. The women, who are encouraged to contribute both toward the development of their own sex and the nation, are also taught skills to enhance their capacity to earn money. In line with its belief in maximizing the potential of persons for the benefit of the country, the YWCA has recently organized workshops on leadership and administration. The YWCA has taken an active stand against the recently promulgated Blasphemy Law and the Hadood *(hudud)* Laws and has organized seminars on these topics. The National News Net and occasional announcements provide members with information about the YWCA.

Bibliography

Fifty Year History of Asian YMCAs (1998). • *Nihon YWCA go-ju-nen no ayumi* (Fifty-year history of the YWCA of Japan) (1955). • *Nenpyo nihon YWCA hachi-ju-nen shi 1905-1984* (Chronological table of the eighty-year history of the YWCA of Japan — 1905-1984) (1985). • *Mizu o kaze o hikari o-nihon YWCA hachi-ju nen 1905-1985* (Water, wind, and light — YWCA of Japan eighty years, 1905-1985) (1987).

LAWRENCE KO, with contributions from THE CHINA GROUP, OCHIAI NORIO, UOKI ASA, WILLIAM PAW, DAW LILIAN KHA NAU, and MERLE JIVANANDHAM

Young, Luther Lisgar

(b. ?; d. Kobe, Japan, Feb 1950). Canadian Presbyterian* missionary to Koreans in Japan.

Young was sent to Korea in 1906 as a missionary of the Canadian Presbyterian Church. His work centered mainly in Hamkyong-do in the northeastern part of Korea. In 1925 Young left his home church in Canada when it joined with the Methodist Church to form the United Church of Canada. He switched his membership to another Canadian Presbyterian church which was not a part of the union and remained a Presbyterian missionary. When his mission territory came under the jurisdiction of the United Church of Canada, he decided to return to Canada in 1927. He stopped briefly in Kobe, Japan*, where he was overjoyed to discover that there were many Koreans seeking a livelihood in Japan. He decided to do missionary work among the Koreans in Japan. He visited many cities and strove to plant churches wherever Koreans were found. After seven years, in 1934 a Korean presbytery comprising more than 50 churches was organized. Young returned to Canada when Japan was waging a new war with the United States and all foreign missionaries, and English-speaking missionaries in particular, were forced to leave Japan.

After the war, Young wanted to return to Japan, but he was not permitted by his church because he was close to retirement age. They relented when he petitioned, and he returned to Japan in 1949 with his former assistants, Mr. and Mrs. Paul Rumball. Young was buried where he desired — in Kobe.

Bibliography

Rhodes, Harry A., *History of the Korea Mission: Presbyterian Church U.S.A., 1884-1934* (1934).

RHEE JONG SUNG

Young-Nak Presbyterian Church

For the past half-century, Young-Nak Presbyterian Church in Seoul, Korea, has been recognized as the model Korean Protestant church. Its founder, Han Kyung-Chik*, has also been considered a model for Korean ministers and church leaders. The establishment of hundreds of Young-Nak Presbyterian churches in Korea and abroad attests to the enormity of its influence in the Korean church and society.

Following the 1945 invasion of Soviet troops into North Korea, Han and 27 refugees fled to the south from the Pyung-Ahn Province, where there was an exceptionally strong community of Christians. This group founded the church on 2 Dec 1945 in Young Nak District, Seoul, Korea. The name of the church at its foundation was Bethany Evangelism Church. This name was given not only because there were several women members in the church whose firm faith and service-oriented life resembled the women of the town of Bethany in the Bible, but also because a women's seminary, of which Han was head, was to be located in the church's vicinity. The church began as a nondenominational, temporary, evangelistic church for refugees from the north. However, when the division between the north and the south became permanent and the members had settled themselves in the south, Bethany Evangelism Church found it necessary to become formally established. On 12 Nov 1946, the name of the church was changed to Young-Nak Presbyterian Church. The term "Young-Nak" had spiritual significance because it is the Chinese acronym for "eternal joy."

Young-Nak Presbyterian Church held to its mission statement, "mission, education and service," and practiced a Bible-centered, evangelical faith and holy living; a nurturing of an ecumenical* spirit between churches; and social responsibility of the church. Before its first anniversary, Young-Nak Presbyterian Church had more than 1,400 registered members, and the following year, in 1947, that number grew to 4,500. Every year thereafter the church experienced an increase of over 1,000 members, and by 1998 it was still growing, with about 60,000 members.

The rapid growth and rise of the church as a national model church could be attributed to the influx of refugees from the Pyung-Ahn Province, but more significantly may be attributed to Han's exceptional ministerial role. His messages were always Bible-centered and plain to everyone. At least 500 daughter churches have been established worldwide, including Young-Nak Presbyterian Church of Los Angeles, which holds 5,000. The church also established a junior and senior high school, through which community leaders are trained. A women's seminary was also established and has made an especially important contribution in the development of Korean women church leaders and workers. Many orphanages, social welfare facilities, and convalescent homes, including Bo-Rin-Won, have also been established. The church, through ministries such as broadcasting, medical* services, military evangelism, and overseas missions, has made great contributions to the expansion of God's kingdom.

Bibliography

Lee Chul-Shin, *The 50-Year History of the Young-Nak Presbyterian Church* (Seoul: Young-Nak Presbyterian Church) (1996). • Lee Jong-Sung, "Rev. Kyung-Chik Han: His Influence on the Korean Church and Korean Theology," unpublished collection of seminar notes delivered on the occasion of the dedication of Kyung-Chik Han Memorial Center (Seoul: Young-Nak Presbyterian Church Publishers).

TIMOTHY KIHO PARK

Yu Guozhen

(Yu Kuo-chen) (b. Zhejrang, Chekiang, 1852; d. 1932). Chinese pastor and founder of the Chinese Jesus Independent Church.

Yu was from Zhejiang and was converted at the age of 16 while studying in a Christian school. After his graduation in 1872, he taught and preached in various places in Zhejiang. In 1894 he became pastor of the Presbyterian* church, Yabeitang, in Shanghai. Ten years later, the church decided to be financially independent. In 1906 Yu started the indigenous Chinese Jesus Independent Church. Its headquarters was established in Shanghai in 1910. A periodical, the *Sheng Bao* (Holy News), was distributed the following year. Yu was elected the lifelong chairman at the first delegates congress of the Chinese Jesus Independent Church in 1920. He retired from the Presbyterian church in 1924 and devoted himself to establishing the Yongzhitang, that is, the National General Independent Hall. Yu was a pioneer of the indigenous church movement in China and one of the first to put "*aiguo* (love country), *aijiao* (love church)" into practice.

Bibliography

"Chinese Independent and Self-Supporting Churches," in *China Mission Yearbook*, Vol. 3 (1912).

CHINA GROUP, translated by PATRICIA SIEW

Yu Rezhang

(David Yui Zek-Tsang) (b. Hubei, China, 25 Nov 1882; d. Shanghai, Jan 1936). Chinese general secretary of the Young Men's Christian Association* (YMCA) in China* for 16 years.

The son of a Christian minister, Yu was taught the Chinese classics as a child. He also studied at Boone University in Wuchang and at St. John's University in Shanghai. He graduated with a bachelor of arts degree from the latter in 1905 and obtained his master's from Harvard University, USA, in 1910.

Upon his return to China, he became headmaster of Boone School in Wuchang and was briefly commissioner for foreign affairs in Hubei. In 1912 he became associate editor of the *Peking Daily News.* He was also a private secretary to Li Yuanhong, first vice president of the new government in Beijing. Yu was appointed national secretary of the YMCA in 1913. When John R. Mott, the well-known leader of the student movement, came to China on a speaking tour in 1913, Yu served as one of his interpreters. In 1915 Yu was adviser and honorary secretary to the Chinese trade commission touring the United States.

In 1916 Yu was appointed acting general secretary of the YMCA. He soon succeeded C. T. Wang* as general secretary and remained at the helm of the YMCA for 16 years. After being selected one of two "citizen representatives" by the Shanghai Chamber of Commerce and the National Federation of Educational Associations, he attended the Washington Conference in 1921. He encouraged the Chinese delegation to redeem the Shandong railway from the Japanese. He headed the fund-raising campaign that remitted the full sum to Japan in 1922.

Yu was elected chairman of the National Christian Council in 1922. He was also involved with the World Student Christian Federation. As a founding chairman of the Institute of Pacific Relations (IPR) in China, he led the Chinese delegation to the second IPR conference in Honolulu in 1927. He also attended the International Missionary Conference in Jerusalem in 1928.

After the Japanese invasion of Manchuria, Yu went on a special mission to the United States in 1932 to raise support for China. In 1933 he suffered a cerebral hemorrhage while in Washington for conferences with Secretary of State Henry L. Stimson. Yu returned to Shanghai and died in Jan 1936.

His best-known phrase, *ren ge jiu guo* (national salvation through the development of individual integrity), underlined his belief that the solution to national problems lay in the character of individuals. This resulted in his emphasis on the training of Chinese youths. He saw the YMCA as a means to strengthen and develop China. In the 1920s, he employed staff through the YMCA to tackle the problem of widespread illiteracy in China. Under his leadership, the YMCA provided moral guidance and made practical contributions toward China's progress.

Bibliography

Boorman, Howard L., ed., *Biographical Dictionary of Republican China,* Vol. 4 (1971). • Garrett, Shirley, *Social Reformers in Urban China: The Chinese YMCA, 1895-1926* (1970).

China Group

Yuasa Hachiro

(b. Akasaka District, Tokyo, Japan, 29 Apr 1890; d. 15 Aug 1981). Educator, doctor of science.

The fifth son of Yuasa Jiro and Hatsuko, Yuasa was raised in the strong Christian faith of his home, and at his baptism in 1905 affirmed, "before God and persons, I strive to be an upright person." After graduating from the regular course at the Doshisha in 1908, he went to the United States. He worked on a pioneer farm in California for three years. He then entered Kansas Agricultural College, where study was difficult for him. After this he went to the graduate school at Illinois State University, majoring in entomology. He received his Ph.D. in 1920 and became an engineer in the state's natural history department. That year he married Ukai Kiyoko. When an agriculture department was established at Kyoto University, he was invited to teach there, but first he served in Germany as a foreign research fellow for the Japanese ministry of education. He then returned to Japan in Jan 1924 to take up the teaching position.

He became a doctor of science in 1931. At an incident at Kyoto University in 1933 in which the essence of the university was being questioned, he supported Takigawa Yukitoki. In Feb 1935, he became the tenth president of Doshisha University, grappling with solutions to the mounting number of internal school problems and battling fascist pressure. In Feb 1937, he worked out the draft for the "Doshisha Educational Platform," working to maintain a constructive school spirit, but he was severely criticized from both within and outside the school and finally labeled a traitor. A number of conflicts with the government resulted in the call for the expulsion of the president. This moved into the *Haizoku Shoko Hikiage* (evacuation of military officer assigned to school), and it became evident that the continuation of Doshisha as an educational institution was in jeopardy, causing Yuasa to resign from the presidency in December of that year.

The next year he attended the meeting of the International Missionary Council at Madras, India, as one of the delegates from Japanese churches. He was a member of the Asia team at that meeting; the team later went to many areas of the United States to spread their message. After this, he continued to appeal for church union and world peace, attending the Christian Peace Conference in Geneva, Switzerland, in 1939 as the only delegate from Japan. He continued to lecture as the danger of war between the United States and Japan became imminent. On the day of the bombing of Pearl Harbor, he delivered a lecture entitled "The Mission of Peace as a Christian."

Even after the beginning of the war, he stayed in the United States working for the revival of world peace. He worked with Japanophiles and Japan missionaries who had returned to the United States to accomplish an end to the war and gain relief for the Japanese in internment camps.

After the war, when he returned to Japan in Oct 1946 to work for world friendship through the United Nations Educational, Scientific and Cultural Organization (UNESCO), he was again called to Doshisha, and in Apr 1947 he became its twelfth president. He worked for both the material and spiritual rebuilding of the school. Yuasa was a member of an international Christian education survey committee and also the vice chair of the board of trustees of the Christian Education League that was working on plans for a comprehensive Christian university. In Sep 1936, he had appealed for the founding of a Japanese Christian scholarly research center, but the time was not ripe. After the war, this idea was brought up again by a group of churches in the United States, and, with the mediation efforts of the National Christian Council in Japan, discussions progressed so that in Jun 1949 the structure for the International Christian University (ICU) was set, and Yuasa was selected its first president. He resigned from Doshisha in Jun 1950.

With the objective of training "international persons of peace to bring about tomorrow's world devoted to free and sincere love," preparations were begun to open a school as an "adventure together with God." He became the president, and the school opened in Apr 1953. With the ideal of creating "a school for tomorrow," he brought together the foundation blocks. In 1962 he became honorary president and chair of the board of trustees, continuing to devote himself to the development of ICU. He then returned to Kyoto, where he chaired the board of trustees of the Young Men's Christian Association* and the International Student Dorm; he also worked with Amnesty International as a representative on the committee to consider the beatings and imprisonments of Kim Dae Jong (see Korea).

In addition to chairing the board of trustees of Niijima Gakuin, he served as trustee, officer, and supporter of a number of different Christian organizations. A lover of folk art, he also served as president of the Kyoto Folk Art Association and as a board member of the Japan Folk Art Association. His collection is stored in the Yuasa Memorial Museum on the ICU campus. His writings include *Mingei no kokoro* (The Heart of Folk Art), 1978, and *Wakamono ni maboroshi o* (A Dream for Youth), 1981. His autobiographical reflections have been edited by the Doshisha University America Research Office as *Aru riberarisuto no kaiso* (The Reflections of a Liberalist), 1977.

Ebisawa Arimichi

Yuen Tiengtk-Yok

(b. Phet Buri, Thailand, 1850; d. 27 Sep 1927). First Thai ordained clergyman and first Thai pastor of First Church, Bangkok, the first Presbyterian* mission church in Thailand*.

Yuen was one of central Thailand's first Thai pastors. His father was a Chinese and his mother a Thai. At the age of 12 or 13, his father left him with the Presbyterian missionary family of Rev. Stephen Mattoon for his education. He eventually trained as a preacher and evangelist and was licensed to preach at the age of 23 or 24. He then worked as a mission evangelist in Ayutthaya for several years. He first married in 1874 and later divorced. His second wife died after giving birth. Yuen then married his third wife, Serm.

Kru (Teacher) Yuen taught at the Harriet House School, also known as Wang Lang Girls' School, for 10 years. In 1895 the Presbyterian Siam Mission pursued a policy of allowing local churches to assume more responsibility for their own leadership and support, and in Jun 1896 the First Church hired him as its pastor. He served the church until his death on 27 Sep 1927. As a pastor he engaged in a wide range of activities including evangelism, and he also aided in the translation of the Bible* into Thai. He was known as a mannerly, patient, and cheerful pastor who was well known both among Christians and more generally.

Bibliography

"Annual Reports," *Siam Outlook,* Vol. 7, No. 3 (Jan 1928). • McFarland, George B., ed., *Historical Sketch of Protestant Missions in Siam, 1828-1928* (1928). • Yuen Tiengtk-Yok, *Autobiography of Yuen Tiengtk-Yok* (1928).

Prasit Pongudom, translated by Herbert R. Swanson

Yuki Ko

(b. Sakaiminato, Tottori Prefecture, Japan, 16 Apr 1896; d. 27 Jan 1985). Minister, hymn writer.

Yuki was raised as the adopted son of Yuki Toramatsu and baptized by Takeda Shunzo on 9 Jul 1911 while a student at Hyogo Prefectural Kobe #2 Junior High School. In the fall of that year, the family moved to Izuhara because of his father's work with Tsushima Mission. Owing to a close brush with death in Oct 1914, he decided to dedicate his life to God's work. He entered the literature department of Kwansei Gakuin. He had begun writing hymns while he was in junior high school and published the first volume of *Seisho shoka* (Singing Scriptures), and all three volumes of *Nichiyo gakko shoka shu* (Collections of Songs for the Sunday School), while a student at Kwansei Gakuin. After graduating, he lived in Minatogawa Mission House and received a practical theological education while lecturing on world history at Kobe Bible School (Kansai Bible Seminary). During his second year of study in 1921, Noguchi Yuka invited him to serve Futaba Independence Church (which later became the United Church of Christ in Japan's Higashi Nakano Church) in Tokyo. He was ordained at this church in 1941 by Shirato Hachiro of the Japan Independent Christian Church Alliance, and served there for his entire pastoral career. He became senior pastor in 1950 and, after his retirement, was an honorary pastor for 14 years.

During this time, he also translated and edited many English hymns, first publishing *Seika* (Hymns) in 1927. He served as editor of a number of hymn collections, including *Sambika* (Hymnal), 1931 edition; *Seinen sambika* (Youth Hymnal), 1941; *Sambika* (Hymnal), 1954 edition; and *Sambika dai ni hen* (Second Hymnal), 1967. He also wrote and translated many hymns, a large number of which are included in the above publications. He was the most important person in the world of hymnody during the Showa period (1926-89). He also translated many of the works of Blaise Pascal, including *Panse josetsu* (Introduction to *Pensées*), 1935; *Pasukaru shohinshu* (Collection of Pascal's Short Works), 1938; and *Pasukaru meisoroku* (Meditations of Pascal), 1938. He made many fine contributions to the research on Pascal, including *Watakushi no Pasukaru taiken* (My Pascal Experience), 1981. His writings and translations include *Kirisuto ni naraite* (Learning from Christ), 1948, revised 1973; *Kono hito o miyo — fukuin, shiso, bunka* (Behold the Man — Gospel, Thought, Culture), 1984; 18 volumes on the Bible and faith; 18 volumes related to Pascal; 17 volumes on liturgy and hymnody; and nine volumes of children's stories, songs, and short songs. The three sections of the present Japanese hymnal include 19 of his poems as hymns and 95 of his translations. A total of about 400 of his hymns have been published. His autobiography, *Deai kara deaie* (From Encounter to Encounter), was published in 1976. KITAMURA SOJI

Yun Tchi Ho

(b. Asan, South Ch'ungch'ong Province, South Korea, 23 Jan 1865; d. 6 Dec 1945). First Korean Methodist* of the Methodist Episcopal Church, South; theologian, educator, politician, and leader of the independence movement.

In 1881, after the Korea-Japanese Treaty of 1876, Yun followed the Korean observation team of envoys to Japan* and studied Western knowledge and English in Tokyo. After his return, he was appointed an official interpreter of the first American consul, L. H. Foote, until he was exiled to China after the failure of his progressive party's *coup d'etat* of the winter of 1884.

In Shanghai he attended the Anglo-Chinese College, a mission school run by the Methodist Episcopal Church, South. There he was baptized on 3 Apr 1887, becoming the first Korean member of that denomination. He was sent to Vanderbilt University in the United States for his theological education, and completed his studies at Emory University. While at Emory, he met Chancellor Candler and urged that the Methodist Episcopal Church, South, become involved in mission work in Korea by contributing $200. Until he returned home in 1895, he taught at his old school in Shanghai. Upon his return to Korea, he was appointed the old Chosun dynasty's civil servant in the ministry of education and of foreign affairs. During the Japanese advance to the peninsula, he participated in the Independence Club as one of its founders and presidents, and in the first Korean-language newspaper, *Toglip Shin Mun* (The Independence). When the Japanese-controlled royal court dismissed the activist groups, he began pastoral work by building a new church on his own property in Koyang, north of Seoul. In 1905 the Korean-Japan protectorate agreement was signed; Yun founded the Anglo-Korean School (later, Songdo High School) with the support of the mission board of the Methodist Episcopal Church, South; and became the school's first principal. When Yonhee Union Christian College was founded, he served as the first president of the college. He was one of the founders of Seoul Young Men's Christian Association* (YMCA) and served as president and secretary. He took part in the World Student Christian Federation and participated in the 1907 Tokyo Conference as the Korean delegation. He attended the World Missionary Conference at Edinburgh, Scotland, the first worldwide ecumenical conference, held in 1910. He also participated in the Jerusalem Conference in 1928 as a Korean YMCA delegate.

In 1910, when the Japanese authorities fabricated the so-called conspiracy case for the attempt to assassinate Japanese governor-general Terauchi, Yun was arrested with other activist groups, interrogated, tortured, and released with death threats. After this, he kept a low profile and concentrated on his work as principal of Songdo High School until the liberation of Korea in 1945.

Yun was a meticulous diary and journal keeper. Part of his journal was published and contains precious historical materials for researchers in the field of modern Korean history. DAVID SUH, with contributions from LEE DUK JOO, translated by KIM IN SOO

Z

Zamora, Hacinto. *See* Gom-Bur-Za

Zamora, Nicolas

(b. 1875; d. 1914). First Filipino-ordained Protestant minister, religious nationalist, and founder of the Evangelical Methodist Church in the Philippines (IEMELIF).

Zamora was the grandnephew of the priest-martyr Jacinto Zamora. He was a Philippine revolutionary army lieutenant colonel in 1896 and was converted in 1899 with father Paulino and two brothers. Becoming a Methodist* evangelist, he was ordained by visiting bishop James Mill Thoburn* in 1900. The prince of Filipino preachers of his time, Zamora spoke in many Catholic churches in Manila which were abandoned by friar curates rounded up for deportation to Spain. Two subdistricts in Manila turned practically all Methodist, and in 1903 Zamora became the first pastor of what is now the Knox Memorial Church.

A nationalist, Zamora resisted the incorporation of the Methodist mission churches into the American Methodist Episcopal Church in 1907. In 1909 he launched the IEMELIF schism, which he led until his death.

Bibliography

Stuntz, H. C., *The Philippines and the Far East* (1904). • Deats, R. L., "Nicolas Zamora: Religious Nationalist," in G. H. Anderson, ed., *Studies in Philippine Church History,* (1969). • Sitoy, T. V., Jr., *Several Springs, One Stream* (1992).

T. Valentino Sitoy, Jr.

Zanin, Mario

(b. Italy, 1890; d. Argentina, 1958). Second Vatican representative to China*.

Ordained a priest in 1913, Zanin worked in various capacities, including as professor of theology and secretary to the bishop. In 1926 he worked in the Propaganda Fide Congregation* ("Congregation for the Evangelization of Peoples") of the Vatican, and on 29 Nov 1933 the pope appointed him the second representative to China. He lived in the Vatican representative mansion built by his predecessor, Celso Costantini*. At the beginning of 1935, Zanin founded the Chong Kuang Publishing Company (*Lumen Agentia,* or "Light News Agency") mainly to disseminate the *Chinese Catholic News,* and in September he convened the first Catholic conference (see Literature and Publishing).

During the war, Zanin publicly exhorted Chinese Catholics (14 Mar 1939) "not to turn left nor right" *(nec ad dexteram nec ad sinistram dec linantes)* — tantamount to a neutral position in the face of Japanese aggression. The relationship between Pope Pius XII and President Jian Jie Shi (Chiang Kai-shek) became closer as China's victory drew near. In Jul 1946, the Vatican and the Jian government established diplomatic ties and exhanged ambassadors. Antonio Riberi* was appointed ambassador to China, and Zanin relinquished his position as Vatican representative to China. He left Shanghai on 10 Aug 1946, returned to the Vatican, and was appointed Vatican ambassador to Chile and, later, Argentina, where he died.

China Group, translated by David Wu

Zarco, Guillermo

(b. ?; d. 1934). Filipino pioneer evangelist, church planter, and pastor.

An outstanding Filipino evangelist and pastor, Zarco was a graduate of the Jesuits'* Ateneo de Manila. After a spiritual crisis, a prodigal life, and opium* addiction, he was converted in 1900 and became a Presbyterian* evangelist.

From 1902 to 1908, he did pioneering work in the provinces of Laguna, Cavite, Batangas, and Tayabas. He was ordained by the Presbytery of Manila in 1906. From 1908 to 1916, he was pastor of Batangas Evangelical Church and minister-on-call for the rest of the churches in the province. His labors resulted in the organization of several churches and the recruitment of four youths for the ministry.

He was called to the pastorate of the Tondo Evangelical Church in 1917, but chronic ill health forced his retirement in 1918 after 17 years in the ministry.

Bibliography

73rd Annual Presbyterian Board Report (1910). • "Filipino Pioneers," *The Philippine Presbyterian,* Vol. 6 (Apr 1915). • "Batangas UCCP 75th Anniversary" (1983). • Sitoy, T. V., Jr., *Several Springs, One Stream* (1992).

T. Valentino Sitoy, Jr.

Zhang Jiashu

(b. Shanghai, China, 1893; d. 25 Feb 1988). First bishop of the Shanghai Diocese elected by Chinese Catholic believers.

Zhang was admitted to the Society of Jesus (Jesuits*) on 4 Nov 1911 after graduating from middle school. He was sent to Europe to study theology and philosophy on Jersey Island. Consecrated as a priest in 1923, he returned to Shanghai on 2 Oct 1925 and taught at his alma mater, Xuhui Middle School. He later became the school's principal but had no authority over the school administration, since he was Chinese. After the establishment of the Chinese People's Republic, Chinese Catholic patriots sponsored the patriotic movement. In 1955 Gong Pinmei, bishop of the Shanghai Diocese, was arrested for treason. Under the sensitive political situation, Zhang decided to cooperate with the People's government. In Jan 1956, he was invited to the Second Session of the Second Chinese People's Political Consultative Conference as a nonvoting delegate. In 1957 he attended the inaugural meeting of the Chinese Catholic Patriotic Association, being elected a member of its standing committee. He was present at the Liturgy for the Self-Ordination of Bishops of the Hankou-Wuchang Dioceses in 1958. On 23 Apr 1960, he was elected bishop of the Shanghai Diocese at the First Representative Assembly of the Shanghai Catholic Church and was consecrated on 27 Apr in the Xujiahui Catholic Church, being entrusted with the task of leading the Catholic Church in Shanghai to become a self-governing church.

Zhang was unjustly treated during the Cultural Revolution. In 1980 he was elected head of the Bishops' Deputation, chairperson of the Religious Affairs Committee, and vice president of the Chinese Catholic Patriotic Association. He served as a member of the standing committee of the Fifth and Sixth Chinese People's Political Consultative Conferences and attended important meetings as a Catholic representative in government affairs. He died of illness at the age of 96. China Group

Zhang Xue Yan

(b. Shantung, China, 1901; d. 1950). Chinese Christian scholar and social activist.

Zhang entered Shantung Wenhua College in 1914 and accepted Christ around that time. During World War I, he went to France and assisted the Allied Forces in translation work. After returning to China in 1919, he was convinced that only armed forces and science could save China; however, his endeavor came to nought. From 1927 to 1929, he worked as assistant editor in Shanghai for the Christian Literature Society. From 1930 to 1933, he studied at Nanking (Nanjing) Theological Seminary. After graduating, he established *Tian Jia Zhuang* in Cheeloo University and founded the magazine *Tian Jia Bi-monthly.* He worked as director *cum* chief editor for 16 years. The aim of this periodical was to serve farmers and to help in the modernization of farms. Its circulation came to several hundred thousand subscribers.

In 1937 Zhang went to the United States for study and earned his doctorate in sociology from Cornell University. He returned to China in 1940 and taught in Cheeloo and Yenching Universities. He also served as chairman of Service to Border Area, and led the team to train teachers stationed in the border area. In 1944, together with some intellectuals who supported democracy, he formed a September 3 Society. After the war against Japan, he returned to Peking (Beijing) and taught at Peking and Yenching Universities. Later, because of his political stance against dictatorship and civil war, he was forced to leave China again; he returned in 1949. He was one of the five representatives from the religious sector to participate in the National Political Consultative Meeting. Zhang supported the idea that Chinese churches should be self-governing, self-supporting, and self-propagating and have their own cultural characteristics. China Group

Zhang Zhijiang

(Paul C. C. Chiang) (b. Hebei, China, 1882; d. Thailand, 1966). Chinese Christian military commander.

Zhang was the son of a landlord and village elder. He learned the classics and sat for the imperial examinations. He was conscripted by the Qing army in 1903. In 1907 he joined a military study society sponsored by Feng Yuxiang and others and came into contact with anti-Manchu officers. Zhang joined Feng's 16th Mixed Brigade in 1912.

In May 1916, Feng forced Chen Yi, governor of Sichuan, to declare the independence of Sichuan, thus hastening the fall of Yuan Shi Kai's regime. Zhang was impressed by the anti-imperialist stand of the Christians in Sichuan. He studied the faith and was converted. He took on the name of Paul and persistently read his Bible and prayed daily throughout his life.

Rising through the ranks, Zhang became commander in chief of the Northwest Army in May 1926. He was subordinate only to Feng Yuxiang, who resigned his post to go to Russia. When Feng returned in August and found his army diminished and demoralized, he resumed his post. Zhang retained his position as defense commissioner of the northwest border.

In 1927 Zhang was Feng's representative at the fourth plenum of the second Central Executive Committee of the Kuomintang in Nanjing. He retired from active service in the military and politics in 1928 and became director of the national traditional sports institute. In 1929 he was chairman of the National Opium* Probation Committee. Then in 1932, he became director of the national institute for martial arts. He traveled to Southeast Asia and elsewhere to promote the traditional martial arts.

During the Sino-Japanese War, Zhang was a member of the People's Political Council. He was politically inactive after the Japanese surrender in 1945. A patriot and a committed Christian, Zhang made generous donations to the Episcopal Church on three occasions. He distributed Bibles to the men under his command and expected his soldiers to read their Bibles and attend Sunday services. There would even be hymns and prayers before each battle.

Bibliography

Boorman, Howard L., ed., *Biographical Dictionary of Republican China,* Vol. 1 (1971). China Group

Zhao Shi-Kuang. *See* Chao, Timothy

Zhao Zhensheng

(b. Jing Xian, Hebei, 1894; d. 1968). First Chinese Catholic bishop of China's Xian Xian (county) Diocese.

Zhao was admitted to the small monastery in Xian Xian Diocese in 1911. Two years later he entered the Xian Xian Society of Jesus*. He was selected for further studies in Belgium, where he received a doctorate in philosophy. In 1924 he was initiated into the priesthood in Belgium. After his return to China, he was first appointed professor of Latin in the small monastery in Xian Xian Diocese. In 1936 he was named priest of the headquarters of parishes in Hejian. In 1938 he was appointed by the papacy as the first Chinese bishop in Xian Xian Diocese. After the founding of the Chinese People's Republic, he gradually dispelled his suspicions and fears about the Chinese Communist Party and attended the First Representative Conference of the Chinese Catholic Church in 1957. He was elected vice chairperson of the Chinese Catholic Patriotic Association and was also elected chairperson of the Hebei Provincial Catholic Patriotic Association at the First Representative Conference of the Hebei Catholic Church. On 20 Apr 1958, he consecrated four "self-chosen" bishops from the dioceses of Yongnian, Yongping, Xuanhua, and Xiwanzi in the Zhangjiazhuang's bishop's cathedral at Xian Xian. Soon after, he consecrated another three "self-chosen" bishops of the Baoding Diocese in the Baoding Catholic Church. He contributed toward the independence and autonomy of the Chinese Catholic Church. During the Cultural Revolution, he was persecuted, arrested, and imprisoned. He died of illness while in prison. In 1981, his wrongful arrest was redressed and his discredited status reinstated posthumously with a memorial meeting held in his honor by the Hebei Provincial Catholic Patriotic Association at Shijiazhuang. China Group

Zhao Zi Chen

(C. T. Chao) (b. Deqing, Zejiang Province, China, 14 Feb 1888; d. Beijing, 21 Nov 1979). Outstanding Chinese scholar, teacher, and interpreter of the Christian faith in the Chinese context.

Although Zhao came from a devout Buddhist family, he studied at a mission middle school. Here he was introduced to the Christian faith and joined the church, although he was not baptized until 1908. In common with other young people at this time of intellectual ferment in the early 1900s, his faith did not preclude his participation in anti-Western and even anti-Christian activities.

He graduated from Suzhou (Soochow) University in 1910, and then, a few years later, went to America where, in the years 1914-17, he received master of arts and master of divinity degrees from Vanderbilt University in Nashville, Tennessee. He returned to China in 1917 and taught at the Methodist* Dongwu University in Suzhou for six years, and then, beginning in 1926, became professor of theology in Yanjing (Yenching) University in Beijing. From 1928 to 1952, he was dean of the Yanjing Graduate School of Religion.

During these years, he participated in the work of the Chinese National Christian Council, attended the meeting of the International Missionary Council (IMC) in 1928 in Jerusalem, and presented a major paper at the Tambaram, Madras, meeting of the IMC in 1938. At the first assembly of the World Council of Churches (WCC) at Amsterdam in 1948, he was elected one of the six presidents of the WCC, representing East Asian churches. He resigned from this post in 1951 because he believed a WCC statement accusing North Korea of invading South Korea was in error. In 1947 Zhao was awarded an honorary doctorate from Princeton University.

In 1949 Zhao participated in the China People's Political Consultation Meeting as one of five representatives from the religious sector. In 1950, at the beginning of the Three-Self Movement, he was one of the 40 people who signed the "Three-Self Manifesto" proclaiming the independence of the Chinese church. In 1956 Zhao was accused of siding with American mission boards in their imperialism toward China and was forced to resign from his position as professor and dean at the School of Religion at Yanjing University. He later continued to participate in the Three-Self Movement and was rehabilitated officially in 1979, a short time before his death.

Zhao was recognized in China by the church before the coming of the new government as one of its leading theologians, an honor he still holds today. He was always concerned with how the church might be thoroughly Chinese. This required that the church be purified both institutionally from its denominationalism and doctrinally from its many nonscientific views. He was also concerned that Christianity be related to Confucianism or, more broadly, to humanism, whether in the traditional Chinese sense or as expressed in the renewed intellectual thought of the mid-1920s.

Zhao went through several phases in this theological journey. In his earlier writings — *Jesus' Philosophy of Life on the Sermon on the Mount* (Chinese, 1926) and *The Life of Jesus* (Chinese, 1935) — he espoused a liberal theological perspective. Later writings — *An Interpretation of Christianity* and *The Life of Paul* (both in Chinese, 1947) — reflect what has been referred to as "a spectacular renunciation of liberal thought." Toward the end of his life, as he saw the accomplishments of China under its new government and as he reflected on what he viewed as the inability of the church to practice its theology, he felt that Christianity was no longer relevant for him.

Bibliography

Covell, Ralph R., *Confucius, the Buddha, and Christ: A History of the Gospel in Chinese* (1986). • Gluer, Winfried, "T. C. Chao 1888-1979: Scholar, Teacher, Gentle Mystic," in *Mission Legacies: Biographical Studies of Leaders of the Modern Missionary Movement,* ed. Gerald Anderson, Robert Coote, Norman Horner, and James Phillips (1994). • Gluer, Winfried, *Christliche Theologie in China: T. C. Chao, 1918-1956* (1979).

Ralph R. Covell, with contributions from the China Group

Zhendan Museum

(Heude Museum). The Zhendan, or Heude, Museum was established by the Society of Jesus* in Shanghai in 1931. It began with a vast collection of animal and plant specimens from China and the Far East, stored in the Xujiahui Museum (the residence of the Xujiahui Society of Jesus) by French Jesuit missionary Heude, who had spent more than 30 years traveling to various places. After Heude's death in 1902, Fredric (Po Yongnian) succeeded him, adding plant and bird specimens from Jiangsu and Anhui Provinces collected over a 25-year period. After Fredric's death (1928), the Shanghai Society of Jesus decided in 1929 to build a formal museum beside Aurora University. The museum was inaugurated in 1931 and named the Heude Museum in French and the Zhendan Museum in Chinese, with Auguste Savio (Song Liangcai), the dean of studies at Aurora University, as curator. He headed the museum until 1933, paying special attention to ornithology and entomology. His successor, Piel (Zheng Bier), a French Jesuit, concentrated on entomology. Another expert of the museum was Belval (Bai Yuheng). In 1951 the People's Government took over the museum and renamed it the Shanghai Research Institute of Entomology.

China Group

Zheng Hefu (Philip Lindel Tsen)

(b. Anhui, China, 7 Jan 1885; d. ca. 1954). First Chinese Anglican* archbishop in China*.

Zheng was born to a poor family. Homeless at 14, he was taken care of by Francis E. Lund, an American Episcopalian missionary. He was baptized in 1901 at St. James Church in Wuhu and confirmed by Bishop James Addison Ingle at the *Zhong Hua Sheng Kung Hui* (Anglican Church in China) a year later. While in St. James High School, Zheng organized the St. Peter's Society, comprising members committed to training for Christian ministry. He completed his studies at Boone College in Wuchang in 1908 and graduated from Boone Divinity School in 1909. He was ordained a deacon in 1909 by Bishop Logan Roots in St. Paul's Cathedral, Hankou, and served as headmaster of St. James High School and as an assistant priest in St. James Church. He was the first priest to be ordained in 1912 by the newly consecrated Bishop Huntington. Zheng was appointed rector of True Light Church at Nanling (near Wuhu) in 1914. He was concurrently general secretary of the Anglican mission board from 1916 to 1921. After relinquishing his church responsibility in Nanling in 1921, he concentrated on raising funds for the mission in Shaanxi. He also became secretary of the interdenominational China for Christ movement started in 1919 by Cheng Chingyi*.

Zheng went to the United States in 1923 and studied for one year each at Virginia Theological School and the divinity school of the Protestant Episcopal Church in Philadelphia. Both later awarded him honorary doctorates, as did several other institutions. He graduated with a master's degree in sociology from the University of Pennsylvania in 1926. He returned home to become dean of Holy Savior in Anhui. In Mar 1927, antiforeign and anti-Christian nationalists killed the vice president of Nanjing University, Dr. J. E. Williams, and ransacked churches. Zheng and his family were forced to evacuate their home. After the Western missionaries were expelled, the church was reopened and Zheng took charge of the Anglican church affairs and property. He was the first Chinese to be elected chairman of the house of delegates at the general synod in Shanghai, 1928, and was consecrated in Feb 1929 as an assistant bishop to William C. White, a Canadian and bishop of Henan. Zheng was the only non-Caucasian at the 1930 Lambeth Conference in England. The conference recognized the Chinese Anglican Church to be an independent province. In 1935 Zheng succeeded White as bishop of Henan and was enthroned at Trinity Cathedral, Kaifeng.

During the Japanese invasion of China, Zheng took over the responsibilities of Arnold Scott and John Wellington, the bishops of North China and Shandong, respectively, when they were interned. Zheng decided to be financially independent of the Canadian church in 1944 and was elected to succeed Scott as chairman of the house of bishops, or archbishop, by the general synod in Aug 1947.

Zheng went to the United States after attending the

1948 Lambeth Conference and suffered a stroke in Philadelphia. He went to recuperate in Canada, where his son, Zheng Jianye (C. Y. Cheng*), was studying at Trinity College. (Cheng was consecrated bishop of Henan in 1951.) Zheng returned to Shanghai in 1948 and retired. He was a supporter of the Three-Self Patriotic Movement* until his death.

Bibliography

Boorman, Howard L., ed., *Biographical Dictionary of Republican China,* Vol. I (1967). China Group

Zheng Jian Ye

(b. 1919; d. 1991). Chinese Anglican bishop and scholar.

Born into the family of a pastor in Anhui Province, Zheng first studied in Shanghai's Dongwu University and then at St. Joseph University Theological Seminary. After his graduation in 1944, he became the secretary of Shanghai's Christian Youth Society. In 1946 he was ordained pastor of St. Peter's Church. In 1948 he went to Toronto University in Canada to study theology. He returned home in 1949 and became editor of *Tianfeng Weekly* and *Protestant Books,* advocating that Chinese churches should be managed independently by Chinese Christians.

Zheng was one of the initiators of the Chinese Christian Three-Self Patriotic Movement* (TSPM). In 1952 he was appointed assistant bishop of the Anglican Church in the Henan District. In 1953 he went to Shanghai again and became executive secretary of the Standing Committee of the Central Committee of the Chinese Anglican Church. He was chosen as a committee member when the TSPM Committee was set up in 1954. After the Cultural Revolution and the establishment of the China Protestant Association in 1980, he was again nominated as vice chairman *cum* executive secretary, taking charge of rebuilding the church and other church affairs.

Zheng also worked hard on research on religious discourse. In 1979 he was chosen for the steering committee and as assistant secretary of the China Religious Association, and in 1982 was chosen by the Shanghai Religious Association to be vice chairman. He was also coeditor of the *Dictionary of Religion,* served on the editorial committee for the *Ci Hai,* and was vice head of the editorial board for the *Chinese Encyclopedia*'s volume on religion.

China Group

Zhou Zhi Yu

(b. Chekiang, China, 1889; d. ?). Zhou was a student of the North China Theological Seminary and Wycliffe College in Toronto. In his younger years, he founded Cheng Tian Middle School, of which he took charge for 11 years. He served as general secretary of the United Society of Christian Endeavor for China *(zhong hua ji-du-jiao mian-li-hui quan guo xie hui)* for 19 years and as director of Shanghai Sheng Jing Xue She for 15 years, beginning in 1933. Zhou was an official delegate to several World Christian Conferences. In 1946 he was ordained a pastor by the Anglican Church, Kiangsu Diocese. In the same year, he was appointed superintendent of *Zhong Guo Ji-du-tu Bu-dao Shi-zi-jun* ("China Christian Mission Crusaders," renamed *Zhong Hua Ji-du-tu Chuan-dao-hui* in 1948). In 1947 he was invited by the council members of the Crusaders to travel to the United States for fund-raising purposes. After his return to China, Zhou founded a magazine, *Zhen Dao,* and also enlarged Shanghai Sheng Jing Xue She into Tai-dong Bible College. In the spring of 1948, Zhou moved to Kweizhou, Kweiyang, together with Tai-dong Bible College, where he took in more students than previously. He subsequently left for Hong Kong. He also served as chairman of the Chinese Home Missionary Society and of *Zhong Hua Wan Guo Du-jing-hui* (China Worldwide Scripture Reading Association). He published a book, *The Christian Life.*

China Group

Zhu Bao Yuan

(b. Jiangsu, 1872; d. 1961). Chinese Anglican* church pastor and initiator of his church's independence movement.

Zhu studied at St. Joseph's Institution in his early years and came to know Christ. In 1894 he graduated with excellent results in English, entered the institution's theology course, and graduated with the school's first class in 1900. He went to Wuti to set up a church and was inducted as pastor in 1902. In the following year, he was transferred to the Church of Our Savior in Shanghai. In 1906 Zhu announced that the church would no longer accept any financial help from the mission board, thereby declaring its independence. He also set up Changshi Secondary School in the vicinity of the church. He went to Columbia University in the United States to further his studies in 1912 and graduated with a master of arts degree. He returned to his original post in Shanghai.

In 1915 the Church of Our Savior, using local architectural design, rebuilt its building. At the dedication ceremony, Zhu had a flag specially made with the words "independence, self-growth, self-governed," and this was hung inside the church. He also organized many patriotic activities in Changshi Secondary School, increased the standard of education, and allowed graduates with good results to enter St. Joseph's University without having to take the entrance exams. He received his doctorate in theology in 1923. He composed a song, "Chinese Church Independence Song," in 1933, which is still widely sung today. With the founding of modern China, Zhu was employed by the Shanghai Archives.

China Group

Zia Ul-Haq, Mohammed

(b. Jullundur, East Pakistan, 12 Aug 1924; d. Pakistan, 17 Aug 1988). Astute politician and longest-serving president of Pakistan*.

An Aryan from a lower-middle-class family, Zia was educated at St. Stephen's College in Delhi and joined the British Army in 1944. In 1976 he was appointed chief of army staff by Zulfiqar Ali Bhutto*, a post he retained until his death in 1988. He assumed the presidency of Pakistan in 1978.

On 17 Aug 1988, General Zia, the longest-serving head of the state of Pakistan, was killed in a still unexplained explosion that brought down the military aircraft taking him from Bahawalpur to Islamabad. Zia's death ended an 11-year reign which was notable for its Islamization* program, but even more so for its foreign policy. Zia fooled all the pundits. He was a gifted balancer and an astute reader of contemporary events. While never overcoming his unpopularity, he managed to steer Pakistan through a difficult decade without loss of direction or purpose. But Zia left behind all the problems that burdened his administration in the years of his rule.

The religious nature of the state in Pakistan has been a matter of debate since the country's founding, and various devices have been used to assuage the demands of those who favored strict Islamization in each of the constitutions devised. Opponents of Islamization, including the minority groups (and especially the Christian minority), often used the words of the founder of the nation-state, Muhammed Ali Jinnah, in his speech to the Constituent Assembly. In this speech, Jinnah saw Pakistan as a state in which Muslims could live under circumstances that would permit them to order their lives according to the Sunna, but that the matter of religion was a personal one and the state had no role to play in enforcing Islamic behavior.

Zia announced in 1978 that the legal system of Pakistan would be based on *Nizam-I-Mustafa* (the law of the Prophet). The ultimate step in a series of steps would be the proclamation that the Shari'a would be the basis of all law in Pakistan. Even though up to his death he never succeeded in carrying this out, and even though many of the punishments inflicted by the Hudud Ordinance were not meted out, yet the spirit of the *Shariat* Laws could be seen in the public floggings. Zia's intentions were to galvanize the Muslim people into a strong Islamic *Ummah*, and he persisted in this endeavor. He decreed the establishment of special *Shariat* courts to adjudicate cases brought under *Shariat* Law. The rules of evidence in Islamic law are so stringent that strong opposition came from women's groups. During this period, women were also angered by Zia's statements concerning the "Islamic dress" and other codes of behavior. Zia also introduced several economic measures according to Islamic law as he saw it. He directed steps to be taken to provide Islamic banking facilities and introduced government collection of *Zakat* (almsgiving) and *Ushr* (a form of agricultural tax).

Concerning Pakistan's foreign policy, Zia took the reins from Zulfiqar Ali Bhutto. In his first few months in office, Zia visited Saudi Arabia, Iran, the United Arab Emirates (UAE), Afghanistan, Kuwait, Turkey, Libya, Jordan, and China*. The purpose of the visits was familiarization and the maintenance of contacts at the highest level with Islamic and other friendly or neighboring states. By contrast, relations with the United States remained in a state of relative tension. Neither the manner in which he had achieved power, his defiant attitude, nor his orthodox Islamic practices were slated to win him many friends in or outside the American government. In relation to two neighboring states — Afghanistan and India — Zia envisioned some sort of peace based on the foundation of genuine Muslim solidarity with the former, while pursing a policy of high-level meetings with the latter. In neither case was his government successful in bringing about a successful treaty because, even today, both the aftermath of the Afghanistan situation and the tension with neighboring India continue.

Bibliography

Burki, Shahid Javed, and Craig Baxter, *Pakistan under the Military* (1991). • Ahmad, Akbar S., *Religion and Politics in a Muslim Society* (1983). • Ahmad, Mushtaq, *Pakistan at the Crossroads* (1985).

Archie Desouza

Ziegenbalg, Bartholomew

(b. 24 Jun 1683; d. ca. 1717). The son of a merchant, Ziegenbalg lost his parents at a very early age. A childhood memory he carried with him was what his mother, Catherine, had spoken to her children on her deathbed. She spoke of her Bible as a great treasure she had collected for them. Two years after his mother's death, his father also died. This tragic loss made a great impression on his heart, and he decided to study theology. His elder sister took care of him, giving him a good education and a good knowledge of the Bible.

Ziegenbalg suffered from hypochondria, and medicines did not help him. As a consequence, his soul suffered along with his physical health, which made him hesitate to accept the call to be a missionary. However, he eventually decided to respond. Along with his friend Plutschau*, Ziegenbalg traveled to a seaport in Denmark ready to go anywhere. Even when many problems arose, they carried on in that willing spirit. They were sent to India as missionaries of the king of Denmark, arriving in 1706.

Ziegenbalg and Plutschau were not liked by the authorities or the chaplain of the ship. Their situation was very unfavorable, and no welcome awaited them. It was three days before they were able to get a boat to take them to shore. They presented themselves at the entrance with their papers addressed to the Danish commandant. They were kept waiting there from 10:00 a.m. until 4:00 p.m. The commandant, J. C. Hassius, permitted them to join the official party to the marketplace, but they were left standing there. A junior official who appeared took pity on them and led them to the home of his in-laws. A few days later, this family found them a house. Ziegenbalg's tasks expanded well beyond his roles as a servant of the king fulfilling the king's wishes. He would not only care for those who by chance lived within the boundaries of the Danish colony, but he felt the Christian calling to carry the Gospel to non-Christians as well. He tried his best to reach beyond Tranquebar*.

Ziegenbalg and his friend began their work by setting themselves to learn Portuguese and Tamil. They found a sphere of work among the German soldiers and the domestic servants of the Europeans. Two churches already existed in Tranquebar, the Roman Catholic* church and the Zion church, which was exclusively reserved for the use of Europeans.

They saw the firstfruits of their labor in the baptism of five Portuguese slaves on 12 May 1707. The missionaries set about erecting a separate church as the center of their mission activities. On 15 Aug 1707, the new church was dedicated. On 5 Sep, they baptized nine adult Tamilians, the first results of their labor among Hindus. Within two years there were 102 believers in the Tamil church. Again in Oct 1718, a second church, called the New Jerusalem Church, was dedicated, which exists even today.

Since Hindus made up the majority of people, Ziegenbalg met more Hindus than any other non-Christians. As soon as he was able to speak Tamil, he entered into religious discussions with Hindus in Tamil and began to preach to them. These conversations with non-Christians often led him to deeper consideration of both theology and philosophy. He learned much which neither he nor other students could have thought of before. Thus through their conversations, Ziegenbalg seemed to have had good contact with the Hindus. The educated Hindus were able to secure a knowledge of Christian concepts and God's revelation in Christ. Later, Schultze and Ziegenbalg offered the opinion that the Hindus must have heard of the incarnation of Christ and used this in their stories of Krishna concerning his divine and human nature. The Brahmins argued that God revealed himself in various ways to different people, so that each person should worship God in the way in which he had revealed himself to that person. On the one hand, Ziegenbalg rejected this idea. He said the incarnation of Jesus was the one and only revelation intended for all humankind and for all times. Ziegenbalg asserted that the Hindu belief in transmigration was one of the strongest prejudices against Christianity.

Ziegenbalg and his fellow missionaries did a considerable amount of work in education and literature*. Education was an essential part of the missionary program. It was not simply the diffusion of knowledge, but was a part of equipping Christians so that they could read the Word of God for themselves and absorb it into their very beings. With that understanding, they started schools. The Portuguese and the Danish schools opened on 21 Nov 1707. On 28 Dec of the same year, a school was opened for Tamil children. A girls school was also opened, which was the first Christian school for Indian girls in the south. In addition, a Tamil free charity school was opened in 1715. The mission was benefited by the contributions from women, and wives of the missionaries voluntarily served the mission's cause. Ziegenbalg "adopted" poor orphaned children. Early in the morning, he found the time to teach them Luther's catechism and other lessons. Another session on catechism was given to the Tamil children from 2:00 to 3:00 p.m. in his bungalow.

Ziegenbalg came to realize the difference between the spoken and the written forms of language. As he penetrated deeper into the classical writings of Indians, he realized that they were a civilized people. He translated into Tamil Luther's short catechism for catechizing the children and followed this instruction with sermons, tracts, and schoolbooks. Within two years of his arrival, Ziegenbalg began the translation of the Bible*, which no one had ever attempted in any Indian language before. At the time of his death, he had gone as far as the book of Ruth. Along with his other writings, he translated hymns, and the first printed hymnbook was published in 1715.

Ziegenbalg's writings were divided into four classes: (1) fourteen books which he had written in Tamil; (2) books written by Catholic authors; (3) books written by Hindus; and (4) books written by Muslims, which he copied out. He also began work on the *Malabar Dictionary*, which contained 20,000 words and expressions. Thus he contributed much to literature.

Three more missionaries came in 1709, namely, Gruendler, Jordan, and Boevengh. They brought a large sum of money and other supplies for the mission. A Latin printing press was donated by the English Society in 1711, of which Gruendler took charge. A Tamil press was presented by German friends who arrived in 1714. These presses greatly facilitated their publication efforts

In 1717 the archbishop of Canterbury wrote a very encouraging letter which contained the following: ". . . you have won a greater honor than all . . . a far magnificent recompense will be given to you, for you shall be taken in the holy company of the prophets, evangelists and apostles; and shall with them shine like the sun and the stars for ever. . . ." But before the letter could reach him, Ziegenbalg had passed away. His death caused universal grief to both Europeans and natives, including the non-Christian "heathen."

Thus we see that, even against bitter opposition and many difficulties, Ziegenbalg paved the way for Protestant missionaries by giving his life for the mission.

Bibliography

Beyreuter, Erich, *Bartholomoeus Ziegenbalg* (1955). • Fenger, J. Ferdinand, *History of the Tranquebar Mission* (1906). • Firth, C. B., *An Introduction to Indian Church History* (1961). • Lehmann, E. Arno, *It Began at Tranquebar* (1956). • Neill, Stephen, *The Story of the Christian Church in India and Pakistan* (1970).

Franklyn J. Balasundaran

Zoroastrianism

National religion of ancient Persia (Iran) during the early development of Christianity (Parthian [238 B.C.E.–225 C.E.] and Sasanian [226-632 C.E.] dynasties).

Zoroastrianism is a prophetic religion that finds its origins in the teachings of Zoroaster (Zartusht or Zarathustra) in the 5th c. B.C.E. The prophet Zoroaster came from west-central Asia during a time (6th c. B.C.E.) of social transformation from nomadic to pastoral and agrarian existence. Zoroaster's reforms and concerns were a strong support for the pastoral life and agrarian bounty. In fact, in Zoroastrianism, one of the great signs of divine blessing is many cattle, abundant crops, and many children. Zoroaster's greatest contribution to religion was the grounding of ethics in the nature of the divine. What we do, how we behave, is rooted in our view of God, creation, redemption, and eschatology.

Zoroastrianism teaches a vertical dualism rather than a horizontal dualism (Greek thought). Thus, running up and down from the lowest bugs, snakes, and amphibians to the highest angels, there are good and evil beings. Spiritual beings are not better or more perfect than physical beings. The good in the universe honor the high lord (Mazda), who is all wise (Ahura). Opposed to Ahura Mazda is the evil god, Angra Mainyu or Ahriman ("Evil Spirit"), who is in a cosmic conflict with Ahura Mazda. This conflict will be resolved through the obedience of humans to Ahura Mazda's creation (to be bountiful and pure) and through an eventual savior who will come and win the final battle (Shaoshyans). Of special concern was the protection of the land from pollution and the people from corruption. Fire was considered divine, and so it purified all that had become corrupt or polluted. The sun, supreme symbol of fire, was honored above all of creation. Thus with its sense of time moving forward, its ethical demands, its supreme god, and its clear eschatology, Zoroastrianism was a dramatic break from the polytheistic worship of nomadic tribesmen of central Asia.

Zoroaster himself was protected by a local ruler, Vishtaspa, who provided freedom for the religion to develop, for the original texts to be recorded (Avesta), and for the religion to take on a unity of prophet and king. In the early Christian era, this royal-religious cooperation under the Parthian Empire did not limit the spread of Christian teachings. The Parthians were broadly Zoroastrian, but they were also powerful warriors more concerned with military conquest. The new Sasanid dynasty (225-632) ushered in a fundamentalist reform wherein the Zoroastrian priests (magi) were making many of the political — and even military — decisions in the name of Ahura Mazda.

Christianity, although it had many similar lines of theological development, was a great threat to the Zoroastrian people as well as the religion. Christians in Asia upheld asceticism and celibacy, but Zoroastrians preached "bounty" and fruitfulness. Christians saw Zoroastrians as "fire worshippers," and Zoroastrians saw Christians as followers of the evil god Ahriman; Christians polluted the earth with dead bodies. And yet Zoroastrians converted to Christianity at a rapid rate in the early Christian centuries. Many of the great Asian patriarchs were converts, and early Asian theologians (e.g., Aphrahat, Narsai) make special mention of the magi (Matt 2), the stars, and the sun. It may have been that in some way the preaching of Jesus was seen as a fulfillment of the longing for a savior (Shaoshyans).

With the Arab invasions of the 7th c., Zoroastrianism, which was closely identified with the conquered Sasanian Empire, went into rapid decline. The close identification with the Shah (king), which had been its strength for centuries, suddenly became the main reason for its decline. Nonetheless, much of the religious spirit and worldly concern of Zoroastrianism was retained in the Persian form of Islam*, which developed in the 8th through 12th cs.

Bibliography

Sacred Books of the East, Vols. 4, 5, 18, 23, 24, 31, 37, 47, trans. E. W. West (1880/1977). • Boyce, Mary, *Zoroastrians: Their Religious Beliefs and Practices* (1979/1986). • Kotwal, Firoze M., and James Boyd, *A Guide to the Zoroastrian Religion* (1982). • Zaehner, R. C., *The Teachings of the Magi: A Compendium of Zoroastrian Beliefs* (1956).

SCOTT W. SUNQUIST

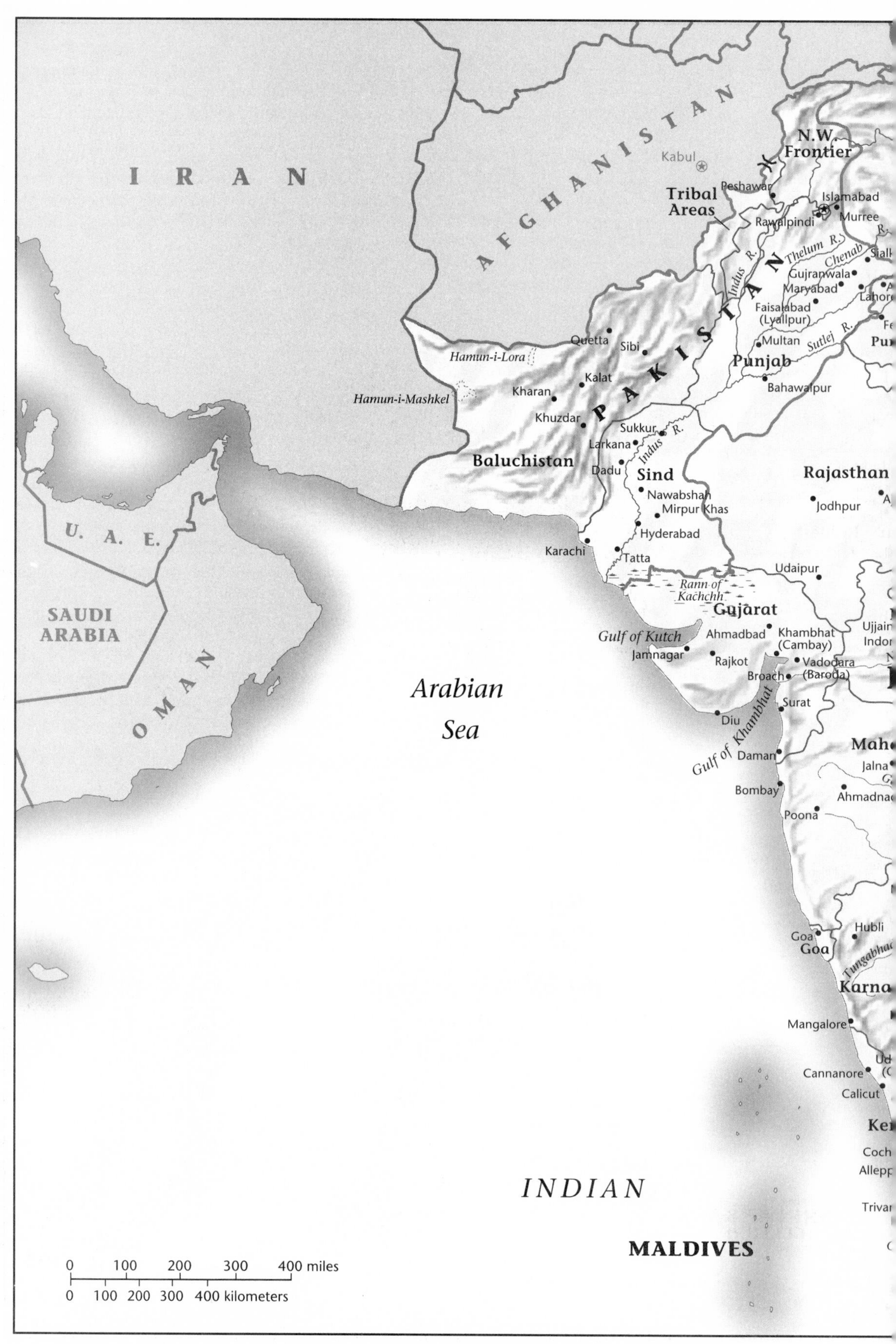

IRAN
AFGHANISTAN
Kabul
N.W. Frontier
Tribal Areas
Peshawar
Islamabad
Rawalpindi
Murree
Thelum R.
Chenab
Indus R.
Gujranwala
Maryabad
Faisalabad (Lyallpur)
PAKISTAN
Quetta
Sibi
Multan
Sutlej R.
Punjab
Bahawalpur
Hamun-i-Lora
Hamun-i-Mashkel
Kharan
Kalat
Khuzdar
Sukkur
Indus R.
Larkana
Baluchistan
Dadu
Sind
Nawabshah
Mirpur Khas
Hyderabad
Karachi
Tatta
Rajasthan
Jodhpur
Udaipur
Rann of Kachchh
Gujarat
Gulf of Kutch
Ahmadbad
Khambhat (Cambay)
Jamnagar
Rajkot
Broach
Vadodara (Baroda)
Surat
Diu
Gulf of Khambhat
Daman
Jalna
Bombay
Poona
Goa
Hubli
Goa
Mangalore
Cannanore
Calicut
U. A. E.
SAUDI ARABIA
OMAN
Arabian Sea
INDIAN
MALDIVES
0 100 200 300 400 miles
0 100 200 300 400 kilometers

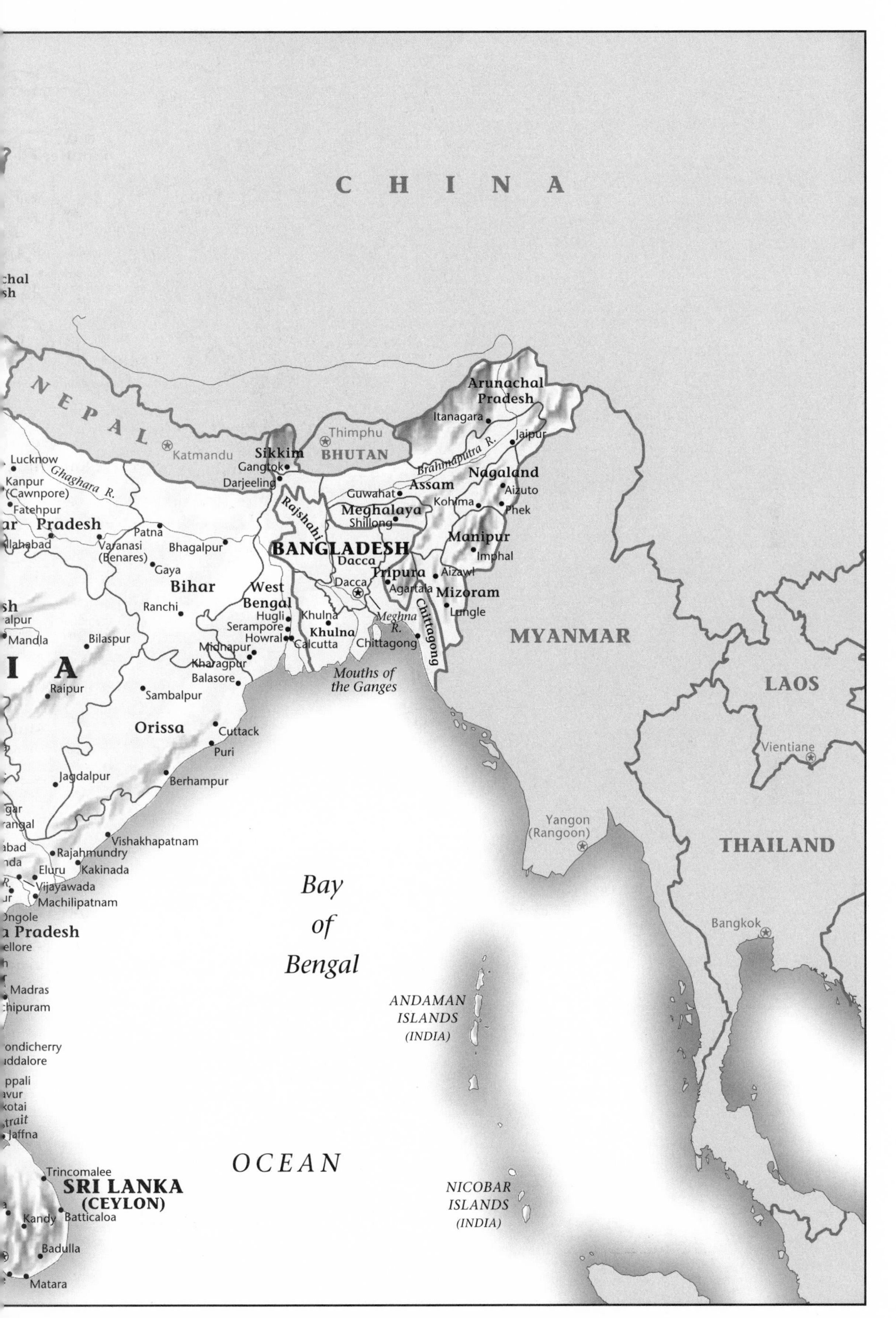

C H I N A
NEPAL
Katmandu
Sikkim
Gangtok
Darjeeling
Thimphu
BHUTAN
Arunachal Pradesh
Itanagara
Jaipur
Brahmaputra R.
Nagaland
Aizuto
Phek
Kohima
Assam
Guwahat
Meghalaya
Shillong
Manipur
Imphal
Rajshahi
BANGLADESH
Dacca
Tripura
Agartala
Aizawl
Mizoram
Lungle
Chittagong
Khulna
Meghna R.
Chittagong
Mouths of the Ganges
MYANMAR
LAOS
Vientiane
Yangon (Rangoon)
THAILAND
Bangkok
Lucknow
Ghaghara R.
Kanpur (Cawnpore)
Fatehpur
Pradesh
Patna
Varanasi (Benares)
Bhagalpur
Gaya
Bihar
West Bengal
Ranchi
Hugli
Serampore
Howral
Calcutta
Midnapur
Kharagpur
Balasore
Mandla
Bilaspur
Raipur
Sambalpur
Orissa
Cuttack
Puri
Jagdalpur
Berhampur
Vishakhapatnam
Rajahmundry
Kakinada
Eluru
Vijayawada
Machilipatnam
Pradesh
Madras
Pondicherry
Jaffna
Bay of Bengal
ANDAMAN ISLANDS (INDIA)
OCEAN
NICOBAR ISLANDS (INDIA)
Trincomalee
SRI LANKA (CEYLON)
Kandy
Batticaloa
Badulla
Matara

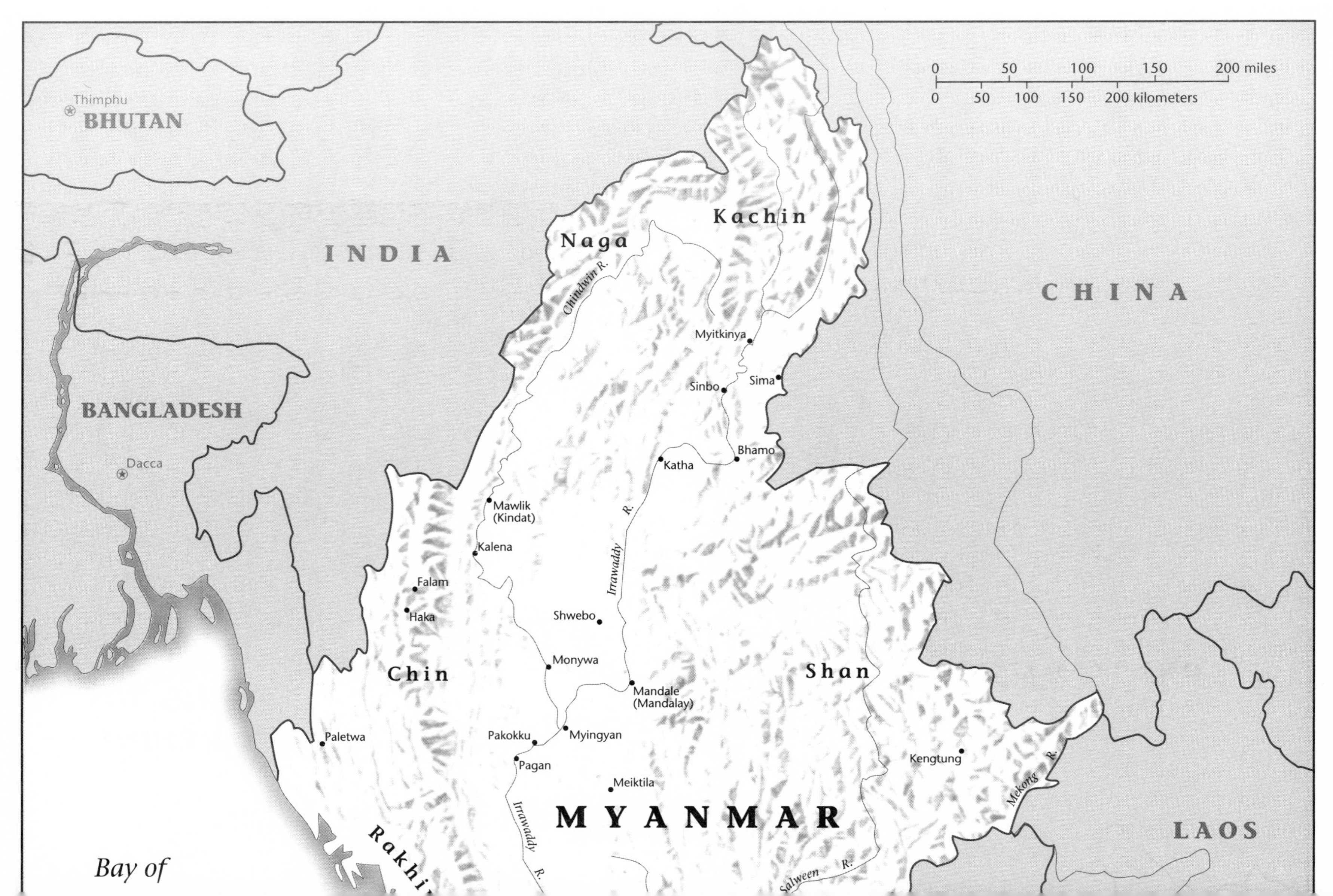

0 50 100 150 200 miles
0 50 100 150 200 kilometers
Thimphu
BHUTAN
INDIA
CHINA
BANGLADESH
Dacca
Naga
Kachin
Chindwin R.
Myitkinya
Sinbo
Sima
Bhamo
Katha
Mawlik (Kindat)
Kalena
Irrawaddy R.
Falam
Haka
Shwebo
Monywa
Chin
Shan
Mandale (Mandalay)
Paletwa
Pakokku
Myingyan
Pagan
Meiktila
Kengtung
Mekong R.
MYANMAR
LAOS
Bay of
Salween R.

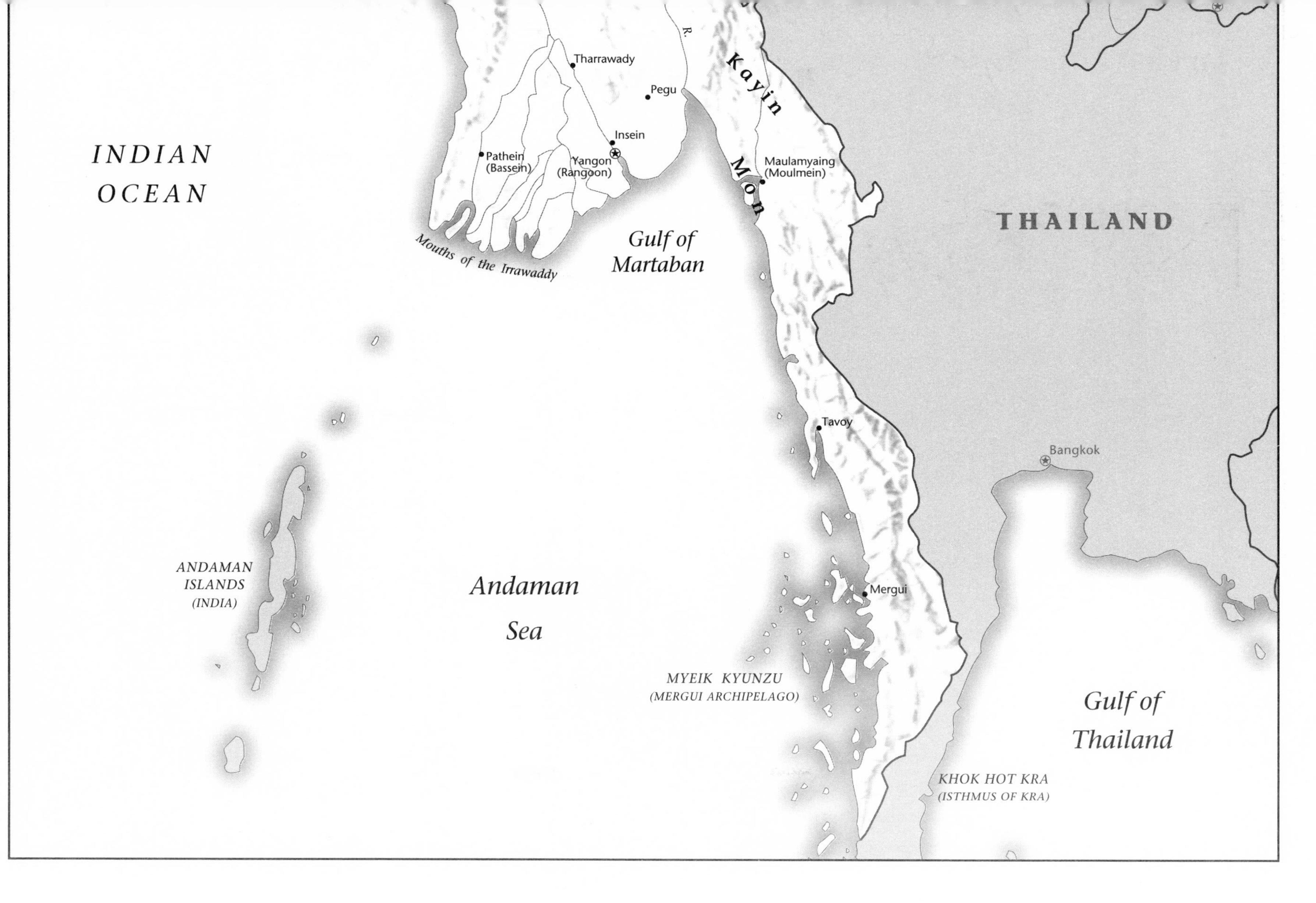
INDIAN
OCEAN
Tharrawady
Pegu
Insein
Pathein
(Bassein)
Yangon
(Rangoon)
R.
Kayin
Mon
Maulamyaing
(Moulmein)
THAILAND
Mouths of the Irrawaddy
Gulf of
Martaban
Tavoy
Bangkok
ANDAMAN
ISLANDS
(INDIA)
Andaman
Sea
Mergui
MYEIK KYUNZU
(MERGUI ARCHIPELAGO)
Gulf of
Thailand
KHOK HOT KRA
(ISTHMUS OF KRA)

0 100 200 300 400 miles
0 100 200 300 400 kilometers
RUSSIA
KAZAKHSTAN
UZBEKISTAN
KYRGYZSTAN
TAJIKISTAN
AFGHANISTAN
PAKISTAN
Xinjiang
Urümqi
Daheyon
Turpan
Aksu
Kashgar
Korla
TAKLIMAKEN
DESERT
Dunhuang
Jiuquan
Golmud
Qinghai
Huang H
Jinsha
Jiang
Tibet
Nu Jiang
Yarlung Zangbo Jiang
Lhasa
Lancang
Jiang
NEPAL
BHUTAN
INDIA
Ganges R.
INDIA
BANGLADESH
Irrawaddy R.
Calcutta
MYANMAR
Bay of
Bengal
Salween R.
THAI

RUSSIA
Heilongjiang
Songhua
Harbin
Vladivostok
Jilin
Sea of Japan
NGOLIA
Mongolia
Chifeng
Shenyang
Liaoning
NORTH KOREA
P'yongyang
Korea Bay
Xiwanxi
Zhangjiakou
Hohhot
Beijing
Tangshan
Dalian
Seoul
Baotou
Bo Hai
Great Wall of China
Baoding
Tianjin
Mouth of Yellow R.
Yantai (Chefoo)
SOUTH KOREA
Hebei
Taiyuan
Huang He
Qingdao
Ningxia
Handan
Jinan
Yellow Sea
Yanan
Shandong
Shanxi
Grand Canal
Mouth of Yellow R. before 1852
JAPAN
Jiangsu
Tongchuan
(Yellow R.)
Kaifeng
Zhengzhou
Xian
Henan
Yangzhou
Bengbu
Nanjing
Suzhou
Shanghai
Hefei
Anhui
Hubei
Hangzhou
Ningbo
Wuhan
Chang Jiang (Yangtze R.)
Zhejiang
Chengdu
Haimen
Poyang Hu
Wenzhou
Chongqing
Nanchang
Changsha
Yiyang
Hunan
Jiangxi
Shaoyang
Fuzhou
Guizhou
Fujian
Guiyang
Quanzhou
Xiamen
Guilin
TAIWAN (FORMOSA)
Guangdong
Xijiang
Guangzhou (Canton)
Shantou
Guangxi
Heifeng
Nanning
Jiangmen
Hong Kong
(Red R.)
Macau
VIETNAM
Zhanjiang
Gulf of Tongking
Haikou
Hainan
South China Sea
PHILIPPINES

RUSSIA
CHINA
HOKKAIDO
Wakkanai
Sapporo
Hakodate
Aomori
Hirosaki
Morioka
Akita
Sendai
Yamagata
Niigata
Aizu
HONSHU
Sea of Japan
Unggi
Musan
Huch'ang
Manp'o
Kimch'aek
Antung
Taedong
Hungnam
Wŏn San
Korea Bay
Pyong-Yang
Haeju
Kang-Wen
Kaesong
Soul

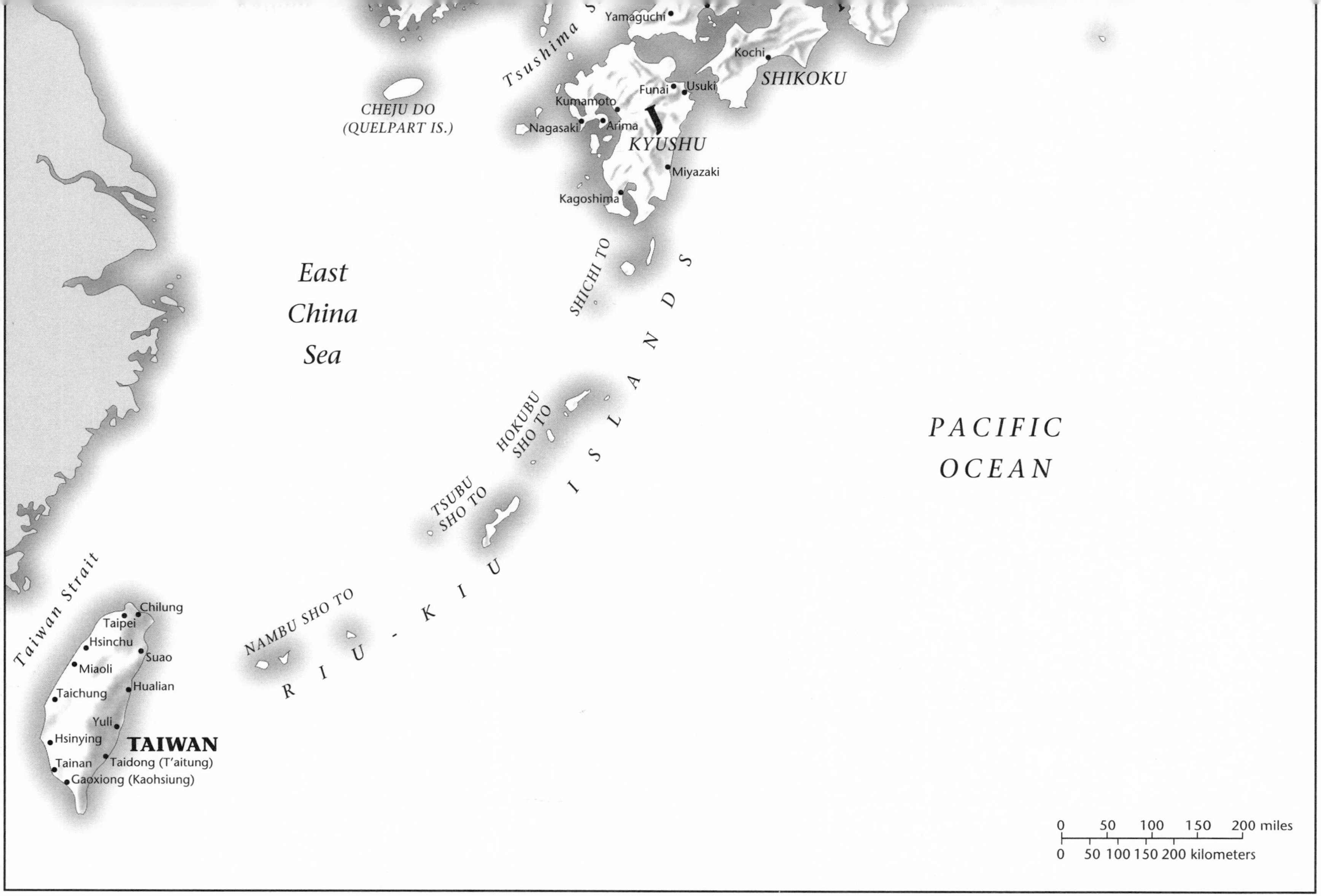

Yamaguchi
Tsushima
Kochi
SHIKOKU
Funai
Usuki
CHEJU DO
(QUELPART IS.)
Kumamoto
Nagasaki
Arima
J
KYUSHU
Miyazaki
Kagoshima
SHICHI TO
East
China
Sea
HOKUBU
SHO TO
TSUBU
SHO TO
RIU - KIU ISLANDS
PACIFIC
OCEAN
NAMBU SHO TO
Taiwan Strait
Chilung
Taipei
Hsinchu
Suao
Miaoli
Hualian
Taichung
Yuli
Hsinying
TAIWAN
Tainan
Taidong (T'aitung)
Gaoxiong (Kaohsiung)
0 50 100 150 200 miles
0 50 100 150 200 kilometers

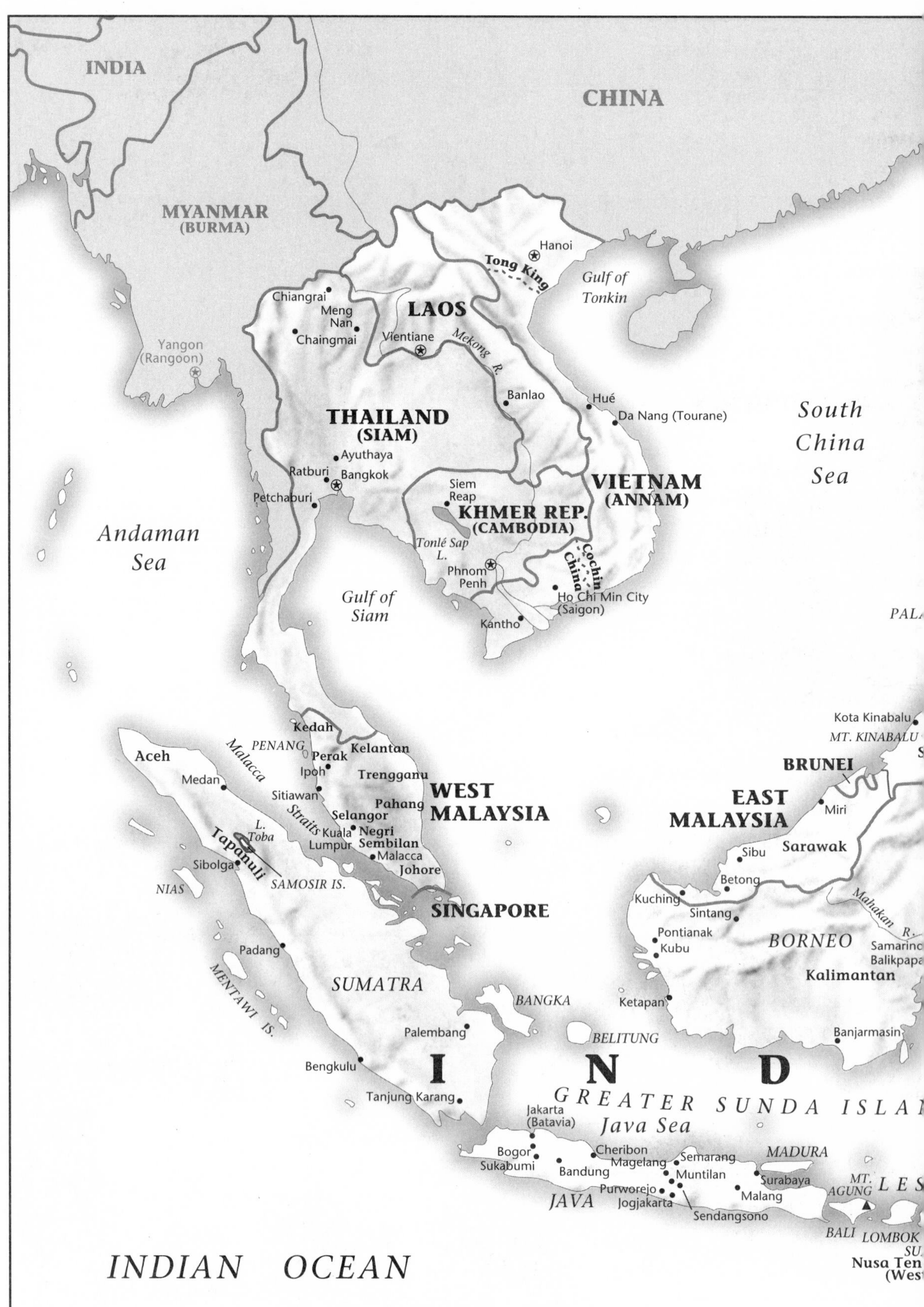

INDIA
CHINA
MYANMAR
(BURMA)
Yangon
(Rangoon)
Hanoi
Tong King
Gulf of
Tonkin
Chiangrai
Meng
Nan
Chaingmai
LAOS
Vientiane
Mekong R.
Banlao
Hué
Da Nang (Tourane)
South
China
Sea
THAILAND
(SIAM)
Ayuthaya
Ratburi
Bangkok
Petchaburi
Siem
Reap
KHMER REP.
(CAMBODIA)
VIETNAM
(ANNAM)
Tonlé Sap
L.
Phnom
Penh
Cochin
China
Ho Chi Min City
(Saigon)
Kantho
Andaman
Sea
Gulf of
Siam
Kedah
PENANG
Perak
Kelantan
Aceh
Malacca
Straits
Ipoh
Trengganu
Medan
Sitiawan
WEST
MALAYSIA
Pahang
Selangor
Kuala
Lumpur
Negri
Sembilan
Malacca
Johore
L.
Toba
Tapanuli
Sibolga
SAMOSIR IS.
NIAS
SINGAPORE
Kota Kinabalu
MT. KINABALU
BRUNEI
EAST
MALAYSIA
Miri
Sarawak
Sibu
Betong
Kuching
Sintang
Mahakam R.
Pontianak
Kubu
BORNEO
Kalimantan
Padang
MENTAWI IS.
SUMATRA
BANGKA
Ketapan
Palembang
BELITUNG
Banjarmasin
Bengkulu
I N D
Tanjung Karang
GREATER SUNDA ISLA
Jakarta
(Batavia)
Java Sea
Bogor
Sukabumi
Cheribon
Magelang
Semarang
MADURA
Bandung
Muntilan
Surabaya
MT.
AGUNG
Purworejo
Jogjakarta
Malang
JAVA
Sendangsono
BALI
LOMBOK
INDIAN OCEAN

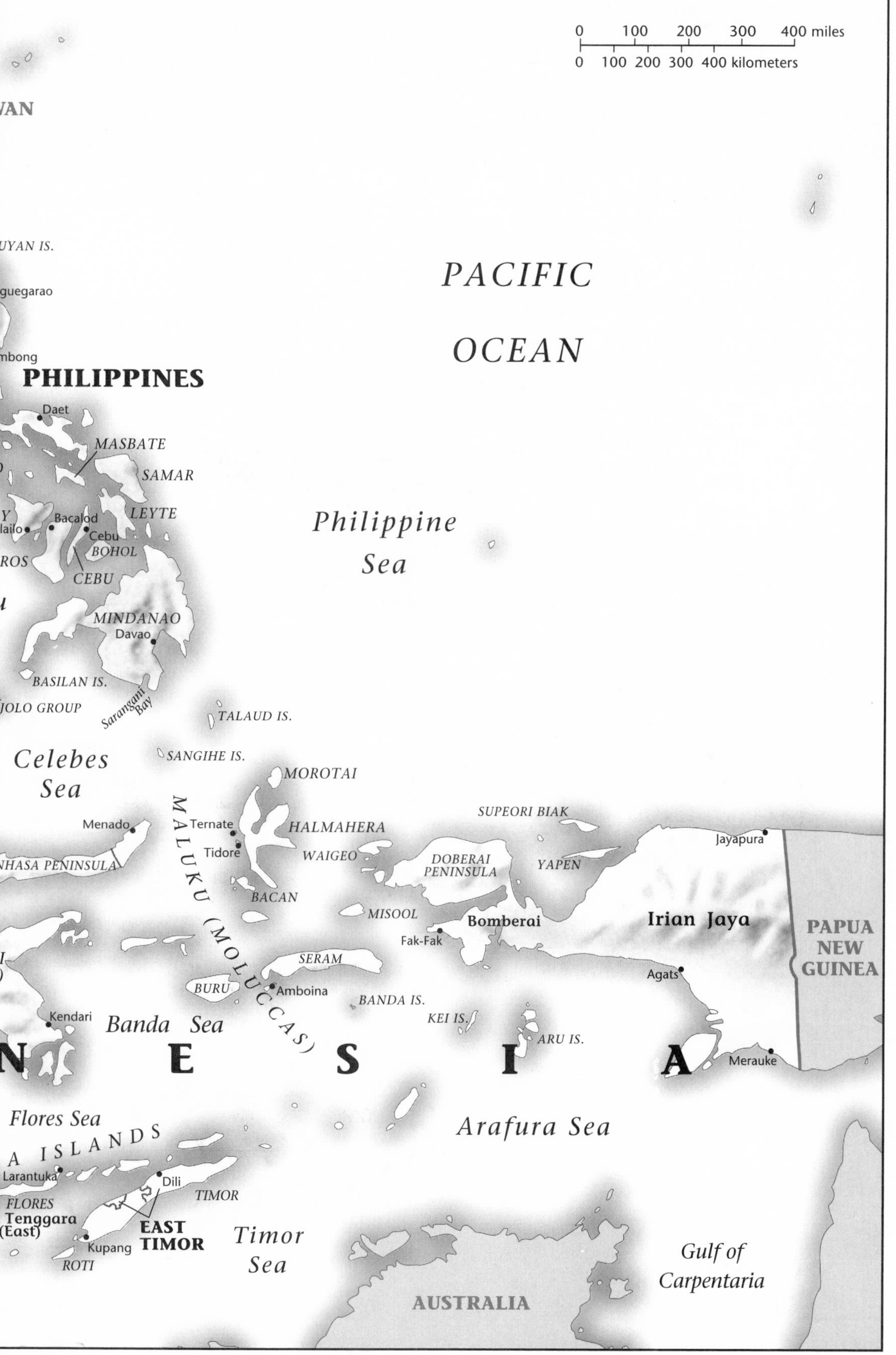

0 100 200 300 400 miles
0 100 200 300 400 kilometers
PACIFIC
OCEAN
PHILIPPINES
Daet
MASBATE
SAMAR
LEYTE
Bacalod
Ilailo
Cebu
BOHOL
CEBU
MINDANAO
Davao
BASILAN IS.
JOLO GROUP
Sarangani Bay
TALAUD IS.
Philippine
Sea
Celebes
Sea
SANGIHE IS.
MOROTAI
Menado
Ternate
Tidore
HALMAHERA
MALUKU (MOLUCCAS)
BACAN
WAIGEO
SUPEORI BIAK
YAPEN
DOBERAI
PENINSULA
Jayapura
MISOOL
Bomberai
Fak-Fak
Irian Jaya
PAPUA
NEW
GUINEA
SERAM
BURU
Amboina
BANDA IS.
KEI IS.
ARU IS.
Agats
Kendari
Banda Sea
N E S I A
Merauke
Flores Sea
Arafura Sea
Larantuka
Dili
FLORES
TIMOR
EAST
TIMOR
Kupang
ROTI
Timor
Sea
Gulf of
Carpentaria
AUSTRALIA